Collectors' Information Bureau®

COLLECTIBLES PRICE GUIDE

&
DIRECTORY TO SECONDARY MARKET DEALERS

Seventh Edition
1997

Collectors' Information Bureau
5065 Shoreline Rd., Suite 200
Barrington, IL 60010

YOUR GUIDE TO CURRENT PRICES AND SECONDARY MARKET DEALERS FOR LIMITED EDITION

Figurines ❖ Architecture ❖ Plates ❖ Dolls
Ornaments ❖ Graphics ❖ Steins ❖ Bells

More Than
50,000
Collectibles
Listed

❖ CONTENTS ❖

1997 C.I.B. Membership	1-2
Introduction	3
10 Most Frequently Asked Questions About Buying and Selling Limited Edition Collectibles	4-5
How to Read the Price Index	6
Collectors' Information Bureau Price Index	
❖ Architecture	7-26
❖ Bells	26-27
❖ Dolls	27-46
❖ Figurines	46-130
❖ Graphics	130-145
❖ Ornaments	145-185
❖ Plates	185-216
❖ Steins	216-218
Directory to Secondary Market Dealers	D1-26
❖ Directory Index by Specialty	D27-28

❖ ACKNOWLEDGMENTS ❖

The staff of the Collectors' Information Bureau would like to express our deep appreciation to our distinguished panel of limited edition retailers and secondary market experts, whose knowledge and dedication to the collectibles industry have helped make this book possible. Although we would like to recognize them by name, they have agreed that to be singled out in this manner may hinder their ability to maintain an unbiased view of the marketplace.

EXECUTIVE DIRECTOR
Peggy Veltri

STAFF
Joan Barcal
Jan Clesen
Susan Knappen
Patricia Rinas
Sharon Scholl
Carol Van Elderen
Debbie Wojtysiak
Cindy Zagumny

DESIGN and GRAPHICS
Kristin E. Wiley, Wright Design

PRINTING
Quebecor Printing-Book Division

Copyright 1997 © by the Collectors' Information Bureau. All rights reserved. No part of this work may be reproduced or used in any form or by any means — graphics, electronic or mechanical, including photocopying or information storage and retrieval systems — without written permission from the copyright holder.

Printed in the United States of America.

ISBN: 0-930785-48-7
Collectors' Information Bureau

ISBN: 0-87069-761-7
Wallace-Homestead Book Company
Krause Publications

❖ 1997 C.I.B. MEMBERSHIP ❖

Established in 1982, the Collectors' Information Bureau (CIB) is a not-for-profit business league whose mission is to serve and educate collectors, members and dealers, and to provide them with credible, comprehensive and authoritative information on limited edition collectibles and their current values. To contact the CIB, write to 5065 Shoreline Rd., Barrington, IL 60010, or call (847) 842-2200.

Ace Product Management Group, Inc.
9053 N. Deerbrook Trail
Brown Deer, WI 53223
(414) 365-5400
Fax: (414) 365-5410

Amazze
1030 Sunnyside Rd.
Vermillion, OH 44089
(800) 543-6759
Fax: (216) 967-5199

Anheuser-Busch, Inc.
2700 So. Broadway
St. Louis, MO 63118
(800) 325-1154
Fax: (314) 577-9656

Annalee Mobilitee Dolls, Inc.
50 Reservoir Rd.
Meredith, NH 03253
(603) 279-3333
Fax: (603) 279-6659

ANRI U.S.
1126 S. Cedar Ridge, Suite 122
P.O. Box 380760
Duncanville, TX 75138-0760
(800) 730-2674
Fax: (972) 283-3522

Arcadian Pewter, Inc.
1802 Broadway, Suite 200
Rockford, IL 61104
(815) 395-8670
Fax: (815) 395-9523

The Art of Glynda Turley
P.O. Box 112
Heber Springs, AR 72543
(800) 203-7620
Fax: (501) 362-5020

The Ashton-Drake Galleries
9200 N. Maryland Ave.
Niles, IL 60714
(800) 634-5164
Fax: (847) 966-3026

BAND Creations, Inc.
28401 N. Ballard
Lake Forest, IL 60045
(800) 535-3242
Fax: (800) 841-5631

The Bradford Exchange
9333 Milwaukee Ave.
Niles, IL 60714
(800) 323-5577

Brandywine Woodcrafts, Inc.
104 Greene Dr.
Yorktown, VA 23692
(757) 898-5031
Fax: (757) 898-6895

Byers' Choice Ltd.
4355 County Line Rd.
Chalfont, PA 18914
(215) 822-6700
Fax: (215) 822-3847

Cardew Design
c/o Devine Corp.
1345 Campus Parkway
Neptune, NJ 07753
(908) 751-0500
Fax: (908) 751-0550

Carlton Cards
One American Rd.
Cleveland, OH 44114
(216) 252-4944
Fax: (216) 252-6751

Cast Art Industries, Inc.
1120 California Ave.
Corona, CA 91719
(800) 932-3020
Fax: (909) 371-0674

Cavanagh Group International
1000 Holcomb Woods Pkwy.
440B
Roswell, GA 30076
(770) 643-1175
Fax: (770) 643-1172

Character Collectibles
10861 Business Dr.
Fontana, CA 92337
(909) 822-9999
Fax: (909) 823-6666

Christina's World
27 Woodcreek Ct.
Deer Park, NY 11729
(516) 242-9664
Fax: (516) 586-1918

Christopher Radko
P.O. Box 745
Ardsley, NY 10502
(800) 71-RADKO

Crystal World
3 Borinski Dr.
Lincoln Park, NJ 07035
(800) 445-4251
Fax: (973) 633-0102

Dave Grossman Creations
1608 N. Warson Rd.
St. Louis, MO 63132
(800) 325-1655
Fax: (314) 423-7620

Dear Artistic Sculpture
P.O. Box 860
Oaks, PA 19456
(610) 666-1650
Fax: (610) 666-1379

Department 56, Inc.
P.O. Box 44456
Eden Prairie, MN 55344-1456
(800) 548-8696

Duncan Royale
1141 S. Acacia St.
Fullerton, CA 92831
(714) 879-1360
Fax: (714) 879-4611

Enesco Corporation
225 Windsor Dr.
Itasca, IL 60143
(800) 4-ENESCO
Fax: (630) 875-5464

Ertl Collectibles Limited
Highways 136 & 20
P.O. Box 500
Dyersville, IA 52040
(319) 875-2000
Fax: (319) 875-5821

Fabergé Collection
35 Danbury Rd.
Wilton, CT 06897
(203) 761-8882
Fax: (203) 834-2178

Fenton Art Glass
700 Elizabeth St.
Williamstown, WV 26187
(304) 375-6122
Fax: (304) 375-6459

Fitz and Floyd Collectibles
13111 No. Central Expressway
Dallas, TX 75243
(972) 918-0098
Fax: (972) 454-1208

FJ Designs Inc./Makers of the Cat's Meow Village
2163 Great Trails Dr.
Wooster, OH 44691-3738
(330) 264-1377
Fax: (330) 264-1481

Flambro Imports
1530 Ellsworth Industrial Dr.
Atlanta, GA 30306
(404) 352-1381
Fax: (404) 352-2150

Forma Vitrum
20414 N. Main St.
Cornelius, NC 28031
(704) 896-9963
Fax: (704) 892-5438

The Franklin Mint
U.S. Route 1
Franklin Center, PA 19091
(610) 459-6000
Fax: (610) 459-6880

Ganz Inc.
908 Niagara Falls Blvd.
N. Tonawanda, NY 14120-2060
(800) 724-5902
Fax: (905) 851-8630

Gartlan USA
575 Rte. 73N., Ste. A-6
West Berlin, NJ 08091
(609) 753-9229
Fax: (609) 753-9280

George Z. Lefton Co.
3622 S. Morgan St.
Chicago, IL 60609
(800) 938-1800
Fax: (773) 254-5437

Georgetown Collection
P.O. Box 9730
Portland, ME 04104-5030
(800) 626-3330
Fax: (207) 775-6457

Goebel of North America
Goebel Plaza
Rt. 31 North
Pennington, NJ 08534
(609) 737-1980
Fax: (609) 737-1545

The Great American® Taylor Collectibles Corp.
110 Sandhills Blvd.
P.O. Box 428
Aberdeen, NC 28315
(910) 944-7447
Fax: (910) 944-7449

The Greenwich Workshop
One Greenwich Place
Shelton, CT 06484
(203) 925-0131
Fax: (203) 925-0262

The Hamilton Collection*
4810 Executive Park Ct.
Jacksonville, FL 32216-6069
(800) 228-2945
Fax: (904) 279-1339

Harbour Lights
1000 North Johnson Ave.
El Cajon, CA 92020
(800) 365-1219
Fax: (619) 579-1911

Harmony Kingdom
232 Neilston St.
Columbus, OH 43215
(614) 469-0600
Fax: (614) 469-0140

Hawthorne Village
9210 North Maryland St.
Niles, IL 60714-1322
(800) 772-4277

Hazle Ceramics
Stallion's Yard, Codham Hall
Gt. Warley
Brentwood, Essex,
United Kingdom CM13 3JT
(011) 441-277-220892
Fax: (011) 441-277-233768

Heritage Artists
560 Sauve West
Montreal, Quebec,
Canada H3L 2A3
(514) 385-7000
Fax: (514) 385-0026

Hudson Creek
321 Central St.
Hudson, MA 01749
(508) 568-1401
Fax: (508) 568-8741

Imperial Graphics, Ltd.
11516 Lake Potomac Dr.
Potomac, MD 20854
(800) 541-7696
Fax: (301) 299-4837

Kurt S. Adler, Inc.
1107 Broadway
New York, NY 10010
(212) 924-0900
Fax: (212) 807-0575

KVK, Inc./Daddy's Long Legs
300 Bank St.
Southlake, TX 76092
(817) 481-4800
Fax: (817) 488-8876

Ladie and Friends, Inc.
220 N. Main St.
Sellersville, PA 18960
(800) 76-DOLLS
Fax: (215) 453-8155

Lee Middleton Original Dolls
1301 Washington Blvd.
Belpre, OH 45714
(614) 423-1717
Fax: (614) 423-5983

Lenox
900 Wheeler Way
Langhorne, PA 19047
(800) 63-LENOX
Fax: (215) 741-6337

Lilliput Lane/Enesco Home
Gallery
P.O. Box 498
Itasca, Il 60143-0498
(630) 875-5633
Fax: (630) 875-5350

Lladró USA, Inc.
1 Lladro Dr.
Moonachie, NJ 07074
(800) 634-9088
Fax: (201) 807-1168

Margaret Furlong Designs
210 State St.
Salem, OR 97301
(503) 363-6004
Fax: (503) 371-0676

Maruri USA Corporation
7541 Woodman Place
Van Nuys, CA 91405
(818) 780-0704
Fax: (818) 780-9871

Media Arts Group, Inc.
521 Charcot Ave.
San Jose, CA 95131
(800) 366-3733
Fax: (408) 324-2035

Michael's Limited
8547 152nd. Ave. N.E.
Redmond, WA 98052
(800) 835-0181
Fax: (425) 861-0608

M.I. Hummel Club*
(Goebel of North America)
Goebel Plaza
P.O. Box 11
Pennington, NJ 08534
(609) 737-1980
Fax: (609) 737-1545

Midwest of Cannon Falls
32057 64th. Ave.
Cannon Falls, MN 55009
(800) 377-3335
Fax: (507) 263-7752

Miss Martha Originals
P.O. Box 5038
Glencoe, AL 35905
(205) 492-0221
Fax: (205) 492-0261

Mr. Sandman
25A Bathurst St.
Toronto, Ontario,
Canada M5V 2P1
(416) 504-9422
Fax: (416) 504-4009

Original Appalachian
Artworks
73 W. Underwood St.
P.O. Box 714
Cleveland, GA 30528
(706) 865-2171
Fax: (706) 865-5862

Our Secret
1701 Broadway N.E.
P.O. Box 26868
Albuquerque, NM 87125
(888) 773-2738
Fax: (800) 242-0385

Pacific Rim Import Corp.
5930 4th Avenue South
Seattle, WA 98108
(206) 767-5000
Fax: (206) 767-5316

Possible Dreams
6 Perry Dr.
Foxboro, MA 02035
(508) 543-6667
Fax: (508) 543-4255

Precious Art
125 W. Ellsworth
Ann Arbor, MI 48108
(313) 663-1885
Fax: (313) 663-2343

Prizm, Inc./Pipka Collectibles
P.O. Box 1106
Manhattan, KS 66505
(888) 427-4752
Fax: (888) 867-4752

Pulaski Furniture, Inc.
One Pulaski Square
Pulaski, VA 24301
(800) 287-4625

Reco International Corp.*
150 Haven Ave.
Port Washington, NY 11010
(516) 767-2400
Fax: (516) 767-2409

Roman, Inc.*
555 Lawrence Ave.
Roselle, IL 60172
(630) 529-3000
Fax: (630) 529-1121

Ron Lee's World of Clowns
330 Carousel Parkway
Henderson, NV 89014
(702) 434-1700
Fax: (702) 434-4310

Royal Copenhagen/
Bing & Grondahl
27 Holland Ave.
White Plains, NY 10603
(800) 431-1992
Fax: (609) 719-1494

Royal Doulton
701 Cottontail Lane
Somerset, NJ 08876
(800) 682-4462
Fax: (908) 356-9467

Sarah's Attic
126-1/2 W. Broad St.
Chesaning, MI 48616
(800) 437-4363
Fax: (517) 845-3477

Seymour Mann, Inc.
230 Fifth Avenue
New York, NY 10001
(212) 683-7262
Fax: (212) 213-4920

Shelia's Inc.
1856 Belgrade Ave.
Charleston, SC 29407
(800) 695-8686
Fax: (803) 556-0040

Shenandoah Designs
204 W. Rail Road
P.O. Box 911
Rural Retreat, VA 24368
(540) 686-6188
Fax: (540) 686-4921

The Society
Giuseppe Armani Art
300 Mac Lane
Keasbey, NJ 08832
(800) 3-ARMANI
Fax: (908) 417-0031

Swarovski America Limited
2 Slater Rd.
Cranston, RI 02920
(800) 426-3088
Fax: (401) 463-8459

The Tudor Mint, Ltd.
P.O. Box 431729
Houston, TX 77243-1729
(800) 455-8715
Fax: (713) 462-0170

United Design Corporation
1600 N. Main
Noble, OK 73068
(800) 727-4883
Fax: (405) 360-4442

WACO Products Corporation
I-80 & New Maple Ave.
P.O. Box 898
Pine Brook, NJ 07058-0898
(973) 882-1820
Fax: (973) 882-3661

The Walt Disney Company
500 South Buena Vista St.
Burbank, CA 91521-6876
(800) WD-CLSIX

Walnut Ridge Collectibles
39048 Webb Dr.
Westland, MI 48185
(800) 275-1765
Fax: (313) 728-5950

*Charter Member

❖ INTRODUCTION ❖

Welcome to the seventh edition of the *Collectibles Price Guide!* This comprehensive, up-to-date index is published each Spring by the Collectors' Information Bureau and reports on current primary and secondary market retail prices for limited edition figurines, architecture, plates, dolls, ornaments, graphics, steins and bells.

The Guide is considered one of the most authoritative and comprehensive price guides available today, listing over 50,000 current market prices. It is an ideal resource for collectors to use in establishing the value of their collections for insurance purposes. It is also a useful guide for those collectors who decide to buy or sell a retired collectible on the secondary market.

Expanded Secondary Market Dealer Directory

This issue of the *Collectibles Price Guide* features a new directory designed to make secondary market transactions more convenient for you. We've added a "Directory to Secondary Market Dealers" at the back of this book to help you find dealers who are secondary market experts in the products that you are looking to buy or sell. And the index, found on pages D27-28, is an easy way to pinpoint the dealer who specializes in particular lines or categories of collectibles. Once you've found the particular dealer that handles your desired products, you're one step closer to a successful secondary market trade!

How We Obtain Our Prices

The *Collectibles Price Guide* is the result of an extensive cooperative effort between the Collectors' Information Bureau's in-house research and development staff, and our national panel of limited edition dealers and secondary market experts. A very systematic procedure for gathering and reporting prices has been developed and refined over the years in order to provide collectors with the most accurate and timely information possible.

The process begins with the C.I.B. research and development staff gathering up-to-date information from collectibles manufacturers on new items, as well as those which have been "retired." This information is entered into a computer and copies are mailed to the C.I.B.'s panel of retailers and exchanges across the United States.

Members of this panel are carefully screened by C.I.B. management for their in-depth knowledge of the marketplace, their stature within the collectibles field, and their dedication to meeting the information needs of collectors everywhere. Through mail and telephone surveys, the panel works with our in-house researchers as a cooperative team to report and analyze actual sales transactions.

Based on these findings, which are checked and rechecked, a price is determined for each entry in which there has been trading activity. Where prices for some items may vary throughout the country, we provide a price range showing a "low" and a "high." All prices are for items in mint condition.

The secondary market in collectibles is a vast, ever-changing market. Some collectibles maintain a steady value for years, while prices for others go up and down so quickly it would be impossible to provide a completely up-to-date price in a printed book. That's why it's very important for anyone who uses the *Collectibles Price Guide* — or any of the other price indexes on the market — to think of it as a general guideline only. Also remember that prices quoted are retail prices, which means that they are the prices which these retail stores or secondary market exchanges have confirmed in a sales transaction, including their profit.

❖ 10 Most Frequently Asked Questions ❖
About Buying and Selling Limited Edition Collectibles

Q. How are prices for limited edition collectibles established on the secondary market?

A. As with most items in an open marketplace, prices are established in response to the supply of and demand for each individual item. Since limited edition pieces are, by definition, limited in the number of pieces available, demand for each piece will impact the market value of the item.

Over time, the "supply" of a particular piece may decrease, as natural disasters and home accidents result in damage or breakage. As the supply shrinks, the price may increase again.

Similarly, items that are in relatively large supply and experience small to moderate demand may see modest or low appreciation on the secondary market. Some items with broad distribution and low demand do not appreciate at all on the secondary market.

These fluctuations in the secondary market value of items are tracked by organizations like the COLLECTORS' INFORMATION BUREAU. Twice a year, the CIB surveys over 300 secondary market dealers and asks them to report back on the actual prices collectors have paid for individual pieces. This input is compiled and reported in the COLLECTIBLES PRICE GUIDE (published each May) and the COLLECTIBLES MARKET GUIDE & PRICE INDEX (published each November).

Q. What does a collector need to know if they are planning to buy or sell on the secondary market?

A. There are 4 things to consider when you begin thinking about buying or selling on the secondary market.

1.) *Know the value of the piece you want to buy or sell.* This information can be found by checking reputable price guides like the CIB's COLLECTIBLES PRICE GUIDE. Since these books list actual prices paid by collectors in recent transactions, they represent an excellent starting point for determining the market value of an item.

2.) *Understand the "terms of sale" used by the secondary market dealer that you're considering.* Individual dealers vary greatly in the services they offer the collectors and the fees they charge for these services. Some dealers buy pieces outright, while others provide a listing service or take goods on consignment. Some dealers charge as little as 10% commission, while others charge upwards of 30% to 50%. In most cases, the buyer pays the fee, however some dealers will ask the seller to pay all or part of the fee.

3.) *Be realistic about the condition of your piece.* Note any markings, mold numbers, etc. Carefully check your piece for any scratches, blemishes or cracks. If you are upfront with the dealer, you'll save yourself time and aggravation. Gather the original paperwork and box. If you don't have these materials, ask the dealer how this will affect the price of the piece you're selling. If you're looking to buy and have no intention of reselling, let the dealer know that you would accept a piece without the original paperwork. But be sure that you will not want to resell the piece later, since this will have an impact on the price you can demand.

4.) *Ask if the piece will be inspected by the dealer.* Many dealers will suggest that you write your initials or some other "code" on the bottom of the piece in pencil. By doing so, you can be sure that the piece you send in is the piece you get back should the sale fall through. Check with the dealer before putting any markings on the piece to ensure that it will not effect the value of the piece.

Q. Does a factory flaw effect the selling price of a piece?

A. As in most things, "visual perfection" is preferred. Usually, factory flaws are not a problem unless they are very pronounced. That's why it is extremely important to inspect each piece you buy...whether it's on the primary market (through a retailer or direct mail) or on the secondary market (at a "swap & sell" or through a dealer/exchange).

And remember, everyone's definition of "perfection" is different. What one collector may find acceptable, another would reject.

Q. Does the presence of an artist's signature on a piece increase its value?

A. Though the presence of a signature is not as important as it used to be, in some cases the value of a signed piece may be 15% to 25% higher than a comparable unsigned piece. Factors that impact the value of a signature include:

1.) *Age of the artist* — Artists who are reaching the end of their career may be doing fewer signings, making a signed piece more valuable to many collectors.

2.) *Accessibility of an artist* — Signatures from artists that rarely make themselves available for signings are often more coveted and therefore add to the value of a signed piece.

3.) *Buyer's preference* — More and more artists are taking to the road for personal appearances. These events give the collector the chance to share a personal experience with the artist. Some collectors prefer to buy unsigned pieces because they plan to have the artist sign the piece for them personally at an upcoming event.

Q. **How important is it to save the original box?**

A. Boxes are very important and the absence of an original box will often result in a lower selling price.

If you have a collectible that breaks and you have your original box, you can buy a replacement piece without the box (since you don't need it) and usually save some money.

On a more practical note, the manufacturer designs the box to afford the best possible protection for the piece during shipment. If you and your collectible move, the original box will be your best shot at getting your collection safely to its new home.

Q. **What steps should I expect to go through in buying or selling collectibles through a secondary market dealer or exchange?**

A. The average secondary market transaction takes about 3 weeks to complete and will usually include the following steps:

1.) *Call the secondary market dealer/exchange and tell them about the piece you want to buy or sell.* Be specific and include the product number if possible.

2.) *If you are looking to buy a piece, the dealer will tell you if they currently have it listed (available from a seller) or in stock, and what the selling price is.* The selling price will usually include a commission or service fee for the dealer/exchange. If you are looking to sell a piece, you should be prepared to tell them your "asking price." This price is the amount of money you expect to clear after the transaction is completed, and should not include the commission. In most cases, the dealer will add the commission on top of your asking price. Keep in mind that you must pay the shipping and insurance charges necessary to get your piece to the dealer/exchange. The buyer will usually pay to have the item shipped to them from the dealer/exchange.

3.) *Once a buyer agrees to pay the price asked, the dealer contacts the seller and has the piece shipped to the dealer for inspection.* At the same time, the buyer sends his/her payment to the dealer.

4.) *After the piece is inspected by the dealer and found to be in acceptable condition, the piece is shipped to the buyer for their inspection.* Before it is shipped, most dealers will put a marking (often invisible) on the bottom of the piece. This is a safeguard to ensure that if the piece is not accepted, the same piece is returned.

5.) *The buyer usually will have a set time-period (3 to 5 days) to either accept or reject the piece.* If the piece is accepted by the buyer, the dealer pays the seller the agreed-upon asking price. If the piece is not acceptable, it is returned to the dealer who can either return it to the seller, or sell it to another buyer for the original asking price.

Q. **It seems that there is a wide range of limited edition products being sold today. Has this resulted in a slow-down in secondary market trading?**

A. Quite the contrary! The increased vitality of the primary market, as seen in the growing number of manufacturers and lines, has resulted in more vigorous trading on the secondary market. There are more collectors than ever before, they are younger and have more disposable income then their predecessors. In many cases, they're getting started later in a series — after the first few issues have retired — so increased demand for earlier pieces is generated. All of this fuels a very strong secondary market.

Q. **Is trading or bartering an option for acquiring limited edition collectibles?**

A. Trading and/or bartering is an alternative to buying and selling on the secondary market. Collectors clubs and "swap and sell" events offer the best avenue for trading or bartering, since you have the opportunity to inspect the piece and negotiate right on the spot.

Q. **If you have a large collection, is it better to sell it as a "collection" or as single pieces?**

A. It is very difficult to sell an entire collection unless it is comprised of all older pieces, since collectors usually have some of the pieces from the collection that they're building. Often, they are looking to supplement their own collection of later issues with some of the earlier pieces that they missed.

It's also typically quite expensive to purchase an entire collection at once, so collectors will add to a collection piece-by-piece as they can afford the investment.

You will usually receive greater value for your collection if you sell it one piece at a time, rather than trying to sell the whole collection at once to one buyer. By listing your collection as individual pieces with a secondary market dealer, you have a better chance of moving all the pieces, though it may take some time.

Q. **Do variations in a piece effect its value?**

A. Variations are not as uncommon as you may think. Usually they do not effect the value of a piece. The exception to this rule is variations that qualify as "mistakes." Misspelling and other obvious mistakes will usually make a piece more valuable.

❖ Collectors' Information Bureau ❖
PRICE INDEX 1997

Limited Edition
Figurines ❖ Architecture ❖ Plates ❖ Dolls ❖ Ornaments ❖ Graphics ❖ Steins ❖ Bells

This index includes thousands of the most widely traded limited editions in today's collectibles market. It is based on surveys and interviews with several hundred of the most experienced and informed limited edition dealers in the United States, as well as many independent market advisors.

HOW TO USE THIS INDEX

Listings are set up using the following format:

❶ Enesco Corporation

❷ Precious Moments Figurines — ❸ S. Butcher

❹	❺	❻	❼	❽	❾
1979	Praise the Lord Anyhow-E1374B	Retrd.	1982	8.00	90-125

❶ Enesco Corporation = Company Name

❷ Precious Moments Figurines = Series Name

❸ S. Butcher = Artist's Name. The word "Various" may also appear here, meaning that several artists have created pieces within the series. The artist's name then appears after the title of the collectible. In some cases, the artist's name will be indicated after the series name "with exceptions noted." If company staff artists have created the piece, no artist name is listed.

❹ 1979 = Year of Issue

❺ Praise the Lord Anyhow-E1374B = Title of the collectible. Many titles also include the model number for further identification purposes.

❻ Retrd. = Edition Limit. In this case, the collectible is no longer available. The edition limit category generally refers to the number of items created with the same name and decoration. Edition limits may indicate a specific number (i.e. 10,000) or the number of firing days for plates (i.e. 100-day, the capacity of the manufacturer to produce collectibles during a given firing period). Refer to "Open," "Suspd.," "Annual," and "Yr. Iss." under "Terms and Abbreviations" below.

❼ 1982 = Year of Retirement. May also indicate the year the manufacturer ceased production of the collectible. If N/A appears in this column, it indicates the information is not available at this time, but research is continuing.
Note: In the plate section, the year of retirement may not be indicated because many plates are limited to firing days and not years.

❽ 8.00 = Original Issue Price in U.S. Dollars

❾ 90-125 = Current Quote Price listed may show a price or price range. Quotes are based on interviews with retailers across the country, who provide their actual sales transactions. Quotes have been rounded up to the nearest dollar. Quote may also reflect a price increase for pieces that are not retired or closed.

A Special Note to Beatrix Potter, Boyds Bears, Cherished Teddies, Disney Classics, Goebel Miniatures, M.I. Hummel and Precious Moments Collectors: *These collectibles are engraved with a special annual mark. This emblem changes with each production year. The secondary market value for each piece varies because of these distinctive yearly markings. Our pricing reflects an average for all years.*

A Special Note to Hallmark Keepsake Ornament Collectors: *All quotes in this section are for ornaments in mint condition in their original box.*

A Special Note to Department 56 Collectors: *Year of Introduction indicates the year in which the piece was designed, sculpted and copyrighted. It is possible these pieces may not be available to the collectors until the following calendar year.*

TERMS AND ABBREVIATIONS

Annual = Issued once a year.
A/P = Artist Proof.
Closed = An item or series no longer in production.
G/P = Gallery Proof.
N/A = Not available at this time.
Open = Not limited by number or time, available until manufacturer stops production, "retires" or "closes" the item or series.

Retrd. = Retired.
S/N = Signed and Numbered.
S/O = Sold Out.
Set = Refers to two or more items issued together for a single price.
Suspd. = Suspended (not currently being produced; may be produced in the future).

Unkn. = Unknown.
Yr. Iss. = Year of issue (limited to a calendar year).
28-day, 10-day, etc. = Limited to this number of production (or firing) days, usually not consecutive.

Copyright 1997 © by Collectors' Information Bureau. All rights reserved. No part of this work may be reproduced or used in any forms or by any means — graphics, electronic or mechanical, including photocopying or information storage and retrieval systems — without written permission from the copyright holder.

ARCHITECTURE

Amazze

Century Lights - S.N. Meyers

YEAR ISSUE		EDITION LIMIT	YEAR RETD.	ISSUE PRICE	*QUOTE U.S.$
1994	Admiralty Head, WA	3,995		66.00	66
1995	Assateague, VA	4,975		62.00	62
1995	Block Island, RI	4,896		86.00	86
1994	Boston Harbor, MA	3,475		58.00	58
1994	Buffalo, NY	3,475		54.00	54
1994	Burrows Island, WA	2,995		66.00	66
1994	Cape Blanco, OR	2,995	1996	58.00	58
1994	Cape Hatteras, NC	10,000		58.00	58
1996	Cape Henry, VA	3,996		62.00	62
1996	Cape Lookout, NC	3,996		62.00	62
1995	Cape May, NJ	4,975		58.00	58
1994	Charlotte-Genesee, NY	3,475		40.00	40
1995	Chicago Harbor, IL	4,250		66.00	66
1994	Coquille River, OR	2,995		66.00	66
1994	Diamond Head, HI	10,000		54.00	54
1996	East Brother Island, CA	3,996		69.00	69
1995	East Quoddy Head, Canada	2,475		58.00	58
1994	Fort Gratiot, MI	3,475		58.00	58
1994	Great Point, MA	2,475		58.00	58
1994	Hilton Head, SC	10,000		54.00	54
1996	Hog Island, RI	3,996		62.00	62
1994	Holland, MI	4,975		66.00	66
1995	Jupiter Inlet, FL	7,500		58.00	58
1995	Lorain Light, OH	3,195		66.00	66
1994	Marblehead, OH	7,500		54.00	54
1994	Montauk Point, NY	3,475		54.00	54
1995	Nauset Beach, MA	4,995		56.00	56
1994	Ned Point, MA	2,475	1996	40.00	40
1994	North Head, WA	2,995		58.00	58
1995	Ocracoke Island Light, NC	3,975		54.00	54
1994	Old Point Loma, CA	4,550		66.00	66
1994	Plymouth, MA	3,475		58.00	58
1994	Ponce De Leon, FL	3,475		54.00	54
1995	Port Isabel, TX	3,975		58.00	58
1995	Rose Island, RI	4,111		68.00	68
1996	Round Island, MI	3,996		69.00	69
1994	Sand Point, MI	3,475		66.00	66
1995	Sandy Hook, NJ	4,975		58.00	58
1995	Split Rock, MN	4,449		66.00	66
1995	St. Augustine, FL	10,000		62.00	62
1995	St. George Reef, CA	4,500		62.00	62
1995	St. Simmons, GA	3,975		56.00	56
1994	Tybee Island, GA	3,475		58.00	58
1994	Umpqua, OR	2,995		58.00	58
1995	West Quoddy Head, ME	4,995		66.00	66
1995	Yaquina Head, OR	4,500		60.00	60

Centuryville - S.N. Meyers

1995	Bed & Breakfast	1,975	1996	56.00	56
1994	Cathedral	2,950	1995	70.00	70
1994	Centuryville B&O	3,250	1996	56.00	56
1994	Cranes Eye Point	3,750	1996	50.00	50
1995	Fire Station	1,975	1996	60.00	60
1994	Foggy Point	4,998	1995	50.00	50
1994	Gothic Church	3,436	1996	60.00	60
1995	Lawrence Keith	1,975	1996	64.00	64
1994	Mr. John Johnson	2,960	1996	50.00	50
1994	Mr. Lyle E. Wilson	2,960	1996	50.00	50
1994	Ms. Hilda Grant	2,960	1996	50.00	50
1995	Ms. Marv William	1,975	1996	60.00	60
1994	Ms. Mary Thompson	2,342	1996	50.00	50
1994	Richard & Jan Smith	2,960	1996	50.00	50
1994	Schoolhouse	3,250	1995	56.00	56
1995	Ship Island Miss	1,975	1995	48.00	48
1995	Sweet Shoppe	1,975	1996	56.00	56
1994	Village Church	3,250	1996	60.00	60

The Chocolate Town, U.S.A.!™ Collection - Innes/Meyers

1996	Chocolate Town™ Cinema	9,988		84.00	84
1996	Chocolate Town™ Post Office	9,988		69.00	69
1996	Hershey's™ 5 and 10 Cent Store	9,988		68.00	68
1996	Hershey's™ Chocolate Shoppe	9,988		76.00	76
1996	Hershey's™ Gallery	9,988		98.00	98
1996	Mr. Goodbar™ Cafe	9,988		66.00	66

Evergreen Village - S.N. Meyers

1994	Candymakers	2,475	1996	36.00	36
1994	Carpenters	2,475	1996	36.00	36
1994	Cobblers	2,475	1996	36.00	36
1994	Cottage Point	2,675	1996	36.00	36
1994	Evergreen Church	2,475	1995	50.00	50
1994	Train Conductors	2,475	1996	36.00	36

Band Creations, Inc.

America's Country Barns - Band Creations

1997	65 Miles Ta Rock City	Open		30.00	30
1996	Double Crib Barn	Open		29.95	30
1996	Dutch Barn	Open		29.95	30
1996	English Barn	Open		29.95	30
1996	Gambrel Roof Barn	Open		29.95	30
1996	Log Barn	Open		29.95	30
1997	Lookout Mountain	Open		30.00	30
1996	Pennsylvania Dutch Barn	Open		29.95	30
1996	Polygonal Barn	Open		29.95	30
1996	Round Barn	Open		29.95	30
1997	See Rock City	Open		30.00	30

America's Covered Bridges - Band Creations

1995	Billie Creek, Parke County, IN	Open		29.95	30
1995	Bridge at the Green, Bennington County, VT	Open		29.95	30
1997	Bridgeton, Park County, IN	Open		39.99	40
1995	Bunker Hill, Catawba County, NC	Open		29.95	30
1995	Burfordville, Cape Giradeai County, MO	Open		39.95	40
1995	Cedar Creek, Ozaukee County, WI	Open		29.95	30
1995	Chiselville, Bennington County, VT	Open		29.95	30
1995	Elder's Mill, Oconee County, GA	Open		29.95	30
1995	Elizabethton, Carter County, TN	Open		29.95	30
1995	Fallasburg, Kent County, MI	Open		29.95	30
1995	Gilliland, Etowah County, AL	Open		29.95	30
1995	Humpback, Allegheny County, VA	Open		29.95	30
1995	Knox, Chester County, PA	Open		29.95	30
1995	Narrows, Parke County, IN	Open		29.95	30
1995	Old Blenheim, Schoharie County, NY	Open		39.95	40
1997	Olin, Ashtabula County, OH	Open		29.95	30
1995	Philippi, Barbour County, WV	Open		39.95	40
1995	Roberts, Proble County, OH	Open		29.95	30
1995	Robyville, Penobscot County, ME	Open		29.95	30
1995	Roseman, Madison County, IA	Open		29.95	30
1997	Sevierville, Sevierville County, TN	Open		39.99	40
1995	Shimenak, Linn County, OR	Open		29.95	30
1995	Thompson Mill, Shelly County, IL	Open		29.95	30
1995	Wawona, Mariposa County, CA	Open		29.95	30
1995	Zumbrota, Goodhue County, MN	Open		29.95	30

America's Weather Vanes - Band Creations

1997	Angel Vane Pinta	Open		35.00	35
1997	Angel Vane, gold -musical	Open		45.00	45
1997	Bird Vane Pinta	Open		35.00	35
1997	Bird Vane, gold -musical	Open		45.00	45
1997	Cow Vane Pinta	Open		35.00	35
1997	Cow Vane, gold -musical	Open		45.00	45
1997	Horse Vane Pinta	Open		35.00	35
1997	Horse Vane, gold -musical	Open		45.00	45
1997	Pig Vane Pinta	Open		35.00	35
1997	Pig Vane, gold -musical	Open		45.00	45
1997	Rooster Vane Pinta	Open		35.00	35
1997	Rooster Vane, gold -musical	Open		45.00	45

Brandywine Collectibles

The Brandywine Neighborhood Association - M. Whiting

1997	Moore House	Yr.Iss.		Gift	N/A

Accessories - M. Whiting

1992	Apple Tree/Tire Swing	Open		10.00	11
1991	Baggage Cart	Open		10.50	11
1990	Bandstand	Closed	1992	10.50	11
1994	Elm Tree with Benches	Open		16.00	17
1988	Flag	Open		10.00	11
1990	Flower Cart	Open		13.00	14
1990	Gate & Arbor	Closed	1992	9.00	9
1990	Gooseneck Lamp	Open		7.50	9
1989	Horse & Carriage	Open		13.00	14
1994	Lamp with Barber Pole	Open		10.50	11
1988	Lampost, Wall & Tree	Open		11.00	12
1989	Mailbox, Tree & Fence	Open		10.00	12
1997	Pickett Fence Display Shelf, 18"	Open		30.00	30
1997	Pickett Fence Display Shelf, 24"	Open		40.00	40
1997	Pickett Fence, 6"	Open		12.00	12
1989	Pumpkin Wagon	Open		11.50	12
1991	Street Sign	Open		8.00	9
1987	Summer Tree with Fence	Open		7.00	7
1991	Town Clock	Open		7.50	9
1992	Tree with Birdhouse	Open		10.00	11
1989	Victorian Gas Light	Open		6.50	7
1990	Wishing Well	Open		10.00	11

Barnsville Collection - M. Whiting

1991	B & O Station	Open		28.00	29
1992	Barnesville Church	Open		44.00	45
1991	Bradfield House	Closed	1996	32.00	32
1990	Candace Bruce House	Closed	1996	30.00	30
1990	Gay 90's Mansion	Closed	1996	32.00	32
1992	Plumtree Bed & Breakfast	Open		44.00	45
1990	Thompson House	Closed	1996	32.00	32
1990	Treat-Smith House	Closed	1996	32.00	32
1991	Whiteley House	Closed	1996	32.00	32

Country Lane - M. Whiting

1995	Berry Farm	Open		30.00	31
1995	Country School	Open		30.00	31
1995	Dairy Farm	Open		30.00	31
1995	Farm House	Open		30.00	31
1995	The General Store	Open		30.00	31

Country Lane II - M. Whiting

1995	Antiques & Crafts	Open		30.00	31
1995	Basketmaker	Open		30.00	31
1995	Country Church	Open		30.00	31
1995	Fishing Lodge	Open		30.00	31
1995	Herb Farm	Open		30.00	31
1995	Olde Mill	Open		30.00	31
1995	Spinners & Weavers	Open		30.00	31

Country Lane III - M. Whiting

1996	Airport	Open		30.00	31
1996	Country Club	Open		30.00	31
1996	Country Fair	Open		30.00	31
1996	Firehouse	Open		30.00	31
1996	Old Orchard	Open		30.00	31
1996	Post Office	Open		30.00	31

Country Lane IV - M. Whiting

1996	Candles & Country	Open		30.00	31
1996	Country Inn	Open		30.00	31
1996	Farmer's Market	Open		30.00	31
1996	Lighthouse	Open		30.00	31
1996	Train Station	Open		30.00	31
1996	Valley Stables	Open		30.00	31

Country Lane V - M. Whiting

1997	Country Curtains & Furniture	Open		31.00	31
1997	Country Music Hall	Open		31.00	31
1997	Little League Field	Open		31.00	31
1997	Noah's Zoo	Open		31.00	31
1997	Quilts & Things	Open		31.00	31
1997	Uncle Joe's Place	Open		31.00	31

Custom Collection - M. Whiting

1988	Burgess Museum	Open		15.50	16
1992	Cumberland County Courthouse	Open		15.00	15
1990	Doylestown Public School	Open		32.00	33
1991	Jamestown Tower	Closed	1991	9.00	9
1990	Jared Coffin House	Open		32.00	33
1989	Lorain Lighthouse	Closed	1992	11.00	11
1992	Loudon County Courthouse	Open		15.00	15
1988	Princetown Monument	Closed	1989	9.70	10
1991	Smithfield VA. Courthouse	Closed	1992	12.00	12
1989	Yankee Candle Co.	Open		13.50	14

Hilton Village - M. Whiting

1987	Dutch House	Closed	1991	8.50	9
1987	English House	Closed	1991	8.50	9
1987	Georgian House	Closed	1991	8.50	9
1987	Gwen's House	Closed	1991	8.50	9
1987	Hilton Firehouse	Closed	1991	8.50	9

Hometown I - M. Whiting

1990	Barber Shop	Closed	1992	14.00	14
1990	General Store	Closed	1992	14.00	14
1990	School	Closed	1992	14.00	14
1990	Toy Store	Closed	1992	14.00	14

Hometown II - M. Whiting

1991	Church	Closed	1993	14.00	14
1991	Dentist	Closed	1993	14.00	14
1991	Ice Cream Shop	Closed	1993	14.00	14
1991	Stitch-N-Sew	Closed	1993	14.00	14

Hometown III - M. Whiting

1991	Basket Shop	Closed	1993	15.50	16
1991	Dairy	Closed	1993	15.50	16
1991	Firehouse	Closed	1993	15.50	16
1991	Library	Closed	1993	15.50	16

Hometown IV - M. Whiting

1992	Bakery	Closed	1994	21.00	21
1992	Country Inn	Closed	1994	21.50	22
1992	Courthouse	Closed	1994	21.50	22
1992	Gas Station	Closed	1994	21.00	21

Hometown V - M. Whiting

1992	Antiques Shop	Closed	1995	22.00	22
1992	Gift Shop	Closed	1995	22.00	22
1992	Pharmacy	Closed	1995	22.00	22
1992	Sporting Goods	Closed	1995	22.00	22
1992	Tea Room	Closed	1995	22.00	22

Hometown VI - M. Whiting

1993	Church	Closed	1995	24.00	24
1993	Diner	Closed	1995	24.00	24
1993	General Store	Closed	1995	24.00	24
1993	School	Closed	1995	24.00	24
1993	Train Station	Closed	1995	24.00	24

Hometown VII - M. Whiting

1993	Candy Shop	Closed	1996	24.00	24
1993	Dress Shop	Closed	1996	24.00	24
1993	Flower Shop	Closed	1996	24.00	24
1993	Pet Shop	Closed	1996	24.00	24
1993	Post Office	Closed	1996	24.00	24
1993	Quilt Shop	Closed	1996	24.00	24

Hometown VIII - M. Whiting

1994	Barber Shop	Closed	1996	28.00	28
1994	Country Store	Closed	1996	28.00	28
1994	Fire Company	Closed	1996	28.00	28
1994	Professional Building	Closed	1996	28.00	28
1994	Sewing Shop	Closed	1996	26.00	26

*Quotes have been rounded up to nearest dollar

Brandywine Collectibles
to The Cat's Meow

ARCHITECTURE

Hometown IX - M. Whiting

YEAR ISSUE		EDITION LIMIT	YEAR RETD.	ISSUE PRICE	*QUOTE U.S. $
1994	Bed & Breakfast	Closed	1997	29.00	30
1994	Cafe/Deli	Closed	1997	29.00	30
1994	Hometown Bank	Closed	1997	29.00	30
1994	Hometown Gazette	Closed	1997	29.00	30
1994	Teddys & Toys	Closed	1997	29.00	30

Hometown X - M. Whiting

YEAR ISSUE		EDITION LIMIT	YEAR RETD.	ISSUE PRICE	*QUOTE U.S. $
1995	Brick Church	Open		29.00	30
1995	The Doll Shoppe	Open		29.00	30
1995	General Hospital	Open		29.00	30
1995	The Gift Box	Open		29.00	30
1995	Police Station	Open		29.00	30

Hometown XI - M. Whiting

YEAR ISSUE		EDITION LIMIT	YEAR RETD.	ISSUE PRICE	*QUOTE U.S. $
1995	Antiques	Open		29.00	30
1995	Church II	Open		29.00	30
1995	Grocer	Open		29.00	30
1995	Pharmacy	Open		29.00	30
1995	School II	Open		29.00	30

Hometown XII - M. Whiting

YEAR ISSUE		EDITION LIMIT	YEAR RETD.	ISSUE PRICE	*QUOTE U.S. $
1996	Bridal & Dress Shoppe	Open		29.00	30
1996	Five & Dime	Open		29.00	30
1996	Hometown Theater	Open		29.00	30
1996	Post Office	Open		29.00	30
1996	Travel Agency	Open		29.00	30

Hometown XIII - M. Whiting

YEAR ISSUE		EDITION LIMIT	YEAR RETD.	ISSUE PRICE	*QUOTE U.S. $
1996	Baby Shoppe	Open		29.00	30
1996	Beauty Shoppe	Open		29.00	30
1996	Gem Shoppe	Open		29.00	30
1996	House of Flowers	Open		29.00	30
1996	Robins & Roses	Open		29.00	30

Hometown XIV - M. Whiting

YEAR ISSUE		EDITION LIMIT	YEAR RETD.	ISSUE PRICE	*QUOTE U.S. $
1997	Bakery	Open		30.00	30
1997	The Corner Store	Open		30.00	30
1997	The Gift Basket	Open		30.00	30
1997	Hook & Ladder	Open		30.00	30
1997	Lawyer	Open		30.00	30
1997	Library	Open		30.00	30
1997	Pottery Barn	Open		30.00	30

North Pole Collection - M. Whiting, unless otherwise noted

YEAR ISSUE		EDITION LIMIT	YEAR RETD.	ISSUE PRICE	*QUOTE U.S. $
1992	3 Winter Trees - D. Whiting	Open		10.50	12
1993	Candy Cane Factory	Open		24.00	26
1991	Claus House	Open		24.00	26
1993	Elf Club	Open		24.00	26
1992	Elves Workshop	Closed	1996	24.00	26
1991	Gingerbread House	Open		24.00	26
1995	New Reindeer Barn	Open		24.00	26
1996	North Pole Chapel	Open		25.50	26
1994	Post Office	Open		25.00	26
1991	Reindeer Barn	Closed	1996	24.00	26
1992	Snowflake Lodge	Open		24.00	26
1992	Snowman with St. Sign	Open		11.50	13
1995	Stocking Shop	Open		24.00	26
1992	Sugarplum Bakery	Open		24.00	26
1993	Teddybear Factory	Open		24.00	26
1993	Town Christmas Tree	Open		20.00	24
1994	Town Hall	Open		25.00	26
1996	Trim-a-Tree Shop	Open		25.50	26

Old Salem Collection - M. Whiting

YEAR ISSUE		EDITION LIMIT	YEAR RETD.	ISSUE PRICE	*QUOTE U.S. $
1987	Boys School	Open		18.50	19
1987	First House	Open		12.80	13
1987	Home Moravian Church	Open		18.50	19
1987	Miksch Tobacco Shop	Closed	1993	12.00	12
1987	Salem Tavern	Open		20.50	21
1987	Schultz Shoemaker	Open		10.50	11
1987	Vogler House	Open		20.50	21
1987	Winkler Bakery	Open		20.50	21

Patriots Collection - M. Whiting

YEAR ISSUE		EDITION LIMIT	YEAR RETD.	ISSUE PRICE	*QUOTE U.S. $
1992	Betsy Ross House	Open		17.50	18
1992	Washingtons Headquarters	Open		24.00	24

Seymour Collection - M. Whiting

YEAR ISSUE		EDITION LIMIT	YEAR RETD.	ISSUE PRICE	*QUOTE U.S. $
1991	Anderson House	Open		20.00	21
1991	Blish Home	Open		20.00	21
1992	Majestic Theater	Open		22.00	23
1991	Seymour Church	Open		19.00	20
1991	Seymour Library	Open		20.00	21

Treasured Times - M. Whiting

YEAR ISSUE		EDITION LIMIT	YEAR RETD.	ISSUE PRICE	*QUOTE U.S. $
1994	Birthday House	750		32.00	33
1994	Halloween House	750		32.00	33
1994	Mother's Day House	750		32.00	33
1994	New Baby Boy House	750		32.00	33
1994	New Baby Girl House	750		32.00	33
1994	Valentine House	750		32.00	33

Victorian Collection - M. Whiting

YEAR ISSUE		EDITION LIMIT	YEAR RETD.	ISSUE PRICE	*QUOTE U.S. $
1989	Broadway House	Closed	1994	22.00	22
1989	Elm House	Closed	1994	25.00	25
1989	Fairplay Church	Closed	1994	19.50	20
1989	Hearts Ease Cottage	Closed	1994	15.30	16
1989	Old Star Hook & Ladder	Closed	1994	23.00	23
1989	Peachtree House	Closed	1994	22.50	23
1989	Seabreeze Cottage	Closed	1994	15.30	16
1989	Serenity Cottage	Closed	1994	15.30	16
1989	Skippack School	Closed	1994	22.50	23

Williamsburg Collection -M. Whiting

YEAR ISSUE		EDITION LIMIT	YEAR RETD.	ISSUE PRICE	*QUOTE U.S. $
1993	Campbell's Tavern	Open		28.00	29
1988	Colonial Capitol	Open		43.50	45
1988	Court House of 1770	Open		26.50	28
1988	Governor's Palace	Open		37.50	39
1993	Kings Arms Tavern	Open		25.00	26
1988	The Magazine	Open		23.50	25
1988	Wythe House	Open		25.00	26

Yorktown Collection - M. Whiting

YEAR ISSUE		EDITION LIMIT	YEAR RETD.	ISSUE PRICE	*QUOTE U.S. $
1987	Custom House	Open		17.50	19
1993	Digges House	Open		22.00	23
1987	Grace Church	Open		19.00	20
1987	Medical Shop	Open		13.00	14
1987	Moore House	Open		22.00	23
1987	Nelson House	Open		22.00	23
1987	Pate House	Open		19.00	20
1987	Swan Tavern	Open		22.00	23

The Cat's Meow

Collector Club Gift - Houses - F. Jones

YEAR ISSUE		EDITION LIMIT	YEAR RETD.	ISSUE PRICE	*QUOTE U.S. $
1989	1989 Betsy Ross House	Retrd.	1989	Gift	200
1990	1990 Amelia Earhart	Retrd.	1990	Gift	100
1991	1991 Limberlost Cabin	Retrd.	1991	Gift	50
1992	1992 Abigail Adams Birthplace	Retrd.	1992	Gift	50
1993	1993 Pearl S. Buck House	Retrd.	1993	Gift	50
1994	1994 Lillian Gish	Retrd.	1994	Gift	30
1995	1995 Eleanor Roosevelt	Retrd.	1995	Gift	N/A
1996	1996 Mother's Day Church	Retrd.	1996	Gift	N/A
1997	1997 Barbara Fritchie House	12/97		Gift	N/A

Collector Club - Famous Authors - F. Jones

YEAR ISSUE		EDITION LIMIT	YEAR RETD.	ISSUE PRICE	*QUOTE U.S. $
1989	Harriet Beecher Stowe	Retrd.	1989	8.75	N/A
1989	Orchard House	Retrd.	1989	8.75	N/A
1989	Longfellow House	Retrd.	1989	8.75	N/A
1989	Herman Melville's Arrowhead	Retrd.	1989	8.75	800
1989	Set	Retrd.	1989	35.00	800

Collector Club - Great Inventors - F. Jones

YEAR ISSUE		EDITION LIMIT	YEAR RETD.	ISSUE PRICE	*QUOTE U.S. $
1990	Thomas Edison	Retrd.	1990	9.25	N/A
1990	Ford Motor Co.	Retrd.	1990	9.25	N/A
1990	Seth Thomas Clock Co.	Retrd.	1990	9.25	75
1990	Wright Cycle Co.	Retrd.	1990	9.25	50
1990	Set	Retrd.	1990	37.00	350-500

Collector Club - American Songwriters - F. Jones

YEAR ISSUE		EDITION LIMIT	YEAR RETD.	ISSUE PRICE	*QUOTE U.S. $
1991	Benjamin R. Hanby House	Retrd.	1991	9.25	N/A
1991	Anna Warner House	Retrd.	1991	9.25	N/A
1991	Stephen Foster Home	Retrd.	1991	9.25	22
1991	Oscar Hammerstein House	Retrd.	1991	9.25	22
1991	Set	Retrd.	1991	37.00	200-300

Collector Club - Signers of the Declaration - F. Jones

YEAR ISSUE		EDITION LIMIT	YEAR RETD.	ISSUE PRICE	*QUOTE U.S. $
1992	Josiah Bartlett Home	Retrd.	1992	9.75	N/A
1992	George Clymer Home	Retrd.	1992	9.75	N/A
1992	Stephen Hopkins Home	Retrd.	1992	9.75	N/A
1992	John Witherspoon Home	Retrd.	1992	9.75	N/A
1992	Set	Retrd.	1992	39.00	150-200

Collector Club -19th Century Master Builders - F. Jones

YEAR ISSUE		EDITION LIMIT	YEAR RETD.	ISSUE PRICE	*QUOTE U.S. $
1993	Henry Hobson Richardson	Retrd.	1993	10.25	25
1993	Samuel Sloan	Retrd.	1993	10.25	25
1993	Alexander Jackson Davis	Retrd.	1993	10.25	25
1993	Andrew Jackson Downing	Retrd.	1993	10.25	25
1993	Set	Retrd.	1993	41.00	100

Collector Club - Williamsburg Merchants - F. Jones

YEAR ISSUE		EDITION LIMIT	YEAR RETD.	ISSUE PRICE	*QUOTE U.S. $
1994	East Carlton Wigmaker	Retrd.	1994	11.15	12
1994	J. Geddy Silversmith	Retrd.	1994	11.15	12
1994	Craig Jeweler	Retrd.	1994	11.15	12
1994	M. Hunter Millinery	Retrd.	1994	11.15	12
1994	Set	Retrd.	1994	44.60	75

Collector Club - Mt. Rushmore Presidential Series - F. Jones

YEAR ISSUE		EDITION LIMIT	YEAR RETD.	ISSUE PRICE	*QUOTE U.S. $
1995	George Washington Birthplace	Retrd.	1995	12.00	12
1995	Metamora Courthouse	Retrd.	1995	12.00	12
1995	Theodore Roosevelt Birthplace	Retrd.	1995	12.00	12
1995	Tuckahoe Plantation	Retrd.	1995	12.00	12
1995	Set	Retrd.	1995	48.00	75

Collector Club - American Holiday Series - F. Jones

YEAR ISSUE		EDITION LIMIT	YEAR RETD.	ISSUE PRICE	*QUOTE U.S. $
1996	And to all a Goodnight	Retrd.	1996	11.00	11
1996	Boo to You	Retrd.	1996	11.00	11
1996	Easter's On Its Way	Retrd.	1996	11.00	11
1996	Let Freedom Ring	Retrd.	1996	11.00	60

Collector Club - The Civil War Generals - F. Jones

YEAR ISSUE		EDITION LIMIT	YEAR RETD.	ISSUE PRICE	*QUOTE U.S. $
1997	Sherman Home	12/97		12.00	12
1997	Jackson Home	12/97		12.00	12
1997	Lee Memorial Chapel	12/97		12.00	12
1997	Grant House	12/97		12.00	12

Accessories - F. Jones

YEAR ISSUE		EDITION LIMIT	YEAR RETD.	ISSUE PRICE	*QUOTE U.S. $
1990	1909 Franklin Limousine	Retrd.	1995	4.00	7
1990	1913 Peerless Touring Car	Retrd.	1995	4.00	7
1990	1914 Fire Pumper	Retrd.	1995	4.00	7
1983	5" Hedge	Retrd.	1988	3.00	20-30
1983	5" Iron Fence	Retrd.	1988	3.00	30
1987	5" Picket Fence	Retrd.	1992	3.00	20-30
1990	5" Wrought Iron Fence	Retrd.	1995	3.00	10-25
1983	8" Hedge	Retrd.	1988	3.25	40
1983	8" Iron Fence	Retrd.	1988	3.25	30-40
1983	8" Picket Fence	Retrd.	1988	3.25	40
1989	Ada Belle	Retrd.	1994	4.00	10-30
1990	Amish Buggy	Retrd.	1995	4.00	8
1991	Amish Garden	Retrd.	1996	4.00	5
1987	Band Stand	Retrd.	1992	6.50	18
1991	Barnyard	Retrd.	1996	4.00	5
1990	Blue Spruce	Retrd.	1995	4.00	10
1990	Bus Stop	Retrd.	1995	4.00	7
1987	Butch & T.J.	Retrd.	1992	4.00	10-20
1986	Cable Car	Retrd.	1991	4.00	9-18
1986	Carolers	Retrd.	1991	4.00	15
1987	Charlie & Co.	Retrd.	1992	4.00	10
1985	Cherry Tree	Retrd.	1990	4.00	50
1991	Chessie Hopper Car	Retrd.	1996	4.00	10
1986	Chickens	Retrd.	1991	3.25	15
1990	Christmas Tree Lot	Retrd.	1995	4.00	10
1989	Clothesline	Retrd.	1994	4.00	9
1988	Colonial Bread Wagon	Retrd.	1993	4.00	12
1991	Concert in the Park	Retrd.	1996	4.00	18
1986	Cows	Retrd.	1991	4.00	15
1986	Dairy Wagon	Retrd.	1991	4.00	15
1986	Ducks	Retrd.	1991	3.25	13
1990	Eugene	Retrd.	1995	4.00	7
1985	Fall Tree	Retrd.	1990	4.00	25
1987	FJ Express	Retrd.	1992	4.00	15
1986	FJ Real Estate Sign	Retrd.	1991	3.00	15
1988	Flower Pots	Retrd.	1993	4.00	11
1988	Gas Light	Retrd.	1993	4.00	10
1990	Gerstenslager Buggy	Retrd.	1995	4.00	7
1989	Harry's Hotdogs	Retrd.	1994	4.00	10
1986	Horse & Carriage	Retrd.	1991	4.00	13
1987	Horse & Sleigh	Retrd.	1992	4.00	13
1986	Ice Wagon	Retrd.	1991	4.00	13
1983	Iron Gate	Retrd.	1988	3.00	40-50
1991	Jack The Postman	Retrd.	1996	3.25	5
1986	Liberty St. Sign	Retrd.	1991	3.25	13
1983	Lilac Bushes	Retrd.	1988	3.00	200-400
1990	Little Red Caboose	Retrd.	1995	4.00	9
1988	Mail Wagon	Retrd.	1993	4.00	10
1988	Main St. Sign	Retrd.	1993	3.25	10
1991	Marble Game	Retrd.	1996	4.00	5
1986	Market St. Sign	Retrd.	1991	3.25	15
1991	Martin House	Retrd.	1996	3.25	5
1987	Nanny	Retrd.	1992	4.00	10
1991	On Vacation	Retrd.	1996	4.00	5
1989	Passenger Train Car	Retrd.	1994	4.00	10
1985	Pine Tree	Retrd.	1990	4.00	30
1988	Pony Express Rider	Retrd.	1993	4.00	11
1991	Popcorn Wagon	Retrd.	1996	4.00	10
1985	Poplar Tree	Retrd.	1990	4.00	25-35
1989	Pumpkin Wagon	Retrd.	1994	3.25	10
1989	Quaker Oats Train Car	Retrd.	1994	4.00	10
1987	Railroad Sign	Retrd.	1992	3.00	13
1990	Red Maple Tree	Retrd.	1995	4.00	10
1989	Rose Trellis	Retrd.	1994	3.25	9
1989	Rudy & Aldine	Retrd.	1994	4.00	9
1990	Santa & Reindeer	Retrd.	1995	4.00	7
1991	Scarey Harry (Scarecrow)	Retrd.	1996	4.00	10
1991	School Bus	Retrd.	1996	4.00	5
1991	Ski Party	Retrd.	1996	4.00	5
1988	Skipjack	Retrd.	1993	6.50	15
1996	Smucker Train Car	Retrd.	1996	5.00	20
1989	Snowmen	Retrd.	1994	4.00	9
1988	Street Clock	Retrd.	1993	4.00	10
1985	Summer Tree	Retrd.	1990	4.00	35
1989	Tad & Toni	Retrd.	1994	4.00	9
1988	Telephone Booth	Retrd.	1993	4.00	10
1986	Touring Car	Retrd.	1991	4.00	10
1990	Tulip Tree	Retrd.	1995	4.00	10
1988	U.S. Flag	Retrd.	1993	4.00	7
1991	USMC War Memorial	Retrd.	1996	6.50	7
1990	Veterinary Wagon	Retrd.	1995	4.00	7
1990	Victorian Outhouse	Retrd.	1995	4.00	7
1991	Village Entrance Sign	Retrd.	1996	6.50	7
1990	Watkins Wagon	Retrd.	1995	4.00	7
1986	Wells, Fargo Wagon	Retrd.	1991	4.00	15
1987	Windmill	Retrd.	1992	3.25	10
1986	Wishing Well	Retrd.	1991	3.25	23
1987	Wooden Gate (two-sided)	Retrd.	1992	3.00	15
1985	Xmas Pine Tree	Retrd.	1990	4.00	25-35
1985	Xmas Pine Tree w/Red Bows	Retrd.	1990	3.00	150-200
1990	Xmas Spruce	Retrd.	1995	4.00	7

Black Heritage Series - F. Jones

YEAR ISSUE		EDITION LIMIT	YEAR RETD.	ISSUE PRICE	*QUOTE U.S. $
1994	Martin Luther King Birthplace	Retrd.	1994	8.00	55

Christmas '83-Williamsburg - F. Jones

YEAR ISSUE		EDITION LIMIT	YEAR RETD.	ISSUE PRICE	*QUOTE U.S. $
1983	Christmas Church	Retrd.	1983	6.00	N/A
1983	Federal House	Retrd.	1983	6.00	N/A
1983	Garrison House	Retrd.	1983	6.00	N/A

*Quotes have been rounded up to nearest dollar

ARCHITECTURE

The Cat's Meow to The Cat's Meow

YEAR ISSUE		EDITION LIMIT	YEAR RETD.	ISSUE PRICE	*QUOTE U.S. $
1983	Georgian House	Retrd.	1983	6.00	450
1983	Set	Retrd.	1983	24.00	N/A

Christmas '84-Nantucket - F. Jones

1984	Christmas Shop	Retrd.	1984	6.50	N/A
1984	Powell House	Retrd.	1984	6.50	350
1984	Shaw House	Retrd.	1984	6.50	350
1984	Wintrop House	Retrd.	1984	6.50	250
1984	Set	Retrd.	1984	26.00	1600

Christmas '85-Ohio Western Reserve - F. Jones

1985	Bellevue House	Retrd.	1985	7.00	175
1985	Gates Mills Church	Retrd.	1985	7.00	200
1985	Olmstead House	Retrd.	1985	7.00	175
1985	Western Reserve Academy	Retrd.	1985	7.00	175
1985	Set	Retrd.	1985	27.00	600-975

Christmas '86-Savannah - F. Jones

1986	J.J. Dale Row House	Retrd.	1986	7.25	150
1986	Lafayette Square House	Retrd.	1986	7.25	140-150
1986	Liberty Inn	Retrd.	1986	7.25	200
1986	Simon Mirault Cottage	Retrd.	1986	7.25	200
1986	Set	Retrd.	1986	29.00	500-600

Christmas '87-Maine - F. Jones

1987	Cappy's Chowder House	Retrd.	1987	7.75	250
1987	Captain's House	Retrd.	1987	7.75	250
1987	Damariscotta Church	Retrd.	1987	7.75	250
1987	Portland Head Lighthouse	Retrd.	1987	7.75	250
1987	Set	Retrd.	1987	31.00	800-1050

Christmas '88-Philadelphia - F. Jones

1988	Elfreth's Alley	Retrd.	1988	7.75	150-200
1988	Graff House	Retrd.	1988	7.75	150-200
1988	The Head House	Retrd.	1988	7.75	150-200
1988	Hill-Physick-Keith House	Retrd.	1988	7.75	150-200
1988	Set	Retrd.	1988	31.00	400-500

Christmas '89-In New England - F. Jones

1989	Hunter House	Retrd.	1989	8.00	50-70
1989	The Old South Meeting House	Retrd.	1989	8.00	80-125
1989	Sheldon's Tavern	Retrd.	1989	8.00	125
1989	The Vermont Country Store	Retrd.	1989	8.00	80-125
1989	Set	Retrd.	1989	32.00	250-350

Christmas '90-Colonial Virginia - F. Jones

1990	Dulany House	Retrd.	1990	8.00	50-100
1990	Rising Sun Tavern	Retrd.	1990	8.00	70-100
1990	Shirley Plantation	Retrd.	1990	8.00	50-75
1990	St. John's Church	Retrd.	1990	8.00	100
1990	St. John's Church (blue)	Retrd.	1990	8.00	150-200
1990	Set	Retrd.	1990	32.00	200-400

Christmas '91-Rocky Mountain - F. Jones

1991	First Presbyterian Church	Retrd.	1991	8.20	30
1991	Tabor House	Retrd.	1991	8.20	55-75
1991	Western Hotel	Retrd.	1991	8.20	25-55
1991	Wheller-Stallard House	Retrd.	1991	8.20	25-55
1991	Set	Retrd.	1991	32.80	100-150

Christmas '92-Hometown - F. Jones

1992	August Imgard House	Retrd.	1992	8.50	25-40
1992	Howey House	Retrd.	1992	8.50	30-50
1992	Overholt House	Retrd.	1992	8.50	30-50
1992	Wayne Co. Courthouse	Retrd.	1992	8.50	25-40
1992	Set	Retrd.	1992	34.00	100-120

Christmas '93-St. Charles - F. Jones

1993	Lewis & Clark Center	Retrd.	1993	9.00	15-20
1993	Newbill-McElhiney House	Retrd.	1993	9.00	15-20
1993	St. Peter's Catholic Church	Retrd.	1993	9.00	15-20
1993	Stone Row	Retrd.	1993	9.00	15-20
1993	Set	Retrd.	1993	36.00	60-85

Christmas '94-New Orleans Series - F. Jones

1994	Beauregard-Keyes House	Retrd.	1994	10.00	14-20
1994	Gallier House	Retrd.	1994	10.00	15
1994	Hermann-Grima House	Retrd.	1994	10.00	14-20
1994	St. Patrick's Church	Retrd.	1994	10.00	20-50
1994	Set	Retrd.	1994	40.00	50

Christmas '95-New York Series - F. Jones

1995	Clement C. Moore House	Retrd.	1995	10.00	15
1995	Fraunces Taver	Retrd.	1995	10.00	15
1995	Fulton Market	Retrd.	1995	10.00	15
1995	St. Marks-In-the-Bowery	Retrd.	1995	10.00	15
1995	Set	Retrd.	1995	40.00	55

Christmas '96-Atlanta Series - F. Jones

1996	Callanwolde	Retrd.	1996	11.00	11
1996	First Baptist Church	Retrd.	1996	11.00	11
1996	Fox Theatre	Retrd.	1996	11.00	11
1996	Swan House	Retrd.	1996	11.00	11

Circus Series - F. Jones

1996	Ferris Wheel	Retrd.	1996	10.00	10
1995	Sideshow	Retrd.	1995	10.00	17

Covered Bridge Series - F. Jones

1995	Creamery Bridge	Retrd.	1995	10.00	17
1996	Kennedy Bridge	Retrd.	1996	10.00	10

Fall - F. Jones

1986	Golden Lamb Buttery	Retrd.	1991	8.00	30-45
1986	Grimm's Farmhouse	Retrd.	1991	8.00	30-40
1986	Mail Pouch Barn	Retrd.	1991	8.00	45-65
1986	Vollant Mills	Retrd.	1991	8.00	30-60
1986	Set	Retrd.	1991	32.00	175

Great Americans Series - F. Jones

1996	Daniel Boone Home	Retrd.	1996	10.00	10

Green Gables Series - F. Jones

1996	Green Gables House	Retrd.	1996	10.00	10

Hagerstown - F. Jones

1988	J Hager House	Retrd.	1993	8.00	18
1988	Miller House	Retrd.	1993	8.00	18
1988	Woman's Club	Retrd.	1993	8.00	18
1988	The Yule Cupboard	Retrd.	1993	8.00	18
1988	Set	Retrd.	1993	32.00	60-75

Liberty St. - F. Jones

1988	County Courthouse	Retrd.	1993	8.00	17-31
1988	Graf Printing Co.	Retrd.	1993	8.00	17-31
1988	Wilton Railway Depot	Retrd.	1993	8.00	17-31
1988	Z. Jones Basketmaker	Retrd.	1993	8.00	20-40

Lighthouse - F. Jones

1990	Admiralty Head	Retrd.	1995	8.00	15
1990	Cape Hatteras Lighthouse	Retrd.	1995	8.00	15
1990	Sandy Hook Lighthouse	Retrd.	1995	8.00	15
1990	Split Rock Lighthouse	Retrd.	1995	8.00	15

Limited Edition Promotional Items - F. Jones

1993	Convention Museum	Retrd.	1993	12.95	13
1993	FJ Factory	Open		12.95	13
1994	FJ Factory/5 Yr. Banner	Retrd.	1994	10.00	18
1993	FJ Factory/Gold Cat Edition	Retrd.	1993	12.95	490
1994	FJ Factory/Home Banner	Retrd.	1994	10.00	10
1990	Frycrest Farm Homestead	Retrd.	1991	10.00	125
1992	Glen Pine	Retrd.	1993	10.00	16-25
1993	Nativity Cat on the Fence	Retrd.	1993	19.95	30

Main St. - F. Jones

1987	Franklin Library	Retrd.	1992	8.00	30
1987	Garden Theatre	Retrd.	1992	8.00	45
1987	Historical Museum	Retrd.	1992	8.00	25
1987	Telegraph/Post Office	Retrd.	1992	8.00	25
1987	Set	Retrd.	1992	32.00	100

Mark Twain's Hannibal Series - F. Jones

1995	Becky Thatcher House	Retrd.	1995	10.00	17
1996	Hickory Stick	Retrd.	1996	10.00	10

Market St. - F. Jones

1989	Schumacher Mills	Retrd.	1993	8.00	17-25
1989	Seville Hardware Store	Retrd.	1993	8.00	17-25
1989	West India Goods Store	Retrd.	1993	8.00	17-25
1989	Yankee Candle Company	Retrd.	1993	8.00	17-35

Martha's Vineyard Series - F. Jones

1995	John Coffin House	Retrd.	1995	10.00	10-15
1996	West Chop Lighthouse	Retrd.	1996	10.00	10

Miscellaneous - F. Jones

1985	Pencil Holder	Retrd.	1988	3.95	210
1985	Recipe Holder	Retrd.	1988	3.95	250
1986	School Desk-blue	Retrd.	1988	12.00	N/A
1986	School Desk-red	Retrd.	1988	12.00	175

Nantucket - F. Jones

1987	Jared Coffin House	Retrd.	1992	8.00	20
1987	Maria Mitchell House	Retrd.	1992	8.00	20
1987	Nantucket Atheneum	Retrd.	1992	8.00	15-35
1987	Unitarian Church	Retrd.	1992	8.00	25
1987	Set	Retrd.	1992	32.00	100

Nautical - F. Jones

1987	H & E Ships Chandlery	Retrd.	1992	8.00	20
1987	Lorain Lighthouse	Retrd.	1992	8.00	20
1987	Monhegan Boat Landing	Retrd.	1992	8.00	25
1987	Yacht Club	Retrd.	1992	8.00	20
1987	Set	Retrd.	1992	32.00	75

Neighborhood Event Series - F. Jones

1995	Peter Seitz Tavern & Stagecoach	Retrd.	1995	12.95	18
1995	Birely Place	Retrd.	1995	12.95	18
1996	Sea-Chimes	Retrd.	1996	12.95	15
1996	Bailey-Gombert House	Retrd.	1996	12.95	13

Ohio Amish - F. Jones

1991	Ada Mae's Quilt Barn	Retrd.	1996	8.00	10
1991	Brown School	Retrd.	1996	8.00	10
1991	Eli's Harness Shop	Retrd.	1996	8.00	10
1991	Jonas Troyer Home	Retrd.	1996	8.00	10

Painted Ladies - F. Jones

1988	Andrews Hotel	Retrd.	1993	8.00	20-30
1988	Lady Amanda	Retrd.	1993	8.00	20-30
1988	Lady Elizabeth	Retrd.	1993	8.00	20
1988	Lady Iris	Retrd.	1993	8.00	20
1988	Set	Retrd.	1993	32.00	70

Postage Stamp Lighthouse Series - F. Jones

1996	The Great Lakes Postage Stamp Lighthouse, set/5	6,000	1996	75.00	75

Roscoe Village - F. Jones

1986	Canal Company	Retrd.	1991	8.00	45-65
1986	Jackson Twp. Hall	Retrd.	1991	8.00	25-45
1986	Old Warehouse Rest.	Retrd.	1991	8.00	30-45
1986	Roscoe General Store	Retrd.	1991	8.00	20-35
1986	Set	Retrd.	1991	32.00	150

Series I - F. Jones

1983	Antique Shop	Retrd.	1988	8.00	100-125
1983	Apothecary	Retrd.	1988	8.00	100-125
1983	Barbershop	Retrd.	1988	8.00	100
1983	Book Store	Retrd.	1988	8.00	50-125
1983	Cherry Tree Inn	Retrd.	1988	8.00	N/A
1983	Federal House	Retrd.	1988	8.00	50-75
1983	Florist Shop	Retrd.	1988	8.00	60-125
1983	Garrison House	Retrd.	1988	8.00	125
1983	Red Whale Inn	Retrd.	1988	8.00	N/A
1983	School	Retrd.	1988	8.00	85-100
1983	Sweetshop	Retrd.	1988	8.00	125
1983	Toy Shoppe	Retrd.	1988	8.00	125
1983	Victorian House	Retrd.	1988	8.00	50-125
1983	Wayside Inn	Retrd.	1988	8.00	N/A
1983	Set of 12 w/1 Inn	Retrd.	1988	96.00	850-1200
1983	Set of 14 w/ 3 Inns	Retrd.	1988	112.00	2000-3000

Series II - F. Jones

1984	Attorney/Bank	Retrd.	1989	8.00	95
1984	Brocke House	Retrd.	1989	8.00	40
1984	Church	Retrd.	1989	8.00	45
1984	Eaton House	Retrd.	1989	8.00	20-35
1984	Grandinere House	Retrd.	1989	8.00	25-75
1984	Millinery/Quilt	Retrd.	1989	8.00	100-150
1984	Music Shop	Retrd.	1989	8.00	75-100
1984	S&T Clothiers	Retrd.	1989	8.00	100-150
1984	Tobacconist/Shoemaker	Retrd.	1989	8.00	75-100
1984	Town Hall	Retrd.	1989	8.00	50-100
1984	Set	Retrd.	1989	96.00	500-700

Series III - F. Jones

1985	Allen-Coe House	Retrd.	1990	8.00	60
1985	Connecticut Ave. FireHouse	Retrd.	1990	8.00	40-75
1985	Dry Goods Store	Retrd.	1990	8.00	50-75
1985	Edinburgh Times	Retrd.	1990	8.00	40-75
1985	Fine Jewelers	Retrd.	1990	8.00	40-50
1985	Hobart-Harley House	Retrd.	1990	8.00	30-40
1985	Kalorama Guest House	Retrd.	1990	8.00	20-35
1985	Main St. Carriage Shop	Retrd.	1990	8.00	50-75
1985	Opera House	Retrd.	1990	8.00	25-50
1985	Ristorante	Retrd.	1990	8.00	50-75
1985	Set	Retrd.	1990	80.00	350-400

Series IV - F. Jones

1986	Bennington-Hull House	Retrd.	1991	8.00	30-40
1986	Chagrin Falls Popcorn Shop	Retrd.	1991	8.00	30-40
1986	Chepachet Union Church	Retrd.	1991	8.00	30-40
1986	John Belville House	Retrd.	1991	8.00	30-40
1986	Jones Bros. Tea Co.	Retrd.	1991	8.00	30-40
1986	The Little House Giftables	Retrd.	1991	8.00	30-40
1986	O'Malley's Livery Stable	Retrd.	1991	8.00	30-40
1986	Vandenberg House	Retrd.	1991	8.00	30-40
1986	Village Clock Shop	Retrd.	1991	8.00	30-40
1986	Westbrook House	Retrd.	1991	8.00	30-40
1986	Set	Retrd.	1991	80.00	320

Series V - F. Jones

1987	Amish Oak/Dixie Shoe	Retrd.	1992	8.00	20-30
1987	Architect/Tailor	Retrd.	1992	8.00	20
1987	Congruity Tavern	Retrd.	1992	8.00	20
1987	Creole House	Retrd.	1992	8.00	20
1987	Dentist/Physician	Retrd.	1992	8.00	20
1987	M. Washington House	Retrd.	1992	8.00	20
1987	Markethouse	Retrd.	1992	8.00	20
1987	Murray Hotel	Retrd.	1992	8.00	20
1987	Police Department	Retrd.	1992	8.00	20
1987	Southport Bank	Retrd.	1992	8.00	20
1987	Set	Retrd.	1992	80.00	200-250

Series VI - F. Jones

1988	Burton Lancaster House	Retrd.	1993	8.00	18-35
1988	City Hospital	Retrd.	1993	8.00	20
1988	First Baptist Church	Retrd.	1993	8.00	18
1988	Fish/Meat Market	Retrd.	1993	8.00	20
1988	Lincoln School	Retrd.	1993	8.00	20
1988	New Masters Gallery	Retrd.	1993	8.00	20
1988	Ohliger House	Retrd.	1993	8.00	15-30
1988	Pruyn House	Retrd.	1993	8.00	20
1988	Stiffenbody Funeral Home	Retrd.	1993	8.00	18
1988	Williams & Sons	Retrd.	1993	8.00	20
1988	Set	Retrd.	1993	80.00	150-175

Series VII - F. Jones

1989	Black Cat Antiques	Retrd.	1994	8.00	15

*Quotes have been rounded up to nearest dollar

Collectors' Information Bureau

9

YEAR ISSUE		EDITION LIMIT	YEAR RETD.	ISSUE PRICE	*QUOTE U.S. $
1989	Hairdressing Parlor	Retrd.	1994	8.00	17
1989	Handcrafted Toys	Retrd.	1994	8.00	20
1989	Justice of the Peace	Retrd.	1994	8.00	15
1989	Octagonal School	Retrd.	1994	8.00	15
1989	Old Franklin Book Shop	Retrd.	1994	8.00	15
1989	Thorpe House Bed & Breakfast	Retrd.	1994	8.00	15
1989	Village Tinsmith	Retrd.	1994	8.00	15
1989	Williams Apothecary	Retrd.	1994	8.00	20
1989	Winkler Bakery	Retrd.	1994	8.00	20
1989	Set	Retrd.	1994	80.00	100

Series VIII - F. Jones

1990	FJ Realty Company	Retrd.	1995	8.00	15
1990	Globe Corner Bookstore	Retrd.	1995	8.00	15
1990	Haberdashers	Retrd.	1995	8.00	15
1990	Medina Fire Department	Retrd.	1995	8.00	15
1990	Nell's Stems & Stitches	Retrd.	1995	8.00	15
1990	Noah's Ark Veterinary	Retrd.	1995	8.00	20
1990	Piccadilli Pipe & Tobacco	Retrd.	1995	8.00	15
1990	Puritan House	Retrd.	1995	8.00	15
1990	Victoria's Parlour	Retrd.	1995	8.00	15
1990	Walldorff Furniture	Retrd.	1995	8.00	15
1990	Set	Retrd.	1995	80.00	100

Series IX - F. Jones

1991	All Saints Chapel	Retrd.	1996	8.00	13
1991	American Red Cross	Retrd.	1996	8.00	13
1991	Central City Opera House	Retrd.	1996	8.00	13
1991	City Hall	Retrd.	1996	8.00	13
1991	CPA/Law Office	Retrd.	1996	8.00	13
1991	Gov. Snyder Mansion	Retrd.	1996	8.00	13
1991	Jeweler/Optometrist	Retrd.	1996	8.00	13
1991	Osbahr's Upholstery	Retrd.	1996	8.00	13
1991	Spanky's Hardware Co.	Retrd.	1996	8.00	13
1991	The Treble Clef	Retrd.	1996	8.00	13

Southern Belles Series - F. Jones

1996	Auburn	Retrd.	1996	10.00	10

Special Item - F. Jones

1996	Discus Thrower	Retrd.	1996	10.00	10
1996	Smithsonian Castle/Stamp Edition	Retrd.	1996	15.00	15
1995	Smokey Bear	Retrd.	1995	8.95	14
1994	Smokey Bear w/ 50th stamp	Retrd.	1994	8.95	13

Tradesman - F. Jones

1988	Buckeye Candy & Tobacco	Retrd.	1993	8.00	20
1988	C.O. Wheel Company	Retrd.	1993	8.00	20
1988	Hermannhof Winery	Retrd.	1993	8.00	20
1988	Jenney Grist Mill	Retrd.	1993	8.00	20
1988	Set	Retrd.	1993	32.00	60

Washington - F. Jones

1991	National Archives	Retrd.	1996	8.00	13
1991	U.S. Capitol	Retrd.	1996	8.00	13
1991	U.S. Supreme Court	Retrd.	1996	8.00	13
1991	White House	Retrd.	1996	8.00	13

Wild West - F. Jones

1989	Drink 'em up Saloon	Retrd.	1993	8.00	20
1989	F.C. Zimmermann's Gun Shop	Retrd.	1993	8.00	20
1989	Marshal's Office	Retrd.	1993	8.00	18
1989	Wells, Fargo & Co.	Retrd.	1993	8.00	18
1989	Wells, Fargo & Co.	Retrd.	1993	32.00	75

Wine Country Series - F. Jones

1996	Charles Krug Winery	Retrd.	1996	10.00	13

Cavanagh Group Intl.

Coca-Cola Brand North Pole Bottling Works - CGI

1995	All in a Day's Work	Open		25.00	25
1996	Art Department	Open		50.00	50
1996	An Artist's Touch	Open		25.00	25
1996	Big Ambitions	Open		25.00	25
1995	Checking His List	Open		30.00	30
1996	Delivery for Mrs. Claus	Open		25.00	25
1996	Elf in Training	Open		25.00	25
1995	An Elf's Favorite Chore	Open		30.00	30
1995	Filling Operations	Open		45.00	45
1995	Front Office	Open		50.00	50
1995	The Kitchen Corner	Open		55.00	55
1995	Maintenance Mischief	Open		25.00	25
1995	Making the Secret Syrup	Open		30.00	30
1996	Oops!	Open		25.00	25
1996	Order Department	Open		55.00	55
1996	Precious Cargo	Open		25.00	25
1995	Quality Control	Open		25.00	25
1996	Shipping Department	Open		55.00	55
1996	Special Delivery	Open		25.00	25
1996	A Stroke of Genius	Open		25.00	25
1995	Top Secret	Open		30.00	30

Coca-Cola Brand Town Square Collection - CGI

1992	Candler's Drugs	Closed	1993	40.00	60-85
1996	Carlson's General Store	Open		40.00	40
1997	Central High	Open		40.00	40
1996	Chandler's Ski Resort	Open		40.00	40
1993	City Hall	Closed	1994	40.00	75-125
1996	Clara's Christmas Shop	Closed	1996	40.00	50-60
1995	Coca-Cola Bottling Works	Closed	1995	40.00	50
1996	Cooper's Tree Farm	Open		20.00	20
1992	Dee's Boarding House	Closed	1993	40.00	400-600
1997	Dew Drop Inn	Open		40.00	40
1996	Diamond Service Station	Closed	1996	40.00	50-70
1992	Dick's Luncheonette	Closed	1993	40.00	60-90
1997	Five and Dime	Open		40.00	40
1994	Flying "A" Service Station	Closed	1996	40.00	50
1992	Gilbert's Grocery	Closed	1993	40.00	90-140
1995	Grist Mill	Closed	1995	40.00	50
1992	Howard Oil	Closed	1993	40.00	140-165
1993	Jacob's Pharmacy	5,000	1993	25.00	400-600
1995	Jenny's Sweet Shoppe	Closed	1995	40.00	50
1995	Lighthouse Point Snack Bar	Closed	1996	40.00	50
1994	McMahon's General Store	Closed	1995	40.00	50
1993	Mooney's Antique Barn	Closed	1994	40.00	75-125
1997	Mrs. Murphy's Chowder House	Open		40.00	40
1994	Plaza Drugs	Closed	1995	20.00	50-60
1993	Route 93 Covered Bridge	Closed	1995	20.00	30-40
1996	Scooter's Drive In	Open		40.00	40
1997	South Station	Open		40.00	40
1994	Station #14 Firehouse	Closed	1996	40.00	50
1994	Strand Theatre	Closed	1996	40.00	50
1993	T. Taylor's Emporium	Closed	1994	40.00	50-60
1993	The Tick Tock Diner	Closed	1995	40.00	60
1996	Town Barber Shop	Open		40.00	40
1994	Town Gazebo	Closed	1995	20.00	30-40
1992	Train Depot	Closed	1993	40.00	250-300
1996	Walton's 5 & 10	Open		40.00	40

Coca-Cola Brand Town Square Collection Accessories - CGI

1992	Ad Car "Coca-Cola"	Closed	1993	9.00	25
1992	After Skating	Closed	1993	8.00	13
1995	Boys with Snowballs	Closed	1995	11.00	17
1992	Bringing It Home	Closed	1993	8.00	20
1994	Checker Players	Closed	1995	15.00	20
1994	Crowley Cab Co.	Closed	1995	11.00	20
1992	Delivery Man	Closed	1993	8.00	22
1992	Delivery Truck "Coca-Cola"	Closed	1993	15.00	32
1993	Extra! Extra!	Closed	1994	7.00	18
1992	Gil the Grocer	Closed	1993	8.00	20
1993	Gone Fishing	Closed	1994	11.00	18
1994	Homeward Bound	Closed	1995	8.00	12
1992	Horse-Drawn Wagon	Closed	1993	12.00	40-60
1995	Lunch Wagon	Closed	1995	15.00	15
1993	Officer Pat	Closed	1995	7.00	13
1993	Old Number Seven	Closed	1995	15.00	20
1994	Sledders	Closed	1995	11.00	14
1994	Sleigh Ride	Closed	1995	15.00	18
1993	Soda Jerk	Closed	1995	7.00	17
1993	Street Vendor	Closed	1994	11.00	22
1992	Thirsty the Snowman	Closed	1993	9.00	22

Department 56

Alpine Village Series - Department 56

1987	Alpine Church 6541-2	Closed	1991	32.00	135-195
1992	Alpine Shops 5618-9, set/2 (Metterniche Wurst, Kukuck Uhren)	Open		75.00	75
1986	Alpine Village 6540-4, set/5 (Apotheke, E. Staubr Backer)	Open		150.00	195
1986	•Bessor Bierkeller 55405	Closed	1996	30.00	30-50
1986	•Gasthof Eisl 55406	Closed	1996	30.00	30-50
1986	•Milch-Kase 55409	Closed	1996	30.00	30-45
1990	Bahnhof 5615-4	Closed	1993	42.00	60-95
1994	Bakery & Chocolate Shop 5614-6	Open		37.50	38
1988	Grist Mill 5953-6	Open		42.00	45
1987	Josef Engel Farmhouse 5952-8	Closed	1989	33.00	750-1050
1995	Kamm Haus 5617-1	Open		42.00	42
1993	Sport Laden 5612-0	Open		50.00	50
1991	St. Nikolaus Kirche 5617-0	Open		37.50	38

Christmas In the City Series - Department 56

1989	5607 Park Avenue Townhouse 5977-3	Closed	1992	48.00	75-100
1989	5609 Park Avenue Townhouse 5978-1	Closed	1992	48.00	75-100
1991	All Saints Corner Church 5542-5	Open		96.00	110
1991	Arts Academy 5543-3	Closed	1993	45.00	60-90
1995	Brighton School 5887-6	Open		52.00	52
1994	Brokerage House 5881-5	Open		48.00	48
1995	Brownstones on the Square 5887-7, set/2 (Beekman House, Pickford Place)	Open		90.00	90
1987	The Cathedral 5962-5	Closed	1990	60.00	300-360
1992	Cathedral Church of St. Mark 5549-2	3,024	1993	120.00	1500-2000
1988	Chocolate Shoppe 5968-4	Closed	1991	40.00	125-160
1987	Christmas In The City 6512-9, set/3	Closed	1990	112.00	500-600
1987	•Bakery 6512-9	Closed	1990	37.50	97-120
1987	•Tower Restaurant 6512-9	Closed	1990	37.50	225-260
1987	•Toy Shop and Pet Store 6512-9	Closed	1990	37.50	215-275
1988	City Hall (small) 5969-2	Closed	1991	65.00	160-195
1988	City Hall (standard) 5969-2	Closed	1991	65.00	150-195
1991	The Doctor's Office 5544-1	Closed	1994	60.00	65-80
1989	Dorothy's Dress Shop 5974-9	12,500	1991	70.00	325-375
1994	First Metropolitan Bank 5882-3	Open		60.00	60
1988	Hank's Market 5970-6	Closed	1992	40.00	70-115
1994	Heritage Museum of Art 5883-1	Open		96.00	96
1991	Hollydale's Department Store 5534-4	Open		75.00	85
1995	Holy Name Church 5887-5	Open		96.00	96
1995	Ivy Terrace Apartments 5887-4	Open		60.00	60
1991	Little Italy Ristorante 5538-7	Closed	1995	50.00	60-95
1987	Palace Theatre 5963-3	Closed	1989	45.00	860-965
1990	Red Brick Fire Station 5536-0	Closed	1995	55.00	60-90
1989	Ritz Hotel 5973-0	Closed	1994	55.00	65-95
1987	Sutton Place Brownstones 5961-7	Closed	1989	80.00	750-895
1992	Uptown Shoppes 5531-0, set/3	Closed	1996	150.00	150
1992	•Haberdashery 55311	Closed	1996	30.00	35-50
1992	•City Clockworks 55313	Closed	1996	30.00	35-70
1992	•Music Emporium 55312	Closed	1996	30.00	40-70
1988	Variety Store 5972-2	Closed	1990	45.00	145-180
1996	Washington Street Post Office 58880	Open		52.00	52
1993	West Village Shops 5880-7, set/2	Closed	1996	90.00	90
1993	•Potters' Tea Seller 58808	Closed	1996	45.00	50-65
1993	•Spring St. Coffee House 58809	Closed	1996	45.00	50-65
1990	Wong's In Chinatown 5537-9	Closed	1994	55.00	65-95

Dickens' Village Series - Department 56

1991	Ashbury Inn 5555-7	Closed	1995	55.00	45-85
1987	Barley Bree 5900-5, set/2 (Farmhouse, Barn)	Closed	1989	60.00	360-373
1990	Bishops Oast House 5567-0	Closed	1992	45.00	55-100
1995	Blenham Street Bank 5833-0	Open		60.00	60
1986	Blythe Pond Mill House 6508-0	Closed	1990	37.00	230-280
1986	By The Pond Mill House 6508-0	Closed	1990	37.00	110-150
1994	Boarding & Lodging School 5810-6	Open		48.00	48
1993	Boarding and Lodging School 5809-2 (Christmas Carol Commemorative Piece)	Yr.Iss.	1993	48.00	125-195
1987	Brick Abbey 6549-8	Closed	1989	33.00	325-395
1996	Butter Tub Barn 58338	Open		48.00	48
1996	Butter Tub Farmhouse 58337	Open		40.00	40
1988	C. Fletcher Public House 5904-8	12,500	1989	35.00	480-575
1986	Chadbury Station and Train 6528-5	Closed	1989	65.00	525-285
1987	Chesterton Manor House 6568-4	7,500	1988	45.00	1300-1600
1986	Christmas Carol Cottages 6500-5, set/3	Closed	1995	75.00	125-150
1986	•The Cottage of Bob Cratchit & Tiny Tim 6500-5	Closed	1995	25.00	40-65
1986	•Fezziwig's Warehouse 6500-5	Closed	1995	25.00	25-50
1986	•Scrooge and Marley Counting House 6500-5	Closed	1995	25.00	33-50
1996	The Christmas Carol Cottages (revisited) 58339	Open		60.00	60
1988	Cobblestone Shops 5924-2, set/3	Closed	1990	95.00	275-375
1988	•Booter and Cobbler 5924-2	Closed	1990	32.00	100-130
1988	•T. Wells Fruit & Spice Shop 5924-2	Closed	1990	32.00	80-100
1988	•The Wool Shop 5924-2	Closed	1990	32.00	140-195
1989	Cobles Police Station 5583-2	Closed	1991	37.50	125-165
1988	Counting House & Silas Thimbleton Barrister 5902-1	Closed	1990	32.00	76-115
1992	Crown & Cricket Inn (Charles Dickens' Signature Series), 5750-9	Yr.Iss.	1992	100.00	135-200
1989	David Copperfield 5550-6, set/3	Closed	1992	125.00	140-185
1989	•Betsy Trotwood's Cottage 5550-6	Closed	1992	42.50	40-80
1989	•Peggotty's Seaside Cottage 5550-6 (green boat)	Closed	1992	42.50	40-75
1989	•Mr. Wickfield Solicitor 5550-6	Closed	1992	42.50	75-100
1989	David Copperfield 5550-6, set/3 with tan boat	Closed	1992	125.00	215-260
1989	Peggotty's Seaside Cottage 5550-6 (tan boat)	Closed	1992	42.50	105-160
1994	Dedlock Arms 5752-5 (Charles Dickens' Signature Series)	Yr.Iss.	1994	100.00	110-165
1985	Dickens' Cottages 6518-8 set/3	Closed	1988	75.00	870-1000
1985	•Stone Cottage 6518-8	Closed	1988	25.00	340-420
1985	•Thatched Cottage 6518-8	Closed	1988	25.00	160-200
1985	•Tudor Cottage 6518-8	Closed	1988	25.00	325-400
1986	Dickens' Lane Shops 6507-2, set/3	Closed	1989	80.00	500-650
1986	•Cottage Toy Shop 6507-2	Closed	1989	27.00	185-220
1986	•Thomas Kersey Coffee House 6507-2	Closed	1989	27.00	145-175
1986	•Tuttle's Pub 6507-2	Closed	1989	27.00	185-240
1984	Dickens' Village Church (cream) 6516-1	Closed	1989	35.00	275-375
1985	Dickens' Village Church (dark) 6516-1	Closed	1989	35.00	125-170
1985	Dickens' Village Church (green) 6516-1	Closed	1989	35.00	275-440
1985	Dickens' Village Church (tan) 6516-1	Closed	1989	35.00	155-195
1985	Dickens' Village Mill 6519-6	2,500	1986	35.00	3700-4400
1995	Dudden Cross Church 5834-3	Open		45.00	45
1995	Dursley Manor, 5832-9	Open		50.00	50
1991	Fagin's Hide-A-Way 5552-2	Closed	1995	68.00	55-95
1989	The Flat of Ebenezer Scrooge 5587-5	Open		37.50	38
1997	Gad's Hill Place (Charles Dickens' Signature Series), 57535	Yr.Iss.		98.00	98
1994	Giggelswick Mutton & Ham, 5822-0	Open		48.00	48
1996	The Grapes Inn, 57534 (Charles Dickens' Signature Series)	Yr.Iss.	1996	120.00	120
1993	Great Denton Mill 5812-2	Open		50.00	50
1989	Green Gate Cottage 5586-7	22,500	1990	65.00	230-290
1994	Hather Harness 5823-8	Open		48.00	48
1992	Hembleton Pewterer, 5800-9	Closed	1995	72.00	55-85
1988	Ivy Glen Church 5927-7	Closed	1991	35.00	65-95

10 Collectors' Information Bureau *Quotes have been rounded up to nearest dollar

YEAR ISSUE		EDITION LIMIT	YEAR RETD.	ISSUE PRICE	*QUOTE U.S.$
1995	J.D. Nichols Toy Shop 5832-8	Open		48.00	48
1987	Kenilworth Castle 5916-1	Closed	1988	70.00	575-775
1992	King's Road Post Office 5801-7	Open		45.00	45
1993	Kingford's Brewhouse 5811-4	Closed	1996	45.00	45-70
1990	Kings Road 5568-9, set/2	Closed	1996	72.00	40-65
1990	•Tutbury Printer 55690	Closed	1996	36.00	43-53
1990	•C.H. Watt Physician 55691	Closed	1996	36.00	50-75
1989	Knottinghill Church 5582-4	Closed	1995	50.00	60-100
1995	The Maltings 5833-5	Open		50.00	50
1996	The Melancholy Tavern (Revisted) 58347	Open		45.00	45
1988	Merchant Shops 5926-9, set/5	1993Closed		150.00	200-260
1988	•Geo. Weeton Watchmaker 5926-9	Closed	1993	30.00	36-70
1988	•The Mermaid Fish Shoppe 5926-9	Closed	1993	30.00	57-75
1988	•Poulterer 5926-9	Closed	1993	30.00	45-70
1988	•Walpole Tailors 5926-9	Closed	1993	30.00	40-70
1988	•White Horse Bakery 5926-9	Closed	1993	30.00	45-75
1996	Mulberrie Court 58345	Open		90.00	90
1991	Nephew Fred's Flat 5557-3	Closed	1994	35.00	65-85
1996	Nettie Quinn Puppets & Marionettes 58344	Open		50.00	50
1988	Nicholas Nickleby 5925-0, set/2	Closed	1991	72.00	150-175
1988	•Nicholas Nickleby Cottage 5925-0	Closed	1991	36.00	65-85
1988	•Wackford Squeers Boarding School 5925-0	Closed	1991	36.00	65-95
1988	Nickolas Nickleby Cottage 5925-0-misspelled	Closed	1991	36.00	65-95
1988	Nickolas Nickleby set/2, 5925-0 misspelled	Closed	1991	36.00	150-200
1986	Norman Church 6502-1	3,500	1987	40.00	3000-3700
1987	The Old Curiosity Shop 5905-6	Open		32.00	42
1992	Old Michaelchurch, 5562-0	Closed	1996	42.00	48-65
1996	The Olde Camden Town Church (Revisited) 58346	Open		55.00	55
1991	Oliver Twist 5553-0, set/2	Closed	1993	75.00	65-140
1991	•Brownlow House 5553-0	Closed	1993	38.00	50-80
1991	•Maylie Cottage 5553-0	Closed	1993	38.00	40-70
1984	The Original Shops of Dickens' Village 6515-3, set of 7	Closed	1988	175.00	1100-1350
1984	•Abel Beesley Butcher 6515-3	Closed	1988	25.00	110-150
1984	•Bean And Son Smithy Shop 6515-3	Closed	1988	25.00	165-195
1984	•Candle Shop 6515-3	Closed	1988	25.00	170-200
1984	•Crowntree Inn 6515-3	Closed	1988	25.00	250-300
1984	•Golden Swan Baker 6515-3	Closed	1988	25.00	155-180
1984	•Green Grocer 6515-3	Closed	1988	25.00	170-190
1984	•Jones & Co. Brush & Basket Shop 6515-3	Closed	1988	25.00	250-295
1993	The Pied Bull Inn (Charles Dickens' Signature Series) 5751-7	Closed	1993	100.00	115-180
1994	Portobello Road Thatched Cottages 5824-6, set/3 (Mr. & Mrs. Pickle, Cobb Cottage, Browning Cottage)	Open		120.00	120
1993	Pump Lane Shoppes 5808-4, set/3	Closed	1996	112.00	112-150
1993	•Bumpstead Nye Cloaks & Canes 58083	Closed	1996	37.35	38-45
1993	•Lomas Ltd. Molasses 58086	Closed	1996	37.35	38-55
1993	•W.M. Wheat Cakes & Puddings 58087	Closed	1996	37.35	38-55
1996	Ramsford Palace 58336, set/17 (Ramsford Palace, Palace Guards, set/2 Accessory, Palace Gate Accessory, Palace Fountain Accessory, Wall Hedge, set/8 Accessory, Corner Wall Topiaries, set/4 Accessory)	27,500	1996	175.00	425-750
1989	Ruth Marion Scotch Woolens 5585-9	17,500	1990	65.00	345-375
1995	Sir John Falstaff Inn 5753-3 (Charles Dickens' Signature Series)	Closed	1995	100.00	110-140
1995	Start A Tradition Set 5832-7, set/13 (The Town Square Carolers Accessory, set/3, 6 Sisal Trees, Bag of Real Plastic Snow, Cobblestone Road)	Closed	1996	85.00	85-110
1995	•Faversham Lamps & Oil	Closed	1996	N/A	N/A
1995	•Morston Steak and Kidney Pie	Closed	1996	N/A	N/A
1989	Theatre Royal 5584-0	Closed	1992	45.00	60-95
1989	Victoria Station 5574-3	Open		100.00	112
1994	Whittlesbourne Church, 5821-1	Open		85.00	85
1995	Wrenbury Shops 5833-1, set/3 (Wrenbury Baker, The Chop Shop, T. Puddlewick Spectacle Shop)	Open		100.00	100

Disney Parks Village Series - Department 56

YEAR ISSUE		EDITION LIMIT	YEAR RETD.	ISSUE PRICE	*QUOTE U.S.$
1994	Fire Station No. 105 5352-0 Disneyland, CA	Closed	1996	45.00	45
1994	Mickey's Christmas Shop 5350-3, set/2 Disney World, FL	Closed	1996	144.00	144
1994	Olde World Antiques 5351-1, set/2 Disney World, FL	Closed	1996	90.00	90
1995	Silversmith 5352-1 Disney World, FL	Closed	1996	50.00	165-235
1995	Tinker Bell's Treasures 5352-2 Disney World, FL	Closed	1996	60.00	175-275

Disney Parks Village Series Accessories - Department 56

YEAR ISSUE		EDITION LIMIT	YEAR RETD.	ISSUE PRICE	*QUOTE U.S.$
1995	The Balloon Seller 5353-9, set/2	Closed	1996	25.00	35-50
1994	Disney Parks Family, set/3 5354-6	Closed	1996	32.50	33
1994	Mickey and Minnie 5353-8, set/2	Closed	1996	22.50	23-35
1994	Olde World Antiques Gate 5355-4	Closed	1996	15.00	15

Event Piece - Heritage Village Collection Accessory - Department 56

YEAR ISSUE		EDITION LIMIT	YEAR RETD.	ISSUE PRICE	*QUOTE U.S.$
1992	Gate House 5530-1	Closed	1992	22.50	40-70
1996	Christmas Bells 98711	Closed	1996	35.00	35-50

Little Town of Bethlehem Series - Department 56

YEAR ISSUE		EDITION LIMIT	YEAR RETD.	ISSUE PRICE	*QUOTE U.S.$
1987	Little Town of Bethlehem 5975-7, set/12	Open		150.00	150

New England Village Series - Department 56

YEAR ISSUE		EDITION LIMIT	YEAR RETD.	ISSUE PRICE	*QUOTE U.S.$
1993	A. Bieler Farm 5648-0, set/2	Closed	1996	92.00	95
1993	•Pennsylvania Dutch Farmhouse 56481	Closed	1996	46.00	46
1993	•Pennsylvania Dutch Barn 56482	Closed	1996	46.00	46-66
1988	Ada's Bed and Boarding House (lemon yellow) 5940-4	Closed	1991	36.00	200-285
1988	Ada's Bed and Boarding House (pale yellow) 5940-4	Closed	1991	36.00	110-145
1996	Apple Valley School 56172	Open		35.00	35
1994	Arlington Falls Church 5651-0	Open		40.00	42
1989	Berkshire House (medium blue) 5942-0	Closed	1991	40.00	135-155
1989	Berkshire House (teal) 5942-0	Closed	1991	40.00	95-125
1993	Blue Star Ice Co. 5647-2	Open		45.00	48
1992	Bluebird Seed and Bulb 5642-1	Closed	1996	48.00	48-60
1996	Bobwhite Cottage 56576	Open		50.00	50
1995	Brewster Bay Cottage 5657-0, set/2 (Jeremiah Brewster House, Thomas T. Julian House)	Open		90.00	90
1994	Cape Keag Cannery 5652-9	Open		48.00	48
1990	Captain's Cottage 5947-1	Closed	1996	40.00	44-55
1988	Cherry Lane Shops 5939-0, set/3	Closed	1990	80.00	260-350
1988	•Anne Shaw Toys 5939-0	Closed	1990	27.00	145-175
1988	•Ben's Barbershop 5939-0	Closed	1990	27.00	100-125
1988	•Otis Hayes Butcher Shop 5939-0	Closed	1990	27.00	70-85
1987	Craggy Cove Lighthouse 5930-7	Closed	1994	35.00	45-75
1995	Chowder House 5657-1	Open		40.00	40
1996	J. Hudson Stoveworks 56574	Open		60.00	60
1986	Jacob Adams Farmhouse and Barn 6538-2	Closed	1989	65.00	450-550
1989	Jannes Mullet Amish Barn 5944-7	Closed	1992	48.00	70-100
1989	Jannes Mullet Amish Farm House 5943-9	Closed	1992	32.00	90-115
1991	McGrebe-Cutters & Sleighs 5640-5	Closed	1995	45.00	50-70
1986	New England Village 6530-7, set/7	Closed	1989	170.00	1100-1280
1986	•Apothecary Shop 6530-7	Closed	1989	25.00	90-105
1986	•Brick Town Hall 6530-7	Closed	1989	25.00	155-200
1986	•General Store 6530-7	Closed	1989	25.00	250-325
1986	•Livery Stable & Boot Shop 6530-7	Closed	1989	25.00	115-140
1986	•Nathaniel Bingham Fabrics 6530-7	Closed	1989	25.00	145-155
1986	•Red Schoolhouse 6530-7	Closed	1989	25.00	245-260
1986	•Steeple Church (Original) 6530-7	Closed	1989	25.00	150-180
1988	Old North Church 5932-3	Open		40.00	45
1995	Pierce Boat Works 5657-3	Open		55.00	55
1994	Pigeonhead Lighthouse 5653-7	Open		50.00	50
1990	Shingle Creek House 5946-3	Closed	1994	37.50	45-60
1990	Sleepy Hollow 5954-4, set/3	Closed	1993	96.00	100-175
1990	•Ichabod Crane's Cottage 5954-4	Closed	1993	32.00	35-60
1990	•Sleepy Hollow School 5954-4	Closed	1993	32.00	65-100
1990	•Van Tassel Manor 5954-4	Closed	1993	32.00	40-70
1990	Sleepy Hollow Church 5955-2	Closed	1993	36.00	45-70
1987	Smythe Woolen Mill 6543-9	7,500	1988	42.00	900-1100
1986	Steeple Church (Second Version) 6539-0	Closed	1990	30.00	75-115
1992	Stoney Brook Town Hall 5644-8	Closed	1995	42.00	42-60
1987	Timber Knoll Log Cabin 6544-7	Closed	1990	28.00	150-175
1987	Weston Train Station 5931-5	Closed	1989	42.00	245-290
1995	Woodbridge Post Office 5657-2	Open		40.00	40
1992	Yankee Jud Bell Casting 5643-0	Closed	1995	44.00	45-60

North Pole Series - Department 56

YEAR ISSUE		EDITION LIMIT	YEAR RETD.	ISSUE PRICE	*QUOTE U.S.$
1994	Beard Barber Shop 5634-0	Open		27.50	28
1992	Elfie's Sleds & Skates 5625-1	Closed	1996	48.00	55-75
1995	Elfin Forge & Assembly Shop 5638-4	Open		65.00	65
1994	Elfin Snow Cone Works 5633-2	Open		40.00	40
1995	Elves' Trade School 5638-7	Open		50.00	50
1993	Express Depot 5627-8	Open		48.00	48
1996	Hall of Records 56392	Open		50.00	50
1991	Neenee's Dolls & Toys 5620-0	Closed	1995	37.50	45-75
1990	North Pole 5601-4, set/2 (Reindeer Barn)	Open		70.00	80
1990	•Elf Bunkhouse 56016	Closed	1996	35.00	40-50
1993	North Pole Chapel 5626-0	Open		45.00	45
1994	North Pole Dolls & Santa's Bear Works 5635-9, set/3 (North Pole Dolls, Santa's Bear Works, Entrance)	Open		96.00	96
1992	North Pole Post Office 5623-5	Open		45.00	50
1991	North Pole Shops 5621-9, set/2	Closed	1995	75.00	100-130
1991	•Orly's Bell & Harness Supply	Closed	1995	37.50	47-75
1991	•Rimpy's Bakery	Closed	1995	37.50	55-75
1992	Obbie's Books & Letrinka's Candy 5624-3	Closed	1996	70.00	70-85
1996	Popcorn & Cranberry House 56388	Open		45.00	45
1996	Route 1, North Pole, Home of Mr. & Mrs. Claus 56391	Open		110.00	110
1996	Santa's Bell Repair 56389	Open		45.00	45
1993	Santa's Lookout Tower 5629-4	Open		45.00	48
1995	Santa's Rooming House 5638-6	Open		50.00	50
1993	Santa's Woodworks 5628-6	Closed	1996	42.00	50-60
1990	Santa's Workshop 5600-6	Closed	1993	72.00	385-500
1996	Start a Tradition Set 56390, set/12 (Candy Cane Elves, set/2 Accessory)	Closed	1996	85.00	85-100
1996	•Candy Cane & Peppermint Shop	Closed	1996	N/A	N/A
1996	•Gift Wrap & Ribbons	Closed	1996	N/A	N/A
1991	Tassy's Mittens & Hassel's Woolies 5622-7	Closed	1995	50.00	60-95
1995	Tin Soldier Shop 5638-3	Open		42.00	42
1995	Weather & Time Observatory 5638-5	Open		50.00	50

The Original Snow Village Collection - Department 56

YEAR ISSUE		EDITION LIMIT	YEAR RETD.	ISSUE PRICE	*QUOTE U.S.$
1986	2101 Maple 5043-1	Closed	1986	32.00	300-350
1990	56 Flavors Ice Cream Parlor 5151-9	Closed	1992	42.00	90-125
1979	Adobe House 5066-6	Closed	1980	18.00	1700-2200
1992	Airport 5439-9	Closed	1996	60.00	60-78
1992	Al's TV Shop 5423-2	Closed	1995	40.00	40-60
1986	All Saints Church 5070-9	Open		38.00	45
1986	Apothecary 5076-8	Closed	1990	34.00	80-100
1981	Bakery 5077-6	Closed	1983	30.00	175-195
1986	Bakery 5077-6	Closed	1991	35.00	70-95
1982	Bank 5024-5	Closed	1983	32.00	445-595
1981	Barn 5074-1	Closed	1984	32.00	350-400
1984	Bayport 5015-6	Closed	1986	30.00	185-235
1986	Beacon Hill House 5065-2	Closed	1988	31.00	135-170
1995	Beacon Hill Victorian 5485-7	Open		60.00	60
1996	Birch Run Ski Chalet 54882	Open		60.00	60
1979	Brownstone 5056-7	Closed	1981	36.00	410-495
1996	Boulder Springs House 54873	Open		60.00	60
1995	Bowling Alley 5485-8	Open		42.00	42
1978	Cape Cod 5013-8	Closed	1980	20.00	275-350
1994	Carmel Cottage 5466-6	Open		48.00	48
1982	Carriage House 5021-0	Closed	1984	28.00	230-325
1986	Carriage House 5071-7	Closed	1988	29.00	99-115
1987	Cathedral Church 5019-9	Closed	1990	50.00	80-105
1980	Cathedral Church 5067-4	Closed	1981	36.00	1800-2500
1982	Centennial House 5020-2	Closed	1984	32.00	245-300
1983	Chateau 5084-9	Closed	1984	35.00	325-425
1995	Christmas Cove Lighthouse 5483-6	Open		60.00	60
1996	Christmas Lake High School 54881	Open		52.00	52
1991	The Christmas Shop 5097-0	Closed	1996	37.50	45-60
1985	Church of the Open Door 5048-2	Closed	1988	34.00	105
1988	Cobblestone Antique Shop 5123-3	Closed	1992	36.00	55-75
1994	Coca-Cola Brand Bottling Plant 5469-0	Open		65.00	65
1995	Coca-Cola Brand Corner Drugstore 5484-4	Open		55.00	55
1989	Colonial Church 5119-5	Closed	1992	60.00	60
1980	Colonial Farm House 5070-9	Closed	1982	30.00	245-275
1984	Congregational Church 5034-2	Closed	1985	28.00	550-600
1988	Corner Cafe 5124-1	Closed	1991	37.00	75-98
1981	Corner Store 5076-8	Closed	1983	30.00	200
1976	Country Church 5004-7	Closed	1979	18.00	285-375
1979	Countryside Church 5051-8 Meadowland Series	Closed	1980	25.00	700-760
1979	Countryside Church 5058-3	Closed	1984	27.50	220-350
1989	Courthouse 5144-6	Closed	1993	65.00	150-175
1992	Craftsman Cottage (American Architecture Series), 5437-2	Closed	1995	55.00	55-75
1987	Cumberland House 5024-5	Closed	1995	42.00	45-65
1993	Dairy Barn 5446-1	Open		55.00	55
1984	Delta House 5012-1	Closed	1986	32.00	220-325
1985	Depot and Train w/2 Train Cars 5051-2	Closed	1988	65.00	75-125
1993	Dinah's Drive-In 5447-0	Closed	1996	45.00	45-69
1989	Doctor's House 5143-8	Closed	1992	56.00	85-100
1991	Double Bungalow 5407-0	Closed	1994	45.00	45-65
1985	Duplex 5050-4	Closed	1987	35.00	110-150
1995	Dutch Colonial 5485-6 (American Architecture Series)	Closed	1996	45.00	45-60
1981	English Church 5078-4	Closed	1982	30.00	265-375
1981	English Cottage 5073-3	Closed	1982	25.00	240-275
1983	English Tudor 5033-4	Closed	1985	30.00	195-225
1987	Farm House 5089-0	Closed	1992	40.00	55-75
1994	Federal House (American Architecture Series) 5465-8	Open		50.00	50
1991	Finklea's Finery: Costume Shop 5405-4	Closed	1993	45.00	50-70
1983	Fire Station 5032-6	Closed	1984	32.00	535-575
1987	Fire Station No. 2 5091-1	Closed	1989	40.00	155-220
1994	Fisherman's Nook Cabins 5461-5, set/2, (Fisherman's Nook Bass Cabin, Fisherman's Nook Trout Cabin)	Open		50.00	50
1994	Fisherman's Nook Resort 5460-7	Open		75.00	75
1982	Flower Shop 5082-2	Closed	1983	25.00	435-455
1976	Gabled Cottage 5002-1	Closed	1979	20.00	300-365
1982	Gabled House 5081-4	Closed	1983	30.00	260-440
1984	Galena House 5009-1	Closed	1985	32.00	275-350
1978	General Store (tan) 5012-0	Closed	1980	25.00	675
1978	General Store (white) 5012-0	Closed	1980	25.00	385-470
1979	Giant Trees 5065-8	Closed	1982	20.00	175-300
1996	Treetop Tree House 54890	Open		35.00	35
1983	Gingerbread House Bank (Non-lighted) 5025-3	Closed	1984	24.00	250-370
1994	Glenhaven House 5468-2	Open		45.00	45
1992	Good Shepherd Chapel & Church School 5424-0, set/2	Closed	1996	72.00	72-90
1983	Gothic Church 5028-8	Closed	1986	36.00	185-250

*Quotes have been rounded up to nearest dollar

ARCHITECTURE

YEAR ISSUE		EDITION LIMIT	YEAR RETD.	ISSUE PRICE	*QUOTE U.S. $
1991	Gothic Farmhouse (American Architecture Series), 5404-6	Open		48.00	48
1983	Governor's Mansion 5003-2	Closed	1985	32.00	200-290
1992	Grandma's Cottage 5420-8	Closed	1996	42.00	45-60
1983	Grocery 5001-6	Closed	1985	35.00	300-350
1996	Harley-Davidson Motorcycle Shop 54886	Open		65.00	65
1992	Hartford House 5426-7	Closed	1995	55.00	60-80
1984	Haversham House 5008-3	Closed	1987	37.00	210-275
1986	Highland Park House 5063-6	Closed	1988	35.00	120-160
1995	Holly Brothers Garage 5485-4	Open		48.00	48
1988	Home Sweet Home/House & Windmill 5126-8	Closed	1991	60.00	100-125
1978	Homestead 5011-2	Closed	1984	30.00	176-260
1991	Honeymooner Motel 5401-1	Closed	1993	42.00	65-75
1993	Hunting Lodge 5445-3	Closed	1996	50.00	55-70
1976	The Inn 5003-9	Closed	1979	20.00	375-440
1989	J. Young's Granary 5149-7	Closed	1992	45.00	65-75
1991	Jack's Corner Barber Shop 5406-2	Closed	1994	42.00	55-80
1987	Jefferson School 5082-2	Closed	1991	36.00	150-200
1989	Jingle Belle Houseboat 5114-4	Closed	1991	42.00	115-130
1988	Kenwood House 5054-7	Closed	1990	50.00	105-150
1979	Knob Hill (gold) 5055-9	Closed	1981	30.00	260-350
1979	Knob Hill 5055-9	Closed	1981	30.00	215-275
1981	Large Single Tree 5080-6	Closed	1989	17.00	25-40
1987	Lighthouse 5030-0	Closed	1988	36.00	430-625
1986	Lincoln Park Duplex 5060-1	Closed	1988	33.00	105
1979	Log Cabin 5057-5	Closed	1981	22.00	345-500
1984	Main Street House 5005-9	Closed	1986	27.00	125-200
1990	Mainstreet Hardware Store 5153-5	Closed	1993	42.00	65-75
1977	Mansion 5008-8	Closed	1979	30.00	390-440
1988	Maple Ridge Inn 5121-7	Closed	1990	55.00	50-85
1994	Marvel's Beauty Salon 5470-4	Open		37.50	38
1986	Mickey's Diner 5078-4	Closed	1987	22.00	625-650
1979	Mission Church 5062-5	Closed	1980	30.00	1000-1100
1979	Mobile Home 5063-3	Closed	1980	18.00	1400-2200
1990	Morningside House 5152-7	Closed	1992	45.00	50
1993	Mount Olivet Church 5442-9	Closed	1996	65.00	65
1976	Mountain Lodge 5001-3	Closed	1979	20.00	295-375
1978	Nantucket 5014-6	Closed	1986	25.00	180-250
1993	Nantucket Renovation 5441-0	Closed	1993	55.00	55-70
1984	New School House 5037-7	Closed	1986	35.00	175-225
1982	New Stone Church 5083-0	Closed	1984	32.00	260-340
1996	Nick's Tree Farm 54871, set/10 (Nick's Tree Farm, Nick The Tree Farmer Accessory)	Open		40.00	40
1989	North Creek Cottage 5120-9	Closed	1992	45.00	45-60
1991	Oak Grove Tudor 5400-3	Closed	1994	42.00	45-60
1994	The Original Snow Village Starter Set 5462-3 (Sunday School Serenade Accessory, 3 assorted Sisal Trees, 1.5 oz. bag of real plastic snow)	Closed	1996	50.00	50-65
1994	•Shady Oak Church	Closed	1996	N/A	N/A
1986	Pacific Heights House 5066-0	Closed	1988	33.00	65-90
1988	Palos Verdes 5141-1	Closed	1990	37.50	60-90
1989	Paramount Theater 5142-0	Closed	1993	42.00	95-140
1984	Parish Church 5039-3	Closed	1986	32.00	205-290
1983	Parsonage 5029-6	Closed	1985	35.00	286-325
1995	Peppermint Porch Day Care 5485-2	Open		45.00	45
1989	Pinewood Log Cabin 5150-0	Closed	1995	37.50	45-60
1982	Pioneer Church 5022-9	Closed	1984	30.00	265-325
1995	Pisa Pizza 5485-1	Open		35.00	35
1985	Plantation House 5047-4	Closed	1987	37.00	80-100
1992	Post Office 5422-4	Closed	1995	35.00	50-80
1990	Prairie House (American Architecture Series), 5156-0	Closed	1993	42.00	50-70
1992	Print Shop & Village News 5425-9	Closed	1994	37.50	45-65
1990	Queen Anne Victorian (American Architecture Series), 5157-8	Closed	1996	48.00	50-65
1986	Ramsey Hill House 5067-9	Closed	1989	36.00	75-125
1987	Red Barn 5081-4	Closed	1992	38.00	75-90
1988	Redeemer Church 5127-6	Closed	1992	42.00	45-60
1996	Reindeer Bus Depot 54874	Open		42.00	42
1985	Ridgewood 5052-0	Closed	1987	35.00	110-175
1984	River Road House 5010-5	Closed	1987	36.00	155-250
1996	Rockabilly Records 54880	Open		45.00	45
1996	Rosita's Cantina 54883	Open		50.00	50
1995	Ryman Auditorium 5485-5	Open		75.00	75
1986	Saint James Church 5068-7	Closed	1988	37.00	130-170
1979	School House 5060-9	Closed	1982	30.00	315-375
1996	The Secret Garden Florist 54885	Open		50.00	50
1988	Service Station 5128-4	Closed	1991	37.50	230-300
1996	Shingle Victorian (American Architecture Series), 54884	Open		55.00	55
1988	Single Car Garage 5125-0	Closed	1990	22.00	33-55
1994	Skate & Ski Shop 5467-4	Open		50.00	50
1982	Skating Pond 5017-2	Closed	1984	25.00	296-360
1978	Skating Rink, Duck Pond (set) 5015-3	Closed	1979	16.00	800-1200
1976	Small Chalet 5006-2	Closed	1979	15.00	300-400
1978	Small Double Trees w/ blue birds 5016-1	Closed	1989	13.50	170
1978	Small Double Trees w/ red birds 5016-1	Closed	1989	13.50	22-30
1996	Smokey Mountain Retreat 54872	Open		65.00	65
1995	Snow Carnival Ice Palace 5485-0	Open		95.00	95
1987	Snow Village Factory 5013-0	Closed	1989	45.00	100-140
1987	Snow Village Resort Lodge 5092-0	Closed	1989	55.00	120-145
1993	Snowy Hills Hospital 5448-8	Closed	1996	48.00	48-63
1986	Sonoma House 5062-8	Closed	1988	33.00	105-150
1991	Southern Colonial (American Architecture Series), 5403-8	Closed	1994	48.00	65-80
1990	Spanish Mission Church 5155-1	Closed	1992	42.00	55-85
1987	Springfield House 5027-0	Closed	1990	40.00	50-80
1985	Spruce Place 5049-0	Closed	1987	33.00	185-285
1987	St. Anthony Hotel & Post Office 5006-7	Closed	1989	40.00	85-130
1992	St. Luke's Church 5421-6	Closed	1994	45.00	45-70
1995	Starbucks Coffee 5485-9	Open		48.00	48
1976	Steepled Church 5005-4	Closed	1979	25.00	415-525
1977	Stone Church (10") 5009-6	Closed	1979	35.00	475-525
1979	Stone Church (8") 5059-1	Closed	1980	32.00	750-990
1980	Stone Mill House 5068-2	Closed	1982	30.00	395-470
1988	Stonehurst House 5140-3	Closed	1994	37.50	40-70
1984	Stratford House 5007-5	Closed	1986	28.00	160-175
1982	Street Car 5019-9	Closed	1984	16.00	275-396
1985	Stucco Bungalow 5045-8	Closed	1986	30.00	310-400
1984	Summit House 5036-9	Closed	1985	28.00	265-345
1982	Swiss Chalet 5023-7	Closed	1984	28.00	350-435
1979	Thatched Cottage 5050-0 Meadowland Series	Closed	1980	30.00	600-750
1980	Town Church 5071-7	Closed	1982	33.00	280-380
1983	Town Hall 5000-8	Closed	1984	32.00	260-400
1986	Toy Shop 5073-3	Closed	1990	36.00	75-95
1980	Train Station w/ 3 Train Cars 5085-6	Closed	1985	100.00	270-300
1996	Treetop Tree House 54890	Open		35.00	35
1984	Trinity Church 5035-0	Closed	1986	32.00	185-275
1979	Tudor House 5061-7	Closed	1981	25.00	250-300
1983	Turn of the Century 5004-0	Closed	1986	36.00	160-240
1986	Twin Peaks 5042-3	Closed	1986	32.00	335-400
1979	Victorian 5054-2	Closed	1982	30.00	245-375
1983	Victorian Cottage 5002-4	Closed	1984	35.00	230-330
1977	Victorian House 5007-0	Closed	1979	30.00	275-400
1983	Village Church 5026-1	Closed	1984	30.00	275-375
1991	Village Greenhouse 5402-0	Closed	1995	35.00	45-65
1988	Village Market 5044-0	Closed	1991	39.00	60-85
1995	Village Police Station 5485-3	Open		48.00	48
1993	Village Public Library 5443-7	Open		55.00	55
1990	Village Realty 5154-3	Closed	1993	42.00	55-60
1992	Village Station 5438-0	Open		65.00	65
1988	Village Station and Train 5122-5	Closed	1992	65.00	80-125
1992	Village Vet and Pet Shop 5427-5	Closed	1995	32.00	45-60
1989	Village Warming House 5145-4	Closed	1992	42.00	48-70
1986	Waverly Place 5041-5	Closed	1986	35.00	240-290
1994	Wedding Chapel 5464-0	Open		55.00	55
1985	Williamsburg House 5046-6	Closed	1988	37.00	125-135
1993	Woodbury House 5444-5	Closed	1996	45.00	45-70
1983	Wooden Church 5031-8	Closed	1985	30.00	270-325
1981	Wooden Clapboard 5072-5	Closed	1984	32.00	170

The Original Snow Village Collection Accessories Retired - Department 56

YEAR ISSUE		EDITION LIMIT	YEAR RETD.	ISSUE PRICE	*QUOTE U.S.$
1987	3 Nuns With Songbooks 5102-0	Closed	1988	6.00	110-130
1988	Apple Girl/Newspaper Boy 5129-2, set/2	Closed	1990	11.00	18-25
1979	Aspen Trees 5052-6, Meadowland Series	Closed	1980	16.00	450-500
1989	Bringing Home The Tree 5169-1	Closed	1992	15.00	20-30
1989	Calling All Cars 5174-8, set/2	Closed	1991	15.00	45-60
1979	Carolers 5064-1	Closed	1986	12.00	95-130
1987	Caroling Family 5105-5, set/3	Closed	1990	20.00	25-35
1980	Ceramic Car 5069-0	Closed	1986	5.00	50
1981	Ceramic Sleigh 5079-2	Closed	1986	5.00	45-55
1993	Check It Out Bookmobile 5451-8, set/3	Closed	1995	25.00	27
1987	Children In Band 5104-7	Closed	1989	15.00	23-30
1989	Choir Kids 5147-0	Closed	1992	15.00	20-32
1993	Christmas at the Farm 5450-0, set/2	Closed	1996	16.00	16
1991	Christmas Cadillac 5413-5	Closed	1994	9.00	14
1987	Christmas Children 5107-1, set/4	Closed	1990	20.00	20-35
1992	Christmas Puppies 5432-1, set/2	Closed	1996	27.50	28
1991	Cold Weather Sports 5410-0, set/4	Closed	1994	27.50	30-45
1991	Come Join The Parade 5411-9	Closed	1992	13.00	18-24
1991	Country Harvest 5415-1	Closed	1993	13.00	20-30
1989	Crack the Whip 5171-3, set/3	Closed	1996	25.00	25
1988	Doghouse/Cat In Garbage Can 5131-4, set/2	Closed	1992	15.00	25-30
1990	Down the Chimney He Goes 5158-6	Closed	1993	6.50	17
1992	Early Morning Delivery 5431-3, set/3	Closed	1995	27.50	32
1985	Family Mom/Kids, Goose/Girl 5057-1	Closed	1988	11.00	25-42
1987	For Sale Sign 5108-0	Closed	1989	3.50	6-12
1990	Fresh Frozen Fish 5163-2, set/2	Closed	1993	20.00	30-40
1986	Girl/Snowman, Boy 5095-4	Closed	1987	11.00	45-70
1988	Hayride 5117-9	Closed	1990	30.00	44-54
1990	Here We Come A Caroling 5161-6, set/3	Closed	1992	18.00	16-30
1990	Home Delivery 5162-4, set/2	Closed	1992	16.00	23-40
1990	A Home For the Holidays 5165-9	Closed	1996	7.00	7
1986	Kids Around The Tree (large) 5094-6	Closed	1990	15.00	42-50
1986	Kids Around The Tree (small) 5094-6	Closed	1990	15.00	30-50
1990	Kids Decorating the Village Sign 5134-9	Closed	1993	13.00	14-25
1989	Kids Tree House 5168-3	Closed	1991	25.00	45-55
1988	Man On Ladder Hanging Garland 5116-0	Closed	1992	7.50	11-17
1984	Monks-A-Caroling (brown) 5040-7	Closed	1988	6.00	24-40
1983	Monks-A-Caroling (butterscotch) 6459-9	Closed	1984	6.00	41-60
1992	Nanny and the Preschoolers 5430-5, set/2	Closed	1994	27.50	22-35
1987	Park Bench (green) 5109-8	Closed	1993	3.00	5
1993	Pint-Size Pony Rides 5453-4, set/3	Closed	1996	37.50	40
1987	Praying Monks 5103-9	Closed	1988	6.00	44
1992	Round & Round We Go! 5433-0, set/2	Closed	1995	18.00	18-30
1985	Santa/Mailbox 5059-8	Closed	1988	11.00	34-40
1994	Santa Comes To Town, 1995 5477-1	Closed	1995	30.00	30-55
1995	Santa Comes To Town, 1996 54862	Closed	1996	32.50	33-44
1988	School Bus, Snow Plow 5137-3, set/2	Closed	1991	16.00	44-55
1988	School Children 5118-7, set/3	Closed	1990	15.00	15-30
1984	Scottie With Tree 5038-5	Closed	1985	3.00	150-180
1979	Sheep, 9 White, 3 Black 5053-4 Meadowland Series	Closed	1980	12.00	400
1986	Shopping Girls w/Packages (large) 5096-2	Closed	1988	11.00	20-40
1986	Shopping Girls w/Packages (small) 5096-2	Closed	1988	11.00	26-36
1985	Singing Nuns 5053-9	Closed	1987	6.00	110-125
1988	Sisal Tree Lot 8183-3	Closed	1991	45.00	82-120
1989	Skate Faster Mom 5170-5	Closed	1991	13.00	16-23
1990	Sleighride 5160-8	Closed	1992	30.00	38-50
1990	Sno-Jet Snowmobile 5159-4	Closed	1993	15.00	18-25
1987	Snow Kids 5113-6, set/4	Closed	1990	20.00	35-55
1985	Snow Kids Sled, Skis 5056-3	Closed	1987	11.00	38-50
1991	Snowball Fort 5414-3, set/3	Closed	1993	28.00	28-38
1982	Snowman With Broom 5018-0	Closed	1990	3.00	5-15
1992	Spirit of Snow Village Airplane 5440-2	Closed	1996	32.50	30-45
1992	Spirit of Snow Village Airplane 5458-5, 2 assorted	Closed	1996	12.50	17
1989	Statue of Mark Twain 5173-0	Closed	1991	15.00	22-36
1990	SV Special Delivery 5197-7, set/2	Closed	1992	16.00	22-35
1989	Through the Woods 5172-1, set/2	Closed	1991	18.00	19-25
1990	A Tree For Me 5164-0, set/2	Closed	1995	8.00	13
1989	US Mailbox 5179-9	Closed	1990	3.50	8-18
1989	US Special Delivery 5148-9, set/2	Closed	1990	16.00	30-48
1989	Village Birds 5180-2, set/6	Closed	1994	3.50	9
1989	Village Gazebo 5146-2	Closed	1995	30.00	32-45
1991	Village Greetings 5418-6, set/3	Closed	1994	5.00	5
1993	Village News Delivery 5459-3, set/2	Closed	1996	15.00	22
1991	Village Marching Band 5412-7, set/3	Closed	1992	30.00	30-50
1988	Water Tower 5133-0	Closed	1991	20.00	65-85
1989	Water Tower-John Deer 568-0	Closed	1991	20.00	600-650
1992	We're Going to a Christmas Pageant 5435-6	Closed	1994	15.00	18
1991	Winter Fountain 5409-7	Closed	1993	25.00	45-55
1992	Winter Playground 5436-4	Closed	1995	20.00	22-28
1988	Woodsman and Boy 5130-6, set/2	Closed	1991	13.00	22-35
1988	Woody Station Wagon 5136-5	Closed	1990	6.50	19-30
1991	Wreaths For Sale 5408-9, set/4	Closed	1994	27.50	28-52

Retired Heritage Village Collection Accessories -Department 56

YEAR ISSUE		EDITION LIMIT	YEAR RETD.	ISSUE PRICE	*QUOTE U.S.$
1991	All Around the Town 5545-0, set/2	Closed	1993	18.00	24-34
1987	Alpine Village Sign 6571-4	Closed	1993	6.00	12-18
1986	Alpine Villagers 6542-0, set/3	Closed	1992	13.00	25-36
1990	Amish Buggy 5949-8	Closed	1992	22.00	44-64
1990	Amish Family 5948-0, set/3	Closed	1992	20.00	25-35
1990	Amish Family, w/Moustache 5948-0, set/3	Closed	1992	20.00	40-50
1987	Automobiles 5964-1, set/3	Closed	1996	22.00	22
1991	Baker Elves 5603-0, set/3	Closed	1995	27.50	28-45
1992	The Bird Seller 5803-3, set/3	Closed	1995	25.00	25-35
1987	Blacksmith 5934-0, set/3	Closed	1990	20.00	65-85
1989	Boulevard 5916-6, set/14	Closed	1993	25.00	43-54
1990	Busy Sidewalks 5535-2, set/4	Closed	1992	28.00	36-50
1992	Buying Bakers Bread 5619-7, set/2	Closed	1995	20.00	25-35
1993	C. Bradford, Wheelwright & Son 5818-1, set/2	Closed	1996	24.00	24
1990	Carolers on the Doorstep 5570-0, set/4	Closed	1993	25.00	28-38
1984	Carolers, w/ Lamppost (bl) 6526-9, set/3	Closed	1990	10.00	28-35
1984	Carolers, w/ Lamppost (wh) 6526-9, set/3	Closed	1990	10.00	70-100
1988	Childe Pond and Skaters 5903-0, set/4	Closed	1991	30.00	60-85
1986	Christmas Carol Figures 6501-3, set/3	Closed	1990	12.50	70-85
1987	Christmas in the City Sign 5960-9	Closed	1993	6.00	10-18
1992	Churchyard Gate and Fence 5563-8, set/3	Closed	1992	15.00	45-60
1988	City Bus & Milk Truck 5983-8, set/2	Closed	1991	15.00	20-38
1988	City Newsstand 5971-4, set/4	Closed	1991	25.00	45-70
1987	City People 5965-0, set/5	Closed	1990	27.50	48-57
1987	City Workers 5967-6, set/4	Closed	1988	15.00	35-48
1991	Come into the Inn, 5560-3	Closed	1994	22.00	28-35
1989	Constables 5579-4, set/3	Closed	1991	17.50	50-65
1986	Covered Wooden Bridge 6531-5	Closed	1990	10.00	28-45
1989	David Copperfield Characters 5551-4, set/5	Closed	1992	32.50	35-40
1987	Dickens' Village Sign 6569-2	Closed	1993	6.00	10-20

*Quotes have been rounded up to nearest dollar

YEAR ISSUE		EDITION LIMIT	YEAR RETD.	ISSUE PRICE	*QUOTE U.S.$
1992	Don't Drop The Presents! 5532-8, set/2	Closed	1995	25.00	25-30
1987	Dover Coach 6590-0	Closed	1990	18.00	50-86
1987	Dover Coach w/o Mustache 6590-0	Closed	1990	18.00	75-95
1989	Farm Animals 5945-5, set/4	Closed	1991	15.00	35-45
1987	Farm People And Animals 5901-3, set/5	Closed	1989	24.00	80-98
1988	Fezziwig and Friends 5928-5, set/3	Closed	1990	12.50	38-53
1991	The Fire Brigade 5546-8, set/2	Closed	1995	20.00	20-30
1991	Fire Truck, "City Fire Dept." 5547-6, set/2	Closed	1995	18.00	25-35
1992	Harvest Seed Cart 5645-6, set/3	Closed	1995	27.50	28-35
1989	Heritage Village Sign 9953-8	Closed	1989	10.00	22
1993	Knife Grinder 5649-9, set/2	Closed	1996	22.50	23
1992	Letters for Santa 5604-9, set/3	Closed	1994	30.00	45-58
1986	Lighted Tree With Children & Ladder 6510-2	Closed	1989	35.00	200-290
1987	Maple Sugaring Shed 6589-7, set/3	Closed	1989	19.00	195-275
1991	Market Day 5641-3,set/3	Closed	1993	35.00	28-45
1987	New England Village Sign 6570-6	Closed	1993	6.00	10-18
1986	New England Winter set 6532-3, set/5	Closed	1990	18.00	32-45
1988	Nicholas Nickleby Characters 5929-3, set/4	Closed	1991	20.00	24-30
1992	The Old Puppeteer 5802-5, set/3	Closed	1995	32.00	25-35
1991	Oliver Twist Characters 5554-9, set/3	Closed	1993	35.00	30-45
1988	One Horse Open Sleigh 5982-0	Closed	1993	20.00	25-45
1989	Organ Grinder 5957-9, set/3	Closed	1991	21.00	28-37
1987	Ox Sled (blue pants) 5951-0	Closed	1989	20.00	100-150
1987	Ox Sled (tan pants) 5951-0	Closed	1989	20.00	205-270
1993	Playing in the Snow 5556-5, set/3	Closed	1996	25.00	28
1989	Popcorn Vendor 5958-7, set/3	Closed	1992	22.00	26-36
1986	Porcelain Trees 6537-4,set/2	Closed	1992	14.00	34
1994	Postern 9871-0, (Dickens' Village Ten Year Accessory Anniversary Piece)	Closed	1994	17.50	20-30
1991	Poultry Market 5559-0, set/3	Closed	1995	32.00	25-35
1988	Red Covered Bridge 5987-0	Closed	1994	17.00	18-25
1989	River Street Ice House Cart 5959-5	Closed	1991	20.00	35-52
1989	Royal Coach 5578-6	Closed	1992	55.00	60-85
1988	Salvation Army Band 5985-4, set/6	Closed	1991	24.00	75-100
1990	Santa's Little Helpers 5610-3, set/3	Closed	1993	28.00	48-65
1987	Shopkeepers 5966-8, set/4	Closed	1988	15.00	24-30
1987	Silo And Hay Shed 5950-1	Closed	1989	18.00	140-175
1987	Skating Pond 6545-5	Closed	1990	24.00	55-75
1990	Sleepy Hollow Characters 5956-0, set/3	Closed	1992	27.50	32-42
1986	Sleighride 6511-0	Closed	1990	19.50	42-65
1988	Snow Children 5938-2	Closed	1994	17.00	19-30
1987	Stone Bridge 6546-3	Closed	1990	12.00	60-75
1990	Tis the Season 5539-5	Closed	1994	12.95	20-25
1992	Town Tinker 5646-4, set/2	Closed	1995	24.00	18-26
1991	Toymaker Elves 5602-2, set/3	Closed	1995	27.50	30-46
1990	Trimming the North Pole 5608-1	Closed	1993	10.00	25-35
1989	U.S. Mail Box and Fire Hydrant 5517-4	Closed	1990	5.00	18
1987	Village Express Train (electric, black),5997-8	Closed	1988	89.95	225-330
1988	Village Express Train 5980-3, set/22	Closed	1996	100.00	118
1993	Village Express Van (black), 9951-1	Closed	1993	25.00	85-125
1993	Village Express Van (gold), 9977-5 (promotional)	Closed	1993	N/A	725-850
1992	Village Express Van 5865-3	Closed	1996	25.00	25
1994	Village Express Van-Bachman's 729-3	Closed	1994	22.50	50-75
1994	Village Express Van-Bronner's 737-4	Closed	1994	22.50	36-54
1995	Village Express Van-Canadian 2163-7	Closed	1995	N/A	37-52
1994	Village Express Van-Christmas Dove 730-7	Closed	1994	25.00	38-55
1994	Village Express Van-European Imports 739-0	Closed	1994	22.50	35-54
1994	Village Express Van-Fortunoff's 735-8	Closed	1994	22.50	110-127
1994	Village Express Van-Limited Edition 733-1	Closed	1994	25.00	87-108
1994	Village Express Van-Lock, Stock & Barrel 731-5	Closed	1994	22.50	100-132
1994	Village Express Van-North Pole City 736-6	Closed	1994	25.00	40-54
1995	Village Express Van-Park West 0755-2	Closed	1995	N/A	50-70
1994	Village Express Van-Robert's Christmas Wonderland 734-0	Closed	1994	22.50	36-58
1994	Village Express Van-Stat's 741-2	Closed	1994	22.50	30-48
1994	Village Express Van-The Incredible Christmas (Pigeon Forge) 732-3	Closed	1994	24.98	41-61
1994	Village Express Van-The Lemon Tree 721-8	Closed	1994	30.00	33-45
1994	Village Express Van-William Glen 738-2	Closed	1994	22.50	37-54
1994	Village Express Van-Windsor Shoppe 740-4	Closed	1994	25.00	31-48
1988	Village Harvest People 5941-2, set/4	Closed	1991	27.50	34-54
1989	Village Sign with Snowman 5572-7	Closed	1994	10.00	12-18
1992	Village Street Peddlers 5804-1, set/2	Closed	1994	16.00	18-27
1985	Village Train Brighton 6527-7, set/3	Closed	1986	12.00	325-425
1988	Village Train Trestle 5981-1	Closed	1990	17.00	45-75
1987	Village Well And Holy Cross 6547-1, set/2	Closed	1989	13.00	113-150
1989	Violet Vendor/Carolers/Chestnut Vendor 5580-8, set/3	Closed	1992	23.00	29-42
1993	Vision of a Christmas Past 5817-3, set/3	Closed	1996	27.50	28
1992	Welcome Home 5533-6, set/3	Closed	1995	27.50	35
1988	Woodcutter And Son 5986-2, set/2	Closed	1990	10.00	42-50
1993	Woodsmen Elves 5630-8, set/3	Closed	1995	27.50	40-52

Village CCP Miniatures - Department 56

YEAR ISSUE		EDITION LIMIT	YEAR RETD.	ISSUE PRICE	*QUOTE U.S.$
1987	Christmas Carol Cottages 6561-7, set/3	Closed	1989	30.00	85-125
1987	•The Cottage of Bob Cratchit & Tiny Tim 6561-7	Closed	1989	10.00	40-50
1987	•Fezziwig's Warehouse 6561-7	Closed	1989	10.00	25
1987	•Scrooge/ Marley Countinghouse 6561-7	Closed	1989	10.00	25-36
1987	Dickens' Chadbury Station & Train 6592-7	Closed	1989	27.50	56-75
1987	Dickens' Cottages 6559-5, set/3	Closed	1989	30.00	275-350
1987	•Stone Cottage 6559-5	Closed	1989	10.00	120-130
1987	•Thatched Cottage 6559-5	Closed	1989	10.00	110-125
1987	•Tudor Cottage 6559-5	Closed	1989	10.00	150-175
1988	Dickens' Kenilworth Castle 6565-0	Closed	1989	30.00	150-175
1987	Dickens' Lane Shops 6591-9, set/3	Closed	1989	30.00	120-140
1987	•Cottage Toy Shop 6591-9	Closed	1989	10.00	28-42
1987	•Thomas Kersey Coffee House 6591-9	Closed	1989	10.00	40-50
1987	•Tuttle's Pub 6591-9	Closed	1989	10.00	55
1987	Dickens' Village Assorted 6560-9, set/3	Closed	1989	48.00	140
1987	•Blythe Pond Mill House 6560-9	Closed	1989	16.00	31
1987	•Dickens Village Church 6560-9	Closed	1989	16.00	42-50
1987	•Norman Church 6560-9	Closed	1989	16.00	90-110
1987	Dickens' Village Assorted 6562-5, set/4	Closed	1989	60.00	300
1987	•Barley Bree Farmhouse 6562-5	Closed	1989	15.00	52
1987	•Brick Abbey 6562-5	Closed	1989	15.00	75-110
1987	•Chesterton Manor House 6562-5	Closed	1989	15.00	110-150
1987	•The Old Curiosity Shop 6562-5	Closed	1989	15.00	65
1987	Dickens' Village Original 6558-7, set/7	Closed	1989	72.00	300
1987	•Abel Beesley Butcher 6558-7	Closed	1989	12.00	25
1987	•Bean and Son Smithy Shop 6558-7	Closed	1989	12.00	40-50
1987	•Candle Shop 6558-7	Closed	1989	12.00	30-36
1987	•Crowntree Inn 6558-7	Closed	1989	12.00	35
1987	•Golden Swan Baker 6558-7	Closed	1989	12.00	24
1987	•Green Grocer 6558-7	Closed	1989	12.00	42-52
1987	•Jones & Co Brush & Basket Shop 6558-7	Closed	1989	12.00	58-72
1987	Little Town of Bethlehem 5976-5, set/12	Closed	1989	85.00	100-200
1988	New England Village Assorted 5937-4, set/6	Closed	1989	85.00	400-500
1988	•Craggy Cove Lighthouse 5937-4	Closed	1989	14.50	95-121
1988	•Jacob Adams Barn 5937-4	Closed	1989	14.50	50-96
1988	•Jacob Adams Farmhouse 5937-4	Closed	1989	14.50	48
1988	•Maple Sugaring Shed 5937-4	Closed	1989	14.50	35-48
1988	•Smythe Wollen Mill 5937-4	Closed	1989	14.50	65-125
1988	•Timber Knoll Log Cabin 5937-4	Closed	1989	14.50	45
1988	New England Village Original 5935-8, set/7	Closed	1989	72.00	600-800
1988	•Apothecary Shop 5935-8	Closed	1989	10.50	42
1988	•Brick Town Hall 5935-8	Closed	1989	10.50	48-60
1988	•General Store 5935-8	Closed	1989	10.50	55
1988	•Livery Stable & Boot Shop 5935-8	Closed	1989	10.50	50-72
1988	•Nathaniel Bingham Fabrics 5935-8	Closed	1989	10.50	65
1988	•Red Schoolhouse 5935-8	Closed	1989	10.50	77-90
1988	•Village Steeple Church 5935-8	Closed	1989	10.50	175-225
1986	Victorian Miniatures, set/2 6564-1	Closed	1987	45.00	275
1986	•Church 6564-1	Closed	1987	22.50	150
1986	•Estate 6564-1	Closed	1987	22.50	175
1986	Victorian Miniatures 6563-3, set/5	Closed	1987	65.00	275
1986	Williamsburg Snowhouse Series, set/6	Closed	1987	60.00	575-650
1986	•Williamsburg Church, White 6566-8	Closed	1987	10.00	75-120
1986	•Williamsburg House Brown Brick 6566-8	Closed	1987	10.00	50-75
1986	•Williamsburg House, Blue 6566-8	Closed	1987	10.00	50-75
1986	•Williamsburg House, Brown Clapboard	Closed	1987	10.00	50-75
1986	•Williamsburg House, Red 6566-8	Closed	1987	10.00	50-80
1986	•Williamsburg House, White 6566-8	Closed	1987	10.00	75-100

Ertl Collectibles

American Country Barn Series - L. Davis

YEAR ISSUE		EDITION LIMIT	YEAR RETD.	ISSUE PRICE	*QUOTE U.S.$
1996	Gambrel Roofed Bank Barn F910	5/97		50.00	50
1996	Western Log Barn F904	7/97		50.00	50
1996	Victorian Barn F909	9/97		50.00	50
1997	Arch Roofed Stone Barn 2483	Yr.Iss.		50.00	50
1997	Round Barn H093	Yr.Iss.		50.00	50
1997	Western Prairie Barn 2484	Yr.Iss.		50.00	50

Farm Country Christmas - L. Davis

YEAR ISSUE		EDITION LIMIT	YEAR RETD.	ISSUE PRICE	*QUOTE U.S.$
1996	Barn H045	Open		90.00	95
1996	Cat & Bird House H053	Open		25.00	25
1997	Chicken House H050	Open		60.00	60
1996	Dinner Bell H091	Open		25.00	25
1996	Farm House H046	Open		85.00	85
1997	Garage H057	Open		65.00	65
1997	Geese H047	Open		35.00	35
1996	Mailbox H056	Open		25.00	25
1996	Silo H052	Open		65.00	65
1996	Smokehouse H054	Open		70.00	70

Signature Edition Barns - L. Davis

YEAR ISSUE		EDITION LIMIT	YEAR RETD.	ISSUE PRICE	*QUOTE U.S.$
1997	George Washington's Barn at Mount Vernon H273	Open		70.00	70

Fitz & Floyd

Charming Tails Squashville Lighted Village - D. Griff

YEAR ISSUE		EDITION LIMIT	YEAR RETD.	ISSUE PRICE	*QUOTE U.S.$
1994	Acorn Street Lamp 87/948	Open		5.00	6
1995	Butternut Squash Dairy 87/562	7,500	1996	45.00	60-120
1996	Candy Apple Candy Store 87/611	9,000		45.00	48
1996	Cantaloupe Cathedral 87/597	Open		45.00	48
1995	Carrot Post Office 87/583	Closed	1996	45.00	45
1994	Chestnut Chapel 87/521	Closed	1996	45.00	45
1995	Great Oak Town Hall 87/584	Open		45.00	48
1994	Leaf Fence 87/947	Open		6.00	7
1995	Mail Box, Bench 87/560	Open		11.00	12
1995	Mushroom Depot 87/563	Open		45.00	48
1994	Old Cob Mill 87/524	7,500		45.00	45
1994	Pumpkin Inn 87/522	Open		45.00	48
1995	Street Light/Sign 87/561	Open		11.00	12
1994	Village Sign 87/533	Open		30.00	31

Flambro Imports

Pleasantville 1893 - J. Berg Victor

YEAR ISSUE		EDITION LIMIT	YEAR RETD.	ISSUE PRICE	*QUOTE U.S.$
1990	1st Church Of Pleasantville	Retrd.	1994	35.00	35
1992	Apothecary/Ice Cream Shop	Open		36.00	36
1992	Ashbey House	Open		40.00	40
1993	Balcomb's Barn	Open		40.00	40
1993	Balcomb's Farm (out buildings)	Open		40.00	40
1993	Balcomb's Farmhouse	Open		40.00	40
1990	The Band Stand	Retrd.	1992	12.00	15
1992	Bank/Real Estate Office	Retrd.	1995	36.00	36
1993	Blacksmith Shop	Open		40.00	40
1991	Court House	Open		36.00	36
1992	Covered Bridge	Retrd.	1995	36.00	36
1990	Department Store	Retrd.	1993	25.00	29
1991	Fire House	Open		40.00	40
1994	Gazebo/Bandstand	Open		25.00	25
1990	The Gerber House	Retrd.	1993	30.00	30
1992	Library	Open		32.00	32
1993	Livery Stable and Residence	Open		40.00	40
1990	Mason's Hotel and Saloon	Open		35.00	35
1991	Methodist Church	Open		40.00	40
1992	Miss Fountains Boarding House	Open		48.00	48
1990	Pleasantville Library	Open		32.00	32
1992	Post Office	Retrd.	1995	40.00	40
1992	Railroad Station	Open		40.00	40
1990	Reverend Littlefield's House	Open		34.00	34
1994	Sacred Heart Catholic Church	Open		40.00	40
1994	Sacred Heart Rectory	Open		40.00	40
1991	School House	Open		36.00	36
1990	Sweet Shoppe & Bakery	Open		40.00	40
1990	Toy Store	Retrd.	1992	30.00	45
1992	Tubbs, Jr. House	Open		40.00	40

Pleasantville 1893 Members Only - J. Berg Victor

YEAR ISSUE		EDITION LIMIT	YEAR RETD.	ISSUE PRICE	*QUOTE U.S.$
1992	Pleasantville Gazette Building	Open		30.00	30

Forma Vitrum

Annual Christmas - B. Job

YEAR ISSUE		EDITION LIMIT	YEAR RETD.	ISSUE PRICE	*QUOTE U.S.$
1995	Confectioner's Cottage 41101	2,500	1995	100.00	110-200
1996	Lollipop Shoppe 41102	2,500	1996	110.00	110

Bed & Breakfast - B. Job

YEAR ISSUE		EDITION LIMIT	YEAR RETD.	ISSUE PRICE	*QUOTE U.S.$
1997	Bavarian Lodge 11306	1,500		225.00	225
1995	Brookview Bed & Breakfast 11303	1,250	1995	295.00	355-450
1996	Edgewater Inn 11305	1,500	1996	310.00	310

Coastal Classics - B. Job

YEAR ISSUE		EDITION LIMIT	YEAR RETD.	ISSUE PRICE	*QUOTE U.S.$
1995	Bayside Beacon Lighthouse 21013	Open		65.00	65
1996	Cape Hope Lighthouse 21014	Open		100.00	100
1993	Carolina Lighthouse 21003	Open		65.00	65
1996	Cozy Cottage 21500	Open		70.00	70
1994	Lookout Point Lighthouse 21012	Open		60.00	60
1993	Maine Lighthouse 21002	Open		50.00	50
1993	Michigan Lighthouse 21001	Open		50.00	50
1994	Patriot's Point 29010	Open		70.00	70
1994	Sailor's Knoll Lighthouse 21011	Open		65.00	65

Coastal Heritage - B. Job

YEAR ISSUE		EDITION LIMIT	YEAR RETD.	ISSUE PRICE	*QUOTE U.S.$
1996	Barnegat (NJ) 25006	2,996		85.00	85
1996	Cape Hatteras (NC) 25102	3,867		120.00	120
1997	Cape Lookout (NC) 25105	1,997		80.00	80
1995	Cape Neddick (ME) 25002	1,995	1995	140.00	155

*Quotes have been rounded up to nearest dollar

Forma Vitrum
to Harbour Lights

ARCHITECTURE

YEAR ISSUE		EDITION LIMIT	YEAR RETD.	ISSUE PRICE	*QUOTE U.S.$
1996	Fire Island (NY) 25005	2,996		150.00	150
1996	Holland Harbor (MI) 25203	1,996		125.00	125
1997	Jupiter (FL) 25104	1,997		80.00	80
1995	Marble Head (OH) 25201	1,995	1995	75.00	90
1996	New London (CT) 25004	2,996		145.00	145
1995	North Head (WA) 25302	1,995	1995	100.00	110
1995	Old Point Loma (CA) 25301	1,995	1995	100.00	110
1996	Peggy's Cove (NS) 25501	2,500		75.00	75
1996	Pigeon Point (CA) 25303	2,996		125.00	125
1995	Portland Head (ME) 25003	1,995	1995	140.00	160
1995	Sandy Hook (NJ) 25001	3,759	1995	140.00	155
1996	Split Rock (MN) 25202	2,996		130.00	130
1996	St. Augustine (FL) 25103	2,996		130.00	130
1995	St. Simon's (GA) 25101	1,995	1995	120.00	130
1997	West Quoddy (ME) 25007	1,997		140.00	140

Special Production - B. Job

1993	The Bavarian Church 11503	Retrd.	1994	90.00	125-200
1994	Gingerbread House 19111	1,020	1994	100.00	175-250
1995	Miller's Mill (Musical) 11304	Open		115.00	115
1993	Pillars of Faith 11504	Retrd.	1994	90.00	135-150

Vitreville™ - B. Job

1997	Breadman's Bakery (Renovation) 11301R	Open		85.00	85
1993	Breadman's Bakery 11301	Retrd.	1996	70.00	72
1993	Candlemaker's Delight 11801	Retrd.	1996	60.00	65
1993	Candymaker's Cottage 11102	Retrd.	1996	65.00	125-175
1994	Community Chapel 19510	Open		95.00	95
1993	Country Church 11502	12,500	1995	100.00	150-225
1993	Doctor's Domain 11201	Open		70.00	74
1995	Fire Station 11403	Open		100.00	100
1996	First Bank & Trust 11405	Open		110.00	110
1997	Klaus Clock Shop 11307	Open		75.00	75
1996	Kramer Building 11404	Open		100.00	100
1994	Maplewood Elementary School 11401	Open		100.00	100
1995	Mayor's Manor 11205	Open		85.00	85
1993	Painter's Place 11202	Open		70.00	74
1993	Pastor's Place 11101	Open		65.00	70
1993	Roofer's Roost 11203	Retrd.	1994	70.00	125-200
1993	Tailor's Townhouse 11204	Retrd.	1995	70.00	125-200
1994	Thompson's Drug 11302	5,000	1995	140.00	160-190
1993	Tiny Town Church 11501	Open		95.00	100
1994	Trinity Church 11511	7,000		130.00	130
1994	Vitreville Post Office 11402	Open		90.00	90
1997	Wildwood Chapel 11505	Open		60.00	60

Woodland Village™ - B. Job

1993	Badger House 31003	Retrd.	1996	80.00	85
1993	Chipmunk House 31005	Retrd.	1996	80.00	85
1993	Owl House 31004	Retrd.	1996	80.00	85
1993	Rabbit House 31001	Retrd.	1996	90.00	94
1993	Racoon House 31002	Retrd.	1996	80.00	85

Geo. Zoltan Lefton Company

Colonial Village - Lefton

1993	Antiques & Curiosities 00723	Open		50.00	50
1995	Applegate-CVRA Exclusive 01327	Closed	1995	50.00	105-125
1997	Ashton House-CVRA Exclusive 10829	Open		50.00	50
1993	Baldwin's Fine Jewelry 00722	Closed	1997	50.00	50
1991	Belle-Union Saloon 07482	Closed	1994	45.00	80-125
1989	Bijou Theatre 06897	Closed	1990	40.00	445-500
1994	Black Sheep Tavern 01003	Open		50.00	50
1993	Blacksmith 00720	Suspd.		47.00	47
1992	Brenner's Apothecary 07961	Open		45.00	50
1996	The Brookfield 11996	5,500		75.00	120
1994	Brown's Book Shop 01001	Open		50.00	50
1993	Burnside 00717	Open		50.00	50
1989	Capper's Millinery 06904	Suspd.		40.00	65-120
1988	City Hall 06340	Suspd.		40.00	70-175
1989	Cobb's Bootery 06903	Suspd.		40.00	65-125
1990	Coffee & Tea Shoppe 07342	Open		45.00	47
1996	Collectors Set 10740	Open		100.00	100
1989	Cole's Barn 06750	Closed	1994	40.00	60-100
1995	Colonial Savings and Loan 01321	Open		50.00	50
1995	Colonial Village News 01002	Open		50.00	50
1990	Country Post Office 07341	Closed	1994	45.00	70-125
1992	County Courthouse 00233	Open		45.00	50
1991	Daisy's Flower Shop 07478	Open		45.00	47
1993	Dentist's Office 00724	Open		50.00	50
1993	Doctor's Office 00721	Open		50.00	50
1992	Elegant Lady Dress Shop 00232	Open		45.00	50
1988	Engine Co. No. 5 Firehouse 06342	Open		40.00	50
1996	Fairbanks House 10397	Open		50.00	50
1988	Faith Church 06333	Closed	1991	40.00	150-250
1990	Fellowship Church 07334	Open		45.00	47
1990	The First Church 07333	Open		45.00	47
1988	First Post Office 06343	Open		40.00	50
1996	Franklin College 10393	Open		50.00	50
1988	Friendship Chapel 06334	Closed	1994	40.00	60-120
1993	Green's Grocery 00725	Open		50.00	50
1988	Greystone House 06339	Closed	1995	40.00	50-125
1989	Gull's Nest Lighthouse 06747	Open		40.00	47
1990	Hampshire House 07336	Open		45.00	50
1996	The Hermitage 10394	Open		55.00	55
1990	Hillside Church 11991	Closed	1991	60.00	450-500
1995	Historical Society Museum 01328	Open		50.00	50
1988	House of Blue Gables 06337	Closed	1995	40.00	50-75
1988	Johnson's Antiques 06346	Closed	1993	40.00	75-125
1993	Joseph House 00718	Open		50.00	50
1993	Kirby House-CVRA Exclusive 00716	Closed	1994	50.00	85-150
1992	Lakehurst House 11992	Closed	1992	55.00	385-415
1996	Lattimore House-CVRA Exclusive 10391	Open		50.00	50
1997	Law Office 10825	Open		50.00	50
1992	Main St. Church 00230	Open		45.00	50
1989	The Major's Manor 06902	Open		40.00	47
1989	Maple St. Church 06748	Closed	1993	40.00	60
1993	Mark Hall 00719	Open		50.00	50
1989	Miller Bros. Silversmiths 06905	Suspd.		40.00	75-175
1997	Montrose Manor 10828	Open		50.00	50
1994	Mt. Zion Church 11994	Closed	1994	70.00	90-125
1990	Mulberry Station 07344	Open		50.00	65
1995	Mundt Manor 01008	Open		50.00	50
1988	New Hope Church (Musical) 06470	Closed	N/A	40.00	125
1990	The Nob Hill 07337	Closed	1995	45.00	50-115
1992	Northpoint School 07960	Open		45.00	50
1994	Notfel Cabin 01320	Open		50.00	50
1995	O'Doul's Ice House 01324	Open		50.00	50
1988	Old Time Station 06335	Closed	1997	40.00	50
1986	Original Set of 6 05818	Unkn.		210.00	N/A
1986	•Charity Chapel 05818 (05895)	Closed	1989	35.00	600-750
1986	•King's Cottage 05818 (05890)	Closed	1997	35.00	50
1986	•McCauley House 05818 (05892)	Closed	1988	35.00	300-365
1986	•Nelson House 05818 (05891)	Closed	1989	35.00	265-365
1986	•Old Stone Church 05818 (05825)	Open		35.00	50
1986	•The Welcome Home 05818 (05824)	Closed	1996	35.00	50
1986	Original Set of 6 05819	Unkn.		210.00	N/A
1986	•Church of the Golden Rule 05819 (05820)	Open		35.00	50
1986	•General Store 05819 (05823)	Closed	1988	35.00	550-750
1986	•Lil Red School House 05819 (05821)	Open		35.00	50
1986	•Penny House 05819 (05893)	Closed	1988	35.00	400-470
1986	•Ritter House 05819 (05894)	Closed	1989	35.00	450
1986	•Train Station 05819 (05822)	Closed	1989	35.00	300-400
1995	Patriot Bridge 01325	Open		50.00	50
1997	Photography Studio 10872	Open		50.00	50
1990	Pierpont-Smithe's Curios 07343	Closed	1993	45.00	65
1997	Potter House 10826	Open		50.00	50
1995	Queensgate 01329	Open		50.00	50
1989	Quincy's Clock Shop 06899	Open		40.00	47
1995	Rainy Days Barn 01323	Open		50.00	50
1994	Real Estate Office -CVRA Exclusive 01006	Open		50.00	50
1988	The Ritz Hotel 06341	Suspd.		40.00	150
1994	Rosamond 00988	Open		50.00	50
1990	Ryman Auditorium-Special Edition 08010	Open		50.00	55
1992	San Sebastian Mission 00231	Closed	1995	45.00	70-120
1991	Sanderson's Mill 07927	Open		45.00	47
1990	Ship's Chandler's Shop 07339	Suspd.		45.00	75
1997	Sir George's Manor 11997	5,500	1997	75.00	75
1994	Smith and Jones Drug Store 01007	Open		50.00	50
1991	Smith's Smithy 07476	Closed	1991	45.00	375-485
1994	Springfield 00989	Open		50.00	50
1993	St. James Cathedral 11993	Closed	1993	75.00	100-225
1996	St. Paul's Church 10735	Open		50.00	50
1993	St. Peter's Church w/Speaker 00715	Open		60.00	60
1996	Stable 10395	Open		33.00	33
1988	The State Bank 06345	Closed	1997	40.00	50
1992	Stearn's Stable 00228	Open		45.00	50
1988	The Stone House 06338	Open		40.00	47
1991	Sweet Shop 07481	Open		45.00	47
1989	Sweetheart's Bridge 06751	Suspd.		40.00	47
1991	The Toy Maker's Shop 07477	Open		45.00	47
1988	Trader Tom's Gen'l Store 06336	Open		40.00	47
1996	Trading Post 10732	Open		50.00	50
1996	Treviso House 10392	Open		50.00	50
1997	Variety Store 10827	Open		50.00	50
1990	The Victoria House 07335	Closed	1993	45.00	75-125
1989	Victorian Apothecary 06900	Closed	1991	40.00	188-288
1991	Victorian Gazebo 07925	Open		45.00	45
1989	The Village Bakery 06898	Open		40.00	47
1989	Village Barber Shop 06901	Open		40.00	47
1986	Village Express 05826	Closed	N/A	27.00	100-145
1992	Village Green Gazebo 00227	Open		22.00	22
1990	Village Hardware 07340	Open		45.00	50
1994	Village Hospital 01004	Open		50.00	50
1992	The Village Inn 07962	Open		45.00	50
1989	Village Library 06752	Open		40.00	47
1988	Village Police Station 06344	Open		40.00	50
1989	Village School 06749	Closed	1991	40.00	145-200
1991	Watt's Candle Shop 07479	Closed	1994	45.00	65-140
1987	Welcome Home 05824	Closed	1997	50.00	50
1994	White's Butcher Shop 01005	Open		50.00	50
1991	Wig Shop 07480	Suspd.		45.00	55-85
1992	Windmilll 00229	Open		45.00	47
1995	Wycoff Manor 11995	5,500		75.00	120
1995	Zachary Peters Cabinet Maker 01322	Open		50.00	50

Colonial Village Special Event - Lefton

1995	Bayside Inn 01326	Yr.Iss.	1995	50.00	100-125
1996	Town Hall 10390	Yr.Iss.	1996	50.00	60
1997	Meeting House 10830	Yr.Iss.		65.00	65

Historic American Lighthouse Collection - Lefton

1995	1716 Boston Lighthouse 08607	7,500	1995	50.00	50
1994	Admirality Head, WA 01126	Open		40.00	40
1997	Alcatraz Island-1854 08649	9,000	1997	55.00	55
1992	Assateaque, VA 00137	Open		40.00	40
1995	Barneget, NJ 01333	Open		40.00	40
1993	Big Sable Point, MI 00885	Open		40.00	40
1996	Block Island, RI 10105	Open		50.00	50
1994	Bodie Island, NC 01118	Open		40.00	40
1993	Boston Harbor, MA 00881	Open		40.00	40
1996	Buffalo, NY 10076	Open		40.00	40
1994	Cana Island, WI 01117	Open		40.00	40
1993	Cape Cod, MA 00882	Open		40.00	40
1994	Cape Florida, FL 01125	Open		40.00	40
1992	Cape Hatteras, NC 00133	Open		40.00	40
1992	Cape Henry, VA 00135	Open		40.00	40
1992	Cape Lookout, NC 00134	Open		40.00	40
1994	Cape May, NJ 01013	Closed	1995	40.00	85
1995	Cape May, NJ 01013R	Open		40.00	40
1996	Cape Neddick, ME 10106	Open		47.00	47
1994	Chicago Harbor, IL 01010	Open		40.00	40
1997	Currituck Beach, NC 10834	Open		40.00	40
1996	Destruction Island, WA 10108	Open		40.00	40
1995	Fire Island, NY 01334	Open		40.00	40
1997	Fort Niagra, NY 10965	Open		40.00	40
1994	Ft. Gratiot, MI 01123	Open		40.00	40
1993	Gray's Harbor, WA 00880	Open		40.00	40
1994	Heceta Head, OR 01122	Open		40.00	40
1996	Holland Harbor, MI 10104	Open		45.00	45
1995	Jupiter Inlet, FL 01336	Open		40.00	40
1996	Key West, FL 10075	Open		40.00	40
1996	Los Angeles Harbor, CA 10109	Open		45.00	45
1993	Marblehead, OH 00879	Open		40.00	40
1993	Montauk, NY 00884	Open		40.00	40
1994	New London Ledge, CT 01119	Open		40.00	40
1994	Ocracoke, NC 01124	Open		40.00	40
1996	Old Cape Henry, VA 08619	7,500	1996	47.00	75
1994	Old Point Loma, CA 01011	Open		40.00	40
1995	Pigeon Point, CA 01289	Open		40.00	40
1997	Point Arena, CA 10968	Open		40.00	40
1995	Point Betsie, MI 01335	Open		47.00	47
1997	Point Bolivar, TX 10967	Open		40.00	40
1995	Point Cabrillo, CA 01330	Open		47.00	47
1993	Point Wilson, WA 00883	Open		40.00	40
1995	Ponce De Leon, FL 01332	Open		40.00	40
1994	Portland Head, ME 01121	Open		40.00	40
1996	Pt. Isabel, TX 10074	Open		40.00	40
1997	Round Island, MI 10969	Open		47.00	47
1992	Sandy Hook, NJ 00132	Open		40.00	40
1994	Split Rock, MN 01009	Open		40.00	40
1994	St. Augustine, FL 01015	Open		40.00	40
1994	St. Simons, GA 01012	Open		40.00	40
1996	Thomas Point, MO 10107	Open		45.00	45
1995	Toledo Harbor, OH 01331	Open		47.00	47
1994	Tybee Island, GA 01014	Open		40.00	40
1992	West Quoddy Head, ME 00136	Open		40.00	40
1993	White Shoal, MI 00878	Open		40.00	40
1997	Wind Point, WI 10966	Open		40.00	40
1994	Yerba Buena, CA 01120	Open		40.00	40

Goebel/M.I. Hummel

M.I. Hummel Bavarian Village Collection - M.I. Hummel

1996	All Aboard (house)	Open		60.00	60
1995	Angel's Duet (house)	Open		50.00	60
1995	The Bench & Tree Set (accessory)	Open		25.00	30
1995	Christmas Mail (house)	Open		50.00	60
1995	Company's Coming (house)	Open		50.00	60
1996	Holiday Fountain (accessory)	Open		35.00	35
1996	Horse With Sled (accessory)	Open		35.00	35
1996	Off for the Holidays (house)	Open		60.00	60
1996	Shoemaker Shop (house)	Open		60.00	60
1995	The Sled & Pine Tree Set (accessory)	Open		25.00	30
1995	The Village Bakery (house)	Open		50.00	60
1995	The Village Bridge (accessory)	Open		25.00	30
1995	Winter's Comfort (house)	Open		50.00	60
1995	The Wishing Well (accessory)	Open		25.00	30

Harbour Lights

Harbour Lights Collector's Society - Harbour Lights

1995	Point Fermin CA 501 (Charter Member Piece)	Retrd.	1996	80.00	130-200
1996	Stonington Harbor CT 502	Retrd.	1997	70.00	70
1996	Spyglass Collection 503	Retrd.	1997	Gift	30
1997	Port Sanilac MI 406	4/98		80.00	80
1997	Amelia Island FL	4/98		Gift	N/A

Event Piece - Harbour Lights

1996	Sunken Rock NY 602	Yr.Iss.	1996	25.00	25
1997	Edgartown MA 603	Yr.Iss.		35.00	35

Chesapeake Series - Harbour Lights

1996	Concord MD 186	9,500		66.00	66
1997	Drum Point MD 180	9,500		99.00	99
1996	Sandy Point MD 167	9,500		70.00	70
1996	Sharp's Island MD 185	9,500		70.00	70
1996	Thomas Point MD 181	9,500	1996	99.00	150-225

*Quotes have been rounded up to nearest dollar

ARCHITECTURE

Harbour Lights to Hawthorne Village

Great Lakes Region - Harbour Lights

Year Issue		Edition Limit	Year Retd.	Issue Price	*Quote U.S. $
1992	Buffalo NY 122	5,500	1996	60.00	120-140
1992	Cana Island WI 119	5,500	1995	60.00	110-155
1996	Charlotte-Genesee NY 165	9,500		77.00	77
1991	Fort Niagara NY 113	5,500	1995	60.00	65-130
1997	Grand Traverse MI 191	9,500		80.00	80
1992	Grosse Point IL 120	5,500	1996	60.00	62
1994	Holland (Big Red) MI 142	5,500	1995	60.00	120-170
1992	Marblehead OH 121	5,500	1995	50.00	110-135
1992	Michigan City IN 123	5,500	1996	60.00	62
1992	Old Mackinac Point MI 118	5,500	1995	65.00	100-160
1995	Round Island MI 153	9,500		85.00	85
1991	Sand Island WI 112	5,500	1996	60.00	75-100
1995	Selkirk NY 157	9,500		75.00	75
1992	Split Rock MI 124 (misspelled)	Closed	1992	60.00	2400-3000
1992	Split Rock MN 124	5,500	1995	60.00	115-140
1995	Tawas Pt. MI 152	5,500	1996	75.00	75
1996	Toledo OH 179	9,500		85.00	85
1995	Wind Point WI 154	9,500		78.00	78

Great Lighthouses of the World - Harbour Lights

Year	Issue	Edition Limit	Year Retd.	Issue Price	*Quote
1997	Barnegat NJ 414	Open		45.00	45
1996	Boston Harbor MA 402	Open		50.00	50
1994	Cape Hatteras NC 401	Open		50.00	50
1997	Cape Neddick ME 410	Open		50.00	50
1997	Point Loma CA 409	Open		50.00	50
1997	Ponce De Leon FL 408	Open		55.00	55
1995	Portland Head ME 404	Open		50.00	50
1996	Sandy Hook NJ 418	Open		50.00	50
1997	Sea Pines (Hilton Head) SC 415	Open		50.00	50
1995	Southeast Block Island RI 403	Open		50.00	50
1997	St. Augustine FL 411	Open		45.00	45
1997	St. Simons GA 416	Open		50.00	50

Gulf Coast Region - Harbour Lights

Year	Issue	Edition Limit	Year Retd.	Issue Price	*Quote
1995	Biloxi MS 149	5,500		60.00	60
1995	Bolivar TX 146	5,500		70.00	70
1997	Middle Bay AL 187	9,500		99.00	99
1995	New Canal LA 148	5,500	1996	65.00	75-95
1995	Pensacola FL 150	9,000		80.00	80
1995	Port Isabel TX 147	5,500		65.00	65

International Series - Harbour Lights

Year	Issue	Edition Limit	Year Retd.	Issue Price	*Quote
1997	La Jument France 192	9,500		68.00	68
1997	Longship UK 193	9,500		68.00	68
1996	Peggy's Cove Canada 169	9,500		68.00	68

Lady Lightkeepers - Harbour Lights

Year	Issue	Edition Limit	Year Retd.	Issue Price	*Quote
1996	Chatham MA 172	9,500		70.00	70
1996	Ida Lewis RI 174	9,500		70.00	70
1996	Matinicus ME 173	9,500		77.00	77
1996	Point Piños CA 170	9,500		70.00	70
1996	Saugerties NY 171	9,500		75.00	75

Northeast Region - Harbour Lights

Year	Issue	Edition Limit	Year Retd.	Issue Price	*Quote
1994	Barnegat NJ 139	5,500	1995	60.00	150-205
1997	Beavertail RI 188	9,500		80.00	80
1991	Boston Harbor MA 117	5,500	1995	60.00	124-160
1995	Brant Point MA 162	9,500		66.00	66
1997	Cape Henry VA 196	9,500		82.00	82
1996	Cape May NJ 168	9,500		75.00	75
1994	Cape Neddick (Nubble) ME 141	5,500	1995	66.00	120-200
1991	Castle Hill RI 116	5,500	1996	60.00	80-100
1996	Fire Island NY 176	9,500		70.00	70
1991	Gt. Captain Island CT 114	5,500	1996	60.00	85
1995	Highland MA 161	9,500		75.00	75
1997	Jeffrey's Hook NY 195	9,500		66.00	66
1992	Minot's Ledge MA 131	5,500	1996	60.00	100-175
1994	Montauk NY 143	5,500		85.00	165-225
1992	Nauset MA 126	5,500	1995	66.00	125-175
1992	New London Ledge CT 129	5,500	1995	66.00	120-150
1996	Pemaquid ME 164	9,500		90.00	90
1992	Portland Breakwater ME 130	5,500	1996	60.00	75-125
1992	Portland Head ME 125	5,500	1994	66.00	500-600
1991	Sandy Hook NJ 104	5,500	1994	60.00	200-245
1996	Scituate MA 166	9,500		77.00	77
1992	Southeast Block Island RI 128	5,500	1994	71.00	190-250
1991	West Quoddy Head ME 103	5,500	1995	60.00	110-160
1992	Whaleback NH 127	5,500	1996	60.00	100

Southeast Region - Harbour Lights

Year	Issue	Edition Limit	Year Retd.	Issue Price	*Quote
1994	Assateague VA 145-mold one	988	1994	69.00	300-425
1994	Assateague VA 145-mold two	4,512	1994	69.00	115-145
1996	Bald Head NC 155	9,500		75.00	75
1996	Bodie NC 159	9,500		77.00	77
1996	Cape Canaveral FL 163	9,500	1996	80.00	100-120
1991	Cape Hatteras NC 102 (w/ house)	Retrd.	1991	60.00	4000-4500
1992	Cape Hatteras NC 102R	5,500	1993	60.00	600-725
1996	Cape Lookout NC 175	9,500		64.00	64
1995	Currituck NC 158	9,500		80.00	80
1993	Hilton Head SC 136	5,500	1994	60.00	300-400
1995	Jupiter FL 151	9,500	1996	77.00	77
1993	Key West FL 134	5,500	1995	60.00	140-195
1993	Ocracoke NC 135	5,500	1995	60.00	150-180
1993	Ponce de Leon FL 132	5,500	1994	60.00	175-225
1993	St. Augustine FL 138	5,500	1994	71.00	425-470
1993	St. Simons GA 137	5,500	1995	66.00	200-225
1993	Tybee GA 133	5,500	1995	60.00	130-175

Special Editions - Harbour Lights

Year	Issue	Edition Limit	Year Retd.	Issue Price	*Quote
1995	Christmas 1995 - Big Bay Point MI 700	5,000	1995	75.00	150-200
1996	Christmas 1996 - Colchester VT 701	8,200	1995	75.00	75
1995	Legacy Light (blue) 601	Retrd.	1996	65.00	150-200
1995	Legacy Light (red) 600	Retrd.	1996	65.00	150-225

Stamp Series - Harbour Lights

Year	Issue	Edition Limit	Year Retd.	Issue Price	*Quote
1995	Marblehead OH 413	Open		50.00	50
1995	Spectacle Reef MI 182	9,500	1996	60.00	60
1995	Split Rock MN 412	Open		60.00	60
1995	St. Joseph MI 183	9,500		60.00	60
1995	Thirty Mile Point NY 184	9,500	1996	62.00	62
1995	Five Piece Matched Numbered Set 400	5,300		275.00	275-350

Tall Towers - Harbour Lights

Year	Issue	Edition Limit	Year Retd.	Issue Price	*Quote
1997	Morris Island - Now, SC 190	9,500		65.00	65
1997	Morris Island - Then, SC 189	9,500		85.00	85

Western Region - Harbour Lights

Year	Issue	Edition Limit	Year Retd.	Issue Price	*Quote
1991	Admirality Head WA 101 (misspelled)	Closed	1994	60.00	120-135
1991	Admiralty Head WA 101	Retrd.	1994	60.00	100-150
1996	Alcatraz CA 177	9,500	1996	77.00	125-175
1991	Burrows Island OR 108 (misspelled)	Closed	1991	60.00	800-1100
1991	Burrows Island WA 108	2,563	1994	60.00	175-275
1991	Cape Blanco OR 109	5,500		60.00	60
1996	Cape Meares OR 160	9,500		68.00	68
1991	Coquille River OR 111	1,138	1993	60.00	2200-2700
1994	Diamond Head HI 140	5,500	1995	60.00	115-150
1994	Heceta Head OR 144	5,500	1995	65.00	75
1996	Mukilteo WA 178	9,500		55.00	55
1991	North Head WA 106	5,500	1996	60.00	60
1991	Old Point Loma CA 105	5,500	1995	60.00	100-130
1995	Pt. Arena CA 156	5,428	1996	80.00	130-200
1991	St. George's Reef CA 115	5,500	1996	60.00	60
1991	Umpqua River OR 107	5,500	1996	60.00	110
1991	Yaquina Head WA 110	5,500	1996	60.00	62

Hawthorne Village

Anne of Green Gables - Hawthorne

Year	Issue	Edition Limit	Year Retd.	Issue Price	*Quote
1996	Arriving at Green Gables	Open		49.95	50

Baseball Stadiums - Hawthorne

Year	Issue	Edition Limit	Year Retd.	Issue Price	*Quote
1996	Wrigley Field-D. Kessinger	Closed	1996	49.95	50
1995	Wrigley Field-Ernie Banks	Open		99.95	100
1996	Wrigley Field-Ernie signature/cert.	Open		49.95	50
1996	Wrigley Field-R. Huntley	Closed	1996	49.95	50
1996	Wrigley Field-R. Rushell	Closed	1996	49.95	50
1996	Wrigley Field-R. Santo	Closed	1996	49.95	50

Beacons of Freedom - Unknown

Year	Issue	Edition Limit	Year Retd.	Issue Price	*Quote
1995	Portland Head Lighthouse	Closed	1996	39.90	40
1996	Sandy Hook Lighthouse	Open		39.90	40
1995	West Quoddy Head Lighthouse	Open		39.90	40

Bedford Falls-Christmas in Bedford Falls (Illuminated) - Hawthorne

Year	Issue	Edition Limit	Year Retd.	Issue Price	*Quote
1995	Baily Bros. Building & Loan	Open		39.90	40
1995	The Old Granville Place	Open		39.90	40

Bedford Falls-It's a Wonderful Life Accessories - Hawthorne

Year	Issue	Edition Limit	Year Retd.	Issue Price	*Quote
1996	George & Mary	Open		21.90	22
1996	Uncle Billy & Clarence	Open		21.90	22

Chestnut Hill Station - K.&H. LeVan

Year	Issue	Edition Limit	Year Retd.	Issue Price	*Quote
1994	Bicycle Shop	Closed	1995	29.90	30
1993	Chestnut Hill Depot	Closed	1994	29.90	30
1993	Parkside Cafe	Closed	1994	29.90	30
1993	Wishing Well Cottage	Closed	1994	29.90	30

Colonial & Main Street Accessories - K.&H. LeVan

Year	Issue	Edition Limit	Year Retd.	Issue Price	*Quote
1996	Colonial Pageant	Open		21.90	22

Colonial Christmas - K.&H. LeVan

Year	Issue	Edition Limit	Year Retd.	Issue Price	*Quote
1996	The Bruton Parish Church	Open		39.90	40
1995	Margaret Hunter's Shop	Open		39.90	40
1995	Market Square Tavern	Open		39.90	40

Concord: The Hometown of American Literature - K.&H. LeVan

Year	Issue	Edition Limit	Year Retd.	Issue Price	*Quote
1993	Alcott's Orchard House	Closed	1995	39.90	40
1992	Emerson's Old Manse	Closed	1995	39.90	40
1991	Hawthorne's Wayside Retreat	Closed	1995	39.90	40

Corinne Layton's Victoriana - C. Layton

Year	Issue	Edition Limit	Year Retd.	Issue Price	*Quote
1996	The Lace Tea Room	Open		34.95	35
1995	May Cottage	Open		29.95	30
1996	Misty River Inn	Open		34.95	35
1996	Rose Manor	Open		29.95	30

Currier & Ives Stocking Holders - C&I Inspired

Year	Issue	Edition Limit	Year Retd.	Issue Price	*Quote
1995	Holder for American Winter	Open		9.90	10
1995	Holder for Early Winter	Open		9.90	10
1995	Holder for Old Grist Mill	Open		9.90	10
1995	Holder for Winter Moonlight	Open		9.90	10
1995	Holder w/American Winter	Open		39.90	40
1995	Holder w/Early Winter	Open		39.90	40
1995	Holder w/Old Grist Mill	Open		39.90	40
1995	Holder w/Winter Moonlight	Open		39.90	40

Currier & Ives Summer - C&I Inspired

Year	Issue	Edition Limit	Year Retd.	Issue Price	*Quote
1995	American Homestead Summer	Closed	1996	29.90	30
1995	Home on the Mississippi	Open		29.90	30

Currier & Ives: The Art of America - C&I Inspired

Year	Issue	Edition Limit	Year Retd.	Issue Price	*Quote
1994	American Homestead Winter	Open		29.90	30
1995	A Cold Morning	Open		29.90	30
1995	Early Winter	Open		29.90	30
1995	Feeding the Chickens	Open		29.90	30
1995	The Old Grist Mill	Open		29.90	30
1994	The Snow Storm	Open		29.90	30
1995	Winter Evenings	Open		29.90	30
1995	Winter Moonlight	Open		29.90	30

England of My Dreams - R. Dowding

Year	Issue	Edition Limit	Year Retd.	Issue Price	*Quote
1994	Mayfair Hill	Closed	1994	59.90	60

The Fairytale Forest - S. Smith

Year	Issue	Edition Limit	Year Retd.	Issue Price	*Quote
1994	Goldilocks and the Three Bears/Figurines	Closed	1996	24.90	25
1994	Goldilocks and the Three Bears/Sculpture	Closed	1996	24.90	25
1994	Little Red Riding Hood/Sculp. & Fig.	Closed	1996	49.80	50

Gone With the Wind (Illuminated) - Hawthorne

Year	Issue	Edition Limit	Year Retd.	Issue Price	*Quote
1994	Atlanta Church	Closed	1996	39.90	40
1995	Butler's Mansion	Open		39.90	40
1994	Kennedy Store	Open		39.90	40
1994	Red Horse Saloon	Open		39.90	40
1993	Tara	Open		39.90	40
1994	Twelve Oaks	Closed	1996	39.90	40

Gone With the Wind Accessories - Hawthorne

Year	Issue	Edition Limit	Year Retd.	Issue Price	*Quote
1995	The Barbeque	Open		24.90	25
1995	The Butlers	Open		24.90	25
1995	Escape	Open		24.90	25
1995	Helping the Wounded	Open		24.90	25
1995	The O'Haras	Open		24.90	25
1995	Rebel Charge	Open		24.90	25
1995	Rhett & Scarlett	Open		24.90	25
1995	The Riding Lesson	Open		24.00	25
1995	Scarlett & Ashley	Open		24.90	25

Gone With the Wind Collection - K.&H. LeVan

Year	Issue	Edition Limit	Year Retd.	Issue Price	*Quote
1993	Against Her Will	Closed	1996	42.90	43
1994	Alone	Closed	1996	45.90	46
1995	Ashley's Safe	Closed	1996	45.90	46
1995	Dignity & Respect	Closed	1996	45.90	46
1994	Hope for a New Tomorrow	Closed	1994	42.90	43
1994	I Have Done Enough	Closed	1996	45.90	46
1993	A Message for Captain Butler	Closed	1996	42.90	43
1995	Revenge on Shantytown	Open		45.90	46
1993	Rhett's Return	Closed	1996	45.90	46
1996	Surrendered at Last	Closed	1996	47.90	50
1994	Swept Away	Closed	1996	45.90	46
1994	Take Me to Tara	Closed	1996	45.90	46
1992	Tara...Scarlett's Pride	Closed	1995	39.90	40
1992	Twelve Oaks: The Romance Begins	Closed	1995	39.90	40

Gone With the Wind Miniatures - Hawthorne

Year	Issue	Edition Limit	Year Retd.	Issue Price	*Quote
1996	Ashley's Safe/Train Station	Open		29.95	30
1996	Message for Capt. Butler/Hope	Open		29.95	30
1996	Revenge/Dignity & Respect	Open		29.95	30
1996	Rhett's Return/Against Her Will	Open		29.95	30
1995	Scarlett's Pride/Romance	Open		29.95	30
1996	Springhouse/Carriage House	Open		29.95	30
1996	Swept Away/Alone	Open		29.95	30
1996	Take Me to Tara/Done Enough	Open		29.95	30
1996	Tara Mill/Stable	Open		29.95	30

Gone With the Wind-Special Edition - Hawthorne

Year	Issue	Edition Limit	Year Retd.	Issue Price	*Quote
1994	Burning of Atlanta	10,000		79.95	80
1995	The Butler Mansion	Open		79.95	80

Helen Steiner Rice Accessories - S. Smith

Year	Issue	Edition Limit	Year Retd.	Issue Price	*Quote
1995	Boy w/Lantern, Singing, lg. Tree	Open		19.90	20
1995	Girl Snowangel, sign, tree	Open		19.90	20
1995	Lamps	Open		19.90	20

Helen Steiner Rice: Windows of Gold - S. Smith

Year	Issue	Edition Limit	Year Retd.	Issue Price	*Quote
1994	Inspiration Point Lighthouse	Open		34.90	35
1994	Peace of Faith	Open		39.90	40
1994	Winter's Warmth	Open		39.90	40

Hershey, PA: An American Dream Comes True - Hawthorne

Year	Issue	Edition Limit	Year Retd.	Issue Price	*Quote
1995	Birthplace of Milton Hershey	Closed	1996	29.90	30
1995	Derry Church School	Open		29.90	30

Hometown America - Rockwell Inspired

Year	Issue	Edition Limit	Year Retd.	Issue Price	*Quote
1992	Evergreen Cottage	Open		34.95	35
1994	Evergreen General Store	Open		39.90	40
1994	Evergreen Valley Church	Open		37.95	38
1993	Evergreen Valley School	Closed	1995	34.90	35
1995	Happy Holidays	Open		39.95	40

*Quotes have been rounded up to nearest dollar

Collectors' Information Bureau

YEAR ISSUE		EDITION LIMIT	YEAR RETD.	ISSUE PRICE	*QUOTE U.S.$
1993	The Village Bakery	Closed	1994	37.95	38
1994	Waiting For Santa	Closed	1995	39.95	40
1994	Woodcutter's Rest	Open		37.95	38

Hummel's Bavarian Village Accessories - Unknown

1996	Evergreen Tree Set	Open		24.90	25
1996	Horse with Sled	Open		29.90	30
1995	Large Tree/Sled	Open		24.90	25
1995	Small Tree/Bench	Open		24.90	25
1995	Village Bridge	Open		24.90	25
1996	The Village Fountain	Open		29.90	30
1995	Wishing Well	Open		24.90	25

Hummel's Bavarian Village Christmas - M.I. Hummel Inspired

1996	All Aboard	Open		49.90	50
1994	Angel's Duet	Open		49.90	50
1994	The Bakery	Open		49.90	50
1995	Christmas Mail	Open		49.90	50
1995	Company's Coming	Open		49.90	50
1996	Little Shoemaker	Open		49.90	50
1996	Off For The Holidays	Open		49.90	50
1995	Winter's Comfort	Open		49.90	50

Inside Gone With the Wind Collection - K.&H. LeVan

1996	Ashley I Love You	Open		39.90	40
1994	Pride and Passion	Open		39.90	40

Kinkade's Candlelight Cottages (Illuminated) - Kinkade-Inspired

1993	Chandler's Cottage	Closed	1994	29.90	30
1992	Olde Porterfield Tea Room	Closed	1994	29.90	30

Kinkade's Candlelight Cottages - Kinkade-Inspired

1994	Candlelit Cottage	Open		29.90	30
1995	Cedar Nook Cottage	Open		29.90	30
1993	Chandler's Cottage	Open		24.90	25
1993	Merritt's Cottage	Open		27.90	28
1992	Olde Porterfield Tea Room	Open		24.90	25
1994	Seaside Cottage	Open		27.90	28
1993	Swanbrooke Cottage	Open		24.90	25
1994	Sweetheart Cottage	Open		27.90	28

Kinkade's Christmas Memories - Kinkade-Inspired

1996	Christmas Tree Cottage	Open		34.90	35
1995	Home Before Christmas	Open		34.90	35
1995	Home to Grandma's	Open		34.90	35
1995	Homespun Holiday	Open		34.90	35
1995	Old Porterfield Gift & Shoppe	Open		34.90	35
1995	Silent Night	Open		34.90	35
1996	Stonehearth Hutch	Open		34.90	35
1995	Warmth of Home	Open		34.90	35

Kinkade's Enchanted Cottages - Kinkade-Inspired

1996	Cottage By the Sea	Open		29.90	30
1995	Heather's Hutch	Open		29.90	30
1995	Julianne's Cottage	Open		29.90	30
1995	McKenna's Cottage	Open		29.90	30
1995	Miller's Cottage	Open		29.90	30
1996	Sweetheart's Cottage	Open		29.90	30

Kinkade's Home for the Holidays - Kinkade-Inspired

1996	Christmas Eve	Open		29.95	30
1996	Moonlit Church	Open		29.95	30
1996	Victorian Christmas	Open		29.95	30
1996	Victorian Homestead	Open		29.95	30

Kinkade's Lamplight Lane - Kinkade-Inspired

1995	Kinkade's Cottage	Open		49.90	50
1996	Stonebrooke Cottage	Open		49.90	50

Kinkade's Lamplight Village (Illuminated) - Kinkade-Inspired

1996	Filkin's Cottage	Open		29.95	30
1996	Grantham's Cottage	Open		29.95	30
1996	Kinkade's Cottage	Open		29.95	30
1996	Lamplight Inn	Open		29.95	30
1996	Stonebrooke Cottage	Open		29.95	30
1996	Windermer Cottage	Open		29.95	30

Kinkade's St. Nicholas Square (Illuminated) - Kinkade-Inspired

1994	Evergreen Apothecary	Closed	1995	39.90	40
1994	The Firehouse	Closed	1995	39.90	40
1994	Holly House Inn	Closed	1995	39.90	40
1994	Kringle Brothers	Closed	1995	39.90	40
1994	Mrs. C. Bakery	Closed	1995	39.90	40
1994	Noel Chapel (free sign in box)	Closed	1996	39.90	40
1994	S.C. Toy Maker	Closed	1996	39.90	40
1993	Town Hall	Closed	1996	39.90	40

Lost Victorians of Old San Francisco - Hawthorne

1992	Empress of Russian Hill	Closed	1993	34.90	35
1991	Grande Dame of Nob Hill	Closed	1994	34.90	35
1993	Princess of Pacific Heights	Closed	1993	34.90	35

Main Street Memories - Unknown

1996	Dairy Queen	Open		39.95	40

Marty Bell-Belshire Village - M. Bell

1996	Gomshall Flower Shop	Open		39.90	40

Marty Bell-Martha's Vineyard - M. Bell

1996	Summerland	Open		39.95	40

Mc-Memories - Hawthorne

1996	Look For the Golden Arches	Open		39.95	40
1995	McDonald's Restaurant	Open		39.95	40

Nativity - Hawthorne

1995	Camels, Beasts & Mary's Donkey	Open		24.90	25
1995	Nativity	Open		39.90	40
1995	Palm Trees	Open		24.90	25
1995	Stable Keeper & Standing Carmel	Open		24.90	25

North Pole Accessories - Hawthorne

1994	Cookies for Kiddies	Open		23.90	24
1994	Getting Ready for Xmas (Santa/Tree)	Open		23.90	24
1994	Letters for Santa Set (Mailman/Deer)	Open		23.90	24
1994	Santa's Helpers Set	Closed	1996	23.90	24
1994	Sweet Delights Set (Elf/Candy Cane)	Open		23.90	24

On the Water - K.&H. LeVan

1995	Artists Delight	Open		34.90	35
1994	Sunrise Cove	Open		34.90	35

P.O. #1, North Pole Collection - G. Hoover

1995	Santa's Candy Shop	Open		39.90	40
1995	Santa's Gift Wrap Central	Closed	1996	39.90	40
1994	Santa's Post Office	Open		39.90	40
1994	Santa's Toy Shoppe with Sign	Open		39.90	40

Peaceable Kingdom - K.&H. LeVan

1993	Squire Boone's Homestead	Closed	1996	34.90	35
1994	White Horse Inn	Closed	1996	34.90	35

Peppercricket Grove - C. Wysocki

1996	Black Bird's Roost	Open		49.90	50
1996	Budzen's Roadside Food Stand	Open		49.90	50
1996	Evening Sled Ride	Open		49.90	50
1995	Peppercricket Farm	Open		44.90	45
1995	Peppercricket Farm, signed	Open		99.90	100
1996	Pumpkin Hollow	Open		49.90	50
1995	Virginia's Nest	Open		49.90	50

Rockwell Minis - Rockwell-Inspired

1996	Church on the Green/The Bank	Open		29.95	30
1996	Country Store/Rockwell Studio	Open		29.95	30
1996	Firehouse/Old Corner House	Open		29.95	30
1996	Grey Stone Church/Plain School	Open		29.95	30
1996	The Parsonage/The Mission House	Open		29.95	30
1996	The Red Lion Inn/Citizen's Hall	Open		29.95	30
1995	Rockwell Residence/Antique Shop	Open		29.95	30
1996	The Town Offices/The Bell Tower	Open		29.95	30
1996	The Train Station/The Library	Open		29.95	30

Rockwell Print Town - Rockwell-Inspired

1996	The Diner	Open		49.95	50

Rockwell's Four Freedoms (Illuminated) - Rockwell-Inspired

1994	Freedom of Worship: Arlington Church	Open		39.90	40
1995	Freedom from Fear: The Rockwell Homestead	Open		39.90	40
1995	Freedom of Speech: Town Hall	Open		39.90	40
1995	Freedom from Want: The Farmhouse	Open		39.90	40
1996	Freedom is Knowledge: The Library	Open		39.90	40
1996	The School	Open		39.90	40

Rockwell's Heart of Stockbridge (Illuminated) - Rockwell-Inspired

1995	Bell Tower	Open		39.90	40
1995	Church on the Green	Open		39.90	40
1996	Citizen's Hall	Open		39.90	40
1995	Firehouse	Open		39.90	40
1995	Rockwell's Home	Open		39.90	40
1995	Rockwell's Studio	Open		39.90	40

Rockwell's Home for the Holidays - Rockwell-Inspired

1992	Bringing Home the Christmas Tree	Closed	1994	34.90	35
1992	Carolers In The Church Yard	Closed	1996	37.90	38
1992	Christmas Eve at the Studio	Closed	1994	34.90	35
1994	A Golden Memory	Closed	1995	41.90	42
1994	Late for the Dance	Closed	1996	41.90	42
1993	Letters to Santa	Closed	1996	39.90	40
1993	Over the River	Closed	1995	37.90	38
1995	Ready & Waiting	Closed	1995	41.90	42
1993	A Room at the Inn	Closed	1996	39.90	40
1993	School's Out	Closed	1994	39.90	40
1993	Three-Day Pass	Closed	1996	37.90	38
1994	A White Christmas	Closed	1995	41.90	42

Rockwell's Hometown Collection - Rockwell-Inspired

1991	The Bell Tower	Closed	1995	36.95	37
1992	Berkshire Playhouse	Closed	1993	42.95	43
1991	The Church on the Green	Closed	1995	39.95	40
1992	Citizen's Hall	Closed	1994	42.95	43
1991	The Fire House	Closed	1995	36.95	37
1991	Grey Stone Church	Closed	1995	34.95	35
1992	The Mission House	Closed	1995	42.95	43
1992	The Old Corner House	Closed	1995	42.95	43
1994	Old Rectory	Closed	1994	42.95	43
1993	Parsonage Cottage	Closed	1995	42.95	43
1993	Plain School	Closed	1995	42.95	43
1990	Rockwell's Residence	Closed	1995	34.95	35
1992	Towne Hall	Closed	1993	39.95	40
1993	Train Station	Closed	1995	42.95	43

Rockwell's Main Street (Illuminated) - Rockwell-Inspired

1993	The Antique Shop	Open		29.90	30
1993	The Bank	Open		29.90	30
1993	The Country Store	Open		29.90	30
1993	The Library	Open		29.90	30
1993	The Red Lion Inn	Open		29.90	30
1993	Rockwell's Studio	Open		29.90	30
1993	The Town Offices	Open		29.90	30

Rockwell's Main Street - Rockwell-Inspired

1992	Bringing Home the Tree	Closed	1994	34.90	35
1992	Carolers in the Churchyard	Closed	1994	37.90	38
1992	Christmas Eve at the Studio	Closed	1993	34.90	35
1995	A Golden Memory	Closed	1995	41.90	42
1994	Late for the Dance	Open		41.90	42
1992	Letters to Santa	Open		39.90	40
1993	Over the River	Closed	1995	37.90	38
1995	Ready & Waiting	Closed	1995	41.90	42
1993	A Room at the Inn	Open		39.90	40
1993	School's Out	Closed	1994	37.90	38
1993	Three-Day Pass	Open		37.90	38
1994	A White Christmas	Closed	1995	41.90	42

Rockwell's Main Street Accessories - Rockwell-Inspired

1996	Around Town	Open		23.90	24
1995	Autumn Trees	Open		29.90	30
1995	Backyard Barbeque	Open		21.90	22
1994	Bringing Home the Tree Set	Open		21.90	22
1996	Charles Dickens Statue	Open		19.90	20
1994	Christmas Shopping Set	Open		21.90	22
1995	Country Farmstand	Open		29.90	30
1994	Decorating the Tree Set	Open		21.90	22
1995	Early Morning Delivery	Open		21.90	22
1996	Festive Holiday Street Lamps	Open		23.90	24
1995	Fire Drill	Open		23.90	24
1996	Footbridge, Bench, & Wishing Well	Open		21.90	22
1994	Greetings & Games Set	Open		21.90	22
1995	Holiday Mail	Open		21.90	22
1995	Last Day of School Before Christmas	Open		21.90	22
1995	Laundry Day	Open		21.90	22
1994	Norman Rockwell & Trio of Carollers	Open		21.90	22
1994	Old Fashioned Street Lights Set	Open		21.90	22
1995	Out for a Stroll	Open		21.90	22
1995	Picking Out a Pumpkin	Open		39.90	40
1995	Refreshments	Open		21.90	22
1994	Roaring Roadsters Set	Open		21.90	22
1994	Shopkeeper & Travelers Set	Open		21.90	22
1995	Sidewalk Sellers	Open		21.90	22
1996	Sidewalk Snacks	Open		21.90	22
1994	The Skating Pond	Closed	1996	23.90	24
1994	Slipping & Sliding Set	Open		21.90	22
1994	Snow Covered Evergreens Set	Open		21.90	22
1995	Snowman & Tree Set	Open		21.90	22
1996	Songs of Joy	Open		21.90	22
1995	Summer Trees	Open		21.90	22
1996	The Swimming Hole	Open		29.90	30
1996	Thompson's Tree Stand	Open		29.90	30
1996	The Village Clock	Open		29.90	30
1994	Village Vehicles Set	Open		21.90	22
1994	Vintage V-8s Set	Open		21.90	22
1996	Winter Swan	Open		21.90	22

Rockwell's Neighborhood Collection - Rockwell-Inspired

1994	Fido's New Home	Closed	1995	29.90	30
1993	The Lemonade Stand	Open		29.90	30
1994	Sidewalk Speedster	Open		29.90	30

Small Town Christmas - C. Wysocki

1996	Christmas Wishes	Open		39.95	40
1996	Winterberry Falls Church	Open		39.95	40
1995	Ye Very Olde Fruitcake Shoppe	Open		39.90	40

Springtime on Main Street - Rockwell-Inspired

1993	Rockwell's Studio	Open		29.95	30

Stonefield Valley - K.&H. LeVan

1992	Church in the Glen	Closed	1994	37.90	38
1993	Ferryman's Cottage	Closed	1994	39.90	40
1993	Hillside Country Store	Closed	1994	39.90	40
1992	Meadowbrook School	Closed	1994	34.90	35
1993	Parson's Cottage	Closed	1994	37.90	38
1992	Springbridge Cottage	Closed	1994	34.90	35
1993	Valley View Farm	Closed	1994	39.90	40
1992	Weaver's Cottage	Closed	1994	37.90	38

*Quotes have been rounded up to nearest dollar

ARCHITECTURE

Hawthorne Village to John Hine N.A. Ltd./Enesco Corporation

Strolling Through Colonial America - K.&H. LeVan

Year Issue		Edition Limit	Year Retd.	Issue Price	*Quote U.S.$
1992	Captain Lee's Grammar School	Closed	1995	39.90	40
1992	Court House on the Green	Closed	1995	37.90	38
1992	Eastbrook Church	Closed	1995	37.90	38
1993	Everett's Joiner Shop	Closed	1993	39.90	40
1992	Higgins' Grist Mill	Closed	1995	37.90	38
1991	Jefferson's Ordinarie	Closed	1995	34.90	35
1992	Millrace Store	Closed	1995	34.90	35
1992	The Village Smithy	Closed	1993	39.90	40

Tara: The Only Thing Worth Fighting For Plantation - K.&H. LeVan

Year	Title	Edition	Year Retd.	Price	Quote
1994	Carriage House	Closed	1996	29.90	30
1993	A Dream Remembered	Closed	1996	29.90	30
1994	Kitchen & Gateway	Closed	1995	29.90	30
1994	The Mill	Closed	1996	29.90	30
1994	Spring House & Hideaway	Closed	1996	29.90	30
1995	The Stable	Closed	1996	29.90	30

Thatcher's Crossing - R. Dowding

Year	Title	Edition	Year Retd.	Price	Quote
1993	Chapel Crossing	Closed	1995	29.90	30
1993	Midsummer's Cottage	Closed	1995	29.90	30
1993	Rose Arbour Cottage	Closed	1994	29.90	30
1994	Woodcutter's Cottage	Closed	1995	29.90	30

Victorian Grove Collection - K.&H. LeVan

Year	Title	Edition	Year Retd.	Price	Quote
1993	Cherry Blossom	Closed	1994	34.90	35
1992	Lilac Cottage	Closed	1995	34.90	35
1992	Rose Haven	Closed	1994	34.90	35

Welcome to Mayberry - Unknown

Year	Title	Edition	Year Retd.	Price	Quote
1996	The Bluebird Diner	Open		39.90	40
1994	The Courthouse	Open		39.90	40
1994	Floyd's Barber Shop	Open		39.90	40
1994	Mayberry Methodist Church	Open		39.90	40
1994	Post Office	Open		39.90	40
1994	The Taylor Home	Open		39.90	40
1994	Wally's Filling Station	Open		39.90	40

Welcome to Mayberry Accessories - Unknown

Year	Title	Edition	Year Retd.	Price	Quote
1995	Andy & Barney	Open		21.90	22
1996	Around Mayberry	Open		23.90	24
1995	Aunt Bee & Opie	Open		21.90	22
1996	Barney's Sidecar	Open		23.90	24
1996	Fishin' with Pa	Open		29.90	30
1996	Gomer at the Station	Open		23.90	24
1996	Have a Great Day	Open		21.90	22
1995	Patrol Car & Gas Pumps	Open		21.90	22
1996	Welcome to Mayberry	Open		23.90	24

Wizard of Oz - Unknown

Year	Title	Edition	Year Retd.	Price	Quote
1995	The Journey Begins (Diorama)	Open		149.50	150

Hazle Ceramics

A Nation of Shopkeepers Collectors' Club - H. Boyles

Year	Title	Edition	Year Retd.	Price	Quote
1995	Anne Frank's "The Hiding Place"	Open		76.00	76

A Nation of Shopkeepers - H. Boyles

Year	Title	Edition	Year Retd.	Price	Quote
1995	Antique Shop	Open		72.00	72
1993	Attorney at Law	Open		72.00	72
1997	Baby Shop	Open		74.00	74
1993	Bagel Bakery	Open		63.00	63
1995	Bakery/Coffee Shop	Open		72.00	72
1992	Bed & Breakfast	Open		72.00	72
1993	Bookshop	Open		72.00	72
1993	Bookshop & Postbox	Open		76.00	76
1996	Bridal Shop	Open		72.00	76
1997	Bridal Shop (Spring)	Open		76.00	76
1991	Chemist	Open		72.00	72
1991	Chocolate Shop	Open		72.00	72
1994	Christmas Ironmonger	300	1996	84.00	84
1996	Christmas Market Hall	Open		86.00	86
1995	Christmas Shop	Open		84.00	84
1990	Clock Shop	Retrd.	1992	54.00	54
1997	Corner Grocers	2,000		90.00	90
1991	Corner Shop	Open		62.00	64
1996	County Bank	200		76.00	76
1996	Dentist	Open		72.00	72
1996	Doctor	Open		72.00	72
1995	Farrers	500		72.00	72
1994	Fine Art Saleroom	Open		124.00	124
1990	Fish & Chips	Open		58.00	64
1990	Florist	Open		58.00	60
1990	Gents Hats	Retrd.	1992	54.00	54
1993	Gift Shop	Retrd.	1997	72.00	72
1991	Greengrocer	Retrd.	1995	62.00	62
1995	Greengrocer (Revised)	Open		64.00	64
1991	Hairdresser	Retrd.	1997	64.00	64
1994	Hardware	1,200	1996	84.00	160
1991	Harvard House	Retrd.	1997	58.00	58
1996	Hat & Shoe Shop	Open		76.00	76
1992	Indian Restaurant	Retrd.	1997	72.00	72
1995	Irish Linen	Open		64.00	64
1996	Jewellers	200		68.00	68
1990	Ladies Hat Shop	Retrd.	1992	54.00	54
1993	Needlewoman	300	1995	72.00	72
1993	Nell Gwynn's House	250	1996	90.00	90
1994	Saddlery	Retrd.	1997	76.00	76
1996	Sally Lunn's	Open		76.00	76
1995	Sewing Room	500	1996	76.00	200
1990	Shoe Shop	Retrd.	1992	54.00	54
1990	Small Post Office	Retrd.	1992	54.00	54
1991	Teashop & Roses	Open		72.00	72
1991	Teashop with Telephone Box	Open		76.00	76
1994	Tom Morris Golf Shop	Retrd.	1997	76.00	76
1995	Tudor Pub-Fox & Hounds	Retrd.	1997	72.00	72
1992	Tudor Pub-Royal Oak	Open		72.00	72
1994	Turret Pub	Open		78.00	78
1995	Turret Pub-King's Head (USA only)	Open		78.00	78
1993	Victorian Post Office	Retrd.	1997	78.00	78
1995	Victorian Pub-Irish	Open		74.00	74
1991	Victorian Pub-Red Lion	Open		74.00	74
1991	Victorian Pub-Victoria & Albert	Retrd.	1997	74.00	74

John Hine N.A. Ltd./Enesco Corporation

David Winter Collectors Guild Exclusives - D. Winter

Year	Title	Edition	Year Retd.	Price	Quote
1987	The Village Scene	Closed	1987	Gift	175-300
1987	Robin Hood's Hideaway	Closed	1987	54.00	250-400
1987	Queen Elizabeth Slept Here	Closed	1987	183.00	225-300
1988	Black Bess Inn	Closed	1988	60.00	175-200
1988	The Pavillion	Closed	1988	52.00	100
1988	Street Scene	Closed	1988	Gift	75-100
1989	Home Guard	Closed	1989	105.00	105
1989	Coal Shed	Closed	1989	112.00	100-150
1990	The Plucked Ducks	Closed	1990	Gift	50
1990	The Cobblers Cottage	Closed	1990	40.00	40-75
1990	The Pottery	Closed	1990	40.00	40-80
1990	Cartwright's Cottage	Closed	1990	45.00	45-75
1991	Pershore Mill	Closed	1991	Gift	45-55
1991	Tomfool's Cottage	Closed	1991	100.00	75-110
1991	Will-O' The Wisp	Closed	1991	120.00	95-120
1992	Irish Water Mill	Closed	1992	Gift	55
1992	Patrick's Water Mill	Closed	1992	Gift	100-200
1992	Candlemaker's	Closed	1992	65.00	70-90
1992	Beekeeper's	Closed	1992	65.00	65-95
1993	On The River Bank	Closed	1993	Gift	45
1993	Thameside	Closed	1993	79.00	60
1993	Swan Upping Cottage	Closed	1993	69.00	50-75
1993	Horatio Persnickety's Amorous Intent	9,900	1993	375.00	250-325
1994	15 Lawnside Road	Closed	1994	Gift	40
1994	While Away Cottage	Closed	1994	70.00	50
1994	Ashe Cottage	Closed	1994	62.00	45-55
1995	Buttercup Cottage	Closed	1995	60.00	50
1995	The Flowershop	Closed	1995	150.00	120-150
1995	Gardener's Cottage	Closed	1995	Gift	45
1996	Punch Stables	Closed	1996	150.00	150
1996	Plough Farmstead	Closed	1996	125.00	125

Special Event Pieces - D. Winter

Year	Title	Edition	Year Retd.	Price	Quote
1992	Birthstone Wishing Well	Closed	1992	40.00	40-65
1993	Birthday Cottage	Closed	1994	55.00	60
1994	Wishing Falls Cottage	Closed	1995	65.00	50-75
1995	Whisper Cottage	Closed	1995	65.00	50-75
1996	Primrose Cottage	Closed	1996	65.00	65

Tour Special Event Piece - D. Winter

Year	Title	Edition	Year Retd.	Price	Quote
1993	Arches Thrice	Closed	1993	150.00	150

Appearance Piece - D. Winter

Year	Title	Edition	Year Retd.	Price	Quote
1994	Winter Arch	Closed	1995	N/A	45
1995	Grumbleweed's Potting Shed	Closed	1995	99.00	100

At The Centre of the Village Collection - D. Winter

Year	Title	Edition	Year Retd.	Price	Quote
1983	The Bakehouse	Closed	1996	31.40	55
1984	The Chapel	Closed	1996	48.80	75-90
1985	The Cooper Cottage	Closed	1993	57.90	70-90
1983	The Green Dragon Inn	Closed	1996	31.40	60
1982	Ivy Cottage	Closed	1992	22.00	55
1980	Little Market	Closed	1994	28.90	40-50
1980	Market Street	Closed	1996	48.80	90
1984	Parsonage	Closed	1994	390.00	450-550
1980	Rose Cottage	Closed	1996	28.90	55
1984	Spinner's Cottage	Closed	1991	28.90	30
1982	The Village Shop	Closed	1992	22.00	35
1980	The Wine Merchant	Closed	1993	28.90	40

British Traditions - D. Winter

Year	Title	Edition	Year Retd.	Price	Quote
1990	Blossom Cottage	Closed	1995	59.00	30-70
1990	The Boat House	Closed	1995	37.50	30-55
1990	Bull & Bush	Closed	1995	37.50	30-50
1990	Burns' Reading Room	Closed	1995	31.00	20-50
1990	Grouse Moor Lodge	Closed	1995	48.00	35-45
1990	Guy Fawkes	Closed	1995	31.00	50
1990	Harvest Barn	Closed	1995	31.00	50
1990	Knight's Castle	Closed	1995	59.00	75-85
1991	The Printers & The Bookbinders	Closed	1994	120.00	150
1990	Pudding Cottage	Closed	1995	78.00	45-65
1990	St. Anne's Well	Closed	1995	48.00	35-50
1990	Staffordshire Vicarage	Closed	1995	48.00	55-70
1990	Stonecutters Cottage	Closed	1995	48.00	50

Cameos - D. Winter

Year	Title	Edition	Year Retd.	Price	Quote
1992	Barley Malt Kilns	Open		12.50	15
1992	Brooklet Bridge	Open		12.50	15
1992	Diorama-Bright	Open		50.00	50
1992	Diorama-Light	Closed	1992	30.00	50
1992	Greenwood Wagon	Open		12.50	15
1992	Lych Gate	Open		12.50	15
1992	Market Day	Open		12.50	15
1992	One Man Jail	Open		12.50	15
1992	Penny Wishing Well	Open		12.50	15
1992	The Potting Shed	Open		12.50	15
1992	Poultry Ark	Open		12.50	15
1992	The Privy	Open		12.50	15
1992	Saddle Steps	Open		12.50	15
1992	Welsh Pig Pen	Open		12.50	15

Carnival Premier Castles-England - D. Winter

Year	Title	Edition	Year Retd.	Price	Quote
1993	Warwick Castle Cottage	Closed	N/A	N/A	325-375
1994	Kingmaker's Castle	Closed	N/A	N/A	310-350
1995	Castle Tower of Windsor	Closed	N/A	N/A	399
1996	Rochester Castle	Closed	N/A	N/A	365

Castle Collection - D. Winter

Year	Title	Edition	Year Retd.	Price	Quote
1995	Bishopsgate	Open		175.00	175
1995	Bishopsgate Premier	3,500		225.00	225
1994	Castle Wall	Open		65.00	65
1996	Christmas Castle	2,950		160.00	160
1996	Guinevere's Castle	4,300		299.00	299
1996	Guinevere's Castle Premier	2,200		350.00	350

Celebration Cottages - D. Winter

Year	Title	Edition	Year Retd.	Price	Quote
1994	Celebration Chapel	Open		75.00	75
1994	Celebration Chapel Premier	3,500		150.00	150
1995	Mother's Cottage	Open		65.00	65
1995	Mother's Cottage Premier	3,500		89.50	90
1994	Spring Hollow	Open		65.00	65
1994	Spring Hollow Premier	3,500		125.00	125
1995	Stork Cottage Boy	Open		65.00	65
1995	Stork Cottage Girl	Open		65.00	65
1994	Sweetheart Haven	Open		60.00	60
1994	Sweetheart Haven Premier	3,500		115.00	115

David Winter Scenes - Cameo Guild, unless otherwise noted

Year	Title	Edition	Year Retd.	Price	Quote
1992	At Rose cottage Vignette - D. Winter	5,000		39.00	39
1992	Daughter - D. Winter	5,000		30.00	30
1992	Father	5,000		45.00	45
1992	Mother	5,000		50.00	50
1992	Son	5,000		30.00	30
1992	At The Bake House Vignette - D. Winter	5,000		35.00	35
1992	Girl Selling Eggs	5,000		30.00	30
1992	Hot Cross Bun Seller	5,000		60.00	60
1992	Lady Customer	5,000		45.00	45
1992	Small Boy And Dog	5,000		45.00	45
1992	Woman At Pump	5,000		45.00	45
1992	At The Bothy Vignette Base - D. Winter	5,000		39.00	39
1992	Farm Hand And Spade	5,000		40.00	40
1992	Farmer And Plough	5,000		60.00	60
1992	Farmer's Wife	5,000		45.00	45
1992	Goose Girl	5,000		45.00	45
1993	Christmas Snow Vignette - D. Winter	5,000		50.00	50
1993	Bob Cratchit And Tiny Tim	5,000		50.00	50
1993	Ebenezer Scrooge	5,000		45.00	45
1993	Fred	5,000		35.00	35
1993	Miss Belle	5,000		35.00	35
1993	Mrs. Fezziwig	5,000		35.00	35
1993	Tom The Street Shoveler	5,000		60.00	60

Dicken's Christmas - D. Winter

Year	Title	Edition	Year Retd.	Price	Quote
1987	Ebenezer Scrooge's Counting House	Closed	1988	96.90	150-225
1988	Christmas in Scotland & Hogmanay	Closed	1988	100.00	80-150
1989	A Christmas Carol	Closed	1989	135.00	80-175
1990	Mr. Fezziwig's Emporium	Closed	1990	135.00	80-135
1991	Fred's Home: "A Merry Christmas, Uncle Ebenezer saids Scrooge's Nephew Fred, and a Happy New Year."	Closed	1991	145.00	80-145
1992	Scrooge's School	Closed	1992	160.00	100-160
1993	Old Joe's Beetling Shop, A Veritable Den of Iniquity!	Closed	1993	175.00	150-190
1994	Scrooge's Family Home	Closed	1994	175.00	140-175
1994	Scrooge's Family Home Premier	Closed	1994	230.00	230
1994	Scrooge's Family Home, Plaque	3,500	1994	125.00	125
1995	Miss Belle's Cottage	Closed	1995	185.00	195
1995	Miss Belle's Cottage Premier	2,200	1995	235.00	235
1995	Miss Belle's Christmas Plaque	4,000	1995	120.00	125
1996	Tiny Tim	Closed	1996	150.00	150
1996	Tiny Tim Premier	2,200	1996	180.00	180
1996	Tiny Tim Christmas Plaque	4,000	1996	110.00	110

Disneyana Convention - John Hine Studio

Year	Title	Edition	Year Retd.	Price	Quote
1992	Cinderella Castle	500	1992	250.00	1100-1200
1993	Sleeping Beauty Castle	500	1993	250.00	400-550
1994	Euro Disney Castle	500	1994	250.00	400

English Village - D. Winter

Year	Title	Edition	Year Retd.	Price	Quote
1994	Cat & Pipe	Open		53.00	53
1994	Chandlery	Open		53.00	53
1994	Church & Vestry	Open		57.00	57
1994	Constabulary	Open		60.00	60
1994	Crystal Cottage	Open		53.00	53
1994	Engine House	Open		55.00	55
1994	Glebe Cottage	Open		53.00	53
1994	Guardian Castle	8,490	1994	275.00	450

*Quotes have been rounded up to nearest dollar

ARCHITECTURE

YEAR ISSUE		EDITION LIMIT	YEAR RETD.	ISSUE PRICE	*QUOTE U.S.$
1994	Guardian Castle Premier	1,500	1994	350.00	400-500
1994	The Hall	Open		55.00	55
1994	One Acre Cottage	Open		55.00	55
1994	The Post Office	Open		53.00	53
1994	The Quack's Cottage	Open		57.00	57
1994	The Rectory	Open		55.00	55
1994	The Seminary	Open		57.00	57
1994	The Smithy	Open		50.00	50
1994	The Tannery	Open		50.00	50

Garden Cottages of England - D. Winter

YEAR ISSUE		EDITION LIMIT	YEAR RETD.	ISSUE PRICE	*QUOTE U.S.$
1995	Spencer Hall Gardens	4,300		395.00	250-315
1995	Spencer Hall Gardens, Premier	2,200		495.00	495
1995	Willow Gardens	4,300	1995	225.00	175-200
1995	Willow Gardens, Premier	2,200	1995	299.00	299

Heart of England Series - D. Winter

YEAR ISSUE		EDITION LIMIT	YEAR RETD.	ISSUE PRICE	*QUOTE U.S.$
1985	The Apothecary Shop	Closed	1995	24.10	35-50
1985	Blackfriars Grange	Closed	1994	24.10	60
1985	Craftsmen's Cottage	Closed	1995	24.10	40
1985	The Hogs Head Tavern	Closed	1995	24.10	40
1985	Meadowbank Cottages	Closed	1995	24.10	30-40
1985	The Schoolhouse	Closed	1995	24.10	50
1985	Shirehall	Closed	1995	24.10	35-50
1985	St. George's Church	Closed	1995	24.10	35-45
1985	The Vicarage	Closed	1995	24.10	45
1985	The Windmill	Closed	1995	37.50	40
1985	Yeoman's Farmhouse	Closed	1995	24.10	35

In The Country Collection - D. Winter

YEAR ISSUE		EDITION LIMIT	YEAR RETD.	ISSUE PRICE	*QUOTE U.S.$
1983	The Bothy	Open		31.40	60
1982	Brookside Hamlet	Closed	1991	74.80	60-70
1981	Drover's Cottage	Open		22.00	35
1983	Fisherman's Wharf	Open		31.40	60
1994	Guardian Gate	Open		150.00	150
1994	Guardian Gate Premier	3,500		199.00	199
1987	John Benbow's Farmhouse	Closed	1993	78.00	80-90
1996	Lover's Tryst	Open		125.00	125
1983	Pilgrim's Rest	Closed	1993	48.80	45-75
1984	Snow Cottage	Closed	1992	24.80	75-135
1986	There was a Crooked House	Open		96.90	100-155
1996	There was a Narrow House	Open		115.00	115
1984	Tollkeeper's Cottage	Closed	1992	87.00	100-120

Irish Collection - D. Winter

YEAR ISSUE		EDITION LIMIT	YEAR RETD.	ISSUE PRICE	*QUOTE U.S.$
1992	Fogartys	Closed	1994	75.00	85
1992	Irish Round Tower	Open		65.00	70
1992	Murphys	Open		100.00	110
1992	O'Donovan's Castle	Open		145.00	170
1991	Only A Span Apart	Closed	1993	80.00	80-95
1991	Secret Shebeen	Closed	1993	70.00	70-90

Landowners - D. Winter

YEAR ISSUE		EDITION LIMIT	YEAR RETD.	ISSUE PRICE	*QUOTE U.S.$
1984	Castle Gate	Closed	1992	155.00	220-250
1982	The Dower House	Closed	1993	22.00	25-50
1988	The Grange	Closed	1989	120.00	800-1050
1985	Squire Hall	Closed	1990	92.30	100-135
1981	Tudor Manor House	Closed	1992	48.80	70-125

Main Collection - D. Winter

YEAR ISSUE		EDITION LIMIT	YEAR RETD.	ISSUE PRICE	*QUOTE U.S.$
1983	The Alms Houses	Closed	1987	59.90	300-450
1992	Audrey's Tea Room	Closed	1992	90.00	125-225
1992	Audrey's Tea Shop	Closed	1992	90.00	225-295
1982	Blacksmith's Cottage	Closed	1986	22.00	250-325
1991	Castle in the Air	Closed	1996	675.00	710
1981	Castle Keep	Closed	1982	30.00	900-1200
1981	Chichester Cross	Closed	1981	50.00	3000-3200
1980	The Coaching Inn	Closed	1983	165.00	3600
1981	Cornish Cottage	Closed	1986	30.00	700
1983	Cornish Tin Mine	Closed	1989	22.00	55-75
1983	Cotton Mill	Closed	1989	41.30	400-600
1981	Double Oast	Closed	1982	60.00	3300
1980	Dove Cottage	Closed	1983	60.00	1250-1690
1982	Fairytale Castle	Closed	1989	115.00	350-500
1986	Falstaff's Manor	10,000	1990	242.00	225-325
1980	The Forge	Closed	1983	60.00	1250-1700
1996	Golf Clubhouse	Open		160.00	160
1996	Haunted House	4,900		325.00	325
1983	The Haybarn	Closed	1987	22.00	200
1985	Hermit's Humble Home	Closed	1988	87.00	175-230
1984	House of the Master Mason	Closed	1988	74.80	200-300
1982	House on Top	Closed	1988	92.30	175-300
1991	Inglenook Cottage	Open		60.00	75
1988	Jim'll Fixit	Closed	1988	350.00	2500-3000
1994	Kingmaker's Castle	Closed	1994	225.00	225
1980	Little Forge	Closed	1983	40.00	1200-1500
1980	Little Mill	Closed	1980	40.00	750-950
1980	Little Mill-remodeled	Closed	1983	Unkn.	1600
1992	Mad Baron Fourthrite's Folly	Closed	1992	275.00	200
1980	Mill House	Closed	1980	50.00	2500
1980	Mill House-remodeled	Closed	1983	50.00	1250
1982	Miner's Cottage	Closed	1987	22.00	175-250
1991	Moonlight Haven	Open		120.00	155
1982	Moorland Cottage	Closed	1987	22.00	200-250
1995	Newtown Millhouse	4,500		195.00	195
1981	The Old Curiosity Shop	Closed	1983	40.00	950-1300
1980	Quayside	Closed	1985	60.00	1100-1500
1994	Quindene Manor	3,000	1994	695.00	750-950
1994	Quindene Manor Premier	1,500	1994	850.00	900
1982	Sabrina's Cottage	Closed	1982	30.00	2000-2350
1981	St. Paul's Cathedral	Closed	1982	40.00	1500-1900
1985	Suffolk House	Closed	1989	48.80	60-100
1980	Three Duck Inn	Closed	1983	60.00	1500-1800
1981	Tythe Barn	Closed	1986	39.30	1350
1981	The Village	Open		362.00	580
1991	The Weaver's Lodgings	Open		65.00	75
1995	Welcome Home Cottage	Closed	1995	99.00	125-150
1995	Welcome Home Cottage Military	Closed	1995	99.00	99
1982	William Shakespeare's Birthplace (large)	Closed	1984	60.00	950
1983	Woodcutter's Cottage	Closed	1988	87.00	275

Midlands Collection - D. Winter

YEAR ISSUE		EDITION LIMIT	YEAR RETD.	ISSUE PRICE	*QUOTE U.S.$
1988	Bottle Kilns	Closed	1991	78.00	80-100
1988	Coal Miner's Row	Open		90.00	120
1988	Derbyshire Cotton Mill	Closed	1994	65.00	90-125
1988	The Gunsmiths	Open		78.00	100
1988	Lacemaker's Cottage	Open		120.00	155
1988	Lock-keepers Cottage	Open		65.00	85

Porridge Pot Alley - D. Winter

YEAR ISSUE		EDITION LIMIT	YEAR RETD.	ISSUE PRICE	*QUOTE U.S.$
1995	Cob's Bakery	Open		125.00	125
1995	Cob's Bakery Premier	3,500		165.00	165
1995	Porridge Pot Arch	Open		50.00	50
1995	Sweet Dreams	Open		79.00	79
1995	Sweet Dreams Premier	3,500		99.00	99
1995	Tartan Teahouse	Open		99.00	99
1995	Tartan Teahouse Premier	3,500		129.00	129

Regions Collection - D. Winter

YEAR ISSUE		EDITION LIMIT	YEAR RETD.	ISSUE PRICE	*QUOTE U.S.$
1981	Cotswold Cottage	Open		22.00	35
1982	Cotswold Village	Closed	1990	59.90	50-100
1983	Hertford Court	Closed	1992	87.00	80-150
1985	Kent Cottage	Open		48.80	110
1981	Single Oast	Closed	1993	22.00	30-50
1981	Stratford House	Open		47.80	130
1981	Sussex Cottage	Open		22.00	35
1981	Triple Oast (old version)	Closed	1994	59.90	115-155

Scottish Collection - D. Winter

YEAR ISSUE		EDITION LIMIT	YEAR RETD.	ISSUE PRICE	*QUOTE U.S.$
1986	Crofter's Cottage	Closed	1989	51.00	75
1989	Gatekeeper's Cottage	Open		65.00	85
1990	Gillie's Cottage	Open		65.00	85
1989	The House on the Loch	Closed	1994	65.00	85-90
1989	MacBeth's Castle	Open		200.00	200-260
1982	Old Distillery	Closed	1993	312.00	375
1992	Scottish Crofter's	Open		42.00	65

Seaside Boardwalk - D. Winter

YEAR ISSUE		EDITION LIMIT	YEAR RETD.	ISSUE PRICE	*QUOTE U.S.$
1995	The Barnacle Theatre	4,500		175.00	175
1995	Dock Accessory	Open		Gift	N/A
1995	The Fisherman's Shanty	Open		110.00	110
1995	Harbour Master's Watch-House	Open		125.00	125
1995	Jolly Roger Tavern	Open		199.00	199
1995	Lodgings and Sea Bathing	Open		165.00	165
1995	Trinity Lighthouse	Open		135.00	135
1995	Waterfront Market	Open		125.00	125

Sherwood Forest Collection - D. Winter

YEAR ISSUE		EDITION LIMIT	YEAR RETD.	ISSUE PRICE	*QUOTE U.S.$
1995	Friar Tuck's Sanctum	Open		45.00	45
1995	King Richard's Bower	Open		45.00	45
1995	Little John's Riverloft	Open		45.00	45
1995	Loxley Castle	Open		150.00	150
1995	Maid Marian's Retreat	Open		49.50	50
1995	Much's Mill	Open		45.00	45
1995	Sherwood Forest Diorama	Open		100.00	100
1995	Will Scarlett's Den	Open		49.50	50

Shires Collection - D. Winter

YEAR ISSUE		EDITION LIMIT	YEAR RETD.	ISSUE PRICE	*QUOTE U.S.$
1993	Berkshire Milking Byre	Closed	1995	38.00	40
1993	Buckinghamshire Bull Pen	Closed	1994	38.00	40
1993	Cheshire Kennels	Closed	1995	36.00	40
1993	Derbyshire Dovecote	Closed	1995	36.00	25-40
1993	Gloucestershire Greenhouse	Closed	1995	40.00	25-40
1993	Hampshire Hutches	Closed	1995	34.00	25-40
1993	Lancashire Donkey Shed	Closed	1995	38.00	25-40
1993	Oxfordshire Goat Yard	Closed	1994	32.00	25-40
1993	Shropshire Pig Shelter	Closed	1995	32.00	25-40
1993	Staffordshire Stable	Closed	1995	36.00	25-40
1993	Wiltshire Waterwheel	Closed	1995	34.00	25-40
1993	Yorkshire Sheep Fold	Closed	1995	38.00	25-40

Tiny Series - D. Winter

YEAR ISSUE		EDITION LIMIT	YEAR RETD.	ISSUE PRICE	*QUOTE U.S.$
1980	Anne Hathaway's Cottage	Closed	1982	Unkn.	500
1980	Cotswold Farmhouse	Closed	1982	Unkn.	450-525
1980	Crown Inn	Closed	1982	Unkn.	525
1980	St. Nicholas' Church	Closed	1982	Unkn.	525
1980	Sulgrave Manor	Closed	1982	Unkn.	450-525
1980	William Shakespeare's Birthplace	Closed	1982	Unkn.	475-550

Welsh Collection - D. Winter

YEAR ISSUE		EDITION LIMIT	YEAR RETD.	ISSUE PRICE	*QUOTE U.S.$
1993	A Bit of Nonsense	Open		50.00	50
1993	Pen-y-Craig	Open		88.00	90
1993	Tyddyn Siriol	Closed	1994	88.00	60-90
1993	Y' Ddraig Goch	Closed	1994	88.00	60-90

West Country Collection - D. Winter

YEAR ISSUE		EDITION LIMIT	YEAR RETD.	ISSUE PRICE	*QUOTE U.S.$
1988	Cornish Engine House	Open		120.00	155
1988	Cornish Harbour	Open		120.00	155
1986	Devon Combe	Closed	1994	73.00	85-110
1987	Devon Creamery	Open		62.90	110
1986	Orchard Cottage	Closed	1991	91.30	100-150
1987	Smuggler's Creek	Open		390.00	520
1987	Tamar Cottage	Open		45.30	75
1996	Wreckers Cottages	4,300		225.00	225
1996	Wreckers Cottages Premier	2,200		275.00	275

Winterville Collection - D. Winter

YEAR ISSUE		EDITION LIMIT	YEAR RETD.	ISSUE PRICE	*QUOTE U.S.$
1996	At Home with Comfort & Joy	5,750		110.00	110
1996	At Home with Comfort & Joy Premier	1,750		145.00	145
1994	The Christmastime Clockhouse	Open		165.00	165
1994	The Christmastime Clockhouse Premier	3,500	1994	215.00	215
1995	St. Stephen's	5,750		150.00	150
1995	St. Stephen's Premier	1,750	1995	195.00	195
1994	Toymaker	Open		135.00	135
1994	Toymaker Premier	3,500	1994	175.00	175
1995	Winterville Square	Open		75.00	75
1995	Ye Merry Gentlemen's Lodgings	5,750		125.00	125
1995	Ye Merry Gentlemen's Lodgings Premier	1,750	1995	170.00	170

Lilliput Lane Ltd./Enesco Corporation

Collectors Club Specials - Various

YEAR ISSUE		EDITION LIMIT	YEAR RETD.	ISSUE PRICE	*QUOTE U.S.$
1986	Packhorse Bridge - D. Tate	Retrd.	1987	Gift	675
1986	Packhorse Bridge (dealer) - D. Tate	Retrd.	1987	Gift	450-750
1986	Crendon Manor - D. Tate	Retrd.	1989	285.00	850
1986	Gulliver - Unknown	Retrd.	1986	65.00	325
1987	Little Lost Dog - D. Tate	Retrd.	1988	Gift	225-450
1987	Yew Tree Farm - D. Tate	Retrd.	1988	160.00	230
1988	Wishing Well - D. Tate	Retrd.	1989	Gift	105
1989	Dovecot - D. Tate	Retrd.	1990	Gift	95
1989	Wenlock Rise - D. Tate	Retrd.	1989	175.00	150
1990	Cosy Corner - D. Tate	Retrd.	1991	Gift	75-175
1990	Lavender Cottage - D. Tate	Retrd.	1991	50.00	50-90
1990	Bridle Way - D. Tate	Retrd.	1991	100.00	150-225
1991	Puddlebrook - D. Tate	Retrd.	1992	Gift	60-100
1991	Gardeners Cottage - D. Tate	Retrd.	1992	120.00	175
1991	Wren Cottage - D. Tate	Retrd.	1993	13.95	70-110
1992	Pussy Willow - D. Tate	Retrd.	1993	Gift	50-95
1992	Forget-Me-Not - D. Tate	Retrd.	1993	130.00	175-250
1993	The Spinney - Lilliput Lane	Retrd.	1994	Gift	100-125
1993	Heaven Lea Cottage - Lilliput Lane	Retrd.	1994	150.00	250
1993	Curlew Cottage - Lilliput Lane	Retrd.	1995	18.95	50-65
1994	Petticoat Cottage - Lilliput Lane	Retrd.	1995	Gift	70
1994	Woodman's Retreat - Lilliput Lane	Retrd.	1995	135.00	150-200
1995	Thimble Cottage - Lilliput Lane	Retrd.	1996	Gift	N/A
1995	Porlock Down - Lilliput Lane	Retrd.	1996	135.00	135-150
1996	Wash Day - Lilliput Lane	Retrd.	1997	Gift	N/A
1996	Meadowsweet Cottage - Lilliput Lane	Retrd.	1997	110.00	110
1996	Nursery Cottage - Lilliput Lane	Retrd.	1997	Gift	N/A
1996	Winnows - Lilliput Lane	Retrd.	1997	22.50	23
1997	Hampton Moat - Lilliput Lane	4/98		Gift	N/A
1997	Hampton Manor - Lilliput Lane	4/98		100.00	100
1997	Cider Apple Cottage - Lilliput Lane	4/98		Gift	N/A

Anniversary Collection - Lilliput Lane

YEAR ISSUE		EDITION LIMIT	YEAR RETD.	ISSUE PRICE	*QUOTE U.S.$
1992	Honeysuckle Cottage	Yr.Iss.	1992	195.00	300-450
1993	Cotman Cottage	Yr.Iss.	1993	220.00	250
1994	Watermeadows	Yr.Iss.	1994	189.00	200-250
1995	Gertrude's Garden	Yr.Iss.	1995	192.00	250
1996	Cruck End	Yr.Iss.	1996	130.00	130
1997	Summer Days	Yr.Iss.		165.00	165

South Bend Dinner Collection - Various

YEAR ISSUE		EDITION LIMIT	YEAR RETD.	ISSUE PRICE	*QUOTE U.S.$
1989	Commemorative Medallion - D. Tate	Retrd.	1989	N/A	130-200
1990	Rowan Lodge - D. Tate	Retrd.	1990	N/A	200-400
1991	Gamekeepers Cottage - D. Tate	Retrd.	1991	N/A	250-400
1992	Ashberry Cottage - D. Tate	Retrd.	1992	N/A	200-400
1993	Magnifying Glass - Lilliput Lane	Retrd.	1993	N/A	N/A

Special Event Collection - Lilliput Lane

YEAR ISSUE		EDITION LIMIT	YEAR RETD.	ISSUE PRICE	*QUOTE U.S.$
1990	Rowan Lodge	Retrd.	1990	50.00	120
1991	Gamekeepers Cottage	Retrd.	1991	75.00	200
1992	Ploughman's Cottage	Retrd.	1992	75.00	75
1993	Aberford Gate	Retrd.	1993	95.00	150
1994	Leagrave Cottage	Retrd.	1994	75.00	75
1995	Vanbrugh Lodge	Retrd.	1995	60.00	75
1996	Amberly Rose	Retrd.	1996	45.00	45
1997	Dormouse Cottage	Yr.Iss.		60.00	60

American Collection - D. Tate

YEAR ISSUE		EDITION LIMIT	YEAR RETD.	ISSUE PRICE	*QUOTE U.S.$
1984	Adobe Church	Retrd.	1985	22.50	700-1100
1984	Adobe Village	Retrd.	1985	60.00	900-1500
1984	Cape Cod	Retrd.	1985	22.50	570-910
1984	Country Church	Retrd.	1985	22.50	500-800
1984	Covered Bridge	Retrd.	1985	22.50	1000-2000
1984	Forge Barn	Retrd.	1985	22.50	550-660
1984	General Store	Retrd.	1985	22.50	600-800
1984	Grist Mill	Retrd.	1985	22.50	500-785
1984	Light House	Retrd.	1985	22.50	650-800
1984	Log Cabin	Retrd.	1985	22.50	625-1000
1984	Midwest Barn	Retrd.	1985	22.50	275
1984	San Francisco House	Retrd.	1985	22.50	850
1984	Wallace Station	Retrd.	1985	22.50	400

Blaise Hamlet Classics - Lilliput Lane

YEAR ISSUE		EDITION LIMIT	YEAR RETD.	ISSUE PRICE	*QUOTE U.S.$
1993	Circular Cottage	Retrd.	1995	95.00	125-175
1993	Dial Cottage	Retrd.	1995	95.00	125-175
1993	Diamond Cottage	Retrd.	1995	95.00	95

*Quotes have been rounded up to nearest dollar

ARCHITECTURE

Lilliput Lane Ltd./Enesco Corporation to Lilliput Lane Ltd./Enesco Corporation

YEAR ISSUE		EDITION LIMIT	YEAR RETRD.	ISSUE PRICE	*QUOTE U.S. $
1993	Double Cottage		Retrd. 1995	95.00	95
1993	Jasmine Cottage		Retrd. 1995	95.00	125-175
1993	Oak Cottage		Retrd. 1995	95.00	105
1993	Rose Cottage		Retrd. 1995	95.00	150
1993	Sweet Briar Cottage		Retrd. 1995	95.00	125-175
1993	Vine Cottage		Retrd. 1995	95.00	135

Blaise Hamlet Collection - D. Tate

1989	Circular Cottage		Retrd. 1993	110.00	150-200
1990	Dial Cottage		Retrd. 1993	110.00	150-175
1989	Diamond Cottage		Retrd. 1993	110.00	125-175
1991	Double Cottage		Retrd. 1996	200.00	200-250
1991	Jasmine Cottage		Retrd. 1996	140.00	110-150
1989	Oak Cottage		Retrd. 1993	110.00	150-200
1991	Rose Cottage		Open	140.00	110-140
1990	Sweetbriar Cottage		Retrd. 1995	110.00	125-175
1990	Vine Cottage		Retrd. 1995	110.00	135-150

Christmas Collection - Various

1992	Chestnut Cottage		Retrd. 1996	46.50	35-50
1992	Cranberry Cottage		Retrd. 1996	46.50	35-50
1988	Deer Park Hall - D. Tate		Retrd. 1989	120.00	200-250
1993	The Gingerbread Shop		Retrd. 1997	50.00	35-50
1992	Hollytree House		Retrd. 1996	46.50	35-50
1991	The Old Vicarage at Christmas - D. Tate		Retrd. 1992	180.00	180-300
1993	Partridge Cottage		Retrd. 1997	50.00	35-50
1994	Ring O' Bells		Open	50.00	35-50
1993	St. Joseph's Church		Open	70.00	50-70
1994	St. Joseph's School		Open	50.00	35-50
1989	St. Nicholas Church - D. Tate		Retrd. 1990	130.00	155
1994	The Vicarage		Open	50.00	35-50
1990	Yuletide Inn - D. Tate		Retrd. 1991	145.00	150-200

Christmas Lodge Collection - Lilliput Lane

1993	Eamont Lodge		Retrd. 1993	185.00	200-300
1992	Highland Lodge		Retrd. 1993	180.00	200-300
1995	Kerry Lodge		Retrd. 1995	160.00	120-160
1994	Snowdon Lodge		Retrd. 1994	175.00	175

Christmas Special - Lilliput Lane

1996	St. Stephen's Church		Yr.Iss.	100.00	100
1997	Christmas Party		Yr.Iss.	150.00	150

Countryside Scene Plaques - D. Simpson

1989	Bottle Kiln		Retrd. 1991	49.50	50
1989	Cornish Tin Mine		Retrd. 1991	49.50	50
1989	Country Inn		Retrd. 1991	49.50	50
1989	Cumbrian Farmhouse		Retrd. 1991	49.50	50
1989	Lighthouse		Retrd. 1991	49.50	50
1989	Norfolk Windmill		Retrd. 1991	49.50	50
1989	Oasthouse		Retrd. 1991	49.50	50
1989	Old Smithy		Retrd. 1991	49.50	50
1989	Parish Church		Retrd. 1991	49.50	50
1989	Post Office		Retrd. 1991	49.50	50
1989	Village School		Retrd. 1991	49.50	50
1989	Watermill		Retrd. 1991	49.50	50

Disneyana Convention - R. Day

1995	Fire Station 105	501	1995	195.00	425-550
1996	The Hall of Presidents	500	1996	225.00	650

Dutch Collection - D. Tate

1991	Aan de Amstel		Open	79.00	60-85
1991	Begijnhof		Open	55.00	35-60
1991	Bloemenmarkt		Open	79.00	60-85
1991	De Branderij		Open	72.50	55-80
1991	De Diamantair		Open	79.00	60-85
1991	De Pepermolen		Open	55.00	35-60
1991	De Wolhandelaar		Open	72.50	55-80
1991	De Zijdewever		Open	79.00	60-85
1991	Rembrant van Rijn		Open	120.00	85-130
1991	Rozengracht		Retrd. 1995	72.50	50-80

English Cottages - D. Tate, unless otherwise noted

1982	Acorn Cottage-Mold 1		Retrd. 1983	30.00	250-350
1983	Acorn Cottage-Mold 2		Retrd. 1987	30.00	60
1996	The Anchor - Lilliput Lane		Open	85.00	85
1982	Anne Hathaway's-Mold 1		Retrd. 1983	40.00	2500
1983	Anne Hathaway's-Mold 2		Retrd. 1984	40.00	400-600
1984	Anne Hathaway's-Mold 3		Retrd. 1987	40.00	375
1989	Anne Hathaway's-Mold 4		Retrd. 1997	130.00	130-150
1991	Anne of Cleves		Retrd. 1996	360.00	250-395
1997	Appleby East - Lilliput Lane		Open	70.00	70
1994	Applejack Cottage - Lilliput Lane		Open	45.00	35-45
1982	April Cottage-Mold 1		Retrd. 1984	Unkn.	350-500
1982	April Cottage-Mold 2		Retrd. 1989	Unkn.	100
1991	Armada House		3/97	175.00	130-185
1989	Ash Nook		Retrd. 1995	47.50	60
1986	Bay View		Retrd. 1988	39.50	90-125
1987	Beacon Heights - Lilliput Lane		Retrd. 1992	125.00	150
1989	Beehive Cottage		Retrd. 1995	72.50	95
1997	Best Friends - Lilliput Lane		Open	25.00	25
1996	Birchwood Cottage - Lilliput Lane		Open	55.00	55
1993	Birdlip Bottom - Lilliput Lane		Open	80.00	50-80
1996	Blue Boar - Lilliput Lane		Open	85.00	85
1996	Bluebell Farm - Lilliput Lane		Open	250.00	250
1992	Bow Cottage		Retrd. 1996	128.00	135
1996	Boxwood Cottage - Lilliput Lane		Open	30.00	30
1990	Bramble Cottage		Retrd. 1995	55.00	100
1988	Bredon House		Retrd. 1990	145.00	150-275
1989	The Briary		Retrd. 1995	47.50	60
1982	Bridge House-Mold 1		Retrd. N/A	15.95	450
1982	Bridge House-Mold 2		Retrd. 1990	15.95	175
1991	Bridge House-Mold 3		Open	25.00	20-30
1988	Brockbank		Retrd. 1993	58.00	90
1985	Bronte Parsonage		Retrd. 1987	72.00	80
1982	Burnside		Retrd. 1985	30.00	600
1990	Buttercup Cottage		Retrd. 1992	40.00	65
1989	Butterwick		Retrd. 1996	52.50	60-70
1995	Button Down - Lilliput Lane		Open	37.50	30-38
1996	Calendar Cottage - Lilliput Lane		Open	55.00	55
1994	Camomile Lawn - Lilliput Lane		Open	125.00	90-125
1982	Castle Street		Retrd. 1986	130.00	240-350
1993	Cat's Coombe Cottage - Lilliput Lane		Retrd. 1995	95.00	95
1996	Chalk Down - Lilliput Lane		Open	35.00	35
1991	Chatsworth View		Retrd. 1996	250.00	170-275
1995	Cherry Blossom Cottage - Lilliput Lane		Open	128.00	95-128
1990	Cherry Cottage		Retrd. 1995	33.50	45
1989	Chiltern Mill		Retrd. 1995	87.50	110
1989	Chine Cot-Mold 1		Retrd. 1989	36.00	N/A
1989	Chine Cot-Mold 2		Retrd. 1995	35.00	35-50
1995	Chipping Combe - Lilliput Lane	3,000		525.00	525
1992	The Chocolate House - Lilliput Lane		Open	130.00	90-140
1985	Clare Cottage		Retrd. 1993	30.00	30
1993	Cley-next-the-sea - Lilliput Lane	2,500		725.00	725
1987	Clover Cottage		Retrd. 1994	27.50	58
1982	Coach House		Retrd. 1985	100.00	1100-1895
1986	Cobblers Cottage - D. Hall		Retrd. 1994	42.00	65
1990	Convent in The Woods		Retrd. 1994	175.00	200-250
1983	Coopers		Retrd. 1986	15.00	440-825
1996	Cradle Cottage - Lilliput Lane		Open	100.00	100
1994	Creel Cottage - Lilliput Lane		Retrd. 1997	35.00	35-40
1996	Crispin Cottage - Lilliput Lane		Open	50.00	50
1988	Crown Inn		Retrd. 1990	120.00	120-215
1996	The Cuddy - Lilliput Lane		Open	30.00	30
1991	Daisy Cottage		Open	37.50	30-40
1982	Dale Farm-Mold 1		Retrd. 1986	30.00	1300
1982	Dale Farm-Mold 2		Retrd. 1986	30.00	875
1986	Dale Head		Retrd. 1988	75.00	85-200
1982	Dale House		Retrd. 1986	25.00	840
1996	The Dalesman - Lilliput Lane		Open	95.00	95
1992	Derwent-le-Dale - Lilliput Lane		Open	75.00	55-80
1983	Dove Cottage-Mold 1		Retrd. 1984	35.00	725-1800
1984	Dove Cottage-Mold 2		Retrd. 1988	35.00	55-85
1991	Dovetails		Retrd. 1996	90.00	100
1982	Drapers-Mold 1		Retrd. 1000	15.95	3000
1982	Drapers-Mold 2		Retrd. 1983	15.95	4025
1995	Duckdown Cottage - Lilliput Lane		Retrd. 1997	95.00	70-95
1994	Elm Cottage - Lilliput Lane		Retrd. 1997	65.00	50-65
1985	Farriers		Retrd. 1990	40.00	55-85
1991	Farthing Lodge		Retrd. 1996	37.50	40
1996	Fiddlers Folly - Lilliput Lane		Open	35.00	35
1992	Finchingfields - Lilliput Lane		Retrd. 1995	82.50	85
1985	Fisherman's Cottage		Retrd. 1989	30.00	60
1989	Fiveways		Retrd. 1995	42.50	55
1991	The Flower Sellers		Retrd. 1995	110.00	110
1996	Flowerpots - Lilliput Lane		Open	55.00	55
1987	Four Seasons - M. Adkinson		Retrd. 1991	70.00	125
1993	Foxglove Fields - Lilliput Lane		Retrd. 1997	130.00	85-130
1996	Fry Days - Lilliput Lane		Open	70.00	70
1996	Fuchsia Cottage - Lilliput Lane		Open	30.00	30
1987	The Gables - Lilliput Lane		Retrd. 1992	145.00	175
1997	Golden Years - Lilliput Lane		Open	25.00	25
1996	Gossip Gate - Lilliput Lane		Open	170.00	170
1992	Granny Smiths		Retrd. 1996	60.00	45-65
1997	Granny's Bonnet - Lilliput Lane		Open	25.00	25
1992	Grantchester Meadows - Lilliput Lane		Retrd. 1996	275.00	195-275
1989	Greensted Church		Open	72.50	95
1994	Gulliver's Gate - Lilliput Lane		Open	45.00	35-45
1997	Halcyon Days - Lilliput Lane		Open	150.00	150
1996	Harriet's Cottage - Lilliput Lane		Open	85.00	85
1989	Helmere Cottage		Retrd. 1994	65.00	80-125
1992	High Ghyll Farm - Lilliput Lane		Open	360.00	250-395
1982	Holly Cottage		Retrd. 1988	42.50	85
1987	Holme Dyke		Retrd. 1990	50.00	65
1996	Honey Pot Cottage - Lilliput Lane		Open	60.00	60
1982	Honeysuckle Cottage		Retrd. 1987	45.00	200
1991	Hopcroft Cottage		Retrd. 1995	120.00	130
1987	Inglewood		Retrd. 1994	27.50	40
1987	Izaak Waltons Cottage		Retrd. 1995	75.00	80-125
1991	John Barleycorn Cottage		Retrd. 1995	130.00	140
1993	Junk and Disorderly - Lilliput Lane		Open	150.00	110-150
1987	Keepers Lodge		Retrd. 1995	75.00	90-120
1985	Kentish Oast		Retrd. 1990	55.00	75-125
1990	The King's Arms		Retrd. 1995	450.00	550
1991	Lace Lane		Retrd. 1997	90.00	70-95
1995	Ladybird Cottage - Lilliput Lane		Open	40.00	35-40
1982	Lakeside House-Mold 1		Retrd. 1983	40.00	1500
1982	Lakeside House-Mold 2		Retrd. 1986	40.00	810-940
1991	Lapworth Lock		Retrd. 1995	82.50	85-100
1995	Larkrise - Lilliput Lane		Open	50.00	45-50
1995	Lazy Days - Lilliput Lane		Open	60.00	60
1994	Lenora's Secret - Lilliput Lane	2,500	1995	350.00	400-500
1995	Little Hay - Lilliput Lane		Open	55.00	50-55
1996	Little Lupins - Lilliput Lane		Open	40.00	40
1995	Little Smithy - Lilliput Lane		Open	65.00	60-65
1996	Loxdale Cottage - Lilliput Lane		Open	35.00	35
1987	Magpie Cottage		Retrd. 1990	70.00	100-115
1993	Marigold Meadow - Lilliput Lane		Open	120.00	80-120
1991	Micklegate Antiques		Open	90.00	80-95
1995	Milestone Cottage - Lilliput Lane		Open	40.00	35-40
1983	Millers		Retrd. 1986	15.00	120-150
1983	Miners-Mold 1		Retrd. 1985	15.00	590
1983	Miners-Mold 2		Retrd. 1985	15.00	400-500
1991	Moonlight Cove		Retrd. 1996	82.50	60-85
1985	Moreton Manor		Retrd. 1989	55.00	65-100
1990	Mrs. Pinkerton's Post Office		Open	72.50	70-85
1992	The Nutshell - Lilliput Lane		Retrd. 1995	70.00	80
1982	Oak Lodge-Mold 1		Retrd. N/A	40.00	1000
1982	Oak Lodge-Mold 2		Retrd. 1987	40.00	65-100
1992	Oakwood Smithy		Open	450.00	300-475
1982	Old Curiosity Shop		Retrd. 1989	62.50	100-150
1982	Old Mine		Retrd. 1983	15.95	6500
1993	Old Mother Hubbard's - Lilliput Lane		Open	185.00	120-185
1982	The Old Post Office		Retrd. 1986	35.00	500
1984	Old School House		Retrd. 1985	25.00	1000-1400
1991	Old Shop at Bignor		Retrd. 1995	215.00	220
1989	Olde York Toll		Retrd. 1991	82.50	125
1994	Orchard Farm Cottage - Lilliput Lane		Open	145.00	110-145
1985	Ostlers Keep		Retrd. 1991	55.00	75
1990	Otter Reach		Retrd. 1996	33.50	30-45
1997	Out of the Storm - Lilliput Lane	3,000		1250.00	1250
1991	Paradise Lodge		Retrd. 1996	130.00	95-140
1990	Pargetters Retreat		Retrd. 1990	75.00	115
1991	Pear Tree House		Retrd. 1995	82.50	85
1995	Penny's Post - Lilliput Lane		Open	55.00	50-55
1991	Periwinkle Cottage		Retrd. 1996	165.00	165-220
1995	Pipit Toll - Lilliput Lane		Open	64.00	50-64
1992	Pixie House		Retrd. 1995	55.00	60
1997	The Poppies - Lilliput Lane		Open	50.00	50
1996	Potter's Beck - Lilliput Lane		Open	35.00	35
1991	The Priest's House		Retrd. 1995	180.00	195-225
1991	Primrose Hill		Retrd. 1996	46.50	50
1992	Puffin Row		Open	128.00	95-135
1996	Purbeck Stores - Lilliput Lane		Open	55.00	35-55
1996	Railway Cottage - Lilliput Lane		Open	60.00	60
1983	Red Lion Inn		Retrd. 1987	125.00	360
1996	Reflections of Jade - Lilliput Lane	3,950		350.00	350
1988	Rising Sun		Retrd. 1992	58.00	84-105
1987	Riverview		Retrd. 1994	27.50	35-55
1990	Robin's Gate		Retrd. 1996	33.50	35
1997	Rose Bouquet - Lilliput Lane		Open	25.00	25
1996	Rosemary Cottage - Lilliput Lane		Open	70.00	70
1988	Royal Oak		Retrd. 1991	145.00	150-300
1990	Runswick House		Open	63.50	55-85
1992	Rustic Root House		Retrd. 1997	110.00	80-120
1995	The Rustlings - Lilliput Lane		Open	128.00	95-128
1987	Rydal View		Retrd. 1989	220.00	200
1994	Saddlers Inn - M. Adkinson		Retrd. 1997	50.00	75-125
1994	Saffron House - Lilliput Lane		Open	220.00	170-220
1985	Sawrey Gill		Retrd. 1992	30.00	125-200
1991	Saxham St. Edmunds		Retrd. 1994	1550.00	1850
1988	Saxon Cottage		Retrd. 1989	245.00	200-400
1986	Scroll on the Wall		Retrd. 1987	55.00	150
1987	Secret Garden - M. Adkinson		Retrd. 1994	145.00	245-300
1988	Ship Inn - Lilliput Lane		Retrd. 1991	210.00	228-325
1988	Smallest Inn		Retrd. 1991	42.50	125
1996	Sore Paws - Lilliput Lane		Open	70.00	70
1996	The Spindles - Lilliput Lane		Open	85.00	85
1988	Spring Bank		Retrd. 1991	42.00	50-70
1994	Spring Gate Cottage - Lilliput Lane		Retrd. 1997	130.00	95-130
1996	St. John the Baptist - Lilliput Lane		Open	75.00	75
1989	St. Lawrence Church		Open	110.00	85-140
1988	St. Marks		Retrd. 1991	75.00	150-225
1985	St. Mary's Church		Retrd. 1988	40.00	75-125
1989	St. Peter's Cove		Retrd. 1991	1375.00	1500-2000
1993	Stocklebeck Mill - Lilliput Lane		Open	325.00	195-325
1982	Stone Cottage-Mold 1		Retrd. 1983	40.00	1500
1982	Stone Cottage-Mold 2		Retrd. 1986	40.00	185
1986	Stone Cottage-Mold 3		Retrd. 1986	40.00	200
1992	Stoneybeck		Retrd. 1992	45.00	60-75
1993	Stradling Priory - Lilliput Lane		Retrd. 1997	130.00	85-130
1990	Strawberry Cottage		Open	36.00	35-45
1987	Street Scene No. 1 - Unknown		Retrd. 1987	40.00	120
1987	Street Scene No. 2 - Unknown		Retrd. 1987	45.00	120
1987	Street Scene No. 3 - Unknown		Retrd. 1987	45.00	120
1987	Street Scene No. 4 - Unknown		Retrd. 1987	45.00	120
1987	Street Scene No. 5 - Unknown		Retrd. 1987	45.00	120
1987	Street Scene No. 6 - Unknown		Retrd. 1987	40.00	120
1987	Street Scene No. 7 - Unknown		Retrd. 1987	45.00	120
1987	Street Scene No. 8 - Unknown		Retrd. 1987	45.00	120
1987	Street Scene No. 9 - Unknown		Retrd. 1987	45.00	120
1987	Street Scene No. 10 - Unknown		Retrd. 1987	45.00	120
1987	Street Scene Set - Unknown		Retrd. 1987	425.00	800-1000
1990	Sulgrave Manor		Retrd. 1992	120.00	125-195
1987	Summer Haze		Retrd. 1993	90.00	110
1994	Sunnyside - Lilliput Lane		Retrd. 1997	40.00	35-40
1982	Sussex Mill		Retrd. 1986	25.00	325-450
1988	Swan Inn		Retrd. 1992	120.00	175-225
1994	Sweet Pea Cottage - Lilliput Lane		Retrd. 1997	40.00	35-40
1997	Sweet William - Lilliput Lane		Open	25.00	25
1988	Swift Hollow		Retrd. 1990	75.00	90
1990	Tanglewood Lodge		Retrd. 1992	97.00	150-200
1987	Tanners Cottage		Retrd. 1992	27.50	45
1994	Teacaddy Cottage - Lilliput Lane		Open	79.00	60-79
1983	Thatcher's Rest		Retrd. 1988	185.00	250
1986	Three Feathers		Retrd. 1989	115.00	200-250
1991	Tillers Green		Retrd. 1995	60.00	65
1984	Tintagel		Retrd. 1988	39.50	110-170

*Quotes have been rounded up to nearest dollar

Lilliput Lane Ltd./Enesco Corporation
to Lilliput Lane Ltd./Enesco Corporation

ARCHITECTURE

YEAR ISSUE		EDITION LIMIT	YEAR RETD.	ISSUE PRICE	*QUOTE U.S. $
1994	Tired Timbers - Lilliput Lane	Open		80.00	60-80
1989	Titmouse Cottage	Retrd.	1995	92.50	120
1993	Titwillow Cottage - Lilliput Lane	Retrd.	1997	70.00	45-70
1983	Toll House	Retrd.	1987	15.00	75-165
1995	Tranquillity	2,500	1995	425.00	425
1983	Troutbeck Farm	Retrd.	1987	125.00	300
1983	Tuck Shop	Retrd.	1986	35.00	650-900
1986	Tudor Court - Lilliput Lane	Retrd.	1992	260.00	350-400
1994	Two Hoots - Lilliput Lane	Retrd.	1997	75.00	55-75
1989	Victoria Cottage	Retrd.	1993	52.50	80
1991	Village School	Retrd.	1996	120.00	85-130
1997	Walton Lodge - Lilliput Lane	Open		65.00	65
1983	Warwick Hall-Mold 1	Retrd.	1983	185.00	3000-4000
1983	Warwick Hall-Mold 2	Retrd.	1985	185.00	1300-1800
1985	Watermill	Retrd.	1993	40.00	50-75
1994	Waterside Mill - Lilliput Lane	Open		65.00	50-65
1987	Wealden House	Retrd.	1990	125.00	140
1992	Wedding Bells - Lilliput Lane	Open		75.00	50-80
1991	Wellington Lodge	Retrd.	1995	55.00	60
1992	Wheyside Cottage - Lilliput Lane	Open		46.50	35-50
1989	Wight Cottage	Retrd.	1994	52.50	65
1982	William Shakespeare-Mold 1	Retrd.	1983	55.00	1500-3000
1983	William Shakespeare-Mold 2	Retrd.	1986	55.00	240
1986	William Shakespeare-Mold 3	Retrd.	1989	55.00	215
1989	William Shakespeare-Mold 4	Retrd.	1992	130.00	150
1996	Windy Ridge - Lilliput Lane	Open		50.00	50
1991	Witham Delph	Retrd.	1994	110.00	120
1983	Woodcutters	Retrd.	1987	15.00	140-300
1997	Yorkvale Cottage - Lilliput Lane	Open		50.00	50

English Tea Room Collection - Lilliput Lane

YEAR ISSUE		EDITION LIMIT	YEAR RETD.	ISSUE PRICE	*QUOTE U.S. $
1995	Bargate Cottage Tea Room	Open		160.00	120-160
1995	Bo-Peep Tea Rooms	Open		120.00	85-120
1995	Grandma Batty's Tea Room	Open		120.00	90-120
1995	Kendal Tea House	Open		120.00	85-120
1995	New Forest Teas	Open		160.00	120-160
1996	Swalesdale Teas	Open		85.00	85

Founders Collection - Lilliput Lane

YEAR ISSUE		EDITION LIMIT	YEAR RETD.	ISSUE PRICE	*QUOTE U.S. $
1996	The Almonry	Yr.Iss.		275.00	275

Framed English Plaques - D. Tate

YEAR ISSUE		EDITION LIMIT	YEAR RETD.	ISSUE PRICE	*QUOTE U.S. $
1990	Ashdown Hall	Retrd.	1991	59.50	70
1990	Battleview	Retrd.	1991	59.50	70
1990	Cat Slide Cottage	Retrd.	1991	59.50	70
1990	Coombe Cot	Retrd.	1991	59.50	70
1990	Fell View	Retrd.	1991	59.50	70
1990	Flint Fields	Retrd.	1991	59.50	70
1990	Huntingdon House	Retrd.	1991	59.50	70
1990	Jubilee Lodge	Retrd.	1991	59.50	70
1990	Stowside	Retrd.	1991	59.50	70
1990	Trevan Cove	Retrd.	1991	59.50	70

Framed Irish Plaques - D. Tate

YEAR ISSUE		EDITION LIMIT	YEAR RETD.	ISSUE PRICE	*QUOTE U.S. $
1990	Ballyteag House	Retrd.	1991	59.50	70
1990	Crockuna Croft	Retrd.	1991	59.50	70
1990	Pearses Cottages	Retrd.	1991	59.50	70
1990	Shannons Bank	Retrd.	1991	59.50	70

Framed Scottish Plaques - D. Tate

YEAR ISSUE		EDITION LIMIT	YEAR RETD.	ISSUE PRICE	*QUOTE U.S. $
1990	Barra Black House	Retrd.	1991	59.50	70
1990	Fife Ness	Retrd.	1991	59.50	70
1990	Kyle Point	Retrd.	1991	59.50	70
1990	Preston Oat Mill	Retrd.	1991	59.50	70

French Collection - D. Tate

YEAR ISSUE		EDITION LIMIT	YEAR RETD.	ISSUE PRICE	*QUOTE U.S. $
1991	L' Auberge d'Armorique	Open		220.00	170-250
1991	La Bergerie du Perigord	Open		230.00	170-250
1991	La Cabane du Gardian	Open		55.00	45-60
1991	La Chaumiere du Verger	Open		120.00	95-130
1991	La Maselle de Nadaillac	Open		130.00	95-140
1991	La Porte Schoenenberg	Open		75.00	60-85
1991	Le Manoir de Champfleuri	Open		265.00	215-295
1991	Le Mas du Vigneron	Open		120.00	85-130
1991	Le Petite Montmartre	Open		130.00	95-140
1991	Locmaria	Open		65.00	50-90

German Collection - D. Tate

YEAR ISSUE		EDITION LIMIT	YEAR RETD.	ISSUE PRICE	*QUOTE U.S. $
1992	Alte Schmiede	Open		175.00	120-185
1987	Das Gebirgskirchlein	Open		120.00	120-140
1988	Das Rathaus	Open		140.00	140-160
1992	Der Bücherwurm	Open		140.00	100-160
1988	Der Familienschrein	Retrd.	1991	52.50	100
1988	Die Kleine Backerei	Retrd.	1994	68.00	80
1987	Haus Im Rheinland	Open		220.00	215-250
1987	Jaghutte	Open		82.50	83-95
1987	Meersburger Weinstube	Open		82.50	70-95
1987	Moselhaus	Open		140.00	140-160
1987	Nurnberger Burgerhaus	Open		140.00	140-160
1992	Rosengartenhaus	Open		120.00	90-130
1987	Schwarzwaldhaus	Open		140.00	120-160
1992	Strandvogthaus	Open		120.00	90-130

Historic Castles of England - Lilliput Lane

YEAR ISSUE		EDITION LIMIT	YEAR RETD.	ISSUE PRICE	*QUOTE U.S. $
1994	Bodiam Castle	Open		129.00	95-129
1994	Castell Coch	Open		149.00	120-149
1995	Penkill Castles	Open		130.00	115-130
1994	Stokesay Castle	Open		99.00	85-99

Irish Cottages - D. Tate

YEAR ISSUE		EDITION LIMIT	YEAR RETD.	ISSUE PRICE	*QUOTE U.S. $
1989	Ballykerne Croft	Retrd.	1996	75.00	70-75
1987	Donegal Cottage	Retrd.	1992	29.00	60
1989	Hegarty's Home	Retrd.	1992	68.00	75
1989	Kennedy Homestead	Retrd.	1996	33.50	30-45
1989	Kilmore Quay	Retrd.	1992	68.00	100
1989	Limerick House	Retrd.	1992	110.00	160-170
1989	Magilligan's	Retrd.	1996	33.50	30-45
1989	O'Lacey's Store	Retrd.	1996	68.00	60-85
1989	Pat Cohan's Bar	Retrd.	1996	110.00	125
1989	Quiet Cottage	Retrd.	1992	72.50	120
1989	St. Columba's School	Retrd.	1996	47.50	40-60
1989	St. Kevin's Church	Retrd.	1996	55.00	55-70
1989	St. Patrick's Church	Retrd.	1993	185.00	185
1989	Thoor Ballylee	Retrd.	1992	105.00	160-170

Lakeland Bridge Plaques - D. Simpson

YEAR ISSUE		EDITION LIMIT	YEAR RETD.	ISSUE PRICE	*QUOTE U.S. $
1989	Aira Force	Retrd.	1991	35.00	35
1989	Ashness Bridge	Retrd.	1991	35.00	35
1989	Birks Bridge	Retrd.	1991	35.00	35
1989	Bridge House	Retrd.	1991	35.00	105-120
1989	Hartsop Packhorse	Retrd.	1991	35.00	35
1989	Stockley Bridge	Retrd.	1991	35.00	35

Lakeland Christmas - Lilliput Lane

YEAR ISSUE		EDITION LIMIT	YEAR RETD.	ISSUE PRICE	*QUOTE U.S. $
1995	Langdale Cottage	Open		48.00	35-48
1995	Patterdale Cottage	Open		48.00	35-48
1995	Rydal Cottage	Open		44.75	35-45
1996	All Saints Watermillock	Open		50.00	50
1996	Borrowdale School	Open		35.00	35
1996	Millbeck Cottage	Open		35.00	35

London Plaques - D. Simpson

YEAR ISSUE		EDITION LIMIT	YEAR RETD.	ISSUE PRICE	*QUOTE U.S. $
1989	Big Ben	Retrd.	1991	39.50	40
1989	Buckingham Palace	Retrd.	1991	39.50	40
1989	Piccadilly Circus	Retrd.	1991	39.50	40
1989	Tower Bridge	Retrd.	1991	39.50	40
1989	Tower of London	Retrd.	1991	39.50	40
1989	Trafalgar Square	Retrd.	1991	39.50	40

Ray Day/American Landmark Series - R. Day

YEAR ISSUE		EDITION LIMIT	YEAR RETD.	ISSUE PRICE	*QUOTE U.S. $
1992	16.9 Cents Per Gallon	Open		150.00	95-150
1995	Afternoon Tea	1,995		495.00	495
1994	Birdsong	Open		120.00	85-120
1990	Country Church	Retrd.	1992	82.50	170
1989	Countryside Barn	Retrd.	1992	75.00	150-200
1990	Covered Memories	Retrd.	1993	110.00	200-300
1989	Falls Mill	Retrd.	1992	130.00	225-325
1991	Fire House 1	Open		87.50	85-140
1994	Fresh Bread	Open		150.00	95-150
1992	Gold Miners' Claim	Retrd.	1997	110.00	95-120
1992	Gold Miners' Claim (no snow)	Retrd.	N/A	95.00	750
1990	Great Point Light	Open		39.50	45-55
1994	Harvest Mill	3,500		395.00	395
1994	Holy Night	Open		225.00	170-225
1992	Home Sweet Home	Open		120.00	95-130
1990	Hometown Depot	Retrd.	1993	68.00	100-125
1989	Mail Pouch Barn	Retrd.	1993	75.00	100-200
1990	Pepsi Cola Barn	Retrd.	1991	87.00	175-225
1990	Pioneer Barn	Retrd.	1991	30.00	75
1991	Rambling Rose	Retrd.	1995	60.00	100
1990	Riverside Chapel	Retrd.	1993	82.50	135-155
1990	Roadside Coolers	Retrd.	1994	75.00	110-145
1991	School Days	Retrd.	1997	60.00	60-80
1993	See Rock City	Open		60.00	35-60
1993	Shave and A Haircut	Retrd.	1997	160.00	95-160
1990	Sign Of The Times	Retrd.	1996	27.50	35
1993	Simply Amish	Open		160.00	110-160
1992	Small Town Library	Retrd.	1995	130.00	140
1994	Spring Victorian	Open		250.00	170-250
1991	Victoriana	Retrd.	1992	295.00	325-500
1992	Winnie's Place	Retrd.	1993	395.00	550-750

Ray Day/Christmas in America - R. Day

YEAR ISSUE		EDITION LIMIT	YEAR RETD.	ISSUE PRICE	*QUOTE U.S. $
1996	Home For the Holidays	2,596		495.00	495
1997	Let Heaven & Nature Sing	Yr.Iss.		150.00	150
1997	To Grandmother's House We Go	Yr.Iss.		150.00	150

Ray Day/Coca Cola Country - R. Day

YEAR ISSUE		EDITION LIMIT	YEAR RETD.	ISSUE PRICE	*QUOTE U.S. $
1996	A Cherry Coke...Just the Prescription	Open		95.00	95
1997	Country Canvas	Open		15.00	15
1996	Country Fresh Pickins	Open		150.00	150
1996	Fill'er Up & Check the Oil	Open		125.00	125
1996	Hazards of the Road	Open		50.00	50
1996	Hook, Line & Sinker	Open		95.00	95
1997	The Lunch Line	Open		40.00	40
1997	Mmmmm...Just Like Home	Open		125.00	125
1997	Oh By Gosh, By Golly	Yr.Iss.		85.00	85
1997	Saturday Night Jive	Open		95.00	95
1996	We've Got it or They Don't Make it	Open		95.00	95
1997	Wet Your Whistle	Open		40.00	40

Ray Day/The Allegiance Collection - R. Day

YEAR ISSUE		EDITION LIMIT	YEAR RETD.	ISSUE PRICE	*QUOTE U.S. $
1997	Home of the Brave	Open		75.00	75
1997	I Pledge Allegiance	Open		75.00	75
1997	In Remembrance	Open		75.00	75
1997	One Nation Under God	Open		75.00	75

Scottish Collection - D. Tate, unless otherwise noted

YEAR ISSUE		EDITION LIMIT	YEAR RETD.	ISSUE PRICE	*QUOTE U.S. $
1985	7 St. Andrews Square - A. Yarrington	Retrd.	1986	15.95	85-120
1995	Amisfield Tower - Lilliput Lane	Open		55.00	50-55
1989	Blair Atholl	Retrd.	1992	275.00	375
1985	Burns Cottage	Retrd.	1988	35.00	70-95
1989	Carrick House	Open		47.50	35-60
1990	Cawdor Castle	3,000	1992	295.00	325-475
1989	Claypotts Castle	Retrd.	1997	72.50	70-95
1989	Craigievar Castle	Retrd.	1991	185.00	300-525
1984	The Croft (renovated)	Retrd.	1991	36.00	65-100
1982	The Croft (without sheep)	Retrd.	1984	29.00	800-1250
1989	Culloden Cottage	Open		36.00	35-45
1992	Culross House	Retrd.	1997	90.00	70-95
1992	Duart Castle	3,000	1997	450.00	475
1987	East Neuk	Retrd.	1991	29.00	60-75
1993	Edzell Summer House - Lilliput Lane	Retrd.	1997	110.00	70-110
1990	Eilean Donan	Open		145.00	145-185
1992	Eriskay Croft	Open		50.00	40-55
1990	Fishermans Bothy	Open		36.00	35-45
1990	Glenlochie Lodge	Retrd.	1993	110.00	120
1990	Hebridean Hame	Retrd.	1992	55.00	65-120
1989	Inverlochie Hame	Open		47.50	40-60
1989	John Knox House	Retrd.	1992	68.00	150-200
1989	Kenmore Cottage	Retrd.	1993	87.00	110
1990	Kinlochness	Retrd.	1993	79.00	85-125
1990	Kirkbrae Cottage	Retrd.	1993	55.00	70-95
1994	Ladybank Lodge - Lilliput Lane	Open		80.00	60-80
1992	Mair Haven	Open		46.50	35-50
1985	Preston Mill-Mold 1	Retrd.	1986	45.00	175-200
1986	Preston Mill-Mold 2	Retrd.	1992	62.50	78
1989	Stockwell Tenement	Retrd.	1996	62.50	63-80

Specials - Various

YEAR ISSUE		EDITION LIMIT	YEAR RETD.	ISSUE PRICE	*QUOTE U.S. $
1985	Bermuda Cottage (3 Colors) - D. Tate	Retrd.	1991	29.00	40-50
1985	Bermuda Cottage (3 Colors)-set - D. Tate	Retrd.	1991	87.00	175-345
1983	Bridge House Dealer Sign - D. Tate	Retrd.	1984	N/A	375
1988	Chantry Chapel - D. Tate	Retrd.	1991	N/A	200-250
1983	Cliburn School - D. Tate	Retrd.	1984	Gift	6000-7000
1987	Clockmaker's Cottage - D. Tate	Retrd.	1990	40.00	200-235
1996	Cornflower Cottage	Retrd.	1996	N/A	100
1993	Counting House Corner (mounted) - Lilliput Lane	Retrd.	1993	N/A	N/A
1993	Counting House Corner - Lilliput Lane	3,093	1993	N/A	N/A
1987	Guildhall - D. Tate	Retrd.	1989	N/A	145
1996	Honeysuckle Plaque (with doves) - Lilliput Lane	Retrd.	1996	N/A	90
1996	Honeysuckle Plaque (without doves) - Lilliput Lane	Retrd.	1996	N/A	N/A
1989	Mayflower House - D. Tate	Retrd.	1990	79.50	120-175
1991	Rose Cottage Skirsgill-Mold 1 - Lilliput Lane	200	1991	N/A	700
1991	Rose Cottage Skirsgill-Mold 2 - Lilliput Lane	Retrd.	1991	N/A	250-300
1994	Rose Cottage Skirsgill-Mold 3 - Lilliput Lane	Open		N/A	N/A
1991	Settler's Surprise - Lilliput Lane	Open		135.00	135
1986	Seven Dwarf's Cottage - D. Tate	Retrd.	1986	146.80	700-1100
1994	Wycombe Toll House - Lilliput Lane	Retrd.	1994	33.00	240-330

Studley Royal Collection - Lilliput Lane

YEAR ISSUE		EDITION LIMIT	YEAR RETD.	ISSUE PRICE	*QUOTE U.S. $
1994	Banqueting House	5,000		65.00	65
1995	Fountains Abbey	3,500		395.00	395
1994	Octagon Tower	5,000		85.00	85
1994	St. Mary's Church	5,000		115.00	115
1994	Temple of Piety	5,000		95.00	95

Unframed Plaques - D. Tate

YEAR ISSUE		EDITION LIMIT	YEAR RETD.	ISSUE PRICE	*QUOTE U.S. $
1989	Large Lower Brockhampton	Retrd.	1991	120.00	120
1989	Large Somerset Springtime	Retrd.	1991	130.00	130
1989	Medium Cobble Combe Cottage	Retrd.	1991	68.00	68
1989	Medium Wishing Well	Retrd.	1991	75.00	75
1989	Small Stoney Wall Lea	Retrd.	1991	47.50	48
1989	Small Woodside Farm	Retrd.	1991	47.50	48

Victorian Shops - Various

YEAR ISSUE		EDITION LIMIT	YEAR RETD.	ISSUE PRICE	*QUOTE U.S. $
1997	Apothecary	Open		90.00	90
1997	Book Shop	Open		75.00	75
1997	Haberdashery	Open		90.00	90
1997	Horologist	Open		75.00	75
1997	Pawnbroker	Open		75.00	75
1997	Tailor	Open		90.00	90

Village Shop Collection - Various

YEAR ISSUE		EDITION LIMIT	YEAR RETD.	ISSUE PRICE	*QUOTE U.S. $
1995	The Baker's Shop	Open		120.00	85-120
1995	The Chine Shop	Open		120.00	85-120
1992	The Greengrocers - D. Tate	Open		120.00	80-130
1993	Jones The Butcher	Open		120.00	80-120
1992	Penny Sweets	Open		130.00	80-130
1993	Toy Shop	Open		120.00	80-120

Welsh Collection - Various

YEAR ISSUE		EDITION LIMIT	YEAR RETD.	ISSUE PRICE	*QUOTE U.S. $
1986	Brecon Bach - D. Tate	Retrd.	1993	42.00	60
1991	Bro Dawel - D. Tate	Open		37.50	30-40
1985	Hermitage - D. Tate	Retrd.	1986	30.00	175-300
1987	Hermitage Renovated - D. Tate	Retrd.	1990	42.50	75
1992	St. Govan's Chapel	Open		75.00	50-80
1991	Tudor Merchant - D. Tate	Retrd.	1997	90.00	70-95
1991	Ugly House - D. Tate	Open		55.00	50-60

A Year In An English Garden - Lilliput Lane

YEAR ISSUE		EDITION LIMIT	YEAR RETD.	ISSUE PRICE	*QUOTE U.S. $
1994	Autumn Hues	Open		120.00	85-120
1995	Spring Glory	Open		120.00	85-120
1995	Summer Impressions	Open		120.00	85-120

*Quotes have been rounded up to nearest dollar

ARCHITECTURE

Lilliput Lane Ltd./Enesco Corporation to Michael's Limited

YEAR ISSUE		EDITION LIMIT	YEAR RETD.	ISSUE PRICE	*QUOTE U.S.$
1994	Winter's Wonder	Open		120.00	85-120

Lowell Davis Farm Club

Davis Farm Set - L. Davis

YEAR ISSUE		EDITION LIMIT	YEAR RETD.	ISSUE PRICE	*QUOTE U.S.$
1985	Barn 25352	Closed	1987	47.50	425
1985	Chicken House 25358	Closed	1987	19.00	50
1985	Corn Crib and Sheep Pen 25354	Closed	1987	25.00	65
1985	Garden and Wood Shed 25359	Closed	1987	25.00	65
1985	Goat Yard and Studio 25353	Closed	1987	32.50	85
1985	Hen House 25356	Closed	1987	32.50	80
1985	Hog House 25355	Closed	1987	27.50	85
1985	Main House 25351	Closed	1987	42.50	100
1985	Privy 25348	Closed	1987	12.50	35
1985	Remus' Cabin 25350	Closed	1987	42.50	95
1985	Smoke House 25357	Closed	1987	12.50	65
1985	Windmill 25349	Closed	1987	25.00	45

Davis Route 66 - L. Davis

YEAR ISSUE		EDITION LIMIT	YEAR RETD.	ISSUE PRICE	*QUOTE U.S.$
1992	Fresh Squeezed? (w/ wooden base) 25609	350	1995	600.00	700
1992	Fresh Squeezed? 25608	2,500	1995	450.00	550
1992	Going To Grandma's 25619	Closed	1995	80.00	80
1993	Home For Christmas 25621	Closed	1995	80.00	80
1991	Just Check The Air 25600	350	1995	700.00	750
1991	Just Check The Air 25603	2,500	1995	550.00	550
1993	Kickin' Himself 25622	Closed	1995	80.00	80
1991	Little Bit Of Shade 25602	Closed	1995	100.00	100
1991	Nel's Diner 25601	350	1995	700.00	700
1991	Nel's Diner 25604	2,500	1995	550.00	550
1992	Quiet Day at Maple Grove 25618	Closed	1995	130.00	130
1992	Relief 25605	Closed	1995	80.00	80
1993	Summer Days 25607	Yr.Iss.	1995	100.00	100
1992	Welcome Mat (w/ wooden base) 25606	1,500	1995	400.00	400
1992	What Are Pals For? 25620	Closed	1995	100.00	100

Michael's Limited

Collectors' Corner - B. Baker

YEAR ISSUE		EDITION LIMIT	YEAR RETD.	ISSUE PRICE	*QUOTE U.S.$
1993	City Cottage (Membership House)-rose/grn.1682	Retrd.	1994	35.00	110-125
1993	Brian's First House (Redemption House)-red1496	Retrd.	1994	71.00	150-175
1994	Gothic Cottage (Membership Sculpture) 1571	Retrd.	1995	35.00	75-95
1994	Duke of Gloucester Street (Redemption House) 1459	Retrd.	1995	108.00	150-165
1995	Marie's Cottage-grey (Membership Sculpture) 1942	Retrd.	1996	35.00	75
1995	Welcome Home-brick (Redemption House) 1599	Retrd.	1996	65.00	95
1996	Queen Ann Cottage-rose/blue (Membership Sculpture) 1676	Retrd.	1997	39.00	39
1996	Oak Street-brick/brown (Redemption House) 1685	9/97		65.00	65
1997	Michael's Garage (Redemption House) 1720	3/98		34.50	35
1997	Michael's House-blue (Membership Sculpture) 1719	3/98		40.00	40

Signing Piece - B. Baker

YEAR ISSUE		EDITION LIMIT	YEAR RETD.	ISSUE PRICE	*QUOTE U.S.$
1995	Joe's Newstand 1348	Yr.Iss.	1995	27.00	27
1996	Yellow Rose Cottage 1444	Yr.Iss.	1996	62.00	62
1997	Umbrella Shop 1179	Yr.Iss.		29.50	30

Brian Baker's Déjà Vu Collection - B. Baker

YEAR ISSUE		EDITION LIMIT	YEAR RETD.	ISSUE PRICE	*QUOTE U.S.$
1988	Adam Colonial Cottage-blue/white 1515	Retrd.	1992	53.00	53
1993	Admiralty Head Lighthouse-white 1532	Retrd.	1995	62.00	62
1992	Alpine Ski Lodge-brown/white 1012	Retrd.	1993	62.00	92
1988	Andulusian Village-white 1060	Retrd.	1993	53.00	63
1992	Angel of the Sea-blue/white 1587	Open		67.00	67
1996	Angel of the Sea-blue/white 1592	Open		69.00	69
1992	Angel of the Sea-mauve/white 1586	Open		67.00	67
1996	Angel of the Sea-mauve/white 1591	Open		69.00	69
1989	Antebellum Mansion-blue/rose 1505	Retrd.	1993	53.00	73
1988	Antebellum Mansion-blue/white 1519	Retrd.	1988	49.00	49
1989	Antebellum Mansion-peach 1506	Retrd.	1991	49.00	56
1988	Antebellum Mansion-peach 1517	Retrd.	1988	49.00	49
1988	Antebellum Mansion-white/green 1518	Retrd.	1988	49.00	49
1994	Barber Shop 1164	Retrd.	1996	53.00	53
1987	Bavarian Church-white 1021	Retrd.	1988	38.00	38
1987	Bavarian Church-yellow 1020	Retrd.	1988	38.00	38
1987	The Bernese Guesthouse -golden br. 1010	Retrd.	1990	49.00	49
1989	Blumen Shop-white/brown 1023	Retrd.	1993	53.00	73
1997	Bourbon Street Cottage 1718	Open		41.00	41
1997	Bracket Cottage-blue 1714	Open		37.00	37
1997	Bracket Cottage-cream 1715	Open		37.00	37
1996	Brick & Brackets-brick 1933	Open		65.00	65
1994	Cabbagetown 1704	Open		65.00	65
1996	Cape Cottage-grey/white 1442	Open		63.00	63
1997	Cape May Gingerbread-cream 1594	Open		48.00	48
1997	Cape May Gingerbread-rose 1593	Open		48.00	48
1997	Carpenter's Gothic-blue 1575	Open		40.00	40
1997	Carpenter's Gothic-rose 1576	Open		40.00	40
1988	Casa Chiquita-natural 1400	Retrd.	1992	53.00	60
1994	Castle in the Clouds 1090	Retrd.	1995	75.00	85
1993	Charleston Single House -blue/white 1583	Open		60.00	60
1993	Charleston Single House -peach/white 1584	Open		60.00	60
1996	Chateau in the Woods-stone 1683	Yr.Iss.	1996	79.00	79
1997	Chesapeake Lighthouse 1595	Open		43.00	43
1994	Christmas at Church 1223	Retrd.	1996	63.00	63
1988	Christmas House-blue 1225	Retrd.	1992	51.00	51
1990	Classic Victorian-blue/white 1555	Retrd.	1994	60.00	80
1990	Classic Victorian-peach 1557	Retrd.	1994	60.00	80
1990	Classic Victorian-rose/blue 1556	Retrd.	1994	60.00	80
1991	Colonial Color-brown 1508	Retrd.	1993	62.00	82
1991	Colonial Cottage-white/bue 1509	Retrd.	1994	59.00	80
1987	Colonial House-blue 1510	Retrd.	1988	49.00	70
1987	Colonial House-wine 1511	Retrd.	1987	40.00	60
1997	Colonial Merchant 1452	Open		37.00	37
1987	Colonial Store-brick 1512	Retrd.	1993	53.00	73
1997	Conch House-blue 1670	Open		48.00	48
1997	Conch House-cream 1671	Open		48.00	48
1993	Corner Grocery-brick 1141	Open		67.00	67
1987	The Cottage House-blue 1531	Retrd.	1988	42.00	42
1987	The Cottage House-white 1530	Retrd.	1993	47.00	67
1989	Country Barn-blue 1528	Retrd.	1991	49.00	70
1989	Country Barn-red 1527	Retrd.	1993	53.00	73
1994	Country Bridge 1513	Open		69.00	69
1996	Country Christmas-red 1219	Open		68.00	68
1988	Country Church-white/blue 1522	Retrd.	1994	49.00	50-70
1992	Country Station-blue/rust 1156	Open		64.00	64
1994	Country Store 1122	Retrd.	1996	61.00	61
1994	Craftsman Cottage-cream 1478	Open		56.00	56
1994	Craftsman Cottage-grey 1477	Retrd.	1995	56.00	56
1989	Deja Vu Sign-ivory/brown 1600	Retrd.	1991	21.00	24-29
1992	Deja Vu Sign-ivory/brown 1999	Retrd.	1996	21.00	21
1993	Dinard Mansion-beige/brick 1005	Retrd.	1996	67.00	67
1996	Dixie Landing-white 1740	Open		68.00	68
1997	Eaton Street Gingerbread-blue 1672	Open		48.00	48
1997	Eaton Street Gingerbread-white 1673	Open		48.00	48
1994	Ellis Island 1250	Retrd.	1996	62.00	62
1993	Enchanted Cottage-natural 1205	Retrd.	1995	63.00	68
1988	Fairy Tale Cottage-white/brown 1200	Retrd.	1992	46.00	46
1997	Farm Country-red 1494	Open		43.00	43
1997	Farm Country-white 1495	Open		43.00	43
1987	The Farm House-beige/blue 1525	Retrd.	1991	49.00	49
1987	The Farm House-spiced tan 1526	Retrd.	1991	49.00	49
1992	Firehouse-brick 1140	Open		60.00	60
1992	Flower Store-tan/green 1145	Open		67.00	67
1988	French Colonial Cottage-beige 1516	Retrd.	1990	42.00	65
1997	French Quarter Townhouse-cream/teal 1717	Open		40.00	40
1997	French Quarter Townhouse -rose/blue 1716	Open		40.00	40
1988	Georgian Colonial House -white/blue 1514	Retrd.	1992	53.00	53
1990	Gothic Victorian-blue/mauve 1534	Retrd.	1991	47.00	52-54
1988	Gothic Victorian-peach 1536	Retrd.	1992	51.00	60
1988	Gothic Victorian-sea green 1537	Retrd.	1990	47.00	47
1993	Grandpa's Barn-brown 1498	Open		63.00	63
1988	Hampshire House-brick 1040	Retrd.	1988	49.00	60
1989	Hampshire House-brick 1041	Retrd.	1990	49.00	56
1996	Harbor Sentry-white 1590	Open		59.00	59
1989	Henry VIII Pub-white/brown 1043	Retrd.	1993	56.00	76
1993	Homestead Christmas-red 1224	Retrd.	1995	57.00	57
1987	Hotel Couronne (original)wh./br. 1000	Retrd.	1988	49.00	49
1989	Hotel Couronne-white/brown 1003	Retrd.	1992	55.00	55
1987	Italianate Victorian-brown 1543	Retrd.	1990	52.00	52
1987	Italianate Victorian-lavendar 1550	Retrd.	1988	45.00	45
1987	Italianate Victorian-mauve/blue 1545	Retrd.	1991	49.00	49
1989	Italianate Victorian-peach/teal 1552	Retrd.	1991	51.00	62
1989	Italianate Victorian-rose/blue 1551	Retrd.	1991	51.00	55-58
1987	Italianate Victorian-rust/blue 1544	Retrd.	1988	49.00	49
1987	Japanese House-white/brown 1100	Retrd.	1988	47.00	47
1996	Japanese Tea House-brown/white 1101	Open		59.00	59
1987	The Lighthouse-white 1535	Retrd.	1992	53.00	60
1991	Log Cabin-brown 1501	Retrd.	1994	55.00	75
1992	Looks Like Nantucket-grey 1451	Open		59.00	59
1995	Main Street Cafe-blue 1142	Open		61.00	61
1997	Main Street Church 1163	Open		49.00	49
1993	Mansard Lady-blue/rose 1606	Open		64.00	64
1993	Mansard Lady-tan/green 1607	Open		64.00	64
1995	Maple Lane-blue/white 1904	Open		72.00	72
1995	Maple Lane-desert/white 1905	Open		72.00	72
1991	Mayor's Mansion-blue/peach 1585	Retrd.	1994	57.00	77
1996	Mediterranean Ave-cream/tile 1741	Open		65.00	65
1995	Mesa Manor 1733	Open		75.00	75
1994	Mission Dolores (no umbrella) 1435	Retrd.	N/A	47.00	75
1994	Mission Dolores 1435	Open		47.00	47
1993	Monday's Wash-cream/blue 1450	Retrd.	1996	62.00	62
1993	Monday's Wash-white/blue 1449	Retrd.	1996	62.00	62
1995	Mountain Homestead-brown 1401	Open		78.00	78
1997	Mountain Meadows-brown 1497	Open		52.00	52
1994	Mukilteo Lighthouse 1569	Open		55.00	55
1989	Norwegian House-brown 1051	Retrd.	1990	51.00	58
1997	Oak Bluff-brown 1573	Open		42.00	42
1997	Oak Bluff-grey 1572	Open		42.00	42
1990	Old Country Cottage-blue 1502	Retrd.	1992	51.00	58
1990	Old Country Cottage-peach 1504	Retrd.	1991	47.00	65
1990	Old Country Cottage-red 1503	Retrd.	1992	51.00	65
1996	Old Glory-brick 1567	Open		59.00	59
1994	The Old School House 1439	Open		61.00	61
1987	Old West General Store-white/grey 1520	Retrd.	1991	50.00	68
1987	Old West General Store-yellow/white 1521	Retrd.	1988	50.00	50
1993	Old West Hotel-cream 1120	Retrd.	1996	62.00	62
1995	Old West Sheriff-red 1125	Open		56.00	56
1995	Old White Church-white 1424	Open		65.00	65
1988	One Room School House-red 1524	Retrd.	1993	53.00	73
1994	Orleans Cottage-white/blue 1447	Retrd.	1996	63.00	63
1994	Orleans Cottage-white/red 1448	Retrd.	1996	63.00	63
1990	Palm Villa-desert/green 1421	Retrd.	1995	54.00	61
1990	Palm Villa-white/blue 1420	Retrd.	1995	54.00	61
1994	Paris by the Bay 1004	Retrd.	1996	55.00	55
1989	Parisian Apartment-beige/blue 1002	Retrd.	1993	53.00	73
1987	Parisian Apartment-golden brown 1001	Retrd.	1993	53.00	73
1995	Peggy's Cove Light-white 1533	Open		56.00	56
1996	Pennridge-white/stone 1429	Open		70.00	70
1997	Point Fermin Lighthouse 1568	Yr.Iss.		54.00	54
1994	Police Station-stone 1147	Open		55.00	55
1993	Post Office-light green 1146	Open		60.00	60
1987	Queen Ann Victorian-peach/green 1540	Retrd.	1993	53.00	73
1987	Queen Ann Victorian-rose 1541	Retrd.	1993	53.00	73
1987	Queen Ann Victorian-rust/green 1542	Retrd.	1988	49.00	49
1995	Quiet Neighborhood-cream/blue 1623	Open		71.00	71
1995	Quiet Neighborhood-rose/blue 1622	Open		71.00	71
1995	River Belle Steamer-white 1092	Open		70.00	70
1994	Riverside Mill 1507	Open		65.00	65
1988	Roeder Gate, Rothenburg-brown 1022	Retrd.	1990	49.00	49
1992	Rose Cottage-grey 1443	Open		59.00	59
1996	Ruby's Watch-blue/white 1630	Open		56.00	56
1996	Ruby's Watch-cream/white 1631	Open		56.00	56
1994	San Francisco Stick-brick/teal 1625	Retrd.	1996	61.00	61
1994	San Francisco Stick-cream/blue 1624	Retrd.	1996	61.00	61
1995	Scenic Route 100-red/green 1426	Open		71.00	71
1995	Scenic Route 100-red/yellow 1425	Open		71.00	71
1996	Seaside Cottage-blue/white1691	Open		64.00	64
1996	Seaside Cottage-rose/white 1690	Open		64.00	64
1988	Second Empire House-sea grn./desert 1539	Retrd.	1991	50.00	50
1988	Second Empire House-white/blue 1538	Retrd.	1993	54.00	74
1993	Smuggler's Cove-grey/brown 1529	Open		72.00	72
1987	Snow Cabin-brown/white 1500	Retrd.	1994	51.00	70
1995	Southern Exposure-cream/rose 1582	Open		62.00	62
1995	Southern Exposure-tan/green 1581	Open		62.00	62
1995	Southern Mansion-brick 1744	Yr.Iss.	1995	79.00	79
1995	St. Nicholas Church-white/blue 1409	Open		56.00	56
1993	Steiner Street-peach/green 1674	Open		63.00	63
1993	Steiner Street-rose/blue 1675	Open		63.00	63
1993	The Stone House-stone/blue 1453	Open		63.00	63
1988	Stone Victorians-browns 1554	Retrd.	1994	56.00	76
1993	Sunday Afternoon-brick 1523	Retrd.	1995	62.00	62
1989	Swedish Home-Swed.red 1050	Retrd.	1990	51.00	58
1991	Teddy's Place-teal/rose 1570	Open		61.00	61
1994	Towered Lady-blue/rose 1688	Open		65.00	65
1994	Towered Lady-rose 1689	Open		65.00	65
1992	Tropical Fantasy-blue/coral 1410	Open		67.00	67
1992	Tropical Fantasy-rose/blue 1411	Open		67.00	67
1992	Tropical Fantasy-yellow/teal 1412	Open		67.00	67
1996	Tropical Paradise-white/brown 1115	Open		65.00	65
1995	Tudor Christmas-red brick 1221	Open		67.00	67
1995	Tudor Home-tan brick 1222	Open		67.00	67
1987	Turreted Victorian-beige/blue 1546	Retrd.	1992	55.00	55
1987	Turreted Victorian-peach 1547	Retrd.	1992	55.00	57
1987	Ultimate Victorian-lt. blue/rose 1549	Retrd.	1993	60.00	80
1987	Ultimate Victorian-maroon/slate 1548	Retrd.	1993	60.00	80
1989	Ultimate Victorian-peach/green 1553	Retrd.	1993	60.00	65
1992	Victorian Bay View-cream/teal 1564	Open		63.00	63
1992	Victorian Bay View-rose/blue 1563	Open		63.00	63
1992	Victorian Charm-cream 1588	Retrd.	1996	61.00	61
1992	Victorian Charm-mauve 1589	Retrd.	1996	61.00	61
1990	Victorian Country Estate-desert/br. 1560	Retrd.	1994	62.00	82
1990	Victorian Country Estate-peach/blue 1562	Retrd.	1994	62.00	82
1990	Victorian Country Estate-rose/blue 1561	Retrd.	1994	62.00	82
1991	Victorian Farmhouse-goldenbrown 1565	Retrd.	1994	59.00	90
1995	Victorian Living-clay/white 1927	Open		70.00	70
1995	Victorian Living-teal/tan 1926	Open		70.00	70
1992	Victorian Tower House-blue/maroon 1558	Open		63.00	63
1992	Victorian Tower House-peach/blue 1559	Open		63.00	63

*Quotes have been rounded up to nearest dollar

YEAR ISSUE		EDITION LIMIT	YEAR RETD.	ISSUE PRICE	*QUOTE U.S. $
1996	Village Pharmacy-brick 1157	Open		65.00	65
1997	Waterfront Property-brown 1737	Open		37.00	37
1996	Willow Road-brick 1713	Open		68.00	68
1991	Wind and Roses-brick 1470	Open		63.00	63
1989	Windmill on the Dike-beige/green 1034	Retrd.	1994	60.00	90

Brian Baker's Déjà Vu Collection Accessories - B. Baker

YEAR ISSUE		EDITION LIMIT	YEAR RETD.	ISSUE PRICE	*QUOTE U.S. $
1995	Apple Tree 1317	Open		36.00	36
1996	Autumn Birch 1323	Open		26.00	26
1996	Autumn Flame 1328	Open		29.00	29
1996	Banana Tree 1318	Open		36.00	36
1997	Beach Umbrella 1362	Open		28.00	28
1997	Beauford's Friends-red 1337	Open		32.00	32
1997	Beauford's Friends-white 1336	Open		32.00	32
1997	Bird Bath 1302	Open		18.00	18
1996	Blue Spruce 1352	Open		24.00	24
1995	Cactus Garden 1334	Open		27.50	28
1995	Coconut Palms 1319	Open		25.00	25
1997	Courtyard Garden 1303	Open		18.00	18
1995	Date Palm 1320	Open		24.00	24
1995	Doghouse 1306	Open		23.00	23
1997	End of Harvest 1316	Open		21.00	21
1996	Farm Truck 1357	Open		47.00	47
1996	Forest Fir 1358	Open		24.00	24
1996	Forest Giant 1333	Open		36.00	36
1996	Garden Trellis 1308	Open		24.00	24
1996	Hemlock 1344	Open		24.00	24
1995	House For Sale 1307	Open		24.00	24
1996	Huckleberry's Cat 1343	Open		20.00	20
1995	In The Park 1340	Open		30.00	30
1996	Japanese Bridge 1330	Open		34.00	34
1996	Japanese Pine 1331	Open		36.00	36
1996	Large Blue Spruce 1361	Open		24.00	24
1995	Long Picket Fence 1309	Open		23.00	23
1995	Members Only 1312	Open		46.00	46
1995	Outhouse 1305	Open		26.00	26
1995	Rope Swing 1311	Open		36.00	36
1995	Route 1 1313	Open		28.00	28
1997	Shade Tree 1355	Open		21.00	21
1995	Short Picket Fence 1310	Open		20.00	20
1997	Spanish Moss 1314	Open		21.00	21
1996	Summer Birch 1322	Open		26.00	26
1996	Summer Shade 1327	Open		29.00	29
1997	Swamp Cypress 1349	Open		21.00	21
1996	Tom's Fence 1342	Open		20.00	20
1997	Wall Flowers 1304	Open		14.00	14
1995	Weeping Willow 1326	Open		39.00	39
1995	Windy Day 1321	Open		35.00	35
1996	Winter Green 1360	Open		24.00	24
1996	Winter Mantel 1351	Open		24.00	24

Limited Editions From Brian Baker - B. Baker

YEAR ISSUE		EDITION LIMIT	YEAR RETD.	ISSUE PRICE	*QUOTE U.S. $
1993	American Classic-rose 1566	500	1993	99.00	450-550
1987	Amsterdam Canal-brown, S/N 1030	1,000	1993	79.00	200-225
1994	Hill Top Mansion 1598	1,200	1995	97.00	97
1993	James River Plantation-brick 1454	Retrd.	1994	108.00	300-400
1996	London 1045	1,200		119.00	119
1994	Painted Ladies 1190	1,200	1996	125.00	125
1995	Philadelphia-brick 1441	1,500		110.00	110
1997	Riverside Plantation 1739	1,200		60.00	60
1994	White Point 1596	700	1996	100.00	150

Midwest of Cannon Falls

Cottontail Lane Figurines and Accessories - Midwest

YEAR ISSUE		EDITION LIMIT	YEAR RETD.	ISSUE PRICE	*QUOTE U.S. $
1993	Arbor w/ Fence Set 02188-0	Open		14.00	15
1993	Birdbath, Bench & Mailbox, 02184-2	Retrd.	1993	4.00	4
1994	Birdhouse, Sundial & Bunny Fountain, 3 asst. 00371-8	Suspd.		4.50	12
1993	Bridge & Gazebo, 2 asst. 02182-9	Retrd.	1996	11.50	12
1997	Bunnies on an Afternoon Stroll 18656-5	Open		5.00	5
1996	Bunnies Sitting in Gazebo 15801-2	Open		10.00	10
1996	Bunny Band Quartet, set/4 15799-2	Open		16.00	16
1995	Bunny Chef, 2 asst. 12433-8	Open		4.50	5
1993	Bunny Child Collecting Eggs, 2 asst. 02880-3	Retrd.	1993	4.20	14
1996	Bunny Children Working in Garden, 2 asst. 15796-1	Open		3.50	4
1997	Bunny Clown, 2 asst. 18659-6	Open		4.00	4
1995	Bunny Couple at Cafe Table 12444-4	Open		7.00	7
1993	Bunny Couple on Bicycle 02978-7	Retrd.	1993	5.30	6
1997	Bunny Flower Girl & Ring Bearer, 2 asst. 18651-0	Open		3.50	4
1995	Bunny Kids at Carrot Juice Stand 12437-6	Open		5.30	6
1997	Bunny Kissing Booth 18660-2	Open		9.00	9
1994	Bunny Marching Band, 6 asst. 00355-8	Open		4.20	5
1995	Bunny Minister, Soloist, 2 asst. 12434-8	Open		5.00	5
1996	Bunny Picnicking, set/4 15798-5	Open		15.00	15
1995	Bunny Playing Piano 12439-0	Open		5.30	6
1995	Bunny Playing, 2 asst. 12442-0	Open		6.50	7
1995	Bunny Popcorn, Balloon Vendor, 2 asst. 12443-7	Open		6.70	7
1994	Bunny Preparing for Easter, 3 asst. 02971-8	Retrd.	1996	4.20	5
1994	Bunny Shopping Couple, 2 asst. 10362-3	Open		4.20	5
1997	Bunny Throwing Pie 18657-2	Open		3.00	3
1997	Bunny Vendor 18658-9	Open		4.00	4
1997	Carrot Fence 19625-0	Open		10.00	10
1994	Cobblestone Road 10072-1	Retrd.	1996	9.00	9
1994	Cone-Shaped Tree Set 10369-2	Retrd.	1996	7.50	8
1997	Cotton Candy Vendor Bunny 18661-9	Open		5.00	5
1994	Cottontail Lane Sign 10063-9	Open		5.00	5
1994	Easter Bunny Figure, 2 asst. 00356-5	Open		4.20	5
1994	Egg Stand & Flower Cart, 2 asst. 10354-8	Open		6.00	6
1995	Electric Street Lamppost, set/4 12461-1	Retrd.	1996	25.00	25
1996	Garden Shopkeeper, set/2 15800-5	Open		10.00	10
1996	Garden Table with Potted Plants and Flowers 15802-9	Open		9.00	9
1996	Garden with Waterfall and Pond 15797-8	Retrd.	1996	15.00	15
1997	Just Married Getaway Car 18650-3	Open		10.00	10
1993	Lamppost, Birdhouse & Mailbox, 3 asst. 02187-3	Retrd.	1993	4.50	5
1995	Mayor Bunny and Bunny with Flag Pole, 2 asst. 12441-3	Open		5.50	6
1995	Outdoor Bunny, 3 asst. 12435-2	Open		5.00	5
1994	Policeman, Conductor Bunny, 2 asst.00367-1	Open		4.20	5
1995	Professional Bunny, 3 asst. 12438-3	Open		5.00	5
1995	Street Sign, 3 asst. 12433-8	Open		4.50	5
1993	Strolling Bunny, 2 asst. 02976-3	Retrd.	1993	4.20	5
1995	Strolling Bunny, 2 asst. 12440-6	Open		5.50	6
1994	Sweeper & Flower Peddler Bunny Couple, 2 asst. 00359-6	Open		4.20	5
1997	Ticket Vendor 18654-1	Open		10.00	10
1994	Topiary Trees, 3 asst. 00346-6	Retrd.	1994	2.50	3
1994	Train Station Couple, 2 asst. 00357-2	Open		4.20	5
1994	Tree & Shrub, 2 asst. 00382-4	Open		5.00	5
1996	Tree with Painted Flowers, set/3 15924-8	Open		20.00	20
1993	Trees, 3 asst. 02194-1	Retrd.	1994	6.20	7
1997	Wedding Bunny Couple 18652-7	Open		5.00	5
1994	Wedding Bunny Couple, 2 asst. 00347-3	Open		4.20	5

Cottontail Lane Houses - Midwest

YEAR ISSUE		EDITION LIMIT	YEAR RETD.	ISSUE PRICE	*QUOTE U.S. $
1997	Arcade Booth (lighted) 18655-8	Open		33.00	33
1993	Bakery (lighted) 01396-0	Open		43.00	45
1996	Bandshell (lighted) 15753-4	Open		50.00	50
1994	Bed & Breakfast House (lighted) 00337-4	Open		43.00	45
1995	Boutique and Beauty Shop (lighted) 12301-0	Open		45.00	45
1996	Bungalow (lighted) 15752-7	Open		45.00	45
1997	Bunny Chapel (lighted) 18653-4	Open		40.00	40
1995	Cafe (lighted) 12303-4	Open		45.00	45
1997	Carousel (lighted & musical) 18649-7	5,000		47.00	47
1995	Cathedral (lighted) 12302-7	Open		47.00	47
1994	Chapel (lighted) 00331-2	3,000	1993	43.00	125-250
1993	Church (lighted) 01385-4	3,000	1993	42.00	125-140
1992	Confectionary Shop (lighted) 06335-5	Retrd.	1994	43.00	70-90
1993	Cottontail Inn (lighted) 01394-6	Retrd.	1996	43.00	45
1996	Fire Station w/Figures, set/6 (lighted) 15830-2	5,000		90.00	90
1992	Flower Shop (lighted) 06333-9	Retrd.	1994	43.00	75-90
1994	General Store (lighted) 00340-4	Open		43.00	45
1993	Painting Studio (lighted) 01395-5	Retrd.	1994	43.00	50-90
1993	Rose Cottage (lighted) 01386-1	Retrd.	1994	43.00	90
1995	Rosebud Manor (lighted) 12304-1	3,500	1994	45.00	100-125
1993	Schoolhouse (lighted) 01378-6	Open		43.00	45
1992	Springtime Cottage (lighted) 06329-8	Retrd.	1994	43.00	90-110
1996	Town Garden Shoppe (lighted) 15751-0	Open		45.00	45
1995	Town Hall (lighted) 12300-3	Open		45.00	45
1994	Train Station (lighted) 00330-5	Open		43.00	45
1997	Tunnel of Love w/Swan (lighted)18648-0	Open		40.00	40
1992	Victorian House (lighted) 06332-1	Open		43.00	45

Creepy Hollow Figurines and Accessories - Midwest

YEAR ISSUE		EDITION LIMIT	YEAR RETD.	ISSUE PRICE	*QUOTE U.S. $
1994	Black Picket Fence 10685-3	Retrd.	1996	13.50	20
1996	Bone Fence 16961-2	Open		9.50	10
1992	Bride of Frankenstein 06663-8	Retrd.	1993	5.00	65-115
1995	Cemetery Gate 13366-8	Open		16.00	16
1996	Covered Bridge 16664-2	Open		22.00	22
1994	Creepy Hollow Sign 10647-1	Open		5.50	6
1993	Dracula (standing) 06707-9	Retrd.	1994	7.30	35-75
1996	Dragon 16936-0	Open		8.50	9
1995	Flying Witch, Ghost, 2 asst. 13362-0	Retrd.	1996	11.00	11
1993	Frankenstein 06704-8	Retrd.	1994	6.00	25-50
1997	Garden Statue, 2 asst. 19827-8	Open		7.50	8
1994	Ghost, 3 asst. 10652-5	Open		6.00	6
1996	Ghostly King 16659-8	Open		8.00	8
1995	Ghoul Usher 13515-0	Open		6.50	7
1995	Ghoulish Organist Playing Organ 13363-7	Open		13.00	13
1995	Grave Digger, 2 asst. 13360-6	Open		10.00	10
1996	Gypsy 16656-7	Open		8.00	8
1996	Gypsy Witch 16655-0	Open		8.00	8
1992	Halloween Sign, 2 asst. 06709-3	Retrd.	1995	6.00	25
1992	•Keep Out 06709-3	Retrd.	1995	N/A	14
1992	•Ghost Town 06709-3	Retrd.	1995	N/A	N/A
1997	Haunted Lighted Trees, 2 asst. 21458-9	Open		24.00	24
1993	Haunted Tree, 2 asst. 05892-3	Open		7.00	7
1996	Headless Horseman 16658-1	Open		11.00	11
1995	Hearse with Monsters 13364-4	Open		15.00	15
1993	Hinged Dracula's Coffin 08545-5	Retrd.	1995	11.00	40
1995	Hinged Tomb 13516-7	Retrd.	1995	15.00	40-50
1995	Hunchback 13359-0	Open		9.00	9
1996	Inn Keeper 16660-4	Open		7.00	7
1994	Mad Scientist 10646-4	Open		6.00	7
1993	Mummy 06705-5	Retrd.	1994	6.00	25-50
1997	Mummy Box 19846-9	Open		8.00	8
1994	Outhouse 10648-8	Suspd.		7.00	25
1994	Phantom of the Opera 10645-7	Open		6.00	7
1997	Potted Plant, 3 asst. 19826-1	Open		7.50	8
1993	Pumpkin Head Ghost 06661-4	Retrd.	1993	5.50	32-45
1993	Pumpkin Patch Sign, 2 asst. 05898-5	Retrd.	1995	6.50	25
1993	•Dead End 05898-5	Retrd.	1995	N/A	15
1993	•Pumpkin Patch 05898-5	Retrd.	1995	N/A	N/A
1995	Pumpkin Street Lamp, set/4 13365-1	Retrd.	1996	25.00	25
1993	Resin Skeleton 06651-5	Retrd.	1994	5.50	50-75
1995	Road of Bones 13371-2	Open		9.00	9
1996	School Teacher 16657-4	Open		8.00	8
1997	Sea Captains, 2 asst. 19823-0	Open		7.50	8
1997	Servant, 2 asst. 19825-4	Open		7.50	8
1997	Siren on Rock, 3 asst. 19824-7	Open		7.50	8
1996	Skeleton Butler 16661-1	Open		7.00	7
1997	Skeleton in Dinghy 19821-6	Open		12.00	12
1994	Street Sign, 2 asst. 10644-0	Retrd.	1996	5.70	25
1995	Street Sign, 3 asst. 13357-6	Retrd.	1996	5.50	25
1995	Theatre Goer, set/2 13358-3	Open		9.00	15
1995	Ticket Seller 13361-3	Open		10.00	10
1994	Tombstone Sign, 3 asst. 10642-6	Suspd.		3.50	4
1993	Trick or Treater, 3 asst. 08591-2	Retrd.	1995	5.50	20
1994	Werewolf 10643-4	Open		6.00	7
1992	Witch 06706-2	Retrd.	1996	6.00	30
1997	Witch with Telescope 19822-3	Open		7.50	8

Creepy Hollow Houses - Midwest

YEAR ISSUE		EDITION LIMIT	YEAR RETD.	ISSUE PRICE	*QUOTE U.S. $
1995	Bewitching Belfry (lighted) 13355-2	Open		50.00	50
1993	Blood Bank (lighted) 08548-6	Retrd.	1996	40.00	65-85
1997	Cape Odd Lighthouse (lighted) 19569-7	Open		45.00	45
1996	Castle (lighted) 16959-9	5,000		50.00	50
1994	Cauldron Cafe (lighted) 10649-5	Retrd.	1996	40.00	70
1992	Dr. Frankenstein's House (lighted) 01621-3	Retrd.	1995	40.00	95-115
1992	Dracula's Castle (lighted) 01627-5	Retrd.	1995	40.00	95-115
1997	Dreary dale Manor House (lighted & sound activated) 19568-0	5,000		50.00	50
1997	Eerie Eatery House (lighted) 19571-0	Open		45.00	45
1995	Funeral Parlor (lighted) 13356-9	Open		50.00	50
1996	Gypsy Wagon (lighted) 16663-5	Open		45.00	45
1993	Haunted Hotel (lighted) 08549-3	Retrd.	1996	40.00	75
1996	Jack-O' Lant-Inn (lighted) 16665-9	Open		45.00	45
1994	Medical Ghoul School (lighted) 10651-8	Open		40.00	43
1992	Mummy's Mortuary (lighted) 01641-1	Retrd.	1995	40.00	95-115
1997	Norman's Bait & Tackle House (lighted) 19572-7	Open		36.00	36
1994	Phantom's Opera (lighted) 10650-1	Retrd.	1996	40.00	75
1996	School House (lighted) 16662-8	Open		45.00	45
1997	Shipwreck House (lighted) 19570-3	Open		45.00	45
1993	Shoppe of Horrors (lighted) 08550-9	Retrd.	1995	40.00	95-110
1995	Skeleton Cinema (lighted) 13354-5	5,000	1995	50.00	100
1992	Witches Cove (lighted) 01665-7	Retrd.	1995	40.00	75-115

Mr. Sandman

Zanandia Castles - J. Willis

YEAR ISSUE		EDITION LIMIT	YEAR RETD.	ISSUE PRICE	*QUOTE U.S. $
1997	Azurine	Open		40.00	40
1997	Balinore	Open		40.00	40
1997	Castle of the Grove	Open		14.00	14
1997	Comet's Spear	Open		30.00	30
1997	The Fairy Folk Palace	Open		20.00	20
1997	Gate Tower of the Heart	Open		30.00	30
1997	Guardian of the Crystal	Open		20.00	20
1997	Knight's Reward	Open		14.00	14
1997	Legend's Lair	Open		30.00	30
1997	Maiden's Gate	Open		14.00	14
1997	My Lady's Retreat	Open		20.00	20
1997	The Queen's Keep	Open		20.00	20
1997	Quinz Castle	Open		14.00	14
1997	The Sorcerer's Eye	Open		20.00	20
1997	Stargazer's Castle	Open		20.00	20
1997	Tower of Dreams	Open		30.00	30
1997	West Tower of Zanandia	Open		20.00	20

Pacific Rim Import Corp.

Bristol Township - P. Sebern unless otherwise noted

YEAR ISSUE		EDITION LIMIT	YEAR RETD.	ISSUE PRICE	*QUOTE U.S. $
1990	Bedford Manor	Open		30.00	30
1990	Black Swan Millinery	Open		30.00	30

*Quotes have been rounded up to nearest dollar

YEAR ISSUE		EDITION LIMIT	YEAR RETD.	ISSUE PRICE	*QUOTE U.S.$
1991	Bridgestone Church	Retrd.	1993	30.00	30
1990	Bristol Books	Open		35.00	35
1995	Bristol Channel Lighthouse	Open		30.00	30
1996	Bristol Somerset Cathedral - Pacific Rim Team	Open		50.00	50
1990	Bristol Township Sign	Open		10.00	10
1993	Chesterfield House	Open		30.00	30
1990	Coventry House	Retrd.	1995	30.00	30
1991	Elmstone House	Retrd.	1993	30.00	45
1991	Flower Shop	Open		30.00	30
1993	Foxdown Manor	Open		30.00	30
1990	Geo. Straith Grocer - R. S. Benson	Open		25.00	25
1991	Hardwicke House	Retrd.	1993	30.00	45
1990	High Gate Mill	Open		40.00	40
1990	Iron Horse Livery	Retrd.	1993	30.00	30
1991	Kilby Cottage	Retrd.	1993	30.00	45
1995	Kings Gate School - Pacific Rim Team	Open		30.00	30
1990	Maps & Charts	Open		25.00	25
1991	Pegglesworth Inn	Retrd.	1995	40.00	40
1990	Queen's Road Church	Open		40.00	40
1994	Shotwick Inn/Surgery	Open		35.00	35
1990	Silversmith	Open		30.00	30
1996	Somerset Cathedral - Pacific Rim Team	Open		50.00	50
1990	Southwick Church	Retrd.	1996	30.00	30
1994	Surrey Road Church	Open		40.00	40
1990	Trinity Church	Retrd.	1993	30.00	30
1990	Violin Shop	Open		30.00	30
1990	Wexford Manor	Open		25.00	25

Bristol Waterfront - P. Sebern unless otherwise noted

YEAR ISSUE		EDITION LIMIT	YEAR RETD.	ISSUE PRICE	*QUOTE U.S.$
1992	Admiralty Shipping	Open		30.00	30
1992	Avon Fish Co.	Open		30.00	30
1995	Bristol Channel Lighthouse - Pacific Rim Team	Open		30.00	30
1993	Bristol Point Lighthouse	Open		45.00	45
1994	Bristol Tattler	Retrd.	1996	40.00	40
1992	Chandler	Open		30.00	30
1992	Customs House	Open		40.00	40
1992	Hawke Exports	Open		40.00	40
1993	Lower Quay Chapel	Open		40.00	40
1994	Portshead Lighthouse	Open		30.00	30
1992	Quarter Deck Inn	Open		40.00	40
1992	Regent Warehouse	Open		40.00	40
1993	Rusty Knight Inn	Open		35.00	35

Possible Dreams

Crinkle Village - Staff

YEAR ISSUE		EDITION LIMIT	YEAR RETD.	ISSUE PRICE	*QUOTE U.S.$
1997	Crinkle Barn 659654	Open		43.30	44
1996	Crinkle Castle (lighted) 659652	Open		70.00	70
1996	Crinkle Church (lighted) 659651	Open		70.00	70
1997	Crinkle Claus Village Display 965006	Open		10.00	10
1996	Crinkle Cottage (lighted) 659653	Open		70.00	70
1997	Crinkle Farm House 659657	Open		43.30	44
1997	Crinkle Grist Mill 659656	Open		43.30	44
1997	Crinkle Inn 659655	Open		43.30	44
1996	Crinkle Workshop (lighted) 659650	Open		70.00	70
1996	Santa Castle 659019	Open		15.00	15
1996	Santa Christmas House 659017	Open		15.00	15
1996	Santa Church 659020	Open		15.00	15
1996	Santa Farm House 659018	Open		15.00	15
1996	Santa Palace 659016	Open		15.00	15
1996	Santa Windmill 659021	Open		15.00	15

Rhodes Studio

Rockwell's Hometown - Rockwell-Inspired, unless otherwise noted

YEAR ISSUE		EDITION LIMIT	YEAR RETD.	ISSUE PRICE	*QUOTE U.S.$
1991	Bell Tower	Closed	N/A	36.95	37
1992	The Berkshire Playhouse	Closed	N/A	42.95	43
1991	Church On The Green	Closed	N/A	39.95	40
1992	Citizen's Hall	Closed	N/A	42.95	43
1991	Firehouse	Closed	N/A	36.95	37
1991	Greystone Church - Rhodes	Closed	N/A	34.95	35
1992	Mission House	Closed	N/A	42.95	43
1992	Old Corner House	Closed	1994	42.95	43
1991	Rockwell's Residence - Rhodes	Closed	N/A	34.95	35
1992	Town Hall	Closed	N/A	39.95	40

Rockwell's Main Street - Rockwell-Inspired

YEAR ISSUE		EDITION LIMIT	YEAR RETD.	ISSUE PRICE	*QUOTE U.S.$
1990	The Antique Shop	150-day		28.00	150
1991	The Bank	150-day		36.00	36
1990	The Country Store	150-day		32.00	36
1991	The Library	150-day		36.00	36
1991	Red Lion Inn	150-day		39.00	39
1990	Rockwell's Studio	150-day		28.00	85
1990	The Town Offices	150-day		32.00	38

Shelia's Collectibles

Shelia's Collectors' Society - S. Thompson

YEAR ISSUE		EDITION LIMIT	YEAR RETD.	ISSUE PRICE	*QUOTE U.S.$
1993	Anne Peacock House SOC01	Retrd.	1994	16.00	50-110
1993	Susan B. Anthony CGA93	Retrd.	1994	Gift	80-115
1993	Anne Peacock House Print	Retrd.	1994	Gift	75
1994	Seaview Cottage SOC02	Retrd.	1995	17.00	70-90
1994	Helen Keller's Birthplace-Ivy Green CGA94	Retrd.	1995	Gift	50-75
1994	Collector's Society T-Shirt	Retrd.	1995	Gift	N/A
1995	Pink Lady SOC03	Retrd.	1996	20.00	40-65
1995	Red Cross CGA95	Retrd.	1996	Gift	40-65
1995	Collector's Society T-Shirt & Collector's Society Pin	Retrd.	1996	Gift	N/A
1996	Tinker Toy House SOC04	6/97		20.00	20
1996	Tatman House CGA96	4/97		Gift	N/A
1996	Tinker Toy House Ornament	4/97		Gift	N/A
1997	25 Meeting St. SOC97	3/98		26.00	26
1997	23 Meeting Street CGA97	12/97		Gift	N/A
1997	25 Meeting Street Ornament OCS02	12/97		Gift	N/A

Signing & Event Pieces - S. Thompson

YEAR ISSUE		EDITION LIMIT	YEAR RETD.	ISSUE PRICE	*QUOTE U.S.$
1994	Star Barn SOP01	Retrd.	1994	24.00	40-60
1995	Shelia's Real Estate Office SOP02	Retrd.	1995	20.00	45
1996	Thompson's Mercantile SOP03	Retrd.	1996	24.00	30
1997	27 Meeting St. SOP97	12/97		26.00	26

Accessories - S. Thompson

YEAR ISSUE		EDITION LIMIT	YEAR RETD.	ISSUE PRICE	*QUOTE U.S.$
1994	Amish Quilt Line COL12	Retrd.	1994	18.00	32-45
1993	Apple Tree COL09	Retrd.	1996	12.00	20-30
1996	Autumn Tree ACC09	Open		14.00	14
1996	Barber Gazebo ACC05	Open		13.00	13
1997	Crepe Myrtle ACC13	Open		15.00	15
1993	Dogwood Tree COL08	Retrd.	1996	12.00	20-30
1992	Fence 5" COL04	Retrd.	1993	9.00	30
1992	Fence 7" COL05	Retrd.	1995	10.00	35-45
1995	Flower Garden ACC02	Open		13.00	13
1994	Formal Garden COL13	Retrd.	1994	18.00	30-50
1992	Gazebo With Victorian Lady COL02	Retrd.	1995	11.00	30-50
1996	Grazing Cows ACC04	Open		12.00	12
1992	Lake With Swan COL06	Retrd.	1993	11.00	25-35
1997	Magnolia Tree ACC11	Open		15.00	15
1992	Oak Bower COL03	Retrd.	1993	11.00	25-50
1996	Palm Tree ACC07	Open		14.00	14
1995	Real Estate Sign ACC03	Open		12.00	12
1997	Sabal Palm ACC12	Open		14.00	14
1996	Sailboat ACC06	Open		12.00	12
1996	Spring Tree ACC10	Open		14.00	14
1996	Summertime Picket Fence ACC08	Open		12.00	12
1994	Sunrise At 80 Meeting COL10	Retrd.	1994	18.00	30
1992	Tree With Bush COL07	Retrd.	1996	10.00	15-30
1994	Victorian Arbor COL11	Retrd.	1994	18.00	30-45
1997	White Dogwood ACC14	Open		15.00	15
1995	Wisteria Arbor ACC01	Open		12.00	12
1992	Wrought Iron Gate With Magnolias COL01	Retrd.	1993	11.00	40-50

American Barns - S. Thompson

YEAR ISSUE		EDITION LIMIT	YEAR RETD.	ISSUE PRICE	*QUOTE U.S.$
1995	Casey Barn AP BAR04	Retrd.	1997	18.00	26-35
1995	Casey Barn BAR04	Retrd.	1997	18.00	18
1995	Mail Pouch Barn AP BAR03	Retrd.	1996	18.00	26-40
1995	Mail Pouch Barn BAR03	Open		18.00	18
1996	Mr. Peanut Barn BAR05	Open		19.00	19
1996	Mr. Peanut Barn, AP BAR05	97	1996	24.00	30-40
1995	Pennsylvania Dutch Barn AP BAR02	Retrd.	1995	20.00	40
1995	Pennsylvania Dutch Barn BAR02	Retrd.	1996	18.00	25-55
1994	Rock City Barn AP BAR01	Retrd.	1994	20.00	26-40
1994	Rock City Barn BAR01	Open		18.00	18

Amish Village - S. Thompson

YEAR ISSUE		EDITION LIMIT	YEAR RETD.	ISSUE PRICE	*QUOTE U.S.$
1994	Amish Barn (renovated) AMS04II	Open		17.00	17
1993	Amish Barn AMS04	Retrd.	1997	17.00	30
1993	Amish Barn, AP AMS04	Retrd.	1993	20.00	40
1997	Amish Barnraising AMS09	Open		22.00	22
1994	Amish Buggy (renovated) AMS05II	Open		12.00	12
1993	Amish Buggy AMS05	Retrd.	1997	12.00	12
1993	Amish Buggy, AP AMS05	Retrd.	1993	16.00	33
1997	Amish Corn Cribs AMS07	Open		18.00	18
1997	Amish Farmhouse AMS08	Open		22.00	22
1994	Amish Home (renovated) AMS01II	Open		17.00	17
1993	Amish Home AMS01	Retrd.	1997	17.00	33
1993	Amish Home, AP AMS01	Retrd.	1993	20.00	25-35
1994	Amish School (renovated) AMS02II	Open		15.00	15
1993	Amish School AMS02	Retrd.	1997	15.00	30
1993	Amish School, AP AMS02	Retrd.	1993	20.00	25-35
1997	Amish Schoolhouse AMS10	Open		18.00	18
1994	Covered Bridge (renovated) AMS03II	Open		16.00	16
1993	Covered Bridge AMS03	Retrd.	1997	16.00	30
1993	Covered Bridge, AP AMS03	Retrd.	1993	20.00	30
1995	Roadside Stand AMS06	Open		17.00	17
1995	Roadside Stand, AP AMS06	Retrd.	1995	24.00	30-40

Arkansas Ladies - S. Thompson

YEAR ISSUE		EDITION LIMIT	YEAR RETD.	ISSUE PRICE	*QUOTE U.S.$
1996	Handford Terry House ARK02	Open		19.00	19
1996	Pillow-Thompson House ARK04	Open		19.00	19
1996	Rosalie House ARK01	Open		19.00	19
1996	Wings ARK03	Open		19.00	19

Art Deco - S. Thompson

YEAR ISSUE		EDITION LIMIT	YEAR RETD.	ISSUE PRICE	*QUOTE U.S.$
1996	Berkeley Shore DEC03	Open		19.00	19
1996	Berkeley Shore, AP DEC03	95	1996	24.00	30-40
1996	The Carlyle DEC02	Open		19.00	19
1996	The Carlyle, AP DEC02	97	1996	24.00	30-40
1996	Hotel Webster DEC01	Open		19.00	19
1996	Hotel Webster, AP DEC01	99	1996	24.00	30-40
1996	Marlin DEC04	Open		19.00	19
1996	Marlin, AP DEC04	89	1996	24.00	24

Atlanta - S. Thompson

YEAR ISSUE		EDITION LIMIT	YEAR RETD.	ISSUE PRICE	*QUOTE U.S.$
1995	Fox Theatre ATL06	Open		19.00	19
1995	Hammond's House ATL05	Retrd.	1997	18.00	25-35
1996	Margaret Mitchell House ATL07	Open		19.00	19
1996	Margaret Mitchell House, AP ATL07	89	1996	24.00	30-40
1995	Swan House ATL03	Open		18.00	18
1995	Tullie Smith House ATL01	Retrd.	1997	17.00	20-30
1995	Victorian Playhouse ATL02	Retrd.	1997	17.00	20-30
1995	Wren's Nest ATL04	Open		19.00	19

Charleston - S. Thompson

YEAR ISSUE		EDITION LIMIT	YEAR RETD.	ISSUE PRICE	*QUOTE U.S.$
1994	#2 Meeting Street (renovated) CHS06II	Open		16.00	16
1991	#2 Meeting Street CHS06	Retrd.	1997	15.00	25-35
1990	90 Church St. CHS17	Retrd.	1993	12.00	30-60
1994	Ashe House (renovated) CHS51II	Open		16.00	16
1993	Ashe House CHS51	Retrd.	1997	16.00	25-35
1991	Beth Elohim Temple CHS20	Retrd.	1993	15.00	28
1994	The Citadel (renovated) CHS22II	Open		16.00	16
1993	The Citadel CHS22	Retrd.	1997	16.00	20-40
1993	City Hall (No banner) CHS21	Retrd.	1993	15.00	50-100
1993	City Hall (without Spuleto colors) CHS21	Retrd.	1993	15.00	200
1993	City Hall CHS21	Retrd.	1993	15.00	100-200
1991	City Market (closed gates) CHS07	Retrd.	1991	15.00	60-100
1991	City Market (open gates) CHS07	Open		15.00	15
1994	City Market (renovated) CHS07II	Open		15.00	15
1994	College of Charleston (renovated) CHS40II	Retrd.	1996	16.00	30
1993	College of Charleston CHS40	Retrd.	1996	16.00	31
1993	College of Charleston, AP CHS40	Retrd.	1993	20.00	40
1992	Dock Street Theater (chimney) CHS08	Retrd.	1993	15.00	30-60
1991	Dock Street Theater (no chimney) CHS08	Retrd.	1992	15.00	60
1994	Edmonston-Alston (renovated) CHS04II	Retrd.	1995	16.00	60
1991	Edmonston-Alston CHS04	Retrd.	1995	15.00	65
1990	Exchange Building CHS15	Retrd.	1994	15.00	30-60
1990	Heyward-Washington House CHS02	Retrd.	1993	15.00	40
1994	John Rutledge House Inn (renovated) CHS50II	Open		16.00	16
1993	John Rutledge House Inn CHS50	Retrd.	1997	16.00	25-35
1991	Magnolia Plantation House (beige curtains) CHS03	Retrd.	1996	16.00	35-65
1994	Magnolia Plantation House (renovated) CHS03II	Retrd.	1996	16.00	30-60
1991	Magnolia Plantation House (white curtains) CHS03	Retrd.	1996	16.00	25-55
1990	Manigault House CHS01	Retrd.	1993	15.00	25-40
1990	Middleton Plantation CHS19	Retrd.	1991	9.00	210-300
1990	Pink House CHS18	Retrd.	1993	12.00	25-40
1990	Powder Magazine CHS16	Retrd.	1991	9.00	175-230
1994	Single Side Porch (renovated) CHS30II	Open		16.00	16
1993	Single Side Porch CHS30	Retrd.	1997	16.00	20-30
1993	Single Side Porch, AP CHS30	Retrd.	1993	20.00	40
1990	St. Michael's Church CHS14	Retrd.	1994	15.00	30-65
1994	St. Philip's Church (renovated) CHS05II	Retrd.	1996	15.00	26
1991	St. Philip's Church CHS05	Retrd.	1996	15.00	26
1991	St. Phillip's Church (misspelling Phillips) CHS05	Retrd.	1996	15.00	15

Charleston Battery - S. Thompson

YEAR ISSUE		EDITION LIMIT	YEAR RETD.	ISSUE PRICE	*QUOTE U.S.$
1996	22 South Battery CHB01	Open		19.00	19
1996	22 South Battery, AP CHB01	109	1996	24.00	40
1996	24 South Battery CHB02	Open		19.00	19
1996	24 South Battery, AP CHB02	99	1996	24.00	40
1996	26 South Battery CHB03	Open		19.00	19
1996	26 South Battery, AP CHB03	74	1996	24.00	40
1996	28 South Battery CHB04	Open		19.00	19
1996	28 South Battery, AP CHB04	74	1996	24.00	40

Charleston Gold Seal - S. Thompson

YEAR ISSUE		EDITION LIMIT	YEAR RETD.	ISSUE PRICE	*QUOTE U.S.$
1988	90 Church St. CHS17	Retrd.	1990	9.00	50
1988	CHS31 Rainbow Row-rust	Retrd.	1990	9.00	N/A
1988	CHS32 Rainbow Row-tan	Retrd.	1990	9.00	N/A
1988	CHS33 Rainbow Row-cream	Retrd.	1990	9.00	N/A
1988	CHS34 Rainbow Row-green	Retrd.	1990	9.00	N/A
1988	CHS35 Rainbow Row-lavender	Retrd.	1990	9.00	N/A
1988	CHS36 Rainbow Row-pink	Retrd.	1990	9.00	N/A
1988	CHS37 Rainbow Row-blue	Retrd.	1990	9.00	N/A
1988	CHS38 Rainbow Row-lt. yellow	Retrd.	1990	9.00	N/A
1988	CHS39 Rainbow Row-lt. pink	Retrd.	1990	9.00	N/A
1988	Exchange Building CHS15	Retrd.	1990	9.00	N/A
1988	Middleton Plantation CHS19	Retrd.	1990	9.00	150
1988	Pink House CHS18	Retrd.	1990	9.00	36
1988	Powder Magazine CHS16	Retrd.	1990	9.00	250
1988	St. Michael's Church CHS14	Retrd.	1990	9.00	N/A

Charleston II - S. Thompson

YEAR ISSUE		EDITION LIMIT	YEAR RETD.	ISSUE PRICE	*QUOTE U.S.$
1995	Boone Hall Plantation CHS56	Open		18.00	18
1995	Boone Hall Plantation, AP CHS56	Retrd.	1995	24.00	40-60
1994	Drayton House CHS52	Open		18.00	18
1994	Drayton House, AP CHS52	Retrd.	1994	24.00	40-60
1996	Huguenot Church CHS58	Open		19.00	19
1996	Huguenot Church, AP CHS58	95	1996	24.00	40-60
1996	Magnolia Garden CHS57	Open		19.00	19
1995	O'Donnell's Folly CHS55	Open		18.00	18

*Quotes have been rounded up to nearest dollar

Shelia's Collectibles
to Shelia's Collectibles

ARCHITECTURE

Year	Issue	Edition Limit	Year Retd.	Issue Price	*Quote U.S.$
1995	O'Donnell's Folly, AP CHS55	Retrd.	1995	24.00	40-60
1996	Sotille CHS59	Open		19.00	19
1996	Sotille, AP CHS59	98	1996	24.00	40-60

Charleston III - S. Thompson

Year	Issue	Edition Limit	Year Retd.	Issue Price	*Quote U.S.$
1997	South of Broad, Cream CHS65	Open		18.00	18
1997	South of Broad, Dark Pink CHS64	Open		18.00	18
1997	South of Broad, Lavender CHS63	Open		18.00	18
1997	South of Broad, Light Pink CHS66	Open		18.00	18
1997	South of Broad, Tan CHS62	Open		18.00	18

Charleston Public Buildings - S. Thompson

Year	Issue	Edition Limit	Year Retd.	Issue Price	*Quote U.S.$
1997	Bethel United Methodist Church CHS61	Open		21.00	21
1997	Summerall Chapel CHS60	Open		21.00	21

Charleston Rainbow Row - S. Thompson

Year	Issue	Edition Limit	Year Retd.	Issue Price	*Quote U.S.$
1990	CHS31 Rainbow Row-rust	Retrd.	1993	9.00	50
1990	CHS32 Rainbow Row-cream	Retrd.	1993	9.00	35-65
1990	CHS33 Rainbow Row-tan	Retrd.	1993	9.00	20-40
1990	CHS34 Rainbow Row-green	Retrd.	1993	9.00	25
1990	CHS35 Rainbow Row-lavender	Retrd.	1993	9.00	35
1990	CHS36 Rainbow Row-pink	Retrd.	1993	9.00	30-50
1990	CHS37 Rainbow Row-blue	Retrd.	1993	9.00	25-40
1990	CHS38 Rainbow Row-lt. yellow	Retrd.	1993	9.00	25-40
1990	CHS39 Rainbow Row-lt. pink	Retrd.	1993	9.00	25
1993	CHS41 Rainbow Row-aurora	Open		13.00	13
1994	CHS41II Rainbow Row-aurora (renovated)	Open		13.00	13
1993	CHS42 Rainbow Row-off-white	Open		13.00	13
1994	CHS42II Rainbow Row-off-white (renovated)	Open		13.00	13
1993	CHS43 Rainbow Row-cream	Open		13.00	13
1994	CHS43II Rainbow Row-cream (renovated)	Open		13.00	13
1993	CHS44 Rainbow Row-green	Open		13.00	13
1994	CHS44II Rainbow Row-green (renovated)	Open		13.00	13
1993	CHS45 Rainbow Row-lavender	Open		13.00	13
1994	CHS45II Rainbow Row-lavender (renovated)	Open		13.00	13
1993	CHS46 Rainbow Row-pink	Open		13.00	13
1994	CHS46II Rainbow Row-pink (renovated)	Open		13.00	13
1993	CHS47 Rainbow Row-blue	Open		13.00	13
1994	CHS47II Rainbow Row-blue (renovated)	Open		13.00	13
1993	CHS48 Rainbow Row-yellow	Open		13.00	13
1994	CHS48 Rainbow Row-yellow (renovated)	Open		13.00	13
1993	CHS49 Rainbow Row-gray	Open		13.00	13
1994	CHS49II Rainbow Row-gray (renovated)	Open		13.00	13
1993	Rainbow Row Sign	Retrd.	N/A	12.50	25

Colored Metal Accessories - S. Thompson

Year	Issue	Edition Limit	Year Retd.	Issue Price	*Quote U.S.$
1997	Burma Shave Sign: Past...Schoolhouse, set/6 CMA01	Open		17.00	17
1997	Burma Shave Sign: Don't Lose Your Head, set/6 CMA02	Open		17.00	17
1997	Daimler 1910 Car CMA03	Open		18.00	18

Dicken's Village - S. Thompson

Year	Issue	Edition Limit	Year Retd.	Issue Price	*Quote U.S.$
1991	Butcher Shop XMS03	Retrd.	1993	15.00	30
1991	Evergreen Tree XMS08	Retrd.	1993	11.00	20-40
1991	Gazebo & Carolers XMS06	Retrd.	1993	12.00	20-40
1991	Scrooge & Marley's Shop XMS01	Retrd.	1993	15.00	25-40
1991	Scrooge's Home XMS05	Retrd.	1993	15.00	20-30
1991	Toy Shoppe XMS04	Retrd.	1993	15.00	30-60
1991	Victorian Apartment Building XMS02	Retrd.	1993	15.00	30
1992	Victorian Church XMS09	Retrd.	1993	15.00	40-55
1991	Victorian Skaters XMS07	Retrd.	1993	12.00	30-60
1992	Set	Retrd.	1993	125.00	210-285

Galveston - S. Thompson

Year	Issue	Edition Limit	Year Retd.	Issue Price	*Quote U.S.$
1995	Beissner House GLV04	Open		18.00	18
1995	Dancing Pavillion GLV03	Open		18.00	18
1995	Frenkel House GLV01	Open		18.00	18
1995	Reymershoffer House GLV02	Open		18.00	18

George Barber - S. Thompson

Year	Issue	Edition Limit	Year Retd.	Issue Price	*Quote U.S.$
1996	Newton House GFB03	Open		19.00	19
1996	Phillippi House GFB02	Open		19.00	19
1996	Pine Crest GFB04	Open		19.00	19
1996	Renaissance GFB01	Open		19.00	19

Ghost House Series - S. Thompson

Year	Issue	Edition Limit	Year Retd.	Issue Price	*Quote U.S.$
1996	31 Legare St. GHO06	Open		19.00	19
1995	Gaffos House GHO04	Open		19.00	19
1994	Inside-Outside House GHO01	Retrd.	1996	18.00	30
1994	Inside-Outside House, AP GHO01	Retrd.	1994	20.00	40-50
1996	Kings Tavern GHO05	Open		19.00	19
1996	Kings Tavern, AP GHO05	102	1996	24.00	24
1994	Pirates' House GHO02	Retrd.	1996	18.00	30-70
1994	Pirates' House, AP GHO02	Retrd.	1994	20.00	40-80
1995	Red Castle GHO03	Open		19.00	19

Gone with the Wind - S. Thompson

Year	Issue	Edition Limit	Year Retd.	Issue Price	*Quote U.S.$
1995	Aunt Pittypat's GWW03	Retrd.	1996	24.00	28-35
1995	Aunt Pittypat's, AP GWW03	Retrd.	1995	30.00	40-55
1995	General Store GWW04	Retrd.	1996	24.00	30
1995	General Store, AP GWW04	Retrd.	1995	30.00	25-60
1995	Loew's Grand GWW05	Retrd.	1995	24.00	40-75
1995	Loew's Grand, AP GWW05	Retrd.	1995	30.00	60-125
1996	Silhouette GWW06	Retrd.	1996	16.00	28
1995	Tara GWW01	Retrd.	1996	24.00	30
1995	Tara, AP GWW01	Retrd.	1995	30.00	30-60
1995	Twelve Oaks GWW02	Retrd.	1996	24.00	30
1995	Twelve Oaks, AP GWW02	Retrd.	1995	30.00	40-55
1995	Set of 5, AP	Retrd.	1995	150.00	250

Inventor Series - S. Thompson

Year	Issue	Edition Limit	Year Retd.	Issue Price	*Quote U.S.$
1993	Ford Motor Company (green) INV01	Retrd.	1993	17.00	30-50
1993	Ford Motor Company (grey) INV01	Retrd.	1994	17.00	30
1993	Ford Motor Company, AP INV01	Retrd.	1993	20.00	45-70
1993	Menlo Park Laboratory (cream) INV02	Retrd.	1993	16.00	30-50
1993	Menlo Park Laboratory (grey) INV02	Retrd.	1994	16.00	30-40
1993	Menlo Park Laboratory, AP INV02	Retrd.	1993	20.00	35-70
1993	Noah Webster House INV03	Retrd.	1994	15.00	30-50
1993	Noah Webster House, AP INV03	Retrd.	1993	20.00	40-70
1993	Wright Cycle Shop INV04	Retrd.	1994	17.00	30-50
1993	Wright Cycle Shop, AP INV04	Retrd.	1993	20.00	40-70

Jazzy New Orleans Series - S. Thompson

Year	Issue	Edition Limit	Year Retd.	Issue Price	*Quote U.S.$
1994	Beauregard-Keys House JNO04	Retrd.	1996	18.00	40
1994	Beauregard-Keys House, AP JNO04	Retrd.	1994	20.00	45-65
1994	Gallier House JNO02	Open		18.00	18
1994	Gallier House, AP JNO02	Retrd.	1994	20.00	50
1994	La Branche Building JNO01	Open		18.00	18
1994	La Branche Building, AP JNO01	Retrd.	1994	20.00	50
1994	LePretre House JNO03	Open		18.00	18
1994	LePretre House, AP JNO03	Retrd.	1994	20.00	50

Key West - S. Thompson

Year	Issue	Edition Limit	Year Retd.	Issue Price	*Quote U.S.$
1995	Artist House KEY06	Open		19.00	19
1995	Artist House, AP KEY06	Retrd.	1995	24.00	40
1995	Eyebrow House KEY01	Open		18.00	18
1995	Eyebrow House, AP KEY01	Retrd.	1995	24.00	40
1995	Hemingway House KEY07	Open		19.00	19
1995	Hemingway House, AP KEY07	Retrd.	1995	24.00	40
1995	Illingsworth Gingerbread House KEY05	Open		19.00	19
1995	Illingsworth Gingerbread House, AP KEY05	Retrd.	1995	24.00	40
1995	Shotgun House KEY03	Retrd.	1997	17.00	17
1995	Shotgun House, AP KEY03	Retrd.	1995	24.00	45
1995	Shotgun Sister KEY04	Retrd.	1997	17.00	17
1995	Shotgun Sister, AP KEY04	Retrd.	1995	24.00	50
1995	Southernmost House KEY02	Open		19.00	19
1995	Southernmost House, AP KEY02	Retrd.	1995	24.00	40
1996	Southernmost Point KEY08	Open		12.00	12

Ladies By The Sea - S. Thompson

Year	Issue	Edition Limit	Year Retd.	Issue Price	*Quote U.S.$
1996	Abbey II LBS01	Open		19.00	19
1996	Abbey II, AP LBS01	93	1996	24.00	40
1996	Centennial Cottage LBS02	Open		19.00	19
1996	Centennial Cottage, AP LBS02	94	1996	24.00	40
1996	Hall Cottage LBS04	Open		19.00	19
1996	Hall Cottage, AP LBS04	108	1996	24.00	40
1996	Heart Blossom LBS03	Open		19.00	19
1996	Heart Blossom, AP LBS03	107	1996	24.00	40

Lighthouse Series - S. Thompson

Year	Issue	Edition Limit	Year Retd.	Issue Price	*Quote U.S.$
1991	Anastasia Lighthouse (burgundy) FL103	Retrd.	1991	15.00	25-75
1991	Anastasia Lighthouse (red) FL103	Retrd.	1994	15.00	30-75
1993	Assateague Island Light LTS07	Retrd.	1997	17.00	25
1994	Assateague Island Light, AP LTS07	Retrd.	1994	20.00	40
1995	Cape Hatteras Light LTS09	Retrd.	1997	17.00	30
1995	Cape Hatteras Light, AP LTS09	Retrd.	1995	24.00	30-60
1991	Cape Hatteras Lighthouse NC103	Retrd.	1994	15.00	25-60
1994	Charleston Light (renovated) LTS01	Retrd.	1995	15.00	30-50
1993	Charleston Light LTS01	Retrd.	1995	15.00	30-40
1993	New London Ledge Light LTS08	Retrd.	1996	17.00	29
1994	New London Ledge Light, AP LTS08	Retrd.	1994	20.00	55
1993	Round Island Light LTS06	Retrd.	1997	17.00	25
1994	Round Island Light, AP LTS06	Retrd.	1994	20.00	40-60
1990	Stage Harbor Lighthouse NEW06	Retrd.	1993	15.00	140
1993	Thomas Point Light LTS05	Retrd.	1997	17.00	29
1994	Thomas Point Light, AP LTS05	Retrd.	1994	20.00	50
1990	Tybee Lighthouse SAV07	Retrd.	1994	15.00	36-70

Limited Edition American Gothic - S. Thompson

Year	Issue	Edition Limit	Year Retd.	Issue Price	*Quote U.S.$
1993	Gothic Revival Cottage ACL01	Retrd.	1993	20.00	25-40
1993	Mele House ACL04	Retrd.	1993	20.00	40
1993	Perkins House ACL02	Retrd.	1993	20.00	40
1993	Rose Arbor ACL05	Retrd.	1993	14.00	40
1993	Roseland Cottage ACL03	Retrd.	1993	20.00	40
1993	Set of 5	Retrd.	1993	94.00	140

Limited Edition Barber Houses - S. Thompson

Year	Issue	Edition Limit	Year Retd.	Issue Price	*Quote U.S.$
1995	Banta House	4,000	1995	24.00	35-55
1995	Greenman House	4,000	1995	24.00	35-55
1995	Riley-Cutler House	4,000	1995	24.00	35-50
1995	Weller House	4,000	1995	24.00	35-55

Limited Edition Mail-Order Victorians (Barber Houses) - S. Thompson

Year	Issue	Edition Limit	Year Retd.	Issue Price	*Quote U.S.$
1994	Brehaut House ACL09	3,300	1994	24.00	30-70
1994	Goeller House ACL08	3,300	1994	24.00	30-70
1994	Henderson House ACL07	3,300	1994	24.00	40-70
1994	Titman House ACL06	3,300	1994	24.00	40-70
1994	Set of 4	3,300	1994	96.00	145-250

Limited Pieces - S. Thompson

Year	Issue	Edition Limit	Year Retd.	Issue Price	*Quote U.S.$
1991	Bridgetown Library NJ102	Retrd.	N/A	16.00	40-65
1993	Comly-Rich House XXX01	Retrd.	N/A	12.00	25-75
1991	Delphos City Hall OH101	Retrd.	N/A	15.00	65-95
1991	Historic Burlington County Clubhouse NJ101	Retrd.	N/A	16.00	40-65
1991	Mark Twain Boyhood Home MO101	Retrd.	N/A	15.00	N/A
1990	Newton County Court House GA101	Retrd.	N/A	16.00	65-100

Mackinac - S. Thompson

Year	Issue	Edition Limit	Year Retd.	Issue Price	*Quote U.S.$
1996	Amberg Cottage MAK01	Open		19.00	19
1996	Amberg Cottage, AP MAK01	102	1996	24.00	45
1996	Anne Cottage MAK02	Open		19.00	19
1996	Anne Cottage, AP MAK02	95	1996	24.00	45
1996	Grand Hotel (3 pc. set) MAK05	Open		57.00	57
1996	Rearick Cottage MAK03	Open		19.00	19
1996	Rearick Cottage, AP MAK03	103	1996	24.00	45
1996	Windermere Hotel MAK04	Open		19.00	19
1996	Windermere Hotel, AP MAK04	105	1996	24.00	45

Martha's Vineyard - S. Thompson

Year	Issue	Edition Limit	Year Retd.	Issue Price	*Quote U.S.$
1994	Alice's Wonderland (renovated) MAR08II	Open		16.00	40
1993	Alice's Wonderland MAR08	Open		16.00	40
1993	Alice's Wonderland, AP MAR08	Retrd.	1993	20.00	30
1995	Blue Cottage MAR13	Open		17.00	17
1995	Blue Cottage, AP MAR13	Retrd.	1995	24.00	30-40
1997	Butterfly Cottage MAR14	Open		20.00	20
1994	Campground Cottage (renovated) MAR07II	Retrd.	1995	16.00	25
1993	Campground Cottage MAR07	Retrd.	1995	16.00	30-50
1993	Campground Cottage, AP MAR07	Retrd.	1993	20.00	25-50
1994	Gingerbread Cottage-grey (renovated) MAR09II	Retrd.	1996	16.00	25-35
1993	Gingerbread Cottage-grey AP MAR09	Retrd.	1993	20.00	30-50
1993	Gingerbread Cottage-grey MAR09	Retrd.	1996	16.00	30-50
1995	Trails End MAR11	Open		17.00	17
1995	Trails End, AP MAR11	Retrd.	1995	24.00	30-40
1995	White Cottage MAR12	Open		17.00	17
1995	White Cottage, AP MAR12	Retrd.	1995	24.00	30-40
1994	Wood Valentine (renovated) MAR10II	Open		16.00	16
1993	Wood Valentine MAR10	Open		16.00	16
1993	Wood Valentine, AP MAR10	Retrd.	1993	20.00	30-40

National Trust Houses - S. Thompson

Year	Issue	Edition Limit	Year Retd.	Issue Price	*Quote U.S.$
1997	Cliveden NHP03	Open		24.00	24
1997	Drayton Hall NHP01	Open		24.00	24
1997	Montpelier NHP02	Open		24.00	24

New England - S. Thompson

Year	Issue	Edition Limit	Year Retd.	Issue Price	*Quote U.S.$
1991	Faneuil Hall NEW09	Retrd.	1993	15.00	30-75
1990	Longfellow's House NEW01	Retrd.	1993	15.00	25-60
1990	Malden Mass. Victorian Inn NEW05	Retrd.	1992	10.00	60-75
1990	Martha's Vineyard Cottage -blue/mauve MAR06	Retrd.	1993	15.00	40-70
1990	Martha's Vineyard Cottage -blue/orange MAR05	Retrd.	1993	15.00	50
1990	Motif #1 Boathouse NEW02	Retrd.	1993	15.00	25-60
1990	Old North Church NEW04	Retrd.	1993	15.00	40-90
1990	Paul Revere's Home NEW03	Retrd.	1993	15.00	35-80
1991	President Bush's Home NEW07	Retrd.	1993	15.00	45-90
1991	Wedding Cake House NEW08	Retrd.	1993	15.00	35-70

North Carolina - S. Thompson

Year	Issue	Edition Limit	Year Retd.	Issue Price	*Quote U.S.$
1990	Josephus Hall House NC101	Retrd.	1993	15.00	25
1990	Presbyterian Bell Tower NC102	Retrd.	1993	15.00	20-30
1991	The Tryon Palace NC104	Retrd.	1993	15.00	25-45

Old-Fashioned Christmas - S. Thompson

Year	Issue	Edition Limit	Year Retd.	Issue Price	*Quote U.S.$
1994	Conway Scenic Railroad Station OFC04	Retrd.	1997	18.00	29
1994	Conway Scenic Railroad Station AP OFC04	Retrd.	1994	20.00	35-45
1994	Dwight House OFC02	Retrd.	1996	18.00	29
1994	Dwight House, AP OFC02	Retrd.	1994	20.00	50-85
1994	General Merchandise OFC03	Retrd.	1997	18.00	29
1994	General Merchandise, AP OFC03	Retrd.	1994	20.00	40-50
1994	Old First Church OFC01	Retrd.	1997	18.00	29
1994	Old First Church, AP OFC01	Retrd.	1994	20.00	40-50
1994	Set of 4 1994 AP	Retrd.	1994	80.00	199
1995	Christmas Inn OFC05	Retrd.	1997	18.00	29
1995	Town Square Tree OFC06	Retrd.	1997	18.00	29

Painted Ladies I - S. Thompson

Year	Issue	Edition Limit	Year Retd.	Issue Price	*Quote U.S.$
1990	The Abbey LAD08	Retrd.	1992	10.00	115-150
1990	Atlanta Queen Anne LAD07	Retrd.	1992	10.00	60-150
1990	Cincinnati Gothic LAD05	Retrd.	1992	10.00	60-100
1990	Colorado Queen Anne LAD04	Retrd.	1992	10.00	50-100
1990	Illinois Queen Anne LAD06	Retrd.	1991	10.00	385-450
1990	San Francisco Italianate-yellow LAD03	Retrd.	1992	10.00	125-150
1990	San Francisco Stick House-blue LAD02	Retrd.	1991	10.00	60-80
1990	San Francisco Stick House-yellow LAD01	Retrd.	1991	10.00	85-125

*Quotes have been rounded up to nearest dollar

ARCHITECTURE

Shelia's Collectibles to Silvestri, Inc.

YEAR ISSUE		EDITION LIMIT	YEAR RETD.	ISSUE PRICE	*QUOTE U.S.$
1990	Painted Ladies I Sign	Retrd.	N/A	12.50	30

Painted Ladies II - S. Thompson

YEAR ISSUE		EDITION LIMIT	YEAR RETD.	ISSUE PRICE	*QUOTE U.S.$
1994	Cape May Gothic (renovated) LAD13II	Retrd.	1995	16.00	35
1992	Cape May Gothic LAD13	Retrd.	1995	15.00	25-35
1994	Cape May Victorian Pink House (renovated) LAD16II	Retrd.	1996	16.00	30
1992	Cape May Victorian Pink House LAD16	Retrd.	1996	15.00	30
1994	The Gingerbread Mansion (renovated) LAD09II	Retrd.	1994	16.00	25-35
1992	The Gingerbread Mansion LAD09	Retrd.	1993	15.00	25-35
1994	Morningstar Inn (renovated) LAD15II	Retrd.	1994	16.00	25-35
1992	Morningstar Inn LAD15	Retrd.	1994	15.00	25-35
1994	Pitkin House (renovated) LAD10II	Retrd.	1996	16.00	30
1992	Pitkin House LAD10	Retrd.	1996	15.00	40
1994	Queen Anne Townhouse (renovated) LAD12II	Retrd.	1994	16.00	35
1992	Queen Anne Townhouse LAD12	Retrd.	1994	15.00	25-35
1994	The Victorian Blue Rose (renovated) LAD14II	Retrd.	1996	16.00	30-60
1992	The Victorian Blue Rose LAD14	Retrd.	1996	15.00	21
1994	The Young-Larson House (renovated) LAD11II	Retrd.	1996	16.00	35
1992	The Young-Larson House LAD11	Retrd.	1996	15.00	25-45

Painted Ladies III - S. Thompson

YEAR ISSUE		EDITION LIMIT	YEAR RETD.	ISSUE PRICE	*QUOTE U.S.$
1994	Cape May Green Stockton Row (renovated) LAD20II	Retrd.	1995	16.00	25-35
1993	Cape May Green Stockton Row LAD20	Retrd.	1995	16.00	25-40
1994	Cape May Linda Lee (renovated) LAD17II	Retrd.	1996	16.00	30
1993	Cape May Linda Lee LAD17	Retrd.	1996	16.00	25-40
1994	Cape May Pink Stockton Row (renovated)LAD19II	Open		16.00	16
1993	Cape May Pink Stockton Row LAD19	Open		16.00	16
1994	Cape May Tan Stockton Row (renovated)LAD18II	Open		16.00	16
1993	Cape May Tan Stockton Row LAD18	Open		16.00	16
1996	Cream Stockton LAD22	Open		19.00	19
1996	Cream Stockton, AP LAD22	101	1996	24.00	24
1995	Steiner Cottage LAD21	Open		17.00	17
1995	Steiner Cottage, AP LAD21	Retrd.	1995	24.00	40

Panaramic Lights - S. Thompson

YEAR ISSUE		EDITION LIMIT	YEAR RETD.	ISSUE PRICE	*QUOTE U.S.$
1996	Jeffrys Hook Light PLH02	Open		19.00	19
1996	Jeffrys Hook Light, AP PLH02	97	1996	24.00	30
1996	New Canal Light PLH03	Open		19.00	19
1996	New Canal Light, AP PLH03	104	1996	24.00	40
1996	Quoddy Head Light PLH04	Open		19.00	19
1996	Quoddy Head Light, AP PLH04	102	1996	24.00	30
1996	Split Rock Light PLH01	Open		19.00	19
1996	Split Rock Light, AP PLH01	105	1996	24.00	40

Philadelphia - S. Thompson

YEAR ISSUE		EDITION LIMIT	YEAR RETD.	ISSUE PRICE	*QUOTE U.S.$
1990	"Besty" Ross House (misspelling) PHI03	Retrd.	1990	15.00	20-45
1990	Betsy Ross House PHI03	Retrd.	1993	15.00	60-100
1990	Carpenter's Hall PHI01	Retrd.	1993	15.00	40-55
1990	Elphreth's Alley PHI05	Retrd.	1993	15.00	30-55
1990	Graff House PHI07	Retrd.	1993	15.00	40-60
1990	Independence Hall PHI04	Retrd.	1993	15.00	75-90
1990	Market St. Post Office PHI02	Retrd.	1993	15.00	35-65
1990	Old City Hall PHI08	Retrd.	1993	15.00	35-45
1990	Old Tavern PHI06	Retrd.	1993	15.00	35-45

Plantations - S. Thompson

YEAR ISSUE		EDITION LIMIT	YEAR RETD.	ISSUE PRICE	*QUOTE U.S.$
1996	Dickey House PLA05	Open		19.00	19
1995	Farley PLA04	Retrd.	1996	18.00	18
1995	Farley, AP PLA04	Retrd.	1995	24.00	40-65
1995	Longwood PLA02	Open		19.00	19
1995	Longwood, AP PLA02	Retrd.	1995	24.00	30-40
1995	Merry Sherwood PLA03	Open		18.00	18
1995	Merry Sherwood, AP PLA03	Retrd.	1995	24.00	30-40
1995	San Francisco PLA01	Open		19.00	19
1995	San Francisco, AP PLA01	Retrd.	1995	24.00	40-50

San Francisco - S. Thompson

YEAR ISSUE		EDITION LIMIT	YEAR RETD.	ISSUE PRICE	*QUOTE U.S.$
1995	Brandywine SF101	Open		18.00	18
1995	Brandywine, AP SF101	Retrd.	1995	24.00	30-40
1995	Eclectic Blue SF103	Open		19.00	19
1995	Eclectic Blue, AP SF103	Retrd.	1995	24.00	40-50
1995	Edwardian Green SF104	Open		18.00	18
1995	Edwardian Green, AP SF104	Retrd.	1995	24.00	30-40
1995	Queen Rose SF102	Open		19.00	19
1995	Queen Rose, AP SF102	Retrd.	1995	24.00	30-40

Savannah - S. Thompson

YEAR ISSUE		EDITION LIMIT	YEAR RETD.	ISSUE PRICE	*QUOTE U.S.$
1990	Andrew Low Mansion SAV02	Retrd.	1994	15.00	30-60
1996	Asendorf SAV13	Open		19.00	19
1996	Asendorf, AP SAV13	100	1996	24.00	30-40
1994	Catherdral of St. John (renovated) SAV09II	Retrd.	1995	16.00	30-40
1992	Catherdral of St. John SAV09	Retrd.	1995	16.00	35-55
1994	Chestnut House SAV11	Open		18.00	18
1994	Chestnut House, AP SAV11	Retrd.	1994	24.00	25-50
1990	Davenport House SAV03	Retrd.	1994	15.00	25-50
1990	Herb House SAV05	Retrd.	1993	15.00	25-75
1994	Juliette Low House (renovated) SAV04II	Open		15.00	15
1990	Juliette Low House (w/logo) SAV04	Open		15.00	15
1990	Juliette Low House (w/o logo) SAV04	Retrd.	1990	15.00	125
1995	Mercer House SAV12	Open		18.00	18
1995	Mercer House, AP SAV12	Retrd.	1995	24.00	25-75
1990	Mikve Israel Temple SAV06	Retrd.	1994	15.00	35-75
1994	Olde Pink House (renovated) SAV01II	Retrd.	1996	15.00	30-60
1990	Olde Pink House SAV01	Retrd.	1996	15.00	25-55
1994	Owens Thomas House (renovated) SAV10II	Retrd.	1996	16.00	25-35
1993	Owens Thomas House AP SAV10	Retrd.	1993	20.00	75
1993	Owens Thomas House SAV10	Retrd.	1996	16.00	35-55
1990	Savannah Gingerbread House I SAV08	Retrd.	1990	15.00	300-350
1990	Savannah Gingerbread House II SAV08	Retrd.	1992	15.00	375

Shadow Play Silhouettes - S. Thompson

YEAR ISSUE		EDITION LIMIT	YEAR RETD.	ISSUE PRICE	*QUOTE U.S.$
1996	Girl w/Hoop & Boy w/Dog SPO03	Open		12.00	15
1996	Horse and Carriage SPO01	Open		15.00	20
1996	Victorian Couple & Bicycle SPO02	Open		15.00	20

Shadow Play Silhouettes Accessories - S. Thompson

YEAR ISSUE		EDITION LIMIT	YEAR RETD.	ISSUE PRICE	*QUOTE U.S.$
1997	Lamp Post, set/2 SPO07	Open		12.00	12

Shadow Play Silhouettes II - S. Thompson

YEAR ISSUE		EDITION LIMIT	YEAR RETD.	ISSUE PRICE	*QUOTE U.S.$
1996	Amish Buggy SPO04	Open		19.50	20
1996	Amish Clothesline SPO05	Open		19.50	20
1996	Amish Couple and Amish Boy SPO06	Open		15.00	15

Show Pieces - S. Thompson

YEAR ISSUE		EDITION LIMIT	YEAR RETD.	ISSUE PRICE	*QUOTE U.S.$
1995	Baldwin House SHW01	Retrd.	1995	20.00	40
1996	The Winnie Watson House SHW02	Retrd.	1996	20.00	26

South Carolina - S. Thompson

YEAR ISSUE		EDITION LIMIT	YEAR RETD.	ISSUE PRICE	*QUOTE U.S.$
1991	All Saints' Church SC105	Retrd.	1993	15.00	30-55
1990	The Governer's Mansion (misspelling) SC102	Retrd.	1990	15.00	30
1994	The Governor's Mansion (renovated) SC102II	Retrd.	1995	15.00	35
1990	The Governor's Mansion SC102	Retrd.	1995	15.00	30
1994	The Hermitage (renovated) SC101II	Retrd.	1995	15.00	30
1990	The Hermitage SC101	Retrd.	1995	15.00	37
1994	The Lace House (renovated) SC103II	Retrd.	1995	15.00	15
1990	The Lace House SC103	Retrd.	1995	15.00	40-50
1994	The State Capitol (renovated) SC104II	Retrd.	1994	15.00	55
1991	The State Capitol SC104	Retrd.	1994	15.00	30

South Carolina Ladies - S. Thompson

YEAR ISSUE		EDITION LIMIT	YEAR RETD.	ISSUE PRICE	*QUOTE U.S.$
1996	Cinnamon Hill SCL04	Open		19.00	19
1996	Cinnamon Hill, AP SCL04	93	1996	24.00	40
1996	Davis-Johnsey House SCL02	Open		19.00	19
1996	Davis-Johnsey House, AP SCL02	104	1996	24.00	40
1996	Inman House SCL01	Open		19.00	19
1996	Inman House, AP SCL01	107	1996	24.00	40
1996	Montgomery House SCL03	Open		19.00	19
1996	Montgomery House, AP SCL03	105	1996	24.00	40

St. Augustine - S. Thompson

YEAR ISSUE		EDITION LIMIT	YEAR RETD.	ISSUE PRICE	*QUOTE U.S.$
1991	Anastasia Lighthousekeeper's House FL104	Retrd.	1993	15.00	45-85
1991	Mission Nombre deDios FL105	Retrd.	1993	15.00	50-75
1991	Old City Gates FL102	Retrd.	1993	15.00	35
1991	The "Oldest House" FL101	Retrd.	1993	15.00	35-65

Texas - S. Thompson

YEAR ISSUE		EDITION LIMIT	YEAR RETD.	ISSUE PRICE	*QUOTE U.S.$
1990	The Alamo TEX01	Retrd.	1993	15.00	200-235
1990	Mission Concepcion TEX04	Retrd.	1993	15.00	50-75
1990	Mission San Francisco TEX03	Retrd.	1993	15.00	35-75
1990	Mission San Jose' TEX02	Retrd.	1993	15.00	40-75
1990	Texas Sign	Retrd.	N/A	12.50	20

Victorian Springtime - S. Thompson

YEAR ISSUE		EDITION LIMIT	YEAR RETD.	ISSUE PRICE	*QUOTE U.S.$
1993	Heffron House VST03	Retrd.	1996	17.00	26-35
1993	Heffron House, AP VST03	Retrd.	1993	20.00	50-60
1993	Jacobsen House VST04	Retrd.	1996	17.00	23-35
1993	Jacobsen House, AP VST04	Retrd.	1993	20.00	50-60
1993	Ralston House VST01	Retrd.	1996	17.00	30-50
1993	Ralston House, AP VST01	Retrd.	1993	20.00	50-60
1993	Sessions House VST02	Retrd.	1996	17.00	35
1993	Sessions House, AP VST02	Retrd.	1993	20.00	50-60
1993	Set of 4, AP	Retrd.	1993	100.00	180

Victorian Springtime II - S. Thompson

YEAR ISSUE		EDITION LIMIT	YEAR RETD.	ISSUE PRICE	*QUOTE U.S.$
1995	Dragon House VST07	Retrd.	1997	18.00	30
1995	Dragon House, AP VST07	Retrd.	1995	24.00	50
1995	E.B. Hall House VST08	Retrd.	1997	19.00	30
1995	E.B. Hall House, AP VST08	Retrd.	1995	24.00	50
1995	Gibney Home VST09	Retrd.	1997	18.00	30
1995	Gibney Home, AP VST09	Retrd.	1995	24.00	50
1995	Ray Home VST05	Retrd.	1997	18.00	30
1995	Ray Home, AP VST05	Retrd.	1995	24.00	50
1995	Victoria VST06	Retrd.	1997	18.00	30
1995	Victoria, AP VST06	Retrd.	1995	24.00	50

Victorian Springtime III - S. Thompson

YEAR ISSUE		EDITION LIMIT	YEAR RETD.	ISSUE PRICE	*QUOTE U.S.$
1996	Clark House VST14	Open		19.00	45
1996	Clark House, AP VST14	96	1996	24.00	45-55
1996	Goodwill House VST13	Open		19.00	19
1996	Goodwill House, AP VST13	88	1996	24.00	45
1996	Queen-Anne Mansion VST12	Open		19.00	19
1996	Queen-Anne Mansion, AP VST12	103	1996	24.00	30-45
1996	Sheppard House VST11	Open		19.00	19
1996	Sheppard House, AP VST11	98	1996	24.00	45
1996	Urfer House VST10	Open		19.00	19
1996	Urfer House, AP VST10	71	1996	24.00	45

Victorian Springtime IV - S. Thompson

YEAR ISSUE		EDITION LIMIT	YEAR RETD.	ISSUE PRICE	*QUOTE U.S.$
1997	Allyn Mansion VST19	Open		22.00	22
1997	Halstead House VST16	Open		22.00	22
1997	Harvard House VST15	Open		22.00	22
1997	Rosewood VST18	Open		22.00	22
1997	Zabriskie House VST17	Open		22.00	22

Washington D.C. - S. Thompson

YEAR ISSUE		EDITION LIMIT	YEAR RETD.	ISSUE PRICE	*QUOTE U.S.$
1992	Cherry Trees DC005	Retrd.	1993	12.00	40-70
1992	Library of Congress DC002	Retrd.	1993	16.00	40-60
1991	National Archives DC001	Retrd.	1993	16.00	40
1991	Washington Monument DC004	Retrd.	1993	16.00	35-40
1992	White House DC003	Retrd.	1993	16.00	150-200
1992	Set of 5	Retrd.	1993	76.00	250-350

West Coast Lighthouse Series - S. Thompson

YEAR ISSUE		EDITION LIMIT	YEAR RETD.	ISSUE PRICE	*QUOTE U.S.$
1995	East Brother Light WCL01	Open		19.00	19
1995	East Brother Light, AP WCL01	Retrd.	1995	24.00	40
1995	Mukilteo Light WCL02	Open		18.00	18
1995	Mukilteo Light, AP WCL02	Retrd.	1995	24.00	40
1995	Point Fermin Light WCL04	Open		18.00	18
1995	Point Fermin Light, AP WCL04	Retrd.	1995	24.00	40
1995	Yaquina Bay Light WCL03	Open		18.00	18
1995	Yaquina Bay Light, AP WCL03	Retrd.	1995	24.00	40

Williamsburg - S. Thompson

YEAR ISSUE		EDITION LIMIT	YEAR RETD.	ISSUE PRICE	*QUOTE U.S.$
1990	Apothecary WIL09	Retrd.	1994	12.00	25
1994	Bruton Parish Church (renovated) WIL13II	Open		15.00	15
1992	Bruton Parish Church WIL13	Retrd.	1997	15.00	35
1995	Capitol WIL15	Open		18.00	18
1995	Capitol, AP WIL15	Retrd.	1995	24.00	35-45
1994	Courthouse (renovated) WIL11II	Retrd.	1995	15.00	25
1990	Courthouse WIL11	Retrd.	1995	15.00	25-35
1990	The Golden Ball Jeweler WIL07	Retrd.	1994	12.00	25
1997	Govenor's Palace Formal Entrance WIL17	Open		22.00	22
1994	Governor's Palace (renovated) WIL04II	Open		15.00	15
1990	Governor's Palace WIL04	Retrd.	1997	15.00	25-35
1994	Homesite (renovated) WIL12II	Retrd.	1996	15.00	25
1990	Homesite WIL12	Retrd.	1996	15.00	25-35
1994	King's Arm Tavern (renovated) WIL10II	Retrd.	1995	15.00	45
1990	King's Arm Tavern WIL10	Retrd.	1995	15.00	40-55
1990	Milliner WIL06	Retrd.	1994	12.00	25-45
1990	Nicolson Shop WIL08	Retrd.	1994	12.00	25
1990	The Printing Offices WIL05	Retrd.	1993	12.00	25
1995	Raleigh Tavern WIL14	Open		18.00	18
1995	Raleigh Tavern, AP WIL14	Retrd.	1995	24.00	35-45
1997	Taylor House WIL16	Open		21.00	21

Silvestri, Inc.

Holiday Hamlet®-Accessories - V. Balcou

YEAR ISSUE		EDITION LIMIT	YEAR RETD.	ISSUE PRICE	*QUOTE U.S.$
1993	Blizzard Express Train	Open		95.00	95
1993	Carols in the Snow	Open		30.00	30
1993	Christmas Tree, large	Open		45.00	45
1993	Christmas Tree, small	Open		30.00	30
1994	Hand Car	Open		35.00	35
1993	Silent Night Singers	Closed	1994	30.00	35
1993	Village Sign	Open		40.00	40
1993	Village Square Clock	Open		50.00	50

Holiday Hamlet®-Figurines - V. Balcou

YEAR ISSUE		EDITION LIMIT	YEAR RETD.	ISSUE PRICE	*QUOTE U.S.$
1993	Baby Squirrel	Closed	1995	15.00	30
1993	Bell Choir Bunny	Open		15.00	15
1993	Bell Choir Fox	Open		10.00	10
1994	Blessed Mother/Joseph Players	Open		25.00	25
1993	Christmas Carolers	Open		20.00	20
1993	Christmas Carolers, waterglobe	Open		45.00	45
1993	Christmas Treats	Open		15.00	15
1993	The Conductor	Open		10.00	10
1993	Delivering Gifts	Open		20.00	20
1993	Dollmaker	Open		15.00	15
1993	Dollmaker's Apprentice	Closed	1994	15.00	30
1993	Dr. B. Well	Open		15.00	15
1993	Dr. Quack & Patient	Open		15.00	15
1993	Gathering Apples	Open		15.00	15
1993	Gathering Pine Boughs	Open		10.00	10
1994	Holiday Hamlet, waterglobe	Open		75.00	75
1994	Little Angels	Open		30.00	30
1993	Mr. Grizzly	Open		20.00	20
1994	Mr. Winterberry, Pie Vendor	2,500	1995	25.00	50
1993	Mrs. Grizzly	Open		20.00	20
1993	Nanny Rabbit & Bunnies	Open		20.00	20
1993	Old Royal Elf	Open		20.00	20
1993	The Parson	Open		10.00	10
1993	Pastry Vendor	Open		10.00	10
1994	Poor Shepherds	Open		15.00	15
1994	The Porter	Closed	1995	25.00	25
1994	Proud Mother/Father	Open		20.00	20

*Quotes have been rounded up to nearest dollar

Silvestri, Inc.
to Kirk Stieff

ARCHITECTURE/BELLS

YEAR ISSUE		EDITION LIMIT	YEAR RETD.	ISSUE PRICE	*QUOTE U.S.$
1993	Santa Claus	Open		25.00	25
1993	Skaters	Open		20.00	20
1993	Squirrel Family	Closed	1994	15.00	30
1994	Three Wisemen	Open		20.00	20
1993	Tying the Christmas Garland	Closed	1994	20.00	20
1993	Waving Elf	Open		10.00	10
1993	Welcome Banner	Open		20.00	20
1993	Welcoming Elf	Closed	1995	10.00	10

Holiday Hamlet®-Lighted Houses - V. Balcou

1994	Christmas Pageant Stage	Open		75.00	75
1993	Doctor's Office	Open		75.00	75
1993	Dollmaker's Cottage	Open		125.00	125
1993	Holiday Hamlet Chapel	Open		75.00	75
1993	Holiday Manor	Closed	1994	75.00	125
1994	Mr. Winterberry's Pie Shop	2,500	1995	100.00	200-350
1993	Railroad Station	Closed	1994	125.00	300-475
1994	Snowman Supply Hut	Open		65.00	65
1993	Stocking Stuffer's Workshop	Open		45.00	45
1993	Tavern in the Woods	Closed	1995	125.00	200-350
1993	Toymaker's Workshop	Open		45.00	45
1994	Whistlestop Junction Train Stop	Open		65.00	65
1994	World's Best Snowman	Open		55.00	55

BELLS

Ace Product Management Group, Inc.

Harley-Davidson Crystal Christmas Bells - Ace

1988	Crystal Bell 99212-89V	Yr.Iss.	1988	29.95	30
1989	Crystal Bell 99212-90V	Yr.Iss.	1989	29.95	30
1990	Crystal Bell 99212-91V	Yr.Iss.	1990	29.95	30
1991	Crystal Bell 99212-92V	Yr.Iss.	1991	32.95	33
1992	Crystal Bell 99212-93Z	Yr.Iss.	1992	38.00	38

Harley-Davidson Porcelain Holiday Bells - Ace

1993	Checking It Twice 99411-94Z	Yr.Iss.	1993	25.00	25
1994	Santa's Predicament 99439-95Z	Yr.Iss.	1994	25.00	25
1995	Finding The Way 99449-96Z	Yr.Iss.	1995	25.00	25

Artists of the World

DeGrazia Bells - T. DeGrazia

1980	Festival of Lights	5,000	N/A	40.00	90-125
1980	Los Ninos	7,500	N/A	40.00	80-125
1980	Los Ninos (signed)	500	N/A	80.00	200-250

Belleek

Belleek Bells - Belleek

1988	Bell, 1st Ed.	Yr.Iss.	1988	38.00	38
1989	Tower, 2nd Ed.	Yr.Iss.	1989	35.00	35
1990	Leprechaun, 3rd Ed.	Yr.Iss.	1990	30.00	30
1991	Church, 4th Ed.	Yr.Iss.	1991	32.00	32
1992	Cottage, 5th Ed.	Yr.Iss.	1992	30.00	30
1993	Pub, 6th Ed.	Yr.Iss.	1993	30.00	30
1994	Castle, 7th Ed.	Yr.Iss.	1994	30.00	30
1995	Georgian House, 8th Ed.	Yr.Iss.	1995	30.00	30
1996	Cathedral, 9th Ed.	Yr.Iss.	1996	30.00	30

Twelve Days of Christmas - Belleek

1991	A Partridge in a Pear Tree	Yr.Iss.	1991	30.00	30
1992	Two Turtle Doves	Yr.Iss.	1992	30.00	30
1993	Three French Hens	Yr.Iss.	1993	30.00	30
1994	Four Calling Birds	Yr.Iss.	1994	30.00	30
1995	Five Golden Rings	Yr.Iss.	1995	30.00	30

Cherished Teddies/Enesco Corporation

Cherished Teddies Bell - P. Hillman

1992	Angel Bell 906530	Suspd.		20.00	40-85

Dave Grossman Creations

Norman Rockwell Collection - Rockwell-Inspired

1975	Faces of Christmas NRB-75	Retrd.	N/A	12.50	35
1976	Drum for Tommy NRB-76	Retrd.	N/A	12.00	30
1976	Ben Franklin (Bicentennial)	Retrd.	N/A	12.50	25
1980	Leapfrog NRB-80	Retrd.	N/A	50.00	60

Fenton Art Glass Company

American Classic Series - M. Dickinson

1986	Jupiter Train, 6 1/2" on Opal Satin	5,000	1986	50.00	50
1986	Studebaker-Garford Car, 6 1/2" on Opal Satin	5,000	1986	50.00	50

Artist Series - Various

1982	After The Snow - D. Johnson	15,000	1982	14.50	20
1983	Winter Chapel - D. Johnson	15,000	1984	15.00	20
1985	Flying Geese - D. Johnson	15,000	1985	15.00	20
1986	The Hummingbird - D. Johnson	15,000	1986	15.00	20
1987	Out in the Country - L. Everson	15,000	1987	15.00	20
1988	Serenity - F. Burton	5,000	1988	16.50	20
1989	Househunting - D. Barbour	5,000	1989	16.50	20

Childhood Treasurers Series - Various

1983	Teddy Bear, 4 1/2" - D. Johnson	15,000	1983	15.00	20
1984	Hobby Horse, 4 1/2" - L. Everson	15,000	1984	15.00	20
1985	Clown, 4 1/2" - L. Everson	15,000	1985	17.50	20
1986	Playful Kitten, 4 1/2" - L. Everson	15,000	1986	15.00	20
1987	Frisky Pup, 4 1/2" - D. Barbour	15,000	1987	15.00	20
1988	Castles in the Air, 4 1/2" - D. Barbour	5,000	1988	16.50	20
1989	A Child's Cuddly Friend, 4 1/2" - D. Johnson	5,000	1989	16.50	20

Christmas - Various

1978	Christmas Morn - M. Dickinson	Yr.Iss.	1978	25.00	25
1979	Nature's Christmas - K. Cunningham	Yr.Iss.	1979	30.00	30
1980	Going Home - D. Johnson	Yr.Iss.	1980	32.50	33
1981	All Is Calm - D. Johnson	Yr.Iss.	1981	35.00	35
1982	Country Christmas - R. Spindler	Yr.Iss.	1982	35.00	35
1983	Anticipation - D. Johnson	7,500	1983	35.00	35
1984	Expectation - D. Johnson	7,500	1984	37.50	38
1985	Heart's Desire - D. Johnson	7,500	1986	37.50	38
1987	Sharing The Spirit - L. Everson	Yr.Iss.	1987	37.50	38
1987	Cardinal in the Churchyard - D. Johnson	4,500	1987	29.50	30
1988	A Chickadee Ballet - D. Johnson	4,500	1988	29.50	30
1989	Downy Pecker - Chisled Song - D. Johnson	4,500	1989	29.50	30
1990	A Blue Bird in Snowfall - D. Johnson	4,500	1990	29.50	30
1990	Sleigh Ride - F. Burton	3,500	1990	39.00	39
1991	Christmas Eve - F. Burton	3,500	1991	35.00	35
1992	Family Tradition - F. Burton	3,500	1992	39.00	39
1993	Family Holiday - F. Burton	3,500	1993	39.50	40
1994	Silent Night - F. Burton	2,500	1994	45.00	45
1995	Our Home Is Blessed - F. Burton	2,500	1995	45.00	45
1996	Star of Wonder - F. Burton	2,500	1996	48.00	48

Christmas Limited Edition - M. Reynolds, unless otherwise noted

1992	Winter on Twilight Blue, 6 1/2"	2,500	1992	29.50	30
1993	Manager Scene on Ruby, 6 1/2"	2,500	1993	39.50	40
1993	Reindeer on Blue, 6 1/2"	2,500	1993	30.00	30
1993	Floral on Green-Musical, 6 1/2"	2,500	1993	39.50	40
1994	Magnolia on Gold, 6 1/2"	1,000	1994	35.00	35
1994	Angel on Ivory, 6 1/2"	1,000	1994	39.50	40
1994	Partridge on Ruby-Musical, 6 1/2"	1,000	1994	48.50	49
1995	Bow & Holly on Ivory, 6 1/2"	900	1995	39.50	40
1995	Chickadee on Gold, 6 1/2"	900	1995	39.50	40
1995	Iced Poinsettia on Ruby, 5 1/2"	900	1995	45.00	45
1995	Angel, Heavenly Bell, 5 3/4" - R. Spindler	1,900	1995	35.00	35
1996	Holly Berries on Gold, 6 1/2"	1,500	1996	39.50	40
1996	Golden Partridge on Spruce, 6 1/2"	1,500	1996	35.00	35
1996	Moonlit Meadow on Ruby, 6 1/2" - R. Spindler	1,500	1996	45.00	45
1996	Nativity Scene on Ivory, 6 1/2" - R. Spindler	1,500	1996	49.00	49
1996	Golden Winged Angel, Hndpt. 6 1/2"	1,500	1996	39.50	40
1996	Golden Winged Angel, 6"	2,000	1996	39.50	40

Connoisseur Bell - Various

1983	Bell, Burmese Handpainted - L. Everson	2,000	1983	50.00	125
1983	Craftsman Bell, White Satin Carnival - Fenton	3,500	1983	25.00	50
1984	Bell, Famous Women's Ruby Satin Irid. - Fenton	3,500	1984	25.00	50
1985	Bell, 6 1/2" Burmese, Hndpt. - L. Everson	2,500	1985	55.00	125
1986	Bell, Burmese-Shells, Hndpt. - D. Barbour	2,500	1986	60.00	125
1988	Bell, 7" Wisteria, Hndpt. - L. Everson	4,000	1988	45.00	85
1989	Bell, 7" Handpainted Rosalene Satin - L. Everson	3,500	1989	50.00	75
1991	Bell, 7" Roses on Rosalene, Hndpt. - M. Reynolds	2,000	1991	50.00	60

Designer Series - Various

1983	Lighthouse Point, 6" - M. Dickinson	1,000	1983	55.00	65
1983	Down Home, 6" - G. Finn	1,000	1983	55.00	60
1984	Smoke 'N Cinders, 6" - M. Dickinson	1,250	1984	55.00	75
1984	Majestic Flight, 6" - B. Cumberledge	1,250	1984	55.00	55
1985	In Season, 6" - M. Dickinson	1,250	1985	55.00	55
1985	Nature's Grace, 6" - B. Cumberland	1,250	1985	55.00	55
1985	Statue of Liberty, 6" - S. Bryan	1,250	1985	55.00	55
1986	Statue of Liberty, 6" - S. Bryan	1,250	1986	55.00	55
1996	Floral Medallion, 6" - M. Reynolds	2,500	1996	60.00	60
1996	Gardenia, 7" - R. Spindler	2,500	1996	55.00	55
1996	Gilded Berry, 6 1/2" - F. Burton	2,500	1996	60.00	60
1996	Wild Rose, 5 1/2" - K. Plauche	2,500	1996	50.00	50
1997	Butterflies, 6" - M. Reynolds	2,500		59.00	59
1997	Feathers, 6 3/4" - R. Spindler	2,500		59.00	59
1997	Forest Cottage, 7" - F. Burton	2,500		59.00	59
1997	Roses on Ribbons, 6 1/2" - K. Plauche	2,500		59.00	59

Mary Gregory - M. Reynolds

1993	Bell, 6" Ruby	Closed	1993	49.00	65
1994	Bell, 6" Ruby - Loves Me, Loves Me Not	Closed	1994	49.00	65
1995	Bell, 6 1/2"	Closed	1995	49.00	65

Mother's Day Series - Various

1980	New Born - L. Everson	Closed	1980	25.00	25
1981	Gentle Fawn - L. Everson	Closed	1981	27.50	28
1982	Nature's Awakening - L. Everson	Closed	1982	28.50	29
1983	Where's Mom - L. Everson	Closed	1983	28.50	29
1984	Precious Panda - L. Everson	Closed	1984	28.50	29
1985	Mother's Little Lamb - L. Everson	Closed	1985	35.00	35
1990	White Swan - L. Everson	Closed	1990	35.00	35
1990	White Swan (Musical) - L. Everson	Closed	1990	45.00	45
1991	Mother's Watchful Eye - M. Reynolds	Closed	1991	35.00	35
1992	Let's Play With Mom - M. Reynolds	Closed	1992	37.50	38
1993	Mother Deer - M. Reynolds	Closed	1993	39.50	40
1994	Loving Puppy - M. Reynolds	Closed	1994	39.50	40

Valentine's Day Series - M. Reynolds

1992	Bell, 6" Vining Hearts Hndpt. Opal Irid.	Closed	1992	35.00	35

Goebel/M.I. Hummel

M.I. Hummel Collectibles Annual Bells - M. I. Hummel

1978	Let's Sing 700	Closed	N/A	50.00	75-100
1979	Farewell 701	Closed	N/A	70.00	75
1980	Thoughtful 702	Closed	N/A	85.00	75
1981	In Tune 703	Closed	N/A	85.00	85-100
1982	She Loves Me, She Loves Me Not 704	Closed	N/A	90.00	125
1983	Knit One 705	Closed	N/A	90.00	125
1984	Mountaineer 706	Closed	N/A	90.00	125
1985	Sweet Song 707	Closed	N/A	90.00	125
1986	Sing Along 708	Closed	N/A	100.00	150-200
1987	With Loving Greetings 709	Closed	N/A	110.00	175-200
1988	Busy Student 710	Closed	N/A	120.00	130-175
1989	Latest News 711	Closed	N/A	135.00	175-200
1990	What's New? 712	Closed	N/A	140.00	200
1991	Favorite Pet 713	Closed	N/A	150.00	150-200
1992	Whistler's Duet 714	Closed	N/A	160.00	175-225

Gorham

Currier & Ives - Mini Bells - Currier & Ives

1976	Christmas Sleigh Ride	Annual	1976	9.95	35
1977	American Homestead	Annual	1977	9.95	25
1978	Yule Logs	Annual	1978	12.95	20
1979	Sleigh Ride	Annual	1979	14.95	20
1980	Christmas in the Country	Annual	1980	14.95	20
1981	Christmas Tree	Annual	1981	14.95	18
1982	Christmas Visitation	Annual	1982	16.50	18
1983	Winter Wonderland	Annual	1983	16.50	18
1984	Hitching Up	Annual	1984	16.50	18
1985	Skaters Holiday	Annual	1985	17.50	18
1986	Central Park in Winter	Annual	1986	17.50	18
1987	Early Winter	Annual	1987	19.00	19

Mini Bells - N. Rockwell

1981	Tiny Tim	Annual	1981	19.75	20
1982	Planning Christmas Visit	Annual	1982	20.00	20

Various - N. Rockwell

1975	Sweet Song So Young	Annual	1975	19.50	50
1975	Santa's Helpers	Annual	1975	19.50	50
1975	Tavern Sign Painter	Annual	1975	19.50	30
1976	Flowers in Tender Bloom	Annual	1976	19.50	40
1976	Snow Sculpture	Annual	1976	19.50	45
1977	Fondly Do We Remember	Annual	1977	19.50	55
1977	Chilling Chore (Christmas)	Annual	1977	19.50	35
1978	Gaily Sharing Vintage Times	Annual	1978	22.50	23
1978	Gay Blades (Christmas)	Annual	1978	22.50	23
1979	Beguiling Buttercup	Annual	1979	24.50	45
1979	A Boy Meets His Dog (Christmas)	Annual	1979	24.50	50
1980	Flying High	Annual	1980	27.50	28
1980	Chilly Reception (Christmas)	Annual	1980	27.50	28
1981	Sweet Serenade	Annual	1981	27.50	45
1981	Ski Skills (Christmas)	Annual	1981	27.50	45
1982	Young Mans Fancy	Annual	1982	29.50	30
1982	Coal Season's Coming	Annual	1982	29.50	30
1983	Christmas Medley	Annual	1983	29.50	30
1983	The Milkmaid	Annual	1983	29.50	30
1984	Tiny Tim	Annual	1984	29.50	50
1984	Young Love	Annual	1984	29.50	50
1984	Marriage License	Annual	1984	32.50	33
1984	Yarn Spinner	5,000	1984	32.50	33
1985	Yuletide Reflections	5,000	1985	32.50	50
1986	Home For The Holidays	5,000	1986	32.50	33
1986	On Top of the World	5,000	1986	32.50	45
1987	Merry Christmas Grandma	5,000	1987	32.50	33
1987	The Artist	5,000	1987	32.50	33
1988	The Homecoming	15,000	1988	37.50	38

Kirk Stieff

Bell - Kirk Stieff

1992	Santa's Workshop	3,000		40.00	40
1993	Santa's Reindeer	Closed	N/A	30.00	30

Musical Bells - Kirk Stieff

1977	Annual Bell 1977	Closed	N/A	17.95	60-100

*Quotes have been rounded up to nearest dollar

YEAR	ISSUE	EDITION LIMIT	YEAR RETD.	ISSUE PRICE	*QUOTE U.S.$
1978	Annual Bell 1978	Closed	N/A	17.95	30-75
1979	Annual Bell 1979	Closed	N/A	17.95	30-50
1980	Annual Bell 1980	Closed	N/A	19.95	30-50
1981	Annual Bell 1981	Closed	N/A	19.95	30-50
1982	Annual Bell 1982	Closed	N/A	19.95	30-50
1983	Annual Bell 1983	Closed	N/A	19.95	30-40
1984	Annual Bell 1984	Closed	N/A	19.95	30
1985	Annual Bell 1985	Closed	N/A	19.95	30
1986	Annual Bell 1986	Closed	N/A	19.95	30
1987	Annual Bell 1987	Closed	N/A	19.95	30
1988	Annual Bell 1988	Closed	N/A	22.50	30
1989	Annual Bell 1989	Closed	N/A	25.00	30
1990	Annual Bell 1990	Closed	N/A	27.00	30
1991	Annual Bell 1991	Closed	N/A	28.00	30
1992	Annual Bell 1992	Closed	N/A	30.00	30
1993	Annual Bell 1993	Closed	N/A	30.00	30
1994	Annual Bell 1994	Open	N/A	30.00	30

Lenox China

Songs of Christmas - Unknown

YEAR	ISSUE	EDITION LIMIT	YEAR RETD.	ISSUE PRICE	*QUOTE U.S.$
1991	We Wish You a Merry Christmas	Yr.Iss.	1992	49.00	49
1992	Deck the Halls	Yr.Iss.	1993	53.00	53
1993	Jingle Bells	Yr.Iss.	1994	57.00	57
1994	Silver Bells	Yr.Iss.	1995	62.00	62
1995	Hark The Herald Angels Sing	Yr.Iss.	1996	62.50	63

Lenox Crystal

Annual Bell Series - Lenox

YEAR	ISSUE	EDITION LIMIT	YEAR RETD.	ISSUE PRICE	*QUOTE U.S.$
1987	Partridge Bell	Yr.Iss.	1990	45.00	45
1988	Angel Bell	Open	1991	45.00	45
1989	St. Nicholas Bell	Open	1991	45.00	45
1990	Christmas Tree Bell	Open	1993	49.00	49
1991	Teddy Bear Bell	Yr.Iss.	1992	49.00	49
1992	Snowman Bell	Yr.Iss.	1993	49.00	49
1993	Nutcracker Bell	Yr.Iss.	1994	49.00	49
1994	Candle Bell	Yr.Iss.	1995	49.00	49
1995	Bell	Yr.Iss.	1996	49.50	50
1996	Bell	Yr.Iss.		49.50	50

Lladró

Lladró Bell - Lladró

YEAR	ISSUE	EDITION LIMIT	YEAR RETD.	ISSUE PRICE	*QUOTE U.S.$
XX	Crystal Wedding Bell L4500	Closed	1985	35.00	195

Lladró Christmas Bell - Lladró

YEAR	ISSUE	EDITION LIMIT	YEAR RETD.	ISSUE PRICE	*QUOTE U.S.$
1987	Christmas Bell - L5458M	Annual	1987	29.50	70-85
1988	Christmas Bell - L5525M	Annual	1988	32.50	45-85
1989	Christmas Bell - L5616M	Annual	1989	32.50	125-150
1990	Christmas Bell - L5641M	Annual	1990	34.50	60
1991	Christmas Bell - L5803M	Annual	1991	37.50	45-60
1992	Christmas Bell - L5913M	Annual	1992	37.50	45-60
1993	Christmas Bell - L6010M	Annual	1993	37.50	50-60
1994	Christmas Bell - L6139M	Annual	1994	39.50	45-65
1995	Christmas Bell - L6206M	Annual	1995	39.50	45-55
1996	Christmas Bell - L6297M	Annual	1996	39.50	40
1997	Christmas Bell - L6441M	Annual		40.00	40

Lladró Limited Edition Bell - Lladró

YEAR	ISSUE	EDITION LIMIT	YEAR RETD.	ISSUE PRICE	*QUOTE U.S.$
1994	Eternal Love 7542M	Annual	1994	95.00	95

Lowell Davis Farm Club

RFD Bell - L. Davis

YEAR	ISSUE	EDITION LIMIT	YEAR RETD.	ISSUE PRICE	*QUOTE U.S.$
1979	Blossom	Closed	1983	65.00	400
1979	Kate	Closed	1983	65.00	375-400
1979	Willy	Closed	1983	65.00	375
1979	Caruso	Closed	1983	65.00	275
1979	Wilbur	Closed	1983	65.00	375-400
1979	Old Blue Lead	Closed	1983	65.00	275
1993	Cow Bell "Blossom"	Closed	1994	65.00	75
1993	Mule Bell "Kate"	Closed	1994	65.00	75
1993	Goat Bell "Willy"	Closed	1994	65.00	75
1993	Rooster Bell "Caruso"	Closed	1994	65.00	75
1993	Pig Bell "Wilbur"	Closed	1994	65.00	75
1993	Dog Bell "Old Blue and Lead"	Closed	1994	65.00	75

Memories of Yesterday/Enesco Corporation

Annual Bells - M. Attwell

YEAR	ISSUE	EDITION LIMIT	YEAR RETD.	ISSUE PRICE	*QUOTE U.S.$
1990	Here Comes the Bride-God Bless Her 523100	Suspd.		25.00	25
1994	Time For Bed 525243	Open		25.00	25

Precious Moments/Enesco Corporation

Annual Bells - S. Butcher

YEAR	ISSUE	EDITION LIMIT	YEAR RETD.	ISSUE PRICE	*QUOTE U.S.$
1981	Let the Heavens Rejoice E-5622	Yr.Iss.	1981	15.00	175-225
1982	I'll Play My Drum for Him E-2358	Yr.Iss.	1982	17.00	65-75
1983	Surrounded With Joy E-0522	Yr.Iss.	1983	18.00	45-75
1984	Wishing You a Merry Christmas E-5393	Yr.Iss.	1984	19.00	45
1985	God Sent His Love 15873	Yr.Iss.	1985	19.00	35-45
1986	Wishing You a Cozy Christmas 102318	Yr.Iss.	1986	20.00	40
1987	Love is the Best Gift of All 109835	Yr.Iss.	1987	22.50	35
1988	Time To Wish You a Merry Christmas 115304	Yr.Iss.	1988	25.00	43
1989	Oh Holy Night 522821	Yr.Iss.	1989	25.00	35
1990	Once Upon A Holy Night 523828	Yr.Iss.	1990	25.00	35
1991	May Your Christmas Be Merry 524182	Yr.Iss.	1991	25.00	35
1992	But The Greatest Of These Is Love 527726	Yr.Iss.	1992	25.00	40
1993	Wishing You The Sweetest Christmas 530174	Yr.Iss.	1993	25.00	40
1994	You're As Pretty as a Christmas Tree 604216	Yr.Iss.	1994	27.50	30-45

Various Bells - S. Butcher

YEAR	ISSUE	EDITION LIMIT	YEAR RETD.	ISSUE PRICE	*QUOTE U.S.$
1981	Jesus Loves Me (B) E-5208	Suspd.		15.00	40-50
1981	Jesus Loves Me (G) E-5209	Suspd.		15.00	50
1981	Prayer Changes Things E-5210	Suspd.		15.00	50-60
1981	God Understands E-5211	Retrd.	1984	15.00	45-60
1981	We Have Seen His Star E-5620	Suspd.		15.00	50-60
1981	Jesus Is Born E-5623	Suspd.		15.00	50-65
1982	The Lord Bless You and Keep You E-7175	Suspd.		17.00	35-65
1982	The Lord Bless You and Keep You E-7176	Suspd.		17.00	55-65
1982	The Lord Bless You and Keep You E-7179	Suspd.		22.50	65-85
1982	Mother Sew Dear E-7181	Suspd.		17.00	35-45
1982	The Purr-fect Grandma E-7183	Suspd.		17.00	50-60

Reed & Barton

Noel Musical Bells - Reed & Barton

YEAR	ISSUE	EDITION LIMIT	YEAR RETD.	ISSUE PRICE	*QUOTE U.S.$
1980	Bell 1980	Closed	1980	20.00	60-80
1981	Bell 1981	Closed	1981	22.50	30-60
1982	Bell 1982	Closed	1982	22.50	25-50
1983	Bell 1983	Closed	1983	22.50	25-60
1984	Bell 1984	Closed	1984	22.50	25-60
1985	Bell 1985	Closed	1985	25.00	25-55
1986	Bell 1986	Closed	1986	25.00	25-60
1987	Bell 1987	Closed	1987	25.00	25-60
1988	Bell 1988	Closed	1988	25.00	25-60
1989	Bell 1989	Closed	1989	25.00	25-60
1990	Bell 1990	Closed	1990	27.50	30
1991	Bell 1991	Closed	1991	30.00	30
1992	Bell 1992	Closed	1992	30.00	30-45
1993	Bell 1993	Yr.Iss.	1993	30.00	30-40
1994	Bell 1994	Yr.Iss.	1994	30.00	30-45
1995	Bell 1995	Yr.Iss.	1995	30.00	30
1996	Bell 1996	Yr.Iss.	1996	35.00	35

Yuletide Bell - Reed & Barton

YEAR	ISSUE	EDITION LIMIT	YEAR RETD.	ISSUE PRICE	*QUOTE U.S.$
1981	Yuletide Holiday	Closed	1981	14.00	25
1982	Little Shepherd	Closed	1982	14.00	25
1983	Perfect Angel	Closed	1983	15.00	25
1984	Drummer Boy	Closed	1984	15.00	25
1985	Caroler	Closed	1985	16.50	25
1986	Night Before Christmas	Closed	1986	16.50	25
1987	Jolly St. Nick	Closed	1987	16.50	25
1988	Christmas Morning	Closed	1988	16.50	25
1989	The Bell Ringer	Closed	1989	16.50	25
1990	The Wreath Bearer	Closed	1990	18.50	20
1991	A Special Gift	Closed	1991	22.50	25
1992	My Special Friend	Closed	1992	22.50	25
1993	My Christmas Present	Yr.Iss.	1993	22.50	25
1994	Holiday Wishes	Yr.Iss.	1994	22.50	25
1995	Christmas Puppy	Yr.Iss.	1995	20.00	20
1996	Yuletide Bell	Yr.Iss.	1996	22.50	23

River Shore

Norman Rockwell Single Issues - N. Rockwell

YEAR	ISSUE	EDITION LIMIT	YEAR RETD.	ISSUE PRICE	*QUOTE U.S.$
1981	Grandpa's Guardian	7,000		45.00	45
1981	Looking Out to Sea	7,000		45.00	95
1981	Spring Flowers	347		175.00	175

Rockwell Children Series I - N. Rockwell

YEAR	ISSUE	EDITION LIMIT	YEAR RETD.	ISSUE PRICE	*QUOTE U.S.$
1977	First Day of School	7,500		30.00	75
1977	Flowers for Mother	7,500		30.00	60
1977	Football Hero	7,500		30.00	75
1977	School Play	7,500		30.00	75

Rockwell Children Series II - N. Rockwell

YEAR	ISSUE	EDITION LIMIT	YEAR RETD.	ISSUE PRICE	*QUOTE U.S.$
1978	Dressing Up	15,000		35.00	50
1978	Five Cents A Glass	15,000		35.00	40
1978	Future All American	15,000		35.00	52
1978	Garden Girl	15,000		35.00	40

Roman, Inc.

Annual Nativity Bell - I. Spencer

YEAR	ISSUE	EDITION LIMIT	YEAR RETD.	ISSUE PRICE	*QUOTE U.S.$
1990	Nativity	Closed	N/A	15.00	15
1991	Flight Into Egypt	Closed	N/A	15.00	15
1992	Gloria in Excelsis Deo	Closed	N/A	15.00	15
1993	Three Kings of Orient	Closed	N/A	15.00	15

F. Hook Bells - F. Hook

YEAR	ISSUE	EDITION LIMIT	YEAR RETD.	ISSUE PRICE	*QUOTE U.S.$
1985	Beach Buddies	15,000		25.00	28
1986	Sounds of the Sea	15,000		25.00	28
1987	Bear Hug	15,000		25.00	28

The Masterpiece Collection - Various

YEAR	ISSUE	EDITION LIMIT	YEAR RETD.	ISSUE PRICE	*QUOTE U.S.$
1979	Adoration - F. Lippe	Open		20.00	20
1980	Madonna with Grapes - P. Mignard	Open		25.00	25
1981	The Holy Family - G. Notti	Open		25.00	25
1982	Madonna of the Streets - R. Ferruzzi	Open		25.00	25

Seymour Mann, Inc.

Connoisseur Christmas Collection - Bernini™

YEAR	ISSUE	EDITION LIMIT	YEAR RETD.	ISSUE PRICE	*QUOTE U.S.$
1996	Cardinal CLT-312	Open		15.00	15
1996	Chickadee CLT-302	Open		15.00	15
1996	Dove CLT-307	Open		15.00	15

Connoisseur Collection - Bernini™

YEAR	ISSUE	EDITION LIMIT	YEAR RETD.	ISSUE PRICE	*QUOTE U.S.$
1995	Bluebird CLT-15	Closed	1996	15.00	15
1995	Canary CLT-12	Open		15.00	15
1995	Cardinal CLT-9	Open		15.00	15
1995	Dove CLT-3	Open		15.00	15
1995	Hummingbird CLT-6	Open		15.00	15
1995	Pink Rose CLT-72	Open		15.00	15
1995	Robin CLT-18	Open		15.00	15
1995	Swan CLT-52	Open		15.00	15
1996	Butterfly/Lily CLT-332	Open		15.00	15
1996	Hummingbirds, Morning Glory, blue CLT-322B	Open		15.00	15
1996	Hummingbirds, Morning Glory, pink CLT-322	Open		15.00	15
1996	Magnolia CLT-78	Open		15.00	15
1996	Roses/Forget-Me-Not CLT-342	Open		15.00	15

DOLLS

All God's Children

Anika Series - M. Root

YEAR	ISSUE	EDITION LIMIT	YEAR RETD.	ISSUE PRICE	*QUOTE U.S.$
1996	Anika - 2600	5,000	1996	175.00	175
1997	Skating Anika - 2601	7,500		125.00	125

Annalee Mobilitee Dolls, Inc.

Doll Society-Animals - A. Thorndike

YEAR	ISSUE	EDITION LIMIT	YEAR RETD.	ISSUE PRICE	*QUOTE U.S.$
1985	10" Penguin and Chick	3,000	N/A	29.95	225
1986	10" Unicorn	3,000	N/A	36.95	350
1987	7" Kangaroo	3,000	N/A	37.45	450
1988	5" Owl	3,000	N/A	37.45	300
1989	7" Polar Bear	3,000	N/A	37.50	300
1990	10" Thorndike Chicken	3,000	N/A	37.50	275

Doll Society-Folk Heroes - A. Thorndike

YEAR	ISSUE	EDITION LIMIT	YEAR RETD.	ISSUE PRICE	*QUOTE U.S.$
1984	10" Johnny Appleseed	1,500	N/A	80.00	1000
1984	10" Robin Hood	1,500	N/A	90.00	850
1985	10" Annie Oakley	1,500	N/A	95.00	700
1986	10" Mark Twain	2,500	N/A	117.50	500
1987	10" Ben Franklin	2,500	N/A	119.50	525
1988	10" Sherlock Holmes	2,500	N/A	119.50	500
1989	10" Abraham Lincoln	2,500	N/A	119.50	500
1990	10" Betsy Ross	2,500	N/A	119.50	450
1991	10" Christopher Columbus	1,132	N/A	119.50	300
1992	10" Uncle Sam	1,034	N/A	87.50	200
1993	10" Pony Express Rider	Yr.Iss.	N/A	97.50	N/A
1994	10" Bean Nose Santa	Yr.Iss.	N/A	119.50	N/A
1995	10" Pocahontas	Yr.Iss.	N/A	87.50	88
1996	10" Fabulous 50's Couple	Yr.Iss.		150.00	150

Doll Society-Logo Kids - A. Thorndike

YEAR	ISSUE	EDITION LIMIT	YEAR RETD.	ISSUE PRICE	*QUOTE U.S.$
1985	Christmas Logo w/Cookie	3,562	1986	N/A	675
1986	Sweetheart Logo	6,271	1987	N/A	275
1987	Naughty Logo	1,100	1988	N/A	425
1988	Raincoat Logo	13,646	1989	N/A	200
1989	Christmas Morning Logo	16,641	1990	N/A	150
1990	Clown Logo	20,049	1991	N/A	150
1991	Reading Logo	26,516	1992	N/A	125
1992	Back to School Logo	17,524	1993	N/A	90
1993	Ice Cream Logo	Yr.Iss.	1994	N/A	N/A
1994	Dress Up Santa Logo	Yr.Iss	1995	N/A	N/A
1995	Goin' Fishin' Logo	Yr.Iss	1995	N/A	30
1996	7" Little Mae Flower Logo	Yr.Iss		N/A	30

Assorted Dolls - A. Thorndike

YEAR	ISSUE	EDITION LIMIT	YEAR RETD.	ISSUE PRICE	*QUOTE U.S.$
1987	3" Baby Witch	3,645	1987	13.95	275
1987	3" Bride and Groom	1,053	1987	38.95	375
1983	3" PJ Kid (designer series)	2,360	1983	10.95	200
1971	3" Reindeer Head	N/A	1976	1.00	200
1991	3" Water Baby in Pond Lily	3,720	1991	14.95	175
1987	3" Duck on Flexible Flyer Sled	5,425	1994	21.95	300
1984	5" E.P. Boy Bunny	2,583	1984	11.95	200
1984	5" E.P. Girl Bunny	2,790	1984	11.95	200
1983	5" Easter Parade Girl Bunny w/ Music Box	1,167	1983	29.95	400
1963	5" Elf (Lilac)	N/A	1963	2.50	325
1959	5" Man (Special Order)	N/A	1959	N/A	1525
1956	5" Miniature Girl	N/A	1956	N/A	1000
1956	5" Miniature Man	N/A	1956	N/A	1600
1954	5" Sloppy Painter Boy	N/A	1954	N/A	2700
1954	5" Sloppy Painter Girl	N/A	1954	N/A	3400
1960	5" Wee Skis	N/A	N/A	3.95	325

*Quotes have been rounded up to nearest dollar

Annalee Mobilitee Dolls, Inc.
to Annalee Mobilitee Dolls, Inc.

DOLLS

YEAR ISSUE		EDITION LIMIT	YEAR RETD.	ISSUE PRICE	*QUOTE U.S.$
1978	7" Airplane Pilot Mouse	2,308	1981	6.95	425
1964	7" Angel in a Blanket	N/A	1964	2.45	325
1984	7" Angel on Star	772	1984	32.95	475
1983	7" Angel w/Musical Instrument on Music Box	N/A	1983	29.95	425
1960	7" Angel w/Paper Wings	N/A	1966	N/A	400
1970	7" Artist Mouse	298	1974	3.95	400
1950	7" Baby Angel	N/A	1950	2.45	1650
1960	7" Baby Angel (yellow feather hair)	N/A	1962	N/A	350
1964	7" Baby Angel Flying w/Halo	N/A	1964	2.45	450
1962	7" Baby Angel on Cloud	N/A	1963	2.45	500-700
1962	7" Baby Angel w/Star	N/A	1962	2.00	225
1980	7" Baby in Bassinet	12,215	1983	13.95	275
1968	7" Baby in Christmas Bag	N/A	1968	2.95	350
1968	7" Baby in Santa's Hat	N/A	1969	2.95	500
1975	7" Baby Mouse	N/A	1975	5.50	150
1971	7" Baby w/Bottle	N/A	1971	N/A	300
1965	7" Baby w/Bow	N/A	1965	N/A	325
1979	7" Ballerina	4,700	1979	7.45	275
1967	7" Ballerina Mouse	N/A	1968	3.95	450
1980	7" Ballooning Santa	N/A	1983	49.95	350
1970	7" Bartender Mouse	289	1973	3.95	400
1971	7" Baseball Player Mouse	1,085	1975	5.50	175
1969	7" Bather-Boy	N/A	1969	N/A	475
1969	7" Bather-Girl	N/A	1969	5.95	800
1987	7" BBQ Mouse	1,798	1987	17.95	300
1975	7" Beautician Mouse	1,349	1975	5.50	600
1974	7" Black Santa w/ Oversized Bag	1,638	1975	5.45	550
1977	7" Boating Mouse	1,186	1977	5.95	175
1964	7" Boudoir Puff Baby Angel	N/A	1965	3.95	400
1984	7" Boy w/ Firecracker	1,893	1984	19.95	400
1966	7" Bride & Groom Mice	N/A	1966	3.95	600
1979	7" Bunny	3,125	1979	6.95	175
1970	7" Bunny (yellow)	3,215	1973	3.95	375
1987	7" Bunny in 10" Carrot Balloon	624	1987	49.95	375
1974	7" Camper in Tent Mouse	468	1974	5.45	325
1976	7" Card Playing Girl Mouse	2,878	1977	5.50	275
1968	7" Caroller Boy Mouse w/ Music	N/A	1969	4.45	400
1978	7" Carpenter Mouse	1,494	1978	6.95	350
1974	7" Carpenter Mouse	2,687	1978	5.45	275
1983	7" Cheerleader Mouse	N/A	1983	11.95	450
1970	7" Christmas Baby on Hat Box	1,894	1971	2.95	350
1965	7" Christmas Dumb Bunny	N/A	1965	3.95	775
1975	7" Christmas Mouse in Santa Mitten	3,959	1976	5.45	375
1977	7" Christmas Mouse in Santa's Mitten	15,916	1979	7.95	175
1975	7" Colonial Boy Mouse	12,739	1976	5.45	350
1975	7" Colonial Girl Mouse	9,338	1976	5.45	350
1965	7" Colored Mouse (Peek)	N/A	1965	3.95	550
1982	7" Cowboy Mouse	3,776	1983	12.95	300
1982	7" Cowgirl Mouse	3,116	1983	12.95	300
1984	7" Cupid in Hanging Heart	2,445	1985	32.95	375
1984	7" Dentist Mouse	2,362	1985	14.95	400
1983	7" Devil Mouse	12,222	1986	13.95	300
1976	7" Diet Time Mouse	3,399	1977	6.00	200
1992	7" Disney Kid	300	1992	59.95	400
1985	7" Dress-Up Boy	1,174	1985	18.95	225
1985	7" Dress-Up Girl	1,536	1985	18.95	225
1993	7" Eric & Shane Boating in Hawaii	100	1993	105.00	750
1979	7" Fishing Mouse	N/A	1979	7.95	275
1972	7" Football Mouse	744	1974	3.95	300
1991	7" Fun in the Sun Kid	300	1991	80.00	300
1962	7" Furcapped Baby	N/A	1962	2.45	400
1967	7" Garden Club Baby	N/A	1969	2.95	800
1974	7" Gardener Mouse	485	1980	5.45	400
1969	7" Gardener Mouse	N/A	1973	4.45	300
1979	7" Gardener Mouse	1,939	1980	7.95	325
1992	7" Gnome w/ Mushroom	1,691	1992	35.95	350
1967	7" Gnome w/ Pajama Suit	N/A	1970	2.95	400
1965	7" Gnome w/ Vest	N/A	1965	2.45	675
1965	7" Hangover Mouse	N/A	1987	3.95	375
1987	7" Hangover Mouse	1,548	1987	13.95	175
1974	7" Hiker Mouse	423	1975	5.45	375
1977	7" Hobo Mouse	1,004	1977	5.95	275
1980	7" Hockey Mouse	2,477	1981	9.95	250
1985	7" Hockey Player Kid	1,578	1985	18.95	400
1974	7" Hunter Mouse w/ Bird	690	1975	5.45	325
1981	7" I'm Late Bunny	100	1981	N/A	475
1991	7" Indian Boy	3,371	1994	29.95	350
1985	7" Kid w/ Kite	1,084	1985	17.95	300
1965	7" Lawyer Mouse	N/A	1965	3.95	350
1966	7" M/M Indoor Santa	N/A	1966	5.95	450
1970	7" M/M Santa on Ski Bob	N/A	1970	5.95	600
1983	7" M/M Santa w/ Basket	5,105	1983	25.95	300
1980	7" M/M Santa w/ Pot Belly Stove	6,552	1980	20.94	325
1970	7" M/M Tuckered Santa w/ Hot Water Bottle	1,761	1971	6.45	200
1967	7" M/M Tuckered Santa w/ Hot Water Bottle	N/A	1968	5.95	400
1959	7" Man (special order)	N/A	1959	N/A	1200
1956	7" Man (special order)	N/A	1956	N/A	1900
1993	7" Mississippi Levee Mouse	341	1993	N/A	400
1973	7" Monkey (Boy)	370	1973	4.50	850
1973	7" Monkey (Girl)	370	1973	4.50	600
1992	7" Mouse on Cheese	14,923	1993	25.95	225
1982	7" Mouse w/ Strawberry	10,267	1985	12.95	175
1982	7" Mr. A.M. Mouse	3,724	1983	11.95	150
1970	7" Mr. Holly Mouse	1,726	1970	3.95	225
1977	7" Mr. Santa Mouse	7,197	1979	6.00	300
1967	7" Mrs. Holly Mouse	N/A	1976	3.95	350
1967	7" Mrs. Santa w/ Fur-Trimmed Cape	N/A	1973	2.95	450
1971	7" Naughty Angel	12,359	1971	10.95	275
1976	7" Needlework Mouse	3,566	1978	6.95	400
1964	7" Nude Angel Bath Puff	N/A	1965	3.95	275
1970	7" Painter Mouse	349	1970	3.95	400
1968	7" Patches Pam	N/A	1968	2.95	850
1979	7" Quilting Mouse	213	1979	N/A	375
1991	7" Santa in Tub w/ Rubber Duckie	5,373	1991	33.95	200
1971	7" Santa Mailman	8,296	1974	5.50	375
1972	7" Santa on Ski-Bob w/ Oversized Bag	7,590	1974	7.95	400
1978	7" Santa w/ 10" Reindeer Trimming Christmas Tree	1,621	1978	18.45	425
1981	7" Santa w/ 18" Moon	N/A	1981	6.95	200
1963	7" Santa w/ Fur Trimmed Suit	N/A	1967	2.95	400
1969	7" Santa w/ Oversized Bag	N/A	1970	3.95	350
1979	7" Santa w/ Pot Belly Stove	11,551	1979	7.95	375
1971	7" Santa w/ Skis and Poles	N/A	1978	5.45	300
1983	7" Santa w/ Sleigh	1,290	1983	14.95	275
1989	7" Science Center Mouse	500	1989	75.00	525
1970	7" Secretary Mouse	727	1972	3.95	150
1972	7" Secretary Mouse	727	1974	3.95	500
1970	7" Sherriff Mouse	11	1970	3.95	650
1991	7" Sherriff Mouse #92	1,191	1992	49.50	700
1965	7" Singing Mouse	N/A	1965	3.95	600
1978	7" Skateboard Mouse	3,733	1979	7.00	200
1979	7" Skateboard Mouse	1,821	1979	7.95	275
1976	7" Ski Mouse	10,375	1981	6.95	225
1974	7" Ski Mouse	1,603	1974	5.45	225
1954	7" Sloppy Painter Boy	N/A	1954	N/A	900
1974	7" Sloppy Painter Mouse	349	1974	5.45	550
1992	7" Spring Skunk	1,590	1993	22.95	375
1971	7" Swimmer Mouse w/ Inner Tube	267	1971	3.95	325
1967	7" Tuckered Mr. & Mrs. Santa Water Bottle	N/A	1969	5.95	400
1973	7" Vacationer Girl Mouse	1,017	1974	4.45	325
1986	7" Witch Mouse w/ Pumpkin Balloon	868	1987	59.95	300
1982	7" Wood Chopper Mouse	1,910	1982	11.95	375
1992	7" Workshop Mouse	6,618	1992	21.95	275
1971	7" Yachtsman Mouse w/ Binnacle	249	1974	3.95	400
1966	7" Yum Yum Bunny	N/A	1966	3.95	600
1968	8" Elephant (Tubby)	N/A	1969	4.95	450
1980	8" Girl BBQ Pig	3,854	1981	9.95	175
1975	8" Lamb	234	1975	8.95	450
1977	8" Rooster	1,642	1977	5.95	350
1959	10" 4th of July Doll	N/A	1959	N/A	1525
1982	10" Annalee Artist	160	1982	295.00	1100
1959	10" Architect	N/A	1959	19.95	1250
1991	10" Aviator Frog w/ Flag	2,110	1991	19.95	425
1957	10" Baby Angel	N/A	1958	8.95	525
1963	10" Ballerina	N/A	1963	5.95	1350
1980	10" Balloon w/ Two 10" Frogs	837	1980	49.95	850
1968	10" Bather (Skinny Minnie w/ Towel)	N/A	1968	5.95	950
1966	10" Bathersome Chick w/ Flippers	N/A	1966	5.95	650
1959	10" Bathing Boy	N/A	1959	5.75	1800
1959	10" Bathing Girl	N/A	1959	7.95	2800
1957	10" Bathing Girl	N/A	1957	N/A	1300
1968	10" Bathing Girl	N/A	1968	5.95	850
1989	10" BBQ Pig	2,471	1989	27.95	325
1964	10" Black (Monk)	N/A	1965	2.95	375
1994	10" Boston Bruins Hockey Player (Signed by team)	2	1994	N/A	500
1966	10" Boy & Girl on Tandem Bike	N/A	1966	20.95	1350
1956	10" Boy Building Boat	N/A	1969	N/A	1550
1950	10" Boy Building Boat	N/A	1950	9.95	1200
1960	10" Boy Building Boat	N/A	1968	12.95	1600
1976	10" Boy in Tire Swing	358	1976	6.95	350
1965	10" Boy on Bike	N/A	1965	N/A	600
1980	10" Boy on Raft	1,087	1981	28.95	450
1955	10" Boy Skier	N/A	1956	10.95	2750
1969	10" Bride & Groom Set	N/A	1969	11.95	800
1967	10" Brown Nun	N/A	1967	2.95	375
1950	10" Calypso Dancer	N/A	1950	N/A	1350
1967	10" Carnaby Street Boy	N/A	1967	3.95	400
1976	10" Caroler Boy	2,898	1976	5.50	400
1960	10" Carpenter	N/A	1965	N/A	575
1987	10" Carrot Balloon w / 7" Bunny in Basket	624	1987	49.95	500
1970	10" Casualty Ski Elf w/ Crutch & Leg in Cast	2,818	1972	4.50	600
1968	10" Cat in Basket	N/A	1968	N/A	700
1959	10" Catcher	N/A	1959	N/A	1900
1967	10" Choir Boy (set/3)	N/A	1967	2.95	725
1971	10" Choir Girl	925	1973	3.95	400
1950	10" Christmas Girl	N/A	1957	N/A	2350
1970	10" Christmas Mushroom w/ 2-7" Gnomes	189	1970	9.95	650
1970	10" Christmas Mushroom w/ 7" Mouse	198	1970	7.95	400
1985	10" Christmas Panda w/ Toybag	6,020	1986	17.95	300
1987	10" Clown	2,699	1987	17.95	450
1981	10" Clown	6,479	1981	9.95	200
1971	10" Clown (black & white)	N/A	1971	2.00	300
1969	10" Clown (bright stripes)	N/A	1971	3.95	350
1969	10" Clown (pink w/green polka dots)	N/A	1969	3.95	525
1971	10" Clown w/ Mushroom	45	1971	7.95	850
1975	10" Colonial Drummer Boy	1,846	1976	5.95	425
1989	10" Country Boy Pig	2,566	1989	25.95	175
1989	10" Country Girl Pig	2,367	1989	25.95	175
1968	10" Cross Country Skier	N/A	1968	7.95	700
1982	10" Cyrano de Bergerac	35	1982	N/A	2300
1961	10" Dalmation	N/A	1961	N/A	1500
1972	10" Democratic Donkey	861	1972	3.95	450
1963	10" Elf	N/A	1963	N/A	350
1960	10" Elf	N/A	1966	N/A	400
1950	10" Elf	N/A	N/A	N/A	900
1954	10" Elf w/ Cap	N/A	1954	N/A	1150
1978	10" Elf w/ Planter	1,978	1978	6.95	275
1967	10" Elf w/ Skis and Poles	48	1971	2.95	425-900
1988	10" Fall Elf	3,183	1988	13.95	125
1959	10" Fisherman & Girl in Boat	N/A	1959	N/A	2550
1986	10" Fishing Bear	2,817	1986	19.95	475
1963	10" Friar	N/A	1963	2.95	500
1959	10" Girl	N/A	1959	N/A	1000
1959	10" Girl and Boy on Tandem Bike	N/A	1959	20.95	2200
1965	10" Girl on Bike	N/A	1965	N/A	600
1955	10" Girl Skier	N/A	1956	10.95	2750
1967	10" Go-Go Boy	N/A	1967	3.95	450
1967	10" Golfer Boy	N/A	1968	5.95	925
1966	10" Golfer Boy	N/A	1966	5.95	1500
1965	10" Golfer Boy Doll	N/A	1965	9.95	700
1966	10" Golfer-Girl Putter	N/A	1968	5.95	925
1957	10" Halloween Girl	N/A	1959	9.95	3200
1965	10" Hiking Doll	N/A	1965	9.95	750
1957	10" Holly Elf	N/A	1957	N/A	1600
1973	10" Holly Hobby (Type Doll)	N/A	1973	N/A	800
1987	10" Huck Finn (#62)	800	1988	102.95	700
1991	10" Husky w/ 5" Puppy in Dog Sled	2,860	1991	54.95	350
1960	10" Impski	N/A	1966	3.95	500
1960	10" Impski (red)	N/A	1966	3.95	325
1960	10" Impski (white)	N/A	1966	3.95	350
1963	10" Indian Boy (special order)	N/A	1963	5.95	1550
1977	10" Jack Frost Elf	5,580	1977	6.00	225
1982	10" Jack Frost Elf w/ 10" Snowflake	N/A	1982	13.50	150
1981	10" Jack Frost Elf w/ 5" Snowflake	5,950	1981	31.95	325
1990	10" Kitten on Sled	238	1991	35.95	350
1959	10" Lawyer	N/A	1959	N/A	3000
1974	10" Leprechaun w/ Sack	8,834	1974	5.45	350
1956	10" Man	N/A	1956	N/A	3000
1959	10" Man (special order)	N/A	1959	N/A	1400
1967	10" Man w/Guitar	N/A	1967	N/A	1000
1964	10" Monk (red robe)	N/A	1965	2.95	800
1965	10" Monk w/ Christmas Tree Planting	N/A	1967	2.95	450
1967	10" Monk w/ Jug	N/A	1969	2.95	375
1967	10" Monk w/ Musical Instrument	N/A	1967	2.95	475
1970	10" Monk w/ Skis and Poles	1,386	1972	3.95	350
1970	10" Mushroom w/ 7" Santa	1,535	1971	7.95	250
1967	10" Nun (green)	N/A	1967	42.95	700
1967	10" Nun w/Basket	N/A	1967	2.95	600
1978	10" Pilgrim Boy	3,461	1978	7.00	300
1994	10" Piper Bear	200	1994	130.00	650
1974	10" Polly Frog Spring Cleaning	580	1974	5.50	325
1965	10" Reindeer	N/A	1965	4.95	425
1975	10" Reindeer w/ 7" Santa	2,429	1976	10.50	400
1964	10" Robin Hood Elf	N/A	1965	2.50	500
1988	10" Scrooge Head	N/A	1988	N/A	325
1984	10" Shriner (special order)	1,000	1984	N/A	875
1987	10" Sitting Frog w/Instrument	2,162	1987	19.95	525
1971	10" Ski Elf	1,262	1971	3.95	275
1987	10" Ski Elf	N/A	1987	19.95	350
1987	10" Skier	1,125	1988	34.95	475
1985	10" Skier (Cross Country)	1,076	1985	33.50	225
1956	10" Skier Girl w/ Broken Leg in Cast	N/A	1957	14.95	1550
1954	10" Sloppy Painter Boy	N/A	1954	N/A	900
1990	10" Spirit of '76	1,080	1990	175.00	550
1992	10" Spring Chicken w/ Boa	N/A	1992	34.95	150
1965	10" Spring Elf	N/A	1965	2.50	375
1954	10" Spring Girl	N/A	1954	N/A	2350
1957	10" Square Dancer (Girl)	N/A	1959	9.95	900
1950	10" Square Dancers (Boy & Girl)	N/A	1959	9.95	2100
1956	10" Square Dancers (set/8)	N/A	1956	59.95	5200
1987	10" State Trooper (#642)	511	1988	134.00	500
1991	10" Summer Santa #1663	1,926	1991	59.95	425
1967	10" Surfer Boy	N/A	1968	5.95	525
1967	10" Surfer Girl	N/A	1968	5.95	625
1989	10" Three Bunnies w/ Maypole	647	1989	190.00	600
1959	10" Two Painters on Scaffold	N/A	1959	39.95	3400
1976	10" Uncle Sam	1,095	1976	5.95	500
1957	10" Valentine Doll	N/A	1957	9.95	1800
1991	10" Victory Ski Doll	1,192	1991	49.50	350
1956	10" Woman	N/A	1956	N/A	2600
1959	10" Woman in Red	N/A	1959	5.75	2200
1959	10" Woman's Head	N/A	1959	N/A	500
1959	10" Wood Sprite	N/A	1967	N/A	750
1966	10" Workshop Elf	N/A	1966	N/A	425
1976	12" Angel	13,338	1979	10.95	350
1960	12" Baby in Green	N/A	1960	N/A	550
1992	12" Bat	2,107	1992	31.95	225
1965	12" Christmas Bonnet Lady Mouse	N/A	1965	9.95	400
1967	12" Country Cousin Boy Mouse	N/A	1967	9.95	500
1990	12" Easter Parade Duck w/ Watering Can	2,891	1990	49.95	300
1967	12" Fancy Nancy Cat	N/A	1967	6.95	1950
1968	12" Gnome w/ Gay Apron	N/A	1968	5.95	900
1968	12" Laura May Cat	N/A	1971	7.95	900
1967	12" Laura May Cat	N/A	1967	6.95	1000
1981	12" Monkey Boy w/ Banana	N/A	1971	23.95	225
1987	12" Mother Mouse w/ 7" Baby Mouse	1,100	1987	43.95	400
1970	12" Mr. Santa Mouse w/ Toybag	N/A	1971	10.95	525

*Quotes have been rounded up to nearest dollar

YEAR ISSUE		EDITION LIMIT	YEAR RETD.	ISSUE PRICE	*QUOTE U.S. $
1988	12" Mrs. Santa Mouse w/ Muff	4,091	1988	31.95	350
1967	12" Mrs. Santa w/ Muff	N/A	1969	9.95	550
1969	12" Myrtle Turtle	N/A	1969	6.95	800
1968	12" Myrtle Turtle	N/A	1969	6.95	2600
1969	12" Nightshirt Boy Mouse	N/A	1976	9.95	550
1957	12" Santa	N/A	1957	N/A	925
1954	12" Santa (Bean Nose)	N/A	1957	19.95	1000
1990	12" Santa Duck	506	1991	49.95	300
1981	12" Santa Monkey	1,800	1981	23.95	600
1982	12" Skunk Boy	935	1982	27.95	225
1982	12" Skunk Girl	936	1982	27.95	225
1967	12" Sneaky Peaky Boy Cat	N/A	1967	6.95	375
1992	12" Spider	3,461	1992	38.95	200
1967	12" Yum-Yum Bunny	N/A	1968	9.95	850
1980	14" Dragon w/ Bush Boy	2,130	1982	32.95	300
1955	14" Fireman	N/A	1955	N/A	4750
1990	15" Christmas Dragon	448	1990	49.95	400
1970	16" Christmas Wreath w/ Santa Head	1,662	1974	9.95	375
1972	16" Democratic Donkey	219	1972	12.95	1600
1972	16" Elephant (Republican)	230	1972	12.95	800
1984	18" Aerobic Girl	622	1984	35.95	375
1988	18" Americana Couple #82	7,258	1988	169.95	700
1990	18" Angel w/ Instrument	398	1990	51.95	325
1978	18" Artist Bunny w/ Brush & Palette	2,023	1979	14.00	300
1985	18" Ballerina Bear	918	1985	39.95	275
1980	18" Ballerina Bunny	7,069	1982	27.95	425
1979	18" Ballerina Bunny	2,315	1982	15.95	450
1984	18" Bear w/ Brush	1,392	1984	39.95	250
1973	18" Bear w/ Butterfly	N/A	1973	10.50	750
1985	18" Bear w/ Honey Pot & Bee	2,032	1986	41.50	600
1974	18" Bell Hop (special order)	3	1974	N/A	1000
1974	18" Bob Cratchet w/ 7" Tiny Tim	984	1974	11.95	425
1977	18" Boy Bunny w/Carrot	1,159	1977	13.50	250
1979	18" Boy Frog	3,524	1981	22.95	175
1977	18" Bunny w/Egg	1,172	1977	13.50	300
1981	18" Butterfly w/ 10" Elf	2,507	1982	27.95	500
1972	18" Candy Kid Boy	4,350	1973	11.95	775
1972	18" Candy Kid Girl	4,350	1973	11.95	775
1975	18" Caroller Boy	1,024	1975	12.00	400
1963	18" Choir Boy	1,470	1963	7.45	550
1973	18" Christmas Panda	437	1973	10.50	600
1979	18" City Boy Bunny w/ Basket	N/A	1979	15.95	300
1975	18" Clown	166	1975	N/A	450
1983	18" Country Girl Bunny w/ Basket	2,905	1983	29.95	400
1990	18" Dragon Kid	269	1990	69.95	325
1984	18" E.P. Girl Bunny	2,952	1984	35.95	350
1976	18" Elephant "Vote '76"	806	1976	8.50	500
1981	18" Escort Fox	657	1981	28.50	650
1984	18" Fawn w/ Wreath	2,080	1984	32.95	375
1979	18" Girl Frog	3,677	1981	22.95	175
1976	18" Gnome	N/A	1976	9.95	750
1979	18" Gnome	15,851	1980	19.95	350
1975	18" Horse	221	1976	16.95	375
1968	18" Indoor Santa	N/A	1968	7.45	375
1975	18" Jockey w/18" Horse	84	1975	30.00	1700
1981	18" Lady Fox	643	1981	28.50	650
1974	18" Martha Cratchet	1,043	1974	11.95	425
1982	18" Monk w/Jug	3,024	1982	26.45	525
1970	18" Mr. & Mrs. Fireside Couple	N/A	1971	7.45	300
1968	18" Mrs. Indoor Santa	N/A	1968	7.45	350
1968	18" Mrs. Santa w/ Boudoir Cap & Apron	N/A	1968	7.45	250
1968	18" Mrs. Santa w/ Hot Water Bottle	N/A	1968	7.45	525
1990	18" Naughty Kid	1,454	1991	69.95	525
1970	18" Patchwork Kid	496	1970	7.45	450
1978	18" Pilgrim Boy	1,213	1978	14.95	275
1964	18" PJ Kid	N/A	1964	6.95	500
1977	18" PJ Kid w/ Stocking	N/A	1977	N/A	425
1979	18" Reindeer w/ Christmas Saddlebags	6,825	1979	20.95	275
1971	18" Santa w/ Vest & Cardholder Sack	3,151	1988	7.95	325
1980	18" Santa Frog w/ Toybag	2,126	1980	24.95	450
1971	18" Santa Fur Kid	1,191	1972	7.45	250
1964	18" Santa Kid	N/A	1965	6.95	450
1990	18" Santa Playing w/ Electric Train	168	1990	119.00	350
1977	18" Scarecrow	2,374	1978	13.50	900
1981	18" Sledding Boy	4,517	1984	N/A	400
1978	18" Snowman w/Bird	9,639	1979	15.95	350
1987	18" Special Mrs. Santa (special order)	341	1987	N/A	400
1990	18" Thorny the Ghost	551	1991	45.45	400
1991	18" Trick or Treat Bunny Kid	625	1991	49.95	275
1976	18" Uncle Sam	345	1976	16.95	500
1985	18" Valentine Bear	2,439	1986	41.50	275
1987	18" Workshop Santa (special order)	1,001	1987	N/A	450
1975	18" Yankee Doodle Dandy w/ 18" Horse	437	1976	28.95	900
1968	18" Yum Yum Bunny	N/A	1968	14.95	1000
1981	22" Christmas Giraffe w/ 10" Elf	1,377	1982	36.95	500
1974	22" Christmas Stocking	8,536	1974	4.95	150
1973	22" Holly Hobby	N/A	1973	N/A	1000
1974	22" Leprchaun	199	1974	11.45	650
1970	22" Monkey (chartreuse)	70	1970	10.95	725
1990	22" Spring Elf (yellow)	1,636	1990	34.95	325
1981	22" Sun Mobile	3,003	1985	36.95	475
1963	24" Bellhop	N/A	1963	13.95	1750
1975	25" Lad w/ Kite	95	1975	28.95	400
1975	25" Lass w/ Flowers	92	1975	28.95	450
1954	26" Elf	N/A	1956	9.95	550
1963	26" Friar	N/A	1963	14.95	2500
1955	26" Woman	N/A	1955	N/A	6500
1979	29" Artist Bunny w/ Brush & Palette	179	1979	42.95	350
1974	29" Bell Hop (special order)	3	1974	29.00	1200
1970	29" Boy Bunny	N/A	1970	24.95	600
1978	29" Caroller Mouse	658	1978	49.95	475
1976	29" Clown (blue w/ white polka dots)	466	1976	29.95	925
1981	29" Dragon w/ 12 Bush Boy	151	1982	69.95	700
1960	29" Fur Trim Santa	N/A	1979	N/A	1000
1971	29" M/M Tuckered w/ 2 18" Kids	811	1972	51.95	800
1974	29" Motorized See-Saw Bunny Set	43	1975	250.00	1600
1977	29" Mr. Santa Mouse w/ Sack	704	1977	49.95	800
1968	29" Mrs. Indoor Santa	N/A	1968	16.95	475
1977	29" Mrs. Santa Mouse w/ Muff	571	1977	49.95	800
1969	29" Mrs. Santa w/ Wired Cardholder Skirt	N/A	1969	18.95	250
1972	29" Mrs. Snow Woman w/ Cardholder Skirt	331	1972	19.95	700
1990	30" Clown	530	1990	99.95	350
1984	30" Santa in Chair w/ 2 18" Kids	940	1984	169.95	1200
1984	30" Snowgirl w/ Muff	685	1984	79.50	1000
1984	32" Monk w/ Grapes	416	1984	78.50	450
1959	33" Boy & Girl on Tandem Bike	N/A	1959	N/A	4500
1960	36" PJ Kid	N/A	1960	N/A	1200
1980	42" Clown	224	1980	74.95	700
1977	42" Scarecrow	365	1978	61.95	2050
1978	48" Mrs. Santa	151	1978	150.00	1450
1978	48" Santa	200	1978	150.00	1450
1986	48" Velour Santa	410	1988	269.95	750
1963	Baby Angel Head w/ Santa Hat	N/A	1963	1.00	350
1965	The Bang Hat (red)	N/A	1965	N/A	175
1963	Bath Puff (yellow)	N/A	1965	1.95	325
1968	Bunny Head Pin On	N/A	1968	1.00	400
1950	Cellist	N/A	N/A	N/A	5250
1976	Colonial Boy Head Pin On	N/A	1976	1.50	275
1976	Colonial Girl Head Pin On	N/A	1976	1.50	275
1972	Donkey Head Pin On	1,371	1972	1.00	300
1972	Elephant Head Pin On	1,384	1972	1.00	325
1962	Fur-Capped Baby on Cloud	N/A	1962	N/A	350
1961	Fur-Capped Head Pin-On	N/A	1962	1.00	225
1960	Head Pin	N/A	N/A	N/A	200
1968	Hippy Head (Boy)	N/A	1969	1.00	350
1968	Hippy Head (Girl)	N/A	1969	1.00	350
1960	Man Head Pin-on	N/A	N/A	N/A	800
1970	Monkey Head Pin-on (boy)	153	1973	1.00	275
1970	Monkey Head Pin-on (girl)	153	1973	1.00	275
1971	Monkey Head Pin-on (hot pink)	N/A	1971	1.00	450
1960	Mouse Head Pin-On	N/A	1976	1.00	250
1970	Mouse Pin	N/A	1970	1.45	150
1971	Snowman Head Pin-on	4,040	1972	1.00	200
1971	Snowman Kid	1,374	1971	3.95	450
1985	Tree Skirt	1,332	1985	24.95	350
1989	Two Bunnies on Flexible Flyer Sled	4,104	1990	52.95	325

ANRI

Disney Dolls - Disney Studios

YEAR ISSUE		EDITION LIMIT	YEAR RETD.	ISSUE PRICE	*QUOTE U.S. $
1990	Daisy Duck, 14"	2,500	1991	895.00	1250
1990	Donald Duck, 14"	2,500	1991	895.00	1250
1989	Mickey Mouse, 14"	2,500	1991	850.00	1000
1989	Minnie Mouse, 14"	2,500	1991	850.00	1000
1989	Pinocchio, 14"	2,500	1991	850.00	895

Ferrandiz Dolls - J. Ferrandiz

YEAR ISSUE		EDITION LIMIT	YEAR RETD.	ISSUE PRICE	*QUOTE U.S. $
1991	Carmen, 14"	1,000	1992	730.00	730
1991	Fernando, 14"	1,000	1992	730.00	730
1989	Gabriel, 14"	1,000	1991	550.00	575
1991	Juanita, 7"	1,500	1992	300.00	300
1990	Margarite, 14"	1,000	1992	575.00	730
1989	Maria, 14"	1,000	1991	550.00	575
1991	Miguel, 7"	1,500	1992	300.00	300
1990	Philipe, 14"	1,000	1992	575.00	680

Sarah Kay Dolls - S. Kay

YEAR ISSUE		EDITION LIMIT	YEAR RETD.	ISSUE PRICE	*QUOTE U.S. $
1991	Annie, 7"	1,500	1993	300.00	300
1989	Bride to Love And To Cherish	750	1992	750.00	790
1989	Charlotte (Blue)	1,000	1991	550.00	575
1990	Christina, 14"	1,000	1993	575.00	730
1989	Eleanor (Floral)	1,000	1991	550.00	575
1989	Elizabeth (Patchwork)	1,000	1991	550.00	575
1988	Emily, 14"	Closed	1989	500.00	500
1990	Faith, 14"	1,000	1993	575.00	685
1989	Groom With This Ring Doll, 14"	750	1992	550.00	730
1989	Helen (Brown), 14"	1,000	1991	550.00	575
1989	Henry, 14"	1,000	1991	550.00	575
1991	Janine, 14"	1,000	1993	750.00	750
1988	Jennifer, 14"	Closed	1989	500.00	500
1991	Jessica, 7"	1,500	1993	300.00	300
1991	Julie, 7"	1,500	1993	300.00	300
1988	Katherine, 14"	Closed	1989	500.00	500
1988	Martha, 14"	Closed	1989	500.00	500
1989	Mary (Red)	1,000	1991	550.00	575
1991	Michelle, 7"	1,500	1993	300.00	300
1991	Patricia, 14"	1,000	1993	730.00	730
1991	Peggy, 7"	1,500	1993	300.00	300
1990	Polly, 14"	1,000	1993	575.00	680
1988	Rachael, 14"	Closed	1989	500.00	500
1988	Rebecca, 14"	Closed	1989	500.00	500
1988	Sarah, 14"	Closed	1989	500.00	500
1990	Sophie, 14"	1,000	1993	575.00	660
1991	Susan, 7"	1,500	1993	300.00	300
1988	Victoria, 14"	Closed	1989	500.00	500

Ashton-Drake Galleries

All I Wish For You - Good-Krüger

YEAR ISSUE		EDITION LIMIT	YEAR RETD.	ISSUE PRICE	*QUOTE U.S. $
1994	I Wish You Love	Closed	1995	49.95	50
1995	I Wish You Faith	12/98		49.95	50
1995	I Wish You Happiness	12/98		49.95	50
1995	I Wish You Wisdom	12/98		49.95	50
1996	I Wish You Charity	12/99		49.95	50
1996	I Wish You Luck	12/99		49.95	50

America the Beautiful - Y. Bello

YEAR ISSUE		EDITION LIMIT	YEAR RETD.	ISSUE PRICE	*QUOTE U.S. $
1995	Billy	Closed	1996	49.95	50
1995	Bobby	Closed	1996	49.95	50

The American Dream - J. Kovacik

YEAR ISSUE		EDITION LIMIT	YEAR RETD.	ISSUE PRICE	*QUOTE U.S. $
1994	Patience	Closed	1995	79.95	80
1994	Hope	Closed	1995	79.95	80

Amish Blessings - J. Good-Krüger

YEAR ISSUE		EDITION LIMIT	YEAR RETD.	ISSUE PRICE	*QUOTE U.S. $
1990	Rebeccah	Closed	1993	68.00	125
1991	Rachel	Closed	1993	69.00	125
1991	Adam	Closed	1993	75.00	125-150
1992	Ruth	Closed	1993	75.00	110
1992	Eli	Closed	1993	79.95	95-125
1993	Sarah	Closed	1994	79.95	125

Amish Inspirations - J. Ibarolle

YEAR ISSUE		EDITION LIMIT	YEAR RETD.	ISSUE PRICE	*QUOTE U.S. $
1994	Ethan	Closed	1995	69.95	70
1994	Mary	Closed	1995	69.95	70
1995	Seth	Closed	1996	74.95	75
1995	Anna	Closed	1996	74.95	75

Anne of Green Gables - J. Kovacik

YEAR ISSUE		EDITION LIMIT	YEAR RETD.	ISSUE PRICE	*QUOTE U.S. $
1995	Anne	12/98		69.95	70
1996	Diana Barry	12/99		69.95	70
1996	Gilbert Blythe	12/00		69.95	70
1996	Josie Pye	12/00		69.95	70

As Cute As Can Be - D. Effner

YEAR ISSUE		EDITION LIMIT	YEAR RETD.	ISSUE PRICE	*QUOTE U.S. $
1993	Sugar Plum	Closed	1994	49.95	75-95
1994	Puppy Love	Closed	1995	49.95	75-95
1994	Angel Face	Closed	1995	49.95	50-75
1995	Patty Cake	12/98		49.95	50

Babies World of Wonder - K. Barry-Hippensteel

YEAR ISSUE		EDITION LIMIT	YEAR RETD.	ISSUE PRICE	*QUOTE U.S. $
1996	Andrew	12/99		59.95	60
1996	Sarah	12/00		59.95	60
1997	Jason	12/01		59.95	60

Baby Book Treasures - K. Barry-Hippensteel

YEAR ISSUE		EDITION LIMIT	YEAR RETD.	ISSUE PRICE	*QUOTE U.S. $
1990	Elizabeth's Homecoming	Closed	1993	58.00	58
1991	Catherine's Christening	Closed	1994	58.00	58
1991	Christopher's First Smile	Closed	1992	63.00	63

Baby Talk - Good-Krüger

YEAR ISSUE		EDITION LIMIT	YEAR RETD.	ISSUE PRICE	*QUOTE U.S. $
1994	All Gone	Closed	1995	49.95	75
1994	Bye-Bye	Closed	1995	49.95	50
1994	Night, Night	Closed	1995	49.95	50

Ballet Recital - P. Bomar

YEAR ISSUE		EDITION LIMIT	YEAR RETD.	ISSUE PRICE	*QUOTE U.S. $
1996	Chloe	12/00		69.95	70
1996	Kylie	12/00		69.95	70
1996	Heidi	12/00		69.95	70

Barely Yours - T. Tomescu

YEAR ISSUE		EDITION LIMIT	YEAR RETD.	ISSUE PRICE	*QUOTE U.S. $
1994	Cute as a Button	Closed	1994	69.95	75-95
1994	Snug as a Bug in a Rug	Closed	1995	75.00	75
1995	Clean as a Whistle	Closed	1996	75.00	75
1995	Pretty as a Picture	Closed	1996	75.00	75
1995	Good as Gold	Closed	1996	75.00	75
1996	Cool As A Cucumber	12/99		75.00	75

Beach Babies - C. Jackson

YEAR ISSUE		EDITION LIMIT	YEAR RETD.	ISSUE PRICE	*QUOTE U.S. $
1996	Carly	12/00		79.95	80
1996	Kyle	12/00		79.95	80

Beautiful Dreamers - G. Rademann

YEAR ISSUE		EDITION LIMIT	YEAR RETD.	ISSUE PRICE	*QUOTE U.S. $
1992	Katrina	Closed	1993	89.00	95-125
1992	Nicolette	Closed	1994	89.95	95
1993	Brigitte	Closed	1994	94.00	94
1993	Isabella	Closed	1994	94.00	94
1993	Gabrielle	Closed	1994	94.00	105

Blessed Are The Children - B. Deval

YEAR ISSUE		EDITION LIMIT	YEAR RETD.	ISSUE PRICE	*QUOTE U.S. $
1996	Blessed Are The Peacemakers	12/99		69.95	70
1996	Blessed Are The Pure of Heart	12/00		69.95	70

Born To Be Famous - K. Barry-Hippensteel

YEAR ISSUE		EDITION LIMIT	YEAR RETD.	ISSUE PRICE	*QUOTE U.S. $
1989	Little Sherlock	Closed	1991	87.00	90
1990	Little Florence Nightingale	Closed	1991	87.00	87-95
1991	Little Davey Crockett	Closed	1994	92.00	92
1992	Little Christopher Columbus	Closed	1993	95.00	95

Boys & Bears - A. Brown

YEAR ISSUE		EDITION LIMIT	YEAR RETD.	ISSUE PRICE	*QUOTE U.S. $
1996	Cody and Cuddle Bear	12/00		62.99	63

*Quotes have been rounded up to nearest dollar

Ashton-Drake Galleries
to Ashton-Drake Galleries

DOLLS

Calendar Babies - Ashton-Drake

YEAR	ISSUE	EDITION LIMIT	YEAR RETD.	ISSUE PRICE	*QUOTE U.S.$
1995	New Year	Open		24.95	25
1995	Cupid	Open		24.95	25
1995	Leprechaun	Open		24.95	25
1995	April Showers	Open		24.95	25
1995	May Flowers	Open		24.95	25
1995	June Bride	Open		24.95	25
1995	Uncle Sam	Open		24.95	25
1995	Sun & Fun	Open		24.95	25
1995	Back to School	Open		24.95	25
1995	Happy Haunting	Open		24.95	25
1995	Thanksgiving Turkey	Open		24.95	25
1995	Jolly Santa	Open		24.95	25

Caught In The Act - M. Tretter

YEAR	ISSUE	EDITION LIMIT	YEAR RETD.	ISSUE PRICE	*QUOTE U.S.$
1992	Stevie, Catch Me If You Can	Closed	1994	49.95	125-145
1993	Kelly, Don't I Look Pretty?	Closed	1994	49.95	75-95
1994	Mikey (Look It Floats)	Closed	1994	55.00	55
1994	Nickie (Cookie Jar)	Closed	1995	59.95	60
1994	Becky (Kleenex Box)	Closed	1995	59.95	60
1994	Sandy	Closed	1995	59.95	60

Children of Christmas - M. Sirko

YEAR	ISSUE	EDITION LIMIT	YEAR RETD.	ISSUE PRICE	*QUOTE U.S.$
1994	The Little Drummer Boy	Closed	1995	79.95	85
1994	The Littlest Angel	Closed	1995	79.95	80
1995	O Christmas Tree	12/98		79.95	80
1995	Sugar Plum Fairy	12/98		79.95	80

Children of Mother Goose - Y. Bello

YEAR	ISSUE	EDITION LIMIT	YEAR RETD.	ISSUE PRICE	*QUOTE U.S.$
1987	Little Bo Peep	Closed	1988	58.00	95-110
1987	Mary Had a Little Lamb	Closed	1989	58.00	110
1988	Little Jack Horner	Closed	1989	63.00	63
1989	Miss Muffet	Closed	1991	63.00	63

Children Of The Sun - M. Severino

YEAR	ISSUE	EDITION LIMIT	YEAR RETD.	ISSUE PRICE	*QUOTE U.S.$
1993	Little Flower	Closed	1994	69.95	75
1993	Desert Star	Closed	1995	69.95	70

A Children's Circus - J. McClelland

YEAR	ISSUE	EDITION LIMIT	YEAR RETD.	ISSUE PRICE	*QUOTE U.S.$
1990	Tommy The Clown	Closed	1993	78.00	78-85
1991	Katie The Tightrope Walker	Closed	1993	78.00	78
1991	Johnnie The Strongman	Closed	1994	83.00	83
1992	Maggie The Animal Trainer	Closed	1994	83.00	83

Christmas Memories - Y. Bello

YEAR	ISSUE	EDITION LIMIT	YEAR RETD.	ISSUE PRICE	*QUOTE U.S.$
1994	Christopher	Closed	1995	59.95	60
1994	Joshua	Closed	1995	59.95	60
1994	Stephanie	Closed	1995	59.95	60

Cindy's Playhouse Pals - C. McClure

YEAR	ISSUE	EDITION LIMIT	YEAR RETD.	ISSUE PRICE	*QUOTE U.S.$
1989	Meagan	Closed	1990	87.00	87
1989	Shelly	Closed	1993	87.00	87
1990	Ryan	Closed	1993	89.00	89
1991	Samantha	Closed	1993	89.00	89

Classic Brides of The Century - E. Williams

YEAR	ISSUE	EDITION LIMIT	YEAR RETD.	ISSUE PRICE	*QUOTE U.S.$
1990	Flora, The 1900s Bride	Closed	1993	145.00	145-195
1991	Jennifer, The 1980s Bride	Closed	1992	149.00	149-195
1993	Kathleen, The 1930s Bride	Closed	1993	149.95	150

Country Sweethearts - M. Tretter

YEAR	ISSUE	EDITION LIMIT	YEAR RETD.	ISSUE PRICE	*QUOTE U.S.$
1996	Millie	12/00		62.99	63

Cuddle Chums - K. Barry-Hippensteel

YEAR	ISSUE	EDITION LIMIT	YEAR RETD.	ISSUE PRICE	*QUOTE U.S.$
1995	Heather	12/98		59.95	60
1995	Jeffrey	12/98		59.95	60

Day in the Life of Emily Ann - A. Tsalkihn

YEAR	ISSUE	EDITION LIMIT	YEAR RETD.	ISSUE PRICE	*QUOTE U.S.$
1996	Breaktime	12/00		82.99	83

Days of the Week - K. Barry-Hippensteel

YEAR	ISSUE	EDITION LIMIT	YEAR RETD.	ISSUE PRICE	*QUOTE U.S.$
1994	Monday	Closed	1995	49.95	50
1995	Tuesday	Closed	1996	49.95	50
1995	Wednesday	Closed	1996	49.95	50
1995	Thursday	Closed	1996	49.95	50
1995	Friday	Closed	1996	49.95	50
1995	Saturday	Closed	1996	49.95	50
1995	Sunday	Closed	1996	49.95	50

Decorating The Tree - M. Tretter

YEAR	ISSUE	EDITION LIMIT	YEAR RETD.	ISSUE PRICE	*QUOTE U.S.$
1996	Trisha	12/00		59.95	60
1996	Patrick	12/00		59.95	60
1996	Ryan	12/00		59.95	60
1996	Melissa	12/00		59.95	60

Deval's Fairytale Princesses - B. Deval

YEAR	ISSUE	EDITION LIMIT	YEAR RETD.	ISSUE PRICE	*QUOTE U.S.$
1996	Cinderella	12/00		92.99	93
1996	Rapunzel	12/00		92.99	93

Dianna Effner's Classic Collection - D. Effner

YEAR	ISSUE	EDITION LIMIT	YEAR RETD.	ISSUE PRICE	*QUOTE U.S.$
1995	Hilary	12/98		79.95	80
1996	Willow	12/99		79.95	80
1996	Emily	12/00		79.95	80

Dianna Effner's Mother Goose - D. Effner

YEAR	ISSUE	EDITION LIMIT	YEAR RETD.	ISSUE PRICE	*QUOTE U.S.$
1990	Mary, Mary, Quite Contrary	Closed	1992	78.00	175-200
1991	The Little Girl With The Curl (Horrid)	Closed	1992	79.00	150-195
1991	The Little Girl With The Curl (Good)	Closed	1993	79.00	125
1992	Little Boy Blue	Closed	1993	85.00	85
1993	Snips & Snails	Closed	1994	85.00	145-200
1993	Sugar & Spice	Closed	1994	89.95	110-125
1993	Curly Locks	Closed	1995	89.95	95

Down The Garden Path - P. Coffer

YEAR	ISSUE	EDITION LIMIT	YEAR RETD.	ISSUE PRICE	*QUOTE U.S.$
1991	Rosemary	Closed	1994	79.00	79
1991	Angelica	Closed	1994	85.00	85

Elvis: Lifetime Of A Legend - L. Di Leo

YEAR	ISSUE	EDITION LIMIT	YEAR RETD.	ISSUE PRICE	*QUOTE U.S.$
1992	'68 Comeback Special	Closed	1994	99.95	100
1994	King of Las Vegas	Closed	1994	99.95	100

European Fairytales - G. Rademann

YEAR	ISSUE	EDITION LIMIT	YEAR RETD.	ISSUE PRICE	*QUOTE U.S.$
1994	Little Red Riding Hood	Closed	1995	79.95	80
1995	Snow White	Closed	1996	79.95	80

Family Ties - M. Tretter

YEAR	ISSUE	EDITION LIMIT	YEAR RETD.	ISSUE PRICE	*QUOTE U.S.$
1994	Welcome Home Baby Brother	Closed	1995	79.95	80
1995	Kiss and Make it Better	Closed	1996	89.95	90
1995	Happily Ever Better	Closed	1996	89.95	90

Flurry of Activity - T. Tomescu

YEAR	ISSUE	EDITION LIMIT	YEAR RETD.	ISSUE PRICE	*QUOTE U.S.$
1996	Making Snowflakes	12/00		72.99	73
1997	Making Icicles	12/01		72.99	73

From The Heart - T. Menzenbach

YEAR	ISSUE	EDITION LIMIT	YEAR RETD.	ISSUE PRICE	*QUOTE U.S.$
1992	Carolin	Closed	1994	79.95	80
1992	Erik	Closed	1994	79.95	80

From This Day Forward - P. Tumminio

YEAR	ISSUE	EDITION LIMIT	YEAR RETD.	ISSUE PRICE	*QUOTE U.S.$
1994	Elizabeth	Closed	1995	89.95	90
1995	Betty	Closed	1996	89.95	90
1995	Beth	Closed	1996	89.95	90
1995	Lisa	Closed	1996	89.95	90

Garden of Inspirations - B. Hanson

YEAR	ISSUE	EDITION LIMIT	YEAR RETD.	ISSUE PRICE	*QUOTE U.S.$
1994	Gathering Violets	Closed	1995	69.95	75
1994	Daisy Chain	Closed	1995	69.95	70
1995	Heart's Bouquet	Closed	1996	74.95	75
1995	Garden Prayer	Closed	1996	74.95	75

Gene - M. Odom

YEAR	ISSUE	EDITION LIMIT	YEAR RETD.	ISSUE PRICE	*QUOTE U.S.$
1995	Premiere	Closed	1996	69.95	95
1995	Red Venus	Closed	1996	69.95	70
1995	Monaco	Closed	1996	69.95	70

Gingham & Bows - S. Freeman

YEAR	ISSUE	EDITION LIMIT	YEAR RETD.	ISSUE PRICE	*QUOTE U.S.$
1995	Gwendolyn	12/98		69.95	70
1996	Mallory	12/99		69.95	70
1996	Ashleigh	12/00		69.95	70
1996	Bridget	12/00		69.95	70

God Hears the Children - B. Conner

YEAR	ISSUE	EDITION LIMIT	YEAR RETD.	ISSUE PRICE	*QUOTE U.S.$
1995	Now I Lay Me Down	12/98		79.95	80
1996	God Is Great, God Is Good	12/99		79.95	80
1996	We Give Thanks For Things We Have	12/99		79.95	80
1996	All Creatures Great & Small	12/00		79.95	80

Growing Up Like Wildflowers - B. Madeja

YEAR	ISSUE	EDITION LIMIT	YEAR RETD.	ISSUE PRICE	*QUOTE U.S.$
1996	Annie	12/99		49.95	50
1996	Bonnie	12/00		49.95	50

Happiness Is... - K. Barry-Hippensteel

YEAR	ISSUE	EDITION LIMIT	YEAR RETD.	ISSUE PRICE	*QUOTE U.S.$
1991	Patricia (My First Tooth)	Closed	1993	69.00	95-125
1992	Crystal (Feeding Myself)	Closed	1994	69.95	100
1993	Brittany (Blowing Kisses)	Closed	1993	69.95	100
1993	Joy (My First Christmas)	Closed	1993	69.95	70-85
1994	Candy Cane (Holly)	Closed	1994	69.95	70
1994	Patrick (My First Playmate)	Closed	1994	69.95	70-85

Happy Thoughts - K. Barry-Hippensteel

YEAR	ISSUE	EDITION LIMIT	YEAR RETD.	ISSUE PRICE	*QUOTE U.S.$
1994	Laughter is the Best Medicine	Closed	1995	59.95	60

Heavenly Inspirations - C. McClure

YEAR	ISSUE	EDITION LIMIT	YEAR RETD.	ISSUE PRICE	*QUOTE U.S.$
1992	Every Cloud Has a Silver Lining	Closed	1994	59.95	75
1993	Wish Upon A Star	Closed	1994	59.95	60
1994	Sweet Dreams	Closed	1994	65.00	65
1994	Luck at the End of Rainbow	Closed	1994	65.00	65
1994	Sunshine	Closed	1994	69.95	70
1994	Pennies From Heaven	Closed	1995	69.95	70

Heritage of American Quilting - J. Lundy

YEAR	ISSUE	EDITION LIMIT	YEAR RETD.	ISSUE PRICE	*QUOTE U.S.$
1994	Eleanor	Closed	1995	79.95	80
1995	Abigail	Closed	1996	79.95	80
1995	Louisa	Closed	1996	84.95	85
1995	Ruth Anne	Closed	1996	84.95	85

Heroines from the Fairy Tale Forests - D. Effner

YEAR	ISSUE	EDITION LIMIT	YEAR RETD.	ISSUE PRICE	*QUOTE U.S.$
1988	Little Red Riding Hood	Closed	1990	68.00	200
1989	Goldilocks	Closed	1991	68.00	75
1990	Snow White	Closed	1992	73.00	175
1991	Rapunzel	Closed	1993	79.00	175-225
1992	Cinderella	Closed	1993	79.00	150-200
1993	Cinderella (Ballgown)	Closed	1994	79.95	150-200

How Little Was I? - S. Bryer

YEAR	ISSUE	EDITION LIMIT	YEAR RETD.	ISSUE PRICE	*QUOTE U.S.$
1995	Brittany	Closed	1996	59.95	60

I Want Mommy - K. Barry-Hippensteel

YEAR	ISSUE	EDITION LIMIT	YEAR RETD.	ISSUE PRICE	*QUOTE U.S.$
1993	Timmy (Mommy I'm Sleepy)	Closed	1994	59.95	145
1993	Tommy (Mommy I'm Sorry)	Closed	1994	59.95	125
1994	Up Mommy (Tammy)	Closed	1994	65.00	65

I'm Just Little - K. Barry-Hippensteel

YEAR	ISSUE	EDITION LIMIT	YEAR RETD.	ISSUE PRICE	*QUOTE U.S.$
1995	I'm a Little Angel	Closed	1996	49.95	50
1995	I'm a Little Devil	Closed	1996	49.95	50
1996	I'm a Little Cutie	12/99		49.95	50

International Festival of Toys and Tots - K. Barry-Hippensteel

YEAR	ISSUE	EDITION LIMIT	YEAR RETD.	ISSUE PRICE	*QUOTE U.S.$
1989	Chen, a Little Boy of China	Closed	1990	78.00	85-150
1989	Natasha	Closed	1992	78.00	80-95
1990	Molly	Closed	1993	83.00	83
1991	Hans	Closed	1993	88.00	88
1992	Miki, Eskimo	Closed	1994	88.00	88

Joy Forever - C. McClure

YEAR	ISSUE	EDITION LIMIT	YEAR RETD.	ISSUE PRICE	*QUOTE U.S.$
1996	Victorian Serenity	12/00		129.95	130
1997	Victorian Bliss	12/01		129.95	130

Joys of Summer - K. Barry-Hippensteel

YEAR	ISSUE	EDITION LIMIT	YEAR RETD.	ISSUE PRICE	*QUOTE U.S.$
1993	Tickles	Closed	1994	49.95	110-120
1993	Little Squirt	Closed	1994	49.95	65
1994	Yummy	Closed	1994	55.00	65
1994	Havin' A Ball	Closed	1994	55.00	65
1994	Lil' Scoop	Closed	1994	55.00	65

Just Caught Napping - A. Brown

YEAR	ISSUE	EDITION LIMIT	YEAR RETD.	ISSUE PRICE	*QUOTE U.S.$
1996	Asleep in the Saddle	12/99		69.95	70
1996	Oatmeal Dreams	12/00		69.95	70
1997	Dog Tired	12/01		69.95	70

The King & I - P.Ryan Brooks

YEAR	ISSUE	EDITION LIMIT	YEAR RETD.	ISSUE PRICE	*QUOTE U.S.$
1991	Shall We Dance	Closed	1992	175.00	200-395

Lasting Traditions - W. Hanson

YEAR	ISSUE	EDITION LIMIT	YEAR RETD.	ISSUE PRICE	*QUOTE U.S.$
1993	Something Old	Closed	1993	69.95	70
1994	Finishing Touch	Closed	1994	69.95	70
1994	Mother's Pearls	Closed	1994	85.00	85
1994	Her Traditional Garter	Closed	1995	85.00	85

Lawton's Nursery Rhymes - W. Lawton

YEAR	ISSUE	EDITION LIMIT	YEAR RETD.	ISSUE PRICE	*QUOTE U.S.$
1994	Little Bo Peep	Closed	1995	79.95	80-95
1994	Little Miss Muffet	Closed	1995	79.95	80
1994	Mary, Mary	Closed	1995	85.00	85
1994	Mary/Lamb	Closed	1995	85.00	85

The Legends of Baseball - Various

YEAR	ISSUE	EDITION LIMIT	YEAR RETD.	ISSUE PRICE	*QUOTE U.S.$
1994	Babe Ruth - T. Tomescu	Closed	1995	79.95	80-110
1994	Lou Gehrig - T. Tomescu	Closed	1995	79.95	80
1995	Ty Cobb - E. Shelton	Closed	1996	79.95	80

Let's Play Mother Goose - K. Barry-Hippensteel

YEAR	ISSUE	EDITION LIMIT	YEAR RETD.	ISSUE PRICE	*QUOTE U.S.$
1994	Cow Jumped Over the Moon	Closed	1995	69.95	70
1994	Hickory, Dickory, Dock	Closed	1995	69.95	95

Little Bits - G. Rademan

YEAR	ISSUE	EDITION LIMIT	YEAR RETD.	ISSUE PRICE	*QUOTE U.S.$
1993	Lil Bit of Sunshine	Closed	1993	39.95	45
1993	Lil Bit of Love	Closed	1994	39.95	40
1994	Lil Bit of Tenderness	Closed	1994	39.95	40
1994	Lil Bit of Innocence	Closed	1994	39.95	40

Little Girls of Classic Literature - W. Lawton

YEAR	ISSUE	EDITION LIMIT	YEAR RETD.	ISSUE PRICE	*QUOTE U.S.$
1995	Pollyanna	12/98		79.95	80
1996	Laura Ingalls	12/99		79.95	80
1996	Rebecca of Sunnybrook Farm	12/99		79.95	80

Little Gymnast - K. Barry-Hippensteel

YEAR	ISSUE	EDITION LIMIT	YEAR RETD.	ISSUE PRICE	*QUOTE U.S.$
1996	Little Gymnast	12/99		59.95	60

Little Handfuls - M. Severino

YEAR	ISSUE	EDITION LIMIT	YEAR RETD.	ISSUE PRICE	*QUOTE U.S.$
1993	Ricky	Closed	1994	39.95	40
1993	Abby	Closed	1995	39.95	40
1993	Josie	Closed	1995	39.95	40

Little House On The Prairie - J. Ibarolle

YEAR	ISSUE	EDITION LIMIT	YEAR RETD.	ISSUE PRICE	*QUOTE U.S.$
1992	Laura	Closed	1993	79.95	95
1993	Mary Ingalls	Closed	1993	79.95	300-395
1993	Nellie Olson	Closed	1994	85.00	145
1993	Almanzo	Closed	1994	85.00	95
1994	Carrie	Closed	1994	85.00	95
1994	Ma Ingalls	Closed	1995	85.00	85
1994	Pa Ingalls	Closed	1995	85.00	85
1995	Baby Grace	Closed	1996	69.95	70

Little Lacy Sleepyheads - J. Wolf

YEAR	ISSUE	EDITION LIMIT	YEAR RETD.	ISSUE PRICE	*QUOTE U.S.$
1996	Jacqueline	12/00		99.99	100

Little Women - W. Lawton

YEAR	ISSUE	EDITION LIMIT	YEAR RETD.	ISSUE PRICE	*QUOTE U.S.$
1994	Jo	Closed	1995	59.95	60
1994	Meg	Closed	1995	59.95	60
1994	Beth	Closed	1996	59.95	60
1994	Amy	Closed	1996	59.95	60
1995	Marmie	Closed	1996	59.95	60

Look At Me - L. Di Leo

YEAR	ISSUE	EDITION LIMIT	YEAR RETD.	ISSUE PRICE	*QUOTE U.S.$
1993	Rose Marie	Closed	1994	49.95	50
1994	Ann Marie	Closed	1994	49.95	50
1994	Lisa Marie	Closed	1995	55.00	55

*Quotes have been rounded up to nearest dollar

DOLLS

Ashton-Drake Galleries to Ashton-Drake Galleries

YEAR ISSUE	EDITION LIMIT	YEAR RETD.	ISSUE PRICE	*QUOTE U.S. $
Lots Of Love - T. Menzenbach				
1993 Hannah Needs A Hug	Closed	1994	49.95	100
1993 Kaitlyn	Closed	1994	49.95	95
1994 Nicole	Closed	1995	55.00	55
1995 Felicia	12/98		55.00	55
Lucky Charmers - C. McClure				
1995 Lucky Star	12/98		69.95	70
1996 Bit O' Luck	12/00		69.95	70
Madonna & Child - B. Deval				
1996 Madonna & Child	12/99		99.95	100
Magic Moments - K. Barry-Hippensteel				
1996 Birthday Boy	12/99		69.95	70
Magical Moments of Summer - Y. Bello				
1995 Whitney	12/98		59.95	60
1996 Zoe	12/99		59.95	60
Mainstreet Saturday Morning - M. Tretter				
1994 Kenny	Closed	1995	69.95	70
1995 Betty	Closed	1996	69.95	70
1995 Donny	Closed	1996	69.95	70
Memories of Yesterday - M. Attwell				
1994 A Friend in Need	Closed	1995	59.95	60-75
1994 Tomorrow is Another Day	Closed	1996	59.95	60
1995 Beauty is in the Eye of the Beholder	Closed	1996	59.95	60
Messages of Hope - T. Tomescu				
1994 Let the Little Children Come to Me	Closed	1995	129.95	130
1995 Good Shepherd	Closed	1996	129.95	130
1995 I Stand at the Door	Closed	1996	129.95	130
1996 Our Father	12/99		129.95	130
Miracle of Life - Y. Bello				
1996 Beautiful Newborn	12/99		49.95	50
1996 Her Very First Smile	12/00		49.95	50
1996 She's Sitting Pretty	12/00		49.95	50
1996 Watch Her Crawl	12/00		49.95	50
Miracles of Jesus - T. Tomescu				
1996 Water Into Wine	12/00		99.95	100
1996 Multiplying the Loaves	12/00		99.95	100
1997 Walking on Water	12/01		99.95	100
Moments To Remember - Y. Bello				
1991 Justin	Closed	1994	75.00	75-85
1992 Jill	Closed	1993	75.00	75-85
1993 Brandon (Ring Bearer)	Closed	1994	79.95	80-90
1993 Suzanne (Flower Girl)	Closed	1994	79.95	80-90
Morning Glories - B. Bambina				
1996 Rosebud	12/00		49.95	50
1996 Dew Drop	12/00		49.95	50
A Mother's Work Is Never Done - T. Menzenbach				
1995 Don't Forget To Wash Behind Your Ears	12/98		59.95	60
1996 A Kiss Will Make It Better	12/99		59.95	60
1996 Who Made This Mess	12/99		59.95	60
My Closest Friend - J. Goodyear				
1991 Boo Bear 'N Me	Closed	1992	78.00	125-135
1991 Me and My Blankie	Closed	1993	79.00	95
1992 My Secret Pal (Robbie)	Closed	1993	85.00	85
1992 My Beary Best Friend	Closed	1993	79.95	85
My Fair Lady - P. Ryan Brooks				
1991 Eliza at Ascot	Closed	1992	125.00	395
My Heart Belongs To Daddy - J. Singer				
1992 Peanut	Closed	1994	49.95	95
1992 Pumpkin	Closed	1994	49.95	60
1994 Princess	Closed	1994	59.95	60
My Little Ballerina - K. Barry-Hippensteel				
1994 My Little Ballerina	Closed	1995	59.95	60
Nostalgic Toys - C. McClure				
1996 Amelia	12/00		79.95	80
1996 Charlotte	12/00		79.95	80
Nursery Newborns - J. Wolf				
1994 It's A Boy	Closed	1995	79.95	80
1994 It's A Girl	Closed	1995	79.95	80
Oh Holy Night - Good-Krüger				
1994 The Holy Family (Jesus, Mary, Joseph)	Closed	1995	129.95	130
1995 The Kneeling King	Closed	1996	59.95	60
1995 The Purple King	Closed	1996	59.95	60
1995 The Blue King	Closed	1996	59.95	60
1995 Shepherd with Pipes	Closed	1996	59.95	60
1995 Shepherd with Lamb	Closed	1996	59.95	60
1995 Angel	Closed	1996	59.95	60
Only At Grandma and Grandpa's - Y. Bello				
1996 I'll Finish The Story	12/99		89.95	90
Our Own Ballet Recital - P. Bomar				
1996 Chloe	12/99		69.95	70
Passports to Friendship - J. Ibarolle				
1995 Serena	12/98		79.95	80
1996 Kali	12/99		79.95	80
1996 Asha	12/99		79.95	80
1996 Liliana	12/00		79.95	80
Patchwork of Love - Good-Krüger				
1995 Warmth of the Heart	12/98		59.95	60
1996 Love One Another	12/99		59.95	60
1996 Family Price	12/99		59.95	60
1996 Simplicity Is Best	12/99		59.95	60
1996 Fondest Memory	12/99		59.95	60
1996 Hard Work Pays	12/99		59.95	60
Perfect Pairs - B. Bambina				
1995 Amber	Closed	1996	59.95	60
1995 Tiffany	Closed	1996	59.95	60
1995 Carmen	Closed	1996	59.95	60
1996 Susie	12/99		59.95	60
Petting Zoo - Y. Bello				
1995 Andy	Closed	1996	59.95	60
1995 Kendra	Closed	1996	59.95	60
1995 Cory	Closed	1996	59.95	60
1995 Maddie	Closed	1996	59.95	60
Polly's Tea Party - S. Krey				
1990 Polly	Closed	1992	78.00	125
1991 Lizzie	Closed	1992	79.00	79
1992 Annie	Closed	1993	83.00	83
Potpourri Babies - A. Brown				
1995 Bubble Trouble	12/98		79.95	80
Precious Memories of Motherhood - S. Kuck				
1989 Loving Steps	Closed	1991	125.00	125-150
1990 Lullaby	Closed	1993	125.00	125
1991 Expectant Moments	Closed	1993	149.00	150
1992 Bedtime	Closed	1993	150.00	150
Precious Papooses - S. Housely				
1995 Sleeping Bear	12/98		79.95	80
1996 Bright Feather	12/99		79.95	80
1996 Cloud Chaser	12/00		79.95	80
1996 Swift Fox	12/00		79.95	80
Pretty in Pastels - J. Goodyear				
1994 Precious in Pink	Closed	1995	79.95	80
Rainbow of Love - Y. Bello				
1994 Blue Sky	Closed	1995	59.95	60
1994 Yellow Sunshine	Closed	1995	59.95	60
1994 Green Earth	Closed	1995	59.95	60
1994 Pink Flower	Closed	1996	59.95	60
1994 Purple Mountain	Closed	1995	59.95	60
1994 Orange Sunset	Closed	1995	59.95	60
Secret Garden - J. Kovacik				
1994 Mary	Closed	1995	69.95	70
1995 Colin	Closed	1996	69.95	70
1995 Martha	Closed	1996	69.95	70
1995 Dickon	Closed	1996	69.95	70
A Sense of Discovery - K. Barry-Hippensteel				
1993 Sweetie (Sense of Discovery)	Closed	1994	59.95	60
Sense of Security - G. Rademann				
1996 Amy	12/00		62.99	63
She Walks in Beauty - S. Bilotto				
1996 Winter Romance	12/00		92.99	93
Siblings Through Time - C. McClure				
1995 Alexandra	Closed	1996	69.95	70
1995 Gracie	Closed	1996	59.95	60
Simple Gifts - Good-Krüger				
1996 Roly Poly Harvest	12/99		49.95	50
Simple Pleasures, Special Days - J. Lundy				
1996 Gretchen	12/99		79.95	80
1996 Molly	12/99		79.95	80
1996 Adeline	12/00		79.95	80
1996 Eliza	12/00		79.95	80
Snow Babies - T. Tomescu				
1995 Beneath the Mistletoe	Closed	1995	69.95	70
1995 Follow the Leader	Closed	1996	75.00	75
1995 Snow Baby Express	Closed	1996	75.00	75
1996 Slip Slidin'	12/00		75.00	75
1996 Learning To Fly	12/00		75.00	75
1996 Catch of the Day	12/00		75.00	75
Someone to Watch Over Me - K. Barry-Hippensteel				
1994 Sweet Dreams	Closed	1995	69.95	70
Night-Night Angel				
1995 Night-Night Angel	Closed	1995	24.95	25
1995 Lullaby Angel	Closed	1996	24.95	25
1995 Sleepyhead Angel	Closed	1996	24.95	25
1995 Stardust Angel	Closed	1996	24.95	25
1995 Tuck-Me-In Angel	Closed	1996	24.95	25
Sooo Big - M. Tretter				
1993 Jimmy	Closed	1994	59.95	60
1994 Kimmy	Closed	1995	59.95	60
Special Edition Tour 1993 - Y. Bello				
1993 Miguel	Closed	1993	69.95	70
1993 Rosa	Closed	1993	69.95	70
Tender Moments - L. Tierney				
1995 Tender Love	Closed	1995	49.95	50
1995 Tender Heart	Closed	1996	49.95	50
1995 Tender Care	Closed	1996	49.95	50
Together Forever - S. Krey				
1994 Kirsten	Closed	1995	59.95	60
1994 Courtney	Closed	1995	59.95	60
1994 Kim	Closed	1995	59.95	60
Treasured Togetherness - M. Tretter				
1994 Tender Touch	Closed	1995	99.95	100
1994 Touch of Love	Closed	1995	99.95	100
Tumbling Tots - K. Barry-Hippensteel				
1993 Roly Poly Polly	Closed	1994	69.95	70
1994 Handstand Harry	Closed	1995	69.95	70
Two Much To Handle - K. Barry-Hippensteel				
1993 Julie (Flowers For Mommy)	Closed	1994	59.95	60
1993 Kevin (Clean Hands)	Closed	1995	59.95	145
Under Her Wings - P. Bomar				
1995 Guardian Angel	12/98		79.95	80
Victorian Dreamers - K. Barry-Hippensteel				
1995 Rock-A-Bye/Good Night	Closed	1996	49.95	50
1995 Victorian Storytime	Closed	1996	49.95	50
Victorian Lace - C. Layton				
1993 Alicia	Closed	1994	79.95	125
1994 Colleen	Closed	1995	70.00	85
1994 Olivia	Closed	1995	79.95	80
Victorian Nursery Heirloom - C. McClure				
1994 Victorian Lullaby	Closed	1995	129.95	130
1995 Victorian Highchair	Closed	1996	129.95	130
1995 Victorian Playtime	Closed	1996	139.95	140
1995 Victorian Bunny Buggy	Closed	1996	139.95	140
Visions Of Our Lady - B. Deval				
1996 Our Lady of Grace	12/99		99.95	100
1996 Our Lady of Lourdes	12/00		99.95	100
What Little Girls Are Made Of - D. Effner				
1994 Peaches and Cream	Closed	1995	69.95	80-130
1995 Lavender & Lace	12/98		69.95	70
1995 Sunshine & Lollipops	12/98		69.95	70
Where Do Babies Come From - T. Tomescu				
1996 Special Delivery	12/99		79.95	80
1996 Fresh From The Patch	12/00		79.95	80
1996 Just Hatched	12/00		79.95	80
Winter Wonderland - K. Barry-Hippensteel				
1994 Annie	Closed	1995	59.95	60
1994 Bobby	Closed	1995	59.95	60
The Wonderful Wizard of Oz - M. Tretter				
1994 Dorothy	Closed	1995	79.95	80
1994 Scarecrow	Closed	1995	79.95	80
1994 Tin Man	Closed	1995	79.95	80
1994 The Cowardly Lion	Closed	1996	79.95	80
Wreathed in Beauty - G. Rademann				
1996 Winter Elegance	12/00		89.95	90
Year Book Memories - Akers/Girardi				
1991 Peggy Sue	Closed	1992	87.00	95
1993 Going Steady (Patty Jo)	Closed	1994	89.95	90
1993 Prom Queen (Betty Jean)	Closed	1993	92.00	92
Yolanda's Heaven Scent Babies - Y. Bello				
1993 Meagan Rose	Closed	1994	49.95	80-95
1993 Daisy Anne	Closed	1995	49.95	50
1993 Morning Glory	Closed	1995	49.95	50
1993 Sweet Carnation	Closed	1995	54.95	55
1993 Lily	Closed	1995	54.95	55
1993 Cherry Blossom	Closed	1995	54.95	55
Yolanda's Lullaby Babies - Y. Bello				
1991 Christy (Rock-a-Bye)	Closed	1993	69.00	75-105
1992 Joey (Twinkle, Twinkle)	Closed	1994	69.00	75
1993 Amy (Brahms Lullaby)	Closed	1994	75.00	75
1993 Eddie (Teddy Bear Lullaby)	Closed	1994	75.00	75
1993 Jacob (Silent Night)	Closed	1994	75.00	75

*Quotes have been rounded up to nearest dollar

Year	Issue	Edition Limit	Year Retd.	Issue Price	*Quote U.S.$
1994	Bonnie (You Are My Sunshine)	Closed	1994	80.00	80

Yolanda's Picture - Perfect Babies - Y. Bello

Year	Issue	Edition Limit	Year Retd.	Issue Price	*Quote U.S.$
1985	Jason	Closed	1988	48.00	700
1986	Heather	Closed	1988	48.00	225-250
1987	Jennifer	Closed	1989	58.00	225-250
1987	Matthew	Closed	1990	58.00	150-195
1987	Sarah	Closed	1990	58.00	95-125
1988	Amanda	Closed	1990	63.00	125
1989	Jessica	Closed	1993	63.00	95
1990	Michael	Closed	1992	63.00	125
1990	Lisa	Closed	1992	63.00	95-110
1991	Emily	Closed	1992	63.00	110
1991	Danielle	Closed	1993	69.00	125

Yolanda's Playtime Babies - Y. Bello

Year	Issue	Edition Limit	Year Retd.	Issue Price	*Quote U.S.$
1993	Lindsey	Closed	1994	59.95	65
1993	Shawna	Closed	1994	59.95	60

Yolanda's Pli'maytime Babies - Y. Bello

Year	Issue	Edition Limit	Year Retd.	Issue Price	*Quote U.S.$
1993	Todd	Closed	1994	59.95	60

Yolanda's Precious Playmates - Y. Bello

Year	Issue	Edition Limit	Year Retd.	Issue Price	*Quote U.S.$
1992	David	Closed	1994	69.95	125
1993	Paul	Closed	1994	69.95	125
1994	Johnny	Closed	1994	69.95	70

Attic Babies

Attic Babies' Collector Club - M. Maschino-Walker

Year	Issue	Edition Limit	Year Retd.	Issue Price	*Quote U.S.$
1992	Burtie Buzbee, SNL	Retrd.	1992	40.00	40
1993	Izzie B. Ruebottom, SNL	277	1993	35.00	35
1994	Sunflower Flossie, SNL	Retrd.	1994	42.00	80
1995	Tricia Kay Yum-Yum, SNL	Retrd.	1995	40.00	50
1996	Baby Savannah, SNL	Retrd.	1996	39.95	40
1997	Fertile Mertle	Yr.Iss.		64.95	65
1997	Optional Bookend Stand	Yr.Iss.		14.95	15

Baggie Collection - M. Maschino-Walker

Year	Issue	Edition Limit	Year Retd.	Issue Price	*Quote U.S.$
1991	Americana Baggie Bear	Retrd.	1994	19.95	22
1991	Americana Baggie Girl	Retrd.	1994	19.95	22
1991	Americana Baggie Rabbit	Retrd.	1994	19.95	22
1991	Americana Baggie Santa	Retrd.	1994	19.95	22
1991	Christmas Baggie Bear	Retrd.	1994	19.95	22
1991	Christmas Baggie Girl	Retrd.	1994	19.95	22
1991	Christmas Baggie Rabbit	Retrd.	1994	19.95	22
1991	Christmas Baggie Santa	Retrd.	1994	19.95	22
1991	Country Baggie Bear	Retrd.	1994	19.95	22
1991	Country Baggie Girl	Retrd.	1994	19.95	22
1991	Country Baggie Rabbit	Retrd.	1994	19.95	22

Mother's Day Angels - M. Maschino-Walker

Year	Issue	Edition Limit	Year Retd.	Issue Price	*Quote U.S.$
1994	Nattie Fae Tucker, SNL	757	1994	64.95	65

Retired Dolls - M. Maschino-Walker

Year	Issue	Edition Limit	Year Retd.	Issue Price	*Quote U.S.$
1994	Abner Abernathy	Retrd.	1995	55.95	75-90
1994	Addie Abernathy	Retrd.	1995	61.95	75-95
1992	Americana Raggedy Santa (1st ed.), SNL	Retrd.	1992	85.95	150
1992	Americana Raggedy Santa (2nd ed.), SNL	Retrd.	1992	89.95	90
1989	Annie Fannie	Retrd.	1992	43.95	70-110
1987	Annie Lee	Retrd.	1996	50.00	50
1990	Anniversary Couple	Retrd.	1996	138.00	138
1992	Artilma Hunnicut	Retrd.	1995	73.95	74
1992	Augie Whippermeyer	Retrd.	1996	66.00	66
1990	Beary Harriete Bear	Retrd.	1995	87.95	88
1990	Beary Harry Bear	Retrd.	1995	87.95	88
1987	Bessie Jo	Retrd.	1989	31.95	98
1987	Beth Sue	Retrd.	1991	27.95	75
1988	Bootsie Wootsie Angel	Retrd.	1996	44.00	44
1989	Bouncing Baby Roy	Retrd.	1995	49.95	65
1991	Buffy Muffy	Retrd.	1996	60.00	60
1988	Bunnifer	Retrd.	1990	39.95	100-160
1988	Buttons	Retrd.	1991	27.95	28
1992	Candy Applebee	Retrd.	1994	15.95	18
1992	Christopher Columbus SNL	Retrd.	1992	79.95	200-250
1989	Cloddy Clyde	Retrd.	1995	69.95	70-140
1989	Cotton Pickin' Ninny	Retrd.	1992	47.95	100
1987	Country Clyde	Retrd.	1988	27.95	28
1992	Daddy's Lil Punkin Patty, SNL	Retrd.	1993	79.95	175
1992	Darcie Duckworth	Retrd.	1995	59.95	60
1987	Dirty Harry	Retrd.	1991	27.95	55-100
1994	Dollie Boots (1st ed.)	100	1994	79.95	300-395
1995	Dollie Boots (2nd ed.)	2,000	1995	84.95	85
1992	Dotin' Dodie	Retrd.	1996	66.00	66
1990	Duckie Dinkle	Retrd.	1991	95.95	96
1992	Durwin Duckworth	Retrd.	1995	59.95	60
1988	Fatty Matty	Retrd.	1996	50.00	50
1988	Fertile Mertle	Retrd.	1996	50.00	50
1988	Fester Chester	Retrd.	1994	39.95	75-100
1989	Flakey Jakey	Retrd.	1995	59.95	76
1989	Flopsy Mopsy	Retrd.	1996	70.00	70
1990	Frannie Farkle	Retrd.	1991	129.95	130
1990	Frizzy Lizzy	Retrd.	1992	95.95	250
1995	Fuzzy Sweezy (1st ed.)	2,000	1995	77.95	78
1990	Gabbie Abbie	Retrd.	1995	109.95	110
1988	Grandpappy Burtie	Retrd.	1996	50.00	75-100
1988	Granny Grunt	Retrd.	1996	50.00	50
1992	Hadden Hobnobber	Retrd.	1996	66.00	66
1988	Hannah Lou	Retrd.	1994	39.95	50
1990	Happy Huck	Retrd.	1992	47.95	102
1993	Happy Pappy Claus SNL	805	1994	73.95	100-135
1987	Harold	Retrd.	1990	27.95	80
1989	Harvey Hog	Retrd.	1996	60.00	60
1995	Hazel Lynora Grimsley	2,000	1995	68.95	69
1989	Heavenly Heather	Retrd.	1992	59.95	100
1988	Heffy Cheffy	Retrd.	1994	75.95	125
1992	Hillary Hobnobber	Retrd.	1996	66.00	66
1990	Homer Hare	Retrd.	1995	147.95	225
1990	Hunnie Bunnie	Retrd.	1995	147.95	148
1989	Itsy Bitsy Mitzy	Retrd.	1995	49.95	50
1993	Itty Bitty Santa	Retrd.	1993	5.95	6
1990	Ivan Ivie	Retrd.	1991	129.95	230
1987	Jacob	Retrd.	1988	27.95	100
1993	Jammy Mammy Claus SNL	653	1994	67.95	85
1987	Jenny Lou	Retrd.	1992	35.95	36
1992	Jessabell	Retrd.	1996	40.00	40
1989	Jingle Jangle Jo	Retrd.	1995	69.95	86
1990	Johnathan Poo Bear	Retrd.	1996	148.00	148
1989	Jolly Jim	Retrd.	1992	31.95	32
1990	Josie Posie Poo Bear	Retrd.	1996	148.00	148
1990	Jumpin Pumkin Jill	Retrd.	1994	55.95	56
1988	Katy	Retrd.	1995	59.95	60
1990	Lampsie Divie Ivie	Retrd.	1991	129.95	285
1995	Lani Frumpet (1st ed.)	2,000	1995	56.95	57
1988	Lazy Daisy	Retrd.	1992	39.95	60
1988	Lazy Liza Jane	Retrd.	1991	47.95	48
1995	Lily Lumpbucket	2,000	1995	61.95	62
1988	Little Dove	Retrd.	1988	39.95	40
1994	Lollie Ann	Retrd.	1994	39.95	75
1987	Maggie Mae	Retrd.	1991	25.95	28
1991	Maizie Mae	Retrd.	1994	51.95	52
1991	Mandi Mae	Retrd.	1994	51.95	52
1991	Memsie Mae	Retrd.	1994	51.95	52
1993	Merry Beary Raggady Santy	1,000	1995	113.95	115-150
1994	Merry Ole Farley Fagan Dooberry, SNL	Retrd.	1994	131.95	200
1987	Messy Tessy	Retrd.	1995	43.95	44
1993	Millie Wilset	2,000	1994	39.95	40
1987	Miss Pitty Pat	Retrd.	1988	27.95	100
1988	Molly Bea	Retrd.	1990	39.95	45-80
1995	Monty Thumpet	2,000	1995	56.95	57
1988	Moosey Matilda	Retrd.	1990	39.95	150-300
1989	Mr. Gardner	Retrd.	1995	109.95	110
1993	Mr. Kno Mo Sno, SNL	1,800	1994	51.95	68
1991	Mr. Raggedy Claus, SNL	Retrd.	1992	69.95	85
1989	Mrs. Gardner	Retrd.	1995	109.95	110
1991	Mrs. Raggedy Claus, SNL	Retrd.	1992	69.95	85
1989	Ms. Waddles	Retrd.	1990	47.95	48
1987	Muslin Bunny	Retrd.	1993	7.95	8
1987	Muslin Teddy	Retrd.	1993	7.95	8
1987	Nasty Cathy	Retrd.	1996	50.00	50
1988	Nathan	Retrd.	1995	59.95	60
1988	Naughty Nellie	Retrd.	1990	31.95	85
1990	Nerdie Nelda	Retrd.	1995	69.95	140
1988	Ninny Nanny	Retrd.	1996	56.00	56
1992	Norville Newton	Retrd.	1996	66.00	66
1994	Old Raggady Noah	2,500	1995	73.95	80-150
1993	Old St. Knickerbocker, SNL	Retrd.	1993	79.95	80
1992	Old St. Nick, SNL	Retrd.	1993	95.95	130
1989	Old Tyme Santy	Retrd.	1989	79.95	80
1995	Pea Pod Sweezy (1st ed.)	2,000	1995	74.95	75
1990	Pearly Rose	Retrd.	1996	110.00	110
1990	Phylbert Farkle	Retrd.	1991	129.95	225
1991	Pippy Pat	Retrd.	1994	47.95	52
1988	Prissy Missy	Retrd.	1990	31.95	32
1987	Rachel	Retrd.	1988	29.95	85
1995	Raggady Cornell G. Hockenberry w/Workbench,set	Retrd.	1996	104.00	130
1995	Raggady Cornell G. Hockenberry Workbench	Retrd.	1996	38.00	38
1995	Raggady Cornell G. Hockenberry, SNL	Retrd.	1996	66.00	66
1987	Raggady Kitty	Retrd.	1988	29.95	30
1995	Raggady Old Wooly Tackitt	2,000	1995	46.95	47
1990	Raggady Ole Chris Cringle (1st ed.)	Retrd.	1990	189.95	262
1990	Raggady Ole Chris Cringle (2nd ed.)	Retrd.	1991	189.95	190
1994	Raggady P. Shagnasty	Retrd.	1995	139.95	195
1988	Raggady Sam (1st ed.)	Retrd.	1991	55.95	115
1991	Raggady Sam (2nd ed.)	500	1995	399.95	500
1987	Raggady Santy (1st ed.)	Retrd.	1988	75.95	250
1990	Raggady Santy (2nd ed.)	Retrd.	1991	89.95	90
1987	Raggady Teddy	Retrd.	1995	9.95	10
1989	Rammy Sammy	Retrd.	1990	43.95	44
1987	Rose Ann	Retrd.	1991	39.95	75
1988	Rotten Wilber	Retrd.	1990	35.95	140
1988	Rufus	Retrd.	1992	35.95	70-80
1989	Sadie Sow	Retrd.	1996	60.00	60
1987	Sally Francis	Retrd.	1993	35.95	62
1987	Sara (muslin)	Retrd.	1992	39.95	180
1987	Sara (satin)	Retrd.	1992	39.95	86
1992	Scary Larry Scarecrow, SNL	Retrd.	1994	79.95	80
1989	Shotgun Pappy	Retrd.	1996	60.00	60
1988	Silly Willie	Retrd.	1990	39.95	76
1992	Sissy Whippermeyer	Retrd.	1996	66.00	66
1989	Skitty Kitty	Retrd.	1991	43.95	140
1990	Sollie Ollie Otis	Retrd.	1991	129.95	130
1995	Spirit of Christmas Santy	Retrd.	1995	87.95	88-130
1988	Spring Santy	Retrd.	1989	47.95	48
1988	Sweet William	Retrd.	1989	35.95	152
1992	Teeny Weenie Christmas Angel	Retrd.	1994	9.95	15
1992	Teeny Weenie Country Angel	Retrd.	1994	9.95	20
1987	Toddy Sue	Retrd.	1990	27.95	87
1995	Tootie Twinkles (1st ed.)	5,000	1995	59.95	60
1989	Tricky Ricky	Retrd.	1996	46.00	46
1988	Tubby Timbo	Retrd.	1996	50.00	50
1990	Verlie Mae	Retrd.	1995	49.95	50
1989	Virtuous Virgie	Retrd.	1996	70.00	70
1988	Wacky Jackie	Retrd.	1990	39.95	40
1989	Wild Wilma	Retrd.	1996	44.00	44
1995	Willa Thumpet	2,000	1995	73.95	74
1991	Winkie Binkie	Retrd.	1993	53.95	54
1992	Witchy Wanda, SNL	Retrd.	1994	79.95	80
1989	Wood Doll, black-large	Retrd.	1991	36.00	36
1989	Wood Doll, white-large	Retrd.	1991	36.00	36
1989	Wood Doll-medium	Retrd.	1991	31.95	32
1989	Wood Doll-small	Retrd.	1991	23.95	24
1990	Yankee Doodle Debbie	Retrd.	1993	95.95	325
1990	Zitty Zelda, SNL	Retrd.	1993	89.95	176

Tour Babies - M. Maschino-Walker

Year	Issue	Edition Limit	Year Retd.	Issue Price	*Quote U.S.$
1992	Tour Baby-old man 1992	Retrd.	1992	19.95	20
1992	Tour Baby-old woman 1992	Retrd.	1992	19.95	20
1992	Tour Baby-young boy 1992	Retrd.	1992	19.95	20
1992	Tour Baby-young girl 1992	Retrd.	1992	19.95	20
1993	Tour Baby 1993	Retrd.	1993	19.95	22
1994	Tour Baby 1994	Retrd.	1994	24.95	25
1995	Tour Baby 1995	Retrd.	1995	26.95	27
1996	Tour Baby 1996	Retrd.	1996	12.95	13

Valentine Collection - M. Maschino-Walker

Year	Issue	Edition Limit	Year Retd.	Issue Price	*Quote U.S.$
1993	Valentine Bear-Girl	Retrd.	1993	39.95	40
1993	Valentine Bear-Boy	Retrd.	1993	39.95	40
1994	Herwin Heaps-O Hugs	613	1994	39.95	50
1994	Lottie Lots-A Hugs	825	1994	39.95	50
1995	Ruthie Claire	Retrd.	1995	39.95	75

Cavanagh Group Intl.

Coca-Cola Brand Heritage Collection - Sundblom

Year	Issue	Edition Limit	Year Retd.	Issue Price	*Quote U.S.$
1997	Hospitality	3,000		200.00	200

The Collectables Inc.

Collector's Club Doll - P. Parkins

Year	Issue	Edition Limit	Year Retd.	Issue Price	*Quote U.S.$
1991	Mandy	Closed	1991	360.00	360
1992	Kallie	Closed	1992	410.00	500
1993	Mommy and Me	Closed	1993	810.00	810
1994	Krystal	Closed	1994	380.00	380
1995	Taylor	Closed	1995	380.00	380

Angel Series - P. Parkins

Year	Issue	Edition Limit	Year Retd.	Issue Price	*Quote U.S.$
1992	Angel on My Shoulder	Closed	1993	530.00	530
1994	Guarding the Way	500	1995	950.00	990
1993	My Guardian Angel	500	1993	590.00	590

Cherished Memories - P. Parkins, unless otherwise noted

Year	Issue	Edition Limit	Year Retd.	Issue Price	*Quote U.S.$
1986	Amy and Andrew	S/O	1986	220.00	325
1988	Brittany	Closed	1988	240.00	300
1990	Cassandra	Closed	1990	500.00	600
1989	Generations	Closed	1989	480.00	500
1988	Heather	Closed	1988	280.00	350
1988	Jennifer	Closed	1988	380.00	500-600
1988	Leigh Ann and Leland	Closed	1988	250.00	400
1988	Tea Time - D. Effner	S/O	1986	380.00	450
1990	Twinkles	Closed	1991	170.00	275

The Collectibles Inc. Dolls - P. Parkins, unless otherwise noted

Year	Issue	Edition Limit	Year Retd.	Issue Price	*Quote U.S.$
1991	Adrianna	Closed	1992	1350.00	1350
1994	Afternoon Delight	500	1995	410.00	450
1995	Alexus	150		770.00	770
1993	Amber	500	1994	330.00	330
1994	Amber Hispanic	500	1994	340.00	340
1992	Angel on My Shoulder (Lillianne w/CeCe)	500	1993	530.00	650
1990	Bassinet Baby	2,000	1990	130.00	375-425
1991	Bethany	Closed	1992	450.00	450
1995	Brianna	150	1995	590.00	590
1995	Christine	350		390.00	390
1990	Danielle	1,000	1990	400.00	475
1994	Earth Angel	500		195.00	195
1993	Haley	500	1994	330.00	330
1990	In Your Easter Bonnet	1,000	1990	350.00	350
1992	Karlie	500	1992	380.00	380
1991	Kelsie	500	1991	320.00	320
1991	Lauren	S/O	1991	490.00	490
1993	Little Dumpling (Black)	500	1994	190.00	190
1993	Little Dumpling (White)	500	1994	190.00	190
1990	Lizbeth Ann - D. Effner	1,000	1990	420.00	500
1994	Madison	250		350.00	420
1994	Madison Sailor	250	1995	370.00	370
1993	Maggie	500	1994	330.00	330
1992	Marissa	300	1992	350.00	350
1992	Marty	250	1992	190.00	190
1992	Matia	250	1992	190.00	190
1989	Michelle	250	1990	270.00	400-450
1992	Missy	Open		59.00	59

*Quotes have been rounded up to nearest dollar

YEAR ISSUE		EDITION LIMIT	YEAR RETD.	ISSUE PRICE	*QUOTE U.S.$
1992	Molly	450	1993	350.00	350
1994	Morgan	250	1995	390.00	390
1994	Morgan in Red	250	1995	390.00	390
1995	A Mother's Love	450		770.00	770
1995	My Little Angel Boy	250		450.00	450
1995	My Little Angel Girl	250		450.00	450
1991	Natasha	Closed	1992	510.00	510
1992	Shelley	300	1992	450.00	450
1987	Storytime By Sarah Jane	S/O	1990	330.00	475-525
1994	Sugar Plum Fairy	500		250.00	250
1987	Tasha	S/O	1987	290.00	1400
1986	Tatiana	S/O	1986	270.00	1000
1989	Welcome Home - D. Effner	1,000	1990	330.00	500-700
1991	Yvette	300	1992	580.00	580

Fairy - P. Parkins

1988	Tabatha	1,500	1989	370.00	425

Mother's Little Treasures - D. Effner

1985	1st Edition	S/O	1985	380.00	1000
1990	2nd Edition	S/O	1990	440.00	500-600

Yesterday's Child - D. Effner, unless otherwise noted

1986	Ashley - P. Parkins	Closed	1987	220.00	275
1983	Chad And Charity	Closed	1984	190.00	250
1982	Cleo	Closed	1983	180.00	250
1982	Columbine	Closed	1983	180.00	250
1982	Jason And Jessica	Closed	1983	150.00	300
1984	Kevin And Karissa	Closed	1985	190.00	250-300
1983	Noel	Closed	1984	190.00	250
1984	Rebecca	Closed	1985	250.00	250-300
1986	Todd And Tiffany	Closed	1987	220.00	320

Department 56

Heritage Village Doll Collection - Department 56

1987	Christmas Carol Dolls 1000-6 set/4 (Tiny Tim, Bob Crachet, Mrs. Crachet, Scrooge)	250	1988	1500.00	1500
1987	Christmas Carol Dolls 5907-2 set/4 (Tiny Tim, Bob Crachet, Mrs. Crachet, Scrooge)	Closed	1993	250.00	265-300
1988	Christmas Carol Dolls 1001-4 set/4 (Tiny Tim, Bob Crachet, Mrs. Crachet, Scrooge)	350	1989	1600.00	1600
1988	Mr. & Mrs. Fezziwig 5594-8 set/2	Open		172.00	172

Snowbabies Dolls - Department 56

1988	Allison & Duncan-Set of 2, 7730-5	Closed	1989	200.00	650-750

Dolls by Jerri

Dolls by Jerri - J. McCloud

1986	Alfalfa	1,000		350.00	350
1986	Allison	1,000		350.00	450
1986	Amber	1,000		350.00	900
1986	Annabelle	300		600.00	585
1986	Ashley	1,000		350.00	500
1986	Audrey	300		550.00	550
1982	Baby David	538		290.00	2000
XX	Boy	1,000		350.00	425
1985	Bride	1,000		350.00	400
1986	Bridgette	300		500.00	500
1985	Candy	1,000		340.00	2000
1986	Cane	1,000		350.00	1200
1986	Charlotte	1,000		330.00	450
1984	Clara	1,000		320.00	1200-1500
1986	Clown-David 3 Yrs. Old	1,000		340.00	450
1986	Danielle	1,000		350.00	500
1986	David-2 Years Old	1,000		330.00	550
1986	David-Magician	1,000		350.00	450
XX	Denise	1,000		380.00	550
1986	Elizabeth	1,000		340.00	350
1984	Emily	1,000		330.00	2500
1986	The Fool	1,000		350.00	350
XX	Gina	1,000		350.00	475
XX	Goldilocks	1,000		370.00	700-800
1989	Goose Girl, Guild	Closed		300.00	700
1986	Helenjean	1,000		350.00	500-650
1988	Holly	1,000		370.00	825
1986	Jacqueline	300		500.00	500
XX	Jamie	800		380.00	450
1986	Joy	1,000		350.00	350
XX	Laura	1,000		350.00	500
1989	Laura Lee	1,000		370.00	575
XX	Little Bo Peep	1,000		340.00	450
XX	Little Miss Muffet	1,000		340.00	450
1986	Lucianna	300		500.00	500
1986	Mary Beth	1,000		350.00	350
XX	Megan	750		420.00	550
XX	Meredith	750		430.00	600
1985	Miss Nanny	1,000		160.00	275
1986	Nobody	1,000		350.00	550-650
1986	Princess and the Unicorn	1,000		370.00	400
1986	Samantha	1,000		350.00	550
1985	Scotty	1,000		340.00	1800
1986	Somebody	1,000		350.00	550-750
1986	Tammy	1,000		350.00	900
1985	Uncle Joe	1,000		160.00	250-300
XX	Uncle Remus	500		290.00	450

YEAR ISSUE		EDITION LIMIT	YEAR RETD.	ISSUE PRICE	*QUOTE U.S.$
1986	Yvonne	300		500.00	500

Elke's Originals, Ltd.

Elke Hutchens - E. Hutchens

1991	Alicia	250		595.00	700-995
1989	Annabelle	250		575.00	1400-1500
1990	Aubra	250		575.00	900-1050
1990	Aurora	250		595.00	900-1050
1991	Bellinda	400		595.00	800-895
1992	Bethany	400		595.00	700-895
1991	Braelyn	400		595.00	1400-1600
1991	Brianna	400		595.00	1000-1200
1992	Cecilia	435		635.00	800-900
1992	Charles	435		635.00	600-900
1992	Cherie	435		635.00	900
1992	Clarissa	435		635.00	800-900
1993	Daphne	435		675.00	700-850
1993	Deidre	435		675.00	700-850
1993	Desirée	435		675.00	700-900
1990	Kricket	500		575.00	400
1992	Laurakaye	435		550.00	550
1990	Little Liebchen	250		475.00	1000
1990	Victoria	500		645.00	645

Ertl Collectibles

Forever Sisters - J. Callander

1997	Julie w/Hope Chest 71	4,500		85.00	85
1997	Kaitlin w/Park Bench 75	4,500		85.00	85
1997	Sara w/Rocking Chair 72	4,500		85.00	85

Girlhood Journeys

1996	Juliet (Medieval Era) 21	Open		64.00	64
1996	Kai (African) 24	Open		64.00	64
1996	Marie (Pre-Rev France) 22	Open		64.00	64
1996	Shannon (Gold Rush Era) 23	Open		64.00	64

LeMutt & FiFi - F. Hoerlein

1997	LeMutt (Black Tie) 244	Open		75.00	75
1997	FiFi (Formal Gown) 272	Open		75.00	75
1997	LeMutt (Skiwear) 249	Open		70.00	70
1997	FiFi (Skating Outfit) 268	Open		70.00	70
1997	LeMutt (Sleepwear) 258	Open		65.00	65
1997	FiFi (Sleepwear) 263	Open		65.00	65
1997	Cher (Sleepwear) 283	Open		24.00	24
1997	Buster (Sleepwear) 292	Open		24.00	24

Ganz

Cowtown - C. Thammavongsa

1994	Buffalo Bull Cody	Open		20.00	20
1994	Old MooDonald	Open		20.00	20
1994	Santa Cows	Open		25.00	25

Little Cheesers/Cheeserville Picnic Collection - G.D.A. Group

1992	Sweet Cicely Musical Doll In Basket	Closed	1996	85.00	85

Georgetown Collection, Inc.

Age of Romance - J. Reavey

1994	Catherine	100-day		150.00	150

American Diary Dolls - L. Mason

1991	Bridget Quinn	Closed	1996	129.25	130
1991	Christina Merovina	100-day		129.25	130
1990	Jennie Cooper	Closed	1996	129.25	130-155
1994	Lian Ying	Closed	1996	130.00	130
1991	Many Stars	100-day		129.25	130
1992	Rachel Williams	100-day		129.25	130
1993	Sarah Turner	100-day		130.00	130
1992	Tulu	100-day		129.25	130

Baby Kisses - T. DeHetre

1992	Michelle	Closed	1996	118.60	119

Blessed Are The Children - J. Reavey

1994	Faith	100-day		83.00	83

Boys Will Be Boys - J. Reavey

1996	Just Like Dad	100-day		96.00	96
1994	Mr. Mischief	100-day		96.00	96

Children of Main St. - G. Braun

1996	Alice	100-day		130.00	130

Children of the Great Spirit - C. Theroux

1993	Buffalo Child	100-day		140.00	140
1994	Golden Flower	100-day		130.00	130
1994	Little Fawn	100-day		114.00	114
1993	Winter Baby	Closed	1996	160.00	160

Class Portraits - J. Kissling

1995	Anna	100-day		140.00	140

YEAR ISSUE		EDITION LIMIT	YEAR RETD.	ISSUE PRICE	*QUOTE U.S.$

The Cottage Garden - P. Phillips

1996	Emily	100-day		131.00	131

Country Quilt Babies - B. Prusseit

1996	Hannah	100-day		104.00	104

Dreams Come True - M. Sirko

1995	Amanda	Closed	1996	120.00	120

Faerie Princess - B. Deval

1989	Faerie Princess	Closed	1996	248.00	248

Fanciful Dreamers - A. Timmerman

1995	Sweetdreams & Moonbeams	100-day		130.00	130

Faraway Friends - S. Skille

1994	Dara	100-day		140.00	140
1993	Kristin	Closed	1996	140.00	140
1994	Mariama	100-day		140.00	140

Favorite Friends - K. Murawska

1995	Christina	100-day		130.00	130
1996	Samantha	100-day		130.00	130

Fuzzy Friends - A. DiMartino

1996	Sandy & Sam	100-day		130.00	130

Georgetown Collection - Various

1995	Buffalo Boy - C. Theroux	100-day		130.00	130
1993	Quick Fox - L. Mason	Closed	1996	138.95	139
1994	Silver Moon - L. Mason	100-day		140.00	140

Gifts From Heaven - B. Prusseit

1994	Good as Gold	100-day		88.00	88
1995	Sweet Pea	100-day		88.00	88

Hearts in Song - J. Galperin

1994	Angelique	100-day		150.00	150
1992	Grace	100-day		149.60	150
1993	Michael	100-day		150.00	150

Heavenly Messages - M. Sirko

1996	David	100-day		104.00	104
1995	Gabrielle	100-day		104.00	104

Kindergarten Kids - V. Walker

1992	Nikki	Closed	1996	129.60	130

Let's Play - T. DeHetre

1992	Eentsy Weentsy Willie	Closed	1996	118.60	119
1992	Peek-A-Boo Beckie	Closed	1996	118.60	119

Linda's Little Ladies - L. Mason

1993	Shannon's Holiday	100-day		169.95	170

Little Artists of Africa - C. Massey

1996	Oluwa Fumike	100-day		131.00	131

Little Bit of Heaven - A. Timmerman

1996	Adriana	100-day		135.00	135
1994	Arielle	100-day		130.00	130
1995	Cupid	100-day		135.00	135
1995	Noelle	100-day		130.00	130

Little Bloomers - J. Reavey

1995	Darling Daisy	100-day		104.00	104

Little Dreamers - A. DiMartino

1994	Beautiful Buttercup	100-day		130.00	130
1995	Julie	100-day		130.00	130
1996	Nicole	100-day		130.00	130

Little Loves - B. Deval

1988	Emma	Closed	1996	139.20	140
1989	Katie	Closed	1996	139.20	140
1990	Laura	Closed	1996	139.20	140
1989	Megan	Closed	1996	138.00	160

Little Performers - M. Sirko

1996	Tickled Pink	100-day		100.00	100

Maud Humphrey's Little Victorians - M. Humphrey

1996	Papa's Little Sailor	100-day		130.00	130

Messengers of the Great Spirit - Various

1994	Noatak - L. Mason	100-day		150.00	150
1994	Prayer for the Buffalo - C. Theroux	100-day		120.00	120

Miss Ashley - P. Thompson

1989	Miss Ashley	Closed	1996	228.00	228

Mommy's World - A. Hollis

1996	Julia	100-day		136.00	136

Naturally Curious Kids - A. Hollis

1996	Jennifer	100-day		100.00	100

Nursery Babies - T. DeHetre

1990	Baby Bunting	Closed	1996	118.20	150

*Quotes have been rounded up to nearest dollar

Collectors' Information Bureau

33

YEAR ISSUE		EDITION LIMIT	YEAR RETD.	ISSUE PRICE	*QUOTE U.S.$
1991	Diddle, Diddle	Closed	1996	118.20	119
1991	Little Girl	Closed	1996	118.20	119
1990	Patty Cake	Closed	1996	118.20	119
1991	Rock-A-Bye Baby	Closed	1996	118.20	119
1991	This Little Piggy	Closed	1996	118.20	119

Nutcracker Sweethearts - S. Skille

1995	Sugar Plum	100-day		130.00	130

Pictures of Innocence - J. Reavey

1994	Clarissa	100-day		137.50	138

Portraits of Enchantment - A. Timmerman

1996	Sleeping Beauty	100-day		150.00	150

Portraits of Perfection - A. Timmerman

1993	Apple Dumpling	100-day		149.60	150
1994	Blackberry Blossom	100-day		149.60	150
1993	Peaches & Cream	100-day		149.60	150
1993	Sweet Strawberry	100-day		149.60	150

Prayers From The Heart - S. Skille

1995	Hope	100-day		115.00	115

Proud Moments - P. Erff

1996	Chelsea	100-day		126.00	126

Reflections of Childhood - L. Mason

1996	Courtney	100-day		152.50	153

Russian Fairy Tales Dolls - B. Deval

1993	Vasilisa	100-day		190.00	190

Small Wonders - B. Deval

1991	Abbey	Closed	1996	97.60	98
1990	Corey	Closed	1996	97.60	98
1992	Sarah	Closed	1996	97.60	98

Songs of Innocence - J. Reavey

1996	Eric	100-day		105.00	105
1995	Kelsey	100-day		104.00	104
1996	Meagan	100-day		104.00	104

Sugar & Spice - L. Mason

1992	Little Sunshine	Closed	1996	141.10	142
1991	Little Sweetheart	Closed	1996	118.25	119
1991	Red Hot Pepper	Closed	1996	118.25	119

Sweethearts of Summer - P. Phillips

1994	Caroline	100-day		140.00	140
1995	Jessica	100-day		140.00	140
1995	Madeleine & Harry	100-day		140.00	140

Sweets For the Sweet - V. Ohms

1996	Elise	100-day		130.00	130

Tansie - P. Coffer

1988	Tansie	Closed	1996	81.00	81

Victorian Fantasies - L. Mason

1995	Amber Afternoon	100-day		150.00	150
1995	Lavender Dreams	100-day		150.00	150
1996	Reflections of Rose	100-day		150.00	150

Victorian Innocence - L. Mason

1994	Annabelle	100-day		130.00	130

Victorian Splendor - J. Reavey

1994	Emily	100-day		130.00	130

What a Beautiful World - R. Hockh

1996	Marisa	100-day		130.00	130
1996	Mora	100-day		126.00	126
1996	Therese & Tino	100-day		155.00	155

Yesterday's Dreams - P. Phillips

1994	Mary Elizabeth	100-day		130.00	130
1996	Sophie	100-day		130.00	130

Goebel of North America

Bob Timberlake Dolls - B. Ball

1996	Abby Liz-911350	2,000		195.00	195
1996	Ann-911352	2,000		195.00	195
1996	Carter-911351	2,000		195.00	195
1996	Kate-911353	2,000		195.00	195

Cindy Guyer Romance Dolls - B. Ball

1996	Cordelia-911824	1,000		225.00	225
1996	Cynthia-911830	1,000		225.00	225
1996	Mackenzie-911825	1,000		225.00	225

Dolly Dingle - B. Ball

1995	Melvis Bumps-911617	1,000		99.00	99

Goebel Dolls - B. Ball

1995	Brother Murphy-911100	2,000		125.00	125

Hummel Dolls - B. Ball

1998	Apple Tree Boy-911213	N/A		250.00	250
1998	Apple Tree Girl-911214	N/A		250.00	250
1996	Little Scholar, 14"-911211	N/A		200.00	200
1997	School Girl, 14"-911212	N/A		200.00	200

United States Historical Society - B. Ball

1995	Mary-911155	1,500		195.00	195

Victoria Ashlea® Birthstone Dolls - K. Kennedy

1995	January-Garnet-912471	2,500	1996	29.50	30
1995	February-Amethyst-912472	2,500	1996	29.50	30
1995	March-Aquamarine-912473	2,500	1996	29.50	30
1995	April-Diamond-912474	2,500	1996	29.50	30
1995	May-Emerald-912475	2,500	1996	29.50	30
1995	June -Lt. Amethyst-912476	2,500	1996	29.50	30
1995	July-Ruby-912477	2,500	1996	29.50	30
1995	August-Peridot-912478	2,500	1996	29.50	30
1995	September-Sapphire-912479	2,500	1996	29.50	30
1995	October-Rosestone-912480	2,500	1996	29.50	30
1995	November-Topaz-912481	2,500	1996	29.50	30
1995	December-Zircon-912482	2,500	1996	29.50	30

Victoria Ashlea® Originals - B. Ball, unless otherwise noted

1985	Adele-901172	Closed	1989	145.00	275
1989	Alexa-912214	Closed	1991	195.00	195
1989	Alexandria-912273	Closed	1991	275.00	275
1987	Alice-901212	Closed	1991	95.00	135
1990	Alice-912296 - K. Kennedy	Closed	1992	65.00	65
1992	Alicia-912388	500	1994	135.00	135
1992	Allison-912358	Closed	1993	160.00	165
1987	Amanda Pouty-901209	Closed	1991	150.00	215
1988	Amanda-912246	Closed	1991	180.00	180
1993	Amanda-912409	2,000	1995	40.00	40
1984	Amelia-933006	Closed	1988	100.00	100
1990	Amie-912313 - K. Kennedy	Closed	1991	150.00	150
1990	Amy-901262	Closed	1993	110.00	110
1990	Angela-912324 - K. Kennedy	Closed	1994	130.00	135
1988	Angelica-912204	Closed	1991	150.00	150
1992	Angelica-912339	1,000	1995	145.00	145
1990	Annabelle-912278	Closed	1992	200.00	200
1988	Anne-912213	Closed	1991	130.00	150
1990	Annette-912333 - K. Kennedy	Closed	1993	85.00	85
1988	April-901239	Closed	1992	225.00	225
1989	Ashlea-901250	Closed	1992	550.00	550
1988	Ashley-901235	Closed	1991	110.00	110
1992	Ashley-911004	Closed	1994	99.00	105
1986	Ashley-912147	Closed	1989	125.00	125
1986	Baby Brook Beige Dress-912103	Closed	1989	60.00	60
1986	Baby Courtney-912124	Closed	1990	120.00	120
1988	Baby Daryl-912200	Closed	1991	85.00	85
1987	Baby Doll-912184	Closed	1990	75.00	75
1988	Baby Jennifer-912210	Closed	1992	75.00	75
1988	Baby Katie-912222	Closed	1993	70.00	70
1986	Baby Lauren Pink-912086	Closed	1991	120.00	120
1987	Baby Lindsay-912190	Closed	1990	80.00	80
1984	Barbara-901108	Closed	1987	57.00	110
1990	Baryshnicat-912298 - K. Kennedy	Closed	1991	25.00	25
1988	Bernice-901245	Closed	1991	90.00	90
1993	Beth-912430 - K. Kennedy	2,000	1996	45.00	45
1992	Betsy-912390	500	1994	150.00	150
1990	Bettina-912310	Closed	1993	100.00	105
1988	Betty Doll-912220	Closed	1993	90.00	90
1987	Bonnie Pouty-901207	Closed	1992	100.00	100
1988	Brandon-901234	Closed	1992	90.00	90
1990	Brandy-912304 - K. Kennedy	Closed	1992	150.00	150
1987	Bride Allison-901218	Closed	1993	180.00	180
1988	Brittany-912207	Closed	1990	130.00	145
1992	Brittany-912365 - K. Kennedy	Closed	1993	140.00	145
1987	Caitlin-901228	Closed	1991	260.00	260
1988	Campbell Kid-Boy-758701	Closed	1988	13.80	14
1988	Campbell Kid-Girl-758700	Closed	1988	13.80	14
1989	Candace-912288 - K. Kennedy	Closed	1992	70.00	70
1992	Carol-912387 - K. Kennedy	1,000	1996	140.00	140
1987	Caroline-912191	Closed	1990	80.00	80
1990	Carolyn-901261 - K. Kennedy	Closed	1993	200.00	200
1992	Cassandra-912355 - K. Kennedy	1,000	1996	165.00	165
1988	Cat Maude-901247	Closed	1993	85.00	85
1986	Cat/Kitty Cheerful Gr Dr-901179	Closed	1990	60.00	60
1987	Catanova-901227	Closed	1991	75.00	75
1988	Catherine-901242	Closed	1992	240.00	240
XX	Charity-912244	Closed	1990	70.00	70
1982	Charleen-912094	Closed	1986	65.00	65
1985	Chauncey-912085	Closed	1988	75.00	110
1988	Christina-901229	Closed	1991	350.00	400
1987	Christine-912168	Closed	1989	75.00	75
1992	Cindy-912384	1,000	1994	185.00	190
1985	Claire-901158	Closed	1988	115.00	160
1984	Claude-901032	Closed	1987	110.00	225
1984	Claudette-901033	Closed	1987	110.00	225
1989	Claudia-901257 - K. Kennedy	Closed	1993	225.00	225
1987	Clementine-901226	Closed	1991	75.00	75
1986	Clown Calypso-912104	Closed	1990	70.00	70
1985	Clown Casey-912078	Closed	1988	40.00	40
1986	Clown Cat Cadwalader-912132	Closed	1988	55.00	55
1987	Clown Champagne-912180	Closed	1989	95.00	95
1986	Clown Christabel-912095	Closed	1988	100.00	150
1985	Clown Christie-912084	Closed	1988	60.00	90
1986	Clown Clarabella-912096	Closed	1989	80.00	80
1986	Clown Clarissa-912123	Closed	1990	75.00	110
1988	Clown Cotton Candy-912199	Closed	1990	67.00	67
1986	Clown Cyd-912093	Closed	1988	70.00	70
1985	Clown Jody-912079	Closed	1988	100.00	150
1982	Clown Jolly-912181	Closed	1991	70.00	70
1986	Clown Kitten-Cleo-912133	Closed	1989	50.00	50
1986	Clown Lollipop-912127	Closed	1989	125.00	225
1984	Clown-901136	Closed	1988	90.00	120
1988	Crystal-912226	Closed	1992	75.00	75
1983	Deborah-901107	Closed	1987	220.00	400
1990	Debra-912319 - K. Kennedy	Closed	1992	120.00	120
1992	Denise-912362 - K. Kennedy	1,000	1994	145.00	175-225
1989	Diana Bride-912277	Closed	1992	180.00	180
1984	Diana-901119	Closed	1987	55.00	135
1988	Diana-912218	Closed	1992	270.00	270
1987	Dominique-901219	Closed	1991	170.00	225
1987	Doreen-912198	Closed	1990	75.00	75
1985	Dorothy-901157	Closed	1988	130.00	275
1992	Dottie-912393 - K. Kennedy	1,000	1996	160.00	160
1988	Elizabeth-901214	Closed	1991	90.00	90
1988	Ellen-901246	Closed	1991	100.00	100
1990	Emily-912303	Closed	1992	150.00	150
1988	Erin-901241	Closed	1991	170.00	170
1990	Fluffer-912293	Closed	1994	135.00	150-225
1985	Garnet-901183	Closed	1988	160.00	295
1990	Gigi-912306 - K. Kennedy	Closed	1994	150.00	150
1986	Gina-901176	Closed	1989	300.00	300
1989	Ginny-912287 - K. Kennedy	Closed	1993	140.00	140
1986	Girl Frog Freda-912105	Closed	1989	20.00	20
1988	Goldilocks-912234 - K. Kennedy	Closed	1992	65.00	65
1986	Googley German Astrid-912109	Closed	1989	60.00	60
1988	Heather-912247	Closed	1990	135.00	150
1990	Heather-912322	Closed	1992	150.00	150
1990	Heidi-901266	2,000	1995	150.00	150
1990	Helene-901249 - K. Kennedy	Closed	1991	160.00	160
1990	Helga-912337	Closed	1994	325.00	325
1984	Henri-901035	Closed	1986	100.00	200
1984	Henrietta-901036	Closed	1986	100.00	200
1992	Hilary-912353	Closed	1993	130.00	135
1992	Holly Belle-912380	500	1994	125.00	125
1982	Holly-901233	Closed	1985	160.00	200
1989	Holly-901254	Closed	1992	180.00	180
1989	Hope Baby w/ Pillow-912292	Closed	1992	110.00	110
1992	Iris-912389 - K. Kennedy	500	1995	165.00	165
1987	Jacqueline-912192	Closed	1990	80.00	80
1990	Jacqueline-912329 - K. Kennedy	Closed	1993	136.00	150-225
1984	Jamie-912061	Closed	1987	65.00	100
1984	Jeannie-901062	Closed	1987	200.00	550
1988	Jennifer-901248	Closed	1991	150.00	150
1988	Jennifer-912221	Closed	1990	80.00	80
1992	Jenny-912374 - K. Kennedy	Closed	1993	150.00	150
1988	Jesse-912231	Closed	1994	110.00	115
1987	Jessica-912195	Closed	1990	120.00	135
1993	Jessica-912410	2,000	1994	40.00	40
1990	Jillian-912323	Closed	1993	150.00	150
1989	Jimmy Baby w/ Pillow-912291 - K. Kennedy	Closed	1992	165.00	165
1989	Jingles-912271	Closed	1991	60.00	60
1990	Joanne-912307 - K. Kennedy	Closed	1991	165.00	165
1987	Joy-912155	Closed	1989	50.00	50
1989	Joy-912289 - K. Kennedy	Closed	1992	110.00	110
1987	Julia-912174	Closed	1989	80.00	80
1990	Julia-912334 - K. Kennedy	Closed	1993	85.00	85
1993	Julie-912435 - K. Kennedy	2,000	1995	45.00	45
1990	Justine-901256	Closed	1992	200.00	200
1988	Karen-912205	Closed	1991	200.00	250
1993	Katie-912412	2,000	1996	40.00	40
1993	Kaylee-912433 - K. Kennedy	2,000	1994	45.00	45
1992	Kelli-912361	1,000	1995	160.00	165
1990	Kelly-912331	Closed	1991	95.00	95
1990	Kimberly-912341	1,000	1996	140.00	145
1987	Kittle Cat-912167	Closed	1989	55.00	55
1987	Kitty Cuddles-901201	Closed	1990	65.00	65
1992	Kris-912345 - K. Kennedy	Closed	1992	160.00	160
1989	Kristin-912285 - K. Kennedy	Closed	1994	90.00	95
1984	Laura-901106	Closed	1987	300.00	575
1988	Laura-912225	Closed	1991	135.00	135
1988	Lauren-912212	Closed	1991	110.00	110
1992	Lauren-912363 - K. Kennedy	1,000	1996	190.00	195
1993	Lauren-912413	2,000	1996	40.00	40
1993	Leslie-912432 - K. Kennedy	2,000	1994	45.00	45
1989	Licorice-912290	Closed	1991	75.00	75
1987	Lillian-901199	Closed	1990	85.00	100
1989	Lindsey-901263	Closed	1991	100.00	100
1989	Lisa-912275	Closed	1991	160.00	160
1989	Loni-912276	Closed	1993	125.00	150-185
1985	Lynn-912144	Closed	1988	90.00	135
1992	Margaret-912354 - K. Kennedy	1,000	1994	150.00	150
1989	Margot-912269	Closed	1991	110.00	110
1989	Maria-912265	Closed	1990	90.00	90
1982	Marie-901231	Closed	1985	95.00	95
1989	Marissa-901252 - K. Kennedy	Closed	1993	225.00	225
1988	Maritta Spanish-912224	Closed	1990	140.00	140
1992	Marjorie-912357	Closed	1993	135.00	135
1990	Marshmallow-912294 - K. Kennedy	Closed	1992	75.00	75
1985	Mary-912126	Closed	1988	60.00	90
1990	Matthew-901251	Closed	1993	100.00	100
1989	Megan-901260	Closed	1993	120.00	120
1987	Megan-912148	Closed	1989	70.00	70
1989	Melanie-912284 - K. Kennedy	Closed	1992	135.00	135
1990	Melinda-912309 - K. Kennedy	Closed	1991	70.00	70

*Quotes have been rounded up to nearest dollar

DOLLS

Goebel of North America to Gorham

YEAR ISSUE		EDITION LIMIT	YEAR RETD.	ISSUE PRICE	*QUOTE U.S.$
1988	Melissa-901230	Closed	1991	110.00	110
1988	Melissa-912208	Closed	1990	125.00	125
1989	Merry-912249	Closed	1990	200.00	200
1987	Michelle-901222	Closed	1991	90.00	90
1985	Michelle-912066	Closed	1989	100.00	225
1992	Michelle-912381 - K. Kennedy	Closed	1992	175.00	175
1985	Millie-912135	Closed	1988	70.00	125
1989	Missy-912283	Closed	1993	110.00	115
1988	Molly-912211 - K. Kennedy	Closed	1992	75.00	75
1990	Monica-912336 - K. Kennedy	Closed	1993	100.00	105
1990	Monique-912335 - K. Kennedy	Closed	1993	85.00	85
1988	Morgan-912239 - K. Kennedy	Closed	1992	75.00	75
1990	Mrs. Katz-912301	Closed	1993	140.00	145
1993	Nadine-912431 - K. Kennedy	2,000	1995	45.00	45
1989	Nancy-912266	Closed	1990	110.00	110
1987	Nicole-901225	Closed	1991	575.00	575
1993	Nicole-912411	2,000	1996	40.00	40
1987	Noel-912170	Closed	1989	125.00	125
1992	Noelle-912360 - K. Kennedy	1,000	1994	165.00	170
1990	Pamela-912302	Closed	1991	95.00	95
1986	Patty Artic Flower Print-901185	Closed	1990	140.00	140
1990	Paula-912316	Closed	1992	100.00	100
1988	Paulette-901244	Closed	1991	90.00	90
1990	Penny-912325 - K. Kennedy	Closed	1993	130.00	150-225
1986	Pepper Rust Dr/Appr-901184	Closed	1990	125.00	200
1985	Phyllis-912067	Closed	1989	60.00	60
1989	Pinky Clown-912268 - K. Kennedy	Closed	1993	70.00	75
1988	Polly-912206	Closed	1990	100.00	125
1990	Priscilla-912300	Closed	1993	185.00	190
1990	Rebecca-901258	Closed	1992	250.00	250
1988	Renae-912245	Closed	1990	120.00	120
1990	Robin-912321	Closed	1993	160.00	165
1985	Rosalind-912087	Closed	1988	145.00	225
1985	Roxanne-901174	Closed	1988	155.00	275
1984	Sabina-901155	Closed	1988	75.00	N/A
1990	Samantha-912314	Closed	1993	185.00	190
1988	Sandy-901240 - K. Kennedy	Closed	1993	115.00	115
1989	Sara-912279	Closed	1991	175.00	175
1988	Sarah w/Pillow-912219	Closed	1991	105.00	105
1987	Sarah-901220	Closed	1992	350.00	350
1993	Sarah-912408	2,000	1996	40.00	40
1993	Shannon-912434 - K. Kennedy	2,000	1996	45.00	45
1990	Sheena-912338	Closed	1992	115.00	115
1984	Sheila-912060	Closed	1988	75.00	135
1990	Sheri-912305 - K. Kennedy	Closed	1992	115.00	115
1992	Sherise-912383 - K. Kennedy	Closed	1992	145.00	145
1989	Sigrid-912282	Closed	1992	145.00	145
1988	Snow White-912235 - K. Kennedy	Closed	1992	65.00	65
1987	Sophia-912173	Closed	1989	40.00	40
1988	Stephanie-912238	Closed	1992	200.00	200
1990	Stephanie-912312	Closed	1993	150.00	150
1984	Stephanie-933012	Closed	1988	115.00	115
1988	Susan-901243	Closed	1991	100.00	100
1990	Susie-912328	Closed	1993	115.00	120
1987	Suzanne-901200	Closed	1990	85.00	100
1989	Suzanne-912286	Closed	1992	120.00	120
1989	Suzy-912295	Closed	1991	110.00	110
1992	Tamika-912382	500	1994	185.00	185
1989	Tammy-912264	Closed	1990	110.00	110
1987	Tasha-901221	Closed	1990	115.00	130
1990	Tasha-912299 - K. Kennedy	Closed	1992	25.00	25
1989	Terry-912281	Closed	1994	125.00	130
1987	Tiffany Pouty-901211	Closed	1991	120.00	160
1990	Tiffany-912326 - K. Kennedy	Closed	1992	180.00	180
1984	Tobie-912023	Closed	1987	30.00	30
1992	Toni-912367 - K. Kennedy	Closed	1993	120.00	120
1990	Tracie-912315	Closed	1993	125.00	125
1992	Trudie-912391	500	1996	135.00	135
1982	Trudy-901232	Closed	1985	100.00	100
1992	Tulip-912385 - K. Kennedy	500	1994	145.00	145
1989	Valerie-901255	Closed	1994	175.00	175
1989	Vanessa-912272	Closed	1991	110.00	110
1984	Victoria-901068	Closed	1987	200.00	1500
1992	Wendy-912330 - K. Kennedy	1,000	1995	125.00	130
1988	Whitney Blk-912232	Closed	1994	62.50	65

Victoria Ashlea® Originals-Birthday Babies - K. Kennedy

YEAR ISSUE		EDITION LIMIT	YEAR RETD.	ISSUE PRICE	*QUOTE U.S.$
1996	January-913017	2,500		30.00	30
1996	February-913018	2,500		30.00	30
1996	March-913019	2,500		30.00	30
1996	April-913020	2,500		30.00	30
1996	May-913021	2,500		30.00	30
1996	June-913022	2,500		30.00	30
1996	July-913023	2,500		30.00	30
1996	August-913024	2,500		30.00	30
1996	September-913025	2,500		30.00	30
1996	October-913026	2,500		30.00	30
1996	November-913027	2,500		30.00	30
1996	December-913028	2,500		30.00	30

Victoria Ashlea® Originals-Collectible Cats - K. Kennedy

YEAR ISSUE		EDITION LIMIT	YEAR RETD.	ISSUE PRICE	*QUOTE U.S.$
1996	Charmer-913005	2,000		39.50	40
1996	Copper-913006	2,000		39.50	40
1996	Cuddles-913007	2,000		39.50	40
1996	Fluffy-913008	2,000		39.50	40
1996	Lollipop-913009	2,000		39.50	40
1996	Mittens-913010	2,000		39.50	40
1996	Patches-913011	2,000		39.50	40
1996	Pebbles-913012	2,000		39.50	40
1996	Pepper-913013	2,000		39.50	40
1996	Ruffles-913014	2,000		39.50	40
1996	Tumbles-913015	2,000		39.50	40
1996	Whiskers-913016	2,000		39.50	40

Victoria Ashlea® Originals-Holiday Babies - K. Kennedy

YEAR ISSUE		EDITION LIMIT	YEAR RETD.	ISSUE PRICE	*QUOTE U.S.$
1996	Boo!-913001	1,000		30.00	30
1996	Happy Easter-913002	1,000		30.00	30
1996	Happy Holidays-913003	1,000		30.00	30
1996	I Love You-913004	1,000		30.00	30

Victoria Ashlea® Originals-Tiny Tot Clowns - K. Kennedy

YEAR ISSUE		EDITION LIMIT	YEAR RETD.	ISSUE PRICE	*QUOTE U.S.$
1994	Danielle-912461	2,000	1996	45.00	45
1994	Lindsey-912463	2,000	1996	45.00	45
1994	Lisa-912458	2,000	1996	45.00	45
1994	Marie-912462	2,000	1996	45.00	45
1994	Megan-912460	2,000	1996	45.00	45
1994	Stacy-912459	2,000	1996	45.00	45

Victoria Ashlea® Originals-Tiny Tot School Girls - K. Kennedy

YEAR ISSUE		EDITION LIMIT	YEAR RETD.	ISSUE PRICE	*QUOTE U.S.$
1994	Andrea- 912456	2,000	1996	47.50	48
1994	Christine- 912450	2,000	1996	47.50	48
1994	Monique- 912455	2,000	1996	47.50	48
1994	Patricia- 912453	2,000	1996	47.50	48
1994	Shawna- 912449	2,000	1996	47.50	48
1994	Susan- 912457	2,000	1996	47.50	48

Goebel/M.I. Hummel

M. I. Hummel Collectible Dolls - M. I. Hummel

YEAR ISSUE		EDITION LIMIT	YEAR RETD.	ISSUE PRICE	*QUOTE U.S.$
1964	Chimney Sweep 1908	Closed	N/A	55.00	120-150
1964	For Father 1917	Closed	N/A	55.00	100-150
1964	Goose Girl 1914	Closed	N/A	55.00	100-150
1964	Gretel 1901	Closed	N/A	55.00	150
1964	Hansel 1902	Closed	N/A	55.00	150
1964	Little Knitter 1905	Closed	N/A	55.00	100-150
1964	Lost Stocking 1926	Closed	N/A	55.00	100-150
1964	Merry Wanderer 1906	Closed	N/A	55.00	125-150
1964	Merry Wanderer 1925	Closed	N/A	55.00	125-150
1964	On Secret Path 1928	Closed	N/A	55.00	100-150
1964	Rosa-Blue Baby 1904/B	Closed	N/A	45.00	100
1964	Rosa-Pink Baby 1904/P	Closed	N/A	45.00	100
1964	School Boy 1910	Closed	N/A	55.00	125-150
1964	School Girl 1909	Closed	N/A	55.00	125-150
1964	Visiting and Invalid 1927	Closed	N/A	55.00	125-150

M. I. Hummel Porcelain Dolls - M. I. Hummel

YEAR ISSUE		EDITION LIMIT	YEAR RETD.	ISSUE PRICE	*QUOTE U.S.$
1984	Birthday Serenade/Boy	Closed	N/A	225.00	275-300
1984	Birthday Serenade/Girl	Closed	N/A	225.00	275-300
1985	Carnival	Closed	N/A	225.00	275-300
1985	Easter Greetings	Closed	N/A	225.00	275-300
1996	Little Scholar 522	Open		200.00	200
1985	Lost Sheep	Closed	N/A	225.00	275-300
1984	On Holiday	Closed	N/A	225.00	275-300
1984	Postman	Closed	N/A	225.00	275-300
1996	School Girl 521	Open		200.00	200
1985	Signs of Spring	Closed	N/A	225.00	275-300

Good-Krüger

Limited Edition - J. Good-Krüger

YEAR ISSUE		EDITION LIMIT	YEAR RETD.	ISSUE PRICE	*QUOTE U.S.$
1990	Alice	Retrd.	1991	250.00	250
1992	Anne with an E	Retrd.	1992	240.00	400
1990	Annie-Rose	Retrd.	1990	219.00	425
1994	Christmas Carols	1,000	1995	240.00	240
1990	Christmas Cookie	Retrd.	1993	199.00	225
1995	Circus Trainer	500	1995	250.00	250
1990	Cozy	Retrd.	1992	179.00	275-375
1990	Daydream	Retrd.	1990	199.00	350
1994	Heidi	1,000	1994	250.00	250
1992	Jeepers Creepers (Porcelain)	Retrd.	1992	725.00	800
1991	Johnny-Lynn	Retrd.	1991	240.00	650-800
1995	Letter to Santa	1,000	1995	250.00	250
1995	Little Princess	1,500	1995	250.00	250
1991	Moppett	Retrd.	1991	179.00	275
1994	Mother's Love	1,000	1994	275.00	275
1994	Stuffed Animal Zoo	1,000	1994	189.00	189
1990	Sue-Lynn	Retrd.	1990	240.00	300
1991	Teachers Pet	Retrd.	1991	199.00	250
1995	Tiny Newborns	500	1995	225.00	225
1991	Victorian Christmas	Retrd.	1992	219.00	275

Gorham

Beverly Port Designer Collection - B. Port

YEAR ISSUE		EDITION LIMIT	YEAR RETD.	ISSUE PRICE	*QUOTE U.S.$
1988	The Amazing Calliope Merriweather 17"	Closed	1990	275.00	1250
1988	Baery Mab 9-1/2"	Closed	1990	110.00	250-300
1987	Christopher Paul Bearkin 10"	Closed	1990	95.00	450
1988	Hollybeary Kringle 15"	Closed	1990	350.00	500
1987	Kristobear Kringle 17"	Closed	1990	200.00	500
1988	Miss Emily 18"	Closed	1990	350.00	1500
1987	Molly Melinda Bearkin 10"	Closed	1990	95.00	250-300
1987	Silver Bell 17"	Closed	1990	175.00	800-1000
1988	T.R. 28-1/2"	Closed	1990	400.00	800-1000
1987	Tedward Jonathan Bearkin 10"	Closed	1990	95.00	350
1987	Tedwina Kimelina Bearkin 10"	Closed	1990	95.00	350
1988	Theodore B. Bear 14"	Closed	1990	175.00	575

Bonnets & Bows - B. Gerardi

YEAR ISSUE		EDITION LIMIT	YEAR RETD.	ISSUE PRICE	*QUOTE U.S.$
1988	Belinda	Closed	1990	195.00	450
1988	Annemarie	Closed	1990	195.00	450
1988	Allessandra	Closed	1990	195.00	350
1988	Lisette	Closed	1990	285.00	495
1988	Bettina	Closed	1994	285.00	495
1988	Ellie	Closed	1994	285.00	495
1988	Alicia	Closed	1994	385.00	700
1988	Bethany	Closed	1994	385.00	1350
1988	Jesse	Closed	1994	525.00	675
1988	Francie	Closed	1994	625.00	800

Celebrations Of Childhood - L. Di Leo

YEAR ISSUE		EDITION LIMIT	YEAR RETD.	ISSUE PRICE	*QUOTE U.S.$
1992	Happy Birthday Amy	Closed	1994	160.00	225

Children Of Christmas - S. Stone Aiken

YEAR ISSUE		EDITION LIMIT	YEAR RETD.	ISSUE PRICE	*QUOTE U.S.$
1989	Clara, 16"	Closed	1994	325.00	650
1990	Natalie, 16"	1,500	1994	350.00	500
1991	Emily	1,500	1994	375.00	400
1992	Virginia	1,500	1994	375.00	400

Dollie And Me - J. Pilallis

YEAR ISSUE		EDITION LIMIT	YEAR RETD.	ISSUE PRICE	*QUOTE U.S.$
1991	Dollie's First Steps	Closed	1994	160.00	225

Gifts of the Garden - S. Stone Aiken

YEAR ISSUE		EDITION LIMIT	YEAR RETD.	ISSUE PRICE	*QUOTE U.S.$
1991	Alisa	Closed	1994	125.00	250
1991	Deborah	Closed	1994	125.00	250
1991	Holly (Christmas)	Closed	1994	150.00	250
1991	Irene	Closed	1994	125.00	250
1991	Joelle (Christmas)	Closed	1994	150.00	250
1991	Lauren	Closed	1994	125.00	250
1991	Maria	Closed	1994	125.00	250
1991	Priscilla	Closed	1994	125.00	250
1991	Valerie	Closed	1994	125.00	250

Gorham Baby Doll Collection - Aiken/Matthews

YEAR ISSUE		EDITION LIMIT	YEAR RETD.	ISSUE PRICE	*QUOTE U.S.$
1987	Christening Day	Closed	1990	245.00	350
1987	Leslie	Closed	1990	245.00	350
1987	Matthew	Closed	1990	245.00	350

Gorham Dolls - S. Stone Aiken, unless otherwise noted

YEAR ISSUE		EDITION LIMIT	YEAR RETD.	ISSUE PRICE	*QUOTE U.S.$
1985	Alexander, 19"	Closed	1990	275.00	400
1981	Alexandria, 18"	Closed	1990	250.00	500
1986	Alissa	Closed	1990	245.00	300
1985	Amelia, 19"	Closed	1990	275.00	325
1982	Baby in Apricot Dress, 16"	Closed	1990	175.00	375
1982	Baby in Blue Dress, 12"	Closed	1990	150.00	300
1982	Baby in White Dress, 18" - Gorham	Closed	1990	250.00	350
1982	Benjamin, 18"	Closed	1990	200.00	600
1981	Cecile, 16"	Closed	1990	200.00	800
1981	Christina, 16"	Closed	1990	200.00	425
1981	Christopher, 19"	Closed	1990	250.00	500
1982	Corrine, 21"	Closed	1990	250.00	500
1981	Danielle, 14"	Closed	1990	150.00	300
1981	Elena, 14"	Closed	1990	150.00	650
1982	Ellice, 18"	Closed	1990	200.00	400
1986	Emily, 14"	Closed	1990	175.00	395
1986	Fleur, 19"	Closed	1990	300.00	450
1985	Gabrielle, 19"	Closed	1990	225.00	350
1983	Jennifer, 19" Bridal Doll	Closed	1990	325.00	750
1982	Jeremy, 23"	Closed	1990	300.00	700
1986	Jessica	Closed	1990	195.00	275
1981	Jillian, 16"	Closed	1990	200.00	400
1986	Julia, 16"	Closed	1990	225.00	350
1987	Juliet	Closed	1990	325.00	400
1982	Kristin, 23"	Closed	1990	300.00	575
1986	Lauren, 14"	Closed	1990	175.00	350
1985	Linda, 19"	Closed	1990	275.00	600
1982	M. Anton, 12" - Unknown	Closed	1990	125.00	175
1982	Melanie, 23"	Closed	1990	300.00	600
1981	Melinda, 14"	Closed	1990	150.00	300
1986	Meredith	Closed	1990	295.00	350
1982	Mlle. Jeanette, 12"	Closed	1990	125.00	175
1982	Mlle. Lucille, 12"	Closed	1990	125.00	375
1982	Mlle. Marsella, 12" - Unknown	Closed	1990	125.00	275
1982	Mlle. Monique, 12"	Closed	1990	125.00	275
1982	Mlle. Yvonne, 12" - Unknown	Closed	1990	125.00	375
1985	Nanette, 19"	Closed	1990	275.00	325
1985	Odette, 19"	Closed	1990	250.00	450
1981	Rosemond, 18"	Closed	1990	250.00	750
1981	Stephanie, 18"	Closed	1990	250.00	2000

Gorham Holly Hobbie Childhood Memories - Holly Hobbie

YEAR ISSUE		EDITION LIMIT	YEAR RETD.	ISSUE PRICE	*QUOTE U.S.$
1985	Mother's Helper	Closed	1990	45.00	175
1985	Best Friends	Closed	1994	45.00	175
1985	First Day of School	Closed	1994	45.00	175
1985	Christmas Wishes	Closed	1994	45.00	175

Gorham Holly Hobbie For All Seasons - Holly Hobbie

YEAR ISSUE		EDITION LIMIT	YEAR RETD.	ISSUE PRICE	*QUOTE U.S.$
1984	Summer Holly 12"	Closed	1994	42.50	195
1984	Fall Holly 12"	Closed	1994	42.50	195
1984	Winter Holly 12"	Closed	1994	42.50	195
1984	Spring Holly 12"	Closed	1994	42.50	195
1984	Set of 4	Closed	1994	170.00	750

Holly Hobbie - Holly Hobbie

YEAR ISSUE		EDITION LIMIT	YEAR RETD.	ISSUE PRICE	*QUOTE U.S.$
1983	Blue Girl, 14"	Closed	1994	80.00	245
1983	Blue Girl, 18"	Closed	1994	115.00	295
1983	Christmas Morning, 14"	Closed	1994	80.00	245

*Quotes have been rounded up to nearest dollar

DOLLS

YEAR	ISSUE	EDITION LIMIT	YEAR RETD.	ISSUE PRICE	*QUOTE U.S.$
1983	Heather, 14"	Closed	1994	80.00	275
1983	Little Amy, 14"	Closed	1994	80.00	245
1983	Robbie, 14"	Closed	1994	80.00	275
1983	Sunday Best, 18"	Closed	1994	115.00	295
1983	Sweet Valentine, 16"	Closed	1994	100.00	295
1983	Yesterday's Memories, 18"	Closed	1994	125.00	375

Joyful Years - B. Gerardi

1989	Katrina	Closed	1994	295.00	375
1989	William	Closed	1994	295.00	375

Kezi Doll For All Seasons - Kezi

1985	Ariel 16"	Closed	1994	135.00	500
1985	Aubrey 16"	Closed	1994	135.00	500
1985	Amber 16"	Closed	1994	135.00	500
1985	Adrienne 16"	Closed	1994	135.00	500
1985	Set of 4	Closed	1994	540.00	1900

Kezi Golden Gifts - Kezi

1984	Charity 16"	Closed	1990	85.00	175
1984	Faith 18"	Closed	1990	95.00	195
1984	Felicity 18"	Closed	1990	95.00	195
1984	Grace 16"	Closed	1990	85.00	175
1984	Hope 16"	Closed	1990	85.00	175
1984	Merrie 16"	Closed	1990	85.00	175
1984	Patience 18"	Closed	1990	95.00	195
1984	Prudence 18"	Closed	1990	85.00	195

Les Belles Bebes Collection - S. Stone Aiken

1993	Camille	1,500	1994	375.00	395
1991	Cherie	Closed	1994	375.00	475
1991	Desiree	1,500	1994	375.00	395

Limited Edition Dolls - S. Stone Aiken

1982	Allison, 19"	Closed	1990	300.00	4500
1983	Ashley, 19"	Closed	1990	350.00	1000
1984	Nicole, 19"	Closed	1990	350.00	875
1984	Holly (Christmas), 19"	Closed	1990	300.00	850
1985	Lydia,19"	Closed	1990	550.00	1800
1985	Joy (Christmas), 19"	Closed	1990	350.00	695
1986	Noel (Christmas), 19"	Closed	1990	400.00	750
1987	Jacqueline, 19"	Closed	1994	500.00	700
1987	Merrie (Christmas), 19"	Closed	1994	500.00	750
1988	Andrew, 19"	Closed	1994	475.00	750
1988	Christa (Christmas), 19"	Closed	1994	550.00	1500
1990	Amey (10th Anniversary Edition)	Closed	1994	650.00	1100

Limited Edition Sister Set - S. Stone Aiken

1988	Kathleen	Closed	1994	550.00	750
1988	Katelin	Set	1994	Set	Set

Little Women - S. Stone Aiken

1983	Amy, 16"	Closed	1994	225.00	500
1983	Beth, 16"	Closed	1994	225.00	500
1983	Jo, 19"	Closed	1994	275.00	575
1983	Meg, 19"	Closed	1994	275.00	650

Precious as Pearls - S. Stone Aiken

1986	Colette	Closed	1994	400.00	1500
1987	Charlotte	Closed	1994	425.00	750
1988	Chloe	Closed	1994	525.00	850
1989	Cassandra	Closed	1994	525.00	1250
XX	Set	Closed	1994	1875.00	4000

Southern Belles - S. Stone Aiken

1985	Amanda, 19"	Closed	1990	300.00	1400
1986	Veronica, 19"	Closed	1990	325.00	750
1987	Rachel, 19"	Closed	1990	375.00	800
1988	Cassie, 19"	Closed	1990	500.00	875

Special Moments - E. Worrell

1991	Baby's First Christmas	Closed	1994	135.00	235
1992	Baby's First Steps	Closed	1994	135.00	135

Sporting Kids - R. Schrubbe

1993	Up At Bat	Closed	1994	49.50	80

Times To Treasure - L. Di Leo

1991	Bedtime	Closed	1994	195.00	250
1993	Playtime	Closed	1994	195.00	250
1990	Storytime	Closed	1994	195.00	250

Valentine Ladies - P. Valentine

1987	Anabella	Closed	1994	145.00	395
1987	Elizabeth	Closed	1994	145.00	450
1988	Felicia	Closed	1994	225.00	325
1987	Jane	Closed	1994	145.00	350
1988	Judith Anne	Closed	1994	195.00	325
1989	Julianna	Closed	1994	225.00	275
1987	Lee Ann	Closed	1994	145.00	325
1988	Maria Theresa	Closed	1994	225.00	350
1987	Marianna	Closed	1994	160.00	400
1987	Patrice	Closed	1994	145.00	325
1988	Priscilla	Closed	1994	195.00	325
1987	Rebecca	Closed	1994	145.00	325
1987	Rosanne	Closed	1994	145.00	325
1989	Rose	Closed	1994	225.00	275
1987	Sylvia	Closed	1994	160.00	350

Victorian Cameo Collection - B. Gerardi

1990	Victoria	1,500	1994	375.00	425
1991	Alexandra	Closed	1994	375.00	425

Victorian Children - S. Stone Aiken

1992	Sara's Tea Time	1,000	1994	495.00	750
1993	Catching Butterflies	1,000	1994	495.00	495

The Victorian Collection - E. Woodhouse

1992	Victoria's Jubilee	Yr.Iss.	1994	295.00	350

H & G Studios

Brenda Burke Dolls - B. Burke

1989	Adelaine	25	1989	1795.00	3600
1989	Alexandra	125	1990	995.00	2000
1989	Alicia	125	1990	895.00	1800
1989	Amanda	25	1989	1995.00	6000
1989	Angelica	50	1989	1495.00	3000
1989	Arabella	500	1990	695.00	1400
1989	Beatrice	85	1991	2395.00	2395
1990	Belinda	12	1990	3695.00	3695
1989	Bethany	45	1990	2995.00	2995
1989	Brittany	75	1990	2695.00	2695
1991	Charlotte	20	1991	2395.00	2395
1991	Clarissa	15	1992	3595.00	3595
1992	Dorothea	500		395.00	395
1993	Giovanna	1	1993	7800.00	7800
1993	Melissa	1	1993	7750.00	7750
1991	Sleigh Ride	20	1991	3695.00	3695
1991	Tender Love	25	1991	3295.00	3295

Hallmark

Special Edition Hallmark Barbie Dolls

1994	Victorian Elegance Barbie	Yr.Iss.	1994	40.00	110-150
1995	Holiday Memories Barbie	Yr.Iss.	1995	45.00	45

Hamilton Collection

Abbie Williams Doll Collection - A. Williams

1992	Molly	Closed	N/A	155.00	200

American Country Doll Collection - T. Tucker

1995	Carson	Open		95.00	95
1995	Bonnie	Open		195.00	195
1996	Patsy	Open		95.00	95
1996	Delaney	Open		95.00	95
1996	Arizona	Open		95.00	95
1996	Kendra	Open		195.00	195

Annual Connossieur Doll - N/A

1992	Lara	7,450		295.00	295

The Antique Doll Collection - Unknown

1989	Nicole	Closed	N/A	195.00	300
1990	Colette	Closed	1996	195.00	195
1991	Lisette	Closed	1996	195.00	225
1991	Katrina	Closed	1996	195.00	195

Baby Portrait Dolls - B. Parker

1991	Melissa	Closed	1993	135.00	175-200
1992	Jenna	Closed	N/A	135.00	200
1992	Bethany	Closed	1996	135.00	150
1993	Mindy	Closed	1996	135.00	150

Belles of the Countryside - C. Heath Orange

1992	Erin	Open		135.00	135
1992	Rose	Open		135.00	135
1993	Lorna	Open		135.00	135
1994	Gwyn	Open		135.00	135

The Bessie Pease Gutmann Doll Collection - B.P. Gutmann

1989	Love is Blind	Closed	N/A	135.00	220
1989	He Won't Bite	Closed	N/A	135.00	135
1991	Virginia	Closed	1996	135.00	135
1991	First Dancing Lesson	Closed	1996	135.00	135
1991	Good Morning	Closed	1996	135.00	135
1991	Love At First Sight	Closed	1996	135.00	135

Best Buddies - C.M. Rolfe

1994	Jodie	Open		69.00	69
1994	Brandy	Open		69.00	69
1995	Joey	Open		69.00	69
1996	Stacey	Open		69.00	69

Boehm Christening - Boehm Studio

1994	Elena's First Portrait	Closed	1996	155.00	250
1994	Elena	Closed	1996	155.00	180

Bridal Elegance - Boehm

1994	Camille	Closed	1996	195.00	225

Bride Dolls - Unknown

1991	Portrait of Innocence	Closed	1996	195.00	210
1992	Portrait of Loveliness	Closed	1996	195.00	250

Brooker Tickler - Harris/Brooker

1995	Nellie	Open		95.00	95
1996	Callie	Open		95.00	95

Brooks Wooden Dolls - P. Ryan Brooks

1993	Waiting For Santa	15,000	1994	135.00	200-250
1993	Are You the Easter Bunny?	15,000		135.00	135
1994	Be My Valentine	Open		135.00	135
1995	Shh! I Only Wanna Peek	Open		135.00	135

Byi Praying Dolls - C. Byi

1996	Mark & Mary	Open		89.95	90

Catherine Mather Dolls - C. Mather

1993	Justine	15,000		155.00	155

Central Park Skaters - Unknown

1991	Central Park Skaters	Closed	1996	245.00	245

A Child's Menagerie - B. Van Boxel

1993	Becky	Closed	1996	69.00	69
1993	Carrie	Closed	1996	69.00	69
1994	Mandy	Closed	1996	69.00	69
1994	Terry	Closed	1996	69.00	69

Children To Cherish - Cybis

1991	A Gift of Innocence	Yr.Iss.	1991	135.00	135
1991	A Gift of Beauty	Closed	1996	135.00	135

Ciambra - M. Ciambra

1995	Chloe	Open		155.00	155
1996	Lydia	Open		155.00	155

Cindy Marschner Rolfe Dolls - C. M. Rolfe

1993	Shannon	Closed	1996	95.00	95
1993	Julie	Open		95.00	95
1993	Kayla	Open		95.00	95
1994	Janey	Open		95.00	95

Cindy Marschner Rolfe Twins - C. M. Rolfe

1995	Shelby & Sydney	Closed	1996	190.00	190

Connie Walser Derek Baby Dolls - C.W. Derek

1990	Jessica	Closed	1993	155.00	300-500
1991	Sara	Closed	1995	155.00	180
1991	Andrew	Closed	1996	155.00	155
1991	Amanda	Closed	1996	155.00	155
1992	Samantha	Closed	1996	155.00	155

Connie Walser Derek Baby Dolls II - C. W. Derek

1992	Stephanie	Closed	1996	95.00	200
1992	Beth	Closed	1996	95.00	160

Connie Walser Derek Baby Dolls III - C. W. Derek

1994	Chelsea	Open		79.00	79
1995	Tina	Open		79.00	79
1995	Tabitha	Open		79.00	79
1995	Ginger	Open		79.00	79

Connie Walser Derek Dolls - C. W. Derek

1992	Baby Jessica	Closed	1996	75.00	75
1993	Baby Sara	Closed	1996	75.00	75

Connie Walser Derek Toddlers - C. W. Derek

1994	Jessie	Closed	1996	79.00	120
1994	Casey	Closed	1996	79.00	120
1995	Angie	Closed	1996	79.00	120
1995	Tori	Open		79.00	79

Daddy's Little Girls - M. Snyder

1992	Lindsay	Closed	1996	95.00	95
1993	Cassie	Closed	1996	95.00	95
1993	Dana	Closed	1996	95.00	120
1994	Tara	Closed	1996	95.00	95

Dey Recital Dolls - P. Dey

1996	Mallory	9,500		195.00	195

Dolls by Autumn Berwick - A. Berwick

1993	Laura	Closed	1995	135.00	135

Dolls By Kay McKee - K. McKee

1992	Shy Violet	Closed	1993	135.00	200-250
1992	Robin	Closed	1995	135.00	135
1993	Katie Did It!	Closed	1995	135.00	135
1993	Ryan	Open		135.00	135

Dolls of America's Colonial Heritage - A. Elekfy

1986	Katrina	Closed	1994	55.00	55
1986	Nicole	Closed	1994	55.00	55
1987	Maria	Closed	1994	55.00	55
1987	Priscilla	Closed	1994	55.00	55
1987	Colleen	Closed	1994	55.00	55
1988	Gretchen	Closed	1994	55.00	55

Elaine Campbell Dolls - E. Campbell

1994	Emma	Closed	1994	95.00	95
1995	Abby	Open		95.00	95
1995	Jana	Open		95.00	95
1995	Molly	Open		95.00	95

*Quotes have been rounded up to nearest dollar

DOLLS

Hamilton Collection to Hamilton Collection

YEAR ISSUE		EDITION LIMIT	YEAR RETD.	ISSUE PRICE	*QUOTE U.S.$

Eternal Friends Doll Collection - Precious Moments
| 1996 | Love One Another | Open | | 135.00 | 135 |
| 1997 | Friendship Hits The Spot | Open | | 135.00 | 135 |

First Recital - N/A
| 1993 | Hillary | Open | | 135.00 | 135 |
| 1994 | Olivia | Open | | 135.00 | 135 |

Grobben Ethnic Babies - J. Grobben
| 1994 | Jasmine | Closed | 1996 | 135.00 | 180 |
| 1995 | Taiya | Closed | 1996 | 135.00 | 160 |

Grothedde Dolls - N. Grothedde
| 1994 | Cindy | Closed | 1996 | 69.00 | 100 |
| 1995 | Holly | Open | | 69.00 | 69 |

Hargrave Dolls - M. Hargrave
| 1994 | Angela | Open | | 79.00 | 79 |
| 1995 | April | Open | | 79.00 | 79 |

Heath Babies - C. Heath Orange
| 1995 | Hayley | Open | | 95.00 | 95 |
| 1996 | Ellie | Open | | 95.00 | 95 |

Heavenly Clowns Doll Collection - K. McKee
| 1996 | Blue Moon | Open | | 95.00 | 95 |

Helen Carr Dolls - H. Carr
1994	Claudia	Open		135.00	135
1995	Jillian	Open		135.00	135
1996	Abigail	Open		135.00	135
1996	Rosalee	Open		135.00	135

Helen Kish II Dolls - H. Kish
| 1992 | Vanessa | Open | | 135.00 | 135 |
| 1994 | Jordan | Open | | 95.00 | 95 |

Holiday Carollers - U. Lepp
| 1992 | Joy | Closed | 1996 | 155.00 | 155 |
| 1993 | Noel | Closed | 1996 | 155.00 | 155 |

Honkytonk Gals Doll Collection - C. Johnston
| 1996 | Kendall | Open | | 95.00 | 95 |
| 1997 | Logan | Open | | 95.00 | 95 |

Huckleberry Hill Kids - B. Parker
1994	Gabrielle	Open		95.00	95
1994	Alexandra	Open		95.00	95
1995	Jeremiah	Open		95.00	95
1996	Sarah	Open		95.00	95

I Love Lucy (Porcelain) - Unknown
1990	Lucy	Closed	N/A	95.00	240-300
1991	Ricky	Closed	N/A	95.00	350
1992	Queen of the Gypsies	Closed	N/A	95.00	245
1992	Vitameatavegamin	Closed	N/A	95.00	200-300

I Love Lucy (Vinyl) - Unknown
1988	Ethel	Closed	N/A	40.00	100
1988	Fred	Closed	N/A	40.00	100
1990	Lucy	Closed	N/A	40.00	100
1991	Ricky	Closed	N/A	40.00	150
1992	Queen of the Gypsies	Open		40.00	40
1992	Vitameatavegamin	Open		40.00	40

I'm So Proud Doll Collection - L. Cobabe
1992	Christina	Closed	1996	95.00	95
1993	Jill	Closed	1996	95.00	120
1994	Tammy	Closed	1996	95.00	95
1994	Shelly	Closed	1996	95.00	115

Inga Manders - I. Manders
1995	Miss Priss	Open		79.00	79
1995	Miss Hollywood	Open		79.00	79
1995	Miss Glamour	Open		79.00	79
1996	Miss Sweetheart	Open		79.00	79

International Children - C. Woodie
1991	Miko	Closed	N/A	49.50	80
1991	Anastasia	Closed	1996	49.50	50
1991	Angelina	Closed	1996	49.50	50
1992	Lian	Closed	1996	49.50	50
1992	Monique	Closed	1996	49.50	50
1992	Lisa	Closed	1996	49.50	50

Jane Zidjunas Party Dolls - J. Zidjunas
1991	Kelly	Closed	1994	135.00	135
1992	Katie	Closed	1994	135.00	135
1993	Meredith	Closed	1994	135.00	135

Jane Zidjunas Sleeping Dolls - J. Zidjunas
| 1995 | Annie | Open | | 79.00 | 79 |
| 1995 | Jamie | Open | | 79.00 | 79 |

Jane Zidjunas Toddler Dolls - J. Zidjunas
1991	Jennifer	Closed	1995	135.00	135
1991	Megan	Closed	1995	135.00	160
1992	Kimberly	Closed	1995	135.00	135
1992	Amy	Closed	1995	135.00	135

Jane Zidjunas Victorian - J. Zidjunas
| 1996 | Constance | 9,500 | | 195.00 | 195 |

Jeanne Wilson Dolls - J. Wilson
| 1994 | Priscilla | Open | | 155.00 | 155 |

Johnston Cowgirls - C. Johnston
1994	Savannah	Open		79.00	79
1994	Skyler	Open		79.00	79
1995	Cheyene	Open		79.00	79
1995	Austin	Open		79.00	79

Join The Parade - N/A
1992	Betsy	Closed	1996	49.50	50
1994	Peggy	Closed	1996	49.50	50
1994	Sandy	Closed	1996	49.50	50
1995	Brian	Closed	1996	49.50	50

Joke Grobben Dolls - J. Grobben
1992	Heather	Closed	1995	69.00	69
1993	Kathleen	Closed	1995	69.00	69
1993	Brianna	Closed	1995	69.00	69
1994	Bridget	Closed	1995	69.00	69

Joke Grobben Tall Dolls - J. Grobben
| 1995 | Jade | Open | | 135.00 | 135 |
| 1996 | Raven | Open | | 135.00 | 135 |

Just Like Mom - H. Kish
1991	Ashley	Closed	1993	135.00	250-300
1992	Elizabeth	Closed	1994	135.00	160
1992	Hannah	Closed	1994	135.00	135
1993	Margaret	Closed	1994	135.00	135

Kay McKee Downsized Dolls - K. McKee
| 1995 | Kyle | Open | | 79.00 | 79 |
| 1996 | Cody | Open | | 79.00 | 79 |

Kay McKee Klowns - K. McKee
| 1993 | The Dreamer | 15,000 | 1995 | 155.00 | 155 |
| 1994 | The Entertainer | 15,000 | 1996 | 155.00 | 180 |

Kuck Fairy - S. Kuck
| 1994 | Tooth Fairy | Closed | 1996 | 135.00 | 135 |

Laura Cobabe Dolls - L. Cobabe
| 1992 | Amber | Closed | 1994 | 195.00 | 225 |
| 1992 | Brooke | Closed | 1994 | 195.00 | 195 |

Laura Cobabe Dolls II - L. Cobabe
| 1993 | Kristen | Closed | 1994 | 75.00 | 75 |

Laura Cobabe Ethnic - L. Cobabe
| 1995 | Nica | Open | | 95.00 | 95 |
| 1996 | Kenu | Open | | 95.00 | 95 |

Laura Cobabe Indians - L. Cobabe
1994	Snowbird	Open		135.00	135
1995	Little Eagle	Open		135.00	135
1995	Desert Bloom	Open		135.00	135
1996	Call of the Coyote	Open		135.00	135

Laura Cobabe Tall Dolls - L. Cobabe
| 1994 | Cassandra | Open | | 195.00 | 195 |
| 1994 | Taylor | Open | | 195.00 | 195 |

Laura Cobabe's Costume Kids - L. Cobabe
1994	Lil' Punkin	Closed	1996	79.00	110
1994	Little Ladybug	Open		79.00	79
1995	Miss Dinomite	Open		79.00	79
1995	Miss Flutterby	Open		79.00	79

Little Gardners - J. Galperin
| 1996 | Daisy | Open | | 95.00 | 95 |

Little Rascals™ - S./J. Hoffman
1992	Spanky	Open		75.00	75
1993	Alfalfa	Open		75.00	75
1994	Darla	Open		75.00	75
1994	Buckwheat	Open		75.00	75
1994	Stymie	Open		75.00	75
1995	Pete The Pup	Open		75.00	75

Littlest Members of the Wedding - J. Esteban
| 1993 | Matthew & Melanie | Closed | 1995 | 195.00 | 195 |

Lucy Dolls - Unknown
| 1996 | Lucy | Open | | 95.00 | 95 |

Maud Humphrey Bogart Dolls - Unknown
| 1992 | Playing Bridesmaid | Closed | N/A | 195.00 | 225 |

Maud Humphrey Bogart Doll Collection - M.H. Bogart
1989	Playing Bride	Closed	N/A	225.00	225
1990	First Party	Closed	N/A	135.00	150
1990	The First Lesson	Closed	N/A	135.00	149
1991	Seamstress	Closed	N/A	135.00	149
1991	Little Captive	Closed	1996	135.00	135
1992	Kitty's Bath	Closed	1996	135.00	135

Mavis Snyder Dolls - M. Snyder
| 1994 | Tara | Closed | 1995 | 95.00 | 95 |

Parker Carousel - B. Parker
| 1996 | Annelise's Musical Ride | 4,500 | | 295.00 | 295 |

Parker Fairy Tale - B. Parker
| 1995 | Claire | Open | | 155.00 | 155 |
| 1996 | Marissa | Open | | 155.00 | 155 |

Parker Levi Toddlers - B. Parker
| 1992 | Courtney | Closed | 1994 | 135.00 | 200 |
| 1992 | Melody | Closed | 1994 | 135.00 | 135 |

Parkins Baby - P. Parkins
| 1995 | Baby Alyssa | Open | | 225.00 | 225 |

Parkins Connisseur - P. Parkins
| 1993 | Faith | Closed | 1995 | 135.00 | 180 |

Parkins Portraits - P. Parkins
1993	Lauren	Closed	1995	79.00	79
1993	Kelsey	Open		79.00	79
1994	Morgan	Open		79.00	79
1994	Cassidy	Closed	1996	79.00	100

Parkins Toddler Angels - P. Parkins
1995	Celeste	Open		135.00	135
1996	Charity	Open		135.00	135
1996	Charisse	Open		135.00	135
1996	Chantelle	Open		135.00	135

Parkins Treasures - P. Parkins
1992	Tiffany	Closed	1994	55.00	120
1992	Dorothy	Closed	1995	55.00	80
1993	Charlotte	Closed	1995	55.00	80
1993	Cynthia	Closed	1995	55.00	80

Phyllis Parkins Dolls - P. Parkins
| 1992 | Swan Princess | 9,850 | 1995 | 195.00 | 220-250 |

Phyllis Parkins II Dolls - P. Parkins
1995	Dakota	Open		135.00	135
1996	Kerrie	Open		135.00	135
1996	Ginny	Open		135.00	135
1000	Dixie	Open		135.00	135

Phyllis Parkins Musical Dolls - P. Parkins
1995	Nite, Nite Pony	Open		95.00	95
1996	Twice As Nice	Open		95.00	95
1996	Sleep Tight, Sweetheart	Open		95.00	95
1996	Cradled in Love	Open		95.00	95

Picnic In The Park - J. Esteban
1991	Rebecca	Closed	1995	155.00	155
1992	Emily	Closed	1995	155.00	155
1992	Victoria	Closed	1995	155.00	155
1993	Benjamin	Closed	1995	155.00	155

Pitter Patter Doll Collection - C. W. Derek
| 1996 | Bobbie Jo | Open | | 79.00 | 79 |
| 1997 | Mary Anne | Open | | 79.00 | 79 |

Precious Moments - S. Butcher
1994	Tell Me the Story of Jesus	Open		79.00	79
1995	God Loveth a Cheerful Giver	Open		79.00	79
1995	Mother Sew Dear	Open		79.00	79
1996	You Are the Type I Love	Open		79.00	79

Precious Moments Christening - S. Butcher
| 1996 | Anna | Open | | 95.00 | 95 |
| 1996 | Elise | Open | | 95.00 | 95 |

Proud Indian Nation - R. Swanson
1992	Navajo Little One	Closed	1993	95.00	200
1993	Dressed Up For The Pow Wow	Closed	1996	95.00	150
1993	Autumn Treat	Open		95.00	95
1994	Out with Mama's Flock	Open		95.00	95

Rachel Cold Toddlers - R. Cold
| 1995 | Jenny | Open | | 95.00 | 95 |
| 1996 | Trudy | Open | | 95.00 | 95 |

The Royal Beauty Dolls - Unknown
| 1991 | Chen Mai | Closed | 1994 | 195.00 | 195 |

Russian Czarra Dolls - Unknown
| 1991 | Alexandra | Closed | N/A | 295.00 | 350 |

Sandra Kuck Dolls - S. Kuck
1993	A Kiss Goodnight	Open		79.00	79
1994	Teaching Teddy	Open		79.00	79
1995	Reading With Teddy	Open		79.00	79
1996	Picnic With Teddy	Open		79.00	79

Santa's Little Helpers - C.W. Derek
| 1992 | Nicholas | Closed | 1996 | 155.00 | 155 |
| 1993 | Hope | Closed | 1996 | 155.00 | 155 |

*Quotes have been rounded up to nearest dollar

Collectors' Information Bureau

DOLLS

Schmidt Babies - J. Schmidt

YEAR	ISSUE	EDITION LIMIT	YEAR RETD.	ISSUE PRICE	*QUOTE U.S.$
1995	Baby	Open		79.00	79
1996	Snookums	Open		79.00	79

Schmidt Dolls - J. Schmidt

YEAR	ISSUE	EDITION LIMIT	YEAR RETD.	ISSUE PRICE	*QUOTE U.S.$
1994	Kaitlyn	Closed	1995	79.00	120
1995	Kara	Closed	1995	79.00	79
1995	Kathy	Open		79.00	79
1996	Karla	Open		79.00	79

Schrubbe Santa Dolls - R. Schrubbe

YEAR	ISSUE	EDITION LIMIT	YEAR RETD.	ISSUE PRICE	*QUOTE U.S.$
1994	Jolly Old St. Nick	Closed	1995	135.00	135

Sentiments From the Garden - M. Severino

YEAR	ISSUE	EDITION LIMIT	YEAR RETD.	ISSUE PRICE	*QUOTE U.S.$
1996	Fairy of Innocence	Open		59.00	59
1997	Fairy of Loveliness	Open		59.00	59

Shelton II Doll - V. Shelton

YEAR	ISSUE	EDITION LIMIT	YEAR RETD.	ISSUE PRICE	*QUOTE U.S.$
1996	Josie	Open		79.00	79

Shelton Indians - V. Shelton

YEAR	ISSUE	EDITION LIMIT	YEAR RETD.	ISSUE PRICE	*QUOTE U.S.$
1995	Little Cloud	Open		95.00	95
1996	Little Basketweaver	Open		95.00	95
1996	Little Warrior	Open		95.00	95
1996	Little Skywatcher	Open		95.00	95

Simon Indians - S. Simon

YEAR	ISSUE	EDITION LIMIT	YEAR RETD.	ISSUE PRICE	*QUOTE U.S.$
1994	Meadowlark	Open		95.00	95
1995	Tashee	Open		95.00	95
1996	Star Dreamer	Open		95.00	95
1996	Sewanka	Open		95.00	95

Songs of the Seasons Hakata Doll Collection - T. Murakami

YEAR	ISSUE	EDITION LIMIT	YEAR RETD.	ISSUE PRICE	*QUOTE U.S.$
1985	Winter Song Maiden	9,800	1991	75.00	75
1985	Spring Song Maiden	9,800	1991	75.00	75
1985	Summer Song Maiden	9,800	1991	75.00	75
1985	Autumn Song Maiden	9,800	1991	75.00	75

Star Trek Doll Collection - E. Daub

YEAR	ISSUE	EDITION LIMIT	YEAR RETD.	ISSUE PRICE	*QUOTE U.S.$
1988	Mr. Spock	Closed	N/A	75.00	150
1988	Captain Kirk	Closed	N/A	75.00	120
1989	Dr. Mc Coy	Closed	N/A	75.00	120
1989	Scotty	Closed	N/A	75.00	120
1990	Sulu	Closed	N/A	75.00	120
1990	Chekov	Closed	N/A	75.00	120
1991	Uhura	Closed	N/A	75.00	120

Storybook Dolls - L. Di Leo

YEAR	ISSUE	EDITION LIMIT	YEAR RETD.	ISSUE PRICE	*QUOTE U.S.$
1991	Alice in Wonderland	Closed	1996	75.00	75

Summertime Beauties - C. Marschner

YEAR	ISSUE	EDITION LIMIT	YEAR RETD.	ISSUE PRICE	*QUOTE U.S.$
1995	Sally	Open		95.00	95
1996	Lacey	Open		95.00	95

Through The Eyes of Virginia Turner - V. Turner

YEAR	ISSUE	EDITION LIMIT	YEAR RETD.	ISSUE PRICE	*QUOTE U.S.$
1992	Michelle	Closed	1993	95.00	150-180
1992	Danielle	Open		95.00	95
1993	Wendy	Closed	1995	95.00	125
1994	Dawn	Closed	1996	95.00	95

Toddler Days Doll Collection - D. Schurig

YEAR	ISSUE	EDITION LIMIT	YEAR RETD.	ISSUE PRICE	*QUOTE U.S.$
1992	Erica	Closed	1995	95.00	125
1993	Darlene	Closed	1995	95.00	95
1994	Karen	Closed	1995	95.00	95
1995	Penny	Closed	1995	95.00	95

Treasured Toddlers - V. Turner

YEAR	ISSUE	EDITION LIMIT	YEAR RETD.	ISSUE PRICE	*QUOTE U.S.$
1992	Whitney	Closed	1996	95.00	200
1993	Natalie	Closed	1996	95.00	150

Vickie Walker 1st's - V. Walker

YEAR	ISSUE	EDITION LIMIT	YEAR RETD.	ISSUE PRICE	*QUOTE U.S.$
1995	Leah	Open		79.00	79
1995	Leslie	Open		79.00	79
1995	Lily	Open		79.00	79
1995	Leanna	Open		79.00	79

Victorian Treasures - C.W. Derek

YEAR	ISSUE	EDITION LIMIT	YEAR RETD.	ISSUE PRICE	*QUOTE U.S.$
1992	Katherine	Closed	1996	155.00	155
1993	Madeline	Closed	1996	155.00	155

Virginia Turner Dolls- V. Turner

YEAR	ISSUE	EDITION LIMIT	YEAR RETD.	ISSUE PRICE	*QUOTE U.S.$
1995	Amelia	Open		95.00	95
1995	Mckenzie	Open		95.00	95
1996	Grace	Open		95.00	95
1996	Alexis	Open		95.00	95

Virginia Turner Little Sisters- V. Turner

YEAR	ISSUE	EDITION LIMIT	YEAR RETD.	ISSUE PRICE	*QUOTE U.S.$
1996	Allie	Open		95.00	95

Wooden Dolls - N/A

YEAR	ISSUE	EDITION LIMIT	YEAR RETD.	ISSUE PRICE	*QUOTE U.S.$
1991	Gretchen	9,850	1995	225.00	280
1991	Heidi	9,850	1995	225.00	250

Wright Indian Dolls - D. Wright

YEAR	ISSUE	EDITION LIMIT	YEAR RETD.	ISSUE PRICE	*QUOTE U.S.$
1994	Sacajawea	Open		135.00	135
1994	Minnehaha	Open		135.00	135
1995	Pine Leaf	Open		135.00	135
1995	Lozen	Open		135.00	135

Year Round Fun - D. Schurig

YEAR	ISSUE	EDITION LIMIT	YEAR RETD.	ISSUE PRICE	*QUOTE U.S.$
1992	Allison	Closed	1995	95.00	95
1993	Christy	Closed	1995	95.00	95
1993	Paula	Closed	1995	95.00	95
1994	Kaylie	Closed	1995	95.00	125

Zolan Dolls - D. Zolan

YEAR	ISSUE	EDITION LIMIT	YEAR RETD.	ISSUE PRICE	*QUOTE U.S.$
1991	A Christmas Prayer	Closed	1993	95.00	250-280
1992	Winter Angel	Closed	1996	95.00	95
1992	Rainy Day Pals	Closed	1996	95.00	125
1992	Quiet Time	Closed	1996	95.00	125
1993	For You	Closed	1996	95.00	125
1993	The Thinker	Closed	1996	95.00	180

Zolan Double Dolls - D. Zolan

YEAR	ISSUE	EDITION LIMIT	YEAR RETD.	ISSUE PRICE	*QUOTE U.S.$
1993	First Kiss	Closed	1995	155.00	155
1994	New Shoes	Closed	1995	155.00	155

Jan McLean Originals

Flowers of the Heart Collection - J. McLean

YEAR	ISSUE	EDITION LIMIT	YEAR RETD.	ISSUE PRICE	*QUOTE U.S.$
1991	Marigold	100	N/A	2400.00	2900-3200
1990	Pansy	100	N/A	2200.00	2800-2900
1990	Pansy (bobbed blonde)	Retrd.	N/A	2200.00	2800-3000
1990	Pansy A/P	Retrd.	N/A	4300	4800
1990	Poppy	100	N/A	2200.00	2700
1991	Primrose	100	N/A	2500.00	2500-2600

Jan McLean Originals - J. McLean

YEAR	ISSUE	EDITION LIMIT	YEAR RETD.	ISSUE PRICE	*QUOTE U.S.$
1991	Lucrezia	15		6000.00	6000
1990	Phoebe I	25	N/A	2700.00	3300-3600

Kurt S. Adler, Inc.

Fleur-dis-Lis Enchanted Garden - J. Mostrom

YEAR	ISSUE	EDITION LIMIT	YEAR RETD.	ISSUE PRICE	*QUOTE U.S.$
1997	Alexandra in Plum W3340	Open		20.00	20
1997	Bonnie in Ribbons W3343	Open		21.00	21
1997	Celeste the Garden Angel W3344	Open		45.00	45
1997	Jenny Lind W3336	Open		28.00	28
1997	Lilac Fairy W3342	Open		22.00	22
1997	Lily Fairy W3342	Open		22.00	22
1997	Marissa In Mauve W3340	Open		20.00	20
1997	Melissa in Lace W3343	Open		21.00	21
1997	Rose Fairy W3342	Open		22.00	22

Fleur-dis-Lis Victorian Manor - J. Mostrom

YEAR	ISSUE	EDITION LIMIT	YEAR RETD.	ISSUE PRICE	*QUOTE U.S.$
1997	Barbara With Muff W3348	Open		30.00	30
1997	Caroling Jane with Book W3338	Open		22.00	22
1997	Jonathan with Horn W3338	Open		22.00	22
1997	Kathryn with Cape W3338	Open		22.00	22
1997	Rebecca Burgundy Skater Lady W3337	Open		32.00	32

Fleur-dis-Lis Winter Dreams - J. Mostrom

YEAR	ISSUE	EDITION LIMIT	YEAR RETD.	ISSUE PRICE	*QUOTE U.S.$
1997	Charlotte with Hat & Cape W3345	Open		22.00	22
1997	George with Box W3345	Open		22.00	22
1997	Sandra with Box W3345	Open		22.00	22

Royal Heritage Collection - J. Mostrom

YEAR	ISSUE	EDITION LIMIT	YEAR RETD.	ISSUE PRICE	*QUOTE U.S.$
1993	Anastasia J5746	3,000	1996	125.00	125
1993	Good King Wenceslas W2928	2,000	1996	130.00	130
1993	Medieval King of Christmas W2981	2,000	1994	390.00	390
1994	Nicholas on Skates J5750	3,000	1996	120.00	120
1994	Sasha on Skates J5749	3,000	1996	130.00	130

Small Wonders - J. Mostrom

YEAR	ISSUE	EDITION LIMIT	YEAR RETD.	ISSUE PRICE	*QUOTE U.S.$
1995	America-Hollie Blue W3162	Open		30.00	30
1995	America-Texas Tyler W3162	Open		30.00	30
1995	Ireland-Cathleen W3082	Open		28.00	28
1995	Ireland-Michael W3082	Open		28.00	28
1995	Kwanza-Mufaro W3161	Retrd.	1996	28.00	28
1995	Kwanza-Shani W3161	Retrd.	1996	28.00	28

When I Grow Up - J. Mostrom

YEAR	ISSUE	EDITION LIMIT	YEAR RETD.	ISSUE PRICE	*QUOTE U.S.$
1995	Dr. Brown W3079	Retrd.	1996	27.00	27
1995	Freddy the Fireman W3163	Open		28.00	28
1995	Melissa the Teacher W3081	Retrd.	1996	28.00	28
1995	Nurse Nancy W3079	Retrd.	1996	27.00	27
1995	Scott the Golfer W3080	Open	1996	28.00	28

KVK, Inc.

Daddy's Long Legs/Collectors Club Members Only - K. Germany

YEAR	ISSUE	EDITION LIMIT	YEAR RETD.	ISSUE PRICE	*QUOTE U.S.$
1993	Faith	2,290	1993	65.00	325-350
1994	Bubby, w/Heart blanket	580	1994	65.00	300-325
1994	Bubby, w/Star blanket	1,537	1994	65.00	250
1994	Sissy	1,963	1995	65.00	250-275
1995	Bull Bishop	1,529	1995	65.00	125-200
1995	Cherry	1,010	1995	65.00	125
1995	Joy (Angel)	Closed	1995	Gift	N/A
1996	Jack	Closed	1996	65.00	100-130
1996	Jill	Closed	1996	65.00	100-130
1996	Carrie (Angel)	Closed	1996	Gift	N/A
1997	Joseph	Yr.Iss.		65.00	65
1997	Mary	Yr.Iss.		65.00	65
1997	Baby Jesus	Yr.Iss.		Gift	N/A

Daddy's Long Legs/Angels - K. Germany

YEAR	ISSUE	EDITION LIMIT	YEAR RETD.	ISSUE PRICE	*QUOTE U.S.$
1995	Demetria	1	1995	2500.00	N/A
1994	Glory	692	1994	118.00	250
1994	Hope	345	1994	118.00	250
1994	Kara	424	1994	76.00	200
1996	Keisha, the Mud Pie Angel	Open		79.95	80
1996	Monica	Open		150.00	150
1994	Precious	824	1994	76.00	200

Daddy's Long Legs/Animals - K. Germany

YEAR	ISSUE	EDITION LIMIT	YEAR RETD.	ISSUE PRICE	*QUOTE U.S.$
1990	Abigail the Cow, blue	3,498	1995	62.00	160-175
1990	Abigail the Cow, red	1,063	1995	68.00	185
1990	Cat in Jump Suit	66	1990	60.00	550
1990	Goat-boy	109	1991	62.00	650
1990	Goat-girl	154	1991	62.00	650
1990	Hugh Hoofner	1,453	1994	68.00	175
1991	Kitty Kat	527	1992	78.00	475-525
1991	Mamie the Pig, blue	425	1992	84.00	500-525
1990	Mamie the Pig, green	425	1992	68.00	500-550
1990	Pig-boy	124	1990	58.00	550-600
1990	Raccoon	123	1990	66.00	600-650
1990	Rachael Rabbit	377	1992	15.00	150
1990	Robby Rabbit	529	1992	44.00	400
1990	Rose Rabbit	684	1992	54.00	600
1990	Roxanne Rabbit	351	1992	52.00	400
1990	Rudy Rabbit	547	1992	54.00	600
1990	Wedding Rabbits	3	1990	240.00	3000

Daddy's Long Legs/Arts & Theater - K. Germany

YEAR	ISSUE	EDITION LIMIT	YEAR RETD.	ISSUE PRICE	*QUOTE U.S.$
1992	Babe Bouchard	Open		98.00	98
1994	Margo	Closed	1996	126.00	150
1990	Mime	57	1990	58.00	1150
1990	Witch Hazel	1,971	1995	86.00	250

Daddy's Long Legs/Babies & Toddlers - K. Germany

YEAR	ISSUE	EDITION LIMIT	YEAR RETD.	ISSUE PRICE	*QUOTE U.S.$
1995	Annie Lee w/blanket	450	1995	150.00	325-350
1995	Annie Lee w/o blanket	100	1995	150.00	275
1997	Baby Hannah	Open		80.00	80
1991	Baby Jesse	Open		18.00	18
1996	Bunny	682	1996	80.00	160

Daddy's Long Legs/Children Around the World - K. Germany

YEAR	ISSUE	EDITION LIMIT	YEAR RETD.	ISSUE PRICE	*QUOTE U.S.$
1995	Lizabeth	Open		76.00	76
1997	Sally	Open		84.00	84
1996	Starr	Open		80.00	80
1995	Su	Open		76.00	76
1996	Teresa	Open		80.00	80

Daddy's Long Legs/Clowns - K. Germany

YEAR	ISSUE	EDITION LIMIT	YEAR RETD.	ISSUE PRICE	*QUOTE U.S.$
1996	Buttons	Closed	1996	80.00	95-125
1993	Cecil	Open		98.00	98
1997	Cricket	Open		94.00	94
1994	Peanut	Open		76.00	76
1995	Sugar (event ed.)	475	1995	120.00	500

Daddy's Long Legs/Community & Family - K. Germany

YEAR	ISSUE	EDITION LIMIT	YEAR RETD.	ISSUE PRICE	*QUOTE U.S.$
1993	Abe	2,483	1995	94.00	135-175
1994	Aunt Fannie	Closed	1996	90.00	100-185
1992	Bessie	Closed	1996	94.00	150
1993	Billye	1,863	1995	98.00	225
1995	Camille	2,000		184.00	184-250
1994	Charles Louis	Closed	1996	90.00	100-180
1992	Doc Moses	2,494	1993	98.00	325
1996	Earl	Closed	1996	98.00	200-350
1996	Ella	Closed	1996	98.00	200-350
1993	Esther	3,000	1993	158.00	350
1992	Ezra	Open		90.00	90
1992	Gracie	Closed	1996	94.00	125-150
1993	Jackie	2,425	1995	98.00	150-200
1992	Jasmine	3,977	1994	90.00	250
1993	Judge	1,866	1995	98.00	225
1991	Junior w/Hat & Banjo	Open		62.00	76
1994	Maxine	Closed	1996	90.00	100-180
1992	Nurse Garnet	1,415	1993	90.00	150-300
1991	Oma Green	Open		90.00	90
1993	Sam	1,813	1995	94.00	125-150
1993	Slats	2,323	1995	98.00	100-150
1990	Sofie	5,548	1992	44.00	350
1994	Uncle Leon	Closed	1996	90.00	100-180

Daddy's Long Legs/Costume Party - K. Germany

YEAR	ISSUE	EDITION LIMIT	YEAR RETD.	ISSUE PRICE	*QUOTE U.S.$
1997	Boots	Open		90.00	90
1996	Gigi	Closed	1996	90.00	100
1995	Gretchen	982	1995	80.00	125
1995	Pistol	1,352	1995	80.00	125-150
1994	Ticker	1,714	1994	76.00	150-225
1994	Wendy	1,609	1994	80.00	200

Daddy's Long Legs/Cultural - K. Germany

YEAR	ISSUE	EDITION LIMIT	YEAR RETD.	ISSUE PRICE	*QUOTE U.S.$
1997	Amani	Open		104.00	104
1995	Kenya	Open		98.00	98
1990	Nettie	Open		70.00	94
1990	Tobias	Open		72.00	94

Daddy's Long Legs/Old West - K. Germany

YEAR	ISSUE	EDITION LIMIT	YEAR RETD.	ISSUE PRICE	*QUOTE U.S.$
1990	Cowboy Buck	1,824	1994	78.00	175-300
1990	Indian, 1st ed.	304	1990	78.00	800

*Quotes have been rounded up to nearest dollar

YEAR ISSUE		EDITION LIMIT	YEAR RETD.	ISSUE PRICE	*QUOTE U.S.$
1992	Lucky the Gambler	939	1992	90.00	450
1990	Miss Lilly	1,664	1994	78.00	175-300
1997	Proud Eagle	1,500		290.00	290
1991	Still River (Indian, 2nd ed.)	1,452	1995	98.00	250
1996	Sweet Savannah	2,000		260.00	260
1996	Wildwood Will	1,000	1996	290.00	475-550

Daddy's Long Legs/Old Woman Who Lived In A Shoe - K. Germany

YEAR ISSUE		EDITION LIMIT	YEAR RETD.	ISSUE PRICE	*QUOTE U.S.$
1997	Hannah	Open		80.00	80
1996	Lovie	Open		98.00	98
1996	William	Open		80.00	80

Daddy's Long Legs/Patriotic - K. Germany

YEAR ISSUE		EDITION LIMIT	YEAR RETD.	ISSUE PRICE	*QUOTE U.S.$
1992	Jeremiah	3,219	1994	90.00	250
1995	Uncle Sam, black	7/97		120.00	120
1991	Uncle Sam, white	729	1991	150.00	1100

Daddy's Long Legs/Santa Claus - K. Germany

YEAR ISSUE		EDITION LIMIT	YEAR RETD.	ISSUE PRICE	*QUOTE U.S.$
1990	Santa-1990, white	48	1990	64.00	1500-1600
1990	Santa-Red Velvet	25	1990	180.00	1650-1700
1990	Santa-Tapestry	25	1990	180.00	1650-1700
1991	Santa-1991, black	1,101	1991	98.00	400
1991	Santa-1991, white	311	1991	98.00	400
1992	Santa-1992, black	511	1993	158.00	375
1992	Santa-1992, special ed.	213	1993	158.00	400-425
1992	Santa-1992, white	166	1993	158.00	375-400
1993	Santa-1993, black	1,112	1994	178.00	325
1994	Santa-1994, Tubbin' Santa	1,859	1995	150.00	200-265
1994	Odessa Claus, 1st ed.	778	1995	144.00	200-225
1995	Santa-1995, black	1,009	1996	160.00	200-225
1995	Santa-1995, white	565	1996	160.00	200-225
1995	Odessa Claus, 2nd ed.	Open		144.00	144
1996	Santa-1996, black	Open		200.00	200

Daddy's Long Legs/Schoolhouse Days - K. Germany

YEAR ISSUE		EDITION LIMIT	YEAR RETD.	ISSUE PRICE	*QUOTE U.S.$
1992	Choo-Choo	3,618	1993	56.00	125
1991	Daphne	1,060	1992	72.00	250
1993	Emily	1,278	1993	80.00	200-225
1991	Iris, Teacher	997	1992	90.00	300
1994	Jane	3,768	1994	70.00	150
1992	Josie	4,132	1993	56.00	125
1994	Julie	Open		76.00	76
1992	Katy	Closed	1996	64.00	85-108
1993	Lucy	1,946	1995	64.00	125
1995	Marcus	1,511	1995	76.00	80-125
1992	Micah	Closed	1996	64.00	85-100
1995	Molly	1,498	1995	76.00	125
1993	Phoebe	2,789	1995	64.00	80-125
1993	Priscilla	501	1993	70.00	350
1995	Skeeter	Open		80.00	80
1993	Timothy	750	1993	76.00	375-400

Daddy's Long Legs/Storybook - K. Germany

YEAR ISSUE		EDITION LIMIT	YEAR RETD.	ISSUE PRICE	*QUOTE U.S.$
1996	Little Miss Muffet	1,117	1996	90.00	125
1994	Little Red Riding Hood	1,824	1994	80.00	175-250
1995	Mary and her Lamb	1,627	1995	80.00	150

Daddy's Long Legs/Sunday School & Church - K. Germany

YEAR ISSUE		EDITION LIMIT	YEAR RETD.	ISSUE PRICE	*QUOTE U.S.$
1993	Cassie	1,521	1993	70.00	75-125
1991	Ms. Hattie	Open		90.00	90
1993	Polly	1,523	1995	70.00	110-125
1991	Rev. Johnson	Open		86.00	86
1993	Ruth	Open		94.00	94
1993	Sister Carter	1,719	1995	94.00	150-195
1992	Sister Mary Kathleen	1,844	1994	98.00	275

Daddy's Long Legs/Wedding Party - K. Germany

YEAR ISSUE		EDITION LIMIT	YEAR RETD.	ISSUE PRICE	*QUOTE U.S.$
1992	James, Groom (originally sold as set/2)	1,295	1992	125.00	325-350
1992	Olivia, Bride (originally sold as set/2)	1,295	1992	125.00	325-350
1992	James, Groom & Olivia, Bride, set	Closed	1992	250.00	700
1996	Joshua, Ringbearer	2,500		98.00	98
1994	Maggie, Flower Girl	2,500	1996	98.00	150
1996	Maurice, Groom	2,500		118.00	118
1994	Victoria, Bride	2,500	1995	178.00	250-275

Ladie and Friends

Lizzie High Society™ Members-Only Dolls - B.&P. Wisber

YEAR ISSUE		EDITION LIMIT	YEAR RETD.	ISSUE PRICE	*QUOTE U.S.$
1993	Audrey High -1301	Closed	1992	59.00	375
1993	Becky High -1330	Closed	1994	96.00	275
1994	Chloe Valentine -1351	Closed	1995	79.00	79
1996	Dottie Bowman -1371	Closed	1996	78.00	78
1997	Ellie Bowman -1396	Yr.Iss.		62.00	62

The Christmas Concert - B.&P. Wisber

YEAR ISSUE		EDITION LIMIT	YEAR RETD.	ISSUE PRICE	*QUOTE U.S.$
1990	Claire Valentine -1262	Open		56.00	60
1993	James Valentine -1310	Open		60.00	63
1992	Judith High -1292	Open		70.00	74
1993	Stephanie Bowman -1309	Open		74.00	77

The Christmas Pageant™ - B.&P. Wisber

YEAR ISSUE		EDITION LIMIT	YEAR RETD.	ISSUE PRICE	*QUOTE U.S.$
1985	"Earth" Angel -1122	Closed	1989	30.00	80-100
1985	"Noel" Angel (1st ed.) -1126	Closed	1989	30.00	100
1989	"Noel" Angel (2nd ed.) -1126	Open		48.00	52
1985	"On" Angel -1121	Closed	1989	30.00	100
1985	"Peace" Angel (1st ed.) -1120	Closed	1989	30.00	100
1989	"Peace" Angel (2nd ed.) -1120	Open		48.00	52
1985	Christmas Wooly Lamb -1133	Closed	1991	11.00	35
1985	Joseph and Donkey -1119	Open		30.00	39
1985	Mary and Baby Jesus -1118	Open		30.00	39
1996	Meredith High -1383	Open		79.50	80
1996	Phillip Valentine -1384	Open		79.50	80
1986	Shepherd -1193	Open		32.00	39
1985	Wiseman #1 -1123	Closed	1996	30.00	39
1985	Wiseman #2 -1124	Closed	1996	30.00	39
1985	Wiseman #3 -1125	Closed	1996	30.00	39
1985	Wooden Creche -1132	Open		28.00	33

The Grummels of Log Hollow™ - B.&P. Wisber

YEAR ISSUE		EDITION LIMIT	YEAR RETD.	ISSUE PRICE	*QUOTE U.S.$
1986	Aunt Gertie Grummel™ -1171	Closed	1988	34.00	70-110
1986	Aunt Hilda Grummel™ -1174	Closed	1988	34.00	70-110
1986	Aunt Polly Grummel™ -1169	Closed	1988	34.00	70-110
1986	Cousin Lottie Grummel™ -1170	Closed	1988	36.00	70-110
1986	Cousin Miranda Grummel™ -1165	Closed	1988	47.00	70-110
1986	Grandma Grummel™ -1173	Closed	1988	45.00	70-110
1986	Grandpa Grummel™ -1176	Closed	1988	36.00	180
1986	The Little Ones -Grummels™ (boy/girl) -1196	Closed	1988	15.00	40
1986	Ma Grummel™ -1167	Closed	1988	36.00	70-110
1986	Pa Grummel™ -1172	Closed	1988	34.00	70-110
1986	Sister Nora Grummel™ -1177	Closed	1988	34.00	70-110
1986	Teddy Bear Bed -1168	Closed	1988	15.00	70-100
1986	Uncle Hollis Grummel™ -1166	Closed	1988	34.00	70-110
1986	Washline -1175	Closed	1988	15.00	70-100

The Little Ones at Christmas-Nativity™ - B.&P. Wisber

YEAR ISSUE		EDITION LIMIT	YEAR RETD.	ISSUE PRICE	*QUOTE U.S.$
1995	Donkey -1362	Open		17.00	18
1995	Little Angel -1359	Open		36.00	37
1995	Little Joseph -1358	Open		31.00	32
1995	Little Mary w/Baby in Manger -1357	Open		33.00	34
1995	Little Ones' Creche -1361	Open		24.00	25
1995	Little Shepherd w/Lamb -1360	Open		45.00	46

The Little Ones at Christmas™ - B.&P. Wisber

YEAR ISSUE		EDITION LIMIT	YEAR RETD.	ISSUE PRICE	*QUOTE U.S.$
1990	Girl (black) w/Basket of Greens -1263	Closed	1996	22.00	27
1990	Girl (white) w/Cookie -1264	Open		22.00	27
1990	Girl (white) w/Gift -1266	Open		22.00	27
1990	Girl (white) w/Tree Garland -1265	Open		22.00	27
1991	Boy (black) w/Santa Photo -1273A	Closed	1996	24.00	29
1991	Boy (white) w/Santa Photo -1273	Closed	1996	24.00	29
1991	Girl (black) w/Santa Photo -1272A	Closed	1996	24.00	29
1991	Girl (white) w/Santa Photo -1272	Closed	1996	24.00	29
1993	Boy Peeking (Alone) -1314	Open		22.00	24
1993	Boy Peeking w/Tree -1313	Open		60.00	63
1993	Girl w/Baking Table -1317	Open		38.00	40
1993	Girl w/Note for Santa -1318	Open		36.00	38
1993	Girl Peeking (Alone) -1316	Open		22.00	24
1993	Girl Peeking w/Tree -1315	Open		60.00	63
1994	Girl w/Greens on Table -1337	Open		46.00	48
1996	Boy Tangled in Lights -1390	Open		31.00	31
1996	Girl Tangled in Lights -1389	Open		35.00	35
1996	Boy with Ornament -1388	Open		26.00	26
1996	Girl with Ornament -1387	Open		30.00	30
1995	Little Santa -1364	Open		50.00	51

The Little Ones™ - B.&P. Wisber

YEAR ISSUE		EDITION LIMIT	YEAR RETD.	ISSUE PRICE	*QUOTE U.S.$
1985	Boy (black) (1st ed.) -1130	Closed	1989	15.00	45-65
1989	Boy (black) (2nd ed.) -1130I	Closed	1994	20.00	23
1985	Boy (white) (1st ed.) -1130	Closed	1989	15.00	45-65
1989	Boy (white) (2nd ed.) -1130H	Closed	1994	20.00	23
1985	Girl (black) (1st ed.) -1130	Closed	1989	15.00	45-65
1989	Girl (black) -country color (2nd ed.) -1130G	Closed	1994	20.00	23
1989	Girl (black) -pastels (2nd ed.) -1130E	Closed	1994	20.00	23
1985	Girl (white) (1st ed.) -1130	Closed	1989	15.00	45-65
1989	Girl (white) -country color (2nd ed.) -1130F	Closed	1994	20.00	23
1989	Girl (white) -pastels (2nd ed.) -1130H	Closed	1994	20.00	23
1993	4th of July Boy -1307	Open		28.00	30
1993	4th of July Girl -1298	Open		30.00	32
1993	Ballerina -1321	Open		40.00	42
1996	Baseball (boy) -1399	Open		44.00	44
1996	Baseball (girl) -1398	Open		44.00	44
1995	Basketweaver -1363	Open		48.00	49
1994	Boy Dyeing Eggs -1327	Open		30.00	32
1993	Boy w/Easter Flowers -1306	Open		30.00	32
1994	Boy w/Pumpkin -1341	Open		29.00	31
1992	Boy w/Sled -1289	Open		30.00	33
1996	Bride -1374	Open		41.50	42
1993	Bunny -1297	Open		36.00	38
1992	Clown -1290	Open		32.00	35
1994	Girl Dyeing Eggs -1326	Open		30.00	32
1996	Girl Hopscotching -1385	Open		45.00	45
1996	Girl in Chair Eating Ice Cream 1400	Open		52.50	53
1993	Girl Picnicking w/ Teddy Bear -1320	Open		34.00	36
1996	Pumpkin Girl -1386	Open		34.00	34
1992	Girl Reading -1286	Open		36.00	39
1996	Girl Rollerskating (black) -1377	Open		40.00	40
1996	Girl Rollerskating (white) -1376	Open		40.00	40
1992	Girl w/Apples -1277	Open		26.00	29
1992	Girl w/Beach Bucket -1275	Open		26.00	29
1992	Girl w/Birthday Gift -1279	Open		26.00	29
1992	Girl w/Christmas Lights -1287	Open		34.00	37
1992	Girl w/Easter Eggs -1276	Open		26.00	29
1993	Girl w/Easter Flowers -1296	Open		34.00	36
1992	Girl w/Kitten and Milk -1280	Open		32.00	35
1992	Girl w/Kitten and Yarn -1278	Open		34.00	37
1994	Girl w/Laundry Basket -1338	Open		38.00	40
1993	Girl w/Mop -1300	Open		36.00	38
1994	Girl w/Pumpkin Wagon -1340	Open		42.00	44
1994	Girl w/Puppy in Tub -1339	Open		43.00	45
1992	Girl w/Snowman -1288	Open		36.00	39
1993	Girl w/Spinning Wheel -1299	Open		36.00	38
1996	Girl w/Sunflower -1373	Open		37.00	37
1992	Girl w/Valentine -1291	Open		30.00	33
1993	Girl w/Violin -1319	Open		28.00	30
1996	Groom -1375	Open		23.50	24
1995	June Fete (boy) -1350	Closed	1997	33.00	33
1995	June Fete (girl) -1349	Closed	1997	33.00	33
1994	Nurse -1328	Open		40.00	42
1994	Teacher -1329	Open		38.00	40

Lizzie High® Dolls - B.&P. Wisber

YEAR ISSUE		EDITION LIMIT	YEAR RETD.	ISSUE PRICE	*QUOTE U.S.$
1987	Abigail Bowman -1199	Closed	1994	40.00	90
1996	Adam Valentine -1380	Open		69.50	70
1987	Addie High -1202	Closed	1996	37.00	43
1990	Albert Valentine -1260	Closed	1995	42.00	45
1986	Alice Valentine (1st ed.) -1148	Closed	1987	32.00	100
1995	Alice Valentine (2nd ed.) -1148	Open		56.00	58
1988	Allison Bowman -1229	Closed	1996	56.00	62
1985	Amanda High (1st ed.) -1111	Closed	1988	30.00	100
1990	Amanda High (2nd ed.) -1111	Closed	1995	54.00	58
1989	Amelia High -1248	Open		45.00	50
1987	Amy Bowman -1201	Closed	1994	37.00	82
1986	Andrew Brown -1157	Closed	1988	45.00	125
1991	Annabelle Bowman -1267	Open		68.00	72
1986	Annie Bowman (1st ed.) -1150	Closed	1989	32.00	100
1993	Annie Bowman (2nd ed.) -1150	Open		68.00	71
1993	Ashley Bowman -1304	Open		48.00	50
1992	Barbara Helen -1274	Closed	1996	58.00	62
1985	Benjamin Bowman (Santa) -1134	Closed	1996	34.00	42
1985	Benjamin Bowman -1129	Closed	1987	30.00	100
1988	Bess High -1241	Closed	1996	45.00	50
1996	Beth Bowman (2nd ed.) -1149A	Open		28.50	29
1988	Betsy Valentine -1245	Closed	1996	42.00	46
1996	Beverly Ann Bowman -1379	Open		69.50	70
1994	Bonnie Valentine -1323	Open		35.00	37
1987	Bridget Bowman (1st ed.) -1222	Closed	1994	40.00	95
1996	Bridget Bowman (2nd ed.) -1222	Open		76.00	76
1992	Carol Anne Bowman -1282	Closed	1994	70.00	142
1986	Carrie High (1st ed.) -1190	Closed	1989	45.00	100
1989	Carrie High (2nd ed.) -1190	Open		46.00	50
1986	Cassie Yocum (1st ed.) -1179	Closed	1988	36.00	150
1993	Cassie Yocum (2nd ed.) -1179	Open		80.00	83
1987	Cat on Chair -1217	Closed	1991	16.00	35
1996	Cecelia Brown (alone) -1366A	Open		27.50	28
1996	Cecelia Brown (w/Mother) -1366	Open		101.00	101
1987	Charles Bowman (1st ed.) -1221	Closed	1990	34.00	100
1992	Charles Bowman (2nd ed.) -1221	Closed	1995	46.00	48
1996	Charlotte High -1370	Open		73.50	74
1985	Christian Bowman -1110	Closed	1987	30.00	100
1994	Christine Bowman -1332	Open		62.00	65
1993	Christmas Tree w/Cats -1293A	Open		42.00	44
1986	Christopher High -1182	Closed	1992	34.00	72
1985	Cora High -1115	Closed	1987	30.00	110
1991	Cynthia High -1127A	Closed	1995	60.00	62
1996	Daniel Brown (alone) -1367A	Open		27.50	28
1996	Daniel Brown (w/Mother) -1367	Open		101.00	101
1988	Daphne Bowman -1235	Closed	1994	38.00	40
1996	Darla High -1394	Open		59.50	60
1996	Darlene Bowman -1368	Open		77.50	78
1986	David Yocum -1195	Closed	1995	33.00	37
1986	Delia Valentine (1st ed.) -1153	Closed	1988	32.00	100
1996	Delia Valentine (2nd ed.) -1153	Open		65.50	66
1991	The Department Store Santa -1270	Closed	1996	76.00	80
1986	Dora Valentine (1st ed.) -1152	Closed	1989	30.00	100
1992	Dora Valentine (2nd ed.) -1152	Open		48.00	51
1986	Edward Bowman (1st ed.) -1158	Closed	1988	45.00	125
1994	Edward Bowman (2nd ed.) -1158	Open		76.00	79
1992	Edwin Bowman -1281	Closed	1994	70.00	71
1995	Edwina High -1343	Open		56.00	58
1985	Elizabeth Sweetland (1st ed.) -1109	Closed	1987	30.00	100
1991	Elizabeth Sweetland (2nd ed.) -1109	Closed	1996	56.00	60
1994	Elsie Bowman -1325	Open		64.00	67
1986	Emily Bowman (1st ed.) -1185	Closed	1990	34.00	100
1990	Emily Bowman (2nd ed.) -1185	Closed	1996	48.00	51
1985	Emma High (1st ed.) -1103	Closed	1988	30.00	100
1996	Emma High (2nd ed.) -1103	Open		69.50	70
1989	Emmy Lou Valentine -1251	Open		45.00	49
1985	Esther Dunn (1st ed.) -1127	Closed	1987	45.00	N/A
1991	Esther Dunn (2nd ed.) -1127	Closed	1995	60.00	62
1988	Eunice High -1240	Closed	1994	56.00	58
1985	Flossie High (1st ed.) -1128	Closed	1988	45.00	100-125
1989	Flossie High (2nd ed.) -1128	Open		54.00	59
1987	The Flower Girl -1204	Closed	1995	17.00	24
1996	Francine Bowman -1381	Open		60.00	60
1993	Francis Bowman -1305	Open		48.00	50
1994	Gilbert High -1335	Open		65.00	68
1996	Glenda Brown -1382	Open		60.00	60
1986	Grace Valentine (1st ed.) -1146	Closed	1989	32.00	100
1991	Grace Valentine (2nd ed.) -1146	Open		48.00	51
1987	Gretchen High -1216	Closed	1994	40.00	44
1994	Gwendolyn High -1342	Open		56.00	59
1985	Hannah Brown -1131	Closed	1988	45.00	125
1988	Hattie Bowman -1239	Closed	1996	40.00	46
1985	Ida Valentine -1116	Closed	1988	30.00	80
1987	Imogene Bowman -1206	Closed	1994	37.00	80
1988	Jacob High -1230	Closed	1994	44.00	46

*Quotes have been rounded up to nearest dollar

Ladie and Friends
to Lawtons

DOLLS

YEAR ISSUE		EDITION LIMIT	YEAR RETD.	ISSUE PRICE	*QUOTE U.S.$
1994	Jamie Bowman -1324	Open		35.00	37
1988	Janie Valentine -1231	Closed	1996	37.00	43
1989	Jason High (alone) -1254A	Closed	1996	20.00	25
1989	Jason High (with Mother) -1254	Closed	1996	58.00	63
1986	Jenny Valentine -1181	Closed	1989	34.00	110
1986	Jeremy Bowman -1192	Closed	1991	36.00	80
1989	Jessica High (alone) -1253A	Closed	1996	20.00	25
1989	Jessica High (with Mother) -1253	Closed	1996	58.00	63
1995	Jillian Bowman ((2nd ed.)) -1180	Open		90.00	92
1986	Jillian Bowman (1st ed.) -1180	Closed	1990	34.00	110
1992	Joanie Valentine -1295	Open		48.00	51
1989	Johann Bowman -1250	Open		40.00	44
1987	Johanna Valentine -1198	Closed	1988	37.00	100
1992	Joseph Valentine -1283	Closed	1995	62.00	64
1994	Josie Valentine -1322	Open		76.00	79
1986	Juliet Valentine (1st ed.) -1147	Closed	1988	32.00	100
1990	Juliet Valentine (2nd ed.) -1147	Closed	1996	48.00	52
1993	Justine Valentine -1302	Open		84.00	87
1986	Karl Valentine (1st ed.) -1161	Closed	1988	30.00	100
1994	Karl Valentine (2nd ed.) -1161	Open		54.00	57
1987	Katie and Barney -1219	Closed	1996	38.00	43
1986	Katie Bowman -1178	Closed	1994	36.00	82
1985	Katrina Valentine -1135	Closed	1989	30.00	100
1988	Kinch Bowman -1237	Closed	1996	47.00	51
1987	Laura Valentine -1223	Closed	1994	36.00	80
1995	Leona High -1355	Open		68.00	70
1986	Little Ghosts -1197	Closed	1996	15.00	20
1987	Little Witch -1225	Closed	1996	17.00	24
1985	Lizzie High® (1st ed.) -1100	Closed	1995	30.00	45
1996	Lizzie High® (2nd ed.) -1100	Open		92.00	92
1996	Lottie Bowman -1395	Open		96.50	97
1985	Louella Valentine -1112	Closed	1991	30.00	100
1996	Louis Bowman -1149B	Open		28.50	29
1989	Lucy Bowman -1255	Open		45.00	49
1985	Luther Bowman (1st ed.) -1108	Closed	1987	30.00	100
1993	Luther Bowman (2nd ed.) -1108	Open		60.00	63
1995	Lydia Bowman -1347	Open		54.00	55
1986	Madaleine Valentine (1st ed.) -1187	Closed	1989	34.00	90
1989	Madaleine Valentine (2nd ed.) -1187	Closed	1996	37.00	41
1986	Maggie High -1160	Closed	1988	30.00	100
1996	Maisie Bowman -1392	Open		57.50	58
1987	Margaret Bowman -1213	Closed	1996	35.00	43
1986	Marie Valentine (1st ed.) -1184	Closed	1990	47.00	125
1992	Marie Valentine (2nd ed.) -1184	Closed	1996	68.00	72
1986	Marisa Valentine (alone) -1194A	Closed	1996	33.00	40
1986	Marisa Valentine (w/ Brother Petey) -1194	Closed	1996	45.00	51
1994	Marisa Valentine -1333	Open		58.00	61
1986	Marland Valentine -1183	Closed	1990	33.00	100
1990	Marlene Valentine -1259	Closed	1995	48.00	51
1986	Martha High -1151	Closed	1989	32.00	75-100
1985	Martin Bowman (1st ed.) -1117	Closed	1992	30.00	43-85
1996	Martin Bowman (2nd ed.) -1117	Open		64.00	64
1988	Mary Ellen Valentine -1236	Closed	1996	40.00	45
1985	Mary Valentine -1105	Closed	1988	30.00	85-100
1996	Matilda High -1393	Open		59.50	60
1986	Matthew Yocum -1186	Closed	1988	33.00	100
1995	Mattie Dunn -1344	Open		56.00	58
1988	Megan Valentine -1227	Closed	1994	44.00	94
1987	Melanie Bowman (1st ed.) -1220	Closed	1990	36.00	125
1992	Melanie Bowman (2nd ed.) -1220	Closed	1995	46.00	48
1996	Melody Valentine -1401	Open		66.50	67
1991	Michael Bowman -1268	Open		52.00	55
1994	Minnie Valentine -1336	Open		64.00	67
1989	Miriam High -1256	Open		46.00	50
1986	Molly Yocum (1st ed.) -1189	Closed	1989	34.00	80-100
1989	Molly Yocum (2nd ed.) -1189	Open		39.00	43
1993	Mommy -1312	Open		48.00	50
1989	Mrs. Claus -1258	Open		42.00	46
1990	Nancy Bowman -1261	Open		48.00	52
1987	Naomi Valentine -1200	Closed	1993	40.00	88
1992	Natalie Valentine -1284	Closed	1995	62.00	64
1995	Nathan Bowman -1354	Open		70.00	72
1985	Nettie Brown (1st ed.) -1102	Closed	1987	30.00	100
1988	Nettie Brown (2nd ed.) -1102	Closed	1995	36.00	39
1985	Nettie Brown (Christmas) (1st ed.) -1114	Closed	1987	30.00	100
1996	Nettie Brown (Christmas) (2nd ed.) -1114	Open		66.00	66
1996	Nicholas Valentine (alone) -1365A	Open		27.50	28
1996	Nicholas Valentine (w/Mother) -1365	Open		101.00	101
1987	Olivia High -1205	Open		37.00	43
1987	Patsy Bowman -1214	Closed	1995	50.00	53
1988	Pauline Bowman -1228	Closed	1996	44.00	50
1993	Pearl Bowman -1303	Open		56.00	59
1989	Peggy Bowman -1252	Closed	1995	58.00	70
1987	Penelope High -1208	Closed	1991	40.00	100
1993	Penny Valentine -1308	Open		60.00	63
1985	Peter Valentine (1st ed.) -1113	Closed	1991	30.00	75
1995	Peter Valentine (2nd ed.) -1113	Open		55.00	57
1988	Phoebe High -1246	Closed	1992	48.00	90
1987	Priscilla High -1226	Closed	1995	56.00	62
1986	Rachel Bowman (1st ed.) -1188	Closed	1989	34.00	100
1989	Rachel Bowman (2nd ed.) -1188	Open		34.00	39
1987	Ramona Brown -1215	Closed	1989	40.00	50
1985	Rebecca Bowman (1st ed.) -1104	Closed	1988	30.00	100
1989	Rebecca Bowman (2nd ed.) -1104	Open		56.00	62
1987	Rebecca's Mother -1207	Closed	1995	37.00	54
1995	Regina Bowman -1353	Open		70.00	72
1995	Robert Bowman -1348	Open		64.00	66
1985	Russell Dunn -1107	Closed	1987	30.00	100

YEAR ISSUE		EDITION LIMIT	YEAR RETD.	ISSUE PRICE	*QUOTE U.S.$
1988	Ruth Anne Bowman -1232	Closed	1994	44.00	92
1985	Sabina Valentine (1st ed.) -1101	Closed	1987	30.00	100
1988	Sabina Valentine (2nd ed.) -1101	Closed	1996	40.00	44
1986	Sadie Valentine -1163	Closed	1996	45.00	50
1986	Sally Bowman (1st ed.) -1155	Closed	1991	32.00	110
1996	Sally Bowman (2nd ed.) -1155	Open		75.50	76
1988	Samantha Bowman -1238	Closed	1996	47.00	51
1989	Santa (with Tub) -1257	Open		58.00	64
1987	Santa Claus (sitting) -1224	Closed	1991	50.00	61
1993	Santa Claus -1311	Open		48.00	50
1991	Santa's Helper -1271	Closed	1996	52.00	55
1986	Sara Valentine -1154	Closed	1994	32.00	38-76
1996	Shannon Fitzpatrick -1391	Open		59.00	59
1994	Shirley Bowman -1334	Open		63.00	66
1986	Sophie Valentine (1st ed.) -1164	Closed	1991	45.00	125
1996	Sophie Valentine (alone) -1164A	Open		27.50	28
1996	Sophie Valentine (w/Mother) (2nd ed.) -1164	Open		101.00	101
1995	St. Nicholas -1356	Open		98.00	100
1986	Susanna Bowman (1st ed.) -1149	Closed	1988	45.00	125
1996	Susanna Bowman (2nd ed.) -1149	Open		49.50	50
1986	Thomas Bowman (1st ed.)-1159	Closed	1987	30.00	100
1996	Thomas Bowman (2nd ed.) -1159	Open		59.50	60
1986	Tillie Brown -1156	Closed	1988	32.00	100
1992	Timothy Bowman -1294	Open		56.00	60
1991	Trudy Valentine -1269	Open		64.00	68
1996	Tucker Bowman -1369	Open		77.50	78
1989	Vanessa High -1247	Closed	1996	45.00	50
1989	Victoria Bowman -1249	Open		40.00	44
1987	The Wedding (Bride) -1203	Closed	1995	37.00	50
1987	The Wedding (Groom) -1203A	Closed	1995	34.00	37
1985	Wendel Bowman (1st ed.) -1106	Closed	1987	30.00	100
1992	Wendel Bowman (2nd ed.) -1106	Closed	1996	60.00	64
1992	Wendy Bowman -1293	Open		78.00	82
1986	William Valentine -1191	Closed	1992	36.00	72
1986	Willie Bowman -1162	Closed	1992	30.00	60

The Pawtuckets of Sweet Briar Lane™ - B.&P. Wisber

1994	Aunt Lillian Pawtucket™ (2nd ed.) -1141	Open		58.00	61
1986	Aunt Lillian Pawtucket™ (1st ed.) -1141	Closed	1989	32.00	110
1987	Aunt Mabel Pawtucket™ -212	Closed	1989	45.00	130
1986	Aunt Minnie Pawtucket™ (1st ed.) -1136	Closed	1989	45.00	110
1994	Aunt Minnie Pawtucket™ (2nd ed.) -1136	Open		72.00	75
1986	Brother Noah Pawtucket™ -1140	Closed	1989	32.00	110
1987	Bunny Bed -1218	Closed	1989	16.00	110
1987	Cousin Alberta Pawtucket™ -1210	Closed	1989	36.00	110
1986	Cousin Clara Pawtucket™ (1st ed.) -1144	Closed	1989	32.00	110
1996	Cousin Clara Pawtucket™ (2nd ed.) -1144	Open		84.00	84
1987	Cousin Isabel Pawtucket™ -1209	Closed	1989	36.00	110
1988	Cousin Jed Pawtucket™ -1234	Closed	1990	34.00	110
1988	Cousin Winnie Pawtucket™ -1233	Closed	1990	49.00	110
1994	Flossie Pawtucket™ -1136A	Open		33.00	35
1986	Grammy Pawtucket™ (1st ed.) -1137	Closed	1989	32.00	110
1994	Grammy Pawtucket™ (2nd ed.) -1137	Open		68.00	71
1995	The Little One Bunnies (1995) -female w/ laundry basket -1211A	Open		33.00	34
1986	The Little One Bunnies -boy (1st ed.) -1145	Closed	1989	15.00	20
1994	The Little One Bunnies -boy (2nd ed.) -1145A	Open		33.00	35
1986	The Little One Bunnies -girl (1st ed.) -1145	Closed	1989	15.00	50
1994	The Little One Bunnies -girl (2nd ed.) -1145	Open		33.00	35
1986	Mama Pawtucket™ (1st ed.) -1142	Closed	1989	34.00	110
1994	Mama Pawtucket™ (2nd ed.) -1142	Open		86.00	89
1986	Pappy Pawtucket™ (1st ed.) -1143	Closed	1989	32.00	110
1995	Pappy Pawtucket™ (2nd ed.) -1143	Open		56.00	58
1994	Pawtucket™ Bunny Hutch -1141A	Open		38.00	40
1995	Pawtucket™ Wash Line -1211B	Open		20.00	21
1987	Sister Clemmie Pawtucket™ (1st ed.) -1211	Closed	1989	34.00	110
1995	Sister Clemmie Pawtucket™ (2nd ed.) -1211	Open		60.00	62
1986	Sister Flora Pawtucket™ (1st ed.) -1139	Closed	1989	32.00	110
1996	Sister Flora Pawtucket™ (2nd ed.) -1139	Open		63.50	64
1986	Uncle Harley Pawtucket™ (1st ed.) -1138	Closed	1989	32.00	110
1994	Uncle Harley Pawtucket™ (2nd ed.) -1138	Open		74.00	77

Special Editions - B.&P. Wisber

1992	Kathryn Bowman™ -1992 (Limited Edition) -1285	3,000	1992	140.00	500
1994	Prudence Valentine™ -1994 (Limited Edition) -1331	4,000	1994	180.00	180
1995	Little Lizzie High® -Anniversary Special Event Edition	Yr.Iss.	1995	40.00	40
1995	Lizzie High® -10th Anniversary Signature Edition -1100A	Yr.Iss.	1995	90.00	90
1996	Little Rebecca Bowman™ -1996 Special Event Edition -1372	Yr.Iss.	1996	37.00	37
1996	Lizzie & The Pawtuckets™ -1378	3,000	1996	180.00	180

YEAR ISSUE		EDITION LIMIT	YEAR RETD.	ISSUE PRICE	*QUOTE U.S.$
1997	Little Amanda High -1997 Special Event Edition -1397	Yr.Iss.		36.00	36

The Thanksgiving Play - B.&P. Wisber

1988	Indian Squaw -1244	Closed	1995	36.00	39
1988	Pilgrim Boy -1242	Closed	1995	40.00	45
1988	Pilgrim Girl -1243	Closed	1995	48.00	51

Lawtons

Guild Dolls - W. Lawton

1989	Baa Baa Black Sheep	1,003	1989	395.00	650-700
1990	Lavender Blue	781	1990	395.00	400
1991	To Market, To Market	683	1991	495.00	600
1992	Little Boy Blue	510	1992	395.00	395
1993	Lawton Logo Doll	575	1993	350.00	500
1994	Wee Handful	540	1994	250.00	295
1995	Uniquely Yours	500	1995	395.00	395
1996	Teddy And Me	Yr.Iss.		450.00	450

Cherished Customs - W. Lawton

1990	The Blessing/Mexico	500	1990	395.00	1000-1200
1992	Carnival/Brazil	750	1992	425.00	495
1992	Cradleboard/Navajo	750	1993	425.00	495
1991	Frolic/Amish	500	1991	395.00	395
1990	Girl's Day/Japan	500	1990	395.00	450
1990	High Tea/Great Britain	500	1990	395.00	500-550
1994	Kwanzaa/Africa	500	1994	425.00	495
1990	Midsommar/Sweden	500	1990	395.00	450
1993	Nalauqataq-Eskimo	500	1993	395.00	450
1991	Ndeko/Zaire	500	1991	395.00	550
1992	Pascha/Ukraine	750	1992	495.00	495
1995	Piping the Haggis	350	1995	495.00	550
1993	Topeng Klana-Java	250	1993	495.00	495

Childhood Classics® - W. Lawton

1983	Alice In Wonderland	100	1983	225.00	2000
1986	Anne Of Green Gables	250	1986	325.00	1600-2400
1991	The Bobbsey Twins: Flossie	350	1991	364.50	500
1991	The Bobbsey Twins: Freddie	350	1991	364.50	500
1985	Hans Brinker	250	1985	325.00	1800
1984	Heidi	250	1984	325.00	650
1991	Hiawatha	500	1991	395.00	500
1989	Honey Bunch	250	1989	350.00	550
1987	Just David	250	1987	325.00	700
1986	Laura Ingalls	250	1986	325.00	500
1991	Little Black Sambo	500	1991	395.00	695
1988	Little Eva	250	1988	350.00	700-900
1989	Little Princess	250	1989	395.00	600
1990	Mary Frances	350	1990	350.00	350
1987	Mary Lennox	250	1987	325.00	550-600
1987	Polly Pepper	250	1987	325.00	450
1986	Pollyanna	250	1986	325.00	1600
1990	Poor Little Match Girl	350	1990	350.00	550
1988	Rebecca	250	1988	350.00	450
1988	Topsy	250	1988	350.00	750

The Children's Hour - W. Lawton

1991	Edith With Golden Hair	500	1991	395.00	475
1991	Grave Alice	500	1991	395.00	475
1991	Laughing Allegra	500	1991	395.00	475

Christmas Dolls - W. Lawton

1988	Christmas Joy	500	1988	325.00	800
1989	Noel	500	1989	325.00	450
1990	Christmas Angel	500	1990	325.00	450
1991	Yuletide Carole	500	1991	395.00	450
1996	The Bird's Christmas Carol	500		450.00	450

Newcomer Collection - W. Lawton

1987	Ellin Elizabeth, Eyes Closed	49	1987	335.00	750-1000
1987	Ellin Elizabeth, Eyes Open	19	1987	335.00	900-1200

Playthings Past - W. Lawton

1989	Edward And Dobbin	500	1989	395.00	495-600
1989	Elizabeth And Baby	500	1989	395.00	495-650
1989	Victoria And Teddy	500	1989	395.00	395

Special Edition - W. Lawton

1993	Flora McFlimsey	250	1993	895.00	1000
1988	Marcella And Raggedy Ann	2,500	1988	395.00	800-950
1994	Mary Chilton	350	1994	395.00	395
1995	Through The Looking Glass	180	1995	N/A	N/A

Special Occasion - W. Lawton

1990	First Birthday	500	1990	295.00	350
1989	First Day Of School	500	1989	325.00	525
1988	Nanthy	500	1988	325.00	525

Sugar 'n' Spice - W. Lawton

1987	Ginger	454	1987	275.00	395-550
1986	Jason	27	1986	250.00	800-1700
1986	Jessica	30	1986	250.00	800-1700
1986	Kersten	103	1986	250.00	550-800
1986	Kimberly	87	1986	250.00	550-800
1987	Marie	208	1987	275.00	450

Timeless Ballads® - W. Lawton

1987	Annabel Lee	250	1987	550.00	600-695
1987	Highland Mary	250	1987	550.00	700-900

*Quotes have been rounded up to nearest dollar

YEAR ISSUE		EDITION LIMIT	YEAR RETD.	ISSUE PRICE	*QUOTE U.S.$
988	She Walks In Beauty	250	1988	550.00	700-800
1987	Young Charlotte	250	1987	550.00	900-950

Wee Bits - W. Lawton

YEAR ISSUE		EDITION LIMIT	YEAR RETD.	ISSUE PRICE	*QUOTE U.S.$
1989	Wee Bit O'Bliss	250	1989	295.00	350
1988	Wee Bit O'Heaven	250	1988	295.00	350
1988	Wee Bit O'Sunshine	250	1988	295.00	350
1988	Wee Bit O'Woe	250	1988	295.00	350
1989	Wee Bit O'Wonder	250	1989	295.00	350

Lee Middleton Original Dolls

Birthday Babies - Lee Middleton

YEAR ISSUE		EDITION LIMIT	YEAR RETD.	ISSUE PRICE	*QUOTE U.S.$
1992	Winter	Retrd.	1994	180.00	180
1992	Fall	Retrd.	1994	170.00	170
1992	Summer	Retrd.	1994	160.00	160
1992	Spring	3,000	1994	170.00	170

Christmas Angel Collection - Lee Middleton

YEAR ISSUE		EDITION LIMIT	YEAR RETD.	ISSUE PRICE	*QUOTE U.S.$
1987	Christmas Angel 1987	4,174	1987	130.00	500-600
1988	Christmas Angel 1988	8,969	1988	130.00	250-300
1989	Christmas Angel 1989	7,500	1991	150.00	225
1990	Christmas Angel 1990	5,000	1991	150.00	200
1991	Christmas Angel 1991	5,000	1992	180.00	225
1992	Christmas Angel 1992	5,000	1995	190.00	200
1993	Christmas Angel 1993-Girl	3,144	1995	190.00	200
1993	Christmas Angel 1993 (set)	1,000	1993	390.00	550
1994	Christmas Angel 1994	5,000		190.00	190
1995	Christmas Angel 1995 (white or black)	3,000		190.00	190

First Collectibles - Lee Middleton

YEAR ISSUE		EDITION LIMIT	YEAR RETD.	ISSUE PRICE	*QUOTE U.S.$
1990	Sweetest Little Dreamer (Asleep)	Retrd.	1993	40.00	40
1990	Day Dreamer (Awake)	Retrd.	1993	42.00	42
1991	Day Dreamer Sunshine	Retrd.	1993	49.00	49
1991	Teenie	Retrd.	1993	59.00	59

First Moments Series - Lee Middleton

YEAR ISSUE		EDITION LIMIT	YEAR RETD.	ISSUE PRICE	*QUOTE U.S.$
1984	First Moments (Sleeping)	40,861	1990	69.00	300
1992	First Moments Awake in Blue	1,230	1994	170.00	170
1992	First Moments Awake in Pink	856	1994	170.00	170
1986	First Moments Blue Eyes	14,494	1990	120.00	150
1987	First Moments Boy	6,075	1989	130.00	160
1986	First Moments Brown Eyes	5,324	1989	120.00	150
1987	First Moments Christening (Asleep)	9,377	1992	160.00	250
1987	First Moments Christening (Awake)	16,384	1992	160.00	180
1993	First Moments Heirloom	1,372	1995	190.00	190
1991	First Moments Sweetness	6,323	1995	180.00	180
1990	First Moments Twin Boy	2,971	1991	180.00	180
1990	First Moments Twin Girl	2,544	1991	180.00	180
1994	Sweetness-Newborn	Retrd.	1995	190.00	190

Limited Edition Vinyl - Lee Middleton

YEAR ISSUE		EDITION LIMIT	YEAR RETD.	ISSUE PRICE	*QUOTE U.S.$
1993	Amanda Springtime	612	1994	180.00	180
1989	Angel Fancy	5,310	1992	120.00	150
1995	Angel Kisses-Belly Dancer	1,000	1995	139.00	139
1990	Angel Locks	8,140	1992	140.00	150
1991	Baby Grace	4,862	1991	190.00	250
1994	Beloved-Happy Birthday (Blue)	1,000		220.00	220
1994	Beloved-Happy Birthday (Pink)	1,000		220.00	220
1992	Beth	1,414	1994	160.00	160
1995	Beth-Flapper	1,000	1995	119.00	119
1995	Bethie Bows	1,000		150.00	150
1995	Bethie Buttons	1,000		150.00	150
1995	The Bride	1,000	1995	250.00	250
1991	Bubba Batboy	3,925	1994	190.00	190
1992	Cottontop Cherish	3,525	1994	180.00	180
1991	Dear One-Sunday Best	1,371	1994	140.00	140
1991	Devan Delightful	4,520	1994	170.00	170
1990	Forever Cherish	5,000	1991	170.00	200
1995	Gordon-Growing Up	1,000		220.00	220
1995	Grace-Growing Up	1,000		220.00	220
1992	Gracie Mae (Blond Hair)	3,660	1995	250.00	250
1992	Gracie Mae (Brown Hair)	2,551	1994	250.00	250
1993	Gracie Mae (Red Velvet)	100	1993	250.00	250
1994	Joey-Newborn	1,000	1995	180.00	180
1991	Johanna	1,388	1994	190.00	200
1994	Johanna-Newborn	2,000		180.00	180
1995	Little Angel-Ballerina	1,000		119.00	119
1985	Little Angel-King-2 (Hand Painted)	Retrd.	1985	40.00	200
1981	Little Angel-Kingdom (Hand Painted)	Retrd.	1981	40.00	300
1995	Little Blessings Awake Boy	1,000		180.00	180
1995	Little Blessings Awake Girl	1,000		180.00	180
1995	Little Blessings Blessed Event	1,500		190.00	190
1995	Little Blessings Sleeping Boy	1,000		180.00	180
1995	Little Blessings Sleeping Girl	1,000		180.00	180
1991	Missy- Buttercup	4,748	1994	160.00	200
1992	Molly Rose	2,981	1994	196.00	196
1991	My Lee Candy Cane	2,240	1994	170.00	170
1993	Patty	4,000	1995	49.00	49
1992	Serenity Berries & Bows	458	1993	250.00	250
1992	Sincerity Petals & Plums	414	1993	250.00	250
1991	Sincerity-Apples n' Spice	1,608	1993	250.00	250
1991	Sincerity-Apricots n' Cream	1,789	1993	250.00	250
1995	Sweetness-Newborn	Retrd.	1995	190.00	190

Porcelain Bears & Bunny - Lee Middleton

YEAR ISSUE		EDITION LIMIT	YEAR RETD.	ISSUE PRICE	*QUOTE U.S.$
1993	Buster Bear	Retrd.	1994	250.00	250
1993	Baby Buster	Retrd.	1994	230.00	230
1993	Bye Baby Bunting	Retrd.	1994	270.00	270

Porcelain Collector Series - Lee Middleton

YEAR ISSUE		EDITION LIMIT	YEAR RETD.	ISSUE PRICE	*QUOTE U.S.$
1992	Beloved & Bé Bé	362	1994	590.00	590
1993	Cherish - Lilac & Lace	141	1994	500.00	500
1992	Sencerity II - Country Fair	253	1994	500.00	500

Porcelain Limited Edition Series - Lee Middleton

YEAR ISSUE		EDITION LIMIT	YEAR RETD.	ISSUE PRICE	*QUOTE U.S.$
1990	Baby Grace	500	1990	500.00	600-650
1994	Blossom	86	1995	500.00	500
1994	Bride	200	1994	1390.00	1500
1988	Cherish -1st Edition	750	1988	350.00	550
1989	Devan	543	1991	500.00	500
1995	Elise - 1860's Civil War	200	1996	1790.00	1800
1991	Johanna	381	1992	500.00	500
1991	Molly Rose	500	1991	500.00	500
1989	My Lee	655	1991	500.00	500
1988	Sincerity -1st Edition -Nettie/Simplicity	750	1988	330.00	350-600
1995	Tenderness - Baby Clown	250	1996	590.00	590
1994	Tenderness-Petite Pierrot	250	1995	500.00	500

Vinyl Collectors Series - Lee Middleton

YEAR ISSUE		EDITION LIMIT	YEAR RETD.	ISSUE PRICE	*QUOTE U.S.$
1987	Amanda - 1st Edition	3,778	1989	140.00	160
1985	Angel Face	20,200	1989	90.00	150
1994	Angel Kisses Boy	Open		98.00	98
1994	Angel Kisses Girl	Open		98.00	98
1986	Bubba Chubbs	5,550	1988	100.00	275
1988	Bubba Chubbs Railroader	7,925	1994	140.00	170
1988	Cherish	14,790	1992	160.00	250
1994	Country Boy	Retrd.	1996	118.00	118
1994	Country Boy (Dark Flesh)	Retrd.	1996	118.00	118
1994	Country Girl	Retrd.	1996	118.00	118
1994	Country Girl (Dark Flesh)	Retrd.	1996	118.00	118
1986	Dear One - 1st Edition	4,935	1988	90.00	250
1989	Devan	8,336	1991	170.00	200
1993	Echo	Retrd.	1995	180.00	180
1995	Hershey's Kisses - Gold	Retrd.	1996	99.50	130
1994	Hershey's Kisses - Silver	Open		99.50	100
1986	Little Angel - 3rd Edition	15,158	1992	90.00	110
1992	Little Angel Boy	Open		130.00	130
1992	Little Angel Girl	Open		130.00	130
1987	Missy	11,855	1991	100.00	120
1989	My Lee	3,794	1991	170.00	170
1992	Polly Ester	2,137	1994	160.00	160
1995	Polly Ester "Sock Hop"	1,000	1995	119.00	119
1995	Polly Ester - Hershey's Country Girl	Retrd.	1995	130.00	150
1988	Sincerity - Limited 1st Ed. - Nettie/Simplicity	3,711	1989	160.00	200-250
1989	Sincerity-Schoolgirl	6,622	1992	180.00	200
1994	Town Boy	Retrd.	1995	118.00	118
1994	Town Boy (Dark Flesh)	Retrd.	1995	118.00	118
1994	Town Girl	Retrd.	1995	118.00	118
1994	Town Girl (Dark Flesh)	Retrd.	1995	118.00	118

Wise Penny Collection - Lee Middleton

YEAR ISSUE		EDITION LIMIT	YEAR RETD.	ISSUE PRICE	*QUOTE U.S.$
1993	Jennifer (Peach Dress)	Retrd.	1995	140.00	140
1993	Jennifer (Print Dress)	Retrd.	1995	140.00	140
1993	Molly Jo	Retrd.	1995	140.00	140
1993	Gordon	Retrd.	1995	140.00	140
1993	Ashley (Brown Hair)	Retrd.	1995	120.00	120
1993	Merry	Retrd.	1995	140.00	140
1993	Grace	Retrd.	1995	140.00	200
1993	Ashley (Blond Hair)	Retrd.	1995	120.00	120
1993	Baby Devan	Retrd.	1995	140.00	140

Mattel

35th Anniversary Dolls by Mattel - Mattel

YEAR ISSUE		EDITION LIMIT	YEAR RETD.	ISSUE PRICE	*QUOTE U.S.$
1994	Blonde	Retrd.	1994	39.99	40-50
1994	Brunette	Retrd.	1994	39.99	65-95
1994	Gift Pack	Retrd.	1994	79.97	125-145

Annual Holiday (white) Barbie Dolls - Mattel

YEAR ISSUE		EDITION LIMIT	YEAR RETD.	ISSUE PRICE	*QUOTE U.S.$
1988	Holiday Barbie	Retrd.	1990	24.95	850-900
1989	Holiday Barbie	Retrd.	1991	N/A	275-300
1990	Holiday Barbie	Retrd.	1991	N/A	195-220
1991	Holiday Barbie	Retrd.	1993	N/A	190-225
1992	Holiday Barbie	Retrd.	1992	N/A	130-150
1993	Holiday Barbie	Retrd.	1993	N/A	125-150
1994	Holiday Barbie	Retrd.	1994	44.95	170-195
1995	Holiday Barbie	Retrd.	1995	44.95	75-140

Bob Mackie Barbie Dolls - B. Mackie

YEAR ISSUE		EDITION LIMIT	YEAR RETD.	ISSUE PRICE	*QUOTE U.S.$
1992	Empress Bride Barbie 4247	Retrd.	1992	232.00	995-1100
1990	Gold Barbie 5405	Retrd.	1990	120.00	660-795
1993	Masquerade	Retrd.	1993	175.00	400-495
1992	Neptune Fantasy Barbie 4248	Retrd.	1993	160.00	950-995
1991	Platinum Barbie 2703	Retrd.	1991	153.00	750
1994	Queen of Hearts	Retrd.	1994	175.00	275-300
1991	Starlight Splendor Barbie 2704	Retrd.	1991	135.00	800-895

Classique Collection - Various

YEAR ISSUE		EDITION LIMIT	YEAR RETD.	ISSUE PRICE	*QUOTE U.S.$
1992	Benefit Ball - C. Spencer	Retrd.	1994	59.95	175-200
1993	City Style - J. Goldblatt	Retrd.	1994	59.95	100-125
1993	Opening Night - J. Goldblatt	Retrd.	1994	59.95	100-125

Golden Jubilee - C. Spencer

YEAR ISSUE		EDITION LIMIT	YEAR RETD.	ISSUE PRICE	*QUOTE U.S.$
1994	Golden Jubliee	Retrd.	1994	299.00	600-990

Great Eras - Mattel

YEAR ISSUE		EDITION LIMIT	YEAR RETD.	ISSUE PRICE	*QUOTE U.S.$
1993	Flapper	Retrd.	1995	54.00	175-195
1993	Gibson Girl	Retrd.	1995	54.00	110-125

Nostalgic Porcelain Barbie Dolls - Mattel

YEAR ISSUE		EDITION LIMIT	YEAR RETD.	ISSUE PRICE	*QUOTE U.S.$
1990	Solo in the Spotlight 7613	Retrd.	1990	198.00	200-240
1990	Sophisticated Lady 5313	Retrd.	1990	198.00	200-300
1989	Wedding Day Barbie 2641	Retrd.	1989	198.00	500-650

The Winter Princess Collection - Mattel

YEAR ISSUE		EDITION LIMIT	YEAR RETD.	ISSUE PRICE	*QUOTE U.S.$
1994	Evergreen Princess	Retrd.	1994	59.95	145-175
1994	Evergreen Princess (Red Head)	Retrd.	1994	59.95	350-500
1995	Peppermint Princess	Retrd.	1995	59.95	70-95
1993	Winter Princess	Retrd.	1993	59.95	400-600

Original Appalachian Artworks

Collectors Club Editions - X. Roberts

YEAR ISSUE		EDITION LIMIT	YEAR RETD.	ISSUE PRICE	*QUOTE U.S.$
1987	Baby Otis	1,275	1987	250.00	500
1989	Anna Ruby	693	1990	250.00	400-650
1990	Lee Ann	468	1991	250.00	400-500
1991	Richard Russell	490	1991	250.00	400-650
1992	Baby Dodd & 'Ittle Bitty	354	1993	250.00	300-500
1993	Patti w/ Cabbage Bud Boutonnier	358	1994	280.00	280
1994	Mother Cabbage	Closed	1995	150.00	150
1995	Rosie	322	1996	275.00	275
1996	Gabriella (Angel)	Closed	1996	265.00	265

BabyLand Career - X. Roberts

YEAR ISSUE		EDITION LIMIT	YEAR RETD.	ISSUE PRICE	*QUOTE U.S.$
1992	BabyLand (Engineer -Career Kid)	Closed	1992	220.00	275-300
1993	BabyLand (Miss BLGH Career 'Kid)	240	1993	220.00	275-300
1994	BabyLand (Child Star Career 'Kid)	241	1994	220.00	250
1995	BabyLand (Career Nurse)	83	1995	210.00	275

BabyLand General Hospital Convention Baby - X. Roberts

YEAR ISSUE		EDITION LIMIT	YEAR RETD.	ISSUE PRICE	*QUOTE U.S.$
1990	Charlie (Amber)	200	1990	175.00	350
1991	Nurse Payne (Garnet)	160	1991	210.00	350-400
1992	Princess Nacoochee (BabyLand)	100	1992	210.00	275
1993	Baby BeBop (BabyLand)	199	1993	210.00	325
1994	Norma Jean (BabyLand)	250	1994	225.00	500
1995	Delta (BabyLand)	200	1994	230.00	230
1996	Marlene (BabyLand)	200	1994	230.00	230

Cabbage Patch Kids (10 Character Kids) - X. Roberts

YEAR ISSUE		EDITION LIMIT	YEAR RETD.	ISSUE PRICE	*QUOTE U.S.$
1982	Amy L.	206	1982	125.00	500-700
1982	Bobbie J.	314	1982	125.00	450-600
1982	Billy B.	201	1982	125.00	450-6
1982	Dorothy J.	126	1982	125.00	700
1982	Gilda R.	105	1982	125.00	700-2500
1982	Marilyn S.	275	1982	125.00	700-800
1982	Otis L.	308	1982	125.00	700
1982	Rebecca R.	301	1982	125.00	700
1982	Sybil S.	502	1982	125.00	450-700
1982	Tyler B.	94	1982	125.00	2000-3000

Cabbage Patch Kids - X. Roberts

YEAR ISSUE		EDITION LIMIT	YEAR RETD.	ISSUE PRICE	*QUOTE U.S.$
1989	Amber (Halloween, Asian)	Closed	1989	175.00	225
1989	Amber (Reg.)	Closed	1990	150.00	225
1989	Amber (Toddler)	Closed	1989	150.00	225
1986	Amethyst	10,000	1986	135.00	200
1986	Amethyst (Show Baby:Rusty)	250	1986	135.00	450
1986	Amethyst (Show Baby:Tiffy)	500	1986	135.00	450
1988	Aquamarine	5,000	1988	150.00	225
1994	BabyLand (Bald)	Closed	1994	210.00	250
1995	BabyLand (Preemie)	Closed	1995	175.00	225
1994	BabyLand (Preemie)	Closed	1994	175.00	225
1992	BabyLand (Reg.)	Closed	1992	190.00	240
1991	BabyLand (Reg.)	969	1991	190.00	240
1994	BabyLand (Reg.)	Closed	1994	210.00	260
1995	BabyLand (Reg.)	Closed	1994	210.00	260
1994	BabyLand (Sweet Sixteen "Casey" Ann	191	1994	260.00	500
1993	Blackberry Preemie	438	1993	175.00	175
1992	Brass	Closed	1992	190.00	190
1992	Brass (Flower Girl Toddler)	Closed	1992	175.00	225
1992	Brass (Garden Party Girl)	Closed	1992	190.00	240
1992	Brass (Hispanic Girl Toddler)	Closed	1992	175.00	225
1992	Brass (Ring Bearer Boy Toddler)	Closed	1992	175.00	225
1992	Brass (Toddler)	Closed	1992	175.00	225
1995	Bucky (California Collectors Club)	105	1995	220.00	220
1983	Champagne (Andre)	1,000	1983	250.00	500
1983	Champagne (Madeira)	1,000	1983	250.00	500
1983	Cleveland "Green"	2,000	1983	125.00	450
1991	Copper	241	1991	190.00	190
1991	Copper (Halloween)	273	1991	190.00	240
1991	Copper (Toddler)	241	1991	175.00	225
1986	Corporate 'Kid	2,000	1986	400.00	400
1991	Crystal	Closed	1991	190.00	190
1991	Crystal (Easter Fashions)	291	1991	190.00	240
1991	Crystal (Toddler)	Closed	1991	175.00	225
1991	Crystal (Valentine Fashions)	439	1991	190.00	240
1991	Crystal (Valentine Toddler Fashions)	67	1991	175.00	225

*Quotes have been rounded up to nearest dollar

Collectors' Information Bureau

41

Original Appalachian Artworks
to Precious Moments/Enesco Corporation

DOLLS

YEAR ISSUE		EDITION LIMIT	YEAR RETD.	ISSUE PRICE	*QUOTE U.S.$
1984	Daddy's Darlins' (Kitten)	500	1984	300.00	400-500
1984	Daddy's Darlins' (Princess)	500	1984	300.00	500-750
1984	Daddy's Darlins' (Pun'kin)	500	1983	300.00	400-500
1984	Daddy's Darlins' (Tootsie)	500	1984	300.00	400-500
1984	Daddy's Darlins', set/4	2,000	1984	1600.00	1000-2000
1992	Diamond	Closed	1993	210.00	210
1992	Diamond (Choir Christmas)	Closed	1992	210.00	260
1992	Diamond (Thanksgiving Indian)	Closed	1992	210.00	260
1992	Diamond (Thanksgiving Toddler Indian)	Closed	1992	195.00	245
1992	Diamond (Toddler)	Closed	1993	195.00	245
1985	Emerald	35,000	1985	135.00	135
1985	Four Seasons (Autumn)	2,000	1985	160.00	160
1985	Four Seasons (Crystal)	2,000	1985	160.00	160
1985	Four Seasons (Morton)	2,000	1985	160.00	160
1985	Four Seasons (Sunny)	2,000	1985	160.00	160
1992	Garden Party Sprout (Babyland "Miss Eula")	140	1992	250.00	500
1992	Garden Party Sprout (Chris' Corner Clown-Daisy)	110	1992	250.00	500
1992	Garden Party Sprout (Cottage of Memories Indian Girl)	80	1992	250.00	500
1992	Garden Party Sprout (Doll House Sweet Dreams)	82	1992	250.00	500
1992	Garden Party Sprout (Hobby City "Tinkerbell")	160	1992	250.00	500
1992	Garden Party Sprout (Wee Heather Victorian-Heather)	62	1992	250.00	500
1991	Garnet	376	1991	190.00	190
1991	Garnet (Father's Day Toddler)	85	1991	175	275
1991	Garnet (Father's Day)	173	1991	190.00	290
1991	Garnet (Mother's Day Girl)	259	1991	190.00	290
1991	Garnet (Mother's Day Toddler Girl)	364	1991	175.00	275
1991	Garnet (Toddler)	49	1991	175.00	175
1993	Georgia Power (Special Stork Delivery)	288	1993	230.00	350
1985	Gold	50,000	1985	135.00	135
1995	Graceland Elvis	500	1995	300.00	300
1993	Happily Ever After (Bride)	343	1993	230.00	275
1993	Happily Ever After (Groom)	343	1993	230.00	275
1994	House of Tyrol (Christina Marie)	1,000	1994	200.00	200
1994	House of Tyrol (Markus Michael)	1,000	1994	200.00	200
1987	Iddy Buds	750	1987	650.00	650
1986	Identical Twins, set/2	5,000	1987	150.00	250
1985	Ivory	45,000	1985	135.00	135
1989	Jade	Closed	1989	150.00	150
1989	Jade (4th of July Fashions)	Closed	1989	150.00	200
1989	Jade (Mother's Day Fashions)	338	1989	150.00	200
1989	Jade (Toddler)	Closed	1989	150.00	200
1992	JC Penney 1992 Catalog Exclusive (Cocoa-Girl)	1,000	1992	200.00	200
1983	KP Darker Green	2,000	1983	125.00	400
1983	KPB Burgundy	10,000	1983	130.00	250
1984	KPF Turquoise	30,000	1984	130.00	130
1984	KPG Bronze	30,000	1984	130.00	130
1984	KPG Coral	35,000	1984	130.00	130
1983	KPP Purple	20,000	1984	130.00	130
1983	KPR Red	2,000	1983	125.00	400
1989	Lapis (Swimsuit Fashions)	Closed	1989	150.00	240
1989	Lapis (Swimsuit Fashions-Toddler)	Closed	1989	150.00	225
1994	Little People 27" (Boy)	300	1994	325.00	750
1993	Little People 27" (Girl)	300	1993	325.00	850
1996	Little People Girls 27"	300	1996	375.00	375
1994	Mt. Laurel (African Inspired Toddler)	Closed	1994	195.00	195
1994	Mt. Laurel (African Inspired) (Reg.)	Closed	1994	210.00	210
1994	Mt. Laurel (Mrs. Pauls)	Closed	1994	198.00	198
1994	Mt. Laurel (Mysterious Barry)	Closed	1994	225.00	225
1994	Mt. Laurel (Northern)	Closed	1995	210.00	210
1994	Mt. Laurel (Twins Baby Sidney & Baby Lanier)	100	1994	390.00	390
1994	Mt. Laurel (Western)	Closed	1994	210.00	210
1994	Mt. Laurel St. Patrick Boys	100	1994	210.00	210
1994	Mt. Laurel St. Patrick Girls	200	1994	210.00	210
1995	Mt. Yonah (Easter)	Closed	1995	215.00	215
1995	Mt. Yonah (Valentine)	Closed	1995	200.00	200
1996	Nacoochee Valley (Easter)	Closed	1996	215.00	215
1996	Nacoochee Valley (Halloween)	Closed	1996	210.00	210
1991	Newborn (BLGH)	909	1991	195.00	195
1992	Newborn (BLGH)	869	1992	195.00	195
1993	Newborn (BLGH)	1,136	1993	195.00	195
1996	Newborn (BLGH)	1,710	1996	195.00	195
1995	Newborn (BLGH)	1,042	1995	195.00	195
1994	Newborn (BLGH)	1,107	1994	195.00	195
1991	Onyx (Thanksgiving Pilgrim)	349	1991	190.00	240
1991	Onyx (Toddler)	297	1991	175.00	225
1991	Onyx 22"	297	1991	190.00	190
1990	Opal (Easter Toddler Fashions)	751	1989	175.00	225
1990	Opal (Garden Fashions)	Closed	1989	175.00	225
1990	Opal (Toddler)	Closed	1990	175.00	175
1990	Pearl	542	1990	190.00	240
1990	Pearl (Toddler)	226	1990	175.00	225
1990	Peridot	680	1990	190.00	190
1990	Peridot (Halloween Toddler Fashions)	588	1990	175.00	225
1990	Peridot (Toddler)	794	1990	175.00	225
1992	Platinum	Closed	1992	210.00	210
1992	Platinum (Best Man)	Closed	1992	220.00	320
1992	Platinum (Maid of Honor)	Closed	1992	220.00	320
1992	Platinum (Summertime 'Kids-Watermelon)	Closed	1992	210.00	210
1992	Platinum (Toddler)	Closed	1992	195.00	195
1985	Preemie (boy)	3,750	1985	150.00	150
1985	Preemie (girl)	11,250	1985	150.00	150
1985	Preemie Twins, set/2	1,500	1985	600.00	600
1990	Quartz (Toddler)	Closed	1989	175.00	175
1990	Quartz (Valentine Toddler Fashions)	Closed	1989	175.00	225
1992	QVC Exclusive (Janeen Sybil)	200	1992	275.00	275
1992	QVC Exclusive (Preemie) (Celeste Diane)	500	1992	250.00	250
1992	QVC Exclusive (Toddler) (Abigail Sydney)	1,000	1992	225.00	225
1985	Rose	40,000	1985	135.00	135
1989	Ruby	1,325	1989	150.00	150
1985	Sapphire	35,000	1985	135.00	135
1992	Silver	Closed	1992	190.00	190
1992	Silver (Asian Toddler)	Closed	1992	175.00	225
1992	Silver (Toddler)	Closed	1992	175.00	175
1992	Silver (Valentine Toddler)	Closed	1992	190.00	240
1995	Skitts Mountain	Closed	1995	210.00	210
1986	Southern Belle "Georgiana"	4,000	1990	160.00	160
1984	Sweetheart (Beau)	750	1984	150.00	400
1984	Sweetheart (Candi)	750	1984	150.00	400
1988	Tiger's Eye	3,653	1989	150.00	150
1988	Tiger's Eye (Easter)	788	1989	150.00	190
1989	Tiger's Eye (Mother's Day)	231	1989	150.00	200-300
1988	Tiger's Eye (Valentine's Day)	328	1989	150.00	200-300
1987	Topaz	5,000	1987	135.00	135
1987	Topaz (Show Baby Iris)	1,500	1985	135.00	450
1993	Unicoi	Closed	1993	210.00	210
1993	Unicoi (Ballerina Toddler)	Closed	1993	195.00	260
1993	Unicoi (Spring Toddler)	Closed	1993	195.00	260
1993	Unicoi (Spring)	Closed	1993	210.00	260
1993	Unicoi (Summer Dinosaur)	Closed	1993	210.00	260
1993	Unicoi (Summer Toddler Dinosaur)	Closed	1993	210.00	260
1993	Unicoi (Toddler)	Closed	1993	210.00	210
1993	White Christmas - Regular Kids (only)	223	1993	210.00	260
1984	World Class	2,500	1984	150.00	400

Cabbage Patch Kids Baby Character - X. Roberts

YEAR ISSUE		EDITION LIMIT	YEAR RETD.	ISSUE PRICE	*QUOTE U.S.$
1990	Baby Amy Loretta Nursery	509	1990	200.00	225
1991	Baby Billy Badd Nursery	306	1991	200.00	225
1991	Baby Bobbie Jo Nursery	393	1991	200.00	225
1988	Baby Dorothy Jane Nursery	2,000	1992	165.00	225
1992	Baby Gilda Roxanne Nursery	351	1992	200.00	225
1988	Baby Marilyn Suzanne Nursery	2,000	1992	165.00	225
1992	Baby Rebecca Ruby Nursery	373	1992	200.00	225
1988	Baby Sybil Sadie Nursery	2,000	1992	165.00	225
1988	Baby Tyler Bo Nursery	2,000	1993	165.00	225

Cabbage Patch Kids Circus Parade - X. Roberts

YEAR ISSUE		EDITION LIMIT	YEAR RETD.	ISSUE PRICE	*QUOTE U.S.$
1987	Big Top Clown-Baby Cakes	2,000	1987	180.00	450-550
1991	Big Top Tot-Mitzi	1,000	1993	220.00	200-400
1989	Happy Hobo-Bashful Billy	1,000	1989	180.00	350

Cabbage Patch Kids International - X. Roberts

YEAR ISSUE		EDITION LIMIT	YEAR RETD.	ISSUE PRICE	*QUOTE U.S.$
1983	American Indian/Pair	500	1983	300.00	1200
1984	Bavarian/Pair	500	1984	300.00	450-800
1983	Hispanic/Pair	500	1983	300.00	400
1983	Irish/Pair	2,000	1985	320.00	320
1983	Oriental/Pair	500	1983	300.00	1000
1987	Polynesian (Lokelina)	1,000	1987	180.00	180
1987	Polynesian (Ohana)	1,000	1987	180.00	180

Cabbage Patch Kids OlympiKids™ - X. Roberts

YEAR ISSUE		EDITION LIMIT	YEAR RETD.	ISSUE PRICE	*QUOTE U.S.$
1996	Baseball Boy	159	1996	275.00	275
1996	Basketball Boy & Girl	199	1996	275.00	275
1996	Basketball Girl	302	1996	275.00	275
1996	Cyclist Boy	126	1996	275.00	275
1996	Equestrian Girl	350	1996	275.00	275
1995	Gymnastics Boy	241	1996	275.00	275
1995	Rowing Girl	205	1996	275.00	275
1995	Soccer Boy & Girl	162	1996	275.00	275
1995	Soccer Girl	262	1996	275.00	275
1996	Softball Girl	140	1996	275.00	275
1995	Track & Field Girl	422	1996	275.00	275
1995	Weight Lifting Boy	158	1996	275.00	275

Cabbage Patch Kids Porcelain - X. Roberts

YEAR ISSUE		EDITION LIMIT	YEAR RETD.	ISSUE PRICE	*QUOTE U.S.$
1994	Porcelain Angel (Angelica)	208	1994	160.00	160
1994	Porcelain Friends (Karen Lee)	59	1994	150.00	150
1994	Porcelain Friends (Kassie Lou)	58	1994	150.00	150
1994	Porcelain Friends (Katie Lyn)	61	1994	150.00	150
1995	Porcelain Peirrot (Sharri Starr)	198	1995	160.00	160

Cabbage Patch Kids Storybook - X. Roberts

YEAR ISSUE		EDITION LIMIT	YEAR RETD.	ISSUE PRICE	*QUOTE U.S.$
1986	Mark Twain (Becky Thatcher)	2,500	1986	160.00	160
1986	Mark Twain (Huck Finn)	2,500	1986	160.00	160
1986	Mark Twain (Tom Sawyer)	2,500	1986	160.00	160
1987	Sleeping Beauty (Prince Charming)	1,250	1991	180.00	180
1987	Sleeping Beauty (Sleeping Beauty)	1,250	1991	180.00	180

Christmas Collection - X. Roberts

YEAR ISSUE		EDITION LIMIT	YEAR RETD.	ISSUE PRICE	*QUOTE U.S.$
1979	X Christmas	1,000	1979	150.00	5500
1980	Christmas-Nicholas/Noel	500	1980	400.00	1200
1982	Christmas-Baby Rudy/Christy Nicole	500	1982	400.00	1600
1983	Christmas-Holly/Berry	1,000	1983	400.00	800
1984	Christmas-Carole/Chris	1,000	1984	400.00	600
1985	Christmas-Baby Sandy/Claude	2,500	1990	400.00	400
1986	Christmas-Hilliary/Nigel	2,000	1990	400.00	425
1987	Christmas-Katrina/Misha	2,000	1990	500.00	500
1988	Christmas-Kelly/Kane	2,000	1993	500.00	500-600
1989	Christmas-Joy	500	1989	250.00	600
1990	Christmas-Krystina	596	1991	250.00	250
1991	Christmas-Nick	700	1991	275.00	275
1992	Christmas-Christy Claus	700	1993	285.00	285
1993	Christmas-Rudolph	500	1993	275.00	275
1994	Christmas-Natalie	500	1994	275.00	275
1995	Christmas-Treena	500	1995	275.00	275
1996	Christmas-Sammy The Snowman	500	1996	275.00	275

Convention Baby - X. Roberts

YEAR ISSUE		EDITION LIMIT	YEAR RETD.	ISSUE PRICE	*QUOTE U.S.$
1989	Ashley (Jade)	200	1989	250.00	600-800
1990	Bradley (Opal)	200	1990	175.00	500-600
1991	Caroline (Garnet)	200	1991	200.00	300
1992	Duke (Brass)	200	1992	225.00	375-400
1993	Ellen (Unicoi)	200	1993	225.00	300-400
1994	Justin (Mt. Laurel)	200	1994	225.00	300-400
1995	Fifi (Mt. Yonah)	200	1995	250.00	450-700
1996	Gina (Nacoochee Valley)	200	1996	275.00	275

Little People - X. Roberts

YEAR ISSUE		EDITION LIMIT	YEAR RETD.	ISSUE PRICE	*QUOTE U.S.$
1978	"A" Blue	1,000	1978	45.00	7000-8500
1978	"B" Red	1,000	1978	80.00	4500-6000
1979	"C" Burgundy	5,000	1979	80.00	1500-1800
1979	"D" Purple	10,000	1979	80.00	1000-1500
1979	"E" Bronze	15,000	1980	80.00	750-850
1982	"PE" New 'Ears Preemie	5,000	1982	140.00	300-450
1981	"PR II" Preemie	10,000	1981	130.00	350-450
1980	"SP" Preemie	5,000	1980	100.00	600-800
1982	"U" Unsigned	21,000	1982	125.00	300-450
1980	"U" Unsigned	73,000	1981	125.00	300-450
1980	Celebrity	5,000	1980	200.00	550
1980	Grand Edition	1,000	1988	1000.00	1000
1978	Helen Blue	Closed	1978	30.00	8000-11000
1981	New 'Ears	15,000	1981	125.00	250
1981	Standing Edition	5,000	1988	300.00	350-375

Our Secret

Little Lops - A. Baggs

YEAR ISSUE		EDITION LIMIT	YEAR RETD.	ISSUE PRICE	*QUOTE U.S.$
1996	Auntie P.J. Rabbitson	6,000		40.00	40
1997	Birdie "Tweetheart" Burlop	6,000		30.00	30
1997	Buffy "Little Tu-Tu" Lopfellow	6,000		16.00	16
1997	Bunny Jean Lopper	6,000		42.00	42
1996	Eujean "The Carrot King" Lopfield	6,000		40.00	40
1996	Gracie "Goodheart" Lopper	6,000		37.00	37
1996	Guardian Angel	6,000		30.00	30
1996	Hare-ison Lopfellow	6,000		34.00	34
1997	Hare-old "Lucky Foot" Lopfellow	6,000		45.00	45
1996	Heavenly Hare	6,000		40.00	40
1996	Hillary Lopfellow	6,000		37.00	37
1996	Jane "Not So Plain" Lopsmith	6,000		30.00	30
1996	Jean-o "Hoppin' Out" Lopfield	6,000		33.00	33
1996	Jeanette "I'm The Momma" Lopfield	6,000		45.00	45
1996	Joey "Wead Me A Sto'ey" Lopsmith	6,000		15.00	15
1996	L'il Angel Wings	6,000		16.00	16
1996	L'il Jeana Lopfield	6,000		15.00	15
1996	L'il Lacy Lopper	6,000		16.00	16
1996	L'il Levi Lopfield	6,000		15.00	15
1996	Mary Jean Lopfield	6,000		33.00	33
1997	Patsy "Junior Lop Scout" Rabbitson	6,000		32.00	32
1996	Pinky Rabbitson	6,000		15.00	15
1996	Tiffany "The Shopper" Lopper	6,000		36.00	36

Precious Moments/Enesco Corporation

Jack-In-The-Boxes - S. Butcher

YEAR ISSUE		EDITION LIMIT	YEAR RETD.	ISSUE PRICE	*QUOTE U.S.$
1991	You Have Touched So Many Hearts 422282	2-Yr.	1993	175.00	175
1991	May You Have An Old Fashioned Christmas 417777	2-Yr.	1993	200.00	200
1990	The Voice of Spring 408735	2-Yr.	1992	200.00	200
1990	Summer's Joy 408743	2-Yr.	1992	200.00	200
1990	Autumn's Praise 408751	2-Yr.	1992	200.00	200
1990	Winter's Song 408778	2-Yr.	1992	200.00	200

Precious Moments Dolls - S. Butcher

YEAR ISSUE		EDITION LIMIT	YEAR RETD.	ISSUE PRICE	*QUOTE U.S.$
1981	Mikey, 18" E-6214B	Suspd.		150.00	200-225
1981	Debbie, 18" E-6214G	Suspd.		150.00	200-225
1982	Cubby, 18" E-7267B	5,000		200.00	350-450
1982	Tammy, 18" E-7267G	5,000		300.00	450-500
1983	Katie Lynne, 16" E-0539	Suspd.		165.00	185
1984	Mother Sew Dear, 18" E-2850	Retrd.	1985	350.00	350
1984	Kristy, 12" E-2851	Suspd.		150.00	175
1984	Timmy, 12" E-5397	Suspd.		125.00	160
1985	Aaron, 12" 12424	Suspd.		135.00	150
1985	Bethany, 12" 12432	Suspd.		135.00	150
1985	P.D., 7" 12475	Suspd.		50.00	80
1985	Trish, 7" 12483	Suspd.		50.00	80
1986	Bong Bong, 13" 100455	12,000		150.00	265
1986	Candy, 13" 100463	12,000		150.00	275
1986	Connie, 12" 102253	7,500		160.00	240
1987	Angie, The Angel of Mercy 12491	12,500		160.00	275
1990	The Voice of Spring 408786	2-Yr.	1992	150.00	150
1990	Summer's Joy 408794	2-Yr.	1992	150.00	150
1990	Autumn's Praise 408808	2-Yr.	1992	150.00	150
1990	Winter's Song 408816	2-Yr.	1992	150.00	170
1991	You Have Touched So Many Hearts 427527	2-Yr.	1993	90.00	90

*Quotes have been rounded up to nearest dollar

YEAR ISSUE		EDITION LIMIT	YEAR RETD.	ISSUE PRICE	*QUOTE U.S.$
1991	May You Have An Old Fashioned Christmas 417785	2-Yr.	1993	150.00	175
1991	The Eyes Of The Lord Are Upon You (Boy Action Musical) 429570	Suspd.		65.00	65
1991	The Eyes Of The Lord Are Upon You (Girl Action Musical) 429589	Suspd.		65.00	65

Reco International

Childhood Doll Collection - S. Kuck

YEAR ISSUE		EDITION LIMIT	YEAR RETD.	ISSUE PRICE	*QUOTE U.S.$
1994	A Kiss Goodnight	Retrd.	1995	79.00	79
1995	Reading With Teddy	Retrd.	1995	79.00	79
1994	Teaching Teddy His Prayers	Open		79.00	79
1996	Teddy's Picnic	Open		79.00	79

Children's Circus Doll Collection - J. McClelland

YEAR ISSUE		EDITION LIMIT	YEAR RETD.	ISSUE PRICE	*QUOTE U.S.$
1991	Johnny The Strongman	Yr.Iss.		83.00	83
1991	Katie The Tightrope Walker	Yr.Iss.		78.00	78
1992	Maggie The Animal Trainer	Yr.Iss.		83.00	83
1991	Tommy The Clown	Yr.Iss.		78.00	78

Christmas Doll Collection - S. Kuck

YEAR ISSUE		EDITION LIMIT	YEAR RETD.	ISSUE PRICE	*QUOTE U.S.$
1996	Carol	Open		135.00	135

Precious Memories of Motherhood - S. Kuck

YEAR ISSUE		EDITION LIMIT	YEAR RETD.	ISSUE PRICE	*QUOTE U.S.$
1993	Bedtime	Retrd.	1994	149.00	149
1992	Expectant Moments	Retrd.	1993	149.00	149
1990	Loving Steps	Retrd.	1992	125.00	150-195
1991	Lullaby	Retrd.	1995	125.00	125

Roman, Inc.

Abbie Williams Collection - E. Williams

YEAR ISSUE		EDITION LIMIT	YEAR RETD.	ISSUE PRICE	*QUOTE U.S.$
1991	Molly	5,000		155.00	155

A Christmas Dream - E. Williams

YEAR ISSUE		EDITION LIMIT	YEAR RETD.	ISSUE PRICE	*QUOTE U.S.$
1990	Carole	5,000		125.00	125
1990	Chelsea	5,000		125.00	125

Classic Brides of the Century - E. Williams

YEAR ISSUE		EDITION LIMIT	YEAR RETD.	ISSUE PRICE	*QUOTE U.S.$
1991	Flora-The 1900's Bride	Yr.Iss.	1991	145.00	145
1992	Jennifer-The 1980's Bride	Yr.Iss.	1992	149.00	149
1993	Kathleen-The 1930's Bride	Yr.Iss.	1993	149.00	149

Ellen Williams Doll - E. Williams

YEAR ISSUE		EDITION LIMIT	YEAR RETD.	ISSUE PRICE	*QUOTE U.S.$
1989	Noelle	5,000		125.00	125
1989	Rebecca 999	7,500		195.00	195

Sarah's Attic, Inc.

Heirlooms from the Attic - Sarah's Attic

YEAR ISSUE		EDITION LIMIT	YEAR RETD.	ISSUE PRICE	*QUOTE U.S.$
1991	Adora 1823	500	1991	90.00	200
1991	All Cloth Muffin blk. Doll 1820	Closed	1991	90.00	200
1991	All Cloth Puffin blk. Doll 1821	Closed	1991	90.00	200
1991	Enos 1822	500	1991	90.00	200
1993	Granny Quilting Lady Doll 3576	Closed	1993	130.00	150
1989	Harmony-Victorian Clown 1464	500	1992	120.00	250
1992	Harpster w/Banjo 3591	Closed	1992	250.00	250
1990	Hickory-Americana 1771	Closed	1993	150.00	170
1990	Hickory-Beachtime 1769	2,000	1993	140.00	150-175
1991	Hickory-Christmas 1810	2,000	1993	150.00	150-175
1990	Hickory-Playtime 1768	2,000	1993	140.00	175
1990	Hickory-School Days 1766	2,000	1993	140.00	175
1991	Hickory-Springtime 1814	2,000	1993	150.00	195
1990	Hickory-Sunday's Best 1770	2,000	1993	150.00	195
1990	Hickory-Sweet Dreams 1767	2,000	1993	140.00	175
1992	Hilary-Victorian 1831	500	1993	200.00	250
1986	Holly Black Angel 0410	Closed	1986	34.00	34
1986	Holly blk. Angel 0410	Retrd.	1986	34.00	200
1992	Kiah Guardian Angel 3570	2,000	1993	170.00	200
1993	Lilla Quilting Lady Doll 3581	Closed	1993	130.00	150
1986	Maggie Cloth Doll 0012	Closed	1989	70.00	120
1986	Matt Cloth Doll 0011	Closed	1989	70.00	120
1993	Millie Quilting Lady Doll 3586	Closed	1993	130.00	130
1992	Peace on Earth Santa 3564	200	1992	175.00	350
1986	Priscilla Doll 0030	Closed	1989	140.00	300
1990	Sassafras-Americana 1685	2,000	1993	150.00	175
1990	Sassafras-Beachtime 1683	2,000	1993	140.00	175
1991	Sassafras-Christmas 1809	2,000	1993	150.00	150-175
1990	Sassafras-Playtime 1682	2,000	1993	140.00	175
1989	Sassafras-School Days 1680	2,000	1993	140.00	175
1991	Sassafras-Springtime 1813	2,000	1993	150.00	195
1990	Sassafras-Sunday's Best 1684	2,000	1993	150.00	175
1990	Sassafras-Sweet Dreams 1681	2,000	1993	140.00	195
1988	Smiley Clown Doll 3050	Closed	1988	126.00	126
1990	Teddy Bear-Americana 1775	Closed	1992	160.00	160
1990	Teddy Bear-School Days 1774	Closed	1992	160.00	160
1986	Twinkie Doll 0039A	Closed	1986	32.00	32
1986	Whimpy Doll 0039E	Closed	1986	32.00	32
1992	Whoopie 3597	Closed	1992	200.00	200
1992	Wooster 3602	Closed	1992	160.00	160

Tattered n' Torn Collection - Sarah's Attic

YEAR ISSUE		EDITION LIMIT	YEAR RETD.	ISSUE PRICE	*QUOTE U.S.$
1994	Belle-Girl Rag Doll 4180	2,500	1996	30.00	30
1994	Britches-Boy Rag Doll 4181	2,500	1996	30.00	30

Seymour Mann, Inc.

Connoisseur Doll Collection - E. Mann

YEAR ISSUE		EDITION LIMIT	YEAR RETD.	ISSUE PRICE	*QUOTE U.S.$
1991	Abby 16" Pink Dress-C3145	Closed	1993	100.00	100
1995	Abby C-3229	2,500	1996	30.00	30
1994	Abby YK-4533	3,500	1995	135.00	135
1991	Abigail EP-3	Closed	1993	100.00	100
1991	Abigal WB-72WM	Closed	1993	75.00	75
1994	Adak PS-412	2,500	1995	150.00	150
1993	Adrienne C-3162	Closed	1994	135.00	135
1995	Aggie PS-435	2,500	1996	80.00	80
1991	Alexis 24" Beige Lace-EP32	Closed	1993	220.00	220
1994	Alice GU-32	2,500	1995	150.00	150
1994	Alice IND-508	2,500	1995	115.00	115
1992	Alice JNC-4013	Closed	1993	90.00	90
1995	Alicia C-3235	2,500	1996	65.00	65
1991	Alicia YK-4215	Closed	1993	90.00	90
1995	Allison CD-18183	2,500		35.00	35
1995	Allison TR-92	2,500	1996	125.00	125
1994	Ally FH-556	2,500	1995	115.00	115
1994	Alyssa C-3201	2,500	1995	110.00	110
1994	Alyssa PP-1	2,500	1996	275.00	300
1991	Amanda Toast-OM-182	Closed	1993	260.00	260
1995	Amanda TR-96	2,500	1996	135.00	135
1989	Amber DOM-281A	Closed	1993	85.00	85
1991	Amelia-TR-47	Closed	1993	105.00	105
1991	Amy C-3147	Closed	1993	135.00	135
1995	Amy GU-300A	2,500	1995	30.00	30
1994	Amy OC-43M	2,500	1996	115.00	115
1992	Amy OM-06	2,500	1993	150.00	200
1990	Anabelle C-3080	Closed	1992	85.00	85
1990	Angel DOM-335	Closed	1992	105.00	105
1995	Angel FH-291DP	2,500		70.00	70
1994	Angel LL-956	2,500	1996	90.00	90
1994	Angel SP-460	2,500	1996	140.00	140
1990	Angela C-3084	Closed	1992	105.00	105
1990	Angela C-3084M	Closed	1992	115.00	115
1995	Angela Doll 556	2,500	1996	35.00	35
1995	Angela FH-511	2,500		85.00	85
1995	Angela OM-87	2,500		150.00	150
1995	Angelica FH-291B	2,500		70.00	70
1994	Angelica FH-291E	2,500		85.00	85
1995	Angelica FH-511B	2,500		85.00	85
1995	Angelina FH-291S	2,500		70.00	70
1994	Angelina FH-291S	2,500		85.00	85
1995	Angeline FH-291WG	2,500		75.00	75
1994	Angeline FH-291WG	2,500		85.00	85
1995	Angeline OM-84	2,500		100.00	100
1994	Angelita FH-291G	2,500		85.00	85
1994	Angelo OC-57	2,500		135.00	135
1990	Anita FH-277G	Closed	1992	65.00	65
1991	Ann TR-52	Closed	1993	135.00	135
1995	Anna Doll 550	2,500		60.00	60
1995	Annette FH-635	2,500		110.00	110
1991	Annette TR-59	Closed	1993	130.00	130
1991	Annie YK-4214	Closed	1993	145.00	145
1991	Antoinette FH-452	Closed	1993	100.00	100
1993	Antonia OM-227	2,500	1993	350.00	350
1994	Antonia OM-42	2,500	1996	150.00	150
1995	April CD-2212B	2,500		50.00	50
1991	Arabella C-3163	Closed	1993	135.00	135
1991	Ariel 34" Blue/White-EP-33	Closed	1993	175.00	175
1995	Ariel OM-81	2,500		185.00	185
1994	Arilene LL-940	2,500	1994	90.00	90
1993	Arlene SP-421	Closed	1993	100.00	100
1988	Ashley C-278	Closed	1990	80.00	80
1989	Ashley C-278	Closed	1993	80.00	80
1990	Ashley FH-325	Closed	1993	75.00	75
1995	Ashley OC-76	2,500		40.00	40
1995	Ashley PS-433	2,500		110.00	110
1994	Atanak PS-414	2,500	1994	150.00	150
1991	Audrey FH-455	2,500	1993	125.00	125
1990	Audrey YK-4089	Closed	1992	125.00	125
1987	Audrina YK-200	Closed	1986	85.00	140
1991	Aurora Gold 22"-OM-181	2,500	1993	260.00	260
1991	Azure AM-15	2,500	1993	175.00	175
1994	Baby Belle C-3193	2,500	1994	150.00	150
1991	Baby Beth DOLL-406P	2,500	1993	27.50	28
1995	Baby Betsy DOLL 336	2,500		75.00	75
1990	Baby Betty YK-4087	Closed	1991	125.00	125
1991	Baby Bonnie SP-341	Closed	1993	55.00	55
1990	Baby Bonnie SP-341	Closed	1991	55.00	55
1991	Baby Bonnie w/Walker Music-DOLL-409	2,500	1993	40.00	40
1991	Baby Brent EP-15	Closed	1993	85.00	110
1991	Baby Carrie DOLL-402P	2,500	1993	27.50	28
1990	Baby Ecru WB-17	Closed	1991	65.00	65
1991	Baby Ellie Ecru Musical DOLL-402E	2,500	1993	27.50	28
1991	Baby Gloria Black Baby PS-289	Closed	1993	75.00	75
1991	Baby John PS-498	Closed	1993	85.00	85
1989	Baby John PS-49B	Closed	1991	85.00	85
1990	Baby Kate WB-19	Closed	1991	85.00	85
1991	Baby Linda DOLL-406E	2,500	1993	27.50	28
1990	Baby Nelly PS-163	Closed	1991	95.00	95
1994	Baby Scarlet C-3194	2,500	1994	115.00	115
1991	Baby Sue DOLL-402B	2,500	1993	27.50	28
1990	Baby Sue DOLL-402B	Closed	1992	27.50	28
1990	Baby Sunshine C-3055	Closed	1992	90.00	90
1995	Barbara PS-439	2,500		65.00	65
1991	Belinda C-3164	Closed	1993	150.00	150
1991	Bernetta EP-40	Closed	1993	115.00	115
1995	Beth OC-74	2,500		40.00	40
1992	Beth OM-05	Closed	1993	135.00	135
1990	Beth YK-4099A/B	Closed	1992	125.00	125
1991	Betsy AM-6	Closed	1993	105.00	105
1995	Betsy C-3224	2,500		45.00	45
1995	Betsy OM-89B	2,500		125.00	175
1995	Betsy RDK-230	2,500		35.00	35
1992	Bette OM-01	2,500	1993	115.00	115
1990	Bettina TR-4	Closed	1991	125.00	125
1991	Bettina YK-4144	Closed	1993	105.00	105
1995	Betty LL-996	2,500	1996	115.00	115
1989	Betty PS27G	Closed	1993	65.00	125
1990	Beverly DOLL-335	Closed	1992	110.00	110
1995	Bianca CD-1450C	2,500		35.00	35
1990	Billie YK-4056V	Closed	1992	65.00	65
1993	Blaine C-3167	Closed	1993	100.00	100
1991	Blaine TR-61	Closed	1993	115.00	115
1994	Blair YK-4532	3,500	1994	150.00	150
1991	Blythe CH-15V	Closed	1993	135.00	135
1991	Bo-Peep w/Lamb C-3128	Closed	1993	105.00	105
1994	Bobbi NM-30	2,500	1994	135.00	135
1994	Brandy YK-4537	3,500	1995	165.00	165
1995	Brenda DOLL 551	2,500		60.00	60
1989	Brett PS27B	Closed	1992	65.00	125
1995	Brianna GU-300B	2,500		30.00	30
1991	Bridget SP-379	2,500	1993	105.00	105
1995	Brie C-3230	2,500		30.00	30
1995	Brie CD-16310C	2,500		30.00	30
1995	Brie OM-89W	2,500		125.00	125
1995	Britt OC-77	2,500		40.00	40
1995	Brittany DOLL 558	2,500		35.00	35
1989	Brittany TK-4	Closed	1990	150.00	150
1988	Brittany TK-5	Closed	1990	120.00	120
1991	Brooke FH-461	2,500	1993	115.00	115
1994	Browyn IND-517	2,500	1994	140.00	140
1991	Bryna AM-100B	2,500	1993	70.00	70
1995	Bryna DOLL 555	2,500		35.00	35
1995	Bunny TR-97	2,500		85.00	85
1995	Burgundy Angel FH-291D	2,500		75.00	75
1994	Cactus Flower Indian LL-944	2,500	1994	105.00	105
1990	Caillin DOLL-11PH	Closed	1992	60.00	60
1995	Caitlin LL-997	2,500		115.00	115
1990	Caitlin YK-4051V	Closed	1992	90.00	90
1994	Callie TR-76	2,500	1994	140.00	140
1994	Calypso LL-942	2,500	1994	150.00	150
1991	Camellia FH-457	2,500	1993	100.00	100
1986	Camelot Fairy C-84	Closed	1988	75.00	225
1993	Camille OM-230	2,500	1994	250.00	250
1995	Candice TR-94	2,500	1995	135.00	135
1995	Carmel TR-93	2,500		125.00	125
1994	Carmen PS-408	2,500	1994	150.00	150
1990	Carole YK-4085W	Closed	1992	125.00	125
1991	Caroline LL-838	2,500	1993	110.00	110
1991	Caroline LL-905	2,500	1993	110.00	110
1995	Carolotta OM-80	2,500		175.00	175
1995	Carrie C-3231	2,500		30.00	30
1994	Casey C-3197	2,500	1995	140.00	140
1995	Catherine RDK-231	2,500		30.00	30
1994	Cathy GU-41	2,500	1994	140.00	140
1995	Cecily Doll 552	2,500		60.00	60
1995	Celene FH-618	2,500		120.00	120
1995	Celestine LL-982	2,500	1996	100.00	100
1990	Charlene YK-4112	Closed	1992	90.00	90
1992	Charlotte FH-484	2,500	1993	115.00	115
1995	Chelsea DOLL 560	2,500		35.00	35
1992	Chelsea IND-397	Closed	1993	85.00	85
1995	Cherry FH-616	2,500	1994	100.00	100
1991	Cheryl TR-49	2,500	1993	120.00	120
1991	Chin Chin YK-4211	Closed	1993	85.00	85
1990	Chin Fa C-3061	Closed	1992	95.00	95
1990	Chinook WB-24	Closed	1992	85.00	85
1994	Chris FH-561	2,500	1994	85.00	85
1994	Chrissie FH-562	2,500	1994	85.00	85
1990	Chrissie WB-2	Closed	1992	75.00	75
1991	Christina PS-261	Closed	1993	115.00	115
1985	Christmas Cheer 125	Closed	1988	40.00	100
1995	Christmas Kitten IND-530	2,500		100.00	100
1991	Cindy Lou FH-464	2,500	1993	85.00	85
1994	Cindy OC-58	2,500	1994	140.00	140
1993	Cinnamon JNC-4014	Closed	1993	90.00	90
1988	Cissie DOM263	Closed	1990	65.00	135
1991	Cissy EP-56	2,500	1993	95.00	95
1995	Clancy GU-54	2,500	1995	80.00	80
1994	Clara IND-518	2,500	1994	140.00	140
1994	Clara IND-524	2,500	1994	150.00	150
1991	Clare DOLL-465	Open	1993	100.00	100
1993	Clare FH-497	2,500	1993	100.00	100
1994	Claudette TR-81	2,500	1995	150.00	150
1991	Claudine C-3146	Closed	1993	95.00	95
1993	Clothilde FH-469	2,500	1993	125.00	125
1995	Cody FH-629	2,500	1995	120.00	120
1991	Colette WB-7	Closed	1993	65.00	65
1991	Colleen YK-4163	Closed	1993	120.00	120
1991	Cookie GU-6	2,500	1993	110.00	110
1994	Copper YK-4546C	3,500		150.00	150
1994	Cora FH-565	2,500		140.00	140
1992	Cordelia OM-09	2,500	1993	250.00	250
1991	Courtney LL-859	2,500	1993	150.00	150
1991	Creole AM-17	2,500	1993	160.00	200
1989	Crying Courtney PS-75	Closed	1992	115.00	115
1991	Crystal YK-4237	3,500	1993	125.00	125

*Quotes have been rounded up to nearest dollar

Collectors' Information Bureau

43

Seymour Mann, Inc.
to Seymour Mann, Inc.

DOLLS

YEAR ISSUE		EDITION LIMIT	YEAR RETD.	ISSUE PRICE	*QUOTE U.S.$
1987	Cynthia DOM-211	Closed	1986	85.00	85
1995	Cynthia GU-300C	2,500		30.00	30
1990	Daisy EP-6	Closed	1992	90.00	90
1994	Dallas PS-403	2,500	1994	150.00	150
1991	Danielle AM-5	Closed	1993	125.00	175
1995	Danielle MER-808	2,500	1996	65.00	65
1995	Danielle PS-432	2,500		100.00	100
1989	Daphne Ecru/Mint Green C3025	Closed	1992	85.00	85
1991	Darcy EP-47	Closed	1993	110.00	110
1991	Darcy FH-451	2,500	1993	105.00	105
1995	Darcy FH-636	2,500	1996	80.00	80
1995	Darcy LL-986	2,500		110.00	110
1991	Daria C-3122	Closed	1993	110.00	110
1995	Darla LL-988	2,500	1996	100.00	100
1991	Darlene DOLL-444	2,500	1993	75.00	75
1994	Daryl LL-947	2,500	1994	150.00	150
1991	Dawn C-3135	Closed	1993	130.00	130
1987	Dawn C185	Closed	1986	75.00	175
1992	Debbie JNC-4006	Open	1993	90.00	90
1994	Dee LL-948	2,500	1994	110.00	110
1992	Deidre FH-473	2,500	1993	115.00	115
1992	Deidre YK-4083	Closed	1993	95.00	95
1994	Delilah C-3195	2,500	1994	150.00	150
1991	Delphine SP-308	Closed	1993	135.00	135
1991	Denise LL-852	2,500	1993	105.00	105
1995	Denise LL-994	2,500	1996	105.00	105
1991	Desiree LL-898	2,500	1993	120.00	120
1995	Diana RDK-221A	2,500		35.00	35
1990	Diane FH-275	Closed	1992	90.00	90
1995	Diane PS-444	2,500		110.00	110
1990	Dianna TK-31	Closed	1992	175.00	175
1995	Dinah OC-79	2,500		40.00	40
1988	Doll Oliver FH392	Closed	1990	100.00	100
1990	Domino C-3050	Closed	1992	145.00	200
1992	Dona FH-494	2,500	1993	100.00	100
1993	Donna DOLL-447	2,500	1993	85.00	85
1995	Donna GU-300D	2,500		30.00	30
1990	Dorothy TR-10	Closed	1992	135.00	150
1990	Dorri DOLL-16PH	Closed	1992	85.00	85
1991	Duanane SP-366	Closed	1993	85.00	85
1995	Dulcie FH-622	2,500		110.00	110
1991	Dulcie YK-4131V	Closed	1993	100.00	100
1991	Dwayne C-3123	Closed	1993	120.00	120
1991	Edie YK-4177	Closed	1993	115.00	115
1990	Eileen FH-367	Closed	1992	100.00	100
1995	Elaine CD-02210	2,500		50.00	50
1995	Eleanor C16669	2,500		35.00	35
1991	Elisabeth and Lisa C-3095	2,500	1993	195.00	195
1989	Elisabeth OM-32	Closed	1990	120.00	120
1991	Elise PS-259	Closed	1993	105.00	105
1991	Elizabeth AM-32	2,500	1993	105.00	105
1989	Elizabeth C-246P	Closed	1990	150.00	200
1995	Elizabeth Doll 553	2,500		35.00	35
1993	Ellen YK-4223	3,500	1994	150.00	150
1995	Ellie FH-621	2,500	1996	125.00	125
1989	Emily PS-48	Closed	1990	110.00	110
1988	Emily YK-243V	Closed	1990	70.00	70
1995	Emma DOLL 559	2,500		35.00	35
1995	Emma GU-300E	2,500		30.00	30
1991	Emmaline Beige/Lilac OM-197	Closed	1993	300.00	300
1991	Emmaline OM-191	2,500	1993	300.00	300
1991	Emmy C-3099	Closed	1993	125.00	125
1991	Erin DOLL-4PH	Closed	1993	60.00	60
1995	Erin RDK-223	2,500		30.00	30
1992	Eugenie OM-225	2,500	1993	300.00	300
1991	Evalina C-3124	Closed	1993	135.00	135
1994	Faith IND-522	2,500	1994	135.00	135
1994	Faith OC-60	2,500	1994	115.00	115
1995	Fawn C-3228	2,500		55.00	55
1995	Felicia GU-300F	2,500		30.00	30
1990	Felicia TR-9	Closed	1992	115.00	115
1991	Fifi AM-100F	Closed	1993	70.00	70
1995	Fleur C-16415	2,500		30.00	30
1991	Fleurette PS-286	2,500	1993	75.00	75
1994	Flora FH-583	2,500	1994	115.00	115
1991	Flora TR-46	Closed	1993	125.00	125
1994	Florette IND-519	2,500	1994	140.00	140
1988	Frances C-233	Closed	1990	80.00	125
1991	Francesca AM-14	2,500	1993	175.00	175
1990	Francesca C-3021	Closed	1992	100.00	175
1994	Gardiner PS-405	2,500		150.00	150
1993	Gena OM-229	Closed	1994	250.00	250
1994	Georgia IND-510	2,500	1995	220.00	220
1995	Georgia IND-528	2,500		125.00	125
1994	Georgia SP-456	2,500		115.00	115
1991	Georgia YK-4131	Closed	1993	100.00	100
1991	Georgia YK-4143	Closed	1993	150.00	150
1990	Gerri Beige YK4094	Closed	1992	95.00	140
1991	Gigi C-3107	Closed	1993	135.00	135
1991	Ginger LL-907	Closed	1993	115.00	115
1995	Ginnie FH-619	2,500		110.00	110
1990	Ginny YK-4119	Closed	1995	100.00	100
1992	Giselle OM-02	Closed	1993	90.00	90
1988	Giselle on Goose FH176	Closed	1990	105.00	225
1991	Gloria AM-100G	2,500	1993	70.00	70
1991	Gloria YK-4166	Closed	1993	105.00	105
1995	Gold Angel FH-511G	2,500		85.00	85
1995	Green Angel FH-511C	2,500		85.00	85
1991	Gretchen DOLL-446	Open	1993	45.00	45
1995	Gretchen FH-620	2,500	1995	120.00	120
1991	Gretel DOLL-434	Closed	1993	60.00	60
1995	Guardian Angel OM-91	2,500		150.00	150
1995	Guardian Angel TR-98	2,500		85.00	85
1991	Hansel and Gretel DOLL-448V	Closed	1993	60.00	60
1989	Happy Birthday C3012	Closed	1990	80.00	125
1993	Happy FH-479	2,500	1994	105.00	105
1995	Happy RDK-238	2,500		25.00	25
1994	Hatty/Matty IND-514	2,500		165.00	165
1995	Heather LL-991	2,500		115.00	115
1995	Heather PS-436	2,500		115.00	115
1994	Heather YK-4531	3,500		165.00	165
1993	Hedy FH-449	Closed	1994	95.00	95
1989	Heidi 260	Closed	1990	50.00	95
1991	Helene AM-29	2,500	1993	150.00	150
1995	Holly CD-16526	2,500		30.00	30
1991	Holly CH-6	Closed	1993	100.00	100
1991	Honey Bunny WB-9	Closed	1993	70.00	70
1991	Honey FH-401	Closed	1993	100.00	100
1994	Honey LL-945	2,500	1996	150.00	150
1991	Hope FH-434	2,500	1993	90.00	90
1990	Hope YK-4118	Closed	1992	90.00	90
1995	Hyacinth C-3227	2,500		130.00	130
1990	Hyacinth DOLL-15PH	Closed	1992	85.00	85
1994	Hyacinth LL-941	2,500	1995	90.00	90
1990	Indian Doll FH-295	Closed	1992	60.00	60
1994	Indian IND-520	2,500		115.00	115
1991	Indira AM-4	2,500	1993	125.00	125
1995	Irene GU-56	2,500		85.00	85
1995	Irina RDK-237	2,500		35.00	35
1993	Iris FH-483	2,500	1994	95.00	95
1991	Iris TR-58	Closed	1993	120.00	120
1995	Ivana RDK-233	2,500		35.00	35
1994	Ivy C-3203	2,500	1996	85.00	85
1991	Ivy PS-307	Closed	1993	75.00	75
1994	Jacqueline C-3202	2,500		150.00	150
1995	Jamaica LL-989	2,500		75.00	75
1993	Jan Dress-Up OM-12	2,500	1994	135.00	175
1994	Jan FH-584R	2,500		115.00	115
1992	Jan OM-012	9,200	1993	135.00	135
1991	Jane PS-243L	Closed	1993	115.00	115
1992	Janet FH-496	2,500	1993	120.00	120
1990	Janette DOLL-385	Closed	1992	85.00	85
1991	Janice OM-194	2,500	1993	300.00	300
1994	Janis FH-584B	2,500		115.00	115
1989	Jaqueline DOLL-254M	Closed	1990	85.00	85
1995	Jennifer PS-446	2,500		145.00	145
1995	Jenny CD-16673B	2,500		35.00	35
1994	Jenny OC-36M	2,500		115.00	115
1995	Jerri PS-434	2,500		100.00	100
1988	Jessica DOM-267	Closed	1990	90.00	90
1991	Jessica FH-423	2,500	1993	95.00	95
1995	Jessica RDK-225	2,500		30.00	30
1992	Jet FH-478	2,500	1993	115.00	150
1995	Jewel TR-100	2,500		110.00	110
1994	Jillian C-3196	2,500		150.00	150
1990	Jillian DOLL-41PH	Closed	1992	90.00	90
1993	Jillian SP-428	Closed	1994	165.00	165
1994	Jo YK-4539	3,500	1995	150.00	150
1988	Joanne Cry Baby PS-50	Closed	1990	100.00	100
1990	Joanne TR-12	Closed	1992	175.00	175
1992	Jodie FH-495	2,500	1993	115.00	115
1995	Joella CD-16779	2,500	1996	35.00	35
1988	Jolie C231	Closed	1990	65.00	150
1994	Jordan SP-455	2,500		150.00	150
1995	Joy CD-1450A	2,500		35.00	35
1991	Joy EP-23V	Closed	1993	130.00	130
1995	Joy TR-99	2,500		85.00	135
1991	Joyce AM-100J	2,500	1993	35.00	35
1991	Julia C-3102	Closed	1993	135.00	135
1995	Julia C-3234	2,500		100.00	100
1995	Julia RDK-222	2,500		35.00	35
1988	Julie C245A	Closed	1990	65.00	160
1990	Julie WB-35	Closed	1992	70.00	70
1988	Juliette Bride Musical C246LTM	Closed	1990	150.00	200
1992	Juliette OM-08	2,500	1993	175.00	175
1991	Juliette OM-192	2,500	1993	300.00	300
1993	Juliette OM-8	2,500	1994	175.00	175
1995	June CD-2212	2,500		50.00	50
1991	Karen EP-24	Closed	1993	115.00	115
1990	Karen PS-198	Closed	1992	150.00	150
1991	Karmela EP-57	2,500	1993	120.00	120
1995	Karyn RDK-224	2,500		35.00	35
1990	Kate C-3060	Closed	1992	95.00	95
1994	Kate OC-55	2,500		150.00	150
1990	Kathy w/Bear-TE1	Closed	1992	70.00	70
1994	Katie IND-511	2,500		110.00	110
1989	Kayoko PS-24	Closed	1991	75.00	175
1991	Kelly AM-8	Closed	1993	125.00	125
1994	Kelly YK-4536	3,500		150.00	150
1995	Kelsey DOLL 561	2,500		35.00	35
1993	Kendra FH-481	2,500	1994	115.00	115
1991	Kerry FH-396	Closed	1993	100.00	100
1994	Kevin MS-25	2,500		150.00	150
1994	Kevin YK-4543	3,500		140.00	140
1990	Kiku EP-4	Closed	1992	100.00	100
1991	Kim AM-100K	2,500	1993	70.00	70
1995	Kimmie CD-15816	2,500		30.00	30
1991	Kinesha SP-402	2,500	1993	110.00	110
1989	Kirsten PS-40G	Closed	1991	70.00	70
1993	Kit SP-426	Closed	1994	55.00	55
1994	Kit YK-4547	3,500		115.00	115
1994	Kitten IND-512	2,500	1996	110.00	110
1995	Kitty IND-527	2,500	1996	40.00	40
1991	Kristi FH-402	Closed	1993	100.00	100
1991	Kyla YK-4137	Closed	1993	95.00	150
1994	Lady Caroline LL-830	2,500		120.00	120
1994	Lady Caroline LL-939	2,500		120.00	120
1994	Laughing Waters PS-410	2,500		150.00	150
1990	Laura DOLL-25PH	Closed	1992	55.00	55
1992	Laura OM-010	2,500	1993	250.00	250
1991	Laura WB-110P	Closed	1993	85.00	85
1990	Lauren SP-300	Closed	1992	85.00	85
1994	Lauren SP-458	2,500		125.00	125
1992	Laurie JNC-4004	Open	1993	90.00	90
1990	Lavender Blue YK-4024	Closed	1992	95.00	135
1991	Leigh DOLL-457	2,500	1993	95.00	95
1991	Leila AM-2	Closed	1993	125.00	125
1995	Lenore FH-617	2,500		120.00	120
1991	Lenore LL-911	2,500	1993	105.00	105
1995	Lenore RDK-229	2,500		50.00	50
1991	Lenore YK-4218	3,500	1995	135.00	135
1995	Leslie LL-983	2,500		105.00	105
1995	Leslie MER-809	2,500		65.00	65
1991	Libby EP-18	Closed	1993	85.00	85
1990	Lien Wha YK-4092	Closed	1992	100.00	150
1991	Lila AM-10	2,500	1993	125.00	125
1991	Lila FH-404	2,500	1993	100.00	125
1995	Lila GU-55	2,500		55.00	55
1995	Lili CD-16888	2,500		30.00	30
1995	Lily FH-630	2,500	1996	120.00	175
1995	Lily in pink stripe IND-533	2,500	1995	85.00	85
1987	Linda C190	Closed	1986	60.00	120
1993	Linda SP-435	Closed	1994	95.00	95
1995	Lindsay PS-442	2,500		175.00	175
1994	Lindsay SP-462	2,500		150.00	150
1991	Lindsey C-3127	Closed	1993	135.00	175
1991	Linetta C-3166	Closed	1993	135.00	135
1990	Ling-Ling DOLL	Closed	1992	50.00	50
1989	Ling-Ling PS-87G	Closed	1991	90.00	90
1988	Lionel FH206B	Closed	1990	50.00	120
1991	Lisa AM-100L	2,500	1993	70.00	70
1990	Lisa Beige Accordion Pleat YK4093	Closed	1992	125.00	125
1990	Lisa FH-379	Closed	1992	100.00	100
1995	Lisette LL-993	2,500		105.00	105
1995	Little Bobby RDK-235	2,500		25.00	25
1991	Little Boy Blue C-3159	Closed	1993	100.00	100
1995	Little Lisa OM-86	2,500		125.00	125
1995	Little Lori RDK-228	2,500		20.00	20
1995	Little Lou RDK-227	2,500		20.00	20
1995	Little Mary RDK-234	2,500		25.00	25
1995	Little Patty PS-429	2,500		50.00	50
1994	Little Red Riding Hood FH-557	2,500		140.00	140
1991	Liz C-3150	2,500	1993	100.00	100
1989	Liz YK-269	Closed	1991	70.00	100
1990	Liza C-3053	Closed	1992	100.00	100
1991	Liza YK-4226	3,500	1993	35.00	35
1991	Lola SP-363	2,500	1993	90.00	90
1990	Lola SP-79	Closed	1992	105.00	105
1991	Loni FH-448	2,500	1993	100.00	100
1990	Loretta FH-321	Closed	1992	90.00	90
1994	Loretta SP-457	2,500		140.00	140
1991	Lori EP-52	2,500	1993	95.00	95
1990	Lori WB-72BM	Closed	1992	75.00	75
1991	Louise LL-908	2,500	1993	105.00	105
1995	Lucie MER-607	2,500		65.00	65
1989	Lucinda DOM-293	Closed	1990	90.00	90
1988	Lucinda DOM-293	Closed	1990	90.00	90
1994	Lucinda PS-406	2,500		150.00	150
1991	Lucy LL-853	Closed	1993	80.00	80
1992	Lydia OM-226	2,500	1993	250.00	250
1993	Lynn FH-498	2,500	1994	120.00	120
1995	Lynn LL-995	2,500	1996	105.00	105
1990	Madame De Pompadour C-3088	Closed	1992	250.00	250
1991	Madeleine C-3106	Closed	1993	95.00	95
1995	Mae PS-431	2,500		70.00	70
1992	Maggie FH-505	Closed	1993	125.00	125
1995	Maggie IND-532	2,500		80.00	80
1990	Maggie PS-151P	Closed	1992	90.00	90
1990	Maggie WB-51	Closed	1992	105.00	105
1994	Magnolia FH-558	2,500		150.00	150
1989	Mai-Ling PS-79	2,500	1991	100.00	100
1994	Maiden PS-409	2,500	1995	150.00	150
1994	Mandy YK-4548	3,500		115.00	115
1989	Marcey YK-4005	3,500	1995	90.00	90
1991	Marcy TR-55	Closed	1993	135.00	135
1987	Marcy YK122	Closed	1986	55.00	100
1989	Margaret 245	Closed	1991	100.00	150
1994	Margaret C-3204	2,500		150.00	150
1994	Maria GU-35	2,500		115.00	115
1990	Maria YK-4116	Closed	1992	85.00	85
1993	Mariah LL-909	Closed	1993	135.00	135
1991	Mariel 18" Ivory-C-3119	Closed	1993	125.00	125
1995	Marielle PS-443	2,500		175.00	175
1995	Marla PS-437	2,500		125.00	125
1995	Martina RDK-232	2,500		35.00	35
1995	Mary Ann FH-633	2,500	1996	110.00	110
1994	Mary Ann TR-79	2,500		125.00	125
1995	Mary Elizabeth OC-51	2,500	1996	50.00	50
1994	Mary Jo FH-552	2,500		150.00	150
1994	Mary Lou FH-565	2,500		135.00	135
1994	Mary OC-56	2,500		135.00	135
1991	Maude AM-100M	2,500	1993	70.00	70
1989	Maureen PS-84	Closed	1990	90.00	90

*Quotes have been rounded up to nearest dollar

YEAR ISSUE		EDITION LIMIT	YEAR RETD.	ISSUE PRICE	*QUOTE U.S.$
1995	Maxine C-3225	2,500		125.00	125
1995	Mc Kenzie LL-987	2,500		100.00	100
1994	Megan C-3192	2,500		150.00	150
1995	Megan RDK-220	2,500		30.00	30
1989	Meimei PS22	Closed	1990	75.00	225
1990	Melanie YK-4115	Closed	1992	80.00	80
1991	Melissa AM-9	Closed	1993	120.00	120
1991	Melissa CH-3	Closed	1993	110.00	110
1990	Melissa DOLL-390	Closed	1992	75.00	75
1989	Melissa LL-794	Closed	1990	95.00	95
1991	Melissa LL-901	Closed	1993	135.00	135
1992	Melissa OM-03	2,500	1993	135.00	135
1991	Meredith FH-391-P	Closed	1993	95.00	95
1995	Meredith MER-806	2,500	1996	65.00	65
1995	Merri MER-810	2,500	1996	65.00	65
1990	Merry Widow 20" C-3040M	Closed	1992	140.00	140
1991	Meryl FH-463	2,500	1993	95.00	95
1991	Michael w/School Books FH-439B	2,500	1993	95.00	95
1988	Michelle & Marcel YK176	Closed	1990	70.00	150
1991	Michelle Lilac/Green EP36	Closed	1993	95.00	95
1991	Michelle w/School Books FH-439G	Closed	1993	95.00	95
1995	Mindi PS-441	2,500	1995	125.00	125
1995	Mindy LL-990	2,500		75.00	75
1995	Miranda C16456B	2,500		30.00	30
1991	Miranda DOLL-9PH	Closed	1993	75.00	75
1995	Miranda TR-91	2,500		135.00	135
1984	Miss Debutante Debi	Closed	1987	75.00	180
1994	Miss Elizabeth SP-459	2,500		150.00	150
1989	Miss Kim PS-25	Closed	1990	75.00	175
1991	Missy DOLL-464	Closed	1993	70.00	70
1994	Missy FH-567	2,500	1996	140.00	140
1991	Missy PS-258	Closed	1993	90.00	90
1991	Mon Yun w/Parasol TR33	2,500	1993	115.00	150
1995	Monica TR-95	2,500		135.00	135
1994	Morning Dew Indian PS-404	2,500		150.00	150
1994	Musical Doll OC-45M	2,500		140.00	140
1991	Nancy 21" Pink w/Rabbit EP-31	Closed	1993	165.00	165
1995	Nancy FH-615	2,500		100.00	100
1992	Nancy JNC-4001	Open	1993	90.00	90
1991	Nancy WB-73	2,500	1993	65.00	65
1990	Nanook WB-23	Closed	1992	75.00	75
1994	Natalie PP-2	2,500		275.00	275
1990	Natasha PS-102	Closed	1992	100.00	100
1995	Natasha TR-90	2,500		125.00	125
1991	Nellie EP-1B	Closed	1993	75.00	75
1991	Nicole AM-12	Closed	1993	135.00	135
1994	Nikki PS-401	2,500	1995	150.00	150
1994	Nikki SP-461	2,500		150.00	150
1993	Nina YK-4232	3,500	1993	135.00	135
1987	Nirmala YK-210	Closed	1995	50.00	50
1994	Noel MS-27	2,500		150.00	150
1994	Noelle C-3199	2,500		195.00	195
1994	Noelle MS-28	2,500		150.00	150
1991	Noelle PS-239V	Closed	1993	95.00	95
1995	Norma C-3226	2,500		135.00	135
1990	Odessa FH-362	Closed	1992	65.00	65
1994	Odetta IND-521	2,500	1995	140.00	140
1993	Oona TR-57	Closed	1993	135.00	135
1994	Oriana IND-515	2,500		140.00	140
1995	Our First Skates RDK-226/BG	2,500		50.00	50
1994	Paige GU-33	2,500		150.00	150
1995	Paige IND-529	2,500		80.00	80
1994	Pamela LL-949	2,500		115.00	115
1995	Pan Pan GU-52	2,500		60.00	60
1994	Panama OM-43	2,500		195.00	195
1989	Patricia/Patrick 215GBB	Closed	1990	105.00	135
1991	Patti DOLL-440	2,500	1993	65.00	65
1995	Patty C-3220	2,500		60.00	60
1994	Patty GU-34	2,500		115.00	115
1991	Patty YK-4221	3,500	1993	125.00	125
1989	Paula PS-56	Closed	1990	75.00	75
1995	Paulette PS-430	2,500		80.00	80
1989	Pauline Bonaparte OM68	Closed	1990	120.00	120
1995	Pauline PS-440	2,500		65.00	65
1988	Pauline YK-230	Closed	1990	90.00	90
1994	Payson YK-4541	3,500		135.00	135
1994	Payton PS-407	2,500	1995	150.00	150
1995	Peaches IND-531	2,500		80.00	80
1994	Pearl IND-523	2,500	1996	275.00	275
1994	Pegeen C-3205	2,500	1996	150.00	150
1994	Peggy TR-75	2,500		185.00	185
1991	Pepper PS-277	Closed	1993	130.00	150
1994	Petula C-3191	2,500		140.00	140
1991	Pia-PS 246L	Closed	1993	115.00	115
1990	Ping-LingDOLL-363RV	Closed	1992	50.00	50
1990	Polly DOLL-22PH	Closed	1992	90.00	90
1990	Princess Fair Skies FH-268B	Closed	1992	75.00	75
1994	Princess Foxfire PS-411	2,500		150.00	150
1994	Princess Moonrise YK-4542	3,500		140.00	140
1990	Princess Red Feather PS-189	Closed	1992	90.00	90
1994	Princess Snow Flower PS-402	2,500	1995	150.00	150
1991	Princess Summer Winds FH-427	2,500	1993	120.00	120
1990	Priscilla WB-50	Closed	1992	105.00	105
1994	Priscilla YK-4538	3,500		135.00	135
1991	Prissy White/Blue C-3140	Closed	1993	100.00	100
1995	Rainie LL-984	2,500	1996	125.00	125
1989	Ramona PS-31B	Closed	1992	80.00	80
1991	Rapunzel C-3157	2,500	1993	150.00	150
1987	Rapunzel C158	Closed	1986	95.00	165
1993	Rebecca C-3177	2,500	1993	135.00	135
1994	Rebecca C-3177	2,500		135.00	135

YEAR ISSUE		EDITION LIMIT	YEAR RETD.	ISSUE PRICE	*QUOTE U.S.$
1989	Rebecca PS-34V	Closed	1992	45.00	45
1991	Red Wing AM-30	2,500	1993	165.00	165
1994	Regina OM-41	2,500		150.00	150
1994	Rita FH-553	2,500	1996	115.00	115
1994	Robby NM-29	2,500		135.00	135
1991	Robin AM-22	Closed	1993	120.00	120
1995	Robin C-3236	2,500		60.00	60
1991	Rosalind C-3090	Closed	1992	150.00	150
1989	Rosie 290M	Closed	1992	55.00	85
1995	Rusty CD-1450B	2,500		35.00	35
1988	Sabrina C-208	Closed	1990	65.00	95
1987	Sabrina C208	Closed	1986	65.00	95
1990	Sabrina C3050	Closed	1992	105.00	105
1987	Sailorette DOM217	Closed	1986	70.00	150
1992	Sally FH-492	2,500	1993	105.00	105
1990	Sally WB-20	Closed	1992	95.00	95
1991	Samantha GU-3	Closed	1992	100.00	100
1995	San San GU-53	2,500		60.00	60
1991	Sandra DOLL-6-PHE	2,500	1992	65.00	65
1992	Sapphires OM-223	2,500	1993	250.00	250
1992	Sara Ann FH-474	2,500	1993	115.00	115
1995	Sarah C-3214	2,500		110.00	110
1994	Saretta SP-423	2,500		100.00	100
1993	Saretta SP-423	2,500	1993	100.00	100
1995	Sasha GU-57	2,500		75.00	75
1991	Scarlett FH-399	2,500	1992	100.00	100
1991	Scarlett FH-436	2,500	1992	135.00	135
1992	Scarlett FH-471	2,500	1993	120.00	120
1991	Shaka SP-401	2,500	1992	110.00	110
1993	Shaka TR-45	2,500	1993	100.00	100
1994	Shaka TR-45	2,500		100.00	100
1991	Sharon 21" Blue EP-34	Closed	1992	120.00	120
1995	Sharon C-3237	2,500		95.00	95
1991	Shau Chen GU-2	2,500	1992	85.00	85
1991	Shelley CH-1	2,500	1992	110.00	110
1995	Shimmering Caroline LL-992	2,500		115.00	115
1990	Shirley WB-37	Closed	1992	65.00	65
1988	Sister Agnes 14" C250	Closed	1990	75.00	75
1988	Sister Ignatius Notre Dame FH184	Closed	1990	75.00	75
1989	Sister Mary C-249	Closed	1992	75.00	125
1990	Sister Mary WB-15	Closed	1992	70.00	70
1994	Sister Suzie IND-509	2,500	1995	95.00	95
1988	Sister Teresa FH187	Closed	1990	80.00	80
1995	Sleeping Beauty OM-88	2,500		115.00	115
1992	Sonja FH-486	2,500	1994	125.00	125
1995	Sophia PS-445	2,500		125.00	125
1990	Sophie OM-1	Closed	1992	65.00	65
1991	Sophie TR-53	2,500	1992	135.00	135
1995	Southern Belle Bride FH-637	2,500		160.00	160
1994	Southern Belle FH-570	2,500		140.00	140
1994	Sparkle OM-40	2,500	1996	150.00	150
1991	Stacy DOLL-6PH	Closed	1992	65.00	65
1995	Stacy FH-634	2,500		110.00	110
1995	Stacy OC-75	2,500		40.00	40
1990	Stacy TR-5	Closed	1992	105.00	105
1991	Stephanie AM-11	Closed	1992	105.00	105
1991	Stephanie FH-467	Closed	1992	95.00	95
1991	Stephanie Pink & White OM-196	Closed	1992	300.00	300
1994	Stephie OC-41M	2,500		115.00	115
1990	Sue Chuen C-3061G	Closed	1992	95.00	95
1992	Sue JNC-4003	Closed	1994	90.00	90
1994	Sue Kwei TR-73	2,500		110.00	110
1994	Sugar Plum Fairy OM-39	2,500	1996	150.00	150
1991	Summer AM-33	Closed	1992	200.00	200
1990	Sunny FH-331	Closed	1992	70.00	70
1989	Sunny PS-59V	Closed	1992	71.00	71
1990	Susan DOLL-364MC	Closed	1992	75.00	75
1995	Suzanna DOLL 554	2,500		35.00	35
1994	Suzanne LL-943	2,500		105.00	105
1994	Suzie GU-38	2,500		135.00	135
1995	Suzie OC-80	2,500		50.00	50
1989	Suzie PS-32	Closed	1992	80.00	80
1993	Suzie SP-422	2,500	1993	164.00	164
1994	Suzie SP-422	2,500		164.00	164
1995	Sweet Pea LL-981	2,500	1996	90.00	90
1991	Sybil 20" Beige C-3131	Closed	1992	135.00	135
1991	Sybil Pink DOLL-12PHMC	2,500	1992	75.00	75
1995	Sylvie CD-16634B	2,500		35.00	35
1995	Tabitha C-3233	2,500		50.00	50
1994	Taffey TR-80	2,500		150.00	150
1994	Tallulah OM-44	2,500		275.00	275
1991	Tamara OM-187	Closed	1992	135.00	135
1990	Tania DOLL-376P	Closed	1992	65.00	65
1989	Tatiana Pink Ballerina M-60	Closed	1991	120.00	175
1994	Teresa C-3198	2,500	1995	110.00	110
1995	Terri OM-78	2,500		150.00	150
1989	Terri PS-104	Closed	1991	85.00	85
1991	Terri TR-62	Closed	1992	75.00	75
1991	Tessa AM-19	Closed	1992	135.00	135
1994	Tiffany OC-44M	2,500	1996	140.00	140
1992	Tiffany OM-014	2,500	1994	150.00	150
1991	Tina AM-16	Closed	1992	130.00	130
1990	Tina DOLL-371	Closed	1992	85.00	85
1995	Tina OM-79	2,500		150.00	150
1990	Tina WB-32	Closed	1992	65.00	65
1994	Tippy LL-946	2,500	1995	110.00	110
1995	Tobey C-3232	2,500		50.00	50
1994	Todd YK-4540	3,500		45.00	45
1990	Tommy-C-3064	Closed	1992	75.00	75
1994	Topaz TR-74	2,500	1995	195.00	195

YEAR ISSUE		EDITION LIMIT	YEAR RETD.	ISSUE PRICE	*QUOTE U.S.$
1988	Tracy C-3006	Closed	1990	95.00	150
1992	Trina OM-011	Closed	1994	165.00	165
1994	Trixie TR-77	2,500		110.00	110
1991	Vanessa AM-34	Closed	1992	90.00	90
1991	Vicki C-3101	Closed	1992	200.00	200
1991	Violet EP-41	Closed	1992	135.00	135
1991	Violet OM-186	2,500	1992	270.00	270
1992	Violette FH-503	2,500	1994	120.00	120
1991	Virginia SP-359	Closed	1992	120.00	120
1994	Virginia TR-78	2,500		195.00	195
1987	Vivian C-201P	Closed	1986	80.00	80
1991	Wah-Ching Watching Oriental Toddler YK-4175	Closed	1992	110.00	110
1995	Wei Lin GU-44	2,500		70.00	70
1994	Wendy MS-26	2,500		150.00	150
1989	Wendy PS-51	Closed	1991	105.00	105
1990	Wendy TE-3	Closed	1992	75.00	75
1985	Wendy-C120	Closed	1987	45.00	150
1990	Wilma PS-174	Closed	1992	75.00	75
1995	Windy in Rose Print FH-626	2,500	1995	200.00	200
1995	Winnie LL-985	2,500	1996	75.00	75
1995	Winter Wonderland RDK-301	2,500		35.00	35
1995	Woodland Sprite OM-90	2,500		100.00	100
1995	Yelena RDK-236	2,500		35.00	35
1990	Yen Yen YK-4091	Closed	1992	95.00	95
1992	Yvette OM-015	2,500	1994	150.00	150

Signature Doll Series - Various

YEAR ISSUE		EDITION LIMIT	YEAR RETD.	ISSUE PRICE	*QUOTE U.S.$
1992	Abigail MS-11 - M. Severino	5,000	1994	125.00	125
1995	Adak PPA-21 - P. Phillips	5,000	1996	110.00	110
1992	Alexandria PAC-19 - P. Aprile	5,000	1995	300.00	300
1991	Alice MS-7 - M. Severino	5,000	1996	120.00	120
1995	Amanda KSFA-1 - K. Fitzpatrick	5,000		175.00	175
1991	Amber MS-1 - M. Severino	Closed	1994	95.00	95
1995	Amelia PAC-28 - P. Aprile	5,000		130.00	130
1995	Amy Rose HKHF-200 - H.K. Hyland	5,000		125.00	125
1992	Baby Cakes Crumbs PK-CRUMBS - P. Kolesar	5,000		17.50	35
1992	Baby Cakes Crumbs/Black PK-CRUMBS/B - P. Kolesar	5,000		17.50	35
1991	Becky MS-2 - M. Severino	5,000	1994	95.00	95
1993	Bonnett Baby MS-17W - M. Severino	5,000	1996	175.00	175
1995	Brad HKH-15 - H.K. Hyland	5,000		85.00	85
1992	Bride & Flower Girl PAC-6 - P. Aprile	5,000	1996	600.00	600
1995	Cara DALI-1 - E. Dali	5,000		400.00	400
1995	Casey PPA-23 - P. Phillips	5,000		85.00	85
1992	Cassandra PAC-8 - P. Aprile	Closed	N/A	450.00	450
1992	Cassie Flower Girl PAC-9 - P. Aprile	Closed	N/A	175.00	175
1992	Celine PAC-11 - P. Aprile	5,000	1995	165.00	165
1991	Clair-Ann PK-252 - P. Kolesar	5,000		100.00	100
1992	Clarissa PAC-3 - P. Aprile	5,000	1996	165.00	165
1991	Daddy's Little Darling MS-8 - M. Severino	5,000		165.00	165
1992	Darla HP-204 - H. Payne	5,000	1996	250.00	250
1992	Dulcie HP-200 - H. Payne	Closed	1993	250.00	250
1991	Enoc PK-100 - P. Kolesar	5,000		100.00	100
1992	Eugenie Bride PAC-1 - P. Aprile	5,000	1996	165.00	165
1995	Ginny LR-2 - L. Randolph	5,000		360.00	360
1993	Grace HKH-2 - H. Kahl-Hyland	5,000	1996	250.00	250
1993	Helene HKH-1 - H. Kahl-Hyland	5,000	1996	250.00	250
1995	Latisha PPA-25 - P. Phillips	5,000	1996	110.00	110
1995	Laurel HKH-17R - H.K. Hyland	5,000		110.00	110
1995	Lauren HKH-202 - H.K. Hyland	5,000	1996	150.00	150
1992	Little Match Girl HP-205 - H. Payne	Closed	1994	150.00	150
1995	Lucy HKH-14 - H.K. Hyland	2,500	1996	105.00	105
1992	Megan MS-12 - M. Severino	5,000	1995	125.00	125
1995	Meredith LR-3 - L. Randolph	5,000		375.00	375
1991	Mikey MS-3 - M. Severino	5,000	1994	95.00	95
1991	Mommy's Rays of Sunshine MS-9 - M. Severino	5,000		165.00	165
1995	Natasha HKH-17P - H.K. Hyland	5,000		110.00	110
1995	Patricia DALI-3 - E. Dali	5,000		280.00	280
1991	Paulette PAC-2 - P. Aprile	5,000		250.00	250
1991	Paulette PAC-4 - P. Aprile	5,000		250.00	250
1992	Pavlova PAC-17 - P. Aprile	5,000	1994	145.00	145
1992	Polly HP-206 - H. Payne	5,000		120.00	120
1991	Precious Baby SB-100 - S. Bilotto	5,000	1996	250.00	250
1991	Precious Pary Time SB-102 - S. Bilotto	5,000		250.00	250
1992	Rebecca Beige Bonnet MS-17B - M. Severino	5,000	1995	175.00	175
1993	Reilly HKH-3 - H. Kahl-Hyland	5,000		260.00	260
1992	Ruby MS-18 - M. Severino	5,000		135.00	135
1995	Shao Ling PPA-22 - P. Phillips	5,000		110.00	110
1991	Sparkle PK-250 - P. Kolesar	5,000	1996	100.00	100
1995	Stacy DALI-2 - E. Dali	5,000		360.00	360
1992	Stacy MS-24 - M. Severino	Closed	1993	110.00	110
1991	Stephie MS-6 - M. Severino	Closed	1994	125.00	125
1991	Su Lin MS-5 - M. Severino	5,000	1994	105.00	105
1995	Suzie HKH-16 - H.K. Hyland	5,000		100.00	100
1991	Sweet Pea PK-251 - P. Kolesar	Closed		100.00	100
1994	Tracy JAG-111 - J. Grammer	5,000	1996	150.00	150
1994	Trevor JAG-112 - J. Grammer	5,000	1996	115.00	115
1992	Violetta PAC-16 - P. Aprile	5,000	1994	165.00	165
1991	Yawning Kate MS-4 - M. Severino	Closed	1994	105.00	105

Susan Wakeen Doll Co. Inc.

The Littlest Ballet Company - S. Wakeen

YEAR ISSUE		EDITION LIMIT	YEAR RETD.	ISSUE PRICE	*QUOTE U.S.$
1985	Cynthia	375		198.00	350

*Quotes have been rounded up to nearest dollar

Susan Wakeen Doll Co. Inc.
to All God's Children

DOLLS/FIGURINES

Year	Issue	Edition Limit	Year Retd.	Issue Price	*Quote U.S.$
1987	Elizabeth	250		425.00	1000
1985	Jeanne	375		198.00	800
1985	Jennifer	250		750.00	750
1987	Marie Ann	50		1000.00	1000
1985	Patty	375		198.00	400-500

Timeless Creations

Barefoot Children - A. Himstedt

Year	Issue	Edition Limit	Year Retd.	Issue Price	*Quote U.S.$
1987	Bastian	Closed	1989	329.00	725
1987	Beckus	Closed	1989	329.00	1200-1500
1987	Ellen	Closed	1989	329.00	825
1987	Fatou	Closed	1989	329.00	995
1987	Fatou (Cornroll)	Closed	1989	329.00	1200-1500
1987	Kathe	Closed	1989	329.00	825
1987	Lisa	Closed	1989	329.00	850-875
1987	Paula	Closed	1989	329.00	825

Blessed Are The Children - A. Himstedt

Year	Issue	Edition Limit	Year Retd.	Issue Price	*Quote U.S.$
1988	Friederike	Closed	1990	499.00	1800-2200
1988	Kasimir	Closed	1990	499.00	1700-1900
1988	Makimura	Closed	1990	499.00	1000-1200
1988	Malin	Closed	1990	499.00	1500-1650
1988	Michiko	Closed	1990	499.00	1300-1450

Faces of Friendship - A. Himstedt

Year	Issue	Edition Limit	Year Retd.	Issue Price	*Quote U.S.$
1991	Liliane (Netherlands)	2-Yr.	1993	598.00	695
1991	Neblina (Switzerland)	2-Yr.	1993	598.00	695
1991	Shireem (Bali)	2-Yr.	1993	598.00	625

Fiene And The Barefoot Babies - A. Himstedt

Year	Issue	Edition Limit	Year Retd.	Issue Price	*Quote U.S.$
1990	Annchen-German Baby Girl	2-Yr.	1992	498.00	700
1990	Fiene-Belgian Girl	2-Yr.	1992	598.00	795
1990	Mo-American Baby Boy	2-Yr.	1992	498.00	625
1990	Taki-Japanese Baby Girl	2-Yr.	1992	498.00	800-1100

Heartland Series - A. Himstedt

Year	Issue	Edition Limit	Year Retd.	Issue Price	*Quote U.S.$
1988	Timi	Closed		329.00	400-500
1988	Toni	Closed		329.00	400-500

Images of Childhood - A. Himstedt

Year	Issue	Edition Limit	Year Retd.	Issue Price	*Quote U.S.$
1993	Kima (Greenland)	2-Yr.	1995	599.00	625
1993	Lona (California)	2-Yr.	1995	599.00	599
1993	Tara (Germany)	2-Yr.	1995	599.00	599

Reflection of Youth - A. Himstedt

Year	Issue	Edition Limit	Year Retd.	Issue Price	*Quote U.S.$
1989	Adrienne (France)	Closed	1991	558.00	800-900
1989	Ayoka (Africa)	Closed	1991	558.00	925
1989	Janka (Hungry)	Closed	1991	558.00	800-900
1989	Kai (German)	Closed	1991	558.00	700-900

Summer Dreams - A. Himstedt

Year	Issue	Edition Limit	Year Retd.	Issue Price	*Quote U.S.$
1992	Enzo	2-Yr.	1994	599.00	599
1992	Jule	2-Yr.	1994	599.00	650-700
1992	Pemba	2-Yr.	1994	599.00	599
1992	Sanga	2-Yr.	1994	599.00	599

FIGURINES

Ace Product Management Group, Inc.

Harley-Davidson Archive Pewter Figurines - Ace

Year	Issue	Edition Limit	Year Retd.	Issue Price	*Quote U.S.$
1994	Catch Of The Day 99450-93Z	1,500	1996	150.00	150
1996	On Patrol 99169-96Z	1,500		150.00	150

Harley-Davidson Christmas Figurines - Ace

Year	Issue	Edition Limit	Year Retd.	Issue Price	*Quote U.S.$
1989	Perfect Tree 99420-90Z	3,000	1989	99.95	100
1990	Mainstreet U.S.A. 9941-91Z	3,000	1990	129.95	130
1991	Joy Of Giving 99423-92Z	3,000	1991	134.95	135
1992	Home For The Holidays 99422-93Z	3,000	1992	145.00	145
1993	Rural Delivery 99423-94Z	3,000	1993	155.00	155
1994	29 Days 'Til Christmas 99089-95Z	3,000	1994	170.00	170
1995	Skating Party 99417-96Z	3,000	1995	185.00	185
1996	Surprise Visit 99934-97Z	3,000		185.00	185
1997	Christmas Vacation 97959-98Z	3,000		190.00	190

Harley-Davidson Mini-Plate Figurines - Ace

Year	Issue	Edition Limit	Year Retd.	Issue Price	*Quote U.S.$
1992	Letters To Santa 99415-93Z	Yr.Iss	1992	25.00	25
1993	Santa's Predicament 99420-94Z	Yr.Iss.	1993	18.00	18
1994	Not A Creature Was Stirring 99447-95Z	Yr.Iss.	1994	20.00	20
1995	Planning The Route 99476-96Z	Yr.Iss.	1995	22.00	22
1996	Reviewing the Plan 99946-97Z	Yr.Iss.	1996	22.00	22
1997	Santa's Workshop 97966-98Z	Yr.Iss.		35.00	35

Harley-Davidson Sculptures - M. Patrick

Year	Issue	Edition Limit	Year Retd.	Issue Price	*Quote U.S.$
1993	90th Anniversary -The Reunion 99215-93Z	2,500	1993	495.00	495
1993	90th Anniversary-Bronze The Reunion 99216-93ZB	90	1993	3495.00	3495
1993	Milwaukee Ride 99497-94Z	1,500	1995	350.00	350
1994	Old Soldier 99403-95Z	1,500	1995	350.00	350
1995	Just Hitched 99079-96Z	1,500	1995	350.00	350
1996	Daytona Bound 99164-96Z	1,500		350.00	350

Harley-Davidson Young Rider Figurines - Ace

Year	Issue	Edition Limit	Year Retd.	Issue Price	*Quote U.S.$
1992	The Jacket 99370-93Z	3,000	1994	25.00	25
1993	Free Wheelin' 99371-93Z	3,000	1995	25.00	25
1993	The Enthusiast 99372-94Z	3,000	1995	25.00	25
1994	Engine Lesson 99376-95Z	3,000	1996	28.00	28
1995	Harley Rides-5 Cents 99377-95Z	3,000	1996	28.00	28
1995	Treehouse Christening 99296-96Z	3,000		32.00	32

Holiday Memories Holiday Music Boxes - Ace

Year	Issue	Edition Limit	Year Retd.	Issue Price	*Quote U.S.$
1994	Under The Mistletoe 99459-95Z	7,500	1994	48.00	48
1995	Late Arrival 99496-96Z	7,500	1995	55.00	55
1996	After the Pageant 99949-97Z	7,500	1996	58.00	58
1997	Roadside Revelation 97962-98Z	7,500		58.00	58

All God's Children

Collectors' Club - M. Root

Year	Issue	Edition Limit	Year Retd.	Issue Price	*Quote U.S.$
1989	Molly -1524	Retrd.	1990	38.00	400-650
1990	Joey -1539	Retrd.	1991	32.00	240-500
1991	Mandy -1540	Retrd.	1992	36.00	275-330
1992	Olivia -1562	Retrd.	1993	36.00	135-270
1993	Garrett -1567	Retrd.	1994	36.00	125-250
1993	Peek-a-Boo	Retrd.	1994	Gift	40-95
1994	Alexandria -1575	Retrd.	1995	36.00	125-145
1994	Lindy	Retrd.	1995	Gift	65-80
1995	Zamika -1581	Retrd.	1996	36.00	75-100
1995	Zizi	Retrd.	1996	Gift	30-45
1996	Donnie -1585	5/97		36.00	36
1996	Dinky	5/97		Gift	N/A

Event Piece - M. Root

Year	Issue	Edition Limit	Year Retd.	Issue Price	*Quote U.S.$
1994	Uriel - 2000	Yr.Iss.	1994	45.00	85-175
1995	Jane - 2001 (ten year Anniversary)	Yr.Iss.	1995	45.00	100-140
1996	Patti - 2002-Spring (rose colored dress for girl, green colored dress for doll)	Yr.Iss.	1996	45.00	55-95
1996	Patti - 2002-Fall (dark blue dress for girl, peach colored dress for doll)	Yr.Iss.	1996	45.00	55-95

All God's Children - M. Root

Year	Issue	Edition Limit	Year Retd.	Issue Price	*Quote U.S.$
1985	Abe - 1357	Retrd.	1988	25.00	1475
1989	Adam - 1526	Open		36.00	37
1987	Amy - 1405W	Retrd.	1996	22.00	55-75
1987	Angel - 1401W	Retrd.	1995	20.00	45-80
1986	Annie Mae 6" -1311	Retrd.	1989	19.00	105-180
1986	Annie Mae 8 1/2" - 1310	Retrd.	1989	27.00	145-250
1987	Aunt Sarah - blue - 1440	Retrd.	1989	45.00	200-300
1987	Aunt Sarah - red - 1440	Retrd.	1989	45.00	300-425
1992	Barney - 1557	Retrd.	1995	32.00	75-100
1988	Bean (Clear Water) - 1521	Retrd.	1992	36.00	225-330
1992	Bean (Painted Water) - 1521	Retrd.	1993	36.00	125-150
1987	Becky - 1402W	Retrd.	1995	22.00	45-80
1987	Becky with Patch - 1402W	Retrd.	N/A	19.00	200-250
1987	Ben - 1504	Retrd.	1988	22.00	350-440
1991	Bessie & Corkie - 1547	Open		70.00	70
1992	Beth - 1558	Retrd.	1995	32.00	75-100
1988	Betsy (Clear Water) - 1513	Retrd.	1992	36.00	225-325
1992	Betsy (Painted Water) - 1513	Retrd.	1993	36.00	125-150
1989	Beverly (sm.) - 1525	Retrd.	1990	50.00	400-650
1991	Billy (lg. stars raised) - 1545	Retrd.	1993	36.00	110-160
1991	Billy (stars imprinted) - 1545	Retrd.	1993	36.00	130-170
1987	Blossom (blue) - 1500	Retrd.	1989	60.00	200-430
1987	Blossom (red) - 1500	Retrd.	1989	60.00	825
1989	Bo - 1530	Retrd.	1994	22.00	60-95
1987	Bonnie & Buttons - 150	Retrd.	1992	24.00	125-175
1985	Booker T - 1320	Retrd.	1988	19.00	1300-1490
1987	Boone - 1510	Retrd.	1989	16.00	75-175
1989	Bootsie - 1529	Retrd.	1994	22.00	60-95
1992	Caitlin - 1554	Retrd.	1994	36.00	85-130
1985	Callie 2 1/4" - 1362	Retrd.	1988	12.00	275-300
1985	Callie 4 1/2" - 1361	Retrd.	1988	19.00	500-535
1988	Calvin - 777	Retrd.	1988	200.00	1750-2150
1987	Cassie - 1503	Retrd.	1989	22.00	110-200
1994	Chantel - 1573	Open		39.00	39
1987	Charity - 1408	Retrd.	1994	28.00	75-135
1996	Charles - 1588	Open		36.00	36
1994	Cheri - 1574	Open		38.00	38
1989	David - 1528	Open		28.00	30
1996	Debi - 1584	Open		N/A	N/A
1991	Dori (green dress) - 1544	Retrd.	N/A	30.00	350-420
1991	Dori (peach dress) - 1544	Open		28.00	30
1987	Eli - 1403W	Open		26.00	28
1985	Emma - 1322	Retrd.	1988	27.00	1750-2000
1992	Faith - 1555	Retrd.	1993	32.00	90-130
1995	Gina - 1579	Open		38.00	38
1987	Ginnie - 1508	Retrd.	1988	22.00	375-450
1986	Grandma - 1323	Retrd.	1987	30.00	3300-3700
1988	Hannah - 1515	Open		36.00	37
1988	Hope - 1519	Open		36.00	37
1987	Jacob - 1407W	Retrd.	1996	26.00	55-80
1989	Jeremy - 1523	800	1993	195.00	750-895
1989	Jerome - 1532	Open		30.00	32
1989	Jessica - 1522	800	1993	195.00	700-890
1989	Jessica and Jeremy -1522-1523	Retrd.	1993	390.00	1800-1950
1987	Jessie (no base) -1501W	Retrd.	1989	19.00	350-450
1989	Jessie - 1501	Open		30.00	32
1988	John - 1514	Retrd.	1990	30.00	160-245
1989	Joseph - 1537	Open		30.00	30
1991	Joy - 1548	Open		30.00	30
1994	Justin - 1576	Open		37.00	37
1989	Kacie - 1533	Open		38.00	38
1988	Kezia - 1518	Retrd.	1997	36.00	37
1986	Lil' Emmie 3 1/2" - 1345	Retrd.	1989	14.00	125-180
1986	Lil' Emmie 4 1/2" - 1344	Retrd.	1989	18.00	160-210
1988	Lisa - 1512	Retrd.	1991	36.00	125-250
1989	Mary - 1536	Open		30.00	30
1988	Maya - 1520	Retrd.	1993	36.00	110-150
1987	Meg (beige dress) - 1505	Retrd.	1988	21.00	1000-1225
1988	Meg (blue dress, long hair) - 1505	Retrd.	1988	21.00	450-500
1988	Meg (blue dress, short hair) - 1505	Retrd.	1988	21.00	875-975
1992	Melissa - 1556	Retrd.	1995	32.00	65-110
1992	Merci - 1559	Open		36.00	37
1986	Michael & Kim - 1517	Open		36.00	38
1988	Moe & Pokey - 1552	Retrd.	1993	16.00	75-110
1987	Moses - 1506	Retrd.	1992	30.00	135-180
1993	Nathaniel - 11569	Open		36.00	36
1991	Nellie - 1546	Retrd.	1993	36.00	135-175
1994	Niambi - 1577	Open		34.00	34
1987	Paddy Paw & Lucy - 1553	Suspd.		24.00	75-100
1987	Paddy Paw & Luke - 1551	Suspd.		24.00	75-100
1988	Peanut -1509	Retrd.	1990	16.00	130-195
1989	Preshus - 1538	Open		24.00	24
1987	Primas Jones (w/base) - 1377	Retrd.	1988	40.00	725-845
1987	Primas Jones - 1377	Retrd.	1988	40.00	600-850
1986	Prissy (Bear) - 1348	Retrd.	1997	18.00	25
1986	Prissy (Moon Pie) - 1347	Open		20.00	32
1986	Prissy with Basket - 1346	Retrd.	1989	16.00	100-175
1986	Prissy with Yarn Hair (6 strands) - 1343	Retrd.	1989	19.00	165-300
1986	Prissy with Yarn Hair (9 strands) - 1343	Retrd.	1989	19.00	450-550
1987	Pud - 1550	Retrd.	1988	11.00	1250-1350
1987	Rachel - 1404W	Open		20.00	28
1992	Rakiya - 1561	Open		36.00	36
1988	Sally -1507	Retrd.	1989	19.00	115-200
1991	Samantha - 1542	Retrd.	1994	38.00	95-140
1991	Samuel - 1541	Retrd.	1994	32.00	100-130
1989	Sasha - 1531	Open		30.00	32
1986	Selina Jane (6 strands) - 1338	Retrd.	1989	21.95	255-300
1986	Selina Jane (9 strands) - 1338	Retrd.	1989	21.95	525-625
1995	Shani - 1583	Open		33.00	33
1996	Shari - 1586	Open		38.00	38
1986	St. Nicholas-B - 1316	Retrd.	1990	30.00	90-175
1986	St. Nicholas-W - 1315	Retrd.	1990	30.00	100-175
1992	Stephen (Nativity Shepherd) - 1563	Open		36.00	36
1988	Sunshine - 1535	Retrd.	1997	38.00	38
1993	Sylvia - 1564	Open		36.00	37
1988	Tansi & Tedi (green socks, collar, cuffs) - 1516	Retrd.	N/A	30.00	250-325
1988	Tansy & Tedi - 1516	Open		N/A	37
1989	Tara - 1527	Open		36.00	37
1989	Tess - 1534	Open		30.00	32
1990	Thaliyah - 778	Retrd.	1990	200.00	1675-1875
1991	Thomas - 1549	Open		30.00	32
1996	Tia - 1587	Retrd.	1997	22.50	23
1987	Tiffany - 1511	Open		32.00	33
1994	Tish - 1572	Open		38.00	38
1986	Toby 3 1/2" - 1332	Retrd.	1989	13.00	95-175
1986	Toby 4 1/2" - 1331	Retrd.	1989	16.00	135-200
1985	Tom - 1353	Retrd.	1988	16.00	350-475
1986	Uncle Bud 6"- 1304	Retrd.	1991	19.00	110-210
1986	Uncle Bud 8 1/2"- 1303	Retrd.	1991	27.00	250-375
1992	Valerie - 1560	Open		36.00	37
1995	William - 1580	Open		38.00	38
1987	Willie - 1406W	Retrd.	1996	22.00	29
1987	Willie - 1406W (no base)	Retrd.	1987	22.00	455
1993	Zack - 1566	Open		34.00	34

All God's Children Ragbabies - M. Root

Year	Issue	Edition Limit	Year Retd.	Issue Price	*Quote U.S.$
1995	Honey - 4005	Open		33.00	33
1995	Issie - 4004	Open		33.00	33
1995	Ivy - 4008	Open		33.00	33
1995	Josie - 4003	Open		33.00	33
1995	Mitzi - 4000	Open		33.00	33
1995	Muffin - 4001	Open		33.00	33
1995	Puddin - 4006	Open		33.00	33
1995	Punkin - 4007	Open		33.00	33
1995	Sweetie - 4002	Open		33.00	33

Angelic Messengers - M. Root

Year	Issue	Edition Limit	Year Retd.	Issue Price	*Quote U.S.$
1994	Cieara - 2500	Open		38.00	38
1996	Demetrious - 2503	Open		38.00	38
1994	Mariah - 2501	Open		38.00	38
1994	Mariah - 2501 (scratched in letters)	Retrd.	N/A	38.00	85-100
1995	Sabrina - 2502	Open		38.00	38

Christmas - M. Root

Year	Issue	Edition Limit	Year Retd.	Issue Price	*Quote U.S.$
1987	1987 Father Christmas-W - 1750	Retrd.	N/A	145.00	625-735
1987	1987 Father Christmas-B - 1751	Retrd.	N/A	145.00	625-735
1988	1988 Father Christmas-W - 1757	Retrd.	N/A	195.00	500-640
1988	1988 Father Christmas-B - 1758	Retrd.	N/A	195.00	500-640
1988	Santa Claus-W - 1767	Retrd.	N/A	185.00	500-650
1988	Santa Claus-B - 1768	Retrd.	N/A	185.00	500-650
1989	1989 Father Christmas-W - 1769	Retrd.	N/A	195.00	500-720
1989	1989 Father Christmas-B - 1770	Retrd.	N/A	195.00	500-700
1990	1990-91 Father Christmas-W - 1771	Retrd.	N/A	195.00	550-675
1990	1990-91 Father Christmas-B - 1772	Retrd.	N/A	195.00	550-675
1991	1991-92 Father Christmas-W - 1773	Retrd.	N/A	195.00	400-500
1991	1991-92 Father Christmas-B - 1774	Retrd.	N/A	195.00	400-500
1992	Father Christmas Bust-W - 1775	Retrd.	N/A	145.00	300-375
1992	Father Christmas Bust-B - 1776	Retrd.	N/A	145.00	300-375

Count Your Blessings - M. Root

Year	Issue	Edition Limit	Year Retd.	Issue Price	*Quote U.S.$
1997	Anna - 2703	Open		24.50	25
1997	Baby Rei - 2700	Open		24.50	25

*Quotes have been rounded up to nearest dollar

FIGURINES

All God's Children to ANRI

YEAR ISSUE		EDITION LIMIT	YEAR RETD.	ISSUE PRICE	*QUOTE U.S.$
1997	Cece - 2701	Open		24.50	25
1997	Leni - 2702	Open		24.50	25
1997	Taci - 2704	Open		24.50	25

Historical Series - M. Root

YEAR ISSUE		EDITION LIMIT	YEAR RETD.	ISSUE PRICE	*QUOTE U.S.$
1994	Augustus Walley (Buffalo Soldier) - 1908	Retrd.	1995	95.00	150-240
1994	Bessie Smith - 1909	Open		70.00	70
1997	Clara Brown - 1912	Open		71.00	71
1992	Dr. Daniel Williams - 1903	Retrd.	1995	70.00	125-180
1992	Frances Harper - 1905	Open		70.00	70
1991	Frederick Douglass - 1902	Open		70.00	70
1992	George Washington Carver - 1907	Open		70.00	70
1989	Harriet Tubman - 1900	Retrd.	1994	65.00	130-200
1992	Ida B. Wells - 1906	Retrd.	1996	70.00	100-160
1992	Mary Bethune (misspelled) - 1904	Retrd.	1992	70.00	250-280
1992	Mary Bethune - 1904	Open		70.00	70
1995	Mary Mahoney - 1911	Open		65.00	65
1995	Richard Allen - 1910	Open		70.00	70
1990	Sojourner Truth - 1901	Open		65.00	65

International Series - M. Root

YEAR ISSUE		EDITION LIMIT	YEAR RETD.	ISSUE PRICE	*QUOTE U.S.$
1987	Juan - 1807	Retrd.	1993	26.00	125-160
1987	Kameko - 1802	Open.		26.00	28
1987	Karl - 1808	Retrd.	1996	26.00	30-45
1987	Katrina - 1803	Retrd.	1993	26.00	125-165
1987	Kelli - 1805	Open		30.00	30
1987	Little Chief - 1804	Open		32.00	32
1993	Minnie - 1568	Open		36.00	36
1987	Pike - 1806	Open		30.00	32
1987	Tat - 1801	Retrd.	1996	30.00	40-80

Little Missionary Series - M. Root

YEAR ISSUE		EDITION LIMIT	YEAR RETD.	ISSUE PRICE	*QUOTE U.S.$
1994	Nakia - 3500	Retrd.	1995	40.00	110-120
1994	Nakia - 3500 (Mat.)	Retrd.	1995	40.00	100-120

Sugar And Spice - M. Root

YEAR ISSUE		EDITION LIMIT	YEAR RETD.	ISSUE PRICE	*QUOTE U.S.$
1987	Blessed are the Peacemakers (Eli) -1403	Retrd.	1988	22.00	535
1987	Friend Show Love (Becky) -1402	Retrd.	1988	22.00	535
1987	Friendship Warms the Heart (Jacob) -1407	Retrd.	1988	22.00	535
1987	God is Love (Angel) -1401	Retrd.	1988	22.00	535
1987	Jesus Loves Me (Amy) -1405	Retrd.	1989	22.00	535
1987	Old Friends are Best (Rachel) - 1404	Retrd.	1988	22.00	535
1987	Sharing with Friends (Willie) - 1406	Retrd.	1988	22.00	535

Through His Eyes - M. Root

YEAR ISSUE		EDITION LIMIT	YEAR RETD.	ISSUE PRICE	*QUOTE U.S.$
1993	Simon & Andrew - 1565	Open		45.00	45
1995	Jewel & Judy - 1582	Open		45.00	45

Amaranth Productions

Christmas Elves - L. West

YEAR ISSUE		EDITION LIMIT	YEAR RETD.	ISSUE PRICE	*QUOTE U.S.$
1988	Bayberry 2304	300	1988	250.00	500
1989	Bayberry 3503	300	1989	278.00	500
1994	Brandy 8103	150	1994	230.00	230
1991	D'Light 4505	350	1992	500.00	500
1993	Dominick 4531	350	1994	420.00	420
1994	Forrest 8101	150	1994	210.00	210
1995	Goldwin 4525	150	1995	950.00	950
1990	Half Note 4603	500	1992	278.00	475
1988	Holly 1988 2302	300	1988	230.00	230
1989	Holly 3501	300	1989	250.00	250
1994	Nate 8102	150	1994	220.00	220
1992	Oliver 2452	200	1993	470.00	470
1992	Patches 4605	500	1993	278.00	515
1992	Pepe Mint 4510	350	1992	850.00	850
1993	Raffael 4530	350	1994	390.00	390
1990	Rocky 4602	500	1992	278.00	278
1991	Rump-Papa-Pum 4604	500	1992	278.00	278
1990	Russell The Wrapper 4500	350	1992	480.00	480
1990	Skeeter 4601	500	1992	278.00	278
1993	T'Winkle 4520	200	1994	950.00	1200-1400
1992	Timothy 2453	200	1994	590.00	590
1988	Wassail 2303	300	1988	250.00	400
1989	Wassail 3502	300	1989	250.00	375
1993	Wolfie 4532	350	1995	390.00	390

Faeries - L. West

YEAR ISSUE		EDITION LIMIT	YEAR RETD.	ISSUE PRICE	*QUOTE U.S.$
1994	Asteroid 4221	300	1995	284.00	284
1992	Baubles 4211	500	1993	284.00	500
1990	Berry 4201	500	1991	278.00	470
1990	Blueberry 4101	500	1990	270.00	270
1995	Borealis 4224	300	1995	310.00	310
1994	Cadence 4222	300	1995	284.00	284
1992	Cardinal 4213	500	1993	284.00	284
1990	Dusty 4103	500	1991	270.00	270
1991	Eggburt 4112	500	1993	278.00	430
1990	Emerald 4102	500	1992	270.00	270
1993	Evergreen 4219	300	1994	284.00	284
1992	Fiddler 4210	500	1993	284.00	430
1995	Figaro 4225	300	1995	310.00	310
1992	Golden Frost 4214	500	1993	284.00	284
1993	Jack 4218	300	1994	284.00	430
1990	Jingles 4202	500	1992	278.00	278
1992	Ludwig 4216	500	1993	284.00	284
1994	Mendicino 7020	200	1995	510.00	510
1991	Mistletoe 4205	500	1993	284.00	430
1991	Raddish 4111	500	1992	278.00	430
1995	Sean-Custom Faerie/Neiman Marcus 101	38	1995	310.00	310
1995	Serenade 4223	300	1995	310.00	310
1990	Snowflake 4203	500	1991	278.00	278
1992	Spring Mist 4215	500	1993	284.00	284
1992	Tealberry 4217	500	1994	284.00	284
1994	Timber 4220	300	1995	284.00	284
1991	Tweetle Berry 4204	500	1992	284.00	284
1995	Winsor-Custom Faerie/Neiman Marcus 100	38	1995	310.00	310
1992	Woodie 4212	500	1993	284.00	284

Father Christmas - L. West

YEAR ISSUE		EDITION LIMIT	YEAR RETD.	ISSUE PRICE	*QUOTE U.S.$
1994	Anniversary Father Christmas 4330	300	1995	750.00	750
1992	Christmas Glory 4310	350	1993	750.00	750
1989	Christmas Majesty 2300	250	1988	750.00	750
1993	Christmas Majesty (Sp Ed.) 4270	100	1993	1590.00	2500
1994	Christmas Peace 4275	100	1995	1450.00	2950
1993	Father Christmas with Staff 4250	200	1994	1300.00	2100
1991	Father Nikolai 4305	500	1993	750.00	750
1989	Grand Father Christmas 3520	300	1991	750.00	750
1993	Special Delivery 4320	350	1993	750.00	750
1994	Victorian Saint Nicholas 4255	150	1995	1300.00	1800-2600
1990	Winter Majesty 4300	350	1992	750.00	950

Forest Fantasies - L. West

YEAR ISSUE		EDITION LIMIT	YEAR RETD.	ISSUE PRICE	*QUOTE U.S.$
1994	Captain Surewood 7025	200	1995	950.00	950
1992	Father Earth 7000	350	1993	830.00	830
1995	Frederick-Music School 7006	100	1995	490.00	490
1993	Hermes 7010	200	1993	790.00	790
1992	Leopole 7002	350	1993	470.00	470
1995	Professer Wind Chime 7005	100	1995	1190.00	1190
1991	Sullivan 4110	350	1992	480.00	480
1990	Telltale and Teabu 7001	350	1993	670.00	1200-1500
1990	Wee Willie 4000	350	1991	480.00	600
1993	Whiskers and Wink 7015	200	1993	590.00	800

Old Time Santa Series - L. West

YEAR ISSUE		EDITION LIMIT	YEAR RETD.	ISSUE PRICE	*QUOTE U.S.$
1992	Old Time Santa-1st in Series 3540	300	1993	530.00	750
1993	Still Fits-2nd in Series 3545	300	1993	700.00	900
1994	Old Time Santa and Tree-3rd in Series 3546	250	1995	650.00	925

Santas - L. West

YEAR ISSUE		EDITION LIMIT	YEAR RETD.	ISSUE PRICE	*QUOTE U.S.$
1992	Classic Santa With Chair 2451	200	1993	1450.00	1850
1988	Kris Kringle Special Edition 1115	50	1988	2000.00	2000
1990	Large Santa 4400	250	1993	700.00	700
1991	Last Minute Details w/ Beard 6005BRD	950	1992	550.00	700
1991	Last Minute Details-M.B. 6005	950	1992	430.00	430
1991	Saint Nick 6000	950	1991	370.00	370
1989	Santa At The North Pole 3535	300	1991	450.00	450
1988	Spencer 2301	150	1991	850.00	850
1994	Standing Santa with Toypack 9002	Retrd.	1994	450.00	450

American Artists

Fred Stone Figurines - F. Stone

YEAR ISSUE		EDITION LIMIT	YEAR RETD.	ISSUE PRICE	*QUOTE U.S.$
1986	Arab Mare & Foal	2,500		150.00	225
1985	The Black Stallion, bronze	1,500		150.00	175
1985	The Black Stallion, porcelain	2,500		125.00	260
1987	Rearing Black Stallion (Bronze)	1,250		175.00	195
1987	Rearing Black Stallion (Porcelain)	3,500		150.00	175
1986	Tranquility	2,500		175.00	275

Anchor Bay

Anchor Bay - Staff

YEAR ISSUE		EDITION LIMIT	YEAR RETD.	ISSUE PRICE	*QUOTE U.S.$
1997	Chesapeake Lightship	Open		N/A	N/A
1997	Chesapeake Lightship (special ed.)	4,000		N/A	N/A
1997	Huron Lightship	Open		N/A	N/A
1997	Huron Lightship (special ed.)	4,000		N/A	N/A
1997	Skipjack	Open		N/A	N/A
1997	Skipjack (special ed.)	4,000		N/A	N/A
1997	Tug	Open		N/A	N/A
1997	Tug (special ed.)	4,000		N/A	N/A

Anheuser-Busch, Inc.

Anheuser-Busch Collectible Figurines - Various

YEAR ISSUE		EDITION LIMIT	YEAR RETD.	ISSUE PRICE	*QUOTE U.S.$
1994	Buddies N4575 - M. Urdahl	7,500		65.00	65
1995	Horseplay F1 - P. Radtke	7,500		65.00	65
1996	"Bud-weis-er Frogs" F4 - A. Busch, Inc.	Open		30.00	30
1996	Something Brewing F-3	7,500		65.00	65
1997	"Gone Fishing" Beagle Puppies F5 - A. Busch, Inc.	7,500		65.00	65

ANRI

Club ANRI - Various

YEAR ISSUE		EDITION LIMIT	YEAR RETD.	ISSUE PRICE	*QUOTE U.S.$
1983	Welcome, 4" - J. Ferrandiz	Yr.Iss.	1984	110.00	395
1984	My Friend, 4" - J. Ferrandiz	Yr.Iss.	1985	110.00	400
1984	Apple of My Eye, 4 1/2" - S. Kay	Yr.Iss.	1985	135.00	385
1985	Harvest Time, 4" - J. Ferrandiz	Yr.Iss.	1986	125.00	175-385
1985	Dad's Helper, 4 1/2" - S. Kay	Yr.Iss.	1986	135.00	150-375
1986	Harvest's Helper, 4" - J. Ferrandiz	Yr.Iss.	1987	135.00	175-335
1986	Romantic Notions, 4" - S. Kay	Yr.Iss.	1987	135.00	175-310
1986	Celebration March, 5" - J. Ferrandiz	Yr.Iss.	1987	165.00	225-295
1987	Will You Be Mine, 4" - J. Ferrandiz	Yr.Iss.	1988	135.00	175-310
1987	Make A Wish, 4" - S. Kay	Yr.Iss.	1988	165.00	215-325
1987	A Young Man's Fancy, 4" - S. Kay	Yr.Iss.	1988	135.00	165-265
1988	Forever Yours, 4" - J. Ferrandiz	Yr.Iss.	1989	170.00	250
1988	I've Got a Secret, 4" - S. Kay	Yr.Iss.	1989	170.00	205
1988	Maestro Mickey, 4 1/2" - Disney Studio	Yr.Iss.	1989	170.00	175
1989	Diva Minnie, 4 1/2" - Disney Studio	Yr.Iss.	1990	190.00	190
1989	I'll Never Tell, 4" - S. Kay	Yr.Iss.	1990	190.00	190
1989	Twenty Years of Love, 4" - J. Ferrandiz	Yr.Iss.	1990	190.00	190
1990	You Are My Sunshine, 4" - J. Ferrandiz	Yr.Iss.	1991	220.00	220
1990	A Little Bashful, 4" - S. Kay	Yr.Iss.	1991	220.00	220
1990	Dapper Donald, 4" - Disney Studio	Yr.Iss.	1991	199.00	199
1991	With All My Heart, 4" - J. Ferrandiz	Yr.Iss.	1992	250.00	250
1991	Kiss Me, 4" - S. Kay	Yr.Iss.	1992	250.00	250
1991	Daisy Duck, 4 1/2" - Disney Studio	Yr.Iss.	1992	250.00	250

ANRI Club - Various

YEAR ISSUE		EDITION LIMIT	YEAR RETD.	ISSUE PRICE	*QUOTE U.S.$
1992	You Are My All, 4" - J. Ferrandiz	Yr.Iss.	1993	260.00	260
1992	My Present For You, 4" - S. Kay	Yr.Iss.	1993	270.00	270
1992	Gift of Love - S. Kay	Yr.Iss.	1993	Gift	N/A
1993	Truly Yours, 4" - J. Ferrandiz	Yr.Iss.	1994	290.00	290
1993	Sweet Thoughts, 4" - S. Kay	Yr.Iss.	1994	300.00	300
1993	Just For You - S. Kay	Yr.Iss.	1994	Gift	N/A
1994	Sweet 'N Shy, 4" - J. Ferrandiz	Yr.Iss.	1994	250.00	250
1994	Snuggle Up, 4" - S. Kay	Yr.Iss.	1994	300.00	300
1994	Dapper 'N Dear, 4" - J. Ferrandiz	Yr.Iss.	1994	250.00	250

ANRI Collectors' Society- Various

YEAR ISSUE		EDITION LIMIT	YEAR RETD.	ISSUE PRICE	*QUOTE U.S.$
1995	On My Own, 4" - S. Kay	Yr.Iss.	1996	175.00	175
1995	Sealed With A Kiss - J. Ferrandiz	Yr.Iss.	1997	275.00	275
1995	ANRI Artists' Tree House - ANRI	Yr.Iss.		695.00	695
1996	On Cloud Nine - J. Ferrandiz	Yr.Iss.	1997	275.00	275
1996	Sweet Tooth - S. Kay	Yr.Iss.	1997	199.50	200
1997	Tell Me A Story - S. Kay	Yr.Iss.		395.00	395

Bernardi Reflections - U. Bernardi

YEAR ISSUE		EDITION LIMIT	YEAR RETD.	ISSUE PRICE	*QUOTE U.S.$
1996	Learning the Skills, 4"	500		275.00	275
1996	Learning the Skills, 6"	250		550.00	550
1994	Master Carver, 4"	500		350.00	350
1994	Master Carver, 6"	250	1995	600.00	600
1995	Planning the Tour, 4"	500		450.00	450
1995	Planning the Tour, 6"	250		300.00	300

Disney Studios Mickey Mouse Thru The Ages - Disney Studios

YEAR ISSUE		EDITION LIMIT	YEAR RETD.	ISSUE PRICE	*QUOTE U.S.$
1991	The Mad Dog, 4"	1,000	1991	500.00	500-600
1990	Steam Boat Willie, 4"	1,000	1990	295.00	450-600

Disney Woodcarving - Disney Studio

YEAR ISSUE		EDITION LIMIT	YEAR RETD.	ISSUE PRICE	*QUOTE U.S.$
1991	Bell Boy Donald, 4" 656029	Closed	1991	250.00	250
1991	Bell Boy Donald, 6" 656110	500	1991	400.00	450-600
1990	Chef Goofy, 2 1/2" 656222	Closed	1991	125.00	150-185
1990	Chef Goofy, 5" 656227	Closed	1991	265.00	275-300
1989	Daisy, 4" 656021	Closed	1991	190.00	250-300
1990	Donald & Daisy, 6" 656108	500	1991	700.00	700-800
1988	Donald Duck, 1 3/4" 656209	Closed	1990	80.00	150
1988	Donald Duck, 2" 656204	Closed	1990	85.00	125-165
1987	Donald Duck, 4" 656004	Closed	1989	150.00	225-300
1988	Donald Duck, 4" 656014	Closed	1990	180.00	225-300
1988	Donald Duck, 6" 656102	500	1988	350.00	525
1989	Donald, 4" 656020	Closed	1991	190.00	250-300
1988	Goofy, 1 3/4" 656210	Closed	1990	80.00	125-175
1988	Goofy, 2" 656205	Closed	1990	85.00	125-175
1987	Goofy, 4" 656005	Closed	1989	150.00	200-300
1988	Goofy, 4" 656015	Closed	1990	180.00	200-300
1989	Goofy, 4" 656022	Closed	1991	190.00	200-300
1988	Goofy, 6" 656103	500	1988	380.00	550-600
1989	Mickey & Minnie Set, 6" 656106	500	1991	700.00	750-950
1989	Mickey & Minnie, 20" matched set	50	1991	7000.00	7000
1987	Mickey & Minnie, 6" 656101	500	1987	625.00	1000
1988	Mickey Mouse, 1 3/4" 656206	Closed	1990	80.00	200-300
1988	Mickey Mouse, 2" 656201	Closed	1990	85.00	175
1990	Mickey Mouse, 2" 656220	Closed	1991	100.00	225-350
1987	Mickey Mouse, 4" 656001	Closed	1989	150.00	225-350
1988	Mickey Mouse, 4" 656011	Closed	1990	180.00	225-325
1990	Mickey Mouse, 4" 656025	Closed	1991	199.00	250-325
1991	Mickey Skating, 2" 656224	Closed	1991	120.00	250-300
1991	Mickey Skating, 4" 656030	Closed	1991	250.00	250-300
1988	Mickey Sorcerer's Apprentice, 2" 656211	Closed	1991	80.00	300-400
1988	Mickey Sorcerer's Apprentice, 4" 656016	Closed	1991	180.00	250
1988	Mickey Sorcerer's Apprentice, 6" 656105	500	1991	350.00	600-700
1989	Mickey, 10" 656800	250	1991	700.00	850-950
1989	Mickey, 20" 656850	50	1991	3500.00	3500
1989	Mickey, 4" 656018	Closed	1991	190.00	300-400
1988	Mini Donald, 1 3/4" 656204	Closed	1991	85.00	150-200
1989	Mini Donald, 2" 656215	Closed	1991	85.00	150-200
1988	Mini Goofy, 1 3/4" 656205	Closed	1991	85.00	175-200
1989	Mini Goofy, 2" 656217	Closed	1991	85.00	175-200
1988	Mini Mickey, 1 3/4" 656201	Closed	1991	85.00	200
1989	Mini Mickey, 2" 656213	Closed	1991	85.00	200
1988	Mini Minnie, 1 3/4" 656202	Closed	1991	85.00	200
1989	Mini Minnie, 2" 656214	Closed	1991	85.00	200
1989	Mini Pluto, 2" 656218	Closed	1991	85.00	100-150

*Quotes have been rounded up to nearest dollar

Collectors' Information Bureau

47

ANRI
to ANRI

FIGURINES

YEAR ISSUE		EDITION LIMIT	YEAR RETD.	ISSUE PRICE	*QUOTE U.S.$
1989	Minnie Daisy, 2" 656216	Closed	1991	85.00	100-150
1988	Minnie Mouse, 2" 656202	Closed	1990	85.00	100-150
1990	Minnie Mouse, 2" 656221	Closed	1991	100.00	150
1987	Minnie Mouse, 4" 656002	Closed	1989	150.00	250-300
1990	Minnie Mouse, 4" 656026	Closed	1991	199.00	250
1988	Minnie Pinocchio, 1 3/4" 656203	Closed	1991	85.00	250-350
1991	Minnie Skating, 2" 656225	Closed	1991	120.00	150
1991	Minnie Skating, 4" 656031	Closed	1991	250.00	350
1989	Minnie, 10" 656801	250	1991	700.00	900
1989	Minnie, 20" 656851	50	1991	3500.00	3500
1989	Minnie, 4" 656019	Closed	1991	190.00	300-350
1988	Pinocchio, 1 3/4" 656208	Closed	1990	80.00	200-300
1989	Pinocchio, 10" 656802	250	1991	700.00	1000
1988	Pinocchio, 2" 656203	Closed	1990	85.00	85
1989	Pinocchio, 2" 656219	Closed	1991	85.00	100
1989	Pinocchio, 20" 656851	50	1991	3500.00	3500
1987	Pinocchio, 4" 656003 (apple)	Closed	1989	150.00	400-450
1988	Pinocchio, 4" 656013	Closed	1990	180.00	199
1989	Pinocchio, 4" 656024	Closed	1991	190.00	199
1989	Pinocchio, 6" 656107	500	1991	350.00	400-500
1988	Pluto, 1 3/4" 656207	Closed	1990	80.00	125-150
1988	Pluto, 4" 656012	Closed	1990	180.00	250-300
1989	Pluto, 4" 656023	Closed	1991	190.00	250-300
1988	Pluto, 6" 656104	500	1991	350.00	475
1990	Sorcerer's Apprentice w/ crystal, 2" 656223	Closed	1991	125.00	500-750
1990	Sorcerer's Apprentice w/ crystal, 4" 656028	Closed	1991	265.00	400-500
1990	Sorcerer's Apprentice w/ crystal, 6" 656109	1,000	1991	475.00	650-850
1990	Sorcerer's Apprentice w/ crystal, 8" 656803	350	1991	790.00	800-900
1990	Sorcerer's Apprentice w/ crystal,16" 656853	100	1991	3500.00	3500

Ferrandiz Boy and Girl - J. Ferrandiz

YEAR ISSUE		EDITION LIMIT	YEAR RETD.	ISSUE PRICE	*QUOTE U.S.$
1983	Admiration, 6"	2,250	1983	220.00	295
1990	Alpine Friend, 3"	1,500	1990	225.00	365
1990	Alpine Friend, 6"	1,500	1990	450.00	610
1990	Alpine Music, 3"	1,500	1990	225.00	225
1990	Alpine Music, 6"	1,500	1990	450.00	580
1989	Baker Boy, 3"	1,500	1989	170.00	170
1989	Baker Boy, 6"	1,500	1989	340.00	340
1978	Basket of Joy, 6"	1,500	1978	140.00	350-450
1983	Bewildered, 6"	2,250	1983	196.00	295
1991	Catalonian Boy, 3"	1,500	1993	227.50	228
1991	Catalonian Boy, 6"	1,500	1993	500.00	500
1991	Catalonian Girl, 3"	1,500	1993	227.50	228
1991	Catalonian Girl, 6"	1,500	1993	500.00	500
1976	Cowboy, 6"	1,500	1976	75.00	500-600
1987	Dear Sweetheart, 3"	2,250	1989	130.00	130
1987	Dear Sweetheart, 6"	2,250	1989	250.00	250
1988	Extra, Extra!, 3"	1,500	1988	145.00	145
1988	Extra, Extra!, 6"	1,500	1988	320.00	320
1979	First Blossom, 6"	2,250	1979	135.00	345-375
1987	For My Sweetheart, 3"	2,250	1989	130.00	130
1987	For My Sweetheart, 6"	2,250	1989	250.00	250
1984	Friendly Faces, 3"	2,250	1984	93.00	110
1984	Friendly Faces, 6"	2,250	1984	210.00	225-295
1980	Friends, 6"	2,250	1980	200.00	300-350
1986	Golden Sheaves, 3"	2,250	1986	125.00	125
1986	Golden Sheaves, 6"	2,250	1986	245.00	245
1982	Guiding Light, 6"	2,250	1982	225.00	275-350
1979	Happy Strummer, 6"	2,250	1979	160.00	395
1976	Harvest Girl, 6"	1,500	1976	75.00	400-800
1977	Leading the Way, 6"	1,500	1977	100.00	300-375
1997	Maria, 4"	Open		285.00	285
1992	May I, Too?, 3"	1,000	1993	230.00	230
1992	May I, Too?, 6"	1,000	1993	440.00	440
1980	Melody for Two, 6"	2,250	1980	200.00	350
1981	Merry Melody, 6"	2,250	1981	210.00	300-350
1997	Miguel, 4"	Open		285.00	285
1989	Pastry Girl, 3"	1,500	1989	170.00	170
1989	Pastry Girl, 6"	1,500	1989	340.00	340
1978	Peace Pipe, 6"	1,500	1978	140.00	325-450
1985	Peaceful Friends, 3"	2,250	1985	120.00	120
1985	Peaceful Friends, 6"	2,250	1985	250.00	295
1986	Season's Bounty, 3"	2,250	1986	125.00	125
1986	Season's Bounty, 6"	2,250	1986	245.00	245
1988	Sunny Skies, 3"	1,500	1988	145.00	145
1988	Sunny Skies, 6"	1,500	1988	320.00	320
1985	Tender Love, 3"	2,250	1985	100.00	125
1985	Tender Love, 6"	2,250	1985	225.00	250
1981	Tiny Sounds, 6"	2,250	1981	210.00	300-350
1982	To Market, 6"	1,500	1982	220.00	295
1977	Tracker, 6"	1,500	1977	100.00	400
1984	Wanderer's Return, 3"	2,250	1984	93.00	135
1984	Wanderer's Return, 6"	2,250	1984	196.00	250
1992	Waste Not, Want Not, 3"	1,000	1993	190.00	200
1992	Waste Not, Want Not, 6"	1,000	1993	430.00	430

Ferrandiz Circus - J. Ferrandiz

YEAR ISSUE		EDITION LIMIT	YEAR RETD.	ISSUE PRICE	*QUOTE U.S.$
1986	Balancing Ballerina, 2 1/2"	Closed	1988	100.00	100
1986	Balancing Ballerina, 5"	3,000	1988	150.00	150
1986	Ballerina on Horse, 2 1/2"	Closed	1988	125.00	125
1986	Ballerina on Horse, 5"	3,000	1988	200.00	200
1986	Cat on Stool, 2 1/2"	Closed	1988	50.00	50
1986	Cat on Stool, 5"	3,000	1988	110.00	110
1986	Clown on Elephant, 2 1/2"	Closed	1988	125.00	125
1986	Clown on Elephant, 5"	3,000	1988	200.00	200
1986	Clown on Unicycle, 2 1/2"	Closed	1988	80.00	80
1986	Clown on Unicycle, 5"	3,000	1988	175.00	175
1987	Clown w/Bunny, 2 1/2"	Closed	1988	80.00	80
1987	Clown w/Bunny, 5"	3,000	1988	175.00	175
1986	Clown w/Sax, 2 1/2"	Closed	1988	80.00	80
1986	Clown w/Sax, 5"	3,000	1988	175.00	175
1987	Clown w/Umbrella, 2 1/2"	Closed	1988	80.00	80
1987	Clown w/Umbrella, 5"	3,000	1988	175.00	175
1986	Lion Tamer, 2 1/2"	Closed	1988	80.00	80
1986	Lion Tamer, 5"	3,000	1988	175.00	175
1986	Ring Master, 2 1/2"	Closed	1988	80.00	80
1986	Ring Master, 5"	3,000	1988	175.00	175

Ferrandiz Message Collection - J. Ferrandiz

YEAR ISSUE		EDITION LIMIT	YEAR RETD.	ISSUE PRICE	*QUOTE U.S.$
1990	Christmas Carillon, 4 1/2"	2,500	1992	299.00	299
1990	Count Your Blessings, 4 1/2"	5,000	1992	300.00	300
1990	God's Creation, 4 1/2"	5,000	1992	300.00	300
1989	God's Miracle, 4 1/2"	5,000	1991	300.00	300
1989	God's Precious Gift, 4 1/2"	5,000	1991	300.00	300
1989	He Guides Us, 4 1/2"	5,000	1991	300.00	300
1989	He is the Light, 4 1/2"	5,000	1991	300.00	300
1989	He is the Light, 9"	5,000	1991	600.00	600
1989	Heaven Sent, 4 1/2"	5,000	1991	300.00	300
1989	Light From Within, 4 1/2"	5,000	1991	300.00	300
1989	Love Knows No Bounds, 4 1/2"	5,000	1991	300.00	300
1989	Love So Powerful, 4 1/2"	5,000	1991	300.00	300

Ferrandiz Mini Nativity Set - J. Ferrandiz

YEAR ISSUE		EDITION LIMIT	YEAR RETD.	ISSUE PRICE	*QUOTE U.S.$
1985	Baby Camel, 1 1/2"	Closed	1993	45.00	53
1985	Camel Guide, 1 1/2"	Closed	1993	45.00	53
1985	Camel, 1 1/2"	Closed	1993	45.00	53
1988	Devotion, 1 1/2"	Closed	1993	53.00	53
1985	Harmony, 1 1/2"	Closed	1993	45.00	53
1984	Infant, 1 1/2"	Closed	1993	Set	Set
1988	Jolly Gift, 1 1/2"	Closed	1992	53.00	53
1984	Joseph, 1 1/2"	Closed	1993	Set	Set
1984	Leading the Way, 1 1/2"	Closed	1993	Set	Set
1988	Long Journey, 1 1/2"	Closed	1993	53.00	53
1984	Mary, 1 1/2"	Closed	1993	300.00	540
1986	Mini Angel, 1 1/2"	Closed	1993	45.00	53
1986	Mini Balthasar, 1 1/2"	Closed	1993	45.00	53
1986	Mini Caspar, 1 1/2"	Closed	1993	45.00	53
1986	Mini Free Ride, plus Mini Lamb, 1 1/2"	Closed	1993	45.00	53
1986	Mini Melchoir, 1 1/2"	Closed	1993	45.00	53
1986	Mini Star Struck, 1 1/2"	Closed	1993	45.00	53
1986	Mini The Hiker, 1 1/2"	Closed	1993	45.00	53
1986	Mini The Stray, 1 1/2"	Closed	1993	45.00	53
1986	Mini Weary Traveller, 1 1/2"	Closed	1993	45.00	53
1984	Ox Donkey, 1 1/2"	Closed	1993	Set	Set
1985	Rest, 1 1/2"	Closed	1993	45.00	53
1985	Reverence, 1 1/2"	Closed	1993	45.00	53
1984	Sheep Kneeling, 1 1/2"	Closed	1993	Set	Set
1984	Sheep Standing, 1 1/2"	Closed	1993	Set	Set
1985	Small Talk, 1 1/2"	Closed	1993	45.00	53
1988	Sweet Dreams, 1 1/2"	Closed	1993	53.00	53
1988	Sweet Inspiration, 1 1/2"	Closed	1992	53.00	53
1985	Thanksgiving, 1 1/2"	Closed	1993	45.00	53

Ferrandiz Shepherds of the Year - J. Ferrandiz

YEAR ISSUE		EDITION LIMIT	YEAR RETD.	ISSUE PRICE	*QUOTE U.S.$
1982	Companions, 6"	2,250	1982	220.00	275-300
1984	Devotion, 3"	2,250	1984	82.50	125
1984	Devotion, 6"	2,250	1984	180.00	200-250
1979	Drummer Boy, 3"	Yr.Iss.	1979	80.00	250
1979	Drummer Boy, 6"	Yr.Iss.	1979	220.00	400-425
1980	Freedom Bound, 3"	Yr.Iss.	1980	90.00	225
1980	Freedom Bound, 6"	Yr.Iss.	1980	225.00	400
1977	Friendship, 3"	Yr.Iss.	1977	53.50	330
1977	Friendship, 6"	Yr.Iss.	1977	110.00	500-675
1983	Good Samaritan, 6"	2,250	1983	220.00	300-320
1981	Jolly Piper, 6"	2,250	1981	225.00	375
1978	Spreading the Word, 3"	Yr.Iss.	1978	115.00	250-275
1978	Spreading the Word, 6"	Yr.Iss.	1978	270.50	500

Ferrandiz Woodcarvings - J. Ferrandiz

YEAR ISSUE		EDITION LIMIT	YEAR RETD.	ISSUE PRICE	*QUOTE U.S.$
1988	Abracadabra, 3"	1,500	1991	145.00	165
1988	Abracadabra, 6"	1,500	1991	315.00	345
1976	Adoration, 12"	Closed	1987	350.00	350
1981	Adoration, 20"	250	1987	3200.00	3200
1976	Adoration, 3"	Closed	1987	45.00	45
1976	Adoration, 6"	Closed	1987	100.00	100
1987	Among Friends, 3"	3,000	1990	125.00	151
1987	Among Friends, 6"	3,000	1990	245.00	291
1969	Angel Sugar Heart, 6"	Closed	1973	25.00	2500
1974	Artist, 3"	Closed	1981	30.00	195
1970	Artist, 6"	Closed	1981	25.00	350
1982	Bagpipe, 3"	Closed	1983	80.00	95
1982	Bagpipe, 6"	Closed	1983	175.00	190
1978	Basket of Joy, 3"	Closed	1984	65.00	120
1984	Bird's Eye View, 3"	Closed	1989	88.00	129
1984	Bird's Eye View, 6"	Closed	1989	216.00	700
1987	Black Forest Boy, 3"	3,000	1990	125.00	151
1987	Black Forest Boy, 6"	3,000	1990	250.00	301
1987	Black Forest Girl, 3"	3,000	1990	125.00	151
1987	Black Forest Girl, 6"	3,000	1990	250.00	300-350
1977	The Blessing, 3"	Closed	1982	45.00	150
1977	The Blessing, 6"	Closed	1982	125.00	250
1988	Bon Appetit, 3"	500	1991	175.00	195
1988	Bon Appetit, 6"	500	1991	395.00	440
1974	The Bouquet, 3"	Closed	1981	35.00	175
1974	The Bouquet, 6"	Closed	1981	75.00	325
1982	Bundle of Joy, 3"	Closed	1990	100.00	300
1982	Bundle of Joy, 6"	Closed	1990	225.00	323
1985	Butterfly Boy, 3"	Closed	1990	95.00	140
1985	Butterfly Boy, 6"	Closed	1990	220.00	322
1976	Catch a Falling Star, 3"	Closed	1983	35.00	150
1976	Catch a Falling Star, 6"	Closed	1983	75.00	250
1986	Celebration March, 11"	750	1987	495.00	495
1986	Celebration March, 20"	200	1987	2700.00	2700
1982	The Champion, 3"	Closed	1985	98.00	110
1982	The Champion, 6"	Closed	1985	225.00	250
1975	Cherub, 2"	Open		32.00	90
1975	Cherub, 4"	Open		32.00	275
1993	Christmas Time, 5"	750		360.00	420
1982	Circus Serenade, 3"	Closed	1988	100.00	160
1982	Circus Serenade, 6"	Closed	1988	220.00	220
1982	Clarinet, 3"	Closed	1983	80.00	100
1982	Clarinet, 6"	Closed	1983	175.00	200
1982	Companions, 3"	Closed	1984	95.00	115
1975	Courting, 3"	Closed	1982	70.00	235
1975	Courting, 6"	Closed	1982	150.00	450
1984	Cowboy, 10"	Closed	1989	370.00	500
1983	Cowboy, 20"	250	1989	2100.00	2100
1976	Cowboy, 3"	Closed	1989	35.00	140-160
1994	Donkey Driver, 3"	Open		160.00	160
1994	Donkey Driver, 6"	Open		360.00	360
1994	Donkey, 3"	Open		200.00	200
1994	Donkey, 6"	Open		450.00	450
1980	Drummer Boy, 3"	Closed	1988	130.00	200
1980	Drummer Boy, 6"	Closed	1988	300.00	400
1970	Duet, 3"	Closed	1991	36.00	165
1970	Duet, 6"	Closed	1991	Unkn.	355
1986	Edelweiss, 10"	Open		500.00	1000
1986	Edelweiss, 20"	250		3300.00	5420
1983	Edelweiss, 3"	Open		95.00	205
1983	Edelweiss, 6"	Open		220.00	500
1982	Encore, 3"	Closed	1984	100.00	115
1982	Encore, 6"	Closed	1984	225.00	235
1979	First Blossom, 3"	Closed	1985	70.00	110
1974	Flight Into Egypt, 3"	Closed	1986	35.00	125
1974	Flight Into Egypt, 6"	Closed	1986	70.00	500
1976	Flower Girl, 3"	Closed	1988	40.00	40
1976	Flower Girl, 6"	Closed	1988	90.00	310
1982	Flute, 3"	Closed	1983	80.00	95
1982	Flute, 6"	Closed	1983	175.00	190
1976	Gardener, 3"	Closed	1984	32.00	195
1976	Gardener, 6"	Closed	1985	65.00	275-350
1975	The Gift, 3"	Closed	1982	40.00	195
1975	The Gift, 6"	Closed	1982	70.00	295
1973	Girl in the Egg, 3"	Closed	1988	30.00	127
1973	Girl in the Egg, 6"	Closed	1988	60.00	272
1973	Girl with Dove, 3"	Closed	1984	30.00	110
1973	Girl with Dove, 6"	Closed	1984	50.00	175-200
1976	Girl with Rooster, 3"	Closed	1982	32.50	175
1976	Girl with Rooster, 6"	Closed	1982	60.00	275
1986	God's Little Helper, 2"	3,500	1991	170.00	255
1986	God's Little Helper, 4"	2,000	1991	425.00	550
1975	Going Home, 3"	Closed	1988	40.00	175
1975	Going Home, 6"	Closed	1988	70.00	325
1986	Golden Blossom, 10"	Open		500.00	1000
1986	Golden Blossom, 20"	250		3300.00	5420
1983	Golden Blossom, 3"	Open		95.00	205
1986	Golden Blossom, 40"	50	1994	8300.00	12950
1983	Golden Blossom, 6"	Open		220.00	500
1982	The Good Life, 3"	Closed	1984	100.00	200
1982	The Good Life, 6"	Closed	1984	225.00	295
1969	The Good Sheperd, 3"	Closed	1988	12.50	121
1971	The Good Shepherd, 10"	Closed	1988	90.00	90
1969	The Good Shepherd, 6"	Closed	1988	25.00	237
1974	Greetings, 3"	Closed	1976	30.00	300
1974	Greetings, 6"	Closed	1976	55.00	475
1982	Guiding Light, 3"	Closed	1984	100.00	115-140
1982	Guitar, 3"	Closed	1983	80.00	95
1982	Guitar, 6"	Closed	1983	175.00	190
1979	Happy Strummer, 3"	Closed	1986	75.00	110
1973	Happy Wanderer, 10"	Closed	1985	120.00	500
1974	Happy Wanderer, 3"	Closed	1986	40.00	105
1974	Happy Wanderer, 6"	Closed	1986	70.00	200
1982	Harmonica, 3"	Closed	1983	80.00	95
1982	Harmonica, 3"	Closed	1983	80.00	95
1982	Harmonica, 6"	Closed	1983	175.00	190
1978	Harvest Girl, 3"	Closed	1986	75.00	110-140
1979	He's My Brother, 3"	Closed	1984	70.00	130
1979	He's My Brother, 6"	Closed	1984	155.00	240
1987	Heavenly Concert, 2"	3,000	1991	200.00	200
1987	Heavenly Concert, 4"	2,000	1991	450.00	550
1969	Heavenly Gardener, 6"	Closed	1973	25.00	2000
1969	Heavenly Quintet, 6"	Closed	1973	25.00	2000
1969	The Helper, 3"	Closed	1987	12.50	13
1969	The Helper, 5"	Closed	1987	25.00	25
1974	Helping Hands, 3"	Closed	1976	30.00	350
1974	Helping Hands, 6"	Closed	1976	55.00	700
1984	High Hopes, 3"	Closed	1986	81.00	81-100
1984	High Hopes, 6"	Closed	1986	170.00	255
1979	High Riding, 3"	Closed	1984	145.00	200
1979	High Riding, 6"	Closed	1984	340.00	475
1974	The Hiker, 3"	Closed	1993	36.00	36
1974	The Hiker, 6"	Closed	1993	80.00	80
1982	Hitchhiker, 3"	Closed	1986	98.00	85-110
1982	Hitchhiker, 6"	Closed	1986	125.00	230
1993	Holiday Greetings, 3"	1,000	1993	200.00	200
1993	Holiday Greetings, 6"	1,000	1993	450.00	450
1975	Holy Family, 3"	Closed	1988	75.00	250
1975	Holy Family, 6"	Closed	1988	200.00	670

48 Collectors' Information Bureau *Quotes have been rounded up to nearest dollar

ANRI
to ANRI

FIGURINES

YEAR ISSUE		EDITION LIMIT	YEAR RETD.	ISSUE PRICE	*QUOTE U.S. $
1996	Homeward Bound, 3"	Open		155.00	155
1996	Homeward Bound, 6"	Open		410.00	410
1977	Hurdy Gurdy, 3"	Closed	1988	53.00	150
1977	Hurdy Gurdy, 6"	Closed	1988	112.00	390
1975	Inspector, 3"	Closed	1981	40.00	250
1975	Inspector, 6"	Closed	1981	80.00	395
1988	Jolly Gift, 3"	Closed	1991	129.00	129
1988	Jolly Gift, 6"	Closed	1991	296.00	296
1981	Jolly Piper, 3"	Closed	1984	100.00	120
1977	Journey, 3"	Closed	1983	67.50	175
1977	Journey, 6"	Closed	1983	120.00	400
1977	Leading the Way, 3"	Closed	1984	62.50	120
1976	The Letter, 3"	Closed	1988	40.00	40
1976	The Letter, 6"	Closed	1988	90.00	600
1982	Lighting the Way, 3"	Closed	1984	105.00	150
1982	Lighting the Way, 6"	Closed	1984	225.00	295
1974	Little Mother, 3"	Closed	1981	136.00	290
1974	Little Mother, 6"	Closed	1981	85.00	285
1989	Little Sheep Found, 3"	Open		120.00	180
1989	Little Sheep Found, 6"	Open		275.00	335
1993	Lots of Gifts, 3"	1,000	1993	200.00	200
1993	Lots of Gifts, 6"	1,000	1993	450.00	450
1975	Love Gift, 3"	Closed	1982	40.00	175
1975	Love Gift, 6"	Closed	1982	70.00	295
1969	Love Letter, 3"	Closed	1982	12.50	150
1969	Love Letter, 6"	Closed	1982	25.00	250
1983	Love Message, 3"	Closed	1990	105.00	151
1983	Love Message, 6"	Closed	1990	240.00	366
1969	Love's Messenger, 6"	Closed	1973	25.00	2000
1992	Madonna With Child, 3"	1,000	1994	190.00	190
1992	Madonna With Child, 6"	1,000	1994	370.00	370
1981	Merry Melody, 3"	Closed	1984	90.00	115
1989	Mexican Boy, 3"	1,500	1993	170.00	175
1989	Mexican Boy, 6"	1,500	1993	340.00	350
1989	Mexican Girl, 3"	1,500	1993	170.00	175
1989	Mexican Girl, 6"	1,500	1993	340.00	350
1975	Mother and Child, 3"	Closed	1983	45.00	150
1975	Mother and Child, 6"	Closed	1983	90.00	295
1981	Musical Basket, 3"	Closed	1984	90.00	115
1981	Musical Basket, 6"	Closed	1984	200.00	225
1986	A Musical Ride, 4"	Closed	1990	165.00	237
1986	A Musical Ride, 8"	Closed	1990	395.00	559
1973	Nature Girl, 3"	Closed	1988	30.00	30
1973	Nature Girl, 6"	Closed	1988	60.00	272
1987	Nature's Wonder, 3"	3,000	1990	125.00	151
1987	Nature's Wonder, 6"	3,000	1990	245.00	291
1974	New Friends, 3"	Closed	1976	30.00	275
1974	New Friends, 6"	Closed	1976	55.00	550
1977	Night Night, 3"	Closed	1983	45.00	120
1977	Night Night, 6"	Closed	1983	67.50	250-315
1992	Pascal Lamb, 3"	1,000	1993	210.00	210
1992	Pascal Lamb, 6"	1,000	1993	460.00	460
1988	Peace Maker, 3"	1,500	1991	180.00	200
1988	Peace Maker, 6"	1,500	1991	360.00	395
1983	Peace Pipe, 10"	Closed	1986	460.00	495
1984	Peace Pipe, 20"	250	1986	2200.00	3500
1979	Peace Pipe, 3"	Closed	1986	85.00	120
1988	Picnic for Two, 3"	500	1991	190.00	210
1988	Picnic for Two, 6"	500	1991	425.00	465
1982	Play It Again, 3"	Closed	1984	100.00	120
1982	Play It Again, 6"	Closed	1984	250.00	255
1977	Poor Boy, 3"	Closed	1986	50.00	110
1977	Poor Boy, 6"	Closed	1986	125.00	215
1977	Proud Mother, 3"	Closed	1988	52.50	150
1977	Proud Mother, 6"	Closed	1988	130.00	350
1971	The Quintet, 10"	Closed	1990	100.00	750
1971	The Quintet, 20"	Closed	1990	Unkn.	4750
1969	The Quintet, 3"	Closed	1990	12.50	175
1969	The Quintet, 6"	Closed	1990	25.00	395
1970	Reverance, 3"	Closed	1991	30.00	30
1970	Reverance, 6"	Closed	1991	56.00	56
1977	Riding Thru the Rain, 10"	Open		400.00	1190
1985	Riding Thru the Rain, 20"	100	1988	3950.00	3950
1977	Riding Thru the Rain, 5"	Open		145.00	470
1976	Rock A Bye, 3"	Closed	1987	60.00	60
1976	Rock A Bye, 6"	Closed	1987	125.00	125
1974	Romeo, 3"	Closed	1981	50.00	250
1974	Romeo, 6"	Closed	1981	85.00	395
1993	Santa and Teddy, 5"	750		360.00	380
1994	Santa Resting on Bag, 5"	750		400.00	400
1987	Serenity, 3"	3,000	1989	125.00	151
1987	Serenity, 6"	3,000	1989	245.00	291
1976	Sharing, 3"	Closed	1983	32.50	130
1976	Sharing, 6"	Closed	1983	32.50	225-275
1984	Shipmates, 3"	Closed	1989	81.00	119
1984	Shipmates, 6"	Closed	1989	170.00	248
1978	Spreading the Word, 3"	Closed	1989	115.00	194
1978	Spreading the Word, 6"	Closed	1989	270.00	495
1980	Spring Arrivals, 10"	Open		435.00	770
1980	Spring Arrivals, 20"	250		2000.00	3360
1973	Spring Arrivals, 3"	Open		30.00	160
1973	Spring Arrivals, 6"	Open		50.00	350
1978	Spring Dance, 12"	Closed	1984	950.00	1750
1978	Spring Dance, 24"	Closed	1984	4750.00	6200
1974	Spring Outing, 3"	Closed	1976	30.00	625
1974	Spring Outing, 6"	Closed	1976	55.00	900
1982	Star Bright, 3"	Closed	1984	110.00	125
1982	Star Bright, 6"	Closed	1984	250.00	295
1982	Star Struck, 10"	Closed	1987	490.00	490
1982	Star Struck, 20"	250	1987	2400.00	2400
1974	Star Struck, 3"	Closed	1987	97.50	98
1974	Star Struck, 6"	Closed	1987	210.00	210
1981	Stepping Out, 3"	Closed	1984	95.00	110-145
1981	Stepping Out, 6"	Closed	1984	220.00	275
1979	Stitch in Time, 3"	Closed	1984	75.00	125
1979	Stitch in Time, 6"	Closed	1984	150.00	235
1975	Stolen Kiss, 3"	Closed	1987	80.00	80
1975	Stolen Kiss, 6"	Closed	1987	150.00	150
1969	Sugar Heart, 3"	Closed	1973	12.50	450
1969	Sugar Heart, 6"	Closed	1973	25.00	525
1975	Summertime, 3"	Closed	1989	35.00	35
1975	Summertime, 6"	Closed	1989	70.00	258
1982	Surprise, 3"	Closed	1988	100.00	150
1982	Surprise, 6"	Closed	1988	225.00	325
1973	Sweeper, 3"	Closed	1981	35.00	130
1973	Sweeper, 6"	Closed	1981	75.00	425
1981	Sweet Arrival Blue, 3"	Closed	1985	105.00	110
1981	Sweet Arrival Blue, 6"	Closed	1985	225.00	255
1981	Sweet Arrival Pink, 3"	Closed	1985	105.00	110
1981	Sweet Arrival Pink, 6"	Closed	1985	225.00	225
1981	Sweet Dreams, 3"	Closed	1990	100.00	140
1982	Sweet Dreams, 6"	Closed	1990	225.00	330
1989	Sweet Inspiration, 3"	Closed	1991	129.00	129
1989	Sweet Inspiration, 6"	Closed	1991	296.00	296
1982	Sweet Melody, 3"	Closed	1985	80.00	90
1982	Sweet Melody, 6"	Closed	1985	198.00	210
1989	Swiss Boy, 3"	Closed	1993	180.00	180
1986	Swiss Boy, 3"	Closed	1993	122.00	162
1989	Swiss Boy, 6"	Closed	1993	380.00	380
1986	Swiss Boy, 6"	Closed	1993	245.00	324
1986	Swiss Girl, 3"	Closed	1993	122.00	122
1989	Swiss Girl, 3"	Closed	1993	200.00	200
1986	Swiss Girl, 6"	Closed	1993	245.00	304
1989	Swiss Girl, 6"	Closed	1993	470.00	470
1971	Talking to Animals, 20"	Closed	1989	Unkn.	3000
1971	Talking to the Animals, 10"	Closed	1989	90.00	600
1969	Talking to the Animals, 3"	Closed	1969	12.50	125
1969	Talking to the Animals, 6"	Closed	1989	45.00	250
1995	Tender Care, 3" 55710/52	Open		125.00	135
1995	Tender Care, 6" 55700/52	Open		275.00	295
1974	Tender Moments, 3"	Closed	1976	30.00	375
1974	Tender Moments, 6"	Closed	1976	55.00	575
1981	Tiny Sounds, 3"	Closed	1984	90.00	105
1982	To Market, 3"	Closed	1984	95.00	115
1977	Tracker, 3"	Closed	1984	70.00	120-200
1982	Treasure Chest w/6 mini figurines	10,000	1984	300.00	300
1980	Trumpeter, 10"	Closed	1986	500.00	500
1984	Trumpeter, 20"	250	1986	2350.00	3050
1973	Trumpeter, 3"	Closed	1986	69.00	115
1973	Trumpeter, 6"	Closed	1986	120.00	240
1980	Umpapa, 4"	Closed	1984	125.00	140
1982	Violin, 3"	Closed	1983	80.00	95
1982	Violin, 6"	Closed	1983	175.00	195
1976	Wanderlust, 3"	Closed	1983	32.50	125
1975	Wanderlust, 6"	Closed	1983	70.00	450
1972	The Weary Traveler, 3"	Closed	1989	24.00	24
1972	The Weary Traveler, 6"	Closed	1989	48.00	48
1988	Winter Memories, 3"	1,500	1991	180.00	195
1988	Winter Memories, 6"	1,500	1991	398.00	440

Limited Edition Couples - J. Ferrandiz

YEAR ISSUE		EDITION LIMIT	YEAR RETD.	ISSUE PRICE	*QUOTE U.S. $
1985	First Kiss, 8"	750	1985	590.00	950
1987	Heart to Heart, 8"	750	1991	590.00	850
1988	A Loving Hand, 8"	750	1991	795.00	850
1986	My Heart Is Yours, 8"	750	1991	590.00	850
1985	Springtime Stroll, 8"	750	1990	590.00	950
1986	A Tender Touch, 8"	750	1990	590.00	850

Lyndon Gaither Christmas Eve Series - L. Gaither

YEAR ISSUE		EDITION LIMIT	YEAR RETD.	ISSUE PRICE	*QUOTE U.S. $
1995	Hitching Prancer, 3 1/2" figurine & ornament	500		499.00	499
1996	Getting Ready, 3 1/2" figurine & ornament	500		499.00	499
1997	Time To go, 5" figurine & ornament	500		595.00	595

Sarah Kay Figurines - S. Kay

YEAR ISSUE		EDITION LIMIT	YEAR RETD.	ISSUE PRICE	*QUOTE U.S. $
1985	Afternoon Tea, 11"	750	1993	650.00	770
1985	Afternoon Tea, 20"	100	1993	3100.00	3500
1985	Afternoon Tea, 4"	4,000	1990	95.00	185
1985	Afternoon Tea, 6"	4,000	1990	195.00	325-365
1987	All Aboard, 1 1/2"	7,500	1990	50.00	90
1987	All Aboard, 4"	4,000	1990	130.00	185
1987	All Aboard, 6"	2,000	1990	265.00	355
1987	All Mine, 1 1/2"	7,500	1988	49.50	95
1987	All Mine, 4"	4,000	1988	130.00	225
1987	All Mine, 6"	4,000	1988	245.00	465
1986	Always By My Side, 1 1/2"	7,500	1988	45.00	95
1986	Always By My Side, 4"	4,000	1988	95.00	195
1986	Always By My Side, 6"	4,000	1988	195.00	375
1990	Batter Up, 1 1/2"	3,750	1991	90.00	95
1990	Batter Up, 4"	2,000		220.00	265
1990	Batter Up, 6"	2,000		440.00	515
1983	Bedtime, 1 1/2"	7,500	1984	45.00	110
1983	Bedtime, 4"	Closed	1987	95.00	230
1983	Bedtime, 6"	4,000	1987	195.00	435
1994	Bubbles & Bows, 4"	1,000		300.00	300
1994	Bubbles & Bows, 6"	1,000		600.00	600
1986	Bunny Hug, 1 1/2"	7,500	1989	45.00	85
1986	Bunny Hug, 4"	4,000	1989	95.00	172
1986	Bunny Hug, 6"	2,000	1989	210.00	395
1989	Cherish, 1 1/2"	Closed	1991	80.00	95
1989	Cherish, 4"	2,000	1994	199.00	290
1989	Cherish, 6"	2,000	1994	398.00	560
1993	Christmas Basket, 4"	1,000		310.00	290
1993	Christmas Basket, 6"	1,000		600.00	580
1994	Christmas Wonder, 4"	1,000		370.00	370
1994	Christmas Wonder, 6"	1,000		700.00	700
1994	Clowning Around, 4"	1,000		300.00	300
1994	Clowning Around, 6"	1,000		550.00	550
1987	Cuddles, 1 1/2"	7,500	1988	49.50	95
1987	Cuddles, 4"	4,000	1988	130.00	225
1987	Cuddles, 6"	4,000	1988	245.00	465
1984	Daydreaming, 1 1/2"	7,500	1984	45.00	125
1984	Daydreaming, 4"	4,000	1988	95.00	235
1984	Daydreaming, 6"	4,000	1988	195.00	445
1991	Dress Up, 1 1/2"	3,750	1991	110.00	110
1991	Dress Up, 4"	2,000	1993	270.00	270
1991	Dress Up, 6"	2,000	1993	550.00	570
1983	Feeding the Chickens, 1 1/2"	7,500	1984	45.00	110
1983	Feeding the Chickens, 4"	Closed	1987	95.00	250
1983	Feeding the Chickens, 6"	4,000	1987	195.00	450
1991	Figure Eight, 1 1/2"	3,750	1991	110.00	110
1991	Figure Eight, 4"	2,000		270.00	365
1991	Figure Eight, 6"	2,000		550.00	660
1984	Finding Our Way, 1 1/2"	7,500	1984	45.00	135
1984	Finding Our Way, 4"	4,000	1988	95.00	245
1984	Finding Our Way, 6"	2,000	1984	210.00	495
1986	Finishing Touch, 1 1/2"	7,500	1989	45.00	85
1986	Finishing Touch, 4"	4,000	1989	95.00	172
1986	Finishing Touch, 6"	4,000	1989	195.00	312
1989	First School Day, 1 1/2"	Closed	1991	85.00	95
1989	First School Day, 4"	2,000	1993	290.00	350
1989	First School Day, 6"	2,000	1993	550.00	650
1989	Fisherboy, 1 1/2"	Closed	1991	85.00	95
1989	Fisherboy, 4"	2,000	1994	220.00	250
1989	Fisherboy, 6"	1,000	1994	440.00	475
1984	Flowers for You, 1 1/2"	7,500	1984	45.00	125
1984	Flowers for You, 4"	4,000	1988	95.00	250
1984	Flowers for You, 6"	4,000	1988	195.00	450
1991	Fore!!, 1 1/2"	3,750	1991	110.00	115
1991	Fore!!, 4"	2,000		270.00	325
1991	Fore!!, 6"	2,000		550.00	580
1992	Free Skating, 4"	1,000		310.00	325
1992	Free Skating, 6"	1,000		590.00	620
1983	From the Garden, 1 1/2"	7,500	1984	45.00	110
1983	From the Garden, 4"	Closed	1987	95.00	235
1983	From the Garden, 6"	4,000	1987	195.00	450
1989	Garden Party, 1 1/2"	Closed	1991	85.00	95
1989	Garden Party, 4"	2,000	1993	220.00	240
1989	Garden Party, 6"	2,000	1993	440.00	475
1985	Giddyap!, 4"	4,000	1990	95.00	250
1985	Giddyap!, 6"	4,000	1990	195.00	325
1988	Ginger Snap, 1 1/2"	Closed	1990	70.00	90
1988	Ginger Snap, 4"	2,000	1990	150.00	185
1988	Ginger Snap, 6"	1,000	1990	300.00	355
1986	Good As New, 1 1/2"	7,500	1991	45.00	90
1986	Good As New, 4"	4,000	1994	95.00	290
1986	Good As New, 6"	4,000	1994	195.00	500
1983	Helping Mother, 1 1/2"	7,500	1983	45.00	110
1983	Helping Mother, 4"	Closed	1983	95.00	300
1983	Helping Mother, 6"	2,000	1983	210.00	495
1988	Hidden Treasures, 1 1/2"	Closed	1990	70.00	90
1988	Hidden Treasures, 4"	2,000	1990	150.00	185
1988	Hidden Treasures, 6"	1,000	1990	300.00	355
1990	Holiday Cheer, 1 1/2"	3,750	1991	90.00	95
1990	Holiday Cheer, 4"	2,000		225.00	320
1990	Holiday Cheer, 6"	1,000		450.00	610
1989	House Call, 1 1/2"	Closed	1991	85.00	95
1989	House Call, 4"	2,000	1991	190.00	195
1989	House Call, 6"	2,000	1991	390.00	390
1993	Innocence, 4"	1,000		345.00	315
1993	Innocence, 6"	1,000		630.00	630
1994	Jolly Pair, 4"	1,000		350.00	350
1994	Jolly Pair, 6"	1,000		650.00	650
1993	Joy to the World, 4"	1,000		310.00	290
1993	Joy to the World, 6"	1,000		600.00	580
1987	Let's Play, 1 1/2"	7,500	1990	49.50	90
1987	Let's Play, 4"	4,000	1990	130.00	185
1987	Let's Play, 6"	2,000	1990	265.00	355
1994	Little Chimney Sweep, 4"	1,000		300.00	310
1994	Little Chimney Sweep, 6"	1,000		600.00	600
1987	Little Nanny, 1 1/2"	7,500	1990	49.50	90
1987	Little Nanny, 4"	4,000	1990	150.00	200
1987	Little Nanny, 6"	4,000	1990	295.00	400
1987	A Loving Spoonful, 1 1/2"	7,500	1991	49.50	90
1987	A Loving Spoonful, 4"	4,000	1994	150.00	290
1987	A Loving Spoonful, 6"	4,000	1994	295.00	550
1992	Merry Christmas, 1 1/2"	3,750	1994	110.00	115
1992	Merry Christmas, 4"	1,000	1994	350.00	350
1992	Merry Christmas, 6"	1,000	1994	580.00	580
1983	Morning Chores, 1 1/2"	7,500	1983	45.00	110
1983	Morning Chores, 4"	Closed	1983	95.00	300
1983	Morning Chores, 6"	2,000	1983	210.00	550
1993	Mr. Santa, 4"	750		375.00	390
1993	Mr. Santa, 6"	750		695.00	730
1993	Mrs. Santa, 4"	750		375.00	390
1993	Mrs. Santa, 6"	750		695.00	730
1993	My Favorite Doll, 4"	1,000		315.00	315
1993	My Favorite Doll, 6"	1,000		600.00	600
1988	My Little Brother, 1 1/2"	Closed	1991	70.00	90
1988	My Little Brother, 4"	2,000	1991	195.00	225
1988	My Little Brother, 6"	2,000	1991	375.00	450

*Quotes have been rounded up to nearest dollar

Collectors' Information Bureau

49

YEAR ISSUE		EDITION LIMIT	YEAR RETD.	ISSUE PRICE	*QUOTE U.S.$
1988	New Home, 1 1/2"	Closed	1991	70.00	90
1988	New Home, 4"	2,000	1991	185.00	240
1988	New Home, 6"	2,000	1991	365.00	500
1985	Nightie Night, 4"	4,000	1990	95.00	185
1985	Nightie Night, 6"	4,000	1990	195.00	325
1984	Off to School, 1 1/2"	7,500	1984	45.00	125
1984	Off to School, 11"	750		590.00	880
1984	Off to School, 20"	100		2900.00	4200
1984	Off to School, 4"	4,000		95.00	240
1984	Off to School, 6"	4,000		195.00	450
1986	Our Puppy, 1 1/2"	7,500	1990	45.00	90
1986	Our Puppy, 4"	4,000	1990	95.00	185
1986	Our Puppy, 6"	2,000	1990	210.00	355
1988	Penny for Your Thoughts, 1 1/2"	Closed	1991	70.00	90
1988	Penny for Your Thoughts, 4"	2,000		185.00	275
1988	Penny for Your Thoughts, 6"	2,000		365.00	570
1983	Playtime, 1 1/2"	7,500	1984	45.00	110
1983	Playtime, 4"	Closed	1987	95.00	250
1983	Playtime, 6"	4,000	1987	195.00	495
1988	Purrfect Day, 4"	2,000	1991	184.00	215
1988	Purrfect Day, 1 1/2"	Closed	1991	70.00	90
1988	Purrfect Day, 6"	2,000	1991	265.00	455
1992	Raindrops, 1 1/2"	3,750	1994	110.00	110
1992	Raindrops, 4"	1,000	1994	350.00	350
1992	Raindrops, 6"	1,000	1994	640.00	640
1988	School Marm, 6"	2,000	1988	398.00	398
1991	Season's Joy, 1 1/2"	3,750	1991	110.00	115
1991	Season's Joy, 4"	2,000		270.00	350
1991	Season's Joy, 6"	1,000		550.00	690
1990	Seasons Greetings, 1 1/2"	3,750	1991	90.00	95
1990	Seasons Greetings, 4"	2,000		225.00	285
1990	Seasons Greetings, 6"	1,000		450.00	610
1990	Shootin' Hoops, 4"	2,000	1993	220.00	250
1990	Shootin' Hoops, 6"	2,000	1993	440.00	450
1990	Shootin' Hoops,1 1/2"	3,750	1991	90.00	95
1985	A Special Day, 4"	4,000	1990	95.00	195
1985	A Special Day, 6"	4,000	1990	195.00	325
1984	Special Delivery, 1 1/2"	7,500	1984	45.00	125
1984	Special Delivery, 4"	4,000	1989	95.00	187
1984	Special Delivery, 6"	4,000	1989	195.00	312-350
1990	Spring Fever, 1 1/2"	3,750	1991	90.00	95
1990	Spring Fever, 4"	2,000		225.00	325
1990	Spring Fever, 6"	2,000		450.00	610
1983	Sweeping, 1 1/2"	7,500	1984	45.00	110
1983	Sweeping, 4"	Closed	1987	95.00	230
1983	Sweeping, 6"	4,000	1987	195.00	435
1986	Sweet Treat, 1 1/2"	7,500	1989	45.00	85
1986	Sweet Treat, 4"	4,000	1989	95.00	172
1986	Sweet Treat, 6"	4,000	1989	195.00	312
1984	Tag Along, 4"	4,000	1988	95.00	225
1984	Tag Along, 6"	4,000	1988	195.00	290
1984	Tag Along,1 1/2"	7,500	1984	45.00	130
1989	Take Me Along, 1 1/2"	Closed	1991	85.00	95
1992	Take Me Along, 11"	400		950.00	950
1992	Take Me Along, 20"	100		4550.00	4550
1989	Take Me Along, 4"	2,000		220.00	285
1989	Take Me Along, 6"	1,000		440.00	565
1993	Ten Roses For You, 4"	1,000		290.00	290
1993	Ten Roses For You, 6"	1,000		525.00	525
1990	Tender Loving Care, 1 1/2"	3,750	1991	90.00	95
1990	Tender Loving Care, 4"	2,000	1993	220.00	240
1990	Tender Loving Care, 6"	2,000	1993	440.00	475
1985	Tis the Season, 4"	4,000	1993	95.00	250
1985	Tis the Season, 6"	2,000	1985	210.00	425
1986	To Love And To Cherish, 1 1/2"	7,500	1989	45.00	85
1986	To Love and To Cherish, 11"	1,000	1989	Unkn.	667
1986	To Love and To Cherish, 20"	200	1989	Unkn.	3600
1986	To Love And To Cherish, 4"	4,000	1989	95.00	172
1986	To Love And To Cherish, 6"	4,000	1989	195.00	312
1991	Touch Down, 1 1/2"	3,750	1994	110.00	110
1991	Touch Down, 4"	2,000	1994	270.00	310
1991	Touch Down, 6"	2,000	1994	550.00	550
1992	Tulips For Mother, 4"	1,000		310.00	325
1992	Tulips For Mother, 6"	1,000		590.00	620
1983	Waiting for Mother, 1 1/2"	7,500	1984	45.00	110
1983	Waiting for Mother, 11"	750	1987	495.00	795
1983	Waiting for Mother, 4"	Closed	1987	95.00	230
1983	Waiting for Mother, 6"	4,000	1987	195.00	445
1984	Wake Up Kiss, 1 1/2"	7,500	1984	45.00	550
1984	Wake Up Kiss, 4"	4,000	1993	95.00	195
1983	Wake Up Kiss, 6"	2,000	1984	210.00	550
1984	Watchful Eye, 4"	4,000	1988	95.00	235
1984	Watchful Eye, 6"	4,000	1988	195.00	445
1984	Watchful Eye,1 1/2"	7,500	1984	45.00	125
1992	Winter Cheer, 4"	2,000	1993	300.00	300
1992	Winter Cheer, 6"	1,000	1993	580.00	580
1991	Winter Surprise, 1 1/2"	3,750	1994	110.00	110
1991	Winter Surprise, 4"	2,000	1994	270.00	290
1991	Winter Surprise, 6"	1,000	1994	550.00	570
1986	With This Ring, 1 1/2"	7,500	1989	45.00	85
1986	With This Ring, 11"	1,000	1989	Unkn.	668
1986	With This Ring, 20"	200	1989	Unkn.	3600
1986	With This Ring, 4"	4,000	1989	95.00	172
1986	With This Ring, 6"	4,000	1989	195.00	312
1989	Yearly Check-Up, 1 1/2"	Closed	1991	85.00	95
1989	Yearly Check-Up, 4"	2,000	1991	190.00	195
1989	Yearly Check-Up, 6"	2,000	1991	390.00	390
1985	Yuletide Cheer, 4"	4,000	1993	95.00	250
1985	Yuletide Cheer, 6"	Closed	1985	210.00	435

Sarah Kay Koalas - S. Kay

YEAR ISSUE		EDITION LIMIT	YEAR RETD.	ISSUE PRICE	*QUOTE U.S.$
1986	Green Thumb, 3"	3,500	1986	81.00	81
1985	Green Thumb, 5"	2,000	1986	165.00	165
1985	Honey Bunch, 3"	3,500	1986	75.00	75
1985	Honey Bunch, 5"	2,000	1986	165.00	165
1985	A Little Bird Told Me, 3"	3,500	1986	75.00	75
1985	A Little Bird Told Me, 5"	2,000	1986	165.00	165
1985	Party Time, 3"	3,500	1986	75.00	75
1985	Party Time, 5"	2,000	1986	165.00	165
1986	Scout About, 3"	3,500	1986	81.00	81
1986	Scout About, 5"	2,000	1986	178.00	178
1986	A Stitch with Love, 3"	3,500	1986	81.00	81
1986	A Stitch with Love, 5"	2,000	1986	178.00	178

Sarah Kay Mini Santas - S. Kay

YEAR ISSUE		EDITION LIMIT	YEAR RETD.	ISSUE PRICE	*QUOTE U.S.$
1992	Father Christmas, 1 1/2"	2,500	1993	110.00	110
1992	A Friend to All, 1 1/2"	2,500	1993	110.00	110
1991	Jolly Santa, 1 1/2"	2,500	1993	110.00	110
1991	Jolly St. Nick, 1 1/2"	2,500	1993	110.00	110
1991	Kris Kringle, 1 1/2"	2,500	1993	110.00	110
1991	Sarah Kay Santa, 1 1/2"	2,500	1993	110.00	110

Sarah Kay Santas - S. Kay

YEAR ISSUE		EDITION LIMIT	YEAR RETD.	ISSUE PRICE	*QUOTE U.S.$
1995	Checking It Twice, 4" 57709	500		250.00	270
1995	Checking It Twice, 6" 57710	250		395.00	450
1992	Father Christmas, 4"	750	1994	350.00	350
1992	Father Christmas, 6"	750	1994	590.00	590
1991	A Friend To All, 4"	750	1994	300.00	300
1991	A Friend To All, 6"	750	1994	590.00	590
1989	Jolly Santa, 12"	150	1990	1300.00	1300
1988	Jolly Santa, 4"	750	1989	235.00	300-350
1988	Jolly Santa, 6"	750	1989	480.00	600
1988	Jolly St. Nick, 4"	750	1989	199.00	300-550
1988	Jolly St. Nick, 6"	750	1989	398.00	850
1990	Kris Kringle Santa, 4"	750	1990	275.00	350
1990	Kris Kringle Santa, 6"	750	1990	550.00	550
1997	Santa's Helper, 4"	500		350.00	350
1997	Santa's Helper, 6"	250		630.00	630
1989	Santa, 4"	750	1990	235.00	350
1989	Santa, 6"	750	1990	480.00	480
1996	Workshop Santa, 4"	500		295.00	295
1996	Workshop Santa, 6"	250		495.00	495

Sarah Kay School Days - S. Kay

YEAR ISSUE		EDITION LIMIT	YEAR RETD.	ISSUE PRICE	*QUOTE U.S.$
1996	Head of the Class, 4"	500		295.00	295
1996	Head of the Class, 6"	250		495.00	495
1997	Homework, 4"	500		315.00	315
1997	Homework, 6"	250		520.00	520
1995	I Know, I Know, 4" 57701	500		250.00	275
1995	I Know, I Know, 6" 57702	250		395.00	450

Sarah Kay Tribute To Mother - S. Kay

YEAR ISSUE		EDITION LIMIT	YEAR RETD.	ISSUE PRICE	*QUOTE U.S.$
1995	Mom's Joy, 5" 57902	250	1995	297.00	297
1997	Storytime, 5 1/2"	250		650.00	650
1996	Sweets for My Sweet, 6"	250		399.00	399

Sarah Kay's First Christmas - S. Kay

YEAR ISSUE		EDITION LIMIT	YEAR RETD.	ISSUE PRICE	*QUOTE U.S.$
1994	Sarah Kay's First Christmas, 4"	500		350.00	350
1994	Sarah Kay's First Christmas, 6"	250	1995	600.00	600
1995	First Christmas Stocking, 4" 57553	500		250.00	250
1995	First Christmas Stocking, 6" 57554	250		395.00	395
1996	All I Want For Christmas, 4" 57555	500		325.00	325
1996	All I Want For Christmas, 6" 57556	250		550.00	550
1997	Christmas Puppy, 4"	500		375.00	375
1997	Christmas Puppy, 6"	250		625.00	625

Arcadian Pewter, Inc.

Arcade Toys - N. Lindblade

YEAR ISSUE		EDITION LIMIT	YEAR RETD.	ISSUE PRICE	*QUOTE U.S.$
1996	A-Express Truck	10,000		45.95	46
1995	Aeroplane Monocoupe	10,000		45.95	46
1996	Ambulance	10,000		45.95	46
1995	Bus-Safety Coach	10,000		45.95	46
1995	Coffee Mill	10,000		49.95	50
1996	Cottage Bank	10,000		29.95	30
1995	Coupe A-Rumble Seat	10,000		49.95	50
1995	Coupe Model T	10,000		45.95	46
1995	Express Flyer Wagon	10,000		45.95	46
1996	Farm Mower	10,000		39.95	40
1995	Fire Engine Auto	10,000		55.95	56
1996	Fire Ladder Truck	10,000		45.95	46
1995	Firewagon (Horsedrawn)	10,000		69.95	70
1995	Mail Box (Special Edition)	2,500		39.95	40
1996	Motorcycle Cop	10,000		45.95	46
1996	No. 1501 Sedan	10,000		29.95	30
1996	No. 1810 Fire Engine	10,000		45.95	46
1996	Plymouth Sedan	10,000		39.95	40
1996	Prancing Horse Bank	10,000		39.95	40
1996	Rocking Chair	10,000		29.95	30
1996	Row Crop Truck	10,000		45.95	46
1995	Sedan A Tudor	10,000		45.95	46
1995	Sedan T-Fordor	10,000		45.95	46
1995	State Bank	10,000	1996	45.95	46
1995	Steamboat	10,000		49.95	50
1996	Toy Policeman Bank	10,000		45.95	46
1995	Tractor	10,000		45.95	46
1995	Truck A-Stakes Sides	10,000		45.95	46
1995	Truck T-Stake Sides	10,000		55.95	56
1996	Two-Man Racer	10,000		45.95	46
1996	Wheelbarrow with Tools	10,000		45.95	46
1996	Wheelbarrow with Toys	10,000		45.95	46

Red Oak II - N. Lindblade

YEAR ISSUE		EDITION LIMIT	YEAR RETD.	ISSUE PRICE	*QUOTE U.S.$
1995	Leapin' Lizard	10,000		89.95	90
1995	Privy	10,000		29.95	30

Armani

G. Armani Society Members Only Figurine - G. Armani

YEAR ISSUE		EDITION LIMIT	YEAR RETD.	ISSUE PRICE	*QUOTE U.S.$
1990	My Fine Feathered Friends (Bonus)122S	Closed	1990	175.00	350
1990	Awakening 591C	Closed	1991	137.50	1200-1800
1991	Peace & Harmony (Bonus) 824C	7,500	1991	300.00	325-360
1991	Ruffles 745E	Closed	1991	139.00	315-450
1992	Ascent 866C	Closed	1992	195.00	400-450
1992	Julie (Bonus) 293P	Closed	1992	90.00	135-200
1992	Juliette (Bonus) 294P	Closed	1992	90.00	225-265
1993	Venus 881E	Closed	1993	225.00	350-550
1993	Lady Rose (Bonus) 197C	Closed	1993	125.00	200-300
1994	Harlequin 1994 Fifth Anniversary 490C	Closed	1994	300.00	350-450
1994	Flora 212C	Closed	1994	225.00	300-450
1994	Aquarius (Bonus) 248C	Closed	1994	125.00	200-300
1995	Melody 656C	Closed	1995	250.00	300-350
1995	Scarlette (Bonus) 698C	Closed	1995	200.00	250-300
1996	Allegra 345C	Closed	1996	250.00	250
1996	Arianna (Bonus) 400C	Closed	1996	125.00	150
1997	It's Mine (Bonus) 136C	Yr.Iss.		280.00	280
1997	Sabrina 110C	Yr.Iss.		275.00	275

G. Armani Society Member Gift - G. Armani

YEAR ISSUE		EDITION LIMIT	YEAR RETD.	ISSUE PRICE	*QUOTE U.S.$
1993	Petite Maternity 939F	Closed	1993	Gift	N/A
1994	Lady w/Dogs 245F	Closed	1994	Gift	55
1995	Lady w/Doves mini 546F	Closed	1995	Gift	45-85
1996	Perfect Match 358F	Closed	1996	Gift	N/A
1997	Quiet Please 446F	Yr.Iss.		Gift	N/A

G. Armani Society Event - G. Armani

YEAR ISSUE		EDITION LIMIT	YEAR RETD.	ISSUE PRICE	*QUOTE U.S.$
1990	Pals (Boy w/ Dog) '90 & '91 409S	Closed	1991	200.00	200
1992	Springtime 961C	Closed	1992	250.00	395-500
1993	Loving Arms 880E	Closed	1993	250.00	395-495
1994	Daisy 202E	Closed	1994	250.00	400-500
1995	Iris 628E	Closed	1995	250.00	300-400
1996	Rose 678C	Closed	1997	250.00	300
1997	Marianne 135C	Yr.Iss.		275.00	275

Capodimonte - G. Armani

YEAR ISSUE		EDITION LIMIT	YEAR RETD.	ISSUE PRICE	*QUOTE U.S.$
1976	Country Girl (Little Shepherdess) 3153	Closed	1991	47.50	150
1997	Gallant Approach 146C	750		1250.00	1250
1977	Napoleon (5464) 464C	Closed	1991	250.00	500
1980	Old Drunk (Richard's Night Out) 3243	Closed	1988	130.00	240
1978	Organ Grinder 3323	Closed	1989	140.00	350
1997	Venetian Night 125C	975		2000.00	2000
1995	Young Hearts 679C	1,500		900.00	1000

Clown Series - G. Armani

YEAR ISSUE		EDITION LIMIT	YEAR RETD.	ISSUE PRICE	*QUOTE U.S.$
1991	Bust of Clown (The Fiddler Clown) 725E	5,000		500.00	575
1984	Clown with Dog 653E	Closed	1991	135.00	150

Commemorative - G. Armani

YEAR ISSUE		EDITION LIMIT	YEAR RETD.	ISSUE PRICE	*QUOTE U.S.$
1992	Discovery of America - Columbus Plaque 867C	2,500	1994	400.00	425
1993	Mother's Day Plaque 899C	Closed	1993	100.00	100
1994	Mother's Day Plaque-The Swing 254C	Closed	1994	100.00	120
1995	Mother's Day Plaque-Love/Peace 538C	Closed	1995	125.00	125
1996	Mother's Day Plaque-Mother's Rosebud 341C	Closed	1996	150.00	150
1997	Mother's Day Figurine-Mother's Angel 155C	Yr.Iss.		175.00	175

Disneyana - G. Armani

YEAR ISSUE		EDITION LIMIT	YEAR RETD.	ISSUE PRICE	*QUOTE U.S.$
1992	Cinderella '92 783C	500	1992	500.00	3300-4500
1993	Snow White '93 199C	2,000	1993	750.00	1000-1500
1994	Ariel (Little Mermaid) '94 505C	1,500	1994	750.00	1100-1500
1995	Beauty and the Beast '95 543C	2,000	1995	975.00	1100-1600
1996	Jasmine & Rajah '96 410C	1,200	1996	800.00	800-1000

Etrusca - G. Armani

YEAR ISSUE		EDITION LIMIT	YEAR RETD.	ISSUE PRICE	*QUOTE U.S.$
1993	Lady with Bag 2149E	Retrd.	1996	350.00	350

Figurine of the Year - G. Armani

YEAR ISSUE		EDITION LIMIT	YEAR RETD.	ISSUE PRICE	*QUOTE U.S.$
1996	Lady Jane 390C	Yr.Iss.	1996	200.00	200-300
1997	April 121C	Yr.Iss.		250.00	250

Florence/Disney - G. Armani

YEAR ISSUE		EDITION LIMIT	YEAR RETD.	ISSUE PRICE	*QUOTE U.S.$
1995	Jiminy Cricket "Special Backstamp" 379C	1,200	1995	300.00	450-600
1996	Jiminy Cricket 379C	Open		300.00	375
1996	Sleeping Beauty (Briar Rose) 106C	Open		650.00	675
1996	Pinocchio & Figaro 464C	Open		500.00	550
1995	Bashful 916C	Open		150.00	155
1995	Doc 326C	Open		150.00	155
1993	Dopey 200C	Open		105.00	155
1997	Fauna 609C	Open		200.00	200
1997	Flora 608C	Open		200.00	200
1995	Grumpy 917C	Open		145.00	155

*Quotes have been rounded up to nearest dollar

Year Issue		Edition Limit	Year Retd.	Issue Price	*Quote U.S.$
1995	Happy 327C	Open		150.00	155
1997	Merryweather 607C	Open		200.00	200
1995	Sleepy 915C	Open		125.00	155
1995	Sneezy 914C	Open		125.00	155
1993	Snow White 209C	Open		400.00	450
1997	Tinkerbell 108C	Open		425.00	425

Florentine Gardens - G. Armani

Year Issue		Edition Limit	Year Retd.	Issue Price	*Quote U.S.$
1992	Abundance 870C	10,000	1996	600.00	675-775
1994	Ambrosia 482C	5,000		435.00	550
1994	Angelica 484C	5,000		575.00	715
1995	Aquarius 426C	5,000		600.00	650
1997	Artemis 126C	5,000		1750.00	1750
1993	Aurora-Lady With Doves 884C	7,500		370.00	400
1997	Bacco & Arianna 419C	5,000		1500.00	1500
1992	Dawn 874C	10,000	1996	500.00	550-700
1995	Ebony 372C	5,000		550.00	600
1994	The Embrace 480C	3,000	1996	1450.00	1800-2300
1993	Freedom-Man And Horse 906C	3,000	1996	850.00	875-1000
1995	Gemini 427C	5,000		600.00	650
1997	Leo 149C	5,000		650.00	650
1993	Liberty-Girl On Horse 903C	5,000	1996	750.00	750-825
1993	Lilac & Roses-Girl w/Flowers 882C	7,500		410.00	440
1993	Lovers 191C	3,000	1996	450.00	550-750
1997	Pisces 171C	5,000		650.00	650
1994	Summertime-Lady on Swing 485C	5,000		650.00	775
1997	Taurus 170C	5,000		650.00	650
1992	Twilight 872C	10,000	1996	560.00	595-700
1992	Vanity 871C	10,000	1996	585.00	625-800
1995	Virgo 425C	5,000		600.00	650
1993	Wind Song-Girl With Sail 904C	5,000		520.00	575

Galleria Collection - G. Armani

Year Issue		Edition Limit	Year Retd.	Issue Price	*Quote U.S.$
1995	Eros 406T	1,500		750.00	775
1994	Grace 1029T	1,000		465.00	485
1994	Joy 1028T	1,000		465.00	485
1993	Leda & The Swan (USA) 1012T	1,000		550.00	600-700
1993	Leda & The Swan 1012T	1,500		550.00	600
1995	Pearl 1019T	1,000		550.00	600
1993	The Sea Wave (USA) 1006T	1,000	1995	500.00	595
1993	The Sea Wave 1006T	1,500	1996	500.00	500
1993	Spring Herald (USA) 1009T	1,000	1995	500.00	595
1993	Spring Herald 1009T	1,500		500.00	500
1993	Spring Water (USA) 1007T	1,000	1995	500.00	595
1993	Spring Water 1007T	1,500		500.00	500
1993	Zephyr (USA) 1010T	1,000	1995	500.00	595
1993	Zephyr 1010T	1,500		500.00	500

Golden Age - G. Armani

Year Issue		Edition Limit	Year Retd.	Issue Price	*Quote U.S.$
1995	Fragrance 340C	3,000		500.00	560
1997	Morning Ride 147C	5,000		770.00	770
1995	Promenade 339C	3,000		600.00	650
1995	Soiree 338C	3,000		600.00	630
1995	Spring Morning 337C	3,000		600.00	650

Gulliver's World - G. Armani

Year Issue		Edition Limit	Year Retd.	Issue Price	*Quote U.S.$
1994	The Barrel 659T	1,000		225.00	255
1994	Cowboy 657T	1,000	1996	125.00	125
1994	Getting Clean 661T	1,000		130.00	150
1994	Ray of Moon 658T	1,000		100.00	100
1994	Serenade 660T	1,000		200.00	235

Impressions - G. Armani

Year Issue		Edition Limit	Year Retd.	Issue Price	*Quote U.S.$
1990	Bittersweet 528C	Retrd.	1996	400.00	430
1990	Bittersweet 528P	Retrd.	1996	275.00	375
1990	Masquerade 527C	Retrd.	1996	400.00	430
1990	Masquerade 527P	Retrd.	1996	300.00	375-475
1990	Mystery 523C	Retrd.	1996	370.00	370

Masterworks - G. Armani

Year Issue		Edition Limit	Year Retd.	Issue Price	*Quote U.S.$
1995	Aurora 680C	1,500	1996	3500.00	3500

Moonlight Masquerade - G. Armani

Year Issue		Edition Limit	Year Retd.	Issue Price	*Quote U.S.$
1991	Lady Clown 742C	7,500	1994	390.00	415-485
1991	Lady Clown with Puppet 743C	7,500	1994	410.00	410-435
1991	Lady Harlequin 740C	7,500	1994	450.00	465
1991	Lady Pierrot 741C	7,500	1994	390.00	495
1991	Queen of Hearts 744C	7,500	1994	450.00	595

My Fair Ladies™ - G. Armani

Year Issue		Edition Limit	Year Retd.	Issue Price	*Quote U.S.$
1994	At Ease 634C	5,000		650.00	715
1990	Can-Can Dancer 589P	Retrd.	1991	460.00	465
1993	Elegance 195C	5,000		525.00	660
1993	Fascination 192C	5,000		500.00	600
1987	Flamenco Dancer 389C	5,000		400.00	600
1997	Garden Delight 157C	3,000		1000.00	1000
1995	Georgia 414C	5,000		550.00	625
1996	Grace 383C	5,000		475.00	515
1995	In Love 382C	5,000		450.00	500
1994	Isadora 633C	3,000		920.00	1050
1987	Lady with Book 384C	5,000		300.00	475
1987	Lady with Fan 387C	5,000		300.00	450
1988	Lady with Great Dane 429C	5,000	1996	385.00	650-750
1987	Lady with Mirror (Compact) 386C	5,000	1993	300.00	750-1000
1987	Lady with Muff 388C	5,000		250.00	375
1990	Lady with Parrot 616C	5,000	1995	460.00	1195-1395
1987	Lady with Peacock 385C	5,000	1992	380.00	2000-3200
1987	Lady with Peacock 385F	Retrd.	1996	230.00	290
1987	Lady with Peacock 385P	Retrd.	1996	300.00	400
1993	Lady with Umbrella-Nellie 196C	5,000		370.00	450
1995	Lara 415C	5,000		450.00	500

Year Issue		Edition Limit	Year Retd.	Issue Price	*Quote U.S.$
1993	Mahogany 194C	5,000	1995	500.00	900-1200
1993	Morning Rose 193C	5,000		450.00	515
1997	Swans Lake 158C	3,000		900.00	900
1989	Two Can-Can Dancers 516C	Retrd.	1993	880.00	1100-2000

Pearls Of The Orient - G. Armani

Year Issue		Edition Limit	Year Retd.	Issue Price	*Quote U.S.$
1990	Chu Chu San 612C	10,000	1994	550.00	550
1990	Lotus Blossom 613C	10,000	1994	475.00	475
1990	Madame Butterfly 610C	10,000	1994	500.00	550
1990	Turnadot 611C	10,000	1994	500.00	550

Premiere Ballerinas - G. Armani

Year Issue		Edition Limit	Year Retd.	Issue Price	*Quote U.S.$
1989	Ballerina 508C	10,000	1994	470.00	530
1989	Ballerina Group in Flight 518C	7,500	1994	780.00	1000-1200
1989	Ballerina with Drape 504C	10,000	1994	500.00	550
1991	Dancer with Peacock 727C	Retrd.	1993	460.00	530
1989	Flying Ballerina 503C	10,000	1994	440.00	500
1989	Kneeling Ballerina 517C	10,000	1994	340.00	400
1989	Two Ballerinas 515C	7,500	1994	670.00	775

Religious - G. Armani

Year Issue		Edition Limit	Year Retd.	Issue Price	*Quote U.S.$
1994	The Assumption 697C	5,000		650.00	725
1983	Choir Boys 900	5,000	1996	400.00	550
1994	Christ Child (Nativity) 1020C	1,000		175.00	195
1987	Crucifix 1158C	10,000	1990	155.00	750-900
1993	Crucifix 786C	7,500		285.00	315
1987	Crucifix 790C	15,000		160.00	250
1991	Crucifix Plaque 711C	15,000	1996	265.00	285
1995	The Crucifixion 780C	5,000		500.00	550
1994	Donkey (Nativity) 1027C	1,000		185.00	210
1995	The Holy Family 788C	5,000		1000.00	1100
1994	La Pieta 802C	5,000		950.00	1100
1994	Madonna (Nativity) 1022C	1,000		365.00	430
1994	Magi King Gold (Nativity) 1023C	1,000		600.00	650
1994	Magi King Incense (Nativity) 1024C	1,000		600.00	650
1994	Magi King Myrrh (Nativity) 1025C	1,000		450.00	500
1995	Moses 606C	2,500		365.00	400
1994	Ox (Nativity) 1026C	1,000		300.00	350
1994	Renaissance Crucifix 1017T	5,000		265.00	275
1994	St. Joseph (Nativity) 1021C	1,000		500.00	550

Siena Collection - G. Armani

Year Issue		Edition Limit	Year Retd.	Issue Price	*Quote U.S.$
1993	Back From The Fields 1002T	1,000	1995	400.00	450-550
1994	Country Boy w/Mushrooms 1014T	2,500		135.00	155
1993	Encountering 1003T	1,000	1995	350.00	400-550
1993	Fresh Fruit 1001T	2,500	1995	155.00	350-500
1993	The Happy Fiddler 1005T	1,000		225.00	225
1993	Mother's Hand 1008T	2,500		250.00	285
1993	Soft Kiss 1000T	2,500	1995	155.00	250-350
1993	Sound The Trumpet! 1004T	1,000	1995	225.00	300-400

Special Events - G. Armani

Year Issue		Edition Limit	Year Retd.	Issue Price	*Quote U.S.$
1994	Black Maternity 502C	3,000		535.00	650
1993	Carriage Wedding 902C	2,500		1000.00	1100
1991	Just Married 827C	5,000		1000.00	1100
1988	Maternity 405C	5,000		415.00	570
1994	Perfect Love 652C	3,000		1200.00	1250
1995	Tenderness 418C	5,000		950.00	1000
1995	Tomorrow's Dream 336C	5,000		700.00	730
1991	Wedding Couple At Threshold 813C	7,500		400.00	475
1991	Wedding Couple Kissing 815C	7,500		500.00	575
1991	Wedding Couple With Bicycle 814C	7,500		600.00	665
1994	Wedding Waltz (black) 501C	3,000		750.00	800
1994	Wedding Waltz (white) 493C	3,000		750.00	875

Special Releases - G. Armani

Year Issue		Edition Limit	Year Retd.	Issue Price	*Quote U.S.$
1989	Bust of Eve 590T	1,000	1991	250.00	550-950
1993	Doctor in Car 848C	2,000	1996	800.00	825
1992	Girl in Car 861C	3,000	1995	900.00	925
1992	Lady with Dove (Dove Dancer) 858E	1,000	1994	320.00	450
1992	Old Couple in Car (Two Hearts Remember) 862C	5,000		1000.00	1000

Valentine - G. Armani

Year Issue		Edition Limit	Year Retd.	Issue Price	*Quote U.S.$
1983	Hoopla 107E	Retrd.	1996	190.00	200

Vanity Fair - G. Armani

Year Issue		Edition Limit	Year Retd.	Issue Price	*Quote U.S.$
1992	Beauty at the Mirror 850P	Retrd.	1996	300.00	350
1992	Beauty w/Perfume 853P	Retrd.	1996	330.00	390

Via Veneto - G. Armani

Year Issue		Edition Limit	Year Retd.	Issue Price	*Quote U.S.$
1994	Alessandra 648C	5,000		355.00	400
1997	Black Orchid 444C	5,000		1100.00	1100
1994	Marina 649C	5,000		450.00	530
1994	Nicole 651C	5,000		500.00	600
1997	Summer Stroll 431C	5,000		650.00	650
1997	Tiger Lily 244C	5,000		1200.00	1200
1994	Valentina 647C	5,000		400.00	440
1997	Whitney 432C	5,000		750.00	750

Wildlife - G. Armani

Year Issue		Edition Limit	Year Retd.	Issue Price	*Quote U.S.$
1997	Alert (Irish Setters) 550S	975		900.00	900
1989	Bird of Paradise 454S	5,000		475.00	550
1991	Bird of Paradise 718S	5,000	1996	500.00	550
1997	Collie 304S	975		500.00	500
1995	Companions (Two Collies) 302S	3,000		900.00	950
1997	Dalmation 552S	975		600.00	600
1997	Early Days (Deer) 557S	975		1200.00	1200
1994	Elegance in Nature (Herons) 226S	3,000		1000.00	1200
1994	The Falconer 224S	3,000		1000.00	1200
1995	Feed Us! (Mother/Baby Owls) 305S	1,500		950.00	1000
1997	First Days (Mare & Foal) 564S	1,500		800.00	800
1991	Flamingo 713S	5,000		430.00	465
1991	Flying Duck 839S	3,000		470.00	530
1993	Galloping Horse 905S	7,500		465.00	500
1991	Great Argus Pheasant 717S	3,000	1996	625.00	650
1995	The Hunt (Falcon) 290S	3,000		850.00	880
1991	Large Owl 842S	5,000		520.00	570
1995	Lone Wolf 285S	3,000		550.00	575
1995	Midnight 284S	3,000		600.00	630
1997	Monarch (Stag) 555S	1,500		1200.00	1200
1997	Mother's Touch (Elephants) 579S	3,000		700.00	700
1997	Nature's Colors (Pheasant) 582S	1,500		1350.00	1350
1997	Nature's Dance (Herons) 576S	750		1750.00	1750
1995	Night Vigil (Owl) 306S	3,000		650.00	675
1995	Nocturne 976S	1,500		1000.00	1100
1989	Peacock 455S	5,000		620.00	700
1989	Peacock 458S	5,000		650.00	730
1997	Please Play (Cocker Spaniels) 312S	975		600.00	600
1997	Pointer 554S	975		700.00	700
1995	Proud Watch (Lion) 278S	1,500		700.00	750
1993	Rampant Horse 907S	7,500		550.00	585
1997	Royal Couple (Afghan Hounds) 310S	975		850.00	850
1994	Running Free (Greyhounds) 972S	3,000		850.00	930
1993	Running Horse 909S	7,500		515.00	550
1997	Shepherd (Dog) 307S	975		450.00	450
1995	Silent Watch (Mtn. Lion) 291S	1,500		700.00	750
1997	Sky Watch (Flying Eagle) 559S	3,000		1200.00	1200
1990	Soaring Eagle 970S	5,000	1996	620.00	725-800
1997	Standing Tall (Heron) 577S	1,500		800.00	800
1991	Swan 714S	5,000		550.00	600
1990	Three Doves 996S	5,000		690.00	750
1997	Trumpeting (Elephant) 578S	3,000		850.00	850
1995	Vantage Point (Eagle) 270S	3,000		600.00	650
1993	Vase with Doves 204S	3,000	1996	375.00	425
1993	Vase with Parrot 736S	3,000	1996	460.00	475
1993	Vase with Peacock 735S	3,000		450.00	500
1995	Wild Hearts (Horses) 282S	3,000		2000.00	2100
1995	Wisdom (Owl) 281S	3,000		1250.00	1300

Armstrong's

Armstrong's/Ron Lee - R. Skelton

Year Issue		Edition Limit	Year Retd.	Issue Price	*Quote U.S.$
1984	Captain Freddie	7,500	N/A	85.00	350-450
1984	Freddie the Torchbearer	7,500	N/A	110.00	375-450

Happy Art - W. Lantz

Year Issue		Edition Limit	Year Retd.	Issue Price	*Quote U.S.$
1982	Woody's Triple Self-Portrait	5,000	N/A	95.00	325

Pro Autographed Ceramic Baseball Card Plaque - Unknown

Year Issue		Edition Limit	Year Retd.	Issue Price	*Quote U.S.$
1985	Brett, Garvey, Jackson, Rose, Seaver, auto, 3-1/4X5	1,000	N/A	150.00	250

The Red Skelton Collection - R. Skelton

Year Issue		Edition Limit	Year Retd.	Issue Price	*Quote U.S.$
1981	Clem Kadiddlehopper	7,500	N/A	75.00	150
1981	Freddie in the Bathtub	7,500	N/A	80.00	100
1981	Freddie on the Green	7,500	N/A	80.00	150
1981	Freddie the Freeloader	7,500	N/A	70.00	150
1981	Jr., The Mean Widdle Kid	7,500	N/A	75.00	150
1981	San Fernando Red	7,500	N/A	75.00	150
1981	Sheriff Deadeye	7,500	N/A	75.00	150

The Red Skelton Porcelain Plaque - R. Skelton

Year Issue		Edition Limit	Year Retd.	Issue Price	*Quote U.S.$
1991	All American	1,500	N/A	495.00	1500
1994	Another Day	1,994	N/A	675.00	725-800
1992	Independance Day?	1,500	N/A	525.00	600-700
1993	Red & Freddie Both Turned 80	1,993	N/A	595.00	1200-1500

Artaffects

Members Only Limited Edition Redemption Offerings - G. Perillo

Year Issue		Edition Limit	Year Retd.	Issue Price	*Quote U.S.$
1983	Apache Brave (Bust)	Closed		50.00	150
1986	Painted Pony	Closed		125.00	175
1991	Chief Crazy Horse	Closed		195.00	250

Limited Edition Free Gifts to Members - G. Perillo

Year Issue		Edition Limit	Year Retd.	Issue Price	*Quote U.S.$
1986	Dolls	Closed		Gift	35
1991	Sunbeam	Closed		Gift	35
1992	Little Shadow	Closed		Gift	35

The Chieftains - G. Perillo

Year Issue		Edition Limit	Year Retd.	Issue Price	*Quote U.S.$
1983	Crazy Horse	5,000		65.00	200
1983	Geronimo	5,000		65.00	135
1983	Joseph	5,000		65.00	250
1983	Red Cloud	5,000		65.00	275
1983	Sitting Bull	5,000		65.00	200

Pride of America's Indians - G. Perillo

Year Issue		Edition Limit	Year Retd.	Issue Price	*Quote U.S.$
1988	Brave and Free	10-day		50.00	150
1989	Dark Eyed Friends	10-day		45.00	75
1989	Kindred Spirits	10-day		45.00	50
1989	Loyal Alliance	10-day		45.00	75
1989	Noble Companions	10-day		45.00	50
1989	Peaceful Comrades	10-day		45.00	50
1989	Small & Wise	10-day		45.00	50
1989	Winter Scouts	10-day		45.00	50

*Quotes have been rounded up to nearest dollar

Special Issue - G. Perillo

Year	Issue	Edition Limit	Year Retd.	Issue Price	*Quote U.S.$
1984	Apache Boy Bust	Closed	N/A	40.00	75
1984	Apache Girl Bust	Closed	N/A	40.00	75
1985	Lovers	Closed	N/A	70.00	125
1984	Papoose	325		500.00	500
1982	The Peaceable Kingdom	950		750.00	750

The Storybook Collection - G. Perillo

Year	Issue	Edition Limit	Year Retd.	Issue Price	*Quote U.S.$
1981	Cinderella	10,000		65.00	95
1982	Goldilocks & 3 Bears	10,000		80.00	110
1982	Hansel and Gretel	10,000		80.00	110
1980	Little Red Ridinghood	10,000		65.00	95

The Tribal Ponies - G. Perillo

Year	Issue	Edition Limit	Year Retd.	Issue Price	*Quote U.S.$
1984	Arapaho	1,500		65.00	175-200
1984	Comanche	1,500		65.00	175-200
1984	Crow	1,500		65.00	175-200

The War Pony - G. Perillo

Year	Issue	Edition Limit	Year Retd.	Issue Price	*Quote U.S.$
1983	Apache War Pony	495		150.00	175-200
1983	Nez Perce War Pony	495		150.00	175-200
1983	Sioux War Pony	495		150.00	175-200

Artists of the World

DeGrazia Annual Christmas Collection - T. DeGrazia

Year	Issue	Edition Limit	Year Retd.	Issue Price	*Quote U.S.$
1992	Feliz Navidad	1,992		195.00	225
1993	Fiesta Angels	1,993	1995	295.00	350-450
1994	Littlest Angel	1,994		165.00	165
1995	Bethlehem Bound	1,995		195.00	195
1996	Christmas Serenade	1,996		145.00	145

DeGrazia Figurine - T. DeGrazia

Year	Issue	Edition Limit	Year Retd.	Issue Price	*Quote U.S.$
1990	Alone	S/O	N/A	395.00	500-750
1988	Beautiful Burden	Closed	1990	175.00	250-300
1990	Biggest Drum	Closed	1992	110.00	130-150
1986	The Blue Boy	Suspd.		70.00	130
1990	Crucifixion	S/O	1995	295.00	400-500
1990	Desert Harvest	S/O	N/A	135.00	150-200
1986	Festival Lights	Suspd.		75.00	110-125
1984	Flower Boy	Closed	1992	65.00	200-300
1988	Flower Boy Plaque	Closed	1990	80.00	85-110
1984	Flower Girl	Suspd.		65.00	250
1984	Flower Girl Plaque	Closed	1985	45.00	85-110
1985	Little Madonna	Closed	1993	80.00	250-300
1988	Los Ninos	S/O	N/A	595.00	1200-1500
1989	Los Ninos (Artist's Edition)	S/O	N/A	695.00	2000-3500
1987	Love Me	Closed	1992	95.00	300-400
1988	Merrily, Merrily, Merrily	Closed	1991	95.00	240-295
1989	My First Arrow	Closed	1992	95.00	300-400
1984	My First Horse	Closed	1990	65.00	300-400
1990	Navajo Boy	Closed	1992	110.00	150-200
1992	Navajo Madonna	Closed	1993	135.00	200-300
1991	Navajo Mother	3,500	1995	295.00	350-400
1985	Pima Drummer Boy	Closed	1991	65.00	200-350
1984	Sunflower Boy	Closed	1985	65.00	250
1990	Sunflower Girl	Closed	1993	95.00	250
1987	Wee Three	Closed	1990	180.00	200-300
1984	White Dove	Closed	1992	45.00	150
1984	Wondering	Closed	1987	85.00	250-300

DeGrazia Nativity Collection - T. DeGrazia

Year	Issue	Edition Limit	Year Retd.	Issue Price	*Quote U.S.$
1988	Christmas Prayer Angel (red)	Closed	1991	70.00	100-250
1990	El Burrito	Closed	N/A	60.00	90-125
1990	Little Prayer Angel (white)	Closed	1992	85.00	300-400
1989	Two Little Lambs	Closed	1992	70.00	220-295

DeGrazia Pendants - R. Olszewski

Year	Issue	Edition Limit	Year Retd.	Issue Price	*Quote U.S.$
1987	Festival of Lights 562-P	Suspd.		90.00	275
1985	Flower Girl Pendant 561-P	Suspd.		125.00	200-300

DeGrazia Village Collection - T. DeGrazia

Year	Issue	Edition Limit	Year Retd.	Issue Price	*Quote U.S.$
1992	The Listener	Closed	1992	48.00	75
1992	Little Feather	Closed	1995	53.00	100-175
1992	Medicine Man	Closed	1995	75.00	100-150
1992	Standing Tall	Closed	1996	65.00	95-150
1992	Telling Tales	Closed	1992	48.00	75
1992	Tiny Treasure	Closed	1995	53.00	100-200
1993	Water Wagon	Closed	1995	295.00	295

DeGrazia: Goebel Miniatures - R. Olszewski

Year	Issue	Edition Limit	Year Retd.	Issue Price	*Quote U.S.$
1988	Adobe Display 948D	Suspd.		45.00	65-90
1990	Adobe Hacienda (lg.) Display 958-D	Suspd.		85.00	95-150
1989	Beautiful Burden 554-P	Suspd.		110.00	125-150
1990	Chapel Display 971-D	Suspd.		95.00	125
1986	Festival of Lights 507-P	Suspd.		85.00	145-200
1985	Flower Boy 502-P	Suspd.		85.00	145-200
1985	Flower Girl 501-P	Suspd.		85.00	145-200
1986	Little Madonna 552-P	Suspd.		93.00	225
1989	Merry Little Indian 508-P (new style)	Suspd.		110.00	150-175
1987	Merry Little Indian 508-P (old style)	Closed		95.00	250-300
1991	My Beautiful Rocking Horse 555-P	Suspd.		110.00	175-200
1985	My First Horse 503-P	Suspd.		85.00	150-165
1986	Pima Drummer Boy 506-P	Suspd.		85.00	250-300
1985	Sunflower Boy 551- P	Suspd.		93.00	150
1985	White Dove 504-P	Suspd.		80.00	125
1985	Wondering 505-P	Suspd.		93.00	150-175

Band Creations, Inc.

Best Friends-Angel Pins - Richards/Penfield

Year	Issue	Edition Limit	Year Retd.	Issue Price	*Quote U.S.$
1996	Angel on Your Shoulder	Open		5.00	5
1996	Aunt	Open		5.00	5
1996	Childcare Angel	Open		5.00	5
1995	Daughter	Open		5.00	5
1996	Daughter-in-law	Open		5.00	5
1995	Friend	Open		5.00	5
1995	Grandmother	Open		5.00	5
1996	Mom-to-Be	Open		5.00	5
1995	Mother	Open		5.00	5
1995	Nurse	Open		5.00	5
1996	Secret Pal	Open		5.00	5
1995	Sister	Open		5.00	5
1996	Sweetheart	Open		5.00	5
1995	Teacher	Open		5.00	5
1995	Teammate	Open		5.00	5
1996	Volunteer	Open		5.00	5

Best Friends-Angel Wishes - Richards/Penfield

Year	Issue	Edition Limit	Year Retd.	Issue Price	*Quote U.S.$
1994	Anniversary	Open		12.00	12
1994	Best Wishes	Open		12.00	12
1994	Bride and Groom	Open		12.00	12
1994	Congratulations	Open		12.00	12
1994	Create A Wish	Open		12.00	12
1994	Get Well	Open		12.00	12
1994	Good Luck	Open		12.00	12
1994	Happy Birthday	Open		12.00	12
1994	Inspirational	Open		12.00	12
1994	New Baby	Open		12.00	12

Best Friends-Angels Of The Month - Richards/Penfield

Year	Issue	Edition Limit	Year Retd.	Issue Price	*Quote U.S.$
1993	January	Open		10.00	10
1993	February	Open		10.00	10
1993	March	Open		10.00	10
1993	April	Open		10.00	10
1993	May	Open		10.00	10
1993	June	Open		10.00	10
1993	July	Open		10.00	10
1993	August	Open		10.00	10
1993	September	Open		10.00	10
1993	October	Open		10.00	10
1993	November	Open		10.00	10
1993	December	Open		10.00	10

Best Friends-Celebrate Around the World Santas - Richards/Penfield

Year	Issue	Edition Limit	Year Retd.	Issue Price	*Quote U.S.$
1996	England	Open		12.00	12
1996	Germany	Open		12.00	12
1996	Mexico	Open		12.00	12
1996	Norway	Open		12.00	12
1996	Russia	Open		12.00	12
1996	United States (African American)	Open		12.00	12
1996	United States (white)	Open		12.00	12

Best Friends-Celebrate Around the World Trees - Richards/Penfield

Year	Issue	Edition Limit	Year Retd.	Issue Price	*Quote U.S.$
1996	Around the World Tree	Open		18.00	18
1996	British Tree	Open		19.50	20
1996	Germany Tree	Open		19.50	20
1996	Scandinavian Tree	Open		19.50	20
1996	United States Tree	Open		19.50	20

Best Friends-Christmas Pageant - Richards/Penfield

Year	Issue	Edition Limit	Year Retd.	Issue Price	*Quote U.S.$
1996	Angel-peace/joy	Open		6.00	6
1996	Bench	Open		4.00	4
1996	Boy with Star	Open		6.00	6
1996	Donkey	Open		4.00	4
1996	Girl with Tree	Open		6.00	6
1996	Joseph	Open		6.00	6
1996	Mary and Baby Jesus	Open		6.00	6
1996	Sheep	Open		4.00	4
1996	Sign	Open		4.00	4
1996	Stage	Open		14.00	14
1996	Christmas Pageant 10 pc set	Open		60.00	60

Best Friends-Coffee-Tea & Me - Richards/Penfield

Year	Issue	Edition Limit	Year Retd.	Issue Price	*Quote U.S.$
1997	Madame Sassafras	Open		19.95	20
1997	Mr. Earl Grey	Open		19.95	20
1997	Ms. Cinnamon Spice	Open		19.95	20
1997	Ms. Lemon Tart	Open		19.95	20
1997	Ms. Passion Flower	Open		19.95	20
1997	Ms. Wild Blueberry	Open		19.95	20

Best Friends-Earth Angels - Richards/Penfield

Year	Issue	Edition Limit	Year Retd.	Issue Price	*Quote U.S.$
1996	Angel Potsitter Bird Nest	Open		10.00	10
1996	Angel Potsitter Front	Open		8.00	8
1996	Angel Potsitter Left	Open		9.00	9
1996	Angel with Aster	Open		10.00	10
1996	Angel with Calendula	Open		10.00	10
1996	Angel with Carnation	Open		10.00	10
1996	Angel with Chrysanthemum	Open		10.00	10
1996	Angel with Gladiolus	Open		10.00	10
1996	Angel with Jonquil	Open		10.00	10
1996	Angel with Larkspur	Open		10.00	10
1996	Angel with Lily of the Valley	Open		10.00	10
1996	Angel with Narcissus	Open		10.00	10
1996	Angel with Rose	Open		10.00	10
1996	Angel with Sweet Pea	Open		10.00	10
1996	Angel with Violet	Open		10.00	10

Best Friends-First Friends Begin At Childhood - Richards/Penfield

Year	Issue	Edition Limit	Year Retd.	Issue Price	*Quote U.S.$
1993	Castles In The Sand (4 pc set)	Retrd.	1996	16.00	16
1993	Checking It Twice (2 pc set)	Retrd.	1996	15.00	15
1993	Dad's Best Pal	Retrd.	1996	15.00	15
1993	Feathered Friends	Retrd.	1996	13.00	13
1993	Fishing Friends	Retrd.	1996	18.00	18
1993	Grandma's Favorite	Retrd.	1996	15.00	15
1993	My "Beary" Best Friend	Retrd.	1996	12.00	12
1993	My Best Friend (2 pc set)	Retrd.	1996	24.00	24
1993	Oh So Pretty	Retrd.	1996	14.00	14
1993	Purr-Fit Friends	Retrd.	1996	12.00	12
1993	Quiet Time	Retrd.	1996	15.00	15
1993	Rainbow Of Friends	Retrd.	1996	24.00	24
1993	Santa's First Visit	Retrd.	1996	15.00	15
1993	Santa's Surprise	Retrd.	1996	14.00	14
1993	Sharing Is Caring	Retrd.	1996	12.00	12
1993	A Wagon Full Of Fun (2 pc set)	Retrd.	1996	15.00	15

Best Friends-Happy Hearts - Richards/Penfield

Year	Issue	Edition Limit	Year Retd.	Issue Price	*Quote U.S.$
1996	Angels in the Snow	Open		35.00	35
1996	Best Friends	Open		35.00	35
1996	A Guiding Star	Open		35.00	35
1996	Just Married	Open		35.00	35
1996	Making New Friends	Open		35.00	35
1996	Thanksgiving Friends	Open		35.00	35

Best Friends-Heavenly Helpers - Richards/Penfield

Year	Issue	Edition Limit	Year Retd.	Issue Price	*Quote U.S.$
1996	Childcare	Open		12.00	12
1996	Emergency Medical Team	Open		12.00	12
1996	Fireman	Open		12.00	12
1996	Nurse	Open		12.00	12
1996	Policeman	Open		12.00	12
1996	Teacher	Open		12.00	12
1996	Volunteer	Open		12.00	12

Best Friends-My Animal Friends & Me - Richards/Penfield

Year	Issue	Edition Limit	Year Retd.	Issue Price	*Quote U.S.$
1997	Bunny Pin	Open		5.00	5
1997	Cat Pin	Open		5.00	5
1997	Cow Pin	Open		5.00	5
1997	Elephant Pin	Open		5.00	5
1997	Frog Pin	Open		5.00	5
1997	Giraffe Pin	Open		5.00	5
1997	Lion Pin	Open		5.00	5
1997	Moose Pin	Open		5.00	5
1997	Mouse Pin	Open		5.00	5
1997	Raccoon Pin	Open		5.00	5
1997	Teddy Bear Pin	Open		5.00	5
1997	Zebra Pin	Open		5.00	5

Best Friends-Noah's Ark - Richards/Penfield

Year	Issue	Edition Limit	Year Retd.	Issue Price	*Quote U.S.$
1995	Animals (set of 10)	Open		20.00	20
1995	Noah's Ark & Raft	Open		42.00	42
1996	Noah's Ark Pin	Open		4.95	5

Best Friends-O Joyful Night Nativity - Richards/Penfield

Year	Issue	Edition Limit	Year Retd.	Issue Price	*Quote U.S.$
1994	3 Kings (set/3)	Open		18.00	18
1994	Angel on Stable (wall)	Open		16.00	16
1996	Camel	Open		6.00	6
1994	Camel and Donkey (set/2)	Retrd.	1996	8.00	8
1995	Camel Standing	Open		6.00	6
1996	Cow	Open		4.00	4
1996	Donkey	Open		4.00	4
1994	Holy Family (Joseph, Mary & Jesus)	Open		16.00	16
1994	Shepherd Boy	Retrd.	1996	8.00	8
1995	Shepherd with Sheep (set/7)	Open		8.00	8

Best Friends-Plant Friends - Richards/Penfield

Year	Issue	Edition Limit	Year Retd.	Issue Price	*Quote U.S.$
1997	Angel	Open		4.00	4
1997	Bee	Open		4.00	4
1997	Christmas	Open		4.00	4
1997	Frog	Open		4.00	4
1997	House	Open		4.00	4
1997	Mr. Santa	Open		4.00	4
1997	Mrs. Santa	Open		4.00	4
1997	Nest	Open		4.00	4
1997	Reindeer	Open		4.00	4
1997	Snowman	Open		4.00	4
1997	Teddy Bear	Open		4.00	4

Best Friends-Rainbow of Friends - Richards/Penfield

Year	Issue	Edition Limit	Year Retd.	Issue Price	*Quote U.S.$
1996	Rainbow of Friends	Open		24.00	24
1996	Rainbow of Friends, music box	Open		17.50	18

Best Friends-RiverSong - Richards/Penfield

Year	Issue	Edition Limit	Year Retd.	Issue Price	*Quote U.S.$
1994	3 Assorted Carolers	Open		22.00	22
1995	Brick House	Open		19.95	20
1993	Carolers Set (3 carolers, 1 lamp post, 1 dog)	Open		30.00	30
1995	Church	Open		19.95	20
1995	Double Angels	Open		8.00	8
1995	Gingerbread House	Open		19.95	20
1995	Skaters Sitting (set/2)	Open		12.00	12
1995	Skaters Standing (set/2)	Open		12.00	12
1995	Snowball Fight (set/3)	Open		15.00	15
1995	Snowmen (set/3)	Open		12.95	13
1995	Stucco House	Open		19.95	20
1995	Wood House	Open		19.95	20

52

Collectors' Information Bureau

*Quotes have been rounded up to nearest dollar

Best Friends-Winter Wonderland - Richards/Penfield

YEAR ISSUE		EDITION LIMIT	YEAR RETD.	ISSUE PRICE	*QUOTE U.S.$
1994	3 Assorted White Trees	Open		18.00	18
1994	Accessories; rabbits, teddies, presents (set/3)	Open		4.00	4
1994	Mr. Santa	Open		9.00	9
1994	Mrs. Santa	Open		9.00	9
1994	Reindeer (1 standing, 1 sitting) (set/2)	Open		10.00	10

Claws & Paws - Richards/Penfield

YEAR ISSUE		EDITION LIMIT	YEAR RETD.	ISSUE PRICE	*QUOTE U.S.$
1997	Basset Hound, 2"	Open		6.00	6
1997	Black Lab, 2"	Open		6.00	6
1997	Cat, 2"	Open		6.00	6
1997	Cocker Spaniel, 2"	Open		6.00	6
1997	Collie, 2"	Open		6.00	6
1997	Dachshund, 2"	Open		6.00	6
1997	Dalmation, 2"	Open		6.00	6
1997	German Shepherd, 2"	Open		6.00	6
1997	Golden Retriever, 2"	Open		6.00	6
1997	Himalayan, 2"	Open		6.00	6
1997	Jack Russ Terrier, 2"	Open		6.00	6
1997	Rottweiler, 2"	Open		6.00	6
1997	Siamese, 2"	Open		6.00	6
1997	Yellow Lab, 2"	Open		6.00	6
1997	Yorshire Terrier, 2"	Open		6.00	6

Country Time Clocks - Band Creations

YEAR ISSUE		EDITION LIMIT	YEAR RETD.	ISSUE PRICE	*QUOTE U.S.$
1996	Cow	Open		23.95	24
1996	Hen	Open		23.95	24
1996	Home Sweet Home	Open		29.50	30
1996	Pig	Open		23.95	24
1996	Water Can	Open		23.95	24

Bing & Grondahl

Centennial Anniversary Commemoratives - F.A. Hallin

YEAR ISSUE		EDITION LIMIT	YEAR RETD.	ISSUE PRICE	*QUOTE U.S.$
1995	Centennial Vase: Behind the Frozen Window	1,250	1995	295.00	295

Boyds Collection Ltd.

The Bearstone Collection™ - G.M. Lowenthal

YEAR ISSUE		EDITION LIMIT	YEAR RETD.	ISSUE PRICE	*QUOTE U.S.$
1994	Agatha & Shelly-'Scardy Cat' 2246	Open		16.25	17-65
1995	Amelia's Enterprise 'Carrot Juice' 2258	Open		16.25	17-50
1995	Angelica...'the Guardian' 2266	Open		17.95	18-45
1995	Angelica...the Guardian Angel Water Globe 2702	Open		37.50	38-50
1993	Arthur...with Red Scarf 2003-03	Retrd.	1994	10.50	65-110
1994	Bailey & Emily...'Forever Friends' 2018	Retrd.	1996	34.00	75-90
1994	Bailey & Wixie 'To Have and To Hold' 2017	Open		15.75	16-200
1994	Bailey at the Beach 2020-09	Retrd.	1995	15.75	110-125
1993	Bailey Bear with Suitcase (old version) 2000	Retrd.	1993	14.20	300-360
1993	Bailey Bear with Suitcase (revised version) 2000	Open		14.20	15-90
1994	Bailey's Birthday 2014	Open		15.95	16-100
1995	Bailey...'The Baker with Sweetie Pie' 2254	Open		12.50	13-65
1995	Bailey...'The Baker with Sweetie Pie' 2254CL	3,600	1995	15.00	150-225
1995	Bailey...'the Cheerleader' 2268	Open		15.95	16-40
1995	Bailey...'The Honeybear' 2260	Open		15.75	16-70
1996	Bailey...Heart's Desire 2272	Open		15.00	15-60
1993	Bailey...in the Orchard 2006	Retrd.	1996	14.20	15-175
1995	Baldwin...as the Child 2403	Open		14.95	15-30
1994	Bessie the Santa Cow 2239	Retrd.	1996	15.75	50-60
1993	Byron & Chedda w/Catmint 2010	Retrd.	1994	14.20	85-125
1994	Celeste...'The Angel Rabbit' 2230	Open		16.25	17-275
1994	Charlotte & Bebe...'The Gardeners' 2229	Retrd.	1995	15.75	50-65
1993	Christian by the Sea 2012	Open		14.20	15-82
1994	Christmas Big Pig, Little Pig BC2256	Retrd.	N/A	N/A	70-100
1994	Clara...'The Nurse' 2231	Open		16.25	17-225
1994	Clarence Angel Bear (rust) 2029-11	Retrd.	1995	12.60	60-82
1995	Cookie Catberg...'Knittin' Kitten' 2250	12/97		18.75	19-55
1994	Cookie the Santa Cat 2237	Retrd.	1995	15.25	45-55
1995	Daphne and Eloise...'Women's Work' 2251	Open		18.00	18-50
1993	Daphne Hare & Maisey Ewe 2011	Retrd.	1995	14.20	85-125
1994	Daphne...The Reader Hare 2226	Open		14.20	15-100
1994	Edmond & Bailey...'Gathering Holly' 2240	Open		24.25	25-160
1994	Elgin the Elf Bear 2236	Open		14.20	15-60
1994	Elliot & Snowbeary 2242	Open		15.25	15-75
1994	Elliot & The Tree 2241	Open		16.25	17-150
1995	Elliot & the Tree Water Globe 2704	Open		35.00	35-60
1996	Elliot...the Hero 2280	Open		16.75	17-45
1996	Emma & Bailey...Afternoon Tea 2277	Open		18.00	18-40
1995	Emma...'the Witchy Bear' 2269	Open		16.75	17-55
1996	Ewell/Walton Manitoba Moosemen BC2228	12,000		24.99	25-60
1993	Father Chrisbear and Son 2008	Retrd.	1993	15.00	225-325
1994	Grenville & Beatrice...'Best Friends' 2016	Open		26.25	27-175
1996	Grenville & Beatrice...True Love 2274	Open		36.00	36-70
1995	Grenville & Knute...Football Buddies 2255	Open		19.95	20-50
1993	Grenville & Neville...'The Sign' (prototype) 2099	Retrd.	1993	15.75	60-100
1993	Grenville & Neville...'The Sign' 2099	Open		15.75	16-60
1994	Grenville the Santabear 2030	Retrd.	1996	14.20	300-450
1994	Grenville the Santabear Musical Waterball 2700	Retrd.	1996	35.75	36-50
1996	Grenville with Matthew & Bailey...Sunday Afternoon 2281	Open		34.50	35-60
1994	Grenville...'The Graduate' 2233	Retrd.	1996	16.25	65-85
1995	Grenville...'The Storyteller' 2265	Retrd.	1995	50.00	70-125
1993	Grenville...with Green Scarf 2003-04	Retrd.	1994	10.50	250-500
1993	Grenville...with Red Scarf 2003-08	Retrd.	1995	10.50	75-110
1994	Homer on the Plate 2225	Open		15.75	16-80
1994	Homer on the Plate BC2210	Open		24.99	25-75
1995	Hop-a-Long...'The Deputy' 2247	Open		14.00	14-50
1994	Juliette Angel Bear (ivory) 2029-10	Retrd.	1995	12.60	50-90
1994	Justina & M. Harrison...'Sweetie Pie' 2015	Open		26.25	27-80
1996	Justina...The Message "Bearer" 2273	Open		16.00	16-45
1994	Knute & The Gridiron 2245	Open		16.25	17-65
1994	Kringle & Bailey with List 2235	Open		14.20	15-60
1996	Kringle And Company 2283	Open		17.45	18-45
1995	Lefty...'On the Mound' 2253	Open		15.00	15-65
1995	Lefty...'On the Mound' BC2056	Open		24.99	25-65
1994	Lucy Big Pig, Little Pig BC2250	Retrd.	1996	24.99	80-95
1996	M. Harrison's Birthday 2275	Open		17.00	35-45
1994	Manheim the 'Eco-Moose' 2243	Open		15.25	16-60
1994	Maynard the Santa Moose 2238	Open		15.25	16-55
1995	Miss Bruin & Bailey 'The Lesson' 2259	Open		18.45	19-100
1996	Momma Mcbear...Anticipation 2282	Open		14.95	15-38
1993	Moriarty-'The Bear in the Cat Suit' 2005	Retrd.	1995	13.75	50-110
1996	Ms. Griz...Monday Morning 2276	Open		34.00	34-110
1996	Ms. Griz...Saturday Night GCC 2284	Open		15.00	15-52
1995	Neville...as Joseph 2401	Open		14.95	15-30
1993	Neville...The 'Bedtime Bear' 2002	Retrd.	1996	14.20	70-98
1996	Noah & Co...Art Builders 2278	Retrd.	1996	61.00	80-130
1996	Noah & Company (waterglobe) 2706	6,000	1996	50.95	125-175
1995	Otis...'Taxtime' 2262	Open		18.75	19-55
1995	Otis...'The Fisherman' 2249-06	Open		15.75	16-50
1994	Sebastian's Prayer 2227	Retrd.	1996	16.25	45-80
1994	Sherlock & Watson-In Disguise 2019	Retrd.	1996	15.75	85-125
1995	Simone & Bailey...'Helping Hands' 2267	Open		[illegible]	[illegible]
1996	Simone and Bailey...Helping Hands 2705	Open		34.80	35-60
1993	Simone De Bearvoire and Her Mom 2001	Retrd.	1996	14.20	100-250
1996	Sir Edmund... Persistence 2279	Open		20.75	21-40
1995	The Stage...the School Pagent 2425	Open		34.95	35-85
1994	Ted & Teddy 2223	12/97		15.75	16-100
1995	Theresa...as Mary 2402	Open		14.95	15-50
1995	Union Jack...'Love Letters' 2263	Open		18.95	19-55
1993	Victoria...'The Lady' 2004	Open		18.40	19-175
1994	Wilson at the Beach 2020-06	12/97		15.75	16-115
1994	Wilson the "Perfesser" 2222	12/97		16.25	17-90
1993	Wilson with Love Sonnets 2007	12/97		12.60	13-400
1995	Wilson...'the Wonderful Wizard of Wuz' 2261	Open		15.95	16-70
1994	Xmas Bear Elf with List BC2051	1,865	1994	24.99	400-550

The Dollstone Collection™ - G.M. Lowenthal

YEAR ISSUE		EDITION LIMIT	YEAR RETD.	ISSUE PRICE	*QUOTE U.S.$
1996	Betsey and Edmund with Union Jack BC35031	Open		24.99	25-60
1995	Betsey & Edmund 3503PE	Retrd.	1995	19.50	45-75
1995	Katherine, Amanda & Edmund 3505PE	Retrd.	1995	19.50	40-75
1995	Meagan 3504PE	Retrd.	1995	19.50	100
1995	Victoria with Samantha 3502PE	Retrd.	1995	19.50	45-75
1995	Set of 4 PE	Retrd.	1995	78.00	300-600
1997	The Amazing Bailey 3518	Yr.Iss.		60.00	60-85
1996	Anne...the Masterpiece 3599	Open		24.25	25-45
1996	Ashley with Chrissie...Dress Up 3506	Open		20.50	21-50
1996	Betsey with Edmond...The Patriots 3503	Open		20.00	20-50
1996	Candice with Matthew...Gathering Apples 3514	Open		18.95	19-45
1996	Christy w/Nicole...Mother's Presence GCC 3516	Open		26.00	26-63
1996	Courtney with Phoebe...over the River and Thru the Woods 3512	Open		24.25	25-55
1996	Emily with Kathleen & Otis...The Future 3508	Open		30.00	30-55
1996	Jean with Elliot & Debbie...The Bakers 3510	Open		19.50	20-50
1996	Jennifer with Priscilla...The Doll in the Attic 3500	Open		20.50	21-55
1996	Karen & Wilson..Skater's Waltz GCC 3515	Open		26.00	26-45
1996	Katherine with Amanda & Edmond...Kind Hearts 3505	Open		20.00	20-55
1996	Mallory w/Patsy & J.B....Trick or Treat 3517	Retrd.	1996	27.00	100-110
1996	Megan with Elliot & Annie...Christmas Carol 3504	Open		19.50	20-45
1996	Megan with Elliot...Christmas Carol (waterglobe) 2720	Open		39.45	40
1996	Michelle with Daisy...Reading is Fun 3511	Open		17.95	18
1996	Patricia with Molly...Attic Treasures 3501	Open		14.00	14-45
1996	Rebecca with Elliot...Birthday 3509	Open		20.50	21-50
1996	Sara & Heather with Elliot & Amelia...Tea for Four 3507	Retrd.	1996	46.00	55-95
1996	Victoria with Samantha...Victorian Ladies 3502	Open		20.00	20-75

The Folkstone Collection™ - G.M. Lowenthal

YEAR ISSUE		EDITION LIMIT	YEAR RETD.	ISSUE PRICE	*QUOTE U.S.$
1995	Abigail...Peaceable Kingdom 2829	Open		18.95	19-30
1996	Alvin T. Mac Barker...Dogface 2872	12/97		19.00	19-30
1994	Angel of Freedom 2820	Retrd.	1996	16.75	40-60
1994	Angel of Love 2821	Retrd.	1996	16.75	45-60
1994	Angel of Peace 2822	Retrd.	1996	16.75	50-60
1996	Athena...The Wedding Angel 28202	Open		19.00	19-30
1994	Beatrice-Birthday Angel 2825	Open		20.00	20-30
1995	Beatrice...the Giftgiver 2836	Open		17.95	18-25
1996	Bernie... I Got Wat I wanted St. Bernard Santa 2873	Open		17.75	18-25
1996	Betty Cocker 2870	Open		19.00	19-30
1995	Boowinkle Vonhindenmoose...2831	Open		17.95	18-35
1996	Buster Goes A' Courtin' 2844	Open		19.00	19-30
1994	Chilly & Son with Dove 2811	Open		17.75	18-40
1996	Cosmos...The Gardening Angel 28201	Open		19.00	19-25
1994	December 26th 3003	12/97		32.00	32
1996	Egon...the Skier 2837	Open		17.75	18-25
1994	Elmer-Cow on Haystacks 2851	Open		19.00	19-30
1996	Elmo "Tex" Beefcake...On the Range 2853	12/97		19.00	19-30
1995	Ernest Hemmingmoose...the Hunter 2835	Open		17.95	18-35
1995	Esmeralda...the Wonderful Witch 2860	Open		17.95	18-35
1996	Fixit...Santa's Faerie 3600	Open		17.45	18-25
1996	Flora & Amelia...The Gardeners 2843	Open		19.00	19-30
1996	Flora, Amelia & Eloise...The Tea Party 2846	Open		19.00	19-35
1994	Florence-Kitchen Angel 2824	Retrd.	1996	20.00	25
1996	G.M.'s Choice, Etheral...Angel of Light 28203-06	7,200	1996	18.25	85-110
1995	Icabod Mooselman...the Pilgrim 2833	Open		17.95	18-30
1994	Ida & Bessie-The Gardeners 2852	Open		19.00	19-25
1996	Illumina...Angel of Light 28203	Open		18.45	19-35
1996	Jean Claude & Jacque...the Skiers (waterglobe) 2710	Open		37.50	38-45
1995	Jean Claude & Jacques...the Skiers 2815	Open		16.95	17-35
1994	Jill-Language of Love 2842	12/97		19.00	19-40
1994	Jingle Moose 2830	Retrd.	1996	17.75	30-60
1994	Jingles & Son with Wreath 2812	Retrd.	1996	17.75	30-60
1994	Lizzie Shopping Angel 2827	Open		20.00	20-25
1996	Loretta Moostein..."Yer Cheatin' Heart" 2854	Open		19.00	19-35
1994	Minerva-Baseball Angel 2826	12/97		20.00	20-28
1994	Myrtle-Believe 2840	Open		20.00	20-28
1995	Na-Nick of the North 2804	Open		17.95	18-30
1996	Nanick & Siegfried the Plan 2807	10,000	1996	32.50	70-95
1996	Nanny...the Snowmom 2817	Open		17.95	18-25
1994	Nicholai with Tree 2800	Open		17.75	18-50
1994	Nicholas with Book 2802	Retrd.	1996	17.75	18-30
1994	Nick on Ice (1st ed. GCC) 3001	3,600	1995	49.95	65
1994	Nick on Ice 3001	12/97		32.95	33
1996	Nick, Siegfried 2807	Yr.Iss.	1996	35.00	70
1996	Nicknoak...Santa with Ark 2806	Open		17.95	18-30
1994	Nikki with Candle 2801	Open		17.75	18-35
1996	No-No Nick...Bad Boy Santa 2805	Open		17.95	18-25
1995	Northbound Wille 2814	Open		16.95	17-35
1994	Oceana-Ocean Angel 2823	Open		16.75	17-70
1994	Peter-The Whopper 2841	12/97		19.00	19-30
1995	Prudence Mooselmaid...the Pilgrim 2834	Open		17.95	18-30
1996	Robin...the Snowbird Lover 2816	Open		17.95	18-25
1994	Rufus-Hoedown 2850	Open		19.00	19-25
1994	Santa's Challenge (1st ed. GCC) 3002	3,600	1995	49.95	65-80
1994	Santa's Challenge 3002	12/97		32.95	33
1994	Santa's Flight Plan (1st ed. GCC) 3000	3,600	1995	49.95	65
1995	Santa's Flight Plan (waterglobe) 2703	Retrd.	1996	37.00	37
1994	Santa's Flight Plan 3000	12/97		32.95	33
1996	Santa's Hobby 3004	12/97		36.00	36
1995	Seraphina with Jacob & Rachael...the Choir Angels 2828	Open		19.95	20-30
1996	Serenity...the Mother's Angel 28204	Open		18.25	19-33
1995	Siegfried and Egon...the Sign 2899	Open		18.95	19-35
1995	Sliknick the Chimney Sweep 2803	Open		17.95	18-45
1996	Sparky McPlug 2871	Open		19.00	19-30
1996	Too Loose Lapin...The Arteest 2845	Open		19.00	19-30
1994	Windy with Book 2810	Retrd.	1996	17.75	30-75

Byers' Choice Ltd.

Accessories - J. Byers

YEAR ISSUE		EDITION LIMIT	YEAR RETD.	ISSUE PRICE	*QUOTE U.S.$
1995	Cat in Hat	Closed	1995	10.00	10
1997	Cat with Milk	Open		18.50	19
1996	Dog with Hat	Closed	1996	18.50	19
1997	Dog with Lollipop	Open		18.50	19
1995	Dog with Sausages	Closed	1995	18.00	20-30

*Quotes have been rounded up to nearest dollar

Byers' Choice Ltd.
to Byers' Choice Ltd.

FIGURINES

Carolers - J. Byers

YEAR ISSUE		EDITION LIMIT	YEAR RETD.	ISSUE PRICE	*QUOTE U.S.$
1988	Children with Skates	Open		40.00	49
1988	Singing Cats	Open		13.50	16
1986	Singing Dogs	Open		13.00	16
1996	Teenagers (Traditional)	Open		46.00	46
1996	Teenagers (Victorian)	Open		49.00	49
1976	Traditional Adult (1976-80)	Closed	1980	N/A	475
1981	Traditional Adult (1981-current)	Open		45.00	45-300
XX	Traditional Adult (undated)	Closed	N/A	N/A	400-700
1978	Traditional Colonial Lady (w/ hands)	Closed	1978	N/A	1500
1986	Traditional Grandparents	Open		35.00	45
1982	Victorian Adult (1st ed.)	Closed	1982	32.00	400
1982	Victorian Adult (2nd ed./dressed alike)	Closed	1983	46.00	300-400
1983	Victorian Adult (assorted) (2nd ed.)	Open		35.00	48
1997	Victorian Adult Shoppers	Open		61.00	61
1982	Victorian Child (1st ed. w/floppy hats)	Closed	1982	32.00	300-375
1983	Victorian Child (2nd ed./sailor suit)	Closed	1983	33.00	300-400
1983	Victorian Child (assorted) (2nd. ed.)	Open		33.00	48
1988	Victorian Grand Parent	Open		40.00	48

Children of The World - J. Byers

YEAR ISSUE		EDITION LIMIT	YEAR RETD.	ISSUE PRICE	*QUOTE U.S.$
1993	Bavarian Boy	Closed	1993	50.00	150-250
1992	Dutch Boy	Closed	1992	50.00	250-350
1992	Dutch Girl	Closed	1992	50.00	250-350
1994	Irish Girl	Closed	1994	50.00	160-250
1997	Mexican Children	Open		50.00	50
1996	Saint Lucia	Open		52.00	52

Cries Of London - J. Byers

YEAR ISSUE		EDITION LIMIT	YEAR RETD.	ISSUE PRICE	*QUOTE U.S.$
1991	Apple Lady (red stockings)	Closed	1991	80.00	900-1100
1991	Apple Lady (red/wh stockings)	Closed	1991	80.00	895-1200
1992	Baker	Closed	1992	62.00	150-250
1993	Chestnut Roaster	Closed	1993	64.00	200-350
1996	Children Buying Gingerbread	Closed	1996	46.00	46
1995	Dollmaker	Closed	1995	64.00	64-70
1994	Flower Vendor	Closed	1994	64.00	100-200
1996	Gingerbread Vendor	Closed	1996	75.00	75
1995	Girl Holding Doll	Closed	1995	48.00	50-90
1997	Milk Maid	Open		67.00	67

Dickens Series - J. Byers

YEAR ISSUE		EDITION LIMIT	YEAR RETD.	ISSUE PRICE	*QUOTE U.S.$
1990	Bob Cratchit & Tiny Tim (1st ed.)	Closed	1990	84.00	125-250
1991	Bob Cratchit & Tiny Tim (2nd ed.)	Open		86.00	275
1991	Happy Scrooge (1st ed.)	Closed	1991	50.00	150-250
1992	Happy Scrooge (2nd ed.)	Closed	1992	50.00	120-225
1986	Marley's Ghost (1st ed.)	Closed	1986	40.00	250-400
1987	Marley's Ghost (2nd ed.)	Closed	1992	42.00	225-325
1985	Mr. Fezziwig (1st ed.)	Closed	1985	43.00	450-750
1986	Mr. Fezziwig (2nd ed.)	Closed	1990	43.00	350-600
1984	Mrs. Cratchit (1st ed.)	Closed	1984	38.00	900-1200
1985	Mrs. Cratchit (2nd ed.)	Open		39.00	49
1985	Mrs. Fezziwig (1st ed.)	Closed	1985	43.00	600-750
1986	Mrs. Fezziwig (2nd ed.)	Closed	1990	43.00	350-550
1983	Scrooge (1st ed.)	Closed	1983	36.00	975-1450
1984	Scrooge (2nd ed.)	Open		38.00	49
1989	Spirit of Christmas Future (1st ed.)	Closed	1989	46.00	275-350
1990	Spirit of Christmas Future (2nd ed.)	Closed	1991	48.00	225-325
1987	Spirit of Christmas Past (1st ed.)	Closed	1987	42.00	350-395
1988	Spirit of Christmas Past (2nd ed.)	Closed	1991	46.00	275-325
1988	Spirit of Christmas Present (1st ed.)	Closed	1988	44.00	275-350
1989	Spirit of Christmas Present (2nd ed.)	Closed	1991	48.00	210-325

Display Figures - J. Byers

YEAR ISSUE		EDITION LIMIT	YEAR RETD.	ISSUE PRICE	*QUOTE U.S.$
1986	Display Adults	Closed	1987	170.00	500-600
1983	Display Carolers	Closed	1983	200.00	500
1985	Display Children (Boy & Girl)	Closed	1987	140.00	1200-1500
1982	Display Drummer Boy-1st	Closed	1983	96.00	800-1200
1985	Display Drummer Boy-2nd	Closed	1986	160.00	400-600
1981	Display Lady	Closed	1981	N/A	2000
1981	Display Man	Closed	1981	N/A	2000
1985	Display Old World Santa	Closed	1985	260.00	500-600
1982	Display Santa	Closed	1983	96.00	600
1990	Display Santa-bayberry	Closed	1990	250.00	350-600
1990	Display Santa-red	Closed	1990	250.00	450-650
1984	Display Working Santa	Closed	1985	260.00	500
1987	Mechanical Boy with Drum	Closed	1987	N/A	700-850
1987	Mechanical Girl with Bell	Closed	1987	N/A	600-750

Musicians - J. Byers

YEAR ISSUE		EDITION LIMIT	YEAR RETD.	ISSUE PRICE	*QUOTE U.S.$
1991	Boy with Mandolin	Closed	1991	48.00	175-275
1985	Horn Player	Closed	1985	38.00	550-750
1985	Horn Player, chubby face	Closed	1985	37.00	500-900
1991	Musician with Accordian	Closed	1991	48.00	200-275
1989	Musician with Clarinet	Closed	1989	44.00	350-650
1992	Musician with French Horn	Closed	1992	52.00	120-225
1990	Musician with Mandolin	Closed	1990	46.00	180-275
1986	Victorian Girl with Violin	Closed	1986	39.00	300-400
1983	Violin Player Man (1st ed.)	Closed	1983	38.00	1500
1984	Violin Player Man (2nd ed.)	Closed	1984	38.00	1500

Nativity - J. Byers

YEAR ISSUE		EDITION LIMIT	YEAR RETD.	ISSUE PRICE	*QUOTE U.S.$
1989	Angel Gabriel	Closed	1991	37.00	150-200
1987	Angel-Great Star (Blonde)	Closed	1991	40.00	210
1987	Angel-Great Star (Brunette)	Closed	1991	40.00	250
1987	Angel-Great Star (Red Head)	Closed	1991	40.00	200-250
1987	Black Angel	Closed	1987	36.00	250-285
1990	Holy Family with stable	Closed	1991	119.00	250-350
1989	King Balthasar	Closed	1991	40.00	95
1989	King Gaspar	Closed	1991	40.00	85-95
1989	King Melchior	Closed	1991	40.00	95
1988	Shepherds	Closed	1991	37.00	95

The Nutcracker - J. Byers, unless otherwise noted

YEAR ISSUE		EDITION LIMIT	YEAR RETD.	ISSUE PRICE	*QUOTE U.S.$
1996	Drosselmeier w/Music Box (1st ed.)	Closed	1996	83.00	83
1997	Drosselmeier w/Music Box (2nd ed.)	Open		83.00	83
1994	Fritz (1st ed.)	Closed	1994	56.00	90-175
1995	Fritz (2nd ed.)	Open		57.00	57
1995	Louise Playing Piano (1st ed.)	Closed	1995	82.00	110
1996	Louise Playing Piano (2nd ed.)	Closed	1996	83.00	83
1993	Marie (1st ed.)	Closed	1993	52.00	110-200
1994	Marie (2nd ed.)	Open		53.00	54
1997	Mouse King - Jeff Byers	Open		70.00	70

Salvation Army Band - J. Byers

YEAR ISSUE		EDITION LIMIT	YEAR RETD.	ISSUE PRICE	*QUOTE U.S.$
1997	Boy with Flag	Open		57.00	57
1995	Girl with War Cry	Open		55.00	55
1996	Man with Bass Drum	Open		60.00	60
1993	Man with Cornet	Open		54.00	56
1992	Woman with Kettle	Open		64.00	67
1992	Woman with Kettle (1st ed.)	Closed	1992	64.00	175
1993	Woman with Tambourine	Closed	1995	58.00	60-95

Santas - J. Byers

YEAR ISSUE		EDITION LIMIT	YEAR RETD.	ISSUE PRICE	*QUOTE U.S.$
1991	Father Christmas	Closed	1992	48.00	150-200
1988	Knecht Ruprecht (Black Peter)	Closed	1989	38.00	135-150
1996	Knickerbocker Santa	Open		58.00	58
1984	Mrs. Claus	Closed	1991	38.00	275-350
1992	Mrs. Claus (2nd ed.)	Closed	1993	50.00	150
1986	Mrs. Claus on Rocker	Closed	1986	73.00	600
1995	Mrs. Claus' Needlework	Closed	1995	70.00	125-200
1994	Old Befana	Open		53.00	54
1978	Old World Santa	Closed	1986	33.00	375
1989	Russian Santa	Closed	1989	85.00	440-600
1988	Saint Nicholas	Closed	1992	44.00	150-200
1997	Santa Feeding Reindeer	Open		64.50	65
1982	Santa in a Sleigh (1st ed.)	Closed	1983	46.00	800
1984	Santa in Sleigh (2nd ed.)	Closed	1985	70.00	750
1997	Shopping Mrs. Santa	Open		59.50	60
1993	Skating Santa	Closed	1993	60.00	100-125
1987	Velvet Mrs. Claus	Open		44.00	53
1978	Velvet Santa	Closed	1993	Unkn.	300
1994	Velvet Santa w/Stocking (2nd ed.)	Open		47.00	51
1986	Victorian Santa	Closed	1989	39.00	250-300
1990	Weihnachtsmann (German Santa)	Closed	1990	56.00	125-185
1992	Working Santa	Closed	1996	52.00	55
1992	Working Santa (1st yr. issue)	Closed	1992	52.00	150-250
1983	Working Santa (1st yr. issue)	Closed	1991	38.00	175-275

Skaters - J. Byers

YEAR ISSUE		EDITION LIMIT	YEAR RETD.	ISSUE PRICE	*QUOTE U.S.$
1991	Adult Skaters	Closed	1994	50.00	100-125
1991	Adult Skaters (1991 ed.)	Closed	1991	50.00	115-130
1993	Boy Skater on Log	Closed	1993	55.00	85-125
1992	Children Skaters	Open		50.00	52
1992	Children Skaters (1992 ed.)	Closed	1992	50.00	150
1993	Grandparent Skaters	Closed	1993	50.00	65-100
1993	Grandparent Skaters (1993 ed.)	Closed	1993	50.00	145
1995	Man Holding Skates	Open		52.00	52
1995	Woman Holding Skates	Open		52.00	52

Special Characters - J. Byers

YEAR ISSUE		EDITION LIMIT	YEAR RETD.	ISSUE PRICE	*QUOTE U.S.$
1996	Actress	Closed	1996	52.00	52
1979	Adult Male "Icabod"	Closed	1979	32.00	2400-2600
1988	Angel Tree Top	100	1988	Unkn.	275-375
1994	Baby in Basket	Closed	1994	7.50	20
1989	Black Boy w/skates	Closed	N/A	N/A	400-450
1989	Black Drummer Boy	Closed	N/A	N/A	500
1989	Black Girl w/skates	Closed	N/A	N/A	400-450
1983	Boy on Rocking Horse	300	1983	85.00	2400-2600
1987	Boy on Sled	Closed	1987	50.00	300-375
1991	Boy with Apple	Closed	1991	41.00	150-275
1994	Boy with Goose	Closed	1995	49.50	60-75
1996	Boy with Lamb	Open		52.00	52
1995	Boy with Skis	Open		49.50	50
1991	Boy with Tree	Closed	1994	49.00	125
1995	Butcher	Closed	1995	54.00	125
1987	Caroler with Lamp	Closed	1987	40.00	175-200
1997	Children with Treats	Open		58.00	58
1984	Chimney Sweep-Adult	Closed	1984	36.00	1200-1500
1991	Chimney Sweep-Child	Closed	1994	50.00	100-125
1982	Choir Children, boy and girl set	Closed	1986	32.00	400-600
1993	Choir Director, lady/music stand	Closed	1995	56.00	60-100
1982	Conductor	Closed	1992	32.00	125
1994	Constable	Closed	1996	53.00	54
1995	Couple in Sleigh	Closed	1995	110.00	150-175
1982	Drummer Boy	Closed	1992	34.00	147-175
1982	Easter Boy	Closed	1983	32.00	450-550
1982	Easter Girl	Closed	1983	32.00	450-550
1997	Gardener	Open		69.50	70
1996	Girl Holding Holly Basket	Open		52.00	52
1991	Girl with Apple	Closed	1991	41.00	125-200
1991	Girl with Apple/coin purse	Closed	1991	41.00	335-350
1989	Girl with Hoop	Closed	1990	44.00	175
1995	Girl with Skis	Open		49.50	50
1982	Icabod	Closed	1982	32.00	1150
1993	Lamplighter	Closed	1996	48.00	50
1993	Lamplighter (1st yr. issue)	Closed	1993	48.00	100-150
1982	Leprechaun	Closed	1982	34.00	1200-2000
1997	Man Feeding Birds on Bench	Open		83.00	83
1988	Mother Holding Baby	Closed	1993	40.00	125-200
1987	Mother's Day	225	1987	125.00	250-400
1988	Mother's Day (Daughter)	Closed	1988	125.00	450-700
1988	Mother's Day (Son)	Closed	1988	125.00	450-600
1989	Mother's Day (with Carriage)	3,000	1989	75.00	450-475
1994	Nanny	Open		66.00	67
1989	Newsboy with Bike	Closed	1992	78.00	200-250
1997	One Man Band	Open		69.50	70
1985	Pajama Children (painted flannel)	Closed	1989	35.00	195-250
1985	Pajama Children (red flannel)	Closed	1989	35.00	200-250
1990	Parson	Closed	1993	44.00	110-125
1996	Pilgrim Adults	Open		53.00	53
1997	Pilgrim Children	Open		53.50	54
1990	Postman	Closed	1993	45.00	150-185
1996	Puppeteer	Open		54.00	54
1994	Sandwich Board Man (red board)	Closed	1994	52.00	100-125
1994	Sandwich Board Man (white board)	Closed	1996	52.00	53
1993	School Kids	Closed	1994	48.00	75-125
1992	Schoolteacher	Closed	1994	48.00	100-125
1995	Shopper-Man	Closed	1995	56.00	75
1995	Shopper-Woman	Closed	1995	56.00	75
1996	Shoppers - Grandparents	Open		56.00	56
1981	Thanksgiving Lady (Clay Hands)	Closed	1981	Unkn.	2000
1981	Thanksgiving Man (Clay Hands)	Closed	1981	Unkn.	2000
1994	Treetop Angel	Closed	1996	50.00	50
1982	Valentine Boy	Closed	1983	32.00	450-550
1982	Valentine Girl	Closed	1983	32.00	450-550
1990	Victorian Girl On Rocking Horse (blonde)	Closed	1991	70.00	150-200
1990	Victorian Girl On Rocking Horse (brunette)	Closed	1991	70.00	175-200
1992	Victorian Mother with Toddler (Fall/Win-green)	Closed	1993	60.00	150-200
1993	Victorian Mother with Toddler (Spr/Sum-blue)	Closed	1993	61.00	150
1992	Victorian Mother with Toddler (Spr/Sum-white)	Closed	1993	60.00	125
1997	Woman w/ Gingerbread House	Open		60.00	60

Store Exclusives-Christmas Loft - J. Byers

YEAR ISSUE		EDITION LIMIT	YEAR RETD.	ISSUE PRICE	*QUOTE U.S.$
1991	Russian Santa	40	1991	100.00	600-650

Store Exclusives-Country Christmas - J. Byers

YEAR ISSUE		EDITION LIMIT	YEAR RETD.	ISSUE PRICE	*QUOTE U.S.$
1988	Toymaker	600	1988	59.00	850-1000

Store Exclusives-Foster's Exclusives - J. Byers

YEAR ISSUE		EDITION LIMIT	YEAR RETD.	ISSUE PRICE	*QUOTE U.S.$
1995	American Boy	100	1995	50.00	500

Store Exclusives-Long's Jewelers - J. Byers

YEAR ISSUE		EDITION LIMIT	YEAR RETD.	ISSUE PRICE	*QUOTE U.S.$
1981	Leprechaun (with bucket)	Closed	N/A	N/A	2000

Store Exclusives-Port-O-Call - J. Byers

YEAR ISSUE		EDITION LIMIT	YEAR RETD.	ISSUE PRICE	*QUOTE U.S.$
1986	Cherub Angel-blue	Closed	1987	N/A	275-400
1986	Cherub Angel-cream	Closed	1987	N/A	400
1986	Cherub Angel-pink	Closed	1987	N/A	275-400
1987	Cherub Angel-rose	Closed	1987	N/A	275-400

Store Exclusives-Snow Goose - J. Byers

YEAR ISSUE		EDITION LIMIT	YEAR RETD.	ISSUE PRICE	*QUOTE U.S.$
1988	Man with Goose	600	1988	60.00	400-650

Store Exclusives-Stacy's Gifts & Collectibles - J. Byers

YEAR ISSUE		EDITION LIMIT	YEAR RETD.	ISSUE PRICE	*QUOTE U.S.$
1987	Santa in Rocking Chair with Boy	100	1987	130.00	1000
1987	Santa in Rocking Chair with Girl	100	1987	130.00	1000

Store Exclusives-Talbots - J. Byers

YEAR ISSUE		EDITION LIMIT	YEAR RETD.	ISSUE PRICE	*QUOTE U.S.$
1990	Victorian Family of Four	Closed	N/A	N/A	375-450
1993	Skating Girl/Boy	Retrd.	N/A	N/A	280-400
1994	Man w/Log Carrier	Closed	N/A	N/A	130-150
1994	Family of Four/Sweaters	Retrd.	N/A	N/A	525-570
1995	Santa in Sleigh	1,625	1995	88.00	150

Store Exclusives-Tudor Cottage Exclusives - J. Byers

YEAR ISSUE		EDITION LIMIT	YEAR RETD.	ISSUE PRICE	*QUOTE U.S.$
1993	Penny Children (boy/girl)	Closed	1993	42.00	500

Store Exclusives-Wayside Country Store Exclusives - J. Byers

YEAR ISSUE		EDITION LIMIT	YEAR RETD.	ISSUE PRICE	*QUOTE U.S.$
1988	Colonial Lady s/n	600	1988	49.00	500-600
1986	Colonial Lamplighter s/n	600	1986	46.00	750
1987	Colonial Watchman s/n	600	1987	49.00	750
1995	Sunday School Boy	150	1995	55.00	225-250
1995	Sunday School Girl	150	1995	55.00	225-250

Store Exclusives-Wooden Soldier - J. Byers

YEAR ISSUE		EDITION LIMIT	YEAR RETD.	ISSUE PRICE	*QUOTE U.S.$
XX	Victorian Lamp Lighter	Closed	N/A	N/A	150-200

Store Exclusives-Woodstock Inn - J. Byers

YEAR ISSUE		EDITION LIMIT	YEAR RETD.	ISSUE PRICE	*QUOTE U.S.$
1987	Skier Boy	200	1987	40.00	250-350
1987	Skier Girl	200	1987	40.00	250-350
1991	Sugarin Kids (Woodstock)	Closed	1991	41.00	300
1988	Woodstock Lady	Closed	1988	41.00	350
1988	Woodstock Man	Closed	1988	41.00	350

Toddlers - J. Byers

YEAR ISSUE		EDITION LIMIT	YEAR RETD.	ISSUE PRICE	*QUOTE U.S.$
1996	Book - "Night Before Christmas"	Open		20.00	20
1996	Doll - "Night Before Christmas"	Open		20.00	20
1993	Gingerbread Boy	Closed	1994	18.50	27
1993	Package	Closed	1993	18.50	35
1992	Shovel	Closed	1993	17.00	35
1994	Skis (snowsuit)	Closed	1996	19.00	20
1994	Sled (black toddler)	Closed	1994	19.00	19
1992	Sled (white toddler)	Closed	1993	17.00	20
1995	Sled (white toddler-2nd ed.)	Closed	1995	19.00	20
1991	Sled with Dog/toddler	Closed	1991	30.00	125

*Quotes have been rounded up to nearest dollar

FIGURINES

YEAR	ISSUE	EDITION LIMIT	YEAR RETD.	ISSUE PRICE	*QUOTE U.S.$
1992	Snowball	Closed	1994	17.00	35
1994	Snowflake	Closed	1994	18.00	18
1993	Teddy Bear	Closed	1993	18.50	35
1997	Toddler Holding Merry Christmas Banner	Open		20.00	20
1997	Toddler in Sleigh	Open		27.50	28
1997	Toddler on Rocking Horse	Open		27.50	28
1997	Toddler with Skis (sweater)	Open		21.50	22
1997	Toddler with Tricycle (sweater)	Open		21.50	22
1994	Tree	Closed	1996	18.00	20
1996	Tricycle (snowsuit)	Closed	1996	20.00	20
1995	Victorian Boy Toddler	Closed	1995	19.50	20
1995	Victorian Girl Toddler	Closed	1995	19.50	20
1995	Wagon	Closed	1996	19.50	20

Calabar Creations

Angelic Pigasus - P. Apsit

YEAR	ISSUE	EDITION LIMIT	YEAR RETD.	ISSUE PRICE	*QUOTE U.S.$
1996	Acapella & Atto AP75424	Open		25.00	25
1995	Adagio AP75364	Open		18.00	18
1996	Adagio Mini Waterglobe AP76053	Open		8.50	9
1994	Alba AP75353	Retrd.	1996	12.00	12
1995	Allegria AP75395	Open		24.00	24
1996	Allegria Mini Waterglobe AP76033	Open		8.50	9
1995	Ambrose AP75374	Open		22.00	22
1996	Ambrose Mini Waterglobe AP76043	Open		8.50	9
1995	Andante AP75384	Open		18.00	18
1994	Angelica AP75315	Open		24.00	24
1996	Angelica Mini Waterglobe AP76063	Open		8.50	9
1995	Angelo AP75335	Open		5.00	5
1994	Angelo AP75335	Open		24.00	24
1996	Angelo Mini Waterglobe AP76083	Open		8.50	9
1996	Anna & Allegria Mini Waterglobe AP76094	Open		20.00	20
1994	Anna AP75324	Retrd.	1995	22.00	22
1996	Anna Mini Waterglobe AP76073	Open		8.50	9
1994	Aria AP75343	Retrd.	1996	12.00	12
1996	Arpeggio AP75414	Open		22.00	22
1995	Signature Piece AP75405	Open		24.00	24

Barkley Crossing - P. Apsit

YEAR	ISSUE	EDITION LIMIT	YEAR RETD.	ISSUE PRICE	*QUOTE U.S.$
1996	Paws I Care BC78601	Open		19.00	19
1996	Dog Tired BC78602	Open		18.00	18
1996	Mother's Little Yelpers BC78603	Open		15.00	15
1996	Our Love is Furever BC78604	Open		24.00	24
1996	Santa Paws BC78605	Open		19.00	19
1996	Supper for the Puppers BC78606	Open		18.00	18
1996	Happy Tails to You BC78607	Open		17.00	17
1996	Some Days Are Just Grreat BC78608	Open		22.00	22
1996	Bow Wow Boo Boo BC78609	Open		18.00	18
1996	Training For Tomorrow BC78610	Open		19.00	19
1996	Bubbles and Barks BC78611	Open		24.00	24
1996	Working My Tail Off BC78612	Open		24.00	24
1996	Set of 8 BC78600	Open		237.00	237
1997	All Creatures Great and Paw BC78613	Open		28.00	28
1997	Achy Breaky Barkley BC78614	Open		25.00	25
1997	Barkley Signature Piece BC78615	Open		23.00	23

Daddy's Girl - P. Apsit

YEAR	ISSUE	EDITION LIMIT	YEAR RETD.	ISSUE PRICE	*QUOTE U.S.$
1994	All Aboard! DA74804	5,000		20.00	20
1994	Discovery DA74816	5,000		28.00	28
1994	Moil DA74834	5,000		20.00	20
1994	Peek-A-Boo DA74843	5,000		20.00	20
1994	Spring Harvest DA74856	5,000		28.00	28
1995	Summer DA74866	5,000	1996	34.00	34
1994	Teddy Talks DA74826	5,000		40.00	40

Days of Innocence - P. Apsit

YEAR	ISSUE	EDITION LIMIT	YEAR RETD.	ISSUE PRICE	*QUOTE U.S.$
1995	Dear God DI74975	5,000		28.00	28
1995	A Letter From Grandma DI74966	5,000		40.00	40
1995	To Grandma's DI74956	5,000		28.00	28

Grandpions - P. Apsit

YEAR	ISSUE	EDITION LIMIT	YEAR RETD.	ISSUE PRICE	*QUOTE U.S.$
1995	Alex the Great OM77144	Open		13.00	13
1995	Alley King OM77313	Open		13.00	13
1995	Blue Baron OM77294	Open		13.00	13
1995	Chained OM77234	Open		13.00	13
1995	Doc OM77184	Open		13.00	13
1996	Dr. Tooth OM 77544	Open		13.00	13
1995	The Finest OM77174	Open		13.00	13
1995	Harleyson OM77164	Open		15.00	15
1996	Hazel (Waitress) OM 77384	Open		13.00	13
1995	Ice Proof OM77133	Open		13.00	13
1995	Lady Hope OM77304	Open		13.00	13
1995	Marathon Man OM77224	Open		13.00	13
1995	Martiny OM77264	Open		13.00	13
1995	Mazuma OM77244	Open		13.00	13
1996	Ms. Brown (Teacher) OM 77374	Open		13.00	13
1996	Ms. Ellie S. Crow (Real Estate Agent) OM 77394	Open		13.00	13
1996	Ms. Will Do (Secretary) OM77404	Open		13.00	13
1995	Oh Gee! OM77203	Open		13.00	13
1995	Old Red OM77154	Open		13.00	13
1995	Peleman OM77274	Open		13.00	13
1995	Ratchet OM77254	Open		13.00	13
1995	Rocky Road OM77283	Open		13.00	13
1995	See The Birdy OM77193	Open		13.00	13
1995	Struck OM77214	Open		13.00	13
1995	Weed Child OM77323	Open		13.00	13

Junior Murphy's Law - P. Apsit

YEAR	ISSUE	EDITION LIMIT	YEAR RETD.	ISSUE PRICE	*QUOTE U.S.$
1995	Extra Topping JM75216	5,000	1996	40.00	40
1995	Fast Food JM75196	5,000	1996	46.00	46
1995	Lucky Me! JM75176	5,000	1996	40.00	40
1995	Milk Fan JM75205	5,000	1996	44.00	44
1995	Robin Tell JM75226	5,000	1996	40.00	40

Little Farmers - P. Apsit

YEAR	ISSUE	EDITION LIMIT	YEAR RETD.	ISSUE PRICE	*QUOTE U.S.$
1994	Apple Delivery LF73127	5,000		54.00	54
1993	Between Chores LF73105	5,000		40.00	40
1993	Caring Friend LF73066	5,000		57.00	57
1993	Going Home LF73027	5,000		64.00	64
1993	It's Not For You LF73038	5,000		64.00	64
1994	LF Signature Piece LF73147	Open		40.00	40
1993	Little Lumber Joe LF73077	5,000		64.00	64
1994	Lunch Express LF73117	5,000		76.00	76
1993	Oops! LF73058	5,000		64.00	64
1993	Piggy Ride LF73097	5,000		45.00	45
1993	Playful Kittens LF73016	5,000		64.00	64
1993	Surprise! LF73046	5,000		60.00	60
1993	True Love LF73087	5,000		45.00	45
1994	Vita-Veggie Vendor LF73137	5,000		62.00	62

Little Professionals - P. Apsit

YEAR	ISSUE	EDITION LIMIT	YEAR RETD.	ISSUE PRICE	*QUOTE U.S.$
1994	Little Angelo LP75057	5,000		38.00	38
1995	Little Count LP75084	5,000		36.00	36
1995	Little Desi LP75135	5,000		18.00	18
1994	Little Florence LP75065	5,000	1996	44.00	44
1995	Little Gypsy LP75115	5,000		18.00	18
1995	Little Louis LP75106	5,000		18.00	18
1994	Little Miss Market LP75046	5,000		40.00	40
1995	Little Red LP75075	5,000	1996	38.00	38
1995	Little Ringo LP75094	5,000		18.00	18

Pig Hollow - P. Apsit

YEAR	ISSUE	EDITION LIMIT	YEAR RETD.	ISSUE PRICE	*QUOTE U.S.$
1994	The After Picture PH75544	Open		12.00	12
1995	Armchair/buttons PH75752	Open		7.00	7
1994	Barn Fun PH75474	Open		15.00	15
1995	Bathroom Vanity PH75703	Open		6.00	6
1995	Double Bed PH75722	Open		9.00	9
1995	Dresser/2-drawer PH75714	Open		8.00	8
1994	Going South PH75533	Open		11.00	11
1994	Just Cute PH75442	Open		9.00	9
1995	Kitchen Counter PH75684	Open		19.00	19
1995	Large Armchair PH75742	Open		8.00	8
1994	Mary Pig PH75524	Open		11.00	11
1994	Move Please PH75462	Open		11.00	11
1994	Nap Time PH75492	Open		11.00	11
1994	Old McPig PH75513	Open		11.00	11
1995	Par PH75674	Retrd.	1996	15.00	15
1995	Pauline PH75873	Open		9.00	9
1995	Pelota PH75612	Open		8.00	8
1995	Pendleton PH75822	Open		10.00	10
1995	Pepin PH75842	Open		9.00	9
1995	Pieball PH75633	Open		9.00	9
1995	Pig Kahuna PH75602	Open		9.00	9
1995	Pigmobile PH75853	Open		34.00	34
1995	Pilar PH75832	Open		9.00	9
1994	Pillow Talk PH75453	Open		12.00	12
1995	Plopsy PH75642	Open		8.00	8
1995	Pluckster PH75812	Open		9.00	9
1995	Poirot PH75622	Open		8.00	8
1995	Poof PH75592	Open		8.00	8
1995	Pot Belly PH75883	Open		12.00	12
1995	Pristine Pig PH75573	Open		10.00	10
1995	Prof PH75583	Open		9.00	9
1995	Proof PH75862	Open		12.00	12
1995	Prude Jr. PH75652	Open		8.00	8
1995	Prude PH75663	Open		9.00	9
1994	Reddie PH75554	Open		12.00	12
1995	Sidetable/1 book PH75773	Open		8.00	8
1995	Sidetable/2 doors PH75782	Open		6.00	6
1994	Signature Piece PH75565	Open		19.00	19
1995	Sofa PH75762	Open		14.00	14
1995	Stove/Oven PH75693	Open		7.00	7
1994	Sweet Corn PH75503	Open		9.00	9
1994	Time For School PH75484	Open		15.00	15
1995	TV Console PH75793	Open		7.00	7
1995	Twin Bed PH75732	Open		9.00	9

Santaventure - P. Apsit

YEAR	ISSUE	EDITION LIMIT	YEAR RETD.	ISSUE PRICE	*QUOTE U.S.$
1994	Almost Done SV73836	5,000	1996	50.00	50
1993	Cart O' Plenty SV73737	5,000		66.00	66
1993	Hooray For Santa SV73757	5,000		59.00	59
1994	In His Dream SV73816	5,000	1996	78.00	78
1994	The Last Mile SV73806	5,000		54.00	54
1993	Nuts For You SV73787	5,000		59.00	59
1993	Pilgrim Santa SV73748	5,000		59.00	59
1993	A Pinch of Advice SV73768	5,000		68.00	68
1994	Reindeer's Strike SV73827	5,000		54.00	54
1993	Santa Tested SV73778	5,000		68.00	68
1993	Santa's Sack Attack SV73796	5,000		60.00	60
1994	Signature Piece SV73577	5,000		60.00	60
1994	Viola! SV73847	5,000		50.00	50

Tee Club - P. Apsit

YEAR	ISSUE	EDITION LIMIT	YEAR RETD.	ISSUE PRICE	*QUOTE U.S.$
1993	Certain-Tee TC73898	5,000		100.00	100
1993	Naugh-Tee TC73908	5,000		56.00	56
1993	Old Tee-Mer TC73887	5,000		78.00	78
1993	Prac-Tees TC73858	5,000		66.00	66
1993	Putt-Teeing TC73868	5,000		66.00	66
1993	Teed-Off TC73877	5,000		60.00	60

Yesterday's Friends - P. Apsit

YEAR	ISSUE	EDITION LIMIT	YEAR RETD.	ISSUE PRICE	*QUOTE U.S.$
1993	Bayou Boys RW74456	3,500		80.00	80
1993	Bluester RW74446	7,500		44.00	44
1993	Buddies RW74466	7,500		50.00	50
1994	Caddle Chris RW74527	7,500		34.00	34
1994	Cornered RW74707	7,500		54.00	54
1993	Dinner For Two RW74496	7,500		38.00	38
1994	Equipment Manager RW74596	7,500		34.00	34
1994	Excess RW74726	7,500		50.00	50
1993	Freewheeling RW74436	7,500		48.00	48
1994	Funny Frog RW74745	7,500		44.00	44
1994	Goose Loose RW74635	7,500		40.00	40
1995	High Fly RW74795	7,500		28.00	28
1993	Hop-a-Long Pete RW74539	3,500		80.00	80
1993	Interference RW74506	7,500		42.00	42
1993	Jazzy Bubble RW74486	7,500		37.00	37
1993	Me Big Chief RW74548	7,500		56.00	56
1993	Mike's Magic RW74475	7,500		37.00	37
1995	Out! RW74766	7,500		34.00	34
1994	Parade RW74716	7,500		60.00	60
1995	Pop Up! RW74755	7,500		34.00	34
1994	Read All About It RW74616	7,500		70.00	70
1994	Read-A-Thon RW74694	7,500		40.00	40
1994	Scrub-a-Swine RW74606	7,500		48.00	48
1994	Signature Piece RW74737	Open		54.00	54
1993	Strike So Sweet RW74517	7,500		42.00	42
1994	Tuba Notes RW74688	7,500		54.00	54
1993	Tug-a-Leg RW74557	7,500		56.00	56
1994	What A Smile RW74626	7,500		40.00	40

Cardew Design

"English Bettys" - P. Cardew

YEAR	ISSUE	EDITION LIMIT	YEAR RETD.	ISSUE PRICE	*QUOTE U.S.$
1995	Cat Got the Cream-Brown Betty	Open		50.00	55
1996	Chess-Black Betty	Open		50.00	55
1996	Gardening-Green Betty	Open		50.00	60
1996	Golf-White Betty	Open		50.00	55
1995	Harvest Pies-Brown Betty	Open		50.00	55
1996	London Touring-Black Betty	Open		50.00	55
1996	Magician-Black Betty	Retrd.	1996	50.00	55
1995	Ploughman's Lunch-Brown Betty	Retrd.	1996	50.00	55
1995	Rise & "Shoe" Shine-Brown Betty	Retrd.	1996	50.00	55
1995	Summer Picnic-Brown Betty	Retrd.	1996	50.00	55
1995	Tea Table-Brown Betty	Open		50.00	60
1996	Teddy Bear's Picnic-Yellow Betty	Open		50.00	60

Cardew Collectors' Club - P. Cardew

YEAR	ISSUE	EDITION LIMIT	YEAR RETD.	ISSUE PRICE	*QUOTE U.S.$
1995	Moving Day	5,000	1997	175.00	175
1995	Tiny Tea Chest	Yr.Iss.	1997	Gift	N/A
1997	Willow Pattern Tea Cup Teapot	Yr.Iss.		45.00	45
1997	Mug One-Cup	Yr.Iss.		Gift	N/A

Event Piece - P. Cardew

YEAR	ISSUE	EDITION LIMIT	YEAR RETD.	ISSUE PRICE	*QUOTE U.S.$
1996	"Travellers Return"	5,000	1996	45.00	45

Limited Edition Full Sized Teapots - P. Cardew

YEAR	ISSUE	EDITION LIMIT	YEAR RETD.	ISSUE PRICE	*QUOTE U.S.$
1996	Charles Atlas Stand	5,000		250.00	375
1997	Classical Fireplace	5,000		175.00	175
1997	Drawing Room Fireplace	5,000		175.00	175
1997	Farmhouse Dresser	5,000		175.00	175
1996	Fireplace	5,000		175.00	175
1996	Gardener's Bench	5,000		175.00	175
1995	Kitchen Sink	5,000		175.00	175
1995	Ladies Dressing Table	5,000		175.00	175
1996	Lilliput Lane Market Stall	Retrd.	1996	250.00	250
1995	Refrigerator	5,000		175.00	175
1997	Rington's Tea Merchant	5,000		250.00	250
1997	Tea Table	5,000		175.00	175
1995	Teapot Market Stall	5,000	1996	199.00	199
1996	Teapot Marktet Stall Mark II	5,000		199.00	199
1996	Teddy Bear's Picnic	5,000		175.00	175
1995	Washing Machine	5,000		175.00	175
1996	Welsh Dresser	5,000		175.00	175

Market Stall Series - P. Cardew

YEAR	ISSUE	EDITION LIMIT	YEAR RETD.	ISSUE PRICE	*QUOTE U.S.$
1993	Antiques Market Stall	Retrd.	1996	160.00	160
1993	China Market Stall	Open		160.00	175
1993	Hardware Market Stall	Open		160.00	175
1995	Shoe Market Stall	Open		160.00	175

One-Cup Teapot Collection - P. Cardew

YEAR	ISSUE	EDITION LIMIT	YEAR RETD.	ISSUE PRICE	*QUOTE U.S.$
1995	50's Stove	Retrd.	1996	45.00	45
1994	Baking Day	Retrd.	1995	45.00	45
1996	Bloomingdales	Open		45.00	45
1995	China Stall	Open		45.00	60
1995	Christmas Presents	Open		45.00	45
1996	Christmas Tree	Open		45.00	60
1994	Crimewriter's Desk	Retrd.	1996	45.00	45
1996	Egg Cup	Open		45.00	45
1996	Fireplace	Open		45.00	45
1996	Gardening	Open		45.00	60
1996	Golf Bag	Open		45.00	45
1996	Grandfather Clock	Open		45.00	45
1997	Hiker's Rest	Open		60.00	60
1995	Kitchen Sink	Retrd.	1996	45.00	45
1995	Lady's Dressing Table	Open		45.00	45

*Quotes have been rounded up to nearest dollar

YEAR ISSUE		EDITION LIMIT	YEAR RETD.	ISSUE PRICE	*QUOTE U.S.$
1995	Moving Day	Open		45.00	60
1996	Outward Bound	Open		45.00	55
1995	Refrigerator	Open		45.00	60
1996	Romance/Heart	Open		45.00	45
1996	Santa Claus	Open		45.00	45
1995	Sewing Machine	Open		45.00	60
1995	Tea Chest	Retrd.	1996	45.00	45
1995	Tea Scoop	Retrd.	1996	45.00	45
1995	Tea Shop Counter	Retrd.	1996	45.00	45
1995	Teddy Bear's Picnic	Open		45.00	60
1995	Toy Box	Retrd.	1996	45.00	45
1997	Valentine	Open		45.00	45
1997	Victorian Fireplace	Open		45.00	45
1995	Victorian Tea Table	Open		45.00	45
1997	Victorian Washstand	Open		45.00	45
1995	Washing Machine	Open		45.00	60
1995	Washing Mangle	Retrd.	1996	45.00	45
1995	Welsh Dresser	Open		45.00	45

Standard Teapots - P. Cardew

1991	50's Stove	Retrd.	1996	140.00	140
1992	Baking Day	Open		140.00	140
1992	Crime Writer's Desk	Open		140.00	140
1992	Sewing Machine	Open		140.00	140
1993	Tea Shop Counter	Retrd.	1995	140.00	140
1991	Toy Box	Retrd.	1996	140.00	140
1992	Victorian Tea Table	Open		140.00	140
1993	Victorian Washstand	Retrd.	1995	140.00	140
1992	Washing Mangle	Retrd.	1996	140.00	140

Tiny Teapots - P. Cardew

1995	50's Stove	Open		12.00	12
1995	Baking Day	Open		12.00	12
1996	Bedside Table	Retrd.	1996	12.00	12
1995	Crime Writer's Desk	Retrd.	1996	12.00	12
1995	Kitchen Sink	Open		12.00	12
1995	Refrigerator	Retrd.	1996	12.00	12
1995	Sewing Machine	Open		12.00	12
1995	Tea Shop Counter	Open		12.00	12
1995	Teddy Bear's Picnic	Retrd.	1996	12.00	12
1995	Toy Box	Retrd.	1996	12.00	12
1995	Victorian Wash Stand	Retrd.	1996	12.00	12
1995	Washing Machine	Retrd.	1996	12.00	12
1995	Washing Mangle	Open		12.00	12
1996	Golf Trolley	Open		12.00	12
1996	Petrol Pump	Open		12.00	12
1996	Heart	Retrd.	1996	12.00	12
1996	Radio	Open		12.00	12
1996	Safe	Retrd.	1996	12.00	12
1996	50's TV	Open		12.00	12
1996	Fireplace	Open		12.00	12
1996	Grandfather's Clock	Open		12.00	12
1996	Lady's Dressing Table	Retrd.	1996	12.00	12
1996	Night Stand	Retrd.	1996	12.00	12
1996	Valentine	Retrd.	1996	12.00	12
1996	Victorian Tea Table	Retrd.	1996	12.00	12
1995	Victorian Washstand	Retrd.	1996	12.00	12
1995	Washing Machine	Retrd.	1996	12.00	12
1996	Welsh Dresser	Open		12.00	12

Two-Cup Teapot Collection - P. Cardew

1997	Anniversary Teatable	Open		75.00	75
1997	Birthday Teatable	Open		75.00	75
1997	Christening Teatable	Open		75.00	75
1997	Jewelery Box	Open		75.00	75
1997	Safe	Open		75.00	75
1997	Sewing Machine	Open		75.00	75
1997	Tea Service Tea Table	Open		75.00	75
1997	Television	Open		75.00	75
1997	Welsh Dresser	Open		75.00	75
1997	Willow Pattern Teatable	Open		75.00	75

Cast Art Industries

Dreamsicles Club - K. Haynes

1993	A Star is Born-CD001	Retrd.	1993	Gift	85-115
1994	Daydream Believer-CD100	Retrd.	1994	29.95	55-82
1994	Join The Fun-CD002	Retrd.	1994	Gift	50
1994	Makin' A List-CD101	Retrd.	1994	47.95	75
1995	Three Cheers-CD003	Retrd.	1995	Gift	50-60
1995	Town Crier-CD102	Retrd.	1995	24.95	25
1995	Snowbound-CD103	Retrd.	1996	24.95	25
1996	Star Shower-CD004	Retrd.	1996	Gift	28
1996	Heavenly Flowers-CD104	Yr.Iss.		24.95	25
1996	Bee-Friended-CD105	Yr.Iss.		24.95	25
1997	Free Spirit-CD005	Yr.Iss.		Gift	N/A

Dreamsicles - K. Haynes

1992	Baby Love-DC147	Retrd.	1995	7.00	10
1991	Best Pals-DC103	Retrd.	1994	15.00	35
1994	Birthday Party-DC171	Suspd.		13.50	14
1992	Bluebird On My Shoulder-DC115	Retrd.	1995	19.00	23
1992	Bundle of Joy-DC142	Retrd.	1995	7.00	10
1993	By the Silvery Moon-DC253	10,000	1994	100.00	188-288
1992	Caroler - Center Scroll-DC216	Retrd.	1995	19.00	22
1992	Caroler - Left Scroll-DC218	Retrd.	1995	19.00	22
1992	Caroler - Right Scroll-DC217	Retrd.	1995	19.00	22
1994	Carousel-DC174	Suspd.		35.00	40
1991	Cherub and Child-DC100	Retrd.	1995	15.00	100
1992	Cherub For All Seasons-DC114	Retrd.	1995	23.00	75-95
1992	Cherub-DC111	10,000	1992	50.00	75
1992	Cherub-DC112	10,000	1993	50.00	100-225
1996	A Child Is Born-DC256	10,000	1996	95.00	95
1992	A Child's Prayer-DC145	Retrd.	1995	7.00	7
1994	Cuddle Blanket-DC153	Retrd.	1995	6.50	7
1992	Cupid's Bow-DC202	Suspd.		27.00	27
1992	Dance Ballerina Dance-DC140	Retrd.	1995	37.00	42
1992	Dream A Little Dream-DC144	Retrd.	1995	7.00	10
1997	Dreamboat-10060 (special edition)	Open		90.00	90
1994	Eager to Please-DC154	Retrd.	1995	6.50	10
1992	Flying Lesson-DC251	10,000	1993	80.00	500-1000
1991	Forever Friends-DC102	Retrd.	1994	15.00	50
1991	Forever Yours-DC110	Retrd.	1995	44.00	75
1994	Good Shepherd-DC104	Suspd.		15.00	15
1996	Heaven's Gate-DC257 (5th Anniversary piece)	15,000		129.00	129
1991	Heavenly Dreamer-DC106	Retrd.	1996	11.50	12
1994	Here's Looking at You-DC172	Retrd.	1995	25.00	35
1994	I Can Read-DC151	Retrd.	1995	6.50	10
1994	International Collectible Exposition Commemorative Figurine	Retrd.	1995	34.95	120
1992	Life Is Good-DC119	Retrd.	1996	10.00	15
1992	Little Darlin'-DC146	Retrd.	1995	7.00	10
1993	Little Dickens-DC127	Retrd.	1995	24.00	25
1992	Littlest Angel-DC143	Retrd.	1995	7.00	10
1993	Long Fellow-DC126	Retrd.	1995	24.00	25
1993	Me And My Shadow-DC116	Retrd.	1996	19.00	22
1991	Mischief Maker-DC105	Retrd.	1996	10.00	10
1993	Miss Morningstar-DC141	Retrd.	1996	25.00	35
1991	Musician w/Cymbals-5154	Suspd.		22.00	22
1991	Musician w/Drums-5152	Suspd.		22.00	22
1991	Musician w/Flute-5153	Suspd.		22.00	22
1991	Musician w/Trumpet-5151	Suspd.		22.00	22
1992	My Funny Valentine-DC201	Suspd.		17.00	28
1995	Nursery Rhyme-DC229	Suspd.		42.00	50
1995	Picture Perfect-DC255	10,000	1995	100.00	125
1994	The Recital-DC254	10,000	1994	135.00	145-225
1994	Side By Side-DC169	Retrd.	1995	31.50	50
1991	Sitting Pretty-DC101	Retrd.	1996	9.50	12
1992	Sleigh Ride-DC122	Suspd.		15.50	16
1994	Snowflake-DC117	Suspd.		10.00	14
1994	Sock Hop-DC222	Suspd.		16.00	16
1991	Speed Racer Box-5750	Suspd.		14.00	14
1994	Sucking My Thumb-DC156	Retrd.	1995	6.50	10
1994	Surprise Gift-DC152	Retrd.	1995	6.50	10
1993	Sweet Dreams-DC125	Retrd.	1995	29.00	45
1994	Sweet Gingerbread-DC223	Suspd.		16.00	16
1996	Tea Party-DC015 (GCC event)	Retrd.	1996	19.00	40
1993	Teeter Tots-DC252	10,000	1993	100.00	170-195
1994	Up All Night-DC155	Retrd.	1995	6.50	10
1991	Wild Flower-DC107	Retrd.	1996	10.00	10

Dreamsicles Calendar Collection - K. Haynes

1994	Winter Wonderland (January) -DC180	Retrd.	1995	24.00	24
1994	Special Delivery (February)-DC181	Retrd.	1995	24.00	27
1994	Ride Like The Wind (March)-DC182	Retrd.	1995	24.00	27
1994	Springtime Frolic (April)-DC183	Retrd.	1995	24.00	27
1994	Love In Bloom (May)-DC184	Retrd.	1995	24.00	27
1994	Among Friends (June)-DC185	Retrd.	1995	24.00	35
1994	Pool Pals (July)-DC186	Retrd.	1995	24.00	27
1994	Nature's Bounty (August)-DC187	Retrd.	1995	24.00	27
1994	School Days (September)-DC188	Retrd.	1995	24.00	27
1994	Autumn Leaves (October)-DC189	Retrd.	1995	24.00	27
1994	Now Give Thanks (November) -DC190	Retrd.	1995	24.00	27
1994	Holiday Magic (December)-DC191	Retrd.	1995	24.00	27

Dreamsicles Christmas - K. Haynes

1992	Baby Love-DX147	Retrd.	1995	7.00	30
1992	Bluebird On My Shoulder-DX115	Retrd.	1995	19.00	19
1992	Bundle of Joy-DX142	Retrd.	1995	7.00	7
1992	Caroler - Center Scroll-DX216	Retrd.	1995	19.00	22
1992	Caroler - Left Scroll-DX218	Retrd.	1995	19.00	22
1992	Caroler - Right Scroll-DX217	Retrd.	1995	19.00	22
1991	Cherub and Child-DX100	Retrd.	1995	14.00	30
1992	A Child's Prayer-DX145	Retrd.	1995	7.00	7
1992	Dream A Little Dream-DX144	Retrd.	1995	7.00	7
1993	The Finishing Touches-DX248 (2nd Ed.)	Retrd.	1994	85.00	125
1991	Forever Yours-DX110	Retrd.	1995	44.00	44
1991	Heavenly Dreamer-DX106	Retrd.	1996	11.00	11
1994	Here's Looking at You-DX172	Retrd.	1995	25.00	35
1994	Holiday on Ice-DX249 (3rd Ed.)	Retrd.	1995	85.00	125
1996	Homeward Bound-DX251 (5th Ed.)	Yr.Iss.		80.00	80
1992	Life Is Good-DX119	Retrd.	1996	10.50	12
1992	Little Darlin'-DX146	Retrd.	1995	7.00	10
1993	Little Dickens-DX127	Retrd.	1995	24.00	25
1992	Little Drummer Boy-DX241	Suspd.		32.00	32
1992	Littlest Angel-DX143	Retrd.	1995	7.00	7
1993	Long Fellow-DX126	Retrd.	1995	24.00	25
1993	Me And My Shadow-DX116	Retrd.	1996	19.50	20
1991	Mischief Maker-DX105	Retrd.	1996	10.50	11
1993	Miss Morningstar-DX141	Retrd.	1996	25.50	28
1995	Poetry In Motion-DX113	Open		82.00	100
1991	Santa Bunny-DX203	Retrd.	1994	32.00	32
1992	Santa In Dreamsicle Land-DX247 (1st Ed.)	Retrd.	1993	85.00	250-300
1991	Santa's Elf-DX240	Retrd.	1996	19.00	22
1995	Santa's Kingdom-DX250 (4th Ed.)	Retrd.	1995	80.00	100
1994	Side By Side-DX169	Retrd.	1995	31.50	32
1991	Sitting Pretty-DX101	Retrd.	1996	10.00	15
1994	Stolen Kiss-DX162	Suspd.		12.50	14
1993	Sweet Dreams-DX125	Retrd.	1995	29.00	29
1991	Wildflower-DX107	Retrd.	1996	10.50	15

Dreamsicles Day Event- K. Haynes

1995	1995 Dreamsicles Event Figurine -DC075	Retrd.	1995	20.00	35
1996	Glad Tidings-DD100	Retrd.	1996	15.95	27
1996	Time to Retire-DD103	Yr.Iss.		15.95	16

Dreamsicles Heavenly Classics - K. Haynes & S. Hackett

1996	Bundles of Love-HC370	327	1996	80.00	80
1995	The Dedication-DC351	10,000	1996	118.00	150-200
1997	Making Memories-10096 (special ed.)	Open		100.00	100

Cavanagh Group Intl.

Coca-Cola Brand Heritage Collection - Various

1995	Always - CGI	Closed	1996	30.00	30
1995	Always-Musical - CGI	Closed	1996	50.00	50
1995	Boy at Well - N. Rockwell	5,000		60.00	60
1995	Boy Fishing - N. Rockwell	5,000		60.00	60
1996	Busy Man's Pause - Sundblom	Open		80.00	80
1994	Calendar Girl 1916-Music Box - CGI	500	1996	60.00	60
1996	Coca-Cola Stand - CGI	Open		45.00	45
1996	Cool Break - CGI	Open		40.00	45
1994	Dear Santa, Please Pause Here - Sundblom	2,500	1995	80.00	85
1994	Dear Santa, Please Pause Here -Musical - Sundblom	2,500	1995	100.00	100
1996	Decorating The Tree - CGI	Closed	1996	45.00	45
1997	Downhill Derby-CGI	10,000		22.50	23
1994	Eight Polar Bears on Wood - CGI	5,000		100.00	100
1994	Eight Polar Bears on Wood -Musical - CGI	10,000		150.00	150
1995	Elaine - CGI	2,500	1996	100.00	100
1994	Extra Bright Refreshment-Snowglobe - Sundblom	2,500	1996	50.00	50
1996	For Me - Sundblom	Open		40.00	40
1997	For Me-Snowglobe - Sundblom	Open		25.00	25
1995	Girl on Swing - CGI	2,500	1996	100.00	100
1996	Gone Fishing - CGI	Open		60.00	60
1994	Good Boys and Girl - Sundblom	2,500	1995	80.00	80
1994	Good Boys and Girls-Musical - Sundblom	2,500	1995	100.00	100
1994	Good Boys and Girls-Snowglobe - Sundblom	2,000	1995	45.00	45
1994	Hilda Clark 1901-Music Box - CGI	500	1996	60.00	60
1994	Hilda Clark 1903-Music Box - CGI	500	1996	60.00	60
1996	Hollywood-Snowglobe - CGI	Open		50.00	50
1995	The Homecoming - S. Stearman	2,500	1995	125.00	125
1995	Hospitality - Sundblom	5,000		35.00	35
1997	I Can Do Anything With You By My Side-Snowglobe - CGI	Open		40.00	40
1997	A Job Well Done Deserves a Coke - CGI	10,000		22.50	23
1997	Mama Look! Is He a Bear Too? - CGI	10,000		22.50	23
1997	On The Road to Adventure -Musical - CGI	Open		15.00	15
1995	Playing with Dad - CGI	Closed	1996	40.00	40
1996	A Refreshing Break - N. Rockwell	Open		60.00	60
1996	Refreshing Treat - CGI	Closed	1996	45.00	45
1994	Santa at His Desk - Sundblom	5,000	1996	80.00	80
1994	Santa at His Desk-Musical - Sundblom	5,000	1996	100.00	100
1994	Santa at His Desk-Snowglobe - Sundblom	Closed	1996	45.00	45
1994	Santa at the Fireplace - Sundblom	5,000	1996	80.00	80
1994	Santa at the Fireplace-Musical - Sundblom	5,000	1996	100.00	100
1994	Santa at the Lamppost-Snowglobe - Sundblom	Closed	1996	50.00	50
1996	Santa with Polar Bear-Snowglobe - CGI	Open		50.00	50
1996	Say Uncle-Snowglobe - CGI	Open		50.00	50
1994	Single Polar Bear on Ice-Snowglobe - CGI	Closed	1996	40.00	50
1996	Sshh!-Musical - Sundblom	Open		55.00	55
1995	They Remember Me-Musical - Sundblom	5,000		50.00	50
1997	A Time to Share-Musical - Sundblom	5,000		100.00	100
1997	Times With Dad are Special - CGI	10,000		22.50	23
1994	Two Polar Bears on Ice - CGI	Open		25.00	25
1994	Two Polar Bears on Ice-Musical -CGI	Closed	1996	45.00	50

Coca-Cola Brand Heritage Collection Polar Bear Cubs - CGI

1996	Balancing Act	Open		16.00	16
1996	The Bear Cub Club	Open		20.00	20
1996	Bearing Gifts of Love and Friendship	10,000		30.00	30
1996	The Big Catch	Open		16.00	16
1997	Caring Is A Special Gift	Open		16.00	16
1996	A Christmas Wish	Open		10.00	10
1997	Dad Showed Me How-Musical	Open		35.00	35
1997	Everybody Needs A Friend	Open		12.00	12
1997	Fire Chief	Open		16.00	16
1996	Friends Are Forever	Open		16.00	16
1997	Friends Double the Joy	Open		30.00	30
1997	Friendship is A Hiddlen Treaure	Open		20.00	20
1997	Friendship is the Best Gift	Open		16.00	16
1997	Friendship is the Perfect Medicine	Open		20.00	20

*Quotes have been rounded up to nearest dollar

FIGURINES

Cavanagh Group Intl. to Cherished Teddies/Enesco Corporation

YEAR ISSUE		EDITION LIMIT	YEAR RETD.	ISSUE PRICE	*QUOTE U.S.$
1997	Friendship Makes Life Bearable	Open		16.00	16
1996	Giving Is Better Than Receiving	Open		12.00	12
1997	Graduation Day	Open		12.00	12
1997	Happy Birthday	Open		12.00	12
1996	A Helping Hand	Open		20.00	20
1997	I Can't Bear To See You Sick	Open		20.00	20
1997	I Get A Kick Out of You	Open		16.00	16
1996	I'm Not Sleepy...Really	Open		10.00	10
1997	Ice Skating-Snowglobe	Open		45.00	45
1996	It's My Turn to Hide	Open		12.00	12
1997	Just For You	Open		16.00	16
1997	Just Like My Dad	Open		16.00	16
1997	Little Boys are Best	Open		16.00	16
1997	Little Girls are Special	Open		16.00	16
1996	Look What I Can Do	Open		12.00	12
1997	Love Bears All Things	Open		12.00	12
1997	Lucky O'Bear and McPuffin	Open		16.00	16
1997	Polar Bear Cub Sign	Open		16.00	16
1996	Ride 'em Cowboy	Open		20.00	20
1997	Seeds of Friendship Grow w/Caring	Open		16.00	16
1996	Skating Rink Romance	Open		16.00	16
1997	Sled Racing-Snowglobe	Open		35.00	35
1996	Snowday Adventure	Open		12.00	12
1996	Sweet Dreams	Open		12.00	12
1997	Thanks For All You Taught Me	Open		16.00	16
1996	To Grandmother's House We Go	Open		12.00	12
1997	Visits with You are Special	Open		20.00	20
1997	We Did It	Open		20.00	20
1996	Who Says Girls Can't Throw	Open		16.00	16
1997	With All My Heart	Open		16.00	16
1997	You're the Greatest	Open		20.00	20

Coca-Cola Brand Musical - Various

YEAR ISSUE		EDITION LIMIT	YEAR RETD.	ISSUE PRICE	*QUOTE U.S.$
1993	Dear Santa, Please Pause Here - Sundblom	Open		50.00	50
1994	Santa's Soda Shop - CGI	Open		50.00	50

Coca-Cola Brand Santa Animations - Sundblom

YEAR ISSUE		EDITION LIMIT	YEAR RETD.	ISSUE PRICE	*QUOTE U.S.$
1991	Ssshh! (1st Ed.)	Closed	1992	99.99	275-365
1992	Santa's Pause for Refreshment (2nd Ed.)	Closed	1993	99.99	200-265
1993	Trimming the Tree (3rd Ed.)	Closed	1994	99.99	175-235
1995	Santa at the Lamppost (4th Ed.)	Closed	1996	110.00	115

Cherished Teddies/Enesco Corporation

Cherished Teddies Club - P. Hillman

YEAR ISSUE		EDITION LIMIT	YEAR RETD.	ISSUE PRICE	*QUOTE U.S.$
1995	Cub E. Bear CT001	Yr.Iss.	1995	Gift	45-75
1995	Mayor Wilson T.Beary CT951	Yr.Iss.	1995	20.00	45-95
1995	Hilary Hugabear CT952	Yr.Iss.	1995	17.50	50-100
1996	R. Harrison Hartford-New Membear CT002	Yr.Iss.	1996	Gift	40
1996	R. Harrison Hartford-Charter Membear CT102	Yr.Iss.	1996	Gift	40-60
1996	Emily E. Claire CT962	Yr.Iss.	1996	17.50	35
1996	Kurtis D. Claw CT961	Yr.Iss.	1996	17.50	35
1997	Lloyd, CT Town Railway Conductor-Membearship (red suitcase) CT003	Yr.Iss.		Gift	N/A
1997	Lloyd, CT Town Railway Conductor-Charter Membear (green suitcase) CT103	Yr.Iss.		Gift	N/A
1997	Bernard and Bernice CT972	Yr.Iss.		17.50	18
1997	Eleanor P. Beary CT971	Yr.Iss.		17.50	18

Cherished Teddies - P. Hillman

YEAR ISSUE		EDITION LIMIT	YEAR RETD.	ISSUE PRICE	*QUOTE U.S.$
1993	Abigail "Inside We're All The Same" 900362	Suspd.		16.00	32-75
1993	Alice "Cozy Warm Wishes Coming Your Way" (9") 903620	Suspd.		100.00	150-200
1993	Alice "Cozy Warm Wishes Coming Your Way" Dated 1993 912875	Yr.Iss.	1993	17.50	80-175
1995	Allison & Alexandria "Two Friends Mean Twice The Love" 127981	Open		25.00	25
1995	Amanda "Here's Some Cheer to Last The Year" 141186	Yr.Iss.	1995	17.50	35-75
1993	Amy "Hearts Quilted With Love" 910732	Open		13.50	15
1996	Andy "You Have A Special Place In My Heart" 176265	Open		18.50	19
1992	Anna "Hooray For You" 950459	Open		22.50	23
1997	Annie, Brittany, Colby, Danny, Ernie "Strike Up The Band And Give Five Cherished Years A Hand" (5th Anniversary) 205354	Yr.Iss.		75.00	75
1994	Baby Boy Jointed (Musical) 699314	Open		60.00	60
1994	Baby Girl Jointed (Musical) 699322	Open		60.00	60
1993	Baby in Cradle (Musical) 914320	Open		60.00	60
1995	Bea "Bee My Friend" 141348	Open		15.00	18
1994	Bear as Bunny Jointed (Musical) 625302	Retrd.	1996	60.00	100-150
1995	Bear Cupid Girl 2AT 103640	Suspd.		15.00	30
1994	Bear Holding Harp (Musical) 916323	Retrd.	1997	40.00	40
1996	Bear In Bunny Outfit Resin Egg Dated 1996 156507	Yr.Iss.	1996	8.50	20
1992	Bear on Rocking Reindeer (Musical) 950815	Suspd.		60.00	65-80
1993	Bear Playing w/Train (Musical) 912964	Open		40.00	40
1994	Bear w/ Goose (Musical) 627445	Retrd.	1997	45.00	80-120
1994	Bear w/Horse (Musical) 628565	Retrd.	1996	150.00	150
1994	Bear w/Rocking Reindeer (Musical) 629618	Open		165.00	165
1994	Bear w/Toy Chest (Musical) 627453	Open		60.00	60
1995	Beary Scary Halloween House 152382	Open		20.00	20
1994	Becky "Springtime Happiness" 916331	Suspd.		20.00	35-45
1992	Benji "Life Is Sweet, Enjoy" 950548	Retrd.	1995	13.50	35-70
1994	Bessie "Some Bunny Loves You" 916404	Suspd.		15.00	150-200
1995	The Best Is Yet To Come 127949	Open		12.50	14
1995	The Best Is Yet To Come 127957	Open		12.50	14
1992	Beth "Bear Hugs" 950637	Retrd.	1995	17.50	35-75
1992	Beth "Happy Holidays, Deer Friend" 950807	Suspd.		22.50	45-55
1994	Betty "Bubblin' Over With Love" 626066	Open		18.50	20
1994	Billy "Everyone Needs A Cuddle", Betsey "First Step To Love" Bobbie "A Little Friendship To Share" 624896	Open		12.50	13
1992	Blossom & Beth "Friends Are Never Far Apart" 950564	Retrd.	1997	50.00	50-75
1992	Blossom & Beth "Friends Are Never Far Apart" w/butterfly 950564	Closed	1992	50.00	150
1995	Boy Bear Cupid 103551	Suspd.		17.50	31-50
1995	Boy Bear Flying Cupid 103608	Suspd.		13.00	25
1993	Boy Praying (Musical) 914304	Open		37.50	38
1994	Boy/Girl in Laundry Basket (Musical) 624926	Open		60.00	60
1994	Boy/Girl in Sled (Musical) 651435	Open		100.00	100
1994	Breanna "Pumpkin Patch Pals" 617180	Open		15.00	15
1994	Bride/Groom (Musical) 699349	Open		50.00	50
1993	Buckey & Brenda "How I Love Being Friends With You" 912816	Retrd.	1995	15.00	60-75
1995	Bunny "Just In Time For Spring" 103802	Open		13.50	14
1996	Butch "Can I Be Your Football Hero?" 156388	Open		15.00	15
1992	Camille "I'd Be Lost Without You" 950424	Retrd.	1996	20.00	35-50
1993	Carolyn "Wishing You All Good Things" 912921	Retrd.	1996	22.50	40-70
1995	Carrie "The Future 'Beareth' All Things" 141321	Open		18.50	19
1993	Charity "I Found A Friend In Ewe" 910678	Retrd.	1996	20.00	175-275
1992	Charlie "The Spirit of Friendshiip Warms The Heart" 950742	Retrd.	1996	22.50	45-75
1993	Chelsea "Good Friends Are A Blessing" 910694	Retrd.	1995	15.00	225-325
1996	Cheryl & Carl "Wishing You A Cozy Christmas" 141216	Open		25.00	25
1995	Christian "My Prayer Is For You" 103837	Open		18.50	19
1995	Christine "My Prayer Is For You" 103845	Open		18.50	19
1992	Christopher "Old Friends Are The Best Friends" 950483	Open		50.00	50
1993	Connie "You're A Sweet Treat" 912794	Retrd.	1996	15.00	35-50
1992	Couple in Basket/Umbrella (Musical) 950645	Retrd.	1997	60.00	60
1994	Courtney "Springtime Is A Blessing From Above" 916390	Retrd.	1996	15.00	60-125
1995	Cupid Baby on Pillow 2 Asst 103659	Suspd.		13.50	14-27
1995	Cupid Boy Sitting 2 Asst 869074	Suspd.		13.50	14-27
1995	Cupid Boy/Girl Double 103594	Suspd.		25.00	30-50
1995	Cupid Boy/Girl Double 2 Asst 869082	Suspd.		18.50	19-36
1993	Daisy "Friendship Blossoms With Love" 910651	Retrd.	1996	15.00	500-900
1996	Daniel "You're My Little Pumpkin" 176214	Open		22.50	23
1996	Debbie "Let's Hear It For Friendship!" 156361	Open		15.00	15
1995	Donald "Friends Are Egg-ceptional Blessings" 103799	Open		20.00	20
1992	Douglas "Let's Be Friends" 950661	Retrd.	1995	20.00	40-65
1995	Earl "Warm Hearted Friends" 131873	Open		17.50	18
1994	Elizabeth & Ashley "My Beary Best Friend" 916277	Retrd.	1996	25.00	50-75
1994	Eric "Bear Tidings Of Joy" 622796	Open		22.50	25
1996	Erica "Friends Are Always Pulling For You" 176028	Open		22.50	23
1994	Faith "There's No Bunny Like You" 916412	Suspd.		20.00	50-100
1993	Freda & Tina "Our Friendship Is A Perfect Blend" 911747	Open		35.00	35
1995	Gail "Catching the First Blooms of Friendship" 103772	Open		20.00	20
1993	Gary "True Friendships Are Scarce" 912786	Suspd.		18.50	38
1995	Girl Bear Cupid 103586	Suspd.		15.00	30
1995	Girl Bear Flying Cupid 103616	Suspd.		13.00	26
1995	Girl Bear on Ottoman Musical 128058	Open		55.00	55
1993	Girl Praying (Musical) 914312	Open		37.50	38
1993	Gretel "We Make Magic, Me And You" 912778	Open		18.50	20
1993	Hans "Friends In Toyland" 912956	Retrd.	1995	20.00	75-125
1993	Heidi & David "Special Friends" 910708	Suspd.		25.00	45-55
1993	Henrietta "A Basketful of Wings" 910686	Suspd.		22.50	120-150
1994	Henry "Celebrating Spring With You" 916420	Suspd.		20.00	35-50
1995	Hope "Our Love Is Ever-Blooming" 103764	Open		20.00	20
1994	Ingrid "Bundled Up With Warm Wishes" Dated 1994 617237	Yr.Iss.	1994	20.00	40-60
1992	Jacob "Wishing For Love" 950734	Suspd		22.50	35-45
1996	Jamie & Ashley "I'm All Wrapped Up In Your Love" 141224	Open		25.00	25
1992	Jasmine "You Have Touched My Heart" 950475	Suspd.		22.50	30-55
1994	Jedediah "Giving Thanks For Friends" 617091	Retrd.	1997	17.50	20-35
1995	Jennifer "Gathering The Blooms of Friendship" 103810	Open		22.50	23
1992	Jeremy "Friends Like You Are Precious And Few" 950521	Retrd.	1995	15.00	25-60
1997	Jessica "A Mother's Heart Is Full of Love" 155438	Open		25.00	25
1996	Jessica "A Mother's Heart Is Full of Love" GCC Early Introduction 155438A	Yr.Iss.	1996	25.00	90-125
1993	Jointed Bear Christmas (Musical) 903337	Suspd.		60.00	75
1992	Joshua "Love Repairs All" 950556	Open		20.00	20
1994	Kathleen "Luck Found Me A Friend In You" 916447	Open		12.50	13
1992	Katie "A Friend Always Knows When You Need A Hug" 950440	Retrd.	1997	20.00	20
1994	Kelly "You're My One And Only" 916307	Suspd.		15.00	40-75
1995	Kevin "Good Luck To You" 103896	Retrd.	1996	12.50	32
1995	Kiss The Hurt And Make It Well 127965	Open		15.00	15
1996	Kittie "You Make Wishes Come True" 1996 Adoption Center Event 131865	Yr.Iss.	1996	17.50	40
1995	Kristen "Hugs of Love And Friendship" 141194	Open		20.00	20
1996	Laura "Friendship Makes It All Better" 156396	Open		15.00	15
1997	Lily "Lilies Bloom With Petals of Hope" Spring Catalog Exclusive 202959A	Yr.Iss.	1996	15.00	15
1996	Linda "ABC And 1 2 3, You're A Friend To Me!" 156426	Open		15.00	15
1996	Lindsey & Lyndon "Walking In A Winter Wonderland" Fall Catalog Exclusive 141178A	Yr.Iss.	1996	30.00	50
1995	Lisa "My Best Is Always You" 103780	Open		20.00	20
1995	Madeline "A Cup Full of Friendship" 135593	Open		20.00	20
1992	Mandy "I Love You Just The Way You Are" [illegible]	Retrd.	1995	15.00	35-65
1995	Margaret "A Cup Full of Love" 103667	Open		20.00	20
1993	Marie "Friendship Is A Special Treat" 910767	Open		20.00	20
1995	Marilyn "A Cup Full of Cheer" 135682	Open		20.00	20
1993	Mary "A Special Friend Warms The Season" 912840	Open		25.00	25
1995	Maureen "Lucky Friend" 135690	Retrd.	1996	12.50	25-35
1995	Melissa "Every Bunny Needs A Friend" 103829	Open		20.00	20
1993	Michael & Michelle "Friendship Is A Cozy Feeling" 910775	Suspd.		30.00	50-60
1993	Miles "I'm Thankful For A Friend Like You" 912751	Open		17.00	18
1995	Millie, Christy, Dorothy "A. Love Me Tender, B. Take Me To Your Heart, C. Love Me True" 128023	Retrd.	1996	37.50	125
1996	Mindy "Friendship Keeps Me On My Toes" 156418	Open		15.00	15
1993	Molly "Friendship Softens A Bumpy Ride" 910759	Retrd.	1996	30.00	60-75
1994	Nancy "Your Friendship Makes My Heart Sing" 916315	Retrd.	1996	15.00	75-125
1992	Nathaniel & Nellie "It's Twice As Nice With You" 950513	Retrd.	1996	30.00	60-75
1994	Nils "Near And Dear For Christmas" 617245	Suspd.		22.50	40-52
1996	Olga "Feel The Peace...Hold The Joy...Share The Love" 182966	Yr.Iss.	1996	50.00	75-95
1994	Oliver & Olivia "Will You Be Mine?" 916641	Suspd.		25.00	40-55
1996	Park Bench w/Bears 1996 National Event Piece CRT240	Yr.Iss.	1996	12.50	22-45
1995	Pat "Falling For You" 141313	Open		22.50	23
1994	Patience "Happiness Is Homemade" 617105	Retrd.	1997	17.50	20-35
1993	Patrice "Thank You For The Sky So Blue" 911429	Open		18.50	20
1993	Patrick "Thank You For A Friend That's True" 911410	Open		18.50	20
1995	Peter "You're Some Bunny Special 104973	Open		17.50	18
1994	Phoebe "A Little Friendship Is A Big Blessing" 617113	Retrd.	1995	13.50	25-40
1993	Priscilla "Love Surrounds Our Friendship" 910724	Retrd.	1997	15.00	30-75
1995	Priscilla & Greta "Our Hearts Belong to You" 128031	19,950		50.00	90-125
1993	Prudence "A Friend To Be Thankful For" 912808	Open		17.00	18
1996	Pumpkins/Corn Stalk/Scarecrow Mini 3 Asst. 176206	Open		15.00	15
1993	Robbie & Rachel "Love Bears All Things" 911402	Open		27.50	30
1996	Robert "Love Keeps Me Afloat" 156272	Open		13.50	14
1997	Ryan "I'm Green With Envy For You" 203041	Open		20.00	20

*Quotes have been rounded up to nearest dollar

YEAR ISSUE		EDITION LIMIT	YEAR RETD.	ISSUE PRICE	*QUOTE U.S. $
1992	Sara "Lov Ya" Jacki Hugs & Kisses", Karen "Best Buddy" 950432	Open		10.00	10
1995	Sculpted Irish Plaque 110981	Open		13.50	14
1994	Sean "Luck Found Me A Friend In You" 916439	Open		12.50	13
1995	Seth & Sarabeth "We're Beary Good Pals" 128015	Open		25.00	25
1996	Sign/Bunny/Basket of Strawberries Mini 3 Asst. 900931	Open		3.50	4
1992	Signage Plaque (Hamilton) 951005	Closed	N/A	15.00	40-75
1992	Signage Plaque 951005	Open		15.00	15
1994	Sonja "Holiday Cuddles" 622818	Open		20.00	20
1994	Stacie "You Lift My Spirit" 617148	Open		18.50	20
1992	Steven "A Season Filled With Sweetness" 951129	Retrd.	1995	20.00	40-75
1996	Stormi "Hark The Herald Angels Sing" 176001	Yr.Iss.	1996	20.00	30-40
1997	Sweetheart Collector Set/3, (Balcony displayer, Romeo "There's No Sweeter Rose Than You" & Juliet "Wherefore Art Thou Romeo?" 203114	Yr.Iss.		60.00	60
1996	Tabitha "You're The Cat's Meow" 176257	Open		15.00	15
1996	Tasha "In Grandmother's Attic" 1996 Adoption Center Exclusive 156353	19,960	1996	50.00	130-140
1994	Taylor "Sail The Seas With Me" 617156	Suspd.		15.00	30-75
1994	Thanksgiving Quilt 617075	Open		12.00	12
1992	Theadore, Samantha & Tyler "Friends Come In All Sizes" 950505	Open		20.00	20
1993	Theadore, Samantha & Tyler "Friendship Weathers All Storms (9") 912883	Suspd.		160.00	160
1993	Theadore, Samantha & Tyler "Friendship Weathers All Storms" (musical) 904546	Suspd.		170.00	175-200
1992	Theadore, Samantha & Tyler "Friendship Weathers All Storms" 950769	Retrd.	1997	20.00	45-75
1992	Theadore, Samantha & Tyler (9") "Friends Come In All Sizes" 951196	Open		130.00	130
1993	Thomas "Chuggin' Along", Jonathon "Sail With Me", Harrison "We're Going Places" 911739	Retrd.	1997	15.00	25-35
1993	Timothy "A Friend Is Forever" 910740	Retrd.	1996	15.00	25-50
1995	Town Tattler Sign 1995 National Event Piece CRT109	Yr.Iss.	1995	6.00	15-25
1993	Tracie & Nicole "Side By Side With Friends" 911372	Open		35.00	35
1996	Trunk Full of Bear Hugs 103977	Open		22.50	23
1995	Tucker & Travis "We're in This Together" 127973	Open		25.00	25
1996	Two Boys By Lamp Post Musical 141089	Open		50.00	50
1995	UK Bears, Bertie "Friends Forever Near or Far" 163457	Open		17.50	18
1995	UK Bears, Duncan "Your Friendship Is Music To My Ears" 163473	Open		17.50	18
1995	UK Bears, Gordon "Keepin' A Watchful Eye on You" 163465	Open		17.50	18
1995	UK Bears, Sherlock "Good Friends Are Hard To Find" 163481	Open		17.50	18
1995	UK Bears, set/4 (Bertie, Gordon, Duncan, Sherlock)	Open		70.00	125-175
1994	Victoria "From My Heart To Yours" 916293	Suspd.		16.50	70-125
1996	Violet "Blessings Bloom When You Are Near" 156280	Open		15.00	15
1994	Willie "Bears Of A Feather Stay Together" 617164	Retrd.	1997	15.00	15
1994	Winona "Little Fair Feather Friend" 617172	Retrd.	1997	15.00	15
1994	Wyatt "I'm Called Little Running Bear" 629707	Open		15.00	15
1994	Wylie "I'm Called Little Friend" 617121	Open		15.00	15
1992	Zachary "Yesterday's Memories Are Today's Treasures" 950491	Retrd.	1997	30.00	30

Special Limited Edition - P. Hillman

YEAR ISSUE		EDITION LIMIT	YEAR RETD.	ISSUE PRICE	*QUOTE U.S. $
1993	Holding On To Someone Special-Collector Appreciation Fig. 916285	Yr.Iss.	1993	20.00	250-350
1994	Priscilla Ann "There's No One Like Hue" Collectible Exposition Exclusive available only at Secaucus and South Bend in 1994 and at Long Beach in 1995	Yr.Iss.	1994	24.00	125-250
1993	Teddy & Roosevelt "The Book of Teddies 1903 1993" 624918	Yr.Iss.	1993	20.00	155-200

Across The Seas - P. Hillman

YEAR ISSUE		EDITION LIMIT	YEAR RETD.	ISSUE PRICE	*QUOTE U.S. $
1996	Bob "Our Friendship Is From Sea To Shining Sea" 202444	Open		15.00	15
1996	Carlos "I Found An Amigo In You" 202339	Open		15.00	15
1996	Claudette "Our Friendship Is Bon Appetit!" 197254	Open		15.00	15
1996	Fernando "You Make Everday A Fiesta" 202355	Open		15.00	15
1996	Johann "I'd Climb The Highest Alp For You" 202436	Open		15.00	15
1996	Katrinka "Tulips Blossom With Friendship" 202401	Open		15.00	15
1996	Kerstin "You're The Swedish of Them All" 197289	Open		15.00	15
1996	Lian "Our Friendship Spans Many Miles" 202347	Open		15.00	15
1996	Lorna "Our Love Is In The Highlands" 202452	Open		15.00	15
1996	Machiko "Love Fans A Beautiful Friendship" 202312	Open		15.00	15
1996	Nadia "From Russia, With Love" 202320	Open		15.00	15
1996	Preston "Riding Across The Great White North" 216739	Open		15.00	15
1996	Rajul "You're The Jewel Of My Heart" 202398	Open		15.00	15
1996	Winston "Friendship Is Elementary My Dear" 202878	Open		15.00	15

Blossoms of Friendship - P. Hillman

YEAR ISSUE		EDITION LIMIT	YEAR RETD.	ISSUE PRICE	*QUOTE U.S. $
1997	Dahlia "You're The Best Pick of the Bunch" 202932	Open		15.00	15
1997	Iris "You're The Iris of My Eye" 202908	Open		15.00	15
1997	Rose "Everything's Coming Up Roses" 202886	Open		15.00	15
1997	Susan "Love Stems From Our Friendship" 202894	Open		15.00	15

By The Sea, By The Sea - P. Hillman

YEAR ISSUE		EDITION LIMIT	YEAR RETD.	ISSUE PRICE	*QUOTE U.S. $
1997	Gregg "Everything Pails in Comparison To Friends" 203505	Open		20.00	20
1997	Jerry "Ready To Make a Splash" 203475	Open		17.50	18
1997	Jim and Joey "Underneath It All We're Forever Friends" 203513	Open		25.00	25
1997	Judy "I'm Your Bathing Beauty" 203491	Open		35.00	35
1997	Sandy "There's Room In My Sand Castle For You" 203467	Open		20.00	20

A Christmas Carol - P. Hillman

YEAR ISSUE		EDITION LIMIT	YEAR RETD.	ISSUE PRICE	*QUOTE U.S. $
1994	Bear Cratchit "And A Very Merry Christmas To You Mr. Scrooge" 617326	Suspd.		17.50	18
1994	Counting House 622788	Suspd.		75.00	75
1994	Cratchit's House 651362	Suspd.		75.00	75
1994	Ebearneezer Scrooge "Bah Humbug!" 617296	Suspd.		17.50	18
1994	Gloria "Ghost of Christmas Past, " Garland "Ghost Of Christmas Present", Gabriel "Ghost of Christmas Yet To Come" 614807	Suspd.		55.00	55
1994	Jacob Bearly "You Will Be Haunted By Three Spirits" 614785	Suspd.		17.50	18
1994	Mrs. Cratchit "A Beary Christmas And Happy New Year!" 617318	Suspd.		18.50	19
1994	Tiny Ted-Bear "God Bless Us Every One" 614777	Suspd.		10.00	10

Circus Tent - P. Hillman

YEAR ISSUE		EDITION LIMIT	YEAR RETD.	ISSUE PRICE	*QUOTE U.S. $
1996	"Seal of Friendship" 137596	Open		10.00	10
1996	Bruno "Step Right Up And Smile" 103713	Open		17.50	18
1996	Claudia "You Take Center Ring With Me" 103721	Open		17.50	18
1996	Clown on Ball Musical 111430	Open		40.00	40
1997	Dudley "Just Clowning Around" 103748	Open		17.50	18
1997	Lion-"You're My Mane Attraction" 203548	Open		12.50	13
1997	Logan "Love Is A Bear Necessity" 103756	Open		17.50	18
1997	Shelby "Friendship Keeps You Popping" 203572	Open		17.50	18
1997	Tonya "Friends Are Bear Essentials" 103942	Open		20.00	20
1996	Wally "You're The Tops With Me" 103934	Open		17.50	18

Down Strawberry Lane - P. Hillman

YEAR ISSUE		EDITION LIMIT	YEAR RETD.	ISSUE PRICE	*QUOTE U.S. $
1997	Diane "I Picked The Beary Best For You" 202991	Yr.Iss.		25.00	25
1996	Ella "Love Grows in My Heart" 156329	Open		15.00	15
1996	Jenna "You're Berry Special To Me" 156337	Open		15.00	15
1996	Matthew "A Dash of Love Sweetens Any Day!" 156299	Open		15.00	15
1996	Tara "You're My Berry Best Friend!" 156310	Open		15.00	15
1996	Thelma "Cozy Tea For Two" 156302	Open		22.50	23

Family - P. Hillman

YEAR ISSUE		EDITION LIMIT	YEAR RETD.	ISSUE PRICE	*QUOTE U.S. $
1994	Father "A Father Is The Bearer Of Strength" 624888	Open		13.50	14
1994	Mother "A Mother's Love Bears All Things" 624861	Open		20.00	20
1994	Older Daughter "Child Of Love" 624845	Open		10.00	10
1994	Older Son "Child Of Pride" 624829	Open		10.00	10
1994	Young Daughter "Child Of Kindness" 624853	Open		9.00	9
1994	Young Son "Child of Hope" 624837	Open		9.00	9

Holiday Dangling - P. Hillman

YEAR ISSUE		EDITION LIMIT	YEAR RETD.	ISSUE PRICE	*QUOTE U.S. $
1996	Holden "Catchin' The Holiday Spirit" 176095	Open		15.00	15
1996	Jeffrey "Striking Up Another Year" Dated 1996 176044	Yr.Iss.	1996	17.50	35
1996	Jolene "Dropping You A Holiday Greeting" 176133	Open		20.00	20
1996	Joy "You Always Bring Joy" 176087	Open		15.00	15
1996	Noel "An Old Fashioned Noel To You" 176109	Open		15.00	15
1996	Nolan "A String Of Good Tidings" 176141	Open		20.00	20

Little Sparkles - P. Hillman

YEAR ISSUE		EDITION LIMIT	YEAR RETD.	ISSUE PRICE	*QUOTE U.S. $
1997	Bear w/January Birthstone Mini Figurine 239720	Open		7.50	8
1997	Bear w/February Birthstone Mini Figurine 239747	Open		7.50	8
1997	Bear w/March Birthstone Mini Figurine 239763	Open		7.50	8
1997	Bear w/April Birthstone Mini Figurine 239771	Open		7.50	8
1997	Bear w/May Birthstone Mini Figurine 239798	Open		7.50	8
1997	Bear w/June Birthstone Mini Figurine 239801	Open		7.50	8
1997	Bear w/July Birthstone Mini Figurine 239828	Open		7.50	8
1997	Bear w/August Birthstone Mini Figurine 239836	Open		7.50	8
1997	Bear w/September Birthstone Mini Figurine 239844	Open		7.50	8
1997	Bear w/October Birthstone Mini Figurine 239852	Open		7.50	8
1997	Bear w/November Birthstone Mini Figurine 239860	Open		7.50	8
1997	Bear w/December Birthstone Mini Figurine 239933	Open		7.50	8

Love Letters From Teddie Mini - P. Hillman

YEAR ISSUE		EDITION LIMIT	YEAR RETD.	ISSUE PRICE	*QUOTE U.S. $
1997	Bear w/ "I Love Bears" Blocks 902950	Open		7.50	8
1997	Bear w/ "I Love Hugs" Blocks 902969	Open		7.50	8
1997	Bear w/ "I Love You" Blocks 156515	Open		7.50	8
1997	Bear w/Heart Dangling Blocks 203084	Open		7.50	8
1997	Bears w/ "Love" Double 203076	Open		13.50	14

Monthly Friends to Cherish - P. Hillman

YEAR ISSUE		EDITION LIMIT	YEAR RETD.	ISSUE PRICE	*QUOTE U.S. $
1993	Jack January Monthly 914754 (Also available through Hamilton Collection)	Open		15.00	15
1993	Phoebe February Monthly 914762 (Also available through Hamilton Collection)	Open		15.00	15
1993	Mark March Monthly 914770 (Also available through Hamilton Collection)	Open		15.00	15
1993	Alan April Monthly 914789 (Also available through Hamilton Collection)	Open		15.00	15
1993	May May Monthly 914797 (Also available through Hamilton Collection)	Open		15.00	15
1993	June June Monthly 914800 (Also available through Hamilton Collection)	Open		15.00	15
1993	Julie July Monthly 914819 (Also available through Hamilton Collection)	Open		15.00	15
1993	Arthur August Monthly 914827 (Also available through Hamilton Collection)	Open		15.00	15
1993	Seth September Monthly 914835 (Also available through Hamilton Collection)	Open		15.00	15
1993	Oscar October Monthly 914843 (Also available through Hamilton Collection)	Open		15.00	15
1993	Nicole November Monthly 914851 (Also available through Hamilton Collection)	Open		15.00	15
1993	Denise December Monthly 914878 (Also available through Hamilton Collection)	Open		15.00	15

Nativity - P. Hillman

YEAR ISSUE		EDITION LIMIT	YEAR RETD.	ISSUE PRICE	*QUOTE U.S. $
1993	"Friendship Pulls Us Through" & "Ewe Make Being Friends Special" 912867	Open		13.50	14
1992	Angie "I Brought The Star" 951137	Open		15.00	15
1995	Celeste "An Angel To Watch Over You" 141267	Open		20.00	20
1992	Creche & Quilt 951218	Open		50.00	50
1992	Maria, Baby & Josh "A Baby Is God's Gift of Love" "Everyone Needs a Daddy"- 950688	Open		35.00	35
1993	Nativity (Musical) 912859	Suspd.		60.00	100-120
1993	Nativity Camel "Friends Like You Are Precious And True" 904309	Retrd.	1997	30.00	30
1994	Nativity Cow "That's What Friends Are For" 651095	Retrd.	1997	22.50	23
1993	Nativity Figurine Gift Set w/Creche 916684	Open		100.00	100
1996	Nativity Prayer Plaque 176362	Open		13.50	14
1994	Ronnie "I'll Play My Drum For You" 912905	Open		13.50	14
1992	Sammy "Little Lambs Are In My Care" 950726	Open		17.50	18
1992	Three Kings-Richard "My Gift Is Loving", Edward "My Gift Is Caring", Wilbur "My Gift Is Sharing" 950718	Open		55.00	55

Nursery Rhyme - P. Hillman

YEAR ISSUE		EDITION LIMIT	YEAR RETD.	ISSUE PRICE	*QUOTE U.S. $
1994	Jack & Jill "Our Friendship Will Never Tumble" 624772	Open		30.00	30

*Quotes have been rounded up to nearest dollar

FIGURINES

Cherished Teddies/Enesco Corporation to Crystal World

YEAR ISSUE		EDITION LIMIT	YEAR RETD.	ISSUE PRICE	*QUOTE U.S.$
1994	Little Bo Peep "Looking For A Friend Like You" 624802	Open		22.50	23
1994	Little Jack Horner "I'm Plum Happy You're My Friend" 624780	Open		20.00	23
1994	Little Miss Muffet "I'm Never Afraid With You At My Side" 624799	Open		20.00	20
1994	Mary, Mary Quite Contrary "Friendship Blooms With Loving Care" 626074	Open		22.50	23
1994	Tom, Tom The Piper's Son "Wherever You Go I'll Follow" 624810	Open		20.00	20

Santa Express - P. Hillman

YEAR ISSUE		EDITION LIMIT	YEAR RETD.	ISSUE PRICE	*QUOTE U.S.$
1996	Car of Toys "Riding Along With Friends and Smiles" 219096	Open		17.50	18
1996	Casey "Friendship Is The Perfect End To The Holidays" 219525	Open		22.50	23
1996	Colin "He Knows If You've Been Bad or Good" 219088	Open		17.50	18
1996	Lionel "All Aboard the Santa Express" 219061	Open		22.50	23
1996	Tony "A First Class Delivery For You" 219487	Open		17.50	18

Santa's Workshop - P. Hillman

YEAR ISSUE		EDITION LIMIT	YEAR RETD.	ISSUE PRICE	*QUOTE U.S.$
1995	Ginger "Painting Your Holidays With Love" 141127	Open		22.50	23
1995	Holly "A Cup of Homemade Love" 141119	Open		18.50	19
1996	Klaus "Bearer of Good Tidings" 176036	Yr.Iss.	1996	20.00	22-40
1995	Meri "Handsewn Holidays" 141135	Open		20.00	20
1995	Nickolas "You're At The Top Of My List" 141100	Yr.Iss.	1995	20.00	35-65
1996	Ornaments/Mailsack/North Pole Sign Mini 3 Asst. 176079	Open		15.00	15
1995	Santa's Workshop Nightlight 141925	Open		75.00	75
1995	Yule "Building a Sturdy Friendship" 141143	Open		22.50	23

Sweetheart Ball - P. Hillman

YEAR ISSUE		EDITION LIMIT	YEAR RETD.	ISSUE PRICE	*QUOTE U.S.$
1996	Craig & Cheri "Sweethearts Forever" 156485	Open		25.00	25
1996	Darla "My Heart Wishes For You" 156469	Open		20.00	20
1996	Darrel "Love Unveils A Happy Heart" 156450	Open		17.50	18
1996	Jilly "Won't You Be My Sweetheart?" 156477	Open		17.50	18
1996	Marian "You're The Hero Of My Heart" 156442	Open		20.00	20
1996	Robin "You Steal My Heart Away" 156434	Open		17.50	18

T Is For Teddies - P. Hillman

YEAR ISSUE		EDITION LIMIT	YEAR RETD.	ISSUE PRICE	*QUOTE U.S.$
1995	Bear w/"A" Block 158488A	Open		5.00	5
1995	Bear w/"B" Block 158488B	Open		5.00	5
1995	Bear w/"C" Block 158488C	Open		5.00	5
1995	Bear w/"D" Block 158488D	Open		5.00	5
1995	Bear w/"E" Block 158488E	Open		5.00	5
1995	Bear w/"F" Block 158488F	Open		5.00	5
1995	Bear w/"G" Block 158488G	Open		5.00	5
1995	Bear w/"H" Block 158488H	Open		5.00	5
1995	Bear w/"I" Block 158488I	Open		5.00	5
1995	Bear w/"J" Block 158488J	Open		5.00	5
1995	Bear w/"K" Block 158488K	Open		5.00	5
1995	Bear w/"L" Block 158488L	Open		5.00	5
1995	Bear w/"M" Block 158488M	Open		5.00	5
1995	Bear w/"N" Block 158488N	Open		5.00	5
1995	Bear w/"O" Block 158488O	Open		5.00	5
1995	Bear w/"P" Block 158488P	Open		5.00	5
1995	Bear w/"Q" Block 158488Q	Open		5.00	5
1995	Bear w/"R" Block 158488R	Open		5.00	5
1995	Bear w/"S" Block 158488S	Open		5.00	5
1995	Bear w/"T" Block 158488T	Open		5.00	5
1995	Bear w/"U" Block 158488U	Open		5.00	5
1995	Bear w/"V" Block 158488V	Open		5.00	5
1995	Bear w/"W" Block 158488W	Open		5.00	5
1995	Bear w/"X" Block 158488X	Open		5.00	5
1995	Bear w/"Y" Block 158488Y	Open		5.00	5
1995	Bear w/"Z" Block 158488Z	Open		5.00	5

Through The Years - P. Hillman

YEAR ISSUE		EDITION LIMIT	YEAR RETD.	ISSUE PRICE	*QUOTE U.S.$
1993	"Beary Special One" Age 1 911348	Open		13.50	14
1993	"Chalking Up Six Wishes" Age 6 911283	Open		16.50	17
1993	"Color Me Five" Age 5 911291	Open		15.00	15
1993	"Cradled With Love" Baby 911356	Open		16.50	17
1993	"Three Cheers For You" Age 3 911313	Open		15.00	15
1993	"Two Sweet Two Bear" Age 2 911321	Open		13.50	14
1993	"Unfolding Happy Wishes Four You" Age 4 911305	Open		15.00	15

We Bear Thanks - P. Hillman

YEAR ISSUE		EDITION LIMIT	YEAR RETD.	ISSUE PRICE	*QUOTE U.S.$
1996	Barbara "Giving Thanks For Our Family" 141305	Open		12.50	13
1996	Dina "Bear In Mind, You're Special" 141275	Open		15.00	15
1996	John "Bear In Mind, You're Special" 141283	Open		15.00	15
1996	Rick "Suited Up For The Holidays" 141291	Open		12.50	13
1996	Table With Food / Dog 141542	Open		30.00	30

Crystal World

Animal Friends Collection - R. Nakai, unless otherwise noted

YEAR ISSUE		EDITION LIMIT	YEAR RETD.	ISSUE PRICE	*QUOTE U.S.$
1983	Alligator	Closed	N/A	46.00	46
1996	Baby Bird Bath	Open		45.00	45
1990	Baby Dinosaur - T. Suzuki	Closed	N/A	50.00	50
1990	Barney Dog - T. Suzuki	Closed	N/A	32.00	32
1984	Beaver	Closed	N/A	30.00	30
1990	Betsy Bunny - T. Suzuki	Closed	N/A	32.00	32
1984	Butterfly	Closed	N/A	36.00	36
1986	Butterfly, mini - N. Mulargia	Closed	N/A	15.00	15
1994	Cheese Mouse	Open		53.00	53
1987	Circus Puppy, large	Closed	N/A	50.00	50
1987	Circus Puppy, small	Closed	N/A	28.00	28
1990	Clara Cow - T. Suzuki	Closed	N/A	32.00	32
1984	Dachshund	Closed	N/A	28.00	28
1986	Dachshund, mini - N. Mulargia	Closed	N/A	15.00	15
1984	Dog	Closed	N/A	28.00	28
1984	Donkey	Closed	N/A	40.00	40
1987	Duckling - T. Suzuki	Closed	N/A	60.00	60
1983	Elephant	Closed	N/A	40.00	40
1985	Elephant, large	Closed	N/A	54.00	54
1995	Fido the Dog - T. Suzuki	Open		27.00	27
1995	Frisky Fido - T. Suzuki	Closed	1996	27.00	27
1986	Frog Mushroom, mini - N. Mulargia	Closed	N/A	15.00	15
1990	Georgie Giraffe - T. Suzuki	Closed	N/A	32.00	32
1990	Henry Hippo - T. Suzuki	Closed	N/A	32.00	32
1984	Hippo, large	Closed	N/A	50.00	50
1984	Hippo, small	Closed	N/A	30.00	30
1990	Jumbo Elephant - T. Suzuki	Open		32.00	32
1984	Kangaroo, large	Closed	N/A	50.00	50
1984	Kangaroo, small	Closed	N/A	34.00	34
1984	Koala Bear	Closed	N/A	50.00	50
1986	Koala, mini - N. Mulargia	Closed	N/A	15.00	15
1984	Koala, small	Closed	N/A	28.00	28
1995	Ling Ling - T. Suzuki	Open		53.00	53
1985	Lion, large	Closed	N/A	60.00	60
1985	Lion, small	Closed	N/A	36.00	36
1990	Mikey Monkey - T. Suzuki	Closed	N/A	32.00	32
1987	Mother Koala and Cub	Closed	N/A	55.00	55
1983	Mouse Standing	Closed	N/A	34.00	34
1983	Mouse, large	Closed	N/A	36.00	36
1983	Mouse, medium	Closed	N/A	[illegible]	28
1986	Mouse, mini - N. Mulargia	Closed	N/A	15.00	15
1983	Mouse, small	Closed	N/A	20.00	20
1994	Mozart - T. Suzuki	Open		48.00	48
1996	Noah and Friends - N. Mulargia	Open		150.00	150
1994	Owls - N. Mulargia	Open		53.00	53
1987	Panda, large	Closed	1995	45.00	45
1987	Panda, small	Closed	N/A	30.00	30
1984	Peacock	Closed	N/A	50.00	50
1984	Penguin	Closed	N/A	34.00	34
1987	Penguin On Cube	Closed	1996	30.00	30
1995	Percy Piglet - T. Suzuki	Open		19.00	19
1993	Pig - N. Mulargia	Closed	1995	50.00	50
1983	Pig, large	Closed	N/A	50.00	50
1983	Pig, medium	Closed	N/A	32.00	32
1983	Pig, small	Closed	N/A	22.00	22
1994	Playful Pup - T. Suzuki	Open		53.00	53
1987	Playful Pup, large	Closed	N/A	85.00	85
1987	Playful Pup, small	Closed	1995	32.00	32
1993	Playful Seal - T. Suzuki	Open		42.00	42
1984	Poodle	Closed	N/A	30.00	30
1987	Poodle, large	Closed	N/A	64.00	64
1987	Poodle, small	Closed	1994	35.00	35
1984	Porcupine	Closed	N/A	42.00	42
1987	Posing Penguin	Closed	N/A	85.00	85
1990	Puppy Love - T. Suzuki	Closed	N/A	45.00	45
1993	Puppy-Gram - T. Suzuki	Open		58.00	58
1987	Rabbit with Carrot, large	Closed	N/A	55.00	55
1987	Rabbit with Carrot, small	Closed	N/A	32.00	32
1983	Rabbit, large	Closed	N/A	50.00	50
1986	Rabbit, mini - N. Mulargia	Closed	N/A	15.00	15
1983	Rabbit, small	Closed	N/A	28.00	28
1985	Racoon	Closed	N/A	50.00	50
1984	Racoon, large	Closed	N/A	44.00	44
1984	Racoon, small	Closed	N/A	30.00	30
1987	Racoon, small	Closed	N/A	30.00	30
1989	Rainbow Dog, mini	Closed	N/A	25.00	25
1989	Rainbow Owl, mini	Closed	N/A	25.00	25
1989	Rainbow Penguin, mini	Closed	N/A	25.00	25
1989	Rainbow Squirrel, mini	Closed	N/A	25.00	25
1987	Rhinoceros	Closed	N/A	55.00	55
1994	Seal	Closed	1996	46.00	46
1987	Snowbunny, large	Closed	N/A	45.00	45
1987	Snowbunny, small	Closed	N/A	25.00	25
1991	Spike	Closed	N/A	50.00	50
1991	Spot	Closed	N/A	50.00	50
1985	Squirrel	Closed	1994	30.00	30
1986	Swan - N. Mulargia, mini	Open		15.00	28
1994	Sweetie - T. Suzuki	Open		28.00	28
1995	Tea Time	Open		50.00	50
1992	Trumpeting Elephant - T. Suzuki	Closed	1996	50.00	50
1993	Turtle	Closed	1996	65.00	65
1983	Turtle, large	Closed	N/A	56.00	56
1983	Turtle, medium	Closed	N/A	38.00	38
1984	Turtle, mini	Closed	N/A	18.00	18
1983	Turtle, small	Closed	N/A	28.00	28
1986	Unicorn	Closed	1994	110.00	110
1987	Walrus	Closed	N/A	70.00	70
1987	Walrus, small - T. Suzuki	Closed	N/A	60.00	60
1996	Wanna Play? - T. Suzuki	Open		65.00	65
1995	Wilbur in Love - N. Mulargia	Closed	1997	90.00	90
1994	Wilbur the Pig - T. Suzuki	Open		48.00	48

Bird Collection - R. Nakai, unless otherwise noted

YEAR ISSUE		EDITION LIMIT	YEAR RETD.	ISSUE PRICE	*QUOTE U.S.$
1986	Bird Bath - N. Mulargia	Closed	1989	54.00	75
1984	Bird Family	Closed	1990	22.00	35
1984	Love Bird	Closed	1988	44.00	65
1986	Love Birds	Closed	1992	54.00	75
1990	Ollie Owl - T. Suzuki	Closed	1993	32.00	40
1983	Owl Standing	Closed	1987	40.00	70
1983	Owl, large	Closed	1987	44.00	75
1983	Owl, small	Closed	1987	22.00	36
1991	Parrot Couple	Closed	1992	90.00	100
1985	Parrot, extra large	Closed	1988	300.00	450
1987	Parrot, large	Closed	1993	130.00	170
1985	Parrot, small	Closed	1989	100.00	110
1987	Parrot, small	Closed	1989	30.00	45
1990	Tree Top Owls - T. Suzuki	Closed	1993	96.00	96
1990	Wise Owl - T. Suzuki	Closed	1993	55.00	65
1990	Wise Owl-Small - T. Suzuki	Closed	1993	40.00	65

By The Beautiful Sea Collection - R. Nakai, unless otherwise noted

YEAR ISSUE		EDITION LIMIT	YEAR RETD.	ISSUE PRICE	*QUOTE U.S.$
1992	Baby Seal - T. Suzuki	Open		21.00	21
1991	Beaver	Closed	1996	47.00	47
1997	Coastal Lighthouse	Open		85.00	85
1983	Crab, large	Closed	N/A	20.00	20
1983	Crab, small	Closed	N/A	28.00	28
1996	Crabbie le Crab	Open		38.00	38
1992	Cute Crab - T. Suzuki	Open		27.00	32
1988	Dancing Dolphin	Closed	N/A	130.00	130
1988	Dolphin, small	Closed	N/A	55.00	55
1993	Extra Large Oyster with Pearl	Closed	1996	75.00	75
1984	Fish	Closed	N/A	36.00	36
1996	Freddy Frog	Open		30.00	30
1996	Frieda Frog	Open		37.00	37
1993	Harbor Lighthouse - N. Mulargia	Open		75.00	79
1988	Hatching Sea Turtle - T. Suzuki	Open		45.00	47
1988	Island Paradise, large	Closed	N/A	90.00	90
1988	Island Paradise, small	Closed	N/A	50.00	50
1988	Lighthouse, large	Closed	1994	150.00	150
1988	Lighthouse, small	Closed	1997	80.00	80
1994	Oscar Otter - T. Suzuki	Closed	1997	53.00	53
1983	Oyster, large	Closed	1994	30.00	30
1983	Oyster, mini	Closed	N/A	12.00	12
1983	Oyster, small	Closed	1994	18.00	18
1987	Palm Tree	Closed	N/A	160.00	160
1996	Pelican	Open		65.00	65
1996	Penguin On Cube	Open		48.00	48
1991	Penguin On Cube	Closed	1996	40.00	40
1996	Playful Dolphin	Open		125.00	125
1996	Playful Dolphin, small	Open		75.00	75
1992	Playful Dolphins - T. Suzuki	Closed	1996	60.00	60
1993	Playful Seal - T. Suzuki	Closed	1997	45.00	45
1993	Sailboat	Open		100.00	115
1994	Seal	Closed	1996	47.00	47
1992	Seaside Pelican - T. Suzuki	Closed	1995	55.00	55
1992	Tropical Fish	Closed	1995	95.00	95
1992	Tuxedo Penguin	Closed	1995	75.00	75
1992	The Whales - T. Suzuki	Closed	1994	60.00	60

By The Lake Collection - R. Nakai, unless otherwise noted

YEAR ISSUE		EDITION LIMIT	YEAR RETD.	ISSUE PRICE	*QUOTE U.S.$
1985	Butterfly Caterpillar	Closed	N/A	40.00	40
1985	Butterfly on Daisy	Closed	N/A	30.00	30
1984	Duck	Closed	N/A	30.00	30
1990	Duck Family	Closed	N/A	70.00	70
1984	Frog & Mushroom	Closed	N/A	46.00	46
1983	Frog, large	Closed	N/A	30.00	30
1983	Frog, mini	Closed	N/A	14.00	14
1983	Frog, small	Closed	N/A	26.00	26
1987	King Swan	Closed	N/A	110.00	110
1986	Love Swan - N. Mulargia	Closed	N/A	70.00	70
1995	Love Swans - N. Mulargia	Open		83.00	83
1996	Love Swans, large - N. Mulargia	Open		252.00	252
1990	Swan Family - T. Suzuki	Closed	N/A	70.00	70
1987	Swan, large	Closed	1996	70.00	70
1985	Swan, large	Closed	N/A	70.00	70
1983	Swan, large	Closed	N/A	44.00	44
1987	Swan, medium	Open		45.00	63
1985	Swan, medium	Closed	N/A	54.00	54
1985	Swan, mini	Open		28.00	29
1985	Swan, small	Closed	N/A	44.00	44
1983	Swan, small	Closed	N/A	28.00	28
1987	Swan, small	Open		32.00	47

Castles and Legends - R. Nakai, unless otherwise noted

YEAR ISSUE		EDITION LIMIT	YEAR RETD.	ISSUE PRICE	*QUOTE U.S.$
1991	Castle In The Sky	Closed	1994	150.00	150
1994	Castle Rainbow Rainbow Mtn. Bs.	Open		1575.00	1575
1994	Castle Royale/Clear Mountain Bs	Open		1300.00	1300
1989	Dragon Baby	Closed	1994	80.00	80
1996	Emerald Castle	Open		105.00	105
1993	Fantasy Castle, large	Open		230.00	245
1993	Fantasy Castle, medium	Open		130.00	142
1992	Fantasy Castle, mini - N. Mulargia	Open		40.00	40
1992	Fantasy Castle, small	Open		85.00	95
1995	Fantasy Coach, large - N. Mulargia	Open		368.00	368

*Quotes have been rounded up to nearest dollar

FIGURINES

YEAR ISSUE		EDITION LIMIT	YEAR RETD.	ISSUE PRICE	*QUOTE U.S. $
1995	Fantasy Coach, medium - N. Mulargia	Open		158.00	158
1995	Fantasy Coach, small - N. Mulargia	Open		100.00	100
1990	I Love You Unicorn - N. Mulargia	Closed	N/A	58.00	58
1987	Ice Castle	Closed	N/A	150.00	150
1988	Imperial Castle	Open		320.00	345
1988	Imperial Ice Castle	Closed	N/A	320.00	320
1989	Magic Fairy	Closed	N/A	40.00	40
1991	Majestic Castle - A. Kato	Open		390.00	390
1995	Mouse Coach, mini - N. Mulargia	Open		52.00	52
1995	Mouse Coach, small - N. Mulargia	Open		95.00	95
1988	Mystic Castle	Open		90.00	90
1988	Mystic Ice Castle	Closed	N/A	90.00	90
1990	Pegasus - N. Mulargia	Closed	N/A	50.00	50
1987	Rainbow Castle	Open		150.00	184
1989	Rainbow Castle, mini	Open		60.00	62
1990	Rainbow Unicorn - N. Mulargia	Open		50.00	58
1989	Star Fairy	Closed	N/A	65.00	65
1989	Starlight Castle	Closed	1994	155.00	155
1995	Treasure Chest	Open		63.00	63
1989	Unicorn & Friend	Closed	N/A	100.00	100
1990	Unicorn - N. Mulargia	Closed	1994	38.00	38

Clown Collection - R. Nakai, unless otherwise noted

YEAR ISSUE		EDITION LIMIT	YEAR RETD.	ISSUE PRICE	*QUOTE U.S. $
1985	Acrobatic Clown	Closed	N/A	50.00	50
1992	Baby Clown - N. Mulargia	Closed	N/A	30.00	30
1985	Baseball Clown	Closed	N/A	54.00	54
1996	Bo-Bo The Clown - N. Mulargia	Open		53.00	53
1984	Clown	Closed	N/A	42.00	42
1985	Clown On Unicycle	Closed	N/A	54.00	54
1985	Clown, small	Closed	N/A	30.00	30
1992	Flower Clown - N. Mulargia	Closed	N/A	70.00	70
1985	Golf Clown	Closed	N/A	54.00	54
1985	Jack In The Box, small	Closed	N/A	24.00	24
1985	Juggler	Closed	N/A	54.00	54
1985	Large Clown	Closed	N/A	42.00	42
1985	Large Jack In The Box	Closed	N/A	64.00	64
1985	Tennis Clown	Closed	N/A	54.00	54

Decorative Item Collection (Paperweights) - Various

YEAR ISSUE		EDITION LIMIT	YEAR RETD.	ISSUE PRICE	*QUOTE U.S. $
1993	100 mm Diamond - R. Nakai	Open		525.00	525
1996	40 mm Diamond - R. Nakai	Open		48.00	48
1993	50 mm Diamond - R. Nakai	Open		70.00	70
1993	75 mm Diamond - R. Nakai	Open		285.00	285
1990	Baseball - I. Nakamura	Closed	N/A	170.00	170
1995	Boston "Cityscape" Paperweight - R. Nakai	Open		105.00	105
1995	Boston Skyline Paperweight, med. - R. Nakai	Open		80.00	80
1989	Chicago - I. Nakamura	Open		150.00	150
1995	Chicago Skyline Clock Paperweight, med. - R. Nakai	Closed	1996	158.00	158
1996	Crystal Egg And Stand - R. Nakai	Open		83.00	83
1997	CyberMouse - N. Mulargia	Open		52.50	53
1991	Dallas Skyline - I. Nakamura	Open		180.00	180
1988	Empire State - G. Veith	Closed	N/A	120.00	120
1996	Fabulous Fifties Jukebox - N. Mulargia	Open		79.00	79
1990	Fishing - I. Nakamura	Closed	N/A	170.00	170
1990	Golfing - I. Nakamura	Closed	N/A	170.00	170
1992	Heart Clock - R. Nakai	Closed	N/A	100.00	100
1993	Manatee - R. Nakai	Open		125.00	130
1992	Manhattan Reflections - R. Nakai	Open		95.00	95
1997	Moravian Star - J. Makoto	Open		85.00	85
1988	N.Y. Skyline - G. Veith	Open		100.00	100
1988	Nativity - R. Nakai	Closed	1994	100.00	100
1992	Niagara Falls Pwght. - R. Nakai	Open		85.00	85
1994	NY "Cityscape" Pwght. - G. Veith	Open		105.00	105
1994	NY Dome Paperweight - G. Veith	Closed	1995	75.00	75
1994	NY Skyline Clock Paperweight - R. Nakai	Closed	1996	158.00	158
1994	NY Skyline Paperweight, med. - G. Veith	Open		80.00	80
1992	NY, small - G. Veith	Open		45.00	45
1995	Philadelphia "Cityscape" Paperweight - R. Nakai	Open		105.00	105
1995	Philadelphia Skyline Paperweight, med. - R. Nakai	Open		80.00	80
1991	Polar Bear - R. Nakai	Open		98.00	98
1994	S.F. Skyline Clock Paperweight - R. Nakai	Closed	1996	158.00	158
1994	San Francisco "Cityscape" Pwght. - G. Veith	Open		105.00	105
1989	San Francisco - I. Nakamura	Open		150.00	150
1994	San Francisco Dome Paperweight - G. Veith	Closed	1995	75.00	75
1995	San Francisco Skyline Clock Paperweight - R. Nakai	Closed	1996	158.00	158
1994	San Francisco Skyline Pwght., med. - G. Veith	Open		80.00	80
1993	San Francisco Skyline, small	Open		45.00	45
1990	Tennis - I. Nakamura	Closed	N/A	170.00	170
1994	Wash. DC "Cityscape" Paperweight - R. Nakai	Open		105.00	105
1994	Wash. DC Skyline Clock Paperweight - R. Nakai	Closed	1996	158.00	158
1994	Wash. DC Skyline Paperweight, med. - G. Veith	Open		80.00	80
1989	Washington - I. Nakamura	Open		150.00	150
1994	Washington DC Dome Paperweight - G. Veith	Closed	1995	75.00	75
1994	Washington Vietnam Memorial Pwt. - R. Nakai	Closed	1996	105.00	105

Fruit Collection - R. Nakai

YEAR ISSUE		EDITION LIMIT	YEAR RETD.	ISSUE PRICE	*QUOTE U.S. $
1993	Apple with Red Heart, medium	Open		37.00	39
1993	Apple with Red Heart, small	Open		21.00	22
1985	Apple, large	Open		44.00	68
1985	Apple, medium	Open		30.00	39
1987	Apple, mini	Open		15.00	16
1985	Apple, small	Open		15.00	15
1991	Large	Closed	N/A	42.00	42
1985	Pear	Closed	N/A	30.00	30
1996	Pineapple	Open		53.00	53
1991	Pineapple, medium	Closed	N/A	27.00	27
1991	Pineapple, small	Closed	N/A	16.00	16
1985	Strawberries	Closed	N/A	28.00	28

The Gambler Collection - R. Nakai, unless otherwise noted

YEAR ISSUE		EDITION LIMIT	YEAR RETD.	ISSUE PRICE	*QUOTE U.S. $
1991	Dice, small	Closed	1997	27.00	27
1991	Lucky 7	Closed	N/A	50.00	50
1997	Lucky Dice	Open		68.25	69
1994	Lucky Roll	Open		95.00	95
1996	One Arm Bandit	Open		70.00	70
1991	Rolling Dice - T. Suzuki	Closed	N/A	110.00	110
1993	Rolling Dice, large	Open		60.00	60
1993	Rolling Dice, medium	Open		48.00	48
1992	Rolling Dice, mini	Open		32.00	32
1993	Rolling Dice, small	Closed	1996	40.00	40
1993	Slot Machine, large - T. Suzuki	Open		83.00	83
1991	Slot Machine, mini	Open		30.00	30
1991	Slot Machine, small - T. Suzuki	Open		58.00	58
1994	Super Slot	Open		295.00	295

Holiday Treasure Collection - R. Nakai, unless otherwise noted

YEAR ISSUE		EDITION LIMIT	YEAR RETD.	ISSUE PRICE	*QUOTE U.S. $
1984	Angel	Closed	N/A	28.00	28
1997	Angel with Heart - T. Suzuki	Open		30.00	30
1995	Angel, large	Open		53.00	53
1985	Angel, large	Closed	N/A	30.00	30
1985	Angel, mini	Closed	1996	16.00	16
1994	Cathedral w/Rainbow Base	Open		104.00	104
1985	Christmas Tree, large	Open		126.00	126
1985	Christmas Tree, mini	Closed	N/A	10.00	10
1985	Christmas Tree, small	Open		50.00	68
1994	Country Church	Open		53.00	53
1994	Country Church w/Rainbow Base	Open		63.00	63
1994	Extra Large Christmas Tree	Open		315.00	315
1996	Frosty	Open		41.00	41
1995	Happy Birthday Cake	Open		63.00	63
1991	Holy Angel Blowing A Trumpet - T. Suzuki	Open		38.00	38
1991	Holy Angel Holding A Candle - T. Suzuki	Open		38.00	38
1991	Holy Angel Playing A Harp - T. Suzuki	Closed	1997	38.00	38
1986	Nativity - N. Mulargia	Open		150.00	179
1991	Nativity, small - T. Suzuki	Open		85.00	90
1987	Rainbow Christmas Tree, large	Closed	1995	40.00	40
1987	Rainbow Christmas Tree, small	Closed	1993	25.00	25
1984	Snowman	Closed	N/A	38.00	38
1990	Trumpeting Angel	Closed	N/A	60.00	60

Kitty Land Collection - T. Suzuki, unless otherwise noted

YEAR ISSUE		EDITION LIMIT	YEAR RETD.	ISSUE PRICE	*QUOTE U.S. $
1991	Calamity Kitty	Open		60.00	60
1984	Cat - R. Nakai	Closed	N/A	36.00	36
1990	Cat N Mouse	Closed	1996	45.00	45
1987	Cat with Ball, large - R. Nakai	Closed	N/A	70.00	70
1992	Country Cat	Open		60.00	62
1990	The Curious Cat	Open		62.00	62
1991	Curious Cat, large	Open		90.00	90
1991	Hello Birdie	Open		65.00	68
1992	Kitten in Basket - C. Kido	Open		35.00	40
1993	Kitty Kare	Closed	1995	70.00	70
1991	Kitty with Butterfly	Closed	N/A	60.00	60
1991	Kitty with Heart	Open		27.00	29
1990	Moonlight Cat - R. Nakai	Closed	1993	100.00	100
1995	Moonlight Kitties	Closed	1997	83.00	83
1991	Peekaboo Kitties	Open		65.00	65
1993	Pinky	Closed	1996	50.00	50
1992	Playful Kitty	Open		32.00	32
1993	Playful Kitty, large	Closed	1996	50.00	50
1989	Rainbow Mini Cat - R. Nakai	Closed	N/A	25.00	25
1991	Rockabye Kitty - R. Nakai	Open		80.00	83
1992	See Saw Pals - A. Kato	Open		40.00	41
1987	Small Cat with Ball - R. Nakai	Closed	1993	32.00	32
1991	Strolling Kitties	Closed	1993	65.00	65

Limited Edition Collection Series - Various

YEAR ISSUE		EDITION LIMIT	YEAR RETD.	ISSUE PRICE	*QUOTE U.S. $
1986	Airplane -T. Suzuki	Closed	1992	400.00	500
1997	Capitol Hill -T. Suzuki	350		1350.00	1350
1995	Classic Motorcycle -T. Suzuki	950		420.00	420
1993	Country Gristmill -T. Suzuki	1,250		320.00	340
1986	Crucifix - N. Mulargia	Closed	1992	300.00	400
1991	Cruise Ship -T. Suzuki	1000		2000.00	2100
1989	Dream Castle - R. Nakai	500		9000.00	10000
1986	The Eiffel Tower -T. Suzuki	2000		1000.00	1300
1988	Eiffel Tower, small -T. Suzuki	2000		500.00	600
1991	Ellis Island - R. Nakai	Closed	1992	450.00	500
1996	The Empire State Bldg. - R. Nakai	475		1315.00	1315
1985	Empire State Bldg., extra large - R. Nakai	Closed	1992	1000.00	1300
1987	Empire State Bldg., lg. - R. Nakai	2000		650.00	700
1993	Enchanted Castle - R. Nakai	750		800.00	895
1989	Grand Castle - R. Nakai	Closed	1996	2500.00	2500
1995	Independence Hall - R. Nakai	750		370.00	370
1987	Manhattanscape - G. Veith	Closed	1992	1000.00	1100
1996	Merry-Go-Round - N. Mulargia	750		280.00	280
1993	Riverboat - N. Mulargia	350		570.00	600
1992	Santa Maria - N. Mulargia	Closed	1993	1000.00	1050
1989	Space Shuttle Launch -T. Suzuki	Closed	1992	900.00	1000
1987	Taj Mahal -T. Suzuki	2000		2000.00	2100
1990	Tower Bridge -T. Suzuki	Closed	1992	600.00	650
1987	US Capitol Bldg., lg. -T. Suzuki	Closed	1992	1000.00	1100
1993	Victorian House - N. Mulargia	Closed	1996	190.00	190
1992	The White House - R. Nakai	200	1993	3000.00	3000

New York Collection - R. Nakai, unless otherwise noted

YEAR ISSUE		EDITION LIMIT	YEAR RETD.	ISSUE PRICE	*QUOTE U.S. $
1995	Chrysler Building	Open		275.00	275
1992	Contemp. Empire State Bldg., large - A. Kato	Closed	1996	475.00	475
1992	Contemp. Empire State Bldg., med.	Open		170.00	170
1992	Contemp. Empire State Bldg., sm.	Closed	1996	95.00	95
1992	Contemp. Empire State Bldg., small MV	Open		95.00	95
1992	Empire State Bldg. w/Windows, mini	Open		74.00	74
1987	Empire State Bldg., medium	Open		250.00	250
1991	Empire State Bldg., mini	Open		60.00	60
1987	Empire State Bldg., small	Open		120.00	120
1993	Holiday Empire State building - N. Mulargia	Open		205.00	205
1989	Liberty Island - N. Mulargia	Open		75.00	75
1990	Manhattan Island	Open		240.00	240
1993	Manhattan Island, sm. - N. Mulargia	Open		105.00	105
1993	Rainbow Contemp. Empire, sm.	Open		95.00	95
1985	The Statue of Liberty	Open		250.00	250
1987	Statue of Liberty, medium	Open		120.00	120
1992	Statue Of Liberty, mini	Open		50.00	50
1987	Statue of Liberty, sm. - N. Mulargia	Open		50.00	50
1992	Twin Towers, small	Open		130.00	130
1991	World Trade Center Bldg.	Open		170.00	170

Nostalgia Collection - Various

YEAR ISSUE		EDITION LIMIT	YEAR RETD.	ISSUE PRICE	*QUOTE U.S. $
1997	Baby Boy Carriage - T. Suzuki	Open		52.50	53
1997	Baby Girl Carriage - T. Suzuki	Open		52.50	53
1997	Clarinet - J. Makoto	Open		235.00	235
1996	Merry-Go-Round, sm. - N. Mulargia	Open		150.00	150
1996	Pinocchio - T. Suzuki	Open		150.00	150
1997	Up and Away - N. Mulargia	Open		39.50	40

Religious Moment Collection - N. Mulargia, unless otherwise noted

YEAR ISSUE		EDITION LIMIT	YEAR RETD.	ISSUE PRICE	*QUOTE U.S. $
1987	Church - T. Suzuki	Closed	N/A	40.00	40
1987	Cross On Mountain	Closed	N/A	30.00	30
1987	Cross On Mountain, large	Closed	N/A	85.00	85
1992	Cross with Rose	Closed	N/A	30.00	30
1987	Cross, small	Closed	1993	40.00	40
1987	Crucifix	Closed	N/A	50.00	50
1987	Crucifix On Mountain	Closed	N/A	40.00	40
1987	Face Of Christ - R. Nakai	Closed	N/A	35.00	35
1992	Peace On Earth - I. Nakamura	Closed	1995	95.00	95
1987	Star Of David - R. Nakai	Closed	1993	40.00	40

Spring Parade Collection - Various

YEAR ISSUE		EDITION LIMIT	YEAR RETD.	ISSUE PRICE	*QUOTE U.S. $
1990	African Violet - I. Nakamura	Open		32.00	32
1996	American Beauty Rose - N. Mulargia	Open		53.00	53
1992	Barrel Cactus - I. Nakamura	Closed	1995	45.00	45
1991	Blossom Bunny - T. Suzuki	Open		42.00	42
1991	Bunnies On Ice - T. Suzuki	Closed	1996	58.00	58
1991	Bunny Buddy with Carrot - T. Suzuki	Open		32.00	32
1992	Candleholder - N. Mulargia	Closed	1995	125.00	125
1991	Cheep Cheep - T. Suzuki	Open		35.00	35
1990	Crocus - R. Nakai	Closed	N/A	45.00	45
1992	Cute Bunny - T. Suzuki	Closed	1995	38.00	38
1995	Desert Cactus - N. Mulargia	Closed	1997	48.00	48
1994	The Enchanted Rose - R. Nakai	Open		126.00	126
1985	Flower Basket - R. Nakai	Closed	1995	36.00	36
1987	Flower Basket, small - R. Nakai	Closed	N/A	40.00	40
1992	Flowering Cactus - I. Nakamura	Closed	1996	58.00	58
1992	Half Dozen Flower Arrangement - N. Mulargia	Closed	1996	20.00	20
1992	Happy Heart - N. Mulargia	Closed	1996	25.00	25
1992	Hummingbird - T. Suzuki	Open		58.00	58
1992	Hummingbird, mini - T. Suzuki	Open		29.00	29
1990	Hyacinth - I. Nakamura	Open		50.00	50
1989	Large Windmill - R. Nakai	Closed	1991	160.00	160
1992	Long Stem Rose - N. Mulargia	Open		35.00	35
1994	Long Stem Rose in Vase - R. Nakai	Open		82.00	82
1992	Loving Hearts - N. Mulargia	Open		35.00	35
1995	Pink Rose - R. Nakai	Closed	1997	53.00	53
1995	Pink Rose in Vase - R. Nakai	Open		41.00	41
1991	Rainbow Butterfly, mini - R. Nakai	Closed	1997	27.00	27
1994	Rainbow Rose - N. Mulargia	Open		82.00	82
1987	Red Rose - R. Nakai	Open		35.00	35
1992	Rose Bouquet - I. Nakamura	Closed	N/A	100.00	100
1996	Rose Bouquet, small - R. Nakai	Open		45.00	45
1993	Songbirds - I. Nakamura	Open		90.00	90
1997	Spring Blossoms - S. Yamada	Open		90.00	90
1995	Spring Butterfly - R. Nakai	Open		62.00	62
1989	Spring Chick - R. Nakai	Open		50.00	53
1992	Spring Flowers - T. Suzuki	Closed	1997	40.00	40
1996	Water Lily, Medium, AB - R. Nakai	Open		210.00	210
1997	Water Lily, small AB - R. Nakai	Open		105.00	105
1992	Waterfront Village - N. Mulargia	Open		190.00	190
1989	Wedding Couple - N. Mulargia	Open		75.00	75

*Quotes have been rounded up to nearest dollar

FIGURINES

Crystal World to Dave Grossman Creations

YEAR ISSUE		EDITION LIMIT	YEAR RETD.	ISSUE PRICE	*QUOTE U.S.$
1985	Wedding Couple - R. Nakai	Closed	N/A	38.00	38
1995	Wedding Couple, med. - N. Mulargia	Open		63.00	63
1992	Wedding Couple, mini - N. Mulargia	Open		30.00	30
1987	White Rose - R. Nakai	Closed	N/A	35.00	35
1989	Windmill, small - R. Nakai	Closed	1993	90.00	90

Teddyland Collection - Various

YEAR ISSUE		EDITION LIMIT	YEAR RETD.	ISSUE PRICE	*QUOTE U.S.$
1995	Baby Bear's Christmas - T. Suzuki	Open		48.00	48
1990	Baron Von Teddy - T. Suzuki	Closed	1993	60.00	60
1987	Beach Teddies - N. Mulargia	Open		60.00	60
1992	Beach Teddies, sm. - N. Mulargia	Open		55.00	55
1992	Billard Buddies - T. Suzuki	Open		70.00	70
1993	Black Jack Teddies - N. Mulargia	Open		97.00	97
1988	Bouquet Teddy, lg. - N. Mulargia	Closed	N/A	50.00	50
1988	Bouquet Teddy, sm. - N. Mulargia	Open		35.00	35
1990	Choo Choo Teddy - T. Suzuki	Closed	1993	100.00	100
1991	Christmas Wreath Teddy - T. Suzuki	Closed	1993	70.00	70
1995	CompuBear - N. Mulargia	Open		63.00	63
1996	Cuddly Bear - R. Nakai	Open		48.00	48
1993	Flower Teddy - T. Suzuki	Open		50.00	50
1995	Fly A Kite Teddy - T. Suzuki	Closed	1997	41.00	41
1995	Get Well Teddy - R. Nakai	Closed	1996	48.00	48
1989	Golfing Teddies - R. Nakai	Open		100.00	100
1991	Gumball Teddy - T. Suzuki	Closed	1996	63.00	63
1989	Happy Birthday Teddy - R. Nakai	Open		50.00	50
1991	Heart Bear - T. Suzuki	Open		27.00	27
1991	High Chair Teddy - T. Suzuki	Closed	1993	75.00	75
1988	I Love You Teddy - N. Mulargia	Open		50.00	50
1994	I Love You Teddy Couple - N. Mulargia	Open		95.00	95
1995	I Love You Teddy w/lg. Heart - R. Nakai	Open		48.00	48
1992	Ice Cream Teddies - N. Mulargia	Open		55.00	55
1997	Jackpot Teddy - T. Suzuki	Open		62.50	63
1987	Loving Teddies - N. Mulargia	Open		75.00	75
1990	Loving Teddies, sm. - N. Mulargia	Open		60.00	60
1991	Luck Of The Irish - R. Nakai	Closed	1993	60.00	60
1991	Merry Christmas Teddy - T. Suzuki	Open		55.00	55
1985	Mother and Cub - R. Nakai	Closed	N/A	64.00	64
1990	Mountaineer Teddy - N. Mulargia	Closed	N/A	80.00	80
1991	My Favorite Picture - T. Suzuki	Open		45.00	45
1992	Patriotic Teddy - N. Mulargia	Open		30.00	30
1991	Play It Again Ted - T. Suzuki	Open		65.00	65
1991	Playground Teddy - R. Kido	Closed	N/A	90.00	90
1989	Rainbow Bear, mini - R. Nakai	Closed	N/A	25.00	25
1990	Rainbow Teddies - N. Mulargia	Closed	1993	95.00	95
1990	Rocking Horse Teddy - N. Mulargia	Closed	N/A	80.00	80
1987	Sailing Teddies - N. Mulargia	Open		100.00	100
1991	Santa Bear Christmas - T. Suzuki	Closed	1997	70.00	70
1991	Santa Bear Sleighride - T. Suzuki	Open		70.00	70
1991	School Bears - H. Serino	Closed	1993	75.00	75
1991	Scuba Bear - T. Suzuki	Closed	1993	65.00	65
1989	Shipwreck Teddies - N. Mulargia	Closed	1993	100.00	100
1992	Singing Baby Bear - T. Suzuki	Open		55.00	55
1987	Skateboard Teddy - R. Nakai	Closed	1993	30.00	30
1987	Skiing Teddy - R. Nakai	Closed	1997	50.00	50
1989	Speedboat Teddies - R. Nakai	Open		90.00	90
1990	Storytime Teddies - T. Suzuki	Open		70.00	70
1987	Surfing Teddy - R. Nakai	Closed	1993	45.00	45
1988	Surfing Teddy, large - R. Nakai	Closed	N/A	80.00	80
1991	Swinging Teddy - N. Mulargia	Open		100.00	100
1988	Teddies At Eight - N. Mulargia	Open		100.00	100
1988	Teddies With Heart - R. Nakai	Open		45.00	45
1989	Teddy Balloon - R. Nakai	Closed	1993	70.00	70
1994	Teddy Bear - R. Nakai	Closed	1997	63.00	63
1987	Teddy Bear Christmas - R. Nakai	Open		100.00	100
1994	Teddy Bear with Rainbow Base - R. Nakai	Open		75.00	75
1983	Teddy Bear, large - R. Nakai	Closed	N/A	68.00	68
1983	Teddy Bear, medium - R. Nakai	Closed	N/A	44.00	44
1983	Teddy Bear, small - R. Nakai	Closed	N/A	28.00	28
1988	Teddy Family - N. Mulargia	Closed	1993	50.00	50
1995	Teddy's Self Portrait - T. Suzuki	Closed	1997	53.00	53
1986	Teddy, mini - N. Mulargia	Closed	N/A	15.00	15
1997	Tee-Shot Teddy - T. Suzuki	Open		22.50	23
1987	Teeter Totter Teddies - N. Mulargia	Closed	1993	65.00	65
1988	Touring Teddies - N. Mulargia	Open		90.00	90
1990	Tricycle Teddy - T. Suzuki	Closed	1993	40.00	40
1991	Trim A Tree Teddy - R. Nakai	Closed	1996	50.00	50
1989	Vanity Teddy - R. Nakai	Closed	1993	100.00	100
1989	Windsurf Teddy - R. Nakai	Closed	1993	85.00	85
1988	Winter Teddies - N. Mulargia	Closed	N/A	90.00	90

The Voyage Collection - Various

YEAR ISSUE		EDITION LIMIT	YEAR RETD.	ISSUE PRICE	*QUOTE U.S.$
1990	Airplane, small - T. Suzuki	Closed	1993	200.00	200
1995	Amish Buggy - R. Nakai	Closed	1997	160.00	160
1995	Amish Buggy w/Wood Base - R. Nakai	Closed	1997	190.00	190
1994	Bermuda Rig Sailboat - R. Nakai	Open		105.00	105
1991	Bi-Plane, mini - T. Suzuki	Open		65.00	65
1992	Cable Car, mini - T. Suzuki	Closed	1996	40.00	40
1991	Cable Car, small - T. Suzuki	Open		70.00	70
1984	Classic Car - T. Suzuki	Closed	N/A	160.00	160
1996	Classic Motorcycle, sm. - T. Suzuki	Open		210.00	210
1995	Cruise Ship, mini - N. Mulargia	Open		105.00	105
1994	Cruise Ship, small - T. Suzuki	Open		575.00	575
1993	Express Train - N. Mulargia	Closed	1993	95.00	95
1992	Fire Engine - T. Suzuki	Open		100.00	100
1997	Grand Cable Car - T. Suzuki	Open		157.50	158
1991	Large Cable Car, lg. - T. Suzuki	Open		130.00	130
1984	Limousine - R. Nakai	Closed	N/A	46.00	46
1994	Mainsail Sailboat - R. Nakai	Open		230.00	230
1990	Orbiting Space Shuttle - T. Suzuki	Open		300.00	300
1991	Orbiting Space Shuttle, sm. - T. Suzuki	Closed	1997	90.00	90
1984	Pickup Track - R. Nakai	Closed	N/A	38.00	38
1991	The Rainbow Express - N. Mulargia	Closed	1993	125.00	125
1994	Riverboat, small - N. Mulargia	Open		210.00	210
1992	Sailing Ship - N. Mulargia	Open		38.00	38
1993	San Francisco Cable Car, lg. - R. Nakai	Open		59.00	59
1993	San Francisco Cable Car, small - R. Nakai	Open		40.00	40
1991	Schooner - N. Mulargia	Closed	1995	95.00	95
1990	Space Shuttle Launch, small - T. Suzuki	Closed	1996	265.00	265
1994	Spinnaker Sailboat - R. Nakai	Open		265.00	265
1984	Sports Car - T. Suzuki	Closed	N/A	140.00	140
1990	Square Rigger - R. Nakai	Open		250.00	250
1995	Tall Ship - R. Nakai	Open		395.00	395
1984	Touring Car - T. Suzuki	Closed	N/A	140.00	140
1984	Tractor Trailer - R. Nakai	Closed	N/A	40.00	40
1990	Train Set, large - T. Suzuki	Closed	N/A	480.00	480
1990	Train Set, small - T. Suzuki	Open		100.00	100

Wonders of the World Collection - R. Nakai, unless otherwise noted

YEAR ISSUE		EDITION LIMIT	YEAR RETD.	ISSUE PRICE	*QUOTE U.S.$
1993	Capitol Building, sm. - N. Mulargia	Open		100.00	100
1991	Chicago Water Tower w/Base -T. Suzuki	Closed	1997	300.00	300
1991	Chicago Water Tower w/o Base -T. Suzuki	Closed	1996	280.00	280
1990	Le Petit Eiffel -T. Suzuki	Open		240.00	240
1995	The Liberty Bell	Open		160.00	160
1993	Sears Tower	Open		150.00	150
1986	Space Needle, large	Closed	N/A	160.00	160
1986	Space Needle, sm. - N. Mulargia	Closed	N/A	50.00	50
1986	Taj Mahal	Open		1050.00	1050
1995	Taj Mahal, medium	Open		790.00	790
1995	Taj Mahal, small	Open		215.00	215
1987	U.S. Capitol Building	Open		250.00	250
1994	White House w/Oct. Mirror, small - N. Mulargia	Open		185.00	185

Dave Grossman Creations

Gone With The Wind Series - Unknown

YEAR ISSUE		EDITION LIMIT	YEAR RETD.	ISSUE PRICE	*QUOTE U.S.$
1987	Ashley GWW-2	Retrd.	1989	65.00	65
1993	Belle Waiting GWW-10	Retrd.	N/A	70.00	70
1997	Bonnie GWW-21	Open		50.00	50
1994	Gerald O'Hara GWW-15	Retrd.	N/A	70.00	70
1988	Mammy GWW-6	Retrd.		70.00	70
1995	Mrs. O'Hara GWW-16	Retrd.	1997	70.00	70
1991	Prissy GWW-8	Open		50.00	50
1993	Rhett & Bonnie GWW-11	Retrd.	N/A	80.00	80
1987	Rhett GWW-4	Retrd.	1989	65.00	65
1996	Rhett in Tuxedo GWW-19	Open		70.00	70
1993	Rhett in White Suit GWW-12	Retrd.	N/A	70.00	70
1990	Scarlett & Rhett on Stairs GWW-50	Retrd.	1992	130.00	130
1990	Scarlett (red dress) GWW-7	Retrd.	1992	70.00	70
1987	Scarlett GWW-1	Retrd.	1989	65.00	65
1997	Scarlett in Atlanta Dress GWW-20	Open		70.00	70
1994	Scarlett in Bar B Que Dress GWW-14	Retrd.	N/A	70.00	70
1996	Scarlett in Blue Dress GWW-18	Open		70.00	70
1992	Scarlett in Green Dress GWW-9	Open		70.00	70
1995	Suellen GWW-17	Retrd.	1997	70.00	70
1987	Tara GWW-5	Retrd.	N/A	70.00	70

Gone With The Wind Series 6" - Unknown

YEAR ISSUE		EDITION LIMIT	YEAR RETD.	ISSUE PRICE	*QUOTE U.S.$
1994	Ashley GWW-102	Open		40.00	40
1995	Mammy GWW-106	Open		40.00	40
1994	Rhett GW-104	Open		40.00	40
1996	Scarlett (B-B-Q Dress) GWW-114	Open		40.00	40
1994	Scarlett GWW-101	Open		40.00	40
1995	Suellen GWW-105	Open		40.00	40

Gone With The Wind-Scarlett & Her Beaus - Unknown

YEAR ISSUE		EDITION LIMIT	YEAR RETD.	ISSUE PRICE	*QUOTE U.S.$
1995	The Kiss GWWL-200	750	1995	150.00	150
1995	The Kiss GWWL-200AP	75	1995	180.00	180
1997	Scarlett & Ashley GWWL-202	750		150.00	150
1997	Scarlett & Ashley GWWL-202AP	75		180.00	180
1996	The Wedding GWWL-201	750	1996	150.00	150
1996	The Wedding GWWL-201AP	75	1996	180.00	180

Lladró-Norman Rockwell Collection Series - Rockwell-Inspired

YEAR ISSUE		EDITION LIMIT	YEAR RETD.	ISSUE PRICE	*QUOTE U.S.$
1982	Court Jester RL-405G	5,000	N/A	600.00	1300
1982	Daydreamer RL-404G	5,000	N/A	450.00	1300-1500
1982	Lladró Love Letter RL-400G	5,000	N/A	650.00	1000-1200
1982	Practice Makes Perfect RL-402G	5,000	N/A	725.00	800-1000
1982	Springtime RL-406G	5,000	N/A	450.00	1450
1982	Summer Stock RL-401G	5,000	N/A	750.00	800-900
1982	Young Love RL-403G	5,000	N/A	450.00	1350-1750

See also Lladró-Norman Rockwell Collection

Norman Rockwell America Collection - Rockwell-Inspired

YEAR ISSUE		EDITION LIMIT	YEAR RETD.	ISSUE PRICE	*QUOTE U.S.$
1989	Bottom of the Sixth NRC-607	Retrd.	N/A	140.00	140
1981	Breaking Home Ties NRV-300	Retrd.	N/A	2000.00	2300
1989	Doctor and Doll NRP-600	Retrd.	N/A	90.00	60
1989	First Day Home NRC-606	Retrd.	N/A	80.00	60
1989	First Haircut NRC-604	Retrd.	N/A	75.00	75
1989	First Visit NRC-605	Retrd.	N/A	110.00	110
1982	Lincoln NRV-301	Retrd.	N/A	300.00	375
1989	Locomotive NRC-603	Retrd.	N/A	110.00	110
1989	Runaway NRP-610	Retrd.	N/A	140.00	140
1982	Thanksgiving NRV-302	Retrd.	N/A	2500.00	2650
1989	Weigh-In NRP-611	Retrd.	N/A	120.00	120

Norman Rockwell America Collection-Lg. Ltd. Edition - Rockwell-Inspired

YEAR ISSUE		EDITION LIMIT	YEAR RETD.	ISSUE PRICE	*QUOTE U.S.$
1975	Baseball NR-102	Retrd.	N/A	125.00	475
1989	Bottom of the Sixth NRP-307	Retrd.	N/A	190.00	190
1982	Circus NR-106	Retrd.	N/A	500.00	500
1974	Doctor and Doll NR-100	Retrd.	N/A	300.00	1400
1989	Doctor and Doll NRP-300	Retrd.	N/A	150.00	150
1981	Dreams of Long Ago NR-105	Retrd.	N/A	500.00	750
1979	Leapfrog NR-104	Retrd.	N/A	440.00	750
1984	Marble Players NR-107	Retrd.	N/A	500.00	750
1975	No Swimming NR-101	Retrd.	N/A	150.00	550-600
1989	Runaway NRP-310	Retrd.	N/A	190.00	190
1974	See America First NR-103	Retrd.	N/A	100.00	500-550
1989	Weigh-In NRP-311	Retrd.	N/A	160.00	175

Norman Rockwell Collection - Rockwell-Inspired

YEAR ISSUE		EDITION LIMIT	YEAR RETD.	ISSUE PRICE	*QUOTE U.S.$
1982	American Mother NRG-42	Retrd.	N/A	100.00	125
1978	At the Doctor NR-29	Retrd.	N/A	108.00	150-275
1979	Back From Camp NR-33	Retrd.	N/A	96.00	120
1973	Back To School NR-02	Retrd.	N/A	20.00	40-45
1975	Barbershop Quartet NR-23	Retrd.	N/A	100.00	1400
1974	Baseball NR-16	Retrd.	N/A	45.00	175
1975	Big Moment NR-21	Retrd.	N/A	60.00	125
1973	Caroller NR-03	Retrd.	N/A	22.50	75
1975	Circus NR-22	Retrd.	N/A	55.00	145
1983	Country Critic NR-43	Retrd.	N/A	75.00	125
1982	Croquet NR-41	Retrd.	N/A	100.00	150
1973	Daydreamer NR-04	Retrd.	N/A	22.50	60
1975	Discovery NR-20	Retrd.	N/A	55.00	175
1973	Doctor & Doll NR-12	Retrd.	N/A	65.00	150-285
1979	Dreams of Long Ago NR-31	Retrd.	N/A	100.00	125
1976	Drum For Tommy NRC-24	Retrd.	N/A	40.00	95
1980	Exasperated Nanny NR-35	Retrd.	N/A	96.00	100
1978	First Day of School NR-27	Retrd.	N/A	100.00	150
1974	Friends In Need NR-13	Retrd.	N/A	45.00	100
1983	Graduate NR-44	Retrd.	N/A	30.00	85
1979	Grandpa's Ballerina NR-32	Retrd.	N/A	100.00	110
1980	Hankerchief NR-36	Retrd.	N/A	110.00	100-110
1973	Lazybones NR-08	Retrd.	N/A	30.00	250
1973	Leapfrog NR-09	Retrd.	N/A	50.00	600-700
1973	Love Letter NR-06	Retrd.	N/A	25.00	60
1973	Lovers NR-07	Retrd.	N/A	45.00	70
1978	Magic Potion NR-28	Retrd.	N/A	84.00	235
1973	Marble Players NR-11	Retrd.	N/A	60.00	425
1973	No Swimming NR-05	Retrd.	N/A	25.00	65-145
1977	Pals NR-25	Retrd.	N/A	60.00	150
1986	Red Cross NR-47	Retrd.	N/A	67.00	100
1973	Redhead NR-01	Retrd.	N/A	20.00	210
1980	Santa's Good Boys NR-37	Retrd.	N/A	90.00	100
1973	Schoolmaster NR-10	Retrd.	N/A	55.00	225
1984	Scotty's Home Plate NR-46	Retrd.	N/A	30.00	60
1983	Scotty's Surprise NRS-20	Retrd.	N/A	25.00	50-60
1974	See America First NR-17	Retrd.	N/A	50.00	150
1981	Spirit of Education NR-38	Retrd.	N/A	96.00	125
1974	Springtime '33 NR-14	Retrd.	N/A	30.00	65
1977	Springtime '35 NR-19	Retrd.	N/A	50.00	65
1974	Summertime '33 NR-15	Retrd.	N/A	45.00	65
1974	Take Your Medicine NR-18	Retrd.	N/A	50.00	100
1979	Teacher's Pet NRA-30	Retrd.	N/A	35.00	100
1980	The Toss NR-34	Retrd.	N/A	110.00	150-225
1982	A Visit With Rockwell NR-40	Retrd.	N/A	120.00	100-120
1988	Wedding March NR-49	Retrd.	N/A	110.00	175
1978	Young Doctor NRD-26	Retrd.	N/A	100.00	120
1987	Young Love NR-48	Retrd.	N/A	70.00	120

Norman Rockwell Collection-Boy Scout Series - Rockwell-Inspired

YEAR ISSUE		EDITION LIMIT	YEAR RETD.	ISSUE PRICE	*QUOTE U.S.$
1981	Can't Wait BSA-01	Retrd.	N/A	30.00	50
1981	Good Friends BSA-04	Retrd.	N/A	58.00	65
1981	Good Turn BSA-05	Retrd.	N/A	65.00	125
1982	Guiding Hand BSA-07	Retrd.	N/A	58.00	60
1981	Physically Strong BSA-03	Retrd.	N/A	56.00	150
1981	Scout Is Helpful BSA-02	Retrd.	N/A	38.00	45
1981	Scout Memories BSA-06	Retrd.	N/A	65.00	100
1983	Tomorrow's Leader BSA-08	Retrd.	N/A	45.00	55

Norman Rockwell Collection-Country Gentlemen Series - Rockwell-Inspired

YEAR ISSUE		EDITION LIMIT	YEAR RETD.	ISSUE PRICE	*QUOTE U.S.$
1982	Bringing Home the Tree CG-02	Retrd.	N/A	60.00	75
1982	The Catch CG-04	Retrd.	N/A	50.00	60
1982	On the Ice CG-05	Retrd.	N/A	50.00	60
1982	Pals CG-03	Retrd.	N/A	36.00	75
1982	Thin Ice CG-06	Retrd.	N/A	50.00	60
1982	Turkey Dinner CG-01	Retrd.	N/A	85.00	90

*Quotes have been rounded up to nearest dollar

Collectors' Information Bureau

61

Norman Rockwell Collection-Huck Finn Series - Rockwell-Inspired

YEAR ISSUE		EDITION LIMIT	YEAR RETD.	ISSUE PRICE	*QUOTE U.S. $
1980	Listening HF-02	Retrd.	N/A	110.00	120
1980	No Kings HF-03	Retrd.	N/A	110.00	110
1979	The Secret HF-01	Retrd.	N/A	110.00	130
1980	Snake Escapes HF-04	Retrd.	N/A	110.00	120

Norman Rockwell Collection-Miniatures - Rockwell-Inspired

YEAR ISSUE		EDITION LIMIT	YEAR RETD.	ISSUE PRICE	*QUOTE U.S. $
1984	At the Doctor's NR-229	Retrd.	N/A	35.00	35
1979	Back To School NR-202	Retrd.	N/A	18.00	25
1982	Barbershop Quartet NR-223	Retrd.	N/A	40.00	50
1980	Baseball NR-216	Retrd.	N/A	40.00	50
1982	Big Moment NR-221	Retrd.	N/A	36.00	40
1979	Caroller NR-203	Retrd.	N/A	20.00	25
1982	Circus NR-222	Retrd.	N/A	35.00	40
1979	Daydreamer NR-204	Retrd.	N/A	20.00	30
1982	Discovery NR-220	Retrd.	N/A	35.00	45
1979	Doctor and Doll NR-212	Retrd.	N/A	40.00	40
1984	Dreams of Long Ago NR-231	Retrd.	N/A	30.00	30
1982	Drum For Tommy NRC-224	Retrd.	N/A	25.00	30
1989	First Day Home MRC-906	Retrd.	N/A	45.00	45
1984	First Day of School NR-227	Retrd.	N/A	35.00	35
1989	First Haircut MRC-904	Retrd.	N/A	45.00	45
1980	Friends In Need NR-213	Retrd.	N/A	30.00	40
1979	Lazybones NR-208	Retrd.	N/A	22.00	50
1979	Leapfrog NR-209	Retrd.	N/A	32.00	32
1979	Love Letter NR-206	Retrd.	N/A	26.00	50
1979	Lovers NR-207	Retrd.	N/A	28.00	30
1984	Magic Potion NR-228	Retrd.	N/A	30.00	40
1979	Marble Players NR-211	Retrd.	N/A	36.00	38
1979	No Swimming NR-205	Retrd.	N/A	22.00	30
1984	Pals NR-225	Retrd.	N/A	25.00	25
1979	Redhead NR-201	Retrd.	N/A	18.00	50
1983	Santa On the Train NR-245	Retrd.	N/A	35.00	55
1979	Schoolmaster NR-210	Retrd.	N/A	34.00	45
1980	See America First NR-217	Retrd.	N/A	28.00	50
1980	Springtime '33 NR-214	Retrd.	N/A	24.00	80
1982	Springtime '35 NR-219	Retrd.	N/A	24.00	30
1980	Summertime '33 NR-215	Retrd.	N/A	22.00	50
1980	Take Your Medicine NR-218	Retrd.	N/A	36.00	40
1984	Young Doctor NRD-226	Retrd.	N/A	30.00	50

Norman Rockwell Collection-Pewter Figurines - Rockwell-Inspired

YEAR ISSUE		EDITION LIMIT	YEAR RETD.	ISSUE PRICE	*QUOTE U.S. $
1980	Back to School FP-02	Retrd.	N/A	25.00	25
1980	Barbershop Quartet FP-23	Retrd.	N/A	25.00	25
1980	Big Moment FP-21	Retrd.	N/A	25.00	25
1980	Caroller FP-03	Retrd.	N/A	25.00	25
1980	Circus FP-22	Retrd.	N/A	25.00	25
1980	Doctor and Doll FP-12	Retrd.	N/A	25.00	25
1980	Figurine Display Rack FDR-01	Retrd.	N/A	60.00	60
1980	Grandpa's Ballerina FP-32	Retrd.	N/A	25.00	25
1980	Lovers FP-07	Retrd.	N/A	25.00	25
1980	Magic Potion FP-28	Retrd.	N/A	25.00	25
1980	No Swimming FP-05	Retrd.	N/A	25.00	25
1980	See America First FP-17	Retrd.	N/A	25.00	25
1980	Take Your Medicine FP-18	Retrd.	N/A	25.00	25

Norman Rockwell Collection-Rockwell Club Series - Rockwell-Inspired

YEAR ISSUE		EDITION LIMIT	YEAR RETD.	ISSUE PRICE	*QUOTE U.S. $
1982	Diary RCC-02	Retrd.	N/A	35.00	75
1984	Gone Fishing RCC-04	Retrd.	N/A	30.00	55
1983	Runaway Pants RCC-03	Retrd.	N/A	65.00	75
1981	Young Artist RCC-01	Retrd.	N/A	96.00	105

Norman Rockwell Collection-Select Collection, Ltd. - Rockwell-Inspired

YEAR ISSUE		EDITION LIMIT	YEAR RETD.	ISSUE PRICE	*QUOTE U.S. $
1982	Boy & Mother With Puppies SC-1001	Retrd.	N/A	27.50	28
1982	Father With Child SC-1005	Retrd.	N/A	22.00	22
1982	Football Player SC-1004	Retrd.	N/A	22.00	22
1982	Girl Bathing Dog SC-1006	Retrd.	N/A	26.50	27
1982	Girl With Dolls In Crib SC-1002	Retrd.	N/A	26.50	27
1982	Helping Hand SC-1007	Retrd.	N/A	32.00	32
1982	Lemonade Stand SC-1008	Retrd.	N/A	32.00	32
1982	Save Me SC-1010	Retrd.	N/A	35.00	35
1982	Shaving Lesson SC-1009	Retrd.	N/A	30.00	30
1982	Young Couple SC-1003	Retrd.	N/A	27.50	28

Norman Rockwell Collection-Tom Sawyer Miniatures - Rockwell-Inspired

YEAR ISSUE		EDITION LIMIT	YEAR RETD.	ISSUE PRICE	*QUOTE U.S. $
1983	First Smoke TSM-02	Retrd.	N/A	40.00	45
1983	Lost In Cave TSM-05	Retrd.	N/A	40.00	50
1983	Take Your Medicine TSM-04	Retrd.	N/A	40.00	45
1983	Whitewashing the Fence TSM-01	Retrd.	N/A	40.00	50

Norman Rockwell Collection-Tom Sawyer Series - Rockwell-Inspired

YEAR ISSUE		EDITION LIMIT	YEAR RETD.	ISSUE PRICE	*QUOTE U.S. $
1976	First Smoke TS-02	Retrd.	N/A	60.00	235
1978	Lost In Cave TS-04	Retrd.	N/A	70.00	175
1977	Take Your Medicine TS-03	Retrd.	N/A	63.00	235
1975	Whitewashing the Fence TS-01	Retrd.	N/A	60.00	235

Norman Rockwell Saturday Evening Post - Rockwell-Inspired

YEAR ISSUE		EDITION LIMIT	YEAR RETD.	ISSUE PRICE	*QUOTE U.S. $
1992	After the Prom NRP-916	Open		75.00	75
1994	Almost Grown Up NRC-609	Open		75.00	75
1993	Baby's First Step NRC-604	Open		100.00	100
1993	Bed Time NRC-606	Retrd.	1997	100.00	100
1990	Bedside Manner NRP-904	Open		65.00	65
1990	Big Moment NRP-906	Retrd.	N/A	100.00	135
1990	Bottom of the Sixth NRP-908	Retrd.	1997	165.00	165
1993	Bride & Groom NRC-605	Open		100.00	100
1991	Catching The Big One NRP-909	Retrd.	1997	75.00	75
1992	Choosin Up NRP-912	Retrd.	N/A	110.00	140-150
1990	Daydreamer NRP-902	Open		55.00	55
1990	Doctor and Doll NRP-907	Retrd.	N/A	110.00	150
1995	First Down NRC-614	Open		130.00	130
1995	First Haircut NRC-610	Open		85.00	85
1994	For A Good Boy NRC-608	Open		100.00	100
1992	Gone Fishing NRP-915	Open		65.00	65
1991	Gramps NRP-910	Open		85.00	85
1994	Little Mother NRC-607	Open		75.00	75
1992	Missed NRP-914	Open		110.00	110
1995	New Arrival NRC-612	Open		90.00	90
1990	No Swimming NRP-901	Retrd.	N/A	50.00	50
1991	The Pharmacist NRP-911	Open		70.00	70
1990	Prom Dress NRP-903	Retrd.	N/A	60.00	60
1990	Runaway NRP-905	Open		130.00	130
1995	Sweet Dreams NRC-611	Open		85.00	85
1994	A Visit with Rockwell (100th Aniversary)-NRP-100	1,994		100.00	100

Norman Rockwell Saturday Evening Post-Miniatures - Rockwell-Inspired

YEAR ISSUE		EDITION LIMIT	YEAR RETD.	ISSUE PRICE	*QUOTE U.S. $
1991	A Boy Meets His Dog BMR-01	Retrd.	N/A	35.00	35
1991	Downhill Daring BMR-02	Retrd.	N/A	40.00	40
1991	Flowers in Tender Bloom BMR-03	Retrd.	N/A	32.00	32
1991	Fondly Do We Remember BMR-04	Retrd.	N/A	30.00	30
1991	In His Spirit BMR-05	Retrd.	N/A	30.00	30
1991	Pride of Parenthood BMR-06	Retrd.	N/A	35.00	35
1991	Sweet Serenade BMR-07	Retrd.	N/A	32.00	32
1991	Sweet Song So Young BMR-08	Retrd.	N/A	30.00	32

Spencer Collin-Admiral's Flag Quarters Series - C. Spencer Collin

YEAR ISSUE		EDITION LIMIT	YEAR RETD.	ISSUE PRICE	*QUOTE U.S. $
1996	Alki Point Light, VA 748G	5,000		74.00	74
1994	Alki Point Light, VA 748M	3,000	1996	74.00	74
1996	Diamond Head Light, CT 749G	5,000		130.00	130
1994	Diamond Head Light, CT 749M	3,000	1996	130.00	130
1996	Hospital Point Light, MA 750G	5,000		71.00	71
1994	Hospital Point Light, MA 750M	3,000	1996	71.00	71
1996	Yerba Buena Light, CA 747G	5,000		101.00	101
1994	Yerba Buena Light, CA 747M	3,000	1996	101.00	101

Spencer Collin-Commemorative Series - C. Spencer Collin

YEAR ISSUE		EDITION LIMIT	YEAR RETD.	ISSUE PRICE	*QUOTE U.S. $
1996	Admirality Head, WA 720G	5,000	1997	118.00	118
1990	Admirality Head, WA 720M	1,500	1996	98.00	110
1996	American Shoals, Fl 722G	5,000		97.00	97
1990	American Shoals, Fl 722M	1,500	1996	90.00	97
1990	Cape Hatteras, NC 718M	1,500	1994	70.00	70
1996	Sandy Hook Light, NJ 721G	5,000		95.00	95
1990	Sandy Hook Light, NJ 721M	1,500	1996	84.00	95
1996	West Quoddy Light, ME 719G	5,000		107.00	107
1990	West Quoddy Light, ME 719M	1,500	1996	95.00	98

Spencer Collin-Gold Label Signature Series - C. Spencer Collin

YEAR ISSUE		EDITION LIMIT	YEAR RETD.	ISSUE PRICE	*QUOTE U.S. $
1997	Holland Light, MI	4,500		70.00	70
1997	Holland Light, MI (signed/gold label)	500		70.00	70
1997	Lightship Nantucket	4,500		120.00	120
1997	Lightship Nantucket (signed/gold label)	500	1997	120.00	120
1997	New Dungeness, WA	4,500		70.00	70
1997	New Dungeness, WA (signed/gold label)	500		70.00	70

Spencer Collin-Lighthouses - C. Spencer Collin

YEAR ISSUE		EDITION LIMIT	YEAR RETD.	ISSUE PRICE	*QUOTE U.S. $
1996	10th Year Anniversary 751G	5,000		100.00	100
1994	10th Year Anniversary 751M	Retrd.	1994	100.00	100
1996	Annisquam Harbor Light, MA 742G	5,000		50.00	50
1993	Annisquam Harbor Light, MA 742M	2,000	1996	45.00	50
1996	Assateague Light, VA 727G	5,000		76.00	76
1991	Assateague Light, VA 727M	Retrd.	1996	69.00	76
1996	Barnegat Light, NJ 723G	5,000		71.00	71
1990	Barnegat Light, NJ 723M	Retrd.	1996	71.00	71
1996	Bass Harbor Light, ME 715G	5,000		103.00	103
1989	Bass Harbor Light, ME 715M	Retrd.	1996	95.00	103
1996	Boston Harbor Light, MA 710G	5,000		61.00	61
1987	Boston Harbor Light, MA 710M	Retrd.	1996	45.00	61
1985	Brant Point Lighthouse, MA 703M	Retrd.	1996	75.00	75
1996	Cape Hatteras Lighthouse, NC 802G	5,000		118.00	118
1995	Cape Hatteras Lighthouse, NC 802M	Retrd.	1996	118.00	118
1996	Cape May Light, NJ 738G	5,000		88.00	88
1992	Cape May Light, NJ 738M	Retrd.	1996	79.00	88
1996	Cape Neddick "Nubble" Light, ME 709G	5,000		95.00	95
1987	Cape Neddick "Nubble" Light, ME 709M	Retrd.	1996	80.00	95
1996	Castle Hill Light, RI 716G	5,000		32.00	32
1990	Castle Hill Light, RI 716M	Retrd.	1996	22.00	32
1985	Chatham Light, MA 706M	Retrd.	1996	68.00	80
1996	Christmas Eve Light 760G	5,000	1997	86.00	86
1995	Christmas Eve Light 760M	Retrd.	1996	86.00	86
1996	Concord Point Light, MD 761G	5,000		60.00	60
1995	Concord Point Light, MD 761M	2,000	1996	60.00	60
1996	Curtis Island Light, ME 734G	5,000		44.00	44
1992	Curtis Island Light, ME 734M	Retrd.	1996	40.00	44
1996	Edgartown Light, MA 801G	5,000		48.00	48
1994	Edgartown Light, MA 801M	Retrd.	1996	48.00	48
1985	Edgartown, MA (1st ed.) 705M	Retrd.	1996	24.00	24
1996	Eggrock Light, ME 731G	5,000		99.00	99
1992	Eggrock Light, ME 731M	Retrd.	1996	91.00	99
1996	Fire Island Light, NY 732G	5,000		122.00	122
1992	Fire Island Light, NY 732M	Retrd.	1996	114.00	122
1996	Fort Gratiot Light, MI 746G	5,000		57.00	57
1994	Fort Gratiot Light, MI 746M	2,000	1996	54.00	57
1996	Goat Island Light, ME 763G	5,000		50.00	50
1995	Goat Island Light, ME 763M	2,000	1996	50.00	50
1990	Great Point Light, MA 717M	Retrd.	1996	36.00	40
1996	Heceta Head Light, OR 753G	5,000		155.00	155
1994	Heceta Head Light, OR 753M	2,000	1996	155.00	155
1996	Highland "Cape Cod" Light, MA 733G	5,000		101.00	101
1992	Highland "Cape Cod" Light, MA 733M	Retrd.	1996	94.00	101
1996	Jeffrey's Hook Light, NY 735G	5,000		50.00	50
1992	Jeffrey's Hook Light, NY 735M	Retrd.	1996	45.00	50
1996	Jupiter Inlet Light, FL 743G	5,000		88.00	88
1993	Jupiter Inlet Light, FL 743M	2,000	1996	82.00	88
1986	Kennebec River Light, ME 707M	Retrd.	1995	23.00	27
1995	Logo Light w/Flashing Beacon 755M	Retrd.	1995	116.00	116
1996	Logo Mini-Plaque 757G	Open		53.00	53
1995	Logo Mini-Plaque 757M	Retrd.	1996	53.00	53
1996	Marblehead Light, OH 724G	5,000		46.00	46
1990	Marblehead Light, OH 724M	Retrd.	1996	36.00	46
1996	Marshall Point Light, ME 741G	5,000		50.00	50
1993	Marshall Point Light, ME 741M	2,000	1996	45.00	50
1996	Minots Ledge Light, MA 714G	5,000		59.00	59
1989	Minots Ledge Light, MA 714M	Retrd.	1996	50.50	59
1996	Monhegan Island Light, ME 730G	5,000		50.00	50
1991	Monhegan Island Light, ME 730M	Retrd.	1996	44.00	50
1996	Montauk Point Light, NY 711G	5,000		88.00	88
1988	Montauk Point Light, NY 711M	Retrd.	1996	80.00	88
1996	Mystic Seaport Light, CT 728G	5,000		32.00	32
1991	Mystic Seaport Light, CT 728M	Retrd.	1996	29.00	32
1986	Nauset Beach Light, MA 708M	Retrd.	1995	32.00	40
1996	New London Ledge Light, CT 745G	5,000		126.00	126
1993	New London Ledge Light, CT 745M	2,000	1996	124.00	126
1996	Nobska Light, MA 729G	5,000		40.00	40
1991	Nobska Light, MA 729M	Retrd.	1996	35.00	40
1996	Old Point Loma Light, CA 726G	5,000		86.00	86
1991	Old Point Loma Light, CA 726M	Retrd.	1996	80.00	86
1996	Peggy's Point Light, Nova Scotia 739G	5,000		44.00	44
1993	Peggy's Point Light, Nova Scotia 739M	Retrd.	1996	38.00	44
1996	Pemaquid Bell House, ME 704G	5,000		29.00	29
1984	Pemaquid Bell House, ME 704M	Retrd.	1996	16.00	29
1996	Personalized Lighthouse 712G	5,000		34.00	34
1988	Personalized Lighthouse 712M	Retrd.	1996	24.00	34
1996	Point Isabel, TX 752G	5,000		55.00	55
1994	Point Isabel, TX 752M	2,000	1996	55.00	55
1997	Polar Light	5,000		60.00	60
1996	Ponce Inlet Light, FL 744G	5,000		90.00	90
1993	Ponce Inlet Light, FL 744M	2,000	1996	83.00	90
1996	Portland Head Light, ME 701G	5,000	1997	82.00	82
1984	Portland Head Light, ME 701M	Retrd.	1996	75.00	75
1984	Portsmouth Light, NH 702M	Retrd.	1994	16.00	16
1996	Rock of Ages Light, MI 725G	5,000		63.00	63
1991	Rock of Ages Light, MI 725M	Retrd.	1996	58.00	63
1996	Round Island Light, MI 758G	5,000		120.00	120
1995	Round Island Light, MI 758M	2,000	1996	120.00	120
1996	Rudolph's Light 759G	5,000	1997	68.00	68
1995	Rudolph's Light 759M	Retrd.	1996	68.00	68
1996	Sand Island Light, AL 740G	5,000		71.00	71
1993	Sand Island Light, AL 740M	Retrd.	1996	65.00	71
1996	Split Rock Lighthouse, MI 737G	5,000		118.00	118
1992	Split Rock Lighthouse, MI 737M	Retrd.	1996	99.00	118
1996	St. Joseph's Pier Lights, MI 762G	5,000		114.00	114
1995	St. Joseph's Pier Lights, MI 762M	2,000	1996	114.00	114
1996	St. Simons Island Light, GA 736G	5,000		124.00	124
1992	St. Simons Island Light, GA 736M	Retrd.	1996	116.00	124
1996	Thomas Point Light, MD 754G	5,000		109.00	109
1995	Thomas Point Light, MD 754M	2,000	1996	109.00	109
1996	Whaleback Light, NH 713G	5,000		38.00	38
1989	Whaleback Light, NH 713M	Retrd.	1996	30.00	38
1995	Willie & Svea's Light 756M	Retrd.	1995	N/A	N/A

Spencer Collin-New England Collection - C. Spencer Collin

YEAR ISSUE		EDITION LIMIT	YEAR RETD.	ISSUE PRICE	*QUOTE U.S. $
1984	Historical Homes, set/10	Retrd.	1990	N/A	N/A
1984	Home Town, set/10	Retrd.	1990	200.00	200
1984	New England Cottages, set/10 w/base	Retrd.	1990	195.00	195
1984	New England Village, set/12 w/base	Retrd.	1990	227.00	227

Dear Artistic Sculpture, Inc.

Art Gallery Collection - A. Belcari

YEAR ISSUE		EDITION LIMIT	YEAR RETD.	ISSUE PRICE	*QUOTE U.S. $
1995	Autumn	3,000		500.00	500
1995	Black Mother Swing	2,000		750.00	750
1995	Canada Geese	1,000		1700.00	1700
1994	Carriage	2,000		1350.00	1350

FIGURINES

Dear Artistic Sculpture, Inc.
to Department 56

YEAR ISSUE		EDITION LIMIT	YEAR RETD.	ISSUE PRICE	*QUOTE U.S. $
1995	Couple on Horse	2,000		1100.00	1100
1993	Eagle Trunk	1,200		1050.00	1050
1993	Eagle Trunk, white	800		500.00	500
1995	Eagle, lg.	2,000		1250.00	1250
1995	Eagle, lg., white	2,000		750.00	750
1992	Eagle, white	1,000		475.00	475
1995	Elk	1,000		700.00	700
1996	Flamingo	3,000		800.00	800
1996	Giraff w/Young	1,000		800.00	800
1994	Group of Doves	2,000		850.00	850
1996	Hawk	1,000		1075.00	1075
1996	Heron	3,000		750.00	750
1995	Horse Head	2,000		650.00	650
1995	Horse Head, bronze	2,000		650.00	650
1994	Lady on Horse	1,000		850.00	850
1994	Lady on Horse	1,000		750.00	750
1996	Macaw	1,000		1650.00	1650
1996	Owls on Books	3,000		1050.00	1050
1995	Peacock	1,000		700.00	700
1996	Peacock, lg.	2,000		1150.00	1150
1996	Pegasus, lg.	3,000		675.00	675
1996	Pegasus, lg., white	3,000		575.00	575
1996	Pelican	1,000		775.00	775
1995	Snow Geese	1,000		1450.00	1450
1995	Spring	3,000		550.00	550
1995	Summer	3,000		500.00	500
1993	Two Eagles	1,200		1050.00	1050
1993	Two Eagles, white	800		450.00	450
1995	Two Gulls	1,000		1100.00	1100
1996	Two Ibis	3,000		1275.00	1275
1995	Two Swans	1,000		1250.00	1250
1995	Winter	3,000		500.00	500

Department 56

All Through The House - Department 56

YEAR ISSUE		EDITION LIMIT	YEAR RETD.	ISSUE PRICE	*QUOTE U.S. $
1992	Aunt Martha With Turkey 9317-3	Closed	1995	27.50	28
1992	Dinner Table 9313-0	Closed	1995	65.00	65
1992	Mr. & Mrs. Bell at Dinner 9314-9, set/2	Closed	1995	40.00	40
1992	Nicholas, Natalie, & Spot The Dog 9315-7, set/3	Closed	1995	45.00	45
1992	Sideboard 9316-5	Closed	1995	45.00	45
1994	Snowman with Plexi Sign 9874-4	Closed	1996	25.00	25

Easter Collectibles - Department 56

YEAR ISSUE		EDITION LIMIT	YEAR RETD.	ISSUE PRICE	*QUOTE U.S. $
1995	Bisque Chick, Large 2464-3	Closed	1996	8.50	10
1995	Bisque Chick, Small 2465-1	Closed	1996	6.50	8
1993	Bisque Duckling, set	Closed	1993	15.00	20-36
1993	Bisque Duckling, Large 3.5" 7282-6	Closed	1993	8.50	15
1993	Bisque Duckling, Small 2.75" 7281-8	Closed	1993	6.50	12
1994	Bisque Fledgling in Nest, Large 2.75" 2400-7	Closed	1994	6.00	10
1994	Bisque Fledgling in Nest, Small 2.5" 2401-5	Closed	1994	5.00	10
1991	Bisque Lamb, set	Closed	1991	12.50	60-78
1991	Bisque Lamb, Large 4" 7392-0	Closed	1991	7.50	25-40
1991	Bisque Lamb, Small 2.5" 7393-8	Closed	1991	5.00	25
1992	Bisque Rabbit, set	Closed	1992	14.00	30-45
1992	Bisque Rabbit, Large 5" 7498-5	Closed	1992	8.00	30
1992	Bisque Rabbit, Small 4" 7499-3	Closed	1992	6.00	18
1996	Bisque Rabbit, Large 2765-0	Open		8.50	9
1996	Bisque Rabbit, Small 2764-2	Open		7.50	8

Merry Makers - Department 56

YEAR ISSUE		EDITION LIMIT	YEAR RETD.	ISSUE PRICE	*QUOTE U.S. $
1991	Charles The Cellist 9355-6	Closed	1995	19.00	19
1991	Clarence The Concertinist 9353-0	Closed	1995	19.00	19
1991	Frederick The Flutist 9352-1	Closed	1995	19.00	19
1991	Horatio The Hornblower 9351-3	Closed	1995	19.00	19
1991	Martin The Mandolinist 9350-5	Closed	1995	19.00	19
1991	Sidney The Singer 9354-8	Closed	1995	19.00	19

Snowbabies - Department 56

YEAR ISSUE		EDITION LIMIT	YEAR RETD.	ISSUE PRICE	*QUOTE U.S. $
1989	All Fall Down 7984-7, set/4	Closed	1991	36.00	46-85
1990	All Tired Out, waterglobe 7937-5	Closed	1992	55.00	45-75
1988	Are All These Mine? 7977-4	Open		10.00	13
1995	Are You On My List? 6875-6	Open		25.00	25
1995	Are You On My List?, waterglobe 6879-7	Open		32.50	33
1986	Best Friends 7958-8	Closed	1989	12.00	100-150
1994	Bringing Starry Pines 6862-4	Open		35.00	35
1992	Can I Help, Too? 6806-3	18,500	1992	48.00	52-100
1993	Can I Open it Now? 6838-1 (Event Piece)	Closed	1993	15.00	30-38
1986	Catch a Falling Star, waterglobe 7967-7	Closed	1987	18.00	500-650
1996	Climb Every Mountain 68816	22,500	1996	75.00	100-130
1986	Climbing on Snowball, Bisque Votive w/Candle 7965-0	Closed	1989	15.00	90-120
1987	Climbing On Tree 7971-5, set/2	Closed	1989	25.00	700-895
1993	Crossing Starry Skies 6834-9	Open		35.00	35
1991	Dancing To a Tune 6808-0, set/3	Closed	1995	30.00	40
1987	Don't Fall Off 7968-5	Closed	1990	12.50	80-100
1987	Down The Hill We Go 7960-0	Open		20.00	23
1989	Finding Fallen Stars 7985-5	6,000	1989	32.50	130-195
1991	Fishing For Dreams 6809-8	Closed	1994	28.00	28-42
1992	Fishing For Dreams, waterglobe 6832-2	Closed	1994	32.50	46-57
1996	Five-Part Harmony 68824	Open		32.50	33
1986	Forest Accessory "Frosty Forest" 7963-4, set/2	Open		15.00	20
1988	Frosty Frolic 7981-2	4,800	1989	35.00	800-1000
1989	Frosty Fun 7983-9	Closed	1991	27.50	39-70
1995	Frosty Pines 76687, set/3	Open		12.50	13
1986	Give Me A Push 7955-3	Closed	1990	12.00	50-75
1986	Hanging Pair 7966-9	Closed	1989	15.00	125-175
1992	Help Me, I'm Stuck 6817-9	Closed	1994	32.50	35-50
1989	Helpful Friends 7982-0	Closed	1993	30.00	30-50
1986	Hold On Tight 7956-1	Open		12.00	14
1995	I Can't Find Him 68800	Open		37.50	38
1995	I Found The Biggest Star of All! 6874-8	Open		16.00	16
1993	I Found Your Mittens 6836-5, set/2	Closed	1996	30.00	30-40
1991	I Made This Just For You 6802-0	Open		15.00	15
1992	I Need A Hug 6813-6	Open		20.00	20
1995	I See You! 6878-0, set/2	Open		27.50	28
1995	I'll Hug You Goodnight, waterglobe 68798	Open		32.50	33
1995	I'll Play A Christmas Tune 68801	Open		16.00	16
1991	I'll Put Up The Tree 6800-4	Closed	1995	24.00	24-35
1993	I'll Teach You A Trick 6835-7	Closed	1996	24.00	24-30
1993	I'm Making an Ice Sculpture 6842-0	Closed	1996	30.00	30-40
1986	I'm Making Snowballs 7962-6	Closed	1992	12.00	25-40
1994	I'm Right Behind You! 6852-7	Open		60.00	60
1996	I'm So Sleepy 68810	Open		16.00	16
1996	It's A Grand Old Flag 68822	Open		25.00	25
1996	It's Snowing! 68821	Open		16.50	17
1989	Icy Igloo 7987-1	Open		37.50	38
1991	Is That For Me 6803-9, set/2	Closed	1993	32.50	33-50
1996	Jack Frost...A Sleighride Through the Stars 68811, set/3	Open		110.00	110
1994	Jack Frost...A Touch of Winter's Magic 6854-3	Open		90.00	95
1992	Join The Parade 6824-1	Closed	1994	37.50	41-51
1992	Just One Little Candle 6823-3	Open		15.00	15
1989	Let It Snow, waterglobe 7992-8	Closed	1993	25.00	35
1993	Let's All Chime In! 6845-4, set/2	Closed	1995	37.50	42-55
1994	Let's Go Skating 6860-8	Open		16.50	17
1992	Let's Go Skiing 6815-2	Closed	1994	15.00	15
1994	Lift Me Higher, I Can't Reach 6863-2	Open		75.00	75
1996	A Little Night Light 68823	Open		32.50	33
1992	Look What I Can Do! 6819-5	Closed	1996	16.50	20
1993	Look What I Found 6833-0	Open		45.00	45
1994	Look What I Found, waterglobe 6872-1	Open		32.50	33
1994	Mickey's New Friend 714-5 (Disney Exclusive)	Retrd.	1995	60.00	500-650
1995	Mush 68805	Open		48.00	48
1993	Now I Lay Me Down to Sleep 6839-0	Open		13.50	14
1996	Once Upon A Time... 68815	Open		25.00	25
1996	Once Upon a Time, music box 68832	Open		30.00	30
1992	Over the Milky Way 6828-4	Closed	1995	32.00	33-42
1995	Parade of Penguins 68804, set/6	Open		15.00	15
1991	Peek-A-Boo, waterglobe 7938-3	Closed	1993	50.00	72
1989	Penguin Parade 7986-3	Closed	1992	25.00	30-48
1994	Pennies From Heaven 6864-0	Open		17.50	18
1994	Planting Starry Pines, waterglobe 6870-5	Closed	1996	32.50	33
1991	Play Me a Tune, waterglobe 7936-7	Closed	1993	50.00	45
1995	Play Me a Tune, music box 68809	Open		37.50	38
1990	Playing Games Is Fun 7947-2	Closed	1993	30.00	35-50
1988	Polar Express 7978-2	Closed	1992	22.00	75-100
1990	Read Me a Story 7945-6	Open		25.00	25
1992	Read Me a Story, waterglobe 6831-4	Closed	1996	32.50	33
1995	Ring The Bells...It's Christmas! 6876-4	Open		40.00	40
1992	Shall I Play For You? 6820-9	Open		16.50	17
1995	Skate With Me, waterglobe 68799	Open		32.50	33
1995	Snowbabies Animated Skating Pond 7668-6, set/14	Open		60.00	60
1993	Snowbabies Picture Frame, Baby's First Smile 6846-2	Open		30.00	30
1987	Snowbabies Riding Sleds, waterglobe 7975-8	Closed	1988	40.00	700
1986	Snowbaby Holding Picture Frame 7970-7, set/2	Closed	1987	15.00	450-660
1986	Snowbaby Nite-Lite 7959-6	Closed	1989	15.00	300-360
1991	Snowbaby Polar Sign 6804-7	Closed	1996	20.00	20-30
1986	Snowbaby Standing, waterglobe 7964-2	Closed	1987	7.50	325-400
1987	Snowbaby with Wings, waterglobe 7973-1	Closed	1988	20.00	425-500
1993	So Much Work To Do 6837-3	Open		18.00	18
1993	Somewhere in Dreamland 6840-3	Open		85.00	85
1993	Somewhere in Dreamland (1 snowflake) 6840-3	Closed	N/A	85.00	110-126
1990	A Special Delivery 7948-0	Closed	1994	15.00	18-25
1996	Stargazing 68817, set/9	Open		40.00	40
1995	Star Gazing 7800 (Starter Set)	Open		40.00	40
1995	A Star in the Box (GCC exclusive) 68803	Closed	1996	18.00	25-45
1992	Starry Pines 6829-2, set/2	Open		17.50	18
1992	Stars-In-A-Row, Tic-Tac-Toe 6822-5	Closed	1995	32.50	32-45
1994	Stringing Fallen Stars 6861-6	Open		25.00	25
1994	There's Another One!, 6853-5	Open		24.00	24
1996	There's No Place Like Home 68820	Open		16.50	17
1991	This Is Where We Live 6805-5	Closed	1994	60.00	60-75
1992	This Will Cheer You Up 6816-0	Closed	1994	30.00	30-50
1988	Tiny Trio 7979-0, set/3	Closed	1990	20.00	150-175
1987	Tumbling In the Snow 7957-0, set/5	Closed	1993	35.00	80-100
1990	Twinkle Little Stars 7942-1, set/2	Closed	1993	37.50	40-55
1992	Wait For Me 6812-8	Closed	1994	48.00	48-60
1991	Waiting For Christmas 6807-1	Closed	1993	27.50	28-45
1993	We Make a Great Pair 6843-8	Open		30.00	30
1990	We Will Make it Shine 7946-4	Closed	1992	45.00	45-70
1994	We'll Plant the Starry Pines 6865-9, set/2	Open		37.50	38
1995	We're Building An Icy Igloo 68802	Open		70.00	70
1995	What Shall We Do Today? 6877-2	Open		32.50	33
1987	When You Wish Upon a Star, music box 7972-3	Closed	1993	30.00	32-45
1996	Which Way's Up 68812	Open		30.00	30
1993	Whistle While You Work, music box 6849-7	Closed	1995	32.50	40
1993	Where Did He Go? 6841-1	Open		35.00	35
1994	Where Did You Come From? 6856-0	Open		40.00	40
1990	Who Are You? 7949-9	12,500	1991	32.50	100-140
1991	Why Don't You Talk To Me 6801-2	Open		24.00	24
1993	Will it Snow Today? 6844-6	Closed	1995	45.00	52-65
1992	Winken, Blinken, and Nod 6814-4	Open		60.00	65
1987	Winter Surprise 7974-0	Closed	1992	15.00	30-45
1990	Wishing on a Star 7943-0	Closed	1994	22.00	30-40
1996	With Hugs & Kisses 68813, set/2	Open		32.50	33
1996	You Are My Lucky Star 68814, set/2	Open		35.00	35
1992	You Can't Find Me! 6818-7	Closed	1996	45.00	45
1992	You Didn't Forget Me 6821-7	Open		32.50	33
1996	You Need Wings Too! 68818	Open		25.00	25
1996	When the Bough Breaks 68819	Open		30.00	30

Snowbabies Pewter Miniatures - Department 56

YEAR ISSUE		EDITION LIMIT	YEAR RETD.	ISSUE PRICE	*QUOTE U.S. $
1989	All Fall Down 7617-1, set/4	Closed	1993	25.00	38-50
1989	Are All These Mine? 7605-8	Closed	1992	7.00	12-20
1989	Best Friends 7604-0	Closed	1994	10.00	11-20
1993	Can I Open it Now?, mini music box 7648-1	Closed	1994	20.00	23-30
1991	Dancing to a Tune 7630-9, set/3	Closed	1993	18.00	18-29
1989	Don't Fall Off! 7603-1	Closed	1994	7.00	10-23
1989	Finding Fallen Stars 7618-0, set/2	Closed	1992	12.50	25-36
1989	Frosty Frolic 7613-9, set/4	Closed	1993	24.00	24-42
1991	Frosty Frolic, music box 7634-1	Closed	1993	110.00	119
1993	Frosty Fun, mini music box 7650-3	Closed	1994	20.00	25-30
1989	Give Me a Push! 7601-5	Closed	1994	7.00	9-15
1989	Helpful Friends 7608-2, set/4	Closed	1992	13.50	18-28
1991	I Made This Just for You! 7628-7	Closed	1994	7.00	14
1991	I'll Put Up The Tree 7627-9	Closed	1996	9.00	9
1989	Icy Igloo, w/tree 7610-4, set/2	Closed	1992	7.50	19-25
1991	Is That For Me? 7631-7, set/2	Closed	1993	12.50	19-25
1992	Join the Parade 7645-7, set/4	Closed	1995	22.50	25-33
1989	Penguin Parade 7616-3, set/4	Closed	1993	12.50	24-34
1993	Penguin Parade, mini music box 7645-5	Closed	1994	20.00	33
1993	Play Me a Tune, mini music box 7651-1	Closed	1994	20.00	30
1990	Playing Games is Fun! 7623-6, set/2	Closed	1993	13.50	24-35
1989	Polar Express 7609-0, set/2	Closed	1992	13.50	26-35
1993	Reading a Story, mini music box 7649-0	Closed	1994	20.00	25-30
1990	A Special Delivery 7624-4	Closed	1993	7.00	13-23
1992	This Will Cheer You Up 7639-2	Closed	1995	13.75	19-23
1989	Tiny Trio 7615-5, set/3	Closed	1993	18.00	25-40
1989	Tumbling in the Snow! 7614-7, set/5	Closed	1992	30.00	58-65
1990	Twinkle Little Stars 7621-0, set/2	Closed	1993	15.00	18-28
1992	Wait For Me! 7641-4, set/4	Closed	1995	22.50	25-34
1991	Waiting for Christmas 7629-5	Closed	1993	13.00	13-25
1989	Winter Surprise! 7607-4	Closed	1994	13.50	14-25
1991	Wishing on a Star 7626-0	Closed	1995	10.00	13-22
1992	You Can't Find Me! 7637-6, set/4	Closed	1996	22.50	23
1992	You Didn't Forget Me! 7643-0, set/3	Closed	1995	17.50	18-25

Winter Silhouette - Department 56

YEAR ISSUE		EDITION LIMIT	YEAR RETD.	ISSUE PRICE	*QUOTE U.S. $
1990	Angel Candle Holder w/Candle 6767-9	Closed	1992	32.50	33
1992	Bedtime Stories Waterglobe 7838-7	Closed	1995	30.00	30
1989	Bringing Home The Tree 7790-9, set/4	Closed	1993	75.00	75
1989	Camel w/glass Votive 6766-0	Closed	1993	25.00	55-65
1987	Carolers 7774-7, set/4	Closed	1993	120.00	130-160
1991	Chimney Sweep 7799-2	Closed	1993	37.50	55
1989	Father Christmas 7788-7	Closed	1993	50.00	50
1991	Grandfather Clock 7797-6	Closed	1995	27.50	28
1988	Joy To The World 5595-6	Closed	1990	42.00	42
1988	Silver Bells Music Box 8271-6	Closed	1990	75.00	140
1988	Skating Couple 7772-0	Closed	1995	35.00	44
1987	Snow Doves 8215-5, set/2	Closed	1992	60.00	60
1992	Snowy White Deer 7837-9, set/2	Closed	1995	55.00	55
1989	Three Kings Candle Holder 6765-2, set/3	Closed	1992	85.00	85
1991	Town Crier 7800-0	Closed	1994	37.50	50

*Quotes have been rounded up to nearest dollar

Disneyana

Disneyana Conventions - Various

YEAR ISSUE		EDITION LIMIT	YEAR RETD.	ISSUE PRICE	*QUOTE U.S.$
1992	1947 Mickey Mouse Plush J20967 - Gund	1,000	1992	50.00	350
1992	Big Thunder Mountain A26648 - R. Lee	100	1992	1650.00	2200-2800
1992	Carousel Horse 022482 - PJ's	250	1992	125.00	275-300
1992	Cinderella 022076 - Armani	500	1992	500.00	3300-4500
1992	Cinderella Castle 022077 - John Hine Studio	500	1992	250.00	1100-1200
1992	Cruella DeVil Doll-porcelain 22554 - J. Wolf	25	1992	3000.00	3000-3500
1992	Disneyana Logo Charger - B. White	25	1992	600.00	2800
1992	Nifty-Nineties Mickey & Minnie 022503 - House of Laurenz	250	1992	650.00	700
1992	Pinocchio - R. Wright	100	1992	750.00	1000-2000
1992	Steamboat Willie-Resin - M. Delle	500	1992	125.00	1400
1992	Tinker Bell 022075 - Lladró	1,500	1992	350.00	2100-2500
1992	Two Merry Wanderers 022074 - Goebel	1,500	1992	250.00	950-1250
1992	Walt's Convertible (Cel) - Disney Art Ed.	500	1992	950.00	2300
1993	1947 Minnie Mouse Plush - Gund	1,000	1993	50.00	100
1993	Alice in Wonderland - Malvern	10	1993	8000.00	N/A
1993	Annette Doll - Alexander Doll	1,000	1993	395.00	600-800
1993	The Band Concert "Maestro Mickey" - Disney Art Ed.	275	1993	2950.00	N/A
1993	The Band Concert-Bronze - B. Toma	25	1993	650.00	3000-3500
1993	Bandleader-Resin - M. Delle	1,500	1993	125.00	250-270
1993	Family Dinner Figurine - C. Boyer	1,000	1993	600.00	950-1250
1993	Jumper from King Arthur Carousel - PJ's	250	1993	125.00	200-250
1993	Mickey & Pluto Charger - White/Rhodes	25	1993	850.00	3000
1993	Mickey Mouse, the Bandleader - Arribas Brothers	25	1993	700.00	2300-2700
1993	Mickey's Dreams - R. Lee	250	1993	400.00	600-900
1993	Peter Pan - Lladró	2,000	1993	400.00	800-1250
1993	Sleeping Beauty Castle - John Hine Studio	500	1993	250.00	400-550
1993	Snow White - Armani	2,000	1993	750.00	1000-1500
1993	Two Little Drummers - Goebel	1,500	1993	325.00	500-800
1993	Walt's Train Celebration - Disney Art Ed.	950	1993	950.00	1800
1994	Ariel - Armani	1,500	1994	750.00	1100-1500
1994	Cinderella/Godmother - Lladró	2,500	1994	875.00	770-1150
1994	Cinderella's Slipper - Waterford	1,200	1994	250.00	350-450
1994	Euro Disney Castle - John Hine Studio	750	1994	250.00	400
1994	Jessica & Roger Charger - White/Rhodes	25	1994	2000.00	3000-4000
1994	Mickey Triple Self Portrait - Goebel Miniatures	500	1994	295.00	900-1200
1994	Minnie Be Patient - Goebel	1,500	1994	395.00	470-550
1994	MM/MN w/House Kinetic - F. Prescott	10	1994	4000.00	N/A
1994	MM/MN/Goofy Limo (Stepin' Out) - Ron Lee	500	1994	500.00	375-500
1994	Scrooge in Money Bin/Bronze - Carl Barks	100	1994	1800.00	3500-4200
1994	Sleeping Beauty - Malvern	10	1994	5500.00	N/A
1994	Sorcerer Mickey-Bronze - B. Toma	100	1994	1000.00	1800-2200
1994	Sorcerer Mickey-Crystal - Arribas Brothers	50	1994	1700.00	2100-2500
1994	Sorcerer Mickey-Resin - M. Delle	2,000	1994	125.00	200
1995	Ah, Venice - M. Pierson	100	1995	2600.00	2600
1995	Ariel's Dolphin Ride - Wyland	250	1995	2500.00	2500
1995	Barbershop Quartet - Goebel Miniatures	750	1995	300.00	375-700
1995	Beauty and the Beast - Armani	2,000	1995	975.00	1100-1600
1995	Brave Little Tailor Charger - White/Rhodes	15	1995	2000.00	2850
1995	Celebrating-Resin - M. Delle	1,500	1995	125.00	200
1995	Donald Duck Mini-Charger - White/Rhodes	1,000	1995	75.00	75
1995	Ear Force One - R. Lee	500	1995	600.00	600
1995	Engine No. One - R. Lee	500	1995	650.00	995
1995	Fire Station #105 - Lilliput Lane	501	1995	195.00	425-550
1995	For Father - Goebel	1,500	1995	450.00	600
1995	Grandpa's Boys - Goebel	1,500	1995	340.00	340
1995	Mad Minnie Charger - White/Rhodes	10	1995	2000.00	4000
1995	Memories - B. Toma	200	1995	1200.00	1300
1995	Neat & Pretty Mickey-Crystal - Arribas	50	1995	1700.00	2900-3200
1995	Neat & Pretty Mickey-Resin - M. Delle	2,000	1995	135.00	200
1995	Plane Crazy - Arribas	50	1995	1750.00	2200-2400
1995	The Prince's Kiss - P Gordon	25	1995	250.00	600
1995	"Proud Pocahontas" Lithograph - D. Struzan	500	1995	195.00	250
1995	Sheriff of Bullet Valley - Barks/Vought	200	1995	1800.00	2500-2600
1995	Showtime - B. Toma	200	1995	1400.00	2000
1995	Simba - Bolae	200	1995	1500.00	1500
1995	Sleeping Beauty Castle Mirror - P. Gordon	250	1995	1200.00	1200
1995	Sleeping Beauty Dance - Lladró	1,000	1995	1280.00	1300-1600
1995	Sleeping Beauty's Tiara - Waterford	1,500	1995	250.00	250-395
1995	Snow White's Apple - Waterford	1,500	1995	225.00	300-500
1995	"Snow White & Friends" Brooch/Pendant - R. Viramontes	25	1995	1500.00	1500
1995	Thru the Mirror - Barks/Vought	200	1995	2600.00	2800-3200
1995	"Uncle Scrooge" Tile - Barks/Vought	50	1995	900.00	2000
1996	Brave Little Taylor - Arribas Brothers	50		1700.00	1700
1996	Brave Little Taylor (resin) - M. Delle	1,500	1996	125.00	175
1996	Brave Little Taylor Inlaid Leather Box - P. Gordon	25	1996	300.00	300
1996	Breakfast of Tycoons-Scrooge (litho) - C. Barks	295	1996	295.00	295
1996	Cinderella's Castle (bronze) - B. Toma	100	1996	1400.00	1400
1996	Flying Dumbo (bronze) - Wolf's Head	N/A	1996	2000.00	2000
1996	Hall of Presidents - Lilliput Lane	500	1996	225.00	650
1996	Heigh Ho - R. Lee	350		500.00	500
1996	Jasmine & Rajah - Armani	N/A	1996	800.00	800-1000
1996	Mickey - Armani	N/A	1996	Gift	N/A
1996	Minnie for Mother - Goebel	1,200		470.00	470
1996	Proud Pongo (w/backstamp) - Walt Disney Classics	1,200	1996	175.00	350-550
1996	Puppy Love - Goebel Miniatures	750	1996	325.00	375-475
1996	Self Control-Donald Duck (bronze) - C. Barks	150	1996	1800.00	1800
1996	Sorcerer - Waterford	1,200	1996	275.00	275
1996	Uncle Scrooge Charger Plate - B. White	25	1996	2500.00	2500

Duncan Royale

Collector Club - Duncan Royale

YEAR ISSUE		EDITION LIMIT	YEAR RETD.	ISSUE PRICE	*QUOTE U.S.$
1991	Today's Nast	Retrd.	1993	80.00	150
1994	Winter Santa	Retrd.	1994	125.00	150
1995	Santa's Gift	Retrd.	1995	100.00	150
1996	Santa's Choir	Retrd.	1996	90.00	90

1990 & 1991 Special Event Piece - Duncan Royale

YEAR ISSUE		EDITION LIMIT	YEAR RETD.	ISSUE PRICE	*QUOTE U.S.$
XX	Nast & Music	Retrd.	1993	79.95	80

Duncan Royale Figurines - Duncan Royale

YEAR ISSUE		EDITION LIMIT	YEAR RETD.	ISSUE PRICE	*QUOTE U.S.$
1996	Guardian Angel	2,500	1996	150.00	150
1996	Peace & Harmony	2,500		200.00	200

Ebony Collection - Duncan Royale

YEAR ISSUE		EDITION LIMIT	YEAR RETD.	ISSUE PRICE	*QUOTE U.S.$
1990	Banjo Man	5,000		80.00	80
1993	Ebony Angel	5,000		170.00	170
1991	Female Gospel Singer	5,000		90.00	90
1990	The Fiddler	5,000		90.00	90
1990	Harmonica Man	5,000		80.00	80
1991	Jug Man	5,000		90.00	90
1992	Jug Tooter	5,000		90.00	90
1992	A Little Magic	5,000		80.00	80
1991	Male Gospel Singer	5,000		90.00	90
1996	O' Happy Day (Youth Gospel)	5,000		70.00	71
1996	Pigskin (Youth Football)	5,000		70.00	71
1991	Preach	5,000		90.00	90
1991	Spoons	5,000	1996	90.00	90

Ebony Collection- History of Africa's Kings & Queens - Duncan Royale

YEAR ISSUE		EDITION LIMIT	YEAR RETD.	ISSUE PRICE	*QUOTE U.S.$
1996	Gbadebo	5,000		350.00	350
1996	Moshesh	5,000		200.00	200
1996	Nandi	5,000		200.00	200
1996	Shaka	5,000		200.00	200
1996	Sunni Ali Bear	5,000		200.00	200
1996	Tenkamenin	5,000		200.00	200

Ebony Collection-Buckwheat - Duncan Royale

YEAR ISSUE		EDITION LIMIT	YEAR RETD.	ISSUE PRICE	*QUOTE U.S.$
1992	O'Tay	5,000		70.00	90
1992	Painter	5,000		80.00	90
1992	Petee & Friend	5,000		90.00	90
1992	Smile For The Camera	5,000	1996	80.00	90

Ebony Collection-Friends & Family - Duncan Royale

YEAR ISSUE		EDITION LIMIT	YEAR RETD.	ISSUE PRICE	*QUOTE U.S.$
1994	Agnes	5,000		100.00	120
1994	Daddy	5,000		120.00	125
1994	Lunchtime	5,000		100.00	100
1994	Millie	5,000		100.00	100
1994	Mommie & Me	5,000		125.00	125

Ebony Collection-Jazzman - Duncan Royale

YEAR ISSUE		EDITION LIMIT	YEAR RETD.	ISSUE PRICE	*QUOTE U.S.$
1992	Bass	5,000		90.00	110
1992	Bongo	5,000		90.00	100
1992	Piano	5,000		130.00	140
1992	Sax	5,000		90.00	100
1992	Trumpet	5,000		90.00	100

Ebony Collection-Jubilee Dancers - Duncan Royale

YEAR ISSUE		EDITION LIMIT	YEAR RETD.	ISSUE PRICE	*QUOTE U.S.$
1993	Bliss	5,000		200.00	200
1993	Fallana	5,000		100.00	100
1993	Keshia	5,000		100.00	100
1993	Lamar	5,000		100.00	100
1993	Lottie	5,000		125.00	125
1993	Wilfred	5,000		100.00	100

Ebony Collection-Special Releases - Duncan Royale

YEAR ISSUE		EDITION LIMIT	YEAR RETD.	ISSUE PRICE	*QUOTE U.S.$
1991	Signature Piece	Open		50.00	50

History of Classic Entertainers - P. Apsit

YEAR ISSUE		EDITION LIMIT	YEAR RETD.	ISSUE PRICE	*QUOTE U.S.$
1987	American	Retrd.	1995	160.00	350
1987	Auguste	Retrd.	1995	220.00	350
1987	Greco-Roman	Retrd.	1995	180.00	350
1987	Grotesque	Retrd.	1995	230.00	350
1987	Harlequin	Retrd.	1995	250.00	350
1987	Jester	Retrd.	1995	410.00	700-800
1987	Pantalone	Retrd.	1995	270.00	300
1987	Pierrot	Retrd.	1995	180.00	225
1987	Pulcinella	Retrd.	1995	220.00	350
1987	Russian	Retrd.	1995	190.00	350
1987	Slapstick	Retrd.	1995	250.00	300
1987	Uncle Sam	Retrd.	1995	160.00	350

History of Classic Entertainers II - P. Apsit

YEAR ISSUE		EDITION LIMIT	YEAR RETD.	ISSUE PRICE	*QUOTE U.S.$
1988	Bob Hope	Retrd.	1995	250.00	250-295
1988	Feste	Retrd.	1995	250.00	250
1988	Goliard	Retrd.	1995	200.00	300
1988	Mime	Retrd.	1995	200.00	300
1988	Mountebank	Retrd.	1995	270.00	300
1988	Pedrolino	Retrd.	1995	200.00	300
1988	Tartaglia	Retrd.	1995	200.00	250
1988	Thomassi	Retrd.	1995	200.00	300
1988	Touchstone	Retrd.	1995	200.00	300
1988	Tramp	Retrd.	1995	200.00	300
1988	White Face	Retrd.	1995	250.00	300
1988	Zanni	Retrd.	1995	200.00	300

History of Classic Entertainers-Special Releases - P. Apsit

YEAR ISSUE		EDITION LIMIT	YEAR RETD.	ISSUE PRICE	*QUOTE U.S.$
1990	Bob Hope-18"	Retrd.	1995	1500.00	1700
1990	Bob Hope-6" porcelain	Retrd.	1995	130.00	130
1990	Mime-18"	Retrd.	1995	1500.00	1500
1988	Signature Piece	Retrd.	1995	50.00	50

History of Pirates and Buccaneers - Duncan Royale

YEAR ISSUE		EDITION LIMIT	YEAR RETD.	ISSUE PRICE	*QUOTE U.S.$
1997	Anne Bonny	5,000		75.00	75
1997	Blackbeard	5,000		75.00	75
1997	Calico Jack	5,000		75.00	75
1997	Captain Morgan	5,000		75.00	75

History of Santa Claus I - P. Apsit

YEAR ISSUE		EDITION LIMIT	YEAR RETD.	ISSUE PRICE	*QUOTE U.S.$
1983	Black Peter	Retrd.	1991	145.00	300
1983	Civil War	10,000	1991	145.00	350-400
1983	Dedt Moroz	Retrd.	1989	145.00	550-650
1983	Kris Kringle	Retrd.	1988	165.00	1100-1250
1983	Medieval	Retrd.	1988	220.00	1200-1800
1983	Nast	Retrd.	1987	90.00	1800-2200
1983	Pioneer	Retrd.	1989	145.00	275-325
1983	Russian	Retrd.	1989	145.00	550-600
1983	Soda Pop	Retrd.	1988	145.00	1250-1600
1983	St. Nicholas	Retrd.	1989	175.00	1100-1400
1983	Victorian	Retrd.	1990	120.00	300-400
1983	Wassail	Retrd.	1991	90.00	150-300

History of Santa Claus II - P. Apsit

YEAR ISSUE		EDITION LIMIT	YEAR RETD.	ISSUE PRICE	*QUOTE U.S.$
1986	Alsace Angel	10,000		250.00	300
1986	Babouska	10,000		170.00	200
1986	Bavarian	10,000		250.00	300
1986	Befana	10,000		200.00	250
1986	Frau Holda	10,000		160.00	180
1986	Lord of Misrule	10,000		160.00	200
1986	The Magi	10,000		350.00	400
1986	Mongolian/Asian	10,000		240.00	300
1986	Odin	10,000	1996	200.00	250
1986	The Pixie	10,000		140.00	175
1986	Sir Christmas	10,000		150.00	175
1986	St. Lucia	10,000		180.00	225

History of Santa Claus III - Duncan Royale

YEAR ISSUE		EDITION LIMIT	YEAR RETD.	ISSUE PRICE	*QUOTE U.S.$
1990	Druid	10,000	1996	250.00	250
1991	Grandfather Frost & Snow Maiden	10,000		400.00	400
1991	Hoteisho	10,000		200.00	200
1991	Judah Maccabee	10,000		300.00	300
1990	Julenisse	10,000		200.00	200
1991	King Wenceslas	10,000		300.00	300
1991	Knickerbocker	10,000		300.00	300
1991	Samichlaus	10,000		350.00	350
1991	Saturnalia King	10,000	1996	200.00	200
1990	St. Basil	10,000		300.00	300
1990	Star Man	10,000		300.00	300
1990	Ukko	10,000	1996	250.00	250

History of Santa Claus I (6") - P. Apsit

YEAR ISSUE		EDITION LIMIT	YEAR RETD.	ISSUE PRICE	*QUOTE U.S.$
1988	Black Peter-6" porcelain	6,000/yr.		40.00	80
1988	Civil War-6" porcelain	6,000/yr.		40.00	80
1988	Dedt Moroz -6" porcelain	6,000/yr.		40.00	80
1988	Kris Kringle-6" porcelain	6,000/yr.		40.00	80
1988	Medieval-6" porcelain	6,000/yr.		40.00	80
1988	Nast-6" porcelain	6,000/yr.		40.00	80
1988	Pioneer-6" porcelain	6,000/yr.		40.00	80
1988	Russian-6" porcelain	6,000/yr.		40.00	80
1988	Soda Pop-6" porcelain	6,000/yr.		40.00	80
1988	St. Nicholas-6" porcelain	6,000/yr.		40.00	80
1988	Victorian-6" porcelain	6,000/yr.		40.00	80
1988	Wassail-6" porcelain	6,000/yr.		40.00	80

History of Santa Claus II (6") - P. Apsit

YEAR ISSUE		EDITION LIMIT	YEAR RETD.	ISSUE PRICE	*QUOTE U.S.$
1988	Alsace Angel-6" porcelain	6,000/yr		80.00	90
1988	Babouska-6" porcelain	6,000/yr		70.00	80
1988	Bavarian-6" porcelain	6,000/yr		90.00	100
1988	Befana-6" porcelain	6,000/yr		70.00	80
1988	Frau Holda-6" porcelain	6,000/yr		50.00	80
1988	Lord of Misrule-6" porcelain	6,000/yr		60.00	80
1988	Magi-6" porcelain	6,000/yr		130.00	150
1988	Mongolian/Asian-6" porcelain	6,000/yr		80.00	90
1988	Odin-6" porcelain	6,000/yr		80.00	90
1988	Pixie-6" porcelain	6,000/yr		50.00	80
1988	Sir Christmas-6" porcelain	6,000/yr		60.00	80
1988	St. Lucia-6" porcelain	6,000/yr		70.00	80

*Quotes have been rounded up to nearest dollar

History of Santa Claus (18") - P. Apsit

YEAR ISSUE		EDITION LIMIT	YEAR RETD.	ISSUE PRICE	*QUOTE U.S.$
1989	Kris Kringle-18"	1,000	1995	1500.00	1500
1989	Medieval-18"	1,000	1995	1500.00	1500
1989	Nast-18"	1,000	1995	1500.00	1500
1989	Russian-18"	1,000	1995	1500.00	1500
1989	Soda Pop-18"	1,000	1995	1500.00	1500
1989	St. Nicholas-18"	1,000	1995	1500.00	1500

History of Santa Claus I -Wood - P. Apsit

YEAR ISSUE		EDITION LIMIT	YEAR RETD.	ISSUE PRICE	*QUOTE U.S.$
1987	Black Peter-8" wood	500	1993	450.00	450
1987	Civil War-8" wood	500	1993	450.00	450
1987	Dedt Moroz-8" wood	500	1993	450.00	450
1987	Kris Kringle-8" wood	500	1993	450.00	450
1987	Medieval-8" wood	500	1993	450.00	1200
1987	Nast-8" wood	500	1993	450.00	1500
1987	Pioneer-8" wood	500	1993	450.00	450
1987	Russian-8" wood	500	1993	450.00	450
1987	Soda Pop-8" wood	500	1993	450.00	850
1987	St. Nicholas-8" wood	500	1993	450.00	700
1987	Victorian-8" wood	500	1993	450.00	450
1987	Wassail-8" wood	500	1993	450.00	450

History Of Santa Claus-Special Releases - Duncan Royale

YEAR ISSUE		EDITION LIMIT	YEAR RETD.	ISSUE PRICE	*QUOTE U.S.$
1992	Nast & Sleigh	5,000		500.00	650
1991	Signature Piece	Open		50.00	50

Painted Pewter Miniatures-Santa 1st Series - Duncan Royale

YEAR ISSUE		EDITION LIMIT	YEAR RETD.	ISSUE PRICE	*QUOTE U.S.$
1986	Black Peter	500		30.00	30
1986	Civil War	500		30.00	30
1986	Dedt Moroz	500		30.00	30
1986	Kris Kringle	500		30.00	30
1986	Medieval	500		30.00	30
1986	Nast	500		30.00	30
1986	Pioneer	500		30.00	30
1986	Russian	500		30.00	30
1986	Soda Pop	500		30.00	30
1986	St. Nicholas	500		30.00	30
1986	Victorian	500		30.00	30
1986	Wassail	500		30.00	30
1986	Set of 12	500		360.00	360-495

Painted Pewter Miniatures-Santa 2nd Series - Duncan Royale

YEAR ISSUE		EDITION LIMIT	YEAR RETD.	ISSUE PRICE	*QUOTE U.S.$
1988	Alsace Angel	500		30.00	30
1988	Babouska	500		30.00	30
1988	Bavarian	500		30.00	30
1988	Befana	500		30.00	30
1988	Frau Holda	500		30.00	30
1988	Lord of Misrule	500		30.00	30
1988	Magi	500		30.00	30
1988	Mongolian	500		30.00	30
1988	Odin	500		30.00	30
1988	Pixie	500		30.00	30
1988	Sir Christmas	500		30.00	30
1988	St. Lucia	500		30.00	30
1988	Set of 12	500		360.00	360-495

Woodland Fairies - Duncan Royale

YEAR ISSUE		EDITION LIMIT	YEAR RETD.	ISSUE PRICE	*QUOTE U.S.$
1988	Almond Blossom	Retrd.	1993	70.00	70
1988	Apple	Retrd.	1994	70.00	70
1988	Calla Lily	Retrd.	1994	70.00	70
1988	Cherry	10,000	1995	70.00	70
1988	Chestnut	10,000	1995	70.00	70
1988	Christmas Tree	Retrd.	1993	70.00	70
1988	Elm	10,000	1995	70.00	70
1988	Guilder Rose	Retrd.	1994	70.00	70
1988	Lime Tree	Retrd.	1993	70.00	70
1988	Mulberry	10,000	1995	70.00	70
1988	Pear Blossom	Retrd.	1993	70.00	70
1988	Pine Tree	10,000	1995	70.00	70
1988	Poplar	10,000	1995	70.00	70
1988	Sycamore	Retrd.	1993	70.00	70

Enchantica

Enchantica Collectors Club - Various

YEAR ISSUE		EDITION LIMIT	YEAR RETD.	ISSUE PRICE	*QUOTE U.S.$
1991	Snappa on Mushroom-2101 - A. Bill	Retrd.	1991	Gift	10-150
1991	Rattajack with Snail-2102 - A. Bill	Retrd.	1991	60.00	85
1992	Jonquil-2103 - A. Hull	Retrd.	1992	Gift	75
1992	Ice Demon-2104 - K. Fallon	Retrd.	1992	85.00	150
1992	Sea Dragon-2106 - A. Bill	Retrd.	1993	99.00	275
1993	White Dragon-2107 - A. Bill	Retrd.	1993	Gift	200
1993	Jonquil's Flight-2108 - A. Bill	Retrd.	1993	140.00	300-375
1994	Verratus-2111 - A. Bill	Retrd.	1994	Gift	60
1994	Mimmer-Spring Fairy-2112 - A. Bill	Retrd.	1994	100.00	165
1994	Gorgoyle Cameo piece-2113 - K. Fallon	Retrd.	1994	Gift	10
1995	Destroyer-2116 - A. Hull	Retrd.	1995	100.00	100
1995	Cloudbreaker-2115 - J. Oliver	Retrd.	1995	Gift	N/A
1996	Sheylag's Trophy-2119	Retrd.	1996	125.00	125
1996	Jacarand-2118 - A. Hull	Retrd.	1996	Gift	N/A
1997	Dragonskeep-2126 - D. Mayer	Yr.Iss.		129.00	129
1997	Silverflame-2125 - A. Bill	Yr.Iss.		Gift	N/A

Retired Enchantica Collection - Various

YEAR ISSUE		EDITION LIMIT	YEAR RETD.	ISSUE PRICE	*QUOTE U.S.$
1994	Anaxorg-Six Leg Dragon-2094 - A. Hull	Retrd.	1995	87.00	87
1990	Arangast - Summer Dragon -2026 - K. Fallon	7,500	1992	165.00	350
1995	Avenger-2154 - A. Bill	450	1996	2900.00	2900
1991	Bledderag, Goblin Twin-2048 - K. Fallon	15,000	1993	115.00	175
1988	Blick Scoops Crystals-2015 - A. Bill	Retrd.	1991	47.00	70
1992	Breen - Carrier Dragon-2053 - K. Fallon	15,000	1993	156.00	175
1992	Cave Dragon-2065 - A. Bill	7,500	1994	200.00	225
1990	Cellandia-Summer Fairy-2029 - K. Fallon	Retrd.	1992	115.00	170
1996	Changeling-2121 - A. Bill	1,250	1996	120.00	120
1989	Chuckwalla-2021 - A. Bill	Retrd.	1994	43.00	60
1994	Coracob-Cobra Dragon-2093 - A. Hull	Retrd.	1995	87.00	87
1994	Daggerback-2114 - K. Fallon	Retrd.	1995	95.00	95
1992	Desert Dragon-2064 - A. Bill	7,500	1994	175.00	200
1994	Dromelaid, Tunnel Serpent-2097 - A. Bill	Retrd.	1997	83.00	83
1994	Escape (5th Anniversary)-2110 - A. Bill	Retrd.	1994	250.00	320
1988	Fantazar- Spring Wizard-2016 - A. Bill	7,500	1991	132.50	400
1991	Flight to Danger-2044 - K. Fallon	450	1991	3000.00	6500
1990	Fossfex - Autumn Fairy-2030 - K. Fallon	Retrd.	1992	115.00	200
1991	Furza - Carrier Dragon-2050 - K. Fallon	15,000	1993	137.50	200
1996	Glostomorg-2122 - A. Bill	Retrd.	1996	250.00	250
1988	Gorgoyle - Spring Dragon-2017 - A. Bill	7,500	1991	132.50	500
1991	Grawlfang '91 Winter Dragon -2046 - A. Bill	15,000	1994	295.00	375
1989	Grawlfang - Winter Dragon-2019 - A. Bill	7,500	1991	132.50	600
1994	Grogoda, She Troll-2150 - A. Bill	2,950	1997	220.00	220
1988	Hepna Pushes Truck-2014 - A. Bill	Retrd.	1994	47.00	75
1988	Hest Checks Crystals-2013 - A. Bill	Retrd.	1994	47.00	75
1989	Hobba, Hellbenders Twin Son -2023 - A. Bill	Retrd.	1992	69.00	150
1993	Ice Dragon-2109 - A. Bill	Retrd.	1994	95.00	100
1992	Jonquil and Snappa-2055 - A. Bill	Retrd.	1995	40.00	40
1988	Jonquil- Dragons Footprint-2004 - A. Bill	Retrd.	1991	55.00	90
1995	Kirrock of Dragon Duel-2159 - A. Bill	1,950	1996	400.00	400
1992	Manu Manu-Peeper-2105 - A. Bill	Retrd.	1993	40.00	60
1994	Mezereon "Grand Corrupter" -2091 - A. Bill	7,500	1995	187.00	187
1994	Necranon-Raptor Dragon-2095 - A. Bill	Retrd.	1995	105.00	105
1991	Ogrod-Ice Troll-2032 - A. Bill	Retrd.	1994	235.00	325
1991	Okra, Goblin Princess-2031 - K. Fallon	Retrd.	1994	105.00	115
1989	Old Yargle-2020 - A. Bill	Retrd.	1994	55.00	75
1992	Olm & Sylphen, Mer-King & Queen-2059 - A. Bill	9,500	1994	350.00	450
1990	Orolan-Summer Wizard-2025 - A. Bill	7,500	1992	165.00	300
1992	Peeper "Sollo Sollo"-2058 - A. Bill	Retrd.	1997	50.00	50
1995	Piasharn-2162 - K. Fallon	2,950	1996	250.00	250
1991	Quillion-Autumn Witch-2045 - A. Bill	15,000	1994	205.00	220
1993	Rattajack "All Alone"-2089 - A. Bill	Retrd.	1995	52.00	52
1991	Rattajack "Bowled Over"-2037 - A. Hull	Retrd.	1997	65.00	65
1993	Rattajack "Gone Fishing"-2090 - A. Bill	Retrd.	1995	77.00	77
1994	Rattajack "Lazybones"-2087 - A. Bill	Retrd.	1997	49.00	49
1993	Rattajack "Soft Landing"-2088 - A. Bill	Retrd.	1995	53.00	53
1992	Rattajack & Snappa-2056 - A. Bill	Retrd.	1995	73.00	73
1988	Rattajack - Circles-2003 - A. Bill	Retrd.	1993	40.00	70
1988	Rattajack - My Ball-2001 - A. Bill	Retrd.	1993	40.00	70
1988	Rattajack - Please-2000 - A. Bill	Retrd.	1993	40.00	65
1988	Rattajack - Terragon Dreams -2002 - A. Bill	Retrd.	1993	40.00	60
1991	Rattajack - Up & Under-2038 - A. Bill	Retrd.	1994	65.00	70
1995	Saberath-2117 - K. Fallon	Retrd.	1995	100.00	100
1991	Samphire-Carrier Dragon-2049 - A. Bill	15,000	1994	137.50	175
1988	Snappa Climbs High-2008 - A. Bill	Retrd.	1993	25.00	65
1988	Snappa Finds a Collar-2009 - A. Bill	Retrd.	1992	25.00	60
1993	Snappa "Flapping"-2082 - A. Bill	Retrd.	1995	32.50	33
1993	Snappa "If The Cap Fits"-2084 - A. Bill	Retrd.	1995	35.00	35
1993	Snappa "Nature Watch"-2086 - A. Bill	Retrd.	1995	28.00	28
1993	Snappa "Rollaball"-2081 - A. Bill	Retrd.	1995	35.00	35
1991	Snappa "Tickled Pink"-2036 - A. Hull	Retrd.	1997	39.50	40
1993	Snappa "w/Enchantica Rose" -2083 - A. Bill	Retrd.	1995	27.00	27
1993	Snappa "What Ball"-2085 - A. Bill	Retrd.	1995	33.00	33
1991	Snappa Caught Napping-2039 - A. Hull	Retrd.	1994	39.50	60
1988	Snappa Dozes Off-2011 - A. Bill	Retrd.	1993	25.00	60
1988	Snappa Hatches Out-2006 - A. Bill	Retrd.	1991	25.00	60
1991	Snappa Nods Off-2043 - A. Hull	Retrd.	1994	30.00	40
1988	Snappa Plays Ball-2010 - A. Bill	Retrd.	1993	25.00	60
1991	Snappa Posing-2042 - A. Hull	Retrd.	1994	30.00	50
1991	Snappa Tumbles-2047 - A. Hull	Retrd.	1994	30.00	40
1988	Snappa's First Feast-2007 - A. Bill	Retrd.	1993	25.00	60
1991	Snappa-Snowdrift-2041 - A. Hull	Retrd.	1994	30.00	40
1991	Snarlgard - Autumn Dragon -2034 - K. Fallon	7,500	1992	337.00	400
1993	Snow Dragon-2066 - A. Bill	7,500	1995	150.00	150
1995	Snowhawk of Dragon Duel-2160 - A. Bill	1,950	1996	400.00	400
1992	Snowthorn & Wargren-2062 - A. Bill	7,500	1997	570.00	570
1992	Sorren & Gart-2054 - K. Fallon	9,500	1994	220.00	350
1992	Spring Wizard and Yim-2060 - A. Bill	9,500	1993	410.00	450
1990	The Swamp Demon-2028 - K. Fallon	Retrd.	1992	69.00	95
1988	Tarbet with Sack-2012 - A. Bill	Retrd.	1991	47.00	60
1992	Thrace-Gladiator-2061 - K. Fallon	9,500	1993	280.00	350
1992	The Throne Citadel-2063 - J. Woodward	950	1994	2000.00	2000
1990	Tuatara-Evil Witch-2027 - A. Bill	9,500	1994	174.00	185
1996	Vladdigor-2171 - A. Bill	2,950	1996	290.00	290
1989	Vrorst - The Ice Sorcerer-2018 - A. Bill	7,500	1991	155.00	650
1991	Vrorst-Ice Sorcerer on Throne-2040 - A. Bill	15,000	1995	500.00	500
1994	Vyzauga-Twin Headed Dragon -2092 - A. Bill	Retrd.	1995	87.00	87
1991	Waxifrade - Autumn Wizard -2033 - K. Fallon	7,500	1992	265.00	400
1995	Wolfarlis-2163 - K. Fallon	2,950	1996	250.00	250
1994	Zadragul, Tunnel Serpent-2151 - A. Bill	Retrd.	1997	83.00	83
1994	Zorganoid-Crab Dragon-2096 - K. Fallon	Retrd.	1995	99.00	99

Ertl Collectibles

Circus World/Museum Collection - Ertl

YEAR ISSUE		EDITION LIMIT	YEAR RETD.	ISSUE PRICE	*QUOTE U.S.$
1997	Bostock & Wombwell's Managerie 2481	3,500		90.00	90
1997	Lion And Mirror Bandwagon 2479	3,500		90.00	90
1997	Pawnee Bill 2478	3,500		90.00	90
1997	Twin Lions 2480	3,500		90.00	90

Ertl Elves - Ertl

YEAR ISSUE		EDITION LIMIT	YEAR RETD.	ISSUE PRICE	*QUOTE U.S.$
1996	Santa's Workshop H113	5,000		70.00	70
1997	Twas Christmas Morn' 2318	5,000		70.00	70

Lowell Davis America - L. Davis

YEAR ISSUE		EDITION LIMIT	YEAR RETD.	ISSUE PRICE	*QUOTE U.S.$
1997	"A Friend In Need" 2525	4,500		50.00	50
1997	"Get One For Me" 2523	4,500		75.00	75
1997	"Last of the Litter" 2497	5,500		60.00	60
1997	"Next" 2496	4,500		70.00	70
1997	"Nine Lives?" 2534	3,500		60.00	60
1997	"Oh! She'll Be Driving Six White Horses..." 2494	3,500		250.00	250
1997	"Sooie" 2521	3,500		160.00	160

Fabregé Collections

Classic Imperial Egg Reproduction Collection - Fabregé

YEAR ISSUE		EDITION LIMIT	YEAR RETD.	ISSUE PRICE	*QUOTE U.S.$
1996	The Imperial Coronation Egg	100		8000.00	8000
1996	The Imperial Czarevitch Egg	500		3000.00	3000
1996	The Imperial Danish Palace Egg	500		3000.00	3000
1996	The Imperial Rose Trellis Egg	500		3000.00	3000
1996	The Imperial Swan Egg, 3 1/2"	950		1000.00	1000
1996	The Imperial Swan Egg, 7"	100		5000.00	5000

Hand Painted Limoges Porcelain Egg Collection - Fabregé

YEAR ISSUE		EDITION LIMIT	YEAR RETD.	ISSUE PRICE	*QUOTE U.S.$
1997	Cat Egg in cobalt blue porcelain	999		350.00	350
1996	Cat Egg in ruby & gold porcelain	999		350.00	350
1997	Frog Egg in light blue porcelain	999		350.00	350
1996	Gold, Enamel and Jeweled Easter Egg	500		500.00	500
1996	Imperial Clover Egg, 2 1/2"	999		250.00	250
1996	Imperial Clover Egg, 5 1/2"	250		1000.00	1000
1995	Imperial Czarevitch Egg	500		750.00	750
1995	Imperial Danish Palace Egg	500		850.00	850
1996	Imperial Gatchina Palace Egg, 3 1/2"	750		500.00	500
1996	Imperial Gatchina Palace Egg, 7"	250		1500.00	1500
1996	Imperial Rose Trellis Egg	500		500.00	500
1996	Imperial Rosebud Egg	500		750.00	750
1996	Palace Egg	999		250.00	250
1996	Swan Egg	999		250.00	250

Imperial Egg Surprise Collection - Fabregé

YEAR ISSUE		EDITION LIMIT	YEAR RETD.	ISSUE PRICE	*QUOTE U.S.$
1996	The American Eagle Egg	999		650.00	650
1996	The Anna Pavlova Ballerina Egg	999		650.00	650
1997	The Baby Egg	999		500.00	500
1996	The Cat Egg	999		500.00	500
1996	The Cinematography Egg	999		650.00	650
1996	The Director's Egg	999		500.00	500
1997	The Easter Rabbit Egg	999		850.00	850
1996	The Golfer Egg	999		500.00	500
1996	The Grizzly Bear Egg	1,500		350.00	350
1996	The Horse and Jockey Egg	999		650.00	650
1996	The Labrador Retriever Egg	999		500.00	500
1996	The Little Frog Egg	1,500		350.00	350
1996	The Little Mouse Egg	1,500		350.00	350
1996	The Noël Egg	999		850.00	850
1996	The Osprey Egg	999		500.00	500

*Quotes have been rounded up to nearest dollar

YEAR ISSUE		EDITION LIMIT	YEAR RETD.	ISSUE PRICE	*QUOTE U.S.$
1996	The Petit Swan Egg	999		500.00	500
1996	The Pig Egg	1,500		350.00	350
1996	The Polo Player Egg	999		650.00	650
1996	The Rabbit Egg	1,500		350.00	350
1996	The Sailfish Egg	999		650.00	650
1996	The Sailing Yacht Egg	999		650.00	650
1996	The Show Jumper Egg	999		650.00	650
1997	The Skier Egg	999		650.00	650
1996	The Stag Egg	999		650.00	650
1996	The Tennis Player Egg	999		500.00	500
1996	The Tennis Trophy Egg	999		650.00	650
1997	The Wedding Egg	999		650.00	650

Renaissance Crystal Egg Collection - Fabregé

YEAR ISSUE		EDITION LIMIT	YEAR RETD.	ISSUE PRICE	*QUOTE U.S.$
1996	Alexandra Egg	999		450.00	450
1995	Basket of Lilies of the Valley Egg	500		600.00	600
1995	Catherine Palace Egg	999		400.00	400
1995	Grand Duchess Egg	999		400.00	400
1995	Grand Romanov Eagle Egg	500		600.00	600
1996	Griphon Egg	500		750.00	750
1995	The Hermitage Egg	500		600.00	600
1996	The Imperial Coronation Egg	999		450.00	450
1995	Imperial Enameled Easter Egg	999		450.00	450
1995	Imperial Fifteenth Anniversary Egg	999		450.00	450
1996	Imperial Gatchina Palace Egg	999		450.00	450
1995	Imperial Lilies of the Valley Egg	999		450.00	450
1996	Imperial Rose Trellis Egg	999		450.00	450
1995	Imperial Rosebud Egg	999		450.00	450
1996	The Nutcracker Ballet Egg	500		600.00	600
1996	Peter Carl Fabregé Potrait Egg	750		750.00	750
1995	Pine Cone Egg 1837-L	999		400.00	400
1995	Pine Cone Egg 1837-LN	999		350.00	350
1996	Ribbon Egg	999		450.00	450
1996	Romanov Eagle Egg (cobalt w/gold)	999		350.00	350
1996	Romanov Eagle Egg (cobalt w/o gold)	999		250.00	250
1996	Romanov Eagle Egg (red cased)	500		750.00	750
1996	Romanov Eagle Egg (red, blue, green)	999		350.00	350
1996	The Romeo and Juliet Ballet Egg	500		600.00	600
1995	Rosebud Red Egg	999		350.00	350
1995	Spring Flower Egg	999		350.00	350
1996	The Swan Lake Egg	500		650.00	650
1995	Winter Palace Egg	999		400.00	400

St. Petersburg Crystal Petit Egg Collection - Fabregé

YEAR ISSUE		EDITION LIMIT	YEAR RETD.	ISSUE PRICE	*QUOTE U.S.$
1995	Coronation Egg	2,500		75.00	75
1995	Leaf Design Egg	2,500		75.00	75
1995	Lens Egg	2,500		75.00	75
1994	Pine Cone Egg	2,500		75.00	75
1996	Primrose Egg	2,500		75.00	75
1996	Rose Trellis Egg	2,500		75.00	75
1994	Star Cut Egg	2,500		75.00	75
1996	Wreath Egg	2,500		75.00	75

Fenton Art Glass Company

Collectors Club - Fenton

YEAR ISSUE		EDITION LIMIT	YEAR RETD.	ISSUE PRICE	*QUOTE U.S.$
1978	Cranberry Opalescent Baskets w/variety of spot moulds	Yr.Iss.	1978	20.00	75-125
1979	Vasa Murrhina Vases (Variety of colors)	Yr.Iss.	1979	25.00	60-110
1980	Velva Rose Bubble Optic "Melon" Vases	Yr.Iss.	1980	30.00	60-110
1981	Amethyst w/White Hanging Hearts Vases	Yr.Iss.	1981	37.50	130-175
1982	Overlay Baskets in pastel shades (Swirl Optic)	Yr.Iss.	1982	40.00	75-110
1983	Cranberry Opalescent 1 pc. Fairy Lights	Yr.Iss.	1983	40.00	150-295
1984	Blue Burmese w/peloton Treatment Vases	Yr.Iss.	1984	25.00	75-150
1985	Overlay Vases in Dusty Rose w/Mica Flecks	Yr.Iss.	1985	25.00	95
1986	Ruby Iridized Art Glass Vase	Yr.Iss.	1986	30.00	100-195
1987	Dusty Rose Overlay/Peach Blow Interior w/dark blue Crest Vase	Yr.Iss.	1987	38.00	75-95
1988	Teal Green and Milk marble Basket	Yr.Iss.	1988	30.00	75-110
1989	Mulberry Opalescent Basket w/Coin Dot Optic	Yr.Iss.	1989	37.50	100-225
1990	Sea Mist Green Opalescent Fern Optic Basket	Yr.Iss.	1990	40.00	50-75
1991	Rosalene Leaf Basket and Peacock & Dahlia Basket	Yr.Iss.	1991	65.00	95
1992	Blue Bubble Optic Vases	Yr.Iss.	1992	35.00	50-75
1993	Cranberry Opalescent "Jonquil" Basket	Yr.Iss.	1993	35.00	70-110
1994	Cranberry Opalescent Jacqueline Pitcher	Yr.Iss.	1994	55.00	85-135
1994	Rosalene Tulip Vase-1994 Convention Pc.	Yr.Iss.	1994	45.00	110
1995	Fairy Light-Blue Burmese-1995 Convention Pc.	Yr.Iss.	1995	45.00	125

Glass Messenger Subscribers Only - M. Reynolds

YEAR ISSUE		EDITION LIMIT	YEAR RETD.	ISSUE PRICE	*QUOTE U.S.$
1996	Basket, Roselle on Cranberry	Yr.Iss.	1996	89.00	89

1983 Connoisseur Collection - Fenton

YEAR ISSUE		EDITION LIMIT	YEAR RETD.	ISSUE PRICE	*QUOTE U.S.$
1983	Basket, 9" Vasa Murrhina	1,000	1983	75.00	125
1983	Craftsman Stein, White Satin Carnival	1,500	1983	35.00	50
1983	Cruet/Stopper Vasa Murrhina	1,000	1983	75.00	195
1983	Epergne Set, 5 pc. Burmese	500	1983	200.00	550-795
1983	Vase, 4 1/2" Sculptured Rose Quartz	2,000	1983	32.50	75-95
1983	Vase, 7" Sculptured Rose Quartz	1,500	1983	50.00	120
1983	Vase, 9" Sculptured Rose Quartz	850	1983	75.00	175-220

1984 Connoisseur Collection - Fenton, unless otherwise noted

YEAR ISSUE		EDITION LIMIT	YEAR RETD.	ISSUE PRICE	*QUOTE U.S.$
1984	Basket, 10" Plated Amberina Velvet	1,250	1984	85.00	195
1984	Candy Box w/cover, 3 pc. Blue Burmese	1,250	1984	75.00	200-250
1984	Cane, 18" Plated Amberina Velvet	Yr.Iss.	1984	35.00	195
1984	Top Hat, 8" Plated Amberina Velvet	1,500	1984	65.00	175-195
1984	Vase, 9" Rose Velvet Hndpt. Floral - L. Everson	750	1984	75.00	150-175
1984	Vase, 9" Rose Velvet-Mother/Child	750	1984	125.00	175-225
1984	Vase, Swan, 8" Gold Azure	1,500	1984	65.00	175-225

1985 Connoisseur Collection - Fenton, unless otherwise noted

YEAR ISSUE		EDITION LIMIT	YEAR RETD.	ISSUE PRICE	*QUOTE U.S.$
1985	Basket, 8 1/2" Buremese, Hndpt. - L. Everson	1,250	1985	95.00	175-200
1985	Epergne Set, 4 pc. Diamond Lace Green Opal.	1,000	1985	95.00	150-195
1985	Lamp, 22" Burmese-Butterfly, Hndpt. - L. Everson	350	1985	300.00	595-695
1985	Punch Set, 14 pc. Green Opalescent	500	1985	250.00	295
1985	Vase, 12" Gabrielle Scul. French Opal.	800	1985	150.00	195
1985	Vase, 7 1/2" Burmese-Shell - D. Barbour	950	1985	135.00	250
1985	Vase, 7 1/2" Chrysanthemums/ Circlet, Hndpt. - L. Everson	1,000	1985	125.00	150

1986 Connoisseur Collection - Fenton, unless otherwise noted

YEAR ISSUE		EDITION LIMIT	YEAR RETD.	ISSUE PRICE	*QUOTE U.S.$
1986	Basket, Top hat Wild Rose/Teal Overlay	1,500	1986	49.00	110
1986	Boudoir Lamp, Cranberry Pearl	750	1986	145.00	250-295
1986	Cruet/Stopper, Cranberry Pearl	1,000	1986	75.00	250-295
1986	Handled Urn, 13" Cranberry Satin	1,000	1986	185.00	450
1986	Handled Vase, 7" French Royale	1,000	1986	100.00	175
1986	Lamp, 20" Burmese Shells Hndpt. - D. Barbour	500	1986	350.00	600-695
1986	Vanity Set, 4 pc. Blue Ridge	1,000	1986	125.00	250-295
1986	Vase 10 1/2" Danielle Sandcarved - R. Delaney	1,000	1986	95.00	195
1986	Vase, 10 1/2" Misty Morn, Hndpt. - L. Everson	1,000	1986	95.00	195

1987 Connoisseur Collection - Various

YEAR ISSUE		EDITION LIMIT	YEAR RETD.	ISSUE PRICE	*QUOTE U.S.$
1987	Pitcher, 8" Enameled Azure Hndpt.- L. Everson	950	1987	85.00	125
1987	Vase, 7 1/4" Blossom/Bows on Cranberry Hndpt.- D. Barbour	950	1987	95.00	175

1988 Connoisseur Collection - Fenton, unless otherwise noted

YEAR ISSUE		EDITION LIMIT	YEAR RETD.	ISSUE PRICE	*QUOTE U.S.$
1988	Basket, Irid. Teal Cased Vasa Murrhina	2,500	1988	65.00	125-150
1988	Candy, Wave Crest, CranberryHndpt. - L. Everson	2,000	1988	95.00	150-195
1988	Pitcher, Cased Cranberry/ Opal Teal Ring	3,500	1988	60.00	125-150
1988	Vase, 6" Cased Cranberry/Opal Teal/Irid.	3,500	1988	50.00	100-125

1989 Connoisseur Collection - Fenton, unless otherwise noted

YEAR ISSUE		EDITION LIMIT	YEAR RETD.	ISSUE PRICE	*QUOTE U.S.$
1989	Basket, 7" Cranberry w/Crystal Ring Hndpt.- L. Everson	2,500	1989	85.00	100-150
1989	Candy Box, w/cover, Cranberry, Hndpt. - L. Everson	2,500	1989	85.00	150-195
1989	Epergne Set 5 pc., Rosalene	2,000	1989	250.00	400-495
1989	Lamp, 21" Rosalene Satin Hndpt. - L. Everson	1,000	1989	250.00	300-395
1989	Pitcher, Diamond Optic, Rosalene	2,500	1989	55.00	100
1989	Vase, Basketweave, Rosalene	2,500	1989	45.00	85
1989	Vase, Pinch, 8" Vasa Murrhina	2,000	1989	65.00	100

1990-85th Anniversary Collection - Various

YEAR ISSUE		EDITION LIMIT	YEAR RETD.	ISSUE PRICE	*QUOTE U.S.$
1990	Basket, 5 1/2" Trees on Burmese, Hndpt. - Piper/F. Burton	Closed	1990	57.50	110
1990	Basket, 7" Raspberry on Burmese, Hndpt. - L. Everson	Closed	1990	75.00	150-195
1990	Cruet/Stopper Petite Floral on Burmese, Hndpt. - L. Everson	Closed	1990	85.00	150-195
1990	Epergne Set, 2 pc. Pt. Floral on Burmese, Hndpt. - L. Everson	Closed	1990	125.00	200-295
1990	Lamp, 20" Rose Burmese, Hndpt. - Piper/D. Barbour	Closed	1990	250.00	350-450
1990	Lamp, 21" Raspberry on Burmese, Hndpt. - L. Everson	Closed	1990	295.00	450
1990	Vase, 6 1/2" Rose Burmese, Hndpt. - Piper/D. Barbour	Closed	1990	45.00	90
1990	Vase, 9" Trees on Burmese, Hndpt. - Piper/F. Burton	Closed	1990	75.00	150-200
1990	Vase, Fan 6" Rose Burmese, Hndpt. - Piper/D. Barbour	Closed	1990	49.50	95
1990	Water Set, 7 pc. Raspberry on Burmese, Hndpt. - L. Everson	Closed	1990	275.00	500-695

1991 Connoisseur Collection - Various

YEAR ISSUE		EDITION LIMIT	YEAR RETD.	ISSUE PRICE	*QUOTE U.S.$
1991	Basket, Floral on Rosalene, Hndpt. - M. Reynolds	1,500	1991	64.00	100
1991	Candy Box, 3 pc. Favrene - Fenton	1,000	1991	90.00	200
1991	Fish, Paperweight, Rosalene - Fenton	2,000	1991	30.00	60
1991	Lamp, 20" Roses on Burmese, Hndpt. - Piper/F. Burton	500	1991	275.00	450
1991	Vase, 7 1/2" Raspberry on Burmese, Hndpt. - L. Everson	1,500	1991	65.00	100
1991	Vase, Floral on Favrene, Hndpt. - M. Reynolds	850	1991	125.00	350
1991	Vase, Fruit on Favrene, Hndpt. - F. Burton	850	1991	125.00	300-350

1992 Connoisseur Collection - Various

YEAR ISSUE		EDITION LIMIT	YEAR RETD.	ISSUE PRICE	*QUOTE U.S.$
1992	Covered Box, Poppy/Daisy, Hndpt. - F. Burton	1,250	1992	95.00	200
1992	Pitcher, 4 1/2" Berries on Burmese, Hndpt. - M. Reynolds	1,500	1992	65.00	120
1992	Pitcher, 9" Empire on Cranberry, Hndpt. - M. Reynolds	950	1992	110.00	200
1992	Vase, 6 1/2" Raspberry on Burmese, Hndpt. - L. Everson	1,500	1992	45.00	95
1992	Vase, 8" Seascape, Hndpt. - F. Burton	750	1992	150.00	175
1992	Vase, Twining Floral Rosalene Satin, Hndpt. - M. Reynolds	950	1992	110.00	175

1993 Connoisseur Collection - Various

YEAR ISSUE		EDITION LIMIT	YEAR RETD.	ISSUE PRICE	*QUOTE U.S.$
1993	Amphora w/Stand, Favrene, Hndpt. - M. Reynolds	850	1993	285.00	350
1993	Bowl, Ruby Stretch w/Gold Scrolls, Hndpt. - M. Reynolds	1,250	1993	95.00	125
1993	Lamp, Spring Woods Reverse Hndpt. - F. Burton	500	1993	595.00	595
1993	Owl Figurine, 6" Favrene - Fenton	1,500	1993	95.00	125
1993	Perfume/Stopper, Rose Trellis Rosalene, Hndpt. - F. Burton	1,250	1993	95.00	125
1993	Vase, 9" Gold Leaves Sandcarved on Plum Irid., - M. Reynolds	950	1993	175.00	225
1993	Vase, Victorian Roses Persian Blue Opal., Hndpt. - M. Reynolds	950	1993	125.00	180

1993 Family Signature Collection - Various

YEAR ISSUE		EDITION LIMIT	YEAR RETD.	ISSUE PRICE	*QUOTE U.S.$
1993	Basket, 8 1/2" Lilacs - Bill Fenton	Closed	1993	65.00	90
1993	Vase, 9" Alpine Thistle/Ruby Carnival - Frank M. Fenton	Closed	1993	105.00	175
1993	Vase, 9" Cottage Scene - Shelley Fenton	Closed	1993	90.00	150
1993	Vase, 10" Vintage on Plum - Don Fenton	Closed	1993	80.00	110
1993	Vase, 11" Cranberry Dec. - George Fenton	Closed	1993	110.00	140

1994 Connoisseur Collection - Various

YEAR ISSUE		EDITION LIMIT	YEAR RETD.	ISSUE PRICE	*QUOTE U.S.$
1994	Bowl, 14" Cranberry Cameo Sandcarved - Reynolds/Delaney	500	1994	390.00	390
1994	Clock, 4 1/2" Favrene, Hndpt. - F. Burton	850	1994	150.00	175
1994	Lamp, Hummingbird Reverse, Hndpt. - F. Burton	300	1994	590.00	750
1994	Pitcher, 10" Lattice on Burmese, Hndpt. - F. Burton	750	1994	165.00	225
1994	Vase, 7" Favrene, Hndpt. - M. Reynolds	850	1994	185.00	200
1994	Vase, 8" Plum Opalescent, Hndpt. - M. Reynolds	750	1994	165.00	175
1994	Vase, 11" Gold Amberina, Hndpt. - M. Reynolds	750	1994	175.00	225

1994 Family Signature Collection - Various

YEAR ISSUE		EDITION LIMIT	YEAR RETD.	ISSUE PRICE	*QUOTE U.S.$
1994	Basket, 7 1/2" Lilacs - Shelley Fenton	Closed	1994	65.00	95
1994	Basket, 8" Stiegel Green - Bill Fenton	Closed	1994	60.00	95
1994	Basket, 8 1/2" Ruby Carnival - Tom Fenton	Closed	1994	60.00	95
1994	Basket, 11" Autumn Gold Opal - Frank Fenton	Closed	1994	70.00	90
1994	Candy w/cover, 9 1/2" Autumn Leaves - Don Fenton	Closed	1994	60.00	75
1994	Pitcher, 6 1/2" Cranberry - Frank M. Fenton	Closed	1994	85.00	125
1994	Vase, 9 1/2" Pansies on Cranberry - Bill Fenton	Closed	1994	95.00	125
1994	Vase, 10" Fuchsia - George Fenton	Closed	1994	95.00	125

1995 Connoisseur Collection - M. Reynolds, unless otherwise noted

YEAR ISSUE		EDITION LIMIT	YEAR RETD.	ISSUE PRICE	*QUOTE U.S.$
1995	Amphora w/stand, 10 1/4" Royal Purple, Hndpt.	890	1995	195.00	300
1995	Ginger Jar, 3 Pc. 8 1/2" Favrene, Hndpt.	790	1995	275.00	400
1995	Lamp, 21" Butterfly/Floral Reverse, Hndpt. - F. Burton	300	1995	595.00	700-800
1995	Pitcher, 9 1/2" Victorian Art Glass, Hndpt.	490	1995	250.00	250
1995	Vase, 7" Aurora Wild Rose, Hndpt.	890	1995	125.00	175

1995 Family Signature Collection - Various

YEAR ISSUE		EDITION LIMIT	YEAR RETD.	ISSUE PRICE	*QUOTE U.S.$
1995	Basket, 8 1/2" Trellis - Lynn Fenton	Closed	1995	85.00	85
1995	Basket, 9 1/2" Coralene Floral - Frank M./Bill Fenton	Closed	1995	75.00	75
1995	Candy w/cover, 9" Red Carnival - Mike Fenton	Closed	1995	65.00	65
1995	Pitcher, 9 1/2" Thistle - Don Fenton	Closed	1995	125.00	125
1995	Vase, 7" Gold Pansies on Cranberry - George Fenton	Closed	1995	75.00	75
1995	Vase, 9" Summer Garden on Spruce - Don Fenton	Closed	1995	85.00	85
1995	Vase, 9 1/2" Golden Flax on Cobalt - Shelley Fenton	Closed	1995	95.00	95

*Quotes have been rounded up to nearest dollar

FIGURINES

Fenton Art Glass Company
to Fenton Art Glass Company

1996 Connoisseur Collection - Various

YEAR ISSUE		EDITION LIMIT	YEAR RETD.	ISSUE PRICE	*QUOTE U.S.$
1996	Covered Box, 7" Mandarin Red, Hndpt. - K. Plauche	1,250	1996	150.00	150
1996	Lamp, 33" Reverse Painted Poppies, Hndpt. - F. Burton	400	1996	750.00	800
1996	Pitcher, 8" Dragonfly on Burmese, Hndpt. - F. Burton	1,450	1996	165.00	165
1996	Vase, 11" Berries on Wildrose, Hndpt. - M. Reynolds	1,250	1996	195.00	195
1996	Vase, 11" Queen's Bird on Burmese, Hndpt. - M. Reynolds	1,350	1996	250.00	250
1996	Vase, 7 1/2" Favrene Cut-Back Sandcarved - M. Reynolds	1,250	1996	195.00	195
1996	Vase, 8" Trout on Burmese, Hndpt. - R. Spindler	1,450	1996	135.00	135

1996 Family Signature Collection - Various

YEAR ISSUE		EDITION LIMIT	YEAR RETD.	ISSUE PRICE	*QUOTE U.S.$
1996	Basket, 7 1/2" Starflower on Cran. Pearl - M. Fenton	Closed	1996	75.00	75
1996	Basket, 8" Mountain Berry - Don Fenton	Closed	1996	85.00	85
1996	Candy Box w/cover Pansies - Shelley Fenton	Closed	1996	65.00	65
1996	Pitcher, 6 1/2" Asters - Lynn Fenton	Closed	1996	70.00	70
1996	Vase, 10" Magnolia & Berry on Spruce - Tom Fenton	Closed	1996	85.00	85
1996	Vase, 11" Meadow Beauty - Nancy Fenton	Closed	1996	95.00	95
1996	Vase, 8 1/2" Blush Rose on Opaline - George Fenton	Closed	1996	75.00	75

1997 Family Signature Collection - Various

YEAR ISSUE		EDITION LIMIT	YEAR RETD.	ISSUE PRICE	*QUOTE U.S.$
1997	Basket, 9" Sweetbriar on Plum Overlay - L. Fenton	4/30		85.00	85
1997	Fairy Light, 7 1/2" Hydrangeas on Topaz - F. Fenton	4/30		125.00	125
1997	Pitcher, 7 1/2" Irisies on Misty Blue - D. Fenton	4/30		85.00	85
1997	Vase, 6" Field Flowers on Champ. Satin - S. Fenton	4/30		55.00	55
1997	Vase, 8" Medallion Collect. Floral on Black - M. Fenton	4/30		75.00	75

American Classic Series - M. Dickinson

YEAR ISSUE		EDITION LIMIT	YEAR RETD.	ISSUE PRICE	*QUOTE U.S.$
1986	Jupiter Train on Opal Satin, Lamp, 23"	1,000	1986	295.00	350
1986	Studebaker-Garford Car on Opal Satin, Lamp, 16"	1,000	1986	235.00	300

Christmas - Various

YEAR ISSUE		EDITION LIMIT	YEAR RETD.	ISSUE PRICE	*QUOTE U.S.$
1978	Christmas Morn, Lamp, 16" - M. Dickinson	Yr.Iss.	1978	100.00	250
1978	Christmas Morn, Fairy Light - M. Dickinson	Yr.Iss.	1978	25.00	75
1979	Nature's Christmas, Lamp, 16" - K. Cunningham	Yr.Iss.	1979	150.00	250
1979	Nature's Christmas, Fairy Light - K. Cunningham	Yr.Iss.	1979	30.00	95
1980	Going Home, Lamp, 16" - D. Johnson	Yr.Iss.	1980	165.00	250
1980	Going Home, Fairy Light - D. Johnson	Yr.Iss.	1980	32.50	65
1981	All Is Calm, Lamp, 16" - D. Johnson	Yr.Iss.	1981	175.00	295
1981	All Is Calm, Lamp, 20" - D. Johnson	Yr.Iss.	1981	225.00	295
1981	All Is Calm, Fairy Light - D. Johnson	Yr.Iss.	1981	35.00	65
1982	Country Christmas, Lamp, 16" - R. Spindler	Yr.Iss.	1982	175.00	295
1982	Country Christmas, Lamp, 21" - R. Spindler	Yr.Iss.	1982	225.00	350
1982	Country Christmas, Fairy Light - R. Spindler	Yr.Iss.	1982	35.00	65
1983	Anticipation, Fairy Light - D. Johnson	7,500	1983	35.00	65
1984	Expectation, Lamp, 10 1/2" - D. Johnson	7,500	1984	75.00	275
1984	Expectation, Fairy Light - D. Johnson	7,500	1984	37.50	65
1985	Heart's Desire, Fairy Light - D. Johnson	7,500	1986	37.50	65
1987	Sharing The Spirit, Fairy Light - L. Everson	Yr.Iss.	1987	37.50	65
1987	Cardinal in the Churchyard, Lamp, 18 1/2" - D. Johnson	500	1987	250.00	295
1987	Cardinal in the Churchyard, Fairy Light - D. Johnson	4,500	1987	29.50	95
1988	A Chickadee Ballet, Lamp, 21" - D. Johnson	500	1988	274.00	295
1988	A Chickadee Ballet, Fairy Light - D. Johnson	4,500	1988	29.50	95
1989	Downy Pecker, Lamp, 16" - Chisled Song - D. Johnson	500	1989	250.00	295
1989	Downy Pecker, Fairy Light - Chisled Song - D. Johnson	4,500	1989	29.50	95
1990	A Blue Bird in Snowfall, Lamp, 21" - D. Johnson	500	1990	250.00	295
1990	A Blue Bird in Snowfall, Fairy Light - D. Johnson	4,500	1990	29.50	95
1990	Sleigh Ride, Lamp, 16" - F. Burton	1,000	1990	250.00	295
1990	Sleigh Ride, Fairy Light - F. Burton	3,500	1990	39.00	75
1991	Christmas Eve, Lamp, 16" - F. Burton	1,000	1991	250.00	295
1991	Christmas Eve, Fairy Light - F. Burton	3,500	1991	39.00	95
1992	Family Tradition, Lamp, 20" - F. Burton	1,000	1992	250.00	295
1992	Family Tradition, Fairy Light - F. Burton	3,500	1992	39.00	75
1993	Family Holiday, Lamp, 16" - F. Burton	1,000	1993	265.00	295
1993	Family Holiday, Fairy Light - F. Burton	3,500	1993	39.00	75
1994	Silent Night, Lamp, 16" - F. Burton	500	1994	275.00	325
1994	Silent Night, Fairy Light - F. Burton	1,500	1994	45.00	45
1994	Silent Night, Egg on Stand - F. Burton	1,500	1994	45.00	45
1995	Our Home Is Blessed, Lamp, 21" - F. Burton	500	1995	275.00	275
1995	Our Home Is Blessed, Egg - F. Burton	1,500	1995	45.00	45
1995	Our Home Is Blessed, Fairy Light - F. Burton	1,500	1995	45.00	45
1996	Star of Wonder, Lamp, 16" - F. Burton	750	1996	175.00	175
1996	Star of Wonder, Egg - F. Burton	1,750	1996	45.00	45
1996	Star of Wonder, Fairy Light - F. Burton	1,750	1996	48.00	48

Christmas Limited Edition - M. Reynolds, unless otherwise noted

YEAR ISSUE		EDITION LIMIT	YEAR RETD.	ISSUE PRICE	*QUOTE U.S.$
1992	Egg, 3 1/2" Manager Scene on Ruby	2,500	1992	30.00	30
1992	Egg, 3 1/2" Poinsettia on Crystal Irid.	2,500	1992	30.00	30
1993	Egg, 3 1/2" Angel on Green	2,500	1993	35.00	35
1993	Egg, 3 1/2" Woods on White	2,500	1993	35.00	35
1994	Egg, 3 1/2" Magnolia on Gold	1,500	1994	35.00	35
1994	Egg, 3 1/2" Partridge on Ruby	1,500	1994	35.00	35
1995	Egg, 3 1/2" Bow & Holly on Ivory	900	1995	35.00	35
1995	Egg, 3 1/2" Chickadee on Gold	900	1995	35.00	35
1995	Egg, 3 1/2" Iced Poinsettia on Ruby	900	1995	39.50	40
1995	Angel, Radiant-Musical Base	900	1995	85.00	85
1995	Pitcher, Golden Holiday Pine Cones	900	1995	79.00	79
1996	Egg, 3 1/2" Holly Berries on Gold	1,500	1996	37.50	38
1996	Egg, 3 1/2" Golden Partridge on Spruce	1,500	1996	35.00	35
1996	Egg, 3 1/2" Moonlit Meadow on Ruby - R. Spindler	1,500	1996	39.50	40
1996	Fairy Light, Nativity Scene on Ivory - R. Spindler	1,500	1996	37.50	38
1996	Fairy Light, Golden Winged Angel	2,000	1996	39.50	40
1996	Egg, 3 1/2" Golden Winged Angel	1,500	1996	37.50	38
1996	Radiant Golden Winged Angel, 7 1/2"	1,000	1996	59.50	60

Collectible Eggs - M. Reynolds, unless otherwise noted

YEAR ISSUE		EDITION LIMIT	YEAR RETD.	ISSUE PRICE	*QUOTE U.S.$
1991	Egg, Gold Design/Salem Blue Irid.	1,500	1991	29.50	30
1991	Egg, Partridge/Seamist Green Irid.	1,500	1991	29.50	30
1991	Egg, Poinsettias/Special Milk Glass	1,500	1991	29.50	30
1991	Egg, Shell/Favrene	1,500	1991	35.00	45
1991	Egg, Skater/Ruby	1,500	1991	29.50	30
1991	Egg, Snow Scene/Sp. Milk	1,500	1991	29.50	30
1991	Egg, White Scene/Black	1,500	1991	29.50	30
1992	Egg, Butterflies/Black	2,500	1992	30.00	30
1992	Egg, Croquet/Clear Carnival	2,500	1992	30.00	30
1992	Egg, Floral & Bronze/Special Milk Glass	2,500	1992	30.00	30
1992	Egg, Iris/Seamist Green	2,500	1992	30.00	30
1992	Egg, Pink Floral/Dusty Rose	2,500	1992	30.00	30
1992	Egg, Unicorn/Twilight Blue	2,500	1992	30.00	30
1993	Egg, Cottage/White Opal	2,500	1993	30.00	30
1993	Egg, Fuchsia Floral/White	2,500	1993	30.00	30
1993	Egg, Paisley/Dusty Rose	2,500	1993	30.00	30
1993	Egg, Sandcarved/Black	1,500	1993	35.00	35
1993	Egg, Scrolling Floral/Green - K. Plauche	2,500	1993	30.00	30
1993	Egg, Sea Gulls/Ocean Blue	2,500	1993	30.00	30
1993	Egg, w/gold on Plum - K. Plauche	2,500	1993	35.00	35
1993	Egg, w/gold on Ruby	2,500	1993	30.00	30
1994	Egg, Cascading Floral/Pink - S. Jackson	2,500	1994	32.50	33
1994	Egg, Metallic Floral/Plum - K. Plauche	2,500	1994	32.50	33
1994	Egg, Enameled Flowers/Blue - F. Burton	2,500	1994	37.50	38
1994	Egg, Scrolls/Gold	2,500	1994	32.50	33
1994	Egg, Spring Landscape/Opal - S. Jackson	2,500	1994	32.50	33
1994	Egg, Tulips/Sea Mist - S. Jackson	2,500	1994	32.50	33
1994	Egg, Violets/Milk Pearl - S. Jackson	2,500	1994	32.50	33
1995	Egg, Floral/Blue	2,500	1995	32.50	33
1995	Egg, Floral/Gold	2,500	1995	32.50	33
1995	Egg, Floral/Green	2,500	1995	32.50	33
1995	Egg, Floral/White	2,500	1995	32.50	33
1995	Egg, Hummingbird/Dusty Rose	2,500	1995	35.00	35
1995	Egg, Scene/White	2,500	1995	32.50	33
1995	Egg, Scrolls/Black	2,500	1995	32.50	33
1996	Egg, Honeysuckle - R. Spindler	2,500	1996	37.50	38
1996	Egg, Hummingbird	2,500	1996	37.50	38
1996	Egg, Butterflies - R. Spindler	2,500	1996	37.50	38
1996	Egg, Morning Glories - R. Spindler	2,500	1996	37.50	38
1996	Egg, Lake Scene	2,500	1996	37.50	38
1996	Egg, Jeweled	2,500	1996	37.50	38
1996	Egg, Fish - R. Spindler	2,500	1996	37.50	38
1997	Egg, Iris/Seamist Green	2,500		45.00	45
1997	Egg, Daisy/Misty Blue	2,500		45.00	45
1997	Egg, Violas/Dusty Rose - K. Plauche	2,500		39.00	39
1997	Egg, Lighthouse/French Opal Irid. - K. Plauche	2,500		45.00	45
1997	Egg, Roses/Ivory Sandblasted	2,500		39.00	39
1997	Egg, Rooster/Spruce - R. Spindler	2,500		39.00	39
1997	Egg, Dolphin/Favrene-Hndpt. & Sandcarved - K. Plauche	2,500		65.00	65

Designer Series - Various

YEAR ISSUE		EDITION LIMIT	YEAR RETD.	ISSUE PRICE	*QUOTE U.S.$
1983	Lighthouse Point, Lamp, 23 1/2", - M. Dickinson	150	1983	350.00	450
1983	Lighthouse Point, Lamp, 25 1/2", - M. Dickinson	150	1983	350.00	575
1983	Down Home, Lamp, 21" - G. Finn	300	1983	300.00	450
1984	Smoke 'N Cinders, Lamp, 16" - M. Dickinson	250	1984	195.00	325
1984	Smoke 'N Cinders, Lamp, 23" - M. Dickinson	250	1984	350.00	400
1984	Majestic Flight, Lamp, 16" - B. Cumberledge	250	1984	195.00	295
1984	Majestic Flight, Lamp, 23 1/2" B. Cumberledge	250	1984	350.00	450
1985	In Season, Lamp, 16" - M. Dickinson	250	1985	225.00	325
1985	In Season, Lamp, 23" - M. Dickinson	250	1985	295.00	395
1985	Nature's Grace, Lamp, 16" - B. Cumberland	250	1985	225.00	325
1985	Nature's Grace, Lamp, 23" - B. Cumberland	295	1985	295.00	400

Easter Series - M. Reynolds

YEAR ISSUE		EDITION LIMIT	YEAR RETD.	ISSUE PRICE	*QUOTE U.S.$
1995	Fairy Light	Closed	1995	49.00	49

Mary Gregory - M. Reynolds

YEAR ISSUE		EDITION LIMIT	YEAR RETD.	ISSUE PRICE	*QUOTE U.S.$
1994	Basket, 7 1/2" Oval	Closed	1994	59.00	65
1995	Basket, 7 1/2" Oval	Closed	1995	65.00	75
1995	Egg on stand, 4" - Butterfly Delight	Closed	1995	37.50	45
1996	Hat Basket on Cranberry, 6 1/2"	2,000	1996	95.00	95
1996	Vase on Cranberry, 9"	1,500	1996	135.00	135
1997	Guest Set, 7" Cranberry	1,500		189.00	189
1997	Fairy Light, 5" Cranberry	1,500		79.00	79
1997	Basket, 8" Cranberry	1,500		115.00	115

Miniatures - Fenton

YEAR ISSUE		EDITION LIMIT	YEAR RETD.	ISSUE PRICE	*QUOTE U.S.$
1996	Epergne, 4 1/2" Opaline	Closed	1996	35.00	35
1996	Punch Bowl Set, 3 3/4" Dusty Rose	Closed	1996	59.00	59
1997	Punch Bowl Set, 3 3/4" Seamist Green	Closed	1997	59.00	59

Mouthblown Eggs - M. Reynolds, unless otherwise noted

YEAR ISSUE		EDITION LIMIT	YEAR RETD.	ISSUE PRICE	*QUOTE U.S.$
1991	Egg, 3 1/2" Mother of Pearl	Closed	1991	49.00	49
1991	Egg, 4 1/2" Mother of Pearl	Closed	1991	59.00	59
1992	Egg, 5" Petal Pink Iridized - F. Burton	Closed	1992	65.00	65
1992	Egg, 5" Seamist Green Iridized - F. Burton	Closed	1992	65.00	65
1993	Egg, 5" Ocean Blue	Closed	1993	69.00	69
1993	Egg, 5" Plum	Closed	1993	69.00	125
1994	Egg, 5" Blue - F. Burton	Closed	1994	75.00	75
1994	Egg, 5" Rose	Closed	1994	75.00	125
1995	Egg, 5" Gold	Closed	1995	75.00	75
1995	Egg, 5" Spruce	Closed	1995	75.00	75
1996	Egg, 5" Cranberry	Closed	1996	95.00	125
1996	Egg, 5" French Opalescent	Closed	1996	75.00	125

Valentine's Day Series - Fenton, unless otherwise noted

YEAR ISSUE		EDITION LIMIT	YEAR RETD.	ISSUE PRICE	*QUOTE U.S.$
1992	Basket, 6" Cranberry Opal/Heart Optic	Closed	1992	50.00	85
1992	Vase, 4" Cranberry Opal/Heart Optic	Closed	1992	35.00	60
1992	Perfume, w/oval stopper Cranberry Opal/Heart Optic	Closed	1992	60.00	125
1993	Basket, 7" Caprice Cranberry Opal/Heart Optic	Closed	1993	59.00	85
1993	Trinket Box, 5" Cranberry Opal/Heart Optic	Closed	1993	79.00	95
1993	Vase, 5 1/2" Melon Cranberry Opal/Heart Optic	Closed	1993	45.00	70
1993	Southern Girl, 8", Hndpt. Opal Satin - M. Reynolds	Closed	1993	49.00	90
1993	Southern Girl, 8", Rose Pearl Irid.	Closed	1993	45.00	95
1994	Basket, 7" Cranberry Opal/Heart Optic	Closed	1994	65.00	95
1994	Vase, 5 1/2" Ribbed Cranberry Opal/Heart Optic	Closed	1994	47.50	60
1994	Perfume, w/ stopper, 5" Cranberry Opal/Heart Optic	Closed	1994	75.00	125
1995	Basket, 8" Melon Cranberry Opal/Heart Optic	Closed	1995	69.00	95
1995	Pitcher, 5 1/2" Melon Cranberry Opal/Heart Optic	Closed	1995	69.00	95
1995	Perfume, w/ heart stopper, Kristen's Floral Hndpt. - M. Reynolds	2,500	1995	49.00	75
1995	Doll, 7", Kristen's Floral Hndpt. Ivory Satin - M. Reynolds	2,500	1995	49.00	70
1996	Basket, 8" Melon Cranberry Opalescent	Closed	1996	75.00	75
1996	Perfume, 5" Melon Cranberry Opalescent	Closed	1996	95.00	95
1996	Fairy Light, 3 pc. Cranberry Opalescent	Closed	1996	135.00	135
1996	Vanity Set, 4 pc. Tea Rose - M. Reynolds	1,500	1996	250.00	250
1996	Doll, w/Musical Base Tea Rose - M. Reynolds	2,500	1996	55.00	55
1997	Pitcher, 6 1/2" Cranberry Opal/Heart Optic	Closed	1997	89.00	89
1997	Puff Box, 4" Cranberry Opal/Heart Optic	Closed	1997	79.00	79
1997	Hat Basket, 7" Cranberry Opal/Heart Optic	Closed	1997	79.00	79
1997	Vanity Set, 7" Burmese Floral & Butterfly Hndpt. - R. Spindler	2,000		225.00	225
1997	Girl Figurine, 8" Burmese Floral Hndpt. - R. Spindler	2,000		75.00	75

*Quotes have been rounded up to nearest dollar

Collectors' Information Bureau

67

Fenton Art Glass Company
to Flambro Imports

FIGURINES

YEAR ISSUE		EDITION LIMIT	YEAR RETD.	ISSUE PRICE	*QUOTE U.S. $
1997	Pendant & Trinket Box, Champagne Satin	2,500		65.00	65

Fitz & Floyd

Charming Tails Autumn Harvest Figurines - D. Griff

YEAR ISSUE		EDITION LIMIT	YEAR RETD.	ISSUE PRICE	*QUOTE U.S. $
1993	Acorn Built For Two 85/403	Open		10.00	12
1996	Bag of Tricks...Or Treats 87/436	Open		15.50	17
1996	Binkey's Acorn Costume 87/429	Open		11.50	13
1995	Candy Apples 85/611	Open		16.00	17
1995	Candy Corn Vampire 85/607	Closed	1996	18.00	25-30
1993	Caps Off to You 85/402	Closed	1996	10.00	20
1996	Chauncey's Pear Costume 87/431	Open		12.00	13
1993	Cornfield Feast 85/399	Closed	1994	15.00	55-80
1993	Fall Frolicking 85/401	Closed	1996	13.00	32
1994	Frosting Pumpkins 85/511	Closed	1996	16.00	30
1995	Garden Naptime 85/615	Closed	1996	18.00	32
1997	Ghost Stories 85/703	Open		18.50	19
1995	Giving Thanks	Open		16.00	17
1997	The Good Witch 85/704	Open		18.50	19
1993	Gourd Slide 85/398	Closed	1996	16.00	16
1994	Harvest Fruit 85/507	Closed	1995	16.00	35-50
1995	Horn of Plenty 85/610	Closed	1996	20.00	21
1996	Indian Impostor 87/446	Open		14.00	15
1994	Jumpin' Jack O' Lanterns 85/512	Closed	1996	16.00	17
1995	Let's Get Crackin' 85/776	Open		20.00	21
1996	Look! No Hands 87/428	Open		15.50	17
1996	Maxine's Pumpkin Costume 87/430	Open		12.00	13
1993	Mouse Candleholder 85/400	Closed	1995	13.00	13
1994	Mouse on Leaf Candleholder 87/503	Closed	1995	17.00	17
1996	Oops, I Missed 87/443	Open		16.00	17
1994	Open Pumpkin 85/508	Closed	1994	15.00	40-63
1994	Painting Leaves 85/514	Closed	1996	16.00	25
1994	Pear Candleholder 85/509	Closed	1995	14.00	45
1996	Pickin' Time 87/438	Open		16.00	17
1996	Pilgrim's Progress 87/445	Open		13.50	15
1995	Pumpkin Pie 85/606	Closed	1996	16.00	25
1994	Pumpkin Slide 85/513	Closed	1995	16.00	40-60
1994	Pumpkin Votive 85/510	Closed	1995	13.50	30-45
1997	Reginald's Gourd Costume 85/701	Open		12.50	13
1995	Reginald's Hideaway 85/777	Closed	1996	14.00	16
1997	Stewart's Apple Costume 85/700	Open		12.50	13
1994	Stump Candleholders 85/516	Closed	1995	20.00	85
1997	Turkey Traveller 85/702	Open		18.50	19
1996	You're Not Scary 87/440	Open		14.00	15
1996	You're Nutty 87/451	Open		12.00	13

Charming Tails Easter Basket Figurines - D. Griff

YEAR ISSUE		EDITION LIMIT	YEAR RETD.	ISSUE PRICE	*QUOTE U.S. $
1995	After the Hunt 87/372	Open		18.00	19
1993	Animals in Eggs 89/313	Closed	1996	11.00	20
1995	Binkey's Bouncing Bundle 87/422	7,500	1995	18.00	35
1994	Bunny Imposter 89/609	Open		12.00	13
1995	Bunny Love 87/424	Open		18.00	19
1993	Duckling in Egg w/Mouse 89/316	Closed	1994	15.00	125-150
1994	Easter Parade 89/615	Closed	1996	10.00	10
1995	Gathering Treats 87/377	Open		12.00	13
1994	Jelly Bean Feast 89/559	Closed	1996	14.00	25
1995	Look Out Below 87/373	Open		20.00	21
1996	No Thanks, I'm Stuffed 88/603	Open		15.00	16
1994	Peek-a-boo 89/753	Closed	1996	12.00	12
1994	Wanna Play? 89/561	2,500	1994	15.00	100-200
1995	Want a Bite? 87/379	Open		18.00	19
1996	What's Hatchin' 88/600	Open		16.00	17

Charming Tails Event Piece - D. Griff

YEAR ISSUE		EDITION LIMIT	YEAR RETD.	ISSUE PRICE	*QUOTE U.S. $
1996	Take Me Home 87/691	Closed	1996	17.00	40

Charming Tails Everyday Figurines - D. Griff

YEAR ISSUE		EDITION LIMIT	YEAR RETD.	ISSUE PRICE	*QUOTE U.S. $
1996	Ach-Choo, Get Well Soon 89/624	Open		12.00	13
1994	After Lunch Snooze 89/558	Open		15.00	16
1996	The Berry Best 87/391	Open		16.00	17
1994	Binkey Growing Carrots 89/605	Closed	1995	15.00	40-50
1993	Binkey in a Lily 89/305	Closed	1996	16.00	40
1994	Binkey in the Berry Patch 89/752	Closed	1996	12.00	12
1995	Binkey's First Cake 98/349	Open		16.00	17
1994	Binkey's New Pal 89/586	Closed	1996	14.00	14
1996	Bunny Buddies 89/619	Open		20.00	21
1994	Bunny w/Carrot Candleholder 89/317	Closed	1995	12.00	12
1994	Butterfly Smelling Zinnia 89/606	Closed	1995	15.00	40-80
1994	Can I Keep Him? 89/600	2,500	1994	13.00	250-300
1995	Catchin' Butterflies 87/423	Open		16.00	17
1996	Cattail Catapult 87/448	Open		16.00	17
1996	Charming Tails Display Sign 87/690	Open		20.00	20
1996	The Chase is On 87/386	Open		16.00	17
1994	Chauncey Growing Tomatoes 89/607	Closed	1995	15.00	40-45
1994	Duckling Votive 89/315	Closed	1994	12.00	35
1995	Feeding Time 98/417	Closed	1996	16.00	16
1996	Flower Friends 89/608	Open		15.00	16
1996	Fragile...Handle with Care 89/601	15,000		18.00	19
1995	Gardening Break 87/364	Open		16.00	17
1994	Get Well Soon 97/719	Open		15.00	16
1994	Good Luck 97/716	Open		15.00	16
1996	Hangin' Around 89/623	Open		18.00	19
1994	Happy Birthday 97/715	Open		15.00	16
1995	Hello, Sweet Pea 87/367	Open		12.00	13
1993	Hide and Seek 89/307	Closed	1994	13.50	115-188
1994	Hope You're Feeling Better 97/723	Open		15.00	17
1996	Hoppity Hop 87/425	Open		16.00	15
1994	How Do You Measure Love 98/461	Closed	1996	15.00	15
1996	I Have a Question for You 89/603	Open		16.00	17
1994	I Love You 97/724	Open		15.00	16
1996	I See Things Clearly Now 89/626	Open		14.00	15
1995	I'm Berry Happy 87/390	Open		15.00	16
1995	I'm Full 87/365	Open		15.00	16
1994	I'm So Sorry 97/720	Open		15.00	17
1994	It's Not the Same Without You 97/721	Open		15.00	16
1996	Just "Plane" Friends 89/627	Open		18.00	19
1993	King of the Mushroom 89/318	Closed	1996	16.00	30
1993	Love Mice 89/314	Closed	1994	15.00	60-85
1994	Mackenzie Growing Beans 89/604	Closed	1995	15.00	35-45
1993	Maxine's Butterfly Ride 89/190	Open		16.50	17
1994	Mender of Broken Hearts 98/460	Closed	1996	15.00	30
1996	Mid-day Snooze 89/617	Open		18.00	19
1995	Mouse in Strawberry 89/562	Closed	1995	12.00	12
1993	Mouse on a Bee 89/191	Closed	1994	16.50	150-250
1993	Mouse on a Dragonfly 89/320	Closed	1994	16.50	125-250
1993	Mouse on a Grasshopper 89/321	Closed	1994	15.00	125-175
1994	New Arrival 97/717	Open		15.00	17
1995	One for Me... 87/360	Open		16.00	17
1995	One for You... 87/361	Open		16.00	17
1995	Picking Peppers 87/369	Open		12.00	13
1993	Rabbit/Daffodil Candleholder 89/312	Closed	1995	13.50	95-107
1994	Reach for the Stars 97/718	Open		15.00	17
1994	Slumber Party 89/560	Closed	1996	16.00	40
1993	Spring Flowers 89/310	Closed	1996	16.00	20-38
1994	Springtime Showers 89/563	Closed	1996	10.00	10
1995	Surrounded By Friends 87/353	Open		16.00	17
1996	Taggin' Along 87/399	Open		14.00	15
1996	Take Time To Reflect 87/396	Open		16.00	17
1994	Thanks for Being There 89/754	Closed	1996	15.00	25
1995	This Is Hot! 87/366	Open		15.00	16
1996	Training Wings 87/398	Open		16.00	17
1995	Tuggin' Twosome 87/362	10,000		18.00	18
1993	Two Peas in a Pod 89/306	Closed	1996	14.00	25-45
1996	The Waterslide 87/384	Open		20.00	21
1994	We'll Weather the Storm Together 97/722	Open		15.00	17
1995	Why, Hello There! 87/357	Open		14.00	15
1995	You Are Not Alone 98/929	Closed	1996	20.00	35-40
1996	You Couldn't Be Sweeter 89/625	Open		16.00	17
1996	You Love me-You Love Me Not 87/395	Open		16.00	17

Charming Tails Everyday Lazy Days of Summer Figurines - D. Griff

YEAR ISSUE		EDITION LIMIT	YEAR RETD.	ISSUE PRICE	*QUOTE U.S. $
1997	The Blossom Bounce 83/704	Open		20.00	20
1997	Building Castles 83/802	Open		17.00	17
1997	Gone Fishin' 83/702	Open		16.00	16
1997	Life's a Picnic With You 83/701	Open		18.00	18
1997	Row Boat Romance 83/801	Open		15.50	16

Charming Tails Musicals and Waterglobes - D. Griff

YEAR ISSUE		EDITION LIMIT	YEAR RETD.	ISSUE PRICE	*QUOTE U.S. $
1994	Jawbreakers Musical 87/542	Closed	1995	40.00	70
1994	Letter to Santa Waterglobe 87/518	Closed	1994	45.00	75
1995	Me Next! Musical 89/555	Closed	1995	45.00	45
1994	Mini Surprise Waterglobe 87/956	Closed	1994	22.00	50
1994	Mouse on Cheese, Waterglobe 92/224	Closed	1995	44.00	44
1994	Mouse on Rubber Duck, Waterglobe 92/225	Closed	1995	44.00	44
1994	My Hero! Waterglobe 89/557	Closed	1995	45.00	45
1995	Pumpkin Playtime Musical 85/778	Closed	1995	35.00	35
1993	Rocking Mice Musical 86/790	Closed	1994	65.00	115
1994	Sailing Away Waterglobe 87/200	Closed	1994	50.00	50
1994	Sharing the Warmth Waterglobe 87/517	Closed	1994	40.00	40
1993	Skating Mice Musical 87/511	Closed	1994	25.00	25
1994	Sweet Dreams Waterglobe 87/534	Closed	1994	40.00	40
1994	Together at Christmas, Mini Waterglobe 87/532	Closed	1995	30.00	30-50
1994	Trimming the Tree Waterglobe 87/516	Closed	1994	45.00	45
1994	Underwater Explorer Waterglobe 89/556	Closed	1995	45.00	45
1994	Up, Up and Away Musical 89/602	Closed	1995	70.00	100-195

Charming Tails Squashville Figurines - D. Griff

YEAR ISSUE		EDITION LIMIT	YEAR RETD.	ISSUE PRICE	*QUOTE U.S. $
1996	Airmail 87/698	Open		16.00	16
1996	All I Can Give You is Me 87/498	Closed	1996	15.00	20
1996	All Snug in Their Beds Waterglobe 87/476	Closed	1996	30.00	50
1997	All The Trimmings 87/703	Yr.Iss.		15.00	15
1996	Angel of Light 87/481	Open		12.00	13
1997	Baby's 1st Christmas 1997 Annual 87/705	Yr.Iss.		18.50	19
1996	Baby's First Christmas Waterglobe 87/475	Closed	1996	28.00	50
1997	Bearing Gifts 87/600	Open		16.00	16
1996	Binkey in a Bed of Flowers 87/426	Closed	1996	15.00	20-25
1995	Binkey Snow Shoeing 87/580	Open		14.00	15
1995	Binkey's 1995 Ice Sculpture 87/572	Yr.Iss.	1995	20.00	25-38
1996	Building a Snowbunny 87/692	Open		16.00	17
1995	Charming Choo-Choo and Cabbose 87/579	Open		35.00	36
1997	Chauncey's Choo Choo Ride 87/707	Open		19.00	19
1996	Chauncey's Noisemakers 87/554	Open		12.00	13
1995	Christmas Pageant Stage 87/546	Open		30.00	31
1996	Christmas Stroll 87/575	Open		16.00	17
1997	Christmas Trio 87/713	Open		15.50	16
1997	Decorating Binkey 87/714	Open		16.00	16
1996	The Drum Major 87/556	Open		12.00	13
1996	Extra! Extra! 87/590	Open		14.00	15
1996	Farmer Mackenzie 87/695	Open		16.00	17
1996	The Float Driver 87/587	Open		12.00	13
1995	Flying Leaf Saucer 87/305	Open		16.00	17
1996	Follow in my Footsteps 87/473	Open		12.00	13
1996	Holiday Trumpeteer 87/555	Open		12.00	13
1995	Holy Family Players 87/547	Open		20.00	21
1994	Hot Doggin' 87/993	Closed	1995	20.00	40-50
1996	Jingle Bells 87/513	Open		15.00	16
1994	Lady Bug Express 87/188	Closed	1994	18.00	120-185
1994	Leaf Vine Ornament Hanger 87/519	Closed	1995	25.00	25
1996	Lil' Drummer Mouse 87/480	Open		12.00	13
1996	Little Drummer Boy 87/557	Open		12.00	13
1994	Mackenzie and Maxine Caroling 87/925	Closed	1995	18.00	50-60
1994	Mackenzie Building a Snowmouse 87/203	7,500	1994	18.00	110-175
1996	Mackenzie Claus on Parade 87/576	Open		22.00	23
1995	Mail Mouse 87/573	Closed	1996	12.00	12
1996	Manger Animals 87/482	Open		20.00	21
1994	Maxine Makin Snow Angels 87/510	Open		20.00	21
1997	Maxine's Snowmobile Ride 87/612	Open		17.00	17
1994	Mice on Vine Basket 87/506	Closed	1995	55.00	55
1994	Mouse Candle Climber 87/189	Closed	1995	8.00	8
1994	Mouse Card Holder 87/501	Closed	1995	13.00	13
1994	Mouse in Tree Hole Candleholder 87/502	Closed	1995	17.00	17
1994	Mouse on Basket 87/529	Closed	1995	50.00	50
1994	Mouse on Vine Candleholder 87/504	Closed	1995	55.00	55
1994	Mouse on Vine Wreath 87/505	Closed	1995	55.00	55
1993	Mouse Star Treetop 87/958	Closed	1995	14.00	14
1996	My New Toy 87/500	Open		14.00	15
1997	Not a Creature Was Stirring 87/704	Open		17.00	17
1996	Oops! Did I Do That? 87/469	Open		14.00	15
1996	Parade Banner 87/543	Open		16.00	17
1995	Pear Taxi 87/565	Closed	1996	16.00	16
1996	Peeking at Presents 87/527	Open		13.00	14
1994	Pyramid with Mice Candleholder 87/509	Closed	1995	40.00	40
1996	Reginald's Newstand 87/591	Open		20.00	21
1997	The Santa Balloon 87/708	Open		25.00	25
1997	Shepherd's set 87/710	Open		12.50	13
1995	Sleigh Ride 87/569	7,500	1995	16.00	50-100
1996	Snack for the Reindeer 87/512	Closed	1996	13.00	13
1995	Snow Plow 87/566	Open		16.00	17
1996	The Snowball Fight 87/570	Open		18.00	17
1995	Stewart's Choo Choo Ride 87/694	Open		17.50	19
1995	Teamwork Helps 87/571	Open		16.00	17
1996	Testing the Lights 87/514	Open		14.00	15
1995	Three Wise Mice 87/548	Open		20.00	21
1996	Town Crier 87/696	Open		14.00	15
1997	Trimming The Tree 87/702	Open		27.50	28
1996	Waiting For Christmas 87/496	14,000		16.00	16
1997	You Melted My Heart 87/472	Open		20.00	21

Flambro Imports

Emmett Kelly Jr. Members Only Figurine - Undisclosed

YEAR ISSUE		EDITION LIMIT	YEAR RETD.	ISSUE PRICE	*QUOTE U.S. $
1990	Merry-Go-Round	Closed	1990	125.00	400-500
1991	10 Years Of Collecting	Closed	1991	100.00	200
1992	All Aboard	Closed	1992	75.00	200
1993	Ringmaster	Closed	1993	125.00	125
1994	Birthday Mail	Closed	1994	100.00	200-250
1995	Salute To Our Vets	Closed	1995	75.00	100-195
1996	I Love You	Closed	1996	95.00	125-200
1997	Filet of Sole	Yr.Iss.		130.00	130

Emmett Kelly Jr. Event Figurine - Undisclosed

YEAR ISSUE		EDITION LIMIT	YEAR RETD.	ISSUE PRICE	*QUOTE U.S. $
1996	EKJ For President	Retrd.	1996	60.00	65-100

EKJ Professionals - Undisclosed

YEAR ISSUE		EDITION LIMIT	YEAR RETD.	ISSUE PRICE	*QUOTE U.S. $
1987	Accountant	Retrd.	1994	50.00	60-100
1991	Barber	Retrd.	1995	50.00	75-100
1988	Bowler	Retrd.	1994	50.00	100
1996	Bowler	Open		55.00	55
1991	Carpenter	Retrd.	1996	50.00	50
1991	The Chef	Retrd.	1994	50.00	100
1995	Coach	Open		55.00	55
1990	Computer Whiz	Open		50.00	50
1997	Computer Whiz (w/garbage can)	Open		55.00	55
1987	Dentist	Retrd.	1995	50.00	75-100
1996	Dentist	Open		55.00	55
1987	Doctor	Retrd.	1995	50.00	100
1995	Doctor	Open		55.00	55
1987	Engineer	Retrd.	1995	50.00	100
1987	Executive	Open		50.00	50
1997	Executive (talking on phone)	Open		55.00	55
1996	Farmer	Open		55.00	55
1995	Fireman	Open		55.00	55
1988	Fireman	Retrd.	1994	50.00	75
1990	Fisherman	Open		50.00	50
1997	Fisherman (w/fish & dog)	Open		55.00	55
1997	Fitness (runaway weight loss)	Open		55.00	55

*Quotes have been rounded up to nearest dollar

FIGURINES

Flambro Imports
to Flambro Imports

YEAR ISSUE		EDITION LIMIT	YEAR RETD.	ISSUE PRICE	*QUOTE U.S.$
1997	Gardener (w/rake)	Open		55.00	55
1995	Golfer	Open		55.00	55
1988	Golfer	Retrd.	1996	50.00	50
1990	Hunter	Open		50.00	50
1997	Hunter (w/orange camouflauge)	Open		55.00	55
1995	Lawyer	Open		55.00	55
1987	Lawyer	Retrd.	1995	50.00	75-100
1988	Mailman	Retrd.	1996	50.00	100
1996	Mailman	Open		55.00	55
1993	On Maneuvers	Open		50.00	50
1991	Painter	Open		50.00	50
1991	Pharmacist	Open		50.00	50
1990	Photographer	Open		50.00	50
1993	Pilot	Open		50.00	50
1991	Plumber	Retrd.	1994	50.00	100
1995	Policeman	Open		55.00	55
1988	Policeman	Retrd.	1994	50.00	75-100
1990	The Putt	Open		50.00	50
1993	Realtor	Open		50.00	50
1988	Skier	Retrd.	1995	50.00	100
1996	Skier	Open		55.00	55
1987	Stockbrocker	Open		50.00	50
1987	Teacher	Retrd.	1995	50.00	75
1993	Veterinarian	Open		50.00	50

Emmett Kelly Jr. - Undisclosed, unless otherwise noted

YEAR ISSUE		EDITION LIMIT	YEAR RETD.	ISSUE PRICE	*QUOTE U.S.$
1995	20th Anniversary of All Star Circus	5,000	1995	240.00	240
1997	25th Anniversary of White House Appearance	5,000		240.00	240
1995	35 Years of Clowning	5,000	1995	240.00	240
1989	65th Birthday Commemorative	1,989	1989	300.00	1200-1600
1993	After The Parade	7,500		190.00	190
1988	Amen	12,000	1991	120.00	325-400
1996	American Circus Extravaganza	5,000		240.00	240
1991	Artist At Work	7,500		285.00	285
1992	Autumn - D. Rust	Retrd.	1996	60.00	75-175
1983	The Balancing Act	10,000	1985	75.00	700-800
1983	Balloons For Sale	10,000	1985	75.00	600-700
1990	Balloons for Sale II	7,500		250.00	250
1986	Bedtime	12,000	1991	98.00	175-250
1984	Big Business	9,500	1987	110.00	800-900
1997	Catch of the Day	5,000		240.00	240
1990	Convention-Bound	7,500		225.00	230
1986	Cotton Candy	12,000	1987	98.00	375
1996	Daredevil Thrill Motor Show	5,000		240.00	240
1988	Dining Out	12,000	1991	120.00	200-275
1984	Eating Cabbage	12,000	1986	75.00	475
1985	Emmett's Fan	12,000	1986	80.00	475
1986	The Entertainers	12,000	1991	120.00	150-200
1986	Fair Game	2,500	1987	450.00	1650
1991	Finishing Touch	7,500		230.00	230
1991	Follow The Leader	7,500		200.00	200
1994	Forest Friends	7,500		190.00	190
1983	Hole In The Sole	10,000	1986	75.00	600-650
1989	Hurdy-Gurdy Man	9,500	1991	150.00	175-300
1985	In The Spotlight	12,000	1989	103.00	200-400
1993	Kittens For Sale	7,500		190.00	190
1994	Let Him Eat Cake	3,500	1995	300.00	450-600
1994	The Lion Tamer	7,500		190.00	190
1981	Looking Out To See	12,000	1982	75.00	2200-2400
1986	Making New Friends	9,500	1988	140.00	350
1989	Making Up	7,500	1995	200.00	250-450
1985	Man's Best Friend	9,500	1989	98.00	550-650
1990	Misfortune?	3,500	1989	350.00	500-600
1987	My Favorite Things	9,500	1988	109.00	600-700
1989	No Loitering	7,500	1994	200.00	300-400
1985	No Strings Attached	9,500	1991	98.00	200-300
1992	No Use Crying	7,500		200.00	200
1987	On The Road Again	9,500	1991	109.00	450
1988	Over a Barrel	9,500	1991	130.00	250-450
1992	Peanut Butter?	7,500		200.00	200
1984	Piano Player	9,500	1988	160.00	550-650
1992	Ready-Set-Go	7,500		200.00	200
1987	Saturday Night	7,500	1988	153.00	500-600
1983	Spirit of Christmas I	3,500	1984	125.00	2600
1984	Spirit of Christmas II	3,500	1985	270.00	500-600
1985	Spirit of Christmas III	3,500	1989	220.00	525
1986	Spirit of Christmas IV	3,500	1989	150.00	400-550
1987	Spirit of Christmas V	2,400	1989	170.00	400-550
1988	Spirit of Christmas VI	2,400	1989	194.00	400-600
1990	Spirit of Christmas VII	3,500	1990	275.00	425
1991	Spirit of Christmas VIII	3,500	1992	250.00	350
1993	Spirit of Christmas IX	3,500		200.00	200
1993	Spirit of Christmas X	3,500		200.00	200
1994	Spirit of Christmas XI	3,500	1995	200.00	225-250
1995	Spirit of Christmas XII	3,500		200.00	200
1996	Spirit of Christmas XIII	3,500		200.00	200
1997	Spirit of Christmas XIV	3,500		200.00	200
1992	Spring - D. Rust	Retrd.	1996	60.00	75-125
1992	Summer - D. Rust	Retrd.	1996	60.00	75-150
1981	Sweeping Up	12,000	1982	75.00	1200-1500
1982	The Thinker	15,000	1986	60.00	1100
1987	Toothache	12,000	1995	98.00	125-200
1990	Watch the Birdie	9,500		200.00	225
1982	Wet Paint	15,000	1983	80.00	600-800
1988	Wheeler Dealer	7,500	1990	160.00	200-300
1982	Why Me?	15,000	1984	65.00	475-600
1992	Winter - D. Rust	Retrd.	1996	60.00	75-125
1983	Wishful Thinking	10,000	1985	65.00	500-700
1993	World Traveler	7,500		190.00	190

Emmett Kelly Jr. A Day At The Fair - Undisclosed

YEAR ISSUE		EDITION LIMIT	YEAR RETD.	ISSUE PRICE	*QUOTE U.S.$
1990	75 Please	Retrd.	1994	65.00	85-125
1991	Coin Toss	Retrd.	1994	65.00	85-125
1990	Look At You	Retrd.	1994	65.00	85-125
1991	Popcorn!	Retrd.	1994	65.00	85-125
1990	Ride The Wild Mouse	Retrd.	1994	65.00	85-125
1990	Step Right Up	Retrd.	1994	65.00	85-125
1992	Stilt Man	Retrd.	1994	65.00	85-125
1990	The Stilt Man	Retrd.	1994	65.00	85-125
1990	Thanks Emmett	Retrd.	1994	65.00	85-125
1990	Three For A Dime	Retrd.	1994	65.00	85-125
1991	The Trouble With Hot Dogs	Retrd.	1994	65.00	85-125
1990	You Can Do It, Emmett	Retrd.	1994	65.00	85-125
1990	You Go First, Emmett	Retrd.	1994	65.00	85-125

Emmett Kelly Jr. Appearance Figurine - Undisclosed

YEAR ISSUE		EDITION LIMIT	YEAR RETD.	ISSUE PRICE	*QUOTE U.S.$
1992	Now Appearing	Open		100.00	100
1993	The Vigilante	Open		75.00	75
1996	Going My Way	Open		90.00	90

Emmett Kelly Jr. Event Figurine - Undisclosed

YEAR ISSUE		EDITION LIMIT	YEAR RETD.	ISSUE PRICE	*QUOTE U.S.$
1997	Send in the Clowns	12/97		70.00	70

Emmett Kelly Jr. Images of Emmett - Undisclosed

YEAR ISSUE		EDITION LIMIT	YEAR RETD.	ISSUE PRICE	*QUOTE U.S.$
1994	Baby's First Christmas	Open		80.00	80
1994	Best of Friends	Open		55.00	55
1994	Healing Heart	Open		90.00	90
1994	Holding The Future	Retrd.	1996	65.00	75-100
1994	Learning Together	Open		85.00	85
1994	Tightrope	Open		70.00	70
1994	Why Me, Again?	Open		60.00	60

Emmett Kelly Jr. Miniatures - Undisclosed

YEAR ISSUE		EDITION LIMIT	YEAR RETD.	ISSUE PRICE	*QUOTE U.S.$
1994	65th Birthday	Retrd.	1994	70.00	85-125
1996	Amen	Open		35.00	35
1986	Balancing Act	Retrd.	1992	25.00	100-140
1986	Balloons for Sale	Retrd.	1993	25.00	100-130
1997	Balloons for Sale II	Open		55.00	55
1995	Bedtime	Open		35.00	35
1997	Big Boss	Open		55.00	55
1988	Big Business	Retrd.	1995	35.00	90-130
1997	Convention Bound	Open		55.00	55
1989	Cotton Candy	Retrd.	1991	30.00	75-100
1995	Dining Out	Open		35.00	35
1987	Eating Cabbage	Retrd.	1990	30.00	50-100
1987	Emmett's Fan	Retrd.	1991	30.00	100-100
1995	The Entertainers	Open		45.00	45
1994	Fair Game	Open		75.00	75
1986	Hole in the Sole	Retrd.	1989	25.00	100-140
1995	Hurdy Gurdy Man	Open		40.00	40
1991	In The Spotlight	Retrd.	1996	35.00	90-125
1986	Looking Out To See	Retrd.	1987	25.00	150
1992	Making New Friends	Retrd.	1996	40.00	50-75
1996	Making Up	Open		55.00	55
1989	Man's Best Friend?	Retrd.	1994	35.00	85-115
1997	Merry Go Round	Open		65.00	65
1996	Misfortune	Open		60.00	60
1990	My Favorite Things	Retrd.	1995	45.00	90-110
1995	No Loitering	Open		50.00	50
1991	No Strings Attached	Retrd.	1996	35.00	50-90
1992	On the Road Again	Numbrd.		35.00	35
1994	Over a Barrel	Open		30.00	30
1992	Piano Player	Numbrd.		50.00	50
1990	Saturday Night	Retrd.	1995	50.00	75-115
1988	Spirit of Christmas I	Retrd.	1990	40.00	150
1992	Spirit of Christmas II	Retrd.	1995	50.00	75-100
1990	Spirit Of Christmas III	Retrd.	1993	50.00	100-150
1993	Spirit of Christmas IV	Numbrd.		40.00	40
1994	Spirit of Christmas V	Open		50.00	50
1996	Spirit of Christmas VI	Open		55.00	55
1997	Spirit of Christmas VII	Open		50.00	50
1986	Sweeping Up	Retrd.	1987	25.00	175
1986	The Thinker	Retrd.	1991	25.00	75-100
1996	The Toothache	Open		35.00	35
1997	Watch the Birdie	Open		55.00	55
1986	Wet Paint	Retrd.	1993	25.00	75-125
1996	Wheeler Dealer	Open		65.00	65
1986	Why Me?	Retrd.	1989	25.00	100-125
1986	Wishful Thinking	Retrd.	1988	25.00	90-120

Emmett Kelly Jr. Real Rags Collection - Undisclosed

YEAR ISSUE		EDITION LIMIT	YEAR RETD.	ISSUE PRICE	*QUOTE U.S.$
1993	Big Business II	Retrd.	1996	140.00	160
1993	Checking His List	Closed	N/A	100.00	175-225
1994	Eating Cabbage 2	3,000		100.00	100
1994	A Good Likeness	3,000		120.00	120
1993	Looking Out To See II	3,000	1996	100.00	100
1994	On in Two	3,000	1996	100.00	100-150
1994	Rudolph Has A Red Nose, Too	3,000	1996	135.00	150-175
1993	Sweeping Up II	3,000	1996	100.00	100-125
1993	Thinker II	3,000	1996	120.00	120-150

Little Emmetts - M. Wu

YEAR ISSUE		EDITION LIMIT	YEAR RETD.	ISSUE PRICE	*QUOTE U.S.$
1996	Balancing Act	Open		25.00	25
1996	Balloons for Sale	Open		25.00	25
1994	Birthday Haul	Open		30.00	30
1995	Dance Lessons	Open		50.00	50
1994	Little Artist Picture Frame	Open		22.00	22
1994	Little Emmett Fishing	Open		35.00	35
1995	Little Emmett Noel, Noel	Open		40.00	40
1994	Little Emmett Shadow Show	Open		40.00	40
1995	Little Emmett Someday	Open		50.00	50
1994	Little Emmett w/Blackboard	Open		30.00	30
1994	Little Emmett, Counting Lession (Musical)	Open		30.00	30
1994	Little Emmett, Country Road (Musical)	Open		35.00	35
1994	Little Emmett, Raindrops (Musical)	Open		35.00	35
1994	Little Emmett, You've Got a Friend (Musical)	Open		33.00	33
1996	Long Distance	Open		50.00	50
1995	Looking Back Musical Waterglobe	Open		75.00	75
1995	Looking Forward Musical Waterglobe	Open		75.00	75
1996	Looking Out To See	Open		25.00	25
1994	Playful Bookends	Open		40.00	40
1996	Sweeping Up	Open		25.00	25
1996	Thinker	Open		25.00	25
1996	Wet Paint	Open		40.00	40
1994	EKJ, Age 1	Open		9.00	9
1994	EKJ, Age2	Open		9.50	10
1994	EKJ, Age 3	Open		12.00	12
1994	EKJ, Age 4	Open		12.00	12
1994	EKJ, Age 5	Open		15.00	15
1994	EKJ, Age 6	Open		15.00	15
1994	EKJ, Age 7	Open		17.00	17
1994	EKJ, Age 8	Open		21.00	21
1994	EKJ, Age 9	Open		22.00	22
1994	EKJ, Age 10	Open		25.00	25
1996	January-New Years	Open		35.00	35
1996	February-Valentine's Day	Open		35.00	35
1996	March-St. Patrick's Day	Open		35.00	35
1996	April-April Showers	Open		35.00	35
1996	May-May Flowers	Open		35.00	35
1996	June-School Is Out	Open		35.00	35
1996	July-Independence Day	Open		35.00	35
1996	August-Summer Picnic	Open		35.00	35
1996	September-School Is In	Open		35.00	35
1996	October-Pumpkins for Fall & Halloween	Open		35.00	35
1996	November-Thanksgiving	Open		35.00	35
1996	December-Snow Sledding w/Friends	Open		35.00	35

Pocket Dragon Collector Club - R. Musgrave

YEAR ISSUE		EDITION LIMIT	YEAR RETD.	ISSUE PRICE	*QUOTE U.S.$
1991	Collecting Butterflies	Retrd.	1992	Gift	165
1992	The Key to My Heart	Retrd.	1993	Gift	125
1993	Want A Bite?	Retrd.	1994	Gift	60-75
1993	Bitsy	Retrd.	1994	Gift	N/A
1994	Friendship Pin	Open		Gift	85
1994	Blue Ribbon Dragon	Retrd.	1995	Gift	50-75
1995	Making Time For You	Retrd.	1996	Gift	50-100
1996	Good News	5/97		Gift	N/A

Pocket Dragon Members Only Pieces - R. Musgrave

YEAR ISSUE		EDITION LIMIT	YEAR RETD.	ISSUE PRICE	*QUOTE U.S.$
1991	A Spot of Tea Won't You Join Us (set)	Retrd.	1992	75.00	350
1991	Wizard's House Print	Retrd.	1993	39.95	80
1992	Book Nook	Retrd.	1993	140.00	195-225
1993	Pen Pals	Retrd.	1994	90.00	125-180
1994	The Best Seat in the House	Retrd.	1995	75.00	105-175
1995	Party Time	Retrd.	1996	75.00	75-125
1996	Looking For The Right Words	5/97		80.00	80

Pocket Dragon Appearance Figurines - R. Musgrave

YEAR ISSUE		EDITION LIMIT	YEAR RETD.	ISSUE PRICE	*QUOTE U.S.$
1993	A Big Hug	Retrd.	1994	35.00	75-95
1994	Packed and Ready	Retrd.	1995	47.00	45-95
1995	Attention to Detail	Retrd.	1996	24.00	24-50
1996	On The Road Again	Open		30.00	30

Pocket Dragon Christmas Editions - R. Musgrave

YEAR ISSUE		EDITION LIMIT	YEAR RETD.	ISSUE PRICE	*QUOTE U.S.$
1992	A Pocket-Sized Tree	Retrd.	1992	18.95	85-105
1993	Christmas Angel	Retrd.	1993	45.00	65-75
1991	I've Been Very Good	Retrd.	1991	37.50	95-125
1989	Putting Me on the Tree	Retrd.	1994	52.50	100-150
1994	Dear Santa	Retrd.	1995	50.00	65-75
1995	Chasing Snowflakes	Retrd.	1995	35.00	35-50
1996	Christmas Skates	Retrd.	1996	36.00	36
1997	Deck The Halls	12/97		39.00	39

Pocket Dragons - R. Musgrave

YEAR ISSUE		EDITION LIMIT	YEAR RETD.	ISSUE PRICE	*QUOTE U.S.$
1990	The Apprentice	Retrd.	1994	22.50	45-75
1989	Attack	Retrd.	1992	45.00	100-125
1989	Baby Brother	Retrd.	1992	19.50	30-75
1993	Bath Time	Retrd.	1995	90.00	90
1993	The Book End	Retrd.	1996	90.00	90
1994	A Book My Size	Open		30.00	30
1992	Bubbles	Retrd.	1996	55.00	55
1995	But I am Too Little!	Open		14.50	15
1994	Butterfly Kissess	Open		29.50	30
1994	Candy Cane	Open		55.00	55
1995	Classical Dragon	Open		80.00	80
1994	Coffee Please	Open		24.00	24
1996	D-Pressing	Open		28.00	28
1997	Daisy	Open		17.00	17
1994	Dance Partner	Open		23.00	23
1992	A Different Drummer	Retrd.	1994	32.50	45-95
1989	Do I Have To?	Retrd.	1996	45.00	50
1991	Dragons in the Attic	Retrd.	1995	120.00	120-200
1997	The Driver	Open		27.50	28
1989	Drowsy Dragon	Retrd.	1996	27.50	30
1995	Elementary My Dear	Open		35.00	35

Flambro Imports
to Ganz

FIGURINES

YEAR ISSUE		EDITION LIMIT	YEAR RETD.	ISSUE PRICE	*QUOTE U.S. $
1989	Flowers For You	Retrd.	1992	42.50	80-125
1991	Friends	Open		55.00	55
1993	Fuzzy Ears	Open		16.50	17
1989	The Gallant Defender	Retrd.	1992	36.50	125
1989	Gargoyle Hoping For Raspberry Teacakes	Retrd.	1990	139.50	250
1994	Gargoyles Just Wanna Have Fun	Open		30.00	30
1989	A Good Egg	Retrd.	1991	36.50	175
1996	He Ain't Heavy...He's My Puffin	Open		34.00	34
1995	Hedgehog's Joke	Open		27.00	27
1996	Hopalong Gargoyle	Open		42.00	42
1993	I Ate the Whole Thing	Retrd.	1996	32.50	33
1991	I Didn't Mean To	Open		32.50	33
1991	I'm A Kitty	Retrd.	1993	37.50	60-72
1996	I'm So Pretty	Open		22.50	23
1994	In Trouble Again	Open		35.00	35
1995	It's a Present	Open		21.00	21
1994	It's Dark Out There	Open		45.00	45
1994	It's Magic	Open		31.00	31
1991	A Joyful Noise	Retrd.	1996	16.50	17
1992	The Juggler	Open		32.50	33
1993	Let's Make Cookies	Retrd.	1996	90.00	90
1992	The Library Cat	Retrd.	1994	38.50	75-95
1993	Little Bit (lapel pin)	Retrd.	1996	16.50	17-27
1993	Little Jewel (brooch)	Retrd.	1994	19.50	25-30
1994	A Little Security	Open		20.00	20
1989	Look at Me	Retrd.	1990	42.50	225
1992	Mitten Toes	Retrd.	1996	16.50	17
1994	My Big Cookie	Open		35.00	35
1992	Nap Time	Open		15.00	15
1997	The Navigator	Open		30.00	30
1989	New Bunny Shoes	Retrd.	1992	28.50	50-85
1989	No Ugly Monsters Allowed	Retrd.	1992	47.50	82-105
1993	Oh Goody!	Open		16.50	17
1996	Oh Happy Day	Open		22.00	22
1990	One-Size-Fits-All	Retrd.	1993	16.50	35
1992	Oops!	Retrd.	1996	16.50	17
1989	Opera Gargoyle	Retrd.	1991	85.00	225-250
1992	Percy	Retrd.	1994	70.00	110
1991	Pick Me Up	Retrd.	1995	16.50	17
1996	Pillow Fight	3,500	1997	157.00	157
1989	Pink 'n' Pretty	Retrd.	1992	23.90	40-75
1994	Playing Dress Up	Open		30.00	30
1991	Playing Footsie	Retrd.	1994	16.50	25
1989	Pocket Dragon Countersign	Retrd.	1991	50.00	200-250
1989	The Pocket Minstrel	Retrd.	1991	36.50	95
1996	Pocket Piper	Open		37.00	37
1992	Pocket Posey	Retrd.	1995	16.50	18
1993	Pocket Rider (brooch)	Retrd.	1995	19.50	20
1991	Practice Makes Perfect	Retrd.	1993	32.50	60-95
1997	Pretty Please	Open		17.00	17
1991	Putt Putt	Retrd.	1993	37.50	50-110
1996	Quartet	Open		80.00	80
1994	Raiding the Cookie Jar	3,500	1995	200.00	200-250
1993	Reading the Good Parts	Open		70.00	70
1996	Red Ribbon	Open		16.50	17
1991	Scales of Injustice	Open		45.00	45
1989	Scribbles	Retrd.	1994	32.50	45
1989	Sea Dragon	Retrd.	1991	45.00	175-225
1995	Sees All, Knows All	Open		35.00	35
1989	Sir Nigel Smythebe-Smoke	Retrd.	1993	120.00	200-225
1991	Sleepy Head	Retrd.	1995	37.50	38
1994	Snuggles	Open		35.00	35
1989	Stalking the Cookie Jar	Open		27.50	28
1989	Storytime at Wizard's House	Retrd.	1993	375.00	500-550
1996	Sweetie Pie	Open		28.00	28
1990	Tag-A-Long	Retrd.	1993	15.00	35-55
1989	Teddy Magic	Retrd.	1991	85.00	85-150
1995	Telling Secrets	Open		48.00	48
1991	Thimble Foot	Retrd.	1994	38.50	50-95
1991	Tickle	Retrd.	1996	27.50	30
1996	Tiny Bit Tired	Open		16.00	16
1989	Toady Goldtrayler	Retrd.	1993	55.00	75-125
1993	Treasure	Open		90.00	90
1995	Tumbly	Open		21.00	21
1991	Twinkle Toes	Retrd.	1995	16.50	20
1992	Under the Bed	2,500	1995	450.00	500-550
1996	The Volunteer	2,500	1996	350.00	350
1989	Walkies	Retrd.	1992	65.00	155-185
1996	Watcha Doin	Open		22.50	23
1995	Watson	Open		22.50	23
1993	We're Very Brave	Retrd.	1996	37.50	38
1989	What Cookie?	Open		38.50	39
1989	Wizardry for Fun and Profit	Retrd.	1992	375.00	425-575
1993	You Can't Make Me	Open		15.00	15
1989	Your Paint is Stirred	Retrd.	1991	42.50	125
1992	Zoom Zoom	Open		37.50	38

Wizards & Dragons - H. Henriksen

YEAR ISSUE		EDITION LIMIT	YEAR RETD.	ISSUE PRICE	*QUOTE U.S. $
1995	Alkmyne	2,500		135.00	135
1996	Apothes	1,500		195.00	195
1996	Archimedes	1,500		195.00	195
1995	Atnanticus	Retrd.	1996	150.00	150
1995	Confrontation	1,500		295.00	295
1996	Conversation	1,500		175.00	175
1996	Laidley Worm	1,500		150.00	150
1995	Pelryn	2,500		175.00	175
1995	Rammis	2,500		150.00	150
1996	Storm Bringer	1,500		150.00	150
1996	Tholief	1,500		250.00	250
1994	The Travellers	1,500		295.00	295

Franklin Mint

Joys of Childhood - N. Rockwell

YEAR ISSUE		EDITION LIMIT	YEAR RETD.	ISSUE PRICE	*QUOTE U.S.$
1976	Coasting Along	3,700		120.00	175
1976	Dressing Up	3,700		120.00	175
1976	The Fishing Hole	3,700		120.00	175
1976	Hopscotch	3,700		120.00	175
1976	The Marble Champ	3,700		120.00	175
1976	The Nurse	3,700		120.00	175
1976	Ride 'Em Cowboy	3,700		120.00	175
1976	The Stilt Walker	3,700		120.00	175
1976	Time Out	3,700		120.00	175
1976	Trick or Treat	3,700		120.00	175

Ganz

Back to Basics Collection - C. Thammavongsa

YEAR ISSUE		EDITION LIMIT	YEAR RETD.	ISSUE PRICE	*QUOTE U.S.$
1996	Back to Basics Cabin	Open		25.00	25
1996	Campfire	Open		23.00	23
1996	Camping Out	Open		17.00	17
1996	Canoe Trip	Open		20.00	20
1996	Cub Scout	Open		8.50	9
1996	Family Picnic	Open		25.00	25
1996	Fishing Buddies	Open		23.00	23
1996	Honey Bear	Open		19.00	19
1996	Nature Walk	Open		15.00	15
1996	Sweet Tooth	Open		15.00	15
1996	Under the Stars	Open		12.00	12
1996	Wild Berries	Open		12.00	12

Blazing Spirits Collection - Ganz

YEAR ISSUE		EDITION LIMIT	YEAR RETD.	ISSUE PRICE	*QUOTE U.S.$
1995	Freedom's Foal	Open		75.00	75
1995	Racing The Wind	Open		55.00	55
1995	Wild Stallion	Open		55.00	55

Carnival Classico Collection - Ganz

YEAR ISSUE		EDITION LIMIT	YEAR RETD.	ISSUE PRICE	*QUOTE U.S.$
1995	Columbina	Closed	1996	52.00	52
1995	Harlequin	Closed	1996	52.00	52
1995	Jester	Closed	1996	52.00	52
1995	Pierrot	Closed	1996	52.00	52
1995	Spaventa	Closed	1996	52.00	52
1995	Tartaglia	Closed	1996	52.00	52

Cock-A-Doodle Corners Collection - C.Thammavongsa

YEAR ISSUE		EDITION LIMIT	YEAR RETD.	ISSUE PRICE	*QUOTE U.S.$
1995	Cock-a-Doodle Corners Sign	Open		16.00	16
1995	Coffee Clutch	Open		24.00	24
1995	Country Courting	Open		20.00	20
1995	Follow the Leader	Open		24.00	24
1995	Fresh-Baked	Open		16.50	17
1995	Great Eggspectations	Open		15.00	15
1995	Hen Packed	Open		17.00	17
1995	Home Remedy	Open		21.00	21
1995	Master Craftsman	Open		18.00	18
1995	New Arrival	Closed	1996	10.00	10
1995	Organically Grown	Open		22.00	22
1995	Poultry Patrol	Open		16.50	17

Cottage Collectibles Christmas Collection - Ganz

YEAR ISSUE		EDITION LIMIT	YEAR RETD.	ISSUE PRICE	*QUOTE U.S.$
1996	Finishing Touch	Open		25.00	25
1996	Our Tree	Open		28.00	28
1996	Snowy Days	Open		28.00	28
1996	Touch of Heaven	Open		20.00	20

Cottage Collectibles Collection - Ganz

YEAR ISSUE		EDITION LIMIT	YEAR RETD.	ISSUE PRICE	*QUOTE U.S.$
1996	All Aboard	Open		20.00	20
1995	Bath Time	Open		17.00	17
1995	Best Friends	Open		16.00	16
1996	Blowing the Blues	Open		17.00	17
1996	Boy's will be Boys	Open		20.00	20
1995	Circus Parade	Open		23.00	23
1996	Derby Day	Open		28.00	28
1996	Everyone Needs A Hug	Open		16.00	16
1996	Extra, Extra	Open		16.00	16
1996	Family Portrait	Open		28.00	28
1995	First Love	Retrd.	1996	20.00	20
1996	First Steps	Open		20.00	20
1996	Fish is Fryin'	Open		23.00	23
1995	Goin' Fishin'	Open		16.00	16
1996	Good Ole Summertime	Open		25.00	25
1996	Good Ole Time	Open		21.00	21
1995	Grandma's Treasures	Open		25.00	25
1995	A Job Well Done...	Open		25.00	25
1996	Maxwell's ABC's	Open		16.00	16
1995	My Favorite Things	Open		16.00	16
1996	My Girl	Open		25.00	25
1996	My Horsey	Open		16.00	16
1996	My Toys	Open		19.00	19
1995	Naptime	Open		23.00	23
1995	Play Time	Open		23.00	23
1996	Round "Em Up	Open		20.00	20
1995	School Days	Open		16.00	16
1996	Sharing	Open		16.00	16
1996	The Sky's the Limit	Open		17.00	17
1996	A Stroll in the Park	Open		28.00	28
1995	Tea Time	Open		23.00	23
1996	True Friends	Open		20.00	20
1996	Uh oh	Open		16.00	16
1996	Yvonne's Treasures	Open		16.00	16

Cottage Collectibles Easter Collection - Ganz

YEAR ISSUE		EDITION LIMIT	YEAR RETD.	ISSUE PRICE	*QUOTE U.S.$
1997	Artist at Work	Open		16.00	16
1997	Carrots for Sale	Open		20.00	20
1997	Sunken Treasures	Open		21.00	21
1997	Sweet Spring	Open		16.00	16

Cottage Collectibles Valentine Collection - Ganz

YEAR ISSUE		EDITION LIMIT	YEAR RETD.	ISSUE PRICE	*QUOTE U.S.$
1996	Be Mine	Open		16.00	16
1996	Can Anyone Spare A Kiss	Open		21.00	21
1996	Lovestruck	Open		16.00	16
1996	Valentines For Me	Open		21.00	21

Cowtown Collection - C.Thammavongsa

YEAR ISSUE		EDITION LIMIT	YEAR RETD.	ISSUE PRICE	*QUOTE U.S.$
1994	Amoolia Steerheart	Open		25.00	25
1995	Bedtime Dairy Tales	Open		19.00	19
1993	Buffalo Bull Cody	Open		15.00	15
1996	Bull Cassidy & The Sundance Calf	Open		20.00	20
1993	Bull Masterson	Open		15.00	15
1993	Bull Rogers	Open		17.00	17
1993	Bull Ruth	Retrd.	1994	13.00	13
1995	Buster Cowtown	Open		15.00	15
1993	Buttermilk & Buttercup	Retrd.	1996	16.00	16
1995	A Calf's Best Friend	Open		12.00	12
1993	Cowlamity Jane	Open		15.00	15
1994	Cowsey Jones & The Cannonbull Express	Open		26.50	27
1993	Daisy Moo	Open		11.00	11
1995	Dracowla	Open		15.00	15
1995	Francowstein	Open		12.50	13
1994	Geronimoo	Open		17.00	17
1993	Gloria Bovine & Rudolph Bullentino	Open		20.00	20
1995	Grandma Mooses	Open		15.00	15
1994	Heiferella	Open		16.50	17
1995	Hicowatha & Moonehaha	Open		18.50	19
1995	Holy Mootrimoony	Open		20.00	20
1995	Jack-Cow-Lantern	Open		11.00	11
1993	Jethro Bovine	Retrd.	1994	15.00	15
1994	King Cowmooamooa	Open		16.50	17
1993	Lil' Orphan Angus	Open		11.00	11
1996	Lone-Wrangler	Open		15.00	15
1994	Ma & Pa Cattle	Open		23.50	24
1993	Moo West	Open		15.00	15
1995	Moother's Li'l Rascow	Open		20.00	20
1993	Old MooDonald	Open		13.50	14
1994	Pocowhantis	Open		16.50	17
1995	Scarecow	Open		11.50	12
1994	Set of Three Cacti	Open		17.00	17
1995	Steershot Annie	Open		16.50	17
1995	Supercow	Open		15.00	15
1994	Tchaicowsky	Open		19.00	19
1996	Tender Loving Cow	Open		12.50	13
1994	Texas Lonesteer	10,000		50.00	50
1995	Will Bull Hickock	Open		17.00	17
1995	Yellowsteer National Park	Open		20.00	20

Cowtown/Christmas Collection - C. Thammavongsa, unless otherwise noted

YEAR ISSUE		EDITION LIMIT	YEAR RETD.	ISSUE PRICE	*QUOTE U.S.$
1994	Billy the Calf	Open		14.00	14
1996	Calf Ton Pickup - Chiemlowski	Open		10.00	10
1994	Christmas Cactus	Open		13.50	14
1995	Ellie-Moo's Angel	Open		11.00	11
1995	Here Comes Santa Cow	Open		17.50	18
1995	John Steere	Closed	1996	11.00	11
1995	Milk & Cookies	Open		14.50	15
1995	Moo Claus	Open		17.00	17
1995	Polar Bull	Open		17.50	18
1994	Saint Nicowlas	Open		16.00	16
1994	Santa Cows	Open		18.00	18
1994	Santa's Little Heifer	Open		12.50	13
1996	Snowbull and Friends - Chiemlowski	Open		18.00	18
1995	Twinkle Twinkle Little Steer	Open		12.00	12

Cowtown/Fall, Halloween Collection - C. Thammavongsa, unless otherwise noted

YEAR ISSUE		EDITION LIMIT	YEAR RETD.	ISSUE PRICE	*QUOTE U.S.$
1995	Dracowla	Open		15.00	15
1996	Footbull Jersey - Chiemlowski	Open		10.00	10
1995	Francowstein	Open		12.50	13
1995	Jack-Cow-Lantern	Open		11.00	11
1996	The Mooflowers - Chiemlowski	Open		20.00	20
1995	Scarecow	Open		11.50	12

Cowtown/Valentine Collection - C.Thammavongsa

YEAR ISSUE		EDITION LIMIT	YEAR RETD.	ISSUE PRICE	*QUOTE U.S.$
1994	I Love Moo	Open		15.00	15
1994	Robin Hoof & Maid Mooian	Open		23.00	23
1994	Romecow & Mooliet	Open		22.00	22
1994	Wanted: A Sweetheart	Open		16.00	16

Ferggie Polliwog & Friends Collection - Ganz/B. Lemaire

YEAR ISSUE		EDITION LIMIT	YEAR RETD.	ISSUE PRICE	*QUOTE U.S.$
1996	Band-Aids	Open		15.00	15
1996	Beach Buddies	Open		14.00	14
1996	Frog Prince	Open		15.00	15
1996	Froggie Tales	Open		19.00	19
1996	Hi-Ho Fishy!	Open		19.00	19
1996	The Jitterbug Band	Open		21.00	21
1996	Lawnmower Man	Open		15.00	15
1996	Leap Frog	Open		15.00	15
1996	Lilypad League	Open		17.00	17

*Quotes have been rounded up to nearest dollar

FIGURINES

Ganz to Ganz

YEAR ISSUE		EDITION LIMIT	YEAR RETD.	ISSUE PRICE	*QUOTE U.S.$
1996	Moonlight Serenade	Open		20.00	20
1996	No Fishing! Sign	Open		16.00	16
1996	No Place Like Home	Open		17.00	17

Grandma's Attic Collection - C.Thammavongsa

YEAR ISSUE		EDITION LIMIT	YEAR RETD.	ISSUE PRICE	*QUOTE U.S.$
1995	Balderdash	Open		25.00	25
1995	Bumblebeary	Open		10.00	10
1995	Coco & Jiffy	Open		11.00	11
1995	Crumples & Creampuff	Open		13.50	14
1995	Dilly-Dally	Open		13.50	14
1995	Dumblekin	Open		19.00	19
1995	Jelly-Belly	Open		12.00	12
1995	Molly-Coddle	Open		16.00	16
1995	Prince Fuddle-Duddle & Princess Dazzle	Open		17.00	17
1995	Sprinkles	Open		15.00	15
1995	Tootoo	Open		10.00	10

Grandma's Attic/Easter, Springtime Collection - C.Thammavongsa

YEAR ISSUE		EDITION LIMIT	YEAR RETD.	ISSUE PRICE	*QUOTE U.S.$
1995	Hucklebeary	Open		14.50	15
1995	Lambie-Pie	Open		14.50	15
1995	Slugger	Open		13.00	13

Grandma's Attic/Valentine Collection - C.Thammavongsa

YEAR ISSUE		EDITION LIMIT	YEAR RETD.	ISSUE PRICE	*QUOTE U.S.$
1995	Abracadabra	Closed	1996	14.00	14
1995	Cuddles	Closed	1996	12.00	12
1995	Skippy and Marmalade	Closed	1996	23.00	23
1995	Tickles and Giggles	Closed	1996	20.00	20

The Lacewing Fairies Collection - Ganz/B. Lemaire

YEAR ISSUE		EDITION LIMIT	YEAR RETD.	ISSUE PRICE	*QUOTE U.S.$
1995	Lacewing Fairies Sign	Open		10.00	10
1995	Liana & Her Spellbounde Prince	Open		37.00	37
1995	Liana - Spirit of the Woodes	Open		30.00	30
1995	Liana - The Butterflye Maiden	Open		26.50	27
1995	Salina - Enchantress of the Sea	Open		35.00	35
1995	Salina - Midsummer Night's Dreame	Open		36.00	36
1995	Salina - the Faerie Queene	Open		37.00	37

Little Cheesers/Collectors' Club Pieces - C.Thammavongsa

YEAR ISSUE		EDITION LIMIT	YEAR RETD.	ISSUE PRICE	*QUOTE U.S.$
1993	Charter Member	Closed	1994	27.00	27
1994	Fireweed Fox	Closed	1995	15.00	15
1995	Welcome to the Club	Closed	1996	27.00	27
1995	The Invention	Closed	1996	15.00	15

Little Cheesers/Cheeserville Fall - C.Thammavongsa

YEAR ISSUE		EDITION LIMIT	YEAR RETD.	ISSUE PRICE	*QUOTE U.S.$
1995	Bewitched	Open		8.50	9
1995	Candy Bandit	Open		8.50	9
1995	Cornucopia	Open		10.00	10
1995	Peace Offering	Open		8.50	9
1995	Pilgrims	Open		15.50	16
1995	Pumpkin Patch	Open		8.00	8

Little Cheesers/Cheeserville Picnic Collection - G.D.A. Group, unless otherwise noted

YEAR ISSUE		EDITION LIMIT	YEAR RETD.	ISSUE PRICE	*QUOTE U.S.$
1991	Auntie Marigold Eating Cookie	Open		13.00	13
1991	Baby Cicely	Retrd.	1995	8.00	8
1991	Baby Truffle	Open		8.00	8
1991	Blossom & Hickory In Love	Open		19.00	19
1995	Cheeserville Tales - C.Thammavongsa	Open		7.50	8
1993	Chuckles The Clown - C.Thammavongsa	Open		16.00	16
1993	Clownin' Around - C.Thammavongsa	Open		10.50	11
1991	Cousin Woody With Bread & Fruit	Open		14.00	14
1991	Fellow With Picnic Hamper	Retrd.	1991	13.00	13
1991	Fellow With Plate Of Cookies	Retrd.	1991	13.00	13
1994	Fiddle-Dee-Dee - C.Thammavongsa	Open		13.00	13
1993	For Someone Special - C.Thammavongsa	Open		13.50	14
1991	Grandmama Thistledown Holding Bread	Open		14.00	14
1991	Grandpapa Thistledown Carrying Basket	Open		13.00	13
1991	Harley Harvestmouse Waving	Open		13.00	13
1991	Harriet Harvestmouse	Retrd.	1993	13.00	13
1995	Hush-A-Bye Baby - C.Thammavongsa	Open		14.00	14
1991	Jenny Butterfield Kneeling	Open		13.00	13
1991	Jeremy Butterfield	Open		13.00	13
1995	Joyful Beginnings - C.Thammavongsa	Open		15.00	15
1991	Lady With Grapes	Retrd.	1991	14.00	14
1993	Little Cheesers Display Plaque - C.Thammavongsa	Open		25.00	25
1991	Little Truffle Eating Grapes	Open		8.00	8
1991	Little Truffle Smelling Flowers	Retrd.	1995	16.50	17
1991	Mama Fixing Sweet Cicely's Hair	Retrd.	1993	16.50	17
1991	Mama With Rolling Pin	Open		13.00	13
1991	Mama Woodsworth With Crate	Retrd.	1992	14.00	14
1991	Marigold Thistledown Picking Up Jar	Open		14.00	14
1991	Medley Meadowmouse With Bouquet	Open		13.00	13
1994	Melody Maker - C.Thammavongsa	Retrd.	1995	17.00	17
1994	Ooom-Pah-Pah - C.Thammavongsa	Open		13.00	13
1991	Papa Woodsworth	Open		13.00	13
1991	Picnic Buddies	Open		19.00	19
1995	Picnic with Papa - C.Thammavongsa	Open		14.00	14
1995	Playtime - C.Thammavongsa	Open		14.00	14
1995	Read Me A Story - C.Thammavongsa	Open		15.00	15
1993	The Storyteller - C.Thammavongsa	10,000		25.00	25
1994	Strummin' Away - C.Thammavongsa	Open		13.00	13
1993	Sunday Drive - C.Thammavongsa	Open		40.00	40
1993	Sweet Dreams - C.Thammavongsa	Open		27.50	28
1994	Swingin' Sax - C.Thammavongsa	Open		13.00	13
1991	Violet With Peaches	Open		13.00	13
1994	Washboard Blues - C.Thammavongsa	Open		13.00	13
1994	What a Hoot! - C.Thammavongsa	Open		13.00	13
1993	Willy's Toe-Tappin' Tunes - C.Thammavongsa	Open		15.00	15
1993	Words Of Wisdom - C.Thammavongsa	Open		14.00	14

Little Cheesers/Cheeserville Picnic Collection Accessories - G.D.A. Group

YEAR ISSUE		EDITION LIMIT	YEAR RETD.	ISSUE PRICE	*QUOTE U.S.$
1994	Mayflower Meadow Base	Open		50.00	50

Little Cheesers/Cheeserville Picnic Mini-Food Accessories - G.D.A. Group

YEAR ISSUE		EDITION LIMIT	YEAR RETD.	ISSUE PRICE	*QUOTE U.S.$
1991	Basket Of Apples	Open		2.25	3
1991	Basket Of Peaches	Open		2.00	2
1991	Blueberry Cake	Retrd.	1994	2.50	3
1991	Bread Basket	Open		2.50	3
1991	Candy	Open		2.00	2
1991	Cherry Mousse	Open		2.00	2
1991	Cherry Pie	Retrd.	1991	2.00	2
1991	Chocolate Cake	Open		2.50	3
1991	Chocolate Cheesecake	Open		2.00	2
1991	Doughnut Basket	Open		2.50	3
1991	Egg Tart	Open		1.00	1
1991	Food Basket With Blue Cloth	Retrd.	1994	6.50	7
1991	Food Basket With Green Cloth	Open		7.50	8
1991	Food Basket With Pink Cloth	Retrd.	1994	6.00	6
1991	Food Basket With Purple Cloth	Open		6.00	6
1991	Food Trolley	Retrd.	1991	12.00	12
1991	Hazelnut Roll	Retrd.	1991	2.00	2
1991	Honey Jar	Retrd.	1991	2.00	2
1991	Hot Dog	Open		2.25	3
1991	Ice Cream Cup	Open		2.00	2
1991	Lemon Cake	Retrd.	1991	2.00	2
1991	Napkin In Can	Retrd.	1991	2.00	2
1991	Set Of Four Bottles	Retrd.	1991	10.00	10
1991	Strawberry Cake	Open		2.00	2
1991	Sundae	Open		2.00	2
1991	Wine Glass	Retrd.	1995	1.25	2

Little Cheesers/Cheeserville Picnic Musicals - G.D.A. Group

YEAR ISSUE		EDITION LIMIT	YEAR RETD.	ISSUE PRICE	*QUOTE U.S.$
1994	The Bandstand Base	Open		48.50	49
1991	Blossom & Hickory Musical Jewelry Box	Closed	1992	65.00	65
1991	Mama & Sweet Cicely Waterglobe	Closed	1992	55.00	55
1991	Medley Meadowmouse Waterglobe	Retrd.	1995	47.00	47
1993	Musical "Secret Treasures" Trinket Box	Open		36.00	36
1991	Musical Basket Trinket Box	Open		30.00	30
1991	Musical Floral Trinket Box	Open		32.00	32
1991	Musical Medley Meadowmouse Cookie Jar	Retrd.	1992	75.00	75
1991	Musical Picnic Base	Open		60.00	60
1991	Musical Sunflower Base	Closed	1993	65.00	65
1991	Musical Violet Woodsworth Cookie Jar	Retrd.	1992	75.00	75
1992	Sweet Cicely Musical Doll Basket	Closed	1996	85.00	85
1993	Wishing Well Musical	Open		50.00	50

Little Cheesers/Christmas Collection - C. Thammavongsa, unless otherwise noted

YEAR ISSUE		EDITION LIMIT	YEAR RETD.	ISSUE PRICE	*QUOTE U.S.$
1991	Abner Appleton Ringing Bell - G.D.A. Group	Retrd.	1993	14.00	14
1993	All I Want For Christmas	Open		18.00	18
1994	Angel	Open		8.00	8
1991	Auntie Blossom With Ornaments - G.D.A. Group	Open		14.00	14
1994	Baby Jesus	Retrd.	1996	6.50	7
1991	Cheeser Snowman - G.D.A. Group	Retrd.	1994	7.50	8
1993	Christmas Greetings	Open		16.50	17
1991	Cousin Woody Playing Flute - G.D.A. Group	Retrd.	1996	14.00	14
1994	First Wiseman	Retrd.	1996	11.00	11
1991	Frowzy Roquefort III Skating - G.D.A. Group	Retrd.	1993	14.00	14
1991	Grandmama & Little Truffle - G.D.A. Group	Retrd.	1993	19.00	19
1991	Grandpapa & Sweet Cicely - G.D.A. Group	Retrd.	1996	19.00	19
1991	Grandpapa Blowing Horn - G.D.A. Group	Retrd.	1994	14.00	14
1991	Great Aunt Rose With Tray - G.D.A. Group	Open		14.00	14
1991	Harley & Harriet Dancing - G.D.A. Group	Retrd.	1993	19.00	19
1991	Hickory Playing Cello - G.D.A. Group	Retrd.	1994	14.00	14
1991	Jenny On Sleigh - G.D.A. Group	Open		16.00	16
1991	Jeremy With Teddy Bear - G.D.A. Group	Open		12.00	12
1994	Joseph	Retrd.	1996	10.00	10
1995	Joy to the World	Open		8.00	8
1991	Little Truffle With Stocking - G.D.A. Group	Open		8.00	8
1991	Mama Pouring Tea - G.D.A. Group	Retrd.	1993	14.00	14
1991	Marigold & Oscar Stealing A Christmas Kiss - G.D.A. Group	Retrd.	1996	19.00	19
1994	Mary	Retrd.	1996	10.00	10
1991	Medley Playing Drum - G.D.A. Group	Open		8.00	8
1991	Myrtle Meadowmouse With Book - G.D.A. Group	Retrd.	1993	14.00	14
1991	Santa Cheeser - G.D.A. Group	Open		13.00	13
1994	Santa's Sleigh	10,000		22.00	22
1994	Second Wiseman	Retrd.	1996	11.00	11
1994	Shepherd	Retrd.	1996	8.50	9
1993	Sleigh Ride	Retrd.	1995	11.00	11
1995	Tending The Flocks	Open		9.00	9
1994	Third Wiseman	Retrd.	1996	10.50	11
1991	Violet w/Snowball - G.D.A. Group	Retrd.	1994	8.00	8

Little Cheesers/Christmas Collection Accessories - C. Thammavongsa, unless otherwise noted

YEAR ISSUE		EDITION LIMIT	YEAR RETD.	ISSUE PRICE	*QUOTE U.S.$
1993	Candleholder-Santa Cheeser	Open		19.00	19
1993	Candy Cane	Open		2.00	2
1994	Christmas Collection Base	Open		50.00	50
1993	Christmas Gift	Open		3.00	3
1993	Christmas Stocking	Open		3.00	3
1991	Christmas Tree - G.D.A. Group	Open		9.00	9
1994	Creche Base	Retrd.	1996	28.50	29
1993	Gingerbread House	Open		3.00	3
1993	Ice Pond Base	Open		5.50	6
1991	Lamp Post - G.D.A. Group	Open		8.50	9
1995	Little Cheeser Tree Topper	Open		34.00	34
1991	Outdoor Scene Base - G.D.A. Group	Retrd.	1993	35.00	35
1991	Parlor Scene Base - G.D.A. Group	Open		37.50	38
1993	Toy Soldier	Open		3.00	3
1993	Toy Train	Open		3.00	3

Little Cheesers/Christmas Collection Musicals - Various

YEAR ISSUE		EDITION LIMIT	YEAR RETD.	ISSUE PRICE	*QUOTE U.S.$
1992	Jenny Butterfield Christmas Waterglobe - GDA/Thammavongsa	Closed	1992	55.00	55
1992	Little Truffle Christmas Waterglobe - G.D.A. Group	Retrd.	1995	45.00	45
1992	Musical Santa Cheeser Roly-Poly - G.D.A. Group	Suspd.		55.00	55
1993	Rotating Round Wood Base "I'll be Home for X'mas" - C.Thammavongsa	Open		30.00	30
1993	Round Wood Base "We Wish You a Merry X'mas" - C.Thammavongsa	Open		25.00	25

Little Cheesers/Circus Party Collection - C.Thammavongsa

YEAR ISSUE		EDITION LIMIT	YEAR RETD.	ISSUE PRICE	*QUOTE U.S.$
1995	Balancing Act	Open		8.00	8
1995	Beep-Beep	Open		13.50	14
1995	Cheeserville Choo-Choo	Open		21.00	21
1995	Easy As Cake	Open		15.00	15
1995	Look Ma-No Hands	Open		18.00	18
1995	Woops!	Open		10.50	11

Little Cheesers/Little Hoppers Collection - C.Thammavongsa

YEAR ISSUE		EDITION LIMIT	YEAR RETD.	ISSUE PRICE	*QUOTE U.S.$
1994	Bubble Bath	Open		7.50	8
1994	Let's Play Ball	Open		7.00	7
1994	Somebunny Loves You	Open		7.50	8
1994	Sweet Nothings	Open		15.00	15
1994	Tender Loving Care	Open		10.00	10
1994	Tricycle Built for Two	Open		16.00	16

Little Cheesers/Springtime In Cheeserville Accessories - C.Thammavongsa

YEAR ISSUE		EDITION LIMIT	YEAR RETD.	ISSUE PRICE	*QUOTE U.S.$
1992	April Showers Bring May Flowers	Open		7.50	8
1992	Decorated With Love	Open		7.50	8
1992	For Somebunny Special	Open		7.50	8

Little Cheesers/Springtime In Cheeserville Musicals - GDA/Thammavongsa

YEAR ISSUE		EDITION LIMIT	YEAR RETD.	ISSUE PRICE	*QUOTE U.S.$
1992	Tulips & Ribbons Musical Trinket Box	Closed	1994	28.00	28

Little Cheesers/Springtime In Cheeserville Collection - C.Thammavongsa

YEAR ISSUE		EDITION LIMIT	YEAR RETD.	ISSUE PRICE	*QUOTE U.S.$
1992	A Basket Full Of Joy	Open		16.00	16
1994	Birthday Party	Retrd.	1995	22.00	22
1993	Blossom Has A Little lamb	Open		16.50	17
1993	First Kiss	Open		24.00	24
1993	For My Sweatheart	Open		22.00	22
1993	Friends Forever	Open		22.00	22
1995	Fuzzy Friends	Open		9.00	9
1993	Gently Down The Stream	10,000		27.00	27
1994	Get Well	Open		22.00	22
1993	Gift From Heaven	Retrd.	1996	10.00	10
1994	Hip Hip Hooray	Open		22.00	22
1992	Hippity-Hop. It's Eastertime!	Open		16.00	16
1993	Hugs & Kisses	Open		11.00	11
1993	I Love You	Open		22.00	22
1995	Little Miracles	Open		8.00	8
1993	Playing Cupid	Open		10.00	10
1992	Springtime Delights	Open		12.00	12
1993	Sugar & Spice	Open		24.00	24
1993	Sunday Stroll	Open		22.00	22
1992	A Wheelbarrow Of Sunshine	Open		17.00	17

Little Cheesers/Valentine Collection - C.Thammavongsa

YEAR ISSUE		EDITION LIMIT	YEAR RETD.	ISSUE PRICE	*QUOTE U.S.$
1993	Ballerina Sweetheart	Retrd.	1996	10.00	10
1995	Be My Angel	Open		10.50	11
1993	First Kiss	Open		24.00	24

*Quotes have been rounded up to nearest dollar

Ganz
to Ganz

FIGURINES

YEAR ISSUE		EDITION LIMIT	YEAR RETD.	ISSUE PRICE	*QUOTE U.S.$
1993	For My Sweetheart	Open		22.00	22
1993	Friends Forever	Open		22.00	22
1993	Gently Down the Stream	10,000		27.00	27
1993	Hugs & Kisses	Open		11.00	11
1993	I Love You	Open		22.00	22
1995	My L'il Sweetheart	Open		9.00	9
1993	Playing Cupid	Open		10.00	10
1993	Sugar & Spice	Open		24.00	24
1993	Sunday Stroll	Open		22.00	22

Little Cheesers/Wedding Collection - GDA/Thammavongsa, unless otherwise noted

YEAR ISSUE		EDITION LIMIT	YEAR RETD.	ISSUE PRICE	*QUOTE U.S.$
1993	The Big Day - C. Thammavongsa	Open		20.00	20
1992	Blossom Thistledown (bride)	Open		16.00	16
1992	Cousin Woody & Little Truffle	Open		20.00	20
1992	Frowzy Roquefort III w/ Gramophone	Open		20.00	20
1992	Grandmama & Grandpapa Thistledown	Retrd.	1994	20.00	20
1992	Great Aunt Rose Beside Table	Open		20.00	20
1992	Harley & Harriet Harvestmouse	Open		20.00	20
1992	Hickory Harvestmouse (groom)	Open		16.00	16
1992	Jenny Butterfield/Sweet Cicely (bridesmaids)	Retrd.	1995	20.00	20
1992	Little Truffle (ringbearer)	Open		10.00	10
1992	Mama & Papa Woodsworth Dancing	Open		20.00	20
1992	Marigold Thistledown & Oscar Bobbins	Open		20.00	20
1992	Myrtle Meadowmouse w/Medley	Closed	1992	20.00	20
1992	Pastor Smallwood	Open		16.00	16
1992	Wedding Procession	Open		40.00	40

Little Cheesers/Wedding Collection Accessories - C. Thammavongsa

YEAR ISSUE		EDITION LIMIT	YEAR RETD.	ISSUE PRICE	*QUOTE U.S.$
1993	Banquet Table	Open		14.00	14
1993	Gazebo Base	Open		42.00	42

Little Cheesers/Wedding Collection Mini-Food Accessories - G.D.A. Group, unless otherwise noted

YEAR ISSUE		EDITION LIMIT	YEAR RETD.	ISSUE PRICE	*QUOTE U.S.$
1992	Bible Trinket Box - GDA/Thammavongsa	Open		16.50	17
1992	Big Chocolate Cake	Retrd.	1994	4.50	5
1992	Bride Candleholder - GDA/Thammavongsa	Open		20.00	20
1992	Cake Trinket Box - GDA/Thammavongsa	Open		14.00	14
1992	Candles	Open		3.00	3
1992	Cherry Jello	Open		3.00	3
1992	Chocolate Pastry	Retrd.	1992	2.00	2
1992	Chocolate Pudding	Open		2.50	3
1992	Flour Bag	Retrd.	1992	2.00	2
1992	Flower Vase	Retrd.	1994	3.00	3
1992	Fruit Salad	Open		3.00	3
1993	Gooseberry Champagne - C. Thammavongsa	Open		3.00	3
1992	Grass Base - GDA/Thammavongsa	Suspd.		3.50	4
1992	Groom Candleholder - GDA/Thammavongsa	Open		20.00	20
1992	Honey Pot	Open		2.00	2
1992	Ring Cake	Open		3.00	3
1992	Salt Can	Retrd.	1992	2.00	2
1992	Souffle	Retrd.	1992	2.50	3
1992	Soup Pot	Open		3.00	3
1992	Tea Pot Set	Retrd.	1994	3.00	3
1992	Teddy Mouse	Retrd.	1994	2.00	2
1993	Wedding Cake - C. Thammavongsa	Open		4.50	5

Little Cheesers/Wedding Collection Musicals - Various

YEAR ISSUE		EDITION LIMIT	YEAR RETD.	ISSUE PRICE	*QUOTE U.S.$
1993	Blossom & Hickory Musical - C. Thammavongsa	Retrd.	1994	50.00	50
1992	Musical Blossom & Hickory Wedding Waterglobe - GDA/Thammavongsa	Open		55.00	55
1992	Musical Wedding Base - GDA/Thammavongsa	Open		32.00	32
1992	Musical Wooden Base For Wedding Processional - G.D.A. Group	Open		25.00	25
1993	White Musical Wood Base For Gazebo Base "Evergreen" - C. Thammavongsa	Open		25.00	25

Magic of Saint Nicholas Collection - Ganz

YEAR ISSUE		EDITION LIMIT	YEAR RETD.	ISSUE PRICE	*QUOTE U.S.$
1996	Holly Jolly Holidays	Open		60.00	60
1996	Magical Melodies	Open		60.00	60
1996	Twinkling Lights	Open		60.00	60

Perfect Little Place Collection - C.Thammavongsa

YEAR ISSUE		EDITION LIMIT	YEAR RETD.	ISSUE PRICE	*QUOTE U.S.$
1995	All Star Angel	Open		14.00	14
1995	Angel Face	Open		15.00	15
1995	Angel's Food	Retrd.	1996	15.00	15
1996	Bless This Marriage	Open		20.00	20
1995	Divine Intervention	Open		15.00	15
1995	Heaven & Nature	Open		14.00	14
1996	Heaven Makes All Things New	Open		18.00	18
1995	Heavenly Grace	Open		14.00	14
1995	Match Made in Heaven	Open		18.00	18
1995	Paradise	Retrd.	1996	13.00	13
1995	Perfect Little Place	Open		16.00	16
1995	Pray the Lord My Soul to Keep	Open		13.00	13
1995	Ride Like The Wind	Open		15.00	15
1996	Showered With Love	Open		16.00	16
1995	Sweet Sleep, Angel Mild	Open		13.50	14

Perfect Little Place/Christmas Collection - C. Thammavongsa, unless otherwise noted

YEAR ISSUE		EDITION LIMIT	YEAR RETD.	ISSUE PRICE	*QUOTE U.S.$
1995	Angel of Light - L. Sunarth	Open		12.00	12
1996	Angels in the Snow	Open		15.00	15
1995	Bearer of Blessings	Open		17.00	17
1996	Celestial Wonders	Open		17.00	17
1995	A Child is Born	Open		21.00	21
1996	Songs of Praise	Open		17.00	17

Perfect Little Place/Cultures of the World Collection - L. Sunarth

YEAR ISSUE		EDITION LIMIT	YEAR RETD.	ISSUE PRICE	*QUOTE U.S.$
1996	Dream Homes	Open		16.00	16
1996	Healing Touch	Open		16.00	16
1996	Praise the Lord	Open		17.00	17
1996	Smooth Sailing	Open		18.00	18
1996	Teacher's Pet	Open		17.00	17
1996	The Three R's	Open		17.50	18

Perfect Little Place/Valentine Collection - Various

YEAR ISSUE		EDITION LIMIT	YEAR RETD.	ISSUE PRICE	*QUOTE U.S.$
1995	Be My Angel - C. Thammavongsa	Open		16.00	16
1996	First Love - L. Sunarth	Open		22.50	23
1996	He Loves me...he loves me not - L. Sunarth	Open		15.50	16
1996	The Proposal - L. Sunarth	Open		15.50	16
1995	Sweet Innocence - C. Thammavongsa	Open		16.00	16
1995	Whispers of Love - C. Thammavongsa	Open		21.00	21

Pigsville Accessories - C.Thammavongsa

YEAR ISSUE		EDITION LIMIT	YEAR RETD.	ISSUE PRICE	*QUOTE U.S.$
1995	Bale of Straw	Open		10.00	10
1994	Barn	Open		35.00	35
1995	Outhouse	Open		10.00	10
1994	Silo	Open		15.00	15

Pigsville Collection - C.Thammavongsa, unless otherwise noted

YEAR ISSUE		EDITION LIMIT	YEAR RETD.	ISSUE PRICE	*QUOTE U.S.$
1993	Bakin' at the Beach	Open		11.00	11
1994	Bedtime	Open		9.50	10
1994	Birthday Surprise	Open		9.50	10
1993	Ice Cream Anyone? - G.D.A. Group	Retrd.	1994	9.00	9
1995	Juke Box	Open		12.00	12
1993	Me & My Ice Cream - G.D.A. Group	Retrd.	1994	17.00	17
1996	Melon Patch	Open		11.00	11
1993	Mother Love - G.D.A. Group	Open		13.00	13
1995	Mr. Fix It	Open		14.00	14
1993	Nap Time - G.D.A. Group	Retrd.	1995	11.00	11
1994	Ole Fishing Hole	Open		16.00	16
1995	Open Roads	Open		14.00	14
1993	P.O.P Display Sign	Open		8.00	8
1995	Paradise	Open		10.00	10
1993	Pig at the Beach - G.D.A. Group	Open		9.00	9
1996	Pig Pen Blues	Open		11.00	11
1996	Pig Tails	Open		10.00	10
1995	Piggy Back	Open		10.50	11
1994	Play Ball	Open		11.50	12
1994	Pretty Piglet	Open		8.00	8
1993	Prima Ballerina	Retrd.	1994	11.00	11
1994	Sandcastle	Open		12.00	12
1995	Scrub-A-Dub-Dub	Open		13.50	14
1995	Seeds of Love	Open		14.50	15
1994	Snacktime	Open		11.50	12
1993	Soap Suds - G.D.A. Group	Open		12.00	12
1994	Special Treat	Open		11.50	12
1993	Squeaky Clean - G.D.A. Group	Retrd.	1995	11.00	11
1994	Storytime	Open		13.00	13
1993	Tipsy - G.D.A. Group	Open		9.00	9
1995	Touchdown	Open		11.00	11
1993	True Love	Open		12.00	12
1994	Wedded Bliss	Open		16.00	16
1993	Wee Little Piggy	Open		8.00	8
1996	Yard Work	Open		13.00	13

Pigsville/Christmas Collection - C.Thammavongsa, unless otherwise noted

YEAR ISSUE		EDITION LIMIT	YEAR RETD.	ISSUE PRICE	*QUOTE U.S.$
1996	Christmas Rush - Chiemlowski	Open		14.00	14
1994	Christmas Trimmings	10,000		24.00	24
1995	Dear Santa	Open		10.00	10
1996	Holiday Hog - Chiemlowski	Open		16.00	16
1994	Joy to the World	Open		10.00	10
1994	Let It Snow	Open		12.00	12
1994	Mistletoe Magic	Open		14.00	14
1995	Mrs. Claus	Open		11.00	11
1995	Oh Christmas Tree	Open		10.50	11
1994	Santa Pig	Open		11.00	11
1995	Tucked into Bed	Open		12.00	12
1994	Yuletide Carols	Open		19.00	19

Pigsville/Fall, Halloween Collection - C.Thammavongsa, unless otherwise noted

YEAR ISSUE		EDITION LIMIT	YEAR RETD.	ISSUE PRICE	*QUOTE U.S.$
1995	Apple Bobbing	Open		10.00	10
1995	Giving Thanks	Open		10.00	10
1996	Hell's Angel - Chiemlowski	Open		10.00	10
1996	Hobo Clown - Chiemlowski	Open		10.00	10
1995	Pumpkin Pig	Open		11.00	11
1995	Scarecrow	Open		11.00	11

Pigsville/Valentine Collection - C.Thammavongsa

YEAR ISSUE		EDITION LIMIT	YEAR RETD.	ISSUE PRICE	*QUOTE U.S.$
1995	Barn Dance	Open		14.50	15
1994	Champagne & Roses	Open		14.00	14
1995	The Hayloft	Open		11.00	11
1994	I Love You	Open		9.50	10
1994	I'm All Yours	Open		11.50	12
1995	Lover's Lane	Open		17.00	17
1994	Lovestruck	Open		10.00	10
1995	Popping The Question	Open		10.00	10
1995	Secret Admirer	Open		11.00	11
1995	Serenade	Open		10.50	11
1994	Sweetheart Pig	Open		8.00	8
1994	Together Forever	Open		15.00	15

Portraits of a People Collection - Ganz/B. Galvin

YEAR ISSUE		EDITION LIMIT	YEAR RETD.	ISSUE PRICE	*QUOTE U.S.$
1996	"Crazy Horse" Chief of Oglala Sioux	Open		35.00	35
1996	"Ouanah Parker" Comanche Chief	Open		24.00	24
1996	"Ouray" Ute Chief Round Plaque	Open		15.00	15
1996	"Pontiac" Ottawa Chief Square Plaque	Open		15.00	15
1996	"Sitting Bull"	Open		33.00	33
1996	"Tecumseh" Shawnee Chief	Open		25.00	25
1996	"White Arrow" Cherokee SW	Open		24.00	24
1996	"Winema" (Toby Riddle)	Open		25.00	25
1996	Cheyenne Buffalo-Horn Bonnet	Open		21.00	21

The Precious Steeples Collection - Ganz/L. Sunarth

YEAR ISSUE		EDITION LIMIT	YEAR RETD.	ISSUE PRICE	*QUOTE U.S.$
1995	Display Sign	Open		15.00	15
1995	Florence Cathedral	Open		40.00	40
1995	Notre Dame Cathedral	Open		40.00	40
1995	St. Patrick's Cathedral	Open		40.00	40
1995	St. Paul's Cathedral	Open		40.00	40
1995	St. Peter's Basilica	Open		40.00	40
1995	Westminster Abbey	Open		40.00	40

Renaissance Angels Christmas Collectibles - Ganz

YEAR ISSUE		EDITION LIMIT	YEAR RETD.	ISSUE PRICE	*QUOTE U.S.$
1995	Angel with Drum	Open		48.00	48
1996	Angel with Drum - 8"	Open		35.00	35
1995	Angel with Harp	Open		48.00	48
1995	Angel with Horn	Open		48.00	48
1995	Angel with Lamp	Open		48.00	48
1996	Angel with Lute - 8"	Open		35.00	35
1996	Angel with Panpipe - 8"	Open		35.00	35
1995	Angel with Violin	Open		48.00	48
1995	Angel with Wreath	Open		48.00	48
1996	Black Renaissance Angel	Open		50.00	50

Renaissance Angels/Angels of Life - Ganz

YEAR ISSUE		EDITION LIMIT	YEAR RETD.	ISSUE PRICE	*QUOTE U.S.$
1996	Angel of Comfort	Open		50.00	50
1996	Angel of Hope and Peace	Open		50.00	50
1996	Angel of Life	Open		50.00	50

Renaissance Angels/Angels Through Time - Ganz

YEAR ISSUE		EDITION LIMIT	YEAR RETD.	ISSUE PRICE	*QUOTE U.S.$
1996	Baroque Angel	Open		60.00	60
1996	Byzantine Angel	Open		60.00	60
1996	Gothic Angel	Open		60.00	60
1996	Renaissance Angel	Open		60.00	60
1996	Rococo Angel	Open		60.00	60
1996	Victorian Angel	Open		60.00	60

Trains Gone By Collection - Ganz

YEAR ISSUE		EDITION LIMIT	YEAR RETD.	ISSUE PRICE	*QUOTE U.S.$
1996	C.P. Huntington Train	3,000		70.00	70
1996	C.P. Huntington Train w/sound	2,000		85.00	85
1995	Display Sign	Open		24.00	24
1995	The General Train	4,000		70.00	70
1995	The General Train with sound	1,000		85.00	85
1995	New York Central Train	3,000		70.00	70
1995	New York Central Train w/sound	2,000		85.00	85
1995	Pennsylvania Train	4,000		70.00	70
1995	Pennsylvania Train with sound	1,000		85.00	85
1995	Santa Fe Train with sound	1,000		85.00	85
1995	Santa FeTrain	4,000		70.00	70

Watching Over You Collection - C.Thammavongsa

YEAR ISSUE		EDITION LIMIT	YEAR RETD.	ISSUE PRICE	*QUOTE U.S.$
1995	Angelic Teachings	Open		42.00	42
1996	It Is Written...	Open		40.00	40
1995	New Borne Babe	Open		40.00	40
1995	Sweet Dreams Little One	Open		38.00	38

Watching Over You Collection Musicals - C.Thammavongsa

YEAR ISSUE		EDITION LIMIT	YEAR RETD.	ISSUE PRICE	*QUOTE U.S.$
1996	Sweet Music Fills the Air	Open		60.00	60

Woodland Santas Collection - C.Thammavongsa

YEAR ISSUE		EDITION LIMIT	YEAR RETD.	ISSUE PRICE	*QUOTE U.S.$
1995	Forest Friends	Open		45.00	45
1995	Lake of the Woods	Open		45.00	45
1995	Santa's Sanctuary	Open		41.00	41

Zoological Zodiac Collection - Ganz/B. Lemaire

YEAR ISSUE		EDITION LIMIT	YEAR RETD.	ISSUE PRICE	*QUOTE U.S.$
1996	Aries	Open		25.00	25
1996	Taurus	Open		25.00	25
1996	Gemini	Open		25.00	25
1996	Cancer	Open		25.00	25
1996	Leo	Open		25.00	25
1996	Virgo	Open		25.00	25
1996	Libra	Open		25.00	25
1996	Scorpio	Open		25.00	25
1996	Sagittarius	Open		25.00	25
1996	Capricorn	Open		25.00	25
1996	Aquarius	Open		25.00	25
1996	Pisces	Open		25.00	25

*Quotes have been rounded up to nearest dollar

Gartlan USA

Members Only Figurine

YEAR ISSUE		EDITION LIMIT	YEAR RETD.	ISSUE PRICE	*QUOTE U.S.$
1990	Wayne Gretzky-Home Uniform - L. Heyda	Closed	1991	75.00	275-500
1991	Joe Montana-Road Uniform - F. Barnum	Closed	1992	75.00	150-300
1991	Kareem Abdul-Jabbar - L. Heyda	Closed	1993	75.00	150-300
1992	Mike Schmidt - J. Slockbower	Closed	1993	79.00	100-225
1993	Hank Aaron - J. Slockbower	Closed	1994	79.00	100-175
1994	Shaquille O'Neal - L. Cella	Closed	1995	39.95	75-150

Kareem Abdul-Jabbar Sky-Hook Collection - L. Heyda

YEAR ISSUE		EDITION LIMIT	YEAR RETD.	ISSUE PRICE	*QUOTE U.S.$
1989	Kareem Abdul-Jabbar "The Captain", signed	1,989	1990	175.00	300-400
1989	Kareem Abdul-Jabbar, A/P	100	1990	200.00	500-600
1989	Kareem Abdul-Jabbar, Commemorative	33	1990	275.00	4000-4700

Leave It To Beaver - Noble Studio

YEAR ISSUE		EDITION LIMIT	YEAR RETD.	ISSUE PRICE	*QUOTE U.S.$
1995	Jerry Mathers, (5")	5,000		49.95	50
1995	Jerry Mathers, (7 1/2"), signed	1,963		195.00	195
1996	Jerry Mathers, A/P (7 1/2"), signed	234		250.00	250

Magic Johnson Gold Rim Collection - R. Sun

YEAR ISSUE		EDITION LIMIT	YEAR RETD.	ISSUE PRICE	*QUOTE U.S.$
1988	Magic Johnson -"Magic in Motion"	1,737	1989	125.00	400-800
1988	Magic Johnson A/P "Magic in Motion", signed	250	1989	175.00	2000-2300
1988	Magic Johnson Commemorative	32	1989	275.00	7500

Mike Schmidt "500th" Home Run Edition - R. Sun

YEAR ISSUE		EDITION LIMIT	YEAR RETD.	ISSUE PRICE	*QUOTE U.S.$
1987	Mike Schmidt "500th" Home Run, A/P signed	20	1988	275.00	1400-1600
1987	Mike Schmidt "500th" Home Run, signed	1,987	1988	150.00	600-750

Plaques - Various

YEAR ISSUE		EDITION LIMIT	YEAR RETD.	ISSUE PRICE	*QUOTE U.S.$
1986	George Brett-"Royalty in Motion", signed - J. Martin	2,000	1987	75.00	275
1987	Mike Schmidt-"Only Perfect", A/P - Paluso	20	1988	200.00	550
1987	Mike Schmidt-"Only Perfect", signed - Paluso	500	1988	150.00	225-400
1985	Pete Rose-"Desire to Win", signed - T. Sizemore	4,192	1986	75.00	325
1986	Reggie Jackson A/P-The Roundtripper, signed - J. Martin	44	1987	175.00	400-475
1986	Reggie Jackson-"The Roundtripper" signed - J. Martin	500	1987	150.00	350-400
1987	Roger Staubach, signed - C. Soileau	1,979	1988	85.00	250-325

Ringo Starr - J. Hoffman

YEAR ISSUE		EDITION LIMIT	YEAR RETD.	ISSUE PRICE	*QUOTE U.S.$
1996	Ringo Starr with drums, (6")	5,000		150.00	150
1996	Ringo Starr, (4")	10,000		49.95	50
1996	Ringo Starr, (8 1/2") A/P signed	250		600.00	600
1996	Ringo Starr, (8 1/2") signed	1,000		350.00	350

Signed Figurines - Various

YEAR ISSUE		EDITION LIMIT	YEAR RETD.	ISSUE PRICE	*QUOTE U.S.$
1991	Al Barlick - V. Bova	1,989	1995	195.00	195
1993	Bob Cousy - L. Heyda	950	1995	150.00	150
1991	Bobby Hull - The Golden Jet - L. Heyda	1,983	1995	250.00	250
1992	Bobby Hull, A/P - L. Heyda	300	1994	350.00	350-500
1991	Brett Hull - The Golden Brett - L. Heyda	1,986	1995	250.00	250
1992	Brett Hull, A/P - L. Heyda	300	1994	350.00	400-600
1989	Carl Yastrzemski-"Yaz" , A/P - L. Heyda	250	1990	150.00	400-700
1989	Carl Yastrzemski-"Yaz" - L. Heyda	1,989	1990	150.00	275-375
1992	Carlton Fisk - J. Slockbower	1,972	1995	225.00	225
1990	Darryl Strawberry - L. Heyda	2,500	1995	225.00	225
1994	Eddie Matthews - R. Sun	1,978	1995	195.00	200
1994	Frank Thomas - D. Carroll	500	1995	225.00	350
1990	George Brett - F. Barnum	2,250	1995	225.00	225-250
1992	Gordie Howe - L. Heyda	2,358	1994	225.00	250-300
1990	Gordie Howe, signed A/P - L. Heyda	250	1994	395.00	395
1992	Hank Aaron - F. Barnum	1,982	1994	225.00	225-300
1992	Hank Aaron Commemorative w/displ. case - F. Barnum	755	1994	275.00	300-400
1991	Hull Matched Figurines - L. Heyda	950	1993	500.00	500
1989	Joe DiMaggio - L. Heyda	2,214	1990	275.00	850-1200
1990	Joe DiMaggio- Pinstripe Yankee Clipper - L. Heyda	325	1990	695.00	1800-2400
1990	Joe DiMaggio- Pinstripe Yankee Clipper, A/P - L. Heyda	12	1990	1500.00	4000-8000
1991	Joe Montana - F. Barnum	2,250	1991	325.00	450-700
1991	Joe Montana, A/P - F. Barnum	250	1991	500.00	700-1100
1989	John Wooden-Coaching Classics - L. Heyda	1,975	1995	175.00	175
1989	John Wooden-Coaching Classics, A/P - L. Heyda	250	1995	350.00	350
1989	Johnny Bench - L. Heyda	1,989	1990	150.00	225
1989	Johnny Bench, A/P - L. Heyda	250	1990	150.00	500-725
1994	Ken Griffey Jr., - J. Slockbower	1,989	1995	225.00	275
1993	Kristi Yamaguchi - K. Ling Sun	950	1995	195.00	195
1990	Luis Aparicio - J. Slockbower	1,984	1995	225.00	225
1991	Monte Irvin - V. Bova	1,973	1995	195.00	195
1991	Negro League, Set/3	950	1995	500.00	650
1985	Pete Rose-"For the Record", signed - H. Reed	4,192	1987	125.00	800-1200
1992	Ralph Kiner - J. Slockbower	1,975	1995	225.00	225
1991	Rod Carew - Hitting Splendor - J. Slockbower	1,991	1995	225.00	225
1994	Sam Snead - L. Cella	950	1995	225.00	225
1994	Shaquille O'Neal - R. Sun	500	1995	225.00	450-600
1992	Stan Musial - J. Slockbower	1,969	1995	325.00	325
1992	Stan Musial, A/P - J. Slockbower	300	1995	425.00	425
1989	Steve Carlton - L. Heyda	3,290	1992	175.00	225-325
1989	Steve Carlton, A/P - L. Heyda	300	1992	350.00	400-500
1989	Ted Williams - L. Heyda	2,654	1990	295.00	450-700
1989	Ted Williams, A/P - L. Heyda	250	1990	650.00	700-1000
1992	Tom Seaver - J. Slockbower	1,992	1995	225.00	250-350
1994	Troy Aikman - V. Davila	500	1995	225.00	400
1991	Warren Spahn - J. Slockbower	1,973	1995	225.00	275
1989	Wayne Gretzky - L. Heyda	1,851	1989	225.00	600-900
1989	Wayne Gretzky, A/P - L. Heyda	300	1989	695.00	1800-2100
1990	Whitey Ford - S. Barnum	2,360	1995	225.00	225
1990	Whitey Ford, A/P - S. Barnum	250	1995	350.00	350
1989	Yogi Berra - F. Barnum	2,150	1994	225.00	225
1989	Yogi Berra, A/P - F. Barnum	250	1994	350.00	350

Genesis

Arctic Collection - K. Cantrell

YEAR ISSUE		EDITION LIMIT	YEAR RETD.	ISSUE PRICE	*QUOTE U.S.$
1995	Arctic Hares	2,500	1995	98.00	98
1995	Arctic Owl	2,500	1995	98.00	98
1995	Arctic Wolves	2,500	1995	98.00	115
1995	Harp Seal	2,500	1995	98.00	98
1995	Polar Bear	2,500	1995	98.00	98

Birds of Prey - K. Cantrell

YEAR ISSUE		EDITION LIMIT	YEAR RETD.	ISSUE PRICE	*QUOTE U.S.$
1994	Bald Eagle	1,250		350.00	350
1994	Great Horned Owl	1,250	1996	350.00	350

Ocean Realm - K. Cantrell

YEAR ISSUE		EDITION LIMIT	YEAR RETD.	ISSUE PRICE	*QUOTE U.S.$
1994	Dolphins	1,250	1996	240.00	265
1994	Humpback Whales	1,250		240.00	250
1994	Manta Ray	1,250	1996	240.00	250
1994	Marlins	1,250	1996	240.00	250
1994	Otters	1,250		240.00	250

Geo. Zoltan Lefton Company

Tobin Fraley Collector Society (Willitts) - T. Fraley

YEAR ISSUE		EDITION LIMIT	YEAR RETD.	ISSUE PRICE	*QUOTE U.S.$
1992	TF-Collector's Society Horse	Closed	1992	35.00	150

Tobin Fraley Collection (Willitts) - T. Fraley

YEAR ISSUE		EDITION LIMIT	YEAR RETD.	ISSUE PRICE	*QUOTE U.S.$
1986	C.W. Parker - C. 1915 5050	Closed	1986	70.00	200-250
1986	Charles Carmel - C. 1914 5000	Closed	1986	75.00	125-200
1986	Charles Carmel - C. 1914 5043	Closed	1986	35.00	70
1986	Charles Looff - C. 1915 5040	Closed	1986	75.00	125-200
1986	Charles Looff - C. 1917 5038	Closed	1986	75.00	125-200
1986	Charles Looff - C. 1917 5044	Closed	1986	35.00	70
1986	Charles Looff/Ram - C. 1915 5234	Closed	1986	35.00	70
1986	D.C. Muller & Brother - C. 1911 5049	Closed	1986	35.00	70
1986	D.C. Muller & Brother - C. 1911 5233	Closed	1986	25.00	60
1986	Four Horse Musical Carousel 5213	Closed	1986	400.00	800-1000
1986	Gustav Dentzel Co. - C. 1905 5036	Closed	1986	75.00	200-275
1986	Gustav Dentzel Co./Cat - C. 1905 5235	Closed	1986	35.00	100-175
1986	Herschell-Spillman Co. - C. 1915 5046	Closed	1986	35.00	70
1986	Herschell-Spillman Co. - C. 1915 5230	Closed	1986	25.00	50
1986	Ptc - C. 1925 5047	Closed	1986	35.00	70
1986	Ptc - C. 1925 5231	Closed	1986	25.00	50
1986	Spillman Engineering - C. 1922 5041	Closed	1986	75.00	200-250
1986	Spillman Engineering - C. 1922 5042	Closed	1986	35.00	70
1986	Stein & Goldstein - C. 1914 5037	Closed	1986	75.00	125-200
1986	Stein & Goldstein - C. 1914 5045	Closed	1986	35.00	70
1986	Wm. Dentzel Co. - C. 1910 5048	Closed	1986	35.00	70
1986	Wm. Dentzel Co. - C. 1910 5051	Closed	1986	70.00	200-400
1986	Wm. Dentzel Co. - C. 1910 5232	Closed	1986	25.00	50

Tobin Fraley-American Carousel Collection (Willitts) - T. Fraley

YEAR ISSUE		EDITION LIMIT	YEAR RETD.	ISSUE PRICE	*QUOTE U.S.$
1987	Charles Carmel - C. 1915 5968	Closed	1987	70.00	125
1987	Charles Carmel - C. 1915 5986	Closed	1987	35.00	70
1987	Charles Looff - C. 1905 5980	Closed	1987	100.00	700-800
1987	Charles Looff - C. 1905 7127	Closed	1987	500.00	800-1000
1987	Charles Looff - C. 1905 7132	Closed	1987	125.00	125
1987	Charles Looff - C. 1909 5966	Closed	1987	70.00	95
1987	Charles Looff - C. 1909 5967	Closed	1987	70.00	95
1987	Charles Looff - C. 1909 5979	Closed	1987	100.00	600-700
1987	Charles Looff - C. 1909 5984	Closed	1987	35.00	70
1987	Charles Looff - C. 1909 5985	Closed	1987	35.00	70
1987	Charles Looff - C. 1909 7126	Closed	1987	500.00	700-900
1987	Charles Looff - C. 1909 7131	Closed	1987	125.00	500-950
1987	Charles Looff - C. 1909 / Rocker 5983	Closed	1987	70.00	175
1987	Charles Looff - C. 1914 5978	Closed	1987	100.00	200
1987	Charles Looff - C. 1914 7125	Closed	1987	500.00	700
1987	Charles Looff - C. 1914 7130	Closed	1987	125.00	250
1987	Daniel Muller - C. 1912 / Rocker 5982	Closed	1987	70.00	130-150
1987	Looff 5972	Closed	1987	400.00	700-900
1987	M.C. Illions - C. 1910 5971	Closed	1987	70.00	125-135
1987	M.C. Illions - C. 1910 5989	Closed	1987	35.00	70
1987	M.C. Illions - C. 1912 5970	Closed	1987	70.00	95
1987	M.C. Illions - C. 1912 5988	Closed	1987	35.00	70
1987	M.C. Illions - C. 1923 5973	Closed	1987	500.00	700-1000
1987	M.C. Illions - C. 1923 6390	Closed	1987	500.00	500
1987	M.C. Illions - C. 1923 7128	Closed	1987	100.00	190-250
1987	M.C. Illions - C. 1923 7129	Closed	1987	125.00	190-250
1987	Ptc - C. 1922 5969	Closed	1987	70.00	125
1987	Ptc - C. 1922 5987	Closed	1987	35.00	100
1987	Ptc - C. 1922 / Rocker 5981	Closed	1987	70.00	140

Tobin Fraley-American Carousel Collection II (Willitts) - T. Fraley

YEAR ISSUE		EDITION LIMIT	YEAR RETD.	ISSUE PRICE	*QUOTE U.S.$
1988	C.W. Parker - C. 1914 8322	Closed	1988	250.00	250
1988	C.W. Parker - C. 1914 8323	Closed	1988	135.00	250-350
1988	C.W. Parker - C. 1914 8468	Closed	1988	165.00	300
1988	Charles Looff - C. 1914 8213	Closed	1988	65.00	200
1988	Charles Looff - C. 1914 8214	Closed	1988	95.00	200
1988	Charles Looff - C. 1914/Snowglobe 8216	Closed	1988	80.00	80
1988	Charles Looff - C. 1917 8320	Closed	1988	250.00	250
1988	Charles Looff - C. 1917 8321	Closed	1988	135.00	250
1988	Charles Looff - C. 1917 8467	Closed	1988	165.00	250
1988	Daniel Muller - C. 1910 8317	Closed	1988	55.00	95
1988	Daniel Muller - C. 1910 8318	Closed	1988	85.00	125
1988	Dentzel - C. 1905 8329	Closed	1988	150.00	500-750
1988	Dentzel - C. 1905 8474	Closed	1988	235.00	235
1988	Dentzel - C. 1905 8475	Closed	1988	135.00	500
1988	Herschell-Spillman Co. - C. 1909 8331	Closed	1988	150.00	500
1988	Herschell-Spillman Co. - C. 1909 8470	Closed	1988	235.00	235
1988	Herschell-Spillman Co. - C. 1909 8471	Closed	1988	135.00	500
1988	Herschell-Spillman Co. - C. 1912 8330	Closed	1988	150.00	400-500
1988	Herschell-Spillman Co. - C. 1912 8472	Closed	1988	235.00	235
1988	Herschell-Spillman Co. - C. 1912 8473	Closed	1988	135.00	500
1988	M.C. Illions - C. 1912-25 8319	Closed	1988	500.00	750-900
1988	M.C. Illions - C. 1919 8324	Closed	1988	235.00	235
1988	M.C. Illions - C. 1919 8325	Closed	1988	235.00	300-400
1988	M.C. Illions - C. 1919 8340	Closed	1988	550.00	600-700
1988	M.C. Illions - C. 1919 8469	Closed	1988	150.00	275
1988	Ptc - C. 1912 8218	Closed	1988	65.00	100-200
1988	Ptc - C. 1912 8219	Closed	1988	95.00	100-200
1988	Ptc - C. 1912/Snowglobe 8221	Closed	1988	80.00	80
1988	Ptc - C. 1918 8222	Closed	1988	65.00	95
1988	Ptc - C. 1918 8223	Closed	1988	[illegible]	120
1988	Ptc - C. 1918 8224	Closed	1988	65.00	120
1988	Ptc - C. 1918 8225	Closed	1988	95.00	120
1988	Ptc - C. 1918 8315	Closed	1988	55.00	100
1988	Ptc - C. 1918 8316	Closed	1988	85.00	100

Tobin Fraley-American Carousel Collection III (Willitts) - T. Fraley

YEAR ISSUE		EDITION LIMIT	YEAR RETD.	ISSUE PRICE	*QUOTE U.S.$
1989	C.W. Parker - C. 1900-25 9024	Closed	1989	32.50	75
1989	C.W. Parker - C. 1900-25 9025	Closed	1989	32.50	75
1989	C.W. Parker - C. 1900-25 9032	Closed	1989	57.50	100-140
1989	C.W. Parker - C. 1900-25 9033	Closed	1989	57.50	100-140
1989	C.W. Parker - C. 1900-25 9034	Closed	1989	57.50	100-140
1989	C.W. Parker - C. 1900-25 9035	Closed	1989	57.50	100-140
1989	C.W. Parker - C. 1900-25 9071	Closed	1989	52.50	100-140
1989	C.W. Parker - C. 1900-25 9072	Closed	1989	52.50	100-140
1989	C.W. Parker - C. 1900-25 9073	Closed	1989	52.50	100-140
1989	C.W. Parker - C. 1900-25 9074	Closed	1989	52.50	100-140
1989	C.W. Parker - C. 1900-25 9075	Closed	1989	37.50	90
1989	C.W. Parker - C. 1900-25 9076	Closed	1989	37.50	90
1989	C.W. Parker - C. 1900-25 9077	Closed	1989	37.50	90
1989	C.W. Parker - C. 1900-25 9078	Closed	1989	37.50	90
1989	C.W. Parker - C. 1900-25 9079	Closed	1989	32.50	75
1989	C.W. Parker - C. 1900-25 9080	Closed	1989	32.50	75
1989	Charles Carmel - C. 1910 9910	Closed	1989	165.00	300-400
1989	Charles Carmel - C. 1915 9018	Closed	1989	80.00	150
1989	Charles Carmel - C. 1915 9019	Closed	1989	80.00	150
1989	Charles Carmel - C. 1915 9070	Closed	1989	165.00	300
1989	Charles Carmel - C. 1915 9088	Closed	1989	57.50	100-140
1989	Charles Carmel - C. 1915 9089	Closed	1989	57.50	58
1989	Charles Carmel - C. 1915 9094	Closed	1989	95.00	120-160
1989	Charles Carmel - C. 1915 9095	Closed	1989	95.00	120-160
1989	Charles Looff - C. 1909 9020	Closed	1989	80.00	125
1989	Charles Looff - C. 1909 9090	Closed	1989	57.50	140
1989	Charles Looff - C. 1909 9096	Closed	1989	95.00	125-160
1989	Charles Looff - C. 1917 9023	Closed	1989	80.00	120
1989	Charles Looff - C. 1917 9093	Closed	1989	57.50	100
1989	Charles Looff - C. 1917 9373	Closed	1989	95.00	125-150
1989	Daniel Muller - C. 1912 9021	Closed	1989	80.00	120
1989	Daniel Muller - C. 1912 9091	Closed	1989	57.50	75
1989	Daniel Muller - C. 1912 9097	Closed	1989	95.00	125-160
1989	M.C. Illions - C. 1922 9911	Closed	1989	165.00	600-850
1989	Ptc - C. 1922 9022	Closed	1989	80.00	95
1989	Ptc - C. 1922 9092	Closed	1989	57.50	75
1989	Ptc - C. 1922 9372	Closed	1989	95.00	160

Tobin Fraley-American Carousel Collection IV (Willitts) - T. Fraley

YEAR ISSUE		EDITION LIMIT	YEAR RETD.	ISSUE PRICE	*QUOTE U.S.$
1990	C.W. Parker - C. 1900-25 4020	Closed	1990	57.50	95
1990	C.W. Parker - C. 1900-25 4021	Closed	1990	57.50	95
1990	C.W. Parker - C. 1900-25 4022	Closed	1990	57.50	95
1990	C.W. Parker - C. 1900-25 4023	Closed	1990	57.50	95
1990	C.W. Parker - C. 1900-25 4024	Closed	1990	57.50	95
1990	C.W. Parker - C. 1900-25 4025	Closed	1990	57.50	95
1990	C.W. Parker - C. 1900-25 4027	Closed	1990	57.50	95

*Quotes have been rounded up to nearest dollar

Geo. Zoltan Lefton Company
to Goebel of North America

FIGURINES

YEAR ISSUE		EDITION LIMIT	YEAR RETD.	ISSUE PRICE	*QUOTE U.S.$
1990	C.W. Parker - C. 1900-25 4028	Closed	1990	37.50	75
1990	C.W. Parker - C. 1900-25 4029	Closed	1990	37.50	75
1990	C.W. Parker - C. 1900-25 4030	Closed	1990	37.50	75
1990	C.W. Parker - C. 1900-25 4031	Closed	1990	37.50	75
1990	C.W. Parker - C. 1900-25 4032	Closed	1990	37.50	75
1990	C.W. Parker - C. 1900-25 4033	Closed	1990	37.50	75
1990	C.W. Parker - C. 1900-25 4034	Closed	1990	37.50	75
1990	C.W. Parker - C. 1900-25 4056	Closed	1990	37.50	75
1990	Charles Carmel - C. 1915 4035	Closed	1990	95.00	95
1990	Charles Carmel - C. 1915 4036	Closed	1990	95.00	95
1990	Charles Carmel - C. 1915 4037	Closed	1990	85.00	85
1990	Charles Carmel - C. 1915 4038	Closed	1990	85.00	85
1990	Charles Carmel - C. 1915/ Complete 40290	Closed	1990	925.00	925
1990	Charles Looff 4053	Closed	1990	85.00	125
1990	Charles Looff 4054	Closed	1990	110.00	150
1990	Charles Looff 4055	Closed	1990	57.50	58
1990	Charles Looff - C. 1917 4003	Closed	1990	85.00	125-175
1990	Charles Looff - C. 1917 4005	Closed	1990	110.00	200
1990	Charles Looff - C. 1917 4007	Closed	1990	57.50	100-125
1990	The Four Seasons 4058	Closed	1990	500.00	800-1000
1990	The Four Seasons - Autumn 4010	Closed	1990	85.00	125
1990	The Four Seasons - Autumn 4014	Closed	1990	57.50	58
1990	The Four Seasons - Autumn 4018	Closed	1990	110.00	150
1990	The Four Seasons - Spring 4008	Closed	1990	85.00	120
1990	The Four Seasons - Spring 4012	Closed	1990	57.50	58
1990	The Four Seasons - Spring 4016	Closed	1990	110.00	150
1990	The Four Seasons - Summer 4009	Closed	1990	85.00	120
1990	The Four Seasons - Summer 4013	Closed	1990	57.50	58
1990	The Four Seasons - Summer 4017	Closed	1990	110.00	150
1990	The Four Seasons - Winter 4011	Closed	1990	85.00	120
1990	The Four Seasons - Winter 4015	Closed	1990	57.50	58
1990	The Four Seasons - Winter 4019	Closed	1990	110.00	300-400
1990	Herschell-Spillman Co. - C. 1912 4002	Closed	1990	85.00	85
1990	Herschell-Spillman Co. - C. 1912 4004	Closed	1990	110.00	110
1990	Herschell-Spillman Co. - C. 1912 4006	Closed	1990	57.50	58
1990	Inspired By Charles Looff 4047	Closed	1990	175.00	175
1990	Inspired By Charles Looff 4049	Closed	1990	185.00	225
1990	Inspired By Ptc 4048	Closed	1990	185.00	185
1990	Inspired By Ptc 4057	Closed	1990	175.00	220
1990	Ornament / Charles Carmel - C. 1915 4050	Closed	1990	25.00	25
1990	Tribute To Barney Illions 4001	Closed	1990	110.00	200

Tobin Fraley-American Carousel Collection V (Willitts) - T. Fraley

YEAR ISSUE		EDITION LIMIT	YEAR RETD.	ISSUE PRICE	*QUOTE U.S.$
1991	Carmel's Carousel Band Organ 4039	Closed	1990	60.00	60
1990	Carmel's Carousel Horses 4035	Closed	1990	90.00	90
1990	Carmel's Carousel Horses 4036	Closed	1990	90.00	90
1990	Carmel's Carousel Horses 4037	Closed	1990	90.00	90
1990	Carmel's Carousel Horses 4038	Closed	1990	90.00	90
1991	Chares Looff - C. 1915 4091	Closed	1991	50.00	100
1991	Charles Looff - C. 1908 4082	Closed	1991	70.00	125
1991	Charles Looff - C. 1908 4088	Closed	1991	50.00	125
1991	Charles Looff - C. 1908 4094	Closed	1991	90.00	150
1991	Charles Looff - C. 1911 4083	Closed	1991	70.00	70
1991	Charles Looff - C. 1911 4089	Closed	1991	50.00	50
1991	Charles Looff - C. 1911 4095	Closed	1991	90.00	90
1991	Charles Looff - C. 1912 4084	Closed	1991	70.00	70
1991	Charles Looff - C. 1912 4090	Closed	1991	50.00	50
1991	Charles Looff - C. 1914 4081	Closed	1991	70.00	125
1991	Charles Looff - C. 1914 4086	Closed	1991	70.00	150
1991	Charles Looff - C. 1914 4087	Closed	1991	50.00	75-125
1991	Charles Looff - C. 1914 4092	Closed	1991	50.00	95
1991	Charles Looff - C. 1914/Snowglobe 4107	Closed	1991	40.00	40
1991	Charles Looff - C. 1915 4085	Closed	1991	70.00	100-125
1991	Charles Looff/John Zalar - C. 1908-14 4080	Closed	1991	500.00	800-1000
1991	Charles Looff/John Zalar - C. 1908-14 4105	Closed	1991	200.00	300-450
1991	The Four Seasons - Autumn 4078	Closed	1991	140.00	170
1991	The Four Seasons - Spring 4076	Closed	1991	140.00	500-600
1991	The Four Seasons - Spring/50 Note Mus. 4104	Closed	1991	450.00	250
1991	The Four Seasons - Summer 4077	Closed	1991	140.00	300-400
1991	The Four Seasons - Winter 4075	Closed	1991	140.00	300-400
1991	Herschel-Spillman Co. - C. 1908-24 4059	Closed	1991	50.00	50
1991	Herschel-Spillman Co. - C. 1908-24 4062	Closed	1991	50.00	50
1991	Herschel-Spillman Co. - C. 1908-24 4065	Closed	1991	50.00	50
1991	Herschel-Spillman Co. - C. 1908-24 4068	Closed	1991	30.00	30
1991	Herschel-Spillman Co. - C. 1908-24 4072	Closed	1991	30.00	30
1991	Herschell-Spillman Co. - C. 1908-24 4060	Closed	1991	50.00	50
1991	Herschell-Spillman Co. - C. 1908-24 4061	Closed	1991	50.00	50
1991	Herschell-Spillman Co. - C. 1908-24 4063	Closed	1991	50.00	50
1991	Herschell-Spillman Co. - C. 1908-24 4064	Closed	1991	50.00	50
1991	Herschell-Spillman Co. - C. 1908-24 4066	Closed	1991	50.00	50
1991	Herschell-Spillman Co. - C. 1908-24 4067	Closed	1991	50.00	30
1991	Herschell-Spillman Co. - C. 1908-24 4069	Closed	1991	30.00	30
1991	Herschell-Spillman Co. - C. 1908-24 4070	Closed	1991	30.00	30
1991	Herschell-Spillman Co. - C. 1908-24 4071	Closed	1991	30.00	30
1991	Herschell-Spillman Co. - C. 1908-24 4073	Closed	1991	30.00	30
1991	Herschell-Spillman Co. - C. 1908-24 4074	Closed	1991	30.00	30

Tobin Fraley-American Carousel Collection VI (Willitts) - T. Fraley

YEAR ISSUE		EDITION LIMIT	YEAR RETD.	ISSUE PRICE	*QUOTE U.S.$
1992	Dentzel - C. 1895 4112	Closed	1992	70.00	70
1992	Dentzel - C. 1895 4116	Closed	1992	50.00	50
1992	Dentzel - C. 1905 4111	Closed	1992	70.00	70
1992	Dentzel - C. 1905 4115	Closed	1992	50.00	50
1992	The Four Elements - 4 Horse Carousel 4118	Closed	1992	500.00	500
1992	The Four Elements - Air 4117	Closed	1992	165.00	200
1992	The Four Elements - Earth 4121	Closed	1992	165.00	185
1992	The Four Elements - Fire 4119	Closed	1992	165.00	250-300
1992	The Four Elements - Water 4120	Closed	1992	165.00	200-300
1992	Ptc - C. 1918 4109	Closed	1992	70.00	70
1992	Ptc - C. 1918 4110	Closed	1992	70.00	70
1992	Ptc - C. 1918 4113	Closed	1992	50.00	50
1992	Ptc - C. 1918 4114	Closed	1992	50.00	50

Tobin Fraley-American Carousel Collection VII (Willitts) - T. Fraley

YEAR ISSUE		EDITION LIMIT	YEAR RETD.	ISSUE PRICE	*QUOTE U.S.$
1993	Am Apirit/Four Horse Carousel 4139	Closed	1993	250.00	250
1993	Am Spirit/Freedom 4136	Closed	1993	175.00	200-400
1993	Am Spirit/Mardi Gras 4135	Closed	1993	175.00	350-450
1993	Am Spirit/Mardi Gras-Snowglobe 4141	Closed	1993	55.00	100-125
1993	Am Spirit/Pathfinder 4138	Closed	1993	175.00	300-400
1993	Am Spirit/Wind Racer 4137	Closed	1993	175.00	300-400
1993	Carousels: The Myth	Closed	1993	25.00	25

Tobin Fraley-Great American Carousel Collection - T. Fraley

YEAR ISSUE		EDITION LIMIT	YEAR RETD.	ISSUE PRICE	*QUOTE U.S.$
1995	Am Spirit/Heartland 8620	4,500		115.00	115
1995	Am Spirit/Heartland 8624	4,500		125.00	125
1995	Am Spirit/Liberty-Lincoln 8621	4,500		115.00	115
1995	Am Spirit/Liberty/Lincoln 8625	4,500		125.00	125
1995	Am Spirit/Sage 8623	4,500		115.00	115
1995	Am Spirit/Sage 8627	4,500		125.00	125
1995	Am Spirit/Southern Bell 8622	4,500		115.00	115
1995	Am Spirit/Southern Bell 8626	4,500		125.00	125

Tobin Fraley-Great American Carousel Collection II - T. Fraley

YEAR ISSUE		EDITION LIMIT	YEAR RETD.	ISSUE PRICE	*QUOTE U.S.$
1996	C.W. Parker - C. 1915 08646	4,500		57.00	57
1996	Charles Carmel - C. 1912 08644	4,500		75.00	75
1996	Charles Carmel - C. 1915 08643	4,500		75.00	75
1996	Charles Looff - C. 1908 08638	2,500		140.00	140
1996	M.C. Illions - C. 1911 08642	4,500		110.00	110
1996	M.C. Illions - C. 1911 18641	4,500		115.00	115
1996	M.C. Illions - C. 1912 08647	4,500		57.00	57
1996	Philadelphia Toboggan Co. - C. 1912 08637	2,500		140.00	140
1996	Philadelphia Toboggan Co. - C. 1914 08648	4,500		57.00	57
1996	Philadelphia Toboggan Co. - C. 1919 08645	4,500		75.00	75
1996	Stein & Goldstein - C. 1910 08639	4,500		115.00	115
1996	Stein & Goldstein - C. 1910 08640	4,500		110.00	110

Tobin Fraley-Hallmark Galleries - T. Fraley

YEAR ISSUE		EDITION LIMIT	YEAR RETD.	ISSUE PRICE	*QUOTE U.S.$
1991	C.W. Parker - C. 1922 QHG0005	Closed	1991	30.00	60
1991	C.W. Parker - C. 1922 QHG0013	Closed	1991	40.00	40
1991	Charles Carmel - C.1914 QHG0008	Closed	1991	30.00	60
1991	Charles Carmel - C.1914 QHG0016	Closed	1991	40.00	40
1991	Charles Looff - C. 1915 QHG0001	Closed	1991	50.00	50
1991	Charles Looff - C. 1915 QHG0006	Closed	1991	30.00	60
1991	Charles Looff - C. 1915 QHG0009	Closed	1991	60.00	60
1991	Charles Looff - C. 1915 QHG0014	Closed	1991	40.00	40
1992	Daniel Müller - C1910 QHG0021	1,200	1992	275.00	450
1991	Display Stand For 4 - 3.5 " Horses QHG0019	Closed	1991	40.00	80
1991	M.C. Illions & Sons - C. 1910 QHG0003	Closed	1991	50.00	50
1991	M.C. Illions & Sons - C. 1910 QHG0011	Closed	1991	60.00	60
1991	Medallion QHG0020	Closed	1991	45.00	45
1991	Philadelphia Toboggan Co. - C. 1910 QHG0007	Closed	1991	30.00	50
1991	Philadelphia Toboggan Co. - C. 1910 QHG0015	Closed	1991	40.00	40
1993	Philadelphia Toboggan Co. - C. 1914 QHG0028	Closed	1993	60.00	100
1993	Philadelphia Toboggan Co. - C. 1919 QHG0027	Closed	1993	60.00	80
1993	Philadelphia Toboggan Co. - C. 1924 QHG0025	Closed	1993	60.00	80
1993	Philadelphia Toboggan Co. - C. 1925 QHG0026	Closed	1993	60.00	80
1991	Philadelphia Toboggan Co. - C. 1928 QHG0002	Closed	1991	50.00	100
1991	Philadelphia Toboggan Co. - C. 1928 QHG0010	Closed	1991	60.00	150
1991	Playland Carousel/4 Horses QHG0017	Closed	1991	195.00	300
1991	Stein & Goldstein 1914 QHG0004	Closed	1991	50.00	50
1991	Stein & Goldstein 1914 QHG0012	Closed	1991	60.00	60

Glynda Turley Prints

Turley - G. Turley

YEAR ISSUE		EDITION LIMIT	YEAR RETD.	ISSUE PRICE	*QUOTE U.S.$
1995	Circle of Friends	4,800		67.00	67
1995	The Courtyard II	4,800		99.00	99
1995	Flowers For Mommy	4,800		85.00	85
1994	Old Mill Stream	4,800		64.00	64
1995	Past Times	4,800		78.00	78
1995	Playing Hookie Again	4,800		83.00	83
1995	Secret Garden II	4,800		95.00	95

Goebel of North America

Charlot Byj Blondes - C. Byj

YEAR ISSUE		EDITION LIMIT	YEAR RETD.	ISSUE PRICE	*QUOTE U.S.$
1968	Bless Us All	Closed	1987	6.00	75
1968	A Child's Prayer	Closed	1987	6.00	50
1968	Evening Prayer	Closed	1986	8.00	60
1969	Her Shining Hour	Closed	1988	14.00	75
1969	Little Prayers Are Best	Closed	1987	12.00	60
1972	Love Bugs	Closed	1986	38.00	200
XX	Love Bugs (music box)	Closed	1986	80.00	325
1968	Madonna of the Doves	Closed	1993	25.00	100
1968	Mother Embracing Child	Closed	N/A	12.00	60
1968	Rock-A-Bye-Baby	Closed	N/A	7.50	150
XX	Rock-A-Bye-Baby (music box)	Closed	1985	50.00	275
1968	Sitting Pretty	Closed	1983	9.00	65
1968	Sleepy Head	Closed	1986	9.00	50
1968	Tender Shepherd	Closed	1974	8.00	350-500
1968	The Way To Pray	Closed	1988	8.50	65

Charlot Byj Redheads - C. Byj

YEAR ISSUE		EDITION LIMIT	YEAR RETD.	ISSUE PRICE	*QUOTE U.S.$
1982	1-2 Ski-Doo	Closed	1986	75.00	150
1985	All Gone	Closed	1988	42.00	100
1987	Almost There	Closed	1988	45.00	100
1987	Always Fit	Closed	1988	45.00	100
1968	Atta Boy	Closed	1984	6.50	50
1972	Baby Sitter	Closed	1983	28.00	125
1972	Bachelor Degree	Closed	1986	18.00	75
1975	Barbeque	Closed	1983	55.00	150
1985	Bedtime Boy	Closed	1987	26.00	100
1985	Bedtime Girl	Closed	1987	26.00	100
1975	Bird Watcher	Closed	1983	48.00	125
1971	Bongo Beat	Closed	1980	18.50	150
1975	Camera Shy	Closed	1983	48.00	125
1984	Captive Audience	Closed	1988	55.00	100
1968	Cheer Up	Closed	1988	8.00	75
1987	Come Along	Closed	1988	47.50	100
1970	Copper Topper	Closed	1986	10.00	75
1968	Daisies Won't Tell	Closed	1986	6.00	75
1983	A Damper on the Camper	Closed	1986	75.00	100
1983	Dear Sirs	Closed	1988	40.00	100
1968	Dropping In	Closed	1988	6.00	75
1968	E-e-eek	Closed	1986	8.00	75
1985	Farm Friends	Closed	1988	46.00	100
1987	Figurine Collector	Closed	1988	64.00	175
1972	First Degree	Closed	1986	18.00	60
1968	Forbidden Fruit	Closed	1978	7.00	50
1975	Fore	Closed	1983	48.00	100
1983	Four Letter Word For Ouch	Closed	1988	40.00	90
1983	A Funny Face From Outer Space	Closed	1987	65.00	100
1968	Gangway	Closed	1986	8.50	60
1968	Good News	Closed	1988	6.00	50
1988	Greetings	Closed	1988	55.00	125
1968	Guess Who	Closed	1979	8.50	60
1983	Heads or Tails	Closed	1986	60.00	75
1968	The Kibitzer	Closed	1983	7.50	50
1975	Lazy Day	Closed	1986	55.00	100
1969	Let It Rain	Closed	1988	26.00	175
1968	Little Miss Coy	Closed	1988	6.00	45
1968	Little Prayers Are Best	Closed	1969	13.00	55
1969	Little Shopper	Closed	1978	13.00	75
1968	Lucky Day	Closed	1986	5.50	60
1984	Not Yet a Vet	Closed	1988	65.00	100
1983	Nothing Beats a Pizza	Closed	1988	55.00	125
1971	The Nurse	Closed	1988	13.00	70
1968	O'Hair For President	Closed	1983	6.00	50
1968	Off Key	Closed	1986	7.50	50
1984	Once Upon a Time	Closed	1988	55.00	85
1984	One Puff's Enough (Yech)	Closed	1988	55.00	90
1968	Oops	Closed	1988	8.00	50
1987	Please Wait	Closed	1988	47.50	100
1968	Plenty of Nothing	Closed	1986	5.50	50
1987	The Practice	Closed	1988	64.00	150
1968	Putting on the Dog	Closed	1986	9.00	60
1968	The Roving Eye	Closed	1986	6.00	50
1972	Say A-a-a-aah	Closed	1986	19.00	100
1982	Sea Breeze	Closed	1986	65.00	90
1988	Shall We Dance?	Closed	1988	72.50	125
1985	Sharing Secrets	Closed	1988	44.00	125
1968	Shear Nonsense	Closed	1986	10.00	50
1970	Skater's Waltz	Closed	1986	15.00	100
XX	Skater's Waltz (Musical)	Closed	1986	70.00	250
1983	Something Tells Me	Closed	1987	40.00	75
1988	A Special Friend (Black Angel)	Closed	1988	55.00	100
1968	Spellbound	Closed	1986	12.00	50
1968	Spring Time	Closed	1983	7.50	50
1968	The Stolen Kiss	Closed	1978	13.00	50
1968	Strike	Closed	1986	6.00	50
1968	Super Service	Closed	1979	9.00	75

*Quotes have been rounded up to nearest dollar

FIGURINES

YEAR ISSUE		EDITION LIMIT	YEAR RETD.	ISSUE PRICE	*QUOTE U.S.$
985	Sweet Snack	Closed	1988	40.00	100
1971	Swinger	Closed	1983	15.00	75
1969	Trim Lass	Closed	1978	14.00	75
1971	Trouble Shooter (This Won't Hurt)	Closed	1986	13.00	70
1975	Wash Day	Closed	1986	55.00	50
1984	Yeah Team	Closed	1987	65.00	125
1968	A Young Man's Fancy	Closed	1988	10.00	100

Co-Boy - G. Skrobek

YEAR ISSUE		EDITION LIMIT	YEAR RETD.	ISSUE PRICE	*QUOTE U.S.$
1981	Al the Trumpet Player	Closed	N/A	45.00	80
1987	Bank-Pete the Pirate	Closed	N/A	80.00	125-150
1987	Bank-Utz the Money Bank	Closed	N/A	80.00	125
1981	Ben the Blacksmith	Closed	N/A	45.00	80
XX	Bert the Soccer Player	Closed	N/A	Unkn.	50-75
1971	Bit the Bachelor	Closed	N/A	16.00	75
1972	Bob the Bookworm	Closed	N/A	20.00	80
1984	Brad the Clockmaker	Closed	N/A	75.00	150
1972	Brum the Lawyer	Closed	N/A	20.00	80
XX	Candy the Baker's Delight	Closed	N/A	Unkn.	90
1980	Carl the Chef	Closed	N/A	49.00	85
1984	Chris the Shoemaker	Closed	N/A	45.00	80
1987	Chuck on His Pig	Closed	N/A	75.00	100
1984	Chuck the Chimney Sweep	Closed	N/A	45.00	80
1987	Clock-Conny the Watchman	Closed	N/A	125.00	150
1987	Clock-Sepp and the Beer Keg	Closed	N/A	125.00	150
1972	Co-Boy Plaque (English)	Closed	N/A	20.00	80-125
1972	Co-Boy Plaque (German)	Closed	N/A	N/A	250
XX	Conny the Night Watchman	Closed	N/A	Unkn.	80-125
1980	Doc the Doctor	Closed	N/A	49.00	85-100
XX	Ed the Wine Cellar Steward	Closed	N/A	Unkn.	75-90
1984	Felix the Baker	Closed	N/A	45.00	80
1971	Fips the Foxy Fisherman	Closed	N/A	16.00	60-75
1971	Fritz the Happy Boozer	Closed	N/A	16.00	90
1981	George the Gourmand	Closed	N/A	45.00	80
1980	Gerd the Diver	Closed	N/A	49.00	125
1978	Gil the Goalie	Closed	N/A	34.00	50-85
1981	Greg the Gourmet	Closed	N/A	45.00	50-90
1981	Greta the Happy Housewife	Closed	N/A	45.00	80
1980	Herb the Horseman	Closed	N/A	49.00	85-100
1984	Herman the Butcher	Closed	N/A	45.00	80
1984	Homer the Driver	Closed	N/A	45.00	80
XX	Jack the Village Pharmacist	Closed	N/A	Unkn.	85
XX	Jim the Bowler	Closed	N/A	Unkn.	50-75
XX	John the Hawkeye Hunter	Closed	N/A	Unkn.	80
1972	Kuni the Painter	Closed	N/A	20.00	80
XX	Mark-Safety First	Closed	N/A	Unkn.	100
1984	Marthe the Nurse	Closed	N/A	45.00	80
XX	Max the Boxing Champ	Closed	N/A	Unkn.	75
1971	Mike the Jam Maker	Closed	N/A	16.00	80
1980	Monty the Mountain Climber	Closed	N/A	49.00	85
1981	Nick the Nightclub Singer	Closed	N/A	45.00	80
1981	Niels the Strummer	Closed	N/A	45.00	80
1978	Pat the Pitcher	Closed	N/A	34.00	50
1984	Paul the Dentist	Closed	N/A	45.00	80
1981	Peter the Accordionist	Closed	N/A	45.00	80
XX	Petrl the Village Angler	Closed	N/A	Unkn.	80
1971	Plum the Pastry Chef	Closed	N/A	16.00	70
1972	Porz the Mushroom Muncher	Closed	N/A	20.00	80
1984	Rick the Fireman	Closed	N/A	45.00	80
1971	Robby the Vegetarian	Closed	N/A	16.00	90
1984	Rudy the World Traveler	Closed	N/A	45.00	80
1971	Sam the Gourmet	Closed	N/A	16.00	60-75
1972	Sepp the Beer Buddy	Closed	N/A	20.00	80
1984	Sid the Vintner	Closed	N/A	45.00	80
1980	Ted the Tennis Player	Closed	N/A	49.00	50-95
1971	Tom the Honey Lover	Closed	N/A	16.00	80
1978	Tommy Touchdown	Closed	N/A	34.00	50-75
XX	Toni the Skier	Closed	N/A	Unkn.	80
1972	Utz the Banker	Closed	N/A	20.00	80
1981	Walter the Jogger	Closed	N/A	45.00	80
1971	Wim the Court Supplier	Closed	N/A	16.00	80

Co-Boys-Culinary - Welling/Skrobek

YEAR ISSUE		EDITION LIMIT	YEAR RETD.	ISSUE PRICE	*QUOTE U.S.$
1994	Mike the Jam Maker 301050	Closed	N/A	25.00	30
1994	Plum the Sweets Maker 301052	Closed	N/A	25.00	30
1994	Robby the Vegetarian 301054	Closed	N/A	25.00	30
1994	Sepp the Drunkard 301051	Closed	N/A	25.00	30
1994	Tom the Sweet Tooth 301053	Closed	N/A	25.00	30

Co-Boys-Professionals - Welling/Skrobek

YEAR ISSUE		EDITION LIMIT	YEAR RETD.	ISSUE PRICE	*QUOTE U.S.$
1994	Brum the Lawyer 301060	Closed	N/A	25.00	25
1994	Conny the Nightwatchman 301062	Closed	N/A	25.00	25
1994	Doc the Doctor 301064	Closed	N/A	25.00	25
1994	John the Hunter 301063	Closed	N/A	25.00	25
1994	Utz the Banker 301061	Closed	N/A	25.00	25

Co-Boys-Sports - Welling/Skrobek

YEAR ISSUE		EDITION LIMIT	YEAR RETD.	ISSUE PRICE	*QUOTE U.S.$
1994	Bert the Soccer Player 301059	Closed	N/A	25.00	25
1994	Jim the Bowler 301057	Closed	N/A	25.00	25
1994	Petri the Fisherman 301055	Closed	N/A	25.00	25
1994	Ted the Tennis Player 301058	Closed	N/A	25.00	25
1994	Toni the Skier 301056	Closed	N/A	25.00	25

Goebel Figurines - N. Rockwell

YEAR ISSUE		EDITION LIMIT	YEAR RETD.	ISSUE PRICE	*QUOTE U.S.$
1963	Advertising Plaque 218	Closed	N/A	Unkn.	750-1000
1963	Boyhood Dreams (Adventurers between Adventures) 202	Closed	N/A	12.00	350-400
1963	Buttercup Test (Beguiling Buttercup) 214	Closed	N/A	10.00	350-400
1963	First Love (A Scholarly Pace) 215	Closed	N/A	30.00	350-400
1963	His First Smoke 208	Closed	N/A	9.00	350-400
1963	Home Cure 211	Closed	N/A	16.00	350-400
1963	Little Veterinarian (Mysterious Malady) 201	Closed	N/A	15.00	350-400
1963	Mother's Helper (Pride of Parenthood) 203	Closed	N/A	15.00	350-400
1963	My New Pal (A Boy Meets His Dog) 204	Closed	N/A	12.00	350-400
1963	Patient Anglers (Fisherman's Paradise) 217	Closed	N/A	18.00	350-400
1963	She Loves Me (Day Dreamer) 213	Closed	N/A	8.00	350-400
1963	Timely Assistance (Love Aid) 212	Closed	N/A	16.00	350-400

Miniatures-Americana Series - R. Olszewski

YEAR ISSUE		EDITION LIMIT	YEAR RETD.	ISSUE PRICE	*QUOTE U.S.$
1982	American Bald Eagle 661-B	Closed	1989	45.00	275-300
1986	Americana Display 951-D	Closed	1995	80.00	105
1989	Blacksmith 667-P	Closed	1989	55.00	125-150
1986	Carrousel Ride 665-B	Closed	1995	45.00	100-150
1985	Central Park Sunday 664-B	Closed	1995	45.00	75
1984	Eyes on the Horizon 663-B	Closed	1995	45.00	80
1981	The Plainsman 660-B	Closed	1989	45.00	200-250
1983	She Sounds the Deep 662-B	Closed	1995	45.00	75
1987	To The Bandstand 666-B	Closed	1995	45.00	75

Miniatures-Bob Timberlake Signature Series - B. Timberlake

YEAR ISSUE		EDITION LIMIT	YEAR RETD.	ISSUE PRICE	*QUOTE U.S.$
1996	Autumn Afternoons Vignette 818061	500		490.00	490

Miniatures-Children's Series - R. Olszewski

YEAR ISSUE		EDITION LIMIT	YEAR RETD.	ISSUE PRICE	*QUOTE U.S.$
1983	Backyard Frolic 633-P	Closed	1995	65.00	100
1980	Blumenkinder-Courting 630-P	Closed	1989	55.00	200-300
1990	Building Blocks Castle (lg.) 968-D	Closed	1995	75.00	100
1987	Carrousel Days (plain base) 637-P	Closed	1989	85.00	750-815
1987	Carrousel Days 637-P	Closed	1989	85.00	220-250
1988	Children's Display (small)	Closed	1995	45.00	60
1989	Clowning Around 636-P (new style)	Closed	1995	85.00	100-145
1986	Clowning Around 636-P (old style)	Closed	N/A	85.00	165-200
1984	Grandpa 634-P	Closed	1995	75.00	100
1988	Little Ballerina 638-P	Closed	1995	85.00	125
1982	Out and About 632-P	Closed	1989	85.00	285-300
1985	Snow Holiday 635-P	Closed	1995	75.00	125
1981	Summer Days 631-P	Closed	1989	65.00	300

Miniatures-Classic Clocks - Larsen

YEAR ISSUE		EDITION LIMIT	YEAR RETD.	ISSUE PRICE	*QUOTE U.S.$
1995	Alexis 818040	2,500		200.00	200
1995	Blinking Admiral 8180402	2,500		200.00	200
1995	Play 818041	2,500		250.00	250

Miniatures-DeGrazia - R. Olszewski

YEAR ISSUE		EDITION LIMIT	YEAR RETD.	ISSUE PRICE	*QUOTE U.S.$
1988	Adobe Display 948D	Closed	N/A	45.00	65-90
1990	Adobe Hacienda (lg.) Display 958-D	Closed	N/A	85.00	95-150
1989	Beautiful Burden 554-P	Closed	N/A	110.00	125-150
1990	Chapel Display 971-D	Closed	N/A	95.00	125
1986	Festival of Lights 507-P	Closed	N/A	85.00	145-200
1985	Flower Boy 502-P	Closed	N/A	85.00	145-200
1985	Flower Girl 501-P	Closed	N/A	85.00	145-200
1986	Little Madonna 552-P	Closed	N/A	93.00	225
1989	Merry Little Indian 508-P (new style)	Closed	N/A	110.00	150-175
1987	Merry Little Indian 508-P (old style)	Closed	N/A	95.00	250-300
1991	My Beautiful Rocking Horse 555-P	Closed	N/A	110.00	175-200
1985	My First Horse 503-P	Closed	N/A	85.00	150-165
1986	Pima Drummer Boy 506-P	Closed	N/A	85.00	250-300
1985	Sunflower Boy 551- P	Closed	N/A	93.00	150
1985	White Dove 504-P	Closed	N/A	80.00	125
1985	Wondering 505-P	Closed	N/A	93.00	150-175

Miniatures-Disney-Cinderella - Disney

YEAR ISSUE		EDITION LIMIT	YEAR RETD.	ISSUE PRICE	*QUOTE U.S.$
1991	Anastasia 172-P	Suspd.		85.00	150-180
1991	Cinderella 176-P	Suspd.		85.00	165-200
1991	Cinderella's Coach Display 978-D	Suspd.		95.00	165-200
1991	Cinderella's Dream Castle 976-D	Suspd.		95.00	200
1991	Drizella 174-P	Suspd.		85.00	160-200
1991	Fairy Godmother 180-P	Suspd.		85.00	165-200
1991	Footman 181-P	Suspd.		85.00	160-200
1991	Gus 177-P	Suspd.		80.00	165-200
1991	Jaq 173-P	Suspd.		80.00	105-165
1991	Lucifer 175-P	Suspd.		80.00	175
1991	Prince Charming 179-P	Suspd.		85.00	200
1991	Stepmother 178-P	Suspd.		85.00	175-185

Miniatures-Disney-Peter Pan - Disney

YEAR ISSUE		EDITION LIMIT	YEAR RETD.	ISSUE PRICE	*QUOTE U.S.$
1994	Captain Hook 188-P	Suspd.		160.00	200-225
1992	John 186-P	Suspd.		90.00	180
1994	Lost Boy-Fox 191-P	Suspd.		130.00	195-225
1994	Lost Boy-Rabbit 192-P	Suspd.		130.00	195-225
1992	Michael 187-P	Suspd.		90.00	155-175
1992	Nana 189-P	Suspd.		95.00	155-175
1994	Neverland Display 997-D	Suspd.		150.00	175-215
1992	Peter Pan 184-P	Suspd.		90.00	150-215
1992	Peter Pan's London 986-D	Suspd.		125.00	175-220
1994	Smee 190-P	Suspd.		140.00	175-195
1992	Wendy 185-P	Suspd.		90.00	150-195

Miniatures-Disney-Pinocchio - Disney

YEAR ISSUE		EDITION LIMIT	YEAR RETD.	ISSUE PRICE	*QUOTE U.S.$
1991	Blue Fairy 693-P	Suspd.		95.00	150-175
1990	Geppetto's Toy Shop Display 965-D	Suspd.		95.00	200
1990	Geppetto/Figaro 682-P	Suspd.		90.00	180
1990	Gideon 683-P	Suspd.		75.00	175
1990	J. Worthington Foulfellow 684-P	Suspd.		95.00	160-195
1990	Jiminy Cricket 685-P	Suspd.		75.00	175-200
1991	Little Street Lamp Display 964-D	Suspd.		65.00	135-180
1992	Monstro The Whale 985-D	Suspd.		120.00	275
1990	Pinocchio 686-P	Suspd.		75.00	195-225
1991	Stromboli 694-P	Suspd.		95.00	175-200
1991	Stromboli's Street Wagon 979-D	Suspd.		105.00	195-210

Miniatures-Disney-Snow White - Disney

YEAR ISSUE		EDITION LIMIT	YEAR RETD.	ISSUE PRICE	*QUOTE U.S.$
1987	Bashful 165-P	Suspd.		60.00	150-175
1991	Castle Courtyard Display 981-D	Suspd.		105.00	155-175
1987	Cozy Cottage Display 941-D	Suspd.		35.00	325-375
1987	Doc 162-P	Suspd.		60.00	150-175
1987	Dopey 167-P	Suspd.		60.00	150-220
1987	Grumpy 166-P	Suspd.		60.00	150-175
1987	Happy 164-P	Suspd.		60.00	150-175
1988	House In The Woods Display 944-D	Suspd.		60.00	175-185
1992	Path In The Woods 996-D	Suspd.		140.00	225-250
1987	Sleepy 163-P	Suspd.		60.00	150-175
1987	Sneezy 161-P	Suspd.		60.00	150-175
1987	Snow White 168-P	Suspd.		60.00	175-225
1990	Snow White's Prince 170-P	Suspd.		80.00	175-225
1992	Snow White's Queen 182-P	Suspd.		100.00	160-180
1992	Snow White's Witch 183-P	Suspd.		100.00	200
1990	The Wishing Well Display 969-D	Suspd.		65.00	200

Miniatures-Disneyana Convention - P. Larsen

YEAR ISSUE		EDITION LIMIT	YEAR RETD.	ISSUE PRICE	*QUOTE U.S.$
1994	Mickey Self Portrait	500	1994	295.00	900-1200
1995	Barbershop Quartet	750	1995	325.00	375-700
1996	Puppy Love	750	1996	325.00	375-475

Miniatures-Historical Series - R. Olszewski

YEAR ISSUE		EDITION LIMIT	YEAR RETD.	ISSUE PRICE	*QUOTE U.S.$
1985	Capodimonte 600-P (new style)	Closed	N/A	90.00	150-200
1980	Capodimonte 600-P (old style)	Closed	1987	90.00	400-500
1983	The Cherry Pickers 602-P	Closed	N/A	85.00	225-250
1990	English Country Garden 970-D	Open		85.00	110
1989	Farmer w/Doves 607-P	Open		85.00	115
1985	Floral Bouquet Pompadour 604-P	Open		85.00	120
1990	Gentleman Fox Hunt 616-P	Closed	N/A	145.00	170-200
1988	Historical Display 943-D	Closed	1996	45.00	65
1981	Masquerade-St. Petersburg 601-P	Closed	1989	65.00	245-260
1987	Meissen Parrot 605-P	Closed	1996	85.00	115
1988	Minton Rooster 606-P	7,500		85.00	115
1984	Moor With Spanish Horse 603-P	Closed	1996	85.00	115
1992	Poultry Seller 608-G	1,500		200.00	245

Miniatures-Jack & The Beanstalk - R. Olszewski

YEAR ISSUE		EDITION LIMIT	YEAR RETD.	ISSUE PRICE	*QUOTE U.S.$
1994	Beanseller 742-P	5,000		200.00	210
1994	Jack & The Beanstalk Display 999-D	5,000		225.00	260
1994	Jack and the Cow 743-P	5,000		180.00	195
1994	Jack's Mom 741-P	5,000		145.00	180

Miniatures-Mickey Mouse - Disney

YEAR ISSUE		EDITION LIMIT	YEAR RETD.	ISSUE PRICE	*QUOTE U.S.$
1990	Fantasia Living Brooms 972-D	Suspd.		85.00	275-325
1990	The Sorcerer's Apprentice 171-P	Suspd.		80.00	225-295
1990	Set	Suspd.		165.00	350-650

Miniatures-Nativity Collection - R. Olszewski

YEAR ISSUE		EDITION LIMIT	YEAR RETD.	ISSUE PRICE	*QUOTE U.S.$
1992	3 Kings Display 987-D	Closed	1996	85.00	105
1992	Balthazar 405-P	Closed	1996	135.00	200
1994	Camel & Tender 819292	Closed	1996	380.00	395
1992	Caspar 406-P	Closed	1996	135.00	200
1993	Final Nativity Display 991-D	Closed	1996	260.00	275
1994	Guardian Angel 407-P	Closed	1996	200.00	225
1991	Holy Family Display 982-D	Closed	1996	85.00	100
1991	Joseph 401-P	Closed	1996	95.00	130
1991	Joyful Cherubs 403-P	Closed	1996	130.00	165
1992	Melchoir 404-P	Closed	1996	135.00	200
1991	Mother/Child 440-P	Closed	1996	120.00	165
1994	Sheep & Shepherd 819290	Closed	1996	230.00	240
1991	The Stable Donkey 402-P	Closed	1996	95.00	125

Miniatures-Night Before Christmas (1st Edition) - R. Olszewski

YEAR ISSUE		EDITION LIMIT	YEAR RETD.	ISSUE PRICE	*QUOTE U.S.$
1990	Eight Tiny Reindeer 691-P	5,000		110.00	135
1990	Mama & Papa 692-P	5,000		110.00	140
1990	St. Nicholas 690-P	5,000		95.00	125
1990	Sugar Plum Boy 687-P	5,000		70.00	100
1990	Sugar Plum Girl 689-P	5,000		70.00	100
1991	Up To The Housetop 966-D	5,000		95.00	115
1990	Yule Tree 688-P	5,000		90.00	110

Miniatures-Oriental Series - R. Olszewski

YEAR ISSUE		EDITION LIMIT	YEAR RETD.	ISSUE PRICE	*QUOTE U.S.$
1986	The Blind Men and the Elephant 643-P	Closed	N/A	70.00	175
1990	Chinese Temple Lion 646-P	Open		90.00	115-150
1987	Chinese Water Dragon 644-P	Closed	N/A	70.00	150-175
1990	Empress' Garden Display 967-D	Open		95.00	135
1982	The Geisha 641-P	Closed	N/A	65.00	150-200
1984	Kuan Yin 640-W (new style)	Closed	N/A	45.00	125-225
1980	Kuan Yin 640-W (old style)	Closed	1992	40.00	225-250
1987	Oriental Display (small) 945-D	Closed	N/A	45.00	70
1985	Tang Horse 642-P	Closed	N/A	65.00	100
1989	Tiger Hunt 645-P	Closed	N/A	85.00	105

Miniatures-Pendants - R. Olszewski

YEAR ISSUE		EDITION LIMIT	YEAR RETD.	ISSUE PRICE	*QUOTE U.S.$
1986	Camper Bialosky 151-P	Closed	1988	95.00	255-275
1991	Chrysanthemum Pendant 222-P	Closed	1996	135.00	155
1991	Daffodil Pendant 221-P	Closed	1996	135.00	155
1990	Hummingbird 697-P	Closed	1996	125.00	155
1988	Mickey Mouse 169-P	5,000	1989	92.00	285-310
1991	Poinsettia Pendant 223-P	Closed	1996	135.00	155
1991	Rose Pendant 220-P	Closed	1996	135.00	155

*Quotes have been rounded up to nearest dollar

Miniatures-Portrait of America/Saturday Evening Post - N. Rockwell

YEAR ISSUE		EDITION LIMIT	YEAR RETD.	ISSUE PRICE	*QUOTE U.S.$
1989	Bottom Drawer 366-P	7,500	1995	85.00	95-110
1988	Bottom of the Sixth 365-P	Closed	1996	85.00	125-200
1988	Check-Up 363-P	Closed	1996	85.00	100-130
1988	The Doctor and the Doll 361-P	Closed	1996	85.00	150-225
1991	Home Coming Vignette-Soldier/Mother 990-D	2,000	1995	190.00	225-250
1988	Marbles Champion (Pewter) 362-P	Closed	1995	85.00	100-150
1988	No Swimming (Pewter) 360-P	Closed	1995	85.00	100-150
1988	Rockwell Display (Pewter) 952-D	Closed	1995	80.00	100-150
1988	Triple Self-Portrait (Pewter) 364-P	Closed	1996	85.00	175-300

Miniatures-Precious Moments Series I - Goebel

YEAR ISSUE		EDITION LIMIT	YEAR RETD.	ISSUE PRICE	*QUOTE U.S.$
1995	Fields of Friendship-Diorama (display)	Open		135.00	135
1995	God Loveth a Cheerful Giver	Open		70.00	70
1995	His Burden is Light	Open		70.00	70
1995	I'm Sending You a White Christmas	5,000		100.00	100
1995	Love Is Kind	Open		70.00	70
1995	Love One Another	Open		70.00	70
1995	Make a Joyful Noise	Open		70.00	70
1995	Praise the Lord Anyhow	Open		70.00	70
1995	Prayer Changes Things	Open		70.00	70

Miniatures-Precious Moments Series II - Goebel

YEAR ISSUE		EDITION LIMIT	YEAR RETD.	ISSUE PRICE	*QUOTE U.S.$
1996	Heart & Home-Diorama (display)	Open		150.00	150
1996	Jesus is the Answer	Open		70.00	70
1996	Jesus is the Light	Open		70.00	70
1996	Jesus Loves Me (boy)	Open		70.00	70
1996	Jesus Loves Me (girl)	Open		70.00	70
1996	Merry Christmas Deer	5,000		100.00	100
1996	O, How I Love Jesus	Open		70.00	70
1996	Smile, God Loves You	Open		70.00	70
1996	Unto Us A Child is born	Open		70.00	70

Miniatures-Precious Moments Series III - Goebel

YEAR ISSUE		EDITION LIMIT	YEAR RETD.	ISSUE PRICE	*QUOTE U.S.$
1997	Come Let Us Adore Him Cameo	Open		70.00	70
1997	God Understands Cameo	Open		70.00	70
1997	He Careth For You Cameo	Open		70.00	70
1997	He Leadeth Me Cameo	Open		70.00	70
1997	Jesus is Born Cameo	Open		70.00	70
1997	Love Lifted Me Cameo	Open		70.00	70
1997	Prayers of Peace Diorama	Open		150.00	150
1997	Process Stick: God Loveth A Cheerful Giver	Open		200.00	200
1997	Tell Me The Story of Jesus	5,000		100.00	100
1997	We Have Seen His Star Cameo	Open		70.00	70

Miniatures-Special Release-Alice in Wonderland - R. Olszewski

YEAR ISSUE		EDITION LIMIT	YEAR RETD.	ISSUE PRICE	*QUOTE U.S.$
1982	Alice In the Garden 670-P	Closed	1982	60.00	600-650
1984	The Cheshire Cat 672-P	Closed	1984	75.00	375-450
1983	Down the Rabbit Hole 671-P	Closed	1983	75.00	450

Miniatures-Special Release-Wizard of Oz - R. Olszewski

YEAR ISSUE		EDITION LIMIT	YEAR RETD.	ISSUE PRICE	*QUOTE U.S.$
1986	The Cowardly Lion 675-P	Closed	1987	85.00	295-325
1992	Dorothy/Glinda 695-P	Closed	1995	135.00	135-195
1992	Good-Bye to Oz Display 980-D	Closed	1996	110.00	130-175
1988	The Munchkins 677-P	Closed	1995	85.00	85-145
1987	Oz Display 942-D	Closed	1994	45.00	550-650
1984	Scarecrow 673-P	Closed	1985	75.00	395-450
1985	Tinman 674-P	Closed	1986	80.00	275-325
1987	The Wicked Witch 676-P	Closed	1995	85.00	120-180

Miniatures-Special Releases - R. Olszewski

YEAR ISSUE		EDITION LIMIT	YEAR RETD.	ISSUE PRICE	*QUOTE U.S.$
1994	Dresden Timepiece 450-P	750		1250.00	1300
1991	Portrait Of The Artist (convention) 658-P	Closed	1991	195.00	450-600
1991	Portrait Of The Artist (promotion) 658-P	Closed	N/A	195.00	210-250
1992	Summer Days Collector Plaque 659-P	Closed	N/A	130.00	130-175

Miniatures-The American Frontier Collection - Various

YEAR ISSUE		EDITION LIMIT	YEAR RETD.	ISSUE PRICE	*QUOTE U.S.$
1987	American Frontier Museum Display 947-D - R. Olszewski	Closed	N/A	80.00	115
1987	The Bronco Buster 350-B - Remington	Closed	N/A	80.00	130-160
1987	Eight Count 310-B - Pounder	Closed	N/A	75.00	95
1987	The End of the Trail 340-B - Frazier	Closed	N/A	80.00	95-150
1987	The First Ride 330-B - Rogers	Closed	N/A	85.00	105
1987	Grizzly's Last Stand 320-B - Jonas	Closed	N/A	65.00	85
1987	Indian Scout and Buffalo 300-B - Bonheur	Closed	N/A	95.00	95-140

Miniatures-Three Little Pigs - R. Olszewski

YEAR ISSUE		EDITION LIMIT	YEAR RETD.	ISSUE PRICE	*QUOTE U.S.$
1991	The Hungry Wolf 681-P	7,500		80.00	110
1991	Little Bricks Pig 680-P	7,500		75.00	110
1989	Little Sticks Pig 678-P	7,500		75.00	110
1990	Little Straw Pig 679-P	7,500		75.00	110
1991	Three Little Pigs House 956-D	7,500		50.00	130

Miniatures-Wildlife Series - R. Olszewski

YEAR ISSUE		EDITION LIMIT	YEAR RETD.	ISSUE PRICE	*QUOTE U.S.$
1985	American Goldfinch 625-P	Closed	N/A	65.00	100
1986	Autumn Blue Jay 626-P	Closed	N/A	65.00	175-200
1992	Autumn Blue Jay 626-P (Archive release)	Closed	N/A	125.00	140
1980	Chipping Sparrow 620-P	Closed	N/A	55.00	350-415
1987	Country Display (small) 940-D	Closed	N/A	45.00	70
1990	Country Landscape (large) 957-D	Closed	N/A	85.00	115
1989	Hooded Oriole 629-P	Closed	N/A	80.00	105
1990	Hummingbird 696-P	Closed	N/A	85.00	175-200
1987	Mallard Duck 627-P	Closed	N/A	75.00	110
1981	Owl-Daylight Encounter 621-P	Closed	N/A	65.00	275-300
1983	Red-Winged Blackbird 623-P	Closed	N/A	65.00	175-200
1988	Spring Robin 628-P	Closed	N/A	75.00	155-185
1982	Western Bluebird 622-P	Closed	N/A	65.00	165-180
1984	Winter Cardinal 624-P	Closed	N/A	65.00	200-275

Miniatures-Winter Lights - Norrgard

YEAR ISSUE		EDITION LIMIT	YEAR RETD.	ISSUE PRICE	*QUOTE U.S.$
1995	Once Upon a Winter Day	Closed	1996	275.00	275

Miniatures-Women's Series - R. Olszewski

YEAR ISSUE		EDITION LIMIT	YEAR RETD.	ISSUE PRICE	*QUOTE U.S.$
1980	Dresden Dancer 610-P	Closed	1989	55.00	250-350
1985	The Hunt With Hounds (new style) 611-P	Closed	N/A	75.00	250-300
1981	The Hunt With Hounds (old style) 611-P	Closed	1984	75.00	300
1986	I Do 615-P	Closed	N/A	85.00	200-300
1983	On The Avenue 613-P	Closed	1995	65.00	175-200
1982	Precious Years 612-P	Closed	N/A	65.00	200-250
1984	Roses 614-P	Closed	1995	65.00	135-175
1989	Women's Display (small) 950-D	Closed	1995	40.00	95-115

Goebel/M.I. Hummel

M.I. Hummel Collectors Club Exclusives - M. I. Hummel, unless otherwise noted

YEAR ISSUE		EDITION LIMIT	YEAR RETD.	ISSUE PRICE	*QUOTE U.S.$
1977	Valentine Gift 387	Closed	N/A	45.00	450-700
1978	Smiling Through Plaque 690	Closed	N/A	50.00	175-225
1979	Bust of Sister-M.I.Hummel HU-3 - G. Skrobek	Closed	N/A	75.00	250-350
1980	Valentine Joy 399	Closed	N/A	95.00	300-365
1981	Daisies Don't Tell 380	Closed	N/A	80.00	275-350
1982	It's Cold 421	Closed	N/A	80.00	160-275
1983	What Now? 422	Closed	N/A	90.00	280-325
1983	Valentine Gift Mini Pendant 248-P - R. Olszewski	Closed	N/A	85.00	275-350
1984	Coffee Break 409	Closed	N/A	90.00	245-300
1985	Smiling Through 408/0	Closed	N/A	125.00	275-350
1986	Birthday Candle 440	Closed	N/A	95.00	245-350
1986	What Now? Mini Pendant 249-P - R. Olszewski	Closed	N/A	125.00	200-300
1987	Morning Concert 447	Closed	N/A	98.00	200-275
1987	Little Cocopah Indian Girl - T. DeGrazia	Closed	N/A	140.00	200-300
1988	The Surprise 431	Closed	N/A	125.00	200-325
1989	Mickey and Minnie - H. Fischer	Closed	N/A	275.00	350-500
1989	Hello World 429	Closed	N/A	130.00	200-300
1990	I Wonder 486	Closed	N/A	140.00	195-250
1991	Gift From A Friend 485	Closed	N/A	160.00	180-250
1991	Miniature Morning Concert w/ Display 269-P - R. Olszewski	Closed	N/A	175.00	175-250
1992	My Wish Is Small 463/0	Closed	N/A	170.00	175-250
1992	Cheeky Fellow 554	Closed	N/A	120.00	130-150
1993	I Didn't Do It 626	Closed	1995	175.00	175-220
1993	Sweet As Can Be 541	Closed	1995	125.00	125-140
1994	Little Visitor 563/0	Closed	1996	180.00	200
1994	Little Troubadour 558	Closed	1996	130.00	140
1994	At Grandpa's 621	10,000	1996	1300.00	1300-1400
1994	Miniature Honey Lover Pendant 247-P	Closed	1996	165.00	75
1995	Country Suitor 760	5/97		195.00	195
1995	Strum Along 557	5/97		135.00	135
1995	A Story From Grandma 620	10,000	1996	1300.00	1300
1996	Valentine Gift Plaque 717	Closed	1996	250.00	250
1996	Celebrate with Song 790	5/98		295.00	295
1996	One, Two, Three 555	5/98		145.00	145
1996	What's New 418	5/97		310.00	310

Sp. Ed. Anniversary Figurines For 5/10/15/20 Year Membership - M.I. Hummel

YEAR ISSUE		EDITION LIMIT	YEAR RETD.	ISSUE PRICE	*QUOTE U.S.$
1990	Flower Girl 548 (5 year)	Open		105.00	140
1990	The Little Pair 449 (10 year)	Open		170.00	220
1991	Honey Lover 312 (15 year)	Open		190.00	230
1996	Behave 339 (20 year)	Open		350.00	350

M.I. Hummel Candleholders - M.I. Hummel

YEAR ISSUE		EDITION LIMIT	YEAR RETD.	ISSUE PRICE	*QUOTE U.S.$
XX	Angel Duet 193	Open		245.00	245
XX	Angel w/Accordian 1/39/0	Open		60.00	60
XX	Angel w/Lute 1/38/0	Open		60.00	60
XX	Angel w/Trumpet 1/40/0	Open		60.00	60
XX	Boy w/Horse 117	Open		60.00	60
XX	Candlelight 192	Open		255.00	255
XX	Girl w/Fir Tree 116	Open		60.00	60
XX	Girl w/Nosegay 115	Open		60.00	60
XX	Lullaby 241/I	Open		210.00	210
XX	Silent Night 54	Open		360.00	360

M.I. Hummel Collectibles Century Collection - M.I. Hummel

YEAR ISSUE		EDITION LIMIT	YEAR RETD.	ISSUE PRICE	*QUOTE U.S.$
1986	Chapel Time 442	Closed	N/A	500.00	1200-2800
1987	Pleasant Journey 406	Closed	N/A	500.00	1800-2300
1988	Call to Worship 441	Closed	N/A	600.00	800-1000
1989	Harmony in Four Parts 471	Closed	N/A	850.00	1350-2000
1990	Let's Tell the World 487	Closed	N/A	875.00	1150-1500
1991	We Wish You The Best 600	Closed	N/A	1300.00	1450-1800
1992	On Our Way 472	Closed	N/A	950.00	1100-1200
1993	Welcome Spring 635	Closed	N/A	1085.00	1250-1450
1994	Rock-A-Bye 574	Closed	N/A	1150.00	1200-1350
1995	Strike Up the Band 668	Closed	N/A	1200.00	1200
1997	Fond Goodbye 660	Yr.Iss.		1450.00	1450
1996	Love's Bounty 751	Yr.Iss.	1996	1200.00	1200

M.I. Hummel Collectibles Christmas Angels - M.I. Hummel

YEAR ISSUE		EDITION LIMIT	YEAR RETD.	ISSUE PRICE	*QUOTE U.S.$
1993	Angel in Cloud 585	Open		25.00	35
1993	Angel with Lute 580	Open		25.00	35
1993	Angel with Trumpet 586	Open		25.00	35
1993	Celestial Musician 578	Open		25.00	35
1993	Festival Harmony with Flute 577	Open		25.00	35
1993	Festival Harmony w/ Mandolin 576	Open		25.00	35
1993	Gentle Song 582	Open		25.00	35
1993	Heavenly Angel 575	Open		25.00	35
1993	Prayer of Thanks 581	Open		25.00	35
1993	Song of Praise 579	Open		25.00	35

M.I. Hummel Collectibles Figurines - M.I. Hummel

YEAR ISSUE		EDITION LIMIT	YEAR RETD.	ISSUE PRICE	*QUOTE U.S.$
1988	The Accompanist 453	Open		Unkn.	115
XX	Adoration 23/I	Open		Unkn.	380
XX	Adoration 23/III	Open		Unkn.	595
XX	Adventure Bound 347	Open		Unkn.	3980
XX	Angel Duet 261	Open		Unkn.	245
XX	Angel Serenade 214/D/I	Open		Unkn.	100
XX	Angel Serenade with Lamb 83	Open		Unkn.	245
XX	Angel with Accordion 238/B	Open		Unkn.	60
XX	Angel with Lute 238/A	Open		Unkn.	60
XX	Angel With Trumpet 238/C	Open		Unkn.	60
XX	Angelic Song 144	Open		Unkn.	165
1995	The Angler 566	Open		Unkn.	350
1989	An Apple A Day 403	Open		Unkn.	310
XX	Apple Tree Boy 142/3/0	Open		Unkn.	160
XX	Apple Tree Boy 142/I	Open		Unkn.	310
XX	Apple Tree Boy 142/V	Open		Unkn.	1350
XX	Apple Tree Boy 142/X	Open		Unkn.	24000
XX	Apple Tree Girl 141/3/0	Open		Unkn.	160
XX	Apple Tree Girl 141/I	Open		Unkn.	310
XX	Apple Tree Girl 141/V	Open		Unkn.	1350
XX	Apple Tree Girl 141/X	Open		Unkn.	24000
XX	Begging His Share 9	Open		Unkn.	280
1991	Art Critic 318	Open		Unkn.	315
XX	Artist, The 304	Open		Unkn.	275
XX	Auf Wiedersehen 153/0	Open		Unkn.	270
XX	Auf Wiedersehen 153/I	Open		Unkn.	330
XX	Autumn Harvest 355	Open		Unkn.	225
XX	Baker 128	Open		Unkn.	225
XX	Baking Day 330	Open		Unkn.	310
XX	Band Leader 129/4/0	Open		Unkn.	115
XX	Band Leader 129	Open		Unkn.	225
XX	Barnyard Hero 195/2/0	Open		Unkn.	185
XX	Barnyard Hero 195/I	Open		Unkn.	350
XX	Bashful 377	Open		Unkn.	225
1990	Bath Time 412	Open		Unkn.	485
XX	Be Patient 197/2/0	Open		Unkn.	225
XX	Be Patient 197/I	Open		Unkn.	330
XX	Begging His Share 9	Open		Unkn.	280
1997	Best Wishes (personalized) 540	Open		180.00	180
XX	Big Housecleaning 363	Open		Unkn.	315
XX	Bird Duet 169	Open		Unkn.	160
XX	Bird Duet (personalized)169	Open		Unkn.	160
XX	Bird Watcher 300	Open		Unkn.	240
1989	Birthday Cake 338	Open		Unkn.	160
1994	Birthday Present 341/3/0	Open		140.00	160
XX	Birthday Serenade 218/2/0	Open		Unkn.	190
XX	Birthday Serenade 218/0	Open		Unkn.	330
XX	Blessed Event 333	Open		Unkn.	350
1996	Blossom Time 608	Open		155.00	155
XX	Bookworm 8	Open		Unkn.	245
XX	Bookworm 3/I	Open		Unkn.	335
XX	Boots 143/0	Open		Unkn.	225
XX	Boots 143/I	Open		Unkn.	360
XX	Botanist, The 351	Open		Unkn.	200
XX	Boy with Accordion 390	Open		Unkn.	100
XX	Boy with Horse 239/C	Open		Unkn.	60
XX	Boy with Toothache 217	Open		Unkn.	230
XX	Brother 95	Open		Unkn.	230
1988	A Budding Maestro 477	Open		Unkn.	120
XX	Builder, The 305	Open		Unkn.	275
XX	Busy Student 367	Open		Unkn.	180
XX	Call to Glory 739/I	Open		250.00	275
1996	Carefree 490	Open		120.00	120
XX	Carnival 328	Open		Unkn.	240
1993	Celestial Musician 188/4/0	Open		Unkn.	115
XX	Celestial Musician 188/0	Open		Unkn.	245
XX	Celestial Musician 188/I	Open		255.00	295
XX	Chick Girl 57/2/0	Open		Unkn.	165
XX	Chick Girl 57/0	Open		Unkn.	185
XX	Chick Girl 57/I	Open		Unkn.	310
XX	Chicken-Licken 385/4/0	Open		Unkn.	115
XX	Chicken-Licken 385	Open		Unkn.	310
XX	Chimney Sweep 12/2/0	Open		Unkn.	130
XX	Chimney Sweep 12/I	Open		Unkn.	245
XX	Christ Child 18	Open		Unkn.	160
1989	Christmas Angel 301	Open		Unkn.	280
1996	Christmas Song 343/4/0	Open		110.00	110
XX	Christmas Song 343	Open		Unkn.	245
XX	Cinderella 337	Open		Unkn.	315
XX	Close Harmony 336	Open		Unkn.	330
1995	Come Back Soon 545	Open		Unkn.	160
XX	Confidentially 314	Open		Unkn.	325
XX	Congratulations 17	Open		Unkn.	225
XX	Coquettes 179	Open		Unkn.	325
1990	Crossroads (Commemorative) 331	20,000	N/A	360.00	700-1000
XX	Crossroads (Original) 331	Open		Unkn.	450
XX	Culprits 56/A	Open		Unkn.	325

*Quotes have been rounded up to nearest dollar

FIGURINES

YEAR ISSUE		EDITION LIMIT	YEAR RETD.	ISSUE PRICE	*QUOTE U.S.$
1989	Daddy's Girls 371	Open		Unkn.	250
1996	Delicious 435/3/0	Open		155.00	155
XX	Doctor 127	Open		Unkn.	170
XX	Doll Bath 319	Open		Unkn.	315
XX	Doll Mother 67	Open		Unkn.	230
XX	Easter Greetings 378	Open		Unkn.	225
XX	Easter Time 384	Open		Unkn.	275
1992	Evening Prayer 495	Open		Unkn.	120
XX	Eventide 99	Open		Unkn.	360
XX	A Fair Measure 345	Open		Unkn.	325
XX	Farm Boy 66	Open		Unkn.	260
1996	Fascination 649/0 (Special Event)	25,000	1996	190.00	200
XX	Favorite Pet 361	Open		Unkn.	315
XX	Feathered Friends 344	Open		Unkn.	310
XX	Feeding Time 199/0	Open		Unkn.	225
XX	Feeding Time 199/I	Open		Unkn.	315
1994	Festival Harmony with Mandolin 172/4/0	Open		95.00	115
XX	Festival Harmony, with Mandolin 172/0	Open		Unkn.	350
XX	Festival Harmony, with Flute 173/4/0	Open		Unkn.	115
XX	Festival Harmony, with Flute 173/0	Open		Unkn.	350
XX	Flower Vendor 381	Open		Unkn.	275
XX	Follow the Leader 369	Open		Unkn.	1320
XX	For Father 87	Open		Unkn.	240
XX	For Mother 257/2/0	Open		Unkn.	130
XX	For Mother 257	Open		Unkn.	225
XX	Forest Shrine 183	Open		Unkn.	595
1993	A Free Flight 569	Open		Unkn.	200
1996	Free Spirit 564	Open		120.00	120
1991	Friend Or Foe 434	Open		Unkn.	245
XX	Friends 136/I	Open		Unkn.	230
XX	Friends 136/V	Open		Unkn.	1350
1993	Friends Together 662/0 (Commemorative)	Open		260.00	300
1993	Friends Together 662/I (Limited)	25,000		475.00	550
1996	From The Heart 761	Open		120.00	120
XX	Gay Adventure 356	Open		Unkn.	220
1995	Gentle Fellowship (Limited) 628	25,000		550.00	550
XX	A Gentle Glow 439	Open		Unkn.	230
XX	Girl with Doll 239/B	Open		Unkn.	60
XX	Girl with Nosegay 239/A	Open		Unkn.	60
XX	Girl with Sheet Music 389	Open		Unkn.	100
XX	Girl with Trumpet 391	Open		Unkn.	100
XX	Going Home 383	Open		Unkn.	350
XX	Going to Grandma's 52/0	Open		Unkn.	275
XX	Good Friends 182	Open		Unkn.	225
XX	Good Hunting 307	Open		Unkn.	270
1997	Good News (personalized) 539	Open		180.00	180
XX	Good Shepherd 42	Open		Unkn.	280
XX	Goose Girl 47/3/0	Open		Unkn.	185
XX	Goose Girl 47/0	Open		Unkn.	260
XX	Goose Girl Sampler 47/3/0	Open		200.00	200
XX	Grandma's Girl 561	Open		Unkn.	160
XX	Grandpa's Boy 562	Open		Unkn.	160
1991	The Guardian 455	Open		Unkn.	180
1991	The Guardian (personalized) 455	Open		Unkn.	180
XX	Guiding Angel 357	Open		Unkn.	100
XX	Happiness 86	Open		Unkn.	150
XX	Happy Birthday 176/0	Open		Unkn.	240
XX	Happy Birthday 176/I	Open		Unkn.	330
XX	Happy Days 150/2/0	Open		Unkn.	190
XX	Happy Days 150/0	Open		Unkn.	330
XX	Happy Days 150/I	Open		Unkn.	500
XX	Happy Traveller 109/0	Open		Unkn.	165
XX	Hear Ye! Hear Ye! 15/2/0	Open		Unkn.	170
XX	Hear Ye! Hear Ye! 15/0	Open		Unkn.	225
XX	Hear Ye! Hear Ye! 15/I	Open		Unkn.	280
1996	Heart and Soul 559	Open		120.00	120
XX	Heavenly Angel 21/0	Open		Unkn.	140
XX	Heavenly Angel 21/0/1/2	Open		Unkn.	245
XX	Heavenly Angel 21/I	Open		Unkn.	295
XX	Heavenly Lullaby 262	Open		Unkn.	210
XX	Heavenly Protection 88/I	Open		Unkn.	495
XX	Heavenly Protection 88/II	Open		Unkn.	800
1995	Hello (Perpetual Calendar) 788A	Open		295.00	295
XX	Hello 124/0	Open		Unkn.	245
XX	Home from Market 198/2/0	Open		Unkn.	170
XX	Home from Market 198/I	Open		Unkn.	240
XX	Homeward Bound 334	Open		Unkn.	360
1990	Horse Trainer 423	Open		Unkn.	245
1989	Hosanna 480	Open		Unkn.	120
1989	I'll Protect Him 483	Open		Unkn.	100
1994	I'm Carefree 633	Open		365.00	400
1989	I'm Here 478	Open		Unkn.	120
1989	In D Major 430	Open		Unkn.	225
XX	In The Meadow 459	Open		Unkn.	225
XX	In Tune 414	Open		Unkn.	310
XX	Is It Raining? 420	Open		Unkn.	300
XX	Joyful 53	Open		Unkn.	140
XX	Joyous News 27/III	Open		Unkn.	245
1995	Just Dozing 451	Open		Unkn.	250
XX	Just Fishing 373	Open		Unkn.	250
XX	Just Resting 112/3/0	Open		Unkn.	165
XX	Just Resting 112/I	Open		Unkn.	310
XX	The Kindergartner 467	Open		Unkn.	225
XX	Kiss Me 311	Open		Unkn.	315
XX	Knit One, Purl One 432	Open		Unkn.	135
XX	Knitting Lesson 256	Open		Unkn.	525
1991	Land in Sight 530	30,000		1600.00	1600
XX	Latest News 184	Open		Unkn.	320
XX	Latest News (personalized) 184	Open		Unkn.	320
XX	Let's Sing 110/0	Open		Unkn.	140
XX	Let's Sing 110/I	Open		Unkn.	185
XX	Letter to Santa Claus 340	Open		Unkn.	360
1993	The Little Architect 410/I	Open		Unkn.	330
XX	Little Bookkeeper 306	Open		Unkn.	315
XX	Little Cellist 89/I	Open		Unkn.	240
XX	Little Drummer 240	Open		Unkn.	165
XX	Little Fiddler 2/4/0	Open		Unkn.	115
XX	Little Fiddler 4	Open		Unkn.	225
XX	Little Fiddler 2/0	Open		Unkn.	245
XX	Little Gabriel 32	Open		Unkn.	165
XX	Little Gardener 74	Open		Unkn.	130
XX	Little Goat Herder 200/0	Open		Unkn.	225
XX	Little Goat Herder 200/I	Open		Unkn.	260
XX	Little Guardian 145	Open		Unkn.	165
XX	Little Helper 73	Open		Unkn.	130
XX	Little Hiker 16/2/0	Open		Unkn.	130
XX	Little Hiker 16/I	Open		Unkn.	245
XX	Little Nurse 376	Open		Unkn.	270
XX	Little Pharmacist 322/E	Open		Unkn.	270
XX	Little Scholar 80	Open		Unkn.	240
XX	Little Shopper 96	Open		Unkn.	160
XX	Little Sweeper 171/4/0	Open		Unkn.	115
1988	Little Sweeper 171/0	Open		Unkn.	160
XX	Little Tailor 308	Open		Unkn.	275
XX	Little Thrifty 118	Open		Unkn.	170
XX	Lost Stocking 374	Open		Unkn.	165
1995	Lucky Boy (Special Event) 335	25,000	1995	190.00	200
XX	The Mail is Here 226	Open		Unkn.	595
1989	Make A Wish 475	Open		Unkn.	225
1996	Making New Friends 2002	Open		595.00	595
XX	March Winds 43	Open		Unkn.	170
XX	Max and Moritz 123	Open		Unkn.	245
XX	Meditation 13/2/0	Open		Unkn.	160
XX	Meditation 13/0	Open		Unkn.	245
XX	Merry Wanderer 11/2/0	Open		Unkn.	160
XX	Merry Wanderer 11/0	Open		Unkn.	225
XX	Merry Wanderer 7/0	Open		Unkn.	310
XX	Merry Wanderer 7/X	Open		Unkn.	24000
XX	Mischief Maker 342	Open		Unkn.	310
1994	Morning Stroll 375/3/0	Open		170.00	195
XX	Mother's Darling 175	Open		Unkn.	240
XX	Mother's Helper 133	Open		Unkn.	225
XX	Mountaineer 315	Open		Unkn.	240
1991	A Nap 534	Open		Unkn.	130
1996	Nimble Fingers w/wooden bench 758	Open		225.00	230
1996	No Thank You 535	Open		120.00	120
XX	Not For You 317	Open		Unkn.	270
XX	On Holiday 350	Open		Unkn.	170
XX	On Secret Path 386	Open		Unkn.	275
1989	One For You, One For Me 482	Open		Unkn.	120
1993	One Plus One 556	Open		Unkn.	145
XX	Ooh My Tooth 533	Open		Unkn.	125
XX	Out of Danger 56/B	Open		Unkn.	325
1993	Parade Of Lights 616	Open		Unkn.	275
XX	The Photographer 178	Open		Unkn.	315
1995	Pixie 768	Open		Unkn.	120
XX	Playmates 58/2/0	Open		Unkn.	165
XX	Playmates 58/0	Open		Unkn.	185
XX	Playmates 58/I	Open		Unkn.	310
1994	The Poet 397/I	Open		220.00	250
1989	Postman 119/2/0	Open		Unkn.	160
XX	Postman Sampler 119/2/0	Open		Unkn.	160
XX	Postman 119	Open		Unkn.	225
1997	Practice Makes Perfect (w/wooden rocker) 771	Open		250.00	250
XX	Prayer Before Battle 20	Open		Unkn.	185
1996	Pretty Please 489	Open		120.00	120
1992	The Professor 320	Open		Unkn.	225
1995	Puppy Love Display Plaque 767	Closed	1995	Unkn.	265
XX	Retreat to Safety 201/2/0	Open		Unkn.	180
XX	Retreat to Safety 201/I	Open		Unkn.	350
XX	Ride into Christmas 396/2/0	Open		Unkn.	260
XX	Ride into Christmas 396/I	Open		Unkn.	485
XX	Ring Around the Rosie 348	Open		Unkn.	2860
XX	The Run-A-Way 327	Open		Unkn.	280
1992	Scamp 553	Open		Unkn.	120
XX	School Boy 82/2/0	Open		Unkn.	160
XX	School Boy 82/0	Open		Unkn.	225
XX	School Boy 82/II	Open		Unkn.	500
XX	School Boys 170/I	Open		Unkn.	1320
XX	School Girl 81/2/0	Open		Unkn.	160
XX	School Girl 81/0	Open		Unkn.	225
XX	School Girls 177/I	Open		Unkn.	1320
1997	School's Out 538	Open		170.00	170
XX	Sensitive Hunter 6/2/0	Open		Unkn.	165
XX	Sensitive Hunter 6/0	Open		Unkn.	225
XX	Sensitive Hunter 6/I	Open		Unkn.	280
XX	Serenade 85/4/0	Open		Unkn.	115
XX	Serenade 85/0	Open		Unkn.	150
XX	Serenade 85/II	Open		Unkn.	500
XX	She Loves Me, She Loves Me Not 174	Open		Unkn.	220
1996	Shepherd Boy 395/0	Open		295.00	295
XX	Shepherd's Boy 64	Open		Unkn.	260
XX	Shining Light 358	Open		Unkn.	100
XX	Sing Along 433	Open		Unkn.	310
XX	Sing With Me 405	Open		Unkn.	350
XX	Singing Lesson 63	Open		Unkn.	135
1995	Sister (Perpetual Calendar) 788B	Open		295.00	295
XX	Sister 98/2/0	Open		Unkn.	160
XX	Sister 98/0	Open		Unkn.	230
XX	Skier 59	Open		Unkn.	225
1990	Sleep Tight 424	Open		Unkn.	245
XX	Smart Little Sister 346	Open		Unkn.	275
XX	Soldier Boy 332	Open		Unkn.	240
XX	Soloist 135/4/0	Open		Unkn.	115
XX	Soloist 135	Open		Unkn.	150
1988	Song of Praise 454	Open		Unkn.	115
1988	Sound the Trumpet 457	Open		Unkn.	120
1988	Sounds of the Mandolin 438	Open		Unkn.	140
XX	Spring Dance 353/0	Open		Unkn.	350
XX	St. George 55	Open		Unkn.	350
XX	Star Gazer 132	Open		Unkn.	230
XX	A Stitch in Time 255/4/0	Open		Unkn.	115
XX	A Stitch in Time 255/I	Open		Unkn.	325
XX	Stormy Weather 71/2/0	Open		Unkn.	330
XX	Stormy Weather 71/I	Open		Unkn.	495
1992	Storybook Time 458	Open		Unkn.	440
XX	Street Singer 131	Open		Unkn.	220
XX	Surprise 94/3/0	Open		Unkn.	170
XX	Surprise 94/I	Open		Unkn.	325
XX	Sweet Greetings 352	Open		Unkn.	200
XX	Sweet Music 186	Open		Unkn.	225
XX	Telling Her Secret 196/0	Open		Unkn.	330
1997	Thanksgiving Prayer 641/4/0	Open		120.00	120
1997	Thanksgiving Prayer 641/0	Open		180.00	180
XX	Thoughtful 415	Open		Unkn.	245
XX	Timid Little Sister 394	Open		Unkn.	485
1995	To Keep You Warm w/ Wooden Chair 759	Open		Unkn.	230
XX	To Market 49/3/0	Open		Unkn.	175
XX	To Market 49/0	Open		Unkn.	325
1997	Trio of Wishes 721	20,000		475.00	475
XX	Trumpet Boy 97	Open		Unkn.	150
1989	Tuba Player 437	Open		Unkn.	300
XX	Tuneful Angel 359	Open		Unkn.	100
1996	A Tuneful Trio	20,000		450.00	475
XX	Umbrella Boy 152/A/0	Open		Unkn.	650
XX	Umbrella Boy 152/A/II	Open		Unkn.	1600
XX	Umbrella Girl 152/B/0	Open		Unkn.	650
XX	Umbrella Girl 152/B/II	Open		Unkn.	1600
XX	Village Boy 51/3/0	Open		Unkn.	130
XX	Village Boy 51/2/0	Open		Unkn.	165
XX	Village Boy 51/0	Open		Unkn.	280
XX	Visiting an Invalid 382	Open		Unkn.	225
XX	Volunteers 50/2/0	Open		Unkn.	245
XX	Volunteers 50/0	Open		Unkn.	330
XX	Waiter 154/0	Open		Unkn.	240
XX	Waiter 154/I	Open		Unkn.	325
1989	Wash Day 321/4/0	Open		Unkn.	115
XX	Wash Day 321/I	Open		Unkn.	325
XX	Watchful Angel 194	Open		Unkn.	340
XX	Wayside Devotion 28/II	Open		Unkn.	450
XX	Wayside Devotion 28/III	Open		Unkn.	600
XX	Wayside Harmony 111/3/0	Open		Unkn.	165
XX	Wayside Harmony 111/I	Open		Unkn.	310
1993	We Come In Peace (Commemorative) 754	Open		385.00	385
XX	We Congratulate 214/E/I	Open		Unkn.	180
XX	We Congratulate 220	Open		Unkn.	170
XX	Weary Wanderer 204	Open		Unkn.	280
1990	What's New? 418	Open		Unkn.	310
XX	Which Hand? 258	Open		Unkn.	225
1992	Whistler's Duet 413	Open		Unkn.	310
XX	Whitsuntide 163	Open		Unkn.	330
1988	A Winter Song 476	Open		Unkn.	125
XX	With Loving Greetings 309	Open		Unkn.	220
XX	Worship 84/0	Open		Unkn.	180

M.I. Hummel Collectibles Figurines Retired - M.I. Hummel

YEAR ISSUE		EDITION LIMIT	YEAR RETD.	ISSUE PRICE	*QUOTE U.S.$
1947	Accordion Boy 185	Closed	1994	Unkn.	200-700
1939	Duet 130	Closed	1995	Unkn.	280-850
1937	Farewell 65 TMK1-5	Closed	1993	Unkn.	250-700
1937	Globe Trotter 79 TMK1-7	Closed	1991	Unkn.	200-500
XX	Happy Pastime 69	Closed	1996	Unkn.	175
1937	Lost Sheep 68/0 TMK1-7	Closed	1992	Unkn.	350
1955	Lost Sheep 68/2/0 TMK2-7	Closed	1992	7.50	125-300
1935	Puppy Love I TMK1-6	Closed	1988	125.00	350-700
1948	Signs Of Spring 203/2/0 TMK2-6	Closed	1990	120.00	250-900
1948	Signs Of Spring 203/I TMK2-6	Closed	1990	155.00	295-750
1935	Strolling Along 5 TMK1-6	Closed	1989	115.00	265-750

M.I. Hummel Collectibles Madonna Figurines - M.I. Hummel

YEAR ISSUE		EDITION LIMIT	YEAR RETD.	ISSUE PRICE	*QUOTE U.S.$
XX	Flower Madonna, color 10/I/II	Open		Unkn.	470
1996	Flower Madonna, white 10 (Commemorative)	Closed	1996	225.00	225
XX	Madonna with Halo, color 45/I/6	Open		Unkn.	135

M.I. Hummel Collectibles Nativity Components - M. I. Hummel, unless otherwise noted

YEAR ISSUE		EDITION LIMIT	YEAR RETD.	ISSUE PRICE	*QUOTE U.S.$
XX	12-Pc. Set Figs. only, Color, 214/A/M/I, B/I, A/K/I, F/I G/I J/I K/I, L/I, M/I, N/I, O/I, 366/I	Open		Unkn.	1680
XX	Angel Serenade 214/D/I	Open		Unkn.	100
XX	Camel Kneeling - Goebel	Open		Unkn.	275
XX	Camel Lying - Goebel	Open		Unkn.	275
XX	Camel Standing - Goebel	Open		Unkn.	275
XX	Donkey 214/J/0	Open		Unkn.	55
XX	Donkey 214/J/I	Open		Unkn.	75

*Quotes have been rounded up to nearest dollar

YEAR ISSUE		EDITION LIMIT	YEAR RETD.	ISSUE PRICE	*QUOTE U.S. $
XX	Flying Angel/color 366/I	Open		Unkn.	140
XX	Good Night 214/C/I	Open		Unkn.	100
XX	Holy Family, 3 Pcs., Color 214/A/M/0, B/0, A/K/0	Open		Unkn.	335
XX	Holy Family, 3 Pcs., Color 214/A/M/I, B/I, A/K/I	Open		Unkn.	460
XX	Infant Jesus 214/A/K/0	Open		Unkn.	45
XX	Infant Jesus 214/A/K/I	Open		Unkn.	70
XX	King, Kneeling 214/M/I	Open		Unkn.	195
XX	King, Kneeling 214M/0	Open		Unkn.	155
XX	King, Kneeling w/ Box 214/N/0	Open		Unkn.	150
XX	King, Kneeling w/Box 214/N/I	Open		Unkn.	175
XX	King, Moorish 214/L/0	Open		Unkn.	165
XX	King, Moorish 214/L/I	Open		Unkn.	200
XX	Lamb 214/O/0	Open		Unkn.	22
XX	Lamb 214/O/I	Open		Unkn.	22
XX	Little Tooter 214/H/II	Open		Unkn.	135
XX	Little Tooter 214/H/0	Open		Unkn.	110
XX	Little Tooter 214/H/I	Open		Unkn.	135
XX	Little Tooter 214/H/O	Open		Unkn.	110
XX	Madonna 214/A/M/0	Open		Unkn.	145
XX	Madonna 214/A/M/I	Open		Unkn.	195
XX	Ox 214/K/0	Open		Unkn.	55
XX	Ox 214/K/I	Open		Unkn.	75
XX	Shepherd Boy 214/G/I	Open		Unkn.	145
XX	Shepherd Kneeling 214/G/0	Open		Unkn.	130
XX	Shepherd Standing 214/F/0	Open		Unkn.	165
XX	Shepherd w/Sheep-1 piece 214/F/I	Open		Unkn.	195
XX	Small Camel Kneeling - Goebel	Open		Unkn.	220
XX	Small Camel Lying - Goebel	Open		Unkn.	220
XX	Small Camel Standing - Goebel	Open		Unkn.	220
XX	St. Joseph 214/B/0	Open		Unkn.	145
XX	St. Joseph color 214/B/I	Open		Unkn.	195
XX	Stable only fits12 or 16-pc. HUM214/II Set	Open		Unkn.	110
XX	Stable only, fits 16-piece HUM260 Set	Open		Unkn.	440
XX	Stable only, fits 3-pc. HUM214 Set	Open		Unkn.	50
XX	We Congratulate 214/E/I	Open		Unkn.	180

M.I. Hummel Disneyana Figurines - M.I. Hummel

YEAR ISSUE		EDITION LIMIT	YEAR RETD.	ISSUE PRICE	*QUOTE U.S. $
1992	Two Merry Wanderers 022074	1,500	1992	250.00	950-1250
1993	Two Little Drummers	1,500	1993	325.00	500-800
1994	Minnie Be Patient	1,500	1994	395.00	470-550
1995	For Father	1,500	1995	450.00	600
1995	Grandpa's Boys	1,500	1995	340.00	340
1996	Minnie For Mother	1,200	1996	470.00	470

M.I. Hummel First Edition Miniatures - M.I. Hummel

YEAR ISSUE		EDITION LIMIT	YEAR RETD.	ISSUE PRICE	*QUOTE U.S. $
1991	Accordion Boy -37225	Suspd.		105.00	105-135
1989	Apple Tree Boy -37219	Suspd.		115.00	130-200
1990	Baker -37222	Suspd.		100.00	105-130
1992	Bavarian Church (Display) -37370	Closed	N/A	60.00	60-70
1988	Bavarian Cottage (Display) -37355	Closed	N/A	60.00	75-90
1990	Bavarian Marketsquare Bridge(Display) -37358	Closed	N/A	110.00	110-125
1988	Bavarian Village (Display) -37356	Closed	N/A	100.00	105
1991	Busy Student -37226	Suspd.		105.00	105-130
1990	Cinderella -37223	Suspd.		115.00	125
1991	Countryside School (Display) -37365	Closed	N/A	100.00	100
1989	Doll Bath -37214	Suspd.		95.00	110
1992	Goose Girl -37238	Suspd.		130.00	180-225
1989	Little Fiddler -37211	Suspd.		90.00	115
1989	Little Sweeper -37212	Suspd.		90.00	115
1990	Marketsquare Flower Stand (Display) -37360	Closed	N/A	35.00	50-80
1990	Marketsquare Hotel (Display) -37359	Closed	N/A	70.00	90-125
1989	Merry Wanderer -37213	Suspd.		95.00	115
1991	Merry Wanderer Dealer Plaque -37229	Closed	N/A	130.00	135
1989	Postman -37217	Suspd.		95.00	120
1991	Roadside Shrine (Display)-37366	Closed	N/A	60.00	60
1992	School Boy -37236	Suspd.		120.00	120-150
1991	Serenade -37228	Suspd.		105.00	105-120
1992	Snow-Covered Mountain (Display)-37371	Closed	N/A	100.00	100
1989	Stormy Weather -37215	Suspd.		115.00	130-150
1992	Trees (Display)-37369	Closed	N/A	40.00	40-50
1989	Visiting an Invalid -37218	Suspd.		105.00	115-130
1990	Waiter -37221	Suspd.		100.00	115-135
1992	Wayside Harmony -37237	Suspd.		140.00	165-180
1991	We Congratulate -37227	Suspd.		130.00	130

M.I. Hummel Fonts - M.I. Hummel

YEAR ISSUE		EDITION LIMIT	YEAR RETD.	ISSUE PRICE	*QUOTE U.S. $
XX	Angel Cloud 205	Open		55.00	55
XX	Angel Duet 146	Open		55.00	55
XX	Angel Facing Left 91/A	Open		45.00	45
XX	Angel Facing Right 91/B	Open		45.00	45
XX	Angel Shrine 147	Open		55.00	55
XX	Angel Sitting 22/0	Open		45.00	45
XX	Angel w/Bird 167	Open		55.00	55
XX	Child Jesus 26/0	Open		45.00	45
XX	Child w/Flowers 36/0	Open		45.00	45
XX	Good Shepherd 35/0	Open		45.00	45
XX	Guardian Angel 248/0	Open		55.00	55
XX	Heavenly Angel 207	Open		55.00	55
XX	Holy Family 246	Open		55.00	55
XX	Madonna & Child 243	Open		55.00	55
XX	White Angel 75	Open		45.00	45
XX	Worship 164	Open		55.00	55

M.I. Hummel Hummel Scapes - M.I. Hummel

YEAR ISSUE		EDITION LIMIT	YEAR RETD.	ISSUE PRICE	*QUOTE U.S.$
1997	Around The Town	Open		75.00	75
1997	Castle On A Hill	Open		75.00	75
1997	Going To Church	Open		75.00	75
1996	Heavenly Harmonies	Open		100.00	100
1996	Home Sweet Home	Open		130.00	130
1996	Little Music Makers	Open		130.00	130
1997	Strolling Through The Park	Open		75.00	75

M.I. Hummel Pen Pals - M.I. Hummel

YEAR ISSUE		EDITION LIMIT	YEAR RETD.	ISSUE PRICE	*QUOTE U.S.$
1995	For Mother 257/5/0	Open		55.00	55
1995	March Winds 43/5/0	Open		55.00	55
1995	One For You, One For Me 482/5/0	Open		55.00	55
1995	Sister 98/5/0	Open		55.00	55
1995	Soloist 135/5/0	Open		55.00	55
1995	Village Boy 151/5/0	Open		55.00	55

M.I. Hummel Tree Toppers - M.I. Hummel

YEAR ISSUE		EDITION LIMIT	YEAR RETD.	ISSUE PRICE	*QUOTE U.S.$
1994	Heavenly Angel 755	Open		450.00	495

M.I. Hummel Vingettes w/Solitary Domes - M.I. Hummel

YEAR ISSUE		EDITION LIMIT	YEAR RETD.	ISSUE PRICE	*QUOTE U.S.$
1992	Bakery Day w/Baker & Waiter 37726	3,000		225.00	225
1992	The Flower Market w/Cinderella 37729	3,000		135.00	135
1993	The Mail Is Here Clock Tower 826504	Open		495.00	575
1995	Ring Around the Rosie Musical 826101	10,000		675.00	675
1992	Winterfest w/Ride Into Christmas 37728	5,000		195.00	195

M.I. Hummel's Temporarily Out of Production (including trademarks) - M.I. Hummel

YEAR ISSUE		EDITION LIMIT	YEAR RETD.	ISSUE PRICE	*QUOTE U.S.$
XX	16-Pc. Set Figs. only, Color, 214/A/M/I, B/I, A/K/I, C/I, D/I, E/I, F/I, G/I, H/I, J/I, K/I, L/I, M/I, N/I, O/I, 366/I	Suspd.		Unkn.	1990
XX	17-Pc. Set Large Color 16 Figs.& Wooden Stable 260 A-R	Suspd.		Unkn.	4540
XX	Angel Serenade 260/E	Suspd.		Unkn.	345-445
XX	Apple Tree Boy 142/X	Suspd.		Unkn.	17000
XX	Apple Tree Girl 141/X	Suspd.		Unkn.	17000
XX	Blessed Child 78/I/83	Suspd.		Unkn.	35
XX	Blessed Child 78/II/83	Suspd.		Unkn.	50
XX	Blessed Child 78/III/83	Suspd.		Unkn.	60
XX	Bookworm 3/II	Suspd.		Unkn.	675-1350
XX	Bookworm 3/III	Suspd.		Unkn.	1195-2100
XX	Celestial Musician 188/I	Suspd.		Unkn.	255-475
XX	Christ Child 18	Suspd.		Unkn.	130-325
XX	Donkey 260/L	Suspd.		Unkn.	135
XX	Festival Harmony, with Flute 173/II	Suspd.		Unkn.	400-1000
XX	Festival Harmony, with Mandolin 172/II	Suspd.		Unkn.	400-1000
XX	Flower Madonna, color 10/III/II	Suspd.		Unkn.	600-750
XX	Flower Madonna, white 10/I/W	Suspd.		Unkn.	165-420
XX	Flower Madonna, white 10/III/W	Suspd.		Unkn.	470-750
XX	Going to Grandma's 52/I	Suspd.		Unkn.	350-900
XX	Good Night 260/D	Suspd.		Unkn.	145
XX	Goose Girl 47/II	Suspd.		Unkn.	410
XX	Happy Traveler 109/II	Suspd.		Unkn.	350-975
XX	Hear Ye! Hear Ye! 15/II	Suspd.		Unkn.	375-1500
XX	Heavenly Angel 21/II	Suspd.		Unkn.	415-1025
XX	Heavenly Protection 88/II	Suspd.		Unkn.	600-900
XX	Hello 124/I	Suspd.		Unkn.	175-385
XX	Holy Child 70	Suspd.		Unkn.	160-400
XX	Hummel Display Plaque 187	Suspd.		Unkn.	125-150
XX	Infant Jesus 260/C	Suspd.		Unkn.	120
1985	Jubilee 416 TMK6	Suspd.		200.00	275-400
XX	King, Kneeling 260/P	Suspd.		Unkn.	480
XX	King, Moorish 260/N	Suspd.		Unkn.	430-500
XX	King, Standing 260/O	Suspd.		Unkn.	300-500
XX	Little Band 392	Suspd.		Unkn.	250-350
XX	Little Cellist 89/II	Suspd.		Unkn.	400-650
XX	Little Fiddler 2/I	Suspd.		Unkn.	260-650
XX	Little Fiddler 2/II	Suspd.		Unkn.	1100-3000
XX	Little Fiddler 2/III	Suspd.		Unkn.	1200-3500
XX	Little Tooter 260/K	Suspd.		Unkn.	170-195
XX	Lullaby 24/III	Suspd.		Unkn.	450-1800
XX	Madonna 260/A	Suspd.		Unkn.	590
XX	Madonna Holding Child, color 151/II	Suspd.		Unkn.	115
XX	Madonna Holding Child, white 151/W	Suspd.		Unkn.	320
XX	Madonna Praying, color 46/III/6	Suspd.		Unkn.	140-400
XX	Madonna Praying, white 46/0/W	Suspd.		Unkn.	40-195
XX	Madonna Praying, white 46/I/W	Suspd.		Unkn.	70-175
XX	Madonna w/o Halo, color 46/I/6	Suspd.		Unkn.	115-300
XX	Madonna w/o Halo, white 45/I/W	Suspd.		Unkn.	70-175
XX	Madonna w/o Halo, white 46/I/W	Suspd.		Unkn.	70-175
XX	Meditation 13/V	Suspd.		Unkn.	1200-5000
XX	Meditation, color 13/II	Suspd.		Unkn.	400-4500
XX	Merry Wanderer 7/II	Suspd.		Unkn.	850-2200
XX	Merry Wanderer 7/III	Suspd.		Unkn.	925-1300
XX	Merry Wanderer 7/X	Suspd.		Unkn.	12000-20000
XX	Merry Wanderer Stepbase 7/I	Suspd.		Unkn.	360-960
1995	Ooh My Tooth (Special Event) 533	Suspd.		Unkn.	125-175
XX	Ox 260/M	Suspd.		Unkn.	135
XX	School Boys 170/III	Suspd.		Unkn.	1600-2000
XX	School Girls 177/III	Suspd.		Unkn.	1500-2200
XX	Sensitive Hunter 6/II	Suspd.		Unkn.	400-1000
XX	Sheep (Lying) 260/R	Suspd.		Unkn.	100
XX	Sheep (Standing) w/ Lamb 260/H	Suspd.		Unkn.	110
XX	Shepherd Boy, Kneeling 260/J	Suspd.		Unkn.	300
XX	Shepherd, Standing 260/G	Suspd.		Unkn.	525
XX	Spring Cheer 72	Suspd.		Unkn.	165-500
XX	Spring Dance 353/I	Suspd.		Unkn.	500-750
XX	St. Joseph 260/B	Suspd.		Unkn.	520
1984	Supreme Protection 364 TMK6	Suspd.		150.00	350
XX	Telling Her Secret 196/I	Suspd.		Unkn.	430-800
XX	To Market 49/I	Suspd.		Unkn.	300-850
XX	Village Boy 51/I	Suspd.		Unkn.	250-650
XX	Volunteers 50/I	Suspd.		Unkn.	430-1400
XX	We Congratulate 260/F	Suspd.		Unkn.	400
XX	Worship 84/V	Suspd.		Unkn.	800-2800

Gorham

(Four Seasons) A Boy And His Dog - N. Rockwell

YEAR ISSUE		EDITION LIMIT	YEAR RETD.	ISSUE PRICE	*QUOTE U.S.$
1972	A Boy Meets His Dog	2,500	1980	200.00	1300-1575
1972	Adventurers Between Adventures	2,500	1980	Set	Set
1972	The Mysterious Malady	2,500	1980	Set	Set
1972	Pride of Parenthood	2,500	1980	Set	Set

(Four Seasons) A Helping Hand - N. Rockwell

YEAR ISSUE		EDITION LIMIT	YEAR RETD.	ISSUE PRICE	*QUOTE U.S.$
1980	Year End Court	2,500	1980	650.00	650-700
1980	Closed For Business	2,500	1980	Set	Set
1980	Swatter's Right	2,500	1980	Set	Set
1980	Coal Seasons Coming	2,500	1980	Set	Set

(Four Seasons) Dad's Boy - N. Rockwell

YEAR ISSUE		EDITION LIMIT	YEAR RETD.	ISSUE PRICE	*QUOTE U.S.$
1981	Ski Skills	2,500	1990	750.00	750-800
1981	In His Spirit	2,500	1990	Set	Set
1981	Trout Dinner	2,500	1990	Set	Set
1981	Careful Aim	2,500	1990	Set	Set

(Four Seasons) Four Ages of Love - N. Rockwell

YEAR ISSUE		EDITION LIMIT	YEAR RETD.	ISSUE PRICE	*QUOTE U.S.$
1974	Gaily Sharing Vintage Times	2,500	1980	300.00	600-1250
1974	Sweet Song So Young	2,500	1980	Set	Set
1974	Flowers In Tender Bloom	2,500	1980	Set	Set
1974	Fondly Do We Remember	2,500	1980	Set	Set

(Four Seasons) Going On Sixteen - N. Rockwell

YEAR ISSUE		EDITION LIMIT	YEAR RETD.	ISSUE PRICE	*QUOTE U.S.$
1978	Chilling Chore	2,500	1980	400.00	650-675
1978	Sweet Serenade	2,500	1980	Set	Set
1978	Shear Agony	2,500	1980	Set	Set
1978	Pilgrimage	2,500	1980	Set	Set

(Four Seasons) Grand Pals - N. Rockwell

YEAR ISSUE		EDITION LIMIT	YEAR RETD.	ISSUE PRICE	*QUOTE U.S.$
1977	Snow Sculpturing	2,500	1980	350.00	1000-1200
1977	Soaring Spirits	2,500	1980	Set	Set
1977	Fish Finders	2,500	1980	Set	Set
1977	Ghostly Gourds	2,500	1980	Set	Set

(Four Seasons) Grandpa and Me - N. Rockwell

YEAR ISSUE		EDITION LIMIT	YEAR RETD.	ISSUE PRICE	*QUOTE U.S.$
1975	Gay Blades	2,500	1980	300.00	800-1000
1975	Day Dreamers	2,500	1980	Set	Set
1975	Goin' Fishing	2,500	1980	Set	Set
1975	Pensive Pals	2,500	1980	Set	Set

(Four Seasons) Life With Father - N. Rockwell

YEAR ISSUE		EDITION LIMIT	YEAR RETD.	ISSUE PRICE	*QUOTE U.S.$
1983	Big Decision	2,500	1990	250.00	250
1983	Blasting Out	2,500	1990	Set	Set
1983	Cheering The Champs	2,500	1990	Set	Set
1983	A Tough One	2,500	1990	Set	Set

(Four Seasons) Me and My Pal - N. Rockwell

YEAR ISSUE		EDITION LIMIT	YEAR RETD.	ISSUE PRICE	*QUOTE U.S.$
1976	A Licking Good Bath	2,500	1980	300.00	1200
1976	Young Man's Fancy	2,500	1980	Set	Set
1976	Fisherman's Paradise	2,500	1980	Set	Set
1976	Disastrous Daring	2,500	1980	Set	Set

(Four Seasons) Old Buddies - N. Rockwell

YEAR ISSUE		EDITION LIMIT	YEAR RETD.	ISSUE PRICE	*QUOTE U.S.$
1984	Shared Success	2,500	1990	250.00	250
1984	Hasty Retreat	2,500	1990	Set	Set
1984	Final Speech	2,500	1990	Set	Set
1984	Endless Debate	2,500	1990	Set	Set

(Four Seasons) Old Timers - N. Rockwell

YEAR ISSUE		EDITION LIMIT	YEAR RETD.	ISSUE PRICE	*QUOTE U.S.$
1982	Canine Solo	2,500	1990	250.00	250
1982	Sweet Surprise	2,500	1990	Set	Set
1982	Lazy Days	2,500	1990	Set	Set
1982	Fancy Footwork	2,500	1990	Set	Set

(Four Seasons) Tender Years - N. Rockwell

YEAR ISSUE		EDITION LIMIT	YEAR RETD.	ISSUE PRICE	*QUOTE U.S.$
1979	New Year Look	2,500	1979	500.00	1200
1979	Spring Tonic	2,500	1979	Set	Set
1979	Cool Aid	2,500	1979	Set	Set
1979	Chilly Reception	2,500	1979	Set	Set

(Four Seasons) Traveling Salesman - N. Rockwell

YEAR ISSUE		EDITION LIMIT	YEAR RETD.	ISSUE PRICE	*QUOTE U.S.$
1985	Horse Trader	2,500	1985	275.00	250-275
1985	Expert Salesman	2,500	1985	Set	Set
1985	Traveling Salesman	2,500	1985	Set	Set
1985	Country Pedlar	2,500	1985	Set	Set

(Four Seasons) Young Love - N. Rockwell

YEAR ISSUE		EDITION LIMIT	YEAR RETD.	ISSUE PRICE	*QUOTE U.S.$
1973	Downhill Daring	2,500	1973	250.00	1100
1973	Beguiling Buttercup	2,500	1973	Set	Set
1973	Flying High	2,500	1973	Set	Set

*Quotes have been rounded up to nearest dollar

YEAR ISSUE		EDITION LIMIT	YEAR RETD.	ISSUE PRICE	*QUOTE U.S.$
1973	A Scholarly Pace	2,500	1973	Set	Set

Miniature Christmas Figurines - Various

YEAR ISSUE		EDITION LIMIT	YEAR RETD.	ISSUE PRICE	*QUOTE U.S.$
1979	Tiny Tim - N. Rockwell	Yr.Iss.	1979	15.00	20
1980	Santa Plans His Trip - N. Rockwell	Yr.Iss.	1980	15.00	15
1981	Yuletide Reckoning - N. Rockwell	Yr.Iss.	1981	20.00	20
1982	Checking Good Deeds - N. Rockwell	Yr.Iss.	1982	20.00	20
1983	Santa's Friend - N. Rockwell	Yr.Iss.	1983	20.00	20
1984	Downhill Daring - N. Rockwell	Yr.Iss.	1984	20.00	20
1985	Christmas Santa - T. Nast	Yr.Iss.	1985	20.00	20
1986	Christmas Santa - T. Nast	Yr.Iss.	1986	25.00	25
1987	Annual Thomas Nast Santa - T. Nast	Yr.Iss.	1987	25.00	25

Miniatures - N. Rockwell

YEAR ISSUE		EDITION LIMIT	YEAR RETD.	ISSUE PRICE	*QUOTE U.S.$
1982	The Annual Visit	Closed	1990	50.00	75
1981	At the Vets	Closed	1990	27.50	40
1987	Babysitter	15,000	1990	75.00	75
1981	Beguiling Buttercup	Closed	1990	45.00	45
1985	Best Friends	Closed	1990	27.50	28
1987	Between The Acts	15,000	1990	60.00	60
1981	Boy Meets His Dog	Closed	1990	37.50	38
1984	Careful Aims	Closed	1990	55.00	55
1987	Cinderella	15,000	1990	70.00	75
1981	Downhill Daring	Closed	1990	45.00	75
1985	Engineer	Closed	1990	55.00	55
1981	Flowers in Tender Bloom	Closed	1990	60.00	60
1986	Football Season	Closed	1990	60.00	60
1981	Gay Blades	Closed	1990	45.00	75
1984	Ghostly Gourds	Closed	1990	60.00	60
1984	Goin Fishing	Closed	1990	60.00	60
1986	The Graduate	Closed	1990	30.00	40
1984	In His Spirit	Closed	1990	60.00	60
1984	Independence	Closed	1990	60.00	80
1986	Lemonade Stand	Closed	1990	60.00	60
1986	Little Angel	Closed	1990	50.00	60
1985	Little Red Truck	Closed	1990	25.00	25
1982	Marriage License	Closed	1990	60.00	75
1987	The Milkmaid	15,000	1990	80.00	85
1986	Morning Walk	Closed	1990	60.00	60
1985	Muscle Bound	Closed	1990	30.00	30
1985	New Arrival	Closed	1990	32.50	35
1984	The Oculist	Closed	1990	60.00	80
1986	The Old Sign Painter	Closed	1990	70.00	80
1984	Pride of Parenthood	Closed	1990	50.00	50
1987	The Prom Dress	15,000	1990	75.00	75
1982	The Runaway	Closed	1990	50.00	50
1984	Shear Agony	Closed	1990	60.00	60
1986	Shoulder Ride	Closed	1990	50.00	65
1981	Snow Sculpture	Closed	1990	45.00	70
1985	Spring Checkup	Closed	1990	60.00	60
1987	Springtime	15,000	1990	65.00	75
1987	Starstruck	15,000	1990	75.00	80
1981	Sweet Serenade	Closed	1990	45.00	45
1981	Sweet Song So Young	Closed	1990	55.00	55
1985	To Love & Cherish	Closed	1990	32.50	35
1982	Triple Self Portrait	Closed	1990	60.00	90-175
1983	Trout Dinner	15,000	1990	60.00	60
1982	Vintage Times	Closed	1990	50.00	50
1986	Welcome Mat	Closed	1990	70.00	75
1984	Years End Court	Closed	1990	60.00	60
1981	Young Man's Fancy	Closed	1990	55.00	55

Parasol Lady - Unknown

YEAR ISSUE		EDITION LIMIT	YEAR RETD.	ISSUE PRICE	*QUOTE U.S.$
1991	On the Boardwalk	Closed	1993	95.00	95
1994	Sunday Promenade	Closed	1993	95.00	95
1994	At The Fair	Closed	1993	95.00	95

Rockwell - N. Rockwell

YEAR ISSUE		EDITION LIMIT	YEAR RETD.	ISSUE PRICE	*QUOTE U.S.$
1983	Antique Dealer RW48	7,500	1990	130.00	200
1982	April Fool's (At The Curiosity Shop) RW39	Closed	1990	55.00	100-110
1974	At The Vets RW4	Closed	1990	25.00	125
1974	Batter Up RW6	Closed	1990	40.00	150-200
1975	Boy And His Dog RW9	Closed	1990	38.00	150
1974	Captain RW8	Closed	1990	45.00	95
1984	Card Tricks	7,500	1990	110.00	180
1978	Choosing Up RW24	Closed	1990	85.00	275
1981	Christmas Dancers RW37	7,500	1990	130.00	195
1988	Confrontation	15,000	1990	75.00	75
1988	Cramming	15,000	1990	80.00	80
1981	Day in the Life Boy II RW34	Closed	1990	75.00	95
1982	A Day in the Life Boy III RW40	Closed	1990	85.00	95
1982	A Day in the Life Girl III RW41	Closed	1990	85.00	150
1988	The Diary	15,000	1990	80.00	80
1988	Dolores & Eddie NRM59	15,000	1990	75.00	80
1986	Drum For Tommy RW53	Annual	1986	90.00	N/A
1983	Facts of Life RW45	7,500	1990	110.00	180
1974	Fishing RW5	Closed	1990	50.00	175
1988	Gary Cooper in Hollywood	15,000	1990	90.00	90
1976	God Rest Ye Merry Gentlemen RW13	Closed	1990	50.00	1000-1500
1988	Home for the Holidays	7,500	1990	100.00	100
1976	Independence RW15	Closed	1990	40.00	150
1980	Jolly Coachman RW33	7,500	1990	75.00	175
1982	Marriage License (10 3/4") RW38	5,000	1990	110.00	400-600
1976	Marriage License (6 1/4") RW16	Closed	1990	50.00	275
1982	Merrie Christmas RW43	7,500	1990	75.00	150
1978	Missed RW23	Closed	1990	85.00	275
1974	Missing Tooth RW2	Closed	1990	30.00	150
1975	No Swimming RW18	Closed	1990	35.00	175
1976	The Oculist RW17	Closed	1990	50.00	175
1978	Oh Yeah RW22	Closed	1990	85.00	275
1975	Old Mill Pond RW11	Closed	1990	45.00	145
1985	The Old Sign Painter	7,500	1990	130.00	210
1977	Pride of Parenthood RW18	Closed	1990	50.00	125
1985	Puppet Maker	7,500	1990	130.00	130-200
1987	Santa Planning His Annual Visit	7,500	1990	95.00	95
1984	Santa's Friend	7,500	1990	75.00	160
1976	Saying Grace (5 1/2") RW12	5,000	1990	75.00	275
1982	Saying Grace (8") RW42	Closed	1990	110.00	500-600
1984	Serenade	7,500	1990	95.00	165
1974	Skating RW7	Closed	1990	37.50	140
1976	Tackled (Ad Stand)	Closed	1990	35.00	125
1982	Tackled (Rockwell Name Signed) RW8662	Closed	1990	45.00	100
1974	Tiny Tim RW3	Closed	1990	30.00	125
1980	Triple Self Portrait (10 1/2") RW32	5,000	1990	300.00	600
1979	Triple Self Portrait (7 1/2") RW27	Closed	1990	125.00	425
1974	Weighing In RW1	Closed	1990	40.00	150
1981	Wet Sport RW36	Closed	1990	85.00	100

Great American Taylor Collectibles

Great American Collectors' Club - L. Smith

YEAR ISSUE		EDITION LIMIT	YEAR RETD.	ISSUE PRICE	*QUOTE U.S.$
1993	William Claus-USA 700s	1,392	1994	35.00	75-125
1994	Winston-England 716	836	1995	35.00	60
1995	Timothy Claus-Ireland 717	946	1996	35.00	50
1996	Palmer-USA 723	12/97		50.00	50
1997	Bowline-USA 734	12/98		50.00	50

Jim Clement Collectors' Club - L. Smith

YEAR ISSUE		EDITION LIMIT	YEAR RETD.	ISSUE PRICE	*QUOTE U.S.$
1995	Kris Jingle 817	Retrd.	1996	70.00	80
1996	Big Catch 830	12/97		60.00	60
1997	Mogul Master 839	12/98		70.00	70

Jim Clement Collection - J. Clement

YEAR ISSUE		EDITION LIMIT	YEAR RETD.	ISSUE PRICE	*QUOTE U.S.$
1994	Americana Patriotic Santa 807	329	1994	20.00	20
1994	Bearded Shorty Santa 812	533	1994	13.50	16
1994	Mrs. Clement's Santa 808	259	1994	17.00	17
1994	Santa High Hat 815	290	1994	30.00	35
1994	Santa w/Tree 804	425	1994	15.00	18
1994	Day After Christmas 809	494	1995	16.50	17
1994	Down the Chimney Santa 814	426	1995	28.00	30
1994	Golfer Santa 806	684	1995	28.00	33
1994	Mr. Egg Santa 802	397	1995	19.50	22
1994	Sm. Hobby Horse Santa 803	468	1995	28.00	33
1994	Big Santa w/Toys 813	510	1996	70.00	75
1994	Night After Christmas 810	776	1996	16.50	17
1994	Noah Santa 805	788	1996	28.00	30
1994	Santa w/Rover 811	537	1996	20.00	20
1994	Tennis Santa 816	656	1996	28.00	29
1995	Doe a Deer 818	12/97		29.00	30
1995	Ho! Ho! Ho! 819	12/97		11.50	12
1995	Mountain Dream 821	12/97		27.00	30
1995	Silent Night 820	12/97		29.00	32
1995	Visions of Sugar Plums 822	12/97		23.00	25
1996	Heading South 828	12/98		32.00	32
1996	Hogan 827	12/98		29.00	29
1996	Night Cats 825	12/98		30.00	30
1996	Radar 826	12/98		13.00	13
1996	Ted 829	12/98		29.00	29
1997	Blarney 833	12/99		27.00	27
1997	Santa Teddy & Toys 834	12/99		25.00	25
1997	Duke N' Duchess 835	12/99		32.00	32
1997	Santa Card Holder 836	12/99		25.00	25
1997	Grandpa 837	12/99		35.00	35

Lamp Collection - J. Clement

YEAR ISSUE		EDITION LIMIT	YEAR RETD.	ISSUE PRICE	*QUOTE U.S.$
1995	Clementine Cat 55LNKS	12/97		70.00	79
1995	Kris Jingle 817LRS	12/97		99.00	99
1995	Toy Soldier 57LSS	12/97		80.00	89
1995	Uncle Sam 56LRS	12/97		80.00	89

Old World Santas - L. Smith

YEAR ISSUE		EDITION LIMIT	YEAR RETD.	ISSUE PRICE	*QUOTE U.S.$
1988	Jangle Claus-Ireland 335s	664	1990	20.00	145-160
1988	Hons Von Claus-Germany 337s	560	1990	20.00	145-160
1988	Ching Chang Claus-China 338s	570	1990	20.00	150-200
1988	Kris Kringle Claus-Switzerland 339s	607	1990	20.00	150-180
1988	Jingle Claus-England 336s	571	1990	20.00	150-180
1989	Rudy Claus-Austria 410s	709	1991	20.00	150
1989	Noel Claus-Belguim 412s	676	1991	20.00	150
1989	Pierre Claus-France 414s	702	1991	20.00	150
1989	Nicholai Claus-Russia 413s	768	1991	20.00	150
1989	Yule Claus-Germany 411s	565	1991	20.00	150
1990	Matts Claus-Sweden 430s	1,243	1992	20.00	95-130
1990	Vander Claus-Holland 433s	1,136	1992	20.00	95-130
1990	Sven Claus-Norway 432s	1,639	1992	20.00	95-130
1990	Cedric Claus-England 434s	1,087	1992	20.00	95-130
1990	Mario Claus-Italy 431s	887	1992	20.00	95-130
1991	Mitch Claus-England 437s	1,962	1993	25.00	80-110
1991	Samuel Claus-USA 436s	2,656	1993	25.00	80-110
1991	Duncan Claus-Scotland 439s	2,754	1993	25.00	65-80
1991	Benjamin Claus-Israel 438s	2,358	1993	25.00	80-110
1991	Boris Claus-Russia 435s	2,588	1993	25.00	80-110
1992	Mickey Claus-Ireland 701s	3,722	1994	25.00	75
1992	Jacques Claus-France 702s	2,792	1994	25.00	75
1992	Terry Claus-Denmark 703s	3,094	1994	25.00	75
1992	José Claus-Spain 704s	2,797	1994	25.00	65-75
1992	Stu Claus-Poland 705s	3,243	1994	25.00	75
1993	Otto Claus-Germany 707s	2,712	1995	27.50	75
1993	Franz Claus-Switzerland 706s	2,708	1995	27.50	75
1993	Bjorn Claus-Sweden 709s	2,749	1995	27.50	75
1993	Ryan Claus-Canada 710s	2,868	1995	27.50	75
1993	Vito Claus-Italy 708s	2,784	1995	27.50	75
1994	Angus Claus-Scotland 713s	4,873	1996	27.50	32
1994	Ivan Claus-Russia 712s	3,176	1996	27.50	32
1994	Desmond Claus-England 715s	3,129	1996	27.50	32
1994	Gord Claus-Canada 714s	3,637	1996	27.50	32
1994	Wilhelm-Holland 711s	3,235	1996	27.50	32
1995	Tomba Claus-South Africa 718s	12/97		29.00	30
1995	Butch Claus-United States 719s	12/97		29.00	30
1995	Lars Claus-Norway 720s	12/97		29.00	30
1995	Stach Claus-Poland 721s	12/97		29.00	30
1995	Raymond Claus-Galapagos Islands 722s	12/97		29.00	30
1996	Gunther-Germany 724s	12/98		30.00	30
1996	Sean-Ireland 725s	12/98		30.00	30
1996	René-France 728s	12/98		30.00	30
1996	Manuel-Mexico 726s	12/98		30.00	30
1996	Zorba-Greece 727s	12/98		30.00	30
1997	Wenceslas-Czech Repub. 729s	12/99		30.00	30
1997	James-England 730s	12/99		30.00	30
1997	McDonald-Scotland 731s	12/99		30.00	30
1997	Gustav-Sweden 732s	12/99		30.00	30
1997	Guido-Italy 733s	12/99		30.00	30

Stars & Stripes Collection - J. Clement

YEAR ISSUE		EDITION LIMIT	YEAR RETD.	ISSUE PRICE	*QUOTE U.S.$
1996	American Glory 555	12/98		36.00	36
1996	Flying Sam 553	12/98		29.00	29
1996	Great American Chicken 552	12/98		39.00	39
1996	Small Sam 554	12/98		29.00	29
1997	Freedom Sam ss8	12/99		50.00	50
1997	Independence Sam ss11	12/99		35.00	35
1997	Robert E. Claus ss7	12/99		30.00	30
1997	Rocket Sam ss10	12/99		35.00	35
1996	Tall Sam 551	12/98		39.00	39
1997	Ulysses S. Claus ss6	12/99		30.00	30

Greenwich Workshop

Bronze - Various

YEAR ISSUE		EDITION LIMIT	YEAR RETD.	ISSUE PRICE	*QUOTE U.S.$
1994	Bird Hunters (Bronze) - J. Christensen	50	N/A	4500.00	4500
1990	The Candleman, AP (Bronze) - J. Christensen	100	N/A	2250.00	4500
1991	Comanche Rider - K. McCarthy	100	N/A	812.50	813
1989	The Fish Walker (Bronze) - J. Christensen	100	N/A	3200.00	4500
1991	Pony Express - K. McCarthy	10	N/A	934.00	934
1994	Thunder of Hooves - K. McCarthy	10	N/A	875.00	875

The Greenwich Workshop Collection - J. Christensen, unless otherwise noted

YEAR ISSUE		EDITION LIMIT	YEAR RETD.	ISSUE PRICE	*QUOTE U.S.$
1996	And They...Crooked House	Open		295.00	295
1996	Another Fish Act	2,500		350.00	350
1997	Bassoonist	1,500		395.00	395
1996	Bed Time Buddies - W. Bullas	Open		75.00	75
1996	Candleman	2,500		295.00	295
1996	Christmas Angel - W. Bullas	1,996	1996	75.00	75
1996	Christmas Elf - W. Bullas	1,996	1996	75.00	75
1997	Consultant - W. Bullas	Open		95.00	95
1996	The Dare Devil - W. Bullas	Open		75.00	75
1996	Ductor - W. Bullas	Open		75.00	75
1996	Fool and His Bunny - W. Bullas	Open		75.00	75
1997	Forest Fish Rider	2,500		175.00	175
1996	He Bought a Crooked Cat	Open		60.00	60
1996	Head of the Class - W. Bullas	Open		75.00	75
1996	Jack Be Nimble	Open		295.00	295
1996	Jailbirds - W. Bullas	Open		75.00	75
1996	Lawrence Pretended Not to Notice...	2,500		350.00	350
1996	Levi Levitates a Stone Fish	2,500		295.00	295
1996	Man Who Minds the Moon	2,500		295.00	295
1996	Mother Goose	Open		275.00	275
1995	Olde World Santa	950	1995	295.00	550
1996	The Oldest Angel	2,500		295.00	295
1996	The Responsible Woman	2,500		595.00	595
1997	The Scholar	1,700		375.00	375
1996	There Was a Crooked Man...	Open		225.00	225
1996	Three Blind Mice: Fluffy	Open		75.00	75
1996	Three Blind Mice: Sniffer	Open		75.00	75
1996	Three Blind Mice: Weevil	Open		75.00	75
1997	Tommy Tucker	1,250		295.00	295
1996	Trick or Treat - W. Bullas	Open		75.00	75
1996	The Trick Rider - W. Bullas	Open		75.00	75
1996	Tweedle Dee	1,250		295.00	295
1996	Tweedle Dum	1,250		295.00	295
1996	Zippo...the Fire Eater - W. Bullas	Open		75.00	75

Hallmark Galleries

Kiddie Car Classics - E. Weirick

YEAR ISSUE		EDITION LIMIT	YEAR RETD.	ISSUE PRICE	*QUOTE U.S.$
1996	1935 Steelcraft by Murray® (Luxury Edition) QHG9029	24,500	1996	65.00	125
1994	1936 Steelcraft Lincoln Zephyr by Murray® QHG9015	19,500	1996	50.00	115-145
1995	1937 Steelcraft Auburn Luxury Ed. QHG9021	24,500	1996	65.00	125-150
1995	1937 Steelcraft Chrysler Airflow by Murray® QHG9024	24,500	1996	65.00	75-95
1992	1940 Murray Airplane QHG9003	14,500	1993	50.00	400-525

*Quotes have been rounded up to nearest dollar

Collectors' Information Bureau

79

Hallmark Galleries
to Hamilton Collection

FIGURINES

YEAR ISSUE		EDITION LIMIT	YEAR RETD.	ISSUE PRICE	*QUOTE U.S.$
1992	1941 Steelcraft Spitfire Airplane QHG9009	19,500	1996	50.00	125-250
1995	1948 Murray Pontiac QHG9026	Open		50.00	50
1995	1950 Murray Torpedo QHG9020	Retrd.	1996	50.00	119
1992	1953 Murray Dump Truck QHG9012	14,500	1993	48.00	190-230
1992	1955 Murray Champion QHG9008	14,500	1993	45.00	275-365
1992	1955 Murray Dump Truck QHG9011	19,500	1996	48.00	95
1993	1955 Murray Fire Chief QHG9006	19,500	1996	45.00	100-138
1992	1955 Murray Fire Truck QHG9001	14,500	1993	50.00	315-475
1992	1955 Murray Fire Truck QHG9010	19,500	1996	50.00	150-250
1993	1955 Murray Ranch Wagon QHG9007	24,500	1996	48.00	80-119
1992	1955 Murray Red Champion QHG9002	19,500	1996	45.00	105
1995	1955 Murray Royal Deluxe QHG9025	29,500	1996	55.00	55-90
1992	1955 Murray Tractor and Trailer QHG9004	14,500	1993	55.00	275
1994	1956 Garton Dragnet Police Car QHG9016	24,500		50.00	50
1994	1956 Garton Kidillac (Sp. Ed.) QHX9094	Retrd.	1994	50.00	50-88
1994	1956 GARTON Mark V QHG9022	24,500		45.00	45
1994	1958 Murray Atomic Missile QHG9018	24,500	1996	55.00	75-150
1995	1959 GARTON Deluxe Kidillac QHG9017	Retrd.	1996	55.00	75-110
1995	1961 GARTON Casey Jones Locomotive QHG9019	Retrd.	1996	55.00	110
1994	1961 Murray Circus Car QHG9014	24,500	1996	48.00	65-100
1994	1961 Murray Speedway Pace Car 4500QHG9013	24,500	1996	45.00	45-100
1995	1962 Murray Super Deluxe Fire Truck QHG9095	Open		55.00	55
1995	1964 GARTON Tin Lizzie QHG9023	Open		50.00	50
1993	1968 Murray Boat Jolly Roger QHG9005	19,500	1996	50.00	85-110

Tender Touches - E. Seale

YEAR ISSUE		EDITION LIMIT	YEAR RETD.	ISSUE PRICE	*QUOTE U.S.$
1990	Baby Bear in Backpack QEC9863	Retrd.	1991	16.00	60
1988	Baby Raccoon QHG7031	Retrd.	1992	20.00	40
1991	Baby's 1st Riding Rocking Bear QEC9349	Retrd.	1991	16.00	45
1989	Bear Decorating Tree QHG7050	Retrd.	1995	18.00	40
1992	Bear Family Christmas QHG7002	9,500	1995	45.00	45-55
1990	Bear Graduate QHG7043	Retrd.	1995	15.00	15
1988	Bear w/ Umbrella QHG7029	Retrd.	1994	16.00	35
1990	Bear's Easter Parade QHG7040	Retrd.	1995	23.00	23
1990	Bears Playing Baseball QHG7039	Retrd.	1994	20.00	20
1990	Bears w/ Gift QEC9461	Retrd.	1991	18.00	50-65
1992	Beaver Growth Chart QHG7007	19,500	1995	20.00	20
1992	Beaver w/ Double Bass QHG7058	Retrd.	1995	18.00	18
1990	Beavers w/Tree QHG7052	Retrd.	1994	23.00	23
1989	Birthday Mouse QHG7010	Retrd.	1993	16.00	45
1992	Breakfast in Bed QHG7059	Retrd.	1995	18.00	18
1989	Bride & Groom QHG7009	Retrd.	1994	20.00	40
1992	Building a Pumpkin Man QHG7061	Retrd.	1995	18.00	18
1990	Bunnies Eating Ice Cream QHG7038	Retrd.	1995	20.00	20
1990	Bunnies w/ Slide QHG7016	Retrd.	1994	20.00	20
1990	Bunny Cheerleader QHG7018	Retrd.	1994	16.00	45
1992	Bunny Clarinet QHG7063	Retrd.	1994	16.00	45
1990	Bunny Hiding Valentine QHG7035	Retrd.	1995	16.00	16
1990	Bunny in Boat QHG7021	Retrd.	1994	18.00	40
1989	Bunny in Flowers QHG7012	Retrd.	1992	16.00	30
1991	Bunny in High Chair QHG7054	Retrd.	1995	16.00	30
1990	Bunny Pulling Wagon QHG7008	Retrd.	1994	23.00	23
1990	Bunny w/ Ice Cream QHG7020	Retrd.	1993	15.00	15
1992	Bunny w/ Kite QHG7006	19,500	1995	19.00	19
1991	Bunny w/ Large Eggs QHG7056	Retrd.	1995	16.00	85
1990	Bunny w/ Stocking QEC9416	Retrd.	1990	15.00	35
1992	Chatting Mice QHG7003	19,500	1995	23.00	45
1989	Chipmunk Praying QEC9431	Retrd.	1991	18.00	35
1989	Chipmunk w/Roses QHG7023	Retrd.	1992	16.00	35
1992	Chipmunks w/Album QHG7057	Retrd.	1995	23.00	35
1991	Christmas Bunny Skiing QHG7046	Retrd.	1995	18.00	18
1990	Dad and Son Bears QHG7015	Retrd.	1992	23.00	33
1992	Delightful Fright QHG7067	19,500	1995	23.00	50-75
1993	Downhill Dash QHG7080	Retrd.	1995	23.00	23
1990	Easter Egg Hunt QEC9866	Retrd.	1991	18.00	275
1993	Easter Stroll QHG7084	Retrd.	1995	21.00	21
1993	Ensemble Chipmunk Kettledrum QHG7087	Retrd.	1994	18.00	18
1991	Father Bear Barbequing QHG7041	Retrd.	1995	23.00	23
1994	Fireman QHG7090	Retrd.	1995	23.00	23
1991	First Christmas Mice @ Piano QEC9357	Retrd.	1991	23.00	23
1992	Fitting Gift QHG7065	Retrd.	1995	23.00	23
1991	Foxes in Rowboat QHG7053	Retrd.	1995	23.00	23
1992	From Your Valentine QHG7071	Retrd.	1995	20.00	20
1993	Garden Capers QHG7078	Retrd.	1995	20.00	20
1994	Golfing QHG7091	Retrd.	1995	23.00	23
1994	Halloween QHG7093	Retrd.	1995	23.00	40
1989	Halloween Trio QEC9714	Retrd.	1990	18.00	85-125
1993	Handling a Big Thirst QHG7076	Retrd.	1995	21.00	21
1994	Happy Campers QHG7092	Retrd.	1995	25.00	25
1994	Jesus, Mary, Joseph QHG7094	Retrd.	1995	23.00	40
1993	Love at First Sight QHG7085	Retrd.	1995	23.00	23
1991	Love-American Gothic-Farmer Raccoons QHG7047	Retrd.	1995	20.00	20
1993	Making A Splash QHG7088	Retrd.	1995	20.00	20
1988	Mice at Tea Party QHG7028	Retrd.	1993	23.00	23
1991	Mice Couple Slow Waltzing QEC9437	Retrd.	1991	20.00	500
1990	Mice in Red Car QEC9886	Retrd.	1991	20.00	75
1988	Mice in Rocking Chair QHG7030	Retrd.	1994	18.00	20
1990	Mice w/Mistletoe QEC9423	Retrd.	1990	20.00	30
1990	Mice w/Quilt QHG7017	Retrd.	1994	20.00	25
1992	Mom's Easter Bonnet QHG7072	Retrd.	1995	18.00	18
1991	Mother Raccoon Reading Bible Stories QHG7042	Retrd.	1994	20.00	20
1989	Mouse at Desk QEC9434	Retrd.	1990	18.00	25
1991	Mouse Couple Sharing Soda QHG7055	Retrd.	1995	23.00	23
1990	Mouse in Pumpkin QEC9473	Retrd.	1991	18.00	130-150
1992	Mouse Matinee QHG7073	Retrd.	1995	22.00	22
1990	Mouse Nurse QHG7037	Retrd.	1995	15.00	15
1988	Mouse w/Heart QHG7024	Retrd.	1993	18.00	18
1989	Mouse w/Violin QHG7049	Retrd.	1992	16.00	30-50
1993	Mr. Repair Bear QHG7075	Retrd.	1995	18.00	18
1992	New World, Ahoy! QHG7068	Retrd.	1995	25.00	30
1992	Newsboy Bear QHG7060	Retrd.	1995	16.00	16
1993	The Old Swimming Hole QHG7086	9,500	1995	45.00	55-95
1990	Pilgrim Bear Praying QEC9466	Retrd.	1991	18.00	35-65
1989	Pilgrim Mouse QEC9721	Retrd.	1990	16.00	50
1993	Playground Go-Round QHG7089	Retrd.	1995	23.00	23
1989	Rabbit Painting Egg QHG7022	Retrd.	1994	18.00	30
1988	Rabbit w/Ribbon QHG7027	Retrd.	1994	15.00	15
1988	Rabbits at Juice Stand QHG7033	Retrd.	1994	23.00	23
1989	Rabbits Ice Skating QEC9391	Retrd.	1991	18.00	28
1988	Rabbits w/Cake QHG7025	Retrd.	1992	20.00	40
1992	Raccoon in Bath QHG7069	Retrd.	1993	18.00	35
1990	Raccoon Mail Carrier QHG7013	Retrd.	1995	16.00	16
1988	Raccoon w/Cake QEC9724	Retrd.	1991	18.00	45
1990	Raccoon Watering Roses QHG7036	Retrd.	1994	20.00	20
1991	Raccoon Witch QHG7045	Retrd.	1994	16.00	20
1988	Raccoons Fishing QHG7034	Retrd.	1994	18.00	18
1992	Raccoons on Bridge QHG7004	19,500	1995	25.00	25
1988	Raccoons Playing Ball QEC9771	Retrd.	1991	18.00	40
1990	Raccoons w/Flag QHG7044	Retrd.	1994	23.00	45
1990	Raccoons w/Wagon QHG7014	Retrd.	1993	23.00	30
1990	Romeo & Juliet Mice QEC9903	Retrd.	1991	25.00	500
1990	Santa in Chimney QHG7051	Retrd.	1994	18.00	18
1989	Santa Mouse in Chair QEC9394	Retrd.	1990	20.00	150
1993	Sculpting Santa QHG7083	Retrd.	1995	20.00	20
1992	Soapbox Racer QHG7005	19,500	1995	23.00	23
1988	Squirrels w/Bandage QHG7032	Retrd.	1993	18.00	18
1992	Stealing a Kiss QHG7066	19,500	1995	23.00	23
1992	Sweet Sharing QHG7062	Retrd.	1995	20.00	20
1992	Swingtime Love QHG7070	Retrd.	1993	21.00	100
1990	Teacher & Student Chipmunks QHG7019	Retrd.	1992	20.00	30
1988	Teacher w/Student QHG7026	Retrd.	1995	18.00	18
1993	Teeter For Two QHG7077	Retrd.	1995	23.00	23
1992	Tender Touches Tree House QHG7001	9,500	1995	55.00	55
1992	Thanksgiving Family Around Table QHG7048	Retrd.	1995	25.00	25
1990	Tucking Baby in Bed QHG7011	Retrd.	1993	18.00	18
1992	Waiting for Santa QHG7064	Retrd.	1995	20.00	20
1993	Woodland Americana-Liberty Mouse QHG7081	Retrd.	1995	21.00	30
1993	Woodland Americana-Patriot George QHG7082	Retrd.	1995	25.00	40
1993	Woodland Americana-Stitching the Stars and Stripes QHG7079	Retrd.	1995	21.00	35
1992	Younger Than Springtime QHG7074	19,500	1995	35.00	50

Hamilton Collection

American Garden Flowers - D. Fryer

YEAR ISSUE		EDITION LIMIT	YEAR RETD.	ISSUE PRICE	*QUOTE U.S.$
1987	Azalea	15,000		75.00	75
1988	Calla Lilly	15,000		75.00	75
1987	Camelia	9,800		55.00	75
1988	Day Lily	15,000		75.00	75
1987	Gardenia	15,000		75.00	75
1989	Pansy	15,000		75.00	75
1988	Petunia	15,000		75.00	75
1987	Rose	15,000		75.00	75

American Wildlife Bronze Collection - H./N. Deaton

YEAR ISSUE		EDITION LIMIT	YEAR RETD.	ISSUE PRICE	*QUOTE U.S.$
1980	Beaver	7,500		60.00	65
1979	Bobcat	7,500		60.00	75
1979	Cougar	7,500		60.00	125
1980	Polar Bear	7,500		60.00	65
1980	Sea Otter	7,500		60.00	65
1979	White-Tailed Deer	7,500		60.00	105

Arrowhead Spirits - M. Richter

YEAR ISSUE		EDITION LIMIT	YEAR RETD.	ISSUE PRICE	*QUOTE U.S.$
1996	Path of the Wolf	28-day		29.95	30
1996	Piercing The Night	28-day		29.95	30
1996	Soul of the Hunter	28-day		29.95	30

A Celebration of Roses - N/A

YEAR ISSUE		EDITION LIMIT	YEAR RETD.	ISSUE PRICE	*QUOTE U.S.$
1989	Brandy	Open		55.00	55
1989	Color Magic	Open		55.00	55
1989	Honor	Open		55.00	55
1989	Miss All-American Beauty	Open		55.00	55
1991	Ole'	Open		55.00	55
1990	Oregold	Open		55.00	55
1991	Paradise	Open		55.00	55
1989	Tiffany	Open		55.00	55

Coral Reef Beauties - Everhart

YEAR ISSUE		EDITION LIMIT	YEAR RETD.	ISSUE PRICE	*QUOTE U.S.$
1996	Coral Paradise	Open		39.95	40
1996	Ocean's Bounty	Open		39.95	40
1996	Sentinel of the Sea	Open		39.95	40

Dreamsicles Heavenly Village - N/A

YEAR ISSUE		EDITION LIMIT	YEAR RETD.	ISSUE PRICE	*QUOTE U.S.$
1996	Flight School	Open		49.95	50
1996	Star Factory	Open		49.95	50

First on Race Day Figurine Collection - N/A

YEAR ISSUE		EDITION LIMIT	YEAR RETD.	ISSUE PRICE	*QUOTE U.S.$
1996	Bill Elliott	Open		45.00	45
1996	Jeff Gordon	Open		45.00	45

Freshwater Challenge - M. Wald

YEAR ISSUE		EDITION LIMIT	YEAR RETD.	ISSUE PRICE	*QUOTE U.S.$
1992	Prized Catch	Open		75.00	75
1991	Rainbow Lure	Open		75.00	75
1991	The Strike	Open		75.00	75
1991	Sun Catcher	Open		75.00	75

Gifts of the Ancient Spirits - S. Kehrli

YEAR ISSUE		EDITION LIMIT	YEAR RETD.	ISSUE PRICE	*QUOTE U.S.$
1996	Talisman of Courage	Open		79.00	79
1996	Talisman of the Buffalo	Open		79.00	79
1996	Talisman of Strength	Open		79.00	79

Gone With The Wind-Porcelain Trading Cards - N/A

YEAR ISSUE		EDITION LIMIT	YEAR RETD.	ISSUE PRICE	*QUOTE U.S.$
1995	Fire and Passion	28-day		14.95	15
1995	Scarlett and Her Suitors	28-day		14.95	15
1996	Portrait of Scarlett	28-day		14.95	15
1996	Portrait of Rhett	28-day		14.95	15
1996	The Proposal	28-day		14.95	15
1996	Scarlett and Mammy	28-day		14.95	15
1996	Rhett at Twelve Oaks	28-day		14.95	15
1996	The Bold Entrance	28-day		14.95	15
1996	Sunset Embrace	28-day		14.95	15
1996	The Jail Scene	28-day		14.95	15
1996	The Exodus	28-day		14.95	15
1996	Anger Turns to Passion	28-day		14.95	15
1996	The Reunion	28-day		14.95	15

Heroes of Baseball-Porcelain Baseball Cards - N/A

YEAR ISSUE		EDITION LIMIT	YEAR RETD.	ISSUE PRICE	*QUOTE U.S.$
1990	Brooks Robinson	Open		19.50	20
1991	Casey Stengel	Open		19.50	20
1990	Duke Snider	Open		19.50	20
1991	Ernie Banks	Open		19.50	20
1991	Gil Hodges	Open		19.50	20
1991	Jackie Robinson	Open		19.50	20
1991	Mickey Mantle	Open		19.50	20
1990	Roberto Clemente	Open		19.50	20
1991	Satchel Page	Open		19.50	20
1991	Whitey Ford	Open		19.50	20
1990	Willie Mays	Open		19.50	20
1991	Yogi Berra	Open		19.50	20

International Santa - N/A

YEAR ISSUE		EDITION LIMIT	YEAR RETD.	ISSUE PRICE	*QUOTE U.S.$
1995	Alpine Santa	Open		55.00	55
1993	Belsnickel	Open		55.00	55
1995	Dedushka Moroz	Open		55.00	55
1992	Father Christmas	Open		55.00	55
1992	Grandfather Frost	Open		55.00	55
1993	Jolly Old St. Nick	Open		55.00	55
1993	Kris Kringle	Open		55.00	55
1994	Pére Nõel	Open		55.00	55
1992	Santa Claus	Open		55.00	55
1994	Yuletide Santa	Open		55.00	55

Jeweled Carousel - M. Griffin

YEAR ISSUE		EDITION LIMIT	YEAR RETD.	ISSUE PRICE	*QUOTE U.S.$
1995	Sapphire Jumper	Open		55.00	55
1996	Ruby Prancer	Open		55.00	55
1996	Emerald Stander	Open		55.00	55
1996	Amethyst Jumper	Open		55.00	55

Kitten Mischief - S. Kehrli

YEAR ISSUE		EDITION LIMIT	YEAR RETD.	ISSUE PRICE	*QUOTE U.S.$
1996	Picnic Pirates	Open		19.95	20
1996	Toy Smugglers	Open		19.95	20
1996	Wet Paint!	Open		19.95	20

Little Friends of the Arctic - M. Adams

YEAR ISSUE		EDITION LIMIT	YEAR RETD.	ISSUE PRICE	*QUOTE U.S.$
1995	The Young Prince	Open		35.00	35
1995	Princely Fishing	Open		35.00	35
1996	Playful Prince	Open		35.00	35
1996	Snoozing Prince	Open		35.00	35
1996	Princely Disguise	Open		35.00	35
1996	Slippery Prince	Open		35.00	35
1996	Prince Charming	Open		35.00	35
1996	Prince of the Mountain	Open		35.00	35
1996	Frisky Prince	Open		35.00	35
1996	Dreamy Prince	Open		35.00	35

Little Messengers - P. Parkins

YEAR ISSUE		EDITION LIMIT	YEAR RETD.	ISSUE PRICE	*QUOTE U.S.$
1996	Love Is Patient	Open		29.95	30

Little Night Owls - D.T. Lyttleton

YEAR ISSUE		EDITION LIMIT	YEAR RETD.	ISSUE PRICE	*QUOTE U.S.$
1990	Barn Owl	Open		45.00	45
1991	Barred Owl	Open		45.00	45
1991	Great Grey Owl	Open		45.00	45
1991	Great Horned Owl	Open		45.00	45

*Quotes have been rounded up to nearest dollar

YEAR ISSUE		EDITION LIMIT	YEAR RETD.	ISSUE PRICE	*QUOTE U.S.$
1991	Short-Eared Owl	Open		45.00	45
1990	Snowy Owl	Open		45.00	45
1990	Tawny Owl	Open		45.00	45
1991	White-Faced Owl	Open		45.00	45

Masters of the Evening Wilderness - N/A

YEAR ISSUE		EDITION LIMIT	YEAR RETD.	ISSUE PRICE	*QUOTE U.S.$
1994	The Great Snowy Owl	Open		37.50	38
1995	Autumn Barn Owls	Open		37.50	38
1995	Great Grey Owl	Open		37.50	38
1995	Great Horned Owl	Open		37.50	38
1996	Barred Owl	Open		37.50	38
1996	Screech Owl	Open		37.50	38
1996	Burrowing Owl	Open		37.50	38
1996	Eagle Owl	Open		37.50	38

Mickey Mantle Collector's Edition-Porcelain Baseball Cards -N/A

YEAR ISSUE		EDITION LIMIT	YEAR RETD.	ISSUE PRICE	*QUOTE U.S.$
1995	1952 Card #311/1969 Card #500	Open		39.90	40
1996	1956 Card #135/1965 Card #350	Open		39.90	40
1996	1953 Card #82/1964 Card #50	Open		39.90	40
1996	1957 Card #95/1959 Card #10	Open		39.90	40
1996	1958 Card #150/1962 Card #318	Open		39.90	40
1996	1959 Card #564/1961 Card #300	Open		39.90	40

Mickey Mantle Figurine Collection - N/A

YEAR ISSUE		EDITION LIMIT	YEAR RETD.	ISSUE PRICE	*QUOTE U.S.$
1995	Mickey Swings Home	Open		45.00	45
1996	The Switch Hitter Connects	Open		45.00	45
1990	The Ultimate Switch Hitter	Open		45.00	45
1996	On Deck	Open		45.00	45
1996	Bunting From the Left	Open		45.00	45

Mickey Mantle Sculpture - N/A

YEAR ISSUE		EDITION LIMIT	YEAR RETD.	ISSUE PRICE	*QUOTE U.S.$
1996	Tribute to a Yankee Legend	Open		195.00	195

Mystic Spirits - S. Douglas

YEAR ISSUE		EDITION LIMIT	YEAR RETD.	ISSUE PRICE	*QUOTE U.S.$
1995	Spirit of the Wolf	Open		55.00	55
1995	Spirit of the Buffalo	Open		55.00	55
1995	Spirit of the Golden Eagle	Open		55.00	55
1996	Spirit of the Bear	Open		55.00	55
1996	Spirit of the Mountain Lion	Open		55.00	55
1996	Hawk Dancer	Open		55.00	55
1996	Wolf Scout	Open		55.00	55
1996	Spirit of the Deer	Open		55.00	55

Nature's Beautiful Bonds - R. Roberts

YEAR ISSUE		EDITION LIMIT	YEAR RETD.	ISSUE PRICE	*QUOTE U.S.$
1996	A Mother's Vigil	Open		29.95	30
1996	A Moment's Peace	Open		29.95	30
1996	A Warm Embrace	Open		29.95	30
1996	Safe By Mother's Side	Open		29.95	30
1996	Curious Cub	Open		29.95	30
1996	Under Mother's Watchful Eye	Open		29.95	30
1996	Time To Rest	Open		29.95	30
1996	Sheltered From Harm	Open		29.95	30

Nature's Majestic Cats - D. Geentz

YEAR ISSUE		EDITION LIMIT	YEAR RETD.	ISSUE PRICE	*QUOTE U.S.$
1995	Tigress and Cubs	Open		55.00	55
1995	Himalayan Snow Leopard	Open		55.00	55
1996	Cougar and Cubs	Open		55.00	55
1996	Pride of the Lioness	Open		55.00	55

Nesting Instincts - R. Willis

YEAR ISSUE		EDITION LIMIT	YEAR RETD.	ISSUE PRICE	*QUOTE U.S.$
1995	By Mother's Side	Open		19.50	20
1995	Learning to Fly	Open		19.50	20
1995	Like Mother, Like Son	Open		19.50	20
1995	A Mother's Pride	Open		19.50	20
1995	Peaceful Perch	Open		19.50	20
1995	Safe and Sound	Open		19.50	20
1995	Under Mother's Wings	Open		19.50	20
1995	A Watchful Eye	Open		19.50	20

Noble American Indian Women - N/A

YEAR ISSUE		EDITION LIMIT	YEAR RETD.	ISSUE PRICE	*QUOTE U.S.$
1994	Falling Star	Open		55.00	55
1995	Lily of the Mohawks	Open		55.00	55
1995	Lozen	Open		55.00	55
1994	Minnehaha	Open		55.00	55
1994	Pine Leaf	Open		55.00	55
1995	Pocahontas	Open		55.00	55
1993	Sacajawea	Open		55.00	55
1993	White Rose	Open		55.00	55

The Noble Swan - G. Granget

YEAR ISSUE		EDITION LIMIT	YEAR RETD.	ISSUE PRICE	*QUOTE U.S.$
1985	The Noble Swan	5,000		295.00	295

Noble Warriors - N/A

YEAR ISSUE		EDITION LIMIT	YEAR RETD.	ISSUE PRICE	*QUOTE U.S.$
1993	Deliverance	Open		135.00	135
1994	Spirit of the Plains	Open		135.00	135
1995	Top Gun	Open		135.00	135
1995	Windrider	Open		135.00	135

The Nolan Ryan Collectors Edition-Porcelain Baseball Cards - N/A

YEAR ISSUE		EDITION LIMIT	YEAR RETD.	ISSUE PRICE	*QUOTE U.S.$
1993	Angels 1972-C #595	Open		19.50	20
1993	Astros 1985-C #7	Open		19.50	20
1993	Mets 1968-C #177	Open		19.50	20
1993	Mets 1969-C #533	Open		19.50	20
1993	Rangers 1990-C #1	Open		19.50	20
1993	Rangers 1992-C #1	Open		19.50	20

North Pole Bears - T. Newsom

YEAR ISSUE		EDITION LIMIT	YEAR RETD.	ISSUE PRICE	*QUOTE U.S.$
1996	All I Want For Christmas	Open		29.95	30
1996	Beary Best Snowman	Open		29.95	30
1996	Beary Started	Open		29.95	30
1996	Papa's Cozy Chair	Open		29.95	30

Ocean Odyssey - W. Youngstrom

YEAR ISSUE		EDITION LIMIT	YEAR RETD.	ISSUE PRICE	*QUOTE U.S.$
1995	Breaching the Waters	Open		55.00	55
1995	Return to Paradise	Open		55.00	55
1995	Riding the Waves	Open		55.00	55
1996	Baja Bliss	Open		55.00	55
1996	Arctic Blue	Open		55.00	55
1996	Splashdown	Open		55.00	55
1996	Free Spirit	Open		55.00	55
1996	Beluga Belles	Open		55.00	55

Playful Penguins - M. Adams

YEAR ISSUE		EDITION LIMIT	YEAR RETD.	ISSUE PRICE	*QUOTE U.S.$
1996	Look Out Below!	Open		37.50	38

Princess of the Plains - N/A

YEAR ISSUE		EDITION LIMIT	YEAR RETD.	ISSUE PRICE	*QUOTE U.S.$
1995	Mountain Princess	Open		55.00	55
1995	Nature's Guardian	Open		55.00	55
1995	Noble Beauty	Open		55.00	55
1994	Noble Guardian	Open		55.00	55
1995	Proud Dreamer	Open		55.00	55
1994	Snow Princess	Open		55.00	55
1994	Wild Flower	Open		55.00	55
1995	Winter's Rose	Open		55.00	55

Protect Nature's Innocents - R. Manning

YEAR ISSUE		EDITION LIMIT	YEAR RETD.	ISSUE PRICE	*QUOTE U.S.$
1995	African Elephant	Open		14.95	15
1995	Giant Panda	Open		14.95	15
1995	Snow Leopard	Open		14.95	15
1995	Rhinoceros	Open		14.95	15
1996	Orangutan	Open		14.95	15
1996	Key Deer	Open		14.95	15
1996	Bengal Tiger	Open		14.95	15
1996	Pygmy Hippo	Open		14.95	15
1996	Gray Wolf	Open		14.95	15
1996	Fur Seal	Open		14.95	15
1996	Gray Kangaroo	Open		14.95	15
1996	Sea Otter	Open		14.95	15

Puppy Playtime Sculpture Collection - J. Lamb

YEAR ISSUE		EDITION LIMIT	YEAR RETD.	ISSUE PRICE	*QUOTE U.S.$
1991	Cabin Fever	Open		29.50	30
1991	Catch of the Day	Open		29.50	30
1990	Double Take	Open		29.50	30
1991	Fun and Games	Open		29.50	30
1991	Getting Acquainted	Open		29.50	30
1991	Hanging Out	Open		29.50	30
1991	A New Leash on Life	Open		29.50	30
1991	Weekend Gardner	Open		29.50	30

Ringling Bros. Circus Animals - P. Cozzolino

YEAR ISSUE		EDITION LIMIT	YEAR RETD.	ISSUE PRICE	*QUOTE U.S.$
1983	Acrobatic Seal	9,800		49.50	50
1983	Baby Elephant	9,800		49.50	55
1983	Miniature Show Horse	9,800		49.50	68
1983	Mr. Chimpanzee	9,800		49.50	50
1984	Parade Camel	9,800		49.50	50
1983	Performing Poodles	9,800		49.50	50
1984	Roaring Lion	9,800		49.50	50
1983	Skating Bear	9,800		49.50	50

Santa Clothtique - Possible Dreams

YEAR ISSUE		EDITION LIMIT	YEAR RETD.	ISSUE PRICE	*QUOTE U.S.$
1992	Checking His List	Open		95.00	95
1993	Last Minute Details	Open		95.00	95
1993	Twas the Nap Before Christmas	Open		95.00	95
1994	Upon the Rooftop	Open		95.00	95
1994	O Tannenbaum!	Open		95.00	95
1995	Baking Christmas Cheer	Open		95.00	95
1995	Santa to the Rescue	Open		95.00	95
1996	Toyshop Tally	Open		95.00	95

Shield of the Mighty Warrior - S. Kehrli

YEAR ISSUE		EDITION LIMIT	YEAR RETD.	ISSUE PRICE	*QUOTE U.S.$
1995	Spirit of the Grey Wolf	Open		45.00	45
1996	Spirit of the Bear	Open		45.00	45
1996	Protection of the Cougar	Open		45.00	45
1996	Protection of the Buffalo	Open		45.00	45
1996	Protection of the Bobcat	Open		45.00	45

Spirit of the Eagle - T. Sullivan

YEAR ISSUE		EDITION LIMIT	YEAR RETD.	ISSUE PRICE	*QUOTE U.S.$
1994	Spirit of Independence	Open		55.00	55
1995	Blazing Majestic Skies	Open		55.00	55
1995	Noble and Free	Open		55.00	55
1995	Proud Symbol of Freedom	Open		55.00	55
1996	Legacy of Freedom	Open		55.00	55
1996	Protector of Liberty	Open		55.00	55

STAR TREK® : Captain James T. Kirk Autographed Wall Plaque - N/A

YEAR ISSUE		EDITION LIMIT	YEAR RETD.	ISSUE PRICE	*QUOTE U.S.$
1995	Captain James T. Kirk	5,000		195.00	195

STAR TREK® : Captain Jean-Luc Picard Autographed Wall Plaque - N/A

YEAR ISSUE		EDITION LIMIT	YEAR RETD.	ISSUE PRICE	*QUOTE U.S.$
1994	Captain Jean-Luc Picard	5,000		195.00	175-200

STAR TREK® : First Officer Spock® Autographed Wall Plaque - N/A

YEAR ISSUE		EDITION LIMIT	YEAR RETD.	ISSUE PRICE	*QUOTE U.S.$
1994	First Officer Spock®	2,500		195.00	195

STAR TREK® : The Spock® Commemorative Wall Plaque - N/A

YEAR ISSUE		EDITION LIMIT	YEAR RETD.	ISSUE PRICE	*QUOTE U.S.$
1993	Spock®/STAR TREK VI The Undiscovered Country	2,500		195.00	195

STAR TREK®: The Next Generation-Porcelain Cards - S. Hillios

YEAR ISSUE		EDITION LIMIT	YEAR RETD.	ISSUE PRICE	*QUOTE U.S.$
1996	Deanna Troi & Data	28-day		39.90	40
1997	Inner Light & All Good Things	28-day		39.90	40
1996	Jean-Luc Picard & Q	28-day		39.90	40
1996	Ship In a Bottle & Best of Both Worlds	28-day		39.90	40
1996	USS Enterprise NCC-1701-D & William T. Riker	28-day		39.90	40
1997	Worf & Klingon Bird-of-Prey	28-day		39.90	40

STAR TREK®: The Voyagers-Porcelain Cards - K. Birdsong

YEAR ISSUE		EDITION LIMIT	YEAR RETD.	ISSUE PRICE	*QUOTE U.S.$
1996	Klingon Bird-of-Prey & Cardassian Galor Warship	28-day		39.90	40
1996	Triple Nacelled USS Enterprise & USS Excelsior	28-day		39.90	40
1996	USS Enterprise NCC-1701 & Klingon Battlecruiser	28-day		39.90	40
1996	USS Enterprise NCC-1701-A & Ferengi Marauder	28-day		39.90	40
1996	USS Enterprise NCC-1701-D & Romulan Warbird	28-day		39.90	40
1996	USS Voyager NCC-74656 & USS Defiant NX-74205	28-day		39.90	40

Star Wars: A New Hope-Porcelain Cards - N/A

YEAR ISSUE		EDITION LIMIT	YEAR RETD.	ISSUE PRICE	*QUOTE U.S.$
1996	Leia in Detention & Luke Skywalker	28-day		39.90	40
1996	Millennium Falcon Cockpit & Capture of Leia's Ship	28-day		39.90	40
1996	Obi-wan Kenobi & C-3PO & R2-D2	28-day		39.90	40

Tropical Treasures - M. Wald

YEAR ISSUE		EDITION LIMIT	YEAR RETD.	ISSUE PRICE	*QUOTE U.S.$
1990	Beaked Coral Butterfly Fish	Open		37.50	38
1990	Blue Girdled Angel Fish	Open		37.50	38
1989	Flag-tail Surgeonfish	Open		37.50	38
1989	Pennant Butterfly Fish	Open		37.50	38
1989	Sail-finned Surgeonfish	Open		37.50	38
1989	Sea Horse	Open		37.50	38
1990	Spotted Angel Fish	Open		37.50	38
1990	Zebra Turkey Fish	Open		37.50	38

Unbridled Spirits - C. DeHaan

YEAR ISSUE		EDITION LIMIT	YEAR RETD.	ISSUE PRICE	*QUOTE U.S.$
1994	Wild Fury	Open		135.00	135

Visions of Christmas - M. Griffin

YEAR ISSUE		EDITION LIMIT	YEAR RETD.	ISSUE PRICE	*QUOTE U.S.$
1995	Gifts From St. Nick	Open		135.00	135
1994	Mrs. Claus' Kitchen	Open		135.00	135
1993	Santa's Delivery	Open		135.00	135
1993	Toys in Progress	Open		135.00	135

Warrior's Quest - S. Kehrli

YEAR ISSUE		EDITION LIMIT	YEAR RETD.	ISSUE PRICE	*QUOTE U.S.$
1996	Cry of the Eagle	Open		95.00	95
1996	Strength of the Wolf	Open		95.00	95

The Way of the Warrior - J. Pyre

YEAR ISSUE		EDITION LIMIT	YEAR RETD.	ISSUE PRICE	*QUOTE U.S.$
1995	One With the Eagle	Open		45.00	45
1996	Star Shooter	Open		45.00	45
1996	Bear Warrior	Open		45.00	45
1996	Beckoning Back the Buffalo	Open		45.00	45
1996	Great Feather Warrior	Open		45.00	45
1996	Calling His Guardian	Open		45.00	45

Wild and Free - C. De Haan

YEAR ISSUE		EDITION LIMIT	YEAR RETD.	ISSUE PRICE	*QUOTE U.S.$
1996	Wild and Free	Open		195.00	195

Wolves of the Wilderness - D. Geenty

YEAR ISSUE		EDITION LIMIT	YEAR RETD.	ISSUE PRICE	*QUOTE U.S.$
1995	A Wolf's Pride	Open		55.00	55
1995	Mother's Watch	Open		55.00	55
1996	Time For Play	Open		55.00	55
1996	Morning Romp	Open		55.00	55
1996	First Adventure	Open		55.00	55
1996	Tumbling Twosome	Open		55.00	55

Harmony Kingdom

Royal Watch Society - Various

YEAR ISSUE		EDITION LIMIT	YEAR RETD.	ISSUE PRICE	*QUOTE U.S.$
1996	Big Blue - P. Calvestert	Open		75.00	75
1996	The Big Day - P. Calvestert	Retrd.	1996	Gift	N/A
1996	Purrfect Fit - D. Lawrence	Retrd.	1996	Gift	N/A
1996	Kit-Purrfect Fit - D. Lawrence /The Big Day - P. Calvestert	Retrd.	1996	Gift	100
1997	Paper Anniversary - P. Calvesbert	Open		17.50	18
1997	Toad Pin - P. Calvesbert	Open		Gift	N/A
1997	Sweet as a Summer Kiss - D. Lawrence	Open		Gift	N/A

Angelique - D. Lawrence

YEAR ISSUE		EDITION LIMIT	YEAR RETD.	ISSUE PRICE	*QUOTE U.S.$
1996	Fleur-de-lis	Open		35.00	35
1996	Gentil Homme	Open		35.00	35
1996	Ingenue	Open		35.00	35
1996	Joie De Vivre	Open		35.00	35

Garden Party - Various

YEAR ISSUE		EDITION LIMIT	YEAR RETD.	ISSUE PRICE	*QUOTE U.S.$
1996	Baroness Trotter - P. Calvesbert	Open		17.50	18
1997	Count Belfry - D. Lawrence	Open		17.50	18
1996	Courtiers At Rest - P. Calvesbert	Open		17.50	18

*Quotes have been rounded up to nearest dollar

Harmony Kingdom
to Hudson Creek

FIGURINES

YEAR ISSUE		EDITION LIMIT	YEAR RETD.	ISSUE PRICE	*QUOTE U.S. $
1997	Duc de Lyon - D. Lawrence	Open		17.50	18
1997	Earl of Oswald - D. Lawrence	Open		17.50	18
1996	Garden Prince - P. Calvesbert	Open		17.50	18
1996	Ladies In Waiting - P. Calvesbert	Open		17.50	18
1997	Lord Busby - D. Lawrence	Open		17.50	18
1997	Major Parker - D. Lawrence	Open		17.50	18
1997	Marquis de Blanc - D. Lawrence	Open		17.50	18
1996	Royal Flotilla - P. Calvesbert	Open		17.50	18
1996	Yeoman Of The Guard - P. Calvesbert	Open		17.50	18

Harmony Circus - D. Lawrence

1996	The Audience	Open		150.00	150
1996	Ball Brothers	Open		35.00	35
1996	Beppo And Barney The Clowns	Open		35.00	35
1996	Circus Ring	Open		100.00	100
1996	Clever Constantine	Open		35.00	35
1996	Great Escapo	Open		35.00	35
1996	Harmony Circus Arch	Open		80.00	80
1996	Henry The Human Cannonball	Open		35.00	35
1996	Il Bendi	Open		35.00	35
1996	Lionel Loveless	Open		35.00	35
1996	Mr. Sediments	Open		35.00	35
1996	Olde Time Carousel	Open		35.00	35
1996	Pavareata The Little Big Girl	Open		35.00	35
1996	The Ringmaster	Open		35.00	35
1996	Road Dogs	Open		35.00	35
1996	Suave St. John	Open		35.00	35
1996	Top Hat	Open		35.00	35
1996	Vlad The Impaler	Open		35.00	35
1996	Winston The Lion Tamer	Open		35.00	35
1996	Matched Number Harmony Circus Set	1,000		890.00	890

Hi-Jinx - P. Calvesbert

1994	Antarctic Antics	Open		100.00	100
1994	Hold That Line	Open		100.00	100
1994	Mad Dogs and Englishmen	Open		100.00	100
1995	Open Mike	Open		100.00	100

Holiday Edition - D. Lawrence, unless otherwise noted

1995	Chatelaine	Retrd.	1995	35.00	60-90
1996	Bon Enfant	Retrd.	1996	35.00	45-50
1996	Nick Of Time - P. Calvesbert	Retrd.	1996	35.00	45
1997	Celeste	12/97		45.00	45

Large Treasure Jest® - P. Calvesbert

1991	Awaiting A Kiss	Open		55.00	55
1990	Drake's Fancy	Open		55.00	55
1995	Holding Court	Open		55.00	55
1991	Horn A' Plenty	Open		55.00	55
1991	Journey Home	Open		55.00	55
1990	Keeping Current	Open		55.00	55
1992	On A Roll	Open		55.00	55
1994	One Step Ahead	Open		55.00	55
1991	Pen Pals	Open		55.00	55
1990	Pondering	Open		55.00	55
1993	Pride And Joy	Open		55.00	55
1990	Quiet Waters	Open		55.00	55
1993	Standing Guard	Open		55.00	55
1993	Step Aside	Open		55.00	55
1991	Straight From The Hip	Open		55.00	55
1991	Sunnyside Up	Open		55.00	55
1991	Tea For Two	Open		55.00	55

Limited Editions - P. Calvesbert

1995	Noah's Lark	5,000		400.00	400
1995	Unbearables	2,500		400.00	400

Lord Byron's Harmony Garden - M. Perry

1997	Chrysanthemum	Open		35.00	35
1997	Cranberry	Open		35.00	35
1997	Daisy	Open		35.00	35
1997	Hyacinth	Open		35.00	35
1997	Hydrangea	Open		35.00	35
1997	Marsh Marigold	Open		35.00	35
1997	Morning Glory	Open		35.00	35
1997	Peace Lily	Open		35.00	35
1997	Rhododendron	Open		35.00	35
1997	Rose	3,600		35.00	35
1997	Snow Drop	Open		35.00	35

Paradoxicals - P. Calvesbert

1995	Paradise Found	Open		35.00	35
1995	Paradise Lost	Open		35.00	35

Rather Large Series - P. Calvesbert

1996	Rather Large Friends	Open		65.00	65
1996	Rather Large Hop	Open		65.00	65
1996	Rather Large Huddle	Open		65.00	65
1996	Rather Large Safari	Open		65.00	65

Small Treasure Jest® - P. Calvesbert

1994	All Angles Covered	Open		35.00	35
1993	All Ears	Retrd.	1996	35.00	45
1993	All Tied Up	Retrd.	1996	35.00	45-90
1993	At Arm's Length	Retrd.	1996	35.00	45
1995	At The Hop	Open		35.00	35
1993	Baby on Board	Open		35.00	35
1993	Back Scratch	Retrd.	1995	35.00	42
1995	Beak To Beak	Open		35.00	35
1996	Brean Sands	Open		35.00	35
1996	Changing of the Guard	Open		35.00	35
1996	Close Shave	Open		35.00	35
1995	Damnable Plot	Open		35.00	35
1993	Day Dreamer	Retrd.	1996	35.00	45
1995	Den Mothers	Retrd.	1996	35.00	45
1994	Dog Days	Open		35.00	35
1995	Ed's Safari	Open		35.00	35
1994	Family Tree	Open		35.00	35
1992	Forty Winks	Retrd.	1996	35.00	90
1997	Friends in High Places	Open		45.00	45
1995	Fur Ball	Open		35.00	35
1994	Group Therapy	Retrd.	1996	35.00	45
1993	Hammin' It Up	Retrd.	1996	35.00	45
1996	Hog Heaven	Open		35.00	35
1995	Horse Play	Retrd.	1996	35.00	45
1997	In Fine Feather	Open		45.00	45
1994	Inside Joke	Open		35.00	35
1993	It's A Fine Day	Retrd.	1996	35.00	45-90
1995	Jersey Belles	Open		35.00	35
1993	Jonah's Hideaway	Retrd.	1996	35.00	45-90
1994	Let's Do Lunch	Retrd.	1995	35.00	90-150
1996	Liberty and Justice	Open		45.00	45
1995	Life's a Picnic	Open		35.00	35
1994	Love Seat	Open		35.00	35
1995	Major's Mousers	Open		45.00	45
1995	Mud Bath	Open		35.00	35
1994	Neighborhood Watch	Open		35.00	35
1993	Of The Same Stripe	Open		35.00	35
1991	Panda	100	1995	35.00	N/A
1997	Photo Finish	Open		45.00	45
1996	Pink Paradise	Open		35.00	35
1994	Play School	Open		35.00	35
1992	Princely Thoughts	Retrd.	1996	35.00	45
1995	Puddle Huddle	Open		35.00	35
1994	Purrfect Friends	Open		35.00	35
1991	Ram	100	1995	35.00	N/A
1993	Reminiscence	Retrd.	1996	35.00	45
1996	Rumble Seat	Open		45.00	45
1993	School's Out	Open		35.00	35
1991	Shark	100	1995	35.00	N/A
1993	Shell Game	Open		35.00	35
1993	Side Steppin'	Retrd.	1996	35.00	45
1997	Sleepy Hollow	Open		35.00	35
1994	Sunday Swim	Open		35.00	35
1993	Swamp Song	Open		35.00	35
1995	Sweet Serenade	Open		35.00	35
1994	Teacher's Pet	Open		35.00	35
1996	Tin Cat	Open		35.00	35
1994	Tongue And Cheek	Open		35.00	35
1994	Too Much of A Good Thing	Open		35.00	35
1993	Top Banana	Retrd.	1996	35.00	45
1996	Trumpeter's Ball	Open		45.00	45
1993	Trunk Show	Retrd.	1996	35.00	45
1995	Unbridled & Groomed	Open		35.00	35
1994	Unexpected Arrival	Open		35.00	35
1994	Untouchable	Retrd.	1995	35.00	150
1997	Whale of a Time	Open		35.00	35
1993	Who'd A Thought	Retrd.	1995	35.00	250
1995	Wise Guys	Open		35.00	35

Special Edition - P. Calvesbert

1995	Primordial Soup	Open		150.00	150

Heritage Artists

Gosset Wildlife Collection - C. Gosset

XX	American Golden Eye 129	1,000	N/A	180.00	180
XX	American Widgeon 118	1,000	N/A	180.00	180
XX	American Widgeon 178	1,000		300.00	300
XX	Arctic Loon 170	1,000		250.00	250
XX	Bald Eagle 180	2,000		360.00	360
XX	Black Duck 143	1,000	N/A	230.00	230
XX	Blue Goose 175	1,000		290.00	290
XX	Blue Winged Teal 166	1,500		260.00	260
XX	Brant 182	2,000		310.00	310
XX	Bufflehead 124 (miniature)	Retrd.	N/A	N/A	N/A
XX	Canada Goose 160	3,000		270.00	270
1995	Canada Goose w/Chicks 184	2,000		310.00	310
XX	Canvasback 122 (miniature)	Retrd.	N/A	N/A	N/A
XX	Canvasback 128	1,000	N/A	180.00	180
XX	Canvasback 161	1,500	N/A	260.00	260
XX	Cinnamon Teal 146	1,000	N/A	230.00	230
XX	Common Loon 117	1,000	N/A	150.00	150
XX	Common Merganser 112	1,000	N/A	180.00	180
XX	Common Merganser Hen & Chick 173	2,000		300.00	300
1996	Cormorant (pair) 186	2,500		500.00	500
XX	Courting Ruddy 135	200	N/A	180.00	180
XX	Dancing Loon 150	3,000	N/A	250.00	250
XX	Female Redhead 131	1,000	N/A	180.00	180
XX	Gadwall 134	1,000	N/A	180.00	180
XX	Giant Canada Goose 152	3,000		280.00	280
XX	Goldeneye 116 (miniature)	Retrd.	N/A	N/A	N/A
XX	Greater Seaup 140	1,000	N/A	180.00	180
XX	Grebe with Young 168	1,500		260.00	260
XX	Green-Winged Teal 163	2,000		260.00	260
XX	Greenwing Teal 121	1,000	N/A	180.00	180
XX	Harlequin 126	1,000	N/A	180.00	180
XX	Hooded Merganser 113	1,000	N/A	180.00	180
XX	King Elder 130	1,000	N/A	180.00	180
XX	Lesser Canada Goose 110	1,000	N/A	180.00	180
XX	Loon 165	2,000		260.00	260
1995	Loon w/Chicks 185	3,000		290.00	290
XX	Loon with Chick 133	1,000	N/A	180.00	180
XX	Loon with Chicks 155	3,000	N/A	270.00	270
XX	Loon with Two Chicks 144	1,500	N/A	250.00	250
XX	Male Bluewing Teal 120	1,000	N/A	180.00	180
XX	Male Common Merganser 174	1,000		290.00	290
XX	Male Loon 142	1,500	N/A	230.00	230
XX	Male Redhead 132	1,000	N/A	180.00	180
1996	Mallard & Hen & 4 Chicks 187	5,000		325.00	325
XX	Mallard 111	1,000	N/A	180.00	180
XX	Mallard Drake 145	1,000	N/A	230.00	230
XX	Mallard Drake 156	3,000	1996	270.00	270
XX	Mallard Hen & 3 Chicks 179	2,000	N/A	N/A	N/A
XX	Mallard Hens & Chicks 159	1,500	N/A	280.00	280
XX	Mandarin 169	2,000	N/A	N/A	N/A
1997	Mating Pintail 188	2,500		325.00	325
1997	Merganser Hen & 2 Chicks 189	2,500		325.00	325
XX	Northern Shoveler 164	1,000		260.00	260
XX	Northern Shoveller 114	1,000	N/A	N/A	N/A
XX	Old Squaw (Summer Plummage) 157	3,000		260.00	260
XX	Old Squaw (Winter Plummage) 158	3,000		260.00	260
XX	Pintail 115 (miniature)	Retrd.	N/A	N/A	N/A
XX	Pintail 119	1,000	N/A	180.00	180
XX	Pintail 148	Retrd.	1996	N/A	N/A
XX	Preening Black Duck 172	2,000		290.00	290
XX	Preening Bluewing Teal 141	1,000	N/A	250.00	250
XX	Preening Gadwall 162	2,000	N/A	260.00	260
XX	Preening Loon 151	3,000		250.00	250
XX	Preening Mallard 183	2,000		310.00	310
XX	Preening Pintail 176	2,000		310.00	310
XX	Preening Wood Duck 153	3,000		250.00	250
XX	Read Head 123 (miniature)	Retrd.	N/A	N/A	N/A
XX	Red-breasted Goose 139	1,000	N/A	180.00	180
XX	Red-Throated Loon 125	1,000	N/A	180.00	180
XX	Ruddy Duck 138	1,000	N/A	180.00	180
XX	Sheller's Elder 137	200	N/A	180.00	180
XX	Sleeping Hooded Merganser 171	1,000	N/A	N/A	N/A
XX	Sleeping Mallard Hen 147	1,000	N/A	250.00	250
XX	Standing Loon & Chicks 177	2,000		296.00	296
XX	Stretched Legged Gadwall 181	2,000		310.00	310
XX	Western Goose 136	1,000	N/A	180.00	180
XX	Widgeon 149	1,500	N/A	250.00	250
XX	Wood Duck 127	1,000	N/A	180.00	180
XX	Wood Duck Drake 167	2,000		260.00	260
XX	Wood Duck Hen 154	3,000	N/A	250.00	250

Heritage Decoys - J.B. Garton

XX	Black Duck	950		195.00	195
XX	Canada Goose	5,000		195.00	195
XX	Green-Winged Teal	5,000		195.00	195
XX	Hen Black Duck	950		195.00	195
XX	Hen Green-Winged Teal	950		195.00	195
XX	Hen Mallard	2,500		195.00	195
XX	Hen Wood Duck	2,500		195.00	195
XX	Mallard Drake	5,000		195.00	195
XX	New Mother Loon	5,000		195.00	195
XX	Preening Pintail	5,000		195.00	195
XX	Red Breasted Merganser	950		195.00	195
XX	Standing Puffin	5,000		195.00	195
XX	Wood Duck	2,500		195.00	195

Hudson Creek

Chilmark - Various

1981	Budweiser Wagon - Keim/Hazen	890	1989	2000.00	3000
1986	Camelot Chess Set - P. Jackson	Retrd.	1991	2250.00	2250
1979	Carousel - R. Sylvan	950	1983	115.00	115
1980	Charge of the 7th Cavalry - B. Rodden	394	1988	600.00	950
1983	Dragon Slayer - D. LaRocca	290	1988	385.00	500
1989	The Great White Whale - A.T. McGrory	Suspd.		1050.00	1050
1994	Herald of Spring - D. LaRocca	Suspd.		295.00	295
1985	Moby Dick - J. Royce	Retrd.	1995	350.00	350
1979	Moses - B. Rodden	2,500	1989	140.00	235
1985	Out of Trouble - A. Petitto	Suspd.		245.00	245
1979	Pegasus - R. Sylvan	527	1981	95.00	175
1993	St. Nicholas - D. Liberty	Suspd.		750.00	750
1979	Unicorn - R. Sylvan	2,500	1982	115.00	550
1994	Woodland Santa - D. Liberty	Suspd.		750.00	750

Chilmark American West - D. Polland, unless otherwise noted

1981	Ambushed	294	1991	2370.00	2700
1987	Apache Attack - F. Barnum	Suspd.		315.00	315
1982	Apache Gan Dancer	Suspd.		115.00	115
1987	Appeal to the Great Spirit - F. Barnum	Retrd.	1995	275.00	275
1982	Arapaho Drummer	Suspd.		115.00	115
1996	Arrow Marker - M. Boyett	Suspd.		395.00	395
1989	Attack on the Iron Horse - M. Boyett	Suspd.		3675.00	3675
1985	Bareback Rider	Suspd.		315.00	315
1985	Bear Meet - S. York	Retrd.	1992	500.00	600-800
1983	Bison's Fury - M. Boyett	Retrd.	1995	495.00	495
1982	Blood Brothers - M. Boyett	717	1991	250.00	610-995

*Quotes have been rounded up to nearest dollar

FIGURINES

Hudson Creek
to Hudson Creek

YEAR ISSUE		EDITION LIMIT	YEAR RETD.	ISSUE PRICE	*QUOTE U.S.$
1979	Border Rustlers	500	1989	1295.00	1500
1983	Bounty Hunter	264	1987	250.00	300-600
1976	Buffalo Hunt	2,250	1980	300.00	1625
1982	Buffalo Prayer	2,500	1989	95.00	225-400
1981	Buffalo Robe	Suspd.		335.00	335
1990	Buffalo Spirit	2,500	1993	110.00	185
1985	Calf Roper	Suspd.		395.00	395
1979	Cavalry Officer - D. LaRocca	500	1985	125.00	400-650
1974	Cheyenne	2,800	1980	200.00	3000
1987	Clash of Cultures - F. Barnum	Suspd.		385.00	385
1976	Cold Saddles, Mean Horses	2,800	1986	200.00	800
1988	Comanche Hostile	Suspd.		290.00	290
1982	Comanche Plains Drummer	Suspd.		115.00	115
1974	Counting Coup	2,800	1980	225.00	1600-2000
1987	Counting Coup - F. Barnum	Suspd.		385.00	385
1979	Cowboy - D. LaRocca	950	1984	125.00	500-750
1982	Crow Medicine Dancer	Suspd.		115.00	115
1974	Crow Scout	3,000	1983	250.00	1000-1700
1978	Dangerous Encounter - B. Rodden	746	1977	475.00	600-950
1989	Death Battle	Suspd.		335.00	335
1985	The Doctor - M. Boyett	Retrd.	1994	750.00	800-950
1981	Dog Soldier	Suspd.		315.00	315
1990	Eagle Dancer (deNatura)	614	1993	300.00	300
1991	Eagle Dancer (pewter)	Suspd.		275.00	275
1994	Enemy Territory - Sullivan	Suspd.		500.00	500
1981	Enemy Tracks	2,500	1988	225.00	720
1984	Eye to Eye	Suspd.		500.00	500
1984	Flat Out for Red River Station - M. Boyett	2,500	1991	3000.00	5000-6500
1982	Flathead War Dancer	Suspd.		115.00	115
1989	Frenchie	Suspd.		280.00	280
1979	Getting Acquainted	950	1988	215.00	800-1100
1994	He Who Taunts the Enemy - M. Boyett	Suspd.		8900.00	8900
1988	Hightailin'	Suspd.		450.00	450
1982	Hopi Kachina Dancer	Suspd.		115.00	115
1985	Horse of A Different Color - S. York	Retrd.	1992	500.00	600-800
1982	Hostile Apache	Suspd.		115.00	115
1991	I Don't Do Fences	Suspd.		115.00	115
1979	Indian Warrior - D. LaRocca	1,186	1988	95.00	400
1989	Jedediah Smith	Suspd.		345.00	345
1982	Jemez Eagle Dancer	2,500	1989	95.00	250-450
1991	Kiowa Princess (deNatura)	444	1993	300.00	300
1991	Kiowa Princess (pewter)	Suspd.		275.00	275
1982	Last Arrow	2,500	1988	95.00	300-400
1991	Lawman	Suspd.		130.00	130
1983	Line Rider	2,500	1988	195.00	975
1979	Mandan Hunter	5,000	1985	65.00	780-900
1988	Marauders	Retrd.	1994	850.00	850
1975	Maverick Calf	2,500	1981	250.00	1300-1700
1989	Mohawk War Party	Suspd.		600.00	600
1976	Monday Morning Wash	2,500	1986	200.00	1000-1300
1979	Mountain Man - D. LaRocca	764	1988	95.00	500-650
1983	The Mustanger	Retrd.	1995	425.00	425
1982	Navajo Kachina Dancer	Suspd.		115.00	115
1983	Now or Never	693	1991	265.00	800
1975	The Outlaws	2,500	1989	450.00	900-1180
1976	Painting the Town	2,250	1983	300.00	1500-1700
1996	The Peace Pipe - M. Boyett	Suspd.		395.00	395
1990	Pequot Wars	950	1990	395.00	800
1981	Plight of the Huntsman - M. Boyett	950	1987	495.00	850
1989	Portugee Philips	Suspd.		280.00	280
1985	Postal Exchange - S. York	Retrd.	1992	300.00	400-600
1990	Red River Wars	950	1990	425.00	700-850
1989	Renegade	Suspd.		315.00	315
1976	Rescue	2,500	1980	275.00	1200-1500
1991	Rodeo Star	Suspd.		90.00	90
1979	Running Battle - B. Rodden	761	1987	400.00	750-900
1990	Running Wolf (deNatura)	720	1993	350.00	350
1991	Running Wolf (pewter)	Suspd.		325.00	325
1982	Sioux War Chief	2,500	1989	95.00	240-480
1981	Sioux War Cry - M. Boyett	Suspd.		385.00	385
1986	Stallions	Suspd.		315.00	315
1985	Steer Wrestling	Suspd.		635.00	635
1991	The Storyteller	Retrd.	1995	150.00	150
1985	Team Roping	Suspd.		660.00	660
1990	Tecumseh's Rebellion	950	1990	350.00	700
1991	A Test of Courage	Suspd.		290.00	290
1983	Too Many Aces	1,717	1993	400.00	600-850
1981	U.S. Marshal	1,500	1986	95.00	450
1993	The Unconquered - M. Boyett	Suspd.		6500.00	6500
1996	War Paint - M. Boyett	Suspd.		395.00	395
1981	War Party	1,066	1991	550.00	975-1150
1981	When War Chiefs Meet	2,500	1988	300.00	800
1983	The Wild Bunch	285	1987	200.00	225-400
1982	Yakima Salmon Fisherman	2,500	1987	200.00	600-750
1991	Yellow Boy (deNatura)	460	1993	350.00	350
1991	Yellow Boy (pewter)	Suspd.		325.00	325

Chilmark American West Christmas Specials - D. Polland

YEAR ISSUE		EDITION LIMIT	YEAR RETD.	ISSUE PRICE	*QUOTE U.S.$
1991	Merry Christmas Neighbor	1,240	1991	395.00	600-750
1992	Merry Christmas My Love	819	1992	350.00	350-450
1993	Almost Home	520	1994	375.00	375
1994	Cowboy Christmas	427	1994	250.00	250

Chilmark American West Event Specials - D. Polland, unless otherwise noted

YEAR ISSUE		EDITION LIMIT	YEAR RETD.	ISSUE PRICE	*QUOTE U.S.$
1991	Uneasy Truce	737	1991	125.00	175-195
1992	Irons In The Fire	612	1992	125.00	150-225
1994	Bacon 'N' Beans Again?	458	1994	150.00	175-225
1994	Buffalo Skull - J. Slockbower	Yr. Iss.	1994	125.00	125
1995	Renegade Apache	Closed	1995	150.00	150

Chilmark American West Guardians of the Plains - J. Slockbower

YEAR ISSUE		EDITION LIMIT	YEAR RETD.	ISSUE PRICE	*QUOTE U.S.$
1993	Noble Elder (MetalART)	Suspd.		350.00	350
1993	Noble Elder (pewter)	Suspd.		275.00	275
1993	Old Storyteller (MetalART)	Suspd.		350.00	350
1993	Old Storyteller (pewter)	Suspd.		275.00	275
1993	Proud Warrior (MetalART)	Suspd.		350.00	350
1993	Proud Warrior (pewter)	Suspd.		275.00	275
1993	Valiant Leader (MetalART)	Suspd.		350.00	350
1993	Valiant Leader (pewter)	Suspd.		275.00	275

Chilmark American West Kindred Spirits Collection - A. McGrory

YEAR ISSUE		EDITION LIMIT	YEAR RETD.	ISSUE PRICE	*QUOTE U.S.$
1994	Brother Wolf	500	1995	500.00	500
1995	Buffalo Hide	500		750.00	750
1996	Secret Hunter	500		500.00	500

Chilmark American West Legacy of Courage - M. Boyett

YEAR ISSUE		EDITION LIMIT	YEAR RETD.	ISSUE PRICE	*QUOTE U.S.$
1983	Along the Cherokee Trace	624	1991	295.00	720
1981	Apache Signals	765	1987	175.00	550-575
1982	Arapaho Sentinel	678	1991	195.00	500
1981	Blackfoot Snow Hunter	984	1988	175.00	650
1981	Buffalo Stalker	1,034	1991	175.00	560
1983	Circling the Enemy	Retrd.	1992	295.00	395
1981	Comanche	1,553	1991	175.00	530-670
1982	Dance of the Eagles	Retrd.	1992	150.00	215
1983	Forest Watcher	658	1991	215.00	540
1981	Iroquois Warfare	1,477	1991	125.00	600
1982	Kiowa Scout	292	1987	195.00	525
1982	Listening For Hooves	883	1991	150.00	400
1982	Mandan Buffalo Dancer	1,494	1991	195.00	450-600
1983	Moment of Truth	1,145	1991	295.00	550-620
1982	Plains Talk-Pawnee	421	1987	195.00	625
1983	Rite of the Whitetail	Retrd.	1992	295.00	400
1982	Shoshone Eagle Catcher	2,500	1985	225.00	1600-2000
1982	The Tracker Nez Perce	686	1988	150.00	575
1981	Unconquered Seminole	1,021	1991	175.00	540
1981	Victor Cheyenne	1,299	1991	175.00	500
1983	A Warrior's Tribute	Retrd.	1992	335.00	635
1983	Winter Hunt	756	1991	295.00	400

Chilmark American West OffCanvas™ - A. T. McGrory

YEAR ISSUE		EDITION LIMIT	YEAR RETD.	ISSUE PRICE	*QUOTE U.S.$
1990	Attack	Suspd.		1295.00	1295
1991	Blanket Signal	350	1993	750.00	850
1993	Buffalo Hunter (MetalART)	Suspd.		295.00	295
1993	Buffalo Hunter (pewter)	Suspd.		225.00	225
1991	Conjuring Back the Buffalo	Suspd.		290.00	290
1991	Dash for the Timber	Suspd.		580.00	580
1991	The Outlier	Suspd.		515.00	515
1993	Pony War Dance (MetalART)	Suspd.		295.00	295
1993	Pony War Dance (pewter)	Suspd.		225.00	225
1990	Smoke Signal	950	1990	345.00	550-700
1992	Trooper of the Southern Plains	Suspd.		310.00	310
1992	The Vanishing American	Suspd.		265.00	265
1990	Vigil	950	1990	345.00	500-700
1990	Warrior	950	1990	300.00	350-600

Chilmark American West Redemption Specials - D. Polland, unless otherwise noted

YEAR ISSUE		EDITION LIMIT	YEAR RETD.	ISSUE PRICE	*QUOTE U.S.$
1983	The Chief	2,459	1984	275.00	1400-1750
1984	Unit Colors	1,394	1985	250.00	1200-1700
1985	Oh Great Spirit	3,180	1986	300.00	1000-1300
1986	Eagle Catcher - M. Boyett	1,840	1987	300.00	850-1200
1987	Surprise Encounter - F. Barnum	1,534	1988	250.00	600-800
1988	I Will Fight No More Forever (Chief Joseph)	3,404	1989	350.00	850
1989	Geronimo	1,866	1990	375.00	650-750
1990	Cochise	1,778	1991	400.00	500-600
1991	Crazy Horse	2,067	1992	295.00	600-700
1992	Strong Hearts to the Front	1,252	1993	425.00	600
1993	Sacred Ground Reclaimed	861	1994	495.00	550-650
1994	Horse Breaking	504	1995	395.00	395
1995	The Rainmaker - M. Boyett	Yr.Iss.		350.00	350

Chilmark American West The Great Chiefs - J. Slockbower

YEAR ISSUE		EDITION LIMIT	YEAR RETD.	ISSUE PRICE	*QUOTE U.S.$
1992	Chief Joseph	750	1992	975.00	15-1900
1993	Crazy Horse	Suspd.		975.00	975
1992	Geronimo	750	1992	975.00	1300-1850
1993	Sitting Bull	750	1996	1075.00	1075

Chilmark American West The Medicine Men - D. Polland

YEAR ISSUE		EDITION LIMIT	YEAR RETD.	ISSUE PRICE	*QUOTE U.S.$
1992	False Face (MetalART)	1,000		550.00	550
1992	False Face (pewter)	500	1992	375.00	375

Chilmark American West The Seekers - A. McGrory

YEAR ISSUE		EDITION LIMIT	YEAR RETD.	ISSUE PRICE	*QUOTE U.S.$
1993	Bear Vision	Suspd.		1375.00	1375
1992	Buffalo Vision	500	1993	1075.00	1075
1993	Eagle Vision	Suspd.		1250.00	1250

Chilmark American West The Warriors - D. Polland

YEAR ISSUE		EDITION LIMIT	YEAR RETD.	ISSUE PRICE	*QUOTE U.S.$
1995	Keeper of the Eastern Door (pewter)	500		375.00	375
1995	Keeper of the Eastern Door (MetalART)	1,000		500.00	500
1993	Son of the Morning Star (MetalART)	1,000		495.00	495
1993	Son of the Morning Star (pewter)	500	1993	375.00	460
1995	Soul of the Forest (pewter)	500		375.00	375
1995	Soul of the Forest (MetalART)	1,000		500.00	500
1992	Spirit of the Wolf (MetalART)	1,000	1996	500.00	500
1992	Spirit of the Wolf (pewter)	500	1993	350.00	850

Chilmark American West To The Great Spirit - T. Sullivan

YEAR ISSUE		EDITION LIMIT	YEAR RETD.	ISSUE PRICE	*QUOTE U.S.$
1993	Gray Elk	950		775.00	775
1992	Shooting Star	950	1994	775.00	775
1994	Thunder Cloud	950		775.00	775
1993	Two Eagles	950		775.00	775

Chilmark American West Works of the Masters - Various

YEAR ISSUE		EDITION LIMIT	YEAR RETD.	ISSUE PRICE	*QUOTE U.S.$
1985	Bronco Buster (lg.) - C. Rousell	766	1989	400.00	400
1987	Bronco Buster - A.T. McGrory	Suspd.		225.00	225
1986	Buffalo Hunt - A. McGrory	172	1989	550.00	800
1984	Cheyenne (Remington) - C. Rousell	285	1988	400.00	600
1988	Cheyenne - A.T. McGrory	Suspd.		265.00	265
1987	Coming Through the Rye - A. McGrory	Retrd.	1995	750.00	750
1986	End of the Trail (lg.) - A. McGrory	Retrd.	1995	450.00	495
1988	End of the Trail (mini) - A. McGrory	2,500	1992	225.00	325
1987	Mountain Man - A.T. McGrory	Suspd.		240.00	240

Chilmark Americana - L. Davis

YEAR ISSUE		EDITION LIMIT	YEAR RETD.	ISSUE PRICE	*QUOTE U.S.$
1994	City Slicker	Suspd.		2500.00	2500
1994	Milkin' Time	Suspd.		295.00	295
1993	Skedaddlin'	350	1995	2000.00	2000
1993	Tin Man	Suspd.		2500.00	2500

Chilmark Civil War - F. Barnum

YEAR ISSUE		EDITION LIMIT	YEAR RETD.	ISSUE PRICE	*QUOTE U.S.$
1993	Abraham Lincoln Bust (bronze)	50	1993	2000.00	2250
1988	Brother Against Brother	Suspd.		265.00	265
1991	Dear Mother	Suspd.		175.00	175
1989	Devil's Den	Suspd.		280.00	280
1988	A Father's Farewell	2,500	1994	150.00	225
1989	Gaines Mill	Suspd.		580.00	580
1988	Johnny Shiloh	2,500	1992	100.00	220-285
1992	Kennesaw Mountain	350	1992	650.00	1500
1993	Lincoln Bust (MetalART)	Suspd.		1250.00	1250
1993	Lincoln Bust (pewter)	Suspd.		950.00	950
1988	Nothing Left	Suspd.		265.00	265
1989	Old Abe	Suspd.		420.00	420
1992	Parson's Battery	500	1993	495.00	650-750
1987	Pickett's Charge	Retrd.	1994	350.00	490-675
1991	Quantrill's Raiders	Suspd.		1000.00	1000
1987	The Rescue	Retrd.	1995	275.00	350-400
1987	Saving The Colors	Retrd.	1992	350.00	485-650
1990	Spangler's Spring	Suspd.		235.00	235

Chilmark Civil War Cavalry Generals - F. Barnum

YEAR ISSUE		EDITION LIMIT	YEAR RETD.	ISSUE PRICE	*QUOTE U.S.$
1993	George Armstrong Custer	950	1996	375.00	375
1992	J.E.B. Stuart	950	1992	375.00	500
1993	Nathan Bedford Forrest	950	1992	375.00	400-650
1994	Philip Sheridan	Suspd.		375.00	375

Chilmark Civil War Christmas Specials - F. Barnum

YEAR ISSUE		EDITION LIMIT	YEAR RETD.	ISSUE PRICE	*QUOTE U.S.$
1992	Merry Christmas Yank	810	1992	350.00	500-600
1993	Silent Night	591	1993	350.00	500-700
1994	Christmas Truce	Retrd.	1994	295.00	325-600
1995	Peace on Earth	Retrd.	1995	350.00	350

Chilmark Civil War Confederates - F. Barnum

YEAR ISSUE		EDITION LIMIT	YEAR RETD.	ISSUE PRICE	*QUOTE U.S.$
1995	The Cavalier (bronze)	75		1500.00	1500
1995	The Cavalier (pewter)	750		625.00	625
1993	The Gentleman Soldier (bronze)	75		1500.00	1500
1993	The Gentleman Soldier (pewter)	750	1995	625.00	625
1994	Old Jack (bronze)	75		1500.00	1500
1994	Old Jack (pewter)	750		625.00	625

Chilmark Civil War Event Specials - F. Barnum

YEAR ISSUE		EDITION LIMIT	YEAR RETD.	ISSUE PRICE	*QUOTE U.S.$
1991	Boots and Saddles	437	1991	95.00	200-450
1992	140th NY Zouave	389	1992	95.00	150-210
1993	Johnny Reb	889	1993	95.00	150-190
1994	Billy Yank	Retrd.	1994	95.00	125
1995	Seaman, CSS Alabama	Retrd.	1995	95.00	95
1996	The Forager	Yr.Iss.	1996	110.00	110

Chilmark Civil War Redemption Specials - F. Barnum

YEAR ISSUE		EDITION LIMIT	YEAR RETD.	ISSUE PRICE	*QUOTE U.S.$
1989	Lee To The Rear	1,088	1990	300.00	700-800
1990	Lee And Jackson	1,040	1991	375.00	550-1000
1991	Stonewall Jackson	1,169	1992	295.00	450
1992	Zouaves 1st Manassas	640	1993	375.00	500-600
1993	Letter to Sarah	Retrd.	1994	395.00	450-700
1994	Angel of Fredericksburg	Retrd.	1995	275.00	275
1995	Rebel Yell	N/A		475.00	475

Chilmark Civil War The Adversaries - F. Barnum

YEAR ISSUE		EDITION LIMIT	YEAR RETD.	ISSUE PRICE	*QUOTE U.S.$
1991	Robert E. Lee	950	1992	350.00	1250-1500
1992	Stonewall Jackson	950	1992	375.00	500-695
1992	Ulysses S. Grant	950	1992	350.00	600-1000
1993	Wm. Tecumseh Sherman	950	1993	375.00	375-675
1993	Set of 4		1993	1450.00	3500-4000

Chilmark Civil War The Commanders - F. Barnum

YEAR ISSUE		EDITION LIMIT	YEAR RETD.	ISSUE PRICE	*QUOTE U.S.$
1994	Grant Bust (bronze)	Suspd.		2000.00	2000
1994	Grant Bust (MetalART)	Suspd.		1000.00	1000

*Quotes have been rounded up to nearest dollar

Collectors' Information Bureau

83

Hudson Creek
to Hudson Creek

FIGURINES

YEAR ISSUE		EDITION LIMIT	YEAR RETD.	ISSUE PRICE	*QUOTE U.S.$
1994	Grant Bust (pewter)	Suspd.		750.00	750
1993	Lee Bust (bronze)	Suspd.		2000.00	2000
1993	Lee Bust (MetalART)	Suspd.		1000.00	1000
1993	Lee Bust (pewter)	Suspd.		750.00	750

Chilmark Civil War Turning Points - F. Barnum

1994	Clashing Sabers	500	1995	600.00	600
1993	The High Tide	500	1993	600.00	900
1996	Last Resort	500		600.00	600
1995	The Swinging Gate	500	1996	600.00	600

Chilmark Wildlife - Various

1980	Affirmed - M. Jovine	145	1987	850.00	1275
1980	Born Free - B. Rodden	950	1988	250.00	675
1978	Buffalo - B. Rodden	950	1986	170.00	375-400
1977	The Challenge - B. Rodden	1,600	1977	175.00	250-300
1981	Clydesdale Wheel Horse - C. Keim	2,808	1989	120.00	430
1991	Cry of Freedom - S. Knight	Suspd.		395.00	395
1994	Down to the Wire - A. Petitto	Suspd.		495.00	495
1980	Duel of the Bighorns - M. Boyett	137	1987	650.00	1200
1988	Eagles Rock - C. Bronson	Suspd.		3100.00	3100
1979	Elephant - D. Polland	750	1987	315.00	450-550
1992	Feeling Free - P. Sedlow	Suspd.		100.00	100
1981	Freedom Eagle - G. deLodzia	2,500	1983	195.00	750-900
1979	Giraffe - D. Polland	414	1981	145.00	145
1991	The Guardian - J. Mullican	Suspd.		450.00	450
1989	High and Mighty - A. McGrory	Suspd.		185.00	200
1988	The Honor and the Glory - S. Knight	Suspd.		345.00	345
1979	Kudu - D. Polland	204	1981	160.00	160
1980	Lead Can't Catch Him - M. Boyett	397	1987	645.00	845
1978	Paddock Walk - A. Petitto	1,277	1991	85.00	215
1980	Prairie Sovereign - M. Boyett	247	1987	550.00	800
1992	Racing the Wind - P. Sedlow	Suspd.		100.00	100
1979	Rhino - D. Polland	142	1981	135.00	135-550
1977	Rise and Shine - B. Rodden	1,500	1977	135.00	200
1980	Ruby-Throated Hummingbird - V. Hayton	500	1983	275.00	350
1976	Running Free - B. Rodden	2,500	1977	75.00	300
1976	Stallion - B. Rodden	2,500	1977	75.00	260
1985	Stretch Run - A. Petitto	Suspd.		250.00	250
1992	Tender Mercies - P. Sedlow	Suspd.		130.00	130
1982	Tender Persuasion - J. Mootry	155	1987	950.00	1250
1992	Untamed - P. Sedlow	Suspd.		100.00	100
1980	Voice of Experience - M. Boyett	174	1987	645.00	850
1985	Wild Stallion - D. Polland	179	1988	145.00	350
1987	Winged Victory - J. Mullican	Suspd.		275.00	315
1982	Wings of Liberty - M. Boyett	950	1986	625.00	1200

Hudson Pewter Figures - P.W. Baston, unless otherwise noted

1972	Benjamin Franklin	Closed	1974	15.00	75-100
1969	Betsy Ross	Closed	1971	30.00	100-125
1969	Colonial Blacksmith	Closed	1971	30.00	100-125
1975	Declaration Wall Plaque	100	1975	Unkn.	300-500
1975	The Favored Scholar - P.W. Baston	6	1975	Unkn.	600-1000
1972	George Washington	Closed	1974	15.00	75-100
1969	George Washington (Cannon)	Closed	1971	35.00	75-100
1972	James Madison	Closed	1974	15.00	50-75
1972	John Adams	Closed	1974	15.00	75-100
1969	John Hancock	Closed	1971	15.00	100-125
1975	Lee's Ninth General Order	Closed	1975	Unkn.	300-400
1975	Lincoln's Gettysburg Address	Closed	1975	Unkn.	300-400
1975	Neighboring Pews	6	1975	Unkn.	600-1000
1975	Spirit of '76 - P.W. Baston	12	1975	Unkn.	750-1500
1972	Thomas Jefferson - P.W. Baston	Closed	1974	15.00	75-100
1975	Washington's Letter of Acceptance - P.W. Baston	Closed	1975	Unkn.	300-400
1975	Weighing the Baby - P.W. Baston	6	1975	Unkn.	600-1000

Mickey & Co. - Staff

1989	"Gold Edition" Hollywood Mickey	Retrd.	1990	200.00	400-750
1994	Be My Valentine	Closed	1994	65.00	75-125
1995	California or Bust! (pewter)	250	1995	1250.00	1750
1994	Christmas Waltz	Closed	1994	65.00	100-200
1997	Daisy-Carousel Ride	2,500		160.00	160
1996	Donald-Carousel Ride	2,500		160.00	160
1995	The Duck (bronze)	50		1375.00	1375
1995	The Duck (MetalART))	200		650.00	650
1995	The Duck (pewter)	300		500.00	500
1989	Fantasia	Retrd.	1995	19.00	19
1996	Getting Out the Vote	Retrd.	1996	99.00	99
1995	Goofy-Carousel Ride	2,500		195.00	195
1988	Happy Birthday Mickey	Yr.Iss.	1989	60.00	150
1989	Hollywood Mickey	Suspd.	1991	165.00	200-300
1996	Hook, Line & Sinker (bronze)	75		3250.00	3250
1996	Hook, Line & Sinker (pewter)	975		1250.00	1250
1994	Lights, Camera, Action (bronze)	50		3250.00	3250
1994	Lights, Camera, Action (pewter)	500		1500.00	1500
1994	Mickey on Parade (bronze)	50	1994	950.00	1450-1600
1994	Mickey on Parade (MetalART))	350	1994	500.00	600-900
1994	Mickey on Parade (pewter)	750	1996	375.00	400
1991	Mickey-Carousel Ride	2,500		150.00	160
1992	Minnie-Carousel Ride	2,500		150.00	160
1994	Mouse in a Million (bronze)	50	1994	1250.00	1500-2000
1994	Mouse in a Million (MetalART))	250	1994	650.00	800-1000
1994	Mouse in a Million (pewter)	500	1994	500.00	600-900
1991	Mouse Waltz	Retrd.	1994	41.00	41
1994	Puttin' on the Ritz (bronze)	50	1994	2000.00	2200
1994	Puttin' on the Ritz (MetalART))	250		1000.00	1000
1994	Puttin' on the Ritz (pewter)	350		750.00	750
1996	Simply Minnie (bronze)	50		1100.00	1100
1996	Simply Minnie (MetalART))	200		600.00	600
1996	Simply Minnie (pewter)	300		450.00	450
1988	Socerer's Apprentice	Retrd.	1995	25.00	25
1986	Socerer's Apprentice (lg.)	Retrd.	1995	25.00	25
1988	Socerer's Apprentice/Music Train	Retrd.	1995	28.00	28
1990	Socerer's Apprentice/No. 9 Birthday Train	Retrd.	1995	25.00	25
1990	Socerer's Apprentice/No. 9 Birthday Train-painted	Retrd.	1995	27.00	27
1988	Sweethearts	Retrd.	1993	45.00	45

Mickey & Co. Annual Christmas Special - Staff

1993	Hanging the Stockings	Annual	1993	295.00	350-395
1994	Trimming the Tree	Annual	1994	350.00	400-425
1995	Holiday Harmony?	Annual	1995	395.00	395
1996	Christmas Tree Safari	Annual		195.00	195

Mickey & Co. Annual Santa - Staff

1993	Checking it Twice	Annual	1993	195.00	300
1994	Just For You	Annual	1994	265.00	300-400
1995	Surprise, Santa!	Annual	1995	225.00	245
1996	Jolly Old St. Mick	Annual		245.00	245

Mickey & Co. Annual Special - Staff

1994	Bicycle Built For Two	Retrd.	1995	195.00	225-400
1995	Riding the Rails	Retrd.	1996	295.00	295

Mickey & Co. Comic Capers - Staff

1995	Crack the Whip (bronze)	50		2000.00	2000
1995	Crack the Whip (pewter)	500		750.00	750
1994	Foursome Follies (bronze)	50	1994	2000.00	2000
1994	Foursome Follies (pewter)	500	1994	750.00	700-1000
1994	Matched Numbrd set	500	1994	N/A	3100-3500
1994	Un-Matched Numbrd set	500	1994	N/A	2700-2900

Mickey & Co. Country Club - Staff

1995	Mouse Trap (bronze)	75		400.00	400
1995	Mouse Trap (pewter)	950		175.00	175
1995	Perfect Form (bronze)	75		450.00	450
1995	Perfect Form (pewter)	950		195.00	195
1995	Teed Off (bronze)	75		400.00	400
1995	Teed Off (pewter)	950		175.00	175
1995	What Birdie? (bronze)	75		400.00	400
1995	What Birdie? (pewter)	950		175.00	175

Mickey & Co. Generations of Mickey - Staff

1987	Antique Mickey	2,500	1990	95.00	700-1200
1990	The Band Concert	2,500		185.00	195
1990	The Band Concert (Painted)	500	1993	215.00	400-600
1990	Disneyland Mickey	2,500		150.00	160
1989	Mickey's Gala Premiere	2,500		150.00	160
1991	The Mouse-1935	1,200		185.00	195
1991	Plane Crazy-1928	2,500		175.00	185
1989	Sorcerer's Apprentice	2,500	1993	150.00	300-600
1989	Steamboat Willie	2,500	1993	165.00	325-425

Mickey & Co. Highway Highjinks - Staff

1997	Coastal Cruisin' (bronze)	25		1650.00	1650
1997	Coastal Cruisin' (MetalART)	350		550.00	550
1996	Get Your Kicks (bronze)	25		1650.00	1650
1996	Get Your Kicks (MetalART)	350	1996	550.00	550

Mickey & Co. Mickey and Friends - Staff

1994	Donald (bronze)	75	1994	325.00	400
1994	Donald (pewter)	1,500		150.00	150
1994	Goofy (bronze)	75	1994	375.00	450
1994	Goofy (pewter)	1,500		175.00	175
1994	Mickey (bronze)	75	1994	325.00	400
1994	Mickey (pewter)	1,500		150.00	150
1994	Minnie (bronze)	75	1994	325.00	400
1994	Minnie (pewter)	1,500		150.00	150
1994	Pluto (bronze)	75	1994	325.00	400
1994	Pluto (pewter)	1,500		150.00	150

Mickey & Co. On the Road - Staff

1994	Beach Bound	350	1994	350.00	800-1300
1992	Cruising	350	1992	275.00	2000-3500
1993	Sunday Drive	350	1993	325.00	1200-1800
1993	Matched Numbrd. set/3	350	1993	950.00	8000-9000
1993	Mixed & Matched Numbrd. set/3	350	1993	950.00	5000-8000

Mickey & Co. Sweethearts - Staff

1994	Jitterbugging	500	1994	450.00	600-900
1995	Mice on Ice	500	1995	425.00	500-700
1994	Rowboat Serenade	500	1994	495.00	500-700

Mickey & Co. Sweethearts Too - Staff

1996	First Date (bronze)	35		750.00	750
1996	First Date (pewter)	500	1996	250.00	250
1997	Love Toons (bronze)	35		1050.00	1050
1997	Love Toons (pewter)	500		350.00	350
1996	Sippin' Soda (bronze)	35		850.00	850
1996	Sippin' Soda (pewter)	500		275.00	275

Mickey & Co. The Sorcerer's Apprentice - Staff

1990	The Whirlpool	Retrd.	1995	225.00	275
1990	The Dream	Retrd.	1995	225.00	240
1990	The Incantation	Retrd.	1995	150.00	175
1990	The Repentant Apprentice	Retrd.	1994	195.00	300-500
1990	The Sorcerer's Apprentice	Retrd.	1995	225.00	240
1990	Matched Numbrd set	Retrd.	1995	225.00	1800-2200

Mickey & Co. Two Wheeling - Staff

1994	Get Your Motor Runnin' (bronze)	50	1994	1200.00	1300-1600
1994	Get Your Motor Runnin' (MetalART)	950	1994	475.00	600-1000
1994	Head Out on the Highway (bronze)	50	1996	1200.00	1200-1300
1994	Head Out on the Highway (MetalART)	950		475.00	475
1995	Looking For Adventure (bronze)	50		1200.00	1200
1995	Looking For Adventure (MetalART)	950		475.00	475

Polland Collectors Society Annual Redemption Special - Various

1995	Thunder Pipe	Closed	1996	395.00	395
1996	Two For the Price of One	Yr.Iss.		260.00	260

Polland Collectors Society Membership Sculptures - D. Polland

1995	Mystic Medicine Man	Closed	1996	Gift	N/A
1996	Training Session	Yr.Iss.		Gift	N/A

See also Polland Studios Collector Society

Sebastian Miniatures Collectors Society - P.W. Baston, unless otherwise noted

1980	S.M.C. Society Plaque ('80 Charter)	11,914	1980	Gift	20-35
1981	S.M.C. Society Plaque	4,957	1981	Gift	20-30
1982	S.M.C. Society Plaque	1,530	1982	Gift	20-30
1983	S.M.C. Society Plaque	1,167	1983	Gift	20-30
1984	S.M.C. Society Plaque	505	1984	Gift	50-75
1984	Self Portrait	Retrd.	1994	Gift	45
1995	Grace - P.W. Baston, Jr.	Annual	1995	Gift	N/A

Sebastian Miniatures Collectors Association - P.W. Baston, Jr.

1996	Ezra	Annual		Gift	N/A

Sebastian Miniatures Member Only - P.W. Baston, Jr.

1989	The Collectors	Yr.Iss.	1990	39.50	40
1992	Christopher Columbus	Yr.Iss.	1993	28.50	29

Sebastian Miniatures Holiday Memories-Member Only - P.W. Baston, Jr.

1990	Thanksgiving Helper	Yr.Iss.	1991	39.50	40
1990	Leprechaun	Yr.Iss.	1991	27.50	35-40
1991	Trick or Treat	Yr.Iss.	1992	25.50	50-75
1993	Father Time	Yr.Iss.	1994	27.50	28
1993	New Year Baby	Yr.Iss.	1994	27.50	28
1994	Look What the Easter Bunny Left Me	Yr.Iss.	1995	27.50	28
1995	On Parade	Yr.Iss.		N/A	N/A

Sebastian Miniature Figurines - P.W. Baston, Jr.

1991	America Salutes Desert Storm -bronze	Retrd.	1994	26.50	100
1991	America Salutes Desert Storm -painted	350	1991	49.50	200-250
1990	America's Hometown	4,750		34.00	34
1994	Boston Light	3,500		45.00	45
1994	Egg Rock Light	3,500		55.00	55
1992	Firefighter	500	1992	28.00	50
1991	Happy Hood Holidays	2,000	1991	32.50	95-105
1983	Harry Hood	1,000	1983	Unkn.	200-250
1992	I Know I Left It Here Somewhere	1,000		28.50	29
1985	It's Hoods (Wagon)	3,250	1985	N/A	75-100
1994	A Job Well Done	1,000		27.50	28
1993	The Lamplighter	1,000		28.00	28
1994	Nubble Light	3,500		45.00	45
1993	Pumpkin Island Light	3,500		55.00	55
1993	Soap Box Derby	500		45.00	45
1986	Statue of Liberty (AT & T)	1,000	1986	N/A	200-225
1987	White House (Gold, Oval Base)	250	1987	17.00	35-50

Sebastian Miniatures America Remembers - P.W. Baston

1979	Family Sing	7,358	1979	29.50	125-150
1980	Family Picnic	16,527	1980	29.50	60-100
1981	Family Reads Aloud	21,027	1981	34.50	50-75
1982	Family Fishing	8,734	1982	34.50	50-100
1983	Family Feast	4,147	1983	37.50	150-175

Sebastian Miniatures Children At Play - P.W. Baston

1979	Building Days Boy	10,000	1980	19.50	30-50
1979	Building Days Girl	10,000	1980	19.50	30-50
1981	Sailing Days Boy	10,000	1981	19.50	30-50
1981	Sailing Days Girl	10,000	1981	19.50	30-50
1982	School Days Boy	10,000	1982	19.50	40-60
1982	School Days Girl	10,000	1982	19.50	40-60
1978	Sidewalk Days Boy	10,000	1980	19.50	40-60
1978	Sidewalk Days Girl	10,000	1980	19.50	40-60
1980	Snow Days Boy	10,000	1980	19.50	40-60
1980	Snow Days Girl	10,000	1980	19.50	40-60

Sebastian Miniatures Christmas - P.W. Baston, Jr.

1993	Caroling With Santa	1,000		29.00	29
1993	Harmonizing With Santa	1,000		27.00	27
1994	Victorian Christmas Skaters	1,000		32.50	33
1995	Midnight Snacks	1,000		28.50	29
1996	Victorian Christmas Santa	1,000		28.50	29

Sebastian Miniatures Exchange Figurines - P.W. Baston, Jr., unless otherwise noted

1984	First Things First	1,267	1985	30.00	45

*Quotes have been rounded up to nearest dollar

YEAR ISSUE		EDITION LIMIT	YEAR RETD.	ISSUE PRICE	*QUOTE U.S.$
1987	It's About Time	576	1988	25.00	40
1986	News Wagon	1,422	1987	35.00	45
1983	Newspaper Boy - P.W. Baston	1,708	1984	28.50	60-95
1985	Newstand	1,454	1986	30.00	45

Sebastian Miniatures Firefighter Collection - P.W. Baston, Jr.

YEAR ISSUE		EDITION LIMIT	YEAR RETD.	ISSUE PRICE	*QUOTE U.S.$
1993	Firefighter No. 1	950	1995	48.00	48
1994	Firefighter No. 2	950		48.00	48
1994	Firefighter No. 3	950		48.00	48
1995	Firefighter No. 4	950		48.00	48

Sebastian Miniatures Jimmy Fund - P.W. Baston, Jr., unless otherwise noted

YEAR ISSUE		EDITION LIMIT	YEAR RETD.	ISSUE PRICE	*QUOTE U.S.$
1993	Boy With Ducks	500	1993	27.50	28
1984	Catcher - P.W. Baston	1,872	1984	24.50	35-75
1987	Football Player	1,270	1988	26.50	27
1995	Girl in Riding Outfit	500		28.00	28
1994	Girl on Bench	500	1994	28.00	28
1985	Hockey Player	1,836	1986	24.50	35-50
1988	Santa	500	1988	32.50	33
1983	Schoolboy - P.W. Baston	3,567	1983	24.50	25-35
1986	Soccer Player	1,166	1987	25.00	25

Sebastian Miniatures Private Label - P.W. Baston Jr.

YEAR ISSUE		EDITION LIMIT	YEAR RETD.	ISSUE PRICE	*QUOTE U.S.$
1993	Adams Academy w/ Steeple	75	N/A	100.00	200-225
1993	Adams Academy w/o Steeple	750	N/A	30.00	30

Sebastian Miniatures Shakespearean-Member Only - P.W. Baston, unless otherwise noted

YEAR ISSUE		EDITION LIMIT	YEAR RETD.	ISSUE PRICE	*QUOTE U.S.$
1984	Anne Boleyn	3,897	1984	17.50	35
1984	Henry VIII	4,578	1984	19.50	35
1985	Falstaff	3,357	1985	19.50	35
1985	Mistress Ford	2,836	1985	17.50	35
1986	Juliet	2,620	1986	17.50	35
1986	Romeo	2,853	1986	19.50	35
1987	Countess Olivia	1,893	1987	19.50	35
1987	Malvolio	2,093	1987	21.50	35
1988	Audrey	1,548	1988	22.50	35
1988	Shakespeare - P.W. Baston, Jr.	Retrd.	1989	23.50	35
1988	Touchstone	1,770	1988	22.50	35
1989	Cleopatra	Retrd.	1989	27.00	35
1989	Mark Antony	Retrd.	1989	27.00	35

Sebastian Miniatures Washington Irving-Member Only - P.W. Baston

YEAR ISSUE		EDITION LIMIT	YEAR RETD.	ISSUE PRICE	*QUOTE U.S.$
1980	Rip Van Winkle	12,005	1983	19.50	35
1981	Ichabod Crane	9,069	1983	19.50	35
1981	Dame Van Winkle	11,217	1983	19.50	35
1982	Brom Bones (Headless Horseman)	6,610	1983	22.50	35
1982	Katrina Van Tassel	7,367	1983	19.50	35
1983	Diedrich Knickerbocker	5,528	1983	22.50	35

June McKenna Collectibles, Inc.

Black Folk Art - J. McKenna

YEAR ISSUE		EDITION LIMIT	YEAR RETD.	ISSUE PRICE	*QUOTE U.S.$
1987	Aunt Bertha -3D	Closed	1991	36.00	75-125
1983	Black Boy With Watermelon, available in 3 colors	Closed	1988	12.00	75-125
1986	Black Butler	Closed	1989	13.00	75
1983	Black Girl With Watermelon, available in 3 colors	Closed	1988	12.00	75-125
1984	Black Man With Pig, available in 3 colors	Closed	1988	13.00	100-150
1984	Black Woman With Broom, available in 3 colors	Closed	1988	13.00	100-125
1989	Delia	Closed	1991	16.00	65
1992	Fishing John -3D	1,000	1997	160.00	160
1989	Jake	Closed	1991	16.00	65
1985	Kids in a Tub -3D	Closed	1990	30.00	110
1985	Kissing Cousins - sill sitter	Closed	1990	36.00	125-175
1990	Let's Play Ball -3D	Closed	1993	45.00	75-100
1987	Lil' Willie -3D	Closed	1991	36.00	75-100
1984	Mammie Cloth Doll	Closed	1988	90.00	450-500
1985	Mammie With Kids -3D	Closed	1990	90.00	175-250
1985	Mammie With Spoon	Closed	1989	13.00	250
1988	Netty	Closed	1991	16.00	65
1984	Remus Cloth Doll	Closed	1988	90.00	375-500
1988	Renty	Closed	1991	16.00	65
1990	Sunday's Best -3D	Closed	1993	45.00	75-100
1987	Sweet Prissy -3D	Closed	1991	36.00	75-100
1992	Sweet Sister Sue -3D	1,000	1997	160.00	160
1990	Tasha	Closed	1991	17.00	65
1985	Toaster Cover	Closed	1988	50.00	350
1990	Tyree	Closed	1991	17.00	65
1987	Uncle Jacob -3D	Closed	1991	36.00	75-100
1985	Watermelon Patch Kids	Closed	1990	24.00	100-150

Carolers - J. McKenna

YEAR ISSUE		EDITION LIMIT	YEAR RETD.	ISSUE PRICE	*QUOTE U.S.$
1985	Boy Caroler	Closed	1989	36.00	75-100
1992	Carolers, Grandparents	Closed	1994	70.00	85
1991	Carolers, Man With Girl	Closed	1994	50.00	65
1991	Carolers, Woman With Boy	Closed	1994	50.00	65
1994	Children Carolers	Closed	1997	90.00	90
1985	Girl Caroler	Closed	1989	36.00	75-100
1985	Man Caroler	Closed	1989	36.00	75-100
1985	Woman Caroler	Closed	1989	36.00	75-100

June McKenna Figurines - J. McKenna

YEAR ISSUE		EDITION LIMIT	YEAR RETD.	ISSUE PRICE	*QUOTE U.S.$
1989	16th Century Santa -3D, blue	Closed	1991	60.00	200-250
1989	16th Century Santa -3D, green	Closed	1989	60.00	250-350
1989	17th Century Santa -3D, red	Closed	1991	70.00	200-250
1993	Angel Name Plaque	Closed	1994	70.00	100
1983	Boy Rag Doll	Closed	1983	12.00	300-450
1985	Bride -3D	Closed	1987	25.00	200
1985	Bride w/o base -3D	Closed	1985	25.00	150-225
1993	Children Ice Skaters	Closed	1994	60.00	75
1992	Choir of Angels	Closed	1993	60.00	100
1992	Christmas Santa -3D	Closed	1993	60.00	100-150
1987	Country Rag Boy (sitting)	Closed	1990	40.00	155
1987	Country Rag Girl (sitting)	Closed	1990	40.00	155
1994	Decorating for Christmas -3D	Closed	1997	70.00	100-125
1985	Father Times -3D	Closed	1991	40.00	175-200
1983	Girl Rag Doll	Closed	1983	12.00	300-450
1993	A Good Night's Sleep -3D	Closed	1995	70.00	100-125
1985	Groom w/o base -3D	Closed	1985	25.00	175-235
1985	Groom-3D	Closed	1987	25.00	150-200
1989	Jolly Ole Santa -3D	Closed	1991	44.00	175-200
1992	Let It Snow	Closed	1997	70.00	85
1986	Little St. Nick -3D	Closed	1990	50.00	175-200
1986	Male Angel -3D	Closed	1986	44.00	1300-1700
1988	Mr. Santa -3D	Closed	1991	44.00	100
1993	Mr. Snowman	Closed	1994	40.00	65
1988	Mrs. Santa -3D	Closed	1989	50.00	200-250
1987	Name Plaque	Closed	1992	50.00	125-150
1990	Noel -3D	Closed	1992	50.00	125
1987	Patriotic Santa -3D	Closed	1989	50.00	300-350
1993	Santa and Friends -3D	Closed	1997	70.00	100-120
1993	Santa Name Plaque	Closed	1995	70.00	100
1993	The Snow Family	Closed	1994	40.00	65
1994	Snowman and Child	Closed	1997	70.00	85
1985	Soldier -3D	Closed	1988	40.00	175-200
1994	Star of Bethlehem-Angel	Closed	1997	40.00	40
1995	A Surprise For Joey -3D	Closed	1997	70.00	70
1992	Taking A Break -3D	Closed	1995	60.00	100-125
1995	Travel Plans	Closed	1997	70.00	70
1984	Tree Topper	Closed	1987	70.00	350-400

Limited Edition - J. McKenna

YEAR ISSUE		EDITION LIMIT	YEAR RETD.	ISSUE PRICE	*QUOTE U.S.$
1988	Bringing Home Christmas	4,000	1990	170.00	300-400
1987	Christmas Eve	4,000	1989	170.00	375-400
1992	Christmas Gathering	4,000	1997	220.00	300
1991	Coming to Town	4,000	1994	220.00	300-350
1983	Father Christmas	4,000	1986	90.00	2500-3000
1987	Kris Kringle	4,000	1990	350.00	675-800
1990	Night Before Christmas	1,500	1993	750.00	750-800
1984	Old Saint Nick	4,000	1986	100.00	600-900
1993	The Patriot	4,000	1997	250.00	300
1988	Remembrance of Christmas Past	4,000	1992	400.00	500-650
1991	Santa's Hot Air Balloon	1,500	1993	800.00	800
1989	Santa's Wardrobe	1,500	1992	750.00	850-1000
1989	Seasons Greetings	4,000	1992	200.00	325-350
1986	Victorian	4,000	1988	150.00	450-650
1990	Wilderness	4,000	1994	200.00	275-300
1985	Woodland	4,000	1987	140.00	500-750

Limited Edition 7" - J. McKenna

YEAR ISSUE		EDITION LIMIT	YEAR RETD.	ISSUE PRICE	*QUOTE U.S.$
1991	Christmas Bishop	7,500	1993	110.00	175-250
1993	Christmas Cheer 1st ed.	7,500	1993	120.00	350-400
1993	Christmas Cheer 2nd. ed.	7,500	1995	120.00	150-200
1990	Christmas Delight	7,500	1992	100.00	150-250
1995	Christmas Lullaby, red	7,500	1996	120.00	125-350
1988	Christmas Memories	7,500	1991	90.00	250
1992	Christmas Wizard	7,500	1994	110.00	150-200
1990	Ethnic Santa	7,500	1992	100.00	175-250
1988	Joyful Christmas	7,500	1991	90.00	175-250
1994	Mrs. Claus, Dancing to the Tune	7,500	1997	120.00	120
1989	Old Fashioned Santa	7,500	1991	100.00	150-200
1989	Santa's Bag of Surprises	7,500	1991	100.00	225-275
1994	Santa's One Man Band	7,500	1997	120.00	120

Limited Edition Flatback - J. McKenna

YEAR ISSUE		EDITION LIMIT	YEAR RETD.	ISSUE PRICE	*QUOTE U.S.$
1991	Bag of Stars	10,000	1993	34.00	45-65
1993	Bells of Christmas	10,000	1995	40.00	45-65
1989	Blue Christmas	10,000	1991	32.00	100
1992	Deck The Halls	10,000	1994	34.00	45-65
1991	Farewell Santa	10,000	1993	34.00	55-65
1992	Good Tidings	10,000	1994	34.00	45-65
1990	Medieval Santa	10,000	1992	34.00	65
1988	Mystical Santa	10,000	1991	30.00	100
1994	Not Once But Twice	10,000	1997	40.00	40
1990	Old Time Santa	10,000	1992	34.00	65
1994	Post Marked North Pole	10,000	1997	40.00	40
1993	Santa's Love	10,000	1995	40.00	55-65
1988	Toys of Joy	10,000	1991	30.00	70-100
1989	Victorian	10,000	1991	32.00	120

Nativity Set - J. McKenna

YEAR ISSUE		EDITION LIMIT	YEAR RETD.	ISSUE PRICE	*QUOTE U.S.$
1988	Nativity - 6/pc. (Mary, Joseph, Baby Jesus, Manger, Guardian Angel & creche)	Closed	1997	130.00	150
1990	Shepherds With Sheep - 2/pc.	Closed	1997	60.00	60
1989	Three Wise Men	Closed	1997	60.00	90

Personal Appearance Figurines - J. McKenna

YEAR ISSUE		EDITION LIMIT	YEAR RETD.	ISSUE PRICE	*QUOTE U.S.$
1989	Father Christmas	Closed	1993	30.00	150-225
1990	Old Saint Nick	Closed	1994	30.00	125-175
1991	Woodland	Closed	1995	35.00	75-125
1992	Victorian	Closed	1996	35.00	50-100
1993	Christmas Eve	Closed	1997	35.00	35
1994	Bringing Home Christmas	4-Yr.		35.00	35
1995	Seasons Greetings	4-Yr.		35.00	35
1996	Wilderness	4-Yr.		35.00	35
1997	Coming To town	4-Yr.		35.00	35

Registered Edition - J. McKenna

YEAR ISSUE		EDITION LIMIT	YEAR RETD.	ISSUE PRICE	*QUOTE U.S.$
1991	Checking His List	Closed	1994	230.00	300-350
1986	Colonial	Closed	1990	150.00	300-400
1992	Forty Winks	Closed	1994	250.00	300
1988	Jolly Ole St. Nick	Closed	1996	170.00	350-450
1994	Say Cheese, Please	Closed	1997	250.00	250
1993	Tomorrow's Christmas	Closed	1995	250.00	275
1990	Toy Maker	Closed	1993	200.00	400
1989	Traditional	Closed	1991	180.00	300-400
1987	White Christmas	Closed	1987	170.00	900-1100

Special Limited Edition - J. McKenna

YEAR ISSUE		EDITION LIMIT	YEAR RETD.	ISSUE PRICE	*QUOTE U.S.$
1996	All Aboard-Logging Car	Yr.Iss.	1997	250.00	250
1995	All Aboard-Toy Car	Closed	1996	250.00	275
1993	Baking Cookies	2,000	1995	450.00	500
1991	Bedtime Stories	2,000	1994	500.00	500
1990	Christmas Dreams	4,000	1992	280.00	400-500
1990	Christmas Dreams (Hassock)	63	1990	280.00	1600-2000
1996	International Santa-German Pelznichol	Yr.Iss.	1997	100.00	100
1989	Last Gentle Nudge	4,000	1991	280.00	350-450
1989	Santa & His Magic Sleigh	4,000	1992	280.00	350-450
1992	Santa's Arrival	2,000	1994	300.00	350-450
1990	Santa's Reindeer	1,500	1993	400.00	400-450
1990	Up On The Rooftop	4,000	1991	280.00	400-450
1994	Welcome to the World	2,000	1995	400.00	450

Victorian Limited Edition - J. McKenna

YEAR ISSUE		EDITION LIMIT	YEAR RETD.	ISSUE PRICE	*QUOTE U.S.$
1990	Edward -3D	1,000	1991	180.00	450
1990	Elizabeth -3D	1,000	1991	180.00	450
1990	Joseph -3D	Closed	1991	50.00	50-250
1990	Victoria -3D	Closed	1991	50.00	50-250

Kurt S. Adler, Inc.

Angel Darlings - N. Bailey

YEAR ISSUE		EDITION LIMIT	YEAR RETD.	ISSUE PRICE	*QUOTE U.S.$
1996	Almost Fits H4765/1	Open		15.00	15
1996	Bottoms Up H4765/6	Open		15.00	15
1996	Buddies H4765/3	Open		15.00	15
1996	Cuddles H4765/5	Open		15.00	15
1996	Dream Builders H4765/4	Open		15.00	15
1997	For You W7951	Open		20.00	20
1996	Peek-A-Boo H4765/2	Open		15.00	15
1997	The Secret W7950	Open		20.00	20
1997	Sharing W7949	Open		20.00	20

Christmas Legends - P.F. Bolinger

YEAR ISSUE		EDITION LIMIT	YEAR RETD.	ISSUE PRICE	*QUOTE U.S.$
1994	Aldwyn of the Greenwood J8196	Retrd.	1996	145.00	145
1994	Berwyn the Grand J8198	Retrd.	1996	175.00	175
1995	Bountiful J8234	Retrd.	1996	164.00	164
1994	Caradoc the Kind J8199	Open		70.00	70
1994	Florian of the Berry Bush J8199	Open		70.00	70
1994	Gustave the Gutsy J8199	Open		70.00	70
1995	Luminatus J8241	Open		136.00	136
1997	Peace Santa J6563	2,500		80.00	80
1994	Silvanus the Cheerful J8197	Retrd.	1996	165.00	165

The Fabriché™ Bear & Friends Series - KSA Design Team

YEAR ISSUE		EDITION LIMIT	YEAR RETD.	ISSUE PRICE	*QUOTE U.S.$
1992	Laughing All The Way J1567	Retrd.	1994	83.00	83
1992	Not A Creature Was Stirring W1534	Retrd.	1996	67.00	67
1993	Teddy Bear Parade W1601	Retrd.	1996	73.00	73

Fabriché™ Angel Series - K.S. Adler

YEAR ISSUE		EDITION LIMIT	YEAR RETD.	ISSUE PRICE	*QUOTE U.S.$
1992	Heavenly Messenger W1584	Retrd.	1994	41.00	41

Fabriché™ Camelot Figure Series - P. Mauk

YEAR ISSUE		EDITION LIMIT	YEAR RETD.	ISSUE PRICE	*QUOTE U.S.$
1994	King Arthur J3372	7,500	1996	110.00	110
1993	Merlin the Magician J7966	7,500	1996	120.00	120
1993	Young Arthur J7967	7,500	1996	120.00	120

Fabriché™ Holiday Figurines - KSA Design Team, unless otherwise noted

YEAR ISSUE		EDITION LIMIT	YEAR RETD.	ISSUE PRICE	*QUOTE U.S.$
1995	All Aboard For Christmas W1679	Retrd.	1996	56.00	56
1994	All Star Santa W1652	Open		56.00	56
1993	All That Jazz W1620	Retrd.	1994	67.00	67
1992	An Apron Full of Love W1582 - M. Rothenberg	Retrd.	1996	75.00	75
1995	Armchair Quarterback W1693	Retrd.	1996	90.00	90
1994	Basket of Goodies W1650	Retrd.	1996	60.00	60
1992	Bringing in the Yule Log W1589 - M. Rothenberg	5,000	1996	200.00	200
1993	Bringing the Gifts W1605	Retrd.	1996	60.00	60
1992	Bundles of Joy W1578	Retrd.	1994	78.00	78
1995	Captain Claus W1680	Open		56.00	56
1994	Checking His List W1643	Retrd.	1996	60.00	60
1993	Checking It Twice W1604	Open		56.00	56
1992	Christmas is in the Air W1590	Retrd.	1995	110.00	125
1997	Christmas Wish List W1773	Open		40.00	40
1995	Diet Starts Tomorrow W1691	Retrd.	1996	60.00	60
1997	Fan Mail W1804 - M. Rothenberg	Open		50.00	50
1995	Father Christmas W1687	Retrd.	1996	56.00	56
1994	Firefighting Friends W1654	Retrd.	1996	72.00	72
1997	For the Mrs. W1800 - V. Antonov	Open		42.00	42
1993	Forever Green W1607	Retrd.	1994	56.00	56
1994	Friendship W1642	Retrd.	1996	65.00	65
1997	Frosty Friends W1807	Open		40.00	40
1995	Gift From Heaven W1694	Retrd.	1996	60.00	60

*Quotes have been rounded up to nearest dollar

Collectors' Information Bureau

85

Kurt S. Adler, Inc.
to Kurt S. Adler, Inc.

FIGURINES

YEAR ISSUE		EDITION LIMIT	YEAR RETD.	ISSUE PRICE	*QUOTE U.S.$
1997	Gifts a Plenty W1775	Open		45.00	45
1992	He Did It Again J7944 - T. Rubel	Retrd.	1996	160.00	160
1993	Here Kitty W1618 - M. Rothenberg	Retrd.	1994	90.00	125
1994	Ho, Ho, Ho Santa W1632	Retrd.	1996	56.00	56
1994	Holiday Express W1636	Open		100.00	100
1997	Holiday on Ice W1805 - M. Rothenberg	Open		135.00	135
1992	Homeward Bound W1568	Retrd.	1996	61.00	65
1997	House Calls W1772	Open		40.00	40
1992	Hugs and Kisses W1531	Retrd.	1994	67.00	67
1992	I'm Late, I'm Late J7947 - T. Rubel	Retrd.	1995	100.00	100
1992	It's Time To Go J7943 - T. Rubel	Retrd.	1994	150.00	150
1995	Kris Kringle W1685	Retrd.	1996	55.00	55
1997	Labor of Love W1774	Open		45.00	45
1994	Mail Must Go Through W1667 - KSA/WRG	Retrd.	1996	110.00	110
1997	Making Waves W1806	Open		55.00	55
1992	Merry Kissmas W1548 - M. Rothenberg	Retrd.	1993	140.00	140
1995	Merry Memories W1735	Open		56.00	56
1994	Merry St. Nick W1641 - Giordano	Open		100.00	100
1995	Mrs. Santa Caroller W1690 - M. Rothenberg	Open		70.00	70
1997	My How You Have Grown W1803 - M. Rothenberg	Open		75.00	75
1995	Night Before Christmas W1692 - Wood River Gallery	Retrd.	1996	60.00	60
1994	Officer Claus W1677	Open		56.00	56
1997	One More Story W1796	Open		55.00	55
1997	Paperwork W1776	Open		56.00	56
1993	Par For The Claus W1603	Open		60.00	60
1994	Peace Santa W1631	Retrd.	1996	60.00	60
1995	Pere Noel W1686	Retrd.	1996	55.00	55
1993	Playtime For Santa W1619	Retrd.	1994	67.00	67
1997	Puppy Love W1808	Open		50.00	50
1994	Santa Calls W1678 - W. Joyce	Retrd.	1996	55.00	55
1995	Santa Caroller W1689 - M. Rothenberg	Open		70.00	70
1991	Santa Fiddler W1549 - M. Rothenberg	Retrd.	1992	100.00	100
1997	Santa on Line W1799	Open		50.00	50
1992	Santa Steals A Kiss & A Cookie W1581 - M. Rothenberg	Retrd.	1994	150.00	175
1992	Santa's Cat Nap W1504 - M. Rothenberg	Retrd.	1992	98.00	110
1994	Santa's Fishtales W1640	Open		60.00	60
1992	Santa's Ice Capades W1588 - M. Rothenberg	Retrd.	1995	110.00	110
1994	Schussing Claus W1651	Retrd.	1996	78.00	78
1992	St. Nicholas The Bishop W1532	Open		78.00	78
1994	Star Gazing Santa W1656 - M. Rothenberg	Open		120.00	120
1993	Stocking Stuffer W1622	Retrd.	1994	56.00	56
1995	Strike Up The Band W1681	Retrd.	1996	55.00	55
1995	Tee Time W1734	Retrd.	1996	60.00	60
1997	Test Drive W1802	Open		45.00	45
1993	Top Brass W1630	Retrd.	1995	67.00	67
1997	Up On The Roof W1783 - Giordano	Open		67.00	67
1997	What a Catch W1801	Open		45.00	45
1993	With All The Trimmings W1616	Open		76.00	76
1995	Woodland Santa W1731 - R. Volpi	Retrd.	1996	67.00	67

Fabriché™ Santa at Home Series - M. Rothenberg

YEAR ISSUE		EDITION LIMIT	YEAR RETD.	ISSUE PRICE	*QUOTE U.S.$
1995	Baby Burping Santa W1732	Retrd.	1996	80.00	80
1994	The Christmas Waltz 1635	Retrd.	1996	135.00	135
1995	Family Portrait W1727	Retrd.	1996	140.00	140
1993	Grandpa Santa's Piggyback Ride W1621	7,500	1996	84.00	84
1995	Santa's Horsey Ride W1728	Open		80.00	80
1994	Santa's New Friend W1655	Open		110.00	110

Fabriché™ Santa's Helpers Series - M. Rothenberg

YEAR ISSUE		EDITION LIMIT	YEAR RETD.	ISSUE PRICE	*QUOTE U.S.$
1993	Little Olde Clockmaker W1629	5,000	1996	134.00	134
1992	A Stitch in Time W1591	5,000		135.00	135

Fabriché™ Smithsonian Museum Series - KSA/Smithsonian

YEAR ISSUE		EDITION LIMIT	YEAR RETD.	ISSUE PRICE	*QUOTE U.S.$
1992	Holiday Drive W1556	Retrd.	1995	155.00	155
1993	Holiday Flight W1617	Retrd.	1995	144.00	144
1992	Peace on Earth Angel Treetop W1583	Retrd.	1995	52.00	52
1992	Peace on Earth Flying Angel W1585	Retrd.	1995	49.00	49
1991	Santa On A Bicycle W1527	Retrd.	1994	150.00	150
1995	Toys For Good Boys and Girls W1696	Retrd.	1996	75.00	75

Fabriché™ Thomas Nast Figurines - KSA Design Team

YEAR ISSUE		EDITION LIMIT	YEAR RETD.	ISSUE PRICE	*QUOTE U.S.$
1992	Caught in the Act W1577	Retrd.	1993	133.00	133
1992	Christmas Sing-A-Long W1576	12,000	1996	110.00	110
1993	Dear Santa W1602	Retrd.	1993	110.00	110
1991	Hello! Little One W1552	12,000	1994	90.00	90

Gallery of Angels - KSA Design Team

YEAR ISSUE		EDITION LIMIT	YEAR RETD.	ISSUE PRICE	*QUOTE U.S.$
1994	Guardian Angel M1099	2,000	1996	150.00	150
1994	Unspoken Word M1100	2,000		150.00	150

Halloween - P.F. Bolinger

YEAR ISSUE		EDITION LIMIT	YEAR RETD.	ISSUE PRICE	*QUOTE U.S.$
1996	Dr. Punkinstein HW535	Open		50.00	50
1996	Eat at Drac's HW493	Open		22.00	22
1996	Pumpkin Grumpkin HW494	Open		18.00	18
1996	Pumpkin Plumpkin HW494	Open		18.00	18
1996	Pumpkins Are Us HW534	Retrd.	1996	17.00	17

Helping Hand Santas - P. Bolinger

YEAR ISSUE		EDITION LIMIT	YEAR RETD.	ISSUE PRICE	*QUOTE U.S.$
1996	Harmonious J6509	Open		115.00	115
1996	Noah J6487	Open		56.00	56
1996	Uncle Sam J6488	Retrd.	1996	56.00	56

Ho Ho Ho Gang - P.F. Bolinger

YEAR ISSUE		EDITION LIMIT	YEAR RETD.	ISSUE PRICE	*QUOTE U.S.$
1997	Behavometer J6555	Open		25.00	25
1996	Box of Chocolate J6510	Open		33.00	33
1997	Boxers or Briefs J6559	Open		25.00	25
1997	Captain Noah J6550	Open		18.00	18
1994	Christmas Goose J8201	Open		22.00	22
1996	Christmas Shopping Santa J6497	Open		22.00	22
1996	Claus-A-Lounger J6478	Open		33.00	33
1995	Cookie Claus J8286	Retrd.	1996	39.00	39
1995	Do Not Disturb J8233	Open		34.00	34
1996	Fire Department North Pole J6508	Open		50.00	50
1996	Fireman Santa J6476	Open		28.00	28
1997	Golf Heaven J6553	Open		25.00	25
1994	Holy Mackerel J8201	Open		22.00	22
1997	Java Jumpstart J6554	Open		15.00	15
1996	Joy of Cooking J6496	Open		28.00	28
1996	Love Santa J6493	Retrd.	1996	18.00	18
1997	Never Say Diet J6578	Open		15.00	15
1995	No Hair Day J8287	Retrd.	1996	50.00	50
1996	Noel Roly Poly J6489	Retrd.	1996	20.00	20
1995	North Pole (large) J8237	Retrd.	1997	56.00	56
1995	North Pole (small) J8238	Open		45.00	45
1997	North Pole Country Club J6557	Open		45.00	45
1996	North Pole Pro-Am J6479	Open		28.00	28
1996	On Strike For More Cookies J6506	Open		33.00	33
1996	Police Department North Pole J6507	Retrd.	1997	50.00	50
1996	Policeman Santa J6475	Open		28.00	28
1994	Santa Cob J8203	Retrd.	1995	28.00	28
1997	Santa With Bear J6556	Open		8.00	8
1997	Santa's Day Off J6558	Open		25.00	25
1996	Save The Reindeer J6498	Open		28.00	28
1997	Snowmen Are Cool J6551	Open		20.00	20
1996	Some Assembly Required J6477	Open		53.00	53
1997	Spring Sale Snowman J6549	Open		20.00	20
1994	Surprise J8201	Retrd.	1997	22.00	22
1994	Will He Make It? J8203	Retrd.	1995	28.00	28
1995	Will Work For Cookies J8235	Open		40.00	40
1997	Winter Fun J6552	Open		25.00	25
1995	Wishful Thinking J8239	Retrd.	1997	32.00	32

Holly Bearies - H. Adler

YEAR ISSUE		EDITION LIMIT	YEAR RETD.	ISSUE PRICE	*QUOTE U.S.$
1996	Angel Bear J7342	Open		14.00	14
1996	Angel Starcatcher (Starlight Foundation) J7222	Retrd.	1996	20.00	20
1997	Angel Starcatcher II (Starlight Foundation) J7222	Yr.Iss.		20.00	20
1997	Bearies Mailing Packages W6443	Open		28.00	28
1997	Charlie The Fisherman W6448	Yr.Iss.		34.00	34
1996	Mother's Day Bear J7318	Retrd.	1996	15.00	15
1997	Sledding Bearies W6445	Open		25.00	25
1996	Teddy Tower J7221	Open		23.00	23

Holly Bearies Calendar Bears - H. Adler

YEAR ISSUE		EDITION LIMIT	YEAR RETD.	ISSUE PRICE	*QUOTE U.S.$
1996	Fergus & Fritzi's Frosty Frolic J7215/Jan	Open		16.00	16
1996	Pinky & Victoria Are Sweeties J7215/Feb	Open		16.00	16
1996	Philo's Pot O Gold J7215/Mar	Open		16.00	16
1996	Sunshine Catching Raindrops J7215/Apr	Open		16.00	16
1996	Petunia & Nathan Plant Posies J7215/May	Open		16.00	16
1996	Thorndike & Filbert Catch Fish J7215/Jun	Open		16.00	16
1996	Clairmont, Dempsey & Pete J7215/Jul	Open		16.00	16
1996	Nicole & Nicholas Sun Bearthing J7215/Aug	Open		16.00	16
1996	Skeeter & Sigourney Start School J7215/Sep	Open		16.00	16
1996	Clara & Carnation The Kitty J7215/Oct	Open		16.00	16
1996	Thorndike All Dressed Up J7215/Nov	Open		16.00	16
1996	Grandma Gladys J7215/Dec	Open		16.00	16

Inspirational - P.F. Bolinger

YEAR ISSUE		EDITION LIMIT	YEAR RETD.	ISSUE PRICE	*QUOTE U.S.$
1997	Angel with Heart J6569	Open		20.00	20
1997	Noah J6487	Open		56.00	56
1997	Saint Francis J6585	Open		56.00	56

Jim Henson's Muppet Nutcrackers - KSA/JHP

YEAR ISSUE		EDITION LIMIT	YEAR RETD.	ISSUE PRICE	*QUOTE U.S.$
1993	Kermit The Frog H1223	Retrd.	1995	90.00	90

Mickey Unlimited - KSA/Disney

YEAR ISSUE		EDITION LIMIT	YEAR RETD.	ISSUE PRICE	*QUOTE U.S.$
1994	Donald Duck Drummer W1671	Retrd.	1996	45.00	45
1993	Donald Duck H1235	Retrd.	1996	90.00	90
1992	Goofy H1216	Retrd.	1996	78.00	78
1994	Mickey Bandleader W1669	Retrd.	1996	45.00	45
1992	Mickey Mouse Soldier H1194	Retrd.	1996	72.00	72
1992	Mickey Mouse Sorcerer H1221	Retrd.	1996	100.00	100
1993	Mickey Mouse w/Gift Boxes W1608	Retrd.	1996	78.00	78
1994	Mickey Santa Nutcracker H1237	Retrd.	1996	90.00	90
1994	Minnie Mouse Soldier Nutcrackers H1236	Retrd.	1996	90.00	90
1994	Minnie With Cymbals W1670	Retrd.	1996	45.00	45
1993	Pinnochio H1222	Retrd.	1996	110.00	110

Old World Santa Series - J. Mostrom

YEAR ISSUE		EDITION LIMIT	YEAR RETD.	ISSUE PRICE	*QUOTE U.S.$
1992	Chelsea Garden Santa W2721	Retrd.	1994	33.50	34
1993	Good King Wenceslas W2928	3,000	1996	134.00	134
1992	Large Black Forest Santa W2717	Retrd.	1994	110.00	110
1992	Large Father Christmas W2719	Retrd.	1994	106.00	106
1993	Medieval King of Christmas W2881	3,000	1994	390.00	390
1992	Mrs. Claus W2714	5,000	1996	37.00	37
1992	Patriotic Santa W2720	3,000	1994	128.00	128
1992	Pere Noel W2723	Retrd.	1994	33.50	34
1992	Small Black Forest Santa W2712	Retrd.	1994	40.00	40
1992	Small Father Christmas W2712	Retrd.	1994	33.50	34
1992	Small Father Frost W2716	Retrd.	1994	43.00	43
1992	Small Grandfather Frost W2718	Retrd.	1994	106.00	106
1992	St. Nicholas W2713	Retrd.	1994	30.00	30
1992	Workshop Santa W2715	5,000		43.00	43

Sesame Street Series - KSA/JHP

YEAR ISSUE		EDITION LIMIT	YEAR RETD.	ISSUE PRICE	*QUOTE U.S.$
1993	Big Bird Fabrich, Figurine J7928	Retrd.	1996	60.00	60
1993	Big Bird Nutcracker H1199	Retrd.	1994	60.00	60

Snow People - P.F. Bolinger

YEAR ISSUE		EDITION LIMIT	YEAR RETD.	ISSUE PRICE	*QUOTE U.S.$
1996	Coola Hula J6430	Retrd.	1996	20.00	20
1996	Snowpoke J6431	Open		28.00	28
1996	Snowy J6429	Open		28.00	28

Steinbach Camelot Smoking Figure Series - KSA/Steinbach

YEAR ISSUE		EDITION LIMIT	YEAR RETD.	ISSUE PRICE	*QUOTE U.S.$
1994	Chief Sitting Bull Smoker ES834	7,500		150.00	150
1993	King Arthur ES832	7,500	1996	175.00	200-350
1992	Merlin The Magician ES830	7,500		150.00	150
1994	Sir Lancelot Smoker ES833	7,500		150.00	150

Steinbach Nutcracker Collectors' Club - KSA/Steinbach

YEAR ISSUE		EDITION LIMIT	YEAR RETD.	ISSUE PRICE	*QUOTE U.S.$
1995	The Town Crier	Retrd.	1996	Gift	N/A
1995	King Wenceslaus	4/97		225.00	225
1997	Mini Chimney Sweep	Yr.Iss.		Gift	N/A
1997	Marek The Royal Guardsman ES856	Yr.Iss.		225.00	225

Steinbach Nutcracker American Inventor Series - KSA/Steinbach

YEAR ISSUE		EDITION LIMIT	YEAR RETD.	ISSUE PRICE	*QUOTE U.S.$
1993	Ben Franklin ES635	12,000	1996	225.00	225

Steinbach Nutcracker American Presidents Series - KSA/Steinbach

YEAR ISSUE		EDITION LIMIT	YEAR RETD.	ISSUE PRICE	*QUOTE U.S.$
1992	Abraham Lincoln ES622	12,000	1995	195.00	250-550
1992	George Washington ES623	12,000	1994	195.00	500-700
1993	Teddy Roosevelt ES644	10,000	1997	225.00	225-275
1996	Thomas Jefferson ES866	7,500		260.00	260

Steinbach Nutcracker Biblical - KSA/Steinbach

YEAR ISSUE		EDITION LIMIT	YEAR RETD.	ISSUE PRICE	*QUOTE U.S.$
1997	Moses ES894	10,000		250.00	250
1996	Noah ES893	10,000		260.00	260

Steinbach Nutcracker Camelot Series - KSA/Steinbach

YEAR ISSUE		EDITION LIMIT	YEAR RETD.	ISSUE PRICE	*QUOTE U.S.$
1992	King Arthur ES621	Retrd.	1993	195.00	500-2000
1991	Merlin The Magician ES610	Retrd.	1991	185.00	2500-5000
1995	Queen Guenevere ES869	10,000		245.00	245
1994	Sir Galahad ES862	12,000	1997	225.00	225
1993	Sir Lancelot ES638	12,000	1997	225.00	225-500

Steinbach Nutcracker Christmas Carol Series - KSA/Steinbach

YEAR ISSUE		EDITION LIMIT	YEAR RETD.	ISSUE PRICE	*QUOTE U.S.$
1997	Ebenezer Scrooge ES896	7,500		250.00	250

Steinbach Nutcracker Christmas Legends Series - KSA/Steinbach

YEAR ISSUE		EDITION LIMIT	YEAR RETD.	ISSUE PRICE	*QUOTE U.S.$
1995	1930s Santa Claus ES891	7,500		245.00	245
1993	Father Christmas ES645	7,500	1996	225.00	225-500
1997	Grandfather Frost ES895	7,500		250.00	250
1994	St. Nicholas, The Bishop ES865	7,500	1995	225.00	300

Steinbach Nutcracker Collection - KSA/Steinbach

YEAR ISSUE		EDITION LIMIT	YEAR RETD.	ISSUE PRICE	*QUOTE U.S.$
1991	Columbus ES697	Retrd.	1992	194.00	225-500
1992	Happy Santa ES601	Open		190.00	220
1984	Oil Sheik	Retrd.	1985	100.00	500

Steinbach Nutcracker Famous Chieftains Series - KSA/Steinbach

YEAR ISSUE		EDITION LIMIT	YEAR RETD.	ISSUE PRICE	*QUOTE U.S.$
1995	Black Hawk ES889	7,500	1996	245.00	245
1993	Chief Sitting Bull ES637	8,500	1995	225.00	300-700
1994	Red Cloud ES864	8,500	1996	225.00	225

Steinbach Nutcracker Mini Series - KSA/Steinbach

YEAR ISSUE		EDITION LIMIT	YEAR RETD.	ISSUE PRICE	*QUOTE U.S.$
1997	King Arthur ES337	15,000		50.00	50
1996	Merlin ES335	15,000		50.00	50
1997	Noah and His Ark ES339	10,000		50.00	50
1996	Robin Hood ES336	10,000		50.00	50
1997	St. Nicholas ES338	15,000		50.00	50

Steinbach Nutcracker Tales of Sherwood Forest - KSA/Steinbach

YEAR ISSUE		EDITION LIMIT	YEAR RETD.	ISSUE PRICE	*QUOTE U.S.$
1995	Friar Tuck ES890	7,500		245.00	245
1997	King Richard the Lion-Hearted ES897	7,500		250.00	250
1992	Robin Hood ES863	7,500	1996	225.00	225-500
1996	Sherif of Nottingham ES892	7,500		260.00	260

*Quotes have been rounded up to nearest dollar

FIGURINES

Kurt S. Adler, Inc. to Legends

Steinbach Nutcracker Three Musketeers - KSA/Steinbach

YEAR ISSUE		EDITION LIMIT	YEAR RETD.	ISSUE PRICE	*QUOTE U.S.$
1996	Aramis ES722	7,500		130.00	130

Vatican Library Collection - Vatican Library

YEAR ISSUE		EDITION LIMIT	YEAR RETD.	ISSUE PRICE	*QUOTE U.S.$
1997	Holy Family Set V29	Open		N/A	N/A
1997	Three Wise Men V30	Open		N/A	N/A

Visions Of Santa Series - KSA Design Team

YEAR ISSUE		EDITION LIMIT	YEAR RETD.	ISSUE PRICE	*QUOTE U.S.$
1992	Santa Coming Out Of Fireplace J1023	Retrd.	1993	29.00	29
1992	Santa Holding Child J826	Retrd.	1993	24.50	25
1992	Santa Spilling Bag Of Toys J1022	7,500	1994	25.50	26
1992	Santa w/ Little Girls On Lap J1024	7,500	1996	24.50	25
1992	Santa w/Sack Holding Toy J827	7,500	1994	24.50	25
1992	Workshop Santa J825	7,500	1994	27.00	27

Zuber Nutcracker Series - KSA/Zuber

YEAR ISSUE		EDITION LIMIT	YEAR RETD.	ISSUE PRICE	*QUOTE U.S.$
1992	The Annapolis Midshipman EK7	5,000	1994	125.00	125
1992	The Bavarian EK16	5,000	1994	130.00	130
1992	Bronco Billy The Cowboy EK1	5,000	1994	125.00	125
1992	The Chimney Sweep EK6	5,000	1993	125.00	125
1992	The Country Singer EK19	5,000	1993	125.00	125
1992	The Fisherman EK17	5,000	1996	125.00	125
1994	The Gardner EK26	2,500	1996	150.00	150
1992	Gepetto, The Toymaker EK9	5,000	1994	125.00	125
1992	The Gold Prospector EK18	5,000	1994	125.00	125
1992	The Golfer EK5	5,000	1994	125.00	125
1993	Herr Drosselmeir Nutcracker EK21	5,000	1996	150.00	300-450
1993	The Ice Cream Vendor EK24	5,000	1996	150.00	150
1992	The Indian EK15	5,000	1994	135.00	135
1994	Jazz Player EK25	2,500		145.00	145
1994	Kurt the Traveling Salesman EK28	2,500	1994	155.00	155
1994	Mouse King EK31	2,500		150.00	150
1993	Napoleon Bonaparte EK23	5,000	1994	150.00	150
1992	The Nor' Easter Sea Captain EK3	5,000		125.00	125
1992	Paul Bunyan The Lumberjack EK2	5,000	1993	125.00	125
1994	Peter Pan EK28	2,500		145.00	145
1992	The Pilgrim EK14	5,000	1994	125.00	125
1993	The Pizzamaker EK22	5,000		150.00	150
1994	Scuba Diver EK27	2,500		150.00	150
1994	Soccer Player EK30	2,500		145.00	145
1992	TheTyrolean EK4	5,000	1994	125.00	125
1992	The West Point Cadet w/Canon EK8	5,000	1994	130.00	130

KVK, Inc.

Daddy's KeepSakes/County Fair Collection - K. Germany

YEAR ISSUE		EDITION LIMIT	YEAR RETD.	ISSUE PRICE	*QUOTE U.S.$
1997	Pete DK97A	3,000		35.00	35
1997	Nick DK97B	3,000		35.00	35
1997	Kelly DK97C	3,000		35.00	35
1997	Nell DK97D	3,000		35.00	35
1997	Penny DK97E	3,000		35.00	35
1997	County Fair Set DKA97A	3,000		175.00	175

Daddy's KeepSakes/Nursery Rhyme Characters - K. Germany

YEAR ISSUE		EDITION LIMIT	YEAR RETD.	ISSUE PRICE	*QUOTE U.S.$
1996	Curly-Locks	3,000		18.95	19
1996	Little Bo Peep	3,000		18.95	19
1996	Little Boy Blue	3,000		16.95	17
1996	Mary, Mary, Quite Contrary	3,000		18.95	19
1996	Old King Cole	3,000		24.95	25
1996	Old Mother Hubbard	3,000		24.95	25
1996	To Market	3,000		18.95	19

Ladie and Friends

Lizzie High® Figurines - B.&P. Wisber

YEAR ISSUE		EDITION LIMIT	YEAR RETD.	ISSUE PRICE	*QUOTE U.S.$
1996	Amanda High -111	2-Yr.		28.00	28
1996	Cassie Yocum -179	2-Yr.		29.50	30
1996	Edward Bowman -158	2-Yr.		28.00	28
1996	Grace Valentine -146	2-Yr.		25.00	25
1996	Katie Bowman -178	2-Yr.		28.00	28
1996	Lizzie High -100	2-Yr.		26.50	27
1996	Lizzie High Sign -090	2-Yr.		37.00	37
1996	Marisa Valentine -333	2-Yr.		25.00	25
1996	Megan Valentine -227	2-Yr.		35.00	35
1996	Minnie Valentine -336	2-Yr.		29.50	30
1996	Nancy Bowman -261	2-Yr.		24.00	24
1996	Natalie Valentine -284	2-Yr.		28.00	28
1996	Rebecca Bowman -104	2-Yr.		37.00	37

Lalique Society of America

Lalique Society Annual Series - Various

YEAR ISSUE		EDITION LIMIT	YEAR RETD.	ISSUE PRICE	*QUOTE U.S.$
1989	Degas Box 10585 - R. Lalique	Yr.Iss.		295.00	725
1990	Hestia Medallion 61051 - M.C. Lalique	Yr.Iss.		295.00	700
1991	Lily of Valley (perfume bottle) 61053 - R. Lalique	Yr.Iss.		275.00	450
1992	La Patineuse (paperweight) 61054 - M.C. Lalique	Yr.Iss.		325.00	375
1993	Enchantment (figurine) 61055 - M.C. Lalique	Yr.Iss.		395.00	395
1994	Eclipse (perfume bottle) - M.C. Lalique	Yr.Iss.		395.00	395

Lance Corporation: See Hudson Creek

Legends

Annual Collectors Edition - C. Pardell

YEAR ISSUE		EDITION LIMIT	YEAR RETD.	ISSUE PRICE	*QUOTE U.S.$
1990	The Night Before	500	1991	990.00	1200-1800
1991	Medicine Gift of Manhood	500	1992	990.00	1500
1992	Spirit of the Wolf	500	1992	950.00	2000
1993	Tomorrow's Warrior	500	1993	590.00	1200
1994	Guiding Hand	500	1994	590.00	875-1100
1995	Gift of the Sacred Calf	500	1995	650.00	650-900
1996	Spirit and Image	500		750.00	750

Collectors Only - Various

YEAR ISSUE		EDITION LIMIT	YEAR RETD.	ISSUE PRICE	*QUOTE U.S.$
1993	Give Us Peace - C. Pardell	1,250	1993	270.00	400-600
1994	First Born - C. Pardell	1,250	1994	350.00	400-600
1994	River Bandits - K. Cantrell	1,250	1995	350.00	400
1995	Sonata - K. Cantrell	1,250	1996	250.00	300-400
1995	Daydreams of Manhood - C. Pardell	2,500	1995	390.00	500
1996	Innocence Remembered - C. Pardell	12/96		490.00	490

American Heritage - D. Edwards

YEAR ISSUE		EDITION LIMIT	YEAR RETD.	ISSUE PRICE	*QUOTE U.S.$
1987	Grizz Country (Bronze)	Retrd.	1990	350.00	350
1987	Grizz Country (Pewter)	Retrd.	1990	370.00	370
1987	Winter Provisions (Bronze)	Retrd.	1990	340.00	340
1987	Winter Provisions (Pewter)	Retrd.	1990	370.00	370
1987	Wrangler's Dare (Bronze)	Retrd.	1990	630.00	630
1987	Wrangler's Dare (Pewter)	Retrd.	1990	660.00	660

American Indian Dance Premier Edition - C. Pardell

YEAR ISSUE		EDITION LIMIT	YEAR RETD.	ISSUE PRICE	*QUOTE U.S.$
1996	Dancing Ground	750		2500.00	2500
1993	Drum Song	750	1995	2800.00	3000-5000
1994	Footprints of the Butterfly	750		1800.00	1990
1994	Image of the Eagle	750		1900.00	2100
1995	Spirit of the Mountain	750		1750.00	1850

American West Premier Edition - C. Pardell

YEAR ISSUE		EDITION LIMIT	YEAR RETD.	ISSUE PRICE	*QUOTE U.S.$
1992	American Horse	950	1995	1300.00	1300
1992	Defending the People	950		1350.00	1450
1991	First Coup	950	1993	1150.00	1500
1993	Four Bears' Challenge	950	1996	990.00	1050
1994	Season of Victory	950		1500.00	1580
1991	Unexpected Rescuer	950	1991	990.00	1500-1700

The Endangered Wildlife Collection - K. Cantrell

YEAR ISSUE		EDITION LIMIT	YEAR RETD.	ISSUE PRICE	*QUOTE U.S.$
1993	Big Pine Survivor	950		390.00	390
1990	Forest Spirit	950	1991	290.00	1500
1991	Mountain Majesty	950		350.00	390
1991	Old Tusker	950		390.00	390
1992	Plains Monarch	950		350.00	390
1994	Prairie Phantom	950		370.00	390
1990	Savannah Prince	950		290.00	350
1993	Silvertip	950		370.00	390
1992	Songs of Autumn	950	1995	390.00	425-625
1992	Spirit Song	950	1992	350.00	500-700
1994	Twilight	950		290.00	310
1992	Unchallenged	950		350.00	390

Endangered Wildlife Eagle Series - K. Cantrell

YEAR ISSUE		EDITION LIMIT	YEAR RETD.	ISSUE PRICE	*QUOTE U.S.$
1989	Aquila Libre	2,500	1995	280.00	400-500
1993	Defiance	2,500		350.00	350
1992	Food Fight	2,500		650.00	750
1989	Outpost	2,500	1995	280.00	350-400
1989	Sentinel	2,500	1993	280.00	400-500
1993	Spiral Flight	2,500		290.00	300
1992	Sunday Brunch	2,500		550.00	650
1989	Unbounded	2,500	1994	280.00	400-450

Gallery Editions - Various

YEAR ISSUE		EDITION LIMIT	YEAR RETD.	ISSUE PRICE	*QUOTE U.S.$
1994	Center Fire - W. Whitten	350		2500.00	2600
1994	Mountain Family - D. Lemon	150	1996	7900.00	8300
1996	On Wings of Eagles - C. Pardell	250		3700.00	3700
1993	Over the Rainbow - K. Cantrell	600	1995	2900.00	3000-3300
1993	Over the Rainbow AP - K. Cantrell	Retrd.	1996	4000.00	5000
1992	Resolute - C. Pardell	250	1992	7950.00	12000-15000
1993	Visionary - C. Pardell	350		7500.00	8300
1993	The Wanderer - K. Cantrell	350		3500.00	3700
1996	Wind on Still Water - C. Pardell	350	1996	2500.00	3500-4500

Hidden Images Collection - D. Lemon

YEAR ISSUE		EDITION LIMIT	YEAR RETD.	ISSUE PRICE	*QUOTE U.S.$
1994	In Search of Bear Rock	350	1995	1300.00	1500
1995	Sensed, But Unseen	350	1995	990.00	1200
1995	Spirit	350		990.00	990

Indian Arts Collection - C. Pardell

YEAR ISSUE		EDITION LIMIT	YEAR RETD.	ISSUE PRICE	*QUOTE U.S.$
1990	Chief's Blanket	1,500	1992	350.00	600-700
1990	Indian Maiden	1,500		240.00	240
1990	Indian Potter	1,500		260.00	260
1990	Kachina Carver	1,500	1993	270.00	400-550
1990	Story Teller	1,500	1993	290.00	450-550

Kachina Dancers Collection - C. Pardell

YEAR ISSUE		EDITION LIMIT	YEAR RETD.	ISSUE PRICE	*QUOTE U.S.$
1991	Ahote	2,500	1996	370.00	390
1991	Angakchina	2,500		370.00	390
1994	Deer Kachina	2,500		390.00	390
1994	Eototo	2,500		390.00	390
1991	Hilili	2,500		390.00	390
1993	Koshari	2,500		370.00	390
1991	Koyemsi	2,500		370.00	390
1992	Kwahu	2,500		390.00	390
1993	Mongwa	2,500	1996	390.00	390
1994	Palhik Mana	2,500		390.00	390
1992	Tawa	2,500		390.00	390
1994	Wiharu	2,500	1996	390.00	390

The Legacies Of The West Premier Edition - C. Pardell

YEAR ISSUE		EDITION LIMIT	YEAR RETD.	ISSUE PRICE	*QUOTE U.S.$
1991	Defiant Comanche	950	1991	1300.00	1400-1900
1993	Eminent Crow	950	1994	1500.00	1500
1994	Enduring	950	1996	1250.00	1350
1992	Esteemed Warrior	950	1992	1750.00	2500-2900
1990	Mystic Vision	950	1990	990.00	2000-3000
1991	No More, Forever	950	1992	1500.00	1800-2200
1992	Rebellious	950		1500.00	1600
1990	Victorious	950	1990	1275.00	2200-3500

The Legendary West Collection - C. Pardell

YEAR ISSUE		EDITION LIMIT	YEAR RETD.	ISSUE PRICE	*QUOTE U.S.$
1992	Beating Bad Odds	2,500		390.00	410
1989	Bustin' A Herd Quitter	2,500		590.00	660
1993	Cliff Hanger	2,500	1996	990.00	1050
1992	Crazy Horse	2,500	1992	390.00	800-1100
1989	Eagle Dancer	2,500		370.00	410
1993	Hunter's Brothers	2,500		590.00	660
1989	Johnson's Last Fight	2,500	1991	590.00	1200-1300
1990	Keeper of Eagles	2,500		370.00	410
1987	Pony Express (Bronze)	2,500	N/A	320.00	320-450
1989	Pony Express (Mixed Media)	2,500		390.00	410
1987	Pony Express (Pewter)	2,500	N/A	320.00	320-450
1989	Sacajawea	2,500	1995	380.00	495
1990	Shhh	2,500		390.00	410
1990	Stand of the Sash Wearer	2,500	1996	390.00	410
1989	Tables Turned	2,500		680.00	750
1990	Unbridled	2,500	1996	290.00	290
1991	Warning	2,500		390.00	410
1989	White Feather's Vision	2,500	1991	390.00	1000-1300

The Legendary West Premier Edition - C. Pardell

YEAR ISSUE		EDITION LIMIT	YEAR RETD.	ISSUE PRICE	*QUOTE U.S.$
1990	Crow Warrior	750	1990	1225.00	2000-3200
1992	The Final Charge	750	1992	1250.00	1500-2000
1989	Pursued	750	1989	750.00	2000-4000
1988	Red Cloud's Coup	750	1988	480.00	5000-5500
1989	Songs of Glory	750	1989	850.00	3500-3900
1991	Triumphant	750	1991	1150.00	1700-2200

North American Wildlife - D. Edwards

YEAR ISSUE		EDITION LIMIT	YEAR RETD.	ISSUE PRICE	*QUOTE U.S.$
1988	Defenders of Freedom (Bronze)	Retrd.	N/A	340.00	340
1988	Defenders of Freedom (Pewter)	Retrd.	N/A	370.00	370
1988	Double Trouble (Bronze)	Retrd.	N/A	300.00	300
1988	Double Trouble (Pewter)	Retrd.	N/A	320.00	320
1988	Downhill Run (Bronze)	Retrd.	N/A	330.00	330
1988	Downhill Run (Pewter)	Retrd.	N/A	340.00	340
1988	Grizzly Solitude (Bronze)	Retrd.	N/A	310.00	310
1988	Grizzly Solitude (Pewter)	Retrd.	N/A	330.00	330
1988	Last Glance (Bronze)	Retrd.	N/A	300.00	300
1988	Last Glance (Pewter)	Retrd.	N/A	320.00	320
1988	The Proud American (Bronze)	Retrd.	N/A	330.00	330
1988	The Proud American (Pewter)	Retrd.	N/A	340.00	340
1988	Ridge Runners (Bronze)	Retrd.	N/A	300.00	300
1988	Ridge Runners (Pewter)	Retrd.	N/A	310.00	310
1988	Sudden Alert (Bronze)	Retrd.	N/A	300.00	300
1988	Sudden Alert (Pewter)	Retrd.	N/A	320.00	320

Special Commissions - Various

YEAR ISSUE		EDITION LIMIT	YEAR RETD.	ISSUE PRICE	*QUOTE U.S.$
1988	Alpha Pair (Bronze) - C. Pardell	Retrd.	N/A	330.00	330
1988	Alpha Pair (Mixed Media) - C. Pardell	S/O	N/A	390.00	500-700
1988	Alpha Pair (Pewter) - C. Pardell	Retrd.	N/A	330.00	330
1991	American Allegiance - D. Edwards	1,250	1996	570.00	625
1995	Father-The Power Within - D. Medina	350		1500.00	1590
1990	Lakota Love Song - C. Pardell	Retrd.	1990	380.00	1950
1987	Mama's Joy (Bronze) - D. Edwards	Retrd.	N/A	200.00	200
1987	Mama's Joy (Pewter) - D. Edwards	Retrd.	N/A	250.00	250
1996	Proud Heritage - K. Cantrell	2,500		290.00	290
1995	Rapture - W. Whitten	350		1750.00	1850
1995	Scent in the Air - K. Cantrell	750		990.00	1050
1991	Symbols of Freedom - K. Cantrell	2,500		490.00	550
1987	Wild Freedom (Bronze) - D. Edwards	Retrd.	N/A	320.00	320
1987	Wild Freedom (Pewter) - D. Edwards	Retrd.	N/A	330.00	330
1992	Yellowstone Bound - K. Cantrell	600	1994	2500.00	3300-3600

Way of the Cat Collection - K. Cantrell

YEAR ISSUE		EDITION LIMIT	YEAR RETD.	ISSUE PRICE	*QUOTE U.S.$
1996	Cat's Cradle	500		790.00	790
1995	Encounter	500	1995	750.00	1000-1600

Way of the Warrior Collection - C. Pardell

YEAR ISSUE		EDITION LIMIT	YEAR RETD.	ISSUE PRICE	*QUOTE U.S.$
1991	Clan Leader	1,600	1994	170.00	225
1991	Elder Chief	1,600	1994	170.00	225
1991	Medicine Dancer	1,600	1994	170.00	225
1991	Rite of Manhood	1,600	1994	170.00	225
1991	Seeker of Visions	1,600	1994	170.00	225
1991	Tribal Defender	1,600	1994	170.00	225

Way of the Wolf Collection - K. Cantrell

YEAR ISSUE		EDITION LIMIT	YEAR RETD.	ISSUE PRICE	*QUOTE U.S.$
1993	Courtship	500	1993	590.00	1500-2000
1995	Gossip Column	500		1250.00	1250
1994	Missed by a Hare	500	1994	700.00	850-1300
1994	Renewal	500	1994	700.00	950-1700
1995	Stink Bomb	500	1995	750.00	950-1100

Wild Realm Premier Edition - C. Pardell

YEAR ISSUE		EDITION LIMIT	YEAR RETD.	ISSUE PRICE	*QUOTE U.S. $
1989	High Spirit	1,600	1996	870.00	1000
1991	Speed Incarnate	1,600	N/A	790.00	790

Lenox, Inc.

Lenox Classics-Away in a Manager - Unknown

YEAR ISSUE		EDITION LIMIT	YEAR RETD.	ISSUE PRICE	*QUOTE U.S. $
1996	Angel	Open		50.00	50
1996	Jesus	Open		40.00	40
1996	Joseph	Open		50.00	50
1996	Mary	Open		50.00	50

Lenox Classics-Barefoot Blessings - Unknown

YEAR ISSUE		EDITION LIMIT	YEAR RETD.	ISSUE PRICE	*QUOTE U.S. $
1997	Bedtime Prayers (Girl Praying)	Open		60.00	60
1996	Cheerful Giver (Girl w/Vegetables)	Open		60.00	60
1996	Gone Fishing (Boy w/Dog)	Open		60.00	60
1997	Making Friends (Girl w/Butterfly)	Open		60.00	60
1996	Morning Chores (Boy w/Cat)	Open		60.00	60
1996	Sharing Secrets (Girl w/Doll)	Open		60.00	60
1996	Spring Surprise (Girl w/Chick)	Open		60.00	60

Lenox Classics-Crystal Cats - Unknown

YEAR ISSUE		EDITION LIMIT	YEAR RETD.	ISSUE PRICE	*QUOTE U.S. $
1997	Crystal Jaguar (Cat in Grass)	Open		160.00	160
1996	Fascination (Cat w/Butterfly)	Open		50.00	50
1997	Morning Stretch (Cat Stretching)	Open		136.00	136
1996	Playtime (Cat w/Ball)	Open		50.00	50
1996	Preen & Serene (Cat Pair)	Open		76.00	76

Lenox Classics-Crystal Eagles - Unknown

YEAR ISSUE		EDITION LIMIT	YEAR RETD.	ISSUE PRICE	*QUOTE U.S. $
1997	The Keeper of the Stars (Patriotic Eagle)	Open		115.00	115
1996	Soaring Majesty (Flying Eagle)	Open		195.00	195
1996	Wings of the Sun (Eagle on Rock)	Open		195.00	195

Lenox Classics-Crystal Elephants - Unknown

YEAR ISSUE		EDITION LIMIT	YEAR RETD.	ISSUE PRICE	*QUOTE U.S. $
1997	Crystal Playmate (Elephant in Grass)	Open		136.00	136
1996	Peanuts & Popcorn (Elephant Pair)	Open		76.00	76

Lenox Classics-Lake/Ocean Friends-Crystal - Unknown

YEAR ISSUE		EDITION LIMIT	YEAR RETD.	ISSUE PRICE	*QUOTE U.S. $
1996	Dolphin's Journey (Mother w/Child)	Open		76.00	76
1996	Glorious Dolphin (Dolphin Jumping Up)	Open		76.00	76
1996	Radiant Dolphin (Dolphin Diving Down)	Open		76.00	76

Lenox Classics-Little Graces - Unknown

YEAR ISSUE		EDITION LIMIT	YEAR RETD.	ISSUE PRICE	*QUOTE U.S. $
1996	Enjoyment (Cherub w/Bell)	5,000		95.00	95
1996	Guidance (Cherub w/Candle)	5,000		95.00	95
1997	Happiness (Cherub Reclining)	5,000		95.00	95
1996	Hope (Cherub w/Star)	5,000		95.00	95
1997	Innocence (Cherub w/Trumpet)	5,000		95.00	95
1996	Knowledge (Cherub w/Book)	5,000		95.00	95
1996	Peace (Cherub w/Dove)	5,000		95.00	95
1996	Tranquility (Cherub w/Harp)	5,000		95.00	95

Lenox Classics-Woodland Animals-Crystal - Unknown

YEAR ISSUE		EDITION LIMIT	YEAR RETD.	ISSUE PRICE	*QUOTE U.S. $
1997	The Keeper of the Wild (Wolf)	Open		100.00	100
1996	Lord & Lady (Wolf Pair)	Open		76.00	76
1996	Satin & Silk (Bunny Pair)	Open		76.00	76

Lladró

Lladró Collectors Society - Lladró

YEAR ISSUE		EDITION LIMIT	YEAR RETD.	ISSUE PRICE	*QUOTE U.S. $
1985	Little Pals S7600	Closed	1985	95.00	2400-3200
1985	LCS Plaque w/blue writing S7601	Closed	N/A	35.00	75-125
1986	Little Traveler S7602	Closed	1986	95.00	1400-2000
1987	Spring Bouquets S7603	Closed	1987	125.00	625-1100
1988	School Days S7604	Closed	1988	125.00	550-800
1988	Flower Song S7607	Closed	1988	175.00	525-800
1989	My Buddy S7609	Closed	1989	145.00	300-600
1990	Can I Play? S7610	Closed	1990	150.00	400-625
1991	Summer Stroll S7611	Closed	1992	195.00	350-600
1991	Picture Perfect S7612	Closed	1991	350.00	450-720
1992	All Aboard S7619	Closed	1993	165.00	300-470
1993	Best Friend S7620	Closed	1993	195.00	250-400
1994	Basket of Love S7622	Closed	1994	225.00	325-350
1995	10 Year Society Anniversary - Ten and Growing S7635	Closed	1995	395.00	500
1995	Afternoon Promenade S7636	Closed	1995	240.00	275-375
1995	Now and Forever (10 year membership piece) S7642	N/A		395.00	395
1996	Innocence In Bloom S7644	Closed	1996	250.00	250
1996	Where Love Begins w/base 7649	4,000	1996	895.00	895
1997	Guardian Angel 6352	4,000		1300.00	1300
1997	Pocket Full of Wishes 7650	Yr.Iss.		360.00	360

Lladró Event Figurines - Lladró

YEAR ISSUE		EDITION LIMIT	YEAR RETD.	ISSUE PRICE	*QUOTE U.S. $
1991	Garden Classic L7617G	Closed	1991	295.00	500-700
1992	Garden Song L7618G	Closed	1992	295.00	400-450
1993	Pick of the Litter L7621G	Closed	1993	350.00	375-500
1994	Little Riders L7623	Closed	1994	250.00	300-350
1995	For A Perfect Performance L7641	Closed	1995	310.00	400-500
1996	Destination Big Top L6245	Closed	1996	225.00	300-400

Capricho - Lladró

YEAR ISSUE		EDITION LIMIT	YEAR RETD.	ISSUE PRICE	*QUOTE U.S. $
1988	Bust w/ Black Veil & base C1538	Open		650.00	1050
1988	Small Bust w/ Veil & base C1539	Open		225.00	490
1987	Orchid Arrangement C1541	Closed	1990	500.00	1700-2100
1987	Iris Arrangement C1542	Closed	1990	800.00	1000-1500
1987	Fan C1546	Closed	1987	650.00	900-1600
1987	Fan C1546.3	Closed	1987	650.00	900-1600
1987	Iris with Vase C1551	Closed	1991	110.00	375
1987	Flowers Chest C1572	Open		550.00	1100
1987	Flat Basket with Flowers C1575	Closed	1991	450.00	850
1989	White Rosary C1647	Closed	1991	290.00	360
1989	Romantic Lady / Black Veil w/base C1666	Closed	1993	420.00	520
XX	White Bust w/ Veil & base C5927	Open		550.00	1000
XX	Special Museum Flower Basket C7606	Closed	1991	N/A	450-750

Crystal Sculptures - Lladró

YEAR ISSUE		EDITION LIMIT	YEAR RETD.	ISSUE PRICE	*QUOTE U.S. $
1983	Frosted Bear, Head Up L04502	Closed	1983	200.00	350
1983	Frosted Bear, Head Down L04503	Closed	1983	205.00	350
1983	Frosted Bear, Head Up L04504	Closed	1983	210.00	350
1983	Frosted Bear, Head Straight L04506	Closed	1983	200.00	350
1983	Frosted Angel w/Guitar L04507	Closed	1983	166.00	375
1983	Frosted Angel w/Cymbal L04508	Closed	1983	165.00	375
1983	Frosted Angel w/Violin L04509	Closed	1983	165.00	375
1983	Frosted Geisha, Praying L04510	Closed	1983	135.00	375
1983	Frosted Geisha/Fan L04511	Closed	1983	135.00	375
1983	Frosted Geisha/Flowers L04512	Closed	1983	135.00	375
1983	Clear Bear, Head Straight L04513	Closed	1983	220.00	400
1983	Clear Bear, Head Up L04514	Closed	1983	230.00	400

Disneyana Limited Edition - Lladró

YEAR ISSUE		EDITION LIMIT	YEAR RETD.	ISSUE PRICE	*QUOTE U.S. $
1992	Tinkerbell LL7518	1,500	1992	350.00	2100-2500
1993	Peter Pan LL7529	3,000	1993	400.00	800-1250
1994	Cinderella and Fairy Godmother LL7553G	2,500	1994	875.00	770-1150
1995	Sleeping Beauty Dance LL7560	1,000	1995	1280.00	1300-1600

Limited Edition - Lladró

YEAR ISSUE		EDITION LIMIT	YEAR RETD.	ISSUE PRICE	*QUOTE U.S. $
1971	Hamlet LL1144	750	1973	125.00	2800-4500
1971	Othello and Desdemona LL1145	750	1973	275.00	2500-3000
1971	Antique Auto LL1146	750	1975	1000.00	6000-10000
1971	Floral LL1184	200	1978	400.00	2200
1971	Floral LL1185	200	1974	475.00	1800
1971	Floral LL1186	200	1976	575.00	2200
1972	Eagles LL1189	750	1978	450.00	3200
1972	Sea Birds with Nest LL1194	500	1975	300.00	2750
1972	Turkey Group LL1196	350	1982	325.00	1800
1972	Peace LL1202	150	1973	550.00	7500
1972	Eagle Owl LL1223	750	1983	225.00	1050
1972	Hansom Carriage LL1225	750	1975	1450.00	9000-11000
1973	Buck Hunters LL1238	800	1976	400.00	3000
1973	Turtle Doves LL1240	850	1976	250.00	2300-2500
1973	The Forest LL1243	500	1976	625.00	3300
1974	Soccer Players LL1266	500	1983	1000.00	7500
1974	Man From LaMancha LL1269	1,500	1977	700.00	3800
1974	Queen Elizabeth II LL1275	250	1985	3650.00	5000
1974	Judge LL1281	1,200	1978	325.00	1250
1974	Partridge LL1290G	800	1974	700.00	1200-2000
1974	The Hunt LL1308	750	1984	4750.00	6900
1974	Ducks at Pond LL1317	1,200	1984	4250.00	5700
1976	Impossible Dream LL1318	1,000	1983	1200.00	4400
1976	Comforting Baby LL1329	750	1978	350.00	1050
1976	Mountain Country Lady LL1330	750	1983	900.00	1700
1976	My Baby LL1331	1,000	1981	275.00	900
1978	Flight of Gazelles LL1352	1,500	1984	1225.00	3100
1978	Car in Trouble LL1375	1,500	1987	3000.00	5250-6500
1978	Fearful Flight LL1377	750		7000.00	18000
1978	Henry VIII LL 1384	1,200	1993	650.00	1000-1250
1981	Venus and Cupid LL1392	750	1993	1100.00	1600-2100
1982	First Date w/base LL1393	1,500		3800.00	5900
1982	Columbus LL1432G	1,200	1988	535.00	1300-1700
1983	Venetian Serenade LL1433	750	1989	2600.00	3900
1985	Festival in Valencia w/base LL1457	3,000	1994	1400.00	2350
1985	Camelot LL1458	3,000	1994	950.00	1500
1985	Napoleon Planning Battle w/base LL1459	1,500	1995	825.00	1450
1985	Youthful Beauty w/base LL1461	5,000		750.00	1200
1985	Flock of Birds w/base LL1462	1,500		1060.00	1750
1985	Classic Spring LL1465	1,500	1995	620.00	975
1985	Classic Fall LL1466	1,500	1995	620.00	975
1985	Valencian Couple on Horse LL1472	3,000		885.00	1550
1985	Coach XVIII Century w/base LL1485	500		14000.00	28000
1986	The New World w/base LL1486	4,000		700.00	1350
1986	Fantasia w/base LL1487	5,000		1500.00	2700
1986	Floral Offering w/base LL1490	3,000		2500.00	4450
1986	Oriental Music w/base LL1491	5,000		1350.00	2445
1986	Three Sisters w/base LL1492	3,000		1850.00	3250
1986	At the Stroke of Twelve w/base LL1493	1,500	1993	4250.00	7000-8000
1986	Hawaiian Festival w/base LL1496	4,000		1850.00	3200
1987	A Sunday Drive w/base LL1510	1,000		3400.00	4000
1987	Listen to Don Quixote w/base LL1520	750		1800.00	2900
1987	A Happy Encounter LL1523	1,500		2900.00	4900
1988	Japanese Vase LL1536	750	1989	2600.00	3450-3750
1988	Garden Party w/base LL1578	500		5500.00	7250
1988	Blessed Lady w/base LL1579	1,000	1991	1150.00	3000
1988	Return to La Mancha w/base LL1580	500		6400.00	8350
1989	Southern Tea LL1597	1,000	1995	1775.00	2300
1989	Kitakami Cruise w/base LL1605	500	1994	5800.00	7500
1989	Mounted Warriors w/base LL1608	500		2850.00	3450
1989	Circus Parade w/base LL1609	1,000		5200.00	6550
1989	"Jesus the Rock" w/base LL1615	1,000		1175.00	1550
1989	Hopeful Group LL1723	1,000	1993	1825.00	1825
1991	Valencian Cruise LL1731	1,000		2700.00	2950
1991	Venice Vows LL1732	1,500		3755.00	4100
1991	Liberty Eagle LL1738	1,500		1000.00	1100
1991	Heavenly Swing LL1739	1,000		1900.00	2050
1991	Columbus, Two Routes LL1740	1,000	1995	1500.00	1650
1991	Columbus Reflecting LL1741	1,000	1994	1850.00	1995
1991	Onward! LL1742	1,000	1993	2500.00	2750-2950
1991	The Prophet LL1743	300		800.00	950
1991	My Only Friend LL1744	200	1993	1400.00	1700-2000
1991	Dawn LL1745	N/A	1993	1200.00	2550
1991	Champion LL1746	300	1994	1800.00	1950
1991	Nesting Doves LL1747	300	1994	800.00	875
1991	Comforting News LL1748	300		1200.00	1345
1991	Baggy Pants LL1749	300	1994	1500.00	1650
1991	Circus Show LL1750	300	1994	1400.00	1525
1991	Maggie LL1751	300	1994	900.00	990
1991	Apple Seller LL1752	300	1994	900.00	1000-1150
1991	The Student LL1753	300		1300.00	1425
1991	Tree Climbers LL1754	300	1994	1500.00	1650
1991	The Princess And The Unicorn LL1755	1,500	1994	1750.00	1950
1991	Outing In Seville LL1756	500		23000.00	24500
1992	Hawaiian Ceremony LL1757	1,000		9800.00	10250
1992	Circus Time LL1758	2,500		9200.00	9650
1992	Tea In The Garden LL1759	2,000		9500.00	9750
1993	Paella Valenciano w/base LL1762	500		10000.00	10000
1993	Trusting Friends w/base LL1763	350		1200.00	1200
1993	He's My Brother w/base LL1764	350		1500.00	1500
1993	The Course of Adventure LL1765	250		1625.00	1625
1993	Ties That Bind LL1766	250		1700.00	1700
1993	Motherly Love LL1767	250		1330.00	1330
1993	Travellers' Respite w/base LL1768	250		1825.00	1825
1993	Fruitful Harvest LL1769	350		1300.00	1300
1993	Gypsy Dancers LL1770	250		2250.00	2500
1993	Country Doctor w/base LL1771	250		1475.00	1700
1993	Back To Back LL1772	350		1450.00	1450
1993	Mischevous Musician LL1773	350		975.00	1045
1993	A Treasured Moment w/base LL1774	350		950.00	965
1993	Oriental Garden w/base LL1775	750		22500.00	22500
1994	Conquered by Love w/base LL1776	2,500		2850.00	2950
1994	Farewell Of The Samurai w/base LL1777	2,500		3950.00	3950
1994	Pegasus w/base LL1778	1,500		1950.00	1950
1994	High Speed w/base LL1779	1,500		3830.00	3830
1994	Indian Princess w/base LL1780	3,000		1630.00	1630
1994	Allegory of Time LL1781	5,000		1290.00	1290
1994	Circus Fanfare w/base LL1783	1,500		14240.00	14240
1994	Flower Wagon w/base LL1784	3,000		3290.00	3290
1994	Cinderella's Arrival w/base LL1785	1,500		25950.00	25950
1994	Floral Figure w/base LL1788	300		2198.00	2198
1994	Natural Beauty LL1795	500		650.00	650
1994	Floral Enchantment w/base LL1796	300		2990.00	2990
1995	Enchanted Outing w/base LL1797	3,000		3950.00	3950
1995	Far Away Thoughts LL1798	1,500		3600.00	3600
1995	Immaculate Virgin w/base LL1799	2,000		2250.00	2250
1995	To the Rim w/base LL1800	1,500		2475.00	2475
1995	Vision of Peace w/base LL1803	1,500		1895.00	1895
1995	Portrait of a Family w/base LL1805	2,500		1750.00	1750
1995	A Family of Love w/base LL1806	2,500		1750.00	1750
1995	A Dream of Peace w/base LL1807	2,000		1160.00	1160
1996	Noah w/base LL1809	1,200		1720.00	1720
1996	Easter Fantasy w/base LL1810	1,000		3500.00	3500
1996	Moses & The Ten Commandments w/base LL1811	1,200		1860.00	1860
1996	La Menina w/base LL1812	1,000		3850.00	3850
1997	Christmas Journey LL1813	1,000		1295.00	1295
1997	Young Beethoven LL1815	2,500		875.00	875
1997	Spring Courtship LL1818	1,500		2,350.00	2350
1970	Girl with Guitar LL2016	750	1982	325.00	1800
1970	Madonna with Child LL2018	300	1974	450.00	1750
1971	Oriental Man LL2021	500	1983	500.00	1850
1971	Three Girls LL2028	500	1976	950.00	3500
1971	Eve at Tree LL2029	600	1976	450.00	3000
1971	Oriental Horse LL2030	350	1983	1100.00	3500-5000
1971	Lyric Muse LL2031	400	1982	750.00	2100
1971	Madonna and Child LL2043	300	1974	400.00	1500
1973	Peasant Woman LL2049	750	1977	200.00	1300
1973	Passionate Dance LL2051	500	1975	375.00	4500
1977	St. Theresa LL2061	1,200	1987	387.50	1400-1600
1977	Concerto LL2063	1,200	1988	500.00	1235
1977	Flying Partridges LL2064	1,200	1987	1750.00	4300
1987	Christopher Columbus w/base LL2176	1,000	1994	1000.00	1350
1990	Invincible w/base LL2188	300		1100.00	1250
1993	Flight of Fancy w/base LL2243	300		1400.00	1400
1993	The Awakening w/base LL2244	300		1200.00	1200
1993	Inspired Voyage w/base LL2245	1,000		4800.00	4800
1993	Days of Yore w/base LL2248	1,000		1950.00	2050
1993	Holiday Glow w/base LL2249	1,500		750.00	750
1993	Autumn Glow w/base LL2250	1,500		750.00	750
1993	Humble Grace w/base LL2255	2,000		2150.00	2150
1983	Dawn w/base LL3000	300		325.00	550
1983	Monks w/base LL3001	300	1993	1675.00	2550
1983	Waiting w/base LL3002	125	1991	1550.00	1900
1983	Indolence LL3003	150		1465.00	2100
1983	Venus in the Bath LL3005	200	1991	1175.00	1450
1987	Classic Beauty w/base LL3012	500		1300.00	1750
1987	Youthful Innocence w/base LL3013	500		1300.00	1750

*Quotes have been rounded up to nearest dollar

FIGURINES

Lladró
to Lladró

YEAR ISSUE		EDITION LIMIT	YEAR RETD.	ISSUE PRICE	*QUOTE U.S. $
1987	The Nymph w/base LL3014	250		1000.00	1450
1987	Dignity w/base LL3015	150		1400.00	1900
1988	Passion w/base LL3016	750		865.00	1200
1988	Muse w/base LL3017	300	1993	650.00	875
1988	Cellist w/base LL3018	300	1993	650.00	875
1988	True Affection w/base LL3019	300		750.00	1025
1989	Demureness w/base LL3020	300	1994	400.00	700
1990	Daydreaming w/base LL3022	500		550.00	775
1990	After The Bath w/base LL3023	300	1991	350.00	1350
1990	Discoveries w/base LL3024	100		1500.00	1750
1991	Resting Nude LL3025	200	1992	650.00	1000-1500
1991	Unadorned Beauty LL3026	200		1700.00	1850
1994	Ebony w/base LL3027	300		1295.00	1295
1994	Modesty w/base LL3028	300		1295.00	1295
1994	Danae LL3029	300		2880.00	2880
1995	Nude Kneeling LL3030	300		975.00	975
1982	Elk LL3501	500	1987	950.00	1200
1978	Nude with Dove LL3503	1,500	1981	250.00	700-1100
1981	The Rescue LL3504	1,500	1987	2900.00	5000
1978	St. Michael w/base LL3515	1,500		2200.00	4690
1980	Turtle Dove Nest w/base LL3519	1,200	1994	3600.00	6050
1980	Turtle Dove Group w/base LL3520	750		6800.00	11900
1981	Philippine Folklore LL3522	1,500	1995	1450.00	2400
1981	Nest of Eagles w/base LL3523	300	1994	6900.00	11500
1981	Drum Beats/Watusi Queen w/base LL3524	1,500	1994	1875.00	3050
1982	Togetherness LL3527	75	1987	375.00	900
1982	Wrestling LL3528	50	1987	950.00	1125
1983	Companionship w/base LL3529	65		1000.00	1790
1983	Anxiety w/base LL3530	125	1993	1075.00	1875
1983	Victory LL3531	90	1988	1500.00	1800
1983	Plentitude LL3532	50	1988	1000.00	1375
1983	The Observer w/base LL3533	115	1993	900.00	1650
1983	In the Distance LL3534	75	1988	525.00	1275
1983	Slave LL3535	50	1988	950.00	1150
1983	Relaxation LL3536	100	1988	525.00	1000
1983	Dreaming w/base LL3537	250	1994	475.00	1475
1983	Youth LL3538	250	1988	525.00	1000
1983	Dantiness LL3539	100	1988	1000.00	1400
1983	Pose LL3540	100	1988	1250.00	1450
1983	Tranquility LL3541	75	1988	1000.00	1400
1983	Yoga LL3542	125	1991	650.00	900
1983	Demure LL3543	100	1988	1250.00	1700
1983	Reflections w/base LL3544	75		650.00	1050
1983	Adoration LL3545	150	1990	1050.00	1600
1983	African Woman LL3546	50	1988	1300.00	2000
1983	Reclining Nude LL3547	75	1988	650.00	875
1983	Serenity w/base LL3548	300	1993	925.00	1550
1983	Reposing LL3549	80	1988	425.00	575
1983	Boxer w/base LL3550	300	1993	850.00	1450
1983	Bather LL3551	300	1988	975.00	1300
1982	Blue God LL3552	1,500	1994	900.00	1575
1982	Fire Bird LL3553	1,500	1994	800.00	1350
1982	Desert People w/base LL3555	750		1680.00	3100
1982	Road to Mandalay LL3556	750	1989	1390.00	2500
1982	Jesus in Tiberias w/base LL3557	1,200		2600.00	4910
1992	The Reader LL3560	200		2650.00	2815
1993	Trail Boss LL3561M	1,500		2450.00	2595
1993	Indian Brave LL3562M	1,500		2250.00	2250
1994	Saint James The Apostle w/base LL3563	1,000		950.00	950
1994	Gentle Moment w/base LL3564	1,000		1795.00	1835
1994	At Peace w/base LL3565	1,000		1650.00	170
1994	Indian Chief w/base LL3566	3,000		1095.00	1095
1994	Trapper w/base LL3567	3,000		950.00	950
1994	American Cowboy w/base LL3568	3,000		950.00	950
1994	A Moment's Pause w/base LL3569	3,500		1495.00	1635
1994	Ethereal Music w/base LL3570	1,000		2450.00	2500
1994	At The Helm w/base LL3571	3,500		1495.00	1495
1995	Proud Warrior w/base LL3572	3,000		995.00	995
1995	Golgotha w/base LL3773	1, 000		1650.00	1650
1996	Playing the Blues w/base LL3576	1,000		2160.00	2160
1997	Man of the Sea LL3577	1,000		1850.00	1850
1997	The Journey LL3700	500		700.00	700
1997	In Concert LL3701	350		1050.00	1050
1997	Pensive Journey LL3702	500		700.00	700
1997	Imagination LL3703	500		750.00	750
1985	Napoleon Bonaparte LL5338	5,000	1994	275.00	650
1985	Beethoven w/base LL5339	3,000	1993	760.00	1300
1985	Thoroughbred Horse w/base LL5340	1,000	1993	625.00	1000
1985	I Have Found Thee, Dulcinea LL5341	750	1990	1460.00	2800
1985	Pack of Hunting Dogs w/base LL5342	3,000	1994	925.00	2000
1985	Love Boat w/base LL5343	3,000		825.00	1350
1986	Fox Hunt w/base LL5362	1,000		5200.00	8750
1986	Rey De Copas w/base LL5366	2,000	1993	325.00	600
1986	Rey De Oros w/base LL5367	2,000	1993	325.00	600
1986	Rey De Espadas w/base LL5368	2,000	1993	325.00	600
1986	Rey De Bastos w/base LL5369	2,000	1993	325.00	600
1986	Pastoral Scene w/base LL5386	750	1995	1100.00	2290
1987	Inspiration LL5413	500	1993	1200.00	2100
1987	Carnival Time w/base LL5423	1,000	1993	2400.00	3900
1989	"Pious" LL5541	1,000	1991	1075.00	1550
1989	Freedom LL5602	1,500	1989	875.00	950
1990	A Ride In The Park LL5718	1,000	1994	3200.00	3500
1991	Youth LL5800	500	1993	650.00	725
1991	Charm LL5801	500	1994	650.00	725
1991	New World Medallion LL5808	5,000	1994	200.00	225
1992	The Voyage of Columbus LL5847	7,500	1994	1450.00	1450-1650
1992	Sorrowful Mother LL5849	1,500		1750.00	1850
1992	Justice Eagle LL5863	1,500		1700.00	1840
1992	Maternal Joy LL5864	1,500		1600.00	1700
1992	Motoring In Style LL5884	1,500		3700.00	3850
1992	The Way Of The Cross LL5890	2,000		975.00	1050
1992	Presenting Credentials LL5911	1,500		19500.00	20500
1992	Young Mozart LL5915	2,500	1994	500.00	1250-1350
1993	Jester's Serenade w/base LL5932	3,000		1995.00	1995
1993	The Blessing w/base LL5942	2,000		1345.00	1345
1993	Our Lady of Rocio w/base LL5951	2,000		3500.00	3500
1993	Where to Sir w/base LL5952	1,500		5250.00	5250
1993	Discovery Mug LL5967	1,992	1994	90.00	90
1993	Graceful Moment w/base LL6033	3,000		1475.00	1475
1993	The Hand of Justice w/base LL6033	1,000		1250.00	1250
1995	Abraham Lincoln w/base LL7554	2,500		2190.00	2190
1996	Statue of Liberty w/base LL7563	2,000		1620.00	1620
1997	George Washington LL7575	2,000		1390.00	1390

Lladró - Lladró

YEAR ISSUE		EDITION LIMIT	YEAR RETD.	ISSUE PRICE	*QUOTE U.S. $
1963	Hunting Dog 308.13	Closed	N/A	N/A	2000
1966	Poodle 325.13	Closed	N/A	N/A	2300
1970	Girl with Pigtails L357.13G	Closed	N/A	N/A	1100
1969	Shepherdess with Goats L1001G	Closed	1987	80.00	675
1969	Shepherdess with Goats L1001M	Closed	1987	80.00	450
1969	Girl's Head L1003G	Closed	1985	150.00	675
1969	Girl's Head L1003M	Closed	1985	150.00	675-800
1969	Pan with Cymbals L1006	Closed	1975	45.00	450-550
1969	Pan with Pipes L1007	Closed	1975	45.00	475-600
1969	Girl With Lamb L1010G	Closed	1993	26.00	200-275
1969	Girl With Pig L1011G	Open		13.00	95
1969	Centaur Girl L1012M	Closed	1989	45.00	400
1969	Centaur Boy L1013M	Closed	1989	45.00	425
1969	Two Women with Water Jugs L1014G	Closed	1985	85.00	400
1969	Dove L1015 G	Closed	1994	21.00	150
1969	Dove L1016 G	Closed	1995	36.00	190
1969	Idyl L1017G	Closed	1991	115.00	700
1969	Idyl L1017M	Closed	1991	115.00	550-615
1969	King Gaspar L1018M	Open		345.00	1895
1969	King Melchior L1019M	Open		345.00	1850
1969	King Baltasar L1020M	Open		345.00	1850
1969	Horse Group L1021G	Closed	1975	950.00	1600
1969	Horse Group/All White L1022M	Open		465.00	2100
1969	Flute Player L1025G	Closed	1978	73.00	750
1969	Clown with Concertina L1027G	Closed	1993	95.00	700
1969	Girl w/Heart L1028G	Closed	1970	37.50	650
1969	Boy w/Bowler L1029G	Closed	1970	37.50	550
1969	Don Quixote w/Stand L1030G	Open		225.00	1450
1969	Sancho Panza L1031G	Closed	1989	65.00	600
1969	Old Folks L1033G	Closed	1985	140.00	1400-1600
1969	Old Folks L1033M	Closed	1985	140.00	1400
1969	Shepherdess with Dog L1034	Closed	1991	30.00	225-275
1969	Girl with Geese L1035G	Closed	1995	37.50	180
1969	Girl With Geese L1035M	Closed	1992	37.50	165
1969	Horseman L1037G	Closed	1970	170.00	2500
1969	Girl with Turkeys L1038G	Closed	1978	95.00	400-550
1969	Violinist and Girl L1039G	Closed	1991	120.00	900-1100
1969	Violinist and Girl L1039M	Closed	1991	120.00	825-1000
1969	Hunters L1048	Closed	1986	115.00	1200-1400
1969	Del Monte (Boy) L1050	Closed	1978	65.00	N/A
1969	Girl with Duck L1052G	Open		30.00	205
1969	Girl with Duck L1052M	Closed	1992	30.00	190
1969	Bird L1053G	Closed	1985	13.00	100
1969	Bird L1054G	Closed	1985	14.00	125
1969	Duck L1056G	Closed	1978	19.00	275
1969	Girl with Pheasant L1055G	Closed	1978	105.00	N/A
1969	Panchito L1059	Closed	1980	28.00	N/A
1969	Bull w/Head Up L1063	Closed	1975	90.00	1100
1969	Deer L1064	Closed	1986	27.50	325
1969	Fox and Cub L1065G	Closed	1985	17.50	400
1969	Basset L1066G	Closed	1981	23.50	600
1969	Old dog L1067G	Closed	1978	40.00	600
1969	Great Dane L1068G	Closed	1989	55.00	500
1969	Afghan (sitting) L1069G	Closed	1985	36.00	625
1969	Beagle Puppy L1070G	Closed	1991	16.50	225-350
1969	Beagle Puppy L1071G	Closed	1992	16.50	275
1969	Beagle Puppy L1071M	Closed	1992	16.50	200-250
1969	Beagle Puppy L1072G	Closed	1991	16.50	250
1969	Dutch Girl L1077G	Closed	1981	57.50	250-450
1969	Herald L1078G	Closed	1970	110.00	1100
1969	Girl With Brush L1081G	Closed	1985	14.50	200-300
1969	Girl Manicuring L1082G	Closed	1985	14.50	200-300
1969	Girl With Doll L1083G	Closed	1985	14.50	200-300
1969	Girl with Mother's Shoe L1084G	Closed	1985	14.50	200-300
1969	Little Green-Grocer L1087G	Closed	1981	40.00	375
1969	Girl Seated with Flowers L1088G	Closed	1989	45.00	700
1971	Lawyer (Face) L1089G	Closed	1973	35.00	950
1971	Girl and Gazelle L1091G	Closed	1975	225.00	1200
1971	Satyr with Snail L1092G	Closed	1975	30.00	425
1969	Beggar L1094G	Closed	1981	65.00	600-675
1971	Girl With Hens L1103G	Closed	1981	50.00	375
1971	La Tarantela L1123G	Closed	1975	550.00	2250
1971	Pelusa Clown L1125G	Closed	1978	70.00	2500
1971	Clown with Violin L1126G	Closed	1978	71.00	1850
1971	Puppy Love L1127G	Open		50.00	330
1971	Dog in the Basket L1128G	Closed	1985	17.50	450
1971	Faun L1131G	Closed	1972	155.00	1500
1971	Horse L1133G	Closed	1972	115.00	900
1971	Bull L1134G	Closed	1972	130.00	1500
1971	Dog and Snail L1139G	Closed	1981	40.00	850
1971	Girl with Bonnet L1147G	Closed	1985	20.00	275
1971	Girl Shampooing L1148G	Closed	1985	20.00	200-300
1971	Dog's Head L1149G	Closed	1981	27.50	450
1971	Elephants (3) L1150G	Open		100.00	795
1971	Elephants (2) L1151G	Open		45.00	420
1971	Dog Playing Guitar L1152G	Closed	1978	32.50	375-550
1971	Dog Playing Guitar L1153G	Closed	1978	32.50	400-550
1971	Dog Playing Bass Fiddle L1154G	Closed	1978	36.50	400-550
1971	Dog w/Microphone L1155G	Closed	1978	35.00	400-550
1971	Dog Playing Bongos L1156	Closed	1978	32.50	400-550
1971	Seated Torero L1162G	Closed	1973	35.00	700
1971	Kissing Doves L1169G	Open		32.00	155
1971	Kissing Doves L1169M	Closed	1992	32.00	150
1971	Kissing Doves L1170G	Closed	1988	25.00	250
1971	Girl With Flowers L1172G	Closed	1993	27.00	375
1971	Girl With Domino L1175G	Closed	1981	34.00	350
1971	Girl With Dice L1176G	Closed	1981	25.00	350
1971	Girl With Ball L1177G	Closed	1981	27.50	350-450
1971	Girl With Accordian L1178G	Closed	1981	34.00	350-450
1971	Clown on Domino L1179G	Closed	1981	34.00	375
1971	Little Girl w/Turkeys L1180G	Closed	1981	55.00	450
1971	Platero and Marcelino L1181G	Closed	1981	50.00	350-450
1972	Little Girl with Cat L1187G	Closed	1989	37.00	250-375
1972	Boy Meets Girl L1188G	Closed	1989	310.00	400
1972	Eskimo L1195G	Open		30.00	135
1972	Horse Resting L1203G	Closed	1981	40.00	600
1972	Attentive Bear, brown L1204G	Closed	1989	16.00	125
1972	Good Bear, brown L1205G	Closed	1989	16.00	120
1972	Bear Seated, brown L1206G	Closed	1989	16.00	100-125
1972	Attentive Polar Bear, white L1207G	Open		16.00	75
1972	Bear, white L1208G	Open		16.00	75
1972	Bear, white L1209G	Open		16.00	75
1972	Round Fish L1210G	Closed	1981	35.00	625
1972	Girl With Doll L1211G	Closed	1993	72.00	440
1972	Woman Carrying Water L1212G	Closed	1983	100.00	475
1972	Little Jug Magno L1222.3G	Closed	1979	35.00	300
1972	Young Harlequin L1229G	Open		70.00	520
1972	Young Harlequin L1229M	Closed	1991	70.00	550
1972	Friendship L1230G	Closed	1991	68.00	475
1972	Friendship L1230M	Closed	1991	68.00	325
1972	Angel with Lute L1231G	Closed	1988	60.00	425
1972	Angel with Clarinet L1232G	Closed	1988	60.00	400
1972	Angel with Flute L1233G	Closed	1988	60.00	450
1972	Little Jesus of Prag L1234G	Closed	1978	70.00	725
1973	Christmas Carols L1239G	Closed	1981	125.00	750
1973	Fluttering Nightingale L1244G	Closed	1981	44.00	375
1973	Girl with Wheelbarrow L1245G	Closed	1981	75.00	500-650
1972	Caress and Rest L1246G	Closed	1990	50.00	300
1974	Happy Harlequin L1247M	Closed	1983	220.00	1100
1974	Honey Lickers L1248G	Closed	1990	100.00	475
1974	The Race L1249G	Closed	1988	450.00	1800-2250
1974	Lovers from Verona L 1250G	Closed	1990	330.00	1300-1600
1974	Pony Ride L1251G	Closed	1979	220.00	1200
1974	Shepherd L1252G	Closed	1981	100.00	500
1974	Sad Chimney Sweep L1253G	Closed	1983	180.00	1200
1974	Hamlet and Yorick L1254G	Closed	1983	325.00	1100-1200
1974	Seesaw L1255G	Closed	1993	110.00	600
1974	Mother with Pups L1257G	Closed	1981	50.00	650
1974	Playing Poodles L1258G	Closed	1981	47.50	800
1974	Poodle L1259G	Closed	1985	27.50	400
1974	Flying Duck L1263G	Open		20.00	90
1974	Flying Duck L1264G	Open		20.00	90
1974	Flying Duck L1265G	Open		20.00	90
1974	Girl with Ducks L1267G	Closed	1993	55.00	300
1974	Reminiscing L1270G	Closed	1988	975.00	1375
1974	Thoughts L1272G	Open		87.50	3490
1974	Lovers in the Park L1274G	Closed	1993	450.00	1365
1974	Christmas Seller L1276G	Closed	1981	120.00	675
1974	Feeding Time L1277G	Closed	1994	120.00	350
1974	Feeding Time L1277M	Closed	N/A	120.00	415
1974	Devotion L1278G	Closed	1990	140.00	475
1974	The Wind L1279M	Open		250.00	830
1974	Playtime L1280G	Closed	1983	110.00	550-700
1974	Afghan Standing L1282G	Closed	1985	45.00	500
1974	Little Gardener L1283G	Open		250.00	785
1974	"My Flowers" L1284G	Open		200.00	550
1974	"My Goodness" L1285G	Closed	1995	190.00	415
1974	Flower Harvest L1286G	Open		200.00	495
1974	Picking Flowers L1287G	Open		170.00	440
1974	Aggressive Duck L1288G	Closed	1995	170.00	475
1974	Good Puppy L1289G	Closed	1985	16.60	225
1974	Victorian Girl on Swing L1297G	Closed	1990	520.00	1650
1974	Birds Resting L1298G	Closed	1985	235.00	975
1974	Birds in Nest L1299G	Closed	1985	120.00	750
1974	Valencian Lady with Flowers L1304G	Open		200.00	625
1974	"On the Farm" L1306G	Closed	1990	130.00	325
1974	Ducklings L1307G	Open		47.50	150
1974	Girl with Cats L1309G	Open		120.00	310
1974	Girl w/Puppies in Basket L1311G	Open		120.00	345
1974	Schoolgirl L1313G	Closed	1990	201.00	650
1974	Girl From Scotland L1315G	Closed	1979	450.00	2800
1976	Collie L1316G	Closed	1981	45.00	400
1976	IBIS L1319G	Open		1550.00	2625
1977	Angel with Tamborine L1320G	Closed	1985	125.00	500
1977	Angel with Lyre L1321G	Closed	1985	125.00	475
1977	Angel with Song L1322G	Closed	1985	125.00	475
1977	Angel with Accordian L1323G	Closed	1985	125.00	400
1977	Angel with Mandolin L1324G	Closed	1985	125.00	400
1976	The Helmsman L1325M	Closed	1988	600.00	900-1200
1976	Playing Cards L1327 M, numbered series	Open		3800.00	6600

*Quotes have been rounded up to nearest dollar

Collectors' Information Bureau

89

Lladró
to Lladró

FIGURINES

YEAR ISSUE		EDITION LIMIT	YEAR RETD.	ISSUE PRICE	*QUOTE U.S.$
1977	Dove Group L1335G	Closed	1990	950.00	1600
1977	Blooming Roses L1339G	Closed	1988	325.00	550
1977	Male Jockey L1341G	Closed	1979	120.00	550
1977	Wrath of Don Quixote L1343G	Closed	1990	250.00	990
1977	Derby L1344G	Closed	1985	1125.00	2500
1978	Sacristan L1345G	Closed	1979	385.00	2300
1978	Under the Willow L1346G	Closed	1990	1600.00	2150
1978	Mermaid on Wave L1347G	Closed	1983	425.00	1850
1978	Pearl Mermaid L1348G	Closed	1983	225.00	1850
1978	Mermaids Playing L1349G	Closed	1983	425.00	3250
1978	In the Gondola L1350G, numbered series	Open		1850.00	3250
1978	Lady with Girl L1353G	Closed	1985	175.00	700
1978	Growing Roses L1354G	Closed	1988	485.00	635
1978	Phyllis L1356G	Closed	1993	75.00	225
1978	Shelley L1357G	Closed	1993	75.00	225
1978	Beth L1358G	Closed	1993	75.00	225
1978	Heather L1359G	Closed	1993	75.00	225
1978	Laura L1360G	Closed	1993	75.00	225
1978	Julia L1361G	Closed	1993	75.00	225
1978	Swinging L1366G	Closed	1988	825.00	1375
1978	Playful Dogs L1367	Closed	1982	160.00	700
1978	Spring Birds L1368G	Closed	1990	1600.00	2500
1978	Anniversary Waltz L1372G	Open		260.00	570
1978	Chestnut Seller L1373G	Closed	1981	800.00	750-900
1978	Waiting in the Park L1374G	Closed	1993	235.00	450
1978	Watering Flowers L1376G	Closed	1990	400.00	1150
1978	Suzy and Her Doll L1378G	Closed	1985	215.00	650
1978	Debbie and Her Doll L1379G	Closed	1985	215.00	600
1978	Cathy and Her Doll L1380G	Closed	1985	215.00	650
1978	Medieval Girl L1381G	Closed	1985	11.80	400-600
1978	Medieval Boy L1382G	Closed	1985	235.00	650-700
1978	A Rickshaw Ride L1383G	Open		1500.00	2150
1978	The Brave Knight L1385G	Closed	1988	350.00	750
1981	St. Joseph L1386G	Open		250.00	385
1981	Mary L1387G	Open		240.00	385
1981	Baby Jesus L1388G	Open		85.00	140
1981	Donkey L1389G	Open		95.00	190
1981	Cow L1390G	Open		95.00	190
1982	Holy Mary L1394G, numbered series	Open		1000.00	1475
1982	Full of Mischief L1395G	Open		420.00	825
1982	Appreciation L1396G	Open		420.00	825
1982	Second Thoughts L1397G	Open		420.00	820
1982	Reverie L1398G	Open		490.00	970
1982	Dutch Woman w/Tulips L1399G	Closed	1988	750.00	750
1982	Valencian Boy L1400G	Closed	1988	298.00	550
1982	Sleeping Nymph L1401G	Closed	1988	210.00	500-600
1982	Daydreaming Nymph L1402G	Closed	1988	210.00	550
1982	Pondering Nymph L1403G	Closed	1988	210.00	550
1982	Matrimony L1404G	Open		320.00	585
1982	Illusion L1413G	Open		115.00	260
1982	Fantasy L1414G	Open		115.00	260
1982	Mirage L1415G	Open		115.00	260
1982	From My Garden L1416G	Open		140.00	295
1982	Nature's Bounty L1417G	Closed	1995	160.00	400
1982	Flower Harmony L1418G	Closed	1995	130.00	270
1982	A Barrow of Blossoms L1419G	Open		390.00	675
1982	Born Free w/base L1420G	Open		1520.00	3140
1982	Mariko w/base L1421G	Closed	1995	860.00	1575
1982	Miss Valencia L1422G	Open		175.00	395
1982	King Melchior L1423G	Open		225.00	440
1982	King Gaspar L1424G	Open		265.00	475
1982	King Balthasar L1425G	Open		315.00	585
1982	Male Tennis Player L1426M	Closed	1988	200.00	350
1982	Female Tennis Player L1427M	Closed	1988	200.00	350
1982	Afternoon Tea L1428G	Open		115.00	275
1982	Afternoon Tea L1428M	Open		115.00	275
1982	Winter Wonderland w/base L1429G	Open		1025.00	2125
1982	High Society L1430G	Closed	1993	305.00	750
1982	The Debutante L1431G	Open		115.00	275
1982	The Debutante L1431M	Open		115.00	275
1983	Vows L1434G	Closed	1991	600.00	900
1983	Blue Moon L1435G	Closed	1988	98.00	350
1983	Moon Glow L1436G	Closed	1988	98.00	400
1983	Moon Light L1437G	Closed	1988	98.00	400-550
1983	Full Moon L1438G	Closed	1988	115.00	675
1983	"How Do You Do!" L1439G	Open		185.00	295
1983	Pleasantries L1440G	Closed	1991	960.00	1900
1983	A Litter of Love L1441G	Open		385.00	645
1983	Kitty Confrontation L1442G	Open		155.00	285
1983	Bearly Love L1443G	Open		55.00	120
1983	Purr-Fect L1444G	Open		350.00	615
1983	Springtime in Japan L1445G	Open		965.00	1800
1983	"Here Comes the Bride" L1446G	Open		518.00	995
1983	Michiko L1447G	Open		235.00	460
1983	Yuki L1448G	Open		285.00	550
1983	Mayumi L1449G	Open		235.00	495
1983	Kiyoko L1450G	Open		235.00	495
1983	Teruko L1451G	Open		235.00	495
1983	On the Town L1452G	Closed	1993	220.00	475
1983	Golfing Couple L1453G	Open		248.00	530
1983	Flowers of the Season L1454G	Open		1460.00	2550
1983	Reflections of Hamlet L1455G	Closed	1988	1000.00	1600
1983	Cranes w/base L1456G	Open		1000.00	1950
1985	A Boy and His Pony L1460G	Closed	1988	285.00	800
1985	Carefree Angel w/Flute L1463G	Closed	1988	220.00	650
1985	Carefree Angel w/Lyre L1464G	Closed	1988	220.00	650
1985	Girl on Carousel Horse L1469G	Open		470.00	935
1985	Boy on Carousel Horse L1470G	Open		470.00	935
1985	Wishing On A Star L1475G	Closed	1988	130.00	375-500
1985	Star Light Star Bright L1476G	Closed	1988	130.00	400
1985	Star Gazing L1477G	Closed	1988	130.00	400
1985	Hawaiian Dancer/Aloha! L1478G	Open		230.00	440
1985	In a Tropical Garden L1479G	Closed	1995	230.00	440
1985	Aroma of the Islands L1480G	Open		260.00	480
1985	Sunning L1481G	Closed	1988	145.00	575
1985	Eve L1482	Closed	1988	145.00	700
1985	Free As a Butterfly L1483G	Closed	1988	145.00	550
1986	Lady of the East w/base L1488G	Closed	1993	625.00	1100
1986	Valencian Children L1489G	Open		700.00	1225
1986	My Wedding Day L1494G	Open		800.00	1495
1986	A Lady of Taste L1495G	Open		575.00	1025
1986	Don Quixote & The Windmill L1497G	Open		1100.00	2050
1986	Tahitian Dancing Girls L1498G	Closed	1995	750.00	1500
1986	Blessed Family L1499G	Open		200.00	395
1986	Ragamuffin L1500G	Closed	1991	125.00	400
1986	Ragamuffin L1500M	Closed	1991	125.00	300
1986	Rag Doll L1501G	Closed	1991	125.00	250-300
1986	Rag Doll L1501M	Closed	1991	125.00	300
1986	Forgotten L1502G	Closed	1991	125.00	300
1986	Forgotten L1502M	Closed	1991	125.00	300
1986	Neglected L1503G	Closed	1991	125.00	425
1986	Neglected L1503M	Closed	1991	125.00	300
1986	The Reception L1504G	Closed	1990	625.00	1050
1986	Nature Boy L1505G	Closed	1991	100.00	275
1986	Nature Boy L1505M	Closed	1991	100.00	N/A
1986	A New Friend L1506G	Closed	1991	110.00	275-325
1986	A New Friend L1506M	Closed	1991	110.00	260
1986	Boy & His Bunny L1507G	Closed	1991	90.00	275
1986	Boy & His Bunny L1507M	Closed	1991	90.00	N/A
1986	In the Meadow L1508G	Closed	1991	100.00	300
1986	In the Meadow L1508M	Closed	1991	100.00	285
1986	Spring Flowers L1509G	Closed	1991	100.00	300
1986	Spring Flowers L1509M	Closed	1991	100.00	285
1987	Cafe De Paris L1511G	Closed	1995	1900.00	2950
1987	Hawaiian Beauty L1512G	Closed	1990	575.00	1000
1987	A Flower for My Lady L1513G	Closed	1990	1150.00	1750
1987	Gaspar 's Page L1514G	Closed	1990	275.00	300-500
1987	Melchior's Page L1515G	Closed	1990	290.00	650
1987	Balthasar's Page L1516G	Closed	1990	275.00	850
1987	Circus Train L1517G	Closed	1994	2900.00	4350
1987	Valencian Garden L1518G	Closed	1991	1100.00	1795
1987	Stroll in the Park L1519G	Open		1600.00	2600
1987	The Landau Carriage L1521G	Open		2500.00	3850
1987	I am Don Quixote! L1522G	Open		2600.00	3950
1987	Valencian Bouquet L1524G	Closed	1991	250.00	400
1987	Valencian Dreams L1525G	Closed	1991	240.00	300-400
1987	Valencian Flowers L1526G	Closed	1991	375.00	550
1987	Tenderness L1527G	Open		260.00	430
1987	I Love You Truly L1528G	Open		375.00	595
1987	Momi L1529G	Closed	1990	275.00	500
1987	Leilani L1530G	Closed	1990	275.00	550
1987	Malia L1531G	Closed	1990	275.00	500
1987	Lehua L1532G	Closed	1990	275.00	600
1987	Not So Fast! L1533G	Open		175.00	265
1988	Little Sister L1534G	Open		180.00	240
1988	Sweet Dreams L1535G	Open		150.00	220
1988	Stepping Out L1537G	Open		230.00	325
1988	Pink Ballet Slippers L1540	Closed	1991	275.00	450-475
1988	White Ballet Slippers L1540.3	Closed	1991	275.00	395
1987	Light Blue Spoon L1548G	Closed	1991	70.00	150
1987	Dark Blue Spoon L1548.1	Closed	1991	70.00	150
1987	White Spoon L1548.3	Closed	1991	70.00	150
1987	Wild Stallions w/base L1566G	Closed	1993	1100.00	1465
1987	Running Free w/base L1567G	Open		1500.00	1600
1987	Grand Dame L1568G	Open		290.00	425
1989	Fluttering Crane L1598G	Open		115.00	145
1989	Nesting Crane L1599G	Open		95.00	115
1989	Landing Crane L1600G	Open		115.00	145
1989	Rock Nymph L1601G	Closed	1995	665.00	795
1989	Spring Nymph L1602G	Closed	1995	665.00	825
1989	Latest Addition L1606G	Open		385.00	480
1989	Flight Into Egypt w/base L1610G	Open		885.00	1150
1989	Courting Cranes L1611G	Open		565.00	695
1989	Preening Crane L1612G	Open		385.00	485
1989	Bowing Crane L1613G	Open		385.00	485
1989	Dancing Crane L1614G	Open		385.00	485
1989	Snow Queen Mask No.11 L1645G	Closed	1991	390.00	450
1989	Medieval Cross No.4 L1652G	Closed	1991	250.00	250
1989	Lavender Lady L1667M	Closed	1991	385.00	550
1989	Lacy Butterfly #1 L1673M	Closed	1991	95.00	200
1989	Beautiful Butterfly #2 L1674M	Closed	1991	100.00	160
1989	Black Butterfly #3 L1675M	Closed	1991	120.00	185
1989	Pink & White Butterfly #4 L1676M	Closed	1991	100.00	175
1989	Black & White Butterfly #5 L1677M	Closed	1991	100.00	175
1989	Large Pink Butterfly #6 L1678M	Closed	1991	100.00	175
1989	Pink & Blue Butterfly #7 L1679M	Closed	1991	80.00	140
1989	Small Pink Butterfly #8 L1680M	Closed	1991	72.50	125
1989	Blue Butterfly #9 L1681M	Closed	1991	185.00	275
1989	Pretty Butterfly #10 L1682M	Closed	1991	185.00	275
1989	Spotted Butterfly #11 L1683M	Closed	1991	175.00	260
1989	Leopard Butterfly #12 L1684M	Closed	1991	165.00	250
1989	Great Butterfly #13 L1685M	Closed	1991	150.00	225
1989	Queen Butterfly #14 L1686M	Closed	1991	125.00	200
1988	Cellist L1700M	Closed	1993	1200.00	1750
1988	Saxophone Player L1701M	Closed	1993	835.00	1840
1988	Boy at the Fair (Decorated) L1708M	Closed	1993	650.00	650
1988	Exodus L1709M	Closed	1993	875.00	875
1988	School Boy L1710M	Closed	1993	750.00	750
1988	School Girl L1711M	Closed	1993	950.00	950
1988	Nanny L1714M	Closed	1993	575.00	700
1988	On Our Way Home (decorated) L1715M	Closed	1993	2000.00	2000
1988	Harlequin with Puppy L1716M	Closed	1993	825.00	1000
1988	Harlequin with Dove L1717M	Closed	1993	900.00	1000
1988	Dress Rehearsal L1718M	Closed	1993	1150.00	1150
1989	Back From the Fair L1719M	Closed	1993	1825.00	1825
1990	Sprite w/base L1720G, numbered series	Open		1200.00	1400
1990	Leprechaun w/base L1721G, numbered series	Open		1200.00	1395
1989	Group Discussion L1722M	Closed	1993	1500.00	1500
1989	Hopeful Group L1723M	Closed	1993	1825.00	1825
1989	Belle Epoque L1724M	Closed	1993	700.00	700
1989	Young Lady w/Parasol L1725M	Closed	1993	950.00	950
1989	Young Lady with Fan L1726M	Closed	1993	750.00	750
1989	Pose L1727M	Closed	1993	725.00	725
1991	Nativity L1730M	Open		725.00	725
1970	Cat L2001G	Closed	1975	27.50	625
1970	Gothic King L2002G	Closed	1975	25.00	450
1970	Gothic Queen L2003G	Closed	1975	25.00	450
1970	Shepherdess w/Lamb L2005M	Closed	1981	100.00	710
1970	Water Carrier Girl Lamp L2006M	Closed	1975	30.00	600
1971	Girl with Dog L2013M	Closed	1975	300.00	2350
1971	Little Eagle Owl L2020M	Closed	1985	15.00	425
1971	Boy/Girl Eskimo L2038.3M	Closed	1994	100.00	275-455
1974	Setter's Head L2045M	Closed	1981	42.50	550
1974	Magistrates L2052M	Closed	1981	135.00	950
1974	Oriental L2056M	Open		35.00	105
1974	Oriental L2057M	Open		30.00	100
1974	Thailandia L2058M	Open		650.00	1885
1974	Muskateer L2059M	Closed	1981	900.00	2000-3000
1977	Monk L2060M	Open		60.00	145
1977	Day Dream L2062M	Closed	1985	400.00	1300
1977	Chinese Farmer w/Staff L2065M	Closed	1985	340.00	1800
1977	Dogs-Bust L2067M	Closed	1979	280.00	800
1977	Thai Dancers L2069M	Open		300.00	745
1977	A New Hairdo L2070M	Closed	1991	1060.00	1430
1977	Graceful Duo L2073M	Closed	1994	775.00	1650
1977	Nuns L2075M	Open		90.00	250
1978	Lonely L2076M	Open		72.50	185
1978	Rain in Spain L2077M	Closed	1990	190.00	475-550
1978	Woman L2080M	Closed	1985	625.00	625
1978	Woman L2081M	Closed	1985	550.00	1400
1978	Carmen L2083M	Closed	1981	275.00	625
1978	Don Quixote Dreaming L2084M	Closed	1985	550.00	2050
1978	The Little Kiss L2086M	Closed	1985	180.00	475
1978	Girl in Rocking Chair L2089	Closed	1981	235.00	600
1978	Saint Francis L2090	Closed	1981	565.00	N/A
1978	Holy Virgin L2092M	Closed	1981	200.00	N/A
1978	Girl Waiting L2093M	Closed	1995	90.00	185
1978	Tenderness L2094M	Open		100.00	205
1978	Duck Pulling Pigtail L2095M	Open		110.00	275
1978	Nosy Puppy L2096M	Closed	1993	190.00	400
1978	Laundress L2109M	Closed	1983	325.00	325-650
1980	Marujita w/Two Ducks L2113M	Closed	1993	240.00	295
1980	Kissing Father L2114M	Closed	1981	575.00	575
1980	Mother's Kiss L2115M	Closed	1981	575.00	700
1980	The Whaler L2121M	Closed	1988	820.00	1050
1981	Lost in Thought L2125M	Closed	1990	210.00	300
1983	Indian Chief L2127M	Closed	1988	525.00	750
1983	Venus L2128M	Open		650.00	1330
1983	Waiting for Santa L2129M	Closed	1985	325.00	600
1983	Egyptian Cat L2130M	Closed	1985	75.00	500
1983	Mother & Son L2131M, numbered series	Open		850.00	1550
1983	Spring Sheperdess L2132M	Closed	1985	450.00	1200
1983	Autumn Sheperdess L2133M	Closed	1985	285.00	N/A
1984	Nautical Watch L2134M	Closed	1988	450.00	800
1984	Mystical Joseph L2135M	Closed	1988	428.00	700
1984	The King L2136M	Closed	1988	570.00	710
1984	Fairy Ballerina L2137M	Closed	1988	500.00	1250
1984	Friar Juniper L2138M	Closed	1993	160.00	400
1984	Aztec Indian L2139M	Closed	1988	553.00	600
1984	Pepita wth Sombrero L2140M	Open		97.50	200
1984	Pedro with Jug L2141M	Open		100.00	205
1984	Sea Harvest L2142M	Closed	1990	535.00	700
1984	Aztec Dancer L2143M	Closed	1988	463.00	650
1984	Leticia L2144M	Closed	1995	100.00	225
1984	Gabriela L2145M	Closed	1994	100.00	250
1984	Desiree L2146M	Closed	1995	100.00	225
1984	Alida L2147M	Closed	1994	100.00	250
1984	Head of Congolese Woman L2148M	Closed	1988	55.00	500-700
1985	Young Madonna L2149M	Closed	1988	400.00	675
1985	A Tribute to Peace w/base L2150M	Open		470.00	930
1985	A Bird on Hand L2151M	Open		118.00	255
1985	Chinese Girl L2152M	Closed	1990	90.00	200-250
1985	Chinese Boy L2153	Closed	1990	90.00	200-250
1985	Hawaiian Flower Vendor L2154M	Open		245.00	460
1985	Arctic inter L2156M	Open		75.00	145
1985	Eskimo Girl w/Cold Feet L2157M	Open		140.00	285
1985	Pensive Eskimo Girl L2158M	Open		100.00	210
1985	Pensive Eskimo Boy L2159M	Open		100.00	210
1985	Flower Vendor L2160M	Closed	1995	110.00	215
1985	Fruit Vendor L2161M	Closed	1994	120.00	230
1985	Fish Vendor L2162M	Closed	1994	110.00	205
1987	Mountain Shepherd L2163M	Open		120.00	210
1987	My Lost Lamb L2164M	Open		100.00	175
1987	Chiquita L2165M	Closed	1993	100.00	170
1987	Paco L2166M	Closed	1993	100.00	170
1987	Fernando L2167M	Closed	1993	100.00	200

*Quotes have been rounded up to nearest dollar

Lladró
to Lladró

FIGURINES

YEAR ISSUE		EDITION LIMIT	YEAR RETD.	ISSUE PRICE	*QUOTE U.S.$
1987	Julio L2168M	Closed	1993	100.00	225
1987	Repose L2169M	Open		120.00	195
1987	Spanish Dancer L2170M	Open		190.00	345
1987	Ahoy Tere L2173M	Open		190.00	325
1987	Andean Flute Player L2174M	Closed	1990	250.00	350
1988	Harvest Helpers L2178M	Open		190.00	265
1988	Sharing the Harvest L2179M	Open		190.00	265
1988	Dreams of Peace w/base L2180M	Open		880.00	1125
1988	Bathing Nymph w/base L2181M	Open		560.00	795
1988	Daydreamer w/base L2182M	Open		560.00	795
1989	Wakeup Kitty L2183M	Closed	1993	225.00	325
1989	Angel and Friend L2184M	Closed	1994	150.00	185
1989	Devoted Reader L2185M	Closed	1994	125.00	160
1989	The Greatest Love L2186M	Open		235.00	320
1989	Jealous Friend L2187M	Closed	1995	275.00	365
1990	Mother's Pride L2189M	Open		300.00	375
1990	To The Well L2190M	Open		250.00	295
1990	Forest Born L2191M	Closed	1991	230.00	450
1990	King Of The Forest L2192M	Closed	1992	290.00	310
1990	Heavenly Strings L2194M	Closed	1993	170.00	235
1990	Heavenly Sounds L2195M	Closed	1993	170.00	235
1990	Heavenly Solo L2196M	Closed	1993	170.00	235
1990	Heavenly Song L2197M	Closed	1993	175.00	185
1990	A King is Born w/base L2198M	Open		750.00	895
1990	Devoted Friends w/base L2199M	Closed	1995	700.00	895
1990	A Big Hug! L2200M	Open		250.00	310
1990	Our Daily Bread L2201M	Closed	1994	150.00	250
1990	A Helping Hand L2202M	Closed	1993	150.00	250
1990	Afternoon Chores L2203M	Closed	1994	150.00	250
1990	Farmyard Grace L2204M	Closed	1993	180.00	300
1990	Prayerful Stitch L2205M	Closed	1994	160.00	250
1990	Sisterly Love L2206M	Open		300.00	375
1990	What A Day! L2207M	Open		550.00	640
1990	Let's Rest L2208M	Open		550.00	665
1991	Long Dy L2209M	Open		295.00	340
1991	Lazy Day L2210M	Open		240.00	260
1991	Patrol Leader L2212M	Closed	1993	390.00	420
1991	Nature's Friend L2213M	Closed	1993	390.00	420
1991	Seaside Angel L2214M	Open		150.00	165
1991	Friends in Flight L2215M	Open		165.00	180
1991	Laundry Day L2216M	Open		350.00	400
1991	Gentle Play L2217M	Closed	1993	380.00	415
1991	Costumed Couple L2218M	Closed	1993	680.00	750
1992	Underfoot L2219M	Open		360.00	410
1992	Free Spirit L2220M	Closed	1994	235.00	245
1992	Spring Beauty L2221M	Closed	1994	285.00	295
1992	Tender Moment L2222M	Open		400.00	450
1992	New Lamb L2223M	Open		365.00	385
1992	Cherish L2224M	Open		1750.00	1850
1992	FriendlySparrow L2225M	Open		295.00	325
1992	Boy's Best Friend L2226M	Open		390.00	410
1992	Artic Allies L2227M	Open		585.00	615
1992	Snowy Sunday L2228M	Open		550.00	625
1992	Seasonal Gifts L2229M	Open		450.00	475
1992	Mary's Child L2230M	Closed	1994	525.00	550
1992	Afternoon Verse L2231M	Open		580.00	595
1992	Poor Little Bear L2232M	Open		250.00	265
1992	Guess What I Have L2233M	Open		340.00	375
1992	Playful Push L2234M	Open		850.00	875
1993	Adoring Mother L2235M	Open		405.00	440
1993	Frosty Outing L2236M	Open		375.00	410
1993	The Old Fishing Hole L2237M	Open		625.00	640
1993	Learning Together L2238M	Open		500.00	500
1993	Valencian Courtship L2239M	Open		880.00	895
1993	Winged Love L2240M	Closed	1995	285.00	310
1993	Winged Harmony L2241M	Closed	1995	285.00	310
1993	Away to School L2242M	Open		465.00	465
1993	Lion Tamer L2246M	Closed	1995	375.00	375
1993	Just Us L2247M	Closed	1995	650.00	650
1993	Noella L2251M	Open		405.00	420
1993	Waiting For Father L2252M	Open		660.00	660
1993	Noisy Friend L2253M	Open		280.00	280
1993	Step Aside L2254M	Open		280.00	280
1994	Solitude L2256M	Open		398.00	435
1994	Constant Companions L2257M	Open		575.00	625
1994	Family Love L2258M	Open		450.00	485
1994	Little Fisherman L2259M	Open		298.00	330
1994	Artic Friends L2260M	Open		345.00	380
1995	Jesus and Joseph L2294M	Open		550.00	550
1995	Peaceful Rest L2295M	Open		390.00	390
1995	Life's Small Wonders L2296M	Open		370.00	370
1995	Elephants L2297M	Open		875.00	875
1995	Hindu Children L2298M	Open		450.00	450
1995	Poetic Moment L2299M	Open		465.00	465
1995	Emperor L2300M	Open		765.00	765
1995	Empress L2301M	Open		795.00	795
1995	Twilight Years L2302M	Open		385.00	385
1995	Not So Fast L2303M	Open		350.00	350
1995	Love in Bloom L2304M	Open		420.00	420
1995	Fragrant Bouquet L2305M	Open		330.00	330
1995	Hurray Now L2306M	Open		310.00	310
1995	Happy Birthday L2307M	Open		150.00	150
1995	Let's Make Up L2308M	Open		265.00	265
1995	Windblown Girl L2309M	Open		320.00	320
1995	Chit-Chat L2310M	Open		270.00	270
1995	Good Night L2311M	Open		280.00	280
1995	Goose Trying to Eat L2312M	Open		325.00	325
1995	Who's the Fairest L2313M	Open		230.00	230
1995	Breezy Afternoon L2314M	Open		220.00	220
1995	On the Green L2315M	Open		575.00	575
1995	Closing Scene L2316M	Open		560.00	560
1995	Talk to Me L2317M	Open		175.00	175
1995	Taking Time L2318M	Open		175.00	175
1995	A Lesson Shared L2319M	Open		215.00	215
1995	Cat Nap L2320M	Open		265.00	265
1995	All Tuckered Out L2321M	Open		275.00	275
1995	Naptime L2322M	Open		275.00	275
1995	Water Girl L2323M	Open		245.00	245
1995	A Basket of Fun L2324M	Open		320.00	320
1995	Spring Splendor L2325M	Open		440.00	440
1995	Physician L2326M	Open		350.00	350
1995	Sad Sax L2327M	Open		225.00	225
1995	Circus Sam L2328M	Open		225.00	225
1995	Daily Chores L2329M	Open		345.00	345
1996	The Shepherdess L2330	Open		410.00	410
1996	Little Peasant Girl (pink) L2331	Open		155.00	155
1996	Little Peasant Girl (blue) L2332	Open		155.00	155
1996	Little Peasant Girl (white) L2333	Open		155.00	155
1996	Asian Melody L2334	Open		690.00	690
1996	Young Fisherman L2335	Open		225.00	225
1996	Young Water Girl L2336	Open		315.00	315
1996	Virgin of Montserrat w/base L2337	Open		1000.00	1000
1996	Sultan's Dream L2338	Open		700.00	700
1996	The Sultan L2339	Open		480.00	480
1996	Oriental Fantasy w/bow L2340	Open		1350.00	1350
1996	Oriental Fantasy w/brooch L2341	Open		1350.00	1350
1996	Returning From the Well w/base L2342	Open		1800.00	1800
1996	Care & Tenderness w/base L2343	Open		860.00	860
1996	Oration L2344	Open		295.00	295
1996	Bedtime Story L2345	Open		360.00	360
1996	Feeding the Ducks L2346	Open		305.00	305
1996	Meditation (blue) L2347	Open		145.00	145
1996	Prayerful Moment (blue) L2348	Open		145.00	145
1996	Sleigh Ride w/base L2349	Open		1520.00	1520
1996	Pensive Clown w/base L2350	Open		680.00	680
1996	Fishing w/Gramps w/base L2351	Open		1025.00	1025
1996	Under My Spell L2352	Open		225.00	225
1996	Shot on Goal w/base L2353	Open		935.00	935
1997	Waiting For Spring L2354	Open		385.00	385
1997	Gabriela L2355	Open		740.00	740
1997	Country Joy L2356	Open		310.00	310
1997	In Search of Water L2357	Open		410.00	410
1997	I'm Sleepy L2358	Open		360.00	360
1997	First Crush L2359	Open		945.00	945
1997	Hunting Butterflies L2360	Open		465.00	465
1997	Cold Weather Companions L2361	Open		380.00	380
1997	Braving The Storm L2362	Open		470.00	470
1997	Pampered Puppy L2363	Open		345.00	345
1997	Melodies L2364	Open		590.00	590
1997	Holy Mother L2365	Open		230.00	230
1997	Bread of Life L2366	Open		230.00	230
1997	Pensive Harlequin L2367	Open		560.00	560
1997	Colombina L2368	Open		585.00	585
1978	Native L3502M	Open		700.00	2450
1978	Letters to Dulcinea L3509M, numbered series	Open		875.00	2175
1978	Horse Heads L3511M	Closed	1990	260.00	700
1978	Girl With Pails L3512M	Open		140.00	285
1978	A Wintry Day L3513M	Closed	1988	525.00	800-1000
1978	Pensive w/ base L3514M	Open		500.00	1050
1978	Jesus Christ L3516M	Closed	1988	1050.00	1450
1978	Nude w/Rose w/ base L3517M	Open		225.00	780
1980	Lady Macbeth L3518M	Closed	1981	385.00	700-1200
1980	Mother's Love L3521M	Closed	1990	1000.00	1100
1981	Weary w/ base L3525M	Open		360.00	685
1982	Contemplation w/ base L3526M	Open		265.00	590
1982	Stormy Sea w/base L3554M	Open		675.00	1445
1984	Innocence w/base/green L3558M	Closed	1991	960.00	1650
1984	Innocence w/base/red L3558.3M	Closed	1987	960.00	1200
1985	Peace Offering w/base L3559M	Open		397.00	665
1969	Marketing Day L4502G	Closed	1985	40.00	400
1969	Girl with Lamb L4505G	Open		20.00	125
1969	Boy with Kid L4506M	Closed	1985	22.50	400
1969	Boy with Lambs L4509G	Closed	1981	37.50	275
1969	Girl w/Parasol and Geese L4510G	Closed	1993	40.00	350
1969	Nude L4511M	Closed	1985	45.00	700
1969	Nude L4512G	Closed	1985	44.00	400
1969	Man on Horse L4515G	Closed	1985	180.00	1000
1969	Female Equestrian L4516G	Open		170.00	745
1969	Boy Student L4517G	Closed	1978	57.50	475
1969	Flamenco Dancers L4519G	Closed	1993	150.00	1200
1970	Boy With Dog L4522M	Closed	1992	25.00	155
1969	Girl With Slippers L4523G	Closed	1993	17.00	125
1969	Girl With Slippers L4523M	Closed	1993	17.00	100
1969	Donkey in Love L4524G	Closed	1985	15.00	350
1969	Donkey in Love L4524M	Closed	1985	15.00	350
1969	Violinist L4527G	Closed	1985	75.00	500
1969	Ballet Lamp L4528G	Closed	1985	120.00	850
1969	Joseph L4533G	Open		60.00	110
1969	Joseph L4533M	Open		60.00	110
1969	Mary L4534G	Open		60.00	85
1969	Mary L4534M	Open		60.00	85
1971	Baby Jesus L4535.3G	Open		60.00	70
1969	Baby Jesus L4535.3M	Open		60.00	70
1969	Angel, Chinese L4536G	Open		45.00	90
1969	Angel, Chinese L4536M	Open		45.00	90
1969	Angel, Black L4537G	Open		13.00	90
1969	Angel, Black L4537M	Open		13.00	90
1969	Angel, Praying L4538G	Open		13.00	90
1969	Angel, Praying L4538M	Open		13.00	90
1969	Angel, Thinking L4539G	Open		13.00	90
1969	Angel, Thinking L4539M	Open		13.00	90
1969	Angel with Horn L4540G	Open		13.00	90
1969	Angel with Horn L4540M	Open		13.00	90
1969	Angel Reclining L4541G	Open		13.00	90
1969	Angel Reclining L4541M	Open		13.00	90
1969	Group of Angels L4542G	Open		31.00	195
1969	Group of Angels L4542M	Open		31.00	195
1969	Troubador L4548G	Closed	1978	67.50	750
1969	Geese Group L4549G	Open		28.50	230
1969	Geese Group L4549M	Closed	1992	28.50	230
1969	Flying Dove L4550G	Open		47.50	265
1969	Flying Dove L4550M	Closed	1992	47.50	165
1969	Ducks, Set/3 asst. L4551-3G	Open		18.00	140
1969	Shepherd L4554	Closed	1972	69.00	N/A
1969	Sad Harlequin L4558G	Closed	1993	110.00	600
1969	Waiting Backstage L4559G	Closed	1993	110.00	500
1970	Llama Group 4561G	Closed	1970	55.00	1600
1969	Couple with Parasol L4563G	Closed	1985	180.00	900
1969	Girl with Geese L4568G	Closed	1993	45.00	350
1969	Girl With Turkey L4569G	Closed	1981	28.50	375
1969	Shepherd Resting L4571G	Closed	1981	60.00	475
1969	Girl with Piglets L4572G	Closed	1985	70.00	425
1969	Girl with Piglets L4572M	Closed	1985	70.00	400
1969	Mother & Child L4575G	Open		50.00	265
1969	New Shepherdess L4576G	Closed	1985	37.50	315
1969	New Shepherd L4577G	Closed	1983	35.00	550
1969	Mardi Gras L4580G	Closed	1975	57.50	1800
1969	Mardi Gras L4580M	Closed	1975	57.50	1800
1969	Girl with Sheep L4584G	Closed	1993	27.00	170
1969	Holy Family L4585G	Closed	1994	18.00	135
1969	Holy Family L4585M	Closed	1994	18.00	135
1969	Madonna L4586G	Closed	1979	32.50	350
1969	White Cockeral L4588G	Closed	1979	17.50	300
1969	Girl with Pitcher L4590G	Closed	1981	47.50	400
1969	Shepherdess w/Basket L4591G	Closed	1993	20.00	275
1969	Lady with Greyhound L4594G	Closed	1981	60.00	700
1969	Fairy L4595G	Closed	1994	27.50	195
1969	Two Horses L4597	Closed	1990	240.00	925-1000
1969	Doctor L4602.3G	Open		33.00	198
1969	Nurse-L4603.3G	Open		35.00	200
1969	Magic Clown with Girl L4605	Closed	1985	160.00	1000
1969	Accordian Player L4606	Closed	1978	60.00	650
1969	Cupid L4607G	Closed	1980	15.00	150
1969	Cook in Trouble L4608	Closed	1985	27.50	650-775
1969	Nuns L4611G	Open		37.50	155
1969	Nuns L4611M	Open		37.50	155
1969	Girl Singer L4612G	Closed	1979	14.00	150
1969	Boy With Cymbals L4613G	Closed	1979	14.00	400
1969	Boy With Guitar L4614G	Closed	1979	19.50	400
1969	Boy with Double Bass L4615G	Closed	1979	22.50	400
1969	Boy With Drum L4616G	Closed	1979	16.50	350
1969	Group of Musicians L4617G	Closed	1979	33.00	500
1969	Clown L4618G	Open		70.00	415
1969	Sea Captain L4621G	Closed	1993	45.00	325
1969	Sea Captain L4621M	Closed	1989	42.50	300
1969	Old Man with Violin L4622G	Closed	1982	45.00	700
1969	Velazquez Bookend L4626G	Closed	1975	90.00	950
1969	Columbus Bookend L4627G	Closed	1975	90.00	950
1969	Angel with Child L4635G	Open		15.00	110
1969	Honey Peddler L4638G	Closed	1978	60.00	575
1969	Cow With Pig L4640	Closed	1981	42.50	750
1969	Pekinese L4641G	Closed	1985	20.00	450
1969	Dog L4642	Closed	1981	22.50	500
1969	Skye Terrier L4643G	Closed	1985	15.00	500
1969	Andalucians Group L4647G	Closed	1990	412.00	1400
1969	Valencian Couple on Horseback L4648	Closed	1990	900.00	1000
1969	Madonna Head L4649G	Open		25.00	155
1969	Madonna Head L4649M	Open		25.00	155
1969	Girl with Calla Lillies L4650G	Open		18.00	145
1969	Cellist L4651G	Closed	1978	70.00	750
1969	Happy Travelers L4652	Closed	1978	115.00	650
1969	Orchestra Conductor L4653G	Closed	1979	95.00	850
1969	The Grandfather L4654G	Closed	1979	75.00	1200
1969	Horses L4655G	Open		110.00	760
1969	Shepherdess L4660G	Closed	1993	21.00	300
1969	Countryman L4664M	Closed	1979	50.00	500
1969	Girl with Basket L4665G	Closed	1979	50.00	450
1969	Girl with Basket L4665M	Closed	1979	50.00	550
1969	Birds L4667G	Closed	1985	25.00	200
1969	Maja Head L4668G	Closed	1985	50.00	650
1969	Baby Jesus L4670BG	Open		18.00	55
1969	Mary L4671G	Open		33.00	75
1969	St. Joseph L4672G	Open		33.00	90
1969	King Melchior L4673G	Open		35.00	95
1969	King Gaspar L4674G	Open		35.00	95
1969	King Balthasar L4675G	Open		35.00	95
1969	Shepherd with Lamb L4676G	Open		14.00	110
1969	Girl with Rooster L4677G	Open		14.00	90
1969	Shepherdess w/Basket L4678G	Open		13.00	90
1969	Donkey L4679G	Open		36.50	100
1969	Cow L4680G	Open		36.50	90
1970	Girl with Milkpail L4682G	Closed	1991	28.00	325
1970	Hebrew Student L4684G	Closed	1985	33.00	500-650
1970	Hebrew Student L4684M	Closed	1985	33.00	600
1970	Gothic Queen L4689	Closed	1975	20.00	700
1970	Troubadour in Love L4699	Closed	1975	60.00	1000
1970	Dressmaker L4700G	Closed	1993	45.00	500
1970	Mother & Child L4701G	Open		45.00	295
1970	Girl Jewelry Dish L4713G	Closed	1978	30.00	550
1970	Girl Jewelry Dish L4713M	Closed	1978	30.00	550
1970	Lady Empire L4719G	Closed	1979	150.00	1000

*Quotes have been rounded up to nearest dollar

Lladró
to Lladró

FIGURINES

YEAR ISSUE		EDITION LIMIT	YEAR RETD.	ISSUE PRICE	*QUOTE U.S.$
1970	Girl With Tulips L4720G	Closed	1978	65.00	600
1970	Hamlet L4729G	Closed	1980	85.00	800
1970	Bird Watcher L4730	Closed	1985	35.00	400-500
1970	German Shepherd w/Pup L4731	Closed	1975	40.00	950
1971	Small Dog L4749	Closed	1985	5.50	200
1971	Romeo and Juliet L4750G	Open		150.00	1250
1971	Doncel With Roses L4757G	Closed	1979	35.00	500
1974	Lady with Dog L4761G	Closed	1993	60.00	400-500
1971	Dentist L4762	Closed	1978	36.00	550
1971	Dentist (Reduced) L4762.3G	Closed	1985	30.00	475
1971	Obstetrician L4763G	Closed	1973	47.50	450
1971	Obstetrician L4763.3G	Open		40.00	255
1971	Don Quixote Vase L4770G	Closed	1975	25.00	750
1971	Don Quixote Vase L4770M	Closed	1975	25.00	750
1971	Rabbit L4772G	Open		17.50	135
1971	Rabbit L4773G	Open		17.50	130
1971	Dormouse L4774	Closed	1983	30.00	375
1972	Girl Tennis Player L4798	Closed	1981	50.00	400
1971	Children, Praying L4779G	Open		36.00	195
1971	Children, Praying L4779M	Closed	1992	36.00	153
1971	Boy with Goat L4780	Closed	1978	80.00	600
1972	Japanese Woman L4799	Closed	1975	45.00	500
1972	Gypsy with Brother L4800G	Closed	1979	36.00	400
1972	The Teacher L4801G	Closed	1978	45.00	500
1972	Fisherman L4802G	Closed	1979	70.00	700
1972	Woman with Umbrella L4805G	Closed	1981	100.00	800
1972	Girl with Dog L4806G	Closed	1981	80.00	500
1972	Geisha L4807G	Closed	1993	190.00	475
1972	Wedding L4808G	Open		50.00	190
1972	Wedding L4808M	Open		50.00	190
1972	Going Fishing L4809G	Open		33.00	160
1972	Young Sailor L4810G	Open		33.00	175
1972	Boy with Pails L4811	Closed	1988	30.00	400
1972	Getting Her Goat L4812G	Closed	1988	55.00	450
1972	Girl with Geese L4815G	Closed	1991	72.00	400
1972	Girl with Geese L4815M	Closed	1991	72.00	295
1972	Little Shepherd w/Goat L4817M	Closed	1981	50.00	475
1972	Burro L4821G	Closed	1979	24.00	450
1974	Peruvian Girl with Baby L4822	Closed	1981	65.00	775
1974	Legionary L4823	Closed	1978	55.00	400-500
1972	Male Golfer L4824G	Open		66.00	295
1972	Veterinarian L4825	Closed	1985	48.00	500
1972	Girl Feeding Rabbit L4826G	Closed	1993	40.00	300
1972	Caressing Calf L4827G	Closed	1981	55.00	475
1972	Cinderella L4828G	Open		47.00	245
1975	Swan L4829G	Closed	1983	16.00	400
1972	You and Me L4830G	Closed	1979	112.50	1000
1972	Romance L4831G	Closed	1981	175.00	1500
1972	Chess Set Pieces L4833.3G	Closed	1985	410	2500
1972	Shepherdess L4835G	Closed	1991	42.00	225-325
1973	Clean Up Time L4838G	Closed	1993	36.00	250-300
1973	Clean Up Time L4838M	Closed	1992	36.00	250
1973	Oriental Flower Arranger/Girl L4840G	Open		90.00	415
1973	Oriental Flower Arranger/Girl L4840M	Open		90.00	515
1974	Girl from Valencia L4841G	Open		35.00	225
1973	Viola Lesson L4842G	Closed	1981	66.00	450
1973	Donkey Ride L4843	Closed	1981	86.00	650
1973	Pharmacist L4844G	Closed	1985	70.00	1650
1973	Classic Dance L4847G	Closed	1985	80.00	600
1973	Feeding The Ducks L4849G	Closed	1995	60.00	270
1973	Feeding The Ducks L4849M	Closed	1992	60.00	250
1973	Aesthetic Pose L4850G	Closed	1985	110.00	650
1973	Lady Golfer L4851M	Closed	1992	70.00	250
1973	Gardner in Trouble L4852	Closed	1981	65.00	500
1974	Cobbler L4853G	Closed	1985	100.00	600
1973	Don Quixote L4854G	Open		40.00	205
1973	Ballerina L4855G	Open		45.00	330
1983	Ballerina, white L4855.3	Closed	1987	110.00	250
1974	Waltz Time L4856G	Closed	1985	65.00	450
1974	Dog L4857G	Closed	1979	40.00	550
1974	Pleasant Encounter L4858M	Closed	1981	60.00	450
1974	Peddler L4859G	Closed	1985	180.00	750
1974	Dutch Girl L4860G	Closed	1985	45.00	250
1974	Horse L4861	Closed	1978	55.00	425
1974	Horse L4862	Closed	1978	55.00	425
1974	Horse L4863	Closed	1978	55.00	400
1974	Embroiderer L4865G	Closed	1994	115.00	700
1974	Girl with Swan and Dog L4866G	Closed	1993	26.00	205
1974	Seesaw L4867G	Open		55.00	350
1974	Girl with Candle L4868G	Open		13.00	90
1974	Girl with Candle L4868M	Closed	1992	13.00	80
1974	Boy Kissing L4869G	Open		13.00	90
1974	Boy Kissing L4869M	Closed	1992	13.00	150-175
1974	Boy Yawning L4870G	Open		13.00	90
1974	Boy Yawning L4870M	Closed	1992	13.00	175
1974	Girl with Guitar L4871G	Open		13.00	90
1974	Girl with Guitar L4871M	Closed	1992	13.00	80
1974	Girl Stretching L4872G	Open		13.00	90
1974	Girl Stretching L4872M	Closed	1992	13.00	80
1974	Girl Kissing L4873G	Open		13.00	90
1974	Girl Kissing L4873M	Closed	1992	13.00	80
1974	Boy & Girl L4874G	Open		25.00	150
1974	Boy & Girl L4874M	Closed	1992	25.00	135
1974	Girl with Jugs L4875G	Closed	1985	40.00	300
1974	Boy Thinking L4876G	Closed	1993	20.00	170
1974	Boy Thinking L4876M	Closed	1992	20.00	120
1974	Boy with Flute L4877G	Closed	1981	60.00	450
1974	Lady with Parasol L4879G	Open		48.00	325
1974	Carnival Couple L4882G	Closed	1995	60.00	300
1974	Carnival Couple L4882M	Closed	1991	60.00	375
1974	Lady w/ Young Harlequin L4883G	Closed	1975	100.00	2350
1974	Seraph's Head No.1 L4884	Closed	1985	10.00	100
1974	Seraph's Head No.2 L4885	Closed	1985	10.00	100
1974	Seraph's Head No.3 L4886	Closed	1985	10.00	100
1974	The Kiss L4888G	Closed	1983	150.00	700
1974	Spanish Policeman L4889G	Open		55.00	310
1974	Watching the Pigs L4892G	Closed	1978	160.00	1000
1976	"My Dog" L4893G	Open		85.00	230
1974	Tennis Player Boy L4894	Closed	1980	75.00	400
1974	Ducks L4895G	Open		45.00	95
1974	Ducks L4895M	Closed	1992	45.00	85
1974	Boy with Snails L4896G	Closed	1979	50.00	400
1974	Boy From Madrid L4898G	Open		55.00	150
1974	Boy From Madrid L4898M	Closed	1992	55.00	130
1974	Boy with Smoking Jacket L4900	Closed	1983	45.00	200
1974	Barrister L4908G	Closed	1985	100.00	585
1974	Girl With Dove L4909G	Closed	1982	70.00	450
1974	Girl With Lantern L4910G	Closed	1990	85.00	300
1974	Young Lady in Trouble L4912G	Closed	1985	110.00	450
1975	Lady with Shawl L4914G	Open		220.00	730
1975	Girl with Pigeons L4915	Closed	1990	110.00	400
1976	Chinese Noblewoman L4916G	Closed	1978	300.00	2000
1974	A Girl at the Pond L4918G	Closed	1985	85.00	425
1976	Gypsy Woman L4919G	Closed	1981	165.00	1150
1974	Country Lass with Dog L4920G	Closed	1995	185.00	495
1974	Country Lass with Dog L4920M	Closed	1992	185.00	495
1974	Chinese Nobleman L4921G	Closed	1978	325.00	2000
1974	Windblown Girl L4922G	Open		150.00	375
1974	Lanquid Clown L4924G	Closed	1983	200.00	1500
1974	Milk For the Lamb L4926G	Closed	1980	185.00	1300
1974	Medieval Lady L4928G	Closed	1980	275.00	925
1974	Sisters L4930	Closed	1981	250.00	625
1974	Children with Fruits L4931G	Closed	1981	210.00	500
1974	Dainty Lady L4934G	Closed	1985	60.00	475
1974	"Closing Scene" L4935G	Open		180.00	520
1983	"Closing Scene"/white L4935.3M	Closed	1987	213.00	265
1974	Spring Breeze L4936G	Open		145.00	410
1976	Golden Wedding L4937M	Retrd.	1981	285.00	600
1976	Baby's Outing L4938G	Open		250.00	725
1977	Missy L4951M	Closed	1985	300.00	600-850
1977	Meditation L4952M	Closed	1979	200.00	N/A
1977	Tavern Drinkers L4956G	Closed	1985	1125.00	3500
1977	Attentive Dogs L4957G	Closed	1981	350.00	1650
1977	Cherub, Puzzled L4959G	Open		40.00	110
1977	Cherub, Smiling L4960G	Open		40.00	110
1977	Cherub, Dreaming L4961G	Open		40.00	110
1977	Cherub, Wondering L4962G	Open		40.00	110
1977	Cherub, Wondering L4962M	Closed	1992	40.00	100
1977	Infantile Candour L4963G	Closed	1979	285.00	1300-1500
1977	Little Red Riding Hood L4965G	Closed	1983	210.00	575
1977	Tennis Player Puppet L4966G	Closed	1985	60.00	250
1977	Soccer Puppet L4967G	Closed	1985	65.00	425
1977	Oympic Puppet L4968	Closed	1983	65.00	800
1977	Cowboy & Sheriff Puppet L4969G	Closed	1985	85.00	650
1977	Skier Puppet L4970G	Closed	1983	85.00	500-900
1977	Hunter Puppet L4971G	Closed	1985	95.00	750
1977	Girl w/Calla Lillies sitting L4972G	Open		65.00	180
1977	Choir Lesson L4973G	Closed	1981	350.00	1850
1977	Dutch Children L4974G	Closed	1981	375.00	1150
1977	Augustina of Aragon L4976G	Closed	1979	475.00	1500-1800
1977	Harlequin Serenade L4977	Closed	1979	185.00	1250
1977	Milkmaid w/Wheelbarrow L4979G	Closed	1981	220.00	950
1977	Ironing Time L4981G	Closed	1985	80.00	350
1978	Naughty Dog L4982G	Closed	1995	130.00	275
1978	Gossip L4984G	Closed	1985	260.00	1000
1978	Mimi L4985G	Closed	1980	110.00	625
1978	Attentive Lady L4986G	Closed	1981	635.00	2200
1978	Oriental Spring L4988G	Open		125.00	325
1978	Sayonara L4989G	Open		125.00	300
1978	Chrysanthemum L4990G	Open		125.00	310
1978	Butterfly L4991G	Open		125.00	295
1978	Dancers Resting L4992G	Closed	1983	350.00	850
1978	Gypsy Venders L4993G	Closed	1985	165.00	475
1978	Ready to Go L4996G	Closed	1981	425.00	1500-1700
1978	Don Quixote & Sancho L4998G	Closed	1983	875.00	2900
1978	Reading L5000G	Open		150.00	275
1978	Elk Family L5001G	Closed	1981	550.00	700
1978	Sunny Day L5003G	Closed	1993	193.00	360
1978	Eloise L5005G	Closed	1978	175.00	550
1978	Naughty L5006G	Open		55.00	150
1978	Bashful L5007G	Open		55.00	150
1978	Static-Girl w/Straw Hat L5008G	Open		55.00	150
1978	Curious-Girl w/Straw Hat L5009G	Open		55.00	150
1978	Coiffure-Girl w/Straw Hat L5010G	Open		55.00	150
1978	Trying on a Straw Hat L5011G	Open		55.00	150
1978	Daughters L5013G	Closed	1991	425.00	900
1978	Genteel L5014G	Closed	1981	725.00	2300
1978	Painful Monkey L5018	Closed	1981	135.00	800
1978	Painful Giraffe L5019	Closed	1981	115.00	800
1978	Painful Elephant L5020	Closed	1981	85.00	850
1978	Painful Bear L5021	Closed	1981	75.00	800
1978	Painful Lion L5022G	Closed	1981	95.00	800
1978	Painful Kangaroo L5023G	Closed	1981	150.00	900
1978	Woman With Scarf L5024G	Closed	1985	141.00	450
1980	A Clean Sweep L5025G	Closed	1985	100.00	450
1980	Planning the Day L5026G	Closed	1985	90.00	275
1979	Flower Curtsy L5027G	Open		230.00	470
1980	Flowers in Pot L5028G	Closed	1985	325.00	575
1980	Boy w/Tricycle & Flowers L5029G	Closed	1985	675.00	1200-1350
1980	Wildflower L5030G	Closed	1994	360.00	695
1979	Little Friskies L5032G	Open		108.00	220
1980	Avoiding the Goose L5033G	Closed	1993	160.00	350
1980	Goose Trying To Eat L5034G	Open		135.00	310
1980	Act II w/base L5035G	Open		700.00	1425
1979	Jockey with Lass L5036G	Open		950.00	2240
1980	Sleighride w/base L5037G	Open		585.00	1140
1979	Girl Bowing L5038G	Closed	1981	185.00	750
1980	Candid L5039G	Closed	1981	145.00	475
1979	Girl Walking L5040G	Closed	1981	150.00	420-450
1980	Girl Kneeling and Tulips L5041G	Closed	1981	160.00	850
1980	Ladies Talking L5042G	Closed	1983	385.00	575-1000
1980	Hind and Baby Deer L5043G	Closed	1981	650.00	3600
1980	Girl with Toy Wagon L5044G	Open		115.00	245
1980	Belinda with Doll L5045G	Closed	1995	115.00	215
1980	Organ Grinder L5046G	Closed	1981	328.00	1600
1980	Teacher Woman L5048G	Closed	1981	115.00	550-675
1980	Dancer L5050G	Open		85.00	205
1980	Samson and Delilah L5051G	Closed	1981	350.00	1600
1980	Clown & Girl/ At the Circus L5052G	Closed	1985	525.00	1250
1980	Festival Time L5053G	Closed	1985	250.00	375
1980	Little Senorita L5054G	Closed	1985	235.00	600
1980	Ship-Boy with Baskets L5055G	Closed	1985	140.00	450
1980	Boy Clown with Clock L5056G	Closed	1985	290.00	850
1980	Boy Clown with Violin and Top Hat L5057G	Closed	1985	270.00	850
1980	Boy Clown w/Concertina L5058G	Closed	1985	290.00	500-600
1980	Boy Clown w/Saxaphone L5059G	Closed	1985	320.00	600
1980	Girl Clown with Trumpet L5060G	Closed	1985	290.00	550
1980	Girl Bending/March Wind L5061G	Closed	1983	370.00	600
1980	Kristina L5062G	Closed	1985	225.00	400
1980	Dutch Girl With Braids L5063G	Closed	1985	265.00	425-450
1980	Dutch Girl, Hands Akimbo L5064G	Closed	1990	255.00	425
1980	Ingrid L5065G	Closed	1990	370.00	800
1980	Ilsa L5066G	Closed	1990	275.00	600
1981	Snow White with Apple L5067G	Closed	1983	450.00	1500
1980	Fairy Godmother L5068G	Closed	1983	625.00	1600
1980	Choir Boy L5070G	Closed	1983	240.00	850
1980	Nostalgia L5071G	Closed	1993	185.00	350
1980	Courtship L5072	Closed	1990	327.00	750
1980	Country Flowers L5073	Closed	1985	315.00	1500
1980	My Hungry Brood L5074G	Open		295.00	415
1980	Little Harlequin "A" L5075G	Closed	1985	217.50	410
1980	Little Harlequin "B" L5076G	Closed	1985	185.00	375
1980	Little Harlequin "C" L5077G	Closed	1985	185.00	500
1980	Teasing the Dog L5078G	Closed	1985	300.00	600
1980	Woman Painting Vase L5079G	Closed	1985	300.00	600-750
1980	Boy Pottery Seller L5080G	Closed	1985	320.00	550
1980	Girl Pottery Seller L5081G	Closed	1985	300.00	550
1980	Flower Vendor L5082G	Closed	1985	750.00	3000
1980	A Good Book L5084G	Closed	1985	175.00	350-525
1980	Mother Amabilis L5086G	Closed	1983	275.00	600
1980	Roses for My Mom L5088G	Closed	1988	645.00	1150
1980	Scare-Dy Cat/Playful Cat L5091G	Open		65.00	95
1980	After the Dance L5092G	Closed	1983	165.00	475
1980	A Dancing Partner L5093G	Closed	1983	165.00	500
1980	Ballet First Step L5094G	Closed	1983	165.00	400
1980	Ballet Bowing L5095G	Closed	1983	165.00	300
1989	Her Ladyship, L5097G	Closed	1991	5900.00	6700
1980	Successful Hunt L5098	Closed	1993	5200.00	5200
1982	Playful Tot L5099G	Closed	1985	58.00	265
1982	Cry Baby L5100G	Closed	1985	58.00	275
1982	Learning to Crawl L5101G	Closed	1985	58.00	275-300
1982	Teething L5102G	Closed	1985	58.00	300
1982	Time for a Nap L5103G	Closed	1985	58.00	275
1982	Natalia L5106G	Closed	1985	85.00	350
1982	Little Ballet Girl L5108G	Closed	1985	85.00	400
1982	Little Ballet Girl L5109G	Closed	1985	85.00	400
1982	Dog Sniffing L5110G	Closed	1985	50.00	450-700
1982	Timid Dog L5111G	Closed	1985	44.00	500-600
1982	Play with Me L5112G	Open		40.00	80
1982	Feed Me L5113G	Open		40.00	80
1982	Pet Me L5114G	Open		40.00	80
1982	Little Boy Bullfighter L5115G	Closed	1985	123.00	400
1982	A Victory L5116G	Closed	1985	123.00	400-500
1982	Proud Matador L5117G	Closed	1985	123.00	500
1982	Girl in Green Dress L5118G	Closed	1985	170.00	650
1982	Girl in Bluish Dress L5119G	Closed	1985	170.00	675
1982	Girl in Pink Dress L5120G	Closed	1985	170.00	650
1982	August Moon L5122G	Closed	1993	185.00	350
1982	My Precious Bundle L5123G	Open		150.00	235
1982	Dutch Couple w/Tulips L5124G	Closed	1985	310.00	950
1982	Amparo L5125G	Closed	1990	130.00	330-350
1982	Sewing A Trousseau L5126G	Closed	1990	185.00	400-600
1982	Marcelina L5127G	Closed	1985	255.00	255
1982	Lost Love L5128G	Closed	1988	400.00	700
1982	Jester w/base L5129G	Open		220.00	445
1982	Pensive Clown w/base L5130G	Open		250.00	445
1982	Cervantes L5132G	Closed	1988	925.00	1175
1982	Trophy with Base L5133G	Closed	1983	250.00	650
1982	Girl Soccer Player L5134G	Closed	1983	140.00	575
1982	Billy Football Player L5135G	Closed	1983	140.00	575
1982	Billy Skier L5136G	Closed	1983	140.00	750
1982	Billy Baseball Player L5137G	Closed	1983	140.00	750
1982	Billy Golfer L5138G	Closed	1983	140.00	1000
1982	A New Doll House L5139G	Closed	1983	185.00	850
1982	Feed Her Son L5140G	Closed	1991	170.00	300
1982	Balloons for Sale L5141G	Open		145.00	250
1982	Comforting Daughter L5142G	Closed	1991	195.00	375
1982	Scooting L5143G	Closed	1988	575.00	850-1000
1982	Amy L5145G	Closed	1985	110.00	1500
1982	"E" is for Ellen L5146G	Closed	1985	110.00	1250
1982	Ivez L5147G	Closed	1985	100.00	600

*Quotes have been rounded up to nearest dollar

Lladró
to Lladró

FIGURINES

YEAR	ISSUE	EDITION LIMIT	YEAR RETD.	ISSUE PRICE	*QUOTE U.S.$
1982	Olivia L5148G	Closed	1985	100.00	400
1982	Ursula L5149G	Closed	1985	100.00	400
1982	Girl's Head L5150G	Closed	1983	435.00	1300
1982	Girl's Head L5151G	Closed	1983	380.00	1400
1982	Girl's Head L5152G	Closed	1983	535.00	2000
1982	Girl's Head L5153G	Closed	1983	475.00	1350
1982	First Prize L5154G	Closed	1985	90.00	170-300
1982	Monks at Prayer L5155M	Open		130.00	275
1982	Susan and the Doves L5156G	Closed	1991	203.00	325-360
1982	Bongo Beat L5157G	Open		135.00	230
1982	A Step In Time L5158G	Open		90.00	195
1982	Harmony L5159G	Open		270.00	495
1982	Rhumba L5160G	Open		113.00	185
1982	Cycling To A Picnic L5161G	Closed	1985	2000.00	2800
1982	Mouse Girl/Mindy L5162G	Closed	1985	125.00	500
1982	Bunny Girl/Bunny L5163G	Closed	1985	125.00	450
1982	Cat Girl/Kitty L5164G	Closed	1985	125.00	450
1982	Sancho with Bottle L5165	Closed	1990	100.00	425
1982	Sea Fever L5166M	Closed	1993	130.00	235
1982	Sea Fever L5166G	Closed	1993	130.00	350
1982	Jesus L5167G	Open		130.00	265
1982	King Solomon L5168G	Closed	1985	205.00	950
1982	Abraham L5169G	Closed	1985	155.00	725-750
1982	Moses L5170G	Open		175.00	395
1982	Madonna with Flowers L5171G	Open		173.00	310
1982	Fish A'Plenty L5172G	Closed	1994	190.00	400
1982	Pondering L5173G	Closed	1993	300.00	700
1982	Roaring 20's L5174G	Closed	1993	173.00	425
1982	Flapper L5175G	Closed	1995	185.00	425
1982	Rhapsody in Blue L5176G	Closed	1985	325.00	1850
1982	Dante L5177G	Closed	1983	263.00	750
1982	Stubborn Mule L5178G	Closed	1993	250.00	500
1983	Three Pink Roses w/base L5179M	Closed	1990	70.00	250
1983	Dahlia L5180M	Closed	1990	65.00	140
1983	Japanese Camelia w/base L5181M	Closed	1990	60.00	90
1983	White Peony L5182M	Closed	1990	85.00	125
1983	Two Yellow Roses L5183M	Closed	1990	57.50	100
1983	White Carnation L5184M	Closed	1990	65.00	100
1983	Lactiflora Peony L5185M	Closed	1990	65.00	100
1983	Begonia L5186M	Closed	1990	67.50	100
1983	Rhododendrom L5187M	Closed	1990	67.50	190
1983	Miniature Begonia L5188M	Closed	1990	80.00	120
1983	Chrysanthemum L5189M	Closed	1990	100.00	150
1983	California Poppy L5190M	Closed	1990	97.50	180
1985	Predicting the Future L5191G	Closed	1985	135.00	450
1984	Lolita L5192G	Open		80.00	165
1984	Juanita L5193G	Open		80.00	165
1984	Roving Photographer L5194G	Closed	1985	145.00	1800
1983	Say "Cheese!" L5195G	Closed	1990	170.00	500
1983	"Maestro, Music Please!" L5196G	Closed	1988	135.00	500
1983	Female Physician L5197	Open		120.00	260
1984	Boy Graduate L5198G	Open		160.00	290
1984	Girl Graduate L5199G	Open		160.00	285
1984	Male Soccer Player L5200G	Closed	1988	155.00	475
1984	Special Male Soccer Player L5200.3G	Closed	1988	150.00	500
1983	Josefa Feeding Duck L5201G	Closed	1991	125.00	250-300
1983	Aracely with Ducks L5202G	Closed	1991	125.00	250-300
1984	Little Jester L5203G	Closed	1993	75.00	300-325
1984	Little Jester L5203M	Closed	1992	75.00	200-250
1983	Sharpening the Cutlery L5204	Closed	1988	210.00	975
1983	Lamplighter L5205G	Open		170.00	395
1983	Yachtsman L5206G	Closed	1994	110.00	210
1983	A Tall Yarn L5207G	Open		260.00	545
1983	Professor L5208G	Closed	1990	205.00	550-750
1983	School Marm L5209G	Closed	1990	205.00	900
1984	Jolie L5210G	Open		105.00	220
1984	Angela L5211G	Open		105.00	220
1984	Evita L5212G	Open		105.00	195
1984	Lawyer L5213G	Open		250.00	570
1984	Architect L5214G	Closed	1990	140.00	450
1984	Fishing w/Gramps w/base L5215G	Open		410.00	850
1984	On the Lake L5216G	Closed	1988	660.00	1000
1984	Spring L5217G	Open		90.00	185
1984	Spring L5217M	Open		90.00	185
1984	Autumn L5218G	Open		90.00	185
1984	Autumn L5218M	Open		90.00	185
1984	Summer L5219G	Open		90.00	185
1984	Summer L5219M	Open		90.00	185
1984	Winter L5220G	Open		90.00	185
1984	Winter L5220M	Open		90.00	185
1984	Sweet Scent L5221G	Open		80.00	145
1984	Sweet Scent L5221M	Open		80.00	145
1984	Pretty Pickings L5222G	Open		80.00	145
1984	Pretty Pickings L5222M	Open		80.00	145
1984	Spring is Here L5223G	Open		80.00	145
1984	Spring is Here L5223M	Open		80.00	145
1984	The Quest L5224G	Open		125.00	295
1984	Male Candleholder L5226	Closed	1985	660.00	1200
1984	Playful Piglets L5228G	Open		80.00	150
1984	Storytime L5229G	Closed	1990	245.00	1000
1984	Graceful Swan L5230G	Open		35.00	90
1984	Swan /Wings Spread L5231G	Open		50.00	125
1984	Playful Kittens L5232G	Open		130.00	280
1984	Charlie the Tramp L5233G	Closed	1991	150.00	750-950
1984	Artistic Endeavor L5234G	Closed	1988	225.00	500-650
1984	Ballet Trio L5235G	Open		785.00	1650
1984	Cat and Mouse L5236G	Open		55.00	98
1984	Cat and Mouse L5236M	Closed	1992	55.00	95
1984	School Chums L5237G	Open		225.00	485
1984	Eskimo Boy with Pet L5238G	Open		55.00	115
1984	Eskimo Boy with Pet L5238M	Closed	1992	55.00	95
1984	Wine Taster L5239G	Open		190.00	395
1984	Lady from Majorca L5240G	Closed	1990	120.00	385
1984	Best Wishes L5244G	Closed	1986	185.00	325
1984	A Thought for Today L5245	Closed	1986	180.00	250
1984	St. Christopher L5246	Closed	1988	265.00	650
1984	Penguin L5247G	Closed	1988	70.00	200
1984	Penguin L5248G	Closed	1988	70.00	200
1984	Penguin L5249G	Closed	1988	70.00	175
1984	Exam Day L5250G	Closed	1994	115.00	210
1984	Torch Bearer L5251G	Closed	1988	100.00	400-500
1984	Dancing the Polka L5252G	Closed	1994	205.00	525
1984	Cadet L5253G	Closed	1984	150.00	550-650
1984	Making Paella L5254G	Closed	1993	215.00	500
1984	Spanish Soldier L5255G	Closed	1988	185.00	475-575
1984	Folk Dancing L5256G	Closed	1990	205.00	525
1984	Vase L5257.30	Closed	1988	55.00	200
1984	Vase L5258.30	Closed	1988	55.00	175
1984	Vase L5261.30	Closed	1988	70.00	125
1984	Vase L5262.30	Closed	1988	70.00	125
1984	Centerpiece-Decorated L5265M	Closed	1990	50.00	175
1985	Bust of Lady from Elche L5269M	Closed	1988	432.00	750
1985	Racing Motor Cyclist L5270G	Closed	1988	360.00	800
1985	Gazelle L5271G	Closed	1988	205.00	425-550
1985	Biking in the Country L5272G	Closed	1990	295.00	850
1985	Civil Guard at Attention L5273G	Closed	1988	170.00	500
1985	Wedding Day L5274G	Open		240.00	435
1985	Weary Ballerina L5275G	Closed	1995	175.00	310
1985	Weary Ballerina L5275M	Closed	1992	175.00	310
1985	Sailor Serenades His Girl L5276G	Closed	1988	315.00	950
1985	Pierrot with Puppy L5277G	Open		95.00	160
1985	Pierrot w/Puppy and Ball L5278G	Open		95.00	160
1985	Pierrot with Concertina L5279G	Open		95.00	160
1985	Hiker L5280G	Closed	1988	195.00	425
1985	Nativity Scene "Haute Relief" L5281M	Closed	1988	210.00	450
1985	Over the Threshold L5282G	Open		150.00	290
1985	Socialite of the Twenties L5283G	Open		175.00	340
1985	Glorious Spring L5284G	Open		355.00	710
1985	Summer on the Farm L5285G	Open		235.00	455
1985	Fall Clean-up L5286G	Open		295.00	565
1985	Winter Frost L5287G	Open		270.00	520
1985	Mallard Duck L5288G	Closed	1994	310.00	520
1985	Little Leaguer Exercising L5289	Closed	1990	150.00	450
1985	Little Leaguer, Catcher L5290	Closed	1990	150.00	450
1985	Little Leaguer on Bench L5291	Closed	1990	150.00	450
1985	Love in Bloom L5292G	Open		225.00	425
1985	Mother and Child and Lamb L5299G	Closed	1988	180.00	750
1985	Medieval Courtship L5300G	Closed	1990	735.00	800
1985	Waiting to Tee Off L5301G	Open		145.00	295
1985	Antelope Drinking L5302	Closed	1988	215.00	600
1985	Playing with Ducks at the Pond L5303G	Closed	1990	425.00	875
1985	Children at Play L5304	Closed	1990	220.00	550
1985	A Visit with Granny L5305G	Closed	1993	275.00	600
1985	Young Street Musicians L5306G	Closed	1988	300.00	1500
1985	Mini Kitten L5307G	Closed	1993	35.00	100
1985	Mini Cat L5308G	Closed	1993	35.00	125
1985	Mini Cocker Spaniel Pup L5309G	Closed	1993	35.00	125
1985	Mini Cocker Spaniel L5310G	Closed	1993	35.00	125
1985	Mini Puppies L5311G	Closed	1990	65.00	175
1985	Mini Bison Resting L5312G	Closed	1990	50.00	150
1985	Mini Bison Attacking L5313G	Closed	1990	57.50	225
1985	Mini Deer L5314G	Closed	1990	40.00	175
1985	Mini Dromedary L5315G	Closed	1990	45.00	150
1985	Mini Giraffe L5316G	Closed	1990	50.00	200
1985	Mini Lamb L5317G	Closed	1990	30.00	175
1985	Mini Seal Family L5318G	Closed	1990	77.50	215
1985	Wistful Centaur Girl L5319G	Closed	1990	157.00	450
1985	Demure Centaur Girl L5320	Closed	1990	157.00	425
1985	Parisian Lady L5321G	Closed	1995	193.00	325
1985	Viennese Lady L5322G	Closed	1994	160.00	295
1985	Milanese Lady L5323G	Closed	1994	180.00	400
1985	English Lady L5324G	Closed	1994	225.00	475
1985	Ice Cream Vendor L5325G	Closed	1995	380.00	650
1985	The Tailor L5326G	Closed	1988	335.00	900-1300
1985	Nippon Lady L5327G	Open		325.00	575
1985	Lady Equestrian L5328G	Closed	1988	160.00	450
1985	Gentleman Equestrian L5329G	Closed	1988	160.00	525
1985	Concert Violinist L5330G	Closed	1988	220.00	400
1985	Gymnast with Ring L5331	Closed	1988	95.00	295
1985	Gymnast Balancing Ball L5332	Closed	1988	95.00	375
1985	Gymnast Exercising w/Ball L5333G	Closed	1988	95.00	350
1985	Aerobics Push-Up L5334G	Closed	1988	110.00	295
1985	Aerobics Floor Exercies L5335G	Closed	1988	110.00	300
1985	"La Giaconda" L5337G	Closed	1988	110.00	400
1986	A Stitch in Time L5344G	Open		425.00	795
1986	A New Hat L5345G	Closed	1990	200.00	375
1986	Nature Girl L5346G	Closed	1988	450.00	1000
1986	Bedtime L5347G	Open		300.00	545
1986	On The Scent L5348G	Closed	1990	47.50	300
1986	Relaxing L5349G	Closed	1990	47.50	150
1986	On Guard L5350G	Closed	1990	50.00	200
1986	Woe is Me L5351G	Closed	1990	45.00	200
1986	Hindu Children L5352G	Open		250.00	445
1986	Eskimo Riders L5353G	Open		150.00	250
1986	Eskimo Riders L5353M	Open		150.00	250
1986	A Ride in the Country L5354G	Closed	1993	225.00	415
1986	Consideration L5355M	Closed	1988	100.00	225
1986	Wolf Hound L5356G	Closed	1990	45.00	225
1986	Oration L5357G	Open		170.00	295
1986	Little Sculptor L5358G	Closed	1990	160.00	325-400
1986	El Greco L5359G	Closed	1990	300.00	550
1986	Sewing Circle L5360G	Closed	1990	600.00	1250-1400
1986	Try This One L5361G	Open		225.00	385
1986	Still Life L5363G	Open		180.00	395
1986	Litter of Fun L5364G	Open		275.00	465
1986	Sunday in the Park L5365G	Open		375.00	625
1986	Can Can L5370G	Closed	1990	700.00	1200-1400
1986	Family Roots L5371G	Open		575.00	935
1986	Lolita L5372G	Closed	1993	120.00	250
1986	Carmencita L5373G	Closed	1993	120.00	250
1986	Pepita L5374G	Closed	1993	120.00	350
1986	Teresita L5375G	Closed	1993	120.00	350
1986	This One's Mine L5376G	Closed	1995	300.00	520
1986	A Touch of Class L5377G	Open		475.00	795
1986	Time for Reflection L5378G	Open		425.00	745
1986	Children's Games L5379G	Closed	1991	325.00	700
1986	Sweet Harvest L5380G	Closed	1990	450.00	850
1986	Serenade L5381	Closed	1990	450.00	625
1986	Lovers Serenade L5382G	Closed	1990	350.00	850
1986	Petite Maiden L5383	Closed	1990	110.00	350
1986	Petite Pair L5384	Closed	1990	225.00	400
1986	Scarecrow & the Lady L5385G	Open		350.00	680
1986	St. Vincent L5387	Closed	1990	190.00	350
1986	Sidewalk Serenade L5388G	Closed	1988	750.00	1100-1300
1986	Deep in Thought L5389G	Closed	1990	170.00	450
1986	Spanish Dancer L5390G	Closed	1990	170.00	450
1986	A Time to Rest L5391G	Closed	1990	170.00	275-375
1986	Balancing Act L5392G	Closed	1990	35.00	200
1986	Curiosity L5393G	Closed	1990	25.00	150
1986	Poor Puppy L5394G	Closed	1990	25.00	250
1986	Valencian Boy L5395G	Closed	1991	200.00	400
1986	The Puppet Painter L5396G	Open		500.00	850
1986	The Poet L5397G	Closed	1988	425.00	900
1986	At the Ball L5398G	Closed	1991	375.00	750
1987	Time To Rest L5399G	Closed	1993	175.00	295
1987	Time To Rest L5399M	Closed	1991	175.00	350
1987	The Wanderer L5400G	Open		150.00	245
1987	My Best Friend L5401G	Closed	1994	150.00	240
1987	Desert Tour L5402G	Closed	1990	950.00	1050
1987	The Drummer Boy L5403G	Closed	1990	225.00	400
1987	Cadet Captain L5404G	Closed	1990	175.00	360
1987	The Flag Bearer L5405G	Closed	1990	200.00	450
1987	The Bugler L5406G	Closed	1990	175.00	375
1987	At Attention L5407G	Closed	1990	175.00	325
1987	Sunday Stroll L5408G	Closed	1990	250.00	600
1987	Courting Time L5409	Closed	1990	425.00	550
1987	Pilar L5410G	Closed	1990	200.00	400
1987	Teresa L5411G	Closed	1990	225.00	430
1987	Isabel L5412G	Closed	1990	225.00	450
1987	Mexican Dancers L5415G	Open		800.00	1195
1987	In the Garden L5416G	Open		200.00	325
1987	Artist's Model L5417	Closed	1990	425.00	475
1987	Short Eared Owl L5418G	Closed	1990	200.00	360
1987	Great Gray Owl L5419G	Closed	1990	190.00	195
1987	Horned Owl L5420G	Closed	1990	150.00	225
1987	Barn Owl L5421G	Closed	1990	120.00	175
1987	Hawk Owl L5422G	Closed	1990	120.00	195-225
1987	Intermezzo L5424	Closed	1990	325.00	550
1987	Studying in the Park L5425G	Closed	1991	675.00	950
1987	Studying in the Park L5425M	Closed	1989	675.00	400-600
1987	One, Two, Three L5426G	Closed	1995	240.00	390
1987	Saint Nicholas L5427G	Closed	1991	425.00	750
1987	Feeding the Pigeons L5428	Closed	1990	490.00	700
1987	Happy Birthday L5429G	Open		100.00	155
1987	Music Time L5430G	Closed	1990	500.00	700
1987	Midwife L5431G	Closed	1990	175.00	650
1987	Midwife L5431M	Closed	1990	175.00	525
1987	Monkey L5432G	Closed	1990	60.00	200
1987	Kangaroo L5433G	Closed	1990	65.00	175-300
1987	Miniature Polar Bear L5434G	Open		65.00	110
1987	Cougar L5435G	Closed	1990	65.00	275
1987	Lion L5436G	Closed	1990	50.00	200-300
1987	Rhino L5437G	Closed	1990	50.00	175
1987	Elephant L5438G	Closed	1990	50.00	250
1987	The Bride L5439G	Closed	1995	250.00	425
1987	Poetry of Love L5442G	Open		500.00	865
1987	Sleepy Trio L5443G	Open		190.00	305
1987	Will You Marry Me? L5447G	Closed	1994	750.00	1250
1987	Naptime L5448G	Open		135.00	250
1987	Naptime L5448M	Open		135.00	250
1987	Goodnight L5449	Open		225.00	375
1987	I Hope She Does L5450G	Open		190.00	345
1988	Study Buddies L5451G	Open		225.00	295
1988	Masquerade Ball L5452G	Closed	1993	220.00	375
1988	Masquerade Ball L5452M	Closed	1992	220.00	265
1988	For You L5453G	Open		450.00	640
1988	For Me? L5454G	Open		290.00	395
1988	Bashful Bather L5455G	Open		150.00	190
1988	Bashful Bather L5455M	Closed	1992	150.00	180
1988	New Playmates L5456G	Open		160.00	230
1988	New Playmates L5456M	Closed	1992	160.00	190
1988	Bedtime Story L5457G	Open		275.00	355
1988	Bedtime Story L5457M	Closed	1992	275.00	330
1988	A Barrow of Fun L5460G	Open		370.00	525
1988	A Barrow of Fun L5460M	Closed	1992	370.00	450
1988	Koala Love L5461G	Closed	1993	115.00	200-300
1988	Practice Makes Perfect L5462G	Open		375.00	545
1988	Look At Me! L5465G	Open		375.00	495
1988	Look At Me! L5465M	Closed	1992	375.00	435
1988	"Chit-Chat" L5466G	Open		150.00	198

*Quotes have been rounded up to nearest dollar

Collectors' Information Bureau
93

FIGURINES

YEAR ISSUE		EDITION LIMIT	YEAR RETD.	ISSUE PRICE	*QUOTE U.S.$
1988	"Chit-Chat" L5466M	Closed	1992	150.00	180
1988	May Flowers L5467G	Open		160.00	215
1988	May Flowers L5467M	Closed	1992	160.00	190
1988	"Who's The Fairest?" L5468G	Open		150.00	200
1988	"Who's The Fairest?" L5468M	Closed	1992	150.00	180
1988	Lambkins L5469G	Closed	1993	150.00	210
1988	Lambkins L5469M	Closed	1989	150.00	195
1988	Tea Time L5470G	Open		280.00	385
1988	Sad Sax L5471G	Open		175.00	205
1988	Circus Sam L5472G	Open		175.00	205
1988	How You've Grown! L5474G	Open		180.00	250
1988	How You've Grown! L5474M	Closed	1992	180.00	215
1988	A Lesson Shared L5475G	Open		150.00	190
1988	A Lesson Shared L5475M	Closed	1992	150.00	170
1988	St. Joseph L5476G	Open		210.00	270
1988	Mary L5477G	Open		130.00	165
1988	Baby Jesus L5478G	Open		55.00	75
1988	King Melchior L5479G	Open		210.00	265
1988	King Gaspar L5480G	Open		210.00	265
1988	King Balthasar L5481G	Open		210.00	265
1988	Ox L5482G	Open		125.00	175
1988	Donkey L5483G	Open		125.00	175
1988	Lost Lamb L5484G	Open		100.00	140
1988	Shepherd Boy L5485G	Open		140.00	190
1988	Debutantes L5486G	Open		490.00	695
1988	Debutantes L5486M	Closed	1992	490.00	635
1988	Ingenue L5487G	Open		110.00	145
1988	Ingenue L5487M	Closed	1992	110.00	130
1988	Sandcastles L5488G	Closed	1993	160.00	300
1988	Sandcastles L5488M	Closed	1992	160.00	200
1988	Justice L5489G	Closed	1993	675.00	950
1988	Flor Maria L5490G	Open		500.00	635
1988	Heavenly Strings L5491G	Closed	1993	140.00	160
1988	Heavenly Cellist L5492G	Closed	1993	240.00	240
1988	Angel with Lute L5493G	Closed	1993	140.00	160
1988	Angel with Clarinet L5494G	Closed	1993	140.00	160
1988	Angelic Choir L5495G	Closed	1993	300.00	550
1988	Recital L5496G	Open		190.00	285
1988	Dress Rehearsal L5497G	Open		290.00	420
1988	Opening Night L5498G	Open		190.00	285
1988	Pretty Ballerina L5499G	Open		190.00	285
1988	Prayerful Moment (blue) L5500G	Open		90.00	110
1988	Time to Sew (blue) L5501G	Open		90.00	110
1988	Time to Sew (white) L5501.3	Closed	1991	90.00	200
1988	Meditation (blue) L5502G	Open		90.00	110
1988	Hurry Now L5503G	Open		180.00	250
1988	Hurry Now L5503M	Closed	1992	180.00	240
1988	Silver Vase No. 20 L5531.4	Closed	1991	135.00	275
1989	Flowers for Sale L5537G	Open		1200.00	1550
1989	Puppy Dog Tails L5539G	Open		1200.00	1595
1989	An Evening Out L5540G	Closed	1991	350.00	450
1989	Melancholy w/base L5542G	Open		375.00	455
1989	"Hello, Flowers" L5543G	Closed	1993	385.00	545
1989	Reaching the Goal L5546G	Open		215.00	275
1989	Only the Beginning L5547G	Open		215.00	275
1989	Pretty Posies L5548G	Closed	1994	425.00	530
1989	My New Pet L5549G	Open		150.00	185
1989	Serene Moment (blue) L5550G	Closed	1993	115.00	250
1989	Serene Moment (white) L5550.3G	Closed	1991	115.00	250
1989	Serene Moment (white) L5550.3M	Closed	1991	115.00	250
1989	Call to Prayer (blue) L5551G	Closed	1993	100.00	250
1989	Call to Prayer (white) L5551.3G	Closed	1991	100.00	250
1989	Call to Prayer (white) L5551.3M	Closed	1991	100.00	250
1989	Morning Chores (blue) L5552G	Closed	1993	115.00	250
1989	Morning Chores (white) L5552G	Closed	1991	115.00	250
1989	Wild Goose Chase L5553G	Open		175.00	230
1989	Pretty and Prim L5554G	Open		215.00	270
1989	"Let's Make Up" L5555G	Open		215.00	265
1989	Wide Tulip Vase L5560G	Closed	1990	110.00	300
1989	Green Clover Vase L5561G	Closed	1991	130.00	225
1989	Sad Parting L5583G	Closed	1991	375.00	525
1989	Daddy's Girl/Father's Day L5584G	Open		315.00	395
1989	Fine Melody w/base L5585G	Closed	1993	225.00	325
1989	Sad Note w/base L5586G	Closed	1993	185.00	375
1989	Wedding Cake L5587G	Open		595.00	750
1989	Blustery Day L5588G	Closed	1993	185.00	260
1989	Pretty Pose L5589G	Closed	1993	185.00	230
1989	Spring Breeze L5590G	Closed	1993	185.00	260
1989	Garden Treasures L5591G	Closed	1993	185.00	230
1989	Male Siamese Dancer L5592G	Closed	1993	345.00	400
1989	Siamese Dancer L5593G	Closed	1993	345.00	420
1989	Playful Romp L5594G	Open		215.00	270
1989	Joy in a Basket L5595G	Open		215.00	270
1989	A Gift of Love L5596G	Open		400.00	495
1989	Summer Soiree L5597G	Open		150.00	180
1989	Bridesmaid L5598G	Open		150.00	180
1989	Coquette L5599G	Open		150.00	180
1989	The Blues w/base L5600G	Closed	1993	265.00	395
1989	"Ole" L5601G	Open		365.00	460
1989	Close To My Heart L5603G	Open		125.00	165
1989	Spring Token L5604G	Open		175.00	230
1989	Floral Treasures L5605G	Open		195.00	250
1989	Quiet Evening L5606G	Closed	1993	125.00	165
1989	Calling A Friend L5607G	Open		125.00	165
1989	Baby Doll L5608G	Open		150.00	180
1989	Playful Friends L5609G	Closed	1995	135.00	170
1989	Star Struck w/base L5610G	Open		335.00	420
1989	Sad Clown w/base L5611G	Open		335.00	420
1989	Reflecting w/base L5612G	Closed	1994	335.00	420
1989	Startled L5614G	Closed	1991	265.00	425
1989	Bathing Beauty L5615G	Closed	1991	265.00	350-475
1989	Candleholder L5625G	Closed	1990	105.00	125
1989	Candleholder L5626	Closed	1990	90.00	125
1989	Lladró Vase L5631G	Closed	1990	150.00	300-350
1990	Water Dreamer Vase L5633G	Closed	1990	150.00	350-400
1990	Cat Nap L5640G	Open		125.00	145
1990	The King's Guard w/base L5642G	Closed	1993	950.00	1100
1990	Cathy L5643G	Open		200.00	235
1990	Susan L5644G	Open		190.00	215
1990	Elizabeth L5645G	Open		190.00	215
1990	Cindy L5646G	Open		190.00	215
1990	Sara L5647G	Open		200.00	230
1990	Courtney L5648G	Open		200.00	230
1990	Nothing To Do L5649G	Open		190.00	220
1990	Anticipation L5650G	Closed	1993	300.00	400
1990	Musical Muse L5651G	Open		375.00	440
1989	Marbella Clock L5652	Closed	1994	125.00	235
1989	Avila Clock L5653	Closed	1995	135.00	135
1990	Venetian Carnival L5658G	Closed	1993	500.00	575
1990	Barnyard Scene L5659G	Open		200.00	450
1990	Sunning In Ipanema L5660G	Closed	1993	370.00	440-525
1990	Traveling Artist L5661G	Closed	1994	250.00	290
1990	May Dance L5662G	Open		170.00	210
1990	Spring Dance L5663G	Open		170.00	300
1990	Giddy Up L5664G	Closed	1994	190.00	230
1990	Hang On! L5665G	Closed	1995	225.00	325
1990	Trino At The Beach L5666G	Closed	1995	390.00	500
1990	Valencian Harvest L5668G	Closed	1993	175.00	350-400
1990	Valencian FLowers L5669G	Closed	1993	370.00	375
1990	Valencian Beauty L5670G	Closed	1993	175.00	325
1990	Little Dutch Gardener L5671G	Closed	1993	400.00	475
1990	Hi There! L5672G	Open		450.00	520
1990	A Quiet Moment L5673G	Open		450.00	520
1990	A Faun And A Friend L5674G	Open		450.00	520
1990	Tee Time L5675G	Closed	1993	280.00	315
1990	Wandering Minstrel L5676G	Closed	1993	270.00	310
1990	Twilight Years L5677G	Open		370.00	420
1990	I Feel Pretty L5678G	Open		190.00	230
1990	In No Hurry L5679G	Closed	1994	550.00	640
1990	Traveling In Style L5680G	Closed	1994	425.00	495
1990	On The Road L5681G	Closed	1991	320.00	450-550
1990	Breezy Afternoon L5682G	Open		180.00	195
1990	Breezy Afternoon L5682M	Open		180.00	195
1990	Beautiful Burro L5683G	Closed	1993	280.00	365
1990	Barnyard Reflections L5684G	Closed	1993	460.00	600
1990	Promenade L5685G	Closed	1994	275.00	325
1990	On The Avenue L5686G	Closed	1994	275.00	325
1990	Afternoon Stroll L5687G	Closed	1994	275.00	350
1990	Dog's Best Friend L5688G	Open		250.00	295
1990	Can I Help? L5689G	Open		250.00	325
1990	Marshland Mates w/base L5691G	Open		950.00	1200
1990	Street Harmonies w/base L5692G	Closed	1993	3200.00	3750
1990	Circus Serenade L5694G	Closed	1994	300.00	375
1990	Concertina L5695G	Closed	1994	300.00	360
1990	Mandolin Serenade L5696G	Closed	1994	300.00	360
1990	Over The Clouds L5697G	Open		275.00	310
1990	Don't Look Down L5698G	Open		330.00	395
1990	Sitting Pretty L5699G	Open		300.00	340
1990	Southern Charm L5700G	Open		675.00	1025
1990	Just A Little Kiss L5701G	Open		320.00	375
1990	Back To School L5702G	Closed	1993	350.00	300-445
1990	Behave! L5703G	Closed	1994	230.00	265
1990	Swan Song L5704G	Closed	1995	350.00	410
1990	The Swan & The Princess L5705G	Closed	1994	350.00	425-450
1990	We Can't Play L5706G	Open		200.00	235
1990	After School L5707G	Closed	1993	280.00	315
1990	My First Class L5708G	Closed	1993	280.00	315
1990	Between Classes L5709G	Closed	1993	280.00	315
1990	Fantasy Friend L5710G	Closed	1993	420.00	495
1990	A Christmas Wish L5711G	Open		350.00	410
1990	Sleepy Kitten L5712G	Open		110.00	130
1990	The Snow Man L5713G	Open		300.00	350
1990	First Ballet L5714G	Open		370.00	420
1990	Mommy, it's Cold! L5715G	Closed	1994	360.00	435-450
1990	Land of The Giants L5716G	Closed	1994	275.00	425
1990	Rock A Bye Baby L5717G	Open		300.00	365
1990	Sharing Secrets L5720G	Open		290.00	335
1990	Once Upon A Time L5721G	Open		550.00	650
1990	Follow Me L5722G	Open		140.00	160
1990	Heavenly Chimes L5723G	Open		100.00	120
1990	Angelic Voice L5724G	Open		125.00	145
1990	Making A Wish L5725G	Open		125.00	145
1990	Sweep Away The Clouds L5726G	Open		125.00	145
1990	Angel Care L5727G	Open		190.00	210
1990	Heavenly Dreamer L5728G	Open		100.00	120
1991	Carousel Charm L5731G	Closed	1994	1700.00	1850
1991	Carousel Canter L5732G	Closed	1994	1700.00	1850
1991	Horticulturist L5733G	Closed	1993	450.00	495
1991	Pilgrim Couple L5734G	Closed	1993	490.00	525
1991	Big Sister L5735G	Open		650.00	685
1991	Puppet Show L5736G	Open		280.00	295
1991	Little Prince L5737G	Closed	1993	295.00	315
1991	Best Foot Forward L5738G	Closed	1994	280.00	305
1991	Lap Full Of Love L5739G	Closed	1995	275.00	295
1991	Alice In Wonderland L5740G	Open		440.00	485
1991	Dancing Class L5741G	Open		340.00	365
1991	Bridal Portrait L5742G	Closed	1995	480.00	560
1991	Don't Forget Me L5743G	Open		150.00	160
1991	Bull & Donkey L5744G	Open		250.00	275
1991	Baby Jesus L5745G	Open		170.00	185
1991	St. Joseph L5746G	Open		350.00	375
1991	Mary L5747G	Open		275.00	295
1991	Shepherd Girl L5748G	Open		150.00	165
1991	Shepherd Boy L5749G	Open		225.00	245
1991	Little Lamb L5750G	Open		40.00	42
1991	Walk With Father L5751G	Closed	1994	375.00	440
1991	Little Virgin L5752G	Closed	1994	295.00	325
1991	Hold Her Still L5753G	Closed	1993	650.00	700
1991	Singapore Dancers L5754G	Closed	1993	950.00	1195
1991	Claudette L5755G	Closed	1993	265.00	350
1991	Ashley L5756G	Closed	1993	265.00	300
1991	Beautiful Tresses L5757G	Closed	1993	725.00	875
1991	Sunday Best L5758G	Open		725.00	785
1991	Presto! L5759G	Closed	1993	275.00	325
1991	Interrupted Nap L5760G	Closed	1995	325.00	425
1991	Out For A Romp L5761G	Closed	1995	375.00	410
1991	Checking The Time L5762G	Closed	1995	560.00	595
1991	Musical Partners L5763G	Closed	1995	625.00	675
1991	Seeds Of Laughter L5764G	Closed	1995	525.00	575
1991	Hats Off To Fun L5765G	Closed	1995	475.00	510
1991	Charming Duet L5766G	Open		575.00	625
1991	First Sampler L5767G	Closed	1995	625.00	680
1991	Academy Days L5768G	Closed	1993	280.00	310
1991	Faithful Steed L5769G	Closed	1994	370.00	395
1991	Out For A Spin L5770G	Closed	1994	390.00	420
1991	The Magic Of Laughter L5771G	Open		950.00	1050
1991	Little Dreamers L5772G	Open		230.00	240
1991	Little Dreamers L5772M	Open		230.00	240
1991	Graceful Offering L5773G	Closed	1995	850.00	895
1991	Nature's Gifts L5774G	Closed	1994	900.00	975
1991	Gift Of Beauty L5775G	Closed	1995	850.00	1100
1991	Lover's Paradise L5779G	Open		2250.00	2450
1991	Walking The Fields L5780G	Closed	1993	725.00	795
1991	Not Too Close L5781G	Closed	1994	365.00	450
1991	My Chores L5782G	Closed	1995	325.00	355
1991	Special Delivery L5783G	Closed	1994	525.00	550
1991	A Cradle Of Kittens L5784G	Open		360.00	385
1991	Ocean Beauty L5785G	Open		625.00	665
1991	Story Hour L5786G	Open		550.00	625
1991	Sophisticate L5787G	Open		185.00	195
1991	Talk Of The Town L5788G	Open		185.00	195
1991	The Flirt L5789G	Open		185.00	195
1991	Carefree L5790G	Open		300.00	325
1991	Fairy Godmother L5791G	Closed	1994	375.00	450
1991	Reverent Moment L5792G	Closed	1994	295.00	320
1991	Precocious Ballerina L5793G	Closed	1995	575.00	625
1991	Precious Cargo L5794G	Closed	1994	460.00	495
1991	Floral Getaway L5795G	Closed	1993	625.00	745
1991	Holy Night L5796G	Closed	1994	330.00	360
1991	Come Out And Play L5797G	Closed	1994	275.00	300
1991	Milkmaid L5798G	Closed	1993	450.00	495
1991	Shall We Dance? L5799G	Closed	1993	600.00	750
1991	Elegant Promenade L5802G	Open		775.00	825
1991	Playing Tag L5804G	Closed	1993	170.00	190
1991	Tumbling L5805G	Closed	1993	130.00	140
1991	Tumbling L5805M	Closed	1992	130.00	140
1991	Tickling L5806G	Closed	1993	130.00	145
1991	Tickling L5806M	Closed	1992	130.00	145
1991	My Puppies L5807G	Closed	1993	325.00	360
1991	Musically Inclined L5810G	Closed	1993	235.00	250
1991	Littlest Clown L5811G	Open		225.00	240
1991	Tired Friend L5812G	Open		225.00	245
1991	Having A Ball L5813G	Open		225.00	240
1991	Curtain Call L5814G	Closed	1994	490.00	520
1991	Curtain Call L5814M	Closed	1994	490.00	520
1991	In Full Relave L5815G	Closed	1994	490.00	520
1991	In Full Relave L5815M	Closed	1994	490.00	520
1991	Prima Ballerina L5816G	Closed	1994	490.00	520
1991	Prima Ballerina L5816M	Closed	1994	490.00	520
1991	Backstage Preparation L5817G	Closed	1994	490.00	520
1991	Backstage Preparation L5817M	Closed	1994	490.00	520
1991	On Her Toes L5818G	Closed	1994	490.00	520
1991	On Her Toes L5818M	Closed	1994	490.00	520
1991	Allegory Of Liberty L5819G	Open		1950.00	2100
1991	Dance Of Love L5820G	Closed	1993	575.00	625
1991	Minstrel's Love L5821G	Closed	1993	525.00	575
1991	Little Unicorn L5826G	Open		275.00	295
1991	Little Unicorn L5826M	Open		275.00	295
1991	I've Got It L5827G	Closed	1995	170.00	180
1991	Next At Bat L5828G	Open		170.00	180
1991	Heavenly Harpist L5830	Yr.Iss.	1991	135.00	200
1991	Jazz Horn L5832G	Open		295.00	310
1991	Jazz Sax L5833G	Open		295.00	315
1991	Jazz Bass L5834G	Open		395.00	425
1991	I Do L5835G	Open		165.00	190
1991	Sharing Sweets L5836G	Open		220.00	245
1991	Sing With Me L5837G	Open		240.00	250
1991	On The Move L5838G	Open		340.00	395
1992	A Quiet Afternoon L5843G	Closed	1995	1050.00	1125
1992	Flirtatious Jester L5844G	Open		890.00	925
1992	Dressing The Baby L5845G	Open		295.00	295
1992	All Tuckered Out L5846G	Open		220.00	255
1992	All Tuckered Out L5846M	Open		220.00	255
1992	The Loving Family L5848G	Closed	1994	950.00	985
1992	Inspiring Muse L5850G	Closed	1994	1200.00	1250
1992	Feathered Fantasy L5851G	Open		1200.00	1250
1992	Easter Bonnets L5852G	Closed	1993	265.00	400
1992	Floral Admiration L5853G	Closed	1994	690.00	825
1992	Floral Fantasy L5854G	Closed	1995	690.00	710
1992	Afternoon Jaunt L5855G	Closed	1993	420.00	440
1992	Circus Concert L5856G	Open		570.00	585
1992	Grand Entrance L5857G	Closed	1994	265.00	275
1992	Waiting to Dance L5858G	Closed	1995	295.00	335

*Quotes have been rounded up to nearest dollar

Lladró
to Lladró

FIGURINES

YEAR ISSUE		EDITION LIMIT	YEAR RETD.	ISSUE PRICE	*QUOTE U.S.$
1992	At The Ball L5859G	Open		295.00	330
1992	Fairy Garland L5860G	Closed	1995	630.00	750
1992	Fairy Flowers L5861G	Closed	1995	630.00	655
1992	Fragrant Bouquet L5862G	Open		350.00	360
1992	Dressing For The Ballet L5865G	Closed	1995	395.00	415
1992	Final Touches L5866G	Closed	1995	395.00	415
1992	Serene Valenciana L5867G	Closed	1994	365.00	385
1992	Loving Valenciana L5868G	Closed	1995	365.00	385
1992	Fallas Queen L5869G	Closed	1995	420.00	440
1992	Olympic Torch w/Fantasy Logo L5870G	Closed	1994	165.00	145
1992	Olympic Champion w/Fantasy Logo L5871G	Closed	1994	165.00	145
1992	Olympic Pride w/Fantasy Logo L5872G	Closed	1994	165.00	495
1992	Modern Mother L5873G	Open		325.00	335
1992	Off We Go L5874G	Closed	1994	365.00	385
1992	Angelic Cymbalist L5876	Yr.Iss.	1992	140.00	165
1992	Guest Of Honor L5877G	Open		195.00	200
1992	Sister's Pride L5878G	Open		595.00	615
1992	Shot On Goal L5879G	Open		1100.00	1150
1992	Playful Unicorn L5880G	Open		295.00	320
1992	Playful Unicorn L5880M	Open		295.00	320
1992	Mischievous Mouse L5881G	Open		285.00	295
1992	Restful Mouse L5882G	Open		285.00	295
1992	Loving Mouse L5883G	Open		285.00	295
1992	From This Day Forward L5885G	Open		265.00	285
1992	Hippity Hop L5886G	Closed	1995	95.00	95
1992	Washing Up L5887G	Closed	1995	95.00	95
1992	That Tickles! L5888G	Closed	1995	95.00	105
1992	Snack Time L5889G	Closed	1995	95.00	105
1992	The Aviator L5891G	Open		375.00	415
1992	Circus Magic L5892G	Open		470.00	495
1992	Friendship In Bloom L5893G	Closed	1995	650.00	685
1992	Precious Petals L5894G	Open		395.00	415
1992	Bouquet of Blossoms L5895G	Open		295.00	295
1992	The Loaves & Fishes L5896G	Open		695.00	760
1992	Trimming The Tree L5897G	Open		900.00	925
1992	Spring Splendor L5898G	Open		440.00	450
1992	Just One More L5899G	Open		450.00	495
1992	Sleep Tight L5900G	Open		450.00	495
1992	Surprise L5901G	Open		325.00	335
1992	Easter Bunnies L5902G	Open		240.00	250
1992	Down The Aisle L5903G	Open		295.00	295
1992	Sleeping Bunny L5904G	Open		75.00	75
1992	Attentive Bunny L5905G	Open		75.00	75
1992	Preening Bunny L5906G	Open		75.00	80
1992	Sitting Bunny L5907G	Open		75.00	80
1992	Just A Little More L5908G	Open		370.00	380
1992	All Dressed Up L5909G	Open		440.00	450
1992	Making A Wish L5910G	Open		790.00	825
1992	Swans Take Flight L5912G	Open		2850.00	2950
1992	Rose Ballet L5919G	Open		210.00	215
1992	Swan Ballet L5920G	Open		210.00	215
1992	Take Your Medicine L5921G	Open		360.00	370
1990	Floral Clock L5924	Closed	1995	N/A	165
1990	Garland Quartz Clock L5926	Closed	1995	195.00	195
1992	Jazz Clarinet L5928G	Open		295.00	295
1992	Jazz Drums L5929G	Open		595.00	610
1992	Jazz Duo L5930G	Open		795.00	885
1993	The Ten Commandments w/Base L5933G	Open		930.00	930
1993	The Holy Teacher L5934G	Open		375.00	375
1993	Nutcracker Suite L5935G	Open		620.00	620
1993	Little Skipper L5936G	Open		320.00	320
1993	Riding The Waves L5941G	Open		405.00	405
1993	World of Fantasy L5943G	Closed	1995	295.00	295
1993	The Great Adventure L5944G	Closed	1994	325.00	325
1993	A Mother's Way L5946G	Open		1350.00	1350
1993	General Practitioner L5947G	Open		360.00	360
1993	Physician L5948G	Open		360.00	360
1993	Angel Candleholder w/Lyre L5949G	Open		295.00	315
1993	Angel Candleholder w/Tambourine L5950G	Open		295.00	315
1993	Sounds of Summer L5953G	Open		125.00	142
1993	Sounds of Winter L5954G	Open		125.00	142
1993	Sounds of Fall L5955G	Open		125.00	142
1993	Sounds of Spring L5956G	Open		125.00	142
1993	The Glass Slipper L5957G	Open		475.00	475
1993	Country Ride w/base L5958G	Open		2850.00	2875
1993	It's Your Turn L5959G	Open		365.00	365
1993	On Patrol L5960G	Open		395.00	445
1993	The Great Teacher w/base L5961G	Open		850.00	850
1993	Angelic Melody L5963	Yr.Iss.	1993	145.00	145-175
1993	The Great Voyage L5964G	Closed	1994	50.00	50
1993	The Clipper Ship w/base L5965M	Open		240.00	250
1993	Flowers Forever w/base L5966G	Open		4150.00	4150
1993	Honeymoon Ride w/base L5968G	Closed	1995	2750.00	2750
1993	A Special Toy L5971G	Open		815.00	815
1993	Before the Dance w/base L5972G	Open		3550.00	3550
1993	Before the Dance w/base L5972M	Open		3550.00	3550
1993	Family Outing w/base L5974G	Open		4275.00	4275
1993	Up and Away w/base L5975G	Open		2850.00	2850
1993	The Fireman L5976G	Open		395.00	445
1993	Revelation w/base (white) L5977G	Closed	1995	310.00	310
1993	Revelation w/base (black) L5978M	Closed	1995	310.00	310
1993	Revelation w/base (sand) L5979M	Closed	1995	310.00	310
1993	The Past w/base (white) L5980G	Closed	1995	310.00	310
1993	The Past w/base (black) L5981M	Closed	1995	310.00	310
1993	The Past w/base (sand) L5982M	Closed	1995	310.00	310
1993	Beauty w/base (white) L5983G	Closed	1995	310.00	310
1993	Beauty w/base (black) L5984M	Closed	1995	310.00	310
1993	Beauty w/base (sand) L5985M	Closed	1995	310.00	310
1993	Sunday Sermon L5986G	Open		425.00	425
1993	Talk to Me L5987G	Open		145.00	165
1993	Taking Time L5988G	Open		145.00	165
1993	A Mother's Touch L5989G	Open		470.00	470
1993	Thoughtful Caress L5990G	Open		225.00	225
1993	Love Story L5991G	Open		2800.00	2800
1993	Unicorn and Friend L5993G	Open		355.00	355
1993	Unicorn and Friend L5993M	Open		355.00	355
1993	Meet My Friend L5994G	Open		695.00	695
1993	Soft Meow L5995G	Open		480.00	515
1993	Bless the Child L5996G	Closed	1994	465.00	465
1993	One More Try L5997G	Open		715.00	715
1993	My Dad L6001G	Closed	1995	550.00	575
1993	Down You Go L6002G	Open		815.00	815
1993	Ready To Learn L6003G	Open		650.00	650
1993	Bar Mitzvah Day L6004G	Open		395.00	430
1993	Christening Day w/base L6005G	Closed	1995	1425.00	1425
1993	Oriental Colonade w/base L6006G	Closed	1995	1875.00	1875
1993	The Goddess & Unicorn w/base L6007G	Open		1675.00	1675
1993	Joyful Event L6008G	Open		825.00	825
1993	Monday's Child (Boy) L6011G	Open		245.00	270
1993	Monday's Child (Girl) L6012G	Open		260.00	290
1993	Tuesday's Child (Boy) L6013G	Open		225.00	250
1993	Tuesday's Child (Girl) L6014G	Open		245.00	270
1993	Wednesday's Child (Boy) L6015G	Open		245.00	270
1993	Wednesday's Child (Girl) L6016G	Open		245.00	270
1993	Thursday's Child (Boy) L6017G	Open		225.00	250
1993	Thursday's Child (Girl) L6018G	Open		245.00	270
1993	Friday's Child (Boy) L6019G	Open		225.00	250
1993	Friday's Child (Girl) L6020G	Open		225.00	250
1993	Saturday's Child (Boy) L6021G	Open		245.00	270
1993	Saturday's Child (Girl) L6022G	Open		245.00	270
1993	Sunday's Child (Boy) L6023G	Open		225.00	250
1993	Sunday's Child (Girl) L6024G	Open		225.00	250
1993	Barnyard See Saw L6025G	Open		500.00	500
1993	My Turn L6026G	Open		515.00	515
1993	Hanukah Lights L6027G	Open		345.00	395
1993	Mazel Tov! L6028G	Open		380.00	395
1993	Hebrew Scholar L6029G	Open		225.00	245
1993	On The Go L6031G	Closed	1995	475.00	485
1993	On The Green L6032G	Open		645.00	645
1993	Monkey Business L6034G	Closed	1994	745.00	745
1993	Young Princess L6036G	Open		240.00	240
1994	Saint James L6084G	Open		310.00	310
1994	Angelic Harmony L6085G	Open		495.00	550
1994	Allow Me L6086G	Open		1625.00	1625
1994	Loving Care L6087G	Open		250.00	270
1994	Communion Prayer (Boy) L6088G	Open		194.00	200
1994	Communion Prayer (Girl) L6089G	Open		198.00	210
1994	Baseball Player L6090G	Open		295.00	310
1994	Basketball Player L6091G	Open		295.00	310
1994	The Prince L6092G	Open		325.00	325
1994	Songbird L6093G	Open		395.00	395
1994	The Sportsman L6096G	Open		495.00	540
1994	Sleeping Bunny With Flowers L6097G	Open		110.00	110
1994	Attentive Bunny With Flowers L6098G	Open		140.00	140
1994	Preening Bunny With Flowers L6099G	Open		140.00	140
1994	Sitting Bunny With Flowers L6100G	Open		110.00	110
1994	Follow Us L6101G	Open		198.00	215
1994	Mother's Little Helper L6102G	Open		275.00	285
1994	Beautiful Ballerina L6103G	Open		250.00	270
1994	Finishing Touches L6104	Open		240.00	250
1994	Spring Joy L6106G	Open		795.00	795
1994	Football Player L6107	Open		295.00	310
1994	Hockey Player L6108G	Open		295.00	310
1994	Meal Time L6109G	Open		495.00	515
1994	Medieval Maiden L6110G	Open		150.00	165
1994	Medieval Soldier L6111G	Open		225.00	245
1994	Medieval Lord L6112G	Open		285.00	300
1994	Medieval Lady L6113G	Open		225.00	225
1994	Medieval Princess L6114G	Open		245.00	245
1994	Medieval Prince L6115G	Open		295.00	315
1994	Medieval Majesty L6116G	Open		315.00	325
1994	Constance L6117G	Open		195.00	205
1994	Musketeer Portos L6118G	Open		220.00	230
1994	Musketeer Aramis L6119G	Open		275.00	295
1994	Musketeer Dartagnan L6120G	Open		245.00	270
1994	Musketeer Athos L6121G	Open		245.00	270
1994	A Great Adventure L6122	Open		198.00	215
1994	Out For a Stroll L6123G	Open		198.00	215
1994	Travelers Rest L6124G	Open		275.00	295
1994	Angelic Violinist L6126G	Yr.Iss.	1994	150.00	185
1994	Sweet Dreamers L6127G	Open		280.00	290
1994	Christmas Melodies L6128G	Open		375.00	385
1994	Little Friends L6129G	Open		225.00	235
1996	Spring Enchantment L6130G	Open		245.00	245
1994	Angel of Peace L6131G	Open		345.00	370
1994	Angel with Garland L6133G	Open		345.00	370
1994	Birthday Party L6134G	Open		395.00	425
1994	Football Star L6135	Open		295.00	295
1994	Basketball Star L6136G	Open		295.00	295
1994	Baseball Star L6137G	Open		295.00	295
1994	Globe Paperweight L6138M	Open		95.00	95
1994	Springtime Friends L6140G	Open		485.00	485
1994	Kitty Cart L6141G	Open		750.00	795
1994	Indian Pose L6142G	Open		475.00	475
1994	Indian Dancer L6143G	Open		475.00	475
1995	Caribbean Kiss L6144G	Open		340.00	340
1994	Heavenly Prayer L6145	Open		675.00	695
1994	Spring Angel L6146G	Open		250.00	265
1994	Fall Angel L6147G	Open		250.00	265
1994	Summer Angel L6148G	Open		220.00	220
1994	Winter Angel L6149G	Open		250.00	265
1994	Playing The Flute L6150G	Open		175.00	190
1994	Bearing Flowers L6151G	Open		175.00	190
1994	Flower Gazer L6152G	Open		175.00	190
1994	American Love L6153G	Open		225.00	225
1994	African Love L6154G	Open		225.00	225
1994	European Love L6155G	Open		225.00	225
1994	Asian Love L6156G	Open		225.00	225
1994	Polynesian Love L6157G	Open		225.00	225
1995	Fiesta Dancer L6163G	Open		285.00	285
1994	Wedding Bells L6164G	Open		175.00	185
1995	Pretty Cargo L6165G	Open		500.00	500
1995	Dear Santa L6166G	Open		250.00	250
1995	Delicate Bundle L6167G	Open		275.00	275
1994	The Apollo Landing L6168G	Closed	1995	450.00	450
1995	Seesaw Friends L6169G	Open		795.00	795
1995	Under My Spell L6170G	Open		195.00	195
1995	Magical Moment L6171G	Open		180.00	180
1995	Coming of Age L6172G	Open		345.00	345
1995	A Moment's Rest L6173G	Open		130.00	130
1995	Graceful Pose L6174G	Open		195.00	195
1995	Graceful Pose L6174M	Open		195.00	195
1995	White Swan L6175G	Open		90.00	90
1995	Communion Bell L6176G	Open		85.00	85
1995	Asian Scholar L6177G	Open		315.00	315
1995	Little Matador L6178G	Open		245.00	245
1995	Peaceful Moment L6179G	Open		385.00	385
1995	Sharia L6180G	Open		235.00	235
1995	Velisa L6181G	Open		180.00	180
1996	Wanda L6182	Open		205.00	205
1995	Preparing For The Sabbath L6183G	Open		385.00	385
1995	For a Better World L6186G	Open		575.00	575
1995	European Boy L6187G	Open		185.00	185
1995	Asian Boy L6188G	Open		225.00	225
1995	African Boy L6189G	Open		195.00	195
1995	Polynesian Boy L6190G	Open		250.00	250
1995	All American L6191G	Open		225.00	225
1995	American Indian Boy L6192G	Open		225.00	225
1995	Summer Serenade L6193G	Open		375.00	375
1995	Summer Serenade L6193M	Open		375.00	375
1996	Christmas Wishes L6194	Open		245.00	245
1995	Carnival Companions L6195G	Open		650.00	650
1995	Seaside Companions L6196G	Open		230.00	230
1995	Seaside Serenade L6197G	Open		275.00	275
1995	Soccer Practice L6198G	Open		195.00	195
1995	In The Procession L6199G	Open		250.00	250
1995	In The Procession L6199M	Open		250.00	250
1995	Bridal Bell L6200G	Open		125.00	125
1995	Cuddly Kitten L6201G	Open		270.00	270
1995	Daddy's Little Sweetheart L6202G	Open		595.00	595
1995	Grace and Beauty L6204G	Open		325.00	325
1995	Grace and Beauty L6204M	Open		325.00	325
1995	Graceful Dance L6205G	Open		340.00	340
1995	Reading the Torah L6208G	Open		535.00	535
1995	The Rabbi L6209G	Open		250.00	250
1995	Gentle Surprise L6210G	Open		125.00	125
1995	New Friend L6211G	Open		120.00	120
1995	Little Hunter L6212G	Open		115.00	115
1995	Lady Of Nice L6213G	Open		198.00	198
1995	Lady Of Nice L6213M	Open		198.00	198
1995	Leo L6214G	Open		198.00	198
1995	Virgo L6215G	Open		198.00	198
1995	Aquarius L6216G	Open		198.00	198
1995	Sagittarius L6217G	Open		198.00	198
1995	Taurus L6218G	Open		198.00	198
1995	Gemini L6219G	Open		198.00	198
1995	Libra L6220G	Open		198.00	198
1995	Aries L6221G	Open		198.00	198
1995	Capricorn L6222G	Open		198.00	198
1995	Pisces L6223G	Open		198.00	198
1995	Cancer L6224G	Open		198.00	198
1995	Scorpio L6225G	Open		198.00	198
1995	Snuggle Up L6226G	Open		170.00	170
1995	Trick or Treat L6227G	Open		250.00	250
1995	Special Gift L6228G	Open		265.00	265
1995	Contented Companion L6229G	Open		195.00	195
1995	Oriental Dance L6230G	Open		198.00	198
1995	Oriental Lantern L6231G	Open		198.00	198
1995	Oriental Beauty L6232G	Open		198.00	198
1995	Chef's Apprentice L6233G	Open		260.00	260
1995	Chef's Apprentice L6233M	Open		260.00	260
1995	The Great Chef L6234G	Open		195.00	195
1995	The Great Chef L6234M	Open		195.00	195
1995	Dinner is Served L6235G	Open		185.00	185
1995	Dinner is Served L6235M	Open		185.00	185
1995	Lady of Monaco L6236G	Open		250.00	250
1995	Lady of Monaco L6236M	Open		250.00	250
1995	The Young Jester-Mandolin L6237G	Open		235.00	235
1995	The Young Jester-Mandolin L6237M	Open		235.00	235
1995	The Young Jester-Trumpet L6238G	Open		235.00	235
1995	The Young Jester-Trumpet L6238M	Open		235.00	235
1995	The Young Jester-Singer L6239G	Open		235.00	235
1995	The Young Jester-Singer L6239M	Open		235.00	235
1995	Graceful Ballet L6240G	Open		795.00	795

*Quotes have been rounded up to nearest dollar

YEAR ISSUE		EDITION LIMIT	YEAR RETD.	ISSUE PRICE	*QUOTE U.S.$
1995	Graceful Ballet L6240M	Open		795.00	795
1995	Allegory of Spring L6241G	Open		735.00	735
1995	Allegory of Spring L6241M	Open		735.00	735
1996	Winged Companions L6242G	Open		270.00	270
1996	Winged Companions L6242M	Open		270.00	270
1996	Sweet Symphony L6243	Open		450.00	450
1996	Pumpkin Ride L6244	Open		695.00	695
1996	Sunday's Best L6246	Open		370.00	370
1995	Challenge L6247M	Yr.Iss.	1995	350.00	350
1995	Regatta L6248G	Yr.Iss.	1995	695.00	695
1995	Delphica w/base L6249	Open		1200.00	1200
1996	Springtime Harvest L6250	Open		760.00	760
1997	Wind of Peace L6251	Open		310.00	310
1996	Nature's Beauty w/base L6252	Open		770.00	770
1996	Making Rounds L6256	Open		295.00	295
1996	Pierrot in Preparation L6257	Open		195.00	195
1996	Pierrot in Love L6258	Open		195.00	195
1996	Pierrot Rehearsing L6259	Open		195.00	195
1996	Our Lady "Caridid Del Cobre" w/base L6268	Open		1355.00	1355
1996	Diana Goddess of the Hunt w/base L6269	Open		1550.00	1550
1996	Commencement L6270	Open		200.00	200
1996	Cap and Gown L6271	Open		200.00	200
1996	Going Forth L6272	Open		200.00	200
1996	Pharmacist L6273	Open		290.00	290
1996	Daisy L6274	Open		150.00	150
1996	Rose L6275	Open		150.00	150
1996	Iris L6276	Open		150.00	150
1996	Young Mandolin Player L6278	Open		330.00	330
1996	Flowers of Paris L6279	Open		525.00	525
1996	Paris in Bloom L6280	Open		525.00	525
1996	Coqueta L6281G	Open		435.00	435
1996	Coqueta L6281M	Open		435.00	435
1996	Medic L6282G	Open		225.00	225
1996	Medic L6282M	Open		225.00	225
1996	Temis L6283G	Open		435.00	435
1996	Temis L6283M	Open		435.00	435
1996	Quione L6284G	Open		435.00	435
1996	Quione L6284M	Open		435.00	435
1996	Dreams of Aladdin w/base L6285	Open		1440.00	1440
1996	Tennis Champion w/base L6286G	Open		350.00	350
1996	Tennis Champion w/base L6286M	Open		350.00	350
1996	Restless Dove L6287G	Open		105.00	105
1996	Restless Dove L6287M	Open		105.00	105
1996	Taking Flight L6288G	Open		150.00	150
1996	Taking Flight L6288M	Open		150.00	150
1996	Peaceful Dove L6289G	Open		105.00	105
1996	Peaceful Dove L6289M	Open		105.00	105
1996	Proud Dove L6290G	Open		105.00	105
1996	Proud Dove L6290M	Open		105.00	105
1996	Love Nest L6291G	Open		260.00	260
1996	Love Nest L6291M	Open		260.00	260
1997	Summer Egg L6293	Open		365.00	365
1996	Sweethearts L6296	Open		900.00	900
1996	Little Bear L6299	Open		285.00	285
1996	Rubber Ducky L6300	Open		285.00	285
1996	Care & Tenderness w/base L6301	Open		850.00	850
1996	Thena L6302G	Open		485.00	485
1996	Thena L6302M	Open		485.00	485
1996	Tuba Player L6303	Open		315.00	315
1996	Bass Drummer L6304	Open		400.00	400
1996	Trumpet Player L6305	Open		270.00	270
1996	Majorette L6306	Open		310.00	310
1996	Young Nurse L6307	Open		185.00	185
1996	Natural Wonder L6308	Open		220.00	220
1996	Nature's Treasures L6309	Open		220.00	220
1996	Nature's Song L6310	Open		230.00	230
1996	Cupid L6311	Open		200.00	200
1996	The Harpist L6312	Open		820.00	820
1996	Lost in Dreams L6313	Open		420.00	420
1996	Little Sailor Boy L6314	Open		225.00	225
1996	Dreaming of You L6315	Open		1280.00	1280
1996	Carnevale L6316	Open		840.00	840
1996	Making House Calls L6317	Open		260.00	260
1996	Little Distraction L6318	Open		350.00	350
1996	Beautiful Rhapsody L6319	Open		450.00	450
1996	Architect L6320	Open		330.00	330
1996	Serenading Colombina L6322	Open		415.00	415
1996	Stage Presence L6323	Open		355.00	355
1996	Princess of Peace L6324	Open		830.00	830
1996	Curtains Up L6325	Open		255.00	255
1996	Virgin of Carmen w/base L6326	Open		1270.00	1270
1996	Medieval Romance w/base L6327	Open		2250.00	2250
1996	Venice Festival w/base L6328	Open		5350.00	5350
1996	Blushing Bride L6329G	Open		370.00	370
1996	Blushing Bride L6329M	Open		370.00	370
1996	Refreshing Pause L6330	Open		170.00	170
1996	Bridal Bell L6331	Open		155.00	155
1996	Concerto L6332	Open		490.00	490
1996	Medieval Chess Set L6333	Open		2120.00	2120
1997	Little Fireman L6334	Open		185.00	185
1997	Poodle L6337	Open		150.00	150
1997	I'm Sleepy L6338	Open		360.00	360
1996	Country Sounds L6339	Open		750.00	750
1996	Sweet Country L6340	Open		750.00	750
1997	Little Veterinarian L6348	Open		210.00	210
1997	Little Maestro L6349	Open		165.00	165
1997	Hunting Butterflies L6350	Open		425.00	425
1997	Tokens of Love L6351	Open		385.00	385
1997	A World of Love L6353	Open		450.00	450
1997	Attentive Polar Bear w/Flowers L6354	Open		100.00	100
1997	Polar Bear Resting w/Flowers L6355	Open		100.00	100
1997	Polar Bear Seated w/Flowers L6356	Open		100.00	100
1997	Kissing Doves w/Flowers L6359	Open		225.00	225
1997	St. Joseph The Carpenter L6363	Open		1050.00	1050
1997	A Dream Come True L6364	Open		550.00	550
1997	Spring Flirtation L6365	Open		395.00	395
1997	Little Policeman L6367	Open		185.00	185
1997	Little Artist L6368	Open		175.00	175
1997	Indian Maiden L6369	Open		600.00	600
1997	Country Chores L6370	Open		260.00	260
1997	En Pointe L6371	Open		390.00	390
1997	Palace Dance L6373	Open		700.00	700
1997	Pas De Deux L6374	Open		725.00	725
1997	New Arrival L6382	Open		265.00	265
1997	The Ascension L6383	Open		775.00	775
1997	A Quiet Moment L6384	Open		270.00	270
1997	A Passionate Dance L6387	Open		890.00	890
1997	The Bouquet L6389	Open		95.00	95
1997	The Encounter L6391	Open		150.00	150
1997	The Kiss L6392	Open		150.00	150
1997	Morning Delivery L6398	Open		160.00	160
1997	Generous Gesture L6399	Open		345.00	345
1997	Daydreams L6400	Open		325.00	325
1997	Little Ballerina L6402	Open		200.00	200
1997	Breathless L6403	Open		235.00	235
1997	Sister w/Sax L6404G	Open		180.00	180
1997	Sister w/Sax L6404M	Open		180.00	180
1997	Sister Singing L6405G	Open		165.00	165
1997	Sister Singing L6405M	Open		165.00	165
1997	Sister w/Guitar L6406G	Open		200.00	200
1997	Sister w/Guitar L6406M	Open		200.00	200
1997	Sister w/Tambourine L6407G	Open		185.00	185
1997	Sister w/Tambourine L6407M	Open		185.00	185
1997	A Surprise Visit L6409	Open		190.00	190
1997	Would You Be Mine? L6410	Open		190.00	190
1997	Bath Time L6411	Open		195.00	195
1997	Joy of Life L6412	Open		215.00	215
1997	Spirit of Youth L6413	Open		215.00	215
1997	It's A Boy! L6415	Open		125.00	125
1997	It's A Girl! L6416	Open		125.00	125
1997	Unlikely Friends L6417	Open		125.00	125
1997	So Beautiful! L6418G	Open		325.00	325
1997	So Beautiful! L6418M	Open		325.00	325
1997	Arms Full of Love L6419	Open		180.00	180
1997	Off To Bed L6421	Open		145.00	145
1997	My Chubby Kitty L6422	Open		135.00	135
1997	Precious Papoose L6423	Open		240.00	240
1997	Ceremonial Princess L6424	Open		240.00	240
1997	A Flower For You L6427	Open		320.00	320
1997	My First Step L6428	Open		165.00	165
1997	Ready To Roll L6429	Open		165.00	165
1997	Little Lawyer L6431	Open		210.00	210
1997	Pensive Harlequin L6434	Open		495.00	495
1997	Colombina L6435	Open		525.00	525
1997	Time For Bed L6440	Open		160.00	160
1985	Lladró Plaque L7116	Open		17.50	18
1985	Lladró Plaque L7118	Closed	N/A	17.00	18
1992	Special Torch L7513G	Open		165.00	165
1992	Special Champion L7514G	Open		165.00	165
1992	Special Pride L7515G	Open		165.00	165
1993	Courage L7522G	Open		195.00	200
1994	Dr. Martin Luther King, Jr. L7528G	Open		345.00	345
1994	Spike L7543G	Open		95.00	105
1994	Brutus L7544G	Open		125.00	140
1994	Rocky L7545G	Open		110.00	120
1994	Stretch L7546G	Open		125.00	140
1994	Rex L7547G	Open		125.00	140
1994	Snow White L7555G (Disney-back stamp Theme Park issue)	Closed	N/A	295.00	880
1994	Snow White L7555G	Open		295.00	295
1995	Snow White Wishing Well L7558	Open		1500.00	1500
1995	16th Century Globe Paperweight	Open		105.00	105
1989	Starting Forward/Lolo L7605G	Closed	1989	125.00	350
1996	By My Side L7645	Open		250.00	250
1996	Chess Board L8036	Open		145.00	145

Lladró Limited Edition Egg Series - Lladró

YEAR ISSUE		EDITION LIMIT	YEAR RETD.	ISSUE PRICE	*QUOTE U.S.$
1993	1993 Limited Edition Egg L6083M	Closed	1993	145.00	240
1994	1994 Limited Edition Egg L7532M	Closed	1994	150.00	175
1995	1995 Limited Edition Egg L7548M	Closed	1995	150.00	155-175
1996	1996 Limited Edition Egg L7550	Closed	1996	155.00	155
1997	1997 Limited Edition Egg L7552	Yr.Iss.		155.00	155

Norman Rockwell Collection - Rockwell-Inspired

YEAR ISSUE		EDITION LIMIT	YEAR RETD.	ISSUE PRICE	*QUOTE U.S.$
1982	Lladró Love Letter L1406 (RL-400G)	5,000	N/A	650.00	1000-1200
1982	Summer Stock L1407 (RL-401G)	5,000	N/A	750.00	800-900
1982	Practice Makes Perfect L1408 (RL-402G)	5,000	N/A	725.00	800-1000
1982	Young Love L1409 (RL-403G)	5,000	N/A	450.00	1350-1750
1982	Daydreamer L1411 (RL-404G)	5,000	N/A	450.00	1300-1500
1982	Court Jester L1405 (RL-405G)	5,000	N/A	600.00	1300
1982	Springtime L1410 (RL-406G)	5,000	N/A	450.00	1450

See also Dave Grossman: Lladró-Norman Rockwell Collection

Lowell Davis Farm Club

Lowell Davis Farm Club - L. Davis

YEAR ISSUE		EDITION LIMIT	YEAR RETD.	ISSUE PRICE	*QUOTE U.S.$
1985	The Bride 221001 / 20993	Yr.Iss.	1985	45.00	400-475
1987	The Party's Over 221002 / 20994	Yr.Iss.	1987	50.00	175
1988	Chow Time 221003 / 20995	Yr.Iss.	1988	55.00	100-150
1989	Can't Wait 221004 / 20996	Yr.Iss.	1989	75.00	125
1990	Pit Stop 221005 / 20997	Yr.Iss.	1990	75.00	125-150
1991	Arrival Of Stanley 221006 / 20998	Yr.Iss.	1991	100.00	100
1991	Don't Pick The Flowers 221007 / 21007	Yr.Iss.	1991	100.00	145
1992	Hog Wild	Yr.Iss.	1992	100.00	100
1992	Check's in the Mail	Yr.Iss.	1992	100.00	110
1993	The Survivor 25371	Yr.Iss.	1993	70.00	70
1994	Summer Days	Yr.Iss.	1994	100.00	100
1995	Dutch Treat	Yr.Iss.	1995	100.00	100
1995	Free Kittens	Yr.Iss.	1995	40.00	40
1996	Sunnyside Up	9/97		55.00	55

Lowell Davis Farm Club Renewal Figurine - L. Davis

YEAR ISSUE		EDITION LIMIT	YEAR RETD.	ISSUE PRICE	*QUOTE U.S.$
1986	Thirsty? 892050 / 92050	Yr.Iss.	1987	Gift	30
1987	Cackle Berries 892051 / 92051	Yr.Iss.	1989	Gift	85
1988	Ice Cream Churn 892052 / 92052	Yr.Iss.	1990	Gift	60
1990	Not A Sharing Soul 892053 / 92053	Yr.Iss.	1991	Gift	50
1991	New Arrival 892054 / 92054	Yr.Iss.	1992	Gift	65
1992	Garden Toad 92055	Yr.Iss.	1993	Gift	50-65
1993	Luke 12:6 25372	Yr.Iss.	1994	Gift	65-75
1994	Feathering Her Nest	Yr.Iss.	1995	Gift	35
1995	After the Rain	Yr.Iss.	1996	Gift	25
1996	A Gift For You	6/97		Gift	N/A
1997	One in the Hand 97011	6/98		Gift	N/A

Davis Cat Tales Figurines - L. Davis

YEAR ISSUE		EDITION LIMIT	YEAR RETD.	ISSUE PRICE	*QUOTE U.S.$
1982	Company's Coming 25205	Closed	1986	60.00	215
1982	Flew the Coop 25207	Closed	1986	60.00	365
1982	On the Move 25206	Closed	1986	70.00	600-650
1982	Right Church, Wrong Pew 25204	Closed	1986	70.00	375

Davis Country Christmas Figurines - L. Davis

YEAR ISSUE		EDITION LIMIT	YEAR RETD.	ISSUE PRICE	*QUOTE U.S.$
1983	Hooker at Mailbox w/Presents 23550	Closed	1984	80.00	750
1984	Country Christmas 23551	Closed	1985	80.00	450
1985	Christmas at Fox Fire Farm 23552	Closed	1986	80.00	275
1986	Christmas at Red Oak 23553	Closed	1987	80.00	225-250
1987	Blossom's Gift 23554	Closed	1988	150.00	400-450
1988	Cutting the Family Christmas Tree 23555	Closed	1989	80.00	350
1989	Peter and the Wren 23556	Closed	1990	165.00	450
1990	Wintering Deer 23557	Closed	1991	165.00	200
1991	Christmas At Red Oak II 23558	Closed	1992	250.00	250
1992	Born on a Starry Night 23559	2,500	1993	225.00	225
1993	Waiting For Mr. Lowell 23606	2,500	1994	250.00	250
1994	Visions of Sugar Plums	2,500	1995	250.00	250
1995	Bah Humbug	2,500	1996	200.00	250

Davis Country Pride - L. Davis

YEAR ISSUE		EDITION LIMIT	YEAR RETD.	ISSUE PRICE	*QUOTE U.S.$
1981	Bustin' with Pride 25202	Closed	1985	100.00	250
1981	Duke's Mixture 25203	Closed	1985	100.00	400-450
1981	Plum Tuckered Out 25201	Closed	1985	100.00	950
1981	Surprise in the Cellar 25200	Closed	1985	100.00	800-1000

Davis Friends of Mine - L. Davis

YEAR ISSUE		EDITION LIMIT	YEAR RETD.	ISSUE PRICE	*QUOTE U.S.$
1992	Cat and Jenny Wren 23633	5,000	1993	170.00	175
1992	Cat and Jenny Wren Mini 23634	Open	1993	35.00	40
1989	Sun Worshippers 23620	5,000	1993	120.00	135
1989	Sun Worshippers Mini 23621	5,000	1993	32.50	40
1990	Sunday Afternoon Treat 23625	5,000	1993	120.00	130
1990	Sunday Afternoon Treat Mini 23626	Closed	1993	32.50	40-50
1991	Warm Milk 23629	Closed	1993	120.00	200
1991	Warm Milk Mini 23630	5,000	1993	32.50	40

Davis Little Critters - L. Davis

YEAR ISSUE		EDITION LIMIT	YEAR RETD.	ISSUE PRICE	*QUOTE U.S.$
1992	Charivari 25707	950	1993	250.00	250
1991	Christopher Critter 25514	1,192	1993	150.00	150
1992	Double Yolker 25516	Yr.Iss.	1993	70.00	70
1989	Gittin' a Nibble 25294	Closed	1993	50.00	60
1991	Great American Chicken Race 25500	2,500	1993	225.00	250
1991	Hittin' The Sack 25510	Closed	1993	70.00	70
1990	Home Squeezins 25504	Closed	1993	90.00	90
1991	Itiskit, Itasket 25511	Closed	1993	45.00	45
1991	Milk Mouse 25503	2,500	1993	175.00	230
1992	Miss Private Time 25517	Yr.Iss.	1993	35.00	35
1990	Outing With Grandpa 25502	2,500	1993	200.00	250
1990	Private Time 25506	Closed	1993	18.00	25
1990	Punkin' Pig 25505	2,500	1993	250.00	300
1991	Punkin' Wine 25501	Closed	1993	100.00	120
1991	Toad Strangler 25509	Closed	1993	57.00	57
1991	When Coffee Never Tasted So Good (Music box) 809225	1,250	1993	800.00	800
1991	When Coffee Never Tasted So Good 25507	1,250	1993	800.00	800
1992	A Wolf in Sheep's Clothing 25518	Yr.Iss.	1993	110.00	110

Davis Pen Pals - L. Davis

YEAR ISSUE		EDITION LIMIT	YEAR RETD.	ISSUE PRICE	*QUOTE U.S.$
1993	The Old Home Place (mini) 25801	Closed	1995	25.00	25
1993	The Old Home Place 25802	1,200	1995	200.00	200

*Quotes have been rounded up to nearest dollar

Davis Promotional Figurine - L. Davis

YEAR ISSUE		EDITION LIMIT	YEAR RETD.	ISSUE PRICE	*QUOTE U.S.$
1991	Leavin' The Rat Race 225512	Yr.Iss.	1991	80.00	150
1992	Hen Scratch Prom 225968	Yr.Iss.	1992	90.00	95
1993	Leapin' Lizard 225969	Yr.Iss.	1993	80.00	80
1994	Don't Forget Me 227130	Yr.Iss.	1994	70.00	70
1995	Nasty Stuff 95103	Yr.Iss.	1995	40.00	50

Davis RFD America - L. Davis

YEAR ISSUE		EDITION LIMIT	YEAR RETD.	ISSUE PRICE	*QUOTE U.S.$
1984	Anybody Home 25239	Closed	1987	35.00	100
1994	Attic Antics	Closed	1995	100.00	150
1982	Baby Blossom 25227	Closed	1984	40.00	325
1982	Baby Bobs 25222	Closed	1984	47.50	250
1985	Barn Cats 25257	Closed	1990	39.50	90
1993	Be My Valentine 27561	Open		35.00	40
1986	Bit Off More Than He Could Chew 25279	Closed	1992	15.00	55
1979	Blossom 25032	Closed	1983	180.00	1800
1993	Blossom 96846 (15th Anniversary)	Closed	1993	80.00	80
1982	Blossom and Calf 25326	Closed	1986	250.00	850
1995	Blossom's Best	750	1995	300.00	400
1987	Bottoms Up 25270	Closed	1992	80.00	105
1989	Boy's Night Out 25339	1,500	1992	190.00	250-300
1982	Brand New Day 25226	Closed	1984	23.50	150-175
1979	Broken Dreams 25035	Closed	1983	165.00	1200-1300
1993	Broken Dreams 96847 (15th Anniversary)	Closed	1993	80.00	80
1988	Brothers 25286	Closed	1990	55.00	70
1984	Catnapping Too? 25247	Closed	1991	70.00	150
1987	Chicken Thief 25338	Closed	1988	200.00	325-375
1983	City Slicker 25329	Closed	1990	150.00	270
1991	Cock Of The Walk 25347	2,500	1993	300.00	300
1986	Comfy? 25273	Open		40.00	80
1994	Companion pc. And Down the Hatch	6 mo.	1994	135.00	145
1994	Companion pc. Open The Lid	6 mo.	1994	135.00	145
1989	Coon Capers 25291	Open		67.50	90
1990	Corn Crib Mouse 25295	Closed	1993	35.00	45
1983	Counting the Days 25233	Closed	1992	40.00	60
1981	Country Boy 25213	Closed	1984	37.50	350-375
1985	Country Cousins 25266	Closed	1995	42.50	90
1982	Country Crook 25280	Closed	1984	37.50	330
1985	Country Crooner 25256	Closed	1995	25.00	50
1984	Country Kitty 25246	Closed	1987	52.00	125
1979	Country Road 25030	Closed	1983	100.00	675
1993	Country Road 96842 (15th Anniversary)	Closed	1993	65.00	65
1984	Courtin' 25220	Closed	1986	45.00	125
1980	Creek Bank Bandit 25000	Closed	1985	37.50	400
1995	Cussin' Up a Storm	Closed	1995	45.00	45
1993	Don't Open Till Christmas 27562	Open		35.00	35
1992	Don't Play With Fire 25319	Open		120.00	120
1985	Don't Play With Your Food 25258	Closed	1992	28.50	50
1981	Double Trouble 25211	Closed	1984	35.00	475
1981	Dry as a Bone 25216	Closed	1984	45.00	300-325
1993	Dry Hole 25374	Closed	1995	30.00	35
1987	Easy Pickins 25269	Closed	1990	45.00	85
1993	End of the Trail 81000A	100	1993	100.00	600
1983	Fair Weather Friend 25236	Closed	1987	25.00	85
1983	False Alarm 25237	Closed	1985	65.00	185
1989	Family Outing 25289	Closed	1995	45.00	60
1994	Favorite Sport 25381	Closed	1995	230.00	230
1985	Feelin' His Oats 25275	1,500	1990	150.00	300-345
1990	Finder's Keepers 25299	Open		39.50	45
1991	First Offense 25304	Closed	1993	70.00	80
1994	First Outing	Open		65.00	65
1988	Fleas 25272	Open		20.00	30
1980	Forbidden Fruit 25022	Closed	1985	25.00	150
1990	Foreplay 25300	Closed	1993	59.50	80
1979	Fowl Play 25033	Closed	1983	100.00	275-325
1993	Fowl Play 96845 (15th Anniversary)	Closed	1993	60.00	60
1992	Free Lunch 25321	Open		85.00	85
1993	The Freeloaders 95042	1,250	1995	230.00	230
1985	Furs Gonna Fly 25335	1,500	1989	145.00	275-425
1994	Get Well 96902	Open		35.00	40
1987	Glutton for Punishment 25268	Closed	1991	95.00	160
1988	Goldie and Her Peeps 25283	Closed	1991	25.00	37
1984	Gonna Pay for His Sins 25243	Closed	1989	27.50	55
1980	Good, Clean Fun 25020	Closed	1989	40.00	150
1984	Gossips 25248	Closed	1987	110.00	265
1992	The Grass is Always Greener 25367	Closed	1995	195.00	195
1991	Gun Shy 25305	Closed	1993	70.00	70
1990	Hanky Panky 25298	Closed	1993	65.00	80
1994	Happy Anniversary 95089	Open		35.00	40
1993	Happy Birthday My Sweet 27560	Open		35.00	40
1988	Happy Hour 25287	Open		57.50	80
1983	Happy Hunting Ground 25330	Closed	1990	160.00	235
1984	Headed Home 25240	Closed	1991	25.00	50
1992	Headed South 25327	Closed	1995	45.00	45
1991	Heading For The Persimmon Grove 25306	Closed	1993	80.00	80
1994	Helpin Himself	Closed	1995	65.00	75
1983	Hi Girls, The Name's Big Jack 25328	Closed	1987	200.00	400-425
1981	Hightailing It 25214	Closed	1984	50.00	400-450
1983	His Eyes Are Bigger Than His Stomach 25332	Closed	1989	235.00	350
1984	His Master's Dog 25244	Closed	1988	45.00	150
1994	Hittin The Trail	1,250	1995	250.00	250
1985	Hog Heaven 25336	1,500	1988	165.00	350-400
1992	The Honeymoon's Over 25370	1,950	1994	300.00	300
1995	Hook, Line & Sinker 25382	Open		35.00	35
1984	Huh? 25242	Closed	1989	40.00	150
1993	I'm Thankful For You 27563	Open		35.00	40
1982	Idle Hours 25230	Closed	1985	37.50	450-475
1993	If You Can't Beat Em Join Em 25379	1,750	1995	250.00	250
1979	Ignorance is Bliss 25031	Closed	1983	165.00	1100
1993	Ignorance is Bliss 96843 (15th Anniversary)	Closed	1993	75.00	75
1988	In a Pickle 25284	Closed	1995	40.00	50
1980	Itching Post 25037	Closed	1988	30.00	100-115
1993	King of The Mountain 25380	750	1995	500.00	500
1991	Kissin' Cousins 25307	Closed	1993	80.00	80
1990	The Last Straw 25301	Closed	1993	125.00	165
1989	Left Overs 25290	Open		90.00	95
1983	Licking Good 25234	Closed	1985	35.00	225
1990	Little Black Lamb (Baba) 25297	Closed	1993	30.00	38
1990	Long Days, Cold Nights 25344	2,500	1993	175.00	190
1991	Long, Hot Summer 25343	1,950	1995	250.00	250
1985	Love at First Sight 25267	Closed	1992	70.00	115
1992	Lowell Davis Profile 25366	Open		75.00	75
1984	Mad As A Wet Hen 25334	Closed	1986	185.00	700-800
1987	Mail Order Bride 25263	Closed	1991	150.00	325-375
1983	Makin' Tracks 25238	Closed	1989	70.00	150-185
1988	Making a Bee Line 25274	Closed	1990	75.00	125
1994	Mama Can Willie Stay For Supper	1,250	1995	200.00	220
1983	Mama's Prize Leghorn 25235	Closed	1988	55.00	135
1986	Mama? 25277	Closed	1991	15.00	45
1989	Meeting of Sheldon 25293	Closed	1992	120.00	125
1980	Milking Time 25023	Closed	1985	20.00	240
1988	Missouri Spring 25278	Closed	1992	115.00	130
1982	Moon Raider 25325	Closed	1986	190.00	325
1995	The Morning After 10000	Closed	1995	60.00	120
1989	Mother Hen 25292	Open		37.50	50
1993	Mother's Day 95088	Open		35.00	40
1982	Moving Day 25225	Closed	1984	43.50	325
1992	My Favorite Chores 25362	1,500	1994	750.00	750
1980	New Day 25025	Closed	1980	20.00	165
1989	New Friend 25288	Closed	1994	45.00	60
1993	No Hunting 25375	1,000	1995	95.00	105
1988	No Private Time 25316	Closed	1992	200.00	300-350
1994	Not a Happy Camper	Open		75.00	75
1994	Oh Mother What is it?	1,000	1995	250.00	250
1992	OH Sheeeit . . . 25363	Closed	1995	120.00	140
1993	Oh Where is He Now 95041	1,250	1995	250.00	250
1984	One for the Road 25241	Closed	1988	37.50	70
1987	The Orphans 25271	Closed	1992	50.00	95
1985	Out-of-Stop 25260	Closed	1989	45.00	90
1985	Ozark Belle 25264	Closed	1990	35.00	70
1992	Ozark's Vittles 25318	Open		60.00	60
1984	Pasture Pals 25245	Closed	1990	52.00	130
1993	Peep Show 25376	Open		35.00	35
1988	Perfect Ten 25282	Closed	1990	95.00	180
1990	Piggin' Out 25345	Closed	1993	190.00	250
1994	Pollywogs 25617	750	1994	750.00	900
1984	Prairie Chorus 25333	Closed	1986	135.00	1200
1996	Proud Papa 96002	Yr.Iss.		250.00	250
1981	Punkin' Seeds 25219	Closed	1984	225.00	1550-1750
1994	Qu'est - Ceque C'est?	Closed	1995	200.00	220
1985	Renoir 25261	Closed	1991	45.00	85
1981	Rooted Out 25217	Closed	1989	45.00	90-115
1992	Safe Haven 25320	Closed	1994	95.00	95
1988	Sawin' Logs 25260	Closed	1993	85.00	105
1981	Scallawags 25221	Closed	1987	65.00	150-200
1992	School Yard Dogs 25369	Closed	1994	100.00	100
1996	See Ya There 96002	Yr.Iss.		330.00	330
1990	Seein' Red (Gus w/shoes) 25296	Closed	1993	35.00	47
1992	She Lay Low 25364	Closed	1995	120.00	120
1993	Sheep Sheerin Time 25388	1,200	1995	500.00	500
1982	A Shoe to Fill 25229	Closed	1986	37.50	175
1979	Slim Pickins 25034	Closed	1983	165.00	750-850
1993	Slim Pickins 96846 (15th Anniversary)	Closed	1993	75.00	85
1992	Snake Doctor 25365	Closed	1995	70.00	70
1991	Sooieee 25360	1,500	1994	350.00	350
1981	Split Decision 25210	Closed	1984	45.00	300-325
1995	Sticks and Stones	Open		30.00	30
1983	Stirring Up Trouble 25331	Closed	1988	160.00	260
1980	Strawberry Patch 25021	Closed	1989	25.00	95
1982	Stray Dog 25223	Closed	1988	35.00	75
1981	Studio Mouse 25215	Closed	1984	60.00	360
1980	Sunday Afternoon 25024	Closed	1985	22.50	225-250
1993	Sweet Tooth 25373	Closed	1995	60.00	60
1982	Thinking Big 25231	Closed	1988	35.00	100
1985	Too Good to Waste on Kids 25262	Closed	1989	70.00	130
1982	Treed 25327	Closed	1988	155.00	320
1989	A Tribute to Hooker 25340	Closed	1992	180.00	225-250
1993	Trick or Treat 27565	Open		35.00	50
1990	Tricks Of The Trade 25346	Closed	1994	300.00	350-375
1987	Two in the Bush 25337	Closed	1988	150.00	320
1994	Two Timer	Closed	1995	95.00	95
1982	Two's Company 25224	Closed	1986	43.50	200-225
1981	Under the Weather 25212	Closed	1991	25.00	85
1995	Uninvited Caller	Closed	1995	35.00	35
1980	Up To No Good 25218	Closed	1984	200.00	850-950
1982	Waiting for His Master 25281	Closed	1986	50.00	300
1994	Warmin' Their Buns	1,250	1995	270.00	270
1991	Washed Ashore 25308	Closed	1993	70.00	70
1982	When Mama Gets Mad 25228	Closed	1986	37.50	350-375
1987	When the Cat's Away 25276	Closed	1990	40.00	60
1988	When Three Foot's a Mile 25315	Closed	1991	230.00	300
1980	Wilbur 25029	Closed	1985	100.00	585
1985	Will You Still Respect Me in the Morning 25265	Closed	1993	35.00	75
1988	Wintering Lamb 25317	Closed	1990	200.00	250-275
1988	Wishful Thinking 25285	Closed	1990	55.00	70
1983	Woman's Work 25232	Closed	1989	35.00	80
1989	Woodscolt 25342	Closed	1992	300.00	400-450
1993	You're a Basket Full of Fun 27564	Open		35.00	35

Davis Special Edition Figurines - L. Davis

YEAR ISSUE		EDITION LIMIT	YEAR RETD.	ISSUE PRICE	*QUOTE U.S.$
1983	The Critics 23600	Closed	1986	400.00	1600-1700
1989	From A Friend To A Friend 23602	1,200	1990	750.00	1200
1985	Home from Market 23601	Closed	1988	400.00	1200
1992	Last Laff 23604	1,200	1994	900.00	900
1990	What Rat Race? 23603	1,200	1994	800.00	1025

Davis Uncle Remus - L. Davis

YEAR ISSUE		EDITION LIMIT	YEAR RETD.	ISSUE PRICE	*QUOTE U.S.$
1981	Brer Bear 25251	Closed	1984	80.00	1000-1200
1981	Brer Coyote 25255	Closed	1984	80.00	500
1981	Brer Fox 25250	Closed	1984	70.00	900-950
1981	Brer Rabbit 25252	Closed	1984	85.00	2000
1981	Brer Weasel 25254	Closed	1984	80.00	700
1981	Brer Wolf 25253	Closed	1984	85.00	500

Maruri USA

African Safari Animals - W. Gaither

YEAR ISSUE		EDITION LIMIT	YEAR RETD.	ISSUE PRICE	*QUOTE U.S.$
1983	African Elephant	Closed	N/A	3500.00	3500
1983	Black Maned Lion	Closed	N/A	1450.00	1450
1983	Cape Buffalo	Closed	N/A	2200.00	2200
1983	Grant's Zebras, pair	500	1995	1200.00	1200
1981	Nyala	300	1995	1450.00	1450
1983	Sable	Closed	N/A	1200.00	1200
1983	Southern Greater Kudu	Closed	N/A	1800.00	1800
1983	Southern Impala	Closed	N/A	1200.00	1200
1983	Southern Leopard	Closed	1994	1450.00	1450
1983	Southern White Rhino	150		3200.00	3200

American Eagle Gallery - Maruri Studios

YEAR ISSUE		EDITION LIMIT	YEAR RETD.	ISSUE PRICE	*QUOTE U.S.$
1985	E-8501	Closed	1989	45.00	75
1985	E-8502	Open		55.00	65
1985	E-8503	Open		60.00	65
1985	E-8504	Open		65.00	75
1985	E-8505	Closed	1989	65.00	150
1985	E-8506	Open		75.00	90
1985	E-8507	Open		75.00	90
1985	E-8508	Closed	1989	75.00	85
1985	E-8509	Closed	1989	85.00	125
1985	E-8510	Open		85.00	95
1985	E-8511	Closed	1989	85.00	125
1985	E-8512	Open		295.00	325
1987	E-8721	Open		40.00	50
1987	E-8722	Open		45.00	55
1987	E-8723	Closed	1989	55.00	60
1987	E-8724	Open		175.00	195
1989	E-8931	Open		55.00	60
1989	E-8932	Open		75.00	80
1989	E-8933	Open		95.00	95
1989	E-8934	Open		135.00	140
1989	E-8935	Open		175.00	185
1989	E-8936	Open		185.00	195
1991	E-9141 Eagle Landing	Open		60.00	60
1991	E-9142 Eagle w/ Totem Pole	Open		75.00	75
1991	E-9143 Pair in Flight	Open		95.00	95
1991	E-9144 Eagle w/Salmon	Open		110.00	110
1991	E-9145 Eagle w/Snow	Open		135.00	135
1991	E-9146 Eagle w/Babies	Open		145.00	145
1995	E-9551 Eagle	Open		60.00	60
1995	E-9552 Eagle	Open		65.00	65
1995	E-9553 Eagle	Open		75.00	75
1995	E-9554 Eagle	Open		80.00	80
1995	E-9555 Eagle	Open		90.00	90
1995	E-9556 Eagle	Open		110.00	110

Americana - W. Gaither

YEAR ISSUE		EDITION LIMIT	YEAR RETD.	ISSUE PRICE	*QUOTE U.S.$
1981	Grizzley Bear and Indian	Closed	N/A	650.00	650
1982	Sioux Brave and Bison	Closed	N/A	985.00	985

Baby Animals - W. Gaither

YEAR ISSUE		EDITION LIMIT	YEAR RETD.	ISSUE PRICE	*QUOTE U.S.$
1981	African Lion Cubs	1,500	1995	195.00	195
1981	Black Bear Cubs	Closed	N/A	195.00	195
1981	Wolf Cubs	Closed	N/A	195.00	195

Birds of Prey - W. Gaither

YEAR ISSUE		EDITION LIMIT	YEAR RETD.	ISSUE PRICE	*QUOTE U.S.$
1981	Screech Owl	300		960.00	960
1981	American Bald Eagle I	Closed	N/A	165.00	1750
1982	American Bald Eagle II	Closed	N/A	245.00	2750
1983	American Bald Eagle III	Closed	N/A	445.00	1750
1984	American Bald Eagle IV	Closed	N/A	360.00	1750
1986	American Bald Eagle V	Closed	N/A	325.00	1250

Eyes Of The Night - Maruri Studios

YEAR ISSUE		EDITION LIMIT	YEAR RETD.	ISSUE PRICE	*QUOTE U.S.$
1988	Double Barn Owl O-8807	Closed	1993	125.00	130
1988	Double Snowy Owl O-8809	Closed	1993	245.00	250
1988	Single Great Horned Owl O-8803	Closed	1993	60.00	65
1988	Single Great Horned Owl O-8808	Closed	1993	145.00	150
1988	Single Screech Owl O-8801	Closed	1993	50.00	55
1988	Single Screech Owl O-8806	Closed	1993	90.00	95
1988	Single Snowy Owl O-8802	Closed	1993	50.00	55
1988	Single Snowy Owl O-8805	Closed	1993	80.00	85
1988	Single Tawny Owl O-8804	Closed	1993	60.00	65

*Quotes have been rounded up to nearest dollar

Gentle Giants - Maruri Studios

YEAR ISSUE		EDITION LIMIT	YEAR RETD.	ISSUE PRICE	*QUOTE U.S.$
1992	Baby Elephant Sitting GG-9252	Open		65.00	65
1992	Baby Elephant Standing GG-9251	Open		50.00	50
1992	Elephant Pair GG-9255	Open		220.00	220
1992	Elephant Pair Playing GG-9253	Open		80.00	80
1992	Mother & Baby Elephant GG-9254	Open		160.00	160

Graceful Reflections - Maruri Studios

YEAR ISSUE		EDITION LIMIT	YEAR RETD.	ISSUE PRICE	*QUOTE U.S.$
1991	Mute Swan w/Baby SW-9152	Closed	1993	95.00	95
1991	Pair-Mute Swan SW-9153	Closed	1993	145.00	145
1991	Pair-Mute Swan SW-9154	Closed	1993	195.00	195
1991	Single Mute Swan SW-9151	Closed	1993	85.00	85

Horses Of The World - Maruri Studios

YEAR ISSUE		EDITION LIMIT	YEAR RETD.	ISSUE PRICE	*QUOTE U.S.$
1993	Arabian HW-9356	Closed	1995	175.00	175
1993	Camargue HW-9354	Closed	1995	150.00	150
1993	Clydesdale HW-9351	Closed	1995	145.00	145
1993	Paint Horse HW-9355	Closed	1995	160.00	160
1993	Quarter Horse HW-9353	Closed	1995	145.00	145
1993	Thoroughbred HW-9352	Closed	1995	145.00	145

Hummingbirds - Maruri Studios

YEAR ISSUE		EDITION LIMIT	YEAR RETD.	ISSUE PRICE	*QUOTE U.S.$
1995	Allen's & Babies w/Rose H-9523	Open		120.00	120
1995	Allen's w/Easter Lily H-9522	Open		95.00	95
1989	Allen's w/Hibiscus H-8906	Open		195.00	195
1989	Anna's w/Lily H-8905	Open		160.00	160
1995	Anna's w/Trumpet Creeper H-9524	Open		130.00	130
1995	Broad-Billed w/Amaryllis H-9526	Open		150.00	150
1989	Calliope w/Azalea H-8904	Open		120.00	120
1989	Ruby-Throated w/Azalea H-8911	Open		75.00	75
1989	Ruby-Throated w/Orchid H-8914	Open		150.00	150
1989	Rufous w/Trumpet Creeper H-8901	Open		70.00	75
1989	Violet-crowned w/Gentian H-8903	Open		90.00	90
1989	Violet-Crowned w/Gentian H-8913	Open		75.00	75
1995	Violet-Crowned w/Iris H-9521	Open		95.00	95
1989	White-eared w/Morning Glory H-8902	Open		85.00	85
1989	White-Eared w/Morning Glory H-8912	Open		75.00	75
1995	White-Eared w/Tulip H-9525	Open		145.00	145

Legendary Flowers of the Orient - Ito

YEAR ISSUE		EDITION LIMIT	YEAR RETD.	ISSUE PRICE	*QUOTE U.S.$
1985	Cherry Blossom	15,000		45.00	55
1985	Chinese Peony	15,000		45.00	55
1985	Chrysanthemum	15,000		45.00	55
1985	Iris	15,000		45.00	55
1985	Lily	15,000		45.00	55
1985	Lotus	15,000		45.00	45
1985	Orchid	15,000		45.00	55
1985	Wisteria	15,000		45.00	55

Majestic Owls of the Night - D. Littleton

YEAR ISSUE		EDITION LIMIT	YEAR RETD.	ISSUE PRICE	*QUOTE U.S.$
1988	Barred Owl	15,000		55.00	55
1987	Burrowing Owl	15,000		55.00	55
1988	Elf Owl	15,000		55.00	55

National Parks - Maruri Studios

YEAR ISSUE		EDITION LIMIT	YEAR RETD.	ISSUE PRICE	*QUOTE U.S.$
1993	Baby Bear NP-9301	Closed	1996	60.00	60
1993	Bear Family NP-9304	Closed	1996	160.00	160
1993	Buffalo NP-9306	Closed	1996	170.00	170
1993	Cougar Cubs NP-9302	Closed	1996	70.00	70
1993	Deer Family NP-9303	Closed	1996	120.00	120
1993	Eagle NP-9307	Closed	1996	180.00	180
1993	Falcon NP-9308	Closed	1996	195.00	195
1993	Howling Wolves NP-9305	Closed	1996	165.00	165

North American Game Animals - W. Gaither

YEAR ISSUE		EDITION LIMIT	YEAR RETD.	ISSUE PRICE	*QUOTE U.S.$
1984	White Tail Deer	950		285.00	285

North American Game Birds - W. Gaither

YEAR ISSUE		EDITION LIMIT	YEAR RETD.	ISSUE PRICE	*QUOTE U.S.$
1983	Bobtail Quail, female	Closed	N/A	375.00	375
1983	Bobtail Quail, male	Closed	N/A	375.00	375
1981	Canadian Geese, pair	Closed	N/A	2000.00	2000
1981	Eastern Wild Turkey	Closed	N/A	300.00	300
1982	Ruffed Grouse	Closed	N/A	1745.00	1745
1983	Wild Turkey Hen with Chicks	Closed	N/A	300.00	300

North American Songbirds - W. Gaither

YEAR ISSUE		EDITION LIMIT	YEAR RETD.	ISSUE PRICE	*QUOTE U.S.$
1982	Bluebird	Closed	N/A	95.00	95
1983	Cardinal, female	Closed	N/A	95.00	95
1982	Cardinal, male	Closed	N/A	95.00	95
1982	Carolina Wren	Closed	N/A	95.00	95
1982	Chickadee	Closed	N/A	95.00	95
1982	Mockingbird	Closed	N/A	95.00	95
1983	Robin	Closed	N/A	95.00	95

North American Waterfowl I - W. Gaither

YEAR ISSUE		EDITION LIMIT	YEAR RETD.	ISSUE PRICE	*QUOTE U.S.$
1981	Blue Winged Teal	200	1996	980.00	980
1981	Canvasback Ducks	Closed	1994	780.00	780
1981	Flying Wood Ducks	Closed	N/A	880.00	880
1981	Mallard Drake	Closed	N/A	2380.00	2380
1981	Wood Duck, decoy	950		480.00	480

North American Waterfowl II - W. Gaither

YEAR ISSUE		EDITION LIMIT	YEAR RETD.	ISSUE PRICE	*QUOTE U.S.$
1982	Bufflehead Ducks Pair	1,500		225.00	225
1982	Goldeneye Ducks Pair	Closed	N/A	225.00	225
1983	Loon	Closed	1989	245.00	245
1981	Mallard Ducks Pair	1,500		225.00	225
1982	Pintail Ducks Pair	Closed	1994	225.00	225
1982	Widgeon, female	Closed	N/A	225.00	225
1982	Widgeon, male	Closed	N/A	225.00	225

Polar Expedition - Maruri Studios

YEAR ISSUE		EDITION LIMIT	YEAR RETD.	ISSUE PRICE	*QUOTE U.S.$
1992	Arctic Fox Cubs Playing-P-9223	Open		65.00	65
1990	Baby Arctic Fox-P-9002	Open		50.00	55
1990	Baby Emperor Penguin-P-9001	Open		45.00	50
1992	Baby Harp Seal-P-9221	Open		55.00	55
1990	Baby Harp Seals-P-9005	Open		65.00	70
1992	Emperor Penguins-P-9222	Open		60.00	60
1990	Mother & Baby Emperor Penguins-P-9006	Open		80.00	85
1990	Mother & Baby Harp Seals-P-9007	Open		90.00	95
1990	Mother & Baby Polar Bears-P-9008	Open		125.00	130
1990	Polar Bear Cub Sliding-P-9003	Open		50.00	55
1990	Polar Bear Cubs Playing-P-9004	Open		60.00	65
1992	Polar Bear Family-P-9224	Open		90.00	90
1990	Polar Expedition Sign-PES-001	Open		18.00	18

Precious Panda - Maruri Studios

YEAR ISSUE		EDITION LIMIT	YEAR RETD.	ISSUE PRICE	*QUOTE U.S.$
1992	Lazy Lunch PP-9202	Open		60.00	60
1992	Mother's Cuddle-PP-9204	Open		120.00	120
1992	Snack Time PP-9201	Open		60.00	60
1992	Tug Of War PP-9203	Open		70.00	70

Santa's World Travels - Maruri Studios

YEAR ISSUE		EDITION LIMIT	YEAR RETD.	ISSUE PRICE	*QUOTE U.S.$
1996	Cat Nap SWT-9603	7,500		85.00	85
1996	Crossing the Tundra SWT-9605	7,500		145.00	145
1996	Desert Trip SWT-9604	7,500		95.00	95
1996	Santa's Safari SWT-9600	5,000		225.00	225
1996	Trusted Friend SWT-9602	7,500		85.00	85
1996	Wild Ride SWT-9601	7,500		75.00	75

Shore Birds - W. Gaither

YEAR ISSUE		EDITION LIMIT	YEAR RETD.	ISSUE PRICE	*QUOTE U.S.$
1984	Pelican	Closed	N/A	260.00	260
1984	Sand Piper	Closed	N/A	285.00	285

Signature Collection - W. Gaither

YEAR ISSUE		EDITION LIMIT	YEAR RETD.	ISSUE PRICE	*QUOTE U.S.$
1985	American Bald Eagle	Closed	N/A	60.00	60
1985	Canada Goose	Closed	N/A	60.00	60
1985	Hawk	Closed	N/A	60.00	60
1985	Pintail Duck	Closed	N/A	60.00	60
1985	Snow Goose	Closed	N/A	60.00	60
1985	Swallow	Closed	N/A	60.00	60

Songbirds Of Beauty - Maruri Studios

YEAR ISSUE		EDITION LIMIT	YEAR RETD.	ISSUE PRICE	*QUOTE U.S.$
1991	Bluebird w/ Apple Blossom SB-9105	Closed	1994	85.00	85
1991	Cardinal w/ Cherry Blossom SB-9103	Closed	1994	85.00	85
1991	Chickadee w/ Roses SB-9101	Closed	1994	85.00	85
1991	Dbl. Bluebird w/ Peach Blossom SB-9107	Closed	1994	145.00	145
1991	Dbl. Cardinal w/ Dogwood SB-9108	Closed	1994	145.00	145
1991	Goldfinch w/ Hawthorne SB-9102	Closed	1994	85.00	85
1991	Robin & Baby w/ Azalea SB-9106	Closed	1994	115.00	115
1991	Robin w/ Lilies SB-9104	Closed	1994	85.00	85

Special Commissions - W. Gaither

YEAR ISSUE		EDITION LIMIT	YEAR RETD.	ISSUE PRICE	*QUOTE U.S.$
1982	Cheetah	Closed	N/A	995.00	995
1983	Orange Bengal Tiger	240		340.00	340
1981	White Bengal Tiger	240		340.00	340

Studio Collection - Maruri Studios

YEAR ISSUE		EDITION LIMIT	YEAR RETD.	ISSUE PRICE	*QUOTE U.S.$
1990	Majestic Eagles-MS-100	Closed	N/A	350.00	800
1991	Delicate Motion-MS-200	3,500	1996	325.00	325
1992	Imperial Panda-MS-300	3,500		350.00	350
1993	Wild Wings-MS-400	3,500		395.00	450
1994	Waltz of the Dolphins-MS-500	3,500		300.00	300
1995	"Independent Spirit" MS-600	3,500		395.00	395

Stump Animals - W. Gaither

YEAR ISSUE		EDITION LIMIT	YEAR RETD.	ISSUE PRICE	*QUOTE U.S.$
1984	Bobcat	Closed	N/A	175.00	175
1984	Chipmunk	Closed	N/A	175.00	175
1984	Gray Squirrel	1,200	1995	175.00	175
1983	Owl	Closed	N/A	175.00	175
1983	Raccoon	Closed	1989	175.00	175
1982	Red Fox	Closed	N/A	175.00	175

Tribal Spirits - Maruri Studios

YEAR ISSUE		EDITION LIMIT	YEAR RETD.	ISSUE PRICE	*QUOTE U.S.$
1996	Bear Healer TS-9653	5,000		140.00	140
1996	Buffalo Hunter TS-9651	5,000		130.00	130
1996	Eagle Messenger TS-9652	5,000		140.00	140
1996	Wolf Guide TS-9654	5,000		150.00	150

Upland Birds - W. Gaither

YEAR ISSUE		EDITION LIMIT	YEAR RETD.	ISSUE PRICE	*QUOTE U.S.$
1981	Mourning Doves	Closed	N/A	780.00	780

Wings of Love Doves - Maruri Studios

YEAR ISSUE		EDITION LIMIT	YEAR RETD.	ISSUE PRICE	*QUOTE U.S.$
1987	D-8701 Single Dove w/ Forget-Me-Not	Closed	1994	45.00	55
1987	D-8702 Double Dove w/ Primrose	Open		55.00	65
1987	D-8703 Single Dove w/Buttercup	Closed	1994	65.00	70
1987	D-8704 Double Dove w/Daisy	Open		75.00	85
1987	D-8705 Single Dove w/Blue Flax	Closed	1994	95.00	95
1987	D-8706 Double Dove w/Cherry Blossom	Open		175.00	195
1990	D-9021 Double Dove w/Gentian	Open		50.00	55
1990	D-9022 Double Dove w/Azalea	Open		75.00	75
1990	D-9023 Double Dove w/Apple Blossom	Open		115.00	120
1990	D-9024 Double Dove w/Morning Glory	Open		150.00	160

Wonders of the Sea - Maruri Studios

YEAR ISSUE		EDITION LIMIT	YEAR RETD.	ISSUE PRICE	*QUOTE U.S.$
1994	Dolphin WS-9401	Open		70.00	70
1994	Great White Shark WS-9406	Open		90.00	90
1994	Green Sea Turtle WS-9405	Open		85.00	85
1994	Humpback Mother & Baby WS-9409	Open		150.00	150
1994	Manatee & Baby WS-9403	Open		75.00	75
1994	Manta Ray WS-9404	Open		80.00	80
1994	Orca Mother & Baby WS-9410	Open		150.00	150
1994	Sea Otter & Baby WS-9402	Open		75.00	75
1994	Three Dolphins WS-9408	Open		135.00	135
1994	Two Dolphins WS-9407	Open		120.00	120

Maud Humphrey Bogart/Enesco Corporation

Maud Humphrey Bogart Collectors' Club Members Only - M. Humphrey

YEAR ISSUE		EDITION LIMIT	YEAR RETD.	ISSUE PRICE	*QUOTE U.S.$
1991	Friends For Life MH911	Closed	N/A	60.00	65
1992	Nature's Little Helper MH921	Closed	N/A	65.00	60-65
1993	Sitting Pretty MH931	Closed	N/A	60.00	60

Maud Humphrey Bogart - Symbol Of Membership - M. Humphrey

YEAR ISSUE		EDITION LIMIT	YEAR RETD.	ISSUE PRICE	*QUOTE U.S.$
1991	A Flower For You H5596	Closed	N/A	Unkn.	35
1992	Sunday Best M0002	Closed	N/A	Unkn.	30-53
1993	Playful Companions M0003	Closed	N/A	Unkn.	65

Maud Humphrey Bogart - M. Humphrey

YEAR ISSUE		EDITION LIMIT	YEAR RETD.	ISSUE PRICE	*QUOTE U.S.$
1988	Tea And Gossip H1301	Retrd.	N/A	65.00	75-110
1988	Cleaning House H1303	Retrd.	N/A	60.00	65-90
1988	Susanna H 1305	Retrd.	N/A	60.00	100-125
1988	Little Chickadees H1306	Retrd.	N/A	65.00	90
1988	The Magic Kitten H1308	Retrd.	N/A	66.00	50-80
1988	Seamstress H1309	Retrd.	N/A	66.00	80-94
1988	A Pleasure To Meet You H1310	Retrd.	N/A	65.00	90
1988	My First Dance H1311	Retrd.	N/A	60.00	100-130
1988	Sarah H1312	Retrd.	N/A	60.00	250
1988	Sealed With A Kiss H1316	Retrd.	N/A	45.00	60-70
1988	Special Friends H1317	Retrd.	N/A	66.00	75-90
1988	School Days H1318	Retrd.	N/A	42.50	55-70
1988	Gift Of Love H1319	Retrd.	N/A	65.00	80
1988	My 1st Birthday H1320	Retrd.	N/A	47.00	80
1989	Winter Fun H1354	Retrd.	N/A	46.00	65
1992	Stars and Stripes Forever 910201	Retrd.	N/A	75.00	80
1993	Playing Mama (5th Anniv.) 915963	Retrd.	N/A	80.00	110
1993	Playing Mama (Event) 915963R	Retrd.	N/A	80.00	90-110

Memories of Yesterday/Enesco Corporation

Memories of Yesterday Society Figurines - M. Attwell

YEAR ISSUE		EDITION LIMIT	YEAR RETD.	ISSUE PRICE	*QUOTE U.S.$
1991	Welcome To Your New Home MY911	Yr.Iss.		30.00	45
1991	I Love My Friends MY921	Yr.Iss.		32.50	35
1993	Now I'm The Fairest Of Them All MY931	Yr.Iss.		35.00	35
1993	A Little Love Song for You MY941	Yr.Iss.		35.00	35
1994	Wot's All This Talk About Love MY942	Yr.Iss.		27.50	28
1995	Sharing the Common Thread of Love MY951	Yr.Iss.		100.00	100
1995	A Song For You From One That's True MY952	Yr.Iss.		37.50	38
1996	You've Got My Vote MY961	Yr.Iss.		40.00	40
1996	Peace, Heavenly Peace MY962	Yr.Iss.		30.00	30
1997	We Take Care of One Another MY971	Yr.Iss.		45.00	45
1997	You Mean the World to Me MY972	Yr.Iss.		40.00	40

Memories of Yesterday Exclusive Membership Figurine - M. Attwell

YEAR ISSUE		EDITION LIMIT	YEAR RETD.	ISSUE PRICE	*QUOTE U.S.$
1991	We Belong Together S0001	Yr.Iss.		Gift	35
1992	Waiting For The Sunshine S0002	Yr.Iss.		Gift	35
1993	I'm The Girl For You S0003	Yr.Iss.		Gift	40
1994	Blowing a Kiss to a Dear I Miss S0004	Yr.Iss.		Gift	N/A
1995	Time to Celebrate S0005	Yr.Iss.		Gift	N/A
1996	Forget-Me-Not! S0006	Yr.Iss.		Gift	N/A
1997	Holding On To Childhood Memories S0007	Yr.Iss.		Gift	N/A

Memories of Yesterday Exclusive Charter Membership Figurine - M. Attwell

YEAR ISSUE		EDITION LIMIT	YEAR RETD.	ISSUE PRICE	*QUOTE U.S.$
1992	Waiting For The Sunshine S0102	Yr.Iss.		Gift	N/A
1993	I'm The Girl For You S0103	Yr.Iss.		Gift	N/A
1994	Blowing a Kiss to a Dear I Miss S0104	Yr.Iss.		Gift	N/A
1995	Time to Celebrate S0105	Yr.Iss.		Gift	N/A
1996	Forget-Me-Not! S0106	Yr.Iss.		Gift	N/A
1997	Holding On To Childhood Memories S0107	Yr.Iss.		Gift	N/A

Memories of Yesterday 10th Anniversary Celebration - M. Attwell

YEAR ISSUE		EDITION LIMIT	YEAR RETD.	ISSUE PRICE	*QUOTE U.S.$
1997	Meeting Friends Along The Way Figurine 270407	Yr.Iss.		85.00	85
1997	Meeting Friends Along The Way Covered Box 277746	Yr.Iss.		10.00	10

*Quotes have been rounded up to nearest dollar

Memories of Yesterday - M. Attwell

YEAR ISSUE		EDITION LIMIT	YEAR RETD.	ISSUE PRICE	*QUOTE U.S.$
1995	A Friend Like You Is Hard To Find 101176	Open		45.00	45
1995	A Helping Hand For You 101192	Open		40.00	40
1995	Won't You Skate With Me? 134864	5,000		35.00	35
1995	Dear Old Dear, Wish You Were Here 134872	5,000		37.50	38
1995	You're My Sunshine On A Rainy Day 137626	Open		37.50	38
1995	Boo-Boo's Band Set/5 137758	Open		25.00	25
1996	We're In Trouble Now! 162299	7,500		37.50	38
1996	A Basket Full of Love 162582	Open		50.00	50
1997	You're My Bouquet of Blessings 162604	5,000		30.00	30
1996	Just Longing To See You 162620	7,500		27.50	28
1996	We Are All His Children 162639	Open		30.00	30
1996	Just Like Daddy 162698	7,500		27.50	28
1996	How Good of God To Make Us All 164135	5,000		50.00	50
1997	In the Hands of a Guardian Angel 209856	5,000		50.00	50
1997	There's Always a Rainbow 209864	5,000		38.00	38
1997	I Know You Can Do It 209821	5,000		35.00	35
1990	Collection Sign 513156	Closed	1993	7.00	7
1989	Blow Wind, Blow 520012	Open		40.00	40
1990	Hold It! You're Just Swell 520020	Suspd.		50.00	50
1990	Kiss The Place And Make It Well 520039	Suspd.		50.00	50
1989	Let's Be Nice Like We Was Before 520047	Suspd.		50.00	50
1991	Who Ever Told Mother To Order Twins? 520063	Open		33.50	34
1989	I'se Spoken For 520071	Retrd.	1991	30.00	30-50
1993	You Do Make Me Happy 520098	Open		27.50	28
1990	Where's Muvver? 520101	Retrd.	1994	30.00	30
1990	Here Comes The Bride And Groom God Bless 'Em! 520136 (musical)	Suspd.		80.00	80
1989	Daddy, I Can Never Fill Your Shoes 520187	Open		30.00	30
1989	This One's For You, Dear 520195	Suspd.		50.00	50
1989	Should I . . . ? 520209	Suspd.		50.00	50
1990	Luck At Last! He Loves Me 520217	Retrd.	1992	35.00	36-58
1989	Here Comes The Bride-God Bless Her! 9" 520527	Retrd.	1990	95.00	95-100
1989	We's Happy! How's Yourself? 520616	Retrd.	1991	70.00	85-150
1989	Here Comes The Bride & Groom (musical) God Bless 'Em 520896	Open		50.00	50
1989	The Long and Short of It [illegible]	Retrd.	1994	32.50	33
1989	As Good As His Mother Ever Made 522392	Open		32.50	32-40
1989	Must Feed Them Over Christmas 522406	Retrd.	1996	38.50	39
1989	Knitting You A Warm & Cozy Winter 522414	Suspd.		37.50	38
1989	Joy To You At Christmas 522449	Retrd.	1996	45.00	45
1989	For Fido And Me 522457	Open		70.00	70
1991	Wishful Thinking 522597	Open		45.00	45
1991	Why Don't You Sing Along? 522600	Retrd.	1995	55.00	55
1995	You Brighten My Day With A Smile 522627	Open		30.00	30
1991	Tying The Knot 522678	Open		60.00	60
1991	Wherever I Am, I'm Dreaming of You 522686	Suspd.		40.00	40
1993	Will You Be Mine? 522694	Open		30.00	30
1991	Sitting Pretty 522708	Retrd.	1993	40.00	50
1993	Here's A Little Song From Me To You Musical 522716	Open		70.00	70
1992	A Whole Bunch of Love For You 522732	Retrd.	1996	40.00	40
1992	I'se Such A Good Little Girl Sometimes 522759	Suspd.		30.00	30
1992	Things Are Rather Upside Down 522775	Suspd.		30.00	30
1991	Pull Yourselves Together Girls, Waists Are In 522783	Open		30.00	30
1993	Bringing Good Luck To You 522791	Retrd.	1996	30.00	30
1995	I Comfort Fido And Fido Comforts Me 522813	5,000		50.00	50
1992	A Kiss From Fido 523119	Suspd.		35.00	35
1994	Bless 'Em! 523127	Open		35.00	35
1994	Bless 'Em! 523232	Open		35.00	35
1990	I'm Not As Backwards As I Looks 523240	Open		32.50	33
1990	I Pray The Lord My Soul To Keep 523259	Open		25.00	25
1990	He Hasn't Forgotten Me 523267	Suspd.		30.00	30
1990	Time For Bed 9" 523275	Retrd.	1991	95.00	125
1991	Just Thinking 'bout You 523461 (musical)	Suspd.		70.00	70
1992	Now Be A Good Dog Fido 524581	Open		45.00	45
1991	Them Dishes Nearly Done 524611	Suspd.		50.00	50
1995	Join Me For A Little Song 524654	5,000		37.50	38
1990	Let Me Be Your Guardian Angel 524670	Open		32.50	33
1990	A Lapful Of Luck 524689	Open		15.00	15
1990	Not A Creature Was Stirrin' 524697	Suspd.		45.00	45
1990	I'se Been Painting 524700	Suspd.		37.50	38
1992	The Future-God Bless 'Em! 524719	Open		37.50	38
1990	A Dash of Something With Something For the Pot 524727	Open		55.00	55
1991	Opening Presents Is Much Fun! 524735	Suspd.		37.50	38
1992	You'll Always Be My Hero 524743	Open		50.00	50
1990	Got To Get Home For The Holidays 524751(musical)	Retrd.	1994	100.00	100
1990	Hush-A-Bye Baby 524778	Open		80.00	80
1990	The Greatest Treasure The World Can Hold 524808	Open		50.00	50
1994	With A Heart That's True, I'll Wait For You 524816	Retrd.	1996	50.00	50
1990	Hoping To See You Soon 524824	Suspd.		30.00	30
1991	I Must Be Somebody's Darling 524832	Retrd.	1993	30.00	30
1991	We All Loves A Cuddle 524832	Retrd.	1992	30.00	35
1991	He Loves Me 9" 525022	Retrd.	1992	100.00	100
1993	Now I Lay Me Down To Sleep 525413 (musical)	Suspd.		65.00	65
1992	Making Something Special For You 525472	Suspd.		45.00	45
1991	I'm As Comfy As Can Be 525480	Suspd.		50.00	50
1992	I'm Hopin' You're Missing Me Too 525499	Suspd.		55.00	55
1993	The Jolly Ole Sun Will Shine Again 525502	Retrd.	1994	55.00	55
1991	Friendship Has No Boundaries (Special Understamp) 525545	Yr.Iss.	1991	30.00	30-50
1992	Home's A Grand Place To Get Back To Musical 525553	Retrd.	1995	100.00	100
1991	Give It Your Best Shot 525561	Open		35.00	35
1992	I Pray the Lord My Soul To Keep (musical) 525596	Suspd.		65.00	65
1991	Could You Love Me For Myself Alone? 525618	Retrd.	1994	30.00	30
1996	Whenever I Get A Moment-I Think of You 525626	7,500		37.50	38
1992	Good Night and God Bless You In Every Way! 525634	Suspd.		50.00	50
1992	Five Years Of Memories 525669 (Five Year Anniversary Figurine)	Yr.Iss.	1992	50.00	65
1992	Five Years Of Memories Celebrating Our Five Years 1992 525669A	500		N/A	N/A
1996	Loving You One Stitch At A Time 525677	5,000		50.00	50
1993	May Your Flowers Be Even Better Than The Pictures On The Packets 525685	Open		37.50	38
1995	Let's Sail Away Together 525707	Open		32.50	33
1993	You Won't Catch Me Being A Golf Widow 525715	Open		30.00	30
1995	Good Friends Are Great Gifts 525723	Open		50.00	50
1994	Taking After Mother 525731	Open		40.00	40
1994	Too Shy For Words 525758	Retrd.	1996	50.00	50
1991	Good Morning, Little Boo-Boo 525766	Retrd.	1996	40.00	40
1992	Hurry Up For the Last Train to Fairyland 525863	Suspd.		40.00	40
1992	I'se So Happy You Called 526401	Retrd.	1993	100.00	100
1994	Pleasant Dreams and Sweet Repose-(musical) 526592	Open		80.00	80
1996	Put Your Best Foot Forward 526983	5,000		50.00	50
1994	Bobbed 526991	Retrd.	1995	32.50	33
1996	Can I Keep Her, Mommy? 527025	Open		13.50	14
1992	Time For Bed 527076	Open		30.00	30
1991	S'no Use Lookin' Back Now! 527203	Yr.Iss.	1991	75.00	75
1992	Collection Sign 527300	Open		30.00	30
1993	Having A Wash And Brush Up 527424	Open		35.00	35
1994	Having a Good Ole Laugh 527432	Open		50.00	50
1993	A Bit Tied Up Just Now-But Cheerio 527467	Open		45.00	45
1992	Send All Life's Little Worries Skipping 527505	Open		30.00	30
1994	Don't Wait For Wishes to Come True-Go Get Them! 527645	Open		37.50	38
1993	Hullo! Did You Come By Underground? 527653	Yr.Iss.	1993	40.00	40
1993	Hullo! Did You Come By Underground? Commemorative Issue: 1913 1993 527653A	500		N/A	N/A
1993	Look Out-Something Good Is Coming Your Way! 528781	Suspd.		37.50	38
1992	Merry Christmas, Little Boo-Boo 528803	Open		37.50	38
1994	Do Be Friends With Me 529117	Open		40.00	40
1994	Good Morning From One Cheery Soul To Another 529141	Open		30.00	30
1994	May Your Birthday Be Bright And Happy 529575	Open		35.00	35
1996	God Bless Our Future 529583	5,000		45.00	45
1993	Strikes Me, I'm Your Match 529656	Open		27.50	28
1993	Wot's All This Talk About Love? 529737	Retrd.	1994	100.00	100
1994	Thank God For Fido 529753	2-Yr.		100.00	100
1994	Making the Right Connection 529907	Yr.Iss.	1994	30.00	30
1994	Still Going Strong 530344	Open		27.50	28
1993	Do You Know The Way To Fairyland? 530379	Retrd.	1996	50.00	50
1996	We'd Do Anything For You, Dear 530905	5,000		50.00	50
1994	Comforting Thoughts 531367	Open		32.50	33
1995	Love To You Always 602752	Open		30.00	30
1995	Wherever You Go, I'll Keep In Touch 602760	Retrd.	1996	30.00	30
1995	Love Begins With Friendship 602914	Open		50.00	50
1994	The Nativity Pageant 602949	Open		90.00	90
1995	May You Have A Big Smile For A Long While 602965	Open		30.00	30
1995	Love To You Today 602973	Open		30.00	30
1996	You Warm My Heart 603007	7,500		35.00	35

Memories of Yesterday Charter 1988 - M. Attwell

YEAR ISSUE		EDITION LIMIT	YEAR RETD.	ISSUE PRICE	*QUOTE U.S.$
1988	Mommy, I Teared It 114480	Open		25.00	40-143
1988	Now I Lay Me Down To Sleep 114499	Open		20.00	25-65
1988	We's Happy! How's Yourself? 114502	Retrd.	1996	40.00	45-60
1988	Hang On To Your Luck! 114510	Suspd.		25.00	27-70
1988	How Do You Spell S-O-R-R-Y? 114529	Retrd.	1990	25.00	50-95
1988	What Will I Grow Up To Be? 114537	Suspd.		40.00	45
1988	Can I Keep Her Mommy? 114545	Retrd.	1995	25.00	27-70
1988	Hush! 114553	Retrd.	1990	45.00	75-125
1988	It Hurts When Fido Hurts 114561	Retrd.	1992	30.00	32-75
1988	Anyway, Fido Loves Me 114588	Suspd.		30.00	32-75
1988	If You Can't Be Good, Be Careful 114596	Retrd.	1993	50.00	55-90
1988	Welcome Santa 114960	Suspd.		45.00	50-100
1988	Special Delivery 114979	Retrd.	1991	30.00	32-70
1988	How 'bout A Little Kiss? 114987	Retrd.	1995	25.00	27-85
1988	Waiting For Santa 114995	Open		40.00	40-50
1988	Dear Santa. . . 115002	Suspd.		50.00	50
1988	I Hope Santa Is Home . . . 115010	Open		30.00	33-45
1988	It's The Thought That Counts 115029	Suspd.		25.00	29-75
1988	Is It Really Santa? 115347	Retrd.	1996	50.00	55-60
1988	He Knows If You've Been Bad Or Good 115355	Suspd.		40.00	45-75
1988	Now He Can Be Your Friend, Too! 115363	Suspd.		45.00	50-70
1988	We Wish You A Merry Christmas 115371 (musical)	Suspd.		70.00	70
1988	Good Morning Mr. Snowman 115401	Retrd.	1992	75.00	80-170
1988	Mommy, I Teared It, 9" 115924	Retrd.	1990	85.00	140-195

Memories of Yesterday Event Item Only - M. Attwell

YEAR ISSUE		EDITION LIMIT	YEAR RETD.	ISSUE PRICE	*QUOTE U.S.$
1994	I'll Always Be Your Truly Friend 525693	Yr.Iss.	1994	30.00	30
1995	Wrapped In Love And Happiness 602930	Yr.Iss.	1995	35.00	35
1996	A Sweet Treat For You 115126	Yr.Iss.	1996	30.00	30
1997	Mommy, I Teared It 114480A	Yr.Iss.		28.00	28

Alice in Wonderland - M. Attwell

YEAR ISSUE		EDITION LIMIT	YEAR RETD.	ISSUE PRICE	*QUOTE U.S.$
1997	Alice in Wonderland Collector Set 225254	3,000		150.00	150

Comforting Thoughts - M. Attwell

YEAR ISSUE		EDITION LIMIT	YEAR RETD.	ISSUE PRICE	*QUOTE U.S.$
1997	You Make My Heart Feel Glad 209880	5,000		30.00	30

Exclusive Heritage Dealer Figurine - M. Attwell

YEAR ISSUE		EDITION LIMIT	YEAR RETD.	ISSUE PRICE	*QUOTE U.S.$
1991	A Friendly Chat and a Cup of Tea 525510	Yr.Iss.	1991	50.00	100
1993	I'm Always Looking Out For You 527440	Yr.Iss.	1993	55.00	55
1994	Loving Each Other Is The Nicest Thing We've Got 522430	Yr.Iss.	1994	60.00	60
1995	A Little Help From Fairyland 529133	1,995	1995	55.00	55
1995	Friendship Is Meant To Be Shared 602922	Yr.Iss.	1995	50.00	50
1995	Bedtime Tales-set 153400	2,000	1996	60.00	60
1996	Tucking My Dears All Safe Away 130095	Yr.Iss.	1996	50.00	50
1996	I Do Like My Holiday Crews 522805	1,996		100.00	100
1996	Peter Pan Collector's Set 174564	1,000		150.00	150
1997	Every Stitch is Sewn With Kindness 209910	Yr.Iss.		50.00	50
1997	We're Going to Be Great Friends 525537	1,997		50.00	50

Friendship - M. Attwell

YEAR ISSUE		EDITION LIMIT	YEAR RETD.	ISSUE PRICE	*QUOTE U.S.$
1996	I'll Miss You 179183	Open		25.00	25
1996	I Love You This Much! 179191	Open		25.00	25
1996	Thinking of You 179213	Open		25.00	25
1996	You And Me 179205	Open		25.00	25

Holiday Snapshots - M. Attwell

YEAR ISSUE		EDITION LIMIT	YEAR RETD.	ISSUE PRICE	*QUOTE U.S.$
1995	I'll Help You Mommy 144673	Open		25.00	25
1995	Isn't She Pretty? 144681	Open		25.00	25
1995	I Didn't Mean To Do It 144703	Open		25.00	25
1995	Can I Open Just One? 144711	Open		25.00	25

A Loving Wish For You - M. Attwell

YEAR ISSUE		EDITION LIMIT	YEAR RETD.	ISSUE PRICE	*QUOTE U.S.$
1995	Happiness Is Our Wedding Wish 135178	Open		25.00	25
1995	A Blessed Day For You 135186	Open		25.00	25
1995	Wishing You A Bright Future 135194	Open		25.00	25
1995	An Anniversary Is Love 135208	Open		25.00	25
1995	A Birthday Wish For You 135216	Open		25.00	25
1995	Bless You, Little One 135224	Open		25.00	25
1996	You Are My Shining Star 164585	Open		25.00	25
1996	You Brighten My Days 164615	Open		25.00	25

Memories Of A Special Day - M. Attwell

YEAR ISSUE		EDITION LIMIT	YEAR RETD.	ISSUE PRICE	*QUOTE U.S.$
1994	Monday's Child... 531421	Open		35.00	35
1994	Tuesday's Child... 531448	Open		35.00	35
1994	Wednesday's Child... 531405	Open		35.00	35

*Quotes have been rounded up to nearest dollar

Memories of Yesterday/Enesco Corp.
to Midwest of Cannon Falls

FIGURINES

YEAR ISSUE		EDITION LIMIT	YEAR RETD.	ISSUE PRICE	*QUOTE U.S.$
1994	Thursday's Child... 531413	Open		35.00	35
1994	Friday's Child... 531391	Open		35.00	35
1994	Saturday's Child... 531383	Open		35.00	35
1994	Sunday's Child... 531480	Open		35.00	35
1994	Collector's Commemorative Edition Set of 7, Hand-numbered 528056	1,994	1994	250.00	250

Nativity - M. Attwell

1994	Nativity Set of 4 602949	Open		90.00	90
1995	Innkeeper 602892	Open		27.50	28
1996	Shepherd 602906	Open		27.50	28

Once Upon A Fairy Tale™... - M. Attwell

1992	Mother Goose 526428	18,000		50.00	50
1993	Mary, Mary Quite Contrary 526436	18,000		45.00	45
1993	Little Miss Muffett 526444	18,000		50.00	50
1992	Simple Simon 526452	18,000		35.00	35
1992	Mary Had A Little Lamb 526479	18,000		45.00	45
1994	Tweedle Dum & Tweedle Dee 526460	10,000		50.00	50

A Penny For Your Thoughts - M. Attwell

1997	You're Nice 204722	Open		20.00	20
1997	Now Do You Love Me Or Do You Don't 204730	Open		20.00	20
1997	Roses Are Red, Violets Are Blue-Violets Are Sweet, An' So Are You 204757	Open		20.00	20

Peter Pan - M. Attwell

1996	John 165441	Open		25.00	25
1996	Michael 165425	Open		30.00	30
1996	Peter Pan 164666	Open		25.00	25
1996	Wendy 164674	Open		25.00	25

Special Edition - M. Attwell

1989	As Good As His Mother Ever Made 523925	9,600	1989	32.50	114-150
1988	Mommy, I Teared It 523488	10,000	1988	25.00	175-325
1990	A Lapful of Luck 525014	5,000	1990	30.00	114-180
1990	Set of Three	N/A		87.50	735

When I Grow Up - M. Attwell

1995	When I Grow Up, I Want To Be A Doctor 102997	Open		25.00	25
1995	When I Grow Up, I Want To Be A Mother 103195	Open		25.00	25
1995	When I Grow Up, I Want To Be A Ballerina 103209	Open		25.00	25
1995	When I Grow Up, I Want To Be A Teacher 103357	Open		25.00	25
1995	When I Grow Up, I Want To Be A Fireman 103462	Open		25.00	25
1995	When I Grow Up, I Want To Be A Nurse 103535	Open		25.00	25
1996	When I Grow Up, I Want To Be A Businessman 164623	Open		25.00	25
1996	When I Grow Up, I Want To Be A Businesswoman 164631	Open		25.00	25

Midwest of Cannon Falls

Americana Nutcracker Collection - Midwest

1997	Uncle Sam 21166-3	500		170.00	170

Belenes Puig Nativity Collection - J.P. Llobera

1989	Angel 02087-6	Open		50.00	55
1989	Baby Jesus 02085-2	Open		62.00	62
1989	Donkey 02082-1	Open		26.00	26
1989	Joseph 02086-9	Open		62.00	62
1989	Mother Mary 02084-5	Open		62.00	62
1985	Nativity, set/6: Holy Family, Angel, Animals 6 3/4" 00205-6	Open		250.00	250
1989	Ox 02083-8	Open		26.00	26
1990	Resting Camel 04025-6	Open		115.00	115
1986	Sheep, set/3 00475-3	Open		28.00	28
1987	Shepherd & Angel Scene, set/7 06084-1	Open		305.00	305
1989	Shepherd Carrying Lamb 02092-0	Open		56.00	56
1989	Shepherd with Staff 02091-3	Open		56.00	56
1985	Shepherd, set/2 00458-6	Open		110.00	110
1988	Standing Camel 08792-3	Open		115.00	115
1989	Wise Man with Frankincense 02088-3	Open		66.00	66
1989	Wise Man with Frankincense on Camel 02077-7	Open		155.00	156
1989	Wise Man with Gold 02089-0	Open		66.00	66
1989	Wise Man with Gold on Camel 02075-3	Open		155.00	156
1989	Wise Man with Myrrh 02090-6	Open		66.00	66
1989	Wise Man with Myrrh on Camel 02076-0	Open		155.00	156
1985	Wise Men, set/3 00459-3	Open		185.00	185

Cooperstown Collection - Midwest

1997	Chicago Cubs Baseball Player 22868-5	Open		180.00	180
1997	Chicago White Sox Baseball Player 22867-8	Open		180.00	180
1997	New York Yankees Baseball Player 22869-2	Open		180.00	180

Eddie Walker Collection - E. Walker

1995	Noah's Ark Set 15155-6	2,500	1996	175.00	175
1997	North Pole Express Train Set 21569-2	7,500		200.00	200
1996	Santa in Sleigh with Reindeer 17803-4	6,000	1996	180.00	180
1997	Signature Santa-1997 21919-5	Yr.Iss.		50.00	50

Leo R. Smith III Collection - L. R. Smith

1997	American Heritage Santa 21318-6	750		110.00	110
1996	Angel of the Morning 18232-1	1,000		48.00	50
1995	Angel with Lion and Lamb 13990-5	1,500	1995	125.00	175
1995	Circle of Nature Wreath 16120-3	500	1996	200.00	200
1991	Cossack Santa 01092-1	1,700	1993	103.00	185
1993	Dancing Santa 09042-8	5,000	1995	170.00	170
1992	Dreams of Night Buffalo 07999-7	1,062	1996	250.00	270
1991	Fisherman Santa 03311-1	4,000	1995	270.00	350-475
1993	Folk Angel 05444-4	2,095	1995	145.00	250
1995	Gardening Angel 16118-0	2,500	1996	130.00	150
1997	Gardening Santa 21320-9	1,000		110.00	110
1994	Gift Giver Santa 12056-9	1,500	1996	180.00	180
1993	Gnome Santa on Deer 05206-8	1,463	1996	270.00	270
1992	Great Plains Santa 08049-8	5,000	1994	270.00	400-500
1995	Hare Leaping Over the Garden 16121-0	750	1996	100.00	100
1996	Jolly Boatman Santa 17794-5	1,500		180.00	180
1992	Leo Smith Name Plaque 07881-5	5,000		12.00	12
1995	Maize Maiden Angel 13992-9	2,500	1996	45.00	50
1991	Milkmaker 03541-2	5,000	1994	170.00	184
1992	Ms. Liberty 07866-2	5,000	1994	190.00	250-300
1994	Old-World Santa 12053-8	1,500	1994	75.00	200-250
1995	Orchard Santa 13989-9	1,500	1996	125.00	125
1995	Otter Wall Hanging 16122-7	750	1996	150.00	200
1995	Owl Lady 13988-2	1,000	1995	100.00	105
1991	Pilgrim Man 03313-5	5,000	1994	84.00	200
1991	Pilgrim Riding Turkey 03312-8	1,811	1994	230.00	350-500
1991	Pilgrim Woman 03315-9	5,000	1995	84.00	200
1996	Prairie Moon Market 17793-8	750		300.00	300
1993	Santa Fisherman 08979-8	1,748		250.00	300
1996	Santa in Red Convertible 17790-7	2,000		100.00	100
1995	Santa in Sleigh 13987-5	1,500	1996	125.00	250
1992	Santa of Peace 07328-5	5,000	1994	250.00	350-400
1997	Santa on Horse 21327-8	1,000		150.00	150
1994	Santa Skier 12054-5	1,500	1995	190.00	200
1997	Snow King 21319-3	1,000		100.00	100
1996	Snowflake in Nature Santa 17791-4	1,500		125.00	125
1994	Star of the Roundup Cowboy 11966-1	1,500	1996	100.00	100
1991	Stars and Stripes Santa 01743-2	5,000	1994	190.00	350-400
1995	Sunbringer Santa 13991-2	1,500	1996	125.00	125
1996	SW Bach Santa 17792-1	1,500		125.00	125
1991	Tis a Witching Time 03544-3	609	1991	140.00	1500
1991	Toymaker 03540-5	5,000	1994	120.00	200
1997	Victorian Santa 21317-9	1,000		130.00	130
1993	Voyageur 09043-5	788	1996	170.00	170
1994	Weatherwise Angel 12055-2	1,500	1996	150.00	150
1995	Wee Willie Santa 13993-6	2,500	1995	50.00	50
1997	White Nite Nick 21316-2	1,000		130.00	130
1992	Woodland Brave 07867-9	1,500	1993	87.00	350-450
1991	Woodsman Santa 03310-4	5,000	1995	230.00	300-350

Ore Mountain "A Christmas Carol" Nutcrackers - Midwest

1993	Bob Cratchit, 09421-1	5,000	1995	120.00	130
1994	Ghost of Christmas Future, 10449-1	1,500	1995	116.00	125
1994	Ghost of Christmas Past, 10447-7	1,500	1995	116.00	125
1993	Ghost of Christmas Present 12041-5	1,500	1996	116.00	200
1994	Marley's Ghost, 10448-4	1,500	1995	116.00	125
1993	Scrooge, 05522-9	2,500	1995	104.00	125

Ore Mountain "Nutcracker Fantasy" Nutcrackers - Midwest

1995	Clara, 12801-5	5,000		125.00	137
1991	Clara, 8" 01254-3	Retrd.	1995	77.00	100
1994	Herr Drosselmeyer, 10456-9	5,000		110.00	137
1988	Herr Drosselmeyer, 14 1/2" 07506-7	Retrd.	1996	75.00	115
1993	The Mouse King, 05350-8	5,000		100.00	125
1988	The Mouse King, 10" 07509-8	Open		60.00	85
1994	Nutcracker Prince, 11001-0	5,000		104.00	125
1988	The Prince, 12 3/4" 07507-4	Open		75.00	105
1988	The Toy Soldier, 11" 07508-1	Retrd.	1996	70.00	95
1995	Toy Soldier, 12804-6	5,000		125.00	125

Ore Mountain Easter Nutcrackers - Midwest

1992	Bunny Painter, 06480-1	Retrd.	1993	77.00	80
1991	Bunny with Egg, 00145-5	Retrd.	1993	77.00	80
1984	March Hare, 00312-1	Retrd.	1993	77.00	80

Ore Mountain Nutcracker Collection - Midwest

1995	American Country Santa, 13195-4	Retrd.	1996	165.00	170
1997	Angel w/Horn 21178-6	Open		250.00	250
1996	Angel with Candle 17010-6	Open		220.00	240
1994	Annie Oakley, 10464-4	Retrd.	1995	128.00	130
1996	Attorney 17012-0	Open		120.00	130
1995	August the Strong, 13185-5	Retrd.	1996	190.00	190
1997	Ballerina 21180-9	Open		165.00	165
1995	Barbeque Dad, 13193-0	Retrd.	1996	176.00	176
1994	Baseball Player, 10459-0	Retrd.	1995	111.00	120
1995	Basketball Player, 12784-1	Retrd.	1996	135.00	135
1995	Beefeater, 12797-1	Retrd.	1996	175.00	177
1997	Bell-shaped Hunter 21172-4	Open		130.00	130
1997	Bell-shaped Santa 21169-4	Open		130.00	130
1994	Black Santa, 10460-6	Retrd.	1995	74.00	74
1993	Cat Witch, 09426-6	Retrd.	1995	93.00	93
1994	Cavalier, 12952-4	Open		80.00	100
1994	Cavalier, 12953-1	Open		65.00	80
1994	Cavalier, 12958-6	Open		57.00	70
1996	Chimney Sweep 17043-4	Open		120.00	120
1995	Chimney Sweep, 00326-8	Open		70.00	76
1992	Christopher Columbus, 00152-3	Retrd.	1992	80.00	80
1991	Clown, 03561-0	Retrd.	1994	115.00	118
1994	Confederate Soldier, 12837-4	Retrd.	1996	93.00	110
1996	Count Dracula 17050-2	Open		150.00	150
1989	Country Santa, 09326-9	Retrd.	1995	95.00	150
1996	Cow Farmer 17054-0	Open		120.00	145
1992	Cowboy, 00298-8	Retrd.	1995	97.00	150
1997	Doctor 21173-1	Open		75.00	75
1995	Downhill Santa Skier, 13197-8	Open		145.00	150
1996	Drummer 17044-1	Open		120.00	120
1996	East Coast Santa 17047-2	Open		200.00	220
1990	Elf, 04154-3	Retrd.	1993	70.00	73
1996	Emergency Medical Technician 17013-7	Open		140.00	140
1994	Engineer, 10454-5	Retrd.	1995	108.00	108
1992	Farmer, 01109-6	Retrd.	1994	65.00	77
1996	Female Farmer 17011-3	1,000		145.00	180
1997	Fireman 21170-0	Open		75.00	75
1993	Fireman with Dog, 06592-1	Retrd.	1996	134.00	145
1997	Fisherman 21168-7	Open		165.00	165
1989	Fisherman, 09327-6	Retrd.	1995	90.00	100
1996	Frankenstein 17009-0	Open		170.00	190
1997	Gardener 21165-6	Open		160.00	160
1994	Gardening Lady, 10450-7	Retrd.	1996	104.00	112
1993	Gepetto Santa, 09417-4	Retrd.	1995	115.00	115
1989	Golfer, 09325-2	Retrd.	1994	85.00	90
1996	Guard 17046-5	Open		120.00	120
1995	Handyman, 12806-0	Retrd.	1996	136.00	137
1996	Harlequin Santa 17174-5	Open		150.00	160
1997	Hippie 21184-7	Open		145.00	145
1995	Hockey Player, 12783-4	Retrd.	1996	155.00	155
1995	Hunter Nutcracker 12785-8	Retrd.	1996	136.00	136
1992	Indian, 00195-0	Retrd.	1994	96.00	100
1995	Jack Frost, 12803-9	Open		150.00	150
1997	Jazz Musician 21177-9	Open		200.00	200
1995	Jolly St. Nick with Toys, 13709-3	Retrd.	1996	135.00	135
1995	King Richard the Lionhearted, 12798-8	Retrd.	1996	165.00	165
1996	King with Sceptor 17045-8	Open		120.00	120
1995	Law Scholar, 12789-6	Retrd.	1996	127.00	127
1996	Male Farmer 17015-1	1,000		145.00	145
1990	Merlin the Magician, 04207-6	Retrd.	1995	67.00	75
1994	Miner, 10493-4	Retrd.	1995	110.00	120
1994	Nature Lover, 10446-0	Retrd.	1995	112.00	112
1997	Noah 21181-6	Open		150.00	150
1988	Nordic Santa, 08872-2	Retrd.	1995	84.00	110
1996	Northwoods Santa 17048-9	Open		200.00	220
1991	Nutcracker-Maker, 03601-3	Retrd.	1993	62.00	65
1995	Peddler, 12805-3	Retrd.	1996	140.00	140
1995	Pierre Le Chef, 12802-2	Retrd.	1996	147.00	147
1992	Pilgrim, 00188-2	Retrd.	1994	96.00	100
1994	Pinecone Santa, 10461-3	Retrd.	1994	92.00	92
1984	Pinocchio, 00160-8	Retrd.	1996	60.00	68
1995	Pizza Baker, 13194-7	Retrd.	1996	170.00	170
1997	Policeman 21171-7	Open		75.00	75
1997	Portly Carpenter 21287-5	Open		150.00	150
1997	Portly Chef 21163-2	Open		150.00	150
1997	Portly Santa w/Gifts 21164-9	Open		150.00	150
1996	Prince 17038-0	Open		120.00	120
1994	Prince Charming, 10457-6	Retrd.	1994	125.00	130
1994	Pumpkin Head Scarecrow, 10451-1	Retrd.	1996	127.00	140
1994	Regal Prince, 10452-1	Retrd.	1996	140.00	152
1992	Ringmaster, 00196-7	Retrd.	1993	135.00	137
1995	Riverboat Gambler, 12787-2	Retrd.	1996	137.00	140
1995	Royal Lion, 13985-1	Retrd.	1996	130.00	140
1995	Santa at Workbench, 13335-4	Retrd.	1996	130.00	130
1994	Santa in Nightshirt, 10462-0	Retrd.	1995	108.00	120
1996	Santa One-Man Band Musical 17051-9	Open		170.00	175
1988	Santa w/Tree & Toys, 07666-8	Retrd.	1993	76.00	87
1993	Santa with Animals, 09424-2	Retrd.	1994	117.00	117
1994	Santa with Basket, 10472-9	Retrd.	1996	80.00	100
1992	Santa with Skis, 01305-2	Retrd.	1994	100.00	110
1990	Sea Captain, 04157-4	Retrd.	1994	86.00	95
1997	Skier 21176-2	Open		180.00	180
1997	Skiing Santa 21252-3	Open		170.00	170
1994	Snow King, 10470-5	Retrd.	1995	108.00	120
1997	Snowman 21183-0	Open		130.00	130
1994	Soccer Player, 10494-1	Retrd.	1995	97.00	107
1994	Sorcerer, 10471-2	Retrd.	1995	100.00	100
1996	Sports Fan 17173-8	Open		120.00	125
1994	Sultan King, 10455-2	Retrd.	1995	130.00	145
1995	Teacher, 13196-1	Retrd.	1996	165.00	165
1994	Toy Vendor, 11987-7	Retrd.	1996	124.00	145
1990	Uncle Sam, 04206-9	Retrd.	1993	50.00	62
1994	Union Soldier, 12836-7	Retrd.	1996	93.00	105
1996	Victorian Santa 17172-1	Open		180.00	185
1992	Victorian Santa, 00187-5	Retrd.	1994	130.00	140
1996	Western 17049-6	Open		250.00	250
1997	White Santa with Wreath 21175-5	Open		175.00	175
1993	White Santa, 09533-1	Retrd.	1995	100.00	100
1990	Windsor Club, 04160-4	Retrd.	1994	85.00	87
1990	Witch, 04159-8	Retrd.	1995	75.00	76

*Quotes have been rounded up to nearest dollar

FIGURINES

Midwest of Cannon Falls
to Old World Christmas

YEAR ISSUE		EDITION LIMIT	YEAR RETD.	ISSUE PRICE	*QUOTE U.S.$
1990	Woodland Santa, 04191-8	Retrd.	1995	105.00	150

Wendt and Kuhn Collection - Wendt/Kuhn

YEAR ISSUE		EDITION LIMIT	YEAR RETD.	ISSUE PRICE	*QUOTE U.S.$
1989	Angel at Piano 09403-7	Open		31.00	37
1983	Angel Brass Musicians, set/6 00470-8	Open		92.00	110
1983	Angel Conductor on Stand 00469-2	Open		21.00	28
1990	Angel Duet in Celestial Stars 04158-1	Retrd.	1994	60.00	63
1983	Angel Percussion Musicians set/6 00443-2	Open		110.00	145
1979	Angel Playing Violin 00403-6	Retrd.	1994	34.00	35
1980	Angel Pulling Wagon 00553-8	Retrd.	1995	43.00	50
1983	Angel String & Woodwind Musicians, set/6 00465-4	Open		108.00	140
1983	Angel String Musicians, set/6 00455-5	Retrd.	1995	105.00	120
1979	Angel Trio, set/3 00471-5	Open		140.00	185
1981	Angel w/Tree & Basket 01190-8	Retrd.	1993	24.00	25
1976	Angel with Sled 02940-4	Retrd.	1994	36.50	38
1981	Angels at Cradle, set/4 01193-5	Open		73.00	92
1996	Angels Bearing Gifts 17039-7	Open		120.00	130
1984	Angels Bearing Toys, set/6 00451-7	Retrd.	1995	97.00	110
1979	Bavarian Moving Van 02854-4	Open		134.00	174
1991	Birdhouse 01209-3	Retrd.	1994	22.50	23
1996	Blueberry Children 17040-3	Open		110.00	120
1991	Boy on Rocking Horse, 2 asst. 01202-4	Retrd.	1994	35.00	36
1994	Busy Elf, 3 asst. 12856-5	Open		22.00	25
1987	Child on Skis, 2 asst. 06083-4	Retrd.	1994	28.00	29
1987	Child on Sled 06085-8	Retrd.	1994	25.50	27
1994	Child with Flowers Set 12947-0	Retrd.	1996	45.00	50
1991	Display Base for Wendt und Kuhn Figures, 12 1/2 x 2" 01214-7	Open		32.00	45
1997	Flower Children Place Card Holder, set/6 22736-7	Open		150.00	150
1991	Flower Children, set/6 01213-0	Open		130.00	157
1979	Girl w/Cradle, set/2 01203-1	Retrd.	1994	37.50	40
1979	Girl w/Porridge Bowl 01198-0	Open		29.00	34
1979	Girl w/Scissors 01197-3	Open		25.00	32
1983	Girl w/Wagon 01196-6	Retrd.	1994	27.00	29
1991	Girl with Doll 01200-0	Open		31.50	37
1980	Little People Napkin Rings 6 asst. 03504-7	Open		21.00	28
1988	Lucia Parade Figures, set/3 07667-5	Retrd.	1995	75.00	80
1978	Madonna w/Child 01207-9	Open		120.00	153
1979	Magarita Angels, set/6 02938-1	Open		94.00	125
1983	Margarita Birthday Angels, set/3 00100-7	Retrd.	1995	44.00	[illegible]
1979	Pied Piper and Children, set/7 02843-8	Retrd.	1994	120.00	130
1981	Santa w/Angel in Sleigh 01192-8	Retrd.	1995	52.00	60
1976	Santa with Angel 00473-9	Open		50.00	55
1994	Santa with Tree 12942-5	Open		29.00	34
1994	Sun, Moon, Star Set 12943-2	Open		69.00	128
1992	Wendt und Kuhn Display Sign w/ Sitting Angel 07535-7	Retrd.	1996	20.00	23
1991	White Angel with Violin 01205-5	Retrd.	1993	25.50	27

Wendt and Kuhn Collection Music Boxes - Wendt/Kuhn

YEAR ISSUE		EDITION LIMIT	YEAR RETD.	ISSUE PRICE	*QUOTE U.S.$
1978	Angel at Pipe Organ 01929-0	Open		176.00	230
1996	Angel Musicians Music Box 17036-6	Open		260.00	270
1994	Angel Under Stars Crank Music Box 12974-6	300		150.00	190
1991	Angels & Santa Around Tree 01211-6	Open		300.00	370
1996	Children Around Tree Music Box 17037-3	Open		330.00	350
1976	Girl Rocking Cradle 09215-6	Retrd.	1994	180.00	190
1978	Rotating Angels 'Round Cradle 01911-5	Open		270.00	336

Wendt and Kuhn Figurines Candleholders - Wendt/Kuhn

YEAR ISSUE		EDITION LIMIT	YEAR RETD.	ISSUE PRICE	*QUOTE U.S.$
1976	Angel Candleholder Pair 00472-2	Open		70.00	94
1991	Angel with Friend Candleholder 01191-1	Retrd.	1994	33.30	34
1994	Angel with Wagon Candleholder 12860-2	Open		35.00	44
1980	Large Angel Candleholder Pair 01201-7	Retrd.	1994	270.00	277
1996	Orchestra Stand Candleholder 17042-7	Open		130.00	145
1986	Pair of Angels Candleholder 01204-8	Retrd.	1994	30.00	32
1987	Santa Candleholder 06082-7	Retrd.	1994	53.00	54
1991	Small Angel Candleholder Pair 01195-9	Retrd.	1994	60.00	63
1991	White Angel Candleholder 01206-2	Retrd.	1994	28.00	29

Miss Martha's Collection/Enesco Corporation

Miss Martha's Collection - M. Root

YEAR ISSUE		EDITION LIMIT	YEAR RETD.	ISSUE PRICE	*QUOTE U.S.$
1993	Erin-Don't Worry Santa Won't Forget Us 307246	Retrd.	1994	55.00	110
1993	Amber-Mr. Snowman! (waterglobe) 310476	Closed	1994	50.00	100
1993	Kekisha-Heavenly Peace Musical 310484	Closed	1994	60.00	120
1993	Whitney-Let's Have Another Party 321559	Closed	1994	45.00	90
1993	Megan-My Birthday Cake! 321567	Closed	1994	60.00	100-120
1993	Doug-I'm Not Showin' Off 321575	Closed	1994	40.00	80
1993	Francie-Such A Precious Gift! 321583	Closed	1994	50.00	100
1993	Alicia-A Blessing From God 321591	Closed	1994	40.00	80
1993	Anita-It's For You, Mama! 321605	Closed	1994	45.00	80
1994	Jeffrey-Bein' A Fireman Sure Is Hot & Thirsty Work 350206	Closed	1994	40.00	80
1993	Jess-I Can Fly 350516	Retrd.	1994	45.00	90
1993	Ruth-Littlest Angel Figurine 350524	Closed	1994	40.00	80
1993	Stephen-I'll Be The Best Shepherd In The World! 350540	Closed	1994	40.00	80
1993	Jonathon-Maybe I Can Be Like Santa 350559	Closed	1994	45.00	90
1994	Charlotte-You Can Be Whatever You Dream 353191	Closed	1994	40.00	70-90
1992	Lillie-Christmas Dinner! 369373	Retrd.	1993	55.00	110
1992	Eddie-What A Nice Surprise! 369381	Retrd.	1994	50.00	100
1992	Kekisha-Heavenly Peace 421456	Closed	1994	40.00	80
1992	Angela-I Have Wings 421464	Closed	1994	45.00	90
1992	Amber-Mr. Snowman 421472	Retrd.	1993	60.00	120
1992	Mar/Jsh/Christopher-Hush Baby! It's Your B-day! Musical 431362	Closed	1994	80.00	160
1992	Carrie-God Bless America 440035	Closed	1994	45.00	90
1993	Hallie-Sing Praises To The Lord 443166	Retrd.	1993	60.00	100-120
1991	Jana-Plant With Love 443174	Closed	1994	40.00	80
1991	Hallie-Sing Praises To The Lord 443182	Closed	1994	37.50	75
1992	Belle/Maize-Not Now, Muffin 443204	Retrd.	1993	50.00	100
1991	Sammy/Leisha-Sister's First Day Of School 443190	Retrd.	1993	55.00	90-110
1991	Nate-Hope You Hear My Prayer, Lord 443212	Closed	1994	17.50	55
1991	Sadie-They Can't Find Us Here 443220	Retrd.	1993	45.00	90
1992	Patsy-Clean Clothes For Dolly 443239	Retrd.	1993	50.00	100
1991	Dawn-Pretty Please, Mama 443247	Closed	1994	40.00	80
1991	Tonya-Hush, Puppy Dear 443255	Closed	1994	50.00	90-100
1991	Jenny/Jeremiah-Birthday Biscuits, With Love... 443263	Retrd.	1993	60.00	100-120
1991	Suzi-Mama, Watch Me! 443271	Retrd.	1993	35.00	60-70
1992	Mattie-Sweet Child 443298	Retrd.	1993	30.00	60
1992	Sara Lou-Here, Lammie 443301	Retrd.	1993	50.00	90-100
1992	Angel Tree Topper 446521	Closed	1994	80.00	225
1992	Mar/Jsh/Christopher-Hush, Baby! It's Your B-day Figurine 448354	Closed	1994	55.00	110

Mr. Sandman

Bearhugs - J. Willis

YEAR ISSUE		EDITION LIMIT	YEAR RETD.	ISSUE PRICE	*QUOTE U.S.$
1997	After All These Years, brown	Open		8.00	8
1997	After All These Years, white	Open		8.00	8
1996	Best Buddies, brown	Open		8.00	8
1996	Best Buddies, white	Open		8.00	8
1997	Family Portrait, brown	Open		8.00	8
1997	Family Portrait, white	Open		8.00	8
1997	Horsing Around, brown	Open		8.00	8
1997	Horsing Around, white	Open		8.00	8
1997	Lean on Me, brown	Open		8.00	8
1997	Lean on Me, white	Open		8.00	8
1996	Mama's Love, brown	Open		8.00	8
1996	Mama's Love, white	Open		8.00	8
1997	Once Upon A Time, brown	Open		8.00	8
1997	Once Upon A Time, white	Open		8.00	8
1996	Reunited, brown	Open		8.00	8
1996	Reunited, white	Open		8.00	8
1997	Rock-A-Bye, brown	Open		8.00	8
1997	Rock-A-Bye, white	Open		8.00	8
1997	Tickle Time, brown	Open		8.00	8
1997	Tickle Time, white	Open		8.00	8
1996	Two Step, brown	Open		8.00	8
1996	Two Step, white	Open		8.00	8
1997	You're The Best, brown	Open		8.00	8
1997	You're The Best, white	Open		8.00	8

Museum Collections, Inc.

American Family I - N. Rockwell

YEAR ISSUE		EDITION LIMIT	YEAR RETD.	ISSUE PRICE	*QUOTE U.S.$
1979	Baby's First Step	22,500		90.00	200-225
1980	Birthday Party	22,500		110.00	150
1981	Bride and Groom	22,500		110.00	125
1980	First Haircut	22,500		90.00	150
1980	First Prom	22,500		90.00	135
1980	Happy Birthday, Dear Mother	22,500		90.00	135
1980	Little Mother	22,500		110.00	125
1981	Mother's Little Helpers	22,500		110.00	135
1980	The Student	22,500		110.00	175
1980	Sweet Sixteen	22,500		90.00	125
1980	Washing Our Dog	22,500		110.00	125
1980	Wrapping Christmas Presents	22,500		90.00	125

Christmas - N. Rockwell

YEAR ISSUE		EDITION LIMIT	YEAR RETD.	ISSUE PRICE	*QUOTE U.S.$
1980	Checking His List	Yr.Iss.		65.00	110
1983	High Hopes	Yr.Iss.		95.00	175
1981	Ringing in Good Cheer	Yr.Iss.		95.00	100
1984	Space Age Santa	Yr.Iss.		65.00	100
1982	Waiting for Santa	Yr.Iss.		95.00	110

Classic - N. Rockwell

YEAR ISSUE		EDITION LIMIT	YEAR RETD.	ISSUE PRICE	*QUOTE U.S.$
1984	All Wrapped Up	Closed		65.00	90-95
1980	Bedtime	Closed		65.00	90-95
1984	The Big Race	Closed		65.00	90-95
1983	Bored of Education	Closed		65.00	90-95
1983	Braving the Storm	Closed		65.00	150
1980	The Cobbler	Closed		65.00	125
1982	The Country Doctor	Closed		65.00	90-95
1981	A Dollhouse for Sis	Closed		65.00	90-95
1982	Dreams in the Antique Shop	Closed		65.00	90-95
1983	A Final Touch	Closed		65.00	90-95
1980	For A Good Boy	Closed		65.00	125
1984	Goin' Fishin'	Closed		65.00	90-95
1983	High Stepping	Closed		65.00	90-95
1982	The Kite Maker	Closed		65.00	100
1980	Lighthouse Keeper's Daughter	Closed		65.00	125
1980	Memories	Closed		65.00	150
1981	The Music Lesson	Closed		65.00	135
1981	Music Master	Closed		65.00	90-95
1981	Off to School	Closed		65.00	90-95
1981	Puppy Love	Closed		65.00	90-95
1984	Saturday's Hero	Closed		65.00	90-95
1983	A Special Treat	Closed		65.00	90-95
1982	Spring Fever	Closed		65.00	90-95
1980	The Toymaker	Closed		65.00	125
1981	While The Audience Waits	Closed		65.00	85
1983	Winter Fun	Closed		65.00	90-95
1982	Words of Wisdom	Closed		65.00	90-95

Commemorative - N. Rockwell

YEAR ISSUE		EDITION LIMIT	YEAR RETD.	ISSUE PRICE	*QUOTE U.S.$
1985	Another Masterpiece by Norman Rockwell	5,000		125.00	200-250
1981	Norman Rockwell Display	5,000		125.00	200-250
1983	Norman Rockwell, America's Artist	5,000		125.00	200-250
1984	Outward Bound	5,000		125.00	200-250
1986	The Painter and the Pups	5,000		125.00	250
1982	Spirit of America	5,000		125.00	200-250

Old World Christmas

Collectibles - O.W.C., unless otherwise noted

YEAR ISSUE		EDITION LIMIT	YEAR RETD.	ISSUE PRICE	*QUOTE U.S.$
1992	Candle Arch with Church 862	Retrd.	1993	28.50	50
1991	Carved Deer at Feeder, set/3 86104	Retrd.	1996	35.00	35
1990	Carved Deer w/Tree 8653	Retrd.	1996	12.00	12
1991	Carved Goats, set/3 86123 - Helbig	Retrd.	1996	55.00	55
1992	Church w/Choir Candle 8699	Retrd.	1996	40.00	40
1986	Hansel & Gretel Bank 86898	Retrd.	1996	35.00	[illegible]
[illegible]	Large Seiffener Candle Arch 8616	Retrd.	1994	450.00	495
1991	Nativity, 12 pc. 8657	Retrd.	1996	145.00	145
1990	Shaved Wood Tree 86020 - K.W.O	Retrd.	1996	12.00	12
1992	Weather House 86109	Retrd.	1994	31.50	37

Halloween - E.M. Merck

YEAR ISSUE		EDITION LIMIT	YEAR RETD.	ISSUE PRICE	*QUOTE U.S.$
1988	Black Cat on Wire 9208	Retrd.	1992	8.35	13
1989	Black Cat/Witch with Cart (A) 9251	Retrd.	1994	10.00	12
1989	Cast Iron Scarecrow 9218	Retrd.	1994	32.50	39
1987	Ghost Light 9205	Retrd.	1992	37.00	150-195
1989	Ghost Votive 9211	Retrd.	1994	8.50	12
1988	Haunted House Waterglobe 9206	Retrd.	1989	22.50	32
1987	Haunted House with Lights 9203	Retrd.	1994	99.50	150-200
1988	Large Pumpkin Bowl 9273	Retrd.	1994	18.50	20
1987	Lighted Ghost Dish 9204	Retrd.	1994	45.00	50
1988	Pumpkin Head on Wire 9207	Retrd.	1992	7.35	12
1987	Pumpkin Light with Ghosts 9201	Retrd.	1994	39.50	45
1987	Pumpkin Light w/Scarecrow 9202	Retrd.	1991	37.00	45
1988	Pumpkin Taper Holder 9272	Retrd.	1992	5.65	9
1988	Pumpkin Votive 9271	Retrd.	1991	8.90	12
1989	Witch on Moon Night Light 9212	Retrd.	1994	37.50	95
1988	Witch Taper Holder 9282	Retrd.	1993	11.00	19
1988	Witch Votive Holder 9281	Retrd.	1994	29.50	350

Night Lights - E.M. Merck

YEAR ISSUE		EDITION LIMIT	YEAR RETD.	ISSUE PRICE	*QUOTE U.S.$
1986	ABC Block 529713	Retrd.	1994	37.00	50
1986	Angel 529703	Retrd.	1992	18.00	125-150
1990	Father Christmas 529721	Retrd.	1992	45.00	200-400
1993	Father Christmas w/Toys 529727	Retrd.	1995	65.00	70
1985	Santa 529701	Retrd.	1987	37.00	600-750
1988	Santa Hugging Tree 529717	Retrd.	1990	42.00	400-625
1986	Santa in Chimney 529707	Retrd.	1988	37.00	400-650
1989	Santa on Locomotive 529719	Retrd.	1991	42.00	300-500
1992	Santa with Nutcracker 529725	Retrd.	1992	45.00	300-495
1991	Santa with Stocking 529723	Retrd.	1993	45.00	300-395
1987	Santa with Tree 529715	Retrd.	1989	39.50	300-600
1986	Snowman 529709	Retrd.	1988	37.00	200-225
1986	Teddy Bear 529711	Retrd.	1991	37.00	225

Nutcrackers - E.M. Merck, unless otherwise noted

YEAR ISSUE		EDITION LIMIT	YEAR RETD.	ISSUE PRICE	*QUOTE U.S.$
1987	Austrian Musketeer 72048 - K.W.O.	Retrd.	1995	57.50	58
1993	Bohemian Beekeeper 7264	Retrd.	1995	110.00	110
1993	Brandenburger Guard 7250	Retrd.	1994	110.00	125
1987	British Guard 72041 - K.W.O.	Retrd.	1995	60.00	60
1992	Carved Hunter 72213 - O.W.C.	Retrd.	1992	150.00	200-250
1993	Exceptional Guard 7231 - K.W.O.	50	1995	995.00	1100
1992	Exceptional King 7230	50	1994	950.00	1200-1400
1994	Exceptional Santa 7232 - Merten	Retrd.	1995	995.00	1200
1993	Falkensteiner Wizard 7261	Retrd.	1995	110.00	110
1991	Inlaid Natural King 7214 - O.W.C.	Retrd.	1992	150.00	195
1991	Inlaid Natural Muskateer 7225 - O.W.C.	Retrd.	1992	150.00	225-300
1992	Large Bavarian Duke 72242 - K.W.O.	Retrd.	1995	130.00	130
1992	Large British Guard 72141 - K.W.O.	Retrd.	1994	90.00	95

*Quotes have been rounded up to nearest dollar

Collectors' Information Bureau

101

FIGURINES

YEAR ISSUE		EDITION LIMIT	YEAR RETD.	ISSUE PRICE	*QUOTE U.S.$
1992	Large Carved Santa 7223 - K.W.O.	Retrd.	1994	175.00	180
1992	Large Dutch Guard 72140 - K.W.O.	Retrd.	1994	90.00	96
1991	Large Hunter 7228 - K.W.O.	Retrd.	1994	97.50	105
1993	Large King 72033 - K.W.O.	Retrd.	1994	79.95	85
1992	Large Prussian King 72244 - K.W.O.	Retrd.	1994	130.00	135
1992	Large Prussian Sargeant 72145 - K.W.O.	Retrd.	1995	90.00	90
1992	Large Saxon Duke 72241 - K.W.O.	Retrd.	1995	130.00	130
1992	Large Snow Prince 7277	Retrd.	1992	100.00	115
1989	Prussian Corporal 72047 - K.W.O.	Retrd.	1990	42.50	43
1987	Prussian Sergeant 72045 - K.W.O.	Retrd.	1995	60.00	60
1993	Rostocker Pirate 7252	Retrd.	1995	110.00	110
1993	Saalfelder Shepherd 7263	Retrd.	1995	110.00	110
1993	Seiffener Santa 7257	Retrd.	1994	110.00	115
1992	Skier 7294	Retrd.	1992	82.50	83
1993	Teddy Bear 7296	Retrd.	1994	135.00	150
1993	Tegernsee Golfer 7259	Retrd.	1995	135.00	135

Paper Maché - E.M. Merck

YEAR ISSUE		EDITION LIMIT	YEAR RETD.	ISSUE PRICE	*QUOTE U.S.$
1988	52 cm. Father Christmas 9652	Retrd.	1990	175.00	195
1988	Assorted Father Christmas 9615	Retrd.	1989	44.00	50
1989	Assorted Santas 9691	Retrd.	1991	35.00	43
1988	Blue Father Christmas 9602	Retrd.	1988	19.50	27
1988	Father Christmas (A) 9600	Retrd.	1988	19.50	27
1989	Father Christmas 9612	Retrd.	1989	38.50	45
1988	Father Christmas with Gifts 9610	Retrd.	1988	32.50	40
1989	Father Christmas w/Pack 9638	Retrd.	1989	40.00	47
1988	Red Father Christmas 9601	Retrd.	1988	19.50	25
1989	Santa in Sleigh 9672	Retrd.	1989	39.50	45
1988	Small Traditional Belznickel 9662	Retrd.	1994	35.00	40
1988	Traditional Belznickel 9661	Retrd.	1994	40.00	50
1988	White Father Christmas 9603	Retrd.	1988	19.50	30
1988	White Father Christmas 9616	Retrd.	1989	50.00	55

Porcelain Christmas - E.M. Merck

YEAR ISSUE		EDITION LIMIT	YEAR RETD.	ISSUE PRICE	*QUOTE U.S.$
1987	Angels, Set/3 9421	Retrd.	1987	15.50	21
1988	Bear on Skates Music Box 9492	Retrd.	1988	44.00	50
1988	Bunny on Skies Music Box 9491	Retrd.	1988	44.00	50
1987	Cast Iron Santa 9419	Retrd.	1993	35.00	47
1987	Cast Iron Santa on Horse 9418	Retrd.	1993	37.50	48
1987	Four Castles of Germany 9450	Retrd.	1988	31.00	52
1995	Mr. C's Roadster 9708	Retrd.	1994	9.95	14
1988	Penguin w/Gifts Music Box 9493	Retrd.	1988	44.00	65
1987	Roly-Poly Santa 9440	Retrd.	1987	27.00	35
1987	Santa Head Night Light 9412	Retrd.	1989	19.00	30
1987	Santa Head Stocking Holder 9414	Retrd.	1987	18.00	25
1987	Santa Head Votive 9411	Retrd.	1988	10.00	20
1987	Santa in Chimney Music Box 9413	Retrd.	1987	44.00	47
1988	Santa in Swing 9473	Retrd.	1988	6.25	12
1988	Santa on Polar Bear 9471	Retrd.	1988	6.25	12
1988	Santa on Teeter-Totter 9475	Retrd.	1988	6.25	12
1988	Santa Visiting Igloo 9476	Retrd.	1988	6.25	15
1988	Santa Visiting Lighthouse 9472	Retrd.	1988	6.25	12
1988	Santa with Angel 9474	Retrd.	1988	6.25	15
1995	Swinging into the Season 9705	Retrd.	1994	10.50	13

Pyramids - O.W.C., unless otherwise noted

YEAR ISSUE		EDITION LIMIT	YEAR RETD.	ISSUE PRICE	*QUOTE U.S.$
1992	3-Tier Forest 882	Retrd.	1995	225.00	225
1992	3-Tier Nativity 883	Retrd.	1995	250.00	250
1991	3-Tier Painted Nativity 8818	Retrd.	1993	225.00	260
1992	5ft Hand-Carved 884007	Retrd.	1992	1295.00	1325
1992	6ft Hand-Carved 884006	Retrd.	1992	4000.00	4500-5000
1991	Camel Caravan 8812	Retrd.	1995	92.50	93
1986	Deer w/Tree, Wall Pyramid 88137	Retrd.	1993	65.00	65
1992	Detailed Nativity 8851	Retrd.	1993	175.00	195
1991	Mini-Pyramid, Angels 8811	Retrd.	1993	22.50	23
1992	Mini-Pyramid, Santa 8820	Retrd.	1994	32.50	40
1992	Miniature Choir 885	Retrd.	1995	35.00	35
1992	Miniature Forest 884	Retrd.	1994	35.00	40
1992	Miniature Music Band 886	Retrd.	1993	30.00	30
1991	Musical 4-Tier 8815	Retrd.	1991	775.00	825
1992	Natural with Deer 8821	Retrd.	1995	65.00	65
1992	Santa with Angels 887	Retrd.	1993	175.00	195
1991	Santa with Train 8817	Retrd.	1991	62.50	95
1992	Small Choir 8879	Retrd.	1993	68.50	75
1992	Small Nativity 8822	Retrd.	1995	110.00	110
1992	Small Nativity 889	Retrd.	1993	82.00	90
1991	White 3-Tier 8816	Retrd.	1992	225.00	250
1992	White with Angels 8824	Retrd.	1993	55.00	75

Smoking Men - O.W.C., unless otherwise noted

YEAR ISSUE		EDITION LIMIT	YEAR RETD.	ISSUE PRICE	*QUOTE U.S.$
1992	Alpenhorn Player 7058	Retrd.	1995	70.00	70
1988	Antique Style Coachman 70053 - K.W.O.	Retrd.	1988	28.00	35
1988	Antique Style Cook 70052 - K.W.O.	Retrd.	1989	27.50	33
1986	Artist 7020 - E.M. Merck	Retrd.	1993	55.00	60
1991	Baker 7044	Retrd.	1992	49.50	55
1992	Basket Peddler 7040	Retrd.	1993	130.00	140
1991	Bavarian Hunter 7032	Retrd.	1994	79.50	85
1991	Beer Drinker 7033	Retrd.	1994	67.50	72
1991	Bird Seller 7014	Retrd.	1992	50.00	55
1991	Butcher 7043	Retrd.	1992	49.50	55
1986	Carved Hunter 70100	Retrd.	1991	90.00	97
1992	Carved Hunter 7054	Retrd.	1993	200.00	245
1992	Carved King 7072	Retrd.	1995	68.50	69
1992	Carved Shepherd 7053	Retrd.	1993	150.00	195
1992	Carved Woodsman 7015	Retrd.	1994	67.50	75
1991	Champion Archer 7041	Retrd.	1995	67.50	68
1989	Chimney Sweep 7017 - E.M. Merck	Retrd.	1993	55.00	55
1992	Clock Salesman 7039	Retrd.	1992	275.00	495
1990	Coachman 70062 - K.W.O.	Retrd.	1996	50.00	50
1991	Coachman 7057	Retrd.	1992	60.00	72
1991	Cook 7025	Retrd.	1993	55.00	60
1992	Farmer 7026	Retrd.	1993	55.00	60
1992	Farmer with Crate 7023	Retrd.	1994	150.00	175
1992	Father Christmas 70113-1	Retrd.	1989	45.00	60
1986	Father Christmas 702	Retrd.	1994	60.00	63
1991	Father Christmas 7051	Retrd.	1995	80.00	80
1993	Father Christmas 7063	Retrd.	1993	45.00	50
1986	Father Christmas w/Toys 7010	Retrd.	1992	60.00	68
1991	Fisherman 7029	Retrd.	1993	55.00	58
1991	Frosty Snowman 703	Retrd.	1993	22.50	31
1991	Gardener 7045	Retrd.	1992	49.50	56
1991	Gardner 7016 - E.M. Merck	Retrd.	1993	55.00	59
1992	Grandma 702622	Retrd.	1993	42.50	48
1985	Grandpa 702615	Retrd.	1993	42.50	46
1986	Hunter 701	Retrd.	1992	30.00	36
1991	Hunter 7018 - E.M. Merck	Retrd.	1993	55.00	60
1992	Hunter with Crate 7021	Retrd.	1994	150.00	180
1991	Ice Skater 7038 - E.M. Merck	Retrd.	1992	60.00	63
1992	Innkeeper 70268	Retrd.	1993	54.00	58
1991	Innkeeper 7037	Retrd.	1995	60.00	60
1992	King 70229 - E.M. Merck	Retrd.	1993	95.00	104
1986	Large Old World Santa 70203	Retrd.	1988	77.50	83
1992	Minstrel 7061	Retrd.	1994	85.00	85
1991	Mountain Climber 7036	Retrd.	1995	67.50	68
1991	Natural Father Christmas 7012	Retrd.	1992	60.00	69
1991	Natural Santa 706	Retrd.	1992	40.00	48
1991	Nightwatchman 7027	Retrd.	1993	55.00	59
1985	Nightwatchman 7034	Retrd.	1993	32.50	41
1986	Old World Santa 70204	Retrd.	1988	42.50	47
1991	Postman 7028	Retrd.	1993	55.00	59
1991	Prussian Soldier 7056	Retrd.	1993	60.00	63
1989	Santa 7086	Retrd.	1992	55.00	61
1991	Santa Claus 705	Retrd.	1993	45.00	51
1992	Santa in Crate 707	Retrd.	1994	165.00	215
1986	Santa Smoker/Candleholder 704	Retrd.	1994	55.00	58
1986	Skier 702616	Retrd.	1992	54.00	62
1992	Skier 7059	Retrd.	1995	59.50	60
1986	Small Old World Santa 70202	Retrd.	1988	37.50	44
1992	Small Santa 7011	Retrd.	1995	37.50	38
1985	Snowman 702621	Retrd.	1991	30.00	38
1991	Snowman on Skis 7092	Retrd.	1992	30.00	39
1988	Snowman with Bird 708	Retrd.	1993	26.00	35
1992	St. Peter 70228	Retrd.	1993	95.00	105
1991	Toy Peddler 7030	Retrd.	1993	60.00	60
1991	Toy Peddler 7055	Retrd.	1993	60.00	66
1992	Toy Peddler 7060	Retrd.	1994	110.00	150
1992	Tyrolian 702613	Retrd.	1993	45.00	50
1992	Witch 70543 - E.M. Merck	Retrd.	1993	49.50	56
1991	Wood Worker 7031	Retrd.	1994	79.50	85
1987	Woodcarver 70043 - K.W.O.	Retrd.	1990	40.00	47
1991	Woodsman 7013	Retrd.	1993	60.00	64
1991	Woodsman 7019 - E.M. Merck	Retrd.	1993	55.00	60

Olszewski Studios

Olszewski Studios - R. Olszewski

YEAR ISSUE		EDITION LIMIT	YEAR RETD.	ISSUE PRICE	*QUOTE U.S.$
1994	The Grand Entrance SM1	1,500	1994	225.00	325
1994	The Grand Entrance A/P SM1	120	1994	450.00	575
1994	Tinker's Treasure Chest SM2	Closed	1994	235.00	450-495
1994	Tinker's Treasure Chest A/P SM2	120	1994	470.00	470
1994	To Be (included w/Treasure Chest) SM3	Closed	1994	Set	Set
1994	To Be (included w/Treasure Chest) A/P SM3	120	1994	Set	Set
1994	The Little Tinker SM4	750	1995	235.00	295
1994	The Little Tinker A/P SM4	100	1995	470.00	470
1995	Special Treat SM5	800	1995	220.00	225
1995	Special Treat A/P SM5	100	1995	440.00	440
1995	Mocking Bird with Peach Blossoms SM6	800	1995	230.00	230
1995	Mocking Bird with Peach Blossoms A/P SM6	100	1995	460.00	460
1995	Lady With An Urn (brown, green, pink, blue dress) SM7	250	1995	235.00	235
1995	Lady With An Urn (brown, green, pink, blue dress) A/P SM7	124	1995	470.00	470
1995	Castle of Gleaming White Porcelain SM8	750	1995	285.00	285
1995	Castle of Gleaming White Porcelain A/P SM8	100	1995	570.00	570
1996	Spring Dance SM9	750	1996	210.00	210
1996	Spring Dance A/P SM9	100	1996	420.00	420
1996	Oriental Lovers SM11	750	1996	240.00	240
1996	Oriental Lovers A/P SM11	100	1996	480.00	480
1996	Dashing Through the Snow SM12	500	1996	480.00	480
1996	Dashing Through the Snow A/P SM12	100	1996	960.00	960
1996	The Viceroy SM13	750	1996	235.00	235
1996	The Viceroy A/P SM13	100	1996	470.00	470
1996	Little Red Riding Hood SM14	750	1996	225.00	225
1996	Little Red Riding Hood A/P SM14	100	1996	450.00	450
1996	The Departure (Sterling) SM1S	375	1996	325.00	325
1996	The Departure (Sterling) A/P SM1S	27	1996	650.00	650

Pacific Rim Import Corp.

Bunny Toes - Pacific Rim Team, unless otherwise noted

YEAR ISSUE		EDITION LIMIT	YEAR RETD.	ISSUE PRICE	*QUOTE U.S.$
1997	Annie on the Swing	Open		30.00	30
1995	Annie w/Strawberries - P. Sebern	Open		15.00	15
1997	Betsy Sews the Flag	Open		13.00	13
1996	Betsy-Celebrate	1,440		15.00	15
1995	Bunny Gazebo	Open		50.00	50
1995	Bunny Toes Sign - P. Sebern	Open		20.00	20
1995	Garden Trellis	Open		30.00	30
1995	Hannah Strolls With Carriage	Open		15.00	15
1995	Hannah With Maximillian	Retrd.	1997	13.00	13
1997	Hannah's Pride and Joy	Open		17.00	17
1997	Justin on Parade	Open		13.00	13
1996	Justin-Stars & Stripes	1,440		15.00	15
1994	Mazie at Play	Open		13.00	13
1997	Mazie Frolics	Open		15.00	15
1997	Miss Amanda's Class	Open		20.00	20
1997	Oh, Christmas Tree	Open		20.00	20
1994	Phoebe Goes Ballooning	Open		7.00	7
1995	Rustic Garden Accessory Group (6 pcs) - P. Sebern	Open		40.00	40
1994	Sophie Pops Out	Open		7.00	7
1997	Sophie Trims the Tree	Open		20.00	20
1995	Spring Garden Accessory Group (6 pcs) - P. Sebern	Open		40.00	40
1994	Sweethearts (lighted)	Open		50.00	50
1994	Tillie Making a Wreath	Open		13.00	13
1995	Tillie With Her Bike	Open		15.00	15
1997	Timothy & Tille Give Thanks	Open		20.00	20
1995	Timothy With Eggs	Open		13.00	13
1994	Timothy With Flower Cart	Open		17.00	17
1994	Timothy With Tulips	Open		13.00	13
1995	Tommy's Joy Ride - P. Sebern	Open		15.00	15
1994	Wendell at the Mail Box	Open		17.00	17
1995	Wendell Play The Cello	Open		13.00	13
1994	Wendell With Eggs in Hat	Open		13.00	13
1995	Wendell With Flowers	Retrd.	1997	13.00	13
1994	Willis & Skeeter	Open		17.00	17
1995	Willis & Skeeter Gardening	Open		15.00	15
1997	Winifred & Wendell Caroling	Open		20.00	20
1995	Winifred Paints Eggs	Open		15.00	15
1994	Winifred With Blooms	Open		13.00	13

Bunny Toes Birthday Bunnies - P. Sebern

YEAR ISSUE		EDITION LIMIT	YEAR RETD.	ISSUE PRICE	*QUOTE U.S.$
1995	Anabell Gliding Along	Open		20.00	20
1995	Beth Back to School	Open		20.00	20
1995	Callie Bundle Up	Open		20.00	20
1995	Carly Striking a Pose	Open		20.00	20
1995	Charlotte Best of the Bunch	Open		20.00	20
1995	Chester Sharing With Friends	Open		20.00	20
1995	Christopher & Cory The Best Shot	Open		20.00	20
1995	Dinah Irresistible	Open		20.00	20
1995	Douglas Frosty Friends	Open		20.00	20
1995	Goldie Taking Turns	Open		20.00	20
1995	Harvey Giddy-Up and Go	Open		20.00	20
1995	Jeremy Clear Sailing	Open		20.00	20
1995	Joey Autumn Chores	Open		20.00	20
1995	Maggie Joy of Giving	Open		20.00	20
1995	Molly Sweet Wishes	Open		20.00	20
1995	Nicholas Between Tides	Open		20.00	20
1995	Penelope Wishful Thinking	Open		20.00	20
1995	Phoebe First Outing	Open		20.00	20
1995	Pieter Higher Education	Open		20.00	20
1995	Russel & Robby Sharing the Harvest	Open		20.00	20
1995	Violet Thank You Notes	Open		20.00	20
1995	Wilbur Lazy Daze	Open		20.00	20
1995	Wiley Winter Games	Open		20.00	20
1995	Zachary Waitin' on the Wind	Open		20.00	20

When Grandma Was a Girl - Pacific Rim Team

YEAR ISSUE		EDITION LIMIT	YEAR RETD.	ISSUE PRICE	*QUOTE U.S.$
1996	Amanda with 5 Kittens	Open		20.00	20
1996	Ballerina Rebecca	Open		17.00	17
1996	Billy & Josie Bathe Pigs	Open		25.00	25
1996	Eliza & Mama	Open		25.00	25
1996	Ella, Cats & Fishbowl	Open		25.00	25
1996	Jen, Bess & Ann Skip Rope	Open		35.00	35
1996	Jonathan at Bat	Open		15.00	15
1996	Joshua & Grandpa	Open		25.00	25
1996	Mary, Claire & Wagon	Open		35.00	35
1996	Naomi & Hannah	Open		25.00	25
1996	Rose, Luke & Luster	Open		30.00	30
1996	Ruth & Abigail (Musical)	Open		35.00	35
1996	Verna & Thomas at Play	Open		25.00	25

Pemberton & Oakes

Zolan's Children - D. Zolan

YEAR ISSUE		EDITION LIMIT	YEAR RETD.	ISSUE PRICE	*QUOTE U.S.$
1982	Erik and the Dandelion	17,000		48.00	90
1983	Sabina in the Grass	6,800		48.00	115
1985	Tender Moment	10,000		29.00	80
1984	Winter Angel	8,000		28.00	150

PenDelfin

PenDelfin Family Circle Collectors' Club - J. Heap

YEAR ISSUE		EDITION LIMIT	YEAR RETD.	ISSUE PRICE	*QUOTE U.S.$
1993	Herald	Closed	1993	Gift	50
1993	Bosun	Closed	1993	50.00	100-150
1994	Buttons	Closed	1994	Gift	30
1994	Puffer	Closed	1995	85.00	85
1995	Bellman	Closed	1995	Gift	N/A
1995	Georgie and the Dragon	Closed	1995	125.00	125
1996	Newsie	Closed	1996	Gift	N/A
1996	Delia	Closed	1996	125.00	125

*Quotes have been rounded up to nearest dollar

YEAR ISSUE		EDITION LIMIT	YEAR RETD.	ISSUE PRICE	*QUOTE U.S.$
1997	Tom	Yr.Iss.		Gift	N/A
1997	Woody	Yr.Iss.		125.00	125

40th Anniversary Piece - PenDelfin

YEAR ISSUE		EDITION LIMIT	YEAR RETD.	ISSUE PRICE	*QUOTE U.S.$
1994	Aunt Ruby	10,000		275.00	275

Event Piece - J. Heap

YEAR ISSUE		EDITION LIMIT	YEAR RETD.	ISSUE PRICE	*QUOTE U.S.$
1994	Walmsley	Retrd.	1995	75.00	75
1995	Runaway	Retrd.	1995	90.00	90
1996	Event Piece	Retrd.	1996	85.00	85
1997	Event Piece	Yr.Iss.		N/A	N/A

Nursery Rhymes - Various

YEAR ISSUE		EDITION LIMIT	YEAR RETD.	ISSUE PRICE	*QUOTE U.S.$
1956	Little Bo Peep - J. Heap	Retrd.	1959	2.00	N/A
1956	Little Jack Horner - J. Heap	Retrd.	1959	2.00	N/A
1956	Mary Mary Quite Contrary - J. Heap	Retrd.	1959	2.00	N/A
1956	Miss Muffet - J. Heap	Retrd.	1959	2.00	N/A
1956	Tom Tom the Piper's Son - J. Heap	Retrd.	1959	2.00	N/A
1956	Wee Willie Winkie - J. Heap	Retrd.	1959	2.00	N/A

Retired Figurines - Various

YEAR ISSUE		EDITION LIMIT	YEAR RETD.	ISSUE PRICE	*QUOTE U.S.$
1985	Apple Barrel - J. Heap	Retrd.	1992	N/A	15-25
1963	Aunt Agatha - J. Heap	Retrd.	1965	N/A	1500-2000
1955	Balloon Woman - J. Heap	Retrd.	1956	1.00	N/A
1964	Bandstand - J. Heap	Retrd.	N/A	70.00	85
1967	The Bath Tub - J. Heap	Retrd.	1975	4.50	70-100
1955	Bell Man - J. Heap	Retrd.	1956	1.00	N/A
1984	Blossom - D. Roberts	Retrd.	1989	35.00	60-75
1955	Bobbin Woman - J. Heap	Retrd.	1956	N/A	N/A
1964	Bongo - D. Roberts	Retrd.	1987	31.00	75-150
1966	Cakestand - J. Heap	Retrd.	1972	2.00	250-500
1953	Cauldron Witch - J. Heap	Retrd.	1959	3.50	N/A
1959	Cha Cha - J. Heap	Retrd.	1961	N/A	1000-1200
1990	Charlotte - D. Roberts	Retrd.	1992	25.00	75-90
1989	Chirpy - D. Roberts	Retrd.	1992	31.50	60-100
1985	Christmas Set - D. Roberts	2,000	1989	N/A	450-550
1962	Cornish Prayer (Corny) - J. Heap	Retrd.	1965	N/A	500-900
1980	Crocker - D. Roberts	Retrd.	1989	20.00	60-75
1963	Cyril Squirrel - J. Heap	Retrd.	1965	N/A	750-1300
1955	Daisy Duck - J. Heap	Retrd.	1958	N/A	N/A
1956	Desmond Duck - J. Heap	Retrd.	1958	2.50	N/A
1964	Dodger - J. Heap	Retrd.	1996	24.00	28
1955	Elf - J. Heap	Retrd.	1956	1.00	N/A
1954	Fairy Jardiniere - N/A	Retrd.	1958	N/A	N/A
1953	The Fairy Shop - J. Heap	Retrd.	1958	N/A	N/A
1961	Father Mouse (grey) - J. Heap	Retrd.	1966	N/A	500-750
1955	Flying Witch - J. Heap	Retrd.	1956	1.00	N/A
[illegible]	Forty Winks - D. Roberts	Retrd.	1996	57.00	57
1969	The Gallery Series: Wakey, Pieface, Poppet, Robert, Dodger - J. Heap	Retrd.	1971	N/A	200-400
1961	Grand Stand (mold 1) - J. Heap	Retrd.	1969	35.00	400-775
1992	Grand Stand (mold 2)- J. Heap	Retrd.	1996	150.00	150
1960	Gussie - J. Heap	Retrd.	1968	N/A	400
1989	Honey - D. Roberts	Retrd.	1993	40.00	60
1988	Humphrey Go-Kart - J. Heap	Retrd.	1994	70.00	100
1986	Jim-Lad - D. Roberts	Retrd.	1992	22.50	45-75
1985	Jingle - D. Roberts	Retrd.	1992	11.25	25-45
1986	Little Mo - D. Roberts	Retrd.	1994	35.00	43
1961	Lollipop (grey) (Mouse) - J. Heap	Retrd.	1966	N/A	500-700
1960	Lucy Pocket - J. Heap	Retrd.	1967	4.20	300-400
1956	Manx Kitten - J. Heap	Retrd.	1958	2.00	N/A
1955	Margot - J. Heap	Retrd.	1961	2.00	350-550
1967	Maud - J. Heap	Retrd.	1970	N/A	300-550
1961	Megan - J. Heap	Retrd.	1967	3.00	400-500
1956	Midge (Replaced by Picnic Midge) - J. Heap	Retrd.	1965	2.00	300-600
1966	Milk Jug Stand - J. Heap	Retrd.	1972	2.00	250-500
1960	Model Stand - J. Heap	Retrd.	1964	4.00	400-750
1961	Mother Mouse (grey) - J. Heap	Retrd.	1966	N/A	450-800
1965	Mouse House (bronze) - J. Heap	Retrd.	1969	N/A	300-400
1965	Mouse House (stoneware) - J. Heap	Retrd.	N/A	N/A	500-700
1965	Muncher - D. Roberts	Retrd.	1983	26.00	60-100
1981	Nipper - D. Roberts	Retrd.	1989	20.50	75
1955	Old Adam - J. Heap	Retrd.	1956	4.00	N/A
1955	Old Father (remodeled)- J. Heap	Retrd.	1970	50.	700-1000
1957	Old Mother - J. Heap	Retrd.	1978	6.25	550-800
1984	Oliver - D. Roberts	Retrd.	1996	25.00	30
1955	Original Father - J. Heap	Retrd.	1960	50.00	1000-1500
1956	Original Robert - J. Heap	Retrd.	1967	2.50	200-400
1953	Pendle Witch (stoneware) - J. Heap	Retrd.	1957	4.00	800-1200
1967	Phumf - J. Heap	Retrd.	1985	24.00	75
1955	Phynnodderee (Commissioned-Exclusive) - J. Heap	Retrd.	N/A	1.00	N/A
1966	Picnic Basket - J. Heap	Retrd.	1968	2.00	350-600
1965	Picnic Stand - J. Heap	Retrd.	1985	62.50	150-175
1967	Picnic Table - J. Heap	Retrd.	1972	N/A	250-600
1966	Pieface - D. Roberts	Retrd.	1987	31.00	60-75
1965	Pixie Bods - J. Heap	Retrd.	1967	N/A	N/A
1953	Pixie House - J. Heap	Retrd.	1958	N/A	N/A
1962	Pooch - D. Roberts	Retrd.	1987	24.50	60-75
1958	Rabbit Book Ends - J. Heap	Retrd.	1965	10.00	1500-2000
1983	The Raft - J. Heap	Retrd.	1997	70.00	80
1954	Rhinegold Lamp - J. Heap	Retrd.	1956	21.00	N/A
1967	Robert w/lollipop - D. Roberts	Retrd.	1979	12.00	100-250
1978	Rocky (mold 2) - J. Heap	Retrd.	1997	N/A	N/A
1959	Rocky - J. Heap	Retrd.	N/A	32.00	37
1959	Rolly - J. Heap	Retrd.	1997	17.50	22
1957	Romeo & Juliet - J. Heap	Retrd.	1959	11.00	N/A
1960	Shiner w/black eye - J. Heap	Retrd.	1967	2.50	300-500
1981	Shrimp Stand - D. Roberts	Retrd.	1994	70.00	80
1985	Solo - D. Roberts	Retrd.	1993	40.00	50-75
1960	Squeezy - J. Heap	Retrd.	1970	2.50	300-550
1957	Tammy - D. Roberts	Retrd.	1987	24.50	75
1987	Tennyson - D. Roberts	Retrd.	1994	35.00	42
1956	Timber Stand - J. Heap	Retrd.	1982	35.00	150-200
1953	Tipsy Witch - J. Heap	Retrd.	1959	3.50	N/A
1955	Toper - J. Heap	Retrd.	1956	1.00	N/A
1971	Totty - J. Heap	Retrd.	1981	21.00	150-250
1959	Uncle Soames - J. Heap	Retrd.	1985	105.00	300-400
1991	Wordsworth - D. Roberts	Retrd.	1993	60.00	75

Polland Studios

Collector Society - D. Polland

YEAR ISSUE		EDITION LIMIT	YEAR RETD.	ISSUE PRICE	*QUOTE U.S.$
1987	I Come In Peace	Closed	1987	35.00	400-600
1987	Silent Trail	Closed	1987	300.00	1300
1987	I Come In Peace, Silent Trail-Matched Numbered Set	Closed	1987	335.00	15-1895
1988	The Hunter	Closed	1988	35.00	545
1988	Disputed Trail	Closed	1988	300.00	700-1045
1988	The Hunter, Disputed Trail-Matched Numbered Set	Closed	1988	335.00	11-1450
1989	Crazy Horse	Closed	1989	35.00	300-470
1989	Apache Birdman	Closed	1989	300.00	700-970
1989	Crazy Horse, Apache Birdman-Matched Numbered Set	Closed	1989	335.00	13-1700
1990	Chief Pontiac	Closed	1990	35.00	420
1990	Buffalo Pony	Closed	1990	300.00	600-800
1990	Chief Pontiac, Buffalo Pony-Matched Numbered Set	Closed	1990	335.00	900-1350
1991	War Drummer	Closed	1991	35.00	330
1991	The Signal	Closed	1991	350.00	730
1991	War Drummer, The Signal-Matched Numbered Set	Closed	1991	385.00	900-1150
1992	Cabinet Sign	Closed	1992	35.00	125
1992	Warrior's Farewell	Closed	1992	350.00	400
1992	Cabinet Sign, Warrior's Farewell-Matched Numbered Set	Closed	1992	385.00	465
1993	Mountain Man	Closed	1993	35.00	125
1993	Blue Bonnets & Yellow Ribbon	Closed	1993	350.00	350-400
1993	Mountain Man, Blue Bonnets & Yellow Ribbon-Matched Numbered Set	Closed	1993	385.00	385
1994	The Wedding Robe	Closed	1995	45.00	45
1994	The Courtship Race	Closed	1995	375.00	375
1994	The Wedding Robe, The Courtship Race-Matched Numbered Set	Closed	1995	385.00	420

See also Hudson Creek Polland Collectors Society

Possible Dreams

Santa Claus Network® Collectors Club - Staff

YEAR ISSUE		EDITION LIMIT	YEAR RETD.	ISSUE PRICE	*QUOTE U.S.$
1992	The Gift Giver 805001	Closed	1993	Gift	40
1993	Santa's Special Friend 805050	Closed	1993	59.00	59
1993	Special Delivery 805002	Closed	1994	Gift	N/A
1994	On a Winter's Eve 805051	Closed	1994	65.00	65
1994	Jolly St. Nick 805003	Closed	1995	Gift	N/A
1995	Marionette Santa 805052	Closed	1995	50.00	50
1995	Checking His List 805004	Closed	1996	Gift	N/A
1996	A Tree For the Children 805054	Yr.Iss.		40.00	40
1996	A Cookie From Santa 805005	Yr.Iss.		Gift	N/A

The Citizens of Londonshire® - Unknown

YEAR ISSUE		EDITION LIMIT	YEAR RETD.	ISSUE PRICE	*QUOTE U.S.$
1990	Admiral Waldo 713407	Open		65.00	68
1992	Albert 713426	Closed	1994	65.00	68
1991	Bernie 713414	Open		68.00	71
1992	Beth 713417	Open		35.00	37
1992	Christopher 713418	Open		35.00	37
1992	Countess of Hamlett 713419	Open		65.00	68
1992	David 713423	Open		37.50	39
1992	Debbie 713422	Open		37.50	39
1990	Dianne 713413	Open		33.00	35
1990	Dr. Isaac 713409	Closed	1995	65.00	68
1989	Earl of Hamlett 713400	Closed	1994	65.00	68
1992	Jean Claude 713421	Open		35.00	37
1989	Lady Ashley 713405	Open		65.00	68
1989	Lord Nicholas 713402	Open		72.00	76
1989	Lord Winston of Riverside 713403	Closed	1994	65.00	68
1994	Maggie 713428	Closed	1994	57.00	57
1990	Margaret of Foxcroft 713408	Open		65.00	68
1992	Nicole 713420	Open		35.00	37
1993	Nigel As Santa 713427	Open		53.50	56
1990	Officer Kevin 713406	Closed	1994	65.00	68
1990	Phillip 713412	Open		33.00	35
1992	Rebecca 713424	Open		35.00	37
1992	Richard 713425	Open		35.00	37
1989	Rodney 713404	Open		65.00	68
1991	Sir Red 713415	Closed	1994	72.00	76
1989	Sir Robert 713401	Open		65.00	68
1992	Tiffany Sorbet 713416	Open		65.00	68
1990	Walter 713410	Closed	1994	33.00	35
1990	Wendy 713411	Closed	1994	33.00	35

Clothtique® American Artist Collection™ - Various

YEAR ISSUE		EDITION LIMIT	YEAR RETD.	ISSUE PRICE	*QUOTE U.S.$
1996	The 12 Days of Christmas 15052 - M. Monterio	Open		48.00	48
1991	Alpine Christmas 15003 - J. Brett	Closed	1994	129.00	135
1992	An Angel's Kiss 15008 - J. Griffith	Closed	1995	85.00	125
1993	A Beacon of Light 15022 - J. Vaillancourt	Closed	1996	60.00	63
1993	A Brighter Day 15024 - J. St. Denis	Open		67.50	70
1994	Captain Claus 15030 - M. Monteiro	Closed	1996	77.00	77
1995	Christmas Caller 15035 - J. Vaillancourt	Open		57.50	58
1992	Christmas Company 15011 - T. Browning	Closed	1995	77.00	125
1996	Christmas Light 15055 - D. Wenzel	Open		53.50	54
1996	Christmas Stories 15054 - T. Browning	Open		63.50	64
1994	Christmas Surprise 15033 - M. Alvin	Open		88.00	88
1997	Cookie Maker 15063 - T. Browning	Open		55.00	55
1995	Country Sounds 15042 - M. Monteiro	Open		74.00	74
1997	Downhill Thrills 15058 - T. Browning	Open		49.00	49
1996	Dressed For the Holidays 15050 - J. Vaillancourt	Open		27.00	27
1993	Easy Putt 15018 - T. Browning	Closed	1996	110.00	135
1991	Father Christmas 15007 - J. Vaillancourt	Closed	1995	59.50	90
1993	Father Earth 15017 - M. Monteiro	Open		77.00	80
1995	Fresh From The Oven 15051 - M. Alvin	Open		49.00	49
1991	A Friendly Visit 15005 - T. Browning	Closed	1994	99.50	105
1997	The Fun Seekers 15064 - T. Browning	Open		48.00	48
1994	The Gentle Craftsman 15031 - J. Griffith	Closed	1996	81.00	99
1994	Gifts from the Garden 15032 - J. Griffith	Closed	1996	77.00	92
1995	Giving Thanks 15045 - M. Alvin	Open		45.50	46
1995	A Good Round 15041 - T. Browning	Open		73.00	73
1992	Heralding the Way 15014 - J. Griffith	Closed	1995	72.00	75
1993	Ice Capers 15025 - T. Browning	Closed	1996	99.50	105
1993	Just Scooting Along 15023 - J. Vaillancourt	Open		79.50	83
1997	Last Minute Prep 15060 - D. Wenzel	Open		52.50	53
1992	Lighting the Way 15012 - L. Bywaters	Closed	1996	85.00	106
1991	The Magic of Christmas 15001 - L. Bywaters	Closed	1994	132.00	139
1997	Morning Brew 15056 - J. Cleveland	Open		44.50	45
1992	Music Makers 15010 - T. Browning	Closed	1995	135.00	155
1993	Nature's Love 15016 - M. Alvin	Closed	1996	75.00	79
1995	A New Suit For Santa 15053 - T. Browning	Open		90.00	90
1997	North Country Weather 15057 - J. Cleveland	Open		40.00	40
[illegible]	Not a Creature Was Stirring 15046 - J. Cleveland	Open		44.00	44
1992	Out of the Forest 15013 - J. Vaillancourt	Closed	1995	60.00	68
1995	Patchwork Santa 15039 - J. Cleveland	Open		67.50	68
1992	Peace on Earth 15009 - M. Alvin	Closed	1995	87.50	92
1997	Peaceable Kingdom 15061 - J. Griffith	Open		78.80	79
1991	A Peaceful Eve 15002 - L. Bywaters	Closed	1994	99.50	105
1995	Ready For Christmas 15049 - T. Browning	Open		95.00	95
1995	Refuge From The Storm15047 - M. Monterio	Open		49.00	49
1995	Riding High 15040 - L. Nillson	Open		115.00	115
1994	Santa and Feathered Friend 15026 - D. Wenzel	Open		84.00	84
1995	Santa and the Ark 15038 - J. Griffith	Open		71.50	72
1992	Santa in Rocking Chair 713090 - M. Monteiro	Closed	1995	85.00	100
1997	Santa on the Green 15062 - T. Browning	Open		41.00	41
1991	Santa's Cuisine 15006 - T. Browning	Closed	1994	138.00	148
1995	Southwest Santa 15043 - V. Wiseman	Closed	1996	65.00	89
1994	Spirit of Christmas Past 15036 - J. Vaillancourt	Open		79.00	79
1994	Spirit of Santa 15028 - T. Browning	Closed	1996	68.00	68
1995	The Storyteller 15029 - T. Browning	Open		76.00	76
1993	Strumming the Lute 15015 - M. Alvin	Open		79.00	83
1995	Sunflower Santa 15044 - J. Griffith	Open		75.00	75
1994	Tea Time 15034 - M. Alvin	Open		90.00	90
1994	Teddy Love 15037 - J. Griffith	Open		89.00	89
1994	A Touch of Magic 15027 - T. Browning	Open		95.00	95
1991	Traditions 15004 - T. Blackshear	Closed	1994	50.00	75
1993	The Tree Planter 15020 - J. Griffith	Open		79.50	84
1995	Visions of Sugar Plums 15048 - J. Griffith	Open		50.00	50
1993	The Workshop 15019 - T. Browning	Closed	1995	140.00	175
1997	Yuletide Gardner 15059 - J. Griffith	Open		50.00	50

Clothtique® Limited Edition Santas - Unknown

YEAR ISSUE		EDITION LIMIT	YEAR RETD.	ISSUE PRICE	*QUOTE U.S.$
1988	Father Christmas 3001	10,000	1993	240.00	550-650
1988	Kris Kringle 3002	10,000	1992	240.00	550-650
1988	Patriotic Santa 3000	10,000	1994	240.00	550-650
1989	Traditional Santa 40's 3003	10,000	1994	240.00	550-650

Clothtique® Pepsi® Santa Collection - Various

YEAR ISSUE		EDITION LIMIT	YEAR RETD.	ISSUE PRICE	*QUOTE U.S.$
1994	Holiday Host 3605 - Unknown	Open		62.00	62
1995	Jolly Traveler 3606 - B. Prata	Open		90.00	90
1990	Pepsi Cola Santa 1940's 3601 - Unknown	Closed	1996	68.00	74
1992	Pepsi Santa Sitting 3603 - Unknown	Closed	1994	84.00	95

Possible Dreams
to Possible Dreams

FIGURINES

YEAR ISSUE		EDITION LIMIT	YEAR RETD.	ISSUE PRICE	*QUOTE U.S.$
1991	Rockwell Pepsi Santa 1952 3602 - N. Rockwell	Closed	1994	75.00	82

Clothtique® Santas Collection - Staff, unless otherwise noted

YEAR ISSUE		EDITION LIMIT	YEAR RETD.	ISSUE PRICE	*QUOTE U.S.$
1992	1940's Traditional Santa 713049	Closed	1994	44.00	65
1992	African American Santa 713056	Closed	1995	65.00	68
1993	African-American Santa w/ Doll 713102	Open		40.00	42
1997	Autograph For a Fan 713143	Open		39.00	39
1989	Baby's First Christmas 713042	Closed	1992	42.00	46
1995	Baby's First Noel 713120	Open		62.00	62
1988	Carpenter Santa 713033	Closed	1992	38.00	44
1997	Celtic Sounds 713162	Open		46.00	46
1994	Christmas Cheer 713109	Open		58.00	58
1994	A Christmas Guest 713112	Open		79.00	79
1994	Christmas is for Children 713115	Open		62.00	62
1986	Christmas Man 713027	Closed	1989	34.50	35
1987	Colonial Santa 713032	Closed	1990	38.00	40
1997	Doctor Claus 713157	Open		35.00	35
1995	Down Hill Santa 713123	Open		66.50	67
1997	Down the Chimney He Came 713154	Open		42.50	43
1997	Easy Ridin' Santa 713159	Open		37.50	38
1992	Engineer Santa 713057	Closed	1995	130.00	137
1993	European Santa 713095	Closed	1996	53.00	69
1989	Exhausted Santa 713043	Closed	1992	60.00	65
1991	Father Christmas 713087	Closed	1993	43.00	47
1995	Finishing Touch 713121	Open		54.70	55
1993	Fireman & Child 713106	Open		55.00	58
1992	Fireman Santa 713053	Closed	1996	60.00	68
1996	For Someone Special 713142	Open		39.00	39
1995	Frisky Friend 713130	Open		45.50	46
1988	Frontier Santa 713034	Closed	1991	40.00	42
1995	Ginger Bread Baker 713135	Open		35.00	35
1994	Good Tidings 713107	Closed	1996	51.00	69
1997	Grampa Claus 713146	Open		41.40	42
1990	Harlem Santa 713046	Closed	1994	46.00	55
1995	Heaven Sent 713138	Open		50.00	50
1993	His Favorite Color 713098	Closed	1996	48.00	50
1995	Ho: Ho-Hole in One 713131	Open		43.00	43
1994	Holiday Friend 713110	Open		104.00	104
1997	Holiday Gourmet 713147	Open		39.10	40
1997	Holiday Traffic 713148	Open		47.50	48
1995	Home Spun Holidays 713128	Open		49.50	50
1995	Hook Line and Santa 713129	Open		49.70	50
1996	Jumping Jack Santa 713139	Open		45.50	46
1991	Kris Kringle 713088	Closed	1993	43.00	46
1997	Leprechaun 713153	Open		18.50	19
1993	A Long Trip 713105	Open		95.00	100
1993	May Your Wishes Come True 713096	Closed	1996	59.00	62
1993	The Modern Shopper 713103	Closed	1996	40.00	42
1994	A Most Welcome Visitor 713113	Open		63.00	63
1994	Mrs. Claus 713118	Open		58.00	58
1991	Mrs. Claus in Coat 713078	Closed	1995	47.00	71
1989	Mrs. Claus w/doll 713041	Closed	1992	42.00	43
1992	Nicholas 713052	Closed	1994	57.50	60
1997	North Pole Polka 713163	Open		46.00	46
1997	North Pole Prescription 713164	Open		65.60	66
1997	On Christmas Pond 713156	Open		52.30	53
1994	Our Hero 713116	Open		62.00	62
1989	Pelze Nichol 713039	Closed	1993	40.00	47
1995	Pet Project 713134 - L. Craven	Open		37.00	37
1994	Playmates 713111	Closed	1996	104.00	104
1994	Puppy Love 713117	Open		62.00	62
1988	Russian St. Nicholas 713036	Closed	1996	40.00	43
1997	A Sacred Gift 713150	Open		36.00	36
1990	Santa "Please Stop Here" 713045	Closed	1992	63.00	72
1991	Santa Decorating Christmas Tree 713079	Closed	1992	60.00	60
1991	Santa in Bed 713076	Closed	1994	76.00	139
1997	Santa O' Claus 713165	Open		41.50	175
1997	Santa on Line 713151	Open		55.20	56
1992	Santa on Motorbike 713054	Closed	1994	115.00	130
1992	Santa on Reindeer 713058	Closed	1995	75.00	83
1992	Santa on Sled 713050	Closed	1994	75.00	79
1992	Santa on Sleigh 713091	Closed	1995	79.00	83
1991	Santa Shelf Sitter 713089	Closed	1995	55.50	60
1990	Santa w/Blue Robe 713048	Closed	1992	46.00	69
1989	Santa w/Embroidered Coat 713040	Closed	1991	43.00	46
1993	Santa w/Groceries 713099	Closed	1996	47.50	50
1986	Santa w/Pack 713026	Closed	1989	34.50	35
1997	Santa's Better Half 713155	Open		35.80	36
1997	Santa's Grab Bag 713158	Open		47.50	48
1996	Shamrock Santa 713140	Open		41.50	42
1991	Siberian Santa 713077	Closed	1993	49.00	96
1990	Skiing Santa 713047	Closed	1993	62.00	65
1995	Sounds of Christmas 713127	Closed	1996	57.50	58
1995	A Special Treat 713122	Open		50.50	51
1988	St. Nicholas 713035	Closed	1991	40.00	169
1995	The Stockings Were Hung 713126	Open		N/A	N/A
1997	Test Ride 713149	Open		47.10	48
1995	Three Alarm Santa 713137	Open		42.50	43
1987	Traditional Deluxe Santa 713030	Closed	1990	38.00	38
1986	Traditional Santa 713028	Closed	1989	34.50	125
1989	Traditional Santa 713038	Closed	1992	42.00	43
1991	The True Spirit of Christmas 713075	Closed	1992	97.00	97
1987	Ukko 713031	Closed	1990	38.00	38
1995	Victorian Evergreen 713125	Open		49.00	49
1995	Victorian Puppeteer 713124	Open		51.50	52
1993	Victorian Santa 713097	Closed	1996	55.50	58
1988	Weihnachtsman 713037	Closed	1991	40.00	43
1994	A Welcome Visit 713114	Closed	1996	62.00	62
1997	Winter Wanderer 713152	Open		56.90	57
1990	Workbench Santa 713044	Closed	1993	72.00	95
1994	Yuletide Journey 713108	Open		58.00	58

Clothtique® Saturday Evening Post J. C. Leyendecker - J. Leyendecker

YEAR ISSUE		EDITION LIMIT	YEAR RETD.	ISSUE PRICE	*QUOTE U.S.$
1991	Hugging Santa 3599	Closed	1994	129.00	150
1996	Hugging Santa 3650 (smaller re-issue)	Open		52.50	53
1992	Santa on Ladder 3598	Closed	1995	135.00	150
1996	Santa on Ladder 3651 (smaller re-issue)	Open		59.00	59
1991	Traditional Santa 3600	Closed	1992	100.00	125
1996	Traditional Santa 3652 (smaller re-issue)	Open		66.00	66

Clothtique® Saturday Evening Post Norman Rockwell - N. Rockwell

YEAR ISSUE		EDITION LIMIT	YEAR RETD.	ISSUE PRICE	*QUOTE U.S.$
1992	Balancing the Budget 3064	Open		120.00	126
1989	Christmas "Dear Santa" 3050	Closed	1992	160.00	180
1996	Christmas "Dear Santa" 3050 (smaller re-issue)	Open		70.50	71
1989	Christmas "Santa with Globe" 3051	Closed	1992	154.00	175
1996	Santa With Globe 3101 (smaller re-issue)	Open		73.00	73
1991	Doctor and Doll 3055	Closed	1995	196.00	206
1991	The Gift 3057	Closed	1996	160.00	168
1991	Gone Fishing 3054	Closed	1995	250.00	263
1997	Gone Fishing 3104 (smaller re-issue)	Open		67.70	68
1991	Gramps at the Reins 3058	Open		290.00	305
1990	Hobo 3052	Open		159.00	167
1990	Love Letters 3053	Open		172.00	180
1991	Man with Geese 3059	Open		120.00	126
1992	Marriage License 3062	Open		195.00	205
1996	Not a Creature was Stirring (smaller re-issue)	Open		44.00	44
1991	Santa Plotting His Course 3060	Open		160.00	168
1992	Santa's Helpers 3063	Closed	1994	170.00	179
1997	Santa's Helpers 3103 (smaller re-issue)	Open		64.90	65
1991	Springtime 3056	Closed	1996	130.00	137
1992	Triple Self Portrait 3061	Closed	1995	230.00	250
1997	Triple Self Portrait 3105 (smaller re-issue)	Open		65.70	66

Clothtique® Signature Series® - Stanley/Chang

YEAR ISSUE		EDITION LIMIT	YEAR RETD.	ISSUE PRICE	*QUOTE U.S.$
1995	Department Store Santa, USA/Circa 1940s 721001	Open		108.00	108
1995	Father Christmas, England/Circa 1890s 721002	Open		90.00	90
1996	St. Nicholas, Myra/Circa 1300s 721004	Open		99.00	99
1996	Kriss Kringle, USA/Circa 1840s 721005	Open		99.00	99

Crinkle Angels - Staff

YEAR ISSUE		EDITION LIMIT	YEAR RETD.	ISSUE PRICE	*QUOTE U.S.$
1996	Crinkle Angel w/Candle 659405	Open		19.80	20
1996	Crinkle Angel w/Dove 659403	Open		19.80	20
1996	Crinkle Angel w/Harp 659402	Open		19.80	20
1996	Crinkle Angel w/Lamb 659401	Open		19.80	20
1996	Crinkle Angel w/Lantern 659400	Open		19.80	20
1996	Crinkle Angel w/Mandolin 659404	Open		19.80	20

Crinkle Claus - Staff

YEAR ISSUE		EDITION LIMIT	YEAR RETD.	ISSUE PRICE	*QUOTE U.S.$
1995	American Santa 657224	Open		15.50	16
1997	Appalachian Light 659030	Open		8.30	9
1995	Arctic Santa 659107	Open		15.70	16
1995	Austrian Santa 659103	Open		15.80	16
1997	Bavarian Crinkle 659029	Open		8.30	9
1997	Bedtime Story 659910	Open		31.40	32
1995	Bell Shape Santa 659008	Retrd.	1996	23.50	24
1996	Bishop of Maya 659111	Open		19.90	20
1996	Bishop of Maya Plaque 659306	Open		19.90	20
1996	Black Forest Gift Giver 659114	Open		19.90	20
1996	Black Forest Gift Giver Plaque 659302	Open		19.90	20
1997	Blarney Stone Crinkle 659125	Open		13.40	14
1997	Brazilian Fiesta 659028	Open		8.30	9
1997	British Jubilee 659027	Open		8.30	9
1996	Buckets of Fruit for Good Girls & Boys 659903	5,000		45.00	45
1997	Buckingham Crinkle 659126	Open		13.40	14
1995	Candle Stick Santa 659121	Open		15.80	16
1996	Carrying The Torch	Open		19.80	20
1996	Catch of The Day 659504	Open		19.90	20
1996	Celtic Santa 659110	Open		19.90	20
1996	Celtic Santa Plaque 659305	Open		19.90	20
1996	Choo-Choo For The Children 659904	5,000		25.00	25
1997	Christmas King Crinkle 659123	Open		13.40	14
1997	Christmas Tree Crinkle 659036	Open		16.30	17
1995	Christmas Tree Santa 659117	Open		19.90	20
1997	Christmas Wilderness 659603	Open		46.80	47
1995	Crescent Moon Santa 659119	Open		19.00	19
1997	Crinkle Ark 660301	Open		57.00	57
1997	Crinkle Bears 660303	Open		14.90	15
1996	Crinkle Claus w/Dome-German Santa 659601	Open		45.00	45
1996	Crinkle Claus w/Dome-Santa/Chimney 659600	Open		45.00	45
1996	Crinkle Claus w/Dome-St. Nicholas 659602	Open		45.00	45
1997	Crinkle Horses 660305	Open		13.30	14
1997	Crinkle Locomotive & Coal Car 660201	Open		42.00	42
1997	Crinkle Noah 660302	Open		10.30	11
1997	Crinkle Reindeer 660306	Open		13.30	14
1997	Crinkle Sheep 660304	Open		10.80	11
1996	A Crown of Antlers	Open		19.70	20
1996	Dashing Through The Snow 659902	5,000		45.00	45
1996	Display Figurine-965003	Open		11.00	11
1997	Down The Chimney 659911	Open		31.10	32
1995	English Santa 659100	Open		15.80	16
1996	Feeding His Forest Friends 659905	5,000		27.50	28
1997	Filled With Joy 659908	Open		31.00	31
1997	Fjord Crinkle 659124	Open		13.40	14
1997	Flickering Crinkle 659035	Open		14.00	14
1995	Forest Santa 657225	Open		15.50	16
1995	French Santa 659108	Open		15.70	16
1995	German Santa 659105	Open		15.80	16
1995	Hard Boiled Santa 659115	Open		13.70	14
1995	High Hat Santa 657134	Open		13.40	14
1997	High Ho 659025	Open		13.20	14
1997	High Note 659023	Open		13.20	14
1997	Highland Piper 659026	Open		8.30	9
1997	Holiday Cane Crinkle 659034	Open		14.00	14
1995	Hour Glass Santa 659118	Open		15.00	15
1996	Iceland Visitor 659112	Open		19.90	20
1996	Iceland Visitor Plaque 659303	Open		19.90	20
1995	Italian Santa 659106	Open		15.70	16
1995	Jolly St. Nick 659012	Open		15.00	15
1997	Kelly Crinkle 659132	Open		16.00	16
1997	Kelly Crinkle 659712	Open		7.80	8
1996	Learned Gentleman	Open		19.80	20
1996	Lighting The Way	Open		19.80	20
1997	Lisbon Traveler 659033	Open		8.30	9
1996	Low & Behold	Open		13.90	14
1997	Madrid Crinkle 659131	Open		16.00	16
1997	Madrid Crinkle 659708	Open		7.80	8
1997	Mediterranean Treasures 659032	Open		8.30	9
1996	Merry Old England 659113	Open		19.90	20
1996	Merry Old England Plaque 659301	Open		19.90	20
1997	Moscow Crinkle 659128	Open		16.00	16
1997	Moscow Crinkle 659711	Open		7.80	8
1997	Munich Crinkle 659130	Open		16.00	16
1997	Munich Crinkle 659710	Open		7.80	8
1996	The Music Man	Open		19.80	20
1995	Netherlands Santa 659102	Open		15.70	16
1997	North Pole Artisan 659907	Open		30.00	30
1996	Northland Santa 659109	Open		19.90	20
1996	Northland Santa Plaque 659304	Open		19.90	20
1997	Pamplona Crinkle 659122	Open		13.40	14
1997	Paris Crinkle 659709	Open		7.80	8
1995	Pine Cone Santa 657226	Open		15.50	16
1996	Rag/Doll Delivery 659906	5,000		34.50	35
1997	Rocking Crinkle 659039	Open		17.60	18
1995	Roly Poly Santa 3.5" 657138	Retrd.	1996	12.50	13
1995	Roly Poly Santa 4" 659009	Retrd.	1996	23.00	23
1996	Running Down The List 659901	5,000		33.00	33
1995	Russian Santa 3.5" 659101	Open		15.70	16
1995	Russian Santa 4" 657228	Retrd.	1996	15.50	16
1995	Santa on Bag 657508	Retrd.	1996	15.00	15
1995	Santa on Roof 659006	Open		28.50	29
1995	Santa Sitting Pretty 659116	Open		13.90	14
1995	Santa w/Book 659010	Open		13.80	14
1995	Santa w/Candy Cane 4.5" 657139	Retrd.	1996	13.00	13
1996	Santa w/Candy Cane 5" 657142	Retrd.	1996	27.00	27
1996	Santa w/Candy Cane 6.5" 657135	Retrd.	1996	17.50	18
1995	Santa w/Cane & Bag 657230	Retrd.	1996	12.00	12
1995	Santa w/Gifts 657143	Retrd.	1996	27.00	27
1995	Santa w/Lantern & Bag 657229	Retrd.	1996	15.50	16
1995	Santa w/Lantern 5" 657136	Retrd.	1996	12.50	13
1995	Santa w/Lantern 5" 657144	Retrd.	1996	27.00	27
1995	Santa w/Noah's Ark 657227	Open		15.50	16
1995	Santa w/Patchwork Bag 657232	Open		19.00	19
1995	Santa w/Stars 657140	Retrd.	1996	14.00	14
1995	Santa w/Teddy Bear 657231	Open		16.00	16
1995	Santa w/Tree 659011	Retrd.	1996	14.20	15
1995	Santa w/Wreath 657141	Retrd.	1996	16.30	17
1995	Santa's Candy Surprise	Open		27.00	27
1995	Scandinavian Santa 659104	Open		15.80	16
1997	Slavic Crinkle 659133	Open		16.00	16
1997	Slavic Crinkle 659713	Open		7.80	8
1995	Slimline Santa 657137	Retrd.	1996	12.00	12
1997	Something For Everyone 659909	Open		31.10	32
1997	Starburst Crinkle 659038	Open		14.20	15
1995	Tall Santa	Open		17.50	18
1995	Tick Tock Santa 659120	Open		15.00	15
1995	Tip Top Santa 659007	Retrd.	1996	23.50	24
1996	To The Rescue	Open		19.90	20
1997	Top of the List 659022	Open		13.20	14
1997	Top of the Tree 659024	Open		13.20	14
1997	Top Spin Crinkle 659037	Open		13.70	14
1997	Vatican Crinkle 659127	Open		13.40	14

*Quotes have been rounded up to nearest dollar

YEAR ISSUE		EDITION LIMIT	YEAR RETD.	ISSUE PRICE	*QUOTE U.S.$
1996	Well Rounded Santa	Open		13.70	14
1997	West Coast Beat 659031	Open		8.30	9

Crinkle Cousins - Staff

YEAR ISSUE		EDITION LIMIT	YEAR RETD.	ISSUE PRICE	*QUOTE U.S.$
1995	Crinkle Cousin w/Clock 659002	Open		15.50	16
1995	Crinkle Cousin w/Clown 659004	Open		15.50	16
1995	Crinkle Cousin w/Dolls 659003	Open		15.50	16
1995	Crinkle Cousin w/Lantern 659001	Open		15.50	16
1995	Crinkle Cousin w/Teddy 659005	Open		15.50	16

Crinkle Crackers - Staff

YEAR ISSUE		EDITION LIMIT	YEAR RETD.	ISSUE PRICE	*QUOTE U.S.$
1995	Admiral Crinkle Cracker 659212	Open		18.50	19
1995	Captain Crinkle Cracker 659211	Retrd.	1996	13.00	13
1995	Corporal Crinkle Cracker 659214	Retrd.	1996	14.60	15
1995	French Crinkle Cracker 659203	Open		22.00	22
1995	French Lieutenant Crinkle Cracker 659205	Open		13.50	14
1995	General Crinkle Cracker 659213	Retrd.	1996	15.50	16
1995	Lieutenant Crinkle Cracker 659209	Open		26.50	27
1995	Major Crinkle Cracker 659215	Open		14.50	15
1995	Private Crinkle Cracker 659210	Retrd.	1996	15.00	15
1995	Roly Poly French Crinkle Cracker 659204	Open		13.90	14
1995	Roly Poly Russian Crinkle Cracker 659207	Open		13.50	14
1995	Roly Poly Sergeant Crinkle Cracker 659216	Open		13.50	14
1995	Roly Poly U.S. Crinkle Cracker 659201	Open		13.90	14
1995	Russian Crinkle Cracker 4" 659208	Open		13.50	14
1995	Russian Crinkle Cracker 7.75" 659206	Open		29.50	30
1995	U.S. Crinkle Cracker 3.75" 659202	Open		13.50	14
1995	U.S.Crinkle Cracker 7.5" 659200	Open		29.00	29

Crinkle Professionals - Staff

YEAR ISSUE		EDITION LIMIT	YEAR RETD.	ISSUE PRICE	*QUOTE U.S.$
1996	Baseball Player 659507	Open		19.50	20
1996	Doctor 659500	Open		19.50	20
1996	Fireman 659503	Open		19.50	20
1996	Fisherman 659504	Open		19.50	20
1996	Football Player 659506	Open		19.50	20
1996	Golfer 659505	Open		19.50	20
1996	Hockey Player 659508	Open		19.50	20
1997	Lawyer 659511	Open		19.50	20
1996	Policeman 659502	Open		19.50	20
1996	Postman 659501	Open		19.50	20
1996	Soccer Player 659509	Open		19.50	20
1997	Teacher 659510	Open		19.50	20
1997	Tennis Player 659512	Open		19.50	20

Floristine Angels® - B. Sargent

YEAR ISSUE		EDITION LIMIT	YEAR RETD.	ISSUE PRICE	*QUOTE U.S.$
1996	Angel of Happiness 668002	Open		100.00	100
1996	An Angel's Prayer 668003	Open		98.00	98
1997	Blissful Ballet 668008	Open		72.40	73
1996	Celestial Garden 668001	Open		98.00	98
1996	Heavenly Harmony 668006	Open		100.00	100
1996	Lessons From Above 668005	Open		100.00	100
1996	My Guardian Angel 668004	Open		112.00	112
1997	My Inspiration 668007	Open		37.70	38
1997	Sacred Virgil 668009	Open		47.10	48

The Thickets at Sweetbriar® - B. Ross

YEAR ISSUE		EDITION LIMIT	YEAR RETD.	ISSUE PRICE	*QUOTE U.S.$
1995	Angel Dear 350123	Open		32.00	32
1996	Autumn Peppergrass 350135	Open		31.00	31
1993	The Bride-Emily Feathers 350112	Open		30.00	30
1995	Buttercup 350121	Open		32.00	32
1995	Cecily Pickwick 350125	Open		32.00	32
1995	Clem Jingles 350130	Open		37.00	37
1993	Clovis Buttons 350101	Closed	1996	24.15	25
1996	Dainty Whiskers 350136	Open		30.00	30
1996	Goody Pringle 350134	Open		31.00	31
1993	The Groom-Oliver Doone 350111	Closed	1996	30.00	30
1993	Jewel Blossom 350106	Open		36.75	37
1995	Katy Hollyberry 350124	Closed	1996	35.00	35
1995	Kris Krinkle 350414	Open		12.50	13
1994	Lady Slipper 350116	Open		20.00	20
1993	Lily Blossom 350105	Closed	1996	36.75	37
1996	Lily Blossom 350201 (musical)	Closed	1996	59.50	60
1993	Maude Tweedy 350100	Closed	1994	26.25	27
1996	Merry Heart 350131	Open		30.00	30
1994	Morning Dew 350113	Open		30.00	30
1993	Morning Glory 350104	Open		30.45	31
1993	Mr. Claws 350109	Closed	1996	34.00	34
1993	Mrs. Claws 350110	Closed	1996	34.00	34
1993	Orchid Beasley 350103	Closed	1996	26.25	27
1995	Parsley Divine 350129	Open		37.00	37
1996	Patience Finney 350133	Open		31.00	31
1993	Peablossom Thorndike 350102	Closed	1994	26.25	27
1995	Penny Pringle 350128	Open		32.00	32
1995	Pittypat 350122	Open		32.00	32
1994	Precious Petals 350115	Open		34.00	34
1993	Raindrop 350108	Closed	1996	47.25	48
1995	Riley Pickens 350127	Open		32.00	32
1993	Rose Blossom 350107	Open		36.75	37
1994	Sunshine 350118	Open		33.00	33
1994	Sweetie Flowers 350114	Closed	1996	33.00	33
1995	Tillie Lilly 350120	Open		32.00	32
1995	Timmy Evergreen 350126	Open		29.00	29
1996	Velvet Winterberry 350132	Open		30.00	30
1995	Violet Wiggles 350119	Open		32.00	32

Precious Art/Panton

Krystonia Collector's Club - Panton

YEAR ISSUE		EDITION LIMIT	YEAR RETD.	ISSUE PRICE	*QUOTE U.S.$
1989	Pultzr	Retrd.	1990	55.00	550-600
1989	Key	Retrd.	1990	Gift	90-150
1991	Dragons Play	Retrd.	1992	65.00	150-250
1991	Kephrens Chest	Retrd.	1992	Gift	100-135
1992	Vaaston	Retrd.	1993	65.00	150-225
1992	Lantern	Retrd.	1993	Gift	40-80
1993	Sneaking A Peak	Retrd.	1994	Gift	40-80
1993	Spreading His Wings	Retrd.	1994	60.00	80-150
1994	All Tuckered Out	Retrd.	1995	65.00	83
1994	Filler-Up	Retrd.	1995	Gift	30-40
1995	Twingnuk	Retrd.	1996	55.00	55-75
1995	Kappah Krystal	Retrd.	1996	Gift	30-50
1996	Quinzet	Yr.Iss	1997	38.00	38
1996	Holy Dragons	Yr.Iss	1997	65.00	65
1996	Frobbit	Yr.Iss	1997	Gift	30.00
1996	Glowing Mashal	2/98		Gift	30.00
1997	Almost There	5/98		75.00	75

Fair Maidens - Panton

YEAR ISSUE		EDITION LIMIT	YEAR RETD.	ISSUE PRICE	*QUOTE U.S.$
1994	Faithful Companion	1,000	1994	325.00	350-425
1995	Safe Passage	1,000	1996	350.00	350

World of Krystonia - Panton

YEAR ISSUE		EDITION LIMIT	YEAR RETD.	ISSUE PRICE	*QUOTE U.S.$
1992	Azael -3811	Retrd.	1995	85.00	87
1989	Babul -1402	Retrd.	1995	25.00	30
1994	Boll-3912	Retrd.	1994	52.00	90-150
1989	Caught At Last! -1107	Retrd.	1992	150.00	200-250
1991	Charcoal Cookie -3451	Retrd.	1996	38.00	38-45
1993	Cuda Tree - 705	Retrd.	1997	35.00	35
1991	Culpy -3441	Retrd.	1996	38.00	38
1992	Dubious Alliance -1109	Retrd.	1995	195.00	200
1995	Enough Is Enough -1114	1,500	1996	250.00	250
1992	Escublar (Classic Moment) - 1110	7,500	1997	170.00	170
1991	Flayla w/Sumbly -1105	Retrd.	1995	104.00	104
1980	Gateway to Kystonia-3301	Retrd.	1994	35.00	50-75
1989	Gorph In Bucket -2801	Retrd.	1996	20.00	20-26
1989	Gorphylia -2802	Retrd.	1996	18.00	22
1987	Grackene -1051	Retrd.	1995	50.00	50
1989	Graffyn on Grunch (waterglobe) -9006	Retrd.	1992	42.00	150-180
1987	Groc -1041	Retrd.	1995	50.00	50
1987	Grumblypeg Grunch -1081	Retrd.	1992	52.00	110-150
1989	Kephren -2702	Retrd.	1994	56.00	65
1989	Krystonia Sign -701	Retrd.	1993	10.00	45-95
1989	Large Bags -703	Retrd.	1996	12.00	12
1987	Large Graffyn on Grumblypeg Grunch -1011	Retrd.	1992	52.00	95-125
1991	Large Grunch's Toothache -1082	Retrd.	1994	76.00	80
1987	Large Haapf -1901	Retrd.	1991	38.00	90-150
1987	Large Krak N'Borg -3001	Retrd.	1990	240.00	500-750
1987	Large Moplos -1021	Retrd.	1991	90.00	175-250
1987	Large Myzer -1201	Retrd.	1991	50.00	90-150
1987	Large N' Chakk -2101	Retrd.	1995	140.00	140
1987	Large N'Borg -1092	Retrd.	1994	98.00	140
1988	Large N'Grall -2201	Retrd.	1990	108.00	200-250
1987	Large Rueggan -1701	Retrd.	1989	55.00	150-250
1987	Large Stoope -1103	15,000	1996	98.00	100-140
1987	Large Turfen -1601	Retrd.	1991	50.00	85-100
1987	Large Wodema -1301	Retrd.	1990	50.00	100-200
1991	Maj-Dron Migration -1108	Retrd.	1994	145.00	155
1988	Medium N'Grall -2202	Retrd.	1994	70.00	80
1988	Medium Rueggan -1702	Retrd.	1993	48.00	50-75
1987	Medium Stoope -1101	Retrd.	1990	52.00	100-225
1987	Medium Wodema -1302	Retrd.	1993	44.00	50-75
1992	Mini N' Grall -611	Retrd.	1995	27.00	27
1992	N' Leila-3801	Retrd.	1994	60.00	80-90
1991	N'Borg-Mini -609	Retrd.	1994	29.00	29
1990	N'Chakk-Mini -607	Retrd.	1994	29.00	30-60
1989	N'Tormet -2601	15,000	1996	60.00	75
1990	Owhey (waterglobe) -9004	Retrd.	1995	42.00	110-250
1987	Owhey -1071	Retrd.	1990	32.00	95-140
1990	Shadra -3401	Retrd.	1994	30.00	55-70
1987	Shepf - 1151	15,000	1997	70.00	70
1989	Small Bags -704	Retrd.	1996	4.00	4
1987	Small Graffyn/Grunch -1012	Retrd.	1989	45.00	120-250
1987	Small Groc -1042B	Retrd.	1987	24.00	2000-4000
1987	Small Krak N' Borg -3003	Retrd.	1993	60.00	140
1987	Small N' Borg -1091	Retrd.	1989	50.00	200-300
1987	Small N' Tormet -2602	Retrd.	1993	44.00	50-60
1988	Small Rueggau -1703	Retrd.	1995	42.00	42-52
1989	Small Scrolls -702	Retrd.	1996	4.00	4
1987	Small Shepf -1152	Retrd.	1990	40.00	80-120
1987	Small Stoope -1102	Retrd.	1995	46.00	46
1988	Small Tulan Captain -2502	Retrd.	1991	44.00	65-95
1987	Spyke -1061	Retrd.	1993	50.00	60-95
1989	Stoope (waterglobe) -9003	Retrd.	1991	40.00	200-300
1988	Tarnhold-Med. -3202	Retrd.	1992	120.00	175
1987	Tarnhold-Small -3203	Retrd.	1995	60.00	60
1988	Tokkel -2401	Retrd.	1995	42.00	45
1989	Tulan -2501	15,000	1996	60.00	70

Precious Moments/Enesco Corporation

Precious Moments Collectors Club Welcome Gift - S. Butcher

YEAR ISSUE		EDITION LIMIT	YEAR RETD.	ISSUE PRICE	*QUOTE U.S.$
1982	But Love Goes On Forever -Plaque E-0202	Yr.Iss.	1982	N/A	80-100
1983	Let Us Call the Club to Order E-0303	Yr.Iss.	1983	N/A	50-65
1984	Join in on the Blessings E-0404	Yr.Iss.	1984	N/A	50-60
1985	Seek and Ye Shall Find E-0005	Yr.Iss.	1985	N/A	40-60
1986	Birds of a Feather Collect Together E-0006	Yr.Iss.	1986	N/A	35-45
1987	Sharing Is Universal E-0007	Yr.Iss.	1987	N/A	40
1988	A Growing Love E-0008	Yr.Iss.	1988	N/A	35-55
1989	Always Room For One More C-0009	Yr.Iss.	1989	N/A	40-60
1990	My Happiness C-0010	Yr.Iss.	1990	N/A	40-50
1991	Sharing the Good News Together C-0011	Yr.Iss.	1991	N/A	30-65
1992	The Club That's Out Of This World C-0012	Yr.Iss.	1992	N/A	40
1993	Loving, Caring, and Sharing Along the Way C-0013	Yr.Iss.	1993	N/A	35-45
1994	You Are the End of My Rainbow C-0014	Yr.Iss.	1994	N/A	35-40
1995	You're The Sweetest Cookie In The Batch C-0015	Yr.Iss.	1995	N/A	28-35
1996	You're As Pretty As A Picture C-0016	Yr.Iss.	1996	N/A	30
1997	A Special Toast To Precious Moments C-0017	Yr.Iss.		N/A	N/A

Precious Moments Inscribed Charter Member Renewal Gift - S. Butcher

YEAR ISSUE		EDITION LIMIT	YEAR RETD.	ISSUE PRICE	*QUOTE U.S.$
1981	But Love Goes on Forever E-0001	Yr.Iss.	1981	N/A	150-190
1982	But Love Goes on Forever-Plaque E-0102	Yr.Iss.	1982	N/A	70-125
1983	Let Us Call the Club to Order E-0103	Yr.Iss.	1983	25.00	50-85
1984	Join in on the Blessings E-0104	Yr.Iss.	1984	25.00	50-70
1985	Seek and Ye Shall Find E-0105	Yr.Iss.	1985	25.00	40-70
1986	Birds of a Feather Collect Together E-0106	Yr.Iss.	1986	25.00	40-60
1987	Sharing Is Universal E-0107	Yr.Iss.	1987	25.00	40-60
1988	A Growing Love E-0108	Yr.Iss.	1988	25.00	40-55
1989	Always Room For One More C-0109	Yr.Iss.	1989	35.00	35-55
1990	My Happiness C-0110	Yr.Iss.	1990	N/A	40-55
1991	Sharing The Good News Together C-0111	Yr.Iss.	1991	N/A	45
1992	The Club That's Out Of This World C-0112	Yr.Iss.	1992	N/A	45
1993	Loving, Caring, and Sharing Along the Way C-0113	Yr.Iss.	1993	N/A	40
1994	You Are the End of My Rainbow C-0114	Yr.Iss.	1994	N/A	30-50
1995	You're The Sweetest Cookie In The Batch C-0115	Yr.Iss.	1995	N/A	35
1996	You're As Pretty As A Picture C-0116	Yr.Iss.	1996	N/A	N/A
1997	A Special Toast To Precious Moments C-0117	Yr.Iss.		N/A	N/A

Precious Moments Special Edition Members' Only - S. Butcher

YEAR ISSUE		EDITION LIMIT	YEAR RETD.	ISSUE PRICE	*QUOTE U.S.$
1981	Hello, Lord, It's Me Again PM-811	Yr.Iss.	1981	25.00	350-500
1982	Smile, God Loves You PM-821	Yr.Iss.	1982	25.00	215-240
1983	Put on a Happy Face PM-822	Yr.Iss.	1983	25.00	200-300
1983	Dawn's Early Light PM-831	Yr.Iss.	1983	27.50	80-90
1984	God's Ray of Mercy PM-841	Yr.Iss.	1984	25.00	60-90
1984	Trust in the Lord to the Finish PM-842	Yr.Iss.	1984	25.00	58-95
1985	The Lord is My Shepherd PM-851	Yr.Iss.	1985	25.00	80-140
1985	I Love to Tell the Story PM-852	Yr.Iss.	1985	27.50	65-85
1986	Grandma's Prayer PM-861	Yr.Iss.	1986	25.00	80-110
1986	I'm Following Jesus PM-862	Yr.Iss.	1986	25.00	60-90
1987	Feed My Sheep PM-871	Yr.Iss.	1987	25.00	45-95
1987	In His Time PM-872	Yr.Iss.	1987	25.00	45-75
1987	Loving You Dear Valentine PM-873	Yr.Iss.	1987	25.00	40-55
1987	Loving You Dear Valentine PM-874	Yr.Iss.	1987	25.00	40-50
1988	God Bless You for Touching My Life PM-881	Yr.Iss.	1988	27.50	50-60
1988	You Just Can't Chuck A Good Friendship PM-882	Yr.Iss.	1988	27.50	40-45
1989	You Will Always Be My Choice PM-891	Yr.Iss.	1989	27.50	35-55
1989	Mow Power To Ya PM-892	Yr.Iss.	1989	27.50	45-65
1990	Ten Years And Still Going Strong PM-901	Yr.Iss.	1990	30.00	35-85
1990	You Are A Blessing To Me PM-902	Yr.Iss.	1990	30.00	55-65
1991	One Step At A Time PM-911	Yr.Iss.	1991	33.00	40-55
1991	Lord, Keep Me In TeePee Top Shape PM-912	Yr.Iss.	1991	33.00	45-60
1992	Only Love Can Make A Home PM-921	Yr.Iss.	1992	30.00	50-90
1992	Sowing The Seeds of Love PM-922	Yr.Iss.	1992	30.00	40
1993	His Little Treasure PM-931	Yr.Iss.	1993	30.00	40-65
1993	Loving PM-932	Yr.Iss.	1993	30.00	50-95
1994	Caring PM-941	Yr.Iss.	1994	35.00	55
1994	Sharing PM-942	Yr.Iss.	1994	35.00	55-70
1994	You Fill The Pages of My Life (figurine/book) PMB034	Yr.Iss.	1994	67.50	68
1995	You're One In A Million To Me PM-951	Yr.Iss.	1995	35.00	35-40
1995	Always Take Time To Pray PM-952	Yr.Iss.	1995	35.00	35-40
1996	Teach Us To Love One Another PM-961	Yr.Iss.	1996	40.00	40
1996	Our Club Is Soda-licious PM-962	Yr.Iss.	1996	35.00	35

*Quotes have been rounded up to nearest dollar

YEAR ISSUE		EDITION LIMIT	YEAR RETD.	ISSUE PRICE	*QUOTE U.S.$
1997	You Will Always Be A Treasure To Me PM971	Yr.Iss.		50.00	50
1997	Blessed Are The Merciful PM972	Yr.Iss.		40.00	40

Precious Moments Club 5th Anniversary Commemorative Edition - S. Butcher

YEAR ISSUE		EDITION LIMIT	YEAR RETD.	ISSUE PRICE	*QUOTE U.S.$
1985	God Bless Our Years Together 12440	Yr.Iss.	1985	175.00	280-365

Precious Moments Club 10th Anniversary Commemorative Edition - S. Butcher

YEAR ISSUE		EDITION LIMIT	YEAR RETD.	ISSUE PRICE	*QUOTE U.S.$
1988	The Good Lord Has Blessed Us Tenfold 114022	Yr.Iss.	1988	90.00	145-190

Precious Moments Club 15th Anniversary Commemorative Edition - S. Butcher

YEAR ISSUE		EDITION LIMIT	YEAR RETD.	ISSUE PRICE	*QUOTE U.S.$
1993	15 Happy Years Together: What A Tweet 530786	Yr.Iss.	1993	100.00	110
1995	A Perfect Display of 15 Happy Years 127817	Yr.Iss.	1995	100.00	125

Precious Moments - S. Butcher

YEAR ISSUE		EDITION LIMIT	YEAR RETD.	ISSUE PRICE	*QUOTE U.S.$
1983	Sharing Our Season Together E-0501	Suspd.		50.00	125-160
1983	Jesus is the Light that Shines E-0502	Suspd.		23.00	40-70
1983	Blessings from My House to Yours E-0503	Suspd.		27.00	80-95
1983	Christmastime Is for Sharing E-0504	Retrd.	1989	37.00	60-95
1983	Surrounded with Joy E-0506	Retrd.	1987	21.00	60-80
1983	God Sent His Son E-0507	Suspd.		32.50	70-85
1983	Prepare Ye the Way of the Lord E-0508	Suspd.		75.00	140-150
1983	Bringing God's Blessing to You E-0509	Suspd.		35.00	80-100
1983	Tubby's First Christmas E-0511	Suspd.		12.00	25-40
1983	It's a Perfect Boy E-0512	Suspd.		18.50	60
1983	Onward Christian Soldiers E-0523	Open		24.00	35-65
1983	You Can't Run Away from God E-0525	Retrd.	1989	28.50	85-90
1983	He Upholdeth Those Who Fall E-0526	Suspd.		35.00	85-115
1987	His Eye Is On The Sparrow E-0530	Retrd.	1987	28.50	90-130
1979	Jesus Loves Me E-1372B	Open		7.00	28-55
1979	Jesus Loves Me E-1372G	Open		7.00	28-55
1979	Smile, God Loves You E-1373B	Retrd.	1984	7.00	50-70
1979	Jesus is the Light E-1373G	Retrd.	1988	7.00	50-70
1979	Praise the Lord Anyhow E-1374B	Retrd.	1982	8.00	90-135
1979	Make a Joyful Noise E-1374G	Open		8.00	28-50
1979	Love Lifted Me E-1375A	Retrd.	1993	11.00	60-85
1979	Prayer Changes Things E-1375B	Suspd.		11.00	150-170
1979	Love One Another E-1376	Open		10.00	40-70
1979	He Leadeth Me E-1377A	Suspd.		9.00	85-140
1979	He Careth For You E-1377B	Suspd.		9.00	85-120
1979	God Loveth a Cheerful Giver E-1378	Retrd.	1981	11.00	900-975
1979	Love is Kind E-1379A	Suspd.		8.00	85-135
1979	God Understands E-1379B	Suspd.		8.00	90-115
1979	O, How I Love Jesus E-1380B	Retrd.	1984	8.00	90-125
1979	His Burden Is Light E-1380G	Retrd.	1984	8.00	95-110
1979	Jesus is the Answer E-1381	Suspd.		11.50	135-145
1992	Jesus is the Answer E-1381R	Retrd.	1996	55.00	55
1979	We Have Seen His Star E-2010	Suspd.		8.00	75-150
1979	Come Let Us Adore Him E-2011	Retrd.	1981	10.00	100-225
1979	Jesus is Born E-2012	Suspd.		12.00	95-115
1979	Unto Us a Child is Born E-2013	Suspd.		12.00	90-150
1982	May Your Christmas Be Cozy E-2345	Suspd.		23.00	80-110
1982	May Your Christmas Be Warm E-2348	Suspd.		30.00	125-140
1983	Tell Me the Story of Jesus E-2349	Suspd.		30.00	100-120
1982	Dropping in for Christmas E-2350	Suspd.		18.00	70-85
1982	Holy Smokes E-2351	Retrd.	1987	27.00	150-165
1983	O Come All Ye Faithful E-2353	Retrd.	1986	27.50	95-135
1982	I'll Play My Drum for Him E-2356	Suspd.		30.00	75-100
1982	I'll Play My Drum for Him E-2360	Open		16.00	30-38
1982	Christmas Joy from Head to Toe E-2361	Suspd.		25.00	60-75
1982	Camel Figurine E-2363	Open		20.00	33-40
1982	Goat Figurine E-2364	Suspd.		10.00	35-45
1982	The First Noel E-2365	Suspd.		16.00	50-70
1982	The First Noel E-2366	Suspd.		16.00	50-60
1982	Bundles of Joy E-2374	Retrd.	1993	27.50	55-85
1982	Dropping Over for Christmas E-2375	Retrd.	1991	30.00	55-90
1982	Our First Christmas Together E-2377	Suspd.		35.00	75-95
1982	3 Mini Nativity Houses & Palm Tree E-2387	Open		45.00	75-100
1982	Come Let Us Adore Him E-2395 (11pc. set)	Open		80.00	130-150
1980	Come Let Us Adore Him E-2800 (9 pc. set)	Open		70.00	125-170
1980	Jesus is Born E-2801	Suspd.		37.00	175-325
1980	Christmas is a Time to Share E-2802	Suspd.		20.00	70-95
1980	Crown Him Lord of All E-2803	Suspd.		20.00	70-100
1980	Peace on Earth E-2804	Suspd.		20.00	115-150
1980	Wishing You a Season Filled w/ Joy E-2805	Retrd.	1985	20.00	85-125
1984	You Have Touched So Many Hearts E-2821	Suspd.		25.00	43
1984	This is Your Day to Shine E-2822	Retrd.	1988	37.50	80-150
1984	To God Be the Glory E-2823	Suspd.		40.00	110-125
1984	To a Very Special Mom E-2824	Open		27.50	38-55
1984	To a Very Special Sister E-2825	Open		37.50	55
1984	May Your Birthday Be a Blessing E-2826	Suspd.		37.50	75-100
1984	I Get a Kick Out of You E-2827	Suspd.		50.00	175-225
1984	Precious Memories E-2828	Open		45.00	45-70
1984	I'm Sending You a White Christmas E-2829	Open		37.50	55-60
1984	God Bless the Bride E-2832	Open		35.00	50-60
1986	Sharing Our Joy Together E-2834	Suspd.		30.00	40-60
1984	Baby Figurines (set of 6) E-2852	Closed	N/A	15.00	120-140
1984	Boy Standing E-2852A	Suspd.		13.50	25
1984	Girl Standing E-2852B	Suspd.		13.50	25
1984	Boy Sitting Up E-2852C	Suspd.		13.50	25
1984	Girl Sitting Clapping E-2852D	Suspd.		13.50	25
1984	Boy Crawling E-2852E	Suspd.		13.50	25
1984	Girl Laying Down E-2852F	Suspd.		13.50	25
1980	Blessed Are the Pure in Heart E-3104	Suspd.		9.00	40-50
1980	He Watches Over Us All E-3105	Suspd.		11.00	65-90
1980	Mother Sew Dear E-3106	Open		13.00	28-60
1980	Blessed are the Peacemakers E-3107	Retrd.	1985	13.00	75-115
1980	The Hand that Rocks the Future E-3108	Suspd.		13.00	80-90
1980	The Purr-fect Grandma E-3109	Open		13.00	28-60
1980	Loving is Sharing E-3110B	Retrd.	1993	13.00	75-125
1980	Loving is Sharing E-3110G	Open		13.00	30-70
1980	Be Not Weary In Well Doing E-3111	Retrd.	1985	14.00	80-130
1980	God's Speed E-3112	Retrd.	1983	14.00	60-85
1980	Thou Art Mine E-3113	Open		16.00	40-50
1980	The Lord Bless You and Keep You E-3114	Open		16.00	45-55
1980	But Love Goes on Forever E-3115	Open		16.50	38-60
1980	Thee I Love E-3116	Retrd.	1994	16.50	60-110
1980	Walking By Faith E-3117	Open		35.00	70-100
1980	Eggs Over Easy E-3118	Retrd.	1983	12.00	65-110
1980	It's What's Inside that Counts E-3119	Suspd.		13.00	90-125
1980	To Thee With Love E-3120	Suspd.		13.00	75-85
1981	The Lord Bless You and Keep You E-4720	Suspd.		14.00	45-50
1981	The Lord Bless You and Keep You E-4721	Open		14.00	33-45
1981	Love Cannot Break a True Friendship E 4722	Suspd.		22.50	100-125
1981	Peace Amid the Storm E-4723	Suspd.		22.50	85-95
1981	Rejoicing with You E-4724	Open		25.00	45-65
1981	Peace on Earth E-4725	Suspd.		25.00	75-95
1981	Bear Ye One Another's Burdens E-5200	Suspd.		20.00	70-90
1981	Love Lifted Me E-5201	Suspd.		25.00	75-95
1981	Thank You for Coming to My Ade E-5202	Suspd.		22.50	125-140
1981	Let Not the Sun Go Down Upon Your Wrath E-5203	Suspd.		22.50	140-150
1981	To A Special Dad E-5212	Open		20.00	35-45
1981	God is Love E-5213	Suspd.		17.00	60-70
1981	Prayer Changes Things E-5214	Suspd.		35.00	125-160
1984	May Your Christmas Be Blessed E-5376	Suspd.		37.50	55-70
1984	Love is Kind E-5377	Retrd.	1987	27.50	92
1984	Joy to the World E-5378	Suspd.		18.00	50
1984	Isn't He Precious? E-5379	Open		20.00	30-40
1984	A Monarch is Born E-5380	Suspd.		33.00	65-100
1984	His Name is Jesus E-5381	Suspd.		45.00	100-110
1984	For God So Loved the World E-5382	Suspd.		70.00	110-120
1984	Wishing You a Merry Christmas E-5383	Yr.Iss.	1984	17.00	45
1984	I'll Play My Drum for Him E-5384	Open		10.00	16-30
1984	Oh Worship the Lord (B) E-5385	Suspd.		10.00	30-50
1984	Oh Worship the Lord (G) E-5386	Suspd.		10.00	40
1981	Come Let Us Adore Him E-5619	Suspd.		10.00	40
1981	Donkey Figurine E-5621	Open		6.00	15
1981	They Followed the Star E-5624	Open		130.00	200-260
1981	We Three Kings E-5635	Open		40.00	75-90
1981	Rejoice O Earth E-5636	Open		15.00	30-45
1981	The Heavenly Light E-5637	Open		15.00	30-45
1981	Cow with Bell Figurine E-5638	Open		16.00	30-40
1981	Isn't He Wonderful (B) E-5639	Suspd.		12.00	40-70
1981	Isn't He Wonderful (G) E-5640	Suspd.		12.00	45-70
1981	They Followed the Star E-5641	Suspd.		75.00	180-225
1981	Nativity Wall (2 pc. set) E-5644	Open		60.00	120-145
1984	God Sends the Gift of His Love E-6613	Suspd.		22.50	70-150
1982	God is Love, Dear Valentine E-7153	Suspd.		16.00	22-40
1982	God is Love, Dear Valentine E-7154	Suspd.		16.00	22-40
1982	Thanking Him for You E-7155	Suspd.		16.00	60
1982	I Believe in Miracles E-7156	Suspd.		17.00	90-110
1988	I Believe In Miracles E-7156R	Retrd.	1992	22.50	70-85
1982	There is Joy in Serving Jesus E-7157	Retrd.	1986	17.00	40-75
1982	Love Beareth All Things E-7158	Open		25.00	38-45
1982	Lord Give Me Patience E-7159	Suspd.		25.00	45-65
1982	The Perfect Grandpa E-7160	Suspd.		25.00	45-60
1982	His Sheep Am I E-7161	Suspd.		25.00	50-80
1982	Love is Sharing E-7162	Suspd.		25.00	140-170
1982	God is Watching Over You E-7163	Suspd.		27.50	75-105
1982	Bless This House E-7164	Suspd.		45.00	200-250
1982	Let the Whole World Know E-7165	Suspd.		45.00	100-110
1983	Love is Patient E-9251	Suspd.		35.00	65-130
1983	Forgiving is Forgetting E-9252	Suspd.		37.50	75-150
1983	The End is in Sight E-9253	Suspd.		25.00	60-85
1983	Praise the Lord Anyhow E-9254	Retrd.	1994	35.00	75-90
1983	Bless You Two E-9255	Open		21.00	40-50
1983	We are God's Workmanship E-9258	Open		19.00	33-60
1983	We're In It Together E-9259	Suspd.		24.00	65
1983	God's Promises are Sure E-9260	Suspd.		30.00	60-85
1983	Seek Ye the Lord E-9261	Suspd.		21.00	40-50
1983	Seek Ye the Lord E-9262	Suspd.		21.00	50
1983	How Can Two Walk Together Except They Agree E-9263	Suspd.		35.00	130-170
1983	Press On E-9265	Open		40.00	55-75
1983	Animal Collection, Teddy Bear E-9267A	Suspd.		6.50	20-30
1983	Animal Collection, Dog W/ Slippers E-9267B	Suspd.		6.50	18-25
1983	Animal Collection, Bunny W/ Carrot E-9267C	Suspd.		6.50	18-31
1983	Animal Collection, Kitty With Bow E-9267D	Suspd.		6.50	18-22
1983	Animal Collection, Lamb With Bird E-9267E	Suspd.		6.50	20
1983	Animal Collection, Pig W/ Patches E-9267F	Suspd.		6.50	20
1983	Nobody's Perfect E-9268	Retrd.	1990	21.00	60-95
1983	Let Love Reign E-9273	Retrd.	1987	27.50	70-85
1983	Taste and See that the Lord is Good E-9274	Retrd.	1986	22.50	55-90
1983	Jesus Loves Me E-9278	Open		9.00	17-36
1983	Jesus Loves Me E-9279	Open		9.00	17-30
1983	To Some Bunny Special E-9282A	Suspd.		8.00	18-35
1983	You're Worth Your Weight In Gold E-9282B	Suspd.		8.00	15-30
1983	Especially For Ewe E-9282C	Suspd.		8.00	15-35
1983	If God Be for Us, Who Can Be Against Us E-9285	Suspd.		27.50	55-70
1983	Peace on Earth E-9287	Suspd.		37.50	125-170
1997	And A Child Shall Lead Them E-9287R	Open		50.00	50-90
1983	Sending You a Rainbow E-9288	Suspd.		22.50	75-90
1983	Trust in the Lord E-9289	Suspd.		21.00	60-75
1985	Love Covers All 12009	Suspd.		27.50	75-90
1985	Part of Me Wants to be Good 12149	Suspd.		19.00	60-83
1987	This Is The Day Which The Lord Has Made 12157	Suspd.		20.00	50-60
1985	Get into the Habit of Prayer 12203	Suspd.		19.00	35-45
1985	Miniature Clown 12238A	Suspd.		13.50	35
1985	Miniature Clown 12238B	Suspd.		13.50	35
1985	Miniature Clown 12238C	Suspd.		13.50	35
1985	Miniature Clown 12238D	Suspd.		13.50	35
1985	It is Better to Give than to Receive 12297	Suspd.		19.00	200-275
1985	Love Never Fails 12300	Open		25.00	35-80
1985	God Bless Our Home 12319	Open		40.00	55-65
1986	You Can Fly 12335	Suspd.		25.00	60-70
1985	Jesus is Coming Soon 12343	Suspd.		22.50	35-70
1985	Halo, and Merry Christmas 12351	Suspd.		40.00	160
1985	May Your Christmas Be Delightful 15482	Suspd.		25.00	40-50
1985	Honk if You Love Jesus 15490	Open		13.00	20-35
1985	Baby's First Christmas 15539	Yr.Iss.	1985	13.00	25-40
1985	Baby's First Christmas 15547	Yr.Iss.	1985	13.00	25-40
1985	God Sent His Love 15881	Yr.Iss.	1985	17.00	25-40
1986	To My Favorite Paw 100021	Suspd.		22.50	50-60
1987	To My Deer Friend 100048	Open		33.00	50-92
1986	Sending My Love 100056	Suspd.		22.50	40-50
1986	O Worship the Lord 100064	Open		24.00	38-49
1986	To My Forever Friend 100072	Open		33.00	44-65
1987	He's The Healer Of Broken Hearts 100080	Open		33.00	50-59
1987	Make Me A Blessing 100102	Retrd.	1990	35.00	75-120
1986	Lord I'm Coming Home 100110	Open		22.50	33-55
1986	Lord, Keep Me On My Toes 100129	Retrd.	1988	22.50	80-110
1986	The Joy of the Lord is My Strength 100137	Open		35.00	50-75
1986	God Bless the Day We Found You 100145	Suspd.		37.50	90
1995	God Bless the Day We Found You(Girl) 100145R	Open		60.00	60
1986	God Bless the Day We Found You 100153	Suspd.		37.50	45-85
1995	God Bless the Day We Found You(Boy) 100153R	Open		60.00	60
1986	Serving the Lord 100161	Suspd.		19.00	50-70
1986	I'm a Possibility 100188	Retrd.	1993	21.00	65
1987	The Spirit Is Willing But The Flesh Is Weak 100196	Retrd.	1991	19.00	60-80
1987	The Lord Giveth & the Lord Taketh Away 100226	Retrd.	1995	33.50	60-80
1986	Friends Never Drift Apart 100250	Open		35.00	55-60
1986	Help, Lord, I'm In a Spot 100269	Retrd.	1989	18.50	60-90
1986	He Cleansed My Soul 100277	Open		24.00	38-60
1986	Serving the Lord 100293	Suspd.		19.00	35-55
1987	Scent From Above 100528	Retrd.	1991	19.00	60
1987	I Picked A Very Special Mom 100536	Yr.Iss.	1987	40.00	80-100
1986	Brotherly Love 100544	Suspd.		37.00	75-125
1987	No Tears Past The Gate 101826	Open		40.00	70-150
1987	Smile Along The Way 101842	Retrd.	1991	30.00	140-155

*Quotes have been rounded up to nearest dollar

FIGURINES

Precious Moments/Enesco Corporation to Precious Moments/Enesco Corporation

YEAR ISSUE		EDITION LIMIT	YEAR RETD.	ISSUE PRICE	*QUOTE U.S. $
1987	Lord, Help Us Keep Our Act Together 101850	Retrd.	1991	35.00	125-155
1986	O Worship the Lord 102229	Open		24.00	38-42
1986	Shepherd of Love 102261	Open		10.00	16-24
1986	Three Mini Animals 102296	Suspd.		13.50	30
1986	Wishing You a Cozy Christmas 102342	Yr.Iss.	1986	17.00	35-40
1986	Love Rescued Me 102393	Open		21.00	38-40
1986	Angel of Mercy 102482	Open		19.00	19-45
1986	Sharing our Christmas Together 102490	Suspd.		35.00	60-80
1987	We Are All Precious In His Sight 102903	Yr.Iss.	1987	30.00	70-110
1986	God Bless America 102938	Yr.Iss.	1986	30.00	65-75
1986	It's the Birthday of a King 102962	Suspd.		18.50	35-50
1987	I Would Be Sunk Without You 102970	Open		15.00	20-30
1987	My Love Will Never Let You Go 103497	Open		25.00	38-45
1986	I Believe in the Old Rugged Cross 103632	Open		25.00	35-40
1986	Come Let Us Adore Him 104000 (9 pc. set w/cassette)	Open		95.00	130
1987	With this Ring I... 104019	Open		40.00	60-70
1987	Love Is The Glue That Mends 104027	Suspd.		33.50	45-65
1987	Cheers To The Leader 104035	Retrd.	1997	22.50	30-39
1987	Happy Days Are Here Again 104396	Suspd.		25.00	65-75
1987	A Tub Full of Love 104817	Open		22.50	30-42
1987	Sitting Pretty 104825	Suspd.		22.50	40
1987	Have I Got News For You 105635	Suspd.		22.50	30-55
1988	Something's Missing When You're Not Around 105643	Suspd.		32.50	50-65
1987	To Tell The Tooth You're Special 105813	Suspd.		38.50	90-200
1988	Hallelujah Country 105821	Open		35.00	45-55
1987	We're Pulling For You 106151	Suspd.		40.00	55-70
1987	God Bless You Graduate 106194	Open		20.00	33-35
1987	Congratulations Princess 106208	Open		20.00	33-35
1987	Lord Help Me Make the Grade 106216	Suspd.		25.00	65-75
1988	Heaven Bless Your Togetherness 106755	Open		65.00	80-87
1988	Precious Memories 106763	Open		37.50	50-55
1988	Puppy Love Is From Above 106798	Retrd.	1995	45.00	60-75
1988	Happy Birthday Poppy 106836	Suspd.		27.50	45
1988	Sew In Love 106844	Retrd.	1997	45.00	55-75
1987	They Followed The Star 108243	Open		75.00	120
1987	The Greatest Gift Is A Friend 109231	Open		30.00	38-50
1988	Believe the Impossible 109487	Suspd.		35.00	60-90
1988	Happiness Divine 109584	Retrd.	1992	25.00	50-80
1987	Wishing You A Yummy Christmas 109754	Suspd.		35.00	40-55
1987	We Gather Together To Ask The Lord's Blessing 109762	Retrd.	1995	130.00	175-275
1988	Meowie Christmas 109800	Open		30.00	40-50
1987	Oh What Fun It Is To Ride 109819	Open		85.00	110-135
1988	Wishing You A Happy Easter 109886	Open		23.00	35
1988	Wishing You A Basket Full Of Blessings 109924	Open		23.00	30
1988	Sending You My Love 109967	Open		35.00	45-60
1988	Mommy, I Love You 109975	Open		22.50	30-34
1987	Love Is The Best Gift of All 110930	Yr.Iss.	1987	22.50	35-45
1988	Faith Takes The Plunge 111155	Open		27.50	40-50
1988	Tis the Season 111163	Suspd.		27.50	40-50
1987	O Come Let Us Adore Him (4 pc. 9" Nativity) 111333	Suspd.		200.00	225-275
1988	Mommy, I Love You 112143	Open		22.50	30-36
1987	A Tub Full of Love 112313	Open		22.50	30-75
1988	This Too Shall Pass 114014	Open		23.00	28-37
1988	Some Bunny's Sleeping 115274	Suspd.		15.00	20-30
1988	Our First Christmas Together 115290	Suspd.		50.00	60-80
1988	Time to Wish You a Merry Christmas 115339	Yr.Iss.	1988	24.00	35-50
1995	Love Blooms Eternal 127019 (1st in dated cross series)	Yr.Iss.	1995	35.00	35
1995	Dreams Really Do Come True 128309	Open		37.50	38
1995	Another Year More Grey Hares 128686	Open		17.50	18
1995	Happy Hula Days 128694	Open		30.00	30
1995	I Give You My Love Forever True 129100	Open		70.00	70
1997	Love Letters in The Sand 129488	Open		35.00	35
1995	He Covers the Earth With His Beauty 142654	Yr.Iss.	1995	30.00	30
1995	Come Let Us Adore Him 142735 (large nativity)	Open		50.00	50
1995	Come Let Us Adore Him 142743 (small nativity)	Open		35.00	35
1995	Making A Trail to Bethlehem 142751	Open		30.00	30
1995	I'll Give Him My Heart 150088	Open		40.00	40
1995	Soot Yourself To A Merry Christmas 150096	Open		35.00	35
1995	Making Spirits Bright 150118	Open		37.50	38
1996	Standing In The Presence Of The Lord 163732 (2nd in dated cross series)	Yr.Iss.	1996	37.50	38
1996	Take It To The Lord In Prayer 163767	Open		30.00	30
1996	The Sun Is Always Shining Somewhere 163775	Open		37.50	38
1996	Sowing Seeds of Kindness 163856 (1st in Growing In God's Garden Of Love Series)	Open		37.50	38

YEAR ISSUE		EDITION LIMIT	YEAR RETD.	ISSUE PRICE	*QUOTE U.S.$
1996	Some Plant, Some Water, But God Giveth The Increase 176958 (2nd in Growing In God's Garden Of Love Series)	Open		37.50	38
1996	It May Be Greener, But It's Just As Hard to Cut 163899	Open		37.50	38
1996	God's Love Is Reflected In You 175277	15,000		150.00	150
1996	Peace On Earth...Anyway 183342	Yr.Iss.	1996	32.50	33
1996	Angels On Earth-Boy Making Snow Angel 183776	Open		40.00	40
1996	Snowbunny Loves You Like I Do 183792	Open		18.50	19
1996	Sing In Excelsis Deo Tree Topper 183830	Open		125.00	125
1996	Color Your World With Thanksgiving 183857	Open		50.00	50
1996	Shepard/Standing White Lamb/Sitting Black Lamb 3pc. Nativity set 183954	Open		40.00	40
1996	Making a Trail to Bethlehem-Mini Nativity 184004	Open		18.50	19
1996	All Sing His Praises-Large Nativity 184012	Open		32.50	33
1996	Love Makes The World Go 'Round 184209	Yr.Iss.	1996	22.50	23
1997	A Bouquet From God's Garden Of Love 184268 (3rd in God's Garden of Love series)	Open		37.50	38
1997	You're A Life Saver To Me 204854	Open		35.00	35
1996	Wee Three Kings-Mini Nativity set 213624	Open		55.00	55
1997	Lead Me To Calvary 260916 (3rd in dated cross series)	Yr.Iss.		37.50	38
1997	Friends From The Very Beginning 261068	Open		50.00	50
1997	You Have Touched So Many Hearts 261084	Open		37.50	38
1997	Lettuce Pray 261122	Open		17.50	18
1997	Have You Any Room For Jesus 261130	Open		35.00	35
1997	Say I Do 261149	Open		35.00	35
1997	We All Have Our Bad Hair Days 261157	Open		35.00	35
1997	The Lord Is the Hope Of Our Future 261564	Open		40.00	40
1988	Rejoice O Earth 520268	Open		13.00	17-27
1988	Jesus the Savior Is Born 520357	Suspd.		25.00	30-40
1992	The Lord Turned My Life Around 520535	Suspd.		35.00	45
1991	In The Spotlight Of His Grace 520543	Suspd.		35.00	40-56
1990	Lord, Turn My Life Around 520551	Suspd.		35.00	40-50
1992	You Deserve An Ovation 520578	Open		35.00	35
1989	My Heart Is Exposed With Love 520624	Open		45.00	55-60
1989	A Friend Is Someone Who Cares 520632	Retrd.	1995	30.00	60-70
1989	I'm So Glad You Fluttered Into My Life 520640	Retrd.	1991	40.00	275-325
1989	Eggspecially For You 520667	Open		45.00	50
1989	Your Love Is So Uplifting 520675	Open		60.00	65-79
1989	Sending You Showers Of Blessings 520683	Retrd.	1992	32.50	50-90
1989	Just A LineTo Wish You A Happy Day 520721	Suspd.		65.00	80
1989	Friendship Hits The Spot 520748	Open		55.00	60-70
1989	Jesus Is The Only Way 520756	Suspd.		40.00	55-65
1989	Puppy Love 520764	Open		12.50	45-70
1989	Many Moons In Same Canoe, Blessum You 520772	Retrd.	1990	50.00	300-375
1989	Wishing You Roads Of Happiness 520780	Open		60.00	75-100
1989	Someday My Love 520799	Retrd.	1992	40.00	70-85
1989	My Days Are Blue Without You 520802	Suspd.		65.00	90-115
1989	We Need A Good Friend Through The Ruff Times 520810	Suspd.		35.00	40-60
1989	You Are My Number One 520829	Open		25.00	33-42
1989	The Lord Is Your Light To Happiness 520837	Open		50.00	65
1989	Wishing You A Perfect Choice 520845	Open		55.00	60-67
1989	I Belong To The Lord 520853	Suspd.		25.00	30-45
1990	Heaven Bless You 520934	Open		35.00	30-150
1993	There Is No Greater Treasure Than To Have A Friend Like You 521000	Open		30.00	30
1990	That's What Friends Are For 521183	Open		45.00	45-49
1997	Lord, Spare Me 521191	Open		50.00	50
1990	Hope You're Up And OnThe Trail Again 521205	Suspd.		35.00	40-60
1993	The Fruit of the Spirit is Love 521213	Yr.Iss.	1993	30.00	35
1996	Enter His Court With Thanksgiving 521221	Open		35.00	35
1991	Take Heed When You Stand 521272	Suspd.		55.00	60-75
1990	Happy Trip 521280	Suspd.		35.00	35-60
1991	Hug One Another 521299	Retrd.	1995	45.00	50-80
1990	Yield Not To Temptation 521310	Suspd.		27.50	30-45
1990	Faith Is A Victory 521396	Retrd.	1993	25.00	125-185
1990	I'll Never Stop Loving You 521418	Retrd.	1996	37.50	38-53
1991	To A Very Special Mom & Dad 521434	Suspd.		35.00	35-45
1990	Lord, Help Me Stick To My Job 521450	Retrd.	1997	30.00	30-48
1989	Tell It To Jesus 521477	Open		35.00	38-60
1991	There's A Light At The End Of The Tunnel 521485	Suspd.		55.00	70
1991	A Special Delivery 521493	Open		30.00	30

YEAR ISSUE		EDITION LIMIT	YEAR RETD.	ISSUE PRICE	*QUOTE U.S.$
1991	Thumb-body Loves You 521698	Suspd.		55.00	65
1996	My Love Blooms For You 521728	Open		50.00	50-75
1990	Sweep All Your Worries Away 521779	Retrd.	1996	40.00	40-110
1990	Good Friends Are Forever 521817	Open		50.00	50-60
1990	Love Is From Above 521841	Suspd.		45.00	40-50
1989	The Greatest of These Is Love 521868	Suspd.		27.50	35-60
1990	Easter's On Its Way 521892	Open		60.00	40-45
1991	Hoppy Easter Friend 521906	Open		40.00	55-60
1994	Perfect Harmony 521914	Open		55.00	55
1993	Safe In The Arms Of Jesus 521922	Open		30.00	30
1989	Wishing You A Cozy Season 521949	Suspd.		42.50	50-60
1990	High Hopes 521957	Suspd.		30.00	40-45
1991	To A Special Mum 521965	Open		30.00	30-35
1996	Marching To The Beat of Freedom's Drum 521981	Open		35.00	35
1993	To The Apple Of God's Eye 522015	Yr.Iss.	1993	32.50	35
1989	May Your Life Be Blessed With Touchdowns 522023	Open		45.00	50-60
1989	Thank You Lord For Everything 522031	Suspd.		55.00	65-90
1994	Now I Lay Me Down To Sleep 522058	Retrd.	1997	30.00	35
1991	May Your World Be Trimmed With Joy 522082	Suspd.		55.00	55-65
1990	There Shall Be Showers Of Blessings 522090	Open		60.00	70
1992	It's No Yolk When I Say I Love You 522104	Suspd.		60.00	65-90
1989	Don't Let the Holidays Get You Down 522112	Retrd.	1993	42.50	80-100
1989	Wishing You A Very Successful Season 522120	Open		60.00	65-70
1989	Bon Voyage! 522201	Suspd.		75.00	90-125
1989	He Is The Star Of The Morning 522252	Suspd.		55.00	65-75
1989	To Be With You Is Uplifting 522260	Retrd.	1994	20.00	25-40
1991	A Reflection Of His Love 522279	Open		50.00	50
1990	Thinking Of You Is What I Really Like To Do 522287	Suspd.		30.00	30-42
1989	Merry Christmas Deer 522317	Retrd.	1997	50.00	60-90
1996	Sweeter As The Years Go By 522333	Open		60.00	60
1989	Oh Holy Night 522546	Yr.Iss.	1989	25.00	50
1995	Just A Line To Say You're Special 522864	Open		50.00	50
1997	On My Way To A Perfect Day 522872	Open		45.00	45
1989	Isn't He Precious 522988	Suspd.		15.00	20-30
1990	Some Bunny's Sleeping 522996	Suspd.		12.00	25
1989	Jesus Is The Sweetest Name I Know 523097	Suspd.		22.50	30-35
1991	Joy On Arrival 523178	Open		50.00	50-60
1990	The Good Lord Always Delivers 523453	Open		27.50	28-35
1990	This Day Has Been Made In Heaven 523496	Open		30.00	33-40
1990	God Is Love Dear Valentine 523518	Open		27.50	28-40
1991	I Will Cherish The Old Rugged Cross 523534	Yr.Iss.	1991	27.50	35
1992	You Are The Type I Love 523542	Open		40.00	40-50
1993	The Lord Will Provide 523593	Yr.Iss.	1993	40.00	40-55
1991	Good News Is So Uplifting 523615	Open		60.00	65-75
1992	I'm So Glad That God Has Blessed Me With A Friend Like You 523623	Retrd.	1995	50.00	70-80
1994	I Will Always Be Thinking Of You 523631	Retrd.	1996	45.00	55
1990	Time Heals 523739	Open		37.50	38-45
1990	Blessings From Above 523747	Retrd.	1994	45.00	80-100
1994	Just Poppin' In To Say Halo 523755	Open		45.00	45
1991	I Can't Spell Success Without You 523763	Suspd.		40.00	50-75
1990	Once Upon A Holy Night 523836	Yr.Iss.	1990	25.00	35-45
1996	Love Never Leaves A Mother's Arms 523941	Open		40.00	40
1992	My Warmest Thoughts Are You 524085	Retrd.	1996	55.00	75
1991	Good Friends Are For Always 524123	Open		27.50	75
1994	Lord Teach Us to Pray 524158	Yr.Iss.	1994	35.00	40-50
1991	May Your Christmas Be Merry 524166	Yr.Iss.	1991	27.50	38
1995	Walk In The Sonshine 524212	Open		35.00	35
1991	He Loves Me 524263	Yr.Iss.	1991	35.00	40-50
1992	Friendship Grows When You Plant A Seed 524271	Retrd.	1994	40.00	85-100
1993	May Your Every Wish Come True 524298	Open		50.00	50
1991	May Your Birthday Be A Blessing 524301	Open		30.00	33-45
1992	What The World Needs Now 524352	Retrd.	1997	50.00	55
1997	Something Precious From Above 524360	Open		50.00	50
1993	You Are Such A Purr-fect Friend 524395	Open		35.00	35
1991	May Only Good Things Come Your Way 524425	Open		30.00	38
1993	Sealed With A Kiss 524441	Retrd.	1996	50.00	60
1993	A Special Chime For Jesus 524468	Yr.Iss.	1993	32.50	35
1994	God Cared Enough To Send His Best 524476	Retrd.	1996	50.00	60
1990	Happy Birthday Dear Jesus 524875	Suspd.		13.50	20
1992	It's So Uplifting To Have A Friend Like You 524905	Open		40.00	45
1990	We're Going To Miss You 524913	Open		50.00	50

*Quotes have been rounded up to nearest dollar

Precious Moments/Enesco Corporation
to Precious Moments/Enesco Corporation

FIGURINES

YEAR ISSUE		EDITION LIMIT	YEAR RETD.	ISSUE PRICE	*QUOTE U.S.$
1991	Angels We Have Heard On High 524921	Retrd.	1996	60.00	75
1992	Tubby's First Christmas 525278	Open		10.00	10
1991	It's A Perfect Boy 525286	Open		16.50	17
1993	May Your Future Be Blessed 525316	Open		35.00	38
1992	Ring Those Christmas Bells 525898	Retrd.	1996	95.00	115
1992	Going Home 525979	Open		60.00	60
1996	A Prince Of A Guy 526038	Open		35.00	35
1996	Pretty As A Princess 526053	Open		35.00	35
1992	I Would Be Lost Without You 526142	Open		27.50	28
1994	Friends To The Very End 526150	Retrd.	1997	40.00	45-50
1992	You Are My Happiness 526185	Yr.Iss.	1992	37.50	35-80
1994	You Suit Me to a Tee 526193	Open		35.00	35
1994	Sharing Sweet Moments Together 526487	Open		45.00	45-55
1996	The Lord Is With You 526835	Open		27.50	28
1991	We Have Come From Afar 526959	Suspd.		17.50	25
1993	Bless-Um You 527335	Open		35.00	35-42
1992	You Are My Favorite Star 527378	Retrd.	1997	55.00	75
1992	Bring The Little Ones To Jesus 527556	Open		90.00	90-110
1992	God Bless The U.S.A. 527564	Yr.Iss.	1992	32.50	35-45
1993	Tied Up For The Holidays 527580	Suspd.		40.00	42
1993	Bringing You A Merry Christmas 527599	Retrd.	1995	45.00	80-100
1992	Wishing You A Ho Ho Ho 527629	Open		40.00	40-55
1991	You Have Touched So Many Hearts w/personalization kit 527661	Suspd.		37.50	38
1992	But The Greatest of These Is Love 527688	Yr.Iss.	1992	27.50	35
1992	Wishing You A Comfy Christmas 527750	Open		30.00	30
1993	I Only Have Arms For You 527769	Open		15.00	16
1992	This Land Is Our Land 527777	Yr.Iss.	1992	35.00	35-45
1994	Nativity Cart 528072	Open		16.00	16-20
1994	Have I Got News For You 528137	Open		16.00	17
1994	To a Very Special Sister 528633	Open		60.00	60-70
1993	America You're Beautiful 528862	Yr.Iss.	1993	35.00	50
1996	My True Love Gave To Me 529273	Open		40.00	40
1993	Ring Out The Good News 529966	Yr.Iss.	1993	27.50	38
1993	Wishing You the Sweetest Christmas 530166	Yr.Iss.	1993	27.50	40
1994	You're As Pretty As A Christmas Tree 530425	Yr.Iss.	1994	27.50	35
1994	Serenity Prayer Girl 530697	Open		35.00	35
1994	Serenity Prayer Boy 530700	Open		35.00	35
1995	We Have Come From Afar 530913	Open		12.00	12
1995	I Only Have Ice For You 530956	Open		27.50	28-60
1997	Sometimes You're Next To Impossible 530964	Open		50.00	50
1997	Potty Time 531022	Open		25.00	25
1995	What The World Needs Is Love 531065	Open		45.00	45
1994	Money's Not The Only Green Thing Worth Saving 531073	Retrd.	1996	50.00	60
1996	What A Difference You've Made In My Life 531138	Open		50.00	50
1995	Vaya Con Dios (To Go With God) 531146	Open		32.50	33-40
1995	Bless Your Soul 531162	Open		25.00	25-35
1997	Who's Gonna Fill You're Shoes 531634	Open		37.50	38
1996	You Deserve a Halo—Thank You 531693	Open		55.00	55
1994	The Lord is Counting on You 531707	Open		32.50	33-40
1994	Dropping In For The Holidays 531952	Open		40.00	40
1995	Hallelujah For The Cross 532002	Open		35.00	35
1995	Sending You Oceans Of Love 532010	Retrd.	1996	35.00	35
1995	I Can't Bear To Let You Go 532037	Open		50.00	50
1995	Lord Help Me To Stay On Course 532096	Open		35.00	35
1994	The Lord Bless You and Keep You 532118	Open		40.00	45-50
1994	The Lord Bless You and Keep You 532126	Open		30.00	33-40
1994	The Lord Bless You and Keep You 532134	Open		30.00	33
1994	Luke 2:10 11 532916	Open		35.00	35
1994	Nothing Can Dampen The Spirit of Caring 603864	Open		35.00	35
1995	A Poppy For You 604208	Open		35.00	35

Anniversary Figurines - S. Butcher

YEAR ISSUE		EDITION LIMIT	YEAR RETD.	ISSUE PRICE	*QUOTE U.S.$
1984	God Blessed Our Years Together With So Much Love And Happiness E-2853	Open		35.00	50-60
1984	God Blessed Our Year Together With So Much Love And Happiness (1st) E-2854	Open		35.00	50-60
1984	God Blessed Our Years Together With So Much Love And Happiness (5th) E-2855	Suspd.		35.00	50-55
1984	God Blessed Our Years Together With So Much Love And Happiness (10th) E-2856	Suspd.		35.00	50-55
1984	God Blessed Our Years Together With So Much Love And Happiness (25th) E-2857	Open		35.00	50-60
1984	God Blessed Our Years Together With So Much Love And Happiness (40th) E-2859	Suspd.		35.00	50-60
1984	God Blessed Our Years Together With So Much Love And Happiness (50th) E-2860	Open		35.00	50-60
1994	I Still Do 530999	Open		30.00	30
1994	I Still Do 531006	Open		30.00	30

Baby Classics - S. Butcher

YEAR ISSUE		EDITION LIMIT	YEAR RETD.	ISSUE PRICE	*QUOTE U.S.$
1997	Good Friends Are Forever 272422	Open		30.00	30
1997	Make A Joyful Noice 272450	Open		30.00	30
1997	We Are God's Workmanship 272434	Open		25.00	25
1997	I Believe In Miracles 272469	Open		25.00	25
1997	God Loveth A Cheerful Giver 272477	Open		25.00	25
1997	Love Is Sharing 272493	Open		25.00	25
1997	You Have Touched So Many Hearts 272485	Open		25.00	25
1997	Love One Another 272507	Open		30.00	30

Baby's First - S. Butcher

YEAR ISSUE		EDITION LIMIT	YEAR RETD.	ISSUE PRICE	*QUOTE U.S.$
1984	Baby's First Step E-2840	Suspd.		35.00	50-95
1984	Baby's First Picture E-2841	Retrd.	1986	45.00	155-200
1985	Baby's First Haircut 12211	Suspd.		32.50	145-175
1986	Baby's First Trip 16012	Suspd.		32.50	200-300
1989	Baby's First Pet 520705	Suspd.		45.00	70-85
1990	Baby's First Meal 524077	Open		35.00	35-45
1992	Baby's First Word 527238	Open		24.00	24-30
1993	Baby's First Birthday 524069	Open		25.00	25

Birthday Club Figurines - S. Butcher

YEAR ISSUE		EDITION LIMIT	YEAR RETD.	ISSUE PRICE	*QUOTE U.S.$
1986	Fishing For Friends BC-861	Yr.Iss.	1986	10.00	130-160
1987	Hi Sugar BC-871	Yr.Iss.	1987	11.00	85-120
1988	Somebunny Cares BC-881	Yr.Iss.	1988	13.50	45-195
1989	Can't Bee Hive Myself Without You BC-891	Yr.Iss.	1989	13.50	45
1990	Collecting Makes Good Scents BC-901	Yr.Iss.	1990	15.00	35-45
1990	I'm Nuts Over My Collection BC-902	Yr.Iss.	1990	15.00	40
1991	Love Pacifies BC-911	Yr.Iss.	1991	15.00	35
1991	True Blue Friends BC-912	Yr.Iss.	1991	15.00	30
1992	Every Man's Home Is His Castle BC-921	Yr.Iss.	1992	16.50	25-35
1992	I Got You Under My Skin BC-922	Yr.Iss.	1992	16.00	30-40
1993	Put a Little Punch In Your Birthday BC-931	Yr.Iss.	1993	15.00	22
1993	Owl Always Be Your Friend BC-932	Yr.Iss.	1993	16.00	25
1994	God Bless Our Home BC-941	Yr.Iss.	1994	16.00	20-43
1994	Yer A Pel-I-Can Count On BC-942	Yr.Iss.	1994	16.00	25
1995	Making A Point To Say You're Special BC-951	Yr.Iss.	1995	15.00	35
1995	10 Wonderful Years Of Wishes BC-952	Yr.Iss.	1995	50.00	50
1996	There's A Spot In My Heart For You BC-961	Yr.Iss.	1996	15.00	15
1996	You're First In My Heart BC-962	Yr.Iss.	1996	15.00	15

Birthday Club Inscribed Charter Membership Renewal Gift - S. Butcher

YEAR ISSUE		EDITION LIMIT	YEAR RETD.	ISSUE PRICE	*QUOTE U.S.$
1987	A Smile's the Cymbal of Joy B-0102	Yr.Iss.	1987	Unkn.	60-80
1988	The Sweetest Club Around B-0103	Yr.Iss.	1988	Unkn.	50-70
1989	Have A Beary Special Birthday B-0104	Yr.Iss.	1989	Unkn.	30-60
1990	Our Club Is A Tough Act To Follow B-0105	Yr.Iss.	1990	Unkn.	30-40
1991	Jest To Let You Know You're Tops B-0106	Yr.Iss.	1991	Unkn.	45-60
1992	All Aboard For Birthday Club Fun B-0107	Yr.Iss.	1992	Unkn.	30-50
1993	Happiness is Belonging B-0108	Yr.Iss.	1993	Unkn.	20-35
1994	Can't Get Enough of Our Club B-0109	Yr.Iss.	1994	Unkn.	25
1995	Hoppy Birthday B-0110	Yr.Iss.	1995	Unkn.	Unkn.
1996	Scootin' By Just To Say Hi! B-0111	Yr.Iss.	1996	Unkn.	Unkn.

Birthday Club Welcome Gift - S. Butcher

YEAR ISSUE		EDITION LIMIT	YEAR RETD.	ISSUE PRICE	*QUOTE U.S.$
1986	Our Club Can't Be Beat B-0001	Yr.Iss.	1986	Unkn.	70-85
1987	A Smile's The Cymbal of Joy B-0002	Yr.Iss.	1987	Unkn.	55-70
1988	The Sweetest Club Around B-0003	Yr.Iss.	1988	Unkn.	45
1989	Have A Beary Special Birthday B-0004	Yr.Iss.	1989	Unkn.	30-40
1990	Our Club Is A Tough Act To Follow B-0005	Yr.Iss.	1990	Unkn.	25-35
1991	Jest To Let You Know You're Tops B-0006	Yr.Iss.	1991	Unkn.	40-55
1992	All Aboard For Birthday Club Fun B-0007	Yr.Iss.	1992	Unkn.	30-40
1993	Happiness Is Belonging B-0008	Yr.Iss.	1993	Unkn.	20-30
1994	Can't Get Enough of Our Club B-0009	Yr.Iss.	1994	Unkn.	25
1995	Hoppy Birthday B-0010	Yr.Iss.	1995	Unkn.	Unkn.
1996	Scootin' By Just To Say Hi! B-0011	Yr.Iss.	1996	Unkn.	Unkn.

Birthday Series - S. Butcher

YEAR ISSUE		EDITION LIMIT	YEAR RETD.	ISSUE PRICE	*QUOTE U.S.$
1988	Friends To The End 104418	Suspd.		15.00	30
1987	Showers Of Blessings 105945	Retrd.	1993	16.00	35-50
1987	Brighten Someone's Day 105953	Suspd.		12.50	35
1990	To My Favorite Fan 521043	Suspd.		16.00	35
1989	Hello World! 521175	Open		13.50	15-30
1993	Hope You're Over The Hump 521671	Suspd.		16.00	16
1990	Not A Creature Was Stirring 524484	Suspd.		17.00	20-30
1991	Can't Be Without You 524492	Open		16.00	17-29
1991	How Can I Ever Forget You 526924	Open		15.00	17
1992	Let's Be Friends 527270	Retrd.	1996	15.00	15-20
1992	Happy Birdie 527343	Suspd.		8.00	25
1993	Happy Birthday Jesus 530492	Open		20.00	20
1994	Oinky Birthday 524506	Open		13.50	14
1995	Wishing You A Happy Bear Hug 520659	Suspd.		27.50	30
1996	I Haven't Seen Much of You Lately 531057	Open		13.50	14
1997	From The First Time I Spotted You I Knew We'd Be Friends 260940	Open		18.50	19

Birthday Train Figurines - S. Butcher

YEAR ISSUE		EDITION LIMIT	YEAR RETD.	ISSUE PRICE	*QUOTE U.S.$
1988	Isn't Eight Just Great 109460	Open		18.50	23
1988	Wishing You Grr-eatness 109479	Open		18.50	23-30
1985	May Your Birthday Be Warm 15938	Open		10.00	16-25
1985	Happy Birthday Little Lamb 15946	Open		10.00	15-30
1985	Heaven Bless Your Special Day 15954	Open		11.00	18-25
1985	God Bless You On Your Birthday 15962	Open		11.00	18-35
1985	May Your Birthday Be Gigantic 15970	Open		12.50	20-35
1985	This Day Is Something To Roar About 15989	Open		13.50	23-35
1985	Keep Looking Up 15997	Open		13.50	23-30
1985	Bless The Days Of Our Youth 16004	Open		15.00	23-30
1991	May Your Birthday Be Mammoth 521825	Open		25.00	25-35
1991	Being Nine Is Just Divine 521833	Open		25.00	25-35

Bless Those Who Serve Their Country - S. Butcher

YEAR ISSUE		EDITION LIMIT	YEAR RETD.	ISSUE PRICE	*QUOTE U.S.$
1991	Bless Those Who Serve Their Country (Navy) 526568	Suspd.		32.50	125-150
1991	Bless Those Who Serve Their Country (Army) 526576	Suspd.		32.50	50-60
1991	Bless Those Who Serve Their Country (Air Force) 526584	Suspd.		32.50	45-60
1991	Bless Those Who Serve Their Country (Girl Soldier) 527289	Suspd.		32.50	48
1991	Bless Those Who Serve Their Country (Soldier) 527297	Suspd.		32.50	50-60
1991	Bless Those Who Serve Their Country (Marine) 527521	Suspd.		32.50	50-60
1995	You Will Always Be Our Hero 136271	Yr.Iss.	1995	40.00	45

Boys & Girls Club - S. Butcher

YEAR ISSUE		EDITION LIMIT	YEAR RETD.	ISSUE PRICE	*QUOTE U.S.$
1996	Shoot For The Stars And You'll Never Strike Out 521701	Open		60.00	60

Bridal Party - S. Butcher

YEAR ISSUE		EDITION LIMIT	YEAR RETD.	ISSUE PRICE	*QUOTE U.S.$
1984	Bridesmaid E-2831	Open		13.50	22
1985	Ringbearer E-2833	Open		11.00	17-20
1985	Flower Girl E-2835	Open		11.00	17-25
1984	Best Man E-2836	Open		13.50	22-28
1986	Groom E-2837	Open		13.50	20-30
1987	This is the Day That the Lord Hath Made E-2838	N/A		185.00	195
1985	Junior Bridesmaid E-2845	Open		12.50	20-30
1987	Bride E-2846	Open		18.00	25-30
1987	God Bless Our Family (Parents of the Groom) 100498	Open		35.00	50-55
1987	God Bless Our Family (Parents of the Bride) 100501	Open		35.00	50-60
1987	Wedding Arch 102369	Suspd.		22.50	40-55

Calendar Girl - S. Butcher

YEAR ISSUE		EDITION LIMIT	YEAR RETD.	ISSUE PRICE	*QUOTE U.S.$
1988	January 109983	Open		37.50	40-67
1988	February 109991	Open		27.50	38-67
1988	March 110019	Open		27.50	38-50
1988	April 110027	Open		30.00	38-70
1988	May 110035	Open		25.00	30-175
1988	June 110043	Open		40.00	50-70
1988	July 110051	Open		35.00	45-58
1988	August 110078	Open		40.00	45-58
1988	September 110086	Open		27.50	38-50
1988	October 110094	Open		35.00	45-59
1988	November 110108	Open		32.50	38-50
1988	December 110116	Open		27.50	35-75

Clown - S. Butcher

YEAR ISSUE		EDITION LIMIT	YEAR RETD.	ISSUE PRICE	*QUOTE U.S.$
1985	I Get a Bang Out of You 12262	Retrd.	1997	30.00	50-65
1986	Lord Keep Me On the Ball 12270	Open		30.00	45-60
1985	Waddle I Do Without You 12459	Retrd.	1989	30.00	90-100
1986	The Lord Will Carry You Through 12467	Retrd.	1988	30.00	80-110

Commemorative 500th Columbus Anniversary - S. Butcher

YEAR ISSUE		EDITION LIMIT	YEAR RETD.	ISSUE PRICE	*QUOTE U.S.$
1992	This Land Is Our Land 527386	Yr.Iss.	1992	350.00	350-425

Commemorative Easter Seal - S. Butcher

YEAR ISSUE		EDITION LIMIT	YEAR RETD.	ISSUE PRICE	*QUOTE U.S.$
1988	Jesus Loves Me 9" Fig. 104531	1,000		500.00	1800-2000
1987	He Walks With Me 107999	Yr.Iss.	1987	25.00	35-55
1988	Blessed Are They That Overcome 115479	Yr.Iss.	1988	27.50	50-65
1989	Make A Joyful Noise 9" 520322	1,500		N/A	900-950
1989	His Love Will Shine On You 522376	Yr.Iss.	1989	30.00	50-65
1990	You Have Touched So Many Hearts 9" fig. 523283	2,000		500.00	600-775

*Quotes have been rounded up to nearest dollar

YEAR ISSUE		EDITION LIMIT	YEAR RETD.	ISSUE PRICE	*QUOTE U.S.$
1991	We Are God's Workmanship 9" 523879	2,000		N/A	650-725
1990	Always In His Care 524522	Yr.Iss.	1990	30.00	40-55
1992	You Are Such A Purr-fect Friend 9" 526010	2,000		N/A	600-700
1991	Sharing A Gift Of Love 527114	Yr.Iss.	1991	30.00	40-65
1992	A Universal Love 527173	Yr.Iss.	1992	32.50	40-60
1993	Gather Your Dreams 9" 529680	2,000		500.00	600
1993	You're My Number One Friend 530026	Yr.Iss.	1993	30.00	40
1994	It's No Secret What God Can Do 531111	Yr.Iss.	1994	30.00	35
1994	You Are The Rose of His Creation 9" 531243	2,000		N/A	N/A
1995	Take Time To Smell the Flowers 524387	Yr.Iss.	1995	30.00	30
1995	He's Got The Whole World In His Hands 9" 526886	Yr.Iss.	1995	500.00	N/A
1996	He Loves Me 9" 152277	2,000		500.00	N/A
1996	You Can Always Count on Me 526827	Yr.Iss.	1996	30.00	30
1997	Love Is Universal 9" 192376	2,000		N/A	N/A
1997	Give Ability A Chance 192368	Yr.Iss.		30.00	30

Events Figurines - S. Butcher

YEAR ISSUE		EDITION LIMIT	YEAR RETD.	ISSUE PRICE	*QUOTE U.S.$
1988	You Are My Main Event 115231	Yr.Iss.	1988	30.00	45-60
1989	Sharing Begins In The Heart 520861	Yr.Iss.	1989	25.00	55-70
1990	I'm A Precious Moments Fan 523526	Yr.Iss.	1990	25.00	40
1990	Good Friends Are Forever 525049	Yr.Iss.	1990	25.00	N/A
1991	You Can Always Bring A Friend 527122	Yr.Iss.	1991	27.50	45
1992	An Event Worth Wading For 527319	Yr.Iss.	1992	32.50	40
1993	An Event For All Seasons 530158	Yr.Iss.	1993	30.00	40
1994	Memories Are Made of This 529982	Yr.Iss.	1994	30.00	30
1995	Follow Your Heart 528080	Yr.Iss.	1995	30.00	30
1996	Hallelujah Hoedown 163864	Yr.Iss.	1996	32.50	30-45
1997	We're So Hoppy You're Here 261351	Yr.Iss.		32.50	33

Family Christmas Scene - S. Butcher

YEAR ISSUE		EDITION LIMIT	YEAR RETD.	ISSUE PRICE	*QUOTE U.S.$
1985	May You Have the Sweetest Christmas 15776	Suspd.		17.00	25-55
1985	The Story of God's Love 15784	Suspd.		22.50	40-70
1985	Tell Me a Story 15792	Suspd.		10.00	35-40
1985	God Gave His Best 15806	Suspd.		13.00	40-55
1985	Silent Night 15814	Suspd.		37.50	100-130
1986	Sharing Our Christmas Together 102490	Suspd.		40.00	50-60
1990	Have A Beary Merry Christmas 522856	Suspd.		15.00	30
1990	Christmas Fireplace 524883	Suspd.		37.50	55-65

Four Seasons - S. Butcher

YEAR ISSUE		EDITION LIMIT	YEAR RETD.	ISSUE PRICE	*QUOTE U.S.$
1985	The Voice of Spring 12068	Yr.Iss.	1985	30.00	250-325
1985	Summer's Joy 12076	Yr.Iss.	1985	30.00	100-175
1986	Autumn's Praise 12084	Yr.Iss.	1986	30.00	90-105
1986	Winter's Song 12092	Yr.Iss.	1986	30.00	90-105
1986	Set	Yr.Iss.	1986	120.00	550

Growing In Grace - S. Butcher

YEAR ISSUE		EDITION LIMIT	YEAR RETD.	ISSUE PRICE	*QUOTE U.S.$
1995	Infant Angel w/Newspaper 136204	Open		22.50	23
1995	Age 1 Baby With Cake 136190	Open		25.00	25
1995	Age 2 Girl With Blocks 136212	Open		25.00	25
1995	Age 3 Girl With Flowers 136220	Open		25.00	25
1995	Age 4 Girl With Doll 136239	Open		27.50	28
1995	Age 5 Girl w/Lunch Box 136247	Open		27.50	28
1995	Age 6 Girl On Bicycle 136255	Open		30.00	30
1996	Age 7 Girl Dressed As Nurse 163740	Open		32.50	33
1996	Age 8 Girl Shooting Marbles 163759	Open		32.50	33
1995	Age 16 Sweet Sixteen Girl Holding Sixteen Roses 136263	Open		45.00	45
1996	Age 9 Girl w/Charm Bracelet 183865	Open		30.00	30
1996	Age 10 Girl Bowling 183873	Open		37.50	38
1997	Age 11 Girl With Ice Cream Cone 260924	Open		37.50	38
1997	Age 12 Girl/Puppy Holding Clock 260932	Open		37.50	38

Little Moments - S. Butcher

YEAR ISSUE		EDITION LIMIT	YEAR RETD.	ISSUE PRICE	*QUOTE U.S.$
1996	Where Would I Be Without You 139491	Open		20.00	20
1996	All Things Grow With Love 139505	Open		20.00	20
1996	You're The Berry Best 139513	Open		20.00	20
1996	You Make The World A Sweeter Place 139521	Open		20.00	20
1996	You're Forever In My Heart 139548	Open		20.00	20
1996	Birthday Wishes With Hugs & Kisses 139556	Open		20.00	20
1996	You Make My Spirit Soar 139564	Open		20.00	20
1997	January 261203	Open		20.00	20
1997	February 261246	Open		20.00	20
1997	April 261300	Open		20.00	20
1997	March 261270	Open		20.00	20
1997	May 261211	Open		20.00	20
1997	June 261254	Open		20.00	20
1997	July 261289	Open		20.00	20
1997	August 261319	Open		20.00	20
1997	September 261238	Open		20.00	20
1997	October 261262	Open		20.00	20
1997	November 261297	Open		20.00	20
1997	December 261327	Open		20.00	20

Musical Figurines - S. Butcher

YEAR ISSUE		EDITION LIMIT	YEAR RETD.	ISSUE PRICE	*QUOTE U.S.$
1983	Sharing Our Season Together E-0519	Retrd.	1986	70.00	125-150
1983	Wee Three Kings E-0520	Suspd.		60.00	115-140
1983	Let Heaven And Nature Sing E-2346	Suspd.		55.00	110-160
1982	O Come All Ye Faithful E-2352	Suspd.		50.00	135-155
1982	I'll Play My Drum For Him E-2355	Suspd.		45.00	175-200
1980	Christmas Is A Time To Share E-2806	Retrd.	1984	35.00	165-175
1980	Crown Him Lord Of All E-2807	Suspd.		35.00	90-125
1980	Unto Us A Child Is Born E-2808	Suspd.		35.00	95-125
1980	Jesus Is Born E-2809	Suspd.		35.00	130-145
1980	Come Let Us Adore Him E-2810	Suspd.		45.00	120-130
1980	Peace On Earth E-4726	Suspd.		45.00	125
1981	The Hand That Rocks The Future E-5204	Open		30.00	55-75
1981	My Guardian Angel E-5205	Suspd.		22.50	75-90
1981	My Guardian Angel E-5206	Suspd.		22.50	70-90
1984	Wishing You A Merry Christmas E-5394	Suspd.		55.00	100-125
1981	Silent Knight E-5642	Suspd.		45.00	250-300
1981	Rejoice O Earth E-5645	Retrd.	1988	35.00	75-100
1982	The Lord Bless You And Keep You E-7180	Open		55.00	80-115
1982	Mother Sew Dear E-7182	Open		35.00	55-90
1982	The Purr-fect Grandma E-7184	Suspd.		35.00	70-80
1982	Love Is Sharing E-7185	Retrd.	1985	40.00	150-175
1982	Let the Whole World Know E-7186	Suspd.		60.00	155-185
1985	Lord Keep My Life In Tune (B) (2/set) 12165	Suspd.		50.00	90-120
1985	We Saw A Star 12408	Suspd.		50.00	75-105
1987	Lord Keep My Life In Tune (G) (2/set) 12580	Suspd.		50.00	175-200
1985	God Sent You Just In Time 15504	Retrd.	1989	60.00	95-115
1986	Heaven Bless You 100285	Suspd.		45.00	60-75
1986	Our 1st Christmas Together 101702	Retrd.	1992	50.00	85-110
1986	Let's Keep In Touch 102520	Open		85.00	85-100
1988	Peace On Earth 109746	Suspd.		120.00	155-175
1987	I'm Sending You A White Christmas 112402	Retrd.	1993	55.00	80-130
1988	You Have Touched So Many Hearts 112577	Suspd.		50.00	55-65
1991	Lord Keep My Life In Balance 520691	Suspd.		60.00	80-125
1989	The Light Of The World Is Jesus 521507	Open		65.00	65-80
1992	Do Not Open Till Christmas 522244	Suspd.		75.00	85-100
1992	This Day Has Been Made In Heaven 523682	Open		60.00	60
1993	Wishing You Were Here 526916	Open		100.00	100-110

Rejoice in the Lord - S. Butcher

YEAR ISSUE		EDITION LIMIT	YEAR RETD.	ISSUE PRICE	*QUOTE U.S.$
1985	Lord Keep My Life In Tune 12165	Suspd.		37.50	80-120
1985	There's a Song in My Heart 12173	Suspd.		11.00	25-45
1985	Happiness is the Lord 12378	Suspd.		15.00	25-40
1985	Lord Give Me a Song 12386	Suspd.		15.00	23-40
1985	He is My Song 12394	Suspd.		17.50	30-40

Sammy's Circus - S. Butcher

YEAR ISSUE		EDITION LIMIT	YEAR RETD.	ISSUE PRICE	*QUOTE U.S.$
1994	Markie 528099	Suspd.		18.50	19
1994	Dusty 529176	Suspd.		22.50	23
1994	Katie 529184	Suspd.		17.00	17
1994	Tippy 529192	Suspd.		12.00	12
1994	Collin 529214	Suspd.		20.00	20
1994	Sammy 529222	Yr.Iss.	1994	20.00	45
1994	Circus Tent 528196 (Nite-Lite)	Suspd.		90.00	90
1995	Jordan 529168	Suspd.		20.00	20
1996	Jennifer 163708	Suspd.		20.00	20

Spring Catalog - S. Butcher

YEAR ISSUE		EDITION LIMIT	YEAR RETD.	ISSUE PRICE	*QUOTE U.S.$
1993	Happiness Is At Our Fingertips 529931	Yr.Iss.	1993	35.00	60-100
1994	So Glad I Picked You As A Friend 524379	Yr.Iss.	1994	40.00	40
1995	Sending My Love Your Way 528609	Yr.Iss.	1995	40.00	40
1996	Have I Toad You Lately I Love You 521329	Yr.Iss.	1996	30.00	30
1997	Happiness To The Core 261378	Yr.Iss.		37.50	38

Sugartown - S. Butcher

YEAR ISSUE		EDITION LIMIT	YEAR RETD.	ISSUE PRICE	*QUOTE U.S.$
1992	Chapel 529621	Retrd.	1994	85.00	90-100
1992	Christmas Tree 528684	Retrd.	1994	15.00	15
1992	Grandfather 529516	Retrd.	1994	15.00	20
1992	Nativity 529508	Retrd.	1994	20.00	30
1992	Philip 529494	Retrd.	1994	17.00	30
1992	Aunt Ruth & Aunt Dorothy 529486	Retrd.	1994	20.00	25
1992	Sam Butcher 529567 (1st sign)	Yr.Iss.	1992	22.50	150-275
1993	7 pc. Sam's House Collector's Set 531774	Open		189.00	189
1993	Sam's House Night Light 529605	Open		80.00	85
1993	Fence 529796	Open		10.00	10
1993	Sammy 528668	Open		17.00	17
1993	Katy Lynne 529524	Open		20.00	20
1993	Sam Butcher 529842 (2nd sign)	Yr.Iss.	1993	22.50	55
1993	Dusty 529435	Open		17.00	17
1993	Sam's Car 529443	Open		22.50	23
1994	Dr. Sam Sugar 530850	Open		17.00	17
1994	Doctor's Office Night Light 529869	Open		80.00	85
1994	Sam's House 530468	Yr.Iss.	1994	17.50	18
1994	Jan 529826	Open		17.00	17
1994	Sugar & Her Dog House 533165	Open		20.00	20
1994	Stork With Baby Sam 529788	Yr.Iss.	1994	22.50	25-50
1994	Free Christmas Puppies 528064	Open		18.50	19
1994	7 pc. Doctor's Office Collectors Set 529281	Yr.Iss.	1994	189.00	190-225
1994	Leon & Evelyn Mae 529818	Open		20.00	20
1995	Sam the Conductor 150169	Yr.Iss.	1995	20.00	20
1995	Train Station Night Light 150150	Open		50.00	50
1995	Railroad Crossing Sign 150177	Open		12.00	12
1995	Tammy and Debbie 531812	Open		22.50	23
1995	Donny 531871	Open		22.50	23
1995	Luggage Cart With Kitten And Tag 150185	Open		13.00	13
1995	6 pc. Train Station Collector Set 750193	Yr.Iss.	1995	190.00	190
1996	Sugar Town Skating Sign 184020	Yr.Iss.	1996	15.00	15
1996	Skating Pond 184047	Open		40.00	40
1996	Mazie 184055	Open		18.50	19
1996	Cocoa 184063	Open		7.50	8
1996	Leroy 184071	Open		18.50	19
1996	Hank and Sharon 184098	Open		25.00	25
1996	Lighted Warming Hut 192341	Open		60.00	60

Sugartown Enhancements - S. Butcher

YEAR ISSUE		EDITION LIMIT	YEAR RETD.	ISSUE PRICE	*QUOTE U.S.$
1995	Bus Stop 150207	Open		8.50	9
1995	Fire Hydrant 150215	Open		5.00	5
1995	Bird Bath 150223	Open		8.50	9
1995	Sugartown Enhancement Pack, set/5 152269	Open		45.00	45
1996	Tree Night Light 184039	Open		45.00	45
1996	Flag Pole w/Kitten 184136	Open		15.00	15
1996	Wooden Barrel Hot Cocoa Stand 184144	Open		15.00	15
1996	Bonfire with Bunnies 184152	Open		10.00	10
1995	Dog And Kitten On Park Bench 529540	Open		13.00	13
1994	Lamp Post 529559	Open		8.00	8
1994	Mailbox 531847	Open		5.00	5
1995	Street Sign 532185	Open		5.00	5
1994	Village Town Hall Clock 532908	Open		80.00	85
1994	Curved Sidewalk 533149	Open		10.00	10
1994	Straight Sidewalk 533157	Open		10.00	10
1994	Single Tree 533173	Open		10.00	10
1994	Double Tree 533181	Open		10.00	10
1994	Cobble Stone Bridge 533203	Open		17.00	17

To Have And To Hold - S. Butcher

YEAR ISSUE		EDITION LIMIT	YEAR RETD.	ISSUE PRICE	*QUOTE U.S.$
1996	Love Vows To Always Bloom 1st Anniversary Couple With Flowers 129097	Open		70.00	70
1996	A Year Of Blessings-1st Anniversary Couple With Cake 163783	Open		70.00	70
1996	Each Hour Is Precious With You-5th Anniversary Couple With Clock 163791	Open		70.00	70
1996	Ten Years Heart To Heart-10th Anniversary Couple With Pillow 163805	Open		70.00	70
1996	A Silver Celebration To Share-25th Anniversary Couple With Silver Platter 163813	Open		70.00	70
1996	Sharing The Gift of 40 Precious Years-40th Anniversary Couple With Gift Box 163821	Open		70.00	70
1996	Precious Moments To Remember-50th Anniversary Couple With Photo Album 163848	Open		70.00	70

Two By Two - S. Butcher

YEAR ISSUE		EDITION LIMIT	YEAR RETD.	ISSUE PRICE	*QUOTE U.S.$
1993	Noah, Noah's Wife, & Noah's Ark (lighted) 530042	Open		125.00	125-195
1993	Sheep (mini double fig.) 530077	Open		10.00	10
1993	Pigs (mini double fig.) 530085	Open		12.00	12
1993	Giraffes (mini double fig.) 530115	Open		16.00	16
1993	Bunnies (mini double fig.) 530123	Open		9.00	9
1993	Elephants (mini double fig.) 530131	Open		18.00	18
1993	Eight Piece Collector's Set 530948	Open		190.00	190
1994	Llamas 531375	Open		15.00	15
1995	Congratulations You Earned Your Stripes 127809	Open		15.00	15
1996	I'd Goat Anywhere With You 163694	Open		10.00	10

You Are Always There For Me - S. Butcher

YEAR ISSUE		EDITION LIMIT	YEAR RETD.	ISSUE PRICE	*QUOTE U.S.$
1996	Mother Kissing Daughter's Owie 163600	Open		50.00	50
1996	Father Helping Son Bat 163627	Open		50.00	50
1996	Sister Consoling Sister 163635	Open		50.00	50
1997	Mother Kissing Son's Owie 163619	Open		50.00	50
1997	Father Bandaging Daughter's Doll 163597	Open		50.00	50

Prizm, Inc./Pipka

Pipka's Earth Angels - Pipka

YEAR ISSUE		EDITION LIMIT	YEAR RETD.	ISSUE PRICE	*QUOTE U.S.$
1996	Angel of Hearts 13801	5,400		85.00	85
1997	Angel of Roses 13804	5,400		85.00	85
1996	Cottage Angel 13800	5,400		85.00	85
1996	Gardening Angel 13802	5,400		85.00	85
1997	Guardian Angel 13805	5,400		85.00	85
1997	Messenger Angel 13803	5,400		85.00	85

*Quotes have been rounded up to nearest dollar

Pipka's Memories of Christmas - Pipka

YEAR	ISSUE	EDITION LIMIT	YEAR RETD.	ISSUE PRICE	*QUOTE U.S.$
1996	Aussie Santa & Boomer 13906	3,600	1997	85.00	85
1995	Czechoslovakian Santa 13905	3,600	1996	85.00	85
1995	Gingerbread Santa 13903	3,600	1996	85.00	85
1996	Good News Santa 13908	3,600		85.00	85
1995	Midnight Visitor 13902	3,600	1996	85.00	85
1997	Norwegian/Julenisse Santa 13911	3,600	1997	90.00	90
1997	Polish Father Christmas 13917	3,600	1997	90.00	90
1997	Russian Santa 13916	3,600		90.00	90
1995	Santa's Ark 13901	3,600	1997	85.00	85
1997	Santa's Spotted Grey 13914	3,600		90.00	90
1997	St. Nicholas 13912	3,600		90.00	90
1995	Star Catcher Santa 13904	3,600	1996	85.00	85
1995	Starcoat Santa 13900	3,600	1996	85.00	85
1996	Storytime Santa 13909	3,600		85.00	85
1996	Ukrainian Santa 13907	3,600		85.00	85
1997	Where's Rudolph 13915	3,600		90.00	90

Pipka's Reflections of Christmas - Pipka

YEAR	ISSUE	EDITION LIMIT	YEAR RETD.	ISSUE PRICE	*QUOTE U.S.$
1997	Amish Country Santa 6 1/2" 11305	9,700		40.00	40
1997	Better Watch Out Santa 6 1/2" 11304	9,700		40.00	40
1997	Czechoslovakian Santa 6 1/2" 11301	9,700		40.00	40
1997	Midnight Visitor 6 1/2" 11300	9,700		40.00	40
1997	Star Catcher Santa 6 1/2" 11303	9,700		40.00	40
1997	Starcoat Santa 6 1/2" 11302	9,700		40.00	40

Pulaski Furniture, Inc.

Curios Henry Limited Edition Figurine Series - L. Eisen

YEAR	ISSUE	EDITION LIMIT	YEAR RETD.	ISSUE PRICE	*QUOTE U.S.$
1996	Jack Russell Terrier	Yr.Iss.		19.95	20

Reco International

Clown Figurines by John McClelland - J. McClelland

YEAR	ISSUE	EDITION LIMIT	YEAR RETD.	ISSUE PRICE	*QUOTE U.S.$
1988	Mr. Cool	9,500		35.00	35
1987	Mr. Cure-All	9,500		35.00	35
1988	Mr. Heart-Throb	9,500		35.00	35
1987	Mr. Lovable	9,500		35.00	35
1988	Mr. Magic	9,500		35.00	35
1987	Mr. One-Note	9,500		35.00	35
1987	Mr. Tip	9,500		35.00	35

Faces of Love - J. McClelland

YEAR	ISSUE	EDITION LIMIT	YEAR RETD.	ISSUE PRICE	*QUOTE U.S.$
1988	Cuddles	Open		29.50	33
1988	Sunshine	Open		29.50	33

Granget Crystal Sculpture - G. Granget

YEAR	ISSUE	EDITION LIMIT	YEAR RETD.	ISSUE PRICE	*QUOTE U.S.$
1973	Long Earred Owl, Asio Otus	Retrd.	1974	2250.00	2250
XX	Ruffed Grouse	Retrd.	1976	1000.00	1000

Laughables - J. Bergsma

YEAR	ISSUE	EDITION LIMIT	YEAR RETD.	ISSUE PRICE	*QUOTE U.S.$
1997	Angel & Alex	Open		17.50	18
1997	Anna & Abigail	Open		15.00	15
1995	Annie, Geoge & Harry	Open		17.50	18
1996	Ashley	Open		13.50	14
1997	Brie & Benjamin	Open		16.50	17
1995	Cody & Spot	Open		15.00	15
1995	Daffodil & Prince	Open		13.50	14
1995	Daisy & Jeremiah	Open		15.00	15
1996	Felix & Freddie	Open		15.00	15
1997	Harry & Sally	Open		16.50	17
1997	Jenny & Jamie	Open		15.00	15
1995	Joey & Jumper	Open		15.00	15
1996	Jordan & Jessie	Open		15.00	15
1996	Leo & Lindsey	Open		17.50	18
1996	Mattie & Quackers	Open		15.00	15
1995	Merlin & Gemini	Open		15.00	15
1995	Millie & Mittens	Open		15.00	15
1996	Nicholas & Chelsea	Retrd.	1996	15.00	15
1997	Nicky	Open		15.00	15
1995	Patches and Pokey	Open		15.00	15
1995	Patty & Petunia	Open		16.50	17
1996	Peter & Polly	Open		17.50	18
1997	Rocky & Jody	Yr.Iss.		16.50	17
1996	Sammy & Mikey	Open		15.00	15
1995	Sunny	Open		13.50	14
1995	Whiskers & Willie	Open		13.50	14

Porcelains in Miniature by John McClelland - J. McClelland

YEAR	ISSUE	EDITION LIMIT	YEAR RETD.	ISSUE PRICE	*QUOTE U.S.$
XX	Alice	10,000		34.50	35
XX	Autumn Dreams	Open		29.50	30
XX	The Baker	Open		29.50	30
XX	Batter Up	Retrd.	1993	29.50	30
XX	Center Ice	Open		29.50	30
XX	Cheerleader	Open		29.50	30
XX	Chimney Sweep	10,000		34.50	35
XX	The Clown	Open		29.50	30
XX	Club Pro	Open		29.50	30
XX	Country Lass	Open		29.50	30
XX	Cowboy	Open		29.50	30
XX	Cowgirl	Open		29.50	30
XX	Doc	Open		29.50	30
XX	Dressing Up	10,000		34.50	35
XX	The Farmer	Open		29.50	30
XX	Farmer's Wife	Open		29.50	30
XX	The Fireman	Open		29.50	30
XX	First Outing	Open		29.50	30
XX	First Solo	Open		29.50	30
XX	Highland Fling	7,500		34.50	35
XX	John	10,000		34.50	35
XX	Lawyer	Open		29.50	30
XX	Love 40	Open		29.50	30
XX	The Nurse	Open		29.50	30
XX	The Painter	Open		29.50	30
XX	The Policeman	Open		29.50	30
XX	Quiet Moments	Open		29.50	30
XX	Smooth Smailing	Open		29.50	30
XX	Special Delivery	Open		29.50	30
XX	Sudsie Suzie	Open		29.50	30
XX	Tuck-Me-In	Open		29.50	30
XX	Winter Fun	Open		29.50	30

The Reco Angel Collection - J. McClelland

YEAR	ISSUE	EDITION LIMIT	YEAR RETD.	ISSUE PRICE	*QUOTE U.S.$
1986	Adoration	Open		24.00	24
1986	Devotion	Open		15.00	15
1986	Faith	Retrd.	1995	24.00	24
1986	Gloria	Retrd.	1996	12.00	12
1986	Harmony	Retrd.	1994	12.00	12
1986	Hope	Open		24.00	24
1986	Innocence	Retrd.	1996	12.00	12
1986	Joy	Retrd.	1994	15.00	15
1986	Love	Retrd.	1996	12.00	12
1988	Minstral	Retrd.	1995	12.00	12
1986	Peace	Retrd.	1996	24.00	24
1986	Praise	Retrd.	1996	20.00	20
1988	Reverence	Retrd.	1995	12.00	12
1986	Serenity	Retrd.	1996	24.00	24

The Reco Clown Collection - J. McClelland

YEAR	ISSUE	EDITION LIMIT	YEAR RETD.	ISSUE PRICE	*QUOTE U.S.$
1985	Arabesque	Open		12.00	13
1985	Bow Jangles	Open		12.00	13
1985	Curly	Open		12.00	13
1987	Disco Dan	Open		12.00	13
1987	Domino	Open		12.00	13
1987	Happy George	Open		12.00	13
1985	Hobo	Open		12.00	13
1987	The Joker	Open		12.00	13
1987	Jolly Joe	Open		12.00	13
1987	Love	Open		12.00	13
1987	Mr. Big	Open		12.00	13
1985	The Professor	Open		12.00	13
1985	Ruffles	Open		12.00	13
1985	Sad Eyes	Open		12.00	13
1985	Scamp	Open		12.00	13
1987	Smiley	Open		12.00	13
1985	Sparkles	Open		12.00	13
1985	Top Hat	Open		12.00	13
1987	Tramp	Open		12.00	13
1987	Twinkle	Open		12.00	13
1985	Whoopie	Open		12.00	13
1985	Winkie	Retrd.	1994	12.00	13
1987	Wistful	Open		12.00	13
1987	Zany Jack	Open		12.00	13

Reco Creche Collection - J. McClelland

YEAR	ISSUE	EDITION LIMIT	YEAR RETD.	ISSUE PRICE	*QUOTE U.S.$
1988	Cow	Open		15.00	15
1988	Donkey	Open		16.50	17
1987	Holy Family (3 Pieces)	Open		49.00	49
1988	King/Frankincense	Open		22.50	23
1988	King/Gold	Open		22.50	23
1988	King/Myrrh	Open		22.50	23
1987	Lamb	Open		9.50	10
1987	Shepherd-Kneeling	Open		22.50	23
1987	Shepherd-Standing	Open		22.50	23

Sandra Kuck's Treasures - S. Kuck

YEAR	ISSUE	EDITION LIMIT	YEAR RETD.	ISSUE PRICE	*QUOTE U.S.$
1997	Baby Bunnies	Open		20.00	20
1997	Be Good	Open		20.00	20
1997	Christmas Morning	1,200		20.00	20
1997	Playful Kitten	Open		20.00	20
1997	Teacher's Pet	Open		20.00	20
1997	Teddy & Me	Open		20.00	20
1997	Victoria's Garden	Open		20.00	20

Rhodes Studio

Rockwell's Age of Wonder - Rockwell-Inspired

YEAR	ISSUE	EDITION LIMIT	YEAR RETD.	ISSUE PRICE	*QUOTE U.S.$
1992	The Birthday Party	Closed	N/A	39.95	40
1991	Hush-A-Bye	Closed	N/A	34.95	35
1991	School Days	Closed	N/A	36.95	37
1991	Splish Splash	Closed	N/A	34.95	35
1991	Stand by Me	Closed	N/A	36.95	37
1991	Summertime	Closed	N/A	39.95	40

Rockwell's Beautiful Dreamers - Rockwell-Inspired

YEAR	ISSUE	EDITION LIMIT	YEAR RETD.	ISSUE PRICE	*QUOTE U.S.$
1991	Dear Diary	Closed	N/A	37.95	38
1992	Debutante's Dance	Closed	N/A	42.95	43
1991	Secret Sonnets	Closed	N/A	39.95	40
1991	Sitting Pretty	Closed	N/A	37.95	38
1991	Springtime Serenade	Closed	N/A	39.95	40
1992	Walk in the Park	Closed	N/A	42.95	43

Rockwell's Gems of Wisdom - Rockwell-Inspired

YEAR	ISSUE	EDITION LIMIT	YEAR RETD.	ISSUE PRICE	*QUOTE U.S.$
1991	Love Cures All	Closed	N/A	39.95	40
1991	Practice Makes Perfect	Closed	N/A	39.95	40
1991	A Stitch In Time	Closed	N/A	42.95	43

Rockwell's Heirloom Santa Collection - Rockwell-Inspired

YEAR	ISSUE	EDITION LIMIT	YEAR RETD.	ISSUE PRICE	*QUOTE U.S.$
1991	Christmas Dream	150-day		49.95	50
1992	Making His List	Closed	N/A	49.95	50
1990	Santa's Workshop	150-day		49.95	50

Rick Cain Studios

Collectors Guild - R. Cain

YEAR	ISSUE	EDITION LIMIT	YEAR RETD.	ISSUE PRICE	*QUOTE U.S.$
1992	High Point	S/O	1992	82.00	95-125
1992	Visor	Retrd.	1992	Gift	100
1993	Strider	S/O	1993	82.00	175
1993	Star Shadow	Retrd.	1993	Gift	75
1994	Midnight Son	1,225	1994	297.00	500
1994	Arctic Moon II	Retrd.	1994	Gift	75
1995	Family Tree	Retrd.	1995	260.00	260-350
1995	Bonsai	Retrd.	1995	Gift	45-75

Master Series - R. Cain

YEAR	ISSUE	EDITION LIMIT	YEAR RETD.	ISSUE PRICE	*QUOTE U.S.$
1986	Aerial Hunter 1114	5,000	1990	70.40	165-185
1991	Aerial Victor 1707	2,000	1995	115.00	150-175
1993	Arctic Moon 1917	2,000	1993	231.00	1000-1300
1993	Arctic Son 1927	2,000	1993	275.00	550-800
1988	The Balance 1302	5,000	1992	374.00	515-550
1992	Bathing Hole 1901	2,000	1994	102.00	153-165
1988	Blackberry Summer 1201	300	1994	165.00	190
1985	Catchmaster 1104	5,000	1990	184.80	325-500
1990	Dark Feather 1501	2,000	1994	86.00	155
1989	Domain 1205	5,000	1992	187.00	255-300
1986	Dragon Sprout 1112	5,000	1990	92.50	300
1987	Dragonflies Dance 1123	5,000	1992	55.00	85
1986	Elder 1113	2,500	1993	550.00	750-900
1988	Fair Atlantis 1130	5,000	1993	319.00	375
1990	Falcon Lore 1406	5,000	1992	86.00	155-200
1985	Featherview 1103	5,000	1993	151.80	330
1988	Guardian 1301	5,000	1995	325.00	370
1989	Hatchling 1205	1,250	1994	85.00	100
1991	Highland Voyager 1805	2,000	1995	120.00	150
1987	Innerview 1203	1,500	1994	84.00	95
1988	Lady Reflecting 1129	5,000	1995	93.00	105
1992	Leaping Wolf 1904	2,000	1992	143.00	450
1987	Liquid Universe 1117	5,000	1995	540.00	615
1990	Majestic Cradle 1505	900	1995	440.00	500
1994	Moon Walk 1930	2,000	1994	198.00	300
1985	Nightmaster 1105	5,000	1990	184.80	350
1988	Old Man of the Forest 1126	5,000	1992	132.00	200
1988	Orbist 1127	5,000	1992	108.00	150-250
1992	The Pack 1902	2,000	1992	105.50	400
1988	Paradise Found 1124	575	1994	308.00	425
1990	Pathfinder 1403	2,000	1991	101.00	155-200
1992	Power of One 1909	2,000	1995	77.00	95
1992	Prairie Thunder 1903	2,000	1994	110.00	165
1986	Sandmaster 1115	5,000	1995	93.00	105
1990	Scarlett Wing 1404	365	1994	101.00	185
1985	Sea View 1107	5,000	1993	70.40	115
1990	Searchers 1502	2,000	1994	174.00	350
1987	Sentinel Crest 1119	5,000	1994	121.00	140-170
1992	Seven Bears 1908	2,000	1993	231.00	385
1991	Spirit Dog 1702	2,000	1992	198.00	450-625
1992	Spirit Eagle 1908	2,000	1993	121.00	185
1993	Spirit Totem 1922	2,000	1993	286.00	435-475
1993	Steppin' Wolf 1925	2,000	1993	210.00	315
1987	Teller 1120	5,000	1992	308.00	425
1985	Tidemaster 1108	2,500	1994	242.00	275
1986	Tropical Flame 1111	5,000	1992	209.00	290-350
1989	Universes 1204	5,000	1995	115.00	130
1994	Waiting Wolf 1929	2,000	1994	198.00	210-300
1986	Wind Horse 1108	5,000	1992	70.00	100-150
1987	Winged Fortress 1118	5,000	1994	363.00	400
1993	Wolf Trail 1919	2,000	1993	121.00	210
1990	Wood Flight 1401	2,000	1992	105.50	150
1993	Wood Song 1912	2,000	1993	143.00	220-320
1987	Yore Castle 1121	5,000	1992	165.00	225-250

Vision Quest - R. Cain

YEAR	ISSUE	EDITION LIMIT	YEAR RETD.	ISSUE PRICE	*QUOTE U.S.$
1992	Alphascape 1900	2,000	1993	210.00	400

River Shore

Rockwell Single Issues - N. Rockwell

YEAR	ISSUE	EDITION LIMIT	YEAR RETD.	ISSUE PRICE	*QUOTE U.S.$
1982	Grandpa's Guardian	9,500	N/A	125.00	195
1981	Looking Out To Sea	9,500	N/A	85.00	200

Roman, Inc.

American Santas Through the Decades - Galleria Lucchese Studios

YEAR	ISSUE	EDITION LIMIT	YEAR RETD.	ISSUE PRICE	*QUOTE U.S.$
1994	1800 Cloth-like Santa 7"	Closed	1995	49.50	50
1994	1800 Pencil Santa 8"	Closed	1995	29.50	30
1994	1810 Cloth-like Santa 7"	Closed	1995	49.50	50
1994	1810 Pencil Santa 8"	Closed	1995	29.50	30

Catnippers - I. Spencer

YEAR	ISSUE	EDITION LIMIT	YEAR RETD.	ISSUE PRICE	*QUOTE U.S.$
1985	A Baffling Yarn	15,000		45.00	45
1985	Can't We Be Friends	15,000		45.00	45
1985	A Christmas Mourning	15,000		45.00	50
1985	Flora and Felina	15,000		45.00	50
1985	Flying Tiger-Retired	15,000		45.00	45
1985	The Paw that Refreshes	15,000		45.00	45

*Quotes have been rounded up to nearest dollar

FIGURINES

Roman, Inc. to Roman, Inc.

YEAR ISSUE		EDITION LIMIT	YEAR RETD.	ISSUE PRICE	*QUOTE U.S.$
1985	Sandy Claws	15,000		45.00	45
1985	A Tail of Two Kitties	15,000		45.00	45

Ceramica Excelsis - Unknown

YEAR ISSUE		EDITION LIMIT	YEAR RETD.	ISSUE PRICE	*QUOTE U.S.$
1978	Assumption Madonna	5,000		56.00	56
1978	Christ Entering Jerusalem	5,000		96.00	96
1978	Christ in the Garden of Gethsemane	5,000		40.00	60
1977	Christ Knocking at the Door	5,000		60.00	60
1980	Daniel in the Lion's Den	5,000		80.00	80
1980	David	5,000		77.00	77
1978	Flight into Egypt	5,000		59.00	90
1983	Good Shepherd	5,000		49.00	49
1978	Guardian Angel with Boy	5,000		69.00	69
1978	Guardian Angel with Girl	5,000		69.00	69
1983	Holy Family	5,000		72.00	72
1978	Holy Family at Work	5,000		96.00	96
1978	Infant of Prague	5,000		37.50	60
1981	Innocence	5,000		95.00	95
1979	Jesus Speaks in Parables	5,000		90.00	90
1983	Jesus with Children	5,000		74.00	74
1981	Journey to Bethlehem	5,000		89.00	89
1983	Kneeling Santa	5,000		95.00	95
1977	Madonna and Child with Angels	5,000		60.00	60
1977	Madonna with Child	5,000		65.00	65
1979	Moses	5,000		77.00	77
1979	Noah	5,000		77.00	77
1981	Sermon on the Mount	5,000		56.00	56
1983	St. Anne	5,000		49.00	49
1983	St. Francis	5,000		59.50	60
1977	St. Francis	5,000		60.00	60
1981	Way of the Cross	5,000		59.00	59
1980	Way to Emmaus	5,000		155.00	155
1977	What Happened to Your Hand?	5,000		60.00	60

A Child's World 1st Edition - F. Hook

YEAR ISSUE		EDITION LIMIT	YEAR RETD.	ISSUE PRICE	*QUOTE U.S.$
1980	Beach Buddies, signed	15,000		29.00	600
1980	Beach Buddies, unsigned	15,000		29.00	450
1980	Helping Hands	Closed	N/A	45.00	85
1980	Kiss Me Good Night	15,000		29.00	40
1980	My Big Brother	Closed	N/A	39.00	200
1980	Nighttime Thoughts	Closed	N/A	25.00	65
1980	Sounds of the Sea	15,000	N/A	45.00	150

A Child's World 2nd Edition - F. Hook

YEAR ISSUE		EDITION LIMIT	YEAR RETD.	ISSUE PRICE	*QUOTE U.S.$
1981	All Dressed Up	15,000		36.00	70
1981	Cat Nap	15,000	N/A	42.00	125
1981	I'll Be Good	15,000	N/A	36.00	80
1981	Making Friends	15,000		42.00	46
1981	The Sea and Me	15,000	N/A	39.00	80
1981	Sunday School	15,000		39.00	70

A Child's World 3rd Edition - F. Hook

YEAR ISSUE		EDITION LIMIT	YEAR RETD.	ISSUE PRICE	*QUOTE U.S.$
1981	Bear Hug	15,000		42.00	45
1981	Pathway to Dreams	15,000		47.00	50
1981	Road to Adventure	15,000		47.00	50
1981	Sisters	15,000	N/A	64.00	75
1981	Spring Breeze	15,000	N/A	37.50	50
1981	Youth	15,000		37.50	40

A Child's World 4th Edition - F. Hook

YEAR ISSUE		EDITION LIMIT	YEAR RETD.	ISSUE PRICE	*QUOTE U.S.$
1982	All Bundled Up	15,000		37.50	40
1982	Bedtime	15,000		35.00	38
1982	Birdie	15,000		37.50	40
1982	Flower Girl	15,000		42.00	45
1982	My Dolly!	15,000		39.00	40
1982	Ring Bearer	15,000		39.00	40

A Child's World 5th Edition - F. Hook

YEAR ISSUE		EDITION LIMIT	YEAR RETD.	ISSUE PRICE	*QUOTE U.S.$
1983	Brothers	15,000		64.00	70
1983	Finish Line	15,000		39.00	42
1983	Handful of Happiness	15,000		36.00	40
1983	He Loves Me...	15,000		49.00	55
1983	Puppy's Pal	15,000		39.00	42
1983	Ring Around the Rosie	15,000		99.00	105

A Child's World 6th Edition - F. Hook

YEAR ISSUE		EDITION LIMIT	YEAR RETD.	ISSUE PRICE	*QUOTE U.S.$
1984	Can I Help?	15,000		37.50	40
1984	Future Artist	15,000		42.00	45
1984	Good Doggie	15,000		47.00	50
1984	Let's Play Catch	15,000		33.00	35
1984	Nature's Wonders	15,000		29.00	31
1984	Sand Castles	15,000		37.50	40

A Child's World 7th Edition - F. Hook

YEAR ISSUE		EDITION LIMIT	YEAR RETD.	ISSUE PRICE	*QUOTE U.S.$
1985	Art Class	15,000		99.00	105
1985	Don't Tell Anyone	15,000		49.00	50
1985	Look at Me!	15,000		42.00	45
1985	Mother's Helper	15,000		45.00	50
1985	Please Hear Me	15,000		29.00	30
1985	Yummm!	15,000		36.00	39

A Child's World 8th Edition - F. Hook

YEAR ISSUE		EDITION LIMIT	YEAR RETD.	ISSUE PRICE	*QUOTE U.S.$
1985	Chance of Showers	15,000		33.00	35
1985	Dress Rehearsal	15,000		33.00	35
1985	Engine	15,000		36.00	40
1985	Just Stopped By	15,000		36.00	40
1985	Private Ocean	15,000		29.00	31
1985	Puzzling	15,000		36.00	40

A Child's World 9th Edition - F. Hook

YEAR ISSUE		EDITION LIMIT	YEAR RETD.	ISSUE PRICE	*QUOTE U.S.$
1987	Hopscotch	15,000		67.50	70
1987	Li'l Brother	15,000		60.00	65

Classic Brides of the Century - E. Williams

YEAR ISSUE		EDITION LIMIT	YEAR RETD.	ISSUE PRICE	*QUOTE U.S.$
1989	1900-Flora	5,000		175.00	175
1989	1910-Elizabeth Grace	5,000		175.00	175
1989	1920-Mary Claire	5,000		175.00	175
1989	1930-Kathleen	5,000		175.00	175
1989	1940-Margaret	5,000		175.00	175
1989	1950-Barbara Ann	5,000		175.00	175
1989	1960-Dianne	5,000		175.00	175
1989	1970-Heather	5,000		175.00	175
1989	1980-Jennifer	5,000		175.00	175
1992	1990-Stephanie Helen	5,000		175.00	175

Divine Servant - M. Greiner Jr.

YEAR ISSUE		EDITION LIMIT	YEAR RETD.	ISSUE PRICE	*QUOTE U.S.$
1993	Divine Servant, pewter sculpture	Open		200.00	200
1993	Divine Servant, porcelain sculpture	Open		59.50	60
1993	Divine Servant, resin sculpture	Open		250.00	250

Fontanini Collectors' Club Member's Only - E. Simonetti

YEAR ISSUE		EDITION LIMIT	YEAR RETD.	ISSUE PRICE	*QUOTE U.S.$
1991	The Pilgrimage	Yr.Iss.	1991	24.95	25
1992	She Rescued Me	Yr.Iss.	1992	23.50	24
1993	Christmas Symphony	Yr.Iss.	1993	13.50	14
1994	Sweet Harmony	Yr.Iss.	1994	13.50	14
1995	Faith: The Fifth Angel	Yr.Iss.	1995	22.50	23

Fontanini Member's Only Nativity Preview - E. Simonetti

YEAR ISSUE		EDITION LIMIT	YEAR RETD.	ISSUE PRICE	*QUOTE U.S.$
1996	Mara	Yr.Iss.	1996	12.50	13
1997	Benjamin	Yr.Iss.		15.00	15

Fontanini Collector Club Renewal Gift - E. Simonetti

YEAR ISSUE		EDITION LIMIT	YEAR RETD.	ISSUE PRICE	*QUOTE U.S.$
1993	He Comforts Me	Yr.Iss.	1993	12.50	13
1994	I'm Heaven Bound	Yr.Iss.	1994	12.50	13
1995	Gift of Joy	Yr.Iss.	1995	12.50	13

Fontanini Collector Club Symbol of Membership - E. Simonetti

YEAR ISSUE		EDITION LIMIT	YEAR RETD.	ISSUE PRICE	*QUOTE U.S.$
1996	Rosannah - Angel of The Roses	Yr.Iss.	1996	Gift	N/A
1997	Leah - Angel of Light	Yr.Iss.		Gift	N/A

Fontanini Collector Club Special Event Piece - E. Simonetti

YEAR ISSUE		EDITION LIMIT	YEAR RETD.	ISSUE PRICE	*QUOTE U.S.$
1990	Gideon	Closed	1995	15.00	15
1995	Dominica	Closed	1996	15.00	15
1997	Sarah	Yr.Iss.		15.00	15

Fontanini Tour Exclusive - E. Simonetti

YEAR ISSUE		EDITION LIMIT	YEAR RETD.	ISSUE PRICE	*QUOTE U.S.$
1995	Luke	Yr.Iss.		15.00	15

Fontanini Collector Club First Year Welcome Gift - E. Simonetti

YEAR ISSUE		EDITION LIMIT	YEAR RETD.	ISSUE PRICE	*QUOTE U.S.$
1990	I Found Him	Closed	1995	Gift	N/A

Fontanini Heirloom Nativity Limited Edition Figurines - E. Simonetti

YEAR ISSUE		EDITION LIMIT	YEAR RETD.	ISSUE PRICE	*QUOTE U.S.$
1994	14 pc. Golden Edition Heirloom Nativity Set	2,500		375.00	375
1994	Abigail & Peter	Retrd.	1996	29.50	30
1992	Ariel	Retrd.	1992	29.50	30
1995	Gabriela	25,000	1995	18.00	18
1993	Jeshua & Adin	Retrd.	1996	29.50	30
1997	Judah	Yr.Iss.		18.00	18
1996	Raphael	Retrd.	1996	18.00	18

Fontanini Nativity Village 2.5" - E. Simonetti

YEAR ISSUE		EDITION LIMIT	YEAR RETD.	ISSUE PRICE	*QUOTE U.S.$
1996	Inn	Open		29.50	30
1996	King's Tent	Open		17.50	18
1996	Shepherd's Camp	Open		29.50	30
1996	Stable	Open		29.50	30
1996	Town Building	Open		25.00	25
1996	Town Store	Open		25.00	25

Fontanini Nativity Village 5"- E. Simonetti

YEAR ISSUE		EDITION LIMIT	YEAR RETD.	ISSUE PRICE	*QUOTE U.S.$
1996	Bakery	Open		80.00	80
1996	Inn	Open		85.00	85
1997	King's Tent	Open		60.00	60
1997	King's Tent	Open		60.00	60
1996	King's Tent	Open		50.00	50
1997	Marketplace	Open		85.00	85
1997	Pottery Shop	Open		85.00	85
1996	Shepherd's Camp	Open		80.00	80
1996	Stable	Open		75.00	75
1997	Town Gate	Open		85.00	85

Fontanini Nativity Village 7.5" - E. Simonetti

YEAR ISSUE		EDITION LIMIT	YEAR RETD.	ISSUE PRICE	*QUOTE U.S.$
1997	Inn	Open		55.00	55
1997	Lighted Stable	Open		75.00	75
1997	Town Building	Open		65.00	65
1997	Town Gate	Open		40.00	40
1997	Work Shop	Open		65.00	65

Fontanini Retired 5" Collection - E. Simonetti

YEAR ISSUE		EDITION LIMIT	YEAR RETD.	ISSUE PRICE	*QUOTE U.S.$
1985	Aaron	Retrd.	1994	12.50	13
1979	Baby Jesus	Retrd.	1992	5.50	12
1979	Balthazar	Retrd.	1993	5.50	12
1979	Gabriel	Retrd.	1993	5.50	12
1979	Gaspar	Retrd.	1993	5.50	12
1979	Joseph	Retrd.	1992	5.50	12
1979	Josiah	Retrd.	1994	5.50	12
1986	Kneeling Angel	Retrd.	1994	5.50	13
1985	Levi	Retrd.	1994	5.50	13
1979	Mary	Retrd.	1992	5.50	12
1979	Melchior	Retrd.	1993	5.50	12
1986	Micah	Retrd.	1995	5.50	13
1985	Miriam	Retrd.	1994	5.50	12
1986	Mordecai	Retrd.	1995	5.50	13
1986	Standing Angel	Retrd.	1994	5.50	13

Fontanini Retired 7.5" Collection - E. Simonetti

YEAR ISSUE		EDITION LIMIT	YEAR RETD.	ISSUE PRICE	*QUOTE U.S.$
1979	Baby Jesus	Retrd.	1994	13.00	25
1979	Gabriel	Retrd.	1994	13.00	25
1979	Joseph	Retrd.	1994	13.00	25
1982	Kneeling Angel	Retrd.	1995	13.00	25
1979	Mary	Retrd.	1994	13.00	25
1982	Standing Angel	Retrd.	1995	13.00	25

Fontanini, The Collectible Creche - E. Simonetti

YEAR ISSUE		EDITION LIMIT	YEAR RETD.	ISSUE PRICE	*QUOTE U.S.$
1973	10cm., (15 piece Set)	Closed	1992	63.60	89
1973	12cm., (15 piece Set)	Closed	1992	76.50	102
1979	16cm., (15 piece Set)	Closed	1992	178.50	285
1982	17cm., (15 piece Set)	Closed	1992	189.00	305
1973	19cm., (15 piece Set)	Closed	1992	175.50	280
1980	30cm., (15 piece Set)	Closed	1992	670.00	759

Frances Hook's Four Seasons - F. Hook

YEAR ISSUE		EDITION LIMIT	YEAR RETD.	ISSUE PRICE	*QUOTE U.S.$
1984	Winter	12,500		95.00	100
1985	Spring	12,500		95.00	100
1985	Summer	12,500		95.00	100
1985	Fall	12,500		95.00	100

Heartbeats - I. Spencer

YEAR ISSUE		EDITION LIMIT	YEAR RETD.	ISSUE PRICE	*QUOTE U.S.$
1986	Miracle	5,000		145.00	145
1987	Storytime	5,000		145.00	145

Hook - F. Hook

YEAR ISSUE		EDITION LIMIT	YEAR RETD.	ISSUE PRICE	*QUOTE U.S.$
1986	Carpenter Bust	Retrd.	1986	95.00	95
1986	Carpenter Bust-Heirloom Edition	Retrd.	1986	95.00	95
1987	Little Children, Come to Me	15,000		45.00	45
1987	Madonna and Child	15,000		39.50	40
1982	Sailor Mates	2,000		290.00	315
1982	Sun Shy	2,000		290.00	315

Jam Session - E. Rohn

YEAR ISSUE		EDITION LIMIT	YEAR RETD.	ISSUE PRICE	*QUOTE U.S.$
1985	Banjo Player	7,500		145.00	145
1985	Bass Player	7,500		145.00	145
1985	Clarinet Player	7,500		145.00	145
1985	Cornet Player	7,500		145.00	145
1985	Drummer	7,500		145.00	145
1985	Trombone Player	7,500		145.00	145

The Masterpiece Collection - Various

YEAR ISSUE		EDITION LIMIT	YEAR RETD.	ISSUE PRICE	*QUOTE U.S.$
1979	Adoration - F. Lippe	5,000		73.00	73
1981	The Holy Family - G. delle Notti	5,000		98.00	98
1982	Madonna of the Streets - R. Ferruzzi	5,000		65.00	65
1980	Madonna with Grapes - P. Mignard	5,000		85.00	85

The Museum Collection by Angela Tripi - A. Tripi

YEAR ISSUE		EDITION LIMIT	YEAR RETD.	ISSUE PRICE	*QUOTE U.S.$
1995	The Batter	1,000		95.00	95
1993	Be a Clown	1,000		95.00	95
1994	Blackfoot Woman with Baby	1,000		95.00	95
1991	The Caddie	1,000		135.00	135
1992	Checking It Twice	2,500		95.00	95
1991	Christopher Columbus	1,000		250.00	250
1994	Crow Warrior	1,000		195.00	195
1991	The Fiddler	1,000		175.00	176
1992	Flying Ace	1,000		95.00	95
1993	For My Next Trick	1,000		95.00	95
1992	Fore!	1,000		175.00	175
1992	The Fur Trapper	1,000		175.00	175
1991	A Gentleman's Game	1,000	1994	175.00	175
1992	The Gift Giver	2,500		95.00	95
1994	Iroquois Warrior	1,000		95.00	95
1995	Jesus in Gethsemane	1,000		95.00	95
1993	Jesus, The Good Shepherd	1,000		95.00	95
1992	Justice for All	1,000		95.00	95
1992	Ladies' Day	1,000		175.00	175
1992	Ladies' Tee	1,000		250.00	250
1990	The Mentor	1,000		290.00	291
1994	Native American Chief	1,000		95.00	95
1994	Native American Woman-Cherokee Maiden	1,000		95.00	95
1992	Nativity Set-8 pc.	2,500		425.00	425
1995	Nurse	1,000		95.00	95
1993	One Man Band Clown	1,000		95.00	95
1992	Our Family Doctor	1,000		95.00	95
1995	The Pitcher	1,000		95.00	95
1993	Preacher of Peace	1,000		175.00	175
1992	Prince of the Plains	1,000		175.00	175
1993	Public Protector	1,000		95.00	95
1994	Rhapsody	1,000		95.00	95
1993	Right on Schedule	1,000		95.00	95
1993	Road Show	1,000		95.00	95
1995	The Runner	1,000		95.00	95
1994	Serenade	1,000		95.00	95
1994	Sonata	1,000		95.00	95
1991	St. Francis of Assisi	1,000		175.00	175
1992	The Tannenbaum Santa	2,500		95.00	95
1992	The Tap In	1,000		175.00	175
1995	Teacher	1,000		95.00	95
1991	Tee Time at St. Andrew's	1,000	1993	175.00	175
1992	This Way, Santa	2,500		95.00	95

*Quotes have been rounded up to nearest dollar

YEAR ISSUE		EDITION LIMIT	YEAR RETD.	ISSUE PRICE	*QUOTE U.S.$
1992	To Serve and Protect	1,000		95.00	95
1993	Tripi Crucifix-Large	Open		59.00	59
1993	Tripi Crucifix-Medium	Open		35.00	35
1993	Tripi Crucifix-Small	Open		27.50	28

The Richard Judson Zolan Collection - R.J. Zolan

YEAR ISSUE		EDITION LIMIT	YEAR RETD.	ISSUE PRICE	*QUOTE U.S.$
1992	Summer at the Seashore	1,200		125.00	125
1994	Terrace Dancing	1,200		175.00	175

Seraphim Classics™ - Seraphim Studios

YEAR ISSUE		EDITION LIMIT	YEAR RETD.	ISSUE PRICE	*QUOTE U.S.$
1996	Celine - The Morning Star	Open		55.00	55
1997	Chelsea - Summer's Delight	Open		55.00	55
1994	Cymbeline - Peacemaker	Open		49.50	55
1994	Evangeline - Angel of Mercy	Open		49.50	55
1996	Faith - The Easter Angel	Open		55.00	55
1995	Felcia - Adoring Maiden	Open		49.50	55
1994	Francesca - Loving Guardian	Open		65.00	65
1996	Gabriel - Celestial Messenger	Open		59.50	60
1997	Harmony - Love's Guardian	Open		55.00	55
1994	Iris - Rainbow's End	Open		49.50	55
1994	Isabel - Gentle Spirit	Open		49.50	55
1995	Laurice - Wisdom's Child	Open		49.50	55
1994	Lydia - Winged Poet	Open		49.50	55
1996	Mariah - Heavenly Joy	Open		59.50	60
1997	Melody - Heaven's Song	Open		55.00	55
1994	Ophelia - Heart Seeker	Retrd.	1996	49.50	60
1995	Priscilla - Benevolent Guide	Open		49.50	55
1997	Rachael - Children's Joy	Open		55.00	55
1996	Rosalie - Nature's Delight	Open		55.00	55
1997	Sabrina - Eternal Guide	Open		55.00	55
1995	Sepaphina - Heaven's Helper	Retrd.	1996	49.50	60
1996	Serena - Angel of Peace	Open		65.00	65
1997	Tamara - Guardian Angel	Open		55.00	55

Seraphim Classics™ Angels To Watch Over Me - Seraphim Studios

YEAR ISSUE		EDITION LIMIT	YEAR RETD.	ISSUE PRICE	*QUOTE U.S.$
1996	Newborn	Open		39.50	40
1996	Age 1	Open		39.50	40
1996	Age 2	Open		39.50	40
1996	Age 3	Open		39.50	40
1996	Age 4	Open		39.50	40
1996	Age 5	Open		39.50	40

Seraphim Classics™ Glitterdome™ - Seraphim Studios

YEAR ISSUE		EDITION LIMIT	YEAR RETD.	ISSUE PRICE	*QUOTE U.S.$
1995	Francesca - Loving Guardian	Open		50.00	50
1997	Iris - Rainbow's End	Open		50.00	50

Seraphim Classics™ Limited Edition Figurines - Seraphim Studios

YEAR ISSUE		EDITION LIMIT	YEAR RETD.	ISSUE PRICE	*QUOTE U.S.$
1995	Alyssa - Nature's Angel	Closed	1995	145.00	200
1997	Chloe - Nature's Gift	Yr.Iss.		175.00	175
1996	Vanessa - Heavenly Maiden	Closed	1996	150.00	175

Seraphim Classics™ Musical - Seraphim Studios

YEAR ISSUE		EDITION LIMIT	YEAR RETD.	ISSUE PRICE	*QUOTE U.S.$
1994	Francesca - Loving Guardian	Open		75.00	75
1996	Iris - Rainbow's End	Open		65.00	65

Spencer - I. Spencer

YEAR ISSUE		EDITION LIMIT	YEAR RETD.	ISSUE PRICE	*QUOTE U.S.$
1985	Flower Princess	5,000		195.00	195
1985	Moon Goddess	5,000		195.00	195

Ron Lee's World of Clowns

The Ron Lee Collector's Club Gifts - R. Lee

YEAR ISSUE		EDITION LIMIT	YEAR RETD.	ISSUE PRICE	*QUOTE U.S.$
1987	Hooping It Up CCG1	Closed	1987	Gift	145
1988	Pudge CCG2	Closed	1988	Gift	95
1989	Pals CCG3	Closed	1989	Gift	95
1990	Potsie CCG4	Closed	1990	Gift	95
1991	Hi! Ya! CCG5	Closed	1991	Gift	95
1992	Bashful Beau CCG6	Closed	1992	Gift	95
1993	Lit'l Mate CCG7	Closed	1993	Gift	95
1994	Chip Off the Old Block CCG8	Closed	1994	Gift	65
1995	Rock-A-Billy CCG9	Closed	1995	Gift	65
1996	Hey There CCG10	Yr.Iss.		Gift	65

The Ron Lee Collector's Club Renewal Sculptures - R. Lee

YEAR ISSUE		EDITION LIMIT	YEAR RETD.	ISSUE PRICE	*QUOTE U.S.$
1987	Doggin' Along CC1	Yr.Iss.	1987	75.00	138
1988	Midsummer's Dream CC2	Yr.Iss.	1988	97.00	168
1989	Peek-A-Boo Charlie CC3	Yr.Iss.	1989	65.00	150
1990	Get The Message CC4	Yr.Iss.	1990	65.00	150
1991	I'm So Pretty CC5	Yr.Iss.	1991	65.00	150
1992	It's For You CC6	Yr.Iss.	1992	65.00	150
1993	My Son Keven CC7	Yr.Iss.	1993	70.00	150

The Ron Lee Collector's Club Specials - R. Lee

YEAR ISSUE		EDITION LIMIT	YEAR RETD.	ISSUE PRICE	*QUOTE U.S.$
1995	Welcome CCGIVE	500		85.00	85
1995	Have a Ball CCS100	3,500		45.00	45
1995	Two Bagger CCS105	3,500		45.00	45
1995	Skate Freighter CCS110	3,500		45.00	45
1995	Lit'l Thinker CCS115	3,500		45.00	45
1995	Mop of My Heart CCS120	3,500		45.00	45
1995	Dreamin' CCS125	3,500		45.00	45
1995	Ground Breaking Celebration LV ONE	10,000		92.50	93
1995	Scissors LV TWO	500		120.00	120
1996	Lara's Glorious Ride CCS130	350		325.00	325
1996	Hear Ye! Hear Ye! CCGIVE2	500		75.00	75
1996	Extra! Extra! LV THREE	500		110.00	110
1996	Ride That Horse CCS135	2,500		65.00	65
1996	Pickles CCS140	2,500		59.50	60
1996	Gingerbread Man CCS145	1,500		47.50	48
1996	Top Hat and Tail CCS150	1,500		47.50	48
1996	A Doll Story CCS155	1,500		47.50	48
1996	Hats All Folks CCS160	1,500		47.50	48
1996	All Day Sucker CCS165	1,500		47.50	48

Around the World With Hobo Joe - R. Lee

YEAR ISSUE		EDITION LIMIT	YEAR RETD.	ISSUE PRICE	*QUOTE U.S.$
1994	Hobo Joe in Caribbean L412	750	1995	110.00	110
1994	Hobo Joe in Egypt L415	750	1995	110.00	110
1994	Hobo Joe in England L411	750	1995	110.00	110
1994	Hobo Joe in France L407	750	1995	110.00	110
1994	Hobo Joe in Italy L406	750	1995	110.00	110
1994	Hobo Joe in Japan L408	750	1995	110.00	110
1994	Hobo Joe in Norway L413	750	1995	110.00	110
1994	Hobo Joe in Spain L414	750	1995	110.00	110
1994	Hobo Joe in Tahiti L410	750	1995	110.00	110
1994	Hobo Joe in the U.S.A L409	750	1995	110.00	110-125

The Betty Boop Collection - R. Lee

YEAR ISSUE		EDITION LIMIT	YEAR RETD.	ISSUE PRICE	*QUOTE U.S.$
1992	Bamboo Isle BB715	1,500		240.00	240
1992	Boop Oop A Doop BB705	1,500		97.00	97
1992	Harvest Moon BB700	1,500		93.00	93
1992	Max's Cafe BB720	1,500		99.00	99
1992	Spicy Dish BB710	1,500		215.00	215

Center Ring - R. Lee

YEAR ISSUE		EDITION LIMIT	YEAR RETD.	ISSUE PRICE	*QUOTE U.S.$
1994	According To L-431SE	750	1995	125.00	125
1994	Aristocrat L-424SE	750	1995	125.00	125
1994	Barella L-423SE	750	1995	125.00	125-140
1994	Belt-a-Loon L-427SE	750	1995	125.00	125
1994	Boo-Boo L-430SE	750	1995	125.00	125
1994	Bubbles L-422SE	750	1995	125.00	125
1994	Carpetbagger L-421SE	750	1995	125.00	125
1994	Daisy L-417SE	750	1995	125.00	125
1994	Forget-Me-Not L-428SE	750	1995	125.00	125
1994	Glamour Boy L-433SE	750	1995	125.00	125
1994	Hoop-De-Doo L-434SE	750	1995	125.00	125
1994	Hot Dog L-418SE	750	1995	125.00	125
1994	Kandy L-419SE	750	1995	125.00	125
1994	Maid in the USA L-432SE	750	1995	125.00	125-140
1994	Mal-Lett L-426SE	750	1995	125.00	125
1994	Poodles L-420SE	750	1995	125.00	125
1994	Puddles L-416SE	750	1995	125.00	125
1994	Rabbit's Foot L-429SE	750	1995	125.00	125
1994	Ruffles L-435SE	750	1995	125.00	125
1994	Snacks L-425SE	750	1995	125.00	125

The Classics - R. Lee

YEAR ISSUE		EDITION LIMIT	YEAR RETD.	ISSUE PRICE	*QUOTE U.S.$
1991	Huckleberry Hound HB815	2,750	1995	90.00	108
1991	Quick Draw McGraw HB805	2,750	1995	90.00	108
1991	Scooby Doo & Shaggy HB810	2,750	1995	114.00	137
1991	Yogi Bear & Boo Boo HB800	2,750	1995	95.00	114

The Commemorative Collection - R. Lee

YEAR ISSUE		EDITION LIMIT	YEAR RETD.	ISSUE PRICE	*QUOTE U.S.$
1995	April 12th L455	2,500		180.00	180
1995	Between Shows L456	2,500		250.00	250
1995	Filet of Sole L460	2,500		180.00	200
1995	The Highwayman L457	2,500		165.00	165
1995	Just Plain Tired L459	2,500		195.00	225
1995	Practice Swing...Not!! L458	2,500		180.00	205

The E.T. Collection - R. Lee

YEAR ISSUE		EDITION LIMIT	YEAR RETD.	ISSUE PRICE	*QUOTE U.S.$
1992	E.T. ET100	1,500	1995	94.00	113
1993	Flight ET115	1,500	1995	325.00	390
1993	Friends ET110	1,500	1995	125.00	150
1992	It's Mee...E.T. ET105	1,500	1995	94.00	113

The Flintstones - R. Lee

YEAR ISSUE		EDITION LIMIT	YEAR RETD.	ISSUE PRICE	*QUOTE U.S.$
1991	Bedrock Serenade HB130	2,750		250.00	250
1991	Bogey Buddies HB150	2,750		143.00	143
1991	Buffalo Brothers HB170	2,750		134.00	134
1991	The Flinstones HB100	2,750		410.00	410
1991	Joyride-A-Saurus HB140	2,750		107.00	107
1991	Saturday Blues HB120	2,750		105.00	105
1991	Vac-A-Saurus HB160	2,750		105.00	110
1991	Yabba-Dabba-Doo HB110	2,750		230.00	230

History of Golf - R. Lee

YEAR ISSUE		EDITION LIMIT	YEAR RETD.	ISSUE PRICE	*QUOTE U.S.$
1994	20th Century GTA700	10,000		150.00	150
1994	Age of Chivalry GTA400	10,000		150.00	150
1994	Caesar GTA300	10,000		150.00	150
1994	Dawn of Man GTA100	10,000		150.00	150
1994	New Frontiers GTA800	10,000		150.00	150
1994	Old West GTA600	10,000		150.00	150
1994	The Pharaoh GTA200	10,000		150.00	150
1994	Plymouth GTA500	10,000		150.00	150

Holiday Special - R. Lee

YEAR ISSUE		EDITION LIMIT	YEAR RETD.	ISSUE PRICE	*QUOTE U.S.$
1995	Bells, Stars, and Angels XMAS-4	N/A		39.00	39
1995	Gifts From Santa XMAS-5	N/A		39.00	39
1996	Happy Chanukah L489	950		190.00	190
1995	Holiday on Ice XMAS-3	N/A		39.00	39
1996	How Big! So Big! L490	950		197.00	197
1995	Santa's Other Sleigh L461	750		195.00	195
1995	Snowflake XMAS-6	N/A		35.00	35

The Jetsons - R. Lee

YEAR ISSUE		EDITION LIMIT	YEAR RETD.	ISSUE PRICE	*QUOTE U.S.$
1991	4 O'Clock Tea HB550	2,750	1995	203.00	244
1991	Astro: Cosmic Canine HB520	2,750	1995	275.00	330
1991	The Cosmic Couple HB510	2,750	1995	105.00	126
1991	I Rove Roo HB530	2,750	1995	105.00	127
1991	The Jetsons HB500	2,750	1995	500.00	600
1991	Scare-D-Dog HB540	2,750	1995	160.00	192

Lance Burton - R. Lee

YEAR ISSUE		EDITION LIMIT	YEAR RETD.	ISSUE PRICE	*QUOTE U.S.$
1996	Levitation LB100	950		425.00	425

Musical Clowns in Harmony - R. Lee

YEAR ISSUE		EDITION LIMIT	YEAR RETD.	ISSUE PRICE	*QUOTE U.S.$
1994	Aristocrat L-424	750	1995	125.00	125
1994	Barella L-423	750	1995	125.00	125
1994	Bubbles L-422	750	1995	125.00	125
1994	Carpet Bagger L-421	750	1995	125.00	125
1994	Daisy L-417	750	1995	125.00	125
1994	Hot Dog L-418	750	1995	125.00	125
1994	Kandy L-419	750	1995	125.00	125
1994	Poodles L-420	750	1995	125.00	125
1994	Puddles L-416	750	1995	125.00	125
1994	Snacks L-425	750	1995	125.00	125

The Original Ron Lee Collection-1976 - R. Lee

YEAR ISSUE		EDITION LIMIT	YEAR RETD.	ISSUE PRICE	*QUOTE U.S.$
1976	Alligator Bowling 504	Closed	N/A	15.00	75-94
1976	Bear Fishing 511	Closed	N/A	15.00	75-94
1976	Clown and Dog Act 101	Closed	N/A	48.00	100-168
1976	Clown and Elephant Act 107	Closed	N/A	56.00	100-168
1976	Clown Tightrope Walker 104	Closed	N/A	50.00	125-186
1976	Dog Fishing 512	Closed	N/A	15.00	75-94
1976	Frog Surfing 502	Closed	N/A	15.00	75-94
1976	Hippo on Scooter 505	Closed	N/A	15.00	75-94
1976	Hobo Joe Hitchiking 116	Closed	N/A	55.00	78
1976	Hobo Joe with Balloons 120	Closed	N/A	63.00	110
1976	Hobo Joe with Pal 115	Closed	N/A	63.00	175-200
1976	Hobo Joe with Umbrella 117	Closed	N/A	58.00	150-192
1976	Kangaroos Boxing 508	Closed	N/A	15.00	75-94
1976	Owl With Guitar 500	Closed	N/A	15.00	75-94
1976	Penguin on Snowskis 503	Closed	N/A	15.00	75-94
1976	Pig Playing Violin 510	Closed	N/A	15.00	75-94
1976	Pinky Lying Down 112	Closed	N/A	25.00	150-250
1976	Pinky Sitting 119	Closed	N/A	25.00	150-170
1976	Pinky Standing 118	Closed	N/A	25.00	125-270
1976	Pinky Upside Down 111	Closed	N/A	25.00	150
1976	Rabbit Playing Tennis 507	Closed	N/A	15.00	75-94
1976	Turtle On Skateboard 501	Closed	N/A	15.00	75-94

The Original Ron Lee Collection-1977 - R. Lee

YEAR ISSUE		EDITION LIMIT	YEAR RETD.	ISSUE PRICE	*QUOTE U.S.$
1977	Bear On Rock 523	Closed	N/A	18.00	75-96
1977	Koala Bear In Tree 514	Closed	N/A	15.00	50-94
1977	Koala Bear On Log 516	Closed	N/A	15.00	50-94
1977	Koala Bear With Baby 515	Closed	N/A	15.00	50-94
1977	Monkey With Banana 521	Closed	N/A	18.00	75-96
1977	Mouse and Cheese 520	Closed	N/A	18.00	75-96
1977	Mr. Penguin 518	Closed	N/A	18.00	75-102
1977	Owl Graduate 519	Closed	N/A	22.00	60-96
1977	Pelican and Python 522	Closed	N/A	18.00	70-96

The Original Ron Lee Collection-1978 - R. Lee

YEAR ISSUE		EDITION LIMIT	YEAR RETD.	ISSUE PRICE	*QUOTE U.S.$
1978	Bobbi on Unicyle 204	Closed	N/A	45.00	80-118
1978	Bow Tie 222	Closed	N/A	67.50	200-258
1978	Butterfly and Flower 529	Closed	N/A	22.00	40
1978	Clancy, the Cop 210	Closed	N/A	55.00	90-165
1978	Clara-Bow 205	Closed	N/A	52.00	90-148
1978	Coco-Hands on Hips 218	Closed	N/A	70.00	85-250
1978	Corky, the Drummer Boy 202	Closed	N/A	53.00	85-130
1978	Cuddles 208	Closed	N/A	37.00	55-110
1978	Dolphins 525	Closed	N/A	22.00	40-85
1978	Driver the Golfer 211	Closed	N/A	55.00	200-225
1978	Elephant on Ball 214	Closed	N/A	26.00	42-80
1978	Elephant on Stand 213	Closed	N/A	26.00	42-80
1978	Elephant Sitting 215	Closed	N/A	26.00	42-80
1978	Fancy Pants 224	Closed	N/A	55.00	90-120
1978	Fireman with Hose 216	Closed	N/A	62.00	85-170
1978	Hey Rube 220	Closed	N/A	35.00	53-92
1978	Hummingbird 528	Closed	N/A	22.00	40-85
1978	Jeri In a Barrel 219	Closed	N/A	75.00	175
1978	Jocko with Lollipop 221	Closed	N/A	67.50	93-215
1978	Oscar On Stilts 223	Closed	N/A	55.00	90-120
1978	Pierrot Painting 207	Closed	N/A	50.00	80-170
1978	Polly, the Parrot & Crackers 201	Closed	N/A	63.00	100-170
1978	Poppy with Puppet 209	Closed	N/A	60.00	75-140
1978	Prince Frog 526	Closed	N/A	22.00	40-85
1978	Sad Sack 212	Closed	N/A	48.00	62-210
1978	Sailfish 524	Closed	N/A	18.00	40-95
1978	Sea Otter on Back 531	Closed	N/A	22.00	40-85
1978	Sea Otter on Rock 532	Closed	N/A	22.00	40-85
1978	Seagull 527	Closed	N/A	22.00	40-85
1978	Skippy Swinging 239	Closed	N/A	52.00	65-85
1978	Sparky Skating 206	Closed	N/A	55.00	72-260
1978	Tinker Bowing 203	Closed	N/A	37.00	55-110
1978	Tobi-Hands Outstretched 217	Closed	N/A	70.00	98-260
1978	Turtle on Rock 530	Closed	N/A	22.00	40-85

The Original Ron Lee Collection-1979 - R. Lee

YEAR ISSUE		EDITION LIMIT	YEAR RETD.	ISSUE PRICE	*QUOTE U.S.$
1979	Buttons Bicycling 229	Closed	N/A	75.00	110-150
1979	Carousel Horse 232	Closed	N/A	119.00	130-195
1979	Darby Tipping Hat 238	Closed	N/A	35.00	60-140
1979	Darby with Flower 235	Closed	N/A	35.00	60-140
1979	Darby with Umbrella 236	Closed	N/A	35.00	60-140
1979	Darby With Violin 237	Closed	N/A	35.00	60-140
1979	Doctor Sawbones 228	Closed	N/A	75.00	110-150
1979	Fearless Fred in Cannon 234	Closed	N/A	80.00	105-300
1979	Harry and the Hare 233	Closed	N/A	69.00	102-180
1979	Kelly at the Piano 241	Closed	N/A	185.00	285-510
1979	Kelly in Kar 230	Closed	N/A	164.00	210-380

*Quotes have been rounded up to nearest dollar

FIGURINES

Ron Lee's World of Clowns
to Ron Lee's World of Clowns

YEAR ISSUE		EDITION LIMIT	YEAR RETD.	ISSUE PRICE	*QUOTE U.S.$
1979	Kelly's Kar 231	Closed	N/A	75.00	90-280
1979	Lilli 227	Closed	N/A	75.00	105-145
1979	Timmy Tooting 225	Closed	N/A	35.00	52-85
1979	Tubby Tuba 226	Closed	N/A	35.00	50

The Original Ron Lee Collection-1980 - R. Lee

YEAR ISSUE		EDITION LIMIT	YEAR RETD.	ISSUE PRICE	*QUOTE U.S.$
1980	Alexander's One Man Band 261	Closed	N/A	N/A	N/A
1980	Banjo Willie 258	Closed	N/A	68.00	85-195
1980	Carousel Horse 248	Closed	N/A	88.00	115-285
1980	Carousel Horse 249	Closed	N/A	88.00	115-285
1980	Chuckles Juggling 244	Closed	N/A	98.00	105-150
1980	Cubby Holding Balloon 240	Closed	N/A	50.00	65-70
1980	Dennis Playing Tennis 252	Closed	N/A	74.00	95-185
1980	Doctor Jawbones 260	Closed	N/A	85.00	110-305
1980	Donkey What 243	Closed	N/A	60.00	92-250
1980	Emile 257	Closed	N/A	43.00	82-190
1980	Happy Waving 255	Closed	N/A	43.00	82-190
1980	Hobo Joe in Tub 259	Closed	N/A	96.00	240
1980	Horse Drawn Chariot 263	Closed	N/A	N/A	N/A
1980	Jaque Downhill Racer 253	Closed	N/A	74.00	90-210
1980	Jingles Telling Time 242	Closed	N/A	75.00	90-190
1980	Jo-Jo at Make-up Mirror 250	Closed	N/A	86.00	125-185
1980	The Menagerie 262	Closed	N/A	N/A	N/A
1980	Monkey 251	Closed	N/A	60.00	85-210
1980	P. T. Dinghy 245	Closed	N/A	65.00	80-190
1980	Peanuts Playing Concertina 247	Closed	N/A	65.00	150-285
1980	Roni Riding Horse 246	Closed	N/A	115.00	180-290
1980	Ruford 254	Closed	N/A	43.00	80-190
1980	Zach 256	Closed	N/A	43.00	82-190

The Original Ron Lee Collection-1981 - R. Lee

YEAR ISSUE		EDITION LIMIT	YEAR RETD.	ISSUE PRICE	*QUOTE U.S.$
1981	Al at the Bass 284	Closed	N/A	48.00	52-112
1981	Barbella 273	Closed	N/A	N/A	N/A
1981	Bojangles 276	Closed	N/A	N/A	N/A
1981	Bosom Buddies 299	Closed	N/A	135.00	90-280
1981	Bozo On Unicycle 279	Closed	N/A	28.00	99-185
1981	Bozo Playing Cymbols 277	Closed	N/A	28.00	99-185
1981	Bozo Riding Car 278	Closed	N/A	28.00	99-185
1981	Carney and Seal Act 300	Closed	N/A	63.00	75-290
1981	Carousel Horse 280	Closed	N/A	88.00	125-290
1981	Carousel Horse 281	Closed	N/A	88.00	125-290
1981	Cashew On One Knee 275	Closed	N/A	N/A	N/A
1981	Elephant Reading 271	Closed	N/A	N/A	N/A
1981	Executive Hitchiking 267	Closed	N/A	23.00	45-110
1981	Executive Reading 264	Closed	N/A	23.00	45-110
1981	Executive Resting 266	Closed	N/A	23.00	45-110
1981	Executive with Umbrella 265	Closed	N/A	23.00	45-110
1981	Harpo 296	Closed	N/A	120.00	190-350
1981	Hobo Joe Praying 298	Closed	N/A	57.00	65-85
1981	Kevin at the Drums 283	Closed	N/A	50.00	92-150
1981	Larry and His Hotdogs 274	Closed	N/A	76.00	90-200
1981	Louie Hitching A Ride 269	Closed	N/A	47.00	58-135
1981	Louie on Park Bench 268	Closed	N/A	56.00	85-160
1981	Louie On Railroad Car 270	Closed	N/A	77.00	95-180
1981	Mickey With Umbrella 291	Closed	N/A	50.00	75-140
1981	Mickey Tightrope Walker 292	Closed	N/A	50.00	75-140
1981	Mickey Upside Down 293	Closed	N/A	50.00	75-140
1981	My Son Darren 295	Closed	N/A	57.00	72-140
1981	Nicky Sitting on Ball 289	Closed	N/A	39.00	48-92
1981	Nicky Standing on Ball 290	Closed	N/A	39.00	48-92
1981	Perry Sitting With Balloon 287	Closed	N/A	37.00	50-95
1981	Perry Standing With Balloon 288	Closed	N/A	37.00	50-95
1981	Pickles and Pooch 297	Closed	N/A	90.00	200-240
1981	Pistol Pete 272	Closed	N/A	76.00	85-180
1981	Rocketman 294	Closed	N/A	77.00	92-150
1981	Ron at the Piano 285	Closed	N/A	46.00	55-110
1981	Ron Lee Trio 282	Closed	N/A	144.00	280-435
1981	Timothy In Big Shoes 286	Closed	N/A	37.00	50-95

The Original Ron Lee Collection-1982 - R. Lee

YEAR ISSUE		EDITION LIMIT	YEAR RETD.	ISSUE PRICE	*QUOTE U.S.$
1982	Ali on His Magic Carpet 335	Closed	N/A	105.00	150-210
1982	Barnum Feeding Bacon 315	Closed	N/A	120.00	160-270
1982	Beaver Playing Accordian 807	Closed	N/A	23.00	35-92
1982	Benny Pulling Car 310	Closed	N/A	190.00	235-360
1982	Burrito Bandito 334	Closed	N/A	150.00	190-260
1982	Buster in Barrel 308	Closed	N/A	85.00	90-120
1982	Camel 818	Closed	N/A	57.00	75-150
1982	Captain Cranberry 320	Closed	N/A	115.00	145-180
1982	Captain Mis-Adventure 703	Closed	N/A	250.00	300-550
1982	Carney and Dog Act 301	Closed	N/A	63.00	75-149
1982	Charlie Chaplain 701	Closed	N/A	230.00	285-650
1982	Charlie in the Rain 321	Closed	N/A	80.00	90-160
1982	Chico Playing Guitar 336	Closed	N/A	70.00	95-180
1982	Clancy, the Cop and Dog 333	Closed	N/A	115.00	140-250
1982	Clarence - The Lawyer 331	Closed	N/A	100.00	140-230
1982	Denny Eating Ice Cream 305	Closed	N/A	39.00	50-170
1982	Denny Holding Gift Box 306	Closed	N/A	39.00	50-170
1982	Denny Juggling Ball 307	Closed	N/A	39.00	50-170
1982	Dog Playing Guitar 805	Closed	N/A	23.00	35-92
1982	Dr. Painless and Patient 311	Closed	N/A	195.00	240-385
1982	Fireman Watering House 303	Closed	N/A	99.00	99-180
1982	Fish With Shoe 803	Closed	N/A	23.00	35-92
1982	Fox In An Airplane 806	Closed	N/A	23.00	35-92
1982	Georgie Going Anywhere 302	Closed	N/A	95.00	375
1982	Giraffe 816	Closed	N/A	57.00	75-150
1982	Herbie Balancing Hat 327	Closed	N/A	26.00	40-110
1982	Herbie Dancing 325	Closed	N/A	26.00	40-110
1982	Herbie Hands Outstretched 326	Closed	N/A	26.00	40-110
1982	Herbie Legs in Air 329	Closed	N/A	26.00	40-110
1982	Herbie Lying Down 328	Closed	N/A	26.00	40-110
1982	Herbie Touching Ground 330	Closed	N/A	26.00	40-110
1982	Hobo Joe on Cycle 322	Closed	N/A	125.00	170-280
1982	Horse 819	Closed	N/A	57.00	75-150
1982	Kukla and Friend 316	Closed	N/A	100.00	140-210
1982	Laurel & Hardy 700	Closed	N/A	225.00	290-500
1982	Limousine Service 705	Closed	N/A	330.00	375-750
1982	Lion 817	Closed	N/A	57.00	75-150
1982	Marion With Marrionette 317	Closed	N/A	105.00	135-225
1982	Murphy On Unicycle 337	Closed	N/A	115.00	160-288
1982	Nappy Snoozing 346	Closed	N/A	110.00	125-210
1982	Norman Painting Dumbo 314	Closed	N/A	126.00	150-210
1982	Ostrich 813	Closed	N/A	57.00	75-150
1982	Parrot Rollerskating 809	Closed	N/A	23.00	35-92
1982	Pig Brick Layer 800	Closed	N/A	23.00	35-92
1982	Pinball Pal 332	Closed	N/A	150.00	195-287
1982	Quincy Lying Down 304	Closed	N/A	80.00	92-210
1982	Rabbit With Egg 801	Closed	N/A	23.00	35-92
1982	Reindeer 812	Closed	N/A	57.00	75-150
1982	Robin Resting 338	Closed	N/A	110.00	125-210
1982	Ron Lee Carousel	Closed	N/A	1000.00	12500
1982	Rooster 815	Closed	N/A	57.00	75-150
1982	Rooster With Barbell 808	Closed	N/A	23.00	35-92
1982	Sammy Riding Elephant 309	Closed	N/A	90.00	125-250
1982	Seal Blowing His Horns 804	Closed	N/A	23.00	35-92
1982	Self Portrait 702	Closed	N/A	355.00	2500
1982	Slim Charging Bull 313	Closed	N/A	195.00	265-410
1982	Smokey, the Bear 802	Closed	N/A	23.00	35-92
1982	Steppin' Out 704	Closed	N/A	325.00	390-700
1982	Three Man Valentinos 319	Closed	N/A	55.00	70-120
1982	Tiger 814	Closed	N/A	57.00	75-150
1982	Too Loose-L'Artiste 312	Closed	N/A	150.00	180-290
1982	Tou Tou 323	Closed	N/A	70.00	90-190
1982	Toy Soldier 324	Closed	N/A	95.00	250
1982	Turtle With Gun 811	Closed	N/A	57.00	75-150
1982	Two Man Valentinos 318	Closed	N/A	45.00	60-130
1982	Walrus With Umbrella 810	Closed	N/A	23.00	35-92

The Original Ron Lee Collection-1983 - R. Lee

YEAR ISSUE		EDITION LIMIT	YEAR RETD.	ISSUE PRICE	*QUOTE U.S.$
1983	The Bandwagon 707	Closed	N/A	900.00	2000
1983	Beethoven's Fourth Paws 358	Closed	N/A	59.00	110-165
1983	Black Carousel Horse 1001	Closed	N/A	450.00	450-600
1983	Bumbles Selling Balloons 353	Closed	N/A	80.00	170-240
1983	Buster and His Balloons 363	Closed	N/A	47.00	90-125
1983	Captain Freddy 375	Closed	N/A	85.00	425-475
1983	Casey Cruising 351	Closed	N/A	57.00	95-170
1983	Catch the Brass Ring 708	Closed	N/A	510.00	900-1350
1983	Cecil and Sausage 354	Closed	N/A	90.00	200-270
1983	Chef's Cuisine 361	Closed	N/A	57.00	100-110
1983	Chestnut Carousel Horse 1002	Closed	N/A	450.00	700-1100
1983	Cimba the Elephant 706	Closed	N/A	225.00	300-550
1983	Clyde Juggling 339	Closed	N/A	39.00	100-115
1983	Clyde Upside Down 340	Closed	N/A	39.00	100-115
1983	Coco and His Compact 369	Closed	N/A	55.00	145-175
1983	Cotton Candy 377	Closed	N/A	150.00	200-400
1983	Daring Dudley 367	Closed	N/A	65.00	100-200
1983	Door to Door Dabney 373	Closed	N/A	100.00	200-285
1983	Engineer Billie 356	Closed	N/A	190.00	275-550
1983	Flipper Diving 345	Closed	N/A	115.00	200-350
1983	Gazebo 1004	Closed	N/A	750.00	13-1750
1983	Gilbert Tee'd Off 376	Closed	N/A	60.00	200
1983	Hobi in His Hammock 344	Closed	N/A	85.00	175
1983	I Love You From My Heart 360	Closed	N/A	35.00	125
1983	The Jogger 372	Closed	N/A	75.00	120-220
1983	Josephine 370	Closed	N/A	55.00	145-175
1983	Knickers Balancing Feather 366	Closed	N/A	47.00	120-135
1983	The Last Scoop 379	Closed	N/A	175.00	300-475
1983	The Last Scoop 900	Closed	N/A	325.00	300-725
1983	Little Horse - Head Down 342	Closed	N/A	29.00	72
1983	Little Horse - Head Up 341	Closed	N/A	29.00	72
1983	Little Saturday Night 348	Closed	N/A	53.00	200
1983	Lou Proposing 365	Closed	N/A	57.00	120-170
1983	Matinee Jitters 378	Closed	N/A	175.00	200-450
1983	Matinee Jitters 901	Closed	N/A	325.00	425
1983	My Daughter Deborah 357	Closed	N/A	63.00	125-185
1983	No Camping or Fishing 902	Closed	N/A	325.00	350-600
1983	On The Road Again 355	Closed	N/A	220.00	300-650
1983	Riches to Rags 374	Closed	N/A	55.00	200-265
1983	Ride 'em Roni 347	Closed	N/A	125.00	200-375
1983	Rufus and His Refuse 343	Closed	N/A	65.00	192
1983	Say It With Flowers 359	Closed	N/A	35.00	95-110
1983	Singin' In The Rain 362	Closed	N/A	105.00	420
1983	Tatters and Balloons 352	Closed	N/A	65.00	162
1983	Teeter Tottie Scottie 350	Closed	N/A	55.00	105-165
1983	Tottie Scottie 349	Closed	N/A	39.00	75-115
1983	Up, Up and Away 364	Closed	N/A	50.00	300
1983	White Carousel Horse 1003	Closed	N/A	450.00	700-1100
1983	Wilt the Stilt 368	Closed	N/A	49.00	100-155

The Original Ron Lee Collection-1984 - R. Lee

YEAR ISSUE		EDITION LIMIT	YEAR RETD.	ISSUE PRICE	*QUOTE U.S.$
1984	Baggy Pants 387	Closed	N/A	98.00	250-300
1984	Black Circus Horse 711A	Closed	N/A	305.00	350-520
1984	A Bozo Lunch 390	Closed	N/A	148.00	250-400
1984	Bozo's Seal of Approval 389	Closed	N/A	138.00	200-350
1984	Chestnut Circus Horse 710A	Closed	N/A	305.00	350-520
1984	Give a Dog a Bone 383	Closed	N/A	95.00	95-182
1984	Just For You 386	Closed	N/A	110.00	150-250
1984	Look at the Birdy 388	Closed	N/A	138.00	200-300
1984	Mortimer Fishing 382	Closed	N/A	78.00	94
1984	My Fellow Americans 391	Closed	N/A	138.00	250-425
1984	No Camping or Fishing 380	Closed	N/A	175.00	275-450
1984	No Loitering 392	Closed	N/A	113.00	150-250
1984	The Peppermints 384	Closed	N/A	150.00	180-250
1984	Rudy Holding Balloons 713	Closed	N/A	230.00	300-550
1984	Saturday Night 714	Closed	N/A	250.00	600-825
1984	T.K. and OH!! 385	Closed	N/A	85.00	200-325
1984	Tisket and Tasket 393	Closed	N/A	93.00	150-250
1984	Wheeler Sheila 381	Closed	N/A	75.00	175-225
1984	White Circus Horse 709	Closed	N/A	305.00	350-520

The Original Ron Lee Collection-1985 - R. Lee

YEAR ISSUE		EDITION LIMIT	YEAR RETD.	ISSUE PRICE	*QUOTE U.S.$
1985	Bull-Can-Rear-You 422	Closed	N/A	120.00	245
1985	Cannonball 466	Closed	N/A	43.00	100
1985	Catch of the Day 441	Closed	N/A	170.00	365
1985	Clowns of the Caribbean PS101	Closed	N/A	1250.00	2000-2800
1985	Dr. Sigmund Fraud 457	Closed	N/A	98.00	190
1985	Dr. Timothy DeCay 459	Closed	N/A	98.00	185
1985	Duster Buster 461	Closed	N/A	43.00	90
1985	The Finishing Touch 409	Closed	N/A	178.00	305
1985	Fred Figures 903	Closed	N/A	175.00	595
1985	From Riches to Rags 374	Closed	N/A	108.00	250
1985	Get the Picture 456	Closed	N/A	70.00	140
1985	Gilbert TeeOd OFF 376	Closed	N/A	63.00	55-63
1985	Giraffe Getting a Bath 428	Closed	N/A	160.00	350-450
1985	Ham Track 451	Closed	N/A	240.00	430
1985	Hi Ho Blinky 462	Closed	N/A	53.00	105
1985	One Wheel Winky 464	Closed	N/A	43.00	83
1985	Pee Wee With Balloons 435	Closed	N/A	50.00	100
1985	Pee Wee With Umbrella 434	Closed	N/A	50.00	100
1985	Policy Paul 904	Closed	N/A	175.00	190
1985	Rosebuds 433	Closed	N/A	155.00	315
1985	Twas the Night Before 408	Closed	N/A	235.00	405
1985	Whiskers Bathing 749	Closed	N/A	305.00	500-800
1985	Whiskers Hitchhiking 745	Closed	N/A	240.00	800
1985	Whiskers Holding Balloons 746	Closed	N/A	265.00	500-800
1985	Whiskers Holding Umbrella 747	Closed	N/A	265.00	500-800
1985	Whiskers On The Bench 750	Closed	N/A	230.00	695-895
1985	Whiskers Sweeping 744	Closed	N/A	240.00	700-850
1985	Yo Yo Stravinsky-Attoney at Law 458	Closed	N/A	98.00	200

The Original Ron Lee Collection-1986 - R. Lee

YEAR ISSUE		EDITION LIMIT	YEAR RETD.	ISSUE PRICE	*QUOTE U.S.$
1986	Bathing Buddies 450	Closed	N/A	145.00	375
1986	Bums Day at the Beach L105	Closed	N/A	97.00	N/A
1986	Captain Cranberry 469	Closed	N/A	140.00	175-335
1986	Christmas Morning Magic L107	Closed	N/A	99.00	N/A
1986	Getting Even 485	Closed	N/A	85.00	125-225
1986	Hari and Hare 454	Closed	N/A	57.00	85-135
1986	High Above the Big Top L112	Closed	N/A	162.00	475
1986	The Last Stop L106	Closed	N/A	99.00	N/A
1986	Most Requested Toy L108	Closed	N/A	264.00	N/A
1986	Puppy Love's Portrait L113	Closed	N/A	168.00	325
1986	Ride 'Em Peanuts 463	Closed	N/A	55.00	70-135
1986	Wet Paint 436	Closed	N/A	80.00	135

The Original Ron Lee Collection-1987 - R. Lee

YEAR ISSUE		EDITION LIMIT	YEAR RETD.	ISSUE PRICE	*QUOTE U.S.$
1987	First & Main L110	Closed	N/A	368.00	850-895
1987	Happines Is L116	Closed	N/A	155.00	185
1987	Heartbroken Harry L101	Closed	N/A	63.00	125-225
1987	Lovable Luke L102	Closed	N/A	70.00	150
1987	Puppy Love L103	Closed	N/A	71.00	150
1987	Show of Shows L115	Closed	N/A	175.00	N/A
1987	Sugarland Express L109	Closed	N/A	342.00	650-895
1987	Would You Like To Ride? L104	Closed	N/A	246.00	350

The Original Ron Lee Collection-1988 - R. Lee

YEAR ISSUE		EDITION LIMIT	YEAR RETD.	ISSUE PRICE	*QUOTE U.S.$
1988	Anchors-A-Way L120	Closed	N/A	195.00	250
1988	Boulder Bay L124	Closed	N/A	700.00	N/A
1988	Bozorina L118	Closed	N/A	95.00	120
1988	Cactus Pete L125	Closed	N/A	495.00	N/A
1988	Dinner for Two L119	Closed	N/A	140.00	N/A
1988	The Fifth Wheel L117	Closed	N/A	250.00	375
1988	Fore! L122	Closed	N/A	135.00	175
1988	New Ron Lee Carousel	Closed	N/A	7000.00	9500
1988	Pumpkuns Galore L121	Closed	N/A	135.00	160-245
1988	To The Rescue L127	Closed	N/A	130.00	160-550
1988	Together Again L126	Closed	N/A	130.00	210
1988	Tunnel of Love L123	Closed	N/A	490.00	600-800
1988	When You're Hot, You're Hot! L128	Closed	N/A	221.00	295

The Original Ron Lee Collection-1989 - R. Lee

YEAR ISSUE		EDITION LIMIT	YEAR RETD.	ISSUE PRICE	*QUOTE U.S.$
1989	The Accountant L173	Closed	N/A	68.00	150-200
1989	The Baseball Player L189	Closed	N/A	72.00	150-200
1989	The Basketball Player L187	Closed	N/A	68.00	150-200
1989	Be Happy L198	Closed	N/A	160.00	195
1989	Be It Ever So Humble L111	Closed	N/A	900.00	950-1250
1989	The Beautician L183	Closed	N/A	68.00	150-200
1989	Beauty Is In The Eye Of L140	Closed	N/A	190.00	400-475
1989	Birdbrain L206	Closed	N/A	110.00	250
1989	The Bowler L191	Closed	N/A	68.00	150-200
1989	Butt-R-Fly L151	Closed	N/A	47.00	75
1989	Butterflies Are Free L204	Closed	N/A	225.00	250
1989	Candy Apple L155	Closed	N/A	47.00	75
1989	Candy Man L217	Closed	N/A	350.00	595
1989	Catch A Falling Star L148	Closed	N/A	57.00	75
1989	The Chef L178	Closed	N/A	65.00	150-200
1989	The Chiropractor L180	Closed	N/A	68.00	150-200
1989	Circus Little L143	Closed	N/A	990.00	1250
1989	Craps L212	Closed	N/A	530.00	895
1989	Dang It L200	Closed	N/A	47.00	63
1989	The Dentist L175	Closed	N/A	65.00	150-200
1989	The Doctor L170	Closed	N/A	65.00	150-200
1989	Eye Love You L136	Closed	N/A	68.00	150

*Quotes have been rounded up to nearest dollar

Ron Lee's World of Clowns
to Ron Lee's World of Clowns

FIGURINES

YEAR ISSUE		EDITION LIMIT	YEAR RETD.	ISSUE PRICE	*QUOTE U.S.$
1989	The Fireman L169	Closed	N/A	68.00	175
1989	The Fisherman L194	Closed	N/A	72.00	400
1989	The Football Player L186	Closed	N/A	65.00	150-200
1989	Get Well L131	Closed	N/A	79.00	96
1989	The Golfer L188	Closed	N/A	72.00	150-200
1989	The Greatest Little Shoe On Earth L210	Closed	N/A	165.00	200-300
1989	Happy Chanakah L162	Closed	N/A	106.00	125
1989	Hot Diggity Dog L201	Closed	N/A	47.00	50
1989	The Housewife L181	Closed	N/A	75.00	150-200
1989	Hughie Mungus L144	Closed	N/A	250.00	300-825
1989	I Ain't Got No Money L195	Closed	N/A	325.00	895
1989	I Just Called! L153	Closed	N/A	47.00	75
1989	I Pledge Allegiance L134	Closed	N/A	131.00	150-250
1989	I Should've When I Could've L196	Closed	N/A	325.00	895
1989	I-D-D-D-Do! L215	Closed	N/A	180.00	225
1989	If I Were A Rich Man L133	Closed	N/A	315.00	695
1989	If That's Your Drive How's Your Putts L164	Closed	N/A	260.00	N/A
1989	In Over My Head L135	Closed	N/A	95.00	250
1989	Jingles Hitchhiking L209	Closed	N/A	90.00	200
1989	Jingles Holding Balloon L208	Closed	N/A	90.00	200
1989	Jingles With Umbrella L207	Closed	N/A	90.00	175
1989	Just Carried Away L138	Closed	N/A	135.00	230
1989	Just Go! L156	Closed	N/A	47.00	75
1989	The Lawyer 171	Closed	N/A	68.00	150-200
1989	Maestro L132	Closed	N/A	173.00	200
1989	Marcelle L150	Closed	N/A	47.00	N/A
1989	The Mechanic L184	Closed	N/A	68.00	150-200
1989	Memories L197	Closed	N/A	325.00	375
1989	Merry Xmas L159	Closed	N/A	94.00	125
1989	My Affections L157	Closed	N/A	47.00	75
1989	My First Tree L161	Closed	N/A	92.00	125
1989	My Heart Beats For You L137	Closed	N/A	74.00	150
1989	My Last Chip L213	Closed	N/A	550.00	N/A
1989	My Money's OnThe Bull L142	Closed	N/A	187.00	480
1989	The New Self Portrait L218	Closed	N/A	800.00	2000-3000
1989	No Fishing L130	Closed	N/A	247.00	795
1989	Not A Ghost Of A Chance L145	Closed	N/A	195.00	500
1989	The Nurse L168	Closed	N/A	65.00	95
1989	O' Solo Mia L139	Closed	N/A	85.00	90-150
1989	The Optometrist L174	Closed	N/A	65.00	150-200
1989	Over 21 L214	Closed	N/A	550.00	N/A
1989	The Pharmacist L166	Closed	N/A	65.00	N/A
1989	The Photographer L172	Closed	N/A	68.00	150-200
1989	The Plumber L176	Closed	N/A	65.00	150-200
1989	The Policeman L165	Closed	N/A	68.00	150
1989	Rain Bugs Me L203	Closed	N/A	225.00	N/A
1989	The Real Estate Lady L185	Closed	N/A	70.00	250
1989	The Real Estate Man L177	Closed	N/A	65.00	150-200
1989	Rest Stop L149	Closed	N/A	47.00	75
1989	The Salesman L167	Closed	N/A	68.00	N/A
1989	Santa's Dilemma L160	Closed	N/A	97.00	250
1989	The Secretary L179	Closed	N/A	65.00	95
1989	The Serenade L202	Closed	N/A	47.00	N/A
1989	Sh-h-h-h! L146	Closed	N/A	210.00	450
1989	She Loves Me Not L205	Closed	N/A	225.00	250
1989	The Skier L193	Closed	N/A	75.00	150-200
1989	Slots Of Luck L211	Closed	N/A	90.00	300-375
1989	Snowdrifter L163	Closed	N/A	230.00	695
1989	Stormy Weathers L152	Closed	N/A	47.00	N/A
1989	Sunflower L154	Closed	N/A	47.00	75
1989	The Surfer L192	Closed	N/A	72.00	150-200
1989	Tee for Two L141	Closed	N/A	125.00	150
1989	The Tennis Player L190	Closed	N/A	72.00	150-200
1989	Today's Catch L147	Closed	N/A	230.00	350
1989	Two a.m. Blues L199	Closed	N/A	125.00	180-250
1989	The Veterinarian L182	Closed	N/A	72.00	150-200
1989	Wintertime Pals L158	Closed	N/A	90.00	N/A
1989	Wishful Thinking L114	Closed	N/A	230.00	2000-3000
1989	You Must Be Kidding L216	Closed	N/A	N/A	800

The Original Ron Lee Collection-1990 - R. Lee

YEAR ISSUE		EDITION LIMIT	YEAR RETD.	ISSUE PRICE	*QUOTE U.S.$
1990	All Show No Go L238	1,500		285.00	795
1990	The Big Wheel L236	Closed	N/A	240.00	245
1990	Carousel Horse L219	Closed	N/A	150.00	N/A
1990	Carousel Horse L220	Closed	N/A	150.00	N/A
1990	Carousel Horse L221	Closed	N/A	150.00	N/A
1990	Carousel Horse L222	Closed	N/A	150.00	210
1990	Fill'er Up L248	Closed	N/A	280.00	300
1990	Flapper Riding Carousel L223	Closed	N/A	190.00	N/A
1990	Heart of My Heart L246	5,500	1995	55.00	55
1990	Heartbroken Hobo L233	Closed	N/A	116.00	195
1990	Henry 8-3/4 L260	Closed	N/A	37.00	50
1990	Horsin' Around L262	Closed	N/A	37.00	37-50
1990	I Love You L242	5,500	1995	55.00	55
1990	I.Q. Two L253	2,750	1995	33.00	50
1990	Jo-Jo Riding Carousel L226	Closed	N/A	190.00	N/A
1990	Kiss! Kiss! L251	Closed	N/A	37.00	44
1990	L-O-V-E L245	5,500	1995	55.00	66
1990	Loving You L244	5,500	1996	55.00	66
1990	Me Too!! L231	Closed	1995	70.00	96
1990	My Heart's on for You L240	5,500	1995	55.00	66
1990	Na! Na! L252	Closed	N/A	33.00	60
1990	New Pinky Lying Down L228	8,500		42.00	50
1990	New Pinky Sitting L230	8,500		42.00	50
1990	New Pinky Standing L229	8,500		42.00	50
1990	New Pinky Upside Down L227	8,500		42.00	50
1990	Paddle L259	2,750	1995	33.00	50
1990	Par Three L232	2,750	1995	144.00	144
1990	Peaches Riding Carousel L224	Closed	N/A	190.00	225
1990	Pitch L261	2,750	1995	35.00	50
1990	Push and Pull L249	Closed	N/A	260.00	280
1990	Q.T. Pie L257	2,750	1995	37.00	50
1990	Rascal Riding Carousel L225	Closed	N/A	190.00	210
1990	Same To "U" L255	2,750	1995	37.00	50
1990	Scooter L234	Closed	1995	240.00	295
1990	Skiing My Way L239	2,500	1995	400.00	895
1990	Snowdrifter II L250	Closed	N/A	340.00	895-925
1990	Squirt L258	2,750	1995	37.00	50
1990	Stuck on Me L243	5,500	1995	55.00	55
1990	Swinging on a Star L241	5,500	1995	55.00	55
1990	Tandem Mania L235	Closed	N/A	360.00	360
1990	Uni-Cycle L237	Closed	N/A	240.00	245
1990	Watch Your Step L247	2,500	1996	78.00	78
1990	Yo Mama L256	2,750	1995	35.00	50
1990	Your Heaviness L254	2,750	1995	37.00	50

The Original Ron Lee Collection-1991 - R. Lee

YEAR ISSUE		EDITION LIMIT	YEAR RETD.	ISSUE PRICE	*QUOTE U.S.$
1991	Ain't No Havana L315	500	1995	230.00	400
1991	Anywhere? L269	Closed	N/A	125.00	200
1991	Banjo Willie L293	1,750	1996	90.00	90
1991	Business is Business L266	Closed	1995	110.00	190
1991	Clarence Clarinet L289	1,750	1995	42.00	50
1991	Cruising L265	Closed	N/A	170.00	170-175
1991	Droopy Drummer L290	1,750	1995	42.00	50
1991	Eight Ball-Corner Pocket L311	1,750		224.00	250
1991	Fall L282	1,500		120.00	140
1991	Geronimo L304	1,750		127.00	180
1991	Gilbert's Dilemma L270	Closed	N/A	90.00	125
1991	Give Me Liberty L313	Closed	N/A	155.00	200-250
1991	Happy Birthday Puppy Love L278	Closed	N/A	73.00	100
1991	Harley Horn L291	1,750	1995	42.00	50
1991	Hobi Daydreaming L299	1,750	1996	112.00	112
1991	Hook, Line and Sinker L303	1,750		100.00	100
1991	Hot Dawg! L316	500	1995	255.00	255
1991	I'm Singin' In The Rain L268	Closed	N/A	135.00	165
1991	IRS or Bust L285	1,500	1995	122.00	122
1991	Lit'l Snowdrifter L298	1,750	1996	70.00	150
1991	Makin Tracks L283	1,500	1995	142.00	142
1991	Marcelle I L271	2,250	1995	50.00	50
1991	Marcelle II L272	2,250	1995	50.00	100
1991	Marcelle III L273	2,250	1995	50.00	50
1991	Marcelle IV L274	2,250	1995	50.00	50
1991	New Darby Tipping Hat L310	1,250	1995	57.00	57
1991	New Darby with Flower L307	1,250	1995	57.00	57
1991	New Darby with Umbrella L308	1,250	1995	57.00	57
1991	New Darby with Violin L309	1,250	1995	57.00	57
1991	New Harpo L305	1,250	1995	130.00	130
1991	New Toy Soldier L306	1,250	1995	115.00	115
1991	Our Nation's Pride L312	Closed	N/A	150.00	150
1991	Puppy Love Scootin' L275	Closed	N/A	73.00	100
1991	Puppy Love's Free Ride L276	Closed	N/A	73.00	100
1991	Puppy Love's Treat L277	Closed	N/A	73.00	100
1991	Refugee L267	1,750	1995	88.00	88
1991	Sand Trap L301	1,750		100.00	100
1991	Soap Suds Serenade L284	1,750	1996	85.00	85
1991	Spring L280	1,500		95.00	95
1991	Strike!!! L302	1,750		76.00	76
1991	Summer L281	1,500	N/A	95.00	135
1991	Surf's Up L300	1,750		80.00	80
1991	TA DA L294	Closed	N/A	220.00	200-295
1991	Tender-Lee L264	1,750	1995	96.00	96
1991	This Won't Hurt L296	1,750	1995	110.00	110
1991	Tootie Tuba L286	1,750	1995	42.00	50
1991	Trash Can Sam L295	1,750	1995	118.00	118
1991	Truly Trumpet L287	1,750	1995	42.00	50
1991	Trusty Trombone L288	1,750	1995	42.00	50
1991	Two For Fore L297	1,750	1996	120.00	120
1991	United We Stand L314	Closed	N/A	150.00	150
1991	The Visit L263	1,750	1995	100.00	100
1991	Winter L279	1,500		115.00	115

The Original Ron Lee Collection-1992 - R. Lee

YEAR ISSUE		EDITION LIMIT	YEAR RETD.	ISSUE PRICE	*QUOTE U.S.$
1992	Baloony L350	2,500		26.00	27
1992	Beats Nothin' L357	1,500		145.00	145
1992	Beau Regards L342	2,500		26.00	27
1992	Big Wheel Kop RLC1005	1,750	1995	65.00	99
1992	Birdy The Hard Way L352	1,750		85.00	85
1992	Bo-Bo Balancing RLC1003	1,750	1995	75.00	75
1992	Break Point L335	2,500		26.00	27
1992	Brokenhearted Huey RLC1006	1,750	1995	65.00	65
1992	Buster Too PC100	1,500	1995	65.00	65
1992	Cannonball RLC1009	1,750	1995	95.00	125
1992	Clar-A-Bow L336	2,500		26.00	27
1992	Cyclin' Around L322	2,500		26.00	27
1992	Dreams L332	2,500		26.00	27
1992	Dudley's Dog Act RLC1010	1,750	1995	75.00	75
1992	Dunkin' L328	2,500		26.00	27
1992	Fish in Pail L358	1,500	1996	130.00	235
1992	Flyin' High L340	2,500		26.00	27
1992	Forget Me Not L341	2,500		26.00	27
1992	Gassing Up RLC1004	1,750	1995	70.00	70
1992	Go Man Go L344	2,500		26.00	27
1992	Handy Standy L321	2,500		26.00	27
1992	Heel's Up L329	2,500		26.00	27
1992	Hi-Five L339	2,500		26.00	27
1992	Hippolong Cassidy L320	Closed	N/A	166.00	140
1992	Howdy L325	2,500		26.00	27
1992	Jo-Jo Juggling RLC1002	1,750	1995	70.00	70
1992	Juggles L347	2,500		26.00	27
1992	Little Pard L349	2,500		26.00	27
1992	Lolly L326	2,500		26.00	27
1992	Love Ya' Baby L355	1,250		190.00	190
1992	Miles PC105	1,500	1995	65.00	65
1992	My Pal L334	2,500		26.00	27
1992	My Portrait L354	Closed	N/A	315.00	595
1992	Myak Kyak L337	2,500		26.00	27
1992	On My Way L348	2,500		26.00	27
1992	Penny Saver L333	2,500		26.00	27
1992	Popcorn & Cotton Candy RLC1001	1,750	1995	70.00	70
1992	Scrub-A- Dub-Dub L319	Closed	N/A	185.00	195
1992	Seven's Up L356	1,250		165.00	165
1992	Shake Jake L324	2,500		26.00	27
1992	Ship Ahoy L345	2,500		26.00	27
1992	Shufflin' L343	2,500		26.00	27
1992	Snowdrifter Blowin' In Wind L317	1,750	1996	77.50	78
1992	Snowdrifter's Special Delivery L318	1,750	1996	136.00	136
1992	Steamer L338	2,500		26.00	27
1992	Stop Cop L331	2,500		26.00	27
1992	Strike Out L323	2,500		26.00	27
1992	Struttin' L346	2,500		26.00	27
1992	Sure-Footed Freddie RLC1007	1,750	1995	80.00	80
1992	To-Tee L327	2,500		26.00	27
1992	Topper PC110	1,500	1995	65.00	65
1992	Twirp Chirp L330	2,500		26.00	27
1992	Vincent Van Clown L353	Closed	N/A	160.00	160
1992	Walking A Fine Line RMB7000	1,750	1995	65.00	65
1992	Webb-ster PC115	1,500	1995	65.00	65
1992	Wrong Hole Clown L351	1,750		125.00	125

The Original Ron Lee Collection-1993 - R. Lee

YEAR ISSUE		EDITION LIMIT	YEAR RETD.	ISSUE PRICE	*QUOTE U.S.$
1993	Andy Jackson L364	950	1995	87.00	115
1993	Anywhere Warm L398	950	1996	90.00	90
1993	Bellboy L390	950	1995	80.00	80
1993	Blinky Lying Down L384	1,200		45.00	45
1993	Blinky Sitting L383	1,200		45.00	45
1993	Blinky Standing L382	1,200		45.00	45
1993	Blinky Upside Down L385	1,200		45.00	45
1993	Bo-Bo L365	950	1995	95.00	95
1993	Britches L377	750		205.00	205
1993	Bumper Fun L403	750		330.00	330
1993	Buster L368	950	1995	87.00	115
1993	Charkles L381	750	1995	220.00	220
1993	Chattanooga Choo-Choo L374	750		420.00	420
1993	Dave Bomber L360	950	1995	90.00	90
1993	Happy Trails L369	950	1995	90.00	90
1993	Honk Honk L370	950	1995	90.00	90
1993	Hot Buns L376	750		175.00	175
1993	Lollipop L363	950	1995	87.00	120
1993	Merry Go Clown L405	750		375.00	375
1993	Moto Kris L380	750		255.00	255
1993	North Pole L396	950	1995	75.00	75
1993	Piggy Backin' L379	750		205.00	205
1993	Pretzels L372	750		195.00	195
1993	Sailin' L366	950	1995	95.00	95
1993	Scrubs L361	950	1995	87.00	115
1993	Sho-Sho L373	750		115.00	115
1993	Shriner Cop L404	750		175.00	175
1993	Skittles L367	950	1995	95.00	95
1993	Snoozin' L399	950		90.00	90
1993	Soft Shoe L400	750		275.00	275
1993	Sole-Full L375	750		250.00	250
1993	Special Occasion L402	750		280.00	280
1993	Taxi L378	750		470.00	470
1993	Tinker And Toy L359	950	1995	95.00	95
1993	Wagone Hes L371	750		210.00	210
1993	Wanderer L401	750		255.00	255
1993	Yo-Yo L362	950	1995	87.00	115

The Original Ron Lee Collection-1995 - R. Lee

YEAR ISSUE		EDITION LIMIT	YEAR RETD.	ISSUE PRICE	*QUOTE U.S.$
1995	Bar Mitzvah L463	950		270.00	270
1995	Bat Mitzvah L462	950		270.00	270
1995	Batter Up L465	500		270.00	270
1995	Cimba's Last Stand L466	950		165.00	165
1995	Fillet of Sole L460	750		180.00	180
1995	Fore! Anyone! L464	500		275.00	275
1995	Santa's Other Sleigh L461	750		195.00	195

The Original Ron Lee Collection-1996 - R. Lee

YEAR ISSUE		EDITION LIMIT	YEAR RETD.	ISSUE PRICE	*QUOTE U.S.$
1996	7-7-7 L486	1,200		525.00	525
1996	The Bass Drum L478	950		47.00	47
1996	Bunches L482	950		215.00	215
1996	The Clarinet L476	950		47.00	47
1996	Craps L488	1,200		475.00	475
1996	The Cymbols L477	950		47.00	47
1996	Frankie L480	750		95.00	95
1996	The Grand Bandwagon L470	750		1100.00	1100
1996	Hit Me L487	1,200		425.00	425
1996	Jocko KL105	500		375.00	375
1996	Johnnie L481	750		95.00	95
1996	The Juggler KL100	500		350.00	350
1996	Juggling Joel L484	950		150.00	150
1996	Pastime Pals L469	950		135.00	135
1996	Pepe L485	950		220.00	220
1996	Portrait Pals L468	950		135.00	135
1996	Rajah, The Elephant KL110	500		295.00	295
1996	Sleepytime Pals L467	950		115.00	115
1996	The Snare Drum L472	950		47.00	47
1996	The Sousaphone L471	950		47.00	47
1996	Strike It Rich L479	950		110.00	110
1996	Tim-Tim L483	950		125.00	125
1996	The Trombone L475	950		47.00	47

*Quotes have been rounded up to nearest dollar

FIGURINES
Ron Lee's World of Clowns
to Ron Lee's World of Clowns

YEAR ISSUE		EDITION LIMIT	YEAR RETD.	ISSUE PRICE	*QUOTE U.S.$
1996	The Trumpet L474	950		47.00	47
1996	The Tuba L473	950		47.00	47

The Popeye Collection - R. Lee

YEAR ISSUE		EDITION LIMIT	YEAR RETD.	ISSUE PRICE	*QUOTE U.S.$
1992	Liberty P001	1,750	1995	184.00	184
1992	Men!!! P002	1,750	1995	230.00	230
1992	Oh Popeye P005	1,750	1995	230.00	230
1992	Par Excellence P006	1,750	1995	220.00	220
1992	Strong to The Finish P003	1,750	1995	95.00	95
1992	That's My Boy P004	1,750	1995	145.00	145

Premier Dealer Collection - R. Lee

YEAR ISSUE		EDITION LIMIT	YEAR RETD.	ISSUE PRICE	*QUOTE U.S.$
1992	Dream On PD002	Closed	N/A	125.00	170
1992	Framed Again PD001	Closed	N/A	110.00	140
1993	Jake-A-Juggling Balls PD008	500		85.00	90
1993	Jake-A-Juggling Clubs PD007	500		85.00	90
1993	Jake-A-Juggling Cylinder PD006	500		85.00	90
1994	Joe's Feline Friend PD009	500		105.00	105
1994	Just Big Enough PD010	500		115.00	115
1992	Moonlighting PD004	Closed	N/A	125.00	125
1992	Nest to Nothing PD003	Closed	N/A	110.00	125
1994	Off The Toe PD011	500		105.00	120
1993	Pockets PD005	500		175.00	175
1994	Storm Warning PD012	500		115.00	115
1994	Trading Places PD013	500		190.00	190

Rocky & Bullwinkle And Friends Collection - R. Lee

YEAR ISSUE		EDITION LIMIT	YEAR RETD.	ISSUE PRICE	*QUOTE U.S.$
1992	Dudley Do-Right RB610	1,750	1995	175.00	175
1992	KA-BOOM! RB620	1,750	1995	175.00	175
1992	My Hero RB615	1,750	1995	275.00	330
1992	Rocky & Bullwinkle RB600	1,750	1995	120.00	140
1992	The Swami RB605	1,750	1995	175.00	175

The Ron Lee Disney Collection Exclusives - R. Lee

YEAR ISSUE		EDITION LIMIT	YEAR RETD.	ISSUE PRICE	*QUOTE U.S.$
1993	Aladdin MM560	500	1996	550.00	550
1996	Alice In Wonderland MM840	750		295.00	295
1995	Autopia MM770	750		220.00	220
1992	Bambi MM330	2,750		195.00	195
1996	Bambi and Thumper MM990	750		130.00	130
1990	The Bandleader MM100	Closed	N/A	75.00	75
1992	Beauty & The Beast (shadow box) DIS100	500		1650.00	1650
1994	Beauty & The Beast MM610	800	1996	170.00	170
1996	Buzz Light Year MM960	950		135.00	135
1992	Captain Hook MM320	2,750		175.00	175
1995	The Carousel MM730	750		125.00	125
1992	Christmas '92 MM420	1,500		145.00	145
1993	Cinderella's Slipper MM510	1,750	1995	115.00	150-160
1996	A Dalmation Christmas MM970	750		98.00	98
1993	Darkwing Duck MM470	1,750		105.00	105
1991	Decorating Donald MM210	2,750		60.00	60
1992	The Dinosaurs MM370	2,750		195.00	195
1991	Dopey MM120	2,750	1995	80.00	135
1996	Dumbo & The Ringmaster MM860	750		195.00	195
1990	Dumbo MM600	2,750		110.00	110
1995	Fantasyland MM780	750		285.00	285
1992	Finishing Touch MM440	1,500		85.00	85
1993	Flying With Dumbo MM530	1,000		330.00	330
1995	Frontierland MM740	750		160.00	160
1992	Genie MM450	2,750		110.00	110
1991	Goofy MM110	2,750		115.00	115
1991	Goofy's Gift MM230	2,750		70.00	70
1994	Grumpy Playing Organ MM590	800	1995	150.00	200
1995	Home Improvements MM820	750		170.00	170
1996	Hunchback of Notre Dame MM910	950		185.00	185
1991	Jiminy's List MM250	2,750		60.00	60
1991	Lady and the Tramp MM280	1,500	1995	295.00	295
1993	Letters to Santa MM550	1,500		170.00	170
1991	Lion Around MM270	2,750		140.00	140
1994	The Lion King MM640	1,750	1996	170.00	250
1992	Litt'l Sorcerer MM340	2,750		57.00	57
1992	Little Mermaid MM310	2,750		230.00	230
1992	Lumiere & Cogsworth MM350	2,750		145.00	145
1995	Main Street MM710	750		120.00	120
1995	The Matterhorn MM750	750		240.00	240
1991	Mickey & Minnie at the Piano MM180	2,750		195.00	195
1996	Mickey & The Caddie MM890	1,250		195.00	195
1991	Mickey's Adventure MM150	2,750		195.00	195
1990	Mickey's Christmas MM400	2,750		95.00	95
1991	Mickey's Delivery MM220	2,750		70.00	70
1994	Mickey, Brave Little Tailor MM570	1,750	1995	72.00	100
1991	Minnie Mouse MM170	2,750		80.00	80
1994	Minnie, Brave Little Tailor MM580	1,750	1995	72.00	72
1992	Mrs. Potts & Chip MM360	2,750		125.00	125
1991	Mt. Mickey MM900	2,750		175.00	175
1994	New Tinkerbell MM680	300	1995	99.00	99
1994	Official Conscience MM620	300	1995	65.00	65
1995	The People Mover MM760	750		190.00	190
1990	Pinocchio MM500	2,750	1995	85.00	85
1991	Pluto's Treat MM240	2,750		60.00	60
1994	Pongo & Pups MM670	800	1995	124.00	124
1995	Pooh & The Cookie Jar MM830	750		190.00	190
1996	Pooh & The Honey Pot MM870	1,250		120.00	120
1996	Pooh In The Honey Tree MM850	750		300.00	300
1996	Pooh Musical MM950	950		150.00	150
1996	Pooh, Eeyore & Piglet MM880	1,250		150.00	150
1995	Reflections MM810	750	1996	99.00	99
1993	Santa's Workshop MM540	1,500		170.00	170
1994	Snow White & Doc MM630	800		135.00	135
1990	Snow White & Grumpy MM800	2,750		140.00	140
1993	Snow White & The Seven Dwarfs (shadow box) DIS200	250		1800.00	1800
1996	Snow White's 60th Anniversary MM980	750		495.00	495
1990	The Sorcerer MM200	Closed	N/A	85.00	120
1992	Sorcerer's Apprentice MM290	2,750		125.00	125
1990	Steamboat Willie MM300	2,750	1995	95.00	95
1992	Stocking Stuffer MM410	1,500	1996	63.00	63
1991	The Tea Cup Ride (Disneyland Exclusive) MM260	1,250	1996	225.00	225
1994	Tigger on Rabbit MM660	800	1995	110.00	110
1993	Tinker Bell MM490	1,750	1995	85.00	85
1995	The Topiary MM720	750		145.00	145
1996	Toy Story MM930	950		197.00	197
1991	Tugboat Mickey MM160	2,750		180.00	180
1996	TV Buddies MM920	1,250		199.00	199
1991	Two Gun Mickey MM140	2,750		115.00	115
1990	Uncle Scrooge MM700	2,750		110.00	110
1993	Winnie The Pooh MM480	1,750	1996	125.00	150-200
1992	Winnie The Pooh & Tigger MM390	2,750	1995	105.00	105
1992	Wish Upon A Star MM430	1,500		80.00	80
1991	The Witch MM130	2,750		115.00	115
1992	Workin' Out MM380	2,750		95.00	95

The Ron Lee Disneyana Collection Exclusives - R. Lee

YEAR ISSUE		EDITION LIMIT	YEAR RETD.	ISSUE PRICE	*QUOTE U.S.$
1992	Big Thunder Mountain MM460	250	1995	1650.00	2200-2800
1993	Mickey's Dream MM520	250	1993	400.00	600-900
1994	MM/MN/Goofy Limo MM650	500	1994	500.00	375-500
1995	Ear Force One MM790	500	1995	600.00	600
1995	Engine Number One MM690	500	1995	650.00	995
1996	Heigh-ho MM940	350		500.00	500

The Ron Lee Emmett Kelly, Sr. Collection - R. Lee

YEAR ISSUE		EDITION LIMIT	YEAR RETD.	ISSUE PRICE	*QUOTE U.S.$
1991	Emmett Kelly, Sr. Sign E208	Closed	N/A	110.00	110
1991	God Bless America EK206	Closed	N/A	130.00	250
1991	Help Yourself EK202	Closed	N/A	145.00	350
1991	Love at First Sight EK204	Closed	N/A	197.00	197
1991	My Protege EK207	Closed	N/A	160.00	165
1991	Spike's Uninvited Guest EK203	Closed	N/A	165.00	295
1991	That-A-Way EK201	Closed	N/A	125.00	135
1991	Time for a Change EK205	Closed	N/A	190.00	305

The Ron Lee Gallery Collection - R. Lee

YEAR ISSUE		EDITION LIMIT	YEAR RETD.	ISSUE PRICE	*QUOTE U.S.$
1996	Toad Bo Joe KL300	500		195.00	195

The Ron Lee Looney Tunes Collection - R. Lee

YEAR ISSUE		EDITION LIMIT	YEAR RETD.	ISSUE PRICE	*QUOTE U.S.$
1991	1940 Bugs Bunny LT165	Closed	N/A	85.00	100
1991	Bugs Bunny LT150	Closed	N/A	120.00	135
1991	Daffy Duck LT140	Closed	N/A	80.00	80-85
1991	Elmer Fudd LT125	Closed	N/A	87.00	87-90
1991	Foghorn Leghorn & Henry Hawk LT160	Closed	N/A	115.00	115
1991	Marvin the Martian LT170	Closed	N/A	75.00	75
1991	Michigan J. Frog LT110	Closed	N/A	115.00	115
1991	Mt. Yosemite LT180	850		160.00	160-300
1991	Pepe LePew & Penelope LT145	Closed	N/A	115.00	115
1991	Porky Pig LT115	Closed	N/A	97.00	100
1991	Sylvester & Tweety LT135	Closed	N/A	110.00	110-115
1991	Tasmanian Devil LT120	Closed	N/A	105.00	105
1991	Tweety LT155	Closed	N/A	110.00	110-115
1991	Western Daffy Duck LT105	Closed	N/A	87.00	90
1991	Wile E. Coyote & Roadrunner LT175	Closed	N/A	165.00	175
1991	Yosemite Sam LT130	Closed	N/A	110.00	110

The Ron Lee Looney Tunes II Collection - R. Lee

YEAR ISSUE		EDITION LIMIT	YEAR RETD.	ISSUE PRICE	*QUOTE U.S.$
1992	Beep Beep LT220	1,500		115.00	115
1992	Ditty Up LT200	2,750		110.00	110
1992	For Better or Worse LT190	1,500		285.00	285
1992	Leopold & Giovanni LT205	1,500		225.00	225
1992	No Pain No Gain LT210	950		270.00	270
1992	Rackin' Frackin' Varmint LT225	950		260.00	260
1992	Speedy Gonzales LT185	2,750		73.00	73
1992	Van Duck LT230	950		335.00	335
1992	The Virtuosos LT235	950		350.00	350
1992	What The ...? LT195	1,500		240.00	240
1992	What's up Doc? LT215	950		270.00	270

The Ron Lee Looney Tunes III Collection - R. Lee

YEAR ISSUE		EDITION LIMIT	YEAR RETD.	ISSUE PRICE	*QUOTE U.S.$
1992	Bugs Bunny w/ Horse LT245	1,500		105.00	105
1992	Cowboy Bugs LT290	1,500		70.00	70
1992	Daffy Duck w/ Horse LT275	1,500		105.00	105
1992	Elmer Fudd w/ Horse LT270	1,500		105.00	105
1992	Pepe Le Pew w/ Horse LT285	1,500		105.00	105
1992	Porky Pig w/ Horse LT260	1,500		105.00	105
1992	Sylvester w/ Horse LT250	1,500		105.00	105
1992	Tasmanian Devil w/ Horse LT255	1,500		105.00	105
1992	Wile E. Coyote w/ Horse LT280	1,500		105.00	105
1992	Yosemite Sam w/ Horse LT265	1,500		105.00	105

The Ron Lee Looney Tunes IV Collection - R. Lee

YEAR ISSUE		EDITION LIMIT	YEAR RETD.	ISSUE PRICE	*QUOTE U.S.$
1993	Bugs LT330	1,200		79.00	79
1993	A Christmas Carrot LT320	1,200		175.00	175
1993	The Essence of Love LT310	1,200		145.00	145
1993	Martian's Best Friend LT305	1,200		140.00	140
1993	Me Deliver LT295	1,200		110.00	110
1993	Puttin' on the Glitz LT325	1,200		79.00	79
1993	The Rookie LT315	1,200		75.00	75
1993	Yo-Ho-Ho- LT300	1,200		105.00	105

The Ron Lee Looney Tunes V Collection - R. Lee

YEAR ISSUE		EDITION LIMIT	YEAR RETD.	ISSUE PRICE	*QUOTE U.S.$
1994	Bugs LT330	1,200		79.00	79
1994	A Carrot a Day LT350	1,200		85.00	85
1994	Guilty LT345	1,200		80.00	80
1994	Ma Cherie LT340	1,200		185.00	185
1994	No H20 LT355	1,200		160.00	160
1994	Puttin' on the Glitz LT325	1,200		79.00	79
1994	Smashing LT335	1,200		80.00	80
1994	Taz On Ice LT360	1,200		115.00	115

The Ron Lee Looney Tunes VI Collection - R. Lee

YEAR ISSUE		EDITION LIMIT	YEAR RETD.	ISSUE PRICE	*QUOTE U.S.$
1994	Bugs Pharoah LT370	500	1996	130.00	150
1994	Cleopatra's Barge LT400	500	1996	550.00	660
1994	Cruising Down the Nile LT385	500	1996	295.00	410
1994	King Bugs and Friends LT395	500	1996	480.00	550
1994	Ramases & Son LT380	500	1996	230.00	260
1994	Tweety Pharoah LT365	500	1996	110.00	140
1994	Warrior Taz LT375	500	1996	140.00	170
1994	Yosemite's Chariot LT390	500	1996	310.00	360

The Ron Lee Looney Tunes VII Collection - R. Lee

YEAR ISSUE		EDITION LIMIT	YEAR RETD.	ISSUE PRICE	*QUOTE U.S.$
1995	The Baron LT475	750		235.00	235
1995	Daffy Scuba Diving LT470	750		170.00	170
1995	Drive..Drive!! Putt..Putt!! LT450	750		120.00	120
1995	The Great Chase LT485	750		385.00	385
1995	Highway My Way LT460	750		280.00	280
1995	The Hustler LT465	750		397.00	397
1995	Ice Dancing LT440	750		180.00	180
1995	King Pin LT445	750		165.00	165
1995	Slam Dunk LT455	750		190.00	190
1995	Speedy Tweety LT480	750		225.00	225

The Ron Lee Looney Tunes VIII Collection - R. Lee

YEAR ISSUE		EDITION LIMIT	YEAR RETD.	ISSUE PRICE	*QUOTE U.S.$
1996	Bugs Bunny LT490	1,500		49.00	49
1996	Daffy Duck LT520	1,500		49.00	49
1996	Daffy's New York Bistro LT575	750		350.00	350
1996	Foghorn Leghorn LT500	1,500		49.00	49
1996	Liberty Bugs LT590	750		285.00	285
1996	Marvin the Martian LT525	1,500		49.00	49
1996	Michigan J. Frog LT560	1,500		49.00	49
1996	Michigan on Broadway LT585	750		330.00	330
1996	Penelope LT555	1,500		49.00	49
1996	Pepe Le Pew LT550	1,500		49.00	49
1996	Porky Pig LT515	1,500		49.00	49
1996	Roadrunner LT545	1,500		49.00	49
1996	She-Devil LT530	1,500		49.00	49
1996	Speedy Gonzales LT505	1,500		49.00	49
1996	Sylvester LT565	1,500		49.00	49
1996	Tasmanian Devil LT495	1,500		49.00	49
1996	Taz and the Big Apple LT570	750		130.00	130
1996	Taz on Empire State LT580	750		170.00	170
1996	Tweety LT535	1,500		49.00	49
1996	Willie Coyote LT540	1,500		49.00	49
1996	Yosemite Sam LT510	1,500		49.00	49

The Ron Lee Looney Tunes Sports Collection - R. Lee

YEAR ISSUE		EDITION LIMIT	YEAR RETD.	ISSUE PRICE	*QUOTE U.S.$
1996	The Baron LT475	750		235.00	235
1996	The Chase LT485	750		385.00	385
1996	Daffy Scuba Diving LT470	750		170.00	170
1996	The Hustler LT465	750		397.00	397
1996	Ice Dancing LT440	750		180.00	180
1996	King Pin LT445	750		165.00	165
1996	Slam Dunk LT455	750		190.00	190
1996	Speedy Tweety LT480	750		225.00	225

The Ron Lee Looney Tunes Western Collection - R. Lee

YEAR ISSUE		EDITION LIMIT	YEAR RETD.	ISSUE PRICE	*QUOTE U.S.$
1995	Acme Junction LT435	500		290.00	290
1995	Bwanding Iron LT420	500		210.00	210
1995	Heap Big Chief LT415	500		230.00	230
1995	Lit'l Trooper LT405	500		157.00	157
1995	Roadrunner Express LT425	500		240.00	240
1995	Saturday Serenade LT430	500		255.00	255
1995	Whoa!! LT410	500		215.00	215

The Ron Lee Warner Bros. Collection - R. Lee

YEAR ISSUE		EDITION LIMIT	YEAR RETD.	ISSUE PRICE	*QUOTE U.S.$
1995	Animaniacs WBA100	750		170.00	170
1996	Bugs At The Door WB007	500		98.00	98
1996	Bugs Playing Hockey WBSF100	750		106.00	106
1993	Courtly Gent WB003	1,000		102.00	102
1992	Dickens' Christmas WB400	850		198.00	198
1993	Duck Dodgers WB005	1,000		300.00	300
1993	Gridiron Glory WB002	1,000		102.00	102
1993	Hair-Raising Hare WB006	1,000		300.00	300
1993	Hare Under Par WB001	1,000		102.00	102
1993	Home Plate Heroes WB004	1,000		102.00	102
1991	The Maltese Falcon WB100	Closed	N/A	175.00	190
1996	Marvin and The Maggott WB008	750		140.00	140
1995	Pinky And The Brain WB105	750		170.00	170
1991	Robin Hood Bugs WB200	1,000		190.00	190
1996	Speedy Playing Soccer WB009	750		135.00	135
1996	Spokesphibian WB500	750		205.00	205
1996	Sylvester Playing Basketball WBSF150	750		106.00	106
1996	Taz Playing Football WBSF125	750		106.00	106
1996	Wyle Coyote Playing Basketball WBSF175	750		106.00	106
1992	Yankee Doodle Bugs WB300	850		195.00	195

Shriner Clowns - R. Lee

YEAR ISSUE		EDITION LIMIT	YEAR RETD.	ISSUE PRICE	*QUOTE U.S.$
1994	Bubbles L437	1,750		120.00	120
1994	Helping Hand L436	1,750		145.00	145

Sports & Professionals - R. Lee

YEAR ISSUE		EDITION LIMIT	YEAR RETD.	ISSUE PRICE	*QUOTE U.S.$
1994	The Baseball Player L448	2,500		77.00	77

*Quotes have been rounded up to nearest dollar

Ron Lee's World of Clowns
to Royal Doulton

FIGURINES

YEAR ISSUE		EDITION LIMIT	YEAR RETD.	ISSUE PRICE	*QUOTE U.S. $
1994	The Basketball Player L450	2,500		74.00	74
1994	The Chef L441	2,500		74.00	74
1994	The Dentist L446	2,500		70.00	70
1994	The Doctor L439	2,500		70.00	70
1994	The Fireman L444	2,500		90.00	90
1994	The Fisherman L452	2,500		77.00	77
1994	The Football Player L449	2,500		74.00	74
1994	The Golfer L447	2,500		77.00	77
1994	The Hockey Player L454	2,500		80.00	80
1994	The Lawyer L445	2,500		70.00	70
1994	The Nurse L443	2,500		74.00	74
1994	The Pilot L440	2,500		74.00	74
1994	The Policeman L442	2,500		77.00	77
1994	The Skier L453	2,500		77.00	77
1994	The Teacher L438	2,500		70.00	70
1994	The Tennis Player L451	2,500		74.00	74

Superman I - R. Lee

1993	Help Is On The Way SP100	750	1995	280.00	280
1993	Meteor Moment SP115	750	1995	314.00	314
1993	Metropolis SP110	750	1995	320.00	320
1993	Proudly We Wave SP105	750	1995	185.00	185

Superman II - R. Lee

1994	Good and Evil SP135	750	1995	190.00	190
1994	More Powerful SP130	750	1995	420.00	420
1994	Quick Change SP120	750	1995	125.00	125
1994	To The Rescue SP125	750	1995	195.00	195

The Wizard of Oz Collection - R. Lee

1992	The Cowardly Lion WZ425	750	1996	620.00	620
1992	Kansas WZ400	750	1996	550.00	550
1992	The Munchkins WZ405	750	1996	620.00	620
1992	The Ruby Slippers WZ410	750	1996	620.00	620
1992	The Scarecrow WZ415	750	1996	510.00	510
1992	The Tin Man WZ420	750	1996	530.00	530

Wizard of Oz II - R. Lee

1994	The Cowardly Lion WZ445	500		130.00	130
1994	Dorothy WZ430	500		150.00	150
1994	Glinda WZ455	500		225.00	225
1994	The Scarecrow WZ435	500		130.00	130
1994	The Tinman WZ440	500		110.00	110
1994	The Wicked Witch WZ450	500		125.00	125

The Woody Woodpecker And Friends Collection - R. Lee

1992	1940 Woody Woodpecker WL020	1,750	1996	73.00	75
1992	Andy and Miranda Panda WL025	1,750	1996	140.00	140
1992	Birdy for Woody WL005	1,750	1996	117.00	125
1992	Pals WL030	1,750	1996	179.00	179
1992	Peck of My Heart WL010	1,750	1996	370.00	495
1992	Woody Woodpecker WL015	1,750	1996	73.00	73

Royal Doulton

Royal Doulton International Collectors' Club - Various

1980	John Doulton Jug (8 O'Clock) D6656 - E. Griffiths	Yr.Iss.	1981	70.00	125-300
1981	Sleepy Darling Figure HN2953 - P. Parsons	Yr.Iss.	1982	100.00	195
1982	Dog of Fo-Flambe - N/A	Yr.Iss.	1983	50.00	175
1982	Prized Possessions Figure HN2942 - R. Tabbenor	Yr.Iss.	1983	125.00	450-500
1983	Loving Cup - N/A	Yr.Iss.	1984	75.00	150-300
1983	Springtime HN3033 - A. Hughes	Yr.Iss.	1984	125.00	325-400
1984	Sir Henry Doulton Jug D6703 - E. Griffiths	Yr.Iss.	1985	50.00	125-200
1984	Pride & Joy Figure HN2945 - R. Tabbenor	Yr.Iss.	1985	125.00	300-350
1985	Top of the Hill HN2126 - P. Gee	Yr.Iss.	1986	35.00	125-175
1985	Wintertime Figure HN3060 - A. Hughes	Yr.Iss.	1986	125.00	250-350
1986	Albert Sagger Toby Jug - W. Harper	Yr.Iss.	1987	35.00	85
1986	Auctioneer Figure HN2988 - R. Tabbenor	Yr.Iss.	1987	150.00	400
1987	Collector Bunnykins DB54 - D. Lyttleton	Yr.Iss.	1988	40.00	550-650
1987	Summertime Figurine HN3137 - P. Parsons	Yr.Iss.	1988	140.00	200-225
1988	Top of the Hill Miniature Figurine HN2126 - P. Gee	Yr.Iss.	1989	95.00	125-200
1988	Beefeater Tiny Jug - R. Tabbenor	Yr.Iss.	1989	25.00	125-200
1988	Old Salt Tea Pot - N/A	Yr.Iss.	1989	135.00	300-350
1989	Geisha Flambe Figure HN3229 - P. Parsons	Yr.Iss.	1990	195.00	195
1989	Flower Sellers Children Plate - N/A	Yr.Iss.	1990	65.00	70-100
1990	Autumntime Figure HN3231 - P. Parsons	Yr.Iss.	1991	190.00	195
1990	Jester Mini Figure HN3335 - C.J. Noke	Yr.Iss.	1991	115.00	115
1990	Old King Cole Tiny Jug - H. Fenton	Yr.Iss.	1991	35.00	125
1991	Bunny's Bedtime Figure HN3370 - N. Pedley	9,500	1992	195.00	200-300
1991	Charles Dickens Jug D6901 - W. Harper	Yr.Iss.	1992	100.00	125
1991	L'Ambiteuse Figure (Tissot Lady) HN3359 - V. Annand	5,000	1992	295.00	300-350
1991	Christopher Columbus Jug D6911 - S. Taylor	Yr.Iss.	1992	95.00	125
1992	Discovery Figure HN3428 - A. Munslow	Yr.Iss.	1993	160.00	100
1992	King Edward Jug D6923 - W. Harper	Yr.Iss.	1993	250.00	295
1992	Master Potter Bunnykins DB131 - W. Platt	Yr.Iss.	1993	50.00	85
1992	Eliza Farren Prestige Figure HN3442 - N/A	Yr.Iss.	1993	335.00	250-325
1993	Barbara Figure - N/A	Yr.Iss.	1994	285.00	450-510
1993	Lord Mountbatten L/S Jug - S. Taylor	5,000	1994	225.00	225
1993	Punch & Judy Double Sided Jug - S. Taylor	2,500	1994	400.00	465
1993	Flambe Dragon HN3552 - N/A	Retrd.	1994	260.00	260
1994	Diane HN3604 - N/A	Retrd.	1995	250.00	300
1995	Le Bal HN3702 - N/A	Retrd.	1996	350.00	350
1995	George Tinworth Jug, sm. D7000 - W. Harper	Retrd.	1996	99.00	99
1995	Partners in Collecting Bunnykins DB151	Retrd.	1996	45.00	45
1996	Special Delivery Plate - N/A	Retrd.	1996	45.00	60-100
1996	Welcome - N/A	Retrd.	1996	80.00	80
1996	Pamela HN3756 - T. Potts	Retrd.	1996	275.00	275
1996	Mr. Pickwick Jug, sm. D7025 - M. Alcock	Retrd.	1996	138.00	150-250
1996	Winter's Day HN3769 - N. Pedley	6/97		325.00	325
1996	Gifts For All plate - N. Pedley	6/97		40.00	40
1997	Susan HN3871 - N. Pedley	Yr.Iss.		345.00	345
1997	Joy - (1997 membership gift) - N. Pedley	Yr.Iss.		85.00	85
1997	Sir Henry Doulton S/S - W. Harper	Yr.Iss.		157.50	158

Age of Innocence - N. Pedley

1991	Feeding Time HN3373	9,500	1994	245.00	400-440
1992	First Outing HN3377	9,500	1994	275.00	390
1991	Making Friends HN3372	9,500	1994	270.00	300-390
1991	Puppy Love HN3371	9,500	1994	270.00	390

Beatrix Potter Figures - Various

1967	Amiable Guinea Pig P2061 - A. Hallam	Retrd.	1983	29.95	395-425
1992	And This Pig Had None P3319 - M. Alcock	Open		29.95	35
1963	Anna Maria P1851 - A. Hallam	Retrd.	1983	29.95	325-395
1971	Appley Dapply P2333 - A. Hallam	Open		29.95	35
1970	Aunt Pettitoes P2276 - A. Hallam	Retrd.	1993	29.95	125
1989	Babbity Bumble P2971 - W. Platt	Retrd.	1993	29.95	95
1992	Benjamin Ate a Lettuce Leaf P3317 - M. Alcock	Open		29.95	35
1948	Benjamin Bunny P1105 - A. Gredington	Open		29.95	35
1983	Benjamin Bunny Sat on a Bank P2803 - D. Lyttleton	Open		29.95	35
1975	Benjamin Bunny with Peter Rabbit P2509 - A. Musiankowski	Retrd.	1995	39.95	95
1995	Benjamin Bunny-lg. size P3403 - M. Alcock	Open		65.00	75
1991	Benjamin Wakes Up P3234 - A. Hughes-Lubeck	Open		29.95	35
1965	Cecily Parsley P1941 - A. Gredington	Retrd.	1993	29.95	85-125
1979	Chippy Hackee P2627 - D. Lyttleton	Retrd.	1993	29.95	85
1991	Christmas Stocking P3257 - M. Alcock	Retrd.	1994	65.00	95
1985	Cottontail at Lunchtime P2878 - D. Lyttleton	Retrd.	1996	29.95	33
1970	Cousin Ribby P2284 - A. Hallam	Retrd.	1993	29.95	75
1982	Diggory Diggory Delvet P2713 - D. Lyttleton	Open		29.95	35
1955	Dutchess w/Pie P1355 - G. Orwell	Retrd.	1967	29.95	250-375
1995	F.W. Gent-lg. size P3450 - M. Alcock	Open		65.00	73
1977	Fierce Bad Rabbit P2586 - D. Lyttleton	Open		29.95	35
1954	Flopsy Mopsy and Cottontail P1274 - A. Gredington	Open		29.95	35
1990	Foxy Reading Country News P3219 - A. Hughes-Lubeck	6/97		49.95	58
1954	Foxy Whiskered Gentleman P1277 - A. Gredington	Open		29.95	35
1990	Gentleman Mouse Made a Bow P3200 - T. Chawner	Retrd.	1996	29.95	33
1976	Ginger P2559 - D. Lyttleton	Retrd.	1982	29.95	550
1986	Goody and Timmy Tiptoes P2957 - D. Lyttleton	Retrd.	1996	49.95	65
1961	Goody Tiptoes P1675 - A. Gredington	Open		29.95	35
1951	Hunca Munca P1198 - A. Gredington	Open		29.95	35
1992	Hunca Munca Spills the Beads P3288 - M. Alcock	Retrd.	1996	29.95	85
1977	Hunca Munca Sweeping P2584 - D. Lyttleton	Open		29.95	35
1990	Jemema Puddleduck-Foxy Whiskered Gentleman P3193 - T. Chawner	Open		55.00	58
1983	Jemima Puddleduck Made a Feather Nest-P2823 - D. Lyttleton	6/97		29.95	35
1948	Jemima Puddleduck P1092 - A. Gredington	Open		29.95	35
1993	Jemima Puddleduck-lg. size P3373 - M. Alcock	Open		49.95	75
1988	Jeremy Fisher Digging P3090 - T. Chawner	Retrd.	1994	50.00	100-225
1950	Jeremy Fisher P1157 - A. Gredington	Open		29.95	35
1995	Jeremy Fisher-lg. size P3372 - M. Alcock	Open		65.00	75
1990	John Joiner P2965 - G. Tongue	Open		29.95	35
1954	Johnny Townmouse P1276 - A. Gredington	Retrd.	1993	29.95	75
1988	Johnny Townmouse with Bag P3094 - T. Chawner	Retrd.	1994	50.00	250
1990	Lady Mouse Made a Curtsy P3220 - A. Hughes-Lubeck	Open		29.95	35
1950	Lady Mouse P1183 - A. Gredington	Open		29.95	35
1977	Little Black Rabbit P2585 - D. Lyttleton	6/97		29.95	35
1987	Little Pig Robinson Spying P3031 - T. Chawner	Retrd.	1993	29.95	100-225
1991	Miss Dormouse P3251 - M. Alcock	Retrd.	1995	29.95	65
1978	Miss Moppet P1275 - A. Gredington	Open		32.50	35
1990	Mittens & Moppet P3197 - T. Chawner	Retrd.	1994	50.00	75
1989	Mother Ladybird P2966 - W. Platt	Retrd.	1996	29.95	33
1973	Mr. Alderman Ptolemy P2424 - G. Tongue	Open		29.95	35
1965	Mr. Benjamin Bunny P1940 - A. Gredington	Open		29.95	35
1979	Mr. Drake Puddleduck P2628 - D. Lyttleton	Open		29.95	35
1974	Mr. Jackson P2453 - A. Hallam	6/97		29.95	35
1995	Mr. McGregor P3506 - M. Alcock	Open		42.50	45
1988	Mr. Tod P3091 - T. Chawner	Retrd.	1993	29.95	95
1965	Mrs. Flopsy Bunny P1942 - A. Gredington	Open		29.95	35
1997	Mrs. Rabbit and Peter P3646 - W. Platt	Open		67.50	68
1997	Mrs. Rabbit and the Four Bunnies P3672 - S. Ridge	1,997		275.00	275
1992	Mrs. Rabbit Cooking P3278 - M. Alcock	Open		29.95	35
1951	Mrs. Rabbit P1200 - A. Gredington	Open		29.95	35
1976	Mrs. Rabbit with Bunnies P2543 - D. Lyttleton	Open		29.95	35
1995	Mrs. Rabbit-lg. P3398 - M. Alcock	Open		65.00	75
1951	Mrs. Ribby P1199 - A. Gredington	Open		29.95	35
1997	Mrs. Tiggywinkle, lg. P3437 - M. Alcock	Open		75.00	75
1948	Mrs. Tittlemouse P1103 - A. Gredington	Retrd.	1993	29.95	75-110
1992	No More Twist P3325 - M. Alcock	6/97		29.95	35
1986	Old Mr. Bouncer P2956 - D. Lyttleton	Retrd.	1995	29.95	100
1963	Old Mr. Brown P1796 - A. Hallam	Open		29.95	35
1983	Old Mr. Pricklepin P2767 - D. Lyttleton	Retrd.	1982	29.95	95-150
1959	Old Woman Who Lived in a Shoe P1545 - C. Melbourne	Open		29.95	35
1983	Old Woman Who Lived in a Shoe, Knitting P2804 - D. Lyttleton	Open		29.95	35
1991	Peter & The Red Handkerchief P3242 - M. Alcock	Open		39.95	45
1995	Peter in Bed P3473 - M. Alcock	Open		39.95	45
1989	Peter Rabbit in the Gooseberry Net P3157 - D. Lyttleton	Retrd.	1995	39.95	50
1948	Peter Rabbit P1098 - A. Gredington	Open		29.95	35
1993	Peter Rabbit-large size P3356 - M. Alcock	Open		65.00	75
1996	Peter with Daffodils P3597 - A. Hughes-Lubeck	Open		42.50	45
1996	Peter with Postbag P3591 - A. Hughes-Lubeck	Open		42.50	45
1996	Peter w/Red Pocket Handkerchief, lg. P3592 - A. Hughes-Lubeck	Open		75.00	75
1971	Pickles P2334 - A. Hallam	Retrd.	1982	29.95	395-600
1948	Pig Robinson P1104 - A. Gredington	Open		29.95	35
1972	Pig Wig P2381 - A. Hallam	Retrd.	1982	29.95	450-575
1955	Pigling Bland P1365 - G. Orwell	Open		29.95	35
1991	Pigling Eats Porridge P3252 - M. Alcock	Retrd.	1994	50.00	95
1976	Poorly Peter Rabbit P2560 - D. Lyttleton	Open		29.95	35
1981	Rebeccah Puddleduck P2647 - D. Lyttleton	Open		29.95	35
1992	Ribby and the Patty Pan P3280 - M. Alcock	Open		29.95	35
1974	Sally Henry Penney P2452 - A. Hallam	Retrd.	1993	29.95	95
1948	Samuel Whiskers P1106 - A. Gredington	Retrd.	1995	29.95	95
1975	Simpkin P2508 - A. Maslankowski	Retrd.	1983	29.95	650
1973	Sir Isaac Newton P2425 - G. Tongue	Retrd.	1984	29.95	350
1948	Squirrel Nutkin P1102 - A. Gredington	Open		29.95	35
1961	Tabitha Twitchitt P1676 - A. Gredington	Retrd.	1995	29.95	50
1976	Tabitha Twitchitt with Miss Moppett P2544 - D. Lyttleton	Retrd.	1993	29.95	125
1949	Tailor of Gloucester P1108 - A. Gredington	Open		29.95	35
1995	Tailor of Gloucester-large size P3449 - M. Alcock	Open		65.00	75
1948	Tiggy Winkle P1107 - A. Gredington	Open		29.95	35
1985	Tiggy Winkle Takes Tea P2877 - D. Lyttleton	Open		29.95	35
1948	Timmy Tiptoes P1101 - A. Gredington	Open		29.95	35
1949	Timmy Willie P1109 - A. Gredington	Retrd.	1993	29.95	45-195
1986	Timmy Willie Sleeping P2996 - G. Tongue	Retrd.	1996	29.95	33
1948	Tom Kitten P1100 - A. Gredington	Open		29.95	35
1995	Tom Kitten-lg. size P3405 - M. Alcock	Open		65.00	75
1987	Tom Kitten and Butterfly P3030 - T. Chawner	Retrd.	1994	50.00	200
1987	Tom Thumb P2989 - W. Platt	6/97		29.95	35
1955	Tommy Brock P1348 - G. Orwell	Open		29.95	35

British Sporting Heritage - V. Annand

1994	Ascot HN3471	5,000		475.00	475
1996	Croquet HN3470	5,000		475.00	475
1993	Henley HN3367	5,000		475.00	475
1995	Wimbledon HN3366	5,000		475.00	475

*Quotes have been rounded up to nearest dollar

Bunnykins - Various

Year Issue		Edition Limit	Year Retd.	Issue Price	*Quote U.S.$
1995	Bathtime DB148 - M. Alcock	6/97		40.00	42
1987	Be Prepared DB56 - D. Lyttleton	Retrd.	1995	40.00	40-60
1987	Bed Time DB55 - D. Lyttleton	Open		40.00	42
1995	Boy Skater DB152 - M. Alcock	Open		40.00	42
1991	Bride DB101 - A. Hughes	Open		40.00	42
1987	Brownie DB61 - W. Platt	Retrd.	1993	39.00	65
1994	Christmas Surprise DB146 - W. Platt	Open		50.00	53
1990	Cook DB85- W. Platt	Retrd.	1994	35.00	75
1995	Easter Greetings - M. Alcock	Open		50.00	53
1996	Father Bunnykin DB154 - M. Alcock	Retrd.	1996	50.00	70
1988	Father, Mother, Victoria DB68 - M. Alcock	Retrd.	1995	40.00	40
1989	Fireman DB75 - M. Alcock	Open		40.00	42
1990	Fisherman DB84- W. Platt	Retrd.	1993	39.00	95
1996	Gardener DB156 - W. Platt	Open		40.00	42
1995	Girl Skater DB153 - M. Alcock	Open		40.00	42
1995	Goodnight DB157 - S. Ridge	Open		40.00	42
1991	Groom DB102 - M. Alcock	Open		40.00	42
1993	Halloween Bunnykin DB132 - M. Alcock	Open		50.00	53
1983	Happy Birthday DB21 - G. Tongue	6/97		40.00	43
1988	Harry DB73 - M. Alcock	Retrd.	1993	34.00	55-95
1972	Helping Mother DB2 - A. Hallam	Retrd.	1993	34.00	75
1986	Home Run DB43 - D. Lyttleton	Retrd.	1993	39.00	65-95
1990	Ice Cream DB82 - W. Platt	Retrd.	1993	39.00	75
1997	Mother & Baby DB167 - S. Ridge	Open		42.00	42
1996	Mother's Day DB155 - S. Ridge	Open		42.00	42
1982	Mr. Bunnykin Easter Parade (pink ribbons) DB18 - G. Tongue	Retrd.	N/A	39.00	550
1982	Mr. Bunnykin Easter Parade DB18 - G. Tongue	Retrd.	1993	39.00	65
1982	Mrs. Bunnykin Easter Parade (pink ribbons) DB19 - D. Lyttleton	Retrd.	N/A	40.00	650
1982	Mrs. Bunnykin Easter Parade DB19 - D. Lyttleton	Retrd.	1995	40.00	40-65
1995	New Baby DB158 - G. Tongue	Open		40.00	42
1989	Nurse DB74 - M. Alcock	Open		35.00	42
1989	Paper Boy DB77 - M. Alcock	Retrd.	1993	39.00	65
1972	Playtime DB8 - A. Hallam	Retrd.	1993	34.00	55-75
1988	Policeman DB69 - M. Alcock	Open		40.00	42
1988	Polly DB71 - M. Alcock	Retrd.	1993	34.00	40-65
1995	Rainy Day DB147 - M. Alcock	6/97		40.00	42
1997	Sailor Bunnykins DB166 - S. Ridge	Yr.Iss.		52.50	53
1981	Santa Bunnykins DB17 - D. Lyttleton	Retrd.	1995	40.00	40
1987	School Days DB57 - D. Lyttleton	Retrd.	1994	40.00	75
1982	School Master DB60 - W. Platt	Retrd.	1995	40.00	40-55
1974	Sleepytime DB15 - A. Musiankowski	Retrd.	1993	39.00	75
1972	Sleigh Ride DB4 - A. Hallam	Open		40.00	42
1972	Story Time DB9 - A. Hallam	Open		35.00	42
1988	Susan DB70 - M. Alcock	Retrd.	1993	34.00	75
1992	Sweetheart Bunnykin DB130 - W. Platt	6/97		40.00	42
1988	Tom DB72 - M. Alcock	Retrd.	1993	34.00	55-65
1986	Uncle Sam DB50 - D. Lyttleton	Open		40.00	42
1988	William DB69 - M. Alcock	Retrd.	1993	34.00	65

Character Sculptures - Various

Year Issue		Edition Limit	Year Retd.	Issue Price	*Quote U.S.$
1996	Bill Sikes HN3785 - A. Dobson	Retrd.	1996	306.25	307
1996	Bowls Player HN3780 - J. Jones	Retrd.	1996	137.50	138
1993	Captain Hook - R. Tabbenor	Retrd.	1996	250.00	270-325
1995	Cyrano de Bergerac HN3751 - D. Biggs	Retrd.	1996	268.75	269
1994	D' Artagnan - R. Tabbenor	Retrd.	1996	260.00	269
1993	Dick Turpin - R. Tabbenor	Retrd.	1996	250.00	269
1995	Fagin HN3752 - A. Dobson	Retrd.	1996	268.75	269
1995	Gulliver - D. Biggs	Retrd.	1996	285.00	307
1993	Long John Silver - A. Maslankowski	Retrd.	1996	250.00	269
1996	Oliver Twist and Artful Dodger HN3786 - A. Dobson	Retrd.	1996	275.00	275
1994	Pied Piper - A. Maslankowski	Retrd.	1996	260.00	269
1993	Robin Hood - A. Maslankowski	Retrd.	1996	250.00	269
1995	Sherlock Holmes HN3639 - R. Tabbenor	Retrd.	1996	268.75	269
1996	Sir Francis Drake HN3770 - D. Biggs	Retrd.	1996	275.00	275
1995	Wizard HN3722 - A. Maslankowski	Retrd.	1996	306.25	307-330

Diamond Anniversary Tinies - Various

Year Issue		Edition Limit	Year Retd.	Issue Price	*Quote U.S.$
1994	John Barleycorn - C. Noke	2,500	1994	350.00	450-500
1994	Simon The Cellarer - Noke/Fenton	2,500	1994	set	Set
1994	Dick Turpin - W. Harper	2,500	1994	set	Set
1994	Granny - W. Harper	2,500	1994	set	Set
1994	Jester - C. Noke	2,500	1994	set	Set
1994	Parson Brown - W. Harper	2,500	1994	set	Set

Femmes Fatales - P. Davies

Year Issue		Edition Limit	Year Retd.	Issue Price	*Quote U.S.$
1979	Cleopatra HN2868	750	1995	750.00	1350
1984	Eve HN2466	750	1995	1250.00	1300-1500
1981	Helen of Troy HN2387	750	1993	1250.00	1400-1600
1985	Lucrezia Borgia HN2342	750	1993	1250.00	1300-1500
1982	Queen of Sheba HN2328	750	1996	1250.00	1300-1600
1983	Tz'u-Hsi HN2391	750	1996	1250.00	1300-1500

Figure of the Year - Various

Year Issue		Edition Limit	Year Retd.	Issue Price	*Quote U.S.$
1991	Amy HN3316 - P. Gee	Closed	1991	195.00	500-700
1992	Mary HN3375 - P. Gee	Closed	1992	225.00	375-475
1993	Patricia HN3365 - V. Annand	Closed	1993	250.00	350-475
1994	Jennifer HN3447 - P. Gee	Closed	1994	250.00	300-375
1995	Deborah - HN3644 - N. Pedley	Closed	1995	225.00	225
1996	Belle HN3703 - V. Annand	Closed	1996	231.25	235
1997	Jessica HN3850 - N. Pedley	Yr.Iss.		245.00	245

The Four Seasons - V. Annand

Year Issue		Edition Limit	Year Retd.	Issue Price	*Quote U.S.$
1993	Springtime HN3477	Retrd.	1996	325.00	350
1994	Summertime HN3478	Retrd.	1996	325.00	350
1993	Autumntime HN3621	Retrd.	1996	325.00	350
1993	Wintertime HN3622	Retrd.	1996	325.00	350

Gainsborough Ladies - P. Gee

Year Issue		Edition Limit	Year Retd.	Issue Price	*Quote U.S.$
1991	Countess of Sefton HN3010	5,000	1996	650.00	700
1991	Hon Frances Duncombe HN3009	5,000	1996	650.00	650-700
1991	Lady Sheffield HN3008	5,000	1996	650.00	650-700
1990	Mary, Countess Howe HN3007	5,000	1996	650.00	700

Great Lovers - R. Jefferson

Year Issue		Edition Limit	Year Retd.	Issue Price	*Quote U.S.$
1995	Antony and Cleopatra HN3114	150		5250.00	5250
1996	Lancelot and Guinevere HN3112	150		5250.00	5250
1994	Robin Hood & Maid Marian HN3111	150		5250.00	5250
1993	Romeo and Juliet HN3113	150		5250.00	5250

Images - Various

Year Issue		Edition Limit	Year Retd.	Issue Price	*Quote U.S.$
1997	Angel HN3940 - A. Maslankowski	Open		125.00	125
1991	Bride & Groom HN3281 - R. Tabbenor	Open		85.00	99
1991	Bridesmaid HN3280 - R. Tabbenor	Open		85.00	99
1993	Brother & Sister HN3460 - A. Hughes	Open		52.50	112
1991	Brothers HN3191 - E. Griffiths	Open		90.00	112
1981	Family HN2720 - E. Griffiths	Open		187.50	215
1988	First Love HN2747 - D. Tootle	Open		170.00	215
1991	First Steps HN3282 - R. Tabbenor	Open		142.00	215
1993	Gift of Freedom HN3443 - N/A	Open		90.00	112
1997	Graduation HN3942 - A. Maslankowski	Open		125.00	125
1989	Happy Anniversary HN3254 - D. Tootle	Open		187.50	215
1981	Lovers HN2762 - D. Tootle	Open		187.50	215
1980	Mother & Daughter HN2841 - E. Griffiths	Open		187.50	215
1997	Mother and Child HN3938 - A. Maslankowski	Open		125.00	125
1993	Our First Christmas HN3452 - N/A	Open		185.00	215
1989	Over the Threshold HN3274 - R. Tabbenor	Open		187.50	215
1983	Sisters HN3010 - P. Parson	Open		90.00	112
1987	Wedding Day HN2748 - D. Tootle	Open		187.50	215

Limited Edition Figurines - Various

Year Issue		Edition Limit	Year Retd.	Issue Price	*Quote U.S.$
1992	Christopher Columbus HN3392 - A. Maslankowski	1,492	N/A	1950.00	1950
1993	Duke of Wellington HN3432 - A. Maslankowski	1,500	1996	1750.00	1750
1996	Eastern Grace Flambe HN3683 - P. Parsons	2,500	1996	493.75	520
1994	Field Marshal Montgomery HN3405 - N/A	1,944	N/A	1100.00	1100
1993	General Robert E. Lee HN3404 - R. Tabbenor	5,000	1995	1175.00	1175
1997	HM Queen Elizabeth, The Queen Mother HN3944 - A. Maslankowski	5,000		635.00	635
1993	Lt. General Ulysses S. Grant HN3403 - R. Tabbenor	5,000	1995	1175.00	1175
1992	Napoleon at Waterloo HN3429 - A. Maslankowski	1,500	N/A	1900.00	1900
1992	Samurai Warrior HN3402 - R. Tabbenor	950	1995	500.00	500
1997	Sir Henry Doulton HN3891 - R. Tabbenor	1,997		430.00	450
1997	Top o' the Hill Blue HN 3735 - L. Harradine	3,500		370.00	370
1993	Vice Admiral Lord Nelson HN3489 - A. Maslankowski	950	1996	1750.00	1750
1993	Winston S. Churchill HN3433 - A. Maslankowski	5,000		595.00	595

Myths & Maidens - R. Jefferson

Year Issue		Edition Limit	Year Retd.	Issue Price	*Quote U.S.$
1986	Diana The Huntress HN2829	300	N/A	2950.00	3000
1985	Europa & Bull HN2828	300	N/A	2950.00	3000
1984	Juno & Peacock HN2827	300	N/A	2950.00	3000
1982	Lady & Unicorn HN2825	300	N/A	2500.00	2500
1983	Leda & Swan HN2826	300	N/A	2950.00	3000

Prestige Figures - Various

Year Issue		Edition Limit	Year Retd.	Issue Price	*Quote U.S.$
1996	Charge of the Light Brigade HN3718 - A. Maslankowski	Open		17500.00	17500
1982	Columbine HN2738 - D. Tootle	Open		1250.00	1375
1982	Harlequin HN2737 - D. Tootle	Open		1250.00	1375
1964	Indian Brave HN2376 - M. Davis	500	1993	2500.00	5500
1952	Jack Point HN2080 - C.J. Noke	Open		2900.00	3400
1950	King Charles HN2084 - C.J. Noke	Open		2500.00	2500
1964	Matador & Bull HN2324 - M. Davis	Open		21500.00	25200
1952	The Moor HN2082 - C.J. Noke	Open		2500.00	3000
1964	The Palio HN2428 - M. Davis	500	1993	2500.00	6500
1952	Princess Badoura HN2081 - H. Stanton	Open		28000.00	33000
1978	St George and Dragon HN2856 - W.K. Harper	Open		13600.00	14500

Queens of Realm - P. Parsons

Year Issue		Edition Limit	Year Retd.	Issue Price	*Quote U.S.$
1989	Mary, Queen of Scots HN3142	S/O	N/A	550.00	900
1988	Queen Anne HN3141	S/O	N/A	525.00	800
1986	Queen Elizabeth I HN3099	S/O	N/A	495.00	900-1100
1987	Queen Victoria HN3125	S/O	N/A	495.00	1200-1400
1987	Set of 4	S/O	N/A	2065.00	3000

Reynolds Collection - P. Gee

Year Issue		Edition Limit	Year Retd.	Issue Price	*Quote U.S.$
1992	Countess Harrington HN3317	5,000	1995	550.00	595
1993	Countess Spencer HN3320	5,000	1995	595.00	595
1991	Lady Worsley HN3318	5,000	1995	550.00	595
1992	Mrs. Hugh Bonfoy HN3319	5,000	1995	550.00	595

Royal Doulton Figurines - Various

Year Issue		Edition Limit	Year Retd.	Issue Price	*Quote U.S.$
1933	Beethoven HN1778 - R. Garbe	25	1935	N/A	6500
1975	The Jersey Milkmaid HN2057A - L. Harradine	Closed	1981	N/A	225
1987	Life Boatman HN2764 - W. Harper	Closed	1991	N/A	250-350
1924	Tony Weller HN684 - C. Noke	Closed	1938	N/A	1800

Royalty - Various

Year Issue		Edition Limit	Year Retd.	Issue Price	*Quote U.S.$
1986	Duchess Of York HN3086 - E. Griffiths	1,500	1987	495.00	650
1981	Duke Of Edinburgh HN2386 - P. Davis	750	1982	395.00	450
1982	Lady Diana Spencer HN2885 - E. Griffiths	1,500	1982	395.00	600-700
1981	Prince Of Wales HN2883 - E. Griffiths	1,500	1982	395.00	450-650
1981	Prince Of Wales HN2884 - E. Griffiths	1,500	1982	750.00	1000
1982	Princess Of Wales HN2887 - E. Griffiths	1,500	1982	750.00	1500-1700
1973	Queen Elizabeth II HN2502 - P. Davis	750	1975	N/A	1800
1982	Queen Elizabeth II HN2878 - E. Griffiths	2,500	1984	N/A	450-600
1992	Queen Elizabeth II, 2nd. Version HN3440 - P. Gee	3,500	1994	460.00	460
1989	Queen Elizabeth, the Queen Mother as the Duchess of York HN3230 - P. Parsons	9,500	1990	N/A	450
1990	Queen Elizabeth, the Queen Mother HN3189 - E. Griffiths	2,500	1992	N/A	450-700
1980	Queen Mother HN2882 - P. Davis	1,500	1983	650.00	1250

Salvino Inc.

Collector Club Figurines - Salvino

Year Issue		Edition Limit	Year Retd.	Issue Price	*Quote U.S.$
1993	6" Mario Lemieux-Painted Away Uniform (Unsigned)	Closed	N/A	70.00	75-90
1993	Joe Montana-"KC" Away Uniform (Hand Signed)	Closed	N/A	275.00	400

Boston Celtic Greats - Salvino

Year Issue		Edition Limit	Year Retd.	Issue Price	*Quote U.S.$
1991	Larry Bird	S/O	N/A	285.00	350
1993	Larry Bird (Special Edition)	S/O	N/A	375.00	450

Boxing Greats - Salvino

Year Issue		Edition Limit	Year Retd.	Issue Price	*Quote U.S.$
1990	Muhammed Ali	S/O	N/A	250.00	250
1990	Muhammed Ali (Special Edition)	S/O	N/A	375.00	395-500

Brooklyn Dodger - Salvino

Year Issue		Edition Limit	Year Retd.	Issue Price	*Quote U.S.$
1989	Don Drysdale	S/O	N/A	185.00	200-250
1989	Don Drysdale AP	300		200.00	300
1993	Duke Snider	1,000		275.00	275
1990	Roy Campanella	2,000		395.00	325-425
1990	Roy Campanella (Special Edition)	S/O	N/A	550.00	500
1989	Sandy Koufax	S/O	N/A	195.00	225-275
1989	Sandy Koufax AP	500		250.00	300

Collegiate Series - Salvino

Year Issue		Edition Limit	Year Retd.	Issue Price	*Quote U.S.$
1992	Joe Montana	S/O	N/A	275.00	395
1992	OJ Simpson	1,000		275.00	395

Dealer Special Series - Salvino

Year Issue		Edition Limit	Year Retd.	Issue Price	*Quote U.S.$
1992	Joe Namath	S/O	N/A	700.00	700
1992	Mickey Mantle #6	S/O	N/A	700.00	1350
1992	Mickey Mantle #7	S/O	N/A	700.00	1450
1993	Willie Mays	S/O	N/A	700.00	700

Heroes of the Diamond - Salvino

Year Issue		Edition Limit	Year Retd.	Issue Price	*Quote U.S.$
1993	Brooks Robinson	1,000		275.00	275
1992	Mickey Mantle Batting	S/O	N/A	395.00	650-695
1992	Mickey Mantle Batting-Right Hand (Away)	S/O	N/A	545.00	795-1200
1992	Mickey Mantle Batting-Right Hand (Home)	S/O	N/A	545.00	995-1395
1992	Mickey Mantle Fielding	S/O	N/A	395.00	595-650
1991	Rickey Henderson (Away)	600		275.00	275
1991	Rickey Henderson (Home)	S/O	N/A	275.00	275
1991	Rickey Henderson (Special Edition)	550		375.00	375
1992	Willie Mays New York	750		395.00	395
1992	Willie Mays San Francisco	750		395.00	395

Hockey Greats - Salvino

Year Issue		Edition Limit	Year Retd.	Issue Price	*Quote U.S.$
1991	Mario Lemieux	S/O	N/A	275.00	300
1992	Mario Lemieux (Special Editon)	S/O	N/A	285.00	300-400
1994	Wayne Gretzky	S/O	N/A	395.00	395

NFL Superstar - Salvino

Year Issue		Edition Limit	Year Retd.	Issue Price	*Quote U.S.$
1990	Jim Brown	S/O	N/A	275.00	275
1990	Jim Brown (Special Edition)	S/O	N/A	525.00	350-450
1990	Joe Montana	S/O	N/A	275.00	275
1990	Joe Montana (Special Edition)	S/O	N/A	395.00	395

*Quotes have been rounded up to nearest dollar

YEAR ISSUE		EDITION LIMIT	YEAR RETD.	ISSUE PRICE	*QUOTE U.S.$
1993	Joe Montana 49'er	1,000		275.00	300
1993	Joe Montana Chiefs	450		275.00	400
1990	Joe Namath	2,500		275.00	275
1990	Joe Namath (Special Edition)	500		375.00	375-475
1990	OJ Simpson	1,000		250.00	300-400

Racing Legends - Salvino

YEAR ISSUE		EDITION LIMIT	YEAR RETD.	ISSUE PRICE	*QUOTE U.S.$
1991	AJ Foyt	S/O	N/A	250.00	250
1991	Darrell Waltrip	S/O	N/A	250.00	250
1991	Richard Petty	S/O	N/A	250.00	250
1991	Richard Petty (Special Edition)	S/O	N/A	279.00	350-400
1993	Richard Petty Farewell Tour	2,500		275.00	275

Sarah's Attic, Inc.

Collector's Club Promotion - Sarah's Attic

YEAR ISSUE		EDITION LIMIT	YEAR RETD.	ISSUE PRICE	*QUOTE U.S.$
1991	Diamond 3497	Closed	1992	36.00	100
1991	Ruby 3498	Closed	1992	42.00	150
1992	Christmas Love Santa 3522	Closed	1992	45.00	65
1992	Forever Frolicking Friends 3523	Closed	1992	Gift	75
1992	Love One Another 3561	Closed	1992	60.00	60
1992	Sharing Dreams 3562	Closed	1993	75.00	100
1992	Life Time Friends 3563	Closed	1993	75.00	125
1992	Love Starts With Children 3607	Closed	1993	Gift	75
1993	First Forever Friend Celebration 3903	Closed	1993	50.00	50
1993	Pledge of Allegiance 3749	Closed	1993	45.00	90
1993	Love Starts With Children II 3837	Closed	1994	Gift	65
1993	Gem wh. Girl w/Basket 3842	Closed	1994	33.00	150
1993	Rocky blk. Boy w/Marbles 3843	Closed	1994	25.00	65
1994	America Boy 4191	Closed	1994	25.00	25
1994	America Girl 4192	Closed	1994	25.00	25
1994	Forever Friends 4286	Closed	1994	45.00	45
1994	Saturday Night Round Up 4232	Closed	1995	Gift	25
1994	Billy Bob 4233	Closed	1995	38.00	38
1994	Jimmy Dean 4234	Closed	1995	38.00	38
1994	Sally/Jack 4235	Closed	1995	55.00	55
1994	Ellie/T.J. 4236	Closed	1995	55.00	55
1995	Flags in Heaven 4386	Closed	1995	45.00	45
1995	Friends Forever 4444	Closed	1996	60.00	60
1995	Playtime Pals 4446	Closed	1997	65.00	70
1995	Horsin' around 4445	Closed	1997	65.00	65
1996	Abigail 4543	Closed	1996	36.00	36
1996	Aretha 4542	Closed	1996	36.00	36
1997	Basket of Memories 4827	Yr.Iss.		35.00	35
1997	Sharing Memories 4828	Yr.Iss.		85.00	85
1997	Basket of Treasures 4829	Yr.Iss.		35.00	35
1997	Treasured Moments 4830	Yr.Iss.		85.00	85

Angels In The Attic - Sarah's Attic

YEAR ISSUE		EDITION LIMIT	YEAR RETD.	ISSUE PRICE	*QUOTE U.S.$
1989	Abbee-Angel-2336	Closed	1991	10.00	20
1990	Adora Girl Angel Standing 3276	4,000	1990	35.00	125-150
1994	Adora w/Harp 4137	Closed	1996	26.00	26
1991	Angel Adora With Bunny 3390	Closed	1993	50.00	65
1991	Angel Enos With Frog 3391	10,000	1993	50.00	65
1996	Angels on Assignment 4544	Closed	1996	65.00	65
1989	Ashbee-Angel 2337	Closed	1991	10.00	25
1991	Bert Angel 3416	1,000	1992	60.00	120
1990	Billi-Angel 3295	Closed	1991	18.00	22
1993	Blessed is He 3952	1,994	1994	48.00	120
1994	Blessed is He II 4189	2,500		66.00	75
1995	Blessed is He III 4387	4,000		60.00	60
1994	Casey Angel 4245	Closed	1996	32.00	32
1995	Christine 4420	5,000	1996	26.00	26
1990	Cindi-Angel 3296	Closed	1991	18.00	22
1989	Clyde-Angel 2329	Closed	1991	17.00	20
1992	Contentment 3500	500	1992	100.00	200
1995	Dignity 4330	Closed	1996	55.00	55
1992	Enos & Adora-Small 3671	5,000	1993	35.00	60-125
1990	Enos Boy Angel Sitting 3275	4,000	1990	33.00	100
1994	Enos w/Harp 4138	Closed	1996	26.00	26
1989	Floppy-Angel 2330	Closed	1990	10.00	20
1990	Flossy-Angel 3301	Closed	1991	15.00	24
1989	Gramps Angel 2357	Closed	1990	17.00	40
1989	Grams Angel 2356	Closed	1990	17.00	40
1992	Heavenly Caring 3661	2,500	1993	70.00	90
1992	Heavenly Giving 3663	Closed	1993	70.00	90
1992	Heavenly Loving 3664	2,500	1993	70.00	90
1993	Heavenly Peace 3833	2,500	1994	47.00	50
1992	Heavenly Sharing 3662	2,500	1993	70.00	90
1993	Heavenly Uniting 3794	2,500	1994	45.00	45
1992	Hope Angel 3659	Closed	1994	40.00	45
1994	Jonathon Angel 4253	Closed	1996	32.00	32
1994	Jovae Angel 4252	Closed	1996	32.00	32
1996	Karissa wh. Angel 4480	1,200	1996	34.00	34
1996	Karita blk. Angel 4479	1,200	1996	34.00	34
1994	Lacy Angel 4244	Closed	1996	32.00	32
1990	Lena-Angel 3297	Closed	1991	36.00	40
1995	LOL - Baby blk. Girl 4288	Closed	1996	25.00	25
1995	LOL - Birthday wh. Girl 4299	Closed	1996	29.00	29
1995	LOL - Birthday wh. Boy 4303	Closed	1996	29.00	29
1995	LOL - Blk Boy Stocking 4436	Closed	1996	18.00	18
1995	LOL - Blk Boy Trumpet 4432	Closed	1996	18.00	18
1995	LOL - Blk Girl Wreath 4435	Closed	1996	18.00	18
1995	LOL - Bottle wh. Girl 4306	Closed	1995	29.00	29
1995	LOL - Boy Wreath wh. 4434	Closed	1996	18.00	18
1995	LOL - Campfire wh. Girl 4293	Closed	1995	29.00	29
1995	LOL - Canning wh. Girl 4297	Closed	1995	29.00	29
1995	LOL - Fishing blk. Boy 4300	Closed	1996	29.00	29
1995	LOL - Girl Praying wh. 4431	Closed	1996	18.00	18
1995	LOL - Girl Stocking wh. 4433	Closed	1996	18.00	18
1995	LOL - Happiness wh. Girl 4291	Closed	1996	29.00	29
1995	LOL - Ironing wh. Girl 4289	Closed	1996	29.00	29
1995	LOL - Mechanic wh. Boy 4298	Closed	1995	29.00	29
1995	LOL - Mowing blk. Boy 4296	Closed	1995	29.00	29
1995	LOL - Planting wh. Girl 4287	Closed	1996	29.00	29
1995	LOL - Roller Blading wh. Boy 4309	Closed	1996	29.00	29
1995	LOL - Studying blk. Boy 4294	Closed	1996	25.00	25
1995	LOL - Tools wh. Boy 4310	Closed	1995	29.00	29
1995	LOL Mini- blk. Boy, blue 4383	Closed	1996	12.00	12
1995	LOL Mini- blk. Boy, gold 4382	Closed	1996	12.00	12
1995	LOL Mini- blk. Girl, gold 4378	Closed	1996	12.00	12
1995	LOL Mini- blk. Girl, pink 4379	Closed	1996	12.00	12
1995	LOL Mini- wh. Boy, blue 4385	Closed	1996	12.00	12
1995	LOL Mini- wh. Boy, gold 4384	Closed	1996	12.00	12
1995	LOL Mini- wh. Girl, gold 4380	Closed	1996	12.00	12
1995	LOL Mini- wh. Girl, pink 4381	Closed	1996	12.00	12
1995	Louise Angel 4472	Closed	1996	34.00	34
1990	Louise-Angel 3300	Closed	1991	17.00	24
1992	Love 3501	500	1992	80.00	200
1995	Love 4328	Closed	1996	40.00	40
1995	Prayer of Love 4437	500	1995	85.00	170
1992	Priscilla-Angel 3511	5,000	1993	46.00	60
1995	Respect 4329	Closed	1996	32.00	32
1989	Saint Willie Bill 2360	Closed	1991	30.00	40
1989	St. Anne 2323	Closed	1991	29.00	40
1989	St. Gabbe 2322	Closed	1991	30.00	33
1990	Trapper-Angel 3299	Closed	1991	17.00	40
1989	Wendall-Angel 2324	Closed	1991	10.00	45
1989	Wilbur-Angel 2327	Closed	1991	10.00	25
1995	Willie Bill Angel 4471	Closed	1996	34.00	34

Beary Adorables Collection - Sarah's Attic

YEAR ISSUE		EDITION LIMIT	YEAR RETD.	ISSUE PRICE	*QUOTE U.S.$
1987	Abbee Bear 2005	Closed	1989	6.00	12
1987	Alex Bear 2003	Closed	1989	10.00	12
1987	Amelia Bear 2004	Closed	1989	8.00	12
1988	Americana Bear 3047	Closed	1990	50.00	75
1989	Angel Bear 3105	Closed	1990	24.00	25
1988	Arti Boy Bear 6319	Closed	1990	7.00	15
1987	Ashbee Bear 2006	Closed	1989	6.00	12
1990	Belinda 50's Girl Bear 3253	4,000	1991	25.00	35
1989	Betsy Bear w/Flag 3097	Closed	1990	22.00	40
1989	Colonial Bear w/Hat 3098	Closed	1990	22.00	40
1989	Daisy Bear 3101	Closed	1990	48.00	55
1991	Dudley Bear 3355	2,500	1990	32.00	60
1988	Ghost Bear 3028	Closed	1989	9.00	25
1989	Griswald Bear 3102	Closed	1990	48.00	55
1988	Honey Ma Bear 6316	Closed	1990	16.00	20
1988	Marti Girl Bear 6318	Closed	1990	12.00	20
1989	Mikey Bear 3104	Closed	1990	26.00	30
1989	Missy Bear 3103	Closed	1990	26.00	30
1988	Rufus Pa Bear 6317	Closed	1990	15.00	20
1989	Sammy Boy Bear 3111	Closed	1990	12.00	15
1989	Sid Papa Bear 3092	Closed	1990	18.00	25
1989	Sophie Mama Bear 3093	Closed	1990	18.00	25
1989	Spice Bear Crawling 3109	Closed	1990	12.00	15

Black Heritage Collection - Sarah's Attic

YEAR ISSUE		EDITION LIMIT	YEAR RETD.	ISSUE PRICE	*QUOTE U.S.$
1991	Baby Tansy blk.3388	Closed	1993	40.00	50
1993	Bessie Gospel Singer 3754	Closed	1996	40.00	40
1992	Booker T. Washington 3648	3,000	1993	80.00	100
1992	Boys Night Out 3660	2,000	1994	350.00	450-695
1990	Brotherly Love 3336	5,000	1991	80.00	175
1992	Buffalo Soldier 3524	5,000	1993	80.00	125
1991	Caleb w/ Football 3485	6,000	1993	40.00	55
1990	Caleb-Lying Down 3232	Closed	1994	23.00	35
1992	Calvin Prayer Time 3510	5,000	1993	46.00	55
1991	Corporal Pervis 3366	8,000	1993	60.00	125
1992	Esther w/Butter Churn 3536	Closed	1994	70.00	70
1987	Gramps 5104	Closed	1988	16.00	100
1987	Grams 5105	Closed	1988	16.00	100
1992	Granny Wynne & Olivia 3535	5,000	1994	85.00	95
1990	Harpster w/Banjo 3257	4,000	1990	60.00	250
1991	Harpster w/Harmonica II 3384	8,000	1993	60.00	125
1992	Harriet Tubman 3687	3,000	1993	60.00	125
1991	Hattie Quilting 3483	6,000	1993	60.00	125
1990	Hattie-Knitting 3233	4,000	1990	40.00	75-100
1992	Ida B. Wells & Frederick Douglass 3642	3,000	1993	160.00	200-250
1993	Jesse Gospel Singer 3755	Closed	1996	40.00	40
1994	Kitty w/Microphone 4141	Closed	1996	50.00	50
1990	Libby w/Overalls 3259	4,000	1990	36.00	175
1991	Libby w/Puppy 3386	10,000	1993	50.00	100
1995	Love 4187	Closed	1996	50.00	50
1991	Lucas w/Dog 3387	10,000	1993	50.00	100
1990	Lucas w/Overalls 3260	4,000	1990	36.00	175
1996	Mary Eliza Mahoney 4501	1,000	1996	50.00	50
1993	Miles Boy Angel 3752	2,500	1995	27.00	40
1993	Moriah Girl Angel 3759	2,500	1994	27.00	45
1992	Muffy-Prayer Time 3509	5,000	1993	46.00	55
1992	Music Masters 3533	1,000	1992	300.00	350
1992	Music Masters II 3621	1,000	1994	250.00	300
1994	Music Masters III 4142	Closed	1996	80.00	80
1993	Nat Love Cowboy (Isom Dart) 3792	2,500	1993	45.00	250-300
1991	Nighttime Pearl 3362	Closed	1993	50.00	65
1991	Nighttime Percy 3363	Closed	1993	50.00	65
1993	Otis Redding 3793	Closed	1994	70.00	300
1989	Pappy Jake 3100	Closed	1990	40.00	100
1990	Pearl-Blk. Girl Dancing 3291	5,000	1992	45.00	100
1990	Percy-Blk. Boy Dancing 3292	5,000	1993	45.00	100
1992	Porter 3525	5,000	1993	80.00	125
1990	Portia Reading Book 3256	Closed	1991	30.00	45-65
1990	Praise the Lord I (Preacher I) 3277	4,000	1991	55.00	150
1991	Praise the Lord II w/Kids 3376	5,000	1994	100.00	100
1993	Praise the Lord III 3753	2,500	1994	44.00	55
1989	Quilting Ladies 3099	Closed	1991	90.00	250-300
1992	Sojourner Truth 3629	3,000	1993	80.00	125
1995	Tuskegee Airman W.W. II 4405	2,500	1996	60.00	60
1991	Uncle Reuben 3389	8,000	1993	70.00	95
1993	Vanessa Gospel Singer (Upside down book) 3756	Closed	1996	40.00	100
1990	Whoopie & Wooster 3255	4,000	1990	50.00	235
1991	Whoopie & Wooster II 3385	8,000	1993	70.00	95

Classroom Memories - Sarah's Attic

YEAR ISSUE		EDITION LIMIT	YEAR RETD.	ISSUE PRICE	*QUOTE U.S.$
1988	Miss Pritchet 6505	Closed	1993	28.00	35

Cotton Tale Collection - Sarah's Attic

YEAR ISSUE		EDITION LIMIT	YEAR RETD.	ISSUE PRICE	*QUOTE U.S.$
1988	Americana Bunny 3048	Closed	1990	58.00	190
1988	Billi Rabbit 6283	Closed	1990	27.00	35
1987	Bonnie 5727	Closed	1989	30.00	125
1988	Cindi Rabbit 6282	Closed	1990	27.00	35
1987	Clyde 5728	Closed	1989	30.00	125
1989	Cookie Rabbit 3078	Closed	1990	29.00	125
1989	Crumb Rabbit 3077	Closed	1990	29.00	35-43
1989	Nana Rabbit 3080	Closed	1990	50.00	60-75
1990	Ollie Rabbit w/Vest 3239	Closed	1991	75.00	150
1989	Papa Rabbit 3079	Closed	1990	50.00	60-75
1989	Sleepy Rabbit 3088	Closed	1990	16.00	25
1991	Tabitha Victorian Rabbit 3371	Closed	1993	30.00	45
1991	Tessy Victorian Rabbit 3370	Closed	1993	20.00	35
1989	Thelma Rabbit 3084	Closed	1990	33.00	40
1989	Thomas Rabbit 3085	Closed	1990	33.00	40
1991	Toby Victorian Rabbit 3369	Closed	1993	40.00	55
1988	Wendall Mini Rabbit 6268	Closed	1990	8.00	12
1987	Wendall Rabbit 5285	Closed	1989	14.00	25
1988	Wendy Mini Rabbit 6270	Closed	1990	8.00	12
1987	Wendy Rabbit 5286	Closed	1989	15.00	25
1988	Wilbur Mini Rabbit 6269	Closed	1990	8.00	12
1987	Wilbur Rabbit 5287	Closed	1989	13.00	25
1990	Zeb Pa Rabbit w/Carrots 3217	500	1990	18.00	32
1990	Zeb Sailor Dad 3319	Closed	1992	28.00	32
1990	Zeke Boy Rabbit w/Carrots 3219	500	1990	17.00	32
1990	Zelda Ma Rabbit w/Carrots 3218	500	1990	18.00	32
1987	Zoe Girl Rabbit w/Carrots 3220	500	1990	17.00	32

Cuddly Critters Collection - Sarah's Attic

YEAR ISSUE		EDITION LIMIT	YEAR RETD.	ISSUE PRICE	*QUOTE U.S.$
1988	Cow w/Bell 3023	Closed	1990	28.00	28
1989	Madam Donna 2321	Closed	1990	36.00	36
1989	Messieur Pierre 2346	Closed	1990	36.00	36
1993	Waldo Dog-Gospel 3751	2,500	1996	10.00	10

Daisy Collection - Sarah's Attic

YEAR ISSUE		EDITION LIMIT	YEAR RETD.	ISSUE PRICE	*QUOTE U.S.$
1990	Bomber-Tom 3309	Closed	1993	52.00	57
1990	Jack Boy Ball & Glove 3249	Closed	1993	40.00	44
1993	Jack Boy w/Broken Arm 3970	2,000	1994	30.00	60
1990	Jewel-Julie 3310	Closed	1993	62.00	68
1989	Sally Booba 2344	Closed	1993	40.00	60
1990	Sparky-Mark 3307	Closed	1993	55.00	60
1990	Spike-Tim 3308	Closed	1993	46.00	51
1990	Stretch-Mike 3311	Closed	1993	52.00	57

Dreams of Tomorrow - Sarah's Attic

YEAR ISSUE		EDITION LIMIT	YEAR RETD.	ISSUE PRICE	*QUOTE U.S.$
1994	Annie-Nurse 4128	Closed	1996	33.00	33
1991	Benjamin w/Drums 3487	10,000	1993	46.00	55
1992	Bubba-Doctor 3506	6,000	1993	60.00	66
1992	Bubba-Policeman 3685	3,000	1993	46.00	51
1992	Bud-Fireman 3668	6,000	1993	50.00	55
1994	Bud-Police (blue) 4260	Closed	1996	45.00	45
1994	Calvin-Soccer 4275	Closed	1996	36.00	36
1994	Champ-Soccer 4277	Closed	1996	36.00	36
1991	Charity Sewing Flags 3486	10,000	1993	46.00	55
1994	Cupcake-Soccer 4276	Closed	1996	36.00	36
1994	Hewett-Police (blue) 4258	2,000	1996	45.00	45
1994	Joe-Farmer w/Basket 4120	Closed	1996	33.00	33
1994	John-Farmer w/Tractor 4119	Closed	1996	36.00	36
1994	Moose-Football 4273	2,000	1996	36.00	36
1992	Noah-Executive 3508	6,000	1993	46.00	46
1992	Pansy-Ballerina 3682	3,000	1993	46.00	55
1992	Pansy-Nurse 3505	6,000	1993	46.00	51
1993	Rachel-Photographer 3871	2,000	1995	27.00	32
1992	Shelby-Executive 3666	6,000	1993	46.00	50
1994	Shelby-Nurse 4127	Closed	1996	33.00	33
1993	Tillie-Photographer 3870	Closed	1996	27.00	32
1994	Tillie-Soccer 4274	Closed	1996	36.00	36
1993	Twinkie-Pilot 3869	Closed	1996	27.00	35
1994	Whimpy-Fireman 4230	2,000	1996	37.00	37
1992	Willie-Fireman 3667	6,000	1993	46.00	50
1993	Willie-Pilot 3868	Closed	1996	27.00	27
1994	Willie-Police (blue) 4256	2,000	1996	32.00	32

Matt & Maggie - Sarah's Attic

YEAR ISSUE		EDITION LIMIT	YEAR RETD.	ISSUE PRICE	*QUOTE U.S.$
1988	Large Matt 3029	4,000	1989	48.00	58
1986	Maggie 2029	4,000	1989	14.00	28
1989	Maggie Bench Sitter 3083	Closed	1990	32.00	42
1987	Maggie on Heart 5145	Closed	1989	9.00	15
1987	Matt & Maggie w/ Bear 5730	100	1987	100.00	150
1986	Matt 2030	Closed	1989	14.00	28
1989	Matt Bench Sitter 3082	Closed	1990	32.00	42
1987	Matt on Heart 5144	Closed	1989	9.00	15
1989	Mini Maggie 2314	Closed	1989	6.00	12
1989	Mini Matt 2313	Closed	1989	6.00	12

*Quotes have been rounded up to nearest dollar

YEAR ISSUE		EDITION LIMIT	YEAR RETD.	ISSUE PRICE	*QUOTE U.S.$
1988	Small Sitting Maggie 5284	Closed	1989	11.50	35
1988	Small Sitting Matt 5283	Closed	1989	11.50	35
1987	Standing Maggie 2014	Closed	1989	11.00	15
1987	Standing Matt 2013	Closed	1989	11.00	15

Santas Of The Month-Series A - Sarah's Attic

YEAR ISSUE		EDITION LIMIT	YEAR RETD.	ISSUE PRICE	*QUOTE U.S.$
1988	January wh. Santa	Closed	1990	50.00	135-150
1988	January blk. Santa	Closed	1990	50.00	200-300
1988	February wh. Santa	Closed	1990	50.00	135-150
1988	February blk. Santa	Closed	1990	50.00	200-300
1988	March wh. Santa	Closed	1990	50.00	135-150
1988	March blk. Santa	Closed	1990	50.00	200-300
1988	April wh. Santa	Closed	1990	50.00	135-150
1988	April blk. Santa	Closed	1990	50.00	200-300
1988	May wh. Santa	Closed	1990	50.00	135-150
1988	May blk. Santa	Closed	1990	50.00	200-300
1988	June wh. Santa	Closed	1990	50.00	135-150
1988	June blk. Santa	Closed	1990	50.00	200-300
1988	July wh. Santa	Closed	1990	50.00	175
1988	July blk. Santa	Closed	1990	50.00	200-300
1988	August wh. Santa	Closed	1990	50.00	135-150
1988	August blk. Santa	Closed	1990	50.00	200-300
1988	September wh. Santa	Closed	1990	50.00	135-150
1988	September blk. Santa	Closed	1990	50.00	200-300
1988	October wh. Santa	Closed	1990	50.00	135-150
1988	October blk. Santa	Closed	1990	50.00	200-300
1988	November wh. Santa	Closed	1990	50.00	135-150
1988	November blk. Santa	Closed	1990	50.00	200-300
1988	December wh. Santa	Closed	1990	50.00	135-150
1988	December blk. Santa	Closed	1990	50.00	225-375
1988	Mini January wh. Santa	Closed	1990	14.00	33-35
1988	Mini January blk. Santa	Closed	1990	14.00	35
1988	Mini February wh. Santa	Closed	1990	14.00	33-35
1988	Mini February blk. Santa	Closed	1990	14.00	35
1988	Mini March wh. Santa	Closed	1990	14.00	33-35
1988	Mini March blk. Santa	Closed	1990	14.00	35
1988	Mini April wh. Santa	Closed	1990	14.00	33-35
1988	Mini April blk. Santa	Closed	1990	14.00	35
1988	Mini May wh. Santa	Closed	1990	14.00	33-35
1988	Mini May blk. Santa	Closed	1990	14.00	35
1988	Mini June wh. Santa	Closed	1990	14.00	33-35
1988	Mini June blk. Santa	Closed	1990	14.00	35
1988	Mini July wh. Santa	Closed	1990	14.00	40
1988	Mini July blk. Santa	Closed	1990	14.00	50
1988	Mini August wh. Santa	Closed	1990	14.00	33-35
1988	Mini August blk. Santa	Closed	1990	14.00	35
1988	Mini September wh. Santa	Closed	1990	14.00	33-35
1988	Mini September blk. Santa	Closed	1990	14.00	35
1988	Mini October wh. Santa	Closed	1990	14.00	33-35
1988	Mini October blk. Santa	Closed	1990	14.00	35
1988	Mini November wh. Santa	Closed	1990	14.00	33-35
1988	Mini November blk. Santa	Closed	1990	14.00	35
1988	Mini December wh. Santa	Closed	1990	14.00	33-35
1988	Mini December blk. Santa	Closed	1990	14.00	35

Santas Of The Month-Series B - Sarah's Attic

YEAR ISSUE		EDITION LIMIT	YEAR RETD.	ISSUE PRICE	*QUOTE U.S.$
1990	Jan. Santa Winter Fun 7135	Closed	1991	80.00	100
1990	Feb. Santa Cupids Help 7136	Closed	1991	120.00	120
1990	Mar. Santa Irish Delight 7137	Closed	1991	120.00	150
1990	Apr. Santa Spring/Joy 7138	Closed	1991	150.00	150
1990	May Santa Par For Course 7139	Closed	1991	100.00	125
1990	June Santa Graduation 7140	Closed	1991	70.00	70
1990	July Santa God Bless 7141	Closed	1991	100.00	125
1990	Aug. Santa Summers Tranquility 7142	Closed	1991	110.00	130
1990	Sept. Santa Touchdown 7143	Closed	1991	90.00	90
1990	Oct. Santa Seasons Plenty 7144	Closed	1991	120.00	120
1990	Nov. Santa Give Thanks 7145	Closed	1991	100.00	125
1990	Dec. Santa Peace 7146	Closed	1991	120.00	125
1990	Jan. Mrs. Winter Fun 7147	Closed	1991	80.00	100
1990	Feb. Mrs. Cupid's Helper 7148	Closed	1991	110.00	110
1990	March Mrs. Irish Delight7149	Closed	1991	80.00	100
1990	April Mrs. Spring Joy 7150	Closed	1991	110.00	110
1990	May Mrs. Par for the Course 7151	Closed	1991	80.00	100
1990	June Mrs. Graduate 7152	Closed	1991	70.00	100
1990	July Mrs. God Bless America 7153	Closed	1991	100.00	125
1990	Aug. Mrs. Summer Tranquility 7154	Closed	1991	90.00	112
1990	Sept. Mrs. Touchdown 7155	Closed	1991	90.00	100
1990	Oct. Mrs. Seasons of Plenty 7156	Closed	1991	90.00	112
1990	Nov. Mrs. Give Thanks 7157	Closed	1991	90.00	112
1990	Dec. Mrs. Peace 7158	Closed	1991	110.00	137

Sarah's Gang Collection - Sarah's Attic

YEAR ISSUE		EDITION LIMIT	YEAR RETD.	ISSUE PRICE	*QUOTE U.S.$
1989	Baby Rachel 2306	Closed	1994	20.00	30
1990	Baby Rachel-Beachtime 3248	Closed	1992	35.00	50
1988	Cupcake 4027	Closed	1994	20.00	25
1995	Cupcake 4346	Closed	1996	28.00	28
1989	Cupcake Clown 3144	Closed	1989	21.00	35
1987	Cupcake on Heart 5140	Closed	1989	9.00	20
1993	Cupcake w/Snowman 3822	2,500	1994	35.00	40
1989	Cupcake-Americana 2304	Closed	1993	21.00	30
1990	Cupcake-Beachtime 3244	Closed	1992	35.00	53
1986	Cupcake-Original 2034	Closed	1988	14.00	20-75
1989	Cupcake-Small School 2309	Closed	1990	11.00	20
1990	Katie & Whimpy-Beachtime 3243	Closed	1992	60.00	60-75
1995	Katie 4344	Closed	1996	28.00	28
1987	Katie On Heart 5141	Closed	1989	9.00	20
1987	Katie Sitting 2002	Closed	1987	14.00	20
1989	Katie-Americana 2302	Closed	1993	21.00	25
1991	Katie-Bride 3431	Closed	1994	47.00	52
1986	Katie-Original 2032	Closed	1988	14.00	20
1989	Katie-Small Sailor 2307	Closed	1990	14.00	20
1990	Katie-Witch 3312	Closed	1992	40.00	50
1991	Percy-Minister 3440	Closed	1994	50.00	55
1991	Pug-Ringbearer 3439	Closed	1994	40.00	44
1995	Rachel 4348	Closed	1996	28.00	28
1991	Rachel-Flower Girl 3432	Closed	1994	40.00	43
1990	Rachel-Pumpkin 3318	Closed	1992	40.00	50
1991	Rachel-Thanksgiving 3474	10,000	1993	32.00	35
1988	Tillie 4032	Closed	1994	20.00	25
1991	Tillie Masquerade 3412	Closed	1993	45.00	50
1987	Tillie On Heart 5150	Closed	1989	9.00	20
1989	Tillie-Americana 2301	Closed	1993	21.00	25
1990	Tillie-Beachtime 3247	Closed	1992	35.00	53
1990	Tillie-Clown 3316	Closed	1992	40.00	50
1986	Tillie-Original 2027	Closed	1988	14.00	20
1989	Tillie-Small Country 2312	Closed	1992	18.00	26
1995	Twinkie 4347	Closed	1996	28.00	28
1989	Twinkie Clown 3145	Closed	1989	19.00	35
1987	Twinkie On Heart 5143	Closed	1989	9.00	20
1989	Twinkie-Americana 2305	Closed	1993	21.00	25
1990	Twinkie-Beachtime 3245	Closed	1992	35.00	53
1990	Twinkie-Devil 3315	Closed	1992	40.00	50
1986	Twinkie-Original 2033	Closed	1988	14.00	20
1989	Twinkie-Small School 2310	Closed	1990	11.00	20
1991	Tyler-Ring Bearer 3433	Closed	1994	40.00	44
1988	Whimpy 4030	Closed	1994	20.00	25
1995	Whimpy 4345	Closed	1996	28.00	28
1987	Whimpy on Heart 5142	Closed	1989	9.00	20
1987	Whimpy Sitting 2001	Closed	1987	14.00	20
1989	Whimpy-Americana 2303	Closed	1993	21.00	25
1991	Whimpy-Groom 3430	Closed	1994	47.00	52
1986	Whimpy-Original 2031	Closed	1988	14.00	20
1989	Whimpy-Small Sailor 2308	Closed	1990	14.00	20
1991	Whimpy-Thanksgiving 3469	10,000	1993	32.00	35
1988	Willie 4031	Closed	1994	20.00	25
1987	Willie On Heart 5151	Closed	1989	9.00	20
1989	Willie-Americana 2300	Closed	1993	21.00	30
1990	Willie-Beachtime 3246	Closed	1992	35.00	53
1990	Willie-Clown 3317	Closed	1992	40.00	50
1986	Willie-Original 2028	Closed	1988	14.00	20-75
1989	Willie-Small Country 2311	Closed	1992	18.00	26

Sarah's Neighborhood Friends - Sarah's Attic

YEAR ISSUE		EDITION LIMIT	YEAR RETD.	ISSUE PRICE	*QUOTE U.S.$
1991	Babes-Nativity Jesus 3427	Closed	1994	20.00	22
1990	Bubba w/Lantern 3268	Closed	1992	40.00	45
1991	Bubba w/Lemonade Stand 3382	Closed	1992	54.00	108
1991	Bud Nativity (Joseph) 3420	Closed	1994	34.00	36
1990	Bud w/Book 3270	Closed	1992	40.00	45
1991	Dolly Nativity (Jesus) 3418	Closed	1994	20.00	22
1993	Emily & Gideon-Small 3670	Closed	1993	40.00	75
1989	Jennifer & Max 2319	4,000	1990	57.00	85
1991	Pansy-Nativity Angel 3425	Closed	1994	30.00	32
1988	Trudy-w/Teacup 3042	Closed	1990	34.00	50
1990	Tyler Victorian Boy 3327	Closed	1992	40.00	65

Snowflake Collection - Sarah's Attic

YEAR ISSUE		EDITION LIMIT	YEAR RETD.	ISSUE PRICE	*QUOTE U.S.$
1989	Boo Mini Snowman 3200	Closed	1993	6.00	12
1992	Christmas Love-Small 3674	5,000	1992	30.00	33
1989	Flurry 2342	Closed	1993	12.00	20
1990	Old Glory Snowman 3225	4,000	1992	24.00	26
1989	Winter Frolic 3209	Closed	1992	60.00	70

Spirit of America - Sarah's Attic

YEAR ISSUE		EDITION LIMIT	YEAR RETD.	ISSUE PRICE	*QUOTE U.S.$
1988	Betsy Ross 3024	Closed	1992	34.00	60
1991	Bright Sky Mother Indian 3345	Closed	1992	70.00	90-140
1991	Iron Hawk Father Indian 3344	Closed	1992	70.00	90-140
1991	Little Dove Girl Indian 3346	Closed	1992	40.00	60-85
1988	Pilgrim Boy 4009	Closed	1990	12.00	20
1988	Pilgrim Girl 4010	Closed	1990	12.00	24
1994	Shine-Boy Indian 3980	1,000	1994	25.00	50
1994	Siyah-Girl Indian 3979	1,000	1994	25.00	50
1991	Spotted Eagle Boy Indian 3347	Closed	1992	30.00	45-85

Spirit of Christmas Collection - Sarah's Attic

YEAR ISSUE		EDITION LIMIT	YEAR RETD.	ISSUE PRICE	*QUOTE U.S.$
1995	Ahmad - Nativity 4453	Closed	1996	23.00	23
1995	Angelika - Nativity 4456	Closed	1996	25.00	25
1995	Care Basket 4424	5,000	1996	26.00	26
1995	Caring - Boy w/Globe 4423	5,000	1996	29.00	29
1995	Cherish the Children 4466	1,000	1996	70.00	70
1995	Christmas Joy 4331	Closed	1996	60.00	60
1994	Gift of Christmas-wh. Santa 4146	Closed	1996	60.00	60
1994	Gift of Love blk. Santa 4145	Closed	1996	60.00	60
1994	Golden Memories Santa 4254	Closed	1996	70.00	70
1995	Happiness 4426	5,000	1996	34.00	34
1995	Helpfulness 4425	5,000	1996	37.00	37
1995	Ishamael - Nativity 4454	Closed	1996	23.00	23
1995	Jabari - Nativity 4455	Closed	1996	23.00	23
1995	Jarrell - Nativity 4452	Closed	1996	23.00	23
1994	Jeb-Christmas 94 4155	Closed	1994	28.00	30
1995	Joah - Nativity 4451	Closed	1996	23.00	23
1995	Joy to the World 4462	1,000	1996	64.00	64
1995	Joyfulness 4428	5,000	1996	28.00	28
1995	Kindness 4427	5,000	1996	30.00	30
1995	Lakeisha - Nativity 4450	Closed	1996	25.00	25
1993	Let The Be Peace Santa 3797	2,000	1996	70.00	70
1993	Let There Be Love Santa 3796	2,000	1996	70.00	70
1994	LOL-Christmas 4151	Closed	1994	30.00	35
1987	Long Journey 2051	Closed	1989	19.00	35
1987	Mini Santa w/Cane 5123	Closed	1990	8.00	38
1995	Mrs. Santa 4430	5,000	1996	42.00	42
1989	Papa Santa Sitting 3180	Closed	1990	30.00	40
1989	Papa Santa Stocking 3182	Closed	1990	50.00	60
1995	Peace on Earth 4464	1,000	1996	80.00	80
1995	Santa 4429	Closed	1996	45.00	45
1988	Santa in Chimney 4020	4,000	1990	110.00	150
1991	Santa Tex 3392	500	1990	30.00	75
1987	Santa's Workshop 3006	Closed	1990	50.00	100
1991	Sharing Love Santa 3491	3,000	1993	120.00	140
1989	Silent Night 2343	6,000	1991	33.00	50
1995	Tillie-Caroling 4461	5,000	1996	26.00	26
1995	Willie-Caroling 4460	5,000	1996	26.00	26
1989	Woodland Santa 2345	7,500	1990	100.00	150

Tender Moments - Sarah's Attic

YEAR ISSUE		EDITION LIMIT	YEAR RETD.	ISSUE PRICE	*QUOTE U.S.$
1992	Baby Boy Birth blk. 3516	Closed	1993	50.00	55
1992	Baby Boy wh. 1 3527	Closed	1993	60.00	66
1992	Baby Girl blk. 1-2 3517	Closed	1993	50.00	55
1992	Baby Girl wh. 1 3528	Closed	1993	60.00	65
1994	Boy w/Fire Truck wh. 4-5 3960	Closed	1996	40.00	40
1994	Boy w/Hobby Horse blk. 4-5 3958	Closed	1996	33.00	33
1992	Boy wh. 2-3 3624	Closed	1993	60.00	65
1995	Bundle of Joy 4392	Closed	1996	20.00	20
1995	Bundle of Love 4393	Closed	1996	29.00	29
1992	Generations of Love	Closed	1994	293.00	425
1994	Girl on Horse blk. 4-5 3957	Closed	1996	37.00	37
1994	Girl w/Trunk wh. 4-5 3959	Closed	1996	40.00	40
1992	Girl wh. 2-3 3623	Closed	1993	60.00	66
1993	Joy of Motherhood blk. Pregnant Woman 3791	1,000	1994	55.00	70
1993	Little Blessing blk. Couple 3839	2,500	1994	75.00	90
1993	Love of Life blk. Couple 3788	1,000	1993	70.00	75-100
1995	Sweet Dreams 4388	Closed	1996	29.00	29
1993	True Love wh. Couple 3789	1,000	1994	70.00	80

United Hearts Collection - Sarah's Attic

YEAR ISSUE		EDITION LIMIT	YEAR RETD.	ISSUE PRICE	*QUOTE U.S.$
1992	Adora Angel-May 3632	Closed	1993	50.00	75
1991	Adora Christmas-December 3479	Closed	1992	36.00	60
1991	Barney the Great-October 3466	Closed	1992	40.00	48
1991	Bibi & Biff Clowns-October 3467	Closed	1992	35.00	42
1991	Bibi-Miss Liberty Bear-July 3457	Closed	1992	30.00	36
1991	Bubba Beach-August 3461	Closed	1992	34.00	41
1992	Carrotman-January 3619	Closed	1993	30.00	40
1991	Chilly Snowman-January 3443	Closed	1992	33.00	40
1992	Cookie-July 3638	Closed	1993	34.00	34
1991	Crumb on Stool-September 3463	Closed	1992	32.00	39
1992	Cupcake-November 3649	Closed	[illegible]	[illegible]	40
1991	Cupcake-Thanksgiving 3470	Closed	1993	36.00	36
1991	Emily-Springtime May 3452	Closed	1992	53.00	60
1992	Ethan Angel-August 3641	Closed	1993	46.00	60
1991	Gideon-Springtime May 3453	Closed	1992	40.00	43
1991	Hewett w/Leprechaun-March 3448	Closed	1992	56.00	67
1991	Noah w/Pot of Gold-March 3447	Closed	1992	36.00	43
1991	Pansy Beach-August 3459	Closed	1992	34.00	41
1991	Papa Barney & Biff-July 3458	Closed	1992	64.00	76
1991	Sally Booba Graduation-June 3454	Closed	1992	45.00	50
1991	Shelby w/Shamrock-March 3446	Closed	1992	36.00	43
1991	Tillie-January 3441	Closed	1992	32.00	40
1991	Willie-January 3442	Closed	1992	32.00	40

Sebastian Studios

Large Ceramastone Figures - P.W. Baston

YEAR ISSUE		EDITION LIMIT	YEAR RETD.	ISSUE PRICE	*QUOTE U.S.$
1963	Abraham Lincoln Toby Jug	Closed	N/A	Unkn.	600-1000
1963	Anne Boleyn	Closed	N/A	Unkn.	600-1000
1940	Basket	Closed	N/A	Unkn.	300-400
1973	Blacksmith	Closed	N/A	Unkn.	300-400
1940	Breton Man	Closed	N/A	Unkn.	1000-1500
1940	Breton Woman	Closed	N/A	Unkn.	1000-1500
1973	Cabinetmaker	Closed	N/A	Unkn.	300-400
1940	Candle Holder	Closed	N/A	Unkn.	300-400
1940	Caroler	Closed	N/A	Unkn.	300-400
1973	Clockmaker	Closed	N/A	Unkn.	600-1000
1964	Colonial Boy	Closed	N/A	Unkn.	600-1000
1964	Colonial Girl	Closed	N/A	Unkn.	600-1000
1964	Colonial Man	Closed	N/A	Unkn.	600-1000
1964	Colonial Woman	Closed	N/A	Unkn.	600-1000
1963	David Copperfield	Closed	N/A	Unkn.	600-1000
1965	The Dentist	Closed	N/A	Unkn.	600-1000
1963	Dora	Closed	N/A	Unkn.	600-1000
1963	George Washington Toby Jug	Closed	N/A	Unkn.	600-1000
1966	Guitarist	Closed	N/A	Unkn.	600-1000
1963	Henry VIII	Closed	N/A	Unkn.	600-1000
1940	Horn of Plenty	Closed	N/A	Unkn.	300-400
1964	IBM Father	Closed	N/A	Unkn.	600-1000
1964	IBM Mother	Closed	N/A	Unkn.	600-1000
1964	IBM Photographer	Closed	N/A	Unkn.	600-1000
1964	IBM Son	Closed	N/A	Unkn.	600-1000
1964	IBM Woman	Closed	N/A	Unkn.	600-1000
1967	Infant of Prague	Closed	N/A	Unkn.	600-1000
1956	Jell-O Cow Milk Pitcher	Closed	N/A	Unkn.	175-225
1940	Jesus	Closed	N/A	Unkn.	300-400
1963	John F. Kennedy Toby Jug	Closed	N/A	Unkn.	600-1000
1940	Lamb	Closed	N/A	Unkn.	300-400
1947	Large Victorian Couple	Closed	N/A	Unkn.	600-1000
1940	Mary	Closed	N/A	Unkn.	600-1000
1963	Mending Time	Closed	N/A	Unkn.	600-1000
1975	Minuteman	Closed	N/A	Unkn.	600-1000
1978	Mt. Rushmore	Closed	N/A	Unkn.	400-500
1965	N.E. Home For Little Wanderers	Closed	N/A	Unkn.	600-1000
1939	Paul Revere Plaque	Closed	N/A	Unkn.	400-500

*Quotes have been rounded up to nearest dollar

Collectors' Information Bureau

119

Sebastian Studios
to Shenandoah Designs

FIGURINES

YEAR ISSUE		EDITION LIMIT	YEAR RETD.	ISSUE PRICE	*QUOTE U.S. $
1973	Potter	Closed	N/A	Unkn.	300-400
XX	Santa Fe...All The Way	Closed	N/A	Unkn.	600-1000
XX	St. Francis (Plaque)	Closed	N/A	Unkn.	600-1000
1965	Stanley Music Box	Closed	N/A	Unkn.	300-500
1958	Swift Instrument Girl	Closed	N/A	Unkn.	500-750
1963	Tom Sawyer	Closed	N/A	Unkn.	600-1000
1959	Wasp Plaque	Closed	N/A	Unkn.	500-750
1948	Woody at Three	Closed	N/A	Unkn.	600-1000

Sebastian Miniatures - P.W. Baston

YEAR ISSUE		EDITION LIMIT	YEAR RETD.	ISSUE PRICE	*QUOTE U.S. $
1956	77th Bengal Lancer (Jell-O)	Closed	N/A	Unkn.	600-1000
1942	Accordion	Closed	N/A	Unkn.	325-375
1952	Aerial Tramway	Closed	N/A	Unkn.	300-600
1959	Alcoa Wrap PS	Closed	N/A	Unkn.	350-400
1959	Alexander Smith Weaver	Closed	N/A	Unkn.	350-425
1956	Alike, But Oh So Different	Closed	N/A	Unkn.	300-350
1957	Along the Albany Road PS	Closed	N/A	Unkn.	600-1000
1940	Ann Stvyvesant	Closed	N/A	Unkn.	75-100
1940	Annie Oakley	Closed	N/A	Unkn.	75-100
1956	Arthritic Hands (J & J)	Closed	N/A	Unkn.	600-1000
XX	Babe Ruth	Closed	N/A	Unkn.	600-1000
1952	Baby (Jell-O)	Closed	N/A	Unkn.	525-600
1939	Benjamin Franklin	Closed	N/A	Unkn.	75-100
1962	Big Brother Bob Emery	Closed	N/A	Unkn.	600-1000
1953	Blessed Julie Billart	Closed	N/A	Unkn.	400-500
1962	Blue Belle Highlander	Closed	N/A	Unkn.	200-250
1954	Bluebird Girl	Closed	N/A	Unkn.	400-450
XX	Bob Hope	Closed	N/A	Unkn.	600-1000
1957	Borden's Centennial (Elsie the Cow)	Closed	N/A	Unkn.	600-1000
1971	Boston Gas Tank	Closed	N/A	Unkn.	300-500
1953	Boy Jesus in the Temple	Closed	N/A	Unkn.	350-400
1949	Boy Scout Plaque	Closed	N/A	Unkn.	300-350
1940	Buffalo Bill	Closed	N/A	Unkn.	75-100
1961	Bunky Knudsen	Closed	N/A	Unkn.	600-1000
1954	Campfire Girl	Closed	N/A	Unkn.	400-450
1955	Captain Doliber	Closed	N/A	Unkn.	300-350
1968	Captain John Parker	Closed	N/A	Unkn.	300-350
1951	Carl Moore (WEEI)	Closed	N/A	Unkn.	200-300
1951	Caroline Cabot (WEEI)	Closed	N/A	Unkn.	200-350
1940	Catherine LaFitte	Closed	N/A	Unkn.	75-100
1958	CBS Miss Columbia PS	Closed	N/A	Unkn.	600-1000
1951	Charles Ashley (WEEI)	Closed	N/A	Unkn.	200-350
1951	Chief Pontiac	Closed	N/A	Unkn.	400-700
1951	Chiquita Banana	Closed	N/A	Unkn.	350-400
1951	Christopher Columbus	Closed	N/A	Unkn.	250-300
1958	Cliquot Club Eskimo PS	Closed	N/A	Unkn.	10-2300
1957	Colonial Fund Doorway PS	Closed	N/A	Unkn.	600-1000
1958	Commodore Stephen Decatur	Closed	N/A	Unkn.	125-175
1958	Connecticut Bank & Trust	Closed	N/A	Unkn.	225-275
1939	Coronado	Closed	N/A	Unkn.	75-100
1939	Coronado's Senora	Closed	N/A	Unkn.	75-100
XX	Coronation Crown	Closed	N/A	Unkn.	600-1000
1942	Cymbals	Closed	N/A	Unkn.	325-375
1954	Dachshund (Audiovox)	Closed	N/A	Unkn.	300-350
1947	Dahl's Fisherman	Closed	N/A	Unkn.	150-175
1940	Dan'l Boone	Closed	N/A	Unkn.	75-100
1953	Darned Well He Can	Closed	N/A	Unkn.	300-350
1955	Davy Crockett	Closed	N/A	Unkn.	225-275
1939	Deborah Franklin	Closed	N/A	Unkn.	75-100
1948	Democratic Victory	Closed	N/A	Unkn.	350-500
1963	Dia-Mel Fat Man	Closed	N/A	Unkn.	375-400
1947	Dilemma	Closed	N/A	Unkn.	275-300
1967	Doc Berry of Berwick (yellow shirt)	Closed	N/A	Unkn.	300-350
1941	Doves	Closed	N/A	Unkn.	600-1000
1947	Down East	Closed	N/A	Unkn.	125-150
1942	Drum	Closed	N/A	Unkn.	325-375
1941	Ducklings	Closed	N/A	Unkn.	600-1000
1949	Dutchman's Pipe	Closed	N/A	Unkn.	175-225
1951	E. B. Rideout (WEEI)	Closed	N/A	Unkn.	200-350
XX	Eagle Plaque	Closed	N/A	Unkn.	1000-1500
1956	Eastern Paper Plaque	Closed	N/A	Unkn.	350-400
1940	Elizabeth Monroe	Closed	N/A	Unkn.	150-175
1956	Elsie the Cow Billboard	Closed	N/A	Unkn.	600-1000
1949	Emmett Kelly	Closed	N/A	Unkn.	200-300
1949	Eustace Tilly	Closed	N/A	Unkn.	750-1500
1939	Evangeline	Closed	N/A	Unkn.	100-125
1952	The Fat Man (Jell-O)	Closed	N/A	Unkn.	525-600
1952	The Favored Scholar	Closed	N/A	Unkn.	200-300
1959	Fiorello LaGuardia	Closed	N/A	Unkn.	125-175
1947	First Cookbook Author	Closed	N/A	Unkn.	125-150
1952	The First House, Plimoth Plantation	Closed	N/A	Unkn.	150-195
1947	Fisher Pair PS	Closed	N/A	Unkn.	400-1000
1959	Fleischman's Margarine PS	Closed	N/A	Unkn.	225-325
1939	Gabriel	Closed	N/A	Unkn.	100-125
1966	Gardener Man	Closed	N/A	Unkn.	250-300
1966	Gardener Women	Closed	N/A	Unkn.	250-300
1966	Gardeners (Thermometer)	Closed	N/A	Unkn.	300-400
1949	Gathering Tulips	Closed	N/A	Unkn.	225-250
1972	George & Hatchet	Closed	N/A	Unkn.	400-450
1939	George Washington	Closed	N/A	Unkn.	35-75
1949	Giant Royal Bengal Tiger	Closed	N/A	Unkn.	1000-1500
1959	Giovanni Verrazzano	Closed	N/A	Unkn.	125-175
1955	Giraffe (Jell-O)	Closed	N/A	Unkn.	350-375
1956	Girl on Diving Board	Closed	N/A	Unkn.	400-450
1951	Great Stone Face	Closed	N/A	Unkn.	600-1000
1956	The Green Giant	Closed	N/A	Unkn.	400-500
1959	H.P. Hood Co. Cigar Store Indian	Closed	N/A	Unkn.	600-1000
1958	Hannah Duston PS	Closed	N/A	Unkn.	250-325
1940	Hannah Penn	Closed	N/A	Unkn.	100-150
1959	Harvard Trust Co. Town Crier	Closed	N/A	Unkn.	350-400
1958	Harvard Trust Colonial Man	Closed	N/A	Unkn.	275-325
1948	A Harvey Girl	Closed	N/A	Unkn.	250-300
1959	Henry Hudson	Closed	N/A	Unkn.	125-175
1965	Henry Wadsworth Longfellow	Closed	N/A	Unkn.	275-325
1953	Holgrave the Daguerrotypist	Closed	N/A	Unkn.	200-250
1954	Horizon Girl	Closed	N/A	Unkn.	400-450
1942	Horn	Closed	N/A	Unkn.	325-375
1955	Horse Head PS	Closed	N/A	Unkn.	350-375
1947	Howard Johnson Pieman	Closed	N/A	Unkn.	300-450
1957	IBM 305 Ramac	Closed	N/A	Unkn.	400-450
1939	Indian Maiden	Closed	N/A	Unkn.	100-125
1939	Indian Warrior	Closed	N/A	Unkn.	100-125
1960	The Infantryman	Closed	N/A	Unkn.	600-1000
1951	The Iron Master's House	Closed	N/A	Unkn.	350-500
1958	Jackie Gleason	Closed	N/A	Unkn.	600-1000
1963	Jackie Kennedy Toby Jug	Closed	N/A	Unkn.	600-1000
1940	James Monroe	Closed	N/A	Unkn.	150-175
1957	Jamestown Church	Closed	N/A	Unkn.	400-450
1957	Jamestown Ships	Closed	N/A	Unkn.	350-475
1940	Jean LaFitte	Closed	N/A	Unkn.	75-100
1951	Jesse Buffman (WEEI)	Closed	N/A	Unkn.	200-350
1939	John Alden	Closed	N/A	Unkn.	35-50
1963	John F. Kennedy Toby Jug	Closed	N/A	Unkn.	600-1000
1940	John Harvard	Closed	N/A	Unkn.	125-150
1940	John Smith	Closed	N/A	Unkn.	75-150
1958	Jordan Marsh Observer	Closed	N/A	Unkn.	175-275
1948	Jordan Marsh Observer	Closed	N/A	Unkn.	150-175
1951	Jordon Marsh Observer Rides the A.W. Horse	Closed	N/A	Unkn.	300-325
1951	Judge Pyncheon	Closed	N/A	Unkn.	175-225
1954	Kernel-Fresh Ashtray	Closed	N/A	Unkn.	400-450
XX	The King	Closed	N/A	Unkn.	600-1000
1941	Kitten (Sitting)	Closed	N/A	Unkn.	600-1000
1941	Kitten (Sleeping)	Closed	N/A	Unkn.	600-1000
1953	Lion (Jell-O)	Closed	N/A	Unkn.	350-375
1966	Little George	Closed	N/A	Unkn.	350-450
1952	Lost in the Kitchen (Jell-O)	Closed	N/A	Unkn.	350-375
1942	Majorette	Closed	N/A	Unkn.	325-375
1952	Marblehead High School Plaque	Closed	N/A	Unkn.	200-300
1939	Margaret Houston	Closed	N/A	Unkn.	75-100
1960	Marine Memorial	Closed	N/A	Unkn.	300-400
1949	The Mark Twain Home in Hannibal, MO	Closed	N/A	Unkn.	600-1000
1972	Martha & the Cherry Pie	Closed	N/A	Unkn.	350-400
1939	Martha Washington	Closed	N/A	Unkn.	35-75
1948	Mary Lyon	Closed	N/A	Unkn.	250-300
1960	Masonic Bible	Closed	N/A	Unkn.	300-400
1966	Massachusetts SPCA	Closed	N/A	Unkn.	250-350
1957	Mayflower PS	Closed	N/A	Unkn.	300-325
1949	Menotomy Indian	Closed	N/A	Unkn.	175-250
1961	Merchant's Warren Sea Capt.	Closed	N/A	Unkn.	200-250
1960	Metropolitan Life Tower PS	Closed	N/A	Unkn.	350-400
1956	Michigan Millers PS	Closed	N/A	Unkn.	200-275
1951	Mit Seal	Closed	N/A	Unkn.	350-425
1954	Moose (Jell-O)	Closed	N/A	Unkn.	350-375
1951	Mother Parker (WEEI)	Closed	N/A	Unkn.	200-350
1947	Mr. Beacon Hill	Closed	N/A	Unkn.	50-75
1950	Mr. Obocell	Closed	N/A	Unkn.	75-125
1948	Mr. Rittenhouse Square	Closed	N/A	Unkn.	150-175
1948	Mr. Sheraton	Closed	N/A	Unkn.	400-500
1947	Mrs. Beacon Hill	Closed	N/A	Unkn.	50-75
1940	Mrs. Dan'l Boone	Closed	N/A	Unkn.	75-100
1940	Mrs. Harvard	Closed	N/A	Unkn.	125-150
1956	Mrs. Obocell	Closed	N/A	Unkn.	400-450
1948	Mrs. Rittenhouse Square	Closed	N/A	Unkn.	150-175
1959	Mrs. S.O.S.	Closed	N/A	Unkn.	300-350
1958	Mt. Vernon	Closed	N/A	Unkn.	400-500
1957	Nabisco Buffalo Bee	Closed	N/A	Unkn.	600-1000
1957	Nabisco Spoonmen	Closed	N/A	Unkn.	600-1000
1948	Nathaniel Hawthorne	Closed	N/A	Unkn.	175-200
1950	National Diaper Service	Closed	N/A	Unkn.	250-300
1963	Naumkeag Indian	Closed	N/A	Unkn.	225-275
1952	Neighboring Pews	Closed	N/A	Unkn.	200-300
1956	NYU Grad School of Bus. Admin. Bldg.	Closed	N/A	Unkn.	300-350
1951	The Observer & Dame New England	Closed	N/A	Unkn.	325-375
1952	Old Powder House	Closed	N/A	Unkn.	250-300
1953	Old Put Enjoys a Licking	Closed	N/A	Unkn.	300-350
1955	Old Woman in the Shoe (Jell-O)	Closed	N/A	Unkn.	500-600
1957	Olde James Fort	Closed	N/A	Unkn.	250-300
XX	Ortho Gynecic	Closed	N/A	Unkn.	600-1000
1967	Ortho-Novum	Closed	N/A	Unkn.	600-1000
1952	Our Lady of Good Voyage	Closed	N/A	Unkn.	200-250
1954	Our Lady of Laleche	Closed	N/A	Unkn.	300-350
1965	Panti-Legs Girl PS	Closed	N/A	Unkn.	250-300
1949	Patrick Henry	Closed	N/A	Unkn.	100-125
1949	Paul Bunyan	Closed	N/A	Unkn.	150-250
1966	Paul Revere Plaque (W.T. Grant)	Closed	N/A	Unkn.	300-350
1941	Peacock	Closed	N/A	Unkn.	600-1000
1956	Permacel Tower of Tape Ashtray	Closed	N/A	Unkn.	600-1000
1960	Peter Stvyvesant	Closed	N/A	Unkn.	125-175
1940	Peter Stvyvesant	Closed	N/A	Unkn.	75-100
1941	Pheasant	Closed	N/A	Unkn.	600-1000
1950	Phoebe, House of 7 Gables	Closed	N/A	Unkn.	150-175
1940	Pocohontas	Closed	N/A	Unkn.	75-150
1961	Pope John 23rd	Closed	N/A	Unkn.	400-450
1965	Pope Paul VI	Closed	N/A	Unkn.	400-500
1956	Praying Hands	Closed	N/A	Unkn.	250-300
1947	Prince Philip	Closed	N/A	Unkn.	200-300
1947	Princess Elizabeth	Closed	N/A	Unkn.	200-300
1939	Priscilla	Closed	N/A	Unkn.	35-50
1951	Priscilla Fortesue (WEEI)	Closed	N/A	Unkn.	200-350
1946	Puritan Spinner	Closed	N/A	Unkn.	500-1000
1953	R.H. Stearns Chestnut Hill Mall	Closed	N/A	Unkn.	225-275
1954	Rabbit (Jell-O)	Closed	N/A	Unkn.	350-375
1956	Rarical Blacksmith	Closed	N/A	Unkn.	300-500
1948	Republican Victory	Closed	N/A	Unkn.	600-1000
1954	Resolute Ins. Co. Clipper PS	Closed	N/A	Unkn.	300-325
1956	Robin Hood & Friar Tuck	Closed	N/A	Unkn.	400-500
1956	Robin Hood & Little John	Closed	N/A	Unkn.	400-500
1958	Romeo & Juliet	Closed	N/A	Unkn.	400-500
1941	Rooster	Closed	N/A	Unkn.	600-1000
1958	Salem Savings Bank	Closed	N/A	Unkn.	250-300
1939	Sam Houston	Closed	N/A	Unkn.	75-100
1955	Santa (Jell-O)	Closed	N/A	Unkn.	500-600
1949	Sarah Henry	Closed	N/A	Unkn.	100-125
1946	Satchel-Eye Dyer	Closed	N/A	Unkn.	125-150
1953	The Schoolboy of 1850	Closed	N/A	Unkn.	350-400
1952	Scottish Girl (Jell-O)	Closed	N/A	Unkn.	350-375
1954	Scuba Diver	Closed	N/A	Unkn.	400-450
1962	Seaman's Bank for Savings	Closed	N/A	Unkn.	300-350
1951	Seb. Dealer Plaque (Marblehead)	Closed	N/A	Unkn.	300-350
1955	Second Bank-State St. Trust PS	Closed	N/A	Unkn.	300-325
1941	Secrets	Closed	N/A	Unkn.	600-1000
1938	Shaker Lady	Closed	N/A	Unkn.	50-100
1938	Shaker Man	Closed	N/A	Unkn.	50-100
1959	Siesta Coffee PS	Closed	N/A	Unkn.	600-1000
1951	Sir Frances Drake	Closed	N/A	Unkn.	250-300
1948	Sitzmark	Closed	N/A	Unkn.	175-200
1948	Slalom	Closed	N/A	Unkn.	175-200
1960	Son of the Desert	Closed	N/A	Unkn.	200-275
1957	Speedy Alka Seltzer	Closed	N/A	Unkn.	600-1000
1952	St. Joan d'Arc	Closed	N/A	Unkn.	300-350
1961	St. Jude Thaddeus	Closed	N/A	Unkn.	400-500
1954	St. Pius X	Closed	N/A	Unkn.	400-475
1952	St. Sebastian	Closed	N/A	Unkn.	300-350
1953	St. Teresa of Lisieux	Closed	N/A	Unkn.	225-275
1965	State Street Bank Globe	Closed	N/A	Unkn.	250-300
1954	Stimalose (Men)	Closed	N/A	Unkn.	600-1000
1954	Stimalose (Woman)	Closed	N/A	Unkn.	175-200
1952	Stork (Jell-O)	Closed	N/A	Unkn.	425-525
1960	Supp-Hose Lady	Closed	N/A	Unkn.	300-500
1941	Swan	Closed	N/A	Unkn.	600-1000
1954	Swan Boat Brooch-Enpty Seats	Closed	N/A	Unkn.	600-1000
1954	Swan Boat Brooch-Full Seats	Closed	N/A	Unkn.	600-1000
1948	Swedish Boy	Closed	N/A	Unkn.	250-500
1948	Swedish Girl	Closed	N/A	Unkn.	250-500
XX	Sylvania Electric-Bulb Display	Closed	N/A	Unkn.	600-1000
1952	Tabasco Sauce	Closed	N/A	Unkn.	400-500
1956	Texcel Tape Boy	Closed	N/A	Unkn.	350-425
1949	The Thinker	Closed	N/A	Unkn.	175-250
1956	Three Little Kittens (Jell-O)	Closed	N/A	Unkn.	375-400
1947	Tollhouse Town Crier	Closed	N/A	Unkn.	125-175
1961	Tony Piet	Closed	N/A	Unkn.	600-1000
1966	Town Lyne Indian	Closed	N/A	Unkn.	600-1000
1971	Town Meeting Plaque	Closed	N/A	Unkn.	350-400
1942	Tuba	Closed	N/A	Unkn.	325-375
1949	Uncle Mistletoe	Closed	N/A	Unkn.	250-300
1970	Uncle Sam in Orbit	Closed	N/A	Unkn.	350-400
1968	Watermill Candy Plaque	Closed	N/A	Unkn.	600-1000
1952	Weighing the Baby	Closed	N/A	Unkn.	200-300
1954	Whale (Jell-O)	Closed	N/A	Unkn.	350-375
1954	William Penn	Closed	N/A	Unkn.	175-225
1940	William Penn	Closed	N/A	Unkn.	100-150
1939	Williamsburg Governor	Closed	N/A	Unkn.	75-100
1939	Williamsburg Lady	Closed	N/A	Unkn.	75-100
1962	Yankee Clipper Sulfide	Closed	N/A	Unkn.	600-1000

Seymour Mann, Inc.

Christmas Collection - Various

YEAR ISSUE		EDITION LIMIT	YEAR RETD.	ISSUE PRICE	*QUOTE U.S. $
1991	Reindeer Barn Lite Up House CJ-421 - Jaimy	Closed	1993	55.00	55

Doll Art™ Collection - E. Mann

YEAR ISSUE		EDITION LIMIT	YEAR RETD.	ISSUE PRICE	*QUOTE U.S. $
1996	Hope CLT-604P	25,000		30.00	30

Wizard Of Oz - 40th Anniversary - E. Mann

YEAR ISSUE		EDITION LIMIT	YEAR RETD.	ISSUE PRICE	*QUOTE U.S. $
1979	Dorothy, Scarecrow, Lion, Tinman	Closed	1981	7.50	45
1979	Dorothy, Scarecrow, Lion, Tinman, Musical	Closed	1981	12.50	75

Shenandoah Designs

Keeper Klub - Shenandoah Design Team

YEAR ISSUE		EDITION LIMIT	YEAR RETD.	ISSUE PRICE	*QUOTE U.S. $
1996	Keeper of Collectors	Yr.Iss.		35.00	35
1996	Keeper Shelf	Yr.Iss.		Gift	N/A

Christmas Keeper Series - Shenandoah Design Team

YEAR ISSUE		EDITION LIMIT	YEAR RETD.	ISSUE PRICE	*QUOTE U.S. $
1995	Keeper of Christmas 1995	6,000	1995	39.95	85-150
1996	Keeper of Christmas 1996	6,000	1996	39.95	45-75
1997	Keeper of Christmas 1997	6,000		39.95	40

D. Morgans - Shenandoah Design Team

YEAR ISSUE		EDITION LIMIT	YEAR RETD.	ISSUE PRICE	*QUOTE U.S. $
1996	Father Christmas	6,000		99.95	100
1996	Magic Never Ends	6,000		99.95	100
1996	St. Nicholas	6,000		99.95	100
1996	Accessory Group, set/3	2,000		70.00	70

*Quotes have been rounded up to nearest dollar

Keeper Series #1 - Shenandoah Design Team

YEAR ISSUE		EDITION LIMIT	YEAR RETD.	ISSUE PRICE	*QUOTE U.S.$
1993	Keeper of The Bath	Open		29.95	30
1993	Keeper of The Bedchamber	Open		29.95	30
1993	Keeper of The Entry	Open		29.95	30
1993	Keeper of The Hearth	Open		29.95	30
1993	Keeper of The Kitchen	Retrd.	1997	29.95	30
1993	Keeper of The Laundry	Open		29.95	30
1993	Keeper of The Library	Retrd.	1996	29.95	45-50
1993	Keeper of The Nursery	Open		29.95	30

Keeper Series #2 - Shenandoah Design Team

YEAR ISSUE		EDITION LIMIT	YEAR RETD.	ISSUE PRICE	*QUOTE U.S.$
1994	Keeper of The Cowboy Spirit	Open		29.95	30
1994	Keeper of The Home Office	Open		29.95	30
1994	Keeper of The Home Workshop	Open		29.95	30
1994	Keeper of Love	Open		29.95	30
1994	Keeper of Mothers	Retrd.	1997	29.95	30
1994	Keeper of Native Americans	Retrd.	1996	29.95	45-50
1994	Keeper of The Sunroom	Open		29.95	30
1994	Keeper of The Time	Open		29.95	30

Keeper Series #3 - Shenandoah Design Team

YEAR ISSUE		EDITION LIMIT	YEAR RETD.	ISSUE PRICE	*QUOTE U.S.$
1995	Keeper of Bears	Open		29.95	30
1995	Keeper of The Catch	Open		29.95	30
1995	Keeper of Fathers	Open		29.95	30
1995	Keeper of Flight	Open		29.95	30
1995	Keeper of Rails	Open		29.95	30
1995	Keeper of Thanksgiving	Open		29.95	30

Keeper Series #4 - Shenandoah Design Team

YEAR ISSUE		EDITION LIMIT	YEAR RETD.	ISSUE PRICE	*QUOTE U.S.$
1995	Keeper of Birthdays	Open		29.95	30
1995	Keeper of Faith	Open		29.95	30
1995	Keeper of Firefighters	Open		29.95	30
1995	Keeper of The Garden	Open		29.95	30
1995	Keeper of Golfing	Open		29.95	30
1995	Keeper of Music	Open		29.95	30
1995	Keeper of The Sea	Open		29.95	30
1995	Keeper of Trails	Open		29.95	30
1995	Keeper of Woodland Animals	Open		29.95	30

Keeper Series #5 - Shenandoah Design Team

YEAR ISSUE		EDITION LIMIT	YEAR RETD.	ISSUE PRICE	*QUOTE U.S.$
1996	Keeper of The Checkered Flag	Open		29.95	30
1996	Keeper of Friendship	Open		29.95	30
1996	Keeper of Peace	Open		29.95	30
1996	Keeper of Photography	Open		29.95	30
1996	Keeper of Secrets	Open		29.95	30
1996	Keeper of Teachers	Open		29.95	30

Keeper Series #6 - Shenandoah Design Team

YEAR ISSUE		EDITION LIMIT	YEAR RETD.	ISSUE PRICE	*QUOTE U.S.$
1997	Keeper of Cats	Open		29.95	30
1997	Keeper of The Crown Jewels	6,000		39.95	40
1997	Keeper of The Galaxy	Open		29.95	30
1997	Keeper of Halloween	3,500		45.00	45
1997	Keeper of Pubs	Open		29.95	30

Leapers - Shenandoah Design Team

YEAR ISSUE		EDITION LIMIT	YEAR RETD.	ISSUE PRICE	*QUOTE U.S.$
1997	Kiss a Leaper	6,000		49.50	50
1997	Leap of Faith	6,000		49.50	50
1997	Leaper Went A-Courtin'	6,000		49.50	50
1997	Learn and Leap	6,000		49.50	50
1997	To Leap or Not to Leap	6,000		49.50	50
1997	To Leap...To Dream	6,000		49.50	50

Limbies - Shenandoah Design Team

YEAR ISSUE		EDITION LIMIT	YEAR RETD.	ISSUE PRICE	*QUOTE U.S.$
1997	Bruno	6,000		39.95	40
1997	First Bear	6,000		39.95	40
1997	Grace	6,000		39.95	40
1997	Guitarist	6,000		39.95	40
1997	Queen	6,000		39.95	40
1997	Zeus	6,000		49.50	50

Shube's Manufacturing, Inc.

Fantasy - Various

YEAR ISSUE		EDITION LIMIT	YEAR RETD.	ISSUE PRICE	*QUOTE U.S.$
1992	Behold - P. Sedlow	2,500		280.00	280
1987	Castle - N/A	Retrd.	1992	N/A	N/A
1992	Crystal Fortress - Sedlow/Wimberly	2,500		480.00	480
1987	Dragon - N/A	Retrd.	1992	N/A	N/A
1991	Dragon Lord - P. Sedlow	4,500		330.00	330
1991	Guardian of the Crystal - D. Wimberly	2,500		870.00	870
1990	Immortal Power - R. Gonzales	3,500		280.00	280
1991	Keeper of the Fire Lamp - P. Sedlow	4,500		330.00	330
1992	Pinnacle - P. Sedlow	Retrd.	1995	280.00	280
1991	Winged Splendor - P. Sedlow	4,500		420.00	420
1989	Wizard - N/A	Retrd.	1992	N/A	N/A
1991	Wizards Spell - P. Sedlow	4,500		330.00	330

Frontier - P. Sedlow

YEAR ISSUE		EDITION LIMIT	YEAR RETD.	ISSUE PRICE	*QUOTE U.S.$
1991	High Desert Ambush	Retrd.	1995	550.00	550
1991	Summit Confrontation	Retrd.	1995	480.00	480

Limited Edition Figurine - N/A

YEAR ISSUE		EDITION LIMIT	YEAR RETD.	ISSUE PRICE	*QUOTE U.S.$
1990	Entrancing Carousel	4,500		240.00	240

Wildlife - Various

YEAR ISSUE		EDITION LIMIT	YEAR RETD.	ISSUE PRICE	*QUOTE U.S.$
1990	American Eagle - D. Wimberly	S/O	1995	430.00	430
1990	Bugling Monarch (diamond cut) - D. Wimberly	4,500		280.00	280
1990	Bugling Monarch - D. Wimberly	4,500		240.00	240
1993	Catch of the Day (classic pewter) - P. Sedlow	450		240.00	240
1993	Catch of the Day (diamond cut) - P. Sedlow	2,500		330.00	330
1993	Catch of the Day - P. Sedlow	2,500		280.00	280
1991	Dancers of the Land (diamond cut) - D. Wimberly	4,500		480.00	480
1991	Dancers of the Land - D. Wimberly	4,500		430.00	430
1990	Duel - P. Sedlow	Retrd.	1995	280.00	280
1990	Family Frolic - H. Freidland	Retrd.	1992	N/A	N/A
1993	Freedom's Cry (classic pewter) - P. Sedlow	450		280.00	280
1993	Freedom's Cry (diamond cut) - P. Sedlow	1,800		380.00	380
1993	Freedom's Cry - P. Sedlow	1,800		330.00	330
1994	Lobo - P. Sedlow	750		240.00	240
1990	Master of the Night - P. Sedlow	Retrd.	1995	330.00	330
1991	Morning Soliitude - D. Wimberly	Retrd.	1995	330.00	330
1993	Night Song (diamond cut) - P. Sedlow	1,800		430.00	430
1993	Night Song - P. Sedlow	1,800		380.00	380
1993	Soaring Spirit (classic pewter) - D. Wimberly	450		330.00	330
1993	Soaring Spirit (diamond cut) - D. Wimberly	1,800		430.00	430
1993	Soaring Spirit - D. Wimberly	1,800		380.00	380
1990	Unbridled Majesty - P. Sedlow	Retrd.	1992	N/A	N/A
1993	Warhorse (diamond cut) - P. Sedlow	1,800		430.00	430
1993	Warhorse - P. Sedlow	1,800		380.00	380

Sports Impressions/Enesco Corporation

Collectors' Club Members Only - Various

YEAR ISSUE		EDITION LIMIT	YEAR RETD.	ISSUE PRICE	*QUOTE U.S.$
1990	The Mick-Mickey Mantle 5000-1	Yr.Iss.	N/A	75.00	75-100
1991	Rickey Henderson-Born to Run 5001-11	Yr.Iss.	N/A	49.95	50
1991	Nolan Ryan-300 Wins 5002-01	Yr.Iss.	N/A	125.00	125
1991	Willie, Mickey & Duke plate 5003-04	Yr.Iss.	N/A	39.95	50
1992	Babe Ruth 5006-11	Yr.Iss.	N/A	40.00	40
1992	Walter Payton 5015-01	Yr.Iss.	N/A	50.00	50
1993	The 1927 Yankees plate - R.Tanenbaum	Yr.Iss.	N/A	60.00	60

Collectors' Club Symbol of Membership - Sports Impressions

YEAR ISSUE		EDITION LIMIT	YEAR RETD.	ISSUE PRICE	*QUOTE U.S.$
1991	Mick/7 plate 5001-02	Yr.Iss.	N/A	Gift	25-50
1992	USA Basketball team plate 5008-30	Yr.Iss.	N/A	Gift	25
1993	Nolan Ryan porcelain card	Yr.Iss.	N/A	Gift	25

Baseball Superstar Figurines - Sports Impressions

YEAR ISSUE		EDITION LIMIT	YEAR RETD.	ISSUE PRICE	*QUOTE U.S.$
1988	Al Kaline	2,500	N/A	90.00	90
1988	Andre Dawson	2,500	N/A	90.00	90
1988	Bob Feller	2,500	N/A	90.00	90
1992	Cubs Ryne Sandberg Home 1118-23	975	1993	150.00	175
1987	Don Mattingly	Closed	N/A	90.00	250
1987	Don Mattingly (Franklin glove variation)	Closed	N/A	90.00	400-500
1989	Duke Snider	2,500	N/A	90.00	90
1994	Giants Barry Bonds (signed) 1160-46	975	1995	150.00	150
1992	Johnny Bench (hand signed) 1126-23	975	1994	150.00	175
1988	Jose Canseco	Closed	N/A	90.00	125
1987	Keith Hernandez	2,500	N/A	90.00	90
1989	Kirk Gibson	Closed	N/A	90.00	90
1987	Mickey Mantle	Closed	N/A	90.00	100-150
1996	Mickey Mantle "The Greatest Switch Hitter" (hand signed) 1228-46 - T. Treadway	975	1995	395.00	500-875
1990	Nolan Ryan	Closed	N/A	50.00	300
1992	Nolan Ryan Figurine/plate/stand 1134-31	500	1994	260.00	260
1990	Nolan Ryan Kings of K	Closed	N/A	125.00	125
1990	Nolan Ryan Mini	Closed	N/A	50.00	50
1990	Nolan Ryan Supersize	Closed	N/A	250.00	250
1993	Oakland A's Reggie Jackson (signed) 1048-46	975	1994	150.00	275
1993	Rangers Nolan Ryan (signed) 1127-46	975	1994	175.00	225-250
1994	Rangers Nolan Ryan (signed) Farewell 1161-49	975	1994	150.00	250
1990	Ted Williams	Closed	N/A	90.00	100-250
1987	Wade Boggs	Closed	N/A	90.00	100-200
1989	Will Clark	Closed	N/A	90.00	100-200
1993	Yankees Mickey Mantle (signed) 1038-46	975	1993	195.00	350

Basketball Superstar Figurines - Sports Impressions

YEAR ISSUE		EDITION LIMIT	YEAR RETD.	ISSUE PRICE	*QUOTE U.S.$
1993	Julius Erving 76ers (hand signed) 4102-46	975	1994	150.00	150
1993	Julius Erving 76ers (hand signed) 4102-61	76	1994	295.00	295

Football Superstar Figurines - Sports Impressions

YEAR ISSUE		EDITION LIMIT	YEAR RETD.	ISSUE PRICE	*QUOTE U.S.$
1993	Gale Sayers Bears (hand signed) 3029-23	975	1994	150.00	175
1992	John Unitas Colts (hand signed) 3016-23	975	1994	150.00	150
1993	Kenny Stabler Raiders (hand signed) 3026-23	975	1994	150.00	150
1993	Walter Payton Bears (hand signed) 3028-23	975	1994	150.00	175

NASCAR - Sports Impressions

YEAR ISSUE		EDITION LIMIT	YEAR RETD.	ISSUE PRICE	*QUOTE U.S.$
1995	Bill Elliott (hand signed) 8100-46	975		150.00	150
1994	Jeff Gordon (hand signed) 8101-46	975	1995	150.00	150

Plaques - Various

YEAR ISSUE		EDITION LIMIT	YEAR RETD.	ISSUE PRICE	*QUOTE U.S.$
1995	Life of a Legend Mickey Mantle 1228-71 - T. Fogarty	Open		40.00	40
1995	Profiles in Courage Mickey Mantle 1231-62 - M. Petronella	Open		40.00	40

Swarovski America Limited

Collectors Society Editions - Various

YEAR ISSUE		EDITION LIMIT	YEAR RETD.	ISSUE PRICE	*QUOTE U.S.$
1987	Togetherness-The Lovebirds - Schreck/Stocker	Yr.Iss.	1987	150.00	3700-4600
1988	Sharing-The Woodpeckers - A. Stocker	Yr.Iss.	1988	165.00	1400-2200
1988	Mini Cactus	Yr.Iss.	1988	Gift	200-300
1989	Amour-The Turtledoves - A. Stocker	Yr.Iss.	1989	195.00	900-1200
1989	SCS Key Chain	Yr.Iss.	1989	Gift	100-125
1990	Lead Me-The Dolphins - M. Stamey	Yr.Iss.	1990	225.00	1200-1400
1990	Mini Chaton	Yr.Iss.	1990	Gift	70-140
1991	Save Me-The Seals - M. Stamey	Yr.Iss.	1991	225.00	475-575
1991	Dolphin Brooch	Yr.Iss.	1991	75.00	100-150
1991	SCS Pin	Yr.Iss.	1991	Gift	50-75
1992	Care For Me - The Whales - M. Stamey	Yr.Iss.	1992	265.00	450-600
1992	SCS Pen	Yr.Iss.	1992	Gift	50-98
1992	5th Anniversary Edition-The Birthday Cake - G. Stamey	Yr.Iss.	1992	85.00	140-225
1993	Inspiration Africa-The Elephant - M. Zendron	Yr.Iss.	1993	325.00	1200-1550
1993	Elephant Brooch	Yr.Iss.	1993	85.00	125-160
1993	Leather Luggage Tag	Yr.Iss.	1993	Gift	40-70
1994	Inspiration Africa-The Kudu - M. Stamey	Yr.Iss.	1994	295.00	440-550
1994	Leather Double Picture Frame	Yr.Iss.	1994	Gift	20-40
1995	Inspiration Africa-The Lion - A. Stocker	Yr.Iss.	1995	325.00	400-600
1995	Centenary Swan Brooch	Yr.Iss.	1995	125.00	150-225
1995	Miniature Crystal Swan	Yr.Iss.	1995	Gift	65-150
1996	Fabulous Creatures-The Unicorn - M. Zendron	Yr.Iss.	1996	325.00	375-450
1997	Fabulous Creatures-The Dragon - G. Stamey	Yr.Iss.		325.00	325
1997	SCS 10th Anniversary Edition The Squirrel - A. Hirzinger	Yr.Iss.		140.00	140

Swarovski Silver Crystal Worldwide Limited Editions - A. Stocker

YEAR ISSUE		EDITION LIMIT	YEAR RETD.	ISSUE PRICE	*QUOTE U.S.$
1995	Eagle	10,000	1995	1750.00	7500-8700

African Wildlife - Various

YEAR ISSUE		EDITION LIMIT	YEAR RETD.	ISSUE PRICE	*QUOTE U.S.$
1995	Baby Elephant - M. Zendron	Open		155.00	155
1994	Cheetah - M. Stamey	Open		275.00	275
1989	Elephant-Small - A. Stocker	Open		50.00	65

Among Flowers And Foliage - C. Schneiderbauer, unless otherwise noted

YEAR ISSUE		EDITION LIMIT	YEAR RETD.	ISSUE PRICE	*QUOTE U.S.$
1992	Bumblebee	Open		85.00	85
1994	Butterfly on Leaf	Open		75.00	85
1995	Dragonfly	Open		85.00	85
1992	Hummingbird	Open		195.00	210
1996	Snail on Vine-Leaf - E. Mair	Open		65.00	65

Barnyard Friends - Various

YEAR ISSUE		EDITION LIMIT	YEAR RETD.	ISSUE PRICE	*QUOTE U.S.$
1993	Mother Goose - A. Stocker	Open		75.00	75
1993	Tom Gosling - A. Stocker	Open		37.50	38
1993	Dick Gosling - A. Stocker	Open		37.50	38
1993	Harry Gosling - A. Stocker	Open		37.50	38
1984	Medium Pig - M. Schreck	Open		35.00	55
1988	Mini Chicks (Set/3) - G. Stamey	Open		35.00	45
1987	Mini Hen - G. Stamey	Open		35.00	45
1982	Mini Pig - M. Schreck	Open		16.00	30
1987	Mini Rooster - G. Stamey	Open		35.00	55

Beauties of the Lake - Various

YEAR ISSUE		EDITION LIMIT	YEAR RETD.	ISSUE PRICE	*QUOTE U.S.$
1983	Drake-Mini - M. Schreck	Open		20.00	45
1994	Frog - G. Stamey	Open		49.50	50
1996	Goldfish-Mini - M. Stamey	Open		45.00	45
1989	Mallard-Giant - M. Stamey	Open		2000.00	4500
1986	Standing Duck-Mini - A. Stocker	Open		22.00	38
1977	Swan-Large - M. Schreck	Open		55.00	95
1995	Swan-Maxi - A. Hirzinger	Open		4500.00	4500
1977	Swan-Medium - M. Schreck	Open		44.00	85
1989	Swan-Small - M. Schreck	Open		35.00	50
1986	Swimming Duck-Mini - A. Stocker	Open		16.00	38

Centenary Edition - A. Hirzinger

YEAR ISSUE		EDITION LIMIT	YEAR RETD.	ISSUE PRICE	*QUOTE U.S.$
1995	Centenary Swan	Yr.Iss.	1995	150.00	155-175

Commemorative Single Issues - Team

YEAR ISSUE		EDITION LIMIT	YEAR RETD.	ISSUE PRICE	*QUOTE U.S.$
1990	Elephant, 7640NR100 (Introduced by Swarovski America as a commemorative item during Design Celebration/January '90 in Walt Disney World)	Closed	1990	125.00	1000-1200
1993	Elephant, 7640NR100001 (Introduced by Swarovski America as a commemorative item during Design Celebration/January '93 in Walt Disney World)	Closed	1993	150.00	350-450

*Quotes have been rounded up to nearest dollar

Swarovski America Limited
to Swarovski America Limited

FIGURINES

Crystal Melodies - M. Zendron, unless otherwise noted

YEAR ISSUE		EDITION LIMIT	YEAR RETD.	ISSUE PRICE	*QUOTE U.S. $
1993	Grand Piano	Open		250.00	260
1992	Harp	Open		175.00	210
1992	Lute	Open		125.00	140
1996	Violin - G. Stamey	Open		140.00	140

Decorative Items For The Desk (Paperweights) - M. Schreck

YEAR ISSUE		EDITION LIMIT	YEAR RETD.	ISSUE PRICE	*QUOTE U.S. $
1990	Chaton-Giant 7433NR180000	Open		4500.00	4500
1987	Chaton-Large 7433NR80	Open		190.00	260
1987	Chaton-Small 7433NR50	Open		50.00	65
1987	Pyramid-Small Crystal Cal. 7450NR40095	Open		100.00	125
1987	Pyramid-Small Vitrail Med. 7450NR40087	Open		100.00	125

Endangered Species - Various

YEAR ISSUE		EDITION LIMIT	YEAR RETD.	ISSUE PRICE	*QUOTE U.S. $
1993	Baby Panda - A. Stocker	Open		24.50	25
1993	Mother Panda - A. Stocker	Open		120.00	125
1987	Koala - A. Stocker	Open		50.00	65
1989	Mini Koala - A. Stocker	Open		35.00	45
1992	Sitting Baby Beaver - A. Stocker	Open		47.50	50
1993	Mother Kangaroo with Baby - G. Stamey	Open		95.00	95
1981	Turtle-Giant - M. Schreck	Open		2500.00	4500
1977	Turtle-Large - M. Schreck	Open		48.00	75

Exquisite Accents - Various

YEAR ISSUE		EDITION LIMIT	YEAR RETD.	ISSUE PRICE	*QUOTE U.S. $
1995	Angel - A. Stocker	Open		210.00	210
1980	Birdbath - M. Schreck	Open		150.00	210
1996	Blue Flower Jewel Box - G. Stamey	Open		210.00	210
1996	Blue Flower Picture Frame - G. Stamey	Open		260.00	260
1987	Dinner Bell-Medium - M. Schreck	Open		80.00	95
1987	Dinner Bell-Small - M. Schreck	Open		60.00	65
1995	The Orchid-pink - M. Stamey	Open		140.00	140
1995	The Orchid-yellow - M. Stamey	Open		140.00	140
1992	The Rose - M. Stamey	Open		150.00	155
1996	Sleigh - M. Zendron	Open		295.00	295

Fairy Tales - E. Mair

YEAR ISSUE		EDITION LIMIT	YEAR RETD.	ISSUE PRICE	*QUOTE U.S. $
1996	Red Riding Hood	Open		185.00	185
1996	Wolf	Open		155.00	155

Feathered Friends - Various

YEAR ISSUE		EDITION LIMIT	YEAR RETD.	ISSUE PRICE	*QUOTE U.S. $
1995	Baby Lovebirds - A. Stocker	Open		155.00	155
1995	Dove - E. Mair	Open		55.00	55
1993	Pelican - A. Hirzinger	Open		37.50	38

Game of Kings - M. Schreck

YEAR ISSUE		EDITION LIMIT	YEAR RETD.	ISSUE PRICE	*QUOTE U.S. $
1984	Chess Set	Open		950.00	1375

Horses on Parade - M. Zendron

YEAR ISSUE		EDITION LIMIT	YEAR RETD.	ISSUE PRICE	*QUOTE U.S. $
1993	White Stallion	Open		250.00	260

In A Summer Meadow - Various

YEAR ISSUE		EDITION LIMIT	YEAR RETD.	ISSUE PRICE	*QUOTE U.S. $
1994	Field Mice (Set/3) - A. Stocker	Open		42.50	45
1991	Field Mouse - A. Stocker	Open		47.50	50
1985	Hedgehog-Medium - M. Schreck	Open		70.00	85
1987	Hedgehog-Small - M. Schreck	Open		50.00	55
1995	Ladybug - E. Mair	Open		29.50	30
1988	Mini Sitting Rabbit - A. Stocker	Open		35.00	45
1988	Mother Rabbit - A. Stocker	Open		60.00	75
1992	Sparrow - C. Schneiderbauer	Open		29.50	30
1982	Butterfly - Team	Open		44.00	85
1986	Mini Butterfly - Team	Open		16.00	45

Kingdom Of Ice And Snow - Various

YEAR ISSUE		EDITION LIMIT	YEAR RETD.	ISSUE PRICE	*QUOTE U.S. $
1986	Large Polar Bear - A. Stocker	Open		140.00	210
1996	Madame Penguin - A. Stocker	Open		85.00	85
1986	Mini Baby Seal - A. Stocker	Open		30.00	45
1984	Mini Penguin - M. Schreck	Open		16.00	38
1995	Sir Penguin - A. Stocker	Open		85.00	85

Our Candleholders - Various

YEAR ISSUE		EDITION LIMIT	YEAR RETD.	ISSUE PRICE	*QUOTE U.S. $
1996	Blue Flower - G. Stamey	Open		260.00	260
1989	Star-Medium 7600NR143001 - Team	Open		200.00	260
1985	Water Lily-Large 7600NR125 - M. Schreck	Open		200.00	375
1983	Water Lily-Medium 7600NR123 - M. Schreck	Open		150.00	260
1985	Water Lily-Small 7600NR124 - M. Schreck	Open		100.00	175

Our Woodland Friends - Various

YEAR ISSUE		EDITION LIMIT	YEAR RETD.	ISSUE PRICE	*QUOTE U.S. $
1981	Bear-Large - M. Schreck	Open		75.00	95
1985	Bear-Mini - M. Schreck	Open		16.00	55
1987	Fox - A. Stocker	Open		50.00	75
1988	Mini Sitting Fox - A. Stocker	Open		35.00	45
1989	Mushrooms - A. Stocker	Open		35.00	45
1996	Night Owl - A. Hirzinger	Open		85.00	85
1983	Owl-Giant - M. Schreck	Open		1200.00	2000
1979	Owl-Large - M. Schreck	Open		90.00	125
1979	Owl-Mini - M. Schreck	Open		16.00	30
1995	Owlet - A. Hirzinger	Open		45.00	45
1994	Roe Deer Fawn - E. Mair	Open		75.00	75
1985	Squirrel - M. Schreck	Open		35.00	55

Pets' Corner - Various

YEAR ISSUE		EDITION LIMIT	YEAR RETD.	ISSUE PRICE	*QUOTE U.S. $
1993	Beagle Playing - A. Stocker	Open		49.50	50
1990	Beagle Puppy - A. Stocker	Open		40.00	50
1992	Poodle - A. Stocker	Open		125.00	140
1991	Sitting Cat - M. Stamey	Open		75.00	85
1993	Sitting Poodle - A. Stocker	Open		85.00	85
1996	St. Bernard - E. Mair	Open		95.00	95
1995	Tomcat - A. Hirzinger	Open		45.00	45

South Sea - Various

YEAR ISSUE		EDITION LIMIT	YEAR RETD.	ISSUE PRICE	*QUOTE U.S. $
1996	Crab-Mini - M. Stamey	Open		65.00	65
1987	Blowfish-Mini - Team	Open		22.00	30
1986	Blowfish-Small - Team	Open		35.00	55
1991	Butterfly Fish - M. Stamey	Open		150.00	175
1995	Dolphin - M. Stamey	Open		210.00	210
1988	Open Shell w/Pearl - M. Stamey	Open		120.00	175
1993	Sea Horse - M. Stamey	Open		85.00	85
1995	Shell - M. Stamey	Open		45.00	45
1995	Starfish - M. Stamey	Open		29.50	30
1995	Conch - M. Stamey	Open		29.50	30
1995	Maritime Trio (Shell, Starfish, Conch) - M. Stamey	Open		104.00	104
1993	Three South Sea Fish - M. Stamey	Open		135.00	140

Sparkling Fruit - Various

YEAR ISSUE		EDITION LIMIT	YEAR RETD.	ISSUE PRICE	*QUOTE U.S. $
1995	Grapes - Team	Open		375.00	375
1991	Pear - M. Stamey	Open		175.00	185
1981	Pineapple-Giant /Gold - M. Schreck	Open		1750.00	3250
1981	Pineapple-Large /Gold - M. Schreck	Open		150.00	260
1986	Pineapple-Small /Gold - M. Schreck	Open		55.00	85

When We Were Young - Various

YEAR ISSUE		EDITION LIMIT	YEAR RETD.	ISSUE PRICE	*QUOTE U.S. $
1988	Locomotive - G. Stamey	Open		150.00	155
1990	Petrol Wagon - G. Stamey	Open		75.00	95
1988	Tender - G. Stamey	Open		55.00	55
1993	Tipping Wagon - G. Stamey	Open		95.00	95
1988	Wagon - G. Stamey	Open		85.00	95
1990	Airplane - A. Stocker	Open		135.00	155
1996	Baby Carriage - G. Stamey	Open		140.00	140
1993	Kris Bear - M. Zendron	Open		75.00	75
1995	Kris Bear on Skates - M. Zendron	Open		75.00	75
1994	Replica Cat - Team	Open		37.50	38
1994	Replica Hedgehog - Team	Open		37.50	38
1994	Replica Mouse - Team	Open		37.50	38
1994	Starter Set - Team	Open		112.50	113
1994	Sailboat - G. Stamey	Open		195.00	210
1991	Santa Maria - G. Stamey	Open		375.00	375
1994	Rocking Horse - G. Stamey	Open		125.00	125
1995	Train-Mini - G. Stamey	Open		125.00	125

Retired Candleholders - Various

YEAR ISSUE		EDITION LIMIT	YEAR RETD.	ISSUE PRICE	*QUOTE U.S. $
XX	Candleholder 7600NR101	Retrd.	1982	23.00	150-200
XX	Candleholder 7600NR102	Retrd.	1987	35.00	125-175
XX	Candleholder 7600NR103	Retrd.	1988	40.00	150-225
XX	Candleholder 7600NR104	Retrd.	1988	95.00	200-330
XX	Candleholder 7600NR106	Retrd.	1986	85.00	300-450
XX	Candleholder 7600NR107	Retrd.	1986	100.00	400
XX	Candleholder 7600NR109	Retrd.	1986	37.00	150-175
XX	Candleholder 7600NR110	Retrd.	1987	40.00	175-200
XX	Candleholder 7600NR111	Retrd.	1986	100.00	300-600
XX	Candleholder 7600NR112	Retrd.	1986	75.00	300-350
XX	Candleholder 7600NR114	Retrd.	1986	37.00	300-400
XX	Candleholder 7600NR115	Retrd.	1987	185.00	500-600
XX	Candleholder 7600NR116	Retrd.	1986	350.00	1200-1600
XX	Candleholder 7600NR119	Retrd.	1989	N/A	275-350
XX	Candleholder 7600NR122	Retrd.	1988	85.00	250-300
XX	Candleholder 7600NR127	Retrd.	1987	65.00	250-300
XX	Candleholder 7600NR128	Retrd.	1987	100.00	250-300
XX	Candleholder 7600NR129	Retrd.	1987	120.00	350-390
XX	Candleholder 7600NR130	Retrd.	1986	275.00	1200-1800
XX	Candleholder 7600NR131 (Set/6)	Retrd.	N/A	43.00	500-600
XX	Candleholder 7600NR138	Retrd.	1987	160.00	500-700
XX	Candleholder 7600NR139	Retrd.	1987	140.00	500-700
XX	Candleholder 7600NR140	Retrd.	1987	120.00	500-700
XX	Candleholder-Baroque 7600NR121	Retrd.	1987	150.00	250-350
XX	Candleholder-European Style 7600NR103	Retrd.	1991	N/A	450-500
XX	Candleholder-European Style 7600NR108	Retrd.	1990	N/A	350-650
XX	Candleholder-European Style 7600NR141	Retrd.	1991	N/A	500-650
XX	Candleholder-European Style 7600NR142	Retrd.	1990	N/A	250-350
XX	Candleholder-Global-Kg. Sz. 7600NR135	Retrd.	1989	50.00	175-250
XX	Candleholder-Global-Lg. 7600NR134	Retrd.	1991	40.00	80-100
XX	Candleholder-Global-Med. (2) 7600NR133	Retrd.	1991	40.00	70-120
XX	Candleholder-Global-Sm. (4) 7600NR132	Retrd.	1990	60.00	150-250
1990	Candleholder-Neo-Classic-Lg. 7600NR144090 - A. Stocker	Retrd.	1993	220.00	225-275
1990	Candleholder-Neo-Classic-Med. 7600NR144080 - A. Stocker	Retrd.	1993	190.00	225-275
1990	Candleholder-Neo-Classic-Sm. 7600NR144070 - A. Stocker	Retrd.	1993	170.00	200
XX	Candleholder-Pineapple 7600NR136G	Retrd.	1987	150.00	250-400
XX	Candleholder-Pineapple 7600NR136R	Retrd.	1987	150.00	275-450
1987	Candleholder-Star-Lg. 7600NR143000 - Team	Retrd.	1996	250.00	400
XX	Candleholder-w/Flowers-Lg. 7600NR137	Retrd.	1991	150.00	225-275
XX	Candleholder-w/Flowers-Sm. 7600NR120	Retrd.	1987	60.00	350-400
XX	Candleholder-w/Leaves-Sm. 7600NR126	Retrd.	1987	100.00	400

Retired - Various

YEAR ISSUE		EDITION LIMIT	YEAR RETD.	ISSUE PRICE	*QUOTE U.S. $
1992	Angel 6475NR000009	Retrd.	1994	65.00	115-130
1991	Apple 7476NR000001- M. Stamey	Retrd.	1996	175.00	205-225
XX	Apple Photo Stand-Kg. Sz. (Gold) 7504NR060G	Retrd.	1989	120.00	400-600
XX	Apple Photo Stand-Kg. Sz. (Rhodium) 7504NR060R - M. Schreck	Retrd.	1989	120.00	450-600
XX	Apple Photo Stand-Lg. 7504NR050R	Retrd.	1987	80.00	350-400
XX	Apple Photo Stand-Lg. (Gold) 7504NR050G	Retrd.	1991	80.00	250-360
XX	Apple Photo Stand-Sm. (Gold) 7504NR030G	Retrd.	1991	40.00	185-200
XX	Apple Photo Stand-Sm. 7504NR030R	Retrd.	1987	40.00	200-260
XX	Ashtray 7461NR100	Retrd.	1991	45.00	275-350
XX	Ashtray 7501NR061	Retrd.	1981	45.50	900-1200
XX	Bear-Giant Size 7637NR112 - M. Schreck	Retrd.	1988	125.00	1700-2000
XX	Bear-Kg Sz 7637NR92 - M. Schreck	Retrd.	1987	95.00	1250-1600
1984	Bear-Mini 7670NR32 - M. Schreck	Retrd.	1989	16.00	100-200
1982	Bear-Sm 7637NR054000 - M. Schreck	Retrd.	1995	44.00	90-110
1992	Beaver-Baby Lying 7616NR000003 - A. Stocker	Retrd.	1995	47.50	60-70
1985	Bee (Gold) 7553NR100	Retrd.	1989	200.00	1400-1800
1985	Bee (Rhodium) 7553NR200	Retrd.	1987	200.00	1650-2000
XX	Beetle Bottle Opener (Gold) 7505NR76	Retrd.	1984	80.00	1200-1450
XX	Beetle Bottle Opener (Rhodium) 7505NR76	Retrd.	1984	80.00	1000-1650
1987	Birds' Nest 7470NR050000 - Team	Retrd.	1996	90.00	140-240
1984	Blowfish-Lg. 7644NR41	Retrd.	1992	40.00	120-200
1985	Butterfly (Gold) 7551NR100	Retrd.	1989	200.00	1000-1200
1985	Butterfly (Rhodium) 7551NR200	Retrd.	1987	200.00	2100-2400
XX	Butterfly-Mini 7671NR30	Retrd.	1989	16.00	90-175
XX	Cardholders-Lg. , Set/4 7403NR30095	Retrd.	1990	45.00	250-350
XX	Cardholders-Sm., Set/4 7403NR20095	Retrd.	1990	25.00	140-200
1977	Cat-Lg 7634NR70 - M. Schreck	Retrd.	1992	44.00	100-150
XX	Cat-Medium 7634NR52	Retrd.	1987	38.00	350-450
1982	Cat-Mini 7659NR31 - M. Schreck	Retrd.	1992	16.00	45-100
1981	Chess Set/Wooden Board 7550NR432032	Retrd.	1987	950.00	1200-2000
XX	Chicken-Mini 7651NR20	Retrd.	1989	16.00	50-100
XX	Cigarette Box 7503NR050	Retrd.	1982	136.00	1800-2500
XX	Cigarette Holder 7463NR062	Retrd.	1991	85.00	130-180
1991	City Gates 7474NR000023 - G. Stamey	Retrd.	1995	95.00	105-185
1991	City Tower 7474NR000022 - G. Stamey	Retrd.	1995	37.50	50-100
1984	Dachshund-Lg. 7641NR75 - M. Schreck	Retrd.	1992	48.00	80-125
XX	Dachshund-Mini 7672NR42 - A. Stocker	Retrd.	1989	20.00	120-175
1987	Dachshund-Mini 7672NR042000 - A. Stocker	Retrd.	1995	20.00	65-100
1981	Dinner Bell-Lg. 7467NR071000 - M. Schreck	Retrd.	1992	80.00	150-200
XX	Dog (standing) 7635NR70	Retrd.	1991	44.00	80-125
XX	Duck-lg. 7653NR75	Retrd.	1987	44.00	200-350
XX	Duck-Medium 7653NR55	Retrd.	1988	38.00	125-160
XX	Duck-Mini 7653NR45	Retrd.	1989	16.00	85-125
XX	Elephant 7640NR55	Retrd.	1990	90.00	240-325
1988	Elephant-Lg. 7640NR060000 - A. Stocker	Retrd.	1995	70.00	100-225
1984	Falcon Head-Lg. 7645NR100 - M. Schreck	Retrd.	1992	600.00	1200-1500
1986	Falcon Head-Sm. 7645NR45 - M. Schreck	Retrd.	1992	60.00	120-175
1988	Fox-Mini Running 7677NR055000 - A. Stocker	Retrd.	1996	35.00	55
1984	Frog (black eyes) 7642NR48 - M. Schreck	Retrd.	1992	30.00	95-150
1984	Frog (clear eyes) 7642NR48 - M. Schreck	Retrd.	1992	30.00	225-350
XX	Grapes-Large 7550NR30015	Retrd.	1989	250.00	1200-1500
1985	Grapes-Med. 7550NR20029	Retrd.	1995	300.00	395-550
1985	Grapes-Sm. 7550NR20015	Retrd.	1995	200.00	260-385
XX	Hedgehog-Kg. Sz. 7630NR60 - M. Schreck	Retrd.	1987	98.00	350-500
XX	Hedgehog-Lg. 7630NR50 - M. Schreck	Retrd.	1987	65.00	155-225
1985	Hedgehog-Lg. 7630NR70 - M. Schreck	Retrd.	1996	120.00	250
XX	Hedgehog-Med. 7630NR40 - M. Schreck	Retrd.	1987	44.00	155-225
XX	Hedgehog-Sm. 7630NR30 - M. Schreck	Retrd.	1987	38.00	360-540
1988	Hippopotamus 7626NR65 - A. Stocker	Retrd.	1993	70.00	135-175
1989	Hippopotamus-Sm. 7626NR055000 - A. Stocker	Retrd.	1995	70.00	85
1991	Holy Family w/Arch 7475NR001	Retrd.	1994	250.00	250-350
1985	Hummingbird (Gold) 7552NR100	Retrd.	1989	200.00	1200-1600
1985	Hummingbird (Rhodium) 7552NR200	Retrd.	1987	200.00	1700-2200
1990	Kingfisher 7621NR000001 - M. Stamey	Retrd.	1993	75.00	125-175
1991	Kitten 7634NR028000 - M. Stamey	Retrd.	1995	47.50	55
1991	Kiwi 7617NR043000 - M. Stamey	Retrd.	1996	37.50	50

*Quotes have been rounded up to nearest dollar

FIGURINES

Swarovski America Limited
to The Tudor Mint Inc.

YEAR ISSUE		EDITION LIMIT	YEAR RETD.	ISSUE PRICE	*QUOTE U.S.$
XX	Lighter 7462NR062	Retrd.	1991	160.00	325
XX	Lighter 7500NR050	Retrd.	1982	160.00	2230
1986	Mallard 7647NR80 - M. Schreck	Retrd.	1995	80.00	150-200
1992	Mother Beaver 7616NR000001 - A. Stocker	Retrd.	1996	110.00	125
XX	Mouse-Kg. Sz. 7631NR60 - M. Schreck	Retrd.	1987	95.00	575-725
XX	Mouse-Lg. 7631NR50 - M. Schreck	Retrd.	1987	69.00	250-350
1976	Mouse-Med. 7631NR040000 - M. Schreck	Retrd.	1995	48.00	90
XX	Mouse-Mini 7655NR23	Retrd.	1989	16.00	70-125
XX	Mouse-Sm. 7631NR30 - M. Schreck	Retrd.	1992	35.00	70-115
1989	Old Timer Automobile 7473NR000001 - G. Stamey	Retrd.	1995	130.00	175-275
1989	Owl 7621NR000003 - M. Stamey	Retrd.	1993	70.00	150-185
1979	Owl-Sm. 7636NR046000 - M. Schreck	Retrd.	1995	59.00	80
1989	Parrot 7621NR000004 - M. Stamey	Retrd.	1993	70.00	125-185
1987	Partridge 7625NR50 - A. Stocker	Retrd.	1991	85.00	125-200
1984	Penguin-Lg. 7643NR085000 - M. Schreck	Retrd.	1995	44.00	90-115
XX	Picture Frame/Oval 7505NR75G	Retrd.	1990	90.00	350-425
XX	Picture Frame/Square 7506NR60G	Retrd.	1990	100.00	350-425
XX	Pig-Lg. 7638NR65 - M. Schreck	Retrd.	1987	50.00	200-350
1985	Pineapple/Rhodium-Giant 7507NR26002 - M. Schreck	Retrd.	1987	1750.00	2700-3700
1982	Pineapple/Rhodium-Lg. 7507NR105002 - M. Schreck	Retrd.	1987	150.00	400-450
1987	Pineapple/Rhodium-Sm. 7507NR060002 - M. Schreck	Retrd.	1987	55.00	165
XX	Pprwgt-Atomic-Crystal Cal 7454NR60095	Retrd.	1985	80.00	1200-1400
XX	Pprwgt-Atomic-Vitrl Med. 7454NR60087	Retrd.	1985	80.00	1200-1400
XX	Pprwgt-Barrel-Crystal Cal 7453NR60095	Retrd.	1989	80.00	225-525
XX	Pprwgt-Barrel-Vitrl Med. 7453NR60087	Retrd.	1989	80.00	240-285
XX	Pprwgt-Carousel-Crystal Cal 7451NR60095	Retrd.	1985	80.00	1100-1375
XX	Pprwgt-Carousel-Vitrl Med. 7451NR60087	Retrd.	1985	80.00	1200-1400
1982	Pprwgt-Cone Crystal Cal 7452NR60095 - M. Schreck	Retrd.	1993	80.00	240
1982	Pprwgt-Cone Vitrl Med. 7452NR60087 - M. Schreck	Retrd.	1993	80.00	200-250
1981	Pprwgt-Egg 7458NR63069 - M. Schreck	Retrd.	1993	60.00	175-275
XX	Pprwgt-Geometric 7432NR57002N	Retrd.	1991	75.00	175-240
XX	Pprwgt-Octron-Crystal Cal 7456NR41	Retrd.	1992	75.00	150-165
XX	Pprwgt-Octron-Vitrl Med. 7456NR41087	Retrd.	1992	75.00	150-195
XX	Pprwgt-One Ton 7495NR65	Retrd.	1991	75.00	125-160
XX	Pprwgt-Rd.-Berm Blue 7404NR30MM	Retrd.	N/A	15.00	150-250
XX	Pprwgt-Rd.-Berm Blue 7404NR40MM	Retrd.	N/A	20.00	175-300
XX	Pprwgt-Rd.-Berm Blue 7404NR50MM	Retrd.	N/A	40.00	200-350
XX	Pprwgt-Rd.-Crystal Cal 7404NR30095/30MM	Retrd.	1989	15.00	60-75
XX	Pprwgt-Rd.-Crystal Cal 7404NR40095/40MM	Retrd.	1989	20.00	80-125
XX	Pprwgt-Rd.-Crystal Cal 7404NR50095/50MM	Retrd.	1989	40.00	150-200
XX	Pprwgt-Rd.-Crystal Cal 7404NR60095/60MM	Retrd.	1989	50.00	225-250
XX	Pprwgt-Rd.-Green 7404NR30	Retrd.	N/A	15.00	100-250
XX	Pprwgt-Rd.-Green 7404NR40	Retrd.	N/A	20.00	150-240
XX	Pprwgt-Rd.-Green 7404NR50	Retrd.	N/A	40.00	255
XX	Pprwgt-Rd.-Sahara 7404NR30	Retrd.	1983	15.00	200-300
XX	Pprwgt-Rd.-Sahara 7404NR40	Retrd.	1982	20.00	250
XX	Pprwgt-Rd.-Sahara 7404NR50	Retrd.	1983	40.00	300-400
XX	Pprwgt-Rd.-Vitrl Med. 7404NR30087/30MM	Retrd.	1989	15.00	60-70
XX	Pprwgt-Rd.-Vitrl Med. 7404NR40087/40MM	Retrd.	1989	20.00	95-125
XX	Pprwgt-Rd.-Vitrl Med. 7404NR50087/50MM	Retrd.	1989	40.00	100-200
XX	Pprwgt-Rd.-Vitrl Med. 7404NR60087/60MM	Retrd.	1989	50.00	125-225
1987	Pyramid-Lg.-Crystal Cal 7450NR50095 - M. Schreck	Retrd.	1994	90.00	210
1987	Pyramid-Lg.-Vitrl Med. 7450NR50087 - M. Schreck	Retrd.	1994	90.00	180-250
XX	Rabbit-Lg. 7652NR45	Retrd.	1988	38.00	210-330
XX	Rabbit-Mini 7652NR20	Retrd.	1989	16.00	100-120
1988	Rabbit-Mini Lying 7678NR030000 - A. Stocker	Retrd.	1995	35.00	50-100
1988	Rhinoceros 7622NR70 - A. Stocker	Retrd.	1993	70.00	125-165
1990	Rhinoceros-Sm. 7622NR060000 - A. Stocker	Retrd.	1995	70.00	89-95
XX	Salt and Pepper Shakers 7508NR068034	Retrd.	1989	80.00	330-350
XX	Schnapps Glasses, Set/6 7468NR039000	Retrd.	1991	150.00	250-450
1990	Scotch Terrier 7619NR000002 - A. Stocker	Retrd.	1996	60.00	85
1985	Seal-Large 7646NR085000 - M. Schreck	Retrd.	1995	44.00	100-150
1992	Shepherd 7475NR000007	Retrd.	1994	65.00	80-135
1990	Silver Crystal City-Cathedral 7474NR000021 - G. Stamey	Retrd.	1995	95.00	135-225
1990	Silver Crystal City-Houses I& II (Set/2) 7474NR100000 - G. Stamey	Retrd.	1995	75.00	150-185
1990	Silver Crystal City-Houses III & IV (Set/2) 7474NR200000 - G. Stamey	Retrd.	1995	75.00	150-185
1990	Silver Crystal City-Poplars (Set/3) 7474NR020003 - G. Stamey	Retrd.	1995	40.00	95-105
1986	Snail 7648NR030000 - M. Stamey	Retrd.	1995	35.00	60
1991	South Sea Shell 7624NR72000 - M. Stamey	Retrd.	1995	110.00	125-140
XX	Sparrow-Lg. 7650NR32	Retrd.	1988	38.00	125-175
1979	Sparrow-Mini 7650NR20 - M. Schreck	Retrd.	1992	16.00	40-80
XX	Swan-Mini 7658NR27 - M. Schreck	Retrd.	1989	16.00	150-185
XX	Table Magnifyer (no chain) 7510NR01G	Retrd.	1984	70.00	1000-1200
XX	Table Magnifyer (no chain) 7510NR01R	Retrd.	1984	80.00	1025-1200
XX	Table Magnifyer (with chain) 7510NR01R	Retrd.	1984	80.00	1200
1989	Toucan 7621NR000002 - M. Stamey	Retrd.	1993	70.00	120-175
1993	Town Hall 7474NR000027 - G. Stamey	Retrd.	1995	135.00	140-225
XX	Treasure Box (Heart/Butterfly)7465NR52/100	Retrd.	1991	80.00	250-300
XX	Treasure Box (Heart/Flower)7465NR52	Retrd.	1989	80.00	250-300
XX	Treasure Box (Oval/Butterfly)7466NR063100	Retrd.	1989	80.00	250-300
XX	Treasure Box (Oval/Flower) 7466NR063000	Retrd.	1991	80.00	275-375
XX	Treasure Box (Round/Butterfly) 7464NR50/100	Retrd.	1989	80.00	250-300
XX	Treasure Box (Round/Flower) 7464NR50	Retrd.	1991	80.00	210-270
XX	Turtle-King Sz. 7632NR75 - M. Schreck	Retrd.	1988	58.00	205-250
1977	Turtle-Small 7632NR030000 - M. Schreck	Retrd.	1996	35.00	100-200
XX	Vase 7511NR70	Retrd.	1991	50.00	140-250
1989	Walrus 7620NR100000 - M. Stamey	Retrd.	1994	120.00	150-225
1988	Whale 7628NR80 - M. Stamey	Retrd.	1992	70.00	150-240
1992	Wise Men (Set/3) 7475NR200000	Retrd.	1994	175.00	200-300

The Tudor Mint Inc.

Arthurian Legend - M. Locker, unless otherwise noted

YEAR ISSUE		EDITION LIMIT	YEAR RETD.	ISSUE PRICE	*QUOTE U.S.$
1990	3200 Merlin	Open		18.60	34
1990	3201 Into Merlin's Care Mold 1	Closed	N/A	25.40	300-350
1990	3201 Into Merlin's Care Mold 2	Closed	1993	25.40	85
1990	3202 Excaliber - M.L./R.G.	Open		18.60	34
1990	3203 Camelot	Open		25.40	42
1990	3204 King Arthur - M.L./R.G.	Open		18.60	34
1990	3205 Queen Guinevere	Open		18.60	34
1990	3206 Sir Percival & the Grail	Closed	1993	18.60	275-350
1990	3207 Morgan Le Fey	Open		25.40	42
1990	3208 Sir Lancelot	Open		25.40	42
1992	3209 Vigil of Sir Galahad - A. Slocombe	Open		31.45	42
1992	3210 Sir Mordred - R. Gibbons	Open		23.70	34
1992	3211 Return of Excalibur	Open		23.70	34
1993	3212 Sir Gawain - A. Slocombe	Open		25.40	34
1993	3213 King Arthur/Sir Bedevere	Closed	1996	33.90	45-55

Dinosaur Collection - Various

YEAR ISSUE		EDITION LIMIT	YEAR RETD.	ISSUE PRICE	*QUOTE U.S.$
1993	6001 Pteranodon - M. Locker	Closed	1994	25.40	70-85
1993	6002 Triceratops - A. Slocombe	Closed	1994	25.40	50-70
1993	6003 Stegosaurus - A. Slocombe	Closed	1994	25.40	50-70
1993	6004 Brontosaurus - M. Locker	Closed	1994	25.40	50-70
1993	6005 Tyrannosaurus Rex - A. Slocombe	Closed	1994	25.40	50-70
1993	6006 Spinosaurus - R. Gibbons	Closed	1994	25.40	50-70

Hobbit Collection - A. Slocombe, unless otherwise noted

YEAR ISSUE		EDITION LIMIT	YEAR RETD.	ISSUE PRICE	*QUOTE U.S.$
1991	5001 Bilbo Baggins - R. Gibbons	Open		23.70	38
1991	5002 Gandalf	Open		42.41	64
1991	5003 Thorn Oakenshield - R. Gibbons	Closed	1992	23.70	70-88
1991	5004 The Great Goblin - R. Gibbons	Closed	1993	23.70	65-88
1991	5005 Gollum	Open		29.75	46
1991	5006 Beorn	Closed	1992	42.41	100-125
1991	5007 The Elven King	Closed	1992	29.75	150
1991	5008 Smaug the Dragon	Closed	1993	93.41	200-250
1991	5009 Bard - M. Locker	Closed	1992	23.70	125
1991	5010 'Good Morn.' at Bag End - R. Gibbons	Closed	1993	67.90	150-200
1991	5011 Moon Letters	Closed	1992	93.41	150-200
1991	5012 Finding the 'Precious' - R. Gibbons	Closed	1992	67.90	150-200
1991	5013 The Capture of Bilbo	Closed	1992	67.90	150-200
1991	5014 'Riddles in the Dark'	Closed	1992	56.01	150-200
1991	5015 Escape From the Wargs - R. Gibbons	Closed	1992	67.90	150-200
1991	5016 Barrels Out of Bond - M. Locker	Closed	1992	67.90	150-200
1991	5017 The 'Courage of the Bilbo'	Closed	1992	56.01	150-200
1991	5018 Prisoner of Elven King	Closed	1992	67.90	150-200
1991	5019 The Enchanted Door - M. Locker	Closed	1992	93.41	200-250
1991	5020 The Wrath of Beorn - M. Locker	Closed	1992	67.90	200
1991	5021 Journey's End - R. Gibbons	Closed	1993	67.90	200
1991	5022 The Troll's Clearing - R. Gibbons	Closed	1992	251.51	1000-1250
1991	5023 Burglar Steals Smaug's	Closed	1993	254.91	1000-1250
1991	5024 Farewell, King Under meeting - M. Locker	Closed	1992	254.91	1000-1250

Lord of the Rings - Various

YEAR ISSUE		EDITION LIMIT	YEAR RETD.	ISSUE PRICE	*QUOTE U.S.$
1992	5025 Frodo Baggins - R. Gibbons	Open		25.40	38
1992	5026 Bilbo's Tale - M. Locker	Closed	1996	25.40	38
1992	5027 Gimli the Dwarf - M. Locker	Closed	1996	25.40	38
1992	5028 Sam Gamgee - R. Gibbons	Closed	1996	25.40	38
1992	5029 Aragorn (Strider) - A. Slocombe	Open		25.40	38
1992	5030 An Orc - R. Gibbons	Closed	1994	30.51	88
1992	5031 Legolas the Elf - A. Slocombe	Open		30.51	46
1992	5032 The Mirror of Galadriel - R. Gibbons	Open		30.51	46
1992	5033 Saruman - A. Slocombe	Closed	1994	43.78	100-125
1992	5034 The Balrog - R. Gibbons	Open		67.90	100
1992	5035 Gandalf & Shadowfax - M. Locker	Open		67.90	100
1992	5036 A Black Rider - A. Slocombe	Open		67.90	100
1992	5037 Pippin - A. Slocombe	Closed	1994	25.40	75-100
1992	5038 Merry - A. Slocombe	Closed	1994	25.40	75-100
1992	5039 Boromir - R. Gibbons	Closed	1994	25.40	75-100
1992	5040 Treebeard (Fangorn) - R. Gibbons	Closed	1994	43.78	100-150

Myth & Magic Club - Various

YEAR ISSUE		EDITION LIMIT	YEAR RETD.	ISSUE PRICE	*QUOTE U.S.$
1990	9001 The Quest For the Truth - R.G./M.L.	Closed	1991	84.90	675-1100
1991	9002 The Game of Strax - R. Gibbons	Closed	1991	25.40	600-900
1991	9003 The Well of Aspirations - A. Slocombe	Closed	1992	84.90	750-850
1992	9004 Playmates - R. Gibbons	Closed	1992	28.80	100-175
1992	9005 Friends - A. Slocombe	Closed	1993	32.20	100-175
1992	9006 The Enchanted Pool - R. Gibbons	Closed	1993	84.90	225-250
1993	9007 The Mystical Encounter - A. Slocombe	Closed	1994	33.58	60-85
1994	9008 Keeper of the Dragons - R. Gibbons	Closed	1994	84.90	125
1994	9009 The Crystal Shield - M. Locker	Closed	1995	44.00	63
1994	9010 Battle for the Crystal - A. Slocombe	Closed	1995	108.00	150-175
1995	9011 Starstruck - S. Darnley	Closed	1996	44.00	80
1996	9012 Cauldron of Fire - A. Slocombe	Closed	1996	108.00	150-175
1996	9013 When Is It Our Turn? - H.C./S.D.	6/97		44.00	44
1996	9014 The Peacemakers - S.R./A.S.	6/97		N/A	N/A
1990	CC01 The Protector - R. Gibbons	Closed	1991	Gift	500-750
1991	CC02 The Jovial Wizard - M. Locker	Closed	1992	Gift	275-450
1992	CC03 Dragon of Destiny - R. Gibbons	Closed	1993	Gift	200
1993	CC04 Dragon of Methtintdour - A. Slocombe	Closed	1994	Gift	100-125
1994	CC05 The Dreamy Dragon - M. Locker	Closed	1995	Gift	88
1995	CC06 The Regal Dragon - A. Slocombe	Closed	1996	Gift	88
1996	CC07 Contemplation - S.R./M.L.	6/97		Gift	88

Myth & Magic One Year Only Piece - R. Gibbons, unless otherwise noted

YEAR ISSUE		EDITION LIMIT	YEAR RETD.	ISSUE PRICE	*QUOTE U.S.$
1993	OY93 The Flying Dragon - A. Slocombe	Closed	1993	67.90	400
1994	OY94 Dragon of Underworld - R. Gibbons	Closed	1994	70.55	400
1995	OY95 Guardian of the Crystal - A. Slocombe	Closed	1995	84.90	150-175
1996	OY96 The Enchanted Dragon - J. Watson	Closed	1996	114.00	140-175

Myth & Magic Promotion - Various

YEAR ISSUE		EDITION LIMIT	YEAR RETD.	ISSUE PRICE	*QUOTE U.S.$
1993	3601 Dactrius - R.G./M.L./A.S.	Closed	1993	67.90	600-700
1994	3603 Vexius - A. Slocombe	Closed	1994	70.55	122
1995	3606 Viamphe - M. Locker	Closed	1995	73.42	150
1995	3607 Quargon - A. Slocombe	Closed	1995	26.32	88
1996	3609 Aurora - H.C./A.S.	Closed	1996	108.00	125-150
1996	3610 Lepidorus - J.W./R.G.	Closed	1996	48.00	88

Myth & Magic Colleggtibles - R. Gibbons

YEAR ISSUE		EDITION LIMIT	YEAR RETD.	ISSUE PRICE	*QUOTE U.S.$
1996	1049 The Protector	Open		38.00	38
1996	1050 The Supreme Dragon	Open		38.00	38
1996	1051 The Family of Dragons	Open		38.00	38
1996	1052 The Dragon of Justice	Open		38.00	38
1996	1053 The Paternal Dragon	Open		38.00	38
1996	1054 The Sleepy Lizards	Open		38.00	38
1996	1055 The Castle of Unicorns	Open		38.00	38
1996	1056 The Fairy Rider	Open		38.00	38
1996	1057 The Leaping Pegasus	Open		38.00	38
1996	1058 The Fairy Glade	Open		38.00	38
1996	1059 The Damsel & Unicorn	Open		38.00	38
1996	1060 The Wizard's Cauldron	Open		38.00	38

Myth & Magic Extravaganza Study - Various

YEAR ISSUE		EDITION LIMIT	YEAR RETD.	ISSUE PRICE	*QUOTE U.S.$
1992	3600 Sauria - A. Slocombe	Closed	1992	33.90	700
1993	3602 Deinos - R. Gibbons	Closed	1993	33.90	600
1994	3604 Lithia - M. Locker	Closed	1994	31.92	32
1995	3608 Imperia - S. Darnley	Closed	1995	41.25	42

The Tudor Mint Inc.
to The Tudor Mint Inc.

FIGURINES

Myth & Magic Large - Various

YEAR ISSUE		EDITION LIMIT	YEAR RETD.	ISSUE PRICE	*QUOTE U.S. $
1990	3300 The Dragon Master - R. Gibbons	7,500		297.50	404
1990	3301 The Magical Encounter - R. Gibbons	Open		30.50	42
1990	3302 The Keeper of the Magic - R. Gibbons	Closed	1995	59.40	150-175
1990	3303 Summoning the Elements - R. Gibbons	Closed	1993	59.40	350-450
1990	3304 Sorceror's Apprentice - R. Gibbons	Closed	1991	59.40	500-600
1990	3305 The Nest of Dragons - M. Locker	Closed	1993	59.40	175-200
1990	3306 Meeting of the Unicorns - M. Locker	Open		59.40	86
1990	3307 Sentinels at the Portal - R. Gibbons	Closed	1991	59.40	500-600
1990	3308 The VII Seekers of Knowledge - M. Locker	7,500		297.50	404
1990	3309 Le Morte D'Arthur - A. Slocombe	Open		84.90	122
1990	3310 The Magical Vision - A. Slocombe	Closed	1995	84.90	150
1990	3311 The Dance of the Dolphins - R. Gibbons	1,537	1993	297.50	600-700
1991	3312 Altar of Enlightenment - M. Locker	Open		84.90	122
1991	3313 Power of the Crystal - A. Slocombe	3,500		595.00	595
1992	3314 The Awakening - J. Pickering	Closed	1995	64.50	150
1992	3315 The Crystal Dragon - A. Slocombe	Open		101.90	122
1992	3318 The Gathering of the Unicorns - A.S./R.G.	5,000	N/A	314.50	425-485
1993	3319 The Invocation - M. Locker	Closed	1995	84.90	150
1993	3320 The Fighting Dragons - A. Slocombe	Closed		67.90	115-150
1993	3321 The Playful Dolphins - M. Locker	Open		56.95	68
1993	3322 The Dragon of Darkness - A. Slocombe	Open		67.90	90
1994	3323 The Destroyer of the Crystal - S. Darnley	Open		84.90	114
1994	3324 A Tranquil Moment - M. Locker	Open		84.90	114
1994	3325 Great Earth Dragon - R. Gibbons	Open		101.90	136
1995	3326 The Great Sun Dragon - A. Slocombe	Open		136.00	136
1995	3327 The Great Moon Dragon - R. Gibbons	Open		136.00	136
1995	3328 The Great Sea Dragon - M. Locker	Open		136.00	136
1996	3329 The Destroyer of Evil - H.C./R.G.	Open		136.00	136
1996	3330 The Portal of Life - H.C./S.D.	Open		136.00	136
1996	3331 The Warlord - S.R./A.S.	2,500		210.00	210

Myth & Magic Miniatures - R. Gibbons, unless otherwise noted

YEAR ISSUE		EDITION LIMIT	YEAR RETD.	ISSUE PRICE	*QUOTE U.S. $
1989	3500 The Incantation	Closed	1991	8.42	125-165
1989	3501 The Book of Spells - R.G./M.L.	Closed	1995	8.42	28
1989	3502 The Enchanted Castle	Closed	1993	8.42	28
1989	3503 The Cauldron of Light - M.L./R.G	Open		8.42	28
1989	3504 The Winged Serpent	Closed	1995	8.42	28
1989	3505 The White Witch - R.G./M.L.	Closed	1991	8.42	83
1989	3506 The Master Wizard	Closed	1995	8.42	28
1989	3507 The Guardian Dragon	Open		8.42	12
1989	3508 The Unicorn	Open		8.42	12
1989	3509 Pegasus	Open		8.42	12
1989	3510 The Castle of Dreams	Closed	1993	8.42	25
1989	3511 The Light of Knowledge - R.G./M.L.	Closed	1991	8.42	25-80
1990	3512 The Siren	Closed	1991	8.42	200-275
1990	3513 The Crystal Queen	Closed	1992	8.76	28-50
1990	3514 The Astronomer - R.G./M.L.	Closed	1991	8.76	50-100
1990	3515 The Alchemist - R.G./M.L.	Closed	1991	8.76	50-100
1990	3516 The Minotaur	Closed	1991	8.76	150-175
1990	3517 The Grim Reaper - R.G./M.L.	Closed	1995	8.76	25
1990	3518 The Castle of Souls	Closed	1993	8.76	41
1990	3519 The Dragon Gateway	Closed	1995	8.76	25
1990	3520 The Dragon Rider - R.G./M.L.	Closed	1991	8.76	175-220
1990	3521 The Dragon's Kiss	Closed	1992	8.76	65
1990	3522 The Witch & Familiar	Closed	1991	8.76	100
1990	3523 The Oriental Dragon - R.G./M.L.	Closed	1993	8.76	30
1990	3524 The Reborn Dragon	Open		8.76	12
1990	3525 The Fire Dragon - R.G./M.L.	Closed	1994	8.76	28
1990	3526 The Giant Sorceror - R.G./M.L.	Closed	1991	8.76	125-160
1990	3527 The Wizard of Light	Closed	1994	8.76	28
1990	3528 Keeper of the Treasure	Closed	1992	8.76	82
1990	3529 The Old Hag	Closed	1991	8.76	250-375
1991	3530 Mother Nature	Closed	1994	9.44	25
1991	3531 The Earth Wizard - R.G./M.L.	Closed	1992	9.44	74
1991	3532 The Fire Wizard	Closed	1994	9.44	28
1991	3533 The Water Wizard	Closed	1992	9.44	20
1991	3534 The Air Wizard	Closed	1992	9.44	70
1991	3535 The Dragon of the Lake	Closed	1994	9.44	35
1991	3536 The Dragon's Spell - R.G./M.L.	Closed	1991	9.44	20-30
1991	3537 Merlin - M. Locker	Open		9.44	12
1991	3538 Excalibur - M.L./R.G.	Closed	1993	9.44	25
1991	3539 Camelot - M. Locker	Open		9.44	12
1991	3540 King Arthur - M.L./R.G.	Open		9.44	12
1991	3541 Queen Guinevere - M. Locker	Closed	1993	9.44	30
1992	3542 Dragon of the Forest	Closed	1995	10.11	25
1992	3543 Dragon of the Moon	Closed	1995	10.11	25
1992	3544 Wizard of Winter	Closed	1995	10.11	25
1992	3545 Dragon of Wisdom	Closed	1995	10.11	25
1992	3546 Dragon of the Sun - M. Locker	Closed	1995	10.11	25
1992	3547 Dragon of the Clouds - M. Locker	Closed	1995	10.11	25
1993	3548 Moon Wizard - A. Slocombe	Open		10.62	12
1993	3549 Unicorn of Light - A. Slocombe	Open		10.62	12
1993	3550 Return of Excalibur - M. Locker	Closed	1994	10.62	28
1993	3551 Magical Encounter	Open		10.62	12
1993	3552 Ice Dragon - A. Slocombe	Closed	1995	10.62	25
1993	3553 Sleepy Dragon - M. Locker	Open		10.62	12
1994	3554 Keeper of the Skulls	Open		10.80	12
1994	3555 The Dark Dragon - A. Slocombe	Open		10.80	12
1994	3556 Protector of the Young - M.L./R.G.	Open		10.80	12
1994	3557 Dragon of Light - R.G./A.S.	Open		10.80	12
1994	3558 Unicorns of Freedom	Open		10.80	12
1994	3559 Defender of the Crystal	Open		10.80	12
1995	3560 The Loving Dragons - N/A	Open		12.00	12
1995	3561 The Wizard of the Lake - N/A	Open		12.00	12
1995	3562 The Hatch Wings - N/A	Open		12.00	12
1995	3563 The Dragon of the Treasure - N/A	Open		12.00	12
1995	3564 The Armoured Dragon - N/A	Open		12.00	12
1995	3565 The Sword Master - N/A	Open		12.00	12
1996	3566 The Dragon of the Ice Crystals - S. Riley	Open		14.00	14
1996	3567 The Mischievous Dragon - S. Riley	Open		14.00	14
1996	3568 The Summoner of Light - S. Riley	Open		14.00	14
1996	3569 The Proud Pegasus - S. Riley	Open		14.00	14
1996	3570 The Crystal Unicorn - S. Riley	Open		14.00	14
1996	3571 The Majestic Dragon - S. Riley	Open		14.00	14
1996	3572 The Celtic Dragon - H. Coventry	Open		14.00	14
1996	3573 The Dragon Warrior - H. Coventry	Open		14.00	14
1996	3574 The Dragon Thief - J. Watson	Open		14.00	14
1996	3575 The Crystal Serpent - S. Riley	Open		14.00	14
1996	3576 The Dragon's Nest - J. Watson	Open		14.00	14
1996	3577 The Guardian of Light - J. Watson	Open		14.00	14

Myth & Magic Standard - R. Gibbons, unless otherwise noted

YEAR ISSUE		EDITION LIMIT	YEAR RETD.	ISSUE PRICE	*QUOTE U.S. $
1989	3001 The Incantation	Open		16.90	34
1989	3002 The Siren	Closed	1995	16.90	85
1989	3003 The Evil of Greed	Closed	1989	16.90	300-425
1989	3004 The Book of Spells - M. Locker	Open		16.90	34
1989	3005 The Enchanted Castle	Closed	1991	16.90	125-150
1989	3006 The Cauldron of Light - M.L./R.G.	Open		16.90	34
1989	3007 The Winged Serpent	Closed	1991	16.90	100-150
1989	3008 The White Witch - M. Locker	Closed	1991	16.90	100-150
1989	3009 The Master Wizard	Closed	1993	16.90	100-150
1989	3010 The Infernal Demon	Closed	1989	16.90	375
1989	3011 The Warrior Knight Mold 1	Closed	N/A	16.90	400-600
1989	3011 The Warrior Knight Mold 2	Closed	1990	16.90	375
1989	3012 The Deadly Combat	Closed	1989	16.90	375
1989	3013 The Old Hag Mold 1	Closed	N/A	16.90	400-900
1989	3013 The Old Hag Mold 2	Closed	1990	16.90	200-250
1989	3014 The Crystal Queen	Closed	1993	16.90	125
1989	3015 The Astronomer - M. Locker	Closed	1990	16.90	275
1989	3016 The Pipes of Pan	Closed	1990	16.90	225-350
1989	3017 Mischievous Goblin	Closed	1990	16.90	175-250
1989	3018 The Gorgon Medusa - R.G./M.L.	Closed	1990	16.90	200
1989	3019 The Alchemist - M. Locker	Closed	1990	16.90	200-600
1989	3020 The Merman - M. Locker	Closed	1990	16.90	200
1989	3021 The Guardian Dragon	Closed	1995	16.90	85
1989	3022 The Minotaur	Closed	1991	16.90	200-375
1989	3023 The Grim Reaper	Open		16.90	34
1989	3024 The Unicorn	Open		16.90	34
1989	3027 The Castle of Souls	Closed	1995	22.00	88
1989	3028 The Dragon Gateway	Closed	1995	22.00	88
1989	3029 The Dragon Rider - M. Locker	Closed	1995	16.90	88
1989	3030 The Dragon's Kiss Mold 1 - M. Locker	Closed	N/A	16.90	88
1989	3030 The Dragon's Kiss Mold 2 - M. Locker	Closed	1993	16.90	88
1989	3031 The Witch and Familiar	Closed	1990	16.90	250-325
1989	3032 The Oriental Dragon Mold 1 - M. Locker	Closed	N/A	16.90	600
1989	3032 The Oriental Dragon Mold 2 - M. Locker	Closed	N/A	16.90	480
1989	3032 The Oriental Dragon Mold 3 - M. Locker	Closed	1993	16.90	295
1989	3033 The Reborn Dragon	Open		16.90	34
1989	3034 The Fire Dragon - M. Locker	Closed	1993	16.90	90
1989	3035 The Giant Sorceror	Closed	1993	16.90	90
1989	3036 The Wizard of Light	Closed	1995	16.90	85
1989	3037 The Light of Knowledge - M. Locker	Closed	1991	16.90	175-220
1989	3038 Pegasus	Open		16.90	34
1990	3039 The Earth Wizard	Closed	1991	18.60	90
1990	3040 The Fire Wizard	Closed	1994	18.60	90
1990	3041 The Water Wizard	Closed	1991	18.60	90
1990	3042 The Air Wizard	Closed	1991	18.60	90
1990	3043 Mother Nature	Open		18.60	34
1990	3044 The Dragon of the Lake	Closed	1993	26.10	125-225
1990	3045 The Dragon's Spell	Closed	1992	18.60	100
1990	3046 The Keeper of the Treasure	Closed	1995	18.60	90
1990	3047 George & the Dragon	Closed	1990	18.60	550-775
1990	3048 Dragon of the Sea	Closed	1993	18.60	88
1990	3049 Dragon of the Forest	Closed	1994	18.65	88
1990	3050 Dragon of Wisdom	Open		18.60	34
1990	3051 Spirits of the Forest	Closed	1995	18.60	85
1990	3052 Virgin and Unicorn	Closed	1993	26.10	88
1991	3053 The Wizard of Autumn	Open		22.00	34
1991	3054 The Wizard of Winter	Open		22.00	34
1991	3055 The Wizard of Spring - A. Slocombe	Closed	1995	22.00	85
1991	3056 The Wizard of Summer	Open		22.00	85
1991	3057 The Dragon of the Moon	Open		22.00	34
1991	3058 The Sun Dragon - M. Locker	Open		22.00	34
1991	3059 Dragon of the Clouds - M. Locker	Open		22.00	34
1991	3060 The Spirited Pegasus	Closed	1994	22.00	88
1991	3061 The Castle of Spires - A. Slocombe	Closed	1993	29.75	125
1991	3062 The Castle in the Clouds - A. Slocombe	Closed	1992	22.00	88
1991	3063 The Moon Wizard - A. Slocombe	Open		22.00	34
1991	3064 Dragon of the Stars - M. Locker	Closed	1995	29.75	85
1991	3065 The Sorceress of Light - M. Locker	Closed	1994	22.00	88
1991	3066 The Jewelled Dragon - A. Slocombe	Closed	1995	22.00	85
1991	3067 Old Father Time - M. Locker	Closed	1993	29.75	110-125
1991	3068 Runelore	Closed	1996	29.75	88
1992	3069 The Fairy Queen - A. Slocombe	Closed	1993	23.70	88
1992	3070 The Dragon Queen - A. Slocombe	Closed	1996	32.20	55
1992	3071 The Ice Dragon - A. Slocombe	Open		23.70	34
1992	3072 The Sleepy Dragon - M. Locker	Open		23.70	34
1992	3073 Unicorn of Light - A. Slocombe	Open		23.70	34
1992	3074 Starspell - M. Locker	Open		23.70	34
1992	3075 The Visionary	Open		32.20	42
1992	3076 The Crystal Spell - M. Locker	Closed	1995	23.70	75-85
1992	3077 Unicorn Rider - A. Slocombe	Open		23.70	34
1992	3078 The Loremaker - A. Slocombe	Open		23.70	34
1992	3079 Dragon's Enchantress - A. Slocombe	Closed	1994	32.20	85-100
1992	3080 The Leaf Spirit	Closed	1994	23.70	88
1992	3081 The Wizard of the Future	Open		23.70	34
1992	3082 The Swamp Dragon - A. Slocombe	Closed	1996	23.70	45
1992	3083 The Dragon of the Skulls	Closed	1996	23.70	45
1992	3084 The Dark Dragon - A. Slocombe	Open		23.70	34
1992	3085 The Dragon of Light - R.G./A.S.	Open		23.70	34
1993	3092 The Fountain of Light - A. Slocombe	Closed	1995	25.00	88
1993	3093 The Dawn of the Dragon - R. Gibbons	Closed	1996	25.00	34
1993	3094 The Dragon of Prehistory	Closed	1995	25.00	88
1993	3095 Defender of the Crystal - A. Slocombe	Open		25.00	34
1993	3096 Rising of the Phoenix - M. Locker	Closed	1995	25.00	88
1993	3097 The Protector of Young - M. Locker	Open		25.00	34
1993	3098 The Unicorns of Freedom - A. Slocombe	Open		25.00	34
1993	3099 The Keeper of the Skulls	Open		33.60	42
1993	3100 The Wizard of the Serpents - M. Locker	Closed	1996	25.00	45
1993	3101 The Loving Dragons - M. Locker	Open		25.00	34
1993	3102 The Sword Master - A. Slocombe	Open		25.00	34
1993	3103 Dragon of Mystery - M. Locker	Closed	1996	25.00	45
1994	3104 The Wizard of the Skies - M. Locker	Open		25.40	36
1994	3105 The Dragon of the Treasure - A. Slocombe	Open		25.40	36
1994	3106 The Wizard of the Lake	Open		25.40	36
1994	3107 Banishing the Dragon - S. Darnley	Open		25.40	36
1994	3108 The Dragon's Castle	Open		25.40	44
1994	3109 The Mystical Traveller - M. Locker	Open		25.40	36
1994	3110 The Armoured Dragon - S. Darnley	Open		25.40	36
1994	3111 The Hatchlings - S. Darnley	Open		25.40	36
1994	3112 Dragon of Ice Crystals - A. Slocombe	Open		30.50	42

*Quotes have been rounded up to nearest dollar

FIGURINES

The Tudor Mint Inc.
to United Design Corp.

YEAR ISSUE		EDITION LIMIT	YEAR RETD.	ISSUE PRICE	*QUOTE U.S.$
1994	3113 Mischievous Dragon - S. Darnley	Open		25.40	36
1994	3114 The Crystal Unicorn - S. Darnley	Open		30.50	42
1994	3115 Summoner of Light - M. Locker	Open		30.50	42
1994	3116 The Majestic Dragon - A. Slocombe	Open		30.50	42
1994	3117 The Proud Pegasus	Open		25.40	36
1995	3118 The Dragon Warrior - S. Darnley	Open		40.00	42
1995	3119 The Crystal Serpent - M. Locker	Open		54.00	54
1995	3120 The Dragon of the Deep - M. Locker	Open		34.00	34
1995	3121 The Celtic Dragon - A. Slocombe	Open		42.00	42
1995	3122 The Unicorn of Justice - A. Slocombe	Open		34.00	34
1995	3123 The Dragon King - M. Locker	Open		64.00	64
1995	3124 The Castle of Light	Open		34.00	34
1995	3125 The Dragon's Nest - A. Slocombe	Open		42.00	42
1995	3126 The Mischievous Dragonets	Open		42.00	42
1995	3127 The Guardian of Light	Open		54.00	54
1995	3128 The Dragon Thief	Open		42.00	42
1995	3129 The Earth Dragon	Open		54.00	54
1995	3130 The Studious Dragon - A. Slocombe	Open		42.00	42
1995	3131 Finding the Dragonets - M. Locker	Open		34.00	34
1995	3132 Learning to Fly	Open		34.00	34
1995	3133 The Wizard's Best Friend	Open		34.00	34
1995	3134 Reflections - M. Locker	Open		42.00	42
1995	3135 The Lord of the Wizards - A. Slocombe	Open		42.00	42
1995	3136 The Solar Dragon - S. Darnley	Open		54.00	54
1995	3137 The Lunar Dragon	Open		54.00	54
1995	3138 Wizard Mountain	Open		28.00	28
1995	3139 The Crystal Chalice	Open		32.00	32
1995	3140 The Wizard's Scroll - A. Slocombe	Open		28.00	28
1995	3141 The Magic Glade - S. Darnley	Open		32.00	32
1995	3142 The Magic Staff - M. Locker	Open		28.00	28
1995	3143 The Wrong Spell - M. Locker	Open		32.00	32
1996	3144 The Sea Dragon - S. Riley	Open		35.00	35
1996	3145 The First Born - J. Watson	Open		35.00	35
1996	3146 Way Out Dragon - H. Coventry	Open		35.00	35
1996	3147 Dragons At Play - H. Coventry	Open		46.00	46
1996	3148 The Nursery - H. Coventry	Open		35.00	35
1996	3149 Snoozing Wizard - H. Coventry	Open		35.00	35
1996	3150 The Fairy Princess - H. Coventry	Open		46.00	46
1996	3151 Follow Me Kids! - H. Coventry	Open		35.00	35
1996	3152 Don't Push Me! - S. Riley	Open		35.00	35
1996	3153 The Artist - S.R./S.D.	Open		46.00	46
1996	3154 The Magical World - S.R./A.S.	Open		38.00	38
1996	3155 The Biker - S.R./M.L.	Open		38.00	38
1996	3156 Behave! - S.R./R.G.	Open		38.00	38
1996	3157 The Looking Glass - H.C./S.D.	Open		46.00	46
1996	3158 Bestowing the Magic Power - J.W./A.S..	Open		46.00	46
1996	3159 A Bicycle Made For Two - J.W./R.G.	Open		38.00	38
1996	3160 'Out of Tune' - H.C./M.L.	Open		38.00	38
1996	3161 The Holder of the Skull - J.W./A.S.	Open		46.00	46

United Design Corp.

Angels Collection - D. Newburn, unless otherwise noted

1993	Angel of Flight AA-032 - K. Memoli	10,000		100.00	100
1993	Angel w/ Birds AA-034	10,000	1995	75.00	75
1994	Angel w/ Book AA-058	10,000		84.00	84
1994	Angel w/ Christ Child AA-061 - K. Memoli	10,000		84.00	84
1993	Angel w/ Lilies AA-033	10,000	1996	80.00	80
1993	Angel w/ Lilies, Crimson AA-040	10,000		80.00	80
1992	Angel, Lamb & Critters AA-021 - S. Bradford	10,000		90.00	95
1996	Angel, Lion & Fawn AA-093 - K. Memoli	20,000		280.00	280
1992	Angel, Lion & Lamb AA-020 - K. Memoli	10,000	1994	135.00	280
1994	Angel, Roses and Bluebirds AA-054	10,000		65.00	65
1996	Angels, Roses & Doves AA-112	10,000		75.00	75
1993	Autumn Angel AA-035	10,000	1996	70.00	70
1993	Autumn Angel, Emerald AA-041	10,000	1996	70.00	70
1995	Celestial Guardian Angel AA-069 - S. Bradford	10,000		120.00	120
1991	Christmas Angel AA-003 - S. Bradford	10,000	1994	125.00	125
1991	Classical Angel AA-005 - S. Bradford	10,000		79.00	79
1994	Dreaming of Angels AA-060 - K. Memoli	10,000		120.00	120
1996	Dreaming of Angels, pastel AA-111 - K. Memoli	10,000		120.00	120
1994	Earth Angel AA-059 - S. Bradford	10,000		84.00	84
1997	Eyes Toward Heaven AA-132 - K. Memoli	10,000		130.00	130
1991	The Gift AA-009 - S. Bradford	2,500	1991	135.00	650
1992	The Gift '92 AA-018 - S. Bradford	3,500	1992	140.00	295
1993	The Gift '93 AA-037 - S. Bradford	3,500	1993	120.00	225
1994	The Gift '94 AA-057	5,000	1994	140.00	175
1995	The Gift '95 AA-067	5,000	1995	140.00	140
1996	The Gift '96 AA-094	5,000	1996	140.00	140
1997	The Gift '97 AA-128 - P.J. Jonas	7,500		150.00	150
1995	Guardian Angel, Lion & Lamb AA-083 - S. Bradford	10,000		165.00	165
1995	Guardian Angel, Lion & Lamb, lt. AA-068 - S. Bradford	10,000		165.00	165
1994	Harvest Angel AA-063 - S. Bradford	10,000		84.00	84
1991	Heavenly Shepherdess AA-008 - S. Bradford	10,000		99.00	99
1992	Joy To The World AA-016	10,000	1996	90.00	95
1995	A Little Closer to Heaven AA-081 - K. Memoli	10,000		230.00	230
1995	A Little Closer to Heaven, lt. AA-085 - K. Memoli	10,000		230.00	230
1993	Madonna AA-031 - K. Memoli	10,000		100.00	100
1991	Messenger of Peace AA-006 - S. Bradford	10,000		75.00	79
1992	Peaceful Encounter AA-017	10,000		100.00	100
1997	Rejoice AA-130 - K. Memoli	10,000		90.00	90
1997	Rejoice, silver AA-143 - K. Memoli	10,000		90.00	90
1997	Serenity AA-131 - K. Memoli	10,000		90.00	90
1997	Serenity, silver AA-144 - K. Memoli	10,000		90.00	90
1997	Spirit of Winter AA-142 - G.G. Santiago	15,000		200.00	200
1995	Starlight Starbright AA-066	10,000		70.00	70
1991	Trumpeter Angel AA-004 - S. Bradford	10,000		99.00	99
1992	Winter Angel AA-019	10,000		75.00	75
1991	Winter Rose Angel AA-007 - S. Bradford	10,000	1994	65.00	65

Backyard Birds™ - Various

1994	Allen's on Pink Flowers BB-044 - P.J. Jonas	Open		22.00	22
1994	Allen's on Purple Morning Glory BB-051 - P.J. Jonas	Open		22.00	22
1989	Baltimore Oriole BB-024 - S. Bradford	Retrd.	1996	19.50	22
1989	Blue Jay BB-026 - S. Bradford	Open		19.50	22
1989	Blue Jay, Baby BB-027 - S. Bradford	Retrd.	1990	15.00	15
1990	Bluebird (Upright) BB-031 - S. Bradford	Open		20.00	20
1988	Bluebird BB-009 - S. Bradford	Open		15.00	21
1988	Bluebird Hanging BB-017 - S. Bradford	Retrd.	1990	11.00	17
1988	Bluebird, sm. BB-001 - S. Bradford	Open		10.00	11
1994	Broadbill on Blue Morning Glory BB-053 - P.J. Jonas	Open		22.00	22
1994	Broadbill on Trumpet Vine BB-043 - P.J. Jonas	Open		22.00	22
1994	Broadbill on Yellow Fuscia BB-055 - P.J. Jonas	Open		22.00	22
1994	Broadbill Pair on Yellow Flowers BB-048 - P.J. Jonas	Open		30.00	30
1988	Cardinal Hanging BB-018 - S. Bradford	Retrd.	1990	11.00	11
1988	Cardinal, Female BB-011 - S. Bradford	Open		15.00	17
1988	Cardinal, Male BB-013 - S. Bradford	Open		15.00	18
1988	Cardinal, sm. BB-002 - S. Bradford	Open		10.00	11
1990	Cedar Waxwing Babies BB-033 - S. Bradford	Retrd.	1996	22.00	22
1990	Cedar Waxwing BB-032 - S. Bradford	Retrd.	1996	20.00	20
1988	Chickadee BB-010 - S. Bradford	Open		15.00	18
1988	Chickadee Hanging BB-019 - S. Bradford	Retrd.	1990	11.00	11
1988	Chickadee, Small BB-003 - S. Bradford	Open		10.00	11
1990	Evening Grosbeak BB-034 - S. Bradford	Retrd.	1996	22.00	22
1989	Goldfinch BB-028 - S. Bradford	Open		16.50	20
1989	Hoot Owl BB-025 - S. Bradford	Open		15.00	20
1988	Humingbird BB-012 - S. Bradford	Open		15.00	18
1988	Hummingbird Female, sm. BB-005 - S. Bradford	Retrd.	1991	10.00	10
1988	Hummingbird Flying, sm. BB-004 - S. Bradford	Open		10.00	11
1988	Hummingbird sm., Hanging BB-022 - S. Bradford	Retrd.	1990	11.00	11
1988	Hummingbird, lg., Hanging BB-023 - S. Bradford	Retrd.	1990	15.00	15
1990	Indigo Bunting BB-036 - S. Bradford	Retrd.	1996	20.00	20
1990	Indigo Bunting, Female BB-039 - S. Bradford	Retrd.	1996	20.00	20
1994	Magnificent Pair on Trumpet Vine BB-046 - P.J. Jonas	Open		30.00	30
1990	Nuthatch, White-throated BB-037 - S. Bradford	Retrd.	1996	20.00	20
1990	Painted Bunting BB-040 - S. Bradford	Retrd.	1996	20.00	20
1990	Painted Bunting, Female BB-041 - S. Bradford	Retrd.	1996	20.00	20
1990	Purple Finch BB-038 - S. Bradford	Retrd.	1996	20.00	20
1988	Red-winged Blackbird BB-014 - S. Bradford	Retrd.	1991	15.00	17
1988	Robin Babies BB-008 - S. Bradford	Open		15.00	19
1988	Robin Baby, Small BB-006 - S. Bradford	Open		10.00	11
1988	Robin BB-015 - S. Bradford	Open		15.00	21
1988	Robin Hanging BB-020 - S. Bradford	Retrd.	1990	11.00	11
1990	Rose Breasted Grosbeak BB-042 - S. Bradford	Retrd.	1996	20.00	20
1994	Rubythroat on Pink Fuscia BB-054 - P.J. Jonas	Open		22.00	22
1994	Rubythroat on Red Morning Glory BB-052 - P.J. Jonas	Open		22.00	22
1994	Rubythroat on Thistle BB-049 - P.J. Jonas	Open		16.50	17
1994	Rubythroat on Yellow Flowers BB-045 - P.J. Jonas	Open		22.00	22
1994	Rubythroat Pair on Pink Flowers BB-047 - P.J. Jonas	Open		30.00	30
1989	Saw-Whet Owl BB-029 - S. Bradford	Open		15.00	18
1988	Sparrow BB-016 - S. Bradford	Open		15.00	17
1988	Sparrow Hanging BB-021 - S. Bradford	Retrd.	1990	11.00	11
1988	Sparrow, sm. BB-007 - S. Bradford	Retrd.	1996	10.00	11
1989	Woodpecker BB-030 - S. Bradford	Open		16.50	20

Easter Bunny Family™ - D. Kennicutt

1994	All Hidden SEC-045	Retrd.	1996	24.50	25
1989	Auntie Bunny SEC-008	Retrd.	1992	20.00	23
1992	Auntie Bunny w/Cake SEC-033R	Retrd.	1994	20.00	22
1991	Baby in Buggy, Boy SEC-027R	Retrd.	1994	20.00	22
1991	Baby in Buggy, Girl SEC-029R	Retrd.	1994	20.00	22
1994	Babysitter SEC-049	Open		24.50	25
1994	Bath Time SEC-044	Retrd.	1997	24.50	25
1995	Bed Time SEC-057	Open		24.00	24
1992	Boy Bunny w/Large Egg SEC-034R	Retrd.	1994	20.00	22
1991	Bubba In Wheelbarrow SEC-021	Retrd.	1993	20.00	20
1990	Bubba w/Wagon SEC-016	Retrd.	1993	16.50	18
1988	Bunnies, Basket Of SEC-001	Retrd.	1991	13.00	18
1991	Bunny Boy w/Basket SEC-025	Retrd.	1993	20.00	20
1988	Bunny Boy w/Duck SEC-002	Retrd.	1991	13.00	18
1997	Bunny Express SEC-070	Open		27.00	27
1988	Bunny Girl w/Hen SEC-004	Retrd.	1991	13.00	18
1989	Bunny w/Prize Egg SEC-010	Retrd.	1993	19.50	20
1988	Bunny, Easter SEC-003	Retrd.	1991	15.00	18
1993	Christening Day SEC-040	Retrd.	1995	20.00	22
1989	Ducky w/Bonnet, Blue SEC-015	Retrd.	1992	10.00	12
1989	Ducky w/Bonnet, Pink SEC-014	Retrd.	1992	10.00	12
1996	Easter Bunny In Evening Clothes-SEC-064	Open		20.00	20
1992	Easter Bunny w/Back Pack SEC 030	Open		20.00	22
1990	Easter Bunny w/Crystal SEC-017	Retrd.	1995	23.00	25
1993	Easter Bunny, Chocolate Egg SEC-041	Retrd.	1996	23.00	25
1995	Easter Cookies SEC-052	Open		24.00	24
1997	Easter Dress SEC-067	Open		22.00	22
1989	Easter Egg Hunt SEC-012	Retrd.	1995	16.50	22
1996	Easter Pageant - SEC-059	Open		17.00	17
1996	Easter Parade - SEC-063	Open		25.00	25
1993	Egg Roll SEC-036	Open		23.00	25
1991	Fancy Find SEC-028	Retrd.	1995	20.00	22
1996	First Kiss - SEC-061	Open		20.00	20
1995	First Outing SEC-054	Open		19.00	19
1994	First Steps SEC-048	Open		24.50	25
1997	Friendship SEC-068	1,997		22.00	22
1997	The Gardener SEC-069	Open		22.00	22
1994	Gift Carrot SEC-046	Open		22.00	22
1993	Girl Bunny w/Basket SEC-039	Open		20.00	22
1992	Girl Bunny w/Large Egg SEC-035R	Retrd.	1994	20.00	22
1993	Grandma & Quilt SEC-037	Retrd.	1997	23.00	25
1992	Grandma w/ Bible SEC-031	Retrd.	1996	20.00	22
1996	Grandma's Dress Makers Form-1996-SEC-066	Yr.Iss.	1996	25.00	25
1992	Grandpa w/Carrots SEC-032R	Retrd.	1994	20.00	22
1996	Grandpa w/Sunflowers - SEC-065	Open		20.00	20
1990	Hen w/Chick SEC-018	Retrd.	1992	23.00	23
1994	Large Prize Egg SEC-047	Open		22.00	22
1989	Little Sis w/Lolly SEC-009	Retrd.	1992	14.50	18
1993	Lop Ear Dying Eggs SEC-042	Retrd.	1997	23.00	25
1996	Lop Girl w/Gift Box - SEC-060	Open		20.00	20
1991	Lop-Ear w/Crystal SEC-022	Open		23.00	25
1993	Mom Storytime SEC-043	Open		20.00	22
1996	Mom w/Chocolate Egg - SEC-062	Open		25.00	25
1990	Momma Making Basket SEC-019	Retrd.	1992	23.00	23
1990	Mother Goose SEC-020	Retrd.	1992	16.50	20
1991	Nest of Bunny Eggs SEC-023	Open		17.50	22
1995	Printing Lessons SEC-053	Open		19.00	19
1995	Quality Inspection SEC-055	Open		19.00	19
1988	Rabbit, Grandma SEC-005	Retrd.	1991	15.00	20
1988	Rabbit, Grandpa SEC-006	Retrd.	1991	15.00	20
1988	Rabbit, Momma w/Bonnet SEC-007	Retrd.	1991	15.00	20
1989	Rock-A-Bye Bunny SEC-013	Retrd.	1995	20.00	25
1993	Rocking Horse SEC-038	Retrd.	1996	20.00	22
1989	Sis & Bubba Sharing SEC-011	Retrd.	1996	22.50	25
1995	Spring Flying SEC-058	Retrd.	1997	19.00	19
1995	Team Work SEC-051	Open		24.00	24
1995	Two in a Basket SEC-056	Retrd.	1997	24.00	24
1991	Victorian Auntie Bunny SEC-026	Retrd.	1993	20.00	20
1991	Victorian Momma SEC-024	Retrd.	1993	20.00	20
1994	Wheelbarrow SEC-050	Open		24.50	25

Easter Bunny Family™ Babies - D. Kennicutt

1995	Baby in Basket SEC-815	Open		8.00	8
1994	Baby on Blanket, Naptime SEC-807	Open		6.50	7
1996	Baby w/Diaper & Bottle, Blue SEC-825	Open		8.00	8

*Quotes have been rounded up to nearest dollar

United Design Corp.
to United Design Corp.

FIGURINES

YEAR ISSUE		EDITION LIMIT	YEAR RETD.	ISSUE PRICE	*QUOTE U.S.$
1996	Baby w/Diaper & Bottle, Pink SEC-817	Open		8.00	8
1996	Baby w/Diaper & Bottle, Yellow SEC-824	Open		8.00	8
1995	Basket of Carrots SEC-812	Open		8.00	8
1994	Boy Baby w/Blocks SEC-805	Open		6.50	7
1994	Boy w/Baseball Bat SEC-801	Open		6.50	7
1996	Boy w/Baseball Mitt SEC-822	Open		8.00	8
1994	Boy w/Basket and Egg SEC-802	Open		6.50	7
1996	Boy w/Big Teddy SEC-819	Open		8.00	8
1995	Boy w/Butterfly SEC-814	Open		8.00	8
1994	Boy w/Stick Horse SEC-803	Open		6.50	7
1996	Boy w/Train Engine SEC-816	Open		8.00	8
1997	Bubble Bath SEC-828	Open		8.50	9
1996	Dress Up Girl SEC-821	Open		8.00	8
1996	Egg Delivery SEC-823	Open		8.00	8
1995	Gift Egg SEC-808	Open		8.00	8
1996	Girl w/Apron Full SEC-820	Open		8.00	8
1994	Girl w/Big Egg SEC-806	Open		6.50	7
1994	Girl w/Blanket SEC-800	Open		6.50	7
1996	Girl w/Book SEC-818	Open		8.00	8
1994	Girl w/Toy Rabbit SEC-804	Open		6.50	7
1997	Grandpa's Boy SEC-826	Open		8.50	9
1995	Hostess SEC-810	Open		8.00	8
1995	Lop Ear & Flower Pot SEC-809	Open		8.00	8
1997	Soccer Player SEC-829	Open		8.50	9
1995	Spring Flowers SEC-813	Open		8.00	8
1995	Tea Party SEC-811	Open		8.00	8
1997	Thank You SEC-827	Open		8.50	9

Legend of Santa Claus™ - L. Miller, unless otherwise noted

YEAR ISSUE		EDITION LIMIT	YEAR RETD.	ISSUE PRICE	*QUOTE U.S.$
1992	Arctic Santa CF-035 - S. Bradford	7,500		90.00	100-140
1988	Assembly Required CF-017	7,500	1994	79.00	130
1997	Bells of Christmas Morn CF-074 - K. Memoli	7,500		190.00	190
1997	Bells of Christmas Morn, Victorian CF-075 - K. Memoli	7,500		190.00	190
1991	Blessed Flight CF-032 - K. Memoli	7,500	1994	159.00	325
1996	Blessing Santa CF-066 - K. Memoli	10,000		160.00	160
1987	Checking His List CF-009	15,000	1994	75.00	120
1997	A Christmas Galleon CF-073 - K. Memoli	7,500		150.00	150
1989	Christmas Harmony CF-020 - S. Bradford	7,500	1992	85.00	130
1992	The Christmas Tree CF-038	7,500	1995	90.00	90
1993	Dear Santa CF-046 - K. Memoli	7,500	1996	170.00	210
1995	Dear Santa, Vict. CF-063	10,000		170.00	170
1987	Dreaming Of Santa CF-008 - S. Bradford	15,000	1988	65.00	325
1992	Earth Home Santa CF-040 - S. Bradford	7,500		135.00	140
1986	Elf Pair CF-005	10,000	1992	60.00	135
1988	Father Christmas CF-018 - S. Bradford	7,500	1993	75.00	135
1991	For Santa CF-029	7,500		99.00	135
1990	Forest Friends CF-025	7,500	1993	90.00	110
1995	Getting Santa Ready CF-056	10,000		170.00	170
1996	High Country Santa CF-064	15,000		190.00	190
1989	Hitching Up CF-021	7,500	1993	90.00	110
1995	Into the Wind CF-061	10,000		140.00	140
1995	Into the Wind, Vict. CF-062	10,000		140.00	140
1993	Jolly St. Nick CF-045 - K. Memoli	7,500		130.00	130
1993	Jolly St. Nick, Victorian CF-050 - K. Memoli	7,500		120.00	120
1986	Kris Kringle CF-002	10,000	1991	60.00	160
1992	Letters to Santa CF-036	7,500	1995	125.00	185
1997	A Light on the Roof CF-072 - K. Memoli	7,500		160.00	160
1997	A Light on the Roof, Victorian CF-076 - K. Memoli	7,500		160.00	160
1988	Load 'Em Up CF-016 - S. Bradford	7,500	1990	79.00	350
1987	Loading Santa's Sleigh CF-010	15,000	1993	100.00	110
1992	Loads of Happiness CF-041 - K. Memoli	7,500	1996	100.00	110
1994	Long Stocking Dilemma, Victorian CF-055 - K. Memoli	7,500		170.00	170
1994	Longstocking Dilemma CF-052 - K. Memoli	7,500		170.00	170
1987	Mrs. Santa CF-006 - S. Bradford	15,000	1991	60.00	235
1993	The Night Before Christmas CF-043	7,500	1996	100.00	100
1993	Northwoods Santa CF-047 - S. Bradford	7,500	1996	100.00	100
1987	On Santa's Knee-CF007 - S. Bradford	15,000	1994	65.00	120
1996	Pause For a Tale CF-065	10,000		190.00	190
1996	Pause For a Tale, Victorian CF-069 - K. Memoli	10,000		190.00	190
1990	Puppy Love CF-024	7,500	1994	100.00	220
1989	A Purr-Fect Christmas CF-019 - S. Bradford	7,500	1994	95.00	135
1991	Reindeer Walk CF-031 - K. Memoli	7,500		150.00	165
1995	The Ride CF-057	10,000		130.00	130
1986	Rooftop Santa CF-004 - S. Bradford	10,000	1991	65.00	200
1990	Safe Arrival CF-027 - Memoli/Jonas	7,500	1996	150.00	175
1996	Santa & Blitzen CF-067 - K. Memoli	10,000		140.00	140
1996	Santa & Blitzen, Victorian CF-070 - K. Memoli	10,000		140.00	140
1992	Santa and Comet CF-037	7,500	1995	110.00	110
1992	Santa and Mrs. Claus CF-039 - K. Memoli	7,500		150.00	150
1992	Santa and Mrs. Claus, Victorian CF-042 - K. Memoli	7,500		135.00	140
1986	Santa At Rest CF-001	10,000	1988	70.00	600
1991	Santa At Work CF-030	7,500	1995	99.00	175
1987	Santa On Horseback CF-011 - S. Bradford	15,000	1990	75.00	350
1994	Santa Riding Dove CF-053	7,500		120.00	120
1986	Santa With Pups CF-003 - S. Bradford	10,000	1988	65.00	570
1993	Santa's Friends CF-044	7,500	1996	100.00	100
1995	Santa, Dusk & Dawn CF-060	10,000		150.00	150
1988	St. Nicholas CF-015	7,500	1992	75.00	125
1994	Star Santa w/ Polar Bear CF-054 - S. Bradford	7,500		130.00	130
1995	Starlight Express CF-059	10,000		170.00	170
1994	The Story of Christmas CF-051 - K. Memoli	10,000	1996	180.00	250
1996	The Story of Christmas, Victorian CF-068 - K. Memoli	10,000		180.00	180
1993	Victorian Lion & Lamb Santa CF-048 - S. Bradford	7,500		100.00	100
1990	Victorian Santa CF-028 - S. Bradford	7,500	1992	125.00	325
1991	Victorian Santa w/ Teddy CF-033 - S. Bradford	7,500		150.00	160
1990	Waiting For Santa CF-026 - S. Bradford	7,500	1995	100.00	225-250
1997	Wilderness Santa CF-071	10,000		300.00	300

Legend Of The Little People™ - L. Miller

YEAR ISSUE		EDITION LIMIT	YEAR RETD.	ISSUE PRICE	*QUOTE U.S.$
1989	Adventure Bound LL-002	Retrd.	1993	35.00	50
1989	Caddy's Helper LL-007	Retrd.	1993	35.00	50
1991	The Easter Bunny's Cart LL-020	Retrd.	1994	45.00	50
1991	Fire it Up LL-023	Retrd.	1994	50.00	55
1990	Fishin' Hole LL-012	Retrd.	1994	35.00	50
1989	A Friendly Toast LL-003	Retrd.	1993	35.00	50
1990	Gathering Acorns LL-014	Retrd.	1994	100.00	100
1991	Got It LL-021	Retrd.	1994	45.00	50
1990	Hedgehog In Harness LL-010	Retrd.	1994	45.00	50
1990	Husking Acorns LL-008	Retrd.	1994	60.00	65
1991	It's About Time LL-022	Retrd.	1994	55.00	60
1990	A Little Jig LL-018	Retrd.	1994	45.00	50
1990	A Look Through The Spyglass LL-015	Retrd.	1994	40.00	50
1989	Magical Discovery LL-005	Retrd.	1993	45.00	50
1990	Ministral Magic LL-017	Retrd.	1994	45.00	50
1990	A Proclamation LL-013	Retrd.	1994	45.00	55
1989	Spring Water Scrub LL-006	Retrd.	1993	35.00	50
1990	Traveling Fast LL-009	Retrd.	1994	45.00	50
1989	Treasure Hunt LL-004	Retrd.	1993	45.00	50
1991	Viking LL-019	Retrd.	1994	45.00	50
1989	Woodland Cache LL-001	Retrd.	1993	35.00	50
1990	Woodland Scout LL-011	Retrd.	1994	40.00	50
1990	Writing The Legend LL-016	Retrd.	1994	35.00	65

Lil' Doll™ - Various

YEAR ISSUE		EDITION LIMIT	YEAR RETD.	ISSUE PRICE	*QUOTE U.S.$
1992	Clara & The Nutcracker LD-017 - D. Newburn	Retrd.	1994	35.00	35
1991	The Nutcracker LD-006 - P.J. Jonas	Retrd.	1994	35.00	35

Music Makers™ - Various

YEAR ISSUE		EDITION LIMIT	YEAR RETD.	ISSUE PRICE	*QUOTE U.S.$
1991	A Christmas Gift MM-015 - D. Kennicutt	Retrd.	1993	59.00	59
1991	Crystal Angel MM-017 - D. Kennicutt	Retrd.	1993	59.00	59
1991	Dashing Through The Snow MM-013 - D. Kennicutt	Retrd.	1993	59.00	59
1989	Evening Carolers MM-005 - D. Kennicutt	Retrd.	1993	69.00	69
1989	Herald Angel MM-011 - S. Bradford	Retrd.	1993	79.00	79
1991	Nutcracker MM-024 - P.J. Jonas	Retrd.	1994	69.00	69
1991	Peace Descending MM-025 - P.J. Jonas	Retrd.	1993	69.00	69
1991	Renaissance Angel MM-028 - P.J. Jonas	Retrd.	1994	69.00	69
1989	Santa's Sleigh MM-004 - L. Miller	Retrd.	1993	69.00	69
1991	Teddy Bear Band #2 MM-023 - D. Kennicutt	Retrd.	1994	90.00	90
1989	Teddy Bear Band MM-012 - S. Bradford	Retrd.	1993	99.00	100
1989	Teddy Drummers MM-009 - D. Kennicutt	Retrd.	1993	69.00	69
1991	Teddy Soldiers MM-018 - D. Kennicutt	Retrd.	1994	69.00	84
1991	Victorian Santa MM-026 - L. Miller	Retrd.	1993	69.00	69

Party Animals™ - L. Miller, unless otherwise noted

YEAR ISSUE		EDITION LIMIT	YEAR RETD.	ISSUE PRICE	*QUOTE U.S.$
1992	Democratic Donkey ('92) - K. Memoli	Retrd.	1994	20.00	20
1984	Democratic Donkey ('84) - D. Kennicutt	Retrd.	1986	14.50	16
1986	Democratic Donkey ('86)	Retrd.	1988	14.50	15
1988	Democratic Donkey ('88)	Retrd.	1990	14.50	16
1990	Democratic Donkey ('90) - D. Kennicutt	Retrd.	1992	16.00	16
1984	GOP Elephant ('84)	Retrd.	1986	14.50	16
1986	GOP Elephant ('86)	Retrd.	1988	14.50	15
1988	GOP Elephant ('88)	Retrd.	1990	14.50	16
1990	GOP Elephant ('90) - D. Kennicutt	Retrd.	1992	16.00	16
1992	GOP Elephant ('92) - K. Memoli	Retrd.	1994	20.00	20

PenniBears™ - P.J. Jonas

YEAR ISSUE		EDITION LIMIT	YEAR RETD.	ISSUE PRICE	*QUOTE U.S.$
1992	After Every Meal PB-058	Retrd.	1994	22.00	22
1992	Apple For Teacher PB-069	Retrd.	1994	24.00	24
1989	Attic Fun PB-019	Retrd.	1992	20.00	40
1989	Baby Hugs PB-007	Retrd.	1992	20.00	35
1991	Baking Goodies PB-043	Retrd.	1993	26.00	30
1989	Bathtime Buddies PB-023	Retrd.	1992	20.00	25
1992	Batter Up PB-066	Retrd.	1994	22.00	22
1991	Bear Footin' it PB-037	Retrd.	1993	24.00	24
1992	Bear-Capade PB-073	Retrd.	1994	22.00	22
1991	Bearly Awake PB-033	Retrd.	1993	22.00	25
1989	Beautiful Bride PB-004	Retrd.	1992	20.00	35
1993	Big Chief Little Bear PB-088	Retrd.	1996	28.00	28
1989	Birthday Bear PB-018	Retrd.	1992	20.00	40
1991	Boo Hoo Bear PB-050	Retrd.	1994	22.00	22
1990	Boooo Bear PB-025	Retrd.	1993	20.00	22
1991	Bountiful Harvest PB-045	Retrd.	1994	24.00	24
1989	Bouquet Boy PB-003	Retrd.	1992	20.00	45
1989	Bouquet Girl PB-001	Retrd.	1992	20.00	45
1991	Bump-bear-Crop PB-035	Retrd.	1993	26.00	30
1991	Bunny Buddies PB-042	Retrd.	1993	22.00	25
1989	Butterfly Bear PB-005	Retrd.	1992	20.00	45-50
1990	Buttons & Bows PB-012	Retrd.	1992	20.00	45
1992	Christmas Cookies PB-075	Retrd.	1994	22.00	22
1991	Christmas Reinbear PB-046	Retrd.	1994	28.00	28
1992	Cinderella PB-056	Retrd.	1994	22.00	22
1992	Clowning Around PB-065	Retrd.	1994	22.00	22
1989	Cookie Bandit PB-006	Retrd.	1992	20.00	30
1990	Count Bearacula PB-027	Retrd.	1993	22.00	24
1991	Country Lullabye PB-036	Retrd.	1993	24.00	25
1990	Country Quilter PB-030	Retrd.	1993	22.00	30
1990	Country Spring PB-013	Retrd.	1992	20.00	45
1991	Curtain Call PB-049	Retrd.	1994	24.00	24
1992	Decorating The Wreath PB-076	Retrd.	1994	22.00	22
1989	Doctor Bear PB-008	Retrd.	1992	20.00	30
1992	Downhill Thrills PB-070	Retrd.	1994	24.00	24
1990	Dress Up Fun PB-028	Retrd.	1993	22.00	30
1992	Dust Bunny Roundup PB-062	Retrd.	1994	22.00	22
1992	First Prom PB-064	Retrd.	1994	22.00	22
1990	Garden Path PB-014	Retrd.	1992	20.00	45-50
1993	Getting 'Round On My Own PB-085	Retrd.	1996	26.00	26
1990	Giddiap Teddy PB-011	Retrd.	1992	20.00	35
1991	Goodnight Little Prince PB-041	Retrd.	1993	26.00	30
1991	Goodnight Sweet Princess PB-040	Retrd.	1993	26.00	30
1993	Gotta Try Again PB-082	Retrd.	1996	24.00	24
1989	Handsome Groom PB-015	Retrd.	1992	20.00	40
1993	Happy Birthday PB-084	Retrd.	1996	26.00	26
1993	A Happy Camper PB-077	Retrd.	1996	28.00	28
1991	Happy Hobo PB-051	Retrd.	1994	26.00	26
1989	Honey Bear PB-002	Retrd.	1992	20.00	45
1992	I Made It Boy PB-061	Retrd.	1994	22.00	22
1992	I Made It Girl PB-060	Retrd.	1994	22.00	22
1989	Lazy Days PB-009	Retrd.	1992	20.00	25
1992	Lil' Devil PB-071	Retrd.	1994	24.00	24
1991	Lil' Mer-teddy PB-034	Retrd.	1993	24.00	24
1992	Lil' Sis Makes Up PB-074	Retrd.	1994	22.00	22
1993	Little Bear Peep PB-083	Retrd.	1996	24.00	24
1993	Making It Better PB-087	Retrd.	1996	24.00	24
1993	May Joy Be Yours PB-080	Retrd.	1996	24.00	24
1993	My Forever Love PB-078	Retrd.	1996	28.00	28
1989	Nap Time PB-016	Retrd.	1992	20.00	22
1989	Nurse Bear PB-017	Retrd.	1992	20.00	35
1992	On Your Toes PB-068	Retrd.	1994	24.00	24
1989	Petite Mademoiselle PB-010	Retrd.	1992	20.00	40
1991	Pilgrim Provider PB-047	Retrd.	1994	32.00	32
1992	Pot O' Gold PB-059	Retrd.	1994	22.00	22
1992	Puddle Jumper PB-057	Retrd.	1994	24.00	24
1989	Puppy Bath PB-020	Retrd.	1992	20.00	25
1989	Puppy Love PB-021	Retrd.	1992	20.00	25
1993	Rest Stop PB-079	Retrd.	1996	24.00	24
1992	Sandbox Fun PB-063	Retrd.	1994	22.00	22
1990	Santa Bear-ing Gifts PB-031	Retrd.	1993	24.00	30
1993	Santa's Helper PB-081	Retrd.	1996	28.00	28
1990	Scarecrow Teddy PB-029	Retrd.	1993	24.00	25
1992	Smokey's Nephew PB-055	Retrd.	1994	22.00	22
1990	Sneaky Snowball PB-026	Retrd.	1993	20.00	25
1989	Southern Belle PB-024	Retrd.	1992	20.00	35
1992	Spanish Rose PB-053	Retrd.	1994	24.00	24
1990	Stocking Surprise PB-032	Retrd.	1993	22.00	26
1993	Summer Belle PB-086	Retrd.	1996	24.00	24
1991	Summer Sailing PB-039	Retrd.	1993	26.00	30
1991	Sweet Lil 'Sis PB-048	Retrd.	1994	22.00	22
1991	Sweetheart Bears PB-044	Retrd.	1993	28.00	30
1992	Tally Ho! PB-054	Retrd.	1994	22.00	22
1992	Touchdown PB-072	Retrd.	1994	22.00	22
1989	Tubby Teddy PB-022	Retrd.	1992	20.00	22
1991	A Wild Ride PB-052	Retrd.	1994	26.00	26
1992	Will You Be Mine? PB-067	Retrd.	1994	22.00	22
1991	Windy Day PB-038	Retrd.	1993	24.00	24

PenniBears™ Collector's Club Members Only Editions - P.J. Jonas

YEAR ISSUE		EDITION LIMIT	YEAR RETD.	ISSUE PRICE	*QUOTE U.S.$
1990	1990 First Collection PB-C90	Retrd.	1990	26.00	125
1991	1991 Collecting Makes Cents PB-C91	Retrd.	1991	26.00	150
1992	1992 Today's Pleasures, Tomorrow's Treasures PB-C92	Retrd.	1992	26.00	100
1993	1993 Chalkin Up Another Year PB-C93	Retrd.	1993	26.00	35
1994	1994 Artist's Touch-Collector's Treasure PB-C94	Retrd.	1994	26.00	26

Storytime Rhymes & Tales - H. Henriksen

YEAR ISSUE		EDITION LIMIT	YEAR RETD.	ISSUE PRICE	*QUOTE U.S.$
1991	Humpty Dumpty SL-008	Retrd.	1993	64.00	64
1991	Little Jack Horner SL-007	Retrd.	1993	50.00	50
1991	Little Miss Muffet SL-006	Retrd.	1993	64.00	64
1991	Mistress Mary SL-002	Retrd.	1993	64.00	64

*Quotes have been rounded up to nearest dollar

YEAR ISSUE		EDITION LIMIT	YEAR RETD.	ISSUE PRICE	*QUOTE U.S.$
1991	Mother Goose SL-001	Retrd.	1993	64.00	64
1991	Owl & Pussy Cat SL-004	Retrd.	1993	100.00	100
1991	Simple Simon SL-003	Retrd.	1993	90.00	90
1991	Three Little Pigs SL-005	Retrd.	1993	100.00	100

Teddy Angels™ - P.J. Jonas

YEAR ISSUE		EDITION LIMIT	YEAR RETD.	ISSUE PRICE	*QUOTE U.S.$
1995	Bruin & Bluebirds "Nurture nature." BA-013	Open		19.00	19
1995	Bruin Making Valentines "Holidays start within the heart." BA-012	Open		15.00	15
1995	Bruin With Harp Seal "Make your corner of the world a little warmer." BA-021	Open		15.00	15
1995	Bunny's Picnic "Make a feast of friendship." BA-007	Open		19.00	19
1995	Casey & Honey Reading "Friends are the best recipe for relaxation." BA-023	Open		15.00	15
1995	Casey Tucking Honey In "There is magic in the simplest things we do." BA-008	Open		19.00	19
1995	Cowboy Murray "Have a Doo Da Day." BA-002	Open		19.00	19
1995	Honey "Love gives our hearts wings." BA-014	Open		13.00	13
1995	Ivy & Blankie "Nothing is as comfortable as an old friend." BA-003	Open		13.00	13
1995	Ivy In Garden "Celebrate the little things." BA-009	Open		15.00	15
1995	Ivy With Locket "You're always close at heart." BA-028	Open		13.00	13
1995	Murray & Little Bit "Imagination can take you anywhere." BA-004	Open		19.00	19
1995	Murray Mending Bruin "Everybody needs a helping hand." BA-005	Open		15.00	15
1995	Murray With Angel "I believe in you, too." BA-022	Open		22.00	22
1995	Nicholas With Stars "Dreams are never too far away to catch." BA-024	Open		15.00	15
1995	Old Bear "Always remember your way home." BA-011	Open		19.00	19
1995	Old Bear & Little Bit Gardening "The well-watered garden produces a great harvest." BA-026	Open		15.00	15
1995	Old Bear & Little Bit Reading "Love to learn and learn to love." BA-006	Open		15.00	15
1995	Rufus Helps Bird "We could all use a little lift." BA-027	Open		15.00	15
1995	Sweetie "Come tell me all about it." - BA-001	Open		15.00	15
1995	Sweetie With Kitty Cats "Always close-knit." BA-025	Open		15.00	15
1995	Tilli & Murray "Friendship is a bridge between hearts." BA-010	Open		15.00	15

Teddy Angels™ Christmas - P.J. Jonas

YEAR ISSUE		EDITION LIMIT	YEAR RETD.	ISSUE PRICE	*QUOTE U.S.$
1997	Angel & Sweetie BA-029	Open		22.00	22
1995	Casey "You're a bright & shining star." BA-019	Open		13.00	13
1995	Ivy "Enchantment glows in winter snows." BA-020	Open		13.00	13
1995	Sweetie & Santa Bear "Tis the season of surprises." BA-016	Open		22.00	22
1995	Tilli & Doves "A wreath is a circle of love." BA-015	Open		19.00	19

WACO Products Corp.

Melody In Motion/Collector's Society - S. Nakane, unless otherwise noted

YEAR ISSUE		EDITION LIMIT	YEAR RETD.	ISSUE PRICE	*QUOTE U.S.$
1992	Amazing Willie the One-Man Band 07152	Retrd.	1994	130.00	300-650
1992	Willie The Conductor	Retrd.	1994	Gift	35
1993	Charmed Bunnies	Retrd.	1993	Gift	45
1993	Willie The Collector 07170	Retrd.	1995	200.00	300-350
1994	Springtime	Retrd.	1994	Gift	45
1995	Best Friends	Retrd.	1995	Gift	45
1996	Willie The Entertainer 07199	Retrd.	1996	200.00	200
1996	'86 Santa Replica - K. Maeda	Yr. Iss.		Gift	45
1997	Willie on Parade/Drum 07214 - K. Maeda	Yr.Iss.		220.00	220
1997	Willie Sez - K. Maeda	Yr. Iss.		Gift	45

Melody In Motion - S. Nakane, unless otherwise noted

YEAR ISSUE		EDITION LIMIT	YEAR RETD.	ISSUE PRICE	*QUOTE U.S.$
1985	Willie The Trumpeter 07000	Open		90.00	175
1985	Willie The Hobo (Memories) 07001	2,500	1985	90.00	175
1985	Willie The Hobo (Show Me...) 07001	Retrd.	1996	90.00	175
1985	Willie The Whistler (Show Me...) 07002	2,500	1985	90.00	175
1985	Willie The Whistler (Memories) 07002	Open		90.00	175
1985	Salty 'N' Pepper 07010	Retrd.	1992	90.00	700-900
1986	The Cellist 07011	Retrd.	1995	100.00	180
1986	Santa Claus 1986 07012	20,000	1986	100.00	2500
1986	The Guitarist 07013	Retrd.	1994	100.00	300
1986	The Fiddler 07014	Retrd.	1995	100.00	250
1987	Lamppost Willie 07051	Open		85.00	150
1987	The Organ Grinder 07053	Retrd.	1994	100.00	200
1987	Violin Clown 07055	Retrd.	1992	85.00	200
1987	Clarinet Clown 07056	Retrd.	1991	85.00	300
1987	Saxophone Clown 07057	Retrd.	1991	85.00	250
1987	Accordion Clown 07058	Retrd.	1991	85.00	250
1987	Santa Claus 1987 07060	16,000	1987	110.00	700-2000
1987	Balloon Clown 07061	Open		85.00	150
1987	The Carousel (1st ed.) 07065	Retrd.	1993	190.00	260
1987	Madame Violin 07075	Retrd.	1991	130.00	130
1987	Madame Mandolin 07076	Retrd.	1994	130.00	130
1987	Madame Cello 07077	Retrd.	1991	130.00	130
1987	Madame Flute 07078	Retrd.	1992	130.00	130
1987	Madame Harpsichord 07080	Retrd.	1991	130.00	130
1987	Madame Lyre 07081	Retrd.	1994	130.00	130
1988	Madame Harp 07079	Open		130.00	130
1988	Spotlight Clown Cornet 07082	Retrd.	1992	120	250-400
1988	Spotlight Clown Banjo 07083	Retrd.	1992	120.00	200
1988	Spotlight Clown Trombone 07084	Retrd.	1992	120.00	200
1988	Spotlight Clown Bingo 07085	Retrd.	1996	130.00	160
1988	Spotlight Clown Tuba 07086	Retrd.	1992	120.00	200
1988	Spotlight Clown Bass 07087	Retrd.	1994	130.00	160
1988	Peanut Vendor 07088	Retrd.	1994	140.00	200
1988	Ice Cream Vendor 07089	Retrd.	1994	140.00	200
1988	Santa Claus 1988 07090	12,000	1988	130.00	1000
1989	Clockpost Willie 07091	Open		150.00	220
1989	Santa Claus 1989 (Willie) 07092	12,000	1989	130.00	N/A
1989	Lull'aby Willie 07093	Retrd.	1992	170.00	170
1989	The Grand Carousel 07094	Retrd.	1995	3000.00	3000
1989	Grandfather's Clock 07096	Retrd.	1994	200.00	295
1990	Santa Claus 1990 07097	12,000	1990	150.00	300-500
1990	Shoemaker 07130	3,700	1993	110.00	200
1990	Blacksmith 07131	3,700	1993	110.00	200
1990	Woodchopper 07132	3,700	1993	110.00	200
1990	Accordion Boy 07133	4,100	1992	120.00	200
1990	Hunter 07134	Retrd.	1994	110.00	150
1990	Robin Hood 07135 - C. Johnson	2,000	1991	180.00	350
1990	Little John 07136 - C. Johnson	2,000	1992	180.00	300
1990	Clockpost Willie II (European) 07140	Retrd.	1990	N/A	N/A
1990	Clockpost Clown 07141	Open		220.00	220
1990	Lull' A Bye Willie II (European) 07142	Retrd.	1990	N/A	N/A
1991	The Carousel (2nd ed.) 07065	Retrd.	1995	240.00	350
1991	Victoria Park Carousel 07143	Open		300.00	360
1991	Hunter Timepiece 07144	Retrd.	1994	250.00	320
1991	Santa Claus 1991 07146	7,000	1991	150.00	300-450
1992	Wall Street Willie 07147	Open		180.00	240
1991	Willie The Fisherman 07148	Open		150.00	200
1992	King of Clowns Carousel 07149	Open		740.00	850
1992	Golden Mountain Clock 07150	Open		250.00	280
1992	Santa Claus 1992 07151	11,000	1992	160.00	180
1992	Dockside Willie 07153	Open		160.00	190
1993	Wild West Willie 07154	Open		175.00	200
1993	Alarm Clock Post 07155	Open		N/A	N/A
1993	Lamplight Willie 07156	Retrd.	1996	220.00	220
1993	Madame Cello Player, glaze 07157	200	1993	170.00	170
1993	Madame Flute, glaze 07158	200	1993	170.00	170
1993	Madame Harpsichord, glaze	200	1993	170.00	170
1993	Madame Harp, glaze	150	1993	190.00	190
1993	Santa Claus 1993 Coke 07161	6,000	1993	180.00	225
1993	Wall Street (Japanese) 07162	Retrd.	1993	N/A	N/A
1993	Santa Claus 1993 (European) 07163	1,000	1993	N/A	N/A
1993	Willie The Golfer - Alarm 07164	Retrd.	1995	240.00	240
1993	The Artist 07165	Retrd.	1996	240.00	240
1993	Heartbreak Willie 07166	Open		180.00	190
1993	South of the Border 07167	Retrd.	1996	180.00	225
1993	When I Grow Up 07171	Retrd.	1996	200.00	200
1994	Low Press Job-Alarm 07168	Retrd.	1995	240.00	240
1994	Day's End-Alarm 07169	Open		240.00	240
1994	Santa '94 Coca-Cola 07174	9,000	1994	190.00	300
1994	Smooth Sailing 07175	Retrd.	1996	200.00	200
1994	Santa Claus 1994 (European) 07176	700	1994	N/A	N/A
1994	The Longest Drive 07177	Open		150.00	150
1994	Happy Birthday Willie 07178	Open		170.00	170
1994	Chattanooga Choo Choo 07179	Open		180.00	190
1994	Jackpot Willie 07180	Open		180.00	190
1994	Caroler Boy 07189	10,000		172.00	180
1994	Caroler Girl 07190	10,000		172.00	180
1994	Willie the Yodeler 07192	Open		158.00	160
1994	Willie the Golfer- Clock 07264	Open		240.00	240
1994	Day's End-Clock 07269	Open		240.00	240
1995	Campfire Cowboy 07172	Retrd.	1995	180.00	250
1995	Blue Danube Carousel 07173	Open		280.00	300
1995	Willie the Conductor (10th Anniversary) 07181	10,000		220.00	220
1995	Coca-Cola Norman Rockwell 07194	Open		194.00	200
1995	Santa Claus '95 07195	6,000	1995	190.00	300
1995	Gaslight Willie 07197	Open		190.00	190
1995	Coca Cola Polar Bear 07198	6,000		180.00	180
1995	Low Pressure Job-Clock 07268	Open		240.00	240
1995	Willie The Fireman 07271	1,500	1996	200.00	200
1996	The Candy Factory-I Love Lucy 07203 - Willingham/Maeda	Open		250.00	250
1996	Willie On The Road 07204 - K. Maeda	Open		180.00	180
1996	Marionette Clown 07205 - K. Maeda	Open		200.00	200
1996	Willie the Racer 07206 - K. Maeda	Open		180.00	180
1996	Willie the Organ Grinder 07207	3,000		200.00	200
1996	Santa Claus '96 07208 - K. Maeda	7,000		220.00	220
1996	Willie the Champion 07209 - K. Maeda	Open		180.00	180
1996	Willie the Photographer 07211 - K. Maeda	Open		220.00	220
1997	Willie on Parade/Trumpet 07212 - K. Maeda	Open		220.00	220
1997	Willie on Parade/Sousaphone 07213 - K. Maeda	Open		220.00	220
1997	Willie on Parade/Trombone 07215 - K. Maeda	Open		220.00	220
1997	I Love Lucy/Vitameatavegamin 07216 - K. Maeda	Open		N/A	N/A
1997	Side Street Circus/Balancing Dog 07230	Open		110.00	110
1997	Side Street Circus/Juggling 07231	Open		110.00	110
1997	Side Street Circus/Accordian 07232	Open		110.00	110
1997	Side Street Circus/Clarinet 07233	Open		110.00	110
1997	Side Street Circus/Plate Spinning 07234	Open		110.00	110

Walnut Ridge Collectibles

Autumn Figurines - K. Bejma

YEAR ISSUE		EDITION LIMIT	YEAR RETD.	ISSUE PRICE	*QUOTE U.S.$
1996	Black Cat-410	Open		24.00	24
1996	Ghost with Pumpkin-417	Open		30.00	30
1996	Jack-O-Lantern Man-416	Open		40.00	40
1996	Jack-O-Lantern-414	Open		28.00	28
1991	Oak Leaf, set/2-420	Open		28.00	28
1996	Owl-411	Open		22.00	22
1996	Pilgrim Set-400	Open		80.00	80
1996	Pumpkin Kids, set/2-415	Open		56.00	56
1991	Pumpkin, set/3-404	Open		22.00	22
1996	Pumpkin-large-412	Open		48.00	48
1996	Pumpkin-small-413	Open		28.00	28
1996	Turkey-large-419	Open		44.00	44
1996	Turkey-medium-418	Open		36.00	36
1991	Turkey-small-401	Open		20.00	20
1996	Witch-large-407	Open		68.00	68
1996	Witch-medium-408	Open		48.00	48
1996	Witch-small-409	Open		44.00	44

Cat Figurines - K. Bejma

YEAR ISSUE		EDITION LIMIT	YEAR RETD.	ISSUE PRICE	*QUOTE U.S.$
1993	Basket of Kittens-309	Open		70.00	70
1991	Calico Cat-306	Open		40.00	40
1991	Goodrich Cat-300	Open		50.00	50
1994	Tabby Cat-310	Open		50.00	50
1991	Tiny Cat-304	Open		24.00	24

Christmas Figurines - K. Bejma

YEAR ISSUE		EDITION LIMIT	YEAR RETD.	ISSUE PRICE	*QUOTE U.S.$
1996	Alpine Tree-1001	Open		24.00	24
1988	Belsnickle-102	Open		32.00	32
1988	Belsnickle-104	Retrd.	1996	48.00	48
1988	Belsnickle-105	Retrd.	1996	32.00	32
1989	Belsnickle-124	Retrd.	1996	30.00	30
1991	Belsnickle-140	Retrd.	1996	40.00	40
1994	Belsnickle-176	Retrd.	1996	28.00	28
1988	Belsnickle-mini-116	Open		22.00	22
1994	Belsnickle/Tree-174	Open		32.00	32
1994	Children on Sled-172	Open		48.00	48
1995	Crying Snowman-189	Open		44.00	44
1994	Father Christmas-175	Open		28.00	28
1992	Father Christmas-large-161	Open		270.00	270
1988	Father Christmas/Apples-122	Retrd.	1996	48.00	48
1988	Father Christmas/Bag-114	Retrd.	1996	34.00	34
1993	Father Christmas/Bag-163	Retrd.	1996	38.00	38
1994	Father Christmas/Bag-166	Open		30.00	30
1994	Father Christmas/Bag-178	Retrd.	1996	42.00	42
1988	Father Christmas/Basket-100R	Retrd.	1996	120.00	120
1988	Father Christmas/Basket-100W	Retrd.	1996	120.00	120
1994	Father Christmas/Girl/Doll-165	Open		52.00	52
1993	Father Christmas/Holly-164	Open		52.00	52
1990	Father Christmas/Toys/Switch-136	Retrd.	1996	120.00	120
1991	Gnome/Rabbit-148	Retrd.	1996	32.00	32
1990	Jolly St. Nick-135	Retrd.	1996	52.00	52
1994	Primitive Snowman-173	Open		32.00	32
1990	Rocking Santa-129	Retrd.	1996	36.00	36
1992	Santa/Horse-small-158	Open		24.00	24
1991	Santa/Walking Stick-152	Retrd.	1996	56.00	56
1996	Snow Children-1002	Open		56.00	56
1994	Snowflake Belsnickle-177	Open		36.00	36
1994	Snowman & Boy-181	Open		34.00	34
1996	Snowman in Forest-1003	Open		70.00	70
1993	Snowman with Scarf-162	Open		28.00	28
1995	Snowman with Twig Arms-188	Open		32.00	32
1990	Snowman-127	Retrd.	1996	32.00	32
1994	Snowman-large-182	Open		44.00	44
1990	Snowman-medium-131	Open		28.00	28
1991	Snowman-small-139	Retrd.	1996	22.00	22
1996	Snowman/Snowflake Scarf-1004	Open		44.00	44
1992	Snowman/Twigs-156	Open		30.00	30
1995	Tall Tree-190	Open		28.00	28
1992	Tree Set-160	Open		44.00	44
1996	Tree-197	Open		26.00	26
1996	Tree-198	Open		22.00	22
1996	Tree-199	Open		18.00	18
1994	Walking Santa-180	Retrd.	1996	90.00	90

Gossamer Wings - K. Bejma

YEAR ISSUE		EDITION LIMIT	YEAR RETD.	ISSUE PRICE	*QUOTE U.S.$
1994	Addie-167	Open		40.00	40
1995	Alexandra-183	Open		54.00	54
1997	Cecelia-1011	Open		90.00	90
1997	Choirs-1010	Open		76.00	76
1996	Deborah-192	Open		50.00	50
1994	Elizabeth-170	Open		52.00	52
1997	Elysia-1005	Open		54.00	54
1997	Emma-1006	Open		50.00	50
1996	Gabriella-194	Open		64.00	64
1994	Hannah-169	Open		50.00	50
1997	Helena-1009	Open		56.00	56
1995	Julia-184	Open		38.00	38
1996	Kathleen-193	Open		56.00	56

*Quotes have been rounded up to nearest dollar

FIGURINES

YEAR ISSUE		EDITION LIMIT	YEAR RETD.	ISSUE PRICE	*QUOTE U.S.$
1995	Lucia-187	Open		62.00	62
1995	Lydia-185	Open		58.00	58
1994	Meghan-168	Open		46.00	46
1997	Noel-1008	Open		40.00	40
1996	Olivia-196	Open		56.00	56
1997	Sarah-1007	Open		32.00	32
1995	Tatiana-186	Open		58.00	58
1996	Thomas-195	Open		64.00	64
1996	Victoria-191	Open		54.00	54

Herr Belsnickle Collection - K. Bejma

YEAR ISSUE		EDITION LIMIT	YEAR RETD.	ISSUE PRICE	*QUOTE U.S.$
1993	Herr Dieter-807	Open		90.00	90
1993	Herr Franz-805	Open		90.00	90
1993	Herr Fritz-803	Open		100.00	100
1993	Herr Gottfried-806	Open		90.00	90
1994	Herr Gregor-818	Open		90.00	90
1993	Herr Gunther-809	Open		70.00	70
1993	Herr Heinrich-810	Open		60.00	60
1993	Herr Hermann-813	Open		48.00	48
1995	Herr Johann-820	Open		230.00	230
1993	Herr Karl-801	Open		150.00	150
1993	Herr Klaus-800	Open		180.00	180
1993	Herr Ludwig-811	Open		60.00	60
1993	Herr Nicholas-802	Open		130.00	130
1993	Herr Oskar-816	Open		44.00	44
1993	Herr Peter-815	Open		44.00	44
1993	Herr Reiner-812	Open		60.00	60
1994	Herr Rudolph-819	Open		230.00	230
1995	Herr Rutger-822	Open		150.00	150
1995	Herr Sebastian-821	Open		70.00	70
1994	Herr Viktor-817	Open		64.00	64
1993	Herr Wilhelm-804	Open		100.00	100
1993	Herr Willi-814	Open		44.00	44
1993	Herr Wolfgang-808	Open		70.00	70

Limited Edition Christmas Figurines - K. Bejma

YEAR ISSUE		EDITION LIMIT	YEAR RETD.	ISSUE PRICE	*QUOTE U.S.$
1997	Glad Tidings-704	Yr.Iss.		60.00	60

Limited Edition Collector's Series - K. Bejma

YEAR ISSUE		EDITION LIMIT	YEAR RETD.	ISSUE PRICE	*QUOTE U.S.$
1997	Cabbages & Violets-639	350		64.00	64
1996	Christkindl 635	2,000		68.00	68
1996	Christmas Aglow 629	1,000		48.00	48
1996	Dash Away All 628	1,500		108.00	108
1995	Downhill Racer 618	2,500		48.00	48
1994	Egg Cottage 603	1,500		80.00	80
1994	Egyptian Egg/Rabbits 600	1,500		48.00	48
1997	Field of Flowers-636	750		56.00	56
1997	Forever Friends-638	500		52.00	52
1997	The Garden Gate-637	350		56.00	56
1995	Happy Christmas 622	2,000		50.00	50
1995	Hareratio 613	1,500		42.00	42
1994	Hemlocks And Holly 610	750		260.00	260
1996	Hitching a Ride 625	750		44.00	44
1996	Holiday Rider 631	1,000		68.00	68
1995	Holiday Sledding 620	2,500		52.00	52
1994	Holy Night 612	750		250.00	250
1995	Jacqueline 614	1,500		48.00	48
1995	Jeffrey 615	1,500		48.00	48
1994	Keeping Secrets 605	3,500		52.00	52
1994	Kimbra 609	10,000		24.00	24
1996	Life is but a Dream 627	1,000		42.00	42
1994	Lite The Way 604	3,500		52.00	52
1995	Magnolias in Bloom 616	1,500		90.00	90
1996	A Merry Christmas Santa-100A	100		600.00	600
1996	A Midnight Clear 634	1,250		52.00	52
1994	Miles To Go 607	10,000		52.00	52
1995	O' Tannenbaum 621	1,500		56.00	56
1995	Père Noel 619	1,500		90.00	90
1994	Rabbits At Home Egg 602	1,500		80.00	80
1996	Robin Tracks 624	1,000		48.00	48
1995	Santa Express 617	2,000		56.00	56
1996	Sharing The Spirit 630	1,000		90.00	90
1994	Shhh... 606	5,000		44.00	44
1994	Silent Night 611	750		120.00	120
1995	St. Nick's Visit 623	750		380.00	380
1996	The Stocking Was Hung 633	1,500		68.00	68
1994	Strolling Rabbits Egg 601	1,500		80.00	80
1996	Sweet Messenger 632	1,500		52.00	52
1997	To Market, To Market-640	500		50.00	50
1994	Up On The Rooftop 608	5,000		56.00	56
1996	Violets for Mary 626	500		64.00	64

Nativity Collection - K. Bejma

YEAR ISSUE		EDITION LIMIT	YEAR RETD.	ISSUE PRICE	*QUOTE U.S.$
1995	Elephant	Open		120.00	120
1995	Group I Stable, Joseph, Mary, Baby Jesus, Angel	Open		324.00	324
1995	Group II Wise Men, set/3	Open		190.00	190
1995	Group III Shepards and Wanderer, set/4	Open		190.00	190
1995	Group IV Farm Animals, Sheep/2, Goat, Donkey, Cow	Open		130.00	130
1995	Laying Camel	Open		120.00	120
1995	Standing Camel	Open		120.00	120

Spring Figurines - K. Bejma

YEAR ISSUE		EDITION LIMIT	YEAR RETD.	ISSUE PRICE	*QUOTE U.S.$
1991	Bavarian Rabbit Set-226	Open		90.00	90
1996	Bunny in Shamrocks-268	Open		52.00	52
1996	Bunny with Carrots on Base-272	Open		48.00	48
1995	Bunny with Colored Eggs-263	Open		28.00	28
1990	Bunny/Acorns/Carrots-202	Open		32.00	32
1991	Bunny/Basket-227	Retrd.	1996	26.00	26
1993	Bunny/Cabbage-233	Open		24.00	24
1997	Cherub on Rabbit-282	Open		44.00	44
1997	Cherub, large-283	Open		120.00	120
1994	Chick with Egg-257	Open		48.00	48
1994	Chicks, set/3 -260	Open		64.00	64
1995	Country Rabbit,large-265	Open		70.00	70
1996	Egg Wagon-275	Open		44.00	44
1996	Farmer Rabbit w/Carrots-270	Open		56.00	56
1992	Folksy/Rabbit-231	Open		48.00	48
1997	Gypsy-313	Open		56.00	56
1994	Hatching Chick-259	Open		20.00	20
1993	Hatching Rabbit-234	Open		34.00	34
1995	Hiking Bunny w/Egg Basket-262	Open		28.00	28
1994	Lady Vendor Rabbit-256	Open		42.00	42
1994	Laying Sheep-245	Open		44.00	44
1995	Meadow Rabbit-266	Open		90.00	90
1991	Mother Rabbit/Basket-215	Retrd.	1996	48.00	48
1990	Mother Rabbit/Six Babies-200	Open		120.00	120
1990	Mother/Bowl of Eggs-207	Retrd.	1996	30.00	30
1993	Mr. Rabbit/Two Children-244	Retrd.	1996	44.00	44
1994	Professor Rabbit/Chicks-236	Open		30.00	30
1990	Rabbit Holding Basket-220	Retrd.	1996	50.00	50
1994	Rabbit Holding Carrot-253	Open		52.00	52
1994	Rabbit in Flower Garden-246	Open		64.00	64
1996	Rabbit on Scooter-271	Open		44.00	44
1991	Rabbit Riding Rooster-209	Open		36.00	36
1996	Rabbit w/Ferns and Lillies-269	Open		120.00	120
1997	Rabbit w/Paw Up-281	Open		32.00	32
1994	Rabbit with Basket-255	Open		52.00	52
1994	Rabbit with Vest-254	Open		38.00	38
1991	Rabbit/Basket Eggs-224	Open		46.00	46
1991	Rabbit/Basket/Bow-225	Open		46.00	46
1994	Rabbit/Hat/Stick-239	Open		28.00	28
1990	Rabbit/Holding Basket-203	Open		30.00	30
1990	Rabbit/Umbrella-208	Retrd.	1996	30.00	30
1994	Rabbits on See-Saw-252	Open		44.00	44
1990	Running Rabbit-205	Open		32.00	32
1996	Shamrock Cart-273	Open		36.00	36
1990	Sitting Bunny-204	Retrd.	1996	24.00	24
1995	Sitting Bunny-261	Open		24.00	24
1990	Sitting Bunny-large-216	Open		68.00	68
1994	Sitting Rabbit-251	Open		36.00	36
1993	Sitting Rabbit-large-235	Open		44.00	44
1994	Squirrel on Pinecone-249	Open		40.00	40
1996	Squirrel-large-276	Open		48.00	48
1996	Squirrel-medium-277	Open		44.00	44
1994	Standing Chick-258	Open		24.00	24
1994	Standing Rabbit-237	Retrd.	1996	44.00	44
1990	Standing Sheep-211	Retrd.	1996	36.00	36
1997	Striped Cat, small-312	Open		30.00	30
1996	Tan Rabbit w/Basket on Back-267	Open		90.00	90
1990	Two Rabbits/Basket-219	Open		52.00	52
1996	Wheelbarrow Egg-274	Open		48.00	48
1994	Wheelbarrow Rabbit-250	Open		44.00	44
1997	White Kitten-311	Open		40.00	40
1997	White Rabbit, large-278	Open		36.00	36
1997	White Rabbit, medium-279	Open		30.00	30
1997	White Rabbit, small-280	Open		24.00	24
1995	Woodland Rabbit-264	Open		48.00	48

Walnut Ridge Everyday Collection - K. Bejma

YEAR ISSUE		EDITION LIMIT	YEAR RETD.	ISSUE PRICE	*QUOTE U.S.$
1997	Bunch of Violets-5009	Open		30.00	30
1997	Fantail Rooster-5005	Open		64.00	64
1997	Flower Wall Basket-5003	Open		48.00	48
1997	Fruit Topiary, large-5000	Open		150.00	150
1997	Fruit Topiary, medium-5001	Open		120.00	120
1997	Fruit Topiary, small-5002	Open		60.00	60
1997	Hen in Basket-5006	Open		48.00	48
1997	Hen w/Shamrocks-5008	Open		36.00	36
1997	Rooster w/Shamrocks-5007	Open		36.00	36
1997	Rooster, large-5004	Open		120.00	120
1997	Summer Flowers-5010	Open		80.00	80

Walt Disney

Walt Disney Collectors Society - Disney Studios

YEAR ISSUE		EDITION LIMIT	YEAR RETD.	ISSUE PRICE	*QUOTE U.S.$
1993	Jiminy Cricket Kit	Closed	1993	Gift	215-325
1993	Jiminy Cricket 4" / wheel	Closed	1993	Gift	200-250
1993	Jiminy Cricket/clef	Closed	1993	Gift	175-215
1993	Brave Little Tailor 7 1/4" (Animator's Choice)	Closed	1994	160.00	245-300
1994	Cheshire Cat 4 3/4"/ clef	Closed	1994	Gift	90-130
1994	Cheshire Cat 4 3/4"/ flower	Closed	1994	Gift	85-100
1994	Pecos Bill 9 1/2"	Closed	1994	650.00	500-650
1994	Admiral Duck 6 1/4" (Animator's Choice)	Closed	1995	165.00	165-210
1995	Dumbo	Closed	1995	Gift	75-95
1995	Cruella De Vil 10 1/4" (Animator's Choice)	Closed	1995	250.00	300-400
1995	Dumbo Ornament	Closed	1995	20.00	40-75
1995	Slue Foot Sue 41075	Closed	1995	695.00	550-695
1996	Winnie the Pooh 41091	Closed	1996	Gift	65-80
1996	Princess Minnie 41095 (Animator's Choice)	Closed	1996	165.00	165
1996	Winnie the Pooh Ornament 41096	Closed	1996	25.00	25-35
1996	Casey at the Bat 41107	Closed	1996	395.00	395
1997	Magician Mickey "On With the Show" 41134	Yr.Iss.		Gift	75.00
1997	Magician Mickey "On With the Show" Ornament 41135	Yr.Iss.		25.00	25
1997	Mickey's Debut (Steamboat Willie) (5th Anniversary) 41136	Yr.Iss.		175.00	175
1997	Goofy-Moving Day "Oh The World Owes Me a Livin'" 41138 (Animator's Choice)	Yr.Iss.		185.00	185

Classics Collection-Special Event - Disney Studios

YEAR ISSUE		EDITION LIMIT	YEAR RETD.	ISSUE PRICE	*QUOTE U.S.$
1993	Flight of Fancy 3" 41051	Closed	1994	35.00	40-50
1994	Mr. Smee 5" 41062	Closed	1995	90.00	85-125
1994	Mr. Smee 5" 41062 (teal stamp)	Closed	1995	90.00	85-135
1995	Lucky 41080	Closed	1995	40.00	60-75
1995	Wicked Witch 41084	Closed	1996	130.00	150-180
1996	Tinkerbell Ornament	Closed	1996	50.00	75-95
1996	Fairy Godmother 41108	Closed	1996	125.00	135-165
1997	Bring Back Her Heart-Evil Queen 41165	Yr.Iss.		150.00	150

Celebration Series - Disney Studios

YEAR ISSUE		EDITION LIMIT	YEAR RETD.	ISSUE PRICE	*QUOTE U.S.$
1997	Bundle of Joy (Dumbo and Stork) 41153	Open		125.00	125
1997	Happy Birthday, Mickey 41170	Open		95.00	95
1997	Money! Money! Money! 41152	Open		175.00	175

Classics Collection-101 Dalmatians - Disney Studios

YEAR ISSUE		EDITION LIMIT	YEAR RETD.	ISSUE PRICE	*QUOTE U.S.$
1996	Go Get Him Thunder 41129	Open		120.00	120
1996	Lucky w/TV 41131	Open		150.00	150
1996	Patient Perdita 41133	Open		175.00	175
1996	Proud Pongo 41132	Open		175.00	175
1996	Rolly 41130	Open		65.00	65
1996	Opening Title 41169	Open		29.00	29

Classics Collection-3 Caballeros - Disney Studios

YEAR ISSUE		EDITION LIMIT	YEAR RETD.	ISSUE PRICE	*QUOTE U.S.$
1995	Amigo Donald 7" 41076	Retrd.	1996	180.00	180-200
1995	Amigo Jose 7" 41077	Retrd.	1996	180.00	180
1995	Amigo Panchito 7" 41078	Retrd.	1996	180.00	180

Classics Collection-Bambi - Disney Studios

YEAR ISSUE		EDITION LIMIT	YEAR RETD.	ISSUE PRICE	*QUOTE U.S.$
1992	Bambi 6" 41033	Open		195.00	195
1992	Bambi 6" 41033/ wheel	Closed	1992	195.00	220-275
1992	Bambi & Flower 6" 41010	10,000	1993	298.00	400-575
1992	Field Mouse-not touching 5 3/5" 41012	7,500	1993	195.00	1300-1600
1992	Field Mouse-touching 5 3/5" 41012	7,500	1993	195.00	1100-1200
1992	Flower 3" 41034	Open		78.00	78
1992	Flower 3" 41034/ clef	Closed	1992	78.00	100
1992	Flower 3" 41034/ wheel	Closed	1992	78.00	130-150
1992	Friend Owl 8 3/5" 41011	Open		195.00	195
1992	Friend Owl 8 3/5" 41011/ wheel	Closed	1992	195.00	150-225
1992	Thumper 3" 41013	Open		55.00	55
1992	Thumper 3" 41013/ wheel	Closed	1992	55.00	60-85
1992	Thumper's Sisters 3 3/5" 41014	Open		69.00	69
1992	Thumper's Sisters 3 3/5" 41014/wheel	Closed	1992	69.00	70-90
1992	Bambi-Opening Title 41015	Open		29.00	29
1992	Bambi-Opening Title 41015/ wheel	Closed	1992	29.00	35

Classics Collection-Beauty and the Beast - Disney Studios

YEAR ISSUE		EDITION LIMIT	YEAR RETD.	ISSUE PRICE	*QUOTE U.S.$
1997	Tale as Old as Time-Belle and the Beast Dancing 41156	Open		295.00	295

Classics Collection-Cinderella - Disney Studios

YEAR ISSUE		EDITION LIMIT	YEAR RETD.	ISSUE PRICE	*QUOTE U.S.$
1993	A Dress For Cinderelly 41030/ wheel & clef	5,000	1993	800.00	1800-2200
1992	Birds With Sash 6 2/5" 41005	Closed	1994	149.00	160-225
1992	Chalk Mouse 3 2/5" 41006	Closed	1994	65.00	80-125
1992	Cinderella 6" 41000/ clef	Closed	1993	195.00	325-425
1992	Cinderella 6" 41000/ wheel	Closed	1992	195.00	300-400
1995	Cinderella & The Prince 41079	Open		275.00	295
1992	Cinderella, Lucifer, Bruno, Set/3/ wheel & clef	Closed	1993	333.00	500-560
1992	Gus 3 2/5" 41007	Closed	1994	65.00	95-125
1992	Bruno 4 2/5" 41002/ wheel & clef	Closed	1993	69.00	95-150
1992	Jaq 4 1/5" 41008	Closed	1994	65.00	85-125
1992	Lucifer 2 3/5" 41001/ clef	Closed	1993	69.00	96-110
1992	Lucifer 2 3/5" 41001/ wheel	Closed	1993	69.00	96-125
1992	Needle Mouse 5 4/5" 41004	Closed	1994	69.00	95-125
1992	Sewing Book 41003	Closed	1994	69.00	75-95
1992	Sewing Book 41003/ no mark	Closed	1994	69.00	80-100
1992	Cinderella-Opening Title 41009	Open		29.00	29
1992	Cinderella-Opening Title-Technicolor 41009	Closed	1993	29.00	40-50

Classics Collection-Delivery Boy - Disney Studios

YEAR ISSUE		EDITION LIMIT	YEAR RETD.	ISSUE PRICE	*QUOTE U.S.$
1992	Mickey 6" 41020	Open		125.00	135
1992	Mickey 6" 41020/ wheel	Closed	1992	125.00	150-225
1992	Minnie 6" 41021	Open		125.00	135
1992	Minnie 6" 41021/ wheel	Closed	1992	125.00	145-225
1992	Pluto (raised letters) 3 3/5" 41022/ wheel	Closed	1992	125.00	270-360
1992	Pluto 3 3/5" 41022	Open		125.00	125
1992	Pluto 3 3/5" 41022/ wheel	Closed	1992	125.00	175-250
1992	Delivery Boy-Opening Title 41019	Open		29.00	29
1992	Delivery Boy-Opening Title 41019/ clef	Closed	1993	29.00	35-50

Classics Collection-Fantasia - Disney Studios

YEAR ISSUE		EDITION LIMIT	YEAR RETD.	ISSUE PRICE	*QUOTE U.S.$
1993	Blue Centaurette-Beauty in Bloom, 7 1/2" 41041	Retrd.	1995	195.00	175-200
1992	Broom, 5 4/5" 41017	Retrd.	1995	75.00	95-125
1992	Broom, w/water spots 5 4/5" 41017/ wheel	Closed	1992	75.00	150-225
1996	Ben Ali Gator 7 1/2" 41118	Open		185.00	185
1994	Hop Low 2 3/4" 41067	Open		35.00	35
1996	Hyacinth Hippo 5 1/2" 41117	Open		195.00	195

*Quotes have been rounded up to nearest dollar

YEAR ISSUE		EDITION LIMIT	YEAR RETD.	ISSUE PRICE	*QUOTE U.S.$
1993	Love's Little Helpers 8" 41042	Retrd.	1995	290.00	290
1994	Mushroom Dancer-Medium 4 1/4" 41068	Open		50.00	50
1994	Mushroom Dancer-Medium 4 1/4" 41068/ teal stamp	Closed	1994	50.00	50-60
1994	Mushroom Dancer-Large 4 3/4" 41058	Open		60.00	60-75
1994	Mushroom Dancer-Large 4 3/4" 41058/ teal stamp	Closed	1994	60.00	60
1994	Mushroom Dancer-Small 41067	Open		35.00	35
1993	Pink Centaurette-Romantic Reflections 7 1/2" 41040	Retrd.	1995	175.00	175-225
1992	Sorcerer Mickey 5 1/8" 41016	Retrd.	1995	195.00	250-325
1992	Fantasia-Opening Title 41018	Open		29.00	40-50
1992	Fantasia-Opening Title-blank 41018	Closed	1994	29.00	40-55
1992	Fantasia-Opening Title-Technicolor 41018	Closed	1993	29.00	50-75

Classics Collection-Holiday Series - Disney Studios

1995	Presents For My Pals 41086	Closed	1995	150.00	175
1996	Pluto Helps Decorate 41112	Closed	1996	150.00	150
1997	Chip 'n Dale 41163	Yr.Iss.		150.00	150

Classics Collection-Jungle Book - Disney Studios

1997	King of the Swingers (King Louie) 41158	Open		175.00	175
1997	Monkeying Around (Flunky Monkey) 41159	Open		135.00	135
1997	Hula Baloo (Baloo) 41160	Open		185.00	185
1997	Mancub (Mowgirl) 41161	Open		115.00	115
1997	Mowgirl's Protector (Bugheera) 41162	Open		135.00	135
1997	Opening Title 41171	Open		29.00	29

Classics Collection-Lady and The Tramp - Disney Studios

1996	Lady 4 1/2" 41089	Open		120.00	120
1996	Tramp 1/2" 41090	Open		100.00	100
1996	Lady and the Tramp-Opening Title 41099	Open		29.00	29

Classics Collection-Mr. Duck - Disney Studios

1993	Donald & Daisy 6 3/5" 41024/clef	5,000	1993	298.00	475-595
1993	Donald & Daisy 6 3/5" 41024/wheel	5,000	1993	298.00	550-800
1993	Mr. Duck Steps Out-Opening Title 41023	Retrd.	1996	29.00	29
1993	Mr. Duck Steps Out-Opening Title 41023/ clef	Closed	1993	29.00	35
1993	Nephew Duck-Dewey 4" 41025	Retrd.	1996	65.00	65
1993	Nephew Duck-Dewey 4" 41025/ wheel	Closed	1993	65.00	65-100
1993	Nephew Duck-Huey 4" 41049	Retrd.	1996	65.00	65
1993	Nephew Duck-Huey 4" 41049/ clef	Closed	1993	65.00	65-85
1993	Nephew Duck-Louie 4" 41050	Retrd.	1996	65.00	65
1993	Nephew Duck-Louie 4" 41050/ clef	Closed	1993	65.00	65-80
1994	With Love From Daisy 6 1/4" 41060	Retrd.	1996	180.00	180-225

Classics Collection-Peter Pan - Disney Studios

1993	Captain Hook 8" 41044	Open		275.00	275
1993	Captain Hook 8" 41044/ clef	Closed	1994	275.00	650-855
1993	The Crocodile 6 1/4" 41054	Open		315.00	315
1993	Peter Pan 7 1/2" 41043	Open		165.00	165
1993	Peter Pan 7 1/2" 41043/ clef	Closed	1994	165.00	195-220
1993	Tinkerbell 5" 41045/ clef	12,500	1994	215.00	450-650
1993	Tinkerbell 5" 41045/ flower	12,500	1994	215.00	350-425
1993	Peter Pan-Opening Title 41047	Open		29.00	29
1993	Peter Pan-Opening Title 41047/ clef	Closed	1994	29.00	35

Classics Collection-Pinocchio - Disney Studios

1996	Figaro 41111	Open		55.00	55
1996	Geppetto 41114	Open		145.00	145
1996	Jiminy Cricket 41109	Open		85.00	85
1996	Pinocchio 41110	Open		125.00	125
1996	Pinocchio-Opening Title 41116	Open		29.00	29

Classics Collection-Reluctant Dragon - Disney Studios

1996	The Reluctant Dragon 7" 41072	7,500	1996	695.00	775-850

Classics Collection-Sleeping Beauty - Disney Studios

1997	Once Upon a Dream-Briar Rose 41157	12,500		345.00	345

Classics Collection-Snow White - Disney Studios

1994	Snow White 8 1/4" 41063/ flower	Closed	1994	165.00	200-250
1994	Snow White 8 1/4" 41063	Open		165.00	165
1995	Bashful 5" 91069	Open		85.00	85
1995	Doc 5 1/4" 41071	Open		95.00	95
1995	Dopey 5" 41074	Open		95.00	95
1995	Grumpy 7 3/4" 41065	Open		180.00	180
1995	Happy 5 1/2" 41064	Open		125.00	125
1995	Sleepy 3 1/4" 41066	Open		95.00	95
1995	Sneezy 4 1/2" 41073	Open		90.00	90
1995	Snow White-Opening Title 41083	Open		29.00	29

Classics Collection-Song of the South - Disney Studios

1996	Brer Bear 7 1/2" 41112	Closed	1997	175.00	175
1996	Brer Fox 4" 41101	Closed	1997	120.00	120
1996	Brer Rabbit 4 3/4" 41103	Closed	1997	150.00	150
1996	Song of the South-Opening Title 41104	Closed	1997	29.00	29

Classics Collection-Symphony Hour - Disney Studios

YEAR ISSUE		EDITION LIMIT	YEAR RETD.	ISSUE PRICE	*QUOTE U.S.$
1993	Clarabelle 6 4/5" 41027/ wheel	Closed	1993	198.00	240-275
1993	Clarabelle 6 4/5" 41027	Open		198.00	198
1994	Clara Cluck 41061	Open		185.00	185
1993	Goofy 6 4/5" 41026/ clef	Closed	1993	198.00	200-260
1993	Goofy 6 4/5" 41026/ wheel	Closed	1993	198.00	2500-2700
1993	Goofy 6 4/5" 41026	Open		198.00	235
1996	Donald Duck 8 1/4" 41105	Open		225.00	225
1993	Horace 6 4/5" 41028	Open		198.00	198
1993	Horace 6 4/5" 41028/ wheel	Closed	1993	198.00	220-240
1993	Mickey Conductor 7 3/8" 41029	Open		185.00	185
1993	Mickey Conductor 7 3/8" 41029/ wheel	Closed	1993	185.00	220-240
1996	Sylvester Macaroni 41106	12,500		395.00	395
1993	Symphony Hour-Opening Title 41031	Open		29.00	29
1993	Symphony Hour-Opening Title 41031/ clef	Closed	1993	29.00	40

Classics Collection-Three Little Pigs - Disney Studios

1993	Big Bad Wolf 41039 (short straight teeth/cone base) 1st version	S/O	1994	295.00	1000-1300
1993	Big Bad Wolf 41039 (short straight teeth/flat base) 2nd version	S/O	1994	295.00	695-990
1993	Big Bad Wolf 41039 (long/short curved teeth) 3rd version	S/O	1994	295.00	700-750
1996	Big Bad Wolf 41094	Open		225.00	225
1993	Fiddler Pig 4 1/2" 41038	Open		75.00	75
1993	Fiddler Pig 4 1/2" 41038/ clef	Closed	1993	75.00	85-100
1993	Fifer Pig 4 1/2" 41037	Open		75.00	75
1993	Fifer Pig 4 1/2" 41037/ clef	Closed	1993	75.00	85-100
1993	Practical Pig 4 1/2" 41036	Open		75.00	75
1993	Practical Pig 4 1/2" 41036/ clef	Closed	1993	75.00	85
1993	Three Little Pigs-Opening Title 41046	Open		29.00	29
1993	Three Little Pigs-Opening Title 41046/ clef	Closed	1993	29.00	35

Classics Collection-Tribute Series - Disney Studios

1995	Pals Forever 41085	Closed	1995	175.00	175-225
1996	Pocahontas 6 1/2" 41098	Closed	1996	225.00	225-275
1996	Pocahontas 6 1/2" (dealer prototype) 41098	Closed	1996	225.00	400-550
1997	Hunchback of Notre Dame (Quasimodo and Esmeralda)	Open		195.00	195

Disney's Enchanted Places - Disney Studios

1996	Beast's Castle 41225	Open		245.00	245
1996	Captain Hook Ship 41209	Open		475.00	475
1997	A Castle For Cinderella	Open		225.00	225
1996	Cinderella's Coach 41208	Open		265.00	265
1996	Fiddler Pig's Stick House 41204	Open		85.00	85
1996	Fifer Pig's Straw House 41205	Open		85.00	85
1996	Geppetto's Toy Shop 41207	Open		150.00	150
1996	Grandpa's House 41211	Open		125.00	125
1997	King Louie's Temple (Jungle Book)	Open		125.00	125
1997	Pooh Bear's House	Open		150.00	150
1996	Practical Pig's Brick House 41206	Open		115.00	115
1995	Seven Dwarf's Cottage 41200	Open		180.00	180
1995	Seven Dwarf's Jewel Mine 41203	Open		190.00	190
1995	White Rabbit's House 41202	Open		175.00	175
1995	Woodcutter's Cottage 41201	Open		170.00	170

Disney's Enchanted Places Miniatures - Disney Studios

1996	Briar Rose 41214	Open		50.00	50
1996	Captain Hook 41219	Open		50.00	50
1996	Dopey 41215	Open		50.00	50
1996	Fiddler Pig 41224	Open		50.00	50
1996	Fifer Pig 41223	Open		50.00	50
1996	Gus 41218	Open		50.00	50
1996	Peter 41221	Open		50.00	50
1996	Pinocchio 41217	Open		50.00	50
1996	Practical Pig 41216	Open		50.00	50
1996	Snow White 41212	Open		50.00	50
1996	The White Rabbit 41213	Open		50.00	50
1997	Winnie the Pooh	Open		50.00	50

Disneyana - Disney Studios

1996	Proud Pongo	1,200	1996	175.00	350-550

Wee Forest Folk

Animals - A. Petersen, unless otherwise noted

1974	Baby Hippo H-2	Closed	1977	7.00	N/A
1978	Beaver Wood Cutter BV-1 - W. Petersen	Closed	1980	8.00	400-500
1974	Miss and Baby Hippo H-3	Closed	1977	15.00	N/A
1973	Miss Ducky D-1	Closed	1977	6.00	N/A
1974	Miss Hippo H-1	Closed	1977	8.00	N/A
1977	Nutsy Squirrel SQ-1 - W. Petersen	Closed	1977	3.00	N/A
1979	Turtle Jogger TS-1	Closed	1980	4.00	N/A

Bears - A. Petersen

1978	Big Lady Bear BR-4	Closed	1980	7.50	1000
1977	Blueberry Bears BR-1	Closed	1982	8.75	500-700
1977	Boy Blueberry Bear BR-3	Closed	1982	4.50	300-500
1977	Girl Blueberry Bear BR-2	Closed	1982	4.25	300-500
1978	Traveling Bear BR-5	Closed	1980	8.00	500-750

Book / Figurine - W. Petersen

1988	Tom & Eon BK-1	Suspd.	1991	45.00	250

Bunnies - A. Petersen, unless otherwise noted

YEAR ISSUE		EDITION LIMIT	YEAR RETD.	ISSUE PRICE	*QUOTE U.S.$
1977	Batter Bunny B-9	Closed	1982	4.50	275-500
1973	Broom Bunny B-6	Closed	1978	9.50	N/A
1972	Double Bunnies B-1	Closed	1980	4.25	N/A
1972	Housekeeping Bunny B-2	Closed	1980	4.50	N/A
1973	Market Bunny B-8	Closed	1977	9.00	N/A
1973	Muff Bunny B-7	Closed	1977	9.00	N/A
1973	The Professor B-4	Closed	1980	4.75	N/A
1980	Professor Rabbit B-11 - W. Petersen	Closed	1981	14.00	500-600
1973	Sir Rabbit B-3 - W. Petersen	Closed	1980	4.50	500-600
1973	Sunday Bunny B-5	Closed	1978	4.75	N/A
1977	Tennis Bunny BS-1	Closed	1980	3.75	300-400
1985	Tiny Easter Bunny B-12 - D. Petersen	Closed	1992	25.00	75-106
1978	Wedding Bunnies B-10 - W. Petersen	Closed	1981	12.50	900-1100

Christmas Carol Series - A. Petersen

1988	The Fezziwigs CC-7	Closed	1996	65.00	100-175

Cinderella Series - A. Petersen

1988	Cinderella's Slipper (with Prince) C-1	Closed	1989	62.00	250-275
1989	Cinderella's Slipper C-1a	Closed	1994	32.00	80-108
1988	Cinderella's Wedding C-5	Closed	1994	62.00	125-155
1989	The Fairy Godmother C-7	Closed	1994	69.00	135-175
1988	Flower Girl C-6	Closed	1994	22.00	70-85
1988	The Flower Girls C-4	Closed	1994	42.00	85-115
1988	The Mean Stepmother C-3	Closed	1994	32.00	80-145
1988	The Ugly Stepsisters C-2	Closed	1994	62.00	110-150

Fairy Tale Series - A. Petersen

1980	Red Riding Hood & Wolf FT-1	Closed	1982	29.00	1250-1600
1980	Red Riding Hood FT-2	Closed	1982	13.00	400-600

Forest Scene - W. Petersen

1990	Mousie Comes A-Calling FS-3	Closed	1996	128.00	146-200
1988	Woodland Serenade FS-1	Closed	1995	125.00	250-295

Foxes - A. Petersen

1978	Barrister Fox FX-3	Closed	1980	7.50	700-900
1977	Dandy Fox FX-2	Closed	1979	6.00	450-500
1977	Fancy Fox FX-1	Closed	1979	4.75	350-475

Frogs - A. Petersen, unless otherwise noted

1977	Frog Friends F-3 - W. Petersen	Closed	1981	5.75	400-600
1974	Frog on Rock F-2	Closed	1977	6.00	N/A
1977	Grampa Frog F-5 - W. Petersen	Closed	1981	6.00	700-1100
1974	Prince Charming F-1 - W. Petersen	Closed	1977	7.50	N/A
1978	Singing Frog F-6	Closed	1979	5.50	N/A
1977	Spring Peepers F-4	Closed	1979	3.50	N/A

Limited Edition - A. Petersen, unless otherwise noted

1981	Beauty and the Beast (color variations) BB-1 - W. Petersen	Closed	1981	89.00	8000-12000
1985	Helping Hand LTD-2	Closed	1985	62.00	600-750
1984	Postmouster LTD-1 - W. Petersen	Closed	1984	46.00	600-750
1987	Statue in the Park LTD-3 - W. Petersen	Closed	1987	93.00	700-950
1988	Uncle Sammy LTD-4	Closed	1988	85.00	300

Mice - A. Petersen, unless otherwise noted

1988	Aloha! M-158	Closed	1994	32.00	65-105
1982	Arty Mouse M-71	Closed	1991	19.00	85-150
1985	Attic Treasure M-126	Closed	1995	42.00	100-145
1977	Baby Sitter M-19	Closed	1981	5.75	350-450
1982	Baby Sitter M-66	Closed	1993	23.50	100-150
1981	Barrister Mouse M-57	Closed	1982	16.00	500-800
1987	Bat Mouse M-154	Closed	1994	25.00	70-100
1982	Beach Mousey M-76	Closed	1993	19.00	80-95
1981	Blue Devil M-61	Closed	N/A	12.50	175-225
1982	Boy Sweetheart M-81	Closed	1982	13.50	350-500
1975	Bride Mouse M-9	Closed	1978	4.00	N/A
1978	Bridge Club Mouse M-20	Closed	1979	6.00	600-800
1978	Bridge Club Mouse Partner M-21	Closed	1979	6.00	600-800
1984	Campfire Mouse M-109 - W. Petersen	Closed	1986	26.00	350-450
1981	The Carolers M-63	Closed	1981	29.00	900-2000
1980	Carpenter Mouse M-49	Closed	1981	15.00	600-800
1983	Chief Geronimouse M-107a	Closed	1995	21.00	80-100
1978	Chief Nip-a-Way Mouse M-26	Closed	1981	7.00	650-750
1987	Choir Mouse M-147 - W. Petersen	Closed	1990	23.00	80-120
1979	Chris-Miss M-32	Closed	1982	9.00	250-350
1979	Chris-Mouse M-33	Closed	1982	9.00	250-350
1983	Christmas Morning M-92	Closed	1987	35.00	225
1983	Clown Mouse M-98	Closed	1984	22.00	350-450
1986	Come & Get It! M-141	Closed	1988	34.00	125-135
1985	Come Play! M-131	Closed	1991	18.00	65-125
1989	Commencement Day M-161 - W. Petersen	Closed	1996	28.00	45-95
1980	Commo-Dormouse M-42 - W. Petersen	Closed	1981	14.00	600-900
1978	Cowboy Mouse M-25	Closed	1981	6.00	600-950
1981	Doc Mouse & Patient M-55 - W. Petersen	Closed	1981	14.00	650-850
1987	Don't Cry! M-149	Closed	1990	33.00	100-200
1986	Down the Chimney M-143	Closed	1988	48.00	225
1987	Drummer M-153b - W. Petersen	Closed	1989	29.00	50-75
1989	Elf Tales M-163	Closed	1995	48.00	100-125
1985	Family Portrait M-127	Closed	1987	54.00	225-300
1976	Fan Mouse M-10	Closed	1979	5.75	N/A
1974	Farmer Mouse M-5	Closed	1979	3.75	N/A
1983	First Christmas M-93	Closed	1986	16.00	225-350
1984	First Day of School M-112	Closed	1985	27.00	375-400

*Quotes have been rounded up to nearest dollar

Collectors' Information Bureau

129

YEAR ISSUE		EDITION LIMIT	YEAR RETD.	ISSUE PRICE	*QUOTE U.S.$
1986	First Haircut M-137 - W. Petersen	Closed	1992	58.00	150-250
1993	First Kiss! M-192	Closed	1996	65.00	125-175
1980	Fishermouse M-41	Closed	1981	16.00	550-750
1981	Flower Girl M-53	Closed	1983	15.00	350-400
1988	Forty Winks M-159 - W. Petersen	Closed	1996	36.00	75-100
1979	Gardener Mouse M-37	Closed	1981	12.00	600-800
1983	Get Well Soon! M-96	Closed	1983	15.00	500-600
1974	Good Knight Mouse M-4 - W. Petersen	Closed	1977	7.50	N/A
1981	Graduate Mouse M-58	Closed	1988	15.00	95
1991	Grammy-Phone M-176	Closed	1996	75.00	90-125
1992	Greta M-169b	Closed	1993	35.00	65-95
1992	Hans M-169a	Closed	1993	35.00	80-90
1990	Hans & Greta M-169	Closed	1992	64.00	125-180
1983	Harvest Mouse M-104 - W. Petersen	Closed	1984	23.00	400-600
1992	High on the Hog M-186	Closed	1995	52.00	100-140
1976	June Belle M-13	Closed	1979	4.25	400-500
1977	King "Tut" Mouse TM-1	Closed	1979	4.50	600-800
1982	Lamplight Carolers M-86	Closed	1987	35.00	250-300
1982	Little Fire Chief M-77 - W. Petersen	Closed	1984	29.00	600-750
1982	Little Sledders M-85	Closed	1985	24.00	200-300
1982	Littlest Angel M-88	Closed	1986	15.00	125-150
1987	Littlest Witch M-156	Closed	1993	24.00	70-90
1981	Lone Caroler M-64	Closed	1981	15.50	800-1500
1993	Lord & Lady Mousebatten M-195	Closed	1995	85.00	100-200
1995	Lord Mousebatten M-195a	Closed	1996	46.00	75-100
1976	Mama Mouse with Baby M-18	Closed	1979	6.00	375-450
1987	Market Mouse M-150 - W. Petersen	Closed	1993	49.00	110-150
1972	Market Mouse M-1a	Closed	1978	4.25	N/A
1976	May Belle M-12	Closed	1980	4.25	300-400
1983	Merry Chris-Miss M-90	Closed	1985	17.00	250-300
1983	Merry Chris-Mouse M-91	Closed	1985	16.00	250-350
1972	Miss Mouse M-1	Closed	1978	4.25	N/A
1972	Miss Mousey M-2	Closed	1978	4.00	N/A
1972	Miss Mousey w/ Bow Hat M-2b	Closed	1979	4.25	N/A
1972	Miss Mousey w/ Straw Hat M-2a	Closed	1980	4.25	350-450
1973	Miss Nursey Mouse M-3	Closed	1980	4.00	400
1980	Miss Polly Mouse M-46	Closed	1984	23.00	400-500
1982	Miss Teach & Pupil M-73	Closed	1984	29.50	375
1980	Miss Teach M-45	Closed	1980	18.00	700-900
1982	Moon Mouse M-78	Closed	1984	15.50	400-600
1981	Mother's Helper M-52	Closed	1983	11.00	250-300
1979	Mouse Artiste M-39	Closed	1981	12.50	350-500
1979	Mouse Ballerina M-38	Closed	1979	12.50	700-900
1983	Mouse Call M-97 - W. Petersen	Closed	1983	24.00	600-800
1979	Mouse Duet M-29	Closed	1982	25.00	550-700
1986	Mouse on Campus M-139 - W. Petersen	Closed	1988	25.00	95-125
1979	Mouse Pianist M-30	Closed	1984	17.00	450
1985	Mouse Talk M-130	Closed	1993	44.00	100-125
1979	Mouse Violinist M-31	Closed	1984	9.00	300-350
1976	Mouse with Muff M-16	Closed	1977	9.00	N/A
1979	Mousey Baby M-34	Closed	1982	9.50	300-350
1981	Mousey Express M-65	Closed	1993	22.00	115-150
1983	Mousey's Cone M-100	Closed	1994	22.00	75-100
1983	Mousey's Dollhouse M-102	Closed	1985	30.00	400-450
1988	Mousey's Easter Basket M-160	Closed	N/A	32.00	90-115
1982	Mousey's Teddy M-75	Closed	1985	29.00	350
1976	Mrs. Mousey M-15	Closed	1978	4.00	N/A
1976	Mrs. Mousey w/ Hat M-15a	Closed	1979	4.25	N/A
1980	Mrs. Tidy M-51	Closed	1981	19.50	400-500
1980	Mrs. Tidy and Helper M-50	Closed	1981	24.00	550-650
1976	Nightie Mouse M-14	Closed	1979	4.75	400-500
1981	Nursery Mousey M-54	Closed	1982	14.00	350-500
1982	Office Mousey M-68	Closed	1984	23.00	375-450
1983	Pack Mouse M-106 - W. Petersen	Closed	1984	19.00	400-450
1985	Pageant Shepherds M-122	Closed	1985	35.00	200-275
1985	Pageant Wiseman M-121	Closed	1985	58.00	200-275
1981	Pearl Knit Mouse M-59	Closed	1985	20.00	300-350
1984	Pen Pal Mousey M-114	Closed	1985	26.00	350-450
1993	Peter Pumpkin Eater M-190	Closed	1995	98.00	125-200
1984	Peter's Pumpkin M-118	Closed	1992	19.00	70-90
1980	Photographer Mouse M-48 - W. Petersen	Closed	1981	23.00	500-800
1978	Picnic Mice M-23 - W. Petersen	Closed	1979	7.25	700-900
1985	Piggy-Back Mousey M-129 - W. Petersen	Closed	1986	28.00	350
1978	Pirate Mouse M-27	Closed	1979	6.50	800-1100
1980	Pirate Mouse M-47 - W. Petersen	Closed	1981	16.00	500-700
1990	Polly's Parasol M-170	Closed	1993	39.00	75-95
1982	Poorest Angel M-89	Closed	1986	15.00	125-150
1984	Prudence Pie Maker M-119	Closed	1992	18.50	70
1977	Queen "Tut" Mouse TM-2	Closed	1979	4.50	600-800
1979	Raggedy and Mouse M-36	Closed	1981	12.00	350-400
1987	The Red Wagon M-151 - W. Petersen	Closed	1991	54.00	200-250
1979	Rock-a-bye Baby Mouse M-35	Closed	1981	17.00	350-500
1983	Rocking Tot M-103	Closed	1990	19.00	50-90
1983	Rope 'em Mousey M-108	Closed	1984	19.00	300-500
1980	Santa Mouse M-43	Closed	1985	12.00	200-350
1984	Santa's Trainee M-116 - W. Petersen	Closed	1984	36.50	400-550
1982	Say "Cheese" M-72 - W. Petersen	Closed	1983	15.50	400-600
1981	School Marm Mouse M-56	Closed	1981	19.50	600-900
1987	Scooter Mouse M-152 - W. Petersen	Closed	1996	34.00	75-115
1978	Secretary Miss Pell M-22	Closed	1981	4.50	400-600
1976	Shawl Mouse M-17	Closed	1977	9.00	N/A
1987	Skeleton Mousey M-157	Closed	1993	27.00	80-90
1982	Snowmouse & Friend M-84	Closed	1985	23.50	375-450
1990	Stars & Stripes M-168	Closed	1996	34.00	60-85
1985	Sunday Drivers M-132 - W. Petersen	Closed	1994	58.00	250-300
1986	Sweet Dreams M-136	Closed	1992	58.00	225-250
1982	Sweethearts M-79	Closed	1982	26.00	400-500
1982	Tea for Two M-74	Closed	1984	26.00	350-450
1976	Tea Mouse M-11	Closed	1979	5.75	500-800
1984	Tidy Mouse M-113	Closed	1985	38.00	500-700
1978	Town Crier Mouse M-28	Closed	1979	10.50	900
1984	Traveling Mouse M-110	Closed	1987	28.00	300-350
1987	Trumpeter M-153a - W. Petersen	Closed	1989	29.00	50-100
1987	Tuba Player M-153c - W. Petersen	Closed	1989	29.00	50-100
1992	Tuckered Out! M-136a	Closed	1993	46.00	125-175
1975	Two Mice with Candle M-7	Closed	1979	4.50	450-550
1975	Two Tiny Mice M-8	Closed	1979	4.50	450-600
1986	Waltzing Matilda M-135 - W. Petersen	Closed	1993	48.00	95-120
1983	Wash Day M-105	Closed	1984	23.00	350-400
1978	Wedding Mice M-24 - W. Petersen	Closed	1981	7.50	500-600
1982	Wedding Mice M-67 - W. Petersen	Closed	1993	29.50	145-200
1980	Witch Mouse M-44	Closed	1983	12.00	175-275
1984	Witchy Boo! M-120	Closed	1995	21.00	60-100
1974	Wood Sprite M-6a	Closed	1978	4.00	N/A
1974	Wood Sprite M-6b	Closed	1978	4.00	N/A
1974	Wood Sprite M-6c	Closed	1978	4.00	N/A

Minutemice - A. Petersen, unless otherwise noted

YEAR ISSUE		EDITION LIMIT	YEAR RETD.	ISSUE PRICE	*QUOTE U.S.$
1974	Concordian On Drum with Glasses MM-4	Closed	1977	9.00	N/A
1974	Concordian Wood Base w/Hat MM-4b	Closed	1977	8.00	N/A
1974	Concordian Wood Base w/Tan Coat MM-4a	Closed	1977	7.50	N/A
1974	Little Fifer on Drum MM-5b	Closed	1977	8.00	N/A
1974	Little Fifer on Drum with Fife MM-5	Closed	1977	8.00	N/A
1974	Little Fifer on Wood Base MM-5a	Closed	1977	8.00	N/A
1974	Mouse Carrying Large Drum MM-3	Closed	1977	8.00	N/A
1974	Mouse on Drum w/Black Hat MM-2	Closed	1977	9.00	N/A
1974	Mouse on Drum with Fife MM-1	Closed	1977	9.00	N/A
1974	Mouse on Drum with Fife Wood Base MM-1a	Closed	1977	9.00	N/A

Moles - A. Petersen

YEAR ISSUE		EDITION LIMIT	YEAR RETD.	ISSUE PRICE	*QUOTE U.S.$
1978	Mole Scout MO-1	Closed	1980	4.25	300-400

Mouse Sports - A. Petersen, unless otherwise noted

YEAR ISSUE		EDITION LIMIT	YEAR RETD.	ISSUE PRICE	*QUOTE U.S.$
1975	Bobsled Three MS-1	Closed	1977	12.00	N/A
1985	Fishin' Chip MS-14 - W. Petersen	Closed	1992	46.00	250-275
1981	Golfer Mouse MS-10	Closed	1984	15.50	350-450
1977	Golfer Mouse MS-7	Closed	1980	5.25	400-500
1984	Land Ho! MS-12	Closed	1987	36.50	200-300
1976	Mouse Skier MS-3	Closed	1979	4.25	350-500
1975	Skater Mouse MS-2	Closed	1980	4.50	300-400
1980	Skater Mouse MS-8	Closed	1983	16.50	250-550
1977	Skating Star Mouse MS-6	Closed	1979	3.75	250-350
1980	Skier Mouse (Early Colors) MS-9	Closed	1983	13.00	225-300
1984	Tennis Anyone? MS-13	Closed	1988	18.00	225-250
1976	Tennis Star MS-4	Closed	1978	3.75	250-300
1976	Tennis Star MS-5	Closed	1981	3.75	250-300

Owls - A. Petersen, unless otherwise noted

YEAR ISSUE		EDITION LIMIT	YEAR RETD.	ISSUE PRICE	*QUOTE U.S.$
1975	Colonial Owls O-4	Closed	1977	11.50	N/A
1979	Grad Owl O-5 - W. Petersen	Closed	1979	4.25	400-600
1980	Graduate Owl (On Books) O-6 - W. Petersen	Closed	1980	12.00	550
1974	Mr. and Mrs. Owl O-1	Closed	1981	6.00	500-600
1974	Mr. Owl O-3	Closed	1981	3.25	300-400
1974	Mrs. Owl O-2	Closed	1981	3.00	300-400

Piggies - A. Petersen

YEAR ISSUE		EDITION LIMIT	YEAR RETD.	ISSUE PRICE	*QUOTE U.S.$
1978	Boy Piglet/ Picnic Piggy P-6	Closed	1981	4.00	250-300
1978	Girl Piglet/Picnic Piggy P-5	Closed	1981	4.00	250-300
1981	Holly Hog P-11	Closed	1981	25.00	600-800
1978	Jolly Tar Piggy P-3	Closed	1979	4.50	300-350
1978	Miss Piggy School Marm P-1	Closed	1979	4.50	300-600
1980	Nurse Piggy P-10	Closed	1981	15.50	300-400
1978	Picnic Piggies P-4	Closed	1981	7.75	400-600
1980	Pig O' My Heart P-9	Closed	1981	12.00	300-400
1978	Piggy Baker P-2	Closed	1981	4.50	300-350
1980	Piggy Ballerina P-7	Closed	1981	15.50	300-500
1978	Piggy Jogger PS-1	Closed	1981	4.50	400-600
1980	Piggy Policeman P-8	Closed	1981	17.50	300-500

Raccoons - A. Petersen

YEAR ISSUE		EDITION LIMIT	YEAR RETD.	ISSUE PRICE	*QUOTE U.S.$
1978	Bird Watcher Raccoon RC-3	Closed	1981	6.50	600-800
1977	Hiker Raccoon RC-2	Closed	1980	4.50	500-800
1977	Mother Raccoon RC-1	Closed	1980	4.50	400-600
1978	Raccoon Skater RCS-1	Closed	1980	4.75	400-700
1978	Raccoon Skier RCS-2	Closed	1980	6.00	400-600

Rats - A. Petersen, unless otherwise noted

YEAR ISSUE		EDITION LIMIT	YEAR RETD.	ISSUE PRICE	*QUOTE U.S.$
1975	Doc Rat R-2 - W. Petersen	Closed	1980	5.25	500-700
1975	Seedy Rat R-1	Closed	1977	5.25	N/A

Robin Hood Series - A. Petersen

YEAR ISSUE		EDITION LIMIT	YEAR RETD.	ISSUE PRICE	*QUOTE U.S.$
1990	Friar Tuck RH-3	Closed	1994	32.00	50-75
1990	Maid Marion RH-2	Closed	1994	32.00	50-75
1990	Robin Hood RH-1	Closed	1994	37.00	50-75

Single Issues - A. Petersen, unless otherwise noted

YEAR ISSUE		EDITION LIMIT	YEAR RETD.	ISSUE PRICE	*QUOTE U.S.$
1980	Cave Mice - W. Petersen	Closed	N/A	N/A	550-800
1972	Party Mouse in Plain Dress	Closed	N/A	N/A	N/A
1972	Party Mouse in Polka-Dot Dress	Closed	N/A	N/A	N/A
1972	Party Mouse in Sailor Suit	Closed	N/A	N/A	N/A
1972	Party Mouse with Bow Tie	Closed	N/A	N/A	N/A
1980	Screech Owl - W. Petersen	Closed	1982	N/A	N/A

Tiny Teddies - D. Petersen

YEAR ISSUE		EDITION LIMIT	YEAR RETD.	ISSUE PRICE	*QUOTE U.S.$
1984	Boo Bear T-3	Suspd.		20.00	75-125
1987	Christmas Teddy T-10	Suspd.		26.00	125
1984	Drummer Bear T-4	Suspd.		22.00	75-125
1988	Hansel & Gretel Bears @ Witch's House T-11	Open		175.00	175
1986	Huggy Bear T-8	Suspd.		26.00	75-125
1984	Little Teddy T-1	Closed	1986	20.00	75-125
1989	Momma Bear T-12	Suspd.		27.00	100-150
1985	Ride 'em Teddy! T-6	Suspd.		32.00	95-125
1984	Sailor Teddy T-2	Suspd.		20.00	75-125
1984	Santa Bear T-5	Suspd.		27.00	95-125
1985	Seaside Teddy T-7	Suspd.		28.00	75-125
1983	Tiny Teddy TT-1	Closed	1983	16.00	N/A
1987	Wedding Bears T-9	Suspd.		54.00	150-200

Wind in the Willows - A. Petersen, unless otherwise noted

YEAR ISSUE		EDITION LIMIT	YEAR RETD.	ISSUE PRICE	*QUOTE U.S.$
1982	Badger WW-2	Closed	1983	18.00	300-450
1982	Mole WW-1	Closed	1983	18.00	300-450
1982	Ratty WW-4	Closed	1983	18.00	300-450
1982	Toad WW-3 - W. Petersen	Closed	1983	18.00	300-450

GRAPHICS

American Artists

Fred Stone - F. Stone

YEAR ISSUE		EDITION LIMIT	YEAR RETD.	ISSUE PRICE	*QUOTE U.S.$
1979	Affirmed, Steve Cauthen Up	750	N/A	100.00	600
1988	Alysheba	950	N/A	195.00	650
1992	The American Triple Crown I, 1948-1978	1,500		325.00	325
1993	The American Triple Crown II, 1937-1946	1,500		325.00	325
1993	The American Triple Crown III, 1919-1935	1,500		225.00	225
1983	Andalusian, The	750	N/A	150.00	350
1981	Arabians, The	750	N/A	115.00	525
1989	Battle For The Triple Crown	950	N/A	225.00	650
1980	The Belmont-Bold Forbes	500	N/A	100.00	375
1991	Black Stallion	1,500		225.00	250
1988	Cam-Fella	950	N/A	175.00	350
1981	Contentment	750	N/A	115.00	525
1992	Dance Smartly-Pat Day Up	950	N/A	225.00	325
1995	Dancers, canvas litho	350		375.00	375
1995	Dancers, print	Open		60.00	60
1983	The Duel	750	N/A	150.00	400
1985	Eternal Legacy	950	N/A	175.00	950
1980	Exceller-Bill Shoemaker	500	N/A	90.00	800
1990	Final Tribute- Secretariat	1,150	N/A	265.00	1300
1987	The First Day	950	N/A	175.00	225
1991	Forego	1,150		225.00	250
1986	Forever Friends	950	N/A	175.00	725
1985	Fred Stone Paints the Sport of Kings (Book)	750	N/A	265.00	750
1980	Genuine Risk	500	N/A	100.00	700
1991	Go For Wand-A Candle in the Wind	1,150		225.00	225
1986	Great Match Race-Ruffian & Foolish Pleasure	950	N/A	175.00	375
1995	Holy Bull, canvas litho	350		375.00	375
1995	Holy Bull, litho	1,150		225.00	225
1981	John Henry-Bill Shoemaker Up	595	N/A	160.00	1500
1985	John Henry-McCarron Up	750	N/A	175.00	500-750
1995	Julie Krone - Colonial Affair	1,150		225.00	225
1985	Kelso	950	N/A	175.00	750
1980	The Kentucky Derby	750	N/A	100.00	650
1980	Kidnapped Mare-Franfreluche	750	N/A	115.00	575
1987	Lady's Secret	950	N/A	175.00	425
1982	Man O'War "Final Thunder"	750	N/A	175.00	2500-3100
1979	Mare and Foal	500	N/A	90.00	500
1979	The Moment After	500	N/A	90.00	350
1986	Nijinski II	950	N/A	175.00	275
1984	Northern Dancer	950	N/A	175.00	625
1982	Off and Running	750	N/A	125.00	250-350
1990	Old Warriors Shoemaker-John Henry	1,950	N/A	265.00	595
1979	One, Two, Three	500	N/A	100.00	1000
1980	The Pasture Pest	500	N/A	100.00	875
1979	Patience	1,000	N/A	90.00	1200
1989	Phar Lap	950	N/A	195.00	275
1982	The Power Horses	750	N/A	125.00	250
1987	The Rivalry-Alysheba and Bet Twice	950	N/A	195.00	550
1979	The Rivals-Affirmed & Alydar	500	N/A	90.00	500
1983	Ruffian-For Only a Moment	750	N/A	175.00	1100
1983	Secretariat	950	N/A	175.00	995-1200
1989	Shoe Bald Eagle	950	N/A	195.00	675
1981	The Shoe-8,000 Wins	395	N/A	200.00	7000
1980	Spectacular Bid	500	N/A	65.00	350-400
1995	Summer Days, canvas litho	350		375.00	375
1995	Summer Days, litho	1,150		225.00	225
XX	Sunday Silence	950	N/A	195.00	425
1981	The Thoroughbreds	750	N/A	115.00	425
1983	Tranquility	750	N/A	150.00	525

*Quotes have been rounded up to nearest dollar

YEAR ISSUE		EDITION LIMIT	YEAR RETD.	ISSUE PRICE	*QUOTE U.S. $
1984	Turning For Home	750	N/A	150.00	425
1982	The Water Trough	750	N/A	125.00	575

Anheuser-Busch, Inc.

Anheuser-Busch - H. Droog

YEAR ISSUE		EDITION LIMIT	YEAR RETD.	ISSUE PRICE	*QUOTE U.S. $
1994	Gray Wolf Mirror N4570	2,500		135.00	150

Endangered Species Fine Art Prints - B. Kemper

YEAR ISSUE		EDITION LIMIT	YEAR RETD.	ISSUE PRICE	*QUOTE U.S. $
1996	Bald Eagle Print, framed N9995	2,500		159.00	159
1996	Bald Eagle, unframed N9995U	2,500		79.00	79
1996	Cougar Print, framed N9993	2,500		159.00	159
1996	Cougar Print, unframed N9993U	2,500		79.00	79
1996	Gray Wolf Print, framed N9992	2,500		159.00	159
1996	Gray Wolf Print, unframed N9992U	2,500		79.00	79
1996	Panda Print, framed N9994	2,500		159.00	159
1996	Panda Print, unframed N9994U	2,500		79.00	79

Circle Fine Art

Rockwell - N. Rockwell

YEAR ISSUE		EDITION LIMIT	YEAR RETD.	ISSUE PRICE	*QUOTE U.S. $
XX	American Family Folio	200		Unkn.	17500
XX	The Artist at Work	130		Unkn.	3500
XX	At the Barber	200		Unkn.	4900
XX	Autumn	200		Unkn.	3500
XX	Autumn/Japon	25		Unkn.	3600
XX	Aviary	200		Unkn.	4200
XX	Barbershop Quartet	200		Unkn.	4200
XX	Baseball	200		Unkn.	3600
XX	Ben Franklin's Philadelphia	200		Unkn.	3600
XX	Ben's Belles	200		Unkn.	3500
XX	The Big Day	200		Unkn.	3400
XX	The Big Top	148		Unkn.	2800
XX	Blacksmith Shop	200		Unkn.	6300
XX	Bookseller	200		Unkn.	2700
XX	Bookseller/Japon	25		Unkn.	2750
XX	The Bridge	200		Unkn.	3100
XX	Cat	200		Unkn.	3400
XX	Cat/Collotype	200		Unkn.	4000
XX	Cheering	200		Unkn.	3600
XX	Children at Window	200		Unkn.	3600
XX	Church	200		Unkn.	3400
XX	Church/Collotype	200		Unkn.	4000
XX	Circus	200		Unkn.	2650
XX	County Agricultural Agent	200		Unkn.	3900
XX	The Critic	200		Unkn.	4650
XX	Day in the Life of a Boy	200		Unkn.	6200
XX	Day in the Life of a Boy/Japon	25		Unkn.	6500
XX	Debut	200		Unkn.	3600
XX	Discovery	200		Unkn.	5900
XX	Doctor and Boy	200		Unkn.	9400
XX	Doctor and Doll-Signed	200		Unkn.	11900
XX	Dressing Up/Ink	60		Unkn.	4400
XX	Dressing Up/Pencil	200		Unkn.	3700
XX	The Drunkard	200		Unkn.	3600
XX	The Expected and Unexpected	200		Unkn.	3700
XX	Family Tree	200		Unkn.	5900
XX	Fido's House	200		Unkn.	3600
XX	Football Mascot	200		Unkn.	3700
XX	Four Seasons Folio	200		Unkn.	13500
XX	Four Seasons Folio/Japon	25		Unkn.	14000
XX	Freedom from Fear-Signed	200		Unkn.	6400
XX	Freedom from Want-Signed	200		Unkn.	6400
XX	Freedom of Religion-Signed	200		Unkn.	6400
XX	Freedom of Speech-Signed	200		Unkn.	6400
XX	Gaiety Dance Team	200		Unkn.	4300
XX	Girl at Mirror-Signed	200		Unkn.	8400
XX	The Golden Age	200		Unkn.	3500
XX	Golden Rule-Signed	200		Unkn.	4400
XX	Golf	200		Unkn.	3600
XX	Gossips	200		Unkn.	5000
XX	Gossips/Japon	25		Unkn.	5100
XX	Grotto	200		Unkn.	3400
XX	Grotto/Collotype	200		Unkn.	4000
XX	High Dive	200		Unkn.	3400
XX	The Homecoming	200		Unkn.	3700
XX	The House	200		Unkn.	3700
XX	Huck Finn Folio	200		Unkn.	35000
XX	Ichabod Crane	200		Unkn.	6700
XX	The Inventor	200		Unkn.	4100
XX	Jerry	200		Unkn.	4700
XX	Jim Got Down on His Knees	200		Unkn.	4500
XX	Lincoln	200		Unkn.	11400
XX	Lobsterman	200		Unkn.	5500
XX	Lobsterman/Japon	25		Unkn.	5750
XX	Marriage License	200		Unkn.	6900
XX	Medicine	200		Unkn.	3400
XX	Medicine/Color Litho	200		Unkn.	4000
XX	Miss Mary Jane	200		Unkn.	4500
XX	Moving Day	200		Unkn.	3900
XX	Music Hath Charms	200		Unkn.	4200
XX	My Hand Shook	200		Unkn.	4500
XX	Out the Window	200		Unkn.	3400
XX	Out the Window/ Collotype	200		Unkn.	4000
XX	Outward Bound-Signed	200		Unkn.	7900
XX	Poor Richard's Almanac	200		Unkn.	24000
XX	Prescription	200		Unkn.	4900
XX	Prescription/Japon	25		Unkn.	5000
XX	The Problem We All Live With	200		Unkn.	4500
XX	Puppies	200		Unkn.	3700
XX	Raliegh the Dog	200		Unkn.	3900
XX	Rocket Ship	200		Unkn.	3650
XX	The Royal Crown	200		Unkn.	3500
XX	Runaway	200		Unkn.	3800
XX	Runaway/Japon	200		Unkn.	5700
XX	Safe and Sound	200		Unkn.	3800
XX	Saturday People	200		Unkn.	3300
XX	Save Me	200		Unkn.	3600
XX	Saying Grace-Signed	200		Unkn.	7400
XX	School Days Folio	200		Unkn.	14000
XX	Schoolhouse	200		Unkn.	4500
XX	Schoolhouse/Japon	25		Unkn.	4650
XX	See America First	200		Unkn.	5650
XX	See America First/Japon	25		Unkn.	6100
XX	Settling In	200		Unkn.	3600
XX	Shuffelton's Barbershop	200		Unkn.	7400
XX	Smoking	200		Unkn.	3400
XX	Smoking/Collotype	200		Unkn.	4000
XX	Spanking	200		Unkn.	3400
XX	Spanking/ Collotype	200		Unkn.	4000
XX	Spelling Bee	200		Unkn.	6500
XX	Spring	200		Unkn.	3500
XX	Spring Flowers	200		Unkn.	5200
XX	Spring/Japon	25		Unkn.	3600
XX	Study for the Doctor's Office	200		Unkn.	6000
XX	Studying	200		Unkn.	3600
XX	Summer	200		Unkn.	3500
XX	Summer Stock	200		Unkn.	4900
XX	Summer Stock/Japon	25		Unkn.	5000
XX	Summer/Japon	25		Unkn.	3600
XX	The Teacher	200		Unkn.	3400
XX	Teacher's Pet	200		Unkn.	3600
XX	The Teacher/Japon	25		Unkn.	3500
XX	The Texan	200		Unkn.	3700
XX	Then For Three Minutes	200		Unkn.	4500
XX	Then Miss Watson	200		Unkn.	4500
XX	There Warn't No Harm	200		Unkn.	4500
XX	Three Farmers	200		Unkn.	3600
XX	Ticketseller	200		Unkn.	4200
XX	Ticketseller/Japon	25		Unkn.	4400
XX	Tom Sawyer Color Suite	200		Unkn.	30000
XX	Tom Sawyer Folio	200		Unkn.	26500
XX	Top of the World	200		Unkn.	4200
XX	Trumpeter	200		Unkn.	3900
XX	Trumpeter/Japon	25		Unkn.	4100
XX	Two O'Clock Feeding	200		Unkn.	3600
XX	The Village Smithy	200		Unkn.	3500
XX	Welcome	200		Unkn.	3500
XX	Wet Paint	200		Unkn.	3800
XX	When I Lit My Candle	200		Unkn.	4500
XX	White Washing	200		Unkn.	3400
XX	Whitewashing the Fence/Collotype	200		Unkn.	4000
XX	Window Washer	200		Unkn.	4800
XX	Winter	200		Unkn.	3500
XX	Winter/Japon	25		Unkn.	3600
XX	Ye Old Print Shoppe	200		Unkn.	3500
XX	Your Eyes is Lookin'	200		Unkn.	4500

Cross Gallery, Inc.

Bandits & Bounty Hunters - P.A. Cross

YEAR ISSUE		EDITION LIMIT	YEAR RETD.	ISSUE PRICE	*QUOTE U.S. $
1997	Bandits	865		225.00	225
1994	Bounty Hunter	865		225.00	225

The Gift - P.A. Cross

YEAR ISSUE		EDITION LIMIT	YEAR RETD.	ISSUE PRICE	*QUOTE U.S. $
1989	B' Achua Dlubh-bia Bii Noskiiyahi The Gift, Part II	S/O	1989	225.00	650
1993	The Gift, Part III	S/O	1993	225.00	350-1000

Half Breed Series - P.A. Cross

YEAR ISSUE		EDITION LIMIT	YEAR RETD.	ISSUE PRICE	*QUOTE U.S. $
1989	Ach-hua Dlubh: (Body Two), Half Breed	S/O	1989	190.00	1450
1990	Ach-hua Dlubh: (Body Two), Half Breed II	S/O	1990	225.00	800-1100
1991	Ach-hua Dlubh: (Body Two), Half Breed III	S/O	1991	225.00	850
1995	Ach-hua Dlubh: (Body Two), Half Breed IV	865		225.00	225

Limited Edition Original Graphics - P.A. Cross

YEAR ISSUE		EDITION LIMIT	YEAR RETD.	ISSUE PRICE	*QUOTE U.S. $
1991	Bia-A-Hoosh (A Very Special Woman), Stone Lithograph	S/O	1991	500.00	500
1987	Caroline, Stone Lithograph	S/O	1987	300.00	600
1988	Maidenhood Hopi, Stone Lithograph	S/O	1988	950.00	1150
1990	Nighteyes, I, Serigraph	S/O	1990	225.00	425
1989	The Red Capote, Serigraph	S/O	1989	750.00	1150
1989	Rosapina, Etching	74		1200.00	1200
1991	Wooltalkers, Serigraph	275		750.00	750

Limited Edition Prints - P.A. Cross

YEAR ISSUE		EDITION LIMIT	YEAR RETD.	ISSUE PRICE	*QUOTE U.S. $
1991	Ashpahdua Hagay Ashae-Gyoke (My Home & Heart Is Crow)	S/O	1991	225.00	225-350
1983	Ayla-Sah-Xuh-Xah (Pretty Colours, Many Designs)	S/O	1983	150.00	450
1990	Baape Ochia (Night Wind, Turquoise)	S/O	1990	185.00	370
1990	Biaachee-itah Bah-achbeh (Medicine Woman Scout)	S/O	1990	225.00	525
1984	Blue Beaded Hair Ties	S/O	1984	85.00	330
1991	The Blue Shawl	S/O	1991	185.00	275
1987	Caroline	S/O	1987	45.00	145
1989	Chey-ayjeh: Prey	S/O	1989	190.00	325-600
1988	Dance Apache	S/O	1988	190.00	360
1987	Dii-tah-shteh Ee-wihza-ahook (A Coat of much Value)	S/O	1987	90.00	740
1989	The Dreamer	S/O	1989	190.00	600
1987	The Elkskin Robe	S/O	1987	190.00	640
1990	Eshte	S/O	1990	185.00	200
1986	Grand Entry	S/O	1986	85.00	85
1983	Isbaaloo Eetshiileehcheek (Sorting Her Beads)	S/O	1983	150.00	1750
1990	Ishia-Kahda #1 (Quiet One)	S/O	1990	185.00	400
1988	Ma-a-luppis-she-La-dus (She is above everything, nothing can touch her)	S/O	1988	190.00	525
1984	Profile of Caroline	S/O	1984	85.00	185
1986	The Red Capote	S/O	1986	150.00	850
1987	The Red Necklace	S/O	1987	90.00	210
1989	Teesa Waits To Dance	S/O	1989	135.00	180
1984	Thick Lodge Clan Boy: Crow Indian	475		85.00	85
1987	Tina	S/O	1987	45.00	110
1985	The Water Vision	S/O	1985	150.00	325
1984	Whistling Water Clan Girl: Crow Indian	S/O	1984	85.00	85
1993	Winter Girl Bride	1,730		225.00	225
1986	Winter Morning	S/O	1986	185.00	1450
1986	The Winter Shawl	S/O	1986	150.00	1600

Miniature Line - P.A. Cross

YEAR ISSUE		EDITION LIMIT	YEAR RETD.	ISSUE PRICE	*QUOTE U.S. $
1991	BJ	S/O	1995	80.00	80
1993	Braids	447		80.00	80
1993	Daybreak	447		80.00	80
1991	The Floral Shawl	S/O	1995	80.00	80
1991	Kendra	S/O	1995	80.00	80
1993	Ponytails	447		80.00	80
1993	Sundown	447		80.00	80
1991	Watercolour Study #2 For Half Breed	S/O	1995	80.00	80

The Painted Ladies' Suite - P.A. Cross

YEAR ISSUE		EDITION LIMIT	YEAR RETD.	ISSUE PRICE	*QUOTE U.S. $
1992	Acoria (Crow; Seat of Honor)	S/O	1995	185.00	185
1992	Avisola	S/O	1995	185.00	185
1992	Dah-say (Crow; Heart)	S/O	1995	185.00	185
1992	Itza-chu (Apache; The Eagle)	S/O	1995	185.00	185
1992	Kel'hoya (Hopi; Little Sparrow Hawk)	S/O	1995	185.00	185
1992	The Painted Ladies	S/O	1992	225.00	1200
1997	Sus(h)gah-daydus(h) (Crow; Quick)	447		185.00	185
1997	Tze-go-juni (Chiricahua Apache)	447		185.00	185

Star Quilt Series - P.A. Cross

YEAR ISSUE		EDITION LIMIT	YEAR RETD.	ISSUE PRICE	*QUOTE U.S. $
1988	The Quilt Makers	S/O	1988	190.00	1200
1986	Reflections	S/O	1986	185.00	865
1985	Winter Warmth	S/O	1985	150.00	900-1215

Wolf Series - P.A. Cross

YEAR ISSUE		EDITION LIMIT	YEAR RETD.	ISSUE PRICE	*QUOTE U.S. $
1990	Agninaug Amaguut;Inupiag (Women With Her Wolves)	S/O	1993	325.00	350-750
1993	Ahmah-ghut, Tuhtu-loo; Eelahn-nuht Kah-auhk (Wolves and Caribou; My Furs and My Friends)	1,050		255.00	255
1997	Bia Ukbah Chedah Noskiiyah (Woman with wolves at the edge of the water)	865		225.00	225
1989	Biagoht Eecuebeh Hehsheesh-Checah: (Red Ridinghood and Her Wolves), Gift I	S/O	1989	225.00	1500-2500
1985	Dii-tah-shteh Bii-wik; Chedah-bah Iiidah (My Very Own Protective Covering; Walks w/ Wolf Woman)	S/O	1985	185.00	3275
1987	The Morning Star Gives Long Otter His Hoop Medicine Power	S/O	1987	190.00	1800-2500

Enchantica

Retired Enchantica Collection - J. Woodward

YEAR ISSUE		EDITION LIMIT	YEAR RETD.	ISSUE PRICE	*QUOTE U.S. $
1992	"Throne Citadel"-2300	1,500	1995	95.00	95

Flambro Imports

Emmett Kelly Jr. Lithographs - B. Leighton-Jones

YEAR ISSUE		EDITION LIMIT	YEAR RETD.	ISSUE PRICE	*QUOTE U.S. $
1995	All Star Circus	2 Yr.		150.00	150
1994	EKJ 70th Birthday Commemorative	1,994		150.00	150
1994	I Love You	2 Yr.	1996	90.00	90
1994	Joyful Noise	2 Yr.	1996	90.00	90
1994	Picture Worth 1,000 Words	2 Yr.	1996	90.00	90

Gartlan USA

Lithograph - Various

YEAR ISSUE		EDITION LIMIT	YEAR RETD.	ISSUE PRICE	*QUOTE U.S. $
1986	George Brett-"The Swing" - J. Martin	2,000	1990	85.00	200
1991	Joe Montana - M. Taylor	500	1994	495.00	600-700
1989	Kareem Abdul Jabbar-The Record Setter - M. Taylor	1,989	1993	85.00	395
1991	Negro League 1st World Series (print) - Unknown	1,924	1993	109.00	125
1987	Roger Staubach - C. Soileau	1,979	1992	85.00	200-300

Glynda Turley Prints

Turley - Canvas - G. Turley

YEAR ISSUE		EDITION LIMIT	YEAR RETD.	ISSUE PRICE	*QUOTE U.S. $
1996	Abundance III	350		190.00	190
1996	Chrysanthemums and Apples	350		140.00	140

*Quotes have been rounded up to nearest dollar

YEAR ISSUE		EDITION LIMIT	YEAR RETD.	ISSUE PRICE	*QUOTE U.S. $
1992	Courtyard II	200		140.00	140
1994	Courtyard III	350		140.00	140
1988	Elegance	350		130.00	130
1991	Floral Fancy	150		130.00	130
1992	Flower Garden	350		130.00	130
1990	Garden Room	250		130.00	130
1992	The Garden Wreath II	200	1996	130.00	130
1994	The Garden Wreath III	350		140.00	140
1994	Georgia Sweet	350		140.00	140
1992	Grand Glory I	350		160.00	160
1992	Grand Glory II	350		160.00	160
1995	Grand Glory III	350		160.00	160
1995	Grand Glory IV	350		160.00	160
1992	In Full Bloom	200	N/A	160.00	160
1994	In Full Bloom II	350		160.00	160
1995	In Full Bloom III	350		140.00	140
1988	Iris Basket II	350		130.00	130
1990	Iris Basket III	50		130.00	130
1991	Iris Basket IV	25		130.00	130
1989	Iris Parade	350	1996	130.00	130
1988	La Belle IV	25		130.00	130
1995	Little Red River	350		190.00	190
1995	Mabry In Spring	350		160.00	160
1992	Old Mill Stream	350	N/A	130.00	130
1993	Old Mill Stream II	350	N/A	130.00	130
1994	Old Mill Stream III	350		190.00	190
1996	Old Mill Stream IV	350		190.00	190
1988	Once Upon A Time	200		130.00	130
1996	Pears and Roses	350		140.00	140
1989	Petals In Pink	100		190.00	190
1989	Pretty Pickings I	350		130.00	130
1989	Pretty Pickings II	300		130.00	130
1989	Pretty Pickings III	100		130.00	130
1993	Primrose Lane II	300		130.00	130
1995	Remember When	350		190.00	190
1991	Secret Garden	350		130.00	130
1994	Secret Garden II	350		130.00	130
1996	Secret Garden III	350		160.00	160
1991	Simply Southern	350	1996	160.00	160
1992	Southern Sunday	200		140.00	140
1995	Southern Sunday II	350		190.00	190
1993	A Southern Tradition II	350		190.00	190
1994	A Southern Tradition IV	350		190.00	190
1995	A Southern Tradition V	350		190.00	190
1993	Spring's Promise II	300		130.00	130
1988	Spring's Return	350		130.00	130
1995	Summer in Victoria	350		130.00	130
1994	Summer Stroll	350		160.00	160
1990	Sweet Nothings	350		130.00	130
1996	Wreath of Spring	350		140.00	140

Turley - Print - G. Turley

YEAR ISSUE		EDITION LIMIT	YEAR RETD.	ISSUE PRICE	*QUOTE U.S. $
1996	Abundance III	7,500		73.00	73
1996	Abundance III A/P	50		109.50	110
1995	Almost An Angel	7,500		56.00	56
1995	Almost An Angel A/P	50		84.00	84
1986	Attic Curiosity	2,000	N/A	15.00	15
1986	Attic Curiosity A/P	50	N/A	25.00	25
1986	Busy Bodies I	2,000	N/A	25.00	25
1986	Busy Bodies I A/P	50	N/A	40.00	40
1986	Busy Bodies II	2,000	N/A	25.00	25
1986	Busy Bodies II A/P	50	N/A	40.00	40
1986	Callie And Company	2,000	N/A	30.00	30
1986	Callie And Company A/P	50	N/A	50.00	50
1987	Callie And Company II	3,000	N/A	30.00	30
1987	Callie And Company II A/P	50	N/A	50.00	50
1988	Calling On Callie	5,000	1996	30.00	30
1988	Calling On Callie A/P	50		45.00	45
1990	Childhood Memories I	3,500		30.00	30
1990	Childhood Memories I A/P	50		45.00	45
1990	Childhood Memories II	3,500		30.00	30
1990	Childhood Memories II A/P	50		45.00	45
1996	Chrysanthemums and Apples	7,500		64.00	64
1996	Chrysanthemums and Apples A/P	50		192.00	192
1988	Circle of Friends	5,000	1996	25.00	25
1988	Circle Of Friends A/P	50	N/A	40.00	40
1990	The Coming Out Party	3,500		35.00	35
1991	The Courtyard	2,500	N/A	47.00	47
1991	The Courtyard A/P	50	N/A	70.50	71
1992	The Courtyard II	2,500	N/A	50.00	50
1992	The Courtyard II A/P	50		75.00	75
1994	The Courtyard III A/P	50		91.50	92
1990	Dear To My Heart	3,500		35.00	35
1990	Dear To My Heart A/P	50		52.50	53
1988	Elegance	5,000		30.00	30
1988	Elegance A/P	50		45.00	45
1986	A Family Affair	2,500	N/A	25.00	25
1986	A Family Affair A/P	50	N/A	40.00	40
1984	Feeding Time	1,000	N/A	50.00	50
1984	Feeding Time A/P	50	N/A	75.00	75
1984	Feeding Time II	1,000	N/A	25.00	25
1984	Feeding Time II A/P	50	N/A	40.00	40
1987	Fence Row Gathering	3,000	N/A	30.00	30
1987	Fence Row Gathering A/P	50	N/A	50.00	50
1988	Fence Row Gathering II	5,000	N/A	30.00	30
1988	Fence Row Gathering II A/P	50	N/A	50.00	50
1991	Floral Fancy	3,500	N/A	40.00	40
1991	Floral Fancy A/P	50		60.00	60
1992	The Flower Garden	2,500	1996	43.00	43
1992	The Flower Garden A/P	50		64.50	65
1986	Flowers And Lace	3,000	N/A	25.00	25
1986	Flowers And Lace A/P	50	N/A	40.00	40
1988	Flowers For Mommy	5,000	N/A	25.00	25
1988	Flowers For Mommy A/P	50	N/A	40.00	40
1990	Forever Roses	3,500		30.00	30
1990	Forever Roses A/P	50		45.00	45
1987	The Garden Gate	3,000	N/A	30.00	30
1987	The Garden Gate A/P	50	N/A	50.00	50
1990	Garden Room	3,500	N/A	40.00	40
1991	The Garden Wreath	2,500	N/A	47.00	47
1991	The Garden Wreath A/P	50	N/A	60.00	60
1992	The Garden Wreath II	2,500	N/A	50.00	50
1992	The Garden Wreath II A/P	50	N/A	75.00	75
1994	The Garden Wreath III	5,000		61.00	61
1994	The Garden Wreath III A/P	50		91.50	92
1994	Georgia Sweet	2,500		50.00	50
1994	Georgia Sweet A/P	50		75.00	75
1995	Glynda's Garden	7,500		73.00	73
1995	Glynda's Garden A/P	50		109.50	110
1993	Grand Glory I	2,500	N/A	53.00	53
1992	Grand Glory I A/P	50		79.50	80
1993	Grand Glory II	2,500	N/A	53.00	53
1992	Grand Glory II A/P	50		79.50	80
1995	Grand Glory III	7,500		65.00	65
1995	Grand Glory III A/P	50		97.50	98
1995	Grand Glory IV	7,500		65.00	65
1995	Grand Glory IV A/P	50		97.50	98
1984	Heading Home I	1,000	N/A	25.00	25
1984	Heading Home I A/P	50	N/A	40.00	40
1984	Heading Home II	1,000	N/A	25.00	25
1984	Heading Home II A/P	50	N/A	40.00	40
1984	Heading Home III	1,000	N/A	25.00	25
1984	Heading Home III A/P	50	N/A	40.00	40
1987	Heart Wreath	3,000	N/A	25.00	25
1987	Heart Wreath A/P	50	N/A	40.00	40
1988	Heart Wreath II	3,500	N/A	25.00	25
1988	Heart Wreath II A/P	50	N/A	40.00	40
1989	Heart Wreath III	3,500	N/A	25.00	25
1989	Heart Wreath III A/P	50	N/A	40.00	40
1987	Hollyhocks	3,000	N/A	30.00	30
1987	Hollyhocks A/P	50	N/A	50.00	50
1990	Hollyhocks II	3,500	N/A	25.00	25
1990	Hollyhocks II A/P	50	N/A	60.00	60
1995	Hollyhocks III	7,500		69.00	69
1995	Hollyhocks III A/P	50		103.50	104
1992	In Full Bloom	2,500	N/A	53.00	53
1992	In Full Bloom A/P	50	N/A	79.50	80
1994	In Full Bloom II	3,500	N/A	65.00	65
1994	In Full Bloom II A/P	50		97.50	98
1995	In Full Bloom III	7,500		64.00	64
1995	In Full Bloom III A/P	50		96.00	96
1984	In One Ear And Out The Other	950	N/A	50.00	50
1984	In One Ear And Out The Other A/P	50	N/A	75.00	75
1987	Iris Basket	3,000	N/A	30.00	30
1987	Iris Basket A/P	50	N/A	50.00	50
1988	Iris Basket II	3,500	N/A	30.00	30
1988	Iris Basket II A/P	50	N/A	50.00	50
1990	Iris Basket III	3,500	N/A	35.00	35
1990	Iris Basket III A/P	50	N/A	52.50	53
1991	Iris Basket IV	2,500		35.00	35
1991	Iris Basket IV A/P	50		52.50	53
1989	Iris Parade	3,500	1996	35.00	35
1989	Iris Parade A/P	50		52.50	53
1985	La Belle	750	N/A	25.00	25
1985	La Belle A/P	50	N/A	40.00	40
1986	La Belle II	2,000	N/A	25.00	25
1986	La Belle II A/P	50	N/A	40.00	40
1986	La Belle III	3,500	N/A	25.00	25
1986	La Belle III A/P	50	N/A	40.00	40
1988	La Belle IV	5,000	N/A	30.00	30
1988	La Belle IV A/P	50	N/A	50.00	50
1995	Little Red River	7,500		73.00	73
1995	Little Red River A/P	50		109.50	110
1995	Mabry In Spring	7,500		65.00	65
1995	Mabry In Spring A/P	50		97.50	98
1987	Mauve Iris I	3,000	N/A	10.00	10
1987	Mauve Iris I A/P	50	N/A	25.00	25
1987	Mauve Iris II	3,000	N/A	10.00	10
1987	Mauve Iris II A/P	50	N/A	25.00	25
1983	Now I Lay Me	1,000	N/A	50.00	50
1983	Now I Lay Me A/P	50	N/A	75.00	75
1989	Old Favorites	3,500	N/A	35.00	35
1989	Old Favorites A/P	50	N/A	52.50	53
1988	Old Friends	5,000	N/A	30.00	30
1988	Old Friends A/P	50	N/A	50.00	50
1992	Old Mill Stream	2,500	N/A	40.00	40
1992	Old Mill Stream A/P	50		60.00	60
1993	Old Mill Stream II	2,500	N/A	43.00	43
1993	Old Mill Stream II A/P	50		64.50	65
1994	Old Mill Stream III	3,500	N/A	69.00	69
1994	Old Mill Stream III A/P	50		103.50	104
1996	Old Mill Stream IV	7,500		73.00	73
1996	Old Mill Stream IV A/P	50		219.00	219
1988	Once Upon A Time	5,000	N/A	30.00	30
1988	Once Upon A Time A/P	50		45.00	45
1988	Past Times	5,000	N/A	30.00	30
1988	Past Times A/P	50	N/A	50.00	50
1996	Pears and Roses	7,500		64.00	64
1996	Pears and Roses A/P	50		192.00	192
1988	Peeping Tom	5,000	N/A	35.00	35
1988	Peeping Tom A/P	50	N/A	55.00	55
1989	Petals In Pink	3,500	N/A	30.00	30
1989	Petals In Pink A/P	50	N/A	79.50	80
1987	Playing Hookie	3,000	N/A	30.00	30
1987	Playing Hookie A/P	50	N/A	50.00	50
1988	Playing Hookie Again	5,000	N/A	30.00	30
1988	Playing Hookie Again A/P	50	N/A	50.00	50
1988	The Porch	5,000	N/A	30.00	30
1988	The Porch A/P	50	N/A	50.00	50
1989	Pretty Pickings I	3,500	N/A	30.00	30
1989	Pretty Pickings I A/P	50		45.00	45
1989	Pretty Pickings II	3,500		35.00	35
1989	Pretty Pickings II A/P	50		52.50	53
1989	Pretty Pickings III	3,500		30.00	30
1989	Pretty Pickings III A/P	50		45.00	45
1991	Primrose Lane	3,500	N/A	40.00	40
1991	Primrose Lane A/P	50	N/A	60.00	60
1993	Primrose Lane II	2,500	N/A	43.00	43
1993	Primrose Lane II A/P	50		64.50	65
1995	Remember When	7,500		73.00	73
1995	Remember When A/P	50		109.50	110
1983	Sad Face Clown	950	N/A	50.00	50
1983	Sad Face Clown A/P	50	N/A	75.00	75
1991	Secret Garden	3,500	N/A	40.00	40
1991	Secret Garden A/P	50		60.00	60
1994	Secret Garden II A/P	50		79.50	80
1996	Secret Garden III	7,500		65.00	65
1996	Secret Garden III A/P	50		97.50	98
1991	Simply Southern	3,500	N/A	53.00	53
1991	Simply Southern A/P	50	N/A	79.50	80
1985	Snips N Snails	750	N/A	25.00	25
1985	Snips N Snails A/P	50	N/A	40.00	40
1992	Southern Sunday	2,500	N/A	50.00	50
1992	Southern Sunday A/P	50		75.00	75
1995	Southern Sunday II	7,500		73.00	73
1995	Southern Sunday II A/P	50		109.50	110
1993	A Southern Tradition II	3,500	N/A	60.00	60
1993	A Southern Tradition II A/P	50	N/A	90.00	90
1994	A Southern Tradition IV	5,000	N/A	69.00	69
1994	A Southern Tradition IV A/P	50		103.50	104
1995	A Southern Tradition V	7,500		73.00	73
1995	A Southern Tradition V A/P	50		109.50	110
1988	A Special Time	5,000	N/A	30.00	30
1988	A Special Time A/P	50		45.00	45
1993	Spring's Promise II	2,500		43.00	43
1993	Spring's Promise III A/P	50		64.50	65
1988	Spring's Return	5,000		35.00	35
1988	Spring's Return A/P	50		52.50	53
1983	Stepping Out	1,000	N/A	50.00	50
1983	Stepping Out A/P	50	N/A	75.00	75
1985	Sugar N Spice	750	N/A	25.00	25
1985	Sugar N Spice A/P	50	N/A	40.00	40
1987	A Summer Day	3,000	N/A	30.00	30
1987	A Summer Day A/P	50	N/A	50.00	50
1995	Summer In Victoria	7,500		53.00	53
1995	Summer In Victoria A/P	50		79.50	80
1994	Summer Stroll	3,500	N/A	65.00	65
1994	Summer Stroll A/P	50		97.50	98
1990	Sweet Nothings	3,500		40.00	40
1990	Sweet Nothings A/P	50		60.00	60
1987	Victorian Bouquet	3,500	N/A	25.00	25
1987	Victorian Bouquet A/P	50	N/A	40.00	40
1989	Victorian Bouquet II	3,500		25.00	25
1986	White Iris	2,000	N/A	25.00	25
1986	White Iris A/P	50	N/A	40.00	40
1987	Wild Roses	3,000	N/A	30.00	30
1987	Wild Roses A/P	50	N/A	50.00	50
1990	Wild Roses II	3,500		35.00	35
1990	Wild Roses II A/P	50		52.50	53
1996	Wreath of Spring	7,500		64.00	64
1996	Wreath of Spring A/P	50		192.00	192

Greenwich Workshop

Ballantyne - Ballantyne

YEAR ISSUE		EDITION LIMIT	YEAR RETD.	ISSUE PRICE	*QUOTE U.S. $
1995	John's New Pup	850		150.00	150
1995	Kate and Her Fiddle	850		150.00	150
1996	Partners	850		150.00	150

Bama - J. Bama

YEAR ISSUE		EDITION LIMIT	YEAR RETD.	ISSUE PRICE	*QUOTE U.S. $
1996	After the Council	1,000		195.00	195
1993	Art of James Bama Book w/Chester Medicine Crow Fathers Flag Print	2,500	N/A	345.00	345
1981	At a Mountain Man Wedding	1,500	N/A	145.00	145-200
1981	At Burial Gallager and Blind Bill	1,650	N/A	135.00	150
1988	Bittin' Up-Rimrock Ranch	1,250	N/A	195.00	700-800
1992	Blackfeet War Robe	1,000		195.00	195
1995	Blackfoot Ceremonial Headdress (Iris Print)	200		850.00	850
1987	Buck Norris-Crossed Sabres Ranch	1,000	N/A	195.00	700
1990	Buffalo Bill	1,250	N/A	210.00	210
1993	The Buffalo Dance	1,000		195.00	195
1991	Ceremonial Lance	1,250		225.00	225
1996	Cheyene Split Horn Headdress (Iris Print)	200		850.00	850
1994	Cheyenne Dog Soldier	1,000		225.00	225
1991	Chuck Wagon	1,000		225.00	225
1975	Chuck Wagon in the Snow	1,000	N/A	50.00	1125-1395
1992	Coming' Round the Bend	1,000		195.00	195
1978	Contemporary Sioux Indian	1,000	N/A	75.00	1600
1995	A Cowboy Named Anne	1,000		185.00	185
1992	Crow Cavalry Scout	1,000		195.00	195
1977	A Crow Indian	1,000	N/A	65.00	75-95

*Quotes have been rounded up to nearest dollar

Greenwich Workshop
to Greenwich Workshop

GRAPHICS

YEAR ISSUE		EDITION LIMIT	YEAR RETD.	ISSUE PRICE	*QUOTE U.S.$
1982	Crow Indian Dancer	1,250		150.00	150
1988	Crow Indian From Lodge Grass	1,250		225.00	225
1988	Dan-Mountain Man	1,250	N/A	195.00	195
1983	The Davilla Brothers-Bronc Riders	1,250		145.00	145
1983	Don Walker-Bareback Rider	1,250	N/A	85.00	85
1991	The Drift on Skull Creek Pass	1,500		225.00	225
1979	Heritage	1,500	N/A	75.00	275-325
1978	Indian at Crow Fair	1,500	N/A	75.00	75
1988	Indian Wearing War Medicine Bonnet	1,000	N/A	225.00	225
1980	Ken Blackbird	1,500	N/A	95.00	95
1974	Ken Hunder, Working Cowboy	1,000	N/A	55.00	600
1989	Little Fawn-Cree Indian Girl	1,250	N/A	195.00	195
1979	Little Star	1,500	N/A	80.00	900-995
1993	Magua-"The Last of the Mohicans"	1,000		225.00	225
1993	Making Horse Medicine	1,000		225.00	225
1978	Mountain Man	1,000	N/A	75.00	350
1980	Mountain Man 1820-1840 Period	1,500	N/A	115.00	295-375
1979	Mountain Man and His Fox	1,500	N/A	90.00	350
1982	Mountain Man with Rifle	1,250	N/A	135.00	135
1978	A Mountain Ute	1,000	N/A	75.00	500-595
1992	Northern Cheyene Wolf Scout	1,000		195.00	195
1981	Old Arapaho Story-Teller	1,500	N/A	135.00	135
1980	Old Saddle in the Snow	1,500	N/A	75.00	595
1980	Old Sod House	1,500	N/A	80.00	300
1981	Oldest Living Crow Indian	1,500	N/A	135.00	135
1993	On the North Fork of the Shoshoni	1,000		195.00	195
1990	Paul Newman as Butch Cassidy & Video	2,000		250.00	250
1981	Portrait of a Sioux	1,500	N/A	135.00	135
1979	Pre-Columbian Indian with Atlatl	1,500	N/A	75.00	75
1991	Ready to Rendezvous	1,000		225.00	225
1995	Ready to Ride	1,000		185.00	185
1990	Ridin' the Rims	1,250	N/A	210.00	210
1991	Riding the High Country	1,250		225.00	225
1978	Rookie Bronc Rider	1,000	N/A	75.00	150
1976	Sage Grinder	1,000	N/A	65.00	1250-1350
1980	Sheep Skull in Drift	1,500	N/A	75.00	150
1974	Shoshone Chief	1,000	N/A	65.00	650
1982	Sioux Indian with Eagle Feather	1,250	N/A	150.00	150
1992	Sioux Subchief	1,000		195.00	195
1994	Slim Warren, The Old Cowboy	1,000		125.00	125
1983	Southwest Indian Father & Son	1,250		145.00	145
1977	Timber Jack Joe	1,000	N/A	65.00	1295
1988	The Volunteer	1,500		225.00	225
1996	The Warrior (Iris Print)	200		550.00	550
1987	Winter on Trout Creek	1,000	N/A	150.00	300-350
1981	Winter Trapping	1,500	N/A	150.00	520-595
1980	Young Plains Indian	1,500	N/A	125.00	1050-1500
1990	Young Sheepherder	1,500		225.00	225

Bean - A. Bean

YEAR ISSUE		EDITION LIMIT	YEAR RETD.	ISSUE PRICE	*QUOTE U.S.$
1993	Conrad Gordon and Bean:The Fantasy	1,000		385.00	500
1987	Helping Hands	850		150.00	150
1995	Houston, We Have a Problem	1,000		500.00	500
1988	How It Felt to Walk on the Moon	850	N/A	150.00	150
1992	In Flight	850		385.00	385
1994	In The Beginning Apollo 25 C/S	1,000	N/A	450.00	550

Blackshear - T. Blackshear

YEAR ISSUE		EDITION LIMIT	YEAR RETD.	ISSUE PRICE	*QUOTE U.S.$
1994	Beauty and the Beast	1,000		225.00	225
1996	Dance of the Wind & Storm	850		195.00	195
1996	Golden Breeze	850		225.00	225
1993	Hero Frederick Douglass	746		20.00	20
1993	Hero Harriet Tubman	753		20.00	20
1993	Hero Martin Luther King, Jr.	762		20.00	20
1993	Heroes of Our Heritage Portfolio	5,000		35.00	35
1995	Intimacy	550		850.00	1200
1995	Night in Day	850		195.00	195
1994	Swansong	1,000		175.00	175

Blake - B. Blake

YEAR ISSUE		EDITION LIMIT	YEAR RETD.	ISSUE PRICE	*QUOTE U.S.$
1995	The Old Double Diamond	850		175.00	175
1994	West of the Moon	650		195.00	195

Blossom - C. Blossom

YEAR ISSUE		EDITION LIMIT	YEAR RETD.	ISSUE PRICE	*QUOTE U.S.$
1987	After the Last Drift	950		145.00	145
1984	Ah Your Majesty	N/A	N/A	45.00	45
1985	Allerton on the East River	650	N/A	145.00	145
1996	Arthur James Heading Out	850		150.00	150
1988	Black Rock	950		150.00	150
1984	December Moonrise	650	N/A	135.00	135
1984	December Moonrise (remarqued)	25	N/A	175.00	175
1990	Ebb Tide	950		175.00	175
1983	First Out	450	N/A	90.00	600-750
1983	First Out (remarqued)	25	N/A	190.00	800-1000
1987	Gloucester Mackeral Seiners	950		145.00	145
1989	Harbor Light	950		165.00	165
1988	Heading Home	950	N/A	150.00	250
1985	Off Palmer Land	850		145.00	145
1992	Port of Call	850		175.00	175
1986	Potomac By Moonlight	950	N/A	145.00	145
1987	San Francisco-Eve of the Gold Rush	950		150.00	150
1992	Silhouette	850		175.00	175
1986	Southport @ Twilight	950		145.00	145
1985	Tranquil Dawn	650		95.00	95
1994	Traveling in Company	850		175.00	175
1994	Traveling in Company, Remarque	100		415.00	415
1992	Windward	950		175.00	175

YEAR ISSUE		EDITION LIMIT	YEAR RETD.	ISSUE PRICE	*QUOTE U.S.$
1986	Winter Dawn @ Boston Wharf	850		85.00	85

Bralds - B. Bralds

YEAR ISSUE		EDITION LIMIT	YEAR RETD.	ISSUE PRICE	*QUOTE U.S.$
1995	Bag Ladies	2,500	1995	150.00	525-540
1996	Basket Cases	2,500	1996	150.00	150-175
1996	Cabinet Meeting	2,000	1996	150.00	150-200
1996	Cheese	2,000		150.00	150

Bullas - W. Bullas

YEAR ISSUE		EDITION LIMIT	YEAR RETD.	ISSUE PRICE	*QUOTE U.S.$
1995	The Big Game	1,500		95.00	95
1993	Billy the Pig	850		95.00	172
1995	The Chimp Shot	1,000		95.00	95
1994	Clucks Unlimited	850		95.00	95
1995	The Consultant	1,000		95.00	95
1994	Court of Appeals	850	1995	95.00	95
1995	Dog Byte	1,000		95.00	95
1994	Ductor	850		95.00	95
1995	fowl ball...	1,500		95.00	95
1994	Fridays After Five	850		95.00	95
1995	Legal Eagles	1,000		95.00	95
1993	Mr. Harry Buns	850	N/A	95.00	95
1996	The Nerd Dogs	1,500		95.00	95
1993	Our Ladies of the Front Lawn	850		95.00	95
1993	The Pale Prince	850		110.00	110
1993	Sand Trap Pro	850		95.00	95
1993	Some Set of Buns	850		95.00	95
1995	tennis, anyone?	1,000		95.00	95
1993	Wine-Oceros	850		95.00	95
1993	You Rang, Madam?	850		95.00	114
1996	Zippo...The Fire Eater	850		95.00	95

Christensen - J. Christensen

YEAR ISSUE		EDITION LIMIT	YEAR RETD.	ISSUE PRICE	*QUOTE U.S.$
1989	The Annunciation	850	N/A	175.00	200-225
1995	Balancing Act	3,500	N/A	185.00	185
1996	The Bassonist	2,500		125.00	125
1996	The Believer's Etching Edition	1,000		795.00	795
1990	The Burden of the Responsible Man	850	N/A	145.00	900-1000
1991	The Candleman	850	N/A	160.00	200
1993	College of Magical Knowledge	4,500	N/A	185.00	325
1993	College of Magical Knowledge, remarque	500	N/A	252.50	325
1996	Court of the Faeries	3,500		245.00	245
1991	Diggery Diggery Dare-Etching	75	N/A	210.00	400-600
1994	Evening Angels	4,000	N/A	195.00	195
1994	Evening Angels w/Art Furnishings Frame	200	N/A	800.00	800
1989	Fantasies of the Sea-poster	Open		35.00	35
1995	Fishing	2,500	N/A	145.00	145
1993	Getting it Right	4,000	N/A	185.00	185
1985	The Gift For Mrs. Claus	3,500	N/A	80.00	595-800
1991	Jack Be Nimble-Etching	75	N/A	210.00	425
1986	Jonah	850	N/A	95.00	275-325
1991	Lawrence and a Bear	850	N/A	145.00	500-600
1987	Low Tech-Poster	Open		35.00	35
1991	Man in the Moon-Etching	75	N/A	210.00	525
1988	The Man Who Minds the Moon	850	N/A	145.00	450-600
1991	Mother Goose-Etching	75	N/A	210.00	1200-1400
1987	Old Man with a Lot on His Mind	850	N/A	85.00	650-900
1986	Olde World Santa	3,500	N/A	80.00	700-800
1992	The Oldest Angel	850	N/A	125.00	800-1000
1991	Once Upon a Time	1,500	N/A	175.00	1300-1500
1991	Once Upon a Time, remarque	500	N/A	220.00	1400-1600
1996	One Light	1,500		125.00	125
1991	Pelican King	850	N/A	115.00	600-900
1991	Peter Peter Pumpkin Eater-Etching	75	N/A	210.00	450-600
1995	Piscatorial Percussionist	3,000	N/A	125.00	125
1992	The Reponsible Woman	2,500	N/A	175.00	495
1990	Rhymes & Reasons w/Booklet	Open		150.00	150
1990	Rhymes & Reasons w/Booklet, remarque	500	N/A	208.00	350
1993	The Royal Music Barque	2,750	N/A	375.00	375
1992	The Royal Processional	1,500	N/A	185.00	250-425
1992	The Royal Processional, remarque	500	N/A	252.50	350-550
1993	The Scholar	3,250	N/A	125.00	125
1995	Serenade For an Orange Cat	3,000	N/A	125.00	125
1987	The Shakespearean Poster	Open		35.00	35
1995	Sisters of the Sea	2,000	N/A	195.00	195
1994	Six Bird Hunters-Full Camouflage 3	4,662	N/A	165.00	165
1994	Sometimes the Spirit Touches w/book	3,600	N/A	195.00	195
1991	Three Blind Mice-Etching	75	N/A	210.00	2700-3000
1991	Three Wise Men of Gotham-Etching	75	N/A	210.00	600
1991	Tweedle Dee & Tweedle Dum-Etching	75	N/A	210.00	600
1994	Two Angels Discussing Botticelli	2,950	N/A	145.00	145
1990	Two Sisters	650	N/A	325.00	325
1996	The Voyage of the Basset Collector's Edition Book & The Oldest Professor	2,500		195.00	195
1987	Voyage of the Basset w/Journal	850	N/A	225.00	1800-2500
1993	Waiting for the Tide	2,250	N/A	150.00	150
1988	The Widows Mite	850	N/A	145.00	2900-3400
1986	Your Plaice, or Mine?	850	N/A	125.00	200-395

Combes - S. Combes

YEAR ISSUE		EDITION LIMIT	YEAR RETD.	ISSUE PRICE	*QUOTE U.S.$
1992	African Oasis	650	N/A	375.00	650-750
1981	Alert	1,000	N/A	95.00	95
1987	The Angry One	850		95.00	95
1988	Bushwhacker	850	N/A	145.00	145
1983	Chui	275	N/A	250.00	250
1988	Confrontation	850		145.00	145
1988	The Crossing	1,250	N/A	245.00	245
1994	Disdain	850		110.00	110
1980	Facing the Wind	1,500	N/A	75.00	75-125
1993	Fearful Symmetry	850	N/A	110.00	110
1995	Golden Silhouette	950		175.00	175
1990	The Guardian (Silverback)	1,000		185.00	185
1992	The Hypnotist	1,250		145.00	145
1994	Indian Summer	950		175.00	175
1980	Interlude	1,500	N/A	85.00	85
1995	Jungle Phantom	950		175.00	175
1991	Kilimanjaro Morning	850		185.00	185
1981	Leopard Cubs	1,000	N/A	95.00	95
1992	Lookout	1,250		95.00	95
1980	Manyara Afternoon	1,500	N/A	75.00	325
1989	Masai-Longonot, Kenya	850		145.00	145
1992	Midday Sun (Lioness & Cubs)	850		125.00	125
1989	Mountain Gorillas	550	N/A	135.00	135
1995	Mountain Myth	950		175.00	175
1995	Pride	950		175.00	175
1980	Serengeti Monarch	1,500	N/A	85.00	85
1995	Serious Intent	950		175.00	175
1995	Siberian Winter	950		175.00	175
1996	The Siberians	850		175.00	175
1988	Simba	850		125.00	125
1995	Snow Tracker	950		175.00	175
1980	Solitary Hunter	1,500	N/A	75.00	75
1990	Standoff	850	N/A	375.00	600-695
1991	Study in Concentration	850	N/A	185.00	395
1987	Tall Shadows	850	N/A	150.00	825
1985	Tension at Dawn	825	N/A	145.00	900
1985	Tension at Dawn, remarque	25	N/A	275.00	1150-1295
1989	The Watering Hole	850		225.00	225
1986	The Wildebeest Migration	450	N/A	350.00	1295

Crowley - D. Crowley

YEAR ISSUE		EDITION LIMIT	YEAR RETD.	ISSUE PRICE	*QUOTE U.S.$
1981	Afterglow	1,500		110.00	110
1992	Anna Thorne	650		160.00	160
1980	Apache in White	1,500	N/A	85.00	85
1979	Arizona Mountain Man	1,500	N/A	85.00	85
1980	Beauty and the Beast	1,500	N/A	85.00	85
1992	Colors of the Sunset	650		175.00	175
1979	Desert Sunset	1,500	N/A	75.00	75
1978	Dorena	1,000	N/A	75.00	75
1995	The Dreamer	650		150.00	150
1981	Eagle Feathers	1,500	N/A	95.00	95
1988	Ermine and Beads	550	N/A	85.00	85
1989	The Gunfighters	3,000	N/A	35.00	35
1981	The Heirloom	1,000	N/A	125.00	125
1982	Hopi Butterfly	275		350.00	350
1978	Hudson's Bay Blanket	1,000	N/A	75.00	75
1980	The Littlest Apache	275	N/A	325.00	850
1994	Plumes and Ribbons	650		160.00	160
1979	Security Blanket	1,500	N/A	65.00	65
1981	Shannandoah	275	N/A	325.00	325
1978	The Starquilt	1,000	N/A	65.00	500
1986	The Trapper	550		75.00	75

Dawson - J. Dawson

YEAR ISSUE		EDITION LIMIT	YEAR RETD.	ISSUE PRICE	*QUOTE U.S.$
1992	The Attack (Cougars)	850		175.00	175
1993	Berry Contented	850		150.00	150
1993	Berry Contented (Remarque)	100		235.00	235
1994	The Face Off (Right & Left Panel)	850		150.00	150
1993	Looking Back	850		110.00	110
1993	Otter Wise	850		150.00	150
1993	Taking a Break	850	N/A	150.00	150

Doolittle - B. Doolittle

YEAR ISSUE		EDITION LIMIT	YEAR RETD.	ISSUE PRICE	*QUOTE U.S.$
1983	Art of Camouflage, signed	2,000	1983	55.00	395
1980	Bugged Bear	1,000	1980	85.00	3500-3700
1987	Calling the Buffalo	8,500	1987	245.00	825-1000
1983	Christmas Day, Give or Take a Week	4,581	1983	80.00	1025-1150
1988	Doubled Back	15,000	1988	245.00	1095-1250
1996	Drawn From the Heart-Etching Suite	349	1996	750.00	1900-2100
1992	Eagle Heart	48,000	1992	285.00	285
1982	Eagle's Flight	1,500	1982	185.00	2500-2800
1983	Escape by a Hare	1,500	1983	80.00	725-825
1984	Forest Has Eyes, The	8,544	1984	175.00	3300-4000
1980	Good Omen, The	1,000	1980	85.00	2800-3100
1987	Guardian Spirits	13,238	1987	295.00	595-650
1990	Hide and Seek (Composite & Video)	25,000	1990	1200.00	1200
1984	Let My Spirit Soar	1,500	1984	195.00	4500-6000
1979	Pintos	1,000	1979	65.00	6950-7700
1993	Prayer for the Wild Things	65,000	1993	325.00	325
1983	Runs With Thunder	1,500	1983	150.00	900-1200
1983	Rushing War Eagle	1,500	1983	150.00	900-1200
1991	Sacred Circle (Print & Video)	40,192	1991	325.00	375-415
1989	Sacred Ground	69,996	1989	265.00	600-725
1987	Season of the Eagle	36,548	1987	245.00	525-695
1991	The Sentinel	35,000	1991	275.00	475-700
1981	Spirit of the Grizzly	1,500	1981	150.00	3950-4150
1995	Spirit Takes Flight	48,000	1995	225.00	225
1996	Three More for Breakfast	20,000	1996	245.00	275
1986	Two Bears of the Blackfeet	2,650	1986	225.00	825-950
1985	Two Indian Horses	12,253	1985	225.00	3200-3650
1995	Two More Indian Horses	48,000	1995	225.00	425-525
1981	Unknown Presence	1,500	1981	135.00	3000-3100
1992	Walk Softly (Chapbook)	40,192	1992	225.00	275-295
1994	When The Wind Had Wings	57,500	1994	325.00	325
1986	Where Silence Speaks, Doolittle The Art of Bev Doolittle	3,500	1986	650.00	2450-2550
1980	Whoo !?	1,000	1980	75.00	1500-2100

*Quotes have been rounded up to nearest dollar

Greenwich Workshop
to Greenwich Workshop

GRAPHICS

YEAR ISSUE		EDITION LIMIT	YEAR RETD.	ISSUE PRICE	*QUOTE U.S.$
1993	Wilderness? Wilderness!	50,000	1993	65.00	65
1985	Wolves of the Crow	2,650	1985	225.00	1150-1525
1981	Woodland Encounter	1,500	1981	145.00	9200

Dubowski - E. Dubowski

YEAR ISSUE		EDITION LIMIT	YEAR RETD.	ISSUE PRICE	*QUOTE U.S.$
1996	Aspen Flowers	850		145.00	145
1996	Fresh From the Garden	850		145.00	145

Entz - L. Entz

YEAR ISSUE		EDITION LIMIT	YEAR RETD.	ISSUE PRICE	*QUOTE U.S.$
1996	Apple Pie	850		150.00	150
1995	Life's a Dance	850		150.00	150
1996	New Shoes	850		150.00	150

Ferris - K. Ferris

YEAR ISSUE		EDITION LIMIT	YEAR RETD.	ISSUE PRICE	*QUOTE U.S.$
1990	The Circus Outbound	1,000		225.00	225
1991	Farmer's Nightmare	850		185.00	185
1991	Linebacker in the Buff	1,000		225.00	225
1983	Little Willie Coming Home	1,000	N/A	145.00	1750
1994	Real Trouble	1,000		195.00	195
1995	Schweinfurt Again	1,000		195.00	195
1982	Sunrise Encounter	1,000	N/A	145.00	145
1993	A Test of Courage	850		185.00	185
1991	Too Little, Too Late w/Video	1,000		245.00	245

Frederick - R. Frederick

YEAR ISSUE		EDITION LIMIT	YEAR RETD.	ISSUE PRICE	*QUOTE U.S.$
1990	Autumn Leaves	1,250	N/A	175.00	175
1996	Autumn Trail	850		195.00	195
1989	Barely Spring	1,500		165.00	165
1994	Beeline (C)	1,000		195.00	195
1987	Before the Storm (Diptych)	550	N/A	350.00	700-900
1991	Breaking the Ice	2,750	N/A	235.00	235
1989	Colors of Home	1,500	N/A	165.00	275-295
1995	Drifters	850		175.00	175
1985	Early Evening Gathering	475	N/A	325.00	355
1992	An Early Light Breakfast	1,750	N/A	235.00	265-300
1990	Echoes of Sunset	1,750	N/A	235.00	550-750
1987	Evening Shadows (White-Tail Deer)	1,500	N/A	125.00	125
1992	Fast Break	2,250		235.00	235
1992	Fire and Ice (Suite of 2)	1,750		175.00	175
1984	First Moments of Gold	825	N/A	145.00	225
1984	First Moments of Gold, remarque	25	N/A	172.50	265
1984	From Timber's Edge	850	N/A	125.00	140-165
1996	Geyser Basin	850		175.00	175
1989	Gifts of the Land #2	500	N/A	150.00	150
1988	Gifts of the Land w/Wine & Wine Label	500	N/A	150.00	150
1988	Glimmer of Solitude	1,500		145.00	145
1993	Glory Days	1,750		115.00	115
1986	Great Horned Owl	1,250	N/A	115.00	135
1995	High Country Harem	1,000		185.00	185
1985	High Society	950	N/A	115.00	425
1995	Jaywalkers	850		175.00	175
1991	The Long Run	1,750	N/A	235.00	250-295
1991	The Long Run, AP	200	N/A	167.50	495
1985	Los Colores De Chiapas	950	N/A	85.00	85
1994	The Lost World	1,000		175.00	175
1985	Misty Morning Lookout	950	N/A	145.00	145
1984	Misty Morning Sentinel	850	N/A	125.00	145
1989	Monarch of the North	2,000		150.00	150
1990	Morning Surprise	1,750	N/A	165.00	165
1991	Morning Thunder	1,750	N/A	185.00	200
1988	The Nesting Call	2,500		150.00	150
1988	The Nesting Call, remarque	1,000	N/A	165.00	165
1993	New Heights	1,950		195.00	195
1987	Northern Light	1,500	N/A	165.00	165
1986	Out on a Limb	1,250	N/A	145.00	300-375
1993	Point of View	1,000		235.00	235
1992	Rain Forest Rendezvous	1,500	N/A	225.00	225
1988	Rim Walk	1,500	N/A	90.00	90
1988	Shadows of Dusk	1,500	N/A	165.00	165
1990	Silent Watch (High Desert Museum)	2,000	N/A	35.00	35
1994	Snow Pack	1,000		175.00	175
1992	Snowstorm	1,750		195.00	195
1990	Snowy Reflections (Snowy Egret)	1,500		150.00	150
1986	Sounds of Twilight	1,500	N/A	135.00	250-295
1991	Summer's Song (Triptych)	2,500		225.00	225
1993	Temple of the Jaguar	1,500		225.00	225
1988	Timber Ghost w/Mini Wine Label	3,000	N/A	150.00	150
1994	Tropic Moon	850		165.00	165
1987	Tundra Watch (Snowy Owl)	1,500	N/A	145.00	145
1994	Way of the Caribou	1,235		235.00	235
1987	Winter's Brilliance (Cardinal)	1,500	N/A	135.00	135
1986	Winter's Call	1,250	N/A	165.00	550
1986	Winter's Call Raptor, AP	100	N/A	165.00	600
1987	Woodland Crossing (Caribou)	1,500	N/A	145.00	145
1988	World of White	2,500	N/A	150.00	150

Gurney - J. Gurney

YEAR ISSUE		EDITION LIMIT	YEAR RETD.	ISSUE PRICE	*QUOTE U.S.$
1992	Birthday Pageant	2,500	N/A	60.00	60
1992	Birthday Pageant, remarque	300	N/A	275.00	295
1995	Cottage Reflections	3,000		195.00	195
1991	Dinosaur Boulevard	2,000	N/A	125.00	125
1991	Dinosaur Boulevard, remarque	250	N/A	196.00	425
1990	Dinosaur Parade	1,995	1995	125.00	125
1990	Dinosaur Parade, remarque	150	N/A	130.00	2500-2800
1992	Dream Canyon	N/A	N/A	125.00	125
1992	Dream Canyon, remarque	150	N/A	196.00	395
1993	The Excursion	3,500		175.00	175
1993	Garden of Hope	3,500		175.00	175
1990	Morning in Treetown	1,500	N/A	175.00	325
1993	Palace in the Clouds	3,500	N/A	175.00	175
1993	Ring Riders	2,500	N/A	175.00	175
1995	Rumble & Mist	2,500		175.00	175
1995	Santa Claus	2,000		95.00	95
1990	Seaside Romp	1,000	N/A	175.00	395
1992	Skyback Print w/Dinotopia Book	3,500	N/A	295.00	295
1994	Small Wonder	3,299	N/A	75.00	75
1994	Steep Street	3,500		95.00	95
1991	Waterfall City	3,000	N/A	125.00	125
1991	Waterfall City, remarque	250	N/A	186.00	395
1995	The World Beneath Collectors' Book w/ print	3,000		195.00	195

Gustafson - S. Gustafson

YEAR ISSUE		EDITION LIMIT	YEAR RETD.	ISSUE PRICE	*QUOTE U.S.$
1995	The Alice in Wonderland Suite	4,000		195.00	195
1994	Frog Prince	3,500	1994	125.00	150
1993	Goldilocks and the Three Bears	3,500	1993	125.00	300-400
1995	Hansel & Gretel	3,000		125.00	125
1993	Humpty Dumpty	3,500	1993	125.00	125
1995	Jack in the Beanstalk	3,500		125.00	125
1993	Little Red Riding Hood	3,500	1993	125.00	125
1996	Old King Cole	2,750		125.00	125
1994	Pat-A-Cake	4,000	1994	125.00	125
1996	Puss in Boots	2,750		145.00	145
1995	Rumplestiltskin	2,750		125.00	125
1993	Snow White and the Seven Dwarfs	3,500	1993	165.00	225
1995	Touched by Magic	4,000		185.00	185

Hartough - L. Hartough

YEAR ISSUE		EDITION LIMIT	YEAR RETD.	ISSUE PRICE	*QUOTE U.S.$
1996	11th Hole, "White Dogwood", Augusta National Golf Club	850		225.00	225
1995	14th Hole, St. Andrews	850	1995	225.00	225
1996	15th Hole, "Firethorn", Augusta National Golf Club	850		325.00	325
1996	18th Hole, Royal Lytham & St. Annes Golf Club	850		225.00	225
1995	7th Hole, Pebble Beach Golf Links	850		225.00	225

Holm - J. Holm

YEAR ISSUE		EDITION LIMIT	YEAR RETD.	ISSUE PRICE	*QUOTE U.S.$
1996	Slipper Thief	850		95.00	95

Johnson - J. Johnson

YEAR ISSUE		EDITION LIMIT	YEAR RETD.	ISSUE PRICE	*QUOTE U.S.$
1994	Moose River	650		175.00	175
1994	Sea Treasures	650		125.00	125
1994	Winter Thaw	650		150.00	150
1993	Wolf Creek	550	N/A	165.00	200

Kennedy - S. Kennedy

YEAR ISSUE		EDITION LIMIT	YEAR RETD.	ISSUE PRICE	*QUOTE U.S.$
1988	After Dinner Music	2,500	N/A	175.00	230
1995	Alaskan Malamute	1,000		125.00	125
1992	Aurora	2,250	N/A	195.00	195
1991	A Breed Apart	2,750	N/A	225.00	225
1992	Cabin Fever	2,250		175.00	175
1995	Cliff Dwellers	850		175.00	175
1988	Distant Relations	950	N/A	200.00	300
1988	Eager to Run	950	N/A	200.00	1400-1790
1990	Fish Tales	5,500	N/A	225.00	225
1991	In Training	3,350	N/A	165.00	295
1991	In Training, remarque	150	N/A	215.50	345
1996	Keeping Watch	850		150.00	150
1995	The Lesson	1,000		125.00	125
1996	Looking For Trouble	850		125.00	125
1993	Midnight Eyes	1,750		125.00	125
1993	Never Alone	2,250		225.00	225
1993	Never Alone, remarque	250	N/A	272.50	273
1990	On the Edge	4,000		225.00	225
1995	On the Heights	850		175.00	175
1994	Quiet Time Companions-Samoyed	1,000		125.00	125
1994	Quiet Time Companions-Siberian Husky	1,000	N/A	125.00	125
1994	Silent Observers	1,250	N/A	165.00	165
1996	Snow Buddies	850		125.00	125
1989	Snowshoes	4,000	N/A	185.00	185
1994	Spruce and Fur	1,500		165.00	165
1995	Standing Watch	850		175.00	175
1993	The Touch	1,500		115.00	115
1989	Up a Creek	2,500	N/A	185.00	185

Kodera - C. Kodera

YEAR ISSUE		EDITION LIMIT	YEAR RETD.	ISSUE PRICE	*QUOTE U.S.$
1986	The A Team (K10)	850		145.00	145
1995	A.M. Sortie	1,000		225.00	225
1996	Canyon Starliner	850		185.00	185
1991	Darkness Visible (Stealth)	2,671	N/A	40.00	40
1987	Fifty Years a Lady	550	N/A	150.00	450-500
1988	The Great Greenwich Balloon Race	1,000		145.00	145
1990	Green Light-Jump!	650	N/A	145.00	200
1992	Halsey's Surprise	850		95.00	95
1994	Last to Fight	1,000		225.00	225
1995	Lonely Flight to Destiny	1,000	1995	347.00	895-1000
1992	Looking For Nagumo	1,000		225.00	225
1996	The Lost Squadron	850		275.00	275
1992	Memphis Belle/Dauntless Dotty	1,250		245.00	245
1990	A Moment's Peace	1,250		150.00	150
1988	Moonlight Intruders	1,000		125.00	125
1995	Only One Survived	1,000		245.00	245
1989	Springtime Flying in the Rockies	550	N/A	95.00	95
1996	Stratojet Shakedown	1,000		265.00	265
1992	Thirty Seconds Over Tokyo	1,000	N/A	275.00	275
1991	This is No Drill w/Video	1,000		225.00	225
1994	This is No Time to Lose an Engine	850		150.00	150
1994	Tiger's Bite	850		150.00	150
1987	Voyager: The Skies Yield	1,500		225.00	225

Landry - P. Landry

YEAR ISSUE		EDITION LIMIT	YEAR RETD.	ISSUE PRICE	*QUOTE U.S.$
1996	Afternoon Tea (canvas)	450	1996	495.00	495
1993	The Antique Shop	1,250	N/A	125.00	125
1992	Apple Orchard	1,250		150.00	150
1992	Aunt Martha's Country Farm	1,500	N/A	185.00	300
1995	Autumn Market	1,000		185.00	185
1987	Bluenose Country	550	N/A	115.00	175
1992	Boardwalk Promenade	1,250		175.00	175
1989	A Canadian Christmas	1,250		125.00	125
1989	Cape Cod Welcome Cameo	850	N/A	75.00	275
1990	The Captain's Garden	1,000	N/A	165.00	425
1993	Christmas at Mystic Seaport	2,000		125.00	125
1992	Christmas at the Flower Market	2,500		125.00	125
1994	Christmas Carousel Pony	2,000		125.00	125
1990	Christmas Treasures	2,500		165.00	165
1992	Cottage Garden	1,250	N/A	160.00	160
1995	Cottage Reflections	850		135.00	135
1994	An English Cottage	850		150.00	150
1994	Flower Barn	1,000		175.00	175
1988	Flower Boxes	550	N/A	75.00	250
1991	Flower Market	1,500	N/A	185.00	1000
1990	Flower Wagon	1,500	N/A	165.00	165
1994	Flowers For Mary Hope	1,250		165.00	165
1995	Harbor Garden	1,000		160.00	160
1993	Hometown Parade	1,250		165.00	165
1996	It's a Wonderful Christmas	1,250		165.00	165
1996	Joseph's Corner (canvas)	450		495.00	495
1996	Joseph's Corner, Artist Touch (canvas)	100		795.00	795
1995	Lantern Skaters	1,500		135.00	135
1990	Morning Papers	1,250	N/A	135.00	145
1994	Morning Walk	850		135.00	135
1991	Nantucket Colors	1,500		150.00	150
1993	Paper Boy	1,500		150.00	150
1993	A Place in the Park	1,500		185.00	185
1984	Regatta	500	N/A	75.00	150
1984	Regatta, remarque	50	N/A	97.50	145
1990	Seaside Carousel	1,500	N/A	165.00	200
1988	Seaside Cottage	550	N/A	125.00	125
1986	Seaside Mist	450	N/A	85.00	200
1985	The Skaters	500		75.00	75
1985	The Skaters, remarque	50	N/A	97.50	98
1995	Spring Song	2,500		145.00	145
1996	Summer Buddies	950		135.00	135
1991	Summer Concert	1,500		195.00	195
1989	Summer Garden	850	N/A	125.00	400
1995	Summer Mist (Fine Art Original Lithograph)	550		750.00	850
1992	Sunflowers	1,250	N/A	125.00	125
1991	The Toymaker	1,500	N/A	165.00	165
1991	Victorian Memories	1,500	N/A	150.00	150
1996	Winter Memories w/The Captain's Garden Collector's Edition Book	2,000		195.00	195

Lovell - T. Lovell

YEAR ISSUE		EDITION LIMIT	YEAR RETD.	ISSUE PRICE	*QUOTE U.S.$
1988	The Battle of the Crater	1,500	N/A	225.00	225
1988	Berdan's Sharpshooters-Gettysburg	1,500		225.00	225
1986	Blackfeet Wall	450	N/A	325.00	1095-1195
1981	Carson's Boatyard	1,000		150.00	150
1985	Chiricahua Scout	650		90.00	90
1981	The Deceiver	1,000		150.00	150
1990	Dry Goods and Molasses	1,000		225.00	225
1981	Fires Along the Oregon Trail	1,000	N/A	150.00	295
1993	The Handwarmer	1,000		225.00	225
1988	The Hunter	1,000		150.00	150
1982	Invitation to Trade	1,000	N/A	150.00	150
1989	The Lost Rag Doll	1,000		225.00	225
1988	Mr. Bodmer's Music Box	5,000		40.00	40
1975	The Mud Owl's Warning	1,000	N/A	150.00	175
1988	North Country Rider	2,500		95.00	95
1976	Quicksand at Horsehead	1,000		150.00	150
1976	Shotgun Toll	1,000		150.00	150
1983	Sugar in The Coffee	650	N/A	165.00	165
1987	Surrender at Appomattox	1,000	N/A	225.00	1695
1992	Target Practice	2,000		25.00	25
1976	Time of Cold-Maker	1,000		150.00	150
1989	Union Fleet Passing Vicksburg	1,500		225.00	225
1982	Walking Coyote & Buffalo Orphans	650	N/A	165.00	195
1982	The Wheelsoakers	1,000		150.00	150
1984	Winter Holiday	850		95.00	95
1989	Youth's Hour of Glory	1,500		175.00	175

Lyman - S. Lyman

YEAR ISSUE		EDITION LIMIT	YEAR RETD.	ISSUE PRICE	*QUOTE U.S.$
1990	Among The Wild Brambles	1,750	1990	185.00	400-625
1985	Autumn Gathering	850	N/A	115.00	600-850
1996	Beach Bonfire	6,500	1996	225.00	225
1985	Bear & Blossoms (C)	850	N/A	75.00	495-665
1987	Canadian Autumn	1,500	1987	165.00	225-350
1995	Cathedral Snow	4,000	1996	245.00	265
1989	Color In The Snow (Pheasant)	1,500	N/A	165.00	350-495
1996	The Crossing	2,500	1996	195.00	195
1991	Dance of Cloud and Cliff	1,500	1991	225.00	375-495
1991	Dance of Water and Light	3,000	1991	225.00	225
1983	Early Winter In The Mountains	850	N/A	95.00	695-850
1987	An Elegant Couple (Wood Ducks)	1,000	N/A	125.00	250-350
1991	Embers at Dawn	3,500	1991	225.00	1200-1800
1983	End Of The Ridge	850	N/A	95.00	425-575
1990	Evening Light	2,500	1990	225.00	2400-2750
1995	Evening Star w/collector's edition book	9,500	1995	195.00	275
1993	Fire Dance	8,500	1993	235.00	350-540

*Quotes have been rounded up to nearest dollar

GRAPHICS

Greenwich Workshop
to Greenwich Workshop

YEAR ISSUE		EDITION LIMIT	YEAR RETD.	ISSUE PRICE	*QUOTE U.S.$
1984	Free Flight	850	N/A	70.00	95-195
1987	High Creek Crossing	1,000	N/A	165.00	1195-1385
1989	High Light	1,250	1989	165.00	250-425
1986	High Trail At Sunset	1,000	N/A	125.00	675-825
1988	The Intruder	1,500	N/A	150.00	315
1993	Lake of the Shining Rocks	2,250	1993	235.00	400-600
1992	Lantern Light Print w Firelight Chapbook	10,000	1993	195.00	195
1989	Last Light of Winter	1,500	1989	175.00	1195-1400
1995	Midnight Fire	8,500	1996	245.00	245
1994	Moon Fire	7,500	1994	245.00	595-750
1987	Moon Shadows	1,500	N/A	135.00	185
1994	Moonlit Flight on Christmas Night	2,750	1994	165.00	195
1996	Morning Light	8,000	1996	245.00	350-475
1986	Morning Solitude	850	N/A	115.00	500-700
1990	A Mountain Campfire	1,500	1990	195.00	1800-2400
1994	New Kid on the Rock	2,250	1996	185.00	225
1987	New Territory (Grizzly & Cubs)	1,000	N/A	135.00	275-495
1984	Noisy Neighbors	675	N/A	95.00	1195-1395
1984	Noisy Neighbors, remarque	25	N/A	127.50	1800
1994	North Country Shores	3,000	1994	225.00	300-395
1983	The Pass	850	N/A	95.00	800-1000
1989	Quiet Rain	1,500	N/A	165.00	695-995
1988	The Raptor's Watch	1,500	N/A	150.00	675-875
1988	Return Of The Falcon	1,500	N/A	150.00	225-395
1993	Riparian Riches	2,500	1993	235.00	235
1992	River of Light (Geese)	2,950	N/A	225.00	225
1991	Secret Watch (Lynx)	2,250	N/A	150.00	150
1990	Silent Snows	1,750	N/A	210.00	275
1988	Snow Hunter	1,500	N/A	135.00	725-1000
1986	Snowy Throne (C)	850	N/A	85.00	500-795
1993	The Spirit of Christmas	2,750	1993	165.00	250-350
1996	Sunset Fire (PC)	N/A	1996	245.00	300
1995	Thunderbolt	7,000	N/A	235.00	400-550
1987	Twilight Snow (C)	950	N/A	85.00	300-450
1988	Uzumati: Great Bear of Yosemite	1,750	N/A	150.00	200-275
1992	Warmed by the View	8,500	1992	235.00	300-425
1992	Wilderness Welcome	8,500	N/A	235.00	760-835
1992	Wildflower Suite (Hummingbird)	2,250	N/A	175.00	225-325
1992	Woodland Haven	2,500	N/A	195.00	240

Marris - B. Marris

YEAR ISSUE		EDITION LIMIT	YEAR RETD.	ISSUE PRICE	*QUOTE U.S.$
1987	Above the Glacier	850	N/A	145.00	145
1986	Best Friends	850	N/A	85.00	235-295
1994	Big Gray's Barn and Bistro	1,000		125.00	125
1989	Bittersweet	1,000	N/A	135.00	135
1990	Bugles and Trumpets!	1,000	N/A	175.00	175
1996	Catch The Wind	850		165.00	165
1992	The Comeback	1,250		175.00	175
1991	Cops & Robbers	1,000	N/A	165.00	165
1988	Courtship	850	N/A	145.00	145
1995	Dairy Queens	1,000		125.00	125
1995	The Dartmoor Ponies	1,000		165.00	165
1987	Desperados	850	N/A	135.00	135
1996	Dog Days	1,000		165.00	165
1991	End of the Season	1,000		165.00	165
1985	The Fishing Lesson	1,000		145.00	145
1995	The Gift	1,000		125.00	125
1987	Honey Creek Whitetales	850	N/A	145.00	145
1985	Kenai Dusk	1,000	N/A	145.00	800
1994	Lady Marmalade's Bed & Breakfast	1,000		125.00	125
1996	A Little Pig with a Big Heart	1,000	1996	95.00	95
1990	Mom's Shadow	1,000		165.00	165
1994	Moonshine	1,000		95.00	95
1989	New Beginnings	1,000	N/A	175.00	375
1990	Of Myth and Magic	1,500	N/A	175.00	175
1986	Other Footsteps	950		75.00	75
1989	The Playgroud Showoff	850	N/A	165.00	165
1992	Security Blanket	1,250		175.00	175
1993	Spring Fever	1,000		165.00	165
1991	The Stillness (Grizzly & Cubs)	1,000	N/A	165.00	165
1992	Sun Bath	1,000		95.00	95
1992	To Stand and Endure	1,000	N/A	195.00	275-395
1991	Under the Morning Star	1,500		175.00	175
1988	Waiting For the Freeze	1,000	N/A	125.00	125
1995	Where Best Friends Are Welcome	850	1996	95.00	195

McCarthy - F. McCarthy

YEAR ISSUE		EDITION LIMIT	YEAR RETD.	ISSUE PRICE	*QUOTE U.S.$
1996	After the Council	550		850.00	850
1984	After the Dust Storm	1,000	N/A	145.00	295
1982	Alert	1,000	N/A	135.00	135
1984	Along the West Fork	1,000	N/A	175.00	225
1995	Ambush at the Ancient Rocks	1,000		225.00	225
1978	Ambush, The	1,000	N/A	125.00	300
1982	Apache Scout	1,000	N/A	165.00	165
1988	Apache Trackers (C)	1,000	N/A	95.00	95
1992	The Art of Frank McCarthy	10,418	N/A	60.00	60
1982	Attack on the Wagon Train	1,400	N/A	150.00	150
1977	The Beaver Men	1,000	N/A	75.00	350
1980	Before the Charge	1,000	N/A	115.00	150
1978	Before the Norther	1,000	N/A	90.00	325
1990	Below The Breaking Dawn	1,250	N/A	225.00	225
1994	Beneath the Cliff (Petraglyphs)	1,500		295.00	295
1989	Big Medicine	1,000	N/A	225.00	350
1983	Blackfeet Raiders	1,000	N/A	90.00	200
1992	Breaking the Moonlit Silence	650	N/A	375.00	375
1986	The Buffalo Runners	1,000	N/A	195.00	170
1980	Burning the Way Station	1,000	N/A	125.00	250
1993	By the Ancient Trails They Passed	1,000	N/A	245.00	245
1989	Canyon Lands	1,250	N/A	225.00	225
1982	The Challenge	1,000	N/A	175.00	275-450
1995	Charge of the Buffalo Soldiers	1,000	1995	195.00	285
1985	Charging the Challenger	1,000	N/A	150.00	425
1991	The Chase	1,000		225.00	225
1986	Children of the Raven	1,000	N/A	185.00	550
1987	Chiricahua Raiders	1,000	N/A	165.00	225
1977	Comanche Moon	1,000	N/A	75.00	235
1992	Comanche Raider-Bronze	100		812.50	813
1986	Comanche War Trail	1,000	N/A	165.00	170
1989	The Coming Of The Iron Horse	1,500	N/A	225.00	225
1989	The Coming Of The Iron Horse (Print/Pewter Train Special Pub. Ed.)	100	N/A	1500.00	1600-2150
1981	The Coup	1,000	N/A	125.00	500
1981	Crossing the Divide (The Old West)	1,500	N/A	850.00	450-750
1984	The Decoys	450	N/A	325.00	500
1977	Distant Thunder	1,500	N/A	75.00	500
1989	Down From The Mountains	1,500	N/A	245.00	245
1986	The Drive (C)	1,000	N/A	95.00	95-175
1977	Dust Stained Posse	1,000	N/A	75.00	650
1985	The Fireboat	1,000	N/A	175.00	175
1994	Flashes of Lighting-Thunder of Hooves	550		435.00	435
1987	Following the Herds	1,000	N/A	195.00	265
1980	Forbidden Land	1,000	N/A	125.00	125
1978	The Fording	1,000	N/A	75.00	250
1987	From the Rim	1,000	N/A	225.00	225
1981	Headed North	1,000	N/A	150.00	275
1992	Heading Back	1,000		225.00	225
1995	His Wealth	850		225.00	225
1990	Hoka Hey: Sioux War Cry	1,250	N/A	225.00	225
1987	The Hostile Land	1,000	N/A	225.00	235
1976	The Hostiles	1,000	N/A	75.00	475
1984	Hostiles, signed	1,000	N/A	55.00	55
1974	The Hunt	1,000	N/A	75.00	450
1988	In Pursuit of the White Buffalo	1,500	N/A	225.00	425-525
1992	In the Land of the Ancient Ones	1,250	N/A	245.00	265
1983	In The Land Of The Sparrow Hawk People	1,000	N/A	165.00	175
1987	In The Land Of The Winter Hawk	1,000	N/A	225.00	300
1978	In The Pass	1,500	N/A	90.00	265
1985	The Last Crossing	550	N/A	350.00	350
1989	The Last Stand: Little Big Horn	1,500	N/A	225.00	225
1984	Leading the Charge, signed	1,000	N/A	55.00	80
1974	Lone Sentinel	1,000	N/A	55.00	1100
1979	The Loner	1,000	N/A	75.00	225
1974	Long Column	1,000	N/A	75.00	400
1985	The Long Knives	1,000	N/A	175.00	350
1989	Los Diablos	1,250	N/A	225.00	225
1995	Medicine Man	850	1996	165.00	165
1983	Moonlit Trail	1,000	N/A	90.00	295
1992	Navajo Ponies Comanche Warriors	1,000		225.00	225
1978	Night Crossing	1,000	N/A	75.00	200
1974	The Night They Needed a Good Ribbon Man	1,000	N/A	65.00	300
1977	An Old Time Mountain Man	1,000	N/A	65.00	200
1990	On The Old North Trail (Triptych)	650	N/A	550.00	675
1979	On the Warpath	1,000	N/A	75.00	150-175
1983	Out Of The Mist They Came	1,000	N/A	165.00	235
1990	Out Of The Windswept Ramparts	1,250	N/A	225.00	225
1976	Packing In	1,000	N/A	65.00	400
1991	Pony Express	1,000		225.00	225
1979	The Prayer	1,500	N/A	90.00	450
1991	The Pursuit	650	N/A	550.00	550
1981	Race with the Hostiles	1,000	N/A	135.00	135
1987	Red Bull's War Party	1,000	N/A	165.00	165
1979	Retreat to Higher Ground	2,000	N/A	90.00	240-360
1975	Returning Raiders	1,000	N/A	75.00	300
1980	Roar of the Norther	1,000	N/A	90.00	200
1977	Robe Signal	850	N/A	60.00	375
1988	Saber Charge	2,250	N/A	225.00	225-250
1984	The Savage Taunt	1,000	N/A	225.00	275
1985	Scouting The Long Knives	1,400	N/A	195.00	270
1993	Shadows of Warriors (3 Print Suite)	1,000		225.00	225
1994	Show of Defiance	1,000		195.00	195
1993	Sighting the Intruders	1,000		225.00	225
1978	Single File	1,000	N/A	75.00	850
1976	Sioux Warriors	650	N/A	55.00	250
1975	Smoke Was Their Ally	1,000	N/A	75.00	225
1980	Snow Moon	1,000	N/A	115.00	225
1995	Splitting the Herd	550		465.00	465
1986	Spooked	1,400	N/A	195.00	195
1981	Surrounded	1,000	N/A	150.00	350-395
1975	The Survivor	1,000	N/A	65.00	275
1980	A Time Of Decision	1,150	N/A	125.00	225
1978	To Battle	1,000	N/A	75.00	350-400
1985	The Traders	1,000	N/A	195.00	195
1996	The Trek	850		175.00	175
1980	The Trooper	1,000	N/A	90.00	165
1988	Turning The Leaders	1,500	N/A	225.00	225
1983	Under Attack	5,676	N/A	125.00	375-500
1981	Under Hostile Fire	1,000	N/A	150.00	160
1975	Waiting for the Escort	1,000	N/A	75.00	100
1976	The Warrior	650	N/A	55.00	350
1982	The Warriors	1,000	N/A	150.00	150
1984	Watching the Wagons	1,400	N/A	175.00	750
1995	The Way of the Ancient Migrations	1,250		245.00	245
1987	When Omens Turn Bad	1,000	N/A	165.00	425-500
1992	When the Land Was Theirs	1,000		225.00	225
1992	Where Ancient Ones Had Hunted	1,000	N/A	245.00	245
1992	Where Others Had Passed	1,000	N/A	245.00	245
1986	Where Tracks Will Be Lost	550	N/A	350.00	350
1982	Whirling He Raced to Meet the Challenge	1,000	N/A	175.00	400-525
1991	The Wild Ones	1,000	N/A	225.00	225
1990	Winter Trail	1,500	N/A	235.00	235
1993	With Pistols Drawn	1,000		195.00	195

Mitchell - D. Mitchell

YEAR ISSUE		EDITION LIMIT	YEAR RETD.	ISSUE PRICE	*QUOTE U.S.$
1994	Bonding Years	550		175.00	175
1993	Country Church	550		175.00	175
1995	Innocence	1,000		150.00	150
1995	Let Us Pray	850		175.00	175
1993	Psalms 4:1	550	N/A	195.00	195
1996	Return For Honor	850		150.00	150
1992	Rowena	550	N/A	195.00	300

Mo Da-Feng - M. Da-Feng

YEAR ISSUE		EDITION LIMIT	YEAR RETD.	ISSUE PRICE	*QUOTE U.S.$
1990	Family Boat	888		235.00	235
1993	First Journey	650		150.00	150
1989	Fishing Hut	888		235.00	235
1994	Ocean Mist	850		150.00	150

Parker, Ed. - E. Parker

YEAR ISSUE		EDITION LIMIT	YEAR RETD.	ISSUE PRICE	*QUOTE U.S.$
1996	Acadia Tea and Tennis Society	850		135.00	135
1995	The Glorious 4th	850		150.00	150
1996	St. Duffer's Golf Club	850		135.00	135
1995	A Visit From St. Nicholas	850		125.00	125

Parker, Ron. - R. Parker

YEAR ISSUE		EDITION LIMIT	YEAR RETD.	ISSUE PRICE	*QUOTE U.S.$
1995	The Breakfast Club	850		125.00	125
1995	Coastal Morning	850		195.00	195
1995	Evening Solitude	850		195.00	195
1994	Forest Flight	850		195.00	195
1994	Grizzlies at the Falls	850		225.00	225
1994	Morning Flight	4,000		20.00	20
1996	Summer Memories	850		125.00	125
1996	Summer Reading	850		125.00	125
1995	Tea For Two	850		125.00	125

Phillips - W. Phillips

YEAR ISSUE		EDITION LIMIT	YEAR RETD.	ISSUE PRICE	*QUOTE U.S.$
1982	Advantage Eagle	1,000	N/A	135.00	300
1992	Alone No More	850		195.00	195
1988	America on the Move	1,500	N/A	185.00	185
1994	Among the Columns of Thor	1,000		295.00	295
1993	And Now the Trap	850		175.00	175
1986	Changing of the Guard	500		100.00	100
1993	Chasing the Daylight	850		185.00	185
1994	Christmas Leave When Dreams Come True	1,500	N/A	185.00	185
1996	Clipper at the Gate	850		185.00	185
1986	Confrontation at Beachy Head	1,000		150.00	150
1991	Dauntless Against a Rising Sun	850	N/A	195.00	195
1995	Dawn The World Forever Changed	1,000	1996	347.50	348
1995	The Dream Fulfilled	1,750		195.00	195
1991	Fifty Miles Out	1,000		175.00	175
1983	The Giant Begins to Stir	1,250	N/A	185.00	1100-1400
1990	Going in Hot w/Book	1,500		250.00	250
1985	Heading For Trouble	1,000	N/A	125.00	250
1984	Hellfire Corner	1,225	N/A	185.00	600
1984	Hellfire Corner, remarque	25	N/A	225.80	800
1990	Hunter Becomes the Hunted w/video	1,500		265.00	265
1992	I Could Never Be So Lucky Again	850	N/A	295.00	750
1993	If Only in My Dreams	1,000	N/A	175.00	750
1984	Into the Teeth of the Tiger	975	N/A	135.00	925
1984	Into the Teeth of the Tiger, remarque	25	N/A	167.50	2000
1994	Into the Throne Room of God w/book "The Glory of Flight"	750	N/A	195.00	600
1991	Intruder Outbound	1,000		225.00	225
1991	Last Chance	1,000	N/A	165.00	350
1985	Lest We Forget	1,250	N/A	195.00	250
1994	Lethal Encounter	1,000		225.00	225
1996	The Lightkeepers Gift	1,000		175.00	175
1988	The Long Green Line	3,500		185.00	185
1992	The Long Ride Home (P-51D)	850	N/A	195.00	195
1991	Low Pass For the Home Folks, BP	1,000	N/A	175.00	175
1996	The Moonwatchers	1,750		185.00	185
1986	Next Time Get 'Em All	1,500	N/A	225.00	275
1989	No Empty Bunks Tonight	1,500	N/A	165.00	165
1989	No Flying Today	1,500		185.00	185
1989	Over the Top	1,000		165.00	165
1985	The Phantoms and the Wizard	850	N/A	145.00	800
1992	Ploesti: Into the Fire and Fury	850		195.00	195
1987	Range Wars	1,000		160.00	160
1996	Return of the Red Gremlin	1,000		350.00	350
1987	Shore Birds at Point Lobos	1,250	N/A	175.00	175
1989	Sierra Hotel	1,250	N/A	175.00	175
1995	Summer of '45	1,750		195.00	195
1987	Sunward We Climb	1,000		175.00	175
1983	Those Clouds Won't Help You Now	625	N/A	135.00	500
1983	Those Clouds Won't Help You Now, remarque	25	N/A	275.00	675
1987	Those Last Critical Moments	1,250	N/A	185.00	300
1993	Threading the Eye of the Needle	1,000		195.00	195
1996	Thunder and Lightning	850		185.00	185
1986	Thunder in the Canyon	1,000	N/A	165.00	600
1990	A Time of Eagles	1,250	1996	245.00	245
1989	Time to Head Home	1,500		165.00	165
1986	Top Cover for the Straggler	1,000	N/A	145.00	325
1983	Two Down, One to Go	3,000	N/A	15.00	15
1982	Welcome Home Yank	1,000	N/A	135.00	800

*Quotes have been rounded up to nearest dollar

Collectors' Information Bureau

135

Greenwich Workshop
to Hadley House

GRAPHICS

YEAR ISSUE		EDITION LIMIT	YEAR RETD.	ISSUE PRICE	*QUOTE U.S.$
1993	When Prayers are Answered	850		245.00	245
1991	When You See Zeros, Fight Em'	1,500		245.00	245

Poskas - P. Poskas

1996	Yellow Moon Rising	850		175.00	175

Reynolds - J. Reynolds

1994	Arizona Cowboys	850	N/A	195.00	245
1994	Cold Country, Hot Coffee	1,000		185.00	185
1994	The Henry	850	N/A	195.00	195
1995	Mystic of the Plains	1,000		195.00	195
1994	Quiet Place	1,000	N/A	185.00	195
1994	Spring Showers	1,000		225.00	225
1996	A Strange Sign (canvas)	550		750.00	750
1996	The Summit	950		195.00	195

Simpkins - J. Simpkins

1994	All My Love	850		125.00	125
1993	Angels	850		225.00	225
1994	Gold Falls	1,750		195.00	195
1995	Mrs. Tenderhart	1,000		175.00	175
1995	Pavane in Gold	2,500		175.00	175
1996	Pavane von Khint	1,000		195.00	195
1994	Reverence For Life w/border & card	750	N/A	175.00	335
1994	Reverence For Life w/frame	100	N/A	600.00	600
1995	Where Love Resides (Premiere Ed.)	1,000		450.00	450
1995	Where Love Resides (Studio Ed.)	1,000		225.00	225

Smith - T. Smith

1992	The Challenger	1,300		185.00	185
1995	The Refuge	1,000		245.00	245

Terpning - H. Terpning

1992	Against the Coldmaker	1,000	1992	195.00	195
1993	The Apache Fire Makers	1,000	1993	235.00	235
1993	Army Regulations	1,000		235.00	235
1987	Blackfeet Among the Aspen	1,000	1987	225.00	250
1985	Blackfeet Spectators	475	1985	350.00	1095-1200
1988	Blood Man	1,250	1988	95.00	300
1982	CA Set Pony Soldiers/Warriors	1,000	1982	200.00	450-650
1985	The Cache	1,000		175.00	175
1992	Capture of the Horse Bundle	1,250		235.00	235
1982	Chief Joseph Rides to Surrender	1,000	1982	150.00	2600-3000
1996	Color of Sun	1,000		175.00	175
1986	Comanche Spoilers	1,000		195.00	195
1990	Cree Finery	1,000		225.00	225
1996	Crossing Below the Falls	1,000	1996	245.00	245
1983	Crossing Medicine Lodge Creek	1,000	1983	150.00	200-300
1994	Crow Camp, 1864	1,000	1994	235.00	235
1984	Crow Pipe Holder	1,000		150.00	150
1991	Digging in at Sappa Creek MW	650	1991	375.00	375
1994	The Feast	1,850	1994	245.00	285
1992	Four Sacred Drummers	1,000	1992	225.00	225
1988	Hope Springs Eternal-Ghost Dance	2,250		225.00	800-1000
1994	Isdzan-Apache Woman	1,000	1994	175.00	195
1991	The Last Buffalo	1,000		225.00	225
1991	Leader of Men	1,250	1991	235.00	300-500
1984	The Long Shot, signed	1,000	1984	55.00	75
1984	Medicine Man of the Cheyene	450	1984	350.00	2895-3195
1993	Medicine Pipe	1,000	1993	150.00	185
1985	One Man's Castle	1,000		150.00	150
1995	Opening the Sacred Bundle (canvas)	550	1995	850.00	1995-2295
1983	Paints	1,000	1983	140.00	200
1992	Passing Into Womanhood	650	1992	375.00	400
1987	The Ploy	1,000	1987	195.00	600-695
1992	Prairie Knights	1,000	1992	225.00	225
1996	Prairie Shade	1,000		225.00	225
1987	Preparing for the Sun Dance	1,000	1987	175.00	300-375
1988	Pride of the Cheyene	1,250		195.00	195
1993	Profile of Wisdom	1,000		175.00	175
1989	Scout's Report	1,250		225.00	225
1985	The Scouts of General Crook	1,000	1985	175.00	250-275
1988	Search For the Pass	1,000	1988	225.00	250
1982	Search For the Renegades	1,000	1982	150.00	195
1989	Shepherd of the Plains Cameo	1,250		125.00	125
1982	Shield of Her Husband	1,000	1982	150.00	600-900
1983	Shoshonis	1,250	1983	85.00	200-225
1985	The Signal	1,250	1985	90.00	400-600
1981	Sioux Flag Carrier	1,000	1981	125.00	165
1981	Small Comfort	1,000	1981	135.00	400-450
1993	Soldier Hat	1,000		235.00	235
1981	The Spectators	1,000	1981	135.00	195-295
1994	Spirit of the Rainmaker	1,500		235.00	235
1983	Staff Carrier	1,250	1983	90.00	550
1986	Status Symbols	1,000	1986	185.00	1250-1600
1981	Stones that Speak	1,000	1981	150.00	950-1200
1989	The Storyteller w/Video & Book	1,500	1989	950.00	1150
1992	The Strength of Eagles	1,250		235.00	235
1988	Sunday Best	1,250		195.00	195
1995	Talking Robe	1,250		235.00	235
1990	Telling of the Legends	1,250	1990	225.00	800-1200
1986	Thunderpipe and the Holy Man	550	1986	350.00	500-800
1995	Trading Post at Chadron Creek	1,000		225.00	225
1991	Transferring the Medicine Shield	850	1991	375.00	1300-1800
1996	The Trophy (canvas)	1,000		925.00	925
1981	The Victors	1,000	1981	150.00	650-825
1985	The Warning	1,650	1985	175.00	550-750
1986	Watching the Column	1,250	1986	90.00	400
1990	When Careless Spelled Disaster	1,000	1990	225.00	350

YEAR ISSUE		EDITION LIMIT	YEAR RETD.	ISSUE PRICE	*QUOTE U.S.$
1987	Winter Coat	1,250	1987	95.00	175
1996	With Mother Earth	1,250		245.00	245
1984	Woman of the Sioux	1,000	1984	165.00	925-1200

Townsend - B. Townsend

1994	Autumn Hillside	1,000		175.00	175
1993	Dusk	1,250		195.00	195
1995	Gathering of the Herd	1,000		195.00	195
1993	Hailstorm Creek	1,250		195.00	195
1994	Mountain Light	1,000		195.00	195
1992	Open Ridge	1,500	N/A	225.00	225
1993	Out of the Shadows	1,500		195.00	195
1996	Out of the Valley	850		185.00	185
1992	Riverbend	1,000	N/A	185.00	300

Weiss - J. Weiss

1995	All Is Well	1,250		165.00	165
1984	Basset Hound Puppies	1,000	N/A	65.00	200-300
1988	Black Labrador Head Study Cameo	1,000		90.00	90
1984	Cocker Spaniel Puppies	1,000	N/A	75.00	200-295
1992	Cuddle Time	850		95.00	95
1993	A Feeling of Warmth	1,000	N/A	165.00	475
1994	Forever Friends	1,000	1994	95.00	255
1983	Golden Retriever Puppies	1,000	N/A	65.00	900
1988	Goldens at the Shore	850	N/A	145.00	525-725
1995	I Didn't Do It	1,250		125.00	125
1982	Lab Puppies	1,000	N/A	65.00	195-250
1996	New Friends	1,000	1996	125.00	195
1992	No Swimming Lessons Today	1,000		140.00	140
1984	Old English Sheepdog Puppies	1,000	N/A	65.00	200-250
1993	Old Friends	1,000	1993	95.00	700-800
1986	One Morning in October	850	N/A	125.00	525-650
1985	Persian Kitten	1,000	N/A	65.00	80-95
1982	Rebel & Soda	1,000	N/A	45.00	135
1991	Wake Up Call	850		165.00	165
1988	Yellow Labrador Head Study Cameo	1,000		90.00	90

Williams - B.D. Williams

1993	Avant Garde S&N	500	N/A	60.00	60
1993	Avant Garde unsigned	2,603	N/A	30.00	30

Wootton - F. Wootton

1990	Adlertag, 15 August 1940 & Video	1,500	N/A	245.00	245
1993	April Morning:France, 1918	850		245.00	245
1983	The Battle of Britain	850	N/A	150.00	300
1988	Encounter with the Red Baron	850	N/A	165.00	200
1985	Huntsmen and Hounds	650		115.00	115
1982	Knights of the Sky	850	N/A	165.00	375
1993	Last Combat of the Red Baron	850		185.00	185
1992	The Last of the First F. Wooten	850		235.00	235
1994	Peenemunde	850		245.00	245
1986	The Spitfire Legend	850	N/A	195.00	195

Wysocki - C. Wysocki

1987	'Twas the Twilight Before Christmas	7,500	N/A	95.00	150
1988	The Americana Bowl	3,500		295.00	295
1983	Amish Neighbors	1,000	N/A	150.00	1150-1650
1989	Another Year At Sea	2,500	N/A	175.00	450-750
1983	Applebutter Makers	1,000	N/A	135.00	600
1987	Bach's Magnificat in D Minor	2,250	N/A	150.00	650-825
1991	Beauty And The Beast	2,000	N/A	125.00	125
1990	Belly Warmers	2,500		150.00	195-200
1984	Bird House Cameo	1,000	N/A	85.00	300
1985	Birds of a Feather	1,250	N/A	145.00	400
1989	Bostonians And Beans (PC)	6,711	N/A	225.00	650
1979	Butternut Farms	1,000	N/A	75.00	1000
1980	Caleb's Buggy Barn	1,000	N/A	80.00	435
1984	Cape Cod Cold Fish Party	1,000	N/A	150.00	150
1986	Carnival Capers	620		200.00	200
1981	Carver Coggins	1,000	N/A	145.00	900
1989	Christmas Greeting	11,000	N/A	125.00	100
1982	Christmas Print, 1982	2,000	N/A	80.00	500
1984	Chumbuddies, signed	1,000		55.00	55
1985	Clammers at Hodge's Horn	1,000	N/A	150.00	1250
1983	Commemorative Print, 1983	2,000	N/A	55.00	55
1983	Commemorative Print, 1984	2,000		55.00	55
1984	Commemorative Print, 1985	2,000		55.00	55
1985	Commemorative Print, 1986	2,000		55.00	55
1984	Cotton Country	1,000	N/A	150.00	300-350
1983	Country Race	1,000	N/A	150.00	235-395
1986	Daddy's Coming Home	1,250	N/A	150.00	1100-1200
1987	Dahalia Dinalhaven Makes a Dory Deal	2,250	N/A	150.00	300-475
1986	Dancing Pheasant Farms	1,750	N/A	165.00	475
1980	Derby Square	1,000	N/A	90.00	1100
1986	Devilbelly Bay	1,000	N/A	145.00	250
1986	Devilstone Harbor/An American Celebration (Print & Book)	3,500	N/A	195.00	400
1989	Dreamers	3,000	N/A	175.00	425
1992	Ethel the Gourmet	10,179	N/A	150.00	400-530
1979	Fairhaven by the Sea	1,000	N/A	75.00	600
1988	Feathered Critics	2,500		150.00	150
1979	Fox Run	1,000	N/A	75.00	1250-1500
1984	The Foxy Fox Outfoxes the Fox Hunters	1,500	N/A	150.00	425
1992	Frederick the Literate	6,500	N/A	150.00	1695-2195
1989	Fun Lovin' Silly Folks	3,000	N/A	185.00	250-300
1984	The Gang's All Here	Open		65.00	65
1984	The Gang's All Here, remarque	250		90.00	90
1992	Gay Head Light	2,500		165.00	165
1986	Hickory Haven Canal	1,500	N/A	165.00	900-1100

YEAR ISSUE		EDITION LIMIT	YEAR RETD.	ISSUE PRICE	*QUOTE U.S.$
1988	Home Is My Sailor	2,500	N/A	150.00	150
1985	I Love America	2,000		20.00	20
1990	Jingle Bell Teddy and Friends	5,000		125.00	125
1980	Jolly Hill Farms	1,000	N/A	75.00	600
1986	Lady Liberty's Independence Day Enterprising Immigrants	1,500	N/A	140.00	250
1992	Love Letter From Laramie	1,500		150.00	150
1989	The Memory Maker	2,500		165.00	135
1985	Merrymakers Serenade	1,250	N/A	135.00	135
1986	Mr. Swallobark	2,000	N/A	145.00	1200
1982	The Nantucket	1,000	N/A	145.00	275
1981	Olde America	1,500	N/A	125.00	500
1981	Page's Bake Shoppe	1,000	N/A	115.00	275
1983	Plum Island Sound, signed	1,000	N/A	55.00	55
1983	Plum Island Sound, unsigned	Open	N/A	40.00	40
1981	Prairie Wind Flowers	1,000	N/A	125.00	1375-1495
1992	Proud Little Angler	2,750	N/A	150.00	200
1994	Remington w/Book-Heartland	15,000		195.00	195
1990	Robin Hood	2,000		165.00	165
1991	Rockland Breakwater Light	2,500	N/A	165.00	165
1985	Salty Witch Bay	475	N/A	350.00	2400
1991	Sea Captain's Wife Abiding	1,500	N/A	150.00	150
1979	Shall We?	1,000	N/A	75.00	850-1000
1982	Sleepy Town West	1,500	N/A	150.00	550
1984	Storin' Up	450	N/A	325.00	725
1982	Sunset Hills, Texas Wildcatters	1,000	N/A	125.00	150
1984	Sweetheart Chessmate	1,000	N/A	95.00	1200
1983	Tea by the Sea	1,000	N/A	145.00	1000-1300
1993	The Three Sisters of Nauset, 1880	2,500	N/A	165.00	165
1984	A Warm Christmas Love	3,951	N/A	80.00	325
1990	Wednesday Night Checkers	2,500		175.00	175
1991	West Quoddy Head Light, Maine	2,500		165.00	165
1990	Where The Bouys Are	2,750	N/A	175.00	175
1991	Whistle Stop Christmas	5,000		125.00	125
1980	Yankee Wink Hollow	1,000	N/A	95.00	1150
1987	Yearning For My Captain	2,000	N/A	150.00	235-295
1987	You've Been So Long at Sea, Horatio	2,500	N/A	150.00	230

Hadley House

Capser - M. Capser

1993	Briar and Brambles	999		100.00	100
1992	Comes the Dawn	600		100.00	100
1994	Dashing Through the Snow	999		100.00	100
1994	Down the Lane	Open		30.00	30
1995	Enchanted Waters	999		100.00	100
1995	Grapevine Estates	999		100.00	100
1994	The Lifting Fog	Open		30.00	30
1995	Mariner's Point	999		100.00	100
1994	Nappin'	999		100.00	100
1994	A Night's Quiet	999		100.00	100
1995	On Gentle Wings	999		100.00	100
1993	Pickets & Vines	999	1994	100.00	100
1992	Reflections	600	1993	100.00	100
1993	Rock Creek Spring	999		80.00	80
1994	September Blush	999		100.00	100
1992	Silence Unbroken	600		100.00	195
1993	Skyline Serenade	600	1993	100.00	100
1995	Spring Creek Fever	999		100.00	100
1993	A Summer's Glow	999		60.00	60
1994	A Time For Us	999		125.00	125
1994	To Search Again	Open		30.00	30
1992	The Watch	600	1993	100.00	150
1994	The Way Home	Open		30.00	30
1993	Whispering Wings	1,500	1994	100.00	100

Franca - O. Franca

1988	The Apache	950	1990	70.00	175
1990	Blue Navajo	1,500	1991	125.00	210
1990	Blue Tranquility	999	1990	100.00	450
1988	Cacique	950	1990	70.00	150
1990	Cecy	1,500	1992	125.00	225
1990	Destiny	999	1990	100.00	100
1991	Early Morning	3,600		125.00	225
1993	Evening In Taos	4,000		80.00	80
1988	Feathered Hair Ties	600	1988	80.00	1595
1990	Feathered Hair Ties II	999	1990	100.00	200
1991	The Lovers	2,400	1991	125.00	900
1991	The Model	1,500	1991	125.00	495
1992	Navajo Daydream	3,600	1993	175.00	425
1989	Navajo Fantasy	999	1989	80.00	150
1992	Navajo Meditating	4,000		80.00	125
1992	Navajo Reflection	4,000	1992	80.00	225
1990	Navajo Summer	999	1988	100.00	175
1991	Olympia	1,500	1991	125.00	250
1989	Pink Navajo	999	1989	80.00	250
1988	The Red Shawl	600	1990	80.00	300
1991	Red Wolf	1,500	1991	125.00	125
1990	Santa Fe	1,500	1991	125.00	300
1988	Sitting Bull	950	1990	70.00	200
1988	Slow Bull	950	1990	70.00	200
1990	Turqoise Necklace	999	1990	100.00	200
1990	Wind Song	999	1990	100.00	195
1992	Wind Song II	4,000	1992	80.00	175-225
1989	Winter	999	1989	80.00	175
1989	Young Warrior	999	1989	80.00	350-450

Hanks - S. Hanks

1994	All Gone Awry	2,000		150.00	150
1994	All In a Row	2,000	1994	150.00	150

GRAPHICS

Hadley House to Imperial Graphics, Ltd.

YEAR ISSUE	TITLE	EDITION LIMIT	YEAR RETD.	ISSUE PRICE	*QUOTE U.S.$
1995	A Captive Audience	1,500		150.00	150
1995	Cat's Lair	1,500		150.00	150
1993	Catching The Sun	999	1993	150.00	495
1992	Conferring With the Sea	999	1993	125.00	495
1990	Contemplation	999		100.00	150
1995	Country Comfort	999		100.00	100
1995	Drip Castles	4,000		30.00	30
1991	Duet	999	1993	150.00	600
1990	Emotional Appeal	999		150.00	225
1993	Gathering Thoughts	1,500	1995	150.00	345
1992	An Innocent View	999	1992	150.00	300-350
1994	The Journey Is The Goal	1,500	1995	150.00	150
1995	Kali	Open		25.00	25
1993	Little Black Crow	1,500		150.00	150
1994	Michaela and Friends/Book	2,500		200.00	200
1993	The New Arrival	1,500		150.00	200
1995	Pacific Sanctuary	1,500		150.00	150
1993	Peeking Out	Open		40.00	40
1993	Places I Remember	1,500		150.00	150
1990	Quiet Rapport	999		150.00	300
1993	A Sense of Belonging	1,500		150.00	150
1995	Small Miracle	1,500		125.00	125
1992	Sometimes It's the Little Things	999		125.00	225
1994	Southwestern Bedroom	999		150.00	180-225
1992	Stepping Stones	999	1993	150.00	295
1991	Sunday Afternoon	Open		40.00	40
1992	Things Worth Keeping	999	1991	125.00	1495
1993	The Thinkers	1,500		150.00	150
1994	Water Lilies In Bloom	750		295.00	295
1993	When Her Blue Eyes Close	999		100.00	100
1994	Where The Light Shines Brightest	1,500		150.00	150
1991	A World For Our Children	999	1992	125.00	1595

Hulings - C. Hulings

YEAR	TITLE	EDITION LIMIT	YEAR RETD.	ISSUE PRICE	*QUOTE
1990	Ancient French Farmhouse	999		150.00	225
1989	Chechaquene-Morocco Market Square	999	1993	150.00	250
1992	Cuernavaca Flower Market	580		225.00	225
1988	Ile de la Cite-Paris	580	1990	150.00	225
1990	The Lonely Man	999	1993	150.00	150
1988	Ontenlente	580	1989	150.00	425
1991	Place des Ternes	580	1991	195.00	700
1989	Portuguese Vegetable Woman	999	1993	85.00	85
1994	The Red Raincoat	580		225.00	225
1990	Spanish Shawl	999	1994	125.00	125
1993	Spring Flowers	580		225.00	225
1992	Sunday Afternoon	580		195.00	275
1988	Three Cats on a Grapevine	580	1989	65.00	225
1993	Washday In Provence	580		225.00	225

Redlin - T. Redlin

YEAR	TITLE	EDITION LIMIT	YEAR RETD.	ISSUE PRICE	*QUOTE
1981	1981 MN Duck Stamp Print	7,800	1981	125.00	150
1982	1982 MN Trout Stamp Print	960	1982	125.00	600
1983	1983 ND Duck Stamp Print	3,438	1983	135.00	150
1984	1984 Quail Conservation	1,500	1984	135.00	135
1985	1985 MN Duck Stamp	4,385	1985	135.00	135
1985	Afternoon Glow	960	1985	150.00	895-1095
1979	Ageing Shoreline	960	1979	40.00	395
1981	All Clear	960	1981	150.00	395
1994	America, America	29,500		250.00	250
1994	And Crown Thy Good w/Brotherhood	29,500		250.00	250
1977	Apple River Mallards	Retrd.	1977	10.00	100
1981	April Snow	960	1981	100.00	595
1989	Aroma of Fall	6,800	1989	200.00	1600
1987	Autumn Afternoon	4,800	1987	100.00	795
1993	Autumn Evening	29,500		250.00	250
1980	Autumn Run	960	1980	60.00	375
1983	Autumn Shoreline	Retrd.	1983	50.00	325
1978	Back from the Fields	720	1978	40.00	250
1985	Back to the Sanctuary	960	1986	150.00	475
1978	Backwater Mallards	720	1978	40.00	945
1983	Backwoods Cabin	960	1983	150.00	965
1990	Best Friends (AP)	570	1993	1000.00	1895
1982	The Birch Line	960	1982	100.00	1295
1984	Bluebill Point (AP)	240	1984	300.00	785
1988	Boulder Ridge	4,800		150.00	150
1980	Breaking Away	960	1980	60.00	430
1985	Breaking Cover	960	1985	150.00	400
1981	Broken Covey	960	1981	100.00	525
1985	Brousing	960	1985	150.00	895
1994	Campfire Tales	29,500		250.00	250
1988	Catching the Scent	2,400		200.00	200
1986	Changing Seasons-Autumn	960	1986	150.00	425
1987	Changing Seasons-Spring	960	1987	200.00	475
1984	Changing Seasons-Summer	960	1984	150.00	1400
1986	Changing Seasons-Winter	960	1986	200.00	600
1985	Clear View	1,500	1985	300.00	1195
1980	Clearing the Rail	960	1980	60.00	650-850
1984	Closed for the Season	960	1984	150.00	495
1979	Colorful Trio	960	1979	40.00	800
1991	Comforts of Home	22,900	N/A	175.00	300-500
1986	Coming Home	2,400	1986	100.00	1800
1992	The Conservationists	29,500		175.00	175
1988	Country Neighbors	4,800	1988	150.00	600
1980	Country Road	960	1980	60.00	650-745
1987	Deer Crossing	2,400	1987	200.00	1195
1985	Delayed Departure	1,500	1985	150.00	500-1000
1980	Drifting	960	1980	60.00	400
1987	Evening Chores (print & book)	2,400	1988	400.00	775-1000
1985	Evening Company	960	1985	150.00	500
1983	Evening Glow	960	1983	150.00	2250
1987	Evening Harvest	960	1987	200.00	1350
1982	Evening Retreat (AP)	300	1982	400.00	3000
1990	Evening Solitude	9,500	1990	200.00	550-650
1983	Evening Surprise	960	1983	150.00	1000
1990	Evening With Friends	19,500	1991	225.00	1500
1990	Family Traditions	Retrd.	1993	80.00	100
1979	Fighting a Headwind	960	1979	30.00	350
1991	Flying Free	14,500		200.00	200
1993	For Amber Waves of Grain	29,500		250.00	250
1993	For Purple Mountains Majesty	29,500		250.00	250
1995	From Sea to Shining Sea	29,500		250.00	250
1994	God Shed His Grace on Thee	29,500		250.00	250
1987	Golden Retreat (AP)	500	1986	800.00	2000
1995	Harvest Moon Ball	9,500	1995	275.00	275
1986	Hazy Afternoon	2,560	1986	200.00	850
1990	Heading Home	Retrd.	1993	80.00	200
1983	Hidden Point	960	1983	150.00	600
1981	High Country	960	1981	100.00	600
1981	Hightailing	960	1981	75.00	350
1980	The Homestead	960	1980	60.00	640
1988	Homeward Bound	Retrd.	1993	70.00	150
1989	Homeward Bound	Retrd.	1994	80.00	250
1988	House Call	6,800	1990	175.00	1000
1991	Hunter's Haven (A/P)	1,000	N/A	175.00	1000
1989	Indian Summer	4,800	1989	200.00	600-725
1980	Intruders	960	1980	60.00	320
1982	The Landing	Retrd.	1982	30.00	80
1981	The Landmark	960	1981	100.00	400
1984	Leaving the Sanctuary	960	1984	150.00	475
1994	Lifetime Companions	29,500		250.00	250
1988	Lights of Home	9,500	1988	125.00	850
1979	The Loner	960	1979	40.00	300
1990	Master of the Valley	6,800		200.00	200
1988	The Master's Domain	2,400	1988	225.00	800
1988	Moonlight Retreat (A/P)	530	N/A	1000.00	1600
1979	Morning Chores	960	1979	40.00	1350
1984	Morning Glow	960	1984	150.00	1400
1981	Morning Retreat (AP)	240	N/A	400.00	3000
1989	Morning Rounds	6,800	1992	175.00	595
1991	Morning Solitude	12,107	1991	250.00	600
1984	Night Harvest	960	1984	150.00	1795
1985	Night Light	1,500	1985	300.00	1195
1986	Night Mapling	960	1986	200.00	550
1995	A Night on the Town	29,500		150.00	150
1980	Night Watch	2,400	1980	60.00	1000
1984	Nightlight (AP)	360	1984	600.00	2200
1982	October Evening	960	1982	100.00	1000
1989	Office Hours	6,800	1991	175.00	1000
1992	Oh Beautiful for Spacious Skies	29,500		250.00	250
1978	Old Loggers Trail	720	1978	40.00	950-1200
1983	On the Alert	960	1983	125.00	400
1977	Over the Blowdown	Retrd.	1977	20.00	400-600
1978	Over the Rushes	720	1978	40.00	450
1981	Passing Through	960	1981	100.00	225
1983	Peaceful Evening	960	1983	100.00	350
1991	Pleasures of Winter	24,500	1992	150.00	245
1986	Prairie Monuments	960	1986	200.00	795
1988	Prairie Morning	4,800	1988	150.00	500
1984	Prairie Skyline	960	1984	150.00	600
1983	Prairie Springs	960	1983	150.00	595
1987	Prepared for the Season	Retrd.	1994	70.00	100
1990	Pure Contentment	9,500	1989	150.00	400-500
1978	Quiet Afternoon	720	1978	40.00	695
1988	Quiet of the Evening	4,800	1988	150.00	700
1982	Reflections	960	1982	100.00	600
1985	Riverside Pond	960	1985	150.00	525
1984	Rural Route	960	1984	150.00	395
1983	Rushing Rapids	960	1983	125.00	750
1980	Rusty Refuge I	960	1980	60.00	295
1981	Rusty Refuge II	960	1980	100.00	495
1984	Rusty Refuge III	960	1984	150.00	595
1985	Rusty Refuge IV	960	1985	150.00	695
1980	Secluded Pond	960	1980	60.00	295
1982	Seed Hunters	960	1982	100.00	575
1985	Sharing Season I	Retrd.	1993	60.00	150
1986	Sharing Season II	Retrd.	1993	60.00	150
1981	Sharing the Bounty	960	1981	100.00	1500
1994	Sharing the Evening	29,500		175.00	175
1987	Sharing the Solitude	2,400	1987	125.00	900
1986	Silent Flight	960	1986	150.00	335
1980	Silent Sunset	960	1980	60.00	780
1984	Silent Wings Suite (set of 4)	960	1984	200.00	750
1981	Soft Shadows	960	1984	100.00	325
1989	Special Memories (AP)	570		1000.00	1000
1982	Spring Mapling	960	1982	100.00	975
1981	Spring Run-Off	1,700	1981	125.00	695
1980	Spring Thaw	960	1980	60.00	460
1980	Squall Line	960	1980	60.00	300
1978	Startled	720	1978	30.00	995
1986	Stormy Weather	1,500	1986	200.00	550
1992	Summertime	24,900		225.00	225
1984	Sundown	960	1984	300.00	575
1986	Sunlit Trail	960	1986	150.00	350
1984	Sunny Afternoon	960	1984	150.00	700
1987	That Special Time	2,400	1987	125.00	700-1000
1987	Together for the Season	Open		70.00	100
1995	Total Comfort	9,500	1995	275.00	275
1986	Twilight Glow	960	1986	200.00	700
1988	Wednesday Afternoon	6,800	1989	175.00	900
1990	Welcome to Paradise	14,500	1990	150.00	700
1985	Whistle Stop	960	1985	150.00	785
1979	Whitecaps	960	1979	40.00	445
1982	Whitewater	960	1982	100.00	400
1982	Winter Haven	500	1982	85.00	800
1977	Winter Snows	Retrd.	1977	20.00	595
1984	Winter Windbreak	960	1984	150.00	750
1992	Winter Wonderland	29,500	1993	150.00	275

Hamilton Collection

Mickey Mantle - R. Tanenbaum

YEAR	TITLE	EDITION LIMIT	YEAR RETD.	ISSUE PRICE	*QUOTE
1996	An All American Legend-The Mick	Open		95.00	95

Hawthorne Village

Rockwell's Main Street - Rockwell-Inspired

YEAR	TITLE	EDITION LIMIT	YEAR RETD.	ISSUE PRICE	*QUOTE
1993	Rockwell's Main Street	Open		69.95	70

Imperial Graphics, Ltd.

Chang - L. Chang

YEAR	TITLE	EDITION LIMIT	YEAR RETD.	ISSUE PRICE	*QUOTE
1988	Egrets with Lotus S/N	1,950		10.00	10
1988	Flamingos with Catail S/N	1,950		10.00	10

Irvine - G. Irvine

YEAR	TITLE	EDITION LIMIT	YEAR RETD.	ISSUE PRICE	*QUOTE
1995	Pansies	Open		8.00	8
1995	Violets	Open		8.00	8

Lee - H.C. Lee

YEAR	TITLE	EDITION LIMIT	YEAR RETD.	ISSUE PRICE	*QUOTE
1988	Blue Bird of Paradise S/N	950		35.00	35
1988	Cat & Callas S/N	1,950		30.00	30
1990	Double Red Hibiscus S/N	1,950		16.00	16
1988	Hummingbird I S/N	1,950		16.00	16
1988	Hummingbird II S/N	1,950		16.00	16
1990	Maroon & Mauve Peonies S/N	950		60.00	60
1990	Maroon & Peach Peonies S/N	950		60.00	60
1990	Maroon Peony S/N	2,950		20.00	20
1990	Peacock w/Tulip & Peony S/N	1,950		105.00	105
1990	Peonies & Butterflies S/N	2,950		40.00	40
1990	Pink Peony S/N	2,950		20.00	20
1990	Single Red Hibiscus S/N	1,950		16.00	16
1988	White Bird of Paradise S/N	950		35.00	35
1988	White Peacocks w/Peonies S/N	950		65.00	65

Liu - Celestial Symphony Series - L. Liu

YEAR	TITLE	EDITION LIMIT	YEAR RETD.	ISSUE PRICE	*QUOTE
1995	Flute Interlude S/N	5,500		40.00	40
1995	French Horn Melody S/N	5,500		40.00	40
1995	Piano Sonata S/N	5,500		40.00	40
1995	Violin Concerto S/N	5,500		40.00	40

Liu - L. Liu

YEAR	TITLE	EDITION LIMIT	YEAR RETD.	ISSUE PRICE	*QUOTE
1989	Abundance of Lilies (poster)	Closed	1993	30.00	30
XX	Afternoon Nap S/N	1,000		45.00	45
1994	Allen's Hummingbird w/Columbine S/N	3,300	1994	30.00	50
1987	Amaryllis S/N	1,950	N/A	16.00	60
1996	Angel with Harp S/N	5,500		40.00	40
1996	Angel with Trumpet S/N	5,500		40.00	40
1993	Anna's Hummingbird w/Fuchsia S/N	3,300	1993	30.00	30
1989	Autumn Melody S/N	1,950	1993	45.00	45
1990	Azalea Path S/N	2,500		85.00	85
1990	Azalea w/Dogwood S/N	2,500	N/A	55.00	55
1988	Baby Bluebirds S/N	1,950	N/A	16.00	30
1990	Baby Bluebirds w/Plum Tree S/N	2,500	N/A	18.00	18
1988	Baby Chickadees S/N	1,950	N/A	16.00	30
1990	Baby Chickadees w/Pine Tree S/N	2,500	N/A	18.00	18
XX	Basket of Begonias S/N	2,500		40.00	40
1993	Basket of Calla Lilies S/N	3,300	1994	50.00	50
1991	Basket of Grapes & Raspberries S/N	2,500	N/A	25.00	30
1993	Basket of Hydrangi S/N	3,300	1995	50.00	60
1989	Basket of Irises & Lilacs S/N	1,950	N/A	45.00	45
1993	Basket of Magnolias S/N	3,300	1993	50.00	50
1993	Basket of Orchids S/N	3,300		50.00	50
1992	Basket of Pansies & Lilacs S/N	2,950		50.00	50
XX	Basket of Pansies S/N	2,500		40.00	40
1991	Basket of Peonies S/N	2,500		40.00	40
1992	Basket of Roses & Hydrangeas S/N	2,950		50.00	50
1991	Basket of Roses S/N	2,500		40.00	40
1991	Basket of Strawberries & Grapes S/N	2,500		25.00	25
1991	Basket of Sweet Peas S/N	2,500		25.00	25
1989	Basket of Tulips & Lilacs S/N	1,950	N/A	45.00	45
1991	Basket of Wild Roses S/N	2,500	N/A	25.00	25
1991	Baskets of Primroses S/N	2,500		25.00	25
1986	Bearded Irises S/N	1,950	N/A	45.00	45
1994	Berries & Cherries S/N	3,500		30.00	30
1990	Bluebirds & Dandelion S/N	2,500	N/A	40.00	40
1986	Bluebirds w/Plum Blossoms S/N	1,950	N/A	35.00	35
1988	Bluebirds w/Rhododendrons S/N	1,950		40.00	40
1990	Bouquet of Peonies S/N	2,500	N/A	50.00	50
1990	Bouquet of Poppies S/N	2,500	N/A	50.00	50
1992	Bouquet of Roses S/N	2,950	1994	20.00	20
1992	Breath of Spring S/N	2,950		135.00	135
1993	Broad-Billed HB w/Petunias S/N	3,300		30.00	30
1995	Burgundy Irises w/Foxgloves S/N	5,500		60.00	60
1995	Butterfly Garden I S/N	5,500		50.00	50
1995	Butterfly Garden II S/N	5,500		50.00	50
1994	Butterfly Kisses S/N	3,500		50.00	50

*Quotes have been rounded up to nearest dollar

YEAR ISSUE		EDITION LIMIT	YEAR RETD.	ISSUE PRICE	*QUOTE U.S.$
1990	Butterfly w/Clematis S/N	2,500	1994	40.00	40
1990	Butterfly w/Wild Rose S/N	2,500	1993	40.00	50
1987	Calla Lily S/N	1,950		35.00	35
1994	Calliope Hummingbird w/Trumpet Vine S/N	3,300		30.00	30
1990	Cardinal & Queen Anne's Lace S/N	2,500	1994	40.00	40-90
XX	Cat & Hummer S/N	1,000		45.00	45
1989	Cherries & Summer Bouquet S/N	2,500	N/A	45.00	45
1993	Cherub Orchestra S/N	3,300	1994	80.00	90
1991	Cherubim w/Ivy S/N	2,500	1993	20.00	20
1988	Chickadees w/Cherry Blossoms S/N	1,950		40.00	40
1992	Conservatory S/N	2,950	1994	80.00	100
1987	Daylily S/N	1,950	N/A	35.00	35
1989	Daylily w/Hummingbird S/N	2,500	N/A	18.00	18
1987	Dogwood S/N	1,950	N/A	30.00	30
1986	The Dreamer S/N	950		65.00	65
1991	Dried-Floral Bouquet S/N	2,500		25.00	25
1991	The Drying Room S/N	2,500		75.00	75
1992	Early Spring S/N	2,950	1993	85.00	85
1988	Eastern Black Swallowtail w/Milkweed S/N	1,950		45.00	45
1991	Egret's w/Queen Anne's Lace S/N	2,500	1995	60.00	60
1992	Entryway S/N	2,950		40.00	40
1993	Fairy Ballet S/N	3,300		80.00	80
1986	Fall S/N	950		35.00	35
1994	Fancy Fiddle S/N	5,500	1994	80.00	80
1988	Feathered Harmony S/N	1,950	N/A	60.00	60
1991	Field of Irises S/N	2,500	1994	85.00	85
1989	First Landing S/N	1,950	N/A	16.00	25
1991	Floral Arch S/N	2,500	1996	25.00	25
1988	Floral Symphony S/N	1,950	N/A	95.00	95
1990	Forest Azalea S/N	2,500	N/A	55.00	55
1992	Forest Stream S/N	2,950	1995	85.00	85
1992	Fountain S/N	2,950		40.00	40
1986	Free Flight I -Rust Butterfly S/N	950		60.00	60
1986	Free Flight II -Pink Butterfly S/N	950		60.00	60
1989	Fritillaries w/ Violet S/N	2,500		18.00	18
1989	Fruit & Spring Basket S/N	1,500	N/A	45.00	45
1988	Garden Blossoms I S/N	1,950	N/A	35.00	35
1988	Garden Blossoms II S/N	1,950	N/A	35.00	35
1991	Garden Peonies S/N	2,500		60.00	60
1986	Garden Poppies S/N	2,000		45.00	45
1991	Garden Poppies S/N	2,500		60.00	60
1992	Garden Seat S/N	2,950		40.00	40
1991	The Gathering S/N	2,500	N/A	75.00	75
1996	Guardian Angel S/N	5,500		125.00	125
1988	Harmonious Flight S/N	1,950		50.00	50
1994	Heavenly Tulips S/N	3,300	1994	80.00	80
1987	Herons & Irises S/N	1,950		65.00	65
1987	Hibiscus & Hummer S/N	1,950	1995	45.00	45
1988	Hummingbird & Hollyhock S/N	1,950	N/A	40.00	40
1989	Hummingbird & Floral I S/N	2,500	1994	35.00	35
1989	Hummingbird & Floral II S/N	2,500	1994	35.00	35
1996	Hummingbird with Fuchsia S/N	5,500		50.00	50
1996	Hummingbird with Lilac S/N	5,500		50.00	50
1988	Hummingbirds & Iris S/N	1,950	N/A	40.00	40
1989	Hydrangea Bouquet S/N	2,500		30.00	30
1989	Innocents S/N	1,950		16.00	16
1993	Iris Garden II S/N	3,300	1994	105.00	105
1989	Iris Profusion (poster)	Closed	1995	30.00	30
1987	Iris S/N	1,950	N/A	16.00	16
1991	Irises in Bloom S/N	2,500	N/A	85.00	85
1992	Ivy & Fragrant Flowers S/N	3,300	1993	60.00	60
1992	Ivy & Honeysuckle S/N	3,300	1993	50.00	75
1992	Ivy & Sweetpea S/N	3,300	1994	50.00	75
1988	Kingfisher & Iris S/N	1,950		45.00	45
1986	Kingfisher S/N	950		35.00	35
1995	Lilac Breezes S/N	5,500		80.00	80
1986	Lily Pond S/N	950		35.00	35
1987	Lily S/N	1,950	N/A	16.00	16
1994	Love Notes S/N	5,500	1994	80.00	80
1995	Magnolia Path S/N	5,500		135.00	135
1987	Magnolia S/N	1,950	N/A	30.00	30
1995	Magnolias & Day Lilies S/N	5,500		80.00	80
1995	Magnolias & Hydrangeas S/N	5,500		80.00	80
1986	Mauve Veiltail S/N	950		35.00	35
1994	Mermaid Callas S/N	5,500		80.00	80
1996	Messengers of Love S/N	5,500		60.00	60
XX	Misty Valley S/N	1,950		45.00	45
1990	Mixed Irises I S/N	2,500	N/A	50.00	50
1990	Mixed Irises II S/N	2,500	N/A	50.00	50
1988	Moonlight Splendor S/N	1,950	N/A	60.00	60
1987	Morning Glories & Hummer S/N	1,950	N/A	45.00	45
1989	The Morning Room S/N	2,500	N/A	95.00	95
1987	Motherlove S/N	1,950	N/A	45.00	45
1987	Motif Orientale S/N	1,950	N/A	95.00	95
1994	Mystic Bouquet S/N	3,300		80.00	80
1995	Nature's Retreat S/N	5,500		145.00	145
1986	Nuthatch w/Dogwood S/N	1,950	N/A	35.00	35
1992	Old Stone House S/N	2,950	1996	50.00	50
1986	Opera Lady S/N	950	N/A	95.00	95
1989	Orange Tip & Blossoms S/N	2,500		18.00	18
1989	Oriental Screen S/N	2,500	N/A	95.00	95
1996	Oriental Splendor S/N	5,500		145.00	145
1988	Painted Lady w/Thistle S/N	1,950		45.00	45
1988	Pair of Finches S/N	1,950	N/A	35.00	35
1992	Palladian Windows S/N	2,950	1993	80.00	80
1990	Pansies & Ivy S/N	2,500	N/A	18.00	18
1992	Pansies & Lilies of the Valley S/N	2,950	1993	20.00	20
1992	Pansies & Sweet Peas S/N	2,950	1994	20.00	20
1991	Pansies in a Basket S/N	2,500	N/A	25.00	25
1993	Pansies w/Blue Stardrift S/N	2,950	1995	25.00	25

YEAR ISSUE		EDITION LIMIT	YEAR RETD.	ISSUE PRICE	*QUOTE U.S.$
1993	Pansies w/Daisies S/N	2,950		25.00	25
1991	Pansies w/Sweet Pea S/N	2,500	N/A	16.00	16
1991	Pansies w/Violets S/N	2,500	N/A	16.00	16
1987	Parenthood S/N	1,950	N/A	45.00	45
1992	Patio S/N	2,950		40.00	40
1993	Peach & Purple Irises S/N	3,300	1994	50.00	50
1993	Peach & Yellow Roses S/N	3,300		50.00	50
1986	Peach Veiltail S/N	950		35.00	35
1994	Peaches & Fruits S/N	3,500		30.00	30
1991	Peacock Duet-Serigraph S/N	325		550.00	550
1987	Peacock Fantasy S/N	950		65.00	65
1991	Peacock Solo-Serigraph S/N	325		550.00	550
1988	Peonies & Azaleas S/N	1,950	N/A	35.00	35
1988	Peonies & Forsythia S/N	1,950	N/A	35.00	35
1988	Peonies & Waterfall S/N	1,950	N/A	65.00	65
1993	Peonies S/N	3,300	1995	30.00	40
1990	Petunias & Ivy S/N	2,500		18.00	18
1989	Phlox w/Hummingbird S/N	2,500		18.00	18
1990	Potted Beauties S/N	2,500		105.00	105
1996	Potted Pansies S/N	5,500		40.00	40
1996	Potted Petunias S/N	5,500		40.00	40
1996	Protectors of Peace S/N	5,500		60.00	60
1995	Purple Irises w/Foxgloves S/N	5,500		60.00	60
1991	Putti w/Column S/N	2,500		20.00	20
1990	Quiet Moment S/N	2,500	N/A	105.00	175
1989	Romantic Abundance S/N	1,950	N/A	95.00	95
1989	Romantic Garden (poster)	Open		35.00	35
1994	Romantic Reflection S/N	5,950	1996	145.00	185
1993	Rose Bouquet w/Tassel S/N	3,300	1995	25.00	25
1994	Rose Fairies S/N	5,500	1996	80.00	80
1996	Rose Memories S/N	5,500		80.00	80
1989	Roses & Lilacs S/N	2,500		30.00	30
1992	Roses & Violets S/N	2,950	1993	20.00	20
1993	Roses in Bloom S/N	3,300	1995	105.00	105
1990	Royal Garden S/N	1,950		95.00	95
1990	Royal Retreat S/N	1,950	N/A	95.00	95
1995	Ruby Throated Hummingbird w/Hibiscus S/N	5,800		40.00	40
1993	Rufous Hummingbird w/Foxgloves S/N	3,300	1993	30.00	30
1988	Snapdragon S/N	1,950	N/A	16.00	16
1987	Solitude S/N	1,950	N/A	60.00	60
1993	Southern Magnolia S/N	3,300	1995	30.00	30
XX	Spring Blossoms I S/N	1,950		45.00	45
XX	Spring Blossoms II S/N	1,950		45.00	45
1989	Spring Bouquet (poster)	Open		30.00	30
1989	Spring Bouquet (poster-signed)	Open		45.00	45
1996	Spring Bulbs S/N	5,500		50.00	50
1994	Spring Conservatory S/N	3,300		105.00	105
1986	Spring Fairy S/N	950		35.00	35
1990	Spring Floral S/N	2,500	N/A	105.00	105
1995	Spring Garden S/N	5,500		125.00	125
1986	Spring S/N	950		35.00	35
XX	Spring Song S/N	1,950		60.00	60
1986	Spring Tulips S/N	1,950	N/A	45.00	45
1989	Spring Tulips S/N	2,500	N/A	45.00	45
XX	Stream w/Blossoms S/N	1,950		45.00	45
1992	Study for a Breath of Spring S/N	2,950		105.00	105
1996	Summer Bouquet S/N	5,500		50.00	50
1986	Summer Glads S/N	1,950	N/A	45.00	45
1988	Summer Lace w/Blue Chicory S/N	1,950	1991	45.00	45
1987	Summer Lace w/Chicadees S/N	950	N/A	65.00	65
1988	Summer Lace w/Chickadees II S/N	1,950	1991	65.00	65
1988	Summer Lace w/Daisies S/N	1,950	1991	45.00	45
1987	Summer Lace w/Dragon Fly S/N	950	N/A	45.00	45
1987	Summer Lace w/Lady Bug S/N	950	N/A	45.00	45
1989	Summer Rose S/N	2,500	N/A	45.00	45
1986	Summer S/N	950		35.00	35
1987	Swans & Callas S/N	1,950	1994	65.00	65
1991	Swans w/Daylilies S/N	2,500	1993	60.00	60
1989	Swans w/Dogwood S/N	1,950	N/A	65.00	65
1995	Sweet Bounty S/N	5,500		80.00	80
1994	Sweet Delight S/N	3,500		50.00	50
1988	Sweet Pea Floral S/N	1,950	N/A	16.00	16
1986	Three Little Deer S/N	950		35.00	35
1987	Togetherness S/N	1,950	N/A	60.00	60
1988	Trio of Sparrows S/N	1,950	N/A	35.00	35
1993	Tulip Bouquet w/Tassel S/N	3,300	1995	25.00	30
1987	Tulips S/N	1,950	N/A	16.00	16
1993	Two Burgundy Irises S/N	3,300	1994	50.00	50
1990	Two White Irises S/N	2,500	N/A	40.00	40
1992	Victorian Pavilion S/N	2,950		50.00	50
1992	Vintage Bouquet S/N	2,950	1994	135.00	135
1993	Violet Crowned HB w/Morning Glories S/N	3,300	1996	30.00	30
1989	Waterfall w/Dogwood S/N	1,950		45.00	45
1989	Waterfall w/White & Pink Dogwood S/N	1,950		45.00	45
1990	White & Blue Irises S/N	2,500	N/A	40.00	40
1993	White & Burgundy Roses S/N	3,300	1995	50.00	50
1995	White Eared Hummingbird w/Hydrangea S/N	5,800		40.00	40
1991	Wild Flowers w/Single Butterfly S/N	2,500		50.00	50
1991	Wild Flowers w/Two Butterflies S/N	2,500		50.00	50
1986	Winter S/N	950		35.00	35
1996	Wisteria Dreams S/N	5,500		80.00	80
1993	Woodland Path S/N	3,300	1994	135.00	135
1993	Woodland Steps S/N	3,300	1995	85.00	85
1993	Woodland View S/N	3,300	1995	85.00	85
1995	Wreath of Lilies S/N	5,500		55.00	55
1995	Wreath of Pansies S/N	5,500		55.00	55
1994	Wreath of Peonies S/N	3,500		55.00	55

YEAR ISSUE		EDITION LIMIT	YEAR RETD.	ISSUE PRICE	*QUOTE U.S.$
1994	Wreath of Roses S/N	3,500	1995	55.00	80

Liu - The Music Room - L. Liu

1991	The Music Room I S/N	2,500	1992	135.00	850-975
1992	The Music Room II-Nutcracker S/N	4,500	1993	200.00	350-450
1994	The Music Room III-Composer's Retreat S/N	5,500	1994	145.00	275-375
1995	The Music Room IV-Swan Melody S/N	6,500		150.00	150
1996	The Music Room V-Morning Serenade S/N	5,500		145.00	145
1996	Harmonic Duet S/N	5,500		55.00	55
1996	Musical Trio S/N	5,500		55.00	55
1996	Concerto with Guitar S/N	5,500		45.00	45
1996	Concerto with Violin S/N	5,500		45.00	45

Liu - Unframed Canvas Transfers - L. Liu

1996	Angel with Harp S/N	300		145.00	145
1996	Angel with Trumpet S/N	300		145.00	145
1993	Basket of Calla Lilies S/N	300	1995	195.00	195
1993	Basket of Magnolias S/N	300		195.00	195
1993	Cherub Orchestra S/N	300	1995	295.00	400-550
1992	Conservatory S/N	300	1995	295.00	295
1993	Fairy Ballet S/N	300		295.00	295
1994	Fancy Fiddle S/N	300		295.00	295
1996	Guardian Angel S/N	300		395.00	395
1996	Hummingbird with Fuchsia S/N	300		195.00	195
1996	Hummingbird with Lilac S/N	300		195.00	195
1993	Iris Garden II S/N	300	1995	395.00	395-475
1995	Lilac Breezes S/N	300		295.00	295
1994	Love Notes S/N	300		295.00	295
1995	Magnolia Path S/N	300	1996	395.00	395
1994	Mermaid Callas S/N	300		295.00	295
1995	Nature's Retreat S/N	300		395.00	395
1992	Old Stone House S/N	300		195.00	195
1996	Oriental Splendor S/N	300		395.00	395
1992	Palladian Windows S/N	300	1995	295.00	295-395
1996	Potted Pansies S/N	300		145.00	145
1996	Potted Petunias S/N	300		145.00	145
1994	Romantic Reflection S/N	500		395.00	395
1994	Rose Fairies S/N	300		295.00	295
1996	Rose Memories S/N	300		295.00	295
1993	Roses in Bloom S/N	300	1995	395.00	395
1996	Spring Bulbs S/N	300		195.00	195
1994	Spring Conservatory S/N	300		395.00	395
1995	Spring Garden S/N	300		395.00	395
1996	Summer Bouquet S/N	300		195.00	195
1995	Sweet Bounty S/N	300		295.00	295
1992	Victorian Pavillion S/N	300		195.00	195
1992	Vintage Bouquet S/N	300	1995	395.00	395
1996	Wisteria Dreams S/N	300		295.00	295
1993	Woodland Path S/N	300		495.00	495

Liu - Unframed Canvas Transfers Celestial Symphony Series - L. Liu

1995	Flute Interlude S/N	300		145.00	145
1995	French Horn Melody S/N	300		145.00	145
1995	Piano Sonata S/N	300		145.00	145
1995	Violin Concerto S/N	300		145.00	145

Liu - Unframed Canvas Transfers The Music Room Series - L. Liu

1991	The Music Room S/N	300	1992	395.00	700-900
1992	The Music Room II-Nutcracker S/N	300	1993	395.00	600
1994	The Music Room III-Composer's Retreat S/N	300	1994	395.00	500
1995	Music Room IV - Swan Melody S/N	300		425.00	425
1996	Music Room V - Morning Serenade S/N	300		395.00	395
1996	Harmonic Duet S/N	300		195.00	195
1996	Musical Trio S/N	300		195.00	195

McDonald - M. McDonald

1988	Amaryllis Dancer S/N	1,000		55.00	55
1988	Lily Queen S/N	1,000		55.00	55

Lightpost Publishing

Kinkade Member's Only Collectors' Society - T. Kinkade

1992	Skater's Pond	Closed	N/A	295.00	300-500
1992	Morning Lane	Closed	N/A	Gift	350-450
1994	Collector's Cottage I	Closed	1995	315.00	350-500
1994	Painter of Light Book	Closed	1995	Gift	50-80
1995	Lochavan Cottage	Closed	1995	295.00	300-450
1995	Gardens Beyond Autumn Gate -pencil sketch	Closed	1995	Gift	100
1996	Julianne's Cottage-Keepsake Box	Closed	1996	Gift	60
1996	Skater's Pond Sketch Portfolio Edition	Closed	1997	75.00	75
1996	Julianne's Cottage Library Print	Closed	1997	50.00	50
1996	Meadowood Cottage (canvas framed)	4,950	1997	375.00	375
1996	Meadowood Cottage (paper unframed)	950	1997	150.00	150
1997	Simpler Times are Better Times	12/97		Gift	45.00
1997	The Village Inn Library Print	3/98		65.00	65
1997	Collectors' Cottages Portfolio Edition	3/98		175.00	175
1997	Home is Where the Heart Is	3/98		295.00	295

Kinkade-Event Pieces - T. Kinkade

1996	Candlelight Cottage(canvas framed)	7/97		375.00	375

*Quotes have been rounded up to nearest dollar

Lightpost Publishing
to Lightpost Publishing

GRAPHICS

YEAR ISSUE		EDITION LIMIT	YEAR RETD.	ISSUE PRICE	*QUOTE U.S.$
96	Candlelight Cottage(canvas unframed)	7/97		275.00	275
1996	Candlelight Cottage (paper framed)	7/97		325.00	325
1996	Candlelight Cottage (paper unframed)	7/97		150.00	150
1996	Lamplight Village	7/97		Gift	80
1996	We Wish You a Merry Christmas	Closed	1997	70.00	70
1997	Chandler's Cottage Inspirational Print (Mother's Day Event)	Yr.Iss.		80.00	80

Kinkade-Archival Paper/Canvas-Combined Edition -Framed - T. Kinkade

YEAR ISSUE		EDITION LIMIT	YEAR RETD.	ISSUE PRICE	*QUOTE U.S.$
1989	Blue Cottage (Paper)	Retrd.	1993	125.00	200-400
1989	Blue Cottage (Canvas)	Retrd.	1993	495.00	795-995
1990	Moonlit Village (Paper)	Closed	1992	225.00	750-1200
1990	Moonlit Village (Canvas)	Closed	1992	595.00	2450-2800
1986	New York, 1932 (Paper)	Closed	N/A	225.00	750-1450
1986	New York, 1932 (Canvas)	Closed	N/A	595.00	2200-3200
1989	Skating in the Park (Paper) S/N	750	1994	225.00	1150-1500
1989	Skating in the Park (Canvas) S/N	750	1994	595.00	1250-1550

Kinkade-Canvas Editions-Framed - T. Kinkade

YEAR ISSUE		EDITION LIMIT	YEAR RETD.	ISSUE PRICE	*QUOTE U.S.$
1991	Afternoon Light, Dogwood A/P	98	1991	595.00	2050-2250
1991	Afternoon Light, Dogwood S/N	980	N/A	495.00	1600-2100
1992	Amber Afternoon A/P	200	1992	715.00	1350-1800
1992	Amber Afternoon S/N	980	N/A	615.00	1100-1400
1994	Autumn at Ashley's Cottage A/P	395		590.00	675
1994	Autumn at Ashley's Cottage S/N	3,950		440.00	525
1991	The Autumn Gate A/P	200	N/A	695.00	3495-3895
1991	The Autumn Gate R/P	Retrd.	1992	695.00	4000-4200
1991	The Autumn Gate S/N	980	N/A	595.00	2900-3500
1995	Autumn Lane A/P	295	1996	800.00	875
1995	Autumn Lane G/P	1,240		750.00	875
1995	Autumn Lane S/N	2,950		650.00	725
1994	Beacon of Hope A/P	275	1994	765.00	945-1345
1994	Beacon of Hope S/N	2,750	1994	615.00	795-1145
1996	Beginning of a Perfect Day A/P	295	1996	1025.00	1025-1300
1996	Beginning of a Perfect Day G/P	740		1240.00	1300
1996	Beginning of a Perfect Day S/N	2,950		1090.00	1150
1993	Beside Still Waters A/P	400	N/A	745.00	1595-1895
1993	Beside Still Waters G/P	490	N/A	745.00	1695-1995
1993	Beside Still Waters S/N	980	N/A	595.00	1595-1895
1995	Beside Still Waters S/P	Retrd.	N/A	2325.00	2450-2650
1993	Beyond Autumn Gate A/P	600	1993	915.00	3200-3800
1993	Beyond Autumn Gate G/P	500	N/A	915.00	2950-3850
1993	Beyond Autumn Gate S/N	1,750	N/A	815.00	2850-3650
1995	Beyond Autumn Gate S/P	Retrd.	N/A	N/A	4000-6000
1993	The Blessings of Autumn A/P	[illegible]	1994	715.00	995-1295
1993	The Blessings of Autumn G/P	250	1994	715.00	995-1395
1993	The Blessings of Autumn S/N	1,250	1994	615.00	795-1195
1994	The Blessings of Spring A/P	275	1994	665.00	800-895
1994	The Blessings of Spring G/P	685	1994	665.00	800-895
1994	The Blessings of Spring S/N	2,750	1994	515.00	575-695
1995	Blessings of Summer A/P	495		1015.00	1125
1995	Blessings of Summer G/P	1,240		965.00	1125
1995	Blessings of Summer S/N	4,950		865.00	975
1995	Blossom Bridge A/P	295	1996	730.00	775
1995	Blossom Bridge G/P	740		685.00	775
1995	Blossom Bridge S/N	2,950		580.00	625
1992	Blossom Hill Church A/P	200	1994	695.00	800-1200
1992	Blossom Hill Church R/P	Retrd.	1993	695.00	1100-1600
1992	Blossom Hill Church S/N	980	1994	595.00	795-1195
1991	Boston A/P	50	N/A	595.00	1400-2300
1991	Boston S/N	550	N/A	495.00	1100-2000
1992	Broadwater Bridge A/P	200	N/A	595.00	1675-2275
1992	Broadwater Bridge G/P	200	N/A	645.00	1675-2275
1992	Broadwater Bridge S/N	980	N/A	495.00	1500-2000
1995	Brookside Hideaway A/P	395	1995	695.00	695-895
1995	Brookside Hideaway G/P	990	1995	695.00	795-895
1995	Brookside Hideaway S/N	3,950	1996	545.00	600-775
1991	Carmel, Delores Street and the Tuck Box Tea Room A/P	200	1992	745.00	3100-3500
1991	Carmel, Delores Street and the Tuck Box Tea Room R/P	Retrd.	1992	745.00	3200-3600
1991	Carmel, Delores Street and the Tuck Box Tea Room S/N	980	1992	645.00	2900-3600
1989	Carmel, Ocean Avenue A/P	Closed	N/A	795.00	5700
1989	Carmel, Ocean Avenue S/N	Closed	N/A	645.00	3800-5200
1991	Cedar Nook Cottage R/P	200	1991	295.00	700-800
1991	Cedar Nook Cottage S/N	1,960	1991	195.00	445-495
1990	Chandler's Cottage S/N	550	N/A	495.00	2000-2800
1992	Christmas At the Ahwahnee A/P	200	1997	615.00	775
1992	Christmas At the Ahwahnee S/N	980	1997	495.00	625
1990	Christmas Cottage 1990 A/P	550	1990	295.00	1800-2300
1990	Christmas Cottage 1990 S/N	550	N/A	295.00	1350-2050
1991	Christmas Eve A/P	200	1991	495.00	1000-1600
1991	Christmas Eve R/P	Retrd.	1991	495.00	1700-1900
1991	Christmas Eve S/N	980	N/A	395.00	595-1195
1994	Christmas Memories A/P	345	1996	695.00	695-895
1994	Christmas Memories G/P	860		695.00	800-1000
1994	Christmas Memories S/N	3,450	1995	545.00	545-845
1994	Christmas Tree Cottage A/P	395		590.00	675
1994	Christmas Tree Cottage G/P	990		590.00	675
1994	Christmas Tree Cottage S/N	3,950	1996	440.00	525
1996	A Christmas Welcome A/P	295	1996	575.00	575
1996	A Christmas Welcome S/N	2,950		525.00	525
1996	Cobblestone Lane A/P	295	1996	1125.00	1125
1996	Cobblestone Lane S/N	2,950	1996	975.00	1050-1300
1992	Cottage-By-The-Sea A/P	200	1992	695.00	1700-2200
1992	Cottage-By-The-Sea G/P	200	N/A	745.00	1650-2300
1992	Cottage-By-The-Sea S/N	980	N/A	595.00	1400-2000
1992	Country Memories A/P	200	1992	495.00	850-1050
1992	Country Memories G/P	200		545.00	665
1992	Country Memories S/N	980	1994	395.00	695-795
1994	Creekside Trail A/P	198	1994	840.00	875
1994	Creekside Trail G/P	500		840.00	875
1994	Creekside Trail S/N	1,984	1997	690.00	725
1994	Days of Peace A/P	198	1996	840.00	875
1994	Days of Peace G/P	500		840.00	875
1994	Days of Peace S/N	1,984	1997	690.00	725-825
1995	Deer Creek Cottage A/P	295	1996	615.00	675
1995	Deer Creek Cottage G/P	740		565.00	675
1995	Deer Creek Cottage S/N	2,950		465.00	525
1994	Dusk in the Valley A/P	198	1996	840.00	875
1994	Dusk in the Valley G/P	500		840.00	875
1994	Dusk in the Valley S/N	1,984		690.00	725
1994	Emerald Isle Cottage A/P	275	1994	665.00	700-775
1994	Emerald Isle Cottage G/P	685		665.00	775
1994	Emerald Isle Cottage S/N	2,750		515.00	625
1993	End of a Perfect Day I A/P	400	1994	615.00	1600-2300
1993	End of a Perfect Day I G/P	300	N/A	665.00	1700-2300
1993	End of a Perfect Day I S/N	1,250	1994	515.00	1550-2050
1995	End of a Perfect Day I S/P	91	1996	2325	2200-3200
1994	End of a Perfect Day II A/P	275	1994	765.00	1400-2200
1994	End of a Perfect Day II G/P	685	1994	765.00	1395-2300
1994	End of a Perfect Day II S/N	2,750	1995	815.00	1195-2200
1995	End of a Perfect Day III A/P	495	1995	1145.00	1300-1500
1995	End of a Perfect Day III G/P	1,240		1145.00	1245
1995	End of a Perfect Day III S/N	4,950	1996	995.00	1055-1355
1989	Entrance to the Manor House A/P	Closed	1996	595.00	1895
1989	Entrance to the Manor House S/N	550	N/A	495.00	1695
1989	Evening at Merritt's Cottage A/P	Closed	N/A	595.00	2495-2895
1989	Evening at Merritt's Cottage S/N	550	N/A	495.00	2295-2495
1992	Evening at Swanbrooke Cottage Thomashire A/P	Closed	N/A	595.00	1995-2895
1992	Evening at Swanbrooke Cottage Thomashire G/P	Closed	N/A	645.00	1995-3000
1992	Evening at Swanbrooke Cottage Thomashire S/N	980	N/A	495.00	1895-2500
1992	Evening Carolers A/P	200		415.00	525
1992	Evening Carolers G/P	200		415.00	525
1992	Evening Carolers S/N	1,960		295.00	375
1995	Evening in the Forest A/P	495		695.00	775
1995	Evening in the Forest G/P	1,250		645.00	775
1995	Evening in the Forest S/N	4,950		545.00	625
1993	Fisherman's Wharf San Francisco A/P	275	1993	1065.00	1125-1495
1993	Fisherman's Wharf San Francisco G/P	550	N/A	1065.00	1200-1500
1993	Fisherman's Wharf San Francisco S/N	2,750	[illegible]	965.00	[illegible]
1991	Flags Over The Capitol A/P	200		695.00	875
1991	Flags Over The Capitol R/P	Retrd.	N/A	695.00	1000-1300
1991	Flags Over The Capitol S/N	980		595.00	725
1994	Garden Beyond Autumn Gate S/N	Closed	1996	1025.00	1075-1375
1993	The Garden of Promise A/P	300	N/A	715.00	1250-1950
1993	The Garden of Promise G/P	400	N/A	715.00	1900-2250
1993	The Garden of Promise S/N	1,250	1994	615.00	1250-1800
1995	The Garden of Promise S/P	Retrd.	N/A	2800	2400-4000
1992	The Garden Party A/P	200		595.00	775
1992	The Garden Party G/P	200		595.00	775
1992	The Garden Party S/N	980		495.00	625
1993	Glory of Evening A/P	400	1993	365.00	600-900
1993	Glory of Evening G/P	490	N/A	365.00	415
1993	Glory of Evening S/N	1,980	1994	315.00	500-800
1993	Glory of Morning A/P	400	1993	365.00	575-975
1993	Glory of Morning G/P	490	1993	365.00	575-975
1993	Glory of Morning S/N	1,980	1994	315.00	475-845
1993	Glory of Winter A/P	300	1996	715.00	875
1993	Glory of Winter G/P	250		715.00	875
1993	Glory of Winter S/N	1,250		615.00	725
1995	Golden Gate Bridge, San Francisco A/P	395	1996	1240.00	1300-1600
1995	Golden Gate Bridge, San Francisco G/P	990	N/A	1190.00	1300
1995	Golden Gate Bridge, San Francisco S/N	3,950	1996	1090.00	1000-1400
1994	Guardian Castle A/P	475	1996	1015.00	1125
1994	Guardian Castle G/P	1,190		1015.00	1125
1994	Guardian Castle S/N	4,750		865.00	975
1993	Heather's Hutch A/P	400	1993	515.00	550-795
1993	Heather's Hutch G/P	300	N/A	515.00	725-825
1993	Heather's Hutch S/N	1,250	N/A	415.00	595-795
1994	Hidden Arbor A/P	375		665.00	775
1994	Hidden Arbor G/P	685		665.00	775
1994	Hidden Arbor S/N	3,750		515.00	625
1990	Hidden Cottage I A/P	100	N/A	595.00	2000-3000
1990	Hidden Cottage I S/N	550	N/A	495.00	2000-2300
1993	Hidden Cottage II A/P	400	1993	615.00	675-1075
1993	Hidden Cottage II G/P	400	1995	665.00	825-1075
1993	Hidden Cottage II S/N	1,480	1994	515.00	600-895
1994	Hidden Gazebo A/P	240	1994	665.00	765-1100
1994	Hidden Gazebo G/P	600	1994	665.00	795-1095
1994	Hidden Gazebo S/N	2,400	1994	515.00	620-820
1996	Hollyhock House A/P	395		730.00	775
1996	Hollyhock House G/P	990		730.00	775
1996	Hollyhock House S/N	3,850		580.00	625
1991	Home For The Evening A/P	200	1994	295.00	595
1991	Home For The Evening S/N	980	N/A	195.00	495-695
1991	Home For The Holidays A/P	200	1991	695.00	2200-2800
1991	Home For The Holidays R/P	N/A	1991	695.00	3000
1991	Home For The Holidays S/N	980	N/A	595.00	1875-1995
1992	Home is Where the Heart Is A/P	200	N/A	695.00	1800-2200
1992	Home is Where the Heart Is G/P	200	N/A	695.00	1800-2295
1996	Home is Where the Heart Is II A/P	495		875.00	875
1996	Home is Where the Heart Is II S/N	6/97		725.00	725
1992	Home is Where the Heart Is S/N	980	N/A	595.00	1595-1895
1993	Homestead House A/P	300	1996	715.00	750-875
1993	Homestead House G/P	250	N/A	715.00	890
1993	Homestead House S/N	1,250	1996	615.00	725-800
1995	Hometown Chapel A/P	495		1045.00	1125
1995	Hometown Chapel G/P	1,240		995.00	1125
1995	Hometown Chapel S/N	4,950		895.00	975
1996	Hometown Evening A/P	295	1996	1125.00	1125
1996	Hometown Evening S/N	2,950	1996	975.00	975
1995	Hometown Memories I A/P	495	1995	1015.00	925-1325
1995	Hometown Memories I G/P	1,240	N/A	1015.00	1020
1995	Hometown Memories I S/N	4,950	1996	865.00	1075-1375
1996	Hyde Street and the Bay, SF A/P	395	1996	1125.00	1125
1996	Hyde Street and the Bay, SF S/N	3,950	1996	975.00	975
1992	Julianne's Cottage A/P	200	N/A	495.00	1520-1820
1992	Julianne's Cottage G/P	200	N/A	545.00	1450-2095
1992	Julianne's Cottage S/N	980	N/A	395.00	1375-1875
1996	Lamplight Bridge A/P	295	1996	730.00	825-920
1996	Lamplight Bridge G/P	740	N/A	730.00	775
1996	Lamplight Bridge S/N	2,950	1996	580.00	650-850
1993	Lamplight Brooke A/P	400	1994	715.00	1895-2295
1993	Lamplight Brooke G/P	330	1994	715.00	1895-2395
1993	Lamplight Brooke S/N	1,650	1994	615.00	1395-2095
1994	Lamplight Inn A/P	275	1994	765.00	850-995
1994	Lamplight Inn G/P	685	1994	765.00	875-995
1994	Lamplight Inn S/N	2,750	1994	615.00	650-850
1993	Lamplight Lane A/P	200	N/A	695.00	2750-3550
1993	Lamplight Lane G/P	200	1994	695.00	3200-3800
1993	Lamplight Lane S/N	980	N/A	615.00	2700-3500
1995	Lamplight Lane S/P	Retrd.	N/A	N/A	3000-3700
1995	Lamplight Village A/P	495	1995	800.00	1095-1200
1995	Lamplight Village G/P	1,240	N/A	800.00	1145
1995	Lamplight Village S/N	4,950	1995	650.00	900-1200
1995	A Light in the Storm A/P	395	1995	800.00	975
1995	A Light in the Storm G/P	1,240		750.00	750
1995	A Light in the Storm S/N	3,950	1996	650.00	725-825
1996	The Light of Peace A/P	345	1996	1300.00	1300
1996	The Light of Peace S/N	3,450	1996	1150.00	1150
1995	The Lights of Home S/N	2,500	N/A	195.00	195
1996	Lilac Gazebo A/P	295		615.00	675
1996	Lilac Gazebo G/P	740		615.00	675
1996	Lilac Gazebo S/N	2,950		465.00	525
1991	The Lit Path A/P	200	1991	395.00	445
1991	The Lit Path R/P	Retrd.	1991	395.00	495-700
1991	The Lit Path S/N	1,960	1994	195.00	345-495
1995	Main Street Celebration A/P	125	1995	800.00	875
1995	Main Street Celebration S/N	1,250		650.00	725
1995	Main Street Courthouse A/P	125	1995	800.00	875
1995	Main Street Courthouse S/N	1,250		650.00	725
1995	Main Street Matinee A/P	125	1995	800.00	875
1995	Main Street Matinee S/N	1,250		650.00	725
1995	Main Street Trolley A/P	125	1995	800.00	875
1995	Main Street Trolley S/N	1,250		650.00	725
1991	McKenna's Cottage A/P	100	N/A	595.00	795
1991	McKenna's Cottage R/P	200	N/A	615.00	700-1000
1991	McKenna's Cottage S/N	980	1995	495.00	550-695
1992	Miller's Cottage, Thomashire A/P	200	N/A	595.00	1000-1350
1992	Miller's Cottage, Thomashire G/P	200	N/A	595.00	1075-1450
1992	Miller's Cottage, Thomashire S/N	980	1994	495.00	1150-1295
1994	Moonlight Lane I A/P	240	1995	665.00	1150-1295
1994	Moonlight Lane I G/P	600		665.00	775
1994	Moonlight Lane I S/N	2,400		515.00	625
1985	Moonlight on the Riverfront	Retrd.	N/A	N/A	1050-1400
1992	Moonlit Sleigh Ride A/P	200	1995	395.00	500-650
1992	Moonlit Sleigh Ride S/N	1,960	1995	295.00	375-495
1995	Morning Dogwood A/P	495		645.00	725
1995	Morning Dogwood G/P	1,240		645.00	725
1995	Morning Dogwood S/N	4,950		495.00	575
1995	Morning Glory Cottage A/P	495		695.00	775
1995	Morning Glory Cottage G/P	1,240		645.00	775
1995	Morning Glory Cottage S/N	4,950		545.00	625
1990	Morning Light A/P	N/A	N/A	695.00	1500-2400
1992	Olde Porterfield Gift Shoppe A/P	200	1995	595.00	650-850
1992	Olde Porterfield Gift Shoppe G/P	200	N/A	595.00	945
1992	Olde Porterfield Gift Shoppe S/N	980	1994	495.00	550-750
1991	Olde Porterfield Tea Room A/P	200	N/A	595.00	1075-1675
1991	Olde Porterfield Tea Room R/P	Retrd.	1991	595.00	1500-2000
1991	Olde Porterfield Tea Room S/N	980	N/A	495.00	900-1500
1991	Open Gate, Sussex A/P	100	1994	295.00	495
1991	Open Gate, Sussex R/P	Retrd.	1992	295.00	595-795
1991	Open Gate, Sussex S/N	980	1994	195.00	390-425
1993	Paris, City of Lights A/P	600	1994	765.00	1365-1900
1993	Paris, City of Lights G/P	600	N/A	815.00	1195-2095
1993	Paris, City of Lights S/N	1,980	N/A	615.00	1250-1850
1994	Paris, Eiffel Tower A/P	275	1994	945.00	895-1495
1994	Paris, Eiffel Tower G/P	685	1995	945.00	1295-1595
1994	Paris, Eiffel Tower S/N	2,750	1994	795.00	750-1150
1995	Petals of Hope A/P	395		730.00	775
1995	Petals of Hope G/P	990		680.00	775
1995	Petals of Hope S/N	3,950		580.00	625
1996	Pine Cove Cottage A/P	495		875.00	875
1996	Pine Cove Cottage S/N	4,950		725.00	725
1994	The Power & The Majesty A/P	275		765.00	875
1994	The Power & The Majesty G/P	685		765.00	875
1994	The Power & The Majesty S/N	2,750	1996	615.00	725
1991	Pye Corner Cottage A/P	200	N/A	295.00	365-455
1991	Pye Corner Cottage R/P	Retrd.	N/A	295.00	395-595
1991	Pye Corner Cottage S/N	1,960	1996	195.00	300-425
1988	Room with a View	Retrd.	N/A	795.00	895-1200

*Quotes have been rounded up to nearest dollar   Collectors' Information Bureau   139

Lightpost Publishing
to Lightpost Publishing

GRAPHICS

YEAR ISSUE		EDITION LIMIT	YEAR RETD.	ISSUE PRICE	*QUOTE U.S. $
1990	Rose Arbor A/P	98	N/A	595.00	1900
1990	Rose Arbor S/N	935	N/A	495.00	900-1495
1996	Rose Gate A/P	295	1996	615.00	675
1996	Rose Gate G/P	740		615.00	675
1996	Rose Gate S/N	2,950		465.00	525
1994	San Francisco Market Street A/P	750	1994	945.00	995
1994	San Francisco Market Street G/P	1,875	N/A	945.00	945-1045
1994	San Francisco Market Street S/N	7,500		795.00	845
1992	San Francisco, Nob Hill (California St.) A/P	Closed	N/A	715.00	3800-5300
1992	San Francisco, Nob Hill (California St.) P/P	Closed	N/A	815.00	5500-6100
1992	San Francisco, Nob Hill (California St.) S/N	980	N/A	645.00	3400-5200
1989	San Francisco, Union Square A/P	Closed	N/A	795.00	4900-5500
1989	San Francisco, Union Square S/N	Closed	N/A	595.00	4400-5100
1992	Silent Night A/P	200	N/A	495.00	1100-1245
1992	Silent Night G/P	200	N/A	495.00	1095-1295
1992	Silent Night S/N	980	N/A	395.00	795-1095
1995	Simpler Times I A/P	345		840.00	875
1995	Simpler Times I G/P	870		790.00	875
1995	Simpler Times I S/N	3,450		690.00	725
1990	Spring At Stonegate A/P	50	N/A	395.00	600-800
1990	Spring At Stonegate S/N	550	1995	295.00	550-650
1996	Spring Gate A/P	395		1240.00	1300
1996	Spring Gate G/P	990		1240.00	1300
1996	Spring Gate S/N	3,950		1090.00	1150
1994	Spring in the Alps A/P	198		725.00	775
1994	Spring in the Alps G/P	500		725.00	775
1994	Spring in the Alps S/N	1,984	1996	575.00	625
1993	St. Nicholas Circle A/P	420	1995	715.00	850-950
1993	St. Nicholas Circle G/P	350	1995	715.00	850-1050
1993	St. Nicholas Circle S/N	1,750	1994	615.00	715-850
1995	Stepping Stone Cottage A/P	295	1996	840.00	875-920
1995	Stepping Stone Cottage G/P	740		840.00	875
1995	Stepping Stone Cottage S/N	2,950	1996	690.00	725-825
1993	Stonehearth Hutch A/P	300	N/A	515.00	745-845
1993	Stonehearth Hutch G/P	300	1994	515.00	745-895
1993	Stonehearth Hutch S/N	1,650	N/A	415.00	595-795
1993	Studio in the Garden A/P	400	1996	515.00	675
1993	Studio in the Garden G/P	600		515.00	675
1993	Studio in the Garden S/N	1,480	1996	415.00	525
1992	Sunday at Apple Hill A/P	200	1993	595.00	1200-1400
1992	Sunday at Apple Hill G/P	200	N/A	595.00	1250-1500
1992	Sunday at Apple Hill S/N	980	1993	495.00	1125-1195
1996	Sunday Evening Sleigh Ride A/P	295	1996	875.00	875
1996	Sunday Evening Sleigh Ride S/N	2,950	1997	725.00	725
1993	Sunday Outing A/P	200	N/A	595.00	1150-1595
1993	Sunday Outing G/P	200	N/A	595.00	1295-1750
1993	Sunday Outing S/N	980	N/A	495.00	1150-1350
1996	Sunset on Riverbend Farm A/P	495		840.00	875
1996	Sunset on Riverbend Farm G/P	1,240		840.00	875
1996	Sunset on Riverbend Farm S/N	4,950		690.00	725
1992	Sweetheart Cottage I A/P	200	1992	595.00	1295-1400
1992	Sweetheart Cottage I G/P	200	N/A	595.00	1150-1500
1992	Sweetheart Cottage I S/N	980	N/A	495.00	900-1200
1993	Sweetheart Cottage II A/P	400	1993	695.00	1575-1775
1993	Sweetheart Cottage II G/P	490	N/A	745.00	1475-1775
1993	Sweetheart Cottage II S/N	980	N/A	495.00	1475-1775
1994	Sweetheart Cottage III A/P	165	1994	765.00	875-1275
1994	Sweetheart Cottage III G/P	410	1994	765.00	875-1400
1994	Sweetheart Cottage III S/N	1,650	1994	615.00	675-925
1996	Teacup Cottage A/P	295		875.00	875
1996	Teacup Cottage S/N	2,950	1997	725.00	725-825
1996	Venice A/P	495		1240.00	1300
1996	Venice G/P	1,240		1240.00	1300
1996	Venice S/N	4,950		1090.00	1150
1992	Victorian Christmas I A/P	200	1992	695.00	1800-2700
1992	Victorian Christmas I G/P	200	1992	695.00	2600-3000
1992	Victorian Christmas I S/N	980	1992	595.00	1800-2500
1993	Victorian Christmas II A/P	400	1994	715.00	1400-2000
1993	Victorian Christmas II G/P	300	1994	715.00	1500-2100
1993	Victorian Christmas II S/N	980	1994	615.00	1350-1850
1994	Victorian Christmas III A/P	395	1994	800.00	850-875
1994	Victorian Christmas III G/P	990		800.00	875
1994	Victorian Christmas III S/N	3,950		650.00	725-825
1995	Victorian Christmas IV S/N	2,330	1995	650.00	725-895
1991	Victorian Evening	980	1993	495.00	995-1500
1992	Victorian Garden A/P	200	1993	895.00	2225-2695
1992	Victorian Garden G/P	200	1993	895.00	2150-2795
1992	Victorian Garden S/N	980	1993	795.00	2295-2495
1993	Village Inn A/P	400	1996	615.00	775-875
1993	Village Inn G/P	400	N/A	615.00	815-995
1993	Village Inn S/N	1,200	1994	515.00	575-775
1994	The Warmth of Home A/P	345		590.00	675
1994	The Warmth of Home G/P	860		590.00	675
1994	The Warmth of Home S/N	3,450		440.00	525
1992	Weathervane Hutch A/P	200	1995	395.00	425-575
1992	Weathervane Hutch G/P	200	N/A	395.00	615
1992	Weathervane Hutch S/N	1,960	1995	295.00	400-550
1996	Winsor Manor A/P	395		1070.00	1125
1996	Winsor Manor G/P	990		1120.00	1125
1996	Winsor Manor S/N	3,950		920.00	975
1993	Winter's End A/P	400		715.00	875
1993	Winter's End G/P	490		715.00	875
1993	Winter's End S/N	1,450		615.00	725
1991	Woodman's Thatch A/P	200	1995	295.00	495
1991	Woodman's Thatch R/P	200	N/A	295.00	695-795
1991	Woodman's Thatch S/N	1,960	1994	195.00	395-495
1992	Yosemite A/P	200		695.00	875
1992	Yosemite G/P	200		695.00	875
1992	Yosemite S/N	980	1997	595.00	725

Kinkade-Premium Paper-Unframed - T. Kinkade

YEAR ISSUE		EDITION LIMIT	YEAR RETD.	ISSUE PRICE	*QUOTE U.S.$
1991	Afternoon Light, Dogwood A/P	98	N/A	295.00	450-1000
1991	Afternoon Light, Dogwood S/N	980	N/A	185.00	375-775
1992	Amber Afternoon S/N	980	1997	225.00	250-350
1994	Autumn at Ashley's Cottage A/P	245		335.00	350
1994	Autumn at Ashley's Cottage S/N	2,450		185.00	200
1991	The Autumn Gate S/N	980	1994	225.00	750-1200
1995	Autumn Lane A/P	285		400.00	400
1995	Autumn Lane S/N	2,850		250.00	250
1994	Beacon of Hope A/P	275		400.00	400
1994	Beacon of Hope S/N	2,750		235.00	250
1996	Beginning of a Perfect Day A/P	285		475.00	475
1996	Beginning of a Perfect Day S/N	2,850		325.00	325
1993	Beside Still Waters S/N	1,280	1994	185.00	745-1025
1993	Beyond Autumn Gate S/N	1,750	1994	285.00	375-775
1985	Birth of a City S/N	Closed	N/A	150.00	250-950
1993	The Blessings of Autumn S/N	1,250		235.00	250
1994	The Blessings of Spring A/P	275		345.00	375
1994	The Blessings of Spring S/N	2,750		195.00	225
1995	Blessings of Summer A/P	485		450.00	450
1995	Blessings of Summer S/N	4,850		300.00	300
1995	Blossom Bridge A/P	285	1996	375.00	375
1995	Blossom Bridge S/N	2,850		205.00	225
1992	Blossom Hill Church S/N	980		225.00	250
1991	Boston S/N	550	1994	175.00	450-650
1992	Broadwater Bridge S/N	980	1994	225.00	350-425
1995	Brookside Hideaway A/P	385		355.00	375
1995	Brookside Hideaway S/N	3,850		205.00	225
1996	Candlelight Cottage S/N	7/97		150.00	150
1991	Carmel, Delores Street and the Tuck Box Tea Room S/N	980	1994	275.00	450-600
1989	Carmel, Ocean Avenue S/N	Closed	N/A	225.00	1350-2150
1990	Chandler's Cottage S/N	550	N/A	125.00	875-1175
1992	Christmas At the Ahwahnee S/N	980		175.00	225
1990	Christmas Cottage 1990 S/N	550	N/A	95.00	350-650
1991	Christmas Eve S/N	980		125.00	200
1994	Christmas Memories A/P	245		375.00	375
1994	Christmas Memories S/N	2,450		225.00	225
1994	Christmas Tree Cottage A/P	295		335.00	350
1994	Christmas Tree Cottage S/N	2,950		185.00	200
1996	A Christmas Welcome A/P	285		350.00	350
1996	A Christmas Welcome S/N	2,850		200.00	200
1996	Cobblestone Lane A/P	285		450.00	450
1996	Cobblestone Lane S/N	2,850		300.00	300
1992	Cottage-By-The-Sea S/N	980	N/A	250.00	395-595
1992	Country Memories S/N	980		185.00	200
1994	Creekside Trail A/P	198		400.00	400
1994	Creekside Trail S/N	1,984		275.00	250
1984	Dawson S/N	Closed	N/A	150.00	500-1000
1994	Days of Peace A/P	198		400.00	400
1994	Days of Peace S/N	1,984		250.00	250
1995	Deer Creek Cottage A/P	285		335.00	350
1995	Deer Creek Cottage S/N	2,850		185.00	200
1994	Dusk in the Valley A/P	198		400.00	400
1994	Dusk in the Valley S/N	1,984		250.00	250
1994	Emerald Isle Cottage A/P	275		345.00	375
1994	Emerald Isle Cottage S/N	2,750		195.00	225
1993	End of a Perfect Day I S/N	1,250	1994	195.00	450-950
1994	End of a Perfect Day II A/P	275		385.00	450
1994	End of a Perfect Day II S/N	2,750	1996	235.00	350-500
1995	End of a Perfect Day III A/P	485		475.00	475
1995	End of a Perfect Day III S/N	4,850		325.00	400
1989	Entrance to the Manor House S/N	550	N/A	125.00	650-950
1989	Evening at Merritt's Cottage S/N	550	N/A	125.00	750-1100
1992	Evening at Swanbrooke Cottage S/N	980	1994	250.00	500-1000
1992	Evening Carolers S/N	N/A		150.00	150
1995	Evening in the Forest A/P	485		355.00	375
1995	Evening in the Forest S/N	4,850		205.00	225
1985	Evening Service S/N	Closed	N/A	90.00	400-600
1993	Fisherman's Wharf, San Francisco S/N	2,750		305.00	350
1991	Flags Over The Capitol S/N	980		195.00	250
1993	The Garden of Promise S/N	1,250	1994	235.00	450-750
1992	The Garden Party S/N	980		175.00	225
1994	Gardens Beyond Autumn Gate S/N	Closed	1996	325.00	500-550
1993	Glory of Winter S/N	1,250	1996	235.00	250
1995	Golden Gate Bridge, San Francisco A/P	385		475.00	475
1995	Golden Gate Bridge, San Francisco S/N	3,850		325.00	350
1994	Guardian Castle A/P	275	1996	450.00	450
1994	Guardian Castle G/P	685		450.00	450
1994	Guardian Castle S/N	2,750		300.00	300
1993	Heather's Hutch S/N	1,250		175.00	200
1994	Hidden Arbor A/P	275	1996	375.00	375
1994	Hidden Arbor S/N	2,750	N/A	195.00	225-350
1993	Hidden Cottage II S/N	1,480		195.00	225
1990	Hidden Cottage S/N	550	N/A	125.00	1000-1250
1994	Hidden Gazebo A/P	240		345.00	375
1994	Hidden Gazebo, S/N	2,400		195.00	225
1996	Hollyhock House A/P	385		355.00	375
1996	Hollyhock House S/N	3,850		205.00	225
1991	Home For The Evening S/N	980	N/A	100.00	310-400
1991	Home For The Holidays S/N	980	1994	225.00	395-795
1996	Home is Where the Heart Is II A/P	485		400.00	400
1996	Home is Where the Heart Is II S/N	6/97		250.00	250
1992	Home is Where the Heart Is, S/N	980	1994	225.00	575-875
1993	Homestead House S/N	1,250		235.00	250
1996	Hometown Evening A/P	285		450.00	450
1996	Hometown Evening S/N	2,850		300.00	300
1995	Hometown Memories I A/P	485		450.00	450
1995	Hometown Memories I S/N	4,850		300.00	300
1996	Hyde Street and the Bay A/P	385		450.00	450
1996	Hyde Street and the Bay S/N	3,850		300.00	300
1992	Julianne's Cottage S/N	980	N/A	185.00	450-750
1996	Lamplight Bridge A/P	285		355.00	375
1996	Lamplight Bridge S/N	2,850		205.00	225
1993	Lamplight Brook S/N	1,650	1995	235.00	350-750
1994	Lamplight Inn A/P	275	1995	385.00	400
1994	Lamplight Inn S/N	2,750		235.00	250
1993	Lamplight Lane S/N	980	N/A	225.00	500-1000
1995	Lamplight Village A/P	485		400.00	400
1995	Lamplight Village S/N	4,850		250.00	250
1995	A Light in the Storm A/P	385		400.00	400
1995	A Light in the Storm S/N	3,850		250.00	250
1996	The Light of Peace A/P	335		475.00	475
1996	The Light of Peace S/N	3,350		325.00	325
1995	The Lights of Home A/P	250	1996	225.00	225
1996	Lilac Gazebo A/P	285		335.00	380
1996	Lilac Gazebo S/N	2,850		185.00	200
1995	Main Street Celebration A/P	195		400.00	400
1995	Main Street Celebration S/N	1,950		250.00	250
1995	Main Street Courthouse A/P	195		400.00	400
1995	Main Street Courthouse S/N	1,950		250.00	250
1995	Main Street Matinee A/P	195		400.00	400
1995	Main Street Matinee S/N	1,950		250.00	250
1995	Main Street Trolley A/P	195		400.00	400
1995	Main Street Trolley S/N	1,950		250.00	250
1991	McKenna's Cottage S/N	980		150.00	225
1996	Meadowood Cottage S/N	950		95.00	150
1992	Miller's Cottage S/N	980	1995	175.00	225-325
1994	Moonlight Lane I A/P	240		345.00	375
1994	Moonlight Lane I S/N	2,400		195.00	225
1985	Moonlight on the Riverfront S/N	750	N/A	150.00	185-225
1992	Moonlit Sleigh Ride S/N	N/A		150.00	150
1995	Morning Dogwood A/P	485		345.00	350
1995	Morning Dogwood S/N	4,850		195.00	200
1995	Morning Glory Cottage A/P	485		355.00	375
1995	Morning Glory Cottage S/N	4,850		205.00	225
1986	New York, 6th Avenue S/N	Closed	N/A	150.00	1450-2000
1992	Olde Porterfield Gift Shoppe S/N	980		175.00	225
1991	Olde Porterfield Tea Room S/N	980		150.00	225
1991	Open Gate, Sussex S/N	980		100.00	125
1993	Paris, City of Lights S/N	1,980		250.00	250
1994	Paris, Eiffel Tower A/P	275		400.00	400
1994	Paris, Eiffel Tower S/N	2,750		250.00	250
1995	Petals of Hope A/P	385		355.00	375
1995	Petals of Hope S/N	3,850		205.00	225
1996	Pine Cove Cottage A/P	485		400.00	400
1996	Pine Cove Cottage S/N	4,850		250.00	250
1984	Placerville, 1916 S/N	Closed	N/A	90.00	1000
1994	The Power & The Majesty A/P	275		385.00	400
1994	The Power & The Majesty S/N	2,750		235.00	250
1988	Room with a View S/N	Closed	N/A	150.00	350
1990	Rose Arbor S/N	935	1994	125.00	275-875
1996	Rose Gate A/P	285		335.00	350
1996	Rose Gate S/N	2,850		185.00	200
1994	San Francisco Market Street A/P	750		525.00	525
1994	San Francisco Market Street S/N	7,500		375.00	400
1986	San Francisco, 1909 S/N	Closed	N/A	150.00	950-1500
1992	San Francisco, Nob Hill (California St.) S/N	980	N/A	275.00	1000-2000
1989	San Francisco, Union Square S/N	Closed	N/A	225.00	1500-2200
1992	Silent Night S/N	980	1994	175.00	395
1995	Simpler Times I A/P	335		400.00	400
1995	Simpler Times I S/N	3,350		250.00	250
1990	Spring At Stonegate S/N	550	1996	200.00	250-300
1996	Spring Gate A/P	385		475.00	475
1996	Spring Gate S/N	3,850		325.00	325
1994	Spring in the Alps A/P	198	1996	375.00	375
1994	Spring in the Alps S/N	1,984		225.00	225
1993	St. Nicholas Circle S/N	1,750		235.00	250
1995	Stepping Stone Cottage A/P	285		400.00	400
1995	Stepping Stone Cottage S/N	2,850		250.00	250
1993	Stonehearth Hutch S/N	1,650	1995	175.00	200-250
1993	Studio in the Garden S/N	980	1995	175.00	200
1992	Sunday At Apple Hill, S/N	980	1994	175.00	350-400
1996	Sunday Evening Sleigh Ride A/P	285		400.00	400
1996	Sunday Evening Sleigh Ride S/N	2,850		250.00	250
1993	Sunday Outing S/N	980	1995	175.00	260-350
1996	Sunset at Riverbend Farm A/P	485		400.00	400
1996	Sunset at Riverbend Farm S/N	4,850		250	250
1992	Sweetheart Cottage I S/N	980	1995	150.00	250-395
1993	Sweetheart Cottage II S/N	980	1994	150.00	395-450
1993	Sweetheart Cottage III A/P	165	1995	385.00	395-450
1993	Sweetheart Cottage III S/N	1,650		235.00	250
1996	Teacup Cottage A/P	285		400.00	400
1996	Teacup Cottage S/N	2,850		250.00	250
1996	Venice A/P	485		475.00	475
1996	Venice S/N	4,850		325.00	325
1992	Victorian Christmas I S/N	980	N/A	235.00	400-900
1993	Victorian Christmas II S/N	1,650	1996	235.00	250
1994	Victorian Christmas III A/P	295		400.00	400
1994	Victorian Christmas III S/N	2,950		250.00	250
1995	Victorian Christmas IV S/N	750	1995	250.00	295
1991	Victorian Evening, S/N	Retrd.	1993	150.00	250-450
1992	Victorian Garden, S/N	980	1994	275.00	450-950
1993	Village Inn S/N	1,200	1996	195.00	225
1994	The Warmth of Home A/P	245		335.00	350
1994	The Warmth of Home S/N	2,450	1996	185.00	200
1996	Winsor Manor A/P	385		450.00	450
1996	Winsor Manor S/N	3,850		300.00	300

*Quotes have been rounded up to nearest dollar

YEAR ISSUE		EDITION LIMIT	YEAR RETD.	ISSUE PRICE	*QUOTE U.S.$
1993	Winter's End S/N	875		235.00	250
1992	Yosemite S/N	980	1996	225.00	250

Lightpost Publishing/ Recollections

American Heroes Collection-Framed - Recollections

YEAR ISSUE		EDITION LIMIT	YEAR RETD.	ISSUE PRICE	*QUOTE U.S.$
1992	Abraham Lincoln	7,500		150.00	150
1993	Babe Ruth	2,250	1996	95.00	95
1993	Ben Franklin	1,000		95.00	95
1994	Dwight D. Eisenhower	Open		30.00	30
1994	Eternal Love (Civil War)	1,861		195.00	195
1994	Franklin D. Roosevelt	Open		30.00	30
1992	George Washington	7,500		150.00	150
1994	George Washington	Open		30.00	30
1994	John F. Kennedy	Open		30.00	30
1992	John F. Kennedy	7,500		150.00	150
1992	Mark Twain	7,500		150.00	150
1994	A Nation Divided	1,000		150.00	150
1993	A Nation United	1,000		150.00	150

Cinema Classics Collection - Recollections

YEAR ISSUE		EDITION LIMIT	YEAR RETD.	ISSUE PRICE	*QUOTE U.S.$
1993	As God As My Witness Classic Clip	Closed	1995	40.00	40
1994	Attempted Deception Classic Clip	Open		30.00	30
1994	A Chance Meeting Classic Clip	Open		30.00	30
1993	A Dream Remembered Classic Clip	Closed	1995	40.00	40
1993	The Emerald City Classic Clip	Closed	1995	40.00	40
1993	Follow the Yellow Brick Road Classic Clip	Closed	1995	40.00	40
1993	Frankly My Dear Classic Clip	Closed	1995	40.00	40
1994	The Gift Classic Clip	Open		30.00	30
1993	Gone With the Wind-Movie Ticket Classic Clip	2,000		40.00	40
1994	If I Only Had a Brain Classic Clip	Open		30.00	30
1994	If I Only Had a Heart Classic Clip	Open		30.00	30
1994	If I Only Had the Nerve Classic Clip	Open		30.00	30
1993	The Kiss Classic Clip	Closed	1995	40.00	40
1993	Not A Marrying Man	12,500		150.00	150
1993	Over The Rainbow	7,500		150.00	150
1994	The Proposal Classic Clip	Open		30.00	30
1993	The Ruby Slippers Classic Clip	Closed	1995	40.00	40
1993	Scarlett & Her Beaux	12,500		150.00	150
1994	There's No Place Like Home Classic Clip	Open		30.00	30
1993	We're Off to See the Wizard Classic Clip	Closed	1995	40.00	40
1993	You Do Waltz Divinely	12,500		195.00	195
1993	You Need Kissing	12,500		195.00	195

The Elvis Collection - Recollections

YEAR ISSUE		EDITION LIMIT	YEAR RETD.	ISSUE PRICE	*QUOTE U.S.$
1994	Celebrity Soldier/Regular G.I.	Open		30.00	30
1994	Dreams Remembered/Dreams Realized	Open		30.00	30
1994	Elvis the King	2,750		195.00	195
1994	Elvis the Pelvis	2,750		195.00	195
1994	The King/The Servant	Open		30.00	30
1994	Lavish Spender/Generous Giver	Open		30.00	30
1994	Professional Artist/Practical Joker	Open		30.00	30
1994	Public Image/Private Man	Open		30.00	30
1994	Sex Symbol/Boy Next Door	Open		30.00	30
1994	To Elvis with Love	2,750		195.00	195
1994	Vulgar Showman/Serious Musician	Open		30.00	30

Gone With the Wind - Recollections

YEAR ISSUE		EDITION LIMIT	YEAR RETD.	ISSUE PRICE	*QUOTE U.S.$
1995	Final Parting Classic Clip	Open		30.00	30
1995	A Parting Kiss Classic Clip	Open		30.00	30
1995	The Red Dress Classic Clip	Open		30.00	30
1995	Sweet Revenge Classic Clip	Open		30.00	30

The Wizard of Oz - Recollections

YEAR ISSUE		EDITION LIMIT	YEAR RETD.	ISSUE PRICE	*QUOTE U.S.$
1995	Glinda the Good Witch	Open		30.00	30
1995	Toto	Open		30.00	30
1995	The Wicked Witch	Open		30.00	30
1995	The Wizard	Open		30.00	30

Marty Bell

Members Only Collectors Club - M. Bell

YEAR ISSUE		EDITION LIMIT	YEAR RETD.	ISSUE PRICE	*QUOTE U.S.$
1991	Little Thatch Twilight	Closed	1992	288.00	350
1991	Charter Rose, The	Closed	1992	Gift	N/A
1992	Candle At Eventide	Closed	1993	Gift	N/A
1992	Blossom Lane	Closed	1993	288.00	350
1993	Laverstoke Lodge	Closed	1994	328.00	328
1993	Chideock Gate	Closed	1994	Gift	N/A
1994	Hummingbird Hill	Closed	1995	320.00	450-495
1994	The Hummingbird	Closed	1995	Gift	N/A
1995	The Bluebird Victorian	Closed	1996	320.00	340
1995	The Bluebird	Closed	1996	Gift	N/A
1996	Goldfinch Garden	Yr.Iss.		220.00	220
1996	The Goldfinch	Yr.Iss.		Gift	N/A
1997	Wishing Well Garden	Yr.Iss.		180.00	180
1997	The Dove	Yr.Iss.		Gift	N/A

America the Beautiful - M. Bell

YEAR ISSUE		EDITION LIMIT	YEAR RETD.	ISSUE PRICE	*QUOTE U.S.$
1993	Jones Victorian	750	1994	400.00	1300
1995	The Tuck Box Tea Room, Carmel	500	1995	456.00	1295
1993	Turlock Spring	114	1995	700.00	850

Christmas - M. Bell

YEAR ISSUE		EDITION LIMIT	YEAR RETD.	ISSUE PRICE	*QUOTE U.S.$
1989	Fireside Christmas	500	1989	136.00	750
1990	Ready For Christmas	700	1990	148.00	495
1991	Christmas in Rochester	900	1991	148.00	275-350
1992	McCoy's Toy Shoppe	900	1992	148.00	350
1993	Christmas Treasures	900	1993	200.00	200
1995	Tuck Box Christmas	750	1995	250.00	250

England - M. Bell

YEAR ISSUE		EDITION LIMIT	YEAR RETD.	ISSUE PRICE	*QUOTE U.S.$
1987	Alderton Village	500	1988	235.00	650
1992	Antiques of Rye	1,100	1996	220.00	234
1990	Arbor Cottage	900	1990	130.00	150-250
1993	Arundel Row	282	1995	130.00	138
1991	Bay Tree Cottage, Rye	1,100	1992	230.00	230-520
1981	Bibury Cottage	500	1988	280.00	800-1000
1981	Big Daddy's Shoe	700	1989	64.00	150-300
1988	The Bishop's Roses	900	1989	220.00	695
1989	Blush of Spring	1,200	1990	96.00	120-160
1988	Bodiam Twilight	900	1991	520.00	900-1100
1988	Brendon Hills Lane	860	1995	304.00	318
1992	Briarwood	217	1993	220.00	220
1993	Broadway Cottage	122	1995	330.00	350
1987	Broughton Village	900	1988	128.00	400-500
1984	Brown Eyes	312	1993	296.00	400-450
1990	Bryants Puddle Thatch	900	1990	130.00	150-295
1986	Burford Village Store	500	1988	106.00	595
1981	Castle Combe Cottage	500	1988	230.00	895
1993	The Castle Tearoom	900	1993	88.00	200
1987	The Chaplains Garden	500	1987	235.00	1000-2000
1991	Childswickham Morning	305	1993	396.00	396
1987	Chippenham Farm	500	1988	120.00	300-900
1988	Clove Cottage	900	1988	128.00	500
1988	Clover Lane Cottage	1,800	1988	272.00	500
1991	Cobblestone Cottage	652	1995	374.00	404
1993	Coln St. Aldwyn's	1,000	1995	730.00	800-1000
1986	Cotswold Parish Church	500	1988	98.00	1500-2000
1988	Cotswold Twilight	900	1988	128.00	200-495
1991	Cozy Cottage	900	1991	130.00	130
1982	Crossroads Cottage	S/O	1987	38.00	200
1992	Devon Cottage	472	1995	374.00	404
1991	Devon Roses	1,200	1991	96.00	195-500
1991	Dorset Roses	1,200	1991	96.00	250
1987	Dove Cottage Garden	900	1990	260.00	304-495
1987	Driftstone Manor	500	1988	440.00	1500-1800
1987	Ducksbridge Cottage	500	1988	400.00	2000
1987	Eashing Cottage	900	1988	120.00	200-400
1992	East Sussex Roses (Archival)	1,200	1993	96.00	96
1985	Fiddleford Cottage	500	1986	78.00	1950
1988	Friday Street Lane	1,800	1992	280.00	600
1989	The Game Keeper's Cottage	900	1989	560.00	1800-2000
1992	Garlands Flower Shop	900	1992	220.00	350
1988	Ginger Cottage	1,800	1988	320.00	550-800
1989	Glory Cottage	911	1993	96.00	96
1989	Goater's Cottage	900	1991	368.00	400-560
1990	Gomshall Flower Shop	900	1990	396.00	1500-1800
1987	Halfway Cottage	900	1988	260.00	300-500
1992	Hollybush	1,200	1994	560.00	795
1991	Horsham Farmhouse	593	1995	180.00	200
1986	Housewives Choice	500	1987	98.00	750-1000
1988	Icomb Village Garden	900	1988	620.00	1300-1500
1988	Jasmine Thatch	900	1991	272.00	495
1989	Larkspur Cottage	900	1989	220.00	495
1985	Little Boxford	500	1987	78.00	300-900
1991	Little Timbers	900	1992	130.00	130
1987	Little Tulip Thatch	500	1988	120.00	400-700
1990	Little Well Thatch	950	1990	130.00	150-250
1990	Longparish Cottage	900	1991	368.00	650
1990	Longstock Lane	900	1990	130.00	295
1986	Lorna Doone Cottage	500	1987	380.00	3200-3500
1990	Lower Brockhampton Manor	900	1990	640.00	1800
1988	Lullabye Cottage	900	1988	220.00	300-400
1987	May Cottage	900	1988	120.00	200-699
1988	Meadow School	816	1993	220.00	350
1985	Meadowlark Cottage	500	1987	78.00	450-699
1987	Millpond, Stockbridge, The	500	1987	120.00	1100
1987	Morning Glory Cottage	500	1988	120.00	450-599
1988	Morning's Glow	1,800	1989	280.00	320-650
1994	Mother Hubbard's Garden	2-Yr.	1996	230.00	244
1988	Murrle Cottage	1,800	1988	320.00	450-650
1983	Nestlewood	500	1987	300.00	2500
1989	Northcote Lane	1,160	1993	88.00	88
1989	Old Beams Cottage	900	1990	368.00	650
1988	Old Bridge, Grasmere	453	1993	640.00	640
1990	Old Hertfordshire Thatch	900	1990	396.00	2000
1993	Old Mother Hubbard's Cottage	2-Yr.	1995	230.00	250
1989	Overbrook	827	1993	220.00	350
1992	Pangbourne on Thames	900	1994	304.00	675
1984	Penshurst Tea Rooms (Archival)	1,000	1988	335.00	950
1984	Penshurst Tea Rooms (Canvas)	500	1987	335.00	1500-3600
1989	Pride of Spring	1,200	1990	96.00	200-400
1988	Rodway Cottage	900	1989	694.00	700-1500
1989	The Rose Bedroom	515	1993	388.00	388
1990	Sanctuary	900	1992	220.00	450
1982	Sandhills Cottage	S/O	1987	38.00	38
1988	Sandy Lane Thatch	375	1993	380.00	500
1982	School Lane Cottage	S/O	1987	38.00	38
1993	Selborne Cottage	750	1995	300.00	318
1988	Shere Village Antiques	900	1988	272.00	304-699
1981	Spring in the Santa Ynez	500	1991	400.00	1100
1991	Springtime at Scotney	1,200	1992	730.00	950-1200
1989	St. Martin's Ashurst	243	1993	344.00	344
1990	Summer's Garden	900	1991	78.00	400-800
1985	Summers Glow	500	1987	98.00	600-1000
1987	Sunrise Thatch	900	1988	120.00	200-300
1985	Surrey Garden House	500	1986	98.00	850-1499
1985	Sweet Pine Cottage	500	1987	78.00	350-1499
1988	Sweet Twilight	900	1988	220.00	350-600
1990	Sweetheart Thatch	900	1993	220.00	375
1991	Tea Time	900	1991	130.00	300
1994	Tea With Miss Teddy	350	1995	128.00	128
1982	Thatchcolm Cottage	S/O	1987	38.00	38
1989	The Thimble Pub	641	1993	344.00	344
1993	Tithe Barn Cottage	308	1995	368.00	398
1991	Upper Chute	900	1991	496.00	1200
1987	The Vicar's Gate	500	1988	110.00	700-900
1987	Wakehurst Place	900	1988	480.00	1750
1987	Well Cottage, Sandy Lane	500	1988	440.00	650-1500
1991	Wepham Cottage	1,200	1991	396.00	1200
1984	West Kington Dell	500	1988	215.00	650
1992	West Sussex Roses (Archival)	1,200	1993	96.00	96
1990	Weston Manor	900	1995	694.00	742
1987	White Lilac Thatch	900	1988	260.00	400-700
1992	Wild Rose Cottage	155	1993	248.00	248
1985	Windsong Cottage	500	1987	156.00	350-799
1991	Windward Cottage, Rye	1,100	1991	228.00	895
1986	York Garden Shop	500	1988	98.00	250-999

Gardens of the Heart - M. Bell

YEAR ISSUE		EDITION LIMIT	YEAR RETD.	ISSUE PRICE	*QUOTE U.S.$
1995	Cloister Garden	250	1996	488.00	488

Mill Pond Press

Bateman - R. Bateman

YEAR ISSUE		EDITION LIMIT	YEAR RETD.	ISSUE PRICE	*QUOTE U.S.$
1982	Above the River-Trumpeter Swans	950	1984	200.00	750-850
1984	Across the Sky-Snow Geese	950	1985	220.00	695-800
1980	African Amber-Lioness Pair	950	1980	175.00	475
1979	Afternoon Glow-Snowy Owl	950	1979	125.00	300-525
1990	Air, The Forest and The Watch	42,558	N/A	325.00	325
1984	Along the Ridge-Grizzly Bears	950	1984	200.00	700-900
1984	American Goldfinch-Winter Dress	950	1984	75.00	165
1979	Among the Leaves-Cottontail Rabbit	950	1980	75.00	1000
1980	Antarctic Elements	950	1980	125.00	160
1991	Arctic Cliff-White Wolves	13,000	1991	325.00	325
1982	Arctic Evening-White Wolf	950	1982	185.00	1050
1980	Arctic Family-Polar Bears	950	1980	150.00	1000-1150
1992	Arctic Landscape-Polar Bear	5,000	N/A	345.00	195
1992	Arctic Landscape-Polar Bear-Premier Ed.	450		800.00	800
1982	Arctic Portrait-White Gyrfalcon	950	1982	175.00	325
1985	Arctic Tern Pair	950	1985	175.00	185
1981	Artist and His Dog	950	1980	150.00	550
1980	Asleep on Hemlock-Screech Owl	950	1980	125.00	575
1991	At the Cliff-Bobcat	12,500	1991	325.00	325
1992	At the Feeder-Cardinal	950	1992	125.00	200
1987	At the Nest-Secretary Birds	950	1987	290.00	290
1982	At the Roadside-Red-Tailed Hawk	950	1984	185.00	875
1980	Autumn Overture-Moose	950	1980	245.00	2000
1980	Awesome Land-American Elk	950	1980	245.00	2350
1989	Backlight-Mute Swan	950	1989	275.00	450
1983	Bald Eagle Portrait	950	1983	185.00	300-390
1982	Baobab Tree and Impala	950	1986	245.00	300
1980	Barn Owl in the Churchyard	950	1981	125.00	595-690
1989	Barn Swallow and Horse Collar	950	N/A	225.00	225
1982	Barn Swallows in August	950	N/A	245.00	350
1992	Beach Grass and Tree Frog	1,250		345.00	350
1985	Beaver Pond Reflections	950	1985	185.00	265
1984	Big Country, Pronghorn Antelope	950	1985	185.00	185
1986	Black Eagle	950	1986	200.00	200
1993	Black Jaguar-Premier Edition	450	N/A	850.00	1000
1986	Black-Tailed Deer in the Olympics	950	1986	245.00	245
1986	Blacksmith Plover	950	1986	185.00	185
1991	Bluebird and Blossoms	4,500		235.00	235
1991	Bluebird and Blossoms-Prestige Ed.	450		625.00	625
1980	Bluffing Bull-African Elephant	950	1981	135.00	1100
1981	Bright Day-Atlantic Puffins	950	1985	175.00	875
1989	Broad-Tailed Hummingbird Pair	950	1989	225.00	225
1980	Brown Pelican and Pilings	950	1980	165.00	1550
1979	Bull Moose	950	1979	125.00	650
1978	By the Tracks-Killdeer	950	1980	75.00	825-1025
1983	Call of the Wild-Bald Eagle	950	1983	200.00	200
1985	Canada Geese Family(stone lithograph)	260	1985	350.00	795-895
1985	Canada Geese Over the Escarpment	950	1985	135.00	225
1986	Canada Geese With Young	950	1986	195.00	200-265
1981	Canada Geese-Nesting	950	1981	295.00	1395-1595
1993	Cardinal and Sumac	2,510	N/A	235.00	235
1988	Cardinal and Wild Apples	12,183	1988	235.00	235
1989	Catching The Light-Barn Owl	2,000	1990	295.00	295
1988	Cattails, Fireweed and Yellowthroat	950	1988	235.00	275
1989	Centennial Farm	950	1989	295.00	295
1988	The Challenge-Bull Moose	10,671		325.00	325
1980	Chapel Doors	950	1985	135.00	700-850
1986	Charging Rhino	950	1986	325.00	475-575
1982	Cheetah Profile	950	1985	245.00	365
1978	Cheetah With Cubs	950	1980	95.00	365
1988	Cherrywood with Juncos	950	1988	245.00	245
1990	Chinstrap Penguin	810	1991	150.00	150
1992	Clan of the Raven	950	1992	235.00	345-425
1981	Clear Night-Wolves	950	1981	245.00	4400-4600
1988	Colonial Garden	950	1988	245.00	400-525
1987	Continuing Generations-Spotted Owls	950	1987	525.00	475-550
1991	Cottage Lane-Red Fox	950	1991	285.00	250

*Quotes have been rounded up to nearest dollar

Mill Pond Press
to Mill Pond Press

GRAPHICS

YEAR ISSUE		EDITION LIMIT	YEAR RETD.	ISSUE PRICE	*QUOTE U.S.$
1984	Cougar Portrait	950	1984	95.00	290
1979	Country Lane-Pheasants	950	1981	85.00	600
1981	Courting Pair-Whistling Swans	950	1981	245.00	275
1981	Courtship Display-Wild Turkey	950	1981	175.00	225
1980	Coyote in Winter Sage	950	1980	245.00	2250-2500
1992	Cries of Courtship-Red Crowned Cranes	950	1992	350.00	395-550
1980	Curious Glance-Red Fox	950	1980	135.00	800-995
1986	Dark Gyrfalcon	950	1986	225.00	300
1993	Day Lilies and Dragonflies	1,250		345.00	345
1982	Dipper By the Waterfall	950	1985	165.00	485-520
1989	Dispute Over Prey	950		325.00	325
1989	Distant Danger-Raccoon	1,600	1989	225.00	225
1984	Down for a Drink-Morning Dove	950	1985	135.00	260
1978	Downy Woodpecker on Goldenrod Gall	950	1979	50.00	925-1000
1988	Dozing Lynx	950	1988	335.00	1200-1300
1986	Driftwood Perch-Striped Swallows	950	1986	195.00	195
1983	Early Snowfall-Ruffed Grouse	950	1985	195.00	195
1983	Early Spring-Bluebird	950	1984	185.00	625-750
1981	Edge of the Ice-Ermine	950	1981	175.00	400
1982	Edge of the Woods-Whitetail Deer, w/Book	950	1983	745.00	925-1075
1991	Elephant Cow and Calf	950	1991	300.00	400
1986	Elephant Herd and Sandgrouse	950	1986	235.00	320
1991	Encounter in the Bush-African Lions	950	1991	295.00	345
1987	End of Season-Grizzly	950	1987	325.00	595
1991	Endangered Spaces-Grizzly	4,008	1991	325.00	325
1985	Entering the Water-Common Gulls	950	1986	195.00	195
1986	European Robin & Hydrangeas	950	1986	130.00	200-295
1989	Evening Call-Common Loon	950	1989	235.00	495
1980	Evening Grosbeak	950	1980	125.00	695
1983	Evening Idyll-Mute Swans	950	1984	245.00	675
1981	Evening Light-White Gyrfalcon	950	1981	245.00	775-975
1979	Evening Snowfall-American Elk	950	1980	150.00	800-950
1987	Everglades	950	1987	360.00	360
1980	Fallen Willow-Snowy Owl	950	1980	200.00	515-600
1987	Farm Lane and Blue Jays	950	1987	225.00	300-400
1986	Fence Post and Burdock	950	1987	130.00	275
1991	Fluid Power-Orca	290		2500.00	2500
1980	Flying High-Golden Eagle	950	1980	150.00	1000
1982	Fox at the Granary	950	1985	165.00	300
1982	Frosty Morning-Blue Jay	950	1982	185.00	800-900
1982	Gallinule Family	950		135.00	135
1981	Galloping Herd-Giraffes	950	1981	175.00	950-1200
1985	Gambel's Quail Pair	950	1985	95.00	325
1982	Gentoo Penguins and Whale Bones	950	1986	205.00	550-600
1983	Ghost of the North-Great Gray Owl	950	1983	200.00	1550-1700
1982	Golden Crowned Kinglet and Rhododendron	950	1982	150.00	1625-1800
1979	Golden Eagle	950	1981	150.00	250
1985	Golden Eagle Portrait	950	1987	115.00	175
1989	Goldfinch In the Meadow	1,600	1989	150.00	250
1983	Goshawk and Ruffed Grouse	950	1984	185.00	500
1988	Grassy Bank-Great Blue Heron	950	1988	285.00	225
1981	Gray Squirrel	950	1981	180.00	685
1979	Great Blue Heron	950	1980	125.00	700-800
1987	Great Blue Heron in Flight	950	1987	295.00	295-395
1988	Great Crested Grebe	950	1988	135.00	135
1987	Great Egret Preening	950	1987	315.00	600-725
1983	Great Horned Owl in the White Pine	950	1983	225.00	450
1987	Greater Kudu Bull	950	1987	145.00	145
1993	Grizzly and Cubs	2,250		335.00	400
1991	Gulls on Pilings	1,950		265.00	265
1988	Hardwood Forest-White-Tailed Buck	630	1988	300.00	1500-1600
1988	Harlequin Duck-Bull Kelp -Executive Ed.	623	1988	550.00	550
1988	Harlequin Duck-Bull Kelp-Gold Plated	950	1988	300.00	300
1980	Heron on the Rocks	950	1980	75.00	500-800
1981	High Camp at Dusk	950	1985	245.00	465
1979	High Country-Stone Sheep	950	1982	125.00	600
1987	High Kingdom-Snow Leopard	950	1987	325.00	550
1990	Homage to Ahmed	290		3300.00	3300
1984	Hooded Mergansers in Winter	950	1984	210.00	300-400
1984	House Finch and Yucca	950	1984	95.00	195
1986	House Sparrow	950	1986	125.00	225
1987	House Sparrows and Bittersweet	950	1987	220.00	300
1986	Hummingbird Pair Diptych	950	1986	330.00	550
1987	Hurricane Lake-Wood Ducks	950		135.00	200
1981	In for the Evening	950	1981	150.00	1750
1994	In His Prime-Mallard	950	N/A	195.00	250
1984	In the Brier Patch-Cottontail	950	1985	165.00	225-350
1986	In the Grass-Lioness	950	1986	245.00	245
1985	In the Highlands-Golden Eagle	950	1985	235.00	350
1985	In the Mountains-Osprey	950	1987	95.00	200
1992	Intrusion-Mountain Gorilla	2,250		325.00	325
1990	Ireland House	950	1990	265.00	265
1985	Irish Cottage and Wagtail	950	1990	175.00	200
1992	Junco in Winter	1,250	1992	185.00	215
1990	Keeper of the Land	290		3300.00	3300
1993	Kestrel and Grasshopper	1,250		335.00	335
1979	King of the Realm	950	1979	125.00	575
1987	King Penguins	950	1987	130.00	195
1981	Kingfisher and Aspen	950	1981	225.00	700-855
1980	Kingfisher in Winter	950	1981	175.00	825-1000
1980	Kittiwake Greeting	950	1980	75.00	365
1981	Last Look-Bighorn Sheep	950	1986	195.00	225
1987	Late Winter-Black Squirrel	950	1987	165.00	165
1981	Laughing Gull and Horseshoe Crab	950	1981	125.00	125
1982	Leopard Ambush	950	1986	245.00	275-395
1988	Leopard and Thomson Gazelle Kill	950	1988	275.00	275
1985	Leopard at Seronera	950	1985	175.00	290
1980	Leopard in a Sausage Tree	950	1980	150.00	1695-2195
1984	Lily Pads and Loon	950	1984	200.00	1250
1987	Lion and Wildebeest	950	1987	265.00	265
1980	Lion at Tsavo	950	1983	150.00	350
1978	Lion Cubs	950	1981	125.00	300
1987	Lioness at Serengeti	950	1987	325.00	325
1985	Lions in the Grass	950	1985	265.00	700-825
1981	Little Blue Heron	950	1981	95.00	225
1982	Lively Pair-Chickadees	950	1982	160.00	330-400
1983	Loon Family	950	1983	200.00	850
1990	Lunging Heron	1,250	1990	225.00	225
1978	Majesty on the Wing-Bald Eagle	950	1979	150.00	2195-2500
1988	Mallard Family at Sunset	950	1988	235.00	235
1986	Mallard Family-Misty Marsh	950	1986	130.00	130
1986	Mallard Pair-Early Winter	41,740	1986	135.00	200
1985	Mallard Pair-Early Winter 24K Gold	950	1986	1650.00	2000
1986	Mallard Pair-Early Winter Gold ptd.	7,691	1986	250.00	375
1989	Mangrove Morning-Roseate Spoonbills	2,000	1989	325.00	365
1991	Mangrove Shadow-Common Egret	1,250		285.00	285
1993	Marbled Murrelet	55	1993	1200.00	1200
1986	Marginal Meadow	950	1986	220.00	220
1979	Master of the Herd-African Buffalo	950	1980	150.00	1795-1895
1984	May Maple-Scarlet Tanager	950	1984	175.00	625
1982	Meadow's Edge-Mallard	950	1982	175.00	600
1982	Merganser Family in Hiding	950	1982	200.00	575
1994	Meru Dusk-Lesser Kudu	950		135.00	135
1989	Midnight-Black Wolf	25,352	1989	325.00	1195-1395
1980	Mischief on the Prowl-Raccoon	950	1980	85.00	150
1980	Misty Coast-Gulls	950	1980	135.00	420
1984	Misty Lake-Osprey	950	1985	95.00	150-225
1981	Misty Morning-Loons	950	1981	150.00	1100-1300
1986	Moose at Water's Edge	950	1986	130.00	285
1990	Morning Cove-Common Loon	950	1990	165.00	185
1985	Morning Dew-Roe Deer	950	1985	175.00	175
1983	Morning on the Flats-Bison	950	1983	200.00	300
1984	Morning on the River-Trumpeter Swans	950	1984	185.00	320
1990	Mossy Branches-Spotted Owl	4,500	1990	300.00	395-425
1990	Mowed Meadow	950	1990	190.00	190
1986	Mule Deer in Aspen	950	1986	175.00	175
1983	Mule Deer in Winter	950	1983	200.00	275
1988	Muskoka Lake-Common Loons	2,500	1988	265.00	300
1989	Near Glenburnie	950		265.00	265
1983	New Season-American Robin	950	1983	200.00	325
1986	Northern Reflections-Loon Family	8,631	1986	255.00	1300
1985	Old Whaling Base and Fur Seals	950	1985	195.00	300
1987	Old Willow and Mallards	950	1987	325.00	325
1980	On the Alert-Chipmunk	950	1980	60.00	350
1993	On the Brink-River Otters	1,250		345.00	345
1985	On the Garden Wall	950	1985	115.00	300
1985	Orca Procession	950	1985	245.00	2475
1981	Osprey Family	950	1981	245.00	245
1983	Osprey in the Rain	950	1983	110.00	500
1987	Otter Study	950	1987	235.00	275-365
1981	Pair of Skimmers	950	1981	150.00	195
1988	Panda's At Play (stone lithograph)	160	1988	400.00	1200
1994	Path of the Panther	1,950		295.00	295
1984	Peregrine and Ruddy Turnstones	950	1985	200.00	425-500
1985	Peregrine Falcon and White-Throated Swifts	950	1985	245.00	765-850
1987	Peregrine Falcon on the Cliff-Stone Litho	525	1988	350.00	350-780
1983	Pheasant in Cornfield	950	1983	200.00	325
1988	Pheasants at Dusk	950	1988	325.00	500-550
1982	Pileated Woodpecker on Beech Tree	950	1982	175.00	825-900
1990	Pintails in Spring	9,651	1989	135.00	300
1982	Pioneer Memories-Magpie Pair	950	1982	175.00	175
1987	Plowed Field-Snowy Owl	950	1987	145.00	165-280
1990	Polar Bear	290	1990	3300.00	3300
1982	Polar Bear Profile	950	1982	210.00	1700-1900
1982	Polar Bears at Bafin Island	950	1982	245.00	875
1990	Power Play-Rhinoceros	950	1990	320.00	320
1980	Prairie Evening-Short-Eared Owl	950	1983	150.00	325
1994	Predator Portfolio/Black Bear	950		475.00	475
1992	Predator Portfolio/Cougar	950		465.00	465
1993	Predator Portfolio/Grizzly	950		475.00	475
1993	Predator Portfolio/Polar Bear	950		485.00	485
1993	Predator Portfolio/Wolf	950	N/A	475.00	475
1988	Preening Pair-Canada Geese	950	1988	235.00	235
1987	Pride of Autumn-Canada Goose	15,294	1987	135.00	245
1986	Proud Swimmer-Snow Goose	950	1986	185.00	185
1989	Pumpkin Time	950		195.00	195
1982	Queen Anne's Lace and American Goldfinch	950	1982	150.00	700
1984	Ready for Flight-Peregrine Falcon	950	1984	185.00	470
1982	Ready for the Hunt-Snowy Owl	950	1982	245.00	650-770
1993	Reclining Snow Leopard	1,250		335.00	335
1988	Red Crossbills	950	1988	125.00	175
1984	Red Fox on the Prowl	950	1984	245.00	665
1982	Red Squirrel	950	1982	175.00	325
1986	Red Wolf	950	1986	250.00	275
1981	Red-Tailed Hawk by the Cliff	950	1981	245.00	380-425
1981	Red-Winged Blackbird & Rail Fence	950	1981	195.00	315
1984	Reeds	950	1984	185.00	415
1986	A Resting Place-Cape Buffalo	950	1986	265.00	265
1987	Rhino at Ngoro Ngoro	950	1988	325.00	325
1993	River Otter-North American Wilderness	350		325.00	800-925
1993	River Otters	290		1500.00	1500
1986	Robins at the Nest	950	1986	185.00	195
1987	Rocky Point-October	950	1987	195.00	420
1980	Rocky Wilderness-Cougar	950	1980	175.00	975
1990	Rolling Waves-Lesser Scaup	3,330		125.00	125
1993	Rose-breasted Grosbeak	290		450.00	450
1981	Rough-Legged Hawk in the Elm	950	1991	175.00	175
1981	Royal Family-Mute Swans	950	1981	245.00	715
1983	Ruby Throat and Columbine	950	1983	150.00	2000
1987	Ruddy Turnstones	950	1987	175.00	175
1994	Salt Spring Sheep	1,250		235.00	235
1981	Sarah E. with Gulls	950	1981	245.00	2100
1993	Saw Whet Owl and Wild Grapes	950		185.00	185
1991	The Scolding-Chickadees & Screech Owl	12,500		235.00	235
1991	Sea Otter Study	950	1991	150.00	245
1993	Shadow of the Rain Forest	9,000	1993	345.00	395-475
1981	Sheer Drop-Mountain Goats	950	1981	245.00	1900
1988	Shelter	950	1988	325.00	750-875
1992	Siberian Tiger	4,500		325.00	325
1984	Smallwood	950	1985	200.00	700-925
1990	Snow Leopard	290	1990	2500.00	2200-2600
1985	Snowy Hemlock-Barred Owl	950	1985	245.00	245
1994	Snowy Nap-Tiger	950	1994	185.00	475-600
1994	Snowy Owl	150	N/A	265.00	600-750
1987	Snowy Owl and Milkweed	950	1987	235.00	400-575
1983	Snowy Owl on Driftwood	950	1983	245.00	650
1983	Spirits of the Forest	950	1984	170.00	2000
1986	Split Rails-Snow Buntings	950	1986	220.00	220
1980	Spring Cardinal	950	1980	125.00	425
1982	Spring Marsh-Pintail Pair	950	1982	200.00	300
1980	Spring Thaw-Killdeer	950	1980	85.00	245
1982	Still Morning-Herring Gulls	950	1982	200.00	200
1987	Stone Sheep Ram	950	1987	175.00	175
1985	Stream Bank June	950	1986	160.00	175
1984	Stretching-Canada Goose	950	1984	225.00	2300
1985	Strutting-Ring-Necked Pheasant	950	1985	225.00	450
1985	Sudden Blizzard-Red-Tailed Hawk	950	1985	245.00	400
1990	Summer Morning Pasture	950	1990	175.00	175
1984	Summer Morning-Loon	950	1984	185.00	1000
1986	Summertime-Polar Bears	950	1986	225.00	225
1979	Surf and Sanderlings	950	1980	65.00	1300-1600
1981	Swift Fox	950	1981	175.00	175
1986	Swift Fox Study	950	1986	115.00	200
1987	Sylvan Stream-Mute Swans	950	1987	125.00	175
1984	Tadpole Time	950	1985	135.00	400-500
1988	Tawny Owl In Beech	950		325.00	325
1992	Tembo (African Elephant)	1,550		350.00	350
1984	Tiger at Dawn	950	1984	225.00	1700
1983	Tiger Portrait	950	1983	130.00	425
1988	Tree Swallow over Pond	950	1988	290.00	290
1991	Trumpeter Swan Family	290		2500.00	2500
1985	Trumpeter Swans and Aspen	950	1985	245.00	325-450
1979	Up in the Pine-Great Horned Owl	950	1981	150.00	675-795
1980	Vantage Point	950	1980	245.00	795
1993	Vigilance	9,500		330.00	330
1989	Vulture And Wildebeest	550		295.00	295
1981	Watchful Repose-Black Bear	950	1981	245.00	475
1985	Weathered Branch-Bald Eagle	950	1985	115.00	300
1991	Whistling Swan-Lake Erie	1,950		325.00	375
1980	White Encounter-Polar Bear	950	1980	245.00	2500-2950
1990	White on White-Snowshoe Hare	950	1990	195.00	425
1982	White World-Dall Sheep	950	1982	200.00	600
1985	White-Breasted Nuthatch on a Beech Tree	950	1985	175.00	300
1980	White-Footed Mouse in Wintergreen	950	1980	60.00	650
1982	White-Footed Mouse on Aspen	950	1983	90.00	150-225
1992	White-Tailed Deer Through the Birches	10,000		335.00	335
1984	White-Throated Sparrow and Pussy Willow	950	1984	150.00	575
1991	Wide Horizon-Tundra Swans	2,862		325.00	350
1991	Wide Horizon-Tundra Swans Companion	2,862		325.00	325
1986	Wildbeest	950		185.00	185
1982	Willet on the Shore	950	N/A	125.00	195
1979	Wily and Wary-Red Fox	950	1979	125.00	1075
1984	Window into Ontario	950	1984	265.00	1275
1983	Winter Barn	950	1984	170.00	420
1979	Winter Cardinal	950	1979	75.00	2250
1992	Winter Coat	1,250		245.00	575-675
1985	Winter Companion	950	1985	175.00	895
1980	Winter Elm-American Kestrel	950	1980	135.00	800
1986	Winter in the Mountains-Raven	950	1987	200.00	200
1981	Winter Mist-Great Horned Owl	950	1981	245.00	500-550
1980	Winter Song-Chickadees	950	1980	95.00	550
1984	Winter Sunset-Moose	950	1984	245.00	1600
1992	Winter Trackers	4,500	1992	335.00	335
1981	Winter Wren	950	1981	135.00	450
1983	Winter-Lady Cardinal	950	1983	200.00	1025
1979	Winter-Snowshoe Hare	950	1980	95.00	1100
1987	Wise One, The	950	1987	325.00	575
1979	Wolf Pack in Moonlight	950	1979	95.00	2150
1994	Wolf Pair in the Snow	290		795.00	795
1994	Wolverine Porfolio	950		275.00	275
1983	Wolves on the Trail	950	1983	225.00	425
1985	Wood Bison Portrait	950	1985	165.00	225
1983	Woodland Drummer-Ruffed Grouse	950	1984	185.00	235
1981	Wrangler's Campsite-Gray Jay	950	1981	195.00	725
1979	Yellow-Rumped Warbler	950	1980	50.00	435
1978	Young Barn Swallow	950	1979	75.00	575
1983	Young Elf Owl-Old Saguaro	950	1983	95.00	325
1991	Young Giraffe	290		850.00	850

*Quotes have been rounded up to nearest dollar

GRAPHICS

Mill Pond Press
to Mill Pond Press

YEAR ISSUE		EDITION LIMIT	YEAR RETD.	ISSUE PRICE	*QUOTE U.S.$
1989	Young Kittiwake	950		195.00	195
1988	Young Sandhill-Cranes	950	1988	325.00	325
1989	Young Snowy Owl	950	1990	195.00	195

Brenders - C. Brenders

YEAR ISSUE		EDITION LIMIT	YEAR RETD.	ISSUE PRICE	*QUOTE U.S.$
1986	The Acrobat's Meal-Red Squirrel	950	1989	65.00	475
1988	Apple Harvest	950	1989	115.00	525
1989	The Apple Lover	1,500	1990	125.00	250-275
1987	Autumn Lady	950	1989	150.00	825
1991	The Balance of Nature	1,950		225.00	225
1993	Black Sphinx	950		235.00	235
1986	Black-Capped Chickadees	950	1989	40.00	400-625
1990	Blond Beauty	1,950	1990	185.00	185
1986	Bluebirds	950	1989	40.00	150-250
1988	California Quail	950	1989	95.00	225-350
1991	Calm Before the Challenge-Moose	1,950	1991	225.00	225
1987	Close to Mom	950	1988	150.00	1095
1993	Collectors Group (Butterfly Collections)	290		375.00	375
1986	Colorful Playground-Cottontails	950	1989	75.00	625
1989	The Companions	18,036	1989	200.00	525
1994	Dall Sheep Portrait	950		115.00	115
1992	Den Mother-Pencil Sketch	2,500	1992	135.00	135
1992	Den Mother-Wolf Family	25,000	1992	250.00	250
1986	Disturbed Daydreams	950	1989	95.00	425
1987	Double Trouble-Raccoons	950	1988	120.00	650-700
1993	European Group (Butterfly Collections)	290		375.00	375
1993	Exotic Group (Butterfly Collections)	290		375.00	375
1989	Forager's Reward-Red Squirrel	1,250	1989	135.00	135
1988	Forest Sentinel-Bobcat	950	1988	135.00	425-550
1990	Full House-Fox Family	20,106	1990	235.00	500
1990	Ghostly Quiet-Spanish Lynx	1,950	1990	200.00	200
1986	Golden Season-Gray Squirrel	950	1987	85.00	600-700
1986	Harvest Time-Chipmunk	950	1989	65.00	175-300
1988	Hidden In the Pines-Immature Great Hor	950	1988	175.00	1000-1125
1988	High Adventure-Black Bear Cubs	950	1989	105.00	415
1988	A Hunter's Dream	950	1988	165.00	1000
1993	In Northern Hunting Grounds	1,750		375.00	375
1992	Island Shores-Snowy Egret	2,500		250.00	250
1987	Ivory-Billed Woodpecker	950	1989	95.00	775
1988	Long Distance Hunters	950	1988	175.00	895-1095
1989	Lord of the Marshes	1,250	1989	135.00	175
1986	Meadowlark	950	1989	40.00	170-285
1989	Merlins at the Nest	1,250	1989	165.00	235-300
1985	Mighty Intruder	950	1989	95.00	265
1987	Migration Fever-Barn Swallows	950	1989	150.00	325-465
1990	The Monarch is Alive	4,071	1990	265.00	[illegible]
1993	Mother of Pearls	5,000		275.00	275
1990	Mountain Baby-Bighorn Sheep	1,950		165.00	165
1987	Mysterious Visitor-Barn Owl	950	1989	150.00	325
1993	Narrow Escape-Chipmunk	1,750		150.00	150
1991	The Nesting Season-House Sparrow	1,950	1991	195.00	200
1989	Northern Cousins-Black Squirrels	950	1989	150.00	290
1984	On the Alert-Red Fox	950	1986	95.00	250-350
1990	On the Old Farm Door	1,500	1990	225.00	225
1991	One to One-Gray Wolf	10,000	1991	245.00	425
1992	Pathfinder-Red Fox	5,000	1992	245.00	245
1984	Playful Pair-Chipmunks	950	1987	60.00	300-460
1994	Power and Grace	2,500	1994	265.00	485-625
1989	The Predator's Walk	1,250	1989	150.00	175
1992	Red Fox Study	1,250	1992	125.00	125
1994	Riverbank Kestrel	2,500		225.00	300-415
1988	Roaming the Plains-Pronghorns	950	1989	150.00	195
1986	Robins	950	1989	40.00	175
1993	Rocky Camp-Cougar Family	5,000		275.00	275
1993	Rocky Camp-Cubs	950		225.00	225
1992	Rocky Kingdom-Bighorn Sheep	1,750		255.00	255
1991	Shadows in the Grass-Young Cougars	1,950	1991	235.00	235
1990	Shoreline Quartet-White Ibis	1,950		265.00	265
1984	Silent Hunter-Great Horned Owl	950	1987	95.00	450
1984	Silent Passage	950	1988	150.00	475
1990	Small Talk	1,500	1990	125.00	140
1992	Snow Leopard Portrait	1,750	1993	150.00	150
1990	Spring Fawn	1,500	1990	125.00	275
1990	Squirrel's Dish	1,950		110.00	110
1989	Steller's Jay	1,250	1989	135.00	150-175
1991	Study for One to One	1,950		120.00	200
1993	Summer Roses-Winter Wren	1,500	1993	250.00	400-595
1989	The Survivors-Canada Geese	1,500	1989	225.00	400
1994	Take Five-Canadian Lynx	1,500	N/A	245.00	395-475
1988	Talk on the Old Fence	950	1988	165.00	825
1990	A Threatened Symbol	1,950	1990	145.00	175
1994	Tundra Summit-Arctic Wolves	6,061	1994	265.00	265
1984	Waterside Encounter	950	1987	95.00	1000
1987	White Elegance-Trumpeter Swans	950	1989	115.00	500
1993	White Wolves-North American Wilderness Portfolio	350		325.00	475
1988	Witness of a Past-Bison	950	1990	110.00	135
1992	Wolf Scout #1	2,500	1992	105.00	150
1992	Wolf Scout #2	2,500	1992	105.00	135
1991	Wolf Study	950	1991	125.00	150
1987	Yellow-Bellied Marmot	950	1989	95.00	200-335
1989	A Young Generation	1,250	1989	165.00	175-295

Calle - P. Calle

YEAR ISSUE		EDITION LIMIT	YEAR RETD.	ISSUE PRICE	*QUOTE U.S.$
1981	Almost Home	950	1981	150.00	150
1991	Almost There	950	1991	165.00	165
1989	And A Good Book For Company	950	1990	135.00	435
1993	And A Grizzly Claw Necklace	750		150.00	150
1981	And Still Miles to Go	950	1981	245.00	400
1981	Andrew At The Falls	950	1981	150.00	150
1989	The Beaver Men	950		125.00	125
1984	A Brace for the Spit	950	1985	110.00	275
1980	Caring for the Herd	950	1981	110.00	110
1985	The Carrying Place	950	1990	195.00	195
1984	Chance Encounter	950	1986	225.00	325
1981	Chief High Pipe (Color)	950	1981	265.00	265
1980	Chief High Pipe (Pencil)	950	1980	75.00	175
1980	Chief Joseph-Man of Peace	950	1980	135.00	165
1990	Children of Walpi	350		160.00	160
1990	The Doll Maker	950		95.00	95
1982	Emerging from the Woods	950	1987	110.00	110
1981	End of a Long Day	950	1981	150.00	225
1984	Fate of the Late Migrant	950	1985	110.00	375
1983	Free Spirits	950	1985	195.00	475
1983	Free Trapper Study	550	1985	75.00	125-300
1981	Fresh Tracks	950	1981	150.00	150
1981	Friend of Foe	950		125.00	125
1981	Friends	950	1987	150.00	150
1985	The Frontier Blacksmith	950		245.00	245
1989	The Fur Trapper	550		75.00	175
1982	Generations in the Valley	950	1987	245.00	245
1985	The Grandmother	950	1987	400.00	400
1989	The Great Moment	950		350.00	350
1992	Hunter of Geese	950		125.00	125
1993	I Call Him Friend	950		235.00	235
1983	In Search of Beaver	950	1983	225.00	600
1991	In the Beginning . . . Friends	1,250	1993	250.00	275
1987	In the Land of the Giants	950	1988	245.00	900
1990	Interrupted Journey	1,750	1991	265.00	265
1990	Interrupted Journey-Prestige Ed.	290	1991	465.00	465
1987	Into the Great Alone	950	1988	245.00	700-850
1981	Just Over the Ridge	950	1982	245.00	245
1980	Landmark Tree	950	1980	125.00	225
1991	Man of the Fur Trade	550		110.00	110
1984	Mountain Man	550	1988	95.00	225
1993	Mountain Man-North American Wilderness Portfolio	350		325.00	N/A
1989	The Mountain Men	300	1989	400.00	400
1989	Navajo Madonna	650		95.00	95
1988	A New Day	950		150.00	150
1981	One With The Land	950	1981	245.00	250
1992	Out of the Silence	2,500		265.00	265
1992	Out of the Silence-Prestige	290		465.00	465
1981	Pause at the Lower Falls	950	1981	110.00	250
1980	Prayer to the Great Mystery	950	1980	245.00	245
1982	Return to Camp	950	1982	245.00	500
1991	The Silenced Honkers	1,250		250.00	250
1980	Sioux Chief	950	1980	85.00	140
1986	Snow Hunter	950	1988	150.00	225
1980	Something for the Pot	950	1980	175.00	1100
1990	Son of Sitting Bull	950		95.00	675
1985	Storyteller of the Mountains	950	1985	225.00	675
1983	Strays From the Flyway	950	1983	195.00	225
1981	Teton Friends	950	1981	150.00	225
1991	They Call Me Matthew	950		125.00	125
1992	Through the Tall Grass	950		175.00	175
1988	Trapper at Rest	550		95.00	95
1982	Two from the Flock	950	1982	245.00	500
1980	View from the Heights	950	1980	245.00	245
1988	Voyageurs and Waterfowl...Constant	950	1988	265.00	700-900
1980	When Snow Came Early	950	1980	85.00	250-340
1984	When Trails Cross	950	1984	245.00	750
1991	When Trails Grow Cold	2,500		265.00	265
1991	When Trails Grow Cold-Prestige Ed.	290	1991	465.00	465
1994	When Trappers Meet	750		165.00	165
1989	Where Eagles Fly	1,250	1990	265.00	350
1989	A Winter Feast	1,250	1989	265.00	375
1989	A Winter Feast-Prestige Ed.	290	1989	465.00	465
1981	Winter Hunter (Color)	950	1981	245.00	800
1980	Winter Hunter (Pencil)	950	1980	65.00	450
1983	A Winter Surprise	950	1984	195.00	500

Cross - T. Cross

YEAR ISSUE		EDITION LIMIT	YEAR RETD.	ISSUE PRICE	*QUOTE U.S.$
1994	April	750		55.00	55
1994	August	750		55.00	55
1993	Ever Green	750		135.00	135
1993	Flame Catcher	750	1993	185.00	185
1993	Flicker, Flash and Twirl	525		165.00	165
1994	July	750		55.00	55
1994	June	750		55.00	55
1994	March	750		55.00	55
1994	May	750		55.00	55
1992	Shell Caster	750	1993	150.00	150
1993	Sheperds of Magic	750		135.00	135
1993	Spellbound	750		85.00	85
1994	Spring Forth	750		145.00	145
1992	Star Weaver	750	1993	150.00	150
1994	Summer Musings	750		145.00	145
1993	The Summons...And Then They Are One	750	1993	195.00	195
1994	When Water Takes to Air	750		135.00	135
1993	Wind Sifter	750	1993	150.00	150

Daly - J. Daly

YEAR ISSUE		EDITION LIMIT	YEAR RETD.	ISSUE PRICE	*QUOTE U.S.$
1990	The Big Moment	1,500		125.00	125
1991	Cat's Cradle-Prestige Edition	950		450.00	450
1994	Catch of My Dreams	4,500		45.00	45
1994	Childhood Friends	950		110.00	110
1990	Confrontation	1,500	1992	85.00	85
1990	Contentment	1,500	1990	95.00	275
1992	Dominoes	1,500		155.00	155
1992	Favorite Gift	2,500	1992	175.00	175
1987	Favorite Reader	950	1990	85.00	250
1986	Flying High	950	1988	50.00	450-525
1992	The Flying Horse	950		325.00	325
1993	Good Company	1,500		155.00	155
1992	Her Secret Place	1,500	1992	135.00	200
1991	Home Team: Zero	1,500		150.00	150
1991	Homemade	1,500	1992	125.00	125
1990	Honor and Allegiance	1,500	1993	110.00	110
1990	The Ice Man	1,500	1992	125.00	135
1992	The Immigrant Spirit	5,000		125.00	125
1992	The Immigrant Spirit-Prestige Ed.	950		125.00	125
1989	In the Doghouse	1,500	1990	75.00	300-425
1990	It's That Time Again	1,500		120.00	120
1992	Left Out	1,500		110.00	110
1989	Let's Play Ball	1,500	1991	75.00	125
1990	Make Believe	1,500	1990	75.00	275-400
1994	Mud Mates	950		150.00	150
1994	My Best Friends	950		85.00	85
1991	A New Beginning	5,000		125.00	125
1993	The New Citizen	5,000		125.00	125
1993	The New Citizen-Prestige Ed.	950		125.00	125
1987	Odd Man Out	950	1988	85.00	85
1988	On Thin Ice	950	1993	95.00	295
1991	Pillars of a Nation-Charter Ed.	20,000		175.00	175
1992	Playmates	1,500	1992	155.00	350-395
1990	Radio Daze	1,500		150.00	150
1983	Saturday Night	950	1985	85.00	1125
1990	The Scholar	1,500	N/A	110.00	110
1993	Secret Admirer	1,500		150.00	150
1994	Slugger	950		75.00	75
1982	Spring Fever	950	1988	85.00	600
1993	Sunday Afternoon	1,500		150.00	150
1988	Territorial Rights	950	1990	85.00	350
1989	The Thief	1,500	1990	95.00	250
1989	The Thorn	1,500	1990	125.00	350
1988	Tie Breaker	950	1990	95.00	220
1991	Time-Out	1,500	1993	125.00	125
1993	To All a Good Night	1,500		160.00	160
1992	Walking the Rails	1,500		175.00	175
1993	When I Grow Up	1,500		175.00	175
1994	The Wind-Up	950		75.00	75
1988	Wiped Out	1,250	1990	125.00	375-500

Morrissey - D. Morrissey

YEAR ISSUE		EDITION LIMIT	YEAR RETD.	ISSUE PRICE	*QUOTE U.S.$
1994	The Amazing Time Elevator	950		195.00	195
1993	Charting the Skies	1,250	1993	195.00	195
1993	Charting the Skies-Caprice Edition	550	1993	375.00	375
1993	Draft of a Dream	175	1993	250.00	250
1994	The Dreamer's Trunk	1,500		195.00	195
1993	Drifting Closer	1,250		175.00	175
1993	The Mystic Mariner	750	1993	150.00	150
1993	The Redd Rocket	1,250		175.00	375
1994	The Redd Rocket-Pre-Flight	950	1993	110.00	110
1992	The Sandman's Ship of Dreams	750	1993	150.00	150
1994	Sighting off the Stern	950		135.00	135
1993	Sleeper Flight	1,250	1993	195.00	195
1993	The Telescope of Time	5,000		195.00	195

Olsen - G. Olsen

YEAR ISSUE		EDITION LIMIT	YEAR RETD.	ISSUE PRICE	*QUOTE U.S.$
1993	Airship Adventures	750		150.00	150
1993	Angels of Christmas	750	1993	135.00	135
1993	Dress Rehearseal	750	1993	165.00	800
1993	The Fraternity Tree	750		195.00	195
1994	Little Girls Will Mothers Be	750	N/A	135.00	135
1994	Mother's Love	750	1994	165.00	165
1994	Summerhouse	750		165.00	165

Seerey-Lester - J. Seerey-Lester

YEAR ISSUE		EDITION LIMIT	YEAR RETD.	ISSUE PRICE	*QUOTE U.S.$
1994	Abandoned	950		175.00	175
1986	Above the Treeline-Cougar	950	1986	130.00	130
1986	After the Fire-Grizzly	950	1990	95.00	95
1986	Along the Ice Floe-Polar Bears	950		200.00	200
1987	Alpenglow-Artic Wolf	950	1987	200.00	200
1987	Amboseli Child-African Elephant	950		160.00	160
1984	Among the Cattails-Canada Geese	950	1985	130.00	375
1984	Artic Procession-Willow Ptarmigan	950	1988	220.00	500
1990	Artic Wolf Pups	290		500.00	500
1987	Autumn Mist-Barred Owl	950	1987	160.00	160
1987	Autumn Thunder-Muskoxen	950		150.00	150
1985	Awakening Meadow-Cottontail	950		50.00	50
1992	Banyan Ambush- Black Panther	950	1992	235.00	235
1984	Basking-Brown Pelicans	950	1988	115.00	125
1988	Bathing-Blue Jay	950		95.00	95
1987	Bathing-Mute Swan	950	1992	175.00	275
1989	Before The Freeze-Beaver	950		165.00	165
1990	Bittersweet Winter-Cardinal	1,250	1990	150.00	150-175
1992	Black Jade	1,950	1992	275.00	350
1992	Black Magic-Panther	750	1992	195.00	225
1993	Black Wolf-North American Wilderness	350		325.00	N/A
1984	Breaking Cover-Black Bear	950	N/A	130.00	150
1987	Canyon Creek-Cougar	950	1987	195.00	435
1992	The Chase-Snow Leopard	950		200.00	200
1994	Child of the Outback	950		175.00	175
1985	Children of the Forest-Red Fox Kits	950	1985	110.00	325
1985	Children of the Tundra -Artic Wolf Pup	950	1985	110.00	325-395
1988	Cliff Hanger-Bobcat	950		200.00	200

*Quotes have been rounded up to nearest dollar

Collectors' Information Bureau

143

YEAR ISSUE		EDITION LIMIT	YEAR RETD.	ISSUE PRICE	*QUOTE U.S.$
1984	Close Encounter-Bobcat	950	1989	130.00	130
1988	Coastal Clique-Harbor Seals	950		160.00	160
1986	Conflict at Dawn-Heron & Osprey	950	1989	130.00	325
1983	Cool Retreat-Lynx	950	1988	85.00	125
1986	Cottonwood Gold-Baltimore Oriole	950		85.00	85
1985	Cougar Head Study	950		60.00	60
1989	Cougar Run	950	1989	185.00	225
1994	The Courtship	950		175.00	175
1993	Dark Encounter	3,500	N/A	200.00	200
1990	Dawn Majesty	1,250	1991	185.00	225-275
1987	Dawn on the Marsh-Coyote	950		200.00	200
1985	Daybreak-Moose	950		135.00	135
1991	Denali Family-Grizzly Bear	950	1991	195.00	235
1986	Early Arrivals-Snow Buntings	950		75.00	75
1983	Early Windfall-Gray Squirrels	950		85.00	85
1988	Edge of the Forest-Timber Wolves	950	1988	500.00	500-700
1989	Evening Duet-Snowy Egrets	1,250		185.00	185
1991	Evening Encounter-Grizzly & Wolf	1,250		185.00	185
1988	Evening Meadow-American Goldfinch	950		150.00	150
1991	Face to Face	1,250		200.00	200
1985	Fallen Birch-Chipmunk	950	1985	60.00	375
1985	First Light-Gray Jays	950	1985	130.00	175
1983	First Snow-Grizzly Bears	950	1984	95.00	325
1987	First Tracks-Cougar	950		150.00	150
1989	Fluke Sighting-Humback Whales	950	1989	185.00	185
1993	Freedom I	350		500.00	500
1993	Frozen Moonlight	2,500	1993	225.00	200
1985	Gathering-Gray Wolves, The	950	1987	165.00	250
1989	Gorilla	290	1989	400.00	450
1993	Grizzly Impact	950	N/A	225.00	300-385
1990	Grizzly Litho	290	1990	400.00	400-600
1989	Heavy Going-Grizzly	950	1989	175.00	240
1986	Hidden Admirer-Moose	950	1986	165.00	275
1988	Hiding Place-Saw-Whet Owl	950		95.00	95
1989	High and Mighty-Gorilla	950	1989	185.00	185
1986	High Country Champion-Grizzly	950	1986	175.00	375
1984	High Ground-Wolves	950	1984	130.00	225
1987	High Refuge-Red Squirrel	950		120.00	120
1984	Icy Outcrop-White Gyrfalcon	950	1986	115.00	200
1987	In Deep-Black Bear Cub	950	N/A	135.00	135
1990	In Their Presence	1,250		200.00	200
1985	Island Sanctuary-Mallards	950	1987	95.00	150
1986	Kenyan Family-Cheetahs	950		130.00	130
1986	Lakeside Family-Canada Geese	950		75.00	75
1988	Last Sanctuary-Florida Panther	950	1993	175.00	350
1983	Lone Fisherman-Great Blue Heron	950	1985	85.00	375
1993	Loonlight	1,500		225.00	225
1986	Low Tide-Bald Eagles	950		130.00	130
1987	Lying in Wait-Arctic Fox	950		175.00	175
1984	Lying Low-Cougar	950	1986	85.00	550
1991	Monsoon-White Tiger	950	1994	195.00	195
1991	Moonlight Chase-Cougar	1,250		195.00	195-220
1988	Moonlight Fishermen-Raccoons	950	1990	175.00	175
1988	Moose Hair	950	N/A	165.00	225
1988	Morning Display-Common Loons	3,395	1988	135.00	135
1986	Morning Forage-Ground Squirrel	950	1988	75.00	75
1993	Morning Glory-Bald Eagle	1,250	N/A	225.00	225
1984	Morning Mist-Snowy Owl	950	1988	95.00	180
1990	Mountain Cradle	1,250		200.00	200
1988	Night Moves-African Elephants	950		150.00	150
1990	Night Run-Artic Wolves	1,250	1990	200.00	200
1993	Night Specter	1,250		195.00	195
1986	Northwoods Family-Moose	950		75.00	75
1987	Out of the Blizzard-Timber Wolves	950	1987	215.00	450
1992	Out of the Darkness	290		200.00	200
1987	Out of the Mist-Grizzly	950	1990	200.00	375
1991	Out on a Limb-Young Barred Owl	950		185.00	185
1991	Panda Trilogy	950		375.00	375
1993	Phantoms of the Tundra	950		235.00	235
1984	Plains Hunter-Prairie Falcon	950		95.00	95
1990	The Plunge-Northern Sea Lions	1,250		200.00	200
1986	Racing the Storm-Artic Wolves	950	1986	200.00	300
1987	Rain Watch-Belted Kingfisher	950		125.00	125
1993	The Rains-Tiger	950		225.00	225
1992	Ranthambhore Rush	950		225.00	225
1983	The Refuge-Raccoon	950	1983	85.00	275
1992	Regal Majesty	290		200.00	200
1985	Return to Winter-Pintails	950	1990	135.00	135-200
1983	River Watch-Peregrine Falcon	950		85.00	85
1988	Savana Siesta-African Lions	950		165.00	165
1990	Seasonal Greeting-Cardinal	1,250		150.00	150
1993	Seeking Attention	950		200.00	200
1991	Sisters-Artic Wolves	1,250		185.00	185
1989	Sneak Peak	950		185.00	185
1986	Snowy Excursion-Red Squirrel	950		75.00	75
1988	Snowy Watch-Great Gray Owl	950		175.00	175
1989	Softly, Softly-White Tiger	950	1989	220.00	400-500
1991	Something Stirred (Bengal Tiger)	950		195.00	195
1988	Spanish Mist-Young Barred-Owl	950		175.00	175
1984	Spirit of the North-White Wolf	950	1986	130.00	185
1990	Spout	290		500.00	500
1989	Spring Flurry-Adelie Penguins	950		185.00	185
1986	Spring Mist-Chickadees	950	1986	105.00	150
1990	Suitors-Wood Ducks	3,313	1989	135.00	135
1990	Summer Rain-Common Loons	4,500	1990	200.00	200
1990	Summer Rain-Common Loons (Prestige)	450		425.00	425
1987	Sundown Alert-Bobcat	950	N/A	150.00	195
1985	Sundown Reflections-Wood Ducks	950		85.00	85
1990	Their First Season	1,250	1990	200.00	200
1990	Togetherness	1,250		125.00	185
1986	Treading Thin Ice-Chipmunk	950		75.00	75
1988	Tundra Family-Arctic Wolves	950		200.00	200
1985	Under the Pines-Bobcat	950	1986	95.00	275
1989	Water Sport-Bobcat	950	1989	185.00	185
1990	Whitetail Spring	1,250	1990	185.00	185
1988	Winter Grazing-Bison	950		185.00	185
1986	Winter Hiding-Cottontail	950		75.00	75
1983	Winter Lookout-Cougar	950	1985	85.00	600-700
1986	Winter Perch-Cardinal	950	1986	85.00	150
1985	Winter Rendezvous-Coyotes	950	1985	140.00	140
1988	Winter Spirit-Gray Wolf	950		200.00	200
1987	Winter Vigil-Great Horned Owl	950	1990	175.00	175
1993	Wolong Whiteout	950		225.00	225
1986	The Young Explorer-Red Fox Kit	950	N/A	75.00	95

Smith - D. Smith

YEAR ISSUE		EDITION LIMIT	YEAR RETD.	ISSUE PRICE	*QUOTE U.S.$
1993	African Ebony-Black Leopard	1,250		195.00	195
1992	Armada	950		195.00	195
1993	Catching the Scent-Polar Bear	950		175.00	175
1994	Curious Presence-Whitetail Deer	950		195.00	195
1991	Dawn's Early Light-Bald Eagles	950		185.00	185
1993	Echo Bay-Loon Family	1,150		185.00	185
1992	Eyes of the North	2,500		225.00	225
1993	Guardians of the Den	1,500	N/A	195.00	195
1991	Icy Reflections-Pintails	500		250.00	250
1992	Night Moves-Cougar	950		185.00	185
1994	Parting Reflections	950		185.00	185
1993	Shrouded Forest-Bald Eagle	950	N/A	150.00	650
1991	Twilight's Calling-Common Loons	950	1991	175.00	250
1993	What's Bruin	1,750		185.00	185

New Masters Publishing

Bannister - P. Bannister

YEAR ISSUE		EDITION LIMIT	YEAR RETD.	ISSUE PRICE	*QUOTE U.S.$
1982	Amaryllis	500	N/A	285.00	2000
1988	Apples and Oranges	485	N/A	265.00	650
1982	April	300	N/A	200.00	1150
1984	April Light	950	N/A	150.00	650
1987	Autumn Fields	950	N/A	150.00	300
1978	Bandstand	250	N/A	75.00	600
1992	Bed of Roses	663	N/A	265.00	525
1995	Bridesmaids	950	N/A	265.00	530
1991	Celebration	662	N/A	350.00	800
1989	Chapter One	485	N/A	265.00	1500-1700
1991	Crossroads	485	N/A	295.00	600
1993	Crowning Glory	485	N/A	265.00	600
1992	Crystal Bowl	485	N/A	265.00	600
1989	Daydreams	485	N/A	265.00	625
1993	Deja Vu	663	N/A	265.00	1200-1400
1983	The Duchess	500	N/A	250.00	1900
1980	Dust of Autumn	200	N/A	200.00	1225
1981	Easter	300	N/A	260.00	1150
1982	Emily	500	N/A	285.00	1200
1980	Faded Glory	200	N/A	200.00	1225
1984	The Fan Window	950	N/A	195.00	600
1987	First Prize	950	N/A	115.00	275
1988	Floribunda	485	N/A	265.00	675
1994	Fountain	485	N/A	265.00	600
1994	From Russia With Love	950	N/A	165.00	400
1980	Gift of Happiness	200	N/A	200.00	2000
1980	Girl on the Beach	200	N/A	200.00	1400
1990	Good Friends	485	N/A	265.00	750
1988	Guinevere	485	N/A	265.00	1250-1300
1993	Into The Woods	485	N/A	265.00	500
1982	Ivy	500	N/A	285.00	750
1982	Jasmine	500	N/A	285.00	725
1981	Juliet	300	N/A	260.00	5000
1990	Lavender Hill	485	N/A	265.00	775
1992	Love Letters	485	N/A	265.00	550
1988	Love Seat	485	N/A	230.00	500
1989	Low Tide	485	N/A	265.00	650
1995	Magnolias	950	N/A	265.00	1200-1300
1982	Mail Order Brides	500	N/A	325.00	2400
1984	Make Believe	950	N/A	150.00	775
1989	March Winds	485	N/A	265.00	530
1983	Mementos	950	N/A	150.00	1450
1982	Memories	500	N/A	235.00	500
1992	Morning Mist	485	N/A	265.00	500
1981	My Special Place	300	N/A	260.00	2000
1982	Nuance	500	N/A	235.00	500
1994	Once Upon A Time	950	N/A	265.00	600
1983	Ophelia	950	N/A	150.00	700
1989	Peace	485	N/A	265.00	1200
1981	Porcelain Rose	300	N/A	260.00	2000
1982	The Present	500	N/A	260.00	925
1986	Pride & Joy	950	N/A	150.00	300
1991	Pudding & Pies	485	N/A	265.00	500
1987	Quiet Corner	950	N/A	115.00	625
1989	The Quilt	485	N/A	265.00	950
1993	Rambling Rose	485	N/A	265.00	500
1981	Rehearsal	300	N/A	260.00	1900
1990	Rendezvous	485	N/A	265.00	650
1984	Scarlet Ribbons	950	N/A	150.00	325
1980	Sea Haven	300	N/A	260.00	1200
1990	Seascapes	485	N/A	265.00	550
1987	September Harvest	950	N/A	150.00	400
1980	The Silver Bell	200	N/A	200.00	2000
1990	Sisters	485	N/A	265.00	1200
1990	Songbird	485	N/A	265.00	550
1991	String of Pearls	485	N/A	265.00	850
1988	Summer Choices	300	N/A	250.00	850
1991	Teatime	485	N/A	295.00	700
1980	Titania	350	N/A	260.00	950
1991	Wildflowers	485	N/A	295.00	700
1983	Window Seat	950	N/A	150.00	700

Past Impressions

Limited Edition Canvas Transfers - A. Maley

YEAR ISSUE		EDITION LIMIT	YEAR RETD.	ISSUE PRICE	*QUOTE U.S.$
1990	Cafe Royale	100	N/A	665.00	665
1992	Circle of Love	250	N/A	445.00	850
1992	An Elegant Affair	250	N/A	595.00	1095
1992	Evening Performance	100	N/A	295.00	1050
1990	Festive Occasion	100	N/A	595.00	250-300
1990	Gracious Era	100	N/A	645.00	1500-1700
1995	The Letter	250	N/A	465.00	600
1987	Love Letter	75	N/A	445.00	1250
1994	New Years Eve	250	N/A	445.00	600-800
1994	Parisian Beauties	250	N/A	645.00	750
1993	Rags and Riches	250	N/A	445.00	625
1993	The Recital	250	N/A	595.00	900-1400
1990	Romantic Engagement	100	N/A	445.00	1225
1993	Sleigh Bells	250	N/A	595.00	600
1991	Summer Carousel	250	N/A	345.00	600-1100
1994	Summer Elegance	250	N/A	595.00	950
1995	Summer Romance	250	N/A	465.00	575-750
1993	Visiting The Nursery	250	N/A	445.00	1400
1992	A Walk in the Park	250	N/A	595.00	650-1000
1989	Winter Impressions	100	N/A	595.00	775-1100

Limited Edition Paper Prints - A. Maley

YEAR ISSUE		EDITION LIMIT	YEAR RETD.	ISSUE PRICE	*QUOTE U.S.$
1989	Alexandra	750	1994	125.00	125
1989	Beth	750	1994	125.00	125
1988	The Boardwalk	500	N/A	250.00	395
1989	Catherine	750	1994	125.00	200
1987	Day Dreams	500	N/A	200.00	325
1989	English Rose	750	N/A	250.00	400
1990	Festive Occasion	750	N/A	250.00	900
1984	Glorious Summer	350	N/A	150.00	600
1989	In Harmony	750	1995	250.00	250
1988	Joys of Childhood	500	N/A	250.00	320
1987	Love Letter	450	N/A	200.00	200
1988	Opening Night	500	N/A	250.00	2000
1985	Passing Elegance	350	N/A	150.00	900
1987	The Promise	450	N/A	200.00	525
1984	Secluded Garden	350	N/A	150.00	970
1985	Secret Thoughts	350	N/A	150.00	850
1990	Summer Pastime	750	N/A	250.00	375
1986	Tell Me	450	N/A	150.00	800
1988	Tranquil Moment	500	N/A	250.00	325
1989	Victoria	750	1994	125.00	125
1988	Victorian Trio	500	N/A	250.00	350
1986	Winter Romance	450	N/A	150.00	1000

Pemberton & Oakes

Membership-Miniature Lithographs - D. Zolan

YEAR ISSUE		EDITION LIMIT	YEAR RETD.	ISSUE PRICE	*QUOTE U.S.$
1992	Brotherly Love	Retrd.	N/A	18.00	68
1993	New Shoes	Retrd.	N/A	18.00	42
1993	Country Walk	Retrd.	N/A	22.00	40
1994	Enchanted Forest	Retrd.	N/A	22.00	40

Zolan's Children-Lithographs - D. Zolan

YEAR ISSUE		EDITION LIMIT	YEAR RETD.	ISSUE PRICE	*QUOTE U.S.$
1989	Almost Home	Retrd.	N/A	98.00	255
1991	Autumn Leaves	Retrd.	N/A	98.00	120
1993	The Big Catch	Retrd.	N/A	98.00	130
1989	Brotherly Love	Retrd.	N/A	98.00	295
1982	By Myself	Retrd.	N/A	98.00	230
1989	Christmas Prayer	Retrd.	N/A	98.00	175-225
1990	Colors of Spring	Retrd.	N/A	98.00	175-240
1990	Crystal's Creek	Retrd.	N/A	98.00	175
1989	Daddy's Home	Retrd.	N/A	98.00	310
1988	Day Dreamer	Retrd.	N/A	35.00	130
1992	Enchanted Forest	Retrd.	N/A	98.00	110-135
1982	Erik and the Dandelion	Retrd.	N/A	98.00	400
1990	First Kiss	Retrd.	N/A	98.00	240
1991	Flowers for Mother	Retrd.	N/A	98.00	160
1993	Grandma's Garden	Retrd.	N/A	98.00	135
1989	Grandma's Mirror	Retrd.	N/A	98.00	140-195
1990	Laurie and the Creche	Retrd.	N/A	98.00	115-165
1989	Mother's Angels	Retrd.	N/A	98.00	175-240
1992	New Shoes	Retrd.	N/A	98.00	150
1989	Rodeo Girl	Retrd.	N/A	98.00	160
1984	Sabina in the Grass	Retrd.	N/A	98.00	625
1988	Small Wonder	Retrd.	N/A	98.00	250
1989	Snowy Adventure	Retrd.	N/A	98.00	205
1991	Summer Suds	Retrd.	N/A	98.00	140-175
1989	Summer's Child	Retrd.	N/A	98.00	225
1986	Tender Moment	Retrd.	N/A	98.00	275
1988	Tiny Treasures	Retrd.	N/A	150.00	215
1987	Touching the Sky	Retrd.	N/A	98.00	175-225
1988	Waiting to Play	Retrd.	N/A	35.00	135
1988	Winter Angel	Retrd.	N/A	98.00	230

Reco International

Fine Art Canvas Reproduction - J. McClelland

YEAR ISSUE		EDITION LIMIT	YEAR RETD.	ISSUE PRICE	*QUOTE U.S.$
1990	Beach Play	350		80.00	80
1991	Flower Swing	350		100.00	100

*Quotes have been rounded up to nearest dollar

GRAPHICS/ORNAMENTS

Reco International to Armani

YEAR ISSUE		EDITION LIMIT	YEAR RETD.	ISSUE PRICE	*QUOTE U.S.$
1991	Summer Conversation	350		80.00	80

Limited Edition Print - S. Kuck

YEAR ISSUE		EDITION LIMIT	YEAR RETD.	ISSUE PRICE	*QUOTE U.S.$
1986	Ashley	500		85.00	150
1985	Heather	Retrd.	1987	75.00	150
1984	Jessica	Retrd.	1986	60.00	400

McClelland - J. McClelland

YEAR ISSUE		EDITION LIMIT	YEAR RETD.	ISSUE PRICE	*QUOTE U.S.$
XX	I Love Tammy	500		75.00	100
XX	Just for You	300		155.00	155
XX	Olivia	300		175.00	175
XX	Reverie	300		110.00	110
XX	Sweet Dreams	300		145.00	145

Roman, Inc.

Abble Williams - A. Williams

YEAR ISSUE		EDITION LIMIT	YEAR RETD.	ISSUE PRICE	*QUOTE U.S.$
1988	Mary, Mother of the Carpenter	Closed	N/A	100.00	100

The Discovery of America Miniature Art Print - I. Spencer

YEAR ISSUE		EDITION LIMIT	YEAR RETD.	ISSUE PRICE	*QUOTE U.S.$
1991	The Discovery of America	Open		2.00	2

Divine Servant - M. Greiner Jr.

YEAR ISSUE		EDITION LIMIT	YEAR RETD.	ISSUE PRICE	*QUOTE U.S.$
1993	Divine Servant, print of drawing	Open		35.00	35
1994	Divine Servant, print of painting	Closed	1994	150.00	150
1994	Divine Servant, print of painting	Closed	1994	75.00	75
1994	Divine Servant, print of painting w/remarque	Closed	1994	75.00	75
1994	Divine Servant, print of painting w/remarque	Closed	1994	150.00	150

Fishers of Men - M. Greiner, Jr.

YEAR ISSUE		EDITION LIMIT	YEAR RETD.	ISSUE PRICE	*QUOTE U.S.$
1994	Fishers of Men 8x10	Open		10.00	10
1994	Fishers of Men 11x14	Open		20.00	20
1994	Fishers of Men 16x20	Open		35.00	35

Hook - F. Hook

YEAR ISSUE		EDITION LIMIT	YEAR RETD.	ISSUE PRICE	*QUOTE U.S.$
1982	Bouquet	1,200		70.00	350
1981	The Carpenter	Closed	1981	100.00	1000
1981	The Carpenter (remarque)	Closed	1981	100.00	3000
1982	Frolicking	1,200		60.00	350
1982	Gathering	1,200		60.00	350-450
1982	Little Children, Come to Me	1,950		50.00	500
1982	Little Children, Come to Me, remarque	50		100.00	500
1982	Posing	1,200		70.00	350
1982	Poulets	1,200		60.00	350
1982	Surprise	1,200		50.00	350

Portraits of Love - F. Hook

YEAR ISSUE		EDITION LIMIT	YEAR RETD.	ISSUE PRICE	*QUOTE U.S.$
1988	Expectation	2,500		25.00	25
1988	In Mother's Arms	2,500		25.00	25
1988	My Kitty	2,500		25.00	25
1988	Remember When...	2,500		25.00	25
1988	Sharing	2,500		25.00	25
1988	Sunkissed Afternoon	2,500		25.00	25

V.F. Fine Arts

Kuck - S. Kuck

YEAR ISSUE		EDITION LIMIT	YEAR RETD.	ISSUE PRICE	*QUOTE U.S.$
1994	'95 Angel Collection, S/N	750	1995	198.00	198
1995	'96 Angel Collection, S/N	750		198.00	198
1993	Best Friend, proof	250	N/A	175.00	225
1993	Best Friends, Canvas Transfer	250	N/A	500.00	600
1993	Best Friends, S/N	2,500	N/A	145.00	150
1994	Best of Days, S/N	750	1994	160.00	175
1989	Bundle of Joy, S/N	1,000	1989	125.00	250
1993	Buttons & Bows, proof	95	N/A	125.00	150
1993	Buttons & Bows, S/N	950	N/A	95.00	125
1990	Chopsticks, proof	150	1991	120.00	150
1990	Chopsticks, remarque	25	1991	160.00	200
1990	Chopsticks, S/N	1,500	1990	80.00	95
1995	Christmas Magic, S/N	950		80.00	80
1987	The Daisy, proof	90	1988	40.00	175
1987	The Daisy, S/N	900	1988	30.00	125
1989	Day Dreaming, proof	90	1989	225.00	250
1989	Day Dreaming, remarque	50	1989	300.00	395
1989	Day Dreaming, S/N	900	1989	150.00	200
1994	Dear Santa, S/N	950	1994	95.00	125
1992	Duet, Canvas Framed	500	1994	255.00	325
1992	Duet, proof	95	N/A	175.00	200
1992	Duet, S/N	950	N/A	125.00	135
1988	First Recital, proof	25	1988	250.00	750
1988	First Recital, remarque	25	1988	400.00	1000
1988	First Recital, S/N	150	1988	200.00	500
1990	First Snow, proof	50	1990	150.00	250
1990	First Snow, remarque	25	1990	200.00	350
1990	First Snow, S/N	500	1990	95.00	150
1987	The Flower Girl, proof	90	1987	50.00	125
1987	The Flower Girl, S/N	900	1987	40.00	95
1994	Garden Memories, Canvas Transfer	250	N/A	500.00	500
1994	Garden Memories, S/N	2,500	N/A	145.00	175
1991	God's Gift, proof	150	N/A	150.00	175
1991	God's Gift, S/N	1,500	1993	95.00	125
1993	Good Morning, Canvas	250	1993	500.00	500
1993	Good Morning, proof	50	N/A	175.00	200
1993	Good Morning, S/N	2,500	N/A	145.00	165
1996	Hidden Garden, Canvas Transfer	395		379.00	379
1996	Hidden Garden, S/N	950	1996	95.00	95
1995	Homecoming, proof	95	1995	172.50	173
1995	Homecoming, S/N	1,150	1995	125.00	125
1989	Innocence, proof	90	1989	225.00	275
1989	Innocence, remarque	50	1989	300.00	395
1989	Innocence, S/N	900	1989	150.00	220
1992	Joyous Day, Canvas Transfer	250	N/A	250.00	295
1992	Joyous Day, proof	120	N/A	175.00	200
1992	Joyous Day, S/N	1,200	1993	125.00	150
1988	The Kitten, proof	50	1988	150.00	1000
1988	The Kitten, remarque	25	1988	250.00	1200
1988	The Kitten, S/N	350	1988	120.00	1000
1990	Le Beau, proof	150	1990	120.00	225
1990	Le Beau, remarque	25	1990	160.00	275
1990	Le Beau, S/N	1,500	1990	80.00	175
1987	Le Papillion, proof	35	1990	110.00	175
1987	Le Papillion, remarque	7	1990	150.00	250
1987	Le Papillion, S/N	350	1990	90.00	150
1990	Lilly Pond, color remarque	125	1990	500.00	500
1990	Lilly Pond, proof	75	1990	200.00	200
1990	Lilly Pond, S/N	750	1990	150.00	150
1988	Little Ballerina, proof	25	1988	150.00	350
1988	Little Ballerina, remarque	25	1988	225.00	450
1988	Little Ballerina, S/N	150	1988	110.00	275
1987	The Loveseat, proof	90	1987	40.00	150
1987	The Loveseat, S/N	900	1987	30.00	100
1991	Memories, S/N	5,000	1991	195.00	250
1987	Mother's Love, proof	12	1987	225.00	1200
1987	Mother's Love, S/N	150	1987	195.00	750
1988	My Dearest, proof	50	1988	200.00	900
1988	My Dearest, remarque	25	1988	325.00	1200
1988	My Dearest, S/N	350	1988	160.00	700
1995	Night Before Christmas, S/N	1,150		95.00	95
1995	Playful Kitten	950	1995	95.00	95
1989	Puppy, proof	50	1989	180.00	500
1989	Puppy, remarque	50	1989	240.00	750
1989	Puppy, S/N	500	1989	120.00	400
1987	A Quiet Time, proof	90	1987	50.00	100
1987	A Quiet Time, S/N	900	1987	40.00	75
1987	The Reading Lesson, proof	90	1987	70.00	200
1987	The Reading Lesson, S/N	900	1987	60.00	150
1995	Rhapsody & Lace	1,150		95.00	100
1989	Rose Garden, proof	50	1989	150.00	400
1989	Rose Garden, remarque	50	1989	200.00	500
1989	Rose Garden, S/N	500	1989	95.00	390
1986	Silhouette, proof	25	1987	90.00	250
1986	Silhouette, S/N	250	1987	80.00	200
1989	Sisters, proof	90	1989	150.00	550
1989	Sisters, remarque	50	1989	200.00	650
1989	Sisters, S/N	900	1988	95.00	300
1989	Sonatina, proof	90	1989	225.00	700
1989	Sonatina, remarque	50	1989	300.00	850
1989	Sonatina, S/N	900	1989	150.00	400
1986	Summer Reflections, proof	90	1987	70.00	300
1986	Summer Reflections, S/N	900	1987	60.00	250
1986	Tender Moments, proof	50	1986	80.00	300
1986	Tender Moments, S/N	500	1986	70.00	200
1993	Thinking of You, Canvas Transfer	250	1993	500.00	500
1993	Thinking of You, S/N	2,500	N/A	145.00	175
1988	Wild Flowers, proof	50	1988	175.00	300
1988	Wild Flowers, remarque	25	1988	250.00	400
1988	Wild Flowers, S/N	350	1988	160.00	250
1992	Yesterday, Canvas Framed	550	N/A	195.00	200
1992	Yesterday, proof	95	N/A	150.00	150
1992	Yesterday, S/N	950	N/A	95.00	95

ORNAMENTS

Ace Product Management Group, Inc.

Harley-Davidson Child's Ornaments - Ace

YEAR ISSUE		EDITION LIMIT	YEAR RETD.	ISSUE PRICE	*QUOTE U.S.$
1991	For The Young At Heart 99433-92Z	Yr.Iss.	1991	14.95	15
1992	The Gift 99466-93Z	Yr.Iss.	1992	15.00	15
1993	First Harley 99429-94Z	Yr.Iss.	1993	15.00	15
1994	Daddy's Boots 99442-95Z	Yr.Iss.	1994	15.00	15
1995	Little Stocking Stuffer 99448-96Z	Yr.Iss.	1995	15.00	15
1996	1996 Commemorative Ornament 99940-97Z	Yr.Iss.	1996	15.00	15
1997	Christmas Cruise 97968-98Z	Yr.Iss.		17.00	17

Harley-Davidson Christmas Ornaments - Ace

YEAR ISSUE		EDITION LIMIT	YEAR RETD.	ISSUE PRICE	*QUOTE U.S.$
1981	Ornament 99407-82V	Yr.Iss.	1981	5.95	5
1983	Ornament 99407-84V	Yr.Iss.	1983	6.50	7
1984	Ornament 99408-85Z	Yr.Iss.	1984	6.95	7
1985	Ornament 99406-86Z	Yr.Iss.	1985	6.95	7
1986	Ornament 99407-87Z	Yr.Iss.	1986	6.95	7
1987	Ornament 99406-88Z	Yr.Iss.	1987	6.95	7
1988	Ornament 99408-89Z	Yr.Iss.	1988	6.95	7
1989	Ornament 99435-90Z	Yr.Iss.	1989	6.95	7
1990	Ornament 99435-91Z	Yr.Iss.	1990	6.95	7
1991	Skating Party 99436-92Z	Yr.Iss.	1991	6.95	7
1992	Surprise Visit 99437-93Z	Yr.Iss.	1992	7.00	7
1993	Xmas Vacation 99427-94Z	Yr.Iss.	1993	8.00	8

Harley-Davidson Holiday Memories - Ace

YEAR ISSUE		EDITION LIMIT	YEAR RETD.	ISSUE PRICE	*QUOTE U.S.$
1994	Under The Mistletoe 99091-95Z	Yr.Iss.	1994	8.00	8
1995	Late Arrival 99495-96Z	Yr.Iss.	1995	8.00	8
1996	After The Pageant 99948-97Z	Yr.Iss.	1996	8.00	8
1997	Roadside Revelation 97958-98Z	Yr.Iss.		8.00	8

Harley-Davidson Mini-Plate Ornaments - Ace

YEAR ISSUE		EDITION LIMIT	YEAR RETD.	ISSUE PRICE	*QUOTE U.S.$
1989	1989 99440-90Z	Yr.Iss.	1989	10.00	10
1990	Santa's Predicament 99442-91Z	Yr.Iss.	1990	9.95	10
1991	Not A Creature 99443-92Z	Yr.Iss.	1991	10.00	10
1992	Finding The Way 99441.93Z	Yr.Iss.	1992	10.00	10
1993	Pulling Together 99416-94Z	Yr.Iss.	1993	10.00	10
1994	Sorry Guys 99445-95Z	Yr.Iss.	1994	10.00	10
1995	Ratchet The Elf 99480-96Z	Yr.Iss.	1995	10.00	10
1996	Reviewing the Plan 99947-97Z	Yr.Iss.	1996	10.00	10
1997	The More the Merrier 97967-98Z	Yr.Iss.		12.00	12

Harley-Davidson Pewter Ornaments - Ace

YEAR ISSUE		EDITION LIMIT	YEAR RETD.	ISSUE PRICE	*QUOTE U.S.$
1988	Santa's Secret 99409-89Z	Yr.Iss.	1988	6.95	7
1989	Santa's Workshop 99438-90Z	Yr.Iss.	1989	6.95	7
1990	Stocking Stuffer 99438-91Z	Yr.Iss.	1990	8.95	9
1991	Finishing Touches 99439-92Z	Yr.Iss.	1991	10.95	11
1992	Batteries Not Included 99426-93Z	Yr.Iss.	1992	12.00	12
1993	Joy Ride 99428-94Z	Yr.Iss.	1993	12.00	12
1993	90th Anniversary-"The Reunion" 99430-94Z	7,500	1993	35.00	35
1994	Cleared For Takeoff 99463-95Z	Yr.Iss.	1994	14.00	14
1995	Night Flight 99455-96Z	Yr.Iss.	1995	15.00	15
1996	V-Twin 99940-97Z	Yr.Iss.	1996	15.00	15
1997	Letter to Santa 97969-98Z	Yr.Iss.		17.00	17

All God's Children

Angel Dumpling - M. Root

YEAR ISSUE		EDITION LIMIT	YEAR RETD.	ISSUE PRICE	*QUOTE U.S.$
1993	Eric - 1570	Retrd.	1994	22.50	60-90
1994	Erica - 1578	Retrd.	1995	22.50	50-80

Christmas Ornaments - M. Root

YEAR ISSUE		EDITION LIMIT	YEAR RETD.	ISSUE PRICE	*QUOTE U.S.$
1987	Cameo Ornaments (set of 12) - D1912	Retrd.	1988	144.00	1800-2200
1987	Doll Ornaments (set of 24) - D1924	Retrd.	1988	336.00	3000-3500
1993	Santa with Scooty - 1571	Retrd.	1994	22.50	40-60

Amaranth Productions

Christmas Ornaments - L. West

YEAR ISSUE		EDITION LIMIT	YEAR RETD.	ISSUE PRICE	*QUOTE U.S.$
1994	Mr. Santa 8010	500	1995	110.00	110
1994	St. Nick (burgundy) 8020	500	1995	120.00	120
1994	Angel 8030	500	1995	120.00	120
1994	Jester 8040	500	1995	120.00	350
1995	Mrs. Claus 8015	500	1995	110.00	110
1995	Harlequin 8045	500	1995	110.00	110
1995	St. Nick (white) 8025	500	1995	120.00	120

Anheuser-Busch, Inc.

A & Eagle Collector Ornament Series - A.-Busch, Inc.

YEAR ISSUE		EDITION LIMIT	YEAR RETD.	ISSUE PRICE	*QUOTE U.S.$
1991	Budweiser Girl-Circa 1890's N3178	Retrd.	N/A	15.00	15-24
1992	1893 Columbian Exposition N3649	Retrd.	N/A	15.00	15-24
1993	Greatest Triumph N4089	Retrd.	N/A	15.00	15-19

Christmas Ornaments - Various

YEAR ISSUE		EDITION LIMIT	YEAR RETD.	ISSUE PRICE	*QUOTE U.S.$
1992	Clydesdales 3 Mini Plate Ornament N3650 - S. Sampson	Retrd.	N/A	23.00	23
1993	Budweiser Six-Pack Mini Plate Ornament N4220 - M. Urdahl	Retrd.	1994	10.00	10

Annalee Mobilitee Dolls, Inc.

Christmas Ornaments - A. Thorndike

YEAR ISSUE		EDITION LIMIT	YEAR RETD.	ISSUE PRICE	*QUOTE U.S.$
1985	Clown Head	5,701	N/A	6.95	175
1986	3" Clown	3,369	1986	11.95	200
1987	3" Elf	1,950	1989	12.95	325
1992	3" Skier	8,332	N/A	14.45	175

ANRI

Disney Four Star Collection - Disney Studios

YEAR ISSUE		EDITION LIMIT	YEAR RETD.	ISSUE PRICE	*QUOTE U.S.$
1989	Maestro Mickey	Yr.Iss.	1989	25.00	75-95
1990	Minnie Mouse	Yr.Iss.	1990	25.00	50

Ferrandiz Message Collection - J. Ferrandiz

YEAR ISSUE		EDITION LIMIT	YEAR RETD.	ISSUE PRICE	*QUOTE U.S.$
1989	Let the Heavens Ring	1,000	1992	215.00	215
1990	Hear The Angels Sing	1,000	1992	225.00	225

Ferrandiz Woodcarvings - J. Ferrandiz

YEAR ISSUE		EDITION LIMIT	YEAR RETD.	ISSUE PRICE	*QUOTE U.S.$
1988	Heavenly Drummer	1,000	1992	175.00	225
1989	Heavenly Strings	1,000	1992	190.00	190

Sarah Kay's First Christmas - S. Kay

YEAR ISSUE		EDITION LIMIT	YEAR RETD.	ISSUE PRICE	*QUOTE U.S.$
1994	Sarah Kay's First Christmas	500		140.00	195
1995	First Xmas Stocking 57502	500		99.00	195
1996	All I Want for Xmas 57503	500		195.00	195
1997	Christmas Puppy	500		295.00	295

Armani

Christmas - G. Armani

YEAR ISSUE		EDITION LIMIT	YEAR RETD.	ISSUE PRICE	*QUOTE U.S.$
1991	Christmas Ornament 799A	Retrd.	1991	11.50	45
1992	Christmas Ornament 788F	Retrd.	1992	23.50	50-75
1993	Christmas Ornament 982P	Retrd.	1993	25.00	50-75
1994	Christmas Ornament 801P	Retrd.	1994	25.00	40-50

*Quotes have been rounded up to nearest dollar

ORNAMENTS

YEAR ISSUE		EDITION LIMIT	YEAR RETD.	ISSUE PRICE	*QUOTE U.S. $
1995	Christmas Ornament-Gifts & Snow 640P	Retrd.	1995	30.00	30
1996	Christmas Ornament-A Sweet Christmas 355P	Retrd.	1996	30.00	30
1997	Christmas Ornament-Christmas Snow 137F	Yr.Iss.		37.50	38

Artists of the World

De Grazia Annual Ornaments - T. De Grazia

YEAR ISSUE		EDITION LIMIT	YEAR RETD.	ISSUE PRICE	*QUOTE U.S. $
1986	Pima Indian Drummer Boy	Yr.Iss.	1986	28.00	200-400
1987	White Dove	Yr.Iss.	1987	30.00	95-145
1988	Flower Girl	Yr.Iss.	1988	33.00	85-100
1989	Flower Boy	Yr.Iss.	1989	35.00	85-100
1990	Pink Papoose	Yr.Iss.	1990	35.00	85-100
1990	Merry Little Indian	10,000	1990	88.00	100-175
1991	Christmas Prayer (Red)	Yr.Iss.	1991	50.00	75-95
1992	Bearing Gift	Yr.Iss.	1992	55.00	70-100
1993	Lighting the Way	Yr.Iss.	1993	58.00	75-95
1994	Warm Wishes	Yr.Iss.	1994	65.00	70-100
1995	Little Prayer (White)	Yr.Iss.	1995	49.50	65-75
1995	Heavenly Flowers	Yr.Iss.	1995	65.00	65
1995	My Beautiful Rocking Horse	Yr.Iss.	1995	125.00	125-150
1996	Oh Holy Night	Yr.Iss		67.50	70

Attic Babies

Christmas Decorations- M. Maschino-Walker

YEAR ISSUE		EDITION LIMIT	YEAR RETD.	ISSUE PRICE	*QUOTE U.S. $
1993	Raggedy Santa Wreath	Retrd.	1994	101.95	160
1992	Stocking	Retrd.	1994	55.95	56

Wooden Ornaments - M. Maschino-Walker

YEAR ISSUE		EDITION LIMIT	YEAR RETD.	ISSUE PRICE	*QUOTE U.S. $
1993	Angel	Retrd.	1994	21.95	22
1993	Snowman	Retrd.	1994	17.95	18
1993	Stocking	Retrd.	1994	25.95	26

Band Creations, Inc.

Best Friends - Angels - Richards/Penfield

YEAR ISSUE		EDITION LIMIT	YEAR RETD.	ISSUE PRICE	*QUOTE U.S. $
1994	4 Assorted Angel Ornaments	Open		5.00	5
1995	Double Angels	Open		8.00	8
1996	4 Assorted African American Angels	Open		5.00	5

Best Friends-A Star is Born - Richards/Penfield

YEAR ISSUE		EDITION LIMIT	YEAR RETD.	ISSUE PRICE	*QUOTE U.S. $
1995	Baseball Boy	Open		6.00	6
1996	Baseball Boy (African American)	Open		6.00	6
1995	Baseball Girl	Open		6.00	6
1996	Baseball Girl (African American)	Open		6.00	6
1995	Basketball Boy	Open		6.00	6
1996	Basketball Boy (African American)	Open		6.00	6
1995	Basketball Girl	Open		6.00	6
1996	Basketball Girl (African American)	Open		6.00	6
1996	Biker Boy	Open		6.00	6
1996	Biker Girl	Open		6.00	6
1995	Cheerleader Girl	Open		6.00	6
1996	Cheerleader Girl (African American)	Open		6.00	6
1996	Fisher Boy	Open		6.00	6
1996	Fisher Girl	Open		6.00	6
1995	Football Boy	Open		6.00	6
1996	Football Boy (African American)	Open		6.00	6
1995	Golfer Boy	Open		6.00	6
1995	Golfer Girl	Open		6.00	6
1995	Hockey Boy	Open		6.00	6
1996	Skier Boy	Open		6.00	6
1996	Skier Girl	Open		6.00	6
1995	Soccer Boy	Open		6.00	6
1995	Soccer Girl	Open		6.00	6
1995	Swimmer Boy	Open		6.00	6
1995	Swimmer Girl	Open		6.00	6
1996	Tennis Boy	Open		6.00	6
1996	Tennis Girl	Open		6.00	6

Best Friends-Monthly Messengers - Richards/Penfield

YEAR ISSUE		EDITION LIMIT	YEAR RETD.	ISSUE PRICE	*QUOTE U.S. $
1996	January	Open		10.00	10
1996	February	Open		10.00	10
1996	March	Open		10.00	10
1996	April	Open		10.00	10
1996	May	Open		10.00	10
1996	June	Open		10.00	10
1996	July	Open		10.00	10
1996	August	Open		10.00	10
1996	September	Open		10.00	10
1996	October	Open		10.00	10
1996	November	Open		10.00	10
1996	December	Open		10.00	10

Kringle Toppers - Band Creations

YEAR ISSUE		EDITION LIMIT	YEAR RETD.	ISSUE PRICE	*QUOTE U.S. $
1996	America, Santa Claus	Open		10.00	10
1996	Austria, Christkind	Open		10.00	10
1996	England, Father Christmas	Open		10.00	10
1996	France, Pere Noel	Open		10.00	10
1996	Germany, Pelsnickel	Open		10.00	10
1996	Netherlands, St. Nickolas	Open		10.00	10
1996	Russia, Father Frost	Open		10.00	10
1996	Scandinavia, Julnisse	Open		10.00	10

Snowman/Sport Toppers - Band Creations

YEAR ISSUE		EDITION LIMIT	YEAR RETD.	ISSUE PRICE	*QUOTE U.S. $
1996	Beach/Boating	Open		10.00	10
1996	Fishing	Open		10.00	10
1996	Golf	Open		10.00	10
1996	Skiing	Open		10.00	10
1996	Snowman	Open		10.00	10
1996	Tennis	Open		10.00	10

Bing & Grondahl

Christmas - E. Jensen, unless otherwise noted

YEAR ISSUE		EDITION LIMIT	YEAR RETD.	ISSUE PRICE	*QUOTE U.S. $
1985	Christmas Eve at the Farmhouse	Closed	1985	19.50	25
1986	Silent Night, Holy Night	Closed	1986	19.50	30
1987	The Snowman's Christmas Eve	Closed	1987	22.50	25
1988	In the King's Garden	Closed	1988	25.00	25
1989	Christmas Anchorage	Closed	1989	27.00	32
1990	Changing of the Guards	Closed	1990	32.50	35
1991	Copenhagen Stock Exchange	Closed	1991	34.50	35
1992	Christmas at the Rectory - J. Steensen	Closed	1992	36.50	39
1993	Father Christmas in Copenhagen - J. Nielsen	Closed	1993	36.50	39
1994	A Day at the Deer Park - J. Nielsen	Closed	1994	36.50	39
1995	The Towers of Copenhagen - J. Nielsen	Closed	1995	37.50	42
1996	Winter at the Old Mill - J. Nielsen	Closed	1996	37.50	42
1997	Country Christmas - J. Nielsen	Yr.Iss.		37.50	42

Christmas In America - J. Woodson

YEAR ISSUE		EDITION LIMIT	YEAR RETD.	ISSUE PRICE	*QUOTE U.S. $
1986	Christmas Eve in Williamsburg	Closed	1986	12.50	75-100
1987	Christmas Eve at the White House	Closed	1987	15.00	40-60
1988	Christmas Eve at Rockefeller Center	Closed	1988	18.50	30
1989	Christmas in New England	Closed	1989	20.00	25
1990	Christmas Eve at the Capitol	Closed	1990	20.00	30
1991	Independence Hall	Closed	1991	23.50	30
1992	Christmas in San Francisco	Closed	1992	25.00	35
1993	Coming Home For Christmas	Closed	1993	25.00	35
1994	Christmas Eve in Alaska	Closed	1994	25.00	35
1995	Christmas Eve in Mississippi	Closed	1995	25.00	35

Santa Around the World - H. Hansen

YEAR ISSUE		EDITION LIMIT	YEAR RETD.	ISSUE PRICE	*QUOTE U.S. $
1995	Santa in Greenland	Yr.Iss.	1995	25.00	30
1996	Santa in Orient	Yr.Iss.	1996	25.00	30
1997	Santa in Russia	Yr.Iss.		25.00	25

Santa Claus - Unknown

YEAR ISSUE		EDITION LIMIT	YEAR RETD.	ISSUE PRICE	*QUOTE U.S. $
1989	Santa's Workshop	Yr.Iss.	1989	20.00	60
1990	Santa's Sleigh	Yr.Iss.	1990	20.00	60
1991	The Journey	Yr.Iss.	1991	24.00	45
1992	Santa's Arrival	Yr.Iss.	1992	25.00	48
1993	Santa's Gifts	Yr.Iss.	1993	25.00	48
1994	Christmas Stories	Yr.Iss.	1994	25.00	35

Boyds Collection Ltd.

The Bearstone Collection™ - G. M. Lowenthal

YEAR ISSUE		EDITION LIMIT	YEAR RETD.	ISSUE PRICE	*QUOTE U.S. $
1994	'Charity'-Angel Bear with Star 2502	Retrd.	1996	9.45	10
1994	'Faith'-Angel Bear w/ Trumpet 2500	Retrd.	1996	9.45	10
1994	'Hope'-Angel Bear w/ Wreath 2501	Retrd.	1996	9.45	10
1995	'Edmund'...Believe 2505	Open		9.45	10
1995	'Elliot with Tree' 2507	Open		9.45	10
1995	'Manheim' the Moose with Wreath 2506	Open		9.45	10

The Folkstone Collection™ - G.M. Lowenthal

YEAR ISSUE		EDITION LIMIT	YEAR RETD.	ISSUE PRICE	*QUOTE U.S. $
1995	Father Christmas 2553	Open		9.45	10
1995	Jean Claude & Jacque...the Skiers 2561	Open		9.45	10
1995	Jingles the Snowman with Wreath 2562	Open		9.45	10
1995	Nicholai with Tree 2550	Open		9.45	10
1995	Nicholas the Giftgiver 2551	Open		9.45	10
1995	Olaf...Let it Snow 2560	Open		9.45	10
1995	Sliknick in the Chimney 2552	Open		9.45	10

Brandywine Collectibles

Custom Collection - M. Whiting

YEAR ISSUE		EDITION LIMIT	YEAR RETD.	ISSUE PRICE	*QUOTE U.S. $
1989	Lorain Lighthouse	Closed	1992	9.00	9
1994	Smithfield Clerk's Office	Closed	1995	9.00	9
1991	Smithfield VA. Courthouse	Closed	1992	9.00	9

Williamsburg Ornaments - M. Whiting

YEAR ISSUE		EDITION LIMIT	YEAR RETD.	ISSUE PRICE	*QUOTE U.S. $
1988	Apothocary	Closed	1991	9.00	9
1988	Bootmaker	Closed	1991	9.00	9
1989	Cole Shop	Closed	1991	9.00	9
1988	Finnie Quarter	Closed	1991	9.00	9
1989	Gunsmith	Closed	1991	9.00	9
1994	Gunsmith	360	1994	9.50	10
1989	Music Teacher	Closed	1991	9.00	9
1988	Nicolson Shop	Closed	1991	9.00	9
1988	Tarpley's Store	Closed	1991	9.00	9
1988	Wigmaker	Closed	1991	9.00	9
1989	Windmill	Closed	1991	9.00	9

Calabar Creations

Angelic Pigasus - P. Apsit

YEAR ISSUE		EDITION LIMIT	YEAR RETD.	ISSUE PRICE	*QUOTE U.S. $
1995	Adagio AP75361	Open		5.00	5
1995	Alba AP75351	Open		5.00	5
1995	Ambrose AP75372	Open		5.00	5
1995	Andante AP75381	Open		5.00	5
1995	Angelica AP75312	Open		5.00	5
1995	Anna AP75321	Open		5.00	5
1995	Aria AP75341	Open		5.00	5

Carlton Cards

Heirloom Collection Collector's Club - Carlton

YEAR ISSUE		EDITION LIMIT	YEAR RETD.	ISSUE PRICE	*QUOTE U.S. $
1997	Ho-Ho-Hold On! CXOR201W	Yr.Iss.		Gift	N/A
1997	Heavenly Handiwork CXOR202W	Yr.Iss.		14.95	15

Premier Event Ornaments - Carlton

YEAR ISSUE		EDITION LIMIT	YEAR RETD.	ISSUE PRICE	*QUOTE U.S. $
1996	Stirring Up Some Christmas Magic CXOR-500T	Closed	1996	9.95	10
1997	Carousel Dreams CXOR-174W	Yr.Iss.		9.95	10

1988 Summit Heirloom Collection - Carlton

YEAR ISSUE		EDITION LIMIT	YEAR RETD.	ISSUE PRICE	*QUOTE U.S. $
1988	1st Christmas Together 053-047-6	Closed	1988	4.50	5
1988	Animals 053-049-2	Closed	1988	4.50	5
1988	Baby's First Christmas 053-026-3	Closed	1988	5.00	5
1988	Bundles of Joy 053-041-7	Closed	1989	11.00	11
1988	Carousel Magic 053-023-9	Closed	1988	8.00	48-58
1988	Christmas Charmer 053-038-7	Closed	1988	7.50	8
1988	Christmas Confection 053-044-1	Closed	1988	7.00	7
1988	Christmas Dreams 053-012-3	Closed	1988	12.00	12
1988	Christmas Magic 053-022-0	Closed	1988	8.00	8
1988	Christmas Wishes 053-060-3	Closed	1988	4.50	5
1988	Country Cheer 053-919-8	Closed	1988	7.50	38-45
1988	Cozy Kitten 053-053-0	Closed	1988	10.00	10
1988	Cuddly Christmas (A Good Roommate) 053-055-7	Closed	1988	6.50	60
1988	Favorite Things 053-039-5	Closed	1991	10.00	10
1988	Fluffy 053-017-4	Closed	1988	4.50	5
1988	Forever Friends 053-016-6	Closed	1989	9.50	10
1988	Friends Forever 053-032-8	Closed	1988	5.50	6
1988	Giddyap Teddy! 053-019-0	Closed	1988	9.50	10
1988	Grandma Twinkle 053-030-1	Closed	1988	N/A	N/A
1988	Happy Holly Days 053-054-9	Closed	1988	8.00	8
1988	Havin' Fun 053-037-9	Closed	1988	6.50	125-200
1988	Home, Sweet Home 053-015-8	Closed	1988	N/A	N/A
1988	Just Us 053-029-8	Closed	1988	9.50	10
1988	Kiss-Moose 053-025-5	Closed	1996	5.50	6
1988	Little One 053-027-1	Closed	1989	9.50	10
1988	Manger 053-051-4	Closed	1988	5.00	10-15
1988	Merry Christmas Grandson 053-046-8	Closed	1988	7.50	8
1988	Merry Heartwarming 053-048-4	Closed	1988	N/A	N/A
1988	O Holy Night 053-057-3	Closed	1989	9.50	10
1988	Old-Time Santa 053-040-9	Closed	1988	8.50	75
1988	Perky Penguin 053-058-1	Closed	1988	6.50	28
1988	Ring in Christmas 053-020-4	Closed	1988	6.00	6
1988	Roses 053-049-2	Closed	1988	4.50	5
1988	Song of Christmas 053-034-4	Closed	1988	4.50	5
1988	Special Delivery (dated) 053-018-2	Closed	1989	11.00	35
1988	Star of Wonder 053-024-7	Closed	1988	N/A	N/A
1988	The Sweetest Angel 053-043-3	Closed	1988	6.00	6
1988	Teacher's Treat 053-021-2	Closed	1988	5.50	6
1988	Winter Friend 053-056-5	Closed	1989	4.00	24
1988	Wonderland Waltz 053-013-1	Closed	1988	12.00	12
1988	Wood Decoy 053-036-0	Closed	1988	N/A	N/A

1989 Summit/Carlton Heirloom Collection - Carlton

YEAR ISSUE		EDITION LIMIT	YEAR RETD.	ISSUE PRICE	*QUOTE U.S. $
1989	Arctic Antics 058-131-3	Closed	1989	5.50	6
1989	Best Friends 058-109-7	Closed	1989	9.50	10
1989	Bundles of Joy 058-104-6	Closed	1989	11.00	11
1989	Christmas Charmer 058-094-5	Closed	1989	6.50	7
1989	Christmas Confection 058-105-4	Closed	1989	6.50	7
1989	Christmas Dreams 058-096-1	Closed	1989	12.00	12
1989	Christmas Fantasy 058-119-4	Closed	1989	5.00	5
1989	Country Christmas 058-127-5	Closed	1989	5.00	5
1989	A Daughter Is A Joy 058-128-3	Closed	1989	5.00	5
1989	Forever Friends 053-041-7	Closed	1989	9.50	10
1989	Gentle Hearts 058-118-6	Closed	1989	6.50	7
1989	Giddyap Teddy! 058-093-7	Closed	1989	9.50	10
1989	A Gift From Heaven 058-111-9	Closed	1989	8.50	9
1989	Golden Snowflake 058-137-2	Closed	1989	5.00	5
1989	Havin' Fun 058-092-9	Closed	1989	6.50	7
1989	Hello Moon! 058-103-8	Closed	1989	7.50	8
1989	Here Comes Santa! 058-099-6	Closed	1990	7.50	8
1989	Home, Tweet, Home 058-112-7	Closed	1989	9.50	10
1989	Honey Love 058-117-8	Closed	1989	6.50	7
1989	In the Workshop 058-100-3	Closed	1990	11.00	11
1989	Jolly Holiday Bell 058-136-4	Closed	1989	6.50	7
1989	Joy To The World 058-138-0	Closed	1989	7.50	8
1989	Just Us 058-091-0	Closed	1989	9.50	10
1989	Kiss-Moose 058-107-0	Closed	1989	5.50	6
1989	Little Frostee 058-115-1	Closed	1989	8.50	9
1989	Little One 058-098-8	Closed	1989	9.50	10
1989	A Little Shepherd 058-130-5	Closed	1989	5.00	5
1989	Merrie Old Christmas 058-135-6	Closed	1989	5.50	6
1989	Merry Old Santa Claus 053-035-2	Closed	1992	12.00	45
1989	Pa-Rum-Pa-Pum-Pum 058-113-5	Closed	1989	9.50	10
1989	Perky Penguin 058-121-6	Closed	1989	6.50	7
1989	Ring In The Holidays 058-134-9	Closed	1989	7.50	8
1989	School Days 058-125-9	Closed	1989	7.50	8
1989	A Season of Fun 058-108-9	Closed	1989	7.50	8
1989	Season Of Love 058-126-7	Closed	1989	5.00	5
1989	A Sister Is A Friend 058-129-1	Closed	1989	5.00	5
1989	Special Delivery 058-090-2	Closed	1989	11.00	11
1989	To A Special Mom 058-132-1	Closed	1989	7.50	8
1989	Wonderland Waltz 058-095-3	Closed	1989	12.00	12

*Quotes have been rounded up to nearest dollar

1990 Summit/Carlton Collector's Series - Carlton

YEAR ISSUE		EDITION LIMIT	YEAR RETD.	ISSUE PRICE	*QUOTE U.S.$
1990	Christmas Express 102-355-1	Closed	1990	12.00	12
1990	Christmas Go-Round 102-346-2	Closed	1990	13.00	13
1990	Christmas Hello 102-352-7	Closed	1990	13.00	13
1990	A Little Bit Of Christmas 102-340-3	Closed	1990	10.50	11
1990	Santa's Roommate 102-361-6	Closed	1990	7.50	8

1990 Summit/Carlton Heirloom Collection - Carlton

YEAR ISSUE		EDITION LIMIT	YEAR RETD.	ISSUE PRICE	*QUOTE U.S.$
1990	Beary Christmas 102-375-6	Closed	1990	7.50	8
1990	Best Friends 102-376-4	Closed	1990	9.50	10
1990	Bunny Love 102-359-4	Closed	1991	9.50	11
1990	Checkin' It Twice 102-323-4	Closed	1991	12.00	12
1990	Christmas Angel 102-331-4	Closed	1990	7.50	8
1990	Christmas At Heart 102-322-5	Closed	1990	12.00	12
1990	Christmas Blessings 102-353-5	Closed	1991	8.00	8
1990	Christmas Caring 102-338-1	Closed	1990	8.00	8
1990	Christmas Confection 102-337-3	Closed	1990	7.00	7
1990	Christmas Dreams 102-363-2	Closed	1990	12.00	12
1990	Christmas Flight 102-329-2	Closed	1990	6.00	6
1990	Christmas Is Special 102-313-6	Closed	1990	6.50	7
1990	Christmas Means Togetherness 102-369-1	Closed	1990	8.50	9
1990	Christmas Memories 102-347-0	Closed	1990	5.25	6
1990	A Christmas Shared 102-354-3	Closed	1991	10.50	11
1990	Christmas Surprise 102-312-8	Closed	1990	7.50	8
1990	Christmas Whirl 102-378-9	Closed	1990	11.00	11
1990	Cool Yule 102-310-1	Closed	1990	9.50	10
1990	Country Friend 102-326-8	Closed	1990	7.00	7
1990	Cozy Kitten 102-341-1	Closed	1990	10.50	11
1990	Crystal Thoughts 102-335-7	Closed	1990	6.50	7
1990	Favorite Things 102-344-6	Closed	1991	11.00	11
1990	Friendship Is A Gift 102-377-2	Closed	1990	5.50	6
1990	Gentle Hearts 102-330-6	Closed	1990	7.00	7
1990	Giddyap Teddy! 102-364-0	Closed	1990	9.50	10
1990	Giddyap Teddy! 102-365-9	Closed	1990	9.50	10
1990	A Gift From Heaven 102-368-3	Closed	1990	7.50	8
1990	Gifts 'N' Good Wishes 102-345-4	Closed	1990	10.50	11
1990	A Grandmother Is Special 102-382-9	Closed	1990	5.50	6
1990	Grandparents Are Always 102-383-7	Closed	1990	5.25	6
1990	Heavenly Flight 102-358-6	Closed	1990	7.50	8
1990	Hi-Ho Holidays 102-321-7	Closed	1990	9.50	10
1990	A Holiday Hi 102-360-8	Closed	1990	10.00	10
1990	Holiday Magic 102-328-4	Closed	1990	6.50	7
1990	Holiday Purr-fection 102-323-3	Closed	1990	6.50	7
1990	Home For The Holidays 102-357-8	Closed	1990	10.50	11
1990	Home, Tweet, Home 102-374-8	Closed	1990	9.50	10
1990	In The Workshop 102-343-8	Closed	1990	13.00	13
1990	Just Us 102-371-3	Closed	1990	9.50	10
1990	Little Frostee 102-379-9	Closed	1990	8.00	8
1990	Little One 102-367-5	Closed	1990	10.50	11
1990	Love is A Gift 102-320-9	Closed	1990	7.50	8
1990	Merry Little Christmas 102-380-2	Closed	1990	11.00	11
1990	Merry Magic 102-324-1	Closed	1990	6.00	6
1990	A Mother Is Love 102-381-0	Closed	1990	7.50	8
1990	Not A Creature Was Stirring 102-348-9	Closed	1992	13.00	13
1990	The Nutcracker 102-327-6	Closed	1990	9.00	9
1990	Pa-Rum-Pa-Pum-Pum 102-366-7	Closed	1990	9.50	10
1990	Pandabelle 102-386-1	Closed	1990	7.50	8
1990	Peace, Hope, Love 102-333-0	Closed	1990	5.25	6
1990	Perky Penguin 102-332-2	Closed	1990	6.50	7
1990	Remembering Christmas 102-384-5	Closed	1990	9.00	9
1990	Rocking Horse Fun 102-316-0	Closed	1990	10.50	11
1990	Sing A Song Of Christmas 102-336-5	Closed	1990	6.00	6
1990	Sound Of Christmas 102-317-9	Closed	1990	7.00	7
1990	Special Christmas Moments 102-385-3	Closed	1990	8.50	9
1990	A Special Gift Photo Holder 102-314-4	Closed	1990	7.50	8
1990	The Stockings Were Hung 102-349-7	Closed	1990	8.00	8
1990	Thoughts Of Christmas 102-334-9	Closed	1990	5.25	6
1990	Together Forever 102-372-1	Closed	1990	11.00	11
1990	Up On The Roof Top 102-309-8	Closed	1990	11.00	11
1990	Up, Up, Away 102-350-0	Closed	1990	10.00	10
1990	Visions Of Sugar Plums 102-351-9	Closed	1996	9.50	10
1990	Winter Filigree 102-315-2	Closed	1990	6.50	7
1990	Wonderland Waltz 102-370-5	Closed	1990	13.00	13
1990	Wrapped Up In Christmas 102-318-7	Closed	1990	10.00	10
1990	Ziggy 102-319-5	Closed	1990	5.25	6

1991 Carlton Collector's Series - Carlton

YEAR ISSUE		EDITION LIMIT	YEAR RETD.	ISSUE PRICE	*QUOTE U.S.$
1991	Christmas Express 114-826-5	Closed	1991	14.00	14
1991	Christmas Express 114-857-3	Closed	1991	14.00	14
1991	Christmas Go-Round 114-830-3	Closed	1991	14.00	25
1991	A Little Bit Of Christmas 114-831-1	Closed	1991	11.00	11
1991	Santa's Roommate 114-828-1	Closed	1991	8.00	8

1991 Carlton Heirloom Collection - Carlton

YEAR ISSUE		EDITION LIMIT	YEAR RETD.	ISSUE PRICE	*QUOTE U.S.$
1991	And Away We Go 114-879-6	Closed	1992	9.00	9
1991	Bunny Love 114-836-2	Closed	1992	10.00	10
1991	Catch The Christmas Spirit 114-856-7	Closed	1992	8.50	9
1991	Checkin' It Twice 114-844-3	Closed	1991	12.00	12
1991	Christmas Blessing 114-842-7	Closed	1991	8.50	9
1991	Christmas By The Heartful 114-857-5	Closed	1991	9.00	9
1991	Christmas Caring 114-852-4	Closed	1991	8.00	8
1991	Christmas Charmer 114-804-4	Closed	1991	11.00	11
1991	Christmas Couple 114-861-3	Closed	1991	13.00	13
1991	Christmas Cuddles 114-817-6	Closed	1991	10.50	11
1991	Christmas Cutie 114-811-7	Closed	1991	10.00	10
1991	Christmas Darlings 114-806-0	Closed	1991	12.00	12
1991	Christmas Dreams 114-807-9	Closed	1991	13.00	13
1991	Christmas Fantasy 114-872-9	Closed	1991	11.00	11
1991	Christmas Greetings	Closed	1991	10.00	10
1991	Christmas Is In The Air 114-878-8	Closed	1992	11.00	11
1991	A Christmas Shared 114-841-9	Closed	1991	10.50	11
1991	Christmas Sweetie 114-855-9	Closed	1991	9.50	10
1991	A Christmas To Remember 114-822-2	Closed	1991	9.00	9
1991	Christmas Wishes 114-869-9	Closed	1992	14.00	14
1991	Christmastime For Two 114-816-8	Closed	1991	14.00	14
1991	Elfkin 114-870-2	Closed	1992	9.50	10
1991	Favorite Things 114-837-0	Closed	1991	12.00	12
1991	Friends At Heart 114-825-7	Closed	1991	8.00	8
1991	Frosty Friend 114-835-4	Closed	1991	8.50	9
1991	Gentle Hearts 114-866-4	Closed	1991	11.00	11
1991	A Gift From Heaven 114-805-2	Closed	1991	8.00	8
1991	God Bless Us All! 114-858-3	Closed	1992	10.00	10
1991	Happiness Is All Around! 114-876-1	Closed	1992	9.00	9
1991	Happy Christmas To All 114-840-0	Closed	1991	8.50	9
1991	Happy Holidays 114-818-4	Closed	1991	8.00	8
1991	Heavenly Flight 114-853-2	Closed	1991	8.00	8
1991	Here Comes Santa! 114-845-1	Closed	1991	9.00	9
1991	Holiday Beauty 114-860-5	Closed	1991	9.00	9
1991	Holiday Fun 114-867-2	Closed	1991	9.50	10
1991	Holiday Hobby Horse 114-812-5	Closed	1991	10.50	11
1991	Holiday Memories 114-808-7	Closed	1991	9.50	10
1991	Holiday Treat 114-881-8	Closed	1992	10.00	10
1991	Hollie Hobbie Christmas At Heart 114-838-9	Closed	1991	12.00	12
1991	Home For Christmas 114-884-2	Closed	1991	9.50	10
1991	Home For The Holidays 114-839-9	Closed	1991	10.50	11
1991	In The Workshop 114-847-8	Closed	1991	13.00	13
1991	A Jolly Old Elf 114-859-1	Closed	1991	10.00	10
1991	Just Us 114-813-3	Closed	1991	11.00	11
1991	Little Christmas Wishes 114-810-9	Closed	1991	11.00	11
1991	Little Drummer Bear 114-864-8	Closed	1991	9.50	10
1991	Little Starlight 114-868-0	Closed	1991	11.00	11
1991	A Little Taste Of Christmas 114-862-1	Closed	1991	13.00	13
1991	Love Is All Around 114-823-0	Closed	1991	11.00	11
1991	A Mother Is Love 114-819-2	Closed	1991	11.00	11
1991	North Pole Parade 114-874-5	Closed	1991	14.00	14
1991	Not A Creature Was Stirring 114-850-8	Closed	1991	14.00	14
1991	Purr-fect Holidays 114-871-0	Closed	1991	11.00	11
1991	Reindeer Games 114-865-6	Closed	1991	10.00	10
1991	Ring In the Holidays 114-821-4	Closed	1991	10.00	10
1991	Rocking Horse Fun 114-848-6	Closed	1991	11.00	11
1991	Sing A Song Of Christmas 114-873-7	Closed	1991	12.00	12
1991	Small Surprises 114-809-5	Closed	1991	10.50	11
1991	Snowflake Friends 114-824-9	Closed	1991	11.00	11
1991	A Special Gift 114-820-6	Closed	1991	9.00	9
1991	A Special Photo Holder 114-834-6	Closed	1991	9.00	9
1991	Stocking Full Of Love 114-854-0	Closed	1991	9.00	9
1991	There Is A Santa! 114-833-8	Closed	1991	14.00	14
1991	Together Forever 114-814-1	Closed	1991	12.00	12
1991	Up On The Roof Top 114-843-5	Closed	1991	11.00	11
1991	Visions Of Sugar Plums 114-849-4	Closed	1992	9.50	10
1991	The Wonder Of Christmas 114-875-3	Closed	1992	9.00	9

1992 Carlton Collector's Series - Carlton

YEAR ISSUE		EDITION LIMIT	YEAR RETD.	ISSUE PRICE	*QUOTE U.S.$
1992	Christmas Express Caboose (2nd) 120539-0	Closed	1993	15.00	15
1992	Christmas Express Coal Tender (3rd) 120478-5	Closed	1992	15.00	15
1992	Christmas Express Engine (1st) 120477-7	Closed	1992	15.00	15
1992	Christmas Go-Round (3rd) 120479-3	Closed	1992	14.00	14
1992	Christmas Sweets (1st) 120486-6	Closed	1992	11.00	20
1992	Ice Pals (1st) 120483-1	Closed	1992	10.00	10
1992	A Little Bit of Christmas (3rd) 120481-5	Closed	1992	13.00	13
1992	North Pole Parade (1st) 120482-3	Closed	1992	14.00	14
1992	Rodrick & Sam's Winter Fun (1st) 120485-8	Closed	1992	13.00	13

1992 Carlton Heirloom Collection - Carlton

YEAR ISSUE		EDITION LIMIT	YEAR RETD.	ISSUE PRICE	*QUOTE U.S.$
1992	Alpine Adventure 120469-6	Closed	1992	11.00	11
1992	Bundles of Joy 120509-9	Closed	1992	14.00	14
1992	Bunny Love 120519-6	Closed	1992	11.00	11
1992	Catch The Christmas Spirit 120522-6	Closed	1992	8.50	9
1992	Cherished Memories 120457-2	Closed	1992	11.00	11
1992	A Child's Christmas 120532-3	Closed	1992	11.00	11
1992	A Child's Christmas 120533-1	Closed	1992	11.00	11
1992	Christmas Blessing 120513-7	Closed	1992	9.50	10
1992	Christmas Charmer 120441-6	Closed	1992	11.00	11
1992	Christmas Couple 120511-0	Closed	1992	14.00	14
1992	Christmas Cuddles 120461-0	Closed	1992	11.00	11
1992	Christmas Fantasy 120524-2	Closed	1992	11.00	11
1992	The Christmas Star 120527-7	Closed	1992	9.50	10
1992	Christmas Swingtime 120505-6	Closed	1992	10.00	10
1992	A Christmas to Remember 120538-2	Closed	1992	12.00	12
1992	Christmas Twirl 120455-6	Closed	1992	14.00	14
1992	Christmas Warmth 120452-1	Closed	1992	9.00	9
1992	Christmas Whirl 120448-3	Closed	1992	12.00	12
1992	Christmas Wishes 120516-1	Closed	1992	14.00	14
1992	Circle of Love 120439-4	Closed	1992	11.00	11
1992	Cuddly Christmas 120445-9	Closed	1992	10.00	10
1992	Curious Cutie 11.00	Closed	1992	11.00	11
1992	Elfkin 120497-1	Closed	1992	10.00	10
1992	Family Ties 120459-9	Closed	1992	10.00	10
1992	Frosted Fantasy 120502-1	Closed	1992	9.00	9
1992	Frosty Fun 120440-8	Closed	1992	12.00	12
1992	Giddyap, Teddy!	Closed	1992	11.00	11
1992	A Gift From The Heart 120530-7	Closed	1993	9.50	10
1992	Ginger 120476-9	Closed	1992	9.50	10
1992	Happiness Is All Around 120518-8	Closed	1992	9.00	9
1992	Heart Full of Christmas 120446-7	Closed	1992	10.00	10
1992	Heart Full of Love 120463-7	Closed	1992	13.00	13
1992	Heart to Heart 120454-8	Closed	1992	11.00	11
1992	Heartfelt Christmas 120471-8	Closed	1992	10.00	10
1992	Heartwarming Holidays 120528-5	Closed	1992	9.00	9
1992	Heaven Sent 120535-8	Closed	1992	9.50	10
1992	High-Flying Holiday 11.00	Closed	1992	11.00	11
1992	Holiday Harmony 120490-4	Closed	1992	13.00	13
1992	Holiday Heirloom 120450-5	Closed	1992	11.00	11
1992	Holiday Helpers 120491-2	Closed	1992	13.00	13
1992	A Holiday Hi 120525-0	Closed	1992	11.00	11
1992	Holiday Treat 120523-4	Closed	1992	11.00	11
1992	Home, Tweet Home 120468-8	Closed	1992	10.00	10
1992	Honey Bunny Christmas 120494-7	Closed	1992	12.00	12
1992	Jolly Holidays 120456-4	Closed	1992	12.00	12
1992	Joy 120474-2	Closed	1992	9.50	10
1992	Just Us 120460-2	Closed	1992	11.00	11
1992	Kitty Caper 120493-9	Closed	1992	11.00	11
1992	Little Starlight 120537-4	Closed	1992	12.00	12
1992	Made With Love 15.00	Closed	1992	15.00	15
1992	Magic of Christmas 120451-3	Closed	1992	12.00	12
1992	Merry Christmas to All 120506-4	Closed	1992	8.50	9
1992	Merry Marionettes 120487-4	Closed	1992	15.00	15
1992	Noelle 120475-0	Closed	1992	9.50	10
1992	North Pole Putter 120473-4	Closed	1992	11.00	11
1992	Not A Creature Was Stirring	Closed	1992	14.00	14
1992	Picture Perfect 120529-3	Closed	1992	8.50	9
1992	Polar Pals 120512-9	Closed	1992	11.00	11
1992	Pom Pom The Clown 120531-5	Closed	1992	9.50	10
1992	Precious Heart 120444-0	Closed	1992	10.00	10
1992	Purr-fect Holidays 120507-2	Closed	1992	11.00	11
1992	Ringing In Christmas 120536-6	Closed	1992	12.00	12
1992	Rock-A-Bye Baby 120442-4	Closed	1992	13.00	13
1992	Rocking Horse Fun 120504-8	Closed	1992	11.00	11
1992	Santa's Helpers 120495-5	Closed	1992	15.00	15
1992	Santa's Roommate (3rd) 120480-7	Closed	1992	9.00	9
1992	Santa's Surprises 120449-1	Closed	1992	11.00	11
1992	School Days 120472-6	Closed	1992	10.00	10
1992	The Season of Love 120464-5	Closed	1992	9.00	9
1992	A Silver Celebration 120466-1	Closed	1992	10.00	10
1992	Special Surprise 120489-0	Closed	1992	12.00	12
1992	Spirit of St. Nick 120458-0	Closed	1992	10.00	10
1992	Stocking Full of Love 120508-0	Closed	1992	9.00	9
1992	Times to Treasure 120465-3	Closed	1992	9.00	9
1992	Tiny Toy Shop 15.00	Closed	1992	15.00	15
1992	Together Forever 120462-9	Closed	1992	12.00	12
1992	Visions of Sugar Plums 10.00	Closed	1994	10.00	10
1992	Warmhearted Holidays 120526-9	Closed	1992	9.50	10
1992	Winter Funtime 120501-3	Closed	1992	11.00	11
1992	The Wonder of Christmas 120510-2	Closed	1992	10.00	10

1993 Carlton Collector's Series - Carlton

YEAR ISSUE		EDITION LIMIT	YEAR RETD.	ISSUE PRICE	*QUOTE U.S.$
1993	Book of Carols (1st) 126005-7	Closed	1993	13.50	14
1993	Christmas Express Caboose (2nd) 126037-5	Closed	1993	15.00	15
1993	Christmas Express Coal Tender Car (3rd) 126038-3	Closed	1993	15.00	15
1993	Christmas Express Engine (1st) 126036-7	Closed	1993	15.00	15
1993	Christmas Express Reindeer Coach (4th) 126010-3	Closed	1993	15.00	15
1993	Christmas Sweets (2nd) 126035-9	Closed	1993	12.00	12
1993	Christmas-Go-Round (4th) 126013-8	Closed	1993	14.00	14
1993	Ice Pals (2nd) 126006-5	Closed	1993	10.50	11
1993	A Little Bit of Christmas 126007-3	Closed	1993	13.00	13
1993	North Pole Parade (2nd) 126011-1	Closed	1993	14.00	14
1993	Rodrick & Sam's Winter Fun (2nd) 126008-1	Closed	1993	13.00	13
1993	Santa's Roommate (4th) 126039-1	Closed	1993	9.00	9
1993	Santa's Wheels 125986-5	Closed	1993	10.00	10
1993	Sewing Circle Sweetie 126102-9	Closed	1993	12.50	13
1993	Special Surprise 126084-7	Closed	1993	13.00	13
1993	Tiny Toymaker (1st) 126034-0	Closed	1993	12.50	13

1993 Carlton Heirloom Collection - Carlton

YEAR ISSUE		EDITION LIMIT	YEAR RETD.	ISSUE PRICE	*QUOTE U.S.$
1993	10 Yrs. Together Christmas Bell 126002-0	Closed	1993	11.00	11
1993	25 Yrs. Together Christmas Bell 126003-0	Closed	1993	11.00	11
1993	5 Yrs. Together Christmas Bell 126001-4	Closed	1993	11.00	11
1993	Airmail Delivery 126069-3	Closed	1993	12.50	13
1993	All Decked Out 126015-4	Closed	1993	12.50	13
1993	And Away We Go 126073-1	Closed	1993	12.00	12
1993	Baby Kermit's Sleighride 125968-7	Closed	1993	10.50	11
1993	Baby Magic 125981-4	Closed	1993	11.00	11
1993	Baby Miss Piggy's Christmas Star 125966-0	Closed	1993	10.50	11
1993	Beary Merry Balloon 125971-7	Closed	1993	10.00	10
1993	A Beary Snowy Day 126053-7	Closed	1993	18.00	18

*Quotes have been rounded up to nearest dollar

YEAR ISSUE		EDITION LIMIT	YEAR RETD.	ISSUE PRICE	*QUOTE U.S.$
1993	Bundles of Joy 126086-3	Closed	1993	14.50	15
1993	Chef's Delight 126096-0	Closed	1993	11.50	12
1993	Christmas Cuddles 125995-4	Closed	1993	11.00	11
1993	Christmas Fantasy 126094-4	Closed	1993	12.00	12
1993	Christmas Parade 126018-9	Closed	1993	13.00	13
1993	The Christmas Star 126098-7	Closed	1993	9.50	10
1993	Christmas Surprise 125972-5	Closed	1993	10.00	10
1993	Christmas Waltz 126063-4	Closed	1993	16.00	16
1993	Christmas Wishes 126076-6	Closed	1993	14.00	14
1993	Circle of Love 125963-6	Closed	1993	11.00	11
1993	Cozy Moments 125993-8	Closed	1993	11.00	11
1993	Curious Cutie 126070-7	Closed	1993	12.00	12
1993	December 24th Deadline 126059-6	Closed	1993	13.50	14
1993	Do Not Disturb Til Christmas 126044-8	Closed	1993	11.50	12
1993	Festive Lace 125998-5	Closed	1993	8.50	9
1993	Frosty and Friend 125999-7	Closed	1993	10.50	11
1993	A Gift From the Heart 126090-1	Closed	1993	9.50	10
1993	Ginger 126029-4	Closed	1993	10.00	10
1993	Gingerbread Treat 126042-1	Closed	1993	10.50	11
1993	Good Catch! 126040-5	Closed	1993	10.00	10
1993	Happy Home 125991-1	Closed	1993	10.50	11
1993	Heavenly Love 125982-2	Closed	1993	9.50	10
1993	Holiday Harmony 126083-9	Closed	1993	14.00	14
1993	Holiday Helpers 126078-2	Closed	1993	14.00	14
1993	A Holiday Hi 126087-1	Closed	1993	12.00	12
1993	Holiday Treat 126089-8	Closed	1993	12.00	12
1993	Holly Hippo 126101-0	Closed	1993	11.50	12
1993	Home For Christmas 125990-3	Closed	1993	10.00	10
1993	Homemade Happiness 126064-2	Closed	1993	12.50	13
1993	Honeybunny Christmas 126085-5	Closed	1993	12.50	13
1993	Hooked A Good One 126004-9	Closed	1993	11.50	12
1993	It's A Small World 126052-9	Closed	1993	16.00	16
1993	Joy 126028-6	Closed	1993	10.00	10
1993	Just A Few Lines 126048-0	Closed	1993	11.00	11
1993	Just Us 125977-0	Closed	1993	12.00	12
1993	Kermit's Christmas 126032-4	Closed	1993	12.00	12
1993	Kitty Caper 126081-2	Closed	1993	11.00	11
1993	Letter To Santa 126045-6	Closed	1993	12.00	12
1993	Li'l Artist 126056-1	Closed	1993	11.50	12
1993	Li'l Chimney Sweep 126100-2	Closed	1993	11.00	11
1993	Li'l Feathered Friend 126020-0	Closed	1993	8.00	8
1993	Love Birds 125996-2	Closed	1993	13.00	13
1993	Loving Wishes 125987-3	Closed	1993	11.00	11
1993	Made With Love 127072-3	Closed	1993	15.00	15
1993	Magic of the Season 126097-9	Closed	1996	11.50	12
1993	Making Music 126058-8	Closed	1993	11.50	12
1993	Memories to Keep 125985-7	Closed	1993	10.00	10
1993	Merry Marionettes 126095-2	Closed	1993	15.00	15
1993	Miss Piggy's Waltz 126031-6	Closed	1993	12.00	12
1993	A Muppet Christmas 126033-2	Closed	1993	6.50	7
1993	Next Stop, North Pole 125984-9	Closed	1993	11.00	11
1993	Noelle 126030-8	Closed	1993	10.00	10
1993	North Pole Putter 126082-8	Closed	1993	12.00	12
1993	On Top of The Whirl 126067-7	Closed	1993	14.50	15
1993	One Last Touch! 126051-0	Closed	1993	14.00	14
1993	Peppermint Panda 126079-0	Closed	1993	9.50	10
1993	Peppermint Waltz 126047-2	Closed	1993	11.50	12
1993	The Perfect Package 126065-0	Closed	1993	14.00	14
1993	Polar Pals 126093-6	Closed	1993	12.50	13
1993	Pom Pom 126105-3	Closed	1993	10.00	10
1993	Pop-Up Fun! 125964-4	Closed	1993	11.00	11
1993	Precious Heart 125970-9	Closed	1993	10.00	10
1993	Pretty Bubbler 126050-2	Closed	1993	13.00	13
1993	Purr-fect Holidays 126016-2	Closed	1993	12.00	12
1993	Rocking Horse Fun 126017-0	Closed	1993	12.00	12
1993	Santa's Boy 125969-5	Closed	1993	13.00	13
1993	Santa's Helpers 126080-4	Closed	1993	15.00	15
1993	Stocking Full of Love 126082-0	Closed	1993	9.00	9
1993	Sweet Season 125973-3	Closed	1993	10.00	10
1993	Swinging On A Star 126041-3	Closed	1993	10.00	10
1993	Teacher's Pet 126000-6	Closed	1993	7.50	8
1993	Tiny Toyshop 126071-5	Closed	1993	15.00	15
1993	A Token of Love 125983-0	Closed	1993	12.00	12
1993	Trimming The Tree 125988-1	Closed	1993	9.00	9
1993	Two Together 125994-6	Closed	1993	13.50	14
1993	Up on the House Top 126061-8	Closed	1993	17.00	17
1993	Visions of Sugarplums 126075-8	Closed	1994	10.00	10
1993	Waiting For Santa 126066-9	Closed	1994	15.00	15
1993	Wake Me When It's Christmas 126049-9	Closed	1993	13.00	13
1993	Warm 'N Toasty 126054-5	Closed	1993	16.00	16
1993	Warmhearted Holidays 126099-5	Closed	1993	9.50	10
1993	Wee Whatnots 126062-6	Closed	1993	17.50	18
1993	Winter Funtime 126077-4	Closed	1993	11.00	11
1993	Winterland Fun 126055-3	Closed	1993	17.00	17
1993	Wishes On The Way 126068-5	Closed	1993	8.50	9

1994 Carlton Collector's Series - Carlton

YEAR ISSUE		EDITION LIMIT	YEAR RETD.	ISSUE PRICE	*QUOTE U.S.$
1994	Big Fun (1st) ORN001L	Closed	1994	13.50	14
1994	Book Of Carols (2nd) ORN004L	Closed	1994	13.50	14
1994	Christmas Express Caboose (2nd) ORN010L	Closed	1994	15.00	15
1994	Christmas Express Coach (4th) ORN011L	Closed	1994	15.00	15
1994	Christmas Express Engine (1st) ORN009L	Closed	1994	15.00	15
1994	Christmas Express Tanker (5th) ORN012L	Closed	1994	15.00	15
1994	Christmas Go-Round (5th) ORN013L	Closed	1994	15.00	15
1994	Christmas Sweets (3rd) ORN006L	Closed	1994	14.50	15
1994	Ice Pals (3rd) ORN007L	Closed	1994	12.50	13
1994	A Little Bit Of Christmas (5th) ORN014L	Closed	1994	13.50	14
1994	Rodrick & Sam's Winter Fun (3rd) ORN008L	Closed	1994	12.50	13
1994	Santa's Roommate (5th) ORN015L	Closed	1994	10.50	11
1994	Santa's Toy Shop (1st) ORN003L	Closed	1994	17.00	20
1994	Snug In Their Beds (1st) ORN002L	Closed	1994	16.00	16
1994	Tiny Toymaker (2nd) ORN005L	Closed	1994	12.50	13

1994 Carlton Heirloom Collection - Carlton

YEAR ISSUE		EDITION LIMIT	YEAR RETD.	ISSUE PRICE	*QUOTE U.S.$
1994	All Decked Out ORN118L	Closed	1994	12.50	13
1994	Artistic Wishes ORN092L	Closed	1994	14.50	15
1994	Baby's First Christmas ORN022L	Closed	1994	11.50	12
1994	Baby's First Christmas ORN023L	Closed	1994	14.50	15
1994	Baby's First Christmas ORN024L	Closed	1994	13.50	14
1994	Baby's First Christmas ORN025L	Closed	1994	13.50	14
1994	Baby's Second Christmas ORN027L	Closed	1994	10.50	11
1994	A Basketful Of Goodies ORN077L	Closed	1994	10.50	11
1994	Bears On Parade ORN081L	Closed	1995	18.00	18
1994	Beary Merry Wishes ORN075L	Closed	1994	9.50	10
1994	Brother ORN040L	Closed	1994	11.50	12
1994	Bunny Delight ORN112L	Closed	1994	15.00	15
1994	Candy-Gram ORN103L	Closed	1994	8.50	9
1994	Caregiver ORN046L	Closed	1994	11.50	12
1994	Catch The Christmas Spirit ORN116L	Closed	1994	8.50	9
1994	Changin' For Christmas ORN109L	Closed	1994	13.50	14
1994	Chester's Heartfelt Holiday ORN063L	Closed	1994	10.50	11
1995	A Child's Christmas ORN135L	Closed	1994	11.50	12
1994	Child's Fourth Christmas ORN029L	Closed	1994	10.50	11
1994	Child's Third Christmas ORN028L	Closed	1994	10.50	11
1994	Christmas Bell ORN127L	Closed	1994	13.50	14
1994	Christmas By The Heartful ORN021L	Closed	1994	12.50	13
1994	Christmas Catch ORN069L	Closed	1994	11.50	12
1994	Christmas Countdown ORN089L	Closed	1995	14.50	15
1994	Christmas In The Country ORN129L	Closed	1994	8.50	9
1994	Christmas Spin ORN054L	Closed	1994	17.00	17
1994	The Christmas Star ORN076L	Closed	1994	9.50	10
1994	Circle Of Love ORN026L	Closed	1994	11.50	12
1994	Clowning Around ORN090L	Closed	1994	13.50	14
1994	Co-Worker ORN045L	Closed	1994	10.50	11
1994	Dad ORN035L	Closed	1994	12.50	13
1994	Dashing Through The Snow ORN057L	Closed	1994	16.00	16
1994	Daughter N/A	Closed	1994	12.50	13
1994	December 24th Deadline ORN085L	Closed	1994	13.50	14
1994	Downhill Delight ORN070L	Closed	1994	13.50	14
1994	Finishing Touches ORN073L	Closed	1994	12.50	13
1994	First Christmas Together ORN016L	Closed	1994	11.50	12
1994	First Christmas Together ORN017L	Closed	1994	18.00	18
1994	First Christmas Together ORN018L	Closed	1994	13.50	14
1994	Folk Angel ORN132l	Closed	1994	7.50	8
1994	Folk Santa ORN071L	Closed	1994	13.50	14
1994	Friend ORN047L	Closed	1994	9.50	10
1994	Friends Around The World ORN132L	Closed	1994	7.50	8
1994	Gift Exchange ORN078L	Closed	1994	11.50	12
1994	Godchild ORN033L	Closed	1994	10.50	11
1994	Grand-Daughter's First Christmas ORN030L	Closed	1994	11.50	15
1994	Grand-Mother ORN041L	Closed	1994	11.50	12
1994	Grandparents ORN042L	Closed	1994	9.50	10
1994	Grandson's First Christmas ORN031L	Closed	1994	11.50	15
1994	High Flying Fun ORN106L	Closed	1994	12.50	13
1994	High Lights ORN107L	Closed	1994	12.50	13
1994	Holiday Gardner ORN088L	Closed	1994	12.50	13
1994	Holiday Sentiment ORN128L	Closed	1994	11.50	12
1994	Holiday Swing Time ORN108L	Closed	1994	13.50	14
1994	Holiday Time ORN052L	Closed	1995	16.00	16
1994	Homemade Happiness ORN083L	Closed	1994	12.50	13
1994	Hook, Line and Singers ORN067L	Closed	1995	13.50	14
1994	Hoppy Holidays ORN111L	Closed	1994	13.50	14
1994	It's A Small World ORN100L	Closed	1994	16.00	16
1994	Jogging Santa ORN068L	Closed	1995	11.50	12
1994	Juggling Jester ORN050L	Closed	1994	13.50	14
1994	Jumbo Wishes ORN117L	Closed	1994	12.50	13
1994	L'il Artist ORN080L	Closed	1994	11.50	12
1994	Lion & Lamb ORN133L	Closed	1994	13.50	14
1994	Madonna Child ORN131L	Closed	1994	12.50	13
1994	Magic Of The Season ORN124L	Closed	1994	12.50	13
1994	Many Happy Returns ORN061L	Closed	1994	13.50	14
1994	Merry Old Santa ORN074L	Closed	1994	14.50	15
1994	Moo-ey Christmas ORN102L	Closed	1994	8.50	9
1994	Mother ORN034L	Closed	1994	11.50	15
1994	Mouse With Gifts ORN086L	Closed	1994	11.50	12
1994	Music Box Dancers ORN053L	Closed	1994	18.00	18
1994	Nature's Friends ORN125L	Closed	1994	9.50	10
1994	New Home ORN043L	Closed	1994	12.50	13
1994	Noah's Ark ORN134L	Closed	1994	13.50	15
1994	North Pole Pals ORN122L	Closed	1994	14.50	15
1994	O. Opus Tree ORN058L	Closed	1994	12.50	15
1994	Off For A Spin ORN091L	Closed	1994	14.50	15
1994	On Top Of The Whirl ORN097L	Closed	1994	14.50	15
1994	One Last Touch ORN096L	Closed	1994	14.50	15
1994	Our Christmas Together ORN019L	Closed	1994	14.50	15
1994	Our House To Your House ORN044L	Closed	1994	10.50	11
1994	Paddling Pals ORN064L	Closed	1994	11.50	12
1994	Parents ORN036L	Closed	1994	14.50	15
1994	Parents To-Be ORN032L	Closed	1994	11.50	12
1994	Peppermint Waltz ORN119L	Closed	1994	11.50	12
1994	The Perfect Package ORN098L	Closed	1994	14.50	15
1994	Picture Perfect ORN126L	Closed	1994	7.50	8
1994	Playin A Holiday Tune ORN110L	Closed	1995	13.50	14
1994	The Polar Bear Club ORN079L	Closed	1994	13.50	14
1994	Pretty Bubbler ORN084L	Closed	1994	13.50	14
1994	Puffin ORN104L	Closed	1994	11.50	12
1994	Purr-fect Holidays ORN115L	Closed	1994	12.50	13
1994	Rocking Horse Fun ORN123L	Closed	1994	12.50	13
1994	Santa's Hotline ORN114L	Closed	1995	13.50	14
1994	Santa-In-The-Box ORN072L	Closed	1994	15.00	15
1994	Servin' Up Christmas Cheer ORN066L	Closed	1994	10.50	11
1994	Sew Much Love ORN087L	Closed	1994	12.50	13
1994	Sister ORN039L	Closed	1994	10.50	11
1994	SNOWDOME! Winterland Fun ORN113L	Closed	1996	17.00	17
1994	Soccer Star ORN065L	Closed	1995	9.50	10
1994	Son ORN038L	Closed	1994	11.50	12
1994	St. Bernard ORN105L	Closed	1994	8.50	9
1994	Sugar Cone Castle ORN120L	Closed	1994	15.00	15
1994	Surprise! ORN049L	Closed	1994	12.50	13
1994	Sweet Season ORN082L	Closed	1994	10.50	11
1994	Sweetheart ORN020L	Closed	1994	10.50	11
1994	Swinging On A Star ORN094L	Closed	1994	10.50	11
1994	Teacher ORN048L	Closed	1994	7.50	8
1994	Tenderheart Bear ORN062L	Closed	1994	10.50	11
1994	Twinkle, Twinkle Christmas Stars ORN121L	Closed	1995	13.50	14
1994	Twirling Fun ORN051L	Closed	1995	18.00	18
1994	Up On The Housetop ORN055L	Closed	1994	17.00	17
1994	Visions Of Sugarplums ORN095L	Closed	1994	10.50	11
1994	Waiting For Santa ORN099L	Closed	1994	15.00	15
1994	Warm 'N Toasty ORN056L	Closed	1994	16.00	16
1994	Wee Whatnots ORN101L	Closed	1994	17.00	17
1994	Yuletide News ORN093L	Closed	1994	15.00	15
1994	Ziggy ORN059L	Closed	1994	12.50	13
1994	Ziggy ORN060L	Closed	1994	12.50	13

1995 Carlton Collector's Series - Carlton

YEAR ISSUE		EDITION LIMIT	YEAR RETD.	ISSUE PRICE	*QUOTE U.S.$
1995	Book of Carols (3rd) ORN004M	Closed	1995	13.75	14
1995	Christmas Express Handcar (6th) ORN010M	Closed	1995	15.75	18
1995	Christmas Go Round (6th) ORN013M	Closed	1995	15.75	16
1995	Christmas Sweets (4th) ORN006M	Closed	1995	14.75	15
1995	Christmas Town Lane (1st) ORN011M	Closed	1995	14.75	20
1995	Holiday Garden (1st) ORN125M	Closed	1995	14.75	15
1995	Holiday Town (2nd) ORN003M	Closed	1995	17.75	18
1995	Ice Pals (4th) ORN007M	Closed	1995	12.75	13
1995	A Little Bit of Christmas (6th) ORN014M	Closed	1995	13.75	14
1995	Pinecone Cottage (2nd) ORN002M	Closed	1995	16.75	17
1995	Rodrick and Sam's Winter Fun (4th) ORN008M	Closed	1995	12.75	13
1995	Roommate Bear (6th) ORN009M	Closed	1995	12.75	13
1995	Santa's Music Makers (2nd) ORN001M	Closed	1995	13.75	14
1995	Tiny Toymaker (3rd) ORN005M	Closed	1995	12.75	13
1995	Year By Year (1st) ORN126M	Closed	1995	12.75	13

1995 Carlton Heirloom Collection - Carlton

YEAR ISSUE		EDITION LIMIT	YEAR RETD.	ISSUE PRICE	*QUOTE U.S.$
1995	25th Wedding Anniversary ORN056M	Closed	1995	13.75	14
1995	Airmail Delivery ORN100M	Closed	1995	17.75	18
1995	All Around The Workshop ORN074M	Closed	1995	34.00	34
1995	Artistic Wishes ORN092M	Closed	1995	11.75	12
1995	Away In A Manger ORN093M	Closed	1995	11.75	12
1995	Baby Boy's First Christmas ORN025M	Closed	1995	13.75	14
1995	Baby Boy's First Christmas ORN131M	Closed	1995	10.75	11
1995	Baby Girl's First Christmas ORN024M	Closed	1995	14.75	15
1995	Baby Girl's First Christmas ORN130M	Closed	1995	10.75	11
1995	Baby Photoholder ORN026M	Closed	1995	9.75	10
1995	Baby's First Christmas ORN022M	Closed	1995	11.75	12
1995	Baby's First Christmas ORN023M	Closed	1995	14.75	15
1995	Baby's Second Christmas ORN027M	Closed	1995	10.75	11
1995	Bears on Parade ORN081M	Closed	1995	17.75	18
1995	Beary Merry Treasures ORN086M	Closed	1995	13.75	15
1995	Brother ORN040M	Closed	1995	16.75	17
1995	Bunny Delight ORN112M	Closed	1995	13.75	14
1995	Care Bears Bedtime Bear ORN107M	Closed	1995	11.75	12
1995	Caregiver ORN046M	Closed	1995	8.75	9
1995	Changin' for Christmas ORN109M	Closed	1995	18.75	19
1995	Child's Fourth Christmas ORN029M	Closed	1995	10.75	11
1995	Child's Third Christmas ORN028M	Closed	1995	11.75	12
1995	A Christmas Celebration ORN084M	Closed	1995	16.75	17
1995	Christmas Countdown ORN089M	Closed	1996	14.75	15
1995	Christmas is Coming ORN076M	Closed	1995	32.00	32
1995	Christmas Poinsettia ORN079M	Closed	1995	10.75	11
1995	Christmas Spin ORN054M	Closed	1995	14.75	15
1995	The Christmas Star ORN118M	Closed	1995	8.75	9
1995	Clowning Around ORN090M	Closed	1995	13.75	14
1995	Dad ORN035M	Closed	1995	14.75	15
1995	Dancin' Prancin' Bear ORN116M	Closed	1995	14.75	15

*Quotes have been rounded up to nearest dollar

YEAR ISSUE		EDITION LIMIT	YEAR RETD.	ISSUE PRICE	*QUOTE U.S.$
1995	Danglin' Darlin's ORN129M	Closed	1995	8.75	9
1995	Daughter ORN037M	Closed	1995	13.75	14
1995	Do Not Disturb 'Til Christmas ORN049M	Closed	1995	8.75	9
1995	Elvis-Blue Christmas (1st) ORN073M	Closed	1995	25.00	50
1995	A Feeling of Christmas ORN075M	Closed	1995	34.00	34
1995	First Christmas Together ORN012M	Closed	1995	13.75	14
1995	First Christmas Together ORN016M	Closed	1995	11.75	12
1995	First Christmas Together ORN017M	Closed	1995	13.75	14
1995	First Christmas Together ORN018M	Closed	1995	14.75	15
1995	Friend ORN047M	Closed	1995	10.75	11
1995	Get Your Pop-Corn Here! ORN083M	Closed	1996	21.00	21
1995	Gift Exchange ORN078M	Closed	1995	11.75	12
1995	Godchild ORN033M	Closed	1995	10.75	11
1995	Godchild ORN071M	Closed	1995	12.75	13
1995	Godmother ORN015M	Closed	1995	11.75	12
1995	Grandaughter's First Christmas ORN030M	Closed	1995	11.75	12
1995	Grandmother ORN041M	Closed	1995	10.75	11
1995	Grandparents ORN042M	Closed	1995	13.75	14
1995	Grandson's First Christmas ORN031M	Closed	1995	11.75	12
1995	Greetings To You ORN070M	Closed	1995	28.00	28
1995	The Heart of Christmas ORN102M	Closed	1995	12.75	13
1995	Hershey's Express ORN098M	Closed	1995	17.75	18
1995	High-Flyin' Santa ORN077M	Closed	1995	28.00	28
1995	Holiday Gardner ORN088M	Closed	1995	13.75	14
1995	Holiday Harmony ORN128M	Closed	1995	14.75	15
1995	Holiday Time ORN052M	Closed	1995	14.75	15
1995	Hook, Line and Singers ORN067M	Closed	1995	12.75	13
1995	Hoppy Holidays ORN111M	Closed	1995	13.75	14
1995	Juggling Jester ORN050M	Closed	1995	12.75	13
1995	Jukebox Jingles ORN080M	Closed	1995	23.00	23
1995	Li'l Feathered Friend ORN117M	Closed	1995	16.75	17
1995	Love at Christmas ORN021M	Closed	1995	10.75	11
1995	Magic of the Season ORN124M	Closed	1995	14.75	15
1995	Merry Matinee ORN082M	Closed	1995	21.00	21
1995	Merry Meister ORN087M	Closed	1995	18.75	19
1995	Mother ORN034M	Closed	1995	14.75	15
1995	Music Box Dancers ORN053M	Closed	1995	18.75	19
1995	New Home ORN043M	Closed	1995	12.75	13
1995	New Home ORN057M	Closed	1995	12.75	13
1995	North Pole Pals ORN122M	Closed	1995	13.75	14
1995	Off For A Spin ORN091M	Closed	1995	13.75	14
1995	Oh, Sew Merry! ORN064M	Closed	1995	13.75	14
1995	Opus Flashin' Through the Snow! ORN104M	Closed	1995	12.75	13
1995	Our Christmas Together ORN010M	Closed	1995	11.75	12
1995	Our Family Photoholder ORN135M	Closed	1995	9.75	10
1995	Our House To Your House ORN044M	Closed	1995	13.75	14
1995	Parents ORN036M	Closed	1995	15.75	16
1995	Parents To Be ORN032M	Closed	1995	11.75	12
1995	Pet Photoholder ORN055M	Closed	1995	9.75	10
1995	Pillsbury Poppin' Fresh Christmas ORN097M	Closed	1995	13.75	14
1995	Playin' A Holiday Tune ORN110M	Closed	1995	13.75	14
1995	Purr-Fect Holidays ORN115M	Closed	1995	13.75	14
1995	Rocking Horse Fun ORN123M	Closed	1995	9.75	10
1995	Rocky and Bullwinkle Merry Fishmas ORN096M	Closed	1995	15.75	16
1995	Santa's Hotline ORN114M	Closed	1995	13.75	14
1995	Santa's On His Way! ORN127M	Closed	1995	9.75	10
1995	Santa-In-The-Box ORN072M	Closed	1995	15.75	16
1995	Sister ORN039M	Closed	1995	11.75	12
1995	Sister To Sister ORN133M	Closed	1995	13.75	14
1995	A Sleighful Of Joys ORN128M	Closed	1995	15.75	16
1995	Snow Bunnies ORN103M	Closed	1995	12.75	13
1995	Snow Sculpturing ORN105M	Closed	1995	12.75	13
1995	Son ORN038M	Closed	1995	11.75	12
1995	St. Bernard ORN119M	Closed	1995	10.75	11
1995	Stocking Full Of Fun ORN099M	Closed	1995	12.75	13
1995	Sugar Cone Castle ORN120M	Closed	1995	17.75	18
1995	Sweetheart ORN020M	Closed	1995	12.75	13
1995	Swinging Into Christmas ORN085M	Closed	1995	14.75	15
1995	Teacher ORN048M	Closed	1995	8.75	9
1995	To Grandma Photoholder ORN134M	Closed	1995	9.75	10
1995	Twinkle, Twinkle Christmas Star ORN121M	Closed	1995	13.75	14
1995	Twirling Fun ORN051M	Closed	1995	14.75	15
1995	Visit With Santa Photoholder ORN132M	Closed	1995	9.75	10
1995	Volkswagon On Our Merry Way! ORN094M	Closed	1995	21.00	21
1995	Wake Me When It's Christmas ORN106M	Closed	1995	11.75	12
1995	Westward Ho Holidays ORN108M	Closed	1995	17.75	18
1995	The Wisemen's Journey ORN101M	Closed	1995	12.75	13
1995	Workplace Wishes ORN045M	Closed	1995	12.75	13
1995	Ziggy's Merry Tree-Some ORN095M	Closed	1995	13.75	14

1996 Carlton Collector's Series - Carlton

YEAR ISSUE		EDITION LIMIT	YEAR RETD.	ISSUE PRICE	*QUOTE U.S.$
1996	Book of Carols (4th) CXOR-004T	Closed	1996	13.95	14
1996	Candy Cane Cabin (1st) CXOR-108T	Closed	1996	13.95	14
1996	Christmas Go Round (7th) CXOR-011T	Closed	1996	15.95	16
1996	Christmas Sweets (5th) CXOR-005T	Closed	1996	14.95	15
1996	Christmas Tidings (2nd) CXOR-100T	Closed	1996	13.95	14
1996	Country Cow (1st) CXOR-105T	Closed	1996	11.95	12
1996	Gingerbread Farm (3rd) CXOR-110T	Closed	1996	13.95	14
1996	Holiday Fun (3rd) CXOR-101T	Closed	1996	13.95	14
1996	Holiday Garden (2nd) CXOR-010T	Closed	1996	14.95	15
1996	Holiday Recollections (1st) CXOR-099T	Closed	1996	13.95	14
1996	Holiday Town (3rd) CXOR-003T	Closed	1996	18.95	19
1996	Ice Pals (5th) CXOR-006T	Closed	1996	12.95	13
1996	Jolly Old St. Nick (1st) CXOR-015T	Closed	1996	15.95	16
1996	Joy (1st) CXOR-102T	Closed	1996	11.95	12
1996	Joy Is In The Air (1st) CXOR-007T	Closed	1996	16.95	17
1996	Love (3rd) CXOR-104T	Closed	1996	11.95	12
1996	Merry (2nd) CXOR-103T	Closed	1996	11.95	12
1996	Merry Mischief (1st) CXOR-012T	Closed	1996	14.95	15
1996	O Holy Night (1st) CXOR-014T	Closed	1996	17.95	18
1996	Perky Pig (3rd) CXOR-107T	Closed	1996	11.95	12
1996	Pinecone Cottage (3rd) CXOR-002T	Closed	1996	17.95	18
1996	Prancing Pony (3rd)	Closed	1996	11.95	12
1996	Santa's Music Makers (3rd) CXOR-001T	Closed	1996	13.95	14
1996	Song of Hope (2nd) CXOR-097T	Closed	1996	12.95	13
1996	Song of Joy (3rd) CXOR-098T	Closed	1996	12.95	13
1996	Song of Peace (1st) CXOR-096T	Closed	1996	12.95	13
1996	Sugarplum Chapel (2nd) CXOR-109T	Closed	1996	13.95	14
1996	Wonderland Express (1st) CXOR-008T	Closed	1996	15.95	16
1996	Year By Year (2nd) CXOR-013T	Closed	1996	12.95	13

1996 Carlton Heirloom Collection - Carlton

YEAR ISSUE		EDITION LIMIT	YEAR RETD.	ISSUE PRICE	*QUOTE U.S.$
1996	25th Wedding Anniversary CXOR-027T	Closed	1996	14.95	15
1996	All Around The Workshop CXOR-074T	Closed	1996	34.00	34
1996	Another Magical Season CXOR-087T	Closed	1996	15.95	16
1996	Baby Boy's First Christmas CXOR-032T	Closed	1996	13.95	14
1996	Baby Girl's First Christmas CXOR-030T	Closed	1996	13.95	14
1996	Baby Photo Holder CXOR-059T	Closed	1996	9.95	10
1996	Baby's First Christmas CXOR-028T	Closed	1996	14.95	15
1996	Baby's First Christmas CXOR-133T	Closed	1996	15.95	16
1996	Baby's Second Christmas CXOR-036T	Closed	1996	11.95	12
1996	Bainbridge Bear CXOR-031T	Closed	1996	11.95	12
1996	Bainbridge Bear CXOR-033T	Closed	1996	11.95	12
1996	A Brief Message CXOR-086T	Closed	1996	12.95	13
1996	Brother CXOR-049T	Closed	1996	12.95	13
1996	Campbell's, A Hearty Christmas CXOR-090T	Closed	1996	17.95	18
1996	Caregiver CXOR-053T	Closed	1996	10.95	11
1996	A Child's Christmas CXOR-124T	Closed	1996	13.95	14
1996	Child's Fourth Christmas CXOR-038T	Closed	1996	11.95	12
1996	Child's Third Christmas CXOR-037T	Closed	1996	11.95	12
1996	Christmas All Around CXOR-072T	Closed	1996	32.00	32
1996	A Christmas Celebration CXOR-080T	Closed	1996	16.95	17
1996	Christmas Countdown CXOR-024T	Closed	1996	14.95	15
1996	Christmas Kickoff CXOR-113T	Closed	1996	11.95	12
1996	Christmas Town Inn CXOR-009T	Closed	1996	14.95	15
1996	Clubhouse Christmas CXOR-129T	Closed	1996	13.95	14
1996	Counting The Days 'Til Christmas CXOR-118T	Closed	1996	10.95	11
1996	Cozy Little Christmas CXOR-079T	Closed	1996	15.95	16
1996	Cyclin' Santa CXOR-114T	Closed	1996	14.95	15
1996	Dad CXOR-043T	Closed	1996	13.95	14
1996	Dancing 'Til Daylight CXOT-073T	Closed	1996	32.00	32
1996	Daughter CXOR-045T	Closed	1996	13.95	14
1996	Do Not Disturd 'Til Christmas CXOR-121T	Closed	1996	11.95	12
1996	Elvis CXOR-093T	Closed	1996	30.00	30
1996	Finishing Touches CXOR-071T	Closed	1996	28.00	28
1996	First Christmas Together CXOR-019T	Closed	1996	11.95	12
1996	First Christmas Together CXOR-020T	Closed	1996	18.95	19
1996	First Christmas Together CXOR-021T	Closed	1996	14.95	15
1996	First Christmas Together CXOR-022T	Closed	1996	12.95	13
1996	Friend CXOR-054T	Closed	1996	9.95	10
1996	Friend CXOR-055T	Closed	1996	10.95	11
1996	Friends Around The World CXOR-062T	Closed	1996	11.95	12
1996	Get Your Pup-Corn Here! CXOR-078T	Closed	1996	21.00	21
1996	Goal For It! CXOR-116T	Closed	1996	12.95	13
1996	Godchild CXOR-039T	Closed	1996	10.95	11
1996	Godchild CXOR-040T	Closed	1996	13.95	14
1996	Godmother CXOR-052T	Closed	1996	14.95	15
1996	Grandaughter's First Christmas CXOR-034T	Closed	1996	10.95	11
1996	Grandmother CXOR-050T	Closed	1996	14.95	15
1996	Grandparents CXOR-051T	Closed	1996	14.95	15
1996	Grandson's First Christmas CXOR-035T	Closed	1996	10.95	11
1996	Greetings To You CXOR-127T	Closed	1996	28.00	28
1996	Happy Holidaze! CXOR-085T	Closed	1996	15.95	16
1996	Happy, Happy! Joy, Joy! CXOR-091TT	Closed	1996	15.95	16
1996	Hershey's Hugs 'N Kisses CXOR-084T	Closed	1996	15.95	16
1996	High Lights CXOR-120T	Closed	1996	13.95	14
1996	High Powered Holidays! CXOR-095T	Closed	1996	16.95	17
1996	Holiday Debut CXOR-115T	Closed	1996	9.95	10
1996	A Holiday Hello CXOR-075T	Closed	1996	15.95	16
1996	Holiday Hoopla CXOR-119T	Closed	1996	13.95	14
1996	Holiday Sentiment CXOR-029T	Closed	1996	11.95	12
1996	Holiday Surprise! CXOR-08IT	Closed	1996	14.95	15
1996	Holiday Waltz CXOR-070T	Closed	1996	34.00	34
1996	Homerun Holiday CXOR-112T	Closed	1996	12.95	13
1996	It's Showtime! CXOR-077T	Closed	1996	21.00	21
1996	Jukebox Jingles CXOR-067T	Closed	1996	23.95	24
1996	Little Cup of Dreams CXOR-135T	Closed	1996	14.95	15
1996	Little Treasures-Boy CXOR-132T	Closed	1996	11.95	12
1996	Little Treasures-Girl CXOR-131T	Closed	1996	11.95	12
1996	Magic Of The Season CXOR-123T	Closed	1996	12.95	13
1996	Marilyn CXOR-094T	Closed	1996	17.95	18
1996	Merry Birthday CXOR-128T	Open		12.95	13
1996	Mother CXOR-042T	Closed	1996	13.95	14
1996	New Home CXOR-016T	Closed	1996	12.95	13
1996	New Home CXOR-017T	Closed	1996	13.95	14
1996	Noah's Ark CXOR-125T	Closed	1996	13.95	14
1996	Nonstop Wishes CXOR-069T	Closed	1996	28.00	28
1996	North Pole or Bust CXOR-082T	Closed	1996	16.95	17
1996	Our Christmas Together CXOR-025T	Closed	1996	12.95	13
1996	Our Christmas Together CXOR-026T	Closed	1996	13.95	14
1996	Our Family Photo Holder CXOR-061T	Closed	1996	9.95	10
1996	Our House to Your House CXOR-018T	Closed	1996	13.95	14
1996	Paddington Bear, Gliding Into Christmas CXOR-089T	Closed	1996	14.95	15
1996	Parents CXOR-044T	Closed	1996	14.95	15
1996	Parents To Be CXOR-041T	Closed	1996	12.95	13
1996	Pet Photo Holder CXOR-063T	Open		9.95	10
1996	Puppy Pals CXOR-083T	Closed	1996	14.95	15
1996	Purr-Fect Holidays CXOR-122T	Closed	1996	12.95	13
1996	Rocking Horse Fun CXOR-126T	Closed	1996	13.95	14
1996	Santa's Little Friends CXOR-068T	Closed	1996	15.95	16
1996	Santa's Network CXOR-058T	Closed	1996	13.95	14
1996	Season of Giving CXOR-134T	Closed	1996	14.95	15
1996	Sister CXOR-047T	Closed	1996	13.95	14
1996	Sister To Sister CXOR-048T	Closed	1996	14.95	15
1996	Son CXOR-046T	Closed	1996	14.95	15
1996	Sweetheart CXOR-023T	Closed	1996	14.95	15
1996	Sweetheart CXOR-130T	Closed	1996	16.95	17
1996	Teacher CXOR-056T	Closed	1996	9.95	10
1996	Teacher CXOR-057T	Closed	1996	11.95	12
1996	Ten-Pin Christmas CXOR-111T	Closed	1996	10.95	11
1996	Tender Loving Care CXOR-064T	Closed	1996	11.95	12
1996	Tenderheart Bear CXOR-088T	Closed	1996	11.95	12
1996	That's The Spirit! CXOR-117T	Closed	1996	11.95	12
1996	To Grandma Photo Holder CXOR-060T	Closed	1996	9.95	10
1996	To The Rescue CXOR-065T	Closed	1996	12.95	13
1996	Up On The Housetop CXOR-066T	Closed	1996	17.95	18
1996	You're A Winner CXOR-076T	Closed	1996	16.95	17

1997 A Child's Christmas - Carlton

YEAR ISSUE		EDITION LIMIT	YEAR RETD.	ISSUE PRICE	*QUOTE U.S.$
1997	Baby Photo Holder CXOR-041W	Open		13.95	14
1997	Baby's Second Christmas CXOR-036W	Open		12.95	13
1997	Child's Fourth Christmas CXOR-038W	Open		12.95	13
1997	Child's Third Christmas CXOR-037W	Open		12.95	13
1997	Godchild CXOR-039W	Open		11.95	12
1997	Godchild CXOR-040W	Open		13.95	14
1997	Jumpin' Jolly Holidays-Boy CXOR-043W	Open		12.95	13
1997	Jumpin' Jolly Holidays-Girl CXOR-042W	Open		12.95	13

1997 Baby's First Christmas - Carlton

YEAR ISSUE		EDITION LIMIT	YEAR RETD.	ISSUE PRICE	*QUOTE U.S.$
1997	Baby Boy's First Christmas CXOR-032W	Open		15.95	16
1997	Baby Boy's First Christmas CXOR-033W	Open		14.95	15
1997	Baby Girl's First Christmas CXOR-030W	Open		15.95	16
1997	Baby Girl's First Christmas CXOR-031W	Open		14.95	15
1997	Baby's First Christmas CXOR-028W	Open		14.95	15
1997	Granddaughter's First Christmas CXOR-034W	Open		11.95	12
1997	Grandson's First Christmas CXOR-035W	Open		11.95	12

1997 Carlton Collector's Series - Carlton

YEAR ISSUE		EDITION LIMIT	YEAR RETD.	ISSUE PRICE	*QUOTE U.S.$
1997	Book of Carols (5th) CXOR-010W	Open		13.95	14
1997	Christmas Go Round (8th) CXOR-011W	Open		15.95	16
1997	Christmas Sweets (6th) CXOR-005W	Open		14.95	15
1997	Christmas Town Lane (3rd) CXOR-009W	Open		14.95	15
1997	Holiday Town (4th) CXOR-003W	Open		18.95	19
1997	Ice Pals (6th) CXOR-006W	Open		12.95	13
1997	Jolly Old St. Nick (2nd) CXOR-015W	Open		15.95	16
1997	Joy Is In The Air (2nd) CXOR-007W	Open		17.95	18
1997	Merry Mischief (2nd) CXOR-012W	Open		14.95	15
1997	Merry Mobiles (1st) CXOR-002W	Open		13.95	14
1997	Oh Holy Night (2nd) CXOR-014W	Open		18.95	19
1997	Santa's Music Makers (4th) CXOR-001W	Open		14.95	15

*Quotes have been rounded up to nearest dollar

Collectors' Information Bureau

149

ORNAMENTS

YEAR ISSUE		EDITION LIMIT	YEAR RETD.	ISSUE PRICE	*QUOTE U.S. $
1997	Wonderland Express (1st) CXOR-008W	Open		15.95	16
1997	Wonderland Express (2nd) CXOR-004W	Open		13.95	14
1997	Year By Year (3rd) CXOR-013W	Open		12.95	13

1997 Favorite Pastimes - Carlton

1997	Dec. 26th CXOR-120W	Open		14.95	15
1997	From Heaven's Garden CXOR-121W	Open		12.95	13
1997	Fun To Spare CXOR-111W	Open		11.95	12
1997	Goal For It! CXOR-116W	Open		12.95	13
1997	Gridiron Greetings CXOR-113W	Open		12.95	13
1997	Hooked On The Holidays CXOR-114W	Open		14.95	15
1997	Hoopy Holiday CXOR-119W	Open		11.95	12
1997	Sew Very Special CXOR-118W	Open		14.95	15
1997	Star Player CXOR-112W	Open		12.95	13
1997	That's The Spirit! CXOR-117W	Open		11.95	12
1997	Twinkletoes CXOR-115W	Open		9.95	10

1997 Featured Attractions - Carlton

1997	Baby's First Christmas CXOR-029W	Open		32.00	32
1997	The Cherub Tree (Lighted) CXOR-067W	Open		22.00	22
1997	Green Thumb Greetings (Lighted) CXOR-077W	Open		21.50	22
1997	Holiday Hits (Music) CXOR-068W	Open		24.50	25
1997	Is He Here Yet? (Lighted) CXOR-076W	Open		21.50	22
1997	Main Attraction CXOR-080W	Open		36.00	36
1997	Peanut Parade (Lighted) CXOR-075W	Open		22.00	22
1997	Piano Playmates (Music) CXOR-069W	Open		24.50	25
1997	Simpler Times CXOR-079W	Open		22.00	22
1997	To All A Good Night! CXOR-078W	Open		18.50	19
1997	Two By Two (Motion, Lights & Music) CXOR-073W	Open		40.00	40

1997 First Christmas Together - Carlton

1997	First Christmas Together CXOR-019W	Open		17.95	18
1997	First Christmas Together CXOR-020W	Open		16.95	17
1997	First Christmas Together CXOR-021W	Open		10.95	11
1997	First Christmas Together CXOR-022W	Open		13.95	14

1997 For Family - Carlton

1997	Brother CXOR-053W	Open		14.95	15
1997	Dad CXOR-047W	Open		12.95	13
1997	Daughter CXOR-049W	Open		12.95	13
1997	Godmother CXOR-056W	Open		11.95	12
1997	Grandmother CXOR-054W	Open		14.95	15
1997	Grandparents CXOR-055W	Open		15.95	16
1997	Mother CXOR-046W	Open		12.95	13
1997	Our Family Photo Holder CXOR-058W	Open		9.95	10
1997	Parents CXOR-048W	Open		13.95	14
1997	Parents-To-Be CXOR-044W	Open		13.95	14
1997	Parents-To-Be CXOR-045W	Open		12.95	13
1997	Sister CXOR-051W	Open		13.95	14
1997	Sister-To-Sister CXOR-052W	Open		14.95	15
1997	Son CXOR-050W	Open		12.95	13
1997	To Grandma Photo Holder CXOR-057W	Open		12.95	13

1997 Holiday Collections - Carlton

1997	Holiday Magic - Dance of the Jolly Juggler CXOR-105W	Open		13.95	14
1997	Holiday Magic - Flight of Pegasus CXOR-107W	Open		13.95	14
1997	Holiday Magic - Magic of the Snow Fairy CXOR-106W	Open		13.95	14
1997	Northland Journey - Dancer CXOR-096W	Open		13.95	14
1997	Northland Journey - Northland Santa CXOR-098W	Open		13.95	14
1997	Northland Journey - Prancer CXOR-097W	Open		13.95	14
1997	Santa's of the World - England's Father Christmas CXOR-099W	Open		9.95	10
1997	Santa's of the World - Germany's Saint Nikolaus CXOR-100W	Open		9.95	10
1997	Santa's of the World - Mexico's Santa Claus CXOR-101W	Open		9.95	10
1997	Sparkling Christmas - Santa Swirl CXOR-103W	Open		10.95	11
1997	Sparkling Christmas - Snowman Whirl CXOR-104W	Open		10.95	11
1997	Sparkling Christmas - Soldier Twirl CXOR-102W	Open		10.95	11
1997	Touches of Silver - Silvery Bell CXOR-108W	Open		12.95	13
1997	Touches of Silver - Silvery Heart CXOR-110W	Open		12.95	13
1997	Touches of Silver - Silvery Snowflake CXOR-109W	Open		12.95	13

1997 Lasting Love - Carlton

1997	Commemorative Anniversary CXOR-027W	Open		14.95	15
1997	Our Christmas Together CXOR-026W	Open		14.95	15
1997	Our Christmas Together CXOR-25W	Open		17.95	18
1997	Sweetheart CXOR-23W	Open		15.95	16
1997	Sweetheart CXOR-24W	Open		15.95	16

1997 Licensed Characters - Carlton

1997	All Set For Santa (Lassie) CXOR-095W	Open		22.00	22
1997	Baked with Love (Pillsbury) CXOR-082W	Open		14.95	15
1997	Chillin' Out (Opus n' bill) CXOR-085W	Open		13.95	14
1997	Christmas Classics (Elvis) CXOR-093W	Open		30.00	30
1997	Classic Christmas (Mustang) CXOR-094W	Open		16.95	17
1997	Come Back Here! (Tom & Jerry) CXOR-086W	Open		15.95	16
1997	Downhill Daredevils (Rocky & Bullwinkle) CXOR-087W	Open		15.95	16
1997	Frosty's Best Friend (Play Doh) CXOR-081W	Open		14.95	15
1997	Havin' A Ball (Nickelodeon) CXOR-091W	Open		13.95	14
1997	Home For Christmas (Paddington Bear) CXOR-089W	Open		14.95	15
1997	Hugs & Kisses To You (Hershey's) CXOR-084W	Open		15.95	16
1997	M'm M'm from the Kitchen (Campbell's) CXOR-090W	Open		18.95	19
1997	Perfect Present (Nancy & Sluggo) CXOR-083W	Open		22.00	22
1997	Silent Star (Charlie Chaplin) CXOR-092W	Open		17.95	18
1997	Surprise! (Betty Boop) CXOR-088W	Open		22.00	22

1997 Little Heirloom Treasures - Carlton

1997	All Creatures Great and Small CXOR-165W	Open		7.95	8
1997	Beautiful Bell CXOR-151W	Open		7.95	8
1997	Brewing Up Fun CXOR-141W	Open		6.95	7
1997	Christmas in a Nutshell CXOR-160W	Open		5.95	6
1997	Christmas Messenger CXOR-167W	Open		7.95	8
1997	Furry Friend CXOR-156W	Open		6.95	7
1997	Gift Bearer CXOR-154W	Open		7.95	8
1997	Gifts of Nature CXOR-169W	Open		9.95	10
1997	Gliding By CXOR-145W	Open		7.95	8
1997	Heavenly Friends CXOR-139W	Open		7.95	8
1997	Hope You Like It! CXOR-144W	Open		7.95	8
1997	In A Twinkling CXOR-163W	Open		8.95	9
1997	Jennifer's Wish CXOR-158W	Open		7.95	8
1997	Jump For Joy CXOR-152W	Open		7.95	8
1997	Lambkin CXOR-143W	Open		7.95	8
1997	Lighting The Way CXOR-171W	Open		7.95	8
1997	Love Token CXOR-146W	Open		7.95	8
1997	Meow-Y Christmas CXOR-140W	Open		6.95	7
1997	Mother And Child CXOR-161W	Open		5.95	6
1997	The Nutcracker Prince CXOR-149W	Open		5.95	6
1997	Old-Fashioned Fun CXOR-138W	Open		9.95	10
1997	On Track For Christmas CXOR-137W	Open		9.95	10
1997	Partridge in a Pear Tree CXOR-170W	Open		5.95	6
1997	Stocking Stuffers CXOR-166W	Open		6.95	7
1997	Swing Time! CXOR-153W	Open		8.95	9
1997	Tiny Tailor CXOR-159W	Open		6.95	7
1997	Visit From Santa CXOR-147W	Open		7.95	8
1997	Winter Welcome CXOR-162W	Open		5.95	6
1997	Woodland Caroler CXOR-155W	Open		7.95	8

1997 Special People and Moments - Carlton

1997	Caregiver CXOR-059W	Open		11.95	12
1997	Friend CXOR-060W	Open		10.95	11
1997	Friend CXOR-061W	Open		9.95	10
1997	Help's Here CXOR-066W	Open		13.95	14
1997	Love Is The Best Medicine CXOR-065W	Open		12.95	13
1997	Memo To You CXOR-064W	Open		12.95	13
1997	Merry Birthday CXOR-130W	Open		12.95	13
1997	New Home CXOR-016W	Open		14.95	15
1997	New Home CXOR-017W	Open		13.95	14
1997	Our House To Your House CXOR-018W	Open		10.95	11
1997	Teacher CXOR-062W	Open		9.95	10
1997	Teacher CXOR-063W	Open		11.95	12

1997 Traditional - Carlton

1997	A Child's Christmas CXOR-125W	Open		13.95	14
1997	Christmas Goose CXOR-070W	Open		15.95	16
1997	Christmas Ties CXOR-124W	Open		13.95	14
1997	Heavenly Angel CXOR-135W	Open		14.95	15
1997	Holiday Help Wanted CXOR-122W	Open		10.95	11
1997	In The Attic CXOR-132W	Open		15.95	16
1997	The Littlest Cowpoke CXOR-133W	Open		15.95	16
1997	Memories of Christmas Photo holder CXOR-071W	Open		15.95	16
1997	North.Pole Com CXOR-129W	Open		13.95	14
1997	Papa Christmas CXOR-126W	Open		14.95	15
1997	Pet Photo Holder CXOR-128W	Open		9.95	10
1997	Purr-fect Holidays CXOR-123W	Open		12.95	13
1997	Ringing in Christmas CXOR-074W	Open		14.95	15
1997	Rocking Horse Fun CXOR-127W	Open		13.95	14
1997	Toymakers Treasure CXOR-131W	Open		13.95	14
1997	Treasured Keepsake CXOR-134W	Open		15.95	16
1997	Treasured Toy CXOR-072W	Open		15.95	16

The Cat's Meow

1986 Christmas Ornaments - F. Jones

1986	Bancroft House	Retrd.	1986	4.00	40
1986	Chapel	Retrd.	1986	4.00	N/A
1986	Grayling House	Retrd.	1986	4.00	40
1986	Morton House	Retrd.	1986	4.00	N/A
1986	Rutledge House	Retrd.	1986	4.00	75
1986	School	Retrd.	1986	4.00	N/A

1988 Christmas Ornaments - F. Jones

1988	Blacksmith Shop	Retrd.	1988	5.00	60
1988	District #17 School	Retrd.	1988	5.00	60
1988	Globe Corner Bookstore	Retrd.	1988	5.00	60
1988	Kennedy Birthplace	Retrd.	1988	5.00	26-75
1988	Set/4	Retrd.	1988	20.00	175-200

1995 Christmas Ornaments - F. Jones

1995	Carnegie Library	Retrd.	1995	8.75	12
1995	Holly Hill Farmhouse	Retrd.	1995	8.75	12
1995	North Central School	Retrd.	1995	8.75	12
1995	St. James General Store	Retrd.	1995	8.75	12
1995	Unitarian Church	Retrd.	1995	8.75	12
1995	Yaquina Bay Light	Retrd.	1995	8.75	12

1996 Christmas Ornaments - F. Jones

1996	Christ Church	Retrd.	1996	9.00	11
1996	Deerfield Post Office	Retrd.	1996	9.00	11
1996	Gimbel & Sons Country Store	Retrd.	1996	9.00	11
1996	Hook Windmill	Retrd.	1996	9.00	11
1996	Maple Manor	Retrd.	1996	9.00	11
1996	Parsonage	Retrd.	1996	9.00	11

Cavanagh Group Intl.

Coca-Cola Christmas Collectors Society Members' Only - Sundblom, unless otherwise noted

1993	Ho Ho Ho	Closed	1993	Gift	25-35
1994	Fishing Bear - CGI	Closed	1994	Gift	28
1995	Hospitality	Closed	1995	Gift	25
1996	Sprite	Closed	1996	Gift	N/A
1997	Carousel Capers	12/97		Gift	N/A

Coca-Cola Brand Heritage Collection - Sundblom

1995	Christmas Is Love (polyresin)	Open		10.00	10
1996	Hospitality in Your Refrigerator (porcelain & brass)	10,000		25.00	25
1997	It Will Refresh You Too (polyresin)	Open		10.00	10
1996	It Will Refresh You, Too (porcelain & brass)	10,000		25.00	25
1996	Please Pause Here (porcelain & brass)	10,000		25.00	25
1995	Santa at the Mantle (polyresin)	Open		10.00	10
1997	Ssshh! (polyresin)	Open		10.00	10
1995	Ssshhh! (polyresin)	Open		10.00	10
1997	That Extra Something (polyresin)	Open		10.00	10

Coca-Cola Brand Heritage Collection Polar Bear - CGI

1997	Always Family (polyresin)	Open		10.00	10
1996	Baby's First Christmas (porcelain)	Open		12.00	12
1996	Our First Christmas (porcelain)	Open		12.00	12
1997	A Refreshing Break (polyresin)	Open		10.00	10
1996	Stocking Stuffers (porcelain)	Open		12.00	12
1997	Trimming the Tree (polyresin)	Open		10.00	10

Coca-Cola Brand Historical Building - CGI

1991	1930's Service Station	Closed	1994	10.00	20
1991	Early Coca-Cola Bottling Company	Closed	1994	10.00	20
1991	Jacob's Pharmacy	Closed	1994	10.00	20
1991	The Pemberton House	Closed	1994	10.00	20

Coca-Cola Brand North Pole Bottling Works - CGI

1995	Barrel of Bears	Closed	1996	9.00	9
1993	Blast Off	Closed	1995	9.00	15
1993	Delivery for Santa	Closed	1996	9.00	9
1993	Fill 'er Up	Closed	1994	9.00	25-30
1995	Fountain Glass Follies	Open		9.00	9
1993	Ice Sculpting	Closed	1995	9.00	15
1993	Long Winter's Nap	Closed	1995	9.00	15
1993	North Pole Express	Closed	1994	9.00	25-30
1995	North Pole Flying School	Closed	1996	9.00	15
1994	Power Drive	Closed	1996	9.00	13
1996	Refreshing Surprise	Open		9.00	9
1996	Rush Delivery	Open		9.00	9
1994	Santa's Refreshment	Closed	1995	9.00	13
1994	Seltzer Surprise	Closed	1995	9.00	15
1993	Thirsting for Adventure	Closed	1994	9.00	20
1996	To: Mrs. Claus	Open		9.00	9
1994	Tops Off Refreshment	Closed	1995	9.00	12
1993	Tops On Refreshment	Closed	1995	9.00	15

Coca-Cola Brand Polar Bear - CGI

1996	The Christmas Star	Open		9.00	9
1997	Double the Fun	Open		9.00	9
1997	Downhill Racers	Open		9.00	9
1994	Downhill Sledder	Closed	1996	9.00	13
1996	Hollywood	Open		9.00	9
1994	North Pole Delivery	Closed	1995	9.00	13
1995	Polar Bear in Bottle Opener	Open		9.00	9
1994	Skating Coca-Cola Polar Bear	Closed	1995	9.00	13

*Quotes have been rounded up to nearest dollar

YEAR ISSUE		EDITION LIMIT	YEAR RETD.	ISSUE PRICE	*QUOTE U.S.$
1995	Snowboardin' Bear	Open		9.00	9
1994	Vending Machine Mischief	Closed	1996	9.00	9

Coca-Cola Brand Polar Bear Cubs - CGI

YEAR ISSUE		EDITION LIMIT	YEAR RETD.	ISSUE PRICE	*QUOTE U.S.$
1997	Baby's First Christmas	Open		8.00	8
1997	Cookies For Santa	Open		8.00	8
1997	Dreaming of a Magical Christmas	Yr.Iss.		8.00	8
1997	A Refreshing Ice Cold Treat	Open		8.00	8
1997	Stocking Stuffer Surprise	Yr.Iss.		8.00	8
1997	Twas the Night Before Christmas	Open		8.00	8

Coca-Cola Brand Trim A Tree Collection - Sundblom

YEAR ISSUE		EDITION LIMIT	YEAR RETD.	ISSUE PRICE	*QUOTE U.S.$
1990	Away with a Tired and Thirsty Face	Closed	1993	10.00	30
1994	Busy Man's Pause	Closed	1995	10.00	10
1991	Christmas Is Love	Closed	1992	10.00	30
1993	Decorating the Tree	Closed	1994	10.00	20
1993	Extra Bright Refreshment	Closed	1994	10.00	15-20
1994	For Sparkling Holidays	Closed	1996	10.00	10
1997	Good Boys and Girls	Open		9.00	9
1992	Happy Holidays	Closed	1996	10.00	25
1990	Hospitality	Closed	1993	10.00	15
1995	It Will Refresh You Too	Open	1996	10.00	10
1990	Merry Christmas and a Happy New Year	Closed	1991	10.00	40
1996	The Pause That Refreshes	Open		10.00	10
1995	Please Pause Here	Open		10.00	10
1990	Santa on Stool	Closed	1993	10.00	20
1990	Season's Greetings	Closed	1991	10.00	15
1992	Sshhh!	Closed	1993	10.00	20-35
1996	They Remembered Me	Open		10.00	10
1994	Things Go Better with Coke	Closed	1996	10.00	10
1991	A Time to Share	Closed	1993	10.00	25
1993	Travel Refreshed	Closed	1995	10.00	15

Cherished Teddies/Enesco Corporation

Cherished Teddies - P. Hillman

YEAR ISSUE		EDITION LIMIT	YEAR RETD.	ISSUE PRICE	*QUOTE U.S.$
1992	Angel 950777	Suspd.		12.50	55-75
1993	Angel, 3 Asst. 912980	Suspd.		12.50	20-30
1995	Baby Angel on Cloud 141240	Open		13.50	14
1993	Baby Boy (dated) 913014	Yr.Iss.	1993	12.50	25-38
1993	Baby Girl (dated) 913006	Yr.Iss.	1993	12.50	20-38
1992	Bear In Stocking (dated) 950653	Yr.Iss.	1992	16.00	32-60
1996	Bear w/Dangling Mittens 177768	Open		12.50	13
1994	Beary Christmas (dated) 617253	Yr.Iss.	1994	15.00	30-40
1992	Beth On Rocking Reindeer 950793	Suspd.		20.00	40-60
1995	Boy Bear Flying Cupid 103608	Suspd.		13.00	25
1995	Boy/Girl with Banner 141259	Open		13.50	14
1994	Bundled Up For The Holidays (dated) 617229	Open		15.00	25-35
1992	Christmas Sister Bears, 3 asst. 951226	Suspd.		12.50	25
1994	Drummer Boy (dated) 912891	Yr.Iss.	1994	10.00	20-35
1995	Elf Bear W/Doll 625434	Suspd.		12.50	15-25
1995	Elf Bear W/Stuffed Reindeer 625442	Suspd.		12.50	15-25
1995	Elf Bears/Candy Cane 651389	Suspd.		12.50	15-25
1995	Girl Bear Flying Cupid 103616	Suspd.		13.00	25
1993	Girl w/Muff (Alice) (dated) 912832	Yr.Iss.	1993	13.50	30-50
1993	Jointed Teddy Bear 914894	Suspd.		12.50	20-30
1995	Mrs Claus Xmas Holding Tray/Cookies 625426	Suspd.		12.50	25
1996	Santa Bear 2 asst. 176168	Open		12.50	13
1995	Teddies Santa Bear 651370	Open		12.50	13
1995	Teddy w/Ice Skates (dated) 141232	Yr.Iss.	1995	12.50	25
1996	Toy Soldier (dated) 176052	Yr.Iss.	1996	12.50	13

Christina's World

Christina's Connoisseurs' Circle Collector's Club - C. Mallouk

YEAR ISSUE		EDITION LIMIT	YEAR RETD.	ISSUE PRICE	*QUOTE U.S.$
1996	Garden of Eden (champagne) LTD851	200		30.00	30
1996	Snow Village on Matte Purple	12/97		Gift	N/A

1996 Limited Edition Ornaments - C. Mallouk

YEAR ISSUE		EDITION LIMIT	YEAR RETD.	ISSUE PRICE	*QUOTE U.S.$
1996	Chinese Peacock (frosted) Exclusive for Jolly Holiday Gifts Westminister, CA BIR600-J	500		30.00	30
1996	Chinese Peacock on Pearl BIR600	500		30.00	30
1996	Mardi Gras Mask (gold) MAR670	500		30.00	30
1996	Mardi Gras Mask (green) MAR666	500		30.00	30
1996	Mardi Gras Mask (purple) MAR669	500		30.00	30
1996	Mardi Gras Mask (red) MAR668	500		30.00	30
1996	Russian Snow Princess WIN569	500	1997	30.00	30
1996	Vintage Santa GIF316	500	1997	30.00	30
1996	Wisteria in Four Colors Exclusive for Christmas Shop-Savannah, GA WIS096	500		35.00	35

1997 Limited Edition Ornaments - C. Mallouk

YEAR ISSUE		EDITION LIMIT	YEAR RETD.	ISSUE PRICE	*QUOTE U.S.$
1997	Button Santa GIF339	500		30.00	30
1997	Edo Courtesan LTD 853	300		80.00	80
1997	Hans With Tree LTD 850	300		30.00	30
1997	Midnight Mardi Gras MAR671	500		30.00	30
1997	Siberian Santa ICE100	500		30.00	30
1997	Wild Ponies LTD 852	500		30.00	30

Retired Ornaments - C. Mallouk

YEAR ISSUE		EDITION LIMIT	YEAR RETD.	ISSUE PRICE	*QUOTE U.S.$
1994	Antique Gold Alencon Lace LAC402	Retrd.	1997	9.00	9
1994	Baby Duck on Azure Blue ZOO802	Retrd.	1997	12.00	12
1994	Beaded Airplane GIF321	Retrd.	1997	10.00	10
1994	Beaded Dragonfly GIF320	Retrd.	1997	7.00	7
1994	Beaded Model T Car GIF322	Retrd.	1997	24.00	24
1994	Beaded Racing Car GIF325	Retrd.	1997	30.00	30
1994	Beaded Sailboat GIF324	Retrd.	1997	16.00	16
1994	Beaded Train GIF323	Retrd.	1997	16.00	16
1994	Berries and Roses FLO230	Retrd.	1997	8.00	8
1994	Berries and Roses FLO231	Retrd.	1997	10.00	10
1994	Blue Sea w/Golden Ships HUN853	Retrd.	1997	13.00	13
1994	Brocade Flowers on Matte Gold MAT458	Retrd.	1997	12.00	12
1994	Brocade Flowers on Pearl FLO206	Retrd.	1997	8.00	8
1994	Brocade Flowers on Pearl FLO207	Retrd.	1997	12.00	12
1994	By The Sea Assortment in Blue, set/6 SEA335	Retrd.	1997	39.00	39
1994	By The Sea Assortment in white, set/6 SEA340	Retrd.	1997	39.00	39
1994	By The Sea Blue Lighthouse SEA310	Retrd.	1997	10.00	10
1994	Candy Cane Ball, set/6 WIN577	Retrd.	1997	6.00	6
1994	Champagne Alencon Lace LAC405	Retrd.	1997	9.00	9
1994	Clear Ball w/Fiesta of Fruit TUT127	Retrd.	1997	8.00	8
1994	Clear Ball w/Fiesta of Fruit TUT128	Retrd.	1997	10.00	10
1994	Glitter Fans (red) ART999/10	Retrd.	1997	13.00	13
1994	Gold Frost w/Onion Domes (matte) HUN852	Retrd.	1997	13.00	13
1994	Golden Peacock on Burgundy ART910/0	Retrd.	1997	7.00	7
1994	Green Gold Tiger Claws on Red MAR667	Retrd.	1997	18.00	18
1994	Ice Castles Ball LAC409	Retrd.	1997	12.00	12
1994	Ice Castles LAC377	Retrd.	1997	7.00	7
1994	Irridescent White Train Garland WIN570	Retrd.	1997	20.00	20
1994	Little Tree Ball, set/6 WIN579	Retrd.	1997	7.00	7
1994	Mandarin Ball w/Glitter Fans ART995/10	Retrd.	1997	13.00	13
1994	Mandarin Balls ART959	Retrd.	1997	13.00	13
1994	Mandarin Firecrackers ART956	Retrd.	1997	10.00	10
1994	Mandarin Pagoda ART996/10	Retrd.	1997	13.00	13
1994	Mandarin Rockets ART958	Retrd.	1997	6.00	6
1994	Mandarin w/Poinsettias ART989/10	Retrd.	1997	13.00	13
1994	Matte Gold & Chrysanthemums ART976	Retrd.	1997	13.00	13
1994	Native American Mandala OJB833	Retrd.	1997	13.00	13
1994	Peach w/Glitter Mountain (matte) ART992/10	Retrd.	1997	13.00	13
1994	Peacock Feathers on Gold ART966/10	Retrd.	1997	10.00	10
1994	Pearl Spring Garden Ball (matte) FLO527	Retrd.	1997	18.00	18
1994	Pearl White w/Red Onion Domes HUN854	Retrd.	1997	13.00	13
1994	Poinsettia Ribbon Ball GIF318	Retrd.	1997	13.00	13
1994	Red Pinwheel Poinsettia Ball WIN576	Retrd.	1997	8.00	8
1994	Red Tartan Ball GIF301	Retrd.	1997	9.00	9
1994	Red w/Glitter Mountains ART994A/10	Retrd.	1997	13.00	13
1994	Rosetti Madonna ART905/10	Retrd.	1997	13.00	13
1994	Secret Garden Daffodils GAR913	Retrd.	1997	22.00	22
1994	Secret Garden Ladybug Ball GAR906	Retrd.	1997	14.00	14
1994	Shiny Kimono Vin Ball (3 colors) KIM412	Retrd.	1997	16.00	16
1994	Silver White Seurat ART933	Retrd.	1997	13.00	13
1994	Snow Flurry on Clear Red WIN557	Retrd.	1997	16.00	16
1994	Three Ducks in a Row ZOO815	Retrd.	1997	20.00	20
1994	Totem Ball (frosted white) OJB837	Retrd.	1997	10.00	10
1994	Tulip Princess (gold) ART948/10	Retrd.	1997	13.00	13
1994	Victorian Girl Face (3"), set/12 WIN582	Retrd.	1997	5.00	5
1994	Victorian Window Box (burgundy) KIM410	Retrd.	1997	12.00	12
1994	Waterlily on Matte Red ART991/10	Retrd.	1997	13.00	13

Christopher Radko

Christopher Radko Family of Collectors - C. Radko

YEAR ISSUE		EDITION LIMIT	YEAR RETD.	ISSUE PRICE	*QUOTE U.S.$
1993	Angels We Have Heard on High SP1	Retrd.	1993	50.00	400-575
1994	Starbuck Santa SP3	Retrd.	1994	75.00	250-350
1995	Dash Away All SP7	Retrd.	1995	34.00	80-125
1995	Purrfect Present SP8	Retrd.	1995	Gift	60-70
1996	Christmas Magic SP13	Retrd.	1996	50.00	50
1996	Frosty Weather SP14	Retrd.	1996	Gift	N/A
1997	Enchanted Evening SP20	Yr.Iss.		55.00	55
1997	Li'l Miss Angel SP21	Yr.Iss.		Gift	N/A

10 Year Anniversary - C. Radko

YEAR ISSUE		EDITION LIMIT	YEAR RETD.	ISSUE PRICE	*QUOTE U.S.$
1995	On Top of the World SP6	Yr.Iss.	1995	32.00	40-75

1986 Holiday Collection - C. Radko

YEAR ISSUE		EDITION LIMIT	YEAR RETD.	ISSUE PRICE	*QUOTE U.S.$
1986	Alpine Flowers 86-040-0	Retrd.	N/A	16.00	140
1986	Big Top 86-048-1	Retrd.	1988	15.00	180
1986	Deep Sea 41-1	Retrd.	N/A	N/A	39-48
1986	Emerald City 17	Retrd.	N/A	N/A	78
1986	Golden Alpine 86-040-1	Retrd.	N/A	N/A	48
1986	Long Icicle (red) 6	Retrd.	N/A	N/A	90
1986	Midas Touch 49	Retrd.	N/A	N/A	65-125
1986	Roses 86-115	Retrd.	1988	16.00	140
1986	Santa's Cane (pink) 5-1	Retrd.	N/A	N/A	90
1986	Siberian Sleighride 110-1	Retrd.	N/A	N/A	100-115
1986	Three Ribbon Oval 44-0	Retrd.	N/A	N/A	125-150

1987 Holiday Collection - C. Radko

YEAR ISSUE		EDITION LIMIT	YEAR RETD.	ISSUE PRICE	*QUOTE U.S.$
1987	Baby Balloons 87044	Retrd.	1988	6.00	110
1987	Faberge Ball 34	Retrd.	N/A	N/A	48
1987	Grecian Column (red/gold) 520	Retrd.	N/A	N/A	125
1987	Grecian Column (silver) 520	Retrd.	N/A	N/A	125
1987	Kat Koncert 88-067	Retrd.	1994	16.00	140
1987	Memphis 18	Retrd.	N/A	15.00	125
1987	Twin Finial 800	Retrd.	N/A	N/A	130

1988 Holiday Collection - C. Radko

YEAR ISSUE		EDITION LIMIT	YEAR RETD.	ISSUE PRICE	*QUOTE U.S.$
1988	Alpine Flowers 8822	Retrd.	N/A	16.00	85-110
1988	Baby Balloon 8832	Retrd.	N/A	7.95	110-125
1988	Birdhouse 8873	Retrd.	1987	10.00	110-130
1988	Blue Rainbow 8863	Retrd.	N/A	16.00	150
1988	Buds in Bloom (pink) 8824	Retrd.	N/A	16.00	125-140
1988	Celestial (blue) 884	Retrd.	N/A	15.00	65
1988	Celestial 884	Retrd.	N/A	15.00	75
1988	Christmas Fanfare 8850	Retrd.	1988	15.00	150
1988	Circle of Santas 8811	Retrd.	N/A	16.95	150-225
1988	Cornucopia/Pear Branch 8839	Retrd.	N/A	15.00	360
1988	Crescent Moon Santa 881	Retrd.	N/A	15.00	140
1988	Crown Jewels 8874	Retrd.	1993	15.00	150-175
1988	Double Royal Star 8856	Retrd.	1991	23.00	150-200
1988	Exclamation Flask 8871	Retrd.	N/A	7.50	75-95
1988	Faberge Oval 883	Retrd.	N/A	15.00	75-110
1988	Gilded Leaves 8813	Retrd.	N/A	16.00	131-158
1988	Grecian Column 8842	Retrd.	1990	9.95	95
1988	Hot Air Balloon 885	Retrd.	N/A	15.00	150-200
1988	Lilac Sparkle 1814	Retrd.	N/A	15.00	140-150
1988	Mushroom in Winter 8862	Retrd.	1993	12.00	135
1988	Neopolitan Angel 870141	Retrd.	1995	16.00	150
1988	Oz Balloon 872	Retrd.	N/A	18.00	160
1988	Ripples on Oval 8844	Retrd.	1987	6.00	85
1988	Royal Diadem 8860	Retrd.	1987	25.00	135
1988	Royal Porcelain 8812	Retrd.	1991	16.00	135-180
1988	Russian St. Nick 8823	Retrd.	N/A	15.00	125
1988	Satin Scepter 8847	Retrd.	1987	8.95	110
1988	Shiny-Brite 8843	Retrd.	N/A	5.00	36
1988	Simply Cartiere 8817	Retrd.	N/A	16.95	150
1988	Squigglies 889	Retrd.	N/A	15.00	140
1988	Stained Glass 8816	Retrd.	1990	16.00	175
1988	Striped Balloon 8877	Retrd.	N/A	16.95	55-99
1988	Tiger 886	Retrd.	N/A	15.00	335-375
1988	Tree on Ball 8864	Retrd.	N/A	9.00	100-125
1988	Twin Finial 8857	Retrd.	N/A	23.50	135
1988	Zebra 886	Retrd.	N/A	15.00	160-175

1989 Holiday Collection - C. Radko

YEAR ISSUE		EDITION LIMIT	YEAR RETD.	ISSUE PRICE	*QUOTE U.S.$
1989	Alpine Flowers 9-43	Retrd.	N/A	17.00	30
1989	Baroque Angel 9-11	Retrd.	1989	17.00	125-150
1989	Charlie Chaplin (blue hat) 9-55	Retrd.	1990	8.50	60-100
1989	Circle of Santas 9-32	Retrd.	1991	17.00	50-95
1989	Double Top 9-71	Retrd.	1989	7.00	40
1989	Drop Reflector 88	Retrd.	N/A	23.00	90
1989	Elf on Ball (matte) 9-62	Retrd.	1990	9.50	75-125
1989	Fisher Frog 9-65	Retrd.	1991	7.00	75-100
1989	Grecian Urn 9-69	Retrd.	1989	9.00	35
1989	His Boy Elroy 9-104	Retrd.	1991	8.00	100
1989	The Holly 9-49	Retrd.	N/A	17.00	90
1989	Hurricane Lamp 9-67	Retrd.	1989	7.00	45
1989	The Ivy 9-47	Retrd.	N/A	16.50	120
1989	Jester 41	Retrd.	N/A	16.50	120
1989	Joey Clown (light pink) 9-58	Retrd.	1992	9.00	70
1989	Kim Ono 9-57	Retrd.	1990	6.50	50-65
1989	King Arthur (Lt. Blue) 9-103	Retrd.	1991	12.00	60-95
1989	Lilac Sparkle 9-7	Retrd.	1989	17.00	75-125
1989	Lucky Fish 9-73	Retrd.	1989	6.50	45-55
1989	Parachute 9-68	Retrd.	1989	6.50	75-95
1989	Peppermint Stripes 89	Retrd.	N/A	29.00	300
1989	Royal Rooster 9-18	Retrd.	1993	17.00	95
1989	Royal Star Tree Finial 108	Retrd.	N/A	42.00	95
1989	Seahorse 9-54	Retrd.	1992	10.00	125-145
1989	Serpent 9-72	Retrd.	N/A	7.00	30
1989	Shy Kitten 9-66	Retrd.	N/A	7.00	45
1989	Shy Rabbit 9-61	Retrd.	N/A	7.00	40-55
1989	Small Reflector 9-76	Retrd.	N/A	7.50	32
1989	Smiling Sun 9-59	Retrd.	N/A	7.00	45
1989	Songbirds 21	Retrd.	N/A	17.50	240
1989	Tiffany 44	Retrd.	N/A	17.00	450-700
1989	Vineyard 9-51	Retrd.	N/A	17.00	115
1989	Walrus 9-63	Retrd.	1990	8.00	100-130
1989	Zebra 9-10	Retrd.	1991	17.50	100-150

1990 Holiday Collection - C. Radko

YEAR ISSUE		EDITION LIMIT	YEAR RETD.	ISSUE PRICE	*QUOTE U.S.$
1990	Angel on Harp 46	Retrd.	1990	9.00	85
1990	Ballooning Santa 87	Retrd.	1991	20.00	150-250
1990	Bathing Baby 70	Retrd.	N/A	11.00	65
1990	Boy Clown on Reflector 82	Retrd.	N/A	18.00	125
1990	Calla Lilly 38	Retrd.	N/A	7.00	50-85
1990	Candy Trumpet Man (blue) 85-1	Retrd.	N/A	28.00	42
1990	Candy Trumpet Man 85-1	Retrd.	N/A	28.00	95
1990	Carmen Miranda 18	Retrd.	1991	19.00	125
1990	Chimney Sweep Bell 179	Retrd.	N/A	27.00	150
1990	Christmas Cardinals 16	Retrd.	1992	18.00	125
1990	Conch Shell 65	Retrd.	1991	9.00	95-125
1990	Crowned Prince 56	Retrd.	1990	14.00	75-125
1990	Deco Floral 29	Retrd.	N/A	19.00	120
1990	Dublin Pipe 40	Retrd.	1990	14.00	50
1990	Eagle Medallion 67	Retrd.	1990	9.00	50-85

*Quotes have been rounded up to nearest dollar

Christopher Radko
to Christopher Radko

ORNAMENTS

YEAR ISSUE		EDITION LIMIT	YEAR RETD.	ISSUE PRICE	*QUOTE U.S. $
1990	Early Winter 24	Retrd.	1990	10.00	40
1990	Emerald City 92	Retrd.	1990	7.50	65
1990	Fat Lady 35	Retrd.	N/A	7.00	35
1990	Father Christmas 76	Retrd.	N/A	7.00	45
1990	Frog Under Balloon 58	Retrd.	1991	14.00	45-80
1990	Frosty 62	Retrd.	N/A	14.00	70
1990	Golden Puppy 53	Retrd.	1990	8.00	90-125
1990	Google Eyes 44	Retrd.	1990	9.00	100-200
1990	Happy Gnome 77	Retrd.	1991	8.00	75
1990	Holly Ball 4	Retrd.	N/A	19.00	125
1990	Honey Bear 167	Retrd.	N/A	14.00	55
1990	Jester 41	Retrd.	N/A	16.50	120
1990	Joey Clown (red striped) 55	Retrd.	N/A	14.00	90-150
1990	Kim Ono 79	Retrd.	1990	6.00	55
1990	King Arthur (Red) 72	Retrd.	N/A	16.00	110
1990	Lullaby 47	Retrd.	1990	9.00	50
1990	Maracca 94	Retrd.	1990	9.00	125
1990	Mediterranean Sunshine 140	Retrd.	N/A	27.00	34
1990	Mission Ball 26	Retrd.	N/A	18.00	48
1990	Mother Goose (blue bonnet/pink shawl) 52	Retrd.	N/A	10.00	50-75
1990	Nativity 36	Retrd.	1990	6.00	50
1990	Peacock (on snowball) 74	Retrd.	N/A	18.00	75-100
1990	Pierre Le Berry	Retrd.	N/A	10.00	80-150
1990	Polish Folk Dance 13	Retrd.	N/A	19.00	120-150
1990	Praying Angel 37	Retrd.	N/A	5.00	75
1990	Proud Peacock 74	Retrd.	N/A	18.00	90-125
1990	Roly Poly Santa (Red bottom) 69	Retrd.	N/A	13.00	90
1990	Rose Lamp 96	Retrd.	1990	14.00	90
1990	Santa on Ball 80	Retrd.	1991	16.00	100
1990	Silent Movie (black hat) 75	Retrd.	1990	8.50	70-100
1990	Small Nautilus Shell 78	Retrd.	N/A	7.00	22
1990	Smiling Kite 63	Retrd.	1990	14.00	50-100
1990	Snowball Tree 71	Retrd.	1990	17.00	60
1990	Snowman on Ball 45	Retrd.	1990	14.00	75
1990	Southwest Indian Ball 19	Retrd.	N/A	19.00	240
1990	Spin Top 90	Retrd.	N/A	11.00	95
1990	Summer Parasol 88	Retrd.	N/A	7.00	
1990	Sunburst Fish (green/yellow) 68	Retrd.	N/A	13.00	50
1990	Trumpet Player 83	Retrd.	N/A	18.00	100
1990	Tuxedo Penquin 57	Retrd.	1990	8.00	750
1990	Walrus 59	Retrd.	1990	8.50	120
1990	Yarn Fight 23	Retrd.	N/A	17.00	125-150

1991 Holiday Collection - C. Radko

YEAR ISSUE		EDITION LIMIT	YEAR RETD.	ISSUE PRICE	*QUOTE U.S. $
1991	All Weather Santa 137	Retrd.	1992	32.00	250-350
1991	Alladin 29	Retrd.	N/A	14.00	40
1991	Altar Boy 18	Retrd.	1992	16.00	35
1991	Anchor America 65	Retrd.	1992	21.50	55-75
1991	Apache 42	Retrd.	N/A	8.50	50-75
1991	Aspen 76	Retrd.	1992	20.50	45-100
1991	Aztec 141	Retrd.	1991	21.50	100
1991	Aztec Bird 41	Retrd.	1992	20.00	60-120
1991	Ballooning Santa 110	Retrd.	1991	23.00	145-165
1991	Barnum Clown 56	Retrd.	1991	15.00	55-95
1991	Bishop 22	Retrd.	N/A	15.00	50
1991	Blue Rainbow 136	Retrd.	1992	21.50	100-140
1991	Bowery Kid 50	Retrd.	1991	14.50	50
1991	By the Nile 124	Retrd.	1992	21.50	45-65
1991	Chance Encounter 104	Retrd.	1992	13.50	40
1991	Chief Sitting Bull 107	Retrd.	1992	16.00	75
1991	Chimney Santa 12	Retrd.	N/A	14.50	40
1991	Clown Drum 33	Retrd.	1991	14.00	100
1991	Comet 62	Retrd.	1991	9.00	80
1991	Cosette 16	Retrd.	1991	16.00	45-60
1991	Dapper Shoe 89	Retrd.	1991	10.00	45-90
1991	Dawn & Dust 34	Retrd.	N/A	14.00	50-75
1991	Deco Floral 133	Retrd.	1991	22.00	75-125
1991	Deco Sparkle 134	Retrd.	1992	21.00	50-100
1991	Dutch Boy 27	Retrd.	1991	11.00	55
1991	Dutch Girl 28	Retrd.	1991	11.00	55-75
1991	Edwardian Lace 82	Retrd.	1991	21.50	125
1991	Einstein Kite 98	Retrd.	N/A	20.00	75-125
1991	Elephant on Ball (striped) 115	Retrd.	N/A	23.00	250-450
1991	Elf Reflector 135	Retrd.	1992	23.00	50
1991	Evening Santa 20	Retrd.	N/A	14.50	150
1991	Fanfare 126	Retrd.	1992	21.50	98
1991	Fisher Frog 44	Retrd.	1991	11.00	65-125
1991	Florentine 83	Retrd.	N/A	22.00	45-100
1991	Flower Child 90	Retrd.	1991	13.00	65
1991	Frog Under Balloon 53	Retrd.	N/A	16.00	45
1991	Froggy Child 26	Retrd.	N/A	9.00	45
1991	Fruit in Balloon 40	Retrd.	N/A	22.00	90-180
1991	Fu Manchu 11	Retrd.	N/A	15.00	75
1991	Galaxy 120	Retrd.	1991	21.50	95
1991	Grapefruit Tree 113	Retrd.	N/A	23.00	125-225
1991	Harvest 3	Retrd.	N/A	13.50	25
1991	Hatching Duck 35	Retrd.	1991	14.00	50
1991	Hearts & Flowers Finial 158	Retrd.	1993	53.00	253
1991	Her Majesty 39	Retrd.	1991	21.00	100
1991	Her Purse 88	Retrd.	N/A	10.00	55-65
1991	Holly Ball 156	Retrd.	N/A	22.00	60
1991	Irish Laddie 10	Retrd.	1991	12.00	75
1991	Jemima's Child 111	Retrd.	1991	16.00	80-100
1991	King Arthur (Blue) 95	Retrd.	N/A	18.50	55-85
1991	Lion's Head 31	Retrd.	N/A	16.00	45-95
1991	Madeleine's Puppy 25	Retrd.	N/A	11.00	90
1991	Madonna & Child 103	Retrd.	N/A	15.00	125
1991	Melon Slice 99	Retrd.	N/A	18.00	31
1991	Mother Goose 57	Retrd.	N/A	11.00	40
1991	Ms. Maus 94	Retrd.	N/A	14.00	120
1991	Olympiad 125	Retrd.	1992	22.00	125
1991	Patrick's Bunny 24	Retrd.	N/A	11.00	45
1991	Peruvian 74	Retrd.	1991	21.50	100-240
1991	Pierre Le Berry 2	Retrd.	1993	14.00	100-200
1991	Pink Clown on Ball 32	Retrd.	N/A	14.00	55
1991	Pink Elephants 70	Retrd.	N/A	21.50	130-175
1991	Pipe Smoking Monkey 54	Retrd.	1991	11.00	75
1991	Polish Folk Art 116	Retrd.	N/A	20.50	50-75
1991	Prince on Ball (pink/blue/green) 51	Retrd.	1991	15.00	80
1991	Prince Umbrella 21	Retrd.	1991	15.00	100-135
1991	Proud Peacock 37	Retrd.	N/A	23.00	37
1991	Rainbow Bird 92	Retrd.	1991	16.00	35-45
1991	Raspberry & Lime 96	Retrd.	1991	12.00	50
1991	Red Star 129	Retrd.	1992	21.50	50-75
1991	Russian Santa (coral) 112-4	Retrd.	N/A	22.00	60
1991	Russian Santa (white) 112	Retrd.	N/A	22.00	75
1991	Sally Ann 43	Retrd.	1991	8.00	40
1991	Santa Bootie (blue) 55	Retrd.	N/A	10.00	75
1991	Santa Bootie 55	Retrd.	1993	10.00	55
1991	Santa in Winter White (red) 112-2	Retrd.	N/A	22.00	65
1991	Santa in Winter White (silver) 112-1	Retrd.	N/A	22.00	N/A
1991	Shirley 15	Retrd.	1991	16.00	75-125
1991	Shy Elf 1	Retrd.	1991	10.00	45
1991	Sleepy Time Santa 52	Retrd.	N/A	15.00	60-125
1991	Smitty 9	Retrd.	N/A	15.00	125
1991	Star Quilt 139	Retrd.	1991	21.50	50-75
1991	Sunburst Fish 108	Retrd.	N/A	15.00	28
1991	Sunshine 67	Retrd.	N/A	22.00	40
1991	Tabby 46	Retrd.	1991	8.00	30-50
1991	Tiffany 68	Retrd.	1991	22.00	50
1991	Tiger 5	Retrd.	N/A	15.00	60-95
1991	Trigger 114	Retrd.	1991	15.00	150-160
1991	Trumpet Man 100	Retrd.	1992	21.00	95
1991	Tulip Fairy 63	Retrd.	1992	16.00	65
1991	Vienna 1901 127	Retrd.	1992	21.50	200
1991	Villandry 87	Retrd.	1991	21.00	185
1991	Winking St. Nick 102	Retrd.	N/A	16.00	65-95
1991	Woodland Santa 38	Retrd.	N/A	14.00	55-75
1991	Zebra (glittered) 79	Retrd.	1991	22.00	400-500

1992 Holiday Collection - C. Radko

YEAR ISSUE		EDITION LIMIT	YEAR RETD.	ISSUE PRICE	*QUOTE U.S. $
1992	Alpine Flowers 162	Retrd.	1992	28.00	50
1992	Alpine Village 105	Retrd.	N/A	24.00	125
1992	Aspen 120	Retrd.	1992	26.00	50
1992	Barbie's Mom 69	Retrd.	1992	18.00	60-100
1992	Benjamin's Nutcrackers (pr.) 185	Retrd.	N/A	58.00	200-300
1992	Binkie the Clown 168	Retrd.	N/A	12.00	20
1992	Blue Santa 65	Retrd.	N/A	18.00	45
1992	Butterfly Bouquet 119	Retrd.	1992	26.50	125
1992	By the Nile 139	Retrd.	1992	27.00	50-75
1992	Cabaret (see-through) 159	Retrd.	1993	28.00	60
1992	Candy Trumpet Men (pink/blue) 98	Retrd.	N/A	27.00	75
1992	Candy Trumpet Men (red) w/ white glitter 98	Retrd.	1992	27.00	80
1992	Candy Trumpet Men (red) w/o white glitter 98	Retrd.	N/A	27.00	45
1992	Celestial 129	Retrd.	N/A	26.00	100
1992	Cheerful Sun 50	Retrd.	N/A	18.00	40
1992	Chevron 160	Retrd.	1992	28.00	40
1992	Chevron-Tiffany 160	Retrd.	N/A	28.00	98
1992	Chimney Sweep Bell 179	Retrd.	N/A	27.00	150
1992	Choir Boy 114	Retrd.	1992	24.00	50
1992	Christmas Cardinals 123	Retrd.	1992	26.00	100-125
1992	Christmas Rose 143	Retrd.	1992	25.50	45
1992	Circus Lady 54	Retrd.	1992	12.00	25
1992	Clown Snake 62	Retrd.	N/A	22.00	75
1992	Country Scene 169	Retrd.	N/A	12.00	90
1992	Country Star Quilt 176	Retrd.	N/A	12.00	100
1992	Cowboy Santa 94	Retrd.	N/A	24.00	100
1992	Delft Design 124	Retrd.	1992	26.50	170
1992	Diva 73	Retrd.	1992	17.00	100-135
1992	Dolly Madison 115	Retrd.	1992	17.00	65
1992	Downhill Racer 76	Retrd.	1992	34.00	75-140
1992	Elephant on Parade 141	Retrd.	1992	26.00	70-85
1992	Elephant Reflector 181	Retrd.	N/A	17.00	35-75
1992	Elf Reflectors 136	Retrd.	1992	28.00	36
1992	Faberge (pink/lavender) 148	Retrd.	N/A	26.50	45-55
1992	Faith, Hope & Love 183	Retrd.	1992	12.00	30
1992	Festive Smitty	Retrd.	N/A	N/A	80-125
1992	Floral Cascade Tier Drop 175	Retrd.	1992	32.00	50-125
1992	Florentine 131	Retrd.	N/A	27.00	45-75
1992	Flutter By's 201(Set/4)	Retrd.	N/A	11.00	65
1992	Folk Art Set 95	Retrd.	1992	10.00	13
1992	Forest Friends 103	Retrd.	1992	14.00	18
1992	French Country 121	Retrd.	N/A	26.00	50-90
1992	Fruit in Balloon 83	Retrd.	N/A	28.00	250-275
1992	Gabriel's Trumpets 188	Retrd.	N/A	20.00	25
1992	Harlequin Tier Drop 74	Retrd.	1992	36.00	95
1992	Harold Lloyd Reflector 218	Retrd.	1992	70.00	200-450
1992	Her Slipper 56	Retrd.	1992	17.00	22
1992	Holly Finial 200	Retrd.	N/A	70.00	83
1992	Honey Bear 167	Retrd.	N/A	14.00	55
1992	Ice Pear 241	Retrd.	N/A	20.00	50-75
1992	Ice Poppies 127	Retrd.	1992	26.00	60
1992	Jumbo 99	Retrd.	N/A	31.00	45
1992	Kewpie 51	Retrd.	N/A	18.00	65
1992	King of Prussia 149	Retrd.	1992	27.00	100
1992	Kitty Rattle 166	Retrd.	1993	18.00	50-95
1992	Little League 53	Retrd.	1992	20.00	85
1992	The Littlest Snowman (red hat) 67	Retrd.	N/A	14.00	25-75
1992	Locamotive Garland 216	Retrd.	N/A	60.00	120
1992	Mediterranean Sunshine 140	Retrd.	N/A	17.00	34
1992	Merlin Santa 75	Retrd.	N/A	32.00	60
1992	Merry Christmas Maiden 137	Retrd.	1992	26.00	40
1992	Mother Goose 37	Retrd.	N/A	15.00	25
1992	Mr. & Mrs. Claus 59	Retrd.	N/A	18.00	200
1992	Mushroom Elf 87	Retrd.	N/A	18.00	25-45
1992	Neopolitan Angels 152 (Set/3)	Retrd.	1992	27.00	300-400
1992	Norweigian Princess 170	Retrd.	1992	15.00	75-125
1992	Olympiad 132	Retrd.	N/A	26.00	80
1992	Pierre Winterberry 64	Retrd.	1993	17.00	75-175
1992	Pink Lace Ball (See Through) 158	Retrd.	1992	28.00	100-200
1992	Polar Bear 184	Retrd.	N/A	16.00	50
1992	Primary Colors 108	Retrd.	1992	30.00	150
1992	Quilted Hearts (Old Salem Museum) 194	Retrd.	N/A	27.50	55
1992	Rainbow Parasol 90	Retrd.	1992	30.00	100
1992	Royal Scepter 77	Retrd.	1992	36.00	100-200
1992	Russian Imperial 112	Retrd.	1992	25.00	75
1992	Russian Jewel Hearts 146	Retrd.	N/A	27.00	50-125
1992	Russian Star 130	Retrd.	1992	26.00	32-40
1992	Sail Away 215	Retrd.	N/A	22.00	50
1992	Sanke Prince 171	Retrd.	N/A	19.00	40
1992	Santa in Winter White 106	Retrd.	N/A	28.00	65
1992	Seahorse (pink) 92	Retrd.	1992	20.00	86
1992	Serpents of Paradise 97	Retrd.	N/A	13.00	30
1992	Siberian Sleighride (pink) 154	Retrd.	N/A	27.00	100-150
1992	Sitting Bull 93	Retrd.	1992	26.00	75
1992	Sleepytime Santa (pink) 81	Retrd.	N/A	18.00	95
1992	Sloopy Snowman 328	Retrd.	N/A	19.90	75
1992	Snowflakes 209	Retrd.	N/A	10.00	40
1992	Sputniks 134	Retrd.	1992	25.50	75-125
1992	St. Nickcicle 107	Retrd.	N/A	26.00	35-90
1992	Star of Wonder 177	Retrd.	1992	27.00	35
1992	Starbursts 214	Retrd.	N/A	12.00	75
1992	Stardust Joey 110	Retrd.	1992	16.00	75-150
1992	Starlight Santa (powder blue) 180	Retrd.	N/A	18.00	50
1992	Talking Pipe (black stem) 104	Retrd.	N/A	26.00	110
1992	Thunderbolt 178	Retrd.	1993	60.00	75
1992	Tiffany Bright Harlequin 161	Retrd.	1992	28.00	75
1992	Tiffany Pastel Harlequin 163	Retrd.	N/A	28.00	100
1992	To Grandma's House 239	Retrd.	N/A	20.00	55
1992	Topiary 117	Retrd.	N/A	30.00	250-400
1992	Tropical Fish 109	Retrd.	N/A	17.00	60
1992	Tulip Fairy 57	Retrd.	1992	18.00	45
1992	Tuxedo Santa 88	Retrd.	1993	22.00	150-170
1992	Two Sided Santa Reflector 102	Retrd.	1992	28.00	75
1992	Umbrella Santa 182	Retrd.	N/A	60.00	140-190
1992	Victorian Santa & Angel Balloon 122	Retrd.	1992	68.00	500-600
1992	Vienna 1901 128	Retrd.	1992	27.00	150
1992	Virgin Mary 46	Retrd.	1992	20.00	29
1992	Wacko's Brother, Doofus 55	Retrd.	N/A	20.00	75-150
1992	Water Lilies 133	Retrd.	1992	26.00	100
1992	Wedding Bells 217	Retrd.	N/A	40.00	165-225
1992	Winter Kiss 82	Retrd.	N/A	18.00	40
1992	Winter Wonderland 156	Retrd.	1992	26.00	110
1992	Woodland Santa 111	Retrd.	N/A	20.00	55-75
1992	Ziegfeld Follies 126	Retrd.	1992	27.00	100-130

1993 Holiday Collection - C. Radko

YEAR ISSUE		EDITION LIMIT	YEAR RETD.	ISSUE PRICE	*QUOTE U.S. $
1993	1939 World's Fair 149	Retrd.	N/A	26.80	100
1993	Accordian Elf 189	Retrd.	N/A	21.00	65
1993	Aladdin's Lamp 237	Retrd.	N/A	20.00	35-45
1993	Alpine Village 420	Retrd.	1993	23.80	125
1993	Alpine Wings 86	Retrd.	N/A	58.00	108
1993	Anassazi 172	Retrd.	N/A	26.60	75-175
1993	Anchor Santa 407	Retrd.	N/A	32.00	83
1993	Angel of Peace 132	Retrd.	1993	17.00	60-85
1993	Apache 357	Retrd.	1993	13.90	75
1993	Auld Lang Syne 246	Retrd.	N/A	15.00	35
1993	Bavarian Santa 335	Retrd.	N/A	23.00	30
1993	Bedtime Buddy 239	Retrd.	N/A	29.00	90-125
1993	Bell House Boy 291	Retrd.	1993	21.00	32
1993	Beyond the Stars 108	Retrd.	1993	18.50	70-90
1993	Bishop of Myra 327	Retrd.	1993	19.90	50
1993	Blue Top 114	Retrd.	1993	16.00	75
1993	Bowzer 228	Retrd.	N/A	22.80	150
1993	By Jiminy 285	Retrd.	N/A	16.40	45
1993	Calla Lilly 314	Retrd.	N/A	12.90	25
1993	Carnival Rides 303	Retrd.	N/A	18.00	75-95
1993	Celeste 271	Retrd.	N/A	26.00	100-175
1993	Celestial Peacock Finial 322	Retrd.	N/A	69.00	200-295
1993	Center Ring (Exclusive) 192	Retrd.	1993	30.80	38
1993	Centurian 224	Retrd.	1993	25.50	125-225
1993	Chimney Sweep Bell 294	Retrd.	1993	26.00	180
1993	Christmas Express 394 (Garland)	Retrd.	N/A	58.00	220
1993	Christmas Stars 342	Retrd.	N/A	14.00	32
1993	Church Bell 295	Retrd.	N/A	24.00	35
1993	Cinderella's Bluebirds 145	Retrd.	1993	25.90	65-120
1993	Circle of Santas Finial 413	Retrd.	N/A	69.00	100
1993	Circus Seal 249	Retrd.	1993	28.00	95-125
1993	Class Clown 332	Retrd.	N/A	21.00	65
1993	Clowning Around 84	Retrd.	N/A	42.50	68
1993	Confucius 363	Retrd.	1993	19.00	28
1993	Cool Cat 184	Retrd.	N/A	21.00	100-150
1993	Copenhagen 166	Retrd.	1993	26.80	75-100
1993	Country Flowers 205	Retrd.	N/A	16.00	35
1993	Crowned Passion 299	Retrd.	1993	23.00	60
1993	Crystal Rainbow 308	Retrd.	N/A	29.90	200
1993	Deco Snowfall 147	Retrd.	1993	26.80	45
1993	Deer Drop 304	Retrd.	N/A	34.00	150-200
1993	Downhill Racer 195	Retrd.	1993	30.00	60-75

*Quotes have been rounded up to nearest dollar

ORNAMENTS

Christopher Radko
to Christopher Radko

YEAR ISSUE		EDITION LIMIT	YEAR RETD.	ISSUE PRICE	*QUOTE U.S.$
1993	Eggman 241	Retrd.	N/A	22.50	40
1993	Emerald Wizard 279	Retrd.	N/A	18.00	65
1993	Emperor's Pet 253	Retrd.	1993	22.00	95-195
1993	Enchanted Gardens 341	Retrd.	1993	5.50	13
1993	English Kitchen 234	Retrd.	1993	26.00	50
1993	Epiphany 421	Retrd.	N/A	29.00	90
1993	Evening Star Santa 409	Retrd.	1993	59.00	95
1993	Faberge Egg 257	Retrd.	N/A	17.50	45
1993	Fantastia 143	Retrd.	N/A	24.00	130
1993	Far Out Santa 138	Retrd.	N/A	39.00	60
1993	Fiesta Ball 316	Retrd.	N/A	26.40	85
1993	Flora Dora 255	Retrd.	N/A	25.00	90
1993	Fly Boy 235	Retrd.	N/A	33.00	65
1993	Forest Friends 250	Retrd.	1993	28.00	40-75
1993	French Rose 152	Retrd.	1993	26.60	40
1993	Fruit in Balloon 115	Retrd.	N/A	27.90	80
1993	Geisha Girls 261	Retrd.	1993	11.90	60
1993	Glory on High 116	Retrd.	N/A	17.00	150
1993	Gold Fish 158	Retrd.	1993	25.80	75-100
1993	Goofy Fruits 367	Retrd.	N/A	14.00	65
1993	Goofy Garden 191 (Set/4)	Retrd.	N/A	15.00	200-240
1993	Grandpa Bear 260	Retrd.	1993	12.80	13-20
1993	Grecian Urn 231	Retrd.	1993	23.00	50
1993	Guardian Angel 124	Retrd.	N/A	36.00	120
1993	Gypsy Girl 371	Retrd.	1993	16.00	35
1993	Holiday Spice 422	Retrd.	1993	24.00	24
1993	Honey Bear 352	Retrd.	1993	13.90	55
1993	Ice Star Santa 405	Retrd.	1993	38.00	130-150
1993	Jack Frost (blue) 333	Retrd.	N/A	23.00	75
1993	Jaques Le Berry 356	Retrd.	N/A	16.90	100-175
1993	Joey B. Clown 135	Retrd.	N/A	26.00	75-150
1993	Jumbo Spintops 302	Retrd.	N/A	27.00	48
1993	Just Like Grandma's Lg. 200	Retrd.	N/A	7.20	50
1993	Just Like Grandma's Sm. 200	Retrd.	N/A	7.20	30
1993	Kissing Cousins 245 (Pair)	Retrd.	N/A	30.00	100-200
1993	Kitty Rattle 374	Retrd.	1993	17.80	90
1993	Letter to Santa 188	Retrd.	N/A	22.00	55
1993	Light in the Windows 229	Retrd.	1994	24.50	30
1993	Little Doggie 180	Retrd.	1993	7.00	40
1993	Little Eskimo 355	Retrd.	N/A	13.90	21
1993	Majestic Reflector 312	Retrd.	1993	70.00	100
1993	Mediterranean Sunshine 156	Retrd.	N/A	26.90	75
1993	Midas Touch 162	Retrd.	N/A	27.80	68
1993	Monkey Man 97	Retrd.	1993	16.00	100-180
1993	Monterey 290	Retrd.	1993	15.00	75-100
1993	Mooning Over You 106	Retrd.	N/A	17.00	45
1993	Mr. & Mrs. Claus 121	Retrd.	1993	17.90	80-125
1993	Mushroom Elf 267	Retrd.	N/A	17.90	38
1993	Mushroom Santa 212	Retrd.	N/A	28.00	75
1993	Nellie (Italian ornament) 225	Retrd.	1993	27.50	100-200
1993	North Woods 317	Retrd.	1993	26.80	45-100
1993	One Small Leap 222	Retrd.	N/A	26.00	120-250
1993	Pagoda 258	Retrd.	1993	8.00	15
1993	Pennsylvania Dutch 146	Retrd.	1993	26.80	65
1993	Piggly Wiggly 101	Retrd.	N/A	11.00	40
1993	Pineapple Quilt 150	Retrd.	N/A	26.80	65
1993	Pinocchio 248	Retrd.	N/A	26.00	75-100
1993	Pixie Santa 186	Retrd.	N/A	16.00	75
1993	Poinsetta Santa 269	Retrd.	N/A	19.80	76
1993	Polar Bears 112A	Retrd.	1993	15.50	16
1993	Pompadour 344	Retrd.	1993	8.80	25
1993	Prince Albert 263	Retrd.	N/A	23.00	80
1993	Purse 389	Retrd.	1993	15.60	16
1993	Quartet 392	Retrd.	1993	3.60	11
1993	Rainbow Reflector 154	Retrd.	1993	26.60	30-40
1993	Rainbow Shark 277	Retrd.	N/A	18.00	70
1993	Rainy Day Friend 206	Retrd.	N/A	22.00	45-100
1993	Regal Rooster 177	Retrd.	N/A	25.80	75
1993	Rose Pointe Finial 323	Retrd.	1993	34.00	40
1993	Sail by Starlight 339	Retrd.	1993	11.80	14-19
1993	Sailor Man 238	Retrd.	N/A	22.00	140
1993	Santa Baby 112	Retrd.	N/A	18.00	45
1993	Santa in Space 127	Retrd.	N/A	39.00	200
1993	Santa in Winter White 300	Retrd.	N/A	27.90	65
1993	Santa Tree 320	Retrd.	N/A	66.00	240-340
1993	Santa's Helper 329	Retrd.	N/A	16.90	40
1993	Saraband 140	Retrd.	1993	27.80	150-200
1993	Scotch Pine 167	Retrd.	N/A	26.80	95
1993	Serenade Pink 157	Retrd.	1993	26.80	60
1993	Shy Rabbit 280	Retrd.	N/A	14.00	75-90
1993	Siegfred 227	Retrd.	N/A	25.00	60
1993	Silent Night (blue hat) 120	Retrd.	N/A	18.00	75
1993	Silent Night 120	Retrd.	N/A	18.00	75
1993	The Skating Bettinas 242	Retrd.	N/A	29.00	120-160
1993	Ski Baby 99	Retrd.	N/A	21.00	165
1993	Sloopy Snowman 328	Retrd.	1993	19.90	55
1993	Smitty 378	Retrd.	N/A	17.90	90-130
1993	Snow Dance 247	Retrd.	N/A	29.00	90
1993	Snowday Santa 98	Retrd.	1993	20.00	70
1993	Snowman by Candlelight 155	Retrd.	N/A	26.50	60-75
1993	Southern Colonial 171	Retrd.	N/A	26.90	85-135
1993	Spider & the Fly 393	Retrd.	1993	6.40	30
1993	Sporty 345	Retrd.	N/A	20.00	65
1993	St. Nick's Pipe 330	Retrd.	N/A	4.40	75
1993	St. Nickcicle 298	Retrd.	N/A	25.90	35
1993	Star Children 208	Retrd.	1993	18.00	60
1993	Star Fire 175	Retrd.	N/A	26.80	45-75
1993	Starlight Santa 348	Retrd.	N/A	11.90	19
1993	Stocking Stuffers 236	Retrd.	1993	16.00	23
1993	Sunny Side Up 103	Retrd.	N/A	22.00	55
1993	Sweetheart 202	Retrd.	1993	16.00	50-75

YEAR ISSUE		EDITION LIMIT	YEAR RETD.	ISSUE PRICE	*QUOTE U.S.$
1993	Talking Pipe 373	Retrd.	N/A	26.00	55
1993	Texas Star 338	Retrd.	1993	7.50	8
1993	Thomas Nast Santa 217	Retrd.	N/A	23.00	40
1993	Tuxedo Santa 117	Retrd.	1993	21.90	150
1993	Tweeter 94	Retrd.	1993	3.20	6
1993	Twinkle Toes 233	Retrd.	N/A	28.00	59
1993	Twinkle Tree 254	Retrd.	N/A	15.50	45
1993	Twister 214	Retrd.	N/A	16.80	65
1993	U-Boat 353	Retrd.	1993	15.50	50
1993	V.I.P. 230	Retrd.	1993	23.00	100-200
1993	Victorian Santa Reflector 198	Retrd.	N/A	28.00	70
1993	Waddles 95	Retrd.	1993	3.80	65
1993	Winterbirds (pr.) 164	Retrd.	1993	26.80	100

1994 Holiday Collection - C. Radko

YEAR ISSUE		EDITION LIMIT	YEAR RETD.	ISSUE PRICE	*QUOTE U.S.$
1994	Accordion Elf 127	Retrd.	N/A	23.00	65
1994	Andy Gump 48	Retrd.	N/A	18.00	40
1994	Angel Song 141	Retrd.	N/A	45.60	145
1994	Baby Booties (pink) 236	Retrd.	N/A	17.00	35
1994	Batter Up 397	Retrd.	N/A	13.00	25
1994	Bird Brain 254	Retrd.	N/A	33.00	65-95
1994	Bright Heavens Above 136	Retrd.	N/A	56.00	100-125
1994	Candelabra 303	Retrd.	N/A	33.00	85
1994	Castanetta 321	Retrd.	N/A	37.00	105
1994	Chic of Araby 220	Retrd.	N/A	17.00	65
1994	Chubbs & Slim 255	Retrd.	N/A	28.50	45
1994	Cool Cat 219	Retrd.	N/A	26.00	50-100
1994	Corn Husk 336	Retrd.	N/A	13.00	20
1994	Crescent Moons 195	Retrd.	N/A	29.00	75-150
1994	Crock O'Dile 297	Retrd.	N/A	33.00	75
1994	Einstein's Kite 375	Retrd.	N/A	29.90	45
1994	Elephant Prince 170	Retrd.	N/A	14.50	25
1994	Fleet's In 281	Retrd.	N/A	38.00	45
1994	Florentine 190	Retrd.	N/A	29.00	48
1994	French Country 192	Retrd.	N/A	29.00	65-95
1994	French Regency Balloon 393	Retrd.	N/A	32.50	45
1994	Glow Worm 275	Retrd.	N/A	32.00	50-125
1994	Golden Crescendo Finial 384	Retrd.	N/A	42.00	100-125
1994	Hieroglyph 194	Retrd.	N/A	29.00	45-100
1994	Holly Heart 402	Retrd.	N/A	24.00	32
1994	Holly Ribbons Finial 407	Retrd.	N/A	78.00	95
1994	Honey Belle 156	Retrd.	N/A	74.00	100-125
1994	Horse of a Different Color 309	Retrd.	N/A	28.00	140
1994	House Sitting Santa 240	Retrd.	N/A	26.00	30
1994	Ice Man Cometh 63	Retrd.	N/A	22.00	70
1994	Jack Clown 68	Retrd.	N/A	22.00	50
1994	Jockey Pipe 51	Retrd.	N/A	36.00	95-130
1994	Jolly Stripes 210	Retrd.	N/A	28.00	38
1994	Just Like Us 324	Retrd.	N/A	29.50	120-160
1994	Kayo 165	Retrd.	N/A	14.00	25
1994	Kewpie 292	Retrd.	N/A	22.00	40
1994	King of Kings 18	Retrd.	N/A	22.00	45-75
1994	Kissing Cousins (pair) 249	Retrd.	N/A	28.00	200
1994	Kitty Tamer 331	Retrd.	N/A	65.00	350
1994	Leader of the Band 94-915D (wh. pants) - signed	Retrd.	1994	25.00	360
1994	Leader of the Band 94-915D (wh. pants) - unsigned	Retrd.	1994	25.00	120-150
1994	Lemon Twist 28	Retrd.	N/A	14.00	40
1994	Letter to Santa 77	Retrd.	N/A	31.00	55
1994	Little Orphan 47	Retrd.	N/A	18.00	65
1994	The Los Angeles 155	Retrd.	N/A	26.00	45
1994	Martian Holiday 326	Retrd.	N/A	42.00	65-130
1994	Masquerade 45	Retrd.	N/A	16.00	55-75
1994	Medium Nautilus (gold) 103	Retrd.	N/A	16.00	50-75
1994	Moon Martian 298	Retrd.	N/A	26.00	140-175
1994	Moon Mullins 230	Retrd.	N/A	18.00	45
1994	Moon Ride 60	Retrd.	N/A	28.00	68
1994	Mother and Child 83	Retrd.	N/A	28.50	60
1994	Mr. Smedley Drysdale 37	Retrd.	N/A	44.00	180-275
1994	My What Big Teeth	Retrd.	N/A	29.00	80
1994	Nighty Night 299	Retrd.	N/A	36.00	60-120
1994	Old Sour Puss 256	Retrd.	N/A	34.00	60-75
1994	On The Run (Spoon/left side) 247	Retrd.	N/A	45.00	100-125
1994	Over The Waves 261	Retrd.	N/A	38.00	95
1994	Owl Reflector 40	Retrd.	N/A	54.00	75
1994	Papa's Jamboree 427	Retrd.	N/A	29.00	45-75
1994	Partridge Pear Garland 435	Retrd.	N/A	68.00	95
1994	Party Hopper 274	Retrd.	N/A	37.00	165-250
1994	Pickled 317	Retrd.	N/A	26.00	60
1994	Piggly Wiggly 169	Retrd.	N/A	14.00	40
1994	Piglet 294	Retrd.	N/A	13.00	45
1994	Pinecone Santa 118	Retrd.	N/A	29.50	75-100
1994	Pinocchio Gets Hitched 250	Retrd.	N/A	29.50	100-142
1994	Pixie Santa 218	Retrd.	N/A	20.00	50
1994	President Taft 74	Retrd.	N/A	18.00	50
1994	Prince Philip 909	Retrd.	N/A	20.00	150
1994	Private Eye 163	Retrd.	N/A	18.00	35
1994	Quick Draw 330	Retrd.	N/A	65.00	300
1994	Ring Master 61	Retrd.	N/A	22.00	50
1994	Ringing Red Boots 114	Retrd.	N/A	46.00	85
1994	Roly Poly Clown 173	Retrd.	N/A	19.40	75
1994	Royale Finial 382	Retrd.	N/A	64.00	95
1994	Santa Copter 306	Retrd.	N/A	47.00	75
1994	Santa's Helper 131	Retrd.	N/A	19.90	25
1994	Ships Ahoy 263	Retrd.	N/A	38.00	48
1994	Shivers 262	Retrd.	N/A	25.00	200-250
1994	Silent Night 129	Retrd.	N/A	27.00	55
1994	Smiley 52	Retrd.	N/A	16.00	50
1994	Snow Bell 237	Retrd.	N/A	13.00	60
1994	Soldier Boy 142	Retrd.	N/A	19.00	100-125

YEAR ISSUE		EDITION LIMIT	YEAR RETD.	ISSUE PRICE	*QUOTE U.S.$
1994	Squiggles 157	Retrd.	N/A	29.90	45
1994	Stocking Sam 108	Retrd.	N/A	23.00	30-40
1994	Surf's Up 325	Retrd.	N/A	36.00	65
1994	Swami 128	Retrd.	N/A	18.00	25
1994	Sweet Pear 59	Retrd.	N/A	24.00	60
1994	Teddy Roosevelt 232	Retrd.	N/A	22.00	75
1994	Teenage Mermaid 270	Retrd.	N/A	33.00	58
1994	Terrance 53	Retrd.	N/A	16.00	45
1994	Tiny Nautilus (gold) 100	Retrd.	N/A	12.00	45
1994	Valcourt 213	Retrd.	N/A	29.00	95
1994	Vaudeville Sam 57	Retrd.	N/A	18.00	30
1994	Wedded Bliss 94	Retrd.	N/A	88.00	195
1994	Wednesday 120	Retrd.	N/A	42.00	70-95
1994	White Nights 197	Retrd.	N/A	26.00	65-75
1994	Wings and a Snail 301	Retrd.	N/A	32.00	50-125
1994	Winter Frolic 287	Retrd.	N/A	18.00	55
1994	Xenon 304	Retrd.	N/A	38.00	200-250

1995 Holiday Collection - C. Radko

YEAR ISSUE		EDITION LIMIT	YEAR RETD.	ISSUE PRICE	*QUOTE U.S.$
1995	Andrew Jacksons, pair 208	Retrd.	1995	68.00	200
1995	Bringing Home the Bacon 204	Retrd.	N/A	26.00	60
1995	Claudette 17	Retrd.	N/A	N/A	37
1995	Claudette 95-017-0	Retrd.	1995	22.00	90
1995	Dutch Dolls 136	Retrd.	N/A	22.00	40
1995	Farmer Boy 108	Retrd.	N/A	28.00	60
1995	Flying High 8	Retrd.	N/A	22.00	50
1995	Frog Lady 26	Retrd.	N/A	24.00	50
1995	Garden Girls (pair) 39	Retrd.	N/A	18.00	70
1995	Gunther 233	Retrd.	N/A	32.00	90-170
1995	Here Boy 222	Retrd.	N/A	12.00	25-35
1995	Hubbard's the Name 206	Retrd.	N/A	26.00	55-65
1995	Imperial Helmet 240	Retrd.	N/A	22.00	35
1995	Joy To The World 42	Retrd.	N/A	68.00	90
1995	Jumbo Walnut 249	Retrd.	N/A	18.00	35
1995	Kaleidoscope Cone 25	Retrd.	N/A	44.00	66
1995	Little Red 214	Retrd.	N/A	22.00	40
1995	Little Toy Maker 167	Retrd.	N/A	26.00	50
1995	Off to Market 223	Retrd.	N/A	24.00	35
1995	Penelope 197	Retrd.	N/A	26.00	30
1995	Personal Delivery 116	Retrd.	N/A	36.00	70
1995	Sister Act-set 140	Retrd.	N/A	18.00	65
1995	Sweet Madame 192	Retrd.	N/A	48.00	100
1995	Turtle Bird 121	Retrd.	N/A	22.00	40

Event Only - C. Radko

YEAR ISSUE		EDITION LIMIT	YEAR RETD.	ISSUE PRICE	*QUOTE U.S.$
1993	Littlest Snowman 347S (store & C. Radko event)	Retrd.	1993	15.00	90
1994	Roly Poly 94125E (store & C. Radko event)	Retrd.	1994	22.00	35-70
1995	Forever Lucy 91075E (store & C. Radko event)	Retrd.	1995	32.00	45
1996	Poinsettia Elegance 287E (store event)	Retrd.	1996	32.00	32
1996	A Job Well Done SP18 (C. Radko event)	Retrd.	1996	30.00	30
1997	Little Golden Hood 97-261E (store event)	Yr.Iss.		38.00	38

Aids Awareness - C. Radko

YEAR ISSUE		EDITION LIMIT	YEAR RETD.	ISSUE PRICE	*QUOTE U.S.$
1993	A Shy Rabbit's Heart 462	Retrd.	1993	15.00	60-90
1994	Frosty Cares SP5	Retrd.	1994	25.00	60-70
1995	On Wings of Hope SP10	Retrd.	1995	30.00	36-60
1996	A Winter Bear's Heart SP15	Retrd.	1996	34.00	34
1997	A Caring Clown SP22	Yr.Iss.		36.00	36

Cottage Series - C. Radko

YEAR ISSUE		EDITION LIMIT	YEAR RETD.	ISSUE PRICE	*QUOTE U.S.$
1997	Sugar Hill 97-HOU1	10,000		140.00	140

Disney Gallery Ornaments - C. Radko

YEAR ISSUE		EDITION LIMIT	YEAR RETD.	ISSUE PRICE	*QUOTE U.S.$
1997	4th of July Pooh	Open		N/A	N/A
1996	Best Friends DIS10	10,000	1996	60.00	95-150
1996	By Jiminy DIS11	7,500	1996	38.00	60-120
1996	Cruella De Vil DIS13	10,000	1996	55.00	100-160
1996	Holiday Skaters DIS8	Retrd.	1996	42.00	42
1996	Lucky 96DIS14	Retrd.	1996	45.00	100
1995	Mickey's Tree DIS1	2,500	1995	45.00	225-350
1996	Pinocchio DIS9	5,000	1996	45.00	125-185
1997	Pooh Easter	Open		N/A	N/A
1997	Pooh Thanksgiving	Open		N/A	N/A
1997	Pooh Valentine	Open		N/A	N/A
1995	Pooh's Favorite Gift (signed) DIS2	Retrd.	1995	45.00	400
1995	Pooh's Favorite Gift DIS2	2,500	1995	45.00	225-300
1996	Tinker Bell DIS12	10,000		55.00	55
1996	Xmas Eve Mickey 96DIS06	Retrd.	1996	45.00	130

Egyptian Series - C. Radko

YEAR ISSUE		EDITION LIMIT	YEAR RETD.	ISSUE PRICE	*QUOTE U.S.$
1997	Ramses 97-EGY1	15,000		50.00	50

Limited Edition Ornaments - C. Radko

YEAR ISSUE		EDITION LIMIT	YEAR RETD.	ISSUE PRICE	*QUOTE U.S.$
1995	And Snowy Makes Eight 169 (set of 8)	15,000	1996	125.00	125
1996	Russian Rhapsody RUS (Set/6)	7,500	1996	150.00	150-165
1997	Yippy Yi Yo 97-SP25	10,000		70.00	70

Matt Berry Memorial Soccer Fund - C. Radko

YEAR ISSUE		EDITION LIMIT	YEAR RETD.	ISSUE PRICE	*QUOTE U.S.$
1995	Matthew's Game 158-0	Open		12.00	12

Moscow Circus Series - C. Radko

YEAR ISSUE		EDITION LIMIT	YEAR RETD.	ISSUE PRICE	*QUOTE U.S.$
1997	Ivan & Misha 97-CIR1	10,000		90.00	90

Nativity Series - C. Radko

YEAR ISSUE		EDITION LIMIT	YEAR RETD.	ISSUE PRICE	*QUOTE U.S.$
1995	Three Wise Men WM (Set/3)	15,000	1996	90.00	110-195

*Quotes have been rounded up to nearest dollar

YEAR ISSUE		EDITION LIMIT	YEAR RETD.	ISSUE PRICE	*QUOTE U.S. $
1996	Holy Family HF (Set/3)	15,000	1996	70.00	70
1997	Shepherd's Prayer, Gloria 97-NAT3	15,000		90.00	90

Nutcracker Series - C. Radko

YEAR ISSUE		EDITION LIMIT	YEAR RETD.	ISSUE PRICE	*QUOTE U.S. $
1995	Nutcracker Suite I NC1 (Set/3)	15,000	1996	90.00	110-125
1996	Nutcracker Suite II NC2 (Set/3)	15,000		90.00	90
1997	Nutcracker Suite III 97-NC3 (Set/3)	15,000		90.00	90

Patriot Series - C. Radko

YEAR ISSUE		EDITION LIMIT	YEAR RETD.	ISSUE PRICE	*QUOTE U.S. $
1997	LaFayette 97-PAT1	7,500		34.00	34

Pediatrics Cancer Research - C. Radko

YEAR ISSUE		EDITION LIMIT	YEAR RETD.	ISSUE PRICE	*QUOTE U.S. $
1994	A Gifted Santa 70	Retrd.	1994	25.00	80-90
1995	Christmas Puppy Love SP11	Retrd.	1995	30.00	50
1996	Bearly Awake SP16	Retrd.	1996	34.00	50-80
1997	Kitty Cares 97-SP23	Yr.Iss.		30.00	30

Polish Children's Home Fund - C. Radko

YEAR ISSUE		EDITION LIMIT	YEAR RETD.	ISSUE PRICE	*QUOTE U.S. $
1997	Watch Over Me 97-SP26	Yr.Iss.		28.00	28

Rosemont Special - C. Radko

YEAR ISSUE		EDITION LIMIT	YEAR RETD.	ISSUE PRICE	*QUOTE U.S. $
1997	Blue Caroline 96-1521	Yr.Iss.		26.00	26

South Bend Special - C. Radko

YEAR ISSUE		EDITION LIMIT	YEAR RETD.	ISSUE PRICE	*QUOTE U.S. $
1995	Polar Express (lilac) 95-076SB	Retrd.	1995	24.95	50-75

Starlight and Rising Star Store Exclusives - C. Radko

YEAR ISSUE		EDITION LIMIT	YEAR RETD.	ISSUE PRICE	*QUOTE U.S. $
1996	Esquire Santa 96-SP17	750	1996	150.00	150
1997	Regency Santa 97-SP24	2,500		180.00	180

Starlight Store Exclusives - C. Radko

YEAR ISSUE		EDITION LIMIT	YEAR RETD.	ISSUE PRICE	*QUOTE U.S. $
1996	Snowtem Pole (Glass Pheasant) 96155G	Retrd.	1996	33.00	100
1996	White Dolphin (Four Seasons) 96238F	Retrd.	1996	25.00	75
1996	Baby Bear (Christmas Dove) 322-0	N/A		30.00	30
1996	Far Away Places (Christmas Village) 321-0	N/A		40.00	40
1996	Frosty Bear (Christmas House) 326-0	N/A		30.00	30
1996	Kitty Christmas (Tuck's) 323-0	N/A		30.00	30
1996	Little St. Mick (Roger's Gardens) DIS7	N/A	1996	45.00	168
1996	On His Way (Geary's) 319-0	N/A		30.00	30
1996	Ruffles (Christmas Attic) 320-0	N/A		30.00	30
1996	Snow Fun (Vinny's) 324-0	N/A		30.00	30
1996	Tweedle Dee (Glass Pheasant) 325-0	N/A		40.00	40
1996	Winter Kitten (Margo's) 327-0	N/A		30.00	30

Sunday Brunch - C. Radko

YEAR ISSUE		EDITION LIMIT	YEAR RETD.	ISSUE PRICE	*QUOTE U.S. $
1996	Hansel & Gretel and Witch HG1	7,500		50.00	50
1997	Nibble Nibble 97-HG2	7,500		58.00	58

Twelve Days of Christmas - C. Radko

YEAR ISSUE		EDITION LIMIT	YEAR RETD.	ISSUE PRICE	*QUOTE U.S. $
1993	Partridge in a Pear Tree SP2	5,000	1993	35.00	750-1000
1994	Two Turtle Doves SP4	10,000	1994	28.00	125-175
1995	Three French Hens SP9	10,000	1995	34.00	100-135
1995	Three French Hens (signed) SP9	Retrd.	1995	34.00	150-250
1996	Four Calling Birds SP12	10,000		44.00	100-130
1997	Five Gold Rings SP19	10,000		60.00	60

Warner Brothers - C. Radko

YEAR ISSUE		EDITION LIMIT	YEAR RETD.	ISSUE PRICE	*QUOTE U.S. $
1996	Little Angel Tweety WB10	5,000	1996	45.00	75-150
1995	Santa's Bugs Bunny WB1	Retrd.	1995	45.00	85-140
1996	Superman WB7	7,500	1996	48.00	100-155
1996	Sylvester Sprite WB9	5,000	1996	45.00	85-150
1996	Taz & Bugs Stockings WB4	5,000	1996	65.00	65
1995	Taz Angel WB2	Retrd.	1995	40.00	100-190
1996	Trio Tree Topper 96-WB8	5,000		78.00	240
1995	Tweety's Sprite WB3	Retrd.	1995	45.00	125-200

Dave Grossman Creations

Gone With the Wind Ornaments - Various

YEAR ISSUE		EDITION LIMIT	YEAR RETD.	ISSUE PRICE	*QUOTE U.S. $
1987	Ashley - D. Geenty	Closed	N/A	15.00	45
1987	Rhett - D. Geenty	Closed	N/A	15.00	45
1987	Scarlett - D. Geenty	Closed	N/A	15.00	45
1987	Tara - D. Geenty	Closed	N/A	15.00	45
1988	Rhett and Scarlett - D. Geenty	Closed	N/A	20.00	40
1989	Mammy - D. Geenty	Closed	N/A	20.00	20
1990	Scarlett (Red Dress) - D. Geenty	Closed	N/A	20.00	20
1991	Prissy - Unknown	Closed	N/A	20.00	20
1992	Scarlett (Green Dress) - Unknown	Closed	N/A	20.00	20
1993	Rhett (White Suit) GWO-93 - Unknown	Closed	N/A	20.00	20
1994	Gold Plated GWO-00 - Unknown	Open		13.00	13
1994	Scarlett GWO-94 - Unknown	Closed	N/A	20.00	20
1995	The Kiss GWW-95 - Unknown	Yr.Iss.	1995	25.00	25
1994	Scarlett (B-B-Q Dress) GWO-94 - Unknown	Closed	1994	12.00	12
1996	Suellen GWO-95 - Unknown	Closed	1996	12.00	12
1996	Scarlett GWO-96 - Unknown	Closed	1996	12.00	12
1996	1996 Ornament GWW-96 - Unknown	Yr.Iss.	1996	25.00	25
1996	Set of 5 Ornaments GWOS-1 - Unknown	Yr.Iss.	1996	100.00	100
1997	Bonnie GWO-97 - Unknown	Open		12.00	12
1997	Scarlett GWW-97 - Unknown	Yr.Iss.		25.00	25

Ornaments - C. Spencer Collin

YEAR ISSUE		EDITION LIMIT	YEAR RETD.	ISSUE PRICE	*QUOTE U.S. $
1996	Cape Hatteras CSC-01	Yr.Iss.	1997	24.00	24
1997	Nubble Light CSC-O	Yr.Iss.		24.00	24

Rockwell Collection-Annual Rockwell Ball - Rockwell-Inspired

YEAR ISSUE		EDITION LIMIT	YEAR RETD.	ISSUE PRICE	*QUOTE U.S.$
1975	Santa with Feather Quill NRO-01	Retrd.	N/A	3.50	25
1976	Santa at Globe NRO-02	Retrd.	N/A	4.00	25
1977	Grandpa on Rocking Horse NRO-03	Retrd.	N/A	4.00	12
1978	Santa with Map NRO-04	Retrd.	N/A	4.50	12
1979	Santa at Desk w/ Mail Bag NRO-05	Retrd.	N/A	5.00	12
1980	Santa Asleep with Toys NRO-06	Retrd.	N/A	5.00	10
1981	Santa with Boy on Finger NRO-07	Retrd.	N/A	5.00	10
1982	Santa Face on Winter Scene NRO-08	Retrd.	N/A	5.00	10
1983	Coachman with Whip NRO-9	Retrd.	N/A	5.00	10
1984	Christmas Bounty Man NRO-10	Retrd.	N/A	5.00	10
1985	Old English Trio NRO-11	Retrd.	N/A	5.00	10
1986	Tiny Tim on Shoulder NRO-12	Retrd.	N/A	5.00	10
1987	Skating Lesson NRO-13	Retrd.	N/A	5.00	10
1988	Big Moment NRO-14	Retrd.	N/A	5.50	10
1989	Discovery NRO-15	Retrd.	N/A	6.00	10
1990	Bringing Home The Tree NRO-16	Retrd.	N/A	6.00	10
1991	Downhill Daring NRO-17	Retrd.	N/A	6.00	10
1992	On The Ice NRO-18	Retrd.	N/A	6.00	10
1993	Gramps NRO-19	Retrd.	N/A	6.00	10
1994	Triple Self Portrait-Commemorative NRO-20	Retrd.	1994	6.00	10
1994	Merry Christmas NRO-94	Retrd.	1994	6.00	6
1995	Young Love NRO-21	Retrd.	N/A	6.00	6
1996	Christmas Feast NRO-22	Retrd.	1996	6.00	6
1997	Lovers NRO-23	Yr.Iss.		6.00	6

Rockwell Collection-Annual Rockwell Figurine Ornaments - Rockwell-Inspired

YEAR ISSUE		EDITION LIMIT	YEAR RETD.	ISSUE PRICE	*QUOTE U.S.$
1978	Caroler NRX-03	Retrd.	N/A	15.00	45
1979	Drum for Tommy NRX-24	Retrd.	N/A	20.00	30
1980	Santa's Good Boys NRX-37	Retrd.	N/A	20.00	30
1981	Letters to Santa NRX-39	Retrd.	N/A	20.00	30
1982	Cornettist NRX-32	Retrd.	N/A	20.00	30
1983	Fiddler NRX-83	Retrd.	N/A	20.00	30
1984	Christmas Bounty NRX-84	Retrd.	N/A	20.00	30
1985	Jolly Coachman NRX-85	Retrd.	N/A	20.00	30
1986	Grandpa on Rocking Horse NRX-86	Retrd.	N/A	20.00	30
1987	Skating Lesson NRX-87	Retrd.	N/A	20.00	30
1988	Big Moment NRX-88	Retrd.	N/A	20.00	30
1989	Discovery NRX-89	Retrd.	N/A	20.00	30
1990	Bringing Home The Tree NRX-90	Retrd.	N/A	20.00	30
1991	Downhill Daring B NRX-91	Retrd.	N/A	20.00	30
1992	On The Ice	Retrd.	N/A	20.00	30
1993	Granps NRX-93	Retrd.	N/A	24.00	30
1993	Marriage License First Christmas Together NRX-m1	Retrd.	N/A	30.00	30
1994	Merry Christmas NRX-94	Retrd.	N/A	24.00	24
1994	Triple Self-Portrait NRX-TS	Retrd.	N/A	30.00	30
1995	Young Love NRX-95	Retrd.	1995	24.00	45-55
1996	Christmas Feast NRX-96	Retrd.	1996	24.00	24
1997	Lovers NRX-97	Yr.Iss.		24.00	24

Department 56

Bisque Light-Up, Clip-on Ornaments - Department 56

YEAR ISSUE		EDITION LIMIT	YEAR RETD.	ISSUE PRICE	*QUOTE U.S.$
1986	Angelic Lite-up 8260-0	Open		4.00	4
1987	Anniversary Love Birds, (pair) w/brass ribbon 8353-4	Closed	1988	4.00	4
1986	Dessert, 6 asst. 7100-5	Closed	1987	5.00	40
1985	Humpty Dumpty 3525-4	Closed	1986	4.50	5
1990	Owl w/clip 8344-5	Closed	1994	5.00	14
1986	Plum Pudding 7101-3	Closed	1987	4.50	48
1989	Pond-Frog w/clip 8347-0	Closed	1991	5.00	42
1989	Pond-Snail w/clip 8347-0	Closed	1991	5.00	42-57
1988	Rabbit w/clip 8350-0	Open		4.00	17
1987	Shells, set/4 8349-6	Closed	1991	14.00	80-120
1986	Shooting Star 7106-4	Closed	1987	5.50	22
1985	Snowbirds, (pair) w/clip 8357-7	Open		5.00	5
1985	Snowbirds, set/6 8367-4	Closed	1988	15.00	15
1985	Snowbirds, set/8 8358-5	Closed	1988	20.00	20
1985	Snowmen, 3 asst. 8360-7	Closed	1988	10.50	11
1986	Teddy Bear w/clip 8262-7	Closed	1991	5.00	18
1986	Truffles Sampler, set/4 7102-1	Closed	1987	17.50	42
1986	Winged Snowbird 8261-9	Closed	1988	2.50	3
1989	Woodland-Field Mouse w/clip 8348-8	Closed	1991	5.00	42-57
1989	Woodland-Squirrel w/clip 8348-8	Closed	1991	5.00	45

CCP Ornaments-Flat -Department 56

YEAR ISSUE		EDITION LIMIT	YEAR RETD.	ISSUE PRICE	*QUOTE U.S.$
1986	Christmas Carol Houses, set/3 (6504-8)	Closed	1989	13.00	45
1986	-The Cottage of Bob Cratchit & Tiny Tim	Closed	1989	4.35	N/A
1986	-Fezziwig's Warehouse	Closed	1989	4.35	N/A
1986	-Scrooge and Marley Countinghouse	Closed	1989	4.35	N/A
1986	New England Village, set/7 (6536-6)	Closed	1989	25.00	300
1986	-Apothecary Shop	Closed	1989	3.50	25
1986	-Brick Town Hall	Closed	1989	3.50	50
1986	-General Store	Closed	1989	3.50	55
1986	-Livery Stable & Boot Shop	Closed	1989	3.50	25
1986	-Nathaniel Bingham Fabrics	Closed	1989	3.50	25
1986	-Red Schoolhouse	Closed	1989	3.50	40-70
1986	-Steeple Church	Closed	1989	3.50	150-225

Christmas Carol Character Ornaments-Flat -Department 56

YEAR ISSUE		EDITION LIMIT	YEAR RETD.	ISSUE PRICE	*QUOTE U.S.$
1986	Christmas Carol Characters, set/3 (6505-6)	Closed	1987	13.00	45
1986	-Bob Cratchit & Tiny Tim	Closed	1987	4.35	20
1986	-Poulterer	Closed	1987	4.35	20
1986	-Scrooge	Closed	1987	4.35	20

Merry Makers - Department 56

YEAR ISSUE		EDITION LIMIT	YEAR RETD.	ISSUE PRICE	*QUOTE U.S.$
1992	Tolland The Toller 9369-6	Closed	1995	11.00	11

Miscellaneous Ornaments - Department 56

YEAR ISSUE		EDITION LIMIT	YEAR RETD.	ISSUE PRICE	*QUOTE U.S.$
1983	Snow Village Wood Ornaments, set/6, 5099-7	Closed	1984	30.00	N/A
1983	-Carriage House	Closed	1984	5.00	50
1983	-Centennial House	Closed	1984	5.00	100
1983	-Countryside Church	Closed	1984	5.00	125
1983	-Gabled House	Closed	1984	5.00	75
1983	-Pioneer Church	Closed	1984	5.00	75-125
1983	-Swiss Chalet	Closed	1984	5.00	75
1984	Dickens 2-sided Tin Ornaments, set/6, 6522-6	Closed	1985	12.00	440
1984	-Abel Beesley Butcher	Closed	1985	2.00	45
1984	-Bean and Son Smithy Shop	Closed	1985	2.00	45
1984	-Crowntree Inn	Closed	1985	2.00	45
1984	-Golden Swan Baker	Closed	1985	2.00	45
1984	-Green Grocer	Closed	1985	2.00	45
1984	-Jones & Co. Brush & Basket Shop	Closed	1985	2.00	45
1986	Cherub on Brass Ribbon, 8248-1	Closed	1988	8.00	75
1986	Teddy Bear on Brass Ribbon 8263-5	Closed	1988	7.00	75
1988	Balsam Bell Brass Dickens' Candlestick 6244-8	Closed	1989	3.00	15
1988	Christmas Carol- Bob & Mrs. Cratchit 5914-5	Closed	1989	18.00	36-45
1988	Christmas Carol- Scrooge's Head 5912-9	Closed	1989	13.00	30-35
1988	Christmas Carol- Tiny Tim's Head 5913-7	Closed	1989	10.00	25-35
1994	Dickens Village Dedlock Arms 9872-8, (porcelain, gift boxed)	Closed	1994	12.50	15-25
1995	Sir John Falstaff 9870-1 (Charles Dickens' Signature Series)	Closed	1995	15.00	25
1996	The Grapes Inn 98729	Yr.Iss.	1996	15.00	15
1996	Crown & Cricket Inn 98730	Yr.Iss.	1996	15.00	15
1996	The Pied Bull Inn 98731	Yr.Iss.	1996	15.00	15

Snowbabies Mercury Glass Ornaments - Department 56

YEAR ISSUE		EDITION LIMIT	YEAR RETD.	ISSUE PRICE	*QUOTE U.S.$
1996	Snowbaby Drummer The Night Before Christmas 68983	Open		18.00	18
1996	Snowbaby in Package The Night Before Christmas 68986	Open		18.00	18
1996	Snowbaby Jinglebaby The Night Before Christmas 68989	Open		20.00	20
1996	Snowbaby on Moon The Night Before Christmas 68988	Open		18.00	18
1996	Snowbaby On Package The Night Before Christmas 68981	Open		18.00	18
1996	Snowbaby on Snowball The Night Before Christmas 68984	Open		20.00	20
1996	Snowbaby Soldier The Night Before Christmas 68982	Open		18.00	18
1996	Snowbaby With Bell The Night Before Christmas 68987	Open		18.00	18
1996	Snowbaby With Sisal Tree The Night Before Christmas 68990	Open		20.00	20
1996	Snowbaby With Star The Night Before Christmas 68991	Open		18.00	18
1996	Snowbaby With Wreath The Night Before Christmas 68980	Open		18.00	18

Snowbabies Ornaments - Department 56

YEAR ISSUE		EDITION LIMIT	YEAR RETD.	ISSUE PRICE	*QUOTE U.S.$
1996	Baby's 1st Rattle 68828	Open		15.00	15
1994	Be My Baby 6866-7	Open		15.00	15
1986	Crawling, Lite-Up, Clip-On, 7953-7	Closed	1992	7.00	20-30
1994	First Star Jinglebaby, 6858-6	Open		10.00	11
1994	Gathering Stars in the Sky, 6855-1	Open		12.50	13
1996	Jinglebell Jinglebaby 68826	Open		11.00	11
1995	Joy 68807, set/3	Open		32.50	33
1996	Joy to the World, set/2 68829	Open		17.50	18
1994	Juggling Stars in the Sky 6867-5	Open		15.00	15
1994	Just For You Jinglebaby 6869-1	Open		11.00	11
1994	Little Drummer Jinglebaby, 6859-4	Open		10.00	11
1987	Mini, Winged Pair, Lite-Up, Clip-On, 7976-6	Open		9.00	12
1987	Moon Beams, 7951-0	Open		7.50	9
1991	My First Star, 6811-0	Open		7.00	8
1989	Noel, 7988-0	Open		7.50	8
1995	One Little Candle Jinglebaby 68806	Open		11.00	11
1995	Overnight Delivery, 759-5 (Event Piece)	Closed	1995	10.00	25-35
1995	Overnight Delivery, 68808	Open		10.00	10
1990	Penguin, Lite-Up, Clip-On, 7940-5	Closed	1992	5.00	19-25
1990	Polar Bear, Lite-Up, Clip-On, 7941-3	Closed	1992	5.00	13-23
1990	Rock-A-Bye Baby, 7939-1	Closed	1995	7.00	13
1986	Sitting, Lite-Up, Clip-On, 7952-9	Closed	1990	7.00	32-42
1992	Snowbabies Icicle With Star, 6825-0	Closed	1995	16.00	16
1987	Snowbaby Adrift Lite-Up, Clip-On, 7969-3	Closed	1990	8.50	85-125
1996	Snowbaby in my Stocking 68827	Open		10.00	10
1986	Snowbaby on Brass Ribbon, 7961-8	Closed	1989	8.00	125-165
1993	Sprinkling Stars in the Sky, 6848-9	Open		12.50	13
1989	Star Bright, 7990-1	Open		7.50	8
1996	Starry Pine Jinglebaby 68825	Open		11.00	11
1992	Starry, Starry Night, 6830-6	Open		12.50	13

*Quotes have been rounded up to nearest dollar

YEAR ISSUE		EDITION LIMIT	YEAR RETD.	ISSUE PRICE	*QUOTE U.S.$
1994	Stars in My Stocking Jinglebaby 6868-3	Open		11.00	11
1989	Surprise, 7989-8	Closed	1994	12.00	18-25
1991	Swinging On a Star, 6810-1	Open		9.50	10
1988	Twinkle Little Star, 7980-4	Closed	1990	7.00	55-90
1993	Wee...This is Fun!, 6847-0	Open		13.50	14
1986	Winged, Lite-Up, Clip-On, 7954-5	Closed	1990	7.00	30-55

Village Light-Up Ornaments - Department 56

YEAR ISSUE		EDITION LIMIT	YEAR RETD.	ISSUE PRICE	*QUOTE U.S.$
1987	Christmas Carol Cottages, set/3 (6513-7)	Closed	1989	17.00	55-75
1987	•The Cottage of Bob Cratchit & Tiny Tim	Closed	1989	6.00	30
1987	•Fezziwig's Warehouse	Closed	1989	6.00	30
1987	•Scrooge & Marley Countinghouse	Closed	1989	6.00	30
1985	Dickens' Village, set/14 (6521-8, 6520-0)	Closed	1989	84.00	400
1987	Dickens' Village, set/6 (6520-0)	Closed	1989	36.00	100-150
1987	•Barley Bree Farmhouse	Closed	1989	6.00	17-24
1987	•Blythe Pond Mill House	Closed	1989	6.00	30-42
1987	•Brick Abbey	Closed	1989	6.00	85
1987	•Chesterton Manor House	Closed	1989	6.00	40
1987	•Kenilworth Castle	Closed	1989	6.00	35-55
1987	•The Old Curiosity Shop	Closed	1989	6.00	50
1985	Dickens' Village, set/8 (6521-8)	Closed	1989	48.00	200
1985	•Abel Beesley Butcher	Closed	1989	6.00	23
1985	•Bean and Son Smithy Shop	Closed	1989	6.00	25-30
1985	•Candle Shop	Closed	1989	6.00	26
1985	•Crowntree Inn	Closed	1989	6.00	45
1985	•Dickens' Village Church	Closed	1989	6.00	45-55
1985	•Golden Swan Baker	Closed	1989	6.00	18-24
1985	•Green Grocer	Closed	1989	6.00	25-42
1985	•Jones & Co. Brush & Basket Shop	Closed	1989	6.00	25-42
1987	New England Village, set/13 (6533-1, 6534-0)	Closed	1989	78.00	700-750
1987	New England Village, set/6 (6534-0)	Closed	1989	36.00	200-275
1987	•Craggy Cove Lighthouse	Closed	1989	6.00	150-180
1987	•Jacob Adams Barn	Closed	1989	6.00	45-55
1987	•Jacob Adams Farmhouse	Closed	1989	6.00	30-54
1987	•Smythe Woolen Mill	Closed	1989	6.00	80-100
1987	•Timber Knoll Log Cabin	Closed	1989	6.00	85-140
1987	•Weston Train Station	Closed	1989	6.00	46
1986	New England Village, set/7 (6533-1)	Closed	1989	42.00	325
1986	•Apothecary Shop	Closed	1989	6.00	18-24
1986	•Brick Town Hall	Closed	1989	6.00	35
1986	•General Store	Closed	1989	6.00	20-42
1986	•Livery Stable & Boot Shop	Closed	1989	6.00	24-36
1986	•Nathaniel Bingham Fabrics	Closed	1989	6.00	25-35
1986	•Red Schoolhouse	Closed	1989	6.00	90
1986	•Steeple Church	Closed	1989	6.00	132

Duncan Royale

History Of Santa Claus - Duncan Royale

YEAR ISSUE		EDITION LIMIT	YEAR RETD.	ISSUE PRICE	*QUOTE U.S.$
1992	Santa I (set of 12)	Open		144.00	144
1992	Santa II (set of 12)	Open		144.00	144

Ertl Collectibles

Sparrowsville - L. Davis

YEAR ISSUE		EDITION LIMIT	YEAR RETD.	ISSUE PRICE	*QUOTE U.S.$
1996	Bachelor Pad H109	1/98		25.00	25
1997	Cozy Cabin 2493	Open		25.00	25
1996	The Hayloft H108	Open		25.00	25
1996	Hearthside Manor H111	Open		25.00	25
1996	Home Sweet Home H110	Open		25.00	25
1996	Leather Nest H106	Open		25.00	25
1996	Love Nest H107	Open		25.00	25
1996	The Smith's H104	1/98		25.00	25
1996	Snowbirds H103	Open		25.00	25
1997	Stone Haven 2490	Open		25.00	25
1996	Winter Retreat H105	1/98		25.00	25
1997	Winter Squash 2491	Open		25.00	25

Fenton Art Glass Company

Christmas Limited Edition - M. Reynolds

YEAR ISSUE		EDITION LIMIT	YEAR RETD.	ISSUE PRICE	*QUOTE U.S.$
1996	Golden Winged Angel, Hndpt. 3 1/2"	2,000	1996	27.50	28

Fitz & Floyd

Charming Tails Deck The Halls - D. Griff

YEAR ISSUE		EDITION LIMIT	YEAR RETD.	ISSUE PRICE	*QUOTE U.S.$
1992	Catching ZZZ's 86/785	Closed	1995	12.00	20-40
1992	Chickadees on Ball 86/787	Closed	1995	13.50	20-38
1992	Chicks w/Bead Garland 86/791	Closed	1995	17.50	25-65
1992	The Drifters 86/784	Closed	1996	12.00	12
1992	Fresh Fruit 86/789	Closed	1995	12.00	12
1992	Mice/Rabbit Ball, set/2 86/788	Closed	1995	12.00	25
1992	Mice in Leaf Sleigh 86/786	Closed	1995	26.00	26
1993	Bunny & Mouse Bell 87/038	Closed	1995	10.50	11
1993	Hang in There 87/941	Closed	1996	10.00	10
1993	Holiday Wreath 87/939	Closed	1995	12.00	35
1993	Mackenzie Napping 87/940	Closed	1995	12.00	18
1993	Maxine Lights a Candle 87/942	Closed	1995	11.00	25
1993	Mouse on Snowflake (lighted) 87/037	Closed	1995	11.00	15-30
1993	Mouse w/Apple Candleholder 87/044	Closed	1995	13.00	60
1993	Porcelain Mouse Bell 87/036	Closed	1995	5.00	5
1994	Baby's First Christmas 87/184	Yr.Iss.	1994	12.00	28
1994	Binkey & Reginald on Ice 87/924	Closed	1994	10.00	20
1994	Friends in Flight 87/971	Closed	1994	18.00	30-50
1994	The Grape Escape (grape) 87/186	Closed	1995	18.00	18
1994	The Grape Escape (green) 87/186	Closed	1995	18.00	37
1994	High Flying Mackenzie 87/992	Open		20.00	21
1994	Holiday Lights 87/969	Closed	1995	10.00	45
1994	Horsin' Around	Closed	1996	18.00	18
1994	Mackenzie and Binkey's Snack (cherry & plum) 87/187	Closed	1994	12.00	60-120
1994	Mackenzie Blowing Bubbles 87/191	Closed	1994	12.00	48
1994	Mackenzie on Ice 87/970	Closed	1996	10.00	10
1994	Mackenzie's Bubble Ride 87/192	Closed	1996	13.00	20-40
1994	Mackenzie's Snowball (dated) 87/994	Yr.Iss.	1994	10.00	40-60
1994	Maxine and Mackenzie 87/185	Closed	1996	12.00	25
1994	Reginald's Bubble Ride 87/199	Closed	1994	12.00	12
1994	Apple House (lighted) 87/032	Closed	1995	13.00	13
1994	Pear House (lighted) 87/027	Closed	1995	13.00	13
1994	Mouse on Yellow Bulb (lighted) 87/045	Closed	1995	10.00	40
1994	Mouse Star Treetop 87/958	Closed	1995	10.00	40-50
1994	Sticky Situations 87/991	Closed	1996	16.00	30
1995	1995 Annual 87/306	Yr.Iss.	1995	16.00	25
1995	Binkey's Poinsettia 87/303	Open		12.00	13
1995	Christmas Cookies 87/301	Open		10.00	11
1995	Christmas Flowers 87/304	Open		12.00	13
1995	Holiday Balloon Ride 87/299	Closed	1996	16.00	16
1995	Mackenzie's Whirligig 87/300	Open		20.00	21
1995	Peppermint Party 87/314	Open		10.00	11
1995	Reginald in Leaves 87/302	Open		10.00	11
1995	Stewart at Play 87/308	Closed	1995	12.00	12
1995	Stewart's Winter Fun 87/307	Closed	1995	10.00	10
1996	1996 Annual-All Wrapped Up 87/471	Yr.Iss.	1996	12.00	12
1996	Baby's First Christmas 87/850	Yr.Iss.	1996	13.00	30
1996	Our First Christmas (dated)	Yr.Iss.	1996	18.00	30
1996	Christmas Stamps 87/485	Open		12.00	13
1996	Fallen Angel 87/492	Open		12.00	13
1996	Flights of Fancy 87/490	Open		12.00	13
1996	Frequent Flyer 87/491	Open		12.00	13
1996	Letter to Santa 87/486	Open		12.00	13
1996	Stamp Dispenser 87/483	Open		12.00	13
1996	Weeeeee! 87/493	Open		12.00	13
1997	All Lit Up (lighted) 86/660	Open		11.00	11
1997	Chauncey's First Christmas 86/710	Open		9.00	9
1997	Mackenzie In Mitten 86/704	Open		9.00	9
1997	1997 Annual-Mackenzie's Jack in the Box 86/709	Yr.Iss.		10.00	10
1997	Maxine's Angel 86/701	Open		9.00	9
1997	Our First Christmas 86/708	Open		12.50	13
1997	A Special Delivery 86/707	Open		9.00	9

Flambro Imports

Emmett Kelly Jr. Christmas Ornaments - Undis.

YEAR ISSUE		EDITION LIMIT	YEAR RETD.	ISSUE PRICE	*QUOTE U.S.$
1989	65th Birthday	Yr.Iss.	1989	24.00	100-150
1990	30 Years Of Clowning	Yr.Iss.	1990	30.00	135
1991	EKJ With Stocking And Toys	Yr.Iss.	1991	30.00	30
1992	Home For Christmas	Yr.Iss.	1992	24.00	70
1993	Christmas Mail	Yr.Iss.	1993	25.00	70
1994	'70 Birthday Commemorative	Yr.Iss.	1994	24.00	55-90
1995	20th Anniversary All Star Circus	Yr.Iss.	1995	25.00	25
1996	Christmas Pageant	Yr.Iss.	1996	29.00	29
1997	1997 Dated Ornament	Yr.Iss.		30.00	30

Little Emmett Ornaments - M. Wu

YEAR ISSUE		EDITION LIMIT	YEAR RETD.	ISSUE PRICE	*QUOTE U.S.$
1995	Little Emmett Christmas Wrap	Open		11.50	12
1995	Little Emmett Deck the Neck	Open		11.50	12
1996	Little Emmett Singing Carols	Open		13.00	13
1996	Little Emmett Your Present	Open		13.00	13
1996	Little Emmett Baby 1st Christmas	Open		13.00	13
1996	Little Emmett on Rocking Horse	Open		25.00	25

Ganz

Cowtown/The Christmas Collection - C. Thammavongsa

YEAR ISSUE		EDITION LIMIT	YEAR RETD.	ISSUE PRICE	*QUOTE U.S.$
1995	Bells on Cowtail Ring	Open		11.50	12
1994	Bronco Bully	Open		13.00	13
1995	Buckets of Joy	Open		12.00	12
1994	Calf-in-the Box	Open		12.50	13
1994	Christmoos Eve	Open		12.00	12
1995	Dairy Christmas	Open		11.50	12
1994	Downhill Dare Debull	Open		12.00	12
1994	Hallemooah	Open		12.00	12
1995	Holy Cow	Open		12.00	12
1994	Jingle Bull	Open		15.50	16
1994	Li'l Red Gliding Hoof	Open		12.00	12
1994	Little Drummer Calf	Open		12.00	12
1995	Moo, Moo, Moo	Open		11.50	12

Little Cheesers/The Christmas Collection - C. Thammavongsa, unless otherwise noted

YEAR ISSUE		EDITION LIMIT	YEAR RETD.	ISSUE PRICE	*QUOTE U.S.$
1992	Abner Appleton Ornament - GDA/Thammavongsa	Open		15.00	15
1994	All I Want For Christmas	Closed	1994	13.50	14
1994	Angel	Open		8.00	8
1995	Annual Angel 1995	Open		10.50	11
1993	Baby's First X'mas Ornament	Retrd.	1995	12.50	13
1994	Candy Cane Caper	Open		9.00	9
1994	Cheeser Snowman	Closed	1994	5.00	5
1994	Chelsea's Stocking Bell	Open		15.50	16
1994	Cousin Woody Playing Flute	Closed	1994	10.00	10
1993	Dashing Through the Snow	Open		11.00	11
1994	Grandpa Blowing Horn	Closed	1994	10.00	10
1994	Hickory Playing Cello	Closed	1994	10.00	10
1992	Jenny Butterfield - GDA/Thammavongsa	Open		17.00	17
1992	Jeremy With Teddy Bear - GDA/Thammavongsa	Open		13.00	13
1995	Light of the World Bell	Open		16.00	16
1993	Little Stocking Stuffer	Open		10.50	11
1992	Little Truffle - GDA/Thammavongsa	Open		9.50	10
1995	Mama Claus' Special Recipe	Open		11.50	12
1993	Medley Meadowmouse X'mas Bell	Closed	1996	17.00	17
1994	Medley Playing Drum	Closed	1994	5.50	6
1992	Myrtle Meadowmouse - GDA/Thammavongsa	Closed	1996	15.00	15
1995	Noel	Closed	1996	10.50	11
1993	Our First Christmas Together	Open		18.50	19
1994	Peace on Earth	Open		8.00	8
1992	Santa Cheeser - GDA/Thammavongsa	Closed	1996	14.00	14
1993	Santa's Little Helper	Open		11.00	11
1994	Santa's Workshop	Closed	1996	10.00	10
1993	Skating Into Your Heart	Open		10.00	10
1995	Skiing Santa	Open		10.00	10
1994	Sleigh Ride	Closed	1994	9.00	9
1995	Snow Cheeser II	Open		6.50	7
1994	Swinging Into the Season	Closed	1996	11.00	11
1996	Swinging on the Moon - Chiemlowski	Open		10.00	10
1994	Violet With Snowball	Closed	1994	5.50	6

Little Cheesers/The Silverwoods - C. Thammavongsa

YEAR ISSUE		EDITION LIMIT	YEAR RETD.	ISSUE PRICE	*QUOTE U.S.$
1995	Angel Above	Open		8.50	9
1994	Christmas Surprise	Open		8.50	9
1994	Comfort and Joy	Open		6.00	6
1994	Deck the Halls	Closed	1996	9.50	10
1994	Giddy Up!	Open		8.50	9
1995	Harps of Gold	Open		8.50	9
1994	Hickory Dickory Dock	Open		9.50	10
1995	Joyful Sounds	Closed	1996	8.50	9
1994	Mrs. Claus	Closed	1996	9.00	9
1995	Over The Hills	Open		8.50	9
1994	Santa Silverwood	Closed	1996	9.00	9
1994	Xmas Express	Open		8.50	9

Perfect Little Place/Christmas Collection - C.Thammavongsa

YEAR ISSUE		EDITION LIMIT	YEAR RETD.	ISSUE PRICE	*QUOTE U.S.$
1995	Angel of Light	Open		12.00	12

Pigsville/The Christmas Collection - C. Thammavongsa

YEAR ISSUE		EDITION LIMIT	YEAR RETD.	ISSUE PRICE	*QUOTE U.S.$
1994	Caroler	Open		10.00	10
1994	Christmas Treats	Open		9.00	9
1994	Drummer Pig	Open		10.00	10
1995	Fa-La-La-La-La	Open		9.50	10
1995	Heaven Sent	Closed	1996	10.50	11
1994	Joy to the World	Open		10.00	10
1994	Lovestruck	Open		10.50	11
1994	Santa Pig	Open		11.00	11
1994	Wheeeeee! Piggy	Open		9.00	9

The Precious Steeples Collection - Ganz/L. Sunarth

YEAR ISSUE		EDITION LIMIT	YEAR RETD.	ISSUE PRICE	*QUOTE U.S.$
1995	Florence Cathedral	Open		11.00	11
1995	Notre-Dame Cathedral	Open		11.00	11
1995	St. Patrick's Cathedral	Open		11.00	11
1995	St. Paul's Cathedral	Open		11.00	11
1995	St. Peter's Basilica	Open		11.00	11
1995	Westminster Abbey	Open		11.00	11

Trains Gone By/Christmas Collection - Ganz

YEAR ISSUE		EDITION LIMIT	YEAR RETD.	ISSUE PRICE	*QUOTE U.S.$
1996	C.P. Huntington Train	4,896		10.00	10
1996	General Train	4,896		10.00	10
1996	New York Central Train	4,896		10.00	10
1996	Pennsylvania Train	4,896		10.00	10

Gartlan USA

Ringo Starr - M. Taylor

YEAR ISSUE		EDITION LIMIT	YEAR RETD.	ISSUE PRICE	*QUOTE U.S.$
1996	Ringo Starr	Yr.Iss.	1996	19.95	20

Goebel of North America

Angel Bell 3" - Goebel

YEAR ISSUE		EDITION LIMIT	YEAR RETD.	ISSUE PRICE	*QUOTE U.S.$
1994	Angel w/Clarinet - Red	Closed	1994	17.50	18
1995	Angel w/Harp - Blue	Closed	1995	17.50	18
1996	Angel w/Mandolin - Champagne	Closed	1996	18.00	18
1997	Angel w/Accordian-Rose	Yr.Iss.		18.00	18

Angel Bells - 3 Asst. Colors - Goebel

YEAR ISSUE		EDITION LIMIT	YEAR RETD.	ISSUE PRICE	*QUOTE U.S.$
1976	Angel Bell w/Clarinet (3 colors)	Closed	1976	8.00	8
1976	Angel Bell w/Clarinet (white bisque)	Closed	1976	6.00	6
1977	Angel Bell w/Mandolin (3 colors)	Closed	1977	8.50	9
1977	Angel Bell w/Mandolin (white bisque)	Closed	1977	6.50	7
1978	Angel Bell w/Harp (3 colors)	Closed	1978	9.00	9
1978	Angel Bell w/Harp (white bisque)	Closed	1978	7.00	7
1979	Angel Bell w/Accordion (3 colors)	Closed	1979	9.50	10
1979	Angel Bell w/Accordion (white bisque)	Closed	1979	7.50	8
1980	Angel Bell w/Saxaphone (3 colors)	Closed	1980	10.00	10

*Quotes have been rounded up to nearest dollar

YEAR ISSUE		EDITION LIMIT	YEAR RETD.	ISSUE PRICE	*QUOTE U.S.$
1980	Angel Bell w/Saxaphone (white bisque)	Closed	1980	8.00	8
1981	Angel Bell w/Music (3 colors)	Closed	1981	11.00	11
1981	Angel Bell w/Music (white bisque)	Closed	1981	9.00	9
1982	Angel Bell w/French Horn (3 colors)	Closed	1982	11.75	12
1982	Angel Bell w/French Horn (white bisque)	Closed	1982	9.75	10
1983	Angel Bell w/Flute (3 colors)	Closed	1983	12.50	13
1983	Angel Bell w/Flute (white bisque)	Closed	1983	10.50	11
1984	Angel Bell w/Drum (3 colors)	Closed	1984	14.00	14
1984	Angel Bell w/Drum (white bisque)	Closed	1984	12.00	12
1985	Angel Bell w/Trumpet (3 colors)	Closed	1985	14.00	14
1985	Angel Bell w/Trumpet (white bisque)	Closed	1985	12.00	12
1986	Angel Bell w/Bells (3 colors)	Closed	1986	15.00	15
1986	Angel Bell w/Bells (white bisque)	Closed	1986	12.50	13
1987	Angel Bell w/Conductor (3 colors)	Closed	1987	16.50	17
1987	Angel Bell w/Conductor (white bisque)	Closed	1987	13.50	14
1988	Angel Bell w/Candle (3 colors)	Closed	1988	17.50	18
1988	Angel Bell w/Candle (white bisque)	Closed	1988	15.00	15
1989	Angel Bell w/Star (3 colors)	Closed	1989	20.00	20
1989	Angel Bell w/Star (white bisque)	Closed	1989	17.50	18
1990	Angel Bell w/Lantern (3 colors)	Closed	1990	22.50	23
1990	Angel Bell w/Lantern (white bisque)	Closed	1990	20.00	20
1991	Angel Bell w/Teddy (3 colors)	Closed	1991	25.00	25
1991	Angel Bell w/Teddy (white bisque)	Closed	1991	22.50	23
1992	Angel Bell w/Doll (3 colors)	Closed	1992	27.50	28
1992	Angel Bell w/Doll (white bisque)	Closed	1992	25.00	25
1993	Angel Bell w/Rocking Horse (3 colors)	Closed	1993	30.00	30
1993	Angel Bell w/Rocking Horse (white bisque)	Closed	1993	27.50	28
1994	Angel Bell w/Clown (3 colors)	Closed	1994	34.50	35
1994	Angel Bell w/Clown (white bisque)	Closed	1994	29.50	30
1995	Angel Bell w/Train (3 colors)	Closed	1995	37.00	37
1995	Angel Bell w/Train (white bisque)	Closed	1995	30.50	31
1996	Angel Bell w/Puppy (3 colors)	Closed	1996	40.00	40
1996	Angel Bell w/Puppy (white bisque)	Closed	1996	32.00	32
1997	Angel Bell w/Kitten (3 colors)	Open		42.50	43
1997	Angel Bell w/Kitten (white bisque)	Open		32.50	33

Goebel/M.I. Hummel

M.I. Hummel Annual Figurine Ornaments - M.I. Hummel

1988	Flying High 452	Closed	N/A	75.00	95-150
1989	Love From Above 481	Closed	N/A	75.00	75-125
1990	Peace on Earth 484	Closed	N/A	80.00	95-140
1991	Angelic Guide 571	Closed	N/A	95.00	95-140
1992	Light Up The Night 622	Closed	N/A	100.00	100-125
1993	Herald on High 623	Closed	N/A	155.00	155-160

M.I. Hummel Collectibles Christmas Bell Ornaments - M.I. Hummel

1989	Ride Into Christmas 775	Closed	1989	35.00	50-70
1990	Letter to Santa Claus 776	Closed	1990	37.50	40-70
1991	Hear Ye, Hear Ye 777	Closed	1991	40.00	40-70
1992	Harmony in Four Parts 778	Closed	1992	50.00	50-70
1993	Celestial Musician 779	Closed	1993	50.00	50-60
1994	Festival Harmony w/Mandolin 780	Closed	1994	50.00	50-60
1995	Festival Harmony w/Flute 781	Closed	1995	55.00	55
1996	Christmas Song 782	Closed	1996	65.00	65
1997	Thanksgiving Prayer 783	Yr.Iss.		68.00	68

M.I. Hummel Collectibles Miniature Ornaments - M.I. Hummel

1993	Celestial Musician 646	Closed	1993	90.00	110
1994	Festival Harmony w/Mandolin 647	Closed	1994	95.00	110
1995	Festival Harmony w/Flute 648	Closed	1995	100.00	110
1996	Christmas Song 645	Closed	1996	115.00	115
1997	Thanksgiving Prayer 642	Yr.Iss.		120.00	120

Gorham

Annual Crystal Ornaments - Gorham

1985	Crystal Ornament	Closed	1985	22.00	25
1986	Crystal Ornament	Closed	1986	25.00	25
1987	Crystal Ornament	Closed	1987	25.00	25
1988	Crystal Ornament	Closed	1988	28.00	28
1989	Crystal Ornament	Closed	1989	28.00	28
1990	Crystal Ornament	Closed	1990	30.00	30
1991	Crystal Ornament	Closed	1991	35.00	35
1992	Crystal Ornament	Closed	1992	32.50	33
1993	Crystal Ornament	Closed	1993	32.50	33

Annual Snowflake Ornaments - Gorham

1970	Sterling Snowflake	Closed	1970	10.00	300-400
1971	Sterling Snowflake	Closed	1971	10.00	75-175
1972	Sterling Snowflake	Closed	1972	10.00	75-175
1973	Sterling Snowflake	Closed	1973	11.00	75-150
1974	Sterling Snowflake	Closed	1974	18.00	60-100
1975	Sterling Snowflake	Closed	1975	18.00	35-85
1976	Sterling Snowflake	Closed	1976	20.00	55-100
1977	Sterling Snowflake	Closed	1977	23.00	50
1978	Sterling Snowflake	Closed	1978	23.00	50
1979	Sterling Snowflake	Closed	1979	33.00	55-100
1980	Silverplated Snowflake	Closed	1980	15.00	125-175
1981	Sterling Snowflake	Closed	1981	50.00	175-275
1982	Sterling Snowflake	Closed	1982	38.00	60-90
1983	Sterling Snowflake	Closed	1983	45.00	60-100
1984	Sterling Snowflake	Closed	1984	45.00	65-95
1985	Sterling Snowflake	Closed	1985	45.00	65-75
1986	Sterling Snowflake	Closed	1986	45.00	75
1987	Sterling Snowflake	Closed	1987	50.00	75
1988	Sterling Snowflake	Closed	1988	50.00	65
1989	Sterling Snowflake	Closed	1989	50.00	65
1990	Sterling Snowflake	Closed	1990	50.00	60
1991	Sterling Snowflake	Closed	1991	55.00	50-65
1992	Sterling Snowflake	Closed	1992	50.00	60-75
1993	Sterling Snowflake	Closed	1993	50.00	60
1994	Sterling Snowflake	Closed	1994	50.00	60
1995	Sterling Snowflake	Closed	1995	50.00	60

Archive Collectible - Gorham

1988	Victorian Heart	Closed	1988	50.00	60-75
1989	Victorian Wreath	Closed	1989	50.00	50-65
1990	Elizabethan Cupid	Closed	1990	60.00	60
1991	Baroque Angels	Closed	1991	55.00	55-65
1992	Madonna and Child	Closed	1992	50.00	50
1993	Angel With Mandolin	Closed	1993	50.00	50

Baby's First Christmas Crystal - Gorham

1991	Baby's First Rocking Horse	Closed	1994	35.00	35

Greenwich Workshop

The Greenwich Workshop Collection - J. Christensen

1995	The Angel's Gift	Yr.Iss.	1995	50.00	95
1996	A Gift of Light	Yr.Iss.	1996	75.00	75

Hallmark Keepsake Ornaments

1973 Hallmark Keepsake Collection - Keepsake

1973	Betsey Clark (1st Ed.) XHD 110-2	Yr.Iss.	1973	2.50	76-85
1973	Betsey Clark XHD100-2	Yr.Iss.	1973	2.50	112-125
1973	Christmas Is Love XHD106-2	Yr.Iss.	1973	2.50	80
1973	Elves XHD103-5	Yr.Iss.	1973	2.50	75
1973	Manger Scene XHD102-2	Yr.Iss.	1973	2.50	85-125
1973	Santa with Elves XHD101-5	Yr.Iss.	1973	2.50	85

1973 Keepsake Yarn Ornaments - Keepsake

1973	Angel XHD78-5	Yr.Iss.	1973	1.25	23
1973	Blue Girl XHD85-2	Yr.Iss.	1973	1.25	23
1973	Boy Caroler XHD83-2	Yr.Iss.	1973	1.25	30
1973	Choir Boy XHD80-5	Yr.Iss.	1973	1.25	28
1973	Elf XHD79-2	Yr.Iss.	1973	1.25	25
1973	Green Girl XHD84-5	Yr.Iss.	1973	1.25	25
1973	Little Girl XHD82-5	Yr.Iss.	1973	1.25	20
1973	Mr. Santa XHD74-5	Yr.Iss.	1973	1.25	25
1973	Mr. Snowman XHD76-5	Yr.Iss.	1973	1.25	25
1973	Mrs. Santa XHD75-2	Yr.Iss.	1973	1.25	23
1973	Mrs. Snowman XHD77-2	Yr.Iss.	1973	1.25	23
1973	Soldier XHD81-2	Yr.Iss.	1973	1.00	22

1974 Hallmark Keepsake Collection - Keepsake

1974	Angel QX110 -1	Yr.Iss.	1974	2.50	75
1974	Betsey Clark (2nd Ed.) QX 108-1	Yr.Iss.	1974	2.50	47-85
1974	Buttons & Bo (Set/2) QX113-1	Yr.Iss.	1974	3.50	50
1974	Charmers QX109-1	Yr.Iss.	1974	2.50	23-45
1974	Currier & Ives (Set/2) QX112-1	Yr.Iss.	1974	3.50	42-55
1974	Little Miracles (Set/4) QX115-1	Yr.Iss.	1974	4.50	55
1974	Norman Rockwell QX106-1	Yr.Iss.	1974	2.50	45-95
1974	Norman Rockwell QX111-1	Yr.Iss.	1974	2.50	85
1974	Raggedy Ann and Andy(4/set) QX114-1	Yr.Iss.	1974	4.50	75
1974	Snowgoose QX107-1	Yr.Iss.	1974	2.50	75

1974 Keepsake Yarn Ornaments - Keepsake

1974	Angel QX103-1	Yr.Iss.	1974	1.50	28
1974	Elf QX101-1	Yr.Iss.	1974	1.50	23
1974	Mrs. Santa QX100-1	Yr.Iss.	1974	1.50	23
1974	Santa QX105-1	Yr.Iss.	1974	1.50	25
1974	Snowman QX104-1	Yr.Iss.	1974	1.50	23
1974	Soldier QX102-1	Yr.Iss.	1974	1.50	23

1975 Handcrafted Ornaments: Adorable - Keepsake

1975	Betsey Clark QX157-1	Yr.Iss.	1975	2.50	225
1975	Drummer Boy QX161-1	Yr.Iss.	1975	2.50	225-300
1975	Mrs. Santa QX156-1	Yr.Iss.	1975	2.50	275
1975	Raggedy Andy QX160-1	Yr.Iss.	1975	2.50	375
1975	Raggedy Ann QX159-1	Yr.Iss.	1975	2.50	295
1975	Santa QX155-1	Yr.Iss.	1975	2.50	250

1975 Handcrafted Ornaments: Nostalgia - Keepsake

1975	Drummer Boy QX130-1	Yr.Iss.	1975	3.50	115-175
1975	Joy QX132-1	Yr.Iss.	1975	3.50	125-150
1975	Locomotive (dated) QX127-1	Yr.Iss.	1975	3.50	125-175
1975	Peace on Earth (dated) QX131-1	Yr.Iss.	1975	3.50	100-165
1975	Rocking Horse QX128-1	Yr.Iss.	1975	3.50	125-175
1975	Santa & Sleigh QX129-1	Yr.Iss.	1975	3.50	125

1975 Keepsake Property Ornaments - Keepsake

1975	Betsey Clark (3rd Ed.) QX133-1	Yr.Iss.	1975	3.00	26-45
1975	Betsey Clark (Set/2) QX167-1	Yr.Iss.	1975	3.50	25-45
1975	Betsey Clark (Set/4) QX168-1	Yr.Iss.	1975	4.50	50
1975	Betsey Clark QX163-1	Yr.Iss.	1975	2.50	40
1975	Buttons & Bo (Set/4) QX139-1	Yr.Iss.	1975	5.00	50
1975	Charmers QX135-1	Yr.Iss.	1975	3.00	35
1975	Currier & Ives (Set/2) QX137-1	Yr.Iss.	1975	4.00	40
1975	Currier & Ives (Set/2) QX164-1	Yr.Iss.	1975	2.50	35
1975	Little Miracles (Set/4) QX140-1	Yr.Iss.	1975	5.00	40
1975	Marty Links QX136-1	Yr.Iss.	1975	3.00	60
1975	Norman Rockwell QX134-1	Yr.Iss.	1975	3.00	37
1975	Norman Rockwell QX166-1	Yr.Iss.	1975	2.50	45-55
1975	Raggedy Ann and Andy(2/set) QX138-1	Yr.Iss.	1975	4.00	65
1975	Raggedy Ann QX165-1	Yr.Iss.	1975	2.50	50-65

1975 Keepsake Yarn Ornaments - Keepsake

1975	Drummer Boy QX123-1	Yr.Iss.	1975	1.75	25
1975	Little Girl QX126-1	Yr.Iss.	1975	1.75	20
1975	Mrs. Santa QX125-1	Yr.Iss.	1975	1.75	22
1975	Raggedy Andy QX122-1	Yr.Iss.	1975	1.75	40
1975	Raggedy Ann QX121-1	Yr.Iss.	1975	1.75	35
1975	Santa QX124-1	Yr.Iss.	1975	1.75	22

1976 Bicentennial Commemoratives - Keepsake

1976	Bicentennial '76 Commemorative QX211-1	Yr.Iss.	1976	2.50	45-60
1976	Bicentennial Charmers QX198-1	Yr.Iss.	1976	3.00	75-95
1976	Colonial Children (Set/2) 4 QX208-1	Yr.Iss.	1976	4.00	65-95

1976 Decorative Ball Ornaments - Keepsake

1976	Cardinals QX205-1	Yr.Iss.	1976	2.30	45-85
1976	Chickadees QX204-1	Yr.Iss.	1976	2.30	50-65

1976 First Commemorative Ornament - Keepsake

1976	Baby's First Christmas QX211-1	Yr.Iss.	1976	2.50	150

1976 Handcrafted Ornaments: Nostalgia - Keepsake

1976	Drummer Boy QX130-1	Yr.Iss.	1976	3.50	160-175
1976	Locomotive QX222-1	Yr.Iss.	1976	3.50	165
1976	Peace on Earth QX223-1	Yr.Iss.	1976	3.50	95-175
1976	Rocking Horse QX128-1	Yr.Iss.	1976	3.50	165

1976 Handcrafted Ornaments: Tree Treats - Keepsake

1976	Angel QX176-1	Yr.Iss.	1976	3.00	150-195
1976	Reindeer QX 178-1	Yr.Iss.	1976	3.00	115
1976	Santa QX177-1	Yr.Iss.	1976	3.00	195-225
1976	Shepherd QX175-1	Yr.Iss.	1976	3.00	95-115

1976 Handcrafted Ornaments: Twirl-Abouts - Keepsake

1976	Angel QX171-1	Yr.Iss.	1976	4.50	132-165
1976	Partridge QX174-1	Yr.Iss.	1976	4.50	195
1976	Santa QX172-1	Yr.Iss.	1976	4.50	103-125
1976	Soldier QX173-1	Yr.Iss.	1976	4.50	95

1976 Handcrafted Ornaments: Yesteryears - Keepsake

1976	Drummer Boy QX184-1	Yr.Iss.	1976	5.00	122-150
1976	Partridge QX183-1	Yr.Iss.	1976	5.00	115
1976	Santa QX182-1	Yr.Iss.	1976	5.00	165
1976	Train QX181-1	Yr.Iss.	1976	5.00	135-160

1976 Property Ornaments - Keepsake

1976	Betsey Clark (4th Ed.)QX 195-1	Yr.Iss.	1976	3.00	75-100
1976	Betsey Clark (Set/3) QX218-1	Yr.Iss.	1976	4.50	45-65
1976	Betsey Clark QX210-1	Yr.Iss.	1976	2.50	38-42
1976	Charmers (Set/2) QX215-1	Yr.Iss.	1976	3.50	65-75
1976	Currier & Ives QX197-1	Yr.Iss.	1976	3.00	50
1976	Currier & Ives QX209-1	Yr.Iss.	1976	2.50	50
1976	Happy the Snowman (Set/2) QX216-1	Yr.Iss.	1976	3.50	55
1976	Marty Links (Set/2) QX207-1	Yr.Iss.	1976	4.00	45-65
1976	Norman Rockwell QX196-1	Yr.Iss.	1976	3.00	65
1976	Raggedy Ann QX212-1	Yr.Iss.	1976	2.50	65
1976	Rudolph and Santa QX213-1	Yr.Iss.	1976	2.50	75

1976 Yarn Ornaments - Keepsake

1976	Caroler QX126-1	Yr.Iss.	1976	1.75	28
1976	Drummer Boy QX123-1	Yr.Iss.	1976	1.75	23
1976	Mrs. Santa QX125-1	Yr.Iss.	1976	1.75	22
1976	Raggedy Andy QX122-1	Yr.Iss.	1976	1.75	40
1976	Raggedy Ann QX121-1	Yr.Iss.	1976	1.75	35
1976	Santa QX124-1	Yr.Iss.	1976	1.75	24

1977 Christmas Expressions Collection - Keepsake

1977	Bell QX154-2	Yr.Iss.	1977	3.50	35
1977	Mandolin QX157-5	Yr.Iss.	1977	3.50	65
1977	Ornaments QX155-5	Yr.Iss.	1977	3.50	65
1977	Wreath QX156-2	Yr.Iss.	1977	3.50	65

1977 Cloth Doll Ornaments - Keepsake

1977	Angel QX220-2	Yr.Iss.	1977	1.75	40-50
1977	Santa QX221-5	Yr.Iss.	1977	1.75	55-80

1977 Colors of Christmas - Keepsake

1977	Bell QX200-2	Yr.Iss.	1977	3.50	45
1977	Candle QX203-5	Yr.Iss.	1977	3.50	55
1977	Joy QX201-5	Yr.Iss.	1977	3.50	45
1977	Wreath QX202-2	Yr.Iss.	1977	3.50	45-55

1977 Commemoratives - Keepsake

1977	Baby's First Christmas QX131-5	Yr.Iss.	1977	3.50	58-75
1977	First Christmas Together QX132-2	Yr.Iss.	1977	3.50	45-65
1977	For Your New Home QX263-5	Yr.Iss.	1977	3.50	120
1977	Granddaughter QX208-2	Yr.Iss.	1977	3.50	150
1977	Grandmother QX260-2	Yr.Iss.	1977	3.50	150
1977	Grandson QX209-5	Yr.Iss.	1977	3.50	150
1977	Love QX262-2	Yr.Iss.	1977	3.50	95
1977	Mother QX261-5	Yr.Iss.	1977	3.50	75

*Quotes have been rounded up to nearest dollar

ORNAMENTS

Hallmark Keepsake Ornaments to Hallmark Keepsake Ornaments

YEAR ISSUE		EDITION LIMIT	YEAR RETD.	ISSUE PRICE	*QUOTE U.S. $
1977 Decorative Ball Ornaments - Keepsake					
1977	Christmas Mouse QX134-2	Yr.Iss.	1977	3.50	65
1977	Rabbit QX139-5	Yr.Iss.	1977	2.50	95
1977	Squirrel QX138-2	Yr.Iss.	1977	2.50	95
1977	Stained Glass QX152-2	Yr.Iss.	1977	3.50	40-70
1977 Holiday Highlights - Keepsake					
1977	Drummer Boy QX312-2	Yr.Iss.	1977	3.50	38-65
1977	Joy QX310-2	Yr.Iss.	1977	3.50	45
1977	Peace on Earth QX311-5	Yr.Iss.	1977	3.50	65
1977	Star QX313-5	Yr.Iss.	1977	3.50	50
1977 Metal Ornaments - Keepsake					
1977	Snowflake Collection (Set/4) QX 210-2	Yr.Iss.	1977	5.00	95
1977 Nostalgia Collection - Keepsake					
1977	Angel QX182-2	Yr.Iss.	1977	5.00	91-125
1977	Antique Car QX180-2	Yr.Iss.	1977	5.00	65
1977	Nativity QX181-5	Yr.Iss.	1977	5.00	135-140
1977	Toys QX183-5	Yr.Iss.	1977	5.00	140-155
1977 Peanuts Collection - Keepsake					
1977	Peanuts (Set/2) QX163-5	Yr.Iss.	1977	4.00	75
1977	Peanuts QX135-5	Yr.Iss.	1977	3.50	60
1977	Peanuts QX162-2	Yr.Iss.	1977	2.50	60
1977 Property Ornaments - Keepsake					
1977	Betsey Clark (5th Ed.) QX264-2	Yr.Iss.	1977	3.50	460
1977	Charmers QX153-5	Yr.Iss.	1977	3.50	65
1977	Currier & Ives QX130-2	Yr.Iss.	1977	3.50	55
1977	Disney (Set/2) QX137-5	Yr.Iss.	1977	4.00	75
1977	Disney QX133-5	Yr.Iss.	1977	3.50	45
1977	Grandma Moses QX150-2	Yr.Iss.	1977	3.50	100-175
1977	Norman Rockwell QX151-5	Yr.Iss.	1977	3.50	70
1977 The Beauty of America Collection - Keepsake					
1977	Desert QX159-5	Yr.Iss.	1977	2.50	25
1977	Mountains QX158-2	Yr.Iss.	1977	2.50	15
1977	Seashore QX160-2	Yr.Iss.	1977	2.50	50
1977	Wharf QX161-5	Yr.Iss.	1977	2.50	30-50
1977 Twirl-About Collection - Keepsake					
1977	Bellringer QX192-2	Yr.Iss.	1977	6.00	45-55
1977	Della Robia Wreath QX193-5	Yr.Iss.	1977	4.50	91-115
1977	Snowman QX190-2	Yr.Iss.	1977	4.50	60-75
1977	Weather House QX191-5	Yr.Iss.	1977	6.00	85-95
1977 Yesteryears Collection - Keepsake					
1977	Angel QX172-2	Yr.Iss.	1977	6.00	85
1977	House QX170-2	Yr.Iss.	1977	6.00	100-125
1977	Jack-in-the-Box QX171-5	Yr.Iss.	1977	6.00	100-125
1977	Reindeer QX173-5	Yr.Iss.	1977	6.00	106-140
1978 Colors of Christmas - Keepsake					
1978	Angel QX354-3	Yr.Iss.	1978	3.50	40
1978	Candle QX357-6	Yr.Iss.	1978	3.50	85
1978	Locomotive QX356-3	Yr.Iss.	1978	3.50	48
1978	Merry Christmas QX355-6	Yr.Iss.	1978	3.50	50
1978 Commemoratives - Keepsake					
1978	25th Christmas Together QX269-3	Yr.Iss.	1978	3.50	35
1978	Baby's First Christmas QX200-3	Yr.Iss.	1978	3.50	65-85
1978	First Christmas Together QX218-3	Yr.Iss.	1978	3.50	45
1978	For Your New Home QX217-6	Yr.Iss.	1978	3.50	75
1978	Granddaughter QX216-3	Yr.Iss.	1978	3.50	55
1978	Grandmother QX267-6	Yr.Iss.	1978	3.50	50
1978	Grandson QX215-6	Yr.Iss.	1978	3.50	45
1978	Love QX268-3	Yr.Iss.	1978	3.50	55
1978	Mother QX266-3	Yr.Iss.	1978	3.50	25-40
1978 Decorative Ball Ornaments - Keepsake					
1978	Drummer Boy QX252-3	Yr.Iss.	1978	3.50	35
1978	Hallmark's Antique Card Collection Design QX220-3	Yr.Iss.	1978	3.50	40
1978	Joy QX254-3	Yr.Iss.	1978	3.50	30-45
1978	Merry Christmas (Santa) QX202-3	Yr.Iss.	1978	3.50	45-55
1978	Nativity QX253-6	Yr.Iss.	1978	3.50	150
1978	The Quail QX251-6	Yr.Iss.	1978	3.50	45
1978	Yesterday's Toys QX250-3	Yr.Iss.	1978	3.50	55
1978 Handcrafted Ornaments - Keepsake					
1978	Angel QX139-6	Yr.Iss.	1981	4.50	85-95
1978	Angels QX150-3	Yr.Iss.	1978	8.00	345
1978	Animal Home QX149-6	Yr.Iss.	1978	6.00	141-175
1978	Calico Mouse QX137-6	Yr.Iss.	1978	4.50	95
1978	Carrousel Series (1st Ed.) QX146-3	Yr.Iss.	1978	6.00	400
1978	Dough Angel QX139-6	Yr.Iss.	1981	5.50	65-95
1978	Dove QX190-3	Yr.Iss.	1978	4.50	65-85
1978	Holly and Poinsettia Ball QX147-6	Yr.Iss.	1978	6.00	85
1978	Joy QX138-3	Yr.Iss.	1978	4.50	72-85
1978	Panorama Ball QX145-6	Yr.Iss.	1978	6.00	135
1978	Red Cardinal QX144-3	Yr.Iss.	1978	4.50	152-175
1978	Rocking Horse QX148-3	Yr.Iss.	1978	6.00	85
1978	Schneeberg Bell QX152-3	Yr.Iss.	1978	8.00	190
1978	Skating Raccoon QX142-3	Yr.Iss.	1978	6.00	85-95
1978 Holiday Chimes - Keepsake					
1978	Reindeer Chimes QX320-3	Yr.Iss.	1980	4.50	60
1978 Holiday Highlights - Keepsake					
1978	Dove QX310-3	Yr.Iss.	1978	3.50	125
1978	Nativity QX309-6	Yr.Iss.	1978	3.50	70
1978	Santa QX307-6	Yr.Iss.	1978	3.50	75
1978	Snowflake QX308-3	Yr.Iss.	1978	3.50	65
1978 Little Trimmers - Keepsake					
1978	Drummer Boy QX136-3	Yr.Iss.	1978	2.50	55
1978	Praying Angel QX134-3	Yr.Iss.	1978	2.50	90
1978	Santa QX135-6	Yr.Iss.	1978	2.50	63
1978	Set/4 - QX355-6	Yr.Iss.	1978	10.00	400-425
1978	Thimble Series (Mouse) (1st Ed.) QX133-6	Yr.Iss.	1978	2.50	265-295
1978 Peanuts Collection - Keepsake					
1978	Peanuts QX203-6	Yr.Iss.	1978	2.50	50
1978	Peanuts QX204-3	Yr.Iss.	1978	2.50	60
1978	Peanuts QX205-6	Yr.Iss.	1978	3.50	65
1978	Peanuts QX206-3	Yr.Iss.	1978	3.50	50
1978 Property Ornaments - Keepsake					
1978	Betsey Clark (6th Ed.) QX201-6	Yr.Iss.	1978	3.50	60
1978	Disney QX207-6	Yr.Iss.	1978	3.50	60-125
1978	Joan Walsh Anglund QX221-6	Yr.Iss.	1978	3.50	65
1978	Spencer Sparrow QX219-6	Yr.Iss.	1978	3.50	50
1978 Yarn Collection - Keepsake					
1978	Green Boy QX123-1	Yr.Iss.	1979	2.00	25
1978	Green Girl QX126-1	Yr.Iss.	1979	2.00	20
1978	Mr. Claus QX340-3	Yr.Iss.	1979	2.00	23
1978	Mrs. Claus QX125-1	Yr.Iss.	1979	2.00	22
1979 Collectible Series - Keepsake					
1979	Bellringer (1st Ed.) QX147-9	Yr.Iss.	1979	10.00	400
1979	Carousel (2nd Ed.) QX146-7	Yr.Iss.	1979	6.50	165-185
1979	Here Comes Santa (1st Ed.) QX155-9	Yr.Iss.	1979	9.00	425-695
1979	Snoopy and Friends QX141-9	Yr.Iss.	1979	8.00	95
1979	Thimble (2nd Ed.) QX131-9	Yr.Iss.	1980	3.00	150-175
1979 Colors of Christmas - Keepsake					
1979	Holiday Wreath QX353-9	Yr.Iss.	1979	3.50	35-45
1979	Partridge in a Pear Tree QX351-9	Yr.Iss.	1979	3.50	35-45
1979	Star Over Bethlehem QX352-7	Yr.Iss.	1979	3.50	75
1979	Words of Christmas QX350-7	Yr.Iss.	1979	3.50	85
1979 Commemoratives - Keepsake					
1979	Baby's First Christmas QX154-7	Yr.Iss.	1979	8.00	175
1979	Baby's First Christmas QX208-7	Yr.Iss.	1979	3.50	22-35
1979	Friendship QX203-9	Yr.Iss.	1979	3.50	18
1979	Granddaughter QX211-9	Yr.Iss.	1979	3.50	24-35
1979	Grandmother QX252-7	Yr.Iss.	1979	3.50	10
1979	Grandson QX210-7	Yr.Iss.	1979	3.50	35
1979	Love QX258-7	Yr.Iss.	1979	3.50	17-50
1979	Mother QX251-9	Yr.Iss.	1979	3.50	9-22
1979	New Home QX212-7	Yr.Iss.	1979	3.50	45
1979	Our First Christmas Together QX209-9	Yr.Iss.	1979	3.50	65
1979	Our Twenty-Fifth Anniversary QX 250-7	Yr.Iss.	1979	3.50	17-29
1979	Teacher QX213-9	Yr.Iss.	1979	3.50	8-15
1979 Decorative Ball Ornaments - Keepsake					
1979	Behold the Star QX255-9	Yr.Iss.	1979	3.50	40
1979	Black Angel QX207-9	Yr.Iss.	1979	3.50	25
1979	Christmas Chickadees QX204-7	Yr.Iss.	1979	3.50	30
1979	Christmas Collage QX257-9	Yr.Iss.	1979	3.50	22-37
1979	Christmas Traditions QX253-9	Yr.Iss.	1979	3.50	35
1979	The Light of Christmas QX256-7	Yr.Iss.	1979	3.50	18-30
1979	Night Before Christmas QX214-7	Yr.Iss.	1979	3.50	40
1979 Handcrafted Ornaments - Keepsake					
1979	Christmas Eve Surprise QX157-9	Yr.Iss.	1979	6.50	65
1979	Christmas Heart QX140-7	Yr.Iss.	1979	6.50	103-115
1979	Christmas is for Children QX135-9	Yr.Iss.	1980	5.00	83-95
1979	A Christmas Treat QX134-7	Yr.Iss.	1979	5.00	85
1979	The Downhill Run QX145-9	Yr.Iss.	1979	6.50	135-175
1979	The Drummer Boy QX143-9	Yr.Iss.	1979	8.00	90-125
1979	Holiday Scrimshaw QX152-7	Yr.Iss.	1979	4.00	225
1979	Outdoor Fun QX150-7	Yr.Iss.	1979	8.00	125-135
1979	Raccoon QX142-3	Yr.Iss.	1979	6.50	85
1979	Ready for Christmas QX133-9	Yr.Iss.	1979	6.50	95-150
1979	Santa's Here QX138-7	Yr.Iss.	1979	5.00	55-75
1979	The Skating Snowman QX139-9	Yr.Iss.	1980	5.00	65-80
1979 Holiday Chimes - Keepsake					
1979	Reindeer Chimes QX320-3	Yr.Iss.	1979	4.50	75
1979	Star Chimes QX137-9	Yr.Iss.	1979	4.50	75-85
1979 Holiday Highlights - Keepsake					
1979	Christmas Angel QX300-7	Yr.Iss.	1979	3.50	95
1979	Christmas Cheer QX303-9	Yr.Iss.	1979	3.50	95
1979	Christmas Tree QX302-7	Yr.Iss.	1979	3.50	75
1979	Love QX304-7	Yr.Iss.	1979	3.50	80-88
1979	Snowflake QX301-9	Yr.Iss.	1979	3.50	40
1979 Little Trimmer Collection - Keepsake					
1979	Angel Delight QX130-7	Yr.Iss.	1979	3.00	80-95
1979	A Matchless Christmas QX132-7	Yr.Iss.	1979	4.00	67-85
1979	Santa QX135-6	Yr.Iss.	1979	3.00	55
1979	Thimble Series-Mouse QX133-6	Yr.Iss.	1979	3.00	150-225
1979 Property Ornaments - Keepsake					
1979	Betsey Clark (7th Ed.) QX 201-9	Yr.Iss.	1979	3.50	33-40
1979	Joan Walsh Anglund QX205-9	Yr.Iss.	1979	3.50	35
1979	Mary Hamilton QX254-7	Yr.Iss.	1979	3.50	14-25
1979	Peanuts (Time to Trim) QX202-7	Yr.Iss.	1979	3.50	40
1979	Spencer Sparrow QX200-7	Yr.Iss.	1979	3.50	25-40
1979	Winnie-the-Pooh QX206-7	Yr.Iss.	1979	3.50	40
1979 Sewn Trimmers - Keepsake					
1979	Angel Music QX343-9	Yr.Iss.	1980	2.00	20
1979	Merry Santa QX342-7	Yr.Iss.	1980	2.00	20
1979	The Rocking Horse QX340-7	Yr.Iss.	1980	2.00	23
1979	Stuffed Full Stocking QX341-9	Yr.Iss.	1980	2.00	18-25
1979 Yarn Collection - Keepsake					
1979	Green Boy QX123-1	Yr.Iss.	1979	2.00	20
1979	Green Girl QX126-1	Yr.Iss.	1979	2.00	18
1979	Mr. Claus QX340-3	Yr.Iss.	1979	2.00	20
1979	Mrs. Claus QX125-1	Yr.Iss.	1979	2.00	20
1980 Collectible Series - Keepsake					
1980	The Bellringers (2nd Ed.) QX157-4	Yr.Iss.	1980	15.00	61-85
1980	Carrousel (3rd Ed.) QX141-4	Yr.Iss.	1980	7.50	140-165
1980	Frosty Friends (1st Ed.) QX 137-4	Yr.Iss.	1980	6.50	625
1980	Here Comes Santa (2nd Ed.) QX 143-4	Yr.Iss.	1980	12.00	171-195
1980	Norman Rockwell (1st Ed.) QX306-1	Yr.Iss.	1980	6.50	158-250
1980	Snoopy & Friends (2nd Ed.) QX154-1	Yr.Iss.	1980	9.00	75-115
1980	Thimble (3rd Ed.) QX132-1	Yr.Iss.	1980	4.00	100-175
1980 Colors of Christmas - Keepsake					
1980	Joy QX350-1	Yr.Iss.	1980	4.00	22
1980 Commemoratives - Keepsake					
1980	25th Christmas Together QX206-1	Yr.Iss.	1980	4.00	11-22
1980	Baby's First Christmas QX156-1	Yr.Iss.	1980	12.00	50
1980	Baby's First Christmas QX200-1	Yr.Iss.	1980	4.00	23-35
1980	Beauty of Friendship QX303-4	Yr.Iss.	1980	4.00	60
1980	Black Baby's First Christmas QX229-4	Yr.Iss.	1980	4.00	30
1980	Christmas at Home QX210-1	Yr.Iss.	1980	4.00	35
1980	Christmas Love QX207-4	Yr.Iss.	1980	4.00	40
1980	Dad QX214-1	Yr.Iss.	1980	4.00	9-18
1980	Daughter QX212-1	Yr.Iss.	1980	4.00	40
1980	First Christmas Together QX205-4	Yr.Iss.	1980	4.00	43
1980	First Christmas Together QX305-4	Yr.Iss.	1980	4.00	30-55
1980	Friendship QX208-1	Yr.Iss.	1980	4.00	10-20
1980	Granddaughter QX202-1	Yr.Iss.	1980	4.00	35
1980	Grandfather QX231-4	Yr.Iss.	1980	4.00	10-20
1980	Grandmother QX204-1	Yr.Iss.	1980	4.00	20
1980	Grandparents QX213-4	Yr.Iss.	1980	4.00	40
1980	Grandson QX201-4	Yr.Iss.	1980	4.00	18-35
1980	Love QX302-1	Yr.Iss.	1980	4.00	65
1980	Mother and Dad QX230-1	Yr.Iss.	1980	4.00	11-20
1980	Mother QX203-4	Yr.Iss.	1980	4.00	11-23
1980	Mother QX304-1	Yr.Iss.	1980	4.00	35
1980	Son QX211-4	Yr.Iss.	1980	4.00	27-35
1980	Teacher QX209-4	Yr.Iss.	1980	4.00	10-20
1980 Decorative Ball Ornaments - Keepsake					
1980	Christmas Cardinals QX224-1	Yr.Iss.	1980	4.00	35
1980	Christmas Choir QX228-1	Yr.Iss.	1980	4.00	85
1980	Christmas Time QX226-1	Yr.Iss.	1980	4.00	30
1980	Happy Christmas QX222-1	Yr.Iss.	1980	4.00	30
1980	Jolly Santa QX227-4	Yr.Iss.	1980	4.00	30
1980	Nativity QX225-4	Yr.Iss.	1980	4.00	125
1980	Santa's Workshop QX223-4	Yr.Iss.	1980	4.00	15-30
1980 Frosted Images - Keepsake					
1980	Dove QX308-1	Yr.Iss.	1980	4.00	25-39
1980	Drummer Boy QX309-4	Yr.Iss.	1980	4.00	25
1980	Santa QX310-1	Yr.Iss.	1980	4.00	22
1980 Handcrafted Ornaments - Keepsake					
1980	The Animals' Christmas QX150-1	Yr.Iss.	1980	8.00	62
1980	Caroling Bear QX140-1	Yr.Iss.	1980	7.50	116-150
1980	Christmas is for Children QX135-9	Yr.Iss.	1980	5.50	95
1980	A Christmas Treat QX134-7	Yr.Iss.	1980	5.50	75
1980	A Christmas Vigil QX144-1	Yr.Iss.	1980	9.00	95-185
1980	Drummer Boy QX147-4	Yr.Iss.	1980	5.50	58-95
1980	Elfin Antics QX142-1	Yr.Iss.	1980	9.00	225
1980	A Heavenly Nap QX139-4	Yr.Iss.	1981	6.50	39-55
1980	Heavenly Sounds QX152-1	Yr.Iss.	1980	7.50	72-95
1980	Santa 1980 QX146-1	Yr.Iss.	1980	5.50	84-95
1980	Santa's Flight QX138-1	Yr.Iss.	1980	5.50	102-115
1980	Skating Snowman QX139-9	Yr.Iss.	1980	5.50	80
1980	The Snowflake Swing QX133-4	Yr.Iss.	1980	4.00	45
1980	A Spot of Christmas Cheer QX153-4	Yr.Iss.	1980	8.00	149
1980 Holiday Chimes - Keepsake					
1980	Reindeer Chimes QX320-3	Yr.Iss.	1980	5.50	25
1980	Santa Mobile QX136-1	Yr.Iss.	1981	5.50	25-50
1980	Snowflake Chimes QX165-4	Yr.Iss.	1981	5.50	35
1980 Holiday Highlights - Keepsake					
1980	Three Wise Men QX300-1	Yr.Iss.	1980	4.00	30

*Quotes have been rounded up to nearest dollar

Collectors' Information Bureau

Hallmark Keepsake Ornaments to Hallmark Keepsake Ornaments

ORNAMENTS

YEAR ISSUE		EDITION LIMIT	YEAR RETD.	ISSUE PRICE	*QUOTE U.S. $
1980	Wreath QX301-4	Yr.Iss.	1980	4.00	85
1980 Little Trimmers - Keepsake					
1980	Christmas Owl QX131-4	Yr.Iss.	1982	4.00	43
1980	Christmas Teddy QX135-4	Yr.Iss.	1980	2.50	80-135
1980	Clothespin Soldier QX134-1	Yr.Iss.	1980	3.50	40
1980	Merry Redbird QX160-1	Yr.Iss.	1980	3.50	50-65
1980	Swingin' on a Star QX130-1	Yr.Iss.	1980	4.00	65-85
1980	Thimble Series-A Christmas Salute QX131-9	Yr.Iss.	1980	4.00	175
1980 Old-Fashioned Christmas Collection - Keepsake					
1980	In a Nutshell QX469-7	Yr.Iss.	1988	5.50	24-33
1980 Property Ornaments - Keepsake					
1980	Betsey Clark (8th Ed.) QX 215-4	Yr.Iss.	1980	4.00	24-30
1980	Betsey Clark QX307-4	Yr.Iss.	1980	6.50	55
1980	Betsey Clark's Christmas QX194-4	Yr.Iss.	1980	7.50	35
1980	Disney QX218-1	Yr.Iss.	1980	4.00	30
1980	Joan Walsh Anglund QX217-4	Yr.Iss.	1980	4.00	23-25
1980	Marty Links QX221-4	Yr.Iss.	1980	4.00	11-23
1980	Mary Hamilton QX219-4	Yr.Iss.	1980	4.00	20
1980	Muppets QX220-1	Yr.Iss.	1980	4.00	40
1980	Peanuts QX216-1	Yr.Iss.	1980	4.00	40
1980 Sewn Trimmers - Keepsake					
1980	Angel Music QX343-9	Yr.Iss.	1980	2.00	20
1980	Merry Santa QX342-7	Yr.Iss.	1980	2.00	20
1980	The Rocking Horse QX340-7	Yr.Iss.	1980	2.00	22
1980	Stuffed Full Stocking QX341-9	Yr.Iss.	1980	2.00	25
1980 Special Editions - Keepsake					
1980	Checking it Twice QX158-4	Yr.Iss.	1981	20.00	175-195
1980	Heavenly Minstrel QX156-7	Yr.Iss.	1980	15.00	325
1980 Yarn Ornaments - Keepsake					
1980	Angel QX162-1	Yr.Iss.	1981	3.00	10
1980	Santa QX161-4	Yr.Iss.	1981	3.00	9
1980	Snowman QX163-4	Yr.Iss.	1981	3.00	9
1980	Soldier QX164-1	Yr.Iss.	1981	3.00	9
1981 Collectible Series - Keepsake					
1981	Bellringer (3rd Ed.) QX441-5	Yr.Iss.	1981	15.00	70-95
1981	Carrousel (4th Ed.) QX427-5	Yr.Iss.	1981	9.00	62-95
1981	Frosty Friends (2nd Ed.) QX433-5	Yr.Iss.	1981	8.00	413-495
1981	Here Comes Santa (3rd Ed.QX438-2	Yr.Iss.	1981	13.00	205-325
1981	Norman Rockwell (2nd Ed.) QX 511-5	Yr.Iss.	1981	8.50	35-50
1981	Rocking Horse (1st Ed.) QX 422-2	Yr.Iss.	1981	9.00	425
1981	Snoopy and Friends (3rd Ed.) QX436-2	Yr.Iss.	1981	12.00	100-125
1981	Thimble (4th Ed.) QX413-5	Yr.Iss.	1981	4.50	150
1981 Commemoratives - Keepsake					
1981	25th Christmas Together QX504-2	Yr.Iss.	1981	5.50	10-22
1981	25th Christmas Together QX707-5	Yr.Iss.	1981	4.50	10-22
1981	50th Christmas QX708-2	Yr.Iss.	1981	4.50	8-20
1981	Baby's First Christmas QX440-2	Yr.Iss.	1981	13.00	38-50
1981	Baby's First Christmas QX513-5	Yr.Iss.	1981	8.50	11-20
1981	Baby's First Christmas QX516-2	Yr.Iss.	1981	5.50	30
1981	Baby's First Christmas-Black QX602-2	Yr.Iss.	1981	4.50	25
1981	Baby's First Christmas-Boy QX 601-5	Yr.Iss.	1981	4.50	19-25
1981	Baby's First Christmas-Girl QX 600-2	Yr.Iss.	1981	4.50	16-30
1981	Daughter QX607-5	Yr.Iss.	1981	4.50	20-45
1981	Father QX609-5	Yr.Iss.	1981	4.50	8-20
1981	First Christmas Together QX505-5	Yr.Iss.	1981	5.50	12-25
1981	First Christmas Together QX706-2	Yr.Iss.	1981	4.50	29
1981	Friendship QX503-5	Yr.Iss.	1981	5.50	17-30
1981	Friendship QX704-2	Yr.Iss.	1981	4.50	17-30
1981	The Gift of Love QX705-5	Yr.Iss.	1981	4.50	14-25
1981	Godchild QX603-5	Yr.Iss.	1981	4.50	10-20
1981	Granddaughter QX605-5	Yr.Iss.	1981	4.50	13-30
1981	Grandfather QX701-5	Yr.Iss.	1981	4.50	20
1981	Grandmother QX702-2	Yr.Iss.	1981	4.50	11-20
1981	Grandparents QX703-5	Yr.Iss.	1981	4.50	11-20
1981	Grandson QX604-2	Yr.Iss.	1981	4.50	13-30
1981	Home QX709-5	Yr.Iss.	1981	4.50	20
1981	Love QX502-2	Yr.Iss.	1981	5.50	42-50
1981	Mother and Dad QX700-2	Yr.Iss.	1981	4.50	11-17
1981	Mother QX608-2	Yr.Iss.	1981	4.50	6-17
1981	Son QX606-2	Yr.Iss.	1981	4.50	14-30
1981	Teacher QX800-2	Yr.Iss.	1981	4.50	7-15
1981 Crown Classics - Keepsake					
1981	Angel QX507-5	Yr.Iss.	1981	4.50	11-25
1981	Tree Photoholder QX515-5	Yr.Iss.	1981	5.50	17-30
1981	Unicorn QX516-5	Yr.Iss.	1981	8.50	15-27
1981 Decorative Ball Ornaments - Keepsake					
1981	Christmas 1981 QX809-5	Yr.Iss.	1981	4.50	10-25
1981	Christmas in the Forest QX813-5	Yr.Iss.	1981	4.50	145
1981	Christmas Magic QX810-2	Yr.Iss.	1981	4.50	15-25
1981	Let Us Adore Him QX811-5	Yr.Iss.	1981	4.50	28-65
1981	Merry Christmas QX814-2	Yr.Iss.	1981	4.50	13-19
1981	Santa's Coming QX812-2	Yr.Iss.	1981	4.50	12-27
1981	Santa's Surprise QX815-5	Yr.Iss.	1981	4.50	18-25
1981	Traditional (Black Santa) QX801-5	Yr.Iss.	1981	4.50	42-97
1981 Fabric Ornaments - Keepsake					
1981	Calico Kitty QX403-5	Yr.Iss.	1981	3.00	20
1981	Cardinal Cutie QX400-2	Yr.Iss.	1981	3.00	9-20
1981	Gingham Dog QX402-2	Yr.Iss.	1981	3.00	11-20
1981	Peppermint Mouse QX401-5	Yr.Iss.	1981	3.00	35
1981 Frosted Images - Keepsake					
1981	Angel QX509-5	Yr.Iss.	1981	4.00	50-65
1981	Mouse QX508-2	Yr.Iss.	1981	4.00	25
1981	Snowman QX510-2	Yr.Iss.	1981	4.00	25
1981 Hand Crafted Ornaments - Keepsake					
1981	Candyville Express QX418-2	Yr.Iss.	1981	7.50	83-95
1981	Checking It Twice QX158-4	Yr.Iss.	1981	23.00	195
1981	Christmas Dreams QX437-5	Yr.Iss.	1981	12.00	200-225
1981	Christmas Fantasy QX155-4	Yr.Iss.	1982	13.00	68-85
1981	Dough Angel QX139-6	Yr.Iss.	1981	5.50	80
1981	Drummer Boy QX148-1	Yr.Iss.	1981	2.50	43
1981	The Friendly Fiddler QX434-2	Yr.Iss.	1981	8.00	71-80
1981	A Heavenly Nap QX139-4	Yr.Iss.	1981	6.50	50
1981	Ice Fairy QX431-5	Yr.Iss.	1981	6.50	85-100
1981	The Ice Sculptor QX432-2	Yr.Iss.	1982	8.00	90-100
1981	Love and Joy QX425-2	Yr.Iss.	1981	9.00	75-95
1981	Mr. & Mrs. Claus QX448-5	Yr.Iss.	1981	12.00	110-135
1981	Sailing Santa QX439-5	Yr.Iss.	1981	13.00	225-290
1981	Space Santa QX430-2	Yr.Iss.	1981	6.50	67-115
1981	St. Nicholas QX446-2	Yr.Iss.	1981	5.50	40-50
1981	Star Swing QX421-5	Yr.Iss.	1981	5.50	60
1981	Topsy-Turvy Tunes QX429-5	Yr.Iss.	1981	7.50	68-80
1981	A Well-Stocked Stocking QX154-7	Yr.Iss.	1981	9.00	65-85
1981 Holiday Chimes - Keepsake					
1981	Santa Mobile QX136-1	Yr.Iss.	1981	5.50	40
1981	Snowflake Chimes QX165-4	Yr.Iss.	1981	5.50	25
1981	Snowman Chimes QX445-5	Yr.Iss.	1981	5.50	25-30
1981 Holiday Highlights - Keepsake					
1981	Christmas Star QX501-5	Yr.Iss.	1981	5.50	17-30
1981	Shepherd Scene QX500-2	Yr.Iss.	1981	5.50	16-27
1981 Little Trimmers - Keepsake					
1981	Clothespin Drummer Boy QX408-2	Yr.Iss.	1981	4.50	25-45
1981	Jolly Snowman QX407-5	Yr.Iss.	1981	3.50	37-60
1981	Perky Penguin QX409-5	Yr.Iss.	1982	3.50	42-60
1981	Puppy Love QX406-2	Yr.Iss.	1981	3.50	25-40
1981	The Stocking Mouse QX412-2	Yr.Iss.	1981	4.50	80-115
1981 Plush Animals - Keepsake					
1981	Christmas Teddy QX404-2	Yr.Iss.	1981	5.50	24
1981	Raccoon Tunes QX405-5	Yr.Iss.	1981	5.50	15-23
1981 Property Ornaments - Keepsake					
1981	Betsey Clark (9th Ed.)QX 802-2	Yr.Iss.	1981	4.50	23-35
1981	Betsey Clark Cameo QX512-2	Yr.Iss.	1981	8.50	20-30
1981	Betsey Clark QX423-5	Yr.Iss.	1981	9.00	22-32
1981	Disney QX805-5	Yr.Iss.	1981	4.50	15-30
1981	The Divine Miss Piggy QX425-5	Yr.Iss.	1981	12.00	75-95
1981	Joan Walsh Anglund QX804-2	Yr.Iss.	1981	4.50	16-30
1981	Kermit the Frog QX424-2	Yr.Iss.	1981	9.00	78-95
1981	Marty Links QX808-2	Yr.Iss.	1981	4.50	19
1981	Mary Hamilton QX806-2	Yr.Iss.	1981	4.50	10-20
1981	Muppets QX807-5	Yr.Iss.	1981	4.50	15-35
1981	Peanuts QX803-5	Yr.Iss.	1981	4.50	20-40
1982 Brass Ornaments - Keepsake					
1982	Brass Bell QX460-6	Yr.Iss.	1982	12.00	18-25
1982	Santa and Reindeer QX467-6	Yr.Iss.	1982	9.00	40-50
1982	Santa's Sleigh QX478-6	Yr.Iss.	1982	9.00	13-35
1982 Collectible Series - Keepsake					
1982	The Bellringer (4th Ed.) QX455-6	Yr.Iss.	1982	15.00	79-97
1982	Carrousel Series (5th Ed.) QX478-3	Yr.Iss.	1982	10.00	90
1982	Clothespin Soldier (1st Ed.) QX458-3	Yr.Iss.	1982	5.00	123
1982	Frosty Friends (3rd Ed.) QX452-3	Yr.Iss.	1982	8.00	270-300
1982	Here Comes Santa (4th Ed.) QX464-3	Yr.Iss.	1982	15.00	102-150
1982	Holiday Wildlife (1st Ed.) QX313-3	Yr.Iss.	1982	7.00	375-450
1982	Rocking Horse (2nd Ed.) QX 502-3	Yr.Iss.	1982	10.00	425
1982	Snoopy and Friends (4th Ed.) QX478-3	Yr.Iss.	1982	13.00	85-125
1982	Thimble (3rd Ed.) QX451-3	Yr.Iss.	1982	4.50	60-75
1982	Tin Locomotive (1st Ed.) QX460-3	Yr.Iss.	1982	13.00	575-600
1982 Colors of Christmas - Keepsake					
1982	Nativity QX308-3	Yr.Iss.	1982	4.50	37-50
1982	Santa's Flight QX308-6	Yr.Iss.	1982	4.50	49
1982 Commemoratives - Keepsake					
1982	25th Christmas Together QX211-6	Yr.Iss.	1982	4.50	6-20
1982	50th Christmas Together QX212-3	Yr.Iss.	1982	4.50	6-20
1982	Baby's First Christmas (Boy) QX 216-3	Yr.Iss.	1982	4.50	21-30
1982	Baby's First Christmas (Girl) QX 207-3	Yr.Iss.	1982	4.50	20-28
1982	Baby's First Christmas QX302-3	Yr.Iss.	1982	5.50	18-39
1982	Baby's First Christmas QX455-3	Yr.Iss.	1982	13.00	38-50
1982	Baby's First Christmas- Photoholder QX312-6	Yr.Iss.	1982	6.50	22
1982	Christmas Memories QX311-6	Yr.Iss.	1982	6.50	20
1982	Daughter QX204-6	Yr.Iss.	1982	4.50	20-45
1982	Father QX205-6	Yr.Iss.	1982	4.50	8-20
1982	First Christmas Together QX211-3	Yr.Iss.	1982	4.50	39
1982	First Christmas Together QX302-6	Yr.Iss.	1982	5.50	10-30
1982	First Christmas Together QX456-3	Yr.Iss.	1982	8.50	15-45
1982	First Christmas Together-Locket QX456-3	Yr.Iss.	1982	15.00	25-40
1982	Friendship QX208-6	Yr.Iss.	1982	4.50	8-18
1982	Friendship QX304-6	Yr.Iss.	1982	5.50	15-25
1982	Godchild QX222-6	Yr.Iss.	1982	4.50	11-22
1982	Granddaughter QX224-3	Yr.Iss.	1982	4.50	12-28
1982	Grandfather QX207-6	Yr.Iss.	1982	4.50	8-20
1982	Grandmother QX200-3	Yr.Iss.	1982	4.50	7-18
1982	Grandparents QX214-6	Yr.Iss.	1982	4.50	12-18
1982	Grandson QX224-6	Yr.Iss.	1982	4.50	11-30
1982	Love QX209-6	Yr.Iss.	1982	4.50	8-20
1982	Love QX304-3	Yr.Iss.	1982	5.50	20-30
1982	Moments of Love QX209-3	Yr.Iss.	1982	4.50	7-17
1982	Mother and Dad QX222-3	Yr.Iss.	1982	4.50	7-17
1982	Mother QX205-3	Yr.Iss.	1982	4.50	8-19
1982	New Home QX212-6	Yr.Iss.	1982	4.50	8-22
1982	Sister QX208-3	Yr.Iss.	1982	4.50	13-30
1982	Son QX204-3	Yr.Iss.	1982	4.50	11-30
1982	Teacher QX214-3	Yr.Iss.	1982	4.50	6-15
1982	Teacher QX312-3	Yr.Iss.	1982	6.50	10-18
1982	Teacher-Apple QX301-6	Yr.Iss.	1982	5.50	8-14
1982 Decorative Ball Ornaments - Keepsake					
1982	Christmas Angel QX220-6	Yr.Iss.	1982	4.50	10-25
1982	Currier & Ives QX201-3	Yr.Iss.	1982	4.50	10-25
1982	Santa QX221-6	Yr.Iss.	1982	4.50	12-20
1982	Season for Caring QX221-3	Yr.Iss.	1982	4.50	23
1982 Designer Keepsakes - Keepsake					
1982	Merry Christmas QX225-6	Yr.Iss.	1982	4.50	10-22
1982	Old Fashioned Christmas QX227-6	Yr.Iss.	1982	4.50	59
1982	Old World Angels QX226-3	Yr.Iss.	1982	4.50	7-24
1982	Patterns of Christmas QX226-6	Yr.Iss.	1982	4.50	15-22
1982	Stained Glass QX228-3	Yr.Iss.	1982	4.50	12-22
1982	Twelve Days of Christmas QX203-6	Yr.Iss.	1982	4.50	30
1982 Handcrafted Ornaments - Keepsake					
1982	Baroque Angel QX456-6	Yr.Iss.	1982	15.00	175
1982	Christmas Fantasy QX155-4	Yr.Iss.	1982	13.00	59
1982	Cloisonne Angel QX145-4	Yr.Iss.	1982	12.00	95
1982	Cowboy Snowman QX480-6	Yr.Iss.	1982	8.00	53
1982	Cycling Santa QX435-5	Yr.Iss.	1983	20.00	133-150
1982	Elfin Artist QX457-3	Yr.Iss.	1982	9.00	42-50
1982	Embroidered Tree - QX494-6	Yr.Iss.	1982	6.50	40
1982	Ice Sculptor QX432-2	Yr.Iss.	1982	8.00	75
1982	Jogging Santa QX457-6	Yr.Iss.	1982	8.00	32-50
1982	Jolly Christmas Tree QX465-3	Yr.Iss.	1982	6.50	80
1982	Peeking Elf QX419-5	Yr.Iss.	1982	6.50	24-40
1982	Pinecone Home QX461-3	Yr.Iss.	1982	8.00	160-175
1982	Raccoon Surprises QX479-3	Yr.Iss.	1982	9.00	125-132
1982	Santa Bell QX148-7	Yr.Iss.	1982	15.00	38-60
1982	Santa's Workshop QX450-3	Yr.Iss.	1983	10.00	76-85
1982	The Spirit of Christmas QX452-6	Yr.Iss.	1982	10.00	107-175
1982	Three Kings QX307-3	Yr.Iss.	1982	8.50	17-27
1982	Tin Soldier QX483-6	Yr.Iss.	1982	6.50	30-50
1982 Holiday Chimes - Keepsake					
1982	Bell Chimes QX494-3	Yr.Iss.	1982	5.50	21-30
1982	Tree Chimes QX484-6	Yr.Iss.	1982	5.50	30
1982 Holiday Highlights - Keepsake					
1982	Angel QX309-6	Yr.Iss.	1982	5.50	16-30
1982	Christmas Magic QX311-3	Yr.Iss.	1982	5.50	22-30
1982	Christmas Sleigh QX309-3	Yr.Iss.	1982	5.50	55-75
1982 Ice Sculptures - Keepsake					
1982	Arctic Penguin QX300-3	Yr.Iss.	1982	4.00	8-20
1982	Snowy Seal QX300-6	Yr.Iss.	1982	4.00	13-20
1982 Little Trimmers - Keepsake					
1982	Christmas Kitten QX454-3	Yr.Iss.	1983	4.00	36
1982	Christmas Owl QX131-4	Yr.Iss.	1982	4.50	35
1982	Cookie Mouse QX454-6	Yr.Iss.	1982	4.50	49-60
1982	Dove Love QX462-6	Yr.Iss.	1982	4.50	47-55
1982	Jingling Teddy QX477-6	Yr.Iss.	1982	4.00	23-40
1982	Merry Moose QX415-5	Yr.Iss.	1982	5.50	38-60
1982	Musical Angel QX459-6	Yr.Iss.	1982	5.50	112-125
1982	Perky Penguin QX409-5	Yr.Iss.	1982	4.00	35
1982 Property Ornaments - Keepsake					
1982	==Betsey Clark (10th Ed.) QX215-6==	Yr.Iss.	1982	4.50	24-34
1982	Betsey Clark QX305-6	Yr.Iss.	1982	8.50	17-25
1982	Disney QX217-3	Yr.Iss.	1982	4.50	20-35
1982	The Divine Miss Piggy QX425-5	Yr.Iss.	1982	12.00	125
1982	Joan Walsh Anglund QX219-3	Yr.Iss.	1982	4.50	8-20
1982	Kermit the Frog QX495-6	Yr.Iss.	1982	11.00	62-95
1982	Mary Hamilton QX217-6	Yr.Iss.	1982	4.50	10-22
1982	Miss Piggy and Kermit QX218-3	Yr.Iss.	1982	4.50	28-40
1982	Muppets Party QX218-6	Yr.Iss.	1982	4.50	31-40
1982	Norman Rockwell (3rd Ed.) QX305-3	Yr.Iss.	1982	8.50	28
1982	Norman Rockwell QX202-3	Yr.Iss.	1982	4.50	10-28
1982	Peanuts QX200-6	Yr.Iss.	1982	4.50	20-40
1983 Collectible Series - Keepsake					
1983	The Bellringer (5th Ed.)QX 403-9	Yr.Iss.	1983	15.00	85-135

*Quotes have been rounded up to nearest dollar

YEAR ISSUE		EDITION LIMIT	YEAR RETD.	ISSUE PRICE	*QUOTE U.S. $
1983	Carrousel (6th Ed.) QX401-9	Yr.Iss.	1983	11.00	49
1983	Clothespin Soldier (2nd Ed.) QX402-9	Yr.Iss.	1983	5.00	34-50
1983	Frosty Friends (4th Ed.) QX400-7	Yr.Iss.	1983	8.00	215-325
1983	Here Comes Santa (5th Ed.) QX 403-7	Yr.Iss.	1983	13.00	250-295
1983	Holiday Wildlife (2nd Ed.) QX 309-9	Yr.Iss.	1983	7.00	51-75
1983	Porcelain Bear (1st Ed.) QX428-9	Yr.Iss.	1983	7.00	50-73
1983	Rocking Horse (3rd Ed.) QX417-7	Yr.Iss.	1983	10.00	295
1983	Snoopy and Friends (5th Ed.) QX416-9	Yr.Iss.	1983	13.00	95
1983	Thimble (6th Ed.) QX401-7	Yr.Iss.	1983	5.00	28-39
1983	Tin Locomotive (2nd Ed.) QX404-9	Yr.Iss.	1983	13.00	275-295

1983 Commemoratives - Keepsake

1983	25th Christmas Together QX224-7	Yr.Iss.	1983	4.50	18
1983	Baby's First Christmas QX200-7	Yr.Iss.	1983	4.50	23-30
1983	Baby's First Christmas QX200-9	Yr.Iss.	1983	4.50	21-29
1983	Baby's First Christmas QX301-9	Yr.Iss.	1983	7.50	8-18
1983	Baby's First Christmas QX302-9	Yr.Iss.	1983	7.00	7-25
1983	Baby's First Christmas QX402-7	Yr.Iss.	1983	14.00	30-45
1983	Baby's Second Christmas QX226-7	Yr.Iss.	1983	4.50	35
1983	Child's Third Christmas QX226-9	Yr.Iss.	1983	4.50	20-35
1983	Daughter QX203-7	Yr.Iss.	1983	4.50	26-42
1983	First Christmas Together QX208-9	Yr.Iss.	1983	4.50	33
1983	First Christmas Together QX301-7	Yr.Iss.	1983	7.50	15-25
1983	First Christmas Together QX306-9	Yr.Iss.	1983	6.00	22
1983	First Christmas Together QX310-7	Yr.Iss.	1983	6.00	39
1983	First Christmas Together-Brass Locket QX 432-9	Yr.Iss.	1983	15.00	20-40
1983	Friendship QX207-7	Yr.Iss.	1983	4.50	20
1983	Friendship QX305-9	Yr.Iss.	1983	6.00	8-20
1983	Godchild QX201-7	Yr.Iss.	1983	4.50	12-18
1983	Grandchild's First Christmas QX 312-9	Yr.Iss.	1983	6.00	10-23
1983	Grandchild's First Christmas QX430-9	Yr.Iss.	1983	14.00	21-38
1983	Granddaughter QX202-7	Yr.Iss.	1983	4.50	30
1983	Grandmother QX205-7	Yr.Iss.	1983	4.50	19
1983	Grandparents QX429-9	Yr.Iss.	1983	6.50	11-22
1983	Grandson QX201-9	Yr.Iss.	1983	4.50	12-30
1983	Love Is a Song QX223-9	Yr.Iss.	1983	4.50	30
1983	Love QX207-9	Yr.Iss.	1983	4.50	43
1983	Love QX305-7	Yr.Iss.	1983	6.00	9-19
1983	Love QX310-9	Yr.Iss.	1983	6.00	40
1983	Love QX422-7	Yr.Iss.	1983	13.00	20-40
1983	Mom and Dad QX429-7	Yr.Iss.	1983	6.50	14-24
1983	Mother QX306-7	Yr.Iss.	1983	6.00	15-20
1983	New Home QX210-7	Yr.Iss.	1983	4.50	15-32
1983	Sister QX206-9	Yr.Iss.	1983	4.50	23
1983	Son QX202-9	Yr.Iss.	1983	4.50	25-40
1983	Teacher QX224-9	Yr.Iss.	1983	4.50	8-17
1983	Teacher QX304-9	Yr.Iss.	1983	6.00	13
1983	Tenth Christmas Together QX430-7	Yr.Iss.	1983	6.50	12-24

1983 Crown Classics - Keepsake

1983	Enameled Christmas Wreath QX 311-9	Yr.Iss.	1983	9.00	7-15
1983	Memories to Treasure QX303-7	Yr.Iss.	1983	7.00	30
1983	Mother and Child QX302-7	Yr.Iss.	1983	7.50	20-40

1983 Decorative Ball Ornaments - Keepsake

1983	1983 QX220-9	Yr.Iss.	1983	4.50	17-30
1983	Angels QX219-7	Yr.Iss.	1983	5.00	24
1983	The Annunciation QX216-7	Yr.Iss.	1983	4.50	30
1983	Christmas Joy QX216-9	Yr.Iss.	1983	4.50	15-30
1983	Christmas Wonderland QX221-9	Yr.Iss.	1983	4.50	95-125
1983	Currier & Ives QX215-9	Yr.Iss.	1983	4.50	8-19
1983	Here Comes Santa QX217-7	Yr.Iss.	1983	4.50	38
1983	An Old Fashioned Christmas QX2217-9	Yr.Iss.	1983	4.50	33
1983	Oriental Butterflies QX218-7	Yr.Iss.	1983	4.50	30
1983	Season's Greeting QX219-9	Yr.Iss.	1983	4.50	10-22
1983	The Wise Men QX220-7	Yr.Iss.	1983	4.50	42-59

1983 Handcrafted Ornaments - Keepsake

1983	Angel Messenger QX408-7	Yr.Iss.	1983	6.50	89-95
1983	Baroque Angels QX422-9	Yr.Iss.	1983	13.00	130
1983	Bell Wreath QX420-9	Yr.Iss.	1983	6.50	35
1983	Brass Santa QX423-9	Yr.Iss.	1983	9.00	23
1983	Caroling Owl QX411-7	Yr.Iss.	1983	4.50	25-40
1983	Christmas Kitten QX454-3	Yr.Iss.	1983	4.00	35
1983	Christmas Koala QX419-9	Yr.Iss.	1983	4.00	20-33
1983	Cycling Santa QX435-5	Yr.Iss.	1983	20.00	195
1983	Embroidered Heart QX421-7	Yr.Iss.	1983	6.50	25
1983	Embroidered Stocking QX479-6	Yr.Iss.	1983	6.50	10-22
1983	Hitchhiking Santa QX424-7	Yr.Iss.	1983	8.00	33-40
1983	Holiday Puppy QX412-7	Yr.Iss.	1983	3.50	16-30
1983	Jack Frost QX407-9	Yr.Iss.	1983	9.00	60
1983	Jolly Santa QX425-9	Yr.Iss.	1983	3.50	21-35
1983	Madonna and Child QX428-7	Yr.Iss.	1983	12.00	26-45
1983	Mailbox Kitten QX415-7	Yr.Iss.	1983	6.50	40-60
1983	Mountain Climbing Santa QX407-7	Yr.Iss.	1984	6.50	22-40
1983	Mouse in Bell QX419-7	Yr.Iss.	1983	10.00	65
1983	Mouse on Cheese QX413-7	Yr.Iss.	1983	6.50	30-50
1983	Old-Fashioned Santa QX409-9	Yr.Iss.	1983	11.00	40-65
1983	Peppermint Penguin QX408-9	Yr.Iss.	1983	6.50	29-49
1983	Porcelain Doll, Diana QX423-7	Yr.Iss.	1983	9.00	16-32
1983	Rainbow Angel QX416-7	Yr.Iss.	1983	5.50	112-125
1983	Santa's Many Faces QX311-6	Yr.Iss.	1983	6.00	30
1983	Santa's on His Way QX426-9	Yr.Iss.	1983	10.00	35
1983	Santa's Workshop QX450-3	Yr.Iss.	1983	10.00	60
1983	Scrimshaw Reindeer QX424-9	Yr.Iss.	1983	8.00	17-35
1983	Skating Rabbit QX409-7	Yr.Iss.	1983	8.00	47-55
1983	Ski Lift Santa QX418-7	Yr.Iss.	1983	8.00	50-75
1983	Skiing Fox QX420-7	Yr.Iss.	1983	8.00	30-40
1983	Sneaker Mouse QX400-9	Yr.Iss.	1983	4.50	23-40
1983	Tin Rocking Horse QX414-9	Yr.Iss.	1983	6.50	50
1983	Unicorn QX426-7	Yr.Iss.	1983	10.00	40-65

1983 Holiday Highlights - Keepsake

1983	Christmas Stocking QX303-9	Yr.Iss.	1983	6.00	15-40
1983	Star of Peace QX304-7	Yr.Iss.	1983	6.00	20
1983	Time for Sharing QX307-7	Yr.Iss.	1983	6.00	40

1983 Holiday Sculptures - Keepsake

1983	Heart QX307-9	Yr.Iss.	1983	4.00	50
1983	Santa QX308-7	Yr.Iss.	1983	4.00	17-35

1983 Property Ornaments - Keepsake

1983	Betsey Clark (11th Ed.) QX211-9	Yr.Iss.	1983	4.50	30
1983	Betsey Clark QX404-7	Yr.Iss.	1983	6.50	35
1983	Betsey Clark QX440-1	Yr.Iss.	1983	9.00	35
1983	Disney QX212-9	Yr.Iss.	1983	4.50	45
1983	Kermit the Frog QX495-6	Yr.Iss.	1983	11.00	35
1983	Mary Hamilton QX213-7	Yr.Iss.	1983	4.50	40
1983	Miss Piggy QX405-7	Yr.Iss.	1983	13.00	225
1983	The Muppets QX214-7	Yr.Iss.	1983	4.50	40-50
1983	Norman Rockwell (4th Ed.) QX 300-7	Yr.Iss.	1983	7.50	35
1983	Norman Rockwell QX215-7	Yr.Iss.	1983	4.50	50
1983	Peanuts QX212-7	Yr.Iss.	1983	4.50	22-36
1983	Shirt Tales QX214-9	Yr.Iss.	1983	4.50	25

1984 Collectible Series - Keepsake

1984	Art Masterpiece (1st Ed.) QX349-4	Yr.Iss.	1984	6.50	18
1984	The Bellringer (6th & Final Ed.) QX438-4	Yr.Iss.	1984	15.00	30-45
1984	Betsey Clark (12th Ed.) QX249-4	Yr.Iss.	1984	5.00	24-34
1984	Clothespin Soldier (3rd Ed.) QX447-1	Yr.Iss.	1984	5.00	20-30
1984	Frosty Friends (5th Ed.) QX437-1	Yr.Iss.	1984	8.00	60-87
1984	Here Comes Santa (6th Ed.) QX438-4	Yr.Iss.	1984	13.00	61-90
1984	Holiday Wildlife (3rd Ed.) QX 347-4	Yr.Iss.	1984	7.25	20-30
1984	Norman Rockwell (5th Ed.) QX341-1	Yr.Iss.	1984	7.50	24-34
1984	Nostalgic Houses and Shops (1st Ed.) QX 448-1	Yr.Iss.	1984	13.00	180-190
1984	Porcelain Bear (2nd Ed.) QX454-1	Yr.Iss.	1984	7.00	33-50
1984	Rocking Horse (4th Ed.) QX435-4	Yr.Iss.	1984	10.00	65-95
1984	Thimble (7th Ed.) QX430-4	Yr.Iss.	1984	5.00	40-60
1984	Tin Locomotive (3rd Ed.) QX440-4	Yr.Iss.	1984	14.00	62-90
1984	The Twelve Days of Christmas (1st Ed.) QX 3484	Yr.Iss.	1984	6.00	295
1984	Wood Childhood Ornaments (1st Ed.) QX 439-4	Yr.Iss.	1984	6.50	40-50

1984 Commemoratives - Keepsake

1984	Baby's First Christmas QX300-1	Yr.Iss.	1984	7.00	10-20
1984	Baby's First Christmas QX340-1	Yr.Iss.	1984	6.00	20-40
1984	Baby's First Christmas QX438-1	Yr.Iss.	1984	14.00	40-50
1984	Baby's First Christmas QX904-1	Yr.Iss.	1984	16.00	50
1984	Baby's First Christmas-Boy QX240-4	Yr.Iss.	1984	4.50	20-28
1984	Baby's First Christmas-Girl QX340-1	Yr.Iss.	1984	4.50	21-28
1984	Baby's Second Christmas QX241-1	Yr.Iss.	1984	4.50	25-40
1984	Baby-sitter QX253-1	Yr.Iss.	1984	4.50	6-14
1984	Child's Third Christmas QX261-1	Yr.Iss.	1984	4.50	17-30
1984	Daughter QX244-4	Yr.Iss.	1984	4.50	25-35
1984	Father QX257-1	Yr.Iss.	1984	6.00	20
1984	First Christmas Together QX245-1	Yr.Iss.	1984	4.50	11-30
1984	First Christmas Together QX340-4	Yr.Iss.	1984	7.50	12-30
1984	First Christmas Together QX342-1	Yr.Iss.	1984	6.00	10-25
1984	First Christmas Together QX436-4	Yr.Iss.	1984	15.00	15-40
1984	First Christmas Together QX904-4	Yr.Iss.	1984	16.00	41
1984	Friendship QX248-1	Yr.Iss.	1984	4.50	15
1984	From Our Home to Yours QX248-4	Yr.Iss.	1984	4.50	50
1984	The Fun of Friendship QX343-1	Yr.Iss.	1984	6.00	10-35
1984	A Gift of Friendship QX260-4	Yr.Iss.	1984	4.50	25
1984	Godchild QX242-1	Yr.Iss.	1984	4.50	20
1984	Grandchild's First Christmas QX257-4	Yr.Iss.	1984	4.50	7-17
1984	Grandchild's First Christmas QX460-1	Yr.Iss.	1984	11.00	30
1984	Granddaughter QX243-1	Yr.Iss.	1984	4.50	30
1984	Grandmother QX244-1	Yr.Iss.	1984	4.50	13-18
1984	Grandparents QX256-1	Yr.Iss.	1984	4.50	18
1984	Grandson QX242-4	Yr.Iss.	1984	4.50	18-30
1984	Gratitude QX344-4	Yr.Iss.	1984	6.00	12
1984	Heartful of Love QX443-4	Yr.Iss.	1984	10.00	45
1984	Love QX255-4	Yr.Iss.	1984	4.50	25
1984	Love...the Spirit of Christmas QX247-4	Yr.Iss.	1984	4.50	20-42
1984	The Miracle of Love QX342-4	Yr.Iss.	1984	6.00	33
1984	Mother and Dad QX258-1	Yr.Iss.	1984	6.50	12-25
1984	Mother QX343-4	Yr.Iss.	1984	6.00	18
1984	New Home QX245-4	Yr.Iss.	1984	4.50	85
1984	Sister QX259-4	Yr.Iss.	1984	6.50	20-32
1984	Son QX243-4	Yr.Iss.	1984	4.50	10-30
1984	Teacher QX249-1	Yr.Iss.	1984	4.50	6-15
1984	Ten Years Together QX258-4	Yr.Iss.	1984	6.50	11-25
1984	Twenty-Five Years Together QX259-1	Yr.Iss.	1984	6.50	20

1984 Holiday Humor - Keepsake

1984	Bell Ringer Squirrel QX443-1	Yr.Iss.	1984	10.00	20-40
1984	Christmas Owl QX444-1	Yr.Iss.	1984	6.00	20-33
1984	A Christmas Prayer QX246-1	Yr.Iss.	1984	4.50	10-23
1984	Flights of Fantasy QX256-4	Yr.Iss.	1984	4.50	10-20
1984	Fortune Cookie Elf QX452-4	Yr.Iss.	1984	4.50	35-40
1984	Frisbee Puppy QX444-4	Yr.Iss.	1984	5.00	40-50
1984	Marathon Santa QX456-4	Yr.Iss.	1984	8.00	43
1984	Mountain Climbing Santa QX407-7	Yr.Iss.	1984	6.50	35
1984	Musical Angel QX434-4	Yr.Iss.	1984	5.50	70
1984	Napping Mouse QX435-1	Yr.Iss.	1984	5.50	38-50
1984	Peppermint 1984 QX452-1	Yr.Iss.	1984	4.50	50
1984	Polar Bear Drummer QX430-1	Yr.Iss.	1984	4.50	30
1984	Raccoon's Christmas QX447-7	Yr.Iss.	1984	9.00	34-55
1984	Reindeer Racetrack QX254-4	Yr.Iss.	1984	4.50	10-23
1984	Roller Skating Rabbit QX457-1	Yr.Iss.	1985	5.00	18-35
1984	Santa Mouse QX433-4	Yr.Iss.	1984	4.50	47
1984	Santa Star QX450-4	Yr.Iss.	1984	5.50	33-40
1984	Snowmobile Santa QX431-4	Yr.Iss.	1984	6.50	35-40
1984	Snowshoe Penguin QX453-1	Yr.Iss.	1984	6.50	50-60
1984	Snowy Seal QX450-1	Yr.Iss.	1985	4.00	12-24
1984	Three Kittens in a Mitten QX431-1	Yr.Iss.	1985	8.00	32-50

1984 Keepsake Magic Ornaments - Keepsake

1984	All Are Precious QLX704-1	Yr.Iss.	1985	8.00	13-25
1984	Brass Carrousel QLX707-1	Yr.Iss.	1984	9.00	95
1984	Christmas in the Forest QLX703-4	Yr.Iss.	1984	8.00	20
1984	City Lights QLX701-4	Yr.Iss.	1984	10.00	52
1984	Nativity QLX700-1	Yr.Iss.	1985	12.00	18-30
1984	Santa's Arrival QLX702-4	Yr.Iss.	1984	13.00	47-65
1984	Santa's Workshop QLX700-4	Yr.Iss.	1985	13.00	45-62
1984	Stained Glass QLX703-1	Yr.Iss.	1984	8.00	20
1984	Sugarplum Cottage QLX701-1	Yr.Iss.	1986	11.00	45
1984	Village Church QLX702-1	Yr.Iss.	1985	15.00	35-50

1984 Limited Edition - Keepsake

1984	Classical Angel QX459-1	Yr.Iss.	1984	28.00	75-100

1984 Property Ornaments - Keepsake

1984	Betsey Clark Angel QX462-4	Yr.Iss.	1984	9.00	19-35
1984	Currier & Ives QX250-1	Yr.Iss.	1984	4.50	23
1984	Disney QX250-4	Yr.Iss.	1984	4.50	[illegible]
1984	Katybeth QX463-1	Yr.Iss.	1984	9.00	17-33
1984	Kit QX453-4	Yr.Iss.	1984	5.50	28
1984	Muffin QX442-1	Yr.Iss.	1984	5.50	25-33
1984	The Muppets QX251-4	Yr.Iss.	1984	4.50	20-35
1984	Norman Rockwell QX251-4	Yr.Iss.	1984	4.50	35
1984	Peanuts QX252-1	Yr.Iss.	1984	4.50	20-33
1984	Shirt Tales QX252-4	Yr.Iss.	1984	4.50	10-19
1984	Snoopy and Woodstock QX439-1	Yr.Iss.	1984	7.50	95

1984 Traditional Ornaments - Keepsake

1984	Alpine Elf QX452-1	Yr.Iss.	1984	6.00	32-40
1984	Amanda QX432-1	Yr.Iss.	1984	9.00	10-25
1984	Chickadee QX451-4	Yr.Iss.	1984	6.00	33-40
1984	Christmas Memories Photoholder QX300-4	Yr.Iss.	1984	6.50	25
1984	Cuckoo Clock QX455-1	Yr.Iss.	1984	10.00	45-50
1984	Gift of Music QX451-1	Yr.Iss.	1984	15.00	62-95
1984	Holiday Friendship QX445-1	Yr.Iss.	1984	13.00	20-30
1984	Holiday Jester QX437-4	Yr.Iss.	1984	11.00	20-35
1984	Holiday Starburst QX253-4	Yr.Iss.	1984	5.00	20
1984	Madonna and Child QX344-1	Yr.Iss.	1984	6.00	50
1984	Needlepoint Wreath QX459-4	Yr.Iss.	1984	6.50	10-15
1984	Nostalgic Sled QX442-4	Yr.Iss.	1984	6.00	12-30
1984	Old Fashioned Rocking Horse QX346-4	Yr.Iss.	1984	7.50	10-20
1984	Peace on Earth QX341-4	Yr.Iss.	1984	7.50	30
1984	Santa QX458-4	Yr.Iss.	1984	7.50	10-20
1984	Santa Sulky Driver QX436-1	Yr.Iss.	1984	9.00	20-35
1984	A Savior is Born QX254-1	Yr.Iss.	1984	4.50	33
1984	Twelve Days of Christmas QX 415-9	Yr.Iss.	1984	15.00	100-125
1984	Uncle Sam QX449-1	Yr.Iss.	1984	6.00	42-50
1984	White Christmas QX905-1	Yr.Iss.	1984	16.00	70-95

1985 Collectible Series - Keepsake

1985	Art Masterpiece (2nd Ed.) QX377-2	Yr.Iss.	1985	6.75	15
1985	Betsey Clark (13th & final Ed.)) QX263-2	Yr.Iss.	1985	5.00	24-35
1985	Clothespin Soldier (4th Ed.) QX471-5	Yr.Iss.	1985	5.50	20-30
1985	Frosty Friends (6th Ed.) QX482-2	Yr.Iss.	1985	8.50	45-65
1985	Here Comes Santa (7th Ed.) QX496-5	Yr.Iss.	1985	14.00	43-63
1985	Holiday Wildlife (4th Ed.) QX376-5	Yr.Iss.	1985	7.50	20-30
1985	Miniature Creche (1st Ed.) QX482-5	Yr.Iss.	1985	8.75	30-40
1985	Norman Rockwell (6th Ed.) QX374-5	Yr.Iss.	1985	7.50	22-32
1985	Nostalgic Houses and Shops (2nd Ed.) QX497-5	Yr.Iss.	1985	13.75	93-145
1985	Porcelain Bear (3rd Ed.) QX479-2	Yr.Iss.	1985	7.50	36-60
1985	Rocking Horse (5th Ed.) QX493-2	Yr.Iss.	1985	10.75	54-80
1985	Thimble (8th Ed.) QX472-5	Yr.Iss.	1985	5.50	24-35
1985	Tin Locomotive (4th Ed.) QX497-2	Yr.Iss.	1985	14.75	55-80

*Quotes have been rounded up to nearest dollar

Collectors' Information Bureau

159

ORNAMENTS

YEAR ISSUE		EDITION LIMIT	YEAR RETD.	ISSUE PRICE	*QUOTE U.S.$
1985	Twelve Days of Christmas (2nd Ed.) QX371-2	Yr.Iss.	1985	6.50	50-70
1985	Windows of the World (1st Ed.) QX490-2	Yr.Iss.	1985	9.75	82-97
1985	Wood Childhood Ornaments (2nd Ed.) QX472-2	Yr.Iss.	1985	7.00	34-50

1985 Commemoratives - Keepsake

YEAR ISSUE		EDITION LIMIT	YEAR RETD.	ISSUE PRICE	*QUOTE U.S.$
1985	Baby Locket QX401-2	Yr.Iss.	1985	16.00	21-30
1985	Baby's First Christmas QX260-2	Yr.Iss.	1985	5.00	20-35
1985	Baby's First Christmas QX370-2	Yr.Iss.	1985	5.75	22
1985	Baby's First Christmas QX478-2	Yr.Iss.	1985	7.00	18
1985	Baby's First Christmas QX499-2	Yr.Iss.	1985	15.00	55
1985	Baby's First Christmas QX499-5	Yr.Iss.	1985	16.00	22-45
1985	Baby's Second Christmas QX478-5	Yr.Iss.	1985	6.00	25-35
1985	Baby-sitter QX264-2	Yr.Iss.	1985	4.75	10
1985	Child's Third Christmas QX475-5	Yr.Iss.	1985	6.00	25-32
1985	Daughter QX503-2	Yr.Iss.	1985	5.50	13-20
1985	Father QX376-2	Yr.Iss.	1985	6.50	10
1985	First Christmas Together QX261-2	Yr.Iss.	1985	4.75	10-20
1985	First Christmas Together QX370-5	Yr.Iss.	1985	6.75	10-20
1985	First Christmas Together QX400-5	Yr.Iss.	1985	16.75	15-30
1985	First Christmas Together QX493-5	Yr.Iss.	1985	13.00	20-40
1985	First Christmas Together QX507-2	Yr.Iss.	1985	8.00	10-17
1985	Friendship QX378-5	Yr.Iss.	1985	6.75	18
1985	Friendship QX506-2	Yr.Iss.	1985	7.75	15
1985	From Our House to Yours QX520-2	Yr.Iss.	1985	7.75	15
1985	Godchild QX380-2	Yr.Iss.	1985	6.75	15
1985	Good Friends QX265-2	Yr.Iss.	1985	4.75	15-30
1985	Grandchild's First Christmas QX260-5	Yr.Iss.	1985	5.00	15
1985	Grandchild's First Christmas QX495-5	Yr.Iss.	1985	11.00	20
1985	Granddaughter QX263-5	Yr.Iss.	1985	4.75	30
1985	Grandmother QX262-5	Yr.Iss.	1985	4.75	18
1985	Grandparents QX380-5	Yr.Iss.	1985	7.00	15
1985	Grandson QX262-2	Yr.Iss.	1985	4.75	27
1985	Heart Full of Love QX378-2	Yr.Iss.	1985	6.75	10-20
1985	Holiday Heart QX498-2	Yr.Iss.	1985	8.00	18-29
1985	Love at Christmas QX371-5	Yr.Iss.	1985	5.75	25-40
1985	Mother and Dad QX509-2	Yr.Iss.	1985	7.75	10-20
1985	Mother QX372-2	Yr.Iss.	1985	6.75	10-15
1985	New Home QX269-5	Yr.Iss.	1985	4.75	30
1985	Niece QX520-5	Yr.Iss.	1985	5.75	11
1985	Sister QX506-5	Yr.Iss.	1985	7.25	10-20
1985	Son QX502-5	Yr.Iss.	1985	5.50	45
1985	Special Friends QX372-5	Yr.Iss.	1985	5.75	10
1985	Teacher QX505-2	Yr.Iss.	1985	6.00	10-20
1985	Twenty-Five Years Together QX500-5	Yr.Iss.	1985	8.00	10-20
1985	With Appreciation QX375-2	Yr.Iss.	1985	6.75	10

1985 Country Christmas Collection - Keepsake

YEAR ISSUE		EDITION LIMIT	YEAR RETD.	ISSUE PRICE	*QUOTE U.S.$
1985	Country Goose QX518-5	Yr.Iss.	1985	7.75	14
1985	Old-Fashioned Doll QX519-5	Yr.Iss.	1985	15.00	40
1985	Rocking Horse Memories QX518-2	Yr.Iss.	1985	10.00	10-14
1985	Sheep at Christmas QX517-5	Yr.Iss.	1985	8.25	30
1985	Whirligig Santa QX519-2	Yr.Iss.	1985	13.00	15-25

1985 Heirloom Christmas Collection - Keepsake

YEAR ISSUE		EDITION LIMIT	YEAR RETD.	ISSUE PRICE	*QUOTE U.S.$
1985	Charming Angel QX512-5	Yr.Iss.	1985	9.75	10-25
1985	Keepsake Basket QX514-5	Yr.Iss.	1985	15.00	15
1985	Lacy Heart QX511-2	Yr.Iss.	1985	8.75	15-30
1985	Snowflake QX510-5	Yr.Iss.	1985	6.50	10-20
1985	Victorian Lady QX513-2	Yr.Iss.	1985	9.50	25

1985 Holiday Humor - Keepsake

YEAR ISSUE		EDITION LIMIT	YEAR RETD.	ISSUE PRICE	*QUOTE U.S.$
1985	Baker Elf QX491-2	Yr.Iss.	1985	5.75	19-29
1985	Beary Smooth Ride QX480-5	Yr.Iss.	1986	6.50	13-24
1985	Bottlecap Fun Bunnies QX481-5	Yr.Iss.	1985	7.75	33
1985	Candy Apple Mouse QX470-5	Yr.Iss.	1985	6.50	52-75
1985	Children in the Shoe QX490-5	Yr.Iss.	1985	9.50	32-50
1985	Dapper Penguin QX477-2	Yr.Iss.	1985	5.00	30
1985	Do Not Disturb Bear QX481-2	Yr.Iss.	1986	7.75	16-33
1985	Doggy in a Stocking QX474-2	Yr.Iss.	1985	5.50	25-40
1985	Engineering Mouse QX473-5	Yr.Iss.	1985	5.50	15-25
1985	Ice-Skating Owl QX476-5	Yr.Iss.	1985	5.00	15-25
1985	Kitty Mischief QX474-5	Yr.Iss.	1986	5.00	15-25
1985	Lamb in Legwarmers QX480-2	Yr.Iss.	1985	7.00	15-25
1985	Merry Mouse QX403-2	Yr.Iss.	1986	4.50	20-30
1985	Mouse Wagon QX476-2	Yr.Iss.	1985	5.75	37-60
1985	Nativity Scene QX264-5	Yr.Iss.	1985	4.75	30
1985	Night Before Christmas QX449-4	Yr.Iss.	1985	13.00	20-40
1985	Roller Skating Rabbit QX457-1	Yr.Iss.	1985	5.00	19
1985	Santa's Ski Trip QX496-2	Yr.Iss.	1985	12.00	41-60
1985	Skateboard Raccoon QX473-2	Yr.Iss.	1986	6.50	25-43
1985	Snow-Pitching Snowman QX470-2	Yr.Iss.	1986	4.50	23
1985	Snowy Seal QX450-1	Yr.Iss.	1985	4.00	16
1985	Soccer Beaver QX477-5	Yr.Iss.	1986	6.50	15-25
1985	Stardust Angel QX475-2	Yr.Iss.	1985	5.75	24-36
1985	Sun and Fun Santa QX492-2	Yr.Iss.	1985	7.75	40
1985	Swinging Angel Bell QX492-5	Yr.Iss.	1985	11.00	40
1985	Three Kittens in a Mitten QX431-1	Yr.Iss.	1985	8.00	35
1985	Trumpet Panda QX471-2	Yr.Iss.	1985	4.50	15-25

1985 Keepsake Magic Ornaments - Keepsake

YEAR ISSUE		EDITION LIMIT	YEAR RETD.	ISSUE PRICE	*QUOTE U.S.$
1985	All Are Precious QLX704-1	Yr.Iss.	1985	8.00	12-25
1985	Baby's First Christmas QLX700-5	Yr.Iss.	1985	17.00	30-40
1985	Chris Mouse-1st Ed.) QLX703-2	Yr.Iss.	1985	13.00	88
1985	Christmas Eve Visit QLX710-5	Yr.Iss.	1985	12.00	33
1985	Katybeth QLX710-2	Yr.Iss.	1985	10.75	30-43
1985	Little Red Schoolhouse QLX711-2	Yr.Iss.	1985	15.75	70-95
1985	Love Wreath QLX702-5	Yr.Iss.	1985	8.50	19-30
1985	Mr. and Mrs. Santa QLX705-2	Yr.Iss.	1986	15.00	73-90
1985	Nativity 1200 QLX700-1	Yr.Iss.	1985	12.00	18-30
1985	Santa's Workshop QLX700-4	Yr.Iss.	1985	13.00	58
1985	Season of Beauty QLX712-2	Yr.Iss.	1985	8.00	19-29
1985	Sugarplum Cottage QLX701-1	Yr.Iss.	1985	11.00	45
1985	Swiss Cheese Lane QLX706-5	Yr.Iss.	1985	13.00	34-50
1985	Village Church QLX702-1	Yr.Iss.	1985	15.00	35-50

1985 Limited Edition - Keepsake

YEAR ISSUE		EDITION LIMIT	YEAR RETD.	ISSUE PRICE	*QUOTE U.S.$
1985	Heavenly Trumpeter QX405-2	Yr.Iss.	1985	28.00	68-100

1985 Property Ornaments - Keepsake

YEAR ISSUE		EDITION LIMIT	YEAR RETD.	ISSUE PRICE	*QUOTE U.S.$
1985	Betsey Clark QX508-5	Yr.Iss.	1985	8.50	30
1985	A Disney Christmas QX271-2	Yr.Iss.	1985	4.75	30
1985	Fraggle Rock Holiday QX265-5	Yr.Iss.	1985	4.75	23
1985	Hugga Bunch QX271-5	Yr.Iss.	1985	5.00	15-30
1985	Kit the Shepherd QX484-5	Yr.Iss.	1985	5.75	24
1985	Merry Shirt Tales QX267-2	Yr.Iss.	1985	4.75	20
1985	Muffin the Angel QX483-5	Yr.Iss.	1985	5.75	24
1985	Norman Rockwell QX266-2	Yr.Iss.	1985	4.75	28
1985	Peanuts QX266-5	Yr.Iss.	1985	4.75	36
1985	Rainbow Brite and Friends QX 268-2	Yr.Iss.	1985	4.75	15-24
1985	Snoopy and Woodstock QX491-5	Yr.Iss.	1985	7.50	65

1985 Traditional Ornaments - Keepsake

YEAR ISSUE		EDITION LIMIT	YEAR RETD.	ISSUE PRICE	*QUOTE U.S.$
1985	Candle Cameo QX374-2	Yr.Iss.	1985	6.75	15
1985	Christmas Treats QX507-5	Yr.Iss.	1985	5.50	15
1985	Nostalgic Sled QX442-4	Yr.Iss.	1985	6.00	20
1985	Old-Fashioned Wreath QX373-5	Yr.Iss.	1985	7.50	25
1985	Peaceful Kingdom QX373-2	Yr.Iss.	1985	5.75	20-30
1985	Porcelain Bird QX479-5	Yr.Iss.	1985	6.50	29-39
1985	Santa Pipe QX494-2	Yr.Iss.	1985	9.50	10-24
1985	Sewn Photoholder QX379-5	Yr.Iss.	1985	7.00	25-35
1985	The Spirit of Santa Claus (Special Ed.) QX 498-5	Yr.Iss.	1985	23.00	75-95

1986 Christmas Medley Collection - Keepsake

YEAR ISSUE		EDITION LIMIT	YEAR RETD.	ISSUE PRICE	*QUOTE U.S.$
1986	Christmas Guitar QX512-6	Yr.Iss.	1986	7.00	15-25
1986	Favorite Tin Drum QX514-3	Yr.Iss.	1986	8.50	30
1986	Festive Treble Clef QX513-3	Yr.Iss.	1986	8.75	10-28
1986	Holiday Horn QX514-6	Yr.Iss.	1986	8.00	17-33
1986	Joyful Carolers QX513-6	Yr.Iss.	1986	9.75	37

1986 Collectible Series - Keepsake

YEAR ISSUE		EDITION LIMIT	YEAR RETD.	ISSUE PRICE	*QUOTE U.S.$
1986	Art Masterpiece (3rd & Final Ed.) QX350-6	Yr.Iss.	1986	6.75	20-32
1986	Betsey Clark: Home for Christmas (1st Ed.) QX277-6	Yr.Iss.	1986	5.00	20-35
1986	Clothespin Soldier (5th Ed.) QX406-3	Yr.Iss.	1986	5.50	19-29
1986	Frosty Friends (7th Ed.) QX405-3	Yr.Iss.	1986	8.50	63-74
1986	Here Comes Santa (8th Ed.) QX404-3	Yr.Iss.	1986	14.00	43-65
1986	Holiday Wildlife (5th Ed.) QX321-6	Yr.Iss.	1986	7.50	20-30
1986	Miniature Creche (2nd Ed.) QX407-6	Yr.Iss.	1986	9.00	43-59
1986	Mr. and Mrs. Claus (1st Ed.) QX402-6	Yr.Iss.	1986	13.00	89-100
1986	Norman Rockwell (7th Ed.) QX321-3	Yr.Iss.	1986	7.75	20-30
1986	Nostalgic Houses and Shops (3rd Ed.) QX403-3	Yr.Iss.	1986	13.75	250-295
1986	Porcelain Bear (4th Ed.) QX405-6	Yr.Iss.	1986	7.75	27-45
1986	Reindeer Champs (1st Ed.) QX422-3	Yr.Iss.	1986	7.50	128-149
1986	Rocking Horse (6th Ed.) QX401-6	Yr.Iss.	1986	10.75	67-75
1986	Thimble (9th Ed.) QX406-6	Yr.Iss.	1986	5.75	20-30
1986	Tin Locomotive (5th Ed.) QX403-6	Yr.Iss.	1986	14.75	50-80
1986	Twelve Days of Christmas (3rd Ed.) QX378-6	Yr.Iss.	1986	6.50	34-44
1986	Windows of the World (2nd Ed.) QX408-3	Yr.Iss.	1986	10.00	40-64
1986	Wood Childhood Ornaments (3rd Ed.) QX407-3	Yr.Iss.	1986	7.50	21-33

1986 Commemoratives - Keepsake

YEAR ISSUE		EDITION LIMIT	YEAR RETD.	ISSUE PRICE	*QUOTE U.S.$
1986	Baby Locket QX412-3	Yr.Iss.	1986	16.00	27
1986	Baby's First Christmas Photoholder QX379-2	Yr.Iss.	1986	8.00	18-25
1986	Baby's First Christmas QX271-3	Yr.Iss.	1986	5.50	25-30
1986	Baby's First Christmas QX380-3	Yr.Iss.	1986	6.00	20-30
1986	Baby's First Christmas QX412-6	Yr.Iss.	1986	9.00	39
1986	Baby's Second Christmas QX413-3	Yr.Iss.	1986	6.50	22-29
1986	Baby-Sitter QX275-6	Yr.Iss.	1986	4.75	7-12
1986	Child's Third Christmas QX413-6	Yr.Iss.	1986	6.50	20-30
1986	Daughter QX430-6	Yr.Iss.	1986	5.75	38-48
1986	Father QX431-3	Yr.Iss.	1986	6.50	8-15
1986	Fifty Years Together QX400-6	Yr.Iss.	1986	10.00	20
1986	First Christmas Together QX270-3	Yr.Iss.	1986	4.75	27-35
1986	First Christmas Together QX379-3	Yr.Iss.	1986	7.00	22-35
1986	First Christmas Together QX400-3	Yr.Iss.	1986	16.00	17
1986	First Christmas Together QX409-6	Yr.Iss.	1986	12.00	30
1986	Friends Are Fun QX272-3	Yr.Iss.	1986	4.75	40
1986	Friendship Greeting QX427-3	Yr.Iss.	1986	8.00	15
1986	Friendship's Gift QX381-6	Yr.Iss.	1986	6.00	15
1986	From Our Home to Yours QX383-3	Yr.Iss.	1986	6.00	15
1986	Godchild QX271-6	Yr.Iss.	1986	4.75	15
1986	Grandchild's First Christmas QX411-6	Yr.Iss.	1986	10.00	15
1986	Granddaughter QX273-6	Yr.Iss.	1986	4.75	25
1986	Grandmother QX274-3	Yr.Iss.	1986	4.75	8-16
1986	Grandparents QX432-3	Yr.Iss.	1986	7.50	10-23
1986	Grandson QX273-3	Yr.Iss.	1986	4.75	25
1986	Gratitude QX432-6	Yr.Iss.	1986	6.00	10
1986	Husband QX383-6	Yr.Iss.	1986	8.00	14
1986	Joy of Friends QX382-3	Yr.Iss.	1986	6.75	18
1986	Loving Memories QX409-3	Yr.Iss.	1986	9.00	35
1986	Mother and Dad QX431-6	Yr.Iss.	1986	7.50	24
1986	Mother QX382-6	Yr.Iss.	1986	7.00	10-20
1986	Nephew QX381-3	Yr.Iss.	1986	6.25	15
1986	New Home QX274-6	Yr.Iss.	1986	4.75	65
1986	Niece QX426-6	Yr.Iss.	1986	6.00	10
1986	Season of the Heart QX270-6	Yr.Iss.	1986	4.75	10-18
1986	Sister QX380-6	Yr.Iss.	1986	6.75	15
1986	Son QX430-3	Yr.Iss.	1986	5.75	28-35
1986	Sweetheart QX408-6	Yr.Iss.	1986	11.00	50-70
1986	Teacher QX275-3	Yr.Iss.	1986	4.75	6-12
1986	Ten Years Together QX401-3	Yr.Iss.	1986	7.50	25
1986	Timeless Love QX379-6	Yr.Iss.	1986	6.00	30
1986	Twenty-Five Years Together QX410-3	Yr.Iss.	1986	8.00	25

1986 Country Treasures Collection - Keepsake

YEAR ISSUE		EDITION LIMIT	YEAR RETD.	ISSUE PRICE	*QUOTE U.S.$
1986	Country Sleigh QX511-3	Yr.Iss.	1986	10.00	15-30
1986	Little Drummers QX511-6	Yr.Iss.	1986	12.50	18-35
1986	Nutcracker Santa QX512-3	Yr.Iss.	1986	10.00	25-50
1986	Remembering Christmas QX510-6	Yr.Iss.	1986	8.75	30
1986	Welcome, Christmas QX510-3	Yr.Iss.	1986	8.25	20-35

1986 Holiday Humor - Keepsake

YEAR ISSUE		EDITION LIMIT	YEAR RETD.	ISSUE PRICE	*QUOTE U.S.$
1986	Acorn Inn QX424-3	Yr.Iss.	1986	8.50	25-30
1986	Beary Smooth Ride QX480-5	Yr.Iss.	1986	6.50	20
1986	Chatty Penguin QX417-6	Yr.Iss.	1986	5.75	13-25
1986	Cookies for Santa QX414-6	Yr.Iss.	1986	4.50	17-30
1986	Do Not Disturb Bear QX481-2	Yr.Iss.	1986	7.75	15-25
1986	Happy Christmas to Owl QX418-3	Yr.Iss.	1986	6.00	15-25
1986	Heavenly Dreamer QX417-3	Yr.Iss.	1986	5.75	22-35
1986	Jolly Hiker QX483-2	Yr.Iss.	1987	5.00	20-30
1986	Kitty Mischief QX474-5	Yr.Iss.	1986	5.00	25
1986	Li'l Jingler QX419-3	Yr.Iss.	1987	6.75	22-40
1986	Merry Koala QX415-3	Yr.Iss.	1987	5.00	23
1986	Merry Mouse QX403-2	Yr.Iss.	1986	4.50	22
1986	Mouse in the Moon QX416-6	Yr.Iss.	1987	5.50	30
1986	Open Me First QX422-6	Yr.Iss.	1986	7.25	17-32
1986	Playful Possum QX425-3	Yr.Iss.	1986	11.00	33
1986	Popcorn Mouse QX421-3	Yr.Iss.	1986	6.75	45-55
1986	Puppy's Best Friend QX420-3	Yr.Iss.	1986	6.50	17-30
1986	Rah Rah Rabbit QX421-6	Yr.Iss.	1986	7.00	40
1986	Santa's Hot Tub QX426-3	Yr.Iss.	1986	12.00	55-60
1986	Skateboard Raccoon QX473-2	Yr.Iss.	1986	6.50	40
1986	Ski Tripper QX420-6	Yr.Iss.	1986	6.75	12-22
1986	Snow Buddies QX423-6	Yr.Iss.	1986	8.00	38
1986	Snow-Pitching Snowman QX470-2	Yr.Iss.	1986	4.50	23
1986	Soccer Beaver QX477-5	Yr.Iss.	1986	6.50	25
1986	Special Delivery QX415-6	Yr.Iss.	1986	5.00	17-30
1986	Tipping the Scales QX418-6	Yr.Iss.	1986	6.75	15-30
1986	Touchdown Santa QX423-3	Yr.Iss.	1986	8.00	42
1986	Treetop Trio QX424-6	Yr.Iss.	1987	11.00	32
1986	Walnut Shell Rider QX419-6	Yr.Iss.	1987	6.00	18-30
1986	Wynken, Blynken and Nod QX424-6	Yr.Iss.	1986	9.75	42

1986 Lighted Ornament Collection - Keepsake

YEAR ISSUE		EDITION LIMIT	YEAR RETD.	ISSUE PRICE	*QUOTE U.S.$
1986	Baby's First Christmas QLX710-3	Yr.Iss.	1986	19.50	45
1986	Chris Mouse (2nd Ed.) QLX705-6	Yr.Iss.	1986	13.00	75
1986	Christmas Classics (1st Ed.) QLX704-3	Yr.Iss.	1986	17.50	85
1986	Christmas Sleigh Ride QLX701-2	Yr.Iss.	1986	24.50	120-145
1986	First Christmas Together QLX707-3	Yr.Iss.	1986	14.00	43
1986	General Store QLX705-3	Yr.Iss.	1986	15.75	43-60
1986	Gentle Blessings QLX708-3	Yr.Iss.	1986	15.00	110-175
1986	Keep on Glowin' QLX707-6	Yr.Iss.	1987	10.00	37-50
1986	Merry Christmas Bell QLX709-3	Yr.Iss.	1986	8.50	15-25
1986	Mr. and Mrs. Santa QLX705-2	Yr.Iss.	1986	14.50	65-95
1986	Santa and Sparky (1st Ed.) QLX703-3	Yr.Iss.	1986	22.00	95
1986	Santa's On His Way QLX711-5	Yr.Iss.	1986	15.00	63-75
1986	Santa's Snack QLX706-6	Yr.Iss.	1986	10.00	40-60
1986	Sharing Friendship QLX706-3	Yr.Iss.	1986	8.50	17
1986	Sugarplum Cottage QLX701-1	Yr.Iss.	1986	11.00	45
1986	Village Express QLX707-2	Yr.Iss.	1987	24.50	87-125

1986 Limited Edition - Keepsake

YEAR ISSUE		EDITION LIMIT	YEAR RETD.	ISSUE PRICE	*QUOTE U.S.$
1986	Magical Unicorn QX429-3	Yr.Iss.	1986	27.50	86

1986 Property Ornaments - Keepsake

YEAR ISSUE		EDITION LIMIT	YEAR RETD.	ISSUE PRICE	*QUOTE U.S.$
1986	Heathcliff QX436-3	Yr.Iss.	1986	7.50	20-33
1986	Katybeth QX435-3	Yr.Iss.	1986	7.00	25
1986	Norman Rockwell QX276-3	Yr.Iss.	1986	4.75	27
1986	Paddington Bear QX435-6	Yr.Iss.	1986	6.00	31
1986	Peanuts QX276-6	Yr.Iss.	1986	4.75	30
1986	Shirt Tales Parade QX277-3	Yr.Iss.	1986	4.75	18
1986	Snoopy and Woodstock QX434-6	Yr.Iss.	1986	8.00	60
1986	The Statue of Liberty QX384-3	Yr.Iss.	1986	6.00	10-25

1986 Special Edition - Keepsake

YEAR ISSUE		EDITION LIMIT	YEAR RETD.	ISSUE PRICE	*QUOTE U.S.$
1986	Jolly St. Nick QX429-6	Yr.Iss.	1986	22.50	50-75

*Quotes have been rounded up to nearest dollar

1986 Traditional Ornaments - Keepsake

YEAR ISSUE		EDITION LIMIT	YEAR RETD.	ISSUE PRICE	*QUOTE U.S. $
1986	Bluebird QX428-3	Yr.Iss.	1986	7.25	50-60
1986	Christmas Beauty QX322-3	Yr.Iss.	1986	6.00	10
1986	Glowing Christmas Tree QX428-6	Yr.Iss.	1986	7.00	15
1986	Heirloom Snowflake QX515-3	Yr.Iss.	1986	6.75	10-22
1986	Holiday Jingle Bell QX404-6	Yr.Iss.	1986	16.00	45-55
1986	The Magi QX272-6	Yr.Iss.	1986	4.75	23
1986	Mary Emmerling:American Country Collection QX275-2	Yr.Iss.	1986	7.95	25
1986	Memories to Cherish QX427-6	Yr.Iss.	1986	7.50	25
1986	Star Brighteners QX322-6	Yr.Iss.	1986	6.00	19

1987 Artists' Favorites - Keepsake

YEAR ISSUE		EDITION LIMIT	YEAR RETD.	ISSUE PRICE	*QUOTE U.S. $
1987	Beary Special QX455-7	Yr.Iss.	1987	4.75	15-30
1987	December Showers QX448-7	Yr.Iss.	1987	5.50	22-37
1987	Three Men in a Tub QX454-7	Yr.Iss.	1987	8.00	17-30
1987	Wee Chimney Sweep QX451-9	Yr.Iss.	1987	6.25	15-30

1987 Christmas Pizzazz Collection - Keepsake

YEAR ISSUE		EDITION LIMIT	YEAR RETD.	ISSUE PRICE	*QUOTE U.S. $
1987	Christmas Fun Puzzle QX467-9	Yr.Iss.	1987	8.00	15-30
1987	Doc Holiday QX467-7	Yr.Iss.	1987	8.00	40
1987	Happy Holidata QX471-7	Yr.Iss.	1988	6.50	15-30
1987	Holiday Hourglass QX470-7	Yr.Iss.	1987	8.00	25
1987	Jolly Follies QX466-9	Yr.Iss.	1987	8.50	20-40
1987	Mistletoad QX468-7	Yr.Iss.	1988	7.00	22-30
1987	St. Louie Nick QX453-9	Yr.Iss.	1988	7.75	16-33

1987 Collectible Series - Keepsake

YEAR ISSUE		EDITION LIMIT	YEAR RETD.	ISSUE PRICE	*QUOTE U.S. $
1987	Betsey Clark:Home for Christmas (2nd Ed.) QX272-7	Yr.Iss.	1987	5.00	17-25
1987	Clothespin Soldier (6th & Final Ed.) QX480-7	Yr.Iss.	1987	5.50	20-30
1987	Collector's Plate (1st Ed.) QX481-7	Yr.Iss.	1987	8.00	62-75
1987	Frosty Friends (8th Ed.) QX440-9	Yr.Iss.	1987	8.50	43-60
1987	Here Comes Santa (9th Ed.) QX484-7	Yr.Iss.	1987	14.00	48-95
1987	Holiday Heirloom (1st Ed./limited Ed.)QX485-7	Yr.Iss.	1987	25.00	25-47
1987	Holiday Wildlife (6th Ed.) QX371-7	Yr.Iss.	1987	7.50	15-25
1987	Miniature Creche (3rd Ed.) QX481-9	Yr.Iss.	1987	9.00	24-39
1987	Mr. and Mrs. Claus (2nd Ed.) QX483-7	Yr.Iss.	1987	13.25	45-65
1987	Norman Rockwell (8th Ed.) QX370-7	Yr.Iss.	1987	7.75	15-25
1987	Nostalgic Houses and Shops (4th Ed.) QX483-9	Yr.Iss.	1987	14.00	60-80
1987	Porcelain Bear (5th Ed.) QX443-7	Yr.Iss.	1987	7.75	[illegible]
1987	Reindeer Champs (2nd Ed.) QX480-9	Yr.Iss.	1987	7.50	53
1987	Rocking Horse (7th Ed.) QX482-9	Yr.Iss.	1987	10.75	46-70
1987	Thimble (10th Ed.) QX441-9	Yr.Iss.	1987	5.75	20-30
1987	Tin Locomotive (6th Ed.) QX484-9	Yr.Iss.	1987	14.75	45-65
1987	Twelve Days of Christmas (4th Ed.) QX370-9	Yr.Iss.	1987	6.50	27-35
1987	Windows of the World (3rd Ed.) QX482-7	Yr.Iss.	1987	10.00	25-40
1987	Wood Childhood Ornaments (4th Ed.) QX441-7	Yr.Iss.	1987	7.50	17-27

1987 Commemoratives - Keepsake

YEAR ISSUE		EDITION LIMIT	YEAR RETD.	ISSUE PRICE	*QUOTE U.S. $
1987	Baby Locket QX461-7	Yr.Iss.	1987	15.00	30
1987	Baby's First Christmas Photoholder QX4661-9	Yr.Iss.	1987	7.50	30
1987	Baby's First Christmas QX372-9	Yr.Iss.	1987	6.00	20-25
1987	Baby's First Christmas QX411-3	Yr.Iss.	1987	9.75	22-30
1987	Baby's First Christmas-Baby Boy QX274-9	Yr.Iss.	1987	4.75	17-29
1987	Baby's First Christmas-Baby Girl QX274-7	Yr.Iss.	1987	4.75	15-27
1987	Baby's Second Christmas QX460-7	Yr.Iss.	1987	5.75	25-32
1987	Babysitter QX279-7	Yr.Iss.	1987	4.75	10-20
1987	Child's Third Christmas QX459-9	Yr.Iss.	1987	5.75	22-30
1987	Dad QX462-9	Yr.Iss.	1987	6.00	35-40
1987	Daughter QX463-7	Yr.Iss.	1987	5.75	30-36
1987	Fifty Years Together QX443-7	Yr.Iss.	1987	8.00	25
1987	First Christmas Together QX272-9	Yr.Iss.	1987	4.75	10-35
1987	First Christmas Together QX371-9	Yr.Iss.	1987	6.50	15-35
1987	First Christmas Together QX445-9	Yr.Iss.	1987	8.00	20-38
1987	First Christmas Together QX446-7	Yr.Iss.	1987	9.50	20-45
1987	First Christmas Together QX446-9	Yr.Iss.	1987	15.00	20-30
1987	From Our Home to Yours QX279-9	Yr.Iss.	1987	4.75	50
1987	Godchild QX276-7	Yr.Iss.	1987	4.75	20
1987	Grandchild's First Christmas QX460-9	Yr.Iss.	1987	9.00	10-25
1987	Granddaughter QX374-7	Yr.Iss.	1987	6.00	19-25
1987	Grandmother QX277-9	Yr.Iss.	1987	4.75	15
1987	Grandparents QX277-7	Yr.Iss.	1987	4.75	19
1987	Grandson QX276-9	Yr.Iss.	1987	4.75	30
1987	Heart in Blossom QX372-7	Yr.Iss.	1987	6.00	25
1987	Holiday Greetings QX375-7	Yr.Iss.	1987	6.00	13
1987	Husband QX373-9	Yr.Iss.	1987	7.00	12
1987	Love is Everywhere QX278-7	Yr.Iss.	1987	4.75	14-24
1987	Mother and Dad QX462-7	Yr.Iss.	1987	7.00	25
1987	Mother QX373-7	Yr.Iss.	1987	6.50	20
1987	New Home QX376-7	Yr.Iss.	1987	6.00	30
1987	Niece QX275-9	Yr.Iss.	1987	4.75	13
1987	Sister QX474-7	Yr.Iss.	1987	6.00	10-15
1987	Son QX463-9	Yr.Iss.	1987	5.75	47
1987	Sweetheart QX447-9	Yr.Iss.	1987	11.00	16-30
1987	Teacher QX466-7	Yr.Iss.	1987	5.75	21
1987	Ten Years Together QX444-7	Yr.Iss.	1987	7.00	25
1987	Time for Friends QX280-7	Yr.Iss.	1987	4.75	22
1987	Twenty-Five Years Together QX443-9	Yr.Iss.	1987	7.50	15-30
1987	Warmth of Friendship QX375-9	Yr.Iss.	1987	6.00	12
1987	Word of Love QX447-7	Yr.Iss.	1987	8.00	10-22

1987 Holiday Humor - Keepsake

YEAR ISSUE		EDITION LIMIT	YEAR RETD.	ISSUE PRICE	*QUOTE U.S.$
1987	Bright Christmas Dreams QX440-7	Yr.Iss.	1987	7.25	80
1987	Chocolate Chipmunk QX456-7	Yr.Iss.	1987	6.00	45-55
1987	Christmas Cuddle QX453-7	Yr.Iss.	1987	5.75	20-35
1987	Dr. Seuss:The Grinch's Christmas QX278-3	Yr.Iss.	1987	4.75	75-95
1987	Fudge Forever QX449-7	Yr.Iss.	1987	5.00	25-40
1987	Happy Santa QX456-9	Yr.Iss.	1987	4.75	30
1987	Hot Dogger QX471-9	Yr.Iss.	1987	6.50	21-30
1987	Icy Treat QX450-9	Yr.Iss.	1987	4.50	18-30
1987	Jack Frosting QX449-9	Yr.Iss.	1987	7.00	27-50
1987	Jammie Pies QX283-9	Yr.Iss.	1987	4.75	18
1987	Jogging Through the Snow QX457-7	Yr.Iss.	1987	7.25	22-40
1987	Jolly Hiker QX483-2	Yr.Iss.	1987	5.00	18
1987	Joy Ride QX440-7	Yr.Iss.	1987	11.50	45-75
1987	Let It Snow QX458-9	Yr.Iss.	1987	6.50	15-25
1987	Li'l Jingler QX419-3	Yr.Iss.	1987	6.75	22-36
1987	Merry Koala QX415-3	Yr.Iss.	1987	5.00	17
1987	Mouse in the Moon QX416-6	Yr.Iss.	1987	5.50	21
1987	Nature's Decorations QX273-9	Yr.Iss.	1987	4.75	35
1987	Night Before Christmas QX451-7	Yr.Iss.	1988	6.50	19-33
1987	Owliday Wish QX455-9	Yr.Iss.	1988	6.50	14-25
1987	Paddington Bear QX472-7	Yr.Iss.	1987	5.50	20-35
1987	Peanuts QX281-9	Yr.Iss.	1987	4.75	35-40
1987	Pretty Kitten QX448-9	Yr.Iss.	1987	11.00	35
1987	Raccoon Biker QX458-7	Yr.Iss.	1987	7.00	15-30
1987	Reindoggy QX452-7	Yr.Iss.	1988	5.75	20-35
1987	Santa at the Bat QX457-9	Yr.Iss.	1987	7.75	18-30
1987	Seasoned Greetings QX454-9	Yr.Iss.	1987	6.25	15-30
1987	Sleepy Santa QX450-7	Yr.Iss.	1987	6.25	35-40
1987	Snoopy and Woodstock QX472-9	Yr.Iss.	1987	7.25	40-50
1987	Spots 'n Stripes QX452-9	Yr.Iss.	1987	5.50	15-25
1987	Treetop Dreams QX459-7	Yr.Iss.	1988	6.75	15-30
1987	Treetop Trio QX425-6	Yr.Iss.	1987	11.00	25
1987	Walnut Shell Rider QX419-6	Yr.Iss.	1987	6.00	18

1987 Keepsake Collector's Club - Keepsake

YEAR ISSUE		EDITION LIMIT	YEAR RETD.	ISSUE PRICE	*QUOTE U.S.$
1987	Carousel Reindeer QXC580-7	Yr.Iss.	1987	Unkn.	55-65
1987	Wreath of Memories QXC580-9	Yr.Iss.	1988	Unkn.	55

1987 Keepsake Magic Ornaments - Keepsake

YEAR ISSUE		EDITION LIMIT	YEAR RETD.	ISSUE PRICE	*QUOTE U.S.$
1987	Angelic Messengers QLX711-3	Yr.Iss.	1987	18.75	53-60
1987	Baby's First Christmas QLX704-9	Yr.Iss.	1987	13.50	37
1987	Bright Noel QLX705-9	Yr.Iss.	1987	7.00	18-33
1987	Chris Mouse (3rd Ed.) QLX705-7	Yr.Iss.	1987	11.00	60
1987	Christmas Classics (2nd Ed.) QLX702-9	Yr.Iss.	1987	16.00	50-75
1987	Christmas Morning QLX701-3	Yr.Iss.	1988	24.50	33-50
1987	First Christmas Together QLX708-7	Yr.Iss.	1987	11.50	50
1987	Good Cheer Blimp QLX704-6	Yr.Iss.	1987	16.00	52-59
1987	Keeping Cozy QLX704-7	Yr.Iss.	1987	11.75	30-37
1987	Lacy Brass Snowflake QLX709-7	Yr.Iss.	1987	11.50	16-30
1987	Loving Holiday QLX701-6	Yr.Iss.	1987	22.00	38-55
1987	Memories are Forever Photoholder QLX706-7	Yr.Iss.	1987	8.50	33
1987	Meowy Christmas QLX708-9	Yr.Iss.	1987	10.00	45-63
1987	Santa and Sparky (2nd Ed.) QLX701-9	Yr.Iss.	1987	19.50	65-75
1987	Season for Friendship QLX706-9	Yr.Iss.	1987	8.50	11-20
1987	Train Station QLX703-9	Yr.Iss.	1987	12.75	50

1987 Lighted Ornament Collection - Keepsake

YEAR ISSUE		EDITION LIMIT	YEAR RETD.	ISSUE PRICE	*QUOTE U.S.$
1987	Keep on Glowin' QLX707-6	Yr.Iss.	1987	10.00	37
1987	Village Express QLX707-2	Yr.Iss.	1987	24.50	87-120

1987 Limited Edition - Keepsake

YEAR ISSUE		EDITION LIMIT	YEAR RETD.	ISSUE PRICE	*QUOTE U.S.$
1987	Christmas is Gentle QX444-9	Yr.Iss.	1987	17.50	57-85
1987	Christmas Time Mime QX442-9	Yr.Iss.	1987	27.50	46-65

1987 Old-Fashioned Christmas Collection - Keepsake

YEAR ISSUE		EDITION LIMIT	YEAR RETD.	ISSUE PRICE	*QUOTE U.S.$
1987	Country Wreath QX470-9	Yr.Iss.	1987	5.75	30
1987	Folk Art Santa QX474-9	Yr.Iss.	1987	5.25	20-33
1987	In a Nutshell QX469-7	Yr.Iss.	1988	5.50	25-34
1987	Little Whittler QX469-9	Yr.Iss.	1987	6.00	25-33
1987	Nostalgic Rocker QX468-9	Yr.Iss.	1987	6.50	26-33

1987 Special Edition - Keepsake

YEAR ISSUE		EDITION LIMIT	YEAR RETD.	ISSUE PRICE	*QUOTE U.S.$
1987	Favorite Santa QX445-7	Yr.Iss.	1987	22.50	32-45

1987 Traditional Ornaments - Keepsake

YEAR ISSUE		EDITION LIMIT	YEAR RETD.	ISSUE PRICE	*QUOTE U.S.$
1987	Christmas Keys QX473-9	Yr.Iss.	1987	5.75	20-33
1987	Currier & Ives: American Farm Scene QX282-9	Yr.Iss.	1987	4.75	30
1987	Goldfinch QX464-9	Yr.Iss.	1987	7.00	60-85
1987	Heavenly Harmony QX465-9	Yr.Iss.	1987	15.00	35
1987	I Remember Santa QX278-9	Yr.Iss.	1987	4.75	33
1987	Joyous Angels QX465-7	Yr.Iss.	1987	7.75	25
1987	Norman Rockwell:Christmas Scenes QX282-7	Yr.Iss.	1987	4.75	30-35
1987	Promise of Peace QX374-9	Yr.Iss.	1987	6.50	17-25
1987	Special Memories Photoholder QX464-7	Yr.Iss.	1987	6.75	15-27

1988 Artist Favorites - Keepsake

YEAR ISSUE		EDITION LIMIT	YEAR RETD.	ISSUE PRICE	*QUOTE U.S.$
1988	Baby Redbird QX410-1	Yr.Iss.	1988	5.00	20
1988	Cymbals of Christmas QX411-1	Yr.Iss.	1988	5.50	17-30
1988	Little Jack Horner QX408-1	Yr.Iss.	1988	8.00	14-28
1988	Merry-Mint Unicorn QX423-4	Yr.Iss.	1988	8.50	12-22
1988	Midnight Snack QX410-4	Yr.Iss.	1988	6.00	21
1988	Very Strawbeary QX409-1	Yr.Iss.	1988	4.75	20

1988 Christmas Pizzazz Collection - Keepsake

YEAR ISSUE		EDITION LIMIT	YEAR RETD.	ISSUE PRICE	*QUOTE U.S.$
1988	Happy Holidata QX471-7	Yr.Iss.	1988	6.50	15-30
1988	Mistletoad QX468-7	Yr.Iss.	1988	7.00	20-30
1988	St. Louie Nick QX453-9	Yr.Iss.	1988	7.75	15-22

1988 Collectible Series - Keepsake

YEAR ISSUE		EDITION LIMIT	YEAR RETD.	ISSUE PRICE	*QUOTE U.S.$
1988	Betsey Clark: Home for Christmas (3rd Ed.) QX271-4	Yr.Iss.	1988	5.00	18-25
1988	Collector's Plate (2nd Ed.) QX406-1	Yr.Iss.	1988	8.00	50
1988	Five Golden Rings (5th Ed.) QX371-4	Yr.Iss.	1988	6.50	18-30
1988	Frosty Friends (9th Ed.) QX403-1	Yr.Iss.	1988	8.75	45-65
1988	Here Comes Santa (10th Ed.) QX400-1	Yr.Iss.	1988	14.00	47
1988	Holiday Heirloom (2nd Ed.) QX406-4	Yr.Iss.	1988	25.00	24
1988	Holiday Wildlife (7th Ed.QX371-1	Yr.Iss.	1988	7.75	16-25
1988	Mary's Angels (1st Ed.) QX407-4	Yr.Iss.	1988	5.00	45-65
1988	Miniature Creche (4th Ed.) QX403-4	Yr.Iss.	1988	8.50	22-35
1988	Mr. and Mrs. Claus (3rd Ed.) QX401-1	Yr.Iss.	1988	13.00	40-55
1988	Norman Rockwell (9th Ed.) QX370-4	Yr.Iss.	1988	7.75	17
1988	Nostalgic Houses and Shops (5th Ed.) QX401-4	Yr.Iss.	1988	14.50	42-65
1988	Porcelain Bear (6th Ed.) QX404-4	Yr.Iss.	1988	8.00	25-40
1988	Reindeer Champs (3rd Ed.) QX405-1	Yr.Iss.	1988	7.50	27-40
1988	Rocking Horse (8th Ed.) QX402-4	Yr.Iss.	1988	10.75	41-67
1988	Thimble (11th Ed.) QX405-4	Yr.Iss.	1988	5.75	17-25
1988	Tin Locomotive (7th Ed.) QX400-4	Yr.Iss.	1988	14.75	38-60
1988	Windows of the World (4th Ed.) QX402-1	Yr.Iss.	1988	10.00	22-35
1988	Wood Childhood (5th Ed.) QX404-1	Yr.Iss.	1988	7.50	23

1988 Commemoratives - Keepsake

YEAR ISSUE		EDITION LIMIT	YEAR RETD.	ISSUE PRICE	*QUOTE U.S.$
1988	Baby's First Christmas (Boy) QX272-1	Yr.Iss.	1988	4.75	17-25
1988	Baby's First Christmas (Girl) QX272-4	Yr.Iss.	1988	4.75	25
1988	Baby's First Christmas QX372-1	Yr.Iss.	1988	6.00	23
1988	Baby's First Christmas QX470-1	Yr.Iss.	1988	9.75	32-40
1988	Baby's First Christmas QX470-4	Yr.Iss.	1988	7.50	29
1988	Baby's Second Christmas QX471-1	Yr.Iss.	1988	6.00	33
1988	Babysitter QX279-1	Yr.Iss.	1988	4.75	10
1988	Child's Third Christmas QX471-4	Yr.Iss.	1988	6.00	25
1988	Dad QX414-1	Yr.Iss.	1988	7.00	25
1988	Daughter QX415-1	Yr.Iss.	1988	5.75	54
1988	Fifty Years Together QX374-1	Yr.Iss.	1988	6.75	10-20
1988	First Christmas Together QX274-1	Yr.Iss.	1988	4.75	27
1988	First Christmas Together QX373-1	Yr.Iss.	1988	6.75	16-30
1988	First Christmas Together QX489-4	Yr.Iss.	1988	9.00	25-35
1988	Five Years Together QX274-4	Yr.Iss.	1988	4.75	6-22
1988	From Our Home to Yours QX279-4	Yr.Iss.	1988	4.75	17
1988	Godchild QX278-4	Yr.Iss.	1988	4.75	20
1988	Granddaughter QX277-4	Yr.Iss.	1988	4.75	45
1988	Grandmother QX276-4	Yr.Iss.	1988	4.75	15-20
1988	Grandparents QX277-1	Yr.Iss.	1988	4.75	20
1988	Grandson QX278-1	Yr.Iss.	1988	4.75	30-40
1988	Gratitude QX375-4	Yr.Iss.	1988	6.00	12
1988	Love Fills the Heart QX374-4	Yr.Iss.	1988	6.00	18-24
1988	Love Grows QX275-4	Yr.Iss.	1988	4.75	31
1988	Mother and Dad QX414-4	Yr.Iss.	1988	8.00	20
1988	Mother QX375-1	Yr.Iss.	1988	6.50	15-20
1988	New Home QX376-1	Yr.Iss.	1988	6.00	25
1988	Sister QX499-4	Yr.Iss.	1988	8.00	20-32
1988	Son QX415-4	Yr.Iss.	1988	5.75	40-50
1988	Spirit of Christmas QX276-1	Yr.Iss.	1988	4.75	22
1988	Sweetheart QX490-1	Yr.Iss.	1988	9.75	11-22
1988	Teacher QX417-1	Yr.Iss.	1988	6.25	20
1988	Ten Years Together QX275-1	Yr.Iss.	1988	4.75	10-21
1988	Twenty-Five Years Together QX373-4	Yr.Iss.	1988	6.75	10-20
1988	Year to Remember QX416-4	Yr.Iss.	1988	7.00	25

1988 Hallmark Handcrafted Ornaments - Keepsake

YEAR ISSUE		EDITION LIMIT	YEAR RETD.	ISSUE PRICE	*QUOTE U.S.$
1988	Americana Drum QX488-1	Yr.Iss.	1988	7.75	15-30
1988	Arctic Tenor QX472-1	Yr.Iss.	1988	4.00	10-20
1988	Christmas Cardinal QX494-1	Yr.Iss.	1988	4.75	8-20
1988	Christmas Cuckoo QX480-1	Yr.Iss.	1988	8.00	30-40
1988	Christmas Memories QX372-4	Yr.Iss.	1988	6.50	25
1988	Christmas Scenes QX273-1	Yr.Iss.	1988	4.75	24
1988	Cool Juggler QX487-4	Yr.Iss.	1988	6.50	20
1988	Feliz Navidad QX416-1	Yr.Iss.	1988	6.75	18-35
1988	Filled with Fudge QX419-1	Yr.Iss.	1988	4.75	16-33
1988	Glowing Wreath QX492-1	Yr.Iss.	1988	6.00	15
1988	Go For The Gold QX417-4	Yr.Iss.	1988	8.00	16-30
1988	Goin' Cross-Country QX476-4	Yr.Iss.	1988	8.50	26
1988	Gone Fishing QX479-4	Yr.Iss.	1989	5.00	16
1988	Hoe-Hoe-Hoe! QX422-1	Yr.Iss.	1988	5.00	11-20
1988	Holiday Hero QX423-1	Yr.Iss.	1988	5.00	20
1988	Jingle Bell Clown QX477-4	Yr.Iss.	1988	15.00	20-37
1988	Jolly Walrus QX473-1	Yr.Iss.	1988	4.50	23
1988	Kiss from Santa QX482-1	Yr.Iss.	1989	4.50	23-30
1988	Kiss the Claus QX486-1	Yr.Iss.	1988	5.00	10-18

*Quotes have been rounded up to nearest dollar

YEAR ISSUE		EDITION LIMIT	YEAR RETD.	ISSUE PRICE	*QUOTE U.S.$
1988	Kringle Moon QX495-1	Yr.Iss.	1988	5.00	35
1988	Kringle Portrait QX496-1	Yr.Iss.	1988	7.50	22-40
1988	Kringle Tree QX495-4	Yr.Iss.	1988	6.50	20-40
1988	Love Santa QX486-4	Yr.Iss.	1988	5.00	20
1988	Loving Bear QX493-4	Yr.Iss.	1988	4.75	10-20
1988	Nick the Kick QX422-4	Yr.Iss.	1988	5.00	23
1988	Noah's Ark QX490-4	Yr.Iss.	1988	8.50	30-40
1988	Old-Fashioned Church QX498-1	Yr.Iss.	1988	4.00	24
1988	Old-Fashioned School House QX497-1	Yr.Iss.	1988	4.00	23
1988	Oreo QX481-4	Yr.Iss.	1989	4.00	11-20
1988	Par for Santa QX479-1	Yr.Iss.	1988	5.00	20
1988	Party Line QX476-1	Yr.Iss.	1989	8.75	20-30
1988	Peanuts QX280-1	Yr.Iss.	1988	4.75	40-50
1988	Peek-a-boo Kittens QX487-1	Yr.Iss.	1989	7.50	21
1988	Polar Bowler QX478-4	Yr.Iss.	1989	5.00	10-20
1988	Purrfect Snuggle QX474-4	Yr.Iss.	1988	6.25	15-30
1988	Sailing! Sailing! QX491-1	Yr.Iss.	1988	8.50	27
1988	Santa Flamingo QX483-4	Yr.Iss.	1988	4.75	16-33
1988	Shiny Sleigh QX492-4	Yr.Iss.	1988	5.75	20
1988	Slipper Spaniel QX472-4	Yr.Iss.	1988	4.50	10-20
1988	Snoopy and Woodstock QX474-1	Yr.Iss.	1988	6.00	35-46
1988	Soft Landing QX475-1	Yr.Iss.	1988	7.00	15-25
1988	Sparkling Tree QX483-1	Yr.Iss.	1988	6.00	19
1988	Squeaky Clean QX475-4	Yr.Iss.	1988	6.75	13-24
1988	Starry Angel QX494-4	Yr.Iss.	1988	4.75	20
1988	Sweet Star QX418-4	Yr.Iss.	1988	5.00	20-32
1988	Teeny Taster QX418-1	Yr.Iss.	1989	4.75	23-30
1988	The Town Crier QX473-4	Yr.Iss.	1988	5.50	13-24
1988	Travels with Santa QX477-1	Yr.Iss.	1988	10.00	26-40
1988	Uncle Sam Nutcracker QX488-4	Yr.Iss.	1988	7.00	20-40
1988	Winter Fun QX478-1	Yr.Iss.	1988	8.50	17-27

1988 Hallmark Keepsake Ornament Collector's Club - Keepsake

1988	Angelic Minstrel QXC408-4	Yr.Iss.	1988	27.50	45-60
1988	Christmas is Sharing QXC407-1	Yr.Iss.	1988	17.50	31-50
1988	Hold on Tight QXC570-4	Yr.Iss.	1988	Unkn.	75
1988	Holiday Heirloom (2nd Ed.) QXC406-4	Yr.Iss.	1988	25.00	23-37
1988	Our Clubhouse QXC580-4	Yr.Iss.	1988	Unkn.	33-45
1988	Sleighful of Dreams QC580-1	Yr.Iss.	1988	8.00	50-75

1988 Holiday Humor - Keepsake

1988	Night Before Christmas QX451-7	Yr.Iss.	1988	6.50	33-44
1988	Owliday Wish QX455-9	Yr.Iss.	1988	6.50	14-25
1988	Reindoggy QX452-7	Yr.Iss.	1988	5.75	20-25
1988	Treetop Dreams QX459-7	Yr.Iss.	1988	6.75	15-25

1988 Keepsake Magic Ornaments - Keepsake

1988	Baby's First Christmas QLX718-4	Yr.Iss.	1988	24.00	43-60
1988	Bearly Reaching QLX715-1	Yr.Iss.	1988	9.50	40
1988	Chris Mouse (4th Ed.) QLX715-4	Yr.Iss.	1988	8.75	60
1988	Christmas Classics (3rd Ed.) QLX716-1	Yr.Iss.	1988	15.00	30
1988	Christmas is Magic QLX717-1	Yr.Iss.	1988	12.00	35-55
1988	Christmas Morning QLX701-3	Yr.Iss.	1988	24.50	33-50
1988	Circling the Globe QLX712-4	Yr.Iss.	1988	10.50	45
1988	Country Express QLX721-1	Yr.Iss.	1988	24.50	67-75
1988	Festive Feeder QLX720-4	Yr.Iss.	1988	11.50	43-50
1988	First Christmas Together QLX702-7	Yr.Iss.	1988	12.00	37
1988	Heavenly Glow QLX711-4	Yr.Iss.	1988	11.75	19-29
1988	Kitty Capers QLX716-4	Yr.Iss.	1988	13.00	45
1988	Kringle's Toy Shop QLX701-7	Yr.Iss.	1988	25.00	37-65
1988	Last-Minute Hug QLX718-1	Yr.Iss.	1988	19.50	42-49
1988	Moonlit Nap QLX713-4	Yr.Iss.	1988	8.75	21-30
1988	Parade of the Toys QLX719-4	Yr.Iss.	1988	22.00	53
1988	Radiant Tree QLX712-1	Yr.Iss.	1988	11.75	27
1988	Santa and Sparky (3rd Ed.) QLX719-1	Yr.Iss.	1988	19.50	31-42
1988	Skater's Waltz QLX720-1	Yr.Iss.	1988	19.50	36-62
1988	Song of Christmas QLX711-1	Yr.Iss.	1988	8.50	15-30
1988	Tree of Friendship QLX710-4	Yr.Iss.	1988	8.50	23

1988 Keepsake Miniature Ornaments - Keepsake

1988	Baby's First Christmas	Yr.Iss.	1988	6.00	12
1988	Brass Angel	Yr.Iss.	1988	1.50	15-20
1988	Brass Star	Yr.Iss.	1988	1.50	20
1988	Brass Tree	Yr.Iss.	1988	1.50	19
1988	Candy Cane Elf	Yr.Iss.	1988	3.00	20
1988	Country Wreath	Yr.Iss.	1988	4.00	11
1988	Family Home (1st Ed.)	Yr.Iss.	1988	8.50	40-45
1988	First Christmas Together	Yr.Iss.	1988	4.00	11
1988	Folk Art Lamb	Yr.Iss.	1988	2.50	14-23
1988	Folk Art Reindeer	Yr.Iss.	1988	2.50	13-20
1988	Friends Share Joy	Yr.Iss.	1988	2.00	15
1988	Gentle Angel	Yr.Iss.	1988	2.00	15
1988	Happy Santa	Yr.Iss.	1988	4.50	19
1988	Holy Family	Yr.Iss.	1988	8.50	13
1988	Jolly St. Nick	Yr.Iss.	1988	8.00	25-35
1988	Joyous Heart	Yr.Iss.	1988	3.50	22-30
1988	Kittens in Toyland (1st Ed.)	Yr.Iss.	1988	5.00	25-30
1988	Little Drummer Boy	Yr.Iss.	1988	4.50	20-27
1988	Love is Forever	Yr.Iss.	1988	2.00	15
1988	Mother	Yr.Iss.	1988	3.00	12
1988	Penguin Pal (1st Ed.)	Yr.Iss.	1988	3.75	27
1988	Rocking Horse (1st Ed.)	Yr.Iss.	1988	4.50	30-45
1988	Skater's Waltz	Yr.Iss.	1988	7.00	14-22
1988	Sneaker Mouse	Yr.Iss.	1988	4.00	14-20
1988	Snuggly Skater	Yr.Iss.	1988	4.50	27
1988	Sweet Dreams	Yr.Iss.	1988	7.00	18
1988	Three Little Kitties	Yr.Iss.	1988	6.00	13-19

1988 Old Fashioned Christmas Collection - Keepsake

1988	In A Nutshell QX469-7	Yr.Iss.	1988	5.50	24-33

1988 Special Edition - Keepsake

1988	The Wonderful Santacycle QX411-4	Yr.Iss.	1988	22.50	34-45

1989 Artists' Favorites - Keepsake

1989	Baby Partridge QX452-5	Yr.Iss.	1989	6.75	10-15
1989	Bear-i-Tone QX454-2	Yr.Iss.	1989	4.75	10-20
1989	Carousel Zebra QX451-5	Yr.Iss.	1989	9.25	15-20
1989	Cherry Jubilee QX453-2	Yr.Iss.	1989	5.00	16-27
1989	Mail Call QX452-2	Yr.Iss.	1989	8.75	15-20
1989	Merry-Go-Round Unicorn QX447-2	Yr.Iss.	1989	10.75	16-25
1989	Playful Angel QX453-5	Yr.Iss.	1989	6.75	15-25

1989 Collectible Series - Keepsake

1989	Betsey Clark:Home for Christmas (4th Ed.) QX230-2	Yr.Iss.	1989	5.00	30-36
1989	Christmas Kitty (1st Ed.) QX544-5	Yr.Iss.	1989	14.75	26-32
1989	Collector's Plate (3rd Ed.) QX461-2	Yr.Iss.	1989	8.25	20-32
1989	Crayola Crayon (1st Ed.) QX435-2	Yr.Iss.	1989	8.75	45
1989	Frosty Friends (10th Ed.) QX457-2	Yr.Iss.	1989	9.25	32-54
1989	The Gift Bringers (1st Ed.) QX279-5	Yr.Iss.	1989	5.00	20
1989	Hark! It's Herald (1st Ed.) QX455-5	Yr.Iss.	1989	6.75	23-30
1989	Here Comes Santa (11th Ed.) QX458-5	Yr.Iss.	1989	14.75	31-50
1989	Mary's Angels (2nd Ed.) QX454-5	Yr.Iss.	1989	5.75	85-100
1989	Miniature Creche (5th Ed.) QX459-2	Yr.Iss.	1989	9.25	15-24
1989	Mr. and Mrs. Claus (4th Ed.) QX 457-5	Yr.Iss.	1989	13.25	33-50
1989	Nostalgic Houses and Shops (6th Ed.) QX458-2	Yr.Iss.	1989	14.25	60-70
1989	Porcelain Bear (7th Ed.) QX461-5	Yr.Iss.	1989	8.75	20-40
1989	Reindeer Champs (4th Ed.) QX456-2	Yr.Iss.	1989	7.75	17-27
1989	Rocking Horse (9th Ed.) QX462-2	Yr.Iss.	1989	10.75	35-50
1989	Thimble (12th Ed.) QX455-2	Yr.Iss.	1989	5.75	13-25
1989	Tin Locomotive (8th Ed.) QX460-2	Yr.Iss.	1989	14.75	46-60
1989	Twelve Days of Christmas (6th Ed.) QX381-2	Yr.Iss.	1989	6.75	16-20
1989	Windows of the World (5th Ed.) QX462-5	Yr.Iss.	1989	10.75	20-34
1989	Winter Surprise (1st Ed.) QX427-2	Yr.Iss.	1989	10.75	25-33
1989	Wood Childhood Ornaments (6th Ed.) QX459-5	Yr.Iss.	1989	7.75	15-25

1989 Commemoratives - Keepsake

1989	Baby's Fifth Christmas QX543-5	Yr.Iss.	1989	6.75	15-30
1989	Baby's First Christmas Photoholder QX468-2	Yr.Iss.	1989	6.25	50
1989	Baby's First Christmas QX381-5	Yr.Iss.	1989	6.75	18
1989	Baby's First Christmas QX449-2	Yr.Iss.	1989	7.25	75-90
1989	Baby's First Christmas-Baby Boy QX272-5	Yr.Iss.	1989	4.75	16-23
1989	Baby's First Christmas-Baby Girl QX272-2	Yr.Iss.	1989	4.75	23
1989	Baby's Fourth Christmas QX543-2	Yr.Iss.	1989	6.75	15-30
1989	Baby's Second Christmas QX449-5	Yr.Iss.	1989	6.75	25-45
1989	Baby's Third Christmas QX469-5	Yr.Iss.	1989	6.75	17-40
1989	Brother QX445-2	Yr.Iss.	1989	6.25	18
1989	Dad QX442-5	Yr.Iss.	1989	7.25	12-15
1989	Daughter QX443-2	Yr.Iss.	1989	6.25	25-35
1989	Festive Year QX384-2	Yr.Iss.	1989	7.75	10-24
1989	Fifty Years Together Photoholder QX486-2	Yr.Iss.	1989	8.75	12-20
1989	First Christmas Together QX273-2	Yr.Iss.	1989	4.75	20-35
1989	First Christmas Together QX383-2	Yr.Iss.	1989	6.75	17-25
1989	First Christmas Together QX485-2	Yr.Iss.	1989	9.75	17-25
1989	Five Years Together QX273-5	Yr.Iss.	1989	4.75	14-23
1989	Forty Years Together Photoholder QX545-2	Yr.Iss.	1989	8.75	15
1989	Friendship Time QX413-2	Yr.Iss.	1989	9.75	25-33
1989	From Our Home to Yours QX384-5	Yr.Iss.	1989	6.25	8-15
1989	Godchild QX311-2	Yr.Iss.	1989	6.25	15
1989	Granddaughter QX278	Yr.Iss.	1989	4.75	23
1989	Granddaughter's First Christmas QX382-2	Yr.Iss.	1989	6.75	10-23
1989	Grandmother QX277-5	Yr.Iss.	1989	4.75	18
1989	Grandparents QX277-2	Yr.Iss.	1989	4.75	17
1989	Grandson QX278-5	Yr.Iss.	1989	4.75	15-22
1989	Grandson's First Christmas QX382-5	Yr.Iss.	1989	6.75	9-18
1989	Gratitude QX385-2	Yr.Iss.	1989	6.75	14
1989	Language of Love QX383-5	Yr.Iss.	1989	6.25	24
1989	Mom and Dad QX442-5	Yr.Iss.	1989	9.75	17-24
1989	Mother QX440-5	Yr.Iss.	1989	9.75	28
1989	New Home QX275-5	Yr.Iss.	1989	4.75	20
1989	Sister QX279-2	Yr.Iss.	1989	4.75	19
1989	Son QX444-5	Yr.Iss.	1989	6.25	18-25
1989	Sweetheart QX486-5	Yr.Iss.	1989	9.75	33
1989	Teacher QX412-5	Yr.Iss.	1989	5.75	14-24
1989	Ten Years Together QX274-2	Yr.Iss.	1989	4.75	30
1989	Twenty-five Years Together Photoholder QX485-5	Yr.Iss.	1989	8.75	12-17
1989	World of Love QX274-5	Yr.Iss.	1989	4.75	35

1989 Hallmark Handcrafted Ornaments - Keepsake

1989	Peek-a-boo Kittens QX487-1	Yr.Iss.	1989	7.50	21

1989 Hallmark Keepsake Ornament Collector's Club - Keepsake

1989	Christmas is Peaceful QXC451-2	Yr.Iss.	1989	18.50	30-45
1989	Collect a Dream QXC428-5	Yr.Iss.	1989	9.00	57-65
1989	Holiday Heirloom (3rd Ed.) QXC460-5	Yr.Iss.	1989	25.00	29-39
1989	Noelle QXC448-3	Yr.Iss.	1989	19.75	50-60
1989	Sitting Purrty QXC581-2	Yr.Iss.	1989	Unkn.	45
1989	Visit from Santa QXC580-2	Yr.Iss.	1989	Unkn.	38-55

1989 Holiday Traditions - Keepsake

1989	Camera Claus QX546-5	Yr.Iss.	1989	5.75	12-22
1989	A Charlie Brown Christmas QX276-5	Yr.Iss.	1989	4.75	40
1989	Cranberry Bunny QX426-2	Yr.Iss.	1989	5.75	11-18
1989	Deer Disguise QX426-5	Yr.Iss.	1989	5.75	17-25
1989	Feliz Navidad QX439-2	Yr.Iss.	1989	6.75	20-30
1989	The First Christmas QX547-5	Yr.Iss.	1989	7.75	14-16
1989	Gentle Fawn QX548-5	Yr.Iss.	1989	7.75	13-20
1989	George Washington Bicentennial QX386-2	Yr.Iss.	1989	6.75	9-20
1989	Gone Fishing QX479-4	Yr.Iss.	1989	5.75	17
1989	Gym Dandy QX418-5	Yr.Iss.	1989	5.75	10-20
1989	Hang in There QX430-5	Yr.Iss.	1989	5.25	25-35
1989	Here's the Pitch QX545-5	Yr.Iss.	1989	5.75	11-20
1989	Hoppy Holidays QX469-2	Yr.Iss.	1989	7.75	13-24
1989	Joyful Trio QX437-2	Yr.Iss.	1989	9.75	15
1989	A Kiss(tm) From Santa QX482-1	Yr.Iss.	1989	4.50	20
1989	Kristy Claus QX424-5	Yr.Iss.	1989	5.75	12
1989	Norman Rockwell QX276-2	Yr.Iss.	1989	4.75	13-20
1989	North Pole Jogger QX546-2	Yr.Iss.	1989	5.75	11-22
1989	Old-World Gnome QX434-5	Yr.Iss.	1989	7.75	15-30
1989	On the Links QX419-2	Yr.Iss.	1989	5.75	15-23
1989	Oreo® Chocolate Sandwich Cookies QX481-4	Yr.Iss.	1989	4.00	15
1989	Owliday Greetings QX436-5	Yr.Iss.	1989	4.00	13-23
1989	Paddington Bear QX429-2	Yr.Iss.	1989	5.75	14-26
1989	Party Line QX476-1	Yr.Iss.	1989	8.75	27
1989	Peek-a-Boo Kitties QX487-1	Yr.Iss.	1989	7.50	16-22
1989	Polar Bowler QX478-4	Yr.Iss.	1989	5.75	17
1989	Sea Santa QX415-2	Yr.Iss.	1989	5.75	13-30
1989	Snoopy and Woodstock QX433-2	Yr.Iss.	1989	6.75	35-40
1989	Snowplow Santa QX420-5	Yr.Iss.	1989	5.75	12-22
1989	Special Delivery QX432-5	Yr.Iss.	1989	5.25	12-25
1989	Spencer Sparrow, Esq. QX431-2	Yr.Iss.	1990	6.75	14-27
1989	Stocking Kitten QX456-5	Yr.Iss.	1990	6.75	13-22
1989	Sweet Memories Photoholder QX438-5	Yr.Iss.	1989	6.75	25
1989	Teeny Taster QX418-1	Yr.Iss.	1989	4.75	17

1989 Keepsake Magic Collection - Keepsake

1989	Angel Melody QLX720-2	Yr.Iss.	1989	9.50	18-25
1989	The Animals Speak QLX723-2	Yr.Iss.	1989	13.50	78-125
1989	Baby's First Christmas QLX727-2	Yr.Iss.	1989	30.00	45
1989	Backstage Bear QLX721-5	Yr.Iss.	1989	13.50	27
1989	Busy Beaver QLX724-5	Yr.Iss.	1989	17.50	35-50
1989	Chris Mouse (5th Ed.) QLX722-5	Yr.Iss.	1989	9.50	55-62
1989	Christmas Classics (4th Ed.) QLX724-2	Yr.Iss.	1989	13.50	27-43
1989	First Christmas Together QLX734-2	Yr.Iss.	1989	17.50	32-45
1989	Forest Frolics (1st Ed.) QLX728-2	Yr.Iss.	1989	24.50	82-95
1989	Holiday Bell QLX722-2	Yr.Iss.	1989	17.50	29-35
1989	Joyous Carolers QLX729-5	Yr.Iss.	1989	30.00	47-70
1989	Kringle's Toy Shop QLX701-7	Yr.Iss.	1989	24.50	40-60
1989	Loving Spoonful QLX726-2	Yr.Iss.	1989	19.50	31-38
1989	Metro Express QLX727-5	Yr.Iss.	1989	28.00	71-80
1989	Moonlit Nap QLX713-4	Yr.Iss.	1989	8.75	23
1989	Rudolph the Red-Nosed Reindeer QLX725-2	Yr.Iss.	1989	19.50	51-70
1989	Spirit of St. Nick QLX728-5	Yr.Iss.	1989	24.50	60-75
1989	Tiny Tinker QLX717-4	Yr.Iss.	1989	19.50	63
1989	Unicorn Fantasy QLX723-5	Yr.Iss.	1989	9.50	17

1989 Keepsake Miniature Ornaments - Keepsake

1989	Acorn Squirrel QXM568-2	Yr.Iss.	1989	4.50	9
1989	Baby's First Christmas QXM573-2	Yr.Iss.	1989	6.00	11-15
1989	Brass Partridge QXM572-5	Yr.Iss.	1989	3.00	10
1989	Brass Snowflake QXM570-2	Yr.Iss.	1989	4.50	13
1989	Bunny Hug QXM577-5	Yr.Iss.	1989	3.00	8
1989	Country Wreath QXM573-1	Yr.Iss.	1989	4.50	12
1989	Cozy Skater QXM573-5	Yr.Iss.	1989	4.50	11
1989	First Christmas Together QXM564-2	Yr.Iss.	1989	8.50	10
1989	Folk Art Bunny QXM569-2	Yr.Iss.	1989	4.50	10
1989	Happy Bluebird QXM566-2	Yr.Iss.	1989	4.50	13
1989	Holiday Deer QXM577-2	Yr.Iss.	1989	3.00	11
1989	Holy Family QXM561-1	Yr.Iss.	1989	8.50	15
1989	Kittens in Toyland (2nd Ed.) QXM561-2	Yr.Iss.	1989	4.50	15-20
1989	Kitty Cart QXM572-2	Yr.Iss.	1989	3.00	7
1989	The Kringles (1st Ed.) QXM562-2	Yr.Iss.	1989	6.00	26-33
1989	Little Soldier QXM567-5	Yr.Iss.	1989	4.50	10-23
1989	Little Star Bringer QXM562-2	Yr.Iss.	1989	6.00	18
1989	Load of Cheer QXM574-5	Yr.Iss.	1989	6.00	12-20
1989	Lovebirds QXM563-5	Yr.Iss.	1989	6.00	9-15
1989	Merry Seal QXM575-5	Yr.Iss.	1989	6.00	13
1989	Mother QXM564-5	Yr.Iss.	1989	6.00	9-15

*Quotes have been rounded up to nearest dollar

YEAR ISSUE		EDITION LIMIT	YEAR RETD.	ISSUE PRICE	*QUOTE U.S. $
1989	Noel R.R. (1st Ed.) QXM576-2	Yr.Iss.	1989	8.50	30-42
1989	Old English Village (2nd Ed.) QXM561-5	Yr.Iss.	1989	8.50	27-37
1989	Old-World Santa QXM569-5	Yr.Iss.	1989	3.00	8
1989	Penguin Pal (2nd Ed.) QXM560-2	Yr.Iss.	1989	4.50	18
1989	Pinecone Basket QXM573-4	Yr.Iss.	1989	4.50	8
1989	Puppy Cart QXM571-5	Yr.Iss.	1989	3.00	8
1989	Rejoice QXM578-2	Yr.Iss.	1989	3.00	9
1989	Rocking Horse (2nd Ed.) QXM560-5	Yr.Iss.	1989	4.50	23-30
1989	Roly-Poly Pig QXM571-2	Yr.Iss.	1989	3.00	15
1989	Roly-Poly Ram QXM570-5	Yr.Iss.	1989	3.00	13
1989	Santa's Magic Ride QXM563-2	Yr.Iss.	1989	8.50	15-25
1989	Santa's Roadster QXM566-5	Yr.Iss.	1989	6.00	15-20
1989	Scrimshaw Reindeer QXM568-5	Yr.Iss.	1989	4.50	8
1989	Sharing a Ride QXM576-5	Yr.Iss.	1989	8.50	15
1989	Slow Motion QXM575-2	Yr.Iss.	1989	6.00	14
1989	Special Friend QXM565-2	Yr.Iss.	1989	4.50	12
1989	Starlit Mouse QXM565-5	Yr.Iss.	1989	4.50	13
1989	Stocking Pal QXM567-2	Yr.Iss.	1989	4.50	10
1989	Strollin' Snowman QXM574-2	Yr.Iss.	1989	4.50	15
1989	Three Little Kitties QXM569-4	Yr.Iss.	1989	6.00	19

1989 New Attractions - Keepsake

1989	Balancing Elf QX489-5	Yr.Iss.	1989	6.75	21
1989	Cactus Cowboy QX411-2	Yr.Iss.	1989	6.75	33-44
1989	Claus Construction QX488-5	Yr.Iss.	1990	7.75	18-39
1989	Cool Swing QX487-5	Yr.Iss.	1989	6.25	34
1989	Country Cat QX467-2	Yr.Iss.	1989	6.25	17
1989	Festive Angel QX463-5	Yr.Iss.	1989	6.75	13-26
1989	Goin' South QX410-5	Yr.Iss.	1989	4.25	17-24
1989	Graceful Swan QX464-2	Yr.Iss.	1989	6.75	13-20
1989	Horse Weathervane QX463-2	Yr.Iss.	1989	5.75	12
1989	Let's Play QX488-2	Yr.Iss.	1989	7.25	26-35
1989	Nostalgic Lamb QX466-5	Yr.Iss.	1989	6.75	10-15
1989	Nutshell Dreams QX465-5	Yr.Iss.	1989	5.75	14-23
1989	Nutshell Holiday QX465-2	Yr.Iss.	1990	5.75	17-27
1989	Nutshell Workshop QX487-2	Yr.Iss.	1989	5.75	15-23
1989	Peppermint Clown QX450-5	Yr.Iss.	1989	24.75	23-49
1989	Rodney Reindeer QX407-2	Yr.Iss.	1989	6.75	13
1989	Rooster Weathervane QX467-5	Yr.Iss.	1989	5.75	18-24
1989	Sparkling Snowflake QX547-2	Yr.Iss.	1989	7.75	23
1989	TV Break QX409-2	Yr.Iss.	1989	6.25	17
1989	Wiggly Snowman QX489-2	Yr.Iss.	1989	6.75	25-35

1989 Special Edition - Keepsake

1989	The Ornament Express QX580-5	Yr.Iss.	1989	22.00	32-45

1990 Artists' Favorites - Keepsake

1990	Angel Kitty QX4746	Yr.Iss.	1990	8.75	15-25
1990	Donder's Diner QX4823	Yr.Iss.	1990	13.75	22
1990	Gentle Dreamers QX4756	Yr.Iss.	1990	8.75	17-30
1990	Happy Woodcutter QX4763	Yr.Iss.	1990	9.75	17-25
1990	Mouseboat QX4753	Yr.Iss.	1990	7.75	15
1990	Welcome, Santa QX4773	Yr.Iss.	1990	11.75	19-30

1990 Collectible Series - Keepsake

1990	Betsey Clark: Home for Christmas (5th Ed.) QX2033	Yr.Iss.	1990	5.00	15-25
1990	Christmas Kitty (2nd Ed.) QX4506	Yr.Iss.	1990	14.75	21-35
1990	Cinnamon Bear (8th Ed.) QX4426	Yr.Iss.	1990	8.75	21-35
1990	Cookies for Santa (4th Ed.) QX4436	Yr.Iss.	1990	8.75	21-35
1990	CRAYOLA Crayon-Bright Moving Colors (2nd Ed.) QX4586	Yr.Iss.	1990	8.75	43
1990	Fabulous Decade (1st Ed.) QX4466	Yr.Iss.	1990	7.75	35-45
1990	Festive Surrey (12th Ed.) QX4923	Yr.Iss.	1990	14.75	30-42
1990	Frosty Friends (11th Ed.) QX4396	Yr.Iss.	1990	9.75	21-37
1990	The Gift Bringers-St. Lucia (2nd Ed.) QX2803	Yr.Iss.	1990	5.00	14-23
1990	Greatest Story (1st Ed.) QX4656	Yr.Iss.	1990	12.75	26-35
1990	Hark! It's Herald (2nd Ed.) QX4463	Yr.Iss.	1990	6.75	17-27
1990	Heart of Christmas (1st Ed.) QX4726	Yr.Iss.	1990	13.75	64-80
1990	Holiday Home (7th Ed.) QX4696	Yr.Iss.	1990	14.75	65-80
1990	Irish (6th Ed.) QX4636	Yr.Iss.	1990	10.75	20
1990	Mary's Angels-Rosebud (3rd Ed.) QX4423	Yr.Iss.	1990	5.75	31-40
1990	Merry Olde Santa (1st Ed.) QX4736	Yr.Iss.	1990	14.75	72
1990	Popcorn Party (5th Ed.) QX4393	Yr.Iss.	1990	13.75	58-80
1990	Reindeer Champs-Comet (5th Ed.) QX4433	Yr.Iss.	1990	7.75	20-30
1990	Rocking Horse (10th Ed.) QX4646	Yr.Iss.	1990	10.75	85-100
1990	Seven Swans A-Swimming (7th Ed.) QX3033	Yr.Iss.	1990	6.75	20-30
1990	Winter Surprise (2nd Ed.) QX4443	Yr.Iss.	1990	10.75	19-29

1990 Commemoratives - Keepsake

1990	Across The Miles QX3173	Yr.Iss.	1990	6.75	15
1990	Baby's First Christmas QX3036	Yr.Iss.	1990	6.75	10-22
1990	Baby's First Christmas QX4853	Yr.Iss.	1990	9.75	18-25
1990	Baby's First Christmas QX4856	Yr.Iss.	1990	7.75	31-40
1990	Baby's First Christmas-Baby Boy QX2063	Yr.Iss.	1990	4.75	21
1990	Baby's First Christmas-Baby Girl QX2066	Yr.Iss.	1990	4.75	18-25
1990	Baby's First Christmas-Photo Holder QX4843	Yr.Iss.	1990	7.75	23-30
1990	Baby's Second Christmas QX4683	Yr.Iss.	1990	6.75	35
1990	Brother QX4493	Yr.Iss.	1990	5.75	13
1990	Child Care Giver QX3166	Yr.Iss.	1990	6.75	14
1990	Child's Fifth Christmas QX4876	Yr.Iss.	1990	6.75	15-30
1990	Child's Fourth Christmas QX4873	Yr.Iss.	1990	6.75	15-30
1990	Child's Third Christmas QX4866	Yr.Iss.	1990	6.75	18-30
1990	Copy of Cheer QX4486	Yr.Iss.	1990	7.75	17
1990	Dad QX4533	Yr.Iss.	1990	6.75	17
1990	Dad-to-Be QX4913	Yr.Iss.	1990	5.75	19
1990	Daughter QX4496	Yr.Iss.	1990	5.75	19-25
1990	Fifty Years Together QX4906	Yr.Iss.	1990	9.75	18
1990	Five Years Together QX2103	Yr.Iss.	1990	4.75	20
1990	Forty Years Together QX4903	Yr.Iss.	1990	9.75	19
1990	Friendship Kitten QX4142	Yr.Iss.	1990	6.75	17-25
1990	From Our Home to Yours QX2166	Yr.Iss.	1990	4.75	11-20
1990	Godchild QX3167	Yr.Iss.	1990	6.75	11-20
1990	Granddaughter QX2286	Yr.Iss.	1990	4.75	17-27
1990	Granddaughter's First Christmas QX3106	Yr.Iss.	1990	6.75	18-23
1990	Grandmother QX2236	Yr.Iss.	1990	4.75	16
1990	Grandparents QX2253	Yr.Iss.	1990	4.75	16
1990	Grandson QX2293	Yr.Iss.	1990	4.75	20
1990	Grandson's First Christmas QX3063	Yr.Iss.	1990	6.75	16-23
1990	Jesus Loves Me QX3156	Yr.Iss.	1990	6.75	13
1990	Mom and Dad QX4593	Yr.Iss.	1990	8.75	16-26
1990	Mom-to-Be QX4916	Yr.Iss.	1990	5.75	25-33
1990	Mother QX4536	Yr.Iss.	1990	8.75	25-30
1990	New Home QX4343	Yr.Iss.	1990	6.75	25-30
1990	Our First Christmas Together QX2136	Yr.Iss.	1990	4.75	25
1990	Our First Christmas Together QX3146	Yr.Iss.	1990	6.75	13-24
1990	Our First Christmas Together QX4883	Yr.Iss.	1990	9.75	20-35
1990	Our First Christmas Together-Photo Holder Ornament QX4886	Yr.Iss.	1990	7.75	20
1990	Peaceful Kingdom QX2106	Yr.Iss.	1990	4.75	20
1990	Sister QX2273	Yr.Iss.	1990	4.75	18
1990	Son QX4516	Yr.Iss.	1990	5.75	19-27
1990	Sweetheart QX4893	Yr.Iss.	1990	11.75	18-30
1990	Teacher QX4483	Yr.Iss.	1990	7.75	15
1990	Ten Years Together QX2153	Yr.Iss.	1990	4.75	20
1990	Time for Love QX2133	Yr.Iss.	1990	4.75	22
1990	Twenty-Five Years Together QX4896	Yr.Iss.	1990	9.75	18

1990 Holiday Traditions - Keepsake

1990	Spencer Sparrow, Esq. QX431-2	Yr.Iss.	1990	6.75	15
1990	Stocking Kitten QX456-5	Yr.Iss.	1990	6.75	11-15

1990 Keepsake Collector's Club - Keepsake

1990	Armful of Joy QXC445-3	Yr.Iss.	1990	8.00	43
1990	Christmas Limited 1975 QXC476-6	38700	1990	19.75	80-125
1990	Club Hollow QXC445-6	Yr.Iss.	1990	Unkn.	38
1990	Crown Prince QXC560-3	Yr.Iss.	1990	Unkn.	39
1990	Dove of Peace QXC447-6	25400	1990	24.75	50-75
1990	Sugar Plum Fairy QXC447-3	25400	1990	27.75	50-60

1990 Keepsake Magic Ornaments - Keepsake

1990	Baby's First Christmas QLX7246	Yr.Iss.	1990	28.00	50-65
1990	Beary Short Nap QLX7326	Yr.Iss.	1990	10.00	23-33
1990	Blessings of Love QLX7363	Yr.Iss.	1990	14.00	44-50
1990	Children's Express QLX7243	Yr.Iss.	1990	28.00	64-75
1990	Chris Mouse Wreath QLX7296	Yr.Iss.	1990	10.00	30-50
1990	Christmas Memories QLX7276	Yr.Iss.	1990	25.00	47
1990	Deer Crossing QLX7213	Yr.Iss.	1990	18.00	41-50
1990	Elf of the Year QLX7356	Yr.Iss.	1990	10.00	16-25
1990	Elfin Whittler QLX7265	Yr.Iss.	1990	20.00	37-55
1990	Forest Frolics QLX7236	Yr.Iss.	1990	25.00	55
1990	Holiday Flash QLX7333	Yr.Iss.	1990	18.00	25-40
1990	Hop 'N Pop Popper QLX7353	Yr.Iss.	1990	20.00	87-95
1990	Letter to Santa QLX7226	Yr.Iss.	1990	14.00	28-40
1990	The Littlest Angel QLX7303	Yr.Iss.	1990	14.00	30-50
1990	Mrs. Santa's Kitchen QLX7263	Yr.Iss.	1990	25.00	51-85
1990	Our First Christmas Together QLX7255	Yr.Iss.	1990	18.00	30-50
1990	Partridges in a Pear QLX7212	Yr.Iss.	1990	14.00	27-35
1990	Santa's Ho-Ho-Hoedown QLX7256	Yr.Iss.	1990	25.00	90
1990	Song and Dance QLX7253	Yr.Iss.	1990	20.00	60-95
1990	Starlight Angel QLX7306	Yr.Iss.	1990	14.00	27-37
1990	Starship Christmas QLX7336	Yr.Iss.	1990	18.00	35-55

1990 Keepsake Miniature Ornaments - Keepsake

1990	Acorn Wreath QXM5686	Yr.Iss.	1990	6.00	10
1990	Air Santa QXM5656	Yr.Iss.	1990	4.50	10
1990	Baby's First Christmas QXM5703	Yr.Iss.	1990	8.50	17
1990	Basket Buddy QXM5696	Yr.Iss.	1990	6.00	10
1990	Bear Hug QXM5633	Yr.Iss.	1990	6.00	12
1990	Brass Bouquet 600QMX5776	Yr.Iss.	1990	6.00	6
1990	Brass Horn QXM5793	Yr.Iss.	1990	3.00	8
1990	Brass Peace QXM5796	Yr.Iss.	1990	3.00	8
1990	Brass Santa QXM5786	Yr.Iss.	1990	3.00	7
1990	Brass Year QXM5833	Yr.Iss.	1990	3.00	8
1990	Busy Carver QXM5673	Yr.Iss.	1990	4.50	9
1990	Christmas Dove QXM5636	Yr.Iss.	1990	4.50	12
1990	Cloisonne Poinsettia QMX5533	Yr.Iss.	1990	10.75	23
1990	Coal Car QXM5756	Yr.Iss.	1990	8.50	23-30
1990	Country Heart QXM5693	Yr.Iss.	1990	4.50	9
1990	First Christmas Together QXM5536	Yr.Iss.	1990	6.00	12
1990	Going Sledding QXM5683	Yr.Iss.	1990	4.50	12
1990	Grandchild's First Christmas QXM5723	Yr.Iss.	1990	6.00	11
1990	Holiday Cardinal QXM5526	Yr.Iss.	1990	3.00	10
1990	Kittens in Toyland QXM5736	Yr.Iss.	1990	4.50	23-30
1990	The Kringles QXM5753	Yr.Iss.	1990	6.00	22
1990	Lion and Lamb QXM5676	Yr.Iss.	1990	4.50	8
1990	Loving Hearts QXM5523	Yr.Iss.	1990	3.00	8
1990	Madonna and Child QXM5643	Yr.Iss.	1990	6.00	10
1990	Mother QXM5716	Yr.Iss.	1990	4.50	12-20
1990	Nativity QXM5706	Yr.Iss.	1990	4.50	15
1990	Nature's Angels QMX5733	Yr.Iss.	1990	4.50	20-27
1990	Panda's Surprise QXM5616	Yr.Iss.	1990	4.50	12
1990	Penguin Pal QXM5746	Yr.Iss.	1990	4.50	13-20
1990	Perfect Fit QXM5516	Yr.Iss.	1990	4.50	9
1990	Puppy Love QXM5666	Yr.Iss.	1990	6.00	11
1990	Rocking Horse QXM5743	Yr.Iss.	1990	4.50	18-25
1990	Ruby Reindeer QXM5816	Yr.Iss.	1990	6.00	11
1990	Santa's Journey QXM5826	Yr.Iss.	1990	8.50	19
1990	Santa's Streetcar QXM5766	Yr.Iss.	1990	8.50	13-19
1990	School QXM5763	Yr.Iss.	1990	8.50	16-25
1990	Snow Angel QXM5773	Yr.Iss.	1990	6.00	12
1990	Special Friends QXM5726	Yr.Iss.	1990	6.00	12
1990	Stamp Collector QXM5623	Yr.Iss.	1990	4.50	9
1990	Stringing Along QXM5606	Yr.Iss.	1990	8.50	16
1990	Sweet Slumber QXM5663	Yr.Iss.	1990	4.50	10
1990	Teacher QXM5653	Yr.Iss.	1990	4.50	8
1990	Thimble Bells QXM5543	Yr.Iss.	1990	6.00	19-27
1990	Type of Joy QXM5646	Yr.Iss.	1990	4.50	8
1990	Warm Memories QXM5713	Yr.Iss.	1990	4.50	10
1990	Wee Nutcracker QXM5843	Yr.Iss.	1990	8.50	15

1990 New Attractions - Keepsake

1990	Baby Unicorn QX5486	Yr.Iss.	1990	9.75	10-25
1990	Bearback Rider QX5483	Yr.Iss.	1990	9.75	30
1990	Beary Good Deal QX4733	Yr.Iss.	1990	6.75	12
1990	Billboard Bunny QX5196	Yr.Iss.	1990	7.75	13-23
1990	Born to Dance QX5043	Yr.Iss.	1990	7.75	15-25
1990	Chiming In QX4366	Yr.Iss.	1990	9.75	20-25
1990	Christmas Croc QX4373	Yr.Iss.	1990	7.75	13-25
1990	Christmas Partridge QX5246	Yr.Iss.	1990	7.75	15-23
1990	Claus Construction QX4885	Yr.Iss.	1990	7.75	15-20
1990	Country Angel QX5046	Yr.Iss.	1990	6.75	175-195
1990	Coyote Carols QX4993	Yr.Iss.	1990	8.75	17-30
1990	Cozy Goose QX4966	Yr.Iss.	1990	5.75	14
1990	Feliz Navidad QX5173	Yr.Iss.	1990	6.75	17-30
1990	Garfield QX2303	Yr.Iss.	1990	4.75	10-25
1990	Gingerbread Elf QX5033	Yr.Iss.	1990	5.75	17
1990	Goose Cart QX5236	Yr.Iss.	1990	7.75	14
1990	Hang in There QX4713	Yr.Iss.	1990	6.75	15-22
1990	Happy Voices QX4645	Yr.Iss.	1990	6.75	14
1990	Holiday Cardinals QX5243	Yr.Iss.	1990	7.75	14-23
1990	Home for the Owlidays QX5183	Yr.Iss.	1990	6.75	15
1990	Hot Dogger QX4976	Yr.Iss.	1990	7.75	16
1990	Jolly Dolphin QX4683	Yr.Iss.	1990	6.75	20-35
1990	Joy is in the Air QX5503	Yr.Iss.	1990	7.75	20-25
1990	King Klaus QX4106	Yr.Iss.	1990	7.75	12-22
1990	Kitty's Best Pal QX4716	Yr.Iss.	1990	6.75	15-25
1990	Little Drummer Boy QX5233	Yr.Iss.	1990	7.75	20
1990	Long Winter's Nap QX4703	Yr.Iss.	1990	6.75	15-25
1990	Lovable Dears QX5476	Yr.Iss.	1990	8.75	15
1990	Meow Mart QX4446	Yr.Iss.	1990	7.75	16-30
1990	Mooy Christmas QX4933	Yr.Iss.	1990	6.75	27
1990	Norman Rockwell Art QX2296	Yr.Iss.	1990	4.75	23
1990	Nutshell Chat QX5193	Yr.Iss.	1990	6.75	14-25
1990	Nutshell Holiday QX465-2	Yr.Iss.	1990	5.75	17-28
1990	Peanuts QX2233	Yr.Iss.	1990	4.75	15-30
1990	Pepperoni Mouse QX4973	Yr.Iss.	1990	6.75	14-23
1990	Perfect Catch QX4693	Yr.Iss.	1990	7.75	12-19
1990	Polar Jogger QX4666	Yr.Iss.	1990	5.75	9-20
1990	Polar Pair QX4626	Yr.Iss.	1990	5.75	15-30
1990	Polar Sport QX5156	Yr.Iss.	1990	7.75	12-24
1990	Polar TV QX5166	Yr.Iss.	1990	7.75	12-20
1990	Polar V.I.P. QX4663	Yr.Iss.	1990	5.75	12-20
1990	Polar Video QX4633	Yr.Iss.	1990	5.75	10-20
1990	Poolside Walrus QX4986	Yr.Iss.	1990	7.75	13-25
1990	S. Claus Taxi QX4686	Yr.Iss.	1990	11.75	25-35
1990	Santa Schnoz QX4983	Yr.Iss.	1990	6.75	32
1990	Snoopy and Woodstock QX4723	Yr.Iss.	1990	6.75	40
1990	Spoon Rider QX5496	Yr.Iss.	1990	9.75	15
1990	Stitches of Joy QX5186	Yr.Iss.	1990	7.75	16-30
1990	Stocking Kitten QX456-5	Yr.Iss.	1990	6.75	7
1990	Stocking Pals QX5493	Yr.Iss.	1990	10.75	19-25
1990	Three Little Piggies QX4996	Yr.Iss.	1990	7.75	15-30
1990	Two Peas in a Pod QX4926	Yr.Iss.	1990	4.75	25-32

1990 Special Edition - Keepsake

1990	Dickens Caroler Bell-Mr. Ashbourne QX5056	Yr.Iss.	1990	21.75	41-55

1991 Artists' Favorites - Keepsake

1991	Fiddlin' Around QX4387	Yr.Iss.	1991	7.75	17
1991	Hooked on Santa QX4109	Yr.Iss.	1991	7.75	21
1991	Noah's Ark QX4867	Yr.Iss.	1991	13.75	41-50
1991	Polar Circus Wagon QX4399	Yr.Iss.	1991	13.75	27
1991	Santa Sailor QX4389	Yr.Iss.	1991	9.75	18-27
1991	Tramp and Laddie QX4397	Yr.Iss.	1991	7.75	20-40

1991 Club Limited Editions - Keepsake

1991	Galloping Into Christmas QXC4779	28,400	1991	19.75	100-125
1991	Secrets for Santa QXC4797	28,700	1991	23.75	48

1991 Collectible Series - Keepsake

1991	1957 Corvette (1st Ed.) QX4319	Yr.Iss.	1991	12.75	200
1991	Betsey Clark: Home for Christmas (6th Ed.) QX2109	Yr.Iss.	1991	5.00	19-29
1991	Checking His List (6th Ed.) QX4339	Yr.Iss.	1991	13.75	28-49

*Quotes have been rounded up to nearest dollar

Collectors' Information Bureau

163

YEAR ISSUE		EDITION LIMIT	YEAR RETD.	ISSUE PRICE	*QUOTE U.S. $
1991	Christmas Kitty (3rd Ed.) QX4377	Yr.Iss.	1991	14.75	26-32
1991	CRAYOLA CRAYON-Bright Vibrant Carols (3rd Ed.) QX4219	Yr.Iss.	1991	9.75	27-40
1991	Eight Maids A-Milking (8th Ed.) QX3089	Yr.Iss.	1991	6.75	19-29
1991	Fabulous Decade (2nd Ed.) QX4119	Yr.Iss.	1991	7.75	25-40
1991	Fire Station (8th Ed.) QX4139	Yr.Iss.	1991	14.75	42-70
1991	Frosty Friends (12th Ed.) QX4327	Yr.Iss.	1991	9.75	28-42
1991	The Gift Bringers-Christkind (3rd Ed.) QX2117	Yr.Iss.	1991	5.00	20
1991	Greatest Story (2nd Ed.) QX4129	Yr.Iss.	1991	12.75	24-30
1991	Hark! It's Herald (3rd Ed.) QX4379	Yr.Iss.	1991	6.75	19-29
1991	Heart of Christmas (2nd Ed.) QX4357	Yr.Iss.	1991	13.75	27-35
1991	Heavenly Angels (1st Ed.) QX4367	Yr.Iss.	1991	7.75	30-38
1991	Let It Snow! (5th Ed.) QX4369	Yr.Iss.	1991	8.75	19-29
1991	Mary's Angels-Iris (4th Ed.) QX4279	Yr.Iss.	1991	6.75	25-40
1991	Merry Olde Santa (2nd Ed.) QX4359	Yr.Iss.	1991	14.75	60-82
1991	Peace on Earth-Italy (1st Ed.) QX5129	Yr.Iss.	1991	11.75	28
1991	Puppy Love (1st Ed.) QX5379	Yr.Iss.	1991	7.75	45-57
1991	Reindeer Champ-Cupid (6th Ed.) QX4347	Yr.Iss.	1991	7.75	19-29
1991	Rocking Horse (11th Ed.) QX4147	Yr.Iss.	1991	10.75	27-42
1991	Santa's Antique Car (13th Ed.) QX4349	Yr.Iss.	1991	14.75	32-60
1991	Winter Surprise (3rd Ed.) QX4277	Yr.Iss.	1991	10.75	27-35

1991 Commemoratives - Keepsake

1991	Across the Miles QX3157	Yr.Iss.	1991	6.75	13
1991	Baby's First Christmas QX4889	Yr.Iss.	1991	7.75	28-35
1991	Baby's First Christmas QX5107	Yr.Iss.	1991	17.75	32-42
1991	Baby's First Christmas-Baby Boy QX2217	Yr.Iss.	1991	4.75	18
1991	Baby's First Christmas-Baby Girl QX2227	Yr.Iss.	1991	4.75	18
1991	Baby's First Christmas-Photo Holder QX4869	Yr.Iss.	1991	7.75	21-30
1991	Baby's Second Christmas QX4897	Yr.Iss.	1991	6.75	25-35
1991	The Big Cheese QX5327	Yr.Iss.	1991	6.75	18
1991	Brother QX5479	Yr.Iss.	1991	6.75	18
1991	A Child's Christmas QX4887	Yr.Iss.	1991	9.75	17
1991	Child's Fifth Christmas QX4909	Yr.Iss.	1991	6.75	15-30
1991	Child's Fourth Christmas QX4907	Yr.Iss.	1991	6.75	16-30
1991	Child's Third Christmas QX4899	Yr.Iss.	1991	6.75	21-30
1991	Dad QX5127	Yr.Iss.	1991	7.75	19
1991	Dad-to-Be QX4879	Yr.Iss.	1991	5.75	15
1991	Daughter QX5477	Yr.Iss.	1991	5.75	23-40
1991	Extra-Special Friends QX2279	Yr.Iss.	1991	4.75	15
1991	Fifty Years Together QX4947	Yr.Iss.	1991	8.75	18
1991	Five Years Together QX4927	Yr.Iss.	1991	7.75	18
1991	Forty Years Together QX4939	Yr.Iss.	1991	7.75	18
1991	Friends Are Fun QX5289	Yr.Iss.	1991	9.75	17-23
1991	From Our Home to Yours QX2287	Yr.Iss.	1991	4.75	14-23
1991	Gift of Joy QX5319	Yr.Iss.	1991	8.75	18-25
1991	Godchild QX5489	Yr.Iss.	1991	6.75	18
1991	Granddaughter QX2299	Yr.Iss.	1991	4.75	26
1991	Granddaughter's First Christmas QX5119	Yr.Iss.	1991	6.75	14-24
1991	Grandmother QX2307	Yr.Iss.	1991	4.75	19-25
1991	Grandparents QX2309	Yr.Iss.	1991	4.75	15
1991	Grandson QX2297	Yr.Iss.	1991	4.75	18-25
1991	Grandson's First Christmas QX5117	Yr.Iss.	1991	6.75	13-26
1991	Jesus Loves Me QX3147	Yr.Iss.	1991	7.75	14-28
1991	Mom and Dad QX5467	Yr.Iss.	1991	9.75	22
1991	Mom-to-Be QX4877	Yr.Iss.	1991	5.75	17-26
1991	Mother QX5457	Yr.Iss.	1991	9.75	33
1991	New Home QX5449	Yr.Iss.	1991	6.75	19-29
1991	Our First Christmas Together QX2229	Yr.Iss.	1991	4.75	14-25
1991	Our First Christmas Together QX3139	Yr.Iss.	1991	6.75	22
1991	Our First Christmas Together QX4919	Yr.Iss.	1991	8.75	17-35
1991	Our First Christmas Together-Photo Holder QX4917	Yr.Iss.	1991	8.75	25-30
1991	Sister QX5487	Yr.Iss.	1991	6.75	18
1991	Son QX5469	Yr.Iss.	1991	5.75	17
1991	Sweetheart QX4957	Yr.Iss.	1991	9.75	17-25
1991	Teacher QX2289	Yr.Iss.	1991	4.75	12
1991	Ten Years Together QX4929	Yr.Iss.	1991	7.75	17
1991	Terrific Teacher QX5309	Yr.Iss.	1991	6.75	16
1991	Twenty -Five Years Together QX4937	Yr.Iss.	1991	8.75	17
1991	Under the Mistletoe QX4949	Yr.Iss.	1991	8.75	19

1991 Keepsake Collector's Club - Keepsake

1991	Beary Artistic QXC7259	Yr.Iss.	1991	10.00	32-40
1991	Hidden Treasure/Li'l Keeper QXC4769	Yr.Iss.	1991	15.00	38

1991 Keepsake Magic Ornaments - Keepsake

1991	Angel of Light QLT7239	Yr.Iss.	1991	30.00	60
1991	Arctic Dome QLX7117	Yr.Iss.	1991	25.00	45-55
1991	Baby's First Christmas QLX7247	Yr.Iss.	1991	30.00	65-90
1991	Bringing Home the Tree QLX7249	Yr.Iss.	1991	28.00	51-65
1991	Chris Mouse Mail QLX7207	Yr.Iss.	1991	10.00	25-40
1991	Elfin Engineer QLX7209	Yr.Iss.	1991	10.00	23
1991	Father Christmas QLX7147	Yr.Iss.	1991	14.00	29-39
1991	Festive Brass Church QLX7179	Yr.Iss.	1991	14.00	21-32
1991	Forest Frolics QLX7219	Yr.Iss.	1991	25.00	68
1991	Friendship Tree QLX7169	Yr.Iss.	1991	10.00	24
1991	Holiday Glow QLX7177	Yr.Iss.	1991	14.00	23-30
1991	It's A Wonderful Life QLX7237	Yr.Iss.	1991	20.00	60-75
1991	Jingle Bears QLX7323	Yr.Iss.	1991	25.00	45-57
1991	Kringles's Bumper Cars QLX7119	Yr.Iss.	1991	25.00	47-55
1991	Mole Family Home QLX7149	Yr.Iss.	1991	20.00	37-49
1991	Our First Christmas Together QXL7137	Yr.Iss.	1991	25.00	50-60
1991	PEANUTS QLX7229	Yr.Iss.	1991	18.00	65-75
1991	Salvation Army Band QLX7273	Yr.Iss.	1991	30.00	56-80
1991	Santa Special QLX7167	Yr.Iss.	1992	40.00	54-80
1991	Santa's Hot Line QLX7159	Yr.Iss.	1991	18.00	32-42
1991	Ski Trip QLX7266	Yr.Iss.	1991	28.00	50-60
1991	Sparkling Angel QLX7157	Yr.Iss.	1991	18.00	27-37
1991	Toyland Tower QLX7129	Yr.Iss.	1991	20.00	37-45

1991 Keepsake Miniature Ornaments - Keepsake

1991	All Aboard QXM5869	Yr.Iss.	1991	4.50	17
1991	Baby's First Christmas QXM5799	Yr.Iss.	1991	6.00	20
1991	Brass Church QXM5979	Yr.Iss.	1991	3.00	9
1991	Brass Soldier QXM5987	Yr.Iss.	1991	3.00	9
1991	Bright Boxers QXM5877	Yr.Iss.	1991	4.50	16
1991	Busy Bear QXM5939	Yr.Iss.	1991	4.50	12
1991	Cardinal Cameo QXM5957	Yr.Iss.	1991	6.00	17
1991	Caring Shepherd QXM5949	Yr.Iss.	1991	6.00	17
1991	Cool 'n' Sweet QXM5867	Yr.Iss.	1991	4.50	22
1991	Country Sleigh QXM5999	Yr.Iss.	1991	4.50	13
1991	Courier Turtle QXM5857	Yr.Iss.	1991	4.50	14
1991	Fancy Wreath QXM5917	Yr.Iss.	1991	4.50	13
1991	Feliz Navidad QXM5887	Yr.Iss.	1991	6.00	15
1991	Fly By QXM5859	Yr.Iss.	1991	4.50	17
1991	Friendly Fawn QXM5947	Yr.Iss.	1991	6.00	17
1991	Grandchild's First Christmas QXM5697	Yr.Iss.	1991	4.50	14
1991	Heavenly Minstrel QXM5687	Yr.Iss.	1991	9.75	21-30
1991	Holiday Snowflake QXM5997	Yr.Iss.	1991	3.00	12
1991	Inn (4th Ed.) QXM5627	Yr.Iss.	1991	8.50	21-30
1991	Key to Love QXM5689	Yr.Iss.	1991	4.50	16
1991	Kittens in Toyland (4th Ed.) QXM5639	Yr.Iss.	1991	4.50	17
1991	Kitty in a Mitty QXM5879	Yr.Iss.	1991	4.50	13
1991	The Kringles (3rd Ed.) QXM5647	Yr.Iss.	1991	6.00	21
1991	Li'l Popper QXM5897	Yr.Iss.	1991	4.50	16
1991	Love Is Born QXM5959	Yr.Iss.	1991	6.00	18
1991	Lulu & Family QXM5677	Yr.Iss.	1991	6.00	19
1991	Mom QXM5699	Yr.Iss.	1991	6.00	17
1991	N. Pole Buddy QXM5927	Yr.Iss.	1991	4.50	18
1991	Nature's Angels (2nd Ed.) QXM5657	Yr.Iss.	1991	4.50	20
1991	Noel QXM5989	Yr.Iss.	1991	3.00	12
1991	Our First Christmas Together QXM5819	Yr.Iss.	1991	6.00	17
1991	Passenger Car (3rd Ed.) QXM5649	Yr.Iss.	1991	8.50	25-42
1991	Penquin Pal (4th Ed.) QXM5629	Yr.Iss.	1991	4.50	17
1991	Ring-A-Ding Elf QXM5669	Yr.Iss.	1991	8.50	18
1991	Rocking Horse (4th Ed.) QXM5637	Yr.Iss.	1991	4.50	21-30
1991	Seaside Otter QXM5909	Yr.Iss.	1991	4.50	13
1991	Silvery Santa QXM5679	Yr.Iss.	1991	9.75	22
1991	Special Friends QXM5797	Yr.Iss.	1991	8.50	18
1991	Thimble Bells (2nd Ed.) QXM5659	Yr.Iss.	1991	6.00	18-25
1991	Tiny Tea Party (set/6) QXM5827	Yr.Iss.	1991	29.00	143-175
1991	Top Hatter QXM5889	Yr.Iss.	1991	6.00	16
1991	Treeland Trio QXM5899	Yr.Iss.	1991	8.50	17
1991	Upbeat Bear QXM5907	Yr.Iss.	1991	6.00	17
1991	Vision of Santa QXM5937	Yr.Iss.	1991	4.50	14
1991	Wee Toymaker QXM5967	Yr.Iss.	1991	8.50	15
1991	Woodland Babies QXM5667	Yr.Iss.	1991	6.00	22

1991 New Attractions - Keepsake

1991	All-Star QX5329	Yr.Iss.	1991	6.75	20
1991	Basket Bell Players QX5377	Yr.Iss.	1991	7.75	25
1991	Bob Cratchit QX4997	Yr.Iss.	1991	13.75	22-35
1991	Chilly Chap QX5339	Yr.Iss.	1991	6.75	18
1991	Christmas Welcome QX5299	Yr.Iss.	1991	9.75	22
1991	Christopher Robin QX5579	Yr.Iss.	1991	9.75	35-40
1991	Cuddly Lamb QX5199	Yr.Iss.	1991	6.75	20
1991	Dinoclaus QX5277	Yr.Iss.	1991	7.75	16-23
1991	Ebenezer Scrooge QX4989	Yr.Iss.	1991	13.75	27-45
1991	Evergreen Inn QX5389	Yr.Iss.	1991	8.75	15
1991	Fanfare Bear QX5337	Yr.Iss.	1991	8.75	19
1991	Feliz Navidad QX5279	Yr.Iss.	1991	6.75	14-25
1991	Folk Art Reindeer QX5359	Yr.Iss.	1991	8.75	17
1991	GARFIELD QX5177	Yr.Iss.	1991	7.75	20-30
1991	Glee Club Bears QX4969	Yr.Iss.	1991	8.75	18
1991	Holiday Cafe QX5399	Yr.Iss.	1991	8.75	14
1991	Jolly Wolly Santa QX5419	Yr.Iss.	1991	7.75	22-30
1991	Jolly Wolly Snowman QX5427	Yr.Iss.	1991	7.75	21
1991	Jolly Wolly Soldier QX5429`	Yr.Iss.	1991	7.75	20
1991	Joyous Memories-Photoholder QX5369	Yr.Iss.	1991	6.75	16-27
1991	Kanga and Roo QX5617	Yr.Iss.	1991	9.75	45
1991	Look Out Below QX4959	Yr.Iss.	1991	8.75	18
1991	Loving Stitches QX4987	Yr.Iss.	1991	8.75	30
1991	Mary Engelbreit QX2237	Yr.Iss.	1991	4.75	28
1991	Merry Carolers QX4799	Yr.Iss.	1991	29.75	95
1991	Mrs. Cratchit QX4999	Yr.Iss.	1991	13.75	30
1991	Night Before Christmas QX5307	Yr.Iss.	1991	9.75	22
1991	Norman Rockwell Art QX2259	Yr.Iss.	1991	5.00	20-30
1991	Notes of Cheer QX5357	Yr.Iss.	1991	5.75	14
1991	Nutshell Nativity QX5176	Yr.Iss.	1991	6.75	18-25
1991	Nutty Squirrel QX4833	Yr.Iss.	1991	5.75	14
1991	Old-Fashioned Sled QX4317	Yr.Iss.	1991	8.75	18
1991	On a Roll QX5347	Yr.Iss.	1991	6.75	19
1991	Partridge in a Pear Tree QX5297	Yr.Iss.	1991	9.75	18
1991	PEANUTS QX2257	Yr.Iss.	1991	5.00	15-30
1991	Piglet and Eeyore QX5577	Yr.Iss.	1991	9.75	40-50
1991	Plum Delightful QX4977	Yr.Iss.	1991	8.75	19
1991	Polar Classic QX5287	Yr.Iss.	1991	6.75	16-22
1991	Rabbit QX5607	Yr.Iss.	1991	9.75	30
1991	Santa's Studio QX5397	Yr.Iss.	1991	8.75	16
1991	Ski Lift Bunny QX5447	Yr.Iss.	1991	6.75	17
1991	Snoopy and Woodstock QX5197	Yr.Iss.	1991	6.75	39
1991	Snow Twins QX4979	Yr.Iss.	1991	8.75	20
1991	Snowy Owl QX5269	Yr.Iss.	1991	7.75	18
1991	Sweet Talk QX5367	Yr.Iss.	1991	8.75	20
1991	Tigger QX5609	Yr.Iss.	1991	9.75	95-105
1991	Tiny Tim QX5037	Yr.Iss.	1991	10.75	23-40
1991	Up 'N'Down Journey QX5047	Yr.Iss.	1991	9.75	21-28
1991	Winnie-the Pooh QX5569	Yr.Iss.	1991	9.75	55
1991	Yule Logger QX4967	Yr.Iss.	1991	8.75	17-27

1991 Special Edition - Keepsake

1991	Dickens Caroler Bell-Mrs. Beaumont QX5039	Yr.Iss.	1991	21.75	40-50
1991	Starship Enterprise QLX7199	Yr.Iss.	1991	20.00	325-375

1992 Artists' Favorites - Keepsake

1992	Elfin Marionette QX5931	Yr.Iss.	1992	11.75	23
1992	Mother Goose QX4984	Yr.Iss.	1992	13.75	26-35
1992	Polar Post QX4914	Yr.Iss.	1992	8.75	18
1992	Stocked With Joy QX5934	Yr.Iss.	1992	7.75	16-23
1992	Turtle Dreams QX4991	Yr.Iss.	1992	8.75	20-28
1992	Uncle Art's Ice Cream QX5001	Yr.Iss.	1992	8.75	22-30

1992 Collectible Series - Keepsake

1992	1966 Mustang (2nd Ed.) QX4284	Yr.Iss.	1992	12.75	47
1992	Betsey's Country Christmas (1st Ed.) QX2104	Yr.Iss.	1992	5.00	23-30
1992	CRAYOLA CRAYON-Bright Colors (4th Ed.) QX4264	Yr.Iss.	1992	9.75	31-38
1992	Fabulous Decade (3rd Ed.) QX4244	Yr.Iss.	1992	7.75	33-40
1992	Five-and-Ten-Cent Store (9th Ed.) QX4254	Yr.Iss.	1992	14.75	27-45
1992	Frosty Friends (13th Ed.) QX4291	Yr.Iss.	1992	9.75	22-32
1992	The Gift Bringers-Kolyada (4th Ed.) QX2124	Yr.Iss.	1992	5.00	14-22
1992	Gift Exchange (7th Ed.) QX4294	Yr.Iss.	1992	14.75	30-43
1992	Greatest Story (3rd Ed.) QX4251	Yr.Iss.	1992	12.75	18-25
1992	Hark! It's Herald (4th Ed.) QX4464	Yr.Iss.	1992	7.75	18-25
1992	Heart of Christmas (3rd Ed.) QX4411	Yr.Iss.	1992	13.75	30
1992	Heavenly Angels (2nd Ed.) QX4454	Yr.Iss.	1992	7.75	18-30
1992	Kringle Tours (14th Ed.) QX4341	Yr.Iss.	1992	14.75	26-45
1992	Mary's Angels-Lily (5th Ed.) QX4274	Yr.Iss.	1992	6.75	49
1992	Merry Olde Santa (3rd Ed.) QX4414	Yr.Iss.	1992	14.75	37
1992	Nine Ladies Dancing (9th Ed.) QX3031	Yr.Iss.	1992	6.75	18-25
1992	Owliver (1st Ed.) QX4544	Yr.Iss.	1992	7.75	19
1992	Peace On Earth-Spain (2nd Ed.) QX5174	Yr.Iss.	1992	11.75	22
1992	Puppy Love (2nd Ed.) QX4484	Yr.Iss.	1992	7.75	30-42
1992	Reindeer Champs-Donder (7th Ed.) QX5284	Yr.Iss.	1992	8.75	26-35
1992	Rocking Horse (12th Ed.) QX4261	Yr.Iss.	1992	10.75	25-40
1992	Sweet Holiday Harmony (6th Ed.) QX4461	Yr.Iss.	1992	8.75	19-35
1992	Tobin Fraley Carousel (1st Ed.) QX4891	Yr.Iss.	1992	28.00	62-75
1992	Winter Surprise (4th Ed.) QX4271	Yr.Iss.	1992	11.75	30

1992 Collectors' Club - Keepsake

1992	Chipmunk Parcel Service QXC5194	Yr.Iss.	1992	6.75	21
1992	Rodney Takes Flight QXC5081	Yr.Iss.	1992	9.75	22
1992	Santa's Club List QXC7291	Yr.Iss.	1992	15.00	37

1992 Commemoratives - Keepsake

1992	Across the Miles QX3044	Yr.Iss.	1992	6.75	14
1992	Anniversary Year QX4851	Yr.Iss.	1992	9.75	17-26
1992	Baby's First Christmas QX4641	Yr.Iss.	1992	7.75	17-30
1992	Baby's First Christmas QX4644	Yr.Iss.	1992	7.75	24-35
1992	Baby's First Christmas-Baby Boy QX2191	Yr.Iss.	1992	4.75	13-20
1992	Baby's First Christmas-Baby Girl QX2204	Yr.Iss.	1992	4.75	12-20
1992	Baby's First ChristmasQX4581	Yr.Iss.	1992	18.75	38
1992	Baby's Second Christmas QX4651	Yr.Iss.	1992	6.75	20-45
1992	Brother QX4684	Yr.Iss.	1992	6.75	15
1992	A Child's Christmas QX4574	Yr.Iss.	1992	9.75	18
1992	Child's Fifth Christmas QX4664	Yr.Iss.	1992	6.75	15-25
1992	Child's Fourth Christmas QX4661	Yr.Iss.	1992	6.75	20-25
1992	Child's Third Christmas QX4654	Yr.Iss.	1992	6.75	20-30
1992	Dad QX4674	Yr.Iss.	1992	7.75	20
1992	Dad-to-Be QX4611	Yr.Iss.	1992	6.75	17
1992	Daughter QX5031	Yr.Iss.	1992	6.75	20-30
1992	For My Grandma QX5184	Yr.Iss.	1992	7.75	15
1992	For The One I Love QX4884	Yr.Iss.	1992	9.75	20
1992	Friendly Greetings QX5041	Yr.Iss.	1992	7.75	14
1992	Friendship Line QX5034	Yr.Iss.	1992	9.75	27
1992	From Our Home To Yours QX2131	Yr.Iss.	1992	4.75	15
1992	Godchild QX5941	Yr.Iss.	1992	6.75	18
1992	Grandaughter QX5604	Yr.Iss.	1992	6.75	17

*Quotes have been rounded up to nearest dollar

YEAR ISSUE		EDITION LIMIT	YEAR RETD.	ISSUE PRICE	*QUOTE U.S.$
1992	Granddaughter's First Christmas QX4634	Yr.Iss.	1992	6.75	15
1992	Grandmother QX2011	Yr.Iss.	1992	4.75	15
1992	Grandparents QX2004	Yr.Iss.	1992	4.75	18
1992	Grandson QX5611	Yr.Iss.	1992	6.75	16
1992	Grandson's First Christmas QX4621	Yr.Iss.	1992	6.75	18
1992	Holiday Memo QX5044	Yr.Iss.	1992	7.75	14
1992	Love To Skate QX4841	Yr.Iss.	1992	8.75	17
1992	Mom and Dad QX4671	Yr.Iss.	1992	9.75	35
1992	Mom QX5164	Yr.Iss.	1992	7.75	18
1992	Mom-to-Be QX4614	Yr.Iss.	1992	6.75	16-30
1992	New Home QX5191	Yr.Iss.	1992	8.75	19-30
1992	Our First Christmas Together QX4694	Yr.Iss.	1992	8.75	25
1992	Our First Christmas Together QX3011	Yr.Iss.	1992	6.75	17
1992	Our First Christmas Together QX5061	Yr.Iss.	1992	9.75	18-35
1992	Secret Pal QX5424	Yr.Iss.	1992	7.75	14
1992	Sister QX4681	Yr.Iss.	1992	6.75	15
1992	Son QX5024	Yr.Iss.	1992	6.75	17-30
1992	Special Cat QX5414	Yr.Iss.	1992	7.75	16
1992	Special Dog QX5421	Yr.Iss.	1992	7.75	27
1992	Teacher QX2264	Yr.Iss.	1992	4.75	17
1992	V. P. of Important Stuff QX5051	Yr.Iss.	1992	6.75	14
1992	World-Class Teacher QX5054	Yr.Iss.	1992	7.75	20

1992 Easter Ornaments - Keepsake

1992	Easter Parade (1st Ed.) 675QEO8301	Yr.Iss.	1992	6.75	20-30
1992	Egg in Sports (1st Ed.) 675QEO9341	Yr.Iss.	1992	6.75	20-35

1992 Limited Edition Ornaments - Keepsake

1992	Christmas Treasures QXC5464	15,500	1992	22.00	123
1992	Victorian Skater (w/ base) QXC4067	14,700	1992	25.00	75

1992 Magic Ornaments - Keepsake

1992	Angel Of Light QLT7239	Yr.Iss.	1992	30.00	30
1992	Baby's First Christmas QLX7281	Yr.Iss.	1992	22.00	90
1992	Chris Mouse Tales (8th Ed.) QLX7074	Yr.Iss.	1992	12.00	27
1992	Christmas Parade QLX7271	Yr.Iss.	1992	30.00	55
1992	Continental Express QLX7264	Yr.Iss.	1992	32.00	60
1992	The Dancing Nutcracker QLX7261	Yr.Iss.	1992	30.00	54-60
1992	Enchanted Clock QLX7274	Yr.Iss.	1992	30.00	53-60
1992	Feathered Friends QLX7091	Yr.Iss.	1992	14.00	29
1992	Forest Frolics (4th Ed.) QLX7254	Yr.Iss.	1992	28.00	52-65
[illegible]	Good Sledding Ahead QLX72[illegible]	Yr.Iss.	[illegible]	[illegible]	[illegible]
1992	Lighting the Way QLX7231	Yr.Iss.	1992	18.00	39-49
1992	Look! It's Santa QLX7094	Yr.Iss.	1992	14.00	30-50
1992	Nut Sweet Nut QLX7081	Yr.Iss.	1992	10.00	22
1992	Out First Christmas Together QLX7221	Yr.Iss.	1992	20.00	40-45
1992	PEANUTS (2nd Ed.) QLX7214	Yr.Iss.	1992	18.00	45-60
1992	Santa Special QLX7167	Yr.Iss.	1992	40.00	80
1992	Santa Sub QLX7321	Yr.Iss.	1992	18.00	34-40
1992	Santa's Answering Machine QLX7241	Yr.Iss.	1992	22.00	45
1992	Under Construction QLX7324	Yr.Iss.	1992	18.00	35-42
1992	Watch Owls QLX7084	Yr.Iss.	1992	12.00	24-30
1992	Yuletide Rider QLX7314	Yr.Iss.	1992	28.00	52-60

1992 Miniature Ornaments - Keepsake

1992	A+ Teacher QXM5511	Yr.Iss.	1992	3.75	8
1992	Angelic Harpist QXM5524	Yr.Iss.	1992	4.50	13
1992	Baby's First Christmas QXM5494	Yr.Iss.	1992	4.50	18
1992	The Bearymores(1st Ed.) QXM5544	Yr.Iss.	1992	5.75	19
1992	Black-Capped Chickadee QXM5484	Yr.Iss.	1992	3.00	15
1992	Box Car (4th Ed.) Noel R.R. QXM5441	Yr.Iss.	1992	7.00	22
1992	Bright Stringers QXM5841	Yr.Iss.	1992	3.75	14
1992	Buck-A-Roo QXM5814	Yr.Iss.	1992	4.50	12
1992	Christmas Bonus QXM5811	Yr.Iss.	1992	3.00	8
1992	Christmas Copter QXM5844	Yr.Iss.	1992	5.75	5
1992	Church (5th Ed.) Old English V. QXM5384	Yr.Iss.	1992	7.00	25
1992	Coca-Cola Santa QXM5884	Yr.Iss.	1992	5.75	16
1992	Cool Uncle Sam QXM5561	Yr.Iss.	1992	3.00	15
1992	Cozy Kayak QXM5551	Yr.Iss.	1992	3.75	12
1992	Fast Finish QXM5301	Yr.Iss.	1992	3.75	12
1992	Feeding Time QXM5481	Yr.Iss.	1992	5.75	15
1992	Friendly Tin Soldier QXM5874	Yr.Iss.	1992	4.50	15
1992	Friends Are Tops QXM5521	Yr.Iss.	1992	4.50	10
1992	Gerbil Inc. QXM5924	Yr.Iss.	1992	3.75	11
1992	Going Places QXM5871	Yr.Iss.	1992	3.75	10
1992	Grandchild's First Christmas QXM5501	Yr.Iss.	1992	5.75	13
1992	Grandma QXM5514	Yr.Iss.	1992	4.50	14
1992	Harmony Trio-Set/3 QXM5471	Yr.Iss.	1992	11.75	20
1992	Hickory, Dickory, Dock QXM5861	Yr.Iss.	1992	3.75	13
1992	Holiday Holly QXM5364	Yr.Iss.	1992	9.75	20
1992	Holiday Splash QXM5834	Yr.Iss.	1992	5.75	12
1992	Hoop It Up QXM5831	Yr.Iss.	1992	4.50	11
1992	Inside Story QXM5881	Yr.Iss.	1992	7.25	17
1992	Kittens in Toyland (5th Ed.) QXM5391	Yr.Iss.	1992	4.50	15
1992	The Kringles (4th Ed.) QXM5381	Yr.Iss.	1992	6.00	18
1992	Little Town of Bethlehem QXM5864	Yr.Iss.	1992	3.00	18
1992	Minted For Santa QXM5854	Yr.Iss.	1992	3.75	14
1992	Mom QXM5504	Yr.Iss.	1992	4.50	14

YEAR ISSUE		EDITION LIMIT	YEAR RETD.	ISSUE PRICE	*QUOTE U.S.$
1992	Nature's Angels (3rd Ed.) QXM5451	Yr.Iss.	1992	4.50	18
1992	The Night Before Christmas QXM5541	Yr.Iss.	1992	13.75	28-35
1992	Perfect Balance QXM5571	Yr.Iss.	1992	3.00	12
1992	Polar Polka QXM5534	Yr.Iss.	1992	4.50	14
1992	Puppet Show QXM5574	Yr.Iss.	1992	3.00	12
1992	Rocking Horse (5th Ed.) QXM5454	Yr.Iss.	1992	4.50	17
1992	Sew Sew Tiny (set/6) QXM5794	Yr.Iss.	1992	29.00	45-58
1992	Ski For Two QXM5821	Yr.Iss.	1992	4.50	14
1992	Snowshoe Bunny QXM5564	Yr.Iss.	1992	3.75	12
1992	Snug Kitty QXM5554	Yr.Iss.	1992	3.75	13
1992	Spunky Monkey QXM5921	Yr.Iss.	1992	3.00	13
1992	Thimble Bells (3rd Ed.) QXM5461	Yr.Iss.	1992	6.00	19
1992	Visions Of Acorns QXM5851	Yr.Iss.	1992	4.50	15
1992	Wee Three Kings QXM5531	Yr.Iss.	1992	5.75	16
1992	Woodland Babies (2nd Ed.) QXM5444	Yr.Iss.	1992	6.00	14

1992 New Attractions - Keepsake

1992	Bear Bell Champ QX5071	Yr.Iss.	1992	7.75	15-30
1992	Caboose QX5321	Yr.Iss.	1992	9.75	18-25
1992	Cheerful Santa QX5154	Yr.Iss.	1992	9.75	33
1992	Coal Car QX5401	Yr.Iss.	1992	9.75	20
1992	Cool Fliers QX5474	Yr.Iss.	1992	10.75	22
1992	Deck the Hogs QX5204	Yr.Iss.	1992	8.75	22
1992	Down-Under Holiday QX5144	Yr.Iss.	1992	7.75	20
1992	Egg Nog Nest QX5121	Yr.Iss.	1992	7.75	16
1992	Eric the Baker QX5244	Yr.Iss.	1992	8.75	20
1992	Feliz Navidad QX5181	Yr.Iss.	1992	6.75	20
1992	Franz the Artist QX5261	Yr.Iss.	1992	8.75	18-25
1992	Freida the Animals' Friend QX5264	Yr.Iss.	1992	8.75	18-27
1992	Fun on a Big Scale QX5134	Yr.Iss.	1992	10.75	22
1992	GARFIELD QX5374	Yr.Iss.	1992	7.75	17
1992	Genius at Work QX5371	Yr.Iss.	1992	10.75	20
1992	Golf's a Ball QX5984	Yr.Iss.	1992	6.75	27
1992	Gone Wishin' QX5171	Yr.Iss.	1992	8.75	19
1992	Green Thumb Santa QX5101	Yr.Iss.	1992	7.75	16
1992	Hello-Ho-Ho QX5141	Yr.Iss.	1992	9.75	16-23
1992	Holiday Teatime QX5431	Yr.Iss.	1992	14.75	26-30
1992	Holiday Wishes QX5131	Yr.Iss.	1992	7.75	17
1992	Honest George QX5064	Yr.Iss.	1992	7.75	18
1992	Jesus Loves Me QX3024	Yr.Iss.	1992	7.75	15
1992	Locomotive QX5311	Yr.Iss.	1992	9.75	45
1992	Loving Shepherd QX5151	Yr.Iss.	1992	7.75	15
1992	Ludwig the Musician QX5281	Yr.Iss.	1992	8.75	19
1992	Mary Engelbreit Santa Jolly Wolly QX5224	Yr.Iss.	1992	7.75	8
1992	Max the Tailor QX5251	Yr.Iss.	1992	8.75	20
1992	Memories to Cherish QX5161	Yr.Iss.	1992	10.75	20
1992	Merry "Swiss" Mouse QX5114	Yr.Iss.	1992	7.75	15
1992	Norman Rockwell Art QX2224	Yr.Iss.	1992	5.00	16-25
1992	North Pole Fire Fighter QX5104	Yr.Iss.	1992	9.75	21
1992	Otto the Carpenter QX5254	Yr.Iss.	1992	8.75	20
1992	Owl QX5614	Yr.Iss.	1992	9.75	27
1992	Partridge In a Pear Tree QX5234	Yr.Iss.	1992	8.75	19
1992	PEANUTS QX2244	Yr.Iss.	1992	5.00	18-30
1992	Please Pause Here QX5291	Yr.Iss.	1992	14.75	35
1992	Rapid Delivery QX5094	Yr.Iss.	1992	8.75	22
1992	Santa's Hook Shot QX5434	Yr.Iss.	1992	12.75	28
1992	Santa's Roundup QX5084	Yr.Iss.	1992	8.75	22
1992	A Santa-Full! QX5991	Yr.Iss.	1992	9.75	30-40
1992	Silver Star QX5324	Yr.Iss.	1992	28.00	53-60
1992	Skiing 'Round QX5214	Yr.Iss.	1992	8.75	18
1992	SNOOPY and WOODSTOCK QX5954	Yr.Iss.	1992	8.75	25-40
1992	Spirit of Christmas Stress QX5231	Yr.Iss.	1992	8.75	20
1992	Stock Car QX5314	Yr.Iss.	1992	9.75	19
1992	Tasty Christmas QX5994	Yr.Iss.	1992	9.75	19-25
1992	Toboggan Tail QX5459	Yr.Iss.	1992	7.75	16
1992	Tread Bear QX5091	Yr.Iss.	1992	8.75	23

1992 Special Edition - Keepsake

1992	Dickens Caroler Bell-Lord Chadwick (3rd Ed.) QX4554	Yr.Iss.	1992	21.75	40-50

1992 Special Issues - Keepsake

1992	Elvis QX562-4	Yr.Iss.	1992	14.75	25-50
1992	Santa Maria QX5074	Yr.Iss.	1992	12.75	27
1992	Shuttlecraft Galileo 2400QLX733-1	Yr.Iss.	1992	24.00	43-55

1993 Anniversary Edition - Keepsake

1993	Frosty Friends QX5682	Yr.Iss.	1993	20.00	47
1993	Glowing Pewter Wreath QX5302	Yr.Iss.	1993	18.75	37
1993	Shopping With Santa QX5675	Yr.Iss.	1993	24.00	45
1993	Tannenbaum's Dept. Store QX5612	Yr.Iss.	1993	26.00	57

1993 Artists' Favorites - Keepsake

1993	Bird Watcher QX5252	Yr.Iss.	1993	9.75	18
1993	Howling Good Time QX5255	Yr.Iss.	1993	9.75	19
1993	On Her Toes QX5265	Yr.Iss.	1993	8.75	20
1993	Peek-a-Boo Tree QX5245	Yr.Iss.	1993	10.75	22
1993	Wake-Up Call QX5262	Yr.Iss.	1993	8.75	18

1993 Collectible Series - Keepsake

1993	1956 Ford Thunderbird (3rd Ed.) QX5275	Yr.Iss.	1993	12.75	33-40
1993	Betsey's Country Christmas (2nd Ed.) QX2062	Yr.Iss.	1993	5.00	20
1993	Cozy Home (10th Ed.) QX4175	Yr.Iss.	1993	14.75	33-45

YEAR ISSUE		EDITION LIMIT	YEAR RETD.	ISSUE PRICE	*QUOTE U.S.$
1993	CRAYOLA CRAYON-Bright Shining Castle (5th Ed.) QX4422	Yr.Iss.	1993	11.00	26-36
1993	Fabulous Decade (4th Ed.) QX4475	Yr.Iss.	1993	7.75	19
1993	A Fitting Moment (8th Ed.) QX4202	Yr.Iss.	1993	14.75	26-43
1993	Frosty Friends (14th Ed.) QX4142	Yr.Iss.	1993	9.75	22-32
1993	The Gift Bringers-The Magi (5th Ed.) QX2065	Yr.Iss.	1993	5.00	17
1993	Happy Haul-idays (15th Ed.) QX4102	Yr.Iss.	1993	14.75	27-40
1993	Heart Of Christmas (4th Ed.) QX4482	Yr.Iss.	1993	14.75	27
1993	Heavenly Angels (3rd Ed.) QX4945	Yr.Iss.	1993	7.75	18
1993	Humpty-Dumpty (1st Ed.) QX5282	Yr.Iss.	1993	13.75	35-45
1993	Mary's Angels-Ivy (6th Ed.) QX4282	Yr.Iss.	1993	6.75	15-30
1993	Merry Olde Santa (4th Ed.) QX4842	Yr.Iss.	1993	14.75	27-40
1993	Owliver (2nd Ed.) QX5425	Yr.Iss.	1993	7.75	17
1993	Peace On Earth-Poland (3rd Ed.) QX5242	Yr.Iss.	1993	11.75	23
1993	Peanuts (1st Ed.) QX5315	Yr.Iss.	1993	9.75	45-65
1993	Puppy Love (3rd Ed.) QX5045	Yr.Iss.	1993	7.75	28
1993	Reindeer Champs-Blitzen (8th Ed.) QX4331	Yr.Iss.	1993	8.75	24
1993	Rocking Horse (13th Ed.) QX4162	Yr.Iss.	1993	10.75	27-40
1993	Ten Lords A-Leaping (10th Ed.) QX3012	Yr.Iss.	1993	6.75	15-25
1993	Tobin Fraley Carousel (2nd Ed.) QX5502	Yr.Iss.	1993	28.00	40-60
1993	U.S. Christmas Stamps (1st Ed.) QX5292	Yr.Iss.	1993	10.75	30-42

1993 Commemoratives - Keepsake

1993	Across the Miles QX5912	Yr.Iss.	1993	8.75	19
1993	Anniversary Year QX5972	Yr.Iss.	1993	9.75	18
1993	Apple for Teacher QX5902	Yr.Iss.	1993	7.75	16
1993	Baby's First Christmas QX5512	Yr.Iss.	1993	18.75	38
1993	Baby's First Christmas QX5515	Yr.Iss.	1993	10.75	23
1993	Baby's First Christmas QX5522	Yr.Iss.	1993	7.75	23
1993	Baby's First Christmas QX5525	Yr.Iss.	1993	7.75	29-35
1993	Baby's First Christmas-Baby Boy QX2105	Yr.Iss.	1993	4.75	15
1993	Baby's First Christmas-Baby Girl QX2092	Yr.Iss.	1993	4.75	17
1993	Baby's Second Christmas QX5992	Yr.Iss.	1993	6.75	25
1993	Brother QX5542	Yr.Iss.	1993	6.75	13
1993	A Child's Christmas QX5882	Yr.Iss.	1993	9.75	21
1993	Child's Fifth Christmas QX5222	Yr.Iss.	1993	6.75	18
1993	Child's Fourth Christmas QX5215	Yr.Iss.	1993	6.75	15-25
1993	Child's Third Christmas QX5995	Yr.Iss.	1993	6.75	20
1993	Coach QX5935	Yr.Iss.	1993	6.75	15
1993	Dad QX5855	Yr.Iss.	1993	7.75	17
1993	Dad-to-Be QX5532	Yr.Iss.	1993	6.75	15
1993	Daughter QX5872	Yr.Iss.	1993	6.75	18-30
1993	Godchild QX5875	Yr.Iss.	1993	8.75	18
1993	Grandchild's First Christmas QX5552	Yr.Iss.	1993	6.75	14
1993	Granddaughter QX5635	Yr.Iss.	1993	6.75	14
1993	Grandmother QX5665	Yr.Iss.	1993	6.75	13
1993	Grandparents QX2085	Yr.Iss.	1993	4.75	12-20
1993	Grandson QX5632	Yr.Iss.	1993	6.75	13
1993	Mom and Dad QX5845	Yr.Iss.	1993	9.75	18
1993	Mom QX5852	Yr.Iss.	1993	7.75	17
1993	Mom-to-Be QX5535	Yr.Iss.	1993	6.75	15
1993	Nephew QX5735	Yr.Iss.	1993	6.75	13
1993	New Home QX5905	Yr.Iss.	1993	7.75	50
1993	Niece QX5732	Yr.Iss.	1993	6.75	14
1993	Our Christmas Together QX5942	Yr.Iss.	1993	10.75	22
1993	Our Family QX5892	Yr.Iss.	1993	7.75	17
1993	Our First Christmas Together QX3015	Yr.Iss.	1993	6.75	17-25
1993	Our First Christmas Together QX5642	Yr.Iss.	1993	9.75	15-35
1993	Our First Christmas Together QX5952	Yr.Iss.	1993	8.75	18
1993	Our First Christmas Together QX5955	Yr.Iss.	1993	18.75	35
1993	People Friendly QX5932	Yr.Iss.	1993	8.75	16
1993	Sister QX5545	Yr.Iss.	1993	6.75	18-25
1993	Sister to Sister QX5885	Yr.Iss.	1993	9.75	35-50
1993	Son QX5865	Yr.Iss.	1993	6.75	17
1993	Special Cat QX5235	Yr.Iss.	1993	7.75	14
1993	Special Dog QX5962	Yr.Iss.	1993	7.75	15
1993	Star Teacher QX5645	Yr.Iss.	1993	5.75	13
1993	Strange and Wonderful Love QX5965	Yr.Iss.	1993	8.75	16
1993	To My Grandma QX5555	Yr.Iss.	1993	7.75	16
1993	Top Banana QX5925	Yr.Iss.	1993	7.75	18
1993	Warm and Special Friends QX5895	Yr.Iss.	1993	10.75	23

1993 Easter Ornaments - Keepsake

1993	Easter Parade (2nd Ed.) QEO8325	Yr.Iss.	1993	6.75	18
1993	Egg in Sports (2nd Ed.) QEO8332	Yr.Iss.	1993	6.75	20
1993	Springtime Bonnets (1st Ed.) QEO8322	Yr.Iss.	1993	7.75	20-30

1993 Keepsake Collector's Club - Keepsake

1993	It's In The Mail QXC5272	Yr.Iss.	1993	10.00	21
1993	Trimmed With Memories QXC5432	Yr.Iss.	1993	12.00	36

1993 Keepsake Magic Ornaments - Keepsake

1993	Baby's First Christmas QLX7365	Yr.Iss.	1993	22.00	43
1993	Bells Are Ringing QLX7402	Yr.Iss.	1993	28.00	54-65

*Quotes have been rounded up to nearest dollar

YEAR ISSUE		EDITION LIMIT	YEAR RETD.	ISSUE PRICE	*QUOTE U.S.$
1993	Chris Mouse Flight (9th Ed.) QLX7152	Yr.Iss.	1993	12.00	26-35
1993	Dog's Best Friend QLX7172	Yr.Iss.	1993	12.00	23
1993	Dollhouse Dreams QLX7372	Yr.Iss.	1993	22.00	40-50
1993	Forest Frolics (5th Ed.) QLX7165	Yr.Iss.	1993	25.00	47-52
1993	Home On The Range QLX7395	Yr.Iss.	1993	32.00	63-75
1993	The Lamplighter QLX7192	Yr.Iss.	1993	18.00	38
1993	Last-Minute Shopping QLX7385	Yr.Iss.	1993	28.00	41-60
1993	North Pole Merrython QLX7392	Yr.Iss.	1993	25.00	46-50
1993	Our First Christmas Together QLX7355	Yr.Iss.	1993	20.00	38-50
1993	PEANUTS (3rd Ed.) QLX7155	Yr.Iss.	1993	18.00	38-50
1993	Radio News Flash QLX7362	Yr.Iss.	1993	22.00	41-50
1993	Raiding The Fridge QLX7185	Yr.Iss.	1993	16.00	47
1993	Road Runner and Wile E. Coyote QLX7415	Yr.Iss.	1993	30.00	68-75
1993	Santa's Snow-Getter QLX7352	Yr.Iss.	1993	18.00	39
1993	Santa's Workshop QLX7375	Yr.Iss.	1993	28.00	57
1993	Song Of The Chimes QLX7405	Yr.Iss.	1993	25.00	52
1993	Winnie The Pooh QLX7422	Yr.Iss.	1993	24.00	50

1993 Limited Edition Ornaments - Keepsake

1993	Gentle Tidings QXC5442	17,500	1993	25.00	50
1993	Sharing Christmas QXC5435	16,500	1993	20.00	43

1993 Miniature Ornaments - Keepsake

1993	'Round The Mountain QXM4025	Yr.Iss.	1993	7.25	17
1993	Baby's First Christmas QXM5145	Yr.Iss.	1993	5.75	14
1993	The Bearymores (2nd Ed.) QXM5125	Yr.Iss.	1993	5.75	17
1993	Cheese Please QXM4072	Yr.Iss.	1993	3.75	7
1993	Christmas Castle QXM4085	Yr.Iss.	1993	5.75	12
1993	Cloisonne Snowflake QXM4012	Yr.Iss.	1993	9.75	19
1993	Country Fiddling QXM4062	Yr.Iss.	1993	3.75	9
1993	Crystal Angel QXM4015	Yr.Iss.	1993	9.75	40-54
1993	Ears To Pals QXM4075	Yr.Iss.	1993	3.75	8
1993	Flatbed Car (5th Ed.) QXM5105	Yr.Iss.	1993	7.00	19
1993	Grandma QXM5162	Yr.Iss.	1993	4.50	12
1993	I Dream Of Santa QXM4055	Yr.Iss.	1993	3.75	12
1993	Into The Woods QXM4045	Yr.Iss.	1993	3.75	7
1993	The Kringles (5th Ed.) QXM5135	Yr.Iss.	1993	5.75	15
1993	Learning To Skate QXM4122	Yr.Iss.	1993	3.00	8
1993	Lighting A Path QXM4115	Yr.Iss.	1993	3.00	8
1993	March Of The Teddy Bears (1st Ed.) QX2403	Yr.Iss.	1993	4.50	15-23
1993	Merry Mascot QXM4042	Yr.Iss.	1993	3.75	9
1993	Mom QXM5155	Yr.Iss.	1993	4.50	13
1993	Monkey Melody QXM4092	Yr.Iss.	1993	5.75	13
1993	Nature's Angels (4th Ed.) QXM5122	Yr.Iss.	1993	4.50	15
1993	The Night Before Christmas (2nd Ed.) QXM5115	Yr.Iss.	1993	4.50	15-23
1993	North Pole Fire Truck QXM4105	Yr.Iss.	1993	4.75	12
1993	On The Road (1st Ed.) QXM4002	Yr.Iss.	1993	5.75	14-21
1993	Pear-Shaped Tones QXM4052	Yr.Iss.	1993	3.75	7
1993	Pull Out A Plum QXM4095	Yr.Iss.	1993	5.75	13
1993	Refreshing Flight QXM4112	Yr.Iss.	1993	5.75	14
1993	Rocking Horse (6th Ed.) QXM5112	Yr.Iss.	1993	4.50	13-20
1993	Secret Pals QXM5172	Yr.Iss.	1993	3.75	10
1993	Snuggle Birds QXM5182	Yr.Iss.	1993	5.75	13
1993	Special Friends QXM5165	Yr.Iss.	1993	4.50	10
1993	Thimble Bells (4th Ed.) QXM5142	Yr.Iss.	1993	5.75	14
1993	Tiny Green Thumbs, set/6, QXM4032	Yr.Iss.	1993	29.00	38-50
1993	Toy Shop (6th Ed.) QXM5132	Yr.Iss.	1993	7.00	15-21
1993	Visions Of Sugarplums QXM4022	Yr.Iss.	1993	7.25	15
1993	Woodland Babies (3rd Ed.) QXM5102	Yr.Iss.	1993	5.75	13

1993 New Attractions - Keepsake

1993	Beary Gifted QX5762	Yr.Iss.	1993	7.75	18
1993	Big on Gardening QX5842	Yr.Iss.	1993	9.75	18
1993	Big Roller QX5352	Yr.Iss.	1993	8.75	16
1993	Bowling For ZZZ's QX5565	Yr.Iss.	1993	7.75	18
1993	Bugs Bunny QX5412	Yr.Iss.	1993	8.75	25
1993	Caring Nurse QX5785	Yr.Iss.	1993	6.75	18
1993	Christmas Break QX5825	Yr.Iss.	1993	7.75	17-25
1993	Clever Cookie QX5662	Yr.Iss.	1993	7.75	16-26
1993	Curly 'n' Kingly QX5285	Yr.Iss.	1993	10.75	18-25
1993	Dunkin' Roo QX5575	Yr.Iss.	1993	7.75	15
1993	Eeyore QX5712	Yr.Iss.	1993	9.75	20
1993	Elmer Fudd QX5495	Yr.Iss.	1993	8.75	18
1993	Faithful Fire Fighter QX5782	Yr.Iss.	1993	7.75	18
1993	Feliz Navidad QX5365	Yr.Iss.	1993	9.75	18
1993	Fills the Bill QX5572	Yr.Iss.	1993	8.75	17
1993	Great Connections QX5402	Yr.Iss.	1993	10.75	23
1993	He Is Born QX5362	Yr.Iss.	1993	9.75	37
1993	High Top-Purr QX5332	Yr.Iss.	1993	8.75	25
1993	Home For Christmas QX5562	Yr.Iss.	1993	7.75	16
1993	Icicle Bicycle QX5835	Yr.Iss.	1993	9.75	18
1993	Kanga and Roo QX5672	Yr.Iss.	1993	9.75	22
1993	Little Drummer Boy QX5372	Yr.Iss.	1993	8.75	22
1993	Look For Wonder QX5685	Yr.Iss.	1993	12.75	26
1993	Lou Rankin Polar Bear QX5745	Yr.Iss.	1993	9.75	23
1993	Makin' Music QX5325	Yr.Iss.	1993	9.75	18
1993	Making Waves QX5775	Yr.Iss.	1993	9.75	24
1993	Mary Engelbreit QX2075	Yr.Iss.	1993	5.00	15
1993	Maxine QX5385	Yr.Iss.	1993	8.75	17-30
1993	One-Elf Marching Band QX5342	Yr.Iss.	1993	12.75	26
1993	Owl QX5695	Yr.Iss.	1993	9.75	19
1993	PEANUTS QX2072	Yr.Iss.	1993	5.00	13-30
1993	Peep Inside QX5322	Yr.Iss.	1993	13.75	26
1993	Perfect Match QX5772	Yr.Iss.	1993	8.75	18
1993	The Pink Panther QX5755	Yr.Iss.	1993	12.75	26
1993	Playful Pals QX5742	Yr.Iss.	1993	14.75	27
1993	Popping Good Times QX5392	Yr.Iss.	1993	14.75	27
1993	Porky Pig QX5652	Yr.Iss.	1993	8.75	19
1993	Putt-Putt Penguin QX5795	Yr.Iss.	1993	9.75	20
1993	Quick As A Fox QX5792	Yr.Iss.	1993	8.75	16
1993	Rabbit QX5702	Yr.Iss.	1993	9.75	19
1993	Ready For Fun QX5124	Yr.Iss.	1993	7.75	16
1993	Room For One More QX5382	Yr.Iss.	1993	8.75	48
1993	Silvery Noel QX5305	Yr.Iss.	1993	12.75	20-35
1993	Smile! It's Christmas QX5335	Yr.Iss.	1993	9.75	18
1993	Snow Bear Angel QX5355	Yr.Iss.	1993	7.75	16
1993	Snowbird QX5765	Yr.Iss.	1993	7.75	15
1993	Snowy Hideaway QX5312	Yr.Iss.	1993	9.75	15-20
1993	Star Of Wonder QX5982	Yr.Iss.	1993	6.75	33
1993	Superman QX5752	Yr.Iss.	1993	12.75	45-50
1993	The Swat Team QX5395	Yr.Iss.	1993	12.75	27
1993	Sylvester and Tweety QX5405	Yr.Iss.	1993	9.75	32
1993	That's Entertainment QX5345	Yr.Iss.	1993	8.75	18
1993	Tigger and Piglet QX5705	Yr.Iss.	1993	9.75	35-50
1993	Tin Airplane QX5622	Yr.Iss.	1993	7.75	28
1993	Tin Blimp QX5625	Yr.Iss.	1993	7.75	15
1993	Tin Hot Air Balloon QX5615	Yr.Iss.	1993	7.75	16
1993	Water Bed Snooze QX5375	Yr.Iss.	1993	9.75	21
1993	Winnie the Pooh QX5715	Yr.Iss.	1993	9.75	28-35

1993 Showcase Folk Art Americana - Keepsake

1993	Angel in Flight QK1052	Yr.Iss.	1993	15.75	45
1993	Polar Bear Adventure QK1055	Yr.Iss.	1993	15.00	65
1993	Riding in the Woods QK1065	Yr.Iss.	1993	15.75	60
1993	Riding the Wind QK1045	Yr.Iss.	1993	15.75	65
1993	Santa Claus QK1072	Yr.Iss.	1993	16.75	225

1993 Showcase Holiday Enchantment - Keepsake

1993	Angelic Messengers QK1032	Yr.Iss.	1993	13.75	40
1993	Bringing Home the Tree QK1042	Yr.Iss.	1993	13.75	35
1993	Journey to the Forest QK1012	Yr.Iss.	1993	13.75	32
1993	The Magi QK1025	Yr.Iss.	1993	13.75	37
1993	Visions of Sugarplums QK1005	Yr.Iss.	1993	13.75	35

1993 Showcase Old-World Silver - Keepsake

1993	Silver Dove of Peace QK1075	Yr.Iss.	1993	24.75	35
1993	Silver Santa QK1092	Yr.Iss.	1993	24.75	50-60
1993	Silver Sleigh QK1082	Yr.Iss.	1993	24.75	33
1993	Silver Stars and Holly QK1085	Yr.Iss.	1993	24.75	33

1993 Showcase Portraits in Bisque - Keepsake

1993	Christmas Feast QK1152	Yr.Iss.	1993	15.75	31
1993	Joy of Sharing QK1142	Yr.Iss.	1993	15.75	32
1993	Mistletoe Kiss QK1145	Yr.Iss.	1993	15.75	29
1993	Norman Rockwell-Filling the Stockings QK1155	Yr.Iss.	1993	15.75	35
1993	Norman Rockwell-Jolly Postman QK1142	Yr.Iss.	1993	15.75	34

1993 Special Editions - Keepsake

1993	Dickens Caroler Bell-Lady Daphne (4th Ed.) QX5505	Yr.Iss.	1993	21.75	40-50
1993	Julianne and Teddy QX5295	Yr.Iss.	1993	21.75	38-55

1993 Special Issues - Keepsake

1993	Holiday Barbie™ (1st Ed.) QX572-5	Yr.Iss.	1993	14.75	150-175
1993	Messages of Christmas QLX747-6	Yr.Iss.	1993	35.00	56
1993	Star Trek® The Next Generation QLX741-2	Yr.Iss.	1993	24.00	50

1994 Artists' Favorites - Keepsake

1994	Cock-a-Doodle Christmas QX5396	Yr.Iss.	1994	8.95	20-30
1994	Happy Birthday Jesus QX5423	Yr.Iss.	1994	12.95	20-30
1994	Keep on Mowin' QX5413	Yr.Iss.	1994	8.95	17
1994	Kitty's Catamaran QX5416	Yr.Iss.	1994	10.95	18
1994	Making It Bright QX5403	Yr.Iss.	1994	8.95	16

1994 Collectible Series - Keepsake

1994	1957 Chevy (4th Ed.) QX5422	Yr.Iss.	1994	12.95	35
1994	Baseball Heroes-Babe Ruth (1st Ed.) QX5323	Yr.Iss.	1994	12.95	55-65
1994	Betsey's Country Christmas (3rd Ed.) QX2403	Yr.Iss.	1994	5.00	15
1994	Cat Naps (1st Ed.) QX5313	Yr.Iss.	1994	7.95	28-35
1994	CRAYOLA CRAYON-Bright Playful Colors (6th Ed.) QX5273	Yr.Iss.	1994	10.95	21-28
1994	Fabulous Decade (5th Ed.) QX5263	Yr.Iss.	1994	7.95	23
1994	Frosty Friends (15th Ed.) QX5293	Yr.Iss.	1994	9.95	23-33
1994	Handwarming Present (9th Ed.) QX5283	Yr.Iss.	1994	14.95	27-40
1994	Heart of Christmas (5th Ed.) QX5266	Yr.Iss.	1994	14.95	28
1994	Hey Diddle Diddle (2nd Ed.) QX5213	Yr.Iss.	1994	13.95	40
1994	Makin' Tractor Tracks (16th Ed.) QX5296	Yr.Iss.	1994	14.95	45-62
1994	Mary's Angels-Jasmine (7th Ed.) QX5276	Yr.Iss.	1994	6.95	16-25
1994	Merry Olde Santa (5th Ed.) QX5256	Yr.Iss.	1994	14.95	33
1994	Murray Blue Champion (1st Ed.) QX5426	Yr.Iss.	1994	13.95	58-75
1994	Neighborhood Drugstore (11th Ed.) QX5286	Yr.Iss.	1994	14.95	30-40
1994	Owliver (3rd Ed.) QX5226	Yr.Iss.	1994	7.95	18
1994	PEANUTS-Lucy (2nd Ed.) QX5203	Yr.Iss.	1994	9.95	25
1994	Pipers Piping (11th Ed.) QX3183	Yr.Iss.	1994	6.95	20
1994	Puppy Love (4th Ed.) QX5253	Yr.Iss.	1994	7.95	20
1994	Rocking Horse (14th Ed.) QX5016	Yr.Iss.	1994	10.95	25
1994	Tobin Fraley Carousel (3rd Ed.) QX5223	Yr.Iss.	1994	28.00	58
1994	Xmas Stamp (2nd Ed.) QX5206	Yr.Iss.	1994	10.95	23
1994	Yuletide Central (1st Ed.) QX5316	Yr.Iss.	1994	18.95	46-60

1994 Commemoratives - Keepsake

1994	Across the Miles QX5656	Yr.Iss.	1994	8.95	17
1994	Anniversary Year QX5683	Yr.Iss.	1994	10.95	21
1994	Baby's First Christmas Photo QX5636	Yr.Iss.	1994	7.95	18-30
1994	Baby's First Christmas QX5633	Yr.Iss.	1994	18.95	25-40
1994	Baby's First Christmas QX5713	Yr.Iss.	1994	7.95	23-30
1994	Baby's First Christmas QX5743	Yr.Iss.	1994	12.95	27
1994	Baby's First Christmas-Baby Boy QX2436	Yr.Iss.	1994	5.00	15
1994	Baby's First Christmas-Baby Girl QX2433	Yr.Iss.	1994	5.00	15
1994	Baby's Second Christmas QX5716	Yr.Iss.	1994	7.95	22-30
1994	Brother QX5516	Yr.Iss.	1994	6.95	15
1994	Child's Fifth Christmas QX5733	Yr.Iss.	1994	6.95	16-25
1994	Child's Fourth Christmas QX5726	Yr.Iss.	1994	6.95	16-25
1994	Child's Third Christmas QX5723	Yr.Iss.	1994	6.95	16-30
1994	Dad QX5463	Yr.Iss.	1994	7.95	16
1994	Dad-To-Be QX5473	Yr.Iss.	1994	7.95	16-25
1994	Daughter QX5623	Yr.Iss.	1994	6.95	14-25
1994	Friendly Push QX5686	Yr.Iss.	1994	8.95	18
1994	Godchild QX4453	Yr.Iss.	1994	8.95	22
1994	Godparents QX2423	Yr.Iss.	1994	5.00	19
1994	Grandchild's First Christmas QX5676	Yr.Iss.	1994	7.95	17
1994	Granddaughter QX5523	Yr.Iss.	1994	6.95	17
1994	Grandma Photo QX5613	Yr.Iss.	1994	6.95	14
1994	Grandmother QX5673	Yr.Iss.	1994	7.95	19
1994	Grandpa QX5616	Yr.Iss.	1994	7.95	17
1994	Grandparents QX2426	Yr.Iss.	1994	5.00	13
1994	Grandson QX5526	Yr.Iss.	1994	6.95	17
1994	Mom and Dad QX5666	Yr.Iss.	1994	9.95	21
1994	Mom QX5466	Yr.Iss.	1994	7.95	16
1994	Mom-To-Be QX5506	Yr.Iss.	1994	7.95	18
1994	Nephew QX5546	Yr.Iss.	1994	7.95	16
1994	New Home QX5663	Yr.Iss.	1994	8.95	19
1994	Niece QX5543	Yr.Iss.	1994	7.95	16
1994	Our Family QX5576	Yr.Iss.	1994	7.95	19
1994	Our First Christmas Together Photo QX5653	Yr.Iss.	1994	8.95	17-30
1994	Our First Christmas Together QX3186	Yr.Iss.	1994	6.95	16
1994	Our First Christmas Together QX4816	Yr.Iss.	1994	9.95	19
1994	Our First Christmas Together QX5643	Yr.Iss.	1994	9.95	18-30
1994	Our First Christmas Together QX5706	Yr.Iss.	1994	18.95	36-45
1994	Secret Santa QX5736	Yr.Iss.	1994	7.95	18
1994	Sister QX5513	Yr.Iss.	1994	6.95	17
1994	Sister to Sister QX5533	Yr.Iss.	1994	9.95	21
1994	Son QX5626	Yr.Iss.	1994	6.95	14-25
1994	Special Cat QX5606	Yr.Iss.	1994	7.95	16
1994	Special Dog QX5603	Yr.Iss.	1994	7.95	16
1994	Thick 'N' Thin QX5693	Yr.Iss.	1994	10.95	23
1994	Tou Can Love QX5646	Yr.Iss.	1994	8.95	18

1994 Easter Ornaments - Keepsake

1994	Baby's First Easter QEO8153	Yr.Iss.	1994	6.75	18
1994	Carrot Trimmers QEO8226	Yr.Iss.	1994	5.00	5-20
1994	CRAYOLA CRAYON-Colorful Spring QEO8166	Yr.Iss.	1994	7.75	27
1994	Daughter QEO8156	Yr.Iss.	1994	5.75	14
1994	Divine Duet QEO8183	Yr.Iss.	1994	6.75	15
1994	Easter Art Show QEO8193	Yr.Iss.	1994	7.75	16
1994	Egg Car (1st Ed.) QEO8093	Yr.Iss.	1994	7.75	27
1994	Golf (3rd Ed.) QEO8133	Yr.Iss.	1994	6.75	18
1994	Horn (3rd Ed.) QEO8136	Yr.Iss.	1994	6.75	18
1994	Joyful Lamb QEO8206	Yr.Iss.	1994	5.75	14
1994	PEANUTS QEO8176	Yr.Iss.	1994	7.75	26-50
1994	Peeping Out QEO8203	Yr.Iss.	1994	6.75	14
1994	Riding a Breeze QEO8213	Yr.Iss.	1994	5.75	14
1994	Son QEO8163	Yr.Iss.	1994	5.75	15
1994	Springtime Bonnets (2nd Ed.) QEO8096	Yr.Iss.	1994	7.75	23
1994	Sunny Bunny Garden, (Set/3) QEO8146	Yr.Iss.	1994	15.00	28
1994	Sweet as Sugar QEO8086	Yr.Iss.	1994	8.75	19
1994	Sweet Easter Wishes Tender Touches QEO8196	Yr.Iss.	1994	8.75	23
1994	Treetop Cottage QEO8186	Yr.Iss.	1994	9.75	19
1994	Yummy Recipe QEO8143	Yr.Iss.	1994	7.75	20

1994 Keepsake Collector's Club - Keepsake

1994	First Hello QXC4846	Yr.Iss.	1994	5.00	15
1994	Happy Collecting QXC4803	Yr.Iss.	1994	3.00	25
1994	Holiday Pursuit QXC4823	Yr.Iss.	1994	11.75	23
1994	Mrs. Claus' Cupboard QXC4843	Yr.Iss.	1994	55.00	210
1994	On Cloud Nine QXC4853	Yr.Iss.	1994	12.00	28
1994	Sweet Bouquet QXC4806	Yr.Iss.	1994	8.50	23
1994	Tilling Time QXC8256	Yr.Iss.	1994	5.00	20-75

1994 Keepsake Magic Ornaments - Keepsake

1994	Away in a Manager QLX7383	Yr.Iss.	1994	16.00	38
1994	Baby's First Christmas QLX7466	Yr.Iss.	1994	20.00	40
1994	Candy Cane Lookout QLX7376	Yr.Iss.	1994	18.00	50-65

*Quotes have been rounded up to nearest dollar

YEAR ISSUE		EDITION LIMIT	YEAR RETD.	ISSUE PRICE	*QUOTE U.S.$
1994	Chris Mouse Jelly (10th Ed.) QLX7393	Yr.Iss.	1994	12.00	16-30
1994	Conversations With Santa QLX7426	Yr.Iss.	1994	28.00	53
1994	Country Showtime QLX7416	Yr.Iss.	1994	22.00	45
1994	The Eagle Has Landed QLX7486	Yr.Iss.	1994	24.00	45
1994	Feliz Navidad QLX7433	Yr.Iss.	1994	28.00	50-75
1994	Forest Frolics (6th Ed.) QLX7436	Yr.Iss.	1994	28.00	53-60
1994	Gingerbread Fantasy (Sp. Ed.) QLX7382	Yr.Iss.	1994	44.00	88-96
1994	Kringle Trolley QLX7413	Yr.Iss.	1994	20.00	45-50
1994	Maxine QLX7503	Yr.Iss.	1994	20.00	40-50
1994	PEANUTS (4th Ed.) QLX7406	Yr.Iss.	1994	20.00	43
1994	Peekaboo Pup QLX7423	Yr.Iss.	1994	20.00	42
1994	Rock Candy Miner QLX7403	Yr.Iss.	1994	20.00	38
1994	Santa's Sing-Along QLX7473	Yr.Iss.	1994	24.00	40-55
1994	Tobin Fraley (1st Ed.) QLX7496	Yr.Iss.	1994	32.00	65-75
1994	Very Merry Minutes QLX7443	Yr.Iss.	1994	24.00	45
1994	White Christmas QLX7463	Yr.Iss.	1994	28.00	53
1994	Winnie the Pooh Parade QLX7493	Yr.Iss.	1994	32.00	50-65

1994 Limited Editions - Keepsake

YEAR ISSUE		EDITION LIMIT	YEAR RETD.	ISSUE PRICE	*QUOTE U.S.$
1994	Jolly Holly Santa QXC4833	N/A	1994	22.00	47
1994	Majestic Deer QXC4836	N/A	1994	25.00	47

1994 Miniature Ornaments - Keepsake

YEAR ISSUE		EDITION LIMIT	YEAR RETD.	ISSUE PRICE	*QUOTE U.S.$
1994	Babs Bunny QXM4116	Yr.Iss.	1994	5.75	14
1994	Baby's First Christmas QXM4003	Yr.Iss.	1994	5.75	12
1994	Baking Tiny Treats, (Set/6) QXM4033	Yr.Iss.	1994	29.00	58-65
1994	Beary Perfect Tree QXM4076	Yr.Iss.	1994	4.75	9
1994	The Bearymores (3rd Ed.) QXM5133	Yr.Iss.	1994	5.75	13
1994	Buster Bunny QXM5163	Yr.Iss.	1994	5.75	13
1994	Centuries of Santa (1st Ed.) QXM5153	Yr.Iss.	1994	6.00	15-25
1994	Corny Elf QXM4063	Yr.Iss.	1994	4.50	9
1994	Cute as a Button QXM4103	Yr.Iss.	1994	3.75	14
1994	Dazzling Reindeer (Pr. Ed.) QXM4026	Yr.Iss.	1994	9.75	19
1994	Dizzy Devil QXM4133	Yr.Iss.	1994	5.75	13
1994	Friends Need Hugs QXM4016	Yr.Iss.	1994	4.50	13
1994	Graceful Carousel QXM4056	Yr.Iss.	1994	7.75	17
1994	Hamton QXM4126	Yr.Iss.	1994	5.75	12
1994	Hat Shop (7th Ed.) QXM5143	Yr.Iss.	1994	7.00	17
1994	Have a Cookie QXM5166	Yr.Iss.	1994	5.75	15
1994	Hearts A-Sail QXM4006	Yr.Iss.	1994	5.75	13
1994	Jolly Visitor QXM4053	Yr.Iss.	1994	5.75	15
1994	Jolly Wolly Snowman QXM4093	Yr.Iss.	1994	3.75	13
1994	Journey to Bethlehem QXM4036	Yr.Iss.	1994	5.75	13
1994	Just My Size QXM4086	Yr.Iss.	1994	3.75	10
1994	Love Was Born QXM4043	Yr.Iss.	1994	4.50	13
1994	March of the Teddy Bears (2nd Ed.) QXM5106	Yr.Iss.	1994	4.50	15
1994	Melodic Cherub QXM4066	Yr.Iss.	1994	3.75	9
1994	A Merry Flight QXM4073	Yr.Iss.	1994	5.75	12
1994	Mom QXM4013	Yr.Iss.	1994	4.50	11
1994	Nature's Angels (5th Ed.) QXM5126	Yr.Iss.	1994	4.50	12
1994	Night Before Christmas (3rd Ed.) QXM5123	Yr.Iss.	1994	4.50	13
1994	Noah's Ark (Sp. Ed.)) QXM4106	Yr.Iss.	1994	24.50	45-60
1994	Nutcracker Guild (1st Ed.) QXM5146	Yr.Iss.	1994	5.75	15-25
1994	On the Road (2nd Ed.) QXM5103	Yr.Iss.	1994	5.75	15
1994	Plucky Duck QXM4123	Yr.Iss.	1994	5.75	14
1994	Pour Some More QXM5156	Yr.Iss.	1994	5.75	12
1994	Rocking Horse (7th Ed.) QXM5116	Yr.Iss.	1994	4.50	11-18
1994	Scooting Along QXM5173	Yr.Iss.	1994	6.75	14
1994	Stock Car (6th Ed.) QXM5113	Yr.Iss.	1994	7.00	18
1994	Sweet Dreams QXM4096	Yr.Iss.	1994	3.00	14
1994	Tea With Teddy QXM4046	Yr.Iss.	1994	7.25	15

1994 New Attractions - Keepsake

YEAR ISSUE		EDITION LIMIT	YEAR RETD.	ISSUE PRICE	*QUOTE U.S.$
1994	All Pumped Up QX5923	Yr.Iss.	1994	8.95	18
1994	Angel Hare QX5896	Yr.Iss.	1994	8.95	19
1994	Batman QX5853	Yr.Iss.	1994	12.95	30
1994	Beatles Gift Set QX5373	Yr.Iss.	1994	48.00	100
1994	BEATRIX POTTER The Tale of Peter Rabbit QX2443	Yr.Iss.	1994	5.00	20
1994	Big Shot QX5873	Yr.Iss.	1994	7.95	17
1994	Busy Batter QX5876	Yr.Iss.	1994	7.95	18
1994	Candy Caper QX5776	Yr.Iss.	1994	8.95	18
1994	Caring Doctor QX5823	Yr.Iss.	1994	8.95	18
1994	Champion Teacher QX5836	Yr.Iss.	1994	6.95	15
1994	Cheers to You! QX5796	Yr.Iss.	1994	10.95	25
1994	Cheery Cyclists QX5786	Yr.Iss.	1994	12.95	28
1994	Child Care Giver QX5906	Yr.Iss.	1994	7.95	16
1994	Coach QX5933	Yr.Iss.	1994	7.95	18
1994	Colors of Joy QX5893	Yr.Iss.	1994	7.95	18
1994	Cowardly Lion QX5446	Yr.Iss.	1994	9.95	35-80
1994	Daffy Duck QX5415	Yr.Iss.	1994	8.95	20
1994	Daisy Days QX5986	Yr.Iss.	1994	9.95	16-25
1994	Deer Santa Mouse (2) QX5806	Yr.Iss.	1994	14.95	29
1994	Dorothy and Toto QX5433	Yr.Iss.	1994	10.95	55-95
1994	Extra-Special Delivery QX5833	Yr.Iss.	1994	7.95	16
1994	Feelin' Groovy QX5953	Yr.Iss.	1994	7.95	21
1994	A Feline of Christmas QX5816	Yr.Iss.	1994	8.95	27
1994	Feliz Navidad QX5793	Yr.Iss.	1994	8.95	20
1994	Follow the Sun QX5846	Yr.Iss.	1994	8.95	18
1994	Fred and Barney QX5003	Yr.Iss.	1994	14.95	28-40
1994	Friendship Sundae QX4766	Yr.Iss.	1994	10.95	20-25
1994	GARFIELD QX5753	Yr.Iss.	1994	12.95	28
1994	Gentle Nurse QX5973	Yr.Iss.	1994	6.95	18
1994	Harvest Joy QX5993	Yr.Iss.	1994	9.95	16-25
1994	Hearts in Harmony QX4406	Yr.Iss.	1994	10.95	21
1994	Helpful Shepherd QX5536	Yr.Iss.	1994	8.95	18
1994	Holiday Patrol QX5826	Yr.Iss.	1994	8.95	18
1994	Ice Show QX5946	Yr.Iss.	1994	7.95	17
1994	In the Pink QX5763	Yr.Iss.	1994	9.95	22
1994	It's a Strike QX5856	Yr.Iss.	1994	8.95	18
1994	Jingle Bell Band QX5783	Yr.Iss.	1994	10.95	24-30
1994	Joyous Song QX4473	Yr.Iss.	1994	8.95	18
1994	Jump-along Jackalope QX5756	Yr.Iss.	1994	8.95	18
1994	Kickin' Roo QX5916	Yr.Iss.	1994	7.95	16
1994	Kringle's Kayak QX5886	Yr.Iss.	1994	7.95	18
1994	LEGO'S QX5453	Yr.Iss.	1994	10.95	23-30
1994	Lou Rankin Seal QX5456	Yr.Iss.	1994	9.95	20
1994	Magic Carpet Ride QX5883	Yr.Iss.	1994	7.95	23
1994	Mary Engelbreit QX2416	Yr.Iss.	1994	5.00	17
1994	Merry Fishmas QX5913	Yr.Iss.	1994	8.95	18
1994	Mistletoe Surprise (2)QX5996	Yr.Iss.	1994	12.95	27
1994	Norman Rockwell QX2413	Yr.Iss.	1994	5.00	13-20
1994	Open-and-Shut Holiday QX5696	Yr.Iss.	1994	9.95	21
1994	Out of This World Teacher QX5766	Yr.Iss.	1994	7.95	19
1994	Practice Makes Perfect QX5863	Yr.Iss.	1994	7.95	17
1994	Red Hot Holiday QX5843	Yr.Iss.	1994	7.95	18
1994	Reindeer Pro QX5926	Yr.Iss.	1994	7.95	16
1994	Relaxing Moment QX5356	Yr.Iss.	1994	14.95	28-32
1994	Road Runner and Wile E. Coyote QX5602	Yr.Iss.	1994	12.95	28
1994	Scarecrow QX5436	Yr.Iss.	1994	9.95	35-85
1994	A Sharp Flat QX5773	Yr.Iss.	1994	10.95	24
1994	Speedy Gonzales QX5343	Yr.Iss.	1994	8.95	19-25
1994	Stamp of Approval QX5703	Yr.Iss.	1994	7.95	16
1994	Sweet Greeting (2) QX5803	Yr.Iss.	1994	10.95	21
1994	Tasmanian Devil QX5605	Yr.Iss.	1994	8.95	45-60
1994	Thrill a Minute QX5866	Yr.Iss.	1994	8.95	18
1994	Time of Peace QX5813	Yr.Iss.	1994	7.95	15
1994	Tin Man QX5443	Yr.Iss.	1994	9.95	33-85
1994	Tulip Time QX5983	Yr.Iss.	1994	9.95	16-25
1994	Winnie the Pooh/Tigger QX5746	Yr.Iss.	1994	12.95	29-35
1994	Yosemite Sam QX5346	Yr.Iss.	1994	8.95	20
1994	Yuletide Cheer QX5976	Yr.Iss.	1994	9.95	16-25

1994 Premiere Event - Keepsake

YEAR ISSUE		EDITION LIMIT	YEAR RETD.	ISSUE PRICE	*QUOTE U.S.$
1994	Eager for Christmas QX5336	Yr.Iss.	1994	15.00	22

1994 Showcase Christmas Lights - Keepsake

YEAR ISSUE		EDITION LIMIT	YEAR RETD.	ISSUE PRICE	*QUOTE U.S.$
1994	Home for the Holidays QK1123	Yr.Iss.	1994	15.75	32
1994	Moonbeams QK1116	Yr.Iss.	1994	15.75	16
1994	Mother and Child QK1126	Yr.Iss.	1994	15.75	16
1994	Peaceful Village QK1106	Yr.Iss.	1994	15.75	16

1994 Showcase Folk Art Americana Collection - Keepsake

YEAR ISSUE		EDITION LIMIT	YEAR RETD.	ISSUE PRICE	*QUOTE U.S.$
1994	Catching 40 Winks QK1183	Yr.Iss.	1994	16.75	35
1994	Going to Town QK1166	Yr.Iss.	1994	15.75	34
1994	Racing Through the Snow QK1173	Yr.Iss.	1994	15.75	50
1994	Rarin' to Go QK1193	Yr.Iss.	1994	15.75	36
1994	Roundup Time QK1176	Yr.Iss.	1994	16.75	38

1994 Showcase Holiday Favorites - Keepsake

YEAR ISSUE		EDITION LIMIT	YEAR RETD.	ISSUE PRICE	*QUOTE U.S.$
1994	Dapper Snowman QK1053	Yr.Iss.	1994	13.75	14
1994	Graceful Fawn QK1033	Yr.Iss.	1994	11.75	24
1994	Jolly Santa QK1046	Yr.Iss.	1994	13.75	28
1994	Joyful Lamb QK1036	Yr.Iss.	1994	11.75	24
1994	Peaceful Dove QK1043	Yr.Iss.	1994	11.75	24

1994 Showcase Old World Silver Collection - Keepsake

YEAR ISSUE		EDITION LIMIT	YEAR RETD.	ISSUE PRICE	*QUOTE U.S.$
1994	Silver Bells QK1026	Yr.Iss.	1994	24.75	40
1994	Silver Bows QK1023	Yr.Iss.	1994	24.75	40
1994	Silver Poinsettias QK1006	Yr.Iss.	1994	24.75	40
1994	Silver Snowflakes QK1016	Yr.Iss.	1994	24.75	40

1994 Special Edition - Keepsake

YEAR ISSUE		EDITION LIMIT	YEAR RETD.	ISSUE PRICE	*QUOTE U.S.$
1994	Lucinda and Teddy QX4813	Yr.Iss.	1994	21.75	30-43

1994 Special Issues - Keepsake

YEAR ISSUE		EDITION LIMIT	YEAR RETD.	ISSUE PRICE	*QUOTE U.S.$
1994	Barney QLX7506	Yr.Iss.	1994	24.00	27-50
1994	Barney QX5966	Yr.Iss.	1994	9.95	25
1994	Holiday Barbie™ (2nd Ed.) QX5216	Yr.Iss.	1994	14.95	45-55
1994	Klingon Bird of Prey™ QLX7386	Yr.Iss.	1994	24.00	45-50
1994	Mufasa/Simba-Lion King QX5406	Yr.Iss.	1994	14.95	30
1994	Nostalgic-Barbie™ (1st Ed.) QX5006	Yr.Iss.	1994	14.95	35-50
1994	Simba/Nala-Lion King (pr.) QX5303	Yr.Iss.	1994	12.95	26-35
1994	Simba/Sarabi/Mufasa the Lion King QLX7513	Yr.Iss.	1994	20.00	41-70
1994	Simba/Sarabi/Mufasa the Lion King QLX7513	Yr.Iss.	1994	32.00	66
1994	Timon/Pumbaa-Lion King QX5366	Yr.Iss.	1994	8.95	26-35

1995 Anniversary Edition - Keepsake

YEAR ISSUE		EDITION LIMIT	YEAR RETD.	ISSUE PRICE	*QUOTE U.S.$
1995	Pewter Rocking Horse QX6167	Yr.Iss.	1995	20.00	39-45

1995 Artists' Favorite - Keepsake

YEAR ISSUE		EDITION LIMIT	YEAR RETD.	ISSUE PRICE	*QUOTE U.S.$
1995	Barrel-Back Rider QX5189	Yr.Iss.	1995	9.95	26
1995	Our Little Blessings QX5209	Yr.Iss.	1995	12.95	25

1995 Collectible Series - Keepsake

YEAR ISSUE		EDITION LIMIT	YEAR RETD.	ISSUE PRICE	*QUOTE U.S.$
1995	1956 Ford Truck (1st Ed.) QX5527	Yr.Iss.	1995	13.95	30-35
1995	1969 Chevrolet Camaro (5th Ed.) QX5239	Yr.Iss.	1995	12.95	20-35
1995	Bright 'n' Sunny Tepee (7th Ed.) QX5247	Yr.Iss.	1995	10.95	19
1995	Camellia - Mary's Angels (8th Ed.) QX5149	Yr.Iss.	1995	6.95	15
1995	Cat Naps (2nd Ed.) QX5097	Yr.Iss.	1995	7.95	19-30
1995	A Celebration of Angels (1st Ed.) QX5077	Yr.Iss.	1995	12.95	18-35
1995	Christmas Eve Kiss (10th Ed.) QX5157	Yr.Iss.	1995	14.95	28
1995	Fabulous Decade (6th Ed.) QX5147	Yr.Iss.	1995	7.95	18
1995	Frosty Friends (16th Ed.) QX5169	Yr.Iss.	1995	10.95	21-32
1995	Jack and Jill (3rd Ed.) QX5099	Yr.Iss.	1995	13.95	24-30
1995	Lou Gehrig (2nd Ed.) QX5029	Yr.Iss.	1995	12.95	22-35
1995	Merry Olde Santa (6th Ed.) QX5139	Yr.Iss.	1995	14.95	19-35
1995	Murray® Fire Truck (2nd Ed.) QX5027	Yr.Iss.	1995	13.95	30
1995	The PEANUTS Gang (3rd Ed.) QX5059	Yr.Iss.	1995	9.95	20-30
1995	Puppy Love (5th Ed.) QX5137	Yr.Iss.	1995	7.95	19
1995	Rocking Horse (15th Ed.) QX5167	Yr.Iss.	1995	10.95	24-30
1995	Santa's Roadster (17th Ed.) QX5179	Yr.Iss.	1995	14.95	23
1995	St. Nicholas (1st Ed.) QX5087	Yr.Iss.	1995	14.95	30
1995	Tobin Fraley Carousel (4th Ed.) QX5069	Yr.Iss.	1995	28.00	50
1995	Town Church (12th Ed.) QX5159	Yr.Iss.	1995	14.95	26
1995	Twelve Drummers Drumming (12th Ed.) QX3009	Yr.Iss.	1995	6.95	19
1995	U.S. Christmas Stamps (3rd Ed.) QX5067	Yr.Iss.	1995	10.95	23
1995	Yuletide Central (2nd Ed.) QX5079	Yr.Iss.	1995	18.95	23-35

1995 Commemoratives - Keepsake

YEAR ISSUE		EDITION LIMIT	YEAR RETD.	ISSUE PRICE	*QUOTE U.S.$
1995	Across the Miles QX5847	Yr.Iss.	1995	8.95	18
1995	Air Express QX5977	Yr.Iss.	1995	7.95	17
1995	Anniversary Year QX5819	Yr.Iss.	1995	8.95	14
1995	Baby's First Christmas QX5547	Yr.Iss.	1995	18.95	42
1995	Baby's First Christmas QX5549	Yr.Iss.	1995	7.95	18
1995	Baby's First Christmas QX5557	Yr.Iss.	1995	9.95	18
1995	Baby's First Christmas QX5559	Yr.Iss.	1995	7.95	15-25
1995	Baby's First Christmas-Baby Boy QX2319	Yr.Iss.	1995	5.00	13
1995	Baby's First Christmas-Baby Girl QX2317	Yr.Iss.	1995	5.00	15
1995	Baby's Second Christmas QX5567	Yr.Iss.	1995	7.95	17-25
1995	Brother QX5679	Yr.Iss.	1995	6.95	13
1995	Child's Fifth Christmas QX[illegible]	Yr.Iss.	1995	[illegible]	10
1995	Child's Fourth Christmas QX5629	Yr.Iss.	1995	6.95	17-25
1995	Child's Third Christmas QX5627	Yr.Iss.	1995	7.95	17-25
1995	Christmas Fever QX5967	Yr.Iss.	1995	7.95	17
1995	Christmas Patrol QX5959	Yr.Iss.	1995	7.95	17
1995	Dad QX5649	Yr.Iss.	1995	7.95	17
1995	Dad-to-Be QX5667	Yr.Iss.	1995	7.95	16
1995	Daughter QX5677	Yr.Iss.	1995	6.95	19
1995	For My Grandma QX5729	Yr.Iss.	1995	6.95	14
1995	Friendly Boost QX5827	Yr.Iss.	1995	8.95	21
1995	Godchild QX5707	Yr.Iss.	1995	7.95	20
1995	Godparent QX2417	Yr.Iss.	1995	5.00	14
1995	Grandchild's First Christmas QX5777	Yr.Iss.	1995	7.95	15
1995	Granddaughter QX5779	Yr.Iss.	1995	6.95	16
1995	Grandmother QX5767	Yr.Iss.	1995	7.95	26
1995	Grandpa QX5769	Yr.Iss.	1995	8.95	17
1995	Grandparents QX2419	Yr.Iss.	1995	5.00	12
1995	Grandson QX5787	Yr.Iss.	1995	6.95	16
1995	Important Memo QX5947	Yr.Iss.	1995	8.95	18
1995	In a Heartbeat QX5817	Yr.Iss.	1995	8.95	18
1995	Mom and Dad QX5657	Yr.Iss.	1995	9.95	23
1995	Mom QX5647	Yr.Iss.	1995	7.95	17
1995	Mom-to-Be QX5659	Yr.Iss.	1995	7.95	14
1995	New Home QX5839	Yr.Iss.	1995	8.95	18
1995	North Pole 911 QX5957	Yr.Iss.	1995	10.95	23
1995	Number One Teacher QX5949	Yr.Iss.	1995	7.95	16
1995	Our Christmas Together QX5809	Yr.Iss.	1995	9.95	18
1995	Our Family QX5709	Yr.Iss.	1995	7.95	16
1995	Our First Christmas Together QX3177	Yr.Iss.	1995	6.95	19
1995	Our First Christmas Together QX5797	Yr.Iss.	1995	16.95	34
1995	Our First Christmas Together QX5799	Yr.Iss.	1995	8.95	18-25
1995	Our First Christmas Together QX5807	Yr.Iss.	1995	8.95	18
1995	Packed With Memories QX5639	Yr.Iss.	1995	7.95	18
1995	Sister QX5687	Yr.Iss.	1995	6.95	13
1995	Sister to Sister QX5689	Yr.Iss.	1995	8.95	18
1995	Son QX5669	Yr.Iss.	1995	6.95	17
1995	Special Cat QX5717	Yr.Iss.	1995	7.95	15
1995	Special Dog QX5719	Yr.Iss.	1995	7.95	15
1995	Two for Tea QX5829	Yr.Iss.	1995	9.95	32

1995 Easter Ornaments - Keepsake

YEAR ISSUE		EDITION LIMIT	YEAR RETD.	ISSUE PRICE	*QUOTE U.S.$
1995	3 Flowerpot Friends 1495QEO8229	Yr.Iss.	1995	14.95	25
1995	Baby's First Easter QEO8237	Yr.Iss.	1995	7.95	16
1995	Bugs Bunny (Looney Tunes) QEO8279	Yr.Iss.	1995	8.95	19
1995	Bunny w/Crayons (Crayola) QEO8249	Yr.Iss.	1995	7.95	19
1995	Bunny w/Seed Packets (Tender Touches) QEO8259	Yr.Iss.	1995	8.95	19
1995	Bunny w/Water Bucket QEO8253	Yr.Iss.	1995	6.95	14

*Quotes have been rounded up to nearest dollar

Collectors' Information Bureau

167

ORNAMENTS

YEAR ISSUE		EDITION LIMIT	YEAR RETD.	ISSUE PRICE	*QUOTE U.S.$
1995	Collector's Plate (2nd Ed.) QEO8219	Yr.Iss.	1995	7.95	18
1995	Daughter Duck QEO8239	Yr.Iss.	1995	5.95	13
1995	Easter Beagle (Peanuts) QEO8257	Yr.Iss.	1995	7.95	18-25
1995	Easter Egg Cottages (1st Ed.) QEO8207	Yr.Iss.	1995	8.95	25
1995	Garden Club (1st Ed.) QEO8209	Yr.Iss.	1995	7.95	20
1995	Ham n Eggs QEO8277	Yr.Iss.	1995	7.95	16
1995	Here Comes Easter (2nd Ed.) QEO8217	Yr.Iss.	1995	7.95	20
1995	Lily (Religious) QEO8267	Yr.Iss.	1995	6.95	12
1995	Miniature Train QEO8269	Yr.Iss.	1995	4.95	13
1995	Son Duck QEO8247	Yr.Iss.	1995	5.95	16
1995	Springtime Barbie™ (1st Ed.) QEO8069	Yr.Iss.	1995	12.95	35
1995	Springtime Bonnets (3rd Ed.) QEO8227	Yr.Iss.	1995	7.95	17-23

1995 Keepsake Collector's Club - Keepsake

YEAR ISSUE		EDITION LIMIT	YEAR RETD.	ISSUE PRICE	*QUOTE U.S.$
1995	1958 Ford Edsel Citation Convertible QXC4167	Yr.Iss.	1995	12.95	51-75
1995	Brunette Debut-1959 QXC5397	Yr.Iss.	1995	14.95	50-75
1995	Christmas Eve Bake-Off QXC4049	Yr.Iss.	1995	55.00	170
1995	Cinderella's Stepsisters QXC4159	Yr.Iss.	1995	3.75	4
1995	Collecting Memories QXC4117	Yr.Iss.	1995	12.00	16
1995	Cool Santa QXC4457	Yr.Iss.	1995	5.75	12
1995	Cozy Christmas QXC4119	Yr.Iss.	1995	8.50	14
1995	Fishing for Fun QXC5207	Yr.Iss.	1995	10.95	17
1995	A Gift From Rodney QXC4129	Yr.Iss.	1995	5.00	9
1995	Home From the Woods QXC1059	Yr.Iss.	1995	15.95	41-65
1995	May Flower QXC8246	Yr.Iss.	1995	4.95	25

1995 Keepsake Magic Ornaments - Keepsake

YEAR ISSUE		EDITION LIMIT	YEAR RETD.	ISSUE PRICE	*QUOTE U.S.$
1995	Baby's First Christmas QLX7317	Yr.Iss.	1995	22.00	43
1995	Chris Mouse Tree (11th Ed.) QLX7307	Yr.Iss.	1995	12.50	24
1995	Coming to See Santa QLX7369	Yr.Iss.	1995	32.00	65
1995	Forest Frolics (7th Ed.) QLX7299	Yr.Iss.	1995	28.00	55
1995	Fred and Dino QLX7289	Yr.Iss.	1995	28.00	57
1995	Friends Share Fun QLX7349	Yr.Iss.	1995	16.50	36
1995	Goody Gumballs! QLX7367	Yr.Iss.	1995	12.50	31
1995	Headin' Home QLX7327	Yr.Iss.	1995	22.00	47
1995	Holiday Swim QLX7319	Yr.Iss.	1995	18.50	36
1995	Jukebox Party QLX7339	Yr.Iss.	1995	24.50	25
1995	Jumping for Joy QLX7347	Yr.Iss.	1995	28.00	60
1995	My First HOT WHEELS™ QLX7279	Yr.Iss.	1995	28.00	43
1995	PEANUTS (5th Ed.) QLX7277	Yr.Iss.	1995	24.50	45-50
1995	Santa's Diner QLX7337	Yr.Iss.	1995	24.50	33
1995	Space Shuttle QLX7396	Yr.Iss.	1995	24.50	28-50
1995	Superman™ QLX7309	Yr.Iss.	1995	28.00	53
1995	Tobin Fraley Holiday Carousel (2nd Ed.) QLX7269	Yr.Iss.	1995	32.00	60-65
1995	Victorian Toy Box (Special Ed.) QLX7357	Yr.Iss.	1995	42.00	55-66
1995	Wee Little Christmas QLX7329	Yr.Iss.	1995	22.00	43
1995	Winnie the Pooh Too Much Hunny QLX7297	Yr.Iss.	1995	24.50	50

1995 Miniature Ornaments - Keepsake

YEAR ISSUE		EDITION LIMIT	YEAR RETD.	ISSUE PRICE	*QUOTE U.S.$
1995	Alice in Wonderland (1st Ed.) QXM4777	Yr.Iss.	1995	6.75	15
1995	Baby's First Christmas QXM4027	Yr.Iss.	1995	4.75	13
1995	Calamity Coyote QXM4467	Yr.Iss.	1995	6.75	15
1995	Centuries of Santa (2nd Ed.) QXM4789	Yr.Iss.	1995	5.75	13-20
1995	Christmas Bells (1st Ed.) QXM4007	Yr.Iss.	1995	4.75	17
1995	Christmas Wishes QXM4087	Yr.Iss.	1995	3.75	13
1995	Cloisonne Partridge QXM4017	Yr.Iss.	1995	9.75	18
1995	Downhill Double QXM4837	Yr.Iss.	1995	4.75	13
1995	Friendship Duet QXM4019	Yr.Iss.	1995	4.75	13
1995	Furrball QXM4459	Yr.Iss.	1995	5.75	15
1995	Grandpa's Gift QXM4829	Yr.Iss.	1995	5.75	13
1995	Heavenly Praises QXM4037	Yr.Iss.	1995	5.75	13
1995	Joyful Santa QXM4089	Yr.Iss.	1995	4.75	12
1995	Little Beeper QXM4469	Yr.Iss.	1995	5.75	15
1995	March of the Teddy Bears (3rd Ed.) QXM4799	Yr.Iss.	1995	4.75	13
1995	Merry Walruses QXM4057	Yr.Iss.	1995	5.75	15
1995	Milk Tank Car (7th Ed.) QXM4817	Yr.Iss.	1995	6.75	17
1995	Miniature Clothespin Soldier (1st Ed.) QXM4097	Yr.Iss.	1995	3.75	15
1995	A Moustershire Christmas QXM4839	Yr.Iss.	1995	24.50	43-49
1995	Murray® "Champion" (1st Ed.) QXM4079	Yr.Iss.	1995	5.75	17
1995	Nature's Angels (6th Ed.) QXM4809	Yr.Iss.	1995	4.75	17
1995	The Night Before Christmas (4th Ed.) QXM4807	Yr.Iss.	1995	4.75	16
1995	Nutcracker Guild (2nd Ed.) QXM4787	Yr.Iss.	1995	5.75	13-20
1995	On the Road (3rd Ed.) QXM4797	Yr.Iss.	1995	5.75	15
1995	Pebbles and Bamm-Bamm QXM4757	Yr.Iss.	1995	9.75	13
1995	Playful Penguins QXM4059	Yr.Iss.	1995	5.75	17
1995	Precious Creations QXM4077	Yr.Iss.	1995	9.75	18
1995	Rocking Horse (8th Ed.) QXM4827	Yr.Iss.	1995	4.75	13
1995	Santa's Little Big Top (1st Ed.) QXM4779	Yr.Iss.	1995	6.75	15
1995	Santa's Visit QXM4047	Yr.Iss.	1995	7.75	17
1995	Starlit Nativity QXM4039	Yr.Iss.	1995	7.75	19
1995	Sugarplum Dreams QXM4099	Yr.Iss.	1995	4.75	12
1995	Tiny Treasures (set/6) QXM4009	Yr.Iss.	1995	29.00	43-50
1995	Tudor House (8th Ed.) QXM4819	Yr.Iss.	1995	6.75	16
1995	Tunnel of Love QXM4029	Yr.Iss.	1995	4.75	12

1995 New Attractions - Keepsake

YEAR ISSUE		EDITION LIMIT	YEAR RETD.	ISSUE PRICE	*QUOTE U.S.$
1995	Acorn 500 QX5929	Yr.Iss.	1995	10.95	18
1995	Batmobile QX5739	Yr.Iss.	1995	14.95	28
1995	Betty and Wilma QX5417	Yr.Iss.	1995	14.95	26
1995	Bingo Bear QX5919	Yr.Iss.	1995	7.95	18
1995	Bobbin' Along QX5879	Yr.Iss.	1995	8.95	35-40
1995	Bugs Bunny QX5019	Yr.Iss.	1995	8.95	14-20
1995	Catch the Spirit QX5899	Yr.Iss.	1995	7.95	19
1995	Christmas Morning QX5997	Yr.Iss.	1995	10.95	18
1995	Colorful World QX5519	Yr.Iss.	1995	10.95	19
1995	Cows of Bali QX5999	Yr.Iss.	1995	8.95	18
1995	Delivering Kisses QX4107	Yr.Iss.	1995	10.95	21
1995	Dream On QX6007	Yr.Iss.	1995	10.95	22
1995	Dudley the Dragon QX6209	Yr.Iss.	1995	10.95	21
1995	Faithful Fan QX5897	Yr.Iss.	1995	8.95	18
1995	Feliz Navidad QX5869	Yr.Iss.	1995	7.95	18
1995	Forever Friends Bear QX5258	Yr.Iss.	1995	8.95	21
1995	GARFIELD QX5007	Yr.Iss.	1995	10.95	23
1995	Glinda, Witch of the North QX5749	Yr.Iss.	1995	13.95	20-30
1995	Gopher Fun QX5887	Yr.Iss.	1995	9.95	24
1995	Happy Wrappers QX6037	Yr.Iss.	1995	10.95	22
1995	Heaven's Gift QX6057	Yr.Iss.	1995	20.00	40
1995	Hockey Pup QX5917	Yr.Iss.	1995	9.95	25
1995	In Time With Christmas QX6049	Yr.Iss.	1995	12.95	27
1995	Joy to the World QX5867	Yr.Iss.	1995	8.95	19
1995	LEGO® Fireplace w/Santa QX4769	Yr.Iss.	1995	10.95	23
1995	Lou Rankin Bear QX4069	Yr.Iss.	1995	9.95	19
1995	The Magic School Bus™ QX5849	Yr.Iss.	1995	10.95	22
1995	Mary Engelbreit QX2409	Yr.Iss.	1995	5.00	16
1995	Merry RV QX6027	Yr.Iss.	1995	12.95	27
1995	Muletide Greetings QX6009	Yr.Iss.	1995	7.95	16
1995	The Olympic Spirit QX3169	Yr.Iss.	1995	7.95	20
1995	On the Ice QX6047	Yr.Iss.	1995	7.95	21
1995	Perfect Balance QX5927	Yr.Iss.	1995	7.95	16
1995	PEZ® Santa QX5267	Yr.Iss.	1995	7.95	15-25
1995	Polar Coaster QX6117	Yr.Iss.	1995	8.95	22-30
1995	Popeye® QX5257	Yr.Iss.	1995	10.95	20-34
1995	Refreshing Gift QX4067	Yr.Iss.	1995	14.95	28
1995	Rejoice! QX5987	Yr.Iss.	1995	10.95	22
1995	Roller Whiz QX5937	Yr.Iss.	1995	7.95	18
1995	Santa in Paris QX5877	Yr.Iss.	1995	8.95	29
1995	Santa's Serenade QX6017	Yr.Iss.	1995	8.95	18
1995	Santa's Visitors QX2407	Yr.Iss.	1995	5.00	19
1995	Simba, Pumbaa & Timon QX6159	Yr.Iss.	1995	12.95	13-30
1995	Ski Hound QX5909	Yr.Iss.	1995	8.95	19
1995	Surfin' Santa QX6019	Yr.Iss.	1995	9.95	21
1995	Sylvester and Tweety QX5017	Yr.Iss.	1995	13.95	23
1995	Takin' a Hike QX6029	Yr.Iss.	1995	7.95	19
1995	Tennis, Anyone? QX5907	Yr.Iss.	1995	7.95	18
1995	Thomas the Tank Engine-No. 1 QX5857	Yr.Iss.	1995	9.95	28
1995	Three Wishes QX5979	Yr.Iss.	1995	7.95	18
1995	Vera the Mouse QX5537	Yr.Iss.	1995	8.95	17
1995	Waiting Up for Santa QX6106	Yr.Iss.	1995	8.95	18
1995	Water Sports QX6039	Yr.Iss.	1995	14.95	27-35
1995	Wheel of Fortune® QX6187	Yr.Iss.	1995	12.95	23
1995	Winnie the Pooh & Tigger QX5009	Yr.Iss.	1995	12.95	26-35
1995	The Winning Play QX5889	Yr.Iss.	1995	7.95	17-25

1995 Premiere Event - Keepsake

YEAR ISSUE		EDITION LIMIT	YEAR RETD.	ISSUE PRICE	*QUOTE U.S.$
1995	Wish List QX5859	Yr.Iss.	1995	15.00	29

1995 Showcase All Is Bright Collection - Keepsake

YEAR ISSUE		EDITION LIMIT	YEAR RETD.	ISSUE PRICE	*QUOTE U.S.$
1995	Angel of Light QK1159	Yr.Iss.	1995	11.95	23
1995	Gentle Lullaby QK1157	Yr.Iss.	1995	11.95	23

1995 Showcase Angel Bells Collection - Keepsake

YEAR ISSUE		EDITION LIMIT	YEAR RETD.	ISSUE PRICE	*QUOTE U.S.$
1995	Carole QK1147	Yr.Iss.	1995	12.95	25-35
1995	Joy QK1137	Yr.Iss.	1995	12.95	23
1995	Noelle QK1139	Yr.Iss.	1995	12.95	24

1995 Showcase Folk Art Americana Collection - Keepsake

YEAR ISSUE		EDITION LIMIT	YEAR RETD.	ISSUE PRICE	*QUOTE U.S.$
1995	Fetching the Firewood QK1057	Yr.Iss.	1995	15.95	33
1995	Fishing Party QK1039	Yr.Iss.	1995	15.95	33
1995	Guiding Santa QK1037	Yr.Iss.	1995	18.95	45
1995	Learning to Skate QK1047	Yr.Iss.	1995	14.95	36

1995 Showcase Holiday Enchantment Collection - Keepsake

YEAR ISSUE		EDITION LIMIT	YEAR RETD.	ISSUE PRICE	*QUOTE U.S.$
1995	Away in a Manger QK1097	Yr.Iss.	1995	13.95	25
1995	Following the Star QK1099	Yr.Iss.	1995	13.95	25

1995 Showcase Invitation to Tea Collection - Keepsake

YEAR ISSUE		EDITION LIMIT	YEAR RETD.	ISSUE PRICE	*QUOTE U.S.$
1995	Cozy Cottage Teapot QK1127	Yr.Iss.	1995	15.95	30
1995	European Castle Teapot QK1129	Yr.Iss.	1995	15.95	30
1995	Victorian Home Teapot QK1119	Yr.Iss.	1995	15.95	33

1995 Showcase Nature's Sketchbook Collection - Keepsake

YEAR ISSUE		EDITION LIMIT	YEAR RETD.	ISSUE PRICE	*QUOTE U.S.$
1995	Backyard Orchard QK1069	Yr.Iss.	1995	18.95	30
1995	Christmas Cardinal QK1077	Yr.Iss.	1995	18.95	40
1995	Raising a Family QK1067	Yr.Iss.	1995	18.95	30
1995	Violets and Butterflies QK1079	Yr.Iss.	1995	16.95	30

1995 Showcase Symbols of Christmas Collection - Keepsake

YEAR ISSUE		EDITION LIMIT	YEAR RETD.	ISSUE PRICE	*QUOTE U.S.$
1995	Jolly Santa QK1087	Yr.Iss.	1995	15.95	29
1995	Sweet Song QK1089	Yr.Iss.	1995	15.95	29

1995 Showcase Turn-of-the-Century Parade - Keepsake

YEAR ISSUE		EDITION LIMIT	YEAR RETD.	ISSUE PRICE	*QUOTE U.S.$
1995	The Fireman QK1027	Yr.Iss.	1995	16.95	35-45

1995 Special Edition - Keepsake

YEAR ISSUE		EDITION LIMIT	YEAR RETD.	ISSUE PRICE	*QUOTE U.S.$
1995	Beverly and Teddy QX5259	Yr.Iss.	1995	21.75	30

1995 Special Issues - Keepsake

YEAR ISSUE		EDITION LIMIT	YEAR RETD.	ISSUE PRICE	*QUOTE U.S.$
1995	Captain James T. Kirk QXI5539	Yr.Iss.	1995	13.95	18-35
1995	Captain Jean-Luc Picard QXI5737	Yr.Iss.	1995	13.95	18-35
1995	Captain John Smith and Meeko QXI6169	Yr.Iss.	1995	12.95	23
1995	Holiday Barbie™ (3rd Ed.) QXI5057	Yr.Iss.	1995	14.95	30-40
1995	Hoop Stars (1st Ed.) QXI5517	Yr.Iss.	1995	14.95	30-50
1995	Joe Montana (1st Ed.) QXI5759	Yr.Iss.	1995	14.95	35-50
1995	Percy, Flit and Meeko QXI6179	Yr.Iss.	1995	9.95	16
1995	Pocahontas and Captain John Smith QXI6197	Yr.Iss.	1995	14.95	22
1995	Pocahontas QXI6177	Yr.Iss.	1995	12.95	17
1995	Romulan Warbird™ QXI7267	Yr.Iss.	1995	24.00	22-45
1995	The Ships of Star Trek® QXI4109	Yr.Iss.	1995	19.95	17-35
1995	Solo in the Spotlight-Barbie™ (2nd Ed.) QXI5049	Yr.Iss.	1995	14.95	23-30

1995 Special Offer - Keepsake

YEAR ISSUE		EDITION LIMIT	YEAR RETD.	ISSUE PRICE	*QUOTE U.S.$
1995	Charlie Brown QRP4207	Yr.Iss.	1995	3.95	22-35
1995	Linus QRP4217	Yr.Iss.	1995	3.95	19-25
1995	Lucy QRP4209	Yr.Iss.	1995	3.95	17-25
1995	SNOOPY QRP4219	Yr.Iss.	1995	3.95	20-31
1995	Snow Scene QRP4227	Yr.Iss.	1995	3.95	15-25
1995	5-Pc. Set	Yr.Iss.	1995	19.95	60-75

1996 Collectible Series - Keepsake

YEAR ISSUE		EDITION LIMIT	YEAR RETD.	ISSUE PRICE	*QUOTE U.S.$
1996	1955 Chevrolet Cameo (2nd Ed.) QX5241	Yr.Iss.	1996	13.95	14
1996	1959 Cadillac De Ville (6th Ed.) QX5384	Yr.Iss.	1996	12.95	13
1996	700E Hudson Steam Locomotive (1st Ed.) QX5531	Yr.Iss.	1996	18.95	40-55
1996	Bright Flying Colors (8th Ed.) QX5391	Yr.Iss.	1996	10.95	18
1996	Cat Naps (3rd Ed.) QX5641	Yr.Iss.	1996	7.95	8
1996	A Celebration of Angels (2nd Ed.) QX5634	Yr.Iss.	1996	12.95	13
1996	Christkind (2nd Ed.) QX5631	Yr.Iss.	1996	14.95	15
1996	Christy-All God's Children-Martha Holcombe (1st Ed.) QX5564	Yr.Iss.	1996	12.95	13
1996	Cinderella-1995 (1st Ed.) QX6311	Yr.Iss.	1996	14.95	30
1996	Evergreen Santa (Special Ed.) QX5714	Yr.Iss.	1996	22.00	22
1996	Fabulous Decade (7th Ed.) QX5661	Yr.Iss.	1996	7.95	8
1996	Frosty Friends (17th Ed.) QX5681	Yr.Iss.	1996	10.95	11
1996	Mary Had a Little Lamb (4th Ed.) QX5644	Yr.Iss.	1996	13.95	14
1996	Merry Olde Santa (7th Ed.) QX5654	Yr.Iss.	1996	14.95	15
1996	Murray Airplane (3rd Ed.) QX5364	Yr.Iss.	1996	13.95	14
1996	Native American Barbie™ (1st Ed.) QX5561	Yr.Iss.	1996	14.95	15
1996	The PEANUTS Gang (4th Ed.) QX5381	Yr.Iss.	1996	9.95	10
1996	Puppy Love (6th Ed.) QX5651	Yr.Iss.	1996	7.95	8
1996	Rocking Horse (16th Ed.) QX5674	Yr.Iss.	1996	10.95	35
1996	Santa's 4X4 (18th Ed.) QX5684	Yr.Iss.	1996	14.95	15
1996	Satchel Paige (3rd Ed.) QX5304	Yr.Iss.	1996	12.95	13
1996	Victorian Painted Lady (13th Ed.) QX5671	Yr.Iss.	1996	14.95	15
1996	Violet-Mary's Angels (9th Ed.) QX5664	Yr.Iss.	1996	6.95	7
1996	Yuletide Central (3rd Ed.) QX5011	Yr.Iss.	1996	18.95	19

1996 Commemoratives - Keepsake

YEAR ISSUE		EDITION LIMIT	YEAR RETD.	ISSUE PRICE	*QUOTE U.S.$
1996	Baby's First Christmas QX5754	Yr.Iss.	1996	9.95	10
1996	Baby's First Christmas-Beatrix Potter QX5744	Yr.Iss.	1996	18.95	19
1996	Baby's First Christmas-Bessie Pease Gutmann QX5751	Yr.Iss.	1996	10.95	11
1996	Baby's First Christmas-Child's Age Collection QX5764	Yr.Iss.	1996	7.95	8
1996	Baby's First Christmas-Photo Holder QX5761	Yr.Iss.	1996	7.95	8
1996	Baby's Second Christmas - Child's Age Collection QX5771	Yr.Iss.	1996	7.95	20
1996	Child's Fifth Christmas-Child's Age Collection QX5784	Yr.Iss.	1996	6.95	7
1996	Child's Fourth Christmas-Child's Age Collection QX5781	Yr.Iss.	1996	7.95	20
1996	Child's Third Christmas-Child's Age Collection QX5774	Yr.Iss.	1996	7.95	20
1996	Close-Knit Friends QX5874	Yr.Iss.	1996	9.95	10
1996	Dad QX5831	Yr.Iss.	1996	7.95	8
1996	Daughter QX6077	Yr.Iss.	1996	8.95	9
1996	Godchild QX5841	Yr.Iss.	1996	8.95	9
1996	Granddaughter QX5697	Yr.Iss.	1996	7.95	8
1996	Grandma QX5844	Yr.Iss.	1996	8.95	9
1996	Grandpa QX5851	Yr.Iss.	1996	8.95	9
1996	Grandson QX5699	Yr.Iss.	1996	7.95	8
1996	Hearts Full of Love QX5814	Yr.Iss.	1996	9.95	10
1996	Mom and Dad QX5821	Yr.Iss.	1996	9.95	10
1996	Mom QX5824	Yr.Iss.	1996	7.95	8
1996	Mom-to-Be QX5791	Yr.Iss.	1996	7.95	8
1996	New Home QX5881	Yr.Iss.	1996	8.95	9
1996	On My Way-Photo Holder QX5861	Yr.Iss.	1996	7.95	8
1996	Our Christmas Together QX5794	Yr.Iss.	1996	18.95	19
1996	Our Christmas Together-Photo Holder QX5804	Yr.Iss.	1996	8.95	9
1996	Our First Christmas Together QX5811	Yr.Iss.	1996	9.95	10

*Quotes have been rounded up to nearest dollar

YEAR ISSUE		EDITION LIMIT	YEAR RETD.	ISSUE PRICE	*QUOTE U.S.$
1996	Our First Christmas Together -Acrylic QX3051	Yr.Iss.	1996	6.95	7
1996	Our First Christmas Together -Collector's Plate QX5801	Yr.Iss.	1996	10.95	11
1996	Sister to Sister QX5834	Yr.Iss.	1996	9.95	10
1996	Son QX6079	Yr.Iss.	1996	8.95	9
1996	Special Dog Photo Holder QX5864	Yr.Iss.	1996	7.95	8
1996	Thank You, Santa-Photo Holder QX5854	Yr.Iss.	1996	7.95	8

1996 Keepsake Collector's Club - Keepsake

YEAR ISSUE		EDITION LIMIT	YEAR RETD.	ISSUE PRICE	*QUOTE U.S.$
1996	1937 Steelcraft Auburn by Murray QXC4174	Yr.Iss.	1996	15.95	16
1996	1988 Happy Holidays Barbie™ Doll QXC4181	Yr.Iss.	1996	14.95	15
1996	Airmail for Santa QXC4194	Yr.Iss.	1996	8.95	9
1996	Rudolph the Red-Nosed Reindeer QXC7341	Yr.Iss.	1996	N/A	27
1996	Rudolph's Helper QXC4171	Yr.Iss.	1996	N/A	13
1996	Santa QXC4164	Yr.Iss.	1996	N/A	20
1996	Santa's Club Soda #4 QXC4191	Yr.Iss.	1996	8.50	19
1996	Santa's Toy Shop QXC4201	Yr.Iss.	1996	60.00	125
1996	The Wizard of Oz QXC4161	Yr.Iss.	1996	12.95	31

1996 Keepsake Magic Ornaments - Keepsake

YEAR ISSUE		EDITION LIMIT	YEAR RETD.	ISSUE PRICE	*QUOTE U.S.$
1996	Baby's First Christmas QLX7404	Yr.Iss.	1996	22.00	22
1996	Chicken Coop Chorus QLX7491	Yr.Iss.	1996	24.50	25
1996	Chris Mouse Inn (12th Ed.) QLX7371	Yr.Iss.	1996	14.50	15
1996	Father Time QLX7391	Yr.Iss.	1996	24.50	25
1996	Freedom 7 (1st Ed.) QLX7524	Yr.Iss.	1996	24.00	50
1996	THE JETSONS QLX7411	Yr.Iss.	1996	28.00	28
1996	Jukebox Party QLX7339	Yr.Iss.	1996	24.50	25
1996	Let Us Adore Him QLX7381	Yr.Iss.	1996	16.50	17
1996	North Pole Volunteers (Special Ed.) QLX7471	Yr.Iss.	1996	42.00	90
1996	Over the Rooftops QLX7374	Yr.Iss.	1996	14.50	15
1996	PEANUTS-Lucy and Schroeder QLX7394	Yr.Iss.	1996	18.50	19
1996	Pinball Wonder QLX7451	Yr.Iss.	1996	28.00	28
1996	Sharing a Soda QLX7424	Yr.Iss.	1996	24.50	25
1996	Slippery Day QLX7414	Yr.Iss.	1996	24.50	25
1996	STAR WARS-Millennium Falcon QLX7474	Yr.Iss.	1996	24.00	48-55
1996	The Statue of Liberty QLX7421	Yr.Iss.	1996	24.50	25
1996	Tobin Fraley Holiday Carousel (3rd Ed.) QLX7461	Yr.Iss.	1996	32.00	32
1996	Treasured Memories QLX7384	Yr.Iss.	1996	18.50	19
1996	Video Party QLX7431	Yr.Iss.	1996	28.00	28
1996	THE WIZARD OF OZ-Emerald City QLX7454	Yr.Iss.	1996	32.00	55

1996 Miniature Ornaments - Keepsake

YEAR ISSUE		EDITION LIMIT	YEAR RETD.	ISSUE PRICE	*QUOTE U.S.$
1996	African Elephants QXM4224	Yr.Iss.	1996	5.75	14
1996	Centuries of Santa (3rd Ed.) QXM4091	Yr.Iss.	1996	5.75	6
1996	A Child's Gifts QXM4234	Yr.Iss.	1996	6.75	7
1996	Christmas Bear QXM4241	Yr.Iss.	1996	4.75	5
1996	Christmas Bells (2nd Ed.) QXM4071	Yr.Iss.	1996	4.75	15
1996	Cookie Car (8th Ed.) QXM4114	Yr.Iss.	1996	6.75	7
1996	Cool Delivery Coca-Cola QXM4021	Yr.Iss.	1996	5.75	6
1996	GONE WITH THE WIND QXM4211	Yr.Iss.	1996	19.95	40-65
1996	Hattie Chapeau QXM4251	Yr.Iss.	1996	4.75	5
1996	Joyous Angel QXM4231	Yr.Iss.	1996	4.75	5
1996	Long Winter's Nap QXM4244	Yr.Iss.	1996	5.75	6
1996	Loony Tunes Lovables Baby Sylvester QXM4154	Yr.Iss.	1996	5.75	15
1996	Loony Tunes Lovables Baby Tweety QXM4014	Yr.Iss.	1996	5.75	25
1996	Mad Hatter (2nd Ed.) QXM4074	Yr.Iss.	1996	6.75	7
1996	March of the Teddy Bears (4th Ed.) QXM4094	Yr.Iss.	1996	4.75	5
1996	Message for Santa QXM4254	Yr.Iss.	1996	6.75	7
1996	Miniature Clothespin Soldier (2nd Ed.) QXM4144	Yr.Iss.	1996	4.75	5
1996	Murray "Fire Truck" (2nd Ed.) QXM4031	Yr.Iss.	1996	6.75	7
1996	Nature's Angels (7th Ed.) QXM4111	Yr.Iss.	1996	4.75	5
1996	The Night Before Christmas (5th Ed.) QXM4104	Yr.Iss.	1996	5.75	6
1996	The Nutcracker Ballet (1st Ed.) QXM4064	Yr.Iss.	1996	14.75	15
1996	Nutcracker Guild (3rd Ed.) QXM4084	Yr.Iss.	1996	5.75	6
1996	O Holy Night (Special Ed.) QXM4204	Yr.Iss.	1996	24.50	25
1996	On the Road (4th Ed.) QXM4101	Yr.Iss.	1996	5.75	6
1996	Peaceful Christmas QXM4214	Yr.Iss.	1996	4.75	5
1996	Rocking Horse (9th Ed.) QXM4121	Yr.Iss.	1996	4.75	5
1996	Santa's Little Big Top (2nd Ed.) QXM4081	Yr.Iss.	1996	6.75	7
1996	Sparkling Crystal Angel (Precious Ed.) QXM4264	Yr.Iss.	1996	9.75	24
1996	Tiny Christmas Helpers QXM4261	Yr.Iss.	1996	29.00	29
1996	A Tree for WOODSTOCK QXM4767	Yr.Iss.	1996	5.75	15
1996	The Vehicles of STAR WARS QXM4024	Yr.Iss.	1996	19.95	20
1996	Village Mill (9th Ed.) QXM4124	Yr.Iss.	1996	6.75	7
1996	Winnie the Pooh & Tigger QXM4044	Yr.Iss.	1996	9.75	20

1996 New Attractions - Keepsake

YEAR ISSUE		EDITION LIMIT	YEAR RETD.	ISSUE PRICE	*QUOTE U.S.$
1996	Antlers Aweigh! QX5901	Yr.Iss.	1996	9.95	10
1996	Apple for Teacher QX6121	Yr.Iss.	1996	7.95	8
1996	Bounce Pass QX6031	Yr.Iss.	1996	7.95	8
1996	Bowl 'em Over QX6014	Yr.Iss.	1996	7.95	8
1996	BOY SCOUTS OF AMERICA Growth of a Leader QX5541	Yr.Iss.	1996	9.95	10
1996	Child Care Giver QX6071	Yr.Iss.	1996	8.95	9
1996	Christmas Joy QX6241	Yr.Iss.	1996	14.95	15
1996	Christmas Snowman QX6214	Yr.Iss.	1996	9.95	10
1996	Come All Ye Faithful QX6244	Yr.Iss.	1996	12.95	13
1996	Fan-tastic Season QX5924	Yr.Iss.	1996	9.95	10
1996	Feliz Navidad QX6304	Yr.Iss.	1996	9.95	10
1996	Glad Tidings QX6231	Yr.Iss.	1996	14.95	15
1996	Goal Line Glory QX6001	Yr.Iss.	1996	12.95	13
1996	Happy Holi-doze QX5904	Yr.Iss.	1996	9.95	10
1996	High Style QX6064	Yr.Iss.	1996	8.95	9
1996	Hillside Express QX6134	Yr.Iss.	1996	12.95	13
1996	Holiday Haul QX6201	Yr.Iss.	1996	14.95	15
1996	Hurrying Downstairs QX6074	Yr.Iss.	1996	8.95	9
1996	I Dig Golf QX5891	Yr.Iss.	1996	10.95	11
1996	Jackpot Jingle QX5911	Yr.Iss.	1996	9.95	10
1996	Jolly Wolly Ark QX6221	Yr.Iss.	1996	12.95	13
1996	Kindly Shepherd QX6274	Yr.Iss.	1996	12.95	13
1996	Lighting the Way QX6124	Yr.Iss.	1996	12.95	13
1996	A Little Song and Dance QX6211	Yr.Iss.	1996	9.95	10
1996	Little Spooners QX5504	Yr.Iss.	1996	12.95	13
1996	LOONEY TUNES Foghorn Leghorn and Henery Hawk QX5444	Yr.Iss.	1996	13.95	14
1996	LOONEY TUNES Marvin the Martian QX5451	Yr.Iss.	1996	10.95	25
1996	Madonna & Child QX6324	Yr.Iss.	1996	12.95	13
1996	Making His Rounds QX6271	Yr.Iss.	1996	14.95	15
1996	Matchless Memories QX6061	Yr.Iss.	1996	9.95	10
1996	Maxine QX6224	Yr.Iss.	1996	9.95	10
1996	Merry Carpoolers QX5884	Yr.Iss.	1996	14.95	15
1996	Olive Oyl and Swee' Pea QX5481	Yr.Iss.	1996	10.95	20
1996	Peppermint Surprise QX6234	Yr.Iss.	1996	7.95	8
1996	Percy the Small Engine-No. 6. QX6314	Yr.Iss.	1996	9.95	10
1996	PEZ® Snowman QX6534	Yr.Iss.	1996	7.95	8
1996	Polar Cycle QX6034	Yr.Iss.	1996	12.95	13
1996	Prayer for Peace QX6261	Yr.Iss.	1996	7.95	8
1996	Precious Child QX6251	Yr.Iss.	1996	8.95	9
1996	Pup-Tenting QX6011	Yr.Iss.	1996	7.95	8
1996	Regal Cardinal QX6204	Yr.Iss.	1996	9.95	10
1996	Sew Sweet QX5921	Yr.Iss.	1996	8.95	9
1996	SPIDER-MAN QX5757	Yr.Iss.	1996	12.95	13
1996	Star of the Show QX6004	Yr.Iss.	1996	8.95	9
1996	Tamika QX6301	Yr.Iss.	1996	7.95	8
1996	Tender Lovin' Care QX6114	Yr.Iss.	1996	7.95	8
1996	This Big! QX5914	Yr.Iss.	1996	9.95	10
1996	Time for a Treat QX5464	Yr.Iss.	1996	11.95	12
1996	Tonka Mighty Dump Truck QX6321	Yr.Iss.	1996	13.95	14
1996	A Tree for SNOOPY QX5507	Yr.Iss.	1996	8.95	20
1996	Welcome Guest QX5394	Yr.Iss.	1996	14.95	15
1996	Welcome Him QX6264	Yr.Iss.	1996	8.95	9
1996	Winnie the Pooh and Piglet QX5454	Yr.Iss.	1996	12.95	28
1996	THE WIZARD OF OZ Witch of the West QX5554	Yr.Iss.	1996	13.95	14
1996	WONDER WOMAN QX5941	Yr.Iss.	1996	12.95	13
1996	Woodland Santa QX6131	Yr.Iss.	1996	12.95	13
1996	Yogi Bear and Boo Boo QX5521	Yr.Iss.	1996	12.95	13
1996	Yuletide Cheer QX6054	Yr.Iss.	1996	7.95	8
1996	Ziggy QX6524	Yr.Iss.	1996	9.95	10

1996 NFL Ornaments - Keepsake

YEAR ISSUE		EDITION LIMIT	YEAR RETD.	ISSUE PRICE	*QUOTE U.S.$
1996	Arizona Cardinals QSR6484	Yr.Iss.	1996	9.95	10
1996	Atlanta Falcons QSR6364	Yr.Iss.	1996	9.95	10
1996	Browns QSR6391	Yr.Iss.	1996	9.95	10
1996	Buffalo Bills QSR6371	Yr.Iss.	1996	9.95	10
1996	Carolina Panthers QSR6374	Yr.Iss.	1996	9.95	10
1996	Chicago Bears QSR6381	Yr.Iss.	1996	9.95	10
1996	Cincinnati Bengals QSR6384	Yr.Iss.	1996	9.95	10
1996	Dallas Cowboys QSR6394	Yr.Iss.	1996	9.95	10
1996	Denver Broncos QSR6411	Yr.Iss.	1996	9.95	10
1996	Detroit Lions QSR6414	Yr.Iss.	1996	9.95	10
1996	Green Bay Packers QSR6421	Yr.Iss.	1996	9.95	10
1996	Indianapolis Colts QSR6431	Yr.Iss.	1996	9.95	10
1996	Jacksonville Jaguars QSR6434	Yr.Iss.	1996	9.95	10
1996	Kansas City Chiefs QSR6361	Yr.Iss.	1996	9.95	10
1996	Miami Dolphins QSR6451	Yr.Iss.	1996	9.95	10
1996	Minnesota Vikings QSR6454	Yr.Iss.	1996	9.95	10
1996	New England Patriots QSR6461	Yr.Iss.	1996	9.95	10
1996	New Orleans Saints QSR6464	Yr.Iss.	1996	9.95	10
1996	New York Giants QSR6471	Yr.Iss.	1996	9.95	10
1996	New York Jets QSR6474	Yr.Iss.	1996	9.95	10
1996	Oakland Raiders QSR6441	Yr.Iss.	1996	9.95	10
1996	Oilers QSR6424	Yr.Iss.	1996	9.95	10
1996	Philadelphi Eagles QSR6481	Yr.Iss.	1996	9.95	10
1996	Pittsburgh Steelers QSR6491	Yr.Iss.	1996	9.95	10
1996	San Diego Chargers QSR6494	Yr.Iss.	1996	9.95	10
1996	San Francisco 49ers QSR6501	Yr.Iss.	1996	9.95	10
1996	Seattle Seahawks QSR6504	Yr.Iss.	1996	9.95	10
1996	St.Louis Rams QSR6444	Yr.Iss.	1996	9.95	10
1996	Tampa Bay Buccaneers QSR6511	Yr.Iss.	1996	9.95	10
1996	Washington Redskins QSR6514	Yr.Iss.	1996	9.95	10

1996 Premiere Event - Keepsake

YEAR ISSUE		EDITION LIMIT	YEAR RETD.	ISSUE PRICE	*QUOTE U.S.$
1996	Bashful Mistletoe-Merry Minatures QFM8054	Yr.Iss.	1996	12.95	13
1996	Welcome Sign-Tender Touches QX6331	Yr.Iss.	1996	15.00	15

1996 Showcase Cookie Jar Friends Collection - Keepsake

YEAR ISSUE		EDITION LIMIT	YEAR RETD.	ISSUE PRICE	*QUOTE U.S.$
1996	Carmen QK1164	Yr.Iss.	1996	15.95	16
1996	Clyde QK1161	Yr.Iss.	1996	15.95	16

1996 Showcase Folk Art Americana Collection - Keepsake

YEAR ISSUE		EDITION LIMIT	YEAR RETD.	ISSUE PRICE	*QUOTE U.S.$
1996	Caroling Angel QK1134	Yr.Iss.	1996	16.95	35
1996	Mrs. Claus QK1204	Yr.Iss.	1996	18.95	35-45
1996	Santa's Gifts QK1124	Yr.Iss.	1996	18.95	40-50

1996 Showcase Magi Bells Collection - Keepsake

YEAR ISSUE		EDITION LIMIT	YEAR RETD.	ISSUE PRICE	*QUOTE U.S.$
1996	Balthasar (Frankincense) QK1174	Yr.Iss.	1996	13.95	14
1996	Caspar (Myrrh) QK1184	Yr.Iss.	1996	13.95	14
1996	Melchior (Gold) QK1181	Yr.Iss.	1996	13.95	14

1996 Showcase Nature's Sketchbook Collection - Keepsake

YEAR ISSUE		EDITION LIMIT	YEAR RETD.	ISSUE PRICE	*QUOTE U.S.$
1996	The Birds' Christmas Tree QK1114	Yr.Iss.	1996	18.95	19
1996	Christmas Bunny QK1104	Yr.Iss.	1996	18.95	19
1996	The Holly Basket QK1094	Yr.Iss.	1996	18.95	19

1996 Showcase Sacred Masterworks Collection - Keepsake

YEAR ISSUE		EDITION LIMIT	YEAR RETD.	ISSUE PRICE	*QUOTE U.S.$
1996	Madonna and Child QK1144	Yr.Iss.	1996	15.95	16
1996	Praying Madonna QK1154	Yr.Iss.	1996	15.95	16

1996 Showcase The Lanuage of Flowers Collection - Keepsake

YEAR ISSUE		EDITION LIMIT	YEAR RETD.	ISSUE PRICE	*QUOTE U.S.$
1996	Pansy-1st Ed. QK1171	Yr.Iss.	1996	15.95	16

1996 Showcase Turn-of-the-Century Parade Collection - Keepsake

YEAR ISSUE		EDITION LIMIT	YEAR RETD.	ISSUE PRICE	*QUOTE U.S.$
1996	Uncle Sam-2nd Ed. QK1084	Yr.Iss.	1996	16.95	17

1996 Special Issues - Keepsake

YEAR ISSUE		EDITION LIMIT	YEAR RETD.	ISSUE PRICE	*QUOTE U.S.$
1996	101 Dalmatians-Collector's Plate QXI6544	Yr.Iss.	1996	12.95	13
1996	Featuring the Enchanted Evening -Barbie™ Doll (3rd Ed.) QXI6541	Yr.Iss.	1996	14.95	15
1996	Holiday Barbie™ (4th Ed.) QXI5371	Yr.Iss.	1996	14.95	25-35
1996	HUNCHBACK OF NOTRE DAME -Esmeralda and Djali QXI6351	Yr.Iss.	1996	14.95	15
1996	HUNCHBACK OF NOTRE DAME -Laverne, Victor and Hugo QXI6354	Yr.Iss.	1996	12.95	13
1996	THE HUNCHBACK OF NOTRE DAME-Quasimodo QXI6341	Yr.Iss.	1996	9.95	10
1996	It's A Wonderful Life™ (Anniversay Ed.) QXI6531	Yr.Iss.	1996	14.95	15
1996	Larry Bird-Hoop Stars (2nd Ed.) QXI5014	Yr.Iss.	1996	14.95	15
1996	Nolan Ryan-At the Ballpark (1st Ed.) QXI5711	Yr.Iss.	1996	14.95	25-35
1996	OLYMPIC-Cloisonne Medallion QXE4041	Yr.Iss.	1996	9.75	10
1996	OLYMPIC-Invitation to the Games QXE5511	Yr.Iss.	1996	14.95	15
1996	OLYMPIC-IZZY-The Mascot QXE5724	Yr.Iss.	1996	9.95	10
1996	OLYMPIC-Lighting the Flame QXE7444	Yr.Iss.	1996	28.00	28
1996	OLYMPIC-Olympic Triumph QXE5731	Yr.Iss.	1996	10.95	11
1996	OLYMPIC-Parade of Nations -Collector's Plate QXE5741	Yr.Iss.	1996	10.95	11
1996	STAR TREK® THE NEXT GENERATION-Commander William T. Riker QXI5551	Yr.Iss.	1996	14.95	15
1996	STAR TREK®-30 Years QXI7534	Yr.Iss.	1996	45.00	75-100
1996	STAR TREK®-Mr. Spock QXI5544	Yr.Iss.	1996	14.95	15
1996	STAR TREK®-U.S.S.Voyager QXI7544	Yr.Iss.	1996	24.00	24
1996	Troy Aikman-Football Legends (2nd Ed.) QXI5021	Yr.Iss.	1996	14.95	15

1996 Spring Ornaments - Keepsake

YEAR ISSUE		EDITION LIMIT	YEAR RETD.	ISSUE PRICE	*QUOTE U.S.$
1996	Apple Blossom Lane QEO8084	Yr.Iss.	1996	8.95	17
1996	Collector's Plate QEO8221	Yr.Iss.	1996	7.95	14
1996	Daffy Duck, LOONEY TUNES QEO8154	Yr.Iss.	1996	8.95	16
1996	Easter Morning QEO8164	Yr.Iss.	1996	7.95	16
1996	Eggstra Special Surprise, Tender Touches QEO8161	Yr.Iss.	1996	8.95	18
1996	Garden Club QEO8091	Yr.Iss.	1996	7.95	16
1996	Here Comes Easter QEO8094	Yr.Iss.	1996	7.95	17
1996	Hippity-Hop Delivery, CRAYOLA Crayon QEO8144	Yr.Iss.	1996	7.95	17
1996	Joyful Angels QEO8184	Yr.Iss.	1996	9.95	27
1996	Locomotive, Cottontail Express QEO8074	Yr.Iss.	1996	8.95	36-50
1996	Look What I Found! QEO8181	Yr.Iss.	1996	7.95	15
1996	Parade Pals, PEANUTS QEO8151	Yr.Iss.	1996	7.95	16-25
1996	Peter Rabbit™ Beatrix Potter™ QEO8071	Yr.Iss.	1996	8.95	65-95
1996	Pork 'n Beans QEO8174	Yr.Iss.	1996	7.95	8
1996	Springtime Barbie™ QEO8081	Yr.Iss.	1996	12.95	28
1996	Springtime Bonnets QEO8134	Yr.Iss.	1996	7.95	27
1996	Strawberry Patch QEO8171	Yr.Iss.	1996	6.95	15
1996	Strike Up the Band! QEO8141	Yr.Iss.	1996	14.95	21

1997 Collectible Series - Keepsake

YEAR ISSUE		EDITION LIMIT	YEAR RETD.	ISSUE PRICE	*QUOTE U.S.$
1997	1950 Santa Fe F3 Diesel Locomotive-LIONEL (2nd Ed.) QX6145	Yr.Iss.		18.95	19
1997	1953 GMC-All-American Trucks (3rd Ed.) QX6105	Yr.Iss.		13.95	14

*Quotes have been rounded up to nearest dollar

YEAR ISSUE		EDITION LIMIT	YEAR RETD.	ISSUE PRICE	*QUOTE U.S. $
1997	1969 Hurst Oldsmobile 442-Classic American Cars (7th Ed.) QX6102	Yr.Iss.		13.95	14
1997	Bright Rocking Colors-CRAYOLA Crayon (8th Ed.) QX6235	Yr.Iss.		12.95	13
1997	Cafe-Nostalgic Houses and Shops (14th Ed.) QX6245	Yr.Iss.		16.95	17
1997	Cat Naps (4th Ed.) QX6205	Yr.Iss.		8.95	9
1997	A Celebration of Angels (3rd Ed.) QX6175	Yr.Iss.		13.95	14
1997	Chinese Barbie™-Dolls of the World (2nd Ed.) QX6162	Yr.Iss.		14.95	15
1997	The Claus-Mobile-Here Comes Santa (19th Ed.) QX6262	Yr.Iss.		14.95	15
1997	The Clauses on Vacation (1st Ed.) QX6112	Yr.Iss.		14.95	15
1997	Daisy-Mary's Angels (10th Ed.) QX6242	Yr.Iss.		7.95	8
1997	Fabulous Decade (8th Ed.) QX6232	Yr.Iss.		7.95	8
1997	The Flight at Kitty Hawk-Sky's the Limit (1st Ed.) QX5574	Yr.Iss.		14.95	15
1997	Frosty Friends (18th Ed.) QX6255	Yr.Iss.		10.95	11
1997	Jackie Robinson-Baseball Heroes (4th Ed.) QX6202	Yr.Iss.		12.95	13
1997	Kolyada-Christmas Visitors (3rd Ed.) QX6172	Yr.Iss.		14.95	15
1997	Little Boy Blue-Mother Goose (5th Ed.) QX6215	Yr.Iss.		13.95	14
1997	Little Red Riding Hood-1991-Madame Alexander (2nd Ed.) QX6155	Yr.Iss.		14.95	15
1997	Marilyn Monroe (1st Ed.) QX5704	Yr.Iss.		14.95	15
1997	Merry Olde Santa (8th Ed.) QX6225	Yr.Iss.		14.95	15
1997	Murray Dump Truck-Kiddie Car Classics (4th Ed.) QX6195	Yr.Iss.		13.95	14
1997	Nikki-All God's Children-Martha Root (2nd Ed.) QX6142	Yr.Iss.		12.95	13
1997	Puppy Love (7th Ed.) QX6222	Yr.Iss.		7.95	8
1997	Santa Claus-Turn-of-the-Century Parade (3rd Ed.) QX1215	Yr.Iss.		16.95	17
1997	Scarlett O'Hara (1st Ed.) QX6125	Yr.Iss.		14.95	15
1997	Snowdrop Angel-The Language of Flowers (2nd Ed.) QX1095	Yr.Iss.		15.95	16
1997	Snowshoe Rabbits in Winter -Mark Newman-Majestic Wilderness (1st Ed.) QX5694	Yr.Iss.		12.95	13
1997	Yuletide Central (4th Ed.) QX5812	Yr.Iss.		18.95	19

1997 Commemoratives - Keepsake

1997	Baby's First Christmas QX6485	Yr.Iss.		9.95	10
1997	Baby's First Christmas QX6492	Yr.Iss.		9.95	10
1997	Baby's First Christmas QX6535	Yr.Iss.		14.95	15
1997	Baby's First Christmas-Child's Age Collection QX6495	Yr.Iss.		7.95	8
1997	Baby's First Christmas-Photo Holder QX6482	Yr.Iss.		7.95	8
1997	Baby's Second Christmas-Child's Age Collection QX6502	Yr.Iss.		7.95	8
1997	Book of the Year-Photo Holder QX6645	Yr.Iss.		7.95	8
1997	Child's Fifth Christmas-Child's Age Collection QX6515	Yr.Iss.		7.95	8
1997	Child's Fourth Christmas-Child's Age Collection QX6512	Yr.Iss.		7.95	8
1997	Child's Third Christmas-Child's Age Collection QX6505	Yr.Iss.		7.95	8
1997	Dad QX6532	Yr.Iss.		8.95	9
1997	Daughter QX6612	Yr.Iss.		7.95	8
1997	Friendship Blend QX6655	Yr.Iss.		9.95	10
1997	Godchild QX6662	Yr.Iss.		7.95	8
1997	Granddaughter QX6622	Yr.Iss.		7.95	8
1997	Grandma QX6625	Yr.Iss.		8.95	9
1997	Grandson QX6615	Yr.Iss.		7.95	8
1997	Mom and Dad QX6522	Yr.Iss.		9.95	10
1997	Mom QX6525	Yr.Iss.		8.95	9
1997	New Home QX6652	Yr.Iss.		8.95	9
1997	Our Christmas Together QX6475	Yr.Iss.		16.95	17
1997	Our First Chirstmas Together QX6465	Yr.Iss.		10.95	11
1997	Our First Christmas Together Acrylic QX3182	Yr.Iss.		7.95	8
1997	Our First Christmas Together Photo Holder QX6472	Yr.Iss.		8.95	9
1997	Sister to Sister QX6635	Yr.Iss.		9.95	10
1997	Son QX6605	Yr.Iss.		7.95	8
1997	Special Dog-Photo Holder QX6632	Yr.Iss.		7.95	8

1997 Disney Ornaments - Keepsake

1997	101 Dalmatians-Two Tone QXD4015	Yr.Iss.		9.95	10
1997	Bandleader Mickey, Mickey's Holiday Parade (1st Ed.) QXD4022	Yr.Iss.		13.95	14
1997	Cinderella (1st Ed.) QXD4045	Yr.Iss.		14.95	15
1997	Cinderella-Gus & Jaq QXD4052	Yr.Iss.		12.95	13
1997	Donald's Surprising Gift, Hallmark Archives (1st Ed.) QXD4025	Yr.Iss.		12.95	13
1997	Goofy's Ski Adventure QXD4042	Yr.Iss.		12.95	13
1997	Honey of a Gift (Miniature) QXD4255	Yr.Iss.		6.95	7
1997	The Hunchback of Notre Dame Esmeralda & Phoebus QXD6344	Yr.Iss.		14.95	15
1997	Jasmine & Aladdin, Aladdin & King of Thieves QXD4062	Yr.Iss.		14.95	15
1997	The Lion King-Timon & Pumbaa QXD4065	Yr.Iss.		12.95	13
1997	Mickey Snow Angel QXD4035	Yr.Iss.		9.95	10
1997	Mickey's Long Shot QXD6412	Yr.Iss.		10.95	11
1997	New Pair of Skates QXD4032	Yr.Iss.		13.95	14
1997	Snow White (Anniversary Ed.) QXD4055	Yr.Iss.		16.95	17
1997	Waitin' on Santa QXD6365	Yr.Iss.		12.95	13
1997	Winnie the Pooh Plate QXE6835	Yr.Iss.		12.95	13

1997 Keepsake Collector's Club - Keepsake

1997	1937 Steelcraft Airflow by Murray QXC5185	Yr.Iss.		15.95	16
1997	1989 Happy Holidaysr Barbie™ Doll QXC5162	Yr.Iss.		15.95	16
1997	Away to the Window QXC5135	Yr.Iss.		N/A	N/A
1997	Farmer's Market, Tender Touches QXC5182	Yr.Iss.		15.00	15
1997	Happy Christmas to All! QXC5132	Yr.Iss.		N/A	N/A
1997	Jolly Old Santa QXC5145	Yr.Iss.		N/A	N/A
1997	Mrs. Claus (Artist on Tour) QXC5192	Yr.Iss.		14.95	15
1997	Ready for Santa QXC5142	Yr.Iss.		N/A	N/A
1997	Trimming Santa's Tree (Artist on Tour) QXC5175	Yr.Iss.		60.00	60

1997 Keepsake Magic Ornaments - Keepsake

1997	Chris Mouse Luminaria (13th Ed.) QLX7525	Yr.Iss.		14.95	15
1997	Friendship 7-Journeys Into Space (2nd Ed.) QLX7532	Yr.Iss.		24.00	24
1997	Glowing Angel QLX7435	Yr.Iss.		18.95	19
1997	Holiday Serenade QLX7485	Yr.Iss.		24.00	24
1997	Joy to the World QLX7512	Yr.Iss.		14.95	15
1997	Lighthouse Greetings (1st Ed.) QLX7442	Yr.Iss.		24.00	24
1997	The Lincoln Memorial QLX7522	Yr.Iss.		24.00	24
1997	LOONEY TUNES-Decorator Taz QLX7502	Yr.Iss.		30.00	30
1997	Madonna & Child QLX7425	Yr.Iss.		19.95	20
1997	Motorcycle Chums QLX7495	Yr.Iss.		24.00	24
1997	PEANUTS-Snoopy Plays Santa QLX7475	Yr.Iss.		22.00	22
1997	Santa's Secret Gift QLX7455	Yr.Iss.		24.00	24
1997	Santa's Showboat (Special Ed.) QLX7465	Yr.Iss.		42.00	42
1997	Teapot Party QLX7482	Yr.Iss.		18.95	19

1997 Miniature Ornaments - Keepsake

1997	ALICE IN WONDERLAND-White Rabbit (3rd Ed.) QXM4142	Yr.Iss.		6.95	7
1997	Antique Tractors (1st Ed.) QXM4185	Yr.Iss.		6.95	7
1997	Candy Car-Noel R.R. (9th Ed.) QXM4175	Yr.Iss.		6.95	7
1997	Casablanca QXM4272	Yr.Iss.		19.95	20
1997	Centuries of Santa (4th Ed.) QXM4295	Yr.Iss.		5.95	6
1997	Christmas Bells (3rd Ed.) QXM4162	Yr.Iss.		4.95	5
1997	Clothespin Soldier (3rd Ed.) QXM4155	Yr.Iss.		4.95	5
1997	Future Star QXM4232	Yr.Iss.		5.95	6
1997	He Is Born QXM4235	Yr.Iss.		7.95	8
1997	Heavenly Music QXM4292	Yr.Iss.		5.95	6
1997	Home Sweet Home QXM4222	Yr.Iss.		5.95	6
1997	Ice Cold Coca-Cola QXM4252	Yr.Iss.		6.95	7
1997	Murray "Pursuit" Airplane Kiddie Car Classic (3rd Ed.) QXM4132	Yr.Iss.		6.95	7
1997	NOAH'S ARK-Gentle Giraffes QXM4221	Yr.Iss.		5.95	6
1997	THE NUTCRACKER BALLET-Herr Drosselmeyer (2nd Ed.) QXM4135	Yr.Iss.		5.95	6
1997	Nutcracker Guild (4th Ed.) QXM4165	Yr.Iss.		6.95	7
1997	On The Road (5th Ed.) QXM4172	Yr.Iss.		5.95	6
1997	Our Lady of Guadalupe (Precious Ed.) QXM4275	Yr.Iss.		8.95	9
1997	Peppermint Painter QXM4312	Yr.Iss.		4.95	5
1997	Polar Bunnies QXM4332	Yr.Iss.		4.95	5
1997	Rocking Horse (10th Ed.) QXM4302	Yr.Iss.		4.95	5
1997	Santa's Little Big Top (3rd Ed.) QXM4152	Yr.Iss.		6.95	7
1997	Seeds of Joy QXM4242	Yr.Iss.		6.95	7
1997	Sew Talented QXM4195	Yr.Iss.		5.95	6
1997	Shutterbug QXM4212	Yr.Iss.		5.95	6
1997	Snowboard Bunny QXM4315	Yr.Iss.		4.95	5
1997	Snowflake Ballet Series (1st Ed.) QXM4192	Yr.Iss.		5.95	6
1997	Teddy-Bear Style (1st Ed.) QXM4215	Yr.Iss.		5.95	6
1997	Tiny Home Improvers,set/6 QXM4282	Yr.Iss.		29.00	29
1997	Victorian Skater QXM4305	Yr.Iss.		5.95	6
1997	Village Depot-Old English Village (10th Ed.) QXM4182	Yr.Iss.		6.95	7
1997	Welcome Friends (1st Ed.) QXM4205	Yr.Iss.		6.95	7
1997	THE WIZARD OF OZ-King of the Forest QXM4262	Yr.Iss.		24.00	24

1997 NBA Collection - Keepsake

1997	Charlotte Hornets QSR1222	Yr.Iss.		9.95	10
1997	Chicago Bulls QSR1232	Yr.Iss.		9.95	10
1997	Detroit Pistons QSR1242	Yr.Iss.		9.95	10
1997	Houston Rockets QSR1245	Yr.Iss.		9.95	10
1997	Indiana Pacers QSR1252	Yr.Iss.		9.95	10
1997	Los Angeles Lakers QSR1262	Yr.Iss.		9.95	10
1997	New York Knickerbockers QSR1272	Yr.Iss.		9.95	10
1997	Orlando Magic QSR1282	Yr.Iss.		9.95	10
1997	Phoenix Suns QSR1292	Yr.Iss.		9.95	10
1997	Seattle Supersonics QSR1295	Yr.Iss.		9.95	10

1997 New Attractions - Keepsake

1997	All-Round Sports Fan QX6392	Yr.Iss.		8.95	9
1997	All-Weather Walker QX6415	Yr.Iss.		8.95	9
1997	Angel Friend (Archive Collection) QX6762	Yr.Iss.		14.95	15
1997	Biking Buddies QX6682	Yr.Iss.		12.95	13
1997	BOY SCOUTS OF AMERICA -Tomorrow's Leader QX6452	Yr.Iss.		9.95	10
1997	Breezin' Along QX6722	Yr.Iss.		8.95	9
1997	Bucket Brigade QX6382	Yr.Iss.		8.95	9
1997	Catch of the Day QX6712	Yr.Iss.		9.95	10
1997	Christmas Checkup QX6385	Yr.Iss.		7.95	8
1997	Classic Cross QX6805	Yr.Iss.		13.95	14
1997	Clever Camper QX6445	Yr.Iss.		7.95	8
1997	Cycling Santa QX6425	Yr.Iss.		14.95	15
1997	Downhill Run QX6705	Yr.Iss.		9.95	10
1997	Elegance on Ice QX6432	Yr.Iss.		9.95	10
1997	Expressly for Teacher QX6375	Yr.Iss.		7.95	8
1997	Feliz Navidad QX6665	Yr.Iss.		8.95	9
1997	God's Gift of Love QX6792	Yr.Iss.		16.95	17
1997	Heavenly Song (Archive Collection) QX6795	Yr.Iss.		12.95	13
1997	HERSHEYS-Sweet Discovery QX6325	Yr.Iss.		11.95	12
1997	Howdy Doody (Anniversary Ed.) QX6272	Yr.Iss.		12.95	13
1997	The Incredible Hulk QX5471	Yr.Iss.		12.95	13
1997	Jingle Bell Jester QX6695	Yr.Iss.		9.95	10
1997	Juggling Stars QX6595	Yr.Iss.		9.95	9
1997	King Noor-First King-Legend of Three Kings Collection QX6552	Yr.Iss.		12.95	13
1997	Lion and Lamb QX6602	Yr.Iss.		7.95	8
1997	The Lone Ranger QX6265	Yr.Iss.		12.95	13
1997	LOONEY TUNES-Michigan J. Frog QX6332	Yr.Iss.		9.95	10
1997	Love to Sew QX6435	Yr.Iss.		7.95	8
1997	Madonna del Rosario QX6545	Yr.Iss.		12.95	13
1997	Marbles Champion QX6342	Yr.Iss.		10.95	11
1997	Meadow Snowman QX6715	Yr.Iss.		12.95	13
1997	Mr. Potato Head QX6335	Yr.Iss.		10.95	11
1997	Nativity Tree QX6575	Yr.Iss.		14.95	15
1997	The Night Before Christmas -Collector's Choice QX5721	Yr.Iss.		24.00	24
1997	Playful Shepherd QX6592	Yr.Iss.		9.95	10
1997	Porcelain Hinged Box QX6772	Yr.Iss.		14.95	15
1997	Praise Him QX6542	Yr.Iss.		8.95	9
1997	Prize Topiary QX6675	Yr.Iss.		14.95	15
1997	Sailor Bear QX6765	Yr.Iss.		14.95	15
1997	Santa Mail QX6702	Yr.Iss.		10.95	11
1997	Santa's Friend QX6685	Yr.Iss.		12.95	13
1997	Santa's Magical Sleigh QX6672	Yr.Iss.		24.00	24
1997	Santa's Polar Friend QX6755	Yr.Iss.		16.95	17
1997	Santa's Ski Adventure QX6422	Yr.Iss.		12.95	13
1997	Snow Bowling QX6395	Yr.Iss.		6.95	7
1997	Snow Girl QX6562	Yr.Iss.		7.95	8
1997	The Spirit of Christmas-Collector's Plate QX6585	Yr.Iss.		9.95	10
1997	Stealing a Kiss QX6555	Yr.Iss.		14.95	15
1997	Sweet Dreamer QX6732	Yr.Iss.		6.95	7
1997	Swinging in the Snow QX6775	Yr.Iss.		12.95	13
1997	Taking a Break-Coca-Cola QX6305	Yr.Iss.		14.95	15
1997	Tonka Mighty Front Loader QX6362	Yr.Iss.		13.95	14
1997	What a Deal! QX6442	Yr.Iss.		8.95	9
1997	THE WIZARD OF OZ-Miss Gulch QX6372	Yr.Iss.		13.95	14

1997 NFL Ornaments - Keepsake

1997	Arizona Cardinals QSR5505	Yr.Iss.		9.95	10
1997	Atlanta Falcons QSR5305	Yr.Iss.		9.95	10
1997	Baltimore Ravens QSR5352	Yr.Iss.		9.95	10
1997	Buffalo Bills QSR5312	Yr.Iss.		9.95	10
1997	Carolina Panthers QSR5315	Yr.Iss.		9.95	10
1997	Chicago Bears QSR5322	Yr.Iss.		9.95	10
1997	Cincinnati Bengals QSR5325	Yr.Iss.		9.95	10
1997	Dallas Cowboys QSR5355	Yr.Iss.		9.95	10
1997	Denver Broncos QSR5362	Yr.Iss.		9.95	10
1997	Detroit Lions QSR5365	Yr.Iss.		9.95	10
1997	Green Bay Packers QSR5372	Yr.Iss.		9.95	10
1997	Houston Oilers QSR5375	Yr.Iss.		9.95	10
1997	Indianapolis Colts QSR5411	Yr.Iss.		9.95	10
1997	Jacksonville Jaquars QSR5415	Yr.Iss.		9.95	10
1997	Kansas City Chiefs QSR5502	Yr.Iss.		9.95	10
1997	Miami Dolphins QSR5472	Yr.Iss.		9.95	10
1997	Minnesota Vikings QSR5475	Yr.Iss.		9.95	10
1997	New England Patriots QSR5482	Yr.Iss.		9.95	10
1997	New Orleans Saints QSR5485	Yr.Iss.		9.95	10
1997	New York Giants QSR5492	Yr.Iss.		9.95	10
1997	New York Jets QSR5495	Yr.Iss.		9.95	10
1997	Oakland Raiders QSR5422	Yr.Iss.		9.95	10
1997	Philadelphi Eagles QSR5502	Yr.Iss.		9.95	10
1997	Pittsburgh Steelers QSR5512	Yr.Iss.		9.95	10
1997	San Diego Chargers QSR5515	Yr.Iss.		9.95	10
1997	San Francisco 49ers QSR5522	Yr.Iss.		9.95	10
1997	Seattle Seahawks QSR5525	Yr.Iss.		9.95	10
1997	St. Louis Rams QSR5425	Yr.Iss.		9.95	10
1997	Tampa Bay Buccaneers QSR5532	Yr.Iss.		9.95	10
1997	Washington Redskins QSR5535	Yr.Iss.		9.95	10

1997 Premiere Event - Keepsake

1997	The Perfect Tree-Tender Touches QX6572	Yr.Iss.		15.00	15

*Quotes have been rounded up to nearest dollar

1997 Showcase Folk Art Americana Collection - Keepsake

YEAR ISSUE		EDITION LIMIT	YEAR RETD.	ISSUE PRICE	*QUOTE U.S.$
1997	Leading the Way QX6782	Yr.Iss.		16.95	17
1997	Santa's Merry Path QX6785	Yr.Iss.		16.95	10

1997 Showcase Nature's Sketchbook Collection - Keepsake

YEAR ISSUE		EDITION LIMIT	YEAR RETD.	ISSUE PRICE	*QUOTE U.S.$
1997	Garden Bouquet QX6752	Yr.Iss.		14.95	15
1997	Garden Bunnies QEO8702	Yr.Iss.		14.95	15
1997	Honored Guest QX6745	Yr.Iss.		14.95	15

1997 Special Issues - Keepsake

YEAR ISSUE		EDITION LIMIT	YEAR RETD.	ISSUE PRICE	*QUOTE U.S.$
1997	1997 Corvette Miniature QXI4322	Yr.Iss.		6.95	7
1997	1997 Corvette QXI6455	Yr.Iss.		13.95	14
1997	Ariel QXI4072	Yr.Iss.		12.95	13
1997	Barbie™ AND KEN Wedding Day QXI6815	Yr.Iss.		35.00	35
1997	Barbie™ Wedding Day-1959-1962 (4th Ed.) QXI6812	Yr.Iss.		15.95	16
1997	Hank Aaron-At the Ballpark (2nd Ed.) QXI6152	Yr.Iss.		14.95	15
1997	Hercules QXI4005	Yr.Iss.		12.95	13
1997	Holiday Barbie™(5th Ed.) QXI6212	Yr.Iss.		15.95	16
1997	Jeff Gordon-Stock Car Champions (1st Ed.) QXI6165	Yr.Iss.		15.95	16
1997	Joe Namath-Football Legends (3rd Ed.) QXI6182	Yr.Iss.		14.95	15
1997	Magic Johnson-Hoop Stars (3rd Ed.) QXI6832	Yr.Iss.		14.95	15
1997	Megara and Pegasus QXI4012	Yr.Iss.		16.95	17
1997	STAR TREK® U.S.S. Defiant QXI7481	Yr.Iss.		24.00	24
1997	STAR TREK® Dr. Leonard H. McCoy QXI6352	Yr.Iss.		14.95	15
1997	STAR TREK®: THE NEXT GENERATION Commander Date QXI6345	Yr.Iss.		14.95	15
1997	STAR WARS C-3PO & R2-D2 QXI4265	Yr.Iss.		12.95	13
1997	STAR WARS Darth Vader QXI7531	Yr.Iss.		24.00	24
1997	STAR WARS Luke Skywalker (1st Ed.) QXI5484	Yr.Iss.		13.95	14
1997	STAR WARS Yoda QXI6355	Yr.Iss.		9.95	10
1997	Victorian Christmas-Thomas Kinkade (1st Ed.) QXI6135	Yr.Iss.		10.95	11
1997	The Warmth of Home QXI7545	Yr.Iss.		18.95	19
1997	Wayne Gretzky-Hockey Greats (1st Ed.) QXI6275	Yr.Iss.		15.95	16

1997 Spring Ornaments - Keepsake

YEAR ISSUE		EDITION LIMIT	YEAR RETD.	ISSUE PRICE	*QUOTE U.S.$
1997	1935 Steelcraft Streamline Velocipede by Murray® Sidewalk Cruisers QEO8632	Yr.Iss.		12.95	13
1997	Apple Blossom Lane QEO8662	Yr.Iss.		8.95	9
1997	Barbie™ as Rapunzel Doll QEO8635	Yr.Iss.		14.95	15
1997	Bumper Crop, Tender Touches QEO8735	Yr.Iss.		14.95	15
1997	Collector's Plate QEO8675	Yr.Iss.		7.95	8
1997	Colorful Coal Car, Cottontail Express QEO8652	Yr.Iss.		8.95	9
1997	Digging In QEO8712	Yr.Iss.		7.95	8
1997	Eggs-pert Artist, CRAYOLA Crayon QEO8695	Yr.Iss.		8.95	9
1997	Garden Club QEO8665	Yr.Iss.		7.95	8
1997	Gentle Guardian QEO8732	Yr.Iss.		6.95	7
1997	Here Comes Easter QEO8682	Yr.Iss.		7.95	8
1997	Jemima Puddle-duck™ Beatrix Potter™ QEO8645	Yr.Iss.		8.95	9
1997	Joyful Angels QEO8655	Yr.Iss.		10.95	11
1997	A Purr-fect Princess QEO8715	Yr.Iss.		7.95	8
1997	Springtime Barbie™ QEO8642	Yr.Iss.		12.95	13
1997	Springtime Bonnets QEO8672	Yr.Iss.		7.95	8
1997	Swing-Time QEO8705	Yr.Iss.		7.95	8
1997	Victorian Cross QEO8725	Yr.Iss.		8.95	9

Hamilton Collection

Christmas Angels - S. Kuck

YEAR ISSUE		EDITION LIMIT	YEAR RETD.	ISSUE PRICE	*QUOTE U.S.$
1994	Angel of Charity	Open		19.50	20
1995	Angel of Joy	Open		19.50	20
1995	Angel of Grace	Open		19.50	20
1995	Angel of Faith	Open		19.50	20
1995	Angel of Patience	Open		19.50	20
1995	Angel of Glory	Open		19.50	20
1996	Angel of Gladness	Open		19.50	20
1996	Angel of Innocence	Open		19.50	20
1996	Angel of Beauty	Open		19.50	20
1996	Angel of Purity	Open		19.50	20
1996	Angel of Charm	Open		19.50	20
1996	Angel of Kindness	Open		19.50	20

Derek Darlings - N/A

YEAR ISSUE		EDITION LIMIT	YEAR RETD.	ISSUE PRICE	*QUOTE U.S.$
1995	Jessica, Sara, Chelsea (set)	Open		29.85	30

Hand & Hammer

Annual Ornaments - De Matteo

YEAR ISSUE		EDITION LIMIT	YEAR RETD.	ISSUE PRICE	*QUOTE U.S.$
1987	Silver Bells 737	2,700	1987	38.00	66
1988	Silver Bells 792	3,150	1988	39.50	60
1989	Silver Bells 843	3,150	1989	39.50	63
1990	Silver Bells Rev. 964	4,490	1990	39.00	40
1991	Silver Bells 1080	4,100	1991	39.50	40
1992	Silver Bells 1148	4,100	1992	39.50	40
1993	Silver Bells 1311	Retrd.	1993	39.50	40
1994	Silver Bells 1463	Retrd.	1994	39.50	40
1995	Silver Bells 1597	Retrd.	1995	39.50	40
1996	Silver Bells 1795	Retrd.	1996	39.50	40
1997	Silver Bells 1904	Yr.Iss.		39.50	40

Hand & Hammer Ornaments - De Matteo

YEAR ISSUE		EDITION LIMIT	YEAR RETD.	ISSUE PRICE	*QUOTE U.S.$
1996	150 Rose Window 1878	Yr.Iss.		39.50	40
1985	Abigail 613	Suspd.		32.00	50
1992	Andrea 1163	Retrd.	1994	36.00	40
1993	Angel 1993 1405	Suspd.		45.00	50
1996	Angel 1996 1885	Yr.Iss		39.50	40
1985	Angel 607	225	1989	36.00	50
1985	Angel 612	217	1989	32.00	75
1988	Angel 818	Suspd.		32.00	45
1993	Angel Bell 1312	Retrd.	1994	38.00	40
1987	Angel with Lyre 750	Retrd.	1991	32.00	44
1990	Angel with Star 871	Suspd.		38.00	38
1990	Angel with Violin 1024	Suspd.		39.00	60
1990	Angels 1039	Retrd.	1992	36.00	47
1986	Archangel 684	Retrd.	1990	29.00	60
1987	Art Deco Angel 765	Retrd.	1992	38.00	56
1985	Art Deco Deer 620	Suspd.		34.00	55
1985	Audubon Bluebird 615	Suspd.		48.00	125
1985	Audubon Swallow 614	Suspd.		48.00	125
1988	Bank 812	400	1989	40.00	100
1990	Beardsley Angel 1040	Retrd.	1991	34.00	70
1990	Blake Angel 961	Suspd.		36.00	40
1985	Butterfly 646	Retrd.	1989	39.00	56
1983	Calligraphic Deer 511	Suspd.		25.00	38
1994	Canterbury Star 1441	Suspd.		35.00	35
1990	Cardinals 870	Retrd.	1994	39.00	40
1990	Carousel Horse 866	1,915	1992	38.00	40
1991	Carousel Horse 1025	Retrd.	1993	38.00	40
1993	Carousel Horse 1993 1321	Retrd.	1993	38.00	40
1989	Carousel Horse 811	2,150	1990	34.00	43
1985	Cartier Soldier 633	Retrd.	1986	35.00	75
1982	Carved Heart 425	Suspd.		29.00	70
1987	Cat 754	Suspd.		37.00	37
1993	Celebrate America 1352	Retrd.	1994	38.00	38
1993	Cheer Mouse 1359	Retrd.	1994	39.00	39
1983	Cherub 528	295	1987	29.00	56
1985	Cherub 642	815	1989	37.00	60
1992	Chocolate Pot 1208	Retrd.	1994	49.50	75
1990	Church 921	Retrd.	1994	37.00	40
1987	Clipper Ship 756	Suspd.		35.00	55
1991	Columbus 1140	1,500	1993	39.00	50
1988	Coronado 864	Suspd.		38.00	75
1990	Covered Bridge 920	Retrd.	1994	37.00	40
1992	Cowardly Lion 1287	Retrd.	1993	36.00	50
1985	Crane 606	Suspd.		38.00	65
1984	Crescent Angel 559	Suspd.		30.00	60
1990	Currier & Ives Set -Victorian Village 923	2,000	1994	140.00	160
1992	Della Robbia Ornament 1219	Retrd.	1994	39.00	44
1992	Dorothy 1284	Retrd.	1993	36.00	50
1988	Dove 786	112	1991	36.00	60
1985	Eagle 652	375	1989	30.00	125
1988	Eiffel Tower 861	225	1989	38.00	100
1994	Emperor 1439	Retrd.	1995	38.00	50
1996	Faberge Egg 1725	Yr.Iss.		39.50	40
1985	Family 659	915	1989	32.00	53
1990	Farmhouse 919	Retrd.	1994	37.00	40
1991	Fir Tree 1145	Retrd.	1995	39.00	50
1983	Fire Angel 473	315	1985	25.00	53
1990	First Baptist Angel 997	200	1992	35.00	75
1990	First Christmas Bear 940	Suspd.		35.00	40
1982	Fleur de Lys Angel 343	320	1985	28.00	75
1981	Gabriel 320	Suspd.		25.00	60
1981	Gabriel with Liberty Cap 301	275	1986	25.00	60
1985	George Washington 629	Suspd.		35.00	50
1990	Goose & Wreath 868	Retrd.	1993	37.00	40
1989	Goose 857	650	1993	37.00	55
1985	Guardian Angel 616	Suspd.		35.00	48
1986	Hallelujah 686	Suspd.		38.00	56
1985	Halley's Comet 621	432	1990	35.00	75
1990	Heart Angel 959	Suspd.		39.00	39
1995	Heart of Christmas 1682	Yr.Iss.		39.00	39
1996	Heart of Xmas 1866	Yr.Iss.		39.50	40
1985	Herald Angel 641	Retrd.	1989	36.00	60
1985	Hosanna 635	715	1988	32.00	64
1987	Hunting Horn 738	Suspd.		37.00	40
1984	Ibex 584	400	1988	29.00	75
1980	Icicle 009	490	1985	25.00	60
1983	Indian 494	190	1985	29.00	58
1988	Jack in the Box 789	Retrd.	1991	39.50	60
1983	Japanese Snowflake 534	350	1989	29.00	60
1992	Jemima Puddleduck (1992) 1167	Retrd.	1992	39.50	40
1990	Joy 1047	Retrd.	1992	39.00	55
1990	Joy 867	1,140	1993	36.00	40
1990	Koala San Diego Zoo 1095	Suspd.		36.00	40
1995	L&T Santa 1700	Yr.Iss.		39.00	39
1989	L&T Ugly Duckling 917	Retrd.	1995	38.00	75
1985	Lafarge Angel 658	Suspd.		32.00	45
1986	Lafarge Angel 710	Suspd.		31.00	45
1987	Lambs 726	Retrd.	1992	35.00	45
1985	Liberty Bell 611	Suspd.		32.00	50
1990	Locomotive 1100	Suspd.		39.00	50
1982	Madonna & Child 388	175	1985	28.00	75
1985	Madonna 666	227	1990	35.00	75
1988	Madonna 787	600	1992	35.00	60
1988	Madonna 809	Suspd.		39.00	50
1988	Magi 788	Suspd.		39.50	50
1984	Manger 601	Retrd.	1988	29.00	48
1985	Mermaid 622	Retrd.	1995	35.00	75
1989	MFA Angel with Tree 906	Suspd.		36.00	55
1989	MFA Durer Snowflake 907	Suspd.		36.00	44
1989	MFA LaFarge Angel set 937	Suspd.		98.00	110
1989	MFA Noel 905	Suspd.		36.00	44
1991	MFA Snowflake (1991) 1143	Retrd.	1991	36.00	44
1992	MFA Snowflake 1246	Retrd.	1993	39.00	44
1985	Militiaman 608	Suspd.		25.00	38
1990	Mill 922	Retrd.	1994	37.00	40
1987	Minuteman 776	Suspd.		35.00	100
1990	Mole & Rat Wind in Will 944	Suspd.		36.00	36
1991	Mommy & Baby Panda Bear 1079	Retrd.	1993	36.00	40
1991	Mrs. Rabbit (1991) 1086	Retrd.	1991	39.50	40
1993	Mrs. Rabbit (1993) 1325	Retrd.	1993	39.50	40
1984	Mt. Vernon Weathervane 602	Suspd.		32.00	50
1987	Naptime 732	Retrd.	1991	32.00	48
1986	Nativity 679	Retrd.	1991	36.00	55
1988	Nativity 821	Suspd.		32.00	75
1986	Nightingale 716	Retrd.	1995	35.00	75
1984	Nine Hearts 572	275	1985	34.00	66
1987	Noel 731	Suspd.		38.00	40
1989	Nutcracker 1989 872	1,790	1990	38.00	75
1985	Nutcracker 609	510	1989	30.00	55
1986	Nutcracker 681	1,356	1988	37.00	61
1988	Old King Cole 824	Retrd.	1990	34.00	43
1991	Olivers Rocking Horse 1085	Retrd.	1993	37.00	40
1993	Peace 1327	Suspd.		36.00	36
1985	Peacock 603	470	1989	34.00	65
1990	Peter Rabbit (1990) 1018	4,315	1990	39.50	40
1994	Peter Rabbit (1994) 1444	Retrd.	1994	39.50	40
1995	Peter Rabbit (1995) 1598	Yr.Iss.		39.50	40
1996	Peter Rabbit (1996) 1699	Yr.Iss.		39.50	40
1993	Peter Rabbit 100th 1383	Retrd.	1993	39.50	45
1985	Piazza 653	Suspd.		32.00	55
1984	Pineapple 558	Suspd.		30.00	53
1983	Pollock Angel 502	Suspd.		35.00	75
1984	Praying Angel 576	Suspd.		29.00	45
1990	Presidential Homes 990	Suspd.		350.00	400
1989	Presidential Seal 858	Suspd.		39.00	150
1992	Princess & The Pea 1247	Retrd.	1995	39.00	50
1993	Puss In Boots 1396	Suspd.		40.00	44
1987	Reindeer 752	Retrd.	1991	38.00	45
1992	Revere Teapot 1207	Retrd.	1994	49.50	75
1987	Ride a Cock Horse 757	Retrd.	1991	34.00	43
1984	Rosette 571	220	1988	32.00	65
1992	Round Teapot 1206	Retrd.	1994	49.50	55
1981	Roundel 109	220	1985	25.00	60
1986	Salem Lamb 712	Retrd.	1989	32.00	75
1985	Samantha 648	Suspd.		35.00	46
1990	Santa & Reindeer 929	395	1991	39.00	50
1989	Santa (1989) 856	1,715	1989	35.00	60
1990	Santa (1990) 869	2,250	1990	38.00	42
1991	Santa (1991) 1056	3,750	1992	38.00	40
1987	Santa and Sleigh 751	Retrd.	1989	32.00	100
1990	Santa in the Moon 941	Suspd.		38.00	40
1986	Santa Skates 715	Suspd.		36.00	45
1987	Santa Star 739	Retrd.	1991	32.00	48
1988	Santa with Scroll 814	250	1991	34.00	44
1983	Sargent Angel 523	690	1987	29.00	56
1992	Scarecrow 1286	Retrd.	1993	36.00	50
1985	Shepherd 617	1,770	1990	35.00	60
1988	Skaters 790	Retrd.	1991	39.50	50
1994	Smithsonian Angel 1534	Retrd.	1994	39.00	39
1987	Snow Queen 746	Retrd.	1995	35.00	75
1990	Snowflake (1990) 1033	1,415	1990	36.00	45
1993	Snowflake (1993) 1394	Retrd.	1993	40.00	44
1994	Snowflake (1994) 1486	Retrd.	1994	39.00	39
1995	Snowflake (1995) 1652	Yr.Iss.		39.00	40
1986	Snowflake 713	Retrd.	1990	36.00	55
1994	Snowman 1572	Retrd.	1995	39.00	50
1987	Snowman 753	825	1991	38.00	56
1996	Star 1867	Yr.Iss.		39.50	40
1997	Star 1906	Yr.Iss.		39.50	40
1994	Star 1994 1462	Retrd.	1994	39.50	40
1988	Star 806	311	1990	50.00	200
1988	Star 854	275	1990	32.00	75
1988	Star of the East 785	Retrd.	1992	35.00	48
1990	Steadfast Tin Soldier 1050	Retrd.	1995	36.00	75
1982	Straw Star 448	590	1986	25.00	50
1987	Sweetheart Star 740	Retrd.	1991	39.50	58
1985	Teddy 637	Suspd.		37.00	47
1986	Teddy Bear 685	Retrd.	1991	38.00	58
1996	Thayer Angel Smithsonian 1877	Yr.Iss.		39.50	40
1987	Three Crowns 768	Retrd.	1992	35.00	45
1988	Thumbelina 803	Retrd.	1995	35.00	75
1992	Tin Man 1285	Retrd.	1993	36.00	50
1990	Toad Wind in Willows 945	Suspd.		38.00	38
1992	Unicorn 1165	Retrd.	1994	36.00	36
1985	Unicorn 660	Retrd.	1990	37.00	55
1984	USHS 1984 Angel 574	Suspd.		35.00	75
1989	USHS Angel (1989) 901	Suspd.		38.00	75
1991	USHS Angel (1991) 1139	Suspd.		38.00	50
1995	USHS Angel (1995) 1703	Suspd.		39.00	39
1986	USHS Angel 703	Suspd.		35.00	75
1985	USHS Bluebird 631	Suspd.		29.00	38
1987	USHS Gloria Angel 748	Suspd.		39.00	75
1985	USHS Madonna 630	Suspd.		35.00	75
1985	USHS Swallow 632	Suspd.		29.00	38
1986	Victorian Santa 724	250	1988	32.00	45

*Quotes have been rounded up to nearest dollar

Hand & Hammer
to Kurt S. Adler, Inc.

ORNAMENTS

YEAR ISSUE		EDITION LIMIT	YEAR RETD.	ISSUE PRICE	*QUOTE U.S.$
1993	Violin 1340	Retrd.	1993	38.00	90
1991	The Voyages Of Columbus 1141	1,500	1993	39.00	50
1984	Wild Swan 592	Retrd.	1995	35.00	75
1993	Window 1360	Retrd.	1994	38.00	38
1986	Winged Dove 680	Retrd.	1993	35.00	54
1983	Wise Man 549	Retrd.	1988	29.00	56
1986	Wreath 714	Suspd.		36.00	38
1992	Xmas Tree & Heart 1162	Retrd.	1994	36.00	36
1993	Xmas Tree 1395	Suspd.		40.00	44

Harbour Lights

Christmas Ornaments - Harbour Lights

YEAR ISSUE		EDITION LIMIT	YEAR RETD.	ISSUE PRICE	*QUOTE U.S.$
1996	Big Bay Pt. MI 7040	Closed	1996	15.00	15
1996	Burrows Island WA 7043	Closed	1996	15.00	15
1996	Holland MI 7041	Open		15.00	15
1996	Sand Island WI 7042	Closed	1996	15.00	15
1996	Set of 4 702	Open		60.00	60
1996	30 Mile Pt. NY 7044	Closed	1996	15.00	15
1996	Cape Neddick ME 7047	Open		15.00	15
1996	New London Ledge CT 7046	Open		15.00	15
1996	S.E. Block Island RI 7045	Open		15.00	15
1996	Set of 4 703	Open		60.00	60

Hawthorne Village

Gone With the Wind - Hawthorne

YEAR ISSUE		EDITION LIMIT	YEAR RETD.	ISSUE PRICE	*QUOTE U.S.$
1995	Red Horse Saloon/Butler Mansion	Open		29.90	30
1995	Tara/Atlanta Church	Open		29.90	30
1995	Twelve Oaks/Kennedy Store	Open		29.90	30

Kinkade's Candlelight Cottages - Kinkade-Inspired

YEAR ISSUE		EDITION LIMIT	YEAR RETD.	ISSUE PRICE	*QUOTE U.S.$
1995	Cedar Nooke/Candlelit	Open		29.90	30
1995	Olde Porterfield Tea Room/Merritt's	Open		29.90	30
1995	Seaside/Sweetheart	Open		29.90	30
1995	Swanbrooke/Chandler's	Closed	1996	29.90	30

Rockwell's Main Street (Illuminated) - Rockwell-Inspired

YEAR ISSUE		EDITION LIMIT	YEAR RETD.	ISSUE PRICE	*QUOTE U.S.$
1994	Antique Shop & Town Offices	Open		29.90	30
1994	Bank & Library	Open		29.90	30
1994	The Red Lion Inn & Rockwell Residence	Open		29.90	30
1994	Studio & Country Store	Open		29.90	30

Wysocki Ornaments - C. Wysocki

YEAR ISSUE		EDITION LIMIT	YEAR RETD.	ISSUE PRICE	*QUOTE U.S.$
1996	Candy Cane & Rocket	Open		24.95	25
1996	Cardinal & Dove	Open		24.95	25
1996	Chariot & Hearts	Open		24.95	25
1996	Chef & Chimney	Open		24.95	25
1996	Sleigh & Snowman	Open		24.95	25
1996	Snowball & Teddybear	Open		24.95	25

Hudson Creek

Sebastian Christmas Ornaments - P.W. Baston Jr., unless otherwise noted

YEAR ISSUE		EDITION LIMIT	YEAR RETD.	ISSUE PRICE	*QUOTE U.S.$
1943	Madonna of the Chair - P.W. Baston	25	1943	2.00	150-200
1981	Santa Claus - P.W. Baston	5,000	1981	28.50	30
1982	Madonna of the Chair (Reissue of '43) - P.W. Baston	2,165	1982	15.00	30-45
1985	Home for the Holidays	Closed	1993	10.00	13
1986	Holiday Sleigh Ride	Closed	1993	10.00	13
1987	Santa	Closed	1993	10.00	13
1988	Decorating the Tree	Closed	1993	12.50	13
1989	Final Preparations for Christmas	Closed	1993	13.90	14
1990	Stuffing the Stockings	Closed	1993	14.00	14
1990	Christmas Rose-Red on White (Blossom Shop)	Closed	1990	22.00	25-35
1991	Merry Christmas	Closed	1993	14.50	15
1992	Final Check	Closed	1993	14.50	15
1993	Ethnic Santa	Closed	1993	12.50	25-30
1993	Caroling With Santa	Closed	1993	15.00	15
1994	Victorian Christmas Skaters	Closed	1994	17.00	17
1995	Midnight Snacks	Closed	1995	17.00	17
1996	Victorian Christmas Santa	Closed	1996	16.00	16

John Hine N.A. Ltd./Enesco Corporation

David Winter Ornaments - Various

YEAR ISSUE		EDITION LIMIT	YEAR RETD.	ISSUE PRICE	*QUOTE U.S.$
1991	Christmas Carol - D. Winter	Closed	1991	15.00	15
1991	Christmas in Scotland & Hogmanay - D. Winter	Closed	1991	15.00	15
1991	Mr. Fezziwig's Emporium - D. Winter	Closed	1991	15.00	15
1991	Ebenezer Scrooge's Counting House - D. Winter	Closed	1991	15.00	15
1992	Fairytale Castle - D. Winter	Closed	1992	15.00	15
1992	Fred's Home - D. Winter	Closed	1992	15.00	15
1992	Suffolk House - D. Winter	Closed	1992	15.00	15
1992	Tudor Manor - D. Winter	Closed	1992	15.00	15
1993	The Grange - J. Hine Studios	Closed	1993	15.00	15
1993	Scrooge's School - J. Hine Studios	Closed	1993	15.00	15
1993	Tomfool's Cottage - J. Hine Studios	Closed	1993	15.00	15
1993	Will-O The Wisp - J. Hine Studios	Closed	1993	15.00	15
1994	Old Joe's Beetling Shop - J. Hine Studios	Closed	1994	17.50	18
1994	Scrooge's Family Home - J. Hine Studios	Closed	1994	17.50	18
1994	What Cottage - J. Hine Studios	Open		17.50	18
1995	Buttercup Cottage - J. Hine Studios	Open		17.50	18
1995	The Flowershop - J. Hine Studios	Open		17.50	18
1995	Looking for Santa - J. Hine Studios	Open		17.50	18
1995	Miss Belle's Cottage - J. Hine Studios	Closed	1995	17.50	18
1995	Robin's Merry Mouse - J. Hine Studios	Open		17.50	18
1995	Season's Greetings - J. Hine Studios	Open		17.50	18

June McKenna Collectibles, Inc.

Flatback Ornaments - J. McKenna

YEAR ISSUE		EDITION LIMIT	YEAR RETD.	ISSUE PRICE	*QUOTE U.S.$
1988	1776 Santa	Closed	1991	17.00	55-65
1986	Amish Boy, blue	Closed	1989	13.00	100
1986	Amish Boy, pink	Closed	1986	13.00	200-300
1986	Amish Girl, blue	Closed	1989	13.00	100
1986	Amish Girl, pink	Closed	1986	13.00	300
1985	Amish Man	Closed	1989	13.00	100
1985	Amish Woman	Closed	1989	13.00	100-125
1993	Angel of Peace, white or pink	Closed	1994	30.00	50
1984	Angel with Horn	Closed	1988	14.00	150
1995	Angel with Teddy	Closed	1997	30.00	30
1982	Angel With Toys	Closed	1988	14.00	150-175
1995	Angel, Guiding Light, pink, green & white	Closed	1996	30.00	30
1983	Baby Bear in Vest, 5 colors	Closed	1988	11.00	85
1982	Baby Bear, Teeshirt	Closed	1984	11.00	125-175
1985	Baby Pig	Closed	1988	11.00	100-125
1983	Baby, blue trim	Closed	1988	11.00	110
1983	Baby, pink trim	Closed	1988	11.00	70-80
1991	Boy Angel, white	Closed	1992	20.00	100-125
1982	Candy Cane	Closed	1984	10.00	375
1993	Christmas Treat, blue	Closed	1996	30.00	50-65
1982	Colonial Man, 3 colors	Closed	1984	12.00	175
1982	Colonial Woman, 3 colors	Closed	1984	12.00	100-150
1984	Country Boy, 2 colors	Closed	1988	12.00	65
1984	Country Girl, 2 colors	Closed	1988	12.00	65
1993	Elf Bernie	Closed	1994	30.00	30
1995	Elf Danny	Closed	1997	30.00	30
1990	Elf Jeffrey	Closed	1992	17.00	40
1991	Elf Joey	Closed	1993	20.00	30
1994	Elf Ricky	Closed	1995	30.00	30
1992	Elf Scotty	Closed	1993	25.00	30
1994	Elf Tammy	Closed	1995	30.00	30
1988	Elizabeth, sill sitter	Closed	1989	20.00	100-150
1983	Father Bear in Suit, 3 colors	Closed	1988	12.00	85-100
1985	Father Pig	Closed	1988	12.00	100
1993	Final Notes	Closed	1994	30.00	55-65
1991	Girl Angel, white	Closed	1993	20.00	100-125
1983	Gloria Angel	Closed	1984	14.00	400-500
1989	Glorious Angel	Closed	1992	17.00	55-75
1983	Grandma, 4 colors	Closed	1988	12.00	80
1983	Grandpa, 4 colors	Closed	1988	12.00	85
1988	Guardian Angel	Closed	1991	16.00	40
1990	Harvest Santa	Closed	1992	17.00	65
1990	Ho Ho Ho	Closed	1992	17.00	65
1982	Kate Greenaway Boy, 3 colors	Closed	1983	12.00	155
1982	Kate Greenaway Girl, 3 colors	Closed	1983	12.00	125
1982	Mama Bear, Blue Cape	Closed	1984	12.00	100-175
1983	Mother Bear in Dress, 3 colors	Closed	1988	12.00	85-100
1985	Mother Pig	Closed	1988	12.00	100-125
1984	Mr. Claus	Closed	1988	14.00	75
1984	Mrs. Claus	Closed	1988	14.00	75
1994	Mrs. Klaus	Closed	1997	30.00	30
1992	Northpole News	Closed	1993	25.00	55-65
1994	Nutcracker	Closed	1995	30.00	30
1993	Old Lamplighter	Closed	1994	30.00	55-65
1984	Old World Santa, 3 colors	Closed	1989	14.00	75-250
1984	Old World Santa, gold	Closed	1986	14.00	200-275
1982	Papa Bear, Red Cape	Closed	1984	12.00	100-175
1992	Praying Angel	Closed	1993	25.00	30
1985	Primitive Santa	Closed	1989	17.00	145-175
1983	Raggedy Andy, 2 colors	Closed	1983	12.00	250
1983	Raggedy Ann, 2 colors	Closed	1983	12.00	325
1994	Ringing in Christmas	Closed	1995	30.00	45-65
1995	Santa Nutcracker	Closed	1997	30.00	30
1986	Santa with Bag	Closed	1989	16.00	75
1991	Santa with Banner	Closed	1992	20.00	40-65
1992	Santa with Basket	Closed	1993	25.00	40-65
1986	Santa with Bear	Closed	1991	14.00	65
1986	Santa with Bells, blue	Closed	1989	14.00	75
1986	Santa with Bells, green	Closed	1987	14.00	500-700
1988	Santa with Book, blue & red	Closed	1988	17.00	250-300
1991	Santa with Lights, black or white	Closed	1992	20.00	65
1994	Santa with Pipe	Closed	1997	30.00	30
1992	Santa with Sack	Closed	1993	25.00	45-65
1989	Santa with Staff	Closed	1991	17.00	45-65
1982	Santa with Toys	Closed	1988	14.00	100-150
1988	Santa with Toys	Closed	1991	17.00	100
1989	Santa with Tree	Closed	1991	17.00	45-75
1988	Santa with Wreath	Closed	1991	17.00	40-75
1995	Santa's Lil' Helper, brown	Closed	1996	30.00	63
1996	Santa's Lil' Helper, white	Closed	1997	30.00	30
1994	Snow Showers	Closed	1997	30.00	50
1983	St. Nick with Lantern (wooden)	Closed	1988	14.00	75-125
1995	Who's This Frosty?	Closed	1997	30.00	30
1989	Winking Santa	Closed	1991	17.00	75

Santa Head Ornament - J. McKenna

YEAR ISSUE		EDITION LIMIT	YEAR RETD.	ISSUE PRICE	*QUOTE U.S.$
1995	Christmas Kiss	Closed	1997	17.00	20
1995	I Love You, Santa	Closed	1997	17.00	20

Kirk Stieff

Colonial Williamsburg - D. Bacorn

YEAR ISSUE		EDITION LIMIT	YEAR RETD.	ISSUE PRICE	*QUOTE U.S.$
1992	Court House	Open		10.00	10
1989	Doll ornament, silverplate	Closed	N/A	22.00	30
1993	Governors Palace	Open		10.00	10
1988	Lamb, silverplate	Closed	N/A	20.00	25
1992	Prentis Store	Open		10.00	10
1987	Rocking Horse, silverplate	Closed	N/A	20.00	35
1987	Tin Drum, silverplate	Closed	N/A	20.00	28
1983	Tree Top Star, silverplate	Closed	N/A	29.50	35
1984	Unicorn, silverplate	Closed	N/A	22.00	30
1992	Wythe House	Open		10.00	10

Kirk Stieff Ornaments - Various

YEAR ISSUE		EDITION LIMIT	YEAR RETD.	ISSUE PRICE	*QUOTE U.S.$
1994	Angel with Star - J. Ferraioli	Open		8.00	8
1993	Baby's Christmas - D. Bacorn	Open		12.00	12
1993	Bell with Ribbon - D. Bacorn	Open		12.00	12
1992	Cat and Ornament - D. Bacorn	Closed	N/A	10.00	10
1993	Cat with Ribbon - D. Bacorn	Open		12.00	12
1983	Charleston Locomotive - D. Bacorn	Closed	N/A	18.00	20
1993	First Christmas Together - D. Bacorn	Closed	N/A	10.00	10
1993	French Horn - D. Bacorn	Closed	N/A	12.00	12
1992	Guardian Angel - J. Ferraioli	Closed	N/A	13.00	13
1986	Icicle, sterling silver - D. Bacorn	Closed	N/A	35.00	65
1994	Kitten with Tassel - J. Ferraioli	Open		12.00	12
1993	Mouse and Ornament - D. Bacorn	Closed	N/A	10.00	10
1992	Repoussé Angel - J. Ferraioli	Open		13.00	13
1992	Repoussé Wreath - J. Ferraioli	Open		13.00	13
1994	Santa with Tassel - J. Ferraioli	Open		12.00	12
1989	Smithsonian Carousel Horse - Kirk Stieff	Closed	N/A	50.00	50
1989	Smithsonian Carousel Seahorse - Kirk Stieff	Closed	N/A	50.00	50
1994	Teddy Bear - D. Bacorn	Open		8.00	8
1990	Toy Ship - Kirk Stieff	Closed	N/A	23.00	35
1984	Unicorn - D. Bacorn	Closed	N/A	18.00	30
1994	Unicorn - D. Bacorn	Open		8.00	8
1994	Victorian Skaters - D. Bacorn	Open		8.00	8
1994	Williamsburg Wreath - D. Bacorn	Open		15.00	15
1993	Wreath with Ribbon - D. Bacorn	Open		12.00	12

Kurt S. Adler, Inc.

Children's Hour - J. Mostrom

YEAR ISSUE		EDITION LIMIT	YEAR RETD.	ISSUE PRICE	*QUOTE U.S.$
1995	Alice in Wonderland J5751	Retrd.	1996	22.50	23
1995	Bow Peep J5753	Open		27.00	27
1995	Cinderella J5752	Retrd.	1996	28.00	28
1995	Little Boy Blue J5755	Retrd.	1995	18.00	18
1995	Miss Muffet J5753	Open		27.00	27
1995	Mother Goose J5754	Retrd.	1996	27.00	27
1995	Red Riding Hood J5751	Retrd.	1996	22.50	23

Christmas in Chelsea Collection - J. Mostrom

YEAR ISSUE		EDITION LIMIT	YEAR RETD.	ISSUE PRICE	*QUOTE U.S.$
1994	Alice, Marguerite W2973	Retrd.	1996	28.00	28
1992	Allison Sitting in Chair W2812	Retrd.	1994	25.50	26
1992	Allison W2729	Retrd.	1993	21.00	21
1992	Amanda W2709	Retrd.	1994	21.00	21
1992	Amy W2729	Retrd.	1993	21.00	21
1992	Christina W2812	Retrd.	1994	25.50	26
1992	Christopher W2709	Retrd.	1994	21.00	21
1992	Delphinium W2728	Open		20.00	20
1995	Edmond With Violin W3078	Retrd.	1996	32.00	32
1994	Guardian Angel w/Baby W2974	Retrd.	1995	31.00	31
1992	Holly Hock W2728	Open		20.00	20
1992	Holly W2709	Retrd.	1994	21.00	21
1995	Jose With Violin W3078	Retrd.	1996	32.00	32
1995	Pauline With Violin W3078	Retrd.	1996	32.00	32
1992	Peony W2728	Open		20.00	20
1992	Rose W2728	Open		20.00	20

Cornhusk Mice Ornament Series - M. Rothenberg

YEAR ISSUE		EDITION LIMIT	YEAR RETD.	ISSUE PRICE	*QUOTE U.S.$
1994	3" Father Christmas W2976	Open		18.00	18
1994	9" Father Christmas W2982	Open		25.00	25
1995	Angel Mice W3088	Open		10.00	10
1995	Baby's First Mouse W3087	Open		10.00	10
1993	Ballerina Cornhusk Mice W2700	Retrd.	1994	13.50	14
1994	Clara, Prince W2948	Open		16.00	16
1994	Cowboy W2951	Open		18.00	18
1994	Drosselmeir Fairy, Mouse King W2949	Open		16.00	16
1994	Little Pocahontas, Indian Brave W2950	Open		18.00	18
1995	Miss Tammie Mouse W3086	Retrd.	1996	17.00	17
1995	Mr. Jamie Mouse W3086	Retrd.	1996	17.00	17
1995	Mrs. Molly Mouse W3086	Retrd.	1996	17.00	17
1993	Nutcracker Suite Fantasy Cornhusk Mice W2885	Retrd.	1994	15.50	16

Fabriché™ Ornament Series - KS. Adler, unless otherwise noted

YEAR ISSUE		EDITION LIMIT	YEAR RETD.	ISSUE PRICE	*QUOTE U.S.$
1994	All Star Santa W1665	Retrd.	1996	27.00	27
1992	An Apron Full of Love W1594 - M. Rothenberg	Retrd.	1996	27.00	27
1995	Captain Claus W1711	Open		25.00	25
1994	Checking His List W1634	Retrd.	1996	23.50	24
1992	Christmas in the Air W1593	Retrd.	1996	35.50	36
1994	Cookies For Santa W1639	Open		28.00	28
1994	Firefighting Friends W1668	Open		28.00	28
1992	Hello Little One! W1561	Retrd.	1996	22.00	22

*Quotes have been rounded up to nearest dollar

ORNAMENTS
Kurt S. Adler, Inc.
to Kurt S. Adler, Inc.

YEAR ISSUE		EDITION LIMIT	YEAR RETD.	ISSUE PRICE	*QUOTE U.S.$
1994	Holiday Flight W1637 - Smithsonian	Retrd.	1996	40.00	40
1993	Homeward Bound W1596	Retrd.	1996	27.00	27
1992	Hugs And Kisses W1560	Retrd.	1996	22.00	22
1993	Master Toymaker W1595	Retrd.	1996	27.00	27
1992	Merry Chrismouse W1565	Retrd.	1994	10.00	10
1992	Not a Creature Was Stirring W1563	Retrd.	1996	22.00	22
1993	Par For the Claus W1625	Open		27.00	27
1993	Santa With List W1510	Retrd.	1996	20.00	20
1994	Santa's Fishtales W1666	Open		29.00	29
1995	Strike Up The Band W1710	Retrd.	1996	25.00	25

International Christmas - J. Mostrom

YEAR ISSUE		EDITION LIMIT	YEAR RETD.	ISSUE PRICE	*QUOTE U.S.$
1994	Cathy, Johnny W2945	Open		24.00	24
1994	Eskimo-Atom, Ukpik W2967	Retrd.	1996	28.00	28
1994	Germany-Katerina, Hans W2969	Open		27.00	27
1994	Native American-White Dove, Little Wolf W2970	Retrd.	1994	28.00	28
1994	Poland-Marissa, Hedwig W2965	Open		27.00	27
1994	Scotland-Bonnie, Douglas W2966	Open		27.00	27
1994	Spain-Maria, Miguel W2968	Open		27.00	27

Little Dickens - J. Mostrom

YEAR ISSUE		EDITION LIMIT	YEAR RETD.	ISSUE PRICE	*QUOTE U.S.$
1994	Little Bob Crachit W2961	Open		30.00	30
1994	Little Marley's Ghost W2964	Open		33.50	34
1994	Little Mrs. Crachit W2962	Open		27.00	27
1994	Little Scrooge in Bathrobe W2959	Open		30.00	30
1994	Little Scrooge in Overcoat W2960	Open		30.00	30
1994	Little Tiny Tim W2963	Open		22.50	23

Polonaise™ by Komozja - KSA/Komozja, unless otherwise noted

YEAR ISSUE		EDITION LIMIT	YEAR RETD.	ISSUE PRICE	*QUOTE U.S.$
1995	Alarm Clock GP452	Retrd.	1996	25.00	25
1997	Alice Collection 4 pc set GP548	Open		150.00	150
1997	Alice Collection 5 pc set GP547	7,500		175.00	175
1997	Alice in Wonderland GP692	Open		29.95	30
1994	Angel w/Bear GP396	Retrd.	1995	20.20	35-40
1996	Antique Cars boxed set GP522	Open		124.00	124
1997	Babar Elephant GP817	Open		34.95	35
1994	Beer Glass GP366	Open		18.00	18
1996	Betty Boop GP624 - King Features	Open		32.00	32
1995	Blessed Mother GP413	Open		22.50	23
1995	Caesar GP422	Open		22.00	22
1997	Calvary, Gunner, Drummer GP645	Open		29.95	30
1996	Candleholder GP450	Open		20.00	20
1994	Cardinal on Pine Cone GP420	Retrd.	1995	18.00	35
1995	Cat in Boot GP478 - Rothenberg	Open		28.00	28
1994	Cat w/Ball GP390	Retrd.	1995	18.00	35-50
1995	Cat w/Bow GP443	Open		22.50	23
1997	Charlie Brown Peanuts GP824	Open		34.95	35
1995	Christ Child GP414	Open		20.00	20
1997	Christmas in Poland 4pc set GP534	Open		150.00	150
1995	Christmas Tree GP461	Open		22.50	23
1996	Cinderella 4 pc boxed set GP512	Open		134.00	134
1996	Cinderella 6 pc boxed set GP511	7,500	1996	190.00	200
1996	Cinderella Coach GP487	Open		33.00	33
1996	Cinderella GP488	Open		28.00	28
1997	Circus Collection 5 pc set GP545	Open		180.00	180
1997	Circus Ring Master GP691	Open		34.95	35
1997	Circus Strongman GP690	Open		34.95	35
1995	Clara GP408	Open		20.00	20
1995	Clown Head 4.5" GP460	Open		25.00	25
1997	Coca Cola Bear 6 Pack GP803	Open		34.95	35
1997	Coca Cola Bear Skiing GP801	Open		34.95	35
1997	Coca Cola Bear Snowmobile GP802	Open		34.95	35
1997	Coca Cola Bear Truck GP804	Open		37.50	38
1997	Coca Cola 3 pc GP553	Open		130.00	130
1996	Coca Cola 4 pc boxed set GP517	Open		135.00	135
1996	Coca Cola Bear GP630 - Coca Cola	Open		37.00	37
1997	Coca Cola Bottle (golden) GP800	Open		34.95	35
1996	Coca Cola Bottle GP631 - Coca Cola	Open		33.00	33
1996	Coca Cola Bottle Top GP633 - Coca Cola	Open		27.00	27
1996	Coca Cola Disk GP632 - Coca Cola	Open		26.00	26
1996	Coca Cola Vending Machine GP634 - Coca Cola	Open		37.00	37
1996	Cossack GP604	Open		35.00	35
1995	Cowboy Head GP462	Open		30.00	30
1995	Creche GP458 - Stefan	Open		28.00	30
1995	Crocodile GP468	Retrd.	1996	28.00	28
1996	Dice boxed set GP509	Open		60.00	60
1994	Dinosaurs GP397	Retrd.	1996	22.50	23
1994	Dinosaurs-brown GP397	Retrd.	1995	22.50	55
1995	Dove on Ball GP472 - Stefan	Retrd.	1996	30.00	30
1995	Eagle GP453	Open		28.00	28
1994	Egyptian (12 pc boxed set) GP500	Retrd.	1995	214.00	360-420
1997	Egyptian 4 pc set GP515	Open		150.00	150
1996	Egyptian Cat GP351	Open		30.00	30
1996	Egyptian II boxed set GP510	Open		170.00	170
1996	Egyptian Princess GP482	Open		33.00	33
1995	Egyptian set 4 pc. boxed GP500/4	Open		110.00	110
1995	Elephant GP 464	Open		28.00	28
1996	Elves GP611/23	Open		30.00	30
1996	Emerald City GP623	Open		32.00	32
1994	Engine GP353	Open		22.50	23
1997	English Bobbie GP814	Open		29.95	30
1996	Fire Engine GP605	Open		30.00	30
1995	Fish 4 pc. boxed GP506	Open		110.00	110
1997	Four Calling Birds GP828	Open		N/A	N/A
1996	French Hen GP626 - Stefan	Open		33.00	33
1996	Gift Boxes GP614	Open		25.00	25
1997	Gingerbread House GP664	Open		29.95	30
1994	Glass Acorn GP342	Retrd.	1995	11.00	155
1994	Glass Angel GP309	Retrd.	1996	18.00	18
1994	Glass Apple GP339	Retrd.	1995	11.00	15
1997	Glass Big Bird GP699	Open		34.95	35
1994	Glass Church GP369	Open		18.00	18
1997	Glass Circus Seal GP688	Open		29.95	30
1994	Glass Clown 4" GP301	Retrd.	1995	13.50	42
1994	Glass Clown 6" GP303	Retrd.	1995	22.50	40
1994	Glass Clown on Ball 6.5" GP302	Retrd.	1995	22.50	35
1997	Glass Clowns 3/asst. GP682	Open		34.95	35
1994	Glass Doll GP377	Retrd.	1995	13.50	35
1997	Glass Dr. Watson GP813	Open		29.95	30
1994	Glass Gnome GP347	Retrd.	1995	18.00	35
1997	Glass Hat Boxes GP620	Open		27.50	28
1997	Glass Holly Bear GP827	Open		N/A	N/A
1997	Glass Hunter GP667	Open		29.95	30
1994	Glass Knight's Helmet GP304	Retrd.	1995	18.00	18
1997	Glass Krakow Man GP674	Open		29.95	30
1997	Glass Mad Hatter GP696	Open		34.95	35
1994	Glass Nefertiti GP349	Retrd.	1996	27.50	28
1994	Glass Owl GP328	Open		20.00	20
1997	Glass Santa Head GP811	Open		22.50	23
1996	Glass Slipper GP490	Open		20.00	20
1997	Glass Snow White GP660	Open		29.95	30
1997	Glass Star 3/asst. GP671	Open		19.95	20
1997	Glass Star Boy GP676	Open		34.95	35
1997	Glass Tatar Prince GP672	Open		34.95	35
1994	Glass Turkey GP326	Retrd.	1996	20.00	20
1994	Glass White Dice (original -square) GP363	Retrd.	1994	18.00	66-80
1997	Glass Wolf GP666	Open		34.95	35
1996	Glinda the Good Witch GP621	Open		32.00	32
1994	Golden Cherub Head GP372	Retrd.	1994	18.00	75-125
1994	Golden Rocking Horse GP355	Retrd.	1994	22.50	108-125
1997	Gone With The Wind 3 pc boxed set GP557	Open		N/A	N/A
1997	Gone With The Wind Rhett Butler GP815	Open		N/A	N/A
1997	Gone With The Wind Scarlett O'Hara GP805	Open		N/A	N/A
1997	Gone With The Wind Tara GP816	Open		N/A	N/A
1995	Goose w/Wreath GP475 - Stefan	Open		30.00	30
1996	Gramophone GP446	Retrd.	1996	22.50	23
1997	Grand Father Frost GP810COL	Open		50.00	50
1997	Handblown Witch, 7" GP661	Open		34.95	35
1997	Hansel & Gretel GP662	Open		29.95	30
1997	Hansel/Gretel 4 pc set GP538	Open		150.00	150
1997	Herald Rabbit GP693	Open		34.95	35
1995	Herr Drosselmeir GP465 - Rothenberg	Open		30.00	30
1995	Holy Family 3 pc. GP504	Open		84.00	84
1994	Holy Family GP371	Open		28.00	28
1996	Horus GP484	Open		33.00	33
1995	Humpty Dumpty GP477 - Stefan	Open		30.00	30
1995	Icicle Santa GP474 - Stefan	Retrd.	1995	25.00	40-45
1995	Indian Chief GP463	Open		30.00	30
1997	Jewelry Boxes GP637	Open		15.95	16
1997	Just Married GP829	Open		22.50	23
1996	King Balthazar GP607	Open		31.00	31
1996	King Neptune GP496	Open		35.00	35
1997	Krakow Castle GP670	Open		34.95	35
1996	Light Bulb GP449	Retrd.	1996	20.00	20
1996	Little Mermaid GP492	Open		28.00	28
1997	Little Red Riding Hood 4 pc set GP539	Yr.Iss.		110.00	110
1997	Little Red Riding Hood 51/2" GP665	Open		29.95	30
1995	Locomotive GP447	Open		28.00	28
1997	Lucy Peanuts GP825	Open		34.95	35
1997	Madonna Vatican Egg GP830	Open		37.50	38
1994	Madonna w/Child GP370	Open		22.50	23
1997	Magician's Hat GP689	Open		34.95	35
1997	Marilyn Monroe GP818	Open		N/A	N/A
1996	Medieval boxed set GP519	Open		160.00	160
1996	Medieval Dragon GP642	Open		35.00	35
1996	Medieval Knight GP641	Open		35.00	35
1996	Medieval Lady GP643	Open		35.00	35
1994	Merlin GP373	Retrd.	1995	20.00	30
1997	MGM Cowardly Lion GP821	Open		37.50	38
1997	MGM Dorothy GP819	Open		37.50	38
1997	MGM Scarecrow GP822	Open		37.50	38
1997	MGM Tin Man GP820	Open		37.50	38
1997	MGM Wizard of Oz 4 pc. boxed set GP555	Open		N/A	N/A
1995	Mickey Mouse GP392	Retrd.	1995	33.00	178-200
1995	Mickey Mouse GP392 & Minnie Mouse (pr.) GP391,set	Retrd.	1995	66.00	75-125
1995	Minnie Mouse GP391	Retrd.	1995	33.00	50-100
1994	Mouse King GP406	Open		20.00	20
1996	Mummy GP483	Open		33.00	33
1997	Napolionic Soldier GP543	Open		150.00	150
1996	Nefertiti 96 GP485	Open		33.00	33
1994	Night & Day GP307	Open		22.50	23
1995	Noah's Ark GP469	Open		28.00	28
1994	Nutcracker GP404	Open		20.00	20
1995	Nutcracker Suite 4 pc. boxed GP507	Open		110.00	110
1997	NY Ball 5/asst. GP677	Open		24.95	25
1994	Old Fashioned Car GP380	Open		13.50	20
1994	Parrot GP332	Retrd.	1995	15.50	40-48
1995	Partridge in a Pear Tree GP467 - Stefan	Open		33.50	34
1994	Peacock 5" GP324	Retrd.	1996	18.00	18
1994	Peacock on Ball 7.5" GP323	Retrd.	1996	28.00	28
1997	Peanuts 3 pc boxed set GP556	Open		N/A	N/A
1995	Peter Pan 4 pc. boxed set GP503	Open		124.00	124
1995	Peter Pan GP419	Open		22.50	23
1996	Pharaoh GP481	Open		35.00	35
1994	Pierrot Clown GP405	Retrd.	1995	18.00	35
1996	Polanaise Medieval Horse GP640	Open		35.00	35
1997	Polish Mountain Man GP675	Open		29.95	30
1995	Polonaise African-American Santa GP389/1	Open		25.00	25
1995	Polonaise Cardinal GP473 - Stefan	Open		30.00	30
1995	Polonaise House GP455	Retrd.	1996	25.00	25
1995	Polonaise Santa GP389	Open		25.00	25
1996	Prince Charming GP489	Open		28.00	28
1994	Puppy (gold) GP333	Retrd.	1994	15.50	35
1994	Pyramid GP352	Open		22.50	23
1997	Queen of Hearts GP695	Open		34.95	35
1997	Raggedy Andy GP322	Open		24.95	25
1996	Raggedy Ann GP321	Open		28.00	28
1997	Raggedy Ann/Andy GP550	Open		75.00	75
1997	Red Riding Hood 4 pc set GP539	Yr.Iss.		140.00	140
1994	Rocking Horse 5" GP356	Open		22.50	23
1994	Roly-Poly Santa GP317	Open		22.50	23
1995	Roman 4 pc. boxed set GP502/4	Retrd.	1995	110.00	110
1995	Roman 7 pc. boxed set GP502	Retrd.	1995	164.00	195
1995	Roman Centurian GP427	Open		22.50	23
1995	Roman set 4 pc. boxed GP402/4	Retrd.	1995	110.00	145-245
1997	Royal Suite 4 pc set GP552	Open		140.00	140
1997	Royal Suite 4/asst. GP806	Open		29.95	30
1996	Russian 5 pc boxed set GP514	Open		190.00	190
1996	Russian Bishop GP603	Open		35.00	35
1996	Russian Woman GP602	Open		35.00	35
1995	Sailing Ship GP415	Open		30.00	30
1994	Saint Nick GP316	Open		28.00	28
1994	Santa Boot GP375	Open		20.00	20
1996	Santa Car GP367	Open		33.00	33
1994	Santa Head 4" GP315	Retrd.	1995	13.50	14
1994	Santa Head 4.5" GP374	Open		19.00	19
1996	Santa in Airplane GP365	Open		33.00	33
1995	Santa Moon GP454 - Stefan	Open		28.00	28
1995	Santa on Goose on Sled GP479	Open		30.00	30
1995	Santa w/Puppy GP442	Open		25.00	25
1996	Sea Horse GP494	Open		25.00	25
1997	Seven Dwarfs GP611	Open		29.95	30
1995	Shark GP417	Retrd.	1996	18.00	25
1997	Sherlock Holmes 3 pc set GP551	Open		125.00	125
1997	Sherlock Holmes GP812	Open		29.95	30
1997	Smithsonian Astronaut GP826	Open		N/A	N/A
1997	Snoopy Peanuts GP823	Open		37.50	38
1997	Snow White & 7 Dwarfs 8 pc boxed set GP558	Open		300.00	300
1994	Snowman w/Parcel GP313	Open		22.50	23
1994	Snowman w/Specs GP312	Retrd.	1995	20.00	30
1994	Soldier GP407	Retrd.	1995	15.50	175
1994	Sparrow GP329	Retrd.	1995	15.50	20
1994	Sphinx GP350	Retrd.	1995	22.50	65
1996	Sphinx GP480	Open		33.00	33
1994	Spinner Top GP359	Retrd.	1995	9.00	28
1996	St. Basils Cathedral GP600	Open		35.00	35
1995	St. Joseph GP412	Open		22.50	23
1995	Star Santa GP470 - Stefan	Open		25.00	25
1996	Star Snowman GP625 - Stefan	Open		32.00	32
1996	Sting Ray GP495	Retrd.	1996	28.00	28
1994	Swan GP325	Open		20.00	20
1994	Teddy Bear (gold) GP338	Retrd.	1994	13.50	40
1995	Telephone GP448	Retrd.	1996	25.00	25
1996	Three Kings boxed set GP516	Open		144.00	144
1994	Train Coaches GP354	Open		15.50	16
1994	Train Set (boxed) GP501	Open		90.00	90
1995	Treasure Chest GP416	Retrd.	1996	20.00	20
1997	Tropical Fish 4 pc GP517	Open		110.00	110
1994	Tropical Fish GP409	Open		22.50	23
1996	Tsar Ivan GP601	Open		35.00	35
1995	Turtle Doves GP471 - Stefan	Open		25.00	25
1996	Tutenkhamen #2 GP476	Open		35.00	35
1994	Tutenkhamen GP348	Retrd.	1996	28.00	28
1996	Wicked Witch GP606	Open		32.00	32
1996	Winter Boy GP615	Open		22.50	23
1996	Winter Girl GP615	Open		22.50	23
1996	Wizard in Balloon GP622	Open		32.00	32
1995	Wizard of Oz 4 pc. boxed set GP505	Open		124.00	124
1995	Wizard of Oz 6 pc. boxed set GP508	5,000	1995	170.00	250-275
1995	Wizard of Oz Dorothy GP434	Open		25.00	25
1996	Wizard of Oz II boxed set GP518	Open		164.00	164
1995	Wizard of Oz Lion GP433	Open		22.50	23
1995	Wizard of Oz Scarecrow GP435	Open		25.00	25
1995	Wizard of Oz Tinman GP436	Open		25.00	25
1994	Zodiac Sun GP381	Retrd.	1995	22.50	50

Polonaise™ Event Signing Collection - KSA/Komozja

YEAR ISSUE		EDITION LIMIT	YEAR RETD.	ISSUE PRICE	*QUOTE U.S.$
1996	Szlachcic GP673/SIG	Yr.Iss.	1996	35.50	36
1997	Szlachcianka	Yr.Iss.		N/A	N/A

Polonaise™ Vatican Library Collection - Vatican Library

YEAR ISSUE		EDITION LIMIT	YEAR RETD.	ISSUE PRICE	*QUOTE U.S.$
1996	Cherub Bust Glass GP651	Open		39.00	39
1996	Cherubum boxed set, GP 521	Open		160.00	160

*Quotes have been rounded up to nearest dollar

ORNAMENTS

YEAR ISSUE	EDITION LIMIT	YEAR RETD.	ISSUE PRICE	*QUOTE U.S. $
1996 Dancing Cherubs on Ball GP652	Open		40.00	40
1996 Full Body Cherub GP 650	Open		40.00	40
1996 Garden of Mary boxed set, GP 520	Open		150.00	150
1996 Lily Glass GP655	Open		37.00	37
1996 Madonna & Child GP653	Open		37.00	37
1996 Rose Glass GP654	Open		37.00	37

Royal Heritage Collection - J. Mostrom

YEAR ISSUE	EDITION LIMIT	YEAR RETD.	ISSUE PRICE	*QUOTE U.S. $
1993 Anastasia W2922	Retrd.	1994	28.00	28
1996 Angelique Angel Baby W3278	Open		25.00	25
1995 Benjamin J5756	Open		24.50	25
1995 Blythe J5756	Open		24.50	25
1996 Brianna Ivory W7663	Open		25.00	25
1996 Brianna Pink W7663	Open		25.00	25
1993 Caroline W2924	Retrd.	1995	25.50	26
1993 Charles W2924	Retrd.	1995	25.50	26
1993 Elizabeth W2924	Retrd.	1995	25.50	26
1996 Etoile Angel Baby W3278	Open		25.00	25
1996 Francis Winter Boy W3279	Open		28.00	28
1996 Gabrielle in Pink Coat W3276	Open		28.00	28
1996 Giselle w/Bow W3277	Open		28.00	28
1996 Giselle Winter Girl w/Package W3279	Open		28.00	28
1994 Ice Fairy, Winter Fairy W2972	Open		25.50	26
1993 Joella W2979	Retrd.	1993	27.00	27
1993 Kelly W2979	Retrd.	1993	27.00	27
1996 Lady Colette in Sled W3301	Open		32.00	32
1996 Laurielle Lady Skater W3281	Open		36.00	36
1996 Miniotte w/Muff W3279	Open		28.00	28
1996 Monique w/Hat Box W3277	Open		28.00	28
1993 Nicholas W2923	Retrd.	1996	25.50	26
1996 Nicole w/Balloon W3277	Open		28.00	28
1993 Patina W2923	Retrd.	1996	25.50	26
1996 Rene Victorian Lady W3280	Open		36.00	36
1993 Sasha W2923	Retrd.	1996	25.50	26
1994 Snow Princess W2971	Retrd.	1996	28.00	28

Smithsonian Museum Carousel - KSA/Smithsonian

YEAR ISSUE	EDITION LIMIT	YEAR RETD.	ISSUE PRICE	*QUOTE U.S. $
1987 Antique Bunny S3027/2	Retrd.	1992	14.50	15
1992 Antique Camel S3027/12	Open		15.00	15
1989 Antique Cat S3027/6	Retrd.	1995	14.50	15
1992 Antique Elephant S3027/11	Open		14.50	15
1995 Antique Frog S32027/18	Open		15.50	16
1988 Antique Giraffe S3027/4	Retrd.	1993	14.50	15
1987 Antique Goat S3027/1	Retrd.	1992	14.50	15
1991 Antique Horse S3027/10	Open		14.50	15
1993 Antique Horse S3027/14	Open		15.00	15
1988 Antique Horse S3027/3	Retrd.	1993	14.50	15
1989 Antique Lion S3027/5	Retrd.	1994	14.50	15
1994 Antique Pig S3027/16	Open		15.50	16
1994 Antique Reindeer S3027/15	Open		15.50	16
1991 Antique Rooster S3027/9	Retrd.	1994	14.50	15
1990 Antique Seahorse S3027/8	Open		14.50	15
1993 Antique Tiger S3027/13	Open		15.00	15
1990 Antique Zebra S3027/7	Open		14.50	15
1995 Armored Horse S3027/17	Open		15.50	16
1997 Graceful Horse S3027/20	Open		20.00	20
1997 Sea Monster S3027/21	Open		20.00	20

Smithsonian Museum Fabriché™ - KSA/Smithsonian

YEAR ISSUE	EDITION LIMIT	YEAR RETD.	ISSUE PRICE	*QUOTE U.S. $
1992 Holiday Drive W1580	Retrd.	1995	38.00	38
1992 Santa On a Bicycle W1547	Open		31.00	31

Steinbach Ornament Series - KS. Adler

YEAR ISSUE	EDITION LIMIT	YEAR RETD.	ISSUE PRICE	*QUOTE U.S. $
1992 The King's Guards ES300	Open		27.00	27

Lenox China

Annual Ornaments - Lenox

YEAR ISSUE	EDITION LIMIT	YEAR RETD.	ISSUE PRICE	*QUOTE U.S. $
1982 1982 Ball	Yr.Iss.	1983	30.00	50-90
1983 1983 Teardrop Shape	Yr.Iss.	1984	35.00	75
1984 1984 Starburst	Yr.Iss.	1985	38.00	65
1985 1985 Bell	Yr.Iss.	1986	37.50	60
1986 1986 The Three Magi	Yr.Iss.	1987	38.50	50
1987 1987 Dickens Village	Yr.Iss.	1988	39.00	45
1988 1988 Ball	Yr.Iss.	1989	39.00	45
1989 1989 Faberge Egg	Yr.Iss.	1990	39.00	39
1990 1990 Bell	Yr.Iss.	1991	42.00	42
1991 1991 Ornament	Yr.Iss.	1992	39.00	39
1992 1992 Ball	Yr.Iss.	1993	42.00	42
1993 1993 Lantern	Yr.Iss.	1994	45.00	45
1994 1994 Star	Yr.Iss.	1995	39.00	39
1995 1995 Santa	Yr.Iss.	1996	46.50	47
1996 1996 Traditional Ball	Yr.Iss.		46.50	47

Yuletide - Lenox

YEAR ISSUE	EDITION LIMIT	YEAR RETD.	ISSUE PRICE	*QUOTE U.S. $
1994 Cat	Open		19.50	20
1995 Candle	Open		19.95	20
1996 Christmas Angel™	Open		21.00	21

Lilliput Lane Ltd./Enesco Corporation

Christmas Ornaments - Lilliput Lane

YEAR ISSUE	EDITION LIMIT	YEAR RETD.	ISSUE PRICE	*QUOTE U.S. $
1992 Mistletoe Cottage	Retrd.	1992	27.50	40-60
1993 Robin Cottage	Retrd.	1993	35.00	45
1994 Ivy House	Retrd.	1994	35.00	45
1995 Plum Cottage	Retrd.	1995	30.00	40
1996 Fir Tree Cottage	Retrd.	1996	30.00	30
1997 Evergreens	Yr.Iss.		30.00	30

Ray Day/Coca Cola Country - R. Day

YEAR ISSUE	EDITION LIMIT	YEAR RETD.	ISSUE PRICE	*QUOTE U.S. $
1996 Santa's Corner	19,960		35.00	35

Lladró

Angels - Lladró

YEAR ISSUE	EDITION LIMIT	YEAR RETD.	ISSUE PRICE	*QUOTE U.S. $
1994 Joyful Offering L6125G	Yr.Iss.	1994	245.00	265
1995 Angel of the Stars L6132G	Yr.Iss.	1995	195.00	195
1996 Rejoice L6321G	Yr.Iss.		220.00	220

Annual Ornaments - Lladró

YEAR ISSUE	EDITION LIMIT	YEAR RETD.	ISSUE PRICE	*QUOTE U.S. $
1988 Christmas Ball-L1603M	Yr.Iss.	1988	60.00	60-80
1989 Christmas Ball-L5656M	Yr.Iss.	1989	65.00	65
1990 Christmas Ball-L5730M	Yr Iss.	1990	70.00	70
1991 Christmas Ball-L5829M	Yr.Iss.	1991	52.00	68
1992 Christmas Ball-L5914M	Yr.Iss.	1992	52.00	55
1993 Christmas Ball-L6009M	Yr.Iss.	1993	54.00	55
1994 Christmas Ball-L6105M	Yr.Iss.	1994	55.00	55
1995 Christmas Ball-L6207M	Yr.Iss.	1995	55.00	55
1996 Christmas Ball-L6298M	Yr.Iss.	1996	55.00	55
1997 Christmas Ball-L6442M	Yr.Iss.		55.00	55

Cherub Ornaments - Lladró

YEAR ISSUE	EDITION LIMIT	YEAR RETD.	ISSUE PRICE	*QUOTE U.S. $
1995 Surprised Cherub L6253G	Open		120.00	120
1995 Playing Cherub L6254G	Open		120.00	120
1995 Thinking Cherub L6255G	Open		120.00	120

Dove Ornaments - Lladró

YEAR ISSUE	EDITION LIMIT	YEAR RETD.	ISSUE PRICE	*QUOTE U.S. $
1995 Landing Dove L6266G	Open		49.00	49
1995 Flying Dove L6267G	Open		49.00	49

Miniature Ornaments - Lladró

YEAR ISSUE	EDITION LIMIT	YEAR RETD.	ISSUE PRICE	*QUOTE U.S. $
1988 Miniature Angels-L1604G, Set/3	Yr.Iss.	1988	75.00	175-250
1989 Holy Family-L5657G, Set/3	Yr.Iss.	1990	79.50	100
1990 Three Kings-L5729G, Set/3	Yr Iss.	1991	87.50	110
1991 Holy Shepherds-L5809G	Yr.Iss.	1991	97.50	100-110
1993 Nativity Trio-L6095G	Yr.Iss.	1993	115.00	135-150

Ornaments - Lladró

YEAR ISSUE	EDITION LIMIT	YEAR RETD.	ISSUE PRICE	*QUOTE U.S. $
1991 Our First-1991-L5840G	Yr.Iss.	1991	50.00	57
1992 Snowman-L5841G	Yr.Iss.	1994	50.00	60
1992 Santa-L5842G	Yr.Iss.	1994	55.00	60
1992 Baby's First-1992-L5922G	Yr.Iss.	1992	55.00	55
1992 Our First-1992-L5923G	Yr.Iss.	1992	50.00	50
1992 Elf Ornament-L5938G	Yr.Iss.	1994	50.00	57-75
1992 Mrs. Claus-L5939G	Yr.Iss.	1994	55.00	57
1992 Christmas Morning-L5940G	Yr.Iss.	1992	97.50	100
1993 Nativity Lamb-L5969G	Yr.Iss.	1994	85.00	85
1993 Baby's First 1993-L6037G	Yr.Iss.	1993	57.00	57
1993 Our First-L6038G	Yr.Iss.	1993	52.00	57
1996 Santa's Journey-L6265	Yr.Iss.	1996	49.00	49

Toy Ornaments - Lladró

YEAR ISSUE	EDITION LIMIT	YEAR RETD.	ISSUE PRICE	*QUOTE U.S. $
1995 Christmas Tree L6261G	Open		75.00	75
1995 Rocking Horse L6262G	Open		69.00	69
1995 Doll L6263G	Open		69.00	69
1995 Train L6264G	Open		69.00	69

Tree Topper Ornaments - Lladró

YEAR ISSUE	EDITION LIMIT	YEAR RETD.	ISSUE PRICE	*QUOTE U.S. $
1990 Angel Tree Topper-L5719G-Blue	Yr.Iss.	1990	115.00	200-225
1991 Angel Tree Topper-L5831G-Pink	Yr.Iss.	1991	115.00	150
1992 Angel Tree Topper-L5875G -Green	Yr.Iss.	1992	120.00	150
1993 Angel Tree Topper-L5962G -Lavender	Yr.Iss.	1993	125.00	150

Margaret Furlong Designs

Annual Ornaments - M. Furlong

YEAR ISSUE	EDITION LIMIT	YEAR RETD.	ISSUE PRICE	*QUOTE U.S. $
1980 3" Trumpeter Angel	Closed	1994	12.00	75-150
1980 4" Trumpeter Angel	Closed	1994	21.00	160-180
1982 3" Star Angel	Closed	1994	12.00	75-150
1982 4" Star Angel	Closed	1994	21.00	75-160
1984 3" Dove Angel	Closed	1995	12.00	45-90
1984 4" Dove Angel	Closed	1995	21.00	65-95
1988 3" Butterfly Angel	Closed	1996	12.00	45-95
1988 4" Butterfly Angel	Closed	1996	21.00	70-84
1992 3" Noel Angel	Closed	1997	12.00	12
1992 4" Noel Angel	Closed	1997	21.00	21
1996 4" Sunflower Angel	Closed	1996	21.00	21-30
1997 4" Iris Angel	Yr.Iss.		24.00	24

Flora Angelica - M. Furlong

YEAR ISSUE	EDITION LIMIT	YEAR RETD.	ISSUE PRICE	*QUOTE U.S. $
1995 Faith Angel	10,000	1995	45.00	120-150
1996 Hope Angel	10,000	1996	45.00	75-125
1997 Charity Angel	10,000	1997	50.00	50

Gifts from God - M. Furlong

YEAR ISSUE	EDITION LIMIT	YEAR RETD.	ISSUE PRICE	*QUOTE U.S. $
1985 1985 The Charis Angel	3,000	1985	45.00	600-1000
1986 1986 The Hallelujah Angel	3,000	1986	45.00	600-1000
1987 1987 The Angel of Light	3,000	1987	45.00	300-800
1988 1988 The Celestial Angel	3,000	1988	45.00	300-800
1989 1989 Coronation Angel	3,000	1989	45.00	350-800

Joyeux Noel - M. Furlong

YEAR ISSUE	EDITION LIMIT	YEAR RETD.	ISSUE PRICE	*QUOTE U.S. $
1990 1990 Celebration Angel	10,000	1994	45.00	240-300
1991 1991 Thanksgiving Angel	10,000	1994	45.00	240-290
1992 1992 Joyeux Noel Angel	10,000	1994	45.00	100-275
1993 1993 Star of Bethlehem Angel	10,000	1994	45.00	175-275
1994 1994 Messiah Angel	10,000	1994	45.00	300-600

Madonna and Child - M. Furlong

YEAR ISSUE	EDITION LIMIT	YEAR RETD.	ISSUE PRICE	*QUOTE U.S. $
1996 Madonna of the Cross	20.000		80.00	80

Musical Series - M. Furlong

YEAR ISSUE	EDITION LIMIT	YEAR RETD.	ISSUE PRICE	*QUOTE U.S. $
1980 1980 The Caroler	3,000	1980	50.00	400-800
1981 1981 The Lyrist	3,000	1981	45.00	300-800
1982 1982 The Lutist	3,000	1982	45.00	300-900
1983 1983 The Concertinist	3,000	1983	45.00	200-900
1984 1984 The Herald Angel	3,000	1984	45.00	300-900

Victoria - M. Furlong

YEAR ISSUE	EDITION LIMIT	YEAR RETD.	ISSUE PRICE	*QUOTE U.S. $
1994 Victoria Heart	10.000	1996	24.95	50-100
1995 Victoria Lily of the Valley	30,000	1996	25.00	35-75

Memories of Yesterday/Enesco Corporation

Memories of Yesterday Society Member's Only - M. Attwell

YEAR ISSUE	EDITION LIMIT	YEAR RETD.	ISSUE PRICE	*QUOTE U.S. $
1992 With Luck And A Friend, I's In Heaven MY922	Yr.Iss.	1992	16.00	20
1993 I'm Bringing Good Luck -Wherever You Are	Yr.Iss.	1993	16.00	22

Memories of Yesterday - M. Attwell

YEAR ISSUE	EDITION LIMIT	YEAR RETD.	ISSUE PRICE	*QUOTE U.S. $
1988 Baby's First Christmas 1988 520373	Yr.Iss.	1988	13.50	40-60
1988 Special Delivery! 1988 520381	Yr.Iss.	1988	13.50	35-45
1989 Baby's First Christmas 522465	Retrd.	1996	15.00	15-20
1989 A Surprise for Santa 522473 (1989)	Yr.Iss.	1989	13.50	15-25
1989 Christmas Together 522562	Open		15.00	15-25
1995 Happy Landings (Dated 1995) 522619	Yr.Iss.	1995	16.00	16
1990 Time For Bed 524638	Yr.Iss.	1990	15.00	15-30
1990 New Moon 524646	Suspd.		15.00	15-25
1994 Just Dreaming of You 524786	Open		16.00	16
1990 Moonstruck 524794	Retrd.	1992	15.00	25
1991 Just Watchin' Over You 525421	Retrd.	1994	17.50	25
1991 Lucky Me 525448	Retrd.	1993	16.00	22
1993 Wish I Could Fly To You 525790 (dated)	Yr.Iss.	1993	16.00	16
1992 I'll Fly Along To See You Soon 525804 (1992 Dated Bisque)	Yr.Iss.	1992	16.00	16
1991 Star Fishin' 525820	Open		16.00	16
1991 Lucky You 525847	Retrd.	1993	16.00	16
1995 Now I Lay Me Down to Sleep 527009	Open		15.00	15
1995 I Pray the Lord My Soul to Keep 527017	Open		15.00	15
1992 Mommy, I Teared It 527041(Five Year Anniversary Limited Edition)	Yr.Iss.	1992	15.00	20
1991 S'no Use Lookin' Back Now! 527181(dated)	Yr.Iss.	1991	17.50	28
1992 Merry Christmas, Little Boo-Boo 528803	Open		37.50	38
1993 May All Your Finest Dreams Come True 528811	Open		16.00	16
1992 Star Light. Star Bright 528838	Open		16.00	16
1994 Give Yourself a Hug From Me! 529109 ('94 Dated)	Yr. Iss.	1994	17.50	18
1992 Swinging Together 580481(1992 Dated Artplas)	Yr.Iss.	1992	17.50	22
1992 Sailin' With My Friends 587575 (Artplas)	Open		25.00	25
1993 Bringing Good Wishes Your Way 592846 (Artplas)	Open		25.00	25
1994 Bout Time I Came Along to See You 592854 (Artplas)	Open		17.50	18

Event Item Only - Enesco

YEAR ISSUE	EDITION LIMIT	YEAR RETD.	ISSUE PRICE	*QUOTE U.S. $
1993 How 'Bout A Little Kiss? 527068	Closed	1993	16.50	50
1996 Hoping To See You Soon 527033	Yr.Iss.	1996	15.00	15

Friendship - Enesco

YEAR ISSUE	EDITION LIMIT	YEAR RETD.	ISSUE PRICE	*QUOTE U.S. $
1996 I Love You This Much! 185809	Open		13.50	14

Peter Pan - Enesco

YEAR ISSUE	EDITION LIMIT	YEAR RETD.	ISSUE PRICE	*QUOTE U.S. $
1996 Tinkerbell 164682	Open		20.00	20

Midwest of Cannon Falls

Eddie Walker Collection - E. Walker

YEAR ISSUE	EDITION LIMIT	YEAR RETD.	ISSUE PRICE	*QUOTE U.S. $
1997 Santa Holding Reindeer, dated 1997 22284-3	Yr.Iss.		10.00	10

Leo R. Smith III Collection - L.R. Smith

YEAR ISSUE	EDITION LIMIT	YEAR RETD.	ISSUE PRICE	*QUOTE U.S. $
1994 Flying Woodsman Santa 11921-1	2,500	1994	35.00	200-350
1995 Angel of Love 16123-4	3,500	1996	32.00	40
1995 Angel of Peace 16199-9	3,500	1996	32.00	40
1995 Angel of Your Dreams 16130-2	3,500	1996	32.00	33
1995 Partridge Angel 13994-3	3,500	1996	30.00	30
1995 Santa on Reindeer 13780-2	3,500	1996	35.00	75
1996 Angel of Dependability 19218-4	Closed	1996	37.00	37
1996 Angel of Adventure 19219-1	Closed	1996	37.00	37
1996 Angel of Nurturing 19220-7	Closed	1996	37.00	37
1996 Angel of Generosity 19221-4	Closed	1996	37.00	37
1996 Angel of Knowledge 19222-1	Closed	1996	37.00	37
1996 Angel of Sharing 19223-8	Closed	1996	37.00	37
1996 Angel of Guidance 19224-5	Closed	1996	37.00	37
1996 Angel of Pride 19225-2	Closed	1996	37.00	37
1996 Angel of Heaven and Earth 18396-0	3,500		33.00	33

*Quotes have been rounded up to nearest dollar

ORNAMENTS

Midwest of Cannon Falls to Old World Christmas

YEAR ISSUE		EDITION LIMIT	YEAR RETD.	ISSUE PRICE	*QUOTE U.S. $
1996	Angel of Light 18076-1	4,000		33.00	33
1996	Angel of Music 18073-4	3,500		33.00	33
1996	Everyday Angel Ornament Stand 19554-3	Closed	1996	25.00	25
1996	Belsnickle Santa 18074-7	4,000		39.00	39
1997	Santa Riding Bird 19928-2	3,000		35.00	35
1997	Stars & Stripes Santa 19929-9	3,000		35.00	35

Wendt and Kuhn Ornaments - Wendt/Kuhn

YEAR ISSUE		EDITION LIMIT	YEAR RETD.	ISSUE PRICE	*QUOTE U.S. $
1989	Trumpeting Angel Ornament, 2 asst. 09402-0	Retrd.	1995	14.00	17
1991	Angel in Ring Ornament 01208-6	Retrd.	1995	12.00	15
1994	Angel on Moon, Star, 12 asst. 12945-6	Open		20.00	22
1978	Angel Clip-on Ornament 00729-7	Retrd.	1995	20.00	24

Miss Martha's Collection/Enesco Corporation

Miss Martha's Collection - M. Holcombe

YEAR ISSUE		EDITION LIMIT	YEAR RETD.	ISSUE PRICE	*QUOTE U.S. $
1993	Caroline - Always Someone Watching Over Me 350532	Closed	1994	25.00	50
1993	Arianna - Heavenly Sounds H/O 350567	Closed	1994	25.00	50
1992	Baby in Basket 369454	Closed	1994	25.00	50
1992	Baby In Swing 421480	Retrd.	1993	25.00	50
1992	Girl Holding Stocking DTD 1992 421499	Closed	1994	25.00	50
1992	Girl/Bell In Hand 421502	Retrd.	1993	25.00	50

Old World Christmas

Collector Club - E.M. Merck, unless otherwise noted

YEAR ISSUE		EDITION LIMIT	YEAR RETD.	ISSUE PRICE	*QUOTE U.S. $
1993	Mr. & Mrs. Claus set 1490	Retrd.	1993	Gift	100-150
1993	Glass Christmas Maidens, Set/4, 1491	Retrd.	1993	35.00	85-100
1993	Dresdener Drummer Nutcracker 7258	Retrd.	1993	110.00	175-250
1994	Santa in Moon 1492	Retrd.	1994	Gift	40-100
1994	Large Santa in Chimney 1493	Retrd.	1994	42.50	65-95
1995	Large Christmas Carousel 1587 - Inge-Glas	Retrd.	1995	79.50	95
1995	The Konigsee Nutcracker 7284	Retrd.	1995	125.00	200-300
1995	Cherub on Reflector 1545 - Inge-Glas	Retrd.	1995	Gift	27-75
1996	The Baroque Angel Above Reflector 1082	Yr.Iss.		39.50	45
1996	The Saxon Santa Claus Nutcracker 7211	Yr.Iss.		135.00	135-155
1996	The Victorian Christmas Stocking 1554	Yr.Iss.		Gift	20

Angel & Female - E.M. Merck, unless otherwise noted

YEAR ISSUE		EDITION LIMIT	YEAR RETD.	ISSUE PRICE	*QUOTE U.S. $
1991	Angel of Peace 1033	Retrd.	1995	9.25	10
1990	Angel on Disc 1028	Retrd.	1993	11.70	16
1992	Angel on Form 1044	Retrd.	1995	9.70	10
1990	Antique Style Doll Head 1026	Retrd.	1996	8.45	9
1987	Baby 1009	Retrd.	1995	5.25	6
1988	Baby in Bunting 1015	Retrd.	1990	7.70	22
1991	Baby Jesus 1036	Retrd.	1995	9.25	10
1991	Baroque Angel 1031	Retrd.	1995	12.95	13
1985	Caroling Girl 101062	Retrd.	1990	6.65	19
1993	Chubby Mushroom Girl 1057	Retrd.	1996	8.00	8
1986	Clip-on Angel with Wings 1004	Retrd.	1996	10.00	11
1985	Doll Head 103209	Retrd.	1989	6.40	11
1993	Frau Schneemann 1059	Retrd.	1995	16.90	17
1992	Garden Girl 1040	Retrd.	1996	8.25	9
1985	Girl in Blue Dress 1042227	Retrd.	1996	7.00	7
1987	Girl in Grapes 1010	Retrd.	1989	8.45	25
1990	Girl in Polka Dot Dress 1030	Retrd.	1996	12.60	13
1987	Girl on Snowball with Teddy 1007	Retrd.	1995	9.25	15
1988	Girl Under Tree 1014	Retrd.	1995	7.80	8
1985	Girl with Flowers 101069	Retrd.	1993	7.50	13
1992	Girl with White Kitty 1045	Retrd.	1996	9.25	10
1985	Gold Girl with Tree 1010306	Retrd.	1995	8.25	20
1992	Guardian Angel 1043	Retrd.	1995	8.25	15
1992	Honey Child 1042	Retrd.	1995	7.45	8
1988	Large Blue Angel 1012	Retrd.	1994	13.40	17
1988	Large Doll Head 1013	Retrd.	1995	11.60	12
1985	Light Blue Angel with Wings 101052	Retrd.	1994	9.25	14
1986	Little Red Riding Hood 1001	Retrd.	1993	9.90	16
1991	Little Tyrolean Girl 1037	Retrd.	1996	7.00	7
1989	Little Witch 1020	Retrd.	1996	8.35	9
1990	Miniature Mrs. Claus 1027	Retrd.	1995	4.95	5
1986	Mrs. Santa Claus 1003	Retrd.	1989	8.90	32
1987	Mushroom Girl 1006	Retrd.	1994	9.25	12
1989	Pilgrim Girl 1019	Retrd.	1996	9.25	10
1986	Pink Angel with Wings 1002	Retrd.	1988	8.90	16
1990	Praying Girl 1025	Retrd.	1993	7.80	12
1985	Red Girl with Tree 1010309	Retrd.	1995	8.25	13
1989	Small Girl Head 1022	Retrd.	1996	7.00	7
1985	Small Girl with Tree 101029	Retrd.	1995	5.85	6
1989	Victorian Angel 1018	Retrd.	1996	8.35	9
1985	Victorian Girl 101035	Retrd.	1989	5.30	22

Animals - E.M. Merck, unless otherwise noted

YEAR ISSUE		EDITION LIMIT	YEAR RETD.	ISSUE PRICE	*QUOTE U.S. $
1993	Bear Above Reflector 1279	Retrd.	1995	33.75	36
1986	Bear in Crib 1203	Retrd.	1994	9.00	12
1993	Brilliant Butterfly 1267	Retrd.	1996	10.70	11
1993	Buster 1266	Retrd.	1996	8.35	9
1985	Butterfly on Form 1237447	Retrd.	1995	7.80	8
1989	Cat and the Fiddle 1221	Retrd.	1994	7.80	11
1986	Cat in Bag 1204	Retrd.	1995	9.00	9
1985	Cat in Show 121103	Retrd.	1994	7.80	11
1991	Christmas Butterfly 1247	Retrd.	1994	7.00	9
1984	Circus Dog 121021	Retrd.	1994	9.00	12
1989	Fat Fish 1223	Retrd.	1995	5.85	12
1991	Goldfish 1249	Retrd.	1996	7.00	7
1985	Grey Elephant 123420	Retrd.	1995	7.00	7
1993	Grizzly Bear 1265	Retrd.	1995	8.35	9
1988	Jumbo Elephant 1213	Retrd.	1995	9.25	10
1989	King Charles Spaniel 1222	Retrd.	1995	9.90	19
1984	Kitten 121004	Retrd.	1995	7.00	7
1989	Large Fish 1214	Retrd.	1993	6.70	14
1991	Large Puppy with Basket 1241	Retrd.	1993	13.25	22
1985	Large Teddy Bear 121089	Retrd.	1988	13.00	18
1985	Large Three-Sided Head 121088	Retrd.	1994	12.95	30
1985	Matte Gold Bear with Heart 1234356	Retrd.	1996	7.00	7
1986	Monkey 1205	Retrd.	1994	5.85	11
1991	Panda Bear 1242	Retrd.	1996	9.25	15
1993	Pastel Butterfly 1268	Retrd.	1995	8.45	9
1990	Pastel Fish 1234	Retrd.	1996	6.65	7
1985	Pink Pig 121042	Retrd.	1996	7.80	14
1990	Pink Poodle 1227	Retrd.	1994	8.80	15
1986	Playing Cat 1202	Retrd.	1994	8.80	10
1992	Proud Pug 1250	Retrd.	1996	9.25	10
1984	Puppy 121010	Retrd.	1994	7.00	9
1990	Sitting Black Cat 1228	Retrd.	1995	7.00	14
1986	Sitting Dog with Pipe 1206	Retrd.	1995	7.80	11
1991	Sitting Puppy 1246	Retrd.	1994	6.75	15
1985	Small Bunny 121090	Retrd.	1994	5.20	8
1986	Smiling Dog 1207	Retrd.	1994	7.80	10
1985	Snail 121041	Retrd.	1993	6.70	22
1989	Teddy Bear with Bow 1218	Retrd.	1990	6.65	17
1984	Three-Sided: Owl, Dog, Cat 121009	Retrd.	1994	8.55	13
1990	West Highland Terrier 1232	Retrd.	1993	7.45	15
1989	White Kitty 1220	Retrd.	1990	7.45	10
1994	Woodland Squirrel 1291	Retrd.	1995	21.00	21

Bead Garlands - E.M. Merck

YEAR ISSUE		EDITION LIMIT	YEAR RETD.	ISSUE PRICE	*QUOTE U.S. $
1993	Angel Garland 1306	Retrd.	1993	55.00	90-105
1993	Celestial Garland 1303	Retrd.	1993	55.00	95-115
1996	Christmas Candy Garland 1324	Retrd.	1996	110.00	110
1993	Clown & Drum Garland 1301	Retrd.	1993	55.00	75-110
1993	Frog and Fish Garland 1305	Retrd.	1995	55.00	95
1993	Fruit Garland 1302	Retrd.	1993	55.00	70
1993	Pickle Garland 1304	Retrd.	1993	55.00	110
1996	Poinsettia Garland [illegible]	Retrd.	[illegible]	100.00	100
1993	Santa Garland 1308	Retrd.	1995	55.00	95-125
1996	Santa/Candy Christmas Garland 1322	Retrd.	1996	110.00	110
1996	Shiny Gold Garland 1325	Retrd.	1996	135.00	135
1993	Teddy Bear & Heart Garland 1307	Retrd.	1993	55.00	115
1994	Woodland Christmas Garland 1311	Retrd.	1996	65.00	65

Birgit's Christmas Collection - B. Mueller-Blech

YEAR ISSUE		EDITION LIMIT	YEAR RETD.	ISSUE PRICE	*QUOTE U.S. $
1996	Guarding My Children 141	5,000	1996	65.00	95
1996	O' Tannenbaum 131	Retrd.	1996	35.00	55
1996	Old Christmas Barn 133	Retrd.	1996	50.00	80

Butterflies - E.M. Merck

YEAR ISSUE		EDITION LIMIT	YEAR RETD.	ISSUE PRICE	*QUOTE U.S. $
1987	Butterfly, Blue with Blue 1905	Retrd.	1991	20.95	40
1987	Butterfly, Gold with Gold 1906	Retrd.	1991	20.95	40
1987	Butterfly, Orange with Orange 1904	Retrd.	1991	20.95	40
1987	Butterfly, Red with Cream 1903	Retrd.	1991	20.95	40
1987	Butterfly, White with Blue 1902	Retrd.	1991	20.95	40
1987	Butterfly, White with Red 1901	Retrd.	1991	20.95	40

Celestial Figures - E.M. Merck

YEAR ISSUE		EDITION LIMIT	YEAR RETD.	ISSUE PRICE	*QUOTE U.S. $
1993	Comet on Form 2209	Retrd.	1996	7.65	8
1993	High Noon 2211	Retrd.	1996	5.65	6
1985	Large Gold Star w/Glitter 2237139	Retrd.	1993	7.00	10
1990	Shining Sun 2204	Retrd.	1996	7.00	7
1986	Shooting Star on Ball 2201	Retrd.	1993	6.65	12
1985	Sun/Moon 221027	Retrd.	1993	7.00	10

Churches & Houses - E.M. Merck

YEAR ISSUE		EDITION LIMIT	YEAR RETD.	ISSUE PRICE	*QUOTE U.S. $
1985	Bavarian House 201059	Retrd.	1994	8.00	19
1993	Castle Tower 2029	Retrd.	1996	9.45	10
1990	Christmas Chalet 2014	Retrd.	1995	8.00	8
1991	Christmas Shop 2020	Retrd.	1995	9.45	10
1990	Church on Disc 2018	Retrd.	1995	12.50	13
1988	Church/Tree on Form 2008	Retrd.	1995	8.35	9
1986	Farm House 2003	Retrd.	1996	8.45	9
1990	Garden House w/Gnome 2011	Retrd.	1993	7.80	20
1986	Gingerbread House (A) 2001	Retrd.	1989	6.55	16
1986	House with Peacock 2004	Retrd.	1987	7.45	16
1991	Large Lighthouse/Mill 2023	Retrd.	1995	11.00	11
1985	Matte Cream Church 206790-2	Retrd.	1993	6.45	11
1985	Mill 201094	Retrd.	1990	9.45	32
1991	Mission with Sea Gull 2024	Retrd.	1996	9.45	10
1986	Windmill on Form 2006	Retrd.	1988	7.45	26

Clip-On Birds - E.M. Merck

YEAR ISSUE		EDITION LIMIT	YEAR RETD.	ISSUE PRICE	*QUOTE U.S. $
1991	Rooster 1831	Retrd.	1996	10.50	36

Clowns & Male Figures - E.M. Merck, unless otherwise noted

YEAR ISSUE		EDITION LIMIT	YEAR RETD.	ISSUE PRICE	*QUOTE U.S. $
1984	'Shorty Clown' 241011	Retrd.	1988	5.65	14
1984	'Stop' Keystone Cop 241019	Retrd.	1989	6.65	37
1986	Aviator 2402	Retrd.	1994	7.80	20
1986	Baby 2405	Retrd.	1989	6.75	26
1992	Baker 2449	Retrd.	1996	8.35	9
1992	Bavarian 2450	Retrd.	1996	9.25	10
1990	Black Boy 2439	Retrd.	1995	9.00	19
1993	Boxer 2454	Retrd.	1996	7.20	8
1986	Boy Head w/Stocking Cap 2411	Retrd.	1993	5.30	13
1985	Boy in Yellow Sweater 241032	Retrd.	1988	7.00	15
1995	Charlie Chaplin 2487 - Inge-Glas	Retrd.	1995	25.00	65-100
1986	Clip-on Boy Head 2416	Retrd.	1989	6.45	13
1993	Clown Above Ball 2470	Retrd.	1994	42.00	45
1986	Clown Head in Drum 2412	Retrd.	1996	10.25	11
1986	Clown Head w/Burgundy Hat 2418	Retrd.	1994	7.00	10
1984	Clown in Stocking 241006	Retrd.	1988	6.65	20
1985	Dutch Boy 243321	Retrd.	1993	7.55	22
1990	English Bobby 2442	Retrd.	1994	8.80	22
1986	Farm Boy 2414	Retrd.	1989	4.95	21
1985	Fat Boy with Sweater & Cap 2442265	Retrd.	1994	5.85	9
1987	Gnome in Tree 2431	Retrd.	1996	7.80	8
1986	Gnome Under Mushroom 2417	Retrd.	1993	7.00	16
1988	Harpo 2432	Retrd.	1991	6.20	32
1987	Jolly Clown Head 2429	Retrd.	1994	12.95	13
1987	Jolly Snowman 2420	Retrd.	1996	8.00	8
1984	Keystone Cop 241003	Retrd.	1994	9.90	26
1987	King 2421	Retrd.	1995	10.60	11
1989	Leprechaun 2435	Retrd.	1994	7.65	10
1993	Miniature Clown 2464	Retrd.	1995	6.00	6
1993	Monk 2467	Retrd.	1994	7.90	10
1987	Mr. Big Nose 2426	Retrd.	1993	8.00	24
1995	Mr. Sci-Fi 2492 - Inge-Glas	Retrd.	1995	29.50	39
1988	Mushroom Gnome 2430	Retrd.	1989	6.20	13
1986	Pixie with Accordion 2406	Retrd.	1989	4.95	22
1987	Punch 2424	Retrd.	1996	8.70	9
1984	Roly-Poly Keystone Cop 241015	Retrd.	1988	9.90	32
1995	Sailor Boy 2488 - Inge-Glas	Retrd.	1996	7.95	8
1986	Sailor Head 2404	Retrd.	1990	7.45	29
1986	School Boy 2415	Retrd.	1989	4.95	13
1984	Scotsman 241017	Retrd.	1988	6.20	29
1990	Scout 2440	Retrd.	1995	9.25	10
1987	Scrooge 2427	Retrd.	1995	8.55	11
1989	Small Clown Head 2436	Retrd.	1993	6.65	11
1993	Small Snowman 2462	Retrd.	1996	6.00	6
1991	Snowman in Chimney 2447	Retrd.	1996	10.50	11
1990	Snowman on Reflector 2445	Retrd.	1993	10.35	15
1985	Waiter in Tuxedo 241047	Retrd.	1989	7.00	29
1993	Winking Leprechaun 2453	Retrd.	1996	6.55	7

Collector's Editions - E.M. Merck, unless otherwise noted

YEAR ISSUE		EDITION LIMIT	YEAR RETD.	ISSUE PRICE	*QUOTE U.S. $
1994	'94 Santa/Moon on Disc 1512	Retrd.	1994	32.50	45-65
1992	Angel with Tinsel Wire 1522	Retrd.	1993	55.00	75-100
1993	Angel with Wings 1556	Retrd.	1993	12.50	75-100
1993	Christmas Heart 1593	Retrd.	1993	10.00	40-60
1995	Christmas Tree above Star Reflector 1513	2,400	1995	53.00	95
1995	Devil Bell 1599	Retrd.	1995	34.95	95
1992	Flying Peacock with Wings 1550	Retrd.	1995	22.50	34
1992	Flying Songbird with Wings 1551	Retrd.	1995	21.75	34
1993	Hansel and Gretal 1511	2,400	1995	45.00	100-125
1993	Heavenly Angel 1563	Retrd.	1995	20.00	36
1990	Night Before Christmas Ball 1501	500	1993	72.50	125-200
1992	Nutcracker Ornament 1510	Retrd.	1993	33.75	150-200
1995	Parachuting Santa 1547	Retrd.	1995	59.50	60
1993	Santa with Hot Air Balloon 1570	Retrd.	1995	38.85	39
1992	Santa with Tinsel Wire 1521	Retrd.	1993	55.00	80-100
1992	Santa's Departure 1503	500	1994	72.50	100
1991	Santa's Visit 1502	500	1994	72.50	100
1992	Snowman with Tinsel Wire 1523	Retrd.	1993	32.50	85
1995	Special Event Santa 1560	5,000	1995	15.00	35-40
1995	Witch 1582	Retrd.	1995	34.95	700-900

Easter Light Covers - E.M. Merck

YEAR ISSUE		EDITION LIMIT	YEAR RETD.	ISSUE PRICE	*QUOTE U.S. $
1988	Assorted Easter Egg 9331-1	Retrd.	1993	3.95	10
1988	Assorted Pastel Egg 9335-1	Retrd.	1994	2.95	10
1988	Bunny 9333-4	Retrd.	1994	4.20	12
1988	Bunny in Basket 9333-6	Retrd.	1994	4.20	12
1988	Chick 9333-3	Retrd.	1994	4.20	10
1988	Chick in Egg 9333-5	Retrd.	1994	4.20	12
1988	Hen in Basket 9333-1	Retrd.	1994	4.20	10
1988	Rabbit in Egg 9333-2	Retrd.	1994	4.20	12

Fruits & Vegetables - E.M. Merck, unless otherwise noted

YEAR ISSUE		EDITION LIMIT	YEAR RETD.	ISSUE PRICE	*QUOTE U.S. $
1990	Apricot 2831	Retrd.	1995	6.55	7
1990	Cherries on Form 2825	Retrd.	1993	9.00	12
1989	Cucumber 2820	Retrd.	1989	6.65	20
1990	Fruit Basket 2838	Retrd.	1996	7.80	8
1985	Grapes on Form 281038	Retrd.	1987	7.00	20
1994	Grapes with Butterfly 2887	Retrd.	1996	9.50	10
1987	Green Pepper 2812	Retrd.	1995	8.00	8
1985	Large Basket of Grapes 281053	Retrd.	1995	10.35	11
1993	Large Candied Apple 2882	Retrd.	1996	12.95	13
1991	Large Fruit Basket 2849	Retrd.	1995	12.50	13
1984	Large Matte Corn 281033	Retrd.	1995	9.25	10
1985	Large Strawberry 2841432	Retrd.	1993	4.20	19
1990	Large Strawberry w/Flower 2841	Retrd.	1993	10.50	29
1993	Large Sugar Pear 2881	Retrd.	1996	12.95	13
1985	Mr. Apple 281071	Retrd.	1988	6.20	32
1984	Mr. Pear 281023	Retrd.	1993	6.75	14
1987	Onion 2810	Retrd.	1989	8.25	100
1986	Pear with Face 2805	Retrd.	1995	7.00	7

*Quotes have been rounded up to nearest dollar

Old World Christmas
to Old World Christmas

ORNAMENTS

YEAR ISSUE		EDITION LIMIT	YEAR RETD.	ISSUE PRICE	*QUOTE U.S. $
1990	Raspberry 2835	Retrd.	1993	6.20	9
1991	Strawberries/Flower on Form 2851	Retrd.	1994	8.55	10
1990	Strawberry Cluster 2836	Retrd.	1995	5.20	6
1991	Very Large Apple 2848	Retrd.	1993	10.60	15
1991	Very Large Pear 2847	Retrd.	1993	10.60	15

Halloween Light Covers - E.M. Merck

YEAR ISSUE		EDITION LIMIT	YEAR RETD.	ISSUE PRICE	*QUOTE U.S. $
1989	Dancing Scarecrow 9241-3	Retrd.	1994	7.65	12
1987	Devil 9223-5	Retrd.	1993	3.95	15
1987	Ghost w/Pumpkin 9221-2	Retrd.	1994	3.95	10
1987	Haunted House 9223-1	Retrd.	1994	3.95	12
1987	Jack O'Lantern 9221-1	Retrd.	1993	3.95	10
1989	Man in the Moon 9241-5	Retrd.	1993	7.65	28
1989	Pumpkin Face 9241-6	Retrd.	1994	7.65	12
1987	Pumpkin w/Top Hat 9223-6	Retrd.	1994	3.95	12
1987	Sad Pumpkin 9221-5	Retrd.	1993	3.95	12
1987	Scarecrow 9221-3	Retrd.	1993	3.95	10
1987	Six Halloween Light Covers 9221	Retrd.	1994	25.00	56
1987	Six Halloween Light Covers 9223	Retrd.	1993	25.90	56
1987	Skull 9221-6	Retrd.	1994	3.95	12
1987	Smiling Cat 9223-2	Retrd.	1993	3.95	10
1987	Smiling Ghost 9223-4	Retrd.	1994	3.95	10
1989	Spider 9241-1	Retrd.	1994	7.65	10
1987	Standing Witch 9223-3	Retrd.	1994	3.95	12
1987	Witch Head 9221-4	Retrd.	1993	3.95	12
1989	Witch Head 9241-2	Retrd.	1994	7.65	13
1989	Wizard 9241-4	Retrd.	1993	7.65	22

Hanging Birds - E.M. Merck

YEAR ISSUE		EDITION LIMIT	YEAR RETD.	ISSUE PRICE	*QUOTE U.S. $
1986	Large Owl with Stein 1604	Retrd.	1989	10.00	65

Hearts - E.M. Merck

YEAR ISSUE		EDITION LIMIT	YEAR RETD.	ISSUE PRICE	*QUOTE U.S. $
1987	Burgundy Heart with Glitter 3004	Retrd.	1995	6.75	7
1992	Heart with Flowers 3010	Retrd.	1993	9.50	13
1985	Large Matte Red Heart 306925	Retrd.	1995	5.30	6
1985	Pink Heart with Glitter 306767	Retrd.	1995	6.75	7
1986	Small Gold Heart with Star 3001	Retrd.	1993	2.85	9
1988	Valentine 3005	Retrd.	1995	5.75	6

Household Items - E.M. Merck

YEAR ISSUE		EDITION LIMIT	YEAR RETD.	ISSUE PRICE	*QUOTE U.S. $
1986	Black Stocking 3203	Retrd.	1993	9.45	56
1994	Cheers 3222	Retrd.	1996	6.95	7
1994	Christmas Cap 3220	Retrd.	1996	6.50	7
1992	Christmas Shoe 3212	Retrd.	1996	8.25	9
1985	Clip-On Candle 321063	Retrd.	1995	12.95	19
1992	Flapper Purse 3211	Retrd.	1996	9.25	10
1991	Money Bag 3206	Retrd.	1994	7.00	10
1985	Pastel Umbrella (A) 321091	Retrd.	1993	11.00	25
1985	Pocket Watch 326729	Retrd.	1995	5.85	6
1986	Red Stocking 3201	Retrd.	1987	9.00	26
1991	Small Cuckoo Clock 3209	Retrd.	1995	7.00	7
1991	Small Wine Barrel 3210	Retrd.	1993	6.30	15
1985	Very Large Pink Umbrella 321103	Retrd.	1986	29.50	56
1985	Wall Clock 321060	Retrd.	1995	11.00	11
1988	Wine Barrel 3204	Retrd.	1990	7.00	13

Icicles - E.M. Merck

YEAR ISSUE		EDITION LIMIT	YEAR RETD.	ISSUE PRICE	*QUOTE U.S. $
1988	Long Champagne Icicle 3401	Retrd.	1988	7.25	15

Light Covers - E.M. Merck

YEAR ISSUE		EDITION LIMIT	YEAR RETD.	ISSUE PRICE	*QUOTE U.S. $
1984	3 Men in a Tub 529007-1	Retrd.	1986	1.60	15
1986	Angel on Bell 529023-5	Retrd.	1991	3.95	14
1985	Apple 529011-5	Retrd.	1989	3.00	12
1986	Assorted Alphabet Blocks 529043-1	Retrd.	1991	4.50	16
1984	Assorted Animals, set/6 529003	Retrd.	1987	10.35	60
1986	Assorted Bells, set of 6 529023	Retrd.	1993	22.50	60
1988	Assorted Birds 529057-1	Retrd.	1990	3.95	12
1986	Assorted Easter Eggs 529031-1	Retrd.	1993	3.00	12
1988	Assorted Fast Food 529055-1	Retrd.	1991	3.95	18
1984	Assorted Figurals, set of 6 529005	Retrd.	1987	10.35	72
1989	Assorted Fir Cone 529209-1	Retrd.	1991	2.85	12
1993	Assorted Frosty Bell 5275	Retrd.	1993	5.65	10
1985	Assorted Fruit, set of 6 529011	Retrd.	1989	20.00	56
1985	Assorted Heads, set of 6 529009	Retrd.	1988	10.35	60
1986	Assorted Peach Roses 529045-4	Retrd.	1990	3.95	27
1986	Assorted Roses, set/6 529045	Retrd.	1991	22.50	48
1985	Assorted Santas, set/6 529015	Retrd.	1992	20.00	72
1989	Assorted Sea Shells 529301-1	Retrd.	1992	3.50	15
1991	Assorted Snowmen 529305-1	Retrd.	1993	5.55	16
1986	Assorted Yellow Roses 529045-2	Retrd.	1990	3.95	9
1985	Automobile 529019-3	Retrd.	1988	2.70	18
1985	Balloon 529019-2	Retrd.	1988	2.70	15
1984	Bear 519003-3	Retrd.	1987	2.50	12
1986	Blue Father Christmas 529047-3	Retrd.	1992	3.95	16
1993	Blue Man in the Moon 5206	Retrd.	1993	5.50	9
1986	Bunny 529033-4	Retrd.	1993	3.60	10
1986	Bunny in Basket 529033-6	Retrd.	1993	3.60	8
1985	Cable Car 529019-5	Retrd.	1988	2.70	19
1984	Carousel 529005-3	Retrd.	1987	2.70	19
1986	Chick 529033-3	Retrd.	1993	3.60	8
1986	Chick in Egg 529033-5	Retrd.	1993	3.60	8
1988	Christmas Carol 529053	Retrd.	1991	25.00	72
1993	Christmas House 5205	Retrd.	1993	5.50	6
1988	Christmas Tree 529051-4	Retrd.	1992	3.95	12
1984	Church on Ball 529005-6	Retrd.	1987	2.50	12
1985	Clara-The Doll 529017-1	Retrd.	1989	2.70	12
1985	Clear Icicles, set of 6 529205	Retrd.	1989	20.00	48
1984	Clown 529001-5	Retrd.	1986	1.60	16
1988	Clown 529051-6	Retrd.	1991	3.95	15
1985	Clown Head 529009-1	Retrd.	1988	1.60	14
1988	Cornucopia 529049-1	Retrd.	1992	3.95	14
1988	Doll 529051-2	Retrd.	1993	3.95	14
1993	Doll Head 5202	Retrd.	1993	5.65	14
1985	Doll Head 529009-4	Retrd.	1988	1.60	12
1988	Drum 529051-1	Retrd.	1992	3.95	12
1988	Ear of Corn 529049-6	Retrd.	1992	3.95	14
1984	Elephant 529003-4	Retrd.	1987	1.60	14
1985	Father Christmas 529009-5	Retrd.	1990	3.00	15
1986	Father Christmas Set 529047	Retrd.	1992	25.00	72
1984	Flower Basket 529005-1	Retrd.	1987	1.60	12
1989	Frog 529303-6	Retrd.	1993	6.45	10
1993	Frosty Acorn 5276	Retrd.	1994	5.65	8
1993	Frosty Cone 5271	Retrd.	1994	5.65	8
1993	Frosty Icicle 5272	Retrd.	1993	5.65	8
1993	Frosty Red Rose 5277	Retrd.	1993	5.65	9
1993	Frosty Snowman 5270	Retrd.	1993	5.65	9
1993	Frosty Tree 5273	Retrd.	1993	5.65	8
1984	Gnome 529001-1	Retrd.	1986	1.60	8
1985	Grapes 529011-3	Retrd.	1989	3.00	8
1986	Green Father Christmas 529047-2	Retrd.	1992	3.95	16
1984	Hedgehog 529003-5	Retrd.	1987	1.60	19
1986	Hen in Basket 529033-1	Retrd.	1993	3.60	8
1984	House 529005-2	Retrd.	1987	1.60	12
1988	Indian 529049-5	Retrd.	1992	3.95	14
1993	Jolly Santa Head 5201	Retrd.	1993	5.50	10
1985	King 529013-3	Retrd.	1988	2.70	12
1989	Kitten 529303-3	Retrd.	1993	6.45	10
1984	Lil' Boy Blue 529007-5	Retrd.	1986	1.60	16
1985	Lil' Rascal Head 529009-6	Retrd.	1988	1.60	16
1985	Locomotive 529019-4	Retrd.	1988	2.70	19
1993	Man in the Moon 5204	Retrd.	1993	5.50	6
1985	Marie-The Girl 529017-3	Retrd.	1989	2.70	16
1985	Mouse King 529017-5	Retrd.	1989	2.70	16
1984	Mrs. Claus 529001-4	Retrd.	1986	1.60	16
1985	Nutcracker 529017-4	Retrd.	1989	2.70	10
1986	Nutcracker on Bell 529023-6	Retrd.	1993	3.95	15
1985	Nutcracker Suite Figures, set/6 529017	Retrd.	1989	19.00	72
1985	Orange 529011-6	Retrd.	1989	3.00	7
1984	Owl 529003-2	Retrd.	1987	1.60	10
1989	Panda 529303-1	Retrd.	1994	6.45	12
1985	Pastel Icicles 529207	Retrd.	1989	N/A	N/A
1984	Peacock 519003-6	Retrd.	1987	2.70	10
1993	Peacock 5203	Retrd.	1993	5.65	11
1985	Pear 529011-1	Retrd.	1989	3.00	9
1988	Pilgrim Boy 529049-3	Retrd.	1992	3.95	12
1988	Pilgrim Girl 529049-4	Retrd.	1992	3.95	12
1985	Pineapple 529011-4	Retrd.	1989	3.00	15
1985	Pink Heart 529201-3	Retrd.	1989	2.85	9
1989	Puppy 529303-4	Retrd.	1994	6.45	12
1986	Purple Father Christmas 529047-6	Retrd.	1992	3.95	19
1984	Queen of Heart 529007-3	Retrd.	1986	2.70	16
1986	Rabbit in Egg 529033-2	Retrd.	1993	3.60	9
1986	Red Father Christmas 529047-1	Retrd.	1992	3.95	18
1986	Red Father Christmas 529047-4	Retrd.	1992	3.95	18
1985	Red Heart 529201-1	Retrd.	1990	2.85	9
1985	Red Riding Hood 529009-2	Retrd.	1988	1.60	10
1986	Rocking Horse on Bell 529023-4	Retrd.	1990	3.95	14
1985	Roly-Poly Santa 529015-6	Retrd.	1989	3.00	12
1984	Santa Head 529005-4	Retrd.	1987	2.70	16
1985	Santa Head 529009-3	Retrd.	1988	3.00	10
1986	Santa on Bell 529023-3	Retrd.	1990	3.95	16
1984	Santa on Heart 529005-5	Retrd.	1987	3.00	10
1993	Santa with Tree 5207	Retrd.	1993	5.50	6
1985	Santa with Tree 529015-3	Retrd.	1992	3.00	10
1985	School Bus 529019-6	Retrd.	1991	2.70	19
1985	Six Red & White Hearts 529201	Retrd.	1989	15.00	48
1992	Six Snowmen 529305	Retrd.	1993	29.00	72
1984	Snowman 519001-2	Retrd.	1986	2.50	10
1985	Soldier with Drum 529013-1	Retrd.	1988	2.70	14
1985	Soldier with Gun 529013-2	Retrd.	1988	2.70	15
1985	Soldiers, set of 6 529013	Retrd.	1988	17.95	72
1989	Squirrel 529303-2	Retrd.	1994	6.45	9
1984	Standing Santa 529001-3	Retrd.	1987	3.00	12
1988	Stocking 529051-3	Retrd.	1992	3.95	10
1985	Strawberry 529011-2	Retrd.	1989	3.00	9
1993	Sugar Apple 5254	Retrd.	1993	5.50	10
1993	Sugar Fruit Basket 5256	Retrd.	1994	5.65	12
1993	Sugar Grapes 5252	Retrd.	1993	5.50	10
1993	Sugar Pear 5255	Retrd.	1993	5.50	12
1993	Sugar Plum 5253	Retrd.	1993	5.65	10
1985	Sugar Plum Fairy 529017-6	Retrd.	1989	2.70	14
1993	Sugar Strawberry 5251	Retrd.	1993	5.65	12
1989	Swan 529303-5	Retrd.	1994	6.45	12
1986	Teddy Bear 529023-2	Retrd.	1990	3.95	14
1988	Teddy Bear 529051-5	Retrd.	1992	3.95	16
1986	Teddy Bear with Ball 529041-5	Retrd.	1994	3.95	14
1986	Teddy Bear with Candy Cane 529041-1	Retrd.	1992	3.95	14
1986	Teddy Bear with Nightshirt 529041-4	Retrd.	1994	3.95	16
1986	Teddy Bear with Red Heart 529041-2	Retrd.	1992	3.95	16
1986	Teddy Bear with Tree 529041-3	Retrd.	1992	3.95	20
1986	Teddy Bear with Vest 529041-6	Retrd.	1992	3.95	14
1986	Teddy Bears, set of 6 529041	Retrd.	1991	25.00	72
1988	Thanksgiving, set of 6 529049	Retrd.	1992	25.00	72
1988	Toy, set of 6 529051	Retrd.	1992	25.00	72
1985	Transportation Set 529019	Retrd.	1988	17.90	84
1986	Tree on Bell 529023-1	Retrd.	1991	3.95	14
1985	Tug Boat 529019-1	Retrd.	1988	2.70	19
1988	Turkey 529049-2	Retrd.	1992	3.95	8
1986	White Father Christmas 529047-5	Retrd.	1992	3.95	17
1985	White Heart 529201-2	Retrd.	1989	2.85	8

Miscellaneous Forms - E.M. Merck, unless otherwise noted

YEAR ISSUE		EDITION LIMIT	YEAR RETD.	ISSUE PRICE	*QUOTE U.S. $
1990	Assorted Christmas Flowers 3626	Retrd.	1994	8.00	9
1990	Assorted Christmas Stars 3620	Retrd.	1995	7.00	7
1993	Assorted Fantasy Form w/ Wire 3650	Retrd.	1994	20.00	23
1992	Assorted Northern Stars 3640	Retrd.	1995	6.20	7
1992	Assorted Spirals 3636	Retrd.	1995	8.25	9
1992	Christmas Ball with Roses 3634	Retrd.	1995	9.45	10
1986	Flower Basket 3601	Retrd.	1995	10.25	11
1989	Flower with Butterfly 3609	Retrd.	1993	9.75	19
1992	Garden Flowers 3639	Retrd.	1996	9.00	9
1985	Ice Cream Cone 3637164	Retrd.	1988	14.50	24
1990	Large Conical Shell 3629	Retrd.	1993	8.70	18
1991	Large Ribbed Ball w/Roses 3633	Retrd.	1996	7.00	7
1990	Large Sea Shell 3625	Retrd.	1995	8.35	9
1990	Large Snowflake 3622	Retrd.	1995	13.00	13
1993	Lucky Shamrock 3643	Retrd.	1993	7.80	29
1989	Shiny Red Clip-On Tulip 3617	Retrd.	1990	7.45	13

Porcelain Christmas - E.M. Merck

YEAR ISSUE		EDITION LIMIT	YEAR RETD.	ISSUE PRICE	*QUOTE U.S. $
1989	Angel 9435	Retrd.	1994	6.65	12
1995	Angelic Gifts 9712	Retrd.	1995	11.25	12
1988	Bear on Skates 9495	Retrd.	1988	10.00	19
1988	Bunnies on Skies 9494	Retrd.	1988	10.00	19
1987	Father Christmas (A) 9404	Retrd.	1988	11.00	13
1987	Father Christmas w/Cape 9405	Retrd.	1988	11.00	14
1987	Father Christmas w/Toys 9406	Retrd.	1988	11.00	12
1989	Hummingbird 9433	Retrd.	1994	6.65	9
1987	Lighted Angel Tree Top 9420	Retrd.	1992	29.50	37
1989	Nutcracker 9436	Retrd.	1994	6.65	12
1988	Penguin w/Gifts 9496	Retrd.	1988	10.00	19
1989	Rocking Horse 9431	Retrd.	1994	6.65	11
1987	Roly-Poly Santa 9441	Retrd.	1988	6.75	14
1989	Santa 9432	Retrd.	1994	6.65	7
1987	Santa Head 9410	Retrd.	1988	6.55	12
1989	Teddy Bear 9434	Retrd.	1994	6.65	10
1995	Toys Ahoy 9713	Retrd.	1995	11.25	12
1995	Wish Upon a Star 9711	Retrd.	1995	11.25	12

Reflectors - E.M. Merck, unless otherwise noted

YEAR ISSUE		EDITION LIMIT	YEAR RETD.	ISSUE PRICE	*QUOTE U.S. $
1990	Assorted 6 cm Reflectors 4207	Retrd.	1995	7.00	7
1990	Assorted Reflectors with Diamonds 4206	Retrd.	1995	9.95	12
1992	Flower in Reflector 4212	Retrd.	1995	9.25	16
1986	Horseshoe Reflector 4203	Retrd.	1989	7.80	21
1987	Large Drop w/Indents (A) 4204	Retrd.	1994	12.85	25
1995	Patriotic Reflector 4218 - Inge-Glas	Retrd.	1996	8.95	9
1991	Peacock in Reflector 4208	Retrd.	1996	9.25	10
1991	Pears in Reflector 4209	Retrd.	1996	9.25	18
1986	Pink Reflector 4202	Retrd.	1995	9.50	10
1993	Reflector with Tinsel Wire 4215	Retrd.	1995	20.00	20
1992	Scrap Santa in Reflector 4214	Retrd.	1993	8.80	24
1986	Star Pattern Reflector (A) 4201	Retrd.	1994	9.25	14
1990	Strawberry in Reflector 4205	Retrd.	1996	9.25	10

Santas - E.M. Merck, unless otherwise noted

YEAR ISSUE		EDITION LIMIT	YEAR RETD.	ISSUE PRICE	*QUOTE U.S. $
1991	Alpine Santa 4047	Retrd.	1996	7.00	7
1985	Blue Father Christmas 4010498	Retrd.	1995	8.00	8
1990	Blue Victorian St. Nick 4028	Retrd.	1993	9.95	22
1987	Burgundy Father Christmas 4013	Retrd.	1995	7.80	16
1987	Burgundy Santa Claus 4014	Retrd.	1994	13.95	19
1990	Clip-On Victorian St. Nick 4030	Retrd.	1995	11.00	11
1986	Father Christmas Head 4006	Retrd.	1995	7.80	8
1985	Father Christmas Head 403223	Retrd.	1994	7.80	10
1991	Father Christmas on Form 4046	Retrd.	1996	11.00	11
1985	Father Christmas with Basket 403224	Retrd.	1994	7.80	10
1985	Father Christmas w/Tree 401039	Retrd.	1995	8.00	8
1990	Festive Santa Head 4039	Retrd.	1995	11.00	11
1985	Gold Father Christmas 401045	Retrd.	1995	7.45	8
1992	Gold Weihnachtsmann 4052	Retrd.	1996	9.80	10
1986	Green Clip-On Santa 4007	Retrd.	1995	7.80	8
1987	Matte Red Roly-Poly Santa 4012	Retrd.	1995	7.90	8
1991	Old Bavarian Santa 4044	Retrd.	1996	12.50	13
1984	Old Father Christmas Head 401007	Retrd.	1994	7.00	10
1986	Pink Clip-On Santa 4011	Retrd.	1994	8.35	10
1985	Pink Father Christmas 4010499	Retrd.	1995	8.00	8
1984	Roly-Poly Santa 401002	Retrd.	1994	7.90	11
1990	Round Jolly Santa Head 4035	Retrd.	1995	11.00	11
1992	Round Santa Head 4054	Retrd.	1996	9.00	9
1987	Santa Above Ball 4018	Retrd.	1995	13.95	14
1985	Santa and Tree on Form 401026	Retrd.	1995	9.25	10
1987	Santa in Airplane 4017	Retrd.	1995	13.95	14
1986	Santa In Chimney 4005	Retrd.	1995	8.70	18
1985	Santa in Chimney 406912	Retrd.	1989	11.00	26
1991	Santa in Mushroom 4048	Retrd.	1996	8.70	9
1985	Santa in Tree 401054	Retrd.	1995	7.45	8
1993	Santa in Walnut 4058	Retrd.	1996	7.00	7
1986	Santa On Carriage 4003	Retrd.	1988	10.00	29
1986	Santa On Cone 4002	Retrd.	1993	7.90	16
1991	Victorian Father Christmas 4045	Retrd.	1996	10.00	10
1989	Victorian Santa 4021	Retrd.	1995	8.45	9
1990	Victorian Scrap Santa 4043	Retrd.	1993	9.70	21

*Quotes have been rounded up to nearest dollar

Transportation - E.M. Merck, unless otherwise noted

YEAR ISSUE		EDITION LIMIT	YEAR RETD.	ISSUE PRICE	*QUOTE U.S.$
1988	Cable Car 4602	Retrd.	1989	8.45	32
1985	Cable Car 461067	Retrd.	1988	14.95	32
1990	Large Zeppelin 4605	Retrd.	1995	8.25	9
1985	Locomotive 461069	Retrd.	1993	7.00	24
1985	Old-Fashioned Car 463747	Retrd.	1989	6.25	32
1992	Race Car 4609	Retrd.	1995	7.00	7
1986	Rolls Royce 4601	Retrd.	1989	7.90	29
1985	Zeppelin 467265	Retrd.	1996	7.00	7

Tree Tops - E.M. Merck, unless otherwise noted

YEAR ISSUE		EDITION LIMIT	YEAR RETD.	ISSUE PRICE	*QUOTE U.S.$
1987	Angel in Indent Tree Top 5009	Retrd.	1995	27.00	27
1987	Angel w/Crown 5007	Retrd.	1993	50.00	72
1986	Blue Santa 5002	Retrd.	1995	37.50	49
1985	Fancy Gold Spire w/Bells 506266	Retrd.	1993	32.00	46
1985	Fancy Red Spire w/Bells 506269	Retrd.	1993	32.00	46
1992	Large Spire w/Reflectors 5014	Retrd.	1996	69.50	70
1987	Santa in Indent 5008	Retrd.	1995	25.00	25
1993	Very Large Reflector 5017	Retrd.	1996	65.00	65

Trees & Cones - E.M. Merck, unless otherwise noted

YEAR ISSUE		EDITION LIMIT	YEAR RETD.	ISSUE PRICE	*QUOTE U.S.$
1988	Large Mauve & Champagne Cone 4802	Retrd.	1993	11.85	17
1990	Multi-Colored Tree 4812	Retrd.	1994	5.55	9
1990	Pine Cone Man 4811	Retrd.	1996	8.25	9

Pacific Rim Import Corp.

Bristol Waterfront - P. Sebern

YEAR ISSUE		EDITION LIMIT	YEAR RETD.	ISSUE PRICE	*QUOTE U.S.$
1995	Portshead Lighthouse	Open		10.00	10

Patricia Breen Designs

1994 Collection - P. Breen

YEAR ISSUE		EDITION LIMIT	YEAR RETD.	ISSUE PRICE	*QUOTE U.S.$
1994	Magician 94-33	Retrd.	1994	24.00	560
1994	Nesting Instinct 9417-19	Retrd.	1994	N/A	85
1994	Spruce Goose (gold) 94-34	Retrd.	1994	25.00	500-600
1994	St. Petersburg Santa (gold)	Retrd.	1994	20.00	150-175
1994	Woodland Santa (cherry) 94-20	Retrd.	1995	24.00	150

1995 Collection - P. Breen

YEAR ISSUE		EDITION LIMIT	YEAR RETD.	ISSUE PRICE	*QUOTE U.S.$
1995	Amor Angel 9540	2,000	1995	24.00	60-75
1995	Apple Basket (for tree) 9548	2,000	1995	14.00	24
1995	Apple Tree Boy 9547	2,000	1995	24.00	47
1995	Bacchus w/Grapes (lg. grapes) 9553	Retrd.	1995	42.00	92-120
1995	Bacchus w/Grapes (signed) 9553	Retrd.	1995	42.00	87
1995	Bacchus w/Grapes (sm. grapes) 9553	Retrd.	1995	42.00	100-110
1995	Balloon Boy & Balloon (red) Charlecotte 9554	Retrd.	1995	30.00	200
1995	Balloon Boy & Balloon (white, signed) 9554	Retrd.	1995	30.00	72-85
1995	Balloon Boy & Balloon 9554	2,000	1995	30.00	55-72
1995	Beaux Artes Facade (signed) 9551	Retrd.	1995	32.00	150
1995	Beaux Artes Facade 9551	2,000	1995	32.00	85-150
1995	Beeskep & Bee (signed) 9503-2	Retrd.	1995	28.95	85
1995	Beeskep & Bee 9503-2	2,000	1995	28.95	60-90
1995	Dish & Spoon (double face) 9510-11	Retrd.	1995	24.00	90-150
1995	Dish & Spoon (signed) 9510-11	Retrd.	1995	24.00	150
1995	Dish & Spoon 9510-11	2,000	1995	24.00	36-72
1995	Edwina the Victorian Girl 9506-5	2,000	1995	21.00	400-480
1995	Elvis Cat 9509	2,000	1995	32.00	80
1995	Father Time (blue) 9535	Retrd.	1995	20.00	66
1995	Father Time (gold glitter bag) 9535	Retrd.	1995	20.00	120
1995	Father Time (Nordstrom) 9535	2,000	1995	20.00	80-120
1995	Fiddling Cat (signed) 9509-10	Retrd.	1995	20.00	65-100
1995	French Twist 9552	2,000	1995	18.00	120
1995	Gentleman Bug 9502	2,000	1995	12.00	25-45
1995	Giverny (Art Institute of Chicago)	2,000	1995	50.00	300
1995	Henry the Victorian Boy 9506-5	2,000	1995	20.00	55-96
1995	Lady Bug (pink) (signed) 9501-1	200	1995	12.95	72-96
1995	Lady Bug (red) 9501-1	Retrd.	1995	12.95	40-45
1995	Lady Bug (yellow) 9501-1	Retrd.	1995	12.95	160
1995	Laughing Dog 9508-9	2,000	1995	20.00	30-60
1995	Letters To My Beloved (silver) 9537-B	Retrd.	1995	12.95	54-90
1995	Lily of the Valley Egg (Nieman Special)	Retrd.	1995	50.00	180
1995	Monet Trio (Art Institute of Chicago)	Retrd.	1995	78.00	355
1995	Monet Trio, signed (Art Institute of Chicago)	Retrd.	1995	78.00	480-550
1995	Moon & Many Stars 9517-24	2,000	1995	16.95	45-100
1995	Nesting Instinct (red)	Retrd.	1995	20.00	48-75
1995	Night House (glittered) 9519-B	Retrd.	1995	32.00	72-96
1995	Night House 9519-B	2,000	1995	32.00	36-75
1995	Oliver Octopus (green glittered) 9539	Retrd.	1995	30.00	155
1995	Oliver Octopus (lavender) 9539	Retrd.	1995	30.00	130-180
1995	Queen of Hearts (gold) 9518-25	Retrd.	1995	20.00	45
1995	Red Square Santa 9513-16	2,000	1995	22.00	60-95
1995	Rocketboy 9534	2,000	1995	24.95	60-84
1995	Santa Paws (Nordstrom) 9536	Retrd.	1995	28.00	120
1995	Skydiving Santa 9522-35	2,000	1995	18.00	60-132
1995	Snow Man (Nordstrom) 9523-37	Retrd.	1995	21.00	60-120
1995	Snow Man (signed) 9523-37	Retrd.	1995	21.00	50
1995	Snowball Boy (Nordstrom Special)	Retrd.	1995	28.00	125
1995	Snowflake Santa (gold)	Retrd.	1995	28.00	110-120
1995	Snowflake Santa, signed (Event Piece)	Retrd.	1995	28.00	120
1995	St. George and The Dragon 9546 (Fine Art Series)	Retrd.	1995	50.00	350-500
1995	Striped Santa (signed) 9550	Retrd.	1995	24.00	71
1995	Summer Acorn House (signed) 9505-4	Retrd.	1995	24.95	50-95
1995	Sunflower (green) (signed) 9516-23	Retrd.	1995	16.00	105
1995	Sunflower (green) 9516-23	Retrd.	1995	16.00	24-50
1995	Sunflower 9516-23	2,000	1995	16.00	35
1995	Swell Starfish	Retrd.	1995	16.00	75
1995	Valise (black) 9532	Retrd.	1995	30.00	75-119
1995	Valise (red) (Chapel Hill) 9532	Retrd.	1995	30.00	75
1995	Valise (red) (signed-St. Louis Arch) 9532	Retrd.	1995	30.00	90-125
1995	Valise (red) 9532	Retrd.	1995	30.00	65-125
1995	Vincent's Tree 9541	2,000	1995	24.00	55
1995	Winter Acorn House 9504-3	2,000	1995	24.95	35-55
1995	Winter Wizard 9521	2,000	1995	32.00	42
1995	Winter Wizard (gold) 9521	Retrd.	1995	32.00	210
1995	Winter Wizard (Nordstrom) 9521	Retrd.	1995	32.00	83
1995	Winter Wizard (signed) 9521	2,000	1995	32.00	100
1995	Woodland Santa (bordeaux) 9515-20/21	Retrd.	1995	24.00	60-90
1995	Woodland Santa (cherry) 9515-20/21	Retrd.	1995	24.00	65
1995	Woodland Santa (Nordstrom) 9515-20/21	Retrd.	1995	24.00	90-120
1995	Woodland Santa (pink) 9515-20/21	210	1995	24.00	120-150

1996 Collection - P. Breen

YEAR ISSUE		EDITION LIMIT	YEAR RETD.	ISSUE PRICE	*QUOTE U.S.$
1996	Alexandra's Egg (Nieman Marcus)	250	1996	34.00	125
1996	Angel Stocking 9602	2,000	1996	24.00	200-300
1996	Archimbaldo Santa 9603	750	1996	74.00	450
1996	Blow Gabriel Blow 9604	500	1996	60.00	80-108
1996	Chocolate Box Santa (Nordstrom) 9607	Retrd.	1996	32.00	115
1996	Chrysalis Egg (pink) Charlecotte 9608	Retrd.	1996	36.00	45
1996	Chrysalis Egg 9608	2,000	1996	36.00	45
1996	Claude Monet (white) 9595	Retrd.	1996	30.00	270
1996	Faberge Santa (fully glittered) 9630	2,000	1996	28.00	180-275
1996	Frog Prince 9556	2,000	1996	20.00	30
1996	George's Tree 9616	2,000	1996	24.00	35-55
1996	Goldilocks 9618	2,000	1996	28.00	45
1996	Golf Bag w/Doll (gold) [illegible]	Retrd.	1996	34.00	80-200
1996	Grandma Josie's Fridge 9620	2,000	1996	40.00	50-96
1996	Jack Frost (Nordstrom) 9628	Retrd.	1996	30.00	125
1996	Letters to Santa (Wm. Andrews)	70	1996	38.00	96
1996	Little Yellow Taxi (black) 9631	2,000	1996	30.00	144-175
1996	Minsk Santa 9635	2,000	1996	28.00	100
1996	Night Flight Santa (blue moon) 9637	Retrd.	1996	46.00	200-300
1996	Night Flight Santa 9637	2,000	1996	46.00	125-175
1996	Round Midnight (w/Roman numerals) 9639	Retrd.	1996	32.00	190
1996	Santa of the Golden Oaks (green glitter) 9641	Retrd.	1996	34.00	95-175
1996	Santa of the Golden Oaks 9641	2,000	1996	34.00	42-56
1996	Snow Family, set/4	Retrd.	1996	N/A	144
1996	Snowball Boy (blue) (Nordstrom)	Retrd.	1996	N/A	250
1996	Snowflake Santa (citrine) 9645	Retrd.	1996	30.00	80-114
1996	Snowflake Santa (gold) 9645	Retrd.	1996	30.00	90-120
1996	Spiralling Santa 9646	2,000	1996	30.00	100-200
1995	Versailles Balloon (Nordstrom) 9511	Retrd.	1995	22.00	120
1995	Versailles Balloon (red/green) 9511	Retrd.	1995	22.00	150
1996	Victorian Spider & Web 9650	2,000	1996	30.00	45
1996	Woodland Santa (pearl) 9515-20/21	Retrd.	1995	24.00	126
1996	Woodland Santa (pink) Christmas Shop Club Member 9515-20/21	200	1995	24.00	150-200

Possible Dreams

Clothtique® Pepsi® Santa Collection - B. Prata

YEAR ISSUE		EDITION LIMIT	YEAR RETD.	ISSUE PRICE	*QUOTE U.S.$
1995	Yule Pop The Top	Open		7.90	8
1995	Christmas Bells & Bubbles	Open		7.40	8
1995	Holiday Cheer on Top	Open		12.20	13
1995	Get Into The Swing	Open		9.90	10
1995	Unfurl The Fun	Open		7.40	8

Crinkle Claus - Staff

YEAR ISSUE		EDITION LIMIT	YEAR RETD.	ISSUE PRICE	*QUOTE U.S.$
1996	Bishop of Maya-659702	Open		7.80	8
1996	Black Forest Santa-659706	Open		7.80	8
1996	Father Christmas-659703	Open		7.80	8
1996	German Santa-659701	Open		7.80	8
1996	Pere Noel Santa-659705	Open		7.80	8
1996	St. Nicholas-659704	Open		7.80	8

The Thickets at Sweetbriar® - B. Ross

YEAR ISSUE		EDITION LIMIT	YEAR RETD.	ISSUE PRICE	*QUOTE U.S.$
1995	Christmas Whiskers 350400	Closed	1996	11.50	12
1995	Jingle Bells 350407	Closed	1996	12.00	12
1996	Snuggles 350416	Open		11.70	12
1996	Nibbley-Do 350415	Open		10.50	11
1996	Twinkle Tails 350404	Closed	1996	11.50	12
1996	Fickle Tails 350405	Closed	1996	11.50	12
1996	Tinsel Tune 350411	Closed	1996	11.50	12

Precious Moments/Enesco Corporation

Precious Moments - S. Butcher

YEAR ISSUE		EDITION LIMIT	YEAR RETD.	ISSUE PRICE	*QUOTE U.S.$
1983	Surround Us With Joy E-0513	Yr.Iss.	1983	9.00	65
1983	Mother Sew Dear E-0514	Open		9.00	17-25
1983	To A Special Dad E-0515	Suspd.		9.00	30-54
1983	The Purr-fect Grandma E-0516	Open		9.00	17-40
1983	The Perfect Grandpa E-0517	Suspd.		9.00	16-30
1983	Blessed Are The Pure In Heart E-0518	Yr.Iss.	1983	9.00	40
1983	O Come All Ye Faithful E-0531	Suspd.		10.00	40
1983	Let Heaven And Nature Sing E-0532	Retrd.	1986	9.00	35
1983	Tell Me The Story Of Jesus E-0533	Suspd.		9.00	45
1983	To Thee With Love E-0534	Retrd.	1989	9.00	30
1984	Love Is Patient E-0535	Suspd.		9.00	46-59
1984	Love Is Patient E-0536	Suspd.		9.00	55-69
1983	Jesus Is The Light That Shines E-0537	Suspd.		9.00	60-75
1982	Joy To The World E-2343	Suspd.		9.00	35-65
1982	I'll Play My Drum For Him E-2359	Yr.Iss.	1982	9.00	100-115
1982	Baby's First Christmas E-2362	Suspd.		9.00	25-35
1982	The First Noel E-2367	Suspd.		9.00	50-70
1982	The First Noel E-2368	Retrd.	1984	9.00	20-30
1982	Dropping In For Christmas E-2369	Retrd.	1986	9.00	25-35
1982	Unicorn E-2371	Retrd.	1988	10.00	50
1982	Baby's First Christmas E-2372	Suspd.		9.00	35-45
1982	Dropping Over For Christmas E-2376	Retrd.	1985	9.00	50
1982	Mouse With Cheese E-2381	Suspd.		9.00	100-125
1982	Our First Christmas Together E-2385	Suspd.		10.00	15-25
1982	Camel, Donkey & Cow (3 pc. set) E-2386	Suspd.		25.00	65-100
1984	Wishing You A Merry Christmas E-5387	Yr.Iss.	1984	10.00	40
1984	Joy To The World E-5388	Retrd.	1987	10.00	20
1984	Peace On Earth E-5389	Suspd.		10.00	20
1984	May God Bless You With A Perfect Holiday Season E-5390	Suspd.		10.00	20
1984	Love Is Kind E-5391	Suspd.		10.00	24-35
1984	Blessed Are The Pure In Heart E-5392	Yr.Iss.	1984	10.00	15
1981	But Love Goes On Forever E-5627	Suspd.		6.00	90-120
1981	But Love Goes On Forever E-5628	Suspd.		6.00	90-120
1981	Let The Heavens Rejoice E-5629	Yr.Iss.	1981	6.00	200
1981	Unto Us A Child Is Born E-5630	Suspd.		6.00	40-70
1981	Baby's First Christmas E-5631	Suspd.		6.00	40-60
1981	Baby's First Christmas E-5632	Suspd.		6.00	40-50
1981	Come Let Us Adore Him (4pc. set) E-5633	Suspd.		22.00	115-150
1981	Wee Three Kings (3pc. Set) E-5634	Suspd.		19.00	100-129
1981	We Have Seen His Star E-6120	Retrd.	1984	6.00	30-45
1985	Have A Heavenly Christmas 12416	Open		12.00	19-30
1985	God Sent His Love 15768	Yr.Iss.	1985	10.00	35
1985	May Your Christmas Be Happy 15822	Suspd.		10.00	30-40
1985	Happiness Is The Lord 15830	Suspd.		10.00	35
1985	May Your Christmas Be Delightful 15849	Suspd.		10.00	15-25
1985	Honk If You Love Jesus 15857	Suspd.		10.00	15-25
1985	Baby's First Christmas 15903	Yr.Iss.	1985	10.00	35
1985	Baby's First Christmas 15911	Yr.Iss.	1985	10.00	15-25
1986	Shepherd of Love 102288	Suspd.		10.00	15-25
1986	Wishing You A Cozy Christmas 102326	Yr.Iss.	1986	10.00	35
1986	Our First Christmas Together 102350	Yr.Iss.	1986	10.00	20-35
1986	Trust And Obey 102377	Open		10.00	17-25
1986	Love Rescued Me 102385	Open		10.00	17-23
1986	Angel Of Mercy 102407	Open		10.00	17-30
1986	It's A Perfect Boy 102415	Suspd.		10.00	30
1986	Lord Keep Me On My Toes 102423	Retrd.	1990	10.00	20-30
1986	Serve With A Smile 102431	Suspd.		10.00	18-30
1986	Serve With A Smile 102458	Suspd.		10.00	32
1986	Reindeer 102466	Yr.Iss.	1986	11.00	175-200
1986	Rocking Horse 102474	Suspd.		10.00	25
1986	Baby's First Christmas 102504	Yr.Iss.	1986	10.00	30
1986	Baby's First Christmas 102512	Yr.Iss.	1986	10.00	30
1987	Bear The Good News Of Christmas 104515	Yr.Iss.	1987	12.50	15-25
1987	Baby's First Christmas 109401	Yr.Iss.	1987	12.00	37
1987	Baby's First Christmas 109428	Yr.Iss.	1987	12.00	35
1987	Love Is The Best Gift Of All 109770	Yr.Iss.	1987	11.00	35
1987	I'm A Possibility 111120	Suspd.		11.00	20
1987	You Have Touched So Many Hearts 112356	Retrd.	1996	11.00	22
1987	Waddle I Do Without You 112364	Open		11.00	17-30
1987	I'm Sending You A White Christmas 112372	Suspd.		11.00	20
1987	He Cleansed My Soul 112380	Open		12.00	17-25
1987	Our First Christmas Together 112399	Yr.Iss.	1987	11.00	30-35
1988	To My Forever Friend 113956	Open		16.00	19-35
1988	Smile Along The Way 113964	Suspd.		15.00	20-30
1988	God Sent You Just In Time 113972	Suspd.		13.50	25-35
1988	Rejoice O Earth 113980	Retrd.	1991	13.50	20-30
1988	Cheers To The Leader 113999	Suspd.		13.50	35

*Quotes have been rounded up to nearest dollar

YEAR ISSUE		EDITION LIMIT	YEAR RETD.	ISSUE PRICE	*QUOTE U.S. $
1988	My Love Will Never Let You Go 114006	Suspd.		13.50	15-25
1988	Baby's First Christmas 115282	Yr.Iss.	1988	15.00	15-25
1988	Time To Wish You A Merry Christmas 115320	Yr.Iss.	1988	13.00	35-45
1996	Owl Be Home For Christmas 128708	Yr.Iss.	1996	18.50	19
1995	He Covers The Earth With His Beauty 142662	Yr.Iss.	1995	17.00	17
1995	He Covers The Earth With His Beauty (ball) 142689	Yr.Iss.	1995	30.00	30
1995	Our First Christmas Together 142700	Yr.Iss.	1995	18.50	19
1995	Baby's First Christmas 142719	Yr.Iss.	1995	17.50	18
1995	Baby's First Christmas 142727	Yr.Iss.	1995	17.50	18
1995	Joy From Head To Mistletoe 150126	Open		18.50	19
1995	You're "A" Number One In My Book, Teacher 150142	Open		18.50	19
1995	Joy To The World 150320	Open		20.00	20
1996	Joy To The World 153338	Open		20.00	20
1996	Peace On Earth...Anyway (Ball) 183350	Yr.Iss.	1996	30.00	30
1996	Peace On Earth...Anyway 183369	Yr.Iss.	1996	18.50	19
1996	God's Precious Gift 183881	Open		20.00	20
1996	When The Skating's Ruff, Try Prayer 183903	Open		18.50	19
1996	Our First Christmas Together 183911	Yr.Iss.	1996	22.50	23
1996	Baby's First Christmas 183938	Yr.Iss.	1996	17.50	18
1996	Baby's First Christmas 183946	Yr.Iss.	1996	17.50	18
1988	Our First Christmas Together 520233	Yr.Iss.	1988	13.00	21
1988	Baby's First Christmas 520241	Yr.Iss.	1988	15.00	15
1988	You Are My Gift Come True 520276	Yr.Iss.	1988	12.50	25
1988	Hang On For The Holly Days 520292	Yr.Iss.	1988	13.00	25
1992	I'm Nuts About You 520411	Yr.Iss.	1992	15.00	20
1995	Hippo Holy Days 520403	Yr.Iss.	1995	17.00	20
1991	Sno-Bunny Falls For You Like I Do 520438	Yr.Iss.	1991	15.00	15-30
1989	Christmas is Ruff Without You 520462	Yr.Iss.	1989	13.00	25-30
1993	Slow Down & Enjoy The Holidays 520489	Yr.Iss.	1993	16.00	19
1990	Wishing You A Purr-fect Holiday 520497	Yr.Iss.	1990	15.00	20-35
1989	May All Your Christmases Be White 521302 (dated)	Suspd.		15.00	16-25
1989	Our First Christmas Together 521558	Yr.Iss.	1989	17.50	20
1990	Glide Through the Holidays 521566	Retrd.	1992	13.50	20-30
1990	Dashing Through the Snow 521574	Suspd.		15.00	25
1990	Don't Let the Holidays Get You Down 521590	Retrd.	1994	15.00	20
1989	Oh Holy Night 522848	Yr.Iss.	1989	13.50	25-30
1989	Make A Joyful Noise 522910	Suspd.		15.00	17
1989	Love One Another 522929	Open		17.50	19-25
1990	Friends Never Drift Apart 522937	Retrd.	1995	17.50	19-27
1991	Our First Christmas Together 522945	Yr.Iss.	1991	17.50	18-25
1989	I Believe In The Old Rugged Cross 522953	Suspd.		15.00	16-25
1989	Peace On Earth 523062	Yr.Iss.	1989	25.00	65
1989	Baby's First Christmas 523194	Yr.Iss.	1989	15.00	20
1989	Baby's First Christmas 523208	Yr.Iss.	1989	15.00	20
1991	Happy Trails Is Trusting Jesus 523224	Suspd.		15.00	20
1990	May Your Christmas Be A Happy Home 523704	Yr.Iss.	1990	27.50	40
1990	Baby's First Christmas 523798	Yr.Iss.	1990	15.00	25
1990	Baby's First Christmas 523771	Yr.Iss.	1990	15.00	25
1990	Once Upon A Holy Night 523852	Yr.Iss.	1990	15.00	15-25
1992	Good Friends Are For Always 524131	Retrd.	1996	15.00	15
1991	May Your Christmas Be Merry 524174	Yr.Iss.	1991	15.00	25
1990	Bundles of Joy 525057	Yr.Iss.	1990	15.00	30-40
1990	Our First Christmas Together 525324	Yr.Iss.	1990	17.50	18-25
1993	Lord, Keep Me On My Toes 525332	Open		15.00	17-18
1991	May Your Christmas Be Merry (on Base) 526940	Yr.Iss.	1991	30.00	35
1991	Baby's First Christmas (Boy) 527084	Yr.Iss.	1991	15.00	15
1991	Baby's First Christmas (Girl) 527092	Yr.Iss.	1991	15.00	20
1991	The Good Lord Always Delivers 527165	Suspd.		15.00	20
1993	Share in The Warmth of Christmas 527211	Open		15.00	17
1994	Onward Christmas Soldiers 527327	Open		16.00	16
1992	Baby's First Christmas 527475	Yr.Iss.	1992	15.00	15-20
1992	Baby's First Christmas 527483	Yr.Iss.	1992	15.00	17
1992	But The Greatest of These Is Love 527696	Yr.Iss.	1992	15.00	27
1992	But The Greatest of These Is Love 527734 (on Base)	Yr.Iss.	1992	30.00	30-40
1994	Sending You A White Christmas 528218	Open		16.00	16
1994	Bringing You A Merry Christmas 528226	Open		16.00	16
1993	It's So Uplifting to Have a Friend Like You 528846	Open		16.00	17
1992	Our First Christmas Together 528870	Yr.Iss.	1992	17.50	18-25
1994	Our 1st Christmas Together 529206	Yr.Iss.	1994	18.50	19-25
1993	Wishing You the Sweetest Christmas 530190	Yr.Iss.	1993	30.00	35
1993	Wishing You the Sweetest Christmas 530212	Yr.Iss.	1993	15.00	35
1994	Baby's First Christmas 530255	Yr.Iss.	1994	16.00	16
1994	Baby's First Christmas 530263	Yr.Iss.	1994	16.00	16
1994	You're As Pretty As A Christmas Tree 530387	Yr.Iss.	1994	30.00	30
1994	You're As Pretty As A Christmas Tree 530395	Yr.Iss.	1994	16.00	35-40
1993	Our First Christmas Together 530506	Yr.Iss.	1993	17.50	18
1993	Baby's First Christmas 530859	Yr.Iss.	1993	15.00	15
1993	Baby's First Christmas 530867	Yr.Iss.	1993	15.00	15
1994	You Are Always In My Heart 530972	Yr.Iss.	1994	16.00	16-28

Precious Moments Club 15th Anniversary Commemorative Edition - S. Butcher

1993	15 Years Tweet Music Together 530840	Yr.Iss.	1993	15.00	20-30

DSR Open House Weekend Ornaments - S. Butcher

1992	The Magic Starts With You 529648	Yr.Iss.	1992	16.00	25
1993	An Event For All Seasons 529974	Yr.Iss.	1993	15.00	20
1994	Take A Bow Cuz You're My Christmas Star 520470	Yr.Iss.	1994	16.00	25
1995	Merry Chrismoose 150134	Yr.Iss.	1995	17.00	17
1996	Wishing You a Bearie Merry Christmas 531200	Yr.Iss.	1996	17.50	18

Easter Seal Commemorative Ornaments - S. Butcher

1994	It's No Secret What God Can Do 244570	Yr.Iss.	1994	6.50	7
1995	Take Time To Smell The Flowers 128899	Yr.Iss.	1995	7.50	8
1996	You Can Always Count on Me 152579	Yr.Iss.	1996	6.50	7
1997	Give Ability A Chance 192384	Yr.Iss.		6.50	7

Special Edition Members' Only - S. Butcher

1993	Loving, Caring And Sharing Along The Way PM-040 (Club Appreciation)	Yr.Iss.	1993	12.50	15-25
1994	You Are The End of My Rainbow PM-041	Yr.Iss.	1994	15.00	20

Sugartown - S. Butcher

1993	Sugartown Chapel Ornament 530484	Yr.Iss.	1993	17.50	18
1994	Sam's House 530468	Yr.Iss.	1994	17.50	18
1995	Dr. Sugar's Office 530441	Yr.Iss.	1995	17.50	18
1996	Train Station 184101	Yr.Iss.	1996	18.50	19

Reed & Barton

12 Days of Christmas Sterling and Lead Crystal - Reed & Barton

1988	Partridge in a Pear Tree	Yr.Iss.	1988	25.00	30
1989	Two Turtle Doves	Yr.Iss.	1989	25.00	30
1990	Three French Hens	Yr.Iss.	1990	27.50	30
1991	Four Colly birds	Yr.Iss.	1991	27.50	30
1992	Five Golden Rings	Yr.Iss.	1992	27.50	30
1993	Six Geese A Laying	Yr.Iss.	1993	27.50	30
1994	Seven Swans A 'Swimming	Yr.Iss.	1994	27.50	30
1995	Eight Maids A Milking	Yr.Iss.	1995	30.00	30
1996	Nine Ladies Dancing	Yr.Iss.	1996	30.00	30

Carousel Horse - Reed & Barton

1988	Silverplate-1988	Closed	1988	13.50	14
1988	Gold-covered-1988	Closed	1988	15.00	15
1989	Silverplate-1989	Closed	1989	13.50	14
1989	Gold-covered-1989	Closed	1989	15.00	15
1990	Silverplate-1990	Closed	1990	13.50	14
1990	Gold-covered-1990	Closed	1990	15.00	15
1991	Silverplate-1991	Closed	1991	13.50	14
1991	Gold-covered-1991	Closed	1991	15.00	15
1992	Silverplate-1992	Closed	1992	13.50	14
1992	Gold-covered-1992	Closed	1992	15.00	15
1993	Silverplate-1993	Closed	1993	13.50	14
1993	Gold-covered-1993	Closed	1993	15.00	15
1994	Silverplate-1994	Closed	1994	13.50	14
1994	Gold-covered-1994	Closed	1994	15.00	15
1995	Silverplate-1995	Closed	1995	13.50	14
1995	Gold-covered-1995	Closed	1995	15.00	15
1996	Silverplate-1996	Closed	1996	13.50	14
1996	Gold-covered-1996	Closed	1996	15.00	15

Christmas Cross - Reed & Barton

1971	Sterling Silver-1971	Closed	1971	10.00	120-300
1971	24Kt. Gold over Sterling-V1971	Closed	1971	17.50	300
1972	Sterling Silver-1972	Closed	1972	10.00	50-125
1972	24Kt. Gold over Sterling-V1972	Closed	1972	17.50	75-175
1973	Sterling Silver-1973	Closed	1973	10.00	60-85
1973	24Kt. Gold over Sterling-V1973	Closed	1973	17.50	60-85
1974	Sterling Silver-1974	Closed	1974	12.95	45-75
1974	24Kt. Gold over Sterling-V1974	Closed	1974	20.00	45-75
1975	Sterling Silver-1975	Closed	1975	12.95	35
1975	24Kt. Gold over Sterling-V1975	Closed	1975	20.00	50-60
1976	Sterling Silver-1976	Closed	1976	13.95	50
1976	24Kt. Gold over Sterling-V1976	Closed	1976	19.95	45-50
1977	Sterling Silver-1977	Closed	1977	15.00	50
1977	24Kt. Gold over Sterling-V1977	Closed	1977	18.50	45-50
1978	Sterling Silver-1978	Closed	1978	16.00	50
1978	24Kt. Gold over Sterling-V1978	Closed	1978	20.00	45-55
1979	Sterling Silver-1979	Closed	1979	20.00	60
1979	24Kt. Gold over Sterling-V1979	Closed	1979	24.00	32-57
1980	Sterling Silver-1980	Closed	1980	35.00	60
1980	24Kt. Gold over Sterling-V1980	Closed	1980	40.00	45-50
1981	Sterling Silver-1981	Closed	1981	35.00	45
1981	24Kt. Gold over Sterling-V1981	Closed	1981	40.00	45
1982	Sterling Silver-1982	Closed	1982	35.00	65
1982	24Kt. Gold over Sterling-V1982	Closed	1982	40.00	45
1983	Sterling Silver-1983	Closed	1983	35.00	50-100
1983	24Kt. Gold over Sterling-V1983	Closed	1983	40.00	40-45
1984	Sterling Silver-1984	Closed	1984	35.00	45
1984	24Kt. Gold over Sterling-V1984	Closed	1984	45.00	45
1985	Sterling Silver-1985	Closed	1985	35.00	45-80
1985	24Kt. Gold over Sterling-V1985	Closed	1985	40.00	40
1986	Sterling Silver-1986	Closed	1986	38.50	45
1986	24Kt. Gold over Sterling-V1986	Closed	1986	40.00	40
1987	Sterling Silver-1987	Closed	1987	35.00	45
1987	24Kt. Gold over Sterling-V1987	Closed	1987	40.00	40
1988	Sterling Silver-1988	Closed	1988	35.00	45
1988	24Kt. Gold over Sterling-V1988	Closed	1988	40.00	40
1989	Sterling Silver-1989	Closed	1989	35.00	45
1989	24Kt. Gold over Sterling-V1989	Closed	1989	40.00	40
1990	Sterling Silver-1990	Closed	1990	40.00	45
1990	24Kt. Gold over Sterling-1990	Closed	1990	45.00	45
1991	Sterling Silver-1991	Closed	1991	40.00	45
1991	24Kt. Gold over Sterling-1991	Closed	1991	45.00	45
1992	Sterling Silver-1992	Closed	1992	40.00	40
1992	24Kt. Gold over Sterling-1992	Closed	1992	45.00	45
1993	Sterling Silver-1993	Closed	1993	40.00	40
1993	24Kt. Gold over Sterling-1993	Closed	1993	45.00	45
1994	Sterling Silver-1994	Closed	1994	40.00	40
1994	24Kt. Gold over Sterling-1994	Closed	1994	45.00	45
1995	Sterling Silver-1995	Closed	1995	40.00	40
1995	24Kt. Gold over Sterling-1995	Closed	1995	45.00	45
1996	Sterling Silver-1996	Closed	1996	40.00	40
1996	Gold Vermeil-1996	Closed	1996	45.00	45

Holly Ball/Bell - Reed & Barton

1976	1976 Ball	Closed	1976	14.00	40
1977	1977 Ball	Closed	1977	15.00	25
1978	1978 Ball	Closed	1978	15.00	25
1979	1979 Ball	Closed	1979	15.00	35
1980	1980 Bell	Closed	1980	22.50	35
1980	Bell, gold plate, V1980	Closed	1980	25.00	45
1981	1981 Bell	Closed	1981	22.50	30
1981	Bell, gold plate, V1981	Closed	1981	27.50	35
1982	1982 Bell	Closed	1982	22.50	35
1982	Bell, gold plate, V1982	Closed	1982	27.50	50
1983	1983 Bell	Closed	1983	23.50	45-75
1983	Bell, gold plate, V1983	Closed	1983	30.00	75
1984	1984 Bell	Closed	1984	25.00	35
1984	Bell, gold plate, V1984	Closed	1984	28.50	50
1985	1985 Bell	Closed	1985	25.00	75
1985	Bell, gold plate, V1985	Closed	1985	28.50	50
1986	1986 Bell	Closed	1986	25.00	75
1986	Bell, gold plate, V1986	Closed	1986	28.50	50
1987	1987 Bell	Closed	1987	27.50	70
1987	Bell, gold plate, V1987	Closed	1987	30.00	50
1988	1988 Bell	Closed	1988	27.50	40
1988	Bell, gold plate, V1988	Closed	1988	30.00	30
1989	1989 Bell	Closed	1989	27.50	55
1989	Bell, gold plate, V1989	Closed	1989	30.00	30
1990	Bell, gold plate, V1990	Closed	1990	30.00	30
1990	1990 Bell	Closed	1990	27.50	55
1991	Bell, gold plate, V1991	Closed	1991	30.00	30
1991	1991 Bell	Closed	1991	27.50	50
1992	Bell, gold plate, V1992	Closed	1992	30.00	30
1992	Bell, silver plate, 1992	Closed	1992	27.50	45
1993	Bell, gold plate, V1993	Closed	1993	27.50	28
1993	Bell, silver plate, 1993	Closed	1993	30.00	45
1994	Bell, gold plate, 1994	Closed	1994	30.00	30
1994	Bell, silver plate, 1994	Closed	1994	27.50	30
1995	Bell, gold plate, 1995	Closed	1995	30.00	30
1995	Bell, silver plate, 1995	Closed	1995	27.50	30
1996	Bell, gold plate, 1996	Closed	1996	35.00	35
1996	Bell, silver plate, 1996	Closed	1996	30.00	30

Roman, Inc.

Catnippers - I. Spencer

1989	Bow Brummel	Open		15.00	15
1991	Christmas Knight	Open		15.00	15
1988	Christmas Mourning	Open		15.00	15
1991	Faux Paw	Open		15.00	15
1990	Felix Navidad	Open		15.00	15
1989	Happy Holidaze	Open		15.00	15
1991	Holly Days Are Happy Days	Open		15.00	15
1991	Meowy Christmas	Open		15.00	15
1991	Pawtridge in a Purr Tree	Open		15.00	15
1988	Puss in Berries	Open		15.00	15
1988	Ring A Ding-Ding	Open		15.00	15
1989	Sandy Claws	Open		15.00	15
1991	Snow Biz	Open		15.00	15
1990	Sock It to Me Santa	Open		15.00	15
1990	Stuck on Christmas	Open		15.00	15

*Quotes have been rounded up to nearest dollar

The Discovery of America - I. Spencer

Year Issue		Edition Limit	Year Retd.	Issue Price	*Quote U.S.$
1991	Kitstopher Kolumbus	1,992		15.00	15
1991	Queen Kitsabella	1,992		15.00	15

Fontanini Limited Edition Ornaments - E. Simonetti

Year Issue		Edition Limit	Year Retd.	Issue Price	*Quote U.S.$
1995	The Annunciation	20,000		20.00	20
1996	Journey to Bethlehem	20,000		20.00	20
1997	Gloria Angel	Yr.Iss.		20.00	20

Millenium™ Ornament - A. Lucchesi

Year Issue		Edition Limit	Year Retd.	Issue Price	*Quote U.S.$
1992	Silent Night	20,000	1992	20.00	20
1993	The Annunciation	20,000	1993	20.00	20
1994	Peace On Earth	20,000	1994	20.00	20
1995	Cause of Our Joy	20,000	1995	20.00	20
1996	Prince of Peace	30,000	1996	20.00	20
1997	Gentle Love	Yr.Iss.		20.00	20

Museum Collection of Angela Tripi - A. Tripi

Year Issue		Edition Limit	Year Retd.	Issue Price	*Quote U.S.$
1994	1994 Annual Angel Ornament	2,500	1994	49.50	50
1995	1995 Annual Angel Ornament	2,500		49.50	50

Seraphim Classics™ - Seraphim Studios

Year Issue		Edition Limit	Year Retd.	Issue Price	*Quote U.S.$
1995	Isabel - Gentle Spirit	Open		15.00	15
1995	Iris - Rainbow's End	Open		15.00	15
1995	Lydia - Winged Poet	Open		15.00	15
1995	Cymbeline - Peacemaker	Open		15.00	15
1995	Ophelia - Heart Seeker	Open		15.00	15
1995	Evangeline - Angel of Mercy	Open		15.00	15
1996	Laurice - Wisdom's Child	Open		15.00	15
1996	Felicia - Adoring Maiden	Open		15.00	15
1996	Priscilla - Benevolent Guide	Open		15.00	15
1996	Seraphina - Heaven's Helper	Open		15.00	15

Seraphim Collection by Faro - Faro

Year Issue		Edition Limit	Year Retd.	Issue Price	*Quote U.S.$
1994	Rarest of Heaven	20,000		25.00	25
1995	Heaven's Herald	20,000		25.00	25
1996	Flora, Flower of Heaven	20,000		25.00	25
1997	Emily, Heaven's Treasure	Yr.Iss.		25.00	25

Vernon Wilson Signature Series - V. Wilson

Year Issue		Edition Limit	Year Retd.	Issue Price	*Quote U.S.$
1995	We Three Kings	Open		34.00	34

Royal Doulton

Bunnykins - D. Lyttleton

Year Issue		Edition Limit	Year Retd.	Issue Price	*Quote U.S.$
1992	Caroling	Yr.Iss.	1992	10.00	19
1991	Santa Bunny	Yr.Iss.	1991	19.00	19

Christmas Ornaments - Various

Year Issue		Edition Limit	Year Retd.	Issue Price	*Quote U.S.$
1993	Royal Doulton-Together for Christmas - J. James	Yr.Iss.	1993	20.00	20
1993	Royal Albert-Sleighride - N/A	Yr.Iss.	1993	20.00	20
1994	Royal Doulton-Home For Christmas - J. James	Yr.Iss.	1994	20.00	20
1994	Royal Albert-Coaching Inn - N/A	Yr.Iss.	1994	20.00	20
1995	Royal Doulton-Season's Greetings - J. James	Yr.Iss.	1995	20.00	20
1995	Royal Albert-Skating Pond - N/A	Yr.Iss.	1995	20.00	20
1996	Royal Doulton-Night Before Christmas - J. James	Yr.Iss.	1996	20.00	20
1996	Royal Albert-Gathering Winter Fuel - N/A	Yr.Iss.	1996	20.00	20

Shelia's Collectibles

Amish Quilt Ornaments - S. Thompson

Year Issue		Edition Limit	Year Retd.	Issue Price	*Quote U.S.$
1997	Cactus Basket AQO03	Open		16.00	16
1997	Double Irish Chain AQO05	Open		16.00	16
1997	North Carolina Lily AQO04	Open		16.00	16
1997	Pineapple AQO02	Open		16.00	16
1997	Robbing Peter to Pay Paul AQ001	Open		16.00	16
1997	Shoo-Fly AQO06	Open		16.00	16

Historical Ornament Collection - S. Thompson

Year Issue		Edition Limit	Year Retd.	Issue Price	*Quote U.S.$
1995	Blue Cottage (1st ed.) OR001	Retrd.	1996	15.00	25
1996	Blue Cottage (2nd ed.) OR001	Open		15.00	15
1995	Cape Hatteras Light (1st ed.) OR007	Retrd.	1996	15.00	25
1996	Cape Hatteras Light (2nd ed.) OR007	Open		15.00	15
1995	Chestnut House (1st ed.) OR002	Retrd.	1996	15.00	25
1996	Chestnut House (2nd ed.) OR002	Open		15.00	15
1995	Drayton House (1st ed.) OR003	Retrd.	1996	15.00	25
1996	Drayton House (2nd ed.) OR003	Open		15.00	15
1995	East Brother Lighthouse (1st ed.) OR008	Retrd.	1996	15.00	25
1996	East Brother Lighthouse (2nd ed.) OR008	Open		15.00	15
1995	Eclectic Blue (1st ed.) OR004	Retrd.	1996	15.00	25
1996	Eclectic Blue (2nd ed.) OR004	Open		15.00	15
1995	Goeller House (1st ed.) OR005	Retrd.	1996	15.00	25
1996	Goeller House (2nd ed.) OR005	Open		15.00	15
1995	Point Fermin Light (1st ed.) OR009	Retrd.	1996	15.00	25
1996	Point Fermin Light (2nd ed.) OR009	Open		15.00	15
1995	Stockton Row (1st ed.) OR006	Retrd.	1996	15.00	25
1996	Stockton Row (2nd ed.) OR006	Open		15.00	15
1996	Artist House OR015	Open		19.00	19
1996	Capital OR018	Open		19.00	19
1996	Dragon OR010	Open		19.00	19
1996	E.B. Hall House OR011	Open		19.00	19
1996	Mail Pouch Barn OR016	Open		19.00	19
1996	Market OR013	Open		19.00	19
1996	Pink House OR020	Open		19.00	19
1996	Rutledge OR012	Open		19.00	19
1996	St. Philips Church OR022	Open		19.00	19
1996	Thomas Point Light OR019	Open		19.00	19
1996	Titman House OR021	Open		19.00	19
1996	Victoria OR014	Open		19.00	19
1996	White Cottage OR017	Open		19.00	19
1996	Clark House OR023	Open		19.00	19
1996	Urfer House OR024	Open		19.00	19
1996	Queen Anne OR025	Open		19.00	19
1996	Asendorf House OR026	Open		19.00	19
1996	Abbey II OR027	Open		19.00	19
1996	New Canal Light OR028	Open		19.00	19

Historical Ornament Collection II - S. Thompson

Year Issue		Edition Limit	Year Retd.	Issue Price	*Quote U.S.$
1997	Berkeley Shore OR031	Open		21.00	21
1997	The Carlyle OR030	Open		21.00	21
1997	Hotel Webster OR029	Open		21.00	21
1997	Loew's Grand OR033	Open		21.00	21
1997	Magnolia Garden House OR034	Open		21.00	21
1997	Margaret Mitchell OR035	Open		21.00	21
1997	Marlin OR032	Open		21.00	21

Nabisco Ornaments - S. Thompson

Year Issue		Edition Limit	Year Retd.	Issue Price	*Quote U.S.$
1996	Animal Cracker Box, green NAB02	Open		29.00	29
1996	Animal Cracker Box, red NAB01	Open		29.00	29

Our Stars Ornament Collection - S. Thompson

Year Issue		Edition Limit	Year Retd.	Issue Price	*Quote U.S.$
1996	Banta House OSR03	2-Yr.		23.00	23
1996	Greenman House OSR02	2-Yr.		23.00	23
1996	Riley-Cutler House OSR01	2-Yr.		23.00	23
1996	Weller House OSR04	2-Yr.		23.00	23

Swarovski America Limited

Holiday Ornaments - Swarovski

Year Issue		Edition Limit	Year Retd.	Issue Price	*Quote U.S.$
1981	1981 Snowflake 7563NR35	Yr.Iss.		30.00	300-360
1986	1986 Holiday Ornament 92086	Yr.Iss.		N/A	240
1987	1987 Holiday Etching-Candle	Yr.Iss.		20.00	185-250
1988	1988 Holiday Etching-Wreath	Yr.Iss.		25.00	80-120
1989	1989 Holiday Etching-Dove	Yr.Iss.		35.00	240-360
1990	1990 Holiday Etching-Merry Christmas	Yr.Iss.		25.00	125-185
1991	1991 Holiday Ornament-Star	Yr.Iss.		35.00	100-135
1992	1992 Holiday Ornament-Star	Yr.Iss.		37.50	75-125
1993	1993 Holiday Ornament-Star	Yr.Iss.		37.50	90-150
1994	1994 Holiday Ornament-Star	Yr.Iss.		37.50	75-95
1995	1995 Holiday Ornament-Star	Yr.Iss.		40.00	60-75
1996	1996 Holiday Ornament-Snowflake	Yr.Iss.		45.00	70-100

Towle Silversmiths

Christmas Angel Medallions - Towle

Year Issue		Edition Limit	Year Retd.	Issue Price	*Quote U.S.$
1991	1991 Angel	Closed	1991	45.00	60-80
1992	1992 Angel	Closed	1992	45.00	60-80
1993	1993 Angel	Closed	1993	45.00	50-80
1994	1994 Angel	Closed	1994	50.00	50-70
1995	1995 Angel	Closed	1995	50.00	50-60
1996	1996 Angel	Closed	1996	50.00	50

Remembrance Collection - Towle

Year Issue		Edition Limit	Year Retd.	Issue Price	*Quote U.S.$
1990	1990 - Old Master Snowflake	Closed	1990	40.00	40-75
1991	1991 - Old Master Snowflake	Closed	1991	40.00	45-70
1992	1992 - Old Master Snowflake	Closed	1992	40.00	40-65
1993	1993 - Old Master Snowflake	Closed	1993	40.00	45-65
1994	1994 - Old Master Snowflake	Closed	1994	50.00	50-60
1995	1995 - Old Master Snowflake	Closed	1995	50.00	50
1996	1996 - Old Master Snowflake	Closed	1995	50.00	50

Songs of Christmas Medallions - Towle

Year Issue		Edition Limit	Year Retd.	Issue Price	*Quote U.S.$
1978	Silent Night Medallion	Closed	1978	35.00	45-100
1979	Deck The Halls	Closed	1979	35.00	45-100
1980	Jingle Bells	Closed	1980	53.00	45-100
1981	Hark the Hearld Angels Sing	Closed	1981	53.00	125-150
1982	O Christmas Tree	Closed	1982	35.00	50-100
1983	Silver Bells	Closed	1983	40.00	50-65
1984	Let It Snow	Closed	1984	30.00	45-70
1985	Chestnuts Roasting on Open Fire	Closed	1985	35.00	70-80
1986	It Came Upon a Midnight Clear	Closed	1986	35.00	70-80
1987	White Christmas	Closed	1987	35.00	50-100

Sterling Cross - Towle

Year Issue		Edition Limit	Year Retd.	Issue Price	*Quote U.S.$
1994	Sterling Cross	Closed	1994	50.00	50-65
1995	Christmas Cross	Closed	1995	50.00	50
1996	1996 Cross	Closed	1996	50.00	50

Sterling Floral Medallions - Towle

Year Issue		Edition Limit	Year Retd.	Issue Price	*Quote U.S.$
1983	Christmas Rose	Closed	1983	40.00	40
1984	Hawthorn/Glastonbury Thorn	Closed	1984	40.00	40
1985	Poinsettia	Closed	1985	35.00	50-85
1986	Laurel Bay	Closed	1986	35.00	45-70
1987	Mistletoe	Closed	1987	35.00	45-70
1988	Holly	Closed	1988	40.00	45-95
1989	Ivy	Closed	1989	35.00	45-95
1990	Christmas Cactus	Closed	1990	40.00	45-95
1991	Chrysanthemum	Closed	1991	40.00	40-55
1992	Star of Bethlehem	Closed	1992	40.00	45

Sterling Nativity Medallions - Towle

Year Issue		Edition Limit	Year Retd.	Issue Price	*Quote U.S.$
1988	The Angel Appeared	Closed	1988	40.00	75-125
1989	The Journey	Closed	1989	40.00	50-80
1990	No Room at the Inn	Closed	1990	40.00	50-60
1991	Tidings of Joy	Closed	1991	40.00	40-55
1992	Star of Bethlehem	Closed	1992	40.00	40-55
1993	Mother and Child	Closed	1993	40.00	40-55
1994	Three Wisemen	Closed	1994	40.00	60
1995	Newborn King	Closed	1995	40.00	50

Sterling Twelve Days of Christmas Medallions - Towle

Year Issue		Edition Limit	Year Retd.	Issue Price	*Quote U.S.$
1971	Partridge in A Pear Tree	Closed	1971	10.00	300-500
1972	Two Turtle Doves	Closed	1972	10.00	75-125
1973	Three French Hens	Closed	1973	10.00	35-55
1974	Four Colly Birds	Closed	1974	30.00	40-75
1975	Five Gold Rings	Closed	1975	30.00	45-95
1975	Five Gold Rings (vermeil)	Closed	1975	30.00	75-125
1976	Six Geese-a-Laying	Closed	1976	30.00	40-100
1977	Seven Swans-a-Swimming	Closed	1977	35.00	100-125
1977	Seven Swans-a-Swimming (turquoise)	Closed	1977	35.00	45-100
1978	Eight Maids-a-Milking	Closed	1978	37.00	45-100
1979	Nine Ladies Dancing	Closed	1979	37.00	50-100
1980	Ten Lords-a-Leaping	Closed	1980	76.00	80-100
1981	Eleven Pipers Piping	Closed	1981	50.00	50-95
1982	Twelve Drummers Drumming	Closed	1982	35.00	50-95

Twelve Days of Christmas - Towle

Year Issue		Edition Limit	Year Retd.	Issue Price	*Quote U.S.$
1991	Partridge in A Pear Tree In A Wreath	Closed	1991	50.00	70
1992	Two Turtle Doves In A Wreath	Closed	1992	50.00	60
1993	Three French Hens In A Wreath	Closed	1993	50.00	50-90
1994	Four Colly Birds In A Wreath	Closed	1995	50.00	60
1996	Five Gold Rings In A Wreath	Closed	1996	50.00	50
1996	Six Geese A Laying In A Wreath	Closed	1996	50.00	50

Treasury Masterpiece Editions/Enesco

Treasury Ornaments Collectors' Club (formerly known as Enesco Treasury of Christmas Ornaments Collectors' Club) - Enesco, unless otherwise noted

Year Issue		Edition Limit	Year Retd.	Issue Price	*Quote U.S.$
1993	The Treasury Card T0001 - Gilmore	Yr.Iss.	1993	Gift	20
1993	Together We Can Shoot For The Stars TR931 - Hahn	Yr.Iss.	1993	17.50	35
1993	Can't Weights For The Holidays TR932	Yr.Iss.	1993	18.50	35
1994	Seedlings Greetings TR933 - Hahn	Yr.Iss.	1994	22.50	23
1994	Spry Fry (Club) TR934	Yr.Iss.	1994	15.00	15
1995	You're the Perfect Fit T0002 - Hahn	Yr.Iss.	1995	Gift	20
1995	You're the Perfect Fit T0102 (Charter Members) - Hahn	Yr.Iss.	1995	Gift	20
1995	Things Go Better With Coke™ TR951	Yr.Iss.	1995	15.00	15
1995	Buttoning Up Our Holiday Best TR952 - Gilmore	Yr.Iss.	1995	22.50	23
1995	Holiday High-Light TR953 - Gilmore	Yr.Iss.	1995	15.00	15
1995	First Class Christmas TR954 - Gilmore	Yr.Iss.	1995	22.50	23
1996	Yo Ho Holidays T0003	Yr.Iss.	1996	Gift	20
1996	Yo Ho Holidays T0103 (Charter Members)	Yr.Iss.	1996	Gift	20
1996	Coca Colar Choo Choo TR961	Yr.Iss.	1996	35.00	35
1996	Friends Are Tea-riffic TR962	Yr.Iss.	1996	25.00	25
1996	On Track With Coke™ TR963	Yr.Iss.	1996	25.00	25
1996	Riding High TR964 - Hahn	Yr.Iss.	1996	20.00	20
1997	Advent-ures In Ornament Collecting T0004 - Hahn	Yr.Iss.		Gift	N/A
1997	Advent-ures In Ornament Collecting T0104 (Charter Members) - Hahn	Yr.Iss.		Gift	N/A
1997	Coca Cola® Caboose TR971	Yr.Iss.		25.00	25
1997	The Sweetest Nativity TR972 - Hahn	Yr.Iss.		20.00	20

Treasury Masterpiece Editions (formerly known as Enesco Treasury of Christmas Ornaments) - Enesco, unless otherwise noted

Year Issue		Edition Limit	Year Retd.	Issue Price	*Quote U.S.$
1994	To My Favorite V.I.P. 596698	Yr.Iss.	1994	20.00	20
1983	Wide Open Throttle E-0242	3-Yr.	1985	12.00	35
1981	Snow Shoe-In Santa E-6139	2-Yr.	1982	6.00	35
1983	Baby's First Christmas E-0271	Yr.Iss.	1983	6.00	N/A
1983	Grandchild's First Christmas E-0272	Yr.Iss.	1983	5.00	N/A
1983	Baby's First Christmas E-0273	3-Yr.	1985	9.00	N/A
1983	Toy Drum Teddy E-0274	4-Yr.	1986	9.00	N/A
1983	Watching At The Window E-0275	3-Yr.	1985	13.00	N/A
1983	To A Special Teacher E-0276	7-Yr.	1989	5.00	15
1983	Toy Shop E-0277	7-Yr.	1989	8.00	50
1983	Merry Christmas Carousel Horse E-0278	7-Yr.	1989	9.00	20
1981	Look Out Below E-6135	2-Yr.	1982	6.00	N/A
1982	Flyin' Santa Christmas Special 1982 E-6136	Yr.Iss.	1982	9.00	75
1981	Flyin' Santa Christmas Special 1981 E-6136	Yr.Iss.	1981	9.00	N/A
1981	Sawin' Elf Helper E-6138	2-Yr.	1982	6.00	40
1981	Baby's First Christmas 1981 E-6145	Yr.Iss.	1981	6.00	N/A
1981	Our Hero E-6146	2-Yr.	1982	4.00	N/A
1981	Whoops E-6147	2-Yr.	1982	3.50	N/A

*Quotes have been rounded up to nearest dollar

Treasury Masterpiece Editions/Enesco
to Treasury Masterpiece Editions/Enesco

ORNAMENTS

YEAR ISSUE		EDITION LIMIT	YEAR RETD.	ISSUE PRICE	*QUOTE U.S.$
1981	Whoops, It's 1981 E-6148	Yr.Iss.	1981	7.50	75
1981	Not A Creature Was Stirring E-6149	2-Yr.	1982	4.00	25
1984	Joy To The World E-6209	2-Yr.	1985	9.00	35
1984	Letter To Santa E-6210	2-Yr.	1985	5.00	30
1984	Lucy & Me Someone Special Photo Frame E-6211	3-Yr.	1986	5.00	N/A
1984	Lucy & Me Special Friend Photo Frame E-6211	3-Yr.	1986	5.00	N/A
1984	Lucy & Me Teacher Photo Frame E-6211	3-Yr.	1986	5.00	N/A
1984	Lucy & Me Grandma Photo Frame E-6211	3-Yr.	1986	5.00	N/A
1984	Lucy & Me For Baby Photo Frame E-6211	3-Yr.	1986	5.00	N/A
1984	Lucy & Me Grandpa Photo Frame E-6211	3-Yr.	1986	5.00	N/A
1984	Baby's First Christmas 1984 E-6212 - Gilmore	Yr.Iss.	1984	10.00	30
1984	Merry Christmas Mother E-6213	3-Yr.	1986	10.00	30
1984	Baby's First Christmas 1984 E-6215	Yr.Iss.	1984	6.00	N/A
1984	Ferris Wheel Mice E-6216	2-Yr.	1985	9.00	30
1984	Cuckoo Clock E-6217	2-Yr.	1985	8.00	40
1984	Muppet Babies Baby's First Christmas E-6222 - J. Henson	Yr.Iss.	1984	10.00	45
1984	Muppet Babies Baby's First Christmas E-6223 -J. Henson	Yr.Iss.	1984	10.00	45
1984	Garfield Hark! The Herald Angel E-6224 - J. Davis	2-Yr.	1985	7.50	35
1984	Fun in Santa's Sleigh E-6225 - J. Davis	2-Yr.	1985	12.00	35
1984	Deer! Odie E-6226 -J. Davis	2-Yr.	1985	6.00	30
1984	Garfield The Snow Cat E-6227 - J. Davis	2-Yr.	1985	12.00	35
1984	Peek-A-Bear Baby's First Christmas E-6228	3-Yr.	1986	10.00	N/A
1984	Peek-A-Bear Baby's First Christmas E-6229	3-Yr.	1986	9.00	N/A
1984	Owl Be Home For Christmas E-6230	2-Yr.	1985	8.00	23
1984	Santa's Trolley E-6231	3-Yr.	1986	11.00	50
1984	Holiday Penguin E-6240	3-Yr.	1986	1.50	15-20
1984	Little Drummer E-6241	5-Yr.	1988	2.00	N/A
1984	Happy Holidays E-6248	2-Yr.	1985	2.00	5
1984	Christmas Nest E-6249	2-Yr.	1985	3.00	25
1984	Bunny's Christmas Stocking E-6251	Yr.Iss.	1984	2.00	15
1984	Santa On Ice E-6252	3-Yr.	1986	2.50	25
1984	Treasured Memories The New Sled E-6256	2-Yr.	1985	7.00	N/A
1984	Penguins On Ice E-6280	2-Yr.	1985	7.50	N/A
1984	Up On The House Top E-6281	6-Yr.	1989	9.00	N/A
1984	Grandchild's First Christmas (pink) 1984 E-6286	Yr.Iss.	1984	5.00	N/A
1984	Grandchild's First Christmas (blue) 1984 E-6286	Yr.Iss.	1984	5.00	N/A
1984	Godchild's First Christmas E-6287	3-Yr.	1986	7.00	N/A
1984	Santa In The Box E-6292	2-Yr.	1985	6.00	N/A
1984	Carousel Horse E-6913	2-Yr.	1985	1.50	N/A
1983	Arctic Charmer E-6945	2-Yr.	1984	7.00	N/A
1982	Victorian Sleigh E-6946	4-Yr.	1985	9.00	15
1983	Wing-A-Ding Angel E-6948	3-Yr.	1985	7.00	50
1982	A Saviour Is Born This Day E-6949	8-Yr.	1989	4.00	18
1982	Crescent Santa E-6950 - Gilmore	4-Yr.	1985	10.00	50
1982	Baby's First Christmas 1982 E-6952	Yr.Iss.	1982	10.00	N/A
1982	Polar Bear Fun Whoops, It's 1982 E-6953	Yr.Iss.	1982	10.00	75
1982	Holiday Skier E-6954 - J. Davis	5-Yr.	1986	7.00	N/A
1982	Toy Soldier 1982 E-6957	Yr.Iss.	1982	6.50	N/A
1982	Carousel Horses E-6958	3-Yr.	1984	8.00	20-40
1982	Dear Santa E-6959 - Gilmore	8-Yr.	1989	10.00	25
1982	Merry Christmas Grandma E-6975	3-Yr.	1984	5.00	N/A
1982	Penguin Power E-6977	2-Yr.	1983	6.00	15
1982	Bunny Winter Playground 1982 E-6978	Yr.Iss.	1982	10.00	N/A
1982	Baby's First Christmas 1982 E-6979	Yr.Iss.	1982	10.00	N/A
1983	Carousel Horses E-6980	4-Yr.	1986	8.00	N/A
1982	Grandchild's First Christmas 1982 E-6983	Yr.Iss.	1982	5.00	73
1982	Merry Christmas Teacher E-6984	4-Yr.	1985	7.00	N/A
1983	Garfield Cuts The Ice E-8771 - J. Davis	3-Yr.	1985	6.00	45
1984	A Stocking Full For 1984 E-8773 - J. Davis	Yr.Iss.	1984	6.00	N/A
1983	Stocking Full For 1983 E-8773 - J. Davis	Yr.Iss.	1983	6.00	N/A
1985	Santa Claus Balloon 55794	Yr.Iss.	1985	8.50	20
1985	Carousel Reindeer 55808	4-Yr.	1988	12.00	33
1985	Angel In Flight 55816	4-Yr.	1988	8.00	23
1985	Christmas Penguin 55824	4-Yr.	1988	7.50	43
1985	Merry Christmas Godchild 55832 - Gilmore	5-Yr.	1989	8.00	N/A
1985	Baby's First Christmas 55840	2-Yr.	1986	15.00	N/A
1985	Old Fashioned Rocking Horse 55859	2-Yr.	1986	10.00	15
1985	Child's Second Christmas 55867	5-Yr.	1989	11.00	N/A
1985	Fishing For Stars 55875	5-Yr.	1989	9.00	25
1985	Baby Blocks 55883	2-Yr.	1986	12.00	N/A
1985	Christmas Toy Chest 55891	5-Yr.	1989	10.00	N/A
1985	Grandchild's First Christmas 55921	5-Yr.	1989	7.00	30
1985	Joy Photo Frame 55956	Yr.Iss.	1985	6.00	N/A
1985	We Three Kings 55964	Yr.Iss.	1985	4.50	20
1985	The Night Before Christmas 55972	2-Yr.	1986	5.00	N/A
1985	Baby's First Christmas 1985 55980	Yr.Iss.	1985	6.00	N/A
1985	Baby Rattle Photo Frame 56006	2-Yr.	1986	5.00	N/A
1985	Baby's First Christmas 1985 56014 - Gilmore	Yr.Iss.	1985	10.00	N/A
1985	Christmas Plane Ride 56049 - L. Rigg	6-Yr.	1990	10.00	N/A
1985	Scottie Celebrating Christmas 56065	5-Yr.	1989	7.50	25
1985	North Pole Native 56073	2-Yr.	1986	9.00	N/A
1985	Skating Walrus 56081	2-Yr.	1986	9.00	20
1985	Ski Time 56111 - J. Davis	Yr.Iss.	1985	13.00	N/A
1985	North Pole Express 56138 - J. Davis	Yr.Iss.	1985	12.00	N/A
1985	Merry Christmas Mother 56146 - J. Davis	Yr.Iss.	1985	8.50	N/A
1985	Hoppy Christmas 56154 - J. Davis	Yr.Iss.	1985	8.50	N/A
1985	Merry Christmas Teacher 56170 - J. Davis	Yr.Iss.	1985	6.00	N/A
1985	Garfield-In-The-Box 56189 - J. Davis	Yr.Iss.	1985	6.50	25
1985	Merry Christmas Grandma 56197	Yr.Iss.	1985	7.00	N/A
1985	Christmas Lights 56200	2-Yr.	1986	8.00	N/A
1985	Victorian Doll House 56251	Yr.Iss.	1985	13.00	40
1985	Tobaoggan Ride 56286	4-Yr.	1988	6.00	15
1985	St. Nicholas Circa 1910 56359	5-Yr.	1989	6.00	15
1985	Look Out Below 56375	Yr.Iss.	1985	8.50	40
1985	Flying Santa Christmas Special 56383	2-Yr.	1986	10.00	N/A
1985	Sawin Elf Helper 56391	Yr.Iss.	1985	8.00	N/A
1985	Snow Shoe-In Santa 56405	Yr.Iss.	1985	8.00	50
1985	Our Hero 56413	Yr.Iss.	1985	5.50	N/A
1985	Merry Christmas Teacher 56448	Yr.Iss.	1985	9.00	N/A
1985	Not A Creature Was Stirring 56421	2-Yr.	1986	4.00	N/A
1985	A Stocking Full For 1985 56464 - J. Davis	Yr.Iss.	1985	6.00	25
1985	Christmas Tree Photo Frame 56871	4-Yr.	1988	10.00	N/A
1995	How...Do I Love Thee 104949	Yr.Iss.	1995	22.50	23
1995	Swishing You Sweet Greetings 105201	Yr.Iss.	1995	20.00	20
1995	Planely Delicious 109665	Yr.Iss.	1996	20.00	20
1996	Spice Up The Season 111724	Yr. Iss.	1996	20.00	20
1995	Home For The Howl-i-days 111732	Yr.Iss.	1995	20.00	20
1995	Time For Refreshment 111872	Yr.Iss.	1995	20.00	20
1995	Holiday Bike Hike 111937	Yr.Iss.	1995	20.00	20
1996	Santa's Sacks 111945 - Hahn	Yr. Iss.	1996	15.00	18
1995	Ho, Ho, Hole in One! 111953	Yr.Iss.	1995	20.00	20
1995	No Time To Spare at Christmas 111961	Yr.Iss.	1995	20.00	20
1995	Hustling Up Some Cheer 112038	Yr.Iss.	1995	20.00	20
1995	Scoring Big at Christmas 112046	Yr.Iss.	1995	20.00	20
1995	Serving Up the Best 112054	Yr.Iss.	1995	17.50	18
1995	Sea-sons Greetings, Teacher 112070 - Gilmore	Yr.Iss.	1996	17.50	18
1995	Siesta Santa 112089 - Gilmore	Yr.Iss.	1995	25.00	25
1995	We've Shared Sew Much 112097 - Gilmore	Yr.Iss.	1995	25.00	25
1995	Toys To Treasure 112119	Yr.Iss.	1995	20.00	20
1995	To Santa, Post Haste 112151 - Gilmore	Yr.Iss.	1995	15.00	15
1995	Yule Logon For Christmas Cheer 122513	Yr.Iss.	1995	20.00	20
1995	Pretty Up For The Holidays 125830 - Butcher	Yr.Iss.	1995	20.00	20
1995	You Bring The Love to Christmas 125849 - Butcher	Yr.Iss.	1995	15.00	15
1995	Happy Birthday Jesus 125857 - Butcher	Yr.Iss.	1995	15.00	15
1995	Let's Snuggle Together For Christmas 125865 - Butcher	Yr.Iss.	1995	15.00	15
1995	I'm In A Spin Over You 125873 - Butcher	Yr.Iss.	1995	15.00	15
1995	Our First Christmas Together 125881 - Butcher	Yr.Iss.	1995	22.50	23
1995	Twinkle, Twinkle Christmas Star 125903 - Butcher	Yr.Iss.	1995	17.50	18
1995	Bringing Holiday Wishes To You 125911 - Butcher	Yr.Iss.	1995	22.50	23
1995	You Pull The Strings To My Heart 125938 - Butcher	Yr.Iss.	1995	20.00	20
1995	Baby's First Christmas 125946 - Butcher	Yr.Iss.	1995	15.00	15
1995	Baby's First Christmas 125954 - Butcher	Yr.Iss.	1995	15.00	15
1995	Friends Are The Greatest Treasure 125962 - Butcher	20,000	1995	25.00	25
1995	4-Alarm Christmas 128767 - Gilmore	Yr.Iss.	1995	17.50	18
1995	Truckin'/1956 Ford F-100 Truck 128813	Yr.Iss.	1995	25.00	25
1995	1955 Red Ford Thunderbird 128821	19,550	1995	20.00	28
1995	57 HVN/1957 Chevy Bel Air 128848	Yr.Iss.	1995	20.00	22
1995	1965 Chevrolet Corvette Stingray 128856	Yr.Iss.	1995	20.00	22
1995	Mom's Taxi/Dodge Caravan 128872	Yr.Iss.	1995	25.00	25
1995	Choc Full of Wishes 128945	Yr.Iss.	1995	20.00	20
1995	Have a Coke and a Smile™ 128953	Yr.Iss.	1995	22.50	23
1995	Trunk Full of Treasures 128961	20,000	1995	25.00	25
1995	Make Mine a Coke™ 128988	Yr.Iss.	1995	25.00	25
1995	Dashing Through the Snow 128996	Yr.Iss.	1995	20.00	20
1995	Happy Yuleglide 129003	Yr.Iss.	1995	17.50	18
1995	Santa's Speedway 129011	Yr.Iss.	1995	20.00	20
1995	You're My Cup of Tea 129038	Yr.Iss.	1996	20.00	20
1995	Crackin' a Smile 129046	Yr.Iss.	1995	17.50	18
1995	Rx:Mas Greetings 129054	Yr.Iss.	1995	17.50	18
1996	Special Bear-Livery 129062	Yr.Iss.	1996	15.00	15
1995	Merry McMeal 129070	Yr.Iss.	1995	17.50	18
1995	Above the Crowd 129089	Yr.Iss.	1995	20.00	20
1995	Mickey at the Helm 132063	Yr.Iss.	1995	17.50	18
1995	1959 Cadillac Eldorado 132705	Yr.Iss.	1995	20.00	22
1996	Catch Of The Holiday 132888 - Hahn	Yr.Iss.	1996	20.00	20
1995	Jackpot Joy! 132896 - Hahn	Yr.Iss.	1995	17.50	18
1995	Get in the Spirit...Recycle 132918 - Hahn	Yr.Iss.	1996	17.50	18
1995	Miss Merry's Secret 132934 - Hahn	Yr.Iss.	1995	20.00	20
1995	...Good Will Toward Men 132942 - Hahn	19,450	1995	25.00	25
1995	Friendships Bloom Through All Seasons 132950 - Hahn	Yr.Iss.	1995	22.50	23
1995	Merry Monopoly 132969	Yr.Iss.	1996	22.50	23
1995	The Night B 4 Christmas 134848 - Hahn	Yr.Iss.	1995	20.00	20
1996	A Cup Of Cheer 135070 - Gilmore	Yr.Iss.	1996	25.00	25
1995	Bubblin' With Joy 136581	Yr.Iss.	1995	15.00	15
1996	Steppin' With Minnie 136603	Yr.Iss.	1996	13.50	14
1995	Minnie's Merry Christmas 136611	Yr.Iss.	1995	20.00	20
1996	Motorcycle Mickey 136654	Yr.Iss.	1996	25.00	25
1995	Makin' Tracks With Mickey 136662	Yr.Iss.	1995	20.00	20
1995	Mickey's Airmail 136670	Yr.Iss.	1996	20.00	20
1995	Holiday Bound 136689	Yr.Iss.	1996	20.00	20
1995	Goofed-Up! 136697	Yr.Iss.	1996	20.00	20
1995	On The Ball At Christmas 136700	Yr.Iss.	1996	15.00	15
1995	Sweet on You 136719	Yr.Iss.	1995	22.50	23
1995	Nutty About Christmas 137030	Yr.Iss.	1995	22.50	23
1995	Tinkertoy Joy 137049	Yr.Iss.	1996	20.00	20
1995	Starring Roll At Christmas 137057	Yr.Iss.	1995	17.50	18
1995	A Thimble of the Season 137243 - Gilmore	Yr.Iss.	1996	22.50	23
1995	A Little Something Extra...Extra 137251	10,000	1995	25.00	25
1995	The Maze Of Our Lives 139599 - Hahn	Yr.Iss.	1995	17.50	18
1995	A Sip For Good Measure 139610	Yr.Iss.	1995	17.50	18
1995	Christmas Fishes, Dad 139629 - Hahn	Yr.Iss.	1996	17.50	18
1995	Christmas Is In The Bag 139645	Yr.Iss.	1995	17.50	18
1995	Gotta Have a Clue 139653	Yr.Iss.	1995	20.00	20
1995	Fun In Hand 139661	Yr.Iss.	1995	17.50	18
1995	Christmas Cuddle 139688	Yr.Iss.	1996	20.00	20
1995	Dreaming Of the One I Love 139696	Yr.Iss.	1996	25.00	25
1995	Sneaking a Peek 139718	Yr.Iss.	1996	22.50	23
1995	Christmas Eve Mischief 139726	Yr.Iss.	1995	17.50	18
1995	All Tucked In 139734	Yr.Iss.	1995	15.00	15
1995	Merry Christmas To Me 139742	Yr.Iss.	1995	20.00	20
1995	Looking Our Holiday Best 139750	Yr.Iss.	1995	25.00	25
1995	Christmas Vacation 142158	Yr.Iss.	1996	20.00	20
1995	Just Fore Christmas 142174	Yr.Iss.	1996	15.00	15
1995	Christmas Belle 142182	Yr.Iss.	1996	20.00	20
1995	Tail Waggin' Wishes 142190	Yr.Iss.	1995	17.50	18
1995	Holiday Ride 142204	Yr.Iss.	1995	17.50	18
1995	A Carousel For Ariel 142212	Yr.Iss.	1995	17.50	18
1995	On The Move At Christmas 142220 - Hahn	Yr.Iss.	1995	17.50	18
1995	T-Bird 146838	Yr.Iss.	1995	20.00	22
1996	Swinging On A Star 166642	Yr.Iss.	1996	20.00	20
1996	A-Joy Matie, Throw Me A Lifesavers 166677	Yr.Iss.	1996	20.00	20
1996	It's Plane To See...Coke Is It 166723	Yr.Iss.	1996	25.00	25
1996	A Century Of Good Taste 166774	Yr.Iss.	1996	25.00	25
1996	Servin' Up Joy 166847	Yr.Iss.	1996	20.00	20
1996	In-Line To Help Santa 166855	Yr.Iss.	1996	20.00	20
1996	I Love My Daughter 166863	Yr.Iss.	1996	9.00	9
1996	I Love Grandma 166898	Yr.Iss.	1996	9.00	9
1996	I Love Dad 166901	Yr.Iss.	1996	9.00	9
1996	I Love Mom 166928	Yr.Iss.	1996	9.00	9
1996	I Love My Godchild 166936	Yr.Iss.	1996	9.00	9
1996	Baby's 1st Christmas 166944	Yr.Iss.	1996	9.00	9
1996	A Boot Full Of Cheer 166952	Yr.Iss.	1996	20.00	20
1996	Summons For A Merry Christmas 166960	Yr.Iss.	1996	22.50	23
1996	An Appointment With Santa 166979	Yr.Iss.	1996	20.00	20
1996	Play It Again, Nick 166987	Yr.Iss.	1996	17.50	18
1996	Holiday Tinkertoy Tree 166995	Yr.Iss.	1996	17.50	18
1996	A Picture Perfect Pair 167002	Yr.Iss.	1996	25.00	25
1996	Santa's On The Line 167037	Yr.Iss.	1996	25.00	25
1996	Downhill Delivery 167053	Yr.Iss.	1996	25.00	25
1996	On A Roll With Diet Coke 167061	Yr.Iss.	1996	20.00	20
1996	Hold On, Santa! 167088	Yr.Iss.	1996	25.00	25
1996	There's A Friendship Brewing 167096 - Hahn	Yr.Iss.	1996	25.00	25
1996	Tails A' Waggin' 167126	Yr.Iss.	1996	20.00	20
1996	In Store For More 167134	15,000	1996	25.00	25
1996	Jeep Grand Cherokee 167215	Yr.Iss.	1996	22.50	23
1996	Chevy Blazer 167223	Yr.Iss.	1996	22.50	23
1996	Ford Explorer 167231	Yr.Iss.	1996	22.50	23
1996	Dodge Ram Truck 167258	Yr.Iss.	1996	22.50	23
1996	Trees To Please 168378	Yr.Iss.	1996	25.00	25
1996	Plane Crazy 168386	Yr.Iss.	1996	22.50	23

*Quotes have been rounded up to nearest dollar

ORNAMENTS

Treasury Masterpiece Editions/Enesco
to Treasury Masterpiece Editions/Enesco

YEAR ISSUE		EDITION LIMIT	YEAR RETD.	ISSUE PRICE	*QUOTE U.S.$
1996	I Love My Son 168432	Yr.Iss.	1996	9.00	9
1996	#1 Coach 168440	Yr.Iss.	1996	9.00	9
1996	Goin' Fishin' 168459	Yr.Iss.	1996	22.50	23
1996	Gifts From Mickey 168467	Yr.Iss.	1996	20.00	20
1996	All Fired Up For Christmas 168475	Yr.Iss.	1996	25.00	25
1996	Minnie's Mall Haul 168491	Yr.Iss.	1996	25.00	25
1996	A Magic Moment 172197	Yr.Iss.	1996	17.50	18
1996	Happy's Holiday 172200	Yr.Iss.	1996	17.50	18
1996	Sitting Pretty 172219	Yr.Iss.	1996	17.50	18
1996	Life's Sweet Choices 172634	Yr.Iss.	1996	25.00	25
1996	Holiday In Bloom 172669	Yr.Iss.	1996	25.00	25
1996	Have A Cracker Jack Christmas 172979	Yr.Iss.	1996	25.00	25
1996	Hair's The Place 173029 - Hahn	Yr.Iss.	1996	25.00	25
1996	Merry Manicure 173339 - Hahn	Yr.Iss.	1996	25.00	25
1996	100 Years...And Still On A Roll 173770	19,960	1996	17.50	18
1996	Tracking Reindeer Pause 173789 - Hahn	Yr.Iss.	1996	25.00	25
1996	Holiday Dreams Of Green 173797 - Hahn	Yr.Iss.	1996	15.00	15
1996	1965 Ford Mustang 173800	Yr.Iss.	1996	22.50	23
1996	Toyland, Joyland 173878	Yr.Iss.	1996	20.00	20
1996	Tobin's Debut Dancer 173886 - Fraley	20,000	1996	20.00	20
1996	Thou Art My Lamp, O Lord 173894 - Hahn	Yr.Iss.	1996	25.00	25
1996	'Tis The Season To Be Nutty 175234	Yr.Iss.	1996	17.50	18
1996	1956 Chevy Corvette 175269	19,560	1996	22.50	23
1996	A World Of Good Taste 175420	18,600	1996	20.00	20
1996	It's Time For Christmas 175455	Yr.Iss.	1996	25.00	25
1996	15 Years Of Hits 175463	10,000	1996	25.00	25
1996	Sew Darn Cute 176761 - Hahn	Yr.Iss.	1996	25.00	25
1996	Decked Out For Christmas 176796 - Hahn	Yr.Iss.	1996	25.00	25
1996	Campaign For Christmas 176818	19,960	1996	17.50	18
1996	Delivering Holiday Cheers 177318	Yr.Iss.	1996	25.00	25
1996	A Splash Of Cool Yule 213713	Yr.Iss.	1996	20.00	20
1997	100 Years of Soup-erb Good Taste! 265586	Yr.Iss.		20.00	20
1997	Tobin's Graceful Steed 265594 - Fraley	Yr.Iss.		20.00	20
1997	Movin' And Groovin' 270482	Yr.Iss.		22.50	23
1997	Twist And Shout, "Have A Coke!" 277398	Yr.Iss.		22.50	23
1997	Cracker Jack...The Home Run Snack 277401	Yr.Iss.		25.00	25
1997	I'm So Glad I [illegible] A Friend 277428 - Hahn	Yr.Iss.		20.00	20
1997	Workin' Round The Clock 277436	Yr.Iss.		22.50	23
1997	WWW.Holiday.Com 277444	Yr.Iss.		25.00	25
1997	Always Cool With Coke 277967	Yr.Iss.		22.50	23
1997	Weather Or Not...Coke Is It! 277983	Yr.Iss.		20.00	20
1997	Stockin' Up For The Holidays 277991	Yr.Iss.		22.50	23
1997	Home Sweet Home 278017	Yr.Iss.		25.00	25
1997	Ordering Up A Merry Christmas 278068	Yr.Iss.		25.00	25
1997	Best Bet's A 'Vette 278092	Yr.Iss.		22.50	23
1997	Deere Santa 278106	Yr.Iss.		25.00	25
1997	On Track With Santa 278114	Yr.Iss.		20.00	20
1997	Prepare For Battle 278122	Yr.Iss.		25.00	25
1997	Have Your Cake & Bake It, Too 278130	Yr.Iss.		20.00	20
1997	G.I. Love Christmas 278149	Yr.Iss.		20.00	20
1997	Primping Iron 278165 - Hahn	Yr.Iss.		20.00	20
1997	On Course With Santa 278394 - Hahn	Yr.Iss.		20.00	20
1997	Ice Cream Of The Crop 278408	Yr.Iss.		20.00	20
1997	50 Years Of Miracles 278432	Yr.Iss.		20.00	20
1997	Beep Me Up! 278440	Yr.Iss.		20.00	20
1997	Bubbling With Cheer 278467 - Hahn	Yr.Iss.		20.00	20
1997	Fired Up For Christmas 278491 - Hahn	Yr.Iss.		22.50	23
1997	Spare Time For Christmas Fun 280291 - Hahn	Yr.Iss.		25.00	25
1997	Everyone Knows It's Slinky 280992	Yr.Iss.		22.50	23
1997	Cherish The Joy 281263 - Hillman	Yr.Iss.		25.00	25
1997	Ho, Ho, Ho, A Grilling We Will Go! 281301	Yr.Iss.		20.00	20
1997	Hula Hoop Holidays 281336	Yr.Iss.		20.00	20
1997	Howl-A-Day Pet Shoppe 286192 - Hahn	Yr.Iss.		25.00	25
1997	Heading 4-Wheel Merry Christmas 287059	Yr.Iss.		22.50	23
1997	For All You Do, Merry Christmas To You 290858	Yr.Iss.		25.00	25
1997	Play It Again, Santa 295256	Yr.Iss.		20.00	20
1988	Making A Point 489212 - G.G. Santiago	3-Yr.	1990	10.00	N/A
1988	Mouse Upon A Pipe 489220 - G.G. Santiago	2-Yr.	1989	10.00	12
1988	North Pole Deadline 489387	3-Yr.	1990	13.50	25
1988	Christmas Pin-Up 489409	2-Yr.	1989	11.00	30
1988	Airmail For Teacher 489425 - Gilmore	3-Yr.	1990	13.50	N/A
1994	Sending You A Season's Greetings 550140 - Butcher	Yr.Iss.	1994	25.00	25
1994	Goofy Delivery 550639	Yr.Iss.	1994	22.50	23
1994	Happy Howl-idays 550647	Yr.Iss.	1994	22.50	23
1994	Christmas Crusin' 550655	Yr.Iss.	1994	22.50	23
1994	Holiday Honeys 550663	Yr.Iss.	1994	20.00	20
1994	May Your Holiday Be Brightened With Love 550698 - Butcher	Yr.Iss.	1994	15.00	15
1994	May All Your Wishes Come True 550701 - Butcher	Yr.Iss.	1994	20.00	20
1994	Baby's First Christmas 550728 - Butcher	Yr.Iss.	1994	20.00	20
1994	Baby's First Christmas 550736 - Butcher	Yr.Iss.	1994	20.00	20
1994	Our First Christmas Together 550744 - Butcher	Yr.Iss.	1994	25.00	25
1994	Drumming Up A Season Of Joy 550752 - Butcher	Yr.Iss.	1994	18.50	19
1994	Friendships Warm The Holidays 550760 - Butcher	Yr.Iss.	1994	20.00	20
1994	Dropping In For The Holidays 550779 - Butcher	Yr.Iss.	1994	20.00	20
1994	Ringing Up Holiday Wishes 550787 - Butcher	Yr.Iss.	1994	18.50	19
1994	A Child Is Born 550795 - Butcher	Yr.Iss.	1995	25.00	25
1994	Tis The Season To Go Shopping 550817 - Butcher	Yr.Iss.	1994	22.50	23
1994	The Way To A Mouse's Heart 550922	Yr.Iss.	1994	15.00	15
1994	Teed-Off Donald 550930	Yr.Iss.	1994	15.00	15
1994	Holiday Show-Stopper 550949	Yr.Iss.	1995	15.00	15
1994	Answering Christmas Wishes 551023	Yr.Iss.	1994	17.50	18
1994	Pure Christmas Pleasure 551066	Yr.Iss.	1995	20.00	20
1986	First Christmas Together 1986 551171	Yr.Iss.	1986	9.00	15-35
1986	Elf Stringing Popcorn 551198	4-Yr.	1989	10.00	20-30
1986	Christmas Scottie 551201	4-Yr.	1989	7.00	15-30
1986	Santa and Child 551236	4-Yr.	1989	13.50	25-50
1986	The Christmas Angel 551244	4-Yr.	1989	22.50	75
1986	Peace, Love, Joy Carousel Unicorn 551252 - Gilmore	4-Yr.	1989	12.00	38
1986	Have a Heavenly Holiday 551260	4-Yr.	1989	9.00	N/A
1986	Siamese Kitten 551279	4-Yr.	1989	9.00	36
1986	Old Fashioned Doll House 551287	4-Yr.	1989	15.00	N/A
1986	Holiday Fisherman 551309	3-Yr.	1988	8.00	40
1986	Antique Toy 551317	3-Yr.	1988	9.00	10
1986	Time For Christmas 551325 - Gilmore	4-Yr.	1989	13.00	N/A
1986	Christmas Calendar 551333	2-Yr.	1987	7.00	12
1994	Good Tidings, Tidings, Tidings, Tidings 551333	Yr.Iss.	1995	20.00	20
1986	Merry Christmas 551341 - Gilmore	3-Yr.	1988	8.00	50
1994	From Our House To Yours 551384 - Gilmore	Yr.Iss.	1994	25.00	25
1994	Sugar 'N' Spice For Someone Nice 551406 - Gilmore	Yr.Iss.	1994	30.00	30
1994	Toodles 551503 - Zimnicki	Yr.Iss.	1994	25.00	25
1994	Picture Perfect Christmas 551465	Yr.Iss.	1994	15.00	15
1994	A Bough For Belle! 551554	Yr.Iss.	1995	18.50	19
1986	The Santa Claus Shoppe Circa 1905 551562 - J. Grossman	4-Yr.	1989	8.00	15
1994	Ariel's Christmas Surprise! 551570	Yr.Iss.	1994	20.00	20
1994	Merry Little Two-Step 551589	Yr.Iss.	1995	12.50	13
1994	Sweets For My Sweetie 551600	Yr.Iss.	1994	15.00	15
1994	Friends Are The Spice of Life - 551619 - Hahn	Yr.Iss.	1995	20.00	20
1994	Cool Cruise/1964 1/2 Ford Mustang 551635	19,640	1994	20.00	20
1986	Baby Bear Sleigh 551651 - Gilmore	3-Yr.	1988	9.00	30
1994	Special Delivery 561657	Yr.Iss.	1994	20.00	20
1986	Baby's First Christmas 1986 551678 - Gilmore	Yr.Iss.	1986	10.00	20
1986	First Christmas Together 551708	3-Yr.	1988	6.00	10
1986	Baby's First Christmas 551716	3-Yr.	1988	5.50	10
1986	Baby's First Christmas 1986 551724	Yr.Iss.	1986	6.50	30
1994	A Christmas Tail 551759	Yr.Iss.	1995	20.00	20
1994	Merry Mischief- 551767	Yr.Iss.	1994	15.00	15
1994	L'il Stocking Stuffer 551791	Yr.Iss.	1994	17.50	18
1994	Once Upon A Time 551805	Yr.Iss.	1994	15.00	15
1994	Wishing Upon A Star 551813	Yr.Iss.	1994	18.50	19
1994	A Real Boy For Christmas 551821	Yr.Iss.	1995	15.00	15
1986	Peek-A-Bear Grandchild's First Christmas	Yr.Iss.	1986	6.00	23
1986	Peek-A-Bear in Stocking Present 552089	4-Yr.	1989	2.50	N/A
1986	Peek-A-Bear in Box Present 552089	4-Yr.	1989	2.50	N/A
1986	Peek-A-Bear in Shopping Bag Present 552089	4-Yr.	1989	2.50	N/A
1986	Peek-A-Bear in Cloth Bag Present 552089	4-Yr.	1989	2.50	N/A
1986	Merry Christmas (Boy) 552186 - L. Rigg	Yr.Iss.	1986	8.00	N/A
1994	Minnie's Holiday Treasure 552216	Yr.Iss.	1994	12.00	12
1994	Sweet Holidays 552259 - Butcher	Yr.Iss.	1994	12.00	12
1986	Merry Christmas (Girl) 552534 - L. Rigg	Yr.Iss.	1986	8.00	N/A
1986	Lucy & Me Christmas Tree 552542 - L. Rigg	3-Yr.	1988	7.00	25
1986	Santa's Helpers 552607	3-Yr.	1988	2.50	N/A
1986	My Special Friend 552615	3-Yr.	1988	6.00	10
1986	Christmas Wishes From Panda 552623	3-Yr.	1988	6.00	N/A
1986	Lucy & Me Ski Time 552658 - L. Rigg	2-Yr.	1987	6.50	30
1986	Merry Christmas Teacher 552666	3-Yr.	1988	6.50	N/A
1986	Country Cousins Merry Christmas, Mom (Girl on Skates) 552704	3-Yr.	1988	7.00	23
1986	Country Cousins Merry Christmas, Dad (Girl on Skates) 552704	3-Yr.	1988	7.00	23
1986	Country Cousins Merry Christmas, Mom (Boy w/Kite) 552712	4-Yr.	1989	7.00	23
1986	Country Cousins Merry Christmas, Dad (Boy w/Kite) 552712	4-Yr.	1989	7.00	25
1986	Grandmother's Little Angel 552747	4-Yr.	1989	8.00	N/A
1988	Puppy's 1st Christmas 552909	Yr.Iss.	1988	4.00	N/A
1988	Kitty's 1st Christmas 552917	Yr.Iss.	1988	4.00	25
1988	Merry Christmas Puppy 552925	Yr.Iss.	1988	3.50	N/A
1988	Merry Christmas Kitty 552933	Yr.Iss.	1988	3.50	N/A
1986	I Love My Grandparents 553263	Yr.Iss.	1986	6.00	N/A
1986	Merry Christmas Mom & Dad 553271	Yr.Iss.	1986	6.00	N/A
1986	Hollycopter 553344	4-Yr.	1989	13.50	35
1986	From Our House To Your House 553360	3-Yr.	1988	15.00	40
1986	Christmas Rattle 553379	3-Yr.	1988	8.00	35
1986	Bah, Humbug! 553387	4-Yr.	1989	9.00	N/A
1986	God Bless Us Everyone 553395	4-Yr.	1989	10.00	15
1987	Carousel Mobile 553409	3-Yr.	1989	15.00	50
1986	Holiday Train 553417	4-Yr.	1989	10.00	N/A
1986	Lighten Up! 553603 - J. Davis	5-Yr.	1990	10.00	N/A
1986	Gift Wrap Odie 553611 - J. Davis	Yr.Iss.	1986	7.00	20
1986	Merry Christmas 553646	4-Yr.	1989	8.00	N/A
1987	M.V.B. (Most Valuable Bear) Golfing 554219	2-Yr.	1988	3.00	N/A
1987	M.V.B. (Most Valuable Bear) Ice Hockey 554219	2-Yr.	1988	3.00	N/A
1987	M.V.B. (Most Valuable Bear) Skiing 554219	2-Yr.	1988	3.00	N/A
1987	M.V.B. (Most Valuable Bear) Bowling 554219	2-Yr.	1988	3.00	N/A
1988	1st Christmas Together 554537 - Gilmore	3-Yr.	1990	15.00	N/A
1988	An Eye On Christmas 554545 - Gilmore	3-Yr.	1990	22.50	60
1988	A Mouse Check 554553 - Gilmore	3-Yr.	1990	13.50	45
1988	Merry Christmas Engine 554561	2-Yr.	1989	22.50	35
1989	Sardine Express 554588 - Gilmore	2-Yr.	1990	17.50	30
1988	1st Christmas Together 1988 554596	Yr.Iss.	1988	10.00	N/A
1988	Forever Friends 554626 - Gilmore	2-Yr.	1989	12.00	27
1988	Santa's Survey 554642	2-Yr.	1989	35.00	75-100
1989	Old Town Church 554871 - Gilmore	2-Yr.	1990	17.50	20
1988	A Chipmunk Holiday 554898 - Gilmore	3-Yr.	1990	11.00	25
1988	Christmas Is Coming 554901	3-Yr.	1990	12.00	12
1988	Baby's First Christmas 1988 554928	Yr.Iss.	1988	7.50	N/A
1988	Baby's First Christmas 1988 554936 - Gilmore	Yr.Iss.	1988	10.00	25
1988	The Christmas Train 554944	3-Yr.	1990	15.00	N/A
1988	Li'l Drummer Bear 554952 - Gilmore	3-Yr.	1990	12.00	12
1987	Baby's First Christmas 555061	3-Yr.	1989	12.00	N/A
1987	Baby's First Christmas 555088	3-Yr.	1989	7.50	N/A
1987	Baby's First Christmas 555118	3-Yr.	1989	6.00	N/A
1988	Sugar Plum Bearies 555193	Yr.Iss.	1988	4.50	N/A
1987	Garfield Merry Kissmas 555215 - J. Davis	3-Yr.	1989	8.50	30
1988	Sleigh Away 555401	2-Yr.	1989	12.00	N/A
1987	Merry Christmas (Boy) 555428 - L. Rigg	Yr.Iss.	1987	8.00	N/A
1987	Merry Christmas (Girl) 555436 - L. Rigg	Yr.Iss.	1987	8.00	N/A
1987	Lucy & Me Storybook Bear 555444 - L. Rigg	3-Yr.	1989	6.50	N/A
1987	Time For Christmas 555452 - L. Rigg	3-Yr.	1989	12.00	20
1987	Lucy & Me Angel On A Cloud 555487 - L. Rigg	3-Yr.	1989	8.00	35
1987	Teddy's Stocking 555940 - Gilmore	3-Yr.	1989	10.00	N/A
1987	Kitty's Jack-In-The-Box 555959	3-Yr.	1989	11.00	30
1987	Merry Christmas Teacher 555967	3-Yr.	1989	7.50	N/A
1987	Mouse In A Mitten 555975	3-Yr.	1989	7.50	N/A
1987	Boy On A Rocking Horse 555983	3-Yr.	1989	12.00	18
1987	Peek-A-Bear Letter To Santa 555991	2-Yr.	1988	8.00	30
1987	Garfield Sugar Plum Fairy 556009 - J. Davis	3-Yr.	1989	8.50	15
1987	Garfield The Nutcracker 556017 - J. Davis	4-Yr.	1990	8.50	20
1987	Joy To The World Carousel Lion 556025 - Gilmore	3-Yr.	1989	12.00	25
1988	Home Sweet Home 556033 - Gilmore	2-Yr.	1989	15.00	40
1988	Baby's First Christmas 556041	3-Yr.	1990	10.00	20
1988	Little Sailor Elf 556068	2-Yr.	1989	10.00	20
1987	Carousel Goose 556076	3-Yr.	1989	17.00	40
1988	Night Caps Mom 556084	Yr.Iss.	1988	5.50	N/A
1988	Night Caps Dad 556084	Yr.Iss.	1988	5.50	N/A
1988	Night Caps Grandpa 556084	Yr.Iss.	1988	5.50	N/A
1988	Night Caps Grandma 556084	Yr.Iss.	1988	5.50	N/A
1988	Rocking Horse Past Joys 556157	2-Yr.	1989	10.00	20
1987	Partridge In A Pear Tree 556173 - Gilmore	3-Yr.	1989	9.00	35
1987	Skating Santa 1987 556211	Yr.Iss.	1987	13.50	75
1987	Baby's First Christmas 1987 556238 - Gilmore	Yr.Iss.	1987	10.00	25
1987	Baby's First Christmas 1987 556254	Yr.Iss.	1987	7.00	25
1988	Teddy's Suspenders 556262	3-Yr.	1990	8.50	22
1987	Baby's First Christmas (boy) 1987 556297	Yr.Iss.	1987	2.00	N/A
1987	Baby's First Christmas (girl) 1987 556297	Yr.Iss.	1987	2.00	N/A

*Quotes have been rounded up to nearest dollar

Collectors' Information Bureau

181

Treasury Masterpiece Editions/Enesco
to Treasury Masterpiece Editions/Enesco

ORNAMENTS

YEAR ISSUE		EDITION LIMIT	YEAR RETD.	ISSUE PRICE	*QUOTE U.S.$
1987	Beary Christmas Family (Grandma) 556300	2-Yr.	1988	2.00	N/A
1987	Beary Christmas Family (Grandpa) 556300	2-Yr.	1988	2.00	N/A
1987	Beary Christmas Family (Mom) 556300	2-Yr.	1988	2.00	N/A
1987	Beary Christmas Family (Dad) 556300	2-Yr.	1988	2.00	N/A
1987	Beary Christmas Family (Brother) 556300	2-Yr.	1988	2.00	N/A
1987	Beary Christmas Family (Sister)556300	2-Yr.	1988	2.00	N/A
1987	Merry Christmas Teacher (Boy) 556319	2-Yr.	1988	2.00	N/A
1987	Merry Christmas Teacher (Girl) 556319	2-Yr.	1988	2.00	N/A
1987	1st Christmas Together 1987 556335	Yr.Iss.	1987	9.00	18
1987	Katie Goes Ice Skating 556378	3-Yr.	1989	8.00	30
1987	Scooter Snowman 556386	3-Yr.	1989	8.00	30
1987	Santa's List 556394	3-Yr.	1989	7.00	23
1988	Kitty's Bed 556408	3-Yr.	1989	12.00	30
1988	Grandchild's First Christmas 556416	2-Yr.	1989	10.00	N/A
1987	Two Turtledoves 556432 - Gilmore	2-Yr.	1989	9.00	30
1987	Three French Hens 556440 - Gilmore	3-Yr.	1989	9.00	30
1988	Four Calling Birds 556459 - Gilmore	3-Yr.	1990	11.00	30
1988	Teddy Takes A Spin 556467	3-Yr.	1990	13.00	35
1987	Tiny Toy Thimble Mobile 556475	2-Yr.	1988	12.00	35
1987	Bucket O'Love (Puppy's 1st Christmas) 556491	2-Yr.	1988	2.50	N/A
1987	Bucket O'Love (Kitty's 1st Christmas) 556491	2-Yr.	1988	2.50	N/A
1987	Bucket O'Love (Christmas Kitty) 556491	2-Yr.	1988	2.50	N/A
1987	Bucket O'Love (Christmas Puppy) 556491	2-Yr.	1988	2.50	N/A
1987	Puppy Love 556505	3-Yr.	1989	6.00	N/A
1987	Peek-A-Bear My Special Friend 556513	4-Yr.	1990	6.00	30
1987	Our First Christmas Together 556548	3-Yr.	1989	13.00	20
1987	Three Little Bears 556556	3-Yr.	1989	7.50	15
1988	Lucy & Me Mailbox Bear 556564 - L. Rigg	3-Yr.	1990	3.00	N/A
1987	Twinkle Bear 556572 - Gilmore	3-Yr.	1989	8.00	N/A
1988	I'm Dreaming Of A Bright Christmas 556602	Yr.Iss.	1988	2.50	N/A
1988	Christmas Train 557196	2-Yr.	1989	10.00	N/A
1988	Dairy Christmas 557501 - M. Cook	2-Yr.	1989	10.00	30
1988	Merry Christmas (Boy) 557595 - L. Rigg	Yr.Iss.	1988	10.00	N/A
1988	Merry Christmas (Girl) 557609 - L. Rigg	Yr.Iss.	1988	10.00	N/A
1988	Toy Chest Keepsake 558206 - L. Rigg	3-Yr.	1990	12.50	30
1988	Teddy Bear Greetings 558214 - L. Rigg	3-Yr.	1990	8.00	30
1988	Jester Bear 558222 - L. Rigg	2-Yr.	1989	8.00	N/A
1988	Night-Watch Cat 558362 - J. Davis	3-Yr.	1990	13.00	35
1988	Christmas Thim-bell Mouse 558389	Yr.Iss.	1988	4.00	30
1988	Christmas Thim-bell Snowman 558389	Yr.Iss.	1988	4.00	N/A
1988	Christmas Thim-bell Bear 558389	Yr.Iss.	1988	4.00	N/A
1988	Christmas Thim-bell Santa 558389	Yr.Iss.	1988	4.00	N/A
1988	Baby's First Christmas 558397 - D. Parker	3-Yr.	1990	16.00	30
1988	Christmas Tradition 558400 - Gilmore	2-Yr.	1989	10.00	25
1988	Stocking Story 558419 - G.G. Santiago	3-Yr.	1990	10.00	23
1988	Winter Tale 558427 - G.G. Santiago	2-Yr.	1989	6.00	N/A
1988	Party Mouse 558435 - G.G. Santiago	3-Yr.	1990	12.00	30
1988	Christmas Watch 558443 - G.G. Santiago	2-Yr.	1989	11.00	32
1988	Christmas Vacation 558451 - G.G. Santiago	3-Yr.	1990	8.00	23
1988	Sweet Cherub 558478 - G.G. Santiago	3-Yr.	1990	7.00	8
1988	Time Out 558486 - G.G. Santiago	2-Yr.	1989	11.00	N/A
1988	The Ice Fairy 558516 - G.G. Santiago	3-Yr.	1990	23.00	45-55
1988	Santa Turtle 558559	2-Yr.	1989	10.00	35
1988	The Teddy Bear Ball 558567	3-Yr.	1990	10.00	25
1988	Turtle Greetings 558583	2-Yr.	1989	8.50	25
1988	Happy Howladays 558605	Yr.Iss.	1988	7.00	15
1988	Special Delivery 558699 - J. Davis	3-Yr.	1990	9.00	30
1988	Deer Garfield 558702 - J. Davis	3-Yr.	1990	12.00	30
1988	Garfield Bags O' Fun 558761 - J. Davis	Yr.Iss.	1988	3.30	N/A
1988	Gramophone Keepsake 558818	2-Yr.	1989	13.00	20
1988	North Pole Lineman 558834 - Gilmore	2-Yr.	1989	10.00	50
1988	Five Golden Rings 559121 - Gilmore	3-Yr.	1990	11.00	25
1988	Six Geese A-Laying 559148 - Gilmore	3-Yr.	1990	11.00	25
1988	Pretty Baby 559156 - R. Morehead	3-Yr.	1990	12.50	25
1988	Old Fashioned Angel 559164 - R. Morehead	3-Yr.	1990	12.50	20
1988	Two For Tea 559776 - Gilmore	3-Yr.	1990	20.00	35-40
1988	Merry Christmas Grandpa 560065	3-Yr.	1990	8.00	N/A
1990	Reeling In The Holidays 560405 - M. Cook	2-Yr.	1991	8.00	15
1991	Walkin' With My Baby 561029 - M. Cook	2-Yr.	1992	10.00	N/A
1989	Scrub-A-Dub Chipmunk 561037 - M. Cook	2-Yr.	1990	8.00	20
1989	Christmas Cook-Out 561045 - M. Cook	2-Yr.	1990	9.00	20
1989	Bunkie 561835 - S. Zimnicki	3-Yr.	1991	22.50	30
1989	Sparkles 561843 - S. Zimnicki	3-Yr.	1991	17.50	25-28
1992	Sparky & Buffer 561851 - S. Zimnicki	3-Yr.	1994	25.00	25
1989	Popper 561878 - S. Zimnicki	3-Yr.	1991	12.00	25
1989	Seven Swans A-Swimming 562742 - Gilmore	3-Yr.	1991	12.00	23
1989	Eight Maids A-Milking 562750 - Gilmore	3-Yr.	1991	12.00	23
1989	Nine Ladies Dancing 562769 - Gilmore	3-Yr.	1991	15.00	23
1989	Baby's First Christmas 1989 562807	Yr.Iss.	1989	8.00	20
1989	Baby's First Christmas 1989 562815 - Gilmore	Yr.Iss.	1989	10.00	N/A
1989	First Christmas Together 1989 562823	Yr.Iss.	1989	11.00	N/A
1989	Travelin' Trike 562882 - Gilmore	3-Yr.	1991	15.00	15
1989	Victorian Sleigh Ride 562890	3-Yr.	1991	22.50	23
1991	Santa Delivers Love 562904 - Gilmore	2-Yr.	1992	17.50	18
1989	Chestnut Roastin' 562912 - Gilmore	2-Yr.	1990	13.00	13
1990	Th-Ink-In' Of You 562920 - Gilmore	2-Yr.	1991	20.00	30
1989	Ye Olde Puppet Show 562939	2-Yr.	1990	17.50	34
1989	Static In The Attic 562947	2-Yr.	1990	13.00	25
1989	Mistle-Toast 1989 562963 - Gilmore	Yr.Iss.	1989	15.00	25
1989	Merry Christmas Pops 562971 - Gilmore	3-Yr.	1991	12.00	12
1990	North Pole Or Bust 562998 - Gilmore	2-Yr.	1991	25.00	25
1989	By The Light Of The Moon 563005 - Gilmore	3-Yr.	1991	12.00	24
1989	Stickin' To It 563013 - Gilmore	2-Yr.	1990	10.00	12
1989	Christmas Cookin' 563048 - Gilmore	3-Yr.	1991	22.50	25
1989	All Set For Santa 563080 -Gilmore	3-Yr.	1991	17.50	25
1990	Santa's Sweets 563196 - Gilmore	2-Yr.	1991	20.00	20
1990	Purr-Fect Pals 563218	2-Yr.	1991	8.00	8
1989	The Pause That Refreshes 563226	3-Yr.	1991	15.00	75
1989	Ho-Ho Holiday Scrooge 563234 - J. Davis	3-Yr.	1991	13.50	30
1989	God Bless Us Everyone 563242 - J. Davis	3-Yr.	1991	13.50	20
1989	Scrooge With The Spirit 563250 - J. Davis	3-Yr.	1991	13.50	30
1989	A Chains Of Pace For Odie 563269 - J. Davis	3-Yr.	1991	12.00	25
1990	Jingle Bell Rock 1990 563390 - G. Armgardt	Yr.Iss.	1990	13.50	30
1989	Joy Ridin' 563463 - J. Davis	2-Yr.	1990	15.00	30
1989	Just What I Wanted 563668 - M. Peters	3-Yr.	1991	13.50	14
1990	Pucker Up! 563676 - M. Peters	3-Yr.	1992	11.00	11
1989	What's The Bright Idea 563684 - M. Peters	3-Yr.	1991	13.50	14
1990	Fleas Navidad 563978 - M. Peters	3-Yr.	1992	13.50	25
1990	Tweet Greetings 564044 - J. Davis	2-Yr.	1991	15.00	20
1990	Trouble On 3 Wheels 564052 - J. Davis	3-Yr.	1992	20.00	25
1989	Mine, All Mine! 564079 - J. Davis	Yr.Iss.	1989	15.00	25
1989	Star of Stars 564389 - J. Jonik	3-Yr.	1991	9.00	15
1990	Hang Onto Your Hat 564397 - J. Jonik	3-Yr.	1992	8.00	15
1990	Fireplace Frolic 564435 - N. Teiber	2-Yr.	1991	25.00	32
1994	Merry Miss Merry 564508 - Hahn	Yr.Iss.	1994	12.00	12
1994	Santa Delivers 564567	Yr.Iss.	1994	12.00	12
1989	Hoe! Hoe! Hoe! 564761	Yr.Iss.	1989	20.00	35
1991	Double Scoop Snowmouse 564796 - M. Cook	3-Yr.	1993	13.50	14
1990	Christmas Is Magic 564826 - M. Cook	2-Yr.	1991	10.00	10
1990	Lighting Up Christmas 564834 - M. Cook	2-Yr.	1991	10.00	10
1989	Feliz Navidad! 1989 564842 - M. Cook	Yr.Iss.	1989	11.00	40
1989	Spreading Christmas Joy 564850 - M. Cook	3-Yr.	1991	10.00	10
1989	Yuletide Tree House 564915 - J. Jonik	3-Yr.	1991	20.00	20
1990	Brewing Warm Wishes 564974	2-Yr.	1991	10.00	10
1990	Yippie-I-Yuletide 564982 - Hahn	3-Yr.	1992	15.00	15
1990	Coffee Break 564990 - Hahn	3-Yr.	1992	15.00	15
1990	You're Sew Special 565008 - Hahn	Yr.Iss.	1990	20.00	35
1989	Full House Mouse 565016 - Hahn	2-Yr.	1990	13.50	75
1989	I Feel Pretty 565024 - Hahn	3-Yr.	1991	20.00	30
1990	Warmest Wishes 565032 - Hahn	3-Yr.	1992	15.00	15
1990	Baby's Christmas Feast 565040 - Hahn	3-Yr.	1992	13.50	14
1990	Bumper Car Santa 565083 - G.G. Santiago	Yr.Iss.	1990	20.00	40
1989	Special Delivery (Proof Ed.) 565091 - G.G. Santiago	Yr.Iss.	1989	12.00	15
1990	Ho! Ho! Yo-Yo! (Proof Ed.) 565105 - G.G. Santiago	Yr.Iss.	1990	12.00	15
1989	Weightin' For Santa 565148 - G.G. Santiago	3-Yr.	1991	7.50	8
1989	Holly Fairy 565199 - C.M. Baker	Yr.Iss.	1989	15.00	45
1990	The Christmas Tree Fairy 565202 - C.M. Baker	Yr.Iss.	1990	15.00	40
1989	Merry Christmas (Boy) 565210 - L. Rigg	Yr.Iss.	1989	12.00	38
1989	Top Of The Class 565237 - L. Rigg	3-Yr.	1991	11.00	11
1989	Deck The Hogs 565490 - M. Cook	2-Yr.	1990	12.00	14
1989	Pinata Ridin' 565504 - M. Cook	2-Yr.	1990	11.00	N/A
1989	Hangin' In There 1989 565598 - K. Wise	Yr.Iss.	1989	10.00	20
1990	Meow-y Christmas 1990 565601 - K. Wise	Yr.Iss.	1990	10.00	25
1990	Seaman's Greetings 566047	2-Yr.	1991	11.00	24
1990	Hang In There 566055	3-Yr.	1992	13.50	14
1990	Deck The Halls 566063	3-Yr.	1992	12.50	N/A
1991	Pedal Pushin' Santa 566071	Yr.Iss.	1991	20.00	30
1990	Merry Christmas Teacher 566098	2-Yr.	1991	11.00	11
1990	Festive Flight 566101	2-Yr.	1991	11.00	11
1993	I'm Dreaming of a White-Out Christmas 566144	2-Yr.	1994	22.50	23
1990	Santa's Suitcase 566160	3-Yr.	1992	25.00	25
1989	The Purr-Fect Fit! 566462	3-Yr.	1991	15.00	35
1990	Tumbles 1990 566519 - S. Zimnicki	Yr.Iss.	1990	16.00	25
1990	Twiddles 566551 - S. Zimnicki	3-Yr.	1992	15.00	30
1991	Snuffy 566578 - S. Zimnicki	3-Yr.	1993	17.50	18
1990	All Aboard 567671 - Gilmore	2-Yr.	1991	17.50	18
1989	Gone With The Wind 567698	Yr.Iss.	1989	13.50	30
1989	Dorothy 567760	Yr.Iss.	1989	12.00	35
1989	The Tin Man 567779	Yr.Iss.	1989	12.00	12
1989	The Cowardly Lion 567787	Yr.Iss.	1989	12.00	12
1989	The Scarecrow 567795	Yr.Iss.	1989	12.00	12
1990	Happy Holiday Readings 568104	2-Yr.	1991	8.00	8
1989	Merry Christmas (Girl) 568325 - L. Rigg	Yr.Iss.	1989	12.00	N/A
1991	Holidays Ahoy 568368	2-Yr.	1992	12.50	13
1990	Christmas Countdown 568376	3-Yr.	1992	20.00	20
1989	Clara 568406	Yr.Iss.	1989	12.50	20
1990	The Nutcracker 568414	Yr.Iss.	1990	12.50	30
1991	Clara's Prince 568422	Yr.Iss.	1991	12.50	18
1989	Santa's Little Reindear 568430	2-Yr.	1990	15.00	25
1991	Tuba Totin' Teddy 568449	3-Yr.	1993	15.00	15
1990	A Calling Home At Christmas 568457	2-Yr.	1991	15.00	15
1991	Love Is The Secret Ingredient 568562 - L. Rigg	2-Yr.	1992	15.00	15
1990	A Spoonful of Love 568570 - L. Rigg	2-Yr.	1991	10.00	10
1990	Merry Christmas (Boy) 568597 - L. Rigg	Yr.Iss.	1990	13.00	N/A
1990	Merry Christmas (Girl) 568600 - L. Rigg	Yr.Iss.	1990	13.00	N/A
1990	Bearing Holiday Wishes 568619 - L. Rigg	3-Yr.	1992	22.50	23
1992	Moonlight Swing 568627 - L. Rigg	3-Yr.	1994	15.00	15
1990	Smitch 570184 - S. Zimnicki	3-Yr.	1992	22.50	23
1992	Carver 570192 - S. Zimnicki	Yr.Iss.	1992	17.50	18
1991	Twinkle & Sprinkle 570206 - S. Zimnicki	3-Yr.	1993	22.50	23
1990	Blinkie 570214 - S. Zimnicki	3-Yr.	1992	15.00	15
1990	Have A Coke And A Smile™ 571512	3-Yr.	1992	15.00	55
1990	Fleece Navidad 571903 - M. Cook	2-Yr.	1991	13.50	25
1990	Have a Navaho-Ho-Ho 1990 571970 - M. Cook	Yr.Iss.	1990	15.00	35
1990	Cheers 1990 572411 - T. Wilson	Yr.Iss.	1990	13.50	22
1990	A Night Before Christmas 572438 - T. Wilson	2-Yr.	1991	17.50	18
1990	Merry Kissmas 572446 - T. Wilson	2-Yr.	1991	10.00	30
1992	A Rockin' GARFIELD Christmas 572527 - J. Davis	2-Yr.	1993	17.50	18
1991	Here Comes Santa Paws 572535 - J. Davis	3-Yr.	1993	20.00	20
1990	Frosty Garfield 1990 572551 - J. Davis	Yr.Iss.	1990	13.50	35
1990	Pop Goes The Odie 572578 - J. Davis	2-Yr.	1991	15.00	30
1991	Sweet Beams 572586 - J. Davis	2-Yr.	1992	13.50	14
1990	An Apple A Day 572594 - J. Davis	2-Yr.	1991	12.00	12
1990	Dear Santa 572608 - J. Davis	3-Yr.	1992	17.00	17
1991	Have A Ball This Christmas 572616 - J. Davis	Yr.Iss.	1991	15.00	15
1990	Oh Shoosh! 572624 - J. Davis	3-Yr.	1992	17.00	17
1990	Little Red Riding Cat 572632 - J. Davis	Yr.Iss.	1990	13.50	33
1991	All Decked Out 572659 - J. Davis	2-Yr.	1992	13.50	14
1990	Over The Rooftops 572721 - J. Davis	2-Yr.	1991	17.50	28-35
1990	Garfield NFL Los Angeles Rams 572764 - J. Davis	2-Yr.	1991	12.50	13
1993	Born To Shop 572942	Yr.Iss.	1993	26.50	35
1990	Garfield NFL Cincinnati Bengals 573000 - J. Davis	2-Yr.	1991	12.50	13
1990	Garfield NFL Cleveland Browns 573019 - J. Davis	2-Yr.	1991	12.50	13
1990	Garfield NFL Houston Oiliers 573027 - J. Davis	2-Yr.	1991	12.50	13

*Quotes have been rounded up to nearest dollar

ORNAMENTS

Treasury Masterpiece Editions/Enesco
to Treasury Masterpiece Editions/Enesco

YEAR ISSUE		EDITION LIMIT	YEAR RETD.	ISSUE PRICE	*QUOTE U.S.$
1990	Garfield NFL Pittsburg Steelers 573035 - J. Davis	2-Yr.	1991	12.50	13
1990	Garfield NFL Denver Broncos 573043 - J. Davis	2-Yr.	1991	12.50	13
1990	Garfield NFLKansas City Chiefs 573051 - J. Davis	2-Yr.	1991	12.50	13
1990	Garfield NFL Los Angeles Raiders 573078 - J. Davis	2-Yr.	1991	12.50	13
1990	Garfield NFL San Diego Chargers 573086 - J. Davis	2-Yr.	1991	12.50	13
1990	Garfield NFL Seattle Seahawks 573094 - J. Davis	2-Yr.	1991	12.50	13
1990	Garfield NFL Buffalo Bills 573108 - J. Davis	2-Yr.	1991	12.50	13
1990	Garfield NFL Indianapolis Colts 573116 - J. Davis	2-Yr.	1991	12.50	13
1990	Garfield NFL Miami Dolphins 573124 - J. Davis	2-Yr.	1991	12.50	13
1990	Garfield NFL New England Patriots 573132 - J. Davis	2-Yr.	1991	12.50	13
1990	Garfield NFL New York Jets 573140 - J. Davis	2-Yr.	1991	12.50	13
1990	Garfield NFL Atlanta Falcons 573159 - J. Davis	2-Yr.	1991	12.50	13
1990	Garfield NFL New Orleans Saints 573167 - J. Davis	2-Yr.	1991	12.50	13
1990	Garfield NFL San Francisco 49ers 573175 - J. Davis	2-Yr.	1991	12.50	13
1990	Garfield NFL Dallas Cowboys 573183 - J. Davis	2-Yr.	1991	12.50	13
1990	Garfield NFL New York Giants 573191 - J. Davis	2-Yr.	1991	12.50	13
1990	Garfield NFL Philadelphia Eagles 573205 - J. Davis	2-Yr.	1991	12.50	13
1990	Garfield NFL Phoenix Cardinals 573213 - J. Davis	2-Yr.	1991	12.50	13
1990	Garfield NFL Washington Redskins 573221 - J. Davis	2-Yr.	1991	12.50	13
1990	Garfield NFL Chicago Bears 573248 - J. Davis	2-Yr.	1991	12.50	13
1990	Garfield NFL Detroit Lions 573256 - J. Davis	2-Yr.	1991	12.50	13
1990	Garfield NFL Green Bay Packers 573264 - J. Davis	2-Yr.	1991	12.50	13
1990	Garfield NFLMinnesota Vikings 573272 - J. Davis	2-Yr.	1991	12.50	13
1990	Garfield NFL Tampa Bay Buccaneers 573280 - J. Davis	2-Yr.	1991	12.50	13
1991	Tea For Two 573299 - Hahn	3-Yr.	1993	30.00	50
1991	Hot Stuff Santa 573523	Yr.Iss.	1991	25.00	30
1990	Merry Moustronauts 573558 - M. Cook	3-Yr.	1992	20.00	40
1991	Santa Wings It 573612 - J. Jonik	3-Yr.	1993	13.00	13
1990	All Eye Want For Christmas 573617 - Gilmore	3-Yr.	1992	27.50	32
1990	Stuck On You 573655 - Gilmore	2-Yr.	1991	12.50	13
1990	Professor Michael Bear, The One Bear Band 573663 - Gilmore	3-Yr.	1992	22.50	28
1990	A Caroling Wee Go 573671 - Gilmore	3-Yr.	1992	12.00	12
1990	Merry Mailman 573698 - Gilmore	2-Yr.	1991	15.00	30
1990	Deck The Halls 573701 - Gilmore	3-Yr.	1992	22.50	30
1992	Sundae Ride 583707	2-Yr.	1993	20.00	20
1990	You're Wheel Special 573728 - Gilmore	3-Yr.	1992	15.00	15
1991	Come Let Us Adore Him 573736 - Gilmore	2-Yr.	1992	9.00	9
1991	Moon Beam Dreams 573760 - Gilmore	3-Yr.	1993	12.00	12
1991	A Song For Santa 573779 - Gilmore	3-Yr.	1993	25.00	25
1990	Warmest Wishes 573825 - Gilmore	Yr.Iss.	1990	17.50	25
1991	Kurious Kitty 573868 - Gilmore	3-Yr.	1993	17.50	18
1990	Old Mother Mouse 573922 - Gilmore	2-Yr.	1991	17.50	20-32
1990	Railroad Repairs 573930 - Gilmore	2-Yr.	1991	12.50	25
1990	Ten Lords A-Leaping 573949 - Gilmore	3-Yr.	1992	15.00	25
1990	Eleven Drummers Drumming 573957 - Gilmore	3-Yr.	1992	15.00	25
1990	Twelve Pipers Piping 573965 - Gilmore	3-Yr.	1992	15.00	25
1990	Baby's First Christmas 1990 573973 - Gilmore	Yr.Iss.	1990	10.00	N/A
1990	Baby's First Christmas 1990 573981 - Gilmore	Yr.Iss.	1990	12.00	N/A
1991	Peter, Peter Pumpkin Eater 574015 - Gilmore	2-Yr.	1992	20.00	30
1992	The Nutcracker 574023 - Gilmore	3-Yr.	1994	25.00	25
1990	Little Jack Horner 574058 - Gilmore	2-Yr.	1991	17.50	35
1991	Mary, Mary Quite Contrary 574066 - Gilmore	2-Yr.	1992	22.50	33
1992	Humpty Dumpty 574244 - Gilmore	2-Yr.	1993	25.00	25
1991	Through The Years 574252 - Gilmore	Yr.Iss.	1991	17.50	18
1991	Holiday Wing Ding 574333	3-Yr.	1993	22.50	23
1991	North Pole Here I Come 574597	3-Yr.	1993	10.00	10
1991	Christmas Caboose 574856 - Gilmore	2-Yr.	1992	25.00	30
1990	Bubble Trouble 575038 - Hahn	3-Yr.	1992	20.00	35
1991	Merry Mother-To-Be 575046 - Hahn	3-Yr.	1993	13.50	14
1990	A Holiday 'Scent' Sation 575054 - Hahn	3-Yr.	1992	15.00	30
1990	Catch Of The Day 575070 - Hahn	3-Yr.	1992	25.00	25
1990	Don't Open 'Til Christmas 575089 - Hahn	3-Yr.	1992	17.50	18
1990	I Can't Weight 'Til Christmas 575119 - Hahn	3-Yr.	1992	16.50	30
1991	Deck The Halls 575127 - Hahn	2-Yr.	1992	15.00	25
1992	Music Mice-Tro! 575143	2-Yr.	1993	12.00	12
1990	Mouse House 575186	3-Yr.	1992	16.00	16
1991	Dream A Little Dream 575593	2-Yr.	1992	17.50	18
1991	Christmas Two-gether 575615 - L. Rigg	3-Yr.	1993	22.50	23
1992	On Target Two-Gether 575623	Yr.Iss.	1992	17.00	17
1991	Christmas Trimmings 575631	2-Yr.	1992	17.00	17
1991	Gumball Wizard 575658 - Gilmore	2-Yr.	1992	13.00	13
1991	Crystal Ball Christmas 575666 - Gilmore	2-Yr.	1992	22.50	23
1990	Old King Cole 575682 - Gilmore	2-Yr.	1991	20.00	29
1991	Tom, Tom The Piper's Son 575690 - Gilmore	2-Yr.	1992	15.00	33
1992	Rock-A-Bye Baby 575704 - Gilmore	2-Yr.	1993	13.50	14
1992	Queen of Hearts 575712 - Gilmore	2-Yr.	1992	17.50	18
1993	Toy To The World 575763	2-Yr.	1994	25.00	25
1992	Tasty Tidings 575836 - L. Rigg	Yr.Iss.	1992	13.50	14
1991	Tire-d Little Bear 575852 - L. Rigg	Yr.Iss.	1991	12.50	13
1990	Baby Bear Christmas 1990 575860 - L. Rigg	Yr.Iss.	1990	12.00	28
1991	Crank Up The Carols 575887 - L. Rigg	2-Yr.	1992	17.50	18
1990	Beary Christmas 1990 576158 - L. Rigg	Yr.Iss.	1990	12.00	12
1991	Merry Christmas (Boy) 576166 - L. Rigg	Yr.Iss.	1991	13.00	13
1991	Merry Christmas (Girl) 576174 - L. Rigg	Yr.Iss.	1991	13.00	13
1991	Christmas Cutie 576182	3-Yr.	1993	13.50	14
1991	Meow Mates 576220	3-Yr.	1993	12.00	12
1991	Frosty The Snowmant 576425	3-Yr.	1993	15.00	15
1991	Ris-ski Business 576719 - T. Wilson	2-Yr.	1992	10.00	10
1991	Pinocchio 577391 - J. Davis	3-Yr.	1993	15.00	15
1990	Yuletide Ride 1990 577502 - Gilmore	Yr.Iss.	1990	13.50	50
1990	Tons of Toys 577510	Yr.Iss.	1990	13.00	30
1990	McHappy Holidays 577529	2-Yr.	1991	17.50	25
1990	Heading For Happy Holidays 577537	3-Yr.	1992	17.50	18
1990	'Twas The Night Before Christmas 577545	3-Yr.	1992	17.50	18
1990	Over One Million Holiday Wishes! 577553	Yr.Iss.	1990	17.50	30
1990	You Malt My Heart 577596	2-Yr.	1991	25.00	25
1991	All I Want For Christmas 577618	2-Yr.	1992	20.00	20
1992	Bearly Sleepy 578029 - Gilmore	Yr.Iss.	1992	17.50	18
1994	Buttons 'N' Bow Boutique 578363 - Gilmore	Yr.Iss.	1995	22.50	23
1992	Spreading Sweet Joy 580465	Yr.Iss.	1992	13.50	14
1991	Things Go Better With Coke™ 580597	3-Yr.	1993	17.00	25
1991	Christmas To Go 580600 - M. Cook	Yr.Iss.	1991	22.50	23
1991	Have A Mariachi Christmas 580619 - M. Cook	2-Yr.	1992	13.50	14
1993	Bearly Balanced 580724	Yr.Iss.	1993	15.00	15
1992	Ring My Bell 580740 - J. Davis	Yr.Iss.	1992	13.50	14
1992	4 x 4 Holiday Fun 580783 - J. Davis	2-Yr.	1993	20.00	20
1991	Christmas Is In The Air 581453	Yr.Iss.	1991	15.00	15
1991	Holiday Treats 581542	Yr.Iss.	1991	17.50	18
1991	Christmas Is My Goal 581550	2-Yr.	1992	17.50	18
1991	A Quarter Pounder With Cheer® 581569	3-Yr.	1993	20.00	20
1992	The Holidays Are A Hit 581577	2-Yr.	1993	17.50	18
1991	From The Same Mold 581798 - Gilmore	3-Yr.	1993	17.00	17
1991	The Glow Of Christmas 581801	2-Yr.	1992	20.00	20
1992	Tip Top Tidings 581828	2-Yr.	1993	13.00	13
1994	A Sign of Peace 581992	Yr.Iss.	1994	18.50	19
1992	Christmas Lifts The Spirits 582018	2-Yr.	1993	25.00	25
1993	Joyeux Noel 582026	2-Yr.	1994	24.50	25
1992	A Pound Of Good Cheers 582034	2-Yr.	1993	17.50	18
1994	Wishing You Well At Christmas 582050	Yr.Iss.	1994	25.00	25
1994	Ahoy Joy! 582085	Yr.Iss.	1994	20.00	20
1993	Holiday Mew-Sic 582107	2-Yr.	1994	20.00	20
1993	Santa's Magic Ride 582115	2-Yr.	1994	24.00	24
1994	Santa...Phone Home 582166	Yr.Iss.	1994	25.00	25
1993	Warm And Hearty Wishes 582344	Yr.Iss.	1993	17.50	18
1993	Cool Yule 582352	Yr.Iss.	1993	12.00	12
1994	Christmas Swishes 582379	Yr.Iss.	1994	17.50	18
1993	Have A Holly Jell-O Christmas 582387	Yr.Iss.	1993	14.50	45
1994	The Latest Scoop From Santa 582395 - Gilmore	Yr.Iss.	1994	18.50	19
1994	Chiminy Cheer 582409 - Gilmore	Yr.Iss.	1994	22.50	23
1994	Cozy Candlelight Dinner 582417 - Gilmore	Yr.Iss.	1994	25.00	25
1994	Fine Feathered Festivities 582425 - Gilmore	Yr.Iss.	1994	22.50	23
1994	Joy From Head To Hose 582433 - Gilmore	Yr.Iss.	1994	15.00	15
1993	Festive Firemen 582565 - Gilmore	2-Yr.	1994	17.00	17
1991	Lights..Camera..Kissmas! 583626 - Gilmore	Yr.Iss.	1991	15.00	35
1991	All Caught Up In Christmas 583537	2-Yr.	1992	10.00	10
1991	Sweet Steed 583634 - Gilmore	3-Yr.	1993	15.00	15
1992	Sweet as Cane Be 583642 - Gilmore	3-Yr.	1994	15.00	15
1991	Dreamin' Of A White Christmas 583669 - Gilmore	2-Yr.	1992	15.00	15
1991	Merry Millimeters 583677 - Gilmore	3-Yr.	1993	17.00	17
1991	Here's The Scoop 583693	2-Yr.	1992	13.50	20
1991	Happy Meal® On Wheels 583715	3-Yr.	1993	22.50	23
1991	Christmas Kayak 583723	2-Yr.	1992	13.50	14
1993	Light Up Your Holidays With Coke 583758	Yr.Iss.	1993	27.50	28
1992	The Cold, Crisp Taste Of Coke 583766	3-Yr.	1994	17.00	17
1991	Marilyn Monroe 583774	Yr.Iss.	1991	20.00	20
1992	Sew Christmasy 583820	3-Yr.	1994	25.00	25
1991	A Christmas Carol 583928 - Gilmore	3-Yr.	1993	22.50	23
1991	Checking It Twice 583936	2-Yr.	1992	25.00	25
1992	Catch A Falling Star 583944 - Gilmore	2-Yr.	1993	15.00	15
1992	Swingin' Christmas 584096	2-Yr.	1993	15.00	15
1994	Yuletide Yummies 584835 - Gilmore	Yr.Iss.	1994	20.00	20
1993	Pool Hall-idays 584851	2-Yr.	1994	19.00	20
1994	Merry Christmas Tool You, Dad 584886	Yr.Iss.	1994	22.50	23
1994	Exercising Good Taste 584967	Yr.Iss.	1994	17.50	18
1994	Holiday Chew-Chew 584983 - Gilmore	Yr.Iss.	1994	22.50	23
1992	Mc Ho, Ho, Ho 585181	3-Yr.	1994	22.50	23
1991	Merry Christmas Go-Round 585203 - J. Davis	3-Yr.	1993	20.00	20
1992	Holiday On Ice 585254 - J. Davis	3-Yr.	1994	17.50	18
1991	Holiday Hideout 585270 - J. Davis	2-Yr.	1992	15.00	15
1992	Fast Track Cat 585289 - J. Davis	3-Yr.	1994	17.50	18
1992	Holiday Cat Napping 585319 - J. Davis	2-Yr.	1993	20.00	20
1993	Bah Humbug 585394 - Davis	Yr.Iss.	1993	15.00	15
1992	The Finishing Touches 585610 - T. Wilson	2-Yr.	1993	17.50	18
1992	Jolly Ol' Gent 585645 - J. Jonik	3-Yr.	1994	13.50	14
1991	Our Most Precious Gift 585726	Yr.Iss.	1991	17.50	18
1991	Christmas Cheer 585769	2-Yr.	1992	13.50	14
1993	Chimer 585777 - Zimnicki	Yr.Iss.	1993	25.00	25
1993	Sweet Whiskered Wishes 585807	Yr.Iss.	1993	17.00	17
1993	Grade "A" Wishes From Garfield 585823 - Davis	2-Yr.	1994	20.00	20
1992	A Child's Christmas 586358	3-Yr.	1994	25.00	25
1992	Festive Fiddlers 586501	Yr.Iss.	1992	20.00	25
1992	La Luminaria 586579 - M. Cook	2-Yr.	1993	13.50	14
1991	Fired Up For Christmas 586587 - Gilmore	2-Yr.	1992	32.50	33
1991	One Foggy Christmas Eve 586625 - Gilmore	3-Yr.	1993	30.00	30
1991	For A Purr-fect Mom 586641 - Gilmore	Yr.Iss.	1991	12.00	12
1991	For A Special Dad 586668 - Gilmore	Yr.Iss.	1991	17.50	18
1991	With Love 586676 - Gilmore	Yr.Iss.	1991	13.00	13
1991	For A Purr-fect Aunt 586692 - Gilmore	Yr.Iss.	1991	12.00	12
1991	For A Dog-Gone Great Uncle 586706 - Gilmore	Yr.Iss.	1991	12.00	12
1991	Peddling Fun 586714 - Gilmore	Yr.Iss.	1991	16.00	16
1991	Special Keepsakes 586722 - Gilmore	Yr.Iss.	1991	13.50	14
1992	Cozy Chrismas Carriage 586730 - Gilmore	2-Yr.	1993	22.50	23
1992	Small Fry's First Christmas 586749	2-Yr.	1993	17.00	17
1991	Hats Off To Christmas 586757 - Hahn	Yr.Iss.	1991	22.50	23
1992	Friendships Preserved 586765 - Hahn	Yr.Iss.	1992	22.50	23
1995	Sweet Harmony 586773 - Gilmore	Yr.Iss.	1995	17.50	18
1993	Tree For Two 586781 - Gilmore	2-Yr.	1994	17.50	18
1993	A Bright Idea 586803 - Gilmore	2-Yr.	1994	22.50	23
1992	Window Wish List 586854 - Gilmore	2-Yr.	1993	30.00	30
1992	Through The Years 586862 - Gilmore	Yr.Iss.	1992	17.50	18
1993	Baby's First Christmas 1993 586870 - Gilmore	Yr.Iss.	1993	17.50	18
1993	My Special Christmas 586900 - Gilmore	Yr.Iss.	1993	17.50	18
1991	Baby's First Christmas 1991 586935	Yr.Iss.	1991	12.50	13
1992	Baby's First Christmas 1992 586943	Yr.Iss.	1992	12.50	13
1992	Firehouse Friends 586951 - Gilmore	Yr.Iss.	1992	22.50	23
1992	Bubble Buddy 586978 - Gilmore	2-Yr	1993	13.50	14
1992	The Warmth Of The Season 586994	2-Yr.	1993	20.00	20
1993	Baby's First Christmas Dinner 587001	Yr.Iss.	1993	12.00	12
1991	Jugglin' The Holidays 587028	2-Yr.	1992	13.00	13
1991	Santa's Steed 587044	Yr.Iss.	1991	15.00	15
1991	A Decade of Treasures 587052 - Gilmore	Yr.Iss.	1991	37.50	75
1992	It's A Go For Christmas 587095 - Gilmore	2-Yr.	1993	15.00	15
1991	Mr. Mailmouse 587109 - Gilmore	2-Yr.	1992	17.00	17
1992	Post-Mouster General 587117 - Gilmore	2-Yr.	1993	20.00	20
1992	To A Deer Baby 587168	Yr.Iss.	1992	18.50	19
1991	Starry Eyed Santa 587176	2-Yr.	1992	15.00	15
1992	Moon Watch 587184	2-Yr.	1993	20.00	20
1992	Guten Cheers 587192	Yr.Iss.	1992	22.50	23
1992	Put On A Happy Face 588237	2-Yr.	1993	15.00	15
1992	Beginning To Look A Lot Like Christmas 588253	2-Yr.	1993	15.00	15
1992	A Christmas Toast 588261	2-Yr.	1993	20.00	20
1992	Merry Mistle-Toad 588288	2-Yr.	1993	15.00	15
1992	Tic-Tac-Mistle-Toe 588296	3-Yr.	1994	23.00	23
1993	A Pause For Claus 588318	2-Yr.	1994	22.50	23
1992	Heaven Sent 588423 - J. Penchoff	2-Yr.	1993	12.50	13
1992	Holiday Happenings 588555 - Gilmore	3-Yr.	1994	30.00	30

*Quotes have been rounded up to nearest dollar

Collectors' Information Bureau

183

ORNAMENTS

YEAR ISSUE		EDITION LIMIT	YEAR RETD.	ISSUE PRICE	*QUOTE U.S.$
1993	Not A Creature Was Stirring... 588563 - Gilmore	2-Yr.	1994	27.50	28
1992	Seed-son's Greetings 588571 - Gilmore	3-Yr.	1994	27.00	27
1992	Santa's Midnight Snack 588598 - Gilmore	2-Yr.	1993	20.00	20
1992	Trunk Of Treasures 588636	Yr.Iss.	1992	20.00	20
1993	Terrific Toys 588644	Yr.Iss.	1993	20.00	20
1993	Christmas Dancer 588652	Yr.Iss.	1993	15.00	15
1995	Yule Tide Prancer 588660	Yr.Iss.	1995	15.00	15
1994	To The Sweetest Baby 588725 - Gilmore	Yr.Iss.	1994	18.50	19
1995	Baby's Sweet Feast 588733 - Gilmore	Yr.Iss.		17.50	19
1991	Lighting The Way 588776	2-Yr.	1992	20.00	20
1991	Rudolph 588784	2-Yr.	1992	17.50	18
1992	Festive Newsflash 588792	2-Yr.	1993	17.50	18
1992	A-B-C-Son's Greetings 588806	2-Yr.	1993	16.50	17
1992	Hoppy Holidays 588814	Yr.Iss.	1992	13.50	14
1992	Fireside Friends 588830	2-Yr.	1993	20.00	20
1992	Christmas Eve-mergency 588849	2-Yr.	1993	27.00	27
1992	A Sure Sign Of Christmas 588857	2-Yr.	1993	22.50	23
1992	Holidays Give Me A Lift 588865	2-Yr.	1993	30.00	30
1992	Yule Tide Together 588903	2-Yr.	1993	20.00	20
1992	Have A Soup-er Christmas 588911	2-Yr.	1993	17.50	18
1992	Christmas Cure-Alls 588938	2-Yr.	1993	20.00	20
1993	Countin' On A Merry Christmas 588954	2-Yr.	1994	22.50	23
1994	Rockin' Ranger 588970	Yr.Iss.	1994	25.00	25
1994	Peace On Earthworm 588989	Yr.Iss.	1994	20.00	20
1993	To My Gem 589004	Yr.Iss.	1993	27.50	28
1993	Christmas Mail Call 589012	2-Yr.	1994	20.00	20
1993	Spreading Joy 589047	2-Yr.	1994	27.50	28
1993	Pitter-Patter Post Office 589055	2-Yr.	1994	20.00	20
1994	Good Things Crop Up At Christmas 589071	Yr.Iss.	1994	25.00	25
1993	Happy Haul-idays 589098	2-Yr.	1994	30.00	30
1994	Christmas Crossroads 589128	Yr.Iss.	1994	20.00	20
1993	Hot Off ThePress 589292	2-Yr.	1994	27.50	28
1993	Designed With You In Mind 589306	2-Yr.	1994	16.00	16
1992	Dial 'S' For Santa 589373	2-Yr.	1993	25.00	25
1993	Seeing Is Believing 589381 - Gilmore	2-Yr.	1994	20.00	20
1992	Joy To The Whirled 589551 - Hahn	2-Yr.	1993	20.00	20
1992	Merry Make-Over 589586 - Hahn	3-Yr.	1994	20.00	20
1992	Campin' Companions 590282 - Hahn	3-Yr.	1994	20.00	20
1994	Have A Ball At Christmas 590673	Yr.Iss.	1994	15.00	15
1992	Fur-Ever Friends 590797 - Gilmore	2-Yr.	1993	13.50	14
1993	Roundin' Up Christmas Together 590800	Yr.Iss.	1993	25.00	25
1994	Have A Totem-ly Terrific Christmas 590819	Yr.Iss.	1994	30.00	30
1992	Tee-rific Holidays 590827	3-Yr.	1994	25.00	25
1992	Spinning Christmas Dreams 590908 - Hahn	3-Yr.	1994	22.50	23
1992	Christmas Trimmin' 590932	3-Yr.	1994	17.00	17
1993	Toasty Tidings 590940	2-Yr.	1994	20.00	20
1993	Focusing On Christmas 590983 - Gilmore	2-Yr.	1994	27.50	28
1993	Dunk The Halls 591009	2-Yr.	1994	18.50	19
1993	Mice Capades 591386 - Hahn	2-Yr.	1994	26.50	27
1993	25 Points For Christmas 591750	Yr.Iss.	1993	25.00	25
1994	Cocoa 'N' Kisses For Santa- 591939	Yr.Iss.	1995	22.50	23
1994	On The Road With Coke™ 592528	Yr.Iss.	1995	25.00	25
1993	Carving Christmas Wishes 592625 - Gilmore	2-Yr.	1994	25.00	25
1995	A Well, Balanced Meal For Santa 592633	Yr.Iss.	1995	17.50	18
1994	What's Shakin' For Christmas 592668	Yr.Iss.	1994	18.50	19
1994	"A" For Santa 592676	Yr.Iss.	1994	17.50	18
1993	Celebrating With A Splash 592692	Yr.Iss.	1993	17.00	17
1994	Christmas Fly-By 592714	Yr.Iss.	1994	15.00	15
1993	Slimmin' Santa 592722	Yr.Iss.	1993	18.50	24
1993	Plane Ol' Holiday Fun 592773	Yr.Iss.	1993	27.50	28
1995	Salute 593133	Yr.Iss.	1995	22.50	23
1992	Wrappin' Up Warm Wishes 593141	Yr.Iss.	1992	17.50	18
1992	Christmas Biz 593168	2-Yr.	1993	22.50	23
1993	Smooth Move, Mom 593176	Yr.Iss.	1993	20.00	20
1993	Tool TIme, Yule TIme 593192	Yr.Iss.	1993	18.50	19
1993	Speedy 593370 - Zimnicki	2-Yr.	1994	25.00	25
1992	Holiday Take-Out 593508	Yr.Iss.	1992	17.50	18
1992	A Christmas Yarn 593516 - Gilmore	Yr.Iss.	1992	20.00	20
1993	On Your Mark, Set, Is That To Go? 593524	Yr.Iss.	1993	13.50	14
1993	Do Not Open 'Til Christmas 593737 - Hahn	2-Yr.	1994	15.00	15
1993	Greetings In Stereo 593745 - Hahn	Yr.Iss.	1993	19.50	20
1994	Santa...You're The Pops! 593761	Yr.Iss.	1994	22.50	23
1992	Treasure The Earth 593826 - Hahn	2-Yr.	1993	25.00	25
1994	Purdy Packages, Pardner! 593834	Yr.Iss.	1994	20.00	20
1994	Handle With Care 593842	Yr.Iss.	1994	20.00	20
1994	To Coin A Phrase, Merry Christmas 593877	Yr.Iss.	1994	20.00	20
1994	Featured Presentation 593885	Yr.Iss.	1994	20.00	20
1994	Christmas Fishes From Santa Paws 593893	Yr.Iss.	1994	18.50	19
1993	Tangled Up For Christmas 593974	2-Yr.	1994	14.50	15
1992	Toyful' Rudolph 593982	2-Yr.	1993	22.50	23
1992	Take A Chance On The Holidays 594075	3-Yr.	1994	20.00	20
1993	Sweet Season's Eatings 594202	Yr.Iss.	1993	22.50	23
1993	Have A Darn Good Christmas 594229 - Gilmore	2-Yr.	1994	21.00	21
1994	You Melt My Heart 594237 - Gilmore	Yr.Iss.	1994	15.00	15
1993	The Sweetest Ride 594253 - Gilmore	2-Yr.	1994	18.50	19
1994	Finishing First 594342 - Gilmore	Yr.Iss.	1994	20.00	20
1992	Lights..Camera..Christmas! 594369	2-Yr.	1993	20.00	20
1994	Yule Fuel 594385	Yr.Iss.	1994	20.00	20
1992	Spirited Stallion 594407	Yr.Iss.	1992	15.00	15
1993	Have A Cheery Christmas, Sister 594687	Yr.Iss.	1993	13.50	14
1993	Say Cheese 594962 - Gilmore	2-Yr.	1994	13.50	14
1993	Christmas Kicks 594989	Yr.Iss.	1993	17.50	18
1993	Time For Santa 594997 - Gilmore	2-Yr.	1994	17.50	18
1993	Holiday Orders 595004	Yr.Iss.	1993	20.00	20
1993	'Twas The Night Before Christmas 595012	Yr.Iss.	1993	22.50	23
1995	Filled To The Brim 595039 - Gilmore	Yr.Iss.	1995	25.00	25
1994	Toy Tinker Topper 595047 - Gilmore	Yr.Iss.	1994	20.00	20
1993	Sugar Chef Shoppe 595055 - Gilmore	2-Yr.	1994	23.50	24
1993	Merry Mc-Choo-Choo 595063	Yr.Iss.	1993	30.00	30
1993	Merry Christmas, Daughter 595098	Yr.Iss.	1993	20.00	20
1993	Rockin' With Santa 595195	2-Yr.	1994	13.50	14
1994	Santa Claus Is Comin' 595209	Yr.Iss.	1994	20.00	20
1993	Christmas-To-Go 595217	Yr.Iss.	1993	25.50	26
1994	Seasoned With Love 595268	Yr.Iss.	1994	22.50	23
1993	Sleddin' Mr. Snowman 595276	2-Yr.	1994	13.00	13
1993	A Kick Out Of Christmas 595373	2-Yr.	1994	10.00	10
1993	Friends Through Thick And Thin 595381	2-Yr.	1994	10.00	10
1993	See-Saw Sweethearts 595403	2-Yr.	1994	10.00	10
1993	Special Delivery For Santa 595411	2-Yr.	1994	10.00	10
1993	Top Marks For Teacher 595438	2-Yr.	1994	10.00	10
1993	Home Tweet Home 595446	2-Yr.	1994	10.00	10
1993	Clownin' Around 595454	2-Yr.	1994	10.00	10
1993	Heart Filled Dreams 595462	2-Yr.	1994	10.00	10
1993	Merry Christmas Baby 595470	2-Yr.	1994	10.00	10
1994	Sweet Dreams 595489	Yr.Iss.	1994	12.50	13
1994	Peace On Earth 595497	Yr.Iss.	1994	12.50	13
1994	Christmas Two-gether 595500	Yr.Iss.	1994	12.50	13
1994	Santa's L'il Helper 595519	Yr.Iss.	1994	12.50	13
1994	Expecting Joy 595527 - Hahn	Yr.Iss.	1994	12.50	13
1993	Your A Hit With Me, Brother 595535 - Hahn	Yr.Iss.	1993	10.00	10
1993	For A Sharp Uncle 595543	Yr.Iss.	1993	10.00	10
1993	Paint Your Holidays Bright 595551 - Hahn	2-Yr.	1994	10.00	10
1994	Sweet Greetings 595578	Yr.Iss.	1994	12.50	13
1994	Ring In The Holidays 595586 - Hahn	Yr.Iss.	1994	12.50	13
1994	Grandmas Are Sew Special 595594	Yr.Iss.	1994	12.50	13
1994	Holiday Catch 595608 - Hahn	Yr.Iss.	1994	12.50	13
1994	Bubblin' with Joy 595616	Yr.Iss.	1994	12.50	13
1992	A Watchful Eye 595713	Yr.Iss.	1992	15.00	15
1992	Good Catch 595721	Yr.Iss.	1992	12.50	13
1992	Squirrelin' It Away 595748 - Hahn	Yr.Iss.	1992	12.00	12
1992	Checkin' His List 595756	Yr.Iss.	1992	12.50	13
1992	Christmas Cat Nappin' 595764	Yr.Iss.	1992	12.00	12
1992	Bless Our Home 595772	Yr.Iss.	1992	12.00	12
1992	Salute the Season 595780 - Hahn	Yr.Iss.	1992	12.00	12
1992	Fired Up For Christmas 595799	Yr.Iss.	1992	12.00	12
1992	Speedin' Mr. Snowman 595802 - M. Rhyner-Nadig	Yr.Iss.	1992	12.00	12
1992	Merry Christmas Mother Earth 595810 - Hahn	Yr.Iss.	1992	11.00	11
1994	Mine, Mine, Mine 585815 - Davis	Yr.Iss.	1994	20.00	20
1992	Wear The Season With A Smile 595829	Yr.Iss.	1992	10.00	10
1992	Jesus Loves Me 595837 - Hahn	Yr.Iss.	1992	10.00	10
1994	Good Friends Are Forever 595950 - Gilmore	Yr.Iss.	1994	13.50	14
1993	Treasure The Holidays, Man! 596051	Yr.Iss.	1993	22.50	23
1993	Ariel's Under-The-Sea Tree 596078	Yr.Iss.	1993	20.00	20
1993	Here Comes Santa Claws 596086	Yr.Iss.	1993	22.50	35
1993	A Spot of Love 596094	Yr.Iss.	1993	17.50	18
1993	Hearts Aglow 596108	Yr.Iss.	1993	18.50	35
1993	Love's Sweet Dance 596116	Yr.Iss.	1993	25.00	25
1993	Holiday Wishes 596124	Yr.Iss.	1993	15.00	15
1993	Hangin Out For The Holidays 596132	Yr.Iss.	1993	15.00	35
1993	Magic Carpet Ride 596140	Yr.Iss.	1993	20.00	20
1993	Holiday Treasures 596159	Yr.Iss.	1993	18.50	35
1993	Happily Ever After 596167	Yr.Iss.	1993	22.50	23
1993	The Fairest Of Them All 596175	Yr.Iss.	1993	18.50	19
1994	Christmas Tee Time 596256	Yr.Iss.	1995	25.00	25
1994	Have a Merry Dairy Christmas 596264	Yr.Iss.	1994	22.50	23
1994	Happy Holi-date 596272 - Hahn	Yr.Iss.	1995	22.50	23
1994	O' Come All Ye Faithful 596280 - Hahn	Yr.Iss.	1994	15.00	15
1994	One Small Step... 596299 - Hahn	19,690	1994	25.00	45
1993	December 25...Dear Diary 596809 - Hahn	2-Yr.	1994	10.00	10
1994	Building Memories 596876 - Hahn	Yr.Iss.	1994	25.00	25
1994	Open For Business 596906 - Hahn	Yr.Iss.	1994	17.50	18
1993	Wheel Merry Wishes 596930 - Hahn	2-Yr.	1994	15.00	15
1993	Good Grounds For Christmas 596957 - Hahn	Yr.Iss.	1993	24.50	25
1993	Ducking The Season's Rush 597597	Yr.Iss.	1993	17.50	18
1994	Twas The Nite Before Christmas 597643 - Gilmore	Yr.Iss.	1994	18.50	19
1993	Here Comes Rudolph® 597686	2-Yr.	1994	17.50	18
1993	It's Beginning To Look A Lot Like Christmas 597694	Yr.Iss.	1993	22.50	23
1993	Christmas In The Making 597716	Yr.Iss.	1993	20.00	20
1994	I Can Bear-ly Wait For A Coke™ 597724	Yr.Iss.	1995	18.50	19
1993	Mickey's Holiday Treasure 597759	Yr.Iss.	1993	12.00	12
1993	Dream Wheels/1953 Chevrolet Corvette 597856	Yr.Iss.	1993	29.50	50-75
1994	Gallant Greeting- 598313	Yr.Iss.	1994	15.00	20
1994	Merry Menage 598321	Yr.Iss.	1994	20.00	20
1993	All You Add Is Love 598429	Yr.Iss.	1993	18.50	19
1993	Goofy About Skiing 598631	Yr.Iss.	1993	22.50	23
1994	Ski-son's Greetings 599069	Yr.Iss.	1994	20.00	20
1994	Bundle Of Joy 598992	Yr.Iss.	1994	10.00	15
1994	Bundle Of Joy 599018	Yr.Iss.	1994	10.00	10
1994	Have A Dino-mite Christmas 599026 - Hahn	Yr.Iss.	1994	18.50	19
1994	Good Fortune To You 599034	Yr.Iss.	1994	25.00	25
1994	Building a Sew-man 599042	Yr.Iss.	1994	18.50	19
1994	Merry Memo-ries 599050	Yr.Iss.	1994	22.50	23
1994	Holiday Freezer Teaser 599085 - Gilmore	Yr.Iss.	1994	25.00	25
1994	Almost Time For Santa 599093 - Gilmore	Yr.Iss.	1994	25.00	25
1994	Santa's Secret Test Drive 599107 - Gilmore	Yr.Iss.	1994	20.00	20
1994	You're A Wheel Cool Brother 599115 - Gilmore	Yr.Iss.	1994	22.50	23
1994	Hand-Tossed Tidings 599166	Yr.Iss.	1994	17.50	18
1994	Tasty Take Off 599174	Yr.Iss.	1994	20.00	20
1994	Formula For Love 599530 - Olsen	Yr.Iss.	1994	10.00	10
1994	Santa's Ginger-bred Doe 599697 - Gilmore	Yr.Iss.	1994	15.00	15
1994	Nutcracker Sweetheart 599700	Yr.Iss.	1994	15.00	15
1994	Merry Reindeer Ride 599719	Yr.Iss.	1994	20.00	20
1994	Santa's Sing-A-Long 599727 - Gilmore	Yr.Iss.	1994	20.00	20
1994	A Holiday Opportunity 599735	Yr.Iss.	1995	20.00	20
1994	Holiday Stars 599743	Yr.Iss.	1994	20.00	20
1994	The Latest Mews From Home 653977	Yr.Iss.	1994	16.00	16
1989	Tea For Two 693758 - N. Teiber	2-Yr.	1990	12.50	30
1990	Holiday Tea Toast 694770 - N. Teiber	2-Yr.	1991	13.50	14
1991	It's Tea-lightful 694789	2-Yr.	1992	13.50	14
1989	Tea Time 694797 - N. Teiber	2-Yr.	1990	12.50	30
1989	Bottom's Up 1989 830003	Yr.Iss.	1989	11.00	32
1990	Sweetest Greetings 1990 830011 - Gilmore	Yr.Iss.	1990	10.00	27
1990	First Class Christmas 830038 - Gilmore	3-Yr.	1992	10.00	10
1989	Caught In The Act 830046 - Gilmore	3-Yr.	1991	12.50	13
1989	Readin' & Ridin' 830054 - Gilmore	3-Yr.	1991	13.50	34
1991	Beary Merry Mailman 830151 - L. Rigg	3-Yr.	1993	13.50	14
1990	Here's Looking at You! 830259 - Gilmore	2-Yr.	1991	17.50	18
1991	Stamper 830267 - S. Zimnicki	Yr.Iss.	1991	13.50	14
1991	Santa's Key Man 830461 - Gilmore	2-Yr.	1992	11.00	11
1991	Tie-dings Of Joy 830488 - Gilmore	Yr.Iss.	1991	12.00	12
1990	Have a Cool Yule 830496 - Gilmore	3-Yr.	1992	12.00	27
1990	Slots of Luck 830518 - Hahn	2-Yr.	1991	13.50	45-60
1991	Straight To Santa 830534 - J. Davis	2-Yr.	1992	13.50	14
1993	A Toast Ladled With Love 830828 - Hahn	2-Yr.	1994	15.00	15
1991	Letters To Santa 830925 - Gilmore	2-Yr.	1992	15.00	15
1991	Sneaking Santa's Snack 830933 - Gilmore	3-Yr.	1993	13.00	13
1991	Aiming For The Holidays 830941 - Gilmore	2-Yr.	1992	12.00	12
1991	Ode To Joy 830968 - Gilmore	3-Yr.	1993	10.00	10
1991	Fittin' Mittens 830976 - Gilmore	3-Yr.	1993	12.00	12
1992	Merry Kisses 831166	2-Yr.	1993	17.50	18
1992	Christmas Is In The Air 831174	2-Yr.	1993	25.00	25
1992	To The Point 831182	2-Yr.	1993	13.50	14
1992	Poppin' Hoppin' Holidays 831263 - Gilmore	Yr.Iss.	1992	25.00	25
1992	Tankful Tidings 831271 - Gilmore	2-Yr.	1993	30.00	30
1991	The Finishing Touch 831530 - Gilmore	Yr.Iss.	1991	10.00	10
1992	Ginger-Bred Greetings 831581 - Gilmore	Yr.Iss.	1992	12.00	12
1991	A Real Classic 831603 - Gilmore	Yr.Iss.	1991	10.00	10

*Quotes have been rounded up to nearest dollar

YEAR ISSUE		EDITION LIMIT	YEAR RETD.	ISSUE PRICE	*QUOTE U.S.$
1993	Delivered to The Nick In Time 831808 - Gilmore	2-Yr.	1994	13.50	14
1993	Sneaking A Peek 831840 - Gilmore	2-Yr.	1994	10.00	10
1993	Jewel Box Ballet 831859 - Hahn	2-Yr.	1994	20.00	20
1993	A Mistle-Tow 831867 - Gilmore	2-Yr.	1994	15.00	15
1991	Christmas Fills The Air 831921 - Gilmore	3-Yr.	1993	12.00	12
1992	A Gold Star For Teacher 831948 - Gilmore	3-Yr.	1994	15.00	15
1992	A Tall Order 832758 - Gilmore	3-Yr.	1994	12.00	12
1992	Candlelight Serenade 832766 - Gilmore	2-Yr.	1993	12.00	12
1992	Holiday Glow Puppet Show 832774 - Gilmore	3-Yr.	1994	15.00	15
1992	Christopher Columouse 832782 - Gilmore	Yr.Iss.	1992	12.00	12
1992	Cartin' Home Holiday Treats 832790	2-Yr.	1993	13.50	14
1992	Making Tracks To Santa 832804 - Gilmore	2-Yr.	1993	15.00	15
1992	Special Delivery 832812	2-Yr.	1993	12.00	12
1992	A Mug Full Of Love 832928 Gilmore	Yr.Iss.	1992	13.50	14
1993	Grandma's Liddle Griddle 832936 - Gilmore	Yr.Iss.	1993	10.00	10
1992	Have A Cool Christmas 832944 - Gilmore	Yr.Iss.	1992	13.50	14
1992	Knitten' Kittens 832952 - Gilmore	Yr.Iss.	1992	17.50	18
1992	Holiday Honors 833029 - Gilmore	Yr.Iss.	1992	15.00	15
1993	To A Grade "A" Teacher 833037 - Gilmore	2-Yr.	1994	10.00	10
1992	Christmas Nite Cap 834424 - Gilmore	3-Yr.	1994	13.50	14
1993	Have A Cool Christmas 834467 - Gilmore	2-Yr.	1994	10.00	10
1993	For A Star Aunt 834556 - Gilmore	Yr.Iss.	1993	12.00	12
1994	You're A Winner Son! 834564 - Gilmore	Yr.Iss.	1994	18.50	19
1994	Especially For You 834580 - Gilmore	Yr.Iss.	1994	27.50	28
1992	North Pole Peppermint Patrol 840157 - Gilmore	2-Yr.	1993	25.00	25
1992	A Boot-iful Christmas 840165 - Gilmore	Yr.Iss.	1992	20.00	20
1994	Watching For Santa 840432	2-Yr.	1994	25.00	30
1992	Special Delivery 840440	Yr.Iss.	1992	22.50	23
1991	Deck The Halls 860573 - M. Peters	3-Yr.	1993	12.00	12
1991	Bathing Beauty 860581 - Hahn	3-Yr.	1993	13.50	35

United Design Corp.

Angels Collection-Tree Ornaments™ - P.J. Jonas, unless otherwise noted

YEAR ISSUE		EDITION LIMIT	YEAR RETD.	ISSUE PRICE	*QUOTE U.S.$
1992	Angel and Tambourine IBO-422 - S. Bradford	12/97		20.00	20
1992	Angel and Tambourine, ivory IBO-425 - S. Bradford	12/97		20.00	20
1993	Angel Baby w/ Bunny IBO-426 - D. Newburn	Retrd.	1996	23.00	24
1996	Angel w/Doves on Cloud IBO-472	Open		25.00	25
1996	Angel w/Doves on Cloud, blue IBO-473	Open		25.00	25
1991	Angel Waif, ivory IBO-411	Open		15.00	20
1993	Angel Waif, plum IBO-437	Retrd.	1996	20.00	20
1995	Autumn's Bounty IBO-460	12/97		32.00	32
1995	Autumn's Bounty, light IBO-454	12/97		32.00	32
1995	Birds of a Feather IBO-457	Open		27.00	27
1990	Crystal Angel IBO-401	Retrd.	1993	20.00	20
1993	Crystal Angel, emerald IBO-446	12/97		20.00	20
1990	Crystal Angel, ivory IBO-405	12/97		20.00	20
1991	Fra Angelico Drummer, blue IBO-414 - S. Bradford	12/97		20.00	20
1991	Fra Angelico Drummer, ivory IBO-420 - S. Bradford	12/97		20.00	20
1991	Girl Cupid w/Rose, ivory IBO-413 - S. Bradford	12/97		15.00	20
1995	Heavenly Blossoms IBO-458	12/97		27.00	27
1993	Heavenly Harmony IBO-428	12/97		25.00	30
1993	Heavenly Harmony, crimson IBO-433	Open		22.00	30
1993	Little Angel IBO-430 - D. Newburn	Open		18.00	20
1993	Little Angel, crimson IBO-445 - D. Newburn	Retrd.	1996	18.00	20
1992	Mary and Dove IBO-424 - S. Bradford	12/97		20.00	20
1994	Music and Grace IBO-448	Open		24.00	24
1994	Music and Grace, crimson IBO-449	12/97		24.00	24
1994	Musical Flight IBO-450	12/97		28.00	28
1994	Musical Flight, crimson IBO-451	12/97		28.00	28
1991	Peace Descending, ivory IBO-412	12/97		20.00	20
1993	Peace Descending, crimson IBO-436	12/97		20.00	20
1993	Renaissance Angel IBO-429	12/97		24.00	24
1993	Renaissance Angel, crimson IBO-431	12/97		24.00	24
1990	Rose of Sharon IBO-402	Retrd.	1993	20.00	20
1993	Rose of Sharon, crimson IBO-439	12/97		20.00	20
1990	Rose of Sharon, ivory IBO-406	Open		20.00	20
1993	Rosetti Angel, crimson IBO-434	12/97		20.00	24
1991	Rosetti Angel, ivory IBO-410	Open		20.00	24
1995	Special Wishes IBO-456 - D. Newburn	Open		27.00	27
1995	Spring's Rebirth IBO-452	Open		32.00	32
1996	Spring's Rebirth, green IBO-474	Open		25.00	25
1992	St. Francis and Critters IBO-423 - S. Bradford	12/97		20.00	20
1994	Star Flight IBO-447	Open		20.00	20
1990	Star Glory IBO-403	Retrd.	1993	15.00	15
1993	Star Glory, crimson IBO-438	12/97		20.00	20
1990	Star Glory, ivory IBO-407	12/97		15.00	20
1996	Starflight Sapphire IBO-475	Open		20.00	20
1993	Stars & Lace IBO-427	Open		18.00	20
1993	Stars & Lace, Emerald IBO-432	Open		18.00	20
1995	Summer's Glory IBO-453	Open		32.00	32
1996	Summer's Glory, green IBO-476	Open		25.00	25
1995	Tender Time IBO-459	12/97		27.00	27
1990	Victorian Angel IBO-404	Retrd.	1993	15.00	15
1990	Victorian Angel, ivory IBO-408	12/97		15.00	20
1993	Victorian Angel, plum IBO-435	12/97		18.00	20
1993	Victorian Cupid, crimson IBO-440	Open		15.00	20
1991	Victorian Cupid, ivory IBO-409	Open		15.00	20
1995	Winter's Light IBO-455	12/97		32.00	32
1996	Wooden Angel IBO-461 - M. Ramsey	Open		20.00	20

Teddy Angels™ - P.J. Jonas

YEAR ISSUE		EDITION LIMIT	YEAR RETD.	ISSUE PRICE	*QUOTE U.S.$
1995	Casey "You're a bright & shining star." BA-017	Open		13.00	13
1995	Ivy "Enchantment glows in winter snows." BA-018	Open		13.00	13

Wallace Silversmiths

Annual Pewter Bells - Wallace

YEAR ISSUE		EDITION LIMIT	YEAR RETD.	ISSUE PRICE	*QUOTE U.S.$
1992	Angel	Closed	1992	25.00	30
1993	Santa Holding List	Closed	1993	25.00	25
1994	Large Santa Bell	Closed	1994	25.00	25
1995	Santa Bell	Closed	1995	25.00	25
1996	Santa Bell (North Pole)	Yr.Iss.		25.00	25

Annual Silverplated Sleigh Bells - Wallace

YEAR ISSUE		EDITION LIMIT	YEAR RETD.	ISSUE PRICE	*QUOTE U.S.$
1971	1st Edition Sleigh Bell	Closed	1971	12.95	600-1100
1972	2nd Edition Sleigh Bell	Closed	1972	12.95	300-600
1973	3rd Edition Sleigh Bell	Closed	1973	12.95	350-575
1974	4th Edition Sleigh Bell	Closed	1974	13.95	200-300
1975	5th Edition Sleigh Bell	Closed	1975	13.95	100-225
1976	6th Edition Sleigh Bell	Closed	1976	13.95	100-300
1977	7th Edition Sleigh Bell	Closed	1977	14.95	75-200
1978	8th Edition Sleigh Bell	Closed	1978	14.95	50-120
1979	9th Edition Sleigh Bell	Closed	1979	15.95	50-150
1980	10th Edition Sleigh Bell	Closed	1980	18.95	35-75
1981	11th Edition Sleigh Bell	Closed	1981	18.95	45-100
1982	12th Edition Sleigh Bell	Closed	1982	19.95	45-125
1983	13th Edition Sleigh Bell	Closed	1983	19.95	45-125
1984	14th Edition Sleigh Bell	Closed	1984	[illegible]	[illegible]
1985	15th Edition Sleigh Bell	Closed	1985	21.95	50-100
1986	16th Edition Sleigh Bell	Closed	1986	21.95	35-75
1987	17th Edition Sleigh Bell	Closed	1987	21.99	30-60
1988	18th Edition Sleigh Bell	Closed	1988	21.99	30-60
1989	19th Edition Sleigh Bell	Closed	1989	24.99	30-75
1990	20th Edition Sleigh Bell	Closed	1990	25.00	30-55
1990	Special Edition Sleigh Bell, gold	Closed	1990	35.00	30-85
1991	21st Edition Sleigh Bell	Closed	1991	25.00	30
1992	22th Edition Sleigh Bell	Closed	1992	25.00	30
1993	23rd Edition Sleigh Bell	Closed	1993	25.00	35
1994	24th Edition Sleigh Bell	Closed	1994	25.00	25
1994	Sleigh Bell, gold	Closed	1994	35.00	35
1995	25th Edition Sleigh Bell	Closed	1995	30.00	30
1995	Sleigh Bell, gold	Closed	1995	35.00	35
1996	26th Edition Sleigh Bell	Yr.Iss.		30.00	30
1996	Sleigh Bell, gold	Yr.Iss.		35.00	35

Candy Canes - Wallace

YEAR ISSUE		EDITION LIMIT	YEAR RETD.	ISSUE PRICE	*QUOTE U.S.$
1981	Peppermint	Closed	1981	8.95	125-250
1982	Wintergreen	Closed	1982	9.95	50-100
1983	Cinnamon	Closed	1983	10.95	35-75
1984	Clove	Closed	1984	10.95	35-60
1985	Dove Motif	Closed	1985	11.95	35-70
1986	Bell Motif	Closed	1986	11.95	40-100
1987	Teddy Bear Motif	Closed	1987	12.95	40-110
1988	Christmas Rose	Closed	1988	13.99	35-75
1989	Christmas Candle	Closed	1989	14.99	35-45
1990	Reindeer	Closed	1990	16.00	35
1991	Christmas Goose	Closed	1991	16.00	25
1992	Angel	Closed	1992	16.00	25
1993	Snowmen	Closed	1993	16.00	25
1994	Canes	Closed	1994	17.00	20
1995	Santa	Closed	1995	18.00	20
1996	Soldiers	Yr. Iss.		18.00	18

Cathedral Ornaments - Wallace

YEAR ISSUE		EDITION LIMIT	YEAR RETD.	ISSUE PRICE	*QUOTE U.S.$
1988	1988-1st Edition	Closed	1988	24.99	45
1989	1989-2nd Edition	Closed	1989	24.99	30
1990	1990-3rd Edition	Closed	1990	25.00	25

Grande Baroque 12 Day Series - Wallace

YEAR ISSUE		EDITION LIMIT	YEAR RETD.	ISSUE PRICE	*QUOTE U.S.$
1988	Partridge	Closed	1988	39.99	45-75
1989	Two Turtle Doves	Closed	1989	39.99	45-65
1990	Three French Hens	Closed	1990	40.00	45-65
1991	Four Colly Birds	Closed	1991	40.00	50-75
1992	Five Golden Rings	Closed	1992	40.00	45-60
1993	Six Geese-a-Laying	Closed	1993	40.00	50
1994	Seven Swans-a-Swimming	Closed	1994	40.00	40
1995	Eight Maids-a-Milking	Closed	1995	40.00	40
1996	Nine Ladies Dancing	Yr. Iss.		40.00	50

Walnut Ridge Collectibles

Gossamer Wings - K. Bejma

YEAR ISSUE		EDITION LIMIT	YEAR RETD.	ISSUE PRICE	*QUOTE U.S.$
1996	Charity Piece - Glimmer of Hope I	Yr.Iss.	1996	40.00	40
1997	Charity Piece - Glimmer of Hope II	Yr.Iss.		40.00	40

Limited Edition Christmas Ornament - K. Bejma

YEAR ISSUE		EDITION LIMIT	YEAR RETD.	ISSUE PRICE	*QUOTE U.S.$
1996	Snowy, Snowy Night-703	Yr.Iss.	1996	56.00	56

Ornament Collection - K. Bejma

YEAR ISSUE		EDITION LIMIT	YEAR RETD.	ISSUE PRICE	*QUOTE U.S.$
1997	Acorn-68	Open		22.00	22
1994	Angel Bunny-21	Open		26.00	26
1995	Angel Donkey-24	Open		26.00	26
1995	Angel Elephant-23	Open		26.00	26
1996	Angel Frog-40	Open		22.00	22
1997	Angel Holding Child-52	Open		30.00	30
1993	Angel Icicle-9	Retrd.	1996	22.00	22
1994	Angel Kitty-20	Open		26.00	26
1994	Angel Pig-22	Open		26.00	26
1996	Angel w/Star on Wand-35	Open		24.00	24
1997	Angel with 2 Children-53	Open		30.00	30
1997	Angel with Doves-51	Open		30.00	30
1994	Angels, Set/3-15	Open		66.00	66
1995	Angels, Set/3-18	Open		66.00	66
1997	Artichoke-67	Open		22.00	22
1997	Asparagus-66	Open		22.00	22
1997	Baby on Crescent Moon-50	Open		30.00	30
1993	Baby Snowman Icicle-12	Retrd.	1996	22.00	22
1996	Baby's First-33	Open		30.00	30
1997	Bear Angel-61	Open		26.00	26
1996	Black and White Bunny-28	Open		26.00	26
1997	Blue Father Xmas-56	Open		22.00	22
1996	Calico Cat-27	Open		26.00	26
1995	Carrot-cicle-17	Open		22.00	22
1996	Cat-cicle w/Stocking-37	Open		22.00	22
1996	Cat-cicle-36	Open		22.00	22
1993	Cherub Icicle-8	Retrd.	1996	22.00	22
1997	Chili Pepper-62	Open		22.00	22
1997	Corkscrew Santa-58	Open		22.00	22
1997	Corn-65	Open		22.00	22
1996	Crescent Santa-29	Open		28.00	28
1997	Eggplant-64	Open		22.00	22
1993	Father Christmas Icicle-13	Retrd.	1996	22.00	22
1994	Father Christmas, Set/3-16	Open		66.00	66
1993	Father Snowman Icicle-10	Retrd.	1996	22.00	22
1997	Giraffe Angel-41	Open		28.00	28
1996	Golden Father Christmas-38	Open		24.00	24
1997	Golden Top Father Xmas-57	Open		22.00	22
1997	Green Pepper-63	Open		22.00	22
1997	Ice Top Santa-55	Open		24.00	24
1997	Kangaroo Angel-43	Open		26.00	26
1996	Kitty Angel-34	Open		24.00	24
1993	Mother Snowman Icicle-11	Retrd.	1996	22.00	22
1994	Nutcracker-30	Open		22.00	22
1995	Nutcracker-31	Open		22.00	22
1996	Nutcracker-32	Open		22.00	22
1997	Peach-69	Open		22.00	22
1997	Pinetree Santa-54	Open		24.00	24
1997	Polar Bear Angel-42	Open		26.00	26
1995	Reindeer-26	Open		22.00	22
1997	Santa Bell-59	Open		30.00	30
1997	Santa Face, large-45	Open		30.00	30
1993	Santa Icicle-14	Retrd.	1996	22.00	22
1995	Snow Family, set/3-19	Open		66.00	66
1997	Snowman Face-48	Open		24.00	24
1997	Snowman Icicle/Stocking Hat-47	Open		24.00	24
1997	Snowman Icicle/Top Hat-46	Open		24.00	24
1997	Snowman with Cane-49	Open		26.00	26
1996	Snowman, set/2-39	Open		44.00	44
1997	Tricolor Pinecones, set/3-44	Open		48.00	48
1997	Turtle Angel-60	Open		24.00	24

Walt Disney

Classics Collection-Holiday Series - Disney Studios

YEAR ISSUE		EDITION LIMIT	YEAR RETD.	ISSUE PRICE	*QUOTE U.S.$
1995	Presents For My Pals 41087	Closed	1995	50.00	60
1996	Pluto Helps Decorate 41113	Closed	1996	50.00	50
1997	Chip 'n Dale 41190	Yr.Iss.		50.00	50

Disney's Enchanted Places - Disney Studios

YEAR ISSUE		EDITION LIMIT	YEAR RETD.	ISSUE PRICE	*QUOTE U.S.$
1997	Captain Hook's Ship	Open		45.00	45
1997	Cinderella's Coach	Open		45.00	45
1997	Cruella's Car	Open		45.00	45
1996	Grandpa's House 41222	Open		35.00	35
1997	Mickey's Cratchet	Open		50.00	50
1997	Minnie Cratchet	Open		50.00	50
1997	Scrooge McDuck	Open		50.00	50

PLATES

Ace Product Management Group, Inc.

Good Times Together - B. Otero

YEAR ISSUE		EDITION LIMIT	YEAR RETD.	ISSUE PRICE	*QUOTE U.S.$
1995	Road Trip 99276-95Z	10,000		32.00	32

Harley-Davidson Collector Christmas Plates - Ace

YEAR ISSUE		EDITION LIMIT	YEAR RETD.	ISSUE PRICE	*QUOTE U.S.$
1984	1909 V-Twin 99133-85Z	8,500	1984	19.95	20

*Quotes have been rounded up to nearest dollar

Ace Product Management Group, Inc.
to ANRI

PLATES

YEAR	ISSUE	EDITION LIMIT	YEAR RETD.	ISSUE PRICE	*QUOTE U.S.$
1985	Perfect Tree 99134-86Z	8,500	1985	22.50	23
1986	Mainstreet 99136-87Z	8,500	1986	24.95	25
1987	Joy Of Giving 99133-88Z	8,500	1987	24.95	25
1988	Home For The Holidays 99134-89Z	8,500	1988	29.95	30
1989	29 Days Till Xmas 99134-90Z	8,500	1989	34.95	35
1990	Rural Delivery 99134-91Z	8,500	1990	34.95	35
1991	Skating Party 99138-92Z	8,500	1991	34.95	35
1992	A Surprise Visit 99135-93Z	9,500	1992	38.00	38
1993	Christmas Vacation 99287-94Z	9,500	1993	38.00	38

Harley-Davidson Collector Pewter Decade Series - Ace

YEAR	ISSUE	EDITION LIMIT	YEAR RETD.	ISSUE PRICE	*QUOTE U.S.$
1992	Birth Of Legend-1900's 99139-92Z	3,000	1992	120.00	120
1993	Growth Of Sport-1910's 99129-94Z	3,000	1993	125.00	125
1994	Roaring Into The 20's-1920's 99136-95Z	3,000		130.00	130
1995	Growing Stronger With Time -1930's 99294-96Z	3,000		132.00	132

Harley-Davidson Collector Pewter Plates - Ace

YEAR	ISSUE	EDITION LIMIT	YEAR RETD.	ISSUE PRICE	*QUOTE U.S.$
1988	Winter Gathering 99139-89ZP	3,000	1988	74.95	75
1989	1989 Plate 99139-90ZP	3,000	1989	89.95	90
1990	Spring Races 99136-91ZP	3,000	1990	99.95	100
1990	Summer Tradition 99139-91ZP	3,000	1990	99.95	100

Holiday Memories Christmas Plates - B. Otero

YEAR	ISSUE	EDITION LIMIT	YEAR RETD.	ISSUE PRICE	*QUOTE U.S.$
1984	Under The Mistletoe 99090-95Z	15,000	1994	38.00	38
1995	Late Arrival 99415-96Z	15,000	1995	38.00	38
1996	After The Pageant 99933-97Z	15,000	1996	38.00	38
1997	Roadside Revelation 97963-98Z	15,000		38.00	38

American Artists

The Best of Fred Stone-Mares & Foals Series (6 1/2 ") - F. Stone

YEAR	ISSUE	EDITION LIMIT	YEAR RETD.	ISSUE PRICE	*QUOTE U.S.$
1991	Patience	19,500		25.00	25
1992	Water Trough	19,500		25.00	25
1992	Pasture Pest	19,500		25.00	25
1992	Kidnapped Mare	19,500		25.00	25
1993	Contentment	19,500		25.00	25
1993	Arabian Mare & Foal	19,500		25.00	25
1994	Diamond in the Rough	19,500		25.00	25
1995	The First Day	19,500		25.00	25

Famous Fillies Series - F. Stone

YEAR	ISSUE	EDITION LIMIT	YEAR RETD.	ISSUE PRICE	*QUOTE U.S.$
1987	Lady's Secret	9,500		65.00	70
1988	Ruffian	9,500		65.00	90
1988	Genuine Risk	9,500		65.00	65
1992	Go For The Wand	9,500		65.00	80-90

Fred Stone Classic Series - F. Stone

YEAR	ISSUE	EDITION LIMIT	YEAR RETD.	ISSUE PRICE	*QUOTE U.S.$
1986	The Shoe-8,000 Wins	9,500		75.00	80-90
1986	The Eternal Legacy	9,500		75.00	95
1988	Forever Friends	9,500		75.00	85
1989	Alysheba	9,500		75.00	75

Gold Signature Series - F. Stone

YEAR	ISSUE	EDITION LIMIT	YEAR RETD.	ISSUE PRICE	*QUOTE U.S.$
1990	Secretariat Final Tribute, signed	4,500		150.00	375
1990	Secretariat Final Tribute, unsigned	7,500		75.00	100
1991	Old Warriors, signed	4,500		150.00	425
1991	Old Warriors, unsigned	7,500		75.00	100

Gold Signature Series II - F. Stone

YEAR	ISSUE	EDITION LIMIT	YEAR RETD.	ISSUE PRICE	*QUOTE U.S.$
1991	Northern Dancer, double signature	1,500		175.00	250
1991	Northern Dancer, single signature	3,000		150.00	150
1991	Northern Dancer, unsigned	7,500		75.00	75
1991	Kelso, double signature	1,500		175.00	175
1991	Kelso, single signature	3,000		150.00	150
1991	Kelso, unsigned	7,500		75.00	75

Gold Signature Series III - F. Stone

YEAR	ISSUE	EDITION LIMIT	YEAR RETD.	ISSUE PRICE	*QUOTE U.S.$
1992	Dance Smartly-Pat Day, Up, double signature	1,500		175.00	175
1992	Dance Smartly-Pat Day, Up, single signature	3,000		150.00	150
1992	Dance Smartly-Pat Day, Up, unsigned	7,500		75.00	75
1993	American Triple Crown 1937-1946, signed	2,500		195.00	195
1993	American Triple Crown 1937-1946, unsigned	7,500		75.00	75
1993	American Triple Crown 1948-1978, signed	2,500		195.00	195
1993	American Triple Crown 1948-1978, unsigned	7,500		75.00	175
1994	American Triple Crown 1919-1935, signed	2,500		95.00	95
1994	American Triple Crown 1919-1935, unsigned	7,500		75.00	75

Gold Signature Series IV - F. Stone

YEAR	ISSUE	EDITION LIMIT	YEAR RETD.	ISSUE PRICE	*QUOTE U.S.$
1995	Julie Krone - Colonial Affair	7,500		75.00	75
1995	Julie Krone - Colonial Affair, signed	2,500		150.00	150

The Horses of Fred Stone - F. Stone

YEAR	ISSUE	EDITION LIMIT	YEAR RETD.	ISSUE PRICE	*QUOTE U.S.$
1982	Patience	9,500		55.00	60-75
1982	Arabian Mare and Foal	9,500		55.00	55-100
1982	Safe and Sound	9,500		55.00	75-100
1983	Contentment	9,500		55.00	125

Mare and Foal Series - F. Stone

YEAR	ISSUE	EDITION LIMIT	YEAR RETD.	ISSUE PRICE	*QUOTE U.S.$
1986	Water Trough	12,500		49.50	90-125
1986	Tranquility	12,500		49.50	65
1986	Pasture Pest	12,500		49.50	100
1987	The Arabians	12,500		49.50	55

Mare and Foal Series II - F. Stone

YEAR	ISSUE	EDITION LIMIT	YEAR RETD.	ISSUE PRICE	*QUOTE U.S.$
1989	The First Day	Open		35.00	35
1989	Diamond in the Rough	Retrd.		35.00	35

Racing Legends - F. Stone

YEAR	ISSUE	EDITION LIMIT	YEAR RETD.	ISSUE PRICE	*QUOTE U.S.$
1989	Phar Lap	9,500		75.00	75
1989	Sunday Silence	9,500		75.00	75
1990	John Henry-Shoemaker	9,500		75.00	75

Sport of Kings Series - F. Stone

YEAR	ISSUE	EDITION LIMIT	YEAR RETD.	ISSUE PRICE	*QUOTE U.S.$
1984	Man O'War	9,500		65.00	75-100
1984	Secretariat	9,500		65.00	100-200
1985	John Henry	9,500		65.00	75
1986	Seattle Slew	9,500		65.00	65

The Stallion Series - F. Stone

YEAR	ISSUE	EDITION LIMIT	YEAR RETD.	ISSUE PRICE	*QUOTE U.S.$
1983	Black Stallion	19,500		49.50	150
1983	Andalusian	19,500		49.50	150

Anheuser-Busch, Inc.

1992 Olympic Team Series - A-Busch, Inc.

YEAR	ISSUE	EDITION LIMIT	YEAR RETD.	ISSUE PRICE	*QUOTE U.S.$
1991	1992 Olympic Team Winter Plate N3180	Retrd.	1994	35.00	35
1992	1992 Olympic Team Summer Plate N3122	Retrd.	1994	35.00	35

Archives Plate Series - D. Langeneckert

YEAR	ISSUE	EDITION LIMIT	YEAR RETD.	ISSUE PRICE	*QUOTE U.S.$
1992	1893 Columbian Exposition N3477	25-day	1996	27.50	20-35
1992	Ganymede N4004	25-day	1996	27.50	20-50
1995	Budweiser's Greatest Triumph Plate N5195	25-day	1996	27.50	28-50
1995	Mirror of Truth Plate N5196	25-day		27.50	28

Civil War Series - D. Langeneckert

YEAR	ISSUE	EDITION LIMIT	YEAR RETD.	ISSUE PRICE	*QUOTE U.S.$
1992	General Grant N3478	Retrd.	1994	45.00	45
1993	General Robert E. Lee N3590	Retrd.	1994	45.00	45
1993	President Abraham Lincoln N3591	Retrd.	1994	45.00	45

Collector Edition Series - M. Urdahl

YEAR	ISSUE	EDITION LIMIT	YEAR RETD.	ISSUE PRICE	*QUOTE U.S.$
1995	"This Bud's For You" N4945	25-day		27.50	28

Holiday Plate Series - Various

YEAR	ISSUE	EDITION LIMIT	YEAR RETD.	ISSUE PRICE	*QUOTE U.S.$
1989	Winters Day N2295 - B. Kemper	Retrd.	N/A	30.00	50-100
1990	An American Tradition N2767 - S. Sampson	Retrd.	N/A	30.00	35-45
1991	The Season's Best N3034 - S. Sampson	Retrd.	N/A	30.00	30
1992	A Perfect Christmas N3440 - S. Sampson	Retrd.	N/A	27.50	30
1993	Special Delivery N4002 - N. Koerber	Retrd.	N/A	27.50	45-80
1994	Hometown Holiday N4572 - B. Kemper	Retrd.	N/A	27.50	28
1995	Lighting the Way Home N5215 - T. Jester	25-day		27.50	28
1996	Budweiser Clydesdales N5778 - J. Raedeke	25-day		27.50	28

Man's Best Friend Series - M. Urdahl

YEAR	ISSUE	EDITION LIMIT	YEAR RETD.	ISSUE PRICE	*QUOTE U.S.$
1990	Buddies N2615	Retrd.	N/A	30.00	55-100
1990	Six Pack N3005	Retrd.	N/A	30.00	35-45
1992	Something's Brewing N3147	Retrd.	1994	30.00	30
1993	Outstanding in Their Field N4003	Retrd.	1995	27.50	28

Anna-Perenna Porcelain

American Silhouettes Family Series - P. Buckley Moss

YEAR	ISSUE	EDITION LIMIT	YEAR RETD.	ISSUE PRICE	*QUOTE U.S.$
1982	Family Outing	5,000		75.00	95
1982	John and Mary	5,000		75.00	125-195
1984	Homemakers Quilting	5,000		75.00	85-195
1983	Leisure Time	5,000		75.00	85

American Silhouettes Valley Series - P. Buckley Moss

YEAR	ISSUE	EDITION LIMIT	YEAR RETD.	ISSUE PRICE	*QUOTE U.S.$
1982	Frosty Frolic	5,000		75.00	85-95
1984	Hay Ride	5,000		75.00	85
1983	Sunday Ride	5,000		75.00	85-100
1983	Market Day	5,000		75.00	120

American Silhouettes-Childrens Series - P. Buckley Moss

YEAR	ISSUE	EDITION LIMIT	YEAR RETD.	ISSUE PRICE	*QUOTE U.S.$
1981	Fiddlers Two	5,000		75.00	95
1982	Mary With The Lambs	5,000		75.00	125-200
1983	Ring-Around-the-Rosie	5,000		75.00	200
1983	Waiting For Tom	5,000		75.00	175

Annual Christmas Plate - P. Buckley Moss

YEAR	ISSUE	EDITION LIMIT	YEAR RETD.	ISSUE PRICE	*QUOTE U.S.$
1984	Noel, Noel	5,000		67.50	325
1985	Helping Hands	5,000		67.50	100-125
1986	Night Before Christmas	5,000		67.50	75-100
1987	Christmas Sleigh	5,000		75.00	85
1988	Christmas Joy	7,500		75.00	75
1989	Christmas Carol	7,500		80.00	80
1990	Christmas Eve	7,500		80.00	80
1991	The Snowman	7,500		80.00	80
1992	Christmas Warmth	7,500		85.00	85
1993	Joy to the World	7,500		85.00	85
1994	Christmas Night	5,000		85.00	85
1995	Christmas at Home	5,000		85.00	85

The Celebration Series - P. Buckley Moss

YEAR	ISSUE	EDITION LIMIT	YEAR RETD.	ISSUE PRICE	*QUOTE U.S.$
1986	Wedding Joy	5,000		100.00	200-350
1987	The Christening	5,000		100.00	150
1988	The Anniversary	5,000		100.00	100
1990	Family Reunion	5,000		100.00	125

Uncle Tad's Cats - T. Krumeich

YEAR	ISSUE	EDITION LIMIT	YEAR RETD.	ISSUE PRICE	*QUOTE U.S.$
1979	Oliver's Birthday	5,000		75.00	75-100
1980	Peaches & Cream	5,000		75.00	85
1981	Princess Aurora	5,000		80.00	80-85
1981	Walter's Window	5,000		80.00	80-90

ANRI

ANRI Father's Day - Unknown

YEAR	ISSUE	EDITION LIMIT	YEAR RETD.	ISSUE PRICE	*QUOTE U.S.$
1972	Alpine Father & Children	Closed	1972	35.00	100
1973	Alpine Father & Children	Closed	1973	40.00	100
1974	Cliff Gazing	Closed	1974	50.00	100
1975	Sailing	Closed	1975	60.00	90

ANRI Mother's Day - Unknown

YEAR	ISSUE	EDITION LIMIT	YEAR RETD.	ISSUE PRICE	*QUOTE U.S.$
1972	Alpine Mother & Children	Closed	1972	35.00	50
1973	Alpine Mother & Children	Closed	1973	40.00	50
1974	Alpine Mother & Children	Closed	1974	50.00	55
1975	Alpine Stroll	Closed	1975	60.00	65
1976	Knitting	Closed	1976	60.00	65

Christmas - J. Malfertheiner, unless otherwise noted

YEAR	ISSUE	EDITION LIMIT	YEAR RETD.	ISSUE PRICE	*QUOTE U.S.$
1971	St. Jakob in Groden	6,000	1971	37.50	65
1972	Pipers at Alberobello	6,000	1972	45.00	75
1973	Alpine Horn	6,000	1973	45.00	390
1974	Young Man and Girl	6,000	1974	50.00	95
1975	Christmas in Ireland	6,000	1975	60.00	60
1976	Alpine Christmas	6,000	1976	65.00	190
1977	Legend of Heligenblut	6,000	1977	65.00	91
1978	Klockler Singers	6,000	1978	80.00	90
1979	Moss Gatherers - Unknown	6,000	1979	135.00	177
1980	Wintry Churchgoing - Unknown	6,000	1980	165.00	165
1981	Santa Claus in Tyrol - Unknown	6,000	1981	165.00	200
1982	The Star Singers - Unknown	6,000	1982	165.00	165
1983	Unto Us a Child is Born - Unknown	6,000	1983	165.00	310
1984	Yuletide in the Valley - Unknown	6,000	1984	165.00	170
1985	Good Morning, Good Cheer	6,000	1985	165.00	165
1986	A Groden Christmas	6,000	1986	165.00	200
1987	Down From the Alps	6,000	1987	195.00	250
1988	Christkindl Markt	6,000	1988	220.00	230
1989	Flight Into Egypt	6,000	1989	275.00	275
1990	Holy Night	6,000	1990	300.00	300

Disney Four Star Collection - Disney Studios

YEAR	ISSUE	EDITION LIMIT	YEAR RETD.	ISSUE PRICE	*QUOTE U.S.$
1989	Mickey Mini Plate	5,000	1989	40.00	65
1990	Minnie Mini Plate	5,000	1990	40.00	95
1991	Donald Mini Plate	5,000	1991	50.00	55

Ferrandiz Christmas - J. Ferrandiz

YEAR	ISSUE	EDITION LIMIT	YEAR RETD.	ISSUE PRICE	*QUOTE U.S.$
1972	Christ In The Manger	4,000	1972	35.00	200
1973	Christmas	4,000	1973	40.00	225
1974	Holy Night	4,000	1974	50.00	100
1975	Flight into Egypt	4,000	1975	60.00	95
1976	Tree of Life	4,000	1976	60.00	85
1977	Girl with Flowers	4,000	1977	65.00	185
1978	Leading the Way	4,000	1978	77.50	180
1979	The Drummer	4,000	1979	120.00	175
1980	Rejoice	4,000	1980	150.00	160
1981	Spreading the Word	4,000	1981	150.00	150
1982	The Shepherd Family	4,000	1982	150.00	150
1983	Peace Attend Thee	4,000	1983	150.00	150

Ferrandiz Mother's Day Series - J. Ferrandiz

YEAR	ISSUE	EDITION LIMIT	YEAR RETD.	ISSUE PRICE	*QUOTE U.S.$
1972	Mother Sewing	3,000	1972	35.00	200
1973	Alpine Mother & Child	3,000	1973	40.00	150
1974	Mother Holding Child	3,000	1974	50.00	150
1975	Dove Girl	3,000	1975	60.00	150
1976	Mother Knitting	3,000	1976	60.00	200
1977	Alpine Stroll	3,000	1977	65.00	125
1978	The Beginning	3,000	1978	75.00	100-125
1979	All Hearts	3,000	1979	120.00	170
1980	Spring Arrivals	3,000	1980	150.00	165
1981	Harmony	3,000	1981	150.00	150
1982	With Love	3,000	1982	150.00	150

Ferrandiz Wooden Birthday Plates - J. Ferrandiz

YEAR	ISSUE	EDITION LIMIT	YEAR RETD.	ISSUE PRICE	*QUOTE U.S.$
1972	Boy	Unkn.	1972	15.00	100-125
1972	Girl	Unkn.	1972	15.00	160
1973	Boy	Unkn.	1973	20.00	200
1973	Girl	Unkn.	1973	20.00	150
1974	Boy	Unkn.	1974	22.00	160
1974	Girl	Unkn.	1974	22.00	160

Ferrandiz Wooden Wedding Plates - J. Ferrandiz

YEAR	ISSUE	EDITION LIMIT	YEAR RETD.	ISSUE PRICE	*QUOTE U.S.$
1972	Boy and Girl Embracing	Closed	1972	40.00	100-125
1973	Wedding Scene	Closed	1973	40.00	150
1974	Wedding	Closed	1974	48.00	150
1975	Wedding	Closed	1975	60.00	150
1976	Wedding	Closed	1976	60.00	90-150

*Quotes have been rounded up to nearest dollar

Arcadian Pewter, Inc.

Red Oak II - N. Lindblade

YEAR ISSUE		EDITION LIMIT	YEAR RETD.	ISSUE PRICE	*QUOTE U.S.$
1995	Red Oak II	Open		74.95	75

Armstrong's

Classic Memory Collection - R. Skelton

YEAR ISSUE		EDITION LIMIT	YEAR RETD.	ISSUE PRICE	*QUOTE U.S.$
1995	The Donut Dunker (signed)	1,000		375.00	375

Commemorative Issues - R. Skelton

YEAR ISSUE		EDITION LIMIT	YEAR RETD.	ISSUE PRICE	*QUOTE U.S.$
1983	70 Years Young (10 1/2")	15,000		85.00	100-125
1984	Freddie the Torchbearer (8 1/2")	15,000		62.50	63
1994	Red & His Friend	160		700.00	1200

Freedom Collection of Red Skelton - R. Skelton

YEAR ISSUE		EDITION LIMIT	YEAR RETD.	ISSUE PRICE	*QUOTE U.S.$
1990	The All American, (signed)	1,000		195.00	300
1990	The All American	9,000		62.50	63-85
1991	Independence Day? (signed)	1,000		195.00	200
1991	Independence Day?	9,000		62.50	63
1992	Let Freedom Ring, (signed)	1,000		195.00	200
1992	Let Freedom Ring	9,000		62.50	63
1993	Freddie's Gift of Life, (signed)	1,000		195.00	200
1993	Freddie's Gift of Life	9,000		62.50	63

Happy Art Series - W. Lantz

YEAR ISSUE		EDITION LIMIT	YEAR RETD.	ISSUE PRICE	*QUOTE U.S.$
1981	Woody's Triple Self-Portrait, Signed	1,000		100.00	150
1981	Woody's Triple Self-Portrait	9,000		39.50	40
1983	Gothic Woody, Signed	1,000		100.00	150
1983	Gothic Woody	9,000		39.50	40
1984	Blue Boy Woody, Signed	1,000		100.00	150
1984	Blue Boy Woody	9,000		39.50	40

The Signature Collection - R. Skelton

YEAR ISSUE		EDITION LIMIT	YEAR RETD.	ISSUE PRICE	*QUOTE U.S.$
1986	Anyone for Tennis?	9,000		62.50	65
1986	Anyone for Tennis? (signed)	1,000		125.00	450
1987	Ironing the Waves	9,000		62.50	65
1987	Ironing the Waves (signed)	1,000		125.00	300
1988	The Cliffhanger	9,000		62.50	65
1988	The Cliffhanger (signed)	1,000		150.00	300
1988	Hooked on Freddie	9,000		62.50	65
1988	Hooked on Freddie (signed)	1,000		175.00	250

Sports - Schenken

YEAR ISSUE		EDITION LIMIT	YEAR RETD.	ISSUE PRICE	*QUOTE U.S.$
1985	Pete Rose h/s (10 1/4")	1,000		100.00	275
1985	Pete Rose u/s (10 1/4")	10,000		40.00	60

Armstrong's/Crown Parlan

Freddie The Freeloader - R. Skelton

YEAR ISSUE		EDITION LIMIT	YEAR RETD.	ISSUE PRICE	*QUOTE U.S.$
1979	Freddie in the Bathtub	10,000		60.00	135-175
1980	Freddie's Shack	10,000		60.00	70-80
1981	Freddie on the Green	10,000		60.00	60
1982	Love that Freddie	10,000		60.00	60

Freddie's Adventures - R. Skelton

YEAR ISSUE		EDITION LIMIT	YEAR RETD.	ISSUE PRICE	*QUOTE U.S.$
1982	Captain Freddie	15,000		60.00	65
1982	Bronco Freddie	15,000		60.00	65
1983	Sir Freddie	15,000		62.50	63
1984	Gertrude and Heathcliffe	15,000		62.50	80

Artaffects

Club Member Limited Edition Redemption Offerings - G. Perillo

YEAR ISSUE		EDITION LIMIT	YEAR RETD.	ISSUE PRICE	*QUOTE U.S.$
1992	The Pencil	Yr. Iss.		35.00	75
1992	Studies in Black and White (Set/4)	Yr. Iss.		75.00	100
1993	Watcher of the Wilderness	Yr. Iss.		60.00	60

America's Indian Heritage - G. Perillo

YEAR ISSUE		EDITION LIMIT	YEAR RETD.	ISSUE PRICE	*QUOTE U.S.$
1987	Cheyenne Nation	10-day		24.50	38
1988	Arapaho Nation	10-day		24.50	45
1988	Kiowa Nation	10-day		24.50	45
1988	Sioux Nation	10-day		24.50	35
1988	Chippewa Nation	10-day		24.50	35
1988	Crow Nation	10-day		24.50	45
1988	Nez Perce Nation	10-day		24.50	45
1988	Blackfoot Nation	10-day		24.50	35

Chieftains I - G. Perillo

YEAR ISSUE		EDITION LIMIT	YEAR RETD.	ISSUE PRICE	*QUOTE U.S.$
1979	Chief Sitting Bull	7,500		65.00	325
1979	Chief Joseph	7,500		65.00	80-90
1980	Chief Red Cloud	7,500		65.00	120
1980	Chief Geronimo	7,500		65.00	85
1981	Chief Crazy Horse	7,500		65.00	100

Chieftains II - G. Perillo

YEAR ISSUE		EDITION LIMIT	YEAR RETD.	ISSUE PRICE	*QUOTE U.S.$
1983	Chief Pontiac	7,500		70.00	85-150
1983	Chief Victorio	7,500		70.00	150
1984	Chief Tecumseh	7,500		70.00	150
1984	Chief Cochise	7,500		70.00	80-150
1984	Chief Black Kettle	7,500		70.00	150

The Colts - G. Perillo

YEAR ISSUE		EDITION LIMIT	YEAR RETD.	ISSUE PRICE	*QUOTE U.S.$
1985	Appaloosa	5,000		40.00	40
1985	Pinto	5,000		40.00	56
1985	Arabian	5,000		40.00	56
1985	Thoroughbred	5,000		40.00	56

Council of Nations - G. Perillo

YEAR ISSUE		EDITION LIMIT	YEAR RETD.	ISSUE PRICE	*QUOTE U.S.$
1992	Strength of the Sioux	14-day		29.50	35
1992	Pride of the Cheyenne	14-day		29.50	40
1992	Dignity of the Nez Perce	14-day		29.50	35
1992	Courage of the Arapaho	14-day		29.50	38
1992	Power of the Blackfoot	14-day		29.50	35
1992	Nobility of the Algonquin	14-day		29.50	35
1992	Wisdom of the Cherokee	14-day		29.50	40
1992	Boldness of the Seneca	14-day		29.50	35

Indian Bridal - G. Perillo

YEAR ISSUE		EDITION LIMIT	YEAR RETD.	ISSUE PRICE	*QUOTE U.S.$
1990	Yellow Bird (6 1/2")	14-day		25.00	30
1990	Autumn Blossom (6 1/2")	14-day		25.00	30
1990	Misty Waters (6 1/2")	14-day		25.00	30
1990	Sunny Skies (6 1/2")	14-day		25.00	30

Indian Nations - G. Perillo

YEAR ISSUE		EDITION LIMIT	YEAR RETD.	ISSUE PRICE	*QUOTE U.S.$
1983	Blackfoot	7,500		140.00	350
1983	Cheyenne	7,500		set	Set
1983	Apache	7,500		set	Set
1983	Sioux	7,500		set	Set

March of Dimes: Our Children - G. Perillo

YEAR ISSUE		EDITION LIMIT	YEAR RETD.	ISSUE PRICE	*QUOTE U.S.$
1989	A Time to Be Born	150-day		29.00	40

Mother's Love - G. Perillo

YEAR ISSUE		EDITION LIMIT	YEAR RETD.	ISSUE PRICE	*QUOTE U.S.$
1988	Feelings	Yr.Iss.		35.00	55
1989	Moonlight	Yr.Iss.		35.00	65
1990	Pride & Joy	Yr.Iss.		39.50	50
1991	Little Shadow	Yr.Iss.		39.50	45

Motherhood Series - G. Perillo

YEAR ISSUE		EDITION LIMIT	YEAR RETD.	ISSUE PRICE	*QUOTE U.S.$
1983	Madre	10,000		50.00	75
1984	Madonna of the Plains	3,500		50.00	75
1985	Abuela	3,500		50.00	75
1986	Nap Time	3,500		50.00	75

Native American Christmas - G. Perillo

YEAR ISSUE		EDITION LIMIT	YEAR RETD.	ISSUE PRICE	*QUOTE U.S.$
1993	The Little Shepherd	Annual		35.00	55
1994	Joy to the World	Annual		45.00	45

Nature's Harmony - G. Perillo

YEAR ISSUE		EDITION LIMIT	YEAR RETD.	ISSUE PRICE	*QUOTE U.S.$
1982	The Peaceable Kingdom	12,500		100.00	125-200
1982	Zebra	12,500		50.00	50
1982	Bengal Tiger	12,500		50.00	[illegible]
1983	Black Panther	12,500		50.00	70
1983	Elephant	12,500		50.00	80

North American Wildlife - G. Perillo

YEAR ISSUE		EDITION LIMIT	YEAR RETD.	ISSUE PRICE	*QUOTE U.S.$
1989	Mustang	14-day		29.50	35-40
1989	White-Tailed Deer	14-day		29.50	30
1989	Mountain Lion	14-day		29.50	30
1990	American Bald Eagle	14-day		29.50	35
1990	Timber Wolf	14-day		29.50	35
1990	Polar Bear	14-day		29.50	30
1990	Buffalo	14-day		29.50	35-55
1990	Bighorn Sheep	14-day		29.50	30

Perillo Christmas - G. Perillo

YEAR ISSUE		EDITION LIMIT	YEAR RETD.	ISSUE PRICE	*QUOTE U.S.$
1987	Shining Star	Yr.Iss.		29.50	70
1988	Silent Light	Yr.Iss.		35.00	65-80
1989	Snow Flake	Yr.Iss.		35.00	35-65
1990	Bundle Up	Yr.Iss.		39.50	65-75
1991	Christmas Journey	Yr.Iss.		39.50	40-50

Portraits of American Brides - R. Sauber

YEAR ISSUE		EDITION LIMIT	YEAR RETD.	ISSUE PRICE	*QUOTE U.S.$
1986	Caroline	10-day		29.50	45-75
1986	Jacqueline	10-day		29.50	30-75
1987	Elizabeth	10-day		29.50	60
1987	Emily	10-day		29.50	75
1987	Meredith	10-day		29.50	75
1987	Laura	10-day		29.50	45
1987	Sarah	10-day		29.50	45
1987	Rebecca	10-day		29.50	65

Pride of America's Indians - G. Perillo

YEAR ISSUE		EDITION LIMIT	YEAR RETD.	ISSUE PRICE	*QUOTE U.S.$
1986	Brave and Free	10-day		24.50	35-50
1986	Dark-Eyed Friends	10-day		24.50	45
1986	Noble Companions	10-day		24.50	35
1987	Kindred Spirits	10-day		24.50	35
1987	Loyal Alliance	10-day		24.50	75
1987	Small and Wise	10-day		24.50	35
1987	Winter Scouts	10-day		24.50	25-40
1987	Peaceful Comrades	10-day		24.50	40

The Princesses - G. Perillo

YEAR ISSUE		EDITION LIMIT	YEAR RETD.	ISSUE PRICE	*QUOTE U.S.$
1982	Lily of the Mohawks	7,500		50.00	175
1982	Pocahontas	7,500		50.00	100
1982	Minnehaha	7,500		50.00	100
1982	Sacajawea	7,500		50.00	100

Proud Young Spirits - G. Perillo

YEAR ISSUE		EDITION LIMIT	YEAR RETD.	ISSUE PRICE	*QUOTE U.S.$
1990	Protector of the Plains	14-day		29.50	30-45
1990	Watchful Eyes	14-day		29.50	55
1990	Freedom's Watch	14-day		29.50	35-45
1990	Woodland Scouts	14-day		29.50	35-45
1990	Fast Friends	14-day		29.50	35-45
1990	Birds of a Feather	14-day		29.50	30
1990	Prairie Pals	14-day		29.50	35-45
1990	Loyal Guardian	14-day		29.50	30

Special Issue - G. Perillo

YEAR ISSUE		EDITION LIMIT	YEAR RETD.	ISSUE PRICE	*QUOTE U.S.$
1981	Apache Boy	5,000		95.00	175
1983	Papoose	3,000		100.00	125
1983	Indian Style	17,500		50.00	50
1984	The Lovers	Closed	N/A	50.00	100
1984	Navajo Girl	3,500		95.00	175
1986	Navajo Boy	3,500		95.00	175

The Thoroughbreds - G. Perillo

YEAR ISSUE		EDITION LIMIT	YEAR RETD.	ISSUE PRICE	*QUOTE U.S.$
1984	Whirlaway	9,500		50.00	250
1984	Secretariat	9,500		50.00	350
1984	Man o' War	9,500		50.00	150
1984	Seabiscuit	9,500		50.00	150

War Ponies of the Plains - G. Perillo

YEAR ISSUE		EDITION LIMIT	YEAR RETD.	ISSUE PRICE	*QUOTE U.S.$
1992	Nightshadow	75-day		27.00	27
1992	Windcatcher	75-day		27.00	27
1992	Prairie Prancer	75-day		27.00	27
1992	Thunderfoot	75-day		27.00	27
1992	Proud Companion	75-day		27.00	27
1992	Sun Dancer	75-day		27.00	27
1992	Free Spirit	75-day		27.00	27
1992	Gentle Warrior	75-day		27.00	27

The Young Chieftains - G. Perillo

YEAR ISSUE		EDITION LIMIT	YEAR RETD.	ISSUE PRICE	*QUOTE U.S.$
1985	Young Sitting Bull	5,000		50.00	75-100
1985	Young Joseph	5,000		50.00	75-100
1986	Young Red Cloud	5,000		50.00	75-100
1986	Young Geronimo	5,000		50.00	75-100
1986	Young Crazy Horse	5,000		50.00	75-100

Artists of the World

Celebration Series - T. DeGrazia

YEAR ISSUE		EDITION LIMIT	YEAR RETD.	ISSUE PRICE	*QUOTE U.S.$
1993	The Lord's Candle	5,000		39.50	45-75
1993	Pinata Party	5,000		39.50	45-75
1993	Holiday Lullaby	5,000	1995	39.50	50-75
1993	Caroling	5,000	1995	39.50	50-75

Children (Signed) - T. DeGrazia

YEAR ISSUE		EDITION LIMIT	YEAR RETD.	ISSUE PRICE	*QUOTE U.S.$
1978	Los Ninos, signed	500		100.00	1500-2200
1978	White Dove, signed	500		100.00	450-700
1978	Flower Girl, signed	500		100.00	450-700
1979	Flower Boy, signed	500		100.00	450-700
1980	Little Cocopah Girl, signed	500		100.00	450-650
1981	Beautiful Burden, signed	500		100.00	450-650
1981	Merry Little Indian, signed	500		100.00	450-650

Children - T. DeGrazia

YEAR ISSUE		EDITION LIMIT	YEAR RETD.	ISSUE PRICE	*QUOTE U.S.$
1976	Los Ninos	5,000		35.00	1100-1500
1977	White Dove	5,000		40.00	70-200
1978	Flower Girl	9,500		45.00	250-300
1979	Flower Boy	9,500		45.00	250-300
1980	Little Cocopah	9,500		50.00	175
1981	Beautiful Burden	9,500		50.00	150-200
1982	Merry Little Indian	9,500		55.00	150-200
1983	Wondering	10,000		60.00	160
1984	Pink Papoose	10,000		65.00	125
1985	Sunflower Boy	10,000		65.00	125

Children at Play - T. DeGrazia

YEAR ISSUE		EDITION LIMIT	YEAR RETD.	ISSUE PRICE	*QUOTE U.S.$
1985	My First Horse	15,000		65.00	100-150
1986	Girl With Sewing Machine	15,000		65.00	100-150
1987	Love Me	15,000		65.00	100-150
1988	Merrily, Merrily, Merrily	15,000		65.00	75-150
1989	My First Arrow	15,000		65.00	100-150
1990	Away With My Kite	15,000		65.00	100-150

Children Mini-Plates - T. DeGrazia

YEAR ISSUE		EDITION LIMIT	YEAR RETD.	ISSUE PRICE	*QUOTE U.S.$
1980	Los Ninos	5,000		15.00	300
1981	White Dove	5,000		15.00	100
1982	Flower Girl	5,000		15.00	50-100
1982	Flower Boy	5,000		15.00	55-100
1983	Little Cocopah Indian Girl	5,000		15.00	70-100
1983	Beautiful Burden	5,000		20.00	55-100
1984	Merry Little Indian	5,000		20.00	65-100
1984	Wondering	5,000		20.00	50-100
1985	Pink Papoose	5,000		20.00	40-75
1985	Sunflower Boy	5,000		20.00	25-50

Children of the Sun - T. DeGrazia

YEAR ISSUE		EDITION LIMIT	YEAR RETD.	ISSUE PRICE	*QUOTE U.S.$
1987	Spring Blossoms	150-day		34.50	50-100
1987	My Little Pink Bird	150-day		34.50	50-100
1987	Bright Flowers of the Desert	150-day		37.90	75-100
1988	Gifts from the Sun	150-day		37.90	75-100
1988	Growing Glory	150-day		37.90	50-100
1988	The Gentle White Dove	150-day		37.90	75-100
1988	Sunflower Maiden	150-day		39.90	50-75
1989	Sun Showers	150-day		39.90	50-75

Floral Fiesta - T. DeGrazia

YEAR ISSUE		EDITION LIMIT	YEAR RETD.	ISSUE PRICE	*QUOTE U.S.$
1994	Little Flower Vendor	5,000		39.50	40-70
1994	Flowers For Mother	5,000		39.50	40-70
1995	Floral Innocence	5,000		39.50	40-70
1995	Floral Bouquet	5,000		39.50	40-70
1996	Floral Celebration	5,000		39.50	40
1996	Floral Fiesta	5,000		39.50	40

*Quotes have been rounded up to nearest dollar

Holiday (Signed) - T. DeGrazia

Year	Issue	Edition Limit	Year Retd.	Issue Price	*Quote U.S.$
1976	Festival of Lights, signed	500		100.00	600-750
1977	Bell of Hope, signed	500		100.00	450-700
1978	Little Madonna, signed	500		100.00	450-750
1979	The Nativity, signed	500		100.00	500-700
1980	Little Pima Drummer, signed	500		100.00	450-550
1981	A Little Prayer, signed	500		100.00	450-500
1982	Blue Boy, signed	96		100.00	500-900

Holiday - T. DeGrazia

Year	Issue	Edition Limit	Year Retd.	Issue Price	*Quote U.S.$
1976	Festival of Lights	9,500		45.00	200-375
1977	Bell of Hope	9,500		45.00	200-275
1978	Little Madonna	9,500		45.00	200-325
1979	The Nativity	9,500		50.00	225-275
1980	Little Pima Drummer	9,500		50.00	50-125
1981	A Little Prayer	9,500		55.00	65-125
1982	Blue Boy	10,000		60.00	65-125
1983	Heavenly Blessings	10,000		65.00	130
1984	Navajo Madonna	10,000		65.00	135
1985	Saguaro Dance	10,000		65.00	125

Holiday Mini-Plates - T. DeGrazia

Year	Issue	Edition Limit	Year Retd.	Issue Price	*Quote U.S.$
1980	Festival of Lights	5,000		15.00	200-300
1981	Bell of Hope	5,000		15.00	95
1982	Little Madonna	5,000		15.00	95
1982	The Nativity	5,000		15.00	95
1983	Little Pima Drummer	5,000		15.00	25
1983	Little Prayer	5,000		20.00	25
1984	Blue Boy	5,000		20.00	25
1984	Heavenly Blessings	5,000		20.00	25
1985	Navajo Madonna	5,000		20.00	25
1985	Saguaro Dance	5,000		20.00	75

Special Release - T. DeGrazia

Year	Issue	Edition Limit	Year Retd.	Issue Price	*Quote U.S.$
1996	Wedding Party	5,000		49.50	50

Western - T. DeGrazia

Year	Issue	Edition Limit	Year Retd.	Issue Price	*Quote U.S.$
1986	Morning Ride	5,000		65.00	75
1987	Bronco	5,000		65.00	90-150
1988	Apache Scout	5,000		65.00	90-150
1989	Alone	5,000		65.00	90-150

Barbie/Enesco Corporation

Bob Mackie - Enesco

Year	Issue	Edition Limit	Year Retd.	Issue Price	*Quote U.S.$
1996	Queen of Hearts Barbie 157678	Open		25.00	25
1997	Goddess of the Sun 260215	7,500		35.00	35
1997	Moon Goddess 260231	7,500		35.00	35

Bob Mackie JC Penney Exclusive - Enesco

Year	Issue	Edition Limit	Year Retd.	Issue Price	*Quote U.S.$
1995	Queen of Hearts Barbie J1276	7,500	1995	30.00	30
1996	Goddess of the Sun J8768	7,500		30.00	30
1997	Moon Goddess 260266	5,000		30.00	30

Elite Dealer Exclusive - Enesco

Year	Issue	Edition Limit	Year Retd.	Issue Price	*Quote U.S.$
1997	Goddess of the Sun/Moon Goddess Set 270539	2,500		175.00	175

FAO Schwarz Exclusive - Enesco

Year	Issue	Edition Limit	Year Retd.	Issue Price	*Quote U.S.$
1994	Silver Screen Barbie 128805	3,600	1995	30.00	30
1995	Circus Star Barbie 150339	3,600	1995	30.00	30

Glamour - Enesco

Year	Issue	Edition Limit	Year Retd.	Issue Price	*Quote U.S.$
1994	35th Anniversary Barbie 655112	5,000	1994	30.00	30
1995	Barbie Solo In The Spotlight, 1959 114383	5,000	1995	30.00	45
1996	Barbie Enchanted Evening, 1960 175587	10,000	1995	30.00	30
1996	Here Comes The Bride, 1966 170984	Open		30.00	30
1996	Holiday Dance, 1965 188794	10,000		30.00	30
1997	Wedding Day, 1959 260282	7,500		30.00	30

Great Eras - Enesco

Year	Issue	Edition Limit	Year Retd.	Issue Price	*Quote U.S.$
1996	Gibson Girl Barbie 174769	10,000		30.00	30
1996	1920's Flapper Barbie 174777	10,000		30.00	30
1997	1850's Southern Belle 174785	7,500		30.00	30
1997	Egyptian Queen 174793	7,500		30.00	30

Happy Holiday - Enesco

Year	Issue	Edition Limit	Year Retd.	Issue Price	*Quote U.S.$
1994	Happy Holidays Barbie, 1994 115088	5,000	1994	30.00	75-100
1995	Happy Holidays Barbie, 1995 143154	Yr.Iss.	1995	30.00	30
1995	Happy Holidays Barbie, 1988 154180	Yr.Iss.	1995	30.00	30
1996	Happy Holidays Barbie, 1989 188859	Yr.Iss.	1996	30.00	30
1996	Happy Holidays Barbie, 1996 188816	Yr.Iss.	1996	30.00	30

Hollywood Legends - Enesco

Year	Issue	Edition Limit	Year Retd.	Issue Price	*Quote U.S.$
1996	Barbie As Scarlett O'Hara in Green Velvet 171085	10,000	1996	35.00	35
1997	Barbie As Scarlett O'Hara in Red Velvet 260169	7,500		35.00	35
1997	Barbie As Dorothy 260193	7,500		35.00	35

My Fair Lady - Enesco

Year	Issue	Edition Limit	Year Retd.	Issue Price	*Quote U.S.$
1997	Barbie As Eliza Doolittle 270512	7,500		30.00	30

Bareuther

Christmas - H. Mueller, unless otherwise noted

Year	Issue	Edition Limit	Year Retd.	Issue Price	*Quote U.S.$
1967	Stiftskirche	10,000		12.00	85
1968	Kapplkirche	10,000		12.00	25
1969	Christkindlesmarkt	10,000		12.00	18
1970	Chapel in Oberndorf	10,000		12.50	22
1971	Toys for Sale - From Drawing By L. Richter	10,000		12.75	27
1972	Christmas in Munich	10,000		14.50	25
1973	Sleigh Ride	10,000		15.00	35
1974	Black Forest Church	10,000		19.00	19
1975	Snowman	10,000		21.50	30
1976	Chapel in the Hills	10,000		23.50	26
1977	Story Time	10,000		24.50	40
1978	Mittenwald	10,000		27.50	31
1979	Winter Day	10,000		35.00	35
1980	Mittenberg	10,000		37.50	39
1981	Walk in the Forest	10,000		39.50	40
1982	Bad Wimpfen	10,000		39.50	43
1983	The Night before Christmas	10,000		39.50	40
1984	Zeil on the River Main	10,000		42.50	45
1985	Winter Wonderland	10,000		42.50	57
1986	Christmas in Forchheim	10,000		42.50	70
1987	Decorating the Tree	10,000		42.50	85
1988	St. Coloman Church	10,000		52.50	65
1989	Sleigh Ride	10,000		52.50	80-90
1990	The Old Forge in Rothenburg	10,000		52.50	53
1991	Christmas Joy	10,000		56.50	57
1992	Market Place in Heppenheim	10,000		59.50	60
1993	Winter Fun	10,000		59.50	60
1994	Coming Home For Christmas	10,000		59.50	60

Bing & Grondahl

American Christmas Heritage Collection - C. Magadini

Year	Issue	Edition Limit	Year Retd.	Issue Price	*Quote U.S.$
1996	The Statue of Liberty	Yr.Iss.	1996	47.50	48
1997	Christmas Eve at The Lincoln Memorial	Yr.Iss.		47.50	48

Centennial Anniversary Commemoratives - Various

Year	Issue	Edition Limit	Year Retd.	Issue Price	*Quote U.S.$
1995	Centennial Plaquettes: Series of 10-5" plates featuring B&G motifs: 1895, 1905, 1919, 1927, 1932, 1945, 1954, 1967, 1974, 1982	Yr.Iss.	1995	250.00	250
1995	Centennial Plate: Behind the Frozen Window - F.A. Hallin	10,000	1995	39.50	40
1995	Centennial Platter: Towers of Copenhagen - J. Nielsen	7,500	1995	195.00	195

Centennial Collection - Various

Year	Issue	Edition Limit	Year Retd.	Issue Price	*Quote U.S.$
1991	Crows Enjoying Christmas - D. Jensen	Annual	1991	59.50	60
1992	Copenhagen Christmas - H. Vlugenring	Annual	1992	59.50	60-75
1993	Christmas Elf - H. Thelander	Annual	1993	59.50	60-72
1994	Christmas in Church - H. Thelander	Annual	1994	59.50	60-75
1995	Behind The Frozen Window - A. Hallin	Annual	1995	59.50	60

Children's Day Plate Series - Various

Year	Issue	Edition Limit	Year Retd.	Issue Price	*Quote U.S.$
1985	The Magical Tea Party - C. Roller	Annual	1985	24.50	28
1986	A Joyful Flight - C. Roller	Annual	1986	26.50	29-48
1986	The Little Gardeners - C. Roller	Annual	1987	29.50	30-70
1988	Wash Day - C. Roller	Annual	1988	34.50	35-45
1989	Bedtime - C. Roller	Annual	1989	37.00	40-60
1990	My Favorite Dress - S. Vestergaard	Annual	1990	37.00	40-75
1991	Fun on the Beach - S. Vestergaard	Annual	1991	45.00	55-60
1992	A Summer Day in the Meadow - S. Vestergaard	Annual	1992	45.00	45-65
1993	The Carousel - S. Vestergaard	Annual	1993	45.00	45-90
1994	The Little Fisherman - S. Vestergaard	Annual	1994	45.00	45
1995	My First Book - S. Vestergaard	Annual	1995	45.00	50-75
1996	The Little Racers - S. Vestergaard	Annual	1996	45.00	45
1997	Bath Time - S. Vestergaard	Annual		45.00	45

Christmas - Various

Year	Issue	Edition Limit	Year Retd.	Issue Price	*Quote U.S.$
1895	Behind The Frozen Window - F.A. Hallin	Annual	1895	.50	5000-7000
1896	New Moon - F.A. Hallin	Annual	1896	.50	2200-3000
1897	Sparrows - F.A. Hallin	Annual	1897	.75	1100-1700
1898	Roses and Star - F. Garde	Annual	1898	.75	810-975
1899	Crows - F. Garde	Annual	1899	.75	1800-2200
1900	Church Bells - F. Garde	Annual	1900	.75	875-1500
1901	Three Wise Men - S. Sabra	Annual	1901	1.00	525-600
1902	Gothic Church Interior - D. Jensen	Annual	1902	1.00	425-700
1903	Expectant Children - M. Hyldahl	Annual	1903	1.00	412-450
1904	Fredericksberg Hill - C. Olsen	Annual	1904	1.00	175-225
1905	Christmas Night - D. Jensen	Annual	1905	1.00	150-210
1906	Sleighing to Church - D. Jensen	Annual	1906	1.00	90-140
1907	Little Match Girl - E. Plockross	Annual	1907	1.00	125-150
1908	St. Petri Church - P. Jorgensen	Annual	1908	1.00	75-105
1909	Yule Tree - Aarestrup	Annual	1909	1.50	90-135
1910	The Old Organist - C. Ersgaard	Annual	1910	1.50	85-120
1911	Angels and Shepherds - H. Moltke	Annual	1911	1.50	80-108
1912	Going to Church - E. Hansen	Annual	1912	1.50	80-99
1913	Bringing Home the Tree - T. Larsen	Annual	1913	1.50	80-105
1914	Amalienborg Castle - T. Larsen	Annual	1914	1.50	80-105
1915	Dog Outside Window - D. Jensen	Annual	1915	1.50	125-165
1916	Sparrows at Christmas - P. Jorgensen	Annual	1916	1.50	80-90
1917	Christmas Boat - A. Friis	Annual	1917	1.50	75-90
1918	Fishing Boat - A. Friis	Annual	1918	1.50	75-90
1919	Outside Lighted Window - A. Friis	Annual	1919	2.00	65-90
1920	Hare in the Snow - A. Friis	Annual	1920	2.00	75-90
1921	Pigeons - A. Friis	Annual	1921	2.00	70-82
1922	Star of Bethlehem - A. Friis	Annual	1922	2.00	60-90
1923	The Ermitage - A. Friis	Annual	1923	2.00	80-90
1924	Lighthouse - A. Friis	Annual	1924	2.50	80-120
1925	Child's Christmas - A. Friis	Annual	1925	2.50	80-96
1926	Churchgoers - A. Friis	Annual	1926	2.50	80-90
1927	Skating Couple - A. Friis	Annual	1927	2.50	90-117
1928	Eskimos - A. Friis	Annual	1928	2.50	75-84
1929	Fox Outside Farm - A. Friis	Annual	1929	2.50	90-105
1930	Town Hall Square - H. Flugenring	Annual	1930	2.50	90-114
1931	Christmas Train - A. Friis	Annual	1931	2.50	87-96
1932	Life Boat - H. Flugenring	Annual	1932	2.50	75-95
1933	Korsor-Nyborg Ferry - H. Flugenring	Annual	1933	3.00	77-96
1934	Church Bell in Tower - H. Flugenring	Annual	1934	3.00	77-90
1935	Lillebelt Bridge - O. Larson	Annual	1935	3.00	75-100
1936	Royal Guard - O. Larson	Annual	1936	3.00	75-85
1937	Arrival of Christmas Guests - O. Larson	Annual	1937	3.00	80-108
1938	Lighting the Candles - I. Tjerne	Annual	1938	3.00	110-200
1939	Old Lock-Eye, The Sandman - I. Tjerne	Annual	1939	3.00	140-195
1940	Christmas Letters - O. Larson	Annual	1940	4.00	155-220
1941	Horses Enjoying Meal - O. Larson	Annual	1941	4.00	245-300
1942	Danish Farm - O. Larson	Annual	1942	4.00	175-230
1943	Ribe Cathedral - O. Larson	Annual	1943	5.00	175-250
1944	Sorgenfri Castle - O. Larson	Annual	1944	5.00	100-130
1945	The Old Water Mill - O. Larson	Annual	1945	5.00	115-180
1946	Commemoration Cross - M. Hyldahl	Annual	1946	5.00	80-105
1947	Dybbol Mill - M. Hyldahl	Annual	1947	5.00	100-144
1948	Watchman - M. Hyldahl	Annual	1948	5.50	75-105
1949	Landsoldaten - M. Hyldahl	Annual	1949	5.50	75-105
1950	Kronborg Castle - M. Hyldahl	Annual	1950	5.50	110-150
1951	Jens Bang - M. Hyldahl	Annual	1951	6.00	90-125
1952	Thorsvaldsen Museum - B. Pramvig	Annual	1952	6.00	80-120
1953	Snowman - B. Pramvig	Annual	1953	7.50	96-105
1954	Royal Boat - K. Bonfils	Annual	1954	7.00	90-125
1955	Kaulundorg Church - K. Bonfils	Annual	1955	8.00	90-140
1956	Christmas in Copenhagen - K. Bonfils	Annual	1956	8.50	125-180
1957	Christmas Candles - K. Bonfils	Annual	1957	9.00	140-200
1958	Santa Claus - K. Bonfils	Annual	1958	9.50	100-145
1959	Christmas Eve - K. Bonfils	Annual	1959	10.00	120-180
1960	Village Church - K. Bonfils	Annual	1960	10.00	150-220
1961	Winter Harmony - K. Bonfils	Annual	1961	10.50	95-115
1962	Winter Night - K. Bonfils	Annual	1962	11.00	80-120
1963	The Christmas Elf - H. Thelander	Annual	1963	11.00	125-155
1964	The Fir Tree and Hare - H. Thelander	Annual	1964	11.50	35-70
1965	Bringing Home the Tree - H. Thelander	Annual	1965	12.00	50-75
1966	Home for Christmas - H. Thelander	Annual	1966	12.00	45-63
1967	Sharing the Joy - H. Thelander	Annual	1967	13.00	36-65
1968	Christmas in Church - H. Thelander	Annual	1968	14.00	30-45
1969	Arrival of Guests - H. Thelander	Annual	1969	14.00	30-45
1970	Pheasants in Snow - H. Thelander	Annual	1970	14.50	20-27
1971	Christmas at Home - H. Thelander	Annual	1971	15.00	15-27
1972	Christmas in Greenland - H. Thelander	Annual	1972	16.50	15-30
1973	Country Christmas - H. Thelander	Annual	1973	19.50	25-45
1974	Christmas in the Village - H. Thelander	Annual	1974	22.00	27-35
1975	Old Water Mill - H. Thelander	Annual	1975	27.50	25-39
1976	Christmas Welcome - H. Thelander	Annual	1976	27.50	29-39
1977	Copenhagen Christmas - H. Thelander	Annual	1977	29.50	38
1978	Christmas Tale - H. Thelander	Annual	1978	32.00	32-49
1979	White Christmas - H. Thelander	Annual	1979	36.50	30-49
1980	Christmas in Woods - H. Thelander	Annual	1980	42.50	30-49
1981	Christmas Peace - H. Thelander	Annual	1981	49.50	30-49
1982	Christmas Tree - H. Thelander	Annual	1982	54.50	50-60
1983	Christmas in Old Town - H. Thelander	Annual	1983	54.50	53-64
1984	The Christmas Letter - E. Jensen	Annual	1984	54.50	55-75
1985	Christmas Eve at the Farmhouse - E. Jensen	Annual	1985	54.50	55-78
1986	Silent Night, Holy Night - E. Jensen	Annual	1986	54.50	55-78
1987	The Snowman's Christmas Eve - E. Jensen	Annual	1987	59.50	70-77
1988	In the Kings Garden - E. Jensen	Annual	1988	64.50	60-77
1989	Christmas Anchorage - E. Jensen	Annual	1989	59.50	70-108
1990	Changing of the Guards - E. Jensen	Annual	1990	64.50	71-96
1991	Copenhagen Stock Exchange - E. Jensen	Annual	1991	69.50	70-90
1992	Christmas At the Rectory - J. Steensen	Annual	1992	69.50	99-112
1993	Father Christmas in Copenhagen - J. Nielsen	Annual	1993	69.50	75-96
1994	A Day At The Deer Park - J. Nielsen	Annual	1994	72.50	75-84
1995	The Towers of Copenhagen - J. Nielsen	Annual	1995	72.50	75-90
1996	Winter at the Old Mill - J. Nielsen	Annual	1996	74.50	75
1997	Country Christmas - J. Nielsen	Annual		69.50	70

*Quotes have been rounded up to nearest dollar

Christmas In America - J. Woodson

YEAR ISSUE		EDITION LIMIT	YEAR RETD.	ISSUE PRICE	*QUOTE U.S.$
1986	Christmas Eve in Williamsburg	Annual	1986	29.50	65-121
1987	Christmas Eve at the White House	Annual	1987	34.50	35
1988	Christmas Eve at Rockefeller Center	Annual	1988	34.50	60
1989	Christmas In New England	Annual	1989	37.00	55
1990	Christmas Eve at the Capitol	Annual	1990	39.50	55
1991	Christmas Eve at Independence Hall	Annual	1991	45.00	60
1992	Christmas in San Francisco	Annual	1992	47.50	48-60
1993	Coming Home For Christmas	Annual	1993	47.50	48
1994	Christmas Eve In Alaska	Annual	1994	47.50	48-75
1995	Christmas Eve in Mississippi	Annual	1995	47.50	48

Christmas in America Anniversary Plate - J. Woodson

1991	Christmas Eve in Williamsburg	Annual	1991	69.50	75-90
1995	The Capitol - J. Woodson	Annual	1995	74.50	75

Jubilee-5 Year Cycle - Various

1915	Frozen Window - F.A. Hallin	Annual	1915	Unkn.	210-225
1920	Church Bells - F. Garde	Annual	1920	Unkn.	60-110
1925	Dog Outside Window - D. Jensen	Annual	1925	Unkn.	200-300
1930	The Old Organist - C. Ersgaard	Annual	1930	Unkn.	225
1935	Little Match Girl - E. Plockross	Annual	1935	Unkn.	450
1940	Three Wise Men - S. Sabra	Annual	1940	Unkn.	1800
1945	Amalienborg Castle - T. Larsen	Annual	1945	Unkn.	90
1950	Eskimos - A. Friis	Annual	1950	Unkn.	90
1955	Dybbol Mill - M. Hyldahl	Annual	1955	Unkn.	210
1960	Kronborg Castle - M. Hyldahl	Annual	1960	25.00	90-120
1965	Chruchgoers - A. Friis	Annual	1965	25.00	25-75
1970	Amalienborg Castle - T. Larsen	Annual	1970	30.00	30
1975	Horses Enjoying Meal - O. Larson	Annual	1975	40.00	45-60
1980	Yule Tree - Aarestrup	Annual	1980	60.00	50-60
1985	Lifeboat at Work - H. Flugenring	Annual	1985	65.00	65
1990	The Royal Yacht Dannebrog - J. Bonfils	Annual	1990	95.00	85
1995	Centennial Platter - J. Nielsen	7,500	1995	195.00	195
1996	Lifeboat at Work (released a year late) - H. Flugenring	1,000	1996	95.00	95

Mother's Day - Various

1969	Dogs and Puppies - H. Thelander	Annual	1969	9.75	450-800
1970	Bird and Chicks - H. Thelander	Annual	1970	10.00	30
1971	Cat and Kitten - H. Thelander	Annual	1971	11.00	10-20
1972	Mare and Foal - H. Thelander	Annual	1972	12.00	23
1973	Duck and Ducklings - H. Thelander	Annual	1973	13.00	21
1974	Bear and Cubs - H. Thelander	Annual	1974	16.50	20-30
1975	Doe and Fawns - H. Thelander	Annual	1975	19.50	20
1976	Swan Family - H. Thelander	Annual	1976	22.50	[illegible]
1977	Squirrel and Young - H. Thelander	Annual	1977	23.50	25
1978	Heron and Young - H. Thelander	Annual	1978	24.50	25
1979	Fox and Cubs - H. Thelander	Annual	1979	27.50	32
1980	Woodpecker and Young - H. Thelander	Annual	1980	29.50	36
1981	Hare and Young - H. Thelander	Annual	1981	36.50	37
1982	Lioness and Cubs - H. Thelander	Annual	1982	39.50	40-56
1983	Raccoon and Young - H. Thelander	Annual	1983	39.50	47
1984	Stork and Nestlings - H. Thelander	Annual	1984	39.50	48
1985	Bear and Cubs - H. Thelander	Annual	1985	39.50	47
1986	Elephant with Calf - H. Thelander	Annual	1986	39.50	48-60
1987	Sheep with Lambs - H. Thelander	Annual	1987	42.50	83-90
1988	Crested Plover and Young - H. Thelander	Annual	1988	47.50	75-87
1988	Lapwing Mother with Chicks - H. Thelander	Annual	1988	49.50	90
1989	Cow With Calf - H. Thelander	Annual	1989	49.50	60-90
1990	Hen with Chicks - L. Jensen	Annual	1990	52.50	70-93
1991	The Nanny Goat and her Two Frisky Kids - L. Jensen	Annual	1991	54.50	80-112
1992	Panda With Cubs - L. Jensen	Annual	1992	59.50	75-90
1993	St. Bernard Dog and Puppies - A. Therkelsen	Annual	1993	59.50	75-105
1994	Cat with Kittens - A. Therkelsen	Annual	1994	59.50	75-90
1995	Hedgehog with Young - A. Therkelsen	Annual	1995	59.50	60-76
1996	Koala with Young - A. Therkelsen	Annual	1996	59.50	60-75
1997	Goose with Gooslings - L. Didier	Annual		59.50	60

Mother's Day Jubilee-5 Year Cycle - Thelander

1979	Dog & Puppies	Yr.Iss.	1979	55.00	75
1984	Swan Family	Yr.Iss.	1984	65.00	65-100
1989	Mare & Colt	Yr.Iss.	1989	95.00	112
1994	Woodpecker & Young	Yr.Iss.	1994	95.00	95

Olympic - Unknown

1972	Munich, Germany	Closed	1972	20.00	15-30
1976	Montreal, Canada	Closed	1976	29.50	60
1980	Moscow, Russia	Closed	1980	43.00	89
1984	Los Angeles, USA	Closed	1984	45.00	259
1988	Seoul, Korea	Closed	1988	60.00	65-90
1992	Barcelona, Spain	Closed	1992	74.50	80-87

Santa Around the World - H. Hansen

1995	Santa in Greenland	Yr.Iss.	1995	74.50	75
1996	Santa in Orient	Yr.Iss.	1996	74.50	75
1997	Santa in Russia	Yr.Iss.		74.50	75

Santa Claus Collection - H. Hansen

1989	Santa's Workshop	Annual	1989	59.50	60-125
1990	Santa's Sleigh	Annual	1990	59.50	60-100
1991	Santa's Journey	Annual	1991	69.50	70-120
1992	Santa's Arrival	Annual	1992	74.50	60-90
1993	Santa's Gifts	Annual	1993	74.50	75
1994	Christmas Stories	Annual	1994	74.50	75

Statue of Liberty - Unknown

1985	Statue of Liberty	10,000	1985	60.00	75-80

The Bradford Exchange/Russia

The Nutcracker - N. Zaitseva

1993	Marie's Magical Gift	95-day		39.87	47
1993	Dance of Sugar Plum Fairy	95-day		39.87	50
1994	Waltz of the Flowers	95-day		39.87	50
1994	Battle With the Mice King	95-day		39.87	50

The Bradford Exchange/United States

101 Dalmatians - Disney Studios

1993	Watch Dogs	95-day		29.90	30
1994	A Happy Reunion	95-day		29.90	30
1994	Hello Darlings	95-day		32.90	33
1994	Sergeant Tibs Saves the Day	95-day		32.90	33
1994	Halfway Home	95-day		32.90	33
1994	True Love	95-day		32.90	33
1995	Bedtime	95-day		34.90	35
1995	A Messy Good Time	95-day		34.90	35

Aladdin - Disney Studios

1993	Magic Carpet Ride	95-day		29.90	30
1993	A Friend Like Me	95-day		29.90	30
1994	Aladdin in Love	95-day		29.90	30
1994	Traveling Companions	95-day		29.90	30
1994	Make Way for Prince Ali	95-day		29.90	30
1994	Aladdin's Wish	95-day		29.90	30
1995	Bee Yourself	95-day		29.90	30
1995	Group Hug	95-day		29.90	30

Alice in Wonderland - S. Gustafson

1993	The Mad Tea Party	Closed		29.90	65
1993	The Cheshire Cat	Closed		29.90	65
1994	Croquet with the Queen	Closed		29.90	85
1994	Advice from a Caterpillar	Closed		29.90	80

America's Triumph in Space - R. Schaar

1993	The Eagle Has Landed	95-day		29.90	30
1993	The March Toward Destiny	95-day		29.90	30
1994	Flight of Glory	95-day		32.90	33
1994	Beyond the Bounds of Earth	95-day		32.90	[illegible]
1994	Conquering the New Frontier	95-day		32.90	33
1994	Rendezvous With Victory	95-day		34.90	35
1994	The New Explorers	95-day		34.90	35
1994	Triumphant Finale	95-day		34.90	35

American Frontier - C. Wysocki

1993	Timberline Jack's Trading Post	95-day		29.90	30
1994	Dr. Livingwell's Medicine Show	95-day		29.90	30
1994	Bustling Boomtown	95-day		29.90	30
1994	Kirbyville	95-day		29.90	30
1994	Hearty Homesteaders	95-day		29.90	30
1994	Oklahoma or Bust	95-day		29.90	30

Ancient Seasons - M. Silversmith

1995	Edge of Night	95-day		29.90	30

Autumn Encounters - C. Fisher

1995	Woodland Innocents	95-day		29.90	30

Babe Ruth Centennial - P. Heffernan

1994	The 60th Homer	Closed		34.90	55
1995	Ruth's Pitching Debut	Closed		29.90	75
1995	The Final Home Run	Closed		29.90	60
1995	Barnstorming Days	Closed		34.90	45

Baskets of Love - A. Isakov

1993	Andrew and Abbey	Closed		29.90	30
1993	Cody and Courtney	Closed		29.90	45
1993	Emily and Elliott	Closed		32.90	60
1993	Heather and Hannah	Closed		32.90	35
1993	Justin and Jessica	Closed		32.90	33
1993	Katie and Kelly	Closed		34.90	35
1994	Louie and Libby	95-day		34.90	35
1994	Sammy and Sarah	95-day		34.90	35

Battles of American Civil War - J. Griffin

1994	Gettysburg	95-day		29.90	30
1995	Vicksburg	95-day		29.90	30

The Bunny Workshop - J. Maday

1995	Make Today Eggstra Special	95-day		19.95	20

By Gone Days - L. Dubin

1994	Soda Fountain	95-day		29.90	30
1995	Sam's Grocery Store	95-day		29.90	30
1995	Saturday Matinee	95-day		29.90	30
1995	The Corner News Stand	95-day		29.90	30
1995	Main Street Splendor	95-day		29.90	30
1995	The Barber Shop	95-day		29.90	30

Cabins of Comfort River - F. Buchwitz

1995	Comfort by Camplights Fire	95-day		29.90	30

Carousel Daydreams - N/A

1994	Swept Away	Closed		39.90	40
1995	When I Grow Up	Closed		39.90	40
1995	All Aboard	95-day		44.90	45
1995	Hold Onto Your Dreams	95-day		44.90	45
1995	Flight of Fancy	95-day		44.90	45
1995	Big Hopes, Bright Dreams	95-day		49.90	50
1995	Victorian Reverie	95-day		49.90	50
1995	Wishful Thinking	95-day		49.90	50
1995	Dreams of Destiny	95-day		49.90	50
1995	My Favorite Memory	95-day		49.90	50

Charles Wysocki's Peppercricket Grove - C. Wysocki

1993	Peppercricket Farms	95-day		24.90	25
1993	Gingernut Valley Inn	95-day		24.90	25
1993	Budzen's Fruits and Vegetables	95-day		24.90	25
1993	Virginia's Market	95-day		24.90	25
1993	Pumpkin Hollow Emporium	95-day		24.90	25
1993	Liberty Star Farms	95-day		24.90	25
1993	Overflow Antique Market	95-day		24.90	25
1993	Black Crow Antique Shoppe	95-day		24.90	25

Cherished Traditions - M. Lasher

1995	The Wedding Ring	95-day		29.90	30

Cherubs of Innocence - Various

1994	The First Kiss	95-day		29.90	30
1995	Love at Rest	95-day		29.90	30
1995	Thoughts of Love	95-day		32.90	33

Chosen Messengers - G. Running Wolf

1994	The Pathfinders	Closed		29.90	30
1994	The Overseers	Closed		29.90	30
1994	The Providers	Closed		32.90	50
1994	The Surveyors	Closed		32.90	60

A Christmas Carol - L. Garrison

1993	God Bless Us Everyone	Closed		29.90	75
1993	Ghost of Christmas Present	Closed		29.90	70
1994	A Merry Christmas to All	Closed		29.90	90
1994	A Visit From Marley's Ghost	Closed		29.90	60
1994	Remembering Christmas Past	Closed		29.90	70
1994	A Spirit's Warning	Closed		29.90	80
1994	The True Spirit of Christmas	Closed		29.90	75
1994	Merry Christmas, Bob	Closed		29.90	75

Christmas Memories - J. Tanton

1993	A Winter's Tale	Closed		29.90	30
1993	Finishing Touch	Closed		29.90	45
1993	Welcome to Our Home	Closed		29.90	55
1993	A Christmas Celebration	Closed		29.90	60

Classic Melodies from the "Sound of Music" - M. Hampshire

1995	Sing Along with Maria	Closed		29.90	60
1995	A Drop of Golden Sun	Closed		29.90	60-70
1995	The Von Trapp Family Singers	Closed		29.90	60
1995	Alpine Refuge	Closed		29.90	30

The Costuming of A Legend: Dressing Gone With The Wind - D. Klauba

1993	The Red Dress	95-day		29.90	30
1993	The Green Drapery Dress	95-day		29.90	30
1994	The Green Sprigged Dress	95-day		29.90	30
1994	Black & White Bengaline Dress	95-day		29.90	30
1994	Widow's Weeds	95-day		29.90	30
1994	The Country Walking Dress	95-day		29.90	30
1994	Plaid Business Attire	95-day		29.90	30
1994	Orchid Percale Dress	95-day		29.90	30
1994	The Mourning Gown	95-day		29.90	30
1994	The Green Muslin Dress	95-day		29.90	30

A Country Wonderland - W. Goebel

1995	The Quiet Hour	95-day		29.90	30

Deer Friends at Christmas - J. Thornbrugh

1994	All a Glow	Closed		29.90	30
1994	A Glistening Season	Closed		29.90	30
1994	Holiday Sparkle	Closed		29.90	30
1995	Woodland Splendor	95-day		29.90	30
1995	Starry Night	95-day		29.90	30
1995	Radiant Countryside	95-day		29.90	30

Desert Rhythms - M. Cowdery

1994	Partner With A Breeze	95-day		29.90	30
1994	Wind Dancer	95-day		29.90	30
1994	Riding On Air	95-day		29.90	30

Dog Days - J. Gadamus

1993	Sweet Dreams	Closed		29.90	50
1993	Pier Group	Closed		29.90	45
1993	Wagon Train	Closed		32.90	60
1993	First Flush	Closed		32.90	50
1993	Little Rascals	Closed		32.90	70
1993	Where'd He Go	Closed		32.90	70

Elvis: Young & Wild - B. Emmett

1993	The King of Creole	95-day		29.90	30
1993	King of the Road	95-day		29.90	30
1994	Tough But Tender	95-day		32.90	33

*Quotes have been rounded up to nearest dollar

Collectors' Information Bureau

189

YEAR ISSUE		EDITION LIMIT	YEAR RETD.	ISSUE PRICE	*QUOTE U.S. $
1994	With Love, Elvis	95-day		32.90	33
1994	The Picture of Cool	95-day		32.90	33
1994	Kissing Elvis	95-day		34.90	35
1994	The Perfect Take	95-day		34.90	35
1994	The Rockin' Rebel	95-day		34.90	35

Faces of the Wild - D. Parker

1995	The Wolf	95-day		39.90	40

Fairyland - M. Jobe

1994	Trails of Starlight	95-day		29.90	30
1994	Twilight Trio	95-day		29.90	30
1994	Forest Enchantment	95-day		32.90	33
1995	Silvery Splasher	95-day		32.90	33
1995	Magical Mischief	95-day		32.90	33
1995	Farewell to the Night	95-day		34.90	35

Family Circles - R. Rust

1993	Great Gray Owl Family	Closed		29.90	35
1994	Great Horned Owl Family	Closed		29.90	50
1994	Barred Owl Family	Closed		29.90	50
1994	Spotted Owl Family	Closed		29.90	50

Favorite Classic Cars - D. Everhart

1993	1957 Corvette	Closed		54.00	60
1993	1956 Thunderbird	Closed		54.00	75-95
1994	1957 Bel Air	Closed		54.00	100
1994	1965 Mustang	Closed		54.00	100

Field Pup Follies - C. Jackson

1994	Sleeping on the Job	Closed		29.90	35
1994	Hat Check	Closed		29.90	50
1994	Fowl Play	Closed		29.90	50
1994	Tackling Lunch	Closed		29.90	50

Fleeting Encounters - M. Budden

1995	Autumn Retreat	95-day		29.90	30

Floral Frolics - G. Kurz

1994	Spring Surprises	Closed		29.90	45
1994	Bee Careful	Closed		29.90	40
1995	Fuzzy Fun	Closed		32.90	45
1995	Sunny Hideout	Closed		32.90	45

Floral Greetings - L. Liu

1994	Circle of Love	95-day		29.90	30
1994	Circle of Elegance	95-day		29.90	30
1994	Circle of Harmony	95-day		32.90	33
1994	Circle of Joy	95-day		32.90	33
1994	Circle of Romance	95-day		34.90	35
1995	Circle of Inspiration	95-day		34.90	35

Footsteps of the Brave - H. Schaare

1993	Noble Quest	Closed		24.90	25
1993	At Storm's Passage	Closed		24.90	45
1993	With Boundless Vision	Closed		27.90	38
1993	Horizons of Destiny	Closed		27.90	33
1993	Path of His Forefathers	Closed		27.90	45
1993	Soulful Reflection	Closed		29.90	50
1993	The Reverent Trail	Closed		29.90	48
1994	At Journey's End	Closed		34.90	45

Forever Glamorous Barbie - C. Falberg

1995	Enchanted Evening	6/96		49.90	50

Fracé's Kingdom of the Great Cats: Signature Collection - C. Fracé

1994	Mystic Realm	95-day		39.90	40
1994	Snow Leopard	95-day		39.90	40
1994	Emperor of Siberia	95-day		39.90	40
1994	His Domain	95-day		39.90	40
1994	American Monarch	95-day		39.90	40

Freshwater Game Fish of North America - E. Totten

1994	Rainbow Trout	95-day		29.90	30
1995	Largemouth Bass	95-day		29.90	30
1995	Blue Gills	95-day		29.90	30
1995	Northern Pike	95-day		29.90	30
1995	Brown Trout	95-day		29.90	30

Friendship in Bloom - L. Chang

1994	Paws in the Posies	95-day		34.90	35
1995	Cozy Petunia Patch	95-day		34.90	35
1995	Patience & Impatience	95-day		34.90	35

Gallant Men of Civil War - J. P. Strain

1994	Robert E. Lee	95-day		29.90	30
1995	Stonewall Jackson	95-day		29.90	30
1995	Nathan Bedford Forest	95-day		29.90	30
1995	Joshua Chamberlain	95-day		29.90	30
1995	John Hunt Morgan	95-day		29.90	30

Gardens of Innocence - D. Richardson

1994	Hope	95-day		29.90	30
1994	Charity	95-day		29.90	30
1994	Joy	95-day		32.90	33
1994	Faith	95-day		32.90	33
1994	Grace	95-day		32.90	33
1995	Serenity	95-day		34.90	35
1995	Peace	95-day		34.90	35

YEAR ISSUE		EDITION LIMIT	YEAR RETD.	ISSUE PRICE	*QUOTE U.S.$
1995	Patience	95-day		34.90	35

Getting Away From It All - D. Rust

1995	Mountain Hideaway	95-day		29.90	30

Gone With The Wind: A Legend in Stained Glass - M. Phalen

1995	Scarlett Radiance	Closed		39.90	60
1995	Rhett's Bright Promise	95-day		39.90	40
1995	Ashley's Smoldering Fire	95-day		39.90	40
1995	Melanie Lights His World	95-day		39.90	40

Gone With The Wind: Musical Treasures - A. Jenks

1994	Tara: Scarlett's True Love	95-day		29.90	30
1994	Scarlett: Belle of/12 Oaks BBQ	95-day		29.90	30
1995	Charity Bazaar	95-day		32.90	33
1995	The Proposal	95-day		32.90	33

Great Moments in Baseball - S. Gardner

1993	Joe DiMaggio: The Streak	95-day		29.90	30
1993	Stan Musial: 5 Homer Double Header	95-day		29.90	30
1994	Bobby Thomson: Shot Heard Round the World	95-day		32.90	33
1994	Bill Mazeroski: Winning Home Run	95-day		32.90	33
1994	Don Larsen: Perfect Series Game	95-day		32.90	33
1994	J. Robinson: Saved Pennant	95-day		34.90	35
1994	Satchel Paige: Greatest Games	95-day		34.90	35
1994	Billy Martin: The Rescue Catch	95-day		34.90	35
1994	Dizzy Dean: The World Series Shutout	95-day		34.90	35
1995	Carl Hubbell: The 1934 All State	95-day		36.90	37

Great Superbowl Quarterbacks - R. Brown

1995	Joe Montana: King of Comeback	95-day		29.90	30

Guidance From Above - B. Jaxon

1994	Prayer to the Storm	95-day		29.90	30
1995	Appeal to Thunder	95-day		29.90	30
1995	Blessing the Future	95-day		29.90	30

Happy Hearts - J. Daly

1995	Contentment	95-day		29.90	30
1995	Playmates	95-day		29.90	30
1995	Childhood Friends	95-day		32.90	33
1995	Favorite Gift	95-day		32.90	33

Heart to Heart - Various

1995	Thinking of You	95-day		29.90	30

Heaven on Earth - T. Kinkade

1994	I Am the Light of/World	95-day		29.90	30
1995	I Am the Way	95-day		29.90	30
1995	Thy Word is a Lamp	95-day		29.90	30
1995	For Thou Art My Lamp	95-day		29.90	30
1995	In Him Was Life	95-day		29.90	30
1995	But The Path of Just	95-day		29.90	30

Heaven Sent - L. Bogle

1994	Sweet Dreams	95-day		29.90	30
1994	Puppy Dog Tails	95-day		29.90	30
1994	Timeless Treasure	95-day		32.90	33
1995	Precious Gift	95-day		32.90	33

Heirloom Memories - A. Pech

1994	Porcelain Treasure	Closed		29.90	60
1994	Rhythms in Lace	Closed		29.90	65
1994	Pink Lemonade Roses	Closed		29.90	60
1994	Victorian Romance	Closed		29.90	60
1994	Teatime Tulips	Closed		29.90	60
1994	Touch of the Irish	Closed		29.90	50

A Hidden Garden - T. Clausnitzer

1993	Curious Kittens	Closed		29.90	42
1994	Through the Eyes of Blue	Closed		29.90	30
1994	Amber Gaze	95-day		29.90	30
1994	Fascinating Find	95-day		29.90	30

A Hidden World - R. Rust

1993	Two by Night, Two by Light	Closed		29.90	50
1993	Two by Steam, Two in Dream	Closed		29.90	30
1993	Two on Sly, Two Watch Nearby	Closed		32.90	50
1993	Hunter Growls, Spirits Prowl	Closed		32.90	48
1993	In Moonglow One Drinks	Closed		32.90	33
1993	Sings at the Moon, Spirits Sing in Tune	95-day		34.90	35
1994	Two Cubs Play As Spirits Show the Way	95-day		34.90	35
1994	Young Ones Hold on Tight As Spirits Stay in Sight	95-day		34.90	35

Hideaway Lake - R. Rust

1993	Rusty's Retreat	Closed		34.90	35
1993	Fishing For Dreams	Closed		34.90	35
1993	Sunset Cabin	Closed		34.90	48
1993	Echoes of Morning	Closed		34.90	50

Hometown Memories - C. Wysocki

1994	Small Talk at Birdie's Perch	95-day		29.90	30
1995	Tranquil Days/Ravenswhip Cove	95-day		29.90	30
1995	Summer Delights	95-day		29.90	30
1995	Capturing the Moment	95-day		29.90	30

YEAR ISSUE		EDITION LIMIT	YEAR RETD.	ISSUE PRICE	*QUOTE U.S.$
1995	A Farewell Kiss	95-day		29.90	30
1995	Jason Sparkin the Lighthouse Keeper's Daughter	95-day		29.90	30

Hunters of the Spirit - R. Docken

1995	Provider	95-day		29.90	30

Illusions of Nature - M. Bierlinski

1995	A Trio of Wolves	95-day		29.90	30

Keepsakes of the Heart - C. Layton

1993	Forever Friends	Closed		29.90	33
1993	Afternoon Tea	Closed		29.90	37
1993	Riding Companions	Closed		29.90	40
1994	Sentimental Sweethearts	Closed		29.90	60

Kindred Moments - C. Poulin

1995	Sisters Are Blossoms	95-day		29.90	30

Kingdom of the Unicorn - M. Ferraro

1993	The Magic Begins	Closed		29.90	35
1993	In Crystal Waters	Closed		29.90	45
1993	Chasing a Dream	Closed		29.90	45
1993	The Fountain of Youth	Closed		29.90	45

Legend of the White Buffalo - D. Stanley

1995	Mystic Spirit	95-day		29.90	30

Lena Liu's Beautiful Gardens - Inspired by L. Liu

1995	Lily Garden	6/96		39.00	39

The Life of Christ - R. Barrett

1994	The Passion in the Garden	Closed		29.90	50
1994	Jesus Enters Jerusalem	Closed		29.90	30
1994	Jesus Calms the Waters	Closed		32.90	65
1994	Sermon on the Mount	Closed		32.90	50
1994	The Last Supper	Closed		32.90	50
1994	The Ascension	Closed		34.90	40
1994	The Resurrection	Closed		34.90	50
1994	The Crucifixion	Closed		34.90	35

The Light of the World - C. Nick

1995	The Last Supper	95-day		29.90	30

Lincoln's Portraits of Valor - B. Maguire

1993	The Gettysburg Address	95-day		29.90	30
1993	Emancipation Proclamation	95-day		29.90	30
1993	The Lincoln-Douglas Debates	95-day		29.90	30
1993	The Second Inaugural Address	95-day		29.90	30

The Lion King - Disney Studios

1994	The Circle of Life	95-day		29.90	30
1995	Like Father, Like Son	95-day		29.90	30
1995	A Crunchy Feast	95-day		32.90	33

Little Bandits - C. Jagodits

1993	Handle With Care	Closed		29.90	55
1993	All Tied Up	Closed		29.90	55
1993	Everything's Coming Up Daisies	Closed		32.90	45
1993	Out of Hand	Closed		32.90	55
1993	Pupsicles	Closed		32.90	55
1993	Unexpected Guests	Closed		32.90	45

Lords of Forest & Canyon - G. Beecham

1994	Mountain Majesty	95-day		29.90	30
1995	Proud Legacy	95-day		29.90	30
1995	Golden Monarch	95-day		29.90	30
1995	Forest Emperor	95-day		29.90	30

Me & My Shadow - J. Welty

1994	Easter Parade	Closed		29.90	40
1994	A Golden Moment	Closed		29.90	30
1994	Perfect Timing	Closed		29.90	37
1995	Giddyup	Closed		29.90	40

Mickey and Minnie's Through the Years - Disney Studios

1995	Mickey's Birthday Party 1942	95-day		29.90	30
1995	Brave Little Tailor	95-day		29.90	30

A Mother's Love - J. Anderson

1995	Remembrance	95 days		29.90	30

Musical Tribute to Elvis the King - B. Emmett

1994	Rockin' Blue Suede Shoes	95-day		29.90	30
1994	Hound Dog Bop	95-day		29.90	30
1995	Red, White & GI Blues	95-day		32.90	33
1995	American Dream	95-day		32.90	33

Mysterious Case of Fowl Play - H. Bond

1994	Inspector Clawseau	Closed		29.90	40
1994	Glamourpuss	Closed		29.90	38
1994	Sophisicat	Closed		29.90	65
1994	Kool Cat	Closed		29.90	45
1994	Sneakers & High-Top	Closed		29.90	60
1995	Tuxedo	Closed		29.90	75

Mystic Guardians - S. Hill

1993	Soul Mates	95-day		29.90	30
1993	Majestic Messenger	95-day		29.90	30
1993	Companion Spirits	95-day		32.90	33

*Quotes have been rounded up to nearest dollar

The Bradford Exchange/United States
to The Bradford Exchange/United States

PLATES

Year	Issue	Edition Limit	Year Retd.	Issue Price	*Quote U.S.$
1994	Faithful Fellowship	95-day		32.90	33
1994	Spiritual Harmony	95-day		32.90	33
1994	Royal Unity	95-day		32.90	33

Mystic Spirits - V. Crandell

Year	Issue	Edition Limit	Year Retd.	Issue Price	*Quote U.S.$
1995	Moon Shadows	95-day		29.90	30
1995	Midnight Snow	95-day		29.90	30
1995	Arctic Nights	95-day		32.90	33

Native American Legends: Chiefs of Destiny - C. Jackson

Year	Issue	Edition Limit	Year Retd.	Issue Price	*Quote U.S.$
1995	Red Cloud	6/96		44.90	45

Native Beauty - L. Bogle

Year	Issue	Edition Limit	Year Retd.	Issue Price	*Quote U.S.$
1994	The Promise	95-day		29.90	30
1994	Afterglow	95-day		29.90	30
1994	White Feather	95-day		29.90	30
1995	First glance	95-day		29.90	30
1995	Morning Star	95-day		29.90	30
1995	Quiet Time	95-day		29.90	30
1995	Warm Thoughts	95-day		29.90	30

Native Visions - J. Cole

Year	Issue	Edition Limit	Year Retd.	Issue Price	*Quote U.S.$
1995	Bringers of the Storm	95-day		29.90	30
1995	Water Vision	95-day		29.90	30

Nature's Little Treasures - L. Martin

Year	Issue	Edition Limit	Year Retd.	Issue Price	*Quote U.S.$
1994	Garden Whispers	95-day		29.90	30
1994	Wings of Grace	95-day		29.90	30
1994	Delicate Splendor	95-day		32.90	33
1994	Perfect Jewels	95-day		32.90	33
1994	Miniature Glory	95-day		32.90	33
1994	Precious Beauties	95-day		34.90	35
1994	Minute Enchantment	95-day		34.90	35
1994	Rare Perfection	95-day		34.90	35
1995	Misty Morning	95-day		36.90	37

New Horizons - R. Copple

Year	Issue	Edition Limit	Year Retd.	Issue Price	*Quote U.S.$
1993	Building For a New Generation	Closed		29.90	33
1993	The Power of Gold	95-day		29.90	30
1994	Wings of Snowy Grandeur	95-day		32.90	33
1994	Master of the Chase	95-day		32.90	33
1995	Coastal Domain	95-day		32.90	33
1995	Majestic Wings	95-day		32.90	33

Nightsong: The Loon - J. Hansel

Year	Issue	Edition Limit	Year Retd.	Issue Price	*Quote U.S.$
1994	Moonlight Echoes	Closed		29.90	38
1994	Evening Mist	Closed		29.90	60
1994	Nocturnal Glow	Closed		32.90	55
1994	Tranquil Reflections	Closed		32.90	50
1994	Peaceful Waters	Closed		32.90	33
1994	Silently Nestled	Closed		34.90	50
1994	Night Light	Closed		34.90	65
1995	Peaceful Homestead	Closed		34.90	35
1995	Silent Passage	Closed		34.90	35
1995	Tranquil Refuge	95-day		36.90	37
1995	Serene Sanctuary	95-day		36.90	37
1995	Moonlight Cruise	95-day		36.90	37

Nightwatch: The Wolf - D. Ningewance

Year	Issue	Edition Limit	Year Retd.	Issue Price	*Quote U.S.$
1994	Moonlight Serenade	Closed		29.90	30
1994	Midnight Guard	Closed		29.90	45
1994	Snowy Lookout	Closed		29.90	45
1994	Silent Sentries	Closed		29.90	45
1994	Song to the Night	Closed		29.90	45
1994	Winter Passage	Closed		29.90	45

Northern Companions - K. Weisberg

Year	Issue	Edition Limit	Year Retd.	Issue Price	*Quote U.S.$
1995	Midnight Harmony	95-day		29.90	30

Northwoods Spirit - D. Wenzel

Year	Issue	Edition Limit	Year Retd.	Issue Price	*Quote U.S.$
1994	Timeless Watch	95-day		29.90	30
1994	Woodland Retreat	95-day		29.90	30
1995	Forest Echo	95-day		29.90	30
1995	Timberland Gaze	95-day		29.90	30
1995	Evening Respite	95-day		29.90	30

Nosy Neighbors - P. Weirs

Year	Issue	Edition Limit	Year Retd.	Issue Price	*Quote U.S.$
1994	Cat Nap	95-day		29.90	30
1994	Special Delivery	95-day		29.90	30
1995	House Sitting	95-day		29.90	30
1995	Observation Deck	95-day		32.90	33
1995	Surprise Visit	95-day		32.90	33

Notorious Disney Villains - Disney Studios

Year	Issue	Edition Limit	Year Retd.	Issue Price	*Quote U.S.$
1993	The Evil Queen	Closed		29.90	57-65
1994	Maleficent	Closed		29.90	65
1994	Ursella	Closed		29.90	50
1994	Cruella De Vil	Closed		29.90	60

Old Fashioned Christmas with Thomas Kinkade - T. Kinkade

Year	Issue	Edition Limit	Year Retd.	Issue Price	*Quote U.S.$
1993	All Friends Are Welcome	95-day		29.90	35
1993	Winters Memories	95-day		29.90	30
1993	A Holiday Gathering	95-day		32.90	33
1994	Christmas Tree Cottage	95-day		32.90	33
1995	The Best Tradition	95-day		32.90	33

Panda Bear Hugs - W. Nelson

Year	Issue	Edition Limit	Year Retd.	Issue Price	*Quote U.S.$
1993	Rock-A-Bye	Closed		39.90	55
1993	Loving Advice	Closed		39.90	55
1993	A Playful Interlude	Closed		39.90	50
1993	A Taste of Life	Closed		39.90	50

Pathways of the Heart - J. Barnes

Year	Issue	Edition Limit	Year Retd.	Issue Price	*Quote U.S.$
1993	October Radiance	95-day		29.90	30
1993	Daybreak	95-day		29.90	30
1994	Harmony with Nature	95-day		29.90	30
1994	Distant Lights	95-day		29.90	30
1994	A Night to Remember	95-day		29.90	30
1994	Peaceful Evening	95-day		29.90	30

Peace on Earth - D. Geisness

Year	Issue	Edition Limit	Year Retd.	Issue Price	*Quote U.S.$
1993	Winter Lullaby	Closed		29.90	65
1994	Heavenly Slumber	Closed		29.90	45
1994	Sweet Embrace	Closed		32.90	60
1994	Woodland Dreams	Closed		32.90	50
1994	Snowy Silence	Closed		32.90	75
1994	Dreamy Whispers	Closed		32.90	35

Picked from an English Garden - W. Von Schwarzbek

Year	Issue	Edition Limit	Year Retd.	Issue Price	*Quote U.S.$
1994	Inspired by Romance	95-day		29.90	30
1995	Lasting Treasures	95-day		29.90	30
1995	Nature's Wonders	95-day		29.90	30

Pinegrove's Winter Cardinals - S. Timm

Year	Issue	Edition Limit	Year Retd.	Issue Price	*Quote U.S.$
1994	Evening in Pinegrove	95-day		29.90	30
1994	Pinegrove's Sunset	95-day		29.90	30
1994	Pinegrove's Twilight	95-day		29.90	30
1994	Daybreak in Pinegrove	95-day		29.90	30
1994	Pinegrove's Morning	95-day		29.90	30
1994	Afternoon in Pinegrove	95-day		29.90	30
1994	Midnight in Pinegrove	95-day		29.90	30
1994	At Home in Pinegrove	95-day		29.90	30

Portraits of Majesty - Various

Year	Issue	Edition Limit	Year Retd.	Issue Price	*Quote U.S.$
1994	Snowy Monarch	95-day		29.90	30
1995	Reflections of Kings	95-day		29.90	30
1995	Emperor of His Realm	95-day		29.90	30
1995	Solemn Sovereign	95-day		29.90	30

Postcards from Thomas Kinkade - T. Kinkade

Year	Issue	Edition Limit	Year Retd.	Issue Price	*Quote U.S.$
1995	San Francisco	95-day		34.90	35
1995	Paris	95-day		34.90	35
1995	New York City	95-day		34.90	35

Practice Makes Perfect - L. Kaatz

Year	Issue	Edition Limit	Year Retd.	Issue Price	*Quote U.S.$
1994	What's a Mother to Do?	Closed		29.90	40
1994	The Ones That Got Away	Closed		29.90	40
1994	Pointed in the Wrong Direction	Closed		32.90	55
1994	Fishing for Compliments	Closed		32.90	45
1994	Dandy Distraction	Closed		32.90	33
1995	On The Right Track	Closed		34.90	35
1995	More Than a Mouthful	Closed		34.90	35
1995	On the Right Track	95-day		34.90	35
1995	Missing the Point	95-day		34.90	35

Precious Visions - J. Grande

Year	Issue	Edition Limit	Year Retd.	Issue Price	*Quote U.S.$
1994	Brilliant Moment	95-day		29.90	30
1995	Brief Interlude	95-day		29.90	30
1995	Timeless Radiance	95-day		29.90	30
1995	Enduring Elegance	95-day		32.90	33

Promise of a Savior - Various

Year	Issue	Edition Limit	Year Retd.	Issue Price	*Quote U.S.$
1993	An Angel's Message	95-day		29.90	30
1993	Gifts to Jesus	95-day		29.90	30
1993	The Heavenly King	95-day		29.90	30
1993	Angels Were Watching	95-day		29.90	30
1993	Holy Mother and Child	95-day		29.90	30
1994	A Child is Born	95-day		29.90	30

Proud Heritage - M. Amerman

Year	Issue	Edition Limit	Year Retd.	Issue Price	*Quote U.S.$
1994	Mystic Warrior: Medicine Crow	Closed		34.90	35
1994	Great Chief: Sitting Bull	Closed		34.90	35
1994	Brave Leader: Geronimo	Closed		34.90	35
1995	Peaceful Defender: Chief Joseph	95-day		34.90	35

Quiet Moments - K. Daniel

Year	Issue	Edition Limit	Year Retd.	Issue Price	*Quote U.S.$
1994	Time for Tea	95-day		29.90	30
1995	A Loving Hand	95-day		29.90	30
1995	Kept with Care	95-day		29.90	30
1995	Puppy Love	95-day		29.90	30

Radiant Messengers - L. Martin

Year	Issue	Edition Limit	Year Retd.	Issue Price	*Quote U.S.$
1994	Peace	95-day		29.90	30
1994	Hope	95-day		29.90	30
1994	Beauty	95-day		29.90	30
1994	Inspiration	95-day		29.90	30

Reflections of Marilyn - C. Notarile

Year	Issue	Edition Limit	Year Retd.	Issue Price	*Quote U.S.$
1994	All That Glitters	95-day		29.90	30
1994	Shimmering Heat	95-day		29.90	30
1994	Million Dollar Star	95-day		29.90	30
1995	A Twinkle in Her Eye	95-day		29.90	30

Remembering Elvis - N. Giorgio

Year	Issue	Edition Limit	Year Retd.	Issue Price	*Quote U.S.$
1994	The King	95-day		29.90	30
1995	The Legend	95-day		29.90	30

Royal Enchantments - J. Penchoff

Year	Issue	Edition Limit	Year Retd.	Issue Price	*Quote U.S.$
1994	The Gift	Closed		39.90	40
1995	The Courtship	Closed		39.90	40
1995	The Promise	Closed		39.90	40
1995	The Embrace	Closed		39.90	40

Sacred Circle - K. Randle

Year	Issue	Edition Limit	Year Retd.	Issue Price	*Quote U.S.$
1993	Before the Hunt	Closed		29.90	45
1993	Spiritual Guardian	Closed		29.90	30
1993	Ghost Dance	Closed		32.90	60
1994	Deer Dance	Closed		32.90	70
1994	The Wolf Dance	Closed		32.90	45
1994	The Painted Horse	Closed		34.90	35
1994	Transformation Dance	Closed		34.90	48
1994	Elk Dance	Closed		34.90	50

Santa's Little Helpers - B. Higgins Bond

Year	Issue	Edition Limit	Year Retd.	Issue Price	*Quote U.S.$
1994	Stocking Stuffers	Closed		24.90	25
1994	Wrapping Up the Holidays	Closed		24.90	25
1994	Not a Creature Was Stirring	Closed		24.90	25
1995	Cozy Kittens	95-day		24.90	25
1995	Holiday Mischief	95-day		24.90	25
1995	Treats For Santa	95-day		24.90	25

Santa's On His Way - S. Gustafson

Year	Issue	Edition Limit	Year Retd.	Issue Price	*Quote U.S.$
1994	Checking It Twice	95-day		29.90	30
1994	Up, Up & Away	95-day		29.90	30
1995	Santa's First Stop	95-day		29.90	30
1995	Gifts for One and All	95-day		29.90	30

Signs of Spring - J. Thornbrugh

Year	Issue	Edition Limit	Year Retd.	Issue Price	*Quote U.S.$
1994	A Family Feast	95-day		29.90	30
1995	How Fast They Grow	95-day		29.90	30
1995	Our First Home	95-day		29.90	30
1995	Awaiting New Arrivals	95-day		29.90	30

Silent Journey - D. Casey

Year	Issue	Edition Limit	Year Retd.	Issue Price	*Quote U.S.$
1994	Where Paths Cross	95-day		29.90	30
1994	On Eagle's Wings	95-day		29.90	30
1994	Seeing the Unseen	95-day		29.90	30
1995	Where the Buffalo Roam	95-day		29.90	30
1995	Unbridled Majesty	95-day		29.90	30
1995	Wisdom Seeker	95-day		29.90	30
1995	Journey of the Wild	95-day		29.90	30

Soft Elegance - R. Iverson

Year	Issue	Edition Limit	Year Retd.	Issue Price	*Quote U.S.$
1994	Priscilla in Pearls	95-day		29.90	30
1995	Tabitha on Taffeta	95-day		29.90	30
1995	Emily in Emeralds	95-day		29.90	30
1995	Alexandra in Amethysts	95-day		29.90	30

Some Beary Nice Places - J. Tanton

Year	Issue	Edition Limit	Year Retd.	Issue Price	*Quote U.S.$
1994	Welcome to the Library	Closed		29.90	30
1994	Welcome to Our Country Kitchen	Closed		29.90	30
1995	Bearennial Garden	Closed		32.90	33
1995	Welcome to Our Music Conserbeartory	Closed		32.90	33

Soul Mates - L. Bogle

Year	Issue	Edition Limit	Year Retd.	Issue Price	*Quote U.S.$
1995	The Lovers	95-day		29.90	30
1995	The Awakening	95-day		29.90	30

Sovereigns of the Wild - D. Grant

Year	Issue	Edition Limit	Year Retd.	Issue Price	*Quote U.S.$
1993	The Snow Queen	Closed		29.90	40
1994	Let Us Survive	Closed		29.90	35
1994	Cool Cats	Closed		29.90	55
1994	Siberian Snow Tigers	Closed		29.90	30
1994	African Evening	Closed		29.90	45
1994	First Outing	95-day		29.90	30

Superstars of Baseball - T. Sizemore

Year	Issue	Edition Limit	Year Retd.	Issue Price	*Quote U.S.$
1994	Willie "Say Hey" Mays	95-day		29.90	30
1995	Carl "Yaz" Yastrzemski	95-day		29.90	30
1995	Frank "Robby" Robinson	95-day		32.90	33
1995	Bob Gibson	95-day		32.90	33

Superstars of Country Music - N. Giorgio

Year	Issue	Edition Limit	Year Retd.	Issue Price	*Quote U.S.$
1993	Dolly Parton: I Will Always Love You	Closed		29.90	35
1993	Kenny Rogers: Sweet Music Man	Closed		29.90	30
1994	Barbara Mandrell	Closed		32.90	35
1994	Glen Campbell: Rhinestone Cowboy	Closed		32.90	33

Tale of Peter Rabbit & Benjamin Bunny - R. Akers

Year	Issue	Edition Limit	Year Retd.	Issue Price	*Quote U.S.$
1994	A Pocket Full of Onions	Closed		39.00	60
1994	Beside His Cousin	Closed		39.00	50
1995	Round that Corner	Closed		39.00	45
1995	Safely Home	95-day		44.00	44
1995	Mr. McGregor's Garden	95-day		44.00	44
1995	Rosemary Tea and Lavender	95-day		44.00	44
1995	Amongst the Flowerpots	95-day		44.00	44
1995	Upon the Scarecrow	95-day		44.00	44

That's What Friends Are For - A. Isakov

Year	Issue	Edition Limit	Year Retd.	Issue Price	*Quote U.S.$
1994	Friends Are Forever	Closed		29.90	50
1994	Friends Are Comfort	Closed		29.90	55
1994	Friends Are Loving	Closed		29.90	45
1995	Friends Are For Fun	Closed		29.90	65

*Quotes have been rounded up to nearest dollar

Collectors' Information Bureau

191

The Bradford Exchange/United States
to Dave Grossman Creations

PLATES

Thomas Kinkade's Illuminated Cottages - T. Kinkade

YEAR	ISSUE	EDITION LIMIT	YEAR RETD.	ISSUE PRICE	*QUOTE U.S.$
1994	The Flagstone Path	Closed		34.90	35
1995	The Lighted Gate	Closed		37.90	38
1995	Cherry Blossom Hideaway	Closed		34.90	35

Thomas Kinkade's Lamplight Village - T. Kinkade

YEAR	ISSUE	EDITION LIMIT	YEAR RETD.	ISSUE PRICE	*QUOTE U.S.$
1995	Lamplight Brooke	95-day		29.90	30
1995	Lamplight Lane	95-day		29.90	30
1995	Lamplight Inn	95-day		29.90	30

Through a Child's Eyes - K. Noles

YEAR	ISSUE	EDITION LIMIT	YEAR RETD.	ISSUE PRICE	*QUOTE U.S.$
1994	Little Butterfly	Closed		29.90	30
1995	Woodland Rose	Closed		29.90	30
1995	Treetop Wonder	Closed		29.90	30
1995	Little Red Squirrel	Closed		32.90	33
1995	Water Lily	Closed		32.90	33
1995	Prairie Song	Closed		32.90	33

Thundering Waters - F. Miller

YEAR	ISSUE	EDITION LIMIT	YEAR RETD.	ISSUE PRICE	*QUOTE U.S.$
1994	Niagara Falls	Closed		34.90	45
1994	Lower Falls, Yellowstone	Closed		34.90	60
1994	Bridal Veil Falls	Closed		34.90	60
1995	Havasu Falls	Closed		29.90	60

Trains of the Great West - K. Randle

YEAR	ISSUE	EDITION LIMIT	YEAR RETD.	ISSUE PRICE	*QUOTE U.S.$
1993	Moonlit Journey	Closed		29.90	35
1993	Mountain Hideaway	Closed		29.90	45
1993	Early Morning Arrival	Closed		29.90	50
1994	The Snowy Pass	Closed		29.90	42

Triumph in the Air - H. Krebs

YEAR	ISSUE	EDITION LIMIT	YEAR RETD.	ISSUE PRICE	*QUOTE U.S.$
1994	Checkmate!	95-day		34.90	35
1994	One Heck of a Deflection Shot	95-day		34.90	35
1994	Hunting Fever	95-day		34.90	35
1995	Struck by Thunder	95-day		34.90	35

Twilight Memories - J. Barnes

YEAR	ISSUE	EDITION LIMIT	YEAR RETD.	ISSUE PRICE	*QUOTE U.S.$
1995	Winter's Twilight	95-day		29.90	30

Two's Company - S. Eide

YEAR	ISSUE	EDITION LIMIT	YEAR RETD.	ISSUE PRICE	*QUOTE U.S.$
1994	Golden Harvest	95-day		29.90	30
1995	Brotherly Love	95-day		29.90	30
1995	Seeing Double	95-day		29.90	30
1995	Spring Spaniels	95-day		29.90	30

Under A Snowy Veil - C. Sams

YEAR	ISSUE	EDITION LIMIT	YEAR RETD.	ISSUE PRICE	*QUOTE U.S.$
1995	Winter's Warmth	95-day		29.90	30
1995	Snow Mates	95-day		29.90	30
1995	Winter's Dawn	95-day		29.90	30
1995	First Snow	95-day		29.90	30

Untamed Spirits - P. Weirs

YEAR	ISSUE	EDITION LIMIT	YEAR RETD.	ISSUE PRICE	*QUOTE U.S.$
1993	Wild Hearts	Closed		29.90	50
1994	Breakaway	Closed		29.90	50
1994	Forever Free	Closed		29.90	50
1994	Distant Thunder	Closed		29.90	45

Untamed Wilderness - P. Weirs

YEAR	ISSUE	EDITION LIMIT	YEAR RETD.	ISSUE PRICE	*QUOTE U.S.$
1995	Unexpected Encounter	95-day		29.90	30

Vanishing Paradises - G. Dieckhoner

YEAR	ISSUE	EDITION LIMIT	YEAR RETD.	ISSUE PRICE	*QUOTE U.S.$
1994	The Rainforest	Closed		29.90	40
1994	The Panda's World	Closed		29.90	60
1994	Splendors of India	Closed		29.90	60
1994	An African Safari	Closed		29.90	60

Visions from Eagle Ridge - D. Casey

YEAR	ISSUE	EDITION LIMIT	YEAR RETD.	ISSUE PRICE	*QUOTE U.S.$
1995	Assembly of Pride	95-day		29.90	30

Visions of Glory - D. Cook

YEAR	ISSUE	EDITION LIMIT	YEAR RETD.	ISSUE PRICE	*QUOTE U.S.$
1995	Iwo Jima	95-day		29.90	30

Visions of Our Lady - H. Garrido

YEAR	ISSUE	EDITION LIMIT	YEAR RETD.	ISSUE PRICE	*QUOTE U.S.$
1994	Our Lady of Lourdes	95-day		29.90	30
1994	Our Lady of Medjugorje	95-day		29.90	30
1994	Our Lady of Fatima	95-day		29.90	30
1994	Our Lady of Guadeloupe	95-day		29.90	30
1994	Our Lady of Grace	95-day		29.90	30
1994	Our Lady of Mt. Carmel	95-day		29.90	30

Visions of the Sacred - D. Stanley

YEAR	ISSUE	EDITION LIMIT	YEAR RETD.	ISSUE PRICE	*QUOTE U.S.$
1994	Snow Rider	95-day		29.90	30
1994	Spring's Messenger	95-day		29.90	30
1994	The Cheyenne Prophet	95-day		32.90	33
1995	Buffalo Caller	95-day		32.90	33
1995	Journey of Harmony	95-day		32.90	33

A Visit from St. Nick - C. Jackson

YEAR	ISSUE	EDITION LIMIT	YEAR RETD.	ISSUE PRICE	*QUOTE U.S.$
1995	Twas the Night Before Christmas	Closed		49.00	49
1995	Up to the Housetop	Closed		49.00	49
1995	A Bundle of Toys	95-day		54.00	54
1995	The Stockings Were Filled	95-day		54.00	54
1995	Visions of Sugarplums	95-day		54.00	54
1995	To My Wondering Eyes	95-day		59.00	59
1995	A Wink of His Eye	95-day		59.00	59
1995	Happy Christmas To All	95-day		59.00	59

A Visit to Brambly Hedge - J. Barklem

YEAR	ISSUE	EDITION LIMIT	YEAR RETD.	ISSUE PRICE	*QUOTE U.S.$
1994	Summer Story	Closed		39.90	50
1994	Spring Story	Closed		39.90	50
1994	Autumn Story	Closed		39.90	55
1995	Winter Story	Closed		39.90	53

Warm Country Moments - M.A. Lasher

YEAR	ISSUE	EDITION LIMIT	YEAR RETD.	ISSUE PRICE	*QUOTE U.S.$
1994	Mabel's Sunny Retreat	95-day		29.90	30
1994	Annebelle's Simple Pleasures	95-day		29.90	30
1994	Harriet's Loving Touch	95-day		29.90	30
1994	Emily and Alice in a Jam	95-day		29.90	30
1995	Hanna's Secret Garden	95-day		29.90	30

Welcome to the Neighborhood - B. Mock

YEAR	ISSUE	EDITION LIMIT	YEAR RETD.	ISSUE PRICE	*QUOTE U.S.$
1994	Ivy Lane	Closed		29.90	30
1994	Daffodil Drive	Closed		29.90	30
1995	Lilac Lane	Closed		34.90	35
1995	Tulip Terrace	Closed		34.90	35

When All Hearts Come Home - J. Barnes

YEAR	ISSUE	EDITION LIMIT	YEAR RETD.	ISSUE PRICE	*QUOTE U.S.$
1993	Oh Christmas Tree	Closed		29.90	43
1993	Night Before Christmas	Closed		29.90	50
1993	Comfort and Joy	Closed		29.90	48
1993	Grandpa's Farm	95-day		29.90	30
1993	Peace on Earth	95-day		29.90	30
1993	Night Departure	95-day		29.90	30
1993	Supper and Small Talk	95-day		29.90	30
1993	Christmas Wish	95-day		29.90	30

When Dreams Blossom - R. McGinnis

YEAR	ISSUE	EDITION LIMIT	YEAR RETD.	ISSUE PRICE	*QUOTE U.S.$
1994	Dreams to Gather	95-day		29.90	30
1994	Where Friends Dream	95-day		29.90	30
1994	The Sweetest of Dreams	95-day		32.90	33
1994	Dreams of Poetry	95-day		32.90	33
1995	A Place to Dream	95-day		32.90	33
1995	Dreaming of You	95-day		32.90	33

Where Eagles Soar - F. Mittelstadt

YEAR	ISSUE	EDITION LIMIT	YEAR RETD.	ISSUE PRICE	*QUOTE U.S.$
1994	On Freedom's Wing	95-day		29.90	30
1994	Allegiance with the Wind	95-day		29.90	30
1995	Lakeside Eagles	95-day		29.90	30
1995	Lighthouse Eagles	95-day		29.90	30
1995	Noble Legacy	95-day		29.90	30

Windows on a World of Song - K. Daniel

YEAR	ISSUE	EDITION LIMIT	YEAR RETD.	ISSUE PRICE	*QUOTE U.S.$
1993	The Library: Cardinals	Closed		34.90	60
1993	The Den: Black-Capped Chickadees	Closed		34.90	35
1993	The Bedroom: Bluebirds	Closed		34.90	35
1994	The Kitchen: Goldfinches	Closed		34.90	35

Wings of Glory - J. Spurlock

YEAR	ISSUE	EDITION LIMIT	YEAR RETD.	ISSUE PRICE	*QUOTE U.S.$
1995	Pride of America	95-day		29.90	30

Winnie the Pooh and Friends - C. Jackson

YEAR	ISSUE	EDITION LIMIT	YEAR RETD.	ISSUE PRICE	*QUOTE U.S.$
1995	Time For a Little Something	Closed		39.90	40
1995	Bouncing's/Tiggers do Best	Closed		39.90	40
1995	You're a Real Friend	95-day		44.90	45
1995	Silly Old Bear	95-day		44.90	45
1995	Many Happy Returns of the Day	95-day		44.90	45
1996	T is For Tigger	95-day		49.90	50
1996	Nobody is Uncheered w/Balloons	95-day		49.90	50
1996	Do You Think It's a Woozie?	95-day		49.90	50

Winter Shadows - Various

YEAR	ISSUE	EDITION LIMIT	YEAR RETD.	ISSUE PRICE	*QUOTE U.S.$
1995	Canyon Moon	95-day		29.90	30
1995	Shadows of Gray	95-day		29.90	30

Wish You Were Here - T. Kinkade

YEAR	ISSUE	EDITION LIMIT	YEAR RETD.	ISSUE PRICE	*QUOTE U.S.$
1994	End of a Perfect Day	95-day		29.90	30
1994	A Quiet Evening/Riverlodge	95-day		29.90	30
1994	Soft Morning Light	95-day		29.90	30

Woodland Tranquility - G. Alexander

YEAR	ISSUE	EDITION LIMIT	YEAR RETD.	ISSUE PRICE	*QUOTE U.S.$
1994	Winter's Calm	95-day		29.90	30
1995	Frosty Morn	95-day		29.90	30
1995	Crossing Boundaries	95-day		29.90	30

Woodland Wings - J. Hansel

YEAR	ISSUE	EDITION LIMIT	YEAR RETD.	ISSUE PRICE	*QUOTE U.S.$
1994	Twilight Flight	Closed		34.90	35
1994	Gliding on Gilded Skies	Closed		34.90	35
1994	Sunset Voyage	Closed		34.90	35
1995	Peaceful Journey	Closed		34.90	35

The World Beneath the Waves - D. Terbush

YEAR	ISSUE	EDITION LIMIT	YEAR RETD.	ISSUE PRICE	*QUOTE U.S.$
1995	Sea of Light	95-day		29.90	30
1995	All God's Children	95-day		29.90	30
1995	Humpback Whales	95-day		29.90	30

The World of the Eagle - J. Hansel

YEAR	ISSUE	EDITION LIMIT	YEAR RETD.	ISSUE PRICE	*QUOTE U.S.$
1993	Sentinel of the Night	Closed		29.90	48
1994	Silent Guard	Closed		29.90	50
1994	Night Flyer	Closed		32.90	45
1995	Midnight Duty	Closed		32.90	55

A World of Wildlife: Celebrating Earth Day - T. Clausnitzer

YEAR	ISSUE	EDITION LIMIT	YEAR RETD.	ISSUE PRICE	*QUOTE U.S.$
1995	A Delicate Balance	95-day		29.90	30

WWII: A Remembrance - J. Griffin

YEAR	ISSUE	EDITION LIMIT	YEAR RETD.	ISSUE PRICE	*QUOTE U.S.$
1994	D-Day	95-day		29.90	30
1994	The Battle of Midway	95-day		29.90	30
1994	The Battle of The Bulge	95-day		32.90	33
1995	Battle of the Philippines	95-day		32.90	33
1995	Doolittle's Raid Over Tokyo	95-day		32.90	33

Cavanagh Group Intl.

Coca-Cola Brand Heritage Collection - Various

YEAR	ISSUE	EDITION LIMIT	YEAR RETD.	ISSUE PRICE	*QUOTE U.S.$
1995	Boy Fishing - N. Rockwell	5,000		60.00	65
1995	Good Boys and Girls - Sundblom	2,500	1995	60.00	60
1995	Hilda Clark with Roses - CGI	5,000		60.00	65
1996	Travel Refreshed - Sundblom	Open		60.00	60

Cherished Teddies/Enesco Corporation

Cherished Seasons - P. Hillman

YEAR	ISSUE	EDITION LIMIT	YEAR RETD.	ISSUE PRICE	*QUOTE U.S.$
1997	Spring-"Spring Brings A Season of Beauty" 203386	Open		35.00	35
1997	Summer-"Summer Brings A Season of Warmth" 203394	Open		35.00	35
1997	Autumn-"Autumn Brings A Season of Thanksgiving" 203408	Open		35.00	35
1997	Winter "Winter Brings A Season of Joy" 203416	Open		35.00	35

Christmas - P. Hillman

YEAR	ISSUE	EDITION LIMIT	YEAR RETD.	ISSUE PRICE	*QUOTE U.S.$
1995	The Season of Joy 141550	Yr.Iss.		35.00	35
1996	The Season of Peace 176060	Yr.Iss.		35.00	35

Easter - P. Hillman

YEAR	ISSUE	EDITION LIMIT	YEAR RETD.	ISSUE PRICE	*QUOTE U.S.$
1996	Some Bunny Loves You 156590	Yr.Iss.		35.00	35
1997	Springtime Happiness 203009	Yr.Iss.		35.00	35

Mother's Day - P. Hillman

YEAR	ISSUE	EDITION LIMIT	YEAR RETD.	ISSUE PRICE	*QUOTE U.S.$
1996	A Mother's Heart is Full of Love 156493	Yr.Iss.		35.00	35
1997	Our Love Is Ever Blooming 203025	Yr.Iss.		35.00	35

Nursery Rhymes - P. Hillman

YEAR	ISSUE	EDITION LIMIT	YEAR RETD.	ISSUE PRICE	*QUOTE U.S.$
1995	Jack/Jill "Our Friendship Will Never Tumble" 114901	Open		35.00	35
1995	Mary/Lamb "I'll Always Be By Your Side" 128902	Open		35.00	35
1995	Old King Cole "You Wear Your Kindness Like a Crown" 135437	Open		35.00	35
1996	Mother Goose & Friends "Happily Ever After With Friends" 170968	Open		35.00	35
1996	Little Miss Muffet "I'm Never Afraid With You At My Side" 145033	Open		35.00	35
1996	Little Jack Horner "I'm Plum Happy You're My Friend" 151998	Open		35.00	35
1996	Wee Willie Winkie "Good Night, Sleep Tight" 170941	Open		35.00	35
1996	Little Bo Peep "Looking For A Friend Like You" 164658	Open		35.00	35

Sweet Little One - P. Hillman

YEAR	ISSUE	EDITION LIMIT	YEAR RETD.	ISSUE PRICE	*QUOTE U.S.$
1997	Sweet Little One 203726	Yr.Iss.		35.00	35

Dave Grossman Creations

Emmett Kelly Plates - B. Leighton-Jones

YEAR	ISSUE	EDITION LIMIT	YEAR RETD.	ISSUE PRICE	*QUOTE U.S.$
1986	Christmas Carol	Yr.Iss.		20.00	400
1987	Christmas Wreath	Yr.Iss.		20.00	225
1988	Christmas Dinner	Yr.Iss.		20.00	49
1989	Christmas Feast	Yr.Iss.		20.00	39
1990	Just What I Needed	Yr.Iss.		24.00	39
1991	Emmett The Snowman	Yr.Iss.		25.00	45
1992	Christmas Tunes	Yr.Iss.		25.00	35
1993	Downhill-Christmas Plate	Yr.Iss.		30.00	30
1994	Holiday Skater EKP-94	Yr.Iss.		30.00	30
1995	Christmas Tunes EKP-95	Yr.Iss.		30.00	30

Norman Rockwell Collection - Rockwell-Inspired

YEAR	ISSUE	EDITION LIMIT	YEAR RETD.	ISSUE PRICE	*QUOTE U.S.$
1979	Leapfrog NRP-79	Retrd.		50.00	50
1980	Lovers NRP-80	Retrd.		60.00	60
1981	Dreams of Long Ago NRP-81	Retrd.		60.00	60
1982	Doctor and Doll NRP-82	Retrd.		65.00	95
1983	Circus NRP-83	Retrd.		65.00	65
1984	Visit With Rockwell NRP-84	Retrd.		65.00	65
1980	Christmas Trio RXP-80	Retrd.		75.00	75
1981	Santa's Good Boys RXP-81	Retrd.		75.00	75
1982	Faces of Christmas RXP-82	Retrd.		75.00	75
1983	Christmas Chores RXP-83	Retrd.		75.00	75
1984	Tiny Tim RXP-84	Retrd.		75.00	75
1980	Back To School RMP-80	Retrd.		24.00	24
1981	No Swimming RMP-81	Retrd.		25.00	25
1982	Love Letter RMP-82	Retrd.		27.00	30
1983	Doctor and Doll RMP-83	Retrd.		27.00	27
1984	Big Moment RMP-84	Retrd.		27.00	27
1979	Butterboy RP-01	Retrd.		40.00	40
1982	American Mother RGP-42	Retrd.		45.00	45
1983	Dreamboat RGP-83	Retrd.		24.00	30
1978	Young Doctor RDP-26	Retrd.		50.00	65

Norman Rockwell Collection-Boy Scout Plates - Rockwell-Inspired

YEAR	ISSUE	EDITION LIMIT	YEAR RETD.	ISSUE PRICE	*QUOTE U.S.$
1981	Can't Wait BSP-01	Retrd.		30.00	45
1982	Guiding Hand BSP-02	Retrd.		30.00	35
1983	Tomorrow's Leader BSP-03	Retrd.		30.00	45

*Quotes have been rounded up to nearest dollar

Norman Rockwell Collection-Huck Finn Plates - Rockwell-Inspired

YEAR ISSUE		EDITION LIMIT	YEAR RETD.	ISSUE PRICE	*QUOTE U.S.$
1979	Secret HFP-01	Retrd.		40.00	40
1980	ListeningHFP-02	Retrd.		40.00	40
1980	No Kings HFP-03	Retrd.		40.00	40
1981	Snake Escapes HFP-04	Retrd.		40.00	40

Norman Rockwell Collection-Tom Sawyer Plates - Rockwell-Inspired

YEAR ISSUE		EDITION LIMIT	YEAR RETD.	ISSUE PRICE	*QUOTE U.S.$
1975	Whitewashing the Fence TSP-01	Retrd.		26.00	35
1976	First Smoke TSP-02	Retrd.		26.00	35
1977	Take Your Medicine TSP-03	Retrd.		26.00	40
1978	Lost in Cave TSP-04	Retrd.		26.00	40

Saturday Evening Post Collection - Rockwell-Inspired

YEAR ISSUE		EDITION LIMIT	YEAR RETD.	ISSUE PRICE	*QUOTE U.S.$
1991	Downhill Daring BRP-91	Yr.Iss.		25.00	25
1991	Missed BRP-101	Yr.Iss.		25.00	25
1992	Choosin Up BRP-102	Yr.Iss.		25.00	25

Delphi

The Beatles Collection - N. Giorgio

YEAR ISSUE		EDITION LIMIT	YEAR RETD.	ISSUE PRICE	*QUOTE U.S.$
1991	The Beatles, Live In Concert	Closed		24.75	40
1991	Hello America	Closed		24.75	53
1991	A Hard Day's Night	Closed		27.75	60
1992	Beatles '65	Closed		27.75	85
1992	Help	Closed		27.75	50-60
1992	The Beatles at Shea Stadium	150-day		29.75	30
1992	Rubber Soul	150-day		29.75	30
1992	Yesterday and Today	150-day		29.75	30

Cars of the '50's - G. Angelini

YEAR ISSUE		EDITION LIMIT	YEAR RETD.	ISSUE PRICE	*QUOTE U.S.$
1993	'57 Red Corvette	Closed		24.75	40-50
1993	'57 White T-Bird	Closed		24.75	80
1993	'57 Blue Belair	Closed		27.75	50
1993	'59 Cadillac	Closed		27.75	40
1994	'56 Lincoln Premier	Closed		27.75	40
1994	'59 Red Ford Fairlane	Closed		27.75	42

Commemorating The King - M. Stutzman

YEAR ISSUE		EDITION LIMIT	YEAR RETD.	ISSUE PRICE	*QUOTE U.S.$
1993	The Rock and Roll Legend	Closed		29.75	50
1993	Las Vegas, Live	Closed		29.75	45-60
1993	Blues and Black Leather	95-day		29.75	50
1993	Private Presley	95-day		29.75	30
1993	Golden Boy	95-day		29.75	30
1993	Screen Idol	95-day		29.75	30
1993	Outstanding Young Man	95-day		29.75	30
1993	The Tiger: Faith, Spirit & Discipline	95-day		29.75	30

Dream Machines - P. Palma

YEAR ISSUE		EDITION LIMIT	YEAR RETD.	ISSUE PRICE	*QUOTE U.S.$
1988	'56 T-Bird	Closed		24.75	25
1988	'57 'Vette	Closed		24.75	25
1989	'58 Biarritz	Closed		27.75	28
1989	'56 Continental	Closed		27.75	28
1989	'57 Bel Air	Closed		27.75	45
1989	'57 Chrysler 300C	Closed		27.75	28

Elvis on the Big Screen - B. Emmett

YEAR ISSUE		EDITION LIMIT	YEAR RETD.	ISSUE PRICE	*QUOTE U.S.$
1992	Elvis in Loving You	Closed		29.75	45-57
1992	Elvis in G.I. Blues	Closed		29.75	50-75
1992	Viva Las Vegas	Closed		32.75	100
1993	Elvis in Blue Hawaii	Closed		32.75	40
1993	Elvis in Jailhouse Rock	Closed		32.75	36
1993	Elvis in Spinout	Closed		34.75	36
1993	Elvis in Speedway	Closed		34.75	45
1993	Elvis in Harum Scarum	Closed		34.75	35

Elvis Presley: In Performance - B. Emmett

YEAR ISSUE		EDITION LIMIT	YEAR RETD.	ISSUE PRICE	*QUOTE U.S.$
1990	'68 Comeback Special	Closed		24.75	53
1991	King of Las Vegas	Closed		24.75	95
1991	Aloha From Hawaii	Closed		27.75	45
1991	Back in Tupelo, 1956	Closed		27.75	50
1991	If I Can Dream	Closed		27.75	45
1991	Benefit for the USS Arizona	Closed		29.75	40
1991	Madison Square Garden, 1972	Closed		29.75	65
1991	Tampa, 1955	Closed		29.75	45
1991	Concert in Baton Rouge, 1974	Closed		29.75	45
1992	On Stage in Wichita, 1974	Closed		31.75	45
1992	In the Spotlight: Hawaii, '72	Closed		31.75	40
1992	Tour Finale: Indianapolis 1977	Closed		31.75	35

Elvis Presley: Looking At A Legend - B. Emmett

YEAR ISSUE		EDITION LIMIT	YEAR RETD.	ISSUE PRICE	*QUOTE U.S.$
1988	Elvis at/Gates of Graceland	Closed		24.75	70-90
1989	Jailhouse Rock	Closed		24.75	70
1989	The Memphis Flash	Closed		27.75	50-60
1989	Homecoming	Closed		27.75	50-60
1990	Elvis and Gladys	Closed		27.75	45-50
1990	A Studio Session	Closed		27.75	30-40
1990	Elvis in Hollywood	Closed		29.75	50
1990	Elvis on His Harley	Closed		29.75	58-70
1990	Stage Door Autographs	Closed		29.75	40
1991	Christmas at Graceland	Closed		32.75	70
1991	Entering Sun Studio	Closed		32.75	50
1991	Going for the Black Belt	Closed		32.75	50
1991	His Hand in Mine	Closed		32.75	50
1991	Letters From Fans	Closed		32.75	50
1991	Closing the Deal	Closed		34.75	53
1992	Elvis Returns to the Stage	Closed		34.75	50

In the Footsteps of the King - D. Sivavec

YEAR ISSUE		EDITION LIMIT	YEAR RETD.	ISSUE PRICE	*QUOTE U.S.$
1993	Graceland: Memphis, Tenn.	Closed		29.75	35
1994	Elvis' Birthplace: Tupelo, Miss	95-day		29.75	30
1994	Day Job: Memphis, Tenn.	95-day		32.75	33
1994	Flying Circle G. Ranch: Walls, Miss.	95-day		32.75	33
1994	The Lauderdale Courts	95-day		32.75	33
1994	Patriotic Soldier: Bad Nauheim, W. Ger.	95-day		34.75	35

Indiana Jones - V. Gadino

YEAR ISSUE		EDITION LIMIT	YEAR RETD.	ISSUE PRICE	*QUOTE U.S.$
1989	Indiana Jones	Closed		24.75	35
1989	Indiana Jones and His Dad	Closed		24.75	45
1990	Indiana Jones/Dr. Schneider	Closed		27.75	38
1990	A Family Discussion	Closed		27.75	28
1990	Young Indiana Jones	Closed		27.75	50
1991	Indiana Jones/The Holy Grail	Closed		27.75	60

The Magic of Marilyn - C. Notarile

YEAR ISSUE		EDITION LIMIT	YEAR RETD.	ISSUE PRICE	*QUOTE U.S.$
1992	For Our Boys in Korea, 1954	Closed		24.75	35
1992	Opening Night	Closed		24.75	30-50
1993	Rising Star	Closed		27.75	30
1993	Stopping Traffic	Closed		27.75	30-40
1992	Strasberg's Student	Closed		27.75	28
1993	Photo Opportunity	Closed		29.75	45
1993	Shining Star	Closed		29.75	35
1993	Curtain Call	150-day		29.75	30

The Marilyn Monroe Collection - C. Notarile

YEAR ISSUE		EDITION LIMIT	YEAR RETD.	ISSUE PRICE	*QUOTE U.S.$
1989	Marilyn Monroe/7 Year Itch	Closed		24.75	80-90
1990	Diamonds/Girls Best Friend	Closed		24.75	45-90
1991	Marilyn Monroe/River of No Return	Closed		27.75	65-80
1992	How to Marry a Millionaire	Closed		27.75	50-75
1992	There's No Business/Show Business	Closed		27.75	63-85
1992	Marilyn Monroe in Niagra	Closed		29.75	60-75
1992	My Heart Belongs to Daddy	Closed		29.75	50-60
1992	Marilyn Monroe as Cherie in Bus Stop	Closed		29.75	60-80
1992	Marilyn Monroe in All About Eve	Closed		29.75	55-65
1992	Marilyn Monroe in Monkey Business	Closed		31.75	60-83
1992	Marilyn Monroe in Don't Bother to Knock	Closed		31.75	70-80
1992	Marilyn Monroe in We're Not Married	Closed		31.75	65-75

Portraits of the King - D. Zwierz

YEAR ISSUE		EDITION LIMIT	YEAR RETD.	ISSUE PRICE	*QUOTE U.S.$
1991	Love Me Tender	Closed		27.75	40
1991	Are You Lonesome Tonight?	Closed		27.75	48
1991	I'm Yours	Closed		30.75	45
1991	Treat Me Nice	Closed		30.75	45
1992	The Wonder of You	Closed		30.75	32
1992	You're a Heartbreaker	Closed		32.75	33
1992	Just Because	Closed		32.75	40
1992	Follow That Dream	Closed		32.75	33

Department 56

A Christmas Carol - R. Innocenti

YEAR ISSUE		EDITION LIMIT	YEAR RETD.	ISSUE PRICE	*QUOTE U.S.$
1991	The Cratchit's Christmas Pudding 5706-1	18,000	1991	60.00	60-90
1992	Marley's Ghost Appears To Scrooge 5721-5	18,000	1992	60.00	65
1993	The Spirit of Christmas Present 5722-3	18,000	1993	60.00	60
1994	Visions of Christmas Past 5723-1	18,000	1994	60.00	75

Dickens' Village - Department 56

YEAR ISSUE		EDITION LIMIT	YEAR RETD.	ISSUE PRICE	*QUOTE U.S.$
1987	Dickens' Village Porcelain Plates, 5917-0 set/4	Closed	1990	140.00	170-200

Duncan Royale

History of Santa Claus I - S. Morton

YEAR ISSUE		EDITION LIMIT	YEAR RETD.	ISSUE PRICE	*QUOTE U.S.$
1985	Medieval	Retrd.	N/A	40.00	75
1985	Kris Kringle	Retrd.	N/A	40.00	75
1985	Pioneer	10,000	N/A	40.00	40
1986	Russian	Retrd.	N/A	40.00	65
1986	Soda Pop	Retrd.	N/A	40.00	75
1986	Civil War	10,000	N/A	40.00	40
1986	Nast	Retrd.	N/A	40.00	75
1987	St. Nicholas	Retrd.	N/A	40.00	75
1987	Dedt Moroz	10,000	N/A	40.00	45
1987	Black Peter	10,000	N/A	40.00	60
1987	Victorian	Retrd.	N/A	40.00	45
1987	Wassail	Retrd.	N/A	40.00	45
XX	Collection of 12 Plates	Retrd.	N/A	480.00	480

Edna Hibel Studios

Allegro - E. Hibel

YEAR ISSUE		EDITION LIMIT	YEAR RETD.	ISSUE PRICE	*QUOTE U.S.$
1978	Plate & Book	7,500		120.00	150

Arte Ovale - E. Hibel

YEAR ISSUE		EDITION LIMIT	YEAR RETD.	ISSUE PRICE	*QUOTE U.S.$
1980	Takara, gold	300		1000.00	4200
1980	Takara, blanco	700		450.00	1200
1980	Takara, cobalt blue	1,000		595.00	2350
1984	Taro-kun, gold	300		1000.00	2700
1984	Taro-kun, blanco	700		450.00	825
1984	Taro-kun, cobalt blue	1,000		995.00	1050

Christmas Annual - E. Hibel

YEAR ISSUE		EDITION LIMIT	YEAR RETD.	ISSUE PRICE	*QUOTE U.S.$
1985	The Angels' Message	Yr.Iss.		45.00	220
1986	Gift of the Magi	Yr.Iss.		45.00	275
1987	Flight Into Egypt	Yr.Iss.		49.00	250
1988	Adoration of the Shepherds	Yr.Iss.		49.00	175
1989	Peaceful Kingdom	Yr.Iss.		49.00	165
1990	The Nativity	Yr.Iss.		49.00	125

David Series - E. Hibel

YEAR ISSUE		EDITION LIMIT	YEAR RETD.	ISSUE PRICE	*QUOTE U.S.$
1979	Wedding of David & Bathsheba	5,000		250.00	650
1980	David, Bathsheba & Solomon	5,000		275.00	425
1982	David the King	5,000		275.00	295
1982	David the King, cobalt A/P	25		275.00	1200
1984	Bathsheba	5,000		275.00	295
1984	Bathsheba, cobalt A/P	100		275.00	1200

Edna Hibel Holiday - E. Hibel

YEAR ISSUE		EDITION LIMIT	YEAR RETD.	ISSUE PRICE	*QUOTE U.S.$
1991	The First Holiday	Yr.Iss.		49.00	85
1991	The First Holiday, gold	1,000		99.00	150
1992	The Christmas Rose	Yr.Iss.		49.00	70
1992	The Christmas Rose, gold	1,000		99.00	125

Eroica - E. Hibel

YEAR ISSUE		EDITION LIMIT	YEAR RETD.	ISSUE PRICE	*QUOTE U.S.$
1990	Compassion	10,000		49.50	65
1992	Darya	10,000		49.50	50

Famous Women & Children - E. Hibel

YEAR ISSUE		EDITION LIMIT	YEAR RETD.	ISSUE PRICE	*QUOTE U.S.$
1980	Pharaoh's Daughter & Moses, gold	2,500		350.00	625
1980	Pharaoh's Daughter & Moses, cobalt blue	500		350.00	1350
1982	Cornelia & Her Jewels, gold	2,500		350.00	495
1982	Cornelia & Her Jewels, cobalt blue	500		350.00	350
1982	Anna & The Children of the King of Siam, gold	2,500		350.00	495
1982	Anna & The Children of the King of Siam, cobalt blue	500		350.00	1350
1984	Mozart & The Empress Marie Theresa, gold	2,500		350.00	395
1984	Mozart & The Empress Marie Theresa, cobalt blue	500		350.00	975

Flower Girl Annual - E. Hibel

YEAR ISSUE		EDITION LIMIT	YEAR RETD.	ISSUE PRICE	*QUOTE U.S.$
1985	Lily	15,000		79.00	125
1986	Iris	15,000		79.00	150
1987	Rose	15,000		79.00	125
1988	Camellia	15,000		79.00	165
1989	Peony	15,000		79.00	100
1992	Wisteria	15,000		79.00	90

International Mother Love French - E. Hibel

YEAR ISSUE		EDITION LIMIT	YEAR RETD.	ISSUE PRICE	*QUOTE U.S.$
1985	Yvette Avec Ses Enfants	5,000		125.00	225
1991	Liberte, Egalite, Fraternite	5,000		95.00	95

International Mother Love German - E. Hibel

YEAR ISSUE		EDITION LIMIT	YEAR RETD.	ISSUE PRICE	*QUOTE U.S.$
1982	Gesa Und Kinder	5,000		195.00	195
1983	Alexandra Und Kinder	5,000		195.00	195

March of Dimes: Our Children Our Future - E. Hibel

YEAR ISSUE		EDITION LIMIT	YEAR RETD.	ISSUE PRICE	*QUOTE U.S.$
1990	A Time To Embrace	150-day		29.00	29

Mother and Child - E. Hibel

YEAR ISSUE		EDITION LIMIT	YEAR RETD.	ISSUE PRICE	*QUOTE U.S.$
1973	Colette & Child	15,000		40.00	725
1974	Sayuri & Child	15,000		40.00	425
1975	Kristina & Child	15,000		50.00	400
1976	Marilyn & Child	15,000		55.00	400
1977	Lucia & Child	15,000		60.00	350
1981	Kathleen & Child	15,000		85.00	275

Mother's Day - E. Hibel

YEAR ISSUE		EDITION LIMIT	YEAR RETD.	ISSUE PRICE	*QUOTE U.S.$
1992	Molly & Annie	Yr.Iss.		39.00	75
1992	Molly & Annie, gold	2,500		95.00	150
1992	Molly & Annie, platinum	500		275.00	275

Mother's Day Annual - E. Hibel

YEAR ISSUE		EDITION LIMIT	YEAR RETD.	ISSUE PRICE	*QUOTE U.S.$
1984	Abby & Lisa	Yr.Iss.		29.50	200
1985	Erica & Jamie	Yr.Iss.		29.50	200
1986	Emily & Jennifer	Yr.Iss.		29.50	125
1987	Catherine & Heather	Yr.Iss.		34.50	100
1988	Sarah & Tess	Yr.Iss.		34.90	175
1989	Jessica & Kate	Yr.Iss.		34.90	100
1990	Elizabeth, Jorday & Janie	Yr.Iss.		36.90	95
1991	Michele & Anna	Yr.Iss.		36.90	65
1992	Olivia & Hildy	Yr.Iss.		39.90	80

Museum Commemorative - E. Hibel

YEAR ISSUE		EDITION LIMIT	YEAR RETD.	ISSUE PRICE	*QUOTE U.S.$
1977	Flower Girl of Provence	12,750		175.00	425
1980	Diana	3,000		350.00	395

Nobility Of Children - E. Hibel

YEAR ISSUE		EDITION LIMIT	YEAR RETD.	ISSUE PRICE	*QUOTE U.S.$
1976	La Contessa Isabella	12,750		120.00	425
1977	Le Marquis Maurice Pierre	12,750		120.00	225
1978	Baronesse Johanna-Maryke Van Vollendam Tot Marken	12,750		130.00	175
1979	Chief Red Feather	12,750		140.00	200

Nordic Families - E. Hibel

YEAR ISSUE		EDITION LIMIT	YEAR RETD.	ISSUE PRICE	*QUOTE U.S.$
1987	A Tender Moment	7,500		79.00	95

Oriental Gold - E. Hibel

YEAR ISSUE		EDITION LIMIT	YEAR RETD.	ISSUE PRICE	*QUOTE U.S.$
1975	Yasuko	2,000		275.00	3000

*Quotes have been rounded up to nearest dollar

YEAR ISSUE		EDITION LIMIT	YEAR RETD.	ISSUE PRICE	*QUOTE U.S.$
1976	Mr. Obata	2,000		275.00	2100
1978	Sakura	2,000		295.00	1800
1979	Michio	2,000		325.00	1500

Scandinavian Mother & Child - E. Hibel

YEAR ISSUE		EDITION LIMIT	YEAR RETD.	ISSUE PRICE	*QUOTE U.S.$
1987	Pearl & Flowers	7,500		55.00	225
1989	Anemone & Violet	7,500		75.00	95
1990	Holly & Talia	7,500		75.00	85

To Life Annual - E. Hibel

YEAR ISSUE		EDITION LIMIT	YEAR RETD.	ISSUE PRICE	*QUOTE U.S.$
1986	Golden's Child	5,000		99.00	200-275
1987	Triumph! Everyone A Winner	19,500		55.00	60
1988	The Whole Earth Bloomed as a Sacred Place	15,000		85.00	85
1989	Lovers of the Summer Palace	5,000		65.00	75
1992	People of the Fields	5,000		49.00	49

Tribute To All Children - E. Hibel

YEAR ISSUE		EDITION LIMIT	YEAR RETD.	ISSUE PRICE	*QUOTE U.S.$
1984	Giselle	19,500		55.00	95
1984	Gerard	19,500		55.00	95
1985	Wendy	19,500		55.00	70
1986	Todd	19,500		55.00	125

The World I Love - E. Hibel

YEAR ISSUE		EDITION LIMIT	YEAR RETD.	ISSUE PRICE	*QUOTE U.S.$
1981	Leah's Family	17,500		85.00	175-200
1982	Kaylin	17,500		85.00	300
1983	Edna's Music	17,500		85.00	195
1983	O' Hana	17,500		85.00	195

Edwin M. Knowles

Aesop's Fables - M. Hampshire

YEAR ISSUE		EDITION LIMIT	YEAR RETD.	ISSUE PRICE	*QUOTE U.S.$
1988	The Goose That Laid the Golden Egg	Closed		27.90	30
1988	The Hare and the Tortoise	Closed		27.90	30
1988	The Fox and the Grapes	Closed		30.90	31
1989	The Lion And The Mouse	Closed		30.90	32
1989	The Milk Maid And Her Pail	Closed		30.90	31
1989	The Jay And The Peacock	Closed		30.90	31

American Innocents - Marsten/Mandrajji

YEAR ISSUE		EDITION LIMIT	YEAR RETD.	ISSUE PRICE	*QUOTE U.S.$
1986	Abigail in the Rose Garden	Closed		19.50	20
1986	Ann by the Terrace	Closed		19.50	20
1986	Ellen and John in the Parlor	Closed		19.50	20
1986	William on the Rocking Horse	Closed		19.50	27

The American Journey - M. Kunstler

YEAR ISSUE		EDITION LIMIT	YEAR RETD.	ISSUE PRICE	*QUOTE U.S.$
1987	Westward Ho	Closed		29.90	30
1988	Kitchen With a View	Closed		29.90	30
1988	Crossing the River	Closed		29.90	30
1988	Christmas at the New Cabin	Closed		29.90	30

Americana Holidays - D. Spaulding

YEAR ISSUE		EDITION LIMIT	YEAR RETD.	ISSUE PRICE	*QUOTE U.S.$
1978	Fourth of July	Closed		26.00	26
1979	Thanksgiving	Closed		26.00	26
1980	Easter	Closed		26.00	26
1981	Valentine's Day	Closed		26.00	26
1982	Father's Day	Closed		26.00	35
1983	Christmas	Closed		26.00	33
1984	Mother's Day	Closed		26.00	30

Amy Brackenbury's Cat Tales - A. Brackenbury

YEAR ISSUE		EDITION LIMIT	YEAR RETD.	ISSUE PRICE	*QUOTE U.S.$
1987	A Chance Meeting: White American Shorthairs	Closed		21.50	22
1987	Gone Fishing: Maine Coons	Closed		21.50	36
1988	Strawberries and Cream: Cream Persians	Closed		24.90	50
1988	Flower Bed: British Shorthairs	Closed		24.90	25
1988	Kittens and Mittens: Silver Tabbies	Closed		24.90	25
1988	All Wrapped Up: Himalayans	Closed		24.90	40

Annie - W. Chambers

YEAR ISSUE		EDITION LIMIT	YEAR RETD.	ISSUE PRICE	*QUOTE U.S.$
1983	Annie and Sandy	Closed		19.00	19
1983	Daddy Warbucks	Closed		19.00	19
1983	Annie and Grace	Closed		19.00	19
1984	Annie and the Orphans	Closed		21.00	25
1985	Tomorrow	Closed		21.00	21
1986	Annie and Miss Hannigan	Closed		21.00	21
1986	Annie, Lily and Rooster	Closed		24.00	24
1986	Grand Finale	Closed		24.00	24

Baby Owls of North America - J. Thornbrugh

YEAR ISSUE		EDITION LIMIT	YEAR RETD.	ISSUE PRICE	*QUOTE U.S.$
1991	Peek-A-Whoo: Screech Owls	Closed		27.90	35
1991	Forty Winks: Saw-Whet Owls	Closed		29.90	40
1991	The Tree House: Northern Pygmy Owls	Closed		30.90	43
1991	Three of a Kind: Great Horned Owls	Closed		30.90	35
1991	Out on a Limb: Great Gray Owls	Closed		30.90	35
1991	Beginning to Explore: Boreal Owls	Closed		32.90	50
1992	Three's Company: Long Eared Owls	Closed		32.90	40
1992	Whoo's There: Barred Owl	Closed		32.90	50

Backyard Harmony - J. Thornbrugh

YEAR ISSUE		EDITION LIMIT	YEAR RETD.	ISSUE PRICE	*QUOTE U.S.$
1991	The Singing Lesson	Closed		27.90	30
1991	Welcoming a New Day	Closed		27.90	45
1991	Announcing Spring	Closed		30.90	55
1992	The Morning Harvest	Closed		30.90	43
1992	Spring Time Pride	Closed		30.90	55
1992	Treetop Serenade	Closed		32.90	60

YEAR ISSUE		EDITION LIMIT	YEAR RETD.	ISSUE PRICE	*QUOTE U.S.$
1992	At The Peep Of Day	Closed		32.90	45
1992	Today's Discoveries	Closed		32.90	45

Bambi - Disney Studios

YEAR ISSUE		EDITION LIMIT	YEAR RETD.	ISSUE PRICE	*QUOTE U.S.$
1992	Bashful Bambi	Closed		34.90	40
1992	Bambi's New Friends	Closed		34.90	50-60
1992	Hello Little Prince	Closed		37.90	45
1992	Bambi's Morning Greetings	Closed		37.90	45-60
1992	Bambi's Skating Lesson	Closed		37.90	75-90
1993	What's Up Possums?	Closed		37.90	40

Biblical Mothers - E. Licea

YEAR ISSUE		EDITION LIMIT	YEAR RETD.	ISSUE PRICE	*QUOTE U.S.$
1983	Bathsheba and Solomon	Closed		39.50	30
1984	Judgment of Solomon	Closed		39.50	40
1984	Pharaoh's Daughter and Moses	Closed		39.50	40
1985	Mary and Jesus	Closed		39.50	40
1985	Sarah and Isaac	Closed		44.50	45
1986	Rebekah, Jacob and Esau	Closed		44.50	45

Birds of the Seasons - S. Timm

YEAR ISSUE		EDITION LIMIT	YEAR RETD.	ISSUE PRICE	*QUOTE U.S.$
1990	Cardinals In Winter	Closed		24.90	30-55
1990	Bluebirds In Spring	Closed		24.90	40
1991	Nuthatches In Fall	Closed		27.90	35
1991	Baltimore Orioles In Summer	Closed		27.90	40
1991	Blue Jays In Early Fall	Closed		27.90	40-48
1991	Robins In Early Spring	Closed		27.90	35
1991	Cedar Waxwings in Fall	Closed		29.90	40-65
1991	Chickadees in Winter	Closed		29.90	55

Call of the Wilderness - K. Daniel

YEAR ISSUE		EDITION LIMIT	YEAR RETD.	ISSUE PRICE	*QUOTE U.S.$
1991	First Outing	Closed		29.90	32
1991	Howling Lesson	Closed		29.90	65
1991	Silent Watch	Closed		32.90	50
1991	Winter Travelers	Closed		32.90	50
1992	Ahead of the Pack	Closed		32.90	45
1992	Northern Spirits	Closed		34.90	50
1992	Twilight Friends	Closed		34.90	50
1992	A New Future	Closed		34.90	50
1992	Morning Mist	Closed		36.90	95
1992	The Silent One	150-day		36.90	55

Carousel - D. Brown

YEAR ISSUE		EDITION LIMIT	YEAR RETD.	ISSUE PRICE	*QUOTE U.S.$
1987	If I Loved You	Closed		24.90	25
1988	Mr. Snow	Closed		24.90	25
1988	The Carousel Waltz	Closed		24.90	25
1988	You'll Never Walk Alone	Closed		24.90	25

Casablanca - J. Griffin

YEAR ISSUE		EDITION LIMIT	YEAR RETD.	ISSUE PRICE	*QUOTE U.S.$
1990	Here's Looking At You, Kid	Closed		34.90	40
1990	We'll Always Have Paris	Closed		34.90	40
1991	We Loved Each Other Once	Closed		37.90	40
1991	Rick's Cafe Americain	Closed		37.90	40
1991	A Franc For Your Thoughts	Closed		37.90	50
1991	Play it Sam	Closed		37.90	52

Castari Grandparent - J. Castari

YEAR ISSUE		EDITION LIMIT	YEAR RETD.	ISSUE PRICE	*QUOTE U.S.$
1980	Bedtime Story	Closed		18.00	18
1981	The Skating Lesson	Closed		20.00	20
1982	The Cookie Tasting	Closed		20.00	20
1983	The Swinger	Closed		20.00	20
1984	The Skating Queen	Closed		22.00	22
1985	The Patriot's Parade	Closed		22.00	22
1986	The Home Run	Closed		22.00	22
1987	The Sneak Preview	Closed		22.00	22

China's Natural Treasures - T.C. Chiu

YEAR ISSUE		EDITION LIMIT	YEAR RETD.	ISSUE PRICE	*QUOTE U.S.$
1992	The Siberian Tiger	Closed		29.90	40
1992	The Snow Leopard	Closed		29.90	35
1992	The Giant Panda	Closed		32.90	43
1992	The Tibetan Brown Bear	Closed		32.90	40
1992	The Asian Elephant	Closed		32.90	50
1992	The Golden Monkey	Closed		34.90	50

Christmas in the City - A. Leimanis

YEAR ISSUE		EDITION LIMIT	YEAR RETD.	ISSUE PRICE	*QUOTE U.S.$
1992	A Christmas Snowfall	Closed		34.90	35
1992	Yuletide Celebration	Closed		34.90	55
1993	Holiday Cheer	Closed		34.90	60
1993	The Magic of Christmas	Closed		34.90	60

Cinderella - Disney Studios

YEAR ISSUE		EDITION LIMIT	YEAR RETD.	ISSUE PRICE	*QUOTE U.S.$
1988	Bibbidi, Bobbidi, Boo	Closed		29.90	46-60
1988	A Dream Is A Wish Your Heart Makes	Closed		29.90	50
1989	Oh Sing Sweet Nightingale	Closed		32.90	60
1989	A Dress For Cinderelly	Closed		32.90	75-80
1989	So This Is Love	Closed		32.90	50
1990	At The Stroke Of Midnight	Closed		32.90	50
1990	If The Shoe Fits	Closed		34.90	50
1990	Happily Ever After	Closed		34.90	35

Classic Fairy Tales - S. Gustafson

YEAR ISSUE		EDITION LIMIT	YEAR RETD.	ISSUE PRICE	*QUOTE U.S.$
1991	Goldilocks and the Three Bears	Closed		29.90	40
1991	Little Red Riding Hood	Closed		29.90	50
1991	The Three Little Pigs	Closed		32.90	45
1991	The Frog Prince	Closed		32.90	55
1992	Jack and the Beanstalk	Closed		32.90	50
1992	Hansel and Gretel	Closed		34.90	75
1992	Puss in Boots	Closed		34.90	37
1992	Tom Thumb	Closed		34.90	50

Classic Mother Goose - S. Gustafson

YEAR ISSUE		EDITION LIMIT	YEAR RETD.	ISSUE PRICE	*QUOTE U.S.$
1992	Little Miss Muffet	Closed		29.90	30
1992	Mary had a Little Lamb	Closed		29.90	42
1992	Mary, Mary, Quite Contrary	Closed		29.90	50
1992	Little Bo Peep	Closed		29.90	45

Cozy Country Corners - H. H. Ingmire

YEAR ISSUE		EDITION LIMIT	YEAR RETD.	ISSUE PRICE	*QUOTE U.S.$
1990	Lazy Morning	Closed		24.90	40
1990	Warm Retreat	Closed		24.90	40
1991	A Sunny Spot	Closed		27.90	30
1991	Attic Afternoon	Closed		27.90	45
1991	Mirror Mischief	Closed		27.90	50
1991	Hide and Seek	Closed		29.90	40
1991	Apple Antics	Closed		29.90	65
1991	Table Trouble	Closed		29.90	60

Ency. Brit. Birds of Your Garden - K. Daniel

YEAR ISSUE		EDITION LIMIT	YEAR RETD.	ISSUE PRICE	*QUOTE U.S.$
1985	Cardinal	Closed		19.50	35
1985	Blue Jay	Closed		19.50	20
1985	Oriole	Closed		22.50	23
1986	Chickadees	Closed		22.50	23
1986	Bluebird	Closed		22.50	24
1986	Robin	Closed		22.50	23
1986	Hummingbird	Closed		24.50	25
1987	Goldfinch	Closed		24.50	35
1987	Downy Woodpecker	Closed		24.50	30
1987	Cedar Waxwing	Closed		24.90	30

Eve Licea Christmas - E. Licea

YEAR ISSUE		EDITION LIMIT	YEAR RETD.	ISSUE PRICE	*QUOTE U.S.$
1987	The Annunciation	Closed		44.90	45
1988	The Nativity	Closed		44.90	45
1989	Adoration Of The Shepherds	Closed		49.90	45
1990	Journey Of The Magi	Closed		49.90	45
1991	Gifts Of The Magi	Closed		49.90	51
1992	Rest on the Flight into Egypt	Closed		49.90	65

Fantasia: (The Sorcerer's Apprentice) Golden Anniversary - Disney Studios

YEAR ISSUE		EDITION LIMIT	YEAR RETD.	ISSUE PRICE	*QUOTE U.S.$
1990	The Apprentice's Dream	Closed		29.90	50-60
1990	Mischievous Apprentice	Closed		29.90	74
1991	Dreams of Power	Closed		32.90	50
1991	Mickey's Magical Whirlpool	Closed		32.90	45
1991	Wizardry Gone Wild	Closed		32.90	45
1991	Mickey Makes Magic	Closed		34.90	63
1991	The Penitent Apprentice	Closed		34.90	45
1992	An Apprentice Again	Closed		34.90	50

Father's Love - B. Bradley

YEAR ISSUE		EDITION LIMIT	YEAR RETD.	ISSUE PRICE	*QUOTE U.S.$
1984	Open Wide	Closed		19.50	20
1984	Batter Up	Closed		19.50	20
1985	Little Shaver	Closed		19.50	20
1985	Swing Time	Closed		22.50	23

Field Puppies - L. Kaatz

YEAR ISSUE		EDITION LIMIT	YEAR RETD.	ISSUE PRICE	*QUOTE U.S.$
1987	Dog Tired-The Springer Spaniel	Closed		24.90	45
1987	Caught in the Act-The Golden Retriever	Closed		24.90	40-50
1988	Missing/Point/Irish Setter	Closed		27.90	35
1988	A Perfect Set-Labrador	Closed		27.90	40
1988	Fritz's Folly-German Shorthaired Pointer	Closed		27.90	35
1988	Shirt Tales: Cocker Spaniel	Closed		27.90	40-51
1989	Fine Feathered Friends-English Setter	Closed		29.90	30
1989	Command Performance/ Wiemaraner	Closed		29.90	30

Field Trips - L. Kaatz

YEAR ISSUE		EDITION LIMIT	YEAR RETD.	ISSUE PRICE	*QUOTE U.S.$
1990	Gone Fishing	Closed		24.90	25
1991	Ducking Duty	Closed		24.90	25
1991	Boxed In	Closed		27.90	28
1991	Pups 'N Boots	Closed		27.90	28
1991	Puppy Tales	Closed		27.90	28
1991	Pail Pals	Closed		29.90	30
1991	Chesapeake Bay Retrievers	Closed		29.90	30
1991	Hat Trick	Closed		29.90	30

First Impressions - J. Giordano

YEAR ISSUE		EDITION LIMIT	YEAR RETD.	ISSUE PRICE	*QUOTE U.S.$
1991	Taking a Gander	Closed		29.90	40
1991	Two's Company	Closed		29.90	35
1991	Fine Feathered Friends	Closed		32.90	40
1991	What's Up?	Closed		32.90	44
1991	All Ears	Closed		32.90	60
1992	Between Friends	Closed		32.90	34

The Four Ancient Elements - G. Lambert

YEAR ISSUE		EDITION LIMIT	YEAR RETD.	ISSUE PRICE	*QUOTE U.S.$
1984	Earth	Closed		27.50	28
1984	Water	Closed		27.50	28
1985	Air	Closed		29.50	30
1985	Fire	Closed		29.50	35

Frances Hook Legacy - F. Hook

YEAR ISSUE		EDITION LIMIT	YEAR RETD.	ISSUE PRICE	*QUOTE U.S.$
1985	Fascination	Closed		19.50	22-39
1985	Daydreaming	Closed		19.50	22
1986	Discovery	Closed		22.50	22
1986	Disappointment	Closed		22.50	25
1986	Wonderment	Closed		22.50	25
1987	Expectation	Closed		22.50	23

Free as the Wind - M. Budden

YEAR ISSUE		EDITION LIMIT	YEAR RETD.	ISSUE PRICE	*QUOTE U.S.$
1992	Skyward	Closed		29.90	55

*Quotes have been rounded up to nearest dollar

PLATES

Edwin M. Knowles
to Edwin M. Knowles

YEAR ISSUE		EDITION LIMIT	YEAR RETD.	ISSUE PRICE	*QUOTE U.S.$
1992	Aloft	Closed		29.90	55
1992	Airborne	Closed		32.90	35
1993	Flight	Closed		32.90	50
1993	Ascent	Closed		32.90	40
1993	Heavenward	Closed		32.90	45

Friends I Remember - J. Down

YEAR ISSUE		EDITION LIMIT	YEAR RETD.	ISSUE PRICE	*QUOTE U.S.$
1983	Fish Story	Closed		17.50	18
1984	Office Hours	Closed		17.50	18
1985	A Coat of Paint	Closed		17.50	18
1985	Here Comes the Bride	Closed		19.50	20
1985	Fringe Benefits	Closed		19.50	20
1986	High Society	Closed		19.50	20
1986	Flower Arrangement	Closed		21.50	22
1986	Taste Test	Closed		21.50	22

Friends of the Forest - K. Daniel

YEAR ISSUE		EDITION LIMIT	YEAR RETD.	ISSUE PRICE	*QUOTE U.S.$
1987	The Rabbit	Closed		24.50	27
1987	The Raccoon	Closed		24.50	27
1987	The Squirrel	Closed		27.90	30
1988	The Chipmunk	Closed		27.90	30
1988	The Fox	Closed		27.90	30
1988	The Otter	Closed		27.90	30

Garden Secrets - B. Higgins Bond

YEAR ISSUE		EDITION LIMIT	YEAR RETD.	ISSUE PRICE	*QUOTE U.S.$
1993	Nine Lives	Closed		24.90	45
1993	Floral Purr-fume	Closed		24.90	35
1993	Bloomin' Kitties	Closed		24.90	50
1993	Kitty Corner	Closed		24.90	55
1993	Flower Fanciers	Closed		24.90	60
1993	Meadow Mischief	Closed		24.90	35
1993	Pussycat Potpourri	150-day		24.90	25
1993	Frisky Business	150-day		24.90	25

Gone with the Wind - R. Kursar

YEAR ISSUE		EDITION LIMIT	YEAR RETD.	ISSUE PRICE	*QUOTE U.S.$
1978	Scarlett	Closed		21.50	130-175
1979	Ashley	Closed		21.50	60-100
1980	Melanie	Closed		21.50	30-65
1981	Rhett	Closed		23.50	30-65
1982	Mammy Lacing Scarlett	Closed		23.50	35-67
1983	Melanie Gives Birth	Closed		23.50	44-67
1984	Scarlet's Green Dress	Closed		25.50	45-70
1985	Rhett and Bonnie	Closed		25.50	65-90
1985	Scarlett and Rhett: The Finale	Closed		29.50	48-67

Great Cats Of The Americas - L. Cable

YEAR ISSUE		EDITION LIMIT	YEAR RETD.	ISSUE PRICE	*QUOTE U.S.$
1989	The Jaguar	Closed		29.90	40-50
1989	The Cougar	Closed		29.90	47
1989	The Lynx	Closed		30.00	33-50
1990	The Ocelot	Closed		32.90	33-50
1990	The Bobcat	Closed		32.90	33-50
1990	The Jaguarundi	Closed		32.90	33-50
1990	The Margay	Closed		34.90	35-50
1991	The Pampas Cat	Closed		34.90	35-50

Heirlooms And Lace - C. Layton

YEAR ISSUE		EDITION LIMIT	YEAR RETD.	ISSUE PRICE	*QUOTE U.S.$
1989	Anna	Closed		34.90	35
1989	Victoria	Closed		34.90	55
1990	Tess	Closed		37.90	70
1990	Olivia	Closed		37.90	100
1991	Bridget	Closed		37.90	85
1991	Rebecca	Closed		37.90	70

Hibel Christmas - E. Hibel

YEAR ISSUE		EDITION LIMIT	YEAR RETD.	ISSUE PRICE	*QUOTE U.S.$
1985	The Angel's Message	Closed		45.00	45
1986	The Gifts of the Magi	Closed		45.00	45
1987	The Flight Into Egypt	Closed		49.00	49
1988	Adoration of the Shepherd	Closed		49.00	49
1989	Peaceful Kingdom	Closed		49.00	49
1990	Nativity	Closed		49.00	60

Home Sweet Home - R. McGinnis

YEAR ISSUE		EDITION LIMIT	YEAR RETD.	ISSUE PRICE	*QUOTE U.S.$
1989	The Victorian	Closed		39.90	40
1989	The Greek Revival	Closed		39.90	40
1989	The Georgian	Closed		39.90	40
1990	The Mission	Closed		39.90	40

It's a Dog's Life - L. Kaatz

YEAR ISSUE		EDITION LIMIT	YEAR RETD.	ISSUE PRICE	*QUOTE U.S.$
1992	We've Been Spotted	Closed		29.90	30
1992	Literary Labs	Closed		29.90	30
1993	Retrieving Our Dignity	Closed		32.90	33
1993	Lodging a Complaint	150-day		32.90	33
1993	Barreling Along	150-day		32.90	43
1993	Play Ball	150-day		34.90	35
1993	Dogs and Suds	150-day		34.90	35
1993	Paws for a Picnic	150-day		34.90	35

J. W. Smith Childhood Holidays - J. W. Smith

YEAR ISSUE		EDITION LIMIT	YEAR RETD.	ISSUE PRICE	*QUOTE U.S.$
1986	Easter	Closed		19.50	22
1986	Thanksgiving	Closed		19.50	22
1986	Christmas	Closed		19.50	22
1986	Valentine's Day	Closed		22.50	25
1987	Mother's Day	Closed		22.50	25
1987	Fourth of July	Closed		22.50	25

Jerner's Less Traveled Road - B. Jerner

YEAR ISSUE		EDITION LIMIT	YEAR RETD.	ISSUE PRICE	*QUOTE U.S.$
1988	The Weathered Barn	Closed		29.90	37
1988	The Murmuring Stream	Closed		29.90	34
1988	The Covered Bridge	Closed		32.90	50
1989	Winter's Peace	Closed		32.90	38
1989	The Flowering Meadow	Closed		32.90	38

YEAR ISSUE		EDITION LIMIT	YEAR RETD.	ISSUE PRICE	*QUOTE U.S.$
1989	The Hidden Waterfall	Closed		32.90	55

Jewels of the Flowers - T.C. Chiu

YEAR ISSUE		EDITION LIMIT	YEAR RETD.	ISSUE PRICE	*QUOTE U.S.$
1991	Sapphire Wings	Closed		29.90	30
1991	Topaz Beauties	Closed		29.90	40
1991	Amethyst Flight	Closed		32.90	33
1991	Ruby Elegance	Closed		32.90	33
1991	Emerald Pair	Closed		32.90	50
1991	Opal Splendor	Closed		34.90	35
1992	Pearl Luster	Closed		34.90	50
1992	Aquamarine Glimmer	Closed		34.90	35

Keepsake Rhymes - S. Gustafson

YEAR ISSUE		EDITION LIMIT	YEAR RETD.	ISSUE PRICE	*QUOTE U.S.$
1992	Humpty Dumpty	Closed		29.90	30
1993	Peter Pumpkin Eater	Closed		29.90	65
1993	Pat-a-Cake	Closed		29.90	105
1993	Old King Cole	Closed		29.90	85

The King and I - W. Chambers

YEAR ISSUE		EDITION LIMIT	YEAR RETD.	ISSUE PRICE	*QUOTE U.S.$
1984	A Puzzlement	Closed		19.50	20
1985	Shall We Dance?	Closed		19.50	20
1985	Getting to Know You	Closed		19.50	20
1985	We Kiss in a Shadow	Closed		19.50	20

Lady and the Tramp - Disney Studios

YEAR ISSUE		EDITION LIMIT	YEAR RETD.	ISSUE PRICE	*QUOTE U.S.$
1992	First Date	Closed		34.90	70
1992	Puppy Love	Closed		34.90	60
1992	Dog Pound Blues	Closed		37.90	50
1993	Merry Christmas To All	Closed		37.90	55
1993	Double Siamese Trouble	Closed		37.90	65
1993	Ruff House	Closed		39.90	45
1993	Telling Tails	Closed		39.90	40
1993	Moonlight Romance	Closed		39.90	55

Lincoln, Man of America - M. Kunstler

YEAR ISSUE		EDITION LIMIT	YEAR RETD.	ISSUE PRICE	*QUOTE U.S.$
1986	The Gettysburg Address	Closed		24.50	25
1987	The Inauguration	Closed		24.50	25
1987	The Lincoln-Douglas Debates	Closed		27.50	28
1987	Beginnings in New Salem	Closed		27.90	28
1988	The Family Man	Closed		27.90	28
1988	Emancipation Proclamation	Closed		27.90	28

Living with Nature-Jerner's Ducks - B. Jerner

YEAR ISSUE		EDITION LIMIT	YEAR RETD.	ISSUE PRICE	*QUOTE U.S.$
1986	The Pintail	Closed		19.50	25-50
1986	The Mallard	Closed		19.50	35
1987	The Wood Duck	Closed		22.50	33
1987	The Green-Winged Teal	Closed		22.50	30
1987	The Northern Shoveler	Closed		22.90	30
1987	The American Widgeon	Closed		22.90	35
1987	The Gadwall	Closed		24.90	35
1988	The Blue-Winged Teal	Closed		24.90	80

Majestic Birds of North America - D. Smith

YEAR ISSUE		EDITION LIMIT	YEAR RETD.	ISSUE PRICE	*QUOTE U.S.$
1988	The Bald Eagle	Closed		29.90	30
1988	Peregrine Falcon	Closed		29.90	30
1988	The Great Horned Owl	Closed		32.90	33
1989	The Red-Tailed Hawk	Closed		32.90	33
1989	The White Gyrfalcon	Closed		32.90	33
1989	The American Kestral	Closed		32.90	33
1990	The Osprey	Closed		34.90	35
1990	The Golden Eagle	Closed		34.90	35

Mary Poppins - M. Hampshire

YEAR ISSUE		EDITION LIMIT	YEAR RETD.	ISSUE PRICE	*QUOTE U.S.$
1989	Mary Poppins	Closed		29.90	45
1989	A Spoonful of Sugar	Closed		29.90	35
1990	A Jolly Holiday With Mary	Closed		32.90	40
1990	We Love To Laugh	Closed		32.90	40
1991	Chim Chim Cher-ee	Closed		32.90	30
1991	Tuppence a Bag	Closed		32.90	50

Mickey's Christmas Carol - Disney Studios

YEAR ISSUE		EDITION LIMIT	YEAR RETD.	ISSUE PRICE	*QUOTE U.S.$
1992	Bah Humbug!	Closed		29.90	35
1992	What's So Merry About Christmas?	Closed		29.90	40
1993	God Bless Us Every One	Closed		32.90	50
1993	A Christmas Surprise	Closed		32.90	35
1993	Yuletide Greetings	Closed		32.90	35
1993	Marley's Warning	Closed		34.90	50
1993	A Cozy Christmas	150-day		34.90	45
1993	A Christmas Feast	150-day		34.90	70

Musical Moments From the Wizard of Oz - K. Milnazik

YEAR ISSUE		EDITION LIMIT	YEAR RETD.	ISSUE PRICE	*QUOTE U.S.$
1993	Over the Rainbow	Closed		29.90	55
1993	We're Off to See the Wizard	Closed		29.90	65
1993	Munchkin Land	Closed		29.90	70
1994	If I Only Had a Brain	Closed		29.90	75
1994	Ding Dong The Witch is Dead	Closed		29.90	65
1993	The Lullabye League	95-day		29.90	85
1994	If I Were King of the Forest	95-day		29.90	30
1994	Merry Old Land of Oz	95-day		29.90	30

My Fair Lady - W. Chambers

YEAR ISSUE		EDITION LIMIT	YEAR RETD.	ISSUE PRICE	*QUOTE U.S.$
1989	Opening Day at Ascot	Closed		24.90	25
1989	I Could Have Danced All Night	Closed		24.90	25
1989	The Rain in Spain	Closed		27.90	28
1989	Show Me	Closed		27.90	28
1990	Get Me To/Church On Time	Closed		27.90	28
1990	I've Grown Accustomed/Face	Closed		27.90	40

Nature's Child - M. Jobe

YEAR ISSUE		EDITION LIMIT	YEAR RETD.	ISSUE PRICE	*QUOTE U.S.$
1990	Sharing	Closed		29.90	30
1990	The Lost Lamb	Closed		29.90	30
1990	Seems Like Yesterday	Closed		32.90	33
1990	Faithful Friends	Closed		32.90	50
1990	Trusted Companion	Closed		32.90	50
1991	Hand in Hand	Closed		32.90	50

Nature's Nursery - J. Thornbrugh

YEAR ISSUE		EDITION LIMIT	YEAR RETD.	ISSUE PRICE	*QUOTE U.S.$
1992	Testing the Waters	Closed		29.90	50
1993	Taking the Plunge	Closed		29.90	40
1993	Race Ya Mom	Closed		29.90	46
1993	Time to Wake Up	Closed		29.90	45
1993	Hide and Seek	Closed		29.90	45
1993	Piggyback Ride	Closed		29.90	30

Not So Long Ago - J. W. Smith

YEAR ISSUE		EDITION LIMIT	YEAR RETD.	ISSUE PRICE	*QUOTE U.S.$
1988	Story Time	Closed		24.90	25
1988	Wash Day for Dolly	Closed		24.90	25
1988	Suppertime for Kitty	Closed		24.90	26
1988	Mother's Little Helper	Closed		24.90	25

Oklahoma! - M. Kunstler

YEAR ISSUE		EDITION LIMIT	YEAR RETD.	ISSUE PRICE	*QUOTE U.S.$
1985	Oh, What a Beautiful Mornin'	Closed		19.50	20
1986	Surrey with the Fringe on Top'	Closed		19.50	20
1986	I Cain't Say No	Closed		19.50	20
1986	Oklahoma!	Closed		19.50	20

The Old Mill Stream - C. Tennant

YEAR ISSUE		EDITION LIMIT	YEAR RETD.	ISSUE PRICE	*QUOTE U.S.$
1991	New London Grist Mill	Closed		39.90	40
1991	Wayside Inn Grist Mill	Closed		39.90	40
1991	The Red Mill	Closed		39.90	40
1991	Glade Creek Grist Mill	Closed		39.90	40

Old-Fashioned Favorites - M. Weber

YEAR ISSUE		EDITION LIMIT	YEAR RETD.	ISSUE PRICE	*QUOTE U.S.$
1991	Apple Crisp	Closed		29.90	65
1991	Blueberry Muffins	Closed		29.90	65
1991	Peach Cobbler	Closed		29.90	98
1991	Chocolate Chip Oatmeal Cookies	Closed		29.90	180

Once Upon a Time - K. Pritchett

YEAR ISSUE		EDITION LIMIT	YEAR RETD.	ISSUE PRICE	*QUOTE U.S.$
1988	Little Red Riding Hood	Closed		24.90	25
1988	Rapunzel	Closed		24.90	25
1988	Three Little Pigs	Closed		27.90	28
1989	The Princess and the Pea	Closed		27.90	28
1989	Goldilocks and the Three Bears	Closed		27.90	30
1989	Beauty and the Beast	Closed		27.90	45

Pinocchio - Disney Studios

YEAR ISSUE		EDITION LIMIT	YEAR RETD.	ISSUE PRICE	*QUOTE U.S.$
1989	Gepetto Creates Pinocchio	Closed		29.90	55-85
1990	Pinocchio And The Blue Fairy	Closed		29.90	80
1990	It's an Actor's Life For Me	Closed		32.90	45
1990	I've Got No Strings On Me	Closed		32.90	40
1991	Pleasure Island	Closed		32.90	40
1991	A Real Boy	Closed		32.90	50

Portraits of Motherhood - W. Chambers

YEAR ISSUE		EDITION LIMIT	YEAR RETD.	ISSUE PRICE	*QUOTE U.S.$
1987	Mother's Here	Closed		29.50	30
1988	First Touch	Closed		29.50	30

Precious Little Ones - M. T. Fangel

YEAR ISSUE		EDITION LIMIT	YEAR RETD.	ISSUE PRICE	*QUOTE U.S.$
1988	Little Red Robins	Closed		29.90	30
1988	Little Fledglings	Closed		29.90	30
1988	Saturday Night Bath	Closed		29.90	30
1988	Peek-A-Boo	Closed		29.90	32

Proud Sentinels of the American West - N. Glazier

YEAR ISSUE		EDITION LIMIT	YEAR RETD.	ISSUE PRICE	*QUOTE U.S.$
1993	Youngblood	Closed		29.50	55
1993	Cat Nap	Closed		29.90	70
1993	Desert Bighorn Mormon Ridge	Closed		32.90	50
1993	Crown Prince	Closed		32.90	60

Purrfect Point of View - J. Giordano

YEAR ISSUE		EDITION LIMIT	YEAR RETD.	ISSUE PRICE	*QUOTE U.S.$
1992	Unexpected Visitors	Closed		29.90	30
1992	Wistful Morning	Closed		29.90	50
1992	Afternoon Catnap	Closed		29.90	50
1992	Cozy Company	Closed		29.90	35

Pussyfooting Around - C. Wilson

YEAR ISSUE		EDITION LIMIT	YEAR RETD.	ISSUE PRICE	*QUOTE U.S.$
1991	Fish Tales	Closed		24.90	25
1991	Teatime Tabbies	Closed		24.90	25
1991	Yarn Spinners	Closed		24.90	25
1991	Two Maestros	Closed		24.90	32

Romantic Age of Steam - R.B. Pierce

YEAR ISSUE		EDITION LIMIT	YEAR RETD.	ISSUE PRICE	*QUOTE U.S.$
1992	The Empire Builder	Closed		29.90	30
1992	The Broadway Limited	Closed		29.90	35
1992	Twentieth Century Limited	Closed		32.90	50
1992	The Chief	Closed		32.90	60
1992	The Crescent Limited	Closed		32.90	50-65
1993	The Overland Limited	Closed		34.90	35-50
1993	The Jupiter	Closed		34.90	55
1993	The Daylight	Closed		34.90	60

Santa's Christmas - T. Browning

YEAR ISSUE		EDITION LIMIT	YEAR RETD.	ISSUE PRICE	*QUOTE U.S.$
1991	Santa's Love	Closed		29.90	40
1991	Santa's Cheer	Closed		29.90	48
1991	Santa's Promise	Closed		32.90	67
1991	Santa's Gift	Closed		32.90	75
1992	Santa's Surprise	Closed		32.90	55
1992	Santa's Magic	Closed		32.90	55

*Quotes have been rounded up to nearest dollar

Edwin M. Knowles to Ernst Enterprises/Porter & Price, Inc.

PLATES

YEAR ISSUE		EDITION LIMIT	YEAR RETD.	ISSUE PRICE	*QUOTE U.S.$
Season For Song - M. Jobe					
1991	Winter Concert	Closed		34.90	43
1991	Snowy Symphony	Closed		34.90	43
1991	Frosty Chorus	Closed		34.90	60
1991	Silver Serenade	Closed		34.90	65
Seasons of Splendor - K. Randle					
1992	Autumn's Grandeur	Closed		29.90	40
1992	School Days	Closed		29.90	35
1992	Woodland Mill Stream	Closed		32.90	65
1992	Harvest Memories	Closed		32.90	55
1992	A Country Weekend	Closed		32.90	60
1993	Indian Summer	Closed		32.90	55
Shadows and Light: Winter's Wildlife - N. Glazier					
1993	Winter's Children	Closed		29.90	40
1993	Cub Scouts	Closed		29.90	50
1993	Little Snowman	Closed		29.90	50
1993	The Snow Cave	Closed		29.90	40
Singin' In The Rain - M. Skolsky					
1990	Singin' In The Rain	Closed		32.90	33
1990	Good Morning	Closed		32.90	33
1991	Broadway Melody	Closed		32.90	33
1991	We're Happy Again	Closed		32.90	50
Sleeping Beauty - Disney Studios					
1991	Once Upon A Dream	Closed		39.90	50
1991	Awakened by a Kiss	Closed		39.90	90-100
1991	Happy Birthday Briar Rose	Closed		42.90	55
1992	Together At Last	Closed		42.90	50
Small Blessings - C. Layton					
1992	Now I Lay Me Down to Sleep	Closed		29.90	35
1992	Bless Us O Lord For These, Thy Gifts	Closed		29.90	40
1992	Jesus Loves Me, This I Know	Closed		32.90	40
1992	This Little Light of Mine	Closed		32.90	55
1992	Blessed Are The Pure In Heart	Closed		32.90	45
1993	Bless Our Home	Closed		32.90	40
Snow White and the Seven Dwarfs - Disney Studios					
1991	The Dance of Snow White/Seven Dwarfs	Closed		29.90	55
1991	With a Smile and a Song	Closed		29.90	40
1991	A Special Treat	Closed		32.90	40
1992	A Kiss for Dopey	Closed		32.90	45
1992	The Poison Apple	Closed		32.90	57-70
1992	Fireside Love Story	Closed		34.90	50
1992	Stubborn Grumpy	Closed		34.90	35
1992	A Wish Come True	Closed		34.90	37
1993	Time To Tidy Up	Closed		34.50	45
1993	May I Have This Dance?	Closed		36.90	50
1993	A Surprise in the Clearing	Closed		36.50	45
1993	Happy Ending	Closed		36.90	50
Songs of the American Spirit - H. Bond					
1991	The Star Spangled Banner	Closed		29.90	30
1991	Battle Hymn of the Republic	Closed		29.90	45
1991	America the Beautiful	Closed		29.90	35
1991	My Country 'Tis of Thee	Closed		29.90	65
Sound of Music - T. Crnkovich					
1986	Sound of Music	Closed		19.50	28
1986	Do-Re-Mi	Closed		19.50	20-30
1986	My Favorite Things	Closed		22.50	25-35
1986	Laendler Waltz	Closed		22.50	25
1987	Edelweiss	Closed		22.50	23-35
1987	I Have Confidence	Closed		22.50	27
1987	Maria	Closed		24.90	36
1987	Climb Ev'ry Mountain	Closed		24.90	33
South Pacific - E. Gignilliat					
1987	Some Enchanted Evening	Closed		24.50	25
1987	Happy Talk	Closed		24.50	25
1987	Dites Moi	Closed		24.90	25
1988	Honey Bun	Closed		24.90	25
Stately Owls - J. Beaudoin					
1989	The Snowy Owl	Closed		29.90	38
1989	The Great Horned Owl	Closed		29.90	40
1990	The Barn Owl	Closed		32.90	33
1990	The Screech Owl	Closed		32.90	33
1990	The Short-Eared Owl	Closed		32.90	33
1990	The Barred Owl	Closed		32.90	33
1990	The Great Grey Owl	Closed		34.90	35
1991	The Saw-Whet Owl	Closed		34.90	35
Sundblom Santas - H. Sundblom					
1989	Santa By The Fire	Closed		27.90	30
1990	Christmas Vigil	Closed		27.90	35
1991	To All A Good Night	Closed		32.90	60
1992	Santa's on His Way	Closed		32.90	60
A Swan is Born - L. Roberts					
1987	Hopes and Dreams	Closed		24.50	25
1987	At the Barre	Closed		24.50	25
1987	In Position	Closed		24.50	30
1988	Just For Size	Closed		24.50	40

YEAR ISSUE		EDITION LIMIT	YEAR RETD.	ISSUE PRICE	*QUOTE U.S.$
Sweetness and Grace - J. Welty					
1992	God Bless Teddy	Closed		34.90	35
1992	Sunshine and Smiles	Closed		34.90	50
1992	Favorite Buddy	Closed		34.90	45
1992	Sweet Dreams	Closed		34.90	60
Thomas Kinkade's Garden Cottages of England - T. Kinkade					
1991	Chandler's Cottage	Closed		27.90	60
1991	Cedar Nook Cottage	Closed		27.90	45
1991	Candlelit Cottage	Closed		30.90	60
1991	Open Gate Cottage	Closed		30.90	40
1991	McKenna's Cottage	Closed		30.90	50
1992	Woodsman's Thatch Cottage	Closed		32.90	50
1992	Merritt's Cottage	Closed		32.90	60
1992	Stonegate Cottage	Closed		32.90	65
Thomas Kinkade's Home for the Holidays - T. Kinkade					
1991	Sleigh Ride Home	Closed		29.90	50
1991	Home to Grandma's	Closed		29.90	45
1991	Home Before Christmas	Closed		32.90	50
1992	The Warmth of Home	Closed		32.90	55
1992	Homespun Holiday	Closed		32.90	55
1992	Hometime Yuletide	Closed		34.90	55
1992	Home Away From Home	Closed		34.90	75
1992	The Journey Home	Closed		34.90	60
Thomas Kinkade's Home is Where the Heart Is - T. Kinkade					
1992	Home Sweet Home	Closed		29.90	75-85
1992	A Warm Welcome Home	Closed		29.90	60
1992	A Carriage Ride Home	Closed		32.90	60
1993	Amber Afternoon	Closed		32.90	50
1993	Country Memories	Closed		32.90	75-90
1993	The Twilight Cafe	Closed		34.90	50
1993	Our Summer Home	Closed		34.90	60
1993	Hometown Hospitality	Closed		34.90	60
Thomas Kinkade's Thomashire - T. Kinkade					
1992	Olde Porterfield Tea Room	Closed		29.90	40
1992	Olde Thomashire Mill	Closed		29.90	55
1992	Swanbrook Cottage	Closed		32.90	120
1992	Pye Corner Cottage	Closed		32.90	60
1993	Blossom Hill Church	Closed		32.90	50
1993	Olde Garden Cottage	Closed		32.90	70
Thomas Kinkade's Yuletide Memories - T. Kinkade					
1992	The Magic of Christmas	Closed		29.90	75
1992	A Beacon of Faith	Closed		29.90	50
1993	Moonlit Sleighride	Closed		29.90	60
1993	Silent Night	Closed		29.90	60
1993	Olde Porterfield Gift Shoppe	Closed		29.90	60
1993	The Wonder of the Season	Closed		29.90	65
1993	A Winter's Walk	Closed		29.90	45
1993	Skater's Delight	150-day		32.90	55
Tom Sawyer - W. Chambers					
1987	Whitewashing the Fence	Closed		27.50	28
1987	Tom and Becky	Closed		27.50	28
1987	Tom Sawyer the Pirate	Closed		27.90	28
1988	First Pipes	Closed		27.90	30
Under Mother's Wing - J. Beaudoin					
1992	Arctic Spring: Snowy Owls	Closed		29.90	45
1992	Forest's Edge: Great Gray Owls	Closed		29.90	40
1992	Treetop Trio: Long-Eared Owls	Closed		32.90	45
1992	Woodland Watch: Spotted Owls	Closed		32.90	55
1992	Vast View: Saw Whet Owls	Closed		32.90	50
1992	Lofty-Limb: Great Horned Owl	Closed		34.90	50
1993	Perfect Perch: Barred Owls	Closed		34.90	45
1993	Happy Home: Short-Eared Owl	Closed		34.90	50
Upland Birds of North America - W. Anderson					
1986	The Pheasant	Closed		24.50	30-35
1986	The Grouse	Closed		24.50	25
1987	The Quail	Closed		27.50	28
1987	The Wild Turkey	Closed		27.50	28
1987	The Gray Partridge	Closed		27.50	28
1987	The Woodcock	Closed		27.90	28
Wizard of Oz - J. Auckland					
1977	Over the Rainbow	Closed		19.00	43-70
1978	If I Only Had a Brain	Closed		19.00	40
1978	If I Only Had a Heart	Closed		19.00	45
1978	If I Were King of the Forest	Closed		19.00	40-45
1979	Wicked Witch of the West	Closed		19.00	50-65
1979	Follow the Yellow Brick Road	Closed		19.00	50
1979	Wonderful Wizard of Oz	Closed		19.00	50
1980	The Grand Finale	Closed		24.00	45-55
Wizard of Oz: A National Treasure - R. Laslo					
1991	Yellow Brick Road	Closed		29.90	40-55
1992	I Haven't Got a Brain	Closed		29.90	40-55
1992	I'm a Little Rusty Yet	Closed		32.90	45-55
1992	I Even Scare Myself	Closed		32.90	55
1992	We're Off To See the Wizard	Closed		32.90	55-65
1992	I'll Never Get Home	Closed		34.90	55
1992	I'm Melting	Closed		34.90	55-70
1992	There's No Place Like Home	Closed		34.90	55-70

YEAR ISSUE		EDITION LIMIT	YEAR RETD.	ISSUE PRICE	*QUOTE U.S.$
Yesterday's Innocents - J. Wilcox Smith					
1992	My First Book	Closed		29.90	50
1992	Time to Smell the Roses	Closed		29.90	55
1993	Hush, Baby's Sleeping	Closed		32.90	40
1993	Ready and Waiting	Closed		32.90	50

Enchantica

YEAR ISSUE		EDITION LIMIT	YEAR RETD.	ISSUE PRICE	*QUOTE U.S.$
Retired Enchantica Collection - Various					
1992	Winter Dragon-Grawlfang-2200 - J. Woodward	15,000	1993	50.00	75
1992	Spring Dragon-Gorgoyle-2201 - J. Woodward	15,000	1993	50.00	75
1993	Summer Dragon-Arangast-2202 - J. Woodward	15,000	1993	50.00	75
1993	Autumn Dragon-Snarlgard-2203 - J. Woodward	15,000	1993	50.00	75

Ernst Enterprises/Porter & Price, Inc.

YEAR ISSUE		EDITION LIMIT	YEAR RETD.	ISSUE PRICE	*QUOTE U.S.$
A Beautiful World - S. Morton					
1981	Tahitian Dreamer	Retrd.	1987	27.50	30
1982	Flirtation	Retrd.	1987	27.50	30
1984	Elke of Oslo	Retrd.	1987	27.50	30
Classy Cars - S. Kuhnly					
1982	The 26T	Retrd.	1990	24.50	40
1982	The 31A	Retrd.	1990	24.50	40
1983	The Pickup	Retrd.	1990	24.50	40
1984	Panel Van	Retrd.	1990	24.50	40
Commemoratives - S. Morton					
1981	John Lennon	Retrd.	1988	39.50	145
1982	Elvis Presley	Retrd.	1988	39.50	90-120
1982	Marilyn Monroe	Retrd.	1988	39.50	125
1983	Judy Garland	Retrd.	1988	39.50	65-120
1984	John Wayne	Retrd.	1988	39.50	110
Elvira - S. Morton					
1988	Night Rose	90-day		29.50	45
1988	Red Velvet	90-day		29.50	35
1988	Mistress of the Dark	90-day		29.50	35
Elvis Presley - S. Morton					
1987	The King	Retrd.	1991	39.50	125
1987	Loving You	Retrd.	1991	39.50	95
1987	Early Years	Retrd.	1991	39.50	95-125
1987	Tenderly	Retrd.	1991	39.50	95
1988	Forever Yours	Retrd.	1991	39.50	90
1988	Rockin in the Moonlight	Retrd.	1991	39.50	95
1988	Moody Blues	Retrd.	1991	39.50	75-95
1988	Elvis Presley	Retrd.	1991	39.50	90
1989	Elvis Presley-Special Request	Retrd.	1991	150.00	225-250
Hollywood Greats - S. Morton					
1981	Henry Fonda	Retrd.	1988	29.95	55
1981	John Wayne	Retrd.	1988	29.95	100
1981	Gary Cooper	Retrd.	1988	29.95	40-65
1982	Clark Gable	Retrd.	1988	29.95	65
1984	Alan Ladd	Retrd.	1988	29.95	60
Hollywood Walk of Fame - S. Morton					
1989	Jimmy Stewart	Retrd.	1992	39.50	40-50
1989	Elizabeth Taylor	Retrd.	1992	39.50	45
1989	Tom Selleck	Retrd.	1992	39.50	45
1989	Joan Collins	Retrd.	1992	39.50	45
1990	Burt Reynolds	Retrd.	1992	39.50	45
1990	Sylvester Stallone	Retrd.	1992	39.50	45
The Republic Pictures Library - S. Morton					
1991	Showdown With Laredo	28-day		37.50	38
1991	The Ride Home	28-day		37.50	38
1991	Attack at Tarawa	28-day		37.50	45
1991	Thoughts of Angelique	28-day		37.50	45
1992	War of the Wildcats	28-day		37.50	55
1992	The Fighting Seabees	28-day		37.50	45
1992	The Quiet Man	28-day		37.50	40
1992	Angel and the Badman	28-day		37.50	45
1993	Sands of Iwo Jima	28-day		37.50	40
1993	Flying Tigers	28-day		37.50	45-65
1993	The Tribute (12")	28-day		97.50	98
1994	The Tribute (8 1/4") AP	9,500		35.00	35
Seems Like Yesterday - R. Money					
1981	Stop & Smell the Roses	Retrd.	1988	24.50	30
1982	Home by Lunch	Retrd.	1988	24.50	35
1982	Lisa's Creek	Retrd.	1988	24.50	25
1983	It's Got My Name on It	Retrd.	1988	24.50	30
1983	My Magic Hat	Retrd.	1988	24.50	25
1984	Little Prince	Retrd.	1988	24.50	25
Star Trek - S. Morton					
1984	Mr. Spock	Retrd.	1989	29.50	125-200
1985	Dr. McCoy	Retrd.	1989	29.50	75-125
1985	Sulu	Retrd.	1989	29.50	65-100
1985	Scotty	Retrd.	1989	29.50	65-100
1985	Uhura	Retrd.	1989	29.50	65-100
1985	Chekov	Retrd.	1989	29.50	65-100
1985	Captain Kirk	Retrd.	1989	29.50	120-150

*Quotes have been rounded up to nearest dollar

YEAR ISSUE		EDITION LIMIT	YEAR RETD.	ISSUE PRICE	*QUOTE U.S.$
1985	Beam Us Down Scotty	Retrd.	1989	29.50	80-100
1985	The Enterprise	Retrd.	1989	39.50	135-150

Star Trek: Commemorative Collection - S. Morton

1987	The Trouble With Tribbles	Retrd.	1989	29.50	135-150
1987	Mirror, Mirror	Retrd.	1989	29.50	150
1987	A Piece of the Action	Retrd.	1989	29.50	75-150
1987	The Devil in the Dark	Retrd.	1989	29.50	100-150
1987	Amok Time	Retrd.	1989	29.50	100-150
1987	The City on the Edge of Forever	Retrd.	1989	29.50	100-175
1987	Journey to Babel	Retrd.	1989	29.50	80-160
1987	The Menagerie	Retrd.	1989	29.50	80-175

Turn of The Century - R. Money

1981	Riverboat Honeymoon	Retrd.	1987	35.00	40
1982	Children's Carousel	Retrd.	1987	35.00	35
1984	Flower Market	Retrd.	1987	35.00	35
1985	Balloon Race	Retrd.	1987	35.00	35

Women of the West - D. Putnam

1979	Expectations	Retrd.	1986	39.50	40
1981	Silver Dollar Sal	Retrd.	1986	39.50	40
1982	School Marm	Retrd.	1986	39.50	40
1983	Dolly	Retrd.	1986	39.50	40

Fairmont

Famous Clowns - R. Skelton

1976	Freddie the Freeloader	10,000		55.00	275-375
1977	W. C. Fields	10,000		55.00	90
1978	Happy	10,000		55.00	90
1979	The Pledge	10,000		55.00	95

Spencer Special - I. Spencer

1978	Hug Me	10,000		55.00	75-100
1978	Sleep Little Baby	10,000		65.00	65-80

Fenton Art Glass Company

American Classic Series - M. Dickinson

1986	Jupiter Train on Opal Satin	5,000	1986	75.00	75
1986	Studebaker-Garford Car on Opal Satin	5,000	1986	75.00	75

American Craftsman Carnival - Fenton

1970	Glassmaker	Closed	1970	10.00	50-60
1971	Printer	Closed	1971	10.00	50-60
1972	Blacksmith	Closed	1972	10.00	50-60
1973	Shoemaker	Closed	1973	10.00	50-60
1974	Pioneer Cooper	Closed	1974	11.00	50-60
1975	Paul Revere (Patriot & Silversmith)	Closed	1975	12.50	50-60
1976	Gunsmith	Closed	1976	13.50	50-60
1977	Potter	Closed	1977	15.00	50-60
1978	Wheelwright	Closed	1978	15.00	50-60
1979	Cabinetmaker	Closed	1979	15.00	50-60
1980	Tanner	Closed	1980	16.50	50-60
1981	Housewright	Closed	1981	17.50	50-60

Artist Series - Various

1982	After The Snow (31/4") - D. Johnson	15,000	1982	14.50	15
1983	Winter Chapel (3 1/4") - D. Johnson	15,000	1984	15.00	15
1985	Flying Geese (3 1/4") - D. Johnson	15,000	1985	15.00	15
1986	The Hummingbird (3 1/4") - D. Johnson	15,000	1986	15.00	15
1987	Out in the Country (3 1/4") - L. Everson	15,000	1987	15.00	15
1988	Serenity (3 1/4") - F. Burton	5,000	1988	16.50	17
1989	Househunting (3 1/4") - D. Barbour	5,000	1989	16.50	17

Childhood Treasurers Series - Various

1983	Teddy Bear (3 1/4") - D. Johnson	15,000	1983	15.00	15
1984	Hobby Horse (3 1/4") - L. Everson	15,000	1984	15.00	15
1985	Clown (3 1/4") - L. Everson	15,000	1985	17.50	18
1986	Playful Kitten (3 1/4") - L. Everson	15,000	1986	15.00	15
1987	Frisky Pup (3 1/4") - D. Barbour	15,000	1987	15.00	15
1988	Castles in the Air (3 1/4") - D. Barbour	5,000	1988	16.50	17
1989	A Child's Cuddly Friend (3 1/4") - D. Johnson	5,000	1989	16.50	17

Christmas - Various

1979	Nature's Christmas - K. Cunningham	Yr.Iss.	1979	35.00	35
1980	Going Home - D. Johnson	Yr.Iss.	1980	38.50	39
1981	All Is Calm - D. Johnson	Yr.Iss.	1981	42.50	43
1982	Country Christmas - R. Spindler	Yr.Iss.	1982	42.50	43
1983	Anticipation - D. Johnson	7,500	1983	45.00	45
1984	Expectation - D. Johnson	7,500	1984	50.00	50
1985	Heart's Desire - D. Johnson	7,500	1986	50.00	50
1987	Sharing The Spirit - L. Everson	Yr.Iss.	1987	50.00	50
1987	Cardinal in the Churchyard - D. Johnson	4,500	1987	39.50	40
1988	A Chickadee Ballet - D. Johnson	4,500	1988	39.50	40
1989	Downy Pecker - Chisled Song - D. Johnson	4,500	1989	39.50	40
1990	A Blue Bird in Snowfall - D. Johnson	4,500	1990	39.50	40
1990	Sleigh Ride - F. Burton	3,500	1990	45.00	45
1991	Christmas Eve - F. Burton	3,500	1991	45.00	45
1992	Family Tradition - F. Burton	3,500	1992	49.00	49
1993	Family Holiday - F. Burton	3,500	1993	49.00	49
1994	Silent Night - F. Burton	1,500	1994	65.00	65
1995	Our Home Is Blessed - F. Burton	1,500	1995	65.00	65
1996	Star of Wonder - F. Burton	1,750	1996	65.00	65

Christmas In America - Fenton

1970	Little Brown Church in the Vale, Bradford, IA, Blue Satin	Closed	1970	12.50	15
1970	Little Brown Church in the Vale, Bradford, IA, Carnival	Closed	1970	12.50	15
1970	Little Brown Church in the Vale, Bradford, IA, White Satin	Closed	1970	12.50	15
1971	The Old Brick Church, Isle of Wight County, VA, Blue Satin	Closed	1971	12.50	15
1971	The Old Brick Church, Isle of Wight County, VA, Carnival	Closed	1971	12.50	15
1971	The Old Brick Church, Isle of Wight County, VA, White Satin	Closed	1971	12.50	15
1972	The Two Horned Church, Marietta, OH, Blue Satin	Closed	1972	12.50	15
1972	The Two Horned Church, Marietta, OH, Carnival	Closed	1972	12.50	15
1972	The Two Horned Church, Marietta, OH, White Satin	Closed	1972	12.50	15
1973	St. Mary's in the Mountain, Virginia City, NV, Blue Satin	Closed	1973	12.50	15
1973	St. Mary's in the Mountain, Virginia City, NV, Carnival	Closed	1973	12.50	15
1973	St. Mary's in the Mountain, Virginia City, NV, White Satin	Closed	1973	12.50	15
1974	The Nation's Church, Philadelphia, PA, Blue Satin	Closed	1974	13.50	15
1974	The Nation's Church, Philadelphia, PA, Carnival	Closed	1974	13.50	15
1974	The Nation's Church, Philadelphia, PA, White Satin	Closed	1974	13.50	15
1975	Birthplace of Liberty, Richmond, VA, Blue Satin	Closed	1975	13.50	15
1975	Birthplace of Liberty, Richmond, VA, Carnival	Closed	1975	13.50	15
1975	Birthplace of Liberty, Richmond, VA, White Satin	Closed	1975	13.50	15
1976	The Old North Church, Boston, MA, Blue Satin	Closed	1976	15.00	15
1976	The Old North Church, Boston, MA, Carnival	Closed	1976	15.00	15
1976	The Old North Church, Boston, MA, White Satin	Closed	1976	15.00	15
1977	San Carlos Borromeo de Carmelo, Carmel, CA, Blue Satin	Closed	1977	15.00	15
1977	San Carlos Borromeo de Carmelo, Carmel, CA, Carnival	Closed	1977	15.00	15
1977	San Carlos Borromeo de Carmelo, Carmel, CA, White Satin	Closed	1977	15.00	15
1978	The Church of Holy Trinity, Philadelphia, PA, Blue Satin	Closed	1978	15.00	15
1978	The Church of Holy Trinity, Philadelphia, PA, Carnival	Closed	1978	15.00	15
1978	The Church of Holy Trinity, Philadelphia, PA, White Satin	Closed	1978	15.00	15
1979	San Jose Y Miguel de Aguayo, San Antonio, TX, Blue Satin	Closed	1979	15.00	15
1979	San Jose Y Miguel de Aguayo, San Antonio, TX, Carnival	Closed	1979	15.00	15
1979	San Jose Y Miguel de Aguayo, San Antonio, TX, White Satin	Closed	1979	15.00	15
1980	Christ Church, Alexandria, VA, Blue Satin	Closed	1980	16.50	17
1980	Christ Church, Alexandria, VA, Carnival	Closed	1980	16.50	17
1980	Christ Church, Alexandria, VA, White Satin	Closed	1980	16.50	17
1981	San Xavier Del Bac, Tucson, AZ, Blue Satin	Closed	1981	18.50	19
1981	San Xavier Del Bac, Tucson, AZ, Carnival	Closed	1981	18.50	19
1981	San Xavier Del Bac, Tucson, AZ, White Satin	Closed	1981	18.50	19
1981	San Xavier Del Bac, Tucson, AZ, Florentine	Closed	1981	25.00	25

Designer Series - Various

1983	Lighthouse Point - M. Dickinson	1,000	1983	65.00	65
1983	Down Home - G. Finn	1,000	1983	65.00	65
1984	Smoke 'N Cinders - M. Dickinson	1,250	1984	65.00	65
1984	Majestic Flight - B. Cumberledge	1,250	1984	65.00	65
1985	In Season - M. Dickinson	1,250	1985	65.00	65
1985	Nature's Grace - B. Cumberland	1,250	1985	65.00	65
1985	Statue of Liberty - S. Bryan	1,250	1985	65.00	65
1986	Statue of Liberty - S. Bryan	1,250	1986	65.00	65

Easter Series - Various

1995	Covered Hen & Egg Opal Irid. Hndpt. - M. Reynolds	950	1995	95.00	95
1997	Covered Hen & Egg Opal Irid. Hndpt. - R. Spindler	950		115.00	115

Mary Gregory - M. Reynolds

1994	Plate w/stand, 9"	Closed	1994	65.00	65
1995	Plate w/stand, 9"	Closed	1995	65.00	65

Mother's Day Series - Fenton, unless otherwise noted

1971	Madonna w/Sleeping Child, Carnival	Closed	1971	10.75	15
1971	Madonna w/Sleeping Child, Blue Satin	Closed	1971	10.75	15
1972	Madonna of the Goldfinch, Carnival	Closed	1972	12.50	15
1972	Madonna of the Goldfinch, Blue Satin	Closed	1972	12.50	15
1972	Madonna of the Goldfinch, White Satin	Closed	1972	12.50	15
1973	The Small Cowper Madonna, Carnival	Closed	1973	12.50	15
1973	The Small Cowper Madonna, Blue Satin	Closed	1973	12.50	15
1973	The Small Cowper Madonna, White Satin	Closed	1973	12.50	15
1974	Madonna of the Grotto, Carnival	Closed	1974	13.50	15
1974	Madonna of the Grotto, Blue Satin	Closed	1974	13.50	15
1974	Madonna of the Grotto, White Satin	Closed	1974	13.50	15
1975	Taddei Madonna, Blue Satin	Closed	1975	13.50	15
1975	Taddei Madonna, Carnival	Closed	1975	13.50	15
1975	Taddei Madonna, White Satin	Closed	1975	13.50	15
1976	The Holly Night, Cardinal	Closed	1976	13.50	15
1976	The Holly Night, Blue Satin	Closed	1976	13.50	15
1976	The Holly Night, White Satin	Closed	1976	13.50	15
1977	Madonna & Child w/Pomegrantate, Carnival	Closed	1977	15.00	15
1977	Madonna & Child w/Pomegrantate, Blue Satin	Closed	1977	15.00	15
1977	Madonna & Child w/Pomegrantate, White Satin	Closed	1977	15.00	15
1978	The Madonnina, Cardinal	Closed	1978	15.00	15
1978	The Madonnina, Blue Satin	Closed	1978	15.00	15
1978	The Madonnina, White Satin	Closed	1978	15.00	15
1979	Madonna of the Rose Hedge, Carnival	Closed	1979	15.00	15
1979	Madonna of the Rose Hedge, Blue Satin	Closed	1979	15.00	15
1979	Madonna of the Rose Hedge, White Satin	Closed	1979	15.00	15
1979	Madonna of the Rose Hedge, Ruby Carnival	Closed	1979	35.00	35
1980	New Born - L. Everson	Closed	1980	28.50	29
1981	Gentle Fawn - L. Everson	Closed	1981	32.50	33
1982	Nature's Awakening - L. Everson	Closed	1982	35.00	35
1983	Where's Mom - L. Everson	Closed	1983	35.00	35
1984	Precious Panda - L. Everson	Closed	1984	35.00	35
1985	Mother's Little Lamb - L. Everson	Closed	1985	35.00	35
1990	Mother Swan - L. Everson	Closed	1990	45.00	50
1991	Mother's Watchful Eye - M. Reynolds	Closed	1991	45.00	50
1992	Let's Play With Mom - M. Reynolds	Closed	1992	49.50	50
1993	Mother Deer - M. Reynolds	Closed	1993	49.50	50
1994	Loving Puppy - M. Reynolds	Closed	1994	49.50	50

Flambro Imports

Emmett Kelly Jr. Plates - Various

1983	Why Me? Plate I - C. Kelly	10,000	N/A	40.00	450
1984	Balloons For Sale Plate II - C. Kelly	10,000	N/A	40.00	350
1985	Big Business Plate III - C. Kelly	10,000	N/A	40.00	350
1986	And God Bless America IV - C. Kelly	10,000	N/A	40.00	325
1988	Tis the Season - D. Rust	10,000	N/A	50.00	125-150
1989	Looking Back- 65th Birthday - D. Rust	6,500	N/A	50.00	125-150
1991	Winter - D. Rust	10,000	1996	30.00	50-85
1992	Spring - D. Rust	10,000	1996	30.00	50-85
1992	Summer - D. Rust	10,000	1996	30.00	50-85
1992	Autumn - D. Rust	10,000	1996	30.00	30
1993	Santa's Stowaway - D. Rust	10,000	N/A	30.00	40-90
1994	70th Birthday Commemorative - D. Rust	5,000	N/A	30.00	40-90
1995	All Wrapped Up in Christmas - Undisclosed	5,000	N/A	30.00	30

Fountainhead

As Free As The Wind - M. Fernandez

1989	As Free As The Wind	Unkn.		295.00	300-600

The Wings of Freedom - M. Fernandez

1985	Courtship Flight	2,500		250.00	1300-1500
1986	Wings of Freedom	2,500		250.00	1300-1500

Ganz

Watching Over You Collection - C.Thammavongsa

1996	Wings of the Wind	Open		40.00	40

Gartlan USA

Club Gift

1989	Pete Rose (8 1/2") - B. Forbes	Closed	1990	Gift	100-200
1990	Al Barlick (8 1/2") - M. Taylor	Closed	1991	Gift	60-125
1991	Joe Montana (8 1/2") - M. Taylor	Closed	1992	Gift	100-200
1992	Ken Griffey Jr. (8 1/2") - M. Taylor	Closed	1993	Gift	60-75
1993	Gordie Howe (8 1/2") - M. Taylor	Closed	1994	Gift	60-100
1994	Shaquille O'Neal (8 1/2") - M. Taylor	Closed	1995	Gift	60-100
1996	Ringo Starr (8 1/2") - M. Taylor	Yr. Iss.		Gift	30

Bob Cousy - M. Taylor

1994	Signed Plate (10 1/4")	950	1995	175.00	175
1994	Plate (8 1/2")	10,000		30.00	30
1994	Plate (3 1/4")	Open		15.00	15

Brett & Bobby Hull - M. Taylor

1992	Hockey's Golden Boys (10 1/4") signed by both	950	1995	250.00	250-300

*Quotes have been rounded up to nearest dollar

PLATES

Gartlan USA

YEAR ISSUE		EDITION LIMIT	YEAR RETD.	ISSUE PRICE	*QUOTE U.S.$
1992	Hockey's Golden Boys (10 1/4") A/P, signed by both	300	1995	350.00	350
1992	Hockey's Golden Boys (8 1/2")	10,000		30.00	30
1992	Hockey's Golden Boys (3 1/4")	Open		15.00	15

Carl Yastrzemski - M. Taylor
1993	Signed Plate (10 1/4")	950	1995	175.00	175
1993	Plate (8 1/2")	10,000		30.00	30
1993	Plate (3 1/4")	Open		15.00	15

Carlton Fisk - M. Taylor
1993	Signed Plate (10 1/4")	950	1995	175.00	175-200
1993	Plate (8 1/2")	5,000		30.00	30
1993	Plate (3 1/4")	Open		15.00	15

Darryl Strawberry - M. Taylor
1991	Signed Plate (10 1/4")	2,500	1995	150.00	150
1991	Plate (8 1/2")	10,000	1995	40.00	40
1991	Plate (3 1/4")	Retrd.	1995	15.00	15

George Brett Gold Crown Collection - J. Martin
1986	George Brett "Baseball's All Star" (3 1/4")	Open		12.95	15-20
1986	George Brett "Baseball's All Star" (10 1/4") signed	2,000	1988	100.00	200
1986	George Brett "Baseball's All Star" (10 1/4"), A/P signed	24	1988	225.00	N/A

Gordie Howe - M. Taylor
1993	Signed Plate (10 1/4")	2,358	1995	150.00	150-175
1993	Signed Plate (8 1/2")	10,000		30.00	30
1993	Signed Plate (3 1/4")	Open		15.00	15

Joe Montana - M. Taylor
1991	Signed Plate (10 1/4")	2,250	1991	125.00	225-325
1991	Signed Plate (10 1/4") A/P	250	1991	195.00	400-450
1991	Plate (8 1/2")	10,000	1995	30.00	50
1991	Plate (3 1/4")	Open		15.00	15

John Wooden - M. Taylor
1990	Signed Plate (10 1/4")	1,975	1995	150.00	150
1990	Plate (8 1/2")	10,000	1995	30.00	30
1990	Plate (3 1/4")	Retrd.	1995	15.00	15

Johnny Bench - M. Taylor
| 1989 | Signed Plate (10 1/4") | 1,989 | 1991 | 100.00 | 100-250 |
| 1989 | Plate (3 1/4") | Open | | 15.00 | 15 |

Kareem Abdul-Jabbar Sky-Hook Collection - M. Taylor
| 1989 | Kareem Abdul-Jabbar "Path of Glory" (10 1/4"), signed | 1,989 | 1991 | 100.00 | 150-225 |
| 1989 | Plate (3 1/4") | Closed | 1993 | 16.00 | 30 |

Ken Griffey Jr. - M. Taylor
1992	Signed Plate (10 1/4")	1,989	1995	150.00	150-250
1992	Plate (8 1/2")	10,000		30.00	30
1992	Plate (3 1/4")	Open		15.00	15

Kristi Yamaguchi - M. Taylor
1993	Signed Plate (10 1/4")	950	1995	150.00	200-300
1993	Plate (8 1/2")	5,000		30.00	30
1993	Plate (3 1/4")	Open		15.00	15

Leave It To Beaver - M. Taylor
1995	Jerry Mathers, (10 1/4") signed	1,963		125.00	125
1996	Jerry Mathers, (10 1/4") A/P signed	234		175.00	175
1995	Jerry Mathers, (8 1/4")	10,000		39.95	40
1995	Jerry Mathers, (3 1/4") miniature	Open		14.95	15

Luis Aparicio - M. Taylor
1991	Signed Plate (10 1/4")	1,984	1995	150.00	200-250
1991	Plate (8 1/2")	10,000		30.00	30
1991	Plate (3 1/4")	Open		15.00	15

Magic Johnson Gold Rim Collection - R. Winslow
| 1987 | Magic Johnson "The Magic Show" (10 1/4"), signed | 1,987 | 1988 | 100.00 | 300-450 |
| 1987 | Magic Johnson "The Magic Show" (3 1/4") | Closed | 1993 | 14.50 | 25-35 |

Mike Schmidt "500th" Home Run Edition - C. Paluso
1987	Mike Schmidt "Power at the Plate" (10 1/4"), signed	1,987	1988	100.00	300-400
1987	Mike Schmidt "Power at the Plate" (3 1/4")	Open		14.50	19
1987	Mike Schmidt A/P	56	1988	150.00	150

Pete Rose Diamond Collection - Forbes
1988	Pete Rose "The Reigning Legend" (10 1/4"), signed	950	1989	195.00	250-300
1988	Pete Rose "The Reigning Legend" (10 1/4"), signed A/P	50	1989	300.00	395
1988	Pete Rose "The Reigning Legend" (3 1/4")	Open		14.50	15

Pete Rose Platinum Edition - T. Sizemore
| 1985 | Pete Rose "The Best of Baseball" (3 1/4") | Open | | 12.95 | 15-20 |
| 1985 | Pete Rose "The Best of Baseball" (10 1/4") | 4,192 | 1988 | 100.00 | 275-350 |

Ringo Starr - M. Taylor
1996	Ringo Starr, (10 1/4") signed	1,000	1996	225.00	250
1996	Ringo Starr, (10 1/4") A/P signed	250		400.00	400
1996	Ringo Starr, (8 1/4")	10,000		29.95	30
1996	Ringo Starr, (3 1/4") miniature	Open		14.95	15

Rod Carew - M. Taylor
1992	Signed Plate (10 1/4")	950	1995	150.00	150
1992	Plate (8 1/2")	10,000		30.00	30
1992	Plate (3 1/4")	Open		15.00	15

Roger Staubach Sterling Collection - C. Soileau
| 1987 | Roger Staubach (3 1/4" diameter) | Open | | 12.95 | 15-20 |
| 1987 | Roger Staubach (10 1/4" diameter) signed | 1,979 | 1990 | 100.00 | 300 |

Sam Snead - M. Taylor
1994	Signed Plate (10 1/4")	950	1995	100.00	100-150
1994	Plate (8 1/2")	5,000		30.00	30
1994	Plate (3 1/4")	Open		15.00	15

Tom Seaver - M. Taylor
1993	Signed Plate (10 1/4")	1,992	1995	150.00	300
1993	Signed Plate (8 1/2")	10,000		30.00	30
1993	Signed Plate (3 1/4")	Open		15.00	15

Troy Aikman - M. Taylor
1994	Signed Plate (10 1/4")	1,993	1995	225.00	250
1994	Plate (8 1/2")	10,000		30.00	30
1994	Plate (3 1/4")	Open		14.95	15

Wayne Gretzky - M. Taylor
1989	Plate (10 1/4"), signed by Gretzky and Howe	1,851	1989	225.00	250-300
1989	Plate (10 1/4") A/P, signed by Gretzky and Howe	300	1989	300.00	450-500
1989	Plate (8 1/2")	10,000		45.00	45-50
1989	Plate (3 1/4")	Open		15.00	15

Whitey Ford - M. Taylor
1991	Signed Plate (10 1/4")	2,360	1995	150.00	150
1991	Plate (8 1/2")	10,000	1995	30.00	40-70
1991	Plate (3 1/4")	Retrd.	1995	15.00	20

Yogi Berra - M. Taylor
1991	Signed Plate (10 1/4")	2,150	1995	150.00	150
1991	Plate (8 1/2")	10,000		30.00	30
1991	Plate (3 1/4")	Open		15.00	15

Georgetown Collection, Inc.

Children of the Great Spirit - C. Theroux
| 1993 | Buffalo Child | 35-day | | 29.95 | 30 |
| 1993 | Winter Baby | 35-day | | 29.95 | 30 |

Goebel/M.I. Hummel

M.I. Hummel Annual Figural Christmas Plates - M.I. Hummel
1995	Festival Harmony w/Flute 693	Closed	1995	125.00	125
1996	Christmas Song 692	Closed	1996	130.00	130
1997	Thanksgiving Prayer 694	Yr.Iss.		140.00	140

M.I. Hummel Club Exclusive Celebration - M.I. Hummel
1986	Valentine Gift (Hum 738)	Closed		90.00	120-130
1987	Valentine Joy (Hum 737)	Closed		98.00	120-130
1988	Daisies Don't Tell (Hum 736)	Closed		115.00	115-130
1989	It's Cold (Hum 735)	Closed		120.00	120-150

M.I. Hummel Collectibles Anniversary Plates - M.I. Hummel
1975	Stormy Weather 280	Closed		100.00	100-150
1980	Spring Dance 281	Closed		225.00	230
1985	Auf Wiedersehen 282	Closed		225.00	270

M.I. Hummel Collectibles Annual Plates - M.I. Hummel
1971	Heavenly Angel 264	Closed		25.00	500-900
1972	Hear Ye, Hear Ye 265	Closed		30.00	40-80
1973	Glober Trotter 266	Closed		32.50	75-175
1974	Goose Girl 267	Closed		40.00	50-75
1975	Ride into Christmas 268	Closed		50.00	55-80
1976	Apple Tree Girl 269	Closed		50.00	40-60
1977	Apple Tree Boy 270	Closed		52.50	95
1978	Happy Pastime 271	Closed		65.00	80
1979	Singing Lesson 272	Closed		90.00	75-100
1980	School Girl 273	Closed		100.00	100
1981	Umbrella Boy 274	Closed		100.00	100-125
1982	Umbrella Girl 275	Closed		100.00	160
1983	The Postman 276	Closed		108.00	195-240
1984	Little Helper 277	Closed		108.00	108-150
1985	Chick Girl 278	Closed		110.00	110-140
1986	Playmates 279	Closed		125.00	160-225
1987	Feeding Time 283	Closed		135.00	400-500
1988	Little Goat Herder 284	Closed		145.00	145-175
1989	Farm Boy 285	Closed		160.00	160-200
1990	Shepherd's Boy 286	Closed		170.00	250
1991	Just Resting 287	Closed		196.00	196-225
1992	Wayside Harmony 288	Closed		210.00	265
1993	Doll Bath 289	Closed		210.00	240-270
1994	Doctor 290	Closed		225.00	225-250
1995	Come Back Soon 291	Closed		250.00	260

M.I. Hummel Four Seasons - M.I. Hummel
| 1996 | Winter Melody 296 | Yr.Iss. | | 195.00 | 195 |
| 1997 | Springtime Serenade 297 | Yr.Iss. | | 195.00 | 195 |

M.I. Hummel Friends Forever - M.I. Hummel
1992	Meditation 292	Open		180.00	195
1993	For Father 293	Open		195.00	195
1994	Sweet Greetings 294	Open		205.00	205
1995	Surprise 295	Open		210.00	210

M.I. Hummel Little Music Makers - M.I. Hummel
1984	Little Fiddler 744	Closed		30.00	75-100
1985	Serenade 741	Closed		30.00	75-100
1986	Soloist 743	Closed		35.00	75-100
1987	Band Leader 742	Closed		40.00	75-100

M.I. Hummel The Little Homemakers - M.I. Hummel
1988	Little Sweeper (Hum 745)	Closed		45.00	50-100
1989	Wash Day (Hum 746)	Closed		50.00	50-100
1990	A Stitch in Time (Hum 747)	Closed		50.00	60-100
1991	Chicken Licken (Hum 748)	Closed		70.00	70-100

Gorham

(Four Seasons) A Boy and His Dog Plates - N. Rockwell
1971	Boy Meets His Dog	Annual	1971	50.00	175
1971	Adventures Between Adventures	Annual	1971	Set	Set
1971	The Mysterious Malady	Annual	1971	Set	Set
1971	Pride of Parenthood	Annual	1971	Set	Set

(Four Seasons) A Helping Hand Plates - N. Rockwell
1979	Year End Court	Annual	1979	100.00	100
1979	Closed for Business	Annual	1979	Set	Set
1979	Swatter's Rights	Annual	1979	Set	Set
1979	Coal Season's Coming	Annual	1979	Set	Set

(Four Seasons) Dad's Boys Plates - N. Rockwell
1980	Ski Skills	Annual	1980	135.00	135
1980	In His Spirits	Annual	1980	Set	Set
1980	Trout Dinner	Annual	1980	Set	Set
1980	Careful Aim	Annual	1980	Set	Set

(Four Seasons) Four Ages of Love - N. Rockwell
1973	Gaily Sharing Vintage Time	Annual	1973	60.00	135
1973	Flowers in Tender Bloom	Annual	1973	Set	Set
1973	Sweet Song So Young	Annual	1973	Set	Set
1973	Fondly We Do Remember	Annual	1973	Set	Set

(Four Seasons) Going on Sixteen Plates - N. Rockwell
1977	Chilling Chore	Annual	1977	75.00	100
1977	Sweet Serenade	Annual	1977	Set	Set
1977	Shear Agony	Annual	1977	Set	Set
1977	Pilgrimage	Annual	1977	Set	Set

(Four Seasons) Grand Pals Four Plates - N. Rockwell
1976	Snow Sculpturing	Annual	1976	70.00	120
1976	Soaring Spirits	Annual	1976	Set	Set
1976	Fish Finders	Annual	1976	Set	Set
1976	Ghostly Gourds	Annual	1976	Set	Set

(Four Seasons) Grandpa and Me Plates - N. Rockwell
1974	Gay Blades	Annual	1974	60.00	90
1974	Day Dreamers	Annual	1974	Set	Set
1974	Goin' Fishing	Annual	1974	Set	Set
1974	Pensive Pals	Annual	1974	Set	Set

(Four Seasons) Life with Father Plates - N. Rockwell
1982	Big Decision	Annual	1982	100.00	100
1982	Blasting Out	Annual	1982	Set	Set
1982	Cheering the Champs	Annual	1982	Set	Set
1982	A Tough One	Annual	1982	Set	Set

(Four Seasons) Me and My Pals Plates - N. Rockwell
1975	A Lickin' Good Bath	Annual	1975	70.00	90
1975	Young Man's Fancy	Annual	1975	Set	Set
1975	Fisherman's Paradise	Annual	1975	Set	Set
1975	Disastrous Daring	Annual	1975	Set	Set

(Four Seasons) Old Buddies Plates - N. Rockwell
1983	Shared Success	Annual	1983	115.00	115
1983	Endless Debate	Annual	1983	Set	Set
1983	Hasty Retreat	Annual	1983	Set	Set
1983	Final Speech	Annual	1983	Set	Set

(Four Seasons) Old Timers Plates - N. Rockwell
1981	Canine Solo	Annual	1981	100.00	100
1981	Sweet Surprise	Annual	1981	Set	Set
1981	Lazy Days	Annual	1981	Set	Set
1981	Fancy Footwork	Annual	1981	Set	Set

(Four Seasons) Tender Years Plates - N. Rockwell
1978	New Year Look	Annual	1978	100.00	100
1978	Spring Tonic	Annual	1978	Set	Set
1978	Cool Aid	Annual	1978	Set	Set
1978	Chilly Reception	Annual	1978	Set	Set

(Four Seasons) Young Love Plates - N. Rockwell
| 1972 | Downhill Daring | Annual | 1972 | 60.00 | 125 |
| 1972 | Beguiling Buttercup | Annual | 1972 | Set | Set |

PLATES

YEAR ISSUE	EDITION LIMIT	YEAR RETD.	ISSUE PRICE	*QUOTE U.S.$
1972 Flying High	Annual	1972	Set	Set
1972 A Scholarly Pace	Annual	1972	Set	Set

American Artist - R. Donnelly

YEAR ISSUE	EDITION LIMIT	YEAR RETD.	ISSUE PRICE	*QUOTE U.S.$
1976 Apache Mother & Child	9,800	1980	25.00	56

American Landscapes - N. Rockwell

YEAR ISSUE	EDITION LIMIT	YEAR RETD.	ISSUE PRICE	*QUOTE U.S.$
1980 Summer Respite	Annual	1980	45.00	80
1981 Autumn Reflection	Annual	1981	45.00	65
1982 Winter Delight	Annual	1982	50.00	70
1983 Spring Recess	Annual	1983	60.00	75

Barrymore - Barrymore

YEAR ISSUE	EDITION LIMIT	YEAR RETD.	ISSUE PRICE	*QUOTE U.S.$
1971 Quiet Waters	15,000	1980	25.00	25
1972 San Pedro Harbor	15,000	1980	25.00	25
1972 Nantucket, Sterling	1,000	1972	100.00	100
1972 Little Boatyard, Sterling	1,000	1972	100.00	145

Bas Relief - N. Rockwell

YEAR ISSUE	EDITION LIMIT	YEAR RETD.	ISSUE PRICE	*QUOTE U.S.$
1981 Sweet Song So Young	Undis.	1984	100.00	100
1981 Beguiling Buttercup	Undis.	1984	62.50	70
1982 Flowers in Tender Bloom	Undis.	1984	100.00	100
1982 Flying High	Undis.	1984	62.50	65

Boy Scout Plates - N. Rockwell

YEAR ISSUE	EDITION LIMIT	YEAR RETD.	ISSUE PRICE	*QUOTE U.S.$
1975 Our Heritage	18,500	1980	19.50	75
1976 A Scout is Loyal	18,500	1990	19.50	55
1977 The Scoutmaster	18,500	1990	19.50	80
1977 A Good Sign	18,500	1990	19.50	50
1978 Pointing the Way	18,500	1990	19.50	50
1978 Campfire Story	18,500	1990	19.50	25
1980 Beyond the Easel	18,500	1990	45.00	45

Charles Russell - C. Russell

YEAR ISSUE	EDITION LIMIT	YEAR RETD.	ISSUE PRICE	*QUOTE U.S.$
1980 In Without Knocking	9,800	1990	38.00	65
1981 Bronc to Breakfast	9,800	1990	38.00	75
1982 When Ignorance is Bliss	9,800	1990	45.00	85-95
1983 Cowboy Life	9,800	1990	45.00	100

China Bicentennial - Gorham

YEAR ISSUE	EDITION LIMIT	YEAR RETD.	ISSUE PRICE	*QUOTE U.S.$
1972 1776 Plate	18,500	1980	17.50	35
1976 1776 Bicentennial	8,000	1980	17.50	35

Christmas - N. Rockwell

YEAR ISSUE	EDITION LIMIT	YEAR RETD.	ISSUE PRICE	*QUOTE U.S.$
1974 Tiny Tim	Annual	1974	12.50	25-40
1975 Good Deeds	Annual	1975	17.50	25-50
1976 Christmas Trio	Annual	1976	19.50	[illegible]
1977 Yuletide Reckoning	Annual	1977	19.50	45
1978 Planning Christmas Visit	Annual	1978	24.50	30
1979 Santa's Helpers	Annual	1979	24.50	30
1980 Letter to Santa	Annual	1980	27.50	32
1981 Santa Plans His Visit	Annual	1981	29.50	30
1982 Jolly Coachman	Annual	1982	29.50	30
1983 Christmas Dancers	Annual	1983	29.50	35
1984 Christmas Medley	17,500	1984	29.95	30
1985 Home For The Holidays	17,500	1985	29.95	30
1986 Merry Christmas Grandma	17,500	1986	29.95	65
1987 The Homecoming	17,500	1987	35.00	35
1988 Discovery	17,500	1988	37.50	38

Christmas/Children's Television Workshop - Unknown

YEAR ISSUE	EDITION LIMIT	YEAR RETD.	ISSUE PRICE	*QUOTE U.S.$
1981 Sesame Street Christmas	Annual	1981	17.50	18
1982 Sesame Street Christmas	Annual	1982	17.50	18
1983 Sesame Street Christmas	Annual	1983	19.50	20

Encounters, Survival and Celebrations - J. Clymer

YEAR ISSUE	EDITION LIMIT	YEAR RETD.	ISSUE PRICE	*QUOTE U.S.$
1982 A Fine Welcome	7,500	1983	50.00	80
1983 Winter Trail	7,500	1984	50.00	80
1983 Alouette	7,500	1984	62.50	80
1983 The Trader	7,500	1984	62.50	63
1983 Winter Camp	7,500	1984	62.50	75
1983 The Trapper Takes a Wife	7,500	1984	62.50	63

Gallery of Masters - Various

YEAR ISSUE	EDITION LIMIT	YEAR RETD.	ISSUE PRICE	*QUOTE U.S.$
1971 Man with a Gilt Helmet - Rembrandt	10,000	1975	50.00	50
1972 Self Portrait with Saskia - Rembrandt	10,000	1975	50.00	50
1973 The Honorable Mrs. Graham - Gainsborough	7,500	1975	50.00	50

Gorham Museum Doll Plates - Gorham

YEAR ISSUE	EDITION LIMIT	YEAR RETD.	ISSUE PRICE	*QUOTE U.S.$
1984 Lydia	5,000	1984	29.00	125
1984 Belton Bebe	5,000	1984	29.00	55
1984 Christmas Lady	7,500	1984	32.50	33
1985 Lucille	5,000	1985	29.00	35
1985 Jumeau	5,000	1985	29.00	35

Julian Ritter - J. Ritter

YEAR ISSUE	EDITION LIMIT	YEAR RETD.	ISSUE PRICE	*QUOTE U.S.$
1977 Christmas Visit	9,800	1977	24.50	29
1978 Valentine, Fluttering Heart	7,500	1978	45.00	45

Julian Ritter, Fall In Love - J. Ritter

YEAR ISSUE	EDITION LIMIT	YEAR RETD.	ISSUE PRICE	*QUOTE U.S.$
1977 Enchantment	5,000	1977	100.00	100
1977 Frolic	5,000	1977	set	Set
1977 Gutsy Gal	5,000	1977	set	Set
1977 Lonely Chill	5,000	1977	set	Set

Julian Ritter, To Love a Clown - J. Ritter

YEAR ISSUE	EDITION LIMIT	YEAR RETD.	ISSUE PRICE	*QUOTE U.S.$
1978 Awaited Reunion	5,000	1978	120.00	120
1978 Twosome Time	5,000	1978	120.00	120
1978 Showtime Beckons	5,000	1978	120.00	120

YEAR ISSUE	EDITION LIMIT	YEAR RETD.	ISSUE PRICE	*QUOTE U.S.$
1978 Together in Memories	5,000	1978	120.00	120

Leyendecker Annual Christmas Plates - J. C. Leyendecker

YEAR ISSUE	EDITION LIMIT	YEAR RETD.	ISSUE PRICE	*QUOTE U.S.$
1988 Christmas Hug	10,000	1988	37.50	50

Moppet Plates-Anniversary - Unknown

YEAR ISSUE	EDITION LIMIT	YEAR RETD.	ISSUE PRICE	*QUOTE U.S.$
1976 Anniversary	20,000	1977	13.00	13

Moppet Plates-Christmas - Unknown

YEAR ISSUE	EDITION LIMIT	YEAR RETD.	ISSUE PRICE	*QUOTE U.S.$
1973 Christmas	Annual	1973	10.00	35
1974 Christmas	Annual	1974	12.00	12
1975 Christmas	Annual	1975	13.00	13
1976 Christmas	Annual	1976	13.00	15
1977 Christmas	Annual	1977	13.00	14
1978 Christmas	Annual	1978	10.00	10
1979 Christmas	Annual	1979	12.00	12
1980 Christmas	Annual	1980	12.00	12
1981 Christmas	Annual	1981	12.00	12
1982 Christmas	Annual	1982	12.00	12
1983 Christmas	Annual	1983	12.00	12

Moppet Plates-Mother's Day - Unknown

YEAR ISSUE	EDITION LIMIT	YEAR RETD.	ISSUE PRICE	*QUOTE U.S.$
1973 Mother's Day	Annual	1973	10.00	30
1974 Mother's Day	Annual	1974	12.00	20
1975 Mother's Day	Annual	1975	13.00	15
1976 Mother's Day	Annual	1976	13.00	15
1977 Mother's Day	Annual	1977	13.00	15
1978 Mother's Day	Annual	1978	10.00	10

Pastoral Symphony - B. Felder

YEAR ISSUE	EDITION LIMIT	YEAR RETD.	ISSUE PRICE	*QUOTE U.S.$
1982 When I Was a Child	7,500	1983	42.50	50
1982 Gather the Children	7,500	1983	42.50	50
1984 Sugar and Spice	7,500	1985	42.50	50
XX He Loves Me	7,500	1985	42.50	50

Pewter Bicentennial - R. Pailthorpe

YEAR ISSUE	EDITION LIMIT	YEAR RETD.	ISSUE PRICE	*QUOTE U.S.$
1971 Burning of the Gaspee	5,000	1971	35.00	35
1972 Boston Tea Party	5,000	1972	35.00	35

Presidential - N. Rockwell

YEAR ISSUE	EDITION LIMIT	YEAR RETD.	ISSUE PRICE	*QUOTE U.S.$
1976 John F. Kennedy	9,800	1976	30.00	65
1976 Dwight D. Eisenhower	9,800	1976	30.00	35

Remington Western - F. Remington

YEAR ISSUE	EDITION LIMIT	YEAR RETD.	ISSUE PRICE	*QUOTE U.S.$
1973 A New Year on the Cimarron	Annual	1973	25.00	35-50
1973 Aiding a Comrade	Annual	1973	25.00	30-125
1973 The Flight	Annual	1973	25.00	30-95
1973 The Fight for the Water Hole	Annual	1973	25.00	30-125
1975 Old Ramond	Annual	1975	20.00	35-60
1975 A Breed	Annual	1975	20.00	35-65
1976 Cavalry Officer	5,000	1976	37.50	60-75
1976 A Trapper	5,000	1976	37.50	60-75

Silver Bicentennial - Various

YEAR ISSUE	EDITION LIMIT	YEAR RETD.	ISSUE PRICE	*QUOTE U.S.$
1972 1776 Plate - Gorham	500	1972	500.00	500
1972 Burning of the Gaspee - R. Pailthorpe	750	1972	500.00	500
1973 Boston Tea Party - R. Pailthorpe	750	1973	550.00	575

Single Release - F. Quagon

YEAR ISSUE	EDITION LIMIT	YEAR RETD.	ISSUE PRICE	*QUOTE U.S.$
1976 The Black Regiment 1778	7,500	1978	25.00	58

Single Release - N. Rockwell

YEAR ISSUE	EDITION LIMIT	YEAR RETD.	ISSUE PRICE	*QUOTE U.S.$
1974 Weighing In	Annual	1974	12.50	80-99
1974 The Golden Rule	Annual	1974	12.50	30
1975 Ben Franklin	Annual	1975	19.50	35
1976 The Marriage License	Numbrd	1985	37.50	52-75
1978 Triple Self Portrait Memorial	Annual	1978	37.50	50-100
1980 The Annual Visit	Annual	1980	32.50	70
1981 Day in Life of Boy	Annual	1981	50.00	80
1981 Day in Life of Girl	Annual	1981	50.00	80-108

Time Machine Teddies Plates - B. Port

YEAR ISSUE	EDITION LIMIT	YEAR RETD.	ISSUE PRICE	*QUOTE U.S.$
1986 Miss Emily, Bearing Up	5,000	1986	32.50	50
1987 Big Bear, The Toy Collector	5,000	1987	32.50	45
1988 Hunny Munny	5,000	1988	37.50	40

Vermeil Bicentennial - Gorham

YEAR ISSUE	EDITION LIMIT	YEAR RETD.	ISSUE PRICE	*QUOTE U.S.$
1972 1776 Plate	250	1972	750.00	800

Hackett American

Sports - Various

YEAR ISSUE	EDITION LIMIT	YEAR RETD.	ISSUE PRICE	*QUOTE U.S.$
1981 Reggie Jackson h/s - Paluso	Retrd.	N/A	100.00	750-900
1983 Steve Garvey h/s - Paluso	Retrd.	N/A	100.00	150-200
1983 Nolan Ryan h/s - Paluso	Retrd.	N/A	100.00	750
1983 Tom Seaver h/s - Paluso	3,272	N/A	100.00	300
1984 Steve Carlton h/s - Paluso	Retrd.	N/A	100.00	250
1985 Willie Mays h/s - Paluso	Retrd.	N/A	125.00	250-350
1985 Whitey Ford h/s - Paluso	Retrd.	N/A	125.00	250
1985 Hank Aaron h/s - Paluso	Retrd.	N/A	125.00	250-325
1985 Sandy Koufax h/s - Paluso	1,000	N/A	125.00	450
1985 H. Killebrew d/s - Paluso	Retrd.	N/A	125.00	200-250
1985 E. Mathews d/s - Paluso	Retrd.	N/A	125.00	200-250
1986 T. Seaver 300 d/s - Paluso	1,200	N/A	125.00	250
1986 Roger Clemens d/s - Paluso	Retrd.	N/A	125.00	750
1986 Reggie Jackson d/s - Paluso	Retrd.	N/A	125.00	250-325
1986 Wally Joyner d/s - Paluso	Retrd.	N/A	125.00	250
1986 Don Sutton d/s (great events) - Paluso	300	N/A	125.00	250
XX Gary Carter d/s - Simon	Retrd.	N/A	125.00	150
1985 Dwight Gooden u/s - Simon	Retrd.	N/A	55.00	55
XX Arnold Palmer h/s - Alexander	Retrd.	N/A	125.00	200
XX Gary Player h/s - Alexander	Retrd.	N/A	125.00	200-295
1983 Reggie Jackson h/s - Alexander	Retrd.	N/A	125.00	500
1983 Reggie Jackson, proof - Alexander	Retrd.	N/A	250.00	1000-1300
1986 Joe Montana d/s - Alexander	Retrd.	N/A	125.00	600

Hadley House

American Memories Series - T. Redlin

YEAR ISSUE	EDITION LIMIT	YEAR RETD.	ISSUE PRICE	*QUOTE U.S.$
1987 Coming Home	9,500		85.00	85
1988 Lights of Home	9,500	1994	85.00	150
1989 Homeward Bound	9,500		85.00	85
1991 Family Traditions	9,500		85.00	85

Annual Christmas Series - T. Redlin

YEAR ISSUE	EDITION LIMIT	YEAR RETD.	ISSUE PRICE	*QUOTE U.S.$
1991 Heading Home	9,500	1994	65.00	225
1992 Pleasures Of Winter	19,500		65.00	125
1993 Winter Wonderland	19,500		65.00	125
1994 Almost Home	19,500		65.00	125
1995 Sharing the Evening	45-day		29.95	30

Country Doctor Collection - T. Redlin

YEAR ISSUE	EDITION LIMIT	YEAR RETD.	ISSUE PRICE	*QUOTE U.S.$
1995 Wednesday Afternoon	45-day		29.95	30
1995 Office Hours	45-day		29.95	30
1995 House Calls	45-day		29.95	30
1995 Morning Rounds	45-day		29.95	30

Glow Series - T. Redlin

YEAR ISSUE	EDITION LIMIT	YEAR RETD.	ISSUE PRICE	*QUOTE U.S.$
1985 Evening Glow	5,000	1986	55.00	325-450
1985 Morning Glow	5,000	1986	55.00	125-150
1985 Twilight Glow	5,000	1988	55.00	85-125
1988 Afternoon Glow	5,000	1989	55.00	85-125

Lovers Collection - O. Franca

YEAR ISSUE	EDITION LIMIT	YEAR RETD.	ISSUE PRICE	*QUOTE U.S.$
1992 Lovers	9,500		50.00	50

Navajo Visions Suite - O. Franca

YEAR ISSUE	EDITION LIMIT	YEAR RETD.	ISSUE PRICE	*QUOTE U.S.$
1993 Navajo Fantasy	9,500		50.00	50
1993 Young Warrior	9,500		50.00	50

Navajo Woman Series - O. Franca

YEAR ISSUE	EDITION LIMIT	YEAR RETD.	ISSUE PRICE	*QUOTE U.S.$
1990 Feathered Hair Ties	5,000	1994	50.00	50
1991 Navajo Summer	5,000		50.00	50
1992 Turquoise Necklace	5,000		50.00	50
1993 Pink Navajo	5,000		50.00	50

Retreat Series - T. Redlin

YEAR ISSUE	EDITION LIMIT	YEAR RETD.	ISSUE PRICE	*QUOTE U.S.$
1987 Morning Retreat	9,500	1988	65.00	100
1987 Evening Retreat	9,500	1989	65.00	100
1988 Golden Retreat	9,500	1989	65.00	120
1989 Moonlight Retreat	9,500	1993	65.00	85

Seasons - T. Redlin

YEAR ISSUE	EDITION LIMIT	YEAR RETD.	ISSUE PRICE	*QUOTE U.S.$
1994 Autumn Evening	45-day		29.95	30
1995 Spring Fever	45-day		29.95	30
1995 Summertime	45-day		29.95	30
1995 Wintertime	45-day		29.95	30

That Special Time - T. Redlin

YEAR ISSUE	EDITION LIMIT	YEAR RETD.	ISSUE PRICE	*QUOTE U.S.$
1991 Evening Solitude	9,500	1994	65.00	95
1991 That Special Time	9,500	1993	65.00	95
1992 Aroma of Fall	9,500	1994	65.00	95
1993 Welcome To Paradise	9,500		65.00	65

Tranquility - O. Franca

YEAR ISSUE	EDITION LIMIT	YEAR RETD.	ISSUE PRICE	*QUOTE U.S.$
1994 Blue Navajo	9,500		50.00	50
1994 Blue Tranquility	9,500		50.00	50
1994 Navajo Meditating	9,500		50.00	50
1995 Navajo Reflection	9,500		50.00	50

Wildlife Memories - T. Redlin

YEAR ISSUE	EDITION LIMIT	YEAR RETD.	ISSUE PRICE	*QUOTE U.S.$
1994 Best Friends	19,500		65.00	65
1994 Comforts of Home	19,500		65.00	65
1994 Pure Contentment	19,500		65.00	65
1994 Sharing in the Solitude	19,500		65.00	65

Windows to the Wild - T. Redlin

YEAR ISSUE	EDITION LIMIT	YEAR RETD.	ISSUE PRICE	*QUOTE U.S.$
1990 Master's Domain	9,500		65.00	65
1991 Winter Windbreak	9,500		65.00	65
1992 Evening Company	9,500		65.00	65
1994 Night Mapling	9,500		65.00	65

Hamilton Collection

All in a Day's Work - J. Lamb

YEAR ISSUE	EDITION LIMIT	YEAR RETD.	ISSUE PRICE	*QUOTE U.S.$
1994 Where's the Fire?	28-day	1994	29.50	30
1994 Lunch Break	28-day	1994	29.50	30
1994 Puppy Patrol	28-day	1994	29.50	30
1994 Decoy Delivery	28-day	1994	29.50	30
1994 Budding Artist	28-day	1994	29.50	30
1994 Garden Guards	28-day	1994	29.50	30
1994 Saddling Up	28-day	1994	29.50	30
1995 Taking the Lead	28-day	1994	29.50	30

All Star Memories - D. Spindel

YEAR ISSUE	EDITION LIMIT	YEAR RETD.	ISSUE PRICE	*QUOTE U.S.$
1995 The Mantle Story	28-day		35.00	35

*Quotes have been rounded up to nearest dollar

Hamilton Collection
to Hamilton Collection

PLATES

YEAR ISSUE		EDITION LIMIT	YEAR RETD.	ISSUE PRICE	*QUOTE U.S.$
1996	Momentos of the Mick	28-day		35.00	35
1996	Mantle Appreciation Day	28-day		35.00	35
1996	Life of a Legend	28-day		35.00	35
1996	Yankee Pride	28-day		35.00	35
1996	A World Series Tribute	28-day		35.00	35
1996	The Ultimate All Star	28-day		35.00	35
1997	Triple Crown	28-day		35.00	35

America's Greatest Sailing Ships - T. Freeman

YEAR ISSUE		EDITION LIMIT	YEAR RETD.	ISSUE PRICE	*QUOTE U.S.$
1988	USS Constitution	14-day	1991	29.50	50-85
1988	Great Republic	14-day	1991	29.50	50-60
1988	America	14-day	1991	29.50	50-60
1988	Charles W. Morgan	14-day	1991	29.50	50-60
1988	Eagle	14-day	1991	29.50	45
1988	Bonhomme Richard	14-day	1991	29.50	40
1988	Gertrude L. Thebaud	14-day	1991	29.50	45
1988	Enterprise	14-day	1991	29.50	40

The American Civil War - D. Prechtel

YEAR ISSUE		EDITION LIMIT	YEAR RETD.	ISSUE PRICE	*QUOTE U.S.$
1990	General Robert E. Lee	14-day		37.50	75-95
1990	Generals Grant and Lee At Appomattox	14-day		37.50	65
1990	General Thomas "Stonewall" Jackson	14-day		37.50	55-65
1990	Abraham Lincoln	14-day		37.50	65
1991	General J.E.B. Stuart	14-day		37.50	45-65
1991	General Philip Sheridan	14-day		37.50	65
1991	A Letter from Home	14-day		37.50	65
1991	Going Home	14-day		37.50	65
1992	Assembling The Troop	14-day		37.50	75
1992	Standing Watch	14-day		37.50	75

American Water Birds - R. Lawrence

YEAR ISSUE		EDITION LIMIT	YEAR RETD.	ISSUE PRICE	*QUOTE U.S.$
1988	Wood Ducks	14-day		37.50	54
1988	Hooded Mergansers	14-day		37.50	54
1988	Pintail	14-day		37.50	45
1988	Canada Geese	14-day		37.50	45
1988	American Widgeons	14-day		37.50	54
1988	Canvasbacks	14-day		37.50	54
1988	Mallard Pair	14-day		37.50	60
1988	Snow Geese	14-day		37.50	45

The American Wilderness - M. Richter

YEAR ISSUE		EDITION LIMIT	YEAR RETD.	ISSUE PRICE	*QUOTE U.S.$
1995	Gray Wolf	28-day		29.95	30
1995	Silent Watch	28-day		29.95	30
1995	Moon Song	28-day		29.95	30
1995	Silent Pursuit	28-day		29.95	30
1996	Still of the Night	28-day		29.95	30
1996	Nighttime Serenity	28-day		29.95	30
1996	Autumn Solitude	28-day		29.95	30
1996	Arctic Wolf	28-day		29.95	30

Andy Griffith - R. Tanenbaum

YEAR ISSUE		EDITION LIMIT	YEAR RETD.	ISSUE PRICE	*QUOTE U.S.$
1992	Sheriff Andy Taylor	28-day	1994	29.50	60-75
1992	A Startling Conclusion	28-day	1994	29.50	70-85
1993	Mayberry Sing-a-long	28-day	1994	29.50	50-65
1993	Aunt Bee's Kitchen	28-day	1994	29.50	50-65
1993	Surprise! Surprise!	28-day	1994	29.50	50
1993	An Explosive Situation	28-day	1994	29.50	65-75
1993	Meeting Aunt Bee	28-day	1994	29.50	50-60
1993	Opie's Big Catch	28-day	1994	29.50	50-60

The Angler's Prize - M. Susinno

YEAR ISSUE		EDITION LIMIT	YEAR RETD.	ISSUE PRICE	*QUOTE U.S.$
1991	Trophy Bass	14-day		29.50	36
1991	Blue Ribbon Trout	14-day		29.50	33
1991	Sun Dancers	14-day		29.50	30
1991	Freshwater Barracuda	14-day		29.50	36
1991	Bronzeback Fighter	14-day		29.50	36
1991	Autumn Beauty	14-day		29.50	36
1992	Old Mooneyes	14-day		29.50	36
1992	Silver King	14-day		29.50	33

Beauty Of Winter - N/A

YEAR ISSUE		EDITION LIMIT	YEAR RETD.	ISSUE PRICE	*QUOTE U.S.$
1992	Silent Night	28-day		29.50	30
1993	Moonlight Sleighride	28-day		29.50	30

The Best Of Baseball - R. Tanenbaum

YEAR ISSUE		EDITION LIMIT	YEAR RETD.	ISSUE PRICE	*QUOTE U.S.$
1993	The Legendary Mickey Mantle	28-day		29.50	30
1993	The Immortal Babe Ruth	28-day		29.50	30
1993	The Great Willie Mays	28-day		29.50	30
1993	The Unbeatable Duke Snider	28-day		29.50	30
1993	The Extraordinary Lou Gehrig	28-day		29.50	30
1993	The Phenomenal Roberto Clemente	28-day		29.50	30
1993	The Remarkable Johnny Bench	28-day		29.50	30
1993	The Incredible Nolan Ryan	28-day		29.50	30
1993	The Exceptional Brooks Robinson	28-day		29.50	30
1993	The Unforgettable Phil Rizzuto	28-day		29.50	30
1995	The Incomparable Reggie Jackson	28-day		29.50	30

Bialosky® & Friends - P./A.Bialosky

YEAR ISSUE		EDITION LIMIT	YEAR RETD.	ISSUE PRICE	*QUOTE U.S.$
1992	Family Addition	28-day		29.50	33
1993	Sweetheart	28-day		29.50	36
1993	Let's Go Fishing	28-day		29.50	36
1993	U.S. Mail	28-day		29.50	36
1993	Sleigh Ride	28-day		29.50	30
1993	Honey For Sale	28-day		29.50	30
1993	Breakfast In Bed	28-day		29.50	36
1993	My First Two-Wheeler	28-day		29.50	30

Big Cats of the World - D. Manning

YEAR ISSUE		EDITION LIMIT	YEAR RETD.	ISSUE PRICE	*QUOTE U.S.$
1989	African Shade	14-day		29.50	37
1989	View from Above	14-day		29.50	30
1990	On The Prowl	14-day		29.50	30
1990	Deep In The Jungle	14-day		29.50	30
1990	Spirit Of The Mountain	14-day		29.50	30
1990	Spotted Sentinel	14-day		29.50	30
1990	Above the Treetops	14-day		29.50	30
1990	Mountain Dweller	14-day		29.50	30
1992	Jungle Habitat	14-day		29.50	30
1992	Solitary Sentry	14-day		29.50	30

Bundles of Joy - B. P. Gutmann

YEAR ISSUE		EDITION LIMIT	YEAR RETD.	ISSUE PRICE	*QUOTE U.S.$
1988	Awakening	14-day	1991	24.50	75-110
1988	Happy Dreams	14-day	1991	24.50	60-80
1988	Tasting	14-day	1991	24.50	35-50
1988	Sweet Innocence	14-day	1991	24.50	30-50
1988	Tommy	14-day	1991	24.50	35
1988	A Little Bit of Heaven	14-day	1991	24.50	75-95
1988	Billy	14-day	1991	24.50	35
1988	Sun Kissed	14-day	1991	24.50	30

Butterfly Garden - P. Sweany

YEAR ISSUE		EDITION LIMIT	YEAR RETD.	ISSUE PRICE	*QUOTE U.S.$
1987	Spicebush Swallowtail	14-day		29.50	45
1987	Common Blue	14-day		29.50	38
1987	Orange Sulphur	14-day		29.50	35
1987	Monarch	14-day		29.50	45
1987	Tiger Swallowtail	14-day		29.50	30
1987	Crimson Patched Longwing	14-day		29.50	38
1988	Morning Cloak	14-day		29.50	30
1988	Red Admiral	14-day		29.50	38

The Call of the North - J. Tift

YEAR ISSUE		EDITION LIMIT	YEAR RETD.	ISSUE PRICE	*QUOTE U.S.$
1993	Winter's Dawn	28-day		29.50	30
1994	Evening Silence	28-day		29.50	30
1994	Moonlit Wilderness	28-day		29.50	30
1994	Silent Snowfall	28-day		29.50	30
1994	Snowy Watch	28-day		29.50	30
1994	Sentinels of the Summit	28-day		29.50	30
1994	Arctic Seclusion	28-day		29.50	30
1994	Forest Twilight	28-day		29.50	30
1994	Mountain Explorer	28-day		29.50	30
1994	The Cry of Winter	28-day		29.50	30

Call to Adventure - R. Cross

YEAR ISSUE		EDITION LIMIT	YEAR RETD.	ISSUE PRICE	*QUOTE U.S.$
1993	USS Constitution	28-day		29.50	30
1993	The Bounty	28-day		29.50	30
1994	Bonhomme Richard	28-day		29.50	30
1994	Old Nantucket	28-day		29.50	30
1994	Golden West	28-day		29.50	30
1994	Boston	28-day		29.50	30
1994	Hannah	28-day		29.50	30
1994	Improvement	28-day		29.50	30
1995	Anglo-American	28-day		29.50	30
1995	Challenge	28-day		29.50	30

Cameo Kittens - Q. Lemonds

YEAR ISSUE		EDITION LIMIT	YEAR RETD.	ISSUE PRICE	*QUOTE U.S.$
1993	Ginger Snap	28-day		29.50	30
1993	Cat Tails	28-day		29.50	30
1993	Lady Blue	28-day		29.50	30
1993	Tiny Heart Stealer	28-day		29.50	30
1993	Blossom	28-day		29.50	30
1994	Whisker Antics	28-day		29.50	30
1994	Tiger's Temptation	28-day		29.50	30
1994	Scout	28-day		29.50	30
1995	Timid Tabby	28-day		29.50	30
1995	All Wrapped Up	28-day		29.50	30

A Child's Best Friend - B. P. Gutmann

YEAR ISSUE		EDITION LIMIT	YEAR RETD.	ISSUE PRICE	*QUOTE U.S.$
1985	In Disgrace	14-day	1990	24.50	100-175
1985	The Reward	14-day	1990	24.50	60-100
1985	Who's Sleepy	14-day	1990	24.50	90-125
1985	Good Morning	14-day	1990	24.50	60-90
1985	Sympathy	14-day	1990	24.50	55-70
1985	On the Up and Up	14-day	1990	24.50	75-125
1985	Mine	14-day	1990	24.50	95
1985	Going to Town	14-day	1990	24.50	90-125

A Child's Christmas - J. Ferrandiz

YEAR ISSUE		EDITION LIMIT	YEAR RETD.	ISSUE PRICE	*QUOTE U.S.$
1995	Asleep in the Hay	28-day		29.95	30
1995	Merry Little Friends	28-day		29.95	30
1995	Love is Warm All Over	28-day		29.95	30
1995	Little Shepard Family	28-day		29.95	30
1995	Life's Little Blessings	28-day		29.95	30
1995	Happiness is Being Loved	28-day		29.95	30
1995	My Heart Belongs to You	28-day		29.95	30
1996	Lil' Dreamers	28-day		29.95	30

Childhood Reflections - B.P. Gutmann

YEAR ISSUE		EDITION LIMIT	YEAR RETD.	ISSUE PRICE	*QUOTE U.S.$
1991	Harmony	14-day	1990	29.50	65
1991	Kitty's Breakfast	14-day	1990	29.50	40
1991	Friendly Enemies	14-day	1990	29.50	40
1991	Smile, Smile, Smile	14-day	1990	29.50	40
1991	Lullaby	14-day	1990	29.50	40
1991	Oh! Oh! A Bunny	14-day	1990	29.50	30
1991	Little Mother	14-day	1990	29.50	35
1991	Thank You, God	14-day	1990	29.50	40

Children of the American Frontier - D. Crook

YEAR ISSUE		EDITION LIMIT	YEAR RETD.	ISSUE PRICE	*QUOTE U.S.$
1986	In Trouble Again	10-day		24.50	35-45
1986	Tubs and Suds	10-day		24.50	28
1986	A Lady Needs a Little Privacy	10-day		24.50	25-38
1986	The Desperadoes	10-day		24.50	28
1986	Riders Wanted	10-day		24.50	32
1987	A Cowboy's Downfall	10-day		24.50	28
1987	Runaway Blues	10-day		24.50	28
1987	A Special Patient	10-day		24.50	38

Civil War Generals - M. Gnatek

YEAR ISSUE		EDITION LIMIT	YEAR RETD.	ISSUE PRICE	*QUOTE U.S.$
1994	Robert E. Lee	28-day		29.50	45
1994	J.E.B. Stewart	28-day		29.50	45
1994	Joshua L. Chamberlain	28-day		29.50	30
1994	George Armstrong Custer	28-day		29.50	30
1994	Nathan Bedford Forrest	28-day		29.50	30
1994	James Longstreet	28-day		29.50	30
1995	Thomas "Stonewall" Jackson	28-day		29.50	30
1995	Confederate Heroes	28-day		29.50	30

Classic American Santas - G. Hinke

YEAR ISSUE		EDITION LIMIT	YEAR RETD.	ISSUE PRICE	*QUOTE U.S.$
1993	A Christmas Eve Visitor	28-day		29.50	30
1994	Up on the Rooftop	28-day		29.50	30
1994	Santa's Candy Kitchen	28-day		29.50	30
1994	A Christmas Chorus	28-day		29.50	30
1994	An Exciting Christmas Eve	28-day		29.50	30
1994	Rest Ye Merry Gentlemen	28-day		29.50	30
1994	Preparing the Sleigh	28-day		29.50	30
1994	The Reindeer's Stable	28-day		29.50	30
1994	He's Checking His List	28-day		29.50	30

Classic Corvettes - M. Lacourciere

YEAR ISSUE		EDITION LIMIT	YEAR RETD.	ISSUE PRICE	*QUOTE U.S.$
1994	1957 Corvette	28-day		29.50	30
1994	1963 Corvette	28-day		29.50	30
1994	1968 Corvette	28-day		29.50	30
1994	1986 Corvette	28-day		29.50	30
1995	1967 Corvette	28-day		29.50	30
1995	1953 Corvette	28-day		29.50	30
1995	1962 Corvette	28-day		29.50	30
1995	1990 Corvette	28-day		29.50	30

Classic Sporting Dogs - B. Christie

YEAR ISSUE		EDITION LIMIT	YEAR RETD.	ISSUE PRICE	*QUOTE U.S.$
1989	Golden Retrievers	14-day		24.50	50-74
1989	Labrador Retrievers	14-day		24.50	50-70
1989	Beagles	14-day		24.50	35-55
1989	Pointers	14-day		24.50	35-55
1989	Springer Spaniels	14-day		24.50	35-45
1990	German Short-Haired Pointers	14-day		24.50	55
1990	Irish Setters	14-day		24.50	35
1990	Brittany Spaniels	14-day		24.50	48

Classic TV Westerns - K. Milnazik

YEAR ISSUE		EDITION LIMIT	YEAR RETD.	ISSUE PRICE	*QUOTE U.S.$
1990	The Lone Ranger and Tonto	14-day		29.50	75-125
1990	Bonanza™	14-day		29.50	60
1990	Roy Rogers and Dale Evans	14-day		29.50	50-75
1991	Rawhide	14-day		29.50	40
1991	Wild Wild West	14-day		29.50	40-60
1991	Have Gun, Will Travel	14-day		29.50	45
1991	The Virginian	14-day		29.50	40-60
1991	Hopalong Cassidy	14-day		29.50	70

Cloak of Visions - A. Farley

YEAR ISSUE		EDITION LIMIT	YEAR RETD.	ISSUE PRICE	*QUOTE U.S.$
1994	Visions in a Full Moon	28-day		29.50	30
1994	Protector of the Child	28-day		29.50	30
1995	Spirits of the Canyon	28-day		29.50	30
1995	Freedom Soars	28-day		29.50	30
1995	Mystic Reflections	28-day		29.50	30
1995	Staff of Life	28-day		29.50	30
1995	Springtime Hunters	28-day		29.50	30
1996	Moonlit Solace	28-day		29.50	30

Comical Dalmations - Landmark

YEAR ISSUE		EDITION LIMIT	YEAR RETD.	ISSUE PRICE	*QUOTE U.S.$
1996	I Will Not Bark In Class	28-day		29.95	40
1996	The Master	28-day		29.95	30
1996	Spot At Play	28-day		29.95	30
1996	A Dalmation's Dream	28-day		29.95	30
1996	To The Rescue	28-day		29.95	30
1996	Maid For A Day	28-day		29.95	30
1996	Dalmation Celebration	28-day		29.95	30
1996	Concert in D-Minor	28-day		29.95	30

Coral Paradise - H. Bond

YEAR ISSUE		EDITION LIMIT	YEAR RETD.	ISSUE PRICE	*QUOTE U.S.$
1989	The Living Oasis	14-day		29.50	40
1990	Riches of the Coral Sea	14-day		29.50	40
1990	Tropical Pageantry	14-day		29.50	40
1990	Caribbean Spectacle	14-day		29.50	40
1990	Undersea Village	14-day		29.50	40
1990	Shimmering Reef Dwellers	14-day		29.50	40
1990	Mysteries of the Galapagos	14-day		29.50	40
1990	Forest Beneath the Sea	14-day		29.50	40

Cottage Puppies - K. George

YEAR ISSUE		EDITION LIMIT	YEAR RETD.	ISSUE PRICE	*QUOTE U.S.$
1993	Little Gardeners	28-day		29.50	30
1993	Springtime Fancy	28-day		29.50	30
1993	Endearing Innocence	28-day		29.50	30
1994	Picnic Playtime	28-day		29.50	30
1994	Lazy Afternoon	28-day		29.50	30
1994	Summertime Pals	28-day		29.50	30
1994	A Gardening Trio	28-day		29.50	30
1994	Taking a Break	28-day		29.50	30

Council Of Nations - G. Perillo

YEAR ISSUE		EDITION LIMIT	YEAR RETD.	ISSUE PRICE	*QUOTE U.S.$
1992	Strength of the Sioux	14-day		29.50	35

*Quotes have been rounded up to nearest dollar

PLATES

Hamilton Collection
to Hamilton Collection

YEAR ISSUE		EDITION LIMIT	YEAR RETD.	ISSUE PRICE	*QUOTE U.S.$
1992	Pride of the Cheyenne	14-day		29.50	40
1992	Dignity of the Nez Parce	14-day		29.50	35
1992	Courage of the Arapaho	14-day		29.50	38
1992	Power of the Blackfoot	14-day		29.50	35
1992	Nobility of the Algonqui	14-day		29.50	35
1992	Wisdom of the Cherokee	14-day		29.50	40
1992	Boldness of the Seneca	14-day		29.50	35

Country Garden Cottages - E. Dertner

1992	Riverbank Cottage	28-day		29.50	36
1992	Sunday Outing	28-day		29.50	30
1992	Shepherd's Cottage	28-day		29.50	30
1993	Daydream Cottage	28-day		29.50	30
1993	Garden Glorious	28-day		29.50	30
1993	This Side of Heaven	28-day		29.50	33
1993	Summer Symphony	28-day		29.50	30
1993	April Cottage	28-day		29.50	30

Country Kitties - G. Gerardi

1989	Mischief Makers	14-day		24.50	45-65
1989	Table Manners	14-day		24.50	40-55
1989	Attic Attack	14-day		24.50	45
1989	Rock and Rollers	14-day		24.50	45
1989	Just For the Fern of It	14-day		24.50	45
1989	All Washed Up	14-day		24.50	40
1989	Stroller Derby	14-day		24.50	45
1989	Captive Audience	14-day		24.50	40

A Country Season of Horses - J.M. Vass

1990	First Day of Spring	14-day		29.50	40
1990	Summer Splendor	14-day		29.50	35
1990	A Winter's Walk	14-day		29.50	35
1990	Autumn Grandeur	14-day		29.50	30
1990	Cliffside Beauty	14-day		29.50	30
1990	Frosty Morning	14-day		29.50	30
1990	Crisp Country Morning	14-day		29.50	30
1990	River Retreat	14-day		29.50	30

A Country Summer - N. Noel

1985	Butterfly Beauty	10-day		29.50	36
1985	The Golden Puppy	10-day		29.50	30
1986	The Rocking Chair	10-day		29.50	36
1986	My Bunny	10-day		29.50	33
1988	The Piglet	10-day		29.50	30
1988	Teammates	10-day		29.50	30

Curious Kittens - B. Harrison

1990	Rainy Day Friends	14-day		29.50	35
1990	Keeping in Step	14-day		29.50	35
1991	Delightful Discovery	14-day		29.50	35
1991	Chance Meeting	14-day		29.50	35
1991	All Wound Up	14-day		29.50	35
1991	Making Tracks	14-day		29.50	35
1991	Playing Cat and Mouse	14-day		29.50	35
1991	A Paw's in the Action	14-day		29.50	35
1992	Little Scholar	14-day		29.50	35
1992	Cat Burglar	14-day		29.50	35

Dale Earnhardt - Various

1996	The Intimidator - S. Bass	28-day		35.00	35
1996	The Man in Black - R. Tanenbaum	28-day		35.00	35
1996	Silver Select - S. Bass	28-day		35.00	35
1996	Back in Black - R. Tanenbaum	28-day		35.00	35
1996	Ready to Rumble - R. Tanenbaum	28-day		35.00	35

Daughters Of The Sun - K. Thayer

1993	Sun Dancer	28-day		29.50	30
1993	Shining Feather	28-day		29.50	30
1993	Delighted Dancer	28-day		29.50	30
1993	Evening Dancer	28-day		29.50	30
1993	A Secret Glance	28-day		29.50	30
1993	Chippewa Charmer	28-day		29.50	30
1994	Pride of the Yakima	28-day		29.50	30
1994	Radiant Beauty	28-day		29.50	30

Dear to My Heart - J. Hagara

1990	Cathy	14-day		29.50	30-60
1990	Addie	14-day		29.50	30
1990	Jimmy	14-day		29.50	30
1990	Dacy	14-day		29.50	30
1990	Paul	14-day		29.50	30
1991	Shelly	14-day		29.50	30
1991	Jenny	14-day		29.50	30
1991	Joy	14-day		29.50	30

Dolphin Discovery - D. Queen

1995	Sunrise Reverie	28-day		29.50	30
1995	Dolphin's Paradise	28-day		29.50	30
1995	Coral Cove	28-day		29.50	30
1995	Undersea Journey	28-day		29.50	30
1995	Dolphin Canyon	28-day		29.50	30
1995	Coral Garden	28-day		29.50	30
1996	Dolphin Duo	28-day		29.50	30
1996	Underwater Tranquility	28-day		29.50	30

Dreamsicles - K. Haynes

1994	The Flying Lesson	28-day		19.50	20
1995	By the Light of the Moon	28-day		19.50	20
1995	The Recital	28-day		19.50	20
1995	Heavenly Pirouettes	28-day		19.50	20
1995	Blossoms and Butterflies	28-day		19.50	20
1995	Love's Shy Glance	28-day		19.50	20
1996	Wishing Upon a Star	28-day		19.50	20
1996	Rainy Day Friends	28-day		19.50	20
1996	Starboats Ahoy!	28-day		19.50	20
1996	Teeter Tots	28-day		19.50	20
1996	Star Magic	28-day		19.50	20
1996	Heavenly Tea Party	28-day		19.50	20

Dreamsicles Christmas Annual Scuptural - K. Haynes

1996	The Finishing Touches	Open		39.95	40

Dreamsicles Heaven Sent - N/A

1996	Quiet Blessings	28-day		29.95	30
1996	A Heartfelt Embrace	28-day		29.95	30
1996	Earth's Blessings	28-day		29.95	30
1996	A Moment In Dreamland	28-day		29.95	30
1996	Sew Cuddly	28-day		29.95	30
1996	Homemade With Love	28-day		29.95	30
1996	A Sweet Treat	28-day		29.95	30
1996	Pampered And Pretty	28-day		29.95	30

Dreamsicles Life's Little Blessings - K. Haynes

1995	Happiness	28-day		29.95	30
1996	Peace	28-day		29.95	30
1996	Love	28-day		29.95	30
1996	Creativity	28-day		29.95	30
1996	Friendship	28-day		29.95	30
1996	Knowledge	28-day		29.95	30
1996	Hope	28-day		29.95	30
1996	Faith	28-day		29.95	30

Dreamsicles Sculptural - N/A

1995	The Flying Lesson	Open		37.50	38
1996	By The Light of the Moon	Open		37.50	38
1996	The Recital	Open		37.50	38
1996	Teeter Tots	Open		37.50	38
1996	Poetry In Motion	Open		37.50	38
1996	Rock-A-Bye Dreamsicles	Open		37.50	38
1996	The Birth Certificate	Open		37.50	38
1996	Sharing Hearts	Open		37.50	38

Dreamsicles Special Friends - K. Haynes

1995	A Hug From the Heart	28-day		29.95	30
1995	Heaven's Little Helper	28-day		29.95	30
1995	Bless Us All	28-day		[illegible]	[illegible]
1996	Love's Gentle Touch	28-day		29.95	30
1996	The Best Gift of All	28-day		29.95	30
1996	A Heavenly Hoorah!	28-day		29.95	30
1996	A Love Like No Other	28-day		29.95	30
1996	Cuddle Up	28-day		29.95	30

Dreamsicles Special Friends Sculptural - N/A

1995	Heaven's Little Helper	Open		37.50	38
1996	A Hug From The Heart	Open		37.50	38
1996	Bless Us All	Open		37.50	38
1996	The Best Gift of All	Open		37.50	38
1996	A Heavenly Hoorah!	Open		37.50	38
1996	A Love Like No Other	Open		37.50	38

Dreamsicles Sweethearts - K. Haynes

1996	Stolen Kiss	28-day		35.00	35
1996	Sharing Hearts	28-day		35.00	35
1996	Love Letters	28-day		35.00	35
1996	I Love You	28-day		35.00	35
1996	Daisies & Dreamsicles	28-day		35.00	35

Drivers of Victory Lane - R. Tanenbaum

1994	Bill Elliott #11	28-day		29.50	30
1994	Jeff Gordon #24	28-day		29.50	30
1994	Rusty Wallace #2	28-day		29.50	30
1995	Geoff Bodine #7	28-day		29.50	30
1995	Dale Earnhardt #3	28-day		29.50	30
1996	Sterling Martin #4	28-day		29.50	30
1996	Terry Labonte #5	28-day		29.50	30
1996	Ken Scharder #25	28-day		29.50	30
1996	Jeff Gordon #24	28-day		29.50	30
1996	Bill Elliott #94	28-day		29.50	30
1996	Rusty Wallace #2	28-day		29.50	30
1996	Mark Martin #6	28-day		29.50	30
1996	Dale Earnhardt #3	28-day		29.50	30

Easyriders - M. Lacourciere

1995	American Classic	28-day		29.95	30
1995	Symbols of Freedom	28-day		29.95	30
1996	Patriot's Pride	28-day		29.95	30
1996	The Way of the West	28-day		29.95	30
1996	Revival of an Era	28-day		29.95	30
1996	Hollywood Style	28-day		29.95	30
1996	Vietnam Express	28-day		29.95	30
1996	Las Vegas	28-day		29.95	30
1996	Beach Cruising	28-day		29.95	30
1996	New Orleans Scene	28-day		29.95	30

Elvis Remembered - S. Morton

1989	Loving You	90-day		37.50	65-125
1989	Early Years	90-day		37.50	55-75
1989	Tenderly	90-day		37.50	65-95
1989	The King	90-day		37.50	125
1989	Forever Yours	90-day		37.50	75-100
1989	Rockin in the Moonlight	90-day		37.50	100
1989	Moody Blues	90-day		37.50	75-100
1989	Elvis Presley	90-day		37.50	110-130

Enchanted Seascapes - J. Enright

1993	Sanctuary of the Dolphin	28-day		29.50	30
1994	Rhapsody of Hope	28-day		29.50	30
1994	Oasis of the Gods	28-day		29.50	30
1994	Sphere of Life	28-day		29.50	30
1994	Edge of Time	28-day		29.50	30
1994	Sea of Light	28-day		29.50	30
1994	Lost Beneath the Blue	28-day		29.50	30
1994	Blue Paradise	28-day		29.50	30
1995	Morning Odyssey	28-day		29.50	30
1995	Paradise Cove	28-day		29.50	30

English Country Cottages - M. Bell

1990	Periwinkle Tea Room	14-day		29.50	45
1991	Gamekeeper's Cottage	14-day		29.50	75
1991	Ginger Cottage	14-day		29.50	60
1991	Larkspur Cottage	14-day		29.50	45
1991	The Chaplain's Garden	14-day		29.50	33
1991	Lorna Doone Cottage	14-day		29.50	45
1991	Murrle Cottage	14-day		29.50	36
1991	Lullabye Cottage	14-day		29.50	30

Eternal Wishes of Good Fortune - Shuho

1983	Friendship	10-day		34.95	70
1983	Purity and Perfection	10-day		34.95	70
1983	Illustrious Offspring	10-day		34.95	70
1983	Longevity	10-day		34.95	35
1983	Youth	10-day		34.95	70
1983	Immortality	10-day		34.95	70
1983	Marital Bliss	10-day		34.95	70
1983	Love	10-day		34.95	70
1983	Peace	10-day		34.95	70
1983	Beauty	10-day		34.95	70
1983	Fertility	10-day		34.95	35
1983	Fortitude	10-day		34.95	70

Exotic Tigers of Asia - K. Ottinger

1995	Lord of the Rainforest	28-day		29.50	30
1995	Snow King	28-day		29.50	30
1995	Ruler of the Wetlands	28-day		29.50	30
1996	Majestic Vigil	28-day		29.50	30
1996	Keeper of the Jungle	28-day		29.50	30
[illegible]	Eyes of the Jungle	28-day		29.50	30
1996	Sovereign Ruler	28-day		29.50	30
1996	Lord of the Lowlands	28-day		29.50	30

Familiar Spirits - D. Wright

1996	Faithful Guardians	28-day		29.95	30
1996	Sharing Nature's Innocence	28-day		29.95	30
1996	Trusted Friend	28-day		29.95	30
1996	A Friendship Begins	28-day		29.95	30
1996	Winter Homage	28-day		29.95	30
1996	The Blessing	28-day		29.95	30
1996	Healing Powers	28-day		29.95	30

Farmyard Friends - J. Lamb

1992	Mistaken Identity	28-day	1994	29.50	30
1992	Little Cowhands	28-day	1994	29.50	30
1993	Shreading the Evidence	28-day	1994	29.50	30
1993	Partners in Crime	28-day	1994	29.50	30
1993	Fowl Play	28-day	1994	29.50	30
1993	Follow The Leader	28-day	1994	29.50	36
1993	Pony Tales	28-day	1994	29.50	30
1993	An Apple A Day	28-day	1994	29.50	30

Favorite American Songbirds - D. O'Driscoll

1989	Blue Jays of Spring	14-day		29.50	36
1989	Red Cardinals of Winter	14-day		29.50	36
1989	Robins & Apple Blossoms	14-day		29.50	36
1989	Goldfinches of Summer	14-day		29.50	36
1990	Autumn Chickadees	14-day		29.50	36
1990	Bluebirds and Morning Glories	14-day		29.50	36
1990	Tufted Titmouse and Holly	14-day		29.50	30
1991	Carolina Wrens of Spring	14-day		29.50	30

Favorite Old Testament Stories - S. Butcher

1994	Jacob's Dream	28-day		35.00	35
1995	The Baby Moses	28-day		35.00	35
1995	Esther's Gift To Her People	28-day		35.00	35
1995	A Prayer For Victory	28-day		35.00	35
1995	Where You Go, I Will Go	28-day		35.00	35
1995	A Prayer Answered, A Promise Kept	28-day		35.00	35
1996	Joseph Sold Into Slavery	28-day		35.00	35
1996	Daniel In the Lion's Den	28-day		35.00	35
1996	Noah And The Ark	28-day		35.00	35

The Fierce And The Free - F. McCarthy

1992	Big Medicine	28-day		29.50	30
1993	Land of the Winter Hawk	28-day		29.50	30
1993	Warrior of Savage Splendor	28-day		29.50	30
1994	War Party	28-day		29.50	30
1994	The Challenge	28-day		29.50	30
1994	Out of the Rising Mist	28-day		29.50	30
1994	The Ambush	28-day		29.50	35
1994	Dangerous Crossing	28-day		29.50	30

*Quotes have been rounded up to nearest dollar

Hamilton Collection
to Hamilton Collection

PLATES

Flower Festivals of Japan - N. Hara

YEAR	ISSUE	EDITION LIMIT	YEAR RETD.	ISSUE PRICE	*QUOTE U.S.$
1985	Chrysanthemum	10-day		45.00	45
1985	Hollyhock	10-day		45.00	45
1985	Plum Blossom	10-day		45.00	45
1985	Morning Glory	10-day		45.00	45
1985	Cherry Blossom	10-day		45.00	45
1985	Iris	10-day		45.00	45
1985	Lily	10-day		45.00	45
1985	Peach Blossom	10-day		45.00	45

Forging New Frontiers - J. Deneen

YEAR	ISSUE	EDITION LIMIT	YEAR RETD.	ISSUE PRICE	*QUOTE U.S.$
1994	The Race is On	28-day		29.50	30
1994	Big Boy	28-day		29.50	30
1994	Cresting the Summit	28-day		29.50	30
1994	Spring Roundup	28-day		29.50	30
1994	Winter in the Rockies	28-day		29.50	30
1994	High Country Logging	28-day		29.50	30
1994	Confrontation	28-day		29.50	30
1994	A Welcome Sight	28-day		29.50	30

A Garden Song - M. Hanson

YEAR	ISSUE	EDITION LIMIT	YEAR RETD.	ISSUE PRICE	*QUOTE U.S.$
1994	Winter's Splendor	28-day		29.50	30
1994	In Full Bloom	28-day		29.50	30
1994	Golden Glories	28-day		29.50	30
1995	Autumn's Elegance	28-day		29.50	30
1995	First Snowfall	28-day		29.50	30
1995	Robins in Spring	28-day		29.50	30
1995	Summer's Glow	28-day		29.50	30
1995	Fall's Serenade	28-day		29.50	30
1996	Sounds of Winter	28-day		29.50	30
1996	Springtime Haven	28-day		29.50	30

Gardens of the Orient - S. Suetomi

YEAR	ISSUE	EDITION LIMIT	YEAR RETD.	ISSUE PRICE	*QUOTE U.S.$
1983	Flowering of Spring	10-day		19.50	20
1983	Festival of May	10-day		19.50	20
1983	Cherry Blossom Brocade	10-day		19.50	20
1983	Winter's Repose	10-day		19.50	20
1983	Garden Sanctuary	10-day		19.50	20
1983	Summer's Glory	10-day		19.50	20
1983	June's Creation	10-day		19.50	20
1983	New Year's Dawn	10-day		19.50	20
1983	Autumn Serenity	10-day		19.50	20
1983	Harvest Morning	10-day		19.50	20
1983	Tranquil Pond	10-day		19.50	20
1983	Morning Song	10-day		19.50	20

Glory of Christ - C. Micarelli

YEAR	ISSUE	EDITION LIMIT	YEAR RETD.	ISSUE PRICE	*QUOTE U.S.$
1992	The Ascension	48-day		29.50	30
1992	Jesus Teaching	48-day		29.50	30
1993	Last Supper	48-day		29.50	30
1993	The Nativity	48-day		29.50	30
1993	The Baptism of Christ	48-day		29.50	30
1993	Jesus Heals the Sick	48-day		29.50	30
1994	Jesus Walks on Water	48-day		29.50	30
1994	Descent From the Cross	48-day		29.50	30

Glory of the Game - T. Fogarty

YEAR	ISSUE	EDITION LIMIT	YEAR RETD.	ISSUE PRICE	*QUOTE U.S.$
1994	"Hank Aaron's Record-Breaking Home Run"	28-day		29.50	30
1994	"Bobby Thomson's Shot Heard 'Round the World"	28-day		29.50	30
1994	1969 Miracle Mets	28-day		29.50	30
1995	Reggie Jackson: Mr. October	28-day		29.50	30
1995	Don Larsen's Perfect World	28-day		29.50	30
1995	Babe Ruth's Called Shot	28-day		29.50	30
1995	Wille Mays: Greatest Catch	28-day		29.50	30
1995	Bill Mazeroski's Series	28-day		29.50	30
1996	Mickey Mantle's Tape Measure Home Run	28-day		29.50	30

The Golden Age of American Railroads - T. Xaras

YEAR	ISSUE	EDITION LIMIT	YEAR RETD.	ISSUE PRICE	*QUOTE U.S.$
1991	The Blue Comet	14-day		29.50	45
1991	The Morning Local	14-day		29.50	60
1991	The Pennsylvania K-4	14-day		29.50	45-55
1991	Above the Canyon	14-day		29.50	80-90
1991	Portrait in Steam	14-day		29.50	65-75
1991	The Santa Fe Super Chief	14-day		29.50	105
1991	The Big Boy	14-day		29.50	60
1991	The Empire Builder	14-day		29.50	75
1992	An American Classic	14-day		29.50	60
1992	Final Destination	14-day		29.50	60

Golden Discoveries - L. Budge

YEAR	ISSUE	EDITION LIMIT	YEAR RETD.	ISSUE PRICE	*QUOTE U.S.$
1995	Boot Bandits	28-day		29.95	30
1995	Hiding the Evidence	28-day		29.95	30
1995	Decoy Dilemma	28-day		29.95	30
1995	Fishing for Dinner	28-day		29.95	30
1996	Lunchtime Companions	28-day		29.95	30
1996	Friend or Foe?	28-day		29.95	30

Golden Puppy Portraits - P. Braun

YEAR	ISSUE	EDITION LIMIT	YEAR RETD.	ISSUE PRICE	*QUOTE U.S.$
1994	Do Not Disturb!	28-day		29.50	30
1995	Teething Time	28-day		29.50	30
1995	Table Manners	28-day		29.50	30
1995	A Golden Bouquet	28-day		29.50	30
1995	Time For Bed	28-day		29.50	30
1995	Bathtime Blues	28-day		29.50	30
1996	Spinning a Yarn	28-day		29.50	30
1996	Partytime Puppy	28-day		29.50	30

Good Sports - J. Lamb

YEAR	ISSUE	EDITION LIMIT	YEAR RETD.	ISSUE PRICE	*QUOTE U.S.$
1990	Wide Retriever	14-day	1994	29.50	45
1990	Double Play	14-day	1994	29.50	55
1990	Hole in One	14-day	1994	29.50	45
1990	The Bass Masters	14-day	1994	29.50	40
1990	Spotted on the Sideline	14-day	1994	29.50	36
1990	Slap Shot	14-day	1994	29.50	45
1991	Net Play	14-day	1994	29.50	30-45
1991	Bassetball	14-day	1994	29.50	36
1992	Boxer Rebellion	14-day	1994	29.50	35
1992	Great Try	14-day	1994	29.50	39

Great Fighter Planes Of World War II - R. Waddey

YEAR	ISSUE	EDITION LIMIT	YEAR RETD.	ISSUE PRICE	*QUOTE U.S.$
1992	Old Crow	14-day		29.50	35
1992	Big Hog	14-day		29.50	35
1992	P-47 Thunderbolt	14-day		29.50	35
1992	P-40 Flying Tiger	14-day		29.50	35
1992	F4F Wildcat	14-day		29.50	35
1992	P-38F Lightning	14-day		29.50	30
1993	F6F Hellcat	14-day		29.50	30
1993	P-39M Airacobra	14-day		29.50	30
1995	Memphis Belle	14-day		29.50	30
1995	The Dragon and His Tail	14-day		29.50	30
1995	Big Beautiful Doll	14-day		29.50	30
1995	Bats Out of Hell	14-day		29.50	30

Great Mammals of the Sea - Wyland

YEAR	ISSUE	EDITION LIMIT	YEAR RETD.	ISSUE PRICE	*QUOTE U.S.$
1991	Orca Trio	14-day		35.00	45
1991	Hawaii Dolphins	14-day		35.00	45
1991	Orca Journey	14-day		35.00	42
1991	Dolphin Paradise	14-day		35.00	45
1991	Children of the Sea	14-day		35.00	60
1991	Kissing Dolphins	14-day		35.00	39
1991	Islands	14-day		35.00	60
1991	Orcas	14-day		35.00	45

The Greatest Show on Earth - F. Moody

YEAR	ISSUE	EDITION LIMIT	YEAR RETD.	ISSUE PRICE	*QUOTE U.S.$
1981	Clowns	10-day		30.00	32-45
1981	Elephants	10-day		30.00	35
1981	Aerialists	10-day		30.00	45
1981	Great Parade	10-day		30.00	30
1981	Midway	10-day		30.00	30
1981	Equestrians	10-day		30.00	30
1982	Lion Tamer	10-day		30.00	30
1982	Grande Finale	10-day		30.00	45

Growing Up Together - P. Brooks

YEAR	ISSUE	EDITION LIMIT	YEAR RETD.	ISSUE PRICE	*QUOTE U.S.$
1990	My Very Best Friends	14-day		29.50	36
1990	Tea for Two	14-day		29.50	30
1990	Tender Loving Care	14-day		29.50	30
1990	Picnic Pals	14-day		29.50	30
1991	Newfound Friends	14-day		29.50	30
1991	Kitten Caboodle	14-day		29.50	30
1991	Fishing Buddies	14-day		29.50	30
1991	Bedtime Blessings	14-day		29.50	30

The Historic Railways - T. Xaras

YEAR	ISSUE	EDITION LIMIT	YEAR RETD.	ISSUE PRICE	*QUOTE U.S.$
1995	Harper's Ferry	28-day		29.95	30
1995	Horseshoe Curve	28-day		29.95	30
1995	Kentucky's Red River	28-day		29.95	30
1995	Sherman Hill Challenger	28-day		29.95	30
1996	New York Central's 4-6-4 Hudson	28-day		29.95	30
1996	Rails By The Seashore	28-day		29.95	30
1996	Steam in the High Sierras	28-day		29.95	30
1996	Evening Departure	28-day		29.95	30

The I Love Lucy Plate Collection - J. Kritz

YEAR	ISSUE	EDITION LIMIT	YEAR RETD.	ISSUE PRICE	*QUOTE U.S.$
1989	California, Here We Come	14-day	1992	29.50	110-175
1989	It's Just Like Candy	14-day	1992	29.50	165-220
1990	The Big Squeeze	14-day	1992	29.50	100-220
1990	Eating the Evidence	14-day	1992	29.50	100-220
1990	Two of a Kind	14-day	1992	29.50	90-200
1991	Queen of the Gypsies	14-day	1992	29.50	100-200
1992	Night at the Copa	14-day	1992	29.50	100-200
1992	A Rising Problem	14-day	1992	29.50	150-175

James Dean Commemorative Issue - T. Blackshear

YEAR	ISSUE	EDITION LIMIT	YEAR RETD.	ISSUE PRICE	*QUOTE U.S.$
1991	James Dean	14-day		37.50	75

James Dean The Legend - M. Weistling

YEAR	ISSUE	EDITION LIMIT	YEAR RETD.	ISSUE PRICE	*QUOTE U.S.$
1992	Unforgotten Rebel	28-day		29.50	60

Japanese Floral Calendar - Shuho/Kage

YEAR	ISSUE	EDITION LIMIT	YEAR RETD.	ISSUE PRICE	*QUOTE U.S.$
1981	New Year's Day	10-day		32.50	40
1982	Early Spring	10-day		32.50	40
1982	Spring	10-day		32.50	40
1982	Girl's Doll Day Festival	10-day		32.50	40
1982	Buddha's Birthday	10-day		32.50	40
1982	Early Summer	10-day		32.50	40
1982	Boy's Doll Day Festival	10-day		32.50	40
1982	Summer	10-day		32.50	33
1982	Autumn	10-day		32.50	30
1983	Festival of the Full Moon	10-day		32.50	33
1983	Late Autumn	10-day		32.50	33
1983	Winter	10-day		32.50	33

Jeff Gordon - Various

YEAR	ISSUE	EDITION LIMIT	YEAR RETD.	ISSUE PRICE	*QUOTE U.S.$
1996	On The Warpath - S. Bass	28-day		35.00	35
1996	Headed to Victory Lane - R. Tanenbaum	28-day		35.00	35
1996	Gordon Takes the Title - S. Bass	28-day		35.00	35
1996	From Winner to Champion - R. Tanenbaum	28-day		35.00	35

The Jeweled Hummingbirds - J. Landenberger

YEAR	ISSUE	EDITION LIMIT	YEAR RETD.	ISSUE PRICE	*QUOTE U.S.$
1989	Ruby-throated Hummingbirds	14-day		37.50	45
1989	Great Sapphire Wing Hummingbirds	14-day		37.50	45
1989	Ruby-Topaz Hummingbirds	14-day		37.50	45
1989	Andean Emerald Hummingbirds	14-day		37.50	45
1989	Garnet-throated Hummingbirds	14-day		37.50	45
1989	Blue-Headed Sapphire Hummingbirds	14-day		37.50	45
1989	Pearl Coronet Hummingbirds	14-day		37.50	45
1989	Amethyst-throated Sunangels	14-day		37.50	45

Joe Montana - Various

YEAR	ISSUE	EDITION LIMIT	YEAR RETD.	ISSUE PRICE	*QUOTE U.S.$
1996	40,000 Yards - R. Tanenbaum	28-day		35.00	35
1996	Finding a Way to Win - A. Catalano	28-day		35.00	35
1996	Comeback Kid - A. Catalano	28-day		35.00	35
1996	Chief on the Field - Petronella	28-day		35.00	35

Kitten Classics - P. Cooper

YEAR	ISSUE	EDITION LIMIT	YEAR RETD.	ISSUE PRICE	*QUOTE U.S.$
1985	Cat Nap	14-day		29.50	45
1985	Purrfect Treasure	14-day		29.50	40
1985	Wild Flower	14-day		29.50	40
1985	Birdwatcher	14-day		29.50	40
1985	Tiger's Fancy	14-day		29.50	40
1985	Country Kitty	14-day		29.50	40
1985	Little Rascal	14-day		29.50	40
1985	First Prize	14-day		29.50	30

Knick Knack Kitty Cat Sculptural - L. Yencho

YEAR	ISSUE	EDITION LIMIT	YEAR RETD.	ISSUE PRICE	*QUOTE U.S.$
1996	Kittens in the Cupboard	Open		39.95	40
1996	Kittens in the Cushion	Open		39.95	40
1996	Kittens in the Plant	Open		39.95	40
1996	Kittens in the Yarn	Open		39.95	40

The Last Warriors - C. Ren

YEAR	ISSUE	EDITION LIMIT	YEAR RETD.	ISSUE PRICE	*QUOTE U.S.$
1993	Winter of '41	28-day		29.50	30
1993	Morning of Reckoning	28-day		29.50	30
1993	Twilights Last Gleaming	28-day		29.50	30
1993	Lone Winter Journey	28-day		29.50	30
1994	Victory's Reward	28-day		29.50	30
1994	Solitary Hunter	28-day		29.50	30
1994	Solemn Reflection	28-day		29.50	30
1994	Confronting Danger	28-day		29.50	30
1995	Moment of Contemplation	28-day		29.50	30
1995	The Last Sunset	28-day		29.50	30

The Legend of Father Christmas - V. Dezerin

YEAR	ISSUE	EDITION LIMIT	YEAR RETD.	ISSUE PRICE	*QUOTE U.S.$
1994	The Return of Father Christmas	28-day		29.50	30
1994	Gifts From Father Christmas	28-day		29.50	30
1994	The Feast of the Holiday	28-day		29.50	30
1995	Christmas Day Visitors	28-day		29.50	30
1995	Decorating the Tree	28-day		29.50	30
1995	The Snow Sculpture	28-day		29.50	30
1995	Skating on the Pond	28-day		29.50	30
1995	Holy Night	28-day		29.50	30

Legendary Warriors - M. Gentry

YEAR	ISSUE	EDITION LIMIT	YEAR RETD.	ISSUE PRICE	*QUOTE U.S.$
1995	White Quiver and Scout	28-day		29.95	30
1995	Lakota Rendezvous	28-day		29.95	30
1995	Crazy Horse	28-day		29.95	30
1995	Sitting Bull's Vision	28-day		29.95	30
1996	Crazy Horse	28-day		29.95	30
1996	Sitting Bull's Vision	28-day		29.95	30
1996	Noble Surrender	28-day		29.95	30
1996	Sioux Thunder	28-day		29.95	30
1996	Eagle Dancer	28-day		29.95	30
1996	The Trap	28-day		29.95	30

A Lisi Martin Christmas - L. Martin

YEAR	ISSUE	EDITION LIMIT	YEAR RETD.	ISSUE PRICE	*QUOTE U.S.$
1992	Santa's Littlest Reindeer	28-day		29.50	30
1993	Not A Creature Was Stirring	28-day		29.50	30
1993	Christmas Dreams	28-day		29.50	30
1993	The Christmas Story	28-day		29.50	30
1993	Trimming The Tree	28-day		29.50	30
1993	A Taste Of The Holidays	28-day		29.50	30
1993	The Night Before Christmas	28-day		29.50	30
1993	Christmas Watch	28-day		29.50	30
1995	Christmas Presence	28-day		29.50	30
1995	Nose to Nose	28-day		29.50	30

Little Fawns of the Forest - R. Manning

YEAR	ISSUE	EDITION LIMIT	YEAR RETD.	ISSUE PRICE	*QUOTE U.S.$
1995	In the Morning Light	28-day		29.95	30
1995	Cool Reflections	28-day		29.95	30
1995	Nature's Lesson	28-day		29.95	30
1996	A Friendship Blossoms	28-day		29.95	30
1996	Innocent Companions	28-day		29.95	30
1996	New Life, New Day	28-day		29.95	30

Little House on the Prairie - E. Christopherson

YEAR	ISSUE	EDITION LIMIT	YEAR RETD.	ISSUE PRICE	*QUOTE U.S.$
1986	Founder's Day Picnic	10-day		29.50	45
1986	The Woman's Harvest	10-day		29.50	30
1986	The Medicine Show	10-day		29.50	45
1986	Caroline's Eggs	10-day		29.50	30
1986	Mary's Gift	10-day		29.50	30
1986	Bell For Walnut Grove	10-day		29.50	30
1986	Ingalls Family Christmas	10-day		29.50	30
1986	Sweetheart Tree	10-day		29.50	30

*Quotes have been rounded up to nearest dollar

Little Ladies - M.H. Bogart

Year	Issue	Edition Limit	Year Retd.	Issue Price	*Quote U.S.$
1989	Playing Bridesmaid	14-day	1991	29.50	75-125
1990	The Seamstress	14-day	1991	29.50	60-95
1990	Little Captive	14-day	1991	29.50	45
1990	Playing Mama	14-day	1991	29.50	60-85
1990	Susanna	14-day	1991	29.50	50
1990	Kitty's Bath	14-day	1991	29.50	55-75
1990	A Day in the Country	14-day	1991	29.50	45-95
1991	Sarah	14-day	1991	29.50	50
1991	First Party	14-day	1991	29.50	50
1991	The Magic Kitten	14-day	1991	29.50	50

The Little Rascals - Unknown

Year	Issue	Edition Limit	Year Retd.	Issue Price	*Quote U.S.$
1985	Three for the Show	10-day	1989	24.50	40
1985	My Gal	10-day	1989	24.50	25
1985	Skeleton Crew	10-day	1989	24.50	25
1985	Roughin' It	10-day	1989	24.50	25
1985	Spanky's Pranks	10-day	1989	24.50	25
1985	Butch's Challenge	10-day	1989	24.50	25
1985	Darla's Debut	10-day	1989	24.50	25
1985	Pete's Pal	10-day	1989	24.50	25

Little Shopkeepers - G. Gerardi

Year	Issue	Edition Limit	Year Retd.	Issue Price	*Quote U.S.$
1990	Sew Tired	14-day	1989	29.50	30
1991	Break Time	14-day	1989	29.50	30
1991	Purrfect Fit	14-day	1989	29.50	30
1991	Toying Around	14-day	1989	29.50	36
1991	Chain Reaction	14-day	1989	29.50	45
1991	Inferior Decorators	14-day	1989	29.50	36
1991	Tulip Tag	14-day	1989	29.50	36
1991	Candy Capers	14-day	1989	29.50	36

Lore Of The West - L. Danielle

Year	Issue	Edition Limit	Year Retd.	Issue Price	*Quote U.S.$
1993	A Mile In His Mocassins	28-day		29.50	30
1993	Path of Honor	28-day		29.50	30
1993	A Chief's Pride	28-day		29.50	30
1994	Pathways of the Pueblo	28-day		29.50	30
1994	In Her Seps	28-day		29.50	30
1994	Growing Up Brave	28-day		29.50	30
1994	Nomads of the Southwest	28-day		29.50	30
1994	Sacred Spirit of the Plains	28-day		29.50	30
1994	We'll Fight No More	28-day		29.50	30
1994	The End of the Trail	28-day		29.50	30

Love's Messengers - J. Grossman

Year	Issue	Edition Limit	Year Retd.	Issue Price	*Quote U.S.$
1995	To My Love	28-day	1994	29.50	30
1995	Cupid's Arrow	28-day	1994	29.50	30
1995	Love's Melody	28-day	1994	29.50	30
1995	A Token of Love	28-day	1994	29.50	30
1995	Harmony of Love	28-day	1994	29.50	30
1996	True Love's Offering	28-day	1994	29.95	30
1996	Love's In Bloom	28-day	1994	29.95	30
1996	To My Sweetheart	28-day	1994	29.95	30

The Lucille Ball (Official) Commemorative Plate - M. Weistling

Year	Issue	Edition Limit	Year Retd.	Issue Price	*Quote U.S.$
1993	Lucy	28-day	1994	37.50	125-200

Madonna And Child - Various

Year	Issue	Edition Limit	Year Retd.	Issue Price	*Quote U.S.$
1992	Madonna Della Sedia - R. Sanzio	28-day		37.50	38
1992	Virgin of the Rocks - L. DaVinci	28-day		37.50	38
1993	Madonna of Rosary - B. E. Murillo	28-day		37.50	38
1993	Sistine Madonna - R. Sanzio	28-day		37.50	38
1993	Virgin Adoring Christ Child - A. Correggio	28-day		37.50	38
1993	Virgin of the Grape - P. Mignard	28-day		37.50	38
1993	Madonna del Magnificat - S. Botticelli	28-day		37.50	38
1993	Madonna col Bambino - S. Botticelli	28-day		37.50	38

The Magical World of Legends & Myths - J. Shalatain

Year	Issue	Edition Limit	Year Retd.	Issue Price	*Quote U.S.$
1993	A Mother's Love	28-day	1994	35.00	35
1993	Dreams of Pegasus	28-day	1994	35.00	35
1994	Flight of the Pegasus	28-day	1994	35.00	45
1994	The Awakening	28-day	1994	35.00	35
1994	Once Upon a Dream	28-day	1994	35.00	45
1994	The Dawn of Romance	28-day	1994	35.00	35
1994	The Astral Unicorn	28-day	1994	35.00	45
1994	Flight into Paradise	28-day	1994	35.00	35
1995	Pegasus in the Stars	28-day	1994	35.00	35
1995	Unicorn of the Sea	28-day	1994	35.00	35

Majestic Birds of Prey - C.F. Riley

Year	Issue	Edition Limit	Year Retd.	Issue Price	*Quote U.S.$
1983	Golden Eagle	12,500		55.00	65-80
1983	Coopers Hawk	12,500		55.00	60
1983	Great Horned Owl	12,500		55.00	60
1983	Bald Eagle	12,500		55.00	60
1983	Barred Owl	12,500		55.00	60
1983	Sparrow Hawk	12,500		55.00	60
1983	Peregrine Falcon	12,500		55.00	60
1983	Osprey	12,500		55.00	60

Majesty of Flight - T. Hirata

Year	Issue	Edition Limit	Year Retd.	Issue Price	*Quote U.S.$
1989	The Eagle Soars	14-day		37.50	50
1989	Realm of the Red-Tail	14-day		37.50	40
1989	Coastal Journey	14-day		37.50	45
1989	Sentry of the North	14-day		37.50	30-48
1989	Commanding the Marsh	14-day		37.50	38
1990	The Vantage Point	14-day		29.50	45
1990	Silent Watch	14-day		29.50	48

Year	Issue	Edition Limit	Year Retd.	Issue Price	*Quote U.S.$
1990	Fierce and Free	14-day		29.50	45

Man's Best Friend - L. Picken

Year	Issue	Edition Limit	Year Retd.	Issue Price	*Quote U.S.$
1992	Special Delivery	28-day		29.50	30
1992	Making Waves	28-day		29.50	30
1992	Good Catch	28-day		29.50	30
1993	Time For a Walk	28-day		29.50	45
1993	Faithful Friend	28-day		29.50	45
1993	Let's Play Ball	28-day		29.50	36
1993	Sitting Pretty	28-day		29.50	30
1993	Bedtime Story	28-day		29.50	30
1993	Trusted Companion	28-day		29.50	30

Mickey Mantle - R. Tanenbaum

Year	Issue	Edition Limit	Year Retd.	Issue Price	*Quote U.S.$
1996	The Mick	28-day		35.00	35
1996	536 Home Runs	28-day		35.00	35
1996	2,401 Games	28-day		35.00	35
1996	Switch Hitter	28-day		35.00	35
1996	16 Time All Star	28-day		35.00	35
1996	18 World Series Home Runs	28-day		35.00	35
1997	1956-A Crowning Year	28-day		35.00	35
1997	Remembering a Legendary Yankee	28-day		35.00	35

Mike Schmidt - R. Tanenbaum

Year	Issue	Edition Limit	Year Retd.	Issue Price	*Quote U.S.$
1994	The Ultimate Competitor: Mike Schmidt	28-day		29.50	30
1995	A Homerun King	28-day		29.50	30
1995	An All Time, All Star	28-day		29.50	30
1995	A Career Retrospective	28-day		29.50	30

Milestones in Space - D. Dixon

Year	Issue	Edition Limit	Year Retd.	Issue Price	*Quote U.S.$
1994	Moon Landing	28-day		29.50	30
1995	Space Lab	28-day		29.50	30
1995	Maiden Flight of Columbia	28-day		29.50	30
1995	Free Walk in Space	28-day		29.50	30
1995	Lunar Rover	28-day		29.50	30
1995	Handshake in Space	28-day		29.50	30
1995	First Landing on Mars	28-day		29.50	30
1995	Voyager's Exploration	28-day		29.50	30

Mixed Company - P. Cooper

Year	Issue	Edition Limit	Year Retd.	Issue Price	*Quote U.S.$
1990	Two Against One	14-day		29.50	36
1990	A Sticky Situation	14-day		29.50	36
1990	What's Up	14-day		29.50	30
1990	All Wrapped Up	14-day		29.50	36
1990	Picture Perfect	14-day		29.50	30
1991	A Moment to Unwind	14-day		29.50	[illegible]
1991	Ole	14-day		29.50	33
1991	Picnic Prowlers	14-day		29.50	30

Murals From The Precious Moments Chapel - S. Butcher

Year	Issue	Edition Limit	Year Retd.	Issue Price	*Quote U.S.$
1995	The Pearl of Great Price	28-day		35.00	35
1995	The Good Samaritan	28-day		35.00	35
1996	The Prodigal Son	28-day		35.00	35
1996	The Good Shepherd	28-day		35.00	35

Mystic Warriors - C. Ren

Year	Issue	Edition Limit	Year Retd.	Issue Price	*Quote U.S.$
1992	Deliverance	28-day		29.50	30
1992	Mystic Warrior	28-day		29.50	30
1992	Sun Seeker	28-day		29.50	30
1992	Top Gun	28-day		29.50	30
1992	Man Who Walks Alone	28-day		29.50	30
1992	Windrider	28-day		29.50	30
1992	Spirit of the Plains	28-day		29.50	30
1993	Blue Thunder	28-day		29.50	30
1993	Sun Glow	28-day		29.50	30
1993	Peace Maker	28-day		29.50	30

Native American Legends - A. Biffignandi

Year	Issue	Edition Limit	Year Retd.	Issue Price	*Quote U.S.$
1996	Peace Pipe	28-day		29.95	30
1996	Feather-Woman	28-day		29.95	30
1996	Spirit of Serenity	28-day		29.95	30
1996	Enchanted Warrior	28-day		29.95	30
1996	Mystical Serenade	28-day		29.95	30
1996	Legend of Bridal Veil	28-day		29.95	30
1996	Seasons of Love	28-day		29.95	30
1996	A Bashful Courtship	28-day		29.95	30

Nature's Majestic Cats - M. Richter

Year	Issue	Edition Limit	Year Retd.	Issue Price	*Quote U.S.$
1993	Siberian Tiger	28-day		29.50	30
1993	Himalayan Snow Leopard	28-day		29.50	30
1993	African Lion	28-day		29.50	30
1994	Asian Clouded Leopard	28-day		29.50	30
1994	American Cougar	28-day		29.50	30
1994	East African Leopard	28-day		29.50	30
1994	African Cheetah	28-day		29.50	30
1994	Canadian Lynx	28-day		29.50	30

Nature's Nighttime Realm - G. Murray

Year	Issue	Edition Limit	Year Retd.	Issue Price	*Quote U.S.$
1992	Bobcat	28-day		29.50	30
1992	Cougar	28-day		29.50	30
1993	Jaguar	28-day		29.50	30
1993	White Tiger	28-day		29.50	30
1993	Lynx	28-day		29.50	30
1993	Lion	28-day		29.50	30
1993	Snow Leopard	28-day		29.50	30
1993	Cheetah	28-day		29.50	30

Nature's Quiet Moments - R. Parker

Year	Issue	Edition Limit	Year Retd.	Issue Price	*Quote U.S.$
1988	A Curious Pair	14-day		37.50	45-75
1988	Northern Morning	14-day		37.50	55
1988	Just Resting	14-day		37.50	50-75
1989	Waiting Out the Storm	14-day		37.50	38
1989	Creekside	14-day		37.50	38
1989	Autumn Foraging	14-day		37.50	38
1989	Old Man of the Mountain	14-day		37.50	38
1989	Mountain Blooms	14-day		37.50	38

Noble American Indian Women - D. Wright

Year	Issue	Edition Limit	Year Retd.	Issue Price	*Quote U.S.$
1989	Sacajawea	14-day		29.50	45-65
1990	Pocahontas	14-day		29.50	60
1990	Minnehaha	14-day		29.50	40-60
1990	Pine Leaf	14-day		29.50	45
1990	Lily of the Mohawk	14-day		29.50	35-60
1990	White Rose	14-day		29.50	45
1991	Lozen	14-day		29.50	30-50
1991	Falling Star	14-day		29.50	40

Noble Owls of America - J. Seerey-Lester

Year	Issue	Edition Limit	Year Retd.	Issue Price	*Quote U.S.$
1986	Morning Mist	15,000		55.00	45-65
1987	Prairie Sundown	15,000		55.00	60
1987	Winter Vigil	15,000		55.00	50-70
1987	Autumn Mist	15,000		75.00	40-75
1987	Dawn in the Willows	15,000		55.00	60
1987	Snowy Watch	15,000		60.00	60
1988	Hiding Place	15,000		55.00	60
1988	Waiting for Dusk	15,000		55.00	55

Nolan Ryan - R. Tanenbaum

Year	Issue	Edition Limit	Year Retd.	Issue Price	*Quote U.S.$
1994	The Strikeout Express	28-day		29.50	50
1994	Birth of a Legend	28-day		29.50	30
1994	Mr. Fastball	28-day		29.50	30
1994	Million-Dollar Player	28-day		29.50	30
1994	27 Seasons	28-day		29.50	30
1994	Farewell	28-day		29.50	30
1994	The Ryan Express	28-day		29.50	30

Norman Rockwell's Saturday Evening Post Baseball - N. Rockwell

Year	Issue	Edition Limit	Year Retd.	Issue Price	*Quote U.S.$
1992	100th Year of Baseball	Open		19.50	20
1993	The Rookie	Open		19.50	20
1993	The Dugout	Open		19.50	20
1993	Bottom of the Sixth	Open		19.50	20

North American Ducks - R. Lawrence

Year	Issue	Edition Limit	Year Retd.	Issue Price	*Quote U.S.$
1991	Autumn Flight	14-day		29.50	36
1991	The Resting Place	14-day		29.50	30
1991	Twin Flight	14-day		29.50	30
1992	Misty Morning	14-day		29.50	30
1992	Springtime Thaw	14-day		29.50	30
1992	Summer Retreat	14-day		29.50	30
1992	Overcast	14-day		29.50	30
1992	Perfect Pintails	14-day		29.50	30

North American Gamebirds - J. Killen

Year	Issue	Edition Limit	Year Retd.	Issue Price	*Quote U.S.$
1990	Ring-necked Pheasant	14-day		37.50	38
1990	Bobwhite Quail	14-day		37.50	45
1990	Ruffed Grouse	14-day		37.50	38
1990	Gambel Quail	14-day		37.50	42
1990	Mourning Dove	14-day		37.50	45
1990	Woodcock	14-day		37.50	45
1991	Chukar Partridge	14-day		37.50	45
1991	Wild Turkey	14-day		37.50	45

North American Waterbirds - R. Lawrence

Year	Issue	Edition Limit	Year Retd.	Issue Price	*Quote U.S.$
1988	Wood Ducks	14-day		37.50	45
1988	Hooded Mergansers	14-day		37.50	50
1988	Pintails	14-day		37.50	40
1988	Canada Geese	14-day		37.50	40
1989	American Widgeons	14-day		37.50	54
1989	Canvasbacks	14-day		37.50	55
1989	Mallard Pair	14-day		37.50	60
1989	Snow Geese	14-day		37.50	45

The Nutcracker Ballet - S. Fisher

Year	Issue	Edition Limit	Year Retd.	Issue Price	*Quote U.S.$
1978	Clara	28-day		19.50	40
1979	Godfather	28-day		19.50	20
1979	Sugar Plum Fairy	28-day		19.50	45
1979	Snow Queen and King	28-day		19.50	40
1980	Waltz of the Flowers	28-day		19.50	25
1980	Clara and the Prince	28-day		19.50	35-45

Official Honeymooner's Commemorative Plate - D. Bobnick

Year	Issue	Edition Limit	Year Retd.	Issue Price	*Quote U.S.$
1993	The Official Honeymooner's Commemorative Plate	28-day		37.50	175-200

The Official Honeymooners Plate Collection - D. Kilmer

Year	Issue	Edition Limit	Year Retd.	Issue Price	*Quote U.S.$
1987	The Honeymooners	14-day		24.50	125-200
1987	The Hucklebuck	14-day		24.50	125-200
1987	Baby, You're the Greatest	14-day		24.50	125-175
1988	The Golfer	14-day		24.50	95-190
1988	The TV Chefs	14-day		24.50	95-175
1988	Bang! Zoom!	14-day		24.50	95-145
1988	The Only Way to Travel	14-day		24.50	95-175
1988	The Honeymoon Express	14-day		24.50	125-195

On Wings of Eagles - J. Pitcher

Year	Issue	Edition Limit	Year Retd.	Issue Price	*Quote U.S.$
1994	"By Dawn's Early Light"	28-day		29.50	30
1994	Winter's Majestic Flight	28-day		29.50	30
1994	Over the Land of the Free	28-day		29.50	30

*Quotes have been rounded up to nearest dollar

Hamilton Collection
to Hamilton Collection

PLATES

YEAR ISSUE		EDITION LIMIT	YEAR RETD.	ISSUE PRICE	*QUOTE U.S.$
1994	Changing of the Guard	28-day		29.50	30
1995	Free Flight	28-day		29.50	30
1995	Morning Majesty	28-day		29.50	30
1995	Soaring Free	28-day		29.50	30
1994	Majestic Heights	28-day		29.50	30
	Our Cherished Seas - S. Barlowe				
1992	Whale Song	48-day		37.50	38
1992	Lions of the Sea	48-day		37.50	38
1992	Flight of the Dolphins	48-day		37.50	38
1992	Palace of the Seals	48-day		37.50	38
1993	Orca Ballet	48-day		37.50	38
1993	Emperors of the Ice	48-day		37.50	38
1993	Sea Turtles	48-day		37.50	38
1993	Splendor of the Sea	48-day		37.50	38
	Petals and Purrs - B. Harrison				
1988	Blushing Beauties	14-day		24.50	55
1988	Spring Fever	14-day		24.50	38
1988	Morning Glories	14-day		24.50	45
1988	Forget-Me-Not	14-day		24.50	36
1989	Golden Fancy	14-day		24.50	30
1989	Pink Lillies	14-day		24.50	30
1989	Summer Sunshine	14-day		24.50	55
1989	Siamese Summer	14-day		24.50	55
	Pillars of Baseball - A. Hicks				
1995	Babe Ruth	28-day		29.95	30
1995	Lou Gehrig	28-day		29.95	30
1995	Ty Cobb	28-day		29.95	30
1995	Cy Young	28-day		29.95	30
1996	Honus Wagner	28-day		29.95	30
1996	Rogers Hornsby	28-day		29.95	30
1996	Dizzy Dean	28-day		29.95	30
1996	Christy Mathewson	28-day		29.95	30
	Portraits of Childhood - T. Utz				
1981	Butterfly Magic	28-day		24.95	25
1981	Sweet Dreams	28-day		24.95	25
1981	Turtle Talk	28-day		24.95	36
1981	Friends Forever	28-day		24.95	25
	Portraits of Jesus - W. Sallman				
1994	Jesus, The Good Shepherd	28-day		29.50	30
1994	Jesus in the Garden	28-day		29.50	30
1994	Jesus, Children's Friend	28-day		29.50	30
1994	The Lord's Supper	28-day		29.50	30
1994	Christ at Dawn	28-day		29.50	30
1994	Christ at Heart's Door	28-day		29.50	30
1994	Portrait of Christ	28-day		29.50	30
1994	Madonna and Christ Child	28-day		29.50	30
	Portraits of the Bald Eagle - J. Pitcher				
1993	Ruler of the Sky	28-day		37.50	40
1993	In Bold Defiance	28-day		37.50	38
1993	Master Of The Summer Skies	28-day		37.50	38
1993	Spring's Sentinel	28-day		37.50	38
	Portraits of the Wild - J. Meger				
1994	Interlude	28-day		29.50	30
1994	Winter Solitude	28-day		29.50	30
1994	Devoted Protector	28-day		29.50	30
1994	Call of Autumn	28-day		29.50	30
1994	Watchful Eyes	28-day		29.50	30
1994	Babies of Spring	28-day		29.50	30
1994	Rocky Mountain Grandeur	28-day		29.50	30
1995	Unbridled Power	28-day		29.50	30
1995	Moonlight Vigil	28-day		29.50	30
1995	Monarch of the Plains	28-day		29.50	35
1995	Tender Courtship	28-day		29.50	40
	Precious Moments Bible Story - S. Butcher				
1990	Come Let Us Adore Him	28-day		29.50	30
1992	They Followed The Star	28-day		29.50	30
1992	The Flight Into Egypt	28-day		29.50	30
1992	The Carpenter Shop	28-day		29.50	30
1992	Jesus In The Temple	28-day		29.50	30
1992	The Crucifixion	28-day		29.50	30
1993	He Is Not Here	28-day		29.50	30
	Precious Moments Classics - S. Butcher				
1993	God Loveth A Cheerful Giver	28-day		35.00	35
1993	Make A Joyful Noise	28-day		35.00	35
1994	Love One Another	28-day		35.00	35
1994	You Have Touched So Many Hearts	28-day		35.00	35
1994	Praise the Lord Anyhow	28-day		35.00	35
1994	I Believe in Miracles	28-day		35.00	35
1994	Good Friends Are Forever	28-day		35.00	35
1994	Jesus Loves Me	28-day		35.00	35
1995	Friendship Hits the Spot	28-day		35.00	35
1995	To My Deer Friend	28-day		35.00	35
	Precious Moments of Childhood Plates - T. Utz				
1979	Friend in the Sky	28-day		21.50	50
1980	Sand in her Shoe	28-day		21.50	40
1980	Snow Bunny	28-day		21.50	40
1980	Seashells	28-day		21.50	38
1981	Dawn	28-day		21.50	27
1982	My Kitty	28-day		21.50	36
	Precious Moments Words of Love - S. Butcher				
1995	Your Friendship Is Soda-licious	28-day		35.00	35
1996	Your Love Is So Uplifting	28-day		35.00	35
1996	Love Is From Above	28-day		35.00	35
1996	Love Lifted Me	28-day		35.00	35
	Precious Portraits - B. P. Gutmann				
1987	Sunbeam	14-day	1991	24.50	30-45
1987	Mischief	14-day	1991	24.50	30
1987	Peach Blossom	14-day	1991	24.50	30
1987	Goldilocks	14-day	1991	24.50	30-40
1987	Fairy Gold	14-day	1991	24.50	45
1987	Bunny	14-day	1991	24.50	30
	The Prideful Ones - C. DeHaan				
1994	Village Markers	28-day		29.50	30
1994	His Pride	28-day		29.50	30
1994	Appeasing the Water People	28-day		29.50	30
1994	Tribal Guardian	28-day		29.50	30
1994	Autumn Passage	28-day		29.50	30
1994	Winter Hunter	28-day		29.50	30
1994	Silent Trail Break	28-day		29.50	30
1994	Water Breaking	28-day		29.50	30
1994	Crossing at the Big Trees	28-day		29.50	30
1995	Winter Songsinger	28-day		29.50	30
	Princesses of the Plains - D. Wright				
1993	Prairie Flower	28-day		29.50	30-45
1993	Snow Princess	28-day		29.50	30
1993	Wild Flower	28-day		29.50	45
1993	Noble Beauty	28-day		29.50	30
1993	Winter's Rose	28-day		29.50	30
1993	Gentle Beauty	28-day		29.50	30
1994	Nature's Guardian	28-day		29.50	30
1994	Mountain Princess	28-day		29.50	30
1995	Proud Dreamer	28-day		29.50	30
1995	Spring Maiden	28-day		29.50	30
	Proud Indian Families - K. Freeman				
1991	The Storyteller	14-day		29.50	50
1991	The Power of the Basket	14-day		29.50	36
1991	The Naming Ceremony	14-day		29.50	30
1992	Playing With Tradition	14-day		29.50	30
1992	Preparing the Berry Harvest	14-day		29.50	30
1992	Ceremonial Dress	14-day		29.50	30
1992	Sounds of the Forest	14-day		29.50	30
1992	The Marriage Ceremony	14-day		29.50	30
1993	The Jewelry Maker	14-day		29.50	30
1993	Beautiful Creations	14-day		29.50	30
	Proud Innocence - J. Schmidt				
1994	Desert Bloom	28-day		29.50	30
1994	Little Drummer	28-day		29.50	30
1995	Young Archer	28-day		29.50	30
1995	Morning Child	28-day		29.50	30
1995	Wise One	28-day		29.50	30
1995	Sun Blossom	28-day		29.50	30
1995	Laughing Heart	28-day		29.50	30
1995	Gentle Flower	28-day		29.50	30
	The Proud Nation - R. Swanson				
1989	Navajo Little One	14-day		24.50	35-45
1989	In a Big Land	14-day		24.50	25
1989	Out with Mama's Flock	14-day		24.50	25
1989	Newest Little Sheepherder	14-day		24.50	35
1989	Dressed Up for the Powwow	14-day		24.50	35
1989	Just a Few Days Old	14-day		24.50	30
1989	Autumn Treat	14-day		24.50	30
1989	Up in the Red Rocks	14-day		24.50	25
	Puppy Playtime - J. Lamb				
1987	Double Take-Cocker Spaniels	14-day		24.50	75-100
1987	Catch of the Day-Golden Retrievers	14-day		24.50	50
1987	Cabin Fever-Black Labradors	14-day		24.50	50
1987	Weekend Gardener-Lhasa Apsos	14-day		24.50	36
1987	Getting Acquainted-Beagles	14-day		24.50	25
1987	Hanging Out-German Shepherd	14-day		24.50	30-45
1987	New Leash on Life-Mini Schnauzer	14-day		24.50	30-40
1987	Fun and Games-Poodle	14-day		24.50	36
	Quiet Moments Of Childhood - D. Green				
1991	Elizabeth's Afternoon Tea	14-day		29.50	45
1991	Christina's Secret Garden	14-day		29.50	36
1991	Eric & Erin's Storytime	14-day		29.50	30
1992	Jessica's Tea Party	14-day		29.50	33
1992	Megan & Monique's Bakery	14-day		29.50	36
1992	Children's Day By The Sea	14-day		29.50	30
1992	Jordan's Playful Pups	14-day		29.50	33
1992	Daniel's Morning Playtime	14-day		29.50	30
	The Quilted Countryside: A Signature Collection by Mel Steele - M. Steele				
1991	The Old Country Store	14-day		29.50	36
1991	Winter's End	14-day		29.50	36
1991	The Quilter's Cabin	14-day		29.50	45
1991	Spring Cleaning	14-day		29.50	36
1991	Summer Harvest	14-day		29.50	30
1991	The Country Merchant	14-day		29.50	36
1992	Wash Day	14-day		29.50	30
1992	The Antiques Store	14-day		29.50	33
	Remembering Norma Jeane - F. Accornero				
1994	The Girl Next Door	28-day		29.50	30
1994	Her Day in the Sun	28-day		29.50	30
1994	A Star is Born	28-day		29.50	32
1994	Beauty Secrets	28-day		29.50	30
1995	In the Spotlight	28-day		29.50	30
1995	Bathing Beauty	28-day		29.50	30
1995	Young & Carefree	28-day		29.50	30
1995	Free Spirit	28-day		29.50	30
1995	A Country Girl at Heart	28-day		29.50	30
1996	Hometown Girl	28-day		29.50	30
	The Renaissance Angels - L. Bywaters				
1994	Doves of Peace	28-day		29.50	30
1994	Angelic Innocence	28-day		29.50	30
1994	Joy to the World	28-day		29.50	30
1995	Angel of Faith	28-day		29.50	30
1995	The Christmas Star	28-day		29.50	30
1995	Trumpeter's Call	28-day		29.50	30
1995	Harmonious Heavens	28-day		29.50	30
1995	The Angels Sing	28-day		29.50	30
	Rockwell Home of the Brave - N. Rockwell				
1981	Reminiscing	18,000		35.00	53
1981	Hero's Welcome	18,000		35.00	53
1981	Back to his Old Job	18,000		35.00	53
1981	War Hero	18,000		35.00	35
1982	Willie Gillis in Church	18,000		35.00	53
1982	War Bond	18,000		35.00	35
1982	Uncle Sam Takes Wings	18,000		35.00	75
1982	Taking Mother over the Top	18,000		35.00	35
	Romance of the Rails - D. Tutwiler				
1994	Starlight Limited	28-day		29.50	30
1994	Portland Rose	28-day		29.50	30
1994	Orange Blossom Special	28-day		29.50	30
1994	Morning Star	28-day		29.50	30
1994	Crescent Limited	28-day		29.50	30
1994	Sunset Limited	28-day		29.50	30
1994	Western Star	28-day		29.50	30
1994	Sunrise Limited	28-day		29.50	30
1995	The Blue Bonnett	28-day		29.50	30
1995	The Pine Tree Limited	28-day		29.50	30
	Romantic Castles of Europe - D. Sweet				
1990	Ludwig's Castle	19,500		55.00	55
1991	Palace of the Moors	19,500		55.00	55
1991	Swiss Isle Fortress	19,500		55.00	55
1991	The Legendary Castle of Leeds	19,500		55.00	55
1991	Davinci's Chambord	19,500		55.00	55
1991	Eilean Donan	19,500		55.00	55
1992	Eltz Castle	19,500		55.00	55
1992	Kylemore Abbey	19,500		55.00	55
	Romantic Flights of Fancy - Q. Lemonds				
1994	Sunlit Waltz	28-day		29.50	30
1994	Morning Minuet	28-day		29.50	30
1994	Evening Solo	28-day		29.50	30
1994	Summer Sonata	28-day		29.50	30
1995	Twilight Tango	28-day		29.50	30
1995	Sunset Ballet	28-day		29.50	30
1995	Exotic Interlude	28-day		29.50	30
1995	Sunrise Samba	28-day		29.50	30
	Romantic Victorian Keepsake - J. Grossman				
1992	Dearest Kiss	28-day		35.00	35
1992	First Love	28-day		35.00	35
1992	As Fair as a Rose	28-day		35.00	35
1992	Springtime Beauty	28-day		35.00	35
1992	Summertime Fancy	28-day		35.00	35
1992	Bonnie Blue Eyes	28-day		35.00	35
1992	Precious Friends	28-day		35.00	35
1994	Bonnets and Bouquets	28-day		35.00	35
1994	My Beloved Teddy	28-day		35.00	35
1994	A Sweet Romance	28-day		35.00	35
	A Salute to Mickey Mantle - T. Fogarty				
1996	1961 Home Run Duel	28-day		35.00	35
1996	Power at the Plate	28-day		35.00	35
1996	Saluting a Magnificent Yankee	28-day		35.00	35
1996	Triple Crown Achievement	28-day		35.00	35
1996	1953 Grand Slam	28-day		35.00	35
1997	1963's Famous Facade Homer	28-day		35.00	35
1997	Mickey as a Rookie	28-day		35.00	35
1997	A Look Back	28-day		35.00	35
	Santa Takes a Break - T. Newsom				
1995	Santa's Last Stop	28-day		29.95	30
1995	Santa's Railroad	28-day		29.95	30
1995	A Jolly Good Catch	28-day		29.95	30
1995	Simple Pleasures	28-day		29.95	30
1996	Skating On Penguin Pond	28-day		29.95	30
1996	Santa's Sing Along	28-day		29.95	30
1996	Sledding Adventures	28-day		29.95	30
1996	Santa's Sweet Treats	28-day		29.95	30
	The Saturday Evening Post - N. Rockwell				
1989	The Wonders of Radio	14-day		35.00	45
1989	Easter Morning	14-day		35.00	60

*Quotes have been rounded up to nearest dollar

PLATES

Hamilton Collection to Hamilton Collection

YEAR ISSUE		EDITION LIMIT	YEAR RETD.	ISSUE PRICE	*QUOTE U.S.$
1989	The Facts of Life	14-day		35.00	45
1990	The Window Washer	14-day		35.00	45
1990	First Flight	14-day		35.00	54
1990	Traveling Companion	14-day		35.00	35
1990	Jury Room	14-day		35.00	35
1990	Furlough	14-day		35.00	35

Scenes of An American Christmas - B. Perry
1994	I'll Be Home for Christmas	28-day		29.50	30
1994	Christmas Eve Worship	28-day		29.50	30
1994	A Holiday Happening	28-day		29.50	30
1994	A Long Winter's Night	28-day		29.50	30
1994	The Sounds of Christmas	28-day		29.50	30
1994	Dear Santa	28-day		29.50	30
1995	An Afternoon Outing	28-day		29.50	30
1995	Winter Worship	28-day		29.50	30

Seasons of the Bald Eagle - J. Pitcher
1991	Autumn in the Mountains	14-day		37.50	45-75
1991	Winter in the Valley	14-day		37.50	40-65
1991	Spring on the River	14-day		37.50	60
1991	Summer on the Seacoast	14-day		37.50	50

Sharing Life's Most Precious Memories - S. Butcher
1995	Thee I Love	28-day		35.00	35
1995	The Joy of the Lord Is My Strength	28-day		35.00	35
1995	May Your Every Wish Come True	28-day		35.00	35
1996	I'm So Glad That God	28-day		35.00	35
1996	Heaven Bless You	28-day		35.00	35

Sharing the Moments - S. Butcher
1995	You Have Touched So Many Hearts	28-day		35.00	35
1996	Friendship Hits The Spot	28-day		35.00	35
1996	Jesus Love Me	28-day		35.00	35

Single Issues - T. Utz
1983	Princess Grace	21-day		39.50	50

Small Wonders of the Wild - C. Frace
1989	Hideaway	14-day		29.50	45
1990	Young Explorers	14-day		29.50	36-45
1990	Three of a Kind	14-day		29.50	45-75
1990	Quiet Morning	14-day		29.50	36-45
1990	Eyes of Wonder	14-day		29.50	30-45
1990	Ready for Adventure	14-day		29.50	30-45
1990	Uno	14-day		29.50	45
1990	Exploring a New World	14-day		29.50	30-45

Space, The Final Frontier - D. Ward
1996	To Boldly Go...	28-day		37.50	38
1996	Second Star From The Right	28-day		37.50	38
1996	Signs of Intelligence	28-day		37.50	38
1996	Preparing To Cloak	28-day		37.50	38

Spanning America's Railways - D. Tutwiler
1996	Royal York	28-day		29.95	30

Spirit of the Mustang - C. DeHaan
1995	Winter's Thunder	28-day		29.95	30
1995	Moonlit Run	28-day		29.95	30
1995	Morning Reverie	28-day		29.95	30
1995	Autumn Respite	28-day		29.95	30
1996	Spring Frolic	28-day		29.95	30
1996	Dueling Mustangs	28-day		29.95	30
1996	Tranquil Waters	28-day		29.95	30
1996	Summer Squall	28-day		29.95	30

Sporting Generation - J. Lamb
1991	Like Father, Like Son	14-day		29.50	45-55
1991	Golden Moments	14-day		29.50	35
1991	The Lookout	14-day		29.50	30
1992	Picking Up The Scent	14-day		29.50	30
1992	First Time Out	14-day		29.50	40
1992	Who's Tracking Who	14-day		29.50	30
1992	Springing Into Action	14-day		29.50	30
1992	Point of Interest	14-day		29.50	30

STAR TREK: 25th Anniversary Commemorative - T. Blackshear
1991	STAR TREK 25th Anniversary Commemorative Plate	14-day		37.50	180-225
1991	SPOCK	14-day		35.00	100-150
1991	Kirk	14-day		35.00	85-125
1992	McCoy	14-day		35.00	70-120
1992	Uhura	14-day		35.00	65-120
1992	Scotty	14-day		35.00	65-120
1993	Sulu	14-day		35.00	65-120
1993	Chekov	14-day		35.00	65-120
1994	U.S.S. Enterprise NCC-1701	14-day		35.00	150-175

STAR TREK: Deep Space 9 - M. Weistling
1994	Commander Benjamin Sisko	28-day		35.00	35
1994	Security Chief Odo	28-day		35.00	35
1994	Major Kira Nerys	28-day		35.00	45
1994	Space Station	28-day		35.00	35
1994	Proprietor Quark	28-day		35.00	35
1995	Doctor Julian Bashir	28-day		35.00	35
1995	Lieutenant Jadzia Dax	28-day		35.00	35
1995	Chief Miles O'Brien	28-day		35.00	35

STAR TREK: Generations - K. Birdsong
1996	The Ultimate Confrontation	28-day		35.00	35
1996	Kirk's Final Voyage	28-day		35.00	35
1996	Meeting In The Nexus	28-day		35.00	35
1996	Picard's Christmas In The Nexus	28-day		35.00	35
1996	Worf's Ceremony	28-day		35.00	35
1996	The Final Plot/Duras Sisters	28-day		35.00	35

STAR TREK: The Movies - M. Weistling
1994	STAR TREK IV: The Voyage Home	28-day		35.00	35
1994	STAR TREK II: The Wrath of Khan	28-day		35.00	35
1994	STAR TREK VI: The Undiscovered Country	28-day		35.00	35
1995	STAR TREK III: The Search For Spock	28-day		35.00	35
1995	STAR TREK V: The Final Frontier	28-day		35.00	35
1996	Triumphant Return	28-day		35.00	35
1996	Destruction of the Reliant	28-day		35.00	35
1996	STAR TREK I: The Motion Picture	28-day		35.00	35

STAR TREK: The Next Generation - T. Blackshear
1993	Captain Jean-Luc Picard	28-day		35.00	35
1993	Commander William T. Riker	28-day		35.00	35
1994	Lieutenant Commander Data	28-day		35.00	35
1994	Lieutenant Worf	28-day		35.00	35
1994	Counselor Deanna Troi	28-day		35.00	35
1995	Dr. Beverly Crusher	28-day		35.00	35
1995	Lieutenant Commander Laforge	28-day		35.00	35
1996	Ensign W. Crusher	28-day		35.00	35

STAR TREK: The Next Generation The Episodes - K. Birdsong
1994	The Best of Both Worlds	28-day		35.00	35
1994	Encounter at Far Point	28-day		35.00	35
1995	Unification	28-day		35.00	35
1995	Yesterday's Enterprise	28-day		35.00	35
1995	All Good Things	28-day		35.00	35
1995	Descent	28-day		35.00	35
1996	Relics	28-day		35.00	35
1996	Redemption	28-day		35.00	35
1996	The Big Goodbye	28-day		35.00	35
1996	The Inner Light	28-day		35.00	35

STAR TREK: The Original Episodes - J. Martin
1996	The Tholian Web	28-day		35.00	35
1996	Space Seed	28-day		35.00	35
1996	The Menagerie	28-day		35.00	35
1996	City on the Edge	28-day		35.00	35
1996	Journel to Babel	28-day		35.00	35
1996	Trouble With Tribbles	28-day		35.00	35
1996	Where No Man Has Gone	28-day		35.00	35
1996	Devil in the Dark	28-day		35.00	35

STAR TREK: The Power of Command - K. Birdsong
1996	Captain Picard	28-day		35.00	35
1996	Admiral Kirk	28-day		35.00	35
1996	Captain Sisko	28-day		35.00	35
1996	Captain Sulu	28-day		35.00	35
1996	Janeway	28-day		35.00	35
1996	Khan	28-day		35.00	35
1996	General Chang	28-day		35.00	35
1996	Dukat	28-day		35.00	35

STAR TREK: The Voyagers - K. Birdsong
1994	U.S.S. Enterprise NCC-1701	28-day		35.00	35
1994	U.S.S. Enterprise NCC-1701-D	28-day		35.00	35
1994	Klingon Battlecruiser	28-day		35.00	35
1994	Romulan Warbird	28-day		35.00	35
1994	U.S.S. Enterprise NCC-1701-A	28-day		35.00	35
1995	Ferengi Marauder	28-day		35.00	35
1995	Klingon Bird of Prey	28-day		35.00	35
1995	Triple Nacelled U.S.S. Enterprise	28-day		35.00	35
1995	Cardassian Galor Warship	28-day		35.00	35
1995	U.S.S. Excelsior	28-day		35.00	35

STAR TREK: Voyager - D. Curry
1996	The Voyage Begins	28-day		35.00	35
1996	Bonds of Friendship	28-day		35.00	35
1996	Life Signs	28-day		35.00	35
1996	The Vidiians	28-day		35.00	35

Star Wars 10th Anniversary Commemorative - T. Blackshear
1990	Star Wars 10th Anniversary Commemorative Plates	14-day		39.50	125-325

Star Wars Plate Collection - T. Blackshear
1987	Hans Solo	14-day		29.50	125-250
1987	R2-D2 and Wicket	14-day		29.50	75-200
1987	Luke Skywalker and Darth Vader	14-day		29.50	125-225
1987	Princess Leia	14-day		29.50	125-150
1987	The Imperial Walkers	14-day		29.50	150-175
1987	Luke and Yoda	14-day		29.50	125-150
1988	Space Battle	14-day		29.50	350-375
1988	Crew in Cockpit	14-day		29.50	150-250

Star Wars Space Vehicles - S. Hillios
1995	Millenium Falcon	28-day		35.00	35
1995	TIE Fighters	28-day		35.00	35
1995	Red Five X-Wing Fighters	28-day		35.00	35
1995	Imperial Shuttle	28-day		35.00	35
1995	STAR Destroyer	28-day		35.00	35
1996	Snow Speeders	28-day		35.00	35
1996	B-Wing Fighter	28-day		35.00	35
1996	The Slave I	28-day		35.00	35
1996	Medical Frigate	28-day		35.00	35
1996	Jabba's Sail Barge	28-day		35.00	35

Star Wars Trilogy - M. Weistling
1993	Star Wars	28-day		37.50	140
1993	The Empire Strikes Back	28-day		37.50	120-150
1993	Return Of The Jedi	28-day		37.50	125-150

Summer Days of Childhood - T. Utz
1983	Mountain Friends	10-day		29.50	30
1983	Garden Magic	10-day		29.50	30
1983	Little Beachcombers	10-day		29.50	30
1983	Blowing Bubbles	10-day		29.50	30
1983	Birthday Party	10-day		29.50	30
1983	Playing Doctor	10-day		29.50	30
1983	Stolen Kiss	10-day		29.50	30
1983	Kitty's Bathtime	10-day		29.50	30
1983	Cooling Off	10-day		29.50	30
1983	First Cucumber	10-day		29.50	30
1983	A Jumping Contest	10-day		29.50	30
1983	Balloon Carnival	10-day		29.50	30

Symphony of the Sea - R. Koni
1995	Fluid Grace	28-day		29.95	45
1995	Dolphin's Dance	28-day		29.95	30
1995	Orca Ballet	28-day		29.95	30
1995	Moonlit Minuet	28-day		29.95	30
1995	Sailfish Serenade	28-day		29.95	30
1995	Starlit Waltz	28-day		29.95	30
1995	Sunset Splendor	28-day		29.95	30
1995	Coral Chorus	28-day		29.95	30

Those Delightful Dalmations - N/A
1995	You Missed a Spot	28-day		29.95	30
1995	Here's a Good Spot	28-day		29.95	30
1996	The Best Spot	28-day		29.95	30
1996	Spotted in the Headlines	28-day		29.95	30
1996	A Spot In My Heart	28-day		29.95	30
1996	Sweet Spots	28-day		29.95	30
1996	Naptime Already?	28-day		29.95	30
1996	He's In My Spot	28-day		29.95	30
1996	The Serious Studying Spot	28-day		29.95	30
1996	Check Out My Spots	28-day		29.95	30

Timeless Expressions of the Orient - M. Tsang
1990	Fidelity	15,000		75.00	95
1991	Femininity	15,000		75.00	75
1991	Longevity	15,000		75.00	75
1991	Beauty	15,000		55.00	55
1992	Courage	15,000		55.00	55

Treasured Days - H. Bond
1987	Ashley	14-day		29.50	95-145
1987	Christopher	14-day		24.50	30-45
1987	Sara	14-day		24.50	45
1987	Jeremy	14-day		24.50	45
1987	Amanda	14-day		24.50	45
1988	Nicholas	14-day		24.50	45
1988	Lindsay	14-day		24.50	45
1988	Justin	14-day		24.50	45

A Treasury of Cherished Teddies - P. Hillman
1994	Happy Holidays, Friend	28-day		29.50	30
1995	A New Year with Old Friends	28-day		29.50	30
1995	Valentines For You	28-day		29.50	30
1995	Friendship is in the Air	28-day		29.50	30
1995	Showers of Friendship	28-day		29.50	30
1996	Friendship is in Bloom	28-day		29.50	30
1996	Planting the Seeds of Friendship	28-day		29.50	30
1996	A Day in the Park	28-day		29.50	30
1996	Smooth Sailing	28-day		29.50	30
1996	School Days	28-day		29.50	30

Unbridled Spirit - C. DeHaan
1992	Surf Dancer	28-day		29.50	30
1992	Winter Renegade	28-day		29.50	30
1992	Desert Shadows	28-day		29.50	30
1993	Painted Sunrise	28-day		29.50	30
1993	Desert Duel	28-day		29.50	30
1993	Midnight Run	28-day		29.50	30
1993	Moonlight Majesty	28-day		29.50	30
1993	Autumn Reverie	28-day		29.50	30
1993	Blizzard's Peril	28-day		29.50	30
1993	Sunrise Surprise	28-day		29.50	30

Under the Sea - C. Bragg
1993	Tales of Tavarua	28-day		29.50	30
1993	Water's Edge	28-day		29.50	30
1994	Beauty of the Reef	28-day		29.50	30
1994	Rainbow Reef	28-day		29.50	30
1994	Orca Odyssey	28-day		29.50	30
1994	Rescue the Reef	28-day		29.50	30
1994	Underwater Dance	28-day		29.50	30
1994	Gentle Giants	28-day		29.50	30
1995	Undersea Enchantment	28-day		29.50	30

*Quotes have been rounded up to nearest dollar

PLATES

YEAR ISSUE		EDITION LIMIT	YEAR RETD.	ISSUE PRICE	*QUOTE U.S.$
1995	Penguin Paradise	28-day		29.50	30

Undersea Visions - J. Enright

YEAR ISSUE		EDITION LIMIT	YEAR RETD.	ISSUE PRICE	*QUOTE U.S.$
1995	Secret Sanctuary	28-day		29.95	30
1995	Temple of Treasures	28-day		29.95	30
1996	Temple Beneath the Sea	28-day		29.95	30
1996	Lost Kingdom	28-day		29.95	30
1996	Mysterious Ruins	28-day		29.95	30
1996	Last Journey	28-day		29.95	30
1996	Egyptian Dreamscape	28-day		29.95	30
1996	Lost Galleon	28-day		29.95	30

Utz Mother's Day - T. Utz

YEAR ISSUE		EDITION LIMIT	YEAR RETD.	ISSUE PRICE	*QUOTE U.S.$
1983	A Gift of Love	N/A		27.50	38
1983	Mother's Helping Hand	N/A		27.50	28
1983	Mother's Angel	N/A		27.50	28

Vanishing Rural America - J. Harrison

YEAR ISSUE		EDITION LIMIT	YEAR RETD.	ISSUE PRICE	*QUOTE U.S.$
1991	Quiet Reflections	14-day		29.50	45
1991	Autumn's Passage	14-day		29.50	45
1991	Storefront Memories	14-day		29.50	30
1991	Country Path	14-day		29.50	36
1991	When the Circus Came To Town	14-day		29.50	36
1991	Covered in Fall	14-day		29.50	45
1991	America's Heartland	14-day		29.50	33
1991	Rural Delivery	14-day		29.50	33

Victorian Christmas Memories - J. Grossman

YEAR ISSUE		EDITION LIMIT	YEAR RETD.	ISSUE PRICE	*QUOTE U.S.$
1992	A Visit from St. Nicholas	28-day		29.50	30
1993	Christmas Delivery	28-day		29.50	30
1993	Christmas Angels	28-day		29.50	30
1992	With Visions of Sugar Plums	28-day		29.50	30
1993	Merry Olde Kris Kringle	28-day		29.50	30
1993	Grandfather Frost	28-day		29.50	30
1993	Joyous Noel	28-day		29.50	30
1993	Christmas Innocence	28-day		29.50	30
1993	Dreaming of Santa	28-day		29.50	30
1993	Mistletoe & Holly	28-day		29.50	30

Victorian Playtime - M. H. Bogart

YEAR ISSUE		EDITION LIMIT	YEAR RETD.	ISSUE PRICE	*QUOTE U.S.$
1991	A Busy Day	14-day		29.50	30
1992	Little Masterpiece	14-day		29.50	30
1992	Playing Bride	14-day		29.50	60
1992	Waiting for a Nibble	14-day		29.50	30
1992	Tea and Gossip	14-day		29.50	30
1992	Cleaning House	14-day		29.50	30
1992	A Little Persuasion	14-day		29.50	30
1992	Peek-a-Boo	14-day		29.50	30

Warrior's Pride - C. DeHaan

YEAR ISSUE		EDITION LIMIT	YEAR RETD.	ISSUE PRICE	*QUOTE U.S.$
1994	Crow War Pony	28-day		29.50	30
1994	Running Free	28-day		29.50	30
1994	Blackfoot War Pony	28-day		29.50	30
1994	Southern Cheyenne	28-day		29.50	30
1995	Shoshoni War Ponies	28-day		29.50	30
1995	A Champion's Revelry	28-day		29.50	30
1995	Battle Colors	28-day		29.50	30
1995	Call of the Drums	28-day		29.50	30

The West of Frank McCarthy - F. McCarthy

YEAR ISSUE		EDITION LIMIT	YEAR RETD.	ISSUE PRICE	*QUOTE U.S.$
1991	Attacking the Iron Horse	14-day		37.50	60
1991	Attempt on the Stage	14-day		37.50	45
1991	The Prayer	14-day		37.50	54
1991	On the Old North Trail	14-day		37.50	48
1991	The Hostile Threat	14-day		37.50	45
1991	Bringing Out the Furs	14-day		37.50	45
1991	Kiowa Raider	14-day		37.50	45
1991	Headed North	14-day		37.50	39

Wilderness Spirits - P. Koni

YEAR ISSUE		EDITION LIMIT	YEAR RETD.	ISSUE PRICE	*QUOTE U.S.$
1994	Eyes of the Night	28-day		29.95	30
1995	Howl of Innocence	28-day		29.95	30
1995	Midnight Call	28-day		29.95	30
1995	Breaking the Silence	28-day		29.95	30
1995	Moonlight Run	28-day		29.95	30
1995	Sunset Vigil	28-day		29.95	30
1995	Sunrise Spirit	28-day		29.95	30
1996	Valley of the Wolf	28-day		29.95	30

Winged Reflections - R. Parker

YEAR ISSUE		EDITION LIMIT	YEAR RETD.	ISSUE PRICE	*QUOTE U.S.$
1989	Following Mama	14-day		37.50	38
1989	Above the Breakers	14-day		37.50	38
1989	Among the Reeds	14-day		37.50	38
1989	Freeze Up	14-day		37.50	38
1989	Wings Above the Water	14-day		37.50	38
1990	Summer Loon	14-day		29.50	30
1990	Early Spring	14-day		29.50	30
1990	At The Water's Edge	14-day		29.50	30

Winter Rails - T. Xaras

YEAR ISSUE		EDITION LIMIT	YEAR RETD.	ISSUE PRICE	*QUOTE U.S.$
1992	Winter Crossing	28-day		29.50	30
1993	Coal Country	28-day		29.50	35
1993	Daylight Run	28-day		29.50	35
1993	By Sea or Rail	28-day		29.50	35
1993	Country Crossroads	28-day		29.50	35
1993	Timber Line	28-day		29.50	35
1993	The Long Haul	28-day		29.50	35
1993	Darby Crossing	28-day		29.50	35
1995	East Broad Top	28-day		29.50	30
1995	Landsdowne Station	28-day		29.50	30

Winter Wildlife - J. Seerey-Lester

YEAR ISSUE		EDITION LIMIT	YEAR RETD.	ISSUE PRICE	*QUOTE U.S.$
1989	Close Encounters	15,000		55.00	55
1989	Among the Cattails	15,000		55.00	55
1989	The Refuge	15,000		55.00	55
1989	Out of the Blizzard	15,000		55.00	55
1989	First Snow	15,000		55.00	55
1989	Lying In Wait	15,000		55.00	55
1989	Winter Hiding	15,000		55.00	55
1989	Early Snow	15,000		55.00	55

Wizard of Oz Commemorative - T. Blackshear

YEAR ISSUE		EDITION LIMIT	YEAR RETD.	ISSUE PRICE	*QUOTE U.S.$
1988	We're Off to See the Wizard	14-day		24.50	100-200
1988	Dorothy Meets the Scarecrow	14-day		24.50	90-175
1989	The Tin Man Speaks	14-day		24.50	95-150
1989	A Glimpse of the Munchkins	14-day		24.50	125-150
1989	The Witch Casts A Spell	14-day		24.50	110-150
1989	If I Were King Of The Forest	14-day		24.50	95-150
1989	The Great and Powerful Oz	14-day		24.50	95-150
1989	There's No Place Like Home	14-day		24.50	95-195

Wizard of Oz-Fifty Years of Oz - T. Blackshear

YEAR ISSUE		EDITION LIMIT	YEAR RETD.	ISSUE PRICE	*QUOTE U.S.$
1989	Fifty Years of Oz	14-day		37.50	175-300

Wizard of Oz-Portraits From Oz - T. Blackshear

YEAR ISSUE		EDITION LIMIT	YEAR RETD.	ISSUE PRICE	*QUOTE U.S.$
1989	Dorothy	14-day		29.50	175-225
1989	Scarecrow	14-day		29.50	135-200
1989	Tin Man	14-day		29.50	100-200
1990	Cowardly Lion	14-day		29.50	100-200
1990	Glinda	14-day		29.50	100-200
1990	Wizard	14-day		29.50	90-195
1990	Wicked Witch	14-day		29.50	125-250
1990	Toto	14-day		29.50	300-325

The Wonder Of Christmas - J. McClelland

YEAR ISSUE		EDITION LIMIT	YEAR RETD.	ISSUE PRICE	*QUOTE U.S.$
1991	Santa's Secret	28-day		29.50	30
1991	My Favorite Ornament	28-day		29.50	30
1991	Waiting For Santa	28-day		29.50	30
1993	The Caroler	28-day		29.50	30

Woodland Babies - R. Manning

YEAR ISSUE		EDITION LIMIT	YEAR RETD.	ISSUE PRICE	*QUOTE U.S.$
1995	Hollow Hideaway	28-day		29.95	30
1995	A Springtime Adventure	28-day		29.95	30
1995	Amber Eyes	28-day		29.95	30
1996	Peaceful Dreams	28-day		29.95	30
1996	Cozy Nest	28-day		29.95	30
1996	Tree House Trio	28-day		29.95	30

Woodland Encounters - G. Giordano

YEAR ISSUE		EDITION LIMIT	YEAR RETD.	ISSUE PRICE	*QUOTE U.S.$
1991	Want to Play?	14-day		29.50	30
1991	Peek-a-boo!	14-day		29.50	30
1991	Lunchtime Visitor	14-day		29.50	33
1991	Anyone for a Swim?	14-day		29.50	36
1991	Nature Scouts	14-day		29.50	36
1991	Meadow Meeting	14-day		29.50	33
1991	Hi Neighbor	14-day		29.50	30
1992	Field Day	14-day		29.50	36

A World of Puppy Adventures - J. Ren

YEAR ISSUE		EDITION LIMIT	YEAR RETD.	ISSUE PRICE	*QUOTE U.S.$
1995	The Water's Fine	28-day		29.95	30
1996	Swimming Lessons	28-day		29.95	30
1996	Breakfast Is Served	28-day		29.95	30
1996	Laundry Tug O' War	28-day		29.95	30
1996	Did I Do That?	28-day		29.95	30
1996	DeCoy Dismay	28-day		29.95	30
1996	Puppy Picnic	28-day		29.95	30
1996	Sweet Terrors	28-day		29.95	30

The World Of Zolan - D. Zolan

YEAR ISSUE		EDITION LIMIT	YEAR RETD.	ISSUE PRICE	*QUOTE U.S.$
1992	First Kiss	28-day		29.50	50-75
1992	Morning Discovery	28-day		29.50	45
1993	The Little Fisherman	28-day		29.50	45-50
1993	Letter to Grandma	28-day		29.50	45-55
1993	Twilight Prayer	28-day		29.50	60-65
1993	Flowers for Mother	28-day		29.50	45-55

Year Of The Wolf - A. Agnew

YEAR ISSUE		EDITION LIMIT	YEAR RETD.	ISSUE PRICE	*QUOTE U.S.$
1993	Broken Silence	28-day		29.50	30
1993	Leader of the Pack	28-day		29.50	30
1993	Solitude	28-day		29.50	30
1994	Tundra Light	28-day		29.50	30
1994	Guardians of the High Country	28-day		29.50	30
1994	A Second Glance	28-day		29.50	30
1994	Free as the Wind	28-day		29.50	30
1994	Song of the Wolf	28-day		29.50	30
1995	Lords of the Tundra	28-day		29.50	30
1995	Wilderness Companions	28-day		29.50	30

Young Lords of The Wild - M. Richter

YEAR ISSUE		EDITION LIMIT	YEAR RETD.	ISSUE PRICE	*QUOTE U.S.$
1994	Siberian Tiger Club	28-day		29.95	30
1995	Snow Leopard Cub	28-day		29.95	30
1995	Lion Cub	28-day		29.95	30
1995	Clouded Leopard Cub	28-day		29.95	30
1995	Cougar Cub	28-day		29.95	30
1995	Leopard Cub	28-day		29.95	30
1995	Cheetah Cub	28-day		29.95	30
1996	Canadian Lynx Cub	28-day		29.95	30

Hamilton/Boehm

Award Winning Roses - Boehm

YEAR ISSUE		EDITION LIMIT	YEAR RETD.	ISSUE PRICE	*QUOTE U.S.$
1979	Peace Rose	15,000		45.00	100
1979	White Masterpiece Rose	15,000		45.00	75
1979	Tropicana Rose	15,000		45.00	63
1979	Elegance Rose	15,000		45.00	63
1979	Queen Elizabeth Rose	15,000		45.00	63
1979	Royal Highness Rose	15,000		45.00	63
1979	Angel Face Rose	15,000		45.00	63
1979	Mr. Lincoln Rose	15,000		45.00	63

Gamebirds of North America - Boehm

YEAR ISSUE		EDITION LIMIT	YEAR RETD.	ISSUE PRICE	*QUOTE U.S.$
1984	Ring-Necked Pheasant	15,000		62.50	63
1984	Bob White Quail	15,000		62.50	63
1984	American Woodcock	15,000		62.50	63
1984	California Quail	15,000		62.50	63
1984	Ruffed Grouse	15,000		62.50	63
1984	Wild Turkey	15,000		62.50	63
1984	Willow Partridge	15,000		62.50	63
1984	Prairie Grouse	15,000		62.50	63

Hummingbird Collection - Boehm

YEAR ISSUE		EDITION LIMIT	YEAR RETD.	ISSUE PRICE	*QUOTE U.S.$
1980	Calliope	15,000		62.50	80
1980	Broadbilled	15,000		62.50	63
1980	Rufous Flame Bearer	15,000		62.50	80
1980	Broadtail	15,000		62.50	63
1980	Streamertail	15,000		62.50	80
1980	Blue Throated	15,000		62.50	80
1980	Crimson Topaz	15,000		62.50	63
1980	Brazilian Ruby	15,000		62.50	80

Owl Collection - Boehm

YEAR ISSUE		EDITION LIMIT	YEAR RETD.	ISSUE PRICE	*QUOTE U.S.$
1980	Boreal Owl	15,000		45.00	95
1980	Snowy Owl	15,000		45.00	95
1980	Barn Owl	15,000		45.00	80
1980	Saw Whet Owl	15,000		45.00	75
1980	Great Horned Owl	15,000		45.00	75
1980	Screech Owl	15,000		45.00	75
1980	Short Eared Owl	15,000		45.00	75
1980	Barred Owl	15,000		45.00	75

Water Birds - Boehm

YEAR ISSUE		EDITION LIMIT	YEAR RETD.	ISSUE PRICE	*QUOTE U.S.$
1981	Canada Geese	15,000		62.50	65
1981	Wood Ducks	15,000		62.50	65
1981	Hooded Merganser	15,000		62.50	65
1981	Ross's Geese	15,000		62.50	65
1981	Common Mallard	15,000		62.50	65
1981	Canvas Back	15,000		62.50	65
1981	Green Winged Teal	15,000		62.50	65
1981	American Pintail	15,000		62.50	65

Haviland

Twelve Days of Christmas - R. Hetreau

YEAR ISSUE		EDITION LIMIT	YEAR RETD.	ISSUE PRICE	*QUOTE U.S.$
1970	Partridge	30,000		25.00	80
1971	Two Turtle Doves	30,000		25.00	30
1972	Three French Hens	30,000		27.50	30
1973	Four Calling Birds	30,000		28.50	30
1974	Five Golden Rings	30,000		30.00	30
1975	Six Geese a'laying	30,000		32.50	33
1976	Seven Swans	30,000		38.00	38
1977	Eight Maids	30,000		40.00	40
1978	Nine Ladies Dancing	30,000		45.00	45
1979	Ten Lord's a'leaping	30,000		50.00	50
1980	Eleven Pipers Piping	30,000		55.00	55
1981	Twelve Drummers	30,000		60.00	60

Haviland & Parlon

Christmas Madonnas - Various

YEAR ISSUE		EDITION LIMIT	YEAR RETD.	ISSUE PRICE	*QUOTE U.S.$
1972	By Raphael - Raphael	5,000		35.00	42
1973	By Feruzzi - Feruzzi	5,000		40.00	78
1974	By Raphael - Raphael	5,000		42.50	43
1975	By Murillo - Murillo	7,500		42.50	43
1976	By Botticelli - Botticelli	7,500		45.00	45
1977	By Bellini - Bellini	7,500		48.00	48
1978	By Lippi - Lippi	7,500		48.00	53
1979	Madonna of The Eucharist - Botticelli	7,500		49.50	112

Hudson Creek

American Expansion (Hudson Pewter) - P.W. Baston

YEAR ISSUE		EDITION LIMIT	YEAR RETD.	ISSUE PRICE	*QUOTE U.S.$
1975	Spirit of '76 (6" Plate)	4,812	1975	27.50	100-120
1975	American Independence	18,462	N/A	Unkn.	100-125
1975	American Expansion	2,250	N/A	Unkn.	50-75
1975	The American War Between the States	825	N/A	Unkn.	150-200

Sebastian Plates - P.W. Baston

YEAR ISSUE		EDITION LIMIT	YEAR RETD.	ISSUE PRICE	*QUOTE U.S.$
1978	Motif No. 1	4,878	1985	75.00	50-75
1979	Grand Canyon	2,492	1985	75.00	50-75
1980	Lone Cypress	718	1985	75.00	150-175
1980	In The Candy Store	9,098	1985	39.50	40
1981	The Doctor	7,547	1985	39.50	40
1983	Little Mother	2,710	1985	39.50	40
1984	Switching The Freight	706	1985	42.50	80-100

*Quotes have been rounded up to nearest dollar

Hutschenreuther

The Glory of Christmas - W./C. Hallett

YEAR	ISSUE	EDITION LIMIT	YEAR RETD.	ISSUE PRICE	*QUOTE U.S.$
1982	The Nativity	25,000		80.00	125
1983	The Annunciation	25,000		80.00	115
1984	The Shepherds	25,000		80.00	100
1985	The Wiseman	25,000		80.00	100

Gunther Granget - G. Granget

YEAR	ISSUE	EDITION LIMIT	YEAR RETD.	ISSUE PRICE	*QUOTE U.S.$
1972	American Sparrows	5,000		50.00	75-100
1972	European Sparrows	5,000		30.00	65
1973	American Kildeer	2,250		75.00	75
1973	American Squirrel	2,500		75.00	75
1973	European Squirrel	2,500		35.00	50
1974	American Partridge	2,500		75.00	90
1975	American Rabbits	2,500		90.00	90
1976	Freedom in Flight	5,000		100.00	100
1976	Wrens	2,500		100.00	110
1976	Freedom in Flight, Gold	200		200.00	200
1977	Bears	2,500		100.00	100
1978	Foxes' Spring Journey	1,000		125.00	200

Imperial Ching-te Chen

Beauties of the Red Mansion - Z. HuiMin

YEAR	ISSUE	EDITION LIMIT	YEAR RETD.	ISSUE PRICE	*QUOTE U.S.$
1986	Pao-chai	115-day		27.92	30-40
1986	Yuan-chun	115-day		27.92	30-40
1987	Hsi-feng	115-day		30.92	35
1987	Hsi-chun	115-day		30.92	35
1988	Miao-yu	115-day		30.92	34-40
1988	Ying-chun	115-day		30.92	34-40
1988	Tai-yu	115-day		32.92	34-42
1988	Li-wan	115-day		32.92	34-38
1988	Ko-Ching	115-day		32.92	35
1988	Hsiang-yun	115-day		34.92	35
1989	Tan-Chun	115-day		34.92	34-40
1989	Chiao-chieh	115-day		34.92	35

Blessings From a Chinese Garden - Z. Song Mao

YEAR	ISSUE	EDITION LIMIT	YEAR RETD.	ISSUE PRICE	*QUOTE U.S.$
1988	The Gift of Purity	175-day		39.92	40
1989	The Gift of Grace	175-day		39.92	40
1989	The Gift of Beauty	175-day		42.92	43
1989	The Gift of Happiness	175-day		42.92	43
1990	The Gift of Truth	175-day		42.92	43
1990	The Gift of Joy	175-day		42.92	43

Flower Goddesses of China - Z. HuiMin

YEAR	ISSUE	EDITION LIMIT	YEAR RETD.	ISSUE PRICE	*QUOTE U.S.$
1991	The Lotus Goddess	175-day		34.92	35
1991	The Chrysanthemum Goddess	175-day		34.92	35
1991	The Plum Blossom Goddess	175-day		37.92	38
1991	The Peony Goddess	175-day		37.92	38
1991	The Narcissus Goddess	175-day		37.92	62
1991	The Camellia Goddess	175-day		37.92	38

The Forbidden City - S. Fu

YEAR	ISSUE	EDITION LIMIT	YEAR RETD.	ISSUE PRICE	*QUOTE U.S.$
1990	Pavilion of 10,000 Springs	150-day		39.92	40
1990	Flying Kites/Spring Day	150-day		39.92	40
1990	Pavilion/Floating Jade Green	150-day		42.92	43
1991	The Lantern Festival	150-day		42.92	43
1991	Nine Dragon Screen	150-day		42.92	43
1991	The Hall of the Cultivating Mind	150-day		42.92	43
1991	Dressing the Empress	150-day		45.92	46
1991	Pavilion of Floating Cups	150-day		45.92	46

Garden of Satin Wings - J. Xue-Bing

YEAR	ISSUE	EDITION LIMIT	YEAR RETD.	ISSUE PRICE	*QUOTE U.S.$
1992	A Morning Dream	115-day		29.92	35
1993	An Evening Mist	115-day		29.92	37
1993	A Garden Whisper	115-day		29.92	40
1993	An Enchanting Interlude	115-day		29.92	40

Legends of West Lake - J. Xue-Bing

YEAR	ISSUE	EDITION LIMIT	YEAR RETD.	ISSUE PRICE	*QUOTE U.S.$
1989	Lady White	175-day		29.92	30
1990	Lady Silkworm	175-day		29.92	35
1990	Laurel Peak	175-day		29.92	35
1990	Rising Sun Terrace	175-day		32.92	33
1990	The Apricot Fairy	175-day		32.92	33
1990	Bright Pearl	175-day		32.92	33
1990	Thread of Sky	175-day		34.92	35
1991	Phoenix Mountain	175-day		34.92	35
1991	Ancestors of Tea	175-day		34.92	35
1991	Three Pools Mirroring/Moon	175-day		36.92	37
1991	Fly-In Peak	175-day		36.92	40
1991	The Case of the Folding Fans	175-day		36.92	40

Maidens of the Folding Sky - J. Xue-Bing

YEAR	ISSUE	EDITION LIMIT	YEAR RETD.	ISSUE PRICE	*QUOTE U.S.$
1992	Lady Lu	175-day		29.92	35
1992	Mistress Yang	175-day		29.92	35
1992	Bride Yen Chun	175-day		32.92	65
1993	Parrot Maiden	175-day		32.92	70

Scenes from the Summer Palace - Z. Song Mao

YEAR	ISSUE	EDITION LIMIT	YEAR RETD.	ISSUE PRICE	*QUOTE U.S.$
1988	The Marble Boat	175-day		29.92	35
1988	Jade Belt Bridge	175-day		29.92	35
1989	Hall that Dispels the Clouds	175-day		32.92	33
1989	The Long Promenade	175-day		32.92	39
1989	Garden/Harmonious Pleasure	175-day		32.92	33
1989	The Great Stage	175-day		32.92	33
1989	Seventeen Arch Bridge	175-day		34.92	35
1989	Boaters on Kumming Lake	175-day		34.92	35

International Silver

Bicentennial - M. Deoliveira

YEAR	ISSUE	EDITION LIMIT	YEAR RETD.	ISSUE PRICE	*QUOTE U.S.$
1972	Signing Declaration	7,500		40.00	310
1973	Paul Revere	7,500		40.00	160
1974	Concord Bridge	7,500		40.00	115
1975	Crossing Delaware	7,500		50.00	80
1976	Valley Forge	7,500		50.00	65
1977	Surrender at Yorktown	7,500		50.00	60

John Hine N.A. Ltd./Enesco Corporation

David Winter Plate Collection - M. Fisher

YEAR	ISSUE	EDITION LIMIT	YEAR RETD.	ISSUE PRICE	*QUOTE U.S.$
1991	A Christmas Carol	10,000	1993	30.00	30
1991	Cotswold Village Plate	10,000	1993	30.00	30
1992	Chichester Cross Plate	10,000	1993	30.00	30
1992	Little Mill Plate	10,000	1993	30.00	30
1992	Old Curiosity Shop	10,000	1993	30.00	30
1992	Scrooge's Counting House	10,000	1993	30.00	30
1993	Dove Cottage	10,000		30.00	35
1993	Little Forge	10,000		30.00	35

Lalique Society of America

Annual - M. Lalique

YEAR	ISSUE	EDITION LIMIT	YEAR RETD.	ISSUE PRICE	*QUOTE U.S.$
1965	Deux Oiseaux (Two Birds)	2,000		25.00	1250
1966	Rose de Songerie (Dream Rose)	5,000		25.00	75-110
1967	Ballet de Poisson (Fish Ballet)	5,000		25.00	95-100
1968	Gazelle Fantaisie (Gazelle Fantasy)	5,000		25.00	75
1969	Papillon (Butterfly)	5,000		30.00	50
1970	Paon (Peacock)	5,000		30.00	60-70
1971	Hibou (Owl)	5,000		35.00	50-68
1972	Coquillage (Shell)	5,000		40.00	75
1973	Petit Geai (Jayling)	5,000		42.50	100
1974	Sous d'Argent (Silver Pennies)	5,000		47.50	95
1975	Duo de Poisson (Fish Duet)	5,000		50.00	139
1976	Aigle (Eagle)	5,000		60.00	84-90

Lenox Collections

Boehm Birds - E. Boehm

YEAR	ISSUE	EDITION LIMIT	YEAR RETD.	ISSUE PRICE	*QUOTE U.S.$
1970	Wood Thrush	Yr.Iss.	1970	35.00	98-149
1971	Goldfinch	Yr.Iss.	1971	35.00	45
1972	Mountain Bluebird	Yr.Iss.	1972	37.50	45
1973	Meadowlark	Yr.Iss.	1973	50.00	50
1974	Rufous Hummingbird	Yr.Iss.	1974	45.00	50
1975	American Redstart	Yr.Iss.	1975	50.00	50
1976	Cardinals	Yr.Iss.	1976	53.00	53
1977	Robins	Yr.Iss.	1977	55.00	55
1978	Mockingbirds	Yr.Iss.	1978	58.00	58
1979	Golden-Crowned Kinglets	Yr.Iss.	1979	65.00	85
1980	Black-Throated Blue Warblers	Yr.Iss.	1980	80.00	85
1981	Eastern Phoebes	Yr.Iss.	1981	92.50	95

Boehm Woodland Wildlife - E. Boehm

YEAR	ISSUE	EDITION LIMIT	YEAR RETD.	ISSUE PRICE	*QUOTE U.S.$
1973	Racoons	Yr.Iss.	1973	50.00	75
1974	Red Foxes	Yr.Iss.	1974	52.50	75
1975	Cottontail Rabbits	Yr.Iss.	1975	58.50	75
1976	Eastern Chipmunks	Yr.Iss.	1976	62.50	75
1977	Beaver	Yr.Iss.	1977	67.50	75
1978	Whitetail Deer	Yr.Iss.	1978	70.00	75
1979	Squirrels	Yr.Iss.	1979	76.00	76
1980	Bobcats	Yr.Iss.	1980	82.50	83
1981	Martens	Yr.Iss.	1981	100.00	100
1982	River Otters	Yr.Iss.	1982	100.00	100

Lightpost Publishing

Kinkade-Thomas Kinkade Signature Collection - T. Kinkade

YEAR	ISSUE	EDITION LIMIT	YEAR RETD.	ISSUE PRICE	*QUOTE U.S.$
1991	Chandler's Cottage	2,500		49.95	50-75
1991	Cedar Nook	2,500		49.95	40-75
1991	Sleigh Ride Home	2,500		49.95	55-75
1991	Home To Grandma's	2,500		49.95	52-75

Lilliput Lane Ltd./Enesco Corporation

American Landmarks Collection - R. Day

YEAR	ISSUE	EDITION LIMIT	YEAR RETD.	ISSUE PRICE	*QUOTE U.S.$
1990	Country Church	5,000	1996	35.00	35
1990	Riverside Chapel	5,000	1996	35.00	35

Ray Day/Coca Cola Country - R. Day

YEAR	ISSUE	EDITION LIMIT	YEAR RETD.	ISSUE PRICE	*QUOTE U.S.$
1997	Ice Cold Coke	Open		40.00	40
1997	When I Was Your Age...	Open		40.00	40

Lladró

Lladró Plate Collection - Lladró

YEAR	ISSUE	EDITION LIMIT	YEAR RETD.	ISSUE PRICE	*QUOTE U.S.$
1993	The Great Voyage L5964G	Open		50.00	50
1993	Looking Out L5998G	Open		38.00	38
1993	Swinging L5999G	Open		38.00	38
1993	Duck Plate L6000G	Open		38.00	38
1994	Friends L6158	Open		32.00	32
1994	Apple Picking L6159M	Open		32.00	32
1994	Turtledove L6160	Open		32.00	32
1994	Flamingo L6161M	Open		32.00	32

Lowell Davis Farm Club

Davis Cat Tales Plates. - L. Davis

YEAR	ISSUE	EDITION LIMIT	YEAR RETD.	ISSUE PRICE	*QUOTE U.S.$
1982	Right Church, Wrong Pew	12,500	1986	37.50	90
1982	Company's Coming	12,500	1986	37.50	90
1982	On the Move	12,500	1986	37.50	90
1982	Flew the Coop	12,500	1986	37.50	90

Davis Christmas Plates - L. Davis

YEAR	ISSUE	EDITION LIMIT	YEAR RETD.	ISSUE PRICE	*QUOTE U.S.$
1983	Hooker at Mailbox With Present 224-100	7,500	1984	45.00	130
1984	Country Christmas 224-101	7,500	1985	45.00	125
1985	Christmas at Foxfire Farm 224-102	7,500	1986	45.00	150
1986	Christmas at Red Oak 224-103	7,500	1987	45.00	100-150
1987	Blossom's Gift 224-104	7,500	1988	47.50	100
1988	Cutting the Family Christmas Tree 224-105	7,500	1989	47.50	75-100
1989	Peter and the Wren	7,500	1990	47.50	75
1990	Wintering Deer	7,500	1991	47.50	50
1991	Christmas at Red Oak II	7,500	1992	55.00	75
1992	Born On A Starry Night	7,500	1993	55.00	55
1993	Waiting For Mr. Lowell	5,000	1994	55.00	55
1994	Visions of Sugarplums	5,000	1995	55.00	55
1995	Bah Humbug	5,000		55.00	55

Davis Country Pride Plates - L. Davis

YEAR	ISSUE	EDITION LIMIT	YEAR RETD.	ISSUE PRICE	*QUOTE U.S.$
1981	Surprise in the Cellar	7,500	1983	35.00	200-220
1981	Plum Tuckered Out	7,500	1983	35.00	115
1981	Duke's Mixture	7,500	1983	35.00	190
1982	Bustin' with Pride	7,500	1983	35.00	100

Davis Pen Pals - L. Davis

YEAR	ISSUE	EDITION LIMIT	YEAR RETD.	ISSUE PRICE	*QUOTE U.S.$
1993	The Old Home Place 25800	Closed	1995	50.00	50

Davis Red Oak Sampler - L. Davis

YEAR	ISSUE	EDITION LIMIT	YEAR RETD.	ISSUE PRICE	*QUOTE U.S.$
1986	General Store	5,000	1987	45.00	110
1987	Country Wedding	5,000	1988	45.00	125
1989	Country School	5,000	1990	45.00	110
1990	Blacksmith Shop	5,000	1991	52.50	110

Davis Special Edition Plates - L. Davis

YEAR	ISSUE	EDITION LIMIT	YEAR RETD.	ISSUE PRICE	*QUOTE U.S.$
1983	The Critics	12,500	1985	45.00	95
1984	Good Ole Days Privy Set 2	5,000	1986	60.00	185
1986	Home From Market	7,500	1988	55.00	145

March of Dimes

Our Children, Our Future - Various

YEAR	ISSUE	EDITION LIMIT	YEAR RETD.	ISSUE PRICE	*QUOTE U.S.$
1989	A Time for Peace - D. Zolan	150-day		29.00	40-50
1989	A Time To Love - S. Kuck	150-day		29.00	35
1989	A Time To Plant - J. McClelland	150-day		29.00	29
1989	A Time To Be Born - G. Perillo	150-day		29.00	29
1990	A Time To Embrace - E. Hibel	150-day		29.00	29
1990	A Time To Laugh - A. Williams	150-day		29.00	29

Marigold

Sport - Carreno

YEAR	ISSUE	EDITION LIMIT	YEAR RETD.	ISSUE PRICE	*QUOTE U.S.$
1989	Mickey Mantle-handsigned	Retrd.		100.00	695
1989	Mickey Mantle-unsigned	Retrd.		60.00	195
1989	Joe DiMaggio-handsigned	Retrd.		100.00	1200
1989	Joe DiMaggio f/s (blue sig.)	Retrd.		60.00	250
1990	Joe DiMaggio AP-handsigned	Retrd.		N/A	2000

Maruri USA

Eagle Plate Series - W. Gaither

YEAR	ISSUE	EDITION LIMIT	YEAR RETD.	ISSUE PRICE	*QUOTE U.S.$
1984	Free Flight	Closed	1993	150.00	150-198

Memories of Yesterday/Enesco Corporation

Dated Plate Series - Various

YEAR	ISSUE	EDITION LIMIT	YEAR RETD.	ISSUE PRICE	*QUOTE U.S.$
1993	Look Out-Something Good Is Coming Your Way! 530298 - S. Butcher	Yr.Iss.		50.00	50
1994	Pleasant Dreams and Sweet Repose 528102 - M. Atwell	Yr.Iss.		50.00	50
1995	Join Me For a Little Song 134880 - M. Attwell	Yr.Iss.		50.00	50

Museum Collections, Inc.

American Family I - N. Rockwell

YEAR	ISSUE	EDITION LIMIT	YEAR RETD.	ISSUE PRICE	*QUOTE U.S.$
1979	Baby's First Step	9,900		28.50	48
1979	Happy Birthday Dear Mother	9,900		28.50	45
1979	Sweet Sixteen	9,900		28.50	35
1979	First Haircut	9,900		28.50	60
1979	First Prom	9,900		28.50	35
1979	Wrapping Christmas Presents	9,900		28.50	35
1979	The Student	9,900		28.50	35
1979	Birthday Party	9,900		28.50	35
1979	Little Mother	9,900		28.50	35
1979	Washing Our Dog	9,900		28.50	35
1979	Mother's Little Helpers	9,900		28.50	35
1979	Bride and Groom	9,900		28.50	35

*Quotes have been rounded up to nearest dollar

Museum Collections, Inc. to Reco International

PLATES

YEAR ISSUE	EDITION LIMIT	YEAR RETD.	ISSUE PRICE	*QUOTE U.S.$
American Family II - N. Rockwell				
1980 New Arrival	22,500		35.00	50-55
1980 Sweet Dreams	22,500		35.00	38
1980 Little Shaver	22,500		35.00	40
1980 We Missed You Daddy	22,500		35.00	38
1980 Home Run Slugger	22,500		35.00	38
1980 Giving Thanks	22,500		35.00	55
1980 Space Pioneers	22,500		35.00	35
1980 Little Salesman	22,500		35.00	38
1980 Almost Grown up	22,500		35.00	38
1980 Courageous Hero	22,500		35.00	38
1981 At the Circus	22,500		35.00	38
1981 Good Food, Good Friends	22,500		35.00	38
Christmas - N. Rockwell				
1979 Day After Christmas	Yr.Iss		75.00	75
1980 Checking His List	Yr.Iss		75.00	75
1981 Ringing in Good Cheer	Yr.Iss		75.00	75
1982 Waiting for Santa	Yr.Iss		75.00	75
1983 High Hopes	Yr.Iss		75.00	75
1984 Space Age Santa	Yr.Iss		55.00	55
Norman Rockwell Gallery				
Norman Rockwell Centennial - Rockwell Inspired				
1993 The Toymaker	Closed		39.90	65
1993 The Cobbler	Closed		39.90	45-70
Rockwell's Christmas Legacy - Rockwell Inspired				
1992 Santa's Workshop	Closed		49.90	75
1993 Making a List	Closed		49.90	65
1993 While Santa Slumbers	Closed		54.90	60
1993 Visions of Santa	Closed		54.90	60-70
Pemberton & Oakes				
Adventures of Childhood Collection - D. Zolan				
1989 Almost Home	Retrd.		19.60	58
1989 Crystal's Creek	Retrd.		19.60	45
1989 Summer Suds	Retrd.		22.00	40
1990 Snowy Adventure	Retrd.		22.00	37
1991 Forests & Fairy Tales	Retrd.		24.40	35-45
The Best of Zolan in Miniature - D. Zolan				
1985 Sabina	Retrd.		12.50	112
1986 Erik and Dandelion	Retrd.		12.50	100
1986 Tender Moment	Retrd.		12.50	85
1986 Touching the Sky	Retrd.		12.50	83
1987 A Gift for Laurie	Retrd.		12.50	80
1987 Small Wonder	Retrd.		12.50	77
Childhood Discoveries (Miniature) - D. Zolan				
1990 Colors of Spring	Retrd.		14.40	30-40
1990 Autumn Leaves	Retrd.		14.40	45
1991 Enchanted Forest	Retrd.		16.60	35
1991 Just Ducky	Retrd.		16.60	42
1991 Rainy Day Pals	Retrd.		16.60	30
1992 Double Trouble	Retrd.		16.60	36-50
1990 First Kiss	Retrd.		14.40	55
1993 Peppermint Kiss	Retrd.		16.60	25
1995 Tender Hearts	Retrd.		16.60	30
Childhood Friendship Collection - D. Zolan				
1986 Beach Break	Retrd.		19.00	54
1987 Little Engineers	Retrd.		19.00	65
1988 Tiny Treasures	Retrd.		19.00	45-50
1988 Sharing Secrets	Retrd.		19.00	45-70
1988 Dozens of Daisies	Retrd.		19.00	40
1990 Country Walk	Retrd.		19.00	40
Children and Pets - D. Zolan				
1984 Tender Moment	Retrd.		19.00	35-75
1984 Golden Moment	Retrd.		19.00	45-70
1985 Making Friends	Retrd.		19.00	40-60
1985 Tender Beginning	Retrd.		19.00	45
1986 Backyard Discovery	Retrd.		19.00	40-50
1986 Waiting to Play	Retrd.		19.00	45
Children at Christmas - D. Zolan				
1981 A Gift for Laurie	Retrd.		48.00	75
1982 Christmas Prayer	Retrd.		48.00	90
1983 Erik's Delight	Retrd.		48.00	68
1984 Christmas Secret	Retrd.		48.00	66
1985 Christmas Kitten	Retrd.		48.00	65-78
1986 Laurie and the Creche	Retrd.		48.00	75
Christmas (Miniature) - D. Zolan				
1993 Snowy Adventure	Retrd.		16.60	30
1994 Candlelight Magic	Retrd.		16.60	36
Christmas - D. Zolan				
1991 Candlelight Magic	Retrd.		24.80	35-70
Companion to Brotherly Love - D. Zolan				
1989 Sisterly Love	Retrd.		22.00	40-50
Father's Day (Miniature) - D. Zolan				
1994 Two of a Kind	Retrd.		16.60	40
Father's Day - D. Zolan				
1986 Daddy's Home	Retrd.		19.00	60-120
Grandparent's Day - D. Zolan				
1990 It's Grandma & Grandpa	Retrd.		24.40	40
1993 Grandpa's Fence	Retrd.		24.40	45
March of Dimes: Our Children, Our Future - D. Zolan				
1989 A Time for Peace	Retrd.		29.00	40-50
Members Only Single Issue (Miniature) - D. Zolan				
1990 By Myself	Retrd.		14.40	45-55
1993 Summer's Child	Retrd.		16.60	43
1994 Little Slugger	10-day		16.60	37
Membership (Miniature) - D. Zolan				
1987 For You	Retrd.		12.50	102
1988 Making Friends	Retrd.		12.50	75
1989 Grandma's Garden	Retrd.		12.50	72
1990 A Christmas Prayer	Retrd.		14.40	54
1991 Golden Moment	Retrd.		15.00	47
1992 Brotherly Love	Retrd.		15.00	60-90
1993 New Shoes	Retrd.		17.00	40
1994 My Kitty	19-day		Gift	34
Moments To Remember (Miniature) - D. Zolan				
1992 Just We Two	Retrd.		16.60	55
1992 Almost Home	Retrd.		16.60	30-40
1993 Tiny Treasures	Retrd.		16.60	30
1993 Forest Friends	Retrd.		16.60	30
Mother's Day (Miniature) - D. Zolan				
1990 Flowers for Mother	Retrd.		14.40	40
1992 Twilight Prayer	Retrd.		16.60	30
1993 Jessica's Field	Retrd.		16.60	30-40
1994 One Summer Day	Retrd.		16.60	55
Mother's Day - D. Zolan				
1988 Mother's Angels	Retrd.		19.00	60-75
Nutcracker II - Various				
1981 Grand Finale - S. Fisher	Retrd.		24.40	36
1982 Arabian Dancers - S. Fisher	Retrd.		24.40	68
1983 Dew Drop Fairy - S. Fisher	Retrd.		24.40	36
1984 Clara's Delight - S. Fisher	Retrd.		24.40	42
1985 Bedtime for Nutcracker - S. Fisher	Retrd.		24.40	45
1986 The Crowning of Clara - S. Fisher	Retrd.		24.40	36
1987 Dance of the Snowflakes - D. Zolan	Retrd.		24.40	50-75
1988 The Royal Welcome - R. Anderson	Retrd.		24.40	35
1989 The Spanish Dancer - M. Vickers	Retrd.		24.40	45
Plaques - D. Zolan				
1991 New Shoes	Retrd.		18.80	36
1992 Grandma's Garden	Retrd.		18.80	30
1992 Small Wonder	Retrd.		18.80	20
1992 Easter Morning	Retrd.		18.80	25
Single Issues (Miniature) - D. Zolan				
1986 Backyard Discovery	Retrd.		12.50	107
1986 Daddy's Home	Retrd.		12.50	820
1989 Sunny Surprise	Retrd.		12.50	55
1989 My Pumpkin	Retrd.		14.40	60
1991 Backyard Buddies	Retrd.		16.60	35
1991 The Thinker	Retrd.		16.60	39
1993 Quiet Time	Retrd.		16.60	50-66
1994 Little Fisherman	19-day		16.60	36
Special Moments of Childhood Collection - D. Zolan				
1988 Brotherly Love	Retrd.		19.00	70-95
1988 Sunny Surprise	Retrd.		19.00	25-55
1989 Summer's Child	Retrd.		22.00	35-45
1990 Meadow Magic	Retrd.		22.00	25-35
1990 Cone For Two	Retrd.		24.60	30-36
1990 Rodeo Girl	Retrd.		24.60	35
Tenth Anniversary - D. Zolan				
1988 Ribbons and Roses	Retrd.		24.40	30-45
Thanksgiving (Miniature) - D. Zolan				
1993 I'm Thankful Too	Retrd.		16.60	35-75
Thanksgiving - D. Zolan				
1981 I'm Thankful Too	Retrd.		19.00	50-75
Times To Treasure Bone China (Miniature) - D. Zolan				
1993 Little Traveler	Retrd.		16.60	36
1993 Garden Swing	Retrd.		16.60	29
1994 Summer Garden	19-day		16.60	25
1994 September Girl	19-day		16.60	25
Wonder of Childhood - D. Zolan				
1982 Touching the Sky	Retrd.		19.00	25-52
1983 Spring Innocence	Retrd.		19.00	20-45
1984 Winter Angel	Retrd.		22.00	30-60
1985 Small Wonder	Retrd.		22.00	30-50
1986 Grandma's Garden	Retrd.		22.00	27-45
1987 Day Dreamer	Retrd.		22.00	27-50
Yesterday's Children (Miniature) - D. Zolan				
1994 Little Friends	19-day		16.60	40
1994 Seaside Treasures	19-day		16.60	30
Zolan's Children - D. Zolan				
1978 Erik and Dandelion	Retrd.		19.00	90-225
1979 Sabina in the Grass	Retrd.		22.00	70-150
1980 By Myself	Retrd.		24.00	45-60
1981 For You	Retrd.		24.00	30-36
Precious Moments/Enesco Corporation				
Beauty of Christmas Collection - S. Butcher				
1994 You're as Pretty as a Christmas Tree 530409	Yr.Iss		50.00	50
1995 He Covers the Earth With His Beauty 142670	Yr.Iss		50.00	50
1996 Peace On Earth...Anyway 183377	Yr.Iss		50.00	50
Christmas Blessings - S. Butcher				
1990 Wishing You A Yummy Christmas 523801	Yr.Iss		50.00	50
1991 Blessings From Me To Thee 523860	Yr.Iss		50.00	55
1992 But The Greatest of These Is Love 527742	Yr.Iss		50.00	50
1993 Wishing You the Sweetest Christmas 530204	Yr.Iss		50.00	50
Christmas Collection - S. Butcher				
1981 Come Let Us Adore Him E-5646	15,000		40.00	50-65
1982 Let Heaven and Nature Sing E-2347	15,000		40.00	40
1983 Wee Three Kings-E-0538	15,000		40.00	50
1984 Unto Us a Child Is Born E-5395	15,000		40.00	50
Christmas Love Series - S. Butcher				
1986 I'm Sending You a White Christmas 101834	Yr.Iss		45.00	55
1987 My Peace I Give Unto Thee 102954	Yr.Iss		45.00	90
1988 Merry Christmas Deer 520284	Yr.Iss		50.00	55
1989 May Your Christmas Be A Happy Home 523003	Yr.Iss		50.00	55
The Four Seasons Series - S. Butcher				
1985 The Voice of Spring 12106	Yr.Iss		40.00	110-120
1985 Summer's Joy 12114	Yr.Iss		40.00	85-100
1986 Autumn's Praise 12122	Yr.Iss		40.00	53
1986 Winter's Song 12130	Yr.Iss		40.00	58
Inspired Thoughts Series - S. Butcher				
1981 Love One Another E-5215	15,000		40.00	60
1982 Make a Joyful Noise E-7174	15,000		40.00	45
1983 I Believe In Miracles E-9257	15,000		40.00	50
1984 Love is Kind E-2847	15,000		40.00	50
Joy of Christmas Series - S. Butcher				
1982 I'll Play My Drum For Him E-2357	Yr.Iss		40.00	75
1983 Christmastime is for Sharing E-0505	Yr.Iss		40.00	60-75
1984 The Wonder of Christmas E-5396	Yr.Iss		40.00	50
1985 Tell Me the Story of Jesus 15237	Yr.Iss		40.00	90-115
Mother's Day Series - S. Butcher				
1981 Mother Sew Dear E-5217	15,000		40.00	60
1982 The Purr-fect Grandma E-7173	15,000		40.00	45
1983 The Hand that Rocks the Future E-9256	15,000		40.00	40
1984 Loving Thy Neighbor E-2848	15,000		40.00	
1994 Mothers of Yours Is What I Really Like to Do 531766	Yr.Iss		50.00	50
1996 Of All The Mothers I Have Known There's None As Precious As My Own 163716	Yr.Iss		50.00	50
Open Editions - S. Butcher				
1982 Our First Christmas Together E-2378	Suspd.		30.00	45-55
1981 The Lord Bless You and Keep You E-5216	Suspd.		30.00	40-45
1982 Rejoicing with You E-7172	Suspd.		30.00	40
1983 Jesus Loves Me E-9275	Suspd.		30.00	45-48
1983 Jesus Loves Me E-9276	Suspd.		30.00	45
1994 Bring The Little Ones To Jesus 531359	Yr.Iss		50.00	50
Precious Moments - S. Butcher				
1995 He Hath Made Everything Beautiful in His Time 129151	Open		50.00	50
Reco International				
Amish Traditions - B. Farnsworth				
1994 Golden Harvest	95-day		29.50	30
1994 Family Outing	95-day		29.50	30
1994 The Quilting Bee	95-day		29.50	30
1995 Last Day of School	95-day		29.50	30
Barefoot Children - S. Kuck				
1987 Night-Time Story	Retrd.	1994	29.50	45
1987 Golden Afternoon	Retrd.	1996	29.50	30
1988 Little Sweethearts	Retrd.	1995	29.50	40
1988 Carousel Magic	Retrd.	1996	29.50	30
1988 Under the Apple Tree	Retrd.	1995	29.50	45
1988 The Rehearsal	Retrd.	1995	29.50	60
1988 Pretty as a Picture	Retrd.	1993	29.50	45
1988 Grandma's Trunk	Retrd.	1993	29.50	45

Becky's Day - J. McClelland

YEAR ISSUE		EDITION LIMIT	YEAR RETD.	ISSUE PRICE	*QUOTE U.S.$
1985	Awakening	90-day		24.50	25
1985	Getting Dressed	Retrd.	1988	24.50	29
1986	Breakfast	Retrd.	1987	27.50	35
1986	Learning is Fun	Retrd.	1988	27.50	28
1986	Muffin Making	Retrd.	1989	27.50	28
1986	Tub Time	Retrd.	1989	27.50	35
1986	Evening Prayer	Retrd.	1990	27.50	28

Birds of the Hidden Forest - G. Ratnavira

1994	Macaw Waterfall	96-day		29.50	30
1994	Paradise Valley	96-day		29.50	30
1995	Toucan Treasure	96-day		29.50	30

Bohemian Annuals - Factory Artist

1974	1974	Retrd.	1975	130.00	155
1975	1975	Retrd.	1976	140.00	160
1976	1976	Retrd.	1978	150.00	160

Castles & Dreams - J. Bergsma

1992	The Birth of a Dream	48-day		29.50	30
1992	Dreams Come True	48-day		29.50	30
1993	Believe In Your Dreams	48-day		29.50	30
1994	Follow Your Dreams	48-day		29.50	30

A Childhood Almanac - S. Kuck

1985	Fireside Dreams-January	Retrd.	1991	29.50	35-49
1985	Be Mine-February	Retrd.	1992	29.50	35-45
1986	Winds of March-March	Retrd.	1994	29.50	35-50
1985	Easter Morning-April	Retrd.	1992	29.50	35
1985	For Mom-May	Retrd.	1992	29.50	35-45
1985	Just Dreaming-June	Retrd.	1992	29.50	35-55
1985	Star Spangled Sky-July	Retrd.	1995	29.50	35-45
1985	Summer Secrets-August	Retrd.	1991	29.50	35-53
1985	School Days-September	Retrd.	1991	29.50	35-60
1986	Indian Summer-October	Retrd.	1991	29.50	35-45
1986	Giving Thanks-November	Retrd.	1995	29.50	35-49
1985	Christmas Magic-December	Retrd.	1995	35.00	40-70

A Children's Christmas Pageant - S. Kuck

1986	Silent Night	Retrd.	1987	32.50	80-90
1987	Hark the Herald Angels Sing	Retrd.	1988	32.50	45
1988	While Shepherds Watched...	Retrd.	1990	32.50	33
1989	We Three Kings	Yr.Iss.	N/A	32.50	35

The Children's Garden - J. McClelland

1993	Garden Friends	Retrd.	1996	29.50	30
1993	Tea for Three	Retrd.	1996	29.50	30
1993	Puppy Love	Retrd.	1996	29.50	30

Christening Gift - S. Kuck

1995	God's Gift	Open		29.90	30

The Christmas Series - J. Bergsma

1990	Down The Glistening Lane	Retrd.	1996	35.00	35
1991	A Child Is Born	Retrd.	1996	35.00	35
1992	Christmas Day	Retrd.	1996	35.00	35
1993	I Wish You An Angel	Retrd.	1996	35.00	35

Christmas Wishes - J. Bergsma

1994	I Wish You Love	75-day		29.50	30
1995	I Wish You Joy	75-day		29.50	30
1996	I Wish You Peace	75-day		29.50	30

Days Gone By - S. Kuck

1983	Sunday Best	Retrd.	1984	29.50	36-55
1983	Amy's Magic Horse	Retrd.	1985	29.50	30
1984	Little Anglers	Retrd.	1985	29.50	30
1984	Afternoon Recital	Retrd.	1985	29.50	50
1984	Little Tutor	Retrd.	1985	29.50	30
1985	Easter at Grandma's	Retrd.	1985	29.50	30
1985	Morning Song	Retrd.	1986	29.50	30
1985	The Surrey Ride	Retrd.	1987	29.50	30

Dresden Christmas - Factory Artist

1971	Shepherd Scene	Retrd.	1978	15.00	50
1972	Niklas Church	Retrd.	1978	15.00	25
1973	Schwanstein Church	Retrd.	1978	18.00	35
1974	Village Scene	Retrd.	1978	20.00	30
1975	Rothenburg Scene	Retrd.	1978	24.00	30
1976	Village Church	Retrd.	1978	26.00	35
1977	Old Mill	Retrd.	1978	28.00	30

Dresden Mother's Day - Factory Artist

1972	Doe and Fawn	Retrd.	1979	15.00	20
1973	Mare and Colt	Retrd.	1979	16.00	25
1974	Tiger and Cub	Retrd.	1979	20.00	23
1975	Dachshunds	Retrd.	1979	24.00	28
1976	Owl and Offspring	Retrd.	1979	26.00	30
1977	Chamois	Retrd.	1979	28.00	30

Eagle of America - S. Barlowe

1996	Land of The Free	96-day		29.90	30

The Enchanted Norfin Trolls - C. Hopkins

1993	Troll Maiden	Retrd.	1996	19.50	20
1993	The Wizard Troll	Retrd.	1996	19.50	20
1993	The Troll and His Dragon	Retrd.	1996	19.50	20
1994	Troll in Shinning Armor	Retrd.	1996	19.50	20
1994	Minstrel Troll	Retrd.	1996	19.50	20
1994	If Trolls Could Fly	Retrd.	1996	19.50	20
1994	Chef le Troll	Retrd.	1996	19.50	20
1994	Queen of Trolls	Retrd.	1996	19.50	20

Everlasing Friends - S. Kuck

1996	Sharing Secrets	95-day		29.95	30
1996	Sharing Dreams	95-day		29.95	30
1997	Sharing Beauty	95-day		29.95	30

Fishtales - R. Manning

1997	Rainbow River	76-day		29.90	30

The Flower Fairies Year Collection - C.M. Barker

1990	The Red Clover Fairy	Retrd.	1996	29.50	30
1990	The Wild Cherry Blossom Fairy	Retrd.	1996	29.50	30
1990	The Pine Tree Fairy	Retrd.	1996	29.50	30
1990	The Rose Hip Fairy	Retrd.	1996	29.50	30

Four Seasons - J. Poluszynski

1973	Spring	Retrd.	1975	50.00	75
1973	Summer	Retrd.	1975	50.00	75
1973	Fall	Retrd.	1975	50.00	75
1973	Winter	Retrd.	1975	50.00	75

Friends For Keeps - S. Kuck

1996	Puppy Love	95-day		29.95	30
1996	Gone Fishing	95-day		29.95	30
1997	Golden Days	95-day		29.95	30

Furstenberg Christmas - Factory Artist

1971	Rabbits	Retrd.	1977	15.00	30
1972	Snowy Village	Retrd.	1977	15.00	20
1973	Christmas Eve	Retrd.	1977	18.00	35
1974	Sparrows	Retrd.	1977	20.00	30
1975	Deer Family	Retrd.	1977	22.00	30
1976	Winter Birds	Retrd.	1977	25.00	25

Furstenberg Deluxe Christmas - E. Grossberg

1971	Wise Men	Retrd.	1974	45.00	45
1972	Holy Family	Retrd.	1974	45.00	45
1973	Christmas Eve	Retrd.	1974	60.00	65

Furstenberg Easter - Factory Artist

1971	Sheep	Retrd.	1973	15.00	150
1972	Chicks	Retrd.	1975	15.00	60
1973	Bunnies	Retrd.	1976	16.00	80
1974	Pussywillow	Retrd.	1976	20.00	33
1975	Easter Window	Retrd.	1977	22.00	30
1976	Flower Collecting	Retrd.	1977	25.00	25

Furstenberg Mother's Day - Factory Artist

1972	Hummingbirds, Fe	Retrd.	1974	15.00	45
1973	Hedgehogs	Retrd.	1974	16.00	40
1974	Doe and Fawn	Retrd.	1974	20.00	30
1975	Swans	Retrd.	1976	22.00	23
1976	Koala Bears	Retrd.	1976	25.00	30

Furstenberg Olympic - J. Poluszynski

1972	Munich	Retrd.	1972	20.00	75
1976	Montreal	Retrd.	1976	37.50	38

Games Children Play - S. Kuck

1979	Me First	Retrd.	1983	45.00	50
1980	Forever Bubbles	Retrd.	1983	45.00	48
1981	Skating Pals	Retrd.	1983	45.00	48
1982	Join Me	10,000		45.00	45

Gardens of Beauty - D. Barlowe

1988	English Country Garden	Retrd.	1996	29.50	30
1988	Dutch Country Garden	Retrd.	1996	29.50	30
1988	New England Garden	Retrd.	1996	29.50	30
1988	Japanese Garden	Retrd.	1996	29.50	30
1989	Italian Garden	Retrd.	1996	29.50	30
1989	Hawaiian Garden	Retrd.	1996	29.50	30
1989	German Country Garden	Retrd.	1996	29.50	30
1989	Mexican Garden	Retrd.	1996	29.50	30
1992	Colonial Splendor	Retrd.	1994	29.50	30

Gift of Love Mother's Day Collection - S. Kuck

1993	Morning Glory	Retrd.	1994	65.00	65
1994	Memories From The Heart	Retrd.	1994	65.00	65

The Glory Of Christ - C. Micarelli

1992	The Ascension	48-day		29.50	30
1993	Jesus Teaching	48-day		29.50	30
1993	The Last Supper	48-day		29.50	30
1993	The Nativity	48-day		29.50	30
1993	The Baptism Of Christ	48-day		29.50	30
1993	Jesus Heals The Sick	48-day		29.50	30
1994	Jesus Walks On Water	48-day		29.50	30
1994	Descent From The Cross	48-day		29.50	30

God's Own Country - I. Drechsler

1990	Daybreak	Retrd.	1996	30.00	30
1990	Coming Home	Retrd.	1996	30.00	30
1990	Peaceful Gathering	Retrd.	1996	30.00	30
1990	Quiet Waters	Retrd.	1996	30.00	30

The Grandparent Collector's Plates - S. Kuck

1981	Grandma's Cookie Jar	Yr.Iss.		37.50	38
1981	Grandpa and the Dollhouse	Yr.Iss.		37.50	38

Great Stories from the Bible - G. Katz

1987	Moses in the Bulrushes	Retrd.	1994	29.50	30
1987	King Saul & David	Retrd.	1994	29.50	30
1987	Moses and the Ten Commandments	Retrd.	1994	29.50	30-38
1987	Joseph's Coat of Many Colors	Retrd.	1994	29.50	30
1988	Rebekah at the Well	Retrd.	1994	29.50	35
1988	Daniel Reads the Writing on the Wall	Retrd.	1994	29.50	35
1988	The Story of Ruth	Retrd.	1994	29.50	35
1988	King Solomon	Retrd.	1994	29.50	35

Guardians Of The Kingdom - J. Bergsma

1990	Rainbow To Ride On	Retrd.	1993	35.00	37
1990	Special Friends Are Few	17,500		35.00	35
1990	Guardians Of The Innocent Children	17,500		35.00	35
1990	The Miracle Of Love	17,500		35.00	35
1991	The Magic Of Love	17,500		35.00	35
1991	Only With The Heart	17,500		35.00	35
1991	To Fly Without Wings	17,500		35.00	35
1991	In Faith I Am Free	17,500		35.00	35

Guiding Lights - D Hahlbohm

1996	Robbins Reef	96-day		29.90	30
1996	Cape Hateras	96-day		29.90	30

Haven of the Hunters - H. Roe

1994	Eagle's Castle	Retrd.	1996	29.50	30
1994	Sanctuary of the Hawk	Retrd.	1996	29.50	30

Hearts And Flowers - S. Kuck

1991	Patience	120-day		29.50	45
1991	Tea Party	120-day		29.50	55
1992	Cat's In The Cradle	120-day		32.50	45
1992	Carousel of Dreams	120-day		32.50	33
1992	Storybook Memories	120-day		32.50	33
1993	Delightful Bundle	120-day		34.50	35
1993	Easter Morning Visitor	120-day		34.50	35
1993	Me and My Pony	120-day		34.50	40

Imaginary Gardens - S. Somerville

1996	Pussywillows	76-day		29.90	30
1996	Dogwood	76-day		29.90	30

In The Eye of The Storm - W. Lowe

1991	First Strike	Retrd.	1996	29.50	30
1992	Night Force	Retrd.	1996	29.50	30
1992	Tracks Across The Sand	Retrd.	1996	29.50	30
1992	The Storm Has Landed	Retrd.	1996	29.50	30

J. Bergsma Mother's Day Series - J. Bergsma

1990	The Beauty Of Life	Retrd.	1996	35.00	35
1992	Life's Blessing	Retrd.	1996	35.00	35
1993	My Greatest Treasures	Retrd.	1996	35.00	35
1994	Forever In My Heart	Retrd.	1996	35.00	35

King's Christmas - Merli

1973	Adoration	Retrd.	1974	100.00	265
1974	Madonna	Retrd.	1975	150.00	250
1975	Heavenly Choir	Retrd.	1976	160.00	235
1976	Siblings	Retrd.	1978	200.00	225

King's Flowers - A. Falchi

1973	Carnation	Retrd.	1974	85.00	130
1974	Red Rose	Retrd.	1975	100.00	145
1975	Yellow Dahlia	Retrd.	1976	110.00	162
1976	Bluebells	Retrd.	1977	130.00	165
1977	Anemones	Retrd.	1979	130.00	175

King's Mother's Day - Merli

1973	Dancing Girl	Retrd.	1974	100.00	225
1974	Dancing Boy	Retrd.	1975	115.00	250
1975	Motherly Love	Retrd.	1976	140.00	225
1976	Maiden	Retrd.	1978	180.00	200

Kingdom of the Great Cats - P. Jepson

1995	Out of the Mist	36-day		29.50	30
1995	Summit Sanctuary	36-day		29.50	30

Kittens 'N Hats - S. Somerville

1994	Opening Night	48-day		29.50	30
1994	Sitting Pretty	48-day		29.50	30
1995	Little League	48-day		29.50	30

Little Angel Plate Collection - S. Kuck

1994	Angel of Charity	95-day		29.50	30
1994	Angel of Joy	95-day		29.50	30

Little Professionals - S. Kuck

1982	All is Well	Retrd.	1983	39.50	95
1983	Tender Loving Care	Retrd.	1985	39.50	50-75
1984	Lost and Found	Retrd.	1995	39.50	45
1985	Reading, Writing and...	Retrd.	1989	39.50	45

Magic Companions - J. Bergsma

1994	Believe in Love	48-day		29.50	30
1994	Imagine Peace	48-day		29.50	30

*Quotes have been rounded up to nearest dollar

Reco International
to Reco International

PLATES

Year Issue		Edition Limit	Year Retd.	Issue Price	*Quote U.S.$
1995	Live in Harmony	48-day		29.50	30
1995	Trust in Magic	48-day		29.50	30

March of Dimes: Our Children, Our Future - Various

Year Issue		Edition Limit	Year Retd.	Issue Price	*Quote U.S.$
1989	A Time to Love (2nd in Series) - S. Kuck	Retrd.	1993	29.00	40
1989	A Time to Plant (3rd in Series) - J. McClelland	150-day	1993	29.00	50

Marmot Christmas - Factory Artist

Year Issue		Edition Limit	Year Retd.	Issue Price	*Quote U.S.$
1970	Polar Bear, Fe	Retrd.	1971	13.00	60
1971	Buffalo Bill	Retrd.	1972	16.00	55
1972	Boy and Grandfather	Retrd.	1973	20.00	50
1971	American Buffalo	Retrd.	1973	14.50	35
1973	Snowman	Retrd.	1974	22.00	45
1974	Dancing	Retrd.	1975	24.00	30
1975	Quail	Retrd.	1976	30.00	40
1976	Windmill	Retrd.	1978	40.00	40

Marmot Father's Day - Factory Artist

Year Issue		Edition Limit	Year Retd.	Issue Price	*Quote U.S.$
1970	Stag	Retrd.	1970	12.00	100
1971	Horse	Retrd.	1972	12.50	40

Marmot Mother's Day - Factory Artist

Year Issue		Edition Limit	Year Retd.	Issue Price	*Quote U.S.$
1972	Seal	Retrd.	1973	16.00	60
1973	Bear with Cub	Retrd.	1974	20.00	140
1974	Penguins	Retrd.	1975	24.00	50
1975	Raccoons	Retrd.	1976	30.00	45
1976	Ducks	Retrd.	1977	40.00	40

The McClelland Children's Circus Collection - J. McClelland

Year Issue		Edition Limit	Year Retd.	Issue Price	*Quote U.S.$
1982	Tommy the Clown	Retrd.	N/A	29.50	49
1982	Katie, the Tightrope Walker	Retrd.	N/A	29.50	49
1983	Johnny the Strongman	Retrd.	N/A	29.50	39
1984	Maggie the Animal Trainer	Retrd.	N/A	29.50	30

Memories of Childhood - C. Getz

Year Issue		Edition Limit	Year Retd.	Issue Price	*Quote U.S.$
1994	Teatime with Teddy	75-day		29.50	30
1995	Bases Loaded	75-day		29.50	30
1996	Mommy's Little Helper	75-day		29.50	30

Memories Of Yesterday - M. Attwell

Year Issue		Edition Limit	Year Retd.	Issue Price	*Quote U.S.$
1993	Hush	Retrd.	1996	29.50	30
1993	Time For Bed	Retrd.	1996	29.50	30
1993	I'se Been Painting	Retrd.	1996	29.50	30
1993	Just Looking Pretty	Retrd.	1996	29.50	30
1994	Give it Your Best Shot	Retrd.	1996	29.50	30
1994	I Pray The Lord My Soul to Keep	Retrd.	1996	29.50	30
1994	Just Thinking About You	Retrd.	1996	29.50	30
1994	What Will I Grow Up To Be	Retrd.	1996	29.50	30

Moments At Home - S. Kuck

Year Issue		Edition Limit	Year Retd.	Issue Price	*Quote U.S.$
1995	Moments of Caring	95-day		29.90	30
1995	Moments of Tenderness	95-day		29.90	30
1995	Moments of Friendship	95-day		29.90	30
1995	Moments of Sharing	95-day		29.90	30
1995	Moments of Love	95-day		29.90	30
1996	Moments of Reflection	95-day		29.90	30

Moser Christmas - Factory Artist

Year Issue		Edition Limit	Year Retd.	Issue Price	*Quote U.S.$
1970	Hradcany Castle	Retrd.	1971	75.00	170
1971	Karlstein Castle	Retrd.	1972	75.00	80
1972	Old Town Hall	Retrd.	1973	85.00	85
1973	Karlovy Vary Castle	Retrd.	1974	90.00	100

Moser Mother's Day - Factory Artist

Year Issue		Edition Limit	Year Retd.	Issue Price	*Quote U.S.$
1971	Peacocks	Retrd.	1971	75.00	100
1972	Butterflies	Retrd.	1972	85.00	90
1973	Squirrels	Retrd.	1973	90.00	95

Mother Goose - J. McClelland

Year Issue		Edition Limit	Year Retd.	Issue Price	*Quote U.S.$
1979	Mary, Mary	Retrd.	1979	22.50	60-120
1980	Little Boy Blue	Retrd.	1980	22.50	25
1981	Little Miss Muffet	Yr.Iss.		24.50	25
1982	Little Jack Horner	Retrd.	1982	24.50	30-40
1983	Little Bo Peep	Yr.Iss.		24.50	25
1984	Diddle, Diddle Dumpling	Yr.Iss.		24.50	25-40
1985	Mary Had a Little Lamb	Yr.Iss.		27.50	28
1986	Jack and Jill	Retrd.	1988	27.50	40

Mother's Day Collection - S. Kuck

Year Issue		Edition Limit	Year Retd.	Issue Price	*Quote U.S.$
1985	Once Upon a Time	Retrd.	1987	29.50	40-50
1986	Times Remembered	Yr.Iss.		29.50	30
1987	A Cherished Time	Yr.Iss.		29.50	30
1988	A Time Together	Yr.Iss.		29.50	30

Noble and Free - Kelly

Year Issue		Edition Limit	Year Retd.	Issue Price	*Quote U.S.$
1994	Gathering Storm	95-day		29.50	30
1994	Protected Journey	95-day		29.50	30
1994	Moonlight Run	95-day		29.50	30

The Nutcracker Ballet - C. Micarelli

Year Issue		Edition Limit	Year Retd.	Issue Price	*Quote U.S.$
1989	Christmas Eve Party	Retrd.	1994	35.00	35
1990	Clara And Her Prince	14-day		35.00	35
1990	The Dream Begins	14-day		35.00	35
1991	Dance of the Snow Fairies	Retrd.	1994	35.00	35
1992	The Land of Sweets	14-day		35.00	35
1992	The Sugar Plum Fairy	14-day		35.00	35

The Open Road - B. Farnsworth

Year Issue		Edition Limit	Year Retd.	Issue Price	*Quote U.S.$
1997	Lakeside Drive	76-day		29.90	30

Oscar & Bertie's Edwardian Holiday - P.D. Jackson

Year Issue		Edition Limit	Year Retd.	Issue Price	*Quote U.S.$
1991	Snapshot	Retrd.	1996	29.50	30
1992	Early Rise	Retrd.	1996	29.50	30
1992	All Aboard	Retrd.	1996	29.50	30
1992	Learning To Swim	Retrd.	1996	29.50	30

Our Cherished Seas - S. Barlowe

Year Issue		Edition Limit	Year Retd.	Issue Price	*Quote U.S.$
1991	Whale Song	48-day		37.50	38
1991	Lions of the Sea	48-day		37.50	38
1991	Flight of the Dolphins	48-day		37.50	38
1992	Palace of the Seals	48-day		37.50	38
1992	Orca Ballet	48-day		37.50	38
1993	Emperors of the Ice	48-day		37.50	38
1993	Turtle Treasure	48-day		37.50	38
1993	Splendor of the Sea	48-day		37.50	38

Out of The Wild - S. Barlowe

Year Issue		Edition Limit	Year Retd.	Issue Price	*Quote U.S.$
1996	The Pride	76-day		29.90	30

Plate Of The Month Collection - S. Kuck

Year Issue		Edition Limit	Year Retd.	Issue Price	*Quote U.S.$
1990	January	Retrd.	1996	25.00	25
1990	February	Retrd.	1996	25.00	25
1990	March	Retrd.	1996	25.00	25
1990	April	Retrd.	1996	25.00	25
1990	May	Retrd.	1996	25.00	25
1990	June	Retrd.	1996	25.00	25
1990	July	Retrd.	1996	25.00	25
1990	August	Retrd.	1996	25.00	25
1990	September	Retrd.	1996	25.00	25
1990	October	Retrd.	1996	25.00	25
1990	November	Retrd.	1996	25.00	25
1990	December	Retrd.	1996	25.00	25

Precious Angels - S. Kuck

Year Issue		Edition Limit	Year Retd.	Issue Price	*Quote U.S.$
1995	Angel of Grace	95-day		29.90	30
1995	Angel of Happiness	95-day		29.90	30
1995	Angel of Hope	95-day		29.90	30
1995	Angel of Laughter	95-day		29.90	30
1995	Angel of Love	95-day		29.90	30
1995	Angel of Peace	95-day		29.90	30
1995	Angel of Sharing	95-day		29.90	30
1995	Angel of Sunshine	95-day		29.90	30

The Premier Collection - J. McClelland

Year Issue		Edition Limit	Year Retd.	Issue Price	*Quote U.S.$
1991	Love	7,500	1996	75.00	75

Premier Collection - S. Kuck

Year Issue		Edition Limit	Year Retd.	Issue Price	*Quote U.S.$
1991	Puppy	Retrd.	1993	95.00	125-150
1991	Kitten	Retrd.	1992	95.00	100-125
1992	La Belle	7,500	1996	95.00	95
1992	Le Beau	7,500	1996	95.00	95

Royal Mother's Day - Factory Artist

Year Issue		Edition Limit	Year Retd.	Issue Price	*Quote U.S.$
1970	Swan and Young	Retrd.	1971	12.00	80
1971	Doe and Fawn	Retrd.	1972	13.00	55
1972	Rabbits	Retrd.	1973	16.00	40
1973	Owl Family	Retrd.	1974	18.00	40
1974	Duck and Young	Retrd.	1975	22.00	40
1975	Lynx and Cubs	Retrd.	1976	26.00	40
1976	Woodcock and Young	Retrd.	1978	27.50	33
1977	Koala Bear	Retrd.	1978	30.00	30

Royale - Factory Artist

Year Issue		Edition Limit	Year Retd.	Issue Price	*Quote U.S.$
1969	Apollo Moon Landing	Retrd.	1969	30.00	80

Royale Christmas - Factory Artist

Year Issue		Edition Limit	Year Retd.	Issue Price	*Quote U.S.$
1969	Christmas Fair	Retrd.	1970	12.00	125
1970	Vigil Mass	Retrd.	1971	13.00	110
1971	Christmas Night	Retrd.	1972	16.00	50
1972	Elks	Retrd.	1973	16.00	45
1973	Christmas Down	Retrd.	1974	20.00	38
1974	Village Christmas	Retrd.	1975	22.00	60
1975	Feeding Time	Retrd.	1976	26.00	35
1976	Seaport Christmas	Retrd.	1977	27.50	30
1977	Sledding	Retrd.	1978	30.00	30

Royale Father's Day - Factory Artist

Year Issue		Edition Limit	Year Retd.	Issue Price	*Quote U.S.$
1970	Frigate Constitution	Retrd.	1971	13.00	80
1971	Man Fishing	Retrd.	1972	13.00	35
1972	Mountaineer	Retrd.	1973	16.00	55
1973	Camping	Retrd.	1974	18.00	45
1974	Eagle	Retrd.	1975	22.00	35
1975	Regatta	Retrd.	1976	26.00	35
1976	Hunting	Retrd.	1977	27.50	33
1977	Fishing	Retrd.	1978	30.00	30

Royale Game Plates - Various

Year Issue		Edition Limit	Year Retd.	Issue Price	*Quote U.S.$
1972	Setters - J. Poluszynski	Retrd.	1974	180.00	200
1973	Fox - J. Poluszynski	Retrd.	1975	200.00	250
1974	Osprey - W. Schiener	Retrd.	1976	250.00	250
1975	California Quail - W. Schiener	Retrd.	1976	265.00	265

Royale Germania Christmas Annual - Factory Artist

Year Issue		Edition Limit	Year Retd.	Issue Price	*Quote U.S.$
1970	Orchid	Retrd.	1971	200.00	650
1971	Cyclamen	Retrd.	1972	200.00	325
1972	Silver Thistle	Retrd.	1973	250.00	290
1973	Tulips	Retrd.	1974	275.00	310
1974	Sunflowers	Retrd.	1975	300.00	320
1975	Snowdrops	Retrd.	1976	450.00	500

Royale Germania Crystal Mother's Day - Factory Artist

Year Issue		Edition Limit	Year Retd.	Issue Price	*Quote U.S.$
1971	Roses	Retrd.	1971	135.00	650
1972	Elephant and Youngster	Retrd.	1972	180.00	250
1973	Koala Bear and Cub	Retrd.	1973	200.00	225
1974	Squirrels	Retrd.	1974	240.00	250
1975	Swan and Young	Retrd.	1975	350.00	360

Sandra Kuck Mothers' Day - S. Kuck

Year Issue		Edition Limit	Year Retd.	Issue Price	*Quote U.S.$
1995	Home is Where the Heart Is	48-day		35.00	35
1996	Dear To The Heart	48-day		35.00	35

Sculpted Heirlooms - S. Kuck

Year Issue		Edition Limit	Year Retd.	Issue Price	*Quote U.S.$
1996	Best Friends (sculpted plate)	24-mo.		29.95	30
1996	Tea Party (sculpted plate)	24-mo.		29.90	30
1996	Storybook Memories (sculpted plate)	24-mo.		29.90	30
1996	Patience (sculpted plate)	24-mo.		29.90	30

Songs From The Garden - G. Ratnavira

Year Issue		Edition Limit	Year Retd.	Issue Price	*Quote U.S.$
1996	Love Song	76-day		29.90	30
1996	Rhapsody In Blue	76-day		29.90	30
1997	Hummingbirds In Harmony	76-day		29.90	30

The Sophisticated Ladies Collection - A. Fazio

Year Issue		Edition Limit	Year Retd.	Issue Price	*Quote U.S.$
1985	Felicia	21-day		29.50	30
1985	Samantha	21-day	1994	29.50	33
1985	Phoebe	21-day	1994	29.50	33
1985	Cleo	21-day		29.50	30
1986	Cerissa	21-day	1994	29.50	33
1986	Natasha	21-day	1994	29.50	33
1986	Bianka	21-day	1994	29.50	33
1986	Chelsea	21-day	1994	29.50	33

Special Occasions by Reco - S. Kuck

Year Issue		Edition Limit	Year Retd.	Issue Price	*Quote U.S.$
1988	The Wedding	Open		35.00	35
1989	Wedding Day (6 1/2")	Retrd.	1996	25.00	25
1990	The Special Day	Retrd.	1996	25.00	25

Special Occasions-Wedding - C. Micarelli

Year Issue		Edition Limit	Year Retd.	Issue Price	*Quote U.S.$
1991	From This Day Forward (9 1/2")	Open		35.00	35
1991	From This Day Forward (6 1/2")	Retrd.	1996	25.00	25
1991	To Have And To Hold (9 1/2")	Open		35.00	35
1991	To Have And To Hold (6 1/2")	Retrd.	1996	25.00	25

Sugar and Spice - S. Kuck

Year Issue		Edition Limit	Year Retd.	Issue Price	*Quote U.S.$
1993	Best Friends	95-day		29.90	30
1993	Sisters	95-day		29.90	30
1994	Little One	95-day		32.90	33
1994	Teddy Bear Tales	95-day		32.90	33
1994	Morning Prayers	95-day		32.90	33
1995	First Snow	95-day		34.90	35
1994	Garden of Sunshine	95-day		34.90	35
1995	A Special Day	95-day		34.90	35

Tidings Of Joy - S. Kuck

Year Issue		Edition Limit	Year Retd.	Issue Price	*Quote U.S.$
1992	Peace on Earth	Retrd.	1995	35.00	40
1993	Rejoice	Retrd.	1996	35.00	40
1994	Noel	Retrd.	1995	35.00	50

Totems of the West - J. Bergsma

Year Issue		Edition Limit	Year Retd.	Issue Price	*Quote U.S.$
1994	The Watchmen	96-day		29.50	30
1995	Peace At Last	96-day		29.50	30
1995	Never Alone	96-day		35.00	35

Town And Country Dogs - S. Barlowe

Year Issue		Edition Limit	Year Retd.	Issue Price	*Quote U.S.$
1990	Fox Hunt	36-day		35.00	35
1991	The Retrieval	36-day		35.00	35
1991	Golden Fields (Golden Retriever)	36-day		35.00	35
1993	Faithful Companions (Cocker Spaniel)	36-day		35.00	35

Trains of the Orient Express - R. Johnson

Year Issue		Edition Limit	Year Retd.	Issue Price	*Quote U.S.$
1993	The Golden Arrow-England	Retrd.	1996	29.50	30
1994	Austria	Retrd.	1996	29.50	30
1994	Bavaria	Retrd.	1996	29.50	30
1994	Rumania	Retrd.	1996	29.50	30
1994	Greece	Retrd.	1996	29.50	30
1994	Frankonia	Retrd.	1996	29.50	30
1994	Turkey	Retrd.	1996	29.50	30
1994	France	Retrd.	1996	29.50	30

Treasured Songs of Childhood - J. McClelland

Year Issue		Edition Limit	Year Retd.	Issue Price	*Quote U.S.$
1987	Twinkle, Twinkle, Little Star	Retrd.	1990	29.50	30
1988	A Tisket, A Tasket	Retrd.	1991	29.50	30
1988	Baa, Baa, Black Sheep	Retrd.	1991	32.90	33
1989	Round The Mulberry Bush	150-day		32.90	33
1989	Rain, Rain Go Away	Retrd.	1993	32.90	33
1989	I'm A Little Teapot	Retrd.	1993	32.90	33
1989	Pat-A-Cake	150-day		34.90	35
1990	Hush Little Baby	150-day		34.90	35

Up, Up And Away - P. Alexander

Year Issue		Edition Limit	Year Retd.	Issue Price	*Quote U.S.$
1996	Rally At The Grand Canyon	76-day		29.90	30
1996	Gateway To Heaven	76-day		29.90	30

Vanishing Animal Kingdoms - S. Barlowe

Year Issue		Edition Limit	Year Retd.	Issue Price	*Quote U.S.$
1986	Rama the Tiger	21,500	1996	35.00	35
1986	Olepi the Buffalo	21,500	1996	35.00	35

*Quotes have been rounded up to nearest dollar

YEAR ISSUE		EDITION LIMIT	YEAR RETD.	ISSUE PRICE	*QUOTE U.S.$
1987	Coolibah the Koala	21,500	1996	35.00	35
1987	Ortwin the Deer	21,500	1996	35.00	35
1987	Yen-Poh the Panda	21,500	1996	35.00	35
1988	Mamakuu the Elephant	21,500	1996	35.00	35

Victorian Christmas - S. Kuck

YEAR ISSUE		EDITION LIMIT	YEAR RETD.	ISSUE PRICE	*QUOTE U.S.$
1995	Dear Santa	72-day		35.00	35
1996	Night Before Christmas	72-day		35.00	35
1997	Merry Christmas	72-day		35.00	35

Victorian Mother's Day - S. Kuck

YEAR ISSUE		EDITION LIMIT	YEAR RETD.	ISSUE PRICE	*QUOTE U.S.$
1989	Mother's Sunshine	Retrd.	1990	35.00	45-85
1990	Reflection Of Love	Retrd.	1991	35.00	50-80
1991	A Precious Time	Retrd.	1992	35.00	45-75
1992	Loving Touch	Retrd.	1993	35.00	45-49

Western - E. Berke

YEAR ISSUE		EDITION LIMIT	YEAR RETD.	ISSUE PRICE	*QUOTE U.S.$
1974	Mountain Man	Retrd.		165.00	165

Women of the Plains - C. Corcilius

YEAR ISSUE		EDITION LIMIT	YEAR RETD.	ISSUE PRICE	*QUOTE U.S.$
1994	Pride of a Maiden	36-day		29.50	30
1995	No Boundaries	36-day		29.50	30
1995	Silent Companions	36-day		35.00	35

The Wonder of Christmas - J. McClelland

YEAR ISSUE		EDITION LIMIT	YEAR RETD.	ISSUE PRICE	*QUOTE U.S.$
1991	Santa's Secret	Retrd.	1996	29.50	30
1992	My Favorite Ornament	Retrd.	1996	29.50	30
1992	Waiting For Santa	Retrd.	1996	29.50	30
1993	Candlelight Christmas	Retrd.	1995	29.50	55

The World of Children - J. McClelland

YEAR ISSUE		EDITION LIMIT	YEAR RETD.	ISSUE PRICE	*QUOTE U.S.$
1977	Rainy Day Fun	10,000	1977	50.00	50
1978	When I Grow Up	15,000	1978	50.00	55
1979	You're Invited	15,000	1979	50.00	55
1980	Kittens for Sale	15,000	1980	50.00	55

River Shore

Baby Animals - R. Brown

YEAR ISSUE		EDITION LIMIT	YEAR RETD.	ISSUE PRICE	*QUOTE U.S.$
1979	Akiku	20,000		50.00	80
1980	Roosevelt	20,000		50.00	90
1981	Clover	20,000		50.00	65
1982	Zuela	20,000		50.00	65

Little House on the Prairie - E. Christopherson

YEAR ISSUE		EDITION LIMIT	YEAR RETD.	ISSUE PRICE	*QUOTE U.S.$
1985	Founder's Day Picnic	10-day		29.50	45
1985	Women's Harvest	10-day		29.50	45
1985	Medicine Show	10-day		29.50	45
1985	Caroline's Eggs	10-day		29.50	45
1985	Mary's Gift	10-day		29.50	45
1985	A Bell for Walnut Grove	10-day		29.50	45
1985	Ingall's Family	10-day		29.50	45
1985	The Sweetheart Tree	10-day		29.50	45

Norman Rockwell Single Issue - N. Rockwell

YEAR ISSUE		EDITION LIMIT	YEAR RETD.	ISSUE PRICE	*QUOTE U.S.$
1979	Spring Flowers	17,000		75.00	145
1980	Looking Out to Sea	17,000		75.00	195
1982	Grandpa's Guardian	17,000		80.00	80
1982	Grandpa's Treasures	17,000		80.00	80

Rockwell Four Freedoms - N. Rockwell

YEAR ISSUE		EDITION LIMIT	YEAR RETD.	ISSUE PRICE	*QUOTE U.S.$
1981	Freedom of Speech	17,000		65.00	100
1982	Freedom of Worship	17,000		65.00	125
1982	Freedom from Fear	17,000		65.00	200
1982	Freedom from Want	17,000		65.00	425

Rockwell Society

Christmas - N. Rockwell

YEAR ISSUE		EDITION LIMIT	YEAR RETD.	ISSUE PRICE	*QUOTE U.S.$
1974	Scotty Gets His Tree	Yr.Iss.		24.50	75-103
1975	Angel with Black Eye	Yr.Iss.		24.50	40-75
1976	Golden Christmas	Yr.Iss.		24.50	35-50
1977	Toy Shop Window	Yr.Iss.		24.50	50
1978	Christmas Dream	Yr.Iss.		24.50	25
1979	Somebody's Up There	Yr.Iss.		24.50	30-50
1980	Scotty Plays Santa	Yr.Iss.		24.50	25
1981	Wrapped Up in Christmas	Yr.Iss.		25.50	28
1982	Christmas Courtship	Yr.Iss.		25.50	30-60
1983	Santa in the Subway	Yr.Iss.		25.50	30
1984	Santa in the Workshop	Yr.Iss.		27.50	30
1985	Grandpa Plays Santa	Yr.Iss.		27.90	27-35
1986	Dear Santy Claus	Yr.Iss.		27.90	30
1987	Santa's Golden Gift	Yr.Iss.		27.90	32
1988	Santa Claus	Yr.Iss.		29.90	30
1989	Jolly Old St. Nick	Yr.Iss.		29.90	35
1990	A Christmas Prayer	Yr.Iss.		29.90	30
1991	Santa's Helpers	Yr.Iss.		32.90	33
1992	The Christmas Surprise	Yr.Iss.		32.90	35
1993	The Tree Brigade	Yr.Iss.		32.90	44
1994	Christmas Marvel	Yr.Iss.		32.90	84
1995	Filling The Stockings	Yr.Iss.		32.90	55

Colonials-The Rarest Rockwells - N. Rockwell

YEAR ISSUE		EDITION LIMIT	YEAR RETD.	ISSUE PRICE	*QUOTE U.S.$
1985	Unexpected Proposal	150-day		27.90	32-40
1986	Words of Comfort	150-day		27.90	32
1986	Light for the Winter	150-day		30.90	35
1987	Portrait for a Bridegroom	150-day		30.90	35
1987	The Journey Home	150-day		30.90	35
1987	Clinching the Deal	150-day		30.90	35
1988	Sign of the Times	150-day		32.90	35
1988	Ye Glutton	150-day		32.90	35

Coming Of Age - N. Rockwell

YEAR ISSUE		EDITION LIMIT	YEAR RETD.	ISSUE PRICE	*QUOTE U.S.$
1990	Back To School	150-day		29.90	45
1990	Home From Camp	150-day		29.90	47
1990	Her First Formal	150-day		32.90	65
1990	The Muscleman	150-day		32.90	33
1990	A New Look	150-day		32.90	35
1991	A Balcony Seat	150-day		32.90	33
1991	Men About Town	150-day		34.90	35
1991	Paths of Glory	150-day		34.90	35
1991	Doorway to the Past	150-day		34.90	40
1991	School's Out!	150-day		34.90	60

Heritage - N. Rockwell

YEAR ISSUE		EDITION LIMIT	YEAR RETD.	ISSUE PRICE	*QUOTE U.S.$
1977	Toy Maker	Yr.Iss.		14.50	60-100
1978	Cobbler	Yr.Iss.		19.50	35-50
1979	Lighthouse Keeper's Daughter	Yr.Iss.		19.50	35-55
1980	Ship Builder	Yr.Iss.		19.50	31-45
1981	Music maker	Yr.Iss.		19.50	24-42
1982	Tycoon	Yr.Iss.		19.50	25-35
1983	Painter	Yr.Iss.		19.50	20-28
1984	Storyteller	Yr.Iss.		19.50	20-30
1985	Gourmet	Yr.Iss.		19.50	20
1986	Professor	Yr.Iss.		22.90	23-30
1987	Shadow Artist	Yr.Iss.		22.90	23-30
1988	The Veteran	Yr.Iss.		22.90	23-30
1988	The Banjo Player	Yr.Iss.		22.90	30
1990	The Old Scout	Yr.Iss.		24.90	30
1991	The Young Scholar	Yr.Iss.		24.90	30
1992	The Family Doctor	Yr.Iss.		27.90	39-48
1993	The Jeweler	Yr.Iss.		27.90	35-50
1994	Halloween Frolic	Yr.Iss.		27.90	40-50
1995	The Apprentice	Yr.Iss.		29.90	45
1996	Master Violinist	Yr.Iss.		29.90	42

Innocence and Experience - N. Rockwell

YEAR ISSUE		EDITION LIMIT	YEAR RETD.	ISSUE PRICE	*QUOTE U.S.$
1991	The Sea Captain	150-day		29.90	30
1991	The Radio Operator	150-day		29.90	30
1991	The Magician	150-day		32.90	50
1992	The American Heroes	150-day		32.90	33

A Mind of Her Own - N. Rockwell

YEAR ISSUE		EDITION LIMIT	YEAR RETD.	ISSUE PRICE	*QUOTE U.S.$
1986	Sitting Pretty	150-day		24.90	33
1987	Serious Business	150-day		[illegible]	[illegible]
1987	Breaking the Rules	150-day		24.90	30
1987	Good Intentions	150-day		27.90	30
1988	Second Thoughts	150-day		27.90	30
1988	World's Away	150-day		27.90	30
1988	Kiss and Tell	150-day		29.90	30
1988	On My Honor	150-day		29.90	30-45

Mother's Day - N. Rockwell

YEAR ISSUE		EDITION LIMIT	YEAR RETD.	ISSUE PRICE	*QUOTE U.S.$
1976	A Mother's Love	Yr.Iss.		24.50	60
1977	Faith	Yr.Iss.		24.50	48
1978	Bedtime	Yr.Iss.		24.50	35
1979	Reflections	Yr.Iss.		24.50	25
1980	A Mother's Pride	Yr.Iss.		24.50	25-35
1981	After the Party	Yr.Iss.		24.50	25
1982	The Cooking Lesson	Yr.Iss.		24.50	30
1983	Add Two Cups and Love	Yr.Iss.		25.50	26
1984	Grandma's Courting Dress	Yr.Iss.		25.50	26
1985	Mending Time	Yr.Iss.		27.50	28
1986	Pantry Raid	Yr.Iss.		27.90	28
1987	Grandma's Surprise	Yr.Iss.		29.90	35
1988	My Mother	Yr.Iss.		29.90	32-50
1989	Sunday Dinner	Yr.Iss.		29.90	35
1990	Evening Prayers	Yr.Iss.		29.90	30
1991	Building Our Future	Yr.Iss.		32.90	33
1991	Gentle Reassurance	Yr.Iss.		32.90	35
1992	A Special Delivery	Yr.Iss.		32.90	35

Rockwell Commemorative Stamps - N. Rockwell

YEAR ISSUE		EDITION LIMIT	YEAR RETD.	ISSUE PRICE	*QUOTE U.S.$
1994	Triple Self Portrait	95-day		29.90	30
1994	Freedom From Want	95-day		29.90	30
1994	Freedom From Fear	95-day		29.90	30
1995	Freedom of Speech	95-day		29.90	30
1995	Freedom of Worship	95-day		29.90	30

Rockwell on Tour - N. Rockwell

YEAR ISSUE		EDITION LIMIT	YEAR RETD.	ISSUE PRICE	*QUOTE U.S.$
1983	Walking Through Merrie Englande	150-day		16.00	16
1983	Promenade a Paris	150-day		16.00	30
1983	When in Rome	150-day		16.00	16
1984	Die Walk am Rhein	150-day		16.00	16

Rockwell's American Dream - N. Rockwell

YEAR ISSUE		EDITION LIMIT	YEAR RETD.	ISSUE PRICE	*QUOTE U.S.$
1985	A Young Girl's Dream	150-day		19.90	25
1985	A Couple's Commitment	150-day		19.90	25
1985	A Family's Full Measure	150-day		22.90	28
1986	A Mother's Welcome	150-day		22.90	25
1986	A Young Man's Dream	150-day		22.90	25
1986	The Musician's Magic	150-day		22.90	28
1987	An Orphan's Hope	150-day		24.90	28
1987	Love's Reward	150-day		24.90	33

Rockwell's Golden Moments - N. Rockwell

YEAR ISSUE		EDITION LIMIT	YEAR RETD.	ISSUE PRICE	*QUOTE U.S.$
1987	Grandpa's Gift	150-day		19.90	30-40
1987	Grandma's Love	150-day		19.90	35
1988	End of day	150-day		22.90	40
1988	Best Friends	150-day		22.90	25
1989	Love Letters	150-day		22.90	33
1989	Newfound Worlds	150-day		22.90	23
1989	Keeping Company	150-day		24.90	25
1989	Evening's Repose	150-day		24.90	25

Rockwell's Light Campaign - N. Rockwell

YEAR ISSUE		EDITION LIMIT	YEAR RETD.	ISSUE PRICE	*QUOTE U.S.$
1983	This is the Room that Light Made	150-day		19.50	25
1984	Grandpa's Treasure Chest	150-day		19.50	30-35
1984	Father's Help	150-day		19.50	22-30
1984	Evening's Ease	150-day		19.50	25
1984	Close Harmony	150-day		21.50	25
1984	The Birthday Wish	150-day		21.50	25

Rockwell's Rediscovered Women - N. Rockwell

YEAR ISSUE		EDITION LIMIT	YEAR RETD.	ISSUE PRICE	*QUOTE U.S.$
1984	Dreaming in the Attic	100-day		19.50	30-35
1984	Waiting on the Shore	100-day		22.50	23
1984	Pondering on the Porch	100-day		22.50	23
1984	Making Believe at the Mirror	100-day		22.50	23-30
1984	Waiting at the Dance	100-day		22.50	23
1984	Gossiping in the Alcove	100-day		22.50	23
1984	Standing in the Doorway	100-day		22.50	25-35
1984	Flirting in the Parlor	100-day		22.50	30-35
1984	Working in the Kitchen	100-day		22.50	33
1984	Meeting on the Path	100-day		22.50	23
1984	Confiding in the Den	100-day		22.50	23
1984	Reminiscing in the Quiet	100-day		22.50	35-45
XX	Complete Collection	100-day		267.00	267

Rockwell's The Ones We Love - N. Rockwell

YEAR ISSUE		EDITION LIMIT	YEAR RETD.	ISSUE PRICE	*QUOTE U.S.$
1988	Tender Loving Care	150-day		19.90	25-35
1989	A Time to Keep	150-day		19.90	25
1989	The Inventor And The Judge	150-day		22.90	23
1989	Ready For The World	150-day		22.90	25
1989	Growing Strong	150-day		22.90	30
1990	The Story Hour	150-day		22.90	45
1990	The Country Doctor	150-day		24.90	25
1990	Our Love of Country	150-day		24.90	25
1990	The Homecoming	150-day		24.90	25
1991	A Helping Hand	150-day		24.90	25

Rockwell's Treasured Memories - N. Rockwell

YEAR ISSUE		EDITION LIMIT	YEAR RETD.	ISSUE PRICE	*QUOTE U.S.$
1991	Quiet Reflections	150-day		29.90	30
1991	Romantic Reverie	150-day		29.90	30
1991	Tender Romance	150-day		32.90	33
1991	Evening Passage	150-day		32.90	33
1991	Heavenly Dreams	150-day		32.90	34
1991	Sentimental Shores	150-day		32.90	34

Roman, Inc.

Abbie Williams Collection - A. Williams

YEAR ISSUE		EDITION LIMIT	YEAR RETD.	ISSUE PRICE	*QUOTE U.S.$
1991	Legacy of Love	Open		29.50	30
1991	Bless This Child	Open		29.50	30

Catnippers - I. Spencer

YEAR ISSUE		EDITION LIMIT	YEAR RETD.	ISSUE PRICE	*QUOTE U.S.$
1986	Christmas Mourning	9,500		34.50	35
1992	Happy Holidaze	9,500		34.50	35

A Child's Play - F. Hook

YEAR ISSUE		EDITION LIMIT	YEAR RETD.	ISSUE PRICE	*QUOTE U.S.$
1982	Breezy Day	30-day		29.95	39
1982	Kite Flying	30-day		29.95	39
1984	Bathtub Sailor	30-day		29.95	35
1984	The First Snow	30-day		29.95	35

A Child's World - F. Hook

YEAR ISSUE		EDITION LIMIT	YEAR RETD.	ISSUE PRICE	*QUOTE U.S.$
1980	Little Children, Come to Me	15,000		45.00	49

Fontanini Annual Christmas Plate - E. Simonetti

YEAR ISSUE		EDITION LIMIT	YEAR RETD.	ISSUE PRICE	*QUOTE U.S.$
1986	A King Is Born	Yr.Iss.		60.00	60
1987	O Come, Let Us Adore Him	Yr.Iss.		60.00	65
1988	Adoration of the Magi	Yr.Iss.		70.00	75
1989	Flight Into Egypt	Yr.Iss.		75.00	85

Frances Hook Collection-Set I - F. Hook

YEAR ISSUE		EDITION LIMIT	YEAR RETD.	ISSUE PRICE	*QUOTE U.S.$
1982	I Wish, I Wish	15,000		24.95	75
1982	Baby Blossoms	15,000		24.95	35-39
1982	Daisy Dreamer	15,000		24.95	35-39
1982	Trees So Tall	15,000		24.95	35-39

Frances Hook Collection-Set II - F. Hook

YEAR ISSUE		EDITION LIMIT	YEAR RETD.	ISSUE PRICE	*QUOTE U.S.$
1983	Caught It Myself	15,000		24.95	25
1983	Winter Wrappings	15,000		24.95	25
1983	So Cuddly	15,000		24.95	25
1983	Can I Keep Him?	15,000		24.95	25

Frances Hook Legacy - F. Hook

YEAR ISSUE		EDITION LIMIT	YEAR RETD.	ISSUE PRICE	*QUOTE U.S.$
1985	Fascination	100-day		19.50	35-39
1985	Daydreaming	100-day		19.50	35-39
1985	Discovery	100-day		22.50	35-39
1985	Disappointment	100-day		22.50	35-39
1985	Wonderment	100-day		22.50	35-39
1985	Expectation	100-day		22.50	35-39

God Bless You Little One - A. Williams

YEAR ISSUE		EDITION LIMIT	YEAR RETD.	ISSUE PRICE	*QUOTE U.S.$
1991	Baby's First Birthday (Girl)	Open		29.50	30
1991	Baby's First Birthday (Boy)	Open		29.50	30
1991	Baby's First Smile	Open		19.50	20
1991	Baby's First Word	Open		19.50	20
1991	Baby's First Step	Open		19.50	20

*Quotes have been rounded up to nearest dollar

YEAR ISSUE		EDITION LIMIT	YEAR RETD.	ISSUE PRICE	*QUOTE U.S.$
1991	Baby's First Tooth	Open		19.50	20

The Ice Capades Clown - G. Petty

YEAR ISSUE		EDITION LIMIT	YEAR RETD.	ISSUE PRICE	*QUOTE U.S.$
1983	Presenting Freddie Trenkler	30-day		24.50	25

The Lord's Prayer - A. Williams

YEAR ISSUE		EDITION LIMIT	YEAR RETD.	ISSUE PRICE	*QUOTE U.S.$
1986	Our Father	10-day		24.50	25
1986	Thy Kingdom Come	10-day		24.50	25
1986	Give Us This Day	10-day		24.50	25
1986	Forgive Our Trespasses	10-day		24.50	25
1986	As We Forgive	10-day		24.50	25
1986	Lead Us Not	10-day		24.50	25
1986	Deliver Us From Evil	10-day		24.50	25
1986	Thine Is The Kingdom	10-day		24.50	25

The Love's Prayer - A. Williams

YEAR ISSUE		EDITION LIMIT	YEAR RETD.	ISSUE PRICE	*QUOTE U.S.$
1988	Love Is Patient and Kind	14-day		29.50	30
1988	Love Is Never Jealous or Boastful	14-day		29.50	30
1988	Love Is Never Arrogant or Rude	14-day		29.50	30
1988	Love Does Not Insist on Its Own Way	14-day		29.50	30
1988	Love Is Never Irritable or Resentful	14-day		29.50	30
1988	Love Rejoices In the Right	14-day		29.50	30
1988	Love Believes All Things	14-day		29.50	30
1988	Love Never Ends	14-day		29.50	30

The Magic of Childhood - A. Williams

YEAR ISSUE		EDITION LIMIT	YEAR RETD.	ISSUE PRICE	*QUOTE U.S.$
1985	Special Friends	10-day		24.50	25
1985	Feeding Time	10-day		24.50	25
1985	Best Buddies	10-day		24.50	35
1985	Getting Acquainted	10-day		24.50	35
1986	Last One In	10-day		24.50	35
1986	A Handful Of Love	10-day		24.50	35
1986	Look Alikes	10-day		24.50	35
1986	No Fair Peeking	10-day		24.50	35

March of Dimes: Our Children, Our Future - A. Williams

YEAR ISSUE		EDITION LIMIT	YEAR RETD.	ISSUE PRICE	*QUOTE U.S.$
1990	A Time To Laugh	150-day		29.00	39-49

The Masterpiece Collection - Various

YEAR ISSUE		EDITION LIMIT	YEAR RETD.	ISSUE PRICE	*QUOTE U.S.$
1979	Adoration - F. Lippe	5,000		65.00	65
1980	Madonna with Grapes - P. Mignard	5,000		87.50	88
1981	The Holy Family - G. Delle Notti	5,000		95.00	95
1982	Madonna of the Streets - R. Ferruzzi	5,000		85.00	85

Millenium™ Series - Various

YEAR ISSUE		EDITION LIMIT	YEAR RETD.	ISSUE PRICE	*QUOTE U.S.$
1992	Silent Night - Morcaldo/Lucchesi	Closed	1992	49.50	50
1993	The Annunciation - Morcaldo/Lucchesi	5,000	1993	49.50	50
1994	Peace On Earth - Morcaldo/Lucchesi	5,000	1994	49.50	50
1995	Cause of Our Joy - A. Lucchesi	7,500		49.50	50
1996	Prince of Peace - A. Lucchesi	15,000		49.50	50
1997	Gentle Love - A. Lucchesi	Yr.Iss.		49.50	50

Precious Children - A. Williams

YEAR ISSUE		EDITION LIMIT	YEAR RETD.	ISSUE PRICE	*QUOTE U.S.$
1993	Bless Baby Brother	N/A		29.50	30
1993	Blowing Bubbles	N/A		29.50	30
1993	Don't Worry, Mother Duck	N/A		29.50	30
1993	Treetop Discovery	N/A		29.50	30
1993	The Tea Party	N/A		29.50	30
1993	Mother's Little Angel	N/A		29.50	30
1993	Picking Daisies	N/A		29.50	30
1993	Let's Say Grace	N/A		29.50	30

Pretty Girls of the Ice Capades - G. Petty

YEAR ISSUE		EDITION LIMIT	YEAR RETD.	ISSUE PRICE	*QUOTE U.S.$
1983	Ice Princess	30-day		24.50	25

Promise of a Savior - Unknown

YEAR ISSUE		EDITION LIMIT	YEAR RETD.	ISSUE PRICE	*QUOTE U.S.$
1993	An Angel's Message	95-day		29.90	30
1993	Gifts to Jesus	95-day		29.90	30
1993	The Heavenly King	95-day		29.90	30
1993	Angels Were Watching	95-day		29.90	30
1993	Holy Mother & Child	95-day		29.90	30
1993	A Child is Born	95-day		29.90	30

The Richard Judson Zolan Collection - R.J. Zolan

YEAR ISSUE		EDITION LIMIT	YEAR RETD.	ISSUE PRICE	*QUOTE U.S.$
1992	The Butterfly Net	100-day		29.50	30
1994	The Ring	100-day		29.50	30
1994	Terrace Dancing	100-day		29.50	30

Roman Memorial - F. Hook

YEAR ISSUE		EDITION LIMIT	YEAR RETD.	ISSUE PRICE	*QUOTE U.S.$
1984	The Carpenter	Closed	1984	100.00	135

Sepaphim Collection by Faro - Faro

YEAR ISSUE		EDITION LIMIT	YEAR RETD.	ISSUE PRICE	*QUOTE U.S.$
1994	Rosalyn - Rarest of Heaven	7,200	1995	65.00	65
1995	Helena - Heaven's Herald	7,200		65.00	65
1996	Flora - Flower of Heaven	7,200		65.00	65
1997	Emily - Heaven's Treasure	Yr.Iss.		65.00	65

Single Releases - A. Williams

YEAR ISSUE		EDITION LIMIT	YEAR RETD.	ISSUE PRICE	*QUOTE U.S.$
1987	The Christening	Open		29.50	30
1990	The Dedication	Open		29.50	30
1990	The Baptism	Open		29.50	30

The Sweetest Songs - I. Spencer

YEAR ISSUE		EDITION LIMIT	YEAR RETD.	ISSUE PRICE	*QUOTE U.S.$
1986	A Baby's Prayer	30-day		39.50	45
1986	This Little Piggie	30-day		39.50	40
1988	Long, Long Ago	30-day		39.50	40
1989	Rockabye	30-day		39.50	40

Tender Expressions - B. Sargent

YEAR ISSUE		EDITION LIMIT	YEAR RETD.	ISSUE PRICE	*QUOTE U.S.$
1992	Thoughts of You Are In My Heart	100-day		29.50	30

Rosenthal

Christmas - Unknown

YEAR ISSUE		EDITION LIMIT	YEAR RETD.	ISSUE PRICE	*QUOTE U.S.$
1910	Winter Peace	Annual		Unkn.	550
1911	Three Wise Men	Annual		Unkn.	325
1912	Stardust	Annual		Unkn.	255
1913	Christmas Lights	Annual		Unkn.	235
1914	Christmas Song	Annual		Unkn.	350
1915	Walking to Church	Annual		Unkn.	180
1916	Christmas During War	Annual		Unkn.	240
1917	Angel of Peace	Annual		Unkn.	200
1918	Peace on Earth	Annual		Unkn.	200
1919	St. Christopher with Christ Child	Annual		Unkn.	225
1920	Manger in Bethlehem	Annual		Unkn.	325
1921	Christmas in Mountains	Annual		Unkn.	200
1922	Advent Branch	Annual		Unkn.	200
1923	Children in Winter Woods	Annual		Unkn.	200
1924	Deer in the Woods	Annual		Unkn.	200
1925	Three Wise Men	Annual		Unkn.	200
1926	Christmas in Mountains	Annual		Unkn.	195
1927	Station on the Way	Annual		Unkn.	135-175
1928	Chalet Christmas	Annual		Unkn.	185
1929	Christmas in Alps	Annual		Unkn.	225
1930	Group of Deer Under Pines	Annual		Unkn.	225
1931	Path of the Magi	Annual		Unkn.	225
1932	Christ Child	Annual		Unkn.	185
1933	Thru the Night to Light	Annual		Unkn.	190
1934	Christmas Peace	Annual		Unkn.	190
1935	Christmas by the Sea	Annual		Unkn.	190
1936	Nurnberg Angel	Annual		Unkn.	175-200
1937	Berchtesgaden	Annual		Unkn.	195
1938	Christmas in the Alps	Annual		Unkn.	195
1939	Schneekoppe Mountain	Annual		Unkn.	195
1940	Marien Chruch in Danzig	Annual		Unkn.	200-225
1941	Strassburg Cathedral	Annual		Unkn.	200-225
1942	Marianburg Castle	Annual		Unkn.	300
1943	Winter Idyll	Annual		Unkn.	300
1944	Wood Scape	Annual		Unkn.	300
1945	Christmas Peace	Annual		Unkn.	400
1946	Christmas in an Alpine Valley	Annual		Unkn.	240
1947	Dillingen Madonna	Annual		Unkn.	985
1948	Message to the Shepherds	Annual		Unkn.	875
1949	The Holy Family	Annual		Unkn.	185
1950	Christmas in the Forest	Annual		Unkn.	185
1951	Star of Bethlehem	Annual		Unkn.	450
1952	Christmas in the Alps	Annual		Unkn.	195
1953	The Holy Light	Annual		Unkn.	195
1954	Christmas Eve	Annual		Unkn.	195
1955	Christmas in a Village	Annual		Unkn.	195
1956	Christmas in the Alps	Annual		Unkn.	195
1957	Christmas by the Sea	Annual		Unkn.	195
1958	Christmas Eve	Annual		Unkn.	195
1959	Midnight Mass	Annual		Unkn.	75-125
1960	Christmas in a Small Village	Annual		Unkn.	195
1961	Solitary Christmas	Annual		Unkn.	100-200
1962	Christmas Eve	Annual		Unkn.	75-150
1963	Silent Night	Annual		Unkn.	75-150
1964	Christmas Market in Nurnberg	Annual		Unkn.	225
1965	Christmas Munich	Annual		Unkn.	185
1966	Christmas in Ulm	Annual		Unkn.	275
1967	Christmas in Reginburg	Annual		Unkn.	185
1968	Christmas in Bremen	Annual		Unkn.	195
1969	Christmas in Rothenburg	Annual		Unkn.	220
1970	Christmas in Cologne	Annual		Unkn.	175
1971	Christmas in Garmisch	Annual		42.00	100
1972	Christmas in Franconia	Annual		50.00	95
1973	Lubeck-Holstein	Annual		77.00	105
1974	Christmas in Wurzburg	Annual		85.00	100

Nobility of Children - E. Hibel

YEAR ISSUE		EDITION LIMIT	YEAR RETD.	ISSUE PRICE	*QUOTE U.S.$
1976	La Contessa Isabella	12,750		120.00	120
1977	La Marquis Maurice-Pierre	12,750		120.00	120
1978	Baronesse Johanna	12,750		130.00	140
1979	Chief Red Feather	12,750		140.00	180

Oriental Gold - E. Hibel

YEAR ISSUE		EDITION LIMIT	YEAR RETD.	ISSUE PRICE	*QUOTE U.S.$
1976	Yasuko	2,000		275.00	650
1977	Mr. Obata	2,000		275.00	500
1978	Sakura	2,000		295.00	400
1979	Michio	2,000		325.00	375

Wiinblad Christmas - B. Wiinblad

YEAR ISSUE		EDITION LIMIT	YEAR RETD.	ISSUE PRICE	*QUOTE U.S.$
1971	Maria & Child	Undis.		100.00	750
1972	Caspar	Undis.		100.00	290
1973	Melchior	Undis.		125.00	335
1974	Balthazar	Undis.		125.00	300
1975	The Annunciation	Undis.		195.00	195
1976	Angel with Trumpet	Undis.		195.00	195
1977	Adoration of Shepherds	Undis.		225.00	225
1978	Angel with Harp	Undis.		275.00	295
1979	Exodus from Egypt	Undis.		310.00	310
1980	Angel with Glockenspiel	Undis.		360.00	360
1981	Christ Child Visits Temple	Undis.		375.00	375
1982	Christening of Christ	Undis.		375.00	375

Royal Copenhagen

Christmas - Various

YEAR ISSUE		EDITION LIMIT	YEAR RETD.	ISSUE PRICE	*QUOTE U.S.$
1908	Madonna and Child - C. Thomsen	Annual	1908	1.00	3800-4500
1909	Danish Landscape - S. Ussing	Annual	1909	1.00	200-350
1910	The Magi - C. Thomsen	Annual	1910	1.00	145-225
1911	Danish Landscape - O. Jensen	Annual	1911	1.00	165-190
1912	Christmas Tree - C. Thomsen	Annual	1912	1.00	168-210
1913	Frederik Church Spire - A. Boesen	Annual	1913	1.50	140-165
1914	Holy Spirit Church - A. Boesen	Annual	1914	1.50	160-240
1915	Danish Landscape - A. Krog	Annual	1915	1.50	155-200
1916	Shepherd at Christmas - R. Bocher	Annual	1916	1.50	110-130
1917	Our Savior Church - O. Jensen	Annual	1917	2.00	115-150
1918	Sheep and Shepherds - O. Jensen	Annual	1918	2.00	105-150
1919	In the Park - O. Jensen	Annual	1919	2.00	100-150
1920	Mary and Child Jesus - G. Rode	Annual	1920	2.00	100-150
1921	Aabenraa Marketplace - O. Jensen	Annual	1921	2.00	90-125
1922	Three Singing Angels - E. Selschau	Annual	1922	2.00	98-117
1923	Danish Landscape - O. Jensen	Annual	1923	2.00	90-113
1924	Sailing Ship - B. Olsen	Annual	1924	2.00	125-165
1925	Christianshavn - O. Jensen	Annual	1925	2.00	110-160
1926	Christianshavn Canal - R. Bocher	Annual	1926	2.00	100-160
1927	Ship's Boy at Tiller - B. Olsen	Annual	1927	2.00	175
1928	Vicar's Family - G. Rode	Annual	1928	2.00	140
1929	Grundtvig Church - O. Jensen	Annual	1929	2.00	110-135
1930	Fishing Boats - B. Olsen	Annual	1930	2.50	115-145
1931	Mother and Child - G. Rode	Annual	1931	2.50	145-185
1932	Frederiksberg Gardens - O. Jensen	Annual	1932	2.50	120
1933	Ferry and the Great Belt - B. Olsen	Annual	1933	2.50	140-195
1934	The Hermitage Castle - O. Jensen	Annual	1934	2.50	210-280
1935	Kronborg Castle - B. Olsen	Annual	1935	2.50	225-375
1936	Roskilde Cathedral - R. Bocher	Annual	1936	2.50	240-315
1937	Main Street Copenhagen - N. Thorsson	Annual	1937	2.50	200-230
1938	Round Church in Osterlars - H. Nielsen	Annual	1938	3.00	230-420
1939	Greenland Pack-Ice - S. Nielsen	Annual	1939	3.00	335-425
1940	The Good Shepherd - K. Lange	Annual	1940	3.00	375-595
1941	Danish Village Church - T. Kjolner	Annual	1941	3.00	450-575
1942	Bell Tower - N. Thorsson	Annual	1942	4.00	565-800
1943	Flight into Egypt - N. Thorsson	Annual	1943	4.00	500-800
1944	Danish Village Scene - V. Olson	Annual	1944	4.00	295-475
1945	A Peaceful Motif - R. Bocher	Annual	1945	4.00	400-500
1946	Zealand Village Church - N. Thorsson	Annual	1946	4.00	260-300
1947	The Good Shepherd - K. Lange	Annual	1947	4.50	300-400
1948	Nodebo Church - T. Kjolner	Annual	1948	4.50	210-330
1949	Our Lady's Cathedral - H. Hansen	Annual	1949	5.00	225-370
1950	Boeslunde Church - V. Olson	Annual	1950	5.00	340
1951	Christmas Angel - R. Bocher	Annual	1951	5.00	235-435
1952	Christmas in the Forest - K. Lange	Annual	1952	5.00	160-180
1953	Frederiksberg Castle - T. Kjolner	Annual	1953	6.00	163-263
1954	Amalienborg Palace - K. Lange	Annual	1954	6.00	150-195
1955	Fano Girl - K. Lange	Annual	1955	7.00	240-280
1956	Rosenborg Castle - K. Lange	Annual	1956	7.00	210-290
1957	The Good Shepherd - H. Hansen	Annual	1957	8.00	100-160
1958	Sunshine over Greenland - H. Hansen	Annual	1958	9.00	115-230
1959	Christmas Night - H. Hansen	Annual	1959	9.00	125-225
1960	The Stag - H. Hansen	Annual	1960	10.00	125-250
1961	Training Ship - K. Lange	Annual	1961	10.00	155-230
1962	The Little Mermaid - Unknown	Annual	1962	11.00	250-400
1963	Hojsager Mill - K. Lange	Annual	1963	11.00	90-110
1964	Fetching the Tree - K. Lange	Annual	1964	11.00	70-90
1965	Little Skaters - K. Lange	Annual	1965	12.00	55-85
1966	Blackbird - K. Lange	Annual	1966	12.00	40-65
1967	The Royal Oak - K. Lange	Annual	1967	13.00	40-50
1968	The Last Umiak - K. Lange	Annual	1968	13.00	25-39
1969	The Old Farmyard - K. Lange	Annual	1969	14.00	30-48
1970	Christmas Rose and Cat - K. Lange	Annual	1970	14.00	30-51
1971	Hare In Winter - K. Lange	Annual	1971	15.00	25
1972	In the Desert - K. Lange	Annual	1972	16.00	25
1973	Train Homeward Bound - K. Lange	Annual	1973	22.00	29
1974	Winter Twilight - K. Lange	Annual	1974	22.00	27
1975	Queen's Palace - K. Lange	Annual	1975	27.50	27
1976	Danish Watermill - S. Vestergaard	Annual	1976	27.50	30-42
1977	Immervad Bridge - K. Lange	Annual	1977	32.00	33
1978	Greenland Scenery - K. Lange	Annual	1978	35.00	35
1979	Choosing Christmas Tree - K. Lange	Annual	1979	42.50	63-120
1980	Bringing Home the Tree - K. Lange	Annual	1980	49.50	48
1981	Admiring Christmas Tree - K. Lange	Annual	1981	52.50	55-75
1982	Waiting for Christmas - K. Lange	Annual	1982	54.50	55-75
1983	Merry Christmas - K. Lange	Annual	1983	54.50	60-80
1984	Jingle Bells - K. Lange	Annual	1984	54.50	60-80
1985	Snowman - K. Lange	Annual	1985	54.50	95-140
1986	Christmas Vacation - K. Lange	Annual	1986	54.50	65-95
1987	Winter Birds - S. Vestergaard	Annual	1987	59.50	80-98
1988	Christmas Eve in Copenhagen - S. Vestergaard	Annual	1988	59.50	80-120
1989	The Old Skating Pond - S. Vestergaard	Annual	1989	59.50	115
1990	Christmas at Tivoli - S. Vestergaard	Annual	1990	64.50	120-200
1991	The Festival of Santa Lucia - S. Vestergaard	Annual	1991	69.50	90-118
1992	The Queen's Carriage - S. Vestergaard	Annual	1992	69.50	75-110
1993	Christmas Guests - S. Vestergaard	Annual	1993	69.50	90-130
1994	Christmas Shopping - S. Vestergaard	Annual	1994	72.50	83

*Quotes have been rounded up to nearest dollar

Year	Issue	Edition Limit	Year Retd.	Issue Price	*Quote U.S.$
1995	Christmas at the Manor House - S. Vestergaard	Annual	1995	72.50	100-140
1996	Lighting the Street Lamps - S. Vestergaard	Annual	1996	74.50	75-90
1997	Roskilde Cathedral - S. Vestergaard	Annual		69.50	70

Royal Doulton

All God's Children - L. DeWinne

Year	Issue	Edition Limit	Year Retd.	Issue Price	*Quote U.S.$
1978	A Brighter Day	10,000	1984	75.00	75-100
1980	Village Children	10,000	1984	65.00	65
1981	Noble Heritage	10,000	1984	85.00	85
1982	Buddies	10,000	1984	85.00	85
1983	My Little Brother	10,000	1984	95.00	95

American Tapestries - C.A. Brown

Year	Issue	Edition Limit	Year Retd.	Issue Price	*Quote U.S.$
1978	Sleigh Bells	15,000	1983	70.00	70
1979	Pumpkin Patch	15,000	1983	70.00	70
1981	General Store	10,000	1983	95.00	95
1982	Fourth of July	10,000	1983	95.00	95

Behind the Painted Mask - B. Black

Year	Issue	Edition Limit	Year Retd.	Issue Price	*Quote U.S.$
1982	Painted Feelings	10,000	1986	95.00	125-175
1983	Make Me Laugh	10,000	1986	95.00	125-175
1984	Minstrel Serenade	10,000	1986	95.00	125-175
1985	Pleasing Performance	10,000	1986	95.00	125-175

Celebration of Faith - J. Woods

Year	Issue	Edition Limit	Year Retd.	Issue Price	*Quote U.S.$
1982	Rosh Hashanah	7,500	1986	250.00	300-400
1983	Yom Kippur	7,500	1986	250.00	250
1984	Passover	7,500	1986	250.00	250
1985	Chanukah	7,500	1986	250.00	250

Character Plates - N/A

Year	Issue	Edition Limit	Year Retd.	Issue Price	*Quote U.S.$
1979	Old Balloon Seller	Closed	1983	100.00	120
1980	Balloon Man	Closed	1983	125.00	125
1981	Silks and Ribbons	Closed	1983	125.00	140
1982	Biddy Penny Farthing	Closed	1983	125.00	125

Charles Dickens Plates - N/A

Year	Issue	Edition Limit	Year Retd.	Issue Price	*Quote U.S.$
1980	Artful Dodger	Closed	1984	65.00	65
1980	Barkis	Closed	1984	80.00	80
1980	Cap'n Cuttle	Closed	1984	80.00	80
1980	Fagin	Closed	1984	65.00	65
1980	Fat Boy	Closed	1984	65.00	65
1980	Mr. Micawber	Closed	1984	80.00	80
1980	Mr. Pickwick	Closed	1984	80.00	80
1980	Old Peggoty	Closed	1984	65.00	65
1980	Poor Jo	Closed	1984	80.00	80
1980	Sairey Gamp	Closed	1984	80.00	80
1980	Sam Weller	Closed	1984	65.00	65
1980	Sergeant Buz Fuz	Closed	1984	80.00	80
1980	Tony Weller	Closed	1984	65.00	65

Childhood Christmas - N/A

Year	Issue	Edition Limit	Year Retd.	Issue Price	*Quote U.S.$
1983	Silent Night	Yr.Iss.	1983	35.00	75
1984	While Shepherds Watched	Yr.Iss.	1984	39.95	75
1985	Oh Little Town of Bethlehem	Yr.Iss.	1985	39.95	40
1986	We Saw 3 Ships A-Sailing	Yr.Iss.	1986	39.95	40
1987	The Holly and the Ivy	Yr.Iss.	1987	39.95	40

Children of the Pueblo - M. Jungbluth

Year	Issue	Edition Limit	Year Retd.	Issue Price	*Quote U.S.$
1983	Apple Flower	15,000	1985	60.00	100
1984	Morning Star	15,000	1985	60.00	100

Christmas Around the World - N/A

Year	Issue	Edition Limit	Year Retd.	Issue Price	*Quote U.S.$
1972	Old England	15,000	1979	35.00	35
1973	Mexico	15,000	1979	37.50	38
1974	Bulgaria	15,000	1979	37.50	38
1975	Norway	15,000	1979	45.00	45
1976	Holland	15,000	1979	50.00	50
1977	Poland	15,000	1979	50.00	50
1978	America	15,000	1979	55.00	55

Christmas Plates - Various

Year	Issue	Edition Limit	Year Retd.	Issue Price	*Quote U.S.$
1993	Royal Doulton-Together For Christmas - J. James	Yr.Iss.	1993	45.00	50
1993	Royal Albert-Sleighride - N/A	Yr.Iss.	1993	45.00	45
1994	Royal Doulton-Home For Christmas - J. James	Yr.Iss.	1994	45.00	45
1994	Royal Albert-Coaching Inn - N/A	Yr.Iss.	1994	45.00	45
1995	Royal Doulton-Season's Greetings - J. James	Yr.Iss.	1995	45.00	45
1995	Royal Albert-Skating Pond - N/A	Yr.Iss.	1995	45.00	45
1996	Royal Doulton-Night Before Christmas - J. James	Yr.Iss.	1996	45.00	45
1996	Royal Albert-Gathering Winter Fuel - N/A	Yr.Iss.	1996	45.00	45

Commedia Dell Arte - L. Neiman

Year	Issue	Edition Limit	Year Retd.	Issue Price	*Quote U.S.$
1974	Harlequin	15,000	1979	100.00	125-175
1975	Pierrot	15,000	1979	90.00	110-160
1977	Columbine	15,000	1979	80.00	80
1978	Punchinello	15,000	1979	75.00	75

Family Christmas Plates - N/A

Year	Issue	Edition Limit	Year Retd.	Issue Price	*Quote U.S.$
1991	Dad Plays Santa	Closed	1991	60.00	60

Festival Children of the World - B. Burke

Year	Issue	Edition Limit	Year Retd.	Issue Price	*Quote U.S.$
1983	Mariana (Balinese)	15,000	1986	65.00	65
1984	Magdalena (Mexico)	15,000	1986	65.00	65
1985	Michiko (Japanese)	15,000	1986	65.00	65

Flower Garden - H. Vidal

Year	Issue	Edition Limit	Year Retd.	Issue Price	*Quote U.S.$
1975	Spring Harmony	15,000	1981	80.00	80
1976	Dreaming Lotus	15,000	1981	90.00	90
1977	From the Poet's Garden	15,000	1981	75.00	75
1978	Country Bouquet	15,000	1981	75.00	75
1979	From My Mother's Garden	15,000	1981	85.00	90

The Grandest Gift - Mago

Year	Issue	Edition Limit	Year Retd.	Issue Price	*Quote U.S.$
1985	Reunion	10,000	1986	75.00	100
1985	Storytime	10,000	1986	75.00	100

Grandparents - Mago

Year	Issue	Edition Limit	Year Retd.	Issue Price	*Quote U.S.$
1984	Grandfather and Children	15,000	1985	95.00	125

I Remember America - E. Sloane

Year	Issue	Edition Limit	Year Retd.	Issue Price	*Quote U.S.$
1977	Pennsylvania Pastorale	15,000	1982	90.00	90
1978	Lovejoy Bridge	15,000	1982	80.00	80
1979	Four Corners	15,000	1982	75.00	75
1981	Marshland	15,000	1982	95.00	95

Jungle Fantasy - G. Novoa

Year	Issue	Edition Limit	Year Retd.	Issue Price	*Quote U.S.$
1979	The Ark	10,000	1984	75.00	75
1981	Compassion	10,000	1984	95.00	95
1982	Patience	10,000	1984	95.00	95
1983	Refuge	10,000	1984	95.00	95

Log of the Dashing Wave - J. Stobart

Year	Issue	Edition Limit	Year Retd.	Issue Price	*Quote U.S.$
1976	Sailing With the Tide	15,000	1983	115.00	115
1977	Running Free	15,000	1983	110.00	150
1978	Rounding the Horn	15,000	1983	85.00	85
1979	Hong Kong	15,000	1983	75.00	75
1981	Bora Bora	15,000	1983	95.00	95
1982	Journey's End	15,000	1983	95.00	150

Mother and Child - E. Hibel

Year	Issue	Edition Limit	Year Retd.	Issue Price	*Quote U.S.$
1973	Colette and Child	15,000	1982	500.00	500
1974	Sayuri and Child	15,000	1982	175.00	175
1975	Kristina and Child	15,000	1982	125.00	125
1976	Marilyn and Child	15,000	1982	110.00	110
1977	Lucia and Child	15,000	1982	90.00	90
1981	Kathleen and Child	15,000	1982	85.00	125

Portraits of Innocence - F. Masseria

Year	Issue	Edition Limit	Year Retd.	Issue Price	*Quote U.S.$
1980	Panchito	15,000	1987	65.00	100-125
1981	Adrien	15,000	1987	85.00	120
1982	Angelica	15,000	1987	95.00	120
1983	Juliana	15,000	1987	95.00	120
1985	Gabriella	15,000	1987	95.00	120
1986	Francesca	15,000	1987	95.00	150

Ports of Call - D. Kingman

Year	Issue	Edition Limit	Year Retd.	Issue Price	*Quote U.S.$
1975	San Francisco, Fisherman's Wharf	15,000	1979	90.00	90
1976	New Orleans, Royal Street	15,000	1979	80.00	80
1977	Venice, Grand Canal	15,000	1979	65.00	65
1978	Paris, Montmartre	15,000	1979	70.00	70

Reflections of China - C. Chi

Year	Issue	Edition Limit	Year Retd.	Issue Price	*Quote U.S.$
1976	Garden of Tranquility	15,000	1981	90.00	90
1977	Imperial Palace	15,000	1981	80.00	80
1978	Temple of Heaven	15,000	1981	75.00	75
1980	Lake of Mists	15,000	1981	85.00	85

Victorian Era Christmas - N/A

Year	Issue	Edition Limit	Year Retd.	Issue Price	*Quote U.S.$
1977	Winter Fun	Yr.Iss.	1977	55.00	55
1978	Christmas Day	Yr.Iss.	1978	55.00	55
1979	Christmas	Yr.Iss.	1979	25.00	25
1980	Santa's Visit	Yr.Iss.	1980	30.00	30
1981	Christmas Carolers	Yr.Iss.	1981	37.50	38
1982	Santa on Bicycle	Yr.Iss.	1982	39.95	40

Victorian Era Valentines - N/A

Year	Issue	Edition Limit	Year Retd.	Issue Price	*Quote U.S.$
1976	Victorian Boy and Girl	Yr.Iss.	1976	65.00	65
1977	My Sweetest Friend	Yr.Iss.	1977	40.00	40
1978	If I Loved You	Yr.Iss.	1978	40.00	40
1979	My Valentine	Yr.Iss.	1979	35.00	35
1980	Valentine	Yr.Iss.	1980	33.00	33
1981	Valentine Boy and Girl	Yr.Iss.	1981	35.00	35
1982	Angel with Mandolin	Yr.Iss.	1982	39.95	40
1985	My Valentine	Yr.Iss.	1985	39.95	40

Royal Worcester

Birth Of A Nation - P.W. Baston

Year	Issue	Edition Limit	Year Retd.	Issue Price	*Quote U.S.$
1972	Boston Tea Party	10,000		45.00	140-275
1973	Paul Revere	10,000		45.00	140-250
1974	Concord Bridge	10,000		50.00	140
1975	Signing Declaration	10,000		65.00	140
1976	Crossing Delaware	10,000		65.00	140
1977	Washington's Inauguration	1,250		65.00	140

Currier and Ives Plates - P.W. Baston

Year	Issue	Edition Limit	Year Retd.	Issue Price	*Quote U.S.$
1974	Road in Winter	5,570		59.50	55-100
1975	Old Grist Mill	3,200		59.50	55-100
1976	Winter Pastime	1,500		59.50	55-125
1977	Home to Thanksgiving	546		59.50	200-250

Seymour Mann, Inc.

Connoisseur Christmas Collection - Bernini™

Year	Issue	Edition Limit	Year Retd.	Issue Price	*Quote U.S.$
1996	Cardinals CLT-310	25,000		50.00	50
1996	Chickadees CLT-300	25,000		50.00	50
1996	Doves CLT-305	25,000		50.00	50

Connoisseur Collection - Bernini™

Year	Issue	Edition Limit	Year Retd.	Issue Price	*Quote U.S.$
1995	Bluebird CLT-13	25,000	1996	50.00	50
1996	Butterfly/Lily CLT-330	25,000		50.00	50
1995	Canary CLT-10	25,000		50.00	50
1995	Cardinal CLT-7	25,000	1996	50.00	50
1995	Dove Duo CLT-1	25,000		50.00	50
1995	Hummingbird Duo CLT-4	25,000	1996	50.00	50
1996	Hummingbirds, Morning Glory, Blue CLT-320B	25,000		50.00	50
1996	Hummingbirds, Morning Glory, pink CLT-320	25,000		50.00	50
1996	Magnolia CLT-76	25,000		50.00	50
1995	Pink Rose CLT-70	25,000		50.00	50
1995	Robin CLT-16	25,000		50.00	50
1996	Roses/Forget-Me-Not CLT-340	25,000		50.00	50
1995	Swan Duo CLT-50	25,000		50.00	50

Doll Art™ Collection - E. Mann

Year	Issue	Edition Limit	Year Retd.	Issue Price	*Quote U.S.$
1996	Hope CLT-600P	25,000		60.00	60

Sports Impressions/Enesco Corporation

Gold Edition Plates - Various

Year	Issue	Edition Limit	Year Retd.	Issue Price	*Quote U.S.$
XX	A's Jose Canseco Gold (10 1/4") 1028-04 - J. Canseco	2,500	N/A	125.00	125
1990	Andre Dawson - R. Lewis	Closed		150.00	150
1988	Brooks Robinson, signed - R. Simon	Closed		125.00	250
1987	Carl Yastrzemski, signed - R. Simon	Closed		125.00	150
1992	Chicago Bulls '92 World Champions - C. Hayes	Closed		150.00	150
1993	Chicago Bulls 1993 World Championship Gold (10 1/4") 4062-04 - B. Vann	1,993	1994	150.00	150
1987	Darryl Strawberry #1 - R. Simon	Closed		125.00	125
1989	Darryl Strawberry #2 - T. Fogerty	Closed		125.00	125
1986	Don Mattingly - B. Johnson	Closed		125.00	125
1991	Dream Team (1st Ten Chosen) - L. Salk	Closed		150.00	350
1992	Dream Team - R.Tanenbaum	Closed		150.00	175
1992	Dream Team 1992 (8 1/2") 5507-03 - C. Hayes	7,500	1994	60.00	95
1992	Dream Team 1992 Gold (10 1/4") 5509-04 - R. Tanenbaum	1,992	1994	150.00	150
1991	Hawks Dominique Wilkins - J. Catalano	Closed		150.00	195
1990	Joe Montana 49ers Gold (10 1/4") 3000-04 - J. Catalano	1,990	1991	150.00	195
1986	Keith Hernandez - R. Simon	Closed		125.00	175
1991	Larry Bird - J. Catalano	Closed		150.00	195
1988	Larry Bird - R. Simon	Closed		125.00	275
1990	Living Triple Crown - R. Lewis	Closed		150.00	150-225
1993	Magic Johnson (4042-04) - R.Tanenbaum	Closed		150.00	150
1993	Magic Johnson - T. Fogerty	Closed		150.00	150-175
1991	Magic Johnson Lakers Gold (10 1/4") 4007-04 - C.W. Mundy	1,991	1991	150.00	225
1992	Magic Johnson Lakers Gold (10 1/4") 4042-04 - R. Tanenbaum	1,992	1994	150.00	175
1991	Magic Johnson Lakers Platinum (8 1/2") 4007-03 - M. Petronella	5,000	1992	60.00	75
1989	Mantle Switch Hitter - J. Catalano	Closed		150.00	275-300
1991	Michael Jordan - J. Catalano	Closed		150.00	295
1993	Michael Jordan - T. Fogerty	Closed		150.00	200
1992	Michael Jordan Bulls (10 1/4") 4032-04 - R. Tanenbaum	1,991	1992	150.00	225
1993	Michael Jordan Bulls Gold (10 1/4") 4046-04 - T. Fogarty	2,500	1993	150.00	175
1991	Michael Jordan Gold (10 1/4") 4002-04 - J. Catalano	1,991	1992	150.00	150
1991	Michael Jordan Platinum (8 1/2") 4002-03 - M. Petronella	1,991	1993	60.00	95
1995	Mickey Mantle "My Greatest Year 1956" 1229-04 - B. Vann	1,956		100.00	100
1991	Mickey Mantle 7 - B. Simon	Closed		150.00	150-195
1986	Mickey Mantle At Night - R. Simon	Closed		125.00	250
1995	Mickey Mantle double plate set 176923 - T. Treadway	2,401		75.00	75
1987	Mickey, Willie, & Duke, signed - R. Simon	Closed		150.00	500-795
1992	NBA 1st Ten Chosen Platinum (8 1/2") (blue) 5502-03 - J. Catalano	7,500	1993	60.00	95
1992	NBA 1st Ten Chosen Platinum (8 1/2") (red) 5503-03 - C.W. Mundy	7,500	1993	60.00	95
1990	Nolan Ryan 300 Gold 1091-04 - T. Fogarty	1,990	1992	150.00	150
1990	Nolan Ryan 5,000 K's - J. Catalano	1,990		150.00	150-175
1995	Profiles in Courage Mickey Mantle 1231-03 - M. Petronella	Open		30.00	30
1990	Rickey Henderson - R. Lewis	Closed		150.00	150
XX	Roberto Clemente 1090-03 - R. Lewis	10,000	N/A	75.00	75
1994	Shaquille O'Neal , Rookie of the Year - N/A	Open		100.00	100
1993	Shaquille O'Neal Gold (10 1/4") 4047-04 - T. Fogarty	2,500	1994	150.00	150
1987	Ted Williams, signed - R. Simon	Closed		125.00	450-500
1990	Tom Seaver - R. Lewis	Closed		150.00	150
1986	Wade Bogg, signed - B. Johnson	Closed		125.00	150
1989	Will Clark - J. Catalano	Closed		125.00	150

*Quotes have been rounded up to nearest dollar

Sports Impressions/Enesco Corporation
to W.S. George

PLATES

YEAR ISSUE	EDITION LIMIT	YEAR RETD.	ISSUE PRICE	*QUOTE U.S.$
1988 Yankee Tradition - J. Catalano	Closed		150.00	175

The Tudor Mint Inc.

Collector Plates - J. Mulholland

YEAR ISSUE	EDITION LIMIT	YEAR RETD.	ISSUE PRICE	*QUOTE U.S.$
1992 4401 Meeting of Unicorns	Closed	1993	27.10	100
1992 4402 Cauldron of Light	Closed	1993	27.10	100
1992 4403 The Guardian Dragon	Closed	1993	27.10	100
1992 4404 The Dragon's Nest	Closed	1993	27.10	100
1992 Set of 4	Closed	1993	108.40	500

Villeroy & Boch

Flower Fairy - C. Barker

YEAR ISSUE	EDITION LIMIT	YEAR RETD.	ISSUE PRICE	*QUOTE U.S.$
1979 Lavender	21-day		35.00	125
1980 Sweet Pea	21-day		35.00	125
1980 Candytuft	21-day		35.00	89
1981 Heliotrope	21-day		35.00	75
1981 Blackthorn	21-day		35.00	75
1981 Appleblossom	21-day		35.00	95

Russian Fairytales Maria Morevna - B. Zvorykin

YEAR ISSUE	EDITION LIMIT	YEAR RETD.	ISSUE PRICE	*QUOTE U.S.$
1983 Maria Morevna and Tsarevich Ivan	27,500		70.00	70
1983 Koshchey Carries Off Maria Morevna	27,500		70.00	70
1983 Tsarevich Ivan and the Beautiful Castle	27,500		70.00	70

Russian Fairytales The Firebird - B. Zvorykin

YEAR ISSUE	EDITION LIMIT	YEAR RETD.	ISSUE PRICE	*QUOTE U.S.$
1982 In Search of the Firebird	27,500		70.00	55
1982 Ivan and Tsarevna on the Grey Wolf	27,500		70.00	60
1982 The Wedding of Tsarevna Elena the Fair	27,500		70.00	70-100

Russian Fairytales The Red Knight - B. Zvorykin

YEAR ISSUE	EDITION LIMIT	YEAR RETD.	ISSUE PRICE	*QUOTE U.S.$
1981 The Red Knight	27,500		70.00	55-100
1981 Vassilissa and Her Stepsisters	27,500		70.00	55-75
1981 Vassilissa is Presented to the Tsar	27,500		70.00	45-55
1981 Vassilissa is Presented to the Tsar	27,500		70.00	45-55

W.S. George

Alaska: The Last Frontier - H. Lambson

YEAR ISSUE	EDITION LIMIT	YEAR RETD.	ISSUE PRICE	*QUOTE U.S.$
1991 Icy Majesty	Closed		34.50	40
1991 Autumn Grandeur	Closed		34.50	35
1992 Mountain Monarch	Closed		37.50	40
1992 Down the Trail	Closed		37.50	40
1992 Moonlight Lookout	Closed		37.50	60
1992 Graceful Passage	Closed		39.50	60
1992 Arctic Journey	Closed		39.50	66
1992 Summit Domain	Closed		39.50	60

Along an English Lane - M. Harvey

YEAR ISSUE	EDITION LIMIT	YEAR RETD.	ISSUE PRICE	*QUOTE U.S.$
1993 Summer's Bright Welcome	Closed		29.50	50
1993 Greeting the Day	Closed		29.50	60
1993 Friends and Flowers	Closed		29.50	60
1993 Cottage Around the Bend	Closed		29.50	30

America the Beautiful - H. Johnson

YEAR ISSUE	EDITION LIMIT	YEAR RETD.	ISSUE PRICE	*QUOTE U.S.$
1988 Yosemite Falls	Closed		34.50	50
1989 The Grand Canyon	Closed		34.50	30
1989 Yellowstone River	Closed		37.50	41
1989 The Great Smokey Mountains	Closed		37.50	45
1990 The Everglades	Closed		37.50	45
1990 Acadia	Closed		37.50	45
1990 The Grand Tetons	Closed		39.50	55
1990 Crater Lake	Closed		39.50	50

America's Pride - R. Richert

YEAR ISSUE	EDITION LIMIT	YEAR RETD.	ISSUE PRICE	*QUOTE U.S.$
1992 Misty Fjords	Closed		29.50	40
1992 Rugged Shores	Closed		29.50	40
1992 Mighty Summit	Closed		32.50	45
1993 Lofty Reflections	Closed		32.50	60
1993 Tranquil Waters	Closed		32.50	50
1993 Mountain Majesty	Closed		34.50	35
1993 Canyon Climb	Closed		34.50	50
1993 Golden Vista	Closed		34.50	35

Art Deco - M. McDonald

YEAR ISSUE	EDITION LIMIT	YEAR RETD.	ISSUE PRICE	*QUOTE U.S.$
1989 A Flapper With Greyhounds	Closed		39.50	45
1990 Tango Dancers	Closed		39.50	60
1990 Arriving in Style	Closed		39.50	55
1990 On the Town	Closed		39.50	60

Baby Cats of the Wild - C. Fracé

YEAR ISSUE	EDITION LIMIT	YEAR RETD.	ISSUE PRICE	*QUOTE U.S.$
1992 Morning Mischief	Closed		29.50	45
1993 Togetherness	Closed		29.50	45
1993 The Buddy System	Closed		32.50	50
1993 Nap Time	Closed		32.50	50

Bear Tracks - J. Seerey-Lester

YEAR ISSUE	EDITION LIMIT	YEAR RETD.	ISSUE PRICE	*QUOTE U.S.$
1992 Denali Family	Closed		29.50	35
1993 Their First Season	Closed		29.50	45
1993 High Country Champion	Closed		29.50	50
1993 Heavy Going	Closed		29.50	40
1993 Breaking Cover	Closed		29.50	60
1993 Along the Ice Flow	Closed		29.50	55

Beloved Hymns of Childhood - C. Barker

YEAR ISSUE	EDITION LIMIT	YEAR RETD.	ISSUE PRICE	*QUOTE U.S.$
1988 The Lord's My Shepherd	Closed		29.50	40
1988 Away In a Manger	Closed		29.50	35
1989 Now Thank We All Our God	Closed		32.50	33
1989 Love Divine	Closed		32.50	33
1989 I Love to Hear the Story	Closed		32.50	33
1989 All Glory, Laud and Honour	Closed		32.50	33
1990 All People on Earth Do Dwell	Closed		34.50	35
1990 Loving Shepherd of Thy Sheep	Closed		34.50	35

A Black Tie Affair: The Penguin - C. Jagodits

YEAR ISSUE	EDITION LIMIT	YEAR RETD.	ISSUE PRICE	*QUOTE U.S.$
1992 Little Explorer	Closed		29.50	50
1992 Penguin Parade	Closed		29.50	50
1992 Baby-Sitters	Closed		29.50	50
1993 Belly Flopping	Closed		29.50	50

Blessed Are The Children - W. Rane

YEAR ISSUE	EDITION LIMIT	YEAR RETD.	ISSUE PRICE	*QUOTE U.S.$
1990 Let the/Children Come To Me	Closed		29.50	45
1990 I Am the Good Shepherd	Closed		29.50	45
1991 Whoever Welcomes/Child	Closed		32.50	33
1991 Hosanna in the Highest	Closed		32.50	35
1991 Jesus Had Compassion on Them	Closed		32.50	50
1991 Blessed are the Peacemakers	Closed		34.50	55
1991 I am the Vine, You are the Branches	Closed		34.50	50
1991 Seek and You Will Find	Closed		34.50	35

Bonds of Love - B. Burke

YEAR ISSUE	EDITION LIMIT	YEAR RETD.	ISSUE PRICE	*QUOTE U.S.$
1989 Precious Embrace	Closed		29.50	30-40
1990 Cherished Moment	Closed		29.50	30-40
1991 Tender Caress	Closed		32.50	35-45
1992 Loving Touch	Closed		32.50	33-40
1992 Treasured Kisses	Closed		32.50	40-50
1994 Endearing Whispers	Closed		32.50	50-70

The Christmas Story - H. Garrido

YEAR ISSUE	EDITION LIMIT	YEAR RETD.	ISSUE PRICE	*QUOTE U.S.$
1992 Gifts of the Magi	Closed		29.50	45
1993 Rest on the Flight into Egypt	Closed		29.50	50
1993 Journey of the Magi	Closed		29.50	30
1993 The Nativity	Closed		29.50	30
1993 The Annunciation	Closed		29.50	30
1993 Adoration of the Shepherds	Closed		29.50	45

Classic Waterfowl: The Ducks Unlimited - L. Kaatz

YEAR ISSUE	EDITION LIMIT	YEAR RETD.	ISSUE PRICE	*QUOTE U.S.$
1988 Mallards at Sunrise	Closed		36.50	45-50
1988 Geese in the Autumn Fields	Closed		36.50	40
1989 Green Wings/Morning Marsh	Closed		39.50	40
1989 Canvasbacks, Breaking Away	Closed		39.50	40
1989 Pintails in Indian Summer	Closed		39.50	40
1990 Wood Ducks Taking Flight	Closed		39.50	40
1990 Snow Geese Against November Skies	Closed		41.50	42
1990 Bluebills Coming In	Closed		41.50	42

Columbus Discovers America: The 500th Anniversary - J. Penalva

YEAR ISSUE	EDITION LIMIT	YEAR RETD.	ISSUE PRICE	*QUOTE U.S.$
1991 Under Full Sail	Closed		29.50	40
1992 Ashore at Dawn	Closed		29.50	35
1992 Columbus Raises the Flag	Closed		32.50	30
1992 Bringing Together Two Cultures	Closed		32.50	47
1992 The Queen's Approval	Closed		32.50	33
1992 Treasures From The New World	Closed		32.50	50-55

Country Bouquets - G. Kurz

YEAR ISSUE	EDITION LIMIT	YEAR RETD.	ISSUE PRICE	*QUOTE U.S.$
1991 Morning Sunshine	Closed		29.50	45
1991 Summer Perfume	Closed		29.50	30
1992 Warm Welcome	Closed		32.50	50
1992 Garden's Bounty	Closed		32.50	45

Country Nostalgia - M. Harvey

YEAR ISSUE	EDITION LIMIT	YEAR RETD.	ISSUE PRICE	*QUOTE U.S.$
1989 The Spring Buggy	Closed		29.50	30
1989 The Apple Cider Press	Closed		29.50	30
1989 The Vintage Seed Planter	Closed		29.50	30
1989 The Old Hand Pump	Closed		32.50	50
1990 The Wooden Butter Churn	Closed		32.50	40
1990 The Dairy Cans	Closed		32.50	33
1990 The Forgotten Plow	Closed		34.50	35
1990 The Antique Spinning Wheel	Closed		34.50	40

Critic's Choice: Gone With The Wind - P. Jennis

YEAR ISSUE	EDITION LIMIT	YEAR RETD.	ISSUE PRICE	*QUOTE U.S.$
1991 Marry Me, Scarlett	Closed		27.50	35-50
1991 Waiting for Rhett	Closed		27.50	50
1991 A Declaration of Love	Closed		30.50	40-60
1991 The Paris Hat	Closed		30.50	55
1991 Scarlett Asks a Favor	Closed		30.50	55-65
1992 Scarlett Gets Her Way	Closed		32.50	45-60
1992 The Smitten Suitor	Closed		32.50	40-55
1992 Scarlett's Shopping Spree	Closed		32.50	40
1992 The Buggy Ride	Closed		32.50	55
1992 Scarlett Gets Down to Business	Closed		34.50	35
1993 Scarlett's Heart is with Tara	Closed		34.50	40-60
1993 At Cross Purposes	Closed		34.50	45

A Delicate Balance: Vanishing Wildlife - G. Beecham

YEAR ISSUE	EDITION LIMIT	YEAR RETD.	ISSUE PRICE	*QUOTE U.S.$
1992 Tomorrow's Hope	Closed		29.50	40
1993 Today's Future	Closed		29.50	45
1993 Present Dreams	Closed		32.50	35
1993 Eyes on the New Day	Closed		32.50	35

Dr. Zhivago - G. Bush

YEAR ISSUE	EDITION LIMIT	YEAR RETD.	ISSUE PRICE	*QUOTE U.S.$
1990 Zhivago and Lara	Closed		39.50	40
1991 Love Poems For Lara	Closed		39.50	40
1991 Zhivago Says Farewell	Closed		39.50	45
1991 Lara's Love	Closed		39.50	55

The Elegant Birds - J. Faulkner

YEAR ISSUE	EDITION LIMIT	YEAR RETD.	ISSUE PRICE	*QUOTE U.S.$
1988 The Swan	Closed		32.50	35-45
1988 Great Blue Heron	Closed		32.50	33
1989 Snowy Egret	Closed		32.50	33
1989 The Anhinga	Closed		35.50	36
1989 The Flamingo	Closed		35.50	36-45
1990 Sandhill and Whooping Crane	Closed		35.50	36

Enchanted Garden - E. Antonaccio

YEAR ISSUE	EDITION LIMIT	YEAR RETD.	ISSUE PRICE	*QUOTE U.S.$
1993 A Peaceful Retreat	Closed		24.50	40
1993 Pleasant Pathways	Closed		24.50	50
1993 A Place to Dream	Closed		24.50	25
1993 Tranquil Hideaway	Closed		24.50	25

Eyes of the Wild - D. Pierce

YEAR ISSUE	EDITION LIMIT	YEAR RETD.	ISSUE PRICE	*QUOTE U.S.$
1993 Eyes in the Mist	Closed		29.50	55
1993 Eyes in the Pines	Closed		29.50	40
1993 Eyes on the Sly	Closed		29.50	60-73
1993 Eyes of Gold	Closed		29.50	45
1993 Eyes of Silence	Closed		29.50	35
1993 Eyes in the Snow	Closed		29.50	40
1993 Eyes of Wonder	95-day		29.50	55
1994 Eyes of Strength	95-day		29.50	45

The Faces of Nature - J. Kramer Cole

YEAR ISSUE	EDITION LIMIT	YEAR RETD.	ISSUE PRICE	*QUOTE U.S.$
1992 Canyon of the Cat	Closed		29.50	50
1992 Wolf Ridge	Closed		29.50	45
1993 Trail of the Talisman	Closed		29.50	60
1993 Wolfpack of the Ancients	Closed		29.50	50
1993 Two Bears Camp	Closed		29.50	38
1993 Wintering With the Wapiti	Closed		29.50	45
1993 Within Sunrise	Closed		29.50	52
1993 Wambli Okiye	150-day		29.50	30

The Federal Duck Stamp Plate Collection - Various

YEAR ISSUE	EDITION LIMIT	YEAR RETD.	ISSUE PRICE	*QUOTE U.S.$
1990 The Lesser Scaup	Closed		27.50	28
1990 The Mallard	Closed		27.50	38
1990 The Ruddy Ducks	Closed		30.50	31
1990 Canvasbacks	Closed		30.50	31
1991 Pintails	Closed		30.50	31
1991 Wigeons	Closed		30.50	31
1991 Cinnamon Teal	Closed		32.50	33
1991 Fulvous Wistling Duck	Closed		32.50	45
1991 The Redheads	Closed		32.50	45
1991 Snow Goose	Closed		32.50	33

Feline Fancy - H. Ronner

YEAR ISSUE	EDITION LIMIT	YEAR RETD.	ISSUE PRICE	*QUOTE U.S.$
1993 Globetrotters	Closed		34.50	35
1993 Little Athletes	Closed		34.50	40
1993 Young Adventurers	Closed		34.50	45
1993 The Geographers	Closed		34.50	50

Field Birds of North America - D. Bush

YEAR ISSUE	EDITION LIMIT	YEAR RETD.	ISSUE PRICE	*QUOTE U.S.$
1991 Winter Colors: Ring-Necked Pheasant	Closed		39.50	45
1991 In Display: Ruffed Grouse	Closed		39.50	40
1991 Morning Light: Bobwhite Quail	Closed		42.50	50
1991 Misty Clearing: Wild Turkey	Closed		42.50	70
1992 Autumn Moment: American Woodcock	Closed		42.50	50
1992 Season's End: Willow Ptarmigan	Closed		42.50	60

Floral Fancies - C. Callog

YEAR ISSUE	EDITION LIMIT	YEAR RETD.	ISSUE PRICE	*QUOTE U.S.$
1993 Sitting Softly	Closed		34.50	45
1993 Sitting Pretty	Closed		34.50	47
1993 Sitting Sunny	Closed		34.50	35
1993 Sitting Pink	95-day		34.50	35

Flowers From Grandma's Garden - G. Kurz

YEAR ISSUE	EDITION LIMIT	YEAR RETD.	ISSUE PRICE	*QUOTE U.S.$
1990 Country Cuttings	Closed		24.50	40-50
1990 The Morning Bouquet	Closed		24.50	40-50
1991 Homespun Beauty	Closed		27.50	40
1991 Harvest in the Meadow	Closed		27.50	40
1991 Gardener's Delight	Closed		27.50	40
1991 Nature's Bounty	Closed		27.50	60
1991 A Country Welcome	Closed		29.50	55
1991 The Springtime Arrangement	Closed		29.50	50

Flowers of Your Garden - V. Morley

YEAR ISSUE	EDITION LIMIT	YEAR RETD.	ISSUE PRICE	*QUOTE U.S.$
1988 Roses	Closed		24.50	35-60
1988 Lilacs	Closed		24.50	40
1988 Daisies	Closed		27.50	28
1988 Peonies	Closed		27.50	28
1988 Chrysanthemums	Closed		27.50	28
1989 Daffodils	Closed		27.50	28
1989 Tulips	Closed		29.50	30
1989 Irises	Closed		29.50	30

Garden of the Lord - C. Gillies

YEAR ISSUE	EDITION LIMIT	YEAR RETD.	ISSUE PRICE	*QUOTE U.S.$
1992 Love One Another	Closed		29.50	45
1992 Perfect Peace	Closed		29.50	36
1992 Trust In the Lord	150-day		32.50	33
1992 The Lord's Love	150-day		32.50	33
1992 The Lord Bless You	150-day		32.50	33
1992 Ask In Prayer	150-day		34.50	35
1993 Peace Be With You	150-day		34.50	35
1993 Give Thanks To The Lord	150-day		34.50	35

*Quotes have been rounded up to nearest dollar

W.S. George
to W.S. George

PLATES

Gardens of Paradise - L. Chang

Year	Issue	Edition Limit	Year Retd.	Issue Price	*Quote U.S.$
1992	Tranquility	Closed		29.50	40
1992	Serenity	Closed		29.50	40
1993	Splendor	Closed		32.50	40
1993	Harmony	Closed		32.50	55
1993	Beauty	Closed		32.50	40
1993	Elegance	Closed		32.50	50
1993	Grandeur	Closed		32.50	65
1993	Majesty	150-day		32.50	50

Gentle Beginnings - W. Nelson

Year	Issue	Edition Limit	Year Retd.	Issue Price	*Quote U.S.$
1991	Tender Loving Care	Closed		34.50	45
1991	A Touch of Love	Closed		34.50	50
1991	Under Watchful Eyes	Closed		37.50	70-80
1991	Lap of Love	Closed		37.50	60
1992	Happy Together	Closed		37.50	80
1992	First Steps	Closed		37.50	80

Glorious Songbirds - R. Cobane

Year	Issue	Edition Limit	Year Retd.	Issue Price	*Quote U.S.$
1991	Cardinals on a Snowy Branch	Closed		29.50	30
1991	Indigo Buntings and/Blossoms	Closed		29.50	30
1991	Chickadees Among The Lilacs	Closed		32.50	33
1991	Goldfinches in/Thistle	Closed		32.50	33
1991	Cedar Waxwing/Winter Berries	Closed		32.50	33
1991	Bluebirds in a Blueberry Bush	Closed		34.50	35
1991	Baltimore Orioles/Autumn Leaves	Closed		34.50	45
1991	Robins with Dogwood in Bloom	Closed		34.50	45

The Golden Age of the Clipper Ships - C. Vickery

Year	Issue	Edition Limit	Year Retd.	Issue Price	*Quote U.S.$
1989	The Twilight Under Full Sail	Closed		29.50	40
1989	The Blue Jacket at Sunset	Closed		29.50	30
1989	Young America, Homeward	Closed		32.50	45
1990	Flying Cloud	Closed		32.50	33
1990	Davy Crocket at Daybreak	Closed		32.50	35
1990	Golden Eagle Conquers Wind	Closed		32.50	33
1990	The Lightning in Lifting Fog	Closed		34.50	35
1990	Sea Witch, Mistress/Oceans	Closed		34.50	35

Gone With the Wind: Golden Anniversary - H. Rogers

Year	Issue	Edition Limit	Year Retd.	Issue Price	*Quote U.S.$
1988	Scarlett and Her Suitors	Closed		24.50	50-125
1988	The Burning of Atlanta	Closed		24.50	45-90
1988	Scarlett and Ashley After the War	Closed		27.50	50-75
1988	The Proposal	Closed		27.50	60-80
1989	Home to Tara	Closed		27.50	35-50
1989	Strolling in Atlanta	Closed		27.50	35-45
1989	A Question of Honor	Closed		29.50	35-65
1989	Scarlett's Resolve	Closed		29.50	40-70
1989	Frankly My Dear	Closed		29.50	45-85
1989	Melane and Ashley	Closed		32.50	35-55
1990	A Toast to Bonnie Blue	Closed		32.50	45-65
1990	Scarlett and Rhett's Honeymoon	Closed		32.50	40-80

Gone With the Wind: The Passions of Scarlett O'Hara - P. Jennis

Year	Issue	Edition Limit	Year Retd.	Issue Price	*Quote U.S.$
1992	Fiery Embrace	Closed		29.50	50-60
1992	Pride and Passion	Closed		29.50	65
1992	Dreams of Ashley	Closed		32.50	70
1992	The Fond Farewell	Closed		32.50	35
1992	The Waltz	Closed		32.50	35-45
1992	As God Is My Witness	Closed		34.50	45-60
1993	Brave Scarlett	Closed		34.50	35-70
1993	Nightmare	Closed		34.50	40
1993	Evening Prayers	Closed		34.50	35
1993	Naptime	Closed		36.50	40-55
1993	Dangerous Attraction	Closed		36.50	41
1994	The End of An Era	Closed		36.50	37

Grand Safari: Images of Africa - C. Fracé

Year	Issue	Edition Limit	Year Retd.	Issue Price	*Quote U.S.$
1992	A Moment's Rest	Closed		34.50	35
1992	Elephant's of Kilimanjaro	Closed		34.50	50
1992	Undivided Attention	Closed		37.50	45
1993	Quiet Time in Samburu	Closed		37.50	50
1993	Lone Hunter	Closed		37.50	38
1993	The Greater Kudo	Closed		37.50	38

Heart of the Wild - G. Beecham

Year	Issue	Edition Limit	Year Retd.	Issue Price	*Quote U.S.$
1992	A Gentle Touch	Closed		29.50	30
1992	Mother's Pride	Closed		29.50	37
1992	An Afternoon Together	Closed		32.50	50
1993	Quiet Time?	Closed		32.50	50

Hollywood's Glamour Girls - E. Dzenis

Year	Issue	Edition Limit	Year Retd.	Issue Price	*Quote U.S.$
1989	Jean Harlow-Dinner at Eight	Closed		24.50	35-45
1990	Lana Turner-Postman Ring Twice	Closed		29.50	30-40
1990	Carol Lombard-The Gay Bride	Closed		29.50	30-40
1990	Greta Garbo-In Grand Hotel	Closed		29.50	30-40

Hometown Memories - H.T. Becker

Year	Issue	Edition Limit	Year Retd.	Issue Price	*Quote U.S.$
1993	Moonlight Skaters	Closed		29.50	30
1993	Mountain Sleigh Ride	Closed		29.50	40
1993	Heading Home	Closed		29.50	50
1993	A Winter Ride	Closed		29.50	50

Last of Their Kind: The Endangered Species - W. Nelson

Year	Issue	Edition Limit	Year Retd.	Issue Price	*Quote U.S.$
1988	The Panda	Closed		27.50	35-55
1989	The Snow Leopard	Closed		27.50	40-50
1989	The Red Wolf	Closed		30.50	40-50
1989	The Asian Elephant	Closed		30.50	50-60
1990	The Slender-Horned Gazelle	Closed		30.50	50
1990	The Bridled Wallaby	Closed		30.50	50
1990	The Black-Footed Ferret	Closed		33.50	50
1990	The Siberian Tiger	Closed		33.50	60
1991	The Vicuna	Closed		33.50	50
1991	Przewalski's Horse	Closed		33.50	60

Lena Liu's Basket Bouquets - L. Liu

Year	Issue	Edition Limit	Year Retd.	Issue Price	*Quote U.S.$
1992	Roses	Closed		29.50	40
1992	Pansies	Closed		29.50	45
1992	Tulips and Lilacs	Closed		32.50	45
1992	Irises	Closed		32.50	45
1992	Lilies	Closed		32.50	35
1992	Parrot Tulips	Closed		32.50	53
1992	Peonies	Closed		32.50	45
1993	Begonias	150-day		32.50	33
1993	Magnolias	150-day		32.50	33
1993	Calla Lilies	150-day		32.50	33
1993	Orchids	150-day		32.50	33
1993	Hydrangeas	150-day		32.50	33

Lena Liu's Flower Fairies - L. Liu

Year	Issue	Edition Limit	Year Retd.	Issue Price	*Quote U.S.$
1993	Magic Makers	Closed		29.50	30
1993	Petal Playmates	150-day		29.50	30
1993	Delicate Dancers	150-day		32.50	33
1993	Mischief Masters	150-day		32.50	33
1993	Amorous Angels	150-day		32.50	33
1993	Winged Wonders	150-day		34.50	35
1993	Miniature Mermaids	150-day		34.50	35
1993	Fanciful Fairies	150-day		34.50	35

Lena Liu's Hummingbird Treasury - L. Liu

Year	Issue	Edition Limit	Year Retd.	Issue Price	*Quote U.S.$
1992	Ruby-Throated Hummingbird	Closed		29.50	55
1992	Anna's Hummingbird	Closed		29.50	65
1992	Violet-Crowned Hummingbird	Closed		32.50	74-82
1993	Rufous Hummingbird	Closed		32.50	56-80
1993	White-Eared Hummingbird	Closed		32.50	70
1993	Broad-Billed Hummingbird	150-day		34.50	35
1993	Calliope Hummingbird	150-day		34.50	35
1993	The Allen's Hummingbird	150-day		34.50	35

Little Angels - B. Burke

Year	Issue	Edition Limit	Year Retd.	Issue Price	*Quote U.S.$
1992	Angels We Have Heard on High	Closed		29.50	40-65
1992	O Tannenbaum	Closed		29.50	50-70
1993	Joy to the World	Closed		32.50	75
1993	Hark the Herald Angels Sing	Closed		32.50	50-75
1993	It Came Upon a Midnight Clear	Closed		32.50	55
1993	The First Noel	Closed		[illegible]	35

A Loving Look: Duck Families - B. Langton

Year	Issue	Edition Limit	Year Retd.	Issue Price	*Quote U.S.$
1990	Family Outing	Closed		34.50	35
1991	Sleepy Start	Closed		34.50	35
1991	Quiet Moment	Closed		37.50	40
1991	Safe and Sound	Closed		37.50	38
1991	Spring Arrivals	Closed		37.50	38
1991	The Family Tree	Closed		37.50	50

The Majestic Horse - P. Wildermuth

Year	Issue	Edition Limit	Year Retd.	Issue Price	*Quote U.S.$
1992	Classic Beauty: Thoroughbred	Closed		34.50	35
1992	American Gold: The Quarterhorse	Closed		34.50	50
1992	Regal Spirit: The Arabian	Closed		34.50	74
1992	Western Favorite: American Paint Horse	Closed		34.50	60

Melodies in the Mist - A. Sakhavarz

Year	Issue	Edition Limit	Year Retd.	Issue Price	*Quote U.S.$
1993	Early Morning Rain	Closed		34.50	35
1993	Among the Dewdrops	Closed		34.50	38
1993	Feeding Time	Closed		37.50	38
1994	Garden Party	Closed		37.50	38
1994	Spring Rain	Closed		37.50	38
1994	Unpleasant Surprise	Closed		37.50	38

Memories of a Victorian Childhood - Unknown

Year	Issue	Edition Limit	Year Retd.	Issue Price	*Quote U.S.$
1992	You'd Better Not Pout	Closed		29.50	30
1992	Sweet Slumber	Closed		29.50	55
1992	Through Thick and Thin	Closed		32.50	48
1992	An Armful of Treasures	Closed		32.50	65
1993	A Trio of Bookworms	Closed		32.50	60
1993	Pugnacious Playmate	Closed		32.50	55

Nature's Legacy - J. Sias

Year	Issue	Edition Limit	Year Retd.	Issue Price	*Quote U.S.$
1990	Blue Snow at Half Dome	Closed		24.50	35
1991	Misty Morning/Mt. McKinley	Closed		24.50	25
1991	Twilight Reflections on Mount Ranier	Closed		27.50	30
1991	Redwalls of Havasu Canyon	Closed		27.50	28
1991	Autumn Splendor in the Smoky Mountains	Closed		27.50	28
1991	Winter Peace in Yellowstone Park	Closed		29.50	30
1991	Golden Majesty/Rocky Mountains	Closed		29.50	35
1991	Radiant Sunset Over the Everglades	Closed		29.50	30

Nature's Lovables - C. Fracé

Year	Issue	Edition Limit	Year Retd.	Issue Price	*Quote U.S.$
1990	The Koala Bear	Closed		27.50	50
1991	New Arrival	Closed		27.50	50
1991	Chinese Treasure	Closed		27.50	50
1991	Baby Harp Seal	Closed		30.50	50
1991	Bobcat: Nature's Dawn	Closed		30.50	50
1991	Clouded Leopard	Closed		32.50	50
1991	Zebra Foal	Closed		32.50	50
1991	Bandit	Closed		32.50	50

Nature's Playmates - C. Fracé

Year	Issue	Edition Limit	Year Retd.	Issue Price	*Quote U.S.$
1991	Partners	Closed		29.50	30
1991	Secret Heights	Closed		29.50	30
1991	Recess	Closed		32.50	33
1991	Double Trouble	Closed		32.50	33
1991	Pals	Closed		32.50	33
1992	Curious Trio	Closed		34.50	43
1992	Playmates	Closed		34.50	45
1992	Surprise	Closed		34.50	35
1992	Peace On Ice	Closed		36.50	50
1992	Ambassadors	Closed		36.50	40

Nature's Poetry - L. Liu

Year	Issue	Edition Limit	Year Retd.	Issue Price	*Quote U.S.$
1989	Morning Serenade	Closed		24.50	45
1989	Song of Promise	Closed		24.50	30
1990	Tender Lullaby	Closed		27.50	40
1990	Nature's Harmony	Closed		27.50	40
1990	Gentle Refrain	Closed		27.50	28
1990	Morning Chorus	Closed		27.50	28
1990	Melody at Daybreak	Closed		29.50	30
1991	Delicate Accord	Closed		29.50	30
1991	Lyrical Beginnings	Closed		29.50	30
1991	Song of Spring	Closed		32.50	33
1991	Mother's Melody	Closed		32.50	33
1991	Cherub Chorale	Closed		32.50	35

On Golden Wings - W. Goebel

Year	Issue	Edition Limit	Year Retd.	Issue Price	*Quote U.S.$
1993	Morning Light	Closed		29.50	45
1993	Early Risers	Closed		29.50	45
1993	As Day Breaks	Closed		32.50	48
1993	Daylight Flight	Closed		32.50	42
1993	Winter Dawn	Closed		32.50	33
1994	First Light	95-day		34.50	50

On Gossamer Wings - L. Liu

Year	Issue	Edition Limit	Year Retd.	Issue Price	*Quote U.S.$
1988	Monarch Butterflies	Closed		24.50	35-45
1988	Western Tiger Swallowtails	Closed		24.50	40
1988	Red-Spotted Purple	Closed		27.50	40-50
1988	Malachites	Closed		27.50	25
1988	White Peacocks	Closed		27.50	30
1989	Eastern Tailed Blues	Closed		27.50	30
1989	Zebra Swallowtails	Closed		29.50	25
1989	Red Admirals	Closed		29.50	30

On the Wing - T. Humphrey

Year	Issue	Edition Limit	Year Retd.	Issue Price	*Quote U.S.$
1992	Winged Splendor	Closed		29.50	30
1992	Rising Mallard	Closed		29.50	31
1992	Glorious Ascent	Closed		32.50	35
1992	Taking Wing	Closed		32.50	40
1992	Upward Bound	Closed		32.50	40
1993	Wondrous Motion	Closed		34.50	35
1993	Springing Forth	Closed		34.50	55
1993	On The Wing	Closed		34.50	65

On Wings of Snow - L. Liu

Year	Issue	Edition Limit	Year Retd.	Issue Price	*Quote U.S.$
1991	The Swans	Closed		34.50	35
1991	The Doves	Closed		34.50	45
1991	The Peacocks	Closed		37.50	45
1991	The Egrets	Closed		37.50	50
1991	The Cockatoos	Closed		37.50	45
1992	The Herons	Closed		37.50	40

Our Woodland Friends - C. Brenders

Year	Issue	Edition Limit	Year Retd.	Issue Price	*Quote U.S.$
1989	Fascination	Closed		29.00	29
1990	Beneath the Pines	Closed		29.50	30
1990	High Adventure	Closed		32.50	33
1990	Shy Explorers	Closed		32.50	33
1991	Golden Season:Gray Squirrel	Closed		32.50	35
1991	Full House Fox Family	Closed		32.50	45
1991	A Jump Into Life: Spring Fawn	Closed		34.50	35
1991	Forest Sentinel:Bobcat	Closed		34.50	35

Petal Pals - L. Chang

Year	Issue	Edition Limit	Year Retd.	Issue Price	*Quote U.S.$
1992	Garden Discovery	Closed		24.50	40
1992	Flowering Fascination	Closed		24.50	30-40
1993	Alluring Lilies	Closed		24.50	37
1993	Springtime Oasis	Closed		24.50	30
1993	Blossoming Adventure	150-day		24.50	25
1993	Dancing Daffodils	150-day		24.50	25
1993	Summer Surprise	150-day		24.50	25
1993	Morning Melody	150-day		24.50	25

Poetic Cottages - C. Valente

Year	Issue	Edition Limit	Year Retd.	Issue Price	*Quote U.S.$
1992	Garden Paths of Oxfordshire	Closed		29.50	50
1992	Twilight at Woodgreen Pond	Closed		29.50	70
1992	Stonewall Brook Blossoms	Closed		32.50	65
1992	Bedfordshire Evening Sky	Closed		32.50	50
1993	Wisteria Summer	Closed		32.50	50
1993	Wiltshire Rose Arbor	Closed		32.50	50
1993	Alderbury Gardens	Closed		32.50	55
1993	Hampshire Spring Splendor	Closed		32.50	35

Portraits of Christ - J. Salamanca

Year	Issue	Edition Limit	Year Retd.	Issue Price	*Quote U.S.$
1991	Father, Forgive Them	Closed		29.50	65
1991	Thy Will Be Done	Closed		29.50	50
1991	This is My Beloved Son	Closed		32.50	45
1991	Lo, I Am With You	Closed		32.50	50
1991	Become as Little Children	Closed		32.50	55
1992	Peace I Leave With You	Closed		34.50	50
1992	For God So Loved the World	Closed		34.50	50

*Quotes have been rounded up to nearest dollar

Year Issue		Edition Limit	Year Retd.	Issue Price	*Quote U.S.$
1992	I Am the Way, the Truth and the Life	Closed		34.50	50
1992	Weep Not For Me	Closed		34.50	55
1992	Follow Me	Closed		34.50	60

Portraits of Exquisite Birds - C. Brenders

Year Issue		Edition Limit	Year Retd.	Issue Price	*Quote U.S.$
1990	Backyard Treasure/Chickadee	Closed		29.50	30
1990	The Beautiful Bluebird	Closed		29.50	30
1991	Summer Gold: The Robin	Closed		32.50	33
1991	The Meadowlark's Song	Closed		32.50	33
1991	Ivory-Billed Woodpecker	Closed		32.50	33
1991	Red-Winged Blackbird	Closed		32.50	33

Purebred Horses of the Americas - D. Schwartz

Year Issue		Edition Limit	Year Retd.	Issue Price	*Quote U.S.$
1989	The Appalosa	Closed		34.50	35
1989	The Tenesee Walker	Closed		34.50	35
1990	The Quarterhorse	Closed		37.50	38
1990	The Saddlebred	Closed		37.50	38
1990	The Mustang	Closed		37.50	38
1990	The Morgan	Closed		37.50	56

Rare Encounters - J. Seerey-Lester

Year Issue		Edition Limit	Year Retd.	Issue Price	*Quote U.S.$
1993	Softly, Softly	Closed		29.50	40
1993	Black Magic	Closed		29.50	60
1993	Future Song	Closed		32.50	60
1993	High and Mighty	Closed		32.50	55
1993	Last Sanctuary	Closed		32.50	40
1993	Something Stirred	Closed		34.50	45

Romantic Gardens - C. Smith

Year Issue		Edition Limit	Year Retd.	Issue Price	*Quote U.S.$
1989	The Woodland Garden	Closed		29.50	30
1989	The Plantation Garden	Closed		29.50	30
1990	The Cottage Garden	Closed		32.50	33
1990	The Colonial Garden	Closed		32.50	33

Romantic Harbors - C. Vickery

Year Issue		Edition Limit	Year Retd.	Issue Price	*Quote U.S.$
1993	Advent of the Golden Bough	Closed		34.50	42
1993	Christmas Tree Schooner	Closed		34.50	60
1993	Prelude to the Journey	Closed		37.50	55
1993	Shimmering Light of Dusk	Closed		37.50	100

Romantic Roses - V. Morley

Year Issue		Edition Limit	Year Retd.	Issue Price	*Quote U.S.$
1993	Victorian Beauty	Closed		29.50	45
1993	Old-Fashioned Grace	Closed		29.50	50
1993	Country Charm	Closed		32.50	33
1993	Summer Romance	Closed		32.50	33
1993	Pastoral Delight	Closed		32.50	33
1993	Springtime Elegance	95-day		34.50	35
1993	Vintage Splendor	95-day		34.50	35
1994	Heavenly Perfection	95-day		34.50	35

Scenes of Christmas Past - L. Garrison

Year Issue		Edition Limit	Year Retd.	Issue Price	*Quote U.S.$
1987	Holiday Skaters	Closed		27.50	28
1988	Christmas Eve	Closed		27.50	30
1989	The Homecoming	Closed		30.50	31
1990	The Toy Store	Closed		30.50	40
1991	The Carollers	Closed		30.50	40
1992	Family Traditions	Closed		32.50	45
1993	Holiday Past	Closed		32.50	65
1994	A Gathering of Faith	Closed		32.50	50

The Secret World Of The Panda - J. Bridgett

Year Issue		Edition Limit	Year Retd.	Issue Price	*Quote U.S.$
1990	A Mother's Care	Closed		27.50	35
1991	A Frolic in the Snow	Closed		27.50	28
1991	Lazy Afternoon	Closed		30.50	31
1991	A Day of Exploring	Closed		30.50	31
1991	A Gentle Hug	Closed		32.50	35
1991	A Bamboo Feast	Closed		32.50	70

Soaring Majesty - C. Fracé

Year Issue		Edition Limit	Year Retd.	Issue Price	*Quote U.S.$
1991	Freedom	Closed		29.50	30
1991	The Northern Goshhawk	Closed		29.50	30
1991	Peregrine Falcon	Closed		32.50	33
1991	Red-Tailed Hawk	Closed		32.50	33
1991	The Ospray	Closed		32.50	33
1991	The Gyrfalcon	Closed		34.50	35
1991	The Golden Eagle	Closed		34.50	37
1992	Red-Shouldered Hawk	Closed		34.50	35

Sonnets in Flowers - G. Kurz

Year Issue		Edition Limit	Year Retd.	Issue Price	*Quote U.S.$
1992	Sonnet of Beauty	Closed		29.50	33
1992	Sonnet of Happiness	Closed		34.50	40
1992	Sonnet of Love	Closed		34.50	35
1992	Sonnet of Peace	Closed		34.50	55

The Sound of Music: Silver Anniversary - V. Gadino

Year Issue		Edition Limit	Year Retd.	Issue Price	*Quote U.S.$
1991	The Hills are Alive	Closed		29.50	30
1992	Let's Start at the Very Beginning	Closed		29.50	30
1992	Something Good	Closed		32.50	40
1992	Maria's Wedding Day	Closed		32.50	55

Spirit of Christmas - J. Sias

Year Issue		Edition Limit	Year Retd.	Issue Price	*Quote U.S.$
1990	Silent Night	Closed		29.50	30
1991	Jingle Bells	Closed		29.50	30
1991	Deck The Halls	Closed		32.50	35
1991	I'll Be Home For Christmas	Closed		32.50	45
1991	Winter Wonderland	Closed		32.50	33
1991	O Christmas Tree	Closed		32.50	33

Spirits of the Sky - C. Fisher

Year Issue		Edition Limit	Year Retd.	Issue Price	*Quote U.S.$
1992	Twilight Glow	Closed		29.50	40
1992	First Light	Closed		29.50	60
1992	Evening Glimmer	Closed		32.50	75
1992	Golden Dusk	Closed		32.50	35
1993	Sunset Splendor	Closed		32.50	33
1993	Amber Flight	Closed		34.50	42
1993	Winged Radiance	Closed		34.50	48
1993	Day's End	Closed		34.50	35

A Splash of Cats - J. Seerey-Lester

Year Issue		Edition Limit	Year Retd.	Issue Price	*Quote U.S.$
1992	Moonlight Chase: Cougar	Closed		29.50	30

Symphony of Shimmering Beauties - L. Liu

Year Issue		Edition Limit	Year Retd.	Issue Price	*Quote U.S.$
1991	Iris Quartet	Closed		29.50	50-65
1991	Tulip Ensemble	Closed		29.50	45-65
1991	Poppy Pastorale	Closed		32.50	45-50
1991	Lily Concerto	Closed		32.50	40-50
1991	Peony Prelude	Closed		32.50	55
1991	Rose Fantasy	Closed		34.50	40
1991	Hibiscus Medley	Closed		34.50	45
1992	Dahlia Melody	Closed		34.50	45
1992	Hollyhock March	Closed		34.50	45
1992	Carnation Serenade	Closed		36.50	50
1992	Gladiolus Romance	Closed		36.50	50
1992	Zinnia Finale	Closed		36.50	50

Tis the Season - J. Sias

Year Issue		Edition Limit	Year Retd.	Issue Price	*Quote U.S.$
1993	World Dressed in Snow	Closed		29.50	35
1993	A Time for Tradition	Closed		29.50	35
1993	We Shall Come Rejoining	Closed		29.50	40
1993	Our Family Tree	Closed		29.50	40

Tomorrow's Promise - W. Nelson

Year Issue		Edition Limit	Year Retd.	Issue Price	*Quote U.S.$
1992	Curiosity: Asian Elephants	Closed		29.50	30
1992	Playtime Pandas	Closed		29.50	35
1992	Innocence: Rhinos	Closed		32.50	60
1992	Friskiness: Kit Foxes	Closed		32.50	45

Touching the Spirit - J. Kramer Cole

Year Issue		Edition Limit	Year Retd.	Issue Price	*Quote U.S.$
1993	Running With the Wind	Closed		29.50	60
1993	Kindred Spirits	Closed		29.50	35
1993	The Marking Tree	Closed		29.50	50
1993	Wakan Tanka	Closed		29.50	70
1993	He Who Watches	Closed		29.50	60
1994	Twice Traveled Trail	Closed		29.50	45
1994	Keeper of the Secret	95-day		29.50	45
1994	Camp of the Sacred Dogs	95-day		29.50	40

A Treasury of Songbirds - R. Stine

Year Issue		Edition Limit	Year Retd.	Issue Price	*Quote U.S.$
1992	Springtime Splendor	Closed		29.50	45
1992	Morning's Glory	Closed		29.50	45
1992	Golden Daybreak	Closed		32.50	45
1992	Afternoon Calm	Closed		32.50	45
1992	Dawn's Radiance	Closed		32.50	40
1993	Scarlet Sunrise	Closed		34.50	60
1993	Sapphire Dawn	Closed		34.50	50
1995	Alluring Daylight	Closed		34.50	65

The Vanishing Gentle Giants - A. Casay

Year Issue		Edition Limit	Year Retd.	Issue Price	*Quote U.S.$
1991	Jumping For Joy	Closed		32.50	33
1991	Song of the Humpback	Closed		32.50	33
1991	Monarch of the Deep	Closed		35.50	40
1991	Travelers of the Sea	Closed		35.50	55
1991	White Whale of the North	Closed		35.50	45
1991	Unicorn of the Sea	Closed		35.50	40

The Victorian Cat - H. Bonner

Year Issue		Edition Limit	Year Retd.	Issue Price	*Quote U.S.$
1990	Mischief With The Hatbox	Closed		24.50	45
1991	String Quartet	Closed		24.50	45
1991	Daydreams	Closed		27.50	35
1991	Frisky Felines	Closed		27.50	45
1991	Kittens at Play	Closed		27.50	40
1991	Playing in the Parlor	Closed		29.50	57
1991	Perfectly Poised	Closed		29.50	55
1992	Midday Repose	Closed		29.50	55

Victorian Cat Capers - Various

Year Issue		Edition Limit	Year Retd.	Issue Price	*Quote U.S.$
1992	Who's the Fairest of Them All? - F. Paton	Closed		24.50	50-60
1992	Puss in Boots - Unknown	Closed		24.50	40
1992	My Bowl is Empty - W. Hepple	Closed		27.50	35
1992	A Curious Kitty - W. Hepple	Closed		27.50	30
1992	Vanity Fair - W. Hepple	Closed		27.50	28
1992	Forbidden Fruit - W. Hepple	Closed		29.50	55
1993	The Purr-fect Pen Pal - W. Hepple	Closed		29.50	45
1993	The Kitten Express - W. Hepple	Closed		29.50	50

Wild Innocents - C. Fracé

Year Issue		Edition Limit	Year Retd.	Issue Price	*Quote U.S.$
1993	Reflections	Closed		29.50	35
1993	Spiritual Heir	Closed		29.50	50
1993	Lion Cub	Closed		29.50	45
1993	Sunny Spot	Closed		29.50	50
1993	Moonlight Chase-Cougar	Closed		29.50	30

Wild Spirits - T. Hirata

Year Issue		Edition Limit	Year Retd.	Issue Price	*Quote U.S.$
1992	Solitary Watch	Closed		29.50	30
1992	Timber Ghost	Closed		29.50	50
1992	Mountain Magic	Closed		32.50	35
1993	Silent Guard	Closed		32.50	45
1993	Sly Eyes	Closed		32.50	50
1993	Mighty Presence	Closed		34.50	40
1993	Quiet Vigil	Closed		34.50	35
1993	Lone Vanguard	150-day		34.50	35

Wings of Winter - D. Rust

Year Issue		Edition Limit	Year Retd.	Issue Price	*Quote U.S.$
1992	Moonlight Retreat	Closed		29.50	40
1993	Twilight Serenade	Closed		29.50	40
1993	Silent Sunset	Closed		29.50	40
1993	Night Lights	150-day		29.50	30
1993	Winter Haven	150-day		29.50	30
1993	Full Moon Companions	150-day		29.50	30
1993	White Night	150-day		29.50	30
1993	Winter Reflections	150-day		29.50	30

Winter's Majesty - C. Fracé

Year Issue		Edition Limit	Year Retd.	Issue Price	*Quote U.S.$
1992	The Quest	Closed		34.50	35
1992	The Chase	Closed		34.50	35
1993	Alaskan Friend	Closed		34.50	35
1993	American Cougar	Closed		34.50	35
1993	On Watch	Closed		34.50	45
1993	Solitude	Closed		34.50	43

Wonders Of The Sea - R. Harm

Year Issue		Edition Limit	Year Retd.	Issue Price	*Quote U.S.$
1991	Stand By Me	Closed		34.50	35
1991	Heart to Heart	Closed		34.50	35
1991	Warm Embrace	Closed		34.50	40
1991	A Family Affair	Closed		34.50	35

The World's Most Magnificent Cats - C. Fracé

Year Issue		Edition Limit	Year Retd.	Issue Price	*Quote U.S.$
1991	Fleeting Encounter	Closed		24.50	45-50
1991	Cougar	Closed		24.50	45-60
1991	Royal Bengal	Closed		27.50	40-50
1991	Powerful Presence	Closed		27.50	50-60
1991	Jaguar	Closed		27.50	50-60
1991	The Clouded Leopard	Closed		29.50	50-60
1991	The African Leopard	Closed		29.50	50-60
1991	Mighty Warrior	Closed		29.50	60
1992	The Cheetah	Closed		31.50	45-60
1992	Siberian Tiger	Closed		31.50	50-80

Waterford Wedgwood USA

Bicentennial - Unknown

Year Issue		Edition Limit	Year Retd.	Issue Price	*Quote U.S.$
1972	Boston Tea Party	Annual		40.00	40
1973	Paul Revere's Ride	Annual		40.00	115
1974	Battle of Concord	Annual		40.00	55
1975	Across the Delaware	Annual		40.00	105
1975	Victory at Yorktown	Annual		45.00	53
1976	Declaration Signed	Annual		45.00	45

Wedgwood Christmas - Various

Year Issue		Edition Limit	Year Retd.	Issue Price	*Quote U.S.$
1969	Windsor Castle - T. Harper	Annual		25.00	125
1970	Trafalgar Square - T. Harper	Annual		30.00	35
1971	Picadilly Circus - T. Harper	Annual		30.00	30
1972	St. Paul's Cathedral - T. Harper	Annual		35.00	45
1973	Tower of London - T. Harper	Annual		40.00	90
1974	Houses of Parliament - T. Harper	Annual		40.00	40
1975	Tower Bridge - T. Harper	Annual		45.00	45
1976	Hampton Court - T. Harper	Annual		50.00	50
1977	Westminister Abbey - T. Harper	Annual		55.00	60
1978	Horse Guards - T. Harper	Annual		60.00	60
1979	Buckingham Palace - Unknown	Annual		65.00	65
1980	St. James Palace - Unknown	Annual		70.00	70
1981	Marble Arch - Unknown	Annual		75.00	75
1982	Lambeth Palace - Unknown	Annual		80.00	90
1983	All Souls, Langham Palace - Unknown	Annual		80.00	80
1984	Constitution Hill - Unknown	Annual		80.00	80
1985	The Tate Gallery - Unknown	Annual		80.00	80
1986	The Albert Memorial - Unknown	Annual		80.00	110
1987	Guildhall - Unknown	Annual		80.00	85
1988	The Observatory/Greenwich - Unknown	Annual		80.00	90
1989	Winchester Cathedral - Unknown	Annual		88.00	88

STEINS

Ace Product Management Group, Inc.

Harley-Davidson Decade Series - Ace

Year Issue		Edition Limit	Year Retd.	Issue Price	*Quote U.S.$
1993	Birth Of A Legend-1900's 99282-94Z	3,000	1995	180.00	180
1993	Birth Of A Legend-1900's (Signaure) 99712-94Z	500	1995	275.00	275
1994	Growth Of A Sport-1910's 99283-95Z	3,000	1995	180.00	180
1994	Growth Of A Sport-1910's (Signature) 99285-95Z	500	1995	285.00	285
1995	Roaring Into The 20's-1920's 99295-96Z	3,000		185.00	185
1995	Roaring Into The 20's-1920's (Signature) 99291-96Z	500		285.00	285
1996	Growing Stronger With Time-1930's 99170-97Z	3,000		185.00	185
1996	Growing Stronger With Time-1930's (Signature) 99171-97Z	500		285.00	285
1993	8 Ltr Stein 99716-94Z	100	1993	875.00	875

Holiday Memories Holiday Steins - Ace

Year Issue		Edition Limit	Year Retd.	Issue Price	*Quote U.S.$
1994	Under The Mistletoe 99467-95Z	5,000	1994	85.00	85
1995	Late Arrival 99498-96Z	5,000	1995	90.00	90
1996	After The Pageant 99495-97Z	5,000	1996	95.00	95

*Quotes have been rounded up to nearest dollar

STEINS

Ace Product Management Group, Inc. to Anheuser-Busch, Inc.

YEAR ISSUE		EDITION LIMIT	YEAR RETD.	ISSUE PRICE	*QUOTE U.S.$
1997	Roadside Revelation 97965-98Z	5,000		95.00	95

Anheuser-Busch, Inc.

Anheuser-Busch Collectors Club - Various

YEAR ISSUE		EDITION LIMIT	YEAR RETD.	ISSUE PRICE	*QUOTE U.S.$
1995	Budweiser Clydesdales at the Bauernhof CB1 - A. Leon	Yr.Iss.	1996	Gift	75-100
1995	The Brew House Clock Tower CB2 - D. Thompson	Retrd.	1996	150.00	200-300
1996	The World's Largest Brewer CB3 - A. Leon	Yr.Iss.	1996	Gift	35-50
1996	King - A Regal Spirit CB4 - D. Thompson	Retrd.	1997	100.00	100
1997	Pride & Tradition CB5 - J. Turgeon	Yr.Iss.		Gift	35
1997	The Budweiser Girls-Historical Reflections CB6 - D. Curran	4/98		100.00	100

A & Eagle Historical Trademark Series-Giftware Edition - Various

YEAR ISSUE		EDITION LIMIT	YEAR RETD.	ISSUE PRICE	*QUOTE U.S.$
1992	A & Eagle Trademark I (1872) CS201, tin	Retrd.	N/A	31.00	50-125
1993	A & Eagle Trademark I (1872) CS191, boxed	Retrd.	N/A	22.00	30-50
1993	A & Eagle Trademark II (1890s) CS218, tin	Retrd.	N/A	24.00	45-75
1994	A & Eagle Trademark II (1890s) CS219, boxed	Retrd.	N/A	24.00	30-40
1994	A & Eagle Trademark III (1900s) CS238, tin	20,000	1994	28.00	35-60
1995	A & Eagle Trademark III (1900s) CS240, boxed	30,000	1995	25.00	30
1995	A & Eagle Trademark IV (1930s) CS255, tin	20,000	1996	30.00	35-45
1996	A & Eagle Trademark IV (1930s) CS271, boxed	30,000		27.00	27

Anheuser-Busch Founder Series-Premier Collection - A-Busch, Inc.

YEAR ISSUE		EDITION LIMIT	YEAR RETD.	ISSUE PRICE	*QUOTE U.S.$
1993	Adophus Busch CS216	10,000	1996	180.00	180-200
1994	August A. Busch, Sr. CS229	10,000	1996	220.00	165-220
1995	Adolphus Busch III CS265	10,000		220.00	220
1996	August A. Busch, Jr. CS286	10,000		220.00	220

Archives Series-Collector Edition - Various

YEAR ISSUE		EDITION LIMIT	YEAR RETD.	ISSUE PRICE	*QUOTE U.S.$
1992	1893 Columbian Exposition CS169 - D. Langeneckert	75,000	1995	35.00	35-45
1993	Ganymede CS190 - D. Langeneckert	Retrd.	1995	35.00	75-120
1994	Budweiser's Greatest Triumph CS222 - D. Langeneckert	75,000	1996	35.00	45-65
1995	Mirror of Truth Stein CS252 - D. Langeneckert	75,000		35.00	35

Birds of Prey Series-Premier Edition - P. Ford

YEAR ISSUE		EDITION LIMIT	YEAR RETD.	ISSUE PRICE	*QUOTE U.S.$
1991	American Bald Eagle CS164	25,000	1995	125.00	115-155
1992	Peregrine Falcon CS183	25,000	1996	125.00	125-155
1994	Osprey CS212	Retrd.	1994	135.00	650-850
1995	Great Horned Owl CS264	25,000		137.00	137

Bud Label Series-Giftware Edition - A-Busch, Inc.

YEAR ISSUE		EDITION LIMIT	YEAR RETD.	ISSUE PRICE	*QUOTE U.S.$
1989	Budweiser Label CS101	Retrd.	1995	14.00	15-25
1990	Antique Label II CS127	Retrd.	N/A	14.00	15-25
1991	Bottled Beer III CS136	Retrd.	1995	15.00	20
1995	Budweiser Label Stein CS282	Open		19.50	20

Budweiser Military Series-Giftware Edition - M. Watts

YEAR ISSUE		EDITION LIMIT	YEAR RETD.	ISSUE PRICE	*QUOTE U.S.$
1994	Army CS224	Retrd.	1995	19.00	35-55
1994	Air Force CS228	Open		19.00	19
1995	Budweiser Salutes the Navy CS243	Open		19.50	20
1995	Marines stein CS256	Open		22.00	22
1997	Coast Guard stein CS294	Open		22.00	22

Budweiser Opera Card Series-Premiere Collection - A-Busch, Inc.

YEAR ISSUE		EDITION LIMIT	YEAR RETD.	ISSUE PRICE	*QUOTE U.S.$
1997	"Martha" CS300	5,000		169.00	169

Budweiser Racing Series - H. Droog

YEAR ISSUE		EDITION LIMIT	YEAR RETD.	ISSUE PRICE	*QUOTE U.S.$
1993	Budweiser Racing Team CS194	Retrd.	1995	19.00	20-30
1993	Bill Elliott CS196	25,000	1995	150.00	95-150
1993	Bill Elliott, Signature Edition, CS196SE	1,500	1995	295.00	250-300

Civil War Series-Premier Edition - D. Langeneckert

YEAR ISSUE		EDITION LIMIT	YEAR RETD.	ISSUE PRICE	*QUOTE U.S.$
1992	General Grant CS181	25,000	1995	150.00	130-150
1993	General Robert E. Lee CS188	25,000	1995	150.00	130-150
1993	President Abraham Lincoln CS189	25,000	1995	150.00	130-150

Classic Series - A-Busch, Inc.

YEAR ISSUE		EDITION LIMIT	YEAR RETD.	ISSUE PRICE	*QUOTE U.S.$
1988	1st Edition CS93	Retrd.	N/A	34.95	135-175
1989	2nd Edition CS104	Retrd.	N/A	54.95	95-110
1990	3rd Edition CS113	Retrd.	N/A	65.00	40-75
1991	4th Edition CS130	Retrd.	N/A	75.00	40-75

Clydesdales Holiday Series - Various

YEAR ISSUE		EDITION LIMIT	YEAR RETD.	ISSUE PRICE	*QUOTE U.S.$
1980	1st-Budweiser Champion Clydesdales CS19 - A-Busch, Inc.	Retrd.	N/A	9.95	110-135
1981	1st-Budweiser Champion Clydesdales CS19A - A-Busch, Inc.	Retrd.	N/A	N/A	150-250
1981	2nd-Snowy Woodland CS50 - A-Busch, Inc.	Retrd.	N/A	9.95	175-275
1982	3rd-50th Anniversary CS57 - A-Busch, Inc.	Retrd.	N/A	9.95	75-95
1983	4th-Cameo Wheatland CS58 - A-Busch, Inc.	Retrd.	N/A	9.95	35
1984	5th-Covered Bridge CS62 - A-Busch, Inc.	Retrd.	N/A	9.95	17
1985	6th-Snow Capped Mountains CS63 - A-Busch, Inc.	Retrd.	N/A	9.95	15-20
1986	7th-Traditional Horses CS66 - A-Busch, Inc.	Retrd.	N/A	9.95	30-40
1987	8th-Grant's Farm Gates CS70 - A-Busch, Inc.	Retrd.	N/A	9.95	15-30
1988	9th-Cobblestone Passage CS88 - A-Busch, Inc.	Retrd.	N/A	9.95	18
1989	10th-Winter Evening CS89 - A-Busch, Inc.	Retrd.	N/A	12.95	15-20
1990	11th-An American Tradition, CS112, 1990 - S. Sampson	Retrd.	N/A	13.50	13-20
1990	11th-An American Tradition, CS112-SE, 1990 - S. Sampson	Retrd.	N/A	50.00	50-75
1991	12th-The Season's Best, CS133, 1991 - S. Sampson	Retrd.	N/A	14.50	12-20
1991	12th-The Season's Best, CS133-SE Signature Edition, 1991 - S. Sampson	Retrd.	N/A	50.00	40-65
1992	13th-The Perfect Christmas, CS167, 1992 - S. Sampson	Retrd.	N/A	14.50	17
1992	13th-The Perfect Christmas, CS167-SE Signature Edition, 1992 - S. Sampson	Open		50.00	50
1993	14th-Special Delivery, CS192, 1993 - N. Koerber	Retrd.	N/A	15.00	15-30
1993	14th-Special Delivery, CS192-SE Signature Edition, 1993 - N. Koerber	Retrd.	N/A	60.00	100-140
1994	15th-Hometown Holiday, CS211, 1994 - B. Kemper	Retrd.	1994	14.00	15
1994	15th-Hometown Holiday, CS211-SE Signature Edition, 1994 - B. Kemper	Retrd.	N/A	65.00	85-125
1995	16th-Lighting the Way Home, CS263 - T. Jester	Open		17.00	17
1995	16th-Lighting the Way Home, CS263-SE Signature Edition - T. Jester	10,000	1995	75.00	75-115
1996	17th-Budweiser Clydesdales, CS273 - J. Raedeke	Open		17.00	17
1996	17th-Budweiser Clydesdales, CS273-SE Signature Edition - J. Raedeke	10,000		75.00	75

Clydesdales Series-Giftware Edition - A-Busch, Inc.

YEAR ISSUE		EDITION LIMIT	YEAR RETD.	ISSUE PRICE	*QUOTE U.S.$
1987	World Famous Clydesdales CS74	Retrd.	N/A	9.95	20-25
1988	Mare & Foal CS90	Retrd.	N/A	11.50	25-45
1989	Parade Dress CS99	Retrd.	N/A	11.50	50-95
1991	Training Hitch CS131	Retrd.	N/A	13.00	20
1992	Clydesdales on Parade CS161	Retrd.	N/A	16.00	25
1994	Proud and Free CS223	Open		17.00	17
1996	Budweiser Clydesdale Hitch CS292	Open		22.50	23

Collector Edition - J. Tull

YEAR ISSUE		EDITION LIMIT	YEAR RETD.	ISSUE PRICE	*QUOTE U.S.$
1994	Budweiser World Cup Stein CS230	25,000	1994	40.00	40-70

Discover America Series-Collector Edition - A-Busch, Inc.

YEAR ISSUE		EDITION LIMIT	YEAR RETD.	ISSUE PRICE	*QUOTE U.S.$
1990	Nina CS107	100,000	1995	40.00	35-50
1991	Pinta CS129	100,000	1995	40.00	35-50
1992	Santa Maria CS138	100,000	1995	40.00	35-50

Endangered Species Series-Collector Edition - B. Kemper

YEAR ISSUE		EDITION LIMIT	YEAR RETD.	ISSUE PRICE	*QUOTE U.S.$
1989	Bald Eagle CS106 (First)	Retrd.	N/A	24.95	400-500
1990	Asian Tiger CS126 (Second)	Retrd.	N/A	27.50	90-125
1991	African Elephant CS135 (Third)	100,000	1995	29.00	35-50
1992	Giant Panda CS173 (Fourth)	100,000	1996	29.00	35-65
1993	Grizzly CS199 (Fifth)	100,000		29.50	30
1994	Gray Wolf Stein CS226 (Sixth)	100,000		29.50	30
1995	Cougar Stein CS253 (Seventh)	100,000		32.00	32
1996	Gorilla Stein CS283 (Eighth)	100,000		32.00	32

Giftware Edition - A-Busch, Inc.

YEAR ISSUE		EDITION LIMIT	YEAR RETD.	ISSUE PRICE	*QUOTE U.S.$
1992	1992 Rodeo CS184	Retrd.	N/A	18.00	20-30
1993	Bud Man Character Stein CS213	Retrd.	1996	45.00	45-75
1994	"Fore!" Budweiser Golf Bag Stein CS225	Retrd.	1995	16.00	16
1994	"Walking Tall" Budweiser Cowboy Boot Stein CS251	Open		17.50	18
1995	"Play Ball" Baseball Mitt stein CS244	Open		18.00	18
1995	Billiards stein CS278	Open		24.00	24
1996	BUD-WEIS-ER Frog stein CS289	Open		27.95	28
1996	"STRIKE" Bowling stein CS288	Open		24.50	25
1997	Budweiser Salutes Dad CS298	Open		19.95	20

Historical Landmark Series - A-Busch, Inc.

YEAR ISSUE		EDITION LIMIT	YEAR RETD.	ISSUE PRICE	*QUOTE U.S.$
1986	Brew House CS67 (First)	Retrd.	N/A	19.95	35
1987	Stables CS73 (Second)	Retrd.	N/A	19.95	25-40
1988	Grant Cabin CS83 (Third)	Retrd.	N/A	19.95	65-95
1988	Old School House CS84 (Fourth)	Retrd.	N/A	19.95	35

Horseshoe Series - A-Busch, Inc.

YEAR ISSUE		EDITION LIMIT	YEAR RETD.	ISSUE PRICE	*QUOTE U.S.$
1986	Horseshoe CS68	Retrd.	N/A	14.95	40-50
1987	Horsehead CS76	Retrd.	N/A	16.00	35-45
1987	Horseshoe CS77	Retrd.	N/A	16.00	35-75
1987	Horsehead CS78	Retrd.	N/A	14.95	50-75
1988	Harness CS94	Retrd.	N/A	16.00	75

Hunter's Companion Series-Collector Edition - Various

YEAR ISSUE		EDITION LIMIT	YEAR RETD.	ISSUE PRICE	*QUOTE U.S.$
1993	Labrador Retriever CS195 - L. Freeman	50,000	1996	32.50	45-95
1994	The Setter Stein CS205 - S. Ryan	50,000		32.50	33
1995	The Golden Retreiver Stein CS248 - S. Ryan	50,000		34.00	34
1996	Beagle Stein CS272 - S. Ryan	50,000		35.00	35
1997	Springer Spaniel Stein CS296 - S. Ryan	50,000		35.00	35

Limited Edition Series - A-Busch, Inc.

YEAR ISSUE		EDITION LIMIT	YEAR RETD.	ISSUE PRICE	*QUOTE U.S.$
1985	Ltd. Ed. I Brewing & Fermenting CS64	Retrd.	N/A	29.95	150-225
1986	Ltd. Ed. II Aging & Cooperage CS65	Retrd.	N/A	29.95	50-70
1987	Ltd. Ed. III Transportation CS71	Retrd.	N/A	29.95	35-70
1988	Ltd. Ed. IV Taverns & Public Houses CS75	Retrd.	N/A	29.95	35-45
1989	Ltd. Ed.V Festival Scene CS98	Retrd.	N/A	34.95	35-45

Logo Series Steins-Giftware Edition - A-Busch, Inc.

YEAR ISSUE		EDITION LIMIT	YEAR RETD.	ISSUE PRICE	*QUOTE U.S.$
1990	Budweiser CS143	Retrd.	N/A	16.00	12-20
1990	Bud Light CS144	Retrd.	N/A	16.00	12-20
1990	Michelob CS145	Retrd.	N/A	16.00	12-20
1990	Michelob Dry CS146	Retrd.	N/A	16.00	12-20
1990	Busch CS147	Retrd.	N/A	16.00	12-20
1990	A&Eagle CS148	Retrd.	N/A	16.00	12-20
1990	Bud Dry CS156	Open		16.00	12-20

Marine Conservation Series-Collector Edition - B. Kemper

YEAR ISSUE		EDITION LIMIT	YEAR RETD.	ISSUE PRICE	*QUOTE U.S.$
1994	Manatee Stein CS203	25,000		33.50	30-40
1995	Great White Shark Stein CS247	25,000		39.50	30-40
1996	Dolphin Stein CS284	25,000		39.50	30-40

Michelob PGA Series-Collector Edition - A. Leon

YEAR ISSUE		EDITION LIMIT	YEAR RETD.	ISSUE PRICE	*QUOTE U.S.$
1997	Sawgrass CS299	10,000		59.95	60

Octoberfest Series-Giftware Edition - A-Busch, Inc.

YEAR ISSUE		EDITION LIMIT	YEAR RETD.	ISSUE PRICE	*QUOTE U.S.$
1991	1991 Octoberfest N3286	25,000	N/A	19.00	25-35
1992	1992 Octoberfest CS185	35,000		16.00	16
1993	1993 Octoberfest CS202	35,000	N/A	18.00	19

Olympic Centennial Collection - A-Busch, Inc.

YEAR ISSUE		EDITION LIMIT	YEAR RETD.	ISSUE PRICE	*QUOTE U.S.$
1995	1996 U.S. Olympic Team "Gymnastics" Stein CS262	10,000		85.00	85
1995	1996 U.S. Olympic Team "Track & Field" Stein CS246	10,000		85.00	85
1995	Centennial Olympic Games Giftware Stein CS266	Open		25.00	25
1995	Centennial Olympic Games Premier Edition 22" CS267	1,996	1996	500.00	750-1200
1995	Collector's Edition Official Centennial Olympics Games Stein CS259	Retrd.	1996	50.00	50-65

Olympic Team Series 1992-Collector Edition - A-Busch, Inc.

YEAR ISSUE		EDITION LIMIT	YEAR RETD.	ISSUE PRICE	*QUOTE U.S.$
1991	1992 Winter Olympic Stein CS162	25,000	N/A	85.00	50-85
1992	1992 Summer Olympic Stein CS163	Retrd.	1994	85.00	50-85
1992	1992 U.S.Olympic Stein CS168	50,000	N/A	16.00	18

Porcelain Heritage Series-Premier Edition - Various

YEAR ISSUE		EDITION LIMIT	YEAR RETD.	ISSUE PRICE	*QUOTE U.S.$
1990	Berninghaus CS105 - Berninghaus	Retrd.	1994	75.00	75-100
1991	After The Hunt CS155 - A-Busch, Inc.	Retrd.	1994	100.00	85-100
1992	Cherub CS182 - D. Langeneckert	25,000	1996	100.00	85-100

Post Convention Series - A-Busch, Inc.

YEAR ISSUE		EDITION LIMIT	YEAR RETD.	ISSUE PRICE	*QUOTE U.S.$
1982	1st Post Convention Olympic CS53	23,000	1982	N/A	175-300
1982	2nd Post Convention Olympic CS54	23,000	1982	N/A	160-225
1982	3rd Post Convention Olympic CS55	23,000	1982	N/A	175-275
1988	1st Post Convention Heritage CS87	25,000	1988	N/A	95-125
1988	2nd Post Convention Heritage CS102	25,000	1988	N/A	70-120
1989	3rd Post Convention Heritage CS114	25,000	1989	N/A	50-95
1990	4th Post Convention Heritage CS141	25,000	1990	N/A	45-100
1991	5th/Final Post Convention Heritage CS174	25,000	1991	N/A	25-75
1992	1st Advertising Through the Decades 1879-1912 N3989	29,000	1992	N/A	75-100
1993	2nd Advertising Through the Decades 1905-1914 N3990	31,106	1993	N/A	65-100
1994	3rd Advertising Through the Decades 1911-1915 SO85203	31,000	1994	N/A	65-100
1995	4th Advertising Through the Decades 1918-1922 SO95150	31,000	1995	N/A	65-100
1996	5th Advertising Through the Decades 1933-1938 SO95248	31,000	1996	N/A	75-100

Premiere Collection - A. Busch, Inc.

YEAR ISSUE		EDITION LIMIT	YEAR RETD.	ISSUE PRICE	*QUOTE U.S.$
1997	Bud Ice Penquin CS315	10,000		199.00	199
1997	Budweiser Frog CS301	10,000		219.00	219

Sea World Series-Collector Edition - A-Busch, Inc.

YEAR ISSUE		EDITION LIMIT	YEAR RETD.	ISSUE PRICE	*QUOTE U.S.$
1992	Killer Whale CS186	25,000	1996	100.00	75-90
1992	Dolphin CS187	22,500	1996	90.00	65-85

Specialty Steins - A-Busch, Inc.

YEAR ISSUE		EDITION LIMIT	YEAR RETD.	ISSUE PRICE	*QUOTE U.S.$
1975	Bud Man CS1	Retrd.	N/A	N/A	400-475
1976	A&Eagle CS2	Retrd.	N/A	N/A	145-250
1976	A&Eagle Lidded CSL2 (Reference CS28)	Retrd.	N/A	N/A	195-350
1976	Katakombe CS3	Retrd.	N/A	N/A	225-325
1976	Katakombe Lidded CSL3	Retrd.	N/A	N/A	295-395
1976	German Tavern Scene Lidded CS4	Retrd.	N/A	N/A	50-125
1975	Senior Grande Lidded CSL4	Retrd.	N/A	N/A	650-750
1975	German Pilique CS5	Retrd.	N/A	N/A	350-450

*Quotes have been rounded up to nearest dollar

YEAR ISSUE		EDITION LIMIT	YEAR RETD.	ISSUE PRICE	*QUOTE U.S. $
1976	German Pilique Lidded CSL5	Retrd.	N/A	N/A	450-475
1976	Senior Grande CS6	Retrd.	N/A	N/A	450-650
1975	German Tavern Scene CSL6	Retrd.	N/A	N/A	125-225
1975	Miniature Bavarian CS7	Retrd.	N/A	N/A	225-300
1976	Budweiser Centennial Lidded CSL7	Retrd.	N/A	N/A	375-500
1976	U.S. Bicentennial Lidded CSL8	Retrd.	N/A	N/A	350-500
1976	Natural Light CS9	Retrd.	N/A	N/A	195-250
1976	Clydesdales Hofbrau Lidded CSL9	Retrd.	N/A	N/A	225-325
1976	Blue Delft CS11	Retrd.	N/A	N/A	1800-2100
1976	Clydesdales CS12	Retrd.	N/A	N/A	275-375
1976	Budweiser Centennial CS13	Retrd.	N/A	N/A	300-450
1976	U.S. Bicentennial CS14	Retrd.	N/A	N/A	300-475
1976	Clydesdales Grants Farm CS15	Retrd.	N/A	N/A	160-275
1976	German Cities (6 assorted) CS16	Retrd.	N/A	N/A	1500-1800
1976	Americana CS17	Retrd.	N/A	N/A	275-400
1976	Budweiser Label CS18	Retrd.	N/A	N/A	300-475
1980	Budweiser Ladies (4 assorted) CS20	Retrd.	N/A	N/A	1300-2000
1977	Budweiser Girl CS21	Retrd.	N/A	N/A	375-450
1976	Budweiser Centennial CS22	Retrd.	N/A	N/A	350-400
1977	A&Eagle CS24	Retrd.	N/A	N/A	350-395
1976	A&Eagle Barrel CS26	Retrd.	N/A	N/A	100-150
1976	Michelob CS27	Retrd.	N/A	N/A	145-195
1976	A&Eagle Lidded CS28 (Reference CSL2)	Retrd.	N/A	N/A	225-325
1976	Clydesdales Lidded CS29	Retrd.	N/A	N/A	195-275
1976	Coracao Decanter Set (7 piece) CS31	Retrd.	N/A	N/A	495-600
1976	German Wine Set (7 piece) CS32	Retrd.	N/A	N/A	475-600
1976	Clydesdales Decanter CS33	Retrd.	N/A	N/A	1100-1250
1976	Holanda Brown Decanter Set (7 piece) CS34	Retrd.	N/A	N/A	250-395
1976	Holanda Blue Decanter Set (7 piece) CS35	Retrd.	N/A	N/A	450-500
1976	Canteen Decanter Set (7 pc.) CS36	Retrd.	N/A	N/A	N/A
1976	St. Louis Decanter CS37	Retrd.	N/A	N/A	300-400
1976	St. Louis Decanter Set (7 pc.) CS38	Retrd.	N/A	N/A	1100-1200
1980	Wurzburger Hofbrau CS39	Retrd.	N/A	N/A	275-375
1980	Budweiser Chicago Skyline CS40	Retrd.	N/A	N/A	85-150
1978	Busch Gardens CS41	Retrd.	N/A	N/A	195-350
1980	Oktoberfest— "The Old Country" CS42	Retrd.	N/A	N/A	195-350
1980	Natural Light Label CS43	Retrd.	N/A	N/A	150-250
1980	Busch Label CS44	Retrd.	N/A	N/A	125-265
1980	Michelob Label CS45	Retrd.	N/A	N/A	55-110
1980	Budweiser Label CS46	Retrd.	N/A	N/A	55-125
1981	Budweiser Chicagoland CS51	Retrd.	N/A	N/A	45-75
1981	Budweiser Texas CS52	Retrd.	N/A	N/A	45-70
1981	Budweiser California CS56	Retrd.	N/A	N/A	40-50
1983	Budweiser San Francisco CS59	Retrd.	N/A	N/A	160-185
1984	Budweiser 1984 Summer Olympic Games CS60	Retrd.	N/A	N/A	15
1983	Bud Light Baron CS61	Retrd.	N/A	N/A	30-65
1987	Santa Claus CS79	Retrd.	N/A	N/A	65-80
1987	King Cobra CS80	Retrd.	N/A	N/A	225-275
1987	Winter Olympic Games, Lidded CS81	Retrd.	N/A	49.95	65-75
1988	Budweiser Winter Olympic Games CS85	Retrd.	N/A	24.95	20
1988	Summer Olympic Games, Lidded CS91	Retrd.	N/A	54.95	30-60
1988	Budweiser Summer Olympic Games CS92	Retrd.	N/A	54.95	20
1988	Budweiser/ Field&Stream Set (4 piece) CS95	Retrd.	N/A	69.95	225-325
1989	Bud Man CS100	Retrd.	N/A	29.95	45-70
1990	Baseball Cardinal Stein CS125	Retrd.	N/A	30.00	30-55
1991	Bevo Fox Stein CS160	Retrd.	1994	250.00	180-250
1992	Budweiser Racing-Elliot/Johnson N3553 - M. Watts	Retrd.	1995	19.00	25-35

Sports Action Series-Giftware Edition - A-Busch, Inc.

1997	"Play Ball" Baseball stein CS295	Open		29.00	29

Sports History Series-Giftware Edition - A-Busch, Inc.

1990	Baseball, America's Favorite Pastime CS124	Retrd.	N/A	20.00	25-35
1990	Football, Gridiron Legacy CS128	Retrd.	N/A	20.00	25-35
1991	Auto Racing, Chasing The Checkered Flag CS132	100,000	1995	22.00	25
1991	Basketball, Heroes of the Hardwood CS134	100,000		22.00	22
1992	Golf, Par For The Course CS165	100,000	1995	22.00	25
1993	Hockey, Center Ice CS209	100,000		22.00	22

Sports Legend Series-Collector Edition - Various

1991	Babe Ruth CS142 - A-Busch	50,000	1995	85.00	75-85
1992	Jim Thorpe CS171 - M. Caito	50,000	1995	85.00	75-85
1993	Joe Louis CS206 - M. Caito	Retrd.	1994	85.00	85-125

St. Patrick's Day Series-Giftware Edition - A-Busch, Inc.

1991	1991 St. Patrick's Day CS109	Retrd.	N/A	15.00	45-55
1992	1992 St. Patrick's Day CS166	100,000	N/A	15.00	15-23
1993	1993 St. Patrick's Day CS193	Retrd.	N/A	15.30	25-40
1994	Luck O' The Irish CS210	Retrd.	1995	18.00	20
1995	1995 St. Patrick's Day Stein CS242	Retrd.	1995	19.00	19
1996	"Horseshoe" 1996 St. Patrick's Day Stein CS269	Open		19.50	20

Upland Game Birds-Collector Edition - P. Ford

1997	Ruffed Grouse CS316	5,000		75.00	75

Anheuser-Busch, Inc./Gerz Meisterwerke

American Heritage Collection - Gerz

YEAR ISSUE		EDITION LIMIT	YEAR RETD.	ISSUE PRICE	*QUOTE U.S.$
1993	John F. Kennedy Stein GM4	10,000		220.00	220

Gerz Collectorwerke - Various

1993	The Dugout GL1 - A-Busch, Inc.	10,000		110.00	110
1994	Winchester Stein GL2 - A-Busch, Inc.	10,000	1995	120.00	120
1995	"Saturday Evening Post" Christmas Stein #1 GL5 - J.C. Leyendecker	5,000		105.00	105
1996	"Saturday Evening Post" Christmas Stein #2 GL6 - A-Busch, Inc.	5,000		105.00	105

Gerz Collectorwerke Animals of the Prairie - N. Glazier

1997	Buffalo GL11	5,000		149.00	149

Gerz Collectorwerke Call of the Wild - J. Rideout

1996	Wolf Stein GL9	10,000		139.00	139

Gerz Meisterwerke Collection - A-Busch, Inc.

1994	Norman Rockwell-Triple Self Portrait GM6	5,000		250.00	250
1994	Mallard Stein GM7	5,000		220.00	220
1994	Winchester "Model 94" Centennial Stein GM10	5,000		150.00	150
1995	Giant Panda Stein GM8	3,500		210.00	210
1995	Rosie the Riveter Stein GM9	5,000		165.00	165
1996	Winchester Rodeo Stein GM19	5,000		179.00	179
1996	Winchester Pheasant Hunt Stein GM20	3,500		215.00	215
1997	Norman Rockwell-Do Unto Others GM21	7,500		189.00	189

Gerz Meisterwerke First Hunt Series - P. Ford

1992	Golden Retriever GM2	10,000		150.00	150
1994	Springer Spaniel GM5	10,000		170.00	170
1995	Pointer Stein GM16	10,000		190.00	190
1995	Labrador Stein GM17	10,000		190.00	190

Gerz Meisterwerke Holidays Through the Decades - A-Busch, Inc.

1996	Holidays: Decade of the 30's GM18	3,500		169.00	169

Gerz Saturday Evening Post Collection - J.C. Leyendecker

1993	Santa's Mailbag GM1	Retrd.		195.00	250
1993	Santa's Helper GM3	7,500		200.00	200
1994	"All I Want For Christmas" GM13	5,000		220.00	220
1995	Fourth of July Stein GM15	5,000		180.00	180

Working America Series-Gerz Premiere Collection - A. Busch, Inc.

1997	"This Bud's For You" CS318	10,000		209.00	209

Hamilton Collection

Mickey Mantle - R. Tanenbaum

1996	The Legendary Mickey Mantle	Open		39.95	40

The STAR TREK® Tankard Collection - T. Blackshear

1994	SPOCK	Open		49.50	50
1995	Kirk	Open		49.50	50
1995	McCoy	Open		49.50	50
1995	Uhura	Open		49.50	50
1995	Scotty	Open		49.50	50
1995	Sulu	Open		49.50	50
1995	Chekov	Open		49.50	50
1995	U.S.S. Enterprise NCC-1701	Open		49.50	50

Warriors of the Plains Tankards - G. Stewart

1992	Thundering Hooves	Open		125.00	125
1995	Warrior's Choice	Open		125.00	125
1995	Healing Spirits	Open		125.00	125
1995	Battle Grounds	Open		125.00	125

Royal Doulton

Character Jug of the Year - Various

1991	Fortune Teller D6824 - S. Taylor	Closed	1991	130.00	200-275
1992	Winston Churchill D6907 - S. Taylor	Closed	1992	195.00	225
1993	Vice-Admiral Lord Nelson D6932 - S. Taylor	Closed	1993	225.00	225
1994	Captain Hook - M. Alcock	Closed	1994	235.00	235
1995	Captain Bligh D6967 - S. Taylor	Closed	1995	200.00	275
1996	Jesse Owens, lg. D7019 - S. Taylor	Closed	1996	225.00	225
1997	Count Dracula, lg. D7053 - D. Biggs	Yr.Iss.		235.00	250

Character Jugs - Various

1993	Abraham Lincoln - M. Alcock	2,500	1994	190.00	190
1991	Airman, sm. - W. Harper	Retrd.	1996	75.00	75
1996	Albert Einstein, lg.- S. Taylor	Retrd.	1996	225.00	238
1995	Alfred Hitchcock D6987 - D. Biggs	Open		200.00	238
1990	Angler, sm. - S. Taylor	Retrd.	1995	82.50	83
1947	Beefeater, lg. - H. Fenton	Retrd.	1996	137.50	150
1947	Beefeater, sm. - H. Fenton	Retrd.	1996	75.00	75
1995	Charles Dickens D6939 - W. Harper	2,500		500.00	500
1989	Clown, lg.- S. Taylor	Retrd.	1995	205.00	225-250
1991	Columbus, lg.- S. Taylor	Open		137.50	138
1995	Cyrano de Bergerac, lg.- D. Biggs	Open		200.00	210
1983	D'Artagnan, lg.- S. Taylor	Retrd.	1995	150.00	150
1983	D'Artagnan, sm.- S. Taylor	Retrd.	1995	82.50	85-100
1995	Dennis and Gnasher, lg. - S. Ward	Open		212.50	225
1995	Deperate Dan, lg.- S. Ward	Open		212.50	225
1991	Equestrian, sm.- S. Taylor	Retrd.	1995	82.50	83
1995	George Washington - M. Alcock	2,500	1995	200.00	225
1982	George Washington, lg. - S. Taylor	Retrd.	1994	150.00	175
1994	Glenn Miller - M. Alcock	Open		270.00	315
1971	Golfer, lg. - D. Biggs	Retrd.	1995	150.00	150-200
1993	Graduate-Male, sm.- S. Taylor	Retrd.	1995	85.00	85
1986	Guardsman, lg.- S. Taylor	Open		137.50	145
1986	Gurardsman, sm.- S. Taylor	Open		75.00	83
1990	Guy Fawkes, lg. - W. Harper	Retrd.	1996	137.50	150
1975	Henry VIII, lg. - E. Griffiths	Open		137.50	145
1975	Henry VIII, sm. - E. Griffiths	Open		75.00	83
1991	Jockey, sm.- S. Taylor	Retrd.	1995	82.50	83
1995	Judge and Thief Toby D6988 - S. Taylor	Open		185.00	210
1959	Lawyer, lg. - M. Henk	Retrd.	1996	137.50	150
1959	Lawyer, sm. - M. Henk	Retrd.	1996	75.00	83
1990	Leprechaun, lg. - W. Harper	Retrd.	1996	205.00	225
1990	Leprechaun, sm. - W. Harper	Retrd.	1996	75.00	85
1986	London Bobby, lg.- S. Taylor	Open		137.50	145
1986	London Bobby, sm.- S. Taylor	Open		75.00	83
1952	Long John Silver, lg. - M. Henk	Open		137.50	145
1952	Long John Silver, sm. - M. Henk	Open		75.00	83
1960	Merlin, lg. - G. Sharpe	Open		137.50	145
1960	Merlin, sm. - G. Sharpe	Open		75.00	83
1990	Modern Golfer, sm.- S. Taylor	Open		75.00	83
1961	Old Salt, lg.- G. Sharpe	Open		137.50	145
1961	Old Salt, sm.- G. Sharpe	Open		75.00	75
1955	Rip Van Winkle, lg. - M. Henk	Retrd.	1995	150.00	150
1955	Rip Van Winkle, sm. - M. Henk	Retrd.	1995	82.50	83
1991	Sailor, sm. - W. Harper	Retrd.	1996	75.00	83
1984	Santa Claus, lg. - M. Abberley	Open		137.50	145
1984	Santa Claus, sm. - M. Abberley	Open		75.00	83
1993	Shakespeare, sm. - W. Harper	Open		99.00	107
1973	The Sleuth, lg.- A. Moore	Retrd.	1996	137.50	150-200
1973	The Sleuth, sm. - A. Moore	Retrd.	1996	75.00	100
1991	Snooker Player, sm.- S. Taylor	Retrd.	1995	82.50	83
1991	Soldier, sm. - W. Harper	Retrd.	1996	75.00	83
1994	Thomas Jefferson - M. Alcock	2,500	1995	200.00	200
1991	Town Crier, lg. - S. Taylor	Retrd.	1994	170.00	170
1993	Winston Churchill, sm.- S. Taylor	Open		99.00	107
1990	Wizard, lg.- S. Taylor- S. Taylor	Retrd.	1996	175.00	225
1990	Wizard, sm.- S. Taylor	Open		75.00	85
1991	Yeoman of the Guard, lg.- S. Taylor	Open		137.50	145

Great Composers - S. Taylor

1996	Beethoven, lg. D7021	Open		225.00	238
1996	Chopin, lg. D7030	Open		225.00	238
1996	Mozart, lg. D7031	Open		225.00	238
1997	Schubert, lg. D7056	Open		225.00	238
1996	Tchaikovsky, lg. D7022	Open		225.00	238

Limited Edition Character Jugs - Various

1992	Abraham Lincoln D6936 - S. Taylor	2,500	1994	190.00	190
1994	Aladdin's Genie D6971 - D. Biggs	1,500	1994	335.00	350
1996	Angel Miniature - M. Alcock	2,500		77.50	78
1993	Clown Toby - S. Taylor	3,000	1996	175.00	225
1993	Elf Miniature D6942 - W. Harper	2,500	1994	55.00	75
1993	Father Christmas Toby - W. Harper	3,500	1996	125.00	125
1996	Geoffrey Chaucer, lg. - R. Tabbenor	1,500	1996	800.00	800
1995	George Washington, lg. - M. Alcock	2,500	1996	200.00	200
1990	Henry VIII - N/A	Open		150.00	150
1991	Henry VIII - W. Harper	1,991	1992	395.00	1200-1400
1991	Jester - S. Taylor	2,500	1996	125.00	150
1994	King & Queen of Diamonds D6969 - J. Taylor	2,500	1994	260.00	275
1996	King and Queen of Hearts Toby - S. Taylor	2,500		275.00	275
1997	King Arthur, lg. D7055 - R. Tabbenor	1,500		350.00	350
1992	King Charles I D6917 - W. Harper	2,500	1995	450.00	495
1994	Leprechaun Toby - S. Taylor	2,500	1996	150.00	150
1992	Mrs. Claus Miniature D6922 - S. Taylor	2,500	1994	50.00	75
1993	Napoleon, lg. D6941 - S. Taylor	2,000	1994	225.00	225
1994	Oliver Cromwell D6968 - W. Harper	2,500	1994	475.00	475
1996	Pharoah Flambe, lg. - R. Tabbenor	1,500	1996	500.00	500
1991	Santa Claus Miniature D6900 - M. Abberley	5,000	1993	50.00	75
1988	Sir Francis Drake D6805 - P. Gee	Open		N/A	100
1997	Sir Henry Doulton, lg. D7054 - W. Harper	1,997		285.00	285
1992	Snake Charmer - S. Taylor	2,500		210.00	250
1994	Thomas Jefferson - S. Taylor	2,500	1996	200.00	225
1992	Town Crier D6895 - S. Taylor	2,500	1995	175.00	175
1992	William Shakespeare D6933 - W. Harper	2,500	1994	625.00	625

*Quotes have been rounded up to nearest dollar

❖ Collectors' Information Bureau ❖

DIRECTORY TO SECONDARY MARKET DEALERS

The C.I.B. Directory to Secondary Market Dealers is designed to put you in touch with secondary market experts who are in the business of making it easier for you to buy and sell retired collectibles. Together, they have a wealth of knowledge about the field of collectibles and are eager to help you enjoy your hobby even more.

How To Use This Directory

We've organized this directory to make it easy for you to find the dealer you need. Each dealer is listed alphabetically by state. They are also listed in the Directory Index on pages D27 and 28 according to their specialty.

Locating Dealers By Their Specialty

Each dealer has been assigned a locator number in the top right-hand corner of their listing. This number will come in handy when you are looking for a dealer who is an expert in a particular line or company. For example, if you are looking for a dealer to help you buy or sell a Department 56 piece, just turn to the index and look up the Department 56 listing. The numbers you find next to the listing are the locator numbers of the dealers who specialize in Department 56. Once you've found the numbers, look over the individual dealer listings and begin contacting the dealers who most appeal to you.

Locating Dealers By State

Though most dealers are accustomed to doing business on a national basis, you may want to start by contacting dealers closer to home. That's why we've also organized the dealers by state. Within each state listing, dealers are organized in alphabetical order by business name.

Let's Get Started!

Now that you know how to use the directory, you may want to take a moment or two to turn to pages 4-5 and learn the answers to the "10 MOST FREQUENTLY ASKED QUESTIONS ABOUT BUYING AND SELLING LIMITED EDITION COLLECTIBLES." These questions have come to us from collectors like you who want to know more about buying and selling on the secondary market. We've gathered the answers from our panel of secondary market experts. Hopefully, they'll give you the background you need to make the most out of your secondary market transactions!

ABBREVIATIONS

Amex = American Express
Dept. 56 = Department 56
EKJ = Emmett Kelly, Jr.
Ltd. = Limited

MOY = Memories of Yesterday
WFS = Wee Forest Folk
Byers' = Byers' Choice

Directory to Secondary Market Dealers

CAN — LAURA'S COLLECTIBLES [1]
230 Park Avenue
Keskus Harbour Mall
Thunder Bay Ontario, Canada P76-1A2

Phone: (807) 343-4240
Fax: (807) 768-1493
Hours: M-Sat: 9:30-5:30,
Th & F: Open until 9:00PM

Services: Buy outright Barbie dolls (occasionally). No consignments. Will trade. Visa, MasterCard, American Express accepted. Lay-a-way plan available. Will ship anywhere in the world.

Lines: Boyds Bears, Collectible Barbie, Bradford plates, Ashton-Drake dolls, NASCAR, Hockey plates, steins, Gnomes, Lilliput Lane, Seraphim Angels, Disney, Coca-Cola, Star Wars, Star Trek, Canadian Heritage Aircrafts, ERTL, Corgi, Solido Die Casts, Royal Doulton figurines and horses, Upper Deck Authenticated Autographed merchandise, Legends, Memories of Yesterday, Calico Kittens, All sport plates, Occasionally buy, more often sell 1950's to 1980's HOCKEY CARDS.

Noteworthy: Laura's Collectibles has over twenty years of sport card (hockey) experience and knowledge, as well as over ten years of experience and knowledge in Barbie collectibles.

AZ — COLLECTORVILLE AND WHAT THE DICKENS [2]
2885 W. Ribera Place
Tucson, AZ 85742

Phone: (520) 297-7019
Fax: (520) 297-7019 (call first)
AOL: Jlsac3838

Services: Buy/Sell brokerage. 15% commission and cost of shipping charges. Visa, MasterCard and Discover accepted.

Lines: Boyds Bears, Byers' Choice, Charming Tails, Cherished Teddies, Department 56, Disney Classics Collection, Harbour Lights, and Beanie Babies.

Noteworthy: Collectorville, and What the Dickens, has been in existence since 1991. Judith and Kenneth Isaacson, along with Jacquelyn Bunge, have now expanded their secondary market services beyond Disney and Department 56. They currently publish a newsletter for collectors, listing noteworthy and secondary market listings. All sales are handled personally, and items are shipped UPS insured. Besides offering a money back guarantee, Collectorville appraises Department 56 and Disney pieces for all collectors.

AZ — CRYSTAL WORLD [3]
2743 North Campbell Avenue
Tucson, AZ 85719

Phone: (520) 326-5990
Hours: T-F: 10:30-6:00, Sat: 11:00-3:00

Services: We buy/sell, appraise, engrave, design and repair crystal. Brokerage fee applicable. Visa, MasterCard and check.

Lines: Authorized Swarovski/SCS retailer, Crystal World, Austrian faceted sculptures, Abelman Art Glass limited edition clowns, Krystonia.

Noteworthy: In business for over 25 years, we specialize in cut glass, paperweights, custom engraving on wedding and anniversary gifts, corporate presentation awards and trophies expertly created. <u>Attention Swarovski collectors:</u> We pay your membership fee. Now you can purchase your investment collectibles with confidence. All crystal professionally inspected, evaluated and graded for mint condition by William Threm, master glass engraver. Complete crystal showroom of exquisite cut glass and art glass from around the world. We offer repairing on Steuben, Baccarat, Lalique, Waterford, etc. Appraisal services and expert advice of future crystal investments.

AZ — D & A INVESTMENTS [4]
2301 Souchak Drive
Lake Havasu City, AZ 86406

Phone: (520) 453-9076
Fax: (520) 453-9076
Hours: M-F: 9:00-6:00

Services: Buy/sell/trade. Buy outright one item to complete collections. Current price lists available. Visa, MasterCard, money orders and checks accepted. Shipping via UPS insured.

Lines: Specializing in Anheuser-Busch steins, mugs, plates, figurines and other breweriana collectibles. Full line of new and retired product.

Noteworthy: D & A Investments started in breweriana collectibles in 1985. Within a few years, it became a full-time mail order business dealing with collectors throughout the world. We are always willing to share our years of product knowledge, we appreciate your calls. All merchandise sold and shipped by D & A carry a full money back 30-day guarantee. Our goal is to have good product, good service and customer satisfaction.

Directory to Secondary Market Dealers

AZ — 5

Lori's COLLECTIBLES
6121 E. Broadway #134, Tucson, AZ 85711

Phone: (520) 790-6668 (Information)
Hours: T-F: 10:00-6:00, Sat: 10:00-5:00
Closed Sun. and Mon.

Services: Buy outright on selected merchandise. Ship anywhere. Locator service. Will work with other dealers. Call for details.

Lines: Lladro, Hummel, L. Davis, ANRI, Dept. 56, (including Snowbabies, All Through the House, and Merry Makers), Royal Doulton, PM, D. Winter, O. Wieghorst and Zolan lithos, Lilliput, Chilmark, Legends, Bossons, Wideman, DeGrazia, Krystonia, MOY, Rockwell, Gorham, Goebel Miniatures, Tom Clark, Cairn Gnomes, Fontanini, Swarovski, CT and Disney.

Noteworthy: Lori's carries a full line of collectibles, adding about two new lines per year. The store is a Redemption Center for many lines listed above and hosts several open houses during the year. A newsletter is published frequently, and interested collectors can be placed on the mailing list. Lori's offeres personalized service, integrity and fair secondary market prices.

AZ — 6

paper paper paper paper paper paper

PREFERRED DEALER

3160 E. Fort Lowell
Tucson, AZ 85716

Phone: (520) 326-3830
Fax: (520) 326-0750
Hours: M-F: 10:00-5:30, Sat: 10:00-4:00

Services: Secondary market service. Visa, MasterCard accepted. Fax, mail or call-in requests. UPS shipping.

Lines: Byers' Choice Carolers.

Noteworthy: Paper Paper Paper, carries a large selection of retired carolers. Here the collector will find many first and second editions from 1988 to present. They are also an authorized dealer for Byers' Choice Carolers.

CA — 7

Blevins Plates 'n' Things
Collectors Plates, Figurines, Dolls, etc.

301 Georgia St., Vallejo, CA 94590

Phone: (707) 642-7505
Fax: (707) 557-0679
Hours: M-F: 10:00-6:00, Sat: 9:00-5:00,
Closed Sun

Services: Sell only.

Lines: Bradford plates, Hamilton dolls and plates, Memories of Yesterday, Lowell Davis, David Winter, Lilliput Lane, Sports Impressions, Precious Moments, Disney, Enchantica, Goebel Miniatures, Flambro, ANRI, Jan Hagara, Ashton-Drake dolls, Maud Humphrey, lithographs and much more.

Noteworthy: Blevins Plates 'n' Things has grown from an in-home business to a 4,000 square foot store over a period of 15 years. The owners are Larry and Stella Blevins. Years of selling has brought knowledge to the owners and staff. A member of NALED, Blevins is a Redemption Center for numerous collector clubs and hosts artist open houses during the year. They also offer layaways and do brisk mail order business.

CA — 8

City Lights
1202 Morena Blvd.
San Diego, CA 92110
EVERYTHING SHIPS FREE

Phone: (800) 262-5335, (619) 275-1006
Fax: (800) 262-5335
Hours: Open 7 Days

Services: Single pieces or collection bought for cash or will trade. Lay-a-way available. Visa, MasterCard, Discover, American Express accepted. ATM.

Lines: Department 56 (all Villages, Snowbabies, Snowbunnies, All Through The House, Winter Silhouette), Byers' Choice Carolers, Annalee, Fontanini, Cottontail Lane, Creepy Hollow, Margaret Furlong, Christopher Radko, Polanaise, Old World Christmas, Birgits Collections and Seraphim Angels.

Noteworthy: City Lights is a 6,000 square foot store with award winning permanent displays. Everything listed **ships free**. Enormous inventory of both current and retired pieces. Department 56 "Gold Key" dealer, Byers' Choice "Preferred Dealer," Annalee "Doll Society" store, Fontanini "Guild" store, Polanaise "Listed" dealer, Old World Christmas "Collector's Club" store. Knowledgeable staff and friendly efficient service.

Directory to Secondary Market Dealers

CA — 9

Cox Collectibles
2957 Third Avenue
Sacramento, CA 95817

Phone: (916) 456-4151 (800) 895-9920
Hours: T-Sat: 11:00-6:00,
Sun./Mon. by appointment.

Services: Buy/sell/exchange. Listed price plus 10%. Lay-a-way available. Personal checks, Visa, MasterCard, American Express and Discover accepted. Dealer inquiries welcome.

Lines: Sarah's Attic, All God's Children, Daddy's Long Legs, Positive Image, Cherished Teddies, Precious Moments and Boyds Bears.

Noteworthy: Cox Collectibles, the multi-cultural gift and collectible store has a knowledgeable and caring sales staff that is ready to assist you. The store supports most collector clubs and offers special promotions throughout the year.

CA — 10

Crystal Reef

is your primary source on the secondary market for:

Pocket Dragons • Wee Forest Folk
Swarovski • Disney Classics & Disneyana
Tom Clark Gnomes • Lilliput Lane •
David Winter • Pennibears • Armani •
Animation Art • Olszewski • Lladro •
Steiff • Mary Meyer and R. John Wright

© R. John Wright
© Walt Disney Co.
© Annette Peterson

Crystal Reef is one of the largest secondary market exchanges for retired and limited edition collectibles, offering very competitive "True" secondary market values on listed pieces. We do the work of locating and brokering your fine collectibles.

With Crystal Reef, there are no membership, subscription or listing fees, and we provide free secondary market price lists on any of the lines which we represent.

Call us today for a free secondary market price list.

Crystal Reef

Visa * Mastercard * Check * MO
(415) 312-8265
Visit our Web Site at www.crystal-reef.com

CA — 11

Flash Collectibles
560 N. Moorpark Road, Suite 287, Thousand Oaks, CA 91360

Phone: (800) 266-2337 (805) 499-9222
Fax: (805) 376-5541
E-Mail: FLASHCOLL@AOL.COM
Hours: M-F: 10:00-5:00, 24-hour answering service

Services: Buy outright. Consignment and trades. Search service.

Lines: Budweiser, Anheuser-Busch, Strohs, Old Style, Miller, Hamms, Pabst, Coors, steins and plates. New stein importers catalog shows over 800 steins in full color. Features traditional German steins, pewter, character, fire fighters, flasks, Rockwell, Looney Tunes, Superman and Coca-Cola.

Noteworthy: Flash Collectibles started as a part-time business in 1971. By 1973, owners Doug and Natalie Marks were totally consumed by the antiques and collectibles "bug" and opened their first store called The Antique Co. In 1984, the Marks discovered the Anheuser-Busch collectible steins. In 1986, the firm moved to their current location and changed their name to Flash Collectibles. Specializing in mail order beer steins, they offer a free brochure listing their current stock of over 1,000 beer steins. Also featured are movie stills, and an exceptionally large collection of full-color original fruit and vegetable labels.

CA — 12

THE FRAME GALLERY
305 Third Avenue
Chula Vista, CA 91910

Phone: (619) 422-1700
Fax: (619) 422-5860
Hours: M-F: 10:00-5:30
       Sat: 10:00-5:00

Services: Specializes in searching for hard-to-find collectibles. Does not buy outright. Call for details. All major credit cards accepted.

Lines: All collector plates. Also prints, figurines, crystal, and pewter, including Snowbabies, Perillo, Disney Classics, Kinkade, Olszewski, Enesco, Hamilton, Swarovski, Hummels, Rockwell, Kevin Francis, Millpond Press, Hadley House, Somerset House, and autographed celebrity photos, etc.

Noteworthy: The Frame Gallery began as a framing shop, but soon collectors began coming to the store for advice on the art of framing different collectibles. Before long, mother-daughter team Margaret and Jan introduced collectibles to their store. Today, they are a Redemption Center for Disney Classics, Kinkade, Lilliput, Krystonia, Swarovski, Pocket Dragons, Myth & Magic, and Hantel Miniatures. They also carry artists' work of local scenes which are of particular interest to tourists.

Directory to Secondary Market Dealers

CA — 13
THE GOLDEN SWANN
895 Lincoln Way
Auburn, CA 95603

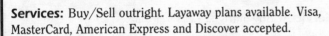

Phone: (800) 272-7926
(916) 823-7739
Fax: (916) 823-1945

Services: Buy/Sell outright. Layaway plans available. Visa, MasterCard, American Express and Discover accepted.

Lines: Lladro, Swarovski, Armani, David Winter Cottages, M.I. Hummel, and all retired collectibles.

Noteworthy: Twenty-one years in the business, The Golden Swann is the largest dealer in Northern California for current and retired pieces of Lladro, Swarovski, Armani, Disney Classics, Mark Hopkins, Country Artists, M.I. Hummel, Maruri, and Genesis. Free membership for all collectors clubs, call for further details. Redemption Center. CALL FOR THE BEST PRICES ON RETIRED ITEMS.

CA — 14
J'S COLLECTIBLES
5827 Encinita Avenue
Temple City, CA 91780

Phone: (818)451-0010
Fax: (818)309-0327
Hours: M-Sat: 10:00-7:00,
24 hr. Message Service

Services: Secondary market service. Large inventory of retired items in stock. Listing service or buy outright from dealers and collectors with prompt payment. Search service provided. Accepts personal checks, money order, Visa and Mastercard. Satisfaction guaranteed.

Lines: Specializes in Swarovski, Disney Classics and Disneyana Convention items.

Noteworthy: One of the dealers with the largest inventory of retired items in stock. Knowledgeable staff provides friendly and helpful service. CIB panel member.

CA — 15
JULIET'S COLLECTIBLES AND WEDDING GARDENS
44060 Margarita Road, Temecula, CA 92592-2746

Phone: (909) 693-1410
Fax: (909) 693-1412
Hours: T-Sat: 10:00-5:30, evenings by appt.

Services: Buy outright, consignment, 90 day layaway. Free shipping in the continental U.S.

Lines: All God's Children, Hummel, Sarah's Attic, Wee Forest Folk, Kinkade, Lena Liu, Sandra Kuck, D. Zolan, G. Harvey, Alan Maley.

Noteworthy: Juliet's Collectibles was opened in 1967 by Juliet Anne Boysen. The store has one of the largest selections of All God's Children retired pieces to be found in California, including most of the Father Christmas pieces and a large selection of Sarah's Attic. They are a Redemption Center for Precious Moments, Sarah's Attic, G. Harvey, and Hummel. They print a quarterly newsletter which collectors can receive just by calling the store. Open houses are hosted when either an artist or a representative comes to the store. Customer service is a most important part of Juliet Anne Boysen's policy. The Wedding Garden, three acres of paradise, is now open. It features gazebos, romantic gardens and over 1,000 beautiful plants.

CA — 16
MCCURRY'S HALLMARK
1779 Tribute Road, Suite C
Sacramento, CA 95815

Phone: (800) 213-0214 (916) 567-9952
Fax: (916) 927-3469
Hours: M-Sat 10:00-9:00, Sun 11-6 (PST)

Dealers for the following: Precious Moments Century Circle Dealer (one of 41 in the U.S.), Department 56 Gold Key Dealer, Cherished Teddies Adoption Center, Boyds Gold Paw, Disney Classics and Hallmark Gold Crown Leadership store.

Secondary Market Lines: Precious Moments, Department 56: (all villages and accessories).

Noteworthy: Started in 1908, McCurry's Hallmark is a family held and operated business, now in the third generation. They have two locations in the major malls, one in the Sunrise Mall and the other in Arden Fair Mall. Between the two stores there is over 7,600 square feet to serve collectors. McCurry's has the largest display of both new and retired Precious Moments in Northern California. They also have one of the most extensive and unique secondary market displays of Department 56.

Directory to Secondary Market Dealers

CA — M.S. Gallery [17]

1304 Glen Dell Drive
San Jose, CA 95125

Phone: (408) 993-0375
24 hr. Answering Service
Hours: M-Sat: 10:00-5:00

Services: Secondary Market Specialist, Buy/Sell. Ship UPS. All major credit cards accepted.

Lines: Lladro, Precious Moments, M.I. Hummel, Jan Hagara, Armani, Swarovski, David Winter, Lilliput, Annalee, Raikes Bears, All God's Children, limited edition plates, Wee Forest Folk, Bradford Exchange, plates and dolls, **Graphics:** P. Buckley Moss, Marty Bell, Donald Zolan, Penni-Ann Cross, Bannister, Sandra Kuck, Corine Layton, Thomas Kinkade, Red Skelton.

Noteworthy: Marie Sider has been selling collectibles since 1980. She has had over 17 years of experience with both primary and secondary market sales. For all your collectible needs call "Marie" she will be anxious to serve you, **"service is her most important product."** CIB panel member.

CA — Rystad's Limited Editions [18]

since 1967

1013 Lincoln Avenue
San Jose, CA 95125

Phone: (408) 279-1960
Fax: (408) 279-1960
Hours: T-Sat: 10:00-5:00

Services: Buy outright. Lists welcome.

Lines: Red Skelton, Rockwell, Hamilton, M.I. Hummel, David Winter, Ashton-Drake, Zolan, Noritake, Lenox, All God's Children, Christopher Radko, Bradford, Snowbabies, Disney Classics, Royal Copenhagen, Bing & Grondahl, Ebony Visions, Boyds Bears.

Noteworthy: Dean Rystad started in the collectibles mail order business in 1967. In 1978, Rystad opened a store, which today features over 4,000 collector plates and figurines. Rystad's specialty is in locating back issues of collectibles. His track record is about 98% of requests. Rystad's is a redemption center for most collector clubs. A new gallery was added recently to feature Red Skelton, Thomas Kinkade, Marty Bell, Sandra Kuck, Jack Terry and Donald Zolan.

CA — SUGARBUSH GIFT GALLERY [19]

1921 W. San Marcos Blvd. #105
San Marcos, CA 92069

Phone: (800) 771-9945, (619) 599-9945
Fax: (619) 599-9945
Hours: M-F: 10:00-6:00, Sat: 10:00-5:00

Services: Secondary Market. Buy outright. Mail your list with asking price. Visa, Master Card, Discover and American Express accepted. Checks and money orders also accepted. 90-day lay-a-way plan available. Ship insured.

Lines: Thomas Kinkade, Dona Gelsinger, Boyds (PAW), Cherished Teddies, Charming Tales, Harbour Lights, Seraphim Angels, Country Artist, Wee Forest Folk and much more.

Noteworthy: Sugarbush Gift Gallery is a primary and secondary source of marketable collectibles, with a knowledgeable and service orientated staff on hand. Member of NALED and CIB panel.

CA — Swan Seekers Network [20]

9740 Campo Road, Suite 134
Spring Valley, CA 91977 USA

Phone: (619) 462-2333
Fax: (619) 462-5517
On line: SWANSEEKERS.COM
Hours: M-Th 9:00 - 5:00 West Coast Time

Services: Second Market Swarovski Brokerage. We offer Swan Seekers Newsletter, published 3 times a year and the Marketplace, (a 'For Sale' and 'Wanted to Buy' retired items list) updated and issued every 2 months **all year round**. We accept Master Card and Visa.

Lines: *Exclusively Swarovski Crystal*

Noteworthy: Swan Seekers Network, established is 1989 is the *FIRST* strictly Swarovski Crystal Brokerage service. Listing your retired items for sale is *free of charge*. We offer UNBIASED information to any interested Swarovski collector. Keep up with what's new and what's happening. Give us a call. We may have what you're looking for. ☺

Directory to Secondary Market Dealers

21 — CA — Un4gettable Collectibles

A Division of Griffith Irrigation

9885 East Dinuba Avenue
Selma, CA 93662-9404
(209) 896-8933

Services: We Buy/Sell/Trade. Exchange and locator service. No cost, no obligation listing. Collectors may send a typed list divided into buy and sell (including prices). Quoted price is the price to the buyer. Layaway available. Personal checks, money orders, Visa, MasterCard, Discover and other Novus cards accepted. All sales handled personally and items are shipped UPS insured. USPS and Federal Express available.

Lines: Rod Bearcloud Berry, Blaylock Originals-Ted Blaylock, J.H. Boone, Cast Art-Dreamsicles and Heavenly Classics, Cody, Creart, Genesis, Legends, Living Stone, Mill Creek, Frank D. Miller-3 dimensional editions, Red Mill, Rick Cain Studios, Riverbend Editions, Tudor Mint-Myth and Magic, Winston Roland.

SECONDARY MARKET SPECIALIST CIB 1997-98

22 — CT — BABE'S BEARS AND DOLLS

32 Walnut Street
Seymour, CT 06483

Phone: (203) 888-6141
Fax: (203) 881-1672
Hours: By appointment.
Telephone or fax 24 hours.
If answered by machine, please leave message, and they'll get back to you.

Services: Buy outright, cash, credit card, checks. Layaways and shipping available.

Lines: Naber Kids dolls, Robert Raikes Bears and dolls, limited edition Beverly Port bears by Gorham. Call for other collectibles they carry.

Noteworthy: Babe's Bears is owned and operated by Jeanette Spinelli and husband Carl, affectionately known as Babe and Papa Bear. Babe and Papa Bear, along with their children, travel to secondary market shows up and down the east coast. Show schedules are available upon request. They carry the full line of limited retired Gorham bears by Beverly Port and are one of the largest dealers of the Robert Raikes Bears, Naber Kids, Wildwood Babies and any upcoming dolls. There is something for collectors of all ages, from children to adult.

SECONDARY MARKET SPECIALIST CIB 1997-98

23 — FL — A RETIRED COLLECTION

550 Harbor Cove Circle
Longboat Key, FL 34228-3544

Phone: (800) 332-8594
(941) 387-0102 (FL)
Fax: (941) 383-8865
On-Line: LladroLady@aol.com
Home Page: http://www.hkproducts.com/lladro-lady
Hours: Mail order: 8:00-9:00 daily.
Visits by appointment

specializing in LLADRÓ a retired collection

Services: Broker service. Representing buyers and sellers. Occasionally buy outright. Dealers and insurance replacement welcome. American Express, Visa, MasterCard and Discover accepted.

Lines: Lladro

Noteworthy: A Retired Collection, specializing in Lladro, was established in 1992 by Janet Gale Hammer. A complimentary Newsletter/Stock & Buy List is published bi-monthly and available upon request. Janet keeps current on Lladro secondary market activities by attending auctions in California and Florida and is a charter member of the Tampa Bay/Sarasota Chapter group and CIB panel member. She is recognized by many as the dominant source for retired Lladro.

SECONDARY MARKET SPECIALIST CIB 1997-98

24 — FL — THE CHRISTMAS PALACE

10600 N.W. 77 Ave.
Hialeah Gardens, FL 33016

Phone: (305) 558-5352
Fax: (305) 558-6718
Hours: M-Sat: 10:00-7:00, Sun: 11:00-6:00 (Off Season)
M-Sat: 10:00-9:00, Sun: 10:00-7:00 (In Season)

Services: No consignments, buy outright. Call for details. Free shipping anywhere in the United States for orders over $50. All major credit cards accepted. No sales tax outside of Florida.

Lines: Department 56 (Villages, Snowbabies, Snowbunnies), Swarovski, Walt Disney Classics, Precious Moments, Armani, Boyds Bears, Ebony Visions by Willits.

Noteworthy: Since 1989, The Christmas Palace has become one of the top collectors' stores in the country. They are one of the largest Department 56 dealers (Gold Key status). Redemption Center for all listed lines.

Directory to Secondary Market Dealers

FL 25

The Christmas Shop
ST. AUGUSTINE, FLORIDA

12 Castillo Drive, St. Augustine, FL 32084

Phone: (904) 824-9898   Fax: (904) 829-8555
Internet: www.tepee.com
Hours: Daily: 9:30-6:00

Services: Consignment, buy outright, paying cash or merchandise.

Lines: M.I. Hummel, Chilmark, Precious Moments, Disney Classics, Department 56, David Winter, Lilliput Lane, Lowell Davis, Perillo, DeGrazia, Alexander Dolls, Cherished Teddies, Harmony Kingdom, Old World Christmas, Greenwich Workshop and more!

Noteworthy: Teepeetown, Inc., founded in 1945, operates The Christmas Shop, The Indian Shop, The Columbia Gift Shop, and the Authentic Old Drugstore. Specializing in fine gifts and collectibles, the Harris' have served the collecting market since 1945 and on advisory boards to such companies as Goebel, Royal Doulton, and Hudson Creek. Well versed on both the primary and secondary markets, the entire staff provides effective aftermarket assistance. The Company now employs a THIRD GENERATION family member to insure credibility and ongoing support for it's customers.

CIB Secondary Market Specialist 1997-98

FL 26

Do You Have a Dream?

Disneyana Exchange Service

Martha's EXCHANGE SERVICE

3961 Kiawa Dr
Orlando, Fl. 32837
Ph: (407) 438-5634
FAX (407) 438-8372

...Then Trust The Experts!
* Call for Your One-time FREE Newsletter
* World's Largest Disney 2ndary Market Brokerage
* Get The Inside "Scoop" Before it Happens
* Over 20,000 listings
* Your Sources for the WDCC, Convention Pieces, Animation Art, Swarovski Crystal, Dept. 56 & More!

Over $1 Million Traded Annually

CIB Secondary Market Specialist 1997-98

FL 27

Donna's Collectibles Exchange

163 Long Leaf Pine Circle
Sanford, FL 32773

Phone: (800) 480-5105
Fax: (407) 323-7747
Hours: M-F: 11:00 AM - 8:00 PM EST

CIB Secondary Market Specialist 1997-98

Services: Secondary Market Buy & Sell listing exchange. Dealer's welcome. Visa & MasterCard Accepted.

Lines: Barbies, Boyd's Collection (Bearstones, Dollstones, Folkstones & Plushes), Breen Ornaments, Charming Tails, Cherished Teddies, Christopher Radko, David Winter, Dept. 56, Forma Vitrum, Harbour Lights, Kiddie Car Classics, Lefton Colonial, Lilliput Lane, Lowell Davis, Maude Humphrey, Muffy's Bears, Raikes Bears, Snowbabies, Swarovski, Walt Disney (Classics, Convention & Videos), Wee Forest Folk & More.

Noteworthy: Donna's Collectibles Exchange is strictly a mail-order business. Subscriptions available for listing updates.

FL 28

HEIRLOOMS OF TOMORROW
750 N.E. 125th Street
North Miami, FL 33161

Phone: (800) 544-2-BUY
       (305) 899-0920
Fax: (305) 899-2877
Hours: M-W & F: 9:30-6:00, Th: 9:30-8:00,
       Sat: 9:00-5:00

Services: Buy outright. Commission. Collectors send a typed list divided into buy and sell.

Lines: ANRI, Hibel, Lladro, Goebel Mini, David Winter, M.I. Hummel, Armani, Swarovski, Department 56, Cabbage Patch, Legends, Bradford, Krystonia, Sarah's Attic, Precious Moments, Memories of Yesterday, Chilmark, Disney Classics, Lilliput Lane, Lowell Davis, cp smithshire, Caithness, Ashton-Drake dolls, Thomas Kinkade, Olszewski, Kuck, Sandridge.

Noteworthy: With over 16 years of experience and literally thousands of items, Heirlooms of Tomorrow is considered one of South Florida's foremost one-stop collectible shops. Family owned and operated since 1980. They have a booming mail order business, and care is taken to ensure that collectibles will arrive safely, as they are shipped worldwide.

CIB Secondary Market Specialist 1997-98

Directory to Secondary Market Dealers

FL — 29

KATHY'S HALLMARK
7709 Seminole Mall
Seminole, FL 33772

Phone: (813) 392-2459
Fax: (813) 392-2459 (call first)
Hours: M-Sat: 10:00-9:00, Sun: 12:00-5:00

Services: Buy and sell outright. Visa, MasterCard, American Express and Discover. Ship via UPS.

Lines: Swarovski, Collector plates, Precious Moments, Cherished Teddies, Hallmark ornaments and Kiddie Car Classics, Snowbabies, Barbie, Dreamsicles, Finnians, Star Wars, and Star Trek.

Noteworthy: Redemption Center for Swarovski, Precious Moments, Cherished Teddies, Dreamsicles, and Hallmark. Many past year ornaments available. Some 5-piece Christmas promotion sets available (i.e. Santa and Reindeer, Snoopy, Bearinger Bears). Call or write for specifics.

FL — 30

VIKING

WORLD SPECIALIST IN BING & GRONDAHL AND ROYAL COPENHAGEN COLLECTIBLES

If you want to buy or sell previous year RC or B&G collectibles, call Viking first! We have been buying and selling RC and B&G since 1948 and have a large inventory, plus a nationwide network of sources. We buy outright, or list your RC and B&G collectibles on our active "Videx" exchange.

CALL US FOR A CURRENT PRICE LIST ON RC AND B&G COLLECTIBLES

We also carry many of the other fine collectibles you love:

Swarovski	Kaiser
Hummel	Wedgwood
Bradford	Edna Hibel
Maruri	Berlin Design

And Many Other Lines

VIKING IMPORT HOUSE, INC.
690 N. E. 13th St., Ft. Lauderdale, FL 33304
CALL US TOLL-FREE (800) 327-2297

GA — 31

JIM RUTHERFORD
P.O. Box 501101
Atlanta, GA 31150

Phone: (770) 754-9060
Fax: (770) 754-9411

Services: Secondary market services, specializing completely in Harbour Lights lighthouses. Annual <u>Survival Guide to Harbour Lights Lighthouses</u> book. Quarterly informational newsletter <u>The Guiding Lights</u> about Harbour Lights, with no-cost, no-obligation listing section.

Lines: Harbour Lights lighthouses

Noteworthy: <u>The 1995 Survival Guide to Harbour Lights Lighthouses</u> was the original definitive information resource on Harbour Lights. It continues to expand each year, and the 1997 edition has the most complete history and analysis of Harbour Lights yet! <u>The Guiding Lights</u> newsletter keeps subscribers current on all breaking Harbour Lights news and secondary trends. Both are MUSTS for any serious Harbour Lights collector! Jim Rutherford is a quoted CIB panel member.

32

Looking for the latest news about collectibles?

ORDER YOUR SUBSCRIPTION to the COLLECTIBLES REPORT

Get a full year of information about new products, artists, clubs and events with the *Collectibles Report*...CIB's quarterly newsletter. Four issues are yours for only $15!

Call (847) 842-2200 today to subscribe.
Or write to: COLLECTORS' INFORMATION BUREAU
5065 SHORELINE ROAD, SUITE 200
BARRINGTON, IL 60010

Directory to Secondary Market Dealers

IA — STAMPS 'N' STUFF™ — 33
2700 University #214, West De Moines, IA 50266-1461

Phone: (515) 224-1737 (Information)
(800) 999-5964 (Orders only)
Fax: (515) 226-1651
E-Mail: b.koepp@earthlink.net
Hours: T-F: 10:00-6:00, Sat: 10:00-4:00

Services: Buy outright. Free buy or sell list on request. Major credit cards accepted. Postage and insurance paid on orders over $300 in the continental U.S.

Lines: Department 56 (Dickens, Christmas in the City, Snow Villages, Alpine, New England, Snowbabies), ANRI, Hummel, Royal Doulton figurines and character jugs, U.S. and foreign stamps and coins.

Noteworthy: In 1977, Stamps 'N' Stuff began as a stamp and coin store in Kalamazoo, MI. Owners Barbara and Jerry Koepp dabbled in antiques, handling furniture and glassware. In 1982 they moved to Des Moines, opened store specializing in collector stamps. In 1990 they were given their first Department 56 building and an obsession was born! They have now moved to a larger store where they can display Department 56, Royal Doulton, Hummel, ANRI and other limited edition collectibles. Already well known at National and Internationl Stamp Exhibitions, they are now attending larger collectible shows in the Midwest. They guarantee your satisfaction.

ID — THREE C'S GIFT GALLERY — 34
350 N. Milwaukee - 1009
Boise, ID 83788

Phone: (800) 847-3302
Fax: (208) 884-1111
Hours: M-F: 10:00-9:00, Sat: 10:00-7:00, Sun: 11:00-6:00

Services: No consignments. Buy outright. Mail your list with asking price. Visa, MasterCard, Discover and American Express.

Lines: Walt Disney Classics, Thomas Kinkade, Swarovski, Chilmark, Legends, David Winter, Snowbabies, M.I.Hummel, Wee Forest Folk, Armani.

Noteworthy: Redemption center for Walt Disney Classics, David Winter, Swarovski, Lilliput Lane, M.I. Hummel, Armani, Chilmark, Legends and Thomas Kinkade.

IL — BRADFORD EXCHANGE — 35
9333 N. Milwaukee Avenue
Niles, IL 60714

Phone: (800) 323-8078
Hours: M-F: 8:00-5:30

Services: The Bradford Exchange matches buyers with sellers by phone or mail. Buyers pay a 4% commission (or $4.00 if the price of the plate is under $100). Sellers are charged a 28.5% commission. Bradford guarantees that once the exchange notifies both parties that a match has occurred, the buyer is guaranteed delivery of a mint-condition plate at the confirmed price, and the seller is guaranteed payment of the confirmed price once his plate has been certified as mint condition.

Lines: Bradford-recommended Collector's plates.

Noteworthy: Founded in 1973, The Bradford Exchange was the first entity to offer an organized secondary market for collector's plates. In 1982, Bradford's computerized Instaquote™ system went into effect, allowing the exchange to electronically match plate buyers with plate sellers from around the country. Bradford tracks the trading activity of more than 4,000 plates eligible for trading on the U.S. exchange, one of 11 offices around the world. Only Bradford-recommended plates may be traded on the exchange.

IL — C. A. Jensen JEWELERS — 36
709 First Street, LaSalle, IL 61301

Phone: (815) 223-0377 (800) 499-5977
Hours: M-Sat: 9:30-5:30

Services: All of our many fine retired collectible lines including china, crystal and silver are new. No outright buying. Checks and credit cards accepted.

Lines: Figurines: Cybis, Boehm, Royal Copenhagen, Bing & Grondahl, Lladro, Hummel, Goebel, Ispanky, Lalique, Baccarrat, Waterford, Lowell Davis, Lilliput Lane, Lenox, ANRI, and Rockwell. Dolls: Gorham musical. Ornaments: Lunt, Kirk Stieff, Wallace, as well as other sterling, wood, and crystal lines. Collector Plates: many discontinued and obscure plates in stock including, Bing & Grondahl, Royal Copenhagen, Bradford, Hummel, and much more.

Noteworthy: C.A. Jensen Jewelers has been in business for 78 years and is second generation, family owned and operated. They house a huge inventory in their 8,000 square foot warehouse and offers many fine collectible lines in their 6,500 square foot store. There are over 3,000 plates on display, of which many are discontinued. Come see for yourself!

Directory to Secondary Market Dealers

IL — COLLECTOR'S COVE — 37
1215 N. Williams Drive, Palatine, IL 60067

Phone: (847) 202-4840
Fax: (847) 776-2205
Hours: Sun: 11-7, M: 9AM - 9PM,
T-Th: 4-9, F: 9AM-9PM,
Sat: 10-7

Services: Secondary market listing service and brokerage. Buy/sell assistance. No cost consignment available and occasionally buy outright. No cost list service, free price quotes and price lists. We ship anywhere - all items guaranteed. Personal checks, Money orders, Visa MasterCard, American Express welcomed. Short term layaways available.

Lines: David Winter, Precious Moments, Cherished Teddies, Disney Classics, Department 56, Lladro, M.I. Hummel, Charming Tails, Krystonia, Lilliput Lane, Collector Plates, Hallmark, Lance and more.

Noteworthy: Collector's Cove is a family run business that deals strictly in the secondary market. Founded and operated by fellow collectors our friendly helpful staff is committed to the customer service and quality that you demand. We specialize in rare and retired collectibles - with over 5000 active listings. CIB panel member and proud member of the Greater Palatine Chamber of Commerce.

IL — 38

The Crystal Connection Ltd.
8510 N. Knoxville Avenue, Suite 218
Peoria • IL 61615-2034
"SWAROVSKI crystal specialist"

Phone: (309) 692-2221 / (800) 692-0708
Fax: (309) 692-2221 (24 hours)
Hours: Mon-Fri: 4:00-9:00, Sat-Sun: 10:00-4:00
(24-hour message service)
E-mail: crystalconnection@worldnet.att.net
Web: www.crystal.org

Services:
- Secondary market brokerage listing service
- Appraisal for insurance and other needs
- *Crystal News* newsletter
- Visa, MasterCard, checks & MO accepted

Lines: Swarovski crystal

Noteworthy: The Crystal Connection Ltd. is operated by Robin Yaw, the world's leading appraiser and authority on Swarovski crystal. He has appeared as a panel speaker on CIB's secondary market seminars and Swarovski's *"Ask The Experts"* shows. He also authors the *Crystal News*, a newsletter written exclusively for Swarovski collectors. Member of the Better Business Bureau (BBB) and the International Society of Appraisers (ISA).

IL — EILENE'S TREASURES — 39
P.O. Box 285
Virden, IL 62690

Phone: (217) 965-3648
Hours: 9:00-8:00 daily

Services: Buy outright. Layaways available. Fair prices. Satisfaction guaranteed.

Lines: Precious Moments, suspended and retired: figurines, bells, ornaments, plates; Memories of Yesterday figurines and ornaments, Hallmark Ornaments, Enesco Treasury Ornaments.

Noteworthy: Eilene Kruse is an expert on Precious Moments marks, as she purchases many early pieces with original marks. She then expanded her business to include other Enesco lines and Hallmark ornaments. Eilene attends four to five ornament and collectible shows in the Illinois area and publishes a price list which is available upon request.

IL — EUROPEAN IMPORTS & GIFTS — 40
7900 N. Milwaukee Avenue
Niles, IL 60714

Phone: (800) 227-8670 (847) 967-5253
Fax: (847) 967-0133
Hours: M-F: 10:00-8:00, Sat: 10:00-5:30,
Sun: 12:00-5:00

Services: No Consignments. Buy outright. Will mail complete listing. Free shipping in the U.S. with purchases over $75. Accepts Visa, MasterCard, American Express and Discover.

Lines: Annalee, ANRI, Armani, Ashton-Drake, Bradford plates, Byers' Choice, Cairn Gnomes, Chilmark, Lowell Davis, Department 56, Walt Disney Classics, Animation Art, Hamilton dolls and plates, Lizzie High, M.I. Hummel, EKJ, Krystonia, S. Kuck, Legends, Lilliput Lane, Lladro, Memories of Yesterday, Michael's Limited, All God's Children, Rockwell, Precious Moments, Royal Doulton, Swarovski, Enesco's Treasury of Christmas ornaments, United Design, WACO, Wee Forest Folk, David Winter, Madame Alexander dolls.

Noteworthy: Established in 1966, European Imports & Gifts is one of the largest dealers in the Midwest. Year round Christmas village.

Directory to Secondary Market Dealers

IL — 41

1-800-445-8745

One FREE call is all you'll need to make!

Gifts International

22341 East Wells Rd.
Canton, IL 61520
Web Site: http://www.RosieWells.com

SPECIALIZING IN THE OLDER:
- Cherished Teddies® Collectibles
- Boyds Collectibles
- Hallmark Ornaments
- Precious Moments® Collectibles
- Secondary Market Price Guides (for above collectibles)
- Beanie Babies™
- Dept. 56

Daisy

Ms. Griz (Pink Dress)

God Loveth A Cheerful Giver

A Cool Yule 1st In Series

Precious Moments® ©1997 PMI, Lic., Enesco. All rights reserved worldwide, Licensee ENESCO CORPORATION. Cherished Teddies ©1991-1997 Priscilla Hillman, Licensee Enesco Corporation. Cherished Teddies® is a registered trademark of Enesco Corporation. ©1997 Hallmark Cards, Inc. ©1997 The Boyds Collection, Ltd.

Secondary Market Specialist CIB 1997-98

IL — 42

Gift Music Ministry
GIFT MUSIC, BOOK & COLLECTIBLES SHOPPE
2501 Chicago Rd., Chicago Heights, IL 60411

Phone: (708) 754-4387 - 24 hours
Hours: M-T&TH-F: 12:00-6:00, Sat: 10:00-2:00CST,
Sun: "See you in Church"

Services: Consignments. Buy outright. Buy/sell brokerage. Donations. Call for information.

Lines: Precious Moments, MOY, Lladro, Hummel, All God's, D. Winter, ANRI, Tom Clark, CT, Dept. 56, EKJ, Lilliput, Hallmark and Enesco ornaments, Rockwell figurines, Fontanini, Remington Bronze, Kurt S. Adler, Midwest, Swarovski, Schmid, Seymour Mann, Wedgwood, Roman, Armani, Disney, Ron Lee, CUI, Possible Dreams, Royal Doulton, Anheuser-Busch, Steinbach, Budweiser, toys, games, books, Bibles, and more.

Noteworthy: They are a nonprofit traveling religious music group, begun by Joe and Terri Schulte in 1980. The store is an outgrowth of this ministry, and their desire is to bring quality religious and inspirational items into more homes and people of various cultures and backgrounds together. Besides being active on the secondary market, the store offers an appraisal service. They accept items and collections for tax donations. They carry wedding, anniversary and Quinciñera invitations and accessories, music, equipment and books, etc.

Secondary Market Specialist CIB 1997-98

IL — 43

STONE'S HALLMARK SHOP
"Specializing in Collectibles"
2508 S. Alpine, Rockford, IL 61108

Phone: (815) 399-4481, (800) 829-6406
Fax: (815) 399-0167
Hours: M-F 9:00AM- 9:00PM,
Sat: 9-5:30, Sun: 11-5

Services: Locator service, lay-a-way, all major credit cards, Hallmark Gold Crown points with purchase. GCC, NALED, and COYNES.

Lines: Dept. 56, Snowbabies, Precious Moments, ANRI, Charming Tails, Boyds, C.T. Adoption Center, Hallmark ornaments, Kiddie Car Classics, David Winter, Lilliput, Armani, All God's, Dreamsicles, Seraphim Angels, Pocket Dragons, Bradford, Ashton-Drake, and Mattel Barbies.

Noteworthy: Stone's is family owned and operated for over forty years and has over 20,000 square feet of fine collectibles. Century Circle Dealer for Enesco and a Gold Key Dealer for Department 56. Redemption Center for most major collectibles. New memberships into most collector clubs are free. Call for details. In-store Department 56 club. Call for application. Some benefits include newsletter, price list, gift with purchase, and priority to limited and retired pieces. Several major artist events held each year.

Secondary Market Specialist CIB 1997-98

IN — 44

COLLECTABLES BY COIN INVESTORS
8275 Broadway Century Mall
Merrillville, IN 46410

Phone: (219) 738-2253
Fax: (219) 738-2363
Hours: M-Sat: 10:00-9:00, Sun: 11:00-5:00

Services: Buy outright. Layaways available. Visa, MasterCard, Discover, and AMEX.

Lines: Bradford Exchange plates, Ashton-Drake dolls, Mattel Barbies, Hawthorne houses, M.I. Hummel, and U.S. Coins.

Noteworthy: Collectables By Coin Investors has been a family owned and operated business for 16 years. As a Bradford dealer since 1990, they carry a complete line of Bradford products. They also carry Hamilton plates, Georgetown dolls, Barbies, and many other collectible doll lines. Over 1,000 plates and 300 dolls are on display for the collector. An Authorized Professional Coin Grading Dealer, offering the collector a free appraisal for coin collections.

Directory to Secondary Market Dealers

IN   **45**

GRAHAM'S CRACKERS
5981 E. 86th Street
Indianapolis, IN 46250

Phone: (800) 442-5727
        (317) 842-5727
Fax: (317) 577-7777
Hours: M-Sat: 10:00-9:00, Sun: 12:00-5:00

Services: Buy retired pieces outright. Call for details. Host many artist appearances and special events throughout the year. Special orders our specialty.

Lines: Department 56 Gold Key Dealer, German Nutcrackers, Lilliput Lane, Mary Englebreit, David Winter, Possible Dreams, Harbour Lights, Sarah's Attic, Precious Moments, Christopher Radko, Boyds Bears, Cherished Teddies, Byers' Choice, Lizzie High, M.I.Hummel, Rick Cain, Fontanini Blue Ribbon Dealer, Lang and Wise, Shelia's, Cat's Meow, North American Bear. Over 90 lines!

Noteworthy: Opened in 1986, now over 20,000 square feet - a Collector's Paradise. Specialize in personal service, exquisite collectibles, collector clubs and seasonal merchandise for **EVERY** holiday. Interested collectors may call to have their name included on the mailing list.

IN   **46**

MARKER'S HUMMELS
P.O. Box 66
603 W. South Street
Bremen, IN 46506

Phone: (219) 546-3111
Hours: M-Sat: Best to call evenings 6:00-9:00

Services: Buy and sell outright. No consignment.

Lines: M.I. Hummel figurines only.

Noteworthy: Marker's has been specializing in M.I. Hummel figurines for over 20 years. They stock current figurines for the beginning collector as well as Crown, Full Bee, and stylized trademarks. Marker's also maintains a stock of rare M.I Hummel figurines which includes internationals. They have a close working relationship with Goebel because of their many trips to Germany, and the staff will be glad to answer any questions about Hummels or Goebel. Marker's recommends a visit to the Donald Stephens Museum in the O'Hare Convention Center to see some of the rare M.I.Hummel figurines they can provide for your collection.

SECONDARY MARKET SPECIALIST CIB 1997-98

IN   **47**

ROSE MARIE'S
1119 Lincoln Avenue
Evansville, IN 47714
MEMBER OF BBB, NALED & GCC

Phone: (800) 637-5734, (812) 423-7557
Fax: (812) 423-7578 (call first)
Home Page: http://www.rosemaries.com
Hours: M-Th & Sat: 10:00-5:00, F: 10:00-7:00,
Nov. & Dec.
       M-F: 10:00-7:00, Sat: 10:00-5:00,
       Sun: 12:00-5:00

Services: Buy/sell exchange. Listed price plus 10%. Accept Visa, MasterCard, American Express and Discover plus 4%. Fully guaranteed. Dealers welcome.

Lines: All Department 56, Disney Classics, Hummel, Armani, Swarovski and many more.

Noteworthy: Looking for a way to aid her missionary sons, Rose Marie Hillenbrand began by selling religious figurines from a restored wardrobe in her living room in 1958. Today, over 38 year later, Rose Marie's specializes in assisting the collector in gift giving and in the acquisition of fine collectibles. The store services and supports over 35 collectors clubs. *Notice to all Collector Club Members, "We pay your club dues for you."* Call for details.

SECONDARY MARKET SPECIALIST CIB 1997-98

KS   **48**

Gifts & Accents
Collectibles Our Specialty

9611 Metcalf Ave. • Metcalf South Mall
Overland Park, KS 66212

Phone: (800) 822-8856   (913) 381-8856
Fax: (913) 381-1986
Hours: Mon - Sat: 10:00 am to 9:00 pm
       Sunday: Noon to 5:30 pm (Central Standard Time)

SECONDARY MARKET SPECIALIST CIB 1997-98

Services: Consignment. Mail your list with asking price. 30% consignment fee. Visa, Mastercard, and Discover.

Lines: Precious Moments

Noteworthy: Gifts & Accents was established in 1980. The store is known for its popular "Swap & Sell" which takes place twice every year; Eight days before Mother's day and the Saturday before Thanksgiving. Typically, a collector will find retired pieces from Precious Moments, Dept. 56, Disney, M.I. Hummel, Boyd's, Cherished Teddies, plates, dolls, cottages, ornaments, and more. Gifts & Accents is a Century Circle Retailer and a member of Gift Creations Concepts.

Directory to Secondary Market Dealers

LA — DICKENS' EXCHANGE, INC. — 49
5150 Highway 22, Suite C-9
Mandeville, LA 70471

Phone: (504) 845-1954
Fax: (504) 845-1873
Hours: M-F: 9:00-5:30, Sat: 10:00-2:00

Services: 10% commission paid by purchaser on consignment listings. Exchange sells outright- no commissions. Call for details.

Lines: Department 56: Snow Village, Dickens Village, Christmas in the City, New England, Alpine, Little Town of Bethlehem, North Pole, Cold Cast Porcelains, Snowbabies and accessories.

Noteworthy: Lynda Blankenship began as a collector of Department 56 collectibles. Eventually this led to the publishing of *The Dickens' Exchange*, a reliable source for Department 56 news and a thriving exchange. Today, Lynda publishes a 32-page newsletter which boasts over 12,000 subscribers! She describes her newsletter as a place for collectors to meet and share their hobby. She is also the author of "Willage Mania", a 353-page color book for Department 56 collectors and co-author of "Display Mania."

MA — FOSTERS' — 50
100 Pleasant Street
South Weymouth, MA 02190

Phone: (800) 439-3546 (617) 337-3546
Fax: (617) 331-6277
Hours: M-Sat: 10:00-5:00, Sun: 12:00-5:00

Services: Consignment. Some outright buying. Call for details. Visa, MasterCard, Discover, and American Express accepted. Fosters' will ship anywhere and has a 30 day layaway plan.

Lines: Byers' Choice Carolers, Cat's Meow, Steiff bears, Thomas Kinkade prints, Christopher Radko ornaments, and Roman angels.

Noteworthy: They are a club Redemption Center for Cat's Meow, Christopher Radko, Lizzie High, June McKenna, Gund, Steiff, and Possible Dreams. For over 25 years Fosters' has been a family run business, located 15 miles south of Boston in the historical village of South Weymouth. They pride themselves on having the largest year-round display of Byers' Choice Carolers on the East coast with an in-store museum of Carolers. Fosters' is a very unique store featuring fine collectibles, country home accessories and furniture.

MA — LINDA'S ORIGINALS & THE YANKEE CRAFTSMEN — 51

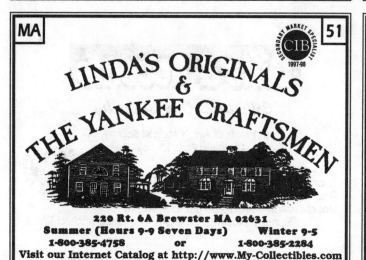

220 Rt. 6A Brewster MA 02631
Summer (Hours 9-9 Seven Days)   Winter 9-5
1-800-385-4758   or   1-800-385-2284
Visit our Internet Catalog at http://www.My-Collectibles.com

Services: Buy Outright, Consignment, On-Line Classified, Listing Service Coming Soon.

Lines: Annalee, Armani, Bennie Babies, Boyds Bears, Byers' Choice, Cats Meow, Cherished Teddies, Cheryl Spencer Lighthouses, Dept 56, D. Winter, Disney Classic, Forma Vitrum, Harbour Light Lighthouses, Harmony Kingdom, Lilliput, Lladro, Margaret Furlong, Possible Dreams, Radko, Stienback, Swarovski, Thomas Kinkade, Wee Forest Folk.

Check Out our Secondary Market Items
For Sale on Byers Choice, Disney and Harbour Lights at our On-Line Catalog.
Enter our Free BI-monthly Contest and you could Win a Free Gift Certificate.
http://www.My-Collectibles.Com

MA — New England Collectibles Exchange — 52

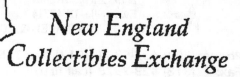

Phone: 1-413-663-3643
Fax: 1-413-663-5140
Email: nece@collectiblesbroker.com
Website: http://www.collectiblesbroker.com
Or Write: 201 Pine Avenue
Clarksburg, Ma. 01247-4640
Hours: M-F 3:00-9:00 ET, Anytime Weekends

Services: Subscribers receive seven newsletters a year which include listings by artist of limited editions and retired pieces. Buyers pay 15% commission, 10% on larger pieces plus shipping costs, there are no seller or listing fees.

Lines: Barbie, Boyds-all pieces, Byers' Choice, Cat's Meow, Charming Tails, Cherished Teddies, Dept.56, Disney Classics, Hallmark, Harbour Lights, Hummel, June McKenna, Lee Sievers, Lefton, Lilliput, Precious Moments, Shelia's, Swarovski, Tim Wolfe, Tom Clark Gnomes and many others.

Noteworthy: Established in 1992, to sell secondary market collectibles, Bob Dorman developed NECE with the rules of courteous, honest, fair and confidential personal service to all buyers and sellers. Serving collectors and retailers - they ship pieces insured worldwide.

Directory to Secondary Market Dealers

MI | AMERICAN BUSINESS CONCEPTS | 53

26455 Van Dyke Avenue, Center Line, MI 48015
Phone: (810) 757-5115
3038 Walton Blvd., Rochester Hills, MI 48309
Phone: (810) 375-2515

Hours: M-F: 9:00AM-9:00PM, Sat: 9:30-6:00, Sun: 12:00-5:00

Services: Buy and sell outright. Some consignment. Locator service. Call for details.

Lines: Hibel, Chilmark, Kaiser, Seraphim Angels, Harbour Lights, Snowbabies, Anheuser-Busch, Department 56, "NAO" Lladro, Steinbach, Maruri, Fraser, Forma Vitrum, Star Trek, M.Cornell Steins, Hummel, CT, Ebony Visions, Thomas Blackshear, Furlong, Premier Kinkade Dealer, Boyds, All God's, Sarah's, Radko, Polonaise, EKJ, Old World Christmas and Lynn Haney.

Noteworthy: American Business Concepts started 45 years ago as an executive gifts, office supplies, and accessories shop. They have since expanded to include many unique collectible lines, including a large selection of collectible Santas. They have a large Hibel line including her oils, stone lithographs, and uniques. Their framing department gives expert care in conservation and museum framing. Collectors are able to enjoy their artwork while it's being preserved.

MI | BONNIE'S HALLMARK | 54

108 N. Mitchell Street
Cadillac, MI 49601

Phone: (800) 968-6260
(616) 775-4282
Fax: (616) 775-7499
Hours: M-Sat: 8:30-9, Sun & Holidays: 10-6

Services: Buy/sell exchange, locator service. Ship UPS, layaways. Free gift wrapping. Accept major credit cards.

Lines: All God's Children, Anchor Bay, Anheuser-Busch Collection Annalee, Boyd's Collection, Charming Tails, Cherished Teddies, Department 56, Disney Classics, Enesco Treasury Ornaments, Hallmark Keepsake Ornaments, Harbour Lights, M.I. Hummel, Kiddie Car Classics, Lilliput Lane, Memories of Yesterday, Precious Moments, Sarah's Attic, Tim Wolfe and Tom Clark Gnomes.

Noteworthy: Gold Crown Hallmark Store. Redemption Center for All God's Children, Anheuser-Busch Collection Annalee, Boyd's Collection, Cherished Teddies, Disney Classics, Enesco Treasury Ornaments, Hallmark Keepsake Ornaments, Harbour Lights, M.I. Hummel, Lilliput Lane, Memories of Yesterday, Precious Moments, Sarah's Attic, Tom Clark Gnomes. Extensively stocked.

MI | 55

DEPARTMENT 56 RETIREES
Harry & June McGowan
6576 Balmoral Terrace, Clarkston, MI 48346

Phone: (810) 623-6664
Fax: (810) 623-6104

Hours: Retired-flexible-daily UPS shipping year-round.
Services: Buy outright, "what's on our price list is in our possession" creating fast delivery. No added commission Visa, MasterCard, Discover and American Express. Free shipping over $500.

Lines: Department 56: Dickens Village, Disney Village, Christmas in the City, New England, Alpine, North Pole and some Snow Village, Snowbabies, Snowbunnies, Merry Makers, Winter Silhouettes; Disney Classics and Lilliput Lane.

Noteworthy: This year will be our 7th annual Home Show with entry fee proceeds and raffles benefitting the Oakland County ChildrensVillage and Salvation Army, etc.

MI | 56

8170 Cooley Lake Road, White Lake, MI 48386
Phone: (800) 893-4494 (248) 360-4155
Fax: (248) 363-1360
On-line: rfe@netquest.com
Hours: M-W: 10:00-8:00, Th-Sat: 10:00-6:00, Sun: 12:00-4:00

Services: Have large stock of items in store. Accept some consignments. Buy outright. Exchange and locator service.

Lines: Cherished Teddies, Dahl Jensen, Disney Classics, Dreamsicles, Harmony Kingdom, Kevin Francis, Krystonia, **Lladro**, **M.I. Hummel**, Norman Rockwell, Pendelfin, Precious Moments, Ron Lee, Royal Copenhagen, **Royal Doulton**, Royal Worcester, **Swarovski**, **Department 56**, **Possible Dreams**, Prizm Pipka Santas, Snowbabies, Creepy Hollow, Crinkle Claus, Margaret Furlong, **Polonaise**, Barbie, Beanie Babies, **Muffy Vanderbear**.

Noteworthy: Owners Stewart and Arlene Richardson have been dealing in antiques and collectibles for 15 years. They have an extensive background in Royal Doulton, M.I. Hummel, Precious Moments and Possible Dreams. In 1993, the Richardsons opened a showroom which stocks over 5,000 figurines.

Directory to Secondary Market Dealers

MN — Collectors Gallery [57]

The Upper Midwest's Premier Collectibles Dealer

Phone: (800) 878-7868 or (612) 738-8351
Fax: (612) 738-6760
E-Mail: dancollect@aol.com
Web Site: collectorsgallery.com
Hours: M-F: 10-9, Sat: 10-6, Sun: 12-5

Services: Competitive buyer of retired collectibles. Please send or fax list with prices desired. We accept Visa, MasterCard, Discover & Am Exp. FREE SHIPPING on all orders over $25.00.

Lines: Department 56, Lladro, Swarovski, David Winter, Armani, Boyd's Bears, JP EDITIONS, Kinkade, Forma Vitrum, Precious Moments, Disney Classics, Snowbabies ... and more!

Noteworthy: Collectors Gallery, with over sixteen years experience, offers the Upper Midwest's largest selection of new and retired collectibles ... and we serve thousands of collectors from coast to coast. Our beautiful new 8,500 square foot store features a Lladro Millenium Gallery and a huge Department 56 Panorama Gallery. All major collector's clubs supported. Member GCC.

We invite you to visit our Web Site for information on current product, new releases, and retired collectibles.

CIB Secondary Market Specialist 1997-98

MO — HOLIDAY MELODY [58]

920 E. Broadway
Columbia, MO 65201

Phone: (573) 442-0298   (573) 657-2920
Fax: (573) 449-8557
Hours: T-Sat: 10:00-5:30 (CST)

Services: Secondary market for European glass Christmas ornaments like Christopher Radko and Breen. Occasionally buy outright. Visa, MasterCard and Discover accepted. Mail us your list or request our list be sent to you.

Lines: Christopher Radko, Old World, Polonaise, Christina's World, Boyds Bears, Harbour Lights, Annalee, Anheuser-Busch steins, Shelias, and Cherished Teddies.

Noteworthy: Melody Link has published *"The Collectors Melody Ornament Newsletter"* since 1994. She has a BS in History, owns a retail Christmas and collectible store, and is raising two children with her husband, Brian, who is a dentist in Columbia. The newsletter focuses on ALL aspects of collecting glass ornaments and offers a <u>FREE</u> swap and sell bulletin board for subscribers. Please call or fax for more information. Holiday Melody is a club redemption center for all of their lines.

CIB Secondary Market Specialist 1997-98

MO — JERDON [59]

311 S. Main
Carthage, MO 64836

Phone: (800) 503-9844 (417) 358-3343
Hours: M-Sat: 10:00-5:00, other hours by appointment

Services: Buy outright. Limited brokerage.

Lines: Precious Moments, Lowell Davis, ANRI, Shelia's, Lefton, Harmony Kingdom, Country Artists, Armani, Lilliput Lane.

Noteworthy: Located halfway between Sam Butcher's Precious Moments Chapel and Lowell Davis' Red Oak II in Carthage, Missouri, and within an hour and a half drive of Branson. Jerdon is a city block deep and is across from one of the most beautiful courthouses in the country. Jerdon handles private liquidation of estates and private collections. We also work with individuals nation wide to handle many of their secondray market needs by telephone. Using the Collectors' Information Bureau's Price Guide helps us to establish a fair and accurate price for buyers and sellers.

CIB Secondary Market Specialist 1997-98

MO — LOWELL DAVIS FARM CLUB [60]

P.O. Box 636
Carthage, MO 64836

Phone: (800) 989-0103
       (417) 359-5600
Fax: (417) 359-8805
Hours: M-Sat: 9:00-5:30

Services: Distribute and promote Lowell Davis Club figurines. Locator and listing service for retired and limited edition Lowell Davis figurines. We provide a "want and sell" list for our club members and collectors which is listed in our club newspaper, "The Farm Club Gazette" which is published quarterly. Call for more information.

Lines: Lowell Davis Club figurines.

Noteworthy: The Lowell Davis Farm Club was purchased in December 1995, by Jerry Truman who moved the club from Boston, MA to Mr. Lowell's farm at Red Oak II in Carthage, MO. This is where Mr. Lowell's new club pieces are distributed. All pieces are now produced at Border Fine Arts in Scotland.

CIB Secondary Market Specialist 1997-98

Directory to Secondary Market Dealers

MT — 61
THE SHIP'S BELL
101 E. 6th Ave.
Helena, MT 59601

Phone: (406) 443-4470
E-mail: AOL-ShirleyLou
Fax: (406) 442-1800
Hours: M-F:11:00-5:30, Sat: 11:00-4:00(MTN)

Services: Available for current and past issues. Payment in money order or certified checks get immediate shipment whereas personal checks have to clear.

Lines: Bradford, Hamilton, Reco, M.I.Hummel, Ernst, Perillo, Villeroy & Boch, Christian Bell, Winston/Rolland, Redlin, Lowell Davis, Ashton-Drake dolls and more.

Noteworthy: Established in 1973, authorized Bradford and Reco dealer. Large plate gallery featured, in addition to other collectible lines. Secondary market specialists for the lines listed above and all other inquiries welcome, as well. Shirley DeWolf and her staff pride themselves on adding a personal touch, as they work with each and every collector.

NC — 62
CALLAHAN'S OF CALABASH
9973 Beach Drive
Calabash, NC 28467

Phone: (800) 344-3816
Fax: (910) 579-7209
Hours: Daily: 9:00-10:00 (Summer),
Daily: 9:00AM-9:00PM (Winter)

Services: Price list available. Items taken on consignment with 15% commission fee added to the selling price.

Lines: As a Department 56 "Gold Key" Dealer, Callahan's specialty is Department 56 Villages, accessories and Snowbabies. They also offer a secondary market for Wee Forest Folk and a growing Christopher Radko market.

Noteworthy: Come visit their 30,000 square foot shopping extravaganza, featuring the 2,000 sq. ft. award winning Department 56 room. In 1996, as a Rising Star Dealer, they are proud to introduce their Christopher Radko Room. Gold-Wing Seraphin Angel dealer.

CIB Secondary Market Specialist 1997-98

NC — 63
THE GREAT AMERICAN BREWERY SHOPPE
128 N. Main Street
Salisbury, NC 28144

Phone: (704) 642-1345   Fax: (704) 642-1377
Hours: T-Sat: 11:00-6:00

Services: Buy/sell/trade. World-wide mail order. MasterCard and Visa accepted. Competitive pricing on newly issued or secondary market steins.

Lines: Budweiser, Anheuser-Busch, Coca-Cola, Coors, Hamm's, Miller, Pabst, Strohs. Large selection of current German steins. Brewery advertising die-cast car, plane and truck banks. American Brewery collector pins with NASCAR and Olympics represented. Liquor advertising and decanters by Jim Beam, McCormick, Ski Country and Wild Turkey, etc.

Noteworthy: The Great American Brewery Shoppe is 3,000 sq. ft., housing the largest selection of new and old Budweiser advertising, steins and toys. Thousands of items for sale include: glassware, gifts, inflatables, mirrors, neons, pool table lights, signs, sports related items, stand-ups, tap knobs, etc. A 25-pg. mail order catalog on steins and Budweiser toys available upon request. They are the one stop shop for licensed Brewery related merchandise. Easy access off I-85, exit 76B. Located in historic downtown Salisbury.

CIB Secondary Market Specialist 1997-98

NJ — 64
PRESTIGE COLLECTIONS
The Mall at Short Hills, Short Hills, NJ 07078
Bridgewater Common, Bridgewater, NJ 08807
The Westchester, White Plains, NY 10601
Garden State Plaza, Paramus, NJ 07652

Phone: (800) 227-7979   Fax: (201) 597-9408
Hours: M-Sat: 10:00-9:30, Sun: 11:00-6:00

Services: Mail your list with asking price, buy outright. Will do in-home or office shows. Lay-a-way, gift wrapping, special orders, and delivery available. Visa, MC, Amex, Discover.

Lines: Millenium Lladro, Armani, Swarovski, Department 56, Snowbabies, Precious Moments, Disney Classics, Lalique, Daum, Caithness, Waterford, Lenox Classics, Boehm, Lilliput, Limoges Boxes, Hummel, Michael's, Harbour Lights, Radko, Kinkade, Cherished Teddies and much more.

Noteworthy: Established in 1977, Prestige Collections has grown to four locations in the finest regional malls in New Jersey and New York. They are a service oriented business that sells fine gifts and collectibles from $5.00-$25,000. Prestige has some of the finest selections of the best brand name collectibles. A Redemption Center for most major collectibles. Artists and collector events throughout the year. They can help you with corporate and personal shopping. JUST CALL!

CIB Secondary Market Specialist 1997-98

Directory to Secondary Market Dealers

NJ — 65

UNIQUE TREASURES
Olde Lafayette Village
Box 106
Lafayette, NJ 07848

Phone: (201) 579-9190
Fax: (201) 729-9745
Hours: M-Sat: 10:00-6:00, Sun: 11:00-6:00
Open Fri. Nights

Services: Buy/sell. Sell for YOU. Appraisals on Tudor Mint. Personal checks, Visa, MasterCard, Discover and American Express accepted.

Lines: Tudor Mint, Cow Town, Pigs Village, Little Cheesers, Lefton lighthouses, Santa's Crystal Valley.

Noteworthy: Tudor Mint Club Members receive discounts except on club and road show pieces. They have been in the industry for over 5 years. Unique Treasures will soon be on the internet.

NY — 66

Collectibly Yours
80 E Route 59
Spring Valley, NY 10977

Phone: (800) 863-7227 (out of N.Y.)
(914) 425-9244
Hours: Tues-Sat: 10:00-6:00, Sun. by chance.
Holiday hours.

Services: Buy outright. Visa, MasterCard, Discover. No appraisals.

Lines: Swarovski, Precious Moments, Lladro, Ebony Visions, M.I.Hummel, Wee Forest Folk, Memories of Yesterday, Cherished Teddies, All God's Children, Collector's plates, Disney Classics, Thomas Kinkade, Lowell Davis, Lilliput Lane, David Winter, Sports Impressions, Department 56: all Villages, accessories, Snowbabies, Merry Makers; Dolls: Yolanda Bello, Annette Himstedt, Ashton-Drake, Cabbage Patch, Robin Woods, Dolls by Jerri, Gorham, Wakeen, Georgetown, Hamilton, North American Bear, Virginia Turner, Wendy Lawton, Madame Alexander.

Noteworthy: Extensive selection of dolls. Department 56 Gold Key dealer, Kinkade Premier Center, NALED, GCC (Gift Creation Concepts). In collectible business since 1978.

NY — 67

Glorious Treasures Ltd.

Mail: 9206 Avenue L #105; Brooklyn, N.Y. 11236
Phone: 718-241-8185   Fax: 718-241-8184
E-Mail: GlorTreas@aol.com
WWW: http://members.aol.com/GlorTreas

Virtually connected and on-line 24 hours a day!

Services: THE worldwide virtual dealer of beautiful and rare collectible and gift items from around the world. Item search and find. Collection and estate apprasials and sales. Items bought and traded as needed. Sales by personal check, money orders, and all major credit cards. All transactions in US funds and instruments only. Sales tax as required by law & shipping extra.

Lines: OLD & NEW: Hamilton and Bradford plates. Ashton-Drake dolls, Hummel, Disney, Schmid, Royal-Doulton, Donald Zolan, Sandra Kuck, Edna Hibel, Gregory Perillo, Francis Hook, Red Skelton, Dave Grossman, Gorham, Norman Rockwell, Anna Perenna, Lowell Davis, Bessie Pease Gutmann, ANRI, Jan Hagara, Maud Humphrey Bogart, Ted DeGrazia, Enesco, Lladro, Goebel, Olszewski and Sebastian miniatures, Emmett Kelly Jr., Fred Stone, Pat Buckley Moss, Terry Redlin, Donald Polland, John McClelland and Cabbage Patch.

Noteworthy: Established in 1977. THEMES: Star Trek, Star Wars, Beatles, Elvis Presley, Gone With The Wind, I Love Lucy, The Honeymooners, Barbie, Wizard of Oz, other popular television and movie subjects.
RELIGIOUS: Roman. BEER: Budweiser & other beer stuff!
SPORTS: Sports Impressions, Gartlan, Scoreboard, Hackett. Rare stamps and coins. Used records/tapes and memorabilia.

Visit our interactive WWW site!

NY — 68

THE LIMITED EDITION
The Gift And Collectible Authority
2170 Sunrise Highway
Merrick, NY 11566

Phone: (800) 645-2864 (516) 623-4400
Fax: (516) 867-3701
http://www.thelimitededition.com
email: tle@thelimitededition
Hours: Mon-Sat: 10:00-6:00, Fri til 9:00pm

Services: No consignments. Buy outright. Mail your list with asking price. Visa, MasterCard, American Express, Discover.

Lines: Annalee, Cherished Teddies, Christopher Radko, Collector Plates, David Winter, Department 56 Villages, Disney Classics, EKJ, Krystonia, Lladro, Hummel, Precious Moments, Snowbabies, Swarovski.

Noteworthy: Over the past 22 years, The Limited Edition has become one of the most important sources of primary and secondary market Collectibles in the country. The Limited Edition has a very knowledgeable and caring sales staff. All purchases are recorded on computer so collectors can be informed of new releases, retired items, limited editions, special offers and more. The Limited Edition is a member of GAA, BBB, NALED & GCC.

Directory to Secondary Market Dealers

NY | 69

Main St., PO Box 201, Essex, NY 12936

Phone: (800) 898-6098 (518) 963-4347
Web Site: http://www.DiscoverHK.com
Hours: 10:00-5:00 (seven days per week) - 24 hour answering service.

Services: Retail store. Worldwide web access for 24 hr. on-line shopping, and secondary market services. Flat fee for shipping and free shipping once total purchases reaches $300. Interest free payment plans available. Accepts personal checks, money orders, Visa, MasterCard and Amex. Enjoy the personalized service your collection deserves.

Lines: Harmony Kingom. Entire line always in stock.

Noteworthy: For three years Natural Goods & Finery has been specializing in Harmony Kingdom collectibles. As a result many loyal customers enjoy knowledge of new issues, rare and retired pieces and low numbered limited editions. They have one of the largest selections in both current and retired pieces. Call for information on joining their "Treasure Jest of the Month Club."

NY | 70

Village Collectors

12 Hart Place
Dix Hills, N.Y. 11746

Phone: 516-242-2457
Fax: 516-243-4607
E-Mail: dcrupi@delphi.com
Hours: M-F Days: Answering Service
Evenings: 5:30 - 10:00 EST
Weekends: 11:00 - 10:00 EST

Services: Offering a complete secondary market service. Including a FREE listing service, consignments, or outright buying of your Department 56 SECONDARY MARKET collectibles, UPS insured shipping, an inspection period, layaways, gift certificates, & gift wrapping. Our commission on listings or consignments is 15%, which is included in our selling price. A FREE price quote or listing is only a call away! We accept Visa, MasterCard, Discover, American Express, & checks.

Lines: All Department 56 Retired or Limited Edition collectibles. Including Villages, Snowbabies & Giftware.

Noteworthy: We started collecting D56 during Christmas of '89 and have been helping collectors find the piece of their dreams since 1992. As my husband always says "Donna collects the little white D56 sticker."
We are always willing to answer your D56 related questions.

OH | 71

Collectible Exchange, Inc.™
Retired & Limited Edition Collectibles

Phone: (800) 752-3208
Fax: (330) 542-9644
Hours: M-F 9:00 a.m. - 8:00 p.m.
Sat: 10:00 a.m. - 4:00 p.m.

Services: International Secondary Market Listing Service. Serving individuals and dealers. No cost no obligation listing service. Personal check, money order, Visa, MasterCard, Discover or American Express accepted. Toll Free 800 Service.

Lines: Boyds Bears, Byers' Choice, Charming Tails, Cherished Teddies, David Winter, Department 56, Disney Classics, Dreamsicles, Emmett Kelly Jr., Forma Vitrum, Hallmark, Harbour Lights, Hummel, Jan Hagara, June McKenna, Kiddie Car Classics, Krystonia, Lefton, Lilliput, Lowell Davis, Lynn West Santas, Maud Humphrey, Memories of Yesterday, Midwest, Olszewski, Precious Moments, Shellia's, Swarovski Crystal, Wee Forest Folk and Wysocki.

Noteworthy: Started in 1989 as the first Independent Nationwide Secondary Service. Has grown to a large scale International Service trading over $2 million annually. Member of original CIB Panel. Referred by many major collectible manufactures.

OH | 72

182 Front Street, Berea, OH 44017

Phone: (216) 826-4169 (800) 344-9299
Fax: (216) 826-0839
E-MAIL: yworrey@aol.com
Hours: M-F: 9:00- 6:00, Sat: 10:00-5:00

Services: Buy/Sell/Trade/ Appraise. MasterCard, Visa, Discover and American Express accepted.

Lines: Royal Doulton, Department 56, M.I. Hummel, Lladro, David Winter, Lilliput Lane, Wee Forest Folk, Walt Disney Classics, Swarovski, Precious Moments, Bing & Grondahl, Royal Copenhagen, and Cherished Teddies.

Noteworthy: Colonial House of Collectibles has been in business for over 23 years. For the past 11 years, they have been located in an 1873 house in the southwest suburb of Cleveland. A year- round Christmas room is always on display. They are a Redemption Center for collector club pieces.

Directory to Secondary Market Dealers

OH — The Exchange — 73

4226 Deepwood Lane
Cincinnati, Ohio 45245-1718

Phone: (800) 792-3885
(513) 752-5708 in Cincinnati
Fax: (513) 752-5253
E-Mail: OrnyChaser@aol.com
Hours: M-F 12-8:00, 24 hour service also available!

"THE ONLY WAY TO FIND COLLECTIBLES"

Services: We locate hard to find collectibles for our customers. If we can't find the piece your searching for, we'll add it to our **NO OBLIGATION** Search List! Dealers Welcome. Check, Money Order, Visa, Master Card or Discover Accepted.

Lines: All God's Children, Anheuser-Busch, Inc., Annalee, Armani, Beanie Babies, Boyds Bears (All lines), Byer's Choice, Charming Tales, Cherished Teddies, Daddy Long Legs, Department 56 Snowbabies and Villages, Hallmark Ornaments, Hummels, Leo Smith, Llardro, Maude Humphrey, Melody In Motion, Merry Miniatures, Precious Moments, Sarah's Attic, Seraphim Angels, Steinbach, Swarovski Crystal, Thomas Blackshear, United Design Santas, Walt Disney Classics and Wee Forest Folks

Noteworthy: The Exchange is owned and operated by Tina Dennis, who also owns the Glass Ornament Exchange. The Exchange will include an appraisal form for each piece purchased. This will enable the Collector to insure their collection for the replacement value, not a value that your Insurance Broker (who probably is very unknowledgeable of the value of collectibles) would put on it. Call today for more details!!

OH — Gift Garden — 74

SINCE 1970
House of Fine Gifts & Collectibles
624 Great Northern Mall
N. Olmsted, OH 44070

Phone: (216) 777-0116 (800) 777-4802
Fax: (216) 777-0116
Website: www.giftgarden.com
Hours: M-Sat: 10:00-9:00, Sun: 11:00-6:00

Services: Buy/sell. No consignments. Visa, MasterCard, Discover and American Express accepted.

Lines: Armani, ANRI, Budweiser, Disney Classics, M.I. Hummel, Swarovski, Pocket Dragons, Robert Olszewski, Animation Art, Emmett Kelly Jr., Ron Lee, Precious Moments, Cherished Teddies, Collector plates, Polanaise, Christopher Radko, and Greenwich Workshop Collection, Chilmark, Legends, Krystonia, Eggspressions, Department 56, Steinbach, and Caithness paperweights.

Noteworthy: Gift Garden has been in business since 1970, serving collectors all over the country. Gift Garden brings the best artists and creations of fine collectibles in the world. Call for further information on our artist events throughout the year. They pay your collector club dues. Call for details on your club.

OH — Glass Ornament Exchange — 75

4226 Deepwood Lane • Cincinnati, Ohio 45245-1718

Phone: (800) 587-2356
(513) 752-3434
Fax: (513) 752-5253
E-Mail: OrnyChaser@aol.com
Hours: M-F 12-8:00, 24 hour service also available!

"Where your collectibles are tomorrow's keepsakes."

Services: We locate your hard to find collectable glass ornaments. If we can't find the piece your searching for, we will add it to our NO OBLIGATION Search List. Dealers Welcome. Check, Money Order, Visa, Master Card or Discover Accepted.

Lines: Christopher Radko, Patricia Breen, Polonaise, Old World, M. Furlong, Lenox, Swarovski and many others.

Noteworthy: The Glass Ornament Exchange is owned and operated by Tina Dennis and is the largest Secondary Broker for glass ornaments. There are over 1,800 Listings, with Radko's dating back to 1986. Starting March 1st, the Glass Ornament Exchange will include an appraisal form for each piece purchased. This will enable the Collector to insure their pieces for the replacement value, not a value that your Insurance Broker (who probably is very unknowledgeable of the value of glass ornaments) would put on it.

Call today for more details!!! 1~ (800) 587 ~ 2356

OH — Little Red Gift House — 76

"a unique treasure of a gift shop"
State Route 113, Birmingham, OH 44816

Phone: (216 or 440) 965-5420
Hours: Tues.-Sat.: 10:00-6:00
Sun.: 12:00-5:00 (except Jan./Feb.)
Closed Mon. (except in Dec.)

Services: Specialist in Norman Rockwell figurines and plates. Occasionally buy Rockwell collections or individual pieces. No consignments. Free appraisals for insurance. Ship UPS daily. Visa and MasterCard accepted.

Lines: Norman Rockwell, M.I. Hummel, Precious Moments, Disney Classics, Thomas Kinkade, Department 56, collector plates, Cherished Teddies, Sports Collectibles, Ray Day, Memories of Yesterday, Seraphim angels, Possible Dreams, Bradford dealer, Anheuser-Busch steins, Emmett Kelly, Amish Heritage, Jan Hagara, Pretty as a Picture.

Noteworthy: Little Red Gift House has become known nationwide as a major source of Norman Rockell collectibles, (both new and older pieces). In stock is a large inventory of retired, discontinued, and limited edition Rockwell figurines. Listing of in-stock Rockwell items is available upon request.

Directory to Secondary Market Dealers

OH — MILLER'S HALLMARK & GIFT GALLERY [77]

1322 North Barron Street, Eaton, Ohio 45320-1016

Phone: (937) 456-4151
Fax: (937) 456-7851
Hours: M-F: 9:00AM-9:00PM,
Sat: 9:00-6:00, Sun: 12:00-5:00

Services: No consignments. Buy outright. Crystal report and brokerage. Collectibles Auctions: some produced on consignment. Expert appraisal services. Call for details.

Lines: Precious Moments, M.I. Hummel, Swarovski, Department 56, Cherished Teddies, Christopher Radko, Hallmark Ornaments, Snowbabies, Boyds Bears, Dreamsicles, Cat's Meow, Memories of Yesterday.

Noteworthy: Miller's Hallmark & Gift Gallery has grown to four stores strong, from a specialty store featuring M.I. Hummel figurines, into a full service Hallmark and collectibles Showcase Gallery. Dean A. Genth is an Associate Member of the American Society of Appraisers and has been appraising M.I. Hummel figurines for over 15 years. Private and personal appraisals are done by Mr. Genth for insurance purposes. The Miller Company and Dean A. Genth have served as counsel to many insurance companies and individuals that need expert advice on matters related to collectibles.

OH — Rochelle's Fine Gifts [78]

364 Franklin Park Mall, Toledo, Ohio 43623

Phone: (800) 458-6585, (419) 472-7673
Hours: M-Sat: 10:00-9:00, Sun: 12:00-6:00

Services: No consignments, buy outright. Mail your list with item number, description, and mold mark (if applicable), and Rochelle's will respond with an offer in writing A.S.A.P. MasterCard, Visa, Discover accepted. Layaway plan available. Free gift wrapping. Redemption Center for most clubs.

Lines: Precious Moments, Cherished Teddies, Boyds Bears, Harbour Lights, Department 56, Disney Classics, Swarovski, and much more.

Noteworthy: Rochelle's is owner operated and celebrating its 20th anniversary this year. The best collectible store in the best mall in northwest Ohio, Rochelle's extensive customer list includes collectors from all 50 states. All purchases are kept in a "customer history" file so collectors can be informed when new items in their collection are available. They are a full service collectible store, carrying most lines, and accept advance reservations and special orders on most items. Rochelle's is a member of NALED and GCC.

OK — PICTORIAL TREASURES [79]

Your Limited Edition Art Print Specialist

Current and Sold-out Prints for over 100 Artists such as **Kinkade, Doolittle, Lyman, Maley, Wysocki**

Pictorial Treasures is the largest secondary market Limited Edition Art Exchange open to both the private collector and retail dealer. Listings are always accepted.
Free price quotes available for over 3000 prints.
All L.E. art prints come with certificates of authenticity.
Call 918 287-2668 today for our lowest price quotes and friendly, reliable service.

Thomas Kinkade Newsletter only $12.95/yr
Bi-monthly articles include special events and appearances, seasonal and collector print favorites, secondary market price lists, what's just sold-out, what's hot, what's new, and more.

PICTORIAL TREASURES
P.O. Box 1586
Pawhuska, OK 74056

Check out our **on-line gallery**
http://www.galstar.com/~rtpeters/
e-mail: rtpeters@galstar.com

OK — RATHBONE'S FLAIR CHRISTMAS & COLLECTIBLES [80]

4734 S. Peoria, Tulsa, OK 74105

Phone: (918) 747-8491
Fax: (918) 749-3045
On-line: www.flairflowers.com
Hours: M-Sat. 9:30-5:30, Sun: 1:00-5:00

Services: Buy/sell outright. Some consignments. Locator service, Visa, MasterCard, Amex and Discover.

Lines: Dept. 56, Armani, Kinkade, Swarovski, Hummels, Lilliput Lane, D.Winter, Byers' Choice, Precious Moments, Sarah's Attic, All God's, Madame Alexander and bears.

Noteworthy: Rathbone's is located in the historical old Brookside Bowling alley in Tulsa, with 18,000 square feet of showroom and 400 feet of showcase, collectors can enjoy Rathbone's spacious surroundings and a wide variety of collectibles. Their year-round Christmas store offers a full line of Christmas decorations including trees, lights and Christmas collectibles. They carry a large selection of giftware including curio cabinets, Grandfather clocks and flower arrangements. An Annual Christmas Open House and special events are held throughout the year with artist signings.

Directory to Secondary Market Dealers

OK — SHIRLEY'S GIFTS, INC. AND COLLECTIBLE EXCHANGE | 81

1021 W. Broadway
Ardmore, OK 73401

Phone (800) 537-2116
(405) 223-2116
Hours: M-Sat: 10:00-6:00

Services: Buy/Sell. Locator service.

Lines: Mattel Barbies, Disney Classics, Swarovski, Chilmark, Lefton, Hummel, Dept. 56, Cherished Teddies, Boyds Bears & Dollstones, Precious Moments, Calico Kittens, Shelia's, Lizzie High, Pocket Dragons, Madame Alexander, Tom Clark, Tim Wolfe, Lee Sievers, Armani, Kinkade, Genesis, Byers' Choice, EKJ, All God's Children, M. Furlong, Dreamsicles, Possible Dreams, Cottontail Lane, Patchville Bunnies, Seraphim Angles, Fontanini, Forma Vitrum and more.

Noteworthy: The store is now a Key Dealer for Cairn Studios, a Showcase Dealer for Department 56, a premier dealer for Swarovski, Charter dealer for Lefton. Shirley's is a Redemption Center for most collectibles and hosts collector events throughtout the year.

OK — WINTER IMAGES | 82

3008 Hilltop
Muskogee, OK 74403

Phone: (918) 683-3488
Fax: (918) 683-2325 (24 hrs.)
E-mail: jeanine@netsites.net
Hours: Weekends and after 4:00PM weekdays

Services: Secondary market exchange, listing retired pieces to buy or sell. Major credit cards accepted. If paying by check, prefer money order or certified check. Order is held for one week if paid by personal check.

Lines: All collectible lines including: David Winter, Precious Moments, Hummel, Hallmark, Lowell Davis, Swarovski, Lladro, DeGrazia, Disney, Department 56, Lilliput Lane, Enesco, Rockwell, Lucy and Me, ANRI, Cherished Teddies, Boyds, Chilmark, Calico Kittens, Tom Clark, Armani, Chapeau Noelle and others.

Noteworthy: Jeanine Vandiver and her children, Jamie and Kirk Brown, began their business in 1992, specializing in David Winter. The business has expanded to a secondary market exchange, helping customers buy and sell in all collectible lines. Winter Images prides itself with personalized service, including insurance appraisals.

OR — CHRISTMAS TREASURES | 83

52959 McKenzie Highway
Blue River, OR 97413

Phone: (800) 820-8189
Orders Only,
(541) 822-3516 Information
Fax: (541) 822-3516
Hours: Daily: 9:00-7:00(PST)

Services: Retail and secondary market. Credit cards accepted.

Lines: Department 56, Byers' Choice, Old World Christmas ornaments and Santa Lights, Christopher Radko, Hallmark, Roman Seraphim Angels, Duncan Royale Santas, Boyds Bears, History of Angels, Melody In Motion Santas, Steinbach Nutcrackers, Christmas Reproducion Memories of Santa, Muffy Vanderbear, V.I.B. and Raikes Christmas Bears, Raggedy Ann and Andy cloth dolls by Applause, Possible Dreams Santas.

Noteworthy: Christmas Treasures brings you the most treasured items for gift giving and collecting. Experience the Old World charm all through the year. Buying outright older retired pieces from the following lines: Byers' Choice, Old World Christmas Santa Lights, Steinbach Nutcrackers and Christmas Reproduction Memories of Santa. Serving customers since 1993.

OR — LITA SALE IMPORT | 84

15565 Eilers Road
Aurora, OR 97002

Phone: (503) 678-1622

Hours: Showroom open by appointment
Services: Buy and Sell outright. Layaway available.

Lines: ANNETTE-HIMSTEDT DOLLS - Exclusive Dealer
STEINBACH NUTCRACKERS
ULBRICHT NUTCRACKERS

Noteworthy: Over 100 limited edition and current nutcrackers and dolls in stock. Call Lita for best prices. Born and raised in Europe, Lita Sale has developed personal relationships with Ulbricht, Steinbach and Himstedt. Trips to the International Toy Fair in Nuremberg, Germany, and the New York Toy Fair, plus visits to artists' homes, studios, and factories, Lita is constantly adding to her inventory of limited collectibles.

Directory to Secondary Market Dealers

PA — BOB LAMSON BEER STEINS, INC. — 85

509 N. 22nd Street
Allentown, PA 18104

Phone: (800) 435-8611
       (610) 435-8611
Fax: (610) 435-8188
Hours: M-F: 9:00AM-9:00PM,
       Sat: 10:00-4:00

Services: Buy/sell/trade. Terms available upon request for larger purchases. Please inquire.

Lines: Anheuser-Busch, Michelob, Budweiser, Bud Light, Coors, Strohs, Miller, steins and related collectibles with beer affiliations, i.e. neons, lights, clocks, signs, tap knobs and mirrors.

Noteworthy: Incorporated in 1990, Bob Lamson Beer Steins, Inc. is owned and operated solely by the Lamson family. The company has a retail store located in Allentown, Pennsylvania, and also ships orders to every state in the nation and to Canada. Collectors should call with any additional questions they have regarding the company. Bob Lamson beer steins is an Anheuser-Busch Collectors Club Redemption Center

PA — CRAYON SOUP — 86

King of Prussia Plaza, King of Prussia, PA 19406

Phone: (610) 265-0458, (800) 552-3760
Fax: (610) 265-2979
Hours: M-Sat: 10:00-9:30,
       Sun: 11:00-6:00

Services: Buy outright

Lines: All God's, Lladro, Dept.-56 (Heritage Village and accessories), Snowbabies, Lilliput, EKJ, David Winter, PM, PenDelfin, Swarovski, Steinbach Nutcrackers, Hummel, MOY, Olszewski Miniatures, Anheuser and German Gentz steins.

Noteworthy: The formation of Crayon Soup in 1982 was a natural, considering that owners Joe and Trish Zawislack had already been collecting for 30 years! The store started in a mall kiosk, with the couple selling stickers and novelties geared toward children. Eventually, the Zawislacks entered the collectibles market. The name, Crayon Soup, was the brainchild of Trish, who formulated the name, thinking the couple would start an educational store for children! Today, the store is a Redemption Center for several collectible lines. Hummel enthusiasts will be delighted to view over 400 Hummels in stock. Crayon Soup hosts 40 collector events including artist appearances and organizes in-store collector clubs. Information on new and retired products and collectors clubs is available free of charge.

PA — LIGHTHOUSE TRADING COMPANY — 87

112 Elio Circle
Limerick, PA 19468

Phone: (610) 409-9336
Fax: (610) 409-9336
On Line: www.lighthousetrading.com
Hours: Mail Order - M-F: 1:30-8:30 (EST)

Services: Buy/sell. Secondary market service. Occasionally buy outright. Dealers welcome. Visa and MasterCard accepted.

Lines: Harbour Lights, Forma Vitrum; (Vitreville, Coastal Heritage), Spencer Collin, and other collectibles.

Noteworthy: Lighthouse Trading Company is owned and operated by Matt Rothman. He keeps current in Harbour Lights, Forma Vitrum and other popular collectibles, offering a personalized secondary market service for collectors to buy and sell their collectibles. Matt has had articles published in national collectible publications and is a contributing Collectors' Information Bureau panel member.

PA — SAM'S STEINS & COLLECTIBLES — 88

2207 Lincoln Highway East RT 30
Lancaster, PA 17602

Phone: (717) 394-6404
Hours: M-W & Sat: 10:00-6:00, Th & F: 10:00-9:00,
       Sun: 11:00-5:00 (Apr.-Dec.)
       T,W & Sat: 10:00-6:00,
       Th & F: 10:00-8:00 (Oct.-May)

Services: Buy outright. Mail order catalog available, send two $.32 stamps.

Lines: Specializes in beer steins: Anheuser-Busch, Miller, Coors, Strohs, Pabst, Hamm's, Yuengling, large selection of German beer steins. Brewery advertising items such as steins, neons, signs, tap markers and mirrors. Sam also carries Cavanagh Coca-Cola Cubs, Ande Rooney Porcelain signs, First Gear, ERTL, and Spec cast collector trucks and banks.

Noteworthy: Sam's Steins & Collectibles, located 1/8 mile from Dutch Wonderland, has been in business since 1967. A collector himself, owner Sam May houses one of the largest displays of beer memorabilia in the United States. Over 900 different U.S. and German steins are on display. See the stein that is in the Guinness Book of Records, four feet tall and holds 8.45 gallons of beer, at Sam's Steins & Collectibles.

Directory to Secondary Market Dealers

PA — 89
WORLDWIDE COLLECTIBLES AND GIFTS
P.O. Box 158, 2 Lakeside Avenue
Berwyn, PA 19312-0158

Phone: (800) 222-1613 (610) 644-2442
Fax: (610) 889-9549
Hours: M-Sat: 10:00-5:00, order desk open 24 hrs.

Services: A 64-page mail order catalog available free, upon request. Call for specific quotes. Prompt payment on all items purchased. Prompt delivery on items ordered.

Lines: Swarovski, Lladro, Department 56, Disney Classics, M.I. Hummel, David Winter, Duncan Royale, Steiff, collector plates, bells, collector club pieces and many others.

Noteworthy: Worldwide Collectibles is a full service company established in 1975. They deal in current and secondary market pieces and maintain a large inventory on all lines carried. The Worldwide staff is actively involved with major insurers for replacement and estimate valuation purposes. Appraisals and references are available on request.

SC — 90

Broughton Christmas Shoppe
1370 Broughton Street, Orangeburg, SC 29115

Phone: (803) 536-4176, (800) 822-5556 (orders only)
Fax: (803) 531-2007
Hours: M-F: 9:00-6:00, Sat: 9:00-5:00,
Sun: 1:30-5:30 (Nov. & Dec. only)

Services: Buy/Sell/Trade/Consignments. Visa, MasterCard, Discover and American Express accepted. Shipping available.

Lines: Department 56 (Snow Village, Dickens Village, New England Village, Alpine Village, North Pole, Christmas in the City, Disney Parks Village, Snowbabies, Snowbunnies, All Through the House, Winter Silhouettes, Merry Makers), Harbour Lights, Shelia's, Keepers, Byers' Choice, and Seraphim Classics.

Noteworthy: Broughton Christmas Shoppe has been in the collectible business for 13 years. A family run business, they cater to collectibles and to their customers. All staff members are collectors themselves, and offer friendly, knowledgable service. Broughton's is a Gold Key Dealer for Department 56 and a Platinum dealer for Shelia's.

SD — 91
RAINBOW HILLS GIFT SHOP
Located in The Chief Restaurant
140 Mt. Rushmore Road
Custer, SD 57730

Phone: (605) 673-4402
Hours: M-Sun: 7:00 AM-8:00 PM

Services: Consignments by listings and locator service. Call for information.

Lines: Legends, Mill Creek, Incolay plates and boxes, and Dreamsicles.

Noteworthy: Rainbow Hills is located in the magnificent Black Hills in the midst of Mt. Rushmore, Crazy Horse and Custer State Park. Rainbow Hills/Chief Enterprises is a family owned and operated gift shop, restaurant, and motel complex that has been serving the collectors' needs for the past 19 years. The Gift shop is a showplace with one of the largest displays of Legends Mixed Media™ sculptures and holds the honor of being one of the top preferred Legends dealers in the nation. Open Houses are held throughtout the year. Rainbow Hills is a Redemption Center and offers unique gifts and collectibles to satisfy any collector.

TN — 92
BARBARA'S GATLINBURG SHOPS
Barbara's Elegants, The John Cody Gallery
The Gatlinburg Shop
511, 716, 963 Parkway, Gatlinburg, TN 37738

Phone: (800) 433-1132
Hours: Daily: 9:00AM-9:00PM

Services: As a service to their customers, Barbara's Gatlinburg Shops try to help both the buyer and the seller. They keep an up-to-date listing of collectibles that customers are interested in selling or buying. Call if you are interested in more information. There is no charge for the listing. They charge 25% if a sale is made.

Lines: All God's Children, Armani, Byers' Choice, Boyd's Bearstone Bears, Cades Cove Cabin, Cairn Gnomes, Cherished Teddies, Chilmark, Christopher Radko, Department 56, David Winter, Dreamsicles, Harmony Kingdom, Hudson, John Cody Prints, Legends, Lilliput Lane, Lladro, Mark Hopkins, Mickey & Co., Sandicast, Swarovski, Wee Forest Folk, plus many more exciting lines!

Noteworthy: Barbara's started in 1977 as a small retailer. They have now grown to three shops with a large mailing list composed of customers from 49 states and several foreign countries. Barbara's ships daily, provides appraisals, and mails brochures and catalogs to customers interested in a particular line. "Our sales consultants are committed to you!"

Directory to Secondary Market Dealers

TN — 93

Classic Endeavors

349 Southshore Drive
Greenback, TN 37742-2301
Phone (423)856-8100
Fax   (423)856-8001
Hours: M-F 11:00 - 5:00 EST

Services: Buy/Sell/Trade! No listing/membership fee. Layaways available. Accepts Visa and MasterCard - no extra fee. Quoted price includes commission - no surprises! 72 hour guarantee. Overseas shipping.

Lines: Harbour Lights, Kinkade (canvas only), Forma Vitrum, Walt Disney Classics Collection, 1990's Disneyana convention memorabilia.

Noteworthy: Established in 1993, **CLASSIC ENDEAVORS, INC.** is owned and operated by Dee Brandt. Ms. Brandt, is also free-lance writer and has had articles published in national collectibles magazines. She recently worked as a consultant on the second Greenbook Guide to the WDCC, which was published in 1996. Associate Member of NALED. Member of CIB's "Panel of Experts".

TX — 94

AMANDA'S FINE GIFTS

265 Central Park Mall
San Antonio, TX 78216-5506

Phone: (800) 441-4458 (210) 525-0412
Hours: M-Sat: 10:00-9:00, Sun: Noon-6:00

Services: 10 month layaway. Consignments. Buy outright when needed. Redemption center for Lladro, Disney, Swarovski, Armani, M.I. Hummel and Lalique Collectors Club. Appraisal service for insurance purposes.

Lines: Lladro, Swarovski, M.I. Hummel, Ron Lee, Armani, Chilmark, Bossons, Disney.

Noteworthy: Barry Harris developed a deep appreciation for Lladro artwork, which eventually led to the purchase of Amanda's Fine Gifts in 1983. Realizing the great potential for offering Lladro artwork and information to collectors, Barry and his staff have become known as experts in the field. The largest Lladro dealer in the southwest, Amanda's has welcomed Lladro family members to the store for artist appearances. Other guests have included Don Polland, Ron Lee, Michael Boyett M.I. Hummel and Armani Artist.

TX — 95

ANTIQUE HAVEN

Route 1, Box 60
Stanton, TX 79782

Phone: (800) 299-3480 (915) 458-3480
Fax: (915) 458-3368 (call first)
Hours: M-Sat: 9:00-5:00

Services: Ten-month layaway. Ship freight free in U.S. Major credit cards accepted. Buy outright. Consignment. Quarterly newsletter.

Lines: All God's Children, Miss Martha's Collection, Endearing Memories, Tom Clark Gnomes, Lee Sievers, Tim Wolfe, Cat's Meow, Daddy's Long Legs, Cherished Teddies, Fenton, Disney Classics, Lowell Davis, Maud Humphrey, Legends and Williraye.

Noteworthy: Antique Haven has been in existence for 29 years and is second generation owned by Vanita and Jerry Waid. They are located 12 miles east of Midland, TX and 5 miles west of Stanton on N. Access Road off Interstate Hwy 20, mile marker 151. They carry European and American antiques, glassware, candles, and many gift items and accessories in addition to specializing in the secondary market and collectibles. They are also a Redemption Center for many collectible lines.

TX — 96

Cola Collection, inc.

**TRY US FIRST, TRY US LAST,
BUT BE SURE TO TRY US!**

COLA COLLECTION carries an excellent & varied stock of secondary market Coca-Cola related Xmas items, including but not limited to, the Cavanaugh Xmas Village buildings & accessories, North Pole Bottling Works components, ornaments, animated Santas & Polar Bears, music boxes, figurines, etc. **We also carry many Enesco Coca-Cola items. Our Coke Xmas Corner remains on display year round.** If we don't have it in stock, chances are we can find it. **You are invited to visit one of the most unique gift shops in the U.S. whenever you are in the Houston area. We ship anywhere in the world. Items in stock are shipped the same day the order is received. All major credit cards accepted. Layaways are invited.**

Phone: (800) 650-8183
           (713) 521-1009
Fax: (713) 521-0227
Hours: M-Sat: 10:00-6:00

Directory to Secondary Market Dealers

VA — 97

Memories In Motion
114 Clark Avenue, Elkton, VA 22827

Phone: (540) 298-9234
Hours: Mail order: 10:00AM-10:00PM(EST)
(work from home-please keep trying)

Services: Secondary Market Dealer. Can help you fill in missing series/family ornaments, etc. Accepts Visa and MasterCard. Worldwide shipping. Buy outright when needed. Refer and sell to other dealers. Call for details.

Lines: Hallmark Ornaments, Kiddie Cars, Cherished Teddies and some Barbie dolls.

Noteworthy: Memories In Motion was started by Bobbie Ann Horne in 1990 from her home in the beautiful Shenandoah Valley of Virginia. This mail order business now has clientele around the world. Bobbie Ann is a charter member of the Hallmark Ornament Collector's Club, serves as a consultant to Hallmark Stores and donates large quantities of ornaments to local charities. She is easy to talk with and specializes in pleasing clients. Her business is a Chamber of Commerce member.

WA — 98

NATALIA'S COLLECTIBLES
19949-130th NE
Woodinville, WA 98072

Phone: (206) 481-4575
Hours: T-Sat: 10:00-7:00

Services: Consignments and buy outright.

Lines: Ashton-Drake dolls, Georgetown dolls, Sarah's Attic, Jan Hagara, Maud Humphrey, Thomas Kinkade, Bradford, Hamilton, Reco, Royal Copenhagen, Bing & Grondahl, Winston Roland, and other limited edition plates.

Noteworthy: Natalia's Collectibles was established as a small store in a quiet garden-type surrounding in 1982. Originally dealing only in limited edition plates on the primary market, the firm soon established themselves in the secondary market for plates. Likewise, as dolls and figurines were added to the store, they assisted their clients with a secondary market outlet. As a Bradford Exchange and NALED member, Natalia's Collectibles is dedicated to friendly expert service in both the primary and secondary markets.

WA — 99

The Second Hand News™
The Independent Guide to Secondary Market Collector Plates

8712 NE 57th Street
Vancouver, WA 98662

Phone: (800) 925-1532   **Fax:** (360) 896-1925
Email: s.gormley@sprynet.com
Hours: 24-hour answering service

Services: Publishes a newsletter six times per year for secondary market collector plates with separate sections for "Plates for Sale" and "Plates Wanted." Subscriptions are $20 a year in the USA, $25 a year foreign and includes 50 free plate listings per issue. Readers interested in buying or selling a listed plate contact the listing party directly to negotiate a deal. Sample copies are $3.

Lines: Bradford, Disney, Bing & Grondahl, Franklin Mint, Hamilton, Goebel, Edwin M. Knowles, Lenox, Pemberton & Oakes, Rockwell Society, Royal Copenhagen, W.S. George, etc.

Noteworthy: The Second Hand News™ was founded in 1993 to enable plate lovers to buy, sell or trade secondary market plates directly with one another, without paying a broker's fee or commission.

WI — 100

Collector's Connection
Secondary Market Services for fine Collectibles
Buy-Sell-Trade & Classified Ads on the Internet

http://www.collectorsconnection.com

816 Eddington Drive
Sun Prairie, WI 53590
608-825-8381
Fax: 608-825-9473
E-mail: connect56@aol.com

Services: All listings & classified ads are available on our web site. Prices include 10% commission. We accept Visa, Mastercard, and checks. Please call or e-mail for current listing/classified rates.

Lines: Boyds, Cherished Teddies, Dept. 56, Charming Tails, Beanie Babies, Swarovski, Hummel, Walt Disney, Lladro, Beatrix Potter, Coca-Cola Town Square, Harbour Lights, Harmony Kingdom, Hallmark, Precious Moments, Muffy, Prints, Plates, Ornaments, Colonial Village, David Winter, Sheila's, Lilliput Lane, Dolls, Armani, & more miscellaneous!

Directory to Secondary Market Dealers

WI — Hum-Haus (101)

3555 South 27th Street, Milwaukee, WI 53221

Phone: (414) 645-HUML (4865)
Fax: (414) 645-8994
Hours: M-F: 5:30-8:00, Sat & Sun: 10:00-5:00

Services: Consignments. Buy outright. Layaway and shipping available.

Lines: Exclusively M.I. Hummel figurines, plates, bells and all Hummel accessories such as cross-stitch, stationery, calendars, books, stained-glass window plaques, ornaments, etc.

Noteworthy: The Hum-Haus opened June 1, 1993, as a retail store. The owners began collecting Hummels as a hobby, with one of the owners interested in Hummels since 1955. Over the years, the collection grew and grew, and as older pieces replaced newer pieces, more and more duplicate Hummels became available for sale. Collectors purchasing Hummels began asking why the owners did not have a store, and so Hum-Haus was formed. Due to a long love of M.I Hummel collectibles, the owners hope to make the store a one-stop shopping establishment for collectors. Hum-Haus offers "full service" to collectors, locating older Hummels as well as retired or limited editon pieces, special orders, consignments and appraisals. Hum-Haus is an authorized dealer and Redemption Center for M.I. Hummel.

WI — RED CROSS GIFTS (102)

122 Walnut Street
Spooner, WI 54801

Phone: (800) 344-9958, (715) 635-6154
Fax: (715) 635-6178
Hours: M-Sat: 9:00-5:00

Services: Locator service for plates, figurines, dolls, bells, and ornaments. No consignments. Layaway and major credit cards accepted.

Lines: Department 56, Precious Moments, Cherished Teddies, Armani, Lladro, Harbour Lights, Emmett Kelly, Forma Vitrum, Seraphim Classics, Dreamsicles, Mickey & Co., Maud Humphrey, Mark Klaus, Fontanini, DeGrazia, Lucy & Me, Kitty Cucumber, Krystonia, Pocket Dragons, Enchantica. Plates; Bradford, Hamilton, Reco, Royal Copenhagen, Bing & Grondahl, Dolls; Ashton-Drake, Hamilton, Gorham, Victoria Ashlea.

Noteworthy: Over 80 years strong and in its' fourth generation, Red Cross Gifts has plenty of experience to offer their collectors. The friendly and helpful staff will assist collectors in finding just what they need. They service over 70 major collectible lines with 1700 collector plates on display. Also a Redemption Center for most collectible lines.

WI — WEMAS OF WISCONSIN, INC. (103)

FORMERLY COTTAGE PARK LTD.
P.O. Box 71
Greendale, WI 53129

Phone: (414) 427-1959
Fax: (414) 427-4468
Hours: M-Sat: 9:00-4:30 (CST)

Services: No consignments. Buy outright if not in our inventory. We accept all major credit cards. Free shipping. Six-month layaway available. All items in mint condition.

Lines: David Winter, Malcom Cooper Pubs, Department 56 (Dickens and Signature series), and Harbour Lights.

Noteworthy: Wemas of Wisconsin has been a secondary market dealer since 1985. We are a Redemption Center for David Winter, Harbour Lights, Harmony Kingdom and Dreamsicles.

104

Looking for the latest news about collectibles?

ORDER YOUR SUBSCRIPTION to the COLLECTIBLES REPORT

Get a full year of information about new products, artists, clubs and events with the *Collectibles Report*...CIB's quarterly newsletter. Four issues are yours for only $15!

Call (847) 842-2200 today to subscribe.

Or write to: COLLECTORS' INFORMATION BUREAU
5065 SHORELINE ROAD, SUITE 200
BARRINGTON, IL 60010

❖ DIRECTORY INDEX BY SPECIALTY ❖

Abelman Art Glass, 3
All God's Children, 9, 15, 17, 18, 40, 42, 43, 53, 54, 66, 73, 80, 81, 86, 92
Amish Heritage, 76
Anchor Bay, 54
Anheuser-Busch, Inc., 4, 11, 42, 53, 54, 58, 63, 73, 76, 85, 86, 88
Animation Art, 10, 26, 40, 74
Annalee Mobilitee Dolls, Inc., 8, 17, 40, 51, 54, 58, 68, 73
ANRI, 5, 7, 28, 33, 36, 40, 42, 43, 59, 67, 74, 82
Armani, 10, 13, 17, 24, 28, 34, 40, 42, 43, 47, 51, 57, 59, 64, 73, 74, 80, 81, 82, 92, 94, 95, 100, 102
Ashton-Drake Dolls, 1, 7, 17, 18, 28, 40, 43, 44, 61, 66, 67, 98, 102
Australian Faceted Sculptures, 3

Baccarat, 36
Bannister, 17
Barbie, 1, 27, 29, 43, 44, 52, 56, 97
Beanie Babies, 2, 41, 56, 73, 100
Bears, 80
Beatrix Potter, 100
Bello, Yolanda, 66
Bells, 89
Berry, Rod Bearcloud, 21
Beverly Port, 22,
Bing & Grondahl, 18, 30, 36, 72, 98, 99, 102
Birgits Collections, 8
Blaylock Originals, 21
Blackshear, Thomas, 53, 73
Boehm Studios, 36, 64
Bossons, 5, 94
Boyds Collection, Ltd., 1, 2, 9, 18, 19, 24, 27, 41, 43, 45, 51, 52, 53, 54, 57, 58, 71, 73, 77, 78, 81, 82, 83, 92, 100
Boyds Dollstones, 27, 52, 73, 81
Boyds Folkstones, 27, 52, 73
Boyds Plushes, 27, 52, 73
Bradford Plates, 1, 7, 17, 18, 28, 35, 36, 40, 43, 44, 61, 67, 76, 98, 99, 102
Patricia Breen Ornaments, 27, 58, 75
Breweriana, 4, 11, 63, 85, 88
Brewery Diecast Car, 63
Bud Light, 85
Budweiser, 11, 42, 63, 74, 85
Byers' Choice Ltd., 2, 6, 8, 40, 45, 50, 51, 52, 71, 73, 80, 81, 83, 90, 92

Cabbage Patch Dolls, 28, 66, 67
Cades Cove Cabin, 92
Cairn Gnomes, 1, 5, 40
Caithness, 28, 64, 74
Calico Kittens, 1, 81, 82
Canadian Heritage Aircrafts, 1
Cat's Meow, 45, 50, 51, 52, 77, 95
Charming Tails, 2, 19, 27, 37, 43, 52, 54, 71, 73, 100
Cherished Teddies, 2, 5, 9, 19, 25, 27, 29, 37, 41, 43, 45, 51, 52, 53, 54, 56, 58, 64, 66, 68, 71, 72, 73, 74, 76, 77, 78, 81, 82, 92, 95, 97, 100, 102
Chilmark, 5, 25, 28, 34, 40, 53, 74, 81, 82, 92, 94
Christian Bell, 61
Christina's World, 58
Christopher Radko, see Radko, Christopher
Classic Carolina Collection, 42

Coca-Cola, 88, 96, 100
Coca-Cola Steins, 1, 63
Cody, 21
Coors, 11, 63, 85, 88
Corgi, 1
Cottontail Lane, 8, 81
Country Artists, 19, 59
Cow Town, 65
cp Smithshire, 28
Creart, 21
Creepy Hollow, 8, 56,
Cross, Penni-Ann, 17
Crystal, 12,
Crystal Ornaments, 36
Crystal World, 3
C.U.I., see Classic Carolina Collection
Cybis, 36

Daddy's Long Legs, 9, 73, 95
David Winter, see Winter, David
Davis, Lowell, 5, 7, 25, 27, 28, 36, 40, 59, 60, 61, 66, 67, 71, 82, 95
Day, Ray, 76
Decanters-Liquor, 63
DeGrazia, 5, 25, 67, 82, 102
Department 56, Inc., 2, 5, 8, 16, 24, 25, 26, 27, 28, 33, 37, 40, 41, 42, 43, 46, 47, 49, 51, 52, 53, 54, 55, 56, 57, 62, 64, 66, 68, 70, 71, 72, 73, 74, 76, 77, 78, 80, 81, 82, 83, 86, 89, 90, 92, 100, 102, 103
Department 56 All Through The House, 5, 8, 90
Department 56 Cold Cast, Porcelains (CCP), 49, 70
Department 56 Disney Village, 55, 90
Department 56 Lite-Ups, 70
Department 56 Merry Makers, 5, 55, 66, 90
Department 56 Snow Babies, 5, 8, 12, 18, 24, 26, 27, 29, 33, 34, 43, 47, 49, 53, 55, 56, 57, 62, 64, 66, 68, 70, 73, 77, 86, 90
Department 56 Snow Bunnies, 8, 24, 55, 90
Department 56 Snow Village, 26, 47, 49, 55, 62, 66, 68, 70, 71, 73, 77, 78, 86, 90
Department 56 Villages, 8, 16, 24, 26, 33, 47, 49, 55, 62, 70, 71, 78, 90
Department 56 Winter Silhouettes, 8, 55, 90
Disney Classic Videos, 27
Disney Classics, 1, 2, 5, 7, 10, 12, 14, 18, 24, 25, 26, 27, 28, 34, 37, 40, 42, 47, 51, 52, 54, 55, 56, 57, 64, 66, 67, 68, 71, 72, 73, 74, 76, 78, 81, 82, 89, 93, 94, 95, 100
Disney Studio Plates, 99
Disneyana, 10, 14, 26, 27, 93
Dolls, 80, 100, 102
Dolls by Jerri, 66
Dreamsicles, 21, 29, 43, 56, 71, 77, 81, 91, 92, 102
Duncan Royale, 83, 89

Ebony Visions, 18, 24, 53, 66
Edna Hibel Studios, 28, 53, 67
Eggspressions, 74
Emmett Kelly Jr.,
  see Kelly, Emmett
Enchantica, 7, 102
Endearing Memories, 95

Enesco, 12, 67, 82
Enesco Coca-Cola, 96
Enesco Treasury Ornaments, 39, 40, 42, 54
Englebreit, Mary, 45
Ernst, 61
Ertl, 1, 88

Fenton, 95
Figurines, 12
Finnians, 29
First Gear, 88
Flambro, 7
Fontanini, 5, 8, 42, 45, 81, 102
Forma Vitrum, 27, 53, 57, 71, 81, 87, 93, 102
Francis, Kevin, 12, 56
Franklin Mint Plates, 99
Fraser, 53

Gartlan, 67
Gelsinger, Dona, 19
Genesis, 21, 81
George Z. Lefton, see Lefton
Georgetown Collection, 66, 98
German Nutcrackers, 45
German Steins, 11, 86, 88
Goebel, 36, 67
Goebel Miniatures, 5, 7, 28
Goebel Plates, 99
Gorham, 5, 66, 102
Gorham Bears, 22
Gorham Musical Dolls, 36
Greenwich Workshop, 25, 74, 79
Grossman, 67
Gutmann, Bessie Pease, 67

Hackett, 67
Hadley House, 12, 79
Hagara, Jan, 7, 17, 67, 71, 76, 98
Hallmark, 37, 52, 71, 82, 83, 100
Hallmark Keepsake Ornaments, 29, 37, 39, 41, 42, 43, 54, 73, 77, 97
Hallmark Plates, 102
Hamilton Collection, 12, 18, 61, 98, 99, 102
Hamilton Dolls, 7, 40, 66, 102
Hamilton Plates, 7, 40, 61, 67, 98, 99
Hamms, 11, 63, 88
Haney, 53
Harbour Lights, 2, 19, 27, 31, 45, 51, 52, 53, 54, 58, 64, 71, 78, 87, 90, 93, 100, 102, 103
Harmony Kingdom, 25, 56, 59, 69, 92, 100
Harvey, G., 15, 79
Hawthorne Houses, 44
Himstedt Dolls, 66, 84
History of Angels, 83
Hockey Plates, 1
Hook, Francis, 67
Hopkins, Mark, 92
Hudson, 92
Hudson Creek, 37
Hummel, M.I., 5, 12, 13, 15, 17, 18, 25, 28, 33, 34, 36, 37, 40, 42, 44, 45, 46, 47, 52, 53, 54, 56, 61, 64, 66, 67, 68, 71, 72, 73, 74, 76, 77, 80, 81, 82, 86, 89, 94, 100, 101
Humphrey, Maud, 7, 27, 67, 71, 73, 95, 98, 102